"Value-packed, accurate,

"Unbeatable . . ."

—*The Washington Post*

LET'S GO:
USA

is the best book for anyone traveling on a budget. Here's why:

No other guidebook has as many budget listings.

In Los Angeles alone we list 15 hotels and hostels that charge less than $36 per night. In Chicago we found eight for less than $28 a night. We tell you how to get there the cheapest way, whether by bus, plane, or thumb, and where to get an inexpensive and satisfying meal once you've arrived. There are hundreds of money-saving tips for everyone plus lots of information on student discounts.

LET'S GO researchers have to make it on their own.

Our Harvard-Radcliffe researchers travel on budgets as tight as your own—no expense accounts, no free hotel rooms.

LET'S GO is completely revised every year.

We don't just update the prices, we go back to the places. If a charming restaurant has become an overpriced tourist trap, we'll replace the listing with a new and better one.

No other budget guidebook includes all this:

Coverage of both the cities and the countryside; directions, addresses, phone numbers, and hours to get you there and back; in-depth information on culture, history, and the people; listings on transportation between and within regions and cities; tips on work, study, sights, nightlife, and special splurges; city and regional maps; and much, much more.

LET'S GO is for anyone who wants to see the USA on a budget.

Books by Harvard Student Agencies, Inc.

Let's Go: London
Let's Go: New York City
Let's Go: Washington, D.C.

Let's Go: Europe
Let's Go: Britain & Ireland
Let's Go: France
Let's Go: Germany, Austria & Switzerland
Let's Go: Greece & Turkey
Let's Go: Italy
Let's Go: Spain & Portugal
Let's Go: Israel & Egypt

Let's Go: USA
Let's Go: California & Hawaii
Let's Go: The Pacific Northwest, Western Canada & Alaska
Let's Go: Mexico

LET'S GO:

The Budget Guide to the

USA

1992

D. Stephen Voss
Editor

David Javerbaum
Miryam C. Segal
Assistant Editors

Written by Harvard Student Agencies, Inc.

ST. MARTIN'S PRESS
NEW YORK

Helping Let's Go

If you have suggestions or corrections, or just want to share your discoveries, drop us a line. We read every piece of correspondence, whether a 10-page letter, a tacky Elvis postcard, or, as in one case, a collage. All suggestions are passed along to our researcher/writers. Please note that mail received after May 5, 1992 will probably be too late for the 1993 book, but will be retained for the following edition. **Address mail to:** *Let's Go: USA;* **Harvard Student Agencies, Inc.; Thayer Hall-B; Harvard University; Cambridge, MA 02138; USA.**

In addition to the invaluable travel advice our readers share with us, many are kind enough to offer their services as researchers or editors. Unfortunately, the charter of Harvard Student Agencies, Inc. enables us to employ only currently enrolled Harvard students.

Maps by David Lindroth, copyright © 1992, 1991, 1990, 1989 by St. Martin's Press, Inc.

Distributed outside the U.S. and Canada by Pan Books Ltd.

ISBN: 0-312-06401-2

First Edition
10 9 8 7 6 5 4 3 2 1

Let's Go: USA is written by Harvard Student Agencies, Inc., Harvard University, Thayer Hall-B, Cambridge, Mass. 02138.

Let's Go ® is a registered trademark of Harvard Student Agencies, Inc.

Editor	D. Stephen Voss
Assistant Editor	David Javerbaum
	Miryam C. Segal
Managing Editor	Andrew Kaplan
Publishing Director	Zanley F. Galton III
Production Manager	Christopher Williams Cowell

Researcher/Writers

Oregon, Washington, British Columbia, Alberta	Hans R. Agrawal
New York, Ontario, Quebec, Vermont	Heather Lynn Bell
California, Nevada	Vanessa Sydney Biddle
Maine, New Brunswick, New Hampshire, Nova Scotia, Prince Edward Island	Ted Hung-Tse Chang
Washington, DC; Maryland; Virginia	Evelyn N. Chi'en
New York, New Jersey	David Chou
New York, New Jersey	Jennifer DeVore
Washington, DC; Maryland; Virginia	Wendy L. Feng
Connecticut, Delaware, Indiana, Kentucky, Massachusetts, New Jersey, Ohio, Pennsylvania, Rhode Island	Jeffrey B. Golden
Alabama, Arkansas, Florida, Georgia, Louisiana, Mississippi, Tennessee	Danna Harman
Illinois, Indiana, Iowa, Florida, Michigan, Minnesota, Missouri, Wisconsin	Melissa Russell Hart
California	Billy Hulkower
Colorado, Kansas, Missouri, Nebraska, Utah, Wyoming	Brett Janis
Alaska	Linda Kern
Hawaii	Kristin N. Kimball
Arizona, New Mexico, Oklahoma, Texas	A. Keven McAlester
Georgia, North Carolina, South Carolina	Kevin D. McFarlane
Idaho, Montana, North Dakota, Oregon, South Dakota, Washington, Wyoming	Chris O'Connor
Washington, British Columbia, The Yukon	Joseph M. Rainsbury
New York, New Jersey	Richard E. Robbins
Michigan	Laurent V. Ruseckas
Washington, DC; Maryland; Virginia	Michelle M. Shih
Oregon, Washington	Aoibheann Sweeney

California, Nevada	L.A. Taggart
Washington, DC; Maryland; Virginia	Karl R. Thompson
Louisiana, Massachusetts	D. Stephen Voss
Florida	Tim Whitmire

Contributors

New York	Christopher Capozzola
Louisiana, Massachusetts	Kathleen J. Elliott
New Brunswick, Nova Scotia, Prince Edward Island	Jack T. Hou

Sales Group Manager	Michael L. Campbell
Sales Group Representatives	Julie Barclay Cotler
	Robert J. Hutter
President	Robert Frost
C.E.O.	Michele Ponti

ACKNOWLEDGMENTS

Sorry for this self-indulgence. I'll start with the researchers, our eyes and ears across two nations. Hardest Worker award goes to front-roller Ted Chang, a grad student in toxicology. You have Ted to thank for the Maritimes—*all* the Maritimes since they are a new addition. Most Efficient award falls upon Melissa Hart, a journalist with the Harvard *Crimson* who completed a very tight Great Lakes itinerary and added a wonderful section on north Michigan. When our south Florida researcher bagged on us, Melissa hopped on a plane and went there to fix things. Heather Bell of Quebec Province was Most Thorough. She researched eastern Canada to the most minute detail, and wrote up Stratford from scratch (but don't blame her for all the corny Shakespeare references). Keven McAlester, a Dallas native who considers *Dallas* a tragedy equal to JFK's assassination, was Funniest Researcher, with constant wry commentary.

Kevin McFarlane, my fellow political scientist, was our Most Grateful researcher; whenever he sent us great copy batches from the Piedmont he thanked us "for the opportunity." Brett Janis was Most Patient, a victim of almost every bureaucratic SNAFU possible within our organization while researching the Lower Rockies. Jeff Golden started out as Most Eager and metamorphosed into Most Underpaid (when he hit New England prices). Chris O'Connor was Mr. Postcards, for sending so many funny ones from the Upper Rockies. Mr. Bleacher Chris Capozzola researched Cooperstown *for free.* Laurent Ruseckas and Tim Whitmire did special write-ups of Detroit/Ann Arbor and Jacksonville respectively. Finally, we need to thank Danna Harman, a former sergeant in the Israeli army and our all-around Best Researcher. The job she did in the Deep South was so amazing that we simply mailed off a check the minute we saw her name on a return address.

On to my co-conspirators. D.J., the New Jersey Editing Machine, was our funny man. His creative influence is the reason much of this book is worth reading. The Schmos, his first cousins, discovered Asuogs'tel while trekking across North Dakota. Miryam, a gutsy New Yorker, was our stabilizing force. We could tell how bad our jokes were by how far back her Winona Ryder eyes rolled. Miryam was the one who took control of our long-term projects and got them done. She's the reason much of the book is worth using to travel (especially in NYC). Finally, office manager Hilary Holmquist did all the *real* work that was necessary to get this book to press.

Two special acknowledgments must be made. The first is to Andrew Kaplan, who as my immediate superior had to catch the flak every time I bucked bureaucratic regulations. Of all the people who worked on this book, I made him suffer the most. The second is to my parents, who did all the suffering before I started the job. Finally, if you are wondering who the Deadhead was, two people are to blame: my wife and best friend Kathleen Elliott, and my water brother, fellow Southerner Normand Modine. Get back truckin' on.

—Steve

I would like to thank Charo, Frank, Dean and Jerry, Wayne, Chip, Elvis, Regis, Kathy Lee, and David Hasselhoff, oddly charismatic star of TV's "Knight Rider." Thanks, guys—you're beautiful.

—D.J.

To The Sisters Levine—SA(rah) and RA(chel), Lev, Maw & Paw, Eliyahu Fuzzball, Devorah & Shmuel, and, of course, Zohara and Mairav.

—Miryam

CONTENTS

x   Contents

LIST OF MAPS

About Let's Go

A generation ago, Harvard Student Agencies, a three-year-old nonprofit corporation dedicated to providing employment to students, was doing a booming business booking charter flights to Europe. One of the extras offered to passengers on these flights was a 20-page mimeographed pamphlet entitled *1960 European Guide,* a collection of tips on continental travel compiled by the HSA staff. The following year, students traveling to Europe researched the first full-fledged edition of *Let's Go: Europe,* a pocket-sized book with tips on budget accommodations, irreverent write-ups of sights, and a decidedly youthful slant.

Throughout the 60s, the series reflected its era: a section of the 1968 *Let's Go: Europe* was entitled "Street Singing in Europe on No Dollars a Day." During the 70s *Let's Go* gradually became a large-scale operation, adding regional European guides and expanding coverage into North Africa and Asia. Now in its 32nd year, *Let's Go* publishes 15 titles covering more than 40 countries. This year *Let's Go* proudly introduces two new guides: *Let's Go: Germany, Austria & Switzerland* and *Let's Go: Washington, D.C.*

Each spring 80 Harvard-Radcliffe students are hired as researcher-writers for the summer months. They train intensively during April and May for their summer tour of duty. Each researcher-writer then hits the road on a shoestring budget for seven weeks, researching six days per week, and overcoming countless obstacles in a glorious quest for better bargains.

Back in a basement deep below Harvard Yard, an editorial staff of 30, a management team of six, and countless typists and proofreaders—all students—spend four months poring over more than 70,000 pages of manuscript as they push the copy through a rigorous editing process. High tech has recently landed in the dungeon: some of the guides are now typeset in-house using sleek black desktop workstations.

And even before the books hit the stands, next year's editions are well underway.

A Note to our Readers

The information for this book is gathered by Harvard Student Agencies' researchers during the late spring and summer months. Each listing is derived from the assigned researcher's opinion based upon his or her visit at a particular time. The opinions are expressed in a candid and forthright manner. Other travelers might disagree. Those traveling at a different time may have different experiences since prices, dates, hours, and conditions are always subject to change. You are urged to check beforehand to avoid inconvenience and surprises. Travel always involves a certain degree of risk, especially in low-cost areas. When traveling, especially on a budget, you should always take particular care to ensure your safety.

AYH-HOSTELS OF DISTINCTION

Houston International Hostel
5302 Crawford
Houston, Texas 77004
713-523-1009

New Orleans International Hostel
2253 Carondelet Street
New Orleans, Louisiana 70130
504-523-3014

Miami Beach International Hostel
1438 Washington Ave.
Miami Beach, Florida 33139
Ph. 305-534-2988 FAX 305-673-0346

Orlando International Hostel
227 North Eola Dr.
Orlando, Florida 32801
Ph. 407-843-8888 FAX 407-841-8867

 MEMBERS INTERNATIONAL YOUTH HOSTEL FEDERATION/AYH

GENERAL INTRODUCTION

A Tourist's Guide to American History

> Travelling is a fool's paradise. . .the wise man stays
> home.
>
> —*Ralph Waldo Emerson*

The United States is a relatively new nation, having severed its colonial bonds only in 1776. America's "old" historical buildings seem quite young—erected long after natural forces had begun eroding Egyptian sphinxes, Incan pyramids, and the Great Wall of China. With that in mind, the term "American history" seems almost ludicrous. But rest assured—the territory now occupied by the United States is by no means historically destitute for the tourist.

Long before the first European explorers and settlers began exploiting the continent's abundant natural resources, a diverse collage of native populations lived in relative peace with the generous land. While these tribes created few towering stone structures, their unique languages, religions and customs reflect ages of accumulated wisdom. Remnants still survive, despite being battered by the forces of assimilation and bastardized in the images of "American" pop culture. Many tourist sites around the United States and Canada, especially those near plots of poor-quality land called "tribal reservations," allow fairly genuine exposure to residual Native-American identity.

The first European tourists to visit the American continent were probably Scandinavians. The Vikings, led by Leif Ericson, explored the Atlantic coast around the year 1000, although few traces mark their legacy. After a dry spell, Europeans again stumbled upon the Americas in 1492. Christopher Columbus, on a grant from Spanish Queen Isabella to find a Western sea route to Oriental riches, found his trip around the world blocked by Hispaniola. Soon Europeans arrived in droves—English religious dissenters to New England, French furriers to Canada and Louisiana, Spanish *conquistadors* to the West, Florida, and Mexico. Each left a legacy of architecture and artifact, which the tourist often can find rubbing shoulders in the same city.

After the end of the expensive Hundred Years' War in 1763, Britain's demands on her colonies grew until a group of revolutionary elites formally rebelled against the monarchy in 1776. The 13 New England colonies, using tactics borrowed from Native-American warriors, successfully beat back the British and established an independent, republican nation. New England tourist sites stress the role of nearby communities and heroes in this "Revolutionary War"—colonial "history trails," war museums and tours of patriots' homes—to the point of nationalistic redundancy.

The United States begged, borrowed, and stole its way across the continent fueled by "Manifest Destiny"—a belief in the God-given superiority of Anglo-America used at various times to justify annihilation of Native Americans, enslavement of Africans, and war against Mexicans. The current social and cultural landscape is less a "melting pot" than a "mixed salad." Collected in pockets around vast expanse

1

of territory is a varied wealth of peoples and cultures—Native American, Western European, African-American, and Cajun French, to name only a few.

The United States has been able to weather the cross-pressures and paradoxes in its cultural history—with one exception. From 1861-65, the North and South of the country fought a vicious war that killed a larger proportion of the population than any other war in which the nation has been involved. It goes by various names—the War over Slavery, the Civil War, the War Between the States, the War for Southern Independence. (The name chosen usually reveals the perspective of the speaker.) When the shooting stopped, the industrial North had beaten the agricultural slave states of the South, and the cultural rift has never completely healed. Numerous tourist sites in the South, as well as a healthy number in the North, still trumpet the glories of hometown heroes in this debilitating domestic conflict. Other sites stress the plight of African- and Native-American slaves, who after the war were emancipated from slavery into more subtle forms of oppression.

After the Civil War, the United States got down to the business of developing the superpower status it currently enjoys. Rapid investment spurred by Social Darwinist "captains of industry" boosted the nation's economic influence, albeit at great cost to workers and farmers. Many of these wealthy industrialists, such as Carnegie, Rockefeller, and Gould, amassed huge estates—including mansions that have since become tourist attractions. This 19th-century system of "free market" capitalism quickly broke down, after cyclical recessions in the 1870s, the 1890s, and especially the 1930s, but American economic dominance did not. During the Great Depression, under the leadership of President Franklin D. Roosevelt, the United States began its transition to a mixed economy—part capitalist, part welfare state. Many of the monuments, buildings, bridges and parks enjoyed by tourists in the United States were built during this period to create work for the American unemployed. Many other buildings open to travelers sport beautiful paintings, sculptures and mosaics created by out-of-work artists employed by the government.

The USA emerged from World War II on the shoulders of a powerful "military-industrial complex" that assured at least temporary continuation of its superpower status. Mutual hostilities between American and Soviet leaders were allowed to escalate, a development that further strengthened the power of these military and industrial leaders and built up the bipolar world dominant during the "Cold War." This global primacy of the United States caused it to become a locus of economic and political dealings. As a result, many sites of international importance are easily within tourists' reach in New York and Washington, D.C.—the United Nations, the New York Stock Exchange, Wall Street, and the Federal Reserve Board, as well as the halls of U.S. government. Of course, the down side of this American economic prominence for tourists is that the dollar is usually strong and wages usually high—vacations often are not cheap. This is especially true as American service-sector employment rises in importance; sites traditionally attractive to vacationers are becoming increasingly commercialized, losing much of the authenticity and spontaneity that made them popular.

But budgetary obstacles should not spoil your vacation in the U.S. One reason is that many regions, especially the poverty-stricken Deep South and the economically depressed Midwest, have remained relatively untouched by American wealth concentrated on the East and West Coasts. These areas, which often have the sites least vulgarized by commercialization, are relatively cheap. The American love of the outdoors has supported numerous inexpensive campgrounds in both isolated and urban areas. Vast and abundant American lands, although suffering from severe environmental irresponsibility, still offer some of the most beautiful, unpopulated, and unspoiled natural tourist sites in the world—and they can be reached relatively cheaply and easily. Finally, you have *Let's Go: USA* on your side. Our researchers have done their best to collect important budgetary strategies and site listings to make your vacation both fulfilling and inexpensive, both exciting and low in stress.

Have a long, strange trip.

—*D. Stephen Voss*

American Culture

American culture is popular. **Very** popular. Not only do this nation's superstars generally become international celebrities, the popular forms that have evolved in the United States in the last 100 years have become dominant in the industrial First World and extremely influential in less-developed nations as well. But despite slurs to the contrary, the United States has also been home to a dazzling array of artists using more traditional forms. Products of American creativity tend to occupy nebulous positions on the spectrum between "high" and "low" art, prime examples being the music of George Gershwin and the paintings of Norman Rockwell. A tourist would be well-advised to study and experience the culture that has thrust Madonna, Thoreau, Schwarzenegger, Copland, Babe Ruth, Warhol, and David Hasselhoff (charismatic star of NBC's "Knight Rider") onto the world stage.

Music

American music—such as country, bluegrass, big band, jazz, blues, and rock and roll—has spread prodigiously from its roots in the South and Midwest. Much of this growth can be attributed to the invention of radio and sound recordings, which made music available to the masses. This music co-exists peaceably with the traditional European classical variety, which can be suffered through at junior-high school concerts and enjoyed at the great music halls that house world-class orchestras in most major American cities. In fact, the 20th century has seen a distinctly American style of classical music develop—no mere appropriation of European forms, but an unmistakably native tradition emerging from such composers as Scott Joplin, Charles Ives, George Gershwin, and the late, great Aaron Copland. The birth of the big Broadway musical has also rewarded Americans with catchy tunes from the pens of Irving Berlin, Cole Porter, Leonard Bernstein, Stephen Sondheim and others.

The best way to get a sense of the broad panoply of United States mellifluity is to scan the radio dial when in or near a megalopolis, or to peruse a well-stocked record store. You can get good first-hand listening experiences in the night clubs, concert halls, and stadiums of any American city, particularly the following:

* for classical music
  New York, Philadelphia, Boston, Chicago, Cleveland and St. Louis.

* for jazz and blues
  New Orleans, St. Louis, Chicago, Kansas City and New York.

* for country
  Nashville, Memphis, Dallas and Houston.

* for rock and roll
  just about anywhere, but especially New York, Los Angeles, Boston, San Francisco, Seattle, Austin, TX, and Minneapolis.

* for rap, a raw, powerful synthesis of rhythm and speech that exploded from the streets of New York City to become the most challenging current style of American music, just turn on your radio or attend a concert anywhere the music hasn't been banned.

Incidentally, the six greatest American rock 'n' roll bands of all time are The Grateful Dead, Velvet Underground, Creedence Clearwater Revival, Steely Dan, R.E.M., and of course, everybody's favorite quintet of heartthrobs, the Old Guys on the Stoop.

Movies

Great films are now considered lasting works of art, unlike great TV shows (with the possible exception of "Knight Rider"), and quite a few of these great films were and are made in America. American films such as *sex, lies, and videotape* and *Paris, Texas* frequently win first prize at the Cannes Film Festival. But for every American *film* that comes out, there are 500 American *movies*—bang 'em up action movies and cop movies and tear-jerker movies and go-with-your-girlfriend horror movies and lots and lots of comedies.

The less popular of these movies are shown quickly on cable TV. The more popular ones are disseminated throughout the civilized and uncivilized world. The latest *Rocky* sequel is translated into Japanese and shown to eager Sylvester Stallone fans in Tokyo. In the United States, the promulgation of movies has been the largest single contributor to the celebrity culture that reveals itself in the tabloids on sale at the local supermarket. Foreign travelers inevitably will find themsleves knee-deep in the movies. A visit to Universal Studios or MGM/Disney Studios in Orlando will prove quite illuminating in your quest to find the *verité* about the *cinema* in America. Hasta la vista, baby.

Sports

Tourists wishing to experience an authentic American mass ritual have two options—they can get invited to the senior prom, or (if they can't find a date) they can attend a sporting event at one of the enormous arenas and stadiums that dot the urban and suburban landscape. Sports and athletic culture have assumed a prominent place in the American mind, especially the male mind, and going to a baseball, American football, basketball, hockey, or other athletic game will give you a taste of some of the peculiarities and pleasures of *Homo Americanus*—among them group identification, vicarious participation, and fermented imbibation. Be sure to buy a hot dog, and see if you can get someone to explain the often incomprehensible rules if you are unfamiliar with them. If you can't fit a trip to a stadium into your schedule, try to watch a game on TV. Invite some friends over to get some *participa-*

tion mystique happening, root root root for the home team, swig down some brewskis, and act like you're an expert. Soon you'll fit right in. Go Giants!

Corporate Culture

Culture and business overlap tremendously in America. When a company becomes large enough, when McDonald's sells its trillionth hamburger or General Motors its billionth car, it ceases to be just a money-making operation. It is an American institution. When Coca-Cola announced plans to change its century-old recipe several years ago, the anguished cries of the *vox populi* seemed to herald revolution. And like much of American culture, big U.S. companies inevitably get their fingers in many foreign pies, as the recent opening of McDonald's and Pizza Hut in Moscow's Red Square indicates. As you journey through the USA, you will begin to appreciate the absolute ubiquity of big business in this country. The significance of individual corporations and products often far transcends what would be justified by their actual quality, even if a company's only intention is to make money.

Which it is.

—David Javerbaum

Literature

Although "American literature" quickly thrived in the United States, rich with the works of giants such as Twain, Dickinson and Poe, American literature faced an identity crisis during its first century. As late as the 19th century, critics—both American and European—denied that the U.S. had a literature separate from the "English literature" of Britain. Yet U.S. writers, even these early authors, have made their mark on the international literary community.

One important literary genre energized by U.S. authors, and especially exploited by macabre master Edgar Allan Poe, is the detective story, still a popular form in contemporary Western culture. Poe, as well as Hawthorne and Melville, is also famous for his use of the short story, a distinctly American genre. Some famous American short story writers include Raymond Carver, John Cheever, Truman Capote, Joyce Carol Oates, and Norman Mailer.

The geographical breadth of the United States has nurtured varying cultural heritages, each offering unique sub-literatures. Faulkner's works, for example, are seen as distinctly Southern, Updike's as expressions of New England; Mark Twain's are associated with the American frontier. The waves of immigration which characterize U.S. demography have resulted in different literatures produced by various ethnic, racial and religious groups. African-American literature has a strong tradition in both poetry and fiction, with contributors including Langston Hughes, Zora Neale Hurston, Leroi Jones, James Baldwin, and Ralph Ellison. Jewish-American writers include Herman Wouk, Bernard Malamud, Cynthia Ozick, and the late Isaac Bashevis Singer.

The history of American literature is shadowed by a distinctly American phenomenon: book banning. As early as the 17th century zealots attempted to ban "obscene" and "blasphemous" books in the colonies of the New World. By the late 1800s, various individuals and organizations turned to the court system and boycotts to enforce their censorious opinions. Works by Faulkner, Hemingway, Anderson, Aiken, Sinclair and Dos Passos all have been banned, at some point and at some place, in the United States. Today, both contemporary and earlier works are the subject of book-banning militants, who have switched their focus to public school libraries.

Visual Art

American art is as diverse and multifaceted as the American experience it depicts. The works of artists such as Edward Hopper and Thomas Hart Benton explore the

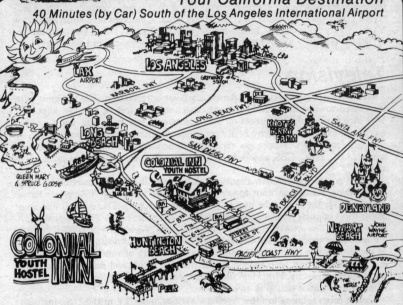

innocence and mythic values of the United States before its emergence as a super-power. The vigorous Abstract Expressionism of Arshile Gorky and Jackson Pollock displays both the swaggering confidence and frenetic insecurity of cold-war America. Pop Art, popularized by Jasper Johns, Robert Rauschenberg, Roy Lichtenstein, and Andy Warhol, uses as its subject matter the icons and motifs of contemporary American life and pop culture, satirizing and exposing what has become since World War II the *de facto* world culture. Cindy Sherman and Robert Mapplethorpe have exposed Americans to personal-as-political photography, despite efforts of self-styled guardians of morality to censor their work. Contemporary American art is often a highly experimental, mixed-media pastiche of audio, video, and performance art which elegantly acknowledges and incorporates advances in technology.

Television

Next to baseball, television is America's favorite recreation. For the most part, it's geared toward the (below) average citizen and it's free (if you can afford the TV). Approximately 98 percent of U.S. homes own television sets, and no one is quite sure exactly how many hours per week Americans spend watching TV. In the past decade, TV culture has expanded tremendously as the four national networks (ABC, NBC, CBS, and Fox) have gained new competition from cable television.

Couch potatoes will watch almost anything, from Brady Bunch reruns to Beach Boys videos. But if you want to see the "best" that American TV culture has to offer, turn on the boob-tube during prime-time (7-10pm). There you'll find some of the most popular hour-long shows and the shorter sit-coms: *The Simpsons, L.A. Law, Cheers.* The growth of cable TV has sprouted 24-hour channels offering nothing but news, sports, movies, kid vid, weather(!), and that most peculiar perennial, MTV, a non-stop music-video whose dazzling display of random, primal images has both shaped and been shaped by the frenzied minds and dark unconscious of the American psyche. Historical time and space stand still before the Siren dance of Madonna, and a nation is awed.

Unlike programming in other Western nations, most TV in the U.S., including news programs, is funded by advertisements. Two-minute breaks for commercials, which are considered the most effective means for businesses to reach potential consumers, interrupt most news and entertainment shows. While this method of funding protects media organizations from government meddling, critics argue the dependence on private corporations has at least an equally deleterious effect.

—*Miryam Segal*

Practical Information: What Every Schmo Needs to Know

In this book, U.S. are listed alphabetically, with cities and intrastate regions alphabetized within each state. Another section covers major portions of seven Canadian provinces and has its own General Introduction. We also provide brief overviews of regions, states, provinces, and major cities. Our maps come in two types: city/state maps and regional maps. The former are located within the sections to which they apply; the latter cluster in a map section at the back of the book. Both sets of maps will give you the general layout of many key travel areas, but you will need more detailed maps when planning a final itinerary.

Let's Go: USA cannot cover every possible attraction north of Mexico in one soft-cover volume. But budget travelers will find this book invaluable. We'll give you the lowdown on what's worth seeing where, and how to do it cheaply. Our guide has the charm of 50 state and several provincial guides without the bulk. We're what every Schmo on the go with no dough needs to know...

Once upon a time, in a sleepy little hamlet in a drowsy little state in a soporific little country named America, there lived a happy little family named the Schmos: Daddy Joe, Momma Flo, son Bo, and daughter Zelda.

One day, Joe Schmo called a pow-wow. The pow-wow came and sat obediently at Joe's knee. Then Joe spoke: "Family," he said, "Your mother and I are going to take a long vacation across America."

"Well, be sure to leave us the car keys and beer money," said Bo.

"No, children, you don't understand. You are going to come with us," said Flo.

"Oh boy oh boy oh boy," sighed Zelda.

"But Ma and Pa," worried Bo, "we have little experience traveling. In fact, we have never left this state before. In fact, we have never left this house before. How are we going to know how to prepare for the trip? Where are we going to stay? How are we going to get around? And where the hell are we going anyway?"

"I'm sure details like these will work themselves out as we go along. All I know is I've managed to save $250 from my job at the pepper mine. That should be enough to last us about two weeks, I'd say," said Joe.

"Well, let's go USA!" said Flo, by way of a segue.

Planning Your Trip

Our friends the Schmos are deciding to play their jaunt across the USA by ear. This is very, very, very DUMB. Planning ahead is the key to an enjoyable, angst-free vacation. Spend time now rather than later figuring out how to have enough money on hand, how to stay in good health, and how to keep in touch with friends back home. In anticipating these and other needs, use your common sense.It's the single most important thing to pack before you travel, and it comes in its own carrying case.

Long-Term Advance Preparations

Sometimes travelers cannot waste time three or even six months in advance of a trip to read the bulky text of a travel guide and make the necessary long-term preparations. With that in mind, we offer you a brief checklist of all the things that simply cannot wait until the week preceding your trip (although they will not be applicable in every case). Be forewarned: Not all of your particular travel needs will be met by this humble effort, and many things that were excluded because they seemed "obvious" to us might not be so apparent to the infrequent or foreign traveler. *You still must plan ahead.*

☐ Plot the dates and locations for the beginning and end of the trip so you can buy plane tickets at cheap advance fares.

☐ Make sure you are properly insured for health, theft and auto problems.

☐ Make an appointment to update inoculations.

☐ Make sure your car gets checked and tuned-up completely.

☐ If applicable and possible, obtain the following to pack for your trip:
   —Two forms of ID, at least one with a picture.
   —An extra set of your prescription eyewear.
   —An extra supply of any prescription drugs, as well as a copy of the prescription.
   —A credit card.
   —Travelers checks.
   —An ATM card that can be used on interstate banking networks.
   —An Atlas of the U.S. and Canada.

Short-Term Advance Preparations

Packing

"We will be gone for about a week or two," said Joe. "How much do you think we should pack?"

"I will pack my entire wardrobe so I can be better prepared for the exigencies of the road," said Flo.

"I will pack my entire compact disc collection in case I want to scream along with my music," said Bo.

"I will pack my carpeting in case the bottoms of my feet are sore and need comfort," said Zelda.

"Well. . . I guess it's better to be safe than sorry. And there should be plenty of room in the Rabbit," said Joe.

Don't be a Schmo. Pack light.

Backpacks are probably your best option. Decent packs can cost more than $100, but they enable you to carry everything in one bag that stays with you at all times. They are also *much* lighter than suitcases. Find a pack which won't grind your shoulders to the bone and can withstand brutal treatment. Be sure to have a smaller pack for day trips so you can have the option of leaving your large pack behind.

The clothes you pack should be durable, comfortable, and already broken in (especially shoes). Be prepared for a wide range of weather conditions. Bring several T-shirts, a sweartshirt or sweater, some shorts and a couple of pairs of jeans, underwear and socks, and you've got a basic wardrobe. A raincoat and a windbreaker are vital accessories, and your footwear should be **waterproof**. But that formal outfit you think you may need—leave it in the closet.

It's a fine line between being prepared and getting a hernia. Nevertheless, there are some things you might want to take along, depending on where and how you plan to travel: first-aid kit, flashlight, pens and stationery, travel alarm, canteen or water bottle, Ziploc bags, sewing kit, safety pins, pocket- or Swiss Army knife, waterproof matches, sunglasses and assorted toiletries.

Money: Bringing It, Sending It, Getting It

"How will we get money on the road?" asked Flo.

"I can pickpocket," said Bo.

"I can shoplift," said Zelda.

Joe looked at his offspring. "Perhaps we can sell the children," he mused.

Traveler's checks are generally the most convenient way to deal with your finances while you travel. They are refundable if lost or stolen, and can be purchased at any bank or directly from the company for a small commission, usually 1%. (The AAA sells American Express checks to its members for no commission.) Buying checks in small denominations is safer and more convenient; make a separate list of their numbers, and keep it on you at all times in a separate pouch or pocket from the checks themselves. Traveler's checks are welcomed and cashed at most American and Canadian tourist establishments, although some low-budget bars and restaurants may not accept them. The most widely-used ones are:

American Express (800-221-7282; outside the U.S., call collect 801-964-6665).

Visa International (800-227-6811; outside the U.S., call collect 415-574-7111).

Don't forget to write.

If your American Express® Travelers Cheques are lost or stolen, we can hand-deliver a refund virtually anywhere you travel. Just give us a call. You'll find it's a lot less embarrassing than calling home.

Bank of America (800-227-3460).

Barclays (800-235-7366).

Citicorp (800-645-6556; outside the U.S., call collect 813-623-4100).

Thomas Cook (800-223-4030 and 800-223-7373). Affiliated with **Mastercard.**

With a major **credit card** you can rent cars, make reservations, and obtain cash advances at most banks. But many places mentioned in *Let's Go* will not honor credit cards. This is just as well—rely on them too much and your trip will no longer deserve the label "budget travel." American Express cardholders pay a hefty annual fee ($55), but membership has its privileges: Local AmEx offices will cash one personal check, domestic or foreign, per person per seven-day period. They can also cancel stolen credit cards, arrange for temporary ID, help change airline, hotel, and car rental reservations, send mailgrams and international cables, and hold your mail if you contact them well in advance (see Keeping in Touch). American Express operates machines at some major airports through which you can purchase traveler's checks with your card. For more info, call the American Express Card Division (800-528-4800) or AmEx Global Assist (800-333-2639). Other popular credit cards are Mastercard (800-223-9920) and Visa (800-227-6811), which offers most of the same services as American Express and is more widely accepted.

Credit cards are also compatible with the latest form of plastic financing—**electronic banking.** At least two banking networks offer 24-hr. service at automated tellers (operated by bank cards) in major cities across the country: the **Cirrus network** (800-424-7787) and the **Plus network** (800-843-7587). When staying in major cities, a bank card may prove as valuable as traveler's checks. The telephone numbers listed for Cirrus and Plus allow you to locate machines in your area. Be warned that the machines are occasionally out of service, and there is a daily withdrawal limit of $300 or less. AmEx, Visa and Mastercard work in these machines, if the operating bank issues the credit card. Check with local banks about these and competing services.

If you run out of money on the road, you have a few options. Most inexpensive for North Americans is to have a **certified check** or **postal money order** mailed to you. Certified checks are redeemable at any bank, while post offices will cash money orders upon presentation of two forms of ID (one with photo). The buyer should keep a receipt to refund lost orders. AmEx offers a money transfer service for cardholders. Romantics can have loved ones in the USA wire them money in minutes via **Western Union** (800-325-6000 or 800-325-4176), but the charge—$40 to send $500—might make even Tchaikovsky or Wagner revert to classicism. You must have a Mastercard or Visa to wire by phone. Money sent from Europe will usually be available within two working days at Western Union offices in the USA, but there is an additional surcharge.

Foreign travelers should plan their trip so that they will not need to have money sent from home. If it has to be done, try to arrange in advance for your bank to send money from your account, on specified days, to correspondent banks in the USA (if it has any). A **cable transfer** is the fastest method of transport, requiring 24 or 48 hours to get to a major city or a bit longer to a more remote location. Cabling costs average $30 for amounts less than $1000, plus the commission charged by your home bank. **Bank drafts** or **international money orders** are cheaper but slower. You pay a commission of $15-20 on the draft, plus the cost of sending it registered air mail. American Express' **Moneygram** service (800-543-4080) will cable up to $10,000 to you within three days. It costs $35 to cable $500, and the fee gets larger with greater amounts. Non-cardholders may use this service for no extra charge, but money can only be sent from England, Germany, and some locations in France—other European and Australian AmEx offices can only receive Moneygrams. Whichever method you use, you and your benefactor need to know the exact name and address of the bank or office to which the money is being sent. As a *last* resort, consulates will wire home for you and deduct the cost from the money you receive. But they will not be very happy about it.

A note about prices quoted in this book: They do not include state or provincial **sales taxes,** which can range from zero to 14%. Many states have special hotel taxes as well; ask before you take the room. For some very basic tipping guidelines, see Currency and Exchange.

Health, Safety, and Insurance

The Schmo vacation started in Minneapolis on a clear winter's day. Unfortunately, Bo Schmo caught a mild cold after spending a few hours walking around town in a bathrobe and thongs. And Zelda's fluorescent orange handbag mysteriously vanished, along with the kindly gentleman in sunglasses with whom she left it for safekeeping.

"Well, look on the bright side," said the optimistic Flo. "At least we were smart enough to buy insurance from that company we saw advertised on TV at 3am."

Health: How Not To Get Sick

Be sure you are up to date on your inoculations, although U.S. water and food are generally safe and no special shots are required. In fact, the weather is the biggest potential threat to a tourist's health. Read about climates in regional and state introductions, and be prepared. In the heat, drink plenty of non-alcoholic, non-caffeinated fluids, wear a hat, and stay indoors in the middle of the afternoon. In the cold, avoid getting wet, and dress warmly. If this advice seems obvious to you, that's a good sign. Not every Schmo is that smart.

Airplane travelers are often plagued by **jet lag.** Jet lag sufferers find they can't sleep well, even though they may be very tired after their flight. The best way to avoid jet lag is to adopt the time of the new region immediately — sleep only when it is nighttime *there.* It's also a good idea not to overeat or drink alcohol until your body has adjusted to the new schedule.

Diabetics, vegetarians, seniors, and the disabled should see the Additional Concerns sections below. Those with medical conditions can obtain a **Medic Alert Identification Tag.** The tag has a 24-hr. hotline and the wearer's condition engraved on it, with lifetime membership included in the price of the tag ($30 for steel, $38 for silver, and, for the fashion-conscious, $48 for gold-plated). Contact Medic Alert Foundation International, P.O. Box 1009, Turlock, CA 95381 (800-ID-ALERT or 800-432-5378).

Safety: How Not to Get Robbed

Unfortunately, violent **crime** and theft occurs more frequently in the U.S. than elsewhere in the civilized world. Consequently, much of any big city is unsafe. Avoid unsupervised, less-populated, poorly lit areas. Look confident, not like a tourist. Don't be afraid to ask for advice about safety from friendly locals. For more info on safe travel, see *Travel Safely: Security and Safeguards at Home and Abroad,* from **Hippocrene Books, Inc.,** 171 Madison Ave., New York NY 10016 (212-685-4371). Women should see Additional Concerns below.

If you do get into trouble, you can call 911, or other emergency numbers listed in the Practical Information sections. **Travel Assistance International,** 1133 15th St. NW, Washington, DC (800-821-2828), provides a 24-hr. hotline for emergencies and referrals. You can buy a year-long travel package for $120, which includes medical and travel insurance, financial assistance, and help in replacing lost passports and visas. **Traveler's Aid International,** 918 16th Street NW #201, Washington, DC 20006 (202-659-9468), charges no fee but requests donations. They provide help for theft, car failure, illness, and other "mobility-related" problems. Local offices are listed under Practical Information.

Wherever you decide to leave your clothing and other stuff, keep your documents, credit cards, and camera with you. Lockers at bus and train stations are safe, and

very useful if you want to sleep outside without most of your bulky possessions. Label *all* your belongings with your name, address, and home phone number.

Insurance: How Not to Get Screwed

Always have proof of medical insurance on your person. Find out about your coverage before you leave. Some homeowner and family policies cover medical costs and theft. **Medicare** covers travel in the U.S., Canada, and Mexico. Canadians may be covered by their home province's health insurance up to 90 days after leaving the country. Students should find out if they are covered by a school policy or a family policy.

Organizations such as AAA and American Express (800-221-7282) offer a variety of insurance plans for travelers. The **Council on International Educational Exchange (CIEE)** (212-661-1414) offers a **Trip-Safe Plan** that provides coverage in the U.S.

The following private firms specialize in travel insurance. You can buy a policy either directly from them or through an agent operating on their behalf:

Access America, Inc., P.O. Box 90310, Richmond, VA 23130-9310 (800-284-8300). A subsidiary of Blue Cross/Blue Shield. Covers on-the-spot hospital admittance costs. 24-hr. hotline. Anything their North American plan does not cover, their international plan will.

Travel Guard International, 1145 Clark St. Stevens Point (715-345-0505). Comprehensive "Travel Guard Gold" package. 24-hr. hotline.

The Traveler's Insurance Co., Ticket and Travel Plans, 9-NB, 1 Tower Sq., Hartford, CT 06183-5040 (800-243-3174, in CT 203-277-2318). Offers the *"Travel Insurance Pak,"* available through most major travel agencies.

Edmund A. Cocco Agency, 220 Broadway, #201, Lynnfield, MA 01940 (800-821-2488). *"Global Care Everywhere"* package has a number of different plan options.

WorldCare Travel Assistance, 1150 Olive St., Suite T-233, Los Angeles, CA 90015 (800-253-1877). A one-year membership is $162, which covers an unlimited number of trips up to 90 days apiece.

If you are an ISIC cardholder (see Documents), you automatically receive $3000 of accident-related coverage and $100 per day of in-patient health coverage for up to 60 days. Canadians and Hawaiians also get generous compensations for death, dismemberment, and repatriation of remains (God forbid a thousand times).

Transportation

The Schmos decided to save money by walking from Minneapolis to Chicago. This was a frugal choice, but a painful one for Flo, who soon ruined her best high heels. At the Wisconsin border, the Schmos rented a Pinto from Rent-a-Recall for $100 a day, but it broke down outside Kenosha. In desperation, they tried hitchhiking. They waited for hours by the side of the road, but nobody stopped. At last, a man in a black van pulled over.

"Want a lift?" he asked.

"Hey, you're famous!" marvelled Bo. "Didn't I see your picture on the wall of the post office?"

The black van mysteriously drove away, and the Schmos decided to fly the rest of the way via General Vicinity Airlines, which flew them to the general vicinity of the Windy City for only $500. A short swim later, the Schmos were in Chicago.

Air Travel

is often cheaper than one might guess. Shuttle service between major cities on the East Coast saves a lot of time and is almost as cheap as the train if you take advantage of special student and senior citizen fares. Check the weekend travel sections of major newspapers for bargain fares, and consider discount travel agencies such as **Travel Avenue,** 641 West Lake St., Suite 201, Chicago, IL 60606-1012 (800-333-3335), which rebates four-fifths of the standard 10% ticket commission.

A few general guidelines for booking a flight: You can save up to 60 percent on fares if you call at least two weeks in advance, especially important during the tourist season or on holidays. Traveling on a weekday (Mon.-Thurs.) usually costs less. The day before your departure, call the airline to reconfirm your flight reservation. Arrive early to ensure you have a seat; airlines usually overbook. (On the other hand, with flexible travel plans, being "bumped" from a flight does not spell doom—you will probably leave on the next flight and receive either a free ticket or a cash bonus. You even might want to bump yourself when the airline asks for volunteers.)

To save money, usually you must buy a round-trip ticket and stay for at least one Sunday and for no longer than three weeks. Look for other restrictions, such as pre-payment (14 days after making your reservation or 14 days before your flight) and 15-100% penalties for reservation changes or cancellations. Ask about "red-eye" (all-night) flights, especially on popular business travel routes. Charter flights run between some U.S. cities; they are more subject to sudden schedule changes but can save money. Talk to a local travel agent or call the airlines' toll-free numbers.

Perhaps the cheapest way to travel is to fly as an **air courier.** You can fly to destinations worldwide for as little as $99 roundtrip. **Courier Air Travel,** 3661 N. Campbell Ave. #342, Tucson, AZ 85719, publishes a 50-page handbook ($8.95) giving step-by-step procedures for traveling as a courier. They also provide names, telephone numbers, and contact points of courier companies.

Automobile Travel

is often the only way to reach certain areas of the U.S., especially in the South or West. Rental rates are usually high, but group travel lowers expenses—check notices on ride boards around college campuses, in newspapers, and the phone book for share-a-ride organizations.

For $15-70 per year (depending on where you live and how many benefits you choose) the **American Automobile Association (AAA)** offers free trip-planning services, emergency road service, great road maps, discounts on car rentals, special insurance, and American Express traveler's checks at no commission or surcharge beyond the value of the checks. For more info, contact your local chapter or dial the national number (800-222-4357). Many major gas companies offer similar services to drivers who have a charge account with them. The **Mobil Auto Club** (800-621-5581) charges members $39 per year for emergency road service (including towing, jump starts, and tire changes). Mobil either dispatches help or reimburses you later, also providing a routing service and up to $5000 insurance on the driver's life at no extra charge.

Always keep spare change and dollar bills in your car for tolls. Before your trip, tune the engine, check the tires, and buy spare fan belts. Your trunk should contain a spare tire and jack, jumper cables, extra oil, flares, and a blanket. If able to repair minor breakdowns and diagnose larger problems, you can avoid expensive service stations except in emergencies. In certain regions it is hard to find mechanics who will work on European cars.

Renting

National auto rental agencies usually allow cars to be picked up in one city and dropped off in another, although often at considerable extra cost (the "drop charge"). Their toll-free numbers allow renters to reserve a reliable car anywhere in the country. Drawbacks include steep prices, high minimum ages for rentals (as high as 25), and credit card requirements. Some national companies are **Alamo** (800-327-9633), **Avis** (800-331-1212), **Budget** (800-527-0700), **Hertz** (800-654-3131), **National** (800-328-4567), **Thrifty** (800-367-2277), and **Dollar** (800-800-4000).

For many local companies, rates often are lower and policies flexible. Some accept cash deposits of $50 or so in lieu of a credit card. Humble companies like **Rent-A-Wreck** (800-421-7253) rent cars past their prime cheaply. Beware: these agencies can have hidden costs (such as high mileage charges). Also, age requirements are still common.

Although basic rental charges run $35-50 per day for a compact car, plus up to 40¢ per mile, many companies offer discount packages. For long distances, buy an unlimited mileage package. Most companies have lower rates on weekends. Drivers' insurance policies cover rented cars, but agencies offer additional, usually expensive, coverage. **American Express** and other credit card companies pay insurance on car rentals charged on the card.

Auto Transport Companies

sometimes can match you with a person who needs a car moved to another city. Give the company your destination and it will tell you when a car will be available. You pay only for gas (usually the first tank is free), tolls, your own living expenses and a refundable deposit. The company's insurance covers any breakdown or damage. Generally, you must be 21 and have a valid driver's license. You also usually must agree to drive 400 mi. or more per day on a fairly direct route; you will be given a time and distance allowance and will be charged for exceeding them. Companies prefer couples and older travelers. Your chances are best for travel from coast to coast or from New York to Miami. **Auto Driveaway**, 310 S. Michigan Ave., Chicago, IL 60604 (800-346-2277) or (312-341-1900), has 90 offices nationwide.

Hitchhiking

in the U.S. is highly risky, although many travelers prefer it. Evaluate the driver carefully. Ask his or her destination before revealing your own. Be especially wary if the driver offers to "drive you anywhere." Make sure you'll be able to open the passenger window or door quickly in case of an emergency. Don't sit between people, and don't let the driver lock your belongings in the trunk.

States prohibit hitching from the actual road (stand on the shoulder), and most states limit it to access ramps and rest stops. Try to keep at least $20 in your wallet to show suspicious police officers you aren't destitute.

Bus Travel

is often the cheapest source of mobility, and can introduce you to people you might never have met on a first-class charter plane flight. For long-range travel you can rely on **Greyhound** or **Trailways.** See our sections on specific cities for bus fares to some nearby destinations. Within specific regions, other bus companies may provide more exhaustive services (for example, **Peter Pan** serves most of New England).

Greyhound sells the **Ameripass,** valid for unlimited travel in the continental U.S. on both Greyhound and Trailways. You can buy passes for seven ($199), 15 ($269), or 30 days ($369) with optional extensions for $10 per day. The Ameripass are valid on your first day of travel. Discounts for children vary according to the age and number of children traveling and the number of adults paying full fares. Foreign students and faculty members are entitled to a discounted Ameripass; see the Getting Around section in Additional Information for Foreign Visitors below. Those with military IDs (both active and retired) can get $159 round-trips anywhere in the U.S.

Greyhound and Trailways offer discounts for specific groups: children accompanied by an adult (ages 5-11 half-fare, 2-4 10% of adult fare, under 2 free); seniors (10% discount Mon.-Thurs., 5% discount Fri.-Sun. except on Ameripass and excursion fares); disabled travelers (companion rides free); and excursion fares (low promotional fares valid for a limited period of time; usually bought 30 days in advance). Fares and discounts change seasonally. See Additional Concerns below.

If you are boarding at a remote "flag stop," be sure you know exactly where the bus stops. Catch the driver's attention by standing on the side of the road and flailing your arms wildly. If the bus speeds on by (usually because of over-crowding), the next less-crowded bus should stop.

You can buy your ticket at the terminal, but arrive early. Ask for info on connections, schedules, and fares, then check the bus schedules and routes to verify the info. When boarding, remember that the company will add a second bus if the first is full. If you decide to cancel, Greyhound and Trailways usually grant refunds. Stopovers are permitted if you want to spend time in cities en route.

You are allowed two pieces of luggage, with a combined weight of up to 100 pounds, for free. Children are allowed half that amount. Identify your belongings clearly, retain your claim check, and watch to make sure your luggage is on the same bus. You usually can take a medium-sized carry-on if it fits into the overhead compartment. Always keep valuables with you inside. Surprisingly efficient air-conditioning brings the temperature down to arctic levels; take a jacket.

Green Tortoise, P.O. Box 24459, San Francisco, CA 94124 (415-821-0803; 800-227-4766 outside CA), runs friendly hostels on wheels. Its proprietors act as hosts and tour guides, running renovated old coaches with foam mattresses, sofa-seats, and dinettes. All prices include transportation, use of the bus at night for sleeping, and tours of the regions through which you pass. Tasty meals are prepared communally. Tours betweeen New York or Boston and San Francisco last 10 to 14 days and cost $279 in either direction plus $75 for food. A "commuter" line runs between Seattle and Los Angeles; hop on at any point. "Loops," which start and finish in San Francisco, go to Yosemite National Park, Northern California, Baja California, the Grand Canyon, and Alaska. The National Park loop hits all the biggies (17 days, $449 plus $121 for food). The Baja trip includes several days on the beach, with sailboats and windsurfers provided for a fee.

Try to use local bus systems to travel within a town. The largest cities also have subways and commuter train lines. In most areas, however, mass public transport remains limited; local buses, while often cheap (fares 25¢-$1.35), are sparse. Call city transit information numbers and track down a public transport map with schedules.

Train Travel

is one of the most comfortable, if slower, ways to tour the country. You can walk from car to car, buy cigarettes, alcohol, and overpriced edibles in the snack car, or shut out the sun to sleep. Travel light; not all stations check baggage and not all trains carry large amounts of it (though most long-distance trains do).

Amtrak (800-872-7245) is not much of a bargain for most intercity trips, although most tickets allow a stopover at no extra cost. Amtrak does offer holiday packages and discounts. Examples: children accompanied by an adult (ages 2-15 half-fare, under 2 free); seniors (25% off one way tickets); round-trips; and circle trips (regional round-trips when returning on a different route). Excursion fares (round-trips during off-peak times) cost little more than the regular one-way tickets, but may not be combined with other discounts, except children's fares.

All-Aboard America promotional fares offer a great way to cover several states. Round-trips between two cities (with two stopovers) cost $189 within one region

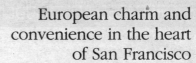

(Western, Central, or Eastern), $269 between two, $339 among three. You have 45 days to complete your pre-planned trip itinerary. The Eastern region is especially generous, allowing, for example, a tour from New York City to Chicago to New Orleans and back on the single-region ticket. Before investing in a ticket, make sure Amtrak reaches all of your destinations, or you may end up spending all the money you saved on local bus or train fares.

When calling for info, use a touch-tone phone Hearing-impaired travelers may use a teletypewriter (800-523-6590; 800-562-6960 in PA).

Bicycle Travel

at an easy pace along rural roads affords a cheap way to get to know a region. Inexperienced bikers might try a few long rides before attempting a full-scale trip. Gathering necessary equipment proves the biggest hassle for a bicycle tour. Look at *Bicycling* magazine for sale prices. **Bike Nashbar,** P.O. Box 3449, Youngstown, OH 44513 (800-627-4227; for catalog 800-945-2453) offers fairly good prices, especially on their own products. It also guarantees to beat the lowest nationally advertised prices. Parts ordered are generally shipped on the same day. Invest in a comfortable bike helmet. See the helmet ratings in the May 1990 *Consumer Reports;* look for a small green "Snell Approved" label, indicating rigorous private testing.

The long-distance cyclist should contact **Bikecentennial,** P.O. Box 8308, Missoula, MT 59807 (406-721-1776), a national non-profit organization that researches and maps long-distance routes across the country and organizes bike tours for members. Its best-known project is the 4450-mi. TransAmerican Bicycle Trail. Bikecentennial also offers members guidebooks, including the *Cyclist's Yellow Pages* ($10 to nonmembers); insurance; maps; route information service; and access to tours. Annual fees are $22, $3 less for students and $3 more for families. **American Youth Hostels, Inc.** (see Accommodations above) also offers complete bike tours at excellent prices.

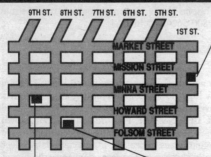

Anyone should be able to fix a bicycle with a few specialized tools. For instructions in the basics of bicycle maintenance and repair, try *The Bike Bag Book* ($3.95 plus $1 shipping), available from Ten Speed Press, P.O. Box 7123, Berkeley, CA 94707 (415-845-8414).

Protect your investment by buying a U-shaped lock ($22-50) made by **Citadel** or **Kryptonite.** For a fee, each company guarantees its locks against the theft of your bike for one or two years.

Accommodations

Too much Schmo money was being spent on hotels. Bo insisted on staying at places with certain stimulating cable TV stations, and Zelda couldn't live in hotels without vibrating beds. This was rapidly draining the wallets of Flo & Joe. "You know," said Flo, "there are other, more affordable lodging alternatives."

"Like what?" gruffed Joe.

"Hostel?"

"No, I'm not. I'm just a little tired. Now, where do you think we should stay?"

"Y?"

"Because I'm asking you, that's why," said Joe.

"Tents?"

"NO! I'M PERFECTLY CALM! NOW GO ON!" vociferated Joe.

"Never mind. I'm sure this is the best way to see the USA on a budget," said Flo, as the kids visited the hotel's private scuba-diving tank.

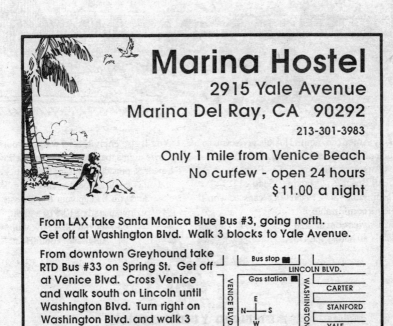

More places.
More fun.

Hostels

are open to everyone regardless of age and offer the least expensive ($10 average) indoor lodgings for those traveling alone, although the U.S. has fewer establishments than Europe. To stay in many hostels, you must be a paid member of **American Youth Hostels, Inc.,** P.O. Box 37613, Washington, DC 20013 (202-783-6161), or 425 Divisadero St. #310, San Francisco, CA 94117 (415-863-9939). Some hostels allow non-members to stay for a small extra fee. One-year AYH memberships for those under 18 cost $10, ages 18-54 $25, over 55 $15, and for families $35. Members often receive discounts on bike rentals and YMCAs. AYH hostels number more than 225, usually well-run dorm-style lodgings. All AYH hostels honor **International Youth Hostel Federation (IYHF)** memberships. The *AYH Handbook,* free with membership, lists and describes all hostels. Hostels are distributed unevenly, with most clustered in the Northeast, the Great Lakes area, Colorado, and the Pacific Northwest—many in out-of-the-way locations.

Some hostels have a maximum length of stay, around three nights. Reservations are useful during peak seasons and in large cities. Many hostels have curfews, sex-segregated rooms and alcohol bans. A few have family accommodations. Guests often share light domestic duties. All require that you buy or rent a sleepsack (two sheets sewn together) to keep the bed clean. Call specific hostels, or look them up in the *AYH Handbook* for details. Not all hostels are AYH—some are members of the **American Association of Independent Hostels (AAIH),** and some advertised "hostels" are actually people renting out basements. We list abbreviations for AYH and other independent organizations, but be sure to check the *AYH Handbook,* since hostel approval is based on frequent inspections.

Hotels and Motels

range widely in price and quality. Although many budget motels preserve single digits in their names, the cellar-level price of a single is now about $25. Nevertheless, budget chain motels cost much less than chains like Holiday Inn that cater to the next-pricier market. Budget chains adhere more to a consistent level of cleanliness and comfort than locally operated competitors. Some even feature heated pools and pay-TVs. But in bigger cities, budget motels usually are inconveniently far from the downtown area. We attempt to list budget inns according to price, safety, and location.

Contact these chains for free directories:

Motel 6 (505-891-6161)

Friendship Inns (800-453-4511)

Super 8 (800-843-1991)

Best Western (800-528-1234)

Comfort and Quality Inns (800-221-2222)

You may also want to consult the *State by State Guide to Budget Motels* ($10) from **Marlor Press,** Contemporary Books, 180 N. Michigan Ave., Chicago, IL 60601 (312-782-9181), or the *National Directory of Budget Motels,* ($5), from **Pilot Books,** 103 Cooper St., Babylon, NY 11702 (516-422-2225).

YMCAs And YWCAs/Bed and Breakfasts/Dorms

If you're planning to stay in a city, don't overlook the **Young Men's Christian Association (YMCA).** Not all YMCA's offer overnight lodgings, but those that do often operate downtown and have relatively low rates (singles around $30, doubles around $45). Rates include use of the library, pool, and other facilities. Reservations are recommended at some YMCAs, though there is a $3 reservation fee. Many YMCAs accept women or families in addition to men. You may have to share a bathroom. Economy packages (2-8 days, $40-270) that include lodging, breakfasts, dinners, and excursions are available in New York, New Orleans, Seattle, Washington, DC, and Hollywood. Write or call The Y's Way, 356 W. 34th St., New York, NY 10001 (212-760-5856).

Few **Young Women's Christian Association (YWCA)** centers provide lodging for travelers—and those that do usually ban dirty, pernicious men from the premises—but they are listed whenever appropriate.

Bed & Breakfasts (B&Bs) and similar guest houses are actually private homes with spare rooms available to travelers. In some areas, they provide the best bargains around, in others, a budget-busting last resort. (In all cases, however, they provide breakfast.) Singles start around $25, doubles slightly higher; rates shoot upward from there. Many B&Bs operate under the auspices of regional associations, which will be listed under Accommodations if individual B&Bs are not. For listings of B&Bs throughout the country, consult *Bed & Breakfast, USA,* ($10.95) by Betty R. Rundback and Nancy Kramer, available in bookstores or through Tourist House Associates, Inc., RD 2, Box 355-A, Greentown, PA 18426 (717-676-3222). Other publications include *The Complete Guide to Bed and Breakfasts, Inns and Guesthouses in the U.S. and Canada,* by Pamela Lanier, from Lanier Publications, P.O. Box 20467, Oakland, CA 94620, and CIEE's (212-661-1414) listings in *Where to Stay USA* ($12.95), which also includes listings for hostels, YMCAs, and dorms. CIEE only lists B&Bs with singles under $30 and doubles under $35, though they allow some leeway in big cities. Since many B&Bs aren't listed in these, check phonebooks and ask travelers.

In New York City, the Y's are your best bed.

There are two YMCA's in the heart of Manhattan, both convenient to everything that makes New York the cultural capital of the world. And there's more good news: At both of them you will find—

- **Clean, comfortable rooms.**
- **Affordable rates—the best value in the city.**
- **Other student guests and young people from here and abroad for congenial company.**
- **Many Y activities available to overnight guests, including gyms, swimming pools and other fitness facilities.**

For reservations in New York and other Y's all over the world, call the ***"Y's Way" Worldwide Reservation System (212-760-5856)***, *or call or write to one of the addresses below.*

The West Side YMCA
5 West 63rd Street
New York, NY 10023
Tel.: 212-787-4400

YMCA OF GREATER NEW YORK

Vanderbilt YMCA
224 East 47th Street
New York, NY 10017
Tel.: 212-755-2410

Please bring this ad with you on check-in and receive a 10% discount from our already low rates.

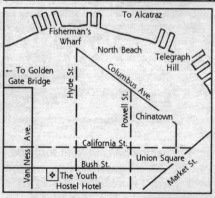

As an alternative to standard B&Bs, contact the **U.S. Servas Committee,** 11 John St. #407, New York, NY 10038 (212-267-0252), an international cooperative system of hosts and travelers. This non-profit organization provides travelers with hosts who provide accommodations for two to three days. Letters of reference and an interview are required. Participation in the program costs $45 per year per traveler, with a $15 deposit on host lists, but travelers and hosts do not exchange money.

Some colleges and universities open their residence halls to travelers during the summer. You may share a bathroom, but rates stay low and facilities should be well-maintained. Contact the school's housing office before your trip.

Camping

gives the best budget alternative for hardier, more adventurous, less monied travelers. Even novices can enjoy tent camping in campgrounds, which cost little (usually under $15 per tent), give flexibility in finding a place to stay, and put you close to breathtaking scenery.

Woodall's Campground Directory ($15; Eastern/Western editions $11; eight regional guides $5 each) covers campsites around the U.S. Also try *Woodall's Tent Camping Guide* ($9.95), and campsite cookbooks. Many bookstores carry the guides, but you can also order them from Woodall Publishing Company, 28167 N. Keith Dr., Lake Forest, IL 60045 (800-323-9076). AAA (800-336-4357) distributes camping information to its members, including a **Kampgrounds of America (KOA)** guidebook. KOA is a coast-to-coast chain of private campgrounds. They are generally more expensive and less scenic than national and state parks and national forests (see below), but usually have uncommon amenities, such as showers, electricity, phones, flush toilets, and sometimes even pools or convenience stores.

Renting equipment might be cheaper for the infrequent camper; check with "outing clubs" in your area. When buying, choose local retailers who give an option to "trade up" for more expensive gear after a brief trial. Many reputable mail-order firms offer prices lower than those in local stores. For the best deals, look around for last year's merchandise, particularly in the fall; tents don't change much, but their prices can go down by as much as 50% after the model "becomes obsolete." Some reliable firms:

Campmor, 810 Rte. 17 N., P.O. Box 997-LG91, Paramus, NJ 07653 (800-526-4784). Name-brand equipment at attractive prices.

L.L. Bean, Freeport, ME 04033 (800-221-4221). Sturdy, high-quality equipment and dedication to customer service. Call for a free catalog. Open 24 hrs.

Cabela's, 812 13th Ave., Sidney, NE 69160 (800-237-4444). Camping, hunting, and fishing supplies.

Recreational Equipment, Inc. (REI), Commercial Sales, P.O. Box 88127, Seattle, WA 98138-2125 (800-426-4840).

Choose your sleeping bag according to the weather in which you'll be camping. Most of the better bags—either down (lighter) or synthetic (cheaper, more water resistant and durable)—have ratings giving the bag's minimum temperature suitability. Expect to pay about $40 for a lightweight synthetic and $150 for a down bag suitable for use in below-freezing temperatures; sub-zero down bags can cost more than $225. Sleeping pads range from $13 for a simple ensolite pad to $60 for the best air mattress.

The best tents are self-supporting, can be set up quickly, and do not require staking. Backpackers and cyclists may wish to pay a bit more for a sophisticated lightweight tent. Expect to pay $225 for a simple two-person tent, $300 for a four-person model. Remember other camping essentials: a battery-operated lantern and a simple plastic groundcloth to protect the tent's floor, a Swiss army knife, toilet paper, bug repellent, calamine lotion, first-aid kit, and cooking gear. Campgrounds often come with grills and allow you to gather firewood for cooking; campstoves, however,

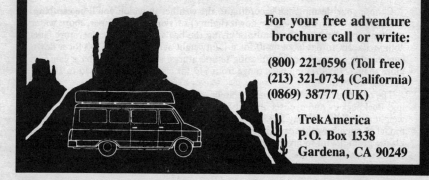

come in all sizes, weights, and fuel types. Coleman's campstoves ($37-80 depending on size, fuel and stove type) are the standard models.

Public Parks and National Forests

offer a convenient alternative to private campgrounds. The U.S. Department of the Interior manages an extensive network of well-organized and -maintained parks, monuments, seashores, historic sites, and scenic rivers. Most **national parks** offer educational ranger talks and guided hikes. Many offer both wilderness and developed tent camping. Others welcome RVs, and a few offer opulent living in lodges. Each area has its own rules; check the visitors' center in each park or contact the regional office or the **National Park Service,** 1849 C Street NW #1013, Washington, DC 20240 (202-343-4747).

Entrance fees range from $3-10 per carload. A variety of passes, however, exempt the cardholder and traveling companions from this fee. Pick up the **Golden Eagle Pass** ($25 per year) at any park entrance, with other passes. Travelers over 62 can obtain the free **Golden Age Passport,** which entitles them to 50% off park user fees as well as free admission. The **Golden Access Passport,** also free, gives disabled persons the same privileges. For info on these programs, call 202-208-4747. For more details about Golden Age discounts see under Senior Citizens.

Plan ahead when visiting the parks. Anticipate summer crowds. Many parks hibernate or offer only limited winter-time services. Reserve lodges months in advance. Since most campgrounds operate on a first-come, first-served basis, arrive early. In camping areas not regulated by a ranger, verify site availability; the most popular parks often leave the "Campground Full" sign up throughout the summer. For a booklet describing less tourist-ridden national parks, write to the Superintendent of Documents (see Publications above). Ask for *The National Parks: Lesser-Known Areas.*

While most **state parks** lack the grandeur of Grand Teton or Yosemite, many provide excellent camping in beautiful settings. You can criss-cross the U.S. and stay at a state park almost every night. Many offer complete facilities and lots of room at prices much lower than those of private campgrounds. Most charge a day-use fee of $2 per person and $5 per vehicle, and camping costs around $10 a night. Some state parks will reserve a percentage of the sites in advance, but generally have vacancies except on summer weekends and holidays. Quality and regulations vary. *Let's Go* Practical Information listings provide information for each state.

National forests offer a worthwhile alternative to the more heavily traveled parks. Often they border a National Park, providing additional campsites and hiking territory. Most offer only primitive camping—no lights, no water, no flush toilets. National forests are rarely crowded, fees nominal or nonexistent. Some areas, such as the Great Plains, have few national forests, and some forests are hard to find. For information, maps, and pamphlets, contact the **U.S. Forest Service,** USDA, 14th St. and Independence Ave. SW, P.O. Box 96090, Washington, DC 20090 (202-447-3706). You can also call (800-283-2267) to reserve a campsite at selected national forests.

Finally, you can call the local Travelers Aid (See Safety and Security above) for info on places to stay in an emergency. The local crisis number (in Practical Information) may also have a list of accommodations.

Additional Concerns

Hiking

Joe wanted to explore the great outdoors, so the four Schmos took a twenty-mile hike. They packed canteens, backpacks, two extra pairs of shoes apiece, a week's supply of rations, and some barbells for working out along the way. It was a long, long walk, and they camped out for a night under the stars. By the time they got back, their feet were blistered, their bodies exhausted, and they had hernias. But they all agreed that hiking was the best way to see the Detroit area.

The title "hiking" covers a wide range of activities, and a hike can be as demanding as you choose. Travel offices, park ranger stations, and outdoor equipment stores will help you plan appropriate hikes. The **Pacific Crest Trail,** snaking through territory from the California/Mexico border all the way up to Canada, and the **Appalachian Trail,** weaving from Georgia to Maine, are only two of a long list of exciting long-distance trails. If you're contemplating a hiking trip, good sources of information include:

American Youth Hostels (see Accommodations above).

Appalachian Trail Conference, P.O. Box 807, Harpers Ferry, WV 25425 (304-535-6331).

Sierra Club, 730 Polk St., San Francisco, CA 94109 (415-776-2211). The club's *Annual Outing Catalog* is available at no cost. They also publish *The Best About Backpacking* ($10.95 plus $3 shipping).

All three groups have local chapters. For topographical maps of any part of the USA, write the **U.S. Geological Survey,** Distribution Branch, P.O. Box 25286, Denver Federal Center, Denver, CO 80225.

General Delivery/Keeping in Touch/Sending Money

Flo's parents Bonnie and Clyde had just made some very fast money in the banking industry, and wanted to send some of it to their daughter. They sent Flo a letter at the post office in a town she'd be driving through. Then they sent her a certified check. These two acts gratified the Schmos, but soon led to the arrest of Bonnie and Clyde by federal authorities. Which confused Flo since, as far as she could tell, Grandma Bonnie and Grandpa Clyde had followed the post office's rules for sending certified checks perfectly.

If you plan to rely on the phone, using a calling card offered by **AT&T** or one of its competitors, such as **MCI** or **Sprint,** is cheaper than calling collect. Visa, Mastercard, and American Express cards also let you charge calls. Be careful, however, to prevent onlookers from seeing your card number; they can, and do, steal numbers and run up huge bills. Calling long distance with coins is incredibly unwieldy, so unless you've just robbed a gumball machine—avoid it.

Western Union (800-325-6000) will deliver a telegram, personally phone it directly to the recipient, or send it through the mail. A 25-word message from New York to Los Angeles would cost $35, $22 and $15, for these respective services.

People back home can send letters through the post office's **General Delivery** service, identical to Poste Restante in Europe. Mail should be addressed:

name of traveler (Viola Lee)

c/o General Delivery

town, state ZIP code (Springfield, IL 62703)The expected arrival date should be marked on the envelope. City introductions in this book give post office locations, as well as ZIP codes, or you can use the ZIP code directory in any post office; large cities may have numerous codes. Post offices close Sunday, and sometimes Saturday. Letters purportedly will be held by General Delivery for up to thirty days. But try to time your arrival to meet your letters. American Express offices also hold mail for cardholders if you contact the specific office in advance.

Travelers with Special Needs

The Schmos had many amusing experiences with the plethoral panoply of special needs. Unfortunately, special needs are a sensitive topic, see, the type of subject a politicallycorrect travel guide such as ours just can't joke about. Who knows, one misplaced attempt at humor could step on any number of phalanges—and all of a sudden we'd have bedlam, with every oversensitive lacto-ovo-vegetarian-rights organization boycotting our vile publication. And that would mean declining profits. So, despite a number of aborted attempts by our culturally imperialistic humor crew, this one section alone will remain Schmoless and humorless. Schmo there.

Senior Travelers

can receive an amazing variety of discounts. All you need is an acceptable ID proving your age (a driver's license, Medicare card, or membership card from a recognized society of retired people will suffice). Pilot Books, 103 Cooper St., Babylon, NY 11702 (516-422-2225) publishes two books that may prove helpful: *Senior Citizen's Guide to Budget Travel in the United States,* by Paige Palmer ($4.95 with postage); and *The International Health Guide for Senior Citizen Travelers,* by W. Robert Lange ($4.95 with postage). *Get Up & Go: A Guide for the Mature Traveler,* by Gene and Adele Malott ($10.95 plus $1.50 postage) is available from Gateway Books, 31 Grand View Ave., San Francisco, CA 94114 (415-821-1928).

The **American Association of Retired Persons** offers its members a tremendous range of services and discounts, many of which aid travelers. Any U.S. resident and spouse over 50 can join for a $5 annual fee. Benefits include group travel programs, as well as discounts on lodging, car and RV rental, and sightseeing. Write to AARP National Headquarters, Special Services Dept., 1909 K St. NW, Washington, DC 20049 (800-227-7737 for membership; 202-662-4850 for special services).

Another organization providing services to those 50 and over is the **National Council of Senior Citizens,** 1331 F St. NW, Washington, DC 20004 (202-347-8800). The NCSC offers hotel and auto rental discounts, a senior citizen newspaper, and use of a discount travel agency, in addition to supplementary medical insurance for members 65 and over. The membership fee is $12 per year for an individual, $16 for a couple or $150 for a lifetime membership.

Elderhostel uses the facilities of over 1500 colleges, universities, and other educational institutions worldwide. Participants in domestic programs spend a week studying subjects ranging from music appreciation to beekeeping at a cost of $270. International programs last two to four weeks at costs ranging from $900-5000 including airfare. The fee covers room, board, tuition, use of campus facilities, and extracurricular activities. Hostelships are available to those requiring financial assistance. You must be at least 60 to enroll and may bring a companion who is over 50; spouses may be any age. For a free catalog listing course descriptions for the current season, contact Elderhostel, 75 Federal St., Boston, MA 02110 (617-426-7788). You can also obtain *Elderhostels: The Students' Choice,* by Mildred Hyman ($15.95 plus $2.75 postage), a guide to the 100 most popular hostels, from John Muir Publications, P.O. Box 613, Santa Fe, NM 87504 (800-888-7504).

Days Inn operates the **September Days Club** for anyone over 50. A $12 annual fee entitles the member and spouse to 15-50% discounts at all Days Inns throughout the U.S. and Canada and 10% off restaurant meals at these locations. Call 800-241-5050.

U.S. citizens and permanent residents 62 and over can obtain a free **Golden Age Passport,** which provides lifetime free admission for the cardholder and passengers in the same car to all U.S. national parks, monuments, historic sites, recreation areas, and national wildlife refuges, in addition to a 50% discount on all national park user fees. Apply in person at any National Park that charges admission. For more info write the U.S. Department of Interior National Park Service, P.O. Box 37127, Washington, DC 20013-7127 (202-208-4747).

For other discounts for senior citizens see Transportation.

Gay and Lesbian Travelers

An excellent source of books geared towards gay and lesbian travelers is **Giovanni's Room**, 345 S. 12th St., Philadelphia, PA 19107 (215-923-2960), which charges $3.50 postage per book in the U.S. All of the following books are available through Giovanni's Room or the address listed under each book:

Gaia's Guide. $12; 9-11 Kensington High St., London W8, England. Annually revised international guide for traveling women, listing lesbian, feminist, and gay information numbers, publications, cultural centers and resources, hotels, and meeting places.

Spartacus International Gay Guide. $28; c/o Bruno Gmünder, Worldwide Advertising Sales, Lutzowstrasse 106, P.O. Box 30 13 45, D-1000, Berlin 30, West Germany. U.S. address: 100 East Biddle St., Baltimore, MD 21202 (301-727-5677). International gay guide for men, listing bars, restaurants, hotels, bookstores, and hotlines throughout the world.

Bob Damron's Address Book. $13; P.O. Box 11270, San Francisco, CA 94101 (415-777-0113). Over 6000 listings of bars, restaurants, guest houses, and services catering to the gay community.

Inn Places: USA and Worldwide Gay Accommodations. $14.95; available from Giovanni's.

The Women's Traveler. $10 plus $4.50 shipping; available from Giovanni's. A travel guide for the lesbian community. Maps of 50 major U.S. cities; listings of bars, restaurants, accommodations, bookstores, and services.

Places of Interest. A series of three books for men ($11), women ($10), and general ($12.50), including maps. Ferrari Publications, P.O. Box 35575, Phoenix, AZ 85069 (602-863-2408).

Wherever possible, *Let's Go: USA* lists local gay and lesbian info lines and community centers. Areas with large gay and lesbian populations include New York City, San Francisco, Los Angeles, New Orleans, Houston, Atlanta, Montréal, and Provincetown, MA.

Disabled Travelers

recently have been able to take advantage of increased vacation-site accessibility. The following books for disabled travelers are available from Twin Peaks Press, P.O. Box 129, Vancouver, WA 98666 (800-637-2256 or 206-694-2462): *Directory for Travel Agencies for the Disabled,* ($19.95); *Travel for the Disabled,* ($14.95); *Wheelchair Vagabond,* ($9.95). Add $2 postage for the first book and $1 for each additional book.

Access to the World: A Travel Guide for the Handicapped, by Louise Weiss ($16.95). Information on tours and organizations. Available from Facts on File, Inc., 460 Park Ave. S., New York, NY 10016 (800-322-8755). The Government Printing Office also publishes relevant pamphlets. If you plan to visit national parks, obtain a free Golden Access Passport at any park entrance entitling you and your family to free admission and a 50% reduction on campsite fees (for address see under Senior Travelers).

All **Red Roof Inns** (800-843-7663) are wheelchair accessible and most have handicapped rooms available. Consult other national motel chains for info (see Hotels and Motels).

Amtrak and all airlines now serve disabled passengers if you notify them in advance. When making reservations, tell the ticket agent what services you'll need.

Ask if there are any restrictions on motorized wheelchairs. Hearing-impaired travelers may use a teletypewriter to contact Amtrak (800-523-6590; 800-562-6960 in PA) and Greyhound (800-345-3109; 800-322-9537 in PA). Bus travel is a feasible and inexpensive option. Greyhound and Trailways have a **Helping Hand Service** that enables disabled travelers to bring along a companion for free; simply show the ticket agent a doctor's letter confirming your need. Both you and your companion receive the standard two-piece, 100-lb. luggage allowance, not counting wheelchairs, seeing-eye dogs, and oxygen tanks. Some major car rental agencies have a few hand-controlled cars; contact them a few days in advance to check on availability at a specific location. Try Avis (800-331-1212), Hertz (800-654-3131), or National (800-328-4567).

Wings on Wheels is the best travel organization for the disabled, providing information and planned tours all over the world. They run a Seattle-based charter bus with on-board wheelchair-accessible facilities, and can arrange "anything for a group, and damn near anything for an individual" at minimal extra cost. They also run White Cane Tours for the blind (with one guide for every three travelers), for the deaf, and for "slow walkers." Contact them at Evergreen Travel, 4114 198th st. SW Suite 13, Lynnwood, WA 98036 (206-776-1184 or 800-435-2288). Send away for their brochures on tourist sights, accommodations, and transportation. For useful guides, write the **Travel Information Center,** Moss Rehabilitation Hospital, 1200 W. Tabor Rd., Philadelphia, PA 19141-3099 (215-456-9600). **Mobility International USA (MIUSA),** P.O. Box 3551, Eugene, OR 97403 (503-343-1284, voice and TDD), provides info on travel programs, accommodations, and organized tours. Membership costs $20 per year. They publish *A World of Options for the 1990's: A Guide to International Educational Exchange, Community Service, and Travel for Persons with Disabilities* ($14 for members, $16 for nonmembers, postage included).

The following organizations also assist disabled travelers:

American Foundation for the Blind, 15 W. 16th St., New York, NY 10011 (800-232-5463, 212-620-2159 in NY). ID cards ($6) and info on discounts; write for an application.

Directions Unlimited, 720 N. Bedford Rd., Bedford Hills, NY 10507 (800-533-5343, 914-241-1700 in NY). Specializes in arranging individual vacations and group tours and cruises for the disabled.

Flying Wheels Travel, 143 West Bridge St., P.O. Box 382, Owatonna, MN 55060 (800-535-6790, 800-722-9351 in MN). Arranges domestic and international trips and cruises for groups and individuals.

The Guided Tour, 613 West Cheltenham Ave., Suite 200, Melrose Park, PA 19176-2414 (215-782-1370, fax 215-635-2637). Year-round travel programs for developmentally- and learning-disabled adults, as well as trips for those with physical disabilities.

Society for the Advancement of Travel for the Handicapped, 347 Fifth Ave., Suite 610, New York, NY 10016 (212-447-7284, fax 212-725-8253). Publishes a quarterly travel newsletter and information booklets, free for members, $2 for nonmembers. Offers advice and assistance on trip planning. Annual membership $45; students and seniors $25.

Whole Persons Tours, P.O. Box 1084, Bayonne, NJ 07002 (201-858-3400). Organizes domestic and international tours and publishes *The Itinerary,* a magazine for disabled travelers. A subscription for one year (6 issues) costs $10; for 2 years (14 issues) $20.

Women Travelers

unfortunately often face dangers above and beyond those of other travelers. To minimize risks, try to appear confident and assertive when under the scrutiny of strangers. Avoid groups of young men when few women are around and always carry enough change for a quick cab ride or phone call. We list emergency numbers, rape crisis hotlines, and women's centers under Practical Information. Never hitchhike alone; even two women hitchhiking together are at risk. Camping alone can be dangerous as well. Try to find centrally located, well-traveled accommodations.

The *Handbook for Women Travellers,* available for £6.95 from Judy Piatkus Publishers Ltd., 5 Windmill St., London W1P 1HF, England (071-631-0710), has additional safety tips.

Vegetarian and Kosher Travelers

Vegetarian travelers can obtain *The International Vegetarian Travel Guide* and *Vegetarian Times Guide to Natural Food Restaurants in the U.S. and Canada.* Each costs $16 plus $2 postage from the **North American Vegetarian Society,** P.O. Box 72, Dolgeville, NY 13329 (516-568-7970).

Kosher travelers should contact synagogues in the larger cities for info on kosher restaurants there. Your own synagogue or college Hillel should have access to lists of Jewish institutions across the continent. *The Jewish Travel Guide* ($11.50 plus $1.50 shipping) lists Jewish institutions, synagogues, and kosher restaurants in over 80 countries. It is available in the U.S. from **Sepher-Hermon Press,** 1265 46th St., Brooklyn, NY 11219 (718-972-9010)

A Once and Future Schmo

The Schmos continued bickering and arguing and fumbling until they got to Cambridge, Massachusetts, where they pahked their cah in Hahvahd Yahd.

"Now where the hell are we?!?" reflected Bo.

"Shut up shut up SHUT UP!!!" philosophized Zelda.

"I will kill you both with my bare hands," pontificated Joe.

"Does anybody want a Spam and peanut butter sandwich?" orated Flo.

Just then, a withered, robed figure approached them holding a red book. He had pale white skin, a hunched back, and the scrunched, glazed eyes of one who has spent hours in front of a computer monitor. But when he spoke, he used a voice imbued with the wisdom of the ages. "I can see by your sunburnt faces, swollen feet, angry scowls, broken down rental car, and general touristic appearance that you have been vacationing without a copy of this." He handed them a copy of the 1992 Let's Go: USA, *and limped off into the sunset.*

The Schmos never found out who that masked man was. But they read the book he gave them, and drew increased strength from it. They found the courage to journey on. Miraculously, the rest of their vacation was cheap and fun.

"We'll never forget that man," cried the joyful children.

Flo and Joe looked at each other and sighed. "Us neither."

And they traveled happily ever after.

Additional Information for Foreign Visitors

Orientation to the United States

The continental U.S. looms large by European standards (3100 by 1800 mi. or 5000 by 2900km), and some areas are largely uninhabited. Except in the Northeast, travel between major urban centers takes hours or even days. The U.S. landscape varies from endless plains to glass-and-steel skyscrapers, from glaciers to deserts. It's best to concentrate travel in particular regions to avoid swallowing the U.S. in undigestable gulps.

To preview what the different areas of the U.S. offer the traveler, scan the cluster of regional introductions after this section. The regions of the U.S. are often as culturally distinct as separate nations; a New Yorker might feel as foreign as an Aussie in Louisiana.

Although you needn't fear a terrorist attack in a U.S. airport, U.S. cities can be more violent and crime-ridden than their European or Asian counterparts. As anywhere, the best advice to foreign travelers in the U.S. is: use common sense. See Safety in the General Introduction for more info. Area-specific safety issues are discussed in the appropriate sections of the book.

U.S. residents tell time on the Latinate 12-hour, not 24-hour, clock. Hours after noon are post meridien or pm (e.g. 2pm); hours before noon are ante meridien or am (e.g. 2am). Noon is 12pm and midnight is 12am; we will use "noon" or "mid."

The Continental U.S. divides into four time zones: Eastern, Central, Mountain, and Pacific. When it's noon Eastern time, it's 11am Central, 10am Mountain, 9am Pacific, and 7am Central Alaskan and Hawaiian. The borders of the time zones are indicated in the map at the beginning of the book. Most areas of the country switch to daylight savings time (one hour ahead of standard) from mid-April to October.

Documents and Formalities

Almost all foreign visitors to the U.S. must have a **passport,** a visitor's **visa,** and proof of plans to leave the U.S. For stays of only a few days, Canadian citizens with proof of citizenship do not need a visa or passport. Mexican citizens with an I-186 form can enter through a U.S. border station, then obtain an I-94 form 25 mi. in from the border. Other travelers will need to apply for visas at a U.S. consulate. International visitors usually obtain a B-1 or B-2 (non-immigrant, pleasure tourist) visa valid for a maximum of six months. Citizens of the U.K., Japan, Italy, Ger-

Only the New York International AYH-Hostel gives you so much for so little, just $18.75* for a comfortable air-conditioned dorm room PLUS a wealth of special services:

- Convenient location, just 1 block from the subway
- 24-hour check-in
- Walking tours, discount tickets to entertainment events and more
- Private garden with volleyball court
- Cafeteria serving breakfast
- Self-service kitchen
- TV lounge and game rooms
- Laundry room
- International student travel store - with discount airfares and travel accessories

For reservations call, fax, or write:

New York International AYH-Hostel
891 Amsterdam Ave. (W. 103rd St.)
New York, NY 10025
Telephone: 212-932-2300   Telefax: 212-932-2574

* For IYHF members; $21.75 more for nonmembers

SAVE $2 ON YOUR FIRST NIGHT

Bring in this book and mention this ad at check-in and save $2 on the overnight rate. Good for 1 person for first night only.

NEW YORK
international
AYH-HOSTEL
891 Amsterdam Avenue
New York, NY 10025
Phone: 212-932-2300

American Youth Hostels
A MEMBER OF THE INTERNATIONAL YOUTH HOSTEL FEDERATION

many, France, the Netherlands, Sweden, and Switzerland—do not need a visa to enter the U.S. They must, however, meet various criteria; they must possess at arrival a ticket to leave the U.S. within 90 days; they must fly on one in a specified group of air carriers. Contact a U.S. consulate for more info.

If you lose your passport in the U.S., you must replace it through your country's embassy. If you lose your visa or I-94 form (arrival/departure certificate attached to visa upon arrival), replace it through the nearest **U.S. Immigration and Naturalization Service** office. A list of offices can be obtained through the INS, Central Office Information Operations Unit, #5044, 425 I St. NW, Washington, DC 20536 (202-633-1900). This advice does not necessarily apply for work or study in the U.S. (see Work and Study below). Separate documentation is required to extend a length of stay in the U.S., also obtained from the INS. An extension must be applied for well before the original departure date.

Foreign students will want an **International Student Identification Card (ISIC)** as proof of student status. These cards entitle the bearer to a variety of student discounts. The ISIC is available at local travel agencies, from the International Student Travel Confederation, from CIEE (see useful organizations), or from **Let's Go Travel Services,** Thayer Hall-B, Harvard University, Cambridge, MA 02138 (617-495-9649). Let's Go Travel also sells American Youth Hostel memberships. The ISIC and the AYH card are available by mail.

Citizens of countries that signed the Geneva Road Traffic Convention of 1949, can legally drive in the U.S. for one year from the date of arrival, providing, of course, that the car driven is registered in the U.S. and that the driver is properly insured. An **international driver's license** may clarify things for a befuddled policeman, but it doesn't change your legal status. Citizens whose countries have not signed the Convention may not drive in the U.S. without obtaining a U.S. license. Most European and many non-European countries are signatories, but check with your national automobile association before you leave.

Come To El Paso...
A Great Way To Discover
The Great Southwest.

Visit El Paso and stay at the Gardner Hotel, an International AYH Hostel. El Paso's 400-plus years of history, dazzling geography and natural attractions, and common border with Mexico make it a perfect stop for people discovering the Great Southwest.

Here are some highlights:

In El Paso
- Spanish Missions
- Franklin Mountains State Park
- 17 Art and Historical Museums
- Tigua Indian Reservation

Near El Paso
- Gila Wilderness Area
- White Sands National Monument
- Hueco Tanks State Park
- Cloudcroft/Ruidoso
- Carlsbad Caverns

In Juarez
- Guadalupe Mission
- Pueblito Mexicano

Near Juarez
- Copper Canyon

Transportation into and throughout Mexico is readily available; buses leave hourly from El Paso.

Call 1-800-351-6024

for information on hotels, restaurants, and attractions. IT'S FREE!

Gardner Hotel/El Paso
International AYH - Hostel
311 E. Franklin Avenue
El Paso, Texas 79901
(915) 532-3661

El Paso

...at the Corner of
Texas and Old Mexico.

**The El Paso Convention & Visitors Bureau
One Civic Center Plaza · El Paso, Texas 79901**

Transportation For Foreign Visitors

Getting Here

The simplest and surest way to find a bargain fare is to have a reliable travel agent guide you through the jungle of travel options. In addition, check the travel sections of major newspapers for special fares, and consult CIEE (see Useful Organizations above) or your national student travel organization—they might have special deals that regular travel agents cannot offer.

From Canada and Mexico

The U.S. and Canada share the world's longest undefended border, easily crossed by U.S. and Canadian citizens alike. (See the Canada General Introduction for details.)

Entering the U.S. from Mexico is a bit more difficult: Mexicans must sometimes have a tourist visa for travel. Contact the U.S. Embassy in Mexico City.

Mexican and American carriers offer many flights between the two countries. Since air travel in the U.S. is relatively expensive, flying on a Mexican airline to one of the border towns and traveling by train or bus from there may cost less. For more info, see *Let's Go: Mexico* or *Let's Go: California and Hawaii*.

Amtrak, Greyhound/Trailways, or one of their subsidiaries connects with all the Mexican border towns. Most buses and trains do no more than cross the Mexico/U.S. border, but connections can be made at: San Diego, CA; Nogales, AZ; and El Paso, Eagle Pass, Laredo, or Brownsville, TX. To drive in the U.S. (see Transportation) you need both a license and insurance; contact your local auto club or the American Automobile Association (800-336-4357) for details.

From Europe

Because of the incredible smorgasbord of flight options from Europe available, flexibility is the best strategy. Direct, regularly scheduled flights are ordinarily far out of any budget traveler's range. Consider leaving from a travel hub; certain cities—such as London, Paris, Amsterdam, and Athens—have competitively-priced flights. The money saved on a flight out of Paris, for example, might exceed the cost of getting to the airport. London is the major travel hub for trans-Atlantic budget flights. Fares to cities only 100 mi. apart may differ by that many dollars. New York is a consistently cheap travel target. Atlanta, Chicago, Los Angeles, Dallas, Seattle, and Toronto, Montréal, and Vancouver in Canada are also competitively priced destinations.

A **charter flight** is usually the most economical option. Departure and return dates must be chosen when the ticket is booked. Changes and cancellations may result in partial or complete forfeiture of the cost of the tickets. Charter companies also reserve the right to change the dates or cost of the ticket, and may even cancel a flight within 48 hours of departure. Check with a travel agent about a charter company's reliability and reputation. The most common problem with charters is delays. To be safe, buy the ticket in advance, and arrive at the airport well before departure time to ensure a seat. A charter flight will, of course, be considerably less swish than a Concorde.

If you decide to take a non-charter flight, you'll be purchasing greater reliability and flexibility. Major airlines offer reduced-fare options. The advantage of flying **standby** is flexibility; standby passengers need only show up at the airport and wait. Standby flights, however, have become increasingly difficult to find. Check with a travel agent for availability. **TWA, British Airways,** and **Pan Am** offer standby from London to most major U.S. cities. Most airlines allow purchase of an open ticket in advance that, depending on seat availability, is confirmed the day of departure. Seat availability is known only on the day of the flight, although some airlines will issue predictions. The worst crunch leaving Europe takes place from mid-June to

early July, while August is uniformly tight for returning flights; at no time can you count on getting a seat right away.

STA Travel is a reliable organization that arranges charter flights; call 800-777-0112 for info, or call the London office from Europe: 44 (071) 937 9971; from the U.S.: 004-41-937-9971. CIEE sponsors two charter services and is another good charter option (**Council Charter** (800-223-7402) and **Council Travel** (212-661-1450; discounts for students and teachers only). Other reliable charter companies include: **DER Tours** (800-937-1234 in the U.S. 44 (71) 408 0111 in London), **Tourlite** (800-272-7600), **Travac** (800-872-8800), **Unitravel** (800-325-2222), and **Canadian Airlines International** (800-426-7000). Many of these organizations have offices throughout Europe. Call the toll-free number and ask for the number of your local office.

Another reduced-fare option is the **Advanced Purchase Excursion Fare (APEX)**. An APEX provides you with confirmed reservations and allows you to arrive and depart from different cities. APEX requires a minimum stay of 7 to 14 days and a maximum stay of 60 to 90 days. You must purchase your ticket 21 days in advance and pay a $50-100 penalty if you change it. For summer travel, book APEX fares early; by June you may have difficulty getting the departure date you want.

Smaller, budget airlines often undercut major carriers by offering bargain fares on regularly scheduled flights. Competition for seats on these smaller carriers during peak season is fierce; book early. Some discount transatlantic airlines include **Icelandair** (800-223-5500; to New York from Luxembourg or London) and **Virgin Atlantic Airways** (800-862-8621; to New York or Newark, NJ from London, Moscow, or Tokyo).

From Asia and Australia

Unfortunately, Asian and Australian travelers have few options for budget air travel to the U.S. Asians and Australians must make do with the APEX. There is about a $100 difference between peak and off-season flights between the U.S. and Japan. U.S. carriers offer cheaper flights than **Japan Airlines.** Some airlines that fly between Australia and the U.S.: **Qantas, Air New Zealand, United, Continental, UTA French Airlines,** and **Canadian Pacific Airlines.** Prices are roughly equivalent among the six, although the cities they serve vary. One compensation for the exorbitant fares is that trans-Pacific flights often allow a stopover in Honolulu.

Customs

All travelers may bring into the U.S. 200 cigarettes, $100 worth of gifts, and all personal belongings duty-free. Travelers 21 or older also may bring up to one liter of alcohol duty-free. You may bring in any amount of currency without a charge, but if you carry over $10,000 you will have to fill out a report form. Travelers should carry prescription drugs in clearly labeled containers, along with a doctor's statement or prescription. Customs officials will often inquire about the amount of money you are carrying and ask your planned departure date to ensure that you will be able to support yourself while in the U.S. For more info, or for the pamphlet called *Know Before You Go,* contact the nearest U.S. Embassy or write to the **U.S. Customs Service,** 1301 Constitution Ave. NW, Washington, DC 20229 (202-566-8195). Remember to check customs regulations in your country to know what you may take with you on your return trip.

Getting Around

In the 1950s, President Dwight D. Eisenhower envisioned an **interstate system,** a federally funded network of highways designed primarily to increase military mobility and subsidize American commerce. Eisenhower's asphalt dream gradually has been realized, although Toyotas far outnumber tanks on the federally funded roads. Even-numbered interstates run east-west and odd run north-south. If the interstate

The 2 Best Kept Secrets In Hollywood

They're tucked away in the "Wilshire Miracle Mile" and Beverly Hills. Two charming and personally managed hide-aways, quietly famous for their high standards and low reasonable rates. ***Now you know the secret too!!!

WILSHIRE-ORANGE HOTEL
6060 W. 8th Street, Los Angeles, Calif. 90036 (213) 931-9533
One block south of Wilshire Blvd., a half block east of Fairfax. Located in a quiet residential community. La Brea tar pits, L.A. County Museum, Farmer's Market, restaurants, buses, and Beverly Hils within walking distance. Many Europeans, Asians, "soon to be stars," relocating entrepreneur set-up bachelor/office. All rooms have color T.V. and refrigerators. Rates from $45.00 (shared bath with one other room), private bath from $54.00 single/double occupancy. $10.00 each additional person. Street parking.

HOTEL DEL FLORES
409 N. Crescent Drive, (P.O. Box 5708) Beverly Hills, Calif. 90210 (213) 274-5115
Splendid location, three blocks east of Rodeo Drive. Twenty-four hour switchboard with phones in each room. Color T.V. Shared bath from $45.00, rates for private bath start from $55.00 single/double occupancy. $10.00 for each additional person. Refrigerators and microwave available. Central to buses, restaurants, and shopping. Area where stars -past, present, and future- live, dine, and play. Metered street parking 8 a.m. to 6 p.m. Weekly and monthly rate available.

To confirm reservations, send $55.00 –include date, time of day, and number of persons– to one of the **HIDDEN HOTELS.**

The Hidden Hotels

has a three-digit number, it is a branch of another interstate (i.e., I-285 is a branch of I-85), often a bypass skirting around a large city. An even digit in the hundred's place means the branch will eventually return to the main interstate; an odd digit means it won't. North-south routes begin on the West Coast with I-5 and end with I-95 on the East Coast. I-10 stretches across the entire southern border, from Los Angeles along the coast of the Gulf of Mexico to Jacksonville, FL. The northern-most east-west route is I-94. The national speed limit of 55mph has been raised to 65mph in some areas, and is enforced to varying degrees in different states (usually the western states are less anal-retentive about these things). The main routes through most towns are **U.S. highways,** which are often locally referred to by non-numerical names. **State highways** are usually less heavily traveled and may lead travelers to American farming communities. U.S. and state highway numbers don't follow any particular numbering pattern. And yes, Americans drive on the right (as opposed to correct) side.

Airlines and bus and train companies offer discounts to foreign visitors within the U.S. **Greyhound/Trailways** offers an **International Ameripass** for foreign students and faculty members. The passes are sold primarily in foreign countries, but may be purchased for a slightly higher price in New York, Los Angeles, San Francisco, or Miami. Prices are $69 for a 4-day pass ($80 in the U.S.) $125 for a 7-day pass ($140 in the U.S.), $199 for a 15-day pass ($215 in the U.S.), and $250 for a 30-day pass. These passes may be extended at the time of purchase for $15 per day. To obtain a pass, you need a valid passport and proof of eligibility. If you are *not* a student or a faculty member, the regular rates for passes are: $199 for seven days, $269 for 15 days, and $369 for 30 days, with optional extensions of $10 per day. Call a local Greyhound for info or to request their *Visit USA Vacation Guide,* which details services for foreigners.

Amtrak's **USA Rail Pass,** similar to the Eurailpass, entitles foreigners to unlimited travel anywhere in the U.S. A 45-day pass costs $299. If you plan to travel only in one particular area, purchase a Regional Rail Pass instead. Each pass serves a single region, including Eastern, Far Western, and Florida ($179 each), and Western ($229). All USA Rail Passes for kids ages 2-11 are half-fare. With a valid passport, you can purchase the USA Rail Pass outside the country or in New York, Boston, Washington D.C., Miami, Los Angeles, or San Francisco. Check with travel agents or Amtrak reps in Europe. If you're already in the U.S. and would like more info, call Amtrak (800-872-7245). Passes are not a bargain unless you plan to make a number of stops. Also remember that many U.S. cities are not accessible by train.

Many major U.S. airlines in the U.S. offer special **Visit USA** air passes and fares to foreign travelers. You purchase these passes outside the U.S., paying one price for a certain number of "flight coupons" good for one flight segment on an airline's domestic system within a certain time period. Some cross-country trips may require two segments. "Visit USA" discount fares are available for specific flights within the U.S. if purchased in one's own country. Most airline passes can be purchased only by those living outside the Western Hemisphere, though some are available for Canadians, Mexicans, and residents of Latin America if they purchase a pass from a travel agent located at least 100 mi. from the U.S. border. "Visit USA" fares are marked by a maze of restrictions and guidelines; consult a travel agent concerning the logistics of these discounts.

Alcohol and Drugs

The U.S. has a long history of trying to curb its citizens' alcohol intake. Some areas of the country are "dry," meaning they do not permit the sale of alcohol at all, and others do not permit selling it on Sundays. Wherever you are, you must be 21 years old to purchase alcoholic beverages legally. If you look under 30, be prepared to show a photo ID (preferably a driver's license or other valid government-issued document). A few select states go so far as to require that you possess a "liquor license" to make a purchase.

Also, many drugs that are legal for either medicinal or recreational purposes in some countries may be illegal in the U.S. See, we have this Drug War going on here. Possession of drugs such as marijuana, cocaine, and most opiate derivatives is punishable by stiff fines and/or imprisonment (unless you are a C.I.A. operative working out of Latin America)—and for students receiving federal aid to attend U.S. universities it could mean termination of all assistance. Check with the U.S. Customs Service (see Customs) about any questionable chemicals before they check you.

Currency and Exchange

U.S. currency uses a decimal system based on the **dollar** ($) or "buck." Paper money ("bills") comes in six denominations, all the same size, shape, and dull green color. The bills now issued are $1, $5, $10, $20, $50, and $100. You occasionally may see denominations of $2 and $500, which are no longer printed but are still acceptable as currency. Some restaurants and retail stores may not accept $50 bills and higher. The dollar divides into 100 cents (¢); fractions such as 35 cents can be represented as 35¢ or $.35. The penny (1¢), the nickel (5¢), the dime (10¢), and the quarter (25¢, "2 bits") are the most common coins. The half-dollar (50¢) and the one-dollar coins (which come in two sizes) are rare but valid currency.

It is nearly impossible to use foreign currency in the U.S., and in some parts of the country you may have trouble exchanging your currency for U.S. dollars. Convert your currency infrequently and in large amounts to minimize fees. Buy U.S. traveler's checks, which can be used in lieu of cash (when an establishment specifies "no checks accepted" this usually refers to checks drawn on a bank account). You may want to bring a U.S.-affiliated credit card such as Interbank (MasterCard), Barclay Card (Visa), or American Express. For more information see Money above.

Personal checks can be very difficult to cash in the U.S; most banks require that you have an account with them to cash one.

Sales tax is the U.S. equivalent of the Value Added Tax. Expect to pay 5-8% depending on the item and place. In addition, a tip of 15-20% is expected by restaurant servers and taxi drivers, although restaurants sometimes include this service charge in the bill. Tip hairdressers 10%, and bellhops at least $1 per bag.

Mail and Telephones

Post offices are usually open weekdays from 8am to 5pm, Saturday from 8am to noon. All close on national holidays. A postcard mailed within the U.S. (including Alaska and Hawaii) or to Mexico costs 19¢; a letter generally costs 29¢. Canada has a special rate of 22¢ for a postcard and 30¢ for a letter. Postcards mailed overseas cost 40¢, letters 50¢; aerograms are available at the post office for 45¢. Mail within the country takes between a day and a week to arrive; to northern Europe, South America and Asia, a week to 10 days; to southern Europe, North Africa, and the Middle East, two to three weeks. Large city post offices offer **International Express Mail** service in case you need to mail something to a major European city in 40 to 72 hours.

The U.S. divides into postal zones, each with a five-digit **ZIP code** particular to a region, city, or part or a city. The normal form of address is as follows:

Ernst Blofeld (name)

S.P.E.C.T.R.E. (name of organization optional)

007 Thunderball Rd. (street address, apartment number)

Somerville, MA 02143 (city, state abbreviation, ZIP)

USA (country)

The leading telephone company **AT&T** competes with other long-distance phone companies such as **MCI** and **Sprint.** Telephone numbers in the U.S. consist of a three-digit area code, a three-digit exchange, and a four-digit number, written as 617-123-4567. Normally only the last seven digits are used in a **local call. Non-local calls** within the area code from which you are dialing require a "1" before the last seven digits, while **long-distance calls** require a "1" and the area code. Canada and much of Mexico share the same system. The area code "800" indicates a toll-free number. For info on specific toll-free numbers, call the toll-free meta-line at 800-555-1212. Be careful—the age of info technology has recently given birth to the "900" number, which is staggeringly expensive to call. Average charges range from $2-5 for the first minute, with a smaller charge for each additional minute. With these lines, you can have phone sex, make donations to political candidates, or listen to the voices of New Kids on the Block—at great cost.

The local telephone directory contains most of the information you will need about telephone usage, including area codes for the U.S., many foreign country codes, and rates. To obtain local phone numbers or area codes of other cities, call directory assistance (411 within your area code, 1-area code-555-1212 elsewhere). From any phone you can reach the **operator** by dialing "0." The operator will help you with rates or other info and give assistance in an emergency. You can reach directory assistance and the operator without payment from any pay phone.

In order to place a call, you must first hear the dial tone, a steady tone meaning that the line is clear. After dialing, you usually will hear an intermittent bell sound that indicates that the call has gone through. You might also hear a "busy signal," which is a rapidly repeating buzzing tone signifying that the person you have called is on the line with someone else.

Pay phones are plentiful, most often stationed on street corners and in public areas. Be wary of private, more expensive pay phones—the rate they charge per call will be printed on the phone. Put your coins (10-25¢ for a local call depending on the region) into the slot and listen for a dial tone before dialing. If there is no answer or if you get a busy signal, you will get your money back, although connecting with answering machines will prevent this. To make a long-distance direct call, dial the number. An operator will tell you the cost of the first three minutes; deposit that amount in the coin slot. The operator will cut in when you must deposit more money. Generally, long-distance rates go down after 5pm on weekdays and are further reduced between 11pm and 8am and on weekends. Look for new pay phones by competitor companies which charge 25¢ for one minute anywhere in the continental U.S.

If you don't have lots of change, you may want to make a **collect call** (i.e. charge the call to the recipient). To do this, first dial "0" and the area code and number you wish to reach; then after a tone, another "0". An operator will cut in and ask to help you. Tell the operator that you wish to place a collect (also known as "station-to-station") call from (your name). You might opt for a **person-to-person** call, which is more expensive than collect. To call person-to-person, you must also give the recipient's name to the operator, but will only be charged if the person you want to speak with is there. With a collect call, another party may accept the charges, and the money will be wasted if the recipient is not at that number. In some areas, particularly rural ones, you may have to tell the operator what number you wish to reach, and she or he will put the call through for you.

You can place **international calls** from any telephone. To call direct, dial the international access code (011), the country code, the city code, and the local number. Country codes may be listed with a zero in front (e.g. 033), but when using 011, drop the zero (e.g. 011-33). In some areas you will have to give the operator the number and he or she will place the call. To find out the cheapest time to call various countries in Europe or the Middle East, call the operator (dial "0"). The cheapest time to call Australia and Japan is between 3am and 2pm, New Zealand 11pm and 10am.

For info on the K.I.T. Toll Saver, a special long-distance deal that allows foreigners to buy flat-rate long-distance credit for calls to anywhere in the world, contact Tad Freidberg at 305-531-0051, or by mail at the Sol Y Mar (see Ft. Lauderdale accommodations).

If a telephone call is impossible, cabling may be the only way to contact someone quickly overseas. A short message will usually reach its destination by the following day. For most overseas telegrams, Western Union charges a base fee of $7, in addition to 40-60¢ per word, including name and address. Exact charges depend on the length of the message and its destination. Call Western Union (800-325-6000) to check rates to specific countries.

Holidays

Government agencies, post offices, and banks usually close on the following holidays. Businesses may also change their hours: **New Year's Day,** January 1; **Martin Luther King, Jr.'s Birthday** the third Monday in January; **Presidents' Day,** the third Monday in February; **Memorial Day,** the last Monday of May and unofficial start of summer; **Independence Day,** the "4th of July"; **Labor Day,** the first Monday of September and unofficial end of summer; **Columbus Day,** the second Monday in October. **Thanksgiving,** the fourth Thursday of November; and **Christmas,** December 25. This list is *not* all-inclusive; very obscure historical events sometimes serve as justification for regional vacation days.

Measurements

The British system of weights and measures is still in use in the U.S., despite recent efforts to convert to the metric system. The following is a list of U.S. units and their metric equivalents:

1 inch = 25 millimeters
1 foot = 0.30 meter
1 yard = 0.91 meter
1 mile = 1.61 kilometers
1 ounce = 25 grams
1 pound = 0.45 kilogram
1 quart(liquid) = 0.94 liter

12 inches equal 1 foot; 3 feet equal 1 yard; 5280 feet equal 1 mile. 16 ounces (weight) equal 1 pound (abbreviated as 1 lb.). 8 ounces (volume) equal 1 cup; 2 cups equal 1 pint; 2 pints equal 1 quart; and 4 quarts equal 1 gallon.

Electric outlets throughout the U.S., Canada, and Mexico provide current at 117 volts, 60 cycles (Hertz). Since European voltage is usually 220, you might need a transformer in order to operate your non-American appliances, including electric systems for disinfecting contact lenses. Transformers are sold to convert specific wattages (e.g. 0-50 watt transformers for razors and radios; larger watt transformers for hair dryers and other appliances). You might also need an adapter to change the shape of the plug; American plugs usually have 2 rectangular prongs; plugs for larger appliances often have a third prong.

The U.S. uses the Fahrenheit temperature scale rather than the Centigrade (Celsius) scale. To convert Fahrenheit to approximate Centigrade temperatures, subtract 32, then divide by 2. Or, just remember that 32° is the freezing point of water, 212° its boiling point, normal human body temperature is 98.6°, and room temperature hovers around 70°.

Work and Study For Foreign Visitors

Working in the U.S. with only a B-2 visa is grounds for deportation. Before a work visa can be issued to you, you must present the U.S. Consulate in your country with a letter from a U.S. employer stating that you have been offered a job and that you have a permanent residence in your home country. The letter must mention you by name and briefly outline the job, its salary, and its employment period. Alternatively, a U.S. employer can obtain an H visa for you (usually an H-2, which means that qualified applicants for the position are not available in the U.S.). For more specific visa info, write the Consumer Information Center, Department 459X, Pueblo, CO 81009 (719-948-3334). Send 50¢ for a brochure on visas for foreigners.

Student travel organizations such as CIEE and its affiliates often assist students in securing work visas. Some have work-exchange programs, while others hire individuals who speak English fluently to act as leaders for tour groups. The CIEE publishes a useful book called *Volunteer! The Comprehensive Guide to Voluntary Service in the U.S. and Abroad* ($6.95 plus $1 postage).

The **Association for International Practical Training (AIPT)** is the umbrella organization for the **International Association for the Exchange of Students for Technology Experience.** AIPT offers on-the-job training in the U.S. to foreign students in agriculture, engineering, architecture, computer science, mathematics, and the sciences. You should have completed two (and preferably three) years in a technical major. You must apply by December 10 for summer placement, six months in advance for other placement. Contact AIPT at IAESTE Trainee Program c/o AIPT 10400 Little Patuxent Pkwy Suite 250 Columbia MD 21044-3510 (301-997-2200 or fax: 301-992-3824). The government agency in your own country that handles educational exchanges and visits to other countries should be able to provide local contacts for suitable organizations.

If you are studying in the U.S., you can take any on-campus job once you have applied for a social security number. Check with your student employment office for job listings and requirements for work clearance. The government has recently begun a strict campaign to prohibit businesses from hiring employees without an H-visa; don't expect leniency. Before being hired, all job applicants must obtain an

I-9 validation, usually processed by the potential employer, by showing proof of U.S. citizenship or a work permit.

Other organizations worth contacting include:

American Friends Service Committee, 1501 Cherry St., Philadelphia, PA 19102 (215-241-7295). Conducts volunteer work camps in Mexican villages. Fluency in Spanish required. $700 participation fee plus travel costs. Can also supply information on volunteer work camps in other regions.

Archaeological Institute of America, 675 Commonwealth Ave., Boston, MA 02215 (617-353-9361). Publishes the *Archaeological Fieldwork Opportunities Bulletin,* available every January.

Central Bureau for Educational Visits and Exchanges, Seymour Mews House, Seymour Mews, London W1H 9PE, England ((071) 486 5101 or fax: (071) 935 5741) Publishes *Working Holidays* (£8.80 including U.K. postage, £10.65 including postage to mainland Europe, £15.85 including airmail postage worldwide).

International Volunteer Service. address: Rte. 2, c/o Innisfree village P.O. Box 506, Crozet, VA 22932 (804-823-1826). Arranges placement in workcamps for young people over 15. In order to avoid placement fees, write to UNESCO's **Coordinating Committee for International Voluntary Service (CCIVS),** 1, rue Miollis, 75105 Paris. They publish a listing of *Workcamp Organizers.*

Volunteers for Peace, 43 Tiffany Rd., Belmont, VT 05730 (802-259-2759). Publishes an annual *International Workcamp Directory* ($10 postpaid, 112 pp) and a free newsletter.

Foreigners who wish to study in the U.S. must apply for either an **F-1 visa** (for exchange students) or a **J-1 visa** (for full-time students enrolled in a degree-granting program). To obtain a J-1, you must fill out an IAP 66 eligibility form, issued by the program in which you will enroll. Neither the F-1 nor J-1 visa specifies any expiration date; instead they are both valid for the "duration of stay," which includes the length of your particular program and a brief grace period thereafter. In order to extend a student visa, fill out an I-538 form. Requests to extend a visa must be submitted 15 to 60 days before the original departure date. Many foreign schools—and most U.S. colleges—have offices that give advice and information on study in the U.S.

Admission offices at almost all U.S. institutions accept applications directly from international students. If English is not your first language, you will generally be required to pass the **Test of English as a Foreign Language and Test of Spoken English (TOEFL/TSE),** administered in many countries. For more info, contact the TOEFL/TSE Application Office, P.O. Box 6155, Princeton, NJ 08541 (609-921-9000).

One excellent info source is the **Institute of International Education (IIE),** which administers many educational exchange programs in the U.S. and abroad. IIE prints *English Language and Orientation Programs in the United States* which describes language and cultural programs (1988 edition $21.95 plus $3 shipping). Contact IIE, 809 United Nations Plaza, New York, NY 10017 (212-883-8200). They are also available through local Fulbright Commission offices, private counseling agencies, or the U.S. International Commission Agency offices in U.S. embassies.

Useful Organizations

When planning your trip, you might contact the **United States Travel and Tourism Administration**—with branches in Australia, Canada, France, Italy, Japan, Mexico, the Netherlands, the U.K. and Germany—which provides abundant free literature. If you can't find the address for the branch in your country, write to the U.S. Travel and Tourism Administration, Department of Commerce, 14th and Constitution Ave. NW, Washington, DC 20230 (202-377-4003). You may also want to write to the tourist offices of the states or cities you'll be visiting (see Practical Information listings). Wherever you write, the more specific your inquiry, the better your chances of getting the information you need. Once you arrive, visit local tourist information centers.

Extremely useful to foreign travelers, the **Council on International Educational Exchange (CIEE)** has affiliates overseas that sell travel literature, hostel cards, and charter airline tickets. Services include issuing the ISIC (see Documents below), the *Student Travel Catalog* ($1 postage), and a publication with accommodations listings, entitled *Where to Stay USA* ($11). They also run **Council Travel,** a budget international travel service. Write to CIEE at 205 E. 42nd St., New York, NY 10017 (800-223-7402 charter flights only; 212-661-1450 for Council Travel; or 212-661-1414), or contact their other offices in Paris, Tokyo, Madrid, and W. Germany.

The **International Student Travel Confederation (ISTC),** of which the CIEE is a member, is a godsend for European students. It arranges charter flights and discount air fares, provides travel insurance, issues a plastic ISIC card, and sponsors the Student Air Travel Association for European students. Write for their Student Travel Guide at ISTC, Weinbergstrasse 31, CH-8006 Zurich, Switzerland (tel. (411) 262 29 96). ISTC has affiliated offices in other countries as well. In Canada, write to **Travel CUTS** (Canadian University Travel Services Limited), 187 College St., Toronto, Ont. M5T 1P7 (416-979-2406). In the U.K., write to London Student Travel, 52 Grosvenor Gardens, London WC1 (tel. (071) 730 34 02).In Australia, contact SSA/STA, 220 Faraday St., Carlton, Melbourne, Victoria 3053 (tel. (03) 347 69 11).

The **Federation of International Youth Travel Organizations (FIYTO)** issues the **International Youth Card (IYC)** to anyone under 26, as well as a free catalog that lists special services and discounts for IYC and ISIC cardholders. Write or call Islands Brygge 81, Copenhagen S, DK 2300 Denmark (tel. (31) 54 60 80).

STA Travel, based in the U.K., has over 100 offices worldwide to help you arrange discounted overseas flights. In the U.S., call 800-777-0112 or write to 7202 Melrose Ave., Los Angeles, CA 90046. Abroad, write to 74 and 86 Old Brompton Rd., London SW7 3LQ, England, or call (071) 937 99 21 for flights to North America.

If you wish to stay in a U.S. home during your vacation, many organizations can help you. The **Experiment in International Living** coordinates homestay programs for international visitors wishing to join a U.S. family for 3-4 weeks. Visitors over 14 live with host families. Homestays are arranged for all times of the year. For the appropriate address in your country, write to the U.S. Headquarters, P.O. Box 676, Kipling Rd., Brattleboro, VT 05302 (800-451-4465 or 802-257-7751). The **Institute of International Education (IIE)** publishes their "Homestay Information Sheet" listing many homestay programs for foreign visitors. Write to them at 809 United Nations Plaza, New York, NY 10017 (212-883-8200). See Accommodations above for information on **Servas,** a similar international travel organization, which coordinates short (2-3 day) homestays.

The Regions of the United States

Dividing the United States into a series of "regions" is a silly task, arbitrary to the point of being useless. Every state is its own region, filled with its own "diversity," as travel guides are excessively wont to point out. Neither economic nor climatic nor ethnic differentiation follows cozy "regional" lines. Most of the regions devised—Great Lakes states, Mid-Atlantic states, Southeastern states—are the result of little more than someone drawing circles on a map and pigeonholing each state in its respective parking space. Because of this, states in *Let's Go: USA* are ordered alphabetically for easy reference, rather than by regions.

However, a few of the regions do have important factors in common. And the arbitrariness of a regional label can sometimes have quite tangible results when decision-makers operate with those arbitrary labels in mind. To the extent gross regional generalizations will help you, here they are.

The Great Lakes

region is generally defined as all states (MN, WI, IL, MI, NY, OH, IA, IN) bordering one of the five Great Lakes. Of course, these same states often are plunked into categories such as the Midwest or the Mid-Atlantic states as well; only Michigan holds an undisputed Great Lakes title.

The presence of so much wilderness and so much water makes the region a strong draw for the hostel-and-campground crowd. As such, the Lakes region stands out as the only area in the central U.S. well-served by **youth hostels.** These hostels tend to lie near established bike trails and access points to canoe routes. Approximately 20 hostels stretch across Michigan from Detroit northwest to the central Lake Michigan shore. Ohio has a well-spaced smattering of hostels, while Minnesota has a cluster around the Twin Cities. Southern Wisconsin has several more. Indiana and Illinois, except for Chicago, are hostel wastelands.

The Great Plains

states (KA, NE, IA, SD, ND, and maybe OK, MO, IL) are known for being flat, agricultural, and sparsely populated—which isn't always true and is about all they have in common. The big highways mostly run east-west, under the presumption most people are passing through from one interesting coast to the other. Don't make the same mistake. These places boast innumerable treasures, from Native-American communities in Oklahoma and the Dakotas to impressive monuments and museums across the stretch. About the only thing this area lacks that the coasts have is beaches and inflationary prices.

The Industrial Northeast

sometimes moonlights as the "Mid-Atlantic States" (OH, PN, IN, NY, MD, DE, NJ, IL, WV). Consisting of just about every northern state not part of "New England," the states in this area enjoyed a long reign as the nation's economic powerhouses—although the shift of economic activity from the Frostbelt to the Sunbelt has resulted in a decline of wealth. Lately, many of these formerly industrial areas have been enjoying a gentrification of sorts, polishing their brass and renovating their colonial sights so that they can rejuvinate the economy with a strong service sector.

Finding reasonably priced **accommodations** in the cities becomes more difficult each year. Older hotels are giving way to luxury conventioneers' inns. Regional Ys are closing residential facilities in many places. Budget hotel chains often skirt the edge of town. **Bed and breakfasts** are sometimes cheaper for longer stays; Philadelphia has the most B&B budget options. In beach areas, look for cottages available on a weekly basis. When in the mood to pamper yourself, consider going to a popular area in the off-season, when rates sometimes drop to one-half to one-third the seasonal cost. In Washington, DC, where "off-season" means every weekend, tickets to area attractions often come with room rental. **Youth hostels** shine bright in an otherwise dismal regional accommodations scene. AYH maintains an excellent chain of hostels in the big cities and a fair smattering on the coastlines.

The Midwest

is a combination of Plains states (IL, MO, IA), industrial northeastern states (IN, OH, IN) and Great Lakes states (WI, MN, MI)—and the label is about as useful as these other ones. Although the states are very agricultural, probably the dominant image for these locations is rust; decaying factories that fueled the United States to greatness earlier in the century but now lie fallow. Of the competing Midwestern stereotypes—"Midwestern farms" and "Midwestern factories"—both are true and false.

If any region can boast the best public universities, the Midwest probably gets the prize. Area universities are paradoxes—both large and respected, successful athletically and successful academically. Whatever distinguishes the big-gun Ivy League schools from universities such as Wisconsin-Madison, Michigan-Ann Arbor, Ilinois and Minnesota, one suspects the difference has a lot more to do with reputation and cost than quality.

Despite the predominant farm and factory mythos for the region, unspoiled wilderness is close by. Although upper peninsula Michigan probably wins in this category hands-down, it is not alone in its impressiveness.

New England

is one of those regions (roughly ME, NH, VT, MA, CT, RI) where the chambers of commerce knew their touristic pigeonhole and played to it. Vacation sites are gauged to give you lots of "history": semi-old buildings, museums, battlegrounds, quaint inns, famous-people sculptures. The colonial theme is big here, since the New England states were among the first in the Union—and because many "historical towns" haven't done anything to warrant your attention since the American Revolution. This nigh-reactionary timbre has wide repurcussions on your vacation experience there. Never known for their cultural diversity, every "rustic" New England town has an Elm Street and a Main Street, a historic Historical Society where a dead President once spent the night, a Town Hall with a town-meeting government, and a nearby Liberal Arts College to preserve the Yankee ideal of higher education.

Browse local bookstores for detailed regional travel guides, or call **New England, USA,** at 76 Summer St., Boston (800-847-4863) for a *New England Travel Planner*. Finding info for your travels is the least of your worries; financing them may prove the greatest. New England, particularly in the wealthy south, offers few budget **accommodations.** Rooms for under $30 are rare. But New England supports no fewer than 29 well-spaced **AYH hostels.** Hostel-like ski lodges in Vermont and Appalachian Mountain Club (AMC) huts (see below) in the White Mountains provide more deals. During fall foliage season (Sept.-Oct.), accommodations prices escalate in Vermont, New Hampshire, and western Massachusetts. You might want to head to the less colorful coast then. For example, fewer tourists hit Cape Cod in fall than in summer, and accommodation prices drop by some 20%. State forests and parks proliferate in New England, and many offer **camping** at low rates ($7-12). But be warned, everything from the state grounds to the tourist attractions slow down or freeze up during the winter months.

Though largely rural, very little of New England (northern Maine excepted) is wild. However, groups such as the AMC still battle developers in attempts to preserve the privately-owned backcountry. The most popular outdoor activities are hiking, bicycling, and canoeing in the spring and autumn, and downhill or cross-country skiing in the winter months. But New England truly shines in fall, when the nation's most brilliant foliage bleeds and burns. The "changing of the leaves," as New Englanders call it, begins at the northern tip in September, completing its cycle around late October in the southern area.

Mark Twain once said that if you don't like the weather in New England, wait ten minutes. Unpredictable at best, the region's weather through March and November may turn particularly dreary. Watch out for black flies, mosquitoes, and swarming greenhead flies in summer, especially in Maine.

The Pacific Northwest

The drive of "manifest destiny" brought 19th-century pioneers to the Pacific Northwest, some of the most beautiful and awe-inspiring territory in the United

States. Lush rainforests, snow-covered mountains, and the deepest lake on the continent all reside in this corner of the country. Oregon's Dunes, Washington's Cascades, miles and miles of the Pacific Crest Trail, and a long, stormy coast inhabited by giant redwoods and sequoias draw the rugged individualist and the novelty-seeking city-slicker alike.

Settled amidst the wildlands of the Pacific Northwest dance cities with all the urban flair of their northeastern counterparts. But unlike New York, Washington, DC, or Boston, the cosmopolitan cities of Seattle and Portland have mountain ranges at their back doors—these are fresh and beautiful communities. The northwestern traveler can hike the Cascade Range by day and club-hop by night, ride Seattle's monorail or a raft down southern Oregon's wild river rapids. For more comprehensive coverage of the Pacific Northwest than can be provided here, please consult *Let's Go: Pacific Northwest, Western Canada, & Alaska.*

The Northwest coastal region remains cool and misty year-round. The densely populated central valleys enjoy a mild climate, with warm summers and rainy winters. The Cascade Range keeps moisture and cool air from reaching eastern Washington and Oregon, where the arid climate resembles that of the Rocky Mountain states.

For info on national parks, contact the **Pacific Northwest Regional Office,** National Park Service, 2001 6th Ave., Seattle, WA 98121 (206-442-0170). The national forest system manages huge expanses of land, including the West Coast's least spoiled natural landscapes, the designated wilderness areas. Reach the **Pacific Northwest Region** at U.S. Forest Service, P.O. Box 3723, Portland, OR 97212. State parks are rarely fully booked even on popular summer weekends. Sites are about $8. All along the West Coast, state parks and forests, especially those by the ocean, offer hiker/biker campsites, where those on two feet or two wheels can camp for $1.

Rocky Mountains

The thousands of towering peaks that have brought the Rocky Mountains their fame shelter spots of unbelievable beauty. Stretching from the Canadian border to central Utah, the mountains hide colorful alpine meadows, forbidding rocky gorges, and relatively unpolluted streams gushing down either side of the Continental Divide. Certain vistas, certain moments of profound silence defy description: don't be surprised if you have trouble squeezing the essence of these "majestic peaks" onto a postcard.

The surrounding states are similarly and grandly spacious. With the whole Rocky Mountain area supporting less than 5% of the U.S. population, much of the land belongs to the public as national parks, forests, and wilderness areas. The stunning Waterton-Glacier International Peace Park lies at Montana's border with Alberta, Canada; Idaho encompasses two impressive backcountry regions and acres of state and national forests; Wyoming and Colorado proudly house Yellowstone and Rocky Mountain National Parks.

Not surprisingly, most residents of the mountain states live close to the land; even in Colorado, the most tourist-laden of the Rockies, agriculture still does bigger business than the trappings of travel. The people of Denver, the only major metropolis in the region, combine big-city sophistication with an appreciation for the area's rich natural endowment. Most other cities are oil towns, ski villages, university seats, or mining towns, leaving commercial centers in something of a short supply. Although acid rain threatens alpine lakes and streams, and dams for the Colorado and Columbia Rivers are proposed every year, the simple truth is that few sections of the high-and-dry Wild West can support big cities. The Rockies most likely will remain eerily empty and relatively unspoiled.

This place is enormous. You can drive for hours through these states without seeing another car; long-time residents think nothing of spending four or five hours behind the wheel in order to do the Sunday shopping. Since switchbacks make up the mountainous roads, a 50-mi. trip can take several hours. The rugged terrain and remoteness of the most interesting parts of the region discourage public transportation. To emphasize the point: If you want to go anywhere, you need a car. Sound brakes and a reliable radiator are essential for successful **car travel.** Take it slow (trapped behind a creeping RV, you may not have any choice), but even with a sturdy two-wheel-drive car you can see almost every famous spot in the Rockies.

The weather in the Rocky Mountains is about as even as the landscape. Winters are invariably tough—extremely cold and snowy—but summers are usually pleasant and warm. Where cold mountain air meets the warm air of the Plains, turbulent weather systems whip up tremendous hail and thunderstorms. The higher mountain passes (9000 ft.) often clog with snow from early October through mid-May. Major highways and interstates remain open year-round.

The high plains rise above 5000 ft., and mountain passes commonly run 8000 ft. above sea level. The thinner air at this altitude means that heavy exertion will tire you out until you become accustomed to the scarcity of oxygen; this usually takes about two weeks. Since less oxygen also means more direct sunlight, beware of severe sunburns. Older cars also may have difficulty accelerating or starting in the morning at this altitude.

Although the nation's growing obsession with all things outdoorsy has made circuses of many Rocky Mountain sights, most of the backcountry is seldom visited. Ask at the nearest ranger station for deserted spots. Better yet, hike into one of the Rockies' little-known ranges, such as the Sawtooths of Idaho, the Wind River Range of Wyoming, or the San Juans of Colorado. Head on up to Glacier National Park and the Canadian Rockies for even more unpopulated beauty.

Most sights worth examining will lie on public land, courtesy of the U.S. Department of the Interior. Access is generally excellent, since both the park service and the forest service maintain well-paved roads throughout their domains. In general, the **National Park Service** manages most areas of truly outstanding natural beauty. The parks now charge hefty entrance fees (generally $5/car). If you plan to visit several, get a **Golden Eagle Passport** (see the General Introduction). The lower-profile **National Forest Service** offers campgrounds in areas spared the throngs of tourists. Camping in undeveloped national forest spots off major roads provides the cheapest way to enjoy the Rockies.

Inquire about the national properties through Rocky Mountain regional offices. The National Park Service is at 12795 W. Alameda Pkwy., P.O. Box 25287, Denver CO 80225 (303-969-2000); send $3 for maps. The National Forest Service office for Colorado and eastern Wyoming is at 11177 W. 8th Ave., P.O. Box 25127, Lakewood, CO 80225 (303-236-9431); for Montana and northern Idaho, the Northern Regional Office, Federal Bldg., P.O. Box 7669, Missoula, MT 59807; for western Wyoming or central and southern Idaho, contact the Intermountain Regional Office, Federal Bldg., 324 25th St., Ogden, UT 84401.

The Confederacy (er, the South)

One quite distinct historical event binds this region together: the Civil War. The "Southern" states seceded from the Union and attempted to form an independent nation, the Confederacy, but were crushed into submission by the United States government. The question remains whether much of this legacy remains. Forget the myth that "the South never forgets." A few remnants of the war do remain: Confederate tourist sites, buildings named after Confederate generals, the Confederate symbols in a few state flags. But most Southerners have no idea when Confederate President Jefferson Davis was born or when any of the major battles (that is, Southern victories) took place.

Now racism is another matter. Southern states, as former slave states, have both higher concentrations of African-Americans and higher concentrations of anti-black prejudices than generally found in the rest of the U.S. But African Americans have been migrating north for many years. The success of the Ku Klux Klan in the Midwest, the slate of black Southern governors with heavy white support, and race-related problems in Boston, New York, and New Jersey blur the seeming regional monopoly on these irritants.

Part of the Civil War was a conflict between the agricultural South and the industrial North. Both labels are slight generalizations, certainly now if they were not then, but the South still has a higher proportion of its population in rural areas than the other regions of the country. The region is also the poorest in the country, although the blame for this may be placed in any number of places—from retarded economic growth caused by the Civil War to the failings of a farming-based economy. To you as tourist, this means cheaper prices but also fewer amenities such as hostels and public transportation that save money on a trip.

With those few similarities aside, very little binds what is called the "South." The Delta states around the Mississippi River basin (LA, MS, AR, MO), the bluegrass states straddling North and South (KY, TN), the Piedmont states on the Atlantic coast (NC, SC, VA), and the Deep South states (AL, GA) all form easily discernable regions. Texas, highly influenced by immigrant Mexicans, is two or three states rolled up into one: the "Southern" state to the east, the desert state to the west, and maybe the Plains state to the north. Florida, shaped by its own Cuban immigration, is several entities itself: cosmopolitan, Catholic Southern Florida; touristy central and coastal Florida; Bible Belt panhandle Florida. Which explains why "Southern historians" and sociologists fight so much over what constitutes "the South."

Southwest

The Anasazi of the 10th and 11th centuries first discovered that the arid lands of the Southwest, with proper management, could support an advanced agricultural civilization. The Navajo, Apache, and Pueblo people later migrated into the region, sharing the land with the Hopi descendants of the Anasazi. Spanish conquest in the early 17th century brought European and *mestizo* colonists to modern-day Texas and New Mexico. European-American conquest of the region quickly followed the Mexican independence in 1821. Begun as a revolt by Mexican and U.S. settlers against Santa Ana's dictatorship, the Texan War of Independence in 1836 led to the Mexican-American War and an opportunity for the U.S. to influence the region. Santa Fe, Nuevo Mexico, became the first foreign capital ever to fall to the U.S.; by 1853, Mexico's beaten government sold the tract of land south of the Gila River that today forms a large part of Arizona and New Mexico.

The legacy of this cultural history still holds throughout the Southwest in the large Hispanic and Native American populations, Spanish and tribal place names, and numerous historical sites. But much of the land retains the tranquility of nature undisturbed by human hands. The lonely grandeur of the desert stretches for miles, and the water- and wind-scored landscape—the cliffs of the Guadalupe Mountains, the gorges of the Colorado and Rio Grande, the redstone arches and twisted spires of southern Utah and northern Arizona—stands as testament to past and present battles waged by erosion.

Try to travel by car, since the Southwest offers no effective substitute. Public transportation serves a few of the cities, but cities are not the reason for venturing to this region. Youth hostels are reproducing, particularly in New Mexico; call ahead or mail in reservations to stay in the more popular ones at the Grand Canyon, Phoenix, Taos, Salt Lake City, and Las Vegas. Many will require an advance deposit to reserve a space.

Travelers can access much of this incredible scenery cheaply and easily since the federal government owns a hefty portion of the region. Well-maintained park service campgrounds dot the region. By all means, gawk at tourist magnets like the Grand Canyon, but also take advantage of the less publicized, less crowded, and more plentiful forest service and Bureau of Land Management (BLM) holdings.

You can wander and camp at will throughout their property almost without cost. Get a free campfire permit at the nearest ranger station before starting out.

The **National Park Service** has two regional offices in the Southwest: the **Southwest Regional Office,** with jurisdiction over New Mexico, Utah, and eastern Arizona (P.O. Box 728, Santa Fe, NM 87504; visitor services at 1220 S. St. Francis Dr.; 505-988-6340); and the **Western Regional Office,** which covers Nevada and most of Arizona (450 Golden Gate Ave., P.O. Box 36063, San Francisco, CA 94102; 415-556-0560). The appropriate **National Forest Regional Offices** are the **Southwestern Office,** Federal Bldg., Albuquerque, NM 87102 (505-842-3292), and the **Intermountain Office,** Federal Bldg., 324 25th St., Ogden, UT 84401 (801-625-5182).

Desert Survival

The body loses a gallon or more of liquid per day in the heat, and water must be replaced. Whether you are driving or hiking, tote two gallons of water per person per day; less is adequate at higher altitudes and during winter months. Drink regularly, even when you're not thirsty. Do not merely drink huge quantities of water after you've become dehydrated—indeed, it may be dangerous. If you're drinking sweet beverages, dilute them with water to avoid a reaction to high sugar content. Alcohol and caffeine cause dehydration; if you indulge, compensate with more liquid. Avoid salt tablets, which shock your system.

Travelers should allow a couple of days to adjust to the climate, especially when planning a hike or other strenuous activity. This warning applies to activity at high altitudes as well as in low-lying deserts. Those new to high-altitude areas may feel drowsy, and one alcoholic beverage will have the same effect as three at a lower altitude. The desert is not the place to sunbathe. A hat, long-sleeved loose-fitting shirts of a light fabric, and long trousers actually keep you cooler and protect you from exposure to the sun.

In winter, nighttime temperatures can drop below freezing at high elevations, even though afternoon temperatures may be in the 60s or 70s. The desert is infamous for its flash floods, mostly during spring and fall. A dry gulch can turn into a violent river with astonishing speed; when camping, try to locate a site well back from moving water.

Those driving in the desert should carry water for the radiator. A two- to five-gallon container should suffice. Drivers should purchase a desert water bag (about $5-10) at a hardware or automotive store; once filled with water, this large canvas bag straps onto the front of the car. If you see the temperature gauge climbing, turn öff the air-conditioning. If an overheating warning light comes on, stop immediately and wait about a half hour before trying again. Don't shut off the engine; the fan will help cool things down under the hood. Turning your car's heater on full force will help cool the engine. Never open the radiator until it has cooled, because internal pressure will cause scalding steam to erupt from it. And never pour cold water on the engine to cool it off; the temperature change may crack the engine block. For any trips off major roads, a board and shovel are useful in case your car gets stuck in sand; the board can be shoved under a tire to gain traction and the shovel can take care of minor quagmires. Letting some air out of your tires can also help you drive free.

Native Americans

Visiting Native-American reservations can either prove an enlightening cultural experience or the imperialistic voyeurism. Avoid the latter by learning about the beliefs, customs, and politics of tribes before you blunder through their territories—considered sovereign areas by the U.S. government. The museums of Flagstaff, the **Pueblo Indian Cultural Center** in Albuquerque, the **University of New Mexico Museum of Anthropology,** Phoenix's **Heard Museum,** and the **Native**

American Folk Art Center in Santa Fe each offer a general background of Southwest Native American life.

Books and museums, however, say little about contemporary tribal life. The overall picture can be bleak; unemployment on the reservations is well above 50%. Although federal law prohibits alcohol on the reservations, wet towns such as Gallup exist just outside their borders and fuel the rampant alcoholism among Native Americans, which combines with wandering livestock to make nighttime driving in these areas very dangerous. Realize as well that reservations are not strictly preservations—many Native Americans live in modern houses, drive trucks, and wear clothes that accord with the image of a Southwestern cowboy.

Despite these drawbacks, the reservations still provide fascinating places to visit. Talk to rangers at national parks and monuments near reservations, who are often unofficial experts on local customs and sights. General stores and gas stations in tribal capitals such as Window Rock are often the best places to find Native Americans who don't mind talking to outsiders. While you may wear shorts on the reservation, avoid tight-fitting or "provocative" clothing. Don't photograph anyone without permission—some residents believe that one's fate is tied up with the artificially-produced likeness. Abide by laws intended to protect customs and rights of privacy; you may be arrested or fined by tribal police when you violate a village ordinance prohibiting non-Native American travel on local trails. Visitors may be deliberately ignored in stores and on roads, particularly by older residents.

Facilities for tourists on most reservations are minimal and overpriced. Camp and picnic if you can; primitive sites are usually free. Many back roads, usually unpaved, are passable only by four-wheel drive.

ALABAMA

Alabama was a popular place for television news crews in the 1950s and 1960s. The African-American battle for civil rights raged here throughout those two ugly decades; journalists could almost always count on Alabama police to provide graphic pictures for national TV of black men getting beaten and black women getting firehosed. Rev. Martin Luther King Jr. shot into national stardom when he took charge of the successful Montgomery bus boycott here. King later led throngs of black and white protestors on a dangerous march from Selma to the Alabama state capital, publicizing the plight of African Americans in this Deep South state. Then in the late 60s and early 70s, Alabama was the launching pad for Gov. George Wallace's "white backlash" campaigns in reaction to African-American advancement.

Of course, these skirmishes were neither the first nor the last race problems to dominate Alabama's social landscape. The Tuskegee Institute, founded in the 19th century by ex-slave Booker T. Washington, constantly struggled with the state's white power structure in its mission to educate African Americans and win them the vote. And today, the Confederate flag still flies over the Capitol in Montgomery.

Nevertheless, to some extent Alabama gets a bad rap. Mobile, on the Gulf Coast, and the more cosmopolitan parts of Alabama's other two largest cities generally escape the negative stereotypes surrounding the state, as of course does Tuskegee. And even so-called "backwoods" Alabama, through its disconcerting conservatism, has preserved a unique rural culture—one in many ways closer to the Anglo society that spawned it than is British culture today.

Practical Information

Capital: Montgomery.

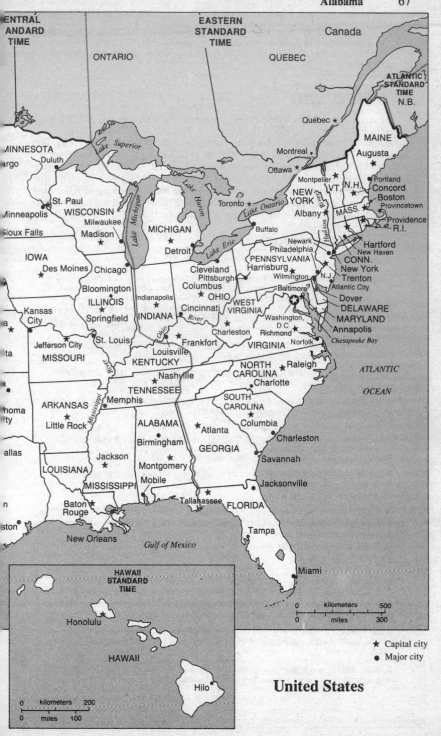

ONTARIO

Canada

QUEBEC

ATLANTIC STANDARD TIME N.B.

MINNESOTA

Lake Superior

Duluth

Québec ★

MAINE

Augusta

argo

Montreal

Fargo

Ottawa

Montpelier

Portland
Concord
Boston
Provincetown

St. Paul

WISCONSIN

Lake Huron

Toronto

Lake Ontario

NEW YORK

VT. N.H.

Minneapolis

Milwaukee

Madison

Lake Michigan

MICHIGAN

Buffalo

Albany

MASS.

Providence
R.I.

Sioux Falls

IOWA

Des Moines

Chicago

Detroit

Lake Erie

Cleveland
Pittsburgh
Columbus

Newark
Philadelphia

Hudson River

Hartford
New Haven

CONN.

New York

Trenton

ILLINOIS

Bloomington

Indianapolis

OHIO

Harrisburg

Wilmington

N.J.

Atlantic City

Kansas City

Springfield

INDIANA

Cincinnati

WEST VIRGINIA

Baltimore

Dover

DELAWARE
MARYLAND

Jefferson City

St. Louis

Ohio River

Frankfort

Charleston

Washington, D.C.

Annapolis

MISSOURI

Louisville

KENTUCKY

Richmond

Norfolk

Chesapeake Bay

Kansas City

Mississippi River

Nashville

VIRGINIA

Raleigh

ATLANTIC

OCEAN

klahoma City

ARKANSAS

TENNESSEE

Memphis

NORTH CAROLINA

Charlotte

Little Rock

SOUTH CAROLINA

Columbia

allas

Jackson

ALABAMA

Atlanta

Charleston

LOUISIANA

Birmingham

GEORGIA

Savannah

MISSISSIPPI

Montgomery

Mobile

Baton Rouge

Tallahassee

FLORIDA

Jacksonville

New Orleans

Gulf of Mexico

Tampa

Miami

kilometers 500
miles 300

HAWAII STANDARD TIME

Honolulu

HAWAII

Hilo

kilometers 200
miles 100

★ Capital city

● Major city

United States

Alabama Bureau of Tourism and Travel, 532 S. Perry St. (242-4169; 800-252-2262 outside AL). Open Mon.-Fri. 8am-5pm. **Travel Council,** 600 Adams Ave. #254, Montgomery 36104 (271-0050). **Division of Parks,** 64 N. Union St., Montgomery 36130 (800-252-7275).

Time Zone: Central (1 hr. behind Eastern). **Postal Abbreviation:** AL

Birmingham

The steel industry built Birmingham, drawing on the coal, iron ore, and limestone deposits which exist naturally in the area's soil. Founded in 1871, the "Magic City" grew rapidly, its population more than tripling between 1900 and 1920. Today, Birmingham's supernatural growth has shot off in different directions. No longer an industrial town, the city's largest employer is the University of Alabama in Birmingham, which includes one of the best hospitals in the U.S., known for its pioneering work in heart surgery. This city of a million people has risen a long way from the days of former police commissioner Eugene "Bull" Connor and his highly publicized racist attacks on nonviolent black protesters in 1963.

Practical Information

Emergency: 911.

Birmingham Visitors Center, 1200 University Blvd. (254-1654). Maps, calendars, and coupons for accommodations. Open Mon.-Sat. 8:30am-5pm, Sun. 1-5pm. Another location at the lower level of **Birmingham Municipal Airport** (254-1640), located east of downtown off Airport Hwy. Open daily 8:30am-8pm. **Greater Birmingham Convention and Visitors Bureau** in the **Chamber of Commerce,** 2027 1st Ave N., 3rd floor (252-9825), downtown. Open Mon.-Fri. 8:30am-5pm. For updated information on city events call **Funline,** 939-3866.

Amtrak: 1819 Morris Ave. (324-3033 or 800-872-7245), downtown. To Montgomery ($11), Atlanta ($30), and Mobile ($53). Open daily 8:30am-4:30pm.

Greyhound/Trailways: 618 N. 19th St. (252-7171). To Montgomery ($15), Atlanta ($19), and Mobile ($40). Open 24 hrs.

Public Transport: Metropolitan Area Express **(MAX),** 252-0101. Runs Mon.-Sat. 7am-6pm. Fare 80¢. **Downtown Area Runabout Transit (DART),** 252-0101. Runs Mon.-Fri. 10am-4pm. Fare 25¢.

Taxi: Yellow Cab of Birmingham, 252-1131. Base fare $2.90, $1.20 each additional mi.

Help Lines: Crisis Center, 323-7777. **Rape Response,** 328-7273.

Post Office: 351 24th St. N. (521-0209). Open Mon.-Fri. 7:30am-7pm. **ZIP code:** 35203.

Area Code: 205.

The downtown area grid system has "avenues" running east-west and "streets" running north-south. Major cultural and government buildings surround **Linn Park,** located between 19th and 21st St. N. on 7th Ave. N. The **University of Alabama in Birmingham (UAB)** extends along University Blvd. and 8th Ave. S. from 11th to 20th St.

Accommodations and Camping

Passport Inn, 820 20th St. S. (252-8041), 2 blocks from UAB. Large, clean rooms, tasteful decor in a convenient location. Singles $30. Doubles $33.

Ranch House, 2127 7th Ave. S. (322-0691). Near busy bars and restaurants; certainly not what its name would suggest. Pleasant rooms with cable TV and wood panellings. Pool. Singles $28. Doubles $32.

Economy Inn, 2224 5th Ave. N. (324-6688). Near some run-down buildings in the middle of downtown. Pool, laundry room. Singles $24. Doubles $29.

Oak Mountain State Park (663-3061), 15 mi. south of Birmingham off I-65 in Pelham. Heavily forested area with 85-acre recreational lake. Sites $8.25 for 1-4 people, with electricity $11.

Birmingham South KOA, 1235 Hwy. 33, (664-8832), 8 mi. south of I-459 on I-65 S. in Pelham. Pool, playground, store. Sites $15, with full hookup $20.

Food

Barbecue remains the local specialty, although more ethnic variations have sprung up downtown. The best places to eat cheaply (and meet other young people) are at **Five Points South,** located at the intersection of Highland Ave. and 20th St. S. Food options there range from pesto pizza with sun-dried tomatoes ($2 per slice) at **Cosmo's Pizza,** 2012 Magnolia Ave. (930-9971), to health-conscious vegetarian lunches and groceries at **The Golden Temple** 1901 11th Ave. S. (933-6333).

Café Bottega, 2240 Highland Ave. S. (939-1000). High-ceilinged and sophisticated, this café serves fresh bread to dip in olive oil and Italian specialties brimming with fresh vegetables and herbs. Marinated pasta with sweet peas and mint $5.25. Open Mon.-Fri. 11am-11pm, Sat. 5-11pm.

Bogue's, 3028 Clairmont Ave. (254-9780). A short-order diner with true Southern fare (cheese omelette and biscuit, $3). Always busy weekend mornings. Open Mon.-Fri. 6am-2pm, Sat.-Sun. 6am-11:30am.

Hickory Pit, Cahaba Heights and White Oak Dr. (967-6004), Cahaba Heights exit off Hwy. 280 S. Specializes in smoky barbecue chicken with your choice of red or white sauce ($4-5). Open Mon.-Thurs. 7am-8pm, Fri.-Sat. 7am-9pm.

Pita Stop, 1106 11th St. S. (328-2748), near UAB and Five Points. Delicious Middle Eastern and vegetarian specialties, felafel sandwiches ($4.25), and dinner plates ($6-8). Open Mon.-Thurs. 11am-9:30pm, Fri.-Sat. 11am-2pm and 5-10:30pm.

Ollie's, 515 University Blvd., near Green Springs Hwy (324-9485). Bible Belt dining in an enormous 50s-style building. Pamphlets query "Is there really a Hell?" while you lustfully consume your beef. Sandwich $1.75, homemade pie $1.50. Open Mon.-Sat. 9:30am-8pm.

Sights

The remnants of Birmingham's steel industry are best exemplified by the gigantic **Sloss Furnaces National Historic Landmark** (324-1911), adjacent to the 1st Ave. N. viaduct off 32nd St. downtown. Though the blast furnaces closed 20 years ago, they now stand as the only preserved example of 20th-century iron-smelting in the world. Concerts, both rock and classical, are often held here at night. (Open Tues.-Sat. 10am-4pm, Sun. noon-4pm. Free guided tours Sat.-Sun. at 1, 2, and 3pm.) The Roman god of the forge, **Vulcan,** Valley Ave. at Hwy. 31 (328-2863), overwhelms Birmingham's skyline as the largest cast-iron statue in the world. Visitors can ride up this tribute to the city's steel industry and survey the city from its observation deck. Vulcan's glowing torch burns red when a car fatality has occured that day, green when none occur. (Open daily 8am-11pm. $1, under 6 free.)

The **Sixteenth Street Baptist Church,** 1530 6th Ave. N. (251-9402) at 16th St. N., was bombed by white segregationists in September 1963, killing four black girls, after a protest push which culminated in Martin Luther King, Jr.'s famous "Letter from a Birmingham Jail." The deaths spurred many protests at the church and in nearby **Kelly-Ingram Park,** at the corner of 5th Ave. and 16th St. N. Today a bronze statue of King stands peacefully in the park; a **Civil Rights Museum** is scheduled to open next door to the park in late 1991.

Facing equally refreshing and urban **Linn Park** is the **Birmingham Museum of Art,** 2000 8th Ave. N. (254-2565). The museum has U.S. paintings and English Wedgwood ceramics, as well as a superb collection of African textiles and sculpture. (Open Tues.-Wed. and Fri.-Sat. 10am-5pm, Thurs. 10am-9pm, Sun. 1-5pm. Closed Mon. Free.)

Antebellum **Arlington,** 331 Cotton Ave. (780-5656), southwest of downtown, houses a fine array of Southern decorative arts from the 19th century. Go west on

1st Ave. N., which becomes Cotton Ave. to reach the stately white Greek Revival building, which also hosts craft fairs throughout the year. (Open Tues.-Sat. 10am-4pm, Sun. 1-4pm. $2, kids $1.)

To learn more about the geology of the area, visit the **Red Mountain Museum and Cut,** 1421 22nd St. S. (933-4104). You can wander a walkway above the highway to see the different level of rock formations inside Red Mountain, and maybe even excavate a fossil or two. The museum indoors has various exhibits on the prehistoric inhabitants of Alabama. (Open Tues.-Sat. 10am-4:30pm, Sun. 1-4:30pm. $1.)

More lively creatures inhabit the **Birmingham Zoo,** 2630 Cahaba Rd. (879-0408), which features special exhibits on different predators and the behavior of social animals. Take zoo exit from U.S. 280 E. (Open daily 9:30am-5pm. $3, kids $1.50.) The zoo neighbors the **Birmingham Botanical Gardens,** 2612 Lane Park Rd. (879-1227). Look for the enormous greenhouse and elegant Japanese gardens, and the giant carp which fill its streams. (Open daily dawn-dusk. Free.)

Entertainment and Nightlife

There ain't much doin' in Birmingham. The historic **Alabama Theater,** 1817 3rd Ave. N. (251-0418), shows old movies on occasional weekends throughout the year. Their organ, the "Mighty Wurlitzer," usually entertains the audience before each showing. (Shows Fri.-Sat. at 7pm, Sun. at 2pm. $4, seniors $3, under 12 $2.) Pick up a free copy of *Fun and Stuff* or see the "Kudzu" in the Friday edition of *The Birmingham Post Herald* for listings of all movies, plays, and clubs in the area.

The **Five Points South** (or **Southside**) area has a high concentration of nightclubs. On cool summer nights many people grab outdoor tables in front of their favorite bars or just hang out by the fountain. Use caution here, and avoid parking or walking in dark alleys near the square.

Music lovers lucky or smart enough to visit Birmingham in the middle of June for **City Stages** (251-1272) will hear everything from country to gospel to big name rock groups, with headliners such as B.B. King and Fats Domino. The three-day festival also includes food, crafts, and children's activities. (Weekend pass $5.) For the hippest licks year-round check out **The Nick,** 2514 10th Ave. S. (322-7550). The poster-covered exterior asserts "the Nick. . .rocks." (Open Mon.-Sat. Live music nightly. Cover $2-5.) For jazz, blues, and even occasional Cajun music, the laid-back **Grundy's Music Room,** 1924 4th Ave. N. (323-3109), actually a basement club, has frequent guest artists. (Open Tues.-Sat. 3pm-until. Call for performance times and cover.) When Grundy's doesn't offer live tunes, you're better off with **The Burly Earl,** 2109 7th Ave. S. (322-5848), specializing in fried finger foods and local acoustic, blues, and sometimes rock sounds. (Restaurant open Mon.-Thurs. 10am-midnight, Fri.-Sat. 10am-2am. Live music Wed.-Thurs. 8:30pm-midnight, Fri.-Sat. 9:30pm-2am.)

Mobile

Mobile (mo-BEEL) is a humid city (the air conditioner was actually invented here) situated on the Gulf of Mexico. Reknowned for its antebellum mansions and the serenity of its azalea-lined streets, Mobile is the oldest of the major cities in Alabama. Named for the Maubilla tribe, a French colony until 1718, Mobile's many influences can also be seen (for free) in the distinct Spanish and English architecture and in the forts around the city.

In many ways Mobile resembles the Mississippi Coast and New Orleans more than it does the rest of Alabama. Beautiful beaches are less than an hour away, and in fact, the first U.S. Mardi Gras took place in Mobile; the celebration still goes on here every year, but on a much smaller scale than in New Orleans.

Practical Information

Emergency: 911.

Fort Condé Information Center, 150 S. Royal St. (434-7304), in a reconstructed French fort near Government St. Open daily 8am-5pm. **Mobile Convention and Visitors Bureau,** 1 St. Louis Center #2002 (433-5100; 800-662-6282 outside AL). Open Mon.-Fri. 8am-5pm.

Travelers Aid: 438-1625. Operated by the Salvation Army; ask for Travelers Services. Lines open Mon.-Fri. 9am-4:30pm.

Greyhound/Trailways: 201 Government Blvd. (432-9793), at S. Conception downtown. To Montgomery (4 hr., $26), New Orleans (3 hr., $29), and Birmingham (6 hr., $40). Open 24 hrs.

Public Transport: Mobile Transit Authority (MTA), 344-5656. Major depots are at Bienville Sq., St. Joseph, and Dauphin St. Operates Mon.-Sat. 5am-7pm. Fare 75¢.

Taxi: Yellow Cab, 476-7711.

Help Lines: Rape Crisis, 473-7273. **Crisis Counseling,** 666-7900. Open 24 hrs.

Post Office: 250 Saint Joseph St. (694-5917). Open Mon.-Fri. 8am-4:30pm, Sat. 8am-noon. ZIP code: 36601.

Area Code: 205.

The downtown district fronts the Mobile River. **Dauphin Street** and **Government Boulevard** are the major east-west routes. **Royal Street** and **St. Joseph Street** are the north-south byways. Some of Mobile's major attractions lie outside downtown. The *U.S.S. Alabama* is off the causeway leading out of the city; Dauphin Island is 30 mi. south.

Accommodations and Camping

Accommodations are both reasonable and accessible, but stop at the Fort Condé Information Center first; they'll make reservations for you at a 10-15% discount. The MTA runs a "Government St." bus regularly which reaches the Government St. motels listed below, but they are all within a 15-minute walk from downtown. For information on the area's many B&Bs, contact **Bed and Breakfast Mobile,** P.O. Box 66261, Mobile 36606 (205-473-2939).

Economy Inn, 1119 Government St. (433-8800). Big beds, clean sheets, a pool and dark-panelled walls. Try to get a ground floor room. Singles $24. Doubles $30.

Oak Tree Inn,55 Church St. (433-6923). In the downtown area. Clean, spacious rooms with wall-to-wall fluffy carpeting. Pool, laundry and free coffee. Singles or doubles $25.

Park Inn, 1500 Government St. at the intersection of Highway 90 and Catherine St. (476-2800). Cable TV, pool and big rooms. Singles or doubles $26.

I-10 Kampground, 400 Theodore Dawes Rd. E. (653-9816), 7½ mi. west on I-10 (exit 13). No public transportation. Pool, kids' playground, and laundry facilities. Sites $14.50.

Food

Because Mobile is on the gulf, both seafood and southern cookin' are regional specialties. As well-known for its atmosphere as for its oysters ($5 for a dozen on the half shell), **Wintzels,** 605 Dauphin St., six blocks west of downtown (433-1004), is covered inside with old anecdotes and sayings. A sign ouside boldly states, "We are famous for absolutely nothing although business is good." (Open Mon.-Thurs. and Sat. 11am-9pm, Fri. 11am-9:45pm.) Business also thrives at the newly-opened **Mayer's,** 278 Dauphin St., two blocks west of Bienville Sq. Friendly service and southern fried chicken at good prices are this diner's specialties. Two pieces of chicken with fries and french bread are $3; also look for daily specials. (Open Mon.-Fri. 7am-3pm.) Farther out of the downtown district, **The Lumber Yard Cafe,** 2617 Dauphin St. (471-1241), serves homemade pizza for $5 and seafood gumbo for $2.

Live bands blare weekends, and the big-screen TV entertains during the week. (Open daily 11am-3am.) **Unknown Jerome's Cafe,** 4400 Old Shell Rd. (343-6796) across from the Jesuit Springhill College, has green and white décor with lots of matching plants and salads ($2-6) and fresh seafood ($7-11). Try the Jack Daniels turtle pie for dessert ($2.50). (Open Mon.-Thurs. 11am-10pm, Fri.-Sat. 11am-11pm.) **Argiro's,** on 1320 Battleship Pkwy. (626-1060), provides both businessmen and sailors with cheap sandwiches ($3-5) and southern specialties such as red beans and rice next to the *U.S.S. Alabama.* (Open daily 6am-10pm.)

Sights and Entertainment

Mobile encompasses four historic districts: **Church Street, DeToni Square, Old Dauphin Way,** and **Oakleigh Garden.** Each offers a unique array of architectural styles. The information center provides maps for walking or driving tours of these former residences of cotton brokers and river pilots as well as the "shotgun" cottages of their servants.

Church St. divides into east and west subdistricts. The homes in the venerable **Church Street East District,** showcase popular U.S. architectural styles of the mid-to late-19th century, including Federal, Greek Revival, Queen Anne, and Victorian. While on Church St., be sure and pass through the **Spanish Plaza,,** Hamilton and Government St., which honors Mobile's sibling city, Malaga, Spain, while recalling Spain's early presence in Mobile. Also of interest in this area is the **Christ Episcopal Church,** 115 S. Conception St. (433-1842), opposite the tourist office at Fort Condé. Dedicated in 1842, the church contains beautiful German, Italian, and Tiffany stained glass windows.

In the **DeToni Historical District,** north of downtown, tour the tastefully restored **Richards-DAR House,** 256 North Joachim St. (434-7320), an award-winning example of antebellum Italianate architectural style. On slow days, the staff may invite you in for tea and cookies. (Open Tues.-Sat. 10am-4pm, Sun. 1-4pm. Tours $3, kids $1.) Brick townhouses with wrought-iron balconies fill the rest of the district.

Words cannot describe how vacant the **Old Dauphin Way** area is today. Once a busy residential area, it seems that now there are more parking lots per square mile than anything else. Attempts at revitalization, with new restaurants and club opening in the Victorian buildings, will hopefully bring new life to the area.

One of the most elegant buildings in Mobile is **Oakleigh,** 350 Oakleigh Place (432-1281) off Government St., with a cantilevered staircase and enormous windows that open onto all the balconies upstairs. Falling away from downtown, take a left on Roper St. Inside, a museum contains furnishings of the early Victorian, Empire, and Regency periods. (Open Mon.-Sat. 10am-4pm, Sun. 2-4pm. Tours every ½ hr.; last tour leaves at 3:30pm. $4, seniors $3, high-schoolers with ID $2, kids $1; tickets sold next door at the simple **Cox-Deasy House.**) For more information on Oakleigh's heyday and on other periods in Mobile's history, visit the **Museum of the City of Mobile,** 355 Government St. (438-7569), which includes an exhibit of Mardi Gras queen costumes from the early 20th century.

The battleship *U.S.S. Alabama,* permanently moored at **Battleship Park** (433-2703), took part in every major World War II battle in the Pacific. The park is at the entrance of the Bankhead Tunnel, 2½ mi. east of town on I-10. Berthed along the port side of this intriguing ship is one of the most famous submarines of the war, the *U.S.S. Drum.* (Open daily 8am-sunset. $5, ages 6-11 $2.50. Parking $1.)

Gray Line of Mobile (432-2229) leads interesting one-hour sight-seeing tours of the downtown historic areas from the **Fort Condé Information Center.** (Tours Mon.-Sat. 10:30am and 2pm, Sun. 2pm. $7, kids $3. A two-hour tour is also available for $15, kids $6.50.)

For nighttime entertainment, stop in at **Trinity's Downtown,** 456 Auditorium Dr. (432-0000), where bands play rock and reggae Wednesday through Saturday nights. (Open Mon.-Thurs. 11am-midnight, Fri.-Sat. 11am-2am.) There's more rock and reggae at **G.T. Henry's,** 462 Dauphin St. (432-0300), on a multi-tiered stage, with crawfish boils on Sundays to boot. (Open nightly from about 10pm. Small cover.)

Montgomery

Capital of the Confederacy for a short time in 1861, this former slave-holding town became the focus of the nationwide civil rights effort a century later, culminating in Martin Luther King's triumphant 1965 march from Selma to the steps of the state capitol. The Dexter Baptist Church (where Reverend King was pastor), the capitol building, and the newly unveiled Civil Rights Memorial testify to the struggles of African Americans here. It is also the home of the Wright brothers' first flight school, the birthplace of Nat King Cole, and the current residence of folk artist Moset.

Practical Information

Emergency: 911.

Visitor Information Center, 401 Madison Ave. (262-0013). Open Mon.-Fri. 8:30am-5pm, Sat.-Sun. 9am-4pm. **Chamber of Commerce,** 41 Commerce St. (834-5200). Open Mon.-Fri. 8:30am-5pm.

Travelers Aid: 265-0568. Operated by Salvation Army, 24 hrs.

Greyhound/Trailways: 210 S. Court St. (264-4518). To Tuskegee (7 per day, 1 hr., $7), Birmingham (7 per day, 3 hr., $15), and Mobile (8 per day, 4 hr., $26). Open 24 hrs.

Public Transport: Montgomery Area Transit System (MATS), 701 N. McDonough St. (262-7321). Operates throughout the metropolitan area Mon.-Sat. 6am-6pm. Fare 80¢, transfers 10¢.

Taxi: Yellow Cab, 262-5225. $1.50 first mi., $1 each additional mi.

Help Lines: Council Against Rape, 264-7273. **Help-A-Crisis,** 279-7837.

Post Office: 135 Catoma St. (244-7576). Open Mon.-Fri. 8am-5pm, Sat. 8am-noon. **ZIP code:** 36104.

Area Code: 205.

Downtown Montgomery follows a grid pattern: **Madison Avenue** and **Dexter Avenue** are the major east-west routes; **Perry Street** and **Lawrence Street** run north-south.

Accommodations and Food

Accommodations are easy to procure for those with a car; I-65 at the Southern Blvd. exit overflows with cheap beds. Two well-maintained budget motels centrally located downtown are the **Capitol Inn,** 205 N. Goldthwaite St. (265-0541), at Heron St. near the bus station on a hill overlooking the city (singles $25, doubles $33) and the venerable, somewhat comfortable **Town Plaza,** 743 Madison Ave. (269-1561), at N. Ripley St. (singles $19, doubles $22). The Plaza, actually closer to the capitol, allows only human adults. Across the street from the Plaza, the **State House Inn,** 924 Madison Ave. (265-0741), is much more fancy, with large rooms, HBO and an enormous pool. Usually pricey, they sometimes offer doubles at $33 as specials. Check at the Information Center. **The Inn South,** 4243 Inn South Ave. (288-7999), has nice new rooms, but is a 10-minute drive from downtown. (Singles $29. Doubles $35.) As an alternative to these inns, contact **Bed and Breakfast Montgomery,** P.O. Box 1026, Montgomery, AL 36101 (264-0056). **KOA Campground,** ¼-mi. south of Hope Hull exit (288-0728), is four mi. from town and has a pool. (Tent sites $11, with water and electricity $15, with A/C $17.50.)

There is rarely an empty seat for the Southern cooking at **The Farmer's Market Cafeteria,** 315 N. McDonough St. Free iced tea and ice cream comes with every inexpensive meal ($3-4). (Open Mon.-Fri. 5am-2pm.) **Chris's Hot Dogs,** 138 Dexter Ave. (265-6850), with over 70 years under its belt, is an even more extablished Montgomery institution. This small diner serves gourmet hot dogs ($1.35) and thick Brunswick stew ($1.50). (Open Mon.-Fri. 8:30am-8pm, Sat. 10am-7pm.) **Martha's Place** at 458 Sayre St. (263-9135) is a new but soon to be legendary family-run down-home restaurant. (Open Mon.-Fri. 11am-3pm and 5-8pm, Sun. 11am-5pm.) At **The China Bowl,** 701 Madison Ave (832-4004), two blocks from the Town Plaza Motel, fast food cooks wok around the clock five ft. from your nose. Large portions include a daily special of one entree, rice, egg roll, and a wanton wonton for $4.20; take-out available. (Open Mon.-Thurs. 11am-9pm, Fri. 11am-9:30pm.) As a final option, head for the Eastdale Hall (off the Atlanta Highway). They have tons of fast-food stalls and Alabama's only shopping-mall ice rink, if you can read that without quaking in your boots ($5, skate rental 50¢).

For a great snack, make your way over to the **Montgomery State Farmers Market,** at the corner of Federal Dr. (US 231) and Coliseum Blvd. (242-5350) and snag a bag of peaches for 75¢. (Open daily 7am-8pm in the spring and summer.)

Sights and Entertainment

Montgomery's newest sight is the **Civil Rights Memorial,** 400 Washington Ave. at Hull St. Maya Lin, architect for the Vietnam Memorial in Washington, also designed this dramatic, though minimalist tribute to 40 men, women, and children who died fighting for civil rights. The outdoor monument bears names and dates of significant events on a circular black marble table over which water and flowers of remembrance continuously flow; a wall frames the table with Martin Luther King's words, ". . .Until Justice rolls down like waters and righteousness like a mighty stream." (Open daily.) The legacy and life of African-American activism and faith can also be seen one block away at the **Dexter Avenue King Memorial Baptist Church,** 454 Dexter Ave. (263-3970), where King preached. At this 112-year-old church, Reverend King and other civil rights leaders organized the 1955 Montgomery bus boycott; 10 years later, King would lead a nationwide civil rights march past the church to the Montgomery capitol. The basement mural chronicles the evolution of King and the nation's struggle during the 1960s. (Open Mon.-Fri. 9am-noon and 1-4pm, Sat. 10am-2pm. Free. Tours available.)

Three blocks north is **Old Alabama Town,** 310 N. Hull St. at Madison (263-4355), an artfully maintained historic district of 19th-century buildings. The complex includes a pioneer homestead, an 1892 grocery, a schoolhouse, an early African-American church, and a freed slave's house. (Open Mon.-Sat. 8:30am-5:30pm, last tour at 3:30pm. Sun. 1:30-3:30pm. $5, ages 5-18 $1.50.)

The Confederate flag flies along with the Stars and Stripes above the **State Capitol,** closed to the public until late 1992 for restoration. But you can visit the nearby **Alabama State History Museum and State Archives,** 624 Washington Ave. (242-4363). On exhibit are many Native American artifacts along with early military swords and medals. Stop by "Grandma's Attic" where you can try on antique furs and play with Tinker Toys. (Open Mon.-Fri. 8am-5pm, Sat.-Sun. 9am-5pm. Free.) Next door to the Archives is the elegant **First White House of the Confederacy,** 644 Washington Ave. (242-1861), which contains many original furnishings from Jefferson Davis's Confederate presidency. (Open Mon.-Fri. 8am-4:30pm, Sat.-Sun. 9am-4:30pm. Free.) Another restored home of interest is the **F. Scott and Zelda Fitzgerald Museum,** 919 Felder Ave. (262-1911), off Carter Hill Rd. Zelda, originally from Montgomery, lived here with Scott from October 1931 to April 1932. The museum contains a few of her paintings and some of his original manuscripts, as well as their strangely monogrammed bath towels. (Open Wed.-Fri. 10am-2pm, Sat.-Sun. 1-5pm.)

Country music fans might want to join the hundreds who make daily pilgrimages to the **Hank Williams Memorial,** located in the Oakwood Cemetery Annex off Upper Wetumpka Rd. For more live entertainment, turn to the renowned **Alabama Shakespeare Festival,** staged at the remarkable $22 million **Wynton M. Blount Cul-**

tural Park, 15 minutes southeast of the downtown area. In addition to Shakespeare, Broadway shows and other plays are staged. Nearby, off Woodmere Blvd., is the **Montgomery Museum of Fine Arts,** 1 Museum Dr. (244-5700). This attractive museum houses a substantial collection of 19th- and 20th-century paintaings and graphics. (Open Tues.-Wed. and Fri.-Sat. 10am-5pm, Thurs. 10am-9pm, Sun. noon-5pm. Free.)

Montgomery shuts down fairly early, but if you're in the mood for some blues and beers, try **1048,** 1048 E. Fairview Ave. (834-1048), near Woodley Ave. (Open Mon.-Fri. 4pm-until and Sat. 6pm-until.) For further information on events in the city, call the chamber of commerce's 24-hr. **FunPhone** (240-9447).

Tuskegee

Late in the 19th century, after Reconstruction, southern states segregated and disenfranchised "emancipated" African Americans. Booker T. Washington, himself a former slave, believed that African Americans could best combat repression through self-education and learning a trade. As a result, the curriculum at Washington's college, now **Tuskegee University,** revolved around practical endeavors such as agriculture and carpentry, with students constructing almost all of the campus buildings. Artist, teacher, and scientist George Washington Carver became head of the Agricultural Department at Tuskegee, where he discovered many practical uses for the peanut, including axle grease and peanut butter.

Today, a more academically-oriented Tuskegee covers over 160 acres and a wide range of subjects; the buildings of Washington's original institute also comprise a national historical site. A walking tour of the campus begins at the **Carver Museum,** with the **Visitor Orientation Center** (727-3200) inside. (Both open daily 9am-5pm. Free.) Down the street from the museum, on old Montgomery Rd., is **The Oaks,** a restored version of Washington's home. Free tours from the museum begin on the hour.

Visitors can stay on campus in the **Dorothy Hall Guest House** (727-8753; singles $24; doubles $29; rooms with shared bath and no A/C $11; reservations are advisable.) During the academic year, the **Dorothy Hall Cafeteria** serves breakfast (Mon.-Fri. 7:30am-9am) and lunch (Mon.-Fri. 11:30am-1pm). For good cafeteria-style home cooking, try **Pierce's** (727-9322), near the intersection of Fonville and E. Martin L. King Dr. a few blocks from campus. The vegetable plate ($2.50) or baked chicken with dressing ($2) are good bets. (Open Mon.-Fri. 6am-4pm, Sat. 7am-noon.)

To get to Tuskegee, take I-85 toward Atlanta and exit at Rte. 81 south. Turn right at the intersection of Rte. 81 and Old Montgomery Rd. onto Rte. 126. **Greyhound** also runs frequently from Montgomery (1 hr., $7).

Tuskegee's **ZIP code** is 36083; the **area code** is 205.

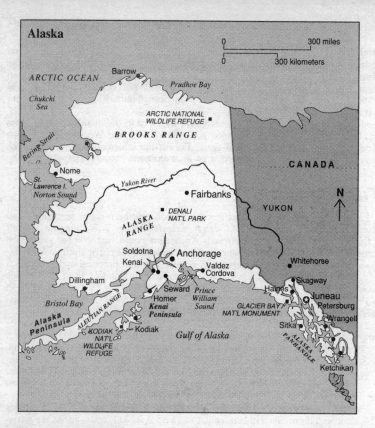

Alaska

ALASKA

Manifest destiny seems to bring out the Hun in the American character, and Alaska, the last U.S. frontier, begs to be exploited. Increased oil extraction from Alaska's rich deposits has reproduced the trappings of 19th-century Klondike gold rush days: a race for big money with soaring prices and impromptu settlements. But America's flowering environmental consciousness blooms even in the Alaskan chill, protecting much of the state's wilderness and wildlife. The few times Alaskans do surrender to the temptation to sell a bit of their beautiful scenery for more synthetic riches, they face the wrath of outside environmental groups, raising the question of sovereignty over the state's abundance.

The generous elbow room provided by vast expanses of misty fjords, mountain lakes, forests, glaciers, and tundra generates a laissez-faire attitude evident in Alaska's liberal marijuana laws and strong Libertarian Party. Only one-fifth of the land is accessible by roads; the float plane is the primary mode of transportation. The rivers teem with salmon. The rocky shores harbor seals while whales sing and hump offshore. Bears of all kinds compete with wolves, lynx, and other carnivores for food and territory, and moose, bighorn sheep, and bald eagles coexist in numbers unheard of elsewhere in the United States. Native Alaskans still live with privacy and autonomy unknown to most other Native Americans, such that Athabascans, Aleuts, Eskimos, Tlingits, and Haidas can still subsist on the land's abundant resources. Even the destructive spill of the Exxon *Valdez's* oil cargo damaged only 1% of Alaska's coastline, just a speck in Alaska's enormity.

76

Although broad enough to accommodate England, France, Spain, and Italy within its borders, Alaska did not host a European visitor until 1741, when the czar of Russia hired Dutch navigator Victor Bering to map out the region near the Kenai Peninsula. Bering died in the effort, but his crew brought home such an abundance of valuable fur that Russian traders soon overran Kodiak Island with traps in hand and rubles in mind. The fur harvest dried up in less than a century, and the czar, dead broke from the Crimean War, decided to sell in 1867 what he considered to be a territory sucked dry of its natural resources. The U.S. bought the vast wasteland for less than 2¢ per acre. Alaska soon became known as "Seward's Icebox," a jab at Secretary of State William Seward for negotiating the purchase. But within 20 years, U.S. prospectors unearthed enough gold to turn Seward's folly into a billion-dollar profit.

The modern development of Alaska began with World War II. In response to the 1941 Japanese occupation of the Aleutian islands, the U.S. military connected Alaska to the lower 48 states by the Alaskan Highway, also building ports and airfields. Many GIs liked what they saw and stayed. The Cold War with Russia led to an increase in military development in Alaska. In the 60s, oil discovered on the Kenai Peninsula and on the north slope of the Brooks Range catalyzed Alaska's growth. The Alaskan pipeline pumped its first barrel of crude 800 mi. from Prudhoe Bay to Valdez in July of 1978. Uproar surrounding the exploitative development of Alaska, while understandable, obscures the fact most of the state retains its pristine beauty.

Although most tourists visit Alaska in its endless summer light, Alaskans maintain that their land is most beautiful in the winter. One reward for the intrepid off-season sojourner is the Aurora Borealis or "Northern Lights." The shimmering spectrums of color dance like smoke from a fire whenever the sky is dark. The brightest displays occur in fall and spring when the earth's tilt toward the sun accentuates their light most.

Practical Information

Capital: Juneau.

Alaska Division of Tourism, Pouch E-101, Juneau 99811 (465-2010). Open Mon.-Fri. 8am-4:30pm. **Alaskan Public Lands Information Center,** Old Federal Building, 4th Ave., Anchorage 99510 (271-2737). Tips on all federal, state, and local parks, refuges, and forests. Open daily 9am-7pm. Branch office in Fairbanks. **Alaska State Division of Parks,** Old Federal Building, Anchorage 99510 (271-2737). Open Mon.-Fri. 8am-4:30pm. **United States Forest Service,** 101 Egan Dr., Juneau 99802 (586-8751). General info regarding national parks and reserves. Open Mon.-Fri. 8am-4:30pm. **National Park Service,** Parks and Forests Information Center, 2525 Gambpell, Anchorage 99503 (261-2643). Open Mon.-Fri. 9am-7pm. **State Department of Fish and Game,** P.O. Box 3-2000, Juneau 99802. Info on hunting and fishing regulations.

Time Zones: Alaska (4 hr. behind Eastern); Aleutian-Hawaii (5 hr. behind Eastern). **Postal Abbreviation:** AK

Physical Characteristics and Climate

Alaska spans 586,412 sq. mi., one-fifth the area of the continental United States, stretching west to a longitude that coincides with New Zealand. It has 33,904 mi. of shoreline (about 1½ times the combined coastlines of the Lower 48). No single temperate zone covers the whole region; Prudhoe Bay differs from Ketchikan as much as Minneapolis does from Atlanta. In general, summer and early fall (June-Sept.) are the best times to visit. Visitors can expect daylight from 6am to 2am in many areas during these months.

Fairbanks, Tok, and the Bush frequently enjoy 95°F hot spells, receiving less than eight in. of precipitation annually. The Interior freezes in its −60° to −80°F temperatures in winter. Farther south, the climate is milder and rainier. Cordova rusts with 167 in. of precipitation annually. Anchorage and other coastal towns in the southcentral are blessed with the Japanese Current, which has a moderating effect on the climate. Average temperatures for Anchorage range from 13°F in January to 57°F in July.

Travelers should prepare for wet, wind, and cold year-round. In summer, those staying below the Arctic Circle probably won't need anything heavier than a light parka or jacket and sweater. For forays into the "Bush" (Alaskans' term for the wilderness), be absolutely certain to bring waterproof boots and sturdy raingear. Wool and polypropylene are staples for socks, underwear, pants, shirts, and hats. The warmest coats and snowsuits are hollofil, not down-filled, garments.

Winter travelers should always expect the chilly unexpected. The National Park Service advises that visitors learn to recognize the symptoms of hypothermia, the gradual lowering of the body temperature; also carry extra dry clothing, blankets, and food. Read Jack London's "To Build a Fire"—if you're an American high school graduate, you already have—to learn how sucky freezing to death can be.

Camping

The U.S. Forest Service maintains more than 178 wilderness log cabins for public use—142 in Tongass National Forest in Southeastern Alaska and 36 in Chugach National Forest in Southcentral Alaska. The cabins are beautifully located and maintained. User permits are required along with a fee of $12 per party per night. Reserve several months in advance. Most cabins have seven-day use limits, except hike-in cabins (3-day max. stay May-Aug.). Cabins sleep six, and usually are accessible only by air, boat, or hiking trail. Facilities at these sites rarely include more than a wood stove and pit toilets. Some cabins provide skiffs (small boats). For maps or further info write to the U.S. Forest Service. For info about free cabins within wildlife ranges, contact the U.S. Fish and Wildlife Service (see Practical Information above).

State-run campgrounds are always free. Often they have toilets and drinking water, but no showers. For info on state campgrounds and waysides, contact the Alaska State Division of Parks (see Practical Information above). Four federal agencies control and manage park lands in Alaska: the U.S. Forest Service (USFS), the Bureau of Land Management (BLM), the National Park Service, and the U.S. Fish and Wildlife Service (see Practical Information above). The USFS maintains numerous campgrounds within the Chugach and Tongass National Forests (sites $5-6.25; 14-day max. stay). The BLM runs about 20 campgrounds throughout the state, all free except the Delta BLM campground on the Alaska Hwy. The National Park Service maintains campgrounds in Mt. Denali National Park, Glacier Bay National Park, and Katmai National Park and Preserve (sites $5-12). Campgrounds managed by the U.S. Fish and Wildlife Service are confined to the Kenai National Wildlife Refuge, Box 2139, Soldotna 99669. Government campgrounds in Alaska rarely have dump stations or electrical hookups.

Most towns, and all those with canneries, have tent cities for seasonal workers. These will cost you a few dollars a night to bunk down, and generally have poor facilities but interesting if fishy communities of student workers.

Remember to leave an itinerary at the offices of parks, hotels, state troopers, guides, and other authorities. This important safety measure takes little time to execute. Alaska looms bigger and more rugged than you can possibly imagine, with weather unpredictable at best.

For additional info about hiking and camping in Alaska, consult one of the following books: *55 Ways of Wilderness* or *Alaska's Parklands,* both published by the Mountaineer Press, or *Adventuring in Alaska,* published by the Sierra Club.

Travel

Anyone who has ever ventured onto Alaska's roads owns a copy of *The Milepost,* published by the Alaska Northwest Publishing Company, 130 2nd Ave. S., Edmond, WA 98020 (907-563-1141; open Mon.-Fri. 8:30am-4:30pm). Each thick volume ($16) packs information about Alaskan and Canadian communities as well as up-to-date ferry schedules and maps of the highways and roads.

Travel in Alaska is easy but expensive. Most Alaskans use **air travel,** often piloting themselves; one in 36 has a pilot's license. Several intrastate airlines run frequent scheduled flights to most places any visitor might be inclined to go: **Alaska Air** (to larger Bush towns and Cordova; 800-426-5292); **Frontier Flying Service** (474-0014); **Markair** (to larger Bush towns, Kodiak, and the Aleutians; 800-426-6784); **ERA Aviation** (southcentral; 243-3300); and **Ryan Air Service** (practically anywhere in the Bush; 248-0695). Many other charters and flight-seeking services are available. Check *The Milepost* (see above) or write **Ketchum Air Service Inc.,** North Shore Lake Hood, Anchorage 99503 (243-5525), to ask about their charters.

The **Alaska Railroad,** the northernmost in North America, connects Seward and Whittier in the south with Anchorage, Fairbanks, and Denali. Service runs from Anchorage to Fairbanks ($117) daily in the summer, once per week in the winter. Given advance notice in the winter, the engineer will drop cargo or passengers along the way. On the way to Fairbanks, trains stop at Denali National Park. The train is the only land route to Whittier (one way $8 from Portage). Passenger service to Seward was recently reintroduced for summer visitors. Advance reservations are required for all except Whittier trips. Write **Alaska Railroad Corporation,** Passenger Services, P.O. Box 7-2111, Anchorage 99510. (Call 265-2623 for schedules, fares, and reservations, 456-4155 in Fairbanks.)

Scheduled **bus service** connects Whitehorse, British Columbia, and Haines with Central Alaska, including Anchorage. Several enterprising van owners run small operations from Haines to Anchorage, synchronized with the ferry. Fares can be as low as $120, but service is often unreliable. The **Alaskan Express,** P.O. Box 100479, Anchorage 99510 (277-5581), runs two buses per week in summer from Anchorage through Whitehorse to Skagway and Haines. You'll need to pay for overnight accommodations. (One-way fare $194; accommodations $90 or tent it.) **Alaska Sightseeing Company,** 533 First Ave., Fairbanks (452-8518), travels daily between Anchorage and Fairbanks for $120. **Alaska Transportation Service** (274-6454) runs between Anchorage and Homer ($40) and Anchorage and Soldotna ($30). **Greyhound** charges well over $300 from Seattle, slightly less from Vancouver. **Bus tours** that often include meals, lodging, and sights otherwise difficult to get to can be a good deal. For example, **Gray Line Tours,** 547 W. 4th Ave., Anchorage 99501 (277-5581), offers a three-day excursion from Whitehorse to Anchorage that includes a sail across Prince William Sound, a train ride from Whittier, and two nights of accommodations. (Singles $329. Doubles $538.)

Driving in Alaska is not for the faint of heart. To the embarrassment of most residents, many major roads in Alaska remain in deplorable condition, and Juneau is the only state capital in the nation that cannot be reached by automobile. Roads reach only a quarter of the state's area. Dust and flying rocks are a major hazard in the summer, as are miserable 10- to 30-mi. patches of gravel. "Frost heaves" from melting and contracting permafrost cause not only dips, but miraculous "twists" on the road. Radiators and headlights should be protected from flying rocks with a wire screen, and a fully functioning spare tire is essential. Winter can actually offer a smoother ride. Active snow crews keep roads as clear as possible, and the packed surface and thinned traffic permit easy driving without summer's mechanical troubles. At the same time, the danger of avalanches and ice is cause for major concern. Check the road conditions before traveling; in Anchorage call 243-7675, or simply tune in to local radio stations. Both winter and summer travelers are advised to let a friend or relative know of their position along the highway several times in the course of a trip. Drivers also should take into account the cost of gas, which varies significantly from station to station.

Many people **hitchhike** instead of depending on buses in Alaska. In fact, state law prohibits moving vehicles from *not* picking up stranded motorists, as the extreme climate can be life-endangering. However, hitchhiking backpackers may only legally thumb on the on-and-off ramps of major highways, not on the highways themselves. Beware of being stranded on lightly traveled stretches of road. A wait of a day or two is not unusual on certain stretches of the Alaska Hwy. Luckily, Alaskans are generally friendly and cooperative, and most rides last at least a day. Women, of course, are always safer traveling in pairs or with a man.

The **Alaska Marine Highway** consists of two ferry systems. The southwest network serves Kodiak Island, Seward, Homer, and the Prince William Sound. The other system runs from Bellingham up the southeast coast to Skagway and stops in Juneau, Ketchikan, Haines, and other towns, many of which are accessible only by plane or on the ferry. The whaled and bald-eagled three-day trip from Bellingham to Skagway features free showers and cafes, historical and ecological lectures, and a heated top-deck solarium where cabinless passengers can sleep (bring a sleeping bag!). Cabins are expensive ($190) and unnecessary—everyone sleeps in the solarium. ($236, ages 6-12 near ½-price, under 6 free.) The southwest ferries are more expensive and less plush, and they ride the open sea, which your alimentary canal will really appreciate.

Anchorage

Anchorage, or "Los Anchorage," as some rural residents prefer to call it, is "big city" Alaska. Only 70 years ago, it was wilderness, but in 1914, railroads began a steady flow of trains, pioneers, and oil, transforming Anchorage into the state's commercial center. Today 250,000 people, half the state's population, live here. Its international airport is among the world's busiest, serving passengers en route to East Asia. Perhaps most remarkable about Anchorage is the fact that everything—the glass and steel for the buildings, food and merchandise, diapers and paperclips—arrives here the same way people do. Everything travels 1,500 mi., either by tortuous drive or by expensive plane or by barge or container ship across one of the roughest seas in the world. Anchorage feels a bit prefabricated, to say the least.

Practical Information

Anchorage Convention and Visitors Bureau, 201 E. 3rd Ave. (274-3531). **Log Cabin Visitor Information Center,** W. 4th Ave. at F St. (274-3531). Open May-Sept. daily 7:30am-7pm; Oct.-April 8:30am-6pm. The **All About Anchorage Line** (276-3200) runs a recorded listing of each day's events. For info on fine arts and dramatic performances, call the **Artsline** (276-2787). Smaller visitor information outlets located in the airport near the baggage claim in the domestic terminal; in the overseas terminal in the central atrium; and in the Valley River Mall, first level.

Alaska Public Lands Information Center, Old Federal Bldg. (271-2737), 4th Ave. between F and G. An astounding conglomeration of 8 state and federal offices (including the **National Park Service, U.S. Forest Service, Division of State Parks,** and **U.S. Fish and Wildlife Service**) under one roof provides the latest information on the entire state. Open daily 9am-7pm.

Anchorage International Airport: a few miles southwest of downtown off International Airport Rd. The People Mover Bus runs 3 times per day to downtown, but the visitors center near the baggage claim can direct you to more frequent routes. **Dynair Charter Service** (243-3310) shuttles downtown for $6; cabs cost about $14.50.

Alaska Railroad: 2nd Ave. (265-2494), at the head of town. To Denali ($78), Fairbanks ($117), and Seward ($36). For more info write to Passenger Service, P.O. Box 107500, Anchorage 99510. Office open daily 8am-8pm; may close if no trains are arriving.

Public Transit: People Mover Bus (343-6543), in the Transit Center on 6th St. between G and H, one block from the hostel. Most buses run from here to all points in the Anchorage Bowl 5am-midnight Cash fare 80¢, tokens 75¢. Office open Mon.-Fri. 8am-5pm.

Taxi: Yellow Cab, 272-2422. **Checker Cab,** 276-1234.

Car Rental: Rent-a-Dent, 512 W. International Airport Rd. (561-0350), at the airport. $35 per day with 50 free mi., 20¢ each additional mi. Open daily 7am-11pm. **Allstar Rent-A-Car,** 512 W. International Airport Rd. (561-0350). $39 per day, unlimited mileage. Reserve 6-7 days in advance. Open daily 7am-10pm.

Alaska Marine Highway: 333 W. 4th St. (272-4482), in the Post Office Mall. No terminal, but ferry tickets and reservations. Open Mon.-Fri. 8am-5pm.

Time Zone: Alaska (4 hr. behind Eastern).

Post Office: W. 4th Ave. and C St. (277-6568), on the lower level in the mall. Open Mon.-Fri. 10:30am-5pm, Sat. 10am-4pm. **ZIP code:** 99510.

Area Code: 907.

The downtown area of Anchorage follows a grid. Numbered avenues run east-west, with addresses designated East or West from **C Street.** North-south streets have letters alphabetically west of **A Street,** and names alphabetically east of A St. The rest of Anchorage spreads out along the major highways. The **University of Alaska-Anchorage** campus lies on 36th Ave. off Northern Lights Blvd.

Accommodations and Camping

Several bed and breakfast referral agencies operate out of Anchorage. Try **Alaska Private Lodgings,** 1236 W. 10th Ave., Anchorage 99511 (258-1717), or **Stay With a Friend,** Box 173, 3605 Arctic Blvd., Anchorage 99503 (344-4006). Both can refer you to singles ($45-50) and doubles ($55-60).

There are several free campgrounds outside the city limits; for info contact the **Alaska Division of Parks,** 3601 C St., 10th Floor, Pouch 7-001 Anchorage 99510, or the **Anchorage Parks and Recreation Dept.,** 2525 Campbell St. #404 (271-2500).

Anchorage Youth Hostel (AYH), 700 H St. (276-3635), 1 block south of the Transit Center downtown. Excellent location. Clean rooms with common areas, kitchens, showers, and laundry. Family rooms in most wings. Lockout 10am-5pm. Midnight curfew. $10, nonmembers $13. Hardly ever full. Local grocery stores drop off boxes and boxes of day-old fruit, pasta and assorted canned goods on Mondays.

Qupquqiag Bed and Breakfast, 3801 Lois Dr. (562-4636) at Spanish Rd. Five min. from the airport. Clean, comfortable rooms. Full breakfast included. Singles $20, with king-sized bed $30.

Heart of Anchorage Bed and Breakfast, 4025 Hillcourt Dr. (243-6814), off Diamond St. near June Lake. Convenient to downtown and close to the airport. Dorm beds $15. Singles $50. Doubles $60. Call ahead for reservations.

Inlet Inn, 7th and H (277-5541), diagonally across from the hostel. Singles $60, doubles $65. Ask for one of the few smaller rooms with shower and toilet but no bathtub. Singles $45. Doubles $48 (which can sleep up to 4). HBO and TV.

Centennial Park, 8300 Glenn Hwy. (333-9711), north of town off Muldoon Rd.; look for the park sign. Take bus #3 or 75 from downtown. Facilities for tents and RVs. Showers, dumpsters, fireplaces, pay phones, and water. 7-day max. stay. Check-in before 6pm in summer. Sites $12, seniors $8.

Lions' Camper Park, 5800 Boniface Pkwy. (333-1495), south of the Glenn Hwy. In Russian Jack Springs Park next to the Municipal Greenhouse. Take bus #12 or 45 to the Boniface Mall and walk 4 blocks. Connected to the city's bike trail system. Ten primitive campsites with water station, fire rings, and showers. Self-contained vehicles only. 7-day max. stay. Open daily 10am-10pm. Sites $12. Open May-Sept.

Food

By virtue of its size and largely imported population, Anchorage wears a culinary coat of many colors. Within blocks of each other stand greasy spoons, Chinese restaurants, and classy hotel-top French eateries. You will also find huge portions of Alaskan sourdough and seafood—halibut, salmon, clams, crab, and snapper. The city's finer restaurants line the hills overlooking Cook Inlet and the Alaska Range.

Tito's Gyros, (279-8961), on 4th St. near McDonald's. Pizza by the slice ($2), a rarity in Alaska. Juicy gyro sandwich ($5.25), and the best ice cream downtown.

Old Anchorage Salmon Bake, 251 K St. (279-8790), in the Bluff at 3rd and K. $17 buys a small snack—salmon and halibut and reindeer sausage and crab legs and salad and beans and sourdough rolls. Smaller *cheechako* meals also available. The light lunch includes salad bar and beans with such orders as salmon burgers ($6.25) or reindeer dogs ($6.50). Open May-Sept. daily 11am-2pm and 4-10pm.

Cyrano's Book Store and Café (274-1173), on D between 4th and 5th. Come here to ghost-write love letters. Classical music, a current *Wall Street Journal*, tall glass of lemonade, and an excellent bowl of chicken gumbo ($6). The best book store in the state next door, and a cutting edge unfranchised cinema downstairs—all under one roof.

Skipper's, at 5 locations: 3960 W. Dimond Blvd., 702 E. Benson Blvd., 5668 DeBarr Rd., 601 E. Dimond Blvd., and 3611 Minnesota Dr. Good enough to make you think you're on Gilligan's Island. Only $5.50 for all the fish fries, chowder, and cole slaw you can fit in your gullet (with shrimp $8). Open daily 11am-11pm.

Wing and Things, 529 I St. (277-9464), at 5th. Unbelievably delicious BBQ chicken wings. Decorated with wing memorabilia and inspirational poetry. Ten wings, celery, and sauce $6. Open daily 10am-9pm.

Sights and Entertainment

Mount Susitna, known to locals as the "Sleeping Lady," watches over Anchorage from Cook Inlet. For a fabulous view of Susitna, as well as the rest of the mountains that form a magnificent backdrop for Anchorage's ever-growing skyline, drive out to **Earthquake Park** at the end of Northern Lights Blvd. Once a fashionable neighborhood, the park now memorializes the disastrous effects of the Good Friday earthquake in 1964, a day Alaskans refer to as "Black Friday." Registering at 9.2 on the current Richter scale, this was the strongest earthquake ever recorded in North America. On a clear day, you can even see **Mount McKinley** far to the north.

The visitors center can set you up with a self-guided walking tour (3-4 hr.) of downtown. The People Mover sponsors less strenuous jaunts. Hop on one of the double-decker buses downtown ($1.50) for a ride through the area. **Gray Line Tours** (274-6454) offers a 3½-hr. tour of Anchorage City (daily at 8am and 3pm; $21).

The **Visual Arts Center**, 5th and G St. (274-9641) showcases the best Alaskan Artists. (Gallery open Mon.-Sat. 10am-5pm. Suggested donation $2.) The **Tundra Times**, a newspaper devoted to Native concerns, operates out of Anchorage. Stop by their office at 411 W. 4th Ave. (274-2512) to learn about the publication's history and aims. (Open Mon.-Fri. 8am-5pm.)

The **Anchorage Museum of History and Art**, 121 W. 7th Ave. (343-4326), at A St., features permanent exhibits of Alaska Native artifacts and art, as well as a Thursday night Alaska wilderness film series (at 3pm). (Open daily 9am-6pm. Admission $3.) To see real, honest-to-goodness Alaskan wildlife in the comfort of urbania, visit the **Alaska Zoo**, mile 2 on O'Malley Rd. (346-2133; open daily 10am-6pm; admission $3.50, seniors and ages 13-18 $2.50, under 13 $1.50).

For a tad more authenticity, head to the close confines of the nonprofit gift shop at the **Alaska Native Medical Center** at 3rd and Gampbell (247-1150). Because many Native Americans pay for medical services with their own arts and handicrafts, the Alaska State Museum in Juneau sent its buyers here last year to outfit its exhibitions. Walrus bone *ulus* (knives; $17-60), fur moccasins, Eskimo parkas, and dolls highlight the selection. (Open Mon.-Fri. 10am-2pm.) Craftworks from Alaska's bush country, similar to those on display at the Museum of History and Art, are sold at the **Alaska Native Arts and Crafts Showroom**, 333 W. 4th Ave. (272-3008; open Mon.-Fri. 10am-7pm, Sat. 10am-5pm).

Anchorageans of all types and incomes party at **Chilkoot Charlie's**, 2435 Spenard Rd. (272-1010), at Fireweed. The six bars have a rocking dance floor and a quiet, "share-my-space" lounge. Ask about the nightly drink specials; otherwise you'll end up paying an outrageous amount to subsidize those who do. (Take bus #7 or 60.) Less crowded and more interesting is **Mr. Whitekey's Fly-by-Night Club**, 3300 Spenard Rd. (279-SPAM), a "sleazy bar serving everything from the world's finest champagnes to a damn fine plate of Spam." The house special gives you anything with Spam at half-price when you order champagne (free with Dom Perignon). Try Spam nachos or Spam and cream cheese on a bagel ($2-6). Monty Python would have loved it. Nightly entertainment ranges from rock to jazz to blues. (Open daily 3pm-2:30am.)

Near Anchorage, **Palmer** is home to the **Alaska State Fairgrounds,** on mile 40.2 on Glen Hwy. Every year the **Alaska State Fair** (745-3247) erupts here with parades, rodeos, livestock, and agricultural sideshows starring cabbages from the set of *Sleeper.* The Fair opens 11 days before and ends on Labor Day. (Open daily 10am-10pm. Admission $6, seniors $2, under 13 $1.)

Denali National Park

Established in 1917 to protect its abundant wildlife, Denali National Park just happened to include Mt. Denali, "The Great One" in Athabascan. Denali, anglicized as **Mt. McKinley,** looms as the tallest mountain in North America and the greatest vertical relief in the world base to summit. About 20,320 ft. above sea level and 18,000 ft. above the meadows below, Denali is so big it makes its own weather; only visible about 20% of the summer, it may make you think you're viewing an optical Aleutian. Missing the mountain doesn't ruin a Denali trip—the park's tundra, taiga, wildlife, and lesser mountains are also worthwhile.

The park is accessible by **Alaska Railroad** (see Anchorage Practical Information) or by car. Some vans and buses run from Anchorage to the park. Try **Alaska Denali Transit** (273-3331, 733-2601, or 766-2869) for $35. Departures to Fairbanks, Sundays at 3pm ($20), to Anchorage, daily at 3pm ($35). A new company, **Moon Bay Express,** (274-6454) runs daily from Denali to Anchorage at 3pm ($20). All visitors should check in at the **Visitor Access Center** (683-1266), less than one mile from Rte. 3. Permits to stay in the park's **campgrounds** are issued here ($10); ride the park's **shuttles** ($3) and enjoy **backcountry camping** (free).

Denali Park has no trails. No trails. Just an 88-mi. bus access road. Get on a bus and ask the driver to stop at the quadrant (for backcountry camping) or campground you've reserved. You could find yourself getting off in a river bed, an ancient glacier path, marshy tundra, or a dense taiga forest. The visit will require some planning, but if you're already familiar with the park's layout, you can reserve your preferred quadrants, campgrounds, and even bus departure times one to three weeks in advance from the Fairbanks or Anchorage offices of the Park: 250 Cushman St., Suite 1A, Fairbanks (451-7352); or 605 W. 4th Ave., Suite 105, Anchorage (271-2737).

If you're not familiar with the park, like most visitors, you have two options. One is camping the first night at the free, no-reservations-required **Morino Campground,** centrally located at the entrance of the park near the Denali Park Hotel, convenience store (with showers for $2) and post office. The next day, take an available park shuttle bus (free with $3 park entrance fee) into the park and survey your camping prospects. The trip takes roughly four hours to the Eielson Visitor Center, and leaves daily every 20 minutes from 5am to 3pm. Go back to Morino that evening, and make reservations at the Visitor Center for your handpicked sites. You may have to wait another day or two to get your first choices, so bring sufficient food—the convenience store has necessary supplies, but is predictably pricey.

The second option is to make reservations based on the very general overview of the park provided here. The first third of the park is varying degrees of taiga forest and tundra. It looks innocuous from the road, but is hellish to hike, like walking on old wet mattresses with bushes growing out of them. The last third or so of the park is mosquito-infested. You may want to camp one night at Wonder Lake Campground for a good glimpse of Denali *sans* clouds, but reserve the last bus out to the campground and the first bus back in the morning, and bring protective netted head gear ($2 in the convenience store, but they sometimes run out). You'll feel like you're at a Star Wars convention, but you'll be able to get out of the tent. Mosquitos start out slow, big and stupid in July and get progressively smaller, faster, wilier and better at biting. By August they're almost gone, but have been replaced by the gnat-sized "no-see-ums" that can crawl through your hair, your clothes and even mosquito netting. They leave painful, swollen rashes. Therefore, prime hiking and camping is probably in the middle third of the park. Especially good locations are Toklat, Marmot Rock, and Polychrome Pass.

There are six **campgrounds** within the park. All have water and some form of toilet facilities (sites $12).

Somewhat Near Denali: Talkeetna and Cantwell

Two small specks of towns on the George Parks Hwy. host the state's two best annual music festivals. **Talkeetna,** 120 mi. south of Denali, is the fly-off point for mountain climbers to Mt. McKinley/Denali, and is known as an unusual enclave of bush pilots and climbers from around the world. Every year in the beginning of August they sponsor the best three-day bluegrass and rock and roll music festival in Alaska. Beards, dogs, children and tie-dye abound. Free, of course. **Cantwell,** 30 mi. south of Denali, hosts a rival, lesser-known bluegrass festival at the end of June. It also lasts three days and is free. Check at the Denali Park Hotel for exact dates. The hotel provides a free shuttle to the Cantwell festival. If you don't want to return at 12:30am, camp at the festival. It may go all "night."

The Kenai Peninsula

The Kenai (KEEN-eye) Peninsula mirrors Alaska in miniature. Like parts of Alaska's interior, Kenai's interior is flat; like the state itself, mountains ring the peninsula. Kenai relies on all three big sectors of Alaska's economy: oil, tourism, and fishing. The Russian influence on the Panhandle can be seen on the town of Kenai, the first Russian settlement in Alaska, and the urban sprawl of Anchorage and Fairbanks mimics road-side towns like Soldotna.

The Peninsula is the place Alaskans, especially those from Anchorage and Fairbanks, go for vacation when they don't go to the towns. Take a hint from the Native Alaskans: find an isolated campsite and fish. (All state-run tent sites $16, 1-day fishing license $10.) Every town can set you up cheaply with the requisite permits and gear. Stay in **USFS Campgrounds,** located every eight or 10 mi. on Seward and Sterling Highways. There are also great spots in between—ask the locals. For more info on hiking, hunting, fishing, camping, and other recreational opportunities, as well as regulations, contact the following: **Kenai Fjords National Park** (see Seward); **Alaska Maritime National Wildlife Refuge** and **Kachemak Bay State Park** (see Homer); **Kenai National Wildlife Refuge** (see Soldotna); **Chugach National Forest,** 201 E. 9th Ave. #206, Anchorage 99501 (261-2500); **State of Alaska, Division of Parks and Outdoor Recreations,** P.O. Box 1247, Soldotna 99669 (262-5581); and **State of Alaska, Department of Fish & Game,** P.O. Box 3150, Soldotna 99669 (262-9368). If you're unclear about which of these offices to contact, check out the **Alaska Public Lands Information Center** (see Anchorage Practical Information) for a referral.

The Kenai Peninsula is serviced by the **Seward** and **Sterling Highways,** as well as the **Alaska Marine Highway,** which runs between Homer, Seward, and Whittier, and extends out to Kodiak Island and Prince William Sound. To reach the peninsula from Anchorage, simply take any of the buses that run onto the New Seward Hwy. (such as the #2 or 9) as far south as possible and hitch. Hitching is common and fairly safe.

Homer

Sing to me, Muse, of the spectacular view as you round Baycrest Hill, which is quite striking, even if you have driven a fjord lately. From the bluff, you can see the sand-and-gravel Spit drooling 4.5 mi. to Kachemak Bay, stopping just short of the Kenai Mountains, fjords and blue glaciers on the other side.

At first glance, the town itself would appear no different from any other college town, complete with health food stores and foreign films. But there is no college in Homer—its lively progressive atmosphere is a result of its combined status as artist's enclave, hearty fishing community, and outpost of traditional Alaskan individualism.

Homer spreads out into three distinct segments: the mainland with its ubiquitous art galleries strung along Pioneer Ave.; the **Spit** lined with campers, fishing charters, harbors and boardwalk-style restaurants and shops; and the wilder, more ruggedly beautiful islands and parks across Kachemak Bay. Things become increasingly lively the farther out you go, and a trip to Homer would be seriously lacking without a visit to the "really interesting stuff" on the other side: **Kachemak Bay State Park,** where the southern end of the Kenai Mountains reaches the sea, offers the area's best hiking trails and wildlife viewing. One also finds the artist-fishing colony **Halibut Cove** there, as well as the **Gull Island** bird rookery, the Russian hippie center **Yukon Island,** the Russian-founded town of **Seldovia,** and much more. **Central Charters,** operating out of the Visitor Center (235-7847) halfway down the Spit, offers inexpensive daily tours to all of the above destinations—and about 500 more (including numerous fishing charters).

Not only one of Alaska's most cherished towns, Homer also has the best museum and art gallery on the peninsula. **Pratt Museum,** 3779 Bartlett St. (235-8635), has exhibits by local artists, extensive living and dead marine mammals, local artifacts, and now a feature on the Valdez oil spill. (Open daily 10am-6pm. Admission $3.)

Colorful, 4½-mi.-long **Homer Spit,** a long walk or a short drive from downtown, is the second-longest spit in the world (and we ain't talkin' watermelon seeds). Boardwalks line its beaches, and shops perched on pilings hawk souvenirs and snacks.

Townsfolk gather at **Smoky Bay Cooperative,** 248 Pioneer Ave. (235-7242), where getting groceries makes a good excuse to hear town gossip. (Open Mon.-Sat. 8am-8pm, Sun. 10am-7:30pm.) Fresh seafood is available at **Icicle Seafood Market,** 842 Fish Dock Rd., at the base of the Spit near the mouth of the Harbor. The name of the **Sourdough Express Bakery and Coffee Shop,** 1316 Ocean Dr. (235-7571), on the main drag to the Spit, says it all, except for the "delicious" added by the clientele. Dine indoors or out on the deck, or just pick up some fresh-baked goods. Try the all-you-can-eat breakfast buffet ($8), which includes a sample of almost everything on the breakfast menu: great sourdough rolls, organic coffee, fresh fruit, sausage gravy and biscuits, bread pudding with blueberries and more. (Open daily 6am-10pm.) **Café Cups,** 162 Pioneer Ave. (235-8330), gathers artists and young travelers with its tasty, unusual sandwiches ($5-7.50) and excellent coffee ($1). Spaces outside, with chess boards and cribbage sets available. (Open Mon.-Fri. 7am-10pm, Sat. 8am-midnight, Sun. 9am-4pm.) **Boardwalk Fish & Chips,** at the end of Cannery Row Boardwalk across from the harbormaster's office, is a local favorite. A big hunk of halibut with chips costs $6.25. (Open daily 11:30am-10pm.)

Nightlife in Homer ranges from beachcombing at low tide in the midnight sun to discovering whether the **Salty Dawg Saloon,** under the log lighthouse at the end of the Spit, ever really closes (open 11am-whenever, as the sign says). For country fare head to **Alice's Champagne Palace,** 196 Pioneer Ave. (235-7650), a wooden barn with rock and roll music (Wed.-Sat. nights). The **Waterfront Bar** has all the character of its name, down to the pool tables, 120 Bunnell Ave. on the water (235-9949; live music Wed.-Sat. 10pm-3am). Yes, moose and calves do pass nearby in summer; you haven't been drinking too much. Those interested in capturing spit in images should check out the **Pier One Theater,** P.O. Box 894, Homer 99603 (235-7333 or 235-7951), performing classic plays on weekend nights from Memorial Day to Labor Day at their theater halfway down the Spit. Mainstage plays Fri. and Sat. nights at 8:15pm, Sun. at 7:15pm. (Admission $6, seniors and kids $5, families $20.)

Homer has two **municipal campgrounds,** one in town, one on the Spit. In town, take Pioneer to Bartlett St., go uphill and take a left onto Fairview. The city allows camping on the edges of the spit, 2 mi. out. Sites ($6, largely uncollected) have neither showers nor hookups. For these amenities, head to the private **Homer Spit Campground** (275-8206), at the spit's tip (sites $3, with full hookup $10-15).

Homer's Mucicipal Spit Camping runs along the beach 50 ft. away from the road, and on the 30-acre fill north of the harbor. It's voluptuously scenic, but windy, and camp high or you'll wake up in the water. **Gerry's Cook Inlet Bed and Breakfast,** technically in Anchor Point at Sterling Hwy mi. 153-5, picks up in Homer (235-2392). In the summer of 1991, Gerry was offering $50 rooms to AYH members for $15.

The visitor center has a list of **bed and breakfasts,** with rooms starting at $50. **Heritage Hotel,** 147 W. Pioneer (235-7787 or 800-478-7789), has rooms with shared baths, with private baths, and smiles. (Rooms $55-70.) The **Ocean Shores Motel,** 300 TAB Crittendon (235-7775), ebbs close to downtown, and has excellent views of the ocean on one side. (Singles from $55.)

Half-way down the Spit is Homer's **visitor center** (235-7847; open Mon.-Sat. 7am-10pm). Beverly Wood literally wrote the book on Homer—*250 Ways to Enjoy Homer.* Her successor Donna Hinkle can set you up with everything from walking tours to expensive halibut charters to stories of Trojan horses. The mogul **Central Charters** operates out of this office, booking most of the tours to the truly interesting and wild side of Kachemak Bay. The **Danny J.** ($35 round-trip) leaves for the artist-fishing colony of Halibut Cove (the most beautiful part of Alaska, according to one researcher) daily at noon. **Kayaking** day trips leave here for Kachemak Bay Park ($75 including kayak, guide and lunch), **Maritime Helicopters** can be booked here for a flight (1 hr., $135) over to the Harding Glacier and a glass of champagne, and **St. Augustine's** Charters also run out of here for a wild-life tour (2½ hr., $32). And there's about 596 more possible odysseys, including prolific halibut day charters ($125-$180).

Homer muses cozily on the southwestern Kenai Peninsula on the north shore of Kachemak Bay. The Sterling Hwy. links it to Anchorage (225.8 mi. away) and the rest of the Kenai Peninsula. To reach the downtown area, bear left off the highway onto Pioneer Ave.; bear right onto Homer Bypass to venture onto the Spit via Spit Rd. The town and the spit are small enough to be crossed on foot, but the long walk from the far end of the spit to downtown covers 6 mi. **Alaska-Denali Transit** (273-3331) will take you from one end to the other for about $40. The **Alaska Marine Highway** serves Homer from Valdez or Cordova, Kodiak, and Seward.

Kenai

Kenai, the second-oldest white settlement in Alaska, is the largest (pop. 6,546) and fastest growing city on the peninsula. Named for the Kenaitze Indians who first settled here, the spot later attracted Russians seeking sea otters and Captain Cook in his quest for a northwest passage. Of strategic interest, the Russian Fort St. Nicholas went up here in 1791, and the U.S. Army erected Fort Kenay in 1889. Only in the 1950s was the area's most valuable resource discovered off shore—black gold. Kenai and Alaska would never be the same. Now the refineries and platforms that ribbon the shore read like a *Who's Who* of the oil world. Vestiges of each era are scattered throughout town: Native American artifacts, a Russian Orthodox church, a U.S. military installation, and oil rigs.

In the spring and early summer, be on the lookout for migrating white beluga whales in **Cook Inlet,** where they feed on sockeye salmon and dodge rigs. The top of the bluff at Alaska and Mission Ave. and the overlook at the end of Forest Dr. are good spots to see these monstrous mammals, as well as the still-active volcanoes Mt. Augustine and Mt. Iliamna, which come out on clear days.

On Overland and Mission St. is the **Holy Assumption Russian Orthodox Church,** the oldest building in Kenai and the oldest standing church in Alaska (1896). This national historic landmark contains a 200-year-old Bible. Call Archpriest Targonsky—as much of a colorful attraction as the church itself—at the rectory (283-4122) for a tour. He levies a "mandatory donation" that varies according to his mood. Usually about $2.

Recreational opportunities in the Kenai area abound, the key word here being "area." Visit Kenai only to get your fishing permits and gear, and get out. It serves visitors best as a hub facilitating fishing in the aquamarine rivers of the peninsula. Check at the Chamber of Commerce for fishing charter info, and with the Forest Service for canoeing and hiking opportunities. The **Captain Cook State Recreation Area,** 30 mi. north of Nikiski at the end of Kenai Spur Rd., offers swimming, canoe landing points on the Swanson River, superb fishing, and free camping. Contact the Kenai Chamber of Commerce for rules and regulations.

For a quick fix, hit **Pizza Paradiso** on Kenai Spur Rd. (283-7008) across from the Kenai Mall, for thick pizza with plenty of toppings (large 'zas from $13.25) and other Italian food. (Open daily 11am-11:30pm. Free delivery.) **Carr's Grocery (283-7829), in the Kenai Mall on Kenai Spur Rd. has a great deli and sandwich bar. (Open 24 hrs., deli closes at 8pm.)**

To save money, head for the city **campground** on Forest Dr. off Kenai Spur Rd., where you can spend three happy days camping for free. Near the beach not far from the center of town, the campground has fireplaces and covered picnic tables. Unfortunately, the noise from motorcycling patrons and other campers is annoying. Hard-sided campers can head for the **Kenai Riverbend Campground,** Porter Rd. (283-9489); take Kalifornsy Beach Rd. off Spur Hwy. Every summer fishers descend to the Kenai Riverbend, one of the best salmon fishing holes in the world. The campground has everything you need: boat launching and rentals, rods and tackle, bait, laundry, and showers. Reservations are often necessary, though not required. (Singles $60. Doubles $65. Camping sites $14, RVs $14, with hookup $16.) The town itself also has two RV parks with full hookups: **Overland RV Park** (283-4648) and **Kenai RV Park** (283-4227), both in Old Kenai near Overland St. The best *beach access* is the sand and gravel paths to the end of Spruce St. Avoid sand trap mud flats at low tide.

Kenai, on the western Kenai Peninsula, preens 148 mi. from Anchorage and 81 mi. north of Homer. It can be reached via Kalifornsky Beach Rd., which joins Sterling Hwy. from Anchorage just south of Soldotna, or Kenai Spur Rd., which runs north through the Nikiski area and east to Soldotna. (Mile markers on Kalifornsky start at Kenai, while mile markers on the Kenai Spur Rd. start at Soldotna.) Both roads boast superb views of the peninsula's lakes and snow-capped peaks. The town's **Chamber of Commerce** and **Visitors Center,** 401 Overland St. (283-7989), meditate in the log cabin on Main St. and Kenai Spur Hwy. (Open Mon.-Fri. 9am-5pm, Sat. 10am-4pm; winter Mon.-Fri. 9am-5pm.) Write to P.O. Box 497. Kenai's **ZIP code** is 99611; the **area code** is 907.

Seward

History-hungry Seward stretches its origins to a small Russian shipyard built nearby by ubiquitous explorer Alexander Baranof in the 1830s. Not until 1903 was a new town built by U.S. railway workers as a supply center and shipping terminal. Today, the town functions primarily as a jump-off point into the magnificent **Kenai Fjords National Park.** Don't stay in the town too long. Seward reassures you with views of Mt. Alice, Mt. Marathon, and Resurrection Bay, just to remind you that you're still amid Alaska's untamed and astonishing natural beauty at the gateway to the Kenai Fjords Park. But downtown Seward is strictly middling, with greasy spoons, overpriced photo developing shops, and a small cinema. Recently, Seward has become enshrined in state consciousness as the beginning of the Iditarod dogsled trail every March.

Seward gives good day hikes. Every 4th of July locals run up nearby **Mt. Marathon,** which offers a great view of the city and ocean. You can walk. The trail begins at the end of Cowell St. **Exit Glacier,** billed as Alaska's kinder, gentler glacier, chills 9 mi. west on the road that starts at Seward Hwy. Mile 3.7 hosts the Exit Glacier 10K Run in mid-May. From the **ranger station** (no phone; open Mon.-Fri. 9am-5pm) only the intrepid should take the 4-mi. steep and slippery trail to the magnificent **Harding Ice Field.** People also flock to Seward for the mid-January **Seward Polar Bear Jump Off** and three days of surrounding festivities.

Known as the gateway to Alaska because of its position at the southern terminus of the railroad, Seward also serves as the point of entry to the **Kenai Fjords National Park.** Much of the park consists of a coastal-mountain system with an abundance of wildlife. The best way to see this area involves a boat on the bay; pick up the list of charters at the Park Service visitors center or from companies along the boardwalk next to the harbormaster's office. Most run $75-100 per day, $55-60 per half-day. For more information, contact **Kenai Fjord Tours** (224-8030), **Kenai Coastal Tours** (224-7114), **Mariah Charters** (243-1238), **Kenai National Park Tours** **(224-8068, 224-8069), or Quest Charters** (224-3025; open in summer daily 6am-10pm).

Fishing tastes heavenly in the Seward area. Salmon and halibut thrive in the bay, grayling and dolly varden right outside of town. Some people just fish off the docks. For a less luck-oriented approach, try a fishing charter with **Mariah** or **Quest,** available for both halibut and salmon throughout the summer. Prices run from $90-100, with all gear provided. Call Quest Charters or Mariah Charters.

Downtown Seward has seafood restaurants, hamburger joints, and pizza parlors galore. Pick up groceries at **Bob's Market,** 207 4th Ave. (Open Mon.-Sat. 9am-7pm, Sun. noon-6pm.) **Bob's Kitchen,** at 4th Ave. and Washington St., serves up the biggest Alaskan breakfast ever—two eggs, two bacon strips, two sausage links, toast, hash browns, biscuit with gravy, and coffee ($5). Bob's a busy guy. (Open daily 6am-8pm.) The **Breeze Inn,** Small Boat Harbor, is not your average hotel restaurant. Breeze in for the huge all-you-can-eat buffet (lunch $8, dinner $11.95). (Open daily 6am-9pm.) Also look for Bob at **Seward Salmon Bake and Bar-B-Q** in the municipal boat harbor, across from the national park center. Serves great salmon ($11.50) and by far the best barbecue in Alaska ($6-8). (Open daily 11am-9pm.)

Seward's three municipal campgrounds are typical: no showers, pleasant view, grassy sites. The best, **City Greenbelt Camping Area,** sits off 7th Ave. (Sites $6.) The nearest full-hookup RV park is **Kenai Fjords** on 4th Ave. (Sites $10.50, with full hookup $15.50.) Bob runs a beautifully restored hotel, the **Van Gilder,** at 308 Adams St. (224-3525), with clean, frontier-style rooms. (Singles $50, with bath $75. Doubles or triples $60, with bath $85.) One step down in price, quality, and Bob is **Tony's Hotel and Bar** (224-3045), on Railway at 4th St. Above the bar are surprisingly clean rooms for $30 per night, $100 per week, $250 per month.

Seward bobsleds on the southeast side of the Kenai Peninsula, in Resurrection Bay. It connects to Anchorage due north on the 127-mi. Seward Hwy. Downtown cross streets are numbered, while the longer north-south avenues are named after U.S. presidents, sequentially, starting with Washington. **Visitor Information** (224-3094) in the streetcar Seward on 3rd and Jefferson, offers an interesting walking tour. (Open daily 11am-5pm.) The **Seward Ranger Station,** 334 4th Ave., has info on local hikes and trails, while the **National Park Visitor's Center,** 1212 4th Ave. (224-3175), near the harbor, has info, films, and exhibits on the Kenai Fjords and western Prince William Sound. (Open daily 8am-7pm.)

Seward's **post office** swears by 5th and Madison. (Open Mon.-Fri. 9:30am-4:30pm, Sat. 10am-2pm.) The **ZIP code** is 99664; the **area code** is 907.

Soldotna

Once merely a fork in the road which people passed on their way to Homer, Kenai, or Seward, Soldotna has just become the center of the Kenai Peninsula's government and recreation. Soldotna is the peninsula's premier fishing spot. World record salmon are consistently caught in the Kenai River, a few minutes from downtown. Kenai Riverbend Campground, halfway between Soldotna and Kenai (see Kenai), offers a $10,000 reward to the person who catches a salmon over the record 97 pounds (see the trophy salmon, shiny and taxidermed, at the Visitors Center). With that kind of cash, you could buy all the *Let's Go* books.

Soldotna is slightly more attractive in itself than Kenai—the restaurants are better and more abundant, and the town abuts an impressive wildlife refuge. But visitors to Soldotna come from Prudhoe Bay and other ends of the earth to fish. Pink, silver, and king salmon, as well as steelhead and dolly varden, swim in the waters all summer long. Numerous **fishing charters** run the river, usually $100-125 for a half-day of halibut or salmon fishing, or $150 for both (contact the Visitors Center for more information). But you shouldn't spend that much when the downtown area is loaded with equipment rental shops that will fully outfit you with everything from bait to licenses for under $15 per day. Just wade into the Kenai and plunk in your line.

When fishing gets too slow-paced, participate in river sports at the **Kenai National Wildlife Refuge.** Dozens of **canoe routes** wend through the forest on one- to four-day journeys. A few places in town, including the Riverbend Campground and **The Sports Den,** will rent you boats (canoes $35 per day, $55 per weekend day). Otherwise, a drive along the highway from downtown will bring you into the wild depths just as quickly; more than one resident puts his boat in the front yard and hangs a "for rent" sign on it. Boat rentals are not cheap, but the experience of gliding through some of the nation's most remote waterways merits the dip into your wallet. For free canoe route maps, write the Refuge Manager, Kenai National Wildlife Refuge, P.O. Box 2139, Soldotna 99669 (262-7021).

So you didn't come just for the fish. The **Damon Memorial Historical Museum,** at mile 3 on Kalifornsky Beach Rd., holds artifacts from Native Alaskan burial grounds and a large diorama. (Admission $1. Open Mon.-Fri. 9am-5pm). The **Kenai National Wildlife Refuge Visitors Center** (262-7021), off Funny River rd. directly across from the visitors center at the top of Ski Hill Rd., is a great source of info on the 197-million-acre refuge for moose, Dall sheep, and other wild animals. (But don't count on seeing anything more than an occasional moose from the panoramic overlook. Most critters are discretely habitating several million acres away.) The center also has dioramas, victims of taxidermy, and several nature trails nearby. Scratch and sniff wooly patches of assorted mammal fur. Or be a loon—pick up a phone and talk to one, or to a wolf for that matter. (Open Mon.-Fri. 8am-4:30pm, Sat.-Sun. 10am-6pm; Sept. 3-May 26 Mon.-Fri. 8am-4pm, Sun.-Sat. 10am-5:30pm.)

Because Soldotna began as a highway crossroads, there's plenty of fast food along the road downtown. Burger-chain prices are slightly higher than in the Lower 48, but budget-oriented visitors may still have to opt for the Big Mac over sit-down dining. **Sal's Klondike Diner,** Sterling Hwy. a ½-mi. from the river, cooks the best dinner in town. Try a sandwich with salad and fries ($4-6). Caffeine addicts will appreciate the Java priced on an hourly basis ($1 per hr.) Breakfast items ($3) are served all day. (Open daily 24 hrs.) **Four Seasons,** 43960 Sterling Hwy., just north of the "Y," has some of the best home-style food in Alaska $6-13. (Open Mon.-Fri. 11am-3pm and 5:30-10pm.)

Backpackers can stay at nearby campgrounds and shell out $2 for hot, clean showers at the **River Terrace RV Park** at the river. **Swiftwater Park Municipal Campground** south of Sterling Hwy. at mi. 94, and **Centennial Park Municipal Campground,** off Kalifornsky Beach Rd. near the visitors center, hunker down in the woods and have boat launches. Conveniently located on the river, the campgrounds feature excellent fishing and tables set aside for cleaning fish. (1-week max. stay. Sites $6.) Indoor accommodations are available at **Duck Inn,** mile 3 on Kalifonsky Beach Rd. (262-5041; write P.O. Box 3634, Soldotna 99669), by the Red Diamond Mall. All rooms have a private bath. (No reservations. $59.50 for 1 or 2 people.)

Soldotna has a sizeable **visitors center,** P.O. Box 236 (262-1337), on the Sterling Hwy. and Kalifornsky Beach Rd., with a sizeable world record king salmon on display. The center serves Soldotna and the less-inhabited regions of the peninsula, such as Ninilchik, Clam Gulch, and the Interior.

Both Sodotna and Kenai locals head to **Nightwatch** (262-7020), on Sterling Hwy. just past the bridge, for nightly live rock and roll. (Open daily 11am-2am.)

Southeastern Alaska (The Panhandle)

The Panhandle flings 500 mi. from the Gulf of Alaska to Prince Rupert, BC. The Tlingit (pronounced KLING-kit) and Haida (pronounced HI-duh) tribes have left a deep mark on this loose network of islands, inlets, and deep saltwater fjords surrounded by deep valleys and rugged mountains. Temperate rain forest conditions, 60-odd major glaciers, and 15,000 bald eagles distinguish the Panhandle.

Southeastern Alaska is one of the few places in the world where the blast of a ferry boat heralds the day's important event. The 1000 islands and 10,000 mi. of coastline in the Alexander Archipelago are connected to each other and to Seattle by ferries run by the Alaska Marine Hwy. While the Interior and the Southcentral regions of Alaska have experienced great urban sprawl (by Alaskan standards), the communities of Southeastern Alaska cling to the coast. Gold Rush days haunt such towns as Juneau; others like Sitka hearken back to the era of the Russian occupation.

The Alaska Marine Hwy. system provides the cheapest, most exciting way to explore the area. The state-run ferries connect Seattle, Ketchikan, Sitka, Juneau, and Haines, as well as some smaller Native American and fishing communities. You can avoid the high price of accommodations in smaller communities by planning your ferry trip at night and sleeping on the deck.

Haines and the Northern Panhandle

North of Juneau, the inside passage grows in magnificence; the mountains become bigger and snowier, the whales and eagles friendlier. The **Alaska Marine Highway** can take you up to Haines ($18 from Juneau, vehicle up to 15 ft. $39). Sleep on the ferry or stay up all night traveling through this land of many glaciers and soaring peaks.

"Haines" was originally "Deishu," or "End of the Trail in Tlingit." Today the most traveled overland route from the interior and the Yukon into SE Alaska terminates here as well—the **Haines Highway.**

The area's main attraction is the convergence of over 3000 bald eagles (more than double the town's population) in the "Council Grounds" on the Chilkat Peninsula from November to January each year. Haines is by far the most strikingly beautiful city on the SE Panhandle with its high bluffs overlooking a turquoise bay and granite mountains, and abundance of superb hiking trails. Walt Disney productions capitalized on this beauty by filming its adaptation of Jack London's **White Fang** here. The movie set still sits on the edge of town.

Backpackers can stay at the exquisitely trimmed **Portage Cove State Park,** ¾-mi. outside of town along Beach Rd., behind the clump of trees. (Pit toilets, water. Sites $6.50.) For indoor accommodations, the **Hotel Halsingland,** Box 1589 MP, Haines 99827 (766-2000), on the parade grounds south of town, is Haines's luxury address. (Singles from $30, with bath $65.) Less luxurious is the **Bear Creek Camp & Hostel (AYH),** Box 1158, Haines 99827 (907-766-2202), on Small Tract Rd. almost 3 mi. outside of town. From downtown, follow 3rd Ave. out Mud Bay Rd. to Small Tract Rd.; call ahead for ferry pickup. (Kitchen. No curfew. $12, nonmembers $14. Cabins $35. Showers $2.50.)

Those wishing to avoid restaurant fare can hit **Howser's Supermarket** on Main St. (open Mon.-Sat. 9am-8pm, Sun. 10am-7pm). The store has a great deli bar, a salad bar with a large pasta selection ($2.99 per lb.), and chicken dinners ($3.99). At **Porcupine Pete's,** Main and 2nd Ave., a slice of pizza and salad ($3.55) prefaces good $1.35 ice cream. (Open daily 11am-10pm.) The **Bamboo Room,** 2nd Ave. near Main St. next to the Pioneer Bar, is a great breakfast spot, always crowded with fishermen on their way out to the nets. (Hot cakes and coffee $5.50, omelettes $6. Open daily 7am-10pm. Breakfast only until 11am.)

The town maintains a **visitor information center,** 2nd Ave. near Willard St. (766-2234 or 800-458-3574), with info on accommodations and nearby parks. Pick up the *Haines is for Hikers* pamphlet. (Open June-Sept. Mon.-Sat. 8am-8pm, Sun.

10:30am-6pm.) The **Alaska Marine Highway Terminal,** 5 Mile Lutake Rd. (766-2111), is 4 mi. (a $7 cab ride) from downtown, or an easy hitchhike connection.

Catch the ever-friendly **Ranger Bill Zack at the State Park Information Office,** 259 Main St. (766-2292), above Helen's shop for *in depth trail suggestions and information.* Your best chances of finding him are Tues.-Sat. 8-8:30am and 4-4:30pm. The **SE Alaska State Fair** lights up the fairgrounds here August 14-18. The **Alaska Bald Eagle Music Festival** runs concurrently.

The **Haines Highway,** one of the most beautiful in the state, winds 40 mi. from Haines through the **Chilkat Range** past bright-blue glaciers, ice-cold waterfalls, and up through the Yukon Territory in Canada. **Chilkat State Park,** a 19-mi. drive up the highway, protects the largest population of bald eagles in North America—3500 all told. From November through January, travelers can see great numbers of eagles perched on birchwoods in the rivers or flying overhead. **Chilkat Guides** (766-2491), P.O. Box 170, leads four-hour raft trips down the Chilkat River when the eagles are flocking. ($60, rubber boots and ponchos provided.)

Gentlemen prefer Haines's **post office** at the corner of 2nd Ave. and Haines Hwy. (open Mon.-Fri. 9am-5:30pm). General Delivery **ZIP code** is 99827; the **area code** is 907.

Juneau

Compressed into a tiny strip of land at the base of noble Mt. Juneau, Alaska's capital city is the only one in the nation inaccessible by highway. This "Little San Francisco" mixes and matches Victorian mansions, log cabins, Russian Orthodox churches, "Federal" style *quonset* huts, and simple frame houses with shutters painted in Norwegian *rosemaling* all set on nearly vertiginous streets leading down to wharf-tourist-mecca.

The styles only hint at the richness of Juneau's history. Tlingit Chief Kowee led Joe Juneau and Richard Harris up Gold Creek to the "mother lode" of gold in October, 1880. By the next summer, boatloads of prospectors found themselves at work in the already-claimed mines. Twenty-five years later Juneau superseded Sitka as capital of the territory of Alaska. Poor Sitka. Mining ended in Juneau in 1941, but by then fishing, lumber, and the government had filled in to support the city's economy. Today, Juneau thrives on government (which from the point-of-view of Alaska's many libertarians means "organized crime") and tourism.

Practical Information

Emergency: 911.

Visitors Information: Davis Log Cabin, 134 3rd St. (586-2284), at Seward St. Open Mon.-Fri. 8:30am-5pm, Sat.-Sun. 10am-5pm; Oct.-May Mon.-Fri. 8:30am-5pm. **Marine Park Kiosk,** Marine Way at Ferry Way, right by the cruise ship unloading dock. Open May-Sept. daily 9am-6pm. **U.S. Forest and National Park Services,** 101 Egan Dr. (586-8751), in Centennial Hall. Makes reservations for USFS cabins in Tongass Forest. Write for application packet (see Camping under Ketchikan). Open daily 8am-5pm.

Juneau International Airport: 9 mi. north of town on Glacier Hwy. **Alaska Air,** in the Baranof Hotel, S. Franklin at 2nd St. (789-0600 or 800-426-0333). To Anchorage, Sitka or Ketchikan.

Public Transport: Capital Transit (789-6901). Runs from downtown to Douglas, the airport, and Mendenhall Glacier. Leaves Marine Park for airport and glacier 5 min. after the hr. every hr. 7am-3pm. From 3-10pm, leaves Marine Park 35 min. after the hr. ($1). **Eagle Express Line** (789-5460) runs vans to the airport ($5); also has an cheap tour of Juneau and Mendenhall Glacier (2½ hr., $25, kids $16) or the glacier alone (45 min., $35). Departs 10:30am and 2:30pm from the Marine Park, and from major hotels in time for all flights.

Alaska Marine Highway: P.O. Box R, Juneau 99811 (465-3940 or 800-642-0066). Ferries dock at the Auke Bay terminal at mile 13.8 Glacier Hwy. To: Bellingham, WA ($216, car and driver $457), Ketchikan ($72, car and driver $151), and Sitka ($24, car and driver $50).

Taxis: Capital Cab, 586-2772. **Taku Taxi,** 586-2121. Both conduct city tours (½hr., $25) and run to Mendenhall (45 min. at glacier, $35).

Car Rental: Rent-a-Wreck, Airport Blvd. (789-4111). $30 per day, 100 free mi., 15¢ each additional mi.

Help Lines: Crisis Line, 586-4337. Open daily 7-11pm.

Post Office: 709 W. 9th St. (586-7138). Open Mon. 8:30am-5pm, Tues.-Fri. 9:30am-5pm, Sat. 9:30am-3:30pm. General Delivery ZIP code: 99801.

Area Code: 907.

Juneau stands on the Gastineau Channel opposite Douglas Island. **Glacier Highway** connects downtown, the airport, the residential area of the Mendenhall Valley, and the ferry terminal.

Accommodations and Camping

For those not interested in Juneau's wonderful hostel, the **Alaska Bed and Breakfast Association**, P.O. Box 3/6500, #169 Juneau 99802 (586-2959), will provide information on rooms in local homes year-round. Most Juneau B&Bs lie uphill, beyond 6th St., offering singles from $45 and doubles from $55. Reservations are recommended.

Juneau International Hostel (AYH), 614 Harris St. (586-9559), at 6th. Clean, friendly, and properly managed. 24 bunk beds. Showers (50¢ per 5 min.), laundry, and kitchen facilities. Curfew 11pm. Lockout 9am-5pm. $8, nonmembers $11. Make reservations well in advance for July and Aug.

Alaska Hotel, 167 S. Franklin St. (586-1000 or 800-327-9347), in the center of downtown. Handsome hotel made of dark wood restored to its 1913 Victorian decor. Singles $40, with bath $55. Doubles $50, with bath $65. Hot tubs noon-4pm $10.50, after 4pm $21. If you're going to splurge, this is the one.

Driftwood Lodge, 435 Willoughby Ave. (586-2280), behind the state office bldg. Courtesy van will whisk you to and from the airport, and daily at 1pm out to Mendenhall Glacier. Efficiency $59-$66. Two bedrooms for 1-4 people $89.

Campgrounds: Run by the forest service (see Practical Information above). 14-day max. stay. Mendenhall Lake Campground, Montana Creek Rd. Take Glacier Hwy. north 9 mi. to Mendenhall Loop Rd.; continue 3½ mi. and take the right fork. By bus, driver will let you off and you can hike the 2 mi. in. Nice view of and trails leading to the glacier. 61 sites. Fireplaces, water, pit toilets. Sites $5. Auke Village Campground, 15 mi. from Juneau on Glacier Hwy. 11 sites. Fireplaces, water, pit toilets. Sites $5.

Food

Travelers on a shoestring should head to the **Foodland Supermarket**, 631 Willoughby Ave., past the Federal Bldg. and near Gold Creek. (Open Mon.-Sat. 9am-7pm, Sun. 10am-6pm.) Or pay a bit more for health food at **Rainbow Foods**, 200 N. Franklin St. Seafood lovers should haunt **Merchants Wharf**, next to Marine Park. Always packed with tourists and locals, **Armadillo Tex-Mex Cafe**, 431 Franklin St., has fantastic "BBQ Hot Link Sausages" ($7) and heaping platefuls of T. Terry's nachos ($4.50). (Open Mon.-Sat. 11am-10pm, Sun. 4-10pm.) Complete with ferns and formica, the upscale **Heritage Cafe And Coffee Co.,** Franklin St. across from the Senate Bldg., is the best place in town for vegetarians to eat, with excellent bottomless coffee ($1) and large sandwiches ($5). (Open Mon.-Fri. 7am-11pm, Thurs. 7am-7pm, Sat.-Sun. 8am-11pm.) Try **Silverbow Inn**, 120 2nd St. (586-4146), downtown, for budget-busting. French and U.S. cuisine served on antique oak tables. Lunch costs $8-13, dinner $13-25. Reservations recommended. (Open Mon.-Fri. 11:30am-2pm, Sat.-Sun. 9am-2pm; off-season daily 5:30-9:30pm.)

Sights

Juneau's greatest attraction is undoubtedly the **Mendenhall Glacier,** about 10 mi. north of downtown. The glacier, descending from the 1500-sq.-mi. Juneau Ice Field to the east, glowers over the valley where most downtown workers reside. At the glacier **visitors center,** rangers explain the relation of the glacier to the ice field and why the glacier is now retreating. Apparently the two have been quarreling of late.

(Open daily 9am-6:30pm.) The rangers give good ecology walks everyday at 10:30am. The best view of the glacier without a helicopter is from the 3½-mi.-long W. Glacier Trail. To reach the glacier, take the local public bus down Glacier Hwy. and up Mendenhall Loop Rd. until it connects with Glacier Spur Rd. From here it's less than a half-hour walk to the visitors center. **Eagle Express Lines** runs excellent tours (see Practical Information), but you can see this hulk on your own. Taking the bus costs only $2 round-trip and you can meander as long as you like.

In Juneau itself, the **Alaska State Museum,** 395 Whittier St. (495-2910), provides a good introduction to the history, ecology, and Native American cultures of "The Great Land." The museum's exhibits cover Alaska's four main Native American cultures: Tlingit, Athabaskan, Eskimo, and Aleut. (Open May 15-Sept. 15 Mon.-Fri. 9am-6pm, Sat.-Sun. 10am-6pm; off-season Tues.-Sat. 10am-4pm. Admission $2, students free.)

The unimpressive **state capitol** building, 4th and Main, offers summer tours daily from 9am to 5pm. Your time is better spent wandering uphill to **St. Nicholas Russian Orthodox Church** on 5th St. between North Franklin and Gold St. Built in 1894, the church is the oldest of its kind in southeastern Alaska. Services, conducted in English, Slavonic, and Tlingit are open to the public. One block farther uphill on 6th St. stands a 45-ft. **totem pole** carved in 1940. Pick up the free **Totem Walking Tour** from the visitor center and discover over a dozen contemporary poles carved by such masters as Ketchikan-based Nathan Jackson.

Finding the best view of downtown is simply a matter of walking to the end of 6th St. and then up a steep 4-mi. trail to the summit of **Mt. Roberts** (3576 ft.). Miners flocked to "them thar hills" in the 1880s after Joe Juneau and Dick Harris found treasure in Gold Creek. Though no longer active in Juneau, the mines are active tourist sights that frequently host salmon bakes. The **Alaska-Juneau Mine** was the largest in its heyday. **Last Chance Basin,** at the end of Basin Rd., now holds Gold Creek's mining museum.

Juneau stalks one of the best hiking centers in the southeast. In addition to the ascent of Mt. Roberts, one popular daytrek is along the first section of the **Perseverance Trail,** which leads past the ruins of the historic **Silverbowl Basin Mine** behind Mt. Roberts. For more details on this as well as several other area hikes, drop by the state museum bookstore, the park service center, or any local bookstore to pick up *Juneau Trails,* published by the Alaska Natural History Association ($2.50). The rangers will provide copies of particular maps in this book at the park service center. (See U.S. Forest and National Park Service under Practical Information.)

During winter the slopes of the **Eaglecrest Ski Area** on Douglas Island (contact 155 S. Seward St., Juneau 99801, 586-5284), offer good skiing. ($30 per day, ages 12-18 $18, under 12 $15.) In summer, the Eaglecrest "Alpine Summer" self-guided nature trail soaks in the mountain scenery of untouched Douglas Island.

At night, tourists head to the **Red Dog Saloon** (463-3777) on S. Franklin. Cateye glasses from the cruise ships mingle right in with backpackers and locals over imported sawdust on the floor. Folksy frontier sayings on the wall and its live music on weekends beat the authenticity. Locals also hang out farther up Franklin: the **Triangle Club** (586-3140), at Front St., attracts a hard-drinking set, while young people and the cruise ship crowd congregate at the **Penthouse,** on the fourth floor of the Senate Bldg. The **Lady Lou Revue** (586-3686), a revival of Gold Rush days, plays multiple shows daily at the Elks Lodge on Franklin. (Admission $18, Children $10.)

Ketchikan

A Ketchikan proverb claims, "If you can't see the top of Deer Mountain, it's raining; if you *can* see the top, it's about to rain." About 164 in. per year marinate this good-sized fishing and lumber town of 14,600, cradled at the watery base of the mountain; locals have to ignore the rain or nothing would ever get done. The southernmost city in Alaska, Ketchikan is also the first port for ferries and cruise ships visiting the state, depositing hordes of students in search of big summer bucks at the canneries. If you're one of them, plan ahead carefully. Job openings follow the fish each season and vary from city to city. **Ketchikan Job Service,** 362 Dock St. (225-5500), is a good place to enquire if you're already in town. Open Mon.-Fri. 7:30am-5pm.

The **Ketchikan Visitors Bureau,** 131 Front St. (225-6166), across from the cruise ship docks downtown, offers maps of a good walking tour. (Open Mon.-Fri. 8am-5pm, and Sat.-Sun. in conjunction with cruise ships.) **Creek Street,** the red-light district that thrived until 1954, preserves Ketchikan's mining boomtown history. This is the only creek where both sailors and salmon went upstream to spawn. Revel in the sordid past of **Dolly's House,** 24 Creek St. (225-6329), a brothel-turned-museum. Hours vary; call ahead. (Admission $2.) Also on the walking tour is the **Totem Heritage Center,** 601 Deermount St., which houses 33 well-preserved totem poles from Tlingit, Tsimshian and Haida villages. (Open Mon.-Sat. 8am-5pm, Sun. 9am-5pm. Admission $2, under 18 free. Sun. afternoon free.) The **Tongass Historical Society Museum,** on Dock St., explains the region's past. (Open mid-May to Sept. Mon.-Sat. 8:30am-5pm, Sun. 1-5pm. Admission $1, under 18 free. Free Sun.) Ketchikan currently has the highest population of Native Alaskans in the southeastern portion of the state. If you can see only one thing in Ketchikan, see **Saxman Native Village,** 2½ mi. south of town, which displays 24 totems, including the world's largest, from original sites at villages in the Inland Passage. (Open daily 9am-5pm and on weekends when cruise ships are in.) The reconstructed Tlinget community house and the 13 totems of the **Totem Bight** lie 13½ mi. north of town along the beach. Without wheels you will have difficulty reaching the rainforest park; taxis charge $9-10 each way to Saxman.

The **Ketchikan Youth Hostel (AYH)** (225-3319), kneels in the United Methodist Church on the corner of Grant and Main St. Kitchen is available; no beds, just comfortable mats on the floor. (Lockout 8:30am-6pm. Lights out 11pm. $5, nonmembers $8. Open June-Aug. No reservations.) The **Ketchikan Bed and Breakfast Network,** P.O. Box 3213 (225-8550), can find you slightly more glamorous accommodations. (Singles $45-70.) Camp on the shores of Ward Lake at the **Signal Creek Campground,** 6 mi. north on Tongass Hwy. from the ferry terminal. (Sites $5. Open in summer.) Privately run **Last Chance Campground,** 2.2 mi. from Signal Creek down Ward Lake, caters mostly to RVs. (Water and pit toilets. Sites $6.)

The supermarket most convenient to downtown is **Tatsuda's,** 633 Stedman, at Deermount St. (225-4125) just beyond the Thomas Basin. (Open 24 hrs.) **Pioneer Pantry,** 124 Front St. (225-3337), across from the visitors bureau, offers clean-cut decor with a few tables and a long bar. Sandwiches ($4.25-7) include salad, fries, or soup. (Open Mon.-Sat. 8am-6pm.)

Frequented by fishermen, **Pancho's Mexican Restaurant,** 834 Water St., a few hundred yards past the tunnel from downtown, will buoy your spirits; large entrees come with chips, salsa, rice, beans, cornbread and dessert ($10-$22.95). The **Ketchikan Café,** 314 Front St., shines with superb views of the Tongass Narrows, melodious classical music and filling dinners ($18). (Open daily 8am-9pm.) **Miss Lillian's** serves great coffee, used books and ambience right next to Dolly's on Creek St. Come up and see her sometime.

Ketchikan sits on an island 235 mi. south of Juneau, 90 mi. north of Prince Rupert, BC, and 600 mi. north of Seattle, WA. The town stretches for 12 mi. but rarely exceeds seven blocks in width.

Just off the coast, **Metlakatla** island and Tsimshian Indian Reserve represents a vanishing autonomous Indian Community. Fly out to visit their two museums and chat with tribal historian Ira Booth. **Taquan Air** offers reasonable daily float plane service for $36 round-trip (225-9668).

The magical **Misty Fjords National Monument** lies 30 mi. east of Ketchikan, accessible by boat or float plane. This 2.2-million-acre park offers great camping, guided tours in summer and workshops year-round. Call the Ketchikan Visitors Bureau or the **Misty Fjords Visitor Center,** on Mill St., for info about tours to the park (over $140). In town, the **Frontier Saloon,** 127 Main St. (225-4407), has live music Tuesday through Sunday in summer. (Open daily 10am-2am.) The **Arctic Bar** (225-4709), on the other side of the tunnel, is a more earthy fishers' haunt. (Open Sun.-Wed. 8am-midnight, Thurs.-Sat. 8am-2am.)

Ketchikan **buses** run about every half-hour from Monday to Saturday 6:45am-6:45pm. (Fare $1, seniors and under 11 75¢.) Ketchikan's **ZIP code** is 99901; the **area code** is 907.

Sitka

Russian explorer Vitus Bering made the first European landfall here in 1741, beginning decades of bloody fighting between Russian settlers and Tlingits. After defeating the Native Americans, the Russians established "New Archangel" as the capital in 1804. The settlement stayed Russia's "Paris of the Pacific" for the next 63 years; visitors came here for the lure of money from sea otter pelts and the trappings of glittering society life. After the U.S. purchased Alaska in 1867, Sitka remained the territory's capital from 1884 until 1906.

The beautiful, onion-domed **Saint Michael's Cathedral** shows much of the earlier colonial influence. Decimated by fire in 1964 but rebuilt in accordance with the original, this Russian Orthodox Church still displays precious icons and vestments. (Open Mon.-Sat. 11am-3pm and when cruise ships in. Donation required.) Historic **Castle Hill**, site of Baranof's Castle and Tlingit forts, offers an incredible view of Mt. Edgecumbe, an inactive volcano known as the "Mt. Fuji of Alaska." The U.S. bought Alaska here in October of 1867.

Stroll down the manicured trails of the **Sitka National Historic Park** (Totem Park, as locals call it), at the end of Lincoln St. (747-6281), one mi. east of St. Michael's. The trails pass by many restored totems on the way to the side of the **Tlingit Fort,** where hammer-wielding chieftain Katlian almost held off the Russians in the battle for Alaska in 1804. The park **visitors center** offers audiovisual presentations and the opportunity to watch native artists in action in the Native American Cultural Center. (Open daily 8am-5pm.) The park service recently restored the **Russian Bishop's House,** across from Crescent Boat Harbor, to duplicate its 1842 appearance when built for its first resident, Bishop Ivan Veniaminor. Unlike at St. Mike's, you can even photograph the beautiful gold and silver icons. (Open daily 8:30am-5pm. Tours every ½-hr.)

The Sitka area offers excellent **hiking** opportunities—make sure to pick up the thick booklet *Sitka Trails* ($1) at the **USFS information booth,** in front of the Centennial Bldg. at Lincoln St. Several outstanding trails include the **Indian River Trail,** an easy 5.5-mi. trek up the valley to the base of **Indian River Falls,** and the 3-mi. uphill trail to the top of **Gavan Hill.** From downtown across the runway at the Japonski Island airport to the old WWII causeway, a fine 3-mi. trek heads past abandoned fortifications all the way to **Makhanati Island.**

Sitka has several bed-and-breakfast homes priced from $35 per person. The **visitors bureau,** Centennial Bldg., 330 Harbor Dr. (747-3225, open Mon.-Sat. 8am-5pm), has a complete list. The small **Sitka Youth Hostel (AYH),** P.O. Box 2645 (747-8356), has army cots in the United Methodist Church on Edgecumbe and Kimsham St. Find the McDonald's, 1 mi. out of town on Halibut Pt. Rd., and walk 100 ft. up Peterson St. to Kimsham. (Kitchen facilities; chore required. Lockout 9am-6pm. Curfew 11pm. $5, nonmembers $8.) **Sitka Hotel,** 118 Lincoln (747-3288), has cheap rooms much cleaner than the building itself. (Singles $43.20, with bath $48.60. Doubles $48.60, with bath $54. Senior discounts available.) The **Sheldon Jackson College** also rents rooms nightly from its campus housing, east end of Lincoln St. (747-8981). Dormitory rooms with bedding, shared bath and no curfew or lockout. Singles $20 and $30, doubles $25 and $35. Register in administration building. The USFS runs the **Starrigaven Creek Campground,** at the end of Halibut Pt. Rd., one mi. from the ferry terminal, 8 mi. from town. (Pit toilets. 14-day max. stay. Sites $6.25.)

For transportation from the ferry terminal, look for the **Orca Tour Buses** with the unmistakeable whale fin on top. They're cheap ($2) to anywhere in town, and will drop you off at your door rather than at the Centennial Bldg.

Pick up your groceries at the **Market Center Grocery** at Sawmill Creek and Baranof St., uphill from the Bishop's House (open Mon.-Sat. 10am-8pm, Sun. noon-6pm), or close to the hostel at **Lakeside Grocery**, 705 Halibut Pt. Rd. (Open Mon.-Sat. 9am-9pm, Sun. 11am-7pm.) Fresh seafood is available from fishers along the docks or at **Sitka Sound Seafood** on Katlian St., which occasionally offers surplus fish for retail sale. **The Bayview Restaurant**, upstairs in the Bayview Trading Company at 407 Lincoln St. (747-5440), cooks up everything from *russkia ribnia blyood* ($7.25) to a Mousetrap sandwich (grilled cheese, $3.75), as well as great burgers. (Open Mon.-Sat. 6am-7:30pm.) **Staton's Steak House**, 228 Harbor Dr., across from the Centennial Bldg., alliterates delicious lunch specials of halibut and french fries ($7). (Open Mon. and Wed. 11am-2pm and 5-9pm; Tues., Thurs. and Sat. 11am-2pm and 5-10pm.)

The **Sitka Music Festival** in June brings world-renowned musicians. Tickets $10 at the Centennial Bldg.

Sitka sits on the western side of Baranof Island, 95 mi. southwest of Juneau and 185 mi. northwest of Ketchikan. The O'Connell Bridge connects downtown to Japonski Island and the airport. Sitka's **post office**, 1207 Sawmill Creek Rd. (747-3381), lies outside of downtown. (Open Mon.-Fri. 9am-5pm.) The **ZIP code** is 99835; the **area code** is 907.

ARIZONA

All who come into this arid zone expose themselves to the unparalleled scenic expanses and plunging depths of the Grand Canyon. Yet to do so while ignoring the other natural wonders of the state is as pleasurable as having sex without foreplay. Indeed, the state seduces with a Caligulastic orgy of natural formations. Canyon de Chelly's steamy cliffs and undulating green valleys elicit blissful moans, as does Monument Valley's thrusting sandstone formations. Native American cliff dwellings and the former mining towns with their abandoned shafts stand erect as an austere reminder of the constant hardships of desert survival in the seminal days before interstates, waterbeds, and No-Tell Motels. The state's esoteric population—a kinky blend of sun-baked, prurient collegians, sperm-whale-saving New-Agers, and sun-loving octogenarians—helps make a visit to Arizona's cities a stimulating, almost orgasmic, experience. We hope it will be as good for you as it was for us.

Practical Information

Capital: Phoenix.

Arizona Office of Tourism, 3507 N. Central Ave. #506, Phoenix 85012 (255-3618). **Arizona State Parks**, 1688 W. Adams St., Phoenix 85007.

Time Zone: Mountain (2 hr. behind Eastern). Arizona (with the exception of the reservations) does not follow Daylight Savings Time; in summer it is one hr. behind the rest of the Mountain Time Zone. **Postal Abbreviation:** AZ

Flagstaff

Flagstaff's mountain-town denizens show signs of schizophrenia. Most of the year they graciously host a handful of skiers and the students of **Northern Arizona University.** Come May, however, the townspeople joyously plunder tourists who use the town as base camp for explorations of the Grand Canyon and other local attractions. Rabid locals aside, Flagstaff does provide a good place to relax for a few days between photography binges; while the mountain elevation cools Flagstaff during the day, renowned local bands heat the town up at night.

Practical Information

Emergency: 911. Police/Medical Assistance, 774-1414.

Visitor Information: Flagstaff Chamber of Commerce, 101 W. Santa Fe Ave. (800-842-7293), across from the Amtrak station. Free city map, National Forest map $2. Open Mon.-Sat. 8am-9pm, Sun. 8am-5pm. Special Events Hotline, 779-3733. 24-hr. recorded message.

Amtrak: 1 E. Sante Fe Ave. (774-8679 or 800-872-7245). One train per day to Los Angeles ($81) and Albuquerque ($76). Open daily 5:45-10am, 11am-2pm, 2:30-6pm, and 7-10:30pm.

Buses: Greyhound, 399 S. Malpais Lane (774-4573), across from NAU campus, 5 blocks southwest of the train station on U.S. 89A. To: Phoenix (5/day, $21); Albuquerque (6/day, $45); Los Angeles (5/day, $75); and Las Vegas via Kingman, AZ (3/day, $51). Terminal open 24 hrs. Gray Line/Nava-Hopi, 774-5003; 800-892-8687 outside AZ. Shuttle buses to the Grand Canyon (3/day, $25 round-trip, $12.90 with Greyhound Ameripass).

Public Transport: Pine County Transit, 970 Old Hwy. 66 (779-6624 or 779-6635). Three routes covering most of town. Fare 75¢; seniors, disabled, and kids 60¢. Runs once per hour. In summer a free trolley runs to the mall Mon.-Sat.

Tours: Gray Line/Nava-Hopi, 774-5003; 800-892-8687 outside AZ. One-day sightseeing tours to: the Grand Canyon ($32); Monument Valley and the Navajo Reservation and Monument ($72); the Hopi Reservation and Painted Desert ($62); and the Museum of N. Arizona, Sunset Crater, Wupatki, and Walnut Canyon (May-Oct.; $30). Kids under 13 ride ½-price on all tours. All tours except Grand Canyon run early April to mid-Nov. Grand Canyon runs year-round. Reservations required. Purchase tickets at the Amtrak and Greyhound stations. Northern Arizona Wilderness Tours, 284 Toho Trail (525-1028). To various National Parks and monuments and Indian villages in vans and open four-wheel drive vehicles.

Camping Equipment Rental: Peace Surplus, 14 W. Santa Fe Ave. (779-4521), 1 block from the hostel. Daily rental of dome tents ($4-8), packs ($5), stoves ($3), plus a good stock of cheap outdoor gear. Open Mon.-Fri. 8:30am-9pm, Sat. 8:30am-7pm, Sun. 9am-6pm.

Bike Rental: Cosmic Cycles, 113 S. San Francisco St. (779-1092), downtown. Mountain bikes $5/day, $20 on weekends. City bikes with wide tires $10/day. Open Mon.-Fri. 9am-6pm, Sun. 11am-4pm.

Taxi: Dream Taxi, (774-2934). Open 24 hrs.; you can dream anytime.

Car Rental: Allstar Rent-A-Car, 602 Mikes Pike (on Hwy. 66; 774-7394 or 800-426-5243). $28/day. 150 free mi., 19¢ each additional mi. Open Mon.-Sat. 7am-7pm, Sun. 9am-1pm. Must be 21 with major credit card or cash deposit.

Post Office: 104 N. Agassiz. Open Mon.-Fri. 9am-3pm. ZIP code: 86001.

Area Code: 602.

The center of Flagstaff is the intersection of **Beaver Street** and **Santa Fe Avenue** (U.S. 89A), where the train station rests. Within ½-mi. of this spot are both bus stations, the three youth hostels, the chamber of commerce, and several inexpensive restaurants. Other commercial establishments lie on **South Sitgreaves Street** (U.S. 89A), near the NAU campus.

Because Flagstaff is a mountain town, it stays cooler than much of the rest of the state, and receives frequent afternoon thundershowers. You can walk around most of downtown, but to get anywhere worth seeing, rent a car or take a tour bus.

Accommodations and Camping

Three competing hostels downtown, as well as other cheap motels on E. Santa Fe Ave., make sleeping in Flagstaff easily affordable. Since the town can get rather chilly even in the summer, be sure to ask for a blanket. Don't expect to find budget lodgings in the vicinity of the the Greyhound station or around the NAU campus, though. Camping in **Cocino National Forest** is a pleasant and inexpensive option.

Downtowner Independent Youth Hostel, 19 S. San Francisco (774-8461). Flexible management will send a Mercedes to shuttle between hostel and bus station. Very clean, well-maintained rooms with wooden floors and comfortable beds. Kitchen, hall baths. Open approximately 7am-9:30pm. Private rooms $10/person, more crowded $8. Linen included. Open mid-May to mid-Aug.

The Weatherford Hotel (AYH), 23 N. Leroux (774-2731). Friendly management and convenient location. Dorm rooms, baths in rooms and halls, kitchen, and a cozy common area; ride board in lobby. Open daily 7am-3pm and 5-11pm; off-season 7am-1pm and 5-10pm. Curfew midnight. Members $9, nonmembers $12. Required sleepsheet $1. Private singles $22. Doubles $24. Guests enjoy ½-off cover at **Charly's,** downstairs, which has live music.

Hotel Du Beau, 19 W. Phoenix (774-6731), just behind the train station. This registered National Landmark hotel, built in 1929, once hosted L.A. film stars and Chicago gangsters. Kitchen, library, nightly videos, gift and necessities shop. No charge to borrow bikes. 4 campsites. $11. Breakfast included.

KOA, 5803 N. Hwy. 89 (526-9926), 6 mi. northeast of Flagstaff. Municipal bus routes stop nearby. Sites $16 for 2 people, with hookup $17. Each additional person $2.50.

You'll probably need a car to reach the public campgrounds that ring the city. Campgrounds at higher elevations close during the winter; many are small and fill up quickly during the summer, particularly on weekends when Phoenicians flock to the mountains. If you stake out your site by 3pm you shouldn't encounter problems. National Forest sites are usually $2-3 per night. Pick up a **Coconino National Forest** map ($2) in Flagstaff at the chamber of commerce. **Lake View,** 13 mi. southeast on Forest Hwy. 3 (U.S. 89A), has 30 sites ($5). **Bonito,** 2 mi. east at Forest Rd. 545, off U.S. 89, has 44 sites at Sunset Crater ($5). All have running water and flush toilets. Those (and only those) who can live without amenities can camp for free on any National Forest land outside the designated campsites, unless you see signs to the contrary. For more info, call the Coconino Forest Service (527-7400; Mon.-Fri. 7:30am-4:30pm; 24-hr. emergency 526-0600).

Food

As befits a college town, cafés and coffeeshops liberally sprinkle Flagstaff, serving a variety of pastries, sandwiches, and hot drinks. Several typical Arizona steakhouses sizzle as well.

Macy's, 14 S. Beaver St. Superb fresh pasta ($3.25-5.25), plus a wide variety of vegetarian entrees, pastries, and espresso-based drinks. Open daily 7am-8pm; food served until 7pm.

Café Express, 16 N. San Francisco, near the Weatherford. Fine danishes ($1.50), plus various sandwiches and coffees. Open daily 7am-9pm.

Alpine Pizza, 7 Leroux St. (779-4109) and 2400 E. Santa Fe Ave. (779-4138). Excellent, huge *calzones* ($4.75) and *strombolis* ($5.50). Alpine with whole wheat crusts and a variety of toppings. Open Mon.-Thurs. 11am-11pm, Fri.-Sat. 11am-mid., Sun. noon-11pm. Must be 21 Tues. and Thurs. after 3pm.

Main St. Bar and Grill, 4 S. San Francisco, (774-1519), across from the Downtowner. When the vegetarian meals and non-alcoholic drinks of the cafés get too healthy, try the delicious brabecued red meat ($2-11), the Buttery Texas Toast, and the calorie-laden but excellent selection of beers. Live music Fri.-Sat. Open Mon.-Sat. 11am-mid., Sun. noon-10pm.

Near Flagstaff

Because most of Flagstaff's legions of tourists are Grand Canyon-bound, they miss the many other (uncrowded) natural wonders surrounding the city. Seventeen mi. north on U.S. 89 lies **Sunset Crater National Monument** (527-7042). This volcanic crater erupted in 1065, forming cinder cones and lava beds; oxidized iron in the cinder gives the pre-nuclear crater its dramatic dusky color. **(Visitors center** open daily 7am-6pm; off-season 8am-5pm; in winter may close due to snow. Admission $3/car or $1/person.) Guided bus trips take off to **O'Leary Peak** three times per day (fare $2; make reservations at the visitors center). From the top you can look down the mouth of Sunset Crater; its treacherous terrain is closed to hiking.

A ½-mi. self-guided tour wanders through the plain's surreal lava formations, 1½ mi. east of the visitors center. All interpretive materials along the trail are also available in Spanish, Dutch, French, and German. Guided tours of the lava tubes begin daily at noon and 3pm; aspiring spelunkers can rent a hard hat and light from the visitors center, don a coat, and explore as far as they dare.

Eighteen mi. north and several hundred feet down from Sunset Crater on a scenic loop road rests **Wupatki National Monument.** The ancestors of the Hopi moved here around 900 AD when they found the black-and-red soil ideal for agriculture. However, by 1215 droughts and overfarming precipitated the abandoning of the pueblos. Seven hundred seventy-six uneventful years later, Wupatki boasts some of the Southwest's most scenic ruins, perched on the sides of arroyos in view of Monument Valley and the San Francisco Peaks just for your vacation pleasure. Four major abandoned pueblos stretch along a 14-mi. park road from U.S. 89 to the visitors center. The largest and most accessible, **Wupatki Ruin,** rises three stories high. Below the ruin, you can see one of Arizona's two stone ballcourts, the sites of ancient games employing a rubber ball and a stone hoop in a circular court. Get info at the **Wupatki Ruin Visitors Center** (774-7000; open daily 7am-7pm, off-season 8am-5pm). When visiting Wupatki or Sunset Crater you can camp at the park's **Bonito Campground,** just across from the Sunset Crater Visitors Center. (Running water, no hookups. Sites $6. Overflow campers can pitch their tents for free in the National Forest.)

In the 13th century, the Sinagua people built more than 300 rooms under hanging ledges in the walls of a 400-ft.-deep canyon. The remaining structures form the **Walnut Canyon National Monument,** 7 mi. east of Flagstaff off I-40. From a glassed-in observation deck in the visitors center you can survey the whole canyon; a stunning variety of plants sprout out of its striated grey walls. A trail snakes down from the visitors center past 25 cliff dwellings; markers along the trail describe aspects of Sinagua life, and identify the plants they used for food, dyes, medicine, and hunting.

Rangers lead hikes down a rugged trail to the original Ranger Cabin and many remote cliff dwellings. These strenuous two-and-a-half-hour hikes leave daily from the visitors center at 10am. Hiking boots and long pants are required. A walk along the main trail takes about 45 minutes. (Open daily 7am-6pm; Labor Day-Memorial Day 8am-5pm. Admission $1 per person.)

The **San Francisco Peaks** are the huge, snow-capped mountains visible to the north of Flagstaff. Sacred to the Hopi, who believe that the Kachina spirits live there, **Humphrey's Peak** is the highest point in Arizona at 12,670 ft. Nearby **Mount Agassiz** has the area's best skiing. The **Fairfield Snow Bowl** operates four lifts from mid-December through mid-April; its 35 trails receive an average of 8½ ft. of powder each winter. Lift tickets cost $19 on weekdays, $26 on weekends. Call the **Fairfield Resort** switchboard (779-1951; 24 hrs.) for information on ski conditions, transportation, and accommodations.

During the summer, the peaks are perfect for hiking. You can see the North Rim of the Grand Canyon, the Painted Desert, and countless square miles of Arizona and Utah from the top of Humphrey's Peak when the air is clear. Those not up to the hike should take the chairlift (20-30 min.) up the mountain (779-1951; runs weekends and holidays 10am-4pm; $7, seniors $5, ages 6-12 $3.50). The vista from the top of the lift proves almost as stunning. Picnic facilities and a cafeteria open from May to October. Since the mountains occupy National Forest land, camping is free, but no organized campsites are available. To reach the peaks, take U.S. 180 about 7 mi. north to the Fairfield Snow Bowl turnoff. **Gray Line/Nava-Hopi** offers a tour of the Museum of Northern Arizona, Walnut Canyon, Sunset Crater, and Wupatki National Monument (see Flagstaff Practical Information), but no other public transportation is available to these sights, or, during the summer, to the San Francisco Peaks.

From Flagstaff to Phoenix

The main thoroughfare between the two cities is I-17. Route 89-A traces a more circular path between Flagstaff and Phoenix, but it makes up for its longer travel time with more awesome scenery, especially in the stretch between Flagstaff and Sedona. A few miles south of Flagstaff, U.S. 89A descends into **Oak Creek Canyon,** a trout-stocked creek bordered by trees and reddish canyon cliffs. You can pull over to swim or fish at several points along the route; look for **Slide Rock,** an algae-covered natural water chute. National forest campsites are scattered along 12 mi. of Oak Creek Canyon on the highway. Arrive early; sites fill quickly. Most of the campgrounds open from April to October. Call the forest service (282-4119) for info. **Manzanita** has a three-day limit, and **Cave Spring** and **Pine Flat** have seven-day limits. All have running water and toilets. (Sites $8.)

Twenty-seven mi. south of Flagstaff, the walls of Oak Creek Canyon open up to reveal the striking red rock formations surrounding **Sedona,** the setting for many western movies. The town itself, an incongruous blend of wealthy retirees and organic trend-followers, boasts a wide variety of restaurants and resort hotels.

Twenty mi. southwest of Sedona (take U.S. 89A to Rte. 279 and continue through the town of Cottonwood) lies **Tuzigoot National Monument,** which consists of a dramatic Sinaguan ruin overlooking the Verde Valley. (Open daily 8am-7pm. Entrance fee $3/vehicle.)

From Sedona, Rte. 179 leads south to I-17. An amazing five-story cliff dwelling sits 10 mi. south back on I-17. **Montezuma Castle National Monument** (567-3322) is a 20-room adobe abode. The dwellings were constructed around 1100 AD, when overpopulation in the Flagstaff area forced the Sinagua south into the Verde Valley along Beaver Creek. Visitors can view the "castle" from a path below. (Path open daily 7am-7pm, visitors center daily 8am-6pm. Admission $3/car.) Eleven mi. away is the little-known **Montezuma Well National Monument.** (Open daily 7am-7pm. Free.)

If you've heard abstract stereotypes about so-called "New Agers" but never met or seen them in action, we've got the place for you. From Montezuma Castle, follow I-17; from the turnoff at Cordes Junction, 28 mi. south, a 3-mi. dirt road leads to **Arcosanti.** When completed around the turn of the century, Arcosanti will be a self-sufficient community embodying Italian architect Paolo Soleri's concept of "arcology," somewhat mysteriously defined as "architecture and ecology working together as one integral process." Budgetarians will appreciate the architect's vision of a city where personal cars are obsolete. The complete city, with its subterranean parks, will surprise even the most imaginative Legoland architect. (Tours daily every hr. 10am-4pm. Open to the public daily 9am-5pm. $4 donation.) For more info, contact Arcosanti, HC 74, P.O. Box 4136, Mayer 86333 (632-7135). **Arizona Central** buses (see Phoenix Practical Information) can drop you off in Cordez Junction, 1½ mi. away from Arcosanti, but no tours go there.

Grand Canyon

Here's the story of a lovely canyon—227 mi. long, 13 mi. wide, and over 1 mi. deep—almost big enough to hold the countless pilgrims that travel to this tourist magnet (such as the Bradys). One day, long before Bobby and Cindy's time, the Colorado River met this mountain range, and decided to disobey the usual laws governing the flow of rivers and curl over the mountains instead of around them. Greg knew that it was much more than a hunch that the river would someday form a canyon in the soft limestone, sandstone, and shale, exposing countless families of strata. The result, as Martha might add jealously, is how the Canyon became a glimpse into the Earth's wonder years. Alice just leers, her thoughts with Sam.

That's the way this became the Grand Canyon National Park, which consists of three areas: the **South Rim,** including Grand Canyon Village; the **North Rim;**

and the canyon gorge itself. The slightly lower, largely more accessible South Rim draws 10 times more Bradys than the higher, more heavily forested North Rim.

The 13-mi. distance that traverses the canyon equals a two-day adventure for sturdy hikers, while the 214 mi. of road prove a good 5-hour drive for those who would rather explore from above. Despite commercial exploitation, the Grand Canyon is still untamed; every year several careless hikers take what locals morbidly refer to as "the 12-second tour."

South Rim

In summer, everything on two legs or four wheels converges from miles around on this side of the Grand Canyon. If you plan to visit during this mobfest, make reservations for lodging or campsites, and mules if you want them, and prepare to battle crowds. During the winter there are fewer tourists; however, many of the canyon's hotels and facilities are closed.

Practical Information

Park Headquarters: 638-7888. Open daily 8am-5pm. Information on programs 24 hrs.

Lodging Reservations: Reservations Dept., Grand Canyon National Park Lodges, Grand Canyon 86023 (638-2401).

Nava-Hopi Bus Lines: 774-5003. Leaves Flagstaff Greyhound station daily at 7am, 9am, and 4pm. Leaves Bright Angel Lodge at Grand Canyon for Flagstaff daily at 9:45am and 5:45pm. Fare $26 round-trip, with Ameripass $13.20, ages 5-12 $12. $2 entrance fee not included.

Transportation Information Desk: In Bright Angel Lodge (638-2631). Reservations for mule rides, bus tours, Phantom Ranch, and taxi. Open daily 6am-6pm.

Equipment Rental: Babbit's General Store, in Mather Center Grand Canyon Village (638-2262 or 638-2234), near Yavapai Lodge. Rents comfortable, adult-sized hiking boots ($5 for the first day), sleeping bags ($5-6), tents ($10), and camping gear. Open daily 8am-8pm. Deposit required.

Weather and Road Conditions: 638-2245. 24-hr. recording.

Post Office: next to Babbit's (638-2512). Open Mon.-Fri. 9am-4:30pm, Sat. 10am-2pm. Lobby open Mon.-Sat. 5am-10pm. **ZIP code:** 86023.

Area Code: 602.

From Flagstaff, the fastest and most scenic route to the South Rim is Hwy. 93 south to I-40 east; Rte. 64 north then takes you to the Desert View entrance in the eastern part of the park. Admission to the Grand Canyon is $20 per car and $2 for travelers using other modes of transportation—even bus passengers must pay. You just might avoid the entrance fee if you enter at sunset.

The National Park Service operates two free **shuttle buses.** The **West Rim Loop** runs between West Rim Junction and Hermit's Rest, with stops at all the scenic vistas along the way (operates Memorial Day-Labor Day every 15 min. 7:30am-sunset). The **Village Loop** covers Bright Angel Lodge, West Rim Junction, the visitors center, Grand Canyon Village, and Yavapai Point (operates year-round every 15 min. 6:30am-9:30pm).

Thanks to the efforts of the park service, the South Rim is quite wheelchair-accessible; pick up the free pamphlet "Access for Visitors" at the visitors center.

Accommodations and Camping

Compared with the six million years it took the Colorado River to cut the Grand Canyon, the six months it takes to get a room on the South Rim is a blink of an eye. Since the hostel closed in 1990, it is now nearly impossible to sleep indoors anywhere near the South Rim without reservations or gobs of cash, though you can check at the visitors center for vacancies.

Most accommodations on the South Rim other than those listed below are outrageously expensive. The campsites listed usually fill by 10am in summer. Campground overflow usually winds up in the **Kaibab National Forest,** adjacent to the park along the southern border, where you can pull off a dirt road and camp for free. Sleeping in cars is not permitted within the park, but is allowed in the Kaibab Forest. The Nava-Hopi bus pauses at Bright Angel Lodge, where you can check your luggage for 50¢ per day. Reservations for Bright Angel Lodge, Maswik Lodge, Trailer Village, and more expensive rooms can be made through Grand Canyon National Park Lodges, P.O. Box 699, Grand Canyon AZ 86023 (602-638-2401). All rooms should be reserved six months in advance for the summer, six weeks for the winter.

> **Bright Angel Lodge,** Grand Canyon Village. Scout-style rustic cabins with plumbing but no heat. Very convenient to Bright Angel Trail and both shuttle buses. Singles $45-52, depending on how much plumbing you want. A few rooms with no plumbing $27. Each additional person $6.

> **Maswik Lodge,** Grand Canyon Village. Small, clean cabins with shower $46 (singles or doubles). Each additional person $8. Reservations required.

> **Mather Campground,** Grand Canyon Village, ½ mi. from the visitors center. Shady, relatively isolated sites without hookups $10. Make reservations through Ticketron outlets 8 weeks in advance.

> **Trailer Village,** next to Mather Campground. Clearly designed with the RV in mind. Campsites resemble driveways and lack seclusion. Sites with hookup $15 for 2 people. Each additional person 50¢.

> **Desert View Campsite,** 25 mi. east of Grand Canyon Village. Sites $8. Open May 15-Oct. 30. No hookups. No reservations accepted; get there early.

> **Ten-X Campground** in the Kaibab National Forest, (638-2443), 10 mi. south of Grand Canyon Village on Hwy. 64. Chemical toilets, water. Sites $9. Open April-Nov. No reservations, no hookups.

> **Phantom Ranch,** on the canyon floor, a 4-hr. hike down the Kaibab Trail. Reservations required 6 months in advance for the April-Oct. season, but check at the Bright Angel Transportation Desk (see above) for last-minute cancellations. The ranch has a snack bar and serves expensive meals; bring your own food to conserve money. Don't show up without reservations—they'll send you back up the trail, on foot. Dorm beds $27. Cabins for 1 or 2 people $58, each additional person $10.

Food

Fast food has not sunk its razor-sharp claws into the rim of the Canyon. While you might find meals for fast-food prices, uniformly bland cuisine is harder to locate. **Babbit's General Store** (638-2262), in Maswik Lodge, is more than just a restaurant—it's a supermarket. Stock up on trail mix, water, and gear. (Open daily 8am-8pm; deli open 8am-7pm.) **The Maswik Cafeteria** also in Maswik Lodge has a variety of inexpensive options grill-made and served in a swish cafeteria atmosphere. (Open daily 6am-10pm.) **Bright Angel Restaurant,** in Bright Angel Lodge (638-6389), has hot sandwiches from $4-6. (Open daily 6:30am-10pm.) The soda fountain at Bright Angel Lodge offers 16 flavors of ice cream ($1) to hikers emerging from the Bright Angel Trail. (Open daily 11am-9pm.)

Activities

Your first glimpse of the canyon will make it clear that the best way to see it is to hike down into it, an enterprise that is much harder than it looks. Much sorrow has come to the plaid-clad, would-be hiker armed with a telephoto lens and an unopened can of Diet Coke—park rangers average over three rescues per day in the National Park with the highest fatality rate in the country. Even the young at heart must remember that what seems to be an easy hike downhill can become a nightmarish 100° journey on the return. Heat exhaustion, the second greatest threat after slipping, is marked by a monstrous headache and termination of sweating. Taking two quarts of water along is an absolute neccesity. A list of hiking safety tips can be found in the **Grand Canyon Guide,** available at the entrance gate and the visitors center, and should be read thoroughly before hitting the trail. Overestimating your limits is a common mistake when it comes to tackling the canyon, and parents should think twice about bringing children more than a mile down the trails—kids have long memories and might exact revenge when they get bigger.

The two trails into the Canyon are the **Bright Angel Trail,** which begins at the Bright Angel Lodge, and **South Kaibab Trail,** originating at Yaki Point. Bright Angel is outfitted to accommodate the average tourist, with its rest houses stationed strategically 1½ mi. and 3 mi. from the rim. **Indian Gardens,** 4½ mi. down offers the tired hiker restrooms, picnic tables, and blessed shade; all three rest stops usually have water in the summer. Kaibab is trickier, steeper, and lacks shade or water, but it rewards the intrepid with a better view of the canyon's hypnotic contours. Consult the *Guide* for a more detailed description of these trails.

If you've made arrangements to spend the night on the canyon floor, the best route is to hike down the Kaibab Trail (3-4 hr., depending on conditions) and back up the Bright Angel (7-8 hr.) the following day. The hikes down Bright Angel Trail to Indian Gardens and Plateau Point, 6 mi. out, where you can look down 1360 ft. to the river, make excellent daytrips. But start early (around 7am) to avoid the worst heat. One local rule: if you meet a mule train, stand quietly by the side of the trail and obey the wrangler's instructions so as not to spook the animals.

If you don't feel up to descending into the canyon, follow the **Rim Trail** east to Grandeur Point and the **Yavapai Geological Museum,** or west to **Hermit's Rest,** using the shuttles as desired. There are no fences or railings between you and oblivion. The Eastern Rim Trail swarms at dusk with sunset-watchers, and the Yavapai Museum at the end of the trail has a sweeping view of the canyon during the day from a glassed-in observation deck. The Western Rim Trail leads to several incredible vistas, notably **Hopi Point,** a favorite for sunsets, and the **Abyss,** where the canyon wall drops almost vertically to the Tonto plateau 3000 ft. below. To watch a sunset, show up at your chosen spot 45 minutes beforehand and face west instead of east, so as to see more than just shadow.

The park service rangers present a variety of free informative talks and hikes. Listings of each day's events are available at the visitors center or in the *Grand Canyon Guide* (10¢), available everywhere in the village. A free presentation, evenings at 8:30pm in the summer and 7:30 in the winter, highlights some aspect of the Grand Canyon in **Mather Amphitheater,** behind the visitors center.

The younger set will be kept busy with the **Grand Canyon Young Adventurer,** a magazine full of stories of the canyon and a variety of puzzles for children 5-12. By finishing all the games inside, the kids can become Junior Rangers, an early civil-service position which just might eventually lead to the presidency.

In addition to the freebies offered by the National Park Service, a variety of commercial tours cover the South Rim. Tours by helicopter, airplane, inflatable raft, and mule soar beyond the reach of most budget travelers. You can book plane and chopper tours at **Tusayan,** 7 mi. south of the Grand Canyon Village. Of the three bus tours, the Sunset and West Rim tours cover places mostly accessible by free shuttle buses. You may decide to take the tour to **West Desert View** (3¾ hr.; 2 per day in summer, 1 per day in winter; tickets $17, children $8.50), which provides the only non-automobile access to Desert View 23 mi. east of the village as well as to the Painted Desert to the east. Contact the Bright Angel Transportation Desk (638-2401) for information on all commercial tours.

North Rim

If you are coming from Utah or Nevada, or if you simply want a more solitary Grand Canyon experience, consider the North Rim. Here things are a bit wilder, a bit cooler, and much more serene—with a view as groovy as that from the South Rim. Unfortunately, public transportation does not reach the North Rim. The only rim-to-rim transportation available is from **Transcanyon,** P.O. Box 348, Grand Canyon, AZ 86023 (638-2820), from late May to mid-Oct. ($50, $85 round-trip. Departs South Rim 1:30pm, arrives at North Rim at 6pm. Call for reservations.) Canyon visitors seem wary of those on foot, making hitching a non-option. From the South

Rim, the North Rim is a 200-mi.-plus, stunningly scenic drive away. Take Rte. 64 east to U.S. 89 north, which runs into Alt. 89; off Alt. 89, take Rte. 67 south to the edge. Between the first snows at the end of October and May 15, Rte. 67 is closed to traffic. Only a snowmobile can get you to the North Rim.

Although you won't find a visitors center on this side of the park, you can direct questions to rangers at the entrance station and to the info desk in **Grand Canyon Lodge** (638-2611; open daily 8am-5pm). The lodge lounges at the very end of Rte. 67. The front desk stays open 24 hrs. The North Rim **emergency** phone (638-7805) is monitored around the clock.

Accommodations, Camping, and Food

Since camping within the confines of the Grand Canyon National Park is limited to designated campgrounds, only a lucky minority of North Rim visitors get to spend the night "right there." If you can't get in-park lodgings, visit the **Kaibab National Forest,** which runs from north of Jacob Lake to the park entrance. Camp in an established site, or pull off the main road onto any forest road and camp for free. Campsite reservations can be made through Ticketron (800-452-1111).

Canyonlands International Youth Hostel, 143 E. South, Kanab, UT 84741 (801-644-5554). It is 1½ hours north of the Grand Canyon on U.S. 89, an equal distance south of Bryce Canyon. Free beverages, large kitchen, newly restored cabins; can accommodate 40. (Office open daily 8-10am and 5-10pm. Non-AYH, but all hostel cards honored; $8, nonmembers $10. Reservations recommended.)

Grand Canyon Lodge, on the edge of the rim. Rooms from $50 for 2 people. Front desk open 24 hrs. Write or call TW Recreational Services, P.O. Box 400, Cedar City, UT 84720 (801-586-7686).

Kaibab Lodge, on Rte. 67 (638-2389), 5 mi. north of the park entrance station. A quiet, secluded lodge with restaurant. Singles $43. Doubles $54. For reservations, contact Kaibab Lodge, North Rim, Rural Rte., Fredonia 85719. Reservations 526-0924 or 800-525-0924. Open late May-Sept.

North Rim Campground, on Rte. 67 near the rim. You really cannot see into the canyon from the pine-covered site, but you know it's there. Near food store, recreation room, and showers. Sites $10. Reserve by writing to North Rim Campground, Grand Canyon National Park, Grand Canyon 86023.

Kaibab National Forest Sites: DeMotte Park Campground, 18 mi. north of the North Rim Entrance Station. No sites; only free "At Large" camping on a first-come, first-served basis. **Jacob Lake Campground,** 32 mi. north of the park entrance, at the junction of U.S. 89A and Rte. 67 (643-7395). 48 sites, $6/night. Reserve in advance.

Both of the eating options on the North Rim are placed strategically at the Grand Canyon Lodge. The restaurant slaps together dinners for $4.50-12 and breakfast for $3.50. A skimpy sandwich at the "buffeteria" costs about $2. North Rim hostelers are far better off eating in Kanab.

Activities

A ½-mi. paved trail takes you from the Grand Canyon Lodge to **Bright Angel Point,** which commands a fantastic view of the Canyon. **Point Imperial,** an 11-mi. drive from the lodge, overlooks Marble Canyon and the Painted Desert.

The North Rim offers nature walks and evening programs, both at the North Rim Campground and at Grand Canyon Lodge. Check at the info desk or campground bulletin boards for schedules. Half-day mule trips ($25) descend into the canyon from Grand Canyon Lodge (628-2292, in winter 801-679-8665; open daily 7:30am-8pm). Ask at the lobby about the much more scenic full-day trips ($52).

On warm evenings, the Grand Canyon Lodge fills with an eclectic group of international travelers, U.S. families, and rugged adventurers. Some frequent the **Lodge Saloon** for drinks, jukebox disco, and the enthusiasm of a young crowd. Others look to the warm air rising from the canyon, a full moon, and the occasional shooting stars for their intoxication at day's end.

Northeastern Arizona

Canyon de Chelly National Monument

While not matching the Grand Canyon's awesome dimensions, Canyon de Chelly more than makes up in beauty what it lacks in size. In the aptly-named Beautiful Valley, the canyon's 30- to 1,000-ft. sandstone cliffs tower over the sandy, fertile valley created by the Chelly River. The oldest ruins in the eroded walls of the Canyon date back to the Anasazi civilization of the 12th century. By the 1800s, the Navajo sought refuge here during hostilities with European Americans. In what was to become a sickening pattern, dozens of Native American women and children were shot by the Spanish in 1805; the sight of the executions is now called Massacre Cave. Kit Carson starved the Navajo out of the Canyon in the 1860s. Today, Navajo farmers once again inhabit the canyon, cultivating the lush soil and living in traditional Navajo dwellings, *hogans.*

The land constituting Canyon de Chelly National Monument is owned by the Navajo Nation and administered by the National Park Service. All but one of the park trails are closed to public travel unless hikers are escorted by Navajo representatives. Although the park service offers free short tours into the canyon, the only way to get far into the canyon or close to the Anasazi ruins is to hire a Navajo guide. Check with the **visitors center** (674-5436), 2 mi. east of Chinle on Navajo Rte. 64, off U.S. 191, which houses a small museum. The staff can arrange for guides and tours at any time of day, although guides usually arrive at the visitors center at about 9am. Guides generally charge $7 per hour to walk or drive into the canyon. Advance reservations are helpful, but you can try dropping in. (Open daily 8am-6pm; off-season 8am-5pm.) To drive into the canyon with a guide, you must provide your own four-wheel-drive vehicle. Horseback tours can be arranged through **Justin's Horse Rental,** on South Rim Dr. (674-5678), at the mouth of the canyon. (Open daily approximately 8am-6pm. Horses "rented" at $7/hr.; mandatory guide "hired" at $7/hr. If you have a philosophical bent, notice that the horse's time is worth as much as the human guide's, and consider the social implications—or at least give a generous tip.) **Twin Trail Tours** (674-3466) also rents horses. For complete service listings, pick up a copy of *Canyon Overlook.*

Seven mi. from the visitors center, the 1-mi. trail to **White House Ruin,** off South Canyon Rd., winds down a 400-ft. face, past a Navajo farm and traditional hogan, through an orchard, and across the stream wash. The only one you can walk without a guide, this trail is best in the spring when you can hike in the canyon heat with the cool stream swirling about your ankles. Take one of the paved **Rim Drives** (North Rim 44 mi., South Rim 36 mi.), which skirt the edge of the 300- to 700-ft. cliffs. The South Rim is the more dramatic. Try to make it all the way to the **Spider Rock Overlook,** 20 mi. from the visitors center, a narrow sandstone monolith that towers hundreds of feet above the canyon floor. Native American lore has it that the whitish rock at the top of Spider Rock contains bleached bones of victims of one of the *kachina* spirits, Spider Woman, or her husband Peter Parker. A written guide to the White House Ruins and the North or South Rim Drives costs 50¢ at the visitors center.

Camp for free in the park's **Cottonwood Campground,** ½ mi. from the visitors center. This giant campground in a pretty cottonwood grove rumbles at night with the din of a hungry army, and stray dogs tend to wander the site. Don't expect to find any budget accommodations in nearby Chinle or anywhere else in Navajo territory. Farmington, NM, and Cortez, CO, are the closest major cities with cheap lodging.

It's impossible to take an ugly approach to the park. The most common route is from Chambers, 75 mi. south of the park, at the intersection of I-40 and U.S. 191. The other approach is from the north, where U.S. 191 leaves U.S. 160 in Colorado near Four Corners, 50 mi. from the monument. Public transportation is unavailable.

Monument Valley and Navajo National Monument

You may have seen the red rock towers of **Monument Valley Navajo Tribal Park** (801-727-3287) in one of numerous westerns filmed here. Rather ironically, the 1000-ft. monoliths helped boost injun-killer John Wayne to heights of movie slaughter. The best and cheapest way to see the valley is via the Park's looping 17-mi. **Valley Drive.** This dirt road winds in and out of the most dramatic monuments, including the famous paired **Mittens** and the slender **Totem Pole.** The gaping ditches, large rocks, and mudholes on this road will do horrible things to your car: Drive at your own risk, and hold your breath. Much of the valley can be reached only in a sturdy four-wheel-drive vehicle or by a long hike. In winter, snow laces the rocky towers, and almost all the tourists flee. Inquire about snow and road conditions at the Flagstaff Chamber of Commerce.

The park entrance is 24 mi. north on U.S. 163 from the town of Kayenta and the intersection with U.S. 160. (Park open May-Sept. daily 7am-8pm; off-season 8am-5pm. Admission $2.50, seniors and kids 6-12 $1.)

Twenty mi. past Kayenta on U.S. 160, Rte. 564 takes you 9 mi. to **Navajo National Monument.** This stunning site consists of three Anasazi cliff-dwellings, including **Keet Seel**, the best-preserved site in the Southwest. Inscription House has closed, and entrance into Keet Seel and **Betatakin**, a 135-room complex, is limited to 25 people per day in ranger-led groups. (Tours daily at 9am, noon, and 2pm; try to make reservations at least two months in advance. Write Navajo National Monument, Tanalea 86044.) For $50, Navajo guides will put you on a horse, lead you down the 8-mi. trail, and leave you with a ranger to explore the 400-year-old ruins left by the Anasazi. Allow a full day for the ride and the strenuous hike. Rangers also lead 5-mi. hikes. You can hike on your own, but you must obtain a permit. The **visitors center** (672-2366) has a craft shop as well as pottery and artifacts displays. (Open daily 8am-6pm; off-season 8am-5pm.)

The Navajo maintain a small campground with water next to the Monument Valley Tribal Park Visitors Center. (Sites $10.) The site at the National Monument has no showers or hookups, but it's free and has the added advantage of nightly ranger talks. If you need hookups, stop at **KOA** (801-727-3280), in Monument Valley, UT, 4 mi. west of Monument Valley Park off U.S. 163. (Sites $14 for 2 people, each additional person $2.)

Navajo and Hopi Reservations

Seeing *Dances With Wolves* can't substitute for the moving experience of visiting a reservation and actually trying to understand the lifestyles and hardships of Native Americans. The Navajo and their neighbors the Hopi, also enclosed by the Navajo Reservation, have lived in this region for centuries. Despite U.S. citizenship, most don't really consider themselves part of a national "melting pot." They, and not the U.S. government, have sovereignty over this large but agriculturally unproductive land.

"Navajo" is actually a European name for these proud, stoic people, who call themselves "Dinee." Reservation politics are lively but obscure, written up only in the *Navajo Times* or in regional sections of Denver, Albuquerque, or Phoenix newspapers. In addition to the town and tribal government, Window Rock features the geological formation that gives the town its name. For a taste of the Dinee's unusual language and even some Native American ritual songs, tune to 660AM, from Window Rock, "The Voice of the Navajo."

The reservations have no central visitors centers. For information on the Hopis, visit their cultural center (see below). The Navajo Nation spreads out more; several tribal parks have their own small information booths. Pick up the excellent *Visitors Guide to the Navajo Nation* ($3), which includes a detailed map.

The "border towns" of **Gallup**, NM, and **Flagstaff**, AZ (see above), provide good entry points to the reservations; you can rent cars in one of these towns. Frequent **Greyhound/Trailways** routes along I-40 serve both. No public transportation goes into or runs within the reservations, with the notable exception of the **Navajo Transit Authority** (729-5457) in Fort Defiance, 6 mi. north of Window Rock. One bus per day leaves Tuba City, AZ, at 6am and travels along Rte. 264 through the Hopi mesa towns (flag stops) to Window Rock, arriving at 9:50am. (Leaves Window Rock heading west at 3:10pm, arriving at 7:50pm. $13.)

US I-40, and state highways 89, 160, and 191, form an imperfect circle through the reservation, with Rte. 264 cutting through to the Hopi reservation and through Window Rock. Hotels charge exorbitant rates, so plan on camping at the national monuments or Navajo campgrounds, some of which also charge guests.

On the Hopi Reservation, the **Hopi Cultural Center** (734-2401), on Rte. 264 in the community of **Second Mesa,** delineates the world of the tribe whose ancestors, the Anasazi, lived here centuries before the Navajo and their cousins the Apache arrived. The center consists of a museum of pottery, photography, and handicrafts, along with four gift shops, a motel, and a restaurant. The motel (734-2401) is expensive but decent and requires reservations two weeks to a month in advance. (Singles $50. Doubles $55.) The restaurant is surprisingly reasonable. Sandwiches cost $4-5 and Native American dishes go for $3-6. (Open daily 6:30am-9pm.)

Inquire at the cultural center or at the Flagstaff Chamber of Commerce for the dates and sites of the **Hopi village dances.** Announced only a few days in advance, these religious ceremonies last from sunrise to sundown. The dances are highly formal occasions; tourists may come to watch, but should not wear shorts, tank tops, or other casual wear. Photography is strictly forbidden.

Petrified Forest National Park and Meteor Crater

On a trip from Flagstaff to New Mexico, Petrified Forest National Park, 107 mi. east on I-40, makes an alluring detour off the Navajo/Hopi reservation circuit. The park includes some of the most scenic areas of the **Painted Desert,** named for the magnificent multicolored bands of rock that cut across its hills. Petrified logs of agate inlaid with quartz and amethyst crystals scatter across the desert floor, creating a stunning kaleidoscope of color. Petrification involves an unlikely set of circumstances: logs must fall into a swamp, be relatively cut off from air and water rapidly, then have each cell replaced by crystal—all in all, about as likely as seeing Tipper Gore at a Mötley Crüe concert.

Entrances are off I-40 to the north and U.S. 180 to the south (entrance fee $5/vehicle). The **Painted Desert Visitors Center,** near the north entrance, shows a film explaining petrification every half hour. A 28-mi. park road through desert landscapes connects the two entrances, winding past piles of petrified logs and Native American ruins. Stop to look at oddly-named **Newspaper Rock,** covered not with newsprint but with Native American petroglyphs; the headlines are a bit out-of-date but still cool to see. At **Blue Mesa,** a hiking trail winds through the desert. **Long Logs Crystal** and **Jasper Forest** contain some of the most exquisite fragments of petrified wood. Picking up fragments of petrified wood in the park is illegal and traditionally unlucky (a result of ancient curses cast by capitalist shamans); if the demons don't getcha then the district attorney will. Those who must take a piece home should buy one at a store along I-40, since the storekeepers are immune to both curses. To camp overnight, make arrangements at the visitors center in the **Rainbow Forest Museum,** at the park's southern entrance (524-6228; open in summer daily 6:30am-7:30pm, in spring and fall 7:30am-6:30pm, in winter 8am-5pm). Public transport does not feed the Petrified Forest; several bus lines do stop in Holbrook, on I-40, 27 mi. away.

Between Flagstaff and the Petrified Forest off I-40 is the privately-owned **Meteor Crater** (602-774-8350), located 35 mi. east of Flagstaff off the Meteor Crater Rd. exit (after which the Crater was named). The meteor crater, the world's largest, was originally believed to be just another ancient volcanic cone. However, geologic tests in the crater and on rock fragments from the surrounding desert proved the hypothesis, once scoffed at, that about 50,000 years ago a huge nickel-iron meteorite crashed through the atmosphere and onto the desert to create the 570-ft. deep pothole. The site was used to train the Apollo astronauts in the 1960s. (Open daily 9am-5pm. Admission $6.)

Phoenix

Rising out of the aptly-named Valley of the Sun, Phoenix, with its monopoly on sunshine, is a haven for frostbitten tourists and sun-loving students in the winter. During these balmy months, golf, spring baseball, and the Fiesta Bowl take advantage of the mild climate; Phoenix's vitality makes it an excellent place to visit. In the summer. . .well, at least the desert air keeps the humidity down. If you just can't start with your baby tonight, that's probably 'cause it's too darn hot. Temperatures are almost always above 100°F (37°C), and at night lows are rarely below 80°F; on any given day from April to October, Phoenix is almost always the hottest major city in the U.S. Prepare for unconditional heat—either condition yourself or condition your air.

Practical Information

Emergency: 911.

Phoenix and Valley of the Sun Convention and Visitors Center, 505 N. 2nd St. (254-6500). Open Mon.-Fri. 8am-5pm. Convenient branch offices downtown on 2nd St. at Adams (open Mon.-Fri. 8am-4:30pm), and in Terminals 2 and 3 at Sky Harbor Airport (open Mon.-Fri. 9am-9pm, Sat.-Sun. 9am-5pm). **Weekly Events Hotline,** 252-5588. 24-hr. recorded information.

Amtrak: 401 W. Harrison (253-0121 or 800-872-7245), 2 blocks south of Jefferson St. at 4th Ave. Dangerous at night. Three per week to Los Angeles ($81) and El Paso ($81). Station open Sun.-Wed. 5:45am-11:30pm, Thurs. and Sat. 3pm-9:30pm.

Greyhound: 5th and Washington St. (248-4040). To Flagstaff (5 per day, $24), Tucson (10 per day, $19.50), and Los Angeles (11 per day, $30). Open 24 hrs. Lockers $1.

Public Transport: Phoenix Transit, 253-5000. Most lines run to and from the **City Bus Terminal,** Central and Washington. Most routes operate Mon.-Fri. 5am-9:30pm, severely reduced service on Sat. Since many lines run only once every ½ hr., expect long, hot waits. Fares 85¢, disabled, seniors, and kids 40¢. To Mesa 85¢. 10-ride pass $7.50, all-day $2.50, disabled and seniors half-price. Pick up free time tables, maps of the bus system, and bus passes at the terminal. Buses running along Central Ave., Washington St., and Jefferson St. downtown cost only 25¢ within a limited zone Mon.-Fri. 9am-3pm. City bus #13 runs between the **Sky Harbor International Airport** and the city (buses leave the airport every ½ hr. Mon.-Fri. 6:20am-8:21pm, Sat. 5:17am-7:17pm, Sun. call Dial-A-Ride). Cab fare to downtown Phoenix costs about $6. **Dial-A-Ride** (271-4545) takes passengers anywhere in Phoenix only on Sun. and holidays 6:30am-6:30pm. Fare $1.50 plus 60¢ for each additional zone; seniors, disabled, and under 12 60¢ plus 30¢ per zone. Call 258-9977 for weekday service in specified areas only. Some buses and Dial-a-Ride vans have wheelchair lifts; call for details.

Car Rental: Rent-a-Wreck, 2422 E. Washington St. (254-1000). $20/day with unlimited mi., 150 mi. radius. Open Mon.-Fri. 7am-6:30pm, Sat.-Sun. 9am-5pm. Must be 21 with credit card or cash deposit. **Associated Rent-a-Car,** 14 S. 22nd St. (275-6992). $22/day with 100 free mi., 20¢ each additional mi. Open Mon.-Thurs. 7am-6pm, Fri. 7am-7pm, Sat. 8am-5pm, Sun. 9am-4pm. Must be 21 with credit card or cash deposit and Arizona driver's license.

Auto Transport Company: Auto Driveaway, 3530 E. Indian School Rd. (952-0339). First tank of gas free. Open Mon.-Fri. 9am-4:30pm, Sun. 9am-5pm. Must be 21 with $200 deposit.

Taxi: Ace Taxi, 254-1999. $2.25 base fare, 90¢/mi. **Yellow Cab,** 252-5252. $2.05 base fare, $1.30/mi.

Help Lines: Center Against Sexual Assault, 241-9010. Open 24 hrs. **Gay and Lesbian Hotline,** 234-2752. **Community Switchboard,** 234-2752.

Post Office: 1441 E. Buckeye (223-3658). Not downtown. Open Mon.-Fri. 8:30am-5:30pm. **ZIP code:** 85026.

Area Code: 602.

The **city bus terminal** at Central Ave. and Washington St. idles in the heart of downtown Phoenix. **Central Avenue** runs north-south; "avenues" are numbered west from Central and "streets" are numbered east. **Washington Street** divides streets north-south.

Accommodations and Camping

In the winter, when temperatures and vacancy signs go down, prices go up; be sure to get reservations if possible. In either season, those without reservations should cruise the 25-mi. row of motels on occasionally decrepit, slightly dangerous East and West **Van Buren Street** or on **Main Street** (Apache Trail) in Tempe and Mesa. The strip is full of 50's ranch-style motels with names like "Kon-Tiki" and "Deserama," as well as your requisite modern chains. In the summer almost all lower their rates and offer gimmicks, making accommodations very cheap. **Bed and Breakfast in Arizona**, P.O. Box 8628, Scottsdale 85252 (995-2831), can help visitors find accommodations in homes in Phoenix and throughout Arizona. (Preferred 2-night min. stay. Singles from $25. Doubles $35. Reservations recommended.)

Metcalf House (AYH), 1026 N. 9th St. (254-9803), a few blocks northeast of downtown. From the city bus terminal, take bus #7 down 7th St. to Roosevelt St., then walk 2 blocks east to 9th St. and turn left—the hostel is ½ block north. About a 20-min. walk from downtown. Dorm-style rooms, wooden bunks, and common showers. Kitchen, porch and common room, laundry. Check-in 7-9:30am and 5-11pm. $9, nonmembers $13. Linen $1. Bike rental $3/day. Sleepsack required.

Motel 6, 2323 E. Van Buren St. (267-7511), near the airport. Other locations north, east, and west of downtown, but this is the central one and, of course, they're all the same. Clean, comfortable rooms. A/C, pool, and TV with free movies. Singles $19. Doubles $25. Prices slightly higher in winter. Best to reserve a few days ahead.

Airport Central Inn, 2247 E. Van Buren St. (244-9341 or 800-492-2904). Nice, large rooms and a pool. In summer, singles from $20, doubles from $25. Winter rates jump significantly.

Budget Lodge Motels, 402 W. Van Buren St. (254-7247), near downtown. A/C, and TV, plus a small pool in the parking lot. Singles $23, weekly $80 in summer, but prices vary by season. Reserve a few weeks ahead in winter.

KOA, 2550 W. Louise (869-8189), 3 mi. north of Bell Rd. on I-17 at Black Canyon City. Sites $15 for 2 people, $18 with hookup. Each additional adult $2.

Food

Rarely will you find several restaurants together amid Phoenix's sprawl. Downtown is fed mainly by small coffeeshops, most of which close on weekends, though **The Mercado**, a faux-Mexican mall on E. Van Buren between 5th and 7th St. contains several inexpensive eateries, most open on weekends. For more variety, just drive down McDowell St.

Bill Johnson's Big Apple, 3757 E. Van Buren (275-2107), 1 of 4 locations. A down-south delight with sawdust on the floor. Sandwiches ($4-6), hearty soups ($2-3). Open daily 6am-11pm.

Tacos de Juárez, 1017 N. 7th St. at Roosevelt (258-1744), near the hostel. Standard Mexican fare at rock-bottom prices. Specializes in tacos. A la carte items all under $3. Open Sun.-Tues. 11am-8pm, Wed. 11am-3pm, Thurs.-Sat. 11am-9pm.

The Matador, 125 E. Adams St. (254-7563), downtown. Standard Mexican dinners $5-8. The deep-fried ice cream is a novelty. Open daily 6am-11pm. Lounge open until 1am.

The Purple Cow, 200 N. Central (253-0861), in the San Carlos Hotel; also in the Park Central Mall. Great for lunch or fro-yo. Open Mon.-Fri. 7am-4pm.

Sights

The **Heard Museum**, 22 E. Monte Vista (252-8848), one block east of Central Ave., has outstanding collections of Navajo handicrafts and promotes the work of contemporary Native American artists and craftspeople, many of whom give free demonstrations. Educate and prepare yourself for the journey among the Southwest's omnipresent Native American artifact vendors. (Guided tours daily. Open Mon.-Sat. 10am-5pm, Sun. noon-5pm. Admission $4, seniors $3, students and kids $1, Native Americans free.) The **Phoenix Art Museum,** 1625 N. Central Ave. (257-1222), three blocks south, has excellent exhibits of European, modern, and U.S. folk art. (Open Tues. and Thurs.-Sat. 10am-5pm, Wed. 10am-9pm, Sun. 1-5pm. Admission $3, seniors $2.50, students $1.50. Free Wed.)

The **Desert Botanical Gardens,** 1201 E. Galvin Way (941-1225), in Papago Park, 5 mi. east of the downtown area, grows a beautiful and colorful collection of cacti and other desert plants. Visit in the morning or late afternoon to avoid the midday heat. (Open daily 8am-sunset. Admission $4, seniors $3.50, kids 5-12 $1. Take bus #3 east to Papago Park.) Also in the park roars the **Phoenix Zoo,** 5810 E. Van Buren St. (273-7771), which includes special sections representing the Arizona desert and the African veldt. (Open daily 7am-4pm; winter 9am-5pm. Admission $6, kids 4-12 $3.)

Just south of Phoenix across the dry Salt River lies Tempe's **Arizona State University (ASU),** where you'll find the **Gammage Memorial Auditorium** (965-3434), at Mill Ave. and Apache Trail, one of the last major buildings designed by Frank Lloyd Wright. Painted in pink and beige to match the surrounding desert, this eccentric edifice's coloration is sure to astound or nauseate you. (20-min. tours daily in winter. Take bus #60, or #22 on weekends.)

Entertainment

Phoenix is the progressive rock and country capital of the Southwest, with an active (though awfully fashion-conscious) nightclub scene. New Music bands with names like Feedhog and Dead Hot Workshop blister the paint on the dark walls of the **Sun Club,** 1001 E. 8th St. (968-5802), in Tempe. (Music nightly at 8 or 9pm. Cover from $3.) **Char's Has the Blues,** 4631 N. 7th Ave. (230-0205), is self-explanatory. Dozens of junior John Lee Hookers rip it up nightly. (Music nightly at 9pm. Cover from $4.) Headbangers find their black leather, big guitar Eldorado in the bottom of the **Mäson Jar,** 2303 E. Indian School (956-6271). (*Heavy* jams nightly at 9 or 10pm. Cover from $3.) The free *New Times Weekly* (271-0040), on local magazine racks, lists club schedules. Pick up a copy of the **Cultural Calendar of Events,** a concise guide covering three months of area entertainment activities.

Near Phoenix

The drive along the **Apache Trail** to Tonto National Monument makes a great daytrip from Phoenix. Take Rte. 60-89 to Apache Junction, about 30 mi. east of Phoenix, then turn right onto Rte. 88, which follows the Apache Trail through the Superstition Mountains. Three mi. after Canyon Lake, the first of three artificial lakes along the trail, lies the good-humored town of **Tortilla Flat,** a way station for hot and dusty travelers. Five mi. east of Tortilla Flat begins a spectacular stretch of scenery. A dangerous dirt road winds its way through 22 mi. of mountains and canyons to **Roosevelt Dam,** an enormous arc of masonry set between two huge red cliffs. Four mi. beyond the dam is the turn-off for **Tonto National Monument** (467-2241), where preserved dwellings of the Saledo tribe are tucked into sheltered caves in the cliffs. A one-hour self-guided hike up the mountainside, through the apartments and back, affords a lovely view of Roosevelt Lake. (Monument open daily 8am-5pm. Admission $3/car or $1/person.)

Tucson and Southwestern Arizona

Immortalized in song by Little Feat ("I've been from Tucson to Tucumcari, Tehachapi to Tonopah") as a western outpost for those willin' to be movin', Tucson at first glance appears indeed to be little more than a glorified truck stop. Dig deeper, though, and you'll find a lot more here than I-10. Settled by the Hohokam and Pima peoples, the region witnessed the arrival of the Spanish in 1776, who built their usual fun-pack of forts and missions in the dry valley. What gives Tucson most of its current flavor, from the huge football stadium to its artsy nightlife, is the University of Arizona, whose summer students have the run of the town in August, when it is HOT. If modern Tucson gets you down, head to the outskirts of town and Saguaro National Monument.

Practical Information

Emergency: 911.

Metropolitan Tucson Convention and Visitors Bureau, 130 S. Scott Ave. (624-1889). Ask for a city bus map, the "Official Visitor's Guide," and the Arizona campground directory. Open Mon.-Fri. 8:30am-5pm, Sat.-Sun. 9am-4pm.

Tucson International Airport: 573-8000. On Valencia Rd., south of downtown. Bus #25 runs once per hr. to the Laos Transit Center, where bus #16 goes downtown. Last bus daily at 7:17pm. **Arizona Stagecoach** (889-1000) has a booth at the airport and will take you downtown for about $10.25 plus tip. Open 24 hrs.

Amtrak: 400 E. Toole at 5th Ave. (623-4442 or 800-872-7245), in a large red-roofed building. Open Sun.-Wed. 7:45am-8:30pm, Thurs. 1:15-8:30pm, Sat. 7:45am-3pm. Three trains per week to: Phoenix ($26), Los Angeles ($97), and El Paso, TX ($69).

Greyhound: 2 S. 4th Ave. (792-0972), downtown between Congress St. and Broadway. To: Phoenix (11/day, $19); Los Angeles (7/day, $52); Albuquerque (6/day, $103, with 30-day advance $68); and El Paso (7/day, $47). Open 24 hrs. Lockers $1.

Sun-Tran: (792-9222). Buses operate Mon.-Fri. 5:30am-10pm, Sat.-Sun. 8am-7pm. Fare 60¢, students 18 and under 40¢, seniors 25¢. The "4th Avenue Trolley" (an eco-friendly, natural-gas burning, trolley-shaped van) runs from downtown, along 4th Ave., and to the university for 25¢. Racks containing maps and schedules at the Congress Hotel, the university visitors center, and elsewhere. "Rider's Information Guide" is particularly helpful.

Car Rental: Care Free (790-2655). $16/day with 100 free mi. per day; within Tucson only. Open Mon.-Fri. 9am-5pm, Sat. 9am-3pm. Must be 21 with major credit card.

Bike Rental: The Bike Shack, 835 Park Ave. (624-3663), across from campus. $15/day. Open Mon.-Thurs. 9:30am-6pm, Fri. 10am-5pm, Sat. 10am-5pm, Sun. noon-4pm.

Post Office: 1501 S. Cherry Bell (620-5157). Open Mon.-Fri. 8:30am-5pm. **ZIP code:** 85726.

Area Code: 602.

Tucson's downtown area is just east of I-10, around the intersection of Broadway (running east-west) and Stone Ave., and includes the train and bus terminals. The **University of Arizona** studies 1 mi. northeast of downtown at the intersection of Park and Speedway Blvd.

Although surrounded by mountains, Tucson itself is quite flat, making most major streets (the downtown area a notable exception) perfectly straight. Streets are marked north, south, east, or west relative to Stone Ave. and Broadway. Avenues run north-south, streets east-west; because some of each are numbered, intersections such as "6th and 6th" are possible.

Accommodations and Camping

There are thousands of good places to stay in Tuscon—in the summer, at least—and almost all offer discounts in the hot months between mid-May and mid-September. The visitor bureau puts out a booklet of summer specials. Tucson's motel row is along **South Freeway,** the frontage road along I-10 just north of the junction with I-19. The historic **Congress Hotel,** 311 E. Congress (622-8848), is conveniently located across from both the Greyhound and the Amtrak stations. The hotel also serves as a hostel, with bunk beds in a small room. Prices are higher in winter and for a renovated room. A café, a bar, and a club swing downstairs. (Hostel

$12, nonmembers $16. Singles $35. Doubles $39.50.) **The Tucson Desert Inn**, I-10 and Congress (624-8151, 800-722-8458 outside AZ), could use new paint and carpeting, but has sunny rooms close to downtown. (Pool. Singles $22. Doubles $30. Winter $10 extra. Seniors 10% discount. Breakfast included.) **Travelodge**, 222 S. Freeway (791-7511, or 800-2555-3050), near downtown, has magnificent, towering palm trees, and drab but bearable rooms. It also has a pool and movies. (Singles $22. Doubles $27. Winter $15 extra. AARP discount.) **Old Pueblo Homestays Bed and Breakfast**, P.O. Box 13603, Tucson 85732 (790-2399; open daily 8am-8pm), arranges overnight stays in private homes. (Singles from $25. Doubles $35-40. Reservations usually required 2 weeks in advance for winter.)

The best place to camp is the **Mount Lemmon Recreation Area** in the **Coronado National Forest**. Campgrounds and picnic areas are two minutes to two hours outside Tucson via the Catalina Hwy. The best unofficial camping in the forest is in Sabino Canyon, on the northeastern outskirts of Tucson. **Rose Canyon**, at 7000 ft., is heavily wooded, comfortably cool, and has a small lake. Sites at higher elevations fill quickly on weekends. (Sites $5 at Rose and Spencer Canyons; General Hitchcock Campground free, but no water available.) For more info, contact the **National Forest Service**, 300 W. Congress Ave. (670-6483), at Granada, seven blocks west of Greyhound. (Open Mon.-Fri. 7:45am-4:30pm.) Among the commercial campgrounds near Tucson, try **Cactus Country RV Park** (574-3000), 10 mi. southeast of Tucson on I-10 off the Houghton Rd. exit. (Sites $12 for 1 or 2 people, with full hookup $16.50. Each additional person $2.)

Food

The downtown business district and the area farther east around the University feature—would you believe it?—excellent Tex-Mex cuisine. Tucson also provides plenty of healthier options for those who've been "El Something"'d out.

Big Ray's Barbeque, 356 E. Grant Rd. (624-RIBS). Welcome to the real deal. Big Ray's not only has some of the most friendly service in town, the BBQ sandwiches ($2.50-4) and homemade sauce are seraphic. Open Mon.-Thurs. 11am-9pm, Fri.-Sat. 11am-10pm, Sun. 1-8pm.

El Charro, 311 N. Court Ave. (622-5465), 4 blocks north of the Civic Center. Flavorful but not fiery sun-dried *carne seca* in various forms (enchilada $4.75). Chips, salsa, and a pitcher of water free with every order. Open daily 11am-10pm.

El Minuto, 354 S. Main Ave. (882-4145), just south of the community center. Colorful atmosphere and impeccable quality. Voted Tucson's best restaurant in 1988. Usually packed with locals. Open daily 11am-2:30am.

Bentley's House of Coffee and Tea, 810 E. University Blvd. (795-0338), near the university. No smoking or styrofoam allowed in this patagonia-clad joint. A wide variety of desserts and non-alcoholic drinks, plus more substantial meals. Open Mon.-Sat. 7am-mid., Sun. 8am-mid.

Entertainment

Tucsonites rock and roll near UA on Speedway Boulevard, and several country music lounges hunker down on North Oracle. The free "Tucson Weekly" (792-3630) comes out on Wednesdays and has arts listings.

Terry & Zeke's, 4376 E. Speedway Blvd. (325-3555). Long-standing institution of great live Texas blues and R&B. A hole-in-the-wall with a great beer selection. Open daily noon-1am.

Berkey's, 5769 E. Speedway (722-0103). A smoke-filled blues and rock club. Open daily noon-1am. Live music Tues.-Sun. at 9pm. Cover Fri.-Sat. $2.

Mudbuggs, 136 N. Park Ave. (882-9844). DJs during the week, live rock (including "Rainer & Das Combo") on weekends. Good stuff. Open Tues.-Sat. 8pm-2am. Cover $2-4.

Hotel Congress Historic Tap Room, 311 E. Congress (622-8848). Frozen in its 1938 incarnation. Eclectic, perhaps even weird, crowd, but very friendly. Open daily 11am-1am. Across the hall, a DJ plays "Mod. . .New Age. . .Alternative" dance music Thurs.-Sat. at **Club Congress**. Occasional live music. Drink specials $1.25. Club opens 9pm.

The **Tucson Parks and Recreation Department** (791-4873) sponsors free concerts periodically throughout the summer. Call for info or check the Thursday evening *Citizen.*

Sights

Most of Tucson's attractions lie some distance outside of town and are generally accessible by car or tour bus only. The city itself offers few diversions. The downtown is not "historic" by East Coast or European standards, with few buildings from before the Civil War; it lays a better claim as "artsy," with galleries and the **Tucson Museum of Art,** 140 N. Main Ave. (624-2333), whose impressive collection concentrates on the pre-Columbian. (Open Tues.-Sat. 10am-4pm, Sun. noon-4pm. Admission $2, seniors and students $1. Free Tues.)

The **University of Arizona,** whose "mall" sits where E. 3rd St. should be, parades another main concentration of in-town attractions. The mall itself is lovely, less for the architecture than the varied—and elaborately irrigated—vegetation. The **UA Visitor's Center,** at Cherry and the Mall (621-5130; events line 621-5784), stocks maps, event calendars, and info on current museum exhibits; the helpful staff answers questions both about the university and Tucson in general. (Open Mon.-Fri. 8am-5pm, Sat. 9am-2pm.) Across the Mall, the **Flandrau Planetarium** (621-7827) has a museum and a public telescope in addition to planetarium shows. (Eccentric hours for museum and shows; call ahead. Museum free; shows $3.75, seniors, students, and kids $3.) Across from Park Ave. from the west end of campus, University Blvd. jams with shops catering to student needs—with clothing, records, and photocopies. **Campus Discount,** 9111 E. University Blvd. prices its fully-flavored sodas as low as 15¢, perhaps out of pure philanthropy. (Open Mon.-Fri. 7:30am-9pm, Sat. 9am-7pm, Sun. 10am-6pm.)

A vibrant local event, the **mariachi mass,** thrills at **St. Augustine,** 192 S. Stone Ave. downtown. The singing and dancing, which are not intended as tourist attractions, take place in Tucson's old white Spanish cathedral. (Sun. 8am mass in Spanish.)

Near Tucson

The natural and man-made attractions which surround Tucson are the city's saving grace for tourists. To the north, a tram takes visitors from the visitors center through **Sabino Canyon** (749-2861), where cliffs and waterfalls make an ideal spot for picnics and day hikes. (Tram daily every ½ hr. 9am-4:30pm.)

If you've ever wondered where to find those tall, pitchforkesque cacti you always see in Westerns and on the Arizona license plate, go to the **Saguaro National Monument** (296-8576), a park devoted to preserving the Saguaro cacti, which can live up to 200 years and grow over 40 ft. tall. Tucson divides this monument into two parts. To the west of the city, the **Tucson Mountain Unit,** on N. Kinney Rd. at Rte. 9 (883-6366), has limited hiking trails for day use only and an auto loop. (Visitors center open daily 8am-5pm. Park open 24 hrs. Free.) Just south of this unit is the **Arizona-Sonora Desert Museum,** 2021 N. Kinney Rd. (883-2702), a naturalist's dream, an up-close look at the flora and fauna of the Sonoran desert, including an excellent walk-though aviary and an underwater look at otters and a beaver the size of a small cow. Take at least two hours to see the museum, the best time to visit being the cool morning hours when the animals have not begun their afternoon siesta. (Open winter daily 8:30am-5pm; summer 7:30am-6pm. Admission $6, ages 6-12 $1.) The way to and from the Tucson Mountain Unit and the Desert Museum goes through **Gates Pass,** whose vistas make it a favorite spot for watching sunrises and sunsets. To the east of the city, the **Rincon Mountain Unit** (296-8576), on the Old Spanish Trail east of Tucson, offers the same services as the Tucson Unit as well as overnight hikes. (Visitors center open daily 8am-5pm. Admission $3/vehicle.)

Pima's **Titan II Missile Museum,** La Canada Dr. (791-2929), in Green Valley, 25 mi. south of Tucson, is a chilling monument built around a deactivated missile silo. (Open Wed.-Sun. 9am-5pm; Nov.-April daily 9am-5pm. Admission $5, seniors and active military $4, ages 10-17 $3.) The Southwest is the desert graveyard for many an outmoded aircraft; low humidity and sparse rainfall preserve the relics. Over 20,000 warplanes, from WWII fighters to Vietnam War jets, are parked in ominous, silent rows on the **Davis-Monthan Air Force Base** (750-4570), 15 mi. southeast of Tucson. Take the Houghton exit off I-10, then travel west on Irvington to Wilmont. (Free tours Mon. and Wed. at 9am. Call ahead for reservations.) You can also view the 2-mi. long graveyard through the airfield fence.

Just next to the Desert Museum lies **Old Tucson,** a movie set attempting to convey the feel of the Old West. More authentic is the small desert town of **Tombstone,** 70 mi. southeast of Tucson. This aptly-named mining town will live forever in Western lore as the sight of the legendary **Shootout at the O.K. Corral** between the Earp brothers and the Clanton gang, as well as the home of such renowned Western figures as Wyatt Earp, Bat Masterson, and Doc Holiday. The **O.K. Corral,** on Allen St. (457-3456) next to City Park, is open to visitors, and doubles as a general tourist info center. (Open daily 8:30am-5pm. Admission $1. Tickets $3; includes a movie screening and a copy of the *Epitaph.*) Tombstone's sheriffs and outlaws, very few of whom died of natural causes, were laid to rot in the **Boothill Cemetery** northeast of downtown. Try to catch the mock gunfights staged every Sunday at 2pm alternately between the O.K. Corral and the town streets. Come prepared to open your wallet; "the town too tough to die" touts an almost irresistible assortment of kitschy curios in several shops. For more info on Tombstone's sights, contact the O.K. Corral or the **Tombstone Tourism Association,** on the corner of 4th and Allen St. (457-2211; open Mon.-Fri. 9am-5pm, Sat.-Sun. 10am-5pm).

ARKANSAS

Arkansas (AR-ken-saw), no relation to Kansas (CAN-zis), is called "the natural state," and so it is. It has all of the quaint slowness and hospitality of any other Southern state, from clean and friendly Little Rock to the old spa town of Hot Springs, without the drearily flat terrain from border to border. The jagged Ozark Mountains tower defiantly over Southern flatlands, offering the Western ranges' unpolluted beauty and excitement without their burdensome distance from the South and East.

Practical Information

Capital: Little Rock.

Arkansas Dept. of Parks and Tourism, 1 Capitol Mall, Little Rock 72201 (501-682-7777 or 800-643-8383). Open Mon.-Fri. 8am-5pm.

Time Zone: Central (1 hr. behind Eastern). **Postal Abbreviation:** AR

Hot Springs

Get out of Little Rock and get to Hot Springs, an old-fashioned spa town in a national park established to preserve the natural springs. Bubbling up from the oak- and hickory-forested Hot Springs Mountain, the 143°F water is totally purified by the time it reaches the surface—NASA used the liquid to protect the Apollo mission moon rocks from bacteria.

Hernando de Soto "discovered" the springs in 1541; Native Americans had been using the Hot Springs as a neutral ground for peaceful tribal meetings. Since then, visitors from Franklin D. Roosevelt to Al Capone have come here to enjoy peace of mind. Hot Springs had its heyday in the 1920s, when the medicinal properties and healing powers of the springs made it one of the country's most popular resorts. The town has declined since the 40s, although the national park, springs, and old-fashioned town are still spiffy. Hot Springs seems like a city that began to become a ghost town but changed its mind halfway through.

The **Fordyce Bathhouse Visitor Center,** 300 Central Ave. (623-1433), offers information and fascinating tours on the surrounding wilderness areas and on the bathhouse itself, both of which are part of the Hot Springs National Park. The **Buckstaff** (623-2308) is the only place you can take a co-ed bath in town (bathing suits are required, wise guy). Baths are $9.50, massages $10. (Open Mon.-Fri. 7-11:45am and 1:30-3pm, Sat. 7-11:45am.) Down the street is the **Hot Springs Health Spa,** N. 500 Reserve (321-9664; bath $9, massage $12; open daily 9am-10pm). The **Arlington** and **Majestic** hotels also have baths open to the public. ($12 bath, $12 massage.)

When you're not bathing in the springs or hiking in the park, try cruising Lake Hamilton on the **Belle of Hot Springs** (525-4438), with one-hour narrated tours alongside the Ouachita Mountains and Lake Hamilton mansions. (Fare $7, kids $3.25.) In town, the **Mountain Valley Spring Water Company,** 150 Central Ave. (623-6671), offers free samples and tours of its national headquarters. The **Magic Springs** amusement park, at 2001 Hwy. 70 E. (624-5411; 800-643-1212 outside AR), has a few musical shows and many kids' rides. (Open summer Sun.-Fri. 10am-6pm, Sat. 10am-11pm. $11, ages 3-11 $10.) From the **Hot Springs Mountain Observatory Tower** (623-6033), located in the national park (turn off Central Ave. to Hwy. 7), you can get a beautiful glimpse of the surrounding mountains and lakes. (Open daily, Nov.-Feb. 9am-5pm, Mar.-Oct. 9am-6pm, May 16-Labor Day 9am-9pm. $3, kids $1.75.)

Nighttime family entertainment percolates throughout Hot Springs. The **Bathhouse Show,** 701 Central Ave. (623-1415), is a two-hour comedic variety show tracing the musical history of Hot Springs from the "boogie-woogie" years to the rock 'n' roll era. (Performances Tues.-Sun. at 8pm. $8, seniors $7.45, kids $4. Reservations recommended.) If you're just a little bit country, the **Rocky Top Jubilee,** 1312 Central Ave. (623-7504), throws in some gospel and lots of comedy with the C&W right in town. (Shows at 8pm. $7.50, seniors $7, kids $3.75. Reservations recommended.) A short drive out of town is the **Music Mountain Jamboree,** 3300 Albert Pike (767-3841) off Hwy. 270 W. Family-style country music shows take place nightly during the summer, and at various times throughout the year. (Shows at 8pm. $8, kids $4. Reservations required.)

Hot Springs has a number of small, inexpensive restaurants. Snack on *beignets* (doughnuts without the hole; 75¢) and *café au lait* (75¢) at **Café New Orleans,** 210 Central Ave. (Open daily until 11:30pm. Live entertainment Fri. and Sat.) **Rod's Pizza Cellar,** at Spring and Broadway (624-7637), serves delicious Italian specialties beneath bright neon for under $7. (Open Tues.-Thurs. 11am-10pm, Fri.-Sat. 11am-midnight, Sun. 11:30am-10pm.) For good ol' country food, try **Maggie's Café,** 362 Central (623-4091). Good Mississippi mud pie ($2) for dessert. (Open 9am-9pm.)

For the budget traveler who has a little stashed away in the ol' moneybelt, the **Arlington Hotel,** at Fountain and Central St. (623-7771), is a world-class resort—of yesteryear—at very reasonable rates. (Singles from $40. Doubles $50. Family rates with 2 double beds from $56.) Walk into a fairy tale at the **Best Motel,** 630 Ouachita (624-5736), which has gingerbread-like cabins, a storybook pool, and relaxing chairs. (Singles $20. Doubles $30.) The **Perry Plaza Motel,** 1007 Park Ave. on Hwy. 7 (623-9814), offers suites with A/C, bedroom, bathroom, and kitchen. ($21 per person, $25 per 2 people, $5 per additional person. Higher during racing season.) The motels clustered along Hwy. 7 and 88 have similar prices, although rates rise during the tourist season (Feb.-April); camping is far cheaper (see State Parks below).

Before touring Hot Springs, you should stop by the **visitors center,** downtown at the corner of Central and Reserve St. (321-2277), and pick up their valuable coupon packets for many attractions and restaurants. (Open Mon.-Sat. 9:30am-5pm, Sun. 1-5pm.) Hot Springs becomes especially crowded during the horse racing season at nearby **Oaklawn** racetrack (Feb.-April). Call 1-800-RACE-OJC (1-800-722-3652) for more information.

Hot Springs's **ZIP code** is 71901; the **area code** is 501.

State Parks Nearby

The 48,000-acre **Lake Ouachita Park** lies on the largest of three clear, beautiful, artificial lakes near Hot Springs. Travel three mi. west of Hot Springs on U.S. 270, then 12 mi. north on Rte. 227. Numerous islands lie just offshore where you can escape from civilization to enjoy the quiet coves and rocky beaches. Fishing is plentiful, and camping available from $5.50 per day (767-9366); fishing boats rent for $6 per day.

By car from Hot Springs you can readily reach **Lake Catherine Park,** which covers over 2,000 acres of Ouachita Mountain, stretching along the shores of beautiful Lake Catherine. Campsites start at $5.50 per day (844-4176). Take exit 97 off I-30 at Malvern and go 12 mi. north on Rte. 171. (Canoe rentals $3.25 per hr., power boats $16 per ½ day, $24 per day.)

Little Rock

Once upon a time, a little rock jutting out into the Arkansas River served as an important landmark for travelers going upstream. Today that little rock is overshadowed by the big city that has grown up around it, a city that serves as the political and geographical center of the state. In 1957, Little Rock was the focus of nationwide controversy, when Governor Orval Faubus led an often violent segregationist movement, using troops to prevent African American students from enrolling in Central High: the "Little Rock Nine" enrolled only under National Guard protection. Today an immaculate and integrated city surrounded by gently sloping hills, Little Rock rolls with a wealth of performing arts, museums, and historical attractions.

Practical Information

Emergency: 911.

Arkansas Dept. of Parks and Tourism, 1 Capitol Mall (800-643-8383 or 682-7777 in-state), in a complex directly behind the capitol building. Open Mon.-Fri. 8am-5pm. **Little Rock Bureau for Conventions and Visitors,** at Markham and Main St. (376-4781 or 800-844-7625), near the Greyhound station. Open Mon.-Fri. 9am-3:30pm; closed for lunch about 11:30am-12:30pm. **Telefun,** 372-3399. Activities listings for Little Rock.

Amtrak: Markham and Victory St. (372-6841 or 800-872-7245), near downtown. One train daily to St. Louis (7 hr., $68) and Dallas (7 hr., $75).

Greyhound/Trailways: 118 E. Washington St. (372-1861), across the river in North Little Rock. Use the walkway over the bridge to get downtown. To St. Louis ($60), New Orleans ($66), and Memphis ($25). More expensive weekends.

Public Transport: Central Arkansas Transit (CAT), 614 Center St. (375-1163). Regular buses Mon.-Sat. every ½ hr. 6am-6:30pm. Fare 80¢, transfers 10¢.

Taxi: Black and White Cab, (374-0333). Base fare $1, $1 per additional mile.

Help Lines: Rape Crisis, 375-5181. Open 24 hrs. **First Call for Help,** 376-4567.

Post Office: 600 W. Capitol at 5th St. (377-6470). Open Mon.-Fri. 7am-5:15pm. **ZIP code:** 72201.

Area Code: 501.

Most of Little Rock's streets were "planned" with no apparent pattern in mind. **Broadway** and **Main** are the major north-south arteries. **Markham** and all streets numbered one to 36 run east-west.

Accommodations and Camping

The Quapaw Inn Bed and Breakfast, 1868 S. Gaines St. (376-6873), 2 blocks west of 17th and Broadway. In a quaint Victorian house. Expensive for 1 person, but *the* place to stay for 2. Extremely friendly proprietor. Huge and delicious breakfast. (Rooms $35-45, each additional person $10.) Call in advance for the *Let's Go* discount ($10).

Little Rock Inn, 6th and Center St. (376-8301), downtown. Large hotel with pool, saloon, laundry room. Attractive rooms, often full. Singles $30. Doubles $33.

Diamond Inn, 322 E. Capitol (376-3661), downtown. Lone travelers might feel uncomfortable in this neighborhood. Spacious and sunny rooms. Nice pool. Singles $24.50. Doubles $32.

Deluxe Inn, 308 Capitol (375-6411), next to the Diamond Inn downtown. The name refers to big rooms, a pool and movie channel more than overall tidiness. Singles $22. Doubles $28.

KOA Campground, Crystal Hill Rd. (758-4598), in North Little Rock 7 mi. from downtown between exit 12 on I-430 and exit 148 on I-48. Pool. Sites from $16, with hookups $18.

Food

Juanita's, 1300 S. Main St (372-1228). The city's best Mexican food in a fun, loud, cantina atmosphere. Reasonable prices (entrees $7-10), nightly entertainment, and a hoppin' bar. Try Margarita night on Mon. ($2.25), or Sat. champagne brunch ($1.25 per glass). Hell, try 'em both. Open Mon.-Thurs. 11am-10pm, Fri. 11am-10:30pm, Sat. noon-10:30pm, Sun. 5:30-9pm.

Solar Cafe, 1706 W. 3rd (375-4747), across from Capitol. Former gas station and future energy source now specializing in healthy soups, sandwiches, and salads ($2.50-4). Open daily 7:30am-10pm.

Hungry's Cafe, 1001 W. 7th St. (372-9720). Raucous joint that revels in solid breakfasts as well as down-home lunch specials with 2 vegetables and bread for under $4. Good cap collection on the wall. Open Mon.-Fri. 6am-2pm.

The Oyster Bar, 3003 W. Markham St. (666-7100). Reasonably priced seafood and "Po'Boy" sandwiches ($4-5). Big screen TV, pool tables, cheap draft beer, and a decidedly laid-back atmosphere where paper towel rolls take the place of napkins. Open Mon.-Thurs. 11am-10pm, Fri.-Sat. 11am-10:30pm. Happy Hour Mon.-Fri. 3-6:30pm.

White Water Tavern, 2500 7th St. (374-3801). Popular gathering place and watering hole serving Southern cooking (full meal under $5). Try the ft.-long hot dog ($2.50). Live music at night. Open Mon.-Sat. 11am-2am, Sun. noon-10pm.

East End Diner, 612 Center St. (376-3515). Blue-suited business luncheon spot. Home-cooked specialties like chicken-fried steak ($4.50), as well as sandwiches and salads. Entrees include 2 veggies and warm biscuits, and run under $5. Open Mon.-Fri. 10:45am-2pm.

Sights

Little Rock's historic downtown district is known as the **Quapaw Quarter.** Pick up free walking tour guides at the **Quapaw Quarter District Office,** 1315 Scott St. (371-0075; open Mon.-Fri. 9am-5pm), or at the visitors bureau. These helpful guides have both labeled maps and brief histories of the historic buildings. Just one block away from the visitors bureau mopes the saucy **Old State House,** 300 W. Markham St. (324-9685), which served as the capitol from 1836 until the ceiling collapsed in 1899 while the legislature was in session. The restored building now provides a good starting point for a downtown tour. (Open Mon.-Sat. 9am-5pm, Sun. 1-5pm. Free.) The functioning **state capitol** (682-5080) at the west end of Capitol St. may look very familiar—it's actually a replica of the U.S. capitol in Washington, DC. Take a free self-guided tour or one of the 45-minute group tours given on the hour. (Open Mon.-Fri. 9am-4pm, Sat. 10am-5pm, Sun. 1-5pm. Call in advance on weekends.) For a look at the history of the townspeople of 19th-century Little Rock, visit the **Arkansas Territorial Restoration,** 214 E. Third St. (371-2348). Tours of four restored buildings include an old grog shop, and a typical old-fashioned print shop. (Open Mon.-Sat. 9am-5pm, Sun. 1-5pm. 50-min. tours every hr. on the hr. $2, seniors $1, kids 50¢. Free first Sun. of month.)

Along the banks of the Arkansas River, you'll find **Riverfront Park,** a pleasant place for a walk, and home to the legendary "Little Rock" itself, which is in fact little and easy to miss. For the best access, cut through the back of the Excelsior Hotel at Markham and Center St. Take a ride on the paddle wheeler **Spirit** (376-4150; 1-hr. cruises $5, kids $2.75; departs from the North Little Rock side of the Arkansas River Tues.-Sat. at 2pm). The town celebrates the waterway annually at **Riverfest,** on Memorial Day weekend.

A mile south of downtown is **MacArthur Park,** elegant home to several interesting museums and title of a Danna Harman. . .er, Donna Summer song. Particularly suited to kids, the **Museum of Science and History** (371-3521), housed in the old arsenal building where General Douglas MacArthur was born, has exhibits on Arkansas history. (Open Mon.-Sat. 9am-4:30pm, Sun. 1-4:30pm. $1. Free Mon.) While in the park don't miss the **Arkansas Arts Center,** 9th and Commerce St. (372-4400), and the **Decorative Arts Museum,** 7th and Rock St. (372-4000), the newest addition to the center and home to a collection of contemporary crafts. (Open Mon.-Sat. 10am-5pm, Sun. noon-5pm. Free.) The **War Memorial Park,** northwest of the state capitol off I-630 at Fair Park Blvd., houses the 40-acre **Little Rock Zoo,** 1 Jonesboro Dr., (666-2406), which simulates the animals' natural habitats. (Open daily 9:30am-4:30pm. $1, kids 50¢.)

The opening scene of *Gone With the Wind* features the **Old Mill Park,** Lakeshore Dr. at Fairway Ave. (758-2445) in North Little Rock, one of the city's most treasured attractions. The WPA constructed this water-powered grist mill during the Depression. (Open daily. Free.) The opening scene of the TV show "Designing Women" also features a Little Rock location—**The Villa Nacre,** 1321 Scott (374-9979), a restored 19th-century house and museum. (Open Sun. 1-5pm, Mon.-Fri. by appointment only. $3, seniors $2.)

Archeologists are uncovering part of Arkansas' past that goes back much farther than the historic homes and parks—all the way to 700 AD. The **Toltec Mounds State Park** (961-9442), 15 mi. east of North Little Rock on Rte. 386, provided the political and religious center of the Plum Bayou people more than 1,000 years ago. (Open Tues.-Sat. 8am-5pm, Sun. noon-5pm. Guided tours at 9:30am, 11am, 12:30pm, and 3:30pm. $2, ages 6-15 $1.) Thirteen mi. west of Little Rock on Rte. 10 and then two mi. north on Rte. 300 is **Pinnacle Mountain State Park** (868-5806), a fairly tame "wilderness park." After the moderately steep 1,000-ft. climb to the top, you can take in a superb summit view. Look for fossils, and bring water on the hike. For more information, contact the Superintendent at Pinnacle Mountain State Park, R 1, Roland Rd., P.O. Box 34, Roland 72135. The park definitely merits a daytrip, but has no camping facilities.

Entertainment and Nightlife

Little Rock has an active cultural life, including a symphony, an opera, and community theaters. Conducted by Robert Henderson, the **Arkansas Symphony,** 2500 N. Tyler (666-1761), performs in Robinson Auditorium from September to May. (Tickets $9-20, students $3.)

The **Arkansas Opera Theatre** makes its new home at the **Wildwood Park for Performing Arts,** 20919 Denny Rd. (821-7275). Besides an opera festival in June, the park hosts kids' theater and jazz concerts throughout the year. The professional **Arkansas Repertory Theatre,** at 6th and Main St. (378-0405), performs both traditional crowd-pleasers and avant-garde works. The **Community Theatre of Little Rock,** 1501 Maryland (376-4582), gives a series of family-oriented plays. For a change of pace, go see the **Rackensack Folklore Society** sing authentic Arkansas folk music at the Arkansas Arts Center. (First Mon. of each month at 7:30pm. Free.)

Live music plays almost nightly at a few spots around the city. Consult the free, bi-weekly *Spectrum,* or the *Nightflying* and *Today* monthlies to find out what's happening. Many good eateries also have good music. **Juanita's,** for example, has rock, reggae, and acoustic music Monday through Saturday, with a blues jam every Tuesday. The **Oyster Bar** gives good jazz every Monday ($3), and the **White Water Tavern** has down-home rock or country every night ($2). (See Food above for all three.)

Ozarks

Beaten by ages of weathering, one of the world's oldest mountain ranges now barely surpasses hill status in height. The terrain, however, is far more than just hilly with twisting switchback roads, steep scenic bluffs, and lush woods which make for a challenging vacationland. Ozark folk culture today is marked by reclusiveness and a fierce concern for preserving a way of life that includes musical and religious elements, such as fiddling and the Baptist Church.

Although settling the land in northern Arkansas and southern Missouri required self-reliance and stubbornness, today's traveler should find things a bit tamer than they were a century ago. The Ozarks have become a major resort area for Missouri, Arkansas, and neighboring states; tacky gift shops have sprung up like kudzu. The scenery, however, remains outstandingly rugged, and provides a beautiful background for long hikes. Arkansas folk love to canoe, fish, and float down the Ozarks' rivers, especially the Buffalo; likeminded travelers should arrive before midsummer, when the rivers begin to run too low for sport.

Few buses venture into the area, but hitching is good, and generally safe. Drivers should follow Rte. 7, 71, or 23 for best access and views. Eureka Springs to Huntsville on Rte. 23 south is a scenic one-hour drive. Also head east or west on Rte. 62 from Eureka Springs for attractive stretches. The **Arkansas Department of Parks and Tourism** (800-643-8383; see Arkansas Practical Information) can help with your trip. If you want to paddle a portion of the **Buffalo National River,** call the ranger station for camping and canoe rental info (449-4311; canoe rental $22 per day, cabin $46 per day), or contact Buffalo Point Concessions, HCR, P.O. Box 388, Yellville 72687 (449-6206). The **Arkansas Bikeways Commission,** 1200 Worthen Bank Bldg., Little Rock 72201, dispenses a bike trail map for the Ozark region. Also, the **Eureka Springs Chamber of Commerce,** (253-8737; 800-643-3546 outside AR) has excellent vacation-planning material.

Ozark culture is alive and well southeast of Eureka Springs, down Rte. 62 to Rte. 14, at the **Ozark Folk Center** (501-269-3851) near **Mountain View.** The center is a living museum of the cabin crafts, music, and lore of the Ozarks. Among the craftspeople practicing their trades in the **Crafts Forum** are a blacksmith, a basket maker, a potter, a gunsmith, and a furniture maker. Trams transport guests to the Crafts Forum from the visitors center. (Open May-Oct. daily 10am-5pm. $4.75, kids $2.75.) Musicians give traditional concerts in the auditorium nightly at 7:30pm. The audience is invited to participate in the jigs. ($5.25, kids $3.25.) Seasonal events include the **Arkansas Folk Festival** and the **Mountain and Hammered Dulcimer Championships** in late April, the **Banjo Weekend** (mid-May), and the **Arkansas Old-Time Fiddlers Association State Championship** (late Sept.). The Fiddlers Championship is quite a sight as hundreds of old pros and young apprentices play authentic music of the Ozarks. Many of the area's people are of Scottish or Irish descent, and the music shows clear signs of its Celtic roots.

Eureka Springs

In the early 19th century, the Osage spread reports of a wonderful spring with magical healing powers. White settlers flocked to the site and quickly established a small town from which they sold bottles of the miraculous water. Built on piety and good marketing, Eureka Springs has since replaced its healing services with scenic and historical tourist attractions. Some faith does survive in **The Great Passion Play** (253-9200), which has brought recent fame to Eureka Springs. Modeled after Germany's Oberammergau Passion Play, which depicts Christ's last days, it is staged in a huge amphitheater atop a hill, drawing up to 4,000 visitors nightly. (Performances April-Oct. Tues.-Wed., Fri.-Sun. 8:30pm. Tickets $8-9, ages 4-11 half-price. For reservations ask at your accommodations, or write P.O. Box 471, Eureka Springs 72632.) The amphitheater is off Rte. 62, just outside of town. **Gray Line Bus Tours** (253-9540) provides transportation to and from the play ($3 per person round-trip). They pick you up and drop you off at your hotel, motel, or campground. The theater is wheelchair-accessible.

The town is filled with tourist-oriented restaurants. The **Gazebo,** in the Best Western Eureka Inn at the junction of Rte. 62 and 23 north (253-9551), is a popular tourist dining spot with 1890s decor. The menu features Southern food and Arkansas catfish, but the best deal is your basic soup, cheese, fruit, and salad bar for $4.50. (Open daily 6:30am-9pm.) Get away from the usual tourist glitz at the **Wagon Wheel,** 84 S. Main St. (253-9934), a country-western bar decorated with antiques. (Open Mon.-Fri. 8am-2am, Sat. 10am-midnight.)

Accommodations in Eureka Springs are not difficult to find, but prices are impossible to foresee. They vary daily according to the crowds, from as low as $18 for singles in August to $45 during April; rates also drop on Mondays and Thursdays when Passion Players take a break. The **King's Hi-Way Inn,** 96 King's Hwy. (253-7311), is friendly and generally reasonable. (Singles $42. Doubles $48.) The best package deal in town is **Keller's Country Dorm,** Rte. 62 (253-8418), five mi. east of town. For $25, you get a dorm bed, breakfast, dinner, and a reserved ticket to the Passion Play (additional nights $9). Call Richard Keller ahead of time to get this rate, generally reserved for church groups of 12 or more but open to individuals. (Open May-Oct.)

There are several campgrounds near Eureka Springs, ranging in price from $5-10. **Pinehaven Campsites,** on Hwy. 62 (253-9052), two mi. east of town, charges $10 per tent and $14 for a full RV hookup. Farther out, but more picturesque, **Lake Leatherwood,** two mi. west on Rte. 62 (253-8624), sees mostly tourists. Rates begin at $7 a tent. The **KOA Campground** (253-8036) is three mi. farther west on Rte. 62, then ¾ mi. south on Rte. 187. Sites $14. (Open April-Oct.)

For extra help in planning your time here, call the **Chamber of Commerce** (800-643-3546 or 253-8737), located on Rte. 62 just north of Rte. 23. (Open May-Oct. daily 9am-5pm; Nov.-April Mon.-Fri. 9am-5pm.) **Gray Line Bus Company** (253-9540) runs two-hour city tours at 9am and 1pm from May 4 to early November. (Fare $8, ages under 12 free.) The buses will pick you up and return you to any motel or campground in Eureka Springs. (Pick-up times approximately 15 min. before tour departure time. Out-of-town pickup approximately 30 min. before departure time.) The town is also accessible by trolley. Check schedules at the chamber of commerce.

Eureka Springs's **ZIP code** is 72632; the **area code** is 501.

CALIFORNIA

Spanish explorers, in search of a fabled strait between the Pacific and Atlantic Oceans, happened upon the Golden State and its 200,000 natives in the 1500s. Hoping to secure the land (and its possible treasures), they quickly named it "California" after an imaginary Amazon island kingdom located just around the corner from Paradise. Although the quixotic quest for Eldorado temporarily turned into a very real 49er Gold Rush with the 1848 discovery of the precious metal at Sutter's Mill, for most of its history California's glittering promise has remained little more than a golden facade for those flocking westward.

Exploited Chinese workers, in the late 19th century, constructed the railroads linking the West to the rest of the country, despite innumerable casualties and American fear of the Yellow Peril. When severe droughts further reduced Depression-era Midwestern farmlands to lifeless "dust bowls," a flood of newcomers arrived to pick the grapes of wrath. Similar misplaced notions of opportunity drew African Americans westward during the great Southern exodus early in the

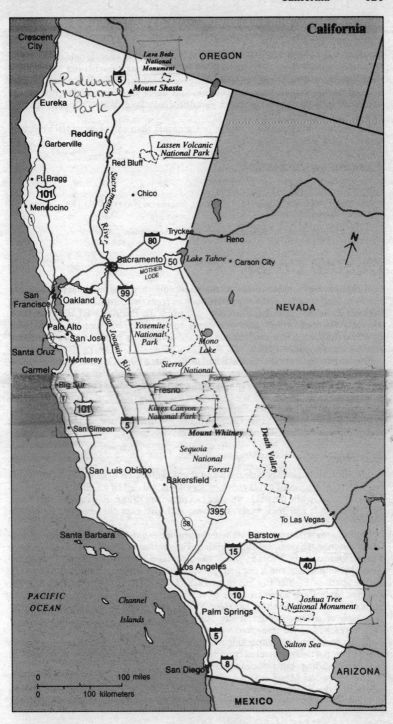

California

Crescent City

OREGON

Lava Beds National Monument

Redwood National Park

Mount Shasta

Eureka

Redding
Garberville

Red Bluff

Lassen Volcanic National Park

Ft. Bragg

101

Chico

Mendocino

Sacramento River

Tryckee

Reno

80

Sacramento

50

Lake Tahoe

Carson City

MOTHER LODE

San Francisco

Oakland

99

NEVADA

Palo Alto

San Jose

San Joaquin River

Yosemite National Park

Mono Lake

Santa Cruz

Monterey

Carmel

Sierra National Forest

Big Sur

Fresno

101

Kings Canyon National Park

San Simeon

5

Mount Whitney

Death Valley

Sequoia National Forest

San Luis Obispo

Bakersfield

395

58

To Las Vegas

Santa Barbara

Barstow

15

40

Los Angeles

PACIFIC OCEAN

Channel Islands

10

Palm Springs

Joshua Tree National Monument

5

Salton Sea

San Diego

8

ARIZONA

MEXICO

0 — 100 miles
0 — 100 kilometers

20th century. Along with California's longstanding Mexican population, many of these later "California Or Bust" groups met hostility from the descendents of earlier fortune-seekers.

Yet no misfortune, not even severe earthquakes, could keep people away, either from the state or from each other; since 1900, the state's population has doubled every 20 years. Today, the accompanying naive industrial expansion has plagued a more mature California with pollution and water shortages. Californians' consumerism may be letting the desert paradise, fool's gold or not, slip like sand between their fingers.

For more comprehensive coverage of California than can be provided here, consult *Let's Go: California and Hawaii.*

Practical Information

Capital: Sacramento.

California Office of Tourism, 1121 L St. #103, Sacramento 95814 (916-322-1396). **National Park Information,** 213-888-3770.

Time Zone: Pacific (3 hr. behind Eastern). **Postal Abbreviation:** CA

Central Coast

Although the popular image of the California dream is manufactured by the media machines of L.A., the image itself comes from the Central Coast. This stretch between La-la-land and San Francisco, linked by the **Pacific Coast Highway (Rte. 1),** embodies California's public-relations soul: rolling surf crashing onto wide beaches, dramatic cliffs and mountains, self-actualizing New Agers, and relaxed fern-bars along surfer huts.

San Simeon anchors the southern end of Big Sur, a 90-mi. strip of sparsely inhabited coastline where Rte. 1 inches motorists right to the edge of jutting cliffs overhanging the ocean. The highway winds its way up the coast to the Monterey Peninsula, where eager merchants try to harness the northern end of Big Sur for tourist consumption, but even they cannot spoil the coast. Just above Monterey, 79 mi. south of San Francisco, Santa Cruz sprinkles its surfer culture and university with a dash of San Francisco's off-beat quirkiness.

Big Sur

Big Sur simultaneously welcomes and shuns visitors. Its dramatic beaches, swirling waters, and acres of moist redwood forest—populated by an abundance of wildlife—invite all, while the fickle weather can prove unsettling. Even as the sun shines, Big Sur's winds can rock buses, tip cows, and give even the cheeriest hippie the blues.

Big Sur area wilderness and state parks provide exquisite natural settings for dozens of outdoor activities, including hiking. The northern end of **Los Padres National Forest,** known as the **Ventana Wilderness,** contains the popular 24-mi. **Pine Ridge Trail.** Pick up a map and a required permit at the USFS **ranger station** (667-2423), ½-mi. south of Pfeiffer Big Sur State Park, 2 mi. north of the post office. **Pfeiffer Big Sur State Park** keeps six trails of varying lengths; pick up a map (25¢) at the park entrance. Try the short but steep **Valley View Trail;** its apex offers a remarkable view of redwood country. Big Sur jealously guards USFS-operated **Pfeiffer Beach,** reached by an unmarked narrow road 1.1 mi. south of Big Sur State Park. Take the road 2 mi. to the parking area, then follow the footpath to the beach. The small cove, partially protected from the Pacific by a huge offshore rock formation, is safe for wading, but riptides make swimming risky.

The Fernwood Motel (see below) includes a bar, a grocery store, a cheap gas pump, and the **Fernwood Burger Bar,** Rte. 1 (667-2422), with a bar. Fish and chips or chicken cost $5-6.50; hamburgers start at $3.25 (Open daily 11:30am-midnight.)

The **Center Deli,** right beside the Big Sur post office, serves the cheapest sandwiches ($2.80-5) in the area. (Open daily 8am-9pm; winter 8am-8pm.) At the Monterey-Salinas Transit bus stop, **Café Amphora** (667-2660), in **Nepenthe Restaurant,** serves coffee and liquor on an outdoor patio spectacularly situated at the edge of a Big Sur cliff. (Open Mon.-Fri. 10am-4pm, Sat.-Sun. 10am-5pm.)

Campgrounds are abundant, beautiful, and cheap. The **Fernwood Motel,** Rte. 1 (667-2422), 2 mi. north of the post office on the Big Sur River, offers friendly management, 65 campsites, and cabins for the tentless. (Registration 8am-midnight. Sites $19, with hookup $21. Motel rooms from $45.) The **Pfeiffer Big Sur State Park** (667-2315), just south of Fernwood and 26 mi. south of Carmel, sometimes fills all 218 developed campsites. (No hookups; hot showers. Sites $16. Reservations 800-444-7275.) **Limekiln** (667-2403), south of Big Sur, runs a private campground with grocery, showers, and beach access. (Sites $15, $5 per additional person. $5 reservation fee.) Los Padres National Forest includes two USFS campgrounds: **Plaskett Creek** (667-2315), south of Limekiln near Jade Cove, and **Kirk Creek,** about 5 mi. north of Jade Cove. (Toilets and running water. Sites $8, hikers $10. No reservations.)

Big Sur stretches between Salmon Cove in the south (17 mi. from San Simeon's Hearst Castle) and Carmel in the north, two groovy hours by car south of the cultivated Monterey Peninsula. For a guide to the area, send a stamped, self-addressed envelope to the **Chamber of Commerce,** P.O. Box 87, Big Sur 93920 (667-2100). The **post office** mails on Rte. 1 (667-2305), next to the Center Deli. Big Sur's **ZIP code** is 93290; the **area code** is 408.

Near Big Sur: Hearst Castle

In San Simeon did William Hearst a stately pleasure dome decree. Popularly known as Hearst Castle (927-2020), the Hearst San Simeon Historic Monument perches high on a hill 5 mi. east of Rte. 1 near San Simeon. Satirized as Charles Foster Kane's "Xanadu" in Orson Welles's *Citizen Kane,* the castle lives up to every adjective ever applied to the state of California itself: opulent, plastic, beautiful, fake, dazzling. It is the American dream/nightmare gone architectural, and a must-experience. Visitors have a choice of four **tours,** each an hour and 45 minutes long. You can take all four in one day, but each costs $12 (ages 6-12 $6, under 6 free if well-behaved—otherwise they meet the fate of Kane's Rosebud). Groups are taken up the hill in old school buses, shepherded around, then taken back down. Tours are given at least once per hour October through March from 8am until 3pm (except tour #4, which runs April-Nov. only), later and more frequently according to demand in summer. To see the Castle in summer, make MISTIX reservations (800-444-7275), since tours sell out quickly. The gates to the visitors center open in summer at 6am, in winter at 7am; tickets go on sale daily at 8am.

Monterey

In the 1940s, John Steinbeck's Monterey swam as a crusty coastal town geared to sardine fishing and canning. When Steinbeck revisited his beloved Cannery Row around 1960, he scornfully wrote that the area had sea-changed into a tourist trap. Cannery Row and Fisherman's Wharf have converted their packing plants to souvenir malls and wax museums. Because residents treat with dignity at least some of the area's history—both as a canning town and former capital of Spanish and Mexican Alta California—visitors should forgive Monterey's crasser side.

The **Monterey Bay Aquarium,** 866 Cannery Row (648-4888), pumps in raw, unfiltered seawater, making the tanks an almost exact duplicate of the environment in the bay—right down to the dozens of species of algae and the simulated waves. In addition to staples such as enormous octopi and docile starfish, the aquarium contains 30-ft. kelps, diving birds, and a clever exhibit that allows otters to be seen from both above and below the water's surface. A jellyfish exhibit will ooze in 1992. The aquarium is sardined with tourists mornings and holidays, but after 3pm things ebb. (Open daily 10am-6pm. Admission $9, seniors and students $6.50, ages 3-12 $4.)

On the waterfront, southeast of the aquarium, lies Steinbeck's **Cannery Row.** Once lined with languishing sardine-packing plants, this ¾-mi. street has magically metamorphosed into a strip of glitzy mini-malls, bars, and discos. To make your visit more endurable, visit one of the **wine tasting** rooms for a free sample of California's Lethe. The **Great Cannery Row Mural,** stretching 400 ft. along Cannery Row's 700 blocks, impressively depicts Monterey in the 30s.

At the south end of the row floats yet another **Fisherman's Wharf,** built in 1846. The fishermen have left, and the wharf now lures tourists with expensive restaurants and shops selling seashells and Steinbeck novels. The best thing about the wharf, and maybe Monterey in general, is the smoked salmon sandwiches ($5.50) sold by local vendors, made with fresh sourdough bread, cream cheese, and plenty of the local salmon (smoked right on the pier).

Monterey State Historic Park envelopes six **historic adobe buildings** headquarted at the **Cooper-Molera complex,** 525 Polk St. (649-7118). Two of the park's buildings are museums near Fisherman's Wharf. In 1846, Commodore John Sloat raised the Stars and Stripes over the **Customs House,** claiming California for the U.S. Today, goods typical of the days when Monterey was the busiest port in Mexican Alta California clutter the place. Next door, the **Pacific House** has a less impressive display of costumes and artifacts. (Both open daily 10am-5pm; winter 10am-4pm. Customs House free. Pacific House $2, ages 6-17 $1.) Farther from the water, the park's other four adobe houses, including the **Robert Louis Stevenson House** and the oddly-landscaped **Casa Soberanes,** are accessible only by tours, given six times daily, five in the winter. (Admission $1 per house, kids 50¢; all six $3.50, kids $2.) For the hardcore history fan, there is a 90-minute **House and Garden Tour** of 10 buildings and five gardens (departs Park headquarters Tues., Thurs., and Fri. at 2pm; $2.75, kids $2). Or buy *The Path of History,* a walking tour book, at the Headquarters ($2). In the same neighborhood as the adobes lies the **Monterey Peninsula Museum of Art,** 559 Pacific St. (372-5477), with a downstairs exhibit of European and American monochrome works from across the centuries, an upstairs collection of Western art including works by Charlie Russell, and another gallery for temporary shows. (Open Tues.-Sat. 10am-4pm, Sun. 1-4pm. Suggested donation $2.)

The huge annual **Monterey Jazz Festival** (373-3366), during the third week in September, comprises five concerts over three days. Season tickets ($80-90) sell out by the end of May. The **Blues Festival** (394-2652) rocks in late June. From late June to early July, **Monterey Bay's Theatrefest** hams it up between the Customs House and the Pacific House. Every Saturday and Sunday, tourists are beguiled by hours of free afternoon theater.

The **Casa de Gutierrez,** 590 Calle Principal, an 1841 structure now serving as a Mexican restaurant, offers a more intimate adobe experience. Many entrees ($7-8) take their names from figures in Monterey's history. Try the heaping Cooper's tostada, a wonderful chicken concoction. (Open Mon.-Thurs. 11am-9pm, Fri.-Sun. 10am-10pm.) For a decadent breakfast, head to **Belleci's,** 470 Alvarado, where the specialty is the *speengie,* a hunk of dough fried before your eyes until crisp outside and fluffy inside, then topped with cinnamon and sugar (75¢) or fruit and whipped cream ($1.50). (Open Mon.-Wed. 8am-4pm, Thurs.-Fri. 7am-4pm.) Aside from the snacks on the wharf, seafood dinners usually run high; however, many restaurants offer money-saving early-bird specials between 4 and 6:30pm. You also don't have to eat at a specifically fish-oriented joint; Thai and Japanese places access the same fresh catch.

The rates at Monterey's hotels and motels vary by day, month, and proximity to events such as the Jazz Festival. The visitor bureau's free *Monterey Peninsula Hotel and Motel Guide* has prices for all area accommodations. Generally, hotels along **Fremont Street** in Monterey and **Lighthouse Avenue** in nearby Pacific Grove are the most reasonable. The **Monterey Peninsula Youth Hostel (AYH)** (649-0375) has no fixed location, but for the past few summers has bunked and debunked in the gym of the Monterey High School on Larkin St. The hostel lacks a kitchen and mattresses lie directly on the floor, but the friendly staff tries to make up for the deficiencies by providing cheap food and lots of info. To reach the high school, take Pacific away from the water, make a right Madison and a left on Larkin St. (Lockout 9am-6pm. Curfew 11pm. Open mid-June to mid-Aug.) **Motel 6**, 2124 N. Fremont St. (646-8585), offers a rare phenomenon: prices that remain constant year-round. (Singles $40. Doubles $45.) As a result, the motel often fills quickly—make reservations as early as possible. The **Paramount Motel**, 3298 Del Monte Blvd. (384-8674) in Marina, 8 mi. north of Monterey, is clean and well-run. (Check-out 11am. Singles $30. Doubles $35. No reservations; arrive by noon to get a room.) The **Veterans Memorial Park Campgroud**, Via del Rey (646-3865), is 1½ mi. from the town center. Take Skyline Dr. off W.R. Holman Hwy. (Rte. 68). From downtown, take Pacific St. south, turn right on Jefferson, and follow the signs; or take bus #3. First-come, first-camped—arrive before 3pm in summer and on winter weekends. (Showers. Sites $10, hikers $2.)

Monterey, 115 mi. south of San Francisco, shares the Monterey Peninsula with Pacific Grove to the west, Ft. Ord and Salinas to the east, and **Carmel-by-the-Sea,** an oversized shopping mall, to the south. Just south of Carmel on Rte. 1 is the **Point Lobos Reserve** (624-4909), a state-run, 1276-acre wildlife sanctuary, popular with skindivers, dayhikers, and naturalists. On weekends a line of cars frequently waits to get in by 8am; park outside the tollbooth and walk or bike in for free. (Open daily 9am-7pm; winter 9am-5pm. Admission $3 per car. Map 50¢. No dogs allowed.)

The **Monterey Peninsula Chamber of Commerce,** 380 Alvarado St. (648-5350), sits on Monterey's main commercial street. Get advance info by writing to P.O. Box 1770, Monterey 93942. (Open Mon.-Fri. 8:30am-5pm.) **Greyhound,** 351 Del Monte Ave. (373-4735), goes to L.A. (4 per day, $47) and San Francisco (4 per day, $18). The **post office** sorts at 565 Hartnell (372-5803; open Mon.-Fri. 9am-5pm). Monterey's **ZIP code** is 93940; the **area code** is 408.

Santa Cruz

Santa Cruz sports an uncalculated hipness that other coastal towns can only envy. Often seen as the epitome of California cool, the town's beaches and bookstores even lure visitors from San Francisco, 75 mi. to the north. Restaurants offer everything from avocado sandwiches to industrial coffee, and the town is catholic enough to embrace both macho surfers and a thriving lesbian community.

The 1989 earthquake epicentered only 10 mi. away from this mellow town, doing serious damage. Tremors destroyed the pleasant Pacific Garden Mall and forced many shops to relocate temporarily to "pavilions" (tents). While some of the shops are still in the pavilions, Santa Cruz has recovered from the quake quickly with the help of a statewide tax increase.

A three-block arcade of ice cream, caramel apples, games, rides, and tacos, the **Boardwalk** (426-7433) dominates Santa Cruz's beach area. The classiest rides are two grizzled war horses: the 1929 **Giant Dipper,** one of the largest wooden roller coasters in the country (rides $2.25), and the 1911 Looff Carousel, accompanied by an 1894 organ ($1.35). (Unlimited rides $16. Boardwalk open May 27-Sept. 2 daily; weekends the rest of the year. Call for hours.)

Broad **Santa Cruz beach** generally jams with high school students from San Jose during summer weekends. When seeking solitude, try the banks of the San Lorenzo River immediately east of the boardwalk. Nude sunbathers should strip on the strip at **Red White and Blue Beach;** take Rte. 1 north to just before Davenport and look for the line of cars to your right. Women should not go alone. ($5 per car.) Those who enjoy tan lines should try the **Bonny Doon Beach,** 11 mi. north of Santa Cruz on Bonny Doon Rd. off Rte. 1, a free but somewhat untamed surfer hangout.

A pleasant 10-minute walk along the beach to the southwest will take you to two madcap and mayhem-filled Santa Cruz museums. The first is the unintentionally amusing **Shroud of Turin Museum,** 544 W. Cliff Dr. (423-7658), at St. Joseph's shrine. Earnest curators shepherd you through many exhibits, including one of only two replicas of Jesus' alleged burial shroud, "casting doubt" on recent Carbon-14 tests that suggest the shroud isn't old enough to have graced anyone's tomb in Biblical times. The Geraldo Rivera video is particularly telling. (Open Sat.-Sun. noon-5pm. Call to visit weekdays.) Just south lies Lighthouse Point, home to the **Santa Cruz Surfing Museum** (429-3429). The cheerful, one-room museum features vintage boards and surfing videos which show little sign of the tragedy that inspired its creation; the lighthouse and gallery were given in memory of a surfer who drowned in a 1965 accident. (Open Wed.-Mon. noon-4pm. Donation.) You can still watch people challenge the sea right below the museum's cliff. The stretch of Pacific along the eastern side of the point offers famous **Steamer Lane,** a hotspot for local surfers for over 100 years.

The 2000-acre **University of California at Santa Cruz (UCSC)** hangs out 5 mi. northwest of downtown. Take bus #1 or ride your bike along a scenic path to the campus. B-movie actor and political dabbler Ronald Reagan's attempt to make it a "riot-proof campus" (without a central point where radicals could spark a crowd) resulted in beautiful, sprawling grounds. University buildings appear intermittently, like startled wildlife, amid spectacular rolling hills and redwood groves. The school itself remains more Berkeley than Berkeley; extracurricular leftist politics supplement a curriculum offering such unique programs as the "History of Consciousness." Guided tours start from the **visitors center** at the base of campus. You need a parking permit when driving on weekdays. (Permits and maps available at the police station, 429-2231.) The UCSC **Arboretum** is one of the finest in the state. (Open daily 9am-5pm. Free.) Directly south of UCSC, the **Natural Bridges State Beach** (423-4609), at the end of W. Cliff Dr., offers a nice beach, tidepools, and tours twice daily during Monarch butterfly season from October to February. "Welcome Back Monarch Day" flutters on October 9, but it's best to visit from November to December, when thousands of the little buggers swarm along the shore. (Open daily 8am-sunset. Parking $3 per day.)

Santa Cruz innkeepers metamorphose winter bargains into summer wallet-drainers. The **Santa Cruz AYH-Hostel,** 511 Broadway (423-8304), is 10 minutes from the beach and a mall. From the bus depot, turn left on Laurel, veer left over the bridge, and you're on Broadway. Reservations are essential during summer; send half of the fee to P.O. Box 1241, Santa Cruz 95601. ($12, members only.) A 10-minute walk north of the boardwalk sits **The Best Inn,** 370 Ocean St. (458-9220), at Broadway. Cross the bridge east from the boardwalk, take Edge Cliff Dr. north until it intersects Ocean St., and follow Ocean north. A bit more tasteful than average, The Best promises A/C, color TV, and pretty quilts. (Singles mid-Sept. to early June $20; mid-June to early Aug. $30; early Aug. to mid-Sept. $40. $10 extra Fri. and Sat. nights. $5 extra for two. No reservations—show up 11am-2pm.) The **American Country Inn,** 645 7th (476-6424), five blocks from the beach just north of Eaton St., is small, pleasant, and off the main drag. (Weekdays $20, with bath $30; weekends $40, with bath $50. Weekly: $150, with bath $170.) The small RV camp in back has full hookup. (Sites $18; weekly $95. Reservations with deposit recommended.)

Reservations for state campgrounds can be made by calling 800-444-7275 at least two weeks in advance. The **New Brighton State Beach** (688-3241), 4 mi. south of Santa Cruz off Rte. 1 near Capitola, offers 112 lovely campsites on a high bluff overlooking the beach. (One-week max. stay. No hookups. Sites $16, $14 in winter. Reservations highly recommended. Take SCMDT "Aptos" bus #54.) The **Henry Cowell Redwoods State Park,** off Rte. 9 (335-9145), commutes 3 mi. south of Felton. Take Graham Hill Rd., or SCMDT buses #30, 34, or 35. (One-week max. stay. Sites $16.) **Big Basin Redwoods State Park,** north of Boulder Creek (338-6132), merits the 45-minute trip from downtown. Take Rte. 9 north to Rte. 236 north, or on weekends take the #35 bus to Big Basin. This spectacular park has 188 sites surrounded by dark red trees. Mountain bikes are available for rental (338-7313) and horseback tours can be arranged. (Showers. 15-day max. stay. Sites $10. Backpackers $1 at special backcountry campsites. Security parking $3 per night. Reservations recommended.)

Santa Cruz is packed with budget restaurants. Hasten to the places with hand-rolled pita bread sandwiches on the menu. The **Food Pavillion,** at Lincoln and Cedar, offers a number of quick, tasty, mall-type lunch choices (open daily 8am-9pm). At **Zachary's,** 819 Pacific Ave. (427-0646), locals crowd in for Breakfast #1: two eggs, great cottage fries, and toast ($3.50). (Open Tues.-Sun. 7am-2:30pm. Arrive before 9am to avoid long waits.) The **Saturn Cafe,** 1230 Mission St. (429-8505), cooks up vegetarian meals at their Santa Cruz best (generally for under $4). Cracked wheat is positively right-wing around here. (Open Mon.-Fri. 11:30am-12:30am, Sat.-Sun. noon-12:30am.) **Zoccoli's Delicatessen,** 1334 Pacific Ave. (423-1711), has great food at great prices. The lunch special of lasagna, salad, garlic bread, salami and cheese slices, and an Italian cookie goes for $4.44. (Open Mon.-Sat. 9am-5:30pm.) Manic **India Joze,** 1001 Cinter St. (427-3554), whips up Middle Eastern, Indian, and Asian dishes daily. Snapper is from $8.50, while veggie options, such as the delicious *kota kari* (Indian pea and cashew dumplings with yogurt and rice) run around $7.75. (Open Sun.-Fri. 8am-2:30pm, 5:30-9:30pm, dessert 9:30-10:30pm; Sat. brunch 10am-2:30pm, dinner 5:30-10pm.) **The Whole Earth,** at UCSC's Redwood Tower Building (426-8255), is simply amazing for a university food service—$4 buys a full meal and a view of the stunning redwoods. (Open during the term Mon.-Fri. 7:30am-8pm, Sat.-Sun. 9am-6pm; in summer Mon.-Fri. 7:30am-4pm.)

Santa Cruz fashions itself a classy operation, and most bars frown on backpacks and sleeping bags. Carding is stringent. The restored ballroom at the boardwalk makes a lovely spot for a drink in the evening, and the boardwalk bandstand also offers free Friday night concerts. The **Kuumbwa Jazz Center,** 320-322 E. Cedar St. (427-2227), has regionally renowned jazz, and welcomes music lovers under 21. (Tickets $5-11.50. Most shows at 8pm.) **The Crow's Nest,** 2218 E. Cliff Dr. (476-4560) at the Santa Cruz Yacht Club, highlights live rock right by the water. (Open nightly; hours and cover vary.) **Blue Lagoon,** 923 Pacific Ave. (423-7117), a relaxed gay bar, swims with a giant aquarium in back, taped music, videos, and dancing. (No cover. Drinks about $1.50. Open daily 4pm-2am.) **Shakespeare Santa Cruz,** Performing Arts Building Complex, UCSC campus (429-2121), features outdoor and indoor modern interpretations of Bill (July-Aug.; tickets for regular performances in the Performing Arts Theatre $12-20.) Watch for occasional free performances. **Whale-watching season** is late winter-early spring; boats depart from the Santa Cruz Municipal Wharf (425-1234; Jan.-April.)

Santa Cruz lies about one hour south of San Francisco on the northern lip of Monterey Bay, along U.S. 101 and Rte. 1, two roads conducive to hitchhiking. **Greyhound/Peerless Stages,** 425 Front St. (423-1800), cruzes to San Francisco (3 per day, $10) and L.A. via Salinas (3 per day, $48) or via San Jose (1 per day, $48). (Open Mon.-Fri. 7:30am-8:10pm; call for weekends hours.) **Santa Cruz Metropolitan District Transit (SCMDT),** 920 Pacific Ave. (425-8600 or 688-8993), serves the city and environs. Pick up a free copy of *Headways* here for route info. (Open Mon.-Fri. 7am-6pm, Sat.-Sun. 9am-1pm and 2-5:30pm.) **Surf City Rentals,** 46 Front St. (423-9050), rents bikes for $6 per hour, $18 per half day. (Open daily 9am-6pm.) The **Santa Cruz Conference and Visitor's Council** santas at 701 Front St. (425-1234 or 800-833-3494). The **post office** dates at 850 Front St. (426-5200; open Mon.-Fri. 9am-5pm). Santa Cruz's **ZIP code** is 95060; the **area code** is 408.

The Desert

Mystics, misanthropes, and mescaline-users have long shared a fascination with the desert's vast spaces and austere scenery. California's desert region has worked its spell on generations of passersby, from the Native Americans of yesterday to today's city slickers disenchanted with smoggy L.A. The fascination stems partly from the desert's seasonal transformations: from a pleasantly warm refuge in winter to a technicolored floral landscape in spring to a blistering wasteland in summer. Considering that only six inches of rain trickle onto the parched sand each year, the desert supports an astonishing array of plant and animal life.

Southern California's desert is on the fringe of the North American Desert, a 500,000-sq.-mi. territory stretching east into Arizona and New Mexico, northeast into Nevada and Utah, and south into Mexico. The California portion claims desert parks, shabby towns around Death Valley, unlikely resorts such as Palm Springs, and dozens of ordinary highway settlements serving as pit stops for those speeding to points beyond.

Orientation

The desert divides roughly into two major regions with different climatic zones. The Sonoran, or **Low Desert,** occupies southeastern California from the Mexican border north to Needles and west to the Borrego Desert; the Mojave, or **High Desert,** spans the southcentral part of the state, bounded by the Sonoran Desert to the south, San Bernardino and the San Joaquin Valley to the west, the Sierra Nevada to the north, and Death Valley to the east.

The Low Desert is flat, dry, and barren. Sparse vegetation makes shade-providing plants a necessary but scarce commodity, one that relies on an even rarer one—water. Humans and animals thrive in the oases in this area, the largest supporting the super-resort of Palm Springs. Despite the arid climate, water from the Colorado River irrigates the Imperial and Coachella Valleys. Other points of interest are Anza-Borrego Desert State Park and the Salton Sea.

By contrast, the High Desert consists of foothills and plains nestled within mountain ranges approaching 5000 ft., making it cooler (by about 10°F in summer) and wetter. Although few resorts have sprung up, Joshua Tree National Monument remains a popular destination for campers. Barstow, the central city of the High Desert, often functions as a rest station on the way to Las Vegas or the Sierras.

Death Valley marks the eastern boundary of the Mojave but might best be considered a region unto itself, containing both high and low desert areas. Major highways cross the desert east-west: I-8 hugs the California-Mexico border, I-10 goes through Indio on its way to Los Angeles, and I-40 crosses Needles to Barstow, where it joins I-15, which runs from Las Vegas and other points east to L.A.

For special health and safety precautions in the desert, see The Regions of the United States.

Barstow

Barstow is an adequate place to prepare for forays into the desert. Once a booming mining town, this desert oasis (pop. 20,000) now thrives on business from local military bases, tourists, and truckers. Stop in at the **California Desert Information Center,** 831 Barstow Rd. (256-8313), for free maps and information on hiking, camping, exploring, and nearby ghost towns, such as the commercialized Calico Ghost Town, Ghost Town Rd. (254-2122), 10 mi. northeast of town on I-15.

What Barstow lacks in charm (and it truly lacks) is made up for by its abundant supply of inexpensive motels and eateries. To prevent a Big Mac attack in this fast-food town, head for the **Barstow Station McDonald's,** on E. Main St. Constructed from old locomotive cars, this Mickey D's serves more burgers per annum than any other U.S. outfit.

The **El Rancho Motel,** 112 E. Main St. (256-2401), convenient to the Greyhound and Amtrak stations, has clean, bright rooms with cable TV, A/C, and pool. (Singles and doubles $27-33.) The **Economy Motel,** 1590 Coolwater Lane (256-1737) off I-40, has singles for $22 and doubles for $32. The **Calico KOA,** I-15 and Ghost Town Rd. (254-2311), is overpopulated with Ghost Town devotees. (Sites for 2 $15, with electricity $19, full hookup $21. Each additional person $2.50.)

Barstow, the western terminus of I-40, orders drinks midway between Los Angeles and Las Vegas on I-15. At the **Amtrak** station, N. 1st St. (800-872-7245), you can get on or off a train—that's all. Two trains per day go to L.A. ($32) and San Diego ($52); one per day ventures to Las Vegas ($43). **Greyhound,** 120 S. 1st St. (256-8757), at W. Main St., goes 13 times a day to L.A. ($17.50) and Las Vegas ($29). (Open daily 8am-6pm.)

Death Valley

Dante, Blake, and Sartre would have been inspired. Nowhere on and few places under the planet can touch the daily summer temperatures here. The *average* high temperature in July is 116°, with a nighttime low of 88°. Ground temperatures hover near an egg-frying 200°. Much of the landscape resembles the Viking photographs of the surface of Mars, with its reddish crags and canyons, immobile and stark. The strangeness of the landscape lends it a certain beauty. The earth-hues of the sands and rocks change hourly in the variable sunlight. The elevation ranges from 11,049-ft. Telescope Peak to Badwater, the lowest point in the hemisphere at 282 ft. below sea level. The region features pure white salt flats on the valley floor, impassable mountain slopes, and huge, shifting sand dunes. Nature appears to have focused all of its extremes and varieties here at a single location.

The region sustains a surprisingly intricate web of Dantean life. Casual tourists and naturalists alike may observe a tremendous variety of desert dwellers, such as the great horned owl, roadrunner, coyote, and kit fox, gecko, chuckwalla, and raven.

Late November through February are the coolest (40-70° in the valley, freezing temperatures and snow in the mountains) and also the wettest months, with infrequent but violent rainstorms which can flood the canyons. Desert wildflowers bloom in March and April, accompanied by moderate temperatures and tempestuous winds that can whip sand and dust into an obscuring mess for hours or even days. Over 50,000 people vie for Death Valley's facilities and sights during the **49ers Encampment** festival, held the last week of October and the first two weeks of November. Other times that bring traffic jams, congested trails and campsites, hour-long lines for gasoline, and four-hour waits at Scotty's Castle include three-day winter holiday weekends, Thanksgiving, Christmas through New Year's Day, and Easter.

Practical Information

Emergency: 911.

Furnace Creek Visitor Center (786-2331), on Rte. 190 in the east-central section of the valley. Simple and informative museum. Slide show every ½-hr., nightly lecture. Office open daily 8am-5pm. Center open daily 8am-5pm; Nov.-Easter 8am-8pm. For info by mail, write the Superintendent, Death Valley National Monument, Death Valley 92328.

Ranger Stations: Grapevine, junction of Rte. 190 and 267 near Scotty's Castle; **Stove Pipe Wells** on Rte. 190; **Wildrose,** Rte. 178, 20 mi. south of Emigrant via Emigrant Canyon Dr.; and **Shoshone,** outside the southeast border of the valley at the junction of Rte. 178 and 127. Weather report, weekly naturalist program, and park info posted at each station. Emergency help too. All open year-round.

Gasoline: Fill up outside Death Valley at Olancha, Shoshone, or Beatty, NV. Otherwise, you'll pay about 20¢ more per gallon at the stations across from the Furnace Creek Visitors Center, in Stove Pipe Wells Village, and at Scotty's Castle (all Chevron). Don't play chicken with the fuel gauge: Death Valley takes no prisoners. **Propane gas** available at the Furnace Creek Chevron; **white gas** at the Furnace Creek Ranch and Stove Pipe Wells Village stores; **diesel fuel** pumped in Las Vegas, Pahrump, and Beatty, NV, and in Lone Pine, Olancha, Ridgecrest, and Trona, CA.

Groceries and Supplies: Furnace Creek Ranch Store. Expensive and well-stocked. Open daily 7am-9pm. **Stove Pipe Wells Village Store.** Same price range. Open daily 7am-8pm. Both sell charcoal and firewood. Ice available at the Furnace Creek Chevron and the Stove Pipe Wells Village Store.

Post Office: Furnace Creek Ranch (786-2223). Open Mon.-Fri. 8:30am-5pm. **ZIP code:** 92328.

Area Code: 619.

Death Valley spans over 2 million isolated acres (1½ times the size of Delaware). However, visitors from the south can reach it with a small detour on the road to Sierra Nevada's Eastern slope; those from the north will find it reasonably convenient on the way to Las Vegas.

There is no regularly scheduled public transportation into Death Valley; only charter buses make the run. Bus tours within Death Valley are monopolized by **Fred Harvey's Death Valley Tours,** the same organization that runs Grand Canyon tours. Excursions begin at Furnace Creek Ranch, which also handles reservations (786-2345, ext. 61; $15-25, children $8-13, small discount for seniors).

The best way to get into and around Death Valley is by **car.** The nearest agencies rent in Las Vegas, Barstow, and Bishop. Be sure to rent a reliable car: this is emphatically *not* the place to cut corners. Upon arrival each vehicle will be charged a $5 entrance fee, valid for seven days.

Of the 13 monument entrances, most visitors choose Rte. 190 from the east. The road is well-maintained, the pass less steep, and more convenient to the visitors center. However, since most of the major sights adjoin the north/south road, a daytripper at the helm of a trusty vehicle should enter from the southeast (Rte. 178 west from Rte. 127 at Shoshone) or the north (direct to Scotty's Castle via NV Rte. 267 from U.S. 95) in order to see more of the monument. Unskilled mountain drivers probably should not attempt to enter via the smaller roads Titus Canyon or Emigrant Canyon Dr., since no guard rails prevent cars from screaming over the canyon's precipitous cliffs.

Eighteen-wheelers have replaced 18-mule teams, but transportation around Death Valley still takes stubborn determination. Radiator water (*not* for drinking) is avaliable at critical points on Rte. 178 and 190 and NV Rte. 374, but not on any unpaved roads. Obey the signs that advise "four-wheel-drive only." Those who do bound along the backcountry trails by four-wheel-drive should carry extra tires, gas, oil, water (both to drink and for the radiator), and spare parts; also leave an itinerary with the visitors center. Be sure to check which roads are closed—especially in summer.

Death Valley has **hiking** trails to challenge the mountain lover, desert daredevil, or backcountry camper. Ask a ranger for advice (see Sights below). Backpackers and dayhikers alike should inform the visitors center of their route, and take appropriate topographic maps. During the summer the National Park Service recommends that valley-floor hikers spend several days prior to the hike acclimating to the heat and low humidity, plan a route along roads where assistance is readily available, and outfit a hiking party of at least two people with another person following in a vehicle to monitor the hikers' progress. Wearing **thick socks** and carrying salve to treat feet parched by the nearly 200°F earth also makes good sense.

Check the weather forecasts before setting out—all roads and trails can disappear during a winter rainstorm. The dryness of the area, plus the lack of any root and soil system to retain moisture, transforms canyon and valley floors into riverbeds for deadly torrents during heavy rains. For other important tips, see Desert Survival, a part of the Southwest introduction in The Regions of the United States.

Accommodations

Fred Harvey's Amfac Consortium retains its vise-like grip on the trendy, resort-style, incredibly overpriced facilities in Death Valley. Look for cheaper accommodations in the towns near Death Valley: Olancha (west), Shoshone (southwest), Tecopa (south), and Beatty, NV (northwest).

The National Park Service maintains nine **campgrounds,** none of which accepts reservations. Call the visitors center to check availability and prepare for a battle if you come during peak periods (see below). Park Service campgrounds include **Mesquite Springs** ($5), **Stove Pipe Wells** ($4), **Emigrant** (free), **Furnace Creek** ($8), **Sunset** ($4), **Texas Springs** ($5), **Wildrose** (free), but camping fees are not pursued with vigor in the summer. All campsites have toilets; all except Thorndike and Mahogany Flat have water; all except Sunset and Stove Pipe Wells have tables. Open fires are prohibited at Stove Pipe Wells, Sunset, and Emigrant; bring a stove. Fires are permitted at Thorndike and Mahogany Flat, though both lack fireplaces; collecting wood, alive or dead, is prohibited anywhere in the monument. **Backcountry camping** is free and legal, as long as you check in at the visitors center and pitch tents at least 1 mi. from main roads and 5 mi. from any established campsite.

Sights

The **Visitors Center and Museum (see Practical Information)** offers info on tours, hikes, and special programs. The nearby museums are amusing as well. If you're interested in astronomy, speak to one of the rangers; some set up telescopes at Zabriskie Point and offer freelance shows. In wildflower season (Feb. to mid-April), tours run to some of the best places for viewing the display. **Hells Gate** and **Jubilee Pass** are especially beautiful, **Hidden Valley** even more so, though it is accessible only by a difficult, 7-mi. four-wheel-drive route from Teakettle Junction (itself 25 mi. south of Ubehebe Crater). Both the **Harmony Borax Works** and the **Borax Museum** are a short drive from the visitors center.

Artist's Drive is a one-way loop off Rte. 178, beginning 10 mi. south of the visitors center. The road twists and winds through rock and dirt canyons on the way to **Artist's Palette,** a rainbow of green, yellow, and red mineral deposits in the hillside. Several mi. south you'll find **Devil's Golf Course,** a huge plane of spiny salt crust left from the evaporation of ancient Lake Manly. Amble across the gigantic links; the salt underfoot sounds like crunching snow. Par is 666. NATAS! NATAS!

Immortalized by the Pink Floyd-soundtracked Antonioni film of the same name, **Zabriskie Point** is a marvelous place from which to view Death Valley's corrugated badlands, particularly at sunrise. The trip up to **Dante's View,** 15 mi. by paved road south off Rte. 190 (take the turn-off beyond Twenty Mule Team Canyon exit), will reward you with views of Badwater, Furnace Creek Ranch, the Panamint Range, and, on a clear day, the Sierra Nevadas. Faintly visible are tracks from 20-mule-team wagons across Devil's Golf Course, itself intricately patterned. Common here are snows in mid-winter and low temperatures anytime but mid-summer.

Joshua Tree National Monument

The low, scorching Sonoran Desert and the higher, cooler Mojave Desert titrate here, producing more than a half-million acres of extraordinarily jumbled scenery. The monument stars the Joshua Tree, a member of the lily and U2 family whose erratic limbs sometimes reach as high as 50 ft. The Mormons who came through here in the 19th century thought the crooked branches resembled the arms of Joshua leading them to the promised land. Spare forests of gangly Joshuas extend for miles in the high central and eastern portions of the monument, punctuated by great piles of quartz monzonite boulders, some over 100 ft. high. This bizarre landscape emerged over millenia as shoots of hot magma pushed to the surface and erosion exposed the rocks to the elements. Together, the two forces have created fantastic textures, shapes, and rock albums. Alongside the natural environment appear vestiges of human existence: ancient rock pictographs, dams built in the 19th century in order to catch the meager rainfall for livestock, and the ruins of gold mines that operated as late as the 1940s.

Over 80% of the monument is designated wilderness area; for those experienced in backcountry desert hiking and camping, Joshua Tree provides some truly remote territory. Hikers should go to one of the visitors centers for the rules and advice on use of isolated areas of the monument, and for a topographic map ($2.50). The wilderness lacks water except when a flash flood comes flushing down a wash, and even this evaporates quickly. Carry at least a gallon of water per person per day; two during the summer months. You must register at roadside boxes before setting out (see maps) to let the monument staff know your location, and to prevent your car from being towed from a roadside parking lot.

Less hardy desert rats can also enjoy Joshua Tree for a day or a weekend in relative comfort. The most popular time, as with other desert parks, is wildflower season (mid-March to mid-May), when the floor of the desert explodes in yucca, verbena, cottonwood, mesquite, and dozens of other floral variations. Summer is the hottest and slowest season. Bear in mind that no off-road driving is permitted.

A drive along the winding road from Twentynine Palms to the town of Joshua Tree (34 mi.) passes by the Wonderland of Rocks, a spectacular concentration of rock formations. The slightly longer drive between Twentynine Palms and I-10 through the monument offers a sampling of both desert landscapes. Along the way on both of these tours, explore as many of the side roads as time allows. Signs indicate whether turnoffs are paved, dirt, or only suitable for four-wheel-drive vehicles. One site not to miss, Key's View off the park road just west of Ryan Campground, offers a stupendous vista. You can see as far as Palm Springs and the Salton Sea on a clear day. Also of note are the palm oases (Twentynine Palms, Forty-nine Palms, Cottonwood Spring, Lost Palms) and the Cholla Cactus Garden off Pinto Basin Rd.

A number of hiking trails lead to the most interesting features of Joshua Tree: five oases, mine ruins, and fine vantage points. Short trails run near picnic areas and campsites. Visitors center brochures describe these trails, which range from a mere 200 yd. (the Cholla Cactus Garden) to 35 mi. (a section of the California Riding and Hiking Trail). The degree of difficulty varies almost as widely; the staff at the visitors center can help you choose. Plan on at least one hour per mi. on even relatively easy trails.

Campgrounds in the monument accept no reservations, except for group sites at Cottonwood, Sheep Pass, and Indian Cove, for which Ticketron handles mandatory reservations. Sites are also available at White Tank (closed in summer), Belle, Black Rock Canyon, Hidden Valley, Ryan, and Jumbo Rocks. All campsites have tables, fireplaces, and pit toilets; all are free except Cottonwood ($6) and Black Rock Canyon ($8), which have the only available water. You must bring your own firewood. If your trip to Joshua Tree is an educational endeavor contributing to a degree, you can secure a fee waiver at one of the group sites; write to the monument on your best official stationery and explain your "bona fide educational/study group" purposes. Backcountry camping is unlimited. Pitch your tent more than 500 ft. from a trail, 1 mi. from a road. (14-day max. stay Oct.-May; 30 days max. in summer. Entrance fee $2 per person or $5 per vehicle, good for a one-week stay at any state park.)

Joshua Tree National Monument occupies a vast area northeast of Palm Springs, about 160 mi. (3-3½ hr. by car) from west L.A. (see our California map). From I-10, the best approaches are via Rte. 62 from the west, leading to the towns of Joshua Tree and Twentynine Palms on the northern side of the monument, and via an unnumbered road that exits the interstate about 25 mi. east of Indio. Desert Stage Lines (367-3581), based in Palm Springs, stops in Twentynine Palms.

The monument's main visitor center offers displays, lectures, and maps at 74485 National Monument Dr., Twentynine Palms 92277 (367-7511), ¼-mi. off Rte. 62. (Open daily 8am-5pm.) Another visitors center sits at the southern gateway approximately 7 mi. north of I-10 (exit 4 mi. west of the town of Chiriaco Summit); an info kiosk adjoins the west entrance on Park Blvd., several mi. southeast of the town of Joshua Tree.

Palm Springs

With Mayor Sonny Bono leading by example next to his swimming pool, Palm Springs continues to be a playground for the nouveau-riche. The beautiful San Jacinto Mountains grind to a halt only blocks from Palm Canyon Drive, the city's main drag. The smog that nowadays begrimes L.A. creeps through the mountains' Gorgonio Pass rarely, and then only with diminished potency. The resulting clear, dry air makes even the summer heat bearable. Medicinal waters bubbling from the town's hot springs have preserved not only the health of the area's opulent residents, but also Palm Springs' resort status. And cheap thrills are available for the budgeter, not the least of which is the vantage of jaw-dropping opulence.

Rising over 5,000 ft., the **Palm Springs Aerial Tramway** works its dramatic way up the side of Mt. San Jacinto to an observation deck that affords excellent views of L.A.'s distant smog. Stairs from the deck lead to a 360° viewing platform, usually covered by snow drifts. The base station is located on Tramway Dr., which intersects Rte. 111 just north of Palm Springs. (Tram operates at least every ½-hr. Mon.-Fri. from 10am, Sat.-Sun. from 8am. Last car 9pm; Nov.-April 7:30pm. Round-trip tram $14, seniors $12, ages under 12 $9. Ride and dine service $4 extra.)

The **Desert Museum**, 101 Museum Dr. (325-7186), behind the Desert Fashion Plaza on Palm Canyon Dr., boasts a collection of Native American art, desert dioramas, and live animals. The gorgeously posh museum also sponsors curator-led field trips ($3) into the canyons, leaving every Friday at 9am; some involve up to 9 mi. of hiking. (Open late Sept.-early June Tues.-Sun. 10am-4pm. Admission $4, seniors $3, under 17 $2, kids with adult free. Free first Tues. of each month.) The four **Indian Canyons** (325-5673) are oases containing a wide variety of desert life and remnants of the Native American communities that once lived there. A permit ($10) is needed to gain entrance to Taquitz, one of the four canyons, available at the front gate at the end of S. Palm Canyon Dr. (Open daily Sept.-July 7, 8am-5pm. Admission $3.50, students and military $2.50, seniors $2, kids 6-12 $1.)

The **Living Desert Reserve** in Palm Desert, 47900 Portola Ave. (346-5694), 1½ mi. south of Rte. 111, display re-creations of various desert environments, from Saharan to Sonoran, along with rare desert fauna such as Arabian oryces and desert unicorns. (Open Sept. to mid-June daily 9am-5pm. Admission $5.50, seniors $5, kids $2.50. Disabled access.) Bizarre **Moorten's Desertland Botanical Gardens**, 1701 S. Palm Canyon Dr. (327-6555), is a botanist's heaven: ocotillo, yucca, prickly pear, and beavertail cactus you can see, smell, and (ouch!) touch.

A **tour of celebrity homes** offers the usual views of celebrities' gardeners at work. You can buy a map downtown and guide yourself, or take a 2½-hr. **Gray Line** tour (325-0974; $14.25, seniors $12.25, kids $8.25; reservations required). Mayor Sonny Bono is in action at the **Palm Springs City Council**, 3200 E. Tahquitz McCallum Way, on the first and third Wednesday of every month. Bono is the less eloquent of the two musical Bonos; be warned that his liberties with the English language make "I Got You Babe" seem stentorian.

Of course, most visitors to Palm Springs have no intention of studying the desert or taking in high culture. Palm Springs means sunning, with no activity more demanding than drinking a gallon of iced tea each day to keep from dehydrating or swimming in the **Olympic-sized pool** at Palm Springs Leisure Center, on Ramon Rd. just east of Sunrise Way (323-8278; open summer daily 11am-5pm, Tues. and Thurs. 7:30-9:30pm; off-season daily 11am-5pm; admission $3, ages 3-13 $2). For complete info about other recreational activies (including tennis, golf and hot-air ballooning), call the Leisure Department (!!!) at 323-8272.

The naturally hot mineral pools of Desert Hot Springs will soak you off well. The **Desert Hot Springs Spa**, 10805 Palm Dr. (329-6495), has pools of different temperatures, a bar, saunas, and house masseurs. (Open daily 8am-10pm. Admission Mon.-Fri. $5, after 3pm $3; Sat.-Sun. $6, after 3pm $3; holidays $7. Refundable $3 lock deposit, $3 towel deposit, plus 50¢ rental.) The **Hacienda Riviera Spa**, 67375 Hacienda (329-7010), attracts younger bathers. (Open Sept.-June daily 9am-5pm; July Wed.-Mon. 9am-5pm. Admission $4, kids $1.) **Oasis Water Park** (825-7873), off Rte. 111 on Gene Autry Trail, is awash with a wave pool and seven water slides, including the seven-story-tall near-free-fall Scorpion. (Admission $15, ages 4-11 $10, under 4 free.)

Palm Springs' cheapest lodgings are at nearby state parks and national forest campgrounds. If you need a room, put your money on either **Motel 6** location: 595 E. Palm Canyon Dr. (325-6129; singles $25, doubles $31) or the more convenient 660 S. Palm Canyon Dr. (327-4700; singles $29, doubles $35). Both locations have a big pool and A/C, and both fill quickly, sometimes up to six months in advance in winter. Some on-the-spot rooms are available around 9am, and no-shows are frequent. The **Mira Loma Hotel**, 1420 N. Indian Ave. (320-1178), has friendly management, a pool, and 12 smartly decorated rooms, all with refrigerators and color

TV. (Singles $35-48, $50-68 in winter. Kids in summer only.) The **Monte Vista Hotel**, 414 N. Palm Canyon Dr. (325-5641), sits smack-dab downtown. (Rooms $45-50; June-Aug. $35-37.50. Suites with kitchens $60-65. Children in summer only.) **Linda Vista Lodge**, 67200 Hacienda Ave. (329-6401) in Desert Hot Springs, is 10 mi. north of Palm Springs, with a heated pool, two naturally heated mineral pools, sauna, mini-golf, refrigerators, and color TV. (Singles and doubles $29-40, more in winter. Suite for 4 with kitchen $100. Stay 3 nights, get the 4th free.)

For those who want to picnic—an excellent idea, given the surroundings—chain supermarkets abound in Palm Springs. **Ralph's**, 1555 S. Palm Canyon Dr. (323-8446), and **Vons**, in the Palm Springs Mall on Tahquitz-McCallum (322-2192), are both reliably low-priced. For sit-down food and the best *comida mexicana* in Palm Springs, try the loud and busy **El Gallito Cafe**, 68820 Grove St., Cathedral City, two blocks west of Date Palm Dr.; look for the Mag Gas station on Rte. 111. The *combinaciones* (2 entrees, beans, rice, and tortillas; $6.25) are fit for a glutton. Take bus #20. (Open Sun.-Fri. 11am-9:30pm, Sat. 10am-9:30pm.) **Carlo's Italian Delicatessen**, 119 S. Indian Ave. (325-5571), serves up reasonably priced (around $5), overgrown sandwiches. (Open Mon.-Thurs. 10am-6pm, Fri.-Sat. 10am-7pm, Sun. 11am-5pm.) The **Hamburger Hamlet**, 105 N. Palm Canyon Dr. (325-3231), alases even the poorest Yorick with scores of southern California burger specialties for around $6.

Palm Springs lies off I-10, 120 mi. east of L.A., just beyond a low pass that marks the edge of the Colorado Desert. The **chamber of commerce** is at 190 W. Amado (325-1577). Ask for a map ($1) and a free copy of *The Desert Guide*. (Open Mon.-Fri. 8am-5pm, Sat. 10am-2pm.) **Amtrak**, on Jackson St. in Indio, 25 mi. southeast of Palm Springs (connect to Greyhound in Indio) sends three trains per week to and from L.A. ($29) with frequent stops along the way. **Greyhound**, 311 N. Indian Ave. (325-2053) is much more convenient (5 per day, $18). **Desert Stage Lines** (367-3581) serves Twenty-nine Palms and Joshua Tree National Monument (3 buses per day, $8.50), with Friday service to L.A. ($20) and San Diego ($23.50). **Sun Bus** (343-3451) is the local bus system, serving all Coachella Valley cities (50¢, plus 25¢ per zone and 25¢ per transfer). Rent a car at **Rent-a-Wreck**, 67501 Rte. 111 (324-1766), for $20 per day, or $120 per week; 700 free mi., 19¢ each additional mi. (must be 21 with major credit card). **Desert Cab** is at 325-2868.

The Palm Springs **post office** disburses, among other things, commemorative mugs at 333 E. Amado Rd. (325-9631; open Mon.-Fri. 8:30am-5pm). Palm Springs' **ZIP code** is 92262; the **area code** is 619.

Los Angeles

Over the last 70 years, the sounds "el-ay" have become an American mantra. L.A. is the flashy oasis at the end of Western desert, and her beauty lies in fabulous wealth fabulously spent, pastel buildings, neon lights, palm trees, and multichromatic gardens.

The sprawling megalopolis controls over 90% of the world's entertainment industry, and culture moguls feel no compunction in pawning their hometown. Its status as backdrop for countless movies and TV shows contributes greatly to the City of Angels' status as a city of myth, a city of self-conscious style, a city (to jaded Easterners such as Woody Allen) of vapidity.

L.A. is now as infamous for its air pollution, earthquakes, and traffic jams as it is famous for its fashion and wealth. Gang warfare, infesting even safer parts of the city such as Zuma Beach, has spread like a plague from L.A. throughout the country. Even the rectitude of the law's enforcers has been called into question. Last year saw the LAPD and chief Darryl Gates, a George Bush supporter, gain national notoriety for the videotaped beating of an African American; a well-publicized investigation criticized the department for condoning violence.

While most of these problems won't affect short-term visitors, others will. L.A. is tough on budget travelers. Nothing is cheap, and public transportation is a frus-

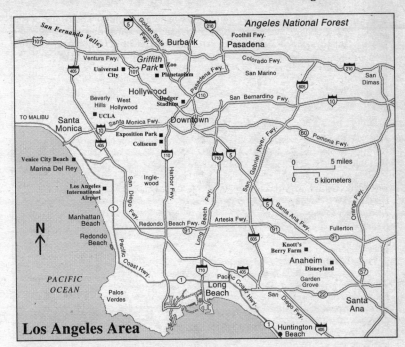

Los Angeles Area

trating oxymoron. Ironically, what saves many travelers from disgruntling experiences is the city's disjointedness. L.A. is only a geographical expression—19 suburbs in search of a city. Find one you like, explore it, and don't worry about the rest of the town.

Practical Information

Emergency: 911.

Los Angeles Convention and Visitors Bureau, 685 S. Figueroa St. 90015 (689-8822), between Wilshire and 7th St. in the Financial District. Hundreds of brochures. Staff speaks Spanish, Filipino, Japanese, French, and German. Good maps for downtown streets, sights, and buses. Publishes *Datelines* and *Artsline,* quarterly guides to Southern California events. *Los Angeles Visitors Guide* and *Lodging Guide* are both free and available by mail (3 weeks delivery lag). Second location in Hollywood at 6541 Hollywood Blvd (461-4213). Open Mon.-Fri. 8am-5pm, Sat. 8:30am-5pm. **Los Angeles Council AYH:** 1434 2nd St., Santa Monica (393-3413). Guidebooks, low-cost flights, rail passes, and ISIC cards. Open Tues.-Sat. 10am-5pm. **Sierra Club:** 3550 W. 6th St., #321 (387-4287). Hiking, biking, and backpacking info. Open Mon.-Fri. 10am-6pm.

American Express: 901 W. 7th St. (627-4800). Open Mon.-Fri. 8am-6pm. Locations in Beverly Hills (at the Beverly Center), Pasadena, Torrance and Costa Mesa. Open Sat. 10am-6pm at 8493 W W. 3rd St. (659-1682).

National Park Service: 30401 Agoura Rd., Agoura Hills (818-597-9192 for local parks Info Center; 818-597-1036 for other offices), in the San Fernando Valley. Info on the Santa Monica Mtns. and other parks. Open Mon.-Sat. 8am-5pm.

Los Angeles County Parks and Recreation: 433 S. Vermont (738-2961). Open Mon.-Fri. 8am-5pm.

Amtrak: Union Station, 800 N. Alameda (624-0171), downtown. To San Francisco (1 per day, 11 hr., $74) and San Diego (8 per day, 3 hr., $24) with stops in San Juan Capistrano, San Clemente, Oceanside, and Del Mar.

Greyhound: 208 E. 6th St. (620-1200), downtown terminal. To: San Diego (20 per day, 2½-3½ hr., $11); Tijuana (16 per day; 3½-4½ hr.; $17, round trip $26); Santa Barbara (11 per

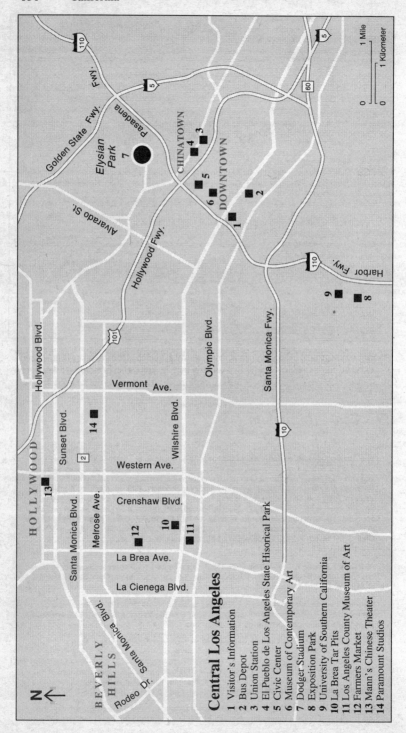

Central Los Angeles

1 Visitor's Information
2 Bus Depot
3 Union Station
4 El Pueblo de Los Angeles State Hisorical Park
5 Civic Center
6 Museum of Contemporary Art
7 Dodger Stadium
8 Exposition Park
9 University of Southern California
10 La Brea Tar Pits
11 Los Angeles County Museum of Art
12 Farmers Market
13 Mann's Chinese Theater
14 Paramount Studios

day; 2-3½ hr.; $12.50, round trip $21); and San Francisco (14 per day, 8½-12½ hr., $40). Occasional special deals for advance purchases. See also Greyhound listings in Hollywood, Santa Monica, and Pasadena below.

RTD Bus Information Line: 626-4455. Customer Service Center at 5301 Wilshire Blvd. (972-6235; open Mon.-Fri. 8am-4:15pm).

Taxi: Checker Cab (482-3456), Independent (213-385-8294), United Independent (213-653-5050), Celebrity Red Top (213-934-6700). Cabbies don't cruise the streets for fares.

Car Rentals:

Penny Rent-A-Car, 12425 Victory Blvd., N. Hollywood (818-786-1733). $14-17 with 75 free mi., 15¢ per mi. after that. $98-111 per week with 500 free mi. Optional insurance (CDW) $5 per day. Must be 21 with major credit card or an international driver's license. Open Mon.-Fri. 7:30am-6pm, Sat. 9am-4pm. **Ugly Duckling,** 920 S. La Brea (933-0522). $19 per day with 100 free mi., $108 per week. CDW $8 per day, $50 per week. Must be 21 with major credit card. Open Mon.-Sat. 9am-6pm. **Avon Rent-A-Car,** 8459 Sunset Blvd. (654-5533). Also at LAX and Sherman Oaks (15719 Ventura Blvd., 818-906-2277). $16.95 and up per day with unlimited mileage, from $101.70 per week. CDW $9 and up per day. Must be 18 with a major credit card; drivers 18-22 face a steep $15 per day surcharge, $5 per day for those 22-25. Open Mon.-Fri. 7:30am-9:30pm.

Automobile transport services: Dependable Car Travel Service, Inc., 18730 Wilshire Blvd., #414, Beverly Hills (659-2922). Must be 18. References from L.A. or destination. Most cars to the northeast, especially N.Y., but also to Florida and Chicago. $150 refundable deposit. Call 1-2 days ahead to reserve. Open Mon.-Fri. 8:30am-5:30pm. **Auto Driveaway,** 3407 W. 6th St. (666-6100). Must be 21 with references in L.A. and destination. Foreign travelers need passport, visa, and an international driver's license rather than references. Photo and either cash deposit ($250), traveler's checks, or money order required. Call a week before departure. Open Mon.-Fri. 9am-5pm.

Green Tortoise (310-392-1990, 415-285-2441 in San Francisco), the northbound "hostel on wheels," leaves L.A. every Sun. night with stops in Venice, Hollywood, and downtown. Arrives in San Francisco ($30) on Mon. morning, Eugene and Portland, Oregon ($69) on Tues. afternoon, and Seattle ($79) on Tues. night. Call for reservations and exact departure location and times. (See Getting There in the General Introduction for more info on tours.)

Tickets: 642-4242 for ~~~~~~~~~~~~~ Open Blue Star ~~~~~~

Weather: 554-1212 for excessively detailed report.

Help Lines: National Gay Advocates Hotline, 800-526-5050. **Rape Crisis,** 392-8381. 24-hr. hotline. **Battered Women's Assistance:** 818-887-6589. 24-hr. hotline. **Ambulance: Los Angeles City Ambulance Emergency Service** (483-6721). **Police:** 626-5273.

Post Office: Main office at Florence Station, 7001 S. Central Ave. (586-1723). Info on rates and schedules, 586-1467. General Delivery, 900 N. Alameda (617-4543), at 9th St. General Delivery ZIP Code: 90055.

Area Codes: Southern half of Los Angeles County (including Westwood and parts of Beverly Hills, Long Beach, Malibu, the Pacific Coast Highway, Santa Monica, UCLA and Westwood, Venice, and parts of West Hollywood) **310,** northern half (including parts of Beverly Hills, Downtown, Hollywood, parts of West Hollywood, and Wilshire District and Hancock Park) **213,** north of Hollywood (including Pasadena and San Marino) **818.**

Hollywood

Area Code: 213.

Police: 1358 N. Wilcox (485-4302).

Visitor Information: The Janes House, 6541 Hollywood Blvd. (461-4213), in Janes House Sq. Provides L.A. visitor guides. Open Mon.-Sat. 9am-5pm. **Hollywood Chamber of Commerce,** 6255 W. Sunset Blvd., #911 (469-8311).

Greyhound: 1409 N. Vine St. (466-6381), 1 block south of Sunset Blvd. To: Santa Barbara (5 per day, $13); San Diego (14 per day, $11); San Francisco (9 per day, $40). Terminal open daily 7:30am-11pm.

Public Transportation: RTD Customer Service Center, 6249 Hollywood Blvd. (972-6000). Free info, maps, timetables, and passes. Open Mon.-Fri. 10am-6pm. **Important buses:** #1 along Hollywood Blvd., #2 and 3 along Sunset Blvd., #4 along Santa Monica Blvd., #10 along Melrose.

Post Office: 1615 Wilcox Ave. (464-2194). Open Mon.-Fri. 8am-5pm, Sat. 8am-1pm. General Delivery ZIP Code: 90028

Area Code: 213.

Santa Monica

Area code: 310.

Police: 1685 Main St. (395-9931).

Visitor Information: 1400 Ocean Ave. (393-7593), in Palisades Park. Local maps, brochures, and info on attractions and events. Open daily 10am-5pm; in winter 10am-4pm.

Public Transportation: Santa Monica Municipal (Big Blue) Bus Lines 1660 7th St. (451-5445), at Olympic. Open Mon.-Fri. 8am-5pm. Bus #10 provides express service between downtown L.A. and downtown Santa Monica for $1.25 (faster than RTD, but so is walking). Pick it up on 7th and Grand. Buses #1 and 2 run between Santa Monica and Venice and are free with a transfer from the #10; otherwise fare 50¢.

Greyhound: 1433 5th St. (395-1708), between Broadway and Santa Monica Blvd. Open Mon.-Fri. 8:30am-5:30pm. To: Santa Barbara (3 per day, 2½ hr., $12.70); San Diego (3 per day, 4½ hr., $19.50); San Francisco (2 per day, 11 hr., $51.20).

Surfboard Rental: Natural Progression Surfboards, 22935½ W. Pacific Hwy., Malibu (456-6302). Boards $20 per day, plus $5 insurance. Wetsuits $8. Also windsurfer rental ($50 per day, plus $5 insurance), and lessons. Open daily 9am-6pm.

Post Office: 5th and Arizona (576-2626). Open Mon.-Fri. 9am-5pm, Sat. 9am-1pm.

Area Code: 213.

Pasadena

Area code: 818.

Police: 207 N. Garfield Ave. (405-4501).

Convention and Visitors Bureau, 171 S. Los Robles Ave. (795-9311), across from the Hilton Hotel. Open Mon.-Fri. 9am-5pm, Sat. 10am-4pm.

Greyhound: 645 E. Walnut (792-5116). Open Mon.-Fri. 8:30am-5:30pm, Sat. 8:30am-3pm, Sun. 9am-3pm. To: Santa Barbara (3 per day, 2½ hr., $11.75); San Diego (3 per day, 4 hr., $16); San Francisco (2 per day, 11 hr., $46).

Post Office: 600 N. Lincoln (304-7122), at Orange. Open Mon. and Fri. 8am-6pm; Tues.-Thurs. 8am-5pm; Sat. 9am-2pm. General Delivery ZIP Code: 91109.

Area Code: 818.

Orientation

Getting There

Los Angeles sprawls along the coast of Southern California, 127 mi. north of San Diego and 403 mi. south of San Francisco. You can still be "in" L.A. even if you're 50 mi. from downtown. Greater L.A. encompasses the urbanized areas of Orange, Riverside, San Bernardino, and Ventura counties.

By Car

General approaches to Greater L.A. are I-5 from the south, California Highway 1, US 101, or I-5 from the north, and I-10 or I-15 from the east. The city itself is crisscrossed by over a dozen freeways. Driving into L.A. can be unnerving if you've never before run the gauntlet of ramps, exits, and four-story directional signs.

By Train and Bus

Amtrak pulls into Union Station, 800 N. Alameda (213-624-0171), at the north-western edge of the heart of downtown Los Angeles. Once the end of the line for westbound rail passengers from all over the U.S., this gloriously designed Spanish colonial-revival building is now sadly deserted. Buses travel out of the station to Pasadena and Longbeach; info about their schedules can be obtained at the station.

Visitors arriving by **Greyhound** will disembark at 208 E. 6th St. (213-620-1200), at Los Angeles St. downtown, in a rough neighborhood. Greyhound also stops in Hollywood, Santa Monica, Pasadena, and other parts of the metropolitan area (see Practical Information). RTD buses #320 and 20 stop on 7th and Hill St., two blocks southwest of the downtown station, and carry passengers westward along Wilshire Blvd. Bus #1 stops at 5th and Broadway, four blocks to the west and one block north, and travels westward along Hollywood Blvd.

By Plane

Los Angeles International Airport (LAX) (310-646-5252) is divided into two levels, the upper serving departures and the lower, arrivals. Nine contiguous terminals are arranged in a large horseshoe, with Terminal 2 serving international carriers. The airport complex is located in Westchester, about 5 mi. southwest of downtown, 10 mi. southeast of Santa Monica, and 1 mi. east of the coast.

Many car rental agencies run shuttle buses directly from the airport to their lots (see Cars). All Rapid Transit District (RTD) service to and from the airport stops at the **transfer terminal** at Vicksburg Ave. and 96th St. To get downtown, take bus #439 (Mon.-Fri. rush hr. only) or #42 (daily 5:30am-11:15pm, from downtown daily 5:45am to 12:10am) from the transfer terminal. To and from UCLA, take express #560; Long Beach, #232; West Hollywood and Beverly Hills, #220. From West Hollywood to Hollywood, take bus #1 (along Hollywood Blvd.), 2 (along Sunset Blvd.), or 4 (along Santa Monica Blvd.).

Metered cabs are costly: $1.95 plus $1.60 per mi. Checker Cab (213-482-3456) fare from the airport to downtown is about $24, to Hollywood $28, and to Disneyland a goofy $85.

A final option, more expensive than the RTD but cheaper than a cab, is one of the many **shuttle vans** which offer door-to-door service from the terminal to different parts of L.A. for a flat rate. The vans pick up outside of baggage claim areas and can be called from the terminal on courtesy phones (see below). For specific info regarding RTD buses, cabs, and shuttles, ask at the kiosks located on the sidewalks directly in front of the terminals.

Getting Around

Before you even think about navigating Los Angeles's 6,500 mi. of streets and 40,000 intersections, get yourself a good map; centerless Los Angeles defies all human comprehension otherwise. The best investment for a stay of at least a week is the *Thomas Guide Los Angeles County Street Guide and Directory* ($48).

Los Angeles is a city of distinctive boulevards; its shopping areas and business centers are distributed along these broad arteries. Streets throughout L.A. are designated east, west, north, and south from First and Main St. at the center of downtown. East-west thoroughfares are the most prominent; use them to get your bearings. Beginning with the northernmost, they are Melrose Ave. and Beverly, Wilshire, Olympic, Pico, Venice, and Washington Boulevards. Melrose is filled with boutiques, galleries, and trendy night spots; Wilshire is studded with large department stores and office buildings; Olympic is residential and the least congested. The important north-south streets of this huge grid, from downtown westward, are Vermont, Normandie, and Western Avenues; Vine Street; Highland, La Brea, and Fairfax Avenues; and La Cienega and Robertson Boulevards.

The area west of downtown is known as the **Wilshire District** after its main boulevard. Wilshire is a continuous wall of tall buildings (called the "Miracle Mile") with bungalows and duplexes huddled in the skyscrapers' shadows. **Hancock Park,** a green park and affluent residential area, covers the northeast portion of the district, on the 5900 block, and harbors the Los Angeles County Museum of Art and the George C. Page Fossil Museum.

Sunset Boulevard runs from the ocean to downtown, with beach communities, lavish wealth, famous nightclubs along "the strip," sleazy motels, the old elegance of Silver Lake, and Chicano murals. Farther north is Hollywood Boulevard, running just beneath the Hollywood Hills, where split-level buildings perched precariously on hillsides house screenwriters, actors, and producers.

Once the sun sets, those on foot outside West L.A. and off well-lit main drags should exercise caution, and not walk alone *anywhere*. Hollywood and the downtown area, east of Western Ave., are considered particularly crime-ridden. Gang- and drug-related crimes have increasingly threatened public safety. Whether walking, riding, or driving, know (or at least pretend like you know) where you are and where you are going.

Public Transportation

Most Angelenos will insist that a car is necessary to live in or visit their city, but the **Southern California Rapid Transit District (RTD)** does work—sort of. With over 200 routes and several independent municipal transit systems complementing RTD, you may need an extra day just to study timetables. Using the RTD to sightsee in L.A. can be frustrating simply because attractions tend to be spread out. Those determined to see *everything* in L.A. should somehow get a car, or at least base yourself centrally, make daytrips, and have plenty of change for the bus.

To familiarize yourself with the RTD, write for a **Riders Kit** (no relation to Kit of *Knight Rider*), RTD, Los Angeles 90001 (this address is sufficient), or stop by one of 10 **customer service centers.** The three downtown are: in ARCO Plaza, 505 S. Flower St., Level B (open Mon.-Fri. 7:30am-3:30pm); at 419 S. Main St. (open Mon.-Fri. 8am-4:30pm); and at 1016 S. Main St. (open Mon.-Sat. 10am-6pm). RTD prints route maps for the different sections of the city, as well as a brochure called *RTD Self-Guide Tours,* which details how to reach the most important sights from downtown. For transit info anywhere in the L.A. area, call 800-2-LA-RIDE (252-7433; lines open daily 5:30am-11:30pm).

Bus service is best downtown and along the major thoroughfares west of downtown. (There is 24-hr. service, for instance, on Wilshire Blvd.) The downtown **DASH shuttle** is only 25¢ and serves Chinatown, Union Station, Olvera Street, City Hall, Little Tokyo, the Music Center, ARCO Plaza, and more. DASH also operates a shuttle on Sunset Blvd. in Hollywood, as well as shuttles in Pacific Palisades, Fairfax (running from Farmer's Market to 3rd and LaBrea), Venice Beach, and Watts. (Downtown DASH operates Mon.-Fri. 6:30am-6:30pm, Sat. 10am-5pm; other DASH shuttles run about the same hours but not on Sat.) Bus service is dismal in the outer reaches of the city, and two-hour journeys are not unusual. The buses, but not transfers, are speedy except in L.A.'s omnipresent traffic.

RTD's **basic fare** is $1.10, disabled passengers 55¢. Additional charges for express buses, buses taking the freeway, sports events, services, etc., can raise the fare to as much as $3. Exact change *required.* Transfers are 25¢, whether you're changing from one RTD line to another or from RTD to another transit authority, such as Santa Monica Municipal Bus Lines, Culver City Municipal Bus Lines, Long Beach Transit, or Orange County Transit District. If you plan to use the buses extensively over a long visit, buy a **bus pass.** Unlimited use for a month costs $42, $25 for college students, $18 for students under 18, and $10 for seniors and the disabled.

Roughly 90% of RTD's lines, marked with the appropriate symbol, are **wheelchair accessible.** For more info call 800-622-7828 (open daily 6am-midnight).

If you don't want to spend tedious hours on an RTD bus to get from one end of the basin to the other, consider paying more to take Greyhound (213-620-1200) to such places as Long Beach, Anaheim and Glendale.

Gray Line Tours, 6541 Hollywood Blvd., Hollywood (213-856-5900), is a more expensive but easier way to reach distant attractions. Costs include transportation and admission: Disneyland $54, Magic Mountain $51, Universal Studios $46, San

Diego Zoo $46, and Sea World $47. Tours leave from the Gray Line office for 200 different locations in summertime.

In a desperate, expensive, last-ditch effort to alleviate the congestion that threatens to choke the city, L.A. has finally started building a subway. The first leg of L.A.'s 300-mi. Metro Rail Plan, the Blue Line, presently runs from 7th St. in Downtown to Long Beach (call 213-626-4455 for info). The Red Line, which will run through downtown and out to the San Fernando Valley, is scheduled to open in 1993. Also in the works are lines to LAX and Pasadena. For information on construction progress call 213-620-RAIL.

Freeways

The freeway is perhaps the most enduring of L.A.'s images. When uncongested, these 10- and 12-lane concrete roadways offer speed and convenience; the trip from downtown to Santa Monica can take as little as 20 minutes. But usually they brim with autos spewing noxious fumes, and movement over the hot concrete is slow.

Perhaps to help them "get in touch with their freeway," Californians refer to the highways by names rather than by numbers. These names are little more than hints of a freeway's route, at best harmless, at worst misleading.

I-405, the **San Diego Freeway.** Roughly parallel to the Pacific Coast Highway (Rte. 1), but approximately 10 mi. inland, it links the San Fernando Valley with Westwood, Beverly Hills, LAX, and Long Beach.

I-10, the **Santa Monica Freeway,** west of downtown. The main commuter link to the western portions of the city: Century City, Westwood and Santa Monica. Called the **San Bernardino Freeway** east of downtown.

I-5, the **Golden State Freeway,** pierces the heart of central California parallel to I-405 and Rte. 1. It comes to within 50 mi. of the coast as it moves through the San Fernando Valley. Called the **Santa Ana Freeway** south of downtown, it serves Anaheim and Orange County.

I-110, called the **Pasadena Freeway** north of downtown (it starts in Pasadena) or the **Harbor Freeway** south of downtown where it runs by USC, Exposition Park, and Watts on its way to San Pedro, is L.A.'s oldest freeway.

U.S. 101, the **Ventura Freeway** from Ventura to North Hollywood, runs inland from Ventura along the outer rim of the Santa Monica Mountains in the San Fernando Valley, serving Thousand Oaks, Woodland Hills, Encino, Van Nuys, Sherman Oaks, Studio City, and North Hollywood. In North Hollywood it veers over the Santa Monica Mountains toward Hollywood, Silver Lake, and downtown, becoming the **Hollywood Freeway.**

Bicycles

The best bike routes are along beaches. The most popular route is the **South Bay Bicycle Path.** It runs from Santa Monica to Torrance (19 mi.), winding over the sandy beaches of the South Bay all the way to San Diego. For maps and advice, write to any **AAA** office. Their local headquarters is at 2601 S. Figueroa (213-741-3111), near Adams, where you can talk to helpful and friendly **Norty Stewart,** "the Source" for bicycling information in Southern California.

Renting a bike has become increasingly expensive. Most shops stand near the piers of the various beaches, especially concentrated on Washington Blvd. near the Venice/Marina Del Rey beach. Those planning extended stays should look into purchasing a used bike; check the classifieds.

Walking and Hitchhiking: Not

The band Missing Persons was bang-on when it sang "Nobody walks in L.A." L.A. pedestrians are a lonely breed. The largely deserted streets of commercial centers will seem eerie to the first-time visitor. Unless you're running in the L.A. Marathon, moving from one part of the city to another on foot is a ludicrous idea—distances are just too great. Nevertheless, some colorful areas such as Melrose, Westwood, and Hollywood are best explored by foot. Venice Beach is a most enjoyable place to walk. Here, you'll be in the company of the thousands of Venetian beach-goers, and Venice's sights and shopping areas are all relatively close to one another. You may also wish to call **Walking Tours of Los Angeles** for tours of El Pueblo de Los Angeles State Historic Park (213-628-1274), City Hall (213-485-4423), or the Music Center (213-972-7483). The **Los Angeles Conservancy** (213-623-8687) offers nine different tours of the downtown area. Tours cost $5; advance reservations required.

Do *not* hitchhike. It is neither safe nor legal on freeways and many streets.

Accommodations

Many inexpensive lodgings in Los Angeles bear a frightening resemblance to the House of Usher. Dozens of flophouses around the Greyhound station charge between $10 and $20 nightly, but those unnerved by skid-row street life should look elsewhere. (Sound glum so far? Welcome to L.A.) Tolerable lodgings fall roughly into four categories: hostels, run-down but safe hotels, residential hotels offering weekly rates (which can save a bundle), and budget motels well off the beaten track. Unless you're set on a specific place, reservations are only necessary for July and August. The useful and comprehensive (though a bit upscale) *L.A. Lodging Guide* is available at the L.A. Visitors Center. **Youth hostel passes** may be obtained from UCLA's Expo Center (310-825-0831).

Los Angeles has no **campgrounds** convenient to public transport. Even motorists face at least a 40-minute commute from campsites to downtown. The only safe place to camp in L.A. County that is even vaguely nearby is **Leo Carrillo State Beach,** on PCH (Rte. 1), 28 mi. northwest of Santa Monica at the Ventura County line (818-706-1310). The beach lays out 134 sites at $9 per night. Sites are first-come, first-served. Dockweiler Beach, just north of LAX, also has a campground with intimate proximity to the airport and its noise.

Downtown

Though busy and relatively safe by day, the downtown area metamorphoses when the workday ends. Never travel alone after dark, especially in the area between Broadway and Main. When renting, don't be afraid to haggle, especially off-season. (The following are all area code 213.)

Royal Host Olympic Motel, 901 W. Olympic Blvd., (626-6255). The ritziest of the budget hotels—beautiful rooms, with bathtubs, balconies, telephone, radio, and color cable TV. Some rooms have kitchens. Singles and doubles $40-45, suites $45-50, but students can get a double for as low as $30.

Hotel Stillwell, 828 S. Grand St. (627-1151). Recently refurbished, this ultra-clean hotel is the most sensible downtown. Rooms bright and pleasantly decorated. Indian restaurant and American grill in hotel, Mexican restaurant next door. A/C, color TV. Singles $35. Doubles $45.

Park Plaza Hotel, 607 S. Park View St. (384-5281), on the west corner of 6th St. across from MacArthur Park. Built in 1927, this eerily grandiose art deco monument has a 3-story marble-floored lobby and a monumental staircase. The Plaza once entertained Bing Crosby and Eleanor Roosevelt, but now caters mainly to semi-permanent residents, especially students from the Otis Art Institute next door. Olympic size pool. A/C, color TV in the clean but small rooms, many under renovation until 1992. Singles $35. Doubles $45. Suite $60. Make reservations at least a week in advance.

Empire 900 Motel, 900 W. Olympic Blvd (748-1322), across the street from the Royal Host. A little rundown and without the amenities of its cross-street neighbor, it does offer $25 singles and $27 doubles.

Orchid Hotel, 819 S. Flower St. (624-5855). Central downtown location and cleanliness make up for the bantam rooms. A/C, color TV. Singles $33.60. Doubles $39.20. Weekly: singles $153.40; doubles $181.50. Reservations recommended.

Budget Inn, 1710 W. 7th St. (483-3470). Location across the Harbor Fwy. from downtown could be a lot better. Rooms, however, are fairly antiseptic. Color TV, swimming pool. Singles $35. Doubles $45. Weekly: singles $175; doubles $225. Make reservations at least a week in advance.

5,300 hostels in 59 countries on 6 continents.

One card.

"The most dynamic travel facilities on earth."

Arthur Frommer, travel writer

"Best of all, hostels provide innumerable oppotunities to meet travelers from all over the world."

Let's Go

The American Youth Hostels card can open doors for you at some of the least expensive, most dynamic and fun-filled travel facilities in Europe...Israel...Japan...Australia... New Zealand...Canada...the USA... anywhere you want to go!   You'll keep costs low...usually $7-$10 a night for a dorm-style room. Plus you'll enjoy global discounts on car rentals, trips and tours, travel books and more. To join, contact any of the 44 American Youth Hostels offices (*see the back of this card for addresses*), or call 202-783-6161.

American Youth Hostels
A MEMBER OF THE INTERNATIONAL YOUTH HOSTEL FEDERATION

American Youth Hostels Office Locations

To get the most out of your hostelling experience, contact the American Youth Hostels office nearest you. All offices provide American Youth Hostels cards, international hostel guidebooks and sheet sleeping sacks. Some even offer railpasses, travel gear and more.

Alaska
P.O. Box 240347
Anchorage, AK 99524

Arizona
1046 E. Lemon St.
Tempe, AZ 85281
602-894-5128
M-F noon-6 pm Mountain

California
P.O. Box 3645
Merced, CA 95344
209-383-0686
M-F noon-4 pm Pacific

425 Divisadero #301
San Francisco, CA 94117
415-863-9939
M-F noon-6 pm Pacific

1434 Second St.
Santa Monica, CA 90401
310-393-3413
Tu-Sa 10 am-5 pm Pacific

335 W. Beech St.
San Diego, CA 92101
619-239-2444
M-F 10 am-6 pm;
Sa 10 am-5 pm Pacific

Colorado
P.O. Box 2370
Boulder, CO 80306
303-442-1166
M, Tu, W 10 am-4 pm;
Th noon-7 pm Mountain

Connecticut
118 Oak Street
Hartford, CT 06106
203-247-6356
M-F 1-4 pm Eastern

D. C.
1017 K St. N.W.
Washington, D.C. 20001
202-783-4943
M-Sa 10 am-6 pm Eastern

Florida
P.O. Box 533097
Orlando, FL 32853-3097
407-649-8761
M-F 9 am-5 pm Eastern

Georgia
223 Ponce De Leon Ave.
Atlanta, GA 30308

Illinois
3036 N. Ashland Ave.
Chicago, IL 60657
312-327-8114
M-W, F 9 am-5 pm;
Th noon-8 pm;
Sa 9 am-1 pm Central

Indiana
8231 Lakeshore Drive
Gary, IN 46403-0016

Iowa
Box 10
Postville, IA 52162
319-864-3923
M-F 8 am-5 pm Central

Maryland
17 W. Mulberry St.
Baltimore, MD 21201
410-576-8880
M-Sa 10 am-6pm Eastern

7420 1/2 Baltimore Blvd.
College Park, MD 20740
301-209-8544
M-Sa 10 am-6 pm Eastern

Massachusetts
1020 Commonwealth Ave.
Boston, MA 02215
617-731-6692
M-W, F noon-6 pm;
Th noon-8 pm Eastern

Michigan
3024 Coolidge
Berkley, MI 48072
313-545-0511
M-F 10 am-5 pm;
W 10 am-8pm Eastern

Minnesota
795 Raymond Ave.
St. Paul, MN 55114-1522
612-659-0407
M-F noon-6 pm Central

Missouri
7187 Manchester Road
St. Louis, MO 63143
314-644-4660
M, Tu, Th, F noon-5 pm;
W 4-7 pm Central

Nebraska
1237 R St. #102
Lincoln, NE 68588
402-472-3265
M-F 8 am-5 pm Central

New Mexico
517 Adams N.W. #4
Albuquerque, NM 87108

New York
P.O. Box 6343
Albany, NY 12206

P.O. Box 1110
Ellicott Station
Buffalo, NY 14203

891 Amsterdam Ave.
New York, NY 10025
212-866-3226
M-F 9 am-5 pm

535 Oak St.
Syracuse, NY 13203
315-472-5788
Daily 5-9 pm Eastern

North Carolina
714 Ninth St. #207
Durham, NC 27705

P.O. Box 10766
Winston-Salem, NC 27103

Ohio
P.O. Box 141015
Cincinnati, OH 45250

P.O. Box 14384
Columbus, OH 43214
614-447-1006
M-W 9:30 am-6 pm;
Th 11 am-7 pm
F 9:30 am-4 pm Eastern

P.O. Box 173
Lima, OH 45802

6093 Stanford Road
Peninsula, OH 44264
216-467-8711
Daily after 5 pm Eastern

6206 Pembridge Drive
Toldedo, OH 43615

Oregon
311 E. 11th Ave.
Eugene, OR 97401
503-683-3685
M-F 11 am-5 pm Pacific

3031 S.E. Hawthorne Blvd.
Portland, OR 97214
503-236-3380
Tu-Sa noon-5 pm Pacific

Pennsylvania
38 S. Third St.
Philadelphia, PA 19106
215-925-6004
M-F noon-6 pm;
Sa 11 am-3 pm Eastern

6300 Fifth Ave.
Pittsburgh, PA 15232-292

Tennessee
P.O. Box 242108
Memphis, TN 38124

Texas
2200 S. Lakeshore Blvd.
Austin, TX 78741
512-444-2294
Daily 8-11 am,
7-10 pm Central

3530 Forest Lane #127
Dallas, TX 75234
214-350-4294
M-F 3-6 pm Central

5302 Crawford
Houston, TX 77004
713-523-1009
Daily 7-10 am,
5-11 pm Central

Washington
419 Queen Anne Ave. N.
#101
Seattle, WA 98109
206-281-7306
M, Tu, Th, F noon-4 pm;
W 3-7 pm Pacific

Wisconsin
2224 W. Wisconsin Ave.
Milwaukee, WI 53233
414-933-1170
M 5-7 pm;
Tu-F 9 am-1 pm Central

National Office
P.O. Box 37613
Washington, D.C.
20013-7613
202-783-6161
M-F 9 am-6 pm Eastern

Hollywood

Jam-packed with activities and blessed with excellent bus service to other areas of L.A., Hollywood is a good tourist base. Hollywood Blvd., east of the main strip, is lined with budget motels, as is Sunset Blvd. Despite its charms, the area gets creepy at night; side streets can be dangerous. (The following are all area code 213.)

Hollywood Wilshire YMCA Hotel and Hostel, 1553 Hudson Ave. (467-4161). By far the best budget lodging in Hollywood. Located 1½ blocks south of Hollywood Blvd., the hotel rooms are clean and light, with no phones, TV, or A/C. They do, however, come with use of gym and pool. Pay phones on each floor. Must be over 18. Visitors allowed 7-10pm. Singles $29. Doubles $39. No reservations. Kitchen, laundry, and lounge. 15-day max. stay. Hostel rate $12 per night.

Hollywood Downtowner Motel, 5601 Hollywood Blvd. (464-7191). Pleasant rooms, swimming pool, helpful management, A/C, telephone, TV. Full kitchen units $2-3 extra (min. 4-night stay for kitchenette rooms). Singles $37, doubles $38-44, cheaper rates in winter. Free parking.

French Cottage Motel, 6757 Sunset Blvd. (464-9144). Not quite what the name suggests, but still a good deal. A/C, color TV, parking, pool. Breakfast included. Singles $32. Doubles $40. Weekly: singles $175; doubles $196.

Hastings Hotel, 6162 Hollywood Blvd. (464-4136). Youth-oriented hotel in the thick of Hollywood, near RTD bus lines. 85 rooms, most with color TV. Singles $30. Doubles $40. Weekly: singles $130; doubles $160.

Beverly Hills, Westside, Wilshire District

The Westside is an attractive part of town, but room rates are generally ugly. Call the **UCLA Off-Campus Housing Office** (825-4491), 100 Sproul Hall, and see if they can find you students who have a spare room (through their "roommate share board").

Hotel Del Flores, 409 N. Crescent Dr., Beverly Hills (310-274-5115), only 3 blocks east of chic Rodeo Dr. and 1 block south of Santa Monica Blvd. Unbelievably inexpensive for Beverly Hills. Renovated in 1991. Communal microwaves and refrigerators. Some rooms with color TV. Singles $40, doubles $45. Weekly: singles $185 and up; doubles $195 and up.

Wilshire Orange Hotel, 6060 W. 8th St. (213-931-9533), in West L.A. near Wilshire Blvd. and Fairfax Ave. Buses #20, 21, 22, and 308 serve Wilshire Blvd. from downtown. Near many major sights in a residential neighborhood. Most rooms have fridges, color TV; all but two with private or semi-private bath. Weekly housekeeping. 2-day min. stay. Singles $45. Doubles $48. Weekly: singles $145; doubles $225.

Crest Motel, 7701 Beverly Blvd. (213-931-8108), near Hollywood and Beverly Hills. An agreeable place, although some bathrooms would make Mr. Clean cringe. Pool, color TV and A/C. Singles $36. Doubles $38. $5 key deposit.

Century City-Westwood Motel, 10604 Santa Monica Blvd. (310-475-4422). Attractive rooms with fridges, color TVs, A/C. Even the bathrooms sparkle. On the southern part of "Little Santa Monica," the smaller road that parallels the divided boulevard. Singles $45, additional person $5; 4 max.

Santa Monica and Venice

The hostels at Venice Beach are budget havens, just about the cheapest way to stay and the most enjoyable way to play in L.A. (Hey, hey!) You may miss the Sunset Strip (and L.A. traffic), but you'll find dazzling beaches, kinky architecture, and a mellow, eccentric sun-worshipping community. The city center is just a short bus ride or drive away. The hostels are a popular destination among foreign students. (The following are all area code 310.)

Venice Beach Cotel, 25 Windward Ave., Venice (399-7649), on the boardwalk between Zephyr Court and 17th Ave. Located close to beaches; shuttle from LAX. To stay in the hostel part you must show your passport and not ask about the name. A lively hostel full of young international travelers. 3-6 people share each tidy, functional room. No food allowed. Bar and social area lively from 7pm-1am. No curfew. $12 per person, with bath $15. Private rooms with and without ocean view $33-49.50.

Santa Monica International AYH Hostel, 1436 2nd St., Santa Monica (393-9913). Opened in June 1990 in the heart of downtown Santa Monica to immediate popularity. Boasts a colossal kitchen, copious common rooms, and a casual, California-cool climate. Curfew 2am. $13.45 per night, AYH members only. $2 rental for bedsheets.

Share-Tel International Hostel, 20 Brooks Ave., Venice (392-0325). ½-block off the boardwalk. Student I.D. or passport required. Family-style atmosphere; pleasant rooms with kitchen facilities and bathroom fit 4-12 each. Kitchen, continental breakfast, safe, linen service, no curfew. $15 per person, $100 per week.

Venice Beach Hostel, 701 Washington St. (306-5180), above Celebrity Cleaners. Relaxed and homey, with a large lounge, cable TV, and sunroof (bathing suits optional). Popular with international travelers. Near bars and nightclubs. Free transportation from LAX. $12 per night, $70 per week. Double rooms $15 per person. Open 24 hrs.

Jim's at The Beach, 17 Brooks Ave., Venice (396-5138), across the street from Share-Tel. Passport required. 6 beds per room max. Clean, bright rooms, kitchen. No curfew. $15 per night, $90 per week.

Marina Hostel, 2915 Yale Ave., Marina Del Rey (301-3983), 3 blocks west from Lincoln Blvd. Near Venice in a quiet residential neighborhood. Privately owned, friendly household with lockers, linen, laundry, and a kitchen with microwave. Some bunks, some floor mattresses. Living room with cable TV. $12 per guest.

Interclub Hostel, 2221 Lincoln Blvd., Venice (305-0250), near Venice Blvd. Passport required. Festive after-hours common-room with many nationalities bumping elbows. Surfer murals on the walls. Rooms sleep 6, or you can sleep in the 30-bed dorm. Mixed-sex accommodations. No lockout during summer, otherwise 11am-4pm. Curfew 4am. Linen. Laundry room. $12 per person plus $5 deposit.

Cadillac Hotel, 401 Ocean Front Walk, Venice (399-8876). A beautiful Art Deco landmark. Airport shuttle service, limited parking. Boardwalk and beach just outside. Private sundeck. No curfew. Shared accommodations $18 per night, private ocean-view rooms $49 and up.

Food

The range of culinary options in L.A. is in direct proportion to the city's ethnic diversity: Jewish and Eastern European food in the Fairfax area; Mexican in East L.A.; Japanese, Chinese, Vietnamese, and Thai around Little Tokyo and Chinatown; seafood along the coast; and Hawaiian, Indian, and Ethiopian scattered throughout. And the range of quality matches the diversity: from the dozens closed each month by the L.A. Department of Health to family-run nooks to glitzy yuppie magnets to celebrity hangouts with stellar prices for the superwealthy.

Sadly, the only cuisine truly indigenous to the area—and the one that best fits L.A. culture—is fast food. The home of the Big Mac, McDonald's, got its start in Southern Cal in the 50s, and Angelenos seem to have spent the intervening years trying to improve upon the recipe; burger joints squat on nearly every corner. To study the phenomenon, try **In 'n Out Burger** (various locations, call 818-287-4377), a family-owned chain that has steadfastly refused to expand beyond the L.A. area. The rewards of such stubborness are evidenced by In 'n Out's burgers and fries, arguably the best in the business. In general, burger places and Mexican restaurants top the budget travelers' dining list in Los Angeles.

The best way to enjoy the natural foods that made California famous is to find a health-food store or co-op that sells organic and small-farm produce. Stands selling just a few items are scattered throughout the San Fernando Valley down to Ventura. Prices are lower than those in the enormous public markets, and the quality superior, although the markets offer greater variety. The **Farmer's Market,** 6333 W. 3rd St. (213-933-9211), at Fairfax in the Wilshire District, has over 160 produce stalls, meat vendors, small restaurants, and sidewalk cafés. The market has become a tourist attraction, so bargains are an endangered species. (Open Mon.-Sat. 9am-7pm, Sun. 10am-6pm; Oct.-May Mon.-Sat. 9am-6:30pm, Sun. 10am-5pm.) A less touristy, less expensive source of produce is the **Grand Central Public Market,** 317 S. Broadway (624-2378), a large baby-blue building downtown. The main market in the Hispanic shopping district, Grand Central has more than 50 stands selling produce, clothing, housewares, costume jewelry, vitamins, and fast food. (Open Mon.-Sat. 9am-6pm, Sunday 10am-6pm.)

Nearby cafés keep the same hours as the markets. The most famous is **Vickman's** at 1228 E. 8th St. (213-622-3852; open Mon.-Fri. 3am-3pm, Sat. 3am-1pm, Sun. 7am-1pm). For listings on late night cafés, restaurants, and combination club/restaurants see Entertainment.

Downtown

The following are all in area code 213.

Philippe's, The Original, 1001 N. Alameda (628-3781), 2 blocks north of Union Station. The sheer variety of food combined with sizeable portions and low prices make this an exemplary locale for mid-day victuals. Philippe's claims to have originated the French-dipped sandwich; varieties include beef, pork, ham, turkey, or lamb ($3-4). Potato salad 65¢ and a glass of iced tea 40¢. Top it off with a large slice of pie ($1.80), and you've got a colossal lunch at this L.A. institution. Open daily 6am-10pm.

The Pantry, 877 S. Figueroa St. (972-9279). Open since the 20s. You may have to share a table with a complete stranger, and the waiter is as likely to insult you as to talk your ear off, but the patrons like it that way. The restaurant seats only 84 yet serves 3,000 meals a day. The owners recently opened a deli/bakery next door (roast beef sandwich $3.85). Be prepared to wait for enormous breakfast specials ($5.95), especially on weekends. Sunday brunch at the Pantry is an L.A. tradition. Open 24 hrs.

La Luz Del Dia, 1 W. Olvera St. (628-7495). This authentic and inexpensive Mexican restaurant is hidden amidst the many tourist-trap Mexican joints along historic Olvera St. Tortillas are made on the premises, and the salsa is sharp. Combo plates ($4). Open Tues.-Sun. 11am-10pm.

Gorky's, 536 E. 8th St. (627-4060). On the southeast edge of downtown. One-of-a-kind restaurant, serving Socialist Realist Russian cuisine (i.e. cafeteria-style) in an avant-garde setting. Entertaining entrees $5-7. Brewery on premises; live music Wed.-Sun. at 8:30pm. Open 24 hrs.

Pacific Restaurant, 859 N. Broadway (626-1688), in Chinatown. The *jook* (rice porridge with scallions and egg, $3.55) and the meat and rice plate ($3.75) are inexpensive and mouthwatering. Open daily 8:30am-9:30pm.

Sushi Bukyu, 318 E. 2nd St. (617-2280), in Little Tokyo. The best Japanese food for the money in Little Tokyo. A la carte menu $2.50-7.50. Full dinner $8-10. Open Thurs.-Tues. 11:30am-midnight.

Hollywood and West Hollywood

Forget those rumors about outrageously priced celebrity hangouts. They're here, but you can ignore them. Hollywood offers the best budget dining in L.A., with good ethnic restaurants. On Melrose, chic cafés and eateries provide outdoor seating so you can see and be seen by the extraordinarily stylized and beautiful Melrosians.

Seafood Bay, 3916 Sunset Blvd., at Sanborn in Silver Lake, east of Hollywood. This modest eatery in a quiet residential area skimps on decor to support a wide variety of seafood at great prices. "Light meals" such as fettucine with clam sauce are filling and run no more than $6. The fish is fantastic, and the accompaniment—sourdough garlic bread, pungent rice pilaf, heaps of sauteed mushrooms—receive the same loving attention. Open Mon.-Thurs. 11:30am-10pm, Fri.-Sat. 11:30am-10:30pm, Sun. 4-10pm.

Lucy's El Adobe Café, 5536 Melrose Ave. (213-462-9421), 1 block east of Gower St. This tiny family-run restaurant is a favorite among downtown politicos and Paramount executives from across the street. Former governor Jerry Brown and Linda Ronstadt allegedly met here. Some of the best Mexican food in town. As you munch on your tostada ($6), glance at the celebrity photos adorning the walls. Full dinners (entree, soup or salad, rice, and beans) $8-10. Open Mon.-Sat. 11:30am-11pm.

Ara's, 4953 Hollywood Blvd. (213-660-3739). Authentic and tantalizing Armenian restaurant. Various kebabs ($7) include pita bread, rice pilaf, and curried vegetables. Open Mon.-Sat. noon-8:30pm.

Chon Doa, 1511 N. Calnenga Blvd. (213-464-8585). Serves excellent Thai food to clubbie clients carbo-boosting for their late-night entertainment. Red noodles $5.75. Curry chicken

$6.75. Open Mon.-Thurs. 11am-11pm, Fri. 11am-midnight, Sat. 5pm-midnight, Sunday 5pm-11pm.

Boardner's Restaurant, 1652 N. Cherokee Ave. (213-462-9621). Boardner's has been serving Americana at nearly the same prices ($3-8) since WWII. Open daily 11am-10pm, drinks 'til 2am.

Beverly Hills, Westside, Wilshire District

Beverly Hills and the Wilshire District offer some of the finest dining in the country; don't expect any bargains. La Brea Ave. and Pico Blvd., however, both offer a wide variety of restaurants. The following are all in area code 310.

Ed Debeure's, 134 N. La Cienoga Blvd. (659-1952), in Beverly Hills. Far and away the most mirthful of the phony 50s diners ("famous since 1984"). Waitresses complete with buttons. Hamburgers $4.55-5.55. Full bar. Open Sun.-Thurs. 11:30am-11pm, Fri.-Sat. 11:30am-1am.

Siam Cottage, 10512 W. Pico Blvd. (838-4012). Therrific Thai food. Lunch special $4.95. Most entrees $4.25-6.50, but the dinner specials are the way to go. Open daily 11am-2:30pm and 5pm-10:30pm.

El Nopal, 10426 National Blvd. (559-4732), in West L.A., between Motor and Overland, just south of the Santa Monica Fwy. Known as "Home of the pregnant burrito." The famed burrito *embarrasado* ($5.50), stuffed with chicken and avocado, lives up to its name—you'll blush with each tasty bite. Smaller burritos $2-3. Tasty tacos and tangy salsa ($1.75). Take-out available. Open Mon.-Sat. 11am-10pm, Sun. 11am-9pm.

Dragon Garden, 2625 S. Robertson (837-3627). Not the best Chinese food in L.A., but you can't beat the $1 per item lunch special (11:30am-4:30pm). The taco stand 2 doors over offers similar-quality food at even better prices. Open Mon.-Sat. 11:30am-9:00pm.

Tommy's Original Hamburgers, 2575 W. Beverly Blvd. (389-9060), Wilshire District. Ignore the multitude of Tommy's knock-offs and head to the winner of the sloppiest chili dog contest (the paper towel dispensers every 2 ft. along the counters aren't just there for looks). Chili dog $1.25, chili burger $1.25, double cheeseburger $2.95. Open 24 hrs.

Westwood

Westwood is filled with chic and convenient eateries perfect before a movie or while shopping, and you'll find everything from felafel to *gelato* in corner shops. The following are all in area code 310.

Sak's Teriyaki, 1121 Glendon Ave. (208-2002), in Westwood. Excellent, low-priced Japanese plates including chicken and beef teriyaki ($3.70-5). Popular with students. Happy Hour special ($2.50) 3-6pm. Open Mon.-Thurs. 11am-10pm, Fri.-Sat. 11am-11pm, Sun. 11am-9pm.

Tacos Tacos, 1084 Glendon Ave. (208-2038), Westwood Village. Trendy "Southwestern Café" with blue corn chicken tacos ($1.75). Try the *horchata* (cinnamon-flavored rice water, $1.25). Open Sun.-Wed. 11am-10:30pm, Thurs.-Sat. 11am-12:30pm.

Numero Uno, 1077 Broxton Ave. (208-5070). All-you-can-eat Pizza and Spaghetti ($4.95) Mon.-Tues. 5pm-11pm. Open Sun.-Thurs. 11am-11:30pm, Fri.-Sat. 11am-1pm.

Lamonica's NY Pizza, 10925 Weyburn Ave. (478-9806). L.A.'s best pizza by the slice ($1.30, 15¢ per topping). They claim to fly the water for their dough cross-country for that authentic New York taste. 12" pizza $8, 75¢ per topping. Open Sun.-Thurs. 11am-10:30pm. Fri.-Sat. 11am-midnight.

Santa Monica and Venice

Unfortunately, most of Santa Monica's eateries are overpriced, and most of Venice's eateries are overgreased. The new **EATZ Café** in Santa Monica Place offers 17 different types of mall food to choose from, a number of which are tasty and reasonably priced. The following are all in area code 310.

Tijuana Restaurant, 11785 W. Olympic Blvd. (473-9293), in West L.A. The menu here looks like a Tijuana jai alai program, but the food is first-rate. A woman stands in the entryway of the dining room hand-making the tortillas for dinner. If you're feeling adventurous, try the *nopalitas,* young cactus served on a tortilla ($2.75). Dinner entrees and combo plates run $7-9. Open Sun.-Thurs. 11am-10pm, Fri.-Sat. 11am-11pm.

Humphrey Yogart Café, 11677 San Vicente Blvd. (207-2206), in Brentwood. Come here for dessert, schweetheart. Start with vanilla frozen yogurt (sweet or tart) and blend in whatever bizarre ingredient combination you wish. A medium with two ingredients is $2.40. Humphrey's also serves sandwiches, soups, and salads. Always crowded. Open Sun. 11am-10:30pm, Mon.-Thurs. 9am-11:30pm, Fri. 9am-11:30pm, Sat. 10am-11:30pm.

Tito's Tacos, 11222 Washington Place (391-5780), in Culver City at Sepulveda, 1 block north of Washington Blvd., virtually *beneath* the San Diego Fwy. The name should have been Tito's Burritos, since the burrito, with its huge hunks of shredded beef, is the star attraction. At a measly $2.10, it's also the most expensive menu item. You can order to go. Plenty of parking. Open daily 9am-11:30pm.

Benita's Frites, 1437 3rd St. Promenade (458-2889), in Santa Monica. French fries served the Belgian way, in a paper cone with *andoulause* sauce (red and green bell peppers, mayonnaise, tomato, and garlic), chili, or peanut curry satay on top ($1.65-2.25, toppings 30-45¢. Open Sun. noon-8pm, Mon. 11:30am-4pm., Tues.-Thurs. 11:30am-10pm, Fri.-Sat. 11:30am-10:30pm.

San Fernando Valley

The entirety of Ventura Blvd. is chock full of restaurants. Lunch in Studio City is your best chance to catch sight of the stars, but *don't ask for autographs.* One notable stop is **Chili John's,** 2018 W. Burbank Blvd. (818-846-3611), in Burbank. The chili recipe hasn't changed since 1900 (a bowl is $3.85). As your mouth burns, check out the wall mountain landscape; it took the former owner/chef over 20 years of in-between-customer moments to paint. Take-out. Open Sept.-June Tues.-Fri. 11am-7pm, Sat. 11am-4pm.

Pasadena

Fair Oaks Ave. and Colorado Blvd., in the Old Town section of Pasadena, are punctuated with cafés and Mexican restaurants. The two notable ones that follow are in area code 818.

Los Tacos, 1 W. California Blvd. (795-9291), enter around the corner of Fair Oaks Blvd. Fast-food Mexican-style. Soft tacos with choice of filling ($1.15). Combo plates ($4.69). A popular weekend stop for local teeny-boppers. Open Sun.-Mon. 9am-10pm, Tues.-Thurs. 9am-1am, Fri.-Sat. 9am-2am.

Mijari's Mexican Restaurant, 145 Palmetto Dr. (792-2763), entrance on Pasadena Ave. Vast, popular, and festive. Combo dinners $5-7. Open Mon.-Thurs. 11am-9pm, Fri.-Sat. 11am-10pm, Sun. 10am-9pm.

Sights

Downtown

The downtown area alone is larger than most cities, a fascinating mélange of neighborhoods. The financial district is a jungle of glass and steel, where gigantic corporate offices of such companies as ARCO, Bank of America, Wells Fargo, and AT&T crowd the busy downtown center (an area bounded roughly by 3rd and 6th St., Figueroa St., and Grand Ave.). The brand new I.M. Pei-designed **First Interstate World Center,** 633 W. 5th St. (955-8151), conspicuously perched atop Bunker Hill, dominates a skyline made famous by the TV show *L.A. Law;* at 73 stories and 1017 ft., it is the tallest building west of the Mississippi River, with curved lines and a cylindrical shape reflecting the trend toward softer form in urban architecture. Across the street is the city's Central Library, an old, pyramid-crowned building currently undergoing renovation.

The **Oviatt Building** at 617 S. Olive St. is the downtown area's Art-Deco masterpiece. The **Times Mirror Building** at 220 W. 1st, with the exception of the 1970s addition, is a classic example of Cal Moderne. The **Civic Center,** a solid wall of bureaucratic architecture bounded by the Hollywood Fwy. (U.S. 101), Grand, 1st, and San Pedro St., runs east from the Music Center. It ends at **City Hall,** 200 N. Spring St. Another of the best-known buildings in the Southland, the hall was cast as the home of the *Daily Planet* in the *Superman* TV series and has an **observation deck** on the 27th floor.

Farther north lies the historic birthplace of Los Angeles. In the place where the original city center once stood, **El Pueblo de Los Angeles State Historic Park** (680-2525; open Mon.-Fri. 10am-8pm) preserves a number of buildings from the Spanish and Mexican eras. Start out at the **docent center,** 130 Paseo de la Plaza. The center offers free walking tours (Tues.-Sat. 10am-1pm on the hour, but call to check first as tours are sometimes cancelled, 628-1274) and a free bus tour of L.A. (1st and 3rd Wed. of each month, make reservations as early as possible; 628-1274) The **Old Plaza,** with its century-old Moreton Bay fig trees and huge bandstand, sprawls at the center of the pueblo. Tours start here and wind their way past the **Avila Adobe** (1818), 10 E. Olvera St., the oldest house in the city (the original adobe has been replaced with concrete in order to meet earthquake regulations), followed by **Pico House,** 500 N. Main St., once L.A.'s most luxurious hotel. Farther down, at 535 N. Main St., the **Plaza Church,** established in 1818, almost melts away from the street with its soft, rose adobe facade. Most tours also include the catacombs that formerly held gambling and opium dens. The **visitors center** is located in the **Sepulveda House** (1887), 622 N. Main St. (628-1274; open Mon.-Fri. 9am-4pm. For interested visitors, they screen *Pueblo of Promise,* an 18-minute history of L.A. **Olvera Street,** one of L.A.'s original roads, has miraculously survived; it is now called Tijuana North by the locals, and one tawdry stand after another sells schlocky Mexican handicrafts. Here L.A.'s large Chicano community celebrates Mexican Independence Day on **Cinco de Mayo.** In December, the Los Posados celebration includes a candlelight procession and the breaking of a piñata (Dec. 16-24; 625-5045). Across Alameda St. from El Pueblo is the grand old **Union Station.**

Bustling **Chinatown** lies north of this area, roughly bordered by Yale, Spring, Ord, and Bernard St. From downtown, take the DASH shuttle. (See Getting Around, Public Transportation.) This once vice-ridden neighborhood taught Roman Polanski's Jake Giddis (played by Mr. L.A. himself, Jack Nicholson) just what a tough old world it is out there. **Little Tokyo,** yet another of downtown L.A.'s ethnic neighborhoods, is centered on 2nd and San Pedro St. on the eastern edge of downtown. The **New Otani Hotel,** 120 S. Los Angeles St., one block south of the Civic Center between 1st and 2nd, rents its lavish Meiji-style rooms for up to $700 per night. For slightly less, you can have a drink in the elegant rooftop garden. The **Japanese Village Plaza,** in the 300 block of E. 2nd St. is the center of the district and is a florid fusion of American shopping mall and Japanese design. The **Japanese American Cultural and Community Center,** 244 S. San Pedro St. (628-2725), was designed by Buckminster Fuller and Isamu Noguchi, who crafted the monumental sculpture for the courtyard. (Administrative offices open Mon.-Fri. 9am-5pm.)

Broadway south of 1st St. is predominantly Mexican. All billboards and store signs are in Spanish, and the **Grand Central Public Market** (see Food) takes a center seat. One of many Spanish-language cinemas housed in old movie palaces is the **Million Dollar Theater,** 307 S. Broadway (239-0939). Peek into the baroque auditorium, and inspect the stars in the sidewalk out front, each bearing the name of a Chicano celebrity, a *rambla de fama* to complement Hollywood's. Across the street, the **Bradbury Building,** 304 S. Broadway, stands as a relic of L.A.'s Victorian past. Uninspiring from the street, this exquisite 1893 office building is mostly lobby. Its ornate staircases and elevators (wrought in iron, wood, and marble) often are bathed in sunlight, which pours in through the glass roof. Crews film period scenes with some regularity here. (Open Mon.-Sat. 10am-5pm. Self-guided tour $1.)

Perhaps the best reason to spend time downtown is to see L.A.'s cultural attractions. Undoubtedly the most striking, chic, and caffeinated museum in the area is the **Museum of Contemporary Art (MOCA),** showcasing art from 1940 to the present. The main museum is located at California Plaza, 250 S. Grand Ave. (626-6222), and is a sleek and geometric architectural marvel. Its collection focuses on Abstract Expressionism, and includes works by Pollock, Calder, Miró, and Giacometti. Its interior is spacious, illuminated by the pyramidal skylights in the ceiling. The second MOCA facility is the **Temporary Contemporary,** 152 N. Central Ave., in Little

Tokyo. The bare warehouse exterior conceals an intriguing collection featuring avant-garde younger artists in a bold setting. One ticket admits you to both locations. DASH shuttles between them for 25¢; the **MOCA Shuttle Bus** teleports you from one to the other for free. (Shuttle operates during all museum hours: open Tues.-Wed. and Fri.-Sun. 11am-6pm, Thurs. 11am-8pm. Admission $4, seniors and students with ID $2, under 12 free. Everyone free Thurs. 5-8pm. Disabled access.) Across from City Hall East, between the Santa Ana Fwy. and Temple in the L.A. Mall, is the **L.A. Children's Museum,** 310 N. Main St. (687-8800), where nothing is behind glass and everything can be fondled. Children are invited to confront their anguish over the depersonalized nature of a contemporary culture dominated by technology by participating in demonstrations of science and stuff. (Open Wed.- Thurs. 2-4pm, Sat.-Sun. 10am-5pm. Admission $4, under 2 free.)

Perhaps the most peculiar and best-hidden of the downtown museums is the **Museum of Neon Art,** 704 Traction Ave. (617-1580), in the artists' neighborhood to the east of Little Tokyo. Exhibits range from neon artwork to other types of electric and kinetic sculpture. Pick up a MONA t-shirt, depicting a neon sculpture of the *Mona Lisa.* Traction Ave. runs east of Alameda St., between 2nd and 3rd St. (Open Tues.-Sat. 11am-5pm. Admission $2.50, seniors and students $1, under 17 free.) Finally, those enticed by the Bradbury Building will want to examine the **Grier-Musser Museum,** which contains an extensive collection of antiques inside a tenderly restored Queen Anne style house. (Open Wed.-Sat. 11am-4pm; adults $3, seniors $2. Located at 403 South Bonnie Brae Avenue, 413-1818.)

Exposition Park

Among the most notable sights near downtown is **Exposition Park,** a once-decrepit area revived for the 1932 Olympics, then a twice-decrepit area revived for the 1984 Olympics. The park, southwest of downtown just off the Harbor Fwy., is bounded by Exposition Blvd., Figueroa St., Vermont Ave., and Santa Barbara Ave. From downtown, take bus #40 or 42 (both from 1st and Broadway) to the park's southern edge. From Hollywood, take #204 down Vermont.

The park is dominated by several major museums, including the **California Museum of Science and Industry,** 700 State Dr. (744-7400). Enter at the corner of Figueroa and Exposition next to the United DC-8 parked out front. Many of the exhibits are either corporate or governmental propaganda; those left to the MSI's own devices are rather amateurish. IBM and Bell Telephone sponsor mathematics and communications, while McDonald's is inexplicably allowed to handle a display on nutrition. One exhibit re-creates an earthquake—complete with a shaking floor and mock news report—to acquaint Southern Californians with their future. The museum also includes the **Kinsey Hall of Health** (*not* run by McDonald's), which has an exhibit on AIDS and uses interactive computer displays to educate visitors about their bodies and the effects of diet, alcohol, and drug use. The **Hall of Economics and Finance** does its best to enliven what even its practitioners call "the dismal science." The **Aerospace Building,** as big as a hangar, exhibits $8 million worth of aircraft, including the Gemini 11 space capsule. New for 1992 is an exhibit on the Science of Toys and Games. (Open daily 10am-5pm. Free. Parking $2, bring quarters.) The museum also runs an **IMAX Theater** (744-2014), which projects films onto a five-story-tall screen and bombards viewers with six-channel surround sound. Films are an hour long, covering such subjects as space flight and the great outdoors. (Showings daily every hr. 10am-9pm. Admission $5.50, over 55, students, and ages 4-17 $4. Call ahead for show info.)

In the same complex, separate from the MSI, is the **California Afro-American Museum,** 600 State Dr. (744-2060), with a permanent sculpture collection, a research library, and a changing assortment of exhibits. (Open daily 10am-5pm. Free. Research library open Mon.-Fri. 10am-5pm.)

The park's other major museum is the **Los Angeles County Natural History Museum,** 900 Exposition Blvd. (744-3466). Exhibits here cover American history from 1472-1914, pre-Columbian cultures, North American and African mammals, and dinosaurs. The **E. Hadley Stuart, Jr. Hall of Gems and Minerals** showcases a dazzling array of precious rocks. (Open Tues.-Sun. 10am-5pm. Admission $5, seniors and students $2.50, ages 5-12 $1, under 5 free.)

Exposition Park also includes the galactic **Los Angeles Memorial Coliseum,** 2601 S. Figueroa St., home of the Los Angeles Raiders and the USC Trojans football teams, and the **Sports Arena,** home of the Los Angeles Clippers basketball team and a common venue for rock concerts.

The **University of Southern California (USC)** campus is opposite Exposition Park on Exposition Blvd. The campus is wide, beautiful and generally safe during the day. The **Fisher Gallery,** 823 Exposition Blvd. (743-2799), includes the Armand Hammer collection of 18th- and 19th-century Dutch paintings. (Open early Sept.-early May Tues.-Sat. noon-5pm. Free.)

To the south and east of the USC campus stretches **Watts,** a neighborhood made notorious by riots in 1965. From the center of what is formally known as the Watts District rise the **Watts Towers,** 1765 E. 107th St. (569-8181), a remarkably impressive work of folk art. Watts resident Simon Rodia singlehandedly built the towers over a period of 33 years. These delicate towers of glistening fretwork, decorated with mosaics of broken glass, ceramic tile, and sea shells, are a truly inspiring testament to the power of one man's extraordinary vision and dedication. Although the towers are a good 7-mi. drive from the nearest tourist attractions at Exposition Park and are in a dangerous part of town, they are worth the trip. (By bus, take RTD #55 from Main St. downtown and get off at Compton Ave. and 108th St. The towers are one block to the east.) For a guided tour of the towers, which are undergoing restoration, call the Watts Towers Arts Center at 569-8181. The center is located at 1727 E. 107th St., right next to the towers, and is open Tues.-Sat. 9am-5pm. (From downtown take the Metro Blue Line and get off at 103 St. Station. Walk on 104th east to Beach, and then south to the corner of 106th and 107th.) The towers are open for exploration Sat.-Sun. from 10am-4pm. During the week the towers undergo restoration, and appointments must be made in advance. Next door, at 1727 E. 107th St. is the **Watts Tower Arts Center** (569-8181), which houses a permanent exhibit of folk instruments, as well as a changing gallery (open Tues.-Sat. 9am-4pm).

Hollywood Park, 1050 S. Prairie Ave. (419-1500), sponsors thoroughbred racing between April and July, and in November and December. The lovely track is landscaped with lagoons and tropical trees, and the facility is complete with restaurants and a children's play area. (Racing held Wed.-Sun. Post time 1:30pm. Admission $3, ages under 18 free.) At the corner of Manchester and Prairie Ave. is the **Great Western Forum** (673-1300), home of Wayne Gretzky's **Los Angeles Kings** hockey team as well as the **Los Angeles Lakers** basketball team, perhaps the most popular of L.A.'s many sports franchises.

Wilshire District and Hancock Park

Wilshire Boulevard, especially the "Miracle Mile" between Highland and Fairfax Ave., played a starring role in Los Angeles' westward suburban expansion. On what was then the end of the boulevard, the Bullocks Corporation gambled on attracting shoppers from downtown and in 1929 erected the massive, bronze-colored **Bullocks Wilshire** at 3050 Wilshire Blvd., near Vermont Ave., now called the **I. Magnin BW Wilshire.** Tours of this Art-Deco landmark are offered by docents of the Los Angeles Conservancy (call 623-2489 to arrange one). The nearby residential neighborhoods and their 20s architecture also are worth exploring. The streets south of Wilshire opposite Hancock Park are lined with Spanish-style bungalows and the occasional modernist manse.

A few mi. further down Wilshire, in **Hancock Park,** an acrid smell pervades the vicinity of the **La Brea Tar Pits,** one of the world's most popular hangouts for fossilized early mammals. Most of the one million bones recovered from the pits between 1913 and 1915 have found jobs on *The Flintstones* and new homes in the **George C. Page Museum of La Brea Discoveries,** 5801 Wilshire Blvd. at Curson and Wilshire (for a fossilized recording 936-2230, for a live person 857-6311). Wilshire buses stop right in front of the museum to make finding a fossil more facile. The museum includes reconstructed Ice Age animals and murals of L.A. Ice Age life, a laboratory where paleontologists work behind plate-glass windows, and a display where you can feel what it's like to stick around in the tar. Archeological digging continues in Pit 91 behind the adjacent county art museum. (Open Tues.-Sun. 10am-5pm. Admission $4, seniors and students $2, kids 75¢. Free 2nd Tues. of each month. Tours of the museum are offered to the public Wed.-Sun. at 2:00pm. Tours of the grounds at 1pm.)

The **Los Angeles County Museum of Art (LACMA)**, 5905 Wilshire Blvd. (857-6000), at the west end of Hancock Park, has a distinguished, comprehensive collection that should rebut those who argue that L.A.'s only culture is in its yogurt. Opened in 1965, the LACMA is the largest museum in the West and still growing. Five major buildings cluster around the **Times Mirror Central Court: a** Japanese pavilion, the Ahmanson Building (the museum's original building and home to most of its non-modern permanent collection), the Hammer Building, the Bing Center, and the Robert O. Anderson Building, a spectacular 1986 addition to the museum, with a facade of salmon-colored sandstone and glass. The museum offers a variety of tours and free talks daily. For schedules, check with the info desk in the Central Court or contact the Docent Council at 857-6108. (Open Tues.-Fri. 10am-5pm, Sat.-Sun. 10am-6pm. Admission $5, seniors and students $3.50, ages 6-17 $1. Free 2nd Tues. of each month.)

Further down the street, at its temporary home in the May Company Building, the **Craft and Folk Art Museum,** 6067 Wilshire Blvd. (938-7197), displays a changing sample of folk art and contemporary crafts in a third floor gallery. (Free. Open Tues.-Sat. 10am-5pm, Sun. 11am-5pm.)

Similar to Jerusalem's famous Yad VaShem Holocaust Memorial is the **Martyrs Memorial and Museum of the Holocaust** (852-1234, ext. 3200), located in the Jewish Community Building, 6505 Wilshire Blvd., just east of Beverly Hills. Horrifying photographs and prisoners' personal items are on display next to paintings and drawings made in the ghettos and death camps. The museum is on the 12th floor; sign in at the security desk. (Open Mon.-Thurs. 8:30am-5pm, Fri. 8:30-3:30pm, Sun. 10am-5pm. Free.)

Hollywood

It's hard to believe that for decades this tiny chunk of a massive city defined glamour on the West Coast. Appropriately, this community that specializes in manufacturing illusions had its origins in deception. In the early days of silent movies, independent producers and directors, many of them Jewish, sought to escape the tight control and restrictions of the conservative anti-semitic Movie Trust based in New York. They began shooting films in the empty groves of Hollywood both to avoid the Trust's surveillance and to take advantage of the steady sunlight and infrequent rain (indoor lighting techniques were not employed at the time). By the early 1920s, all the major studios had moved from the East Coast to this then-obscure suburb. Hollywood quickly became synonymous with the celluloid image. Home to the great stars (Garbo, Gable, Crawford) and the great studios (MGM, Paramount, Warner Bros., 20th Century Fox), Hollywood became an important arbiter of American mores and interpreter of the American Dream. But Hollywood today has lost much of its sparkle. The major studios have moved over the mountains into the San Fernando Valley, where they have more space to weave their ever-more-elaborate fantasies, and blockbusters are increasingly shot elsewhere in the U.S. or overseas. As a result, the Golden Road has turned into Main Street in slacks. Hollywood Boulevard and other thoroughfares, once glittering and glamorous, are now rated X. At night, prostitutes abound; women work Hollywood and Sunset Boulevards, while boys ply their trade on Santa Monica Boulevard (also known as S&M Blvd.). Hollywood is still a fascinating place, but a far cry from the Emerald City it was once thought to be. At 105, the *grand dame* shows her age and survives on memories of her past.

The **Hollywood sign**—those 50-ft.-high, slightly erratic letters perched on Mt. Cahuenga north of Hollywood—stands with New York's Statue of Liberty and

Paris's Eiffel Tower as a universally recognized symbol of its city. The original 1923 sign, which read HOLLYWOODLAND, was an advertisement for a new subdivision in the Hollywood Hills (a caretaker lived behind one of the Ls). Over the years, people came to think of it as a civic monument, and the city, which by 1978 had acquired the sign, reconstructed the crumbling letters leaving off the last syllable. The sign has been a target of pranksters (USC frat boys and Cal Tech hackers) who have made it read everything from "Hollyweed" to "Ollywood," after gap-toothed errand boy Lt. Col. Oliver North. For a closer look at the site, follow Beachwood Dr. up into the hills (bus #208; off Franklin Ave. between Vine St. and Western Ave.). Drive along the narrow twisting streets of the Hollywood Hills for glimpses of the bizarre homes of the Rich and Famous, or detour to **Forest Lawn Memorial Park,** 6300 Forest Lawn Dr. (818-984-1711), on the other side of the hills. The park is a museum of early American history, with a mosaic mural and a collection of statues. (Open daily 9am-5pm. Free.)

Hollywood Boulevard itself, lined with souvenir shops, porno houses, clubs, and theaters, is busy both day and night. The facade of **Mann's Chinese Theater** (formerly Grauman's), 6925 Hollywood Blvd. (464-8111), between Highland and La Brea, is an odd tropical interpretation of a Chinese temple and Hollywood hype at its finest. Tourists always crowd the courtyard, worshipping cement impressions of various parts of the stars' anatomics and trademark possessions (Al Jolson's knees, Trigger's hooves, R2D2's wheels, Jimmy Durante's nose, George Burns' cigar, etc.) If you want to stroll among stars, have a look at the **Walk of Fame** along Hollywood Blvd. and Vine St. More than 2500 bronze-inlaid stars are embedded in the sidewalk, inscribed with names—some familiar, some forgotten—and feets. Across the street and two blocks east is another unique theater, the **UA Egyptian,** 6712 Hollywood Blvd. (467-6167), inspired in 1922 by the then-newly-discovered tomb of King Tut.

Also two blocks east of Mann's is the **Hollywood Wax Museum,** 6767 Hollywood Blvd. (462-8860), where you'll meet over 200 figures from Jesus to Cher. (Open Sun.-Thurs. 10am-midnight, Fri.-Sat. 10am-2am. Admission $7.50, kids $5, seniors $6.) Other Hollywood Blvd. attractions include the original **Frederick's of Hollywood,** 6608 Hollywood Blvd. (466-8506), a purple and pink bastion of tasteful teddies and licorice lingerie, which now houses its own **museum of lingerie** in the back of the store. (Open Mon.-Thurs. 10am-8pm, Fri. 10am-9pm, Sat. 10am-6pm, Sun. noon-5pm. Free.) Down the street, **Larry Edmund's Cinema and Theater Bookshop,** 6658 Hollywood Blvd. (463-3273), sells Ken Schessler's *This Is Hollywood: Guide to Hollywood Murders, Suicides, Graves, Etc.,* a guide to nondescript places made famous by the fact that stars courted, married, fooled around, were discovered, made movies, or committed suicide there. (Open Mon.-Sat. 10am-6pm.)

Hollywood Fantasy Tours, 1651 N. Highland (469-8184), two blocks south of Hollywood Blvd., offers two-hour tours of Tinseltown in double-decker buses with knowledgeable but corny tour guides. (Tours of Beverly Hills and other areas also. Call for info.) The **Hollywood Studio Museum,** 2100 N. Highland Ave. (874-2276), across from the Hollywood Bowl, provides a refreshingly un-Mannesque look at the history of early Hollywood film-making. Back in 1913, when it was a barn, famed director Cecil B. DeMille rented this building as a studio and shot Hollywood's first feature film, *The Straw Man,* there. Antique cameras, costumes, props, and other memorabilia clutter the museum along with vintage film clips. (Open Sat. and Sun. 10am-4pm. Admission $3.50, seniors and students $2.50, kids $1.50. Ample free parking.)

Music is another industry greasing Hollywood's cash-register wheels. The preeminent monument of the modern record industry is the 1954 **Capitol Records Tower,** 1750 Vine St., just north of Hollywood Blvd. The building looks like a stack of records, American architectural kitsch-literalism at its most Californian. More esoteric music and associated paraphernalia can be found at **The Rock Shop,** 6666 Hollywood Blvd. (466-7276), which carries records and tapes, CDs, posters, T-shirts, thousands of buttons, handkerchiefs, tour and promotional merchandise, World War II artifacts, and leather and metal accessories. Isn't that special? Hollywood stars prove less elusive when they are six feet under, and the **Hollywood Cemetery**, at 6000 Santa Monica Blvd. (469-1181), between Vine St. and Western Ave., is the permanent home to the remains of Rudolph Valentino, Douglas Fairbanks, Sr., and other Hollywood notables. (Open daily 8am-5pm.)

The **Hollyhock House,** 4808 Hollywood Blvd. (662-7272), commands a 360° view of Los Angeles and the mountains. Completed in 1922 for eccentric oil heiress Aline Barnsdall, the house remains one of Frank Lloyd Wright's most important works. It is the first building by this pre-eminent modern American architect to reflect the influence of pre-Columbian Mayan temples. The name of the house derives from Barnsdall's favorite flower, which she had Wright reproduce (grudgingly) in abstract all over the house. (Tours Tues.-Thurs. on the hour from 10am-1pm; Sat. and all but the last Sun. each month noon-3pm. Admission $1.50, seniors $1, under 13 free. Buy tickets at the Municipal Art Gallery.) Call to arrange foreign language tours of Hollyhock House (485-4581). About 3 mi. northeast of downtown is **Elysian Park;** with 525 acres of greenery, the park is divine for picnicking. The park largely surrounds and embraces the area of Chavez Ravine, home of **Dodger Stadium** (224-1400) and the Los Angeles Dodgers baseball team. Tickets, which cost from $5 to $10 (all seats have good views of the field), are a hot commodity when the Dodgers are playing well. Purchase in advance if possible, or get a lesson in supply and demand from scalpers outside. Once in the ballpark, grab yourself a Dodger Dog, one of the best dogs in the majors, although a 1991 brouhaha over a change in the wieners' preparation left a bad taste in the mouth of many fans. Sprawling over 4500 acres of hilly terrain is **Griffith Park.** The L.A. Zoo, the Greek Theater, Griffith Observatory and Planetarium, Travel Town, a bird sanctuary, tennis courts, two golf courses, campgrounds, and various hiking trails blanket the dry hills and mountains. This formidable recreational region stretches from the hills above Hollywood north to the intersection of the Ventura and Golden State Freeways. Pick up a map at any of the entrance points. A full day in the Park might include the zoo in the morning, the rest of the park during the afternoon, and the Greek Theater or the planetarium's laser show in the evening. For info, stop by the **visitors center and ranger headquarters,** 4730 Crystal Spring Dr. (665-5188; open daily 6am-10pm).

If you enjoy seeing stars, head for the park's **Observatory and Planetarium** (664-1181, for a recording 664-1191). The white stucco and copper domes of this Art-Deco structure are visible from around the park. You also might remember it from the climactic last scene of the James Dean film, *Rebel Without a Cause.* The exhibits in the Hall of Science are good but no different from other planetarium displays. One of the most interesting is a seismograph that runs continually: if you're there when the Big One comes, you'll know just how big it was. A 12-in. telescope opens the public eye to the sky every clear night from dusk-9:45pm; in winter Tues.-Sun. 7-10pm. (Call the sky report at 663-8171 for more info.) The planetarium also presents popular **Laserium** light shows (997-3624), psychedelic symphonies of colored lasers and music. (Observatory open daily 12:30pm-10pm; winter hours Tues.-Sun. 2-10pm. Free. Hour-long planetarium show Mon.-Fri. at 3 and 7:30pm, Sat.-Sun. also at 4:30pm; in winter Tues.-Fri. 3 and 8pm, Sat.-Sun. also at 4:30pm. Admission $3.50, seniors and under 15 $2.50. Laser shows Sun., Tues.-Thurs. at 6pm and 8:30pm; Fri.-Sat. also at 9:45pm. Admission $6, kids $5.)

A large **bird sanctuary** at the bottom of the observatory hill serves its function well, but if you crave the sight of warm-blooded animals, you might go to the **L.A. Zoo,** at the park's northern end (666-4090). The zoo's 113 acres accommodate 2000 crazy critters, and the facility is consistently ranked among the nation's 10 best. (Open daily 10am-6pm; in winter 10am-5pm. Admission $6, seniors $5, ages 2-12 $2.75, under 2 free. Ticket office closes 1 hr. before zoo.)

On the southern side of the park, below the observatory, the 4500-seat **Greek Theater** (665-5857) hosts a number of concerts in its outdoor amphitheater virtually year-round. Check ads in the *Sunday Times* "Calendar" section for coming attractions. Those with a hankerin' to relive those wild, wild days of yore will enjoy the recently opened **Gene Autry Western Heritage Museum,** 4700 Zoo Dr. (667-2000), also located within Griffith Park at the junction of Golden State (I-5) and Ventura Fwy (Rte. 134). The museum's collection covers both fact and fiction of the Old West, with exhibits on pioneer life and on the history of western films. The Hollywood section includes costumes donated by Robert Redford, Gary Cooper, and Clint Eastwood. Firearms owned by George Custer, Wyatt Earp, Billy the Kid, and Teddy Roosevelt are on display in the historical exhibit. The elaborate displays succeed in evoking the aura of a wilder time. (Open Tues.-Sun. 10am-5pm. Admission $4.75, seniors and students $3.50, kids $2.) To get to the Observatory and Greek Theater, take bus #203 from Hollywood. To reach the Zoo and Travel Town, take bus #97 from downtown. There is no bus service between the northern and southern parts of Griffith Park.

West Hollywood

Once considered a no-man's land between Beverly Hills and Hollywood, West Hollywood was incorporated in 1985 and was one of the first cities in the country to be governed by openly gay officials. There's always a lot going on here, and a list of each month's events can be found in the *L.A. Weekly.*

In the years before incorporation, lax zoning and other liberal laws gave rise to the sybaritic **Sunset Strip,** nurturing bands such as The Doors and Guns 'n' Roses. These days, most of the music on this stretch is heavy metal and hard rock, and weekend nights draw tremendous crowds and traffic jams. Restaurants and comedy clubs flourish here as well.

Melrose Avenue, south of West Hollywood, is lined with swish restaurants, ultra-trendy boutiques, punk clothing pits, and art galleries. The choicest stretch is between La Brea and Fairfax, but the *Repo Man*-like spectre of angst-ridden apocalyptic apathy haunts the whole 3-mi. distance between Highland and Doheny. Packed with pedestrians (mostly locals), especially on weekends, the lively street displays some of L.A.'s most unusual and stylized people. At the corner of Beverly and San Vicente Blvd. is the Los Angeles **Hard Rock Café** (310-276-7605). A pistachio-green '57 Chevy juts out of the roof, unsuccessfully attempting to escape the crowds within. Indiana Jones's leather jacket, one of Pete Townshend's guitars, a 6-ft.-tall martini glass, license plates, and college banners adorn the interior. Expect to tarry for a table every night of the week—over an hour on weekends. Don't you have anything else you could be doing? (Open Sun.-Thurs. 11:30am-midnight, Fri.-Sat. 11:30am-1am.)

North of the Beverly Center, at Melrose and San Vicente, is the **Pacific Design Center,** 8687 Melrose Ave. (310-657-0800), a huge blue-and-green glass complex with a wavey profile (nicknamed **The Blue Whale**). The building, completed in 1976, seems destined for architectural history texts. In addition to some design showrooms, the PDC houses a public plaza with a 350-seat amphitheater, used to stage free summer concerts. Call or inquire at the info desk in the entryway for details about such events. West Hollywood's **Gay Pride Weekend Celebration** (in late June) is usually held at the PDC plaza.

Beverly Hills

Though placed in the midst of Greater Los Angeles, about 2/3 of the way between downtown L.A. and the coast, Beverly Hills remains a steadfast enclave of wealth. Beverly Hills seceded from L.A. in 1914 and has remained in every way distinct from the city ever since. Consider this: the Beverly Hills Post Office (on Beverly Dr.) has *valet parking.* Even the homeless are well-dressed (otherwise they'd be gently escorted to the city's edge by Beverly Hills' remarkably efficient police force). The heart of the city rests in the **Golden Triangle,** a wedge formed by Wilshire and Santa Monica Blvd. centering on **Rodeo Drive,** known for its many opulent clothing boutiques and jewelry shops. You might feel underdressed simply window-shopping. Across the way is the venerable **Beverly Wilshire Hotel,** (310-275-5200) whose old and new wings are connected by El Camino Real, a cobbled street with Louis XIV gates. Inside, hall mirrors reflect the glitter of crystal chandeliers and marble floors. Beverly Hills' new **Civic Center,** completed in September 1990, includes the Beverly Hills Fire Department, Police Station, and library. It took nine years and $120 million to build. Designed by Charles Moore, the Civic Center's Post-Modern pastiche of Spanish Baroque, Art Deco, and Art Moderne is sure to win architectural awards (even the library's parking structure is something to see). The **Beverly Hills Library** (444 N. Rexford Dr.; 213-228-2220) is a case study in the city's overriding priorities—the interior is adorned with marble imported from Thailand, but contains a paltry collection of books.

The scores of other major and minor architectural triumphs and tragedies are as inevitable as new movies and TV shows with the words "Beverly Hills" in the title. A few examples: the **"Greystone Mansion"** (or Doheny House) is a modern-day Versailles. Built by oil mogul Doheny for his son, the Tudor and Jacobean house includes the main building, two gatehouses, glorious gardens, and a stunning view of Los Angeles (905 Loma Vista Drive, just off Doheny Rd.; gardens free, open to the public daily 10am-6pm). The **Virginia Robinson Gardens**, nearby, are open to the public by reservation only (310-276-5367; tours of gardens and the 1911 beaux arts house offered Tues.-Fri. at 10am and 1pm; adults $3, seniors, students and kids $2.25). Back down near Santa Monica, the Gaudiesque dripping ornamentation of the O'Neil House (507 N. Rodeo Dr.) is best seen from the alley behind the house. The Spadena House on the Southeast corner of Carmelita Avenue and Walden Dr. looks as if it belongs to the Wicked Witch of the West.

Those who may be considering hopping on a stargazing **tour bus,** be forewarned: the only people visible on the streets are gardeners, and many of them don't even know whom they're working for. Since you'll never know the difference, some tours feel free to make things up as they go along. A better alternative is the **Beverly Hills Trolley,** which can be picked up at Dayton and Rodeo and runs to Sunset and back every half hour (310-275-2791; $1, Tues.-Sat. 10am-6:15pm).

Just outside of Beverly Hills, the **Beit HaShoa Museum of Tolerance** will be opening in April of 1992 (310-553-9036; 9786 W. Pico Blvd. on the corner of Roxbury). Previously known as the Simon Wiesenthal Center, the museum received $5 million from former Governor Deukmeijian to build a new, larger, structure on the condition that the museum include displays on the Armenian and Native American genocides. The new museum's high-tech wizardry is designed to help visitors explore their own prejudices, with displays on the Holocaust, anti-semitism and prejudice in the U.S., and the U.S. Civil Rights movement. (Hours and prices have not been determined, but are likely to be: admission $5 with student and senior discounts; Mon.-Thurs. 9am-5pm, Fri. 9am-3pm, Sun. 11am-4pm.)

Westwood and UCLA

Welcome to Scooterville! The gargantuan **University of California at Los Angeles** campus (it covers over 400 acres in the foothills of the Santa Monica Mountains, bounded by Sunset, Hilgard, Le Conte, and Gayley) and the dearth of parking spaces make both UCLA and Westwood look like motorbike versions of Disneyland's *autopia*. The school is directly north of Westwood Village and west of Beverly Hills. To reach the campus by car, take the San Diego Fwy. (I-405) north to the Wilshire Blvd./Westwood exit, heading east into Westwood. Take Westwood Blvd. north off Wilshire, heading straight through the center of the village and directly into the campus. By bus, take RTD route #20, 21 (the best, since it goes directly to the campus), 22, 320, or 322 along Wilshire Blvd. to Westwood. Exit at Wilshire and Gayley and walk north to Gayley and Weyburn Ave., where you can pick up a free UCLA Campus Express shuttle to the center of campus. Drivers can find free parking behind the Federal Building and, on Friday and Saturday nights, avoid the 10-minute walk into the village by riding the 10¢ **RTD Shuttle** (Fri. 6:30pm-1:30am, Sat. 11am-1:30am). Those who wish to park on campus may do so by paying $4 at one of the campus info kiosks; you will receive a day permit allowing you to park in the student garages.

The best place to start a tour of UCLA is at the **Visitors Center,** 10945 Le Conte Ave., #147 (206-8147), located in the Ueberroth Olympic Office Building. Free 90-minute walking tours of the campus depart from the visitors center at 10:30am and at 1:30pm Monday to Friday. Campus maps are also available at the info kiosks located at each of the streets leading into the campus.

Royce Hall, situated in the Quadrangle, is the architectural pride and joy of the UCLA Campus, and **Powell Library,** at the campus's south end, is the main undergraduate library and reflects an Islamic influence in its architectural design. At the northernmost reach of the campus, the **Dickson Art Center** (825-1462) houses the Wight Art Gallery, home to the Grunwald Center for the Graphic Arts, as well as frequent internationally recognized exhibitions. (Open Sept.-June Tues. 11am-8pm, Wed.-Fri. 11am-5pm, Sat. and Sun. 1-5pm. Free.) The **Murphy Sculpture Garden,** containing over 70 pieces scattered through five acres, lies directly in front of the Art Center. The collection includes works by Rodin, Matisse, and Miró. Another heralded piece of outdoor artwork is UCLA's **Inverted Fountain,** located between Knudsen Hall and Schoenberg Hall, directly south of Dickson Plaza. Water spouts from the fountain's perimeter and rushes down into the gaping hole in the middle. The **Botanical Gardens** (825-1260), in the southeast corner of the campus, encompass a subtropical canyon where brook-side redwoods and palms mingle (open year-round Mon.-Fri. 8am-5pm, Sat.-Sun. 8am-4pm). There is also a surreally serene **Japanese Garden.** (Open Tues. 10am-1pm, Wed. noon-3pm, by appointment only. Reservations should be made a couple of weeks in advance. Call the visitors center at 825-4574 or 825-4338 to arrange for a tour.)

Ackerman Union, 308 Westwood Plaza (825-7711), stands southwest of the Quadrangle, at the bottom of the hill, the campus info bank. A calendar lists the month's lengthy line-up of movies (first-runs often free), lectures, and campus activities. The Expo Center, on level B, has travel info and a complete **rideboard.** Next door you'll find a bowling alley and enough fast-food joints to satisfy a sumo wrestling team. (Open Mon.-Fri. 8:30am-6pm, Sat. 10am-5pm, Sun. noon-5pm.) The ground floor is swallowed by the **Associated Students Students' Store** (825-0611), the largest on-campus store in the U.S. (Open Mon.-Thurs. 7:45am-7:30pm, Fri. 7:45am-6pm, Sat. 10am-5pm, Sun. noon-5pm.)

The UCLA men's basketball team, which won seven consecutive NCAA championships in the 60s and 70s, plays its home games at **Pauley Pavilion,** located to the west of Dickson Plaza, down Bruin Walk, next to the impressive **Bruin Bear Statue** (depicting the school's mascot). Behind the major ursa is the **UCLA Athletic Hall of Fame** (inside the J.D. Morgan Intercollegiate Athletic Center). The other athletic facilities are clustered around Pauley.

Westwood Village, just south of the campus, with its myriad movie theaters, trendy boutiques, and upscale bistros, is geared more toward the residents of L.A.'s Westside than collegians. Like most college neighborhoods, however, Westwood hums on Friday and Saturday nights when everyone (high schoolers, collegians, tourists, gang members, and police) show up to do their thing.

At 14523 Sunset, hike around **Will Rogers State Historical Park** (454-8212) and take in the panoramic views of the city and the distant Pacific. You can visit the famous horseman's home and eat a picnic brunch while watching polo matches on the grounds on Saturday afternoons (2-5pm) and Sunday mornings (10am-noon). Follow Chautauqua Blvd. inland from PCH to Sunset Blvd., or take bus #2 which runs along Sunset Blvd. (Park open daily 8am-7pm; Rogers's house open daily 10am-5pm.)

Santa Monica

To a resident of turn-of-the-century L.A., a trip to the beach resort of Santa Monica meant a long ride over poor-quality roads. The Red Car electric train shortened the trip considerably, and today it takes about half an hour (with no traffic) on Big Blue express bus #10 or on the Santa Monica Freeway (I-10) from downtown. No longer far away, SaMo is still pretty far out, with an extremely liberal city council and the former Mr. Jane Fonda (Tom Hayden, one of the Chicago Seven) as one of its assemblymen. Its beach is the closest to L.A. proper, and thus crowded and dirty. Still, the magical lure of sun, surf, and sand causes nightmarish summer traffic jams on I-10 and I-405 (beaches to the north and south are much prettier and cleaner). The colorful **Santa Monica Pier** is still a nostalgic and popular, if a bit sleazy, spot. The gem of the pier is the magnificent turn-of the-century carousel, which was featured in *The Sting*. **Palisades Park,** on the bluff overlooking the pier, provides a shaded home for numerous homeless people. With the creation of the **Third Street Promenade** in 1989, and the recent remodeling of its upscale neighbor, **Santa Monica Place** (see Shopping), Santa Monica has recently become one of L.A.'s major walking, movie-seeing, and yuppie mating areas. The Promenade sports some cool cafés, a couple of L.A.'s better bookshops, overpriced bars and restaurants, and a number of fine, fresh street artists (not to mention some water-spouting, ivy-lined, mesh dinosaur sculptures).

Venice

The most unique part of a unique city, Venice is Los Angeles' saving grace for budget travelers. A perennial favorite among foreigners, Venice is wacky on week-days, wild on weekends. A typical Sunday includes trapeze artists, spontaneous rol-lerblade dancing competitions, and your run-of-the-mill clowns, jugglers, comedi-ans, glass-eaters, hemp advocates, bikini-clad skaters, fortune tellers, and choirs of gaping Angelenos. With everyone crowding the beachfront, trying either to see or be seen, life in Venice is, as one hostel brochure aptly puts it, "spontaneous theater."

Venice's story begins just after the turn of the century, when Abbot Kinney dug a series of canals throughout the town and filled them with water, intending to bring the romance and refinement of Venice, Italy, to Southern California. But the water became dirty and oily, and instead of attracting society's upper crust, developed a crust of its own. Venice became home to gamblers, bootleggers, and other assorted rogues. The canals eventually were forgotten and, for the most part, filled in and buried. Skateboarders use some of the others. For a sense of the Venice that Kinney envisioned, head for the traffic circle at Main St. and Windward Ave., three blocks inland from the beach pavilion. This was once a circular canal, the hub of the whole network. The post office on the circle's west side has a small mural inside that sums up Venice's cluttered history in an appropriately jumbled way—with oil derricks seemingly perched on Kinney's shoulders. Back outside on Main St., walk down Windward to its intersection with Pacific Ave. Columns and tiled awnings are all that remain of the grandiose hotels that once housed vacationers from Los Angeles. Health-food shops and vintage clothing stores lie behind the colonnades where se-dans once discharged high-styled passengers. One of the sole surviving canals is at Strong's Dr., off Washington St. Ducks are its liveliest inhabitants.

Venice finally came into its own in the 70s, when the Sexual Revolution spawned a swinging beach community. Although the revolution may have been defeated, Venice's peculiar beach renaissance lives on, a testament to the ongoing allure of the credo, "Do your own thing."**Ocean Front Walk,** Venice's main beach front drag, is a drastic demographic departure from Santa Monica's Promenade. Street people converge on shaded clusters of benches, healthy-types play paddle tennis, and bodybuilders of both sexes pump iron in skimpy outfits at the original **Muscle Beach** (1800 Ocean Front Walk, closest to 18th and Pacific Ave.). This is where the roller-skating craze began, and this is probably where it will breathe its last. Even the police wear shorts while slapping nude sunbathers (hopefully not too hard) with $55 fines. New Wave types, cyclists, joggers, groovy elders (such as the "skate-board grandma"), and bards in Birkenstocks make up the balance of this funky play-ground population. Venders of jewelry, snacks, and beach bric-a-brac overwhelm the boardwalk and are sights themselves. Collect your wits and take in the crowds from a distance at one of the many cafés or juice bars. If your feet don't move you through the crowds fast enough, rent rollerblades or a bike. The cheapest rental place is **Sports and Stuff,** on Washington. (Rollerblades $4 per hour, $8 per day; bikes $2.50 per hour, $5 per day. Open daily 9am-6pm.)

Venice's **street murals** are another free show. Don't miss the brilliant, grafitti-disfigured homage to Botticelli's *Birth of Venus* on the beach pavilion at the end of Windward Ave.: an angelically beautiful woman, wearing short-shorts, a Band-aid top, and roller-skates, boogies out of her seashell. The side wall of a Japanese restaurant on Windward is covered with a perfect imitation of a Japanese Hokusai print of a turbulent sea. Large insect sculptures loom in the rafters of many of the city's posh restaurants. To look at paintings indoors, you might want to stop by **L.A. Louver,** 77 Market St. and 55 N. Venice Blvd. (822-4955), a gallery showing the work of some hip L.A. artists (open Tues.-Sat. noon-5pm).

To get to Venice from downtown L.A., take bus #33 or 333 (or 436 during rush hour). From downtown Santa Monica, take Santa Monica bus #1 or 2.

The Pacific Coast Highway

From Santa Monica, where it temporarily merges with I-10, the **Pacific Coast Highway (PCH)** (Rte. 1) runs northward along the spectacular California coast. Several of L.A. county's best beaches line this stretch of the PCH between Santa Monica and the Ventura County line.

Heading north from Santa Monica, the first major attraction is the **J. Paul Getty Museum,** 17985 PCH (458-2003), set back on a cliff above the ocean. Getty, an oil magnate, built this mansion as a re-creation of the 1st-century Villa dei Papiri in Herculaneum, with a beautiful main peristyle garden, a reflecting pool, and bush-lined paths. Due to the museum's operating agreement with its residential neighbors, access to the museum is more difficult than it could be. The parking lot is small, and reservations are needed, a day in advance most of the time, weeks in advance in summer. You are not permitted to park outside the museum unless you do so at the county lot. Bicyclists and motorcyclists are admitted without reservations. Take RTD #434 (which you can board at Sunset and PCH in Malibu or Ocean and Colorado in Santa Monica) to the museum and mind that you ask for a free **museum pass** from the bus driver. The museum gate is ½-mi. from the bus stop, so be prepared to walk. (Open Tues.-Sun. 10am-5pm. Free.)

The celebrity colony of **Malibu** stretches along the low-20000 blocks of PCH. With their multi-million dollar homes and celebrity neighbors, Malibu residents can afford to be hostile to nonlocals, especially to those from the Valley. The beach lies along the 23200 block of the PCH. You can walk onto the beach via the **Zonker Harris** access way at 22700 PCH, named after the quintessential Californian of Garry Trudeau's comic strip, *Doonesbury.* **Corral State Beach,** an uncrowded, windsurfing, swimming, and scuba-diving beach, lies on the 26000 block of PCH, followed by **Point Dume State Beach,** which is small and generally uncrowded.

North of Point Dume, along the 30000 block of PCH, lies **Zuma,** L.A. County's northernmost and largest county-owned sandbox, with lifeguards, restrooms, and a $5 parking fee. Stations 8 to 12 belong to solitude-seekers. The Valley high-schoolers have staked out 6 and 7, which are the most crowded and lively parts. Zuma 3, 4, and 5 are frequented by families who keep things slightly more sedate. If you don't want to bring food, pick something up at **Trancas Market** (PCH and Trancas Canyon, around Station 12). Evade the beach stands unless you're willing to pay $2.75 for an insipid hamburger or hot dog.

Finally, visitors with cars should not miss **Mulholland Drive,** nature's answer to the roller coaster (south of Big Sur). Twisting and turning for 15 spectacular mi. along the crest of the Santa Monica Mountains, Mulholland stretches from PCH, near the Ventura County line, east to the Hollywood Fwy. and San Fernando Valley. Whoever's driving will have a hard time concentrating—numerous points along the way, especially between Coldwater Canyon and the San Diego Fwy., have compelling views of the entire Los Angeles basin. Avoid Mulholland on late weekend nights, when the road is fraught with drag-racing teenagers and parked cars on Lover's Lane. Racers use both lanes, and four headlights coming at you at 70mph can be an even more arresting sight than all the panoramic lights of what Aldous Huxley called "the city of dreadful joy."

San Fernando Valley

At the end of the Ventura Freeway lies, like, the spiritual center of American suburbia, dude, a seemingly infinite series of heinous communities with tree-lined streets, cookie-cutter homes, lawns, and shopping malls. A most egregious third of L.A.'s population resides here, where the portion of the Valley incorporated into the City of Los Angeles alone covers 140 million acres. The area was settled after city engineer William Mulholland brought water to the valley in 1913. Standing on a hillside overlooking the basin, Mulholland watched the first torrents pour out of the Los Angeles Aqueduct, and proclaimed "There it is; take it!" The city rushed to obey.

Ventura Boulevard, mentioned in the Tom Petty song "Free Falling," is the main commercial thoroughfare. The sprawling valley viewed from the foothills at night, particularly from Mulholland Drive, is spectacular. Once you've finished searching Ventura Blvd. for the ultimate valley hangout (try a Denny's on a weekend night between 2 and 4am), you may want to check out the Valley's only worthwhile tourist spot, the **Mission San Fernando Ray De España.** The mission was founded in 1797 by Padre Fermin Lasuen, but, unfortunately, no structures remain from this period. The old **Iglesia** was destroyed by the 1971 earthquake, and the **Convento** has been covered with stucco, making the cemetery and the park across the street the most intriguing part of the mission. West of the mission, at 10940 Sepulveda, sits the **Andres Pico Adobe,** the former home of Pico, who started the first wave of construction in the valley in 1845 when he built up his own copious tracts of land. The house has been remodeled somewhat.

Pasadena

Pasadena, a suburb about 10 mi. northeast of downtown Los Angeles, offers the perfect antidote to the hectic pace of Greater L.A. Pasadena is placid, with pleasant tree-lined streets and outstanding cultural facilities. You can get there along the Pasadena Fwy. (Rte. 110 North), where drivers are required to merge almost instantaneously with 55-mph traffic from a dead stop.

In the gorge that forms the city's western boundary stands Pasadena's most famous landmark, the **Rose Bowl,** 991 Rosemont Blvd. (818-793-7193, Rose Bowl Event Information Line 577-3106). Home to college football bowl game of the same name, the annual confrontation between the champions of the Big Ten and Pac 10 conferences, the Rose Bowl is also regular-season home to the UCLA Bruins football team. The New Year's Day Rose Bowl game follows the **Tournament of Roses Parade,** which runs along Colorado Blvd. through downtown Pasadena. Thousands line the Pasadena streets (having staked out choice viewing spots days in advance) to watch the flower-covered floats go by. To reach the Rose Bowl, take the Pasadena Fwy. to its end and follow the signs of Arroyo Pkwy.

At the western end of the downtown area (also called Old Pasadena), lies Pasadena's answer to LACMA and the Getty Museum, the **Norton Simon Museum of Art,** 411 W. Colorado Blvd. (449-3730), at Orange Grove Blvd. The collection includes numerous Rodin and Brancusi bronzes, and masterpieces by Rembrandt, Raphael, and Picasso. The ancient Southeast Asian art collection is one of the world's best. Simon's eclectic, slightly idiosyncratic tastes, as well as the well-written descriptions of the works, make this museum more interesting than similar assemblages elsewhere. (Open Thurs.-Sun. noon-6pm. Admission $4, seniors and students $2, under 12 free; wheelchair accessible.) From downtown L.A. take bus #483 from Olive St., anywhere between Venice Blvd. and 1st St., to Colorado Blvd. and Fair Oaks Ave. in Pasadena. The museum is four blocks west. Some of the world's greatest scientific minds do their work at the West Coast rival to the Massachusetts Institute of Technology, the **California Institute of Technology,** 1201 E. California Blvd. (356-6811), about 2½ mi. southeast of downtown. The campus is lush, filled with bush- and olive-tree-lined brick paths. The buildings incorporate a mishmash of Spanish, Italian Renaissance, and modern styles. Caltech, founded in 1891 as Throop University, has amassed a faculty which includes several Nobel prizewinners (Albert Einstein once taught here) and a student body which prides itself both on its high I.Q. and its elaborate and ingenious practical jokes. These range from the mundane (unscrewing all the chairs in a lecture hall and bolting them in backwards) to the audacious (altering the Rose Bowl scoreboard during the big game with the aid of computers).

A half-mile to the south of Cal Tech lies the **Huntington Library, Art Gallery, and Botanical Gardens,** 1151 Oxford Rd., San Marino 91108 (405-2100, ticket info 405-2273). Despite the ban on picnics and sunbathing, families and tourists still flock here on Sundays to stroll around the grounds and visit the library and galleries. The stunning botanical gardens nurture 207 acres of plants, many of them rare. The library houses one of the world's most important collections of rare books and English and American manuscripts, including Benjamin Franklin's handwritten autobiography and the obligatory Gutenberg Bible. The art gallery also is known for its 18th- and 19th-century British paintings. Sentimental favorites on exhibit include Thomas Gainsborough's *Blue Boy* and its companion piece, Sir Thomas Lawrence's *Pinkie.* (Open Tues.-Fri. 1-4:30pm, Sat.-Sun. 10:30am-4:30pm; free, but donation expected.) The museum sits between Huntington Dr. and California Blvd. in San Marino, just south of Pasadena. From downtown L.A., Bus #79 leaves from Olive St., and takes you straight to the library (a 40- to 45-min. trip).

Near Pasadena

Recent remodeling and a spate of innovative exhibits may earn the **Southwest Museum,** 234 Museum Dr. (213-221-2163), the attention it deserves. L.A. offers no better resource to those interested in the history and culture of the Southwest. The museum, housed in a palatial Hispano-Moorish home on a hill, sports a collection of artifacts among the best in the nation, including contemporary Native American art. Take bus #83 along Broadway to Museum Dr. and trek up the hill. Drivers should take the Pasadena Fwy. (Rte. 110) to Ave. 43 and follow the signs. (Open Tues.-Sun. 11am-5pm. Admission $4, seniors and students $2, ages 7-18 $1. Library open Wed.-Sat. 11am-5pm.)

If you don't find any celebrities on the street, you can find many in their graves at the renowned **Forest Lawn** cemetery, 1712 Glendale Ave., Glendale (241-4151). Analyzed by Jessica Mitford as the showy emblem of the "American Way of Death," its grounds include reproductions of many of Michelangelo's works, the "largest religious painting on earth" (the famous 195-ft. version of the *Crucifixion*), a stained-glass *Last Supper,* and innumerable other works of "art." Stop at the entrance for a map of the cemetery's sights, and pick up a guide to the paintings and sculpture at the administration building nearby. (Open daily 8am-5pm.) From downtown, take bus #90 or 91 and disembark just after the bus leaves San Fernando Rd. to turn onto Glendale Ave. Forest Lawn is easily approached from this side of paradise via the Golden State Fwy. or Glendale Fwy. (Rte. 2).

Entertainment

"Vast wasteland" mythology to the contrary, L.A.'s cultural scene is in fact active and diverse. If you're staying in Hollywood or have a car, you can spend all your time in L.A. enjoying a Vampire-like revelry.

Film and Television Studios

All of the major TV studios offer free tickets to show tapings. Some are available on a first-come, first-served basis from the Visitors Information Center of the Greater L.A. Visitor and Convention Bureau or by mail. Some networks won't send tickets to out-of-state addresses, but they will send a guest card or letter that can be redeemed for tickets. Be sure to enclose a self-addressed, stamped envelope. Write: Tickets, Capital City/ABC Inc., 4151 Prospect, Hollywood 90027 (577-7777); CBS Tickets, 7800 Beverly Blvd., Los Angeles 90036 (818-840-3537); NBC-TV, 3000 W. Alameda Ave., Burbank 91523 (840-3537); or FOX Tickets, 100 Universal City Plaza, Bldg. 153, Universal City 91608 (818-506-0043). Tickets also are available to shows produced by Paramount Television, 780 N. Gower St., Hollywood 90038 (213-956-5000). Tickets don't guarantee admittance; arrive a couple of hours early, as seating is also first-come, first-served.

Universal Studios, Universal City (818-508-9600). Hollywood Fwy. to Lankershim. Take bus #424 to Lankershim Blvd. For a hefty fee, the studio will take you for a ride; visit the Bates

Motel and other sets, watch Conan the Barbarian flex his pecs, be attacked by Jaws, get caught in a flash flood, experience an 8.3 earthquake, and witness a variety of special effects and other demonstrations of movie-making magic. No reservations are accepted. Arrive early to secure a ticket. Allow 2½ hr. for the tour and at least an hour for wandering. Tours in Spanish Sat. and Sun. Open summer and holidays 7:30am-10:30pm (last tram leaves at 5pm); Sept.-June Mon.-Fri. 10am-3:30pm, Sat. and Sun. 9:30am-3:30pm. Admission $24.50, ages 3-11 and over 65 $19. Parking $4.

NBC Television Studios Tour, 3000 W. Alameda Ave. (818-840-3572), at Olive Ave. in Burbank, 2 mi. from Universal. Hollywood Fwy. north, exit east on Barham Blvd., which becomes Olive Ave. Take bus #420 from Hill St. downtown. The tour is cancelled but may reopen in 1992. Call for info.

Warner Bros. VIP Tour, 4000 Warner Blvd., Burbank (818-954-1744). Personalized, unstaged tours (max. 12 people) through the Warner Bros. studios. These are technical, 2-hr. treks which chronicle the detailed reality of the movie-making art. No children under 10. Tours Mon.-Fri. 10am and 2pm, additional tours in summer. $22 per person. Reservations required in advance.

Cinema

In the technicolored heaven of Los Angeles, movie theaters cover the city like smog. Foreign films play consistently at the six **Laemmle Theaters** in Beverly Hills, West L.A., Santa Monica, Pasadena, Encino, and downtown.

A unique movie-going treat is the **Mitsubishi IMAX Theater,** at the California Museum of Science and Industry (213-744-2014; see Exposition Park Sights). Movies are shown on a 54×70-ft. screen. The films, of the entertainment-documentary variety, surround the viewer with brilliant sights and sounds. (Admission $5, seniors and under 12 $3.50.)

For film screening info, dial 777-FILM.

Cineplex Odeon Universal City Cinemas, atop the hill at Universal Studios (818-508-0588). Take the Universal Center Dr. exit off the Hollywood Fwy. (U.S. 101). Opened in 1987 as the world's largest cinema complex. The 18 wide-screen theaters, 2 *Parisienne*-style cafés, and opulent decoration put all others to shame. Hooray for Hollywood.

Mann's Chinese, 6925 Hollywood Blvd. (213-464-8111). Hollywood hype to the hilt. For more details, see Hollywood Sights.

Beverly Cineplex (310-652-7760), atop the Beverly Center, on Beverly Dr. at La Cienaga. Unlike most first-run cinemas, the Cineplex screens movies in auditoriums hardly bigger than your living room. But it shows 14 of them every night, a combination of recent hits and artsy discoveries.

Village Theatre, 961 Broxton (310-208-5576), in Westwood. No multiplex nonsense here. One auditorium, one big screen, one great THX sound system, a balcony, and Art-Deco design. Watch the back rows and balcony for late-arriving celebrities.

Comedy

The talent may be imported from New York and other parts of the country, but that doesn't change the fact that L.A.'s comedy clubs are the best in the world (unless you happen to chance upon an amateur night, which is generally a painful experience). Some clubs are open only a few nights weekly. Call ahead to check age restrictions. Cover charges are cheaper during the week, with fewer crowds but just as much fun.

Comedy Store, 8433 Sunset Blvd. (213-656-6225). The shopping mall of comedy clubs, with 3 different rooms, each featuring a different type of comedy. (Each room charges its own cover.) Go to the Main Room for the big-name stuff and the most expensive cover charges (around $14). The Original Room features mid-range comics for $6-8. The Belly Room has the real grab-bag material, often for no cover charge. Over 21 only; 2-drink minimum.

The Improvisation, 8162 Melrose Ave. (213-651-2583). Offers L.A.'s best talent, including, on occasion, Robin Williams or Robert Klein. Their restaurant serves Italian fare. Open nightly, check *L.A. Weekly* for times. Cover $8-10, 2-drink minimum.

Improvisation in Santa Monica, 321 Santa Monica Blvd. (310-394-8664). The beach version of its Hollywood cousin is more laid-back, and brand new. Tex-Mex food in the restaurant, cover $8-10, 2-drink minimum. A third Improvisation is located in Irvine, and a fourth in the Valley.

The Comedy Act Theater, 3339 W. 43rd St. (310-677-4101). A comedy club targeted at an African-American audience, often featuring such nationally known comedians as Robert Townsend and Marsha Warfield. Open Thurs.-Sat. 8:30pm on. Cover $10.

Theater and Classical Music

Los Angeles is blessed with one of the most active theater circuits on the West Coast. About 115 Equity Waiver theaters (under 100 seats) offer a dizzying choice for theatergoers, who can also take in small productions in museums, art galleries, universities, parks, and even garages. During the summer hiatus, TV stars frequently return here to revel in the "legitimate theatre." Mainstream theater merits the high prices for shows that are either Broadway-bound or beginning their national tour after a New York run. The **L.A. Weekly** has comprehensive listings of L.A. theatres both big and small.

Concerts

The commonly used concert venues range from small to massive. The Wiltern Theater (213-381-5005) has presented artists such as Suzanne Vega and The Church. The Hollywood Palladium (213-466-4311) is of comparable size. Mid-size acts head for the Universal Amphitheater (818-890-9421) and the Greek Theater (310-410-1062). Capacious indoor sports arenas, such as the Sports Arena (213-748-6131) or the Forum (310-419-3182), double as concert halls for large shows. Few performers dare to play at the over 100,000-seat L.A. Coliseum. Only U2, Bruce Springsteen, and the Rolling Stones have attempted this feat in recent years.

Bars

L.A. isn't known for its bar scene, but bars do exist, and generally hold a slightly older, and more subdued crowd than do the clubs. Bars on Santa Monica Promenade are presently some of the most popular in L.A.

Molly Malone's, 575 S. Fairfax (213-935-1579). Not your typical Irish pub—showcases some of L.A.'s big up-and-coming bands. Cover varies. Open 10am-1:30pm.

Small's Bar, 5574 Melrose Ave. (213-469-8258), inside what appears to be an auto-body work shop (no sign, just look for the crowds). No cover, no entertainment, just an extremely popular bar. A standard on Thursday nights, especially with the not-yet-famous "industry" folk. Open daily 11am-2am.

Al's Bar, 305 S. Hewitt St. (687-3558), in downtown. One of L.A. nightlife's best-hidden secrets. Wide range of nightly entertainment: traditional rock 'n roll, poetry, experimental bands, performance art and more. Call for info. Open daily 1pm-2:30am.

Clubs

The Club scene is what makes L.A.'s nightlife. With the highest number of bands per capita in the world, most clubs are able to book top-notch bands night after night. The distinction between music clubs and dance clubs is a bit sketchy in L.A. Coupons in *L.A. Weekly* can save you a bundle, and many are also handed out in bushels inside the clubs. To enter the club scene it's best to be 21; the next best option is to look it. Nevertheless, if you're over 18, you'll still find a space to dance. For more extensive listings of gay men's and women's bars contact the Gay and Lesbian Community Services Center (see Practical Information).

Blak and Bloo, 7574 Sunset Blvd. (213-876-1120). Artistic, funky people. Funk, rock, and alternative music. Maybe the only place on Sunset without serious attitude problems. Pool room, 2 bars, 2 dance rooms. Open Tues.-Sun.

Kingston 12, 814 Broadway (451-4423), Santa Monica. L.A.'s only full-time reggae club presents both local and foreign acts. Dreadlocks and fragrant smoke flow freely. Dance floor, 2 bars. Open Wed.-Sun. 8:30pm-2am.

Club Lingerie, 6507 Sunset Blvd., Hollywood (466-8557). The favored music club of all kinds of people. Rock, reggae, ska, and funk. They've got it. Two full bars. Must be 21.

Roxbury, 8225 W. Sunset (213-656-1750). L.A. pretension at its fullest. Contends with *Vertigo* in downtown as the most hotsy-totsy place in the city (you probably won't get in, but it might be fun trying). Jazz room downstairs, huge bar and dancing upstairs. VIP room only admits the wealthy, famous, or startlingly beautiful. Open Tues.-Sat. 7pm-2am.

Whisky A Go-Go, 8901 Sunset Blvd. (310-652-4202). Another venerable spot on the Strip. Like the Roxy, part of L.A.'s music history. The Whisky played host to many progressive bands in the late 70's and early 80's, and was a major part of the punk explosion. Mostly metal nowadays. Full bar, cover varies. No age restrictions.

Roxy, 9009 Sunset Blvd. (310-276-2222). One of the best known of L.A.'s Sunset Strip clubs, the Roxy is filled with record-company types and rockers waiting to be discovered. Many big acts at the height of their popularity play here. Cover varies. No age restrictions.

Gazzarri's, 9039 Sunset Blvd. (310-273-6606). An enormously popular heavy metal club on the Sunset Strip. Don't go if you're disturbed by hordes of long-haired crazies sharing your space. Cover $6-10. Must be 18.

Madame Wong's West, 2900 Wilshire Blvd. (829-7361), Santa Monica. With 2 bands and 2 DJs playing simultaneously 7 nights a week, this is the most music for your money. 3 full bars. Cover $5-8. Must be 21.

The Mayan, 1038 S. Hill St. (746-4287), downtown. House and hip-hop inside a colossal made-over theater. Over 21. Cover $12-15. Open Fri.-Sat. 9pm-4am.

The Palms, 8572 Santa Monica Blvd. (310-652-6188), W. Hollywood's oldest women's bar. Top 40 dancing every night. Full bar. Low cover, if any. 21 and over.

Peanuts, 7969 Santa Moncia Blvd. (213-654-0280). Management varies nightly, and generally offers some of the hottest clubs in L.A. Mostly over 18.

Amusement Parks

For information on Disneyland and Knott's Berry Farm, see Orange County.

Six Flags Magic Mountain, 26101 Magic Mountain Pkwy. (818-367-5965), in Valencia, a 40-min. drive up I-5 from L.A. Not for novices, Magic Mountain has the hairiest roller-coaster in Southern California (hairier even than Disneyland's Space Mountain). Highlights of the park are The Revolution, a smooth metal coaster with a vertical 360° loop; Colossus, the world's largest wooden roller coaster. Free Fall, a simulated no-parachute fall out of the sky; Ninja, a coaster whose cars are suspended on a rail from above and are allowed to swing back and forth as they turn; and the park's newest coaster, the Viper, which is said to approach the limits of what coaster builders can do with G-forces without *really* hurting people. For roller-coaster-o-phobes, there's also a crafts fair area and a children's playland with a Bugs Bunny theme. The truth is, however, that few people over 48-in. tall come to Magic Mountain for the crafts fair or for the love of Bugs Bunny. This becomes especially apparent when you encounter the lines for Colossus on a hot summer afternoon. Open Memorial Day to mid-September, and Christmas and Easter weeks Mon.-Fri. 10am-6pm, Sat. 10am-midnight, Sun. 10am-10pm; mid-September to Memorial Day (save Christmas and Easter holiday weeks) weekends only. Admission $22, seniors $16, children under 48" tall $14. Parking $4.

Raging Waters Park, 111 Raging Waters Dr. (714-592-6453 for recorded message, for directions 714-599-1251), in San Dimas. (Yes, this *is* where Bill and Ted are from.) Near the intersection of the San Bernardino and Foothill Fwy. (I-10 and 210). Beat the heat with 44 acres and 5 million gallons of slides, pools, whitewater rafts, inner-tubes, fake waves, and a fake island (don't fret, they recycle). A cool but costly alternative to the beach. Hurl yourself over the 7-story water-slide "Drop Out" if you dare, or slide through a tropical rain forest. Open Mon.-Fri. 10am-6pm., Sat.-Sun. 10am-7pm. Admission $17, 42"-48" $9, under 2 free.

Seasonal Events

Grunion runs throughout spring and summer. A voyeuristic pleasure: slippery, silver fish squirm onto the beaches (especially San Pedro) to mate. The fish can be caught by hand, but a license is required, oddly, for those over 16, from the Fish and Game Department (310-590-5132) for $10.50, valid until Dec. 31 each year. 1-day license $5.50. Fishing prohibited April-May. Free programs on the Grunion run given at the Cabrillo Marine Museum, San Pedro (310-548-7562).

UCLA Mardi Gras, mid-May, at the athletic field (310-825-8001). Billed as the world's largest collegiate activity (a terrifying thought). Features food, games, and entertainment. (Admission $3, children $1.) Proceeds benefit charity.

Gay Pride Week, late June (213-656-6553). The lesbian and gay community of L.A. comes out in full force. Art, politics, dances, and a big parade all center on the Pacific Design Center, 8687 Melrose Ave., Hollywood. $16 tickets.

Renaissance Pleasure Faire, every weekend from late April-mid June in the city of Devore (818-880-6211). From L.A., take the I-10 east I-15 north, and look for signs as you approach the city. Decked out in their best Elizabethan finery, San Bernardino teenagers are versed in Shakespearian vocab before working at the Faire. Food, games, and music. Open 9am-6pm. Admission $14.50, seniors (over 62) $11.50, children $8.

Northern California

Napa Valley and Wine Country

Transplanted Europeans recognized the Dionysian virtues of this area when California was still a part of Mexico. Prohibition, however, turned the vineyards into fig plantations; only in the last 20 years have vintners resurrected Bacchus there. Today, the wine-tasting carnival lasts from sunup to sundown, dominating the life of small towns in Napa, Sonoma, Dry Creek, Alexander, and Russian River Valley. **Napa Valley** holds the best-known U.S. vineyards. For more info contact the **Napa Chamber of Commerce,** 1556 1st St. (226-7455).

Sonoma offers slightly less-crowded wineries than Napa, as well as more exciting local history. The Sonoma mission, General Vallejo's home, and Jack London's Beauty Ranch all may interest the wine-sodden traveler. Farther north, the **Russian River** flows lazily between small towns and smaller wineries.

Although wine country's heavyweights offer well-organized tours, head to the smaller wineries of Sonoma Valley or Oregon to discuss vintages with the growers themselves. The vineyards listed below are some of the valley's larger operations. To reach the smaller places, pick up a list of vineyards from the chamber of commerce in Napa or look for signs along the roadside.

Robert Mondavi Winery, 7801 St. Helena Hwy. (963-9611), in Oakville. Spirited tours through marvelous catacombs and past towering stacks of oaken barrels with mellowing wine. The best free tour and tasting for the complete novice. Open daily 9am-5pm; May-Sept. 10am-4:30pm. Reservations required. Tours (every 15 min.) fill fast in summer; call before 10am.

Domaine Chandon, California Dr. (944-2280), next to the Veteran's Home in Yountville. One of the finest tours in the valley; available in several languages by prior arrangement. Owned by Moët-Chandon of France (makers of Dom Perignon), and not surprisingly most capable of divulging the secrets of champagne making. Champagne tastings $3-4 per glass at the restaurant attached to the winery. Open daily 11am-6pm; Nov.-April Wed.-Sun. 11am-6pm.

RMS Vineyards, 1250 Cuttings Wharf Rd. (253-9055). For yet another type of Napa grape-based alcohol. New and unique brandy distillery. Tours Mon.-Fri. at 10:30am and 2:30pm. Sales room open until 4pm. Open 9am-4pm daily.

Hanns Kornell Champagne Cellars, 1091 Larkmead Lane (963-2334), 4 mi. north of St. Helena. A one-room testing area with excellent dry champagne (try the Sehr Trocken). Entertaining, informative tours until 3:45pm. Open daily 10am-4pm.

Beaulieu Vineyard, 1960 St. Helena Hwy. (963-2411), in Rutherford. Tour includes a brief, imaginative audio-visual presentation. First tour at 11am, last at 3pm. Tasting daily 10am-4pm.

Clos Du Val Wine Company Ltd., 5330 Silverado Trail (252-6711), in Napa. Outdoor picnic area with whimsical drawings by Ronald Searle. Tours by appointment at 10am and 2pm. Tasting room open all day. Open daily 10am-4pm.

Budget motels amid the valleys are scarce and inaccessible to those without cars. Omnipresent **Motel 6,** 3380 Solano Ave. (257-6111), in Napa at Redwood Rd. off Rte. 29, has rooms with TV and A/C, plus a small pool. (Usually full by 6pm in summer. Singles $35.95. Each additional adult $6.) For the valley's best deal ssslip into the all-wood cabinsss at the **Triple S Ranch,** 4600 Mountain Home Ranch Rd. (942-6730), in Calistoga. (Take Rte. 29 north to Calistoga, my preciousss; turn left on Petrified Forest Rd., and then right on Mountain Home Ranch Rd. Singles $30. Doubles $40. Open April-Oct.) Campers can camp at the **Bothe-Napa Valley State Park**, 3601 St. Helena Hwy. (942-4575; 800-444-7275 for reservations), north of St. Helena on Rte. 29. (Open daily 8am-10:30pm; Oct.-April 9am-5pm. Sites with hot showers $10. Reservations recommended.)

Napa and its neighboring communities support numerous delis where you can pick up inexpensive picnic supplies. The **Jefferson Food Mart** (224-7112), 1704 Jefferson, is open daily 7am-11pm. **Villa Corona Panaderîa-Tortellerîa** (257-8685) 3614 Bel Aire Plaza, behind the Citibank Bldg. Tiny restaurant on alley, off of downtown, with piñataed ceiling. Impressive selection of Mexican beers, drinks, and spices. Large burritos $2.75. Mexican pastries made on premises $1-2. Open 9am-8:30pm daily in summer, 9am-7:30pm winter. Should you tire of the valley's delicate slices of brie on baguette, try the **Hi-Way 29 Diner** (224-6303), 101 Kelly Rd., for hearty greasy-spoon fare. Fluffy frisbee-sized hotcakes cost $2.80. (Open Mon.-Sat. 6am-3pm, Sun. 7am-4pm.)

Route 29 runs through the middle of the valley with the main town of Napa at its southern end and **Calistoga** to the north. Cycling in the area yields the best results; the valley is dead level and no more than 30 mi. long. The **Silverado Trail**, parallel to Rte. 29, is a more scenic and less crowded route than the highway. If you're planning a weekend trip from San Francisco, the 60-mi. trip may take up to 1½ hours on Saturday mornings or Sunday afternoons. If at all possible, try to visit the valley on weekdays and avoid the bus tours with plastic glasses and frantic wine pouring in over-crowded tasting rooms. Rent a bike at **Napa Valley Cyclery**, 4080 Byway E. (255-3377). ($4 first hr., $3 each additional hr., $15 per day. Open Mon.-Sat. 9am-6pm, Sun. 10am-5pm. Major credit card required.) **Greyhound** stops in Napa, Yountville, St. Helena, and Calistoga. (Yountville office on California Dr., 944-8377; open Mon.-Fri. 7am-5pm, Sat.-Sun. 7-11am and 1-5pm. Napa office 1620 Main St., 226-1856; open Mon.-Fri. 7:45am-noon and 1:15-6pm, Sat. 9:15-10:15am.)

Napa's **post office** does its thing at 1625 Trancas St. (255-1621; open Mon.-Fri. 8:30am-5pm). The **ZIP code** is 94558; the **area code** in the valley is 707.

Redwood National Park

Northern California's pride and joy, Redwood National Park (464-6101) flaunts an astonishing variety of flora and fauna in addition to the burly 500-year-old trees themselves. The region's fishing is famous, and the variegated terrain is ideal for hikers and backpackers. The park begins just south of the Oregon border and extends 50 mi. south, hugging the coast for about 40 mi., and encompassing three state parks. The lack of public transport within the park demands of the car-less both perseverance and well-honed hitchhiking skills. Beaches line the coastal trail that marches most of the length of the park; the heavy rains, created by moisture off the Pacific, foster a lush environment of elk, bear, birds, and marine life. Day use of state parks costs $3 per car.

The park divides naturally into five segments—Orick, Prairie Creek, Klamath, Crescent City, and Hiouchi—stacked from south to north along Rte. 101, each with its own ranger station (except Klamath). Although the terrain varies widely, the imposing *Sequoia sempervirens* are always present. **Orick,** the southernmost section of the park, has a **ranger station** about 2 mi. south on U.S. 101 and 1 mi. south of the Shoreline Deli (the Greyhound stop). This area's main attraction is the tall trees grove, an 8-mi. hike from the ranger station. In peak season, a shuttle bus ($3, seniors $1.50, kids $1) runs twice per day from the station to the tall trees trail. From there, you can hike 1.3 mi. to the tallest known tree in the world (367.8 ft.). The average visitor stares at it for 1 minute, 40 seconds. Be sure to leave extra time, since the strenuous return hike is mostly uphill. Backpackers may camp anywhere along the way after obtaining a permit at the ranger station. Orick itself (pop. 400) is a sleepy town brimming over with souvenir stores selling "burl" (tacky, expensive wood carvings).

To the north, the **Klamath** area comprises a thin stretch of park land connecting Prairie Creek with Del Norte State Park. Klamath River, the main attraction here besides the rugged coastline, lures salmon. (Fishing permit required.) The **Prairie Creek** area, equipped with state park campgrounds, is perfect for hikers. Starting at the **Prairie Creek Visitors Center** on U.S. 101 (488-2171), the 10-mi. **James Irvine Trail** winds through magnificent redwoods, around clear and cold creeks, through **Fern Canyon** (famed for its 50-ft. fern walls and mossy bottom), and by a stretch of the Pacific Ocean.

Crescent City is a decent pit stop, but has absolutely nothing else to offer except a maximum-security prison. The well-supplied **Visitors Center** at 1001 Front St. (464-3174) is surprisingly large for such a depressing town (open daily 9am-5pm). Seven mi. south of the city lies the **Del Norte Coast Redwoods State Park,** an extension of the Redwood Forest. The park's magnificent ocean views—along with picnic areas, hiking trails, and nearby fishing—lure enough campers to keep the sites full during peak season. (Tent sites $8, day-use fee $2.) The **Hiouchi** region sits in the northern part of the park inland along Rte. 199 and offers several excellent trails. The **Stout Grove Trail,** an easy ½-mi. walk, boasts the park's stoutest redwood, 16 ft. in diameter. The path is also accessible to the disabled; call 458-3310 for arrangements. **Kayak** trips on the Smith River leave from the **ranger station** on U.S. 199 (458-3134).

If you're not camping, the **Redwood Youth Hostel (AYH),** 14480 U.S. 101, in Klamath 95548 (482-8265), is a great deal. Overlooking the ocean and housed in the historic De Martin House, the Redwood features modern amenities—kitchen, dining room, laundry facilities, two sundecks, and disabled access. Reservations are recommended for summer and weekend stays; they must be made by mail three weeks in advance. ($8, under 18 with parent $4. Family rooms available by reservation. Linen 50¢. Check-in 4:30-9:30pm. Curfew 11pm. Closed 10am-4:30pm.) In Orick, one- or two-person rooms at the **Park Woods Motel,** 121440 Rte. 101 (488-5175), go for $32; two-bedroom units with kitchens are only $40. Crescent City is absolutely not the place to stay; it's as overpriced as national security. Head a little south and stay at **Harbor Motel,** 441 Rte. 101 (464-6111), where large rooms with TVs and free HBO start at $38 ($26 in winter).

Campsites are numerous, ranging from the well equipped (flush toilets and free hot showers; sites $12, hikers $2) to the primitive (outhouses at best; free). Peak season begins in the third week of June and concludes in early September. Try to visit from mid-April to mid-June or September to mid-October, when the park's summer crowds and fogs dissipate. Call MISTIX (800-444-7275) for reservations ($3.75; highly recommended in the peak season).

In Orick, buy some grub at the **Orick Market** (488-3225). Or dine on elk steak ($16), buffalo steak ($15), wild boar roast ($15), and other dainties at **Rolf's Park Cafe** (488-3841), two mi. north of Orick off U.S. 101's Fern Canyon exit, just after the turn-off to Davison Rd. In Crescent City, try the inexpensive seafood at **Harbor View Grotto,** 115 Citizens Dock Rd. (464-3815; open daily noon-10pm) or the Mexican cuisine at **Los Compadres,** Hwy. 101 South (464-7871; open daily 11am-9pm.). Don't leave the area without trying **salmon jerky,** a Native American specialty widely distributed locally.

Greyhound, 1125 Northcrest Dr. (464-2807) in Crescent City, supposedly stops at three places within the park: Shoreline Deli (488-5761), 1 mi. south of Orick on U.S. 101; Paul's Cannery in Klamath on U.S. 101; and the Redwood Hostel. Capricious bus drivers may ignore you. Call the Greyhound station directly preceding your stop to alert the driver of your presence. You can rent town bikes ($4 per hr.) at **Escape Hatch Sport and Cycle,** 960 3rd St. (464-2614; open Mon.-Sat. 9am-5pm). The Crescent City **post office** hunkers at 751 2nd St. (464-2151; open Mon.-Fri. 8:30am-5pm.) The **ZIP code** is 95531. The **area code** for the park region is 707.

Sacramento

A hobo-hangout in the 1960s, **Old Sacramento** has undergone restoration, now attracting cash-besotten tourists with upmarket shops. A pleasant atmosphere pervades a number of historically interesting structures, among them the **B.F. Hastings** building at the corner of 2nd and J St. Dating from 1852, the building houses Wells Fargo's offices, a museum, and the reconstructed chambers of the California Supreme Court. Pick up a self-guided walking tour at the Old Sacramento Visitors Center, or join a tour beginning at the center (1104 Front St., 449-6711, also the phone number for the Visitors Bureau at 1421 K St.).

Before overdosing on souvenir stores and cutesy-pie potpourri gift shops, try the excellent historical museums in Old Sacramento's northern end. The **California State Railroad Museum,** 125 I St. (448-4466), at 2nd St., will delight even those who don't know the difference between a cowcatcher and a caboose. The museum houses a fascinating collection of historical locomotives in its enormous exhibition space. The same ticket admits you to the **Central Pacific Depot and Passenger Station,** at 1st and J St., a reconstruction of a station that once stood here. (Both open daily 10am-5pm. Admission $5, ages 6-17 $2, under 6 free.)

The **Sacramento History Museum,** 101 I St. (449-2057), at Front St., housed in the reconstructed 1854 City Hall, presents scintillating exhibits on California history in a two-story glass-and-chrome extravaganza, with interactive videos. (Open daily 10am-5pm. Guided tours upon request. Adults $2.50, seniors $1.50, ages 6-17 $1, under 6 free.)

Gallery hoppers should enjoy the elegant **Crocker Art Museum,** 216 O St. (449-5423), at 3rd St., housed in a restored Victorian building, with mainly 19th-century European and U.S. oil paintings. One large gallery showcases photography, another contemporary works by California artists. (Open Tues.-Sun. 10am-5pm, Thurs. 10am-9pm. Admission $2.50, seniors and ages 7-18 $1, under 7 free.) Tours available.

Two modern twin towers very nearly replaced the **state capitol,** at 10th St. and Capitol Mall (324-0333), in Capitol Park, when the old and abused structure began to crumble like everything else in the 1970s. But the collective California taxpayer forked out $68 million, and the building was finally restored in 1982 to its glorious 1906 finery: pink and green decor, oak staircases, gilt, and flattering oil paintings of forgotten governors. The "Restoration" tour covers the chambers; the "Historic" delves into the recreated office spaces, decorated as they were decades ago. (Both hr.-long tours daily on the hr. 9am-4pm. Free.) Another tour explores the gardens, including the elaborate Vietnam Memorial, daily at 10am. (Open daily 9am-5pm, fall and winter Sat.-Sun. 10am-5pm. For info, self-guided walking tour brochures, and an excellent free 10-minute film, go to Room B-27 in the basement.

Before the arrival of a certain Ronald Reagan, who demanded more spacious surroundings, the **Old Governor's Mansion,** 16th and H St. (324-0539), fit the bill. This 15-room Victorian masterpiece (c. 1877) housed 13 of California's governors. The building practically bursts with gables and attics, displaying the architectural subtlety of a three-tiered wedding cake. (Open daily 10am-5pm. ½-hr. tours on the hour. Last tour at 4pm. Admission $2, age 6-17 $1, under 6 free.)

Across town at 27th and L St. stands **Sutter's Fort** (324-0539), a reconstruction of the 1839 military settlement that launched Sacramento. All supplies had to be dragged overland from the river to build the settlement, which now contains the **State Indian Museum** (324-0539). Rangers fire the fort's cannon at 11am and 2pm. (Both open daily 10am-5pm. Admission to each $2, under 18 $1.)

Though perhaps a bit disheartened by the dominance of compact discs, vintage vinyl collectors will still enjoy a trip to the original **Tower Records,** at the corner of Landpark Dr. and Broadway (444-3000). Tower Records began in 1941 when an ambitious teenager, Russ Solomon, started selling records in the back of his dad's drugstore; he now owns a national chain of stores. The store's overwhelmingly large selection and late hours are replicated in the adjacent Tower Books, Drugs, Theater, Tobacco, *ad nauseum.* (Record store open daily 9am-midnight.)

The kid in you (or with you) will enjoy the **Sacramento Zoo** (449-5885), at 3930 W. Land Park Dr. (open daily 9am-4pm; admission $3, 3-12 $1.50, under 3 free. 50¢ increase on weekends). If mere animals don't suffice, get off your tuffet and head for the zoo's **Fairytale Town** (449-5233), a 6-acre theme park with puppet shows throughout the day. (Open daily 10am-4:30pm. Admission $2, ages 3-12 $1.50, under 3 free. Take bus #5 or 6 to William Land Park, 3 mi. south of the capitol.) Another kids' place is the **Visionarium**, 2701 K St. (443-7476), on the 2nd level of the Sutter square galleria, an aggressively interactive children's museum billed as "Kids on Kampus." (Open Mon.-Sat. 10am-6pm, Sun. noon-5pm. Admission $2, ages 3-18 $4, under 3 free.)

Downtown Sacramento supports a bunch of breakfast and lunch spots; unfortunately, many close by early afternoon when the government does. Old Sacramento is the place to go for ice cream, light snacks, and classier wining and dining. But the best meals appear in the blocks between 19th St. and 22nd St., concentrated around Capitol St. **Zelda's Original Gourmet Pizza** (447-1400), 1415 21st St., although distant from the town's center, has awesome deep-dish pizza (medium $7.50). (Open Mon.-Thurs. 11:30am-2pm and 5-10pm, Fri. 11:30am-2pm and 5-11:30pm, Sat. 5-11:30pm, Sun. 5-9pm.) In Old Sacramento, **Annabelle's**, 200 J St. (448-6239), boasts an all-you-can-eat lunch buffet ($3.75) which includes pasta, lasagna, pizza, and salad bar. (Open daily 11:30am-8pm.)

Sacramento's supply of motel rooms wanes when one of the city's frequent large conventions is in progress: all but the sleaziest dives are fully booked by midweek. Try to reserve a month in advance. The cheapest places lie near the Greyhound station across from Capitol Park but provide questionable cleanliness and security. Several motels east of Capitol Park, along 15th and 16th St., also average $30 for singles. For even cheaper rates go to West Sacramento, a 20- to 30-minute walk along W. Capitol Ave. from Old Sacramento. Jibboom St., 1 mi. from Old Sacramento, also has a lot of cheap motels. Call the **West Sacramento Motel & Hotel Association** (372-5378) or the **West Sacramento Chamber of Commerce** (372-5378; open Mon.-Fri. 8am-5pm). Yolo buses #40, 41, or 42 go to West Sacramento from the L St. terminal. The quality of rooms even ranges within some of the motels; see your room before paying.

With nine comfortable beds, the **Gold Rush Home Hostel (AYH)** (421-5954), 1421 Tiverton Ave., on the outskirts of town near the zoo, is like visiting your favorite relatives, except they charge you. (Lockout 9am-6pm. $8, nonmembers $10. Reservations required; no walk-ins.) Primarily apartments for the elderly, **Capitol Park Hotel** (441-5361), 1125 9th St., at L St. two blocks from Greyhound, rents some well-worn rooms nightly. The ancient hotel, with a fabulous downtown location, keeps cool with large windows. (Singles $28. Doubles $35.) The **Americana Lodge** (444-3980), 818 15th St., the nicest in the range, features a small pool, A/C, and HBO. Local calls 25¢, check-out 11am. (Singles from $34. Doubles $38. Confirm reservations with advance payment.)

The small, congenial **Sacramento Convention and Visitors Bureau** (449-6711), 1421 K St., between 14th and 15th St., presents a tidy stand of brochures on the corner table. Find the only accommodations guide in the free *Sacramento*, produced by the city. (Open Mon.-Fri. 8am-5pm.) The **Old Sacramento Visitors Center** (449-7611; holidays and weekends 442-7644), 1104 Front St. also has a modest handful of brochures. Open daily 9am-5pm.

Amtrak (444-9131), at 4th and I St., has a huge terminal (open daily 5:15am-11:15pm). Daily trains roll to Reno ($51), Chicago ($202), L.A. ($74), Seattle ($141), and San Francisco ($17). Reservations must be made months in advance for all eastbound and most westbound trains. The **Greyhound** station (444-6800), idles at 715 L St., between 7th and 8th St. in a relatively safe if unpleasant neighborhood. Buses run to Reno (gambler's round-trip special, 3-day min. stay, $19), L.A. ($40), and San Francisco ($10). (Open 24 hrs.) **Sacramento Regional Transit Bus** (321-2877) offers service in downtown Sacramento. ($1 including one transfer, all-day pass $2.50, $1 express buses run Mon.-Fri. 6:30-9am and 3:30-6pm.) An 18.3-mi. **light rail** transit line connects the central business district with the eastern regions of the city. (Trains run every 15 min. 4:30am-1:30am. Fare $1.) The **Yolo Bus Commuter Lines** (371-2877) connect downtown with Old Sacramento, West Sacramento, Davis, and Woodland. (Fare $1, 50¢ surcharge on express buses #43, 44, 45.)

Block numbers in Sacramento correspond to the lettered cross-streets, so 200 3rd St. intersects B St., 1700 C St. is on 17th St., 300 3rd St. intersects C, and so on. The capitol and endless state government buildings occupy the rectilinear downtown area. The **Broadway** area, home of the original Tower Records, lies beyond Z St. The 40 avenues north of Broadway, known as the "fabulous forty," contain the mansions of Sacramento's industrial barons. One housed Ronald Reagan during his term as governor. **West Sacramento** lies, strangely enough, west of downtown, on the other side of the river. With well-marked lanes, the city is a good biker's town. Rent at the **American River Bike Shop**, 9203 Folsom Blvd. (363-6271; $3 per hour, $15 per day).

The **post office** governs at 2000 Royal Oak Dr. (921-0280; on weekends, holidays, and after 5pm, call 921-4564; open Mon.-Fri. 8:30am-5pm). **General Delivery** mail can be picked up at Metro Station, 801 I St. (442-0764), at 8th. (Open Mon.-Fri. 8am-5pm.) The General Delivery **ZIP code** is 95814. The **area code** is 916.

Orange County

Orange County, Los Angeles's neighbor to the south, was part of Los Angeles County until 1861, when "O.C." seceded over a tax dispute. The two since have become sibling rivals. Orange County has a higher per capita income and a less ethnically diverse population than that of Los Angeles. Many O.C. residents live in "planned communities," neighborhoods designed by strict codes governing exactly where schools and shopping centers must be placed as well as what houses must look like. But if regimented living isn't to your taste, head for the coast, where Orange County's fine surf and string of clean, uncrowded beaches, have produced the truest approximation of stereotypical Southern California beach life.

Practical Information

Emergency: 911.

Anaheim Area Visitors and Convention Bureau, 800 W. Katella Ave., Anaheim 92808 (999-8999). In the Anaheim Convention Center. Free brochures. Open Mon.-Fri. 8:30am-5pm.

Airport: John Wayne Orange County, Campus Dr. (755-6500). Flights to and from many major U.S. cities.

Amtrak, 5 stops: 120 E. Santa Fe Ave. (992-0530), in Fullerton, at Harbor Blvd.; 1000 E. Santa Ana (547-8389), in Santa Ana; Santa Fe Depot (661-8835), in San Juan Capistrano; 2150 E. Katella (385-1448), in Anaheim by Anaheim Stadium; unstaffed stop in San Clemente, off I-5, by the municipal pier.

Greyhound, terminals at 2080 S. Harbor (635-5060) in Anaheim, 3 blocks south of Disney (open Mon.-Thurs. 7am-7:30pm, Fri.-Sun. 7am-9:30pm); 1000 E. Santa Ana Blvd. (542-2215), in Santa Ana (open daily 7am-8pm); and 510 Avenida de la Estrella (492-1187), in San Clemente (open Mon.-Thurs. 7:45am-6:30pm, Fri. 7:45am-8pm).

Orange County Transit District (OCTD): 11222 Acacia Parkway (636-7433), in Garden Grove. Thorough service, useful for getting from Santa Ana and Fullerton Amtrak stations to Disneyland, or for beach-hopping along the coast. Long Beach, in L.A. County, serves as the terminus for several OCTD lines. Bus #1 travels the coast from Long Beach down to San Clemente, with service twice per hour from early morning until around 8pm. Schedules available in many public places. Fare 85¢; correct change only. Transfers free. Info center open Mon.-Fri. 6am-7pm; Sat.-Sun. 8am-5pm.

Local RTD Information: 800-2-LA-RIDE (252-7433). Lines open daily 5:30am-midnight. RTD buses run from L.A. to Disneyland and Knott's Berry Farm.

Help lines: Rape Crisis, 836-7400. 24-hr. hotline. Gay-Lesbian Community Service Organization, 534-0862.

Police: 425 S. Harbor Blvd. (999-1900), in Anaheim.

Post Office: 701 N. Loara (520-2602), in Anaheim. One block east of Euclid, 1 block north of Anaheim Plaza. Open Mon.-Fri. 8:30am-5pm. General Delivery ZIP Code: 92803.

Area Code: 714; 213 in Seal Beach.

Accommodations and Camping

Its proximity to Disneyland and the other amusement parks grants **Anaheim** a thriving tourist trade. Because it's fairly remote from L.A.'s other sights, however, the Magic Kingdom is the only reason to stay. Start by contacting the Anaheim Visitors Center, a travel industry dating service, which matches people with rooms they can afford. The road to Disneyland along Harbor Blvd. is lined with economy motels.

The county coast is the other big attraction, and bargain rates can be found at motels scattered along Pacific Coast Hwy. and Newport Beach's Newport Blvd.

Huntington Beach Colonial Inn Youth Hostel, 421 8th St. (536-3315), in Huntington Beach, 4 blocks inland at Pecan. In a large yellow Victorian house shaded by huge palm trees. Nine 2-person rooms, 3 more accommodate 4-5 people. Common showers, bathroom, large kitchen. Reading/TV room. Lockout 9:30am-4:30pm. Curfew 11pm. Late night key rental $1 ($20 deposit). $11 per night. Must have picture ID. Frequented by British, German, and Australian travelers.

Fullerton Hacienda Hostel (AYH), 1700 N. Harbor Blvd. (738-3721), in Fullerton, about a 15-min. drive north of Disneyland. OCTD bus #43 runs up and down Harbor Blvd. to Disneyland, and the hostel managers can arrange car rentals for groups. A white stucco house with a porch swing on an old dairy farm. The house is set back from Harbor Blvd. on a hill with a poorly marked driveway. Separate-sex accommodations can house a total of 15. Kitchen, laundry. 3-day max. stay. Open daily 7:30-9:30am and 4-11pm. Members $13.20, nonmembers $16.20. Linen $1. Reserve one week in advance by mail, and include first night's fee.

Motel 6, 2 Anaheim locations: 921 S. Beach Blvd. (220-2866), and 7450 Katella Ave. (891-0717), both within a 10-min. drive of Disneyland. The excitement of the nearby amusement park permeates the motels osmotically; both have pools filled with couples and their hyperactive, Mickey Mouse-eared children. Not the place to stay if you're seeking peace and quiet. Singles $30-33. Doubles $37-40. Cheaper rates in winter.

Mesa Motel, 415 N. Newport Blvd. (646-3893). A ½-mile to the beach. Small swimming pool, TV, and typical motel rooms. Singles $32. Doubles $36.

State beaches in Orange County with campgrounds are listed below from north to south. Reservations are required for all sites except the Echo Arch Area in San Onofre, made through MISTIX (800-444-7275) a maximum of 56 days in advance.

Bolsa Chica, Rte. 1 (848-1566), 3 mi. west of Huntington Beach. Self-contained vehicles only. 14-day maximum. $14 per vehicle, $12 for senior citizens.

Doheny, Rte. 1 (496-6771), at the south end of Dana Point. Beachside location turns this place into a zoo as suburban families howl out. TVs, lounge furniture, play pens, and more. Beachfront sites $21, otherwise $16.

San Clemente, I-5 (492-3156). 157 sites, 85 developed. Sites $16. Richard Nixon sees you.

San Onofre, I-5 (492-0802), 3 mi. south of San Clemente. 221 campsites along an abandoned stretch of PCH; about 90 suitable for tents. The **Echo Arch Area** has 34 more primitive hike-in sites between the bluffs and the beach. The San Mateo Campground is a brand new park with 140 sites and hot showers. These three areas are the most secluded, and the sight of the most partying (still fairly calm). All three are within mutating distance of the nuclear power plant. Sites $16.

Sights and Food

Among the architectural attractions in Orange County not blessed by Walt Disney is the **Crystal Cathedral,** 12141 Lewis St., Garden Grove. Opinions are split on this shining all-glass structure completed in 1980 by Phillip Johnson and John Burgee; some find it inspiring, others call it garish. It's from the pulpit of this church that Dr. Robert Schuller preaches his weekly TV show, "Hour of Power". With 7000 people moving in and out every Sunday, the Cathedral is also a model of efficiency.

Inland Orange County is graced with a number of attractions, the newest of which is a tribute to everyone's favorite president, Richard Nixon. At **The Richard Nixon Library and Birthplace,** 18001 Yorba Linda Blvd., Yorba Linda (993-3393), you can "enjoy the first lady's garden" and engage in a video conversation with Dick himself. ($3.95, seniors $2, open daily 8:30am-5pm).

Still, recreation and leisure time for residents and visitors of all ages revolves primarily around the ocean. While many of the county's inland cities fall prey to the problems (traffic, crime, etc.) that plague Los Angeles, the coastal towns offer wide beaches and blue skies.

Huntington Beach (area code 714 for all subsequent beaches), served as a port of entry for the surfing craze, which transformed California coast life after being imported from Hawaii by Duke Kahanamoku in the early 1900s. Still popular, the sport culminates each year in the **surfing championships** (536-5486) held in late July. If the surfing championship isn't in town, the best reason to stay in Huntington Beach is the Colonial Inn Youth Hostel (see Accommodations). The careless and carless amuse themselves with beach BBQs or by drinking themselves silly at **Perq's** night club (117 Main St., 960-9996, open daily 11am-1:30pm).

Newport Beach and the surrounding cities inland are the jewels of Orange County, with stunning multi-million-dollar homes lining Newport Harbor, the largest leisure craft harbor in the world. The beach itself displays few signs of ostentatious wealth; it is crowded with young, frequently rowdy, hedonists in neon-colored bikinis and trunks. The area around Newport Pier is a haven for families; the streets from 30th to 56th give way to teenagers and college students sunning, surfing, and playing volleyball. The boardwalk is always a scene in the summer, with beach house renters partying wildly on their porches, especially as their leases expire.

The sands of Newport Beach run south onto the **Balboa Peninsula,** separated from the mainland by Newport Bay. The peninsula is only two to four blocks wide and can be reached from PCH by Balboa Blvd. Several nightspots popular with the disposable-income set reside at the foot of Newport Pier, between 20th and 21st St. **The Crab Cooker,** 2200 Newport Blvd. (673-0100), offers the "world's best seafood," with dinner plates (including rice and potatoes) mostly under $10. (Open Mon.-Sat. 11am-10pm.) Nearby, the **Red Onion,** 2406 Newport Blvd. (675-2244), serves fantastic Mexican food (wide variety of entrees under $10) with a view of the waterfront. Weekends are wild here as residents quest for the perfect margarita. Don't come straight from the beach, though; the code is not strict, but does require that you be fully dressed. (Open daily 11am-2am.) At the end of the peninsula, **The Wedge,** seasonally pounded by waves up to 20 ft., is a bodysurfing mecca. Bodysurfers (ostensibly furloughed from mental institutions) risk a watery grave for this monster ride. Melt into the crowds on Newport Beach and the Balboa Peninsula by hopping on a bicycle or strapping on a pair of rollerskates. Expensive **rental shops** cluster around the Newport Beach pier and at the end of the peninsula, letting bikes ($4-5 per hr., $18-20 per day), skates ($3-6 per hr., $15-18 per day), and boogie boards ($6-7 per day).

North of Newport Beach is **Costa Mesa,** home of the new and dazzling **Orange County Performing Arts Center,** 600 Town Center Dr. (556-2121), on Bristol St. off I-405. The opulent, 3000-seat structure was constructed in 1986 at a cost of $70 million and has enlivened Orange County arts by hosting the American Ballet Theatre and the Kirov Ballet, among other troupes.

More tourists than swallows return every year to **Mission San Juan Capistrano** (493-1424), 3 mi. inland of Dana Point at the junction of Camino Capistrano and Del Obispo Rd. This "jewel of the missions" offers a peek at California's origins as a Spanish colony. Established in 1776 as one of 21 California missions of the Catholic church, it is somewhat run-down today due to an 1812 earthquake. Father Junípero Serra, the mission's founder, officiated from inside the beautiful **Serra Chapel,** the oldest building in the state (1777). The chapel is dark and womby, warmed by the 17th-century Spanish cherrywood altar and the Native American designs painted on walls and ceiling. It's still used by the Catholic Church, so enter quietly and inhale the scent of beeswax candles lit by worshipers. (Open daily 8:30am-7pm; Oct. 1-May 14 8:30am-5pm. Admission $3, ages 6-11 $1.50.) The mission is perhaps best known as a home to the thousands of swallows who return here from their winter migration each year to nest in mid-March. They are scheduled to return to Capistrano on St. Joseph's Day, March 19, but the birds aren't all that religious, and have a tendency to show up whenever there aren't busloads of tourists hanging around. The swallows leave on October 23. The best time to see the birds is when they feed in the early morning or early evening.

The **San Onofre Nuclear Power Plant** helps give **San Onofre State Beach** the warmest water in Southern California. Nevertheless, the beach is a prime surfing area where dozens of wave-riders test the breakers at any given time. The southern end of the beach is frequented by nudists who presumably would be ill-protected should the nearby nuclear plant ever malfunction (drive down as far as you can go on I-5, and walk left on the trail for ¼ to ½ mi.; beach contains both a gay and a straight area). Be forewarned: nude bathing is illegal since it shatters an American myth that people don't have genitalia. For info on the coast farther south, see Near San Diego.

Disneyland

The recent growth of Mike Eisner's Disney empire, with its exclusive Disney cable-TV channel, Touchstone movies, and new studio park in Florida, has breathed new life into one of the world's most famous amusement parks. Opened in 1955 through the vision of Walt Disney, the park's pastel capitalism has delighted even the most hardened cynics. Soviet premier Nikita Kruschev was livid when nationalist Walt barred him from the park at the height of the Cold War.

All this otherworldliness gets disturbing at times, especially with crowds of 75,000 per day jamming the park in search of artificial happiness. But don't worry; Disney euphoria wasn't banned by the Drug War. Admission to the gleaming fantasy world is gained through the **Unlimited Use Passport** ($27.50, ages 3-11 $22.50). The A-E ticket system is now a relic (though if you have any old A-E tickets you can get refunds for them), and visitors have unrestricted entrance to any attraction. The park is open daily in summer from 8am-1am. In the off-season, the park ordinarily closes at 5pm, though hours vary, especially around major holidays; call 714-999-4000 for more information.

Getting There

The park is located at one of the most famous addresses in the world: 1313 Harbor Blvd., in Anaheim in Orange County, bounded by Katella Ave., Harbor Blvd., Ball Rd., and West St. From L.A., take **bus** #460 from 6th and Flower St. downtown, about 1½ hours to the Disneyland Hotel. (Service to the hotel from 4:53am, back to L.A. until 1:20am.) From the hotel, take the free shuttle to Disneyland's portals. Also served by Airport Service, OCTD, Long Beach Transit, and Gray Line (see Public Transportation for prices). If you're **driving,** take the Santa Ana Fwy. to the Katella Ave. exit. Be forewarned, however: while parking in the morning should be painless, leaving in the evening often will not be. In addition, when the park closes early, Disneygoers must contend with L.A.'s maddening, rush-hour traffic.

In the Park

Visitors enter the Magic Kingdom by way of **Main Street, U.S.A.** a collection of shops, arcades, and even a movie theater designed to look like Walt's maudlin turn-of-the-century childhood memories. Main Street, a broad avenue leading to a replica of Sleeping Beauty's castle at the center of the park, includes a bank, an info booth, lockers, and a first aid station. The **Main Street Electrical Parade** makes its way each summer night at 8:45pm and 11pm (with the earlier parade followed by fireworks). Floats and even humans are adorned with thousands of multi-colored lights, making for a potentially shocking nighttime display. This is one of Disneyland's most popular events and people begin lining the sidewalks on Main Street by 7pm.

Four "lands" branch off Main Street. **Tomorrowland,** to your immediate right at the top of Main Street, contains the park's best thrill rides, **Space Mountain** and the George Lucas-produced **Star Tours.** Moving counter-clockwise around the park, next is **Fantasyland,** with the **Matterhorn** rollercoaster, some excellent kids' rides, and the ever-popular **It's A Small World** (a hint: unless you want the cute, but annoying, theme song running through your head for the rest of the day, you may want to save this one for last). Next is **Frontierland,** with the **Thunder Mountain Railroad** coaster and **Tom Sawyer Island.** Last, but not least, is **Adventureland,** with the **Jungle Cruise** and the **Swiss Family Robinson Treehouse.** In addition, tucked between Frontierland and Adventureland are two more areas that aren't official "lands." One is **New Orleans Square,** with **Pirates of the Caribbean,** the **Haunted Mansion,** and some excellent dining. The other is **Critter Country,** with Disneyland's latest super-attraction, **Splash Mountain,** a log ride that climaxes in a wet, five-story drop. Ask about **Hell's Angelland,** due to open next year. (Just kidding. . .)

Food services in the park ranges from sit-down establishments to fast-food eateries such as the Lunch Pad. You can save much time and money by packing a picnic lunch and eating a big breakfast before you leave home. Food in the park is mediocre and generally overpriced. If you're looking for a martini, you'll be left high and dry: alcohol doesn't exist in the Magic Kingdom.

Fall months and weekdays are generally less crowded than summer days and weekends. To avoid long waits, arrive shortly after the park opens. Lines for the most popular attractions are shorter just after opening and late at night; try midday and you'll see why some call it "Disneyline."

Knott Just Disneyland

For more amusing rides and replicas, head to **Knott's Berry Farm,** 8039 Beach Blvd. (714-220-5200 for a recording), at La Palma Ave. in Buena Park just 5 mi. northeast of Disneyland. Take the Santa Ana Fwy. south, exit west on La Palma Ave. Bus #460 stops here on its way to Disneyland. An actual berry farm in its early days, Knott's now cultivates a county-fair atmosphere with a recreated ghost town, Fiesta Village, Roaring Twenties Park, rides, and a replica of Independence Hall. The insane rollercoaster Montezuma's Revenge takes you through a backwards loop. Knott's recently unveiled a $12 million project featuring a Kingdom of the Dinosaurs ride through prehistory and 3 new thrill rides. The Chicken Dinner Restaurant has been serving tender, inexpensive chicken dinners since 1934. Open Sun.-Fri. 9am-midnight, Sat. 9am-1am; in winter Mon.-Fri. 10am-6pm, Sat. 10am-10pm, Sun. 10am-7pm. Admission $22, seniors 60 and over $15, ages 3-11 $10.

Not Knotts

Wild Rivers Waterpark, 8800 Irvine Center Dr., Laguna Hills (714-768-9453), in Orange County, has over 40 water-slide rides, two wave pools, and picnic areas. (Open May-Sept. daily 10am-8pm, Sat.-Sun. 11am-5pm in winter. Admission $16, ages 3-9 $12.)

San Diego

Centuries after its founding on hills of chaparral, San Diego manages to maintain clean air and beaches, a sense of culture and history, and even lush greenery in the face of population growth and water shortages. A solid Navy "industry" cushions the economy; local architecture looks pleasant, not gaudy; and rain and cold winters are virtually unknown. But even "America's Finest City" is challenged with questions of water shortages and immigration surpluses.

San Diego has ample tourist attractions—a world-famous zoo, Sea World, and Old Town—but your most enjoyable destination might simply be a patch of sand at one of the superb beaches. For relief from beach bumming, retreat to the nearby mountains and deserts, or head for Mexico, almost next door.

Practical Information

Emergency: 911.

Visitor Information Center, 11 Horton Plaza (236-1212), downtown at 1st Ave. and F St. They have whatever you need under the counter. Open Mon.-Sat. 8:30am-5:30pm, Sun. 11am-5pm. Old Town and State Park Information, 4002 Wallace Ave. (237-6770), in Old Town Square next to Burguesa. Take the Taylor St. exit off I-8, or bus #5. Historical brochures on the Old Town ($2). Open daily 10am-5pm. National Parks Information, 226-6311. Recorded info. Arts/Entertainment Hotline, 234-2787. Recorded calendar of performances, exhibitions, and other events.

San Diego Council American Youth Hostels: 1031 India St. 92101 (239-2644), 335 W. Beech St. Student travel info, including full lists of hostels. Bike accessories, travel gear, and guides. Sponsors domestic and European trips. Open Mon.-Fri. 10am-6pm, Sat. 10am-5pm.

Travelers Aid: Airport, 231-7361. One station in each terminal. Directions for lost travelers. Open daily 9am-10pm. Downtown office, 1765 4th Ave and Elm St. #201 (232-7991). Open Mon.-Fri. 8:30am-4:30pm.

San Diego International Airport (Lindbergh Field): at the northwestern edge of downtown, across from Harbor Island. Divided into east and west terminals. San Diego Transit "30th and Adams" bus #2 goes downtown ($1.25). Buses run Mon.-Fri. 5am-11:30pm, Sat.-Sun. 6am-midnight.

Amtrak: Santa Fe Depot, 1050 Kettner Blvd. (239-9021, for schedules and info 800-872-7245), at Broadway. To L.A. (8 per day Mon.-Fri. 5:15am-9:15pm; $24, round-trip $38). Info. on bus, trolley, car, and boat transportation available at the station. Ticket office open daily 4:45am-9:15pm.

Greyhound: 120 W. Broadway (239-9171), at 1st Ave. To L.A. (12 per day Mon.-Thurs. 5:30am-midnight; $16, round-trip $25).

Taxi: Yellow Cab, 234-6161. Cab fare downtown around $7.

Car Rental: Rent-A-Wreck, 3309 Midway Dr. (224-8235) $19.95 per day, 100 free mi. per day, 16¢ each additional mi. 125 mi. radius restriction, and cannot drive in Mexico. $2 charge for drivers under 25. Must be 21 with credit card or $200 minimum cash deposit. (Open Mon.-Fri. 8am-5pm, Sat. 8am-3pm, Sun. 10am-3pm.) Aztec Rent-A-Car, 2401 Pacific Hwy. (232-6117). $24 per day, 150 free mi., 25¢ each additional mi. $125 per week with 1000 free mi. Cars may venture south of the border as far as Ensenada with purchase of Mexican insurance ($14 per day). Open Mon.-Fri. 7am-8pm, Sat.-Sun. 8am-5pm. Must be 21 with major credit card.

Driveaway Companies: A-I Automovers, 3650 Clairmont Dr., Suite 5-C, (274-0224) has offices nationwide. Driveaway Service, 3585 Adams Ave. in Normal Heights (280-5454); must be over 21 with $250 deposit. Auto Driveway Co., 4672 Park Blvd. (295-8060) Open Mon.-Fri. 8am-5pm.

Bike Rental: Pennyfarthing's (233-7696), 520 5th Ave., in the Gaslamp Quarter. Bikes $4 per hr., $30 per day. $90 per week. Open daily 9am-6pm. La Jolla Cyclery, 7443 Girard (459-3141), in La Jolla. Limited rental bikes $4 per hr., $16 per day with a 2-hr. min. Tandems $6 per hr., $20 per day. Open Tues.-Fri. 10am-6pm, Sat. 9am-5pm.

Help Lines: Crisis Hotline, 800-479-3339 or 236-3339. Open 24 hrs. **Rape Crisis Hotline,** 233-3088. Open 24 hrs. **Lesbian and Gay Men's Center,** 3780 5th Ave. (692-2077). Open Mon.-Fri. 9am-5pm.

Senior Citizen's Services: 202 C St. (236-6905), in the City Hall Bldg. Provides ID cards so that seniors can take advantage of senior discounts. Plans daytrips and sponsors "nutrition sites" (meals) at 8 locations. Open Mon.-Fri. 8am-5pm.

Community Service Center for the Disabled: 1295 University Ave. (293-3500), Hillcrest. Attendant referral, wheelchair repair and sales, emergency housing, motel/hotel accessibility referral, and **TDD Line** services for the deaf (293-7757). Open Mon.-Fri. 9am-5pm.

Post Office: 2535 Midway Dr. (547-0477), between downtown and Mission Beach. General Delivery. Open Mon.-Fri. 7am-1am, Sat. 8am-4pm. General Delivery **ZIP code:** 92138. Take bus #6, 9, or 35.

Area Code: 619.

Orientation

A group of skyscrapers in the blocks between Broadway and I-5 makes up downtown San Diego. Streets running parallel to the bay (north-south) on the western end of downtown have proper names until they hit Horton Plaza in the east, then they become consecutively numbered avenues. Going east-west are lettered streets; "A" St. is the farthest north, L the farthest south. In their midst, Broadway replaces D St. and runs directly east from the bay. North of A, Ash St. begins a string of alphabetized streets named after plants that continues north all the way to Walnut. Other alphabetical schemes crop up throughout the metro area, the most impressive being Point Loma's complete Addison to Zola literary system.

On the northeastern corner of downtown, **Balboa Park,** larger than the city center, is bounded by 6th Ave. on the west, I-5 and Russ Blvd. on the south, 28th St. on the east, and Upas St. on the north. To the north and east of Balboa Park are the main residential areas. **Hillcrest,** San Diego's most cosmopolitan district and a center for the gay community, lies at the park's northwestern corner, around the intersection of 5th and University Ave.; **University Heights** and **North Park** sit along the major east-west thoroughfares of University Ave., El Cajon Blvd., and Adams Ave.

San Diegan custom is to wait obediently for the walk signal, no matter how clear the coast. Jaywalking is not in vogue; it's illegal (tickets are given occasionally).

The 17-mi. bay, west of downtown, is formed by Coronado Peninsula (jutting northward from Imperial Beach) and Point Loma (dangling down from Ocean Beach). North of Ocean Beach lie Mission Beach (with neighboring Mission Bay), Pacific Beach, and La Jolla.

Getting Around

Buses reach most areas of the city. The public transport systems (San Diego Transit, North County Transit, DART, FAST, and Dial-A-Ride) cover the area from Oceanside in the north to Tijuana in Mexico, and inland to Escondido, Julian, and other towns. Call for **public transit information** (233-3004; daily 5:30am-10pm) or stop by the **Transit Store,** 449 Broadway (234-1060), at 5th Ave. (open daily 8:30am-5:30pm). Pick up the *Transit Rider's Guide,* which lists routes to popular destinations. Fares vary: $1 for North County Transit routes, $1.25 for local routes, $1.50-1.75 for express routes, and $2.25-2.50 for commuter routes. Transfers within San Diego are free; North County transfers cost 25¢. Exact change is required; most city buses accept dollar bills. About 60% of the buses are wheelchair accessible. Visitors age 60 and over with ID receive discounts. Bike racks equip buses on some routes, especially those to the beaches. When you frequent buses, save money by using **Day Tripper** passes, which allow unlimited travel on buses, trolleys, and even the Bay Ferry (1 day $4, 4 days $12). These and the various monthly passes are available at the Transit Store. Most urban routes originate, terminate, or pass through downtown.

The wheelchair-accessible **San Diego Trolley** runs on two lines from a starting point near the Santa Fe Depot on C St., at Kettner. One heads east for **El Cajon.** The other, popularly known as the Tijuana Trolley, runs 16 mi. south to **San Ysidro** at the Mexican border (5am-6pm every 7 min., 6-10pm every 15 min., 10pm-1am every 30 min.). From the border, cabs to the oxymoronic Tijuana Cultural Center or shopping district cost less than $5. The trolley also provides access to local buses in National City, Chula Vista, and Imperial Beach. (Fare 50¢-$2.25 depending on distance, over 60 and disabled passengers 50¢. Transfers free.) You're on the honor system; purchase a ticket from machines at stations and board the trolley. There are no turnstiles or ticket takers, but frequently an inspector will check for tickets.

Accommodations

Lodging rates and the number of tourists skyrocket in summer, particularly on weekends. Reservations can save you time and disappointment; weekly rates can save you money. Consider camping outside San Diego (see Camping). If not, staying downtown will give you access to bus routes that will take you most places.

El Cajon Blvd., a large commercial strip devoted primarily to selling cars, has many inexpensive, bland hotels east of downtown along. Bus #15 offers a sweeping tour of the entire boulevard. Try **Lamplighter Inn Motel,** 6474 El Cajon Blvd. (582-3088 or 800-225-9610; singles $41, doubles $48) or **Aztec Motel,** 6050 El Cajon Blvd. (582-1414 or 800-225-9610; singles $31, doubles $33).

Downtown

Armed Services YMCA (AYH), 500 W. Broadway (232-1133), near train and bus stations. Hostel rooms offer all the comforts of a troop ship: gray walls, metal beds, communal showers. Check-out 9:30am. Dorm rooms $10 (linen not included). Newly renovated singles $22. Doubles $34. Check-out noon. Key deposit $2. AYH membership required for dorms.

YWCA Women's Hostel, 1012 C St. (239-0355), at 10th Ave. Women only. Friendly. Dorm beds for ages 18-34 or older AYH members $7.20, nonmembers $9. Linen $1. Hall bath. Nonmembers singles $19; doubles $32. Key deposit $5. Check-out 11am.

Downtown Inn Hotel, 660 G St. (238-4100), just east of the Gaslamp Quarter. Comfortable, tasteful rooms with microwave/toaster oven, fridge, TV, and ceiling fan. Convenient to buses. Check-out 1pm. Singles $26. Doubles $31-38. Weekly: singles $106; doubles $127-152.

Jim's San Diego, 1425 C St. (235-8341), south of the park at City College trolley. Clean, hostel-type rooms. Management caters to international travelers; passport and $20 deposit required. Kitchen and laundry. $15. Weekly: $90. Breakfast and Sunday BBQ included.

La Pensione on Second, 1546 2nd Ave. (236-9292), downtown. Close to I-5. Pretty rooms with microwave, fridge, and cable TV. Neat art on walls. New European-style building with 24-hr. deli. Singles $24-39. Doubles $29-44. Weekly: singles $125-165; doubles $155-180.

Mission Hills, Hillcrest, Mission Valley

E-Z 8 Motels, 3 locations: 2484 Hotel Circle Pl., Mission Valley (291-8252); 4747 Pacific Hwy., Old Town (294-2512); 3333 Channel Way (223-9500), near the Sports Arena. Three clones, with TV, pool, and A/C. Singles $35. Doubles $40.

Old Town Budget Inn, 4444 Pacific Hwy. (260-8024; for reservations 800-225-9610), near Old Town. Ask for rooms in the old building. Singles $37. Doubles $42. Without A/C $2 less. Microwave and refrigerator $5 more.

South of Downtown and the Beaches

Imperial Beach International Hostel (AYH), 170 Palm Ave. (423-8039). Take bus #901 from the Amtrak station or take the trolley on C St. to Palm St. Station (35 min.). Transfer to bus #933 westward-bound (every hr. on the ½-hr.). In a converted firehouse 2 blocks from the the beach, 5 mi. from Mexico. Quiet and fairly remote, with a well-equipped kitchen and large common area with a TV. Bunkbeds for 36 (more if people share). Open 8-10am and 5:30-12pm. Check-in 5:30-10pm. Curfew 11pm. Members $10, nonmembers $13. Key deposit $2. Make reservations by phone or by sending one night's payment.

Elliot International Hostel (AYH), 3790 Udall St., Point Loma (223-4778). Take bus #35 from downtown; get off at first stop on Voltaire and walk across the street. By car, take I-5 to Sea World exit, then left to Sunset Cliffs Blvd. Take left on Voltaire, right on Warden and look for hostel sign painted on building. Airy 2-story building 1.5 mi. from Ocean Beach. Wooden bunk beds for 60, common room, kitchen. Check-out 10am. Office open 7-10am, 4pm-midnight. Lockout 11am-4pm. Curfew 2am. Talk to Patty for helpful info. Members $12, nonmembers $13. Three night maximum stay, reserve 48 hr. in advance.

Camping

All state campgrounds are open to bikers for $2 nightly; state law requires that no cyclist be turned away because of overcrowding. Only Campland on the Bay lies within city limits. For info on state park camping, call the helpful people at San Elijo Beach (753-5091). MISTIX (800-444-7275) can handle reservations. Most parks fill in summer; make weekend reservations eight weeks in advance.

Campland on the Bay, 2211 Pacific Beach Dr. (274-6260). Take I-5 to Grand Ave. exit and follow the signs, or take bus #30 and get off on Grand at the sign on the left. Expensive and crowded as the only central place to pitch a tent or plug in an RV. Cheapest sites in a "dirt area" with nothing to block the wind coming off the water. Sites $22-41; winter $20-38.

South Carlsbad Beach State Park, Rte. 21 (729-8947), near Leucadia, in north San Diego County. 225 sites, half for tents. On cliffs over the sea. Sites $21, winter $16. Reservations necessary in summer.

San Elijo Beach State Park, Rte. 21 (753-5091), south of Cardiff-by-the-Sea. 271 sites (150 for tents) similar to South Carlsbad to the north. Good landscaping gives the illusion of seclusion. Hiker/biker campsites. Sites $21, $16 in winter. Make reservations for summer.

Food

San Diego has hundreds of fast-food joints, an achievement befitting the birthplace of the genre, but the lunchtime business crowd also has nurtured a multitude of good, cheap restaurants. Pick up cheap, high-quality fruits and vegetables at the **Farmer's Bazaar,** 205 7th Ave. (233-0281), at L St., to complete the feast (open Tues.-Sat. 9am-5:30pm, Sun. 9am-5pm) or Ocean Beach's organic grocery stores on Voltaire Ave. For a wide selection of cheap meals downtown, the food court on the top floor of **Horton Plaza** offers far more than the standard 31 flavors of junk food.

Wong's Nanking Café, 5th and Island (239-2171) in the Gaslamp district. Established in 1949, San Diego's oldest Chinese restaurant. Huge servings for as little as $4. Open Sun.-Thurs. noon-11pm, Fri.-Sat. noon-1am. Closed Wed.

Kansas City Barbeque (231-9680), 610 W. Market St., south of Broadway near the bay. Enjoy decent BBQ in the bar where scenes from *Top Gun* were shot. Dinners with 2 side orders around $8. One-sided sandwiches $4.50 (served only after 10pm). Open daily 11am-2am.

Old Spaghetti Factory (233-4323), 275 5th Ave., in the Gaslamp Quarter. Fresh spaghetti ($4.25-5.85) made in an 1898 building. Open Mon.-Thurs. 5-10pm, Fri.-Sat. 5-11pm, Sun. 4-10pm, for lunch: Mon.-Fri. 11am-2pm.

Filippi's Pizza Grotto, 1747 India St., on a block full of Italian restaurants. Other locations—all family-owned—around town. Subs big enough to threaten the Pacific fleet ($3.25-4.25). Try the homemade sausage. Open Sun.-Fri. 11am-10:45pm, Sat. 11am-11:45pm.

El Indio, 3695 India St., in India St. Colony. Lines all day long, but speedy service and high quality. Large portions; combination plates from $3. Buy a bag of fresh corn tortillas (12 for 55¢) or their "fantabulous" tortilla chips. Open daily Mon.-Thurs. 7am-9pm, Fri.-Sat. 7am-10pm.

Chuey's Café, 1894 Main St. (234-6937), in Barrio Logan. Barrio Logan trolley stop; walk 1 block toward stoplight. A stretch out of downtown but easily reached by trolley. People go out of their way to reach this combination restaurant/cocktail bar/pool hall. Excellent Mexican entrees $4-6. Huge combo plates and *gringo* food too. Open Mon.-Thurs. 11am-8pm, Fri. 11am-10pm, Sat. 11am-4pm.

The Big Kitchen, 3003 Grape St. (234-5789), in Golden Hill. Try the huge waffles ($2.75) or pancakes ($3) served on dishes that Whoopi Goldberg used to clean. Open Mon.-Fri. 6am-2pm, Sat.-Sun. 7am-3pm.

Ichiban, 1449 University Ave. (299-7203). Sushi and other Japanese dishes around $4. Open Mon.-Sat. 11am-2:30pm and 5:30-9pm, Sun. 4-8:30pm.

John's Waffle Shop, 7906 Girard Ave., La Jolla (454-7371). Basic golden waffles $2.50, up to $5.50 for whole grain banana nut waffles. Breakfast and sandwiches average $4.50. Open Mon.-Sat. 7am-3pm, Sun. 8am-3pm.

Julio's, 4502 University Ave. (282-6837). Another of San Diego's dimly lit Mexican restaurants with good food; only its late weekend hours set it apart. Get away for less than a fiver by eating a la carte: big burritos with dressings $3.25 ($2.75 at lunch), 2 enchiladas $4.70. Open Mon.-Thurs. 11am-11pm, Fri.-Sat. 11am-3am, Sun. 9am-11pm.

Sights

In contrast to the rest of Southern California, where pre-fab houses and mobile homes resemble a package of instant, dehydrated city, San Diego's buildings form a tangible record of the city's history. The oldest buildings are the early 19th-century adobes of **Old Town.** Just up Juan St. from Old Town, **Heritage Park** displays old Victorian homes, carefully trimmed gingerbread houses. Extending south from Broadway to the railroad tracks and bounded by 4th and 6th Ave. on the west and east, the **Gaslamp Quarter** houses a notable concentration of pre-1910 commercial buildings now resurrected as upscale shops and restaurants. Well-preserved houses and apartment buildings from 1910 to the 1950s, in styles ranging from Mission Revival to zig-zag Moderne, are found on almost every block. For more relaxing pleasures, head toward the beaches, San Diego's biggest draw. Surfers catch tubular waves, sun-worshippers catch rays, and everybody gets caught up in sun-stimulated serenity. Or heatstroke.

Downtown

Horton Plaza, at Broadway and 4th Ave., centers San Diego's redevelopment. This pastel-colored, multi-faceted, glass and steel shopping center encompasses seven city blocks; its complex architecture, top-floor views of the city and occasional live entertainment set it apart from the average mall. (3-hr. parking free with validation at one of the shops.) Another noteworthy example of local architecture is the **Santa Fe Depot,** Kettner Blvd., a Mission Revival building whose grand arches welcomed visitors to the 1915 exposition. Standing just three blocks west of Horton Plaza, the building now serves as the San Diego Amtrak depot.

Farther south past the Gaslamp Quarter, the **Coronado Bridge** stretches westward from Barrio Logan to the Coronado Peninsula. High enough to allow the Navy's biggest ships to pass underneath, the sleek, sky-blue arc executes a near-90° turn over the waters of San Diego Bay before touching down in Coronado. (Bridge toll $1. Bus #901 and other routes also cross.) When built in 1969, the bridge's eastern end cut a swath through San Diego's largest Chicano community. In response to the threatening division, the community created **Chicano Park** beneath the bridge, taking spiritual possession of the land by painting splendid murals on the piers. The murals, visible from I-5, are heroic in scale and theme, drawing on Hispanic-American, Spanish, Mayan, and Aztec imagery. Take bus #11 or the San Ysidro trolley to Barrio Logan station.

The **Embarcadero,** a fancy Spanish name for a dock, sits at the foot of Broadway on the west side of downtown. **San Diego Harbor Excursion** (234-4111) offers cruises past the Navy ships and under the Coronado Bridge. (7 per day 1 hr., $10,; 5 per day 2 hr., $15. Over 55 and ages 3-11 half-price on all cruises. Whale watching in winter twice daily.) Harbor Excursion also sells tickets for the ferry departing for Coronado (every hr. 9am-10pm, returning on the ½-hr. 9:30am-10:30pm, with one additional trip each way Fri.-Sat. evenings; $1.60). The ferry lands at the Olde Ferry Landing in Coronado on 1st and Orange St., a 10-block trolley ride from the

Hotel del Coronado. **Invader Cruises** (234-8687) offers cruises similar to Harbor Excursion's, but also uses a sailing vessel for some of its tours.

Balboa Park

Balboa Park was established in 1868, when San Diego's population was about 2000. The population is now over a million, but the 1000-plus acre park is relatively unmaimed by city expansion, drawing huge crowds with its concerts, theater, Spanish architecture, entertainers, lush vegetation, and zoo. Bus #7 runs through the park and near the museum and zoo entrances. Or take Laurel St. east from downtown and to one of the many parking lots.

With over 100 acres of exquisitely designed habitats, the **San Diego Zoo** (231-1515) is one of the finest in the world, with flora as exciting as the fauna. They have recently moved to a system of "bioclimactic" areas, in which animals and plants are grouped together by habitat rather than by taxonomy. The stunning **Tiger River** and **Sun Bear Forest** are among the first of these areas to be completed. In addition to the usual elephants and zebras, the zoo houses such unusual creatures as Malay tapirs and everybody's favorite eucalyptus-murderer, the koala. Arrive as early as possible, sit on the left, and take the 40-minute open-air **double-decker bus tour**, which covers 70% of the park and avoids long lines ($3, ages 3-15 $2.50.). The **children's zoo** squawks up a barnyard storm (ages over 2 50¢). The **"skyfari"** aerial tram will make you feel like you're suspended over a box of animal crackers. Most of the zoo is accessible by wheelchair (which can be rented), but steep hills make assistance necessary. (Main zoo entrance open July-Labor Day daily 9am-5pm, must exit by 7pm; Labor Day-June 4 9am-4pm, exit by 6pm. Admission $10.75, ages 3-15 $4. Group rates available. Free on Founder's Day, Oct. 1.)

Balboa Park also has the greatest concentration of museums in the U.S. outside of Washington DC. The park focuses at **Plaza de Panama,** on El Prado St., where the Panama-Pacific International Exposition took place in 1915 and 1916. Designed by Bertram Goodhue in the florid Spanish colonial style, many of the buildings were intended as temporary structures, but their elaborate ornamentation and colorfully tiled roofs make them too beautiful to demolish.

Before exploring El Prado on your own, stop in the House of Hospitality's **information center** (239-0512) which sells simple maps (50¢), more elaborate guides ($1.50), and the **Passport to Balboa Park** ($9). The passport contains six coupons to gain entrance to the park's museums. (Passports also available at participating museums. Open daily 9:30am-4pm.)

The western axis of the plaza stars Goodhue's California State Building, now the **Museum of Man** (239-2001). Covered outside with shiny tiles in a Spanish design, inside the museum recaps millions of years of human evolution with permanent exhibits on primates, the Mayan and Hopi cultures, and other Native American societies. (Open daily 10am-4:30pm. Admission $3 or 2 passport coupons, ages 12-18 $1, 6-11 25¢, under 6 free. Free 3rd Tues. each month.)

Behind the museum, the **Old Globe Theater** (239-2255), the oldest pro theater in California, plays Shakespeare and others nightly (Tues.-Sun., weekend matinees). The **Lowell Davies Outdoor Theater** across the street also draws top name performers. (Matinee tickets from $25, seniors and students $12.50.) The **Spreckels Organ Pavilion** (236-5717; 236-5471 for info) at the south end of the Plaza de Panama opposite the Museum of Art, resounds with free evening concerts (Tues.-Thurs. at 6:30pm).

Ranging from ancient Asian to contemporary Cal, the **San Diego Museum of Art** (232-7931), across the plaza, gathers an eclectic range of art. (Open Tues.-Sun. 10am-4:30pm. Admission $5, seniors $4, ages 6-18 and students with ID $2, under 6 free. Free 1st Tues. each month.) Nearby is the outdoor **Sculpture Court and Garden** (236-1725), with a typically rounded and sensuous Henry Moore presiding over other large abstract blocks. (Open until 4:30pm. Pre-theater dinner 5:30-7pm on Old Globe performance days.)

Farther east along the plaza is the **Botanical Building** (236-5717), a wooden Quonset structure accented by tall palms threatening to burst through the slats of the roof. The scent of jasmine and the gentle play of fountains make this an oasis within an oasis. (Open Sat.-Thurs. 10am-4:30pm. Free.)

Next door, the **Casa de Balboa,** a recent reconstruction of the 1915 Electricity Building, contains several museums.

The Museum of Photographic Arts (239-5262) features works of Southwestern masters and a bookstore that stocks one of the largest collections of photography books in San Diego. (Open Fri.-Wed. 10am-5pm, Thurs. 10am-9pm. Admission $2.50, under 12 free. Free 2nd Tues. each month.)

San Diego Hall of Champions (234-2544) is a slick museum with an astroturf carpet and the square footage of a baseball diamond. (Open Mon.-Sat. 10am-4:30pm, Sun. noon-5pm. Admission $2, over 55 and college students $1, ages 6-17 50¢, under 6 free. Families $5. Free 2nd Tues. each month.)

San Diego Model Railroad Museum (696-0199), downstairs, with its elaborate train sets, gives some idea of what Santa's basement would look like if he had a 10-year-old son. (Open Wed.-Fri. 11am-4pm, Sat.-Sun. 11am-5pm. Admission $1, children free. Free 1st Tues. each month.)

From the end of El Prado St., which is closed to cars, a left onto Village Place St. takes you to **Spanish Village,** a crafts center offering free demonstrations and exhibits for browsers and buyers alike. At the other end of Village Place lies the **Natural History Museum** (232-3821), with exhibits on paleontology and ecology. (Open daily 10am-4:30pm. Admission $4, ages 6-18 $1, under 6 free. Free 1st Tues. each month.)

South of the Natural History Museum is the **Reuben H. Fleet Space Theater and Science Center** (238-1168), where two Omnimax projectors, 153 speakers, and a hemispheric planetarium whisk viewers inside the human body, up with the space shuttle, or 20,000 leagues under the sea. The world's largest motion pictures play here about 10 times per day. (Admission $5.50 or 3 passport coupons, seniors $4, ages 5-15 $3.50, under 5 free.) At 9 and 11pm every night lasers dance on the ceiling of the **Laserium** to the tune of Pink Floyd's "The Wall." (Admission $6, seniors $4.50, children $3.50, under 5 not admitted.) Tickets to the space theater also valid for the **Science Center,** where visitors can play with a cloud chamber, telegraph, light-mixing booth, and other gadgets. (Open Sun.-Thurs. 9:30am-9:30pm, Fri.-Sat. 9:30am-10:30pm. Science Center admission $2 or 1 coupon, ages 5-15 $1. Free 1st Tues. each month.)

For a bit of culture from south of the border follow Park Blvd. south to Pepper Grove, across from the Naval Hospital, to visit the **Centro Cultural de la Raza** (235-6135). The center offers changing exhibits of Chicano and Native American art, along with a permanent collection of murals. (Gallery open Wed.-Sun. noon-5pm. Free.)

Old Town, Mission Valley, and Mission Hills

The high prices and ubiquitous gift shops of **Sea World** (226-3901) won't let you forget it's a commercial venture; this is no San Diego Zoo. Though its famous animal shows range from educational to exploitative, once inside you shouldn't miss seeing five-ton killer whales jump high above water. Sea World also encompasses several impressive, well-lit state-of-the-art aquaria, plus open pools where you can touch and feed various wet critters. (Open daily 9am-dusk, ticket sales end 2 hr. before closing time; mid-June through Labor Day the park remains open until 11pm and adds special shows. Admission $23, ages 3-11 $17.)

The site of the original settlement of San Diego, **Old Town** remained the center of San Diego until the late 19th century. Take bus #4 or 5 from downtown. The Spanish *Presidio,* or military post, started here in 1769. Before becoming a museum, Old Town held the county courthouse, the town gallows, and a busy commercial district. Now the partially enclosed pedestrian mall is an overcrowded, overpriced tourist trap. The state park people offer free walking tours Fri.-Sun. at 2pm, starting at the Casa de Machado y Silvas (237-6770). To appreciate Old Town's buildings on your own, pickup the indispensable visitor center's walking tour ($2). **La Panaderia** serves coffee and Mexican pastries (75¢).

Entertainment

San Diego is not renowned for its nightlife, but a certain amount of spelunking could turn up some action. To find out what's happening consult the mammoth-sized *Reader* (235-3000), a free weekly newspaper listing places, dates, and prices. *Varieties,* a guide to UCSD events, proliferates on campus (try the front desk of any dorm or the campus bookstore). The monthly *San Diego Magazine* ($2) publishes a special annual issue focusing on restaurants and nightlife; this comprehensive guide, usually released in summer, is worth the trouble and cost. *Arts Tix,* 121 Broadway (238-3810), at 1st Ave., offers half-price tickets to shows on the day of performance.

Gorgeous weather and strong community spirit make San Diego an ideal place for local festivals, many of them annual affairs of over 30 years' standing. The visitors bureau (see Practical Information above) publishes a thorough yearly events brochure. A 24-hour **Events Hot Line** (696-8700) lists the latest performances and activites in downtown San Diego.

Diego's, 860 Garnet Ave. (272-1241), Pacific Beach. The young come here en masse for the big dance floor and flood of videos. No dress code, but trendoids get decked out for the evening. Happy Hour Mon.-Fri. 3-6pm. Cover Sun.-Thurs. $3, Fri.-Sat. $5. Open Mon.-Sat. 11am-1:30am, Sun. 10am-10pm.

Confetti's, 5373 Mission Center Rd. (291-8635). A singles saturnalia. Lots of confetti and lots of comparison shopping. Drinks $1.75-3.75. Happy Hour (5-8pm) includes free buffet. Cover Mon.-Wed. $2, Thurs. and Sun. $3, Fri.-Sat. $5. No cover before 8pm. Open Mon.-Fri. 5pm-2am, Sat. 7pm-2am, Sun. 9pm-2am.

The Comedy Store, 916 Pearl St. (454-9176), in La Jolla. Drinks $3. Potluck night Mon.-Tues. at 8pm with local comics. Well-known comedians other evenings. Shows Wed.-Thurs. and Sun. at 8pm ($6), Fri.-Sat. at 8 and 10:30pm ($8-10). Wed.-Thurs. 2-for-1 admission with any college ID. Two-drink minimum enhances performances. Must be 21.

Near San Diego

With 70 mi. of beaches, San Diego even has a place for "man's best friend" at Dog Beach and a resting ground for those wasted and indisposed at Garbage Beach. Sunworshippers glaze the coast from Imperial Beach in the south to La Jolla in the north; it may take a little ingenuity to find room to bask. Chic places like Mission Beach and La Jolla will likely be as packed as funky Ocean Beach come prime sunning time on summer weekends.

The **Hotel del Coronado,** Orange Ave. (435-6611), on the Coronado Peninsula, was built in 1888 as a remote resort. Take the Coronado Bridge from I-5 (toll $1) or bus #910 from downtown. Or take a ferry from San Diego Harbor. Excursions for $1.60. (Every hr. on the hr. See Waterfront Sights.) One of the great hotels of the world, the "Del" has hosted 12 presidents. The 1959 classic *Some Like It Hot* showcased its white verandas and red, circular towers. Wander onto the white, seaweed-free beach in back; it's seldom crowded, even on weekends.

Mission Beach and **Pacific Beach** are more respectable wave-wise than **Ocean Beach,** codename O.B. On San Jose Place, in one of the wind-beaten shacks, screams **Keith's Klothing Kastle.** The proprietor, Keith Nolan, sells his collection of silk Hawaiian shirts from the 40s and 50s at $100 apiece; the San Diego Museum of Art even featured some a few years ago. He also sells vintage Ocean Pacific and Hang Ten beachwear, at more conscionable prices. Hours, like Keith, are unpredictable—open most afternoons and evenings.

Situated on a small rocky promontory, **La Jolla** (pronounced la-HOY-a) was, in the 30s and 40s, the hideaway of wealthy Easterners who built luxurious houses and gardens atop the bluffs overlooking the ocean. Jags, Mercedes, and BMWs purr along Girard Ave. and Prospect St. past boutiques and financial institutions. At the summit of this runway sits the **San Diego Museum of Contemporary Art,** 700 Prospect St. (454-3541), an collection of pop, minimalist, conceptualist, and Californian artwork in galleries overlooking the Pacific. Exhibits change frequently so call ahead for more info. (Open Tues. and Thurs.-Sun. 10am-5pm, Wed. 10am-9pm. Admission $4, seniors and students $2, under 12 50¢. Free Wed. 5-9pm.) Pick up a copy of the *South Coast Gallery Guide* from a sidewalk box for details on other galleries. La Jolla also claims some of the finest beaches in the city. Grassy knolls run right down to the sea at **La Jolla Cove,** and surfers especially dig the waves at **Tourmaline Beach** and **Windansea Beach. At Black's Beach,** people run, sun, and play volleyball in the nude. It is a public beach, not *officially* a nude beach, but you wouldn't know it from the color of most beachcombers' buns. Take I-5 to Genesee Ave., go west and turn left on N. Torrey Pines Rd. until you reach the **Torrey Pines Glider Port** (where clothed hang gliders leap off the cliffs).

Take bus #30 or 34 to La Jolla from downtown San Diego; both the Veteran's Hospital here and the University Towne Centre are transfer points for North County buses.

The University of California at San Diego (UCSD; operator 452-2230, info 534-8273) rests above La Jolla, surrounded on three sides by Torrey Pines Rd., La Jolla Village Dr., and I-5. Despite the thousands of eucalyptus trees and varied architecture, the campus falls somewhere between bland and really bland. Buses #30 and 34 will get you to the campus, but once there a car or bike is invaluable in going from one of the five colleges to the next. An info pavilion on Gilman Dr., just north of La Jolla Village Dr., has campus maps (open daily 7am-8:30pm).

San Francisco

San Francisco—a city whose name evokes images of cable cars, LSD, gay liberation, and Rice-A-Roni. It began as a Spanish mission, and exploded during the Gold Rush that followed 1848's first strike. Although the city emerged from the massive earthquake of 1906 shaken but not stirred, it didn't rebuild and recover completely until the 1930s, when the openings of the Oakland and Golden Gate Bridges ended a long isolation from the rest of the Bay area. The Beat Generation moved here in the 1950s; the 60s saw Haight-Ashbury blossom into the hippie capital of the world; and in the 70s, the gay population emerged as one of the most powerful and visible groups in the city. San Francisco's latest tragedy came when the biggest quake since 1906 killed 62 people, knocked out the Bay Bridge, and cracked Candlestick Park during a World Series game on October 17, 1989.

San Francisco is very much a confederation of neighborhoods; the average San Franciscan thinks in terms of the Mission District, Chinatown, and Nob Hill rather than the city as a whole. Subdivisions follow no discernible logic: a few blocks will take you from ritzy Pacific Heights to the impoverished Western Addition; the crime-ridden Tenderloin abuts the steel-and-glass wonders in the Financial District. Quaint small-scale streets, turreted houses, and extensive parks afford a European air. Everyone leaves inhibitions behind in San Francisco.

Practical Information

Emergency: 911.

Visitor Information Center, Hallidie Plaza (391-2000), at Market and Powell St. beneath street level. Free street maps, events calendars, and the helpful *San Francisco Book.* Open Mon.-Fri. 9am-5:30pm, Sat. 9am-3pm, Sun. 10am-2pm. 24-hr. event and info recordings in English (391-2001), French (391-2003), German (391-2004), Japanese (391-2101), and Spanish (391-2122). **Center for International Educational Exchange (CIEE),** 312 Sutter St. (421-3473), between Stockton St. and Grant Ave. downtown. Student-flight, discount, and lodgings information. ISIC cards. Open Mon.-Tues., Thurs.-Fri. 9am-5pm. **Sierra Club Store,** 730 Polk St. (923-5600), just north of the Civic Center. Tremendous resource for those planning wilderness trips. They prefer and encourage visitors to join the club. Open Mon.-Sat. 10am-5:30pm.

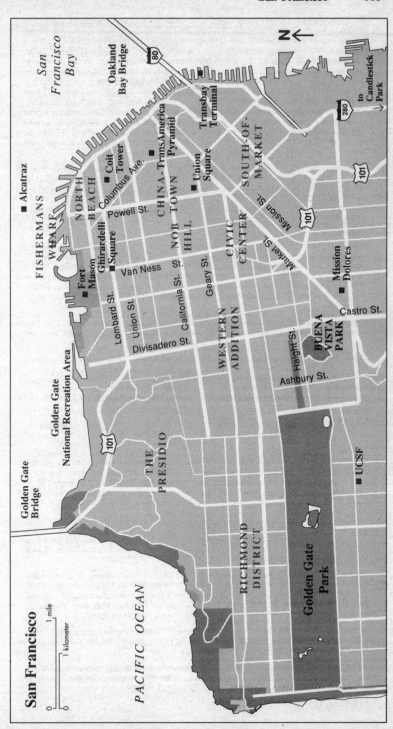

San Francisco

San Francisco Bay

Oakland Bay Bridge

to Candlestick Park

N

Alcatraz

FISHERMANS WHARF

NORTH BEACH

Coit Tower

Columbus Ave.

TransAmerica Pyramid

CHINA-TOWN

Transbay Terminal

SOUTH-OF-MARKET

Union Square

Powell St.

Ghirardelli Square

NOB HILL

Mission St.

Van Ness

Fort Mason

Civic Center

California St.

Geary St.

Market St.

Mission Dolores

Lombard St.

Union St.

Castro St.

Divisadero St.

WESTERN ADDITION

Haight St.

BUENA VISTA PARK

Ashbury St.

Golden Gate Bridge

Golden Gate National Recreation Area

THE PRESIDIO

101

UCSF

PACIFIC OCEAN

RICHMOND DISTRICT

Golden Gate Park

80

280

101

1 mile

1 kilometer

0

San Francisco International Airport (SFO) (721-0800), inconveniently placed on a small nub of land in San Francisco Bay about 15 mi. south of the city center on U.S. 101. **San Mateo County Transit (samTrans)** (800-660-4287) runs two buses from SFO to downtown San Francisco. You can only bring carry-on luggage onto the 35-min. express (#7F) (every ½-hr. 5:30am-1am; $1.25, under 17 75¢, seniors 60¢). On the #7B bus you can carry all the luggage you want (every ½ hr. 5am-12:13am; 1 hr.; $1.20, seniors and under 17 60¢). **Airporter** shuttles (495-8404) run from all three terminals to major hotels and a downtown terminal at 301 Ellis St. (every 20 min. 5:45am-10:50pm, $6). **Taxis** downtown from SFO cost about $25. **Lorrie's Travel and Tour** (334-9000), on the upper level at the west end of all three terminals, provides door-to-door van service to and from the airport. Make reservations only for service to the airport. (Vans run daily 4:30am-11:30pm. $9, seniors $8 ages 2-12 $6, under 2 free.) **Franciscus Adventures** (821-0903) runs a small bus between San Francisco and SFO ($8, $7 per person for groups of five or more). Traffic to the airport can be thick; give yourself some time.

Trains: Amtrak, 425 Mission St. (for ticket info 800-872-7245), 1st floor of Transbay Terminal. Just a boarding area for the free shuttle bus to the actual train station in Oakland on 16th St. (982-8512). Shuttle trip takes 30 min. Open daily 6:45am-10:45pm. **CalTrain,** 4th and Townsend St. (557-8661), 6 blocks south of Market St., is a regional commuter train running to Palo Alto ($3, seniors and disabled $1.50) and San Jose ($3.50, seniors and disabled). The depot is at 4th and Townsend St. and is served by MUNI buses #15, 30, 32, and 42.

Buses: Greyhound, at the Transbay Terminal, 425 Mission St. (558-6789), between Fremont and 1st St. downtown. A regional transport hub. Second floor info center has maps and displays. Free shuttle buses at night. Open daily 5am-12:35am. First St. and Natoma, behind the Transbay Terminal, is the pickup point for **Green Tortoise** (285-2441), the transportation company/mobile commune, which runs trips to L.A. (Fri. night, $30) and Seattle (Mon., Wed., and Fri.-Sat.; $59). Also to New York and Boston (both 14 days, $350). Make reservations in advance.

Gray Line Tours: (558-9400). 3½-hr. bus tours of the city $23.50, ages 5-11 $11.75, plus a variety of other tours departing from Union Square, or the Transbay Terminal for night tours. Reservations required.

Public Transport: San Francisco Municipal Railway (MUNI) (673-6864) operates buses, cable cars, and a combined subway/trolley system. Fares for both buses and trolleys is 85¢, ages 5-17 25¢, seniors and disabled passengers 15¢. Exact coins required. Ask for a free transfer, valid in any direction for several hours, when boarding. MUNI's *San Francisco Street and Transit Map,* available at most bookstores ($1.50), not only contains info on MUNI service, but is also a complete street index and good general street map.

Taxi: Luxor Cabs, 282-4141. **DeSoto Cab Co.,** 673-1414. Small initial charge, $1.90 each additional mi. Both open 24 hrs.

Car Rental: Rent-A-Wreck, 555 Ellis St. (776-8700), between Hyde and Leavenworth St. Used, mid-sized cars $29 per day with 100 free mi., $159 per week with 700 free mi. 20¢ each additional mi. Under 25 $10 extra. Open Mon.-Fri. 8am-6pm, Sat. 9am-4pm , Sun. 9am-1pm. Must be 21 with major credit card. **Bob Leech's Auto Rental,** 435 S. Airport Blvd. (583-3844), South San Francisco. New Toyotas $20 per day with 150 free mi., 10¢ each additional mi. Travelers coming into SFO should call for a ride to the shop. Open Mon.-Fri. 8am-9pm, Sat.-Sun. 9am-5pm. Must be 23 with major credit card.

Auto Driveaway Company, 330 Townsend (777-3740). Open Mon.-Fri. 9am-5pm. Must be 21 with valid license and references. Cash deposit $250. **A-1 Auto,** 1300 Old Bayshore Rd., Burlingame (342-9611). Call 10 days in advance. Open Mon.-Fri. 9am-5pm. Must be 21 with major credit card. Cash deposit $200-300.

Bike Rental: Lincoln Cyclery, 772 Stanyan St. (221-2415), on the east edge of Golden Gate Park. 3-speeds $3 per hr. with $5 deposit, 10-speeds $4 per hr. with $15 deposit. Open Mon. and Wed.-Sat. 9am-5pm, Sun. 11:30am-5pm. Driver's license or major credit card required. **Presidio Bicycle Shop,** 5335 Geary (752-2453), between 17th and 18th Ave. 10-speed or mountain bike $25 per day. Open Mon.-Sat. 10am-6pm, Sun. 11am-4pm.

Help Lines: Rape Crisis Center, 647-7273. **Helpline,** 772-4357. **Gay Switchboard and Counseling Services,** 841-6224. Helpful staff has info on gay community events, local clubs, etc. Open Mon.-Fri. 10am-10pm, Sat. noon-4pm, Sun. 6-9pm.

Post Office: 7th and Mission St. (621-6838), opposite the Greyhound station. Open Mon.-Fri. 9am-5pm, Sat. 9am-1:30pm. **Rincon Annex,** 99 Mission St. Open Mon.-Fri. 7am-6pm, Sat. 9am-2pm. **ZIP code:** 94101.

Area Code: 415.

Getting There

If you're a driver who needs a passenger or vice versa, call the **Berkeley Ride Board** (642-5259) for free, 24-hr. listings. The San Francisco International Hostel and San Francisco State University (469-1842, in the student union; open Mon.-Fri. 7am-10pm, Sat. 10am-4pm) also have ride boards. KALX radio (642-5259), on the Berkeley campus, broadcasts a ride list Monday through Saturday at 10am and 10pm. Call them to put your name and number on the air for free. KSAN radio (986-2825) provides a similar service.

Getting Around

The hilly city of San Francisco, surrounded by water on three sides, is an amalgam of distinct neighborhoods organized along a few central arteries. Each neighborhood is compact enough to explore comfortably on foot. San Francisco once radiated outward from its docks, on the northeast edge of the peninsula just inside the lip of the bay. The city now extends south and west from this point, but many of San Francisco's attractions cluster here, within a wedge formed by **Van Ness Avenue** running north-south, **Market Street** running northeast-southwest, and the **Embarcadero** (waterfront road) curving along the coast. Streets radiating north from Market and west from Market and the Embarcadero are numbered from these thoroughfares, although you should keep in mind that parallel streets do not bear the same block numbers.

At the top of this wedge lies **Fisherman's Wharf,** an area frequented mainly by tourists, and **North Beach,** a district shared by Italian-Americans, artists, and professionals. The focal point of North Beach is Telegraph Hill, topped by Coit Tower and fringed counterclockwise from the northwest to the southeast by Columbus Ave. Across Columbus begin the **Nob Hill** and **Russian Hill** areas, resting places of the city's old money. This fan-shaped area is confined by Columbus along its northeast side, Van Ness along the west, and (roughly) Geary and Bush St. on the south. The core downtown area centers on **Union Square** and then, beyond Jones St., the **Civic Center,** an impressive collection of municipal buildings including City Hall, the Opera House, and Davies Symphony Hall.

Also within this wedge is the **Tenderloin,** which still qualifies as a somewhat seedy region to avoid at night despite the sprouting high-rises. The Tenderloin is roughly bounded by Larkin St. to the west and to the east by Taylor St. extending from Market St. north to Geary. Some of the area's seediness, however, seeps across Market to the area near the Greyhound station (6th and 7th St.).

South-of-Market-Area (SOMA) is home to much of the city's nightlife. SOMA extends inland from the bay to 10th St., at which point the Hispanic **Mission District** begins and spreads south. The **Castro** area, center of the gay community, adjoins the Mission District at 17th and also extends south, centered upon Castro St.

West of Van Ness Ave., the city extends all the way to the ocean side of the peninsula. At the top of Van Ness, the commercially developed **Marina** area embraces a yacht harbor, Fort Mason, and the youth hostel. Fisherman's Wharf lies immediately east. Above the marina rise the wealthy hills of **Pacific Heights. Japantown** is located within the Western Addition. North of **Golden State Park** nods San Francisco's token suburb within the city, the **Richmond District.**

Bay Area Rapid Transit (BART) (778-2278) operates comfortable trains along four lines connecting San Francisco with the East Bay, including Oakland, Berkeley, Concord, and Fremont. One-way fares range from 80¢ to $3. A special excursion deal for $2.60 is designed for tours of the system: you must begin and end at the same station, and your trip must not take more than three hours. (Trains run Mon.-Sat. 6am-midnight, Sun. 9am-midnight.) Maps and schedules are available at the visitor info center and all BART stations. BART stations and trains are wheelchair accessible.

Within San Francisco itself, **cable cars** are a great way to get around—noisy and slow (9½ mph), but indescribably hip. They run promptly and frequently and cover the entire city. Of the three cable lines, the California St. one is by far the least crowded; it runs from the Financial District up Nob Hill. (Fare $2, ages 5-17 75¢, seniors 15¢, under 5 free. Unlimited transfers allowed within a given three-hour period. Cars run daily 7am-1am.)

In San Francisco, cars are not necessary. Furthermore, parking spots are scarce and very expensive. But driving is definitely the best way to explore the outer reaches of the Bay Area. In the city, contending with the hills is the first task; those in a standard-shift car will need to develop a fast clutch foot, since all the hills have stop signs at the crests. The street signs admonishing you to "PREVENT RUN-AWAYS" refer not to wayward youths but rather to cars improperly parked on hills. When parking facing uphill, turn the wheels toward the center of the street; when facing downhill, turn the wheels toward the curb; and *always* park in gear with the brake set. When renting, get an automatic. And remember, in San Francisco cable cars have the right of way.

Accommodations

Unlike most cities, San Francisco has a wide selection of conveniently located, relatively satisfying budget accommodations. But don't expect miracles for these prices. Note that a rapacious 11% bed tax is not included in the prices given below. Most hotels listed here are in areas such as the Tenderloin, the Mission District, Union Square, and downtown, where caution is advised both on the streets and within the buildings, particularly at night.

The International Network Globe Hostel, 10 Hallam Pl. (431-0540), between 7th and 8th St., near Transbay Terminal, just off Folsom St. in the South-of-Market district. Clean and convenient. 4-5 beds per room with chairs and tables. No kitchen, but sundeck and laundry room are good places to meet international students. Serves continental breakfast and dinner. Open 24 hrs. $15. Key deposit $5. Curfew? *Not.*

San Francisco International Hostel (AYH), Bldg. 240, Fort Mason (771-7277). Entrance at Bay and Franklin St., 1 block west of Van Ness Ave. at the northern end of the peninsula. From Transbay Terminal, take MUNI bus #42 to Northpoint and Van Ness, then walk up the hill to Bay St.; follow signs to hostel. One of the largest AYH-affiliated hostels in the nation, with about 160 beds. Clean, well-run, and efficient. Chore-a-day rule enforced. Extensive lounges, large kitchen, spic-and-span food-storage areas, and pay lockers for valuables. Good ride board. Frequented by students, families, and seniors. Crowded in summer. Arrive around 7am or send a night's fee three weeks ahead to reserve a place. 5-day max. stay. Check-in 7am-2pm and 4:30pm-midnight. Lockout 10am-4:30pm. Curfew 2am. Members and non-members $12.

San Francisco Summer Hostel (AYH), 100 McAllister St. (621-5809), near Civic Center BART station and many bus routes. Open in summer only; closes Aug. 11. Laundry and 2 small kitchens. 7-day max. stay. Check-in 7:30am-midnight. Lockout 11am-4:30pm. Curfew 2am. Members $12. Nonmembers $15.

International Guest House, 2976 23rd St. (641-1411), at Harrison St. in the Mission District. Away from the most touristy areas, but 24th St. fairly busy. Strict foreign-travelers-only rule. 2 full kitchens for 28 guests. Common room, TV, stereo, fireplace. 5-day min., no max. stay. No curfew. Bunks $12 for each of the first 10 nights, $11 thereafter. Rooms for couples $20. No reservations.

European Guest House, 761 Minna St. (861-6634), between 8th and 9th St., south of Market in a quiet but run-down neighborhood. Free-wheeling, relaxed, improvised, friendly; people sleep on sofas, mats, cushions. Co-ed rooms. TV room, laundry, kitchen, small info board. Check-in 7am-3am. No curfew. Bed in huge, hot dorm $11. Bunks in 6-bed room $13.

YMCA Hotel, 220 Golden Gate Ave. (885-0460), at Leavenworth St., 1 block north of Market St. Men and women. One of the city's largest lodgings. Spartan rooms. Has the only indoor track in the city. Double locks on all doors. Pool and gym. No curfew. Hostel beds for members only, $16. Singles $32. Doubles $33.50. Breakfast included. $5 key deposit.

YMCA Chinatown, 855 Sacramento St. (982-4412), between Stockton St. and Grant Ave. Near the city center. Men over 18 only. Friendly young staff, pool, and gym. Spartan rooms.

Registration Mon.-Fri. 6:30am-10pm, Sat. 9am-5pm, Sun. 9am-1pm. No curfew. Singles $22.50. Doubles $33.50. 7th day free. Reserve 2 weeks in advance.

El Capitan, 2361 Mission St. (695-1597), north of 20th St. in the Mission District. Rooms clean, impressive facade. Two locked gates. Singles $26, with bath $30. Doubles $32.

Sam Wong Hotel, 615 Broadway (781-6836), between Grant Ave. And Stockton St. in Chinatown. Popular for location. Rooms could use more care, but secure and clean. Singles with toilet $24, with bath $29. Add $2 for double occupancy. Triples with bath $40.

Sutter/Larkin Hotel, 1048 Larkin (474-6820). Take Bus #19 from the Civic Center. Clean and well-maintained. Extremely accommodating manager. Check-in after 10am. Singles with shared bath $20. Doubles $25. Weekly: singles $90, with bath $110, doubles $105.

Olympic Hotel, 140 Mason St. (982-5010) at Ellis St., a few blocks from Union. Caters mostly to Japanese students and Europeans. Comfortable, with atrocious wallpaper. Tends to fill during summer. Singles and doubles $28, with bath $35.

The Red Victorian Bed and Breakfast Inn, 1665 Haight St. (864-1978), 2 blocks east of Golden Gate Park in Haight-Ashbury. 3 mi. from downtown, but close to buses and the "N" trolley. Barely describable—more a state of mind than a hotel. Individually decorated rooms honor butterflies, the nearby Golden Gate Park, and the equally proximate 1960s. Even the 4 hall baths, shared by some of the rooms, have their own names and motifs. If canopied and teddy-bear festooned beds aren't enough to soothe your mind, try the meditation room, the therapeutic massage ($60 per hr.), or a talk with the hotel cat. Downstairs, a newly opened global family network center promotes planetary consciousness with a café, market, and computers. A non-smoking, angst-free environment. Stop by for a tour. Check-in 3-6pm. Checkout 11am. Summer rates $65-125 depending on karma and room size, weekends $5 more; winter $55-120. Extra futon $15. Singles deduct $5, extra persons add $15. Breakfast of fresh bread, pastry, and requisite granola included. Complimentary tea, coffee, popcorn, and cheese in the evenings. Make reservations for summer months. 2-night stay usually required on weekends, man. Weekly rates available.

Pensione International, 875 Post St. (775-3344), east of Hyde St., 4½ blocks west of Union Sq. Very nice rooms with interesting art. Singles $30, with bath $55. Doubles $40, with bath $65. Breakfast included.

Adelaide Inn, 35 Isadora Duncan (441-2261), off Taylor near Post St., 2 blocks west of Union Sq. Warm hosts and jumbled paintings. Does not answer door after 11pm. Steep stairs, no elevator. All rooms with a bright outside exposure. Kitchenette and microwave available. Hall baths. Singles $38. Twin bed or doubles $46. Triples $52. Continental breakfast included. Reservations required.

Grant Plaza, 465 Grant Ave. (434-3883 or 800-472-6899; in CA 800-472-6805), at Pine St. near the Chinatown gate. Excellent location. Recently renovated like a chain motel, but more colorful. Rooms with bath, phones, and color TV. Check-in after 2:30pm. Singles $39. Doubles $45. Twin beds $49. Reservations recommended 2-3 weeks in advance.

The Ansonia, 711 Post St. (673-2670), 3 blocks west of Union Sq. in a nice area. Pretty nice rooms with nice firm mattresses. Nice laundry facilities. Breakfast and dinner nicely included Mon.-Sat. Singles $35, with shared bath $42, with private bath $52. Doubles $47, with bath $60. Weekly: singles $213, with shared bath $250, with private bath $300; doubles $280, with bath $360. Nice student rates for stays of a month or longer if you ask nicely.

Sheehan Hotel, 620 Sutter St. (775-6500 or 800-848-1529), at Mason St. near Union Square. Excellent location near public transport and trendy art galleries. Busy, elegant lobby something of a scene on warm summer evenings. Many international students. Worn, very English rooms; doubles have tea settings. Cable TV, pool, phone, exercise room. Economy singles $40, with bath $55. Economy doubles $50, with bath $60. Additional people $10. Under 12 free with parents. Breakfast included.

Hotel Essex, 684 Ellis St. (474-4664; outside CA 800-45-ESSEX), between Hyde and Larkin St., north of Civic Center. Very friendly. Geared to German travelers; many German-speaking employees. Free coffee. Small rooms with phones. Check-out noon. Singles $39, $46 with bath. Doubles $42, with bath and TV $54. Twin beds $44, with bath and TV $56. Weekly: singles $120-150. Rates slightly higher in summer.

Pacific Bay Inn, 520 Jones St. (673-0234 or 800 445-2631, within CA 800-343-0880), 3 blocks west of Union Sq. Entirely renovated after fire. Pleasant rooms with TV. Singles and doubles $55-65; only $45 if you bring your copy of *Let's Go.* Continental breakfast included.

Food

The pizzas that emerge from the wood ovens of the Bay Area range from North Beach Neapolitan to trendy but tasty goat cheese and *pancetta*. Sourdough is a city landmark, and San Franciscans are as serious about their coffee as they are about the wines of Napa Valley. Head to Chinatown for awesome food and the Mission district for inexpensive gastronomic diversity; elsewhere, cheap eats are few and far between. The Haight has a fabulous selection of bakeries, and Columbus Ave. in North Beach lures visitors to café after café.

Chinatown

House of Nanking, 919 Kearny St. (421-1429). Great food, pleasant atmosphere. Very very popular with workers who walk all the way from the Financial District on their lunch hours. Mu-Shui vegetables ($5), onion cakes ($1.75). Anything made with Tsing-Tao beer is bound to be good. Open Mon.-Sat. 11am-10pm, Sun. 4pm-10pm.

Sam Wo, 813 Washington (982-0596). The late hours, cheap food, and BYOB policy make this restaurant a favorite among students from all over the Bay. Patrons walk through the kitchen to get to their seats. Most dishes $1.25-$4.50. Open Mon.-Sat. 11am-3am, Sun. 12:30-9:30pm.

Dol Ho, 808 Pacific Ave. (392-2828). Perfect for relaxing afternoon tea and *dim sum*. Four *har gow* (steamed shrimp), sweet doughy sesame balls, or pork buns each $1.60. Open daily 8am-4pm.

Yuet Lee, 1300 Stockton at Broadway (982-6020). Not outstanding for atmosphere, but the seafood makes up for it. Seasonal exotic specialties such as sauteed pork stomach with boneless duck feet. Open Mon.-Sun. 11am-3am.

North Beach

Tommaso's, 1042 Kearny St., between Pacific and Broadway, just below Van Ness Ave. For a break from *nouvelle pizza* try some of the very best traditional Italian pizza anywhere. The super deluxe, piled high with mushrooms, peppers, ham, and Italian sausage sates 2 ($13.50). Francis Ford Coppola has been known to occasionally toss pizza dough in front of the huge wood-burning ovens. Long wait worth it. Open Tues.-Sat. 5-10:45pm, Sun. 4-9:45pm.

Bohemian Cigar Store, 566 Columbus Ave., corner of Union Sq. Excellent espresso ($1) and agreeable Italian food. Try their Italian sandwiches (around $5). Open Mon. 10am-11pm, Tues.-Sat. 10am-midnight, Sun. 10am-6pm.

Caffe Trieste, 609 Vallejo St. (392-6739), at Grant. Only a few beatniks now; sip coffee and remember the exciting Eisenhower years when Ginsberg and Ferlinghetti hung out here. Loud live music Sat. 1-4pm. Otherwise settle for a tune from the opera jukebox. Coffees $2.25. Open Sun.-Thurs. 7am-11:30pm, Fri.-Sat. 7am-12:30am.

Marina and Pacific Heights

Bepple's Pies, 1934 Union St. A bit expensive, but perfect pies. Fruit pie slices $3. Another 95¢ for a solid slab of excellent vanilla ice cream. Whole pies $11. Meat pies, Mr. Todd $6. Open Mon.-Wed. 9am-11:30pm, Thurs. 7am-midnight, Fri. 7am-1am, Sat. 9am-1:30am, Sun. 9am-10:30am.

Jackson Fillmore, 2506 Fillmore St. Usually a long wait at this popular and hip *trattoria*, with great southern Italian cuisine and a lively atmosphere. Put your name down and browse the Fillmore scene while you wait. Large portions; you can maybe sneak out for less than $10 per person. Eat lots of tasty breadsticks to fill up. Open Tues.-Thurs. 5:30-10:30pm, Fri.-Sat. 5:30-11pm, Sun. 5-10pm.

Mai's Vietnamese, 1838 Union St. Sidewalk dining on Union St. The crab claws get good marks ($6.75) as does the vegetarian imperial roll ($5). Clear, flavorful crabmeat soup $4. Entrees around $7.50. A romantic spot on warm summer city nights. Open Mon.-Thurs. 11am-10pm, Fri. 11am-11pm, Sat. noon-11pm, Sun. noon-10pm.

Mission District and Castro Street

Café Macondo, 3159 16th St. (863-6517). Central-American food and coffee in a homey, artfully-designed café—you'll feel like you've discovered some wonderful museum. A great place to bring a book while sipping cappuccino ($1.50) and munching sandwiches ($2.75). Open Mon.-Thurs. 11am-10pm, Fri.-Sun. 11am-11pm.

New Dawn, 3174 16th St. at Guerrero (553-8888). Absolutely anything is considered art at this hip restaurant, from the dolly body parts and eggbeaters hanging on the walls to the eardrum-melting music to the chef's magenta mohawk. The menu, mainly breakfast food and burgers, is written around the room on mirrors. Enormous servings. Vegetable home fries ($3), burgers ($3.25). Everything is under $4. Open Mon.-Fri. 8am-3pm, Sat.-Sun. 8am-4:30pm.

La Cumbre, 515 Valencia St. The top. Ample superlative burrito ($2.52, planet-sized $4.83). Open Mon.-Sat. 11am-10pm, Sun. noon-9pm.

Taqueria San Jose, 2830 Mission St., at 24th. Don't be put off by the fast-food-style menu; real care goes into the cooking. Soft, articulate tacos with your choice of meat—a full house of 3 brain and 2 tongue tacos for $3.50. Free chips and guacamole. Open Mon.-Thurs. 8am-1am, Fri.-Sat. 8am-4am.

Manora, 3226 Mission. Attractive Thai restaurant with delicious cuisine at reasonable prices. Especially light with its sauces—food not smothered in peanut butter. The red beef curry ($5.75) gets good reviews. Most dishes under $8. Open 5pm-10pm, Tues.-Fri. also 11:30am-2:30pm.

Haight-Ashbury and Richmond

Cha Cha Cha, 1805 Haight St. Love children join hands with yuppies here. Trendy, but best Latin restaurant in the Haight. Be prepared to wait up to 2 hr. Try the *tapas*. Entrees $5-8. Open Mon.-Thurs. 11:30am-3pm and 5-11:30pm, Fri. 11:30am-3pm and 5:30pm-midnight, Sat. noon-3pm and 5:30pm-midnight, Sun. noon-3pm and 5-11pm.

Ganges, 755 Frederick St. Not exactly in the Haight, but close enough. Veggie Indian food draws health-conscious students from the nearby medical school. Traditional Indian seating in back. Dinners $7.50-11.50. Open Mon.-Sat. 5-9:30pm.

Cambodian House, 5625 Geary Blvd., near 20th Ave. Attractive restaurant, interesting menu. Live music Thurs.-Sat. starting at 7:15pm. Remarkably complex and tasty lunch specials $4. Dinner entrees about $6, seafood $7.50-8. Open Sun.-Thurs. 11am-3pm and 5-10pm, Fri.-Sat. 11am-3pm and 5-10:30pm. Reservations a good idea.

Tassajara Bread Bakery, 1000 Cole St. at Parnassus, 5 blocks south of Haight St. One of the best bakeries in the city. A branch at Fort Mason, but the purist will want to make the pilgrimage to Haight-Ashbury for the original. Open Mon.-Thurs. 7am-7pm, Fri. 7am-10pm, Sat. 8am-10pm, Sun. 8am-2pm.

Chao Kos, 5625 Geary Blvd. (668-5888), near 20th Ave. An attractive restaurant with a mixture of Thai and Cambodian cuisine. Remarkably complex and tasty lunch specials ($3.85). Dinners entrees are about $6, $7.50-8 for seafood. Open Sun.-Thurs. 11am-3pm and 5-10pm, Fri.-Sat. 11am-3pm and 5-10;30pm.

Sights

The way to see the city is not by landmarks or "sights," but by neighborhoods. Whether defined by ethnicity, tax brackets, or topography, or simply a groovy spirit, these communities collectively offer the visitor everything. Off-beat bookstores, Japanese folk festivals, cosmopolitan Union Street, America's most vibrant gay community, Strawberry Hill in Golden Gate Park, the Club Fugazi in North Beach, Haight-Ashbury's tie-dyed crunch. . .we might say they make you leave your heart here, but that would just be dumb.

Downtown

Union Square is the center of San Francisco. Now an established shopping area, the square has a rich and somewhat checkered history. During the Civil War, at a large public meeting here, citizens decided whether San Francisco should secede. The square became the rallying ground of the Unionists, who bore placards reading "The Union, the whole Union, and nothing but the Union."

Even when the Barbary Coast (now the Financial District) stayed down and dirty, Union Square stayed cheaper. **Morton Alley,** in particular, offered off-brand alternatives to the high-priced prostitutes and stiff drinks of the coast; the prices were low, but the action sizzled. At the turn of the century, murders averaged one per week on Morton Alley, and prostitutes with shirts unbuttoned waved to their favorite customers from second-story windows. After the 1906 earthquake and fire destroyed most of the flophouses, a group of proper capitalists moved in and renamed the area **Maiden Lane** in hopes of changing the street's image. The switch worked. Today Maiden Lane, extending two blocks from Union Square's eastern side, boasts smart shops and classy boutiques. Traces of the old street live on, however, in words like "hoodlum," "shanghaied," and "Mickey Finn," all added to the U.S. vocabulary by the people who frequented the area.

The best free ride in town is on the outside elevators of the St. Francis Hotel. As you glide up the building, the entire Bay Area stretches out before you. The "elevator tours" offer an unparalleled view of Coit Tower and the Golden Gate Bridge. The Powell St. cable cars also grant an excellent view of the square.

Financial District

North of Market and east of Kearny, snug against the bay, beats the West's financial heart, or at least one of its ventricles. Try to catch Montgomery Street, the Wall Street of the West, before the workday ends. After 7:30pm, the heart stops, to be resuscitated the next morning.

At the foot of Market St. is **Justin Herman Plaza** with its famous geodesic **Vallaincourt Fountain,** through which you can walk as water flows above you.

San Francisco's most distinctive structure, totally out-of-scale with the surrounding buildings, is the 853-ft. **TransAmerica Pyramid,** at Montgomery St. between Clay and Washington St. Designed mainly to show off the talents of its architects, the building's pyramidal shape and subterranean concrete "anchor" base make it one of the city's most stable, earthquake-resistant buildings. A free observation deck faces north on the 27th floor. (Open Mon.-Fri. 9am-4pm.) Diagonally across from the pyramid is the **Old TransAmerica Building,** 701 Montgomery St., at Washington St., the opulent showpiece of the corporation and a gem of older commercial architecture. Among the best of banking mini-museums in the area, the **Wells Fargo Museum,** 420 Montgomery St. (396-2619), at California St., contains an impressive display of Gold Rush exhibits, including gold nuggets and a 19th-century stagecoach. The affable guide possesses the sort of quiet yet unfathomable expertise usually found only in National Park Service rangers. (Open Mon.-Fri. 9am-5pm.) Nearby the **Chinese Historical Society,** 650 Commercial St. (391-1188), tells the history of the Chinese in California. Gawk at the 1909 parade dragon head and a queue once worn in loyalty to the Manchu Emperor. (Open Wed.-Sun. noon-4pm.)

Chinatown

The largest Chinese community outside of Asia, Chinatown also stays the most densely populated of San Francisco's neighborhoods. Chinatown was founded in the 1880s when bigotry fueled by unemployment engendered a racist outbreak against the "Yellow Peril." To protect themselves, Chinese residents banded together in a small section of the downtown area. As the city grew, speculators tried but failed to take over the increasingly valuable land—especially after the 1906 earthquake leveled the area. Yet Chinatown remains almost exclusively Chinese. **Grant Avenue,** the street Rodgers and Hammerstein wrote a song about, remains the most picturesque part of Chinatown. From the monumental **Chinatown Café,** which straddles Grant at Bush St., and for a few blocks north, Grant cultivates a forest of Chinese banners, signs, and architecture. The less famous streets, such as Jackson, Stockton, and Pacific, give a better feel for this neighborhood where Chinese-newspaper vendors eat their morning noodles out of thermoses. You can watch cookies being shaped by hand at the **Golden Gate Cookie Company,** 56 Ross Alley (781-3956), between Washington and Jackson St. just west of Grant Ave. The **Chinese Culture Center,** 750 Kearny St., 3rd floor (986-1822), houses exhibits of

Chinese-American art and sponsors Heritage and Culinary walking tours of Chinatown. (For schedules and reservations call Tues.-Sat. 9am-5pm.)

Late January and early February feature the indulgent **Chinese New Year** celebrations.

North Beach

As one walks north along Stockton St. or Columbus Ave., supermarkets displaying ginseng give way to those selling provolone; restaurants start luring customers with biscotti instead of roast duck. Lying north of Broadway and east of Columbus, North Beach splits personalities between the bohemian Beats who made it their home—Kerouac, Ginsberg, Ferlinghetti—and the residents of a traditional Italian neighborhood. North Beach bohemianism flourished in the 1950s when the artists and brawlers nicknamed the Beats (short for "beatitude" according to Kerouac) first moved in. Drawn to the area by low rents and cheap bars, the group came to national attention when Ferlinghetti's **City Lights Bookstore** (see Entertainment) published Ginsberg's anguished and ecstatic dream poem *Howl.* The Beats have left. Through the middle of North Beach runs Broadway, the neon netherworld of pornography purveyors. Above it all stands the pleasant old residential district of Telegraph Hill, topped by appropriately named Coit Tower. North Beach is most fun to visit at night as the after-dinner, after-show crowd flocks to the area's numerous cafés for relaxing, ever-present cappuccino.

Between Stockton and Powell lies **Washington Square,** a lush lawn edged by trees. Across Filbert to the north of the square the **Church of St. Peter and St. Paul** beckons tired sight-seers to an island of quiet in its dark, wooden nave. Mrs. Lillie Hitchcock Coit's famous gift to the city, **Coit Tower** (274-0203) looms a few blocks east on Telegraph Hill, the steep mound from which a semaphore signalled the arrival of ships in Gold Rush days. An elevator will take you to the top of the fire-nozzle-shaped Tower for a spectacular 360° view. (Open June-Sept. daily 10am-5pm; Oct.-May daily 9am-4pm. Elevator fare $3, seniors $2, ages 6-12 $1, under 6 free. Last tickets sold ½-hr. before closing.) Parking is limited; leave your car on Washington St. and walk up the Filbert Steps, which rise from the Embarcadero to the eastern base of the tower. The short walk allows excellent views, passing by many gorgeous Art Deco buildings. The **Tattoo Art Museum,** 839 Columbus (775-4991), displays a fantastic collection of tattoo memorabilia, much of which is on owner Lyle Tuttle.

Fisherman's Wharf

Continuing northward, toward the water, one leaves San Francisco proper and enters tourist limbo. "Fisherman's Wharf" maintains 4/5-mi. of porcelain figurines and T-shirt shops. Crowded, very expensive, and quite bland, the wharf manages to provide something to offend almost anyone. The area basically consists of a strip of boutiques flanked by shopping malls on each end; on the west end sits **Ghirardelli Square** (GEAR-a-deli), 900 N. Point St. (Information booth, 775-5500; open daily 10am-9pm). The only remains of Ghirardelli's chocolate factory now lie in the back of the overpriced **Chocolate Factory,** a soda fountain (open daily 10am-midnight). Pricey boutiques now fill the rest of the old factory's red brick buildings, and local musicians and magicians entertain the masses. To escape from this chocolate morass, take one of the **tour boats** or ferries from the wharf. The **Blue & Gold Fleet** (781-7877) and the **Red & White Fleet** (456-2628) take you on technicolor voyages. Blue & Gold's 75-minute tour floats under both the Golden Gate and Bay Bridges, and past the San Francisco Skyline and the Marin Hills, Angel, Alcatraz, and Treasure Islands ($14, seniors and ages 5-18 $7, military and under 5 free). Red & White at Pier 41 offers 45-minute journeys under the Golden Gate Bridge and past Alcatraz ($15, over 55 and ages 12-18 $11, 5-11 $8) while another 45-minute tour circumnavigates Alcatraz, narrated by a former guard. (Summer only. $7.50, seniors $7, ages 5-11 $4.) Red & White boats also discharge passengers at Alcatraz (see below). For a really pleasant escape, try one of the **sailboat charters** that line the wharf. The *Ruby* (861-2165) sails at lunchtime (with sandwiches) daily from May to October, departing from the China Basin building at 12:30pm and returning by

2pm, but call as the schedule often changes (tickets $25, under 10 $12.50). The *Ruby* also takes a 3-hour turn in the bay on Friday and Saturday at 6pm. Reservations are required for sailboat charters. Bring a heavy sweater in summer and a jacket in winter.

A former federal prison, designed to hold those who had made too much trouble within other jails, Alcatraz made life for prisoners extremely harsh. Security was tight—of the 23 escape attempts all were recaptured or killed, save the five "presumed drowned." The prison closed in 1962. Once on Alcatraz, you can wander by yourself or take an audiotape-guided 35-min. tour. Ask about the Native American civil rights takeover in the late 60s. (Departures from Pier 41 in summer every ½-hr. 9:15am-4:15pm, in winter 9:45am-2:45pm. Fare $5.50, seniors $4.60, ages 5-11 $3. Tape tours $3 extra.) Reserve tickets in advance through Ticketron (392-7469) for $1 extra or suffer long lines and risk not getting a ride.

175 Jefferson St. is the home of **Ripley's Believe It or Not!** (771-6188). Unbelievable as it may sound, some of the exhibits, such as the replica of Michelangelo's Pietà made from paper bags, are almost artistic. (Admission $7.50, college students $6, seniors and ages 13-17 $5.50, ages 5-12 $4, under 5 free. Believe it.) The **Wax Museum** (885-4975) at 145 Jefferson St. has dozens and dozens of models of various quality. Jim and Tammy Faye Bakker will make you long for the scandals of yore. (Admission $9, ages 12-17 $7, under 12 $4. Open daily 9am-11pm, 10am-10pm in winter.)

Nob Hill and Russian Hill

Until the earthquake and fire of 1906, railroad magnates occupied the mansions of Nob Hill. Even today, Nob Hill remains one of the nation's most prestigious addresses. Fine buildings line the streets with a certain settled wealth. Sitting atop a hill and peering down upon the working masses can prove a pleasant afternoon diversion. Nearby Russian Hill is named after Russian sailors who died during an expedition in the early 1800s and were buried on the southeast crest.

The notorious **Lombard Street Curves,** on Lombard between Hyde and Leavenworth St. at the top of Russian Hill, afford a fantastic view of the city and harbor—if you can keep your eyes open down this terrifying plunge. Devising transportation on the city's steep streets inspired the vehicles celebrated at the **Cable Car Museum,** at the corner of Washington and Mason St. (474-1887). The building houses the cable-winding terminus for the picturesque cable cars, the working center of the system. (Open daily 10am-6pm; Nov.-March 10am-5pm. Free.)

Grace Cathedral, 1051 Taylor St. (776-6611), crowns Nob Hill. The castings for its portals imitate Ghiberti's on the Baptistry in Florence exactly enough that they were used to restore the originals. Inside, modern murals mix San Franciscan and national historic events with scenes from the lives of the saints. Grace is still in use as a house of worship.

Marina and Pacific Heights

The Marina, Pacific Heights, and the adjoining Presidio Heights are the most sought-after residential addresses in San Francisco. Centered about Union and Sacramento St., Pacific Heights boasts the greatest number of Victorian buildings in the city. The 1906 earthquake and fire left the Heights area west of Van Ness Ave. unscathed. In 1989, the Heights area was not as lucky and sustained serious damage. Victorian restoration has become a full-fledged enterprise; consultants try to determine the original form of fretwork, friezes, fans, columns, corbels, cartouches, rosettes, rococo plaster, and so on. The **Octagon House,** 2645 Gough St. (885-9796), and **Haas-Lilienthal House,** 2007 Franklin St. (441-3004), allow the public a look inside. Rather sedate free tours of the impeccably preserved Octagon House are given on the first Sunday and second and fourth Thursdays of each month between 1 and 4pm. The Haas-Lilienthal House has more regular hours (open Wed. noon-3:15pm, Sun. 11am-4pm; admission $4, seniors and under 18 $2).

For those who prefer shopping to architecture, however, **Union Street** is your salvation. Between Scott and Webster St., Union St. is chock-full of upscale shops, bars, restaurants, and bakeries.

Down from Pacific Heights toward the bay, sits the **Marina** district. **Marina Green** by the water seethes with joggers and walkers and is well-known for spectacularly flown two-line kites. To the west lies the **Palace of Fine Arts,** on Baker St. between Jefferson and Bay St. The strange, domed structure and two curving colonnades are reconstructed remnants of the 1915 Panama Pacific Exposition, which commemorated the opening of the Panama Canal and symbolized San Francisco's completed recovery from the great earthquake. The domed building houses the **Exploratorium** (561-0360), whose hundreds of interactive exhibits may teach even poets a thing or two about the sciences. (Open Wed. 10am-9:30pm, Thurs.-Sun. 10am-5pm. Admission $7, students $5, seniors $3.50, ages 6-17 $3. Admission free 1st Wed. each month.) Inside sits the **Tactile Dome** (561-0362), a pitch-dark maze of tunnels, slides, nooks, and crannies designed to help refine your sense of touch—a wonderful place to bring kids and anyone not afraid of the dark or claustrophobic. (Admission $7. Reservations required for a month in advance. Plenty of free parking.) A short walk from the Exploratorium's main entrance, along the Bay, is the **Wave Organ.** Designed by local artists, the organ is activated by the motion of the waves, and beckons you to sit and meditate to the sound of the water's natural AAUUMMM.

Civic Center

You have two reasons to see the **Civic Center:** the architecture and museums by day, and performing arts at night. The **San Francisco Museum of Modern Art,** Van Ness Ave. (252-4000), at McAllister St. in the Veterans Bldg., displays a collection of 20th-century European and U.S. works. Exhibits scheduled for 1992 include Klee and Pollock. (Open Tues.-Wed. and Fri. 10am-5pm, Thurs. 10am-9pm, Sat.-Sun. 11am-5pm. Admission $4, seniors and students $2, under 13 free. Tues. seniors and students free. Thurs. 5-9pm, seniors and students $1.)

In the evening, **Louise M. Davies Symphony Hall** (431-5400), 201 Van Ness Ave. at Grove St., rings with the sounds of the San Francisco Symphony (box office open 9:30am-5:30pm). Next door, the **War Memorial Opera House,** 301 Van Ness Ave. (864-3330), hosts the San Francisco Opera Company and the San Francisco Ballet. The Civic Center has two other theaters: the **Orpheum,** 1192 Market St. (474-3800), tends to draw flashy shows, while the smaller **Herbst Auditorium,** 401 Van Ness Ave. (552-3656), at McAllister St., hosts string quartets, solo singers, and ensembles. Tours of the symphony hall, opera house, and Herbst Auditorium leave on the hour and half-hour from the Grove St. entrance of the Davies Hall. (½-hr., Mon. 10am-2:30pm. Admission $3, seniors and students $2. For more info, call 552-8338.)

Mission District and Castro Street

Castro Street and the Mission District lie far enough south that both areas may enjoy sunshine when fog blankets Nob Hill. Two thriving cultures make their home in this area: the gay community around Castro St. and the Hispanic community to the east. Although the scene has mellowed considerably from the wild days of the 70s, Castro St. still remains a proud and assertive emblem of gay liberation. In the Hispanic Mission District, the colorful murals along 24th St. reflect the rich cultural influences here of Latin America.

The best way to see Castro St. is to wander, peering into shops or stepping into bars. Two popular hangouts are **Café Flor,** 2298 Market St. (621-8579), and **Café San Marco,** 2367 Market St. (861-3846).

Down the street, **The Names Project,** 2362 Castro (863-1966), sounds a more somber note. This organization has accumulated 12,000 panels for an AIDS memorial quilt, each 3 ft. by 6 ft. section bearing the name and memory of a person who died of AIDS. In addition to housing the project's administration, the building contains a workshop where a victim's friends and relatives can create panels; several are on display. (Open Mon.-Fri. 10am-10pm, Sat.-Sun. noon-8pm.)

At 16th and Dolores St. lies the old heart of San Francisco, **Mission Dolores.** The building, said to be the oldest in the city, turned 200 last year. Father Junípero Serra founded the Mission in 1776, and named it, like San Francisco itself, in honor of St. Francis of Assisi. However, the Mission sat close to a marsh known as *Laguna de Nuestra Señora de los Dolores* (Lagoon of Our Lady of Sorrows) and, despite Serra's wishes, it gradually became known as *Misión de los Dolores.* Exotic bougainvillea, poppies, and birds of paradise bloom in the cemetery, which was featured in Alfred Hitchcock's *Vertigo.* (Admission $1. Open daily 9am-4:30pm, Nov.-April 9am-4pm.)

Haight-Ashbury

The 60s live on in Haight-Ashbury, though more self-consciously than 20 years ago. The Haight willfully preserves an era that many seek to forget. Originally a quiet lower-middle-class neighborhood, the Haight's large Victorian houses—perfect for communal living—and the district's proximity to the University of San Francisco drew a large hippie population in the mid- and late-1960s. LSD flooded the neighborhood, since consciousness-opening was not yet a felony. The hippie scene reached its apogee in 1966-67, when Big Brother and the Holding Company, Jefferson Airplane, and the Appreciative Corpses all lived or played in the neighborhood. During 1967's "Summer of Love," young people from across the country converged on the grassy Panhandle of Golden Gate Park for the celebrated "be-ins." Despite recent gentrification, Haight-Ashbury remains cheap and exciting. Many of the bars and restaurants are remnants of a past era, with faded auras, games in the back rooms, and live-in regulars.

Check out the eclectic shops down Haight St. **Aardvark's Odd Ark,** 1501 Haight St. (621-3141), at Ashbury, has an immense selection of used new wave jackets, good music in the background, and prices that will take you back. (Open Sat.-Mon. 11am-9pm, Wed. 11am-7pm, Thurs. 11am-9pm, Fri. 11am-8pm.) Another used clothing store, **Wasteland,** 1660 Haight St. (863-3150), is worth checking out if only for its great facade and window displays. (Open Mon.-Fri. 11am-6pm, Sat. 11am-7pm, Sun. noon-6pm.) The **Global Family Networking Center,** 1665 Haight St. (864-1978), contains a café, market, and global awareness. The rooms at the Red Vic, upstairs, could be a museum but for the lack of velvet rope and "Do Not Touch" signs (see Accommodations). The offbeat **Holo Gallery,** 1792 Haight St. (668-4656), glows with an amazing collection of holograms, the closest today's USF students come to 60s visions. (Open Mon.-Sat. 11am-6pm. Free.)

Resembling a dense green mountain in the middle of the Haight, **Buena Vista Park** has a predictably bad reputation. Enter at your own risk, and once inside be prepared for those doing their own thing.

MUNI buses #6, 7, 16x, 43, 66, 71, and 73 all serve the area, while Metro line N runs along Carl St., four blocks south.

Golden Gate Park

No visit to San Francisco is complete without a picnic in Golden Gate Park. Frederick Law Olmsted, designer of New York's Central Park, said it couldn't be done when San Francisco's 19th-century leaders asked him to build a park to rival Paris's Bois de Boulogne. But engineer William Hammond Hall and Scottish gardener John McLaren proved him wrong. Hall designed the 1000-acre park—gardens and all—when the land on the city's western side was still shifting sand dunes, and then constructed a mammoth breakwater along the oceanfront to protect the seedling trees and bushes from the sea's burning spray.

The major north-south route through the park is named Park Presidio By-Pass Drive in the north and Cross Over Drive in the south. The **Panhandle,** a thin strip of land bordered by Fell and Oak Street on the north and south respectively, is the oldest part of the park; originally the "carriage entrance," it contains the oldest trees in the park, surrounded by the intriguing Haight-Ashbury. **Park headquarters,** home of info and maps, advises at Fell and Stanyan St. (556-2920), in McLaren Lodge on the eastern edge of the park. (Open Mon.-Fri. 8am-5pm.)

Three museums invigorate the park, all in one large complex on the eastern side between South and John F. Kennedy Dr., where 9th Ave. meets the park.

California Academy of Sciences (221-5100; 750-7145 for a recording; 750-7138 for Laserium), the West Coast's oldest institution of its kind, contains several smaller museums (admission to all $6). The **Steinhart Aquarium** (221-5100) is more lively than the natural history exhibits. The engaging alligator and crocodile pool pales in comparison with the unique Fish Roundabout, a large tank shaped like a doughnut where the fish swim around the visitors. The "Far Side of Science" gallery shows dozens of Gary Larson's best cartoons about nature and scientists. The academy also includes the **Morrison Planetarium** with its shows about white dwarves and black holes. (Additional charge of $2.50, seniors and students $1.25. Schedule changes; call 750-7141.) The Laserium (750-7138) orients its argon laser show to such robust themes as the Summer of '69 and Pink Floyd's *Dark Side of the Moon.* The synesthetic spectacle may be too intense for children under six. (Tickets $6, 5pm matinee $5, seniors and ages 6-12 $4. Academy open daily 10am-7pm; Sept. 2-July 3 10am-5pm. Admission $4, $3 with MUNI Fast Pass or transfer, seniors and ages 12-17 $2, 6-11 $1, under 6 free. Free first Wed. each month until 8:45pm.)

M. H. de Young Museum (750-3600) takes visitors through a 21-room survey of U.S. painting, from the colonial period to the early 20th century, including several works by John Singer Sargent. Mixed in with the survey are some sculptures and pieces of furniture, which include Shaker chairs and a redwood and maple bed made in San Francisco in 1885. Also noteworthy is the museum's glass collection.

Asian Art Museum (668-8921), occupies the west wing of the building, boasting a collection of rare jade and fine porcelain plus bronze works over 3000 years old. Most pieces were donated by Avery Brundage in 1966 in a gift that inaugurated the museum. (Both museums open Wed.-Sun. 10am-5pm. Admission $4, $3 with MUNI Fast Pass or transfer, seniors and ages 12-17 $2, under 12 free.

One admission fee covers the de Young, Asian, and Palace of the Legion of Honor (see Richmond) museums for one day; save your receipt. All free first Wed. each month and 10am-noon on the first Sat.)

Despite its sandy past, the soil of Golden Gate Park appears rich enough today to rival the black earth of the Midwest. Flowers blossom everywhere, particularly in spring and summer. The **Conservatory of Flowers** (386-3150), the oldest building in the park, was allegedly constructed in Ireland and shipped from Dublin via Cape Horn. The delicate and luminescent structure, modeled after Palm House in London's Kew Gardens, houses brilliant displays of tropical plants. (Open daily 9am-6pm; Nov.-March 9am-5pm. Admission $1.50, seniors and ages 6-12 $1, under 6 free.) The **Strybing Arboretum,** on Lincoln Way at 9th Ave. (661-1316), southwest of the academy, shows 5000 varieties of plants. Walk through the Garden of Fragrance for the vision-impaired, with labels in braille and plants chosen especially for their texture and scent. (Tours daily at 1:30pm and at 10:30am Thurs.-Sun. Open Mon.-Fri. 9am-4:30pm, Sat.-Sun. 10am-5pm. Free.) Near the Music Concourse on a path off South Dr., the **Shakespeare Garden** contains almost every flower and plant ever mentioned by the herbalist of Avon. Plaques with the relevant quotations are hung on the back wall; a map helps you find your favorite hyacinths, cowslips, and gillyvors. (Open daily 9am-dusk; winter Tues.-Sun. 9am-dusk. Free.)

A relic of the 1894 California Midwinter Exposition, the **Japanese Tea Garden** is a serene, if overpriced, collection of dark wooden buildings, small pools, graceful footbridges, carefully pruned trees and plants, and tons of tourists. Buy some tea and cookies for $1 and watch the giant goldfish swim placidly in the central pond. (Open daily 9am-6:30pm; Oct.-April 8:30am-5:30pm. Admission $2, seniors and ages 6-12 $1, under 6 free. Free first and last ½-hr. of operation, and all national holidays.)

At the extreme northwestern corner, the **Dutch Windmill** turns and turns again. Rounding out the days of old is the **Carousel** (c. 1912), accompanied by a $50,000 Gebruder band organ. (Open daily 10am-4pm; Oct.-May Wed.-Sun. 10am-4pm. Tickets $1, ages 6-12 25¢, under 6 free.)

Herd of buffalo? A dozen of the shaggy beasts roam a spacious paddock at the western end of John F. Kennedy Dr., near 39th Ave.

To get to the park, hop on bus #5 or 21. On Sundays traffic is banned from park roads, and bicycles and roller skates come out in full force. Bike rental shops are plentiful: skates, though harder to come by, are also available. Numerous MUNI buses cover the streets that surround Golden Gate Park and the north-south Park Presidio By-Pass/Cross Over Dr.

Richmond District

The **Golden Gate Bridge,** a rust-colored symbol of the West's bounding confidence, sways above the entrance to San Francisco Bay. Built in 1937 under the directions of chief engineer Joseph Strauss, the bridge exudes almost indescribable beauty from any angle on or around it.

Lincoln Park, the Richmond district's biggest attraction, grows at the northwest extreme of the city. To get there, follow Clement St. west to 34th Ave., or Geary Blvd. to Point Lobos Ave., or take MUNI bus #1 or 38 to the edge of the Park. The **California Palace of the Legion of Honor** (750-3659), modeled after the Colonnade Hôtel de Salm in Paris, houses San Francisco's major collection of European art. The gallery's particularly strong French collection includes one of the best Rodin inventories in the country, both in plaster and bronze. Downstairs you'll find portions of the **Achenbach Foundation's** extensive graphic arts holdings. (Open Wed.-Sun. 10am-5pm. Admission $4, $3 with MUNI pass or transfer, seniors and ages 12-17 $2, under 12 free. Price includes same-day admission to the de Young and Asian Art Museums in Golden Gate Park. Free first Wed. and Sat. of each month 10am-noon.) Take the **Land's End Path,** running northwest of the cliff edge, for a romantic view of the Golden Gate Bridge.

Entertainment

San Francisco abounds with free publications listing the events in the Bay Area, distributed in record stores, bookshops, and street-corner distribution boxes. The two that natives rely on most are the *San Francisco Bay Guardian* and the *East Bay Express.* For a more detailed listing of Berkeley theater and the Oakland jazz scene, try the *Express.* For listings of the visual and performing arts, listen to the monthly *CenterVoice* (398-1854). The **Entertainment Hotline** is 391-2001 or 391-2002. The *Bay Times* (626-8121), the gay and lesbian paper, also appears monthly. The weekly *Advocate,* whose own pink pages are another thing entirely, offers a large amount of information on San Francisco's gay community.

Clubs

The Paradise Lounge, 1501 Folsom St. (861-6906). 3 stages, 2 floors, 5 bars, and up to 5 live bands a night. Pool tables upstairs. Open daily 3pm-2am.

DNA Lounge, 375 11th St. (626-1409), at the corner of Hanson. The best night for dancing is Wed. Cover rarely exceeds $10. Open 'til 3:30am.

The I-Beam, 1748 Haight St. (668-6023), Haight-Ashbury. Specializes in post-Branca bands and DJs playing high-tech rock. Decor includes shooting light beams and 2 screens full o' clips from cartoons, golden oldies, and Japanese monster flicks. Often free student night Wed. or Thurs. Sun. features a gay tea dance starting at 5pm. Open daily from 9pm. Cover $5-10.

Kimballs', 300 Grove St. (861-5555), at Franklin St. Great jazz musicians scare off the New Age/fusion frauds at this popular club/restaurant. Shows Wed.-Thurs. at 9pm, Sat.-Sun. at 11pm. Cover usually $8-12.

Club DV8, 540 Howard St. (777-1419). 3 floors of sheer dance mania. For the best dancing, stick to the third floor "osmosis." Open until 4am.

Perry's, 1944 Union St. (922-9022). A famous pick-up junction. Lackadaisical by day, hopping at night. Open daily 9am-2am.

Vesuvio Café, 255 Columbus Ave. (362-3370). Watch poets and chess players from the balcony, or hide from them in the subdued bar. Open daily 6am-2am.

Nicki's BBQ, 547 Haight (863-2276), on Lower Haight. D.J. nightly. Mon. features great country music. No cover. Open 11:30am-1:30pm.

Gay and Lesbian Clubs

While less visible than in recent years, gay nightlife in San Francisco still flourishes. Most popular bars thrive in the city's two traditionally gay areas—the Castro (around the intersection of Castro St. and Market St.) and Polk St. (for several blocks north of Geary St.).

The Stud, 399 9th St. (863-6623). A classic club with great dance music. Funk on Mon. No cover on weekdays. Open daily.

The Kennel Club, 628 Divisadero (931-1914). Hosts both "The Box" and "The Q Club". The former offers stupendous dancing and is popular among straights as well. Open Thurs. and Sat. 9pm-2am. "The Q Club", open on Thurs., has dancing for women.

Amelia's, 647 Valencia (552-7788). Dance bar for lesbians. No cover. Open Wed.-Sat. 4pm-2am.

Café San Marco, 2367 Market St. (861-3846). Popular gay bar. Open Mon.-Fri. 2pm-2am, Sat.-Sun. noon-2am.

San Francisco Bay Area

Berkeley

A quarter-century ago Mario Salvo climbed onto a police car and launched the free speech movement that would give Berkeley its lingering reputation for political activism. The legacy of social iconoclasm survives with the image—Ronald Reagan finished fourth here in the 1980 presidential election. While Berkeley maintains its idealistic rhetoric, bourgeois accoutrements such as stylish clothing boutiques and gourmet specialty stores blanket the city. And despite the much-vaunted progressive spirit, Berkeley's liberality has done less to reduce poverty than it has to produce a more confrontational homeless community than found in other urban centers. Last year, when UC-Berkeley moved to build volleyball courts in People's Park, campus, city and Oakland police forces had to join to control protests from the park's transient homeless.

Practical Information

Visitor Information: Chamber of Commerce (549-7000), 1834 University Ave. at Martin Luther King Dr. Open Mon.-Fri. 9am-noon and 1-4pm. **Council on International Educational Exchange (CIEE) Travel Center** (848-8604), 2486 Channing Way at Telegraph Ave. Open Mon.-Tues. and Thurs.-Fri. 9am-5pm, Wed. 10am-5pm. **Recorded Event Calendar,** 676-2222. **U.C. Berkeley Switchboard** (642-6000), 1901 8th St. Info on community events. Irregular hours.

Public Transport: Bay Area Rapid Transit (BART), 465-2278. Berkeley Station at Shattuck Ave. and Center St., close to the west edge of the university. The free university **Humphrey-Go-BART shuttle** (642-5149) connects the BART station with the central and eastern portions of campus. During the school year, the shuttle leaves the station every 10-12 min. 7am-7pm Mon.-Fri.—not on university holidays. **Alameda County Transit (AC Transit),** 839-2882. Buses leave from Transbay Terminal for Berkeley every 30 min. City buses operated by AC Transit run approx. every 20 min. $1, seniors and disabled riders 35¢, ages 5-16 85¢.

Ride Boards: Berkeley Ride Board, ASUC building near the bookstore, on the 1st floor. Or call 642-5259.

Transportation Info: Berkeley TRIP, 644-POOL. Info on public transport, biking, and carpooling. Mostly local transport, but not confined to daily commuting.

Help Lines: Rape Hotline, 845-7273. **Suicide Prevention,** 849-2212 or 889-1333. Both open 24 hrs.

Post Office: 2000 Allston Way (649-3100). Open Mon.-Fri. 8:30am-5pm, Sat. 10am-2pm. ZIP code: 94704.

Area Code: 510.

You can reach Berkeley by crossing the bay on **BART** ($1.85); both the university and Telegraph Ave. are a five-minute walk from the station. The UC-Berkeley campus stretches into the hills, but most buildings reside in the westernmost section near BART.

Lined with bookstores and cafés, **Telegraph Avenue,** which runs south from the student union, is the town's spiritual center. The **downtown** area, around the BART station, contains what few businesses Berkeley will allow. The public library and central post office shelve and sort there. The **Gourmet Ghetto** encompasses the area along Shattuck Ave. and Walnut St. between Virginia and Rose St. West of campus and by the bay lies the **Fourth St. Center,** home to great eating and window shopping. To the northwest of campus, **Solano Avenue** offers countless ethnic restaurants (the best Chinese food in the city), bookstores, and movie theaters as well as more shopping.

Accommodations

The town has no good hostels, and clean, cheap motels are few. Most of the city's hotels are flophouses. You might try renting a **fraternity room** for the night: check the classified ads in the *Daily Californian* for possibilities.

YMCA, 2001 Allston Way (848-6800), at Milvia St. Men over 17 only. No membership needed. Registration 8am-noon. Check-out 11:30am-noon. Small rooms $21.59. Medium rooms $22.80. Pool and basic fitness facilities included. Key deposit $2.

University of California Housing Office (642-5925), 2700 Hearst Ave., in Stern Hall at the northern end of campus. Rents rooms in summer to anyone who claims connection with the school (e.g. considering enrolling). Open daily 7am-11pm. Singles $34. Doubles $44. Call ahead.

Berkeley Capri Motel (845-7090), 1512 University Ave., about 1 mi. west of campus near the North Berkeley BART. Otherwise decent rooms scream for paint and decoration. HBO. Singles $32, two beds $40.

Food

Berkeley supports several exceptional restaurants, many of them budget-busters. The free Berkeley monthly *Bayfood* (652-6115) devotes articles, ads, and recipes to cooking and dining.

Plearn Thai Cuisine, 2050 University Ave. (841-2148), between Shattuck and Milvia. Elegant decor. One of the Bay Area's best. Busy at peak hours. Entrees $5-8.50. Try the Gai-Young chicken ($6.75). Open daily 11:30am-10pm.

Flint's Barbecue (653-0593), 6609 Shattuck Ave., in Oakland. Just over the city line near the Ashby bars. Considered the best BBQ around. Even asbestos-tongued eaters should stick to "medium" or "mild." No seating. Beef or pork ribs $6. Open Sun.-Thurs. 11am-2am, Fri.-Sat. 11am-4am.

Noah's New York Bagels, 3170 College Ave. (654-0944). One of the few kosher restaurants in the area, this popular place gets really packed at lunch, but service is quick and friendly. Choose from an enormous selection of bagels and flavored cream cheeses, like lox, walnut raisin, or vegetables and herbs. Plain bagels 50¢, with cream cheese $1.25. Open Mon.-Fri. 7am-6:30pm, Sat. 7:30am-6pm, Sun. 7:30am-3pm.

Café Intermezzo (849-4592), Telegraph at Haste. The enormous helpings of salad, served with fresh bread, distinguish this café from the multitudes of others along Telegraph. A combination sandwich and salad $4.25 is enough to keep you busy all day. Open Mon.-Fri. 10:30am-9pm.

Zachary's Chicago Pizza, 1853 Solano Ave. (525-5950). Flaky crusts—thick or thin—with interesting toppings, such as pesto and zucchini. Slices with toppings $1.75, pizzas $5-17. One wall displays works by local artists. Open Sun.-Thurs. 11am-9:30pm, Fri.-Sat. 11am-10:30pm.

Mario's La Fiesta, 2444 Telegraph Ave. (848-2588), at Haste St. Great Mexican food and a bopping atmosphere. Large chicken *flauta* combination plates, with rice, beans, guacamole, and chips $7.20. Open daily 10:30am-10:30pm.

The Cheese Board Collective, 1504 Shattuck Ave. (549-3183). A pillar of the Gourmet Ghetto. Add a few hundred cheeses to the excellent French bread for a great picnic. Very generous with samples. 10% discount for customers over 60, 15% for ages over 70, and so on. If you reach 150, they'll pay to eat the cheese. Open Tues.-Fri. 10am-6pm, Sat. 10am-5pm.

Sights

Pass through Sather Gate into **Sproul Plaza** and enter the university's intellectual Arcadia of gracious buildings, grass-covered hills, and sparkling streams. The **information center** (642-4636), in the student union building at Telegraph and Bancroft, has maps and booklets for self-guided tours. (Open Mon.-Fri. 8am-6pm, Sat. 10am-6pm.) Guided tours start at the **visitors center** (642-5215), room 101, University Hall, Oxford St. and University Ave. The Berkeley campus swallows 160 acres, bounded on the south by Bancroft Way, on the west by Oxford St., by Hearst Ave. to the north, and by extensive parkland to the east. The school has an enrollment of over 30,000 and more than 1000 full professors. Imposing **Bancroft Library,** with nearly seven million volumes, is among the nation's largest. Located in the center of campus, the library contains exhibits ranging from California arcana to folio editions of Shakespeare's plays. You can see the tattered bronze plaque left by Sir Francis Drake in the 16th century, vainly claiming California for England. (Open Mon.-Fri. 9am-5pm, Sat. 1-5pm. Free.)

The most dramatic on-campus attraction is **Sather Tower,** the 1914 monument to Berkeley benefactor Jane K. Sather. The 500-ton steel frame is designed to withstand large earthquakes. For 50¢, you can ride to the top of the tower, known affectionately as the *Campanile* because it's modeled after the clock tower in Venice's St. Mark's Square. (Open daily 10am-4:15pm.) The tower's 61 bells are played manually most weekdays at 7:50am, noon, and 6pm, and Sun. 2-2:45pm.

The **University Art Museum,** 2626 Bancroft Way (642-1124; 24-hr. events hotline 642-0808), holds a diverse permanent collection. Innovative directors have put together a number of memorable shows over the years on everything from Cubism to the interaction of U.S. painting and popular 50s culture. (Open Wed.-Sun. 11am-5pm. Admission $5, seniors and ages 6-17 $4. Free Thurs. 11am-noon.)

The **Lawrence Hall of Science** (642-5132) stands above the northeast corner of the campus in a concrete building. Take the free express shuttle from the BART station weekdays during museum hours. Exhibits stress learning science through hands-on use of everyday objects. (Open Mon.-Fri. 10am-4:30pm, Sat.-Sun. 10am-5pm. Admission $3.50; seniors, students, and ages 7-18 $2.50; under 7 free.)

Back in the campus center, the **Worth Ryder Art Gallery** (642-2582), in Kroeber Hall, room 116, displays works of wildly varying quality by students and local artists. (Open Tues.-Thurs. 11am-4pm. Free.)

The **Botanical Gardens** (642-3343), spread over 30 acres in Strawberry Canyon, contain over 10,000 species of plant life. (Open daily 9am-5pm. Free.) The **Berkeley Rose Garden,** on Euclid Ave. at Eunice St. north of the campus, spills from one terrace to another in a vast semi-circular amphitheater. You can see Marin County and the Golden Gate Bridge from the far end. While in bloom, from May through September, the gardens are always open.

Outside of campus stand more museums and noteworthy architecture. The **Judah Magnes Museum,** 2911 Russell St. (849-2710), displays one of the West Coast's leading collections of Judaica. (Open Sun.-Fri. 10am-4pm.) The **Julia Morgan Theater** (845-8542), 2640 College Ave., is housed in a beautiful former church designed by its namesake and constructed of dark redwood and Douglas fir.

People's Park, on Haste St. one block off Telegraph Ave., is an unofficial museum of sorts, featuring a mural that depicts the 60s struggle between the city and local activists over whether to develop it commercially. During that struggle, then-governor Ronald Reagan sent in state police to break a blockade, resulting in the death of one student. In 1989, a rally was held to protest the university's renewed threats to convert the park; some demonstrators began turning over cars, looting stores, and setting fires. The controversy has increased as workers begin construction of University volleyball courts. Presently, crack dealers and the homeless have claimed this dismal site.

Go for an off-beat experience at the **Takara Sake Tasting Room** (540-8250), 708 Addison St. at 4th St. You can request a sample of several varieties, all made with California rice. A narrated slide presentation on *sake* brewing is shown on request. (Open daily noon-6pm.)

A short drive or BART ride (to the Lake Merrit stop) into Oakland will take you to the **Oakland Museum,** 1000 Oak St. (834-2413); a well-designed complex of three galleries devoted to California's artistic, historical, and natural heritage. The top floor houses the **Gallery of California Art** where everything from traditional 19th-century portraits to contemporary works using car doors finds a wall. The gallery also has some splendid Currier cartoons about the Gold Rush. One floor down, the fantastic **Cowell Hall of California History,** takes visitors through California's boom-like social and economic history, using artifacts, costumes, and even vehicles. On the lowest level, the **Hall of California Ecology** uses state-of-the-art fish-simulation technology in its new Aquatic California gallery. (Open Wed.-Sat. 10am-5pm, Sun. noon-7pm. Tours Wed.-Sat. at 2pm. Free. Small fee for special exhibits.)

Entertainment

Hang out with procrastinating students at the **student union** (642-5215). The ticket office, arcade, bowling alleys, and pool tables are all run from a central desk. (Open Mon.-Fri. 8am-6pm, Sat. 10am-6pm; off-season Mon.-Fri. 8am-10pm, Sat. 10am-6pm.) Next door the **Bear's Lair** (843-0373), a student pub, sells pitchers of Bud for $4. (Open Mon.-Thurs. noon-midnight, Fri. 11am-8pm. summer hours: Sat.-Wed. 11am-6pm, live music Thurs. and Fri.) **CAL Performance,** 101 Zellerbach Hall (642-7477), is a university-wide concert and lecture organizer, with info on all the rock, classical, and jazz concerts, lectures, and movies on campus. Ask about non-paying ushering jobs, a good way to see shows for free. Big concerts usually are held in the Greek Theatre (642-5550), a frequent site for Grateful Dead shows, or Zellerbach Hall. (Open Mon.-Fri. 10am-5:30pm, Sat. noon-4pm.)

Starry Plough, 3101 Shattuck Ave. (841-2082). Pub with Irish bands and Anchor Steam on tap. Posters espouse the pro-Irish, anti-nuclear, and U.S.-out-of-Nicaragua points of view. Live bands. Open daily 4pm-2am.

Larry Blake's Downstairs (848-0888), 2367 Telegraph, at Durant Ave., through the college's upstairs dining room and down a flight. An excellent drinking and meeting spot. Sawdust on the floor and live jazz. Drinks from $2. Cover $3-6. Restaurant open Mon.-Sat. 11:30am-2am, Sun. 4pm-2am. Bar open until 1am.

Triple Rock Brewery, 1920 Shattuck Ave. (843-2739). Micro-brewery producing 3 delicious regular beers (2 pale ales and 1 porter) and occasional specials. A bargain at $2.25 per pint. Old beer logos grace the walls. Roof garden, too. After 7pm, you can only stand in the crowded barroom, but in the afternoon, come to meet friendly noncollegiates who really enjoy their beer. Open daily 11am-midnight.

Brennan's (841-0960), 4th St. and University Ave. down by the waterfront. Cheap liquor and large crowds from every part of the city combine for perfect Bacchanalia. Steam tables at one end offer cheap food for the fearless. Great Irish coffee $2.75. Open Sun.-Thurs. 11am-midnight, Fri.-Sat. 11am-2am. Be prepared to stand out if you're female. Food served until 9pm.

U.C. Theater (843-6267), 2036 University Ave., west of Shattuck Ave. Standard reruns, film noir series, studio classics; nicely-matched double feature. Schedules available throughout Berkeley or at the theater. Creative film festivals. Admission $3.50 before 6pm, $5 after 6pm, seniors and children $3.50.

Marin County

The undeveloped hills just west of the Golden Gate Bridge comprise the **Marin Headlands**, part of the Golden Gate National Recreation Area which sprawls across the Bay Area. The view from the Headlands back over the bridge to San Francisco arguably has the most spectacular vista in the Bay Area. You can get to the Headlands (and the viewpoints) easily by car; simply take the Alexander Ave. exit off U.S. 101 and take your first left. You'll go through an underpass and up a hill on your right. You can also take MUNI bus #76. You should consider hiking the ¾-mi. trail that leads from the parking area down to the sheltered (and usually deserted) beach at **Kirby Cove.**

About 5 mi. west along the Panoramic Hwy. off U.S. 101 stands **Muir Woods National Monument,** a congregation of primeval coastal redwoods. A loop road takes you through the most outstanding area. (Open daily 8am-sunset.) The **visitors center** (388-2595), near the entrance, keeps the same hours as the monument. West of Muir Woods lies **Muir Beach,** which offers a tremendous view of San Francisco from its surrounding hills.

North of Muir Woods lies the isolated, largely undiscovered, and utterly beautiful **Mount Tamalpais State Park.** The heavily forested park has a number of challenging trails that lead: to the top of "Mount Tam," the highest peak in the county, and to a natural stone amphitheater. **Stinson Beach,** also in the port, is a local favorite for sunbathing. **Park headquarters** is at 810 Panoramic Hwy. (388-2070). The park opens a half-hour before sunrise and closes a half-hour before sunset.

Encompassing 100 mi. of coastline along most of the western side of Marin, the **Point Reyes National Seashore** juts audaciously into the Pacific from the eastern end of the submerged Pacific Plate. Here the infamous San Andreas Fault comes to an end. The remote position of the point brings heavy fog and strong winds in winter, a special flora and fauna, and crowds of tourists to gawk at it all. For bus info call Golden Gate Transit (332-6600).

Limantour Beach, at the end of Limantour Rd. west of the seashore headquarters, and **McClures Beach,** at the extreme north of the seashore near the end of Pierce Point Rd., are two of the nicest area beaches. Both have high, grassy dunes and long stretches of sandy beach. In summer a free shuttle bus runs to Limantour Beach from seashore headquarters. Strong ocean currents along the point make swimming suicidal. To reach the dramatic **Point Reyes Lighthouse** at the very tip of the point, follow Sir Francis Drake Blvd. to its end and then head right along the long stairway to Sea Lion overlook. From December to February, gray whales occasionally can be spotted off the coast from the overlook.

The **Golden Gate Youth Hostel (AYH)** (331-2777), a few mi. south of Sausalito, sits close to a waterbird sanctuary and houses 66 beds in an old, spacious building that is part of deserted Fort Barry. (Check-in 7-9:30am and 4:30-11pm. From 9:30am-4:30pm, leave your name on a sign-up sheet and return at 4:30pm to claim a bed. Curfew 11pm. $7. Linen 50¢. Reservations best in summer.) By car from San Francisco, take the Alexander Ave. exit off U.S. 101; take the second Sausalito exit if going toward San Francisco. Follow the signs into the Golden Gate National Recreation Area, then follow the hostel signs through the park (about 3 mi.). Golden Gate Transit buses #2, 10, and 20 stop at Alexander Ave. From there, you'll have to hitch. A taxi from San Francisco costs $11-12.

Twenty-five mi. north, the spectacularly situated **Point Reyes Hostel (AYH),** Limantour Rd. (663-881), opens nightly for groups and individuals. You're more likely to get a late-notice room here than in the Golden Gate Hostel, although reservations are advised on weekends. Hiking, wildlife, birdwatching, and Limantour Beach are all within walking distance. Plan ahead to use the well-equipped kitchen since the nearest market hawks its wares 8 mi. away. (Registration 4:30-9:30pm. $8.) By car take the Seashore exit west from Rte. 1. Take Beer Valley Road to Linatour Rd., and follow for 6 mi. until you see a hostel sign. For public transportation info, contact Golden Gate Transit (332-6600) or call the hostel (two buses per day to the hostel).

Lapine campsites on Pt. Reyes reproduce more than in more populated areas. The campground closest to Sausalito hunkers down in **Samuel Taylor State Park** (488-9897), on Sir Francis Drake Blvd. 15 mi. west of San Rafael (itself 10 mi. north of Sausalito on U.S. 101). The park's 60 sites ($14, $12 for seniors) with hot showers stay open year-round. A hiker/biker camp costs $3 per person with a seven-day maximum stay. Make reservations a week in advance from April to September (800-444-7275, 619-452-1950). Four campgrounds (accessible only by foot) line the national seashore in the south, inner-cape portion of Pt. Reyes. All are fairly primitive, with pit toilets, firepits, and tap water; all require permits from the **Point Reyes National Seashore Headquarters,** Bear Valley Rd. (663-1092; open Mon.-Fri. 9am-5pm, Sat.-Sun. 8am-5pm). All camps command exquisite views of the ocean and surrounding hills.

The **Sausalito Chamber of Commerce** (332-0505), 333 Caledonia St., is open Mon.-Fri. 9am-5pm. **Point Reyes National Seashore Headquarters,** on Bear Valley Rd. (663-1092), ½-mi. west of Olema, offers wilderness permits, maps, and campsite reservations. (Open Mon.-Fri. 9am-5pm, Sat.-Sun. 8am-5pm.) Marin has little public transportation. **Golden Gate Transit** (453-2100; 332-6600 in San Francisco) provides daily bus service between San Francisco and Marin County via the Golden Gate Bridge, as well as local service within the county. Buses #10, 20, 30, and 50 run from the Transbay Terminal at 1st and Mission St. in San Francisco ($1.85). The **Golden Gate Ferry** (453-2100, in San Francisco 332-6600) serves Sausalito, departing from the ferry building at the end of Market St. for a 25-minute crossing (Mon.-Fri. 7am-8:25pm, Sat.-Sun. 10:45am-6:55pm). The one-way fare to Sausalito is $3.50, $1.75 for seniors and the disabled. Boats return from Sausalito roughly one hour later than departures.

The **area code** for Marin County is 415.

Sierra Nevada

Sierra Nevada, the highest and steepest mountain range in the contiguous United States, ranges from the heart-stopping sheerness of Yosemite's rock walls to the craggy alpine scenery of Kings Canyon and Sequoia National Parks. The abrupt drop from the eastern slope into Owens Valley produce little breath and less oxygen. At 14,495 ft., Mt. Whitney surmounts all other points in the U.S. outside Alaska.

The **Sequoia National Forest** encompasses the southern tip of the Sierras as they march from Kings Canyon and Sequoia down to the low ranges of the Mojave Desert. The forest includes both popular recreational areas and isolated wilderness. **Forest headquarters** sit in Porterville, 900 W. Grand Ave. (209-784-1500), 15 mi. east of Rte. 99 between Fresno and Bakersfield. The **Sierra National Forest** fills the area between Yosemite, Sequoia, and Kings Canyon. The forest is not exactly "undiscovered"—droves of Californians jam the busier spots at lower elevations, and even the wilderness areas overpopulate in summer. The main **information office** counsels at the Federal Bldg., 1130 O St. #3017, Fresno (209-487-5155; 209-487-5456 for 24-hr. recorded info). Pick up an excellent map ($2.10) of the forests here or in Porterville, or order one from the Three Forest Interpretive Association (3FIA), 13098 E. Wire Grass Lane, Clovis 93612.

Kings Canyon and Sequoia National Park

If your impression of national parks has been formed by the touristy Grand Canyon and Yosemite, you'll thrill to the lack of sightseers in most of Sequoia and Kings Canyon, two separate and enormous parks administered jointly by the National Park Service. Glacier-covered Kings Canyon displays a beautiful array of imposing cliffs and sparkling waterfalls. Home to the deepest canyon walls in the country, turn-outs along the roads offer breathtaking vistas similar to aerial photographs. In Sequoia, the Sierra Crest lifts itself to its greatest heights. Several 14,000-ft. peaks scrape the clouds along the park's eastern border, including Mt. Whitney, the tallest mountain in the contiguous U.S. (14,495 ft.). Both parks contain impressive groves of massive sequoia trees in addition to a large and troublesome bear population. Visitors like to cluster around the largest sequoias, which loom near the entrances to the parks; vast stretches of backcountry remain relatively empty. The "summer season" usually runs from Memorial Day through Labor Day, "snow season" from November through March.

Kings Canyon's **Grant Grove Visitors Center,** 2 mi. east of the Big Stump Entrance by Rte. 180 (335-2315), has books, maps, and exhibits. (Open daily 8am-6pm; winter 8am-5pm.) Sequoia's **Ash Mountain Visitors Center,** Three Rivers 93271 (565-3456), on Rte. 198 out of Visalia, has info on both parks; the **Lodgepole Visitors Center** (565-3341, ext. 631), climbs in the heart of Sequoia, near the big trees and the tourists.

The two parks are accessible to vehicles from the west only. You can reach trailheads into the John Muir Wilderness and Inyo National Forest on the eastern side from spur roads off U.S. 395, but no roads traverse the Sierras here. From Fresno follow Rte. 180 through the foothills; a 60-mi. sojourn takes you to the entrance of the **Grant Grove** section of Kings Canyon. Rte. 180 ends 30 mi. later in the **Cedar Grove,** an island of park land enveloped within Sequoia National Forest. The road into this region closes in winter. From **Visalia,** take Rte. 198 to Sequoia National Park. **Generals Highway** (Rte. 198) connects the Ash Mountain entrance to Sequoia with the **Giant Forest,** and continues to Grant Grove in Kings Canyon.

In summer (June-Nov.), the treacherous road to **Mineral King** opens up the southern parts of Sequoia. From Visalia, take Rte. 198; the turnoff to Mineral King is 3 mi. past Three Rivers, and the **Lookout Point Ranger Station** lies 10 mi. along the Mineral King Rd. Take a break from driving here: Atwell Springs Campground and the nearby town of Silver City are 10 mi. (but 45 min.) farther along. Cold Springs Campground, Mineral King Ranger Station, and several trailheads lie near the end of Mineral King Rd. in a valley framed by 12,000-ft. peaks. The route to Mineral King includes stunning scenery—that is, if you can tear your eyes away from the tortuous road while making 698 turns between Rte. 198 and the Mineral King complex. Allow two hours for the trip from Three Rivers.

Roads can't touch the northern two-thirds of Kings Canyon and the eastern two-thirds of Sequoia; here the backpacker and packhorse have free rein. Check at a ranger station or visitors center for more detailed info.

Sequoia Guest Services, Inc., P.O. Box 789, Three Rivers 93271 (561-3314), has a monopoly on indoor accommodations and food in the parks. Their rustic **cabins** cluster in a little village in Sequoia's Giant Forest, as well as at Grant Grove. (Cabins available May-Oct., $28.50 per person, $3.50 each additional person up to 8.) Most park service **campgrounds** open from mid-May to October (2-week limit year-round). For info about campgrounds, contact a ranger station or call 565-3351 for a recording. Kings Canyon offers sites for $8 at **Sunset, Azalea,** and **Crystal Springs,** all within spitting distance of Grant Grove Village, and at **Sheep Creek, Sentinel, Canyon View,** and **Moraine,** at the Kings River near Cedar Grove. Sequoia has sites without hookups at **Lodgepole** (565-3338), 4 mi. northeast of Giant Forest Village in the heart of Sequoia National Park. (Sites $8-10; free in winter.) Reserve up to eight weeks in advance through Ticketron (800-452-1111) from mid-May to mid-September. Other options are **Atwell Mill** and **Cold Springs,** about 20 mi. along the Mineral King Rd., in the Mineral King area. (Sites $4.)

Lake Tahoe

The tectonic upheaval that brought the Sierras to their present height left a central basin which became the setting for Lake Tahoe, North America's third-deepest lake. Located 118 mi. northeast of Sacramento and 35 mi. southwest of Reno, Tahoe's cerulean waters, surrounded by evergreens and peaks, form an enormous mountain oasis. But the water remains 39°F year-round, so don't plan on doing much sidestroking.

Californian vapidity meets Nevadan avarice along the lake, as the two states split the area's southern shores into two parts—**South Lake Tahoe,** a nature lover's dream, in California, and **Stateline,** a gambling resort, in Nevada. California's **North Lake Tahoe** is a dynamic town rich in campsites.

To see the lake in style, board a boat. The glass bottoms of the *Tahoe Queen* (541-3664) leave from Ski Run Marina (3 per day, $12.50), and the *M.S. Dixie* (588-3508) leaves **Zephyr Cove** (702-588-3833), 4 mi. north of the casino on U.S. 50 (5 per day, $9-30). Several marinas rent out fishing boats, and you can get paddle boats for under $10 per hour. Or share the cost with several people, and rent a motorboat and waterskis ($52 per hr.), or a jet-ski ($45 per hr.), at Zephyr Cove. Rent a wet suit or prepare to hypotherm.

Incline Village, just into Nevada north of Tahoe, holds the famed Ponderosa Ranch (702-831-0691) of *Bonanza* fame, located in the village on Tahoe Blvd. Try the Haywagon Breakfast for a scenic buffet and hayride (daily at 8am). (Open April-Oct. daily 9am-6pm. Admission $5.50, ages 5-11 $4.50, under 5 free.) Both the **Forest Service Fire Lookout** and the **Mount Rose Scenic Overlook** (Rte. 431 from Incline to Reno) afford beautiful views of the lake. The **Heavenly Mountain** chairlift (541-1330) will carry you up 2000 ft. for a bird's-eye view. (Open Mon.-Sat. 10am-10pm, Sun. 9am-10pm.)

For those who prefer to earn their views with boot leather, the U.S. Forest Service (573-2674) produces a series of leaflets and can advise on many different trails. The western side of Tahoe offers the **Tahoe State Recreation Area** (583-3074), **Sugar Pine Point Park** (525-7982), and the **D.L. Bliss** and **Emerald Bay State Parks** (both 525-7277). Magnificent **Emerald Bay** contains Tahoe's only island. A quarter mi. off U.S. 50 at Emerald Bay sits **Vikingsholm** (540-3030), a Scandinavian-style castle built in the 1920s. (Open for tours June-Sept. daily 10am-4pm. Admission $1, kids 50¢.) The ultimate hike, along the 150-mi. **Tahoe Rim Trail,** loops around the entire lake and takes about 15 days (call 576-0676 for info).

Winter draws tourists to Lake Tahoe with nine cross-country areas, 16 ski resorts, and snowmobile routes. **Squaw Valley** (800-545-4350), home of the 1960 Winter Olympics, **Alpine Meadows** (800-824-6348), and **Diamond Peak** own the biggest reputations, but the smaller, less crowded **Homewood** draws rave reviews.

The strip off U.S. 50 on the California side of the state line supports the bulk of Tahoe's 200 motels. Others line the quieter Park Ave. Many other motels have been razed to make room for luxury hotels, and the remaining inexpensive lodgings are booked solid on weekends year-round. The cheapest deals cluster near Stateline on U.S. 50. The standard-issue **Motel 6,** 2375 Lake Tahoe Blvd., 95731 (542-1400), fills quickly, especially on weekends. It has a pool and TV. (Singles $35.15. Each additional adult $6. Make reservations or hope someone cancels.) At the clean, comfortable **Midway Motel,** 3876 U.S. 50 (544-4397), bargain gently for weekday rates. (Double bed $22, weekends $59-95. 2 double beds $30, weekends $75-95.) You also can hit the **Jack Pot Inn,** 3908 U.S. 50 (541-5587), 1 mi. south of the casinos. (Singles $20. Doubles $22. Fri.-Sat. rooms from $35.)

Stateline offers Nevada's usual assortment of cheap casino buffets. Restaurants in California include **Red Hut Waffles,** 2723 U.S. 50 (541-9024), with great breakfasts (open 6am-2pm); **The Siam Restaurant,** 2210 U.S. 50 (544-0370), with large, spicy entrees from $4 (open Mon.-Tues. and Thurs.-Sun. 10am-9:45pm); and **Cantina Los Tres Hombres,** Rte. 89 at 10th St. (544-1233), a margarita playland with free chips and salsa (open 11:30am-10:30pm).

The forest service at the visitors bureau provides up-to-date info on the 30+ campgrounds around Lake Tahoe. Make reservations for state park campgrounds by calling MISTIX at 800-283-2267. Free campgrounds include **Bayview** (544-6420; max. stay 1 night, open June-Sept.), and **Alpine Meadow** (639-2342; tents only; open May-Oct.). **Nevada Beach,** U.S. 50 and Country Rd. (573-2600), 1¾ mi. north of South Lake Tahoe, has a quaint sandy beach. (Sites $10, $12 Sept.-May.)

The **Visitors Bureau and Chamber of Commerce,** 3066 U.S. 50 (541-5255) at San Francisco Ave., has gallons of helpful brochures, maps, and free copies of *101*

Things to Do in Lake Tahoe and *Handbook for the Handicapped.* (Open Mon.-Fri. 8:30am-5pm, Sat.-Sun. 9am-4pm.) The **U.S. Forest Service,** 870 Emerald Bay Rd., S. Lake Tahoe (541-6564), publishes the free, informative *Lake of the Sky Journal* and supervises campgrounds. (Open Mon.-Fri. 8am-4:30pm.) **Greyhound,** 1099 Park Ave. (544-2241), on the state line, has service to San Francisco (10 per day, $28.50) and Sacramento (6 per day, $16.50). **Showboat Lines** sends buses from Reno Airport daily 8:30am-5pm (8 per day, $12.50). **Tahoe Area Regional Transport** (581-6365) connects to the western and northern shores from Tahoma to Incline Village. (Twelve buses daily 6:10am-6pm. Fare $1, unlimited travel day pass $2.50.) **South Tahoe Area Ground Express** (573-2080) STAGEs 24-hour bus service around town, and daily 7-hour jaunts to the beach (1 per ½-hr.; fare $1.25, under 8 free.) For those traveling without luggage, the major hotels all offer free shuttle service along U.S. 50 to and from their casinos. **Harvey's** (702-588-2411) runs a bus daily from 8am to 2am. **Budget** (541-5777), at the airport, rents from $35 per day, with surcharges for drivers under 25. Rent bikes at **Anderson's Bicycle Rental,** 645 Emerald Bay Rd. (541-0500), convenient to the west shore bike trail. (Full day $20, half-day $15. Open daily 8:30am-6:30pm. License required for deposit.) Mopeds are available from **Country Moped,** Rte. 89 S. at 10th St. (544-3500; $10 first hr., less for additional hours; helmets available).

The **post office** registers at 1085 Park Ave. (544-6162), next to the Greyhound station. (Open Mon.-Fri. 8:30am-5pm.) Lake Tahoe's **ZIP code** is 95729; the **area code** is 916 in California, 702 in Nevada.

Mammoth Lakes

The town of Mammoth Lakes is a year-round playground, home to one of the most popular ski resorts in California and unpredictable weather, including occasional snow in June. The intriguing geological oddity **Devil's Postpile National Monument** was formed when lava flows oozed through Mammoth Pass thousands of years ago and then cooled to form columns 40 to 60 ft. high. A pleasant 3-mi. walk away is **Rainbow Falls,** where the middle fork of the San Joaquin River drops 140 ft. past dark cliffs into a glistening green pool. From U.S. 395, the monument and its bubbly hot springs can be reached by a 14-mi. drive past Minaret Summit on Rte. 203. Three mi. south of Mammoth Junction on U.S. 395 bubbles **Hot Creek,** open to bathers. Ask locals about late-night skinny-dips. (Open sunrise to sunset.) None of the more than 100 lakes near town is called "Mammoth Lake." **Lake Mary** is the largest, popular with boaters and fishers; **Twin Lakes** is the closest, 3 mi. from the village on Rte. 203; swimming is allowed only at **Horseshoe Lake,** the trailhead for Mammoth Pass Trail.

Adventurous travelers can enjoy hot-air balloons, snowmobiles, mountain bike paths, and dogsled trails. **Mammoth Adventure Connection** (934-0606) helps you evaluate your options. With 132 downhill runs, over 26 lifts, and oodles of nordic trails, Mammoth is also a skier's paradise. Lift tickets may be bought for several days at a time ($27 per day, $108 for 5 days). They can be purchased at the **Main Lodge** (934-2571) at the base of the mountain on Minaret Road (open Mon.-Fri. 8am-3pm, Sat.-Sun. 7:30am-3pm) or at **Warming Hut II** (934-0771) at the end of Canyon and Lakeview Blvd. (open Mon.-Fri. 8am-5pm, Sat.-Sun. 7:30am-5pm).

Call the Mammoth Ranger District (934-25050) for info on nearly 20 Inyo Forest public **campgrounds** in the area. (Sites $7-9). Otherwise, the **ULLR Lodge** (934-2454), on Minaret Rd. just south of Main St., is the best deal in town. (Winter dorm rooms $17-19. Singles $35, $41 on weekends. Doubles $38, $44 on weekends. Cheaper in summer.) **Motel 6,** 473372 Main St. (934-6660), fills up quickly—book *way* ahead. (Singles $32, each additional person $6. Kids free.)

Chow on chili ($5.50) at the **Brewhouse Grill,** 170 Mountain Blvd. (934-8134; open Tues.-Sat. 11:30am-until, Sun. 5-10:30pm). **Blondie's Kitchen** (934-4048) at the Sierra Center Mall on Old Mammoth Rd. serves mammoth breakfast specials ($3.25; open daily 6:30am-1:30pm).

Mammoth Lakes is located on U.S. 395 about 160 mi. south of Reno and 40 mi. southeast of the eastern entrance to yosemite. Rte. 203 runs through the town as Main St., then veers off to the right as Minaret Summit Rd. The **Visitors Center and Chamber of Commerce** (932-2712) spiels inside Village Center Mall West. (Open Sat.-Thurs. 8am-5pm, Fri. 8am-8pm.) The **Mammoth National Forest Visitor Center** (934-2505) is east off U.S. 395. (Open daily 6am-5pm, Oct.-June 8am-4:30pm.) **Greyhound** (872-2721) stops in front of the Main St. McDonalds and goes once a day to Reno (1am) and L.A. (12:30pm). The **post office** (934-2205) is across from the visitors center. (Open Mon.-Fri. 8:30am-5pm.) The **ZIP code** is 93546; the **area code** is 619.

Yosemite National Park

Two years ago the worst forest fire in the park's 100-year history destroyed more than 22,000 acres in one horrific week. Although this represented only 2% of the park, the destruction is highly visible along Tioga Rd. Father Time, Mother Nature and Uncle Sam are healing the park's wounds, but no fire could boil down the stream of tourists flooding the park every year for a glimpse of its stunning waterfalls, rushing rivers, alpine meadows, and granite cliffs.

Purists bemoan Yosemite's snack shops, delis, photo galleries, and grocery stores. Casual visitors counter that the valley's unique splendor belongs to everyone, not just to backpackers. Fortunately, the embattled valley occupies only a handful of the nearly 1200 square mi. encompassed by this national park. Yosemite graciously manages to accommodate all its suitors.

Practical Information

General Park Information, 372-0265; 372-0200 for 24-hr. recorded info. Advice about accommodations, activities, and weather conditions. TTY users call 372-4726. Open Mon.-Fri. 8am-5pm. **Yosemite Valley Visitors Center,** Yosemite Village (372-4461, ext. 333). Open daily 8am-8pm. **Tuolumne Meadows Visitors Center,** Tioga Rd. (372-0263), 55 mi. from Yosemite Village. Headquarters of high-country activity, with trail info, maps, and special programs. Open summer daily 8am-7:30pm. **Big Oak Flat Information Station,** Rte. 120 W. (379-2445), in the Crane Flat/Tuolumne Sequoia Grove Area. Open summer daily 7:30am-6pm. **Wawona Ranger Station,** Rte. 141 (375-6391), at the southern entrance near the Mariposa Grove. Open Mon.-Fri. 8am-5pm; same hours on weekends in summer. **Backcountry Office,** P.O. Box 577, Yosemite National Park 95389 (372-0308; 372-0307 for 24-hr. recorded info), next to Yosemite Valley Visitors Center. Backcountry and trail info. Open daily 7:30am-7:30pm. Free map of the park and informative free *Yosemite Guide* available at visitors centers. Information folders and maps available in French, German, Japanese, and Spanish. Wilderness permits available at all centers.

Yosemite Park and Curry Co. Room Reservations: 5410 E. Home, Fresno 93727 (252-4848; TTY users 255-8345). Except for campgrounds, YP&C has a monopoly on all the facilities of what has become a full-fledged resort within the park. Contact for info and reservations.

Tour Information: Yosemite Lodge Tour Desk (372-1240), in Yosemite Lodge lobby. Open daily 7:30am-8pm, or contact any other lodge in the park.

Bus Tours: Yosemite Via, 300 Grogan Ave., Merced 95340 (384-1315 or 722-0366). Two trips daily from the Merced Greyhound station to Yosemite ($15; seniors discount). **Yosemite Gray Line (YGL),** P.O. Box 2472, Merced 95344 (383-1563). Picks up morning passengers from Merced's San Fran train, takes them to Yosemite, and returns them in time for the trip back ($15). Also runs to and from Fresno ($18). **Yosemite Transportation System** (372-1240) connects the park with Greyhound in Lee Vining ($32.50). Reservations required; runs July-Labor Day. **Green Tortoise** (415-285-2441) based in San Francisco. Two- or 3-day trip. Buses leave San Francisco at 9pm. "Sleep-aboard" bus arrives at popular sites before the crowds. Two-day trip $79, 3-day trip $99, food $8 per day. Reservations required.

Equipment Rental: Yosemite Mountaineering School, Rte. 120 at Tuolumne Meadows (372-1335; Sept.-May 372-1244). Sleeping bags $4 per day, backpacks $3.50-4 per day, snowshoes $6 per day. License or credit card required.

Bike Rentals: at Yosemite Lodge (372-1208) and Curry Village (372-1200). $4.25 per hr., $15 per day. Both open daily 8am-6pm.

Post Offices: Yosemite Village, next to the visitors center. Open Mon.-Fri. 8:30am-5pm; Sept.-May Mon.-Fri. 8:30am-12:30pm and 1:30-5pm. **Curry Village,** near Registration Office. Open June-Sept. Mon.-Fri. 9am-3pm. **Yosemite Lodge,** open Mon.-Fri. 9am-4pm. General Delivery **ZIP code:** 95389.

Area Code: 209.

Orientation and Sights

Yosemite can be reached by taking Rte. 140 from Merced, Rte. 41 north from Fresno, and Rte. 120 east from Sonoma and west from Lee Vining. Park admission costs $2 on foot, $5 for a seven-day vehicle pass. The best bargain in Yosemite is the free **shuttle bus system.** Comfortable but often crowded, the buses have knowledgeable drivers and huge windows. They operate throughout the valley daily at 10-minute intervals from 7:30am to 10pm. Drivers planning to visit the high-country in spring or fall should have snow tires, also sometimes required in early and late summer. Of the five major approaches to the park, the easiest route is Rte. 140 into Yosemite Valley. The eastern entrance, Tioga Pass, closes during snow season. The road to Mirror Lake and Happy Isles is forbidden to private auto traffic; free shuttle buses serve the road during the summer. In winter, snow closes the road to Glacier Point and sections of Tioga Road. **Biking** is an excellent way to see the Valley. For info on and reservations for **horseback trips,** call 372-1248.

Yosemite National Park divides into several areas. **Yosemite Valley,** the most spectacular, consequently receives the most traffic. Bus tours operate throughout the valley, as well as up to **Glacier Point** and the giant sequoias in the **Mariposa Grove.** Day-hikers often venture up the falls' trails and into **Little Yosemite Valley.** For a moderate hike with varying landscapes, water of all speeds, and an optional ridge or two, head toward **Lake Merced** from Glacier Point and then down toward the **Clark Range.** Weekday hiking almost guarantees privacy. The two main backcountry trailhead areas, **Tuolumne Meadows** and **Happy Isles Nature Center,** are accessible from Yosemite Valley by hitching along Tioga Rd. or by bus (372-1240) after July 1; ask to be let off at the trailhead. Buy both a topographical and a trail route map from a visitors center, namely the *Guide to Yosemite High Sierra Trails* ($2.50). A map of valley trails is also available (50¢). Acquire a wilderness permit from the Backcountry office, the Tuolumne Permit Kiosk (both open daily 7:30am-7:30pm), Big Oak Flat Station (open daily 7am-6pm), or the Wawona Ranger Station (open daily 8am-5pm).

Accommodations and Food

Those who prefer some kind of roof over their heads must call 252-4848 for reservations and info. Clean, sparsely furnished cabins are available at **Yosemite Lodge** (singles or doubles $40-$50, with bath $53.75). Southeast of Yosemite Village, **Curry Village** offers noisy but clean cabins ($40.50, with bath $53.75; canvas-sided cabins $28.50). **Housekeeping Camp** has canvas and concrete units that accommodate up to six people. Bring your own utensils, warm clothes, and industrial-strength bug repellent ($32.35 for 1-4 people). **Tuolumne Meadows,** on Tioga Rd. in the northeast corner of the park, has canvas-sided tent cabins (2 people $32.25; each additional person $5, kids $2.50.) **White Wolf,** west of Tuolumne Meadows on Tioga Rd., has similar cabins ($31.75) and cabins with bath ($54.75).

Most of the park's campgrounds are crowded with trailers and RVs. In Yosemite Valley's drive-in campgrounds, reservations are required from April to November and can be made through Ticketron (900-370-5566) up to eight weeks ahead. Sleeping in cars is emphatically prohibited. With the exception of major holidays, you should be able to camp in one of the first-come, first-served campgrounds provided you arrive at a reasonable hour. **Backcountry camping** (for general info 372-0307) is prohibited in the valley (you'll get slapped with a stiff fine if caught), but it's unrestricted along the high-country trails with a free wilderness permit. Reserve specific sites by mail February through May (write Backcountry Office, P.O. Box 577, Yosemite National Park 95389), or take your chances with the remaining 50% quota held on 24-hr. notice at the Yosemite Valley Visitors Center, the Wawona Ranger

Station, or Big Oak Flat Station. To receive a permit, you must show a planned itinerary (though you needn't follow it exactly). Most hikers stay at the undeveloped mountain campgrounds in the high country for the company and for the **bear lockers,** used for storing food (not bears). These campgrounds often have chemical toilets.

Restaurants in Yosemite are expensive and dull. Buy your own groceries and supplies from the **Yosemite Lodge Store** or the **Village Store** (open daily 8am-10pm; Oct.-May 8am-9pm).

COLORADO

Southwestern Colorado's cliff dwellings around Mesa Verde suggest that Native Americans took their architectural inspiration from the state's rivers, with the Gunnison carving Black Canyon and the Colorado chiseling methodically away at the monoliths of Colorado National Monument. Europeans dug a lot faster and for more pecuniary purposes—silver and gold attracted many of the state's first white immigrants. Even the U.S. military has dug enormous "intelligence" installations into the mountains around Colorado Springs, constructed to survive a nuclear holocaust. There is something for everybody to dig in Colorado.

Back on the surface, skiers worship Colorado's slopes, giving rise to the ubiquitous and oh-so-chic condos of Aspen, Vail, and Crested Butte. As the hub of the state and the entire Rocky Mountain region, Denver provides both an ideal resting place for cross-country travelers and a "culture fix" for people heading to the mountains; Boulder provides a crunchy alternative.

Bus transportation occurs readily throughout the Denver-Boulder area and most of the north, but driving is the way to see the more remote south. Luckily, finding accommodations proves easier; Colorado contains 23 youth hostels and a majority of the Rockies' B&Bs, and offers camping in 13 national forests and eight national parks.

Practical Information

Capital: Denver.

Colorado Board of Tourism, 1625 Broadway #1700, Denver 80202 (592-5510 or 800-433-2656). Open Mon.-Fri. 8am-5pm. **U.S. Forest Service,** Rocky Mountain Region, 11177 W. 8th Ave., Lakewood 80225 (236-9431). Tour maps free, forest maps $3. Open Mon.-Fri. 7:30am-4:30pm. **Ski Country USA,** 1540 Broadway #1300, Denver 80203 (837-0793, open Mon.-Fri. 8am-5:30pm; recorded message 831-7669). **National Park Service,** 1279 W. Alameda Pkwy., P.O. Box 25287, Denver 80255 (969-2000). Handles some reservations for Rocky Mountain National Park. Open Mon.-Fri. 9am-4pm. **Colorado State Parks and Recreation,** 1313 Sherman St. #618, Denver 80203 (866-3437). Guide to state parks and metro area trail guide. Open Mon.-Fri. 8am-5pm.

Hostel Information: AYH, Rocky Mountain Council, 1058 13th St., P.O. Box 2370, Boulder 80306 (303-442-1166).

Bed and Breakfast of Rocky Mountain, 906 S. Pearl, Denver, CO 80209 (800-258-5866). Write for information and a free host list, call for reservations.

Campsite reservation number: 800-365-2267.

Road Conditions: 639-1234 (I-25 and East), 639-1111 (Denver and West).

Time Zone: Mountain (2 hr. behind Eastern). **Postal Abbreviation:** CO

Aspen

A world-renowned hermitage of dedicated musicians and elite skiers, Aspen looms as every budget traveler's worst nightmare. Like countless other resort areas in the Rockies, Aspen was settled first by venturesome miners in search of silver and gold. When the veins of silver began drying up in the 1940s, the shanty settlement went into a 20-year decline. But the Aspen of the 1990s exhibits no signs of its past hardships. With its community of high-browed connoisseurs and wine lovers, some have suggested it has become too exclusive. Well, say Aspenites, tough. The town remains an upper class playground (although liberal enough to embrace the likes of Hunter Thompson and his gonzo lifestyle). In this resort town, low-budget living will probably remain as much a thing of the past as the forsaken mining industry.

Practical Information

Visitors Center, at the Wheeler Opera House, 320 E. Hyman Ave. (925-5656). Pick up free *What to Do in Aspen and Snowmass.* Open daily 8am-7pm; winter 10am-5pm. **Aspen Chamber and Resort Association,** 425 Rio Grand Pl. (925-1940). Open Mon.-Fri. 8:30am-5:30pm. **Aspen District of the White River National Forest Ranger Station,** 806 W. Hallam at N. 7th St. (925-3445). Info for hikers and a map of the whole forest ($3). Open July 7-Sept. 2 Mon.-Sat. 8am-5pm; off-season Mon.-Fri. 8am-5pm. **24-hr. Forest Information,** 920-1664 (recording).

Pitkin County Airport: (920-5380), 4 mi. west of town on Hwy. 82. **Continental** (925-4350) and **United** (925-3400) each offer 8 daily flights from Denver ($122). Roaring Fork buses shuttle visitors into town from the Airport Business Center (50¢).

Public Transport: Roaring Fork Transit Agency, 450 Durant Ave. (925-8484), 1 block from the mall. Service in summer daily 7am-midnight, in winter 7am-1am. Buses to Snowmass, Woody Creek, and other points down valley as far as El Jebel daily 6:15am-12:15am; in winter 6:15am-1am. Five buses per day round-trip to Maroon Bells ($3.50 one way). Free shuttles around town. Out-of-town service 60¢-$2.50.

Taxi: High Mountain, 925-8294. Base fare $2, $2.20 per mi. To airport $12. In winter, call **Aspen Carriage Co.** (925-4289) for a 25-min. horse-drawn sleigh ride for two ($15).

Car Rental: National, (800-227-7368), at the airport. Economy cars $31 per day, $150 per week. 70 free mi., 33¢ each additional mi. Must be 25 with major credit card or cash deposit.

Bike Rental: The Hub, 315 E. Hyman St. (925-7970). Mountain bikes with helmets $6 per hr., $15 per 4 hr., $20 per 8 hr. Open daily 9am-8pm. Must have credit card or $500 deposit.

Weather Line: 831-7669.

Gay Community of Aspen, 925-9249.

Post Office: 235 Puppy Smith Rd. (925-7523). Open Mon.-Fri. 9am-5pm, Sat. 9am-noon. **ZIP code:** 81611.

Area Code: 303.

In the winter, you must take I-70 west to Glenwood Springs before you can pick up CO Rte. 82 south to Aspen, which adds about 70 mi. to the trip. Once in Aspen, you will have no trouble getting around. CO Rte. 82 forms **Main Street,** to the south of which lies the downtown shopping district, and to the north of which lie opulent villas.

Accommodations and Camping

Budget accommodations don't come easy in Aspen, but surrounding national forests offer inexpensive summer camping, and some reasonably priced skiers' dorms double as guest houses in summer. The largest crowds and highest rates arrive during winter. Consider lodging in **Glenwood Springs,** 70 mi. north of Aspen, where inexpensive accommodations are plentiful. Call the **Aspen Chamber Resort Association** (1-800-262-7736) for assistance.

Little Red Ski Haus, 118 E. Cooper (925-3333), 2 blocks west of downtown. Clean, bright, wood-paneled rooms. Vivacious, helpful manager. In winter, dorm bunks $33. Private rooms for 1 or 2 $70. Off-season: dorms $20, private rooms $48. Breakfast included. Wed. night spaghetti dinner $5. Call to ensure vacancies are available.

Aspen International Hostel at the St. Moritz Lodge, 334 W. Hyman Ave. (925-3220). Dorms, shared baths. Pool, jacuzzi, sauna. In winter bunks $26, summer $22, off-season $19.

Alpine Lodge, 1240 Hwy. 82 E. (925-7351), ½-mi. east of town just beyond Independence Pass. B&B run by sweet family. Luxurious private rooms for 2 $35, winter $55. Huge sunny room downstairs with bunks for groups of 4 $55, winter $68. Breakfast included.

Unless 6 ft. of snow covers the ground, try camping in the mountains nearby. Hike well into the forest and camp for free, or use one of the nine **national forest campgrounds** within 15 mi. of Aspen. Maroon Creek offers beautiful campgrounds. Maroon Lake, Silver Bar, Silver Bell, and Silver Queen are on Maroon Creek Rd. just west of Aspen. (3-day max. stay. No reservations; sites fill well before noon. Open July-early Sept.) Southeast of Aspen on Rte. 82 toward Independence Pass are six campgrounds: Difficult, Lincoln Gulch, Dispersed Sites, Weller, Lost Man, and Portal. Ironically, Difficult is the only one with water (14-day max. stay; sites $6). The others are free and have a five-day maximum stay.

Food

The best eateries in Aspen make their meals on Main St. **The Main Street Bakery,** 201 E. Main St. (925-6446), offers sweets, gourmet soups ($3), homemade granola ($3.75), and a reprieve from pretension. (Open Mon.-Sat. 6:30am-9:30pm, Sun. 7:30am-4pm.) Two doors east of the Explore bookstore (see Entertainment and Nightlife below) is the **In and Out House,** 233 E. Main St. (925-6647), a minuscule joint that doles out huge sandwiches on fresh-baked bread ($2-4). (Open Mon.-Fri. 8am-7pm, Sat.-Sun. 8am-4pm.) Built at the height of the silver boom, **The Red Onion,** 420 E. Cooper St. (925-9043), still on its original site after almost 100 years, has lots of antique woodwork to go with burgers and sandwiches ($5-7). Look for a coupon at the visitors center. (Open daily 11:30am-10pm.) The local coffeehouse, **Pour la France,** 411 E. Main St. (920-1151), serves sandwiches ($4.50), good coffee, and pastries, and is ideal for eavesdropping on pretentious conversation. (Open daily 7am-10pm.) **The Popcorn Wagon,** on the corner of Mill and E. Hyman Ave. (925-2718), across from the Wheeler Opera House, sells the only thing you can afford after lodging in Aspen. Great chocolate crepes as well ($1.50). (Open daily 11am-2am.)

Entertainment and Nightlife

Aspen's active après-skiers support an equally active nightlife. Students frequent the **Cooper Street Pier,** 500 E. Cooper St. (925-7758), where a chili dog and fries ($3) and a glass of draft beer (75¢) are the combo of choice. (Restaurant open daily 11am-11pm. Bar open 11am-2pm.) At **The Tippler,** 535 E. Dean Ave. (925-4977), you'll find a more seasoned crowd, also downing 75¢ drafts. (Open daily in winter, Wed.-Sat. in summer; 9am-2am.) **Little Annie's,** 517 E. Hyman Ave. (925-1098), has been known to host the jet set, but usually flies a wider range of patrons. (Restaurant open daily 11:30am-11:30pm. Bar open 11am-2am.) The scene at **Ebbes,** on the third floor at 312 S. Galena (925-6200), changes every time you turn around; business talk, karaoke, TV, student antics, and gay socializing make this one of the liveliest places in town. (Live music Mon.-Sat. 10:30pm-1:30am.) Intellectual discussions, esoteric jokes, and mouth-watering scents fill the air at the **Explore Booksellers and Coffee Shop,** 221 E. Main St. (925-5336). Read as many of the shop's books as you'd like for free, served upstairs over tea and a table. (Open daily 10am-10pm.)

In addition to a plethora of annual artistic rituals, Aspen hosts many seasonal and even nightly cultural events. For tickets and the scoop on dance, theater, and film in the entire Aspen area, call the **Wheeler Opera House Box Office,** 320 E.

Hyman Ave. (925-2750; open Mon.-Sat. 10am-5pm). Tours of the opera house are available 9:30am-3:30pm daily ($2, kids free).

Activities and Sights

The hills surrounding town contain four ski areas; **Aspen Mountain, Buttermilk Mountain,** and **Snowmass Ski Area** (923-1220) sell interchangeable lift tickets. ($40, ages over 70 free, kids $20. Daily hours: Aspen Mtn. 9:30am-3:30pm, Buttermilk Mtn. 9am-4pm, Snowmass 8:30am-3:30pm.) **Aspen Highlands** (925-5300) does not provide interchangeable tickets ($33, seniors with ID and kids $17; open daily 9am-4pm). Favorite slopes include **Sheer Rock Face** at Aspen, **Nipple** at Buttermilk, and **Catholic School** at Snowmass.

Needless to say, you can enjoy the mountains without shelling out money to ski. In the summer ride the **Silver Queen Gondola** ($11) to the top of Aspen mountains. The ghost towns of **Ashcroft** and **Independence** open their doors to visitors in the summer, and hiking in the Maroon Bells and Elk Mountains is permitted when the snow isn't too deep. Maroon and Crater Lakes are popular destinations in this relatively unspoiled area. Shuttles run twice every hour and have been instituted to spare the Maroon Creek Valley from automobile emissions and noise. ($2.50, seniors and kids $1). Free shuttle buses to Highlands leave from Aspen's Rubey Park 15 and 45 minutes after the hour. Biking up to **Maroon Lake** is popular and fairly strenuous. From the trailhead, hike the 1.6-mi. turnpike through aspen groves to **Crater Lake,** and continue through high passes to more distant destinations in the **Maroon Bells-Snowmass Wilderness.** Pick up a topographical map in Aspen before beginning your ascent. The **Ute Mountaineer,** 308 S. Mill St. (925-2849; open daily 9am-8pm), and **Carl's Pharmacy,** 306 E. Main St. (925-3273; open daily 8am-10pm), both sell maps for $2.50.

Undoubtedly Aspen's most famous event, the **Aspen Music Festival** (925-9042) holds sway over the town from late June to August. Free bus transportation goes from Rubey Park downtown to "the Tent," south of town, before and after all concerts. Picnic outside the tent and listen for free; afternoon rehearsals are also free. (Concerts June-late Aug. Free concert held almost every day. Tickets $8-25. Sun. rehearsals $2.) Aspen's only museum, the **Wheeler-Stallard House,** 620 W. Bleecker St. (925-3721), is also home to the symbiotic **Aspen Historical Society.** (Open daily Tues.-Sun. 1-4pm.) Tours include many fascinating details about the mining history of Aspen, including the notorious brownie floor. (Admission $3, kids 50¢.)

Near Aspen: Glenwood Springs

Forty mi. northwest of Aspen on Colorado Rte. 82, **Glenwood Springs** is neither as glitzy nor as overpriced as its larger-than-life neighbor. This tranquil village relies upon the nearby **Glenwood Hot Springs,** 401 N. River Rd. (945-6571), for most of its income. (Open daily 7:30am-10pm. Day charge $5.75, kids $3.50.) Ski 10 mi. west of town at **Sunlight,** 10901 County Rd. 117 (945-7491). Ski passes cost $22 per day for hostelers, including access to the hot springs.

Within walking distance of the springs you'll find the **Glenwood Springs Hostel (AYH),** 1021 Grand Ave. (945-8545), a former Victorian home with spacious dorm and communal areas as well as a full kitchen. The owner, Gary, has a collection of 1100 records. At night, Halka will take you to the local pool hall where you can rack and shoot 'em with the best. Here you can also rent mountain bikes for $8 per day and receive a free ride (by car) from train and bus stations. (Closed 10am-4pm. $10.25, nonmembers $11.50. Linen included.) The Victorian home next door is **Aducci's Inn,** 1023 Grand Ave. (945-9341). Private rooms (1-2 persons) in this B&B cost $28 (weekends $38). Includes breakfast and wine in the evenings. Call for free pick-up from bus and train stations.

The **Amtrak** station thinks it can at 413 7th St. (872-7245; for reservations 800-872-7245). One train daily goes west to Denver (6 hr., $50) and one east to Salt Lake City (7 hr., $78). (Station open daily 9:30am-4:45pm.) **Greyhound** serves Glenwood Springs from a terminal at 118 W. 6th Ave. (945-8501). Four buses run daily to Denver (4 hr., $17) and Grand Junction (2 hr., $8). (Open Mon.-Fri. 6:15am-noon and 4-5pm.) For further information on the town, contact the **Glenwood Springs Chamber Resort Association,** 1102 Grand Ave. (945-6589; open Mon.-Fri. 8:30am-5pm, Sat.-Sun. 10am-2pm; self-service info center open 24 hrs.).

Boulder

Boulder lends itself to the pursuit of both higher knowledge and better karma, as the home of both the University of Colorado and the only accredited Buddhist university in the U.S., the Naropa Institute. Only here can you take summer poetry and mantra workshops lead by Beat guru Allen Ginsberg at the Jack Kerouac School of Disembodied Poets. Boulder's universities also attract a musical mix, from bands with more of an edge, like the Dead Milkmen, to more traditional folk heroes, such as Tracy Chapman and the Indigo Girls. You often can hear top performers in the Pearl Street cafés, surrounded by ceiling fans and iced cappuccino.

The nearby Flatiron Mountains, rising up in big charcoal-colored slabs on the western horizon, beckon rock climbers, while an admirable system of paths make Boulder one of the most bike- and pedestrian-friendly areas around. For those motorists seeking a retreat into nature or tiring of the city's cycle-centricity, Boulder is "on the road" (Colorado Rte. 36) to Rocky Mountain National Park, Estes Park, and Grand Lake.

Practical Information

Emergency: 911.

Boulder Chamber of Commerce/Visitors Service, 2440 Pearl St. (442-1044 or 800-444-0447), at Folsom about 10 blocks from downtown. Take bus #200. Well-equipped, with comprehensive seasonal guides. Open Mon. 9am-5pm, Tues.-Fri. 8:30am-5pm. **University of Colorado Information** (492-6161), 2nd floor of UMC student union. Campus maps. Open Mon.-Thurs. 7am-11pm, Fri.-Sat. 7am-1am, Sun. 11am-11pm. **CU Ride Board,** UMC, Broadway at 16th. Lots of rides, lots of riders—even in the summer.

Public Transport: Boulder Transit Center, 14th and Walnut St. (299-6000). Routes to Denver and Longmont as well as intra-city routes. Buses operate Mon.-Fri. 6am-8pm, Sat.-Sun. 8am-8pm. Fare 50¢, 75¢ Mon.-Fri. 6-9am and 3-6pm. Long-distance: $1.50 to Nederland ("N" bus) and Lyons ("Y" bus); $2 to Golden ("G" bus) and Boulder Foothills or Denver ("H" bus). Several other lines link up with the Denver system (see Denver Practical Information). Get a bus map ($1) at the RTD terminal.

Taxi: Boulder Yellow Cab, 442-2277. $1.20 first ¾-mi., $1.20 each additional mi.

Car Rental: Dollar Rent-a-Car, 2100 30th St. (442-1687). $26 per day, $139 per week. Open Mon.-Fri. 8am-8pm, Sat. 8am-6pm. Must be 21 with major credit card.

Bike Rental: University Bicycles, 839 Pearl St. (444-4196), downtown. 10-speeds and mountain bikes $12 per 3 hr., $16 per day, $20 overnight, with helmet and lock. Open Mon.-Fri. 8:30am-7pm, Sat. 9am-5pm, Sun. 10am-4pm.

Help Lines: Rape Crisis, 443-7300. Open 24 hrs. **Crisis Line,** 447-1665. Open 24 hrs. **Gays, Lesbians, and Friends of Boulder,** 492-8567.

Post Office: 1905 15th St. (938-1100), at Walnut across from the RTD terminal. Open Mon.-Fri. 8:45am-5:15pm, Sat. 9am-noon. General Delivery 8:45am-5:15pm. **ZIP code:** 80302.

Area Code: 303.

Boulder (pop. 83,300) is a small, manageable city. The most developed part of Boulder lies between **Broadway** (Rte. 93) and **28th Street** (Rte. 36), two busy streets running parallel to each other north-south through the city. **Baseline Road,** which connects the Flatirons with the eastern plains, and **Canyon Boulevard** (Rte. 7), which follows the scenic Boulder Canyon up into the mountains, border the main part of the **University of Colorado** campus (CU). The school's surroundings are known locally as the **"Hill."** The pedestrian-only **Pearl Street Mall,** between 11th and 15th St. centers hip life in Boulder. Most east-west roads have names, while north-south streets have numbers; Broadway is a conspicuous exception.

Accommodations and Camping

Though a college town, Boulder doesn't offer many student-rate places to spend the night. In summer, you can rely on the **Boulder International Youth Hostel (AAIH),** 1107 12th St. (442-9304), on the Hill, two blocks west of the CU campus and 15 minutes south of the RTD station. The incredibly friendly atmosphere and laid-back management more than make up for the slight scruffiness of these frat-house rooms. Bring or rent sheets, a towel, and a pillow. (Open 7:30-10am and 5pm-midnight. Curfew midnight in private rooms. $11. Private singles $22, doubles $27. Towels and linen $2. Key deposit $5.) Reservations are recommended at the **Chau-tauqua Association,** 9th St. and Baseline Rd. (442-3282), which offers rooms big enough for two in their lodge for $28 and quaint, highly popular cottages ($39 per night; 4-night min. stay). Guests at this cultural institution can take in films for free. Take bus #203. **The Boulder Mountain Lodge,** 91 Four Mile Canyon Rd. (444-0882), is a 2-mi. drive west on Canyon Rd., near creek-side bike and foot trails. Two comfortable, woody rooms have four and six bunks, respectively. Facilities include phone and TV; hot tub and pool a nice plus. An entire room for one or two people rents for $25, each additional person $12.50. Check-in by 10pm for campsites.)

You'll have an easy time finding camping spots elsewhere. Info on campsites in **Roosevelt National Forest** is available from the Forest Service Station at 2995 Baseline Rd. #16, Boulder 80303 (444-6001; open Mon.-Fri. 8am-5pm). Maps $2. A site at **Kelly Dahl,** 3 mi. south of Nederland on Rte. 119, costs $7. **Rainbow Lakes,** 6 mi. north of Nederland on Rte. 72, then 5 mi. west on Arapahoe Glacier Rd., is free, but no water is available. (Campgrounds open from late May to mid-Sept.) **Peaceful Valley** and **Camp Dick** (north on Rte. 72; $7 per site) have cross-country skiing in the winter and first-come, first-served sites.

Food and Hangouts

The streets on the "Hill" and those along the Pearl St. Mall bristle with good eateries, natural foods markets, cafés, and colorful bars. Many more restaurants and bars line Baseline Rd. As one would expect given the peave-love-nature-touchy-feely climate, Boulder has more restaurants for vegetarians than for carnivores.

When the word went out in 1989 that the **Sink,** 1165 13th St. (444-7465), re-opened, throngs of former "Sink Rats" began to make the pilgrimage back to Boulder; the restaurant still awaits the return of its former janitor, Robert Redford, who quit his job and headed out to California back in the late 1950s. (Open Mon.-Sat. 11am-2am, Sun. 11am-midnight. Food served until 10pm.)

New Age Foods, 1122 Pearl St. Mall (443-0755), at the back of the health food store. The cheapest meals in town, featuring healthful and veggie food. Cafeteria-style restaurant offers soups, large salads, sandwiches, and specials such as lasagna and black-bean burritos. Choose 1 for $2.50, 2 for $3.50. Open Mon.-Fri. 9am-5:30pm, Sat. 9am-4pm. Restaurant open Mon.-Fri. 11am-3pm.

The L.A. Diner (for "Last American"), 1955 28th St. (447-1997). Roller skating staff serve green chili in a silver spaceship of a restaurant. 10-oz. sirloin steak, potato, vegetables, soup or salad $8. Open Mon.-Thurs. 6:30am-midnight, Fri. 6:30am-3am, Sat. 8am-3am, Sun. 8am-midnight.

The Walrus Café, 1911 11th St. (443-9902). Universally popular night spot. Beer $1.50. Open daily 4pm-1:30am.

CU Student Cafeteria, 16th and Broadway, downstairs in the student union (UMC). The large **Alfred Packer Grill** (named after the West's celebrated cannibal) serves burgers ($1.75) and sizeable burritos ($3). Open Mon.-Fri. 7am-7pm, Sat. 10am-4pm, Sun. 11am-4pm.

Harvest Restaurant and Bakery, 1738 Pearl St. (449-6223), at 18th St. inside a little mall. A fine example of mellow, "back-to-nature" Boulder. Very popular among CU students. Try the turkey-cashew salad on toasted whole-wheat bread ($4.65). You can sit at the community table to make friends. Open Sun.-Thurs. 7am-10pm, Fri.-Sat. 7am-11pm.

The Trident Bookstore Café, 940 Pearl St. (443-3133). Boulder's "Buddhist" coffeehouse with Naropa professors and CU students translating poems before class. Order a half-price book with a tall iced coffee ($1.25). Open Mon.-Fri. 6:30am-11pm, Sat.-Sun. 8am-11pm.

Expresso Roma, 110 13th St. (442-5011), on the Hill near the youth hostel. Students head here for jumps of caffeine (85¢) and the almond biscotti (35¢). When the Cabaret Voltaire gets too grating, head for the more peaceful back room. Open daily 7am-midnight.

Sights and Activities

The University of Colorado's intellectuals collaborate with wayward poets and back-to-nature devotees to find innovative things to do. Check out the perennially outrageous street scene on the Mall and the Hill and watch the university's kiosks for the scoop on downtown happenings.

The university's **Cultural Events Board** (492-8409) has the latest word on all CU-sponsored activities. The most massive of these undertakings is the annual **Arts Fest** in mid-July. Phone for tickets or stop by the ticket office in the **University Memorial Center** (492-2736; open Mon.-Sat. 10am-6pm). As part of Arts Fest, the **Colorado Shakespeare Festival** (492-8181) takes place from late June to mid-August. (Previews $8, general admission $10.) Concurrently, the Chautauqua Institute (442-3282; see Accommodations above) hosts the **Colorado Music Festival** (449-1397; 8am-5pm, on concert days 8am-6pm; performances June 23-Aug. 5; tickets $10-22) and the **Boulder Blues Festival** (443-5858; tickets at 444-3601 cost $10-15) held the second week of July. The **Parks and Recreation Department** (441-3400; open Mon.-Fri. 8am-5pm) sponsors free performances in local parks from May to August; dance, classical and modern music, and children's theater are staples. The **Boulder Center for the Visual Arts,** 1750 13th St. (443-2122), focuses on the finest in contemporary regional art and has more wide-ranging exhibits as well. (Open Tues.-Sat. 11am-5pm, Sun. 1-5pm. Free.)

Boulder Public Library, 9th and Arapaho (441-3100), and CU's **Muenzinger Auditorium,** near Folsom and Colorado Ave. (492-1531), both screen international films. Call for times and price. Museums in Boulder don't quite compare with the vitality and spectacle of Pearl St. and the Hill. When the need to see a more formal exhibit overtakes you, the intimate and impressive **Leanin' Tree Museum,** 6055 Longbow Dr. (530-1442), presents an interesting array of Western art and sculpture. (Open Mon.-Fri. 8am-4:30pm. Free.) The small **Naropa Institute** is located at 2130 Arapahoe Ave. (444-0202). Drop by and drop off at one of their many free meditation sessions with Tibetan monks.

The Flatiron Mountains, acting as a backdrop to this bright and vibrant town, offer countless variations on walking, hiking, and biking. Take a stroll or cycle along **Boulder Creek Path,** a beautiful strip of park that lines the creek for 15 mi. Farther back in the mountains lie treacherous, less accessible rocky outcroppings. Trails weave through the 6000-acre **Boulder Mountain Park,** beginning from several sites on the western side of town. **Flagstaff Road** winds its way to the top of the mountains from the far western end of Baseline Rd. The **Boulder Creek Canyon,** accessible from Rte. 119, emits splendid rocky scenery. Nearby **Eldorado Canyon,** as well as the Flatirons themselves, has some of the best rock climbing in the world.

Well-attended running and biking competitions far outnumber any other sports events in the Boulder area. The biggest foot race by far is the 10km Memorial Day challenge known as the **"Bolder Boulder,"** which brings in 30,000 international athletes. The winner takes home $4000. For information on any running event, call the Boulder Roadrunners (499-2061; open daily 9am-6pm).

The **Boulder Brewing Company,** 2880 Wilderness Place (444-8448), offers tours for those who prefer sedentary pleasures to exercise. Yes, they feed you free beer at the end. (25-min. tours Mon.-Fri. at 11am and 2pm and Sat. at 2pm; open Mon.-Fri. 8am-7pm, Sat. 11am-3pm.)

Colorado Springs

The large Victorian houses and wide streets of Colorado Springs' older sections reflect the idle elegance of this long-time resort. Visitors today come for the same reasons that 19th-century travelers did: clean, dry air, and easy access to the mountains—especially Pikes Peak, which surges 14,110 ft. above sea level. The Ute, frequently traveling across the region by the 1600s on their way over the southern front range of the Rockies, stopped in Colorado and Manitou Springs for their healing mineral waters. Tourists now entrench themselves in certain sections of town, especially Manitou Springs to the west; there may be more nearby ghost towns than there ever were cowboys or Native Americans. While tourists pour millions into the Colorado Springs economy during the summer, the U.S. government pours in even more: North American Air Defense Command Headquarters (NORAD) lurks beneath nearby Cheyenne Mountain. Still, the city can serve as a worthwhile day-trip from Denver or as a point of departure for mountain pilgrimages.

Practical Information

Emergency: 911.

Colorado Springs Convention and Visitors Bureau, 104 S. Cascade #104, 80903 (635-7506 or 1-800-368-4748), at Colorado Ave. Check out the *Colorado Springs Pikes Peak Park Region Offical Visitors Guide* and the city bus map. Open Mon.-Sat. 8:30am-5pm, Sun. 9am-3pm; Nov.-March Mon.-Fri. 8:30am-5pm. Manitou Springs Chamber of Commerce, 354 Manitou Ave., Manitou Springs 80829 (685-5089 or 800-642-2567). Near the trailhead for climbing Pikes Peak. Open summer Mon.-Fri. 8:30am-5pm, Sat.-Sun. 8am-4pm. Funfone, 635-1723. Information on current events.

Colorado Springs Airport: 596-0188. Directly east of the downtown area, off Nevada Ave. at the end of Fountain Blvd.

Greyhound/Trailways: 327 S. Weber St. (635-1505). To: Denver (9 per day, 1½-2 hr., $8); Pueblo (8 per day, 50 min., $4.50); Albuquerque, NM (5 per day, 7-9 hr., $55); Kansas City, MO (3 per day, 16-17 hr., $80). Tickets available daily 5am-midnight. Open 4:15am-midnight.

Public Transport: Colorado Springs City Bus Service, 125 E. Kiowa at Nevada (475-9733), 5 blocks from the Greyhound/Trailways station. Serves the city and Widefield, Manitou Springs, Fort Carson, Garden of the Gods, and Peterson AFB. Service Mon.-Fri. 5:45am-6:15pm, Sat. hours vary. Fare 60¢, seniors and kids 25¢; long trips 15¢ extra. Exact change required.

Tours: Gray Line Tours, 3704 Colorado Ave. (633-11810), at the Garden of the Gods Campgrounds. Trips to the U.S. Air Force Academy and Garden of the gods (tickets $15, kids $7.50), Pikes Peak (tickets $20, kids $10) and a nighttime tour of the Cave of the Winds and Seven Falls (prices same as Pikes Peak tour). All tours are 4 hr. Office open daily 7am-11pm.

Taxi: Yellow Cab, 634-5000. $2.90 first mi., $1.25 each additional mi.

Car Rental: Ugly Duckling, 2128 E. Bijou (634-1914). $16 per day, $97 per week. Open Mon.-Fri. 9am-5pm, Sat. 9am-1pm. Must stay in CO and be 21 with major credit card or $200 deposit.

Bike Rental: Holubar Mountaineering, 2626 Colorado Ave. (634-5279). Mountain bikes with helmets $7.50 per half day, $15 per full day, $20 overnight. $300 deposit or credit card. Open Mon.-Fri. 10am-8pm, Sat. 9am-6pm, Sun. noon-5pm.

Help Lines: Crisis Emergency Services, 635-7000. Open 24 hrs. Gay Community Center of Colorado Springs, 512 W. Colorado Ave. (471-4429). Phones answered Mon.-Fri. 6-9pm, Sat. 3-5pm.

Post Office: 201 Pikes Peak Ave. (570-5336), at Nevada Ave. Open Mon.-Fri. 7:30am-5pm. ZIP code: 80903.

Area Code: 719.

Mowed, manicured, broad thoroughfares laid out in a fairly consistent grid make up Colorado Springs. **Nevada Avenue** is the main north-south strip, known for its many bars and restaurants. **Pikes Peak Avenue** serves as the east-west axis, running parallel to **Colorado Avenue,** which connects with U.S. 24 on the city's west side. U.S. 25 from Denver plows through the downtown area. Downtown itself is comprised of the square bounded on the north by Fillmore Ave., on the south by Colorado Ave., on the west by Cascade, and on the east by Nevada Ave. A word of warning—the city's attractions spread out over a wide area, and city bus service is available only Mon.-Sat. from 5:45am-6:15pm.

Accommodations and Camping

Avoid the shabby motels along Nevada Ave. If the youth hostel fails you, head for the establishments along W. Pikes Peak Ave. or a nearby campground. For information on B&Bs, contact Bed and Breakfast of Colorado (see Colorado Practical Information).

Garden of the Gods Youth Hostel (AYH), 3704 W. Colorado Ave. (475-9450). Four-bunk shanties. Showers and bathrooms shared with campground. Swimming pool, jacuzzi, laundry. $8, nonmembers traveling with members $10. Open April-Oct.

Amarillo Motel, 2801 W. Colorado Ave. (635-8539). Take bus #1 West down Colorado Ave. to 34th St. Ask for rooms in the older National Historic Register section. Rooms lack windows, but all have kitchens and TV. Laundry available. Singles $24. Doubles $30. Off-season: $18, $24. Next to the hotel office is **Leisure's Treasures,** the largest display of military relics in the Midwest. (Open Mon.-Sat. 10am-6pm.) Elden Leisure will show you a silver-hilted Civil War sword that you can buy for $6,000, a real bargain for the budget traveler. Look through albums of WWI and WWII snapshots.

Apache Court Motel, 3401 W. Pikes Peak Ave. (471-9440). Take bus #1 west down Colorado Ave. to 34th St., walk 1 block north. Very spiffy pink adobe rooms. Doubles have kitchens. A/C and TV. May-Sept. 15: singles $32, doubles $42. Sept. 6-April: singles $27, doubles $39.

Motel 6, 3228 N. Chestnut St. (520-5400), at Fillmore St. just west of I-25 exit 145. Take bus #8 west. TV, pool, A/C. Some rooms with unobstructed view of Pikes Peak. Singles $30. Doubles $37.

Right in the city is the **Garden of the Gods Campground,** 3704 W. Colorado Ave. (475-9450). Sites are $16.50, with electricity and water $19.50, full hookup $22. Several popular **Pike National Forest** campgrounds lie in the mountains flanking Pikes Peak, generally open May through September. Some clutter around Rte. 67, 5 to 10 mi. north of **Woodland Park,** which is 18 mi. northwest of the Springs on U.S. 24. Others fringe U.S. 24 near the town of Lake George. (Sites $6; fill only on summer weekends.) You can always camp off the road on national forest property for free at least 100 yards from road or stream; the **Forest Service Office,** 601 S. Weber (636-1602), has maps ($3) of the campgrounds and wilderness areas. (Open Mon.-Fri. 7:30am-4:30pm.) Farther afield, you can camp in the **Eleven Mile State Recreation Area** (748-3401 or 800-365-2267), off a spur road from U.S. 24 near Lake George. (Sites $6. Entrance fee $3. Reserve on weekends.) Last resorts include the **Woodland Park KOA** (687-3535), ¼-mi. north of U.S. 24 on Rte. 67, three blocks west on Bowman Ave. (sites $16, with water and electricity $19, full hookup $20; call for reservations) and the **Monument Lake Resort and Campground,** 19750 Mitchell Ave. (481-2223), in nearby Monument (sites $9, with water and electricity $11, full hookup $13).

Food

You can get cheap, straightforward fare downtown, or try the stylish restaurants along W. Colorado Ave.

Poor Richard's Restaurant, 324½ North Tejon (632-7721). The local coffeehouse college hangout. Frozen yogurt and veggie food. Open Mon.-Sat. 10:30am-11pm, Sun 10:30am-10pm.

Kennedy's 26th St. Café, 2601 W. Colorado Ave. One of the cheapest eateries in Colorado Springs. Enormous Ranchman's breakfast (2 eggs, ham, and all the pancakes you can eat) $4. Cheeseburger with large fries $2-3. Open Mon.-Fri. 6:30am-4pm, Sat. 6:30am-3pm.

Meadow Muffins, 2432 W. Colorado Ave. (633-0583), in a converted warehouse. Don't do the Jiffy Burger ($5), named for the peanut butter, but everything else seems safe. Check out the phone booth at the entrance and you'll discover a new definition of a Superman. 89¢ draws. Open daily 11am-2am.

Dale St. Café, 115 Dale St. (578-9898), south of Colorado College between Tejon and Nevada Ave. Where locals go for gourmet pizza. Try a thin-crusted Mediterranean with mozzarella, tomato, and basil ($4.75). Open Mon.-Thurs. 11:30am-9pm, Fri.-Sat. 11:30am-9:30pm.

Henri's, 2427 W. Colorado Ave. (634-9031). Genuine, excellent Mexican food. Popular with locals for 40 years. Fantastic margaritas. Cheese enchiladas ($5), and great free chips. Open Tues.-Sat. 11:30am-10pm, Sun. noon-8pm.

Sights

The town's major attraction looms large on its western horizon; you can see **Pikes Peak** from the town as well as from the quieter expanses of the **Pike National Forest.** You can climb the peak via the 13-mi. **Barr Burro Trail.** The trailhead is in Manitou Springs by the "Manitou Incline" sign. Catch bus #1 to Ruxton. Don't despair if you don't reach the top—explorer Zebulon Pike never reached it either, and they still named the whole mountain after him. Otherwise, pay the fee to drive up the **Pikes Peak Highway** (684-9383), administered by the Colorado Department of Public Works. (Open May-June 10 daily 9am-3pm, June 11-Sept. 2 7am-6:30pm; hours dependent on weather. Admission $4, under 13 $1.) You can also reserve a seat on the **Pikes Peak Cog Railway,** 515 Ruxton Ave. (685-5401; open May-Oct. 8 daily; round-trip $17, ages 5-11 $8). Expect cold weather. At the summit, you'll see Kansas, the Sangre de Cristo Mountains, and the ranges along the Continental Divide. Note that even when the temperature is in the 80s in Colorado Springs, Pikes Peak only warms up to the mid-30s; roads often remain icy through the summer.

Pikes Peak is not Colorado Springs' only outdoor attraction. The **Garden of the Gods City Park,** 1401 Recreation Way (578-6939), composed of red rock monuments that Native Americans believed were the bodies of their enemies thrown down by gods, contains many secluded picnic and hiking areas. (Free. Visitors center open daily 9am-5pm; off-season 10am-4pm.) The oft-photographed "balanced-rock" is at the park's south entrance. For more strenuous hiking, head for the **Cave of the Winds** (685-5444), 6 mi. west of exit 141 off I-25, with guided tours of the fantastically contorted caverns every 15 minutes daily from 9am to 9pm. Just above Manitou Springs on Rte. 24 lies the **Manitou Cliff Dwellings Museum** (685-5242), U.S. 24 bypass, where you can wander through a pueblo of ancient Anasazi buildings. (Open daily May-Sept. 9am-6pm. Admission $3, under 11 $1.50.)

Buried in a hollowed-out cave 1800 ft. below Cheyenne Mountain, the **North American Air Defense Command Headquarters (NORAD)** (554-7321) was designed to survive even a direct nuclear hit. A 3-mi.-long tunnel leads to this telecommunication center, which monitors every plane in the sky. During the Persian Gulf War, all commands to Patriot missiles were sent from this location. The **Peterson Air Force Base,** on the far east side of the city, offers a visitors center and the **Edward J. Peterson Space Command Museum** (554-4915; open Tues.-Fri. 8:30am-4:30pm, Sat. 9:30am-4:30pm; free). Take bus #2.

The **United States Air Force Academy,** a college for future officers, marches 12 mi. north of town on I-25; it's chapel is made of aluminum, steel, and other materials used in airplanes. On weekdays during the school year, uniformed cadets gather at 11:55am near the chapel for the cadet lunch formation—a big production just to chow down. The **visitors center** (472-2000) has self-guided tour maps, info on the many special events, and a 12-minute movie every ½-hr. (Open daily 9am-5pm.)

The **Pioneers' Museum,** downtown at 215 S. Tejon St. (578-6650), covers the settling of Colorado Springs, including a display on the techniques and instruments of a pioneer doctor. (Open Mon.-Sat. 10am-5pm, Sun. 1-5pm.) Everything you ever wanted to know about mining awaits at the **Western Museum of Mining and Industry,** 1025 N. Gate Rd. (598-8850; open Mon.-Sat. 9am-4pm, Sun. noon-4pm; admission $4, students $3.50, ages 5-17 $1.50; closed Dec.-Feb.). Take exit 156-A off I-25. And all your questions about those famous Olympians will be answered at the **U.S. Olympic Complex,** 1750 E. Boulder St. (578-4618 or 578-4644), which offers informative one-hour tours every ½-hr. that include a tear-jerking film. Watch Olympic hopefuls practice in the afternoons. (Open Mon.-Sat. 9am-5pm, Sun. 10am-noon.) Take bus #1 east to Farragut.

For information about the arts in Colorado Springs, drop in at the **Colorado Springs Fine Arts Center,** 30 W. Dale (634-5583; open Tues.-Fri. 9am-5pm, Sat. 10am-5pm, Sun. 1-5pm; admission $2.50, students $1.50), or call **Colorado College** (389-6606), which stocks the city with cultural events, including the **Summer Festival of the Arts.** Tickets and info available at Worner Campus Center, at Cascade and Cache La Poudre St. (Open daily 8am-11pm.)

At night, Colorado College's literati find comfortable reading at **Poor Richard's Espresso Bar,** adjacent to the bookstore (see Food above). The bar occasionally hosts comedy, acoustic performances, and readings. (Open Mon.-Thurs. 7am-midnight, Fri.-Sat. 7am-2am, Sun. 7am-10pm.) The **Dublin House,** 1850 Dominion Way at Academy St. (528-1704), is a popular sports bar, with Sunday night blues downstairs. (Open Mon.-Thurs. 4pm-2am, Fri.-Sun. 11am-2am. Music starts at 9pm. Cover $3.)

Near Colorado Springs: Cripple Creek

Former mining towns pepper the area about Colorado Springs, nostalgic reminders of the state's glory days. In order to pump some life into these forsaken towns, and bring back the spirit of the Old West, the state has decided to introduce limited gambling up on **Cripple Creek** (sung about by The Band), **Central City,** and **Blackhawk.** Hotels and casinos will offer poker, blackjack and slot machines with a $5 maximum bet. If fortune fails you in gambling, look for riches at the **Mollie Kathleen Gold Mine** (689-2465), two hours north of Colorado Springs via Rte. 67 in Cripple Creek. Every 10 minutes during the day, miners lead 40 minute tours down a 1,000-ft.-deep shaft. (Open May-Oct. daily 9am-5pm. Tours $8, kids $3.50.) For info about other activities, try the **Cripple Creek Chamber of Commerce,** P.O. Box 650, Cripple Creek 80813 (689-2169 or 689-2307).

In a car (with good suspension), the most exciting way to reach Cripple Creek is via **Phantom Creek Road.** This route takes off from U.S. 50, 30 mi. southwest of Colorado Springs, and meanders up an ever-narrowing canyon, in which the vertical walls get closer and closer to the road. Finally, near the tourist-haunt mining town of Victor, the road reaches a 9000-ft. highland. Cripple Creek still lies 6 mi. ahead. On the return trip, take the most scenic route over the unpaved **Gold Camp Road** (open only in summer), once described by Teddy Roosevelt as the "trip that bankrupts the English language."

Denver

Gold! In 1858 the word went out from the South Platte River Valley: the South Platte and its smaller neighbor, Cherry Creek, held glittering, drool-inducing money for the taking. Within weeks the rumor of riches drew thousands of miners to northern Colorado, and Denver was born, complete with Colorado's first saloon. (Back then, you didn't get in trouble for serving miners.) Most of the mines have since gone out of business, with cycling shops and sporting goods stores now contributing

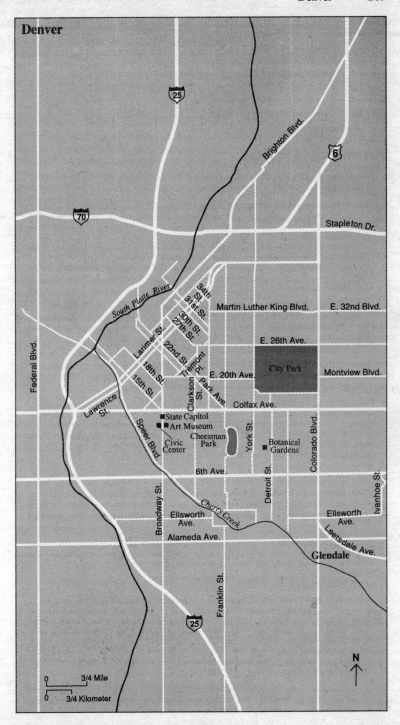

more to Denver's economy than saloons ever did. Colorado's capital is the Rockies' largest and fastest-growing metropolis. Centrally located between Colorado's eastern plains and western ski resorts, Denver today serves as the industrial, commercial, and cultural center of the region—and soon, it will have major-league baseball, too.

A curious mix of transplanted New Yorkers and Chicagoans, rednecked cowpokes, Mexican immigrants, and outdoor enthusiasts comprise Denver's population (1.8 million). After sipping ginseng soda at bohemian hangouts, explore fine museums, numerous parks, and the nation's first symphony in the round, all the while enjoying Denver's glorious mountain view.

Practical Information

Emergency: 911 (Denver), 759-1511 (Glendale), 279-2557 (Golden), 344-2455 (Aurora), 987-7111 (Lakewood), 288-1535 (Commerce City).

Denver and Colorado Convention and Visitors Bureau, 225 West Colfax Ave. (892-1112 or 892-1505), near Civic Center Park just south of the capitol. Open Mon.-Fri. 8am-5pm. Pick up a free copy of the comprehensive *Denver and Colorado Official Visitors Guide.* **Big John's Information Center,** 1055 19th St., at the Greyhound/Trailways station. Big John, an ex-professional basketball player, offers enthusiastic information on hosteling in Colorado. Open Mon.-Sat. 6:15am-noon. **Stapleton Airport Information Center,** located on B, C, D, E concourses. (Open daily 7am-10pm.) Brochures available 24 hrs. **16th St. Ticket Bus,** on the 16th St. Mall at Curtis St. Double-decker bus with visitor information, half-price tickets to local theater performances, and RTD bus info. Open Mon.-Fri. 10am-6pm, Sat. 11am-3pm.

Stapleton International Airport (398-3844 or 800-247-2336), in northeast Denver. Easily accessible from downtown. RTD bus lines #28, 32, 38 serve the airport. Cab fare to downtown $8-12. The 9th busiest airport in the world; delays are common. **Ground Transportation Information** on the 1st floor can arrange transport to surrounding areas such as Estes Park and Vail. Open daily 7am-11pm.

Amtrak: Union Station, at 17th St. and Wynkoop (534-2812), in the northwest corner of downtown. One train per day to: Salt Lake City (14 hr., $103); Omaha, NE (9 hr., $100); Chicago, IL (18 hr., $150); Kansas City (12 hr., $128).

Buses: Greyhound/Trailways, 1055 19th St. (292-6111; 800-531-5332 for Spanish-speaking visitors), downtown. Four per day to: Cheyenne (3 hr., $25); Albuquerque (12 hr., $58); Kansas City (15 hr., $100); Salt Lake City (12 hr., $92). Also comprehensive service within CO. The **Ski Train-Budweiser Eagle Line,** 555 17th St. (296-4754). Leaves from Amtrak Union Station and treks through the Rockies, stopping in Winter Park (Dec.-April only). Departs Denver at 7:15am, Winter Park at 4:15pm; 2 hr.; $25 round-trip.

Public Transport: Regional Transportation District (RTD), 626 E. 16th St. (299-6000). Service within Denver and to Longmont, Evergreen, Conifer, Golden, and the suburbs. Many routes shut down by 9pm or earlier. Fare Mon.-Fri. 6-9am and 4-6pm $1, all other times 50¢, over 65 15¢. Free 16th Street Mall Shuttle covers 14 blocks downtown. Over 20 buses per day to Boulder (45 min., $2.50). Call Mon.-Fri. 6am-8pm, Sat.-Sun. 8am-8pm. Bus maps $1.

Gray Line Tours: At the bus station (289-2841). 2½-hr. tours of Denver twice daily in summer, once during the rest of the year. $15, under 12 $10. The 3½-hr. Denver Mountain Parks tour includes many of the sights outside Denver in nearby Rockies.

Taxi: Zone Cab, 861-2323. **Yellow Cab,** 777-7777. Both $1.20 base fare, $1.20 per mi.

Car Rental: Be wary of renting clunkers in the mountains. **Rent-a-Heap,** 940 S. Jason St. (698-0345) $15 per day, $90 per week, must remain in the metro area, unlimited free mi. Open Mon.-Fri. 8am-5pm, Sat. 8am-1pm. Must have $50 deposit and proof of liability insurance. **Cheap Heaps Rent-a-Car,** 4839 Colifax Ave. (393-0028), 8 blocks east of Colorado Blvd. $13 per day; 30 free mi. per day, 12¢ each additional mi. $15 if you're heading for the mountains. Open Mon.-Fri. 8am-6pm, Sat. 8am-2pm. Must have at least $100 deposit and proof of liability insurance or $7 additional charge for insurance per day. For both, must be at least 21 and not drive out of CO.

Auto Transport Company: Auto Driveaway, 5777 E. Evans Ave. (757-1211); take bus #21 to Hollis and Evans. Open Mon.-Fri. 8:30am-4pm. Must have a $250 cash deposit and a valid drivers license, be at least 21, and have three local references (last requirement waived for foreigners).

Help Lines: Contact Lifeline, 237-4537, open Mon.-Fri. 7am-11pm, Sat.-Sun. 3-11pm. **Rape Crisis,** 430-5656 or 329-9922, open 24 hrs.

Gay and Lesbian Community Center: 1245 E. Colfax Ave. (837-1598). Open daily 10am-10pm.

Post Office: 1823 Stout (297-6016). Open Mon.-Fri. 8am-5pm. **ZIP code:** 80201.

Area Code: 303.

I-25 bifurcates Denver north-south. Traffic sits at a virtual standstill between Denver and Colorado Springs. I-70 links Denver with Grand Junction (250 mi. west) and Kansas City (600 mi. east). Route 285 cuts south through the central Rockies, opening up the Saguache and Sangre de Cristo Ranges to easy exploration.

Broadway divides east Denver from west Denver, and **Ellsworth Avenue** forms the north-south dividing line. Streets west of Broadway progress in alphabetical order, while the streets north of Ellsworth are numbered. Streets downtown run diagonal to those in the rest of the metropolis. Keep in mind that many of the avenues on the eastern side of the city become numbered streets downtown. Most even-numbered thoroughfares downtown run only east-west.

The hub of downtown is the **16th Street Mall.** Few crimes occur in this immediate area, but avoid the east side of town beyond the capitol, the west end of Colfax Ave., and the upper reaches of the *barrio* (25th-34th St.) at night.

Accommodations

A couple of dedicated and generous souls, ex-basketball great "Big John" Schrant and ex-WWII flying ace Leonard Schmitt at the Melbourne Hostel, have helped make Denver a hosteler's heaven, with excellent and inexpensive locations, most within easy reach of downtown.

Melbourne International Hostel (AYH), 607 22nd St. (292-6386), downtown at Welton St. 6 blocks from the 16th St. Mall. Large singles and doubles with refrigerator and sinks. Kitchen and free coffee. Owners Leonard and Mary have, with the help of Hilda and Ilene, created a communal atmosphere where everyone cooks and goes out together at night. Dorms $8, private rooms $15, couples $20. Call ahead.

Big Al's International Hostel, 1714 Humboldt (837-9313). Recently opened, Tami, Sang, and Darren will make you feel part of the family here. Beautiful woodwork and stylish decor. Call ahead for free evening pick-up at bus or train station. Great breakfast included. $8 members, $10 nonmembers.

Denver International Youth Hostel, 630 E. 16th Ave. (832-9996), 10 blocks east of the bus station, 4 blocks north of downtown. Take bus #15 to Washington St., 1 block away. Dorm-style rooms with kitchen and laundry facilities. $7-10.

Franklin House B&B, 1620 Franklin St. (331-9106). European style inn within walking distance of downtown. Free breakfast. Singles $20. Doubles $30, with private bath $40. Triples with 2 beds $45.

Colburn Hotel, 980 Grant St. (837-1261). Take the #2 bus from 17th and Curtis, downtown. Spiffy, family-run hotel with great view of the Rockies and Capitol Hill. A/C, cable, coffee shop. Singles $28. Doubles $33.50.

YMCA, 25 E. 16th St. (861-8300) at Lincoln St. In 3 parts: old section (men only), new section, and family section. For $7, you can use the Olympic-size pool, and other sports facilities. Old section: singles $15, with bath $18; doubles with bath $26. New section: singles $18, with bath $18; doubles $30. Family section: 3-person room $34; 4-person room $40.

Motel 6, 4 locations in the greater Denver area, all with A/C and pool. North: 6 W. 83rd Pl. (429-1550). Northwest: 10300 S. I-70 Frontage Rd. (467-3172). East: 12020 E. 39th Ave. (371-1980). West: 480 Wadsworth Blvd. (232-4924). Singles $27. Doubles from $33.

Camping

Cherry Creek Lake Recreation Area (699-3860; for reservations 671-4500). Take I-25 to exit 200, then west on Rte. 225 for about 3 mi. and south on Parker Rd.—follow the signs. Take the "Parker Road" bus. The 102 sites fill only on summer weekends. Sites $7. Entrance fee $4.

Chatfield Reservoir (791-7275 or 800-365-2267); take Rte. 75 or 85 4 mi. past the center of Littleton to 153 well-developed sites. Sites $7, with electricity $10. Open mid-May to mid-Oct. Make reservations for weekends.

Chief Hosa Campground (526-0364), in Genesee Park off I-70 exit 253. Heated pool, athletic field, laundry, grocery store, showers, and restrooms. Sites $11.50 for 1 person, $13.50 for 2 people, with electricity and water $2 extra. No reservations.

Golden Gate Canyon State Park (592-1502), 20 mi. west of Golden on Rte. 6 past Black Hawk. **Reverend's Ridge Campground.** Developed sites $7. Open late May-late Sept. **Aspen Meadows Campground,** 19 mi. south of Nederland. Sites $6. Entrance fee $3. Contact the Metro-Regional office of the Colorado Division of Parks and Recreation (791-1957; open Mon.-Fri. 9am-5pm) for more info on campgrounds.

National Forest Campgrounds, plentiful in the mountains 25 mi. west of Denver near Idaho Springs, Rte. 103 and 40, and in the region around Deckers, 30 mi. southwest of downtown on Rte. 67. Sites marked, but difficult to find. **Painted Rocks Campground,** on Rte. 67, in the Pikes Peak Ranger District (719-636-1602). Sites $7. **Top of the World,** off Pine Junction on Rte. 126 (236-7386). Free but no water. Most sites open May-Sept. Call ahead or pick up maps at the National Forest's Rocky Mountain Regional Headquarters, 11177 W. 8th Ave., Lakewood (236-9431). Open Mon.-Fri. 8am-5pm.

Food

The *barrio,* north of the mall between 20th and 30th St., proffers some inexpensive—if slightly seedy—bars and Mexican restaurants, while **Sakura Square,** at 19th St. and Larimer, offers several Japanese restaurants surrounding a pleasant rock garden. A young crowd haunts Colfax Ave. in the east, Sheridan, Wadsworth, and Federal Ave. in the west. For those over 21, the cheapest food fries at the Glendale nightclubs around Colorado Ave. and Alameda.

Muddy's Java Café, 2200 Champa St. (298-1631), 2 blocks from the Melbourne hostel. Sultry mocha java den by night, skylit and full of classical music and jazz by day. Meditate on taxi driver Bob Johnson's portraits. Great Belgian waffles ($2.25), turkey sandwiches ($4), and murky specialty coffees. Great after-hours breakfasts daily 11pm-4am. Open Mon.-Fri. 11am-4am, Sat.-Sun. 7pm-4am.

The Market, 1445 Larimer Sq. (534-5140), downtown. Popular for lunch and afternoon iced tea with a young artsy crowd that people-watches from behind salads, pastry, and oversized magazines. Open Mon.-Thurs. 6:45am-6pm, Fri.-Sat. 6:45am-midnight, Sun. 8:30am-6pm.

Paris on the Platte, 1553 Platte St. (455-2451). An artists' hangout and bookstore serving excellent Greek salad ($3.50). Try one of their "boards," with cheese and fruit or meat. Delicious *niçoise,* with marinated tuna, potatoes, green beans, and artichoke hearts ($5-7) and fresh French bread. Open Mon.-Thurs. 11am-1am, Fri. 11am-4am, Sat. 4pm-1am, Sun. 7pm-3am.

The Goodmorning House, 1530 Blake St. A friendly daytime diner with juicy burgers ($3). Large bowl of chili and cornbread to sop it up $2.50. Open Mon.-Fri. 6:30am-3pm, Sat. 7am-2pm.

The Old Spaghetti Factory, 18th and Lawrence (295-1864), 1 block from Larimer St. Part of a national chain. Located in a gorgeously renovated old tramway building. Large, delicious spaghetti dinner only $5. Open Mon.-Fri. 11:30am-2pm and 5-10pm, Sat. 4:45-11pm, Sun. 4-10pm. No credit cards.

City Spirit Café, 1434 Blake St. (575-0022), a few blocks from the north end of the 16th St. Mall. Happy, naive urban scenes in mellow pastels painted directly on the walls, doors, and bar. Specialties or tasty sandwiches $5. Live entertainment most evenings. Open Mon.-Thurs. 11am-midnight, Fri.-Sat. 11am-1am.

The Eggshell, 1520 Blake St. (623-7555). Huge breakfast specials $2. Sandwiches $4-5. Open Mon.-Fri. 6:30am-2pm, Sat.-Sun. 7am-2pm.

Daddy Bruce's Bar-B-Q, 1629 E. 34th St., at Gilpin. Take bus #38. The sign on the back of the owner's truck says: "God loves you. So does Daddy Bruce." With that welcome, wait until you taste the best barbecue in Denver. Lucky parties may meet 87-year-old Daddy himself. Ribs from $2.50. Open Tues.-Sat. 10:30am-10pm.

Sights

With over 300 serene days of sunshine per year, Denver basks in its low humidity air. **City Park,** one of the loveliest of over 205 serene spots throughout the city, lies between 17th and 23rd Ave. from York St. to Colorado Blvd. Nearby, the **Botanic Gardens,** 1005 York St. (331-4000; 331-4010 for 24-hr. info) charges a hefty admission of $4 ($2.50 for seniors) for entrance into the outdoor gardens and conservatory. Take bus #20 or #23 to Colorado Ave. Many people socialize at **Cheesman Park,** four blocks to the south, enjoying the view of the snowy mountains that rise above the Denver skyline. (Take bus #6 or 10.) These parks are terrific for bicycling and strolling during the day, but none are safe after dark. For Denver Parks info, call 698-4900. The **Denver Municipal Band** performs summer concerts at 7:30pm in the parks. Pick up a schedule at the visitors bureau (see Practical Information above). For a wilder park experience from June to September, take I-70 from Golden to Idaho Springs, and then pick up Rte. 103 south over the summit (14,260 ft.) of **Mt. Evans.** Or, journey to **Red Rocks** (see below) or other parts of Denver's 25,000-acre park system. Check with **Denver Parks and Recreation,** 1805 Bryant Ave. (459-4000) about road conditions in fall and winter. (Open Mon.-Fri. 8am-5pm.)

The **16th Street Mall,** a 14-block pedestrian area in the heart of downtown, is a major tourist destination. The shuttle buses which skirt this strip from 6am to 8pm are the only free convenience you'll find here. **Larimer Square,** between 14th and 15th St., has been restored to Victorian elegance, and now houses expensive souvenir shops, galleries, and restaurants. Larimer's wild Octoberfest also draws large crowds.

A gold-plated dome tops the gray Colorado granite of the **capitol building,** on Colfax and Broadway between Grant and 14th St. (866-2604). The lucky 13th step on the west side perches exactly 1 mi. above sea level; the gallery around the dome gives a great view of the Rocky Mountains. (Free tours from the foyer every hr. on the ½-hr. 9am-3:30pm. Open Mon.-Fri. 7am-5:30pm, Sat. 9:30am-3:30pm.)

A modern reminder of Colorado's old silver mining days, the **U.S. Mint,** 320 W. Colfax (844-3332), issues U.S. coins with a small "D" for Denver embossed beneath the date. Free 20-minute tours, every 20 minutes in summer and every 30 minutes in winter, will lead you past a million-dollar pile of gold bars and expose you to the deafening roar of money-making machines that churn out a total of 20 million shiny coins per day. Unfortunately, no free samples are given unless you manage a five-fingered discount. Arrive early in summer, lines often reach around the block. (Open Mon-Fri. 8am-3pm.)

Just a few blocks from the U.S. Mint, and right behind Civic Center Park, stands the **Denver Art Museum,** 100 W. 14th Ave. (575-2793). Architect Gio Ponti designed this six-story "vertical" museum in order to accommodate totem poles and period architecture. The museum's collection of Native American art rivals any in the world. The fabulous third floor of pre-Columbian, pre-Christian art of the Americas resembles an archeological excavation site, with temples, huts, and idols. Call for info on special exhibits. (Museum open Tues.-Sat. 10am-5pm, Sun. noon-5pm. Optional admission $3, seniors and students $1.50.) Housed in the Navarre Building, once the brothel for the Brown Palace, the **Museum of Western Art,** 1727 Tremont Place (296-1880), holds a collection of stellar Russell, Benton, O'Keeffe, and Grant Wood paintings and drawings. The **Brown Palace,** across the street at 321 17th St. (297-3111), is a historic grand hotel that once hosted presidents, generals, and movie stars. **The Black American West Museum and Heritage Center,** 391 California St. (292-2566), will show you a side of frontier history unexplored by John Wayne movies. Come here to learn why supposedly 1/3 of all cowboys were African-American, and other details often left out of textbooks. (Open Wed.-Fri.

10am-2pm, Sat. 10am-5pm, Sun. 2-5pm. Admission $2, seniors $1.50, ages 12-16 75¢, under 12 50¢.)

The **Natural History Museum** (322-7009) in City Park presents amazingly lifelike wildlife sculptures and dioramas. (Open Sat.-Tues. 9am-5pm, Wed.-Fri. 9am-10pm. Admission $4, ages 4-12 $2.) The Natural History Museum complex includes the **Gates Planetarium** with its popular "Laserdrive" show and an **IMAX theater** (370-6300). Combination tickets to the museum, planetarium, and IMAX cost $6.50, seniors and ages 4-12 $4.50. Across the park lies the **Denver Zoo** (331-4110), where you can view the live versions of the museum specimens. (Open daily 10am-6pm. Admission $4, seniors and ages 6-15 $2.)

The dramatic **Red Rocks Amphitheater and Park** (693-1234), 12 mi. west of Denver and south of U.S. 6 on I-70, is carved into red sandstone. As the sun sets over the city, even the most well-known of performers must compete with the natural spectacle behind them. The Grateful Dead, however, who often visit Red Rocks, just become part of the sunset. (For tickets call 623-8497 Mon.-Fri. 8am-5pm. Park admission free. Shows $9-25.) Also, west of Denver in nearby Golden is **Coors Brewery,** 13th and Ford St. (800-642-6116; 277-BEER), the largest brewery in the world. (Free tours Mon.-Sat. 10am-4pm.)

Entertainment and Nightlife

Denver is a "young" city—slews of singles in search of a good time let loose every evening. Although clubs downtown tend to come and go as quickly as the local weather, some have gained a lasting reputation. One tried and true establishment is **Basins Up,** 1427 Larimer St. (623-2104), where you can wallow in live rock music all evening. (Open Mon.-Sat. 8pm-2am. Cover Fri.-Sat. $5. Must be 21 or over.) The "Hill of the Grasshopper," **El Chapultepec,** 20th and Market St. (295-9126), is a great hole-in-the-wall jazz club. (Open daily 7am-2am. No cover.) The magazine *Westwood* has more details on the downtown club scene. For a calendar of alternative art and music events, pick up a copy of *ICON* (455-4643) in the foyer of Muddy's Java Café (see Food above) or downtown. To locate the happening places in the 'burbs, head for Glendale, where the nocturnal bar-hoppers can show you the best places to enjoy a quiet, intimate evening of slam dancing. At **Bangles,** 4501 E. Virginia (377-2702), live bands blare in the evening, and the afternoon volleyball matches often become jubilant free-for-alls after a few pitchers of beer ($4.50). (Open daily 8pm-2am. Volleyball games at 4pm. Cover Wed.-Mon. night $3.) **The Roebucks** play at the small but intimate **Johnson and McArthy's Bar,** 1000 Colfax St. (377-9901). (Open Thurs.-Sun. 8pm-2am.)

Denver's two most popular festivals are the **Greek Festival** and **A Taste of Colorado.** The Greek festival takes place in June, downtown, featuring good Greek food, music, and dancing. An outdoor *fête,* the Taste is the last weekend in August, during which food vendors line the streets near the capitol among open-air concerts.

Mountain Resorts Near Denver

Sixty-eight mi. northwest of Denver on U.S. 40, **Winter Park** nestles among delicious-smelling mountain pines, surrounded by 600 mi. of skiing, hiking, and biking trails. On the town's southern boundary, Olympic cross-country skier Polly runs the **Winter Park Hostel (AYH)** (726-5356), one block from the Greyhound stop and 2 mi. from Amtrak (free shuttle). The hostel features four kitchens, bunks, and three couples' rooms in spotless, cheery trailers. (Nov. to mid-April $10, nonmembers $13; mid-June to Oct. $7, nonmembers $9. Call for reservations in winter. Open June 15-April 15.) **Le Ski Lab,** 7894 US 40, (726-9841) next door offers 25% discounts on bike and ski rentals for hostelers. (Mountain bikes $11 per day, $8 half-day for hostelers; $15 per day, $9 half-day for non-hostelers; skis $6 per day for hostelers, $8 for non-hostelers.) The Lab also cooks up $35 all-day rafting trips down the Colorado river. (Open daily in summer 9am-6pm; in winter 8am-8pm.) The **Winter Park-Fraser Valley Chamber of Commerce,** 50 Vasquez Rd. (726-4118;

from Denver 800-422-0666), provides information about skiing at the Winter Park Mary Jane Ski Area. (Open winter daily 9am-8pm; summer 10am-5pm.) The chamber also serves as the Greyhound/Trailways depot. (From Denver 2 buses per day, 2 hr., $9.) From December through April, the **Ski Train-Budweiser Eagle Line** (296-4754) leaves from Denver's Union Station, 555 17th St. at 7:30am, arriving in Winter Park at 9:30am, and returns to Denver at 4:15pm on weekends only ($25 round-trip).

Those strong of heart and lung should head out to **Frisco,** 55 mi. west of Denver on I-70, for some hiking in the Rockies. Along with Breckenridge, Dillon, Copper Mountain, Keystone, and Silverthorne, Frisco hosts numerous sporting events throughout the year. All six towns fall under the jurisdiction of the **Summit County Chamber of Commerce,** 110 Summit Blvd., P.O. Box 214, Frisco, CO 80443 (668-5800), which provides information on current area events. (Open daily 9am-5pm.) The only reasonable accommodations in the county are at the delightful **Alpen Hütte,** 471 Rainbow Dr. in Silverthorne (468-6336). A bed in the sparsely decorated, gleaming bunk rooms costs $23 during Christmas and March, mid-Nov. to mid-May $18-20, and mid-May to mid-Nov. $12. (Guest rooms closed 9:30am-3:30pm. Reservations recommended.)

Grand Junction

Grand Junction gets its hyperbolic name from the confluence of the Colorado and Gunnison rivers, as well as the Rio Grande and Denver Railroads. As western Colorado's trade and agricultural center, this quiet city serves as a fantastic base for explorations of the Gunnison Valley, the Grand Mesa, and the western San Juans. The car-less traveler will be severely limited in this area without a packed wallet. **Colorado Auto,** 2922 North Ave. (245-5959), rents compact cars for $20 per day with 150 free mi. 25¢ per additional mi. or $135 per wk. with 700 free mi.

Within walking distance from the bus or train station is the old **Melrose Hotel (AYH),** 337 Colorado Ave. between 3rd and 4th St., an immaculate, well-maintained old hotel with oodles of old-fashioned charm. The rooms are spacious with a touch of antique elegance. ($11.25, nonmembers $18, with bath $22.25. Doubles $18, with bath $30.) **Le Master Motel,** 2858 North Ave. (243-3230), has singles as cheap as $17, doubles $24. And there's always **Motel 6,** 776 Horizon Dr. (243-2628), in this case a bit far from downtown. (Singles $31. Doubles $37.) Camping in **Highline State Park** (858-7208), 22 mi. from town and 7 mi. north of exit 15 on I-70, or **Island Acres State Park** (464-0548), 15 mi. east on the banks of the Colorado River, costs $6 per site plus a $3 day pass. A **KOA,** 3238 F Rd. (434-6644), knocks them out in Clifton, just east of Grand Junction off I-70. (Sites $15 for two adults, $3 per additional person, $2.25 for electricity, $2 for sewer.)

Some affordable restaurants conjoin grandly here. **Dos Hombres Restaurant,** 421 Branch Dr. (242-8861), just south of Broadway (Rte. 340) on the southern bank of the Colorado River, serves great Mexican food in a casual, family-style setting. (Combination dinners $3.75-5.25. Open daily 11am-10pm.) During the day, the **B & J Coffee Shop,** 400 Main St. (245-5866), in the back of a downtown dime store, has some charming touches, like Coke in bottles, a soda fountain, and full meals for $4.75, along with thick, iced cinnamon rolls. (Open Mon.-Sat. 6:30am-3:30pm.) For breakfast, go to **Talley's,** 623 Main St. (245-7799) for *huevos rancheros* ($3.75.) (Open Mon.-Sat. 7am-4pm. Sun. 8am-4pm.)

Shopping is plentiful along Main St. Browse through **A Haggle Vendors Emporium,** 510 Main St. (245-7834), for a piece of Americana or the Old West. Items are assembled from 40 different vendors, so look carefully for the best buys. Also along Main St. between 3rd and 7th St., watch for **Art on the Corner,** an outdoor exhibit of discreetly placed sculptures.

For literature on the area, visit the **Tourist Information Center,** 759 Horizon Dr., Suite F (243-1001; open Mon.-Fri. 9am-8pm), or the **Convention and Visitors Bur-**

eau, at 4th and Grand downtown (1-800-962-3547; open Mon.-Fri. 8:30am-5pm). Or contact the **Chamber of Commerce** at 360 Grand Ave.

Grand Junction lies at the grand juncture of U.S. 50 and 24 in northwestern Colorado. U.S. 6 connects these two highways in town. Denver skis 228 mi. to the east; Salt Lake City slithers 240 mi. to the west. The **bus station,** 230 S. 5th S. (242-6012), has service to: Denver (4 per day, 7 hr. $23); Durango (1 per day, $30); Salt Lake City (1 per day, 8 hr., $32); and Los Angeles (4 per day, $104). (Open Mon.-Sat. 3:30am-5:10pm and 9pm-12:30am, Sun. 3:30-7:45am, noon-5:10pm, and 9pm-12:30am.)

Grand Junction's **post office** is at 241 N. 4th St. (244-3401; open Mon.-Fri. 8:30am-5pm, Sat. 9am-12:45pm.) Its **ZIP code** is 81502; its **area code** is 303.

Grand Mesa

Fifty mi. east of Grand Junction lies **Grand Mesa** (Large Table), the world's largest flat-top mountain. An ancient Native American story tells how an enormous eagle who lived on the rim of Grand Mesa snatched up a human child in its beak and flew off. The child's vengeful father found the eagle's nest and tossed out the eaglets, who became lunch for a serpent sunning at the base of the Mesa. In turn, the mother eagle then snatched up the viper, flew to a dizzying height, and tore it to pieces, snake segments careening to the earth to make deep impresssions in Grand Mesa—explaining the area's many lakes. But stodgy, boring geologists claim that some 600 million years ago, a 300-ft.-thick flow of lava covered the area where the mesa now stands. Since then, erosion has worn down the surrounding land by over 5,000 ft., but the lava cap has preserved Grand Mesa's original height.

Whatever the Mesa's origin, this area, as you would expect, offers numerous outdoor attractions, such as fine backcountry hiking. Climbers covet the soft-rock climbs here, including the Monument Spire. A good auto tour also runs all around the rim of the canyon. Stop by the ranger stations on Hwy. 65 and on Land's End Rd. for details on rock climbing and registration. (Both open June-Sept. daily 9am-6pm.) To reach Grand Mesa from Grand Junction, take I-70 eastbound to Plateau Creek, where Rte. 65 cuts off into the long climb through the spruce trees to the top of the mesa. Near the top is the Land's End turn-off leading to the very edge of Grand Mesa, some 12 mi. down a well-maintained dirt road. On a clear day, you can see halfway across Utah.

In addition to the view, the mesa has excellent camping. The National Forest Service maintains a dozen **campsites** on the mesa, including Carp Lake ($6), Island Lake ($5), and Ward Lake ($7)—the rest are free, with water $7. The district **forest service,** 764 Horizon Dr. in Grand Junction (242-8211), disseminates more information. (Open Mon.-Fri. 8am-5pm.) You can buy a map of the mesa's trails, campsites, and trout ponds ($2.50) here, or at **Surplus City,** 200 W. Grand Ave. (242-2818; $4; open Mon.-Fri. 8am-8pm, Sat. 8am-7pm, Sun. 8am-6pm). **Vega State Park** (487-3407), 12 mi. east of Colbrain off Rte. 330, also offers camping in the high country.

European settlers once dismissed the arid, red, fearsome canyons and dry striated sandstone of the **Colorado National Monument** as unusable land. If not for the efforts of intrepid trapper and hunter John Otto, who in 1911 helped petition for the land to become a national monument, the area's natural beauty might very well have been dismissed as a stony wasteland. Facilitate your explorations by renting a mountain bike in nearby Grand Junction at **Cycle Center,** 141 N. 7th St. (242-2541). ($8 per half day, $16 per day. Open Mon.-Fri. 9:30am-6pm, Sat. 9:30am-5pm.)

Saddlehorn Campground offers campsites in the monument on a first-come, first-served basis, with picnic tables, grills, and restrooms. (Sites $6; free in winter.) The **Bureau of Land Management** (243-6552; open Mon.-Fri. 9am-5pm) maintains three less-developed, free "campgrounds" near **Glade Park.** Bring your own water. **Little Dolores Fall,** 10½ mi. west of Glade Park, has fishing and swimming. The monument charges an additional admission fee of $3 per vehicle, $1 per cyclist or hiker. The monument **headquarters and visitors center** (858-3617), near the campground on the Fruita side of the monument, issue backcountry permits. (Open daily 8am-8pm; off-season Mon.-Fri. 8am-4:30pm.)

Great Sand Dunes National Monument

After Colorado's splendid mountains begin to look the same, make a path for the unique mountains of sand at the northwest edge of the **San Luis Valley**. The 700-ft. dunes lap the base of the **Sangre de Christo Range,** representing thousands of years of wind-blown accumulation. The progress of the dunes at passes in the range is checked by the shallow but persistent **Medano Creek.** Visitors can wade across the creek from April to mid-July. For a short hike, head out on Mosca Trail, a ½-mi. jaunt into the desert sands. Try to avoid the intense afternoon heat.

Rangers preside over daily naturalist activities, hikes, and other programs. Full schedules are available at the **visitors center** (719-378-2312), ½-mi. past the entrance gate, where you can also view a 15-minute film on the dunes, shown every half hour. (Open daily 8am-7pm; Sept. 2-May 27 8am-5pm. Entrance fee for vehicles $3, pedestrians and bikers $1.) For more info contact the Superintendent, Great Sand Dunes National Monument, Mosca 81146 (378-2312).

For those who crave more than just the first wave of dunes, the **Oasis** complex (378-2222) on the southern boundary also provides four-wheel-drive tours of the backcountry. The three-hour tour takes the rugged Medano Pass Primitive Road into the nether regions of the monument. (4 tours daily; 3 hr.; $14, under 12 $8. Discounts for seniors.)

Pinyon Flats, the monument's campground, fills quickly in summer. Camping here among the prickly pear cacti is first-come, first-served. Bring mosquito repellent in June. (Sites $7.) If the park's sites are full, you can camp at Oasis. (Sites $9.50 for 2 people, with hookup $14.50. Each additional person $2.50. Showers included.) **Backcountry camping** requires a free permit. For information on nearby National Forest Campgrounds, contact the Rio Grande National Forest Service Office, 1803 W. Hwy. 160, Monte Vista, CO 81144 (852-5941). All developed sites are $7-8.

Great Sand Dunes National Monument blows 32 mi. northeast of Alamosa and 112 mi. west of Pueblo, on Rte. 150 off U.S. 160. **Greyhound/Trailways** sends one bus per day out of Denver to Alamosa (5 hr., $38), with a depot at 513 6th St. (589-4948; open Mon.-Fri. 10am-1pm and 2:30-4:30pm, Sat. 3:30-4:30pm). Hitching to the monument is simple, especially from Rte. 150. The country road from Mosca on Rte. 17 is strictly for four-wheel-drive vehicles. For emergencies within the park, call the **Colorado State Patrol** (589-2503).

Mesa Verde National Park

Fourteen long centuries ago, Native American tribes settled and cultivated the desert mesas of southwestern Colorado. In 1200 AD, they constructed and settled in the cliff dwellings until 1275, when they mysteriously abandoned their shelters. The Navajo tribes that arrived in the area in 1450 named the previous inhabitants the Anasazi, or the "ancient ones." Today only five of the 1000 archeological sites are open to constant touring, because the fragile sandstone wears quickly under human feet. Such caution causes some crowding within the park; arrive early.

Entrance fees to the park are $5 per car, $2 per pedestrian or cyclist. The southern portion of the park divides into the **Chapin Mesa** and the **Wetherill Mesa. The Far View Visitor Center** (529-4593) near the north rim offers info on the park. (Open in summer 8am-5pm.) On Wetherill Mesa, tours run only from June to September and leave from Far View Lodge (6 hr.; $10, under 12 $4). You may take guided tours up ladders and through passageways of the Anasazi dwellings. Spruce Tree House is one of the better-preserved ruins. To get an overview of the Anasazi lifestyle, visit the **Chapin Mesa Museum** (529-4475) at the south end of the park. (Open daily 8am-6:30pm.) At the balcony house ruins, ranger-led guided tours leave every ½-hr. from 9am-6pm daily.

Mesa Verde's only lodging, **Far View Motor Lodge** (529-4421), is extremely expensive, but a few nearby motels can put you up for under $30. Try the **Ute Mountain Motel,** 531 S. Broadway (565-8507) in Cortez, CO. (Singles from $24. Doubles from $34.) However, it's best to stay at the nearby **Durango Hostel** (see Durango). The only camping in Mesa Verde is at **Morfield Campground** (529-4474; off-season 529-4421), 4 mi. inside the park, with some beautiful and secluded sites. In summer, come early to beat the crowds. (Sites $7, with full hookup $15. Showers $1 for 10 min.) Outside the park, ¼ mi. east on Hwy. 160, is the **Double A Campground and R.V. Park** (565-3517; sites $12, with hookup $16.50).

The park's main entrance is off U.S. 160, 36 mi. from Durango and 10 mi. from Cortez. **Greyhound/Trailways** will drop you off on its daily Durango run, but only in the wee hours of the morning. The Durango station is at 275 8th Ave. (259-2755). **Durango Transportation** (259-4818) will take you on a nine-hour tour of the park, from 8:30am-4:30pm ($27, kids $13.50); bring a lunch. Since sights lie up to 40 mi. apart, a car is helpful. Van transportation is also available at the Far View Lodge for self-guided tours with 24-hr. notice.

Mesa Verde's **ZIP code** is 81330; nearby Mancos is 81328. The **area code** is 303.

Rocky Mountain National Park

The Ute shied away from Grand Lake, believing that mists rising from its surface were the spirits of rafters who drowned in a storm. Twelve mi. long and 1 mi. wide, this glacial lake, and today its town, sit in the west end of Rocky Mountain National Park. The longest high road in the states, Trail Ridge Road (U.S. 34), runs 45 mi. through the park from the town of Grand Lake to the town of Estes Park; at the peak of over 2 vertical mi., oxygen is rare and a silence prevails among the low vegetation of the tundra. The sloping cavities of the peaks hold pools of still blue water and even snow in mid-July. In the eastern region of the park, the road ekes by sheer drops of 3000 ft. to rock-lined gorges.

Practical Information

Emergency: 911. Estes Park police 586-4465; Grand Lake police 627-3322.

Visitor Information: Estes Park Chamber of Commerce, P.O. Box 3050, Estes Park 80517, at 500 Big Thompson Hwy. (586-4431 or 800-443-7837). Slightly east of downtown. Open June-Aug. Mon.-Sat. 8am-8pm, Sun. 9am-6pm; off-season Mon.-Sat. 9am-5pm, Sun. 10am-4pm. **Grand Lake Area Chamber of Commerce,** 14700 Hwy. 74 (1-800-462-5253), just outside of the park's west entrance. Open daily 9am-5pm; off-season Mon.-Fri. 10am-5pm.

Park Entrance Fees: $5 per vehicle, $2 per biker or pedestrian, under 16 free. Valid for 7 days.

Park Visitor and Ranger Stations: Park Headquarters and Visitors Center, on Rte. 36 2 mi. west of Estes Park (586-2371), at the Beaver Meadows entrance to the park. Call for park info, or to make sure the Trail Ridge Rd. is open. Headquarters open daily 6am-11pm; 8am-5pm off-season. Visitors center open daily 8am-9pm; off-season Mon.-Fri. 8am-5pm. **Kawuneeche Visitors Center** (627-3471), just outside the park's western entrance. Open daily 7am-7pm; off-season 8am-5pm. **Moraine Park Visitors Center and Museum** (586-3777), on the Bear Lake Rd. Open summer daily 9am-5pm. **Alpine Visitors Center,** at the crest of Trail Ridge Rd. (586-4927). Check out the view of the tundra from the back window. Open June-July 4 daily 10am-4pm, July 5 to mid-Aug. 9am-5pm.

Public Transport: Estes Park Trolley, 586-8866. Red trolleys operate summer daily 9:30am-9pm. Frequent service connects everything you could want to see in Estes Park; guided tour included. $2 round-trip every hour, full day $4. **Charles Limousine** (1-800-950-3274), $20 per person from Denver bus station or airport to Estes. (Open daily 6am-9pm.)

Horse Rental: Sombrero Ranch, 1895 Big Thompson Rd. (586-4577), in Estes Park 2 mi. from downtown on Hwy. 34 E., and on Grand Ave. in Grand Lake (627-3514). $12 for 1 hr., $20 for 2. The breakfast ride (at 7am, $20) includes a 2-hr. ride and a huge breakfast. Call ahead. Hostelers get 10% discount; special rates for those staying at the H Bar G Ranch. Both open daily 7am-5:30pm.

Help Lines: Roads and Weather, 586-9561. **Hearing Impaired Visitors,** 586-8506.

Post Office: Estes Park, 215 W. Riverside (586-8177). Open Mon.-Fri. 9am-5pm, Sat. 10am-12:30pm. **Grand Lake,** 520 Center Dr. (627-3340). Open Mon.-Fri. 8:30am-5pm. **ZIP code:** 80517.

Area Code: 303.

You can reach the National Park most easily from Boulder via Rte. 36 or from Loveland up the **Big Thompson Canyon** via Rte. 34. Busy during the summer, both routes lead to Estes Park as easy hitching or biking trails. From Denver, take the RTD bus (20 per day, 45 min., $2) to its last stop in Boulder, transfer (free) to bus #202 or 204, and hitchhike from U.S. 36 W. In Boulder you can find the entrance to U.S. 36 at 28th and Baseline Rd.

Estes Park lies 65 mi. from Denver, 39 mi. from Boulder, and 31 mi. from Loveland. Hitching within the park is prohibited. With a car, "loop" from Boulder by catching U.S. 36 through Estes Park, pick up Trail Ridge Rd. (U.S. 34), go through Rocky Mountain National Park (45 mi.), stop in Grand Lake, and take U.S. 40 to Winter Park and I-70 back to Denver.

Reach the western side of the park from Granby (50 mi. from I-70) via Rte. 40. One of the most scenic entrances, Rte. 7 approaches the park from the southeast out of Lyons or Nederland, accessing the **Wild Basin Trailhead,** the starting point for some glorious hikes. When Trail Ridge Rd. (open May-Oct.) closes, you can drive from one side of the park to the other through Walden and Fort Collins, via Rte. 125 out of Granby and then Rte. 14 to Fort Collins. Or take the more traveled Rte. 40 over spectacular **Berthoud Pass** to I-70, then Rte. 119 and 72 north to the park. Note: when Trail Ridge Rd. is closed, the drive jumps from 48 to 140 mi.

Accommodations

Although Estes Park and Grand Lake have an overabundance of expensive lodges and motels, there are few good deals on indoor beds near the national park, especially in winter when the hostels close down.

Estes Park

H Bar G Ranch Hostel (AYH), P.O. Box 1260, 80517 (586-3688). Hillside cabins, horses Blackie and Spot, tennis courts, kitchen, and a spectacular view of the front range. Proprietor Lou drives you to the park entrance or into town every morning at 7:30am, and picks you up again at the chamber of commerce. Members only, $7.25. Rent a car for $26 per day. Open late May to mid-Sept. Call ahead.

YMCA of the Rockies, 2515 Tunnel Rd., Estes Park Center 80511 (586-3341), 2 mi. south of the park headquarters on Rte. 66 and 5 mi. from the chamber of commerce. Caters largely to clan gatherings and conventions. Extensive facilities on the 1400-acre complex, as well as daily hikes and other events. Four people can get a cabin from $40, kitchen and bath included. Lodge with bunk beds that sleeps up to 5 $34. Guest membership $3. Families $5.

The Colorado Mountain School, 351 Moraine Ave. (586-5758 or 800-444-0730). Dorm-style accommodations open to travelers unless already booked by mountain-climbing students. Wood bunks with comfortable mattresses $16. Call for reservations.

Grand Lake

Shadowcliff Hostel (AYH), P.O. Box 658, 80447 (627-9220), near the western entrance to the park. Entering Grand Lake, take the left fork after the visitors center on West Protal Rd.; their sign is 2/3 mi. down the road on the left. Beautiful, hand-built pine lodge on a cliff overlooking the lake. Offers easy access to the trails on the western side of the park and to the lakes of Arapahoe National Recreation Area. Kitchen. $7.50, nonmembers $10.50. Private rooms $21-27. Open June-Sept.

Sunset Motel, 505 Grand Ave., (627-3318). Gorgeous singles and doubles $34-36. Each additional person $3.

Camping

Most sites fill up pretty quickly in summer; call ahead or arrive early.

National Park Campgrounds: Moraine Park and **Glacier Basin** ($9) require reservations in summer. First come, first served ($7) at **Aspenglen,** 5 mi. west of Estes Park near the Fall River entrance; tents-only **Longs Peak,** 11 mi. south of Estes Park and 1 mi. off Hwy. 7; and **Timber Creek,** 10 mi. north of Grand Lake on the western side of Trail Ridge. Three-day limit enforced at Longs Peak, one-week limit elsewhere. Timber Creek is the only campground in the western portion of the park. One campground, usually near park headquarters near Estes Park, stays open year-round; the rest close when the snow falls. Reservations can be made at select Ticketrons. In winter, no water but also no charge.

Handicamp: The park's free backcountry campsite for the disabled (586-4459). Open summer daily 7am-7pm.

Backcountry camping: Offices at Park Headquarters (586-2371) and Kawuneeche Visitors Center (627-3471) on the western side of the park at Grand Lake. Open daily 8am-5pm. Get reservations and permits at these offices or write the Backcountry office, Rocky Mountain National Park, Estes Park 80517 (586-0526). No charge for backcountry camping, but many areas in no-fire zones; you may want to bring along a campstove.

Olive Ridge Campground, 15 mi. south of Estes Park on CO Rte. 7, in Roosevelt National Forest. Call 800-283-2267 for reservations. First-come, first-served sites $6. Contact the Roosevelt-Arapahoe National Forest Service Headquarters, 161 2nd St., Estes Park (586-3440). Open June-July daily 8am-noon and 1-5pm; Aug.-May Mon.-Fri. 9am-noon and 1-4pm.

Indian Peaks Wilderness, just south of the park, jointly administered by Roosevelt and Arapahoe National Forests. Permit required for backcountry camping during the summer. On the east slope, contact the Boulder Ranger District, 2915 Baseline Rd. (444-6003; open Mon.-Fri. 8am-5pm). Last chance permits ($4) are available in Nederland at Coast to Coast Hardware (take Hwy. 7 to 72 south; open Mon.-Sat. 9am-9pm). On the west slope, contact the Hot Sulphur Ranger District, 100 U.S. 34, in Granby (887-3331; open May 27-Sept. 2 daily 8am-5pm).

Food

Both towns have surprisingly good food. The establishments below are in Estes Park.

Johnson's Cafe (586-6624), 2 buildings to the right of Safeway, across from the chamber of commerce. Everything made from scratch by the friendly Johnsons. Great waffles $3, sandwiches $3.25, luscious pies $1.75. Open daily 7am-2pm.

O'Shea's, 225 Riverside (586-2815), next to the post office. Great homemade soups $1, full meal daily specials $3.75. Open Mon.-Fri. 7am-3pm, Sat. 7am-2pm.

Polly's Pizza, 181 W. Riverside (586-6081). Free delivery of spicy fresh pizza. 13-in. cheese pizza $6. Open Sun.-Thurs. 11am-midnight, Fri.-Sat. 11am-1am.

Ed's Cantina, 362 E. Elkhorn (586-2919). Best Mexican food in the park area. Combination plate (cheese enchilada, bean burrito, and bean tostada) $5. Open daily 7am-10pm.

Sights and Activities

For those with wheels, the star trail of this park is **Trail Ridge Road.** At its highest point, this 50-mi.-long stretch reaches 12,183 ft. above sea level; much of the road goes above timberline. The round-trip drive takes three hours by car, 12 hours by bicycle. For a closer look at the fragile tundra environment, walk from roadside to the **Forest Canyon Overlook,** or take the half-hour round-trip **Tundra Trail. Fall River Road,** a one-way dirt road merging with Trail Ridge Rd. at the alpine center, offers even more impressive scenery, but also sharp cliffs and tight cutbacks along the road.

Rangers can help plan a hike to suit your interests and abilities. Since the trailheads in the park are already high, just a few hours of hiking will bring you into unbeatable alpine scenery along the Continental Divide. Be aware that the 12,000- to 14,000-ft. altitudes can make your lungs feel as if they're constricted by rubber bands; give your brain a few minutes to adjust to the reduced oxygen levels before starting up the higher trails. Some easy trails include the 3.6-mi. round-trip from **Wild Basin Ranger Station** to Calypso Cascades and the 2.8-mi. round-trip from the Long Peaks Ranger Station to Eugenia Mine. From the nearby Glacier Gorge Junction trailhead, take a short hike to Mills Lake or up to the Loch.

From the town of Grand Lake, a trek into the scenic and remote **North** or **East Inlets** should leave camera-toting tourists behind. Both of these wooded valleys offer excellent trout fishing. The park's gem is prominent **Longs Peak** (14,255 ft.), which dominates the eastern slope. The peak's monumental east face, a 2000-ft. vertical wall known simply as the **Diamond,** is the most challenging rock climbing spot in Colorado.

You can traverse the park on a mountain bike as a fun and challenging alternative to hiking. **Colorado Bicycling Adventures,** 184 E. Elkhorn (586-4241), Estes Park, rents bikes ($5 per hr, $9 for 2 hr., $14 per ½-day, $19 per day; discounts for hostelers; helmets included). Guided mountain bike tours are also offered ($12.50 for 2 hr., $25 for 4 hr.; open daily 9am-8pm; off-season 10am-5pm). The expertise required for the tight turns and sheer drops of the Horseshoe Park/Estes Park Loop make it the least traveled of the three bike routes in the park.

In the winter, tons o' people cross-country ski in the high snows around Bear Lake and Wild Basin. The **Ski Estes Park** ski resort (586-8173) slopes within the park's boundaries, just off Trail Ridge Rd., 10 mi. west of Estes Park. Cross country, snowshoeing, and snowboarding are also available. (Lift tickets $16, lessons $15. Ski, boot, pole rental about $13 per day. Open in winter only.)

During the summer, the three major campgrounds have good nightly amphitheater programs that examine the park's ecology. The visitors centers have information on these and on many enjoyable ranger-led interpretive activities, including nature walks, birding expeditions, and artists' forays.

Of the two towns, **Grand Lake,** Estes's western cousin, draws fewer crowds in the summer. Though inaccessible without a car in the winter, the town offers hairraising snowmobile and cross-country routes. Ask at the visitors center about seasonal events. Camp on the shores of adjacent **Shadow Mountain Lake** and **Lake Granby.**

San Juan Mountain Area

Ask Coloradans about their favorite mountain retreats and they'll most likely name a peak, lake, stream, or town in the San Juan Range of southwestern Colorado. Four national forests—the Uncompahgre (pronounced un-cum-PAH-gray), the Gunnison, the San Juan, and the Rio Grande—encompass this sprawling range.

Durango is an ideal base camp for forages into these mountains. In particular, the **Weminuche Wilderness,** northeast of Durango, tempts the hardy backpacker with a particularly large expanse of hilly terrain. You can hike for miles where wild, sweeping vistas are the rule. Get maps and info on hiking in the San Juans from **Pine Needle Mountaineering,** Main Mall, Durango 81301 (247-8728; open Mon.-Sat. 9am-9pm, Sun. 11am-4pm; winter Mon.-Sat. 9am-6pm, Sun. 11am-4pm; maps $2.50).

The San Juan area is easily accessible on U.S. 50, traveled by hundreds of thousands of tourists each summer. **Greyhound/Trailways** and **Rocky Mountain Stages** service the area, but very poorly. Car travel is the best option in this region.

On a happier note, the San Juans are loaded with AYH hostels and campgrounds, making them one of the most economical places to visit in Colorado.

Black Canyon of the Gunnison National Monument

According to the geologist who first mapped this area, "no other canyon in North America combines the depth, narrowness, sheerness, and somber countenance of the Black Canyon." Sculpted by the Gunnison River, this steely black canyon drops 2500 ft. to the powerful waters still raging today.

The **North Rim** of the canyon is the more remote, accessible only via a 12-mi. dirt road which leaves CO Rte. 92 near the Crawford Reservoir east from Delta or west from Blue Mesa. Seven "overlooks" are along the rim, and a self-guiding nature trail starts from the campground. The better-developed, more-populated **South Rim** is reached from U.S. 50, via Colorado Rte. 347 just outside of Montrose. The 8-mi. scenic drive along this rim boasts spectacular **Chasm View,** where you can peer 2000 ft. down a sheer vertical drop. Inspired hikers can descend to the bottom of the canyon; the least difficult trail (more like a controlled slide) drops 1800 ft. over a distance of 1 mi. At certain points you must hoist yourself up on a chain in order to gain ground. Suffice to say, this hike is not to be undertaken lightly. A backcountry permit and advice from a ranger are required before any descent. But don't let this daunt your spirit of adventure—rangers are helpful and the wild beauty of this canyon climb awaits the brave. Hey, it's Colorado; we're not in Kansas anymore! For more info, call the **visitors center** at 249-1915. (Guided nature walks at 11am and 2pm. Meet at the visitors center. Open Memorial Day-Labor Day daily 8am-7pm, less during the off-season.) A short walk down from the visitors center affords a view startling enough in its steepness to require chest-high rails to protect the dizzy from falling.

Camp in either rim's beautiful desert **campground.** Each has pit toilets and charcoal grills; the southern one has an amphitheater with summer evening programs at 9pm. Water is available, but use it sparingly. (Sites $6.) You can collect wood with some difficulty, or let George Washington collect it at a store on the turn-off from U.S. 50. Backcountry camping and driftwood fires in the canyon bottom are permitted; beware the abundant poison ivy.

The closest town to the Gunnison National Monument is **Montrose,** with administrative offices for the monument located at 2233 E. Main St. (249-7036; open Mon.-Fri. 8am-4:30pm). Look to the **Mesa Hotel,** 10 N. Townsend Ave. (249-3773), at the junction of Rte. 550 and 50, for quaint, clean, cheap rooms. (Singles $15, with bath $20. Doubles $23.) The **Stockman's Café & Bar,** 320 E. Main St. (349-9446), serves hearty Western and Mexican meals across the street. (Open Mon.-Tues., Thurs.-Sun. 7am-11pm.) The town's **visitors center** assists at 2490 S. Townsend Ave. (249-1726; open May-Oct. daily 9am-7pm).

A few mi. south of Montrose on Hwy. 550, the **Ute Indian Museum,** 17253 Chipeta Dr. (249-3098), exhibits among other things costumes from the Bear Dance and the bilingual letters of chief Ouray (leader of the Southern Ute tribe). (Open May 27-Sept. 2 Mon.-Fri. 9am-7pm, Sat. 10am-5pm, Sun. 1-5pm. Admission $2, seniors and kids $1.)

Greyhound serves Montrose, 50 N. Townsend Ave. (249-6673), and Gunnison, 303 Tomichi Ave. in the Changing Hands building (641-0060). Gunnison lies about 55 mi. east of Montrose on U.S. 50. The bus will drop you off at the junction of Rte. 50 and 347, 6 mi. from the canyon. **Western Express Taxi** (249-8880) will drive you in from Montrose for about $14. Entrance to the monument costs $3 for vehicles, $1 for pedestrians and bikers.

Montrose's **ZIP code** is 81401. The **area code** for the region is 303.

Crested Butte

After leading a hunting expedition of several men to Crested Butte in 1873, Alfie Packer returned home alone a few days later appearing strangely pudgier and wealthier. At a trial accusing Packer of murder, robbery, and cannibalism, the presiding judge declared, "This state had seven Democrats, and you ate five of them."

Bizarre politics and anthropophagy aside, Crested Butte is a ski town limited in size by encircling mountains and difficult roads. The town markets itself as the smaller alternative to neighboring Aspen; unfortunately, the prices in Crested Butte are not a smaller alternative. Two routes lead to town, both only accessible to car or mountain bike. Reach Crested Butte from the south by taking I-50 to Gunnison and picking up CO Rte. 135, which heads north 30 mi. to town. From June to October on Hwy. 70 to the north, take CO Rte. 82 15 mi. south from Glenwood Springs to Carbondale, picking up CO Rte. 133, which leads to Crested Butte by turning right shortly after Paonia Reservoir onto seasonal Kebbler Pass, a well-groomed 30 mi. dirt road with incredible scenery.

The **Mount Crested Butte** ski area opens from late November to early April. For a winter brochure and lift reservations contact Crested Butte Vacations, P.O. Box A, Mt. Crested Butte 81225 (800-544-8448). Inquire about their "ski free" offer, good Nov.-Dec. Buses run in season almost non-stop between the mount and Crested Butte, starting at 7am, from the corner of 6th and Elk St. In the summer, buses run hourly from 7:45am until evening.

In summer, Crested Butte has one of the best **4th of July parades** around, with the whole town, including the fire and police departments, making floats and dousing each other with assorted alcoholic beverages. As people recover, Crested Butte hosts an annual **wildflower festival,** (July 4-8), with hikes, art exhibits, and photography workshops. The following week the town eases into "fat tire" or **mountain bike week,** hosting races and instructional camps. In early August, the town hosts a Festival of the Arts. All of these summer festivals, parades, and celebrations attempt to assuage the effects of withdrawal for ski addicts throughout the mild season. For more info, call the **Chamber of Commerce** (349-6438 or 800-545-4505), located at Mt. Crested Butte Town Center, P.O. Box 1288, Crested Butte, CO 81224, or a second facility at Elk and Hwy. 135. (Open daily 9am-5pm.) Get trail maps here as well. **Alpine Outside,** 315 6th St. (349-5011), rents out mountain bikes, with helmets and water bottles, for $8 per ½-day, $15 per day. (Open daily 8am-6pm.)

Crested Butte's nightlife panders to its mostly well-to-do, Ivy League-sweatshirt-wearing clientele. **The Idle Spur** at 225 Elk Ave. (349-5026) brews its own beer on the spot. Food is expensive, but stop by and order the sampler ($4), a collection of six different home-brewed beers. Indian Ale and the Avalanche are two local favorites. (Open daily 3pm-2am.) Do some carbo-loading at **Donita's Cantina,** 4th and Elk, which serves up mouth watering Mexican fare (guacamole $3.25). (Open daily 5-9:30pm.) For coffee, pastries and delicious sandwiches, go to **The Bakery Café** at 3rd and Elk (349-7280; open daily 7:30am-6:30pm.)

Inexpensive lodging would be nearly impossible to find were it not for **The Forest Queen Hotel,** at 2nd and Elk (349-5336), which has resisted the price-hiking trend. Stop by the back room and ask Thelma Cornman about her travels to Iran, Oman, Pakistan, and Spain. (Bunks $13. Doubles $27, with private bath $32. Prices slightly higher in late Dec. and early Jan. Great breakfast included.) **Alpine Outside** (listed above) rents out a "rustic cabin" for $20 per night that can house up to four.

Durango

As Will Rogers once put it, Durango is "out of the way, and glad of it." Despite its increasing popularity as a tourist destination, Durango retains an almost insidiously relaxed small-town atmosphere. Come to see nearby Mesa Verde and to raft down the Animas River, but don't be surprised if you end up staying longer than you expected. Winter is Durango's busiest season, when nearby **Purgatory Resort** (247-9000), 20 mi. north on U.S. 550, hosts skiers of all levels. (Lift tickets $34, kids $17, with one free child per adult.)

Durango is best known for the **Narrow Gauge Railroad,** 479 Main St. (247-2733), which runs along the Animas River Valley to the gilded tourist town of Silverton. Old-fashioned locomotives careen through the San Juans four times per day, leaving Durango at 7:30am, 8:30am, 9:30am, and 10:15am. The six-hour round-trip stops midway for an additional two hours at the small town of Silverton. (Tickets $37, kids $18.75.) If the prospect of sitting all day doesn't sound that great, but you still want to experience the narrow gauge sights, consider buying a one-way train ticket and taking a bus back from Silverton along 550. Buses wait at the Silverton train station to service the weary. (1½-hr., $17.)

To backpack into the scenic **Chicago** and **New York Basins,** buy a round-trip ticket to Needleton ($34). The train will drop you off here on its trip to Silverton. When you decide to leave the high country, return to Needleton and flag the train, but you must have exactly $17 to board if you don't have a return pass. For more info on the train and its services for backpackers, contact the Durango and Silverton Narrow Gauge Railroad, 479 Main St., Durango 81301. (Offices open May-Aug. daily 6am-9pm; Aug.-Oct. 7am-7pm; Oct.-May 8am-5pm.)

For river rafting, **Rivers West,** 520 Main St. (259-5077), has good rates. ($10 for a 1-hr. rapids ride, $19 for 2 hr. plus lunch, $25 for an hr. plus a steak dinner. Kids 20% discount. Daily 8am-9pm.) **Durango Rivertrips,** 720 Main St. (259-0289), organizes two-hour rides for $15 and half-day rides for $23. (Open daily 9am-9pm.) Biking gear is available from **Hassle Free Sports,** 2615 Main St. (259-3874; bikes $8 per hr., $20 per day; open Mon.-Sat. 8:30am-6pm, Sun. 10:30am-5pm; must have driver's license and major credit card).

For provisions, head to **City Market,** on Hwy. 550 one block down 9th St., or at 3130 Main St. (Both open 24 hrs.) Or breakfast with the locals at **Carver's Bakery,** 1022 Main Ave., which has good bread and breakfast specials ($2-4). (Open Mon.-Sat. 6:30am-10pm, Sun. 6:30am-2pm.) The **Durango Diner,** 957 Main St., serves buxom cheeseburgers ($2.50) cooked by a singing chef. (Open Mon.-Sat. 6am-2pm, Sun. 7am-1pm.) Race over to **Pronto,** 150 E. 2nd Ave. (247-1510), for their $4.25 spaghetti dinner or all-you-can-eat specials. **Farquhart's,** 725 Main Ave. (247-9861) serves up delicious burritos for $5.75. Come to this bar at night for the best live music in town; keep an eye open for Walt Richardson and Morningstar. (Music nightly with open jam on Sundays. $2-5 cover. Open daily 11am-2am.)

The simplest way to ensure a pleasant stay in Durango is to rest up at the **Durango Youth Hostel,** 543 E. 2nd Ave. (247-9905 or 247-5477), a quaint old building one block from downtown. David, the host, will help orient you to the area, and will admit that he knew Timothy Leary at Princeton if you ask. (Check-in 5-10pm. Check-out 7-10am. Bunks $10.) The **Central Hotel and Hostel,** 975 Main St. (247-0330), has a TV in each of the clean and pleasant rooms. (Singles $25. Doubles $28.) The **Cottonwood Camper Park,** on U.S. 160 (247-1977), 1/3 mi. west of town, has tent sites ($12, with electricity and water $15, full hookup $16).

Durango parks at the intersection of U.S. 160 (east to Alamosa, 150 mi.) and U.S. 550 (south to Farmington, NM; 45 mi.). Streets run perpendicular to avenues, but everyone calls Main Avenue "Main Street." **Greyhound/Trailways,** 275 E. 8th Ave. (259-2755), serves Grand Junction ($29), Denver ($47), and Albuquerque ($33). (Open Mon.-Fri. 7am-5:30pm, Sat. 7am-noon and 4:30-5:30pm, Sun. 7-10am and 4:30-5:30pm.)

You can pick up care packages at the **Durango Post Office,** 228 8th St. (247-3434; open Mon.-Fri. 8am-5pm, Sat. 9am-noon.) Durango's **ZIP code** is 81301, the **area code** 303.

Ouray

Once upon a time Ouray (pronounced yer-RAY) prospered as, you guessed it, a gold and silver mining town. The surrounding 5000-ft. peaks dwarf this grape-sized hamlet in the Uncompahgre (pronounced un-com-PAH-gray) National Forest. The town itself prepares well for hikers and climbers, with numerous sports shops to equip and keep track of you through their hiker registration service. After a hike or a ski tour, soak in the **Onvis Hot Springs** (626-5324), right off the "Million Dollar Highway" (U.S. 550) on the northern outskirts. (Open daily 10am-10pm, Sun. 9am-7pm; off-season Wed.-Mon. noon-9pm. Admission $5. Clothing optional so loosen up.)

Experience the heritage of Ouray on a tour of the **Bachelor-Syracuse Mine,** County Rd. 14, P.O. Drawer 380 W. (325-4500), just off Hwy. 550. Sit in an ore cart and ride 3350 ft. along a real mine shaft right into the heart of the mountain. The tour provides a unique glimpse into the reasons why miners get subterranean homesick blues. Rides leave on the hour. (Open mid-May to mid-Sept. daily 10am-5pm. Summer hours longer. Admission $7, under 12 $4.) Once you resurface, head to the southwest end of town to see the **Box Canyon Falls,** a 285-ft. cataract. (Open mid-May to mid-Oct. daily 8am-8pm. Admission $1.25, seniors $1, ages 4-12 75¢, under 4 free.)

Many travelers rent a jeep in Ouray and four-wheel over the Imogene Pass to Telluride (see Telluride below). The prices are as steep as the trail, but you'll not likely forget the stupendously beautiful trip past waterfalls, mountain peaks, alpine flowers, ice fields, yellow-bellied marmots, and old mining towns. Reserve a jeep as far in advance as possible. **San Juan Scenic Jeep Tours,** 480 Main St. (325-4444 or 325-4154), rents jeeps for $60 per half day, $80 per day. (Open daily 7am-8pm, off-season 7am-6pm. Credit card or $200 deposit required.) To pedal the mountains, rent a bike ($15 per ½-day, $20 per day; $1 for helmet) at **Downhill Biking,** 825 Main St. (325-4284; open daily 8am-8pm). The Ouray **Visitor Center,** 1222 N. Main (325-4746 or 1-800-228-1876), contains a valuable cache of brochures. (Open summer daily 9am-6pm; rest of year Mon.-Sat. 9am-5pm.)

Polly's Campground (325-4061) perches above Ouray, roughly 1 mi. north on U.S. 550. (Sites $14. Open May-Sept.) The **Ouray KOA** (325-4736) has some streamside sites, and comfortable grassy spots for primitive camping. (Sites $15.25, with electricity and water $17.25, full hookup $18.25.) For indoor accommodation, journey 10 mi. down valley to **Ridgway,** at the intersection of U.S. 550 and Rte. 62, where the **Adobe Inn,** Lidell Dr. (626-5939), has limited room in the back of a small, elegant Mexican restaurant. Free muffin and coffee in the morning. (Bunks $15. Singles $35. Doubles $40.

Ouray's **ZIP code** is 81427; the **area code** is 303.

Telluride

Home to the first bank Butch Cassidy ever robbed (the San Miguel), Telluride has a history right out of a 1930s black-and-white film. Prize fighter Jack Dempsey used to wash dishes in the Senate, a popular saloon/brothel that frequently required Dempsey to serve as bouncer as well. Of course, now it serves delicious Greek food (see below). The **Sheridan Theatre** (see below) hosted actresses Sarah Bernhardt and Lillian Gish on cross-country theater tours, while Vice President William Jennings Bryan delivered his "Cross of Gold" speech in Telluride from the front balcony of the hotel. More recently, in his autobiography *Speak, Memory,* Vladimir Nabokov relates his pursuit through Telluride of a particularly rare type of butterfly. Not so rare (especially after its devaluation) was the silver that attracted all the less aesthetically inclined hoodlums to Telluride in the first place, beginning in 1875.

Today, music lovers, "high-concept" environmentalists, and downhill skiers and mountain bikers inhabit Telluride, lingering for a weekend or several years. These young nomads, with an insatiable appetite for bluegrass, foreign film and outdoor sports, lend Telluride the slightly "groovy" and daredevilish atmosphere of a college town. Self-proclaimed atheists can be spied crossing themselves before tipping their planks down "Spiral Stairs" and "the Plunge," two of the Rockies' most gut-wrenching slopes. For more information, contact the **Telluride Company,** P.O. Box 307, 81435 (728-3856).

Yet neither rockslide nor snowmelt signal the end of the festivities in Telluride. The quality and number of summer arts festivals seems staggering when you consider that only 1500 people call the town home. While get-togethers occur just about every weekend in summer and fall, the most renowned include the **Bluegrass Festival** in late June—last year the likes of James Taylor and the Indigo Girls attracted crowds of 16,000. Although music stores sell tickets ($30 per night) from Grand

Junction to Aspen, people have managed to sneak in. On the weekend of the festivals, you can easily find dishwashing or food-serving jobs in exchange for tickets to the show. Telluride also hosts a **Talking Gourds** poetry fest (late June), a **Composer to Composer** festival (mid-July), and a **Jazz Festival** (early Aug.), among others. You can often hear the music festivals all over town, all day, and deep into the night as you try to sleep. Above all, the **Telluride International Film Festival** (Labor Day weekend), now in its 18th year, draws famous actors and directors from all over the globe. Guests in years past have included Academy Award-winning actor Daniel Day Lewis, Hasty Pudding Award-winning actor Clint Eastwood, and twinly-piqued director David Lynch. The **Visitor Center** is upstairs at **Rose's,** 666 West Colorado Ave. (728-3041), at the entrance to town. (Open Mon.-Fri. 9am-6pm, Sat.-Sun. 9am-5pm.) For 24-hr. recorded info call the **Festival Hotline** (728-6079).

Two blocks from the visitor center lies the **Coonskin Chairlift,** which will haul you up 10,000 ft. for an excellent view of Pikes Peak and the La Sal Mountains. (Open Thurs.-Mon. 10am-2pm. Fare $6, seniors and kids $3.) The biking, hiking and backpacking opportunities around Telluride are endless; ghost towns and lakes tucked behind stern mountain crags fill the wild terrain. For an enjoyable day hike, trek up the San Miguel River Canyon to **Bridal Veil Falls.** Drive to the end of Rte. 145 and hike the steep, misty dirt road to the spectacular waterfall. **Paragon Ski and Sport,** 213 W. Colorado Ave. (728-4525), has camping supplies, bikes, and skis. (Open summer Mon.-Thurs. 9am-7pm, Fri.-Sun. 9am-8pm; winter daily 8am-9pm.) Stop at the local sportshop or **Between the Covers** bookstore, 224 W. Colorado Ave. (728-4504), for trail guides and maps. (Open daily 9am-midnight) To help you page through the complete works of both Henry Miller and Anaïs Nin, charge up with some espresso at the small but chi-chi coffee shop in the rear of the store. Listen for authentic Telluride poetasters.

The **Oak Street Inn (AYH),** 134 N. Oak St. (728-3383), has two-level loft dorms complete with saunas. Beware, even hostels succumb to Colorado gold fever! Bunk rooms are not available during festivals or the Christmas season. ($13.50, nonmembers $25. Showers $3.) When they're out of beds, head for the **New Sheridan Hotel,** 231 W. Colorado (728-4351), where a three-bunk room for one to four people goes for $39. You can **camp** in the east end of town in a town-operated facility with water, restrooms, and showers. (Two-week max. stay. Sites $8.) **Sunshine,** 4 mi. southwest on Rte. 145 toward Cortez, and **Matterhorn,** 10 mi. farther on Rte. 145 (1-800-283-2267), are well-developed national forest campgrounds; the latter can accommodate trailers with hookup. (Two-week max. stay. Sites $7.) Accessible by jeep roads, several free primitive campgrounds locate nearby. During festival times, you can crash just about anywhere in town, and hot showers are mercifully available at the high school ($2 during festivals).

Baked in Telluride, 127 S. Fir St., has enough rich coffee and delicious pastry, pizza, and bagels (42¢) to get you through a festival weekend without sleeping, even if you're already baked in Telluride. (Open daily 6am-10pm.) The **Athena Senate,** 123 S. Spruce (728-3018), serves elegant Greek appetizers, omelettes, gyros ($5), and late night/early morning food. (Open Mon.-Sat. 11am-3am, Sun. 11am-2am; during Bluegrass Fest until 4am.) Delicious Italian fare bakes at **Eddie's Café,** 300 W. Colorado (728-5335) including 8-in. pizzas ($5) and other dinner specials ($7-11). At **Froggies's Popcorn Wagon,** on the corner of Fir and Colorado Ave., sit on the shaded outdoor deck admiring the mountains with a papoose-sized bag of warm buttered popcorn ($1) or fajitas ($3). (Open daily 11am-9pm.)

You can only get to Telluride by car, on Rte. 550 or Rte. 145. Telluride's **post office** stamps and sorts at 101 E. Colorado Ave. (728-3900; open Mon.-Fri. 9am-5pm, Sat. 10am-noon). The **ZIP code** is 81435; the **area code** is 303.

CONNECTICUT

Although it's hard to imagine, Connecticut was once a rugged frontier. The European colonists' westward movement began with the settlement of the Connecticut Valley by Massachusetts Puritans in the 1630s. Nutmeggers were independent from the very beginning—their democratic state constitution motivated the state's nickname, the "Constitution State." Today, Connecticut's original Yankee tradition mingles with present-day urbanity in cities like Hartford and New Haven, where glass skyscrapers overshadow small brick churches and historical landmarks. Connecticut has not lost sight of its Yankee roots, despite the modern conveniences afforded by its status as the state with the highest per-capita income.

Practical Information

Capital: Hartford.

Tourist Information Line: 1-800-282-6863. **Bureau of State Parks and Forests,** 165 Capitol Ave., #265, Hartford 06106 (566-2304). Dispenses topographical maps. Supervises over 100 state parks and forests, many with camping; reservations through this office recommended for July and summer weekends. **Connecticut Forest and Park Association,** 16 Meriden Rd., Rockfall, CT 06481 (346-2372). Hiking and outdoor activities information. **Connecticut Coalition of Bicyclists,** P.O. Box 121, Middletown 06457. Write for a state bike map and *Connecticut Bicycle Directory.*

Time Zone: Eastern. **Postal Abbreviation:** CT

Hartford

The state capitol and the nation's insurance headquarters is at the heart of the city. The gold-domed **Old State House,** 800 Main St. (522-6766) is one nearby landmark which should not be overlooked. Designed by Charles Bullfinch in 1796, the building which housed the state government until 1914 occasionally hosts some interesting historical exhibits. (Open Mon.-Sat. 10am-5pm, Sun. noon-5pm.) Thomas Hooker preached across the street, at the **Center Church and Ancient Burying Grounds,** 675 Main St., and you can see the centuries-old tombstones of his descendants in the graveyard. A block or so west, **Bushnell Park,** bordered by Jewell, Trinity, and Elm St., still maintains one of the country's few extant hand-crafted merry-go-rounds. The **Bushnell Park Carousel,** built in 1914, spins 48 horses and two lovers' chariots to the tunes of a Wurlitzer Organ. (Open April Sat.-Sun. 11am-5pm; May-Sept. 2 Tues.-Sun. 11am-5pm. Admission 25¢.) The **State Capitol,** 210 Capitol Ave., overlooks the park. Also gold-domed, this beautiful building stores frescoes of scenes from Connecticut history. (Free tours available Mon.-Fri. 9am-3pm.)

Fans of American literature won't want to miss engaging tours of the **Mark Twain and Harriet Beecher Stowe Houses** (525-9317), located just west of the city center on Rte. 4 at 77 Forest St. The gaudy Victorian Mark Twain Mansion housed the Missouri-born author for 17 years. Twain composed his controversial masterpiece *Huckleberry Finn* here. Harriet Beecher Stowe lived next door on Nook Farm shortly before her death and well after the publication of *Uncle Tom's Cabin.* (Both houses open June to mid-Oct. and Dec. Mon.-Sat. 9:30am-4pm, Sun. noon-4pm; mid-Oct. to Nov. and Jan.-May Tues.-Sat. 9:30am-4pm, Sun. noon-4pm. Admission includes mandatory guide tour of one or both houses. Twain tour $6.50, seniors $5.50, kids $2.75; Stowe tour $5, seniors $4.50, kids $2.75; both houses $10, kids $4.50.)

Aesthetes should drop by the oldest public art museum in the country, the **Hartford Atheneum,** 600 Main St. (278-2670). The museum has absorbing collections of contemporary and Baroque art, including one of only three Caravaggios in the United States. (Open Tues.-Sun. 11am-5pm. Admission $3, seniors and students

$1.50, under 13 free. Free Thurs. and Sat. from 11am-1pm. Tours Thurs. at 1pm and Sat.-Sun. 2pm.)

There are a number of reasonably priced places to eat in Hartford—scope out food courts in malls, hot dog stands at Bushnell, and restaurants around local schools like Trinity College and the University of Hartford. The city lies at the intersection of I-9, which runs from New Haven to points north, and of I-84, which runs from Boston to points west. The **Greater Hartford Convention and Visitor's Bureau** has two locations: in the **Hartford Civic Center,** One Civic Center Plaza (728-6789), and at the **Old State House,** 800 Main St. (522-6766). Here you can pick up dozens of maps, booklets, and guides to the state's resorts, campgrounds, and many historical sights. Call **Connecticut Transit** (525-9181; basic fare 75¢) with questions about the efficient public transportation.

Hartford's **area code** is 203.

Long Island Sound: New London and Mystic

Connecticut's coastal towns along the Long Island Sound were busy seaports in the days of Melville and Richard Henry Dana, but the dark, musty inns filled with tattooed sailors swapping stories of their journeys have been consigned to history. Today, the coast is important mainly as a resort and sailing base, and maritime enthusiasts in particular will enjoy two former whaling ports, New London and nearby Mystic Seaport. **New London** sits proudly on a hillside overlooking the majestic **Thames River.** Behind stately **Union Station** (designed by H. H. Richardson) lies a **visitors center,** which offers free maps and directions for a "historic walk" through the downtown area. The **Coast Guard Academy** (444-8270; open May-Oct. 9am-5pm), a five-minute drive up Rte. 32, offers free tours through the Coast Guard Museum and the beautiful cadet-training vessel **U.S.S. Eagle** when it is in port. (Open daily 9am-5pm, Sat.-Sun. 10am-5pm.)

Mystic Seaport (572-0711) is a restored 19th-century whaling port. Beyond the interest cooked up by the film *Mystic Pizza,* the main attraction here is the **Charles W. Morgan,** a fully restored, three-masted whaling ship. (Seaport open daily 9am-5pm. Admission $14, ages 5-18 $8.75. Take I-95 5 mi. east from New London and follow signs to Mystic Seaport, or take SEAT bus #2 or 3 from Union Station to Anderson Little ($1), then bus #10 to Mystic ($1).) The **area code** for New London and Mystic is 203.

New Haven

You know you're in the right place when you see a T-shirt that reads "Harvard's a disease—Yale's the cure." But the hype surrounding the centuries-old Ivy League rivalry obscures the fact that Yale was founded in 1738 by a group of clergymen who defected from decadent Harvard in order to create a commercial city with the scriptures as its fundamental law. Today New Haven is simultaneously university town and depressed city. Academic types and a working class population live somewhat uneasily side by side—bumper stickers proclaiming "Tax Yale, Not Us" embellish a number of street signs downtown. But there is more than just political tension here. New Haven has a reputation as something of a battleground, and Yalies tend to stick to areas on or near campus, further widening the rift between town and gown.

New Haven is laid out in nine squares. The central one is **The Green,** which, despite the fact that it lies between **Yale University** and City Hall, is a pleasant escape from the hassles of city life. A small but thriving business district borders the green, consisting mostly of bookstores, boutiques, cheap sandwich places, and other services catering to students and professors. Downtown New Haven, and particularly the Yale campus, is littered with distinctive buildings. The omnipresence of American Collegiate Gothic in spires, towers, and ivy-covered buildings lends the campus a unity of design that its Cambridge cousin lacks.

Yale Information Center, Phelps Gateway, 344 College St. (432-2300), facing the Green, gives organized tours and free campus maps. Pick up a 75¢ walking guide and *The Yale,* a guide to undergraduate life ($2.50). (Open daily 10am-4pm. Free 1-hr. tours Mon.-Fri. at 10:30am and 2pm, Sat.-Sun. at 1:30pm.)

James Gambel Rodgers, a firm believer in the sanctity of printed material, designed **Sterling Memorial Library,** 120 High St. (432-2798). The building looks much like a monastery—even the telephone booths are shaped like confessionals. Rodgers spared no expense to make Yale's library look "authentic," even decapitating the figurines on the library's exterior to replicate those at Oxford, which, because of decay, often fall to the ground and shatter. (Open summer Mon.-Wed. and Fri. 8:30am-5pm, Thurs. 8:30am-10pm, Sat. 10am-5pm; academic year Mon.-Thurs. 8:30am-midnight, Fri. 8:30am-5pm, Sat. 10am-5am, Sun. 1pm-midnight.) The massive **Beinecke Rare Book and Manuscript Library,** 121 Wall St. (432-2977), has no windows. Instead this intriguing modern structure is panelled with Vermont marble cut thin enough to be translucent; supposedly its volumes (including one Gutenberg Bible and an extensive collection of William Carlos Williams's writings) could survive even nuclear war. (Open Mon.-Fri. 8:30am-4:45pm, Sat. 10am-4:45pm.)

Along New Haven's own Wall St., between High and Yale St., the Neo-Gothic sculptured gargoyles on the **Law School** building are actually cops and robbers.

Most of New Haven's museums are on the Yale campus. The **Yale University Art Gallery,** 1111 Chapel St. (432-0600), opened in 1832, claims to be the oldest university art museum in the Western Hemisphere. Its collections of John Trumbull paintings and Italian Renaissance works are especially notable. (Open summer Tues.-Sat. 10am-5pm, Sun. 2-5pm; academic year Tues.-Wed. and Fri.-Sat. 10am-5pm, Thurs. 10am-8pm, Sun. 2-5pm. Free.) The **Yale Center for British Art,** 1080 Chapel St. (432-2800), sponsors some pretty wacky exhibits—two years ago they displayed a collection of snuff boxes. (Open Tues.-Sat. 10am-5pm, Sun. 2-5pm. Free.) The **Peabody Museum of Natural History,** 170 Whitney Ave. (432-5099; 432-5799 for recorded message), houses Rudolph F. Zallinger's Pulitzer Prize-winning mural, which portrays the North American continent as it appeared 70 to 350 million years ago. Other exhibits range from Central American cultural artifacts to a dinosaur hall displaying the skeleton of a Brontosaurus. (Open Mon.-Sat. 10am-5pm, Sun. noon-5pm. Admission $2.50, seniors $2, ages 3-15 $1.)

Food in New Haven is reasonably cheap, catering to the student population.

Atticus Café, 1082 Chapel St. A charming bookstore/café with friendly if harried service. Try their soups served with swell half-loaves of bread ($3-4). Open Mon.-Fri. 8am-midnight, Sat. 9am-midnight, Sun. 9am-9pm.

Naples Pizza, 90 Wall St. A Yale tradition, updated with a video jukebox. Try a pizza with broccoli, pineapple, or white clams ($7.25); wash it down with a pitcher of beer ($5.50). Open June-Aug. Mon.-Wed. 7-10pm, Thurs.-Fri. 7-11pm; Sept.-May Sun.-Thurs. 7pm-1am, Fri.-Sat. 7pm-2am.

Daily Caffe, 376 Elm St. Started by a Yale graduate; quickly becoming the haunt of the university's coffee and cigarette set. Soups and salads under $3, with an impressive selection of *caffes.*

Claire's, 1000 Chapel St. (562-3888). A homey restaurant that touts its gourmet vegetarian menu, but the real draw is Claire's rich cake ($2.25 per slice). Open daily 8am-10pm.

Yankee Doodle Coffee Shop, 258 Elm St. (865-1074). A tiny, diner-like place, squeezed into a 12-ft.-wide slice just across the street from the Yale Boola-Boola Shop. $1.40 gets you eggs, toast, and coffee. Open Mon.-Sat. 6:30am-2:30pm.

Louis Lunch, 263 Crown St. (562-5507). The wife-and-husband team serves the best flame-broiled burger on the East Coast for $2.50. They claim the menu has not changed in 40 years. Open Mon.-Fri. 9-11am and 11:30am-4pm.

New Haven offers plenty of late-night entertainment. Check **Toad's Place,** 300 York St. (562-5589; for recording 777-7431) to see if one of your favorite bands is in town. While you get tickets, grab a draft beer ($1) at the bar. (Box office open daily 11am-6pm; tickets available at bar after 8pm. Bar open Sun.-Thurs. 8pm-1am, Fri.-Sat. 8pm-2am.) **Partner's,** 365 Crown St. (624-5510), is a favorite gay hangout. (Open Sun.-Thurs. 4pm-1am, Fri.-Sat. 4pm-2am.) The **Anchor Bar,** 272 College St. (865-1512), just off the Green, serves everything from Corona to St. Pauli Girl Dark; a local paper recognized its jukebox as the best in the region. (Open Mon.-Thurs. 11am-1am, Fri.-Sat. 10am-2am.)

Once a famous testing ground for Broadway-bound plays, New Haven's thespian community carries on today, but to a much lesser extent. The **Schubert Theater,** 247 College St. (562-5666, 800-228-6622), a large part of the town's on-stage tradition, still produces plays. (Box office open Mon.-Fri. 10am-4:30pm, Sat. noon-3pm.) Across the street, **The Palace,** 246 College St. (399-4233), host concerts and revues. Not to be outdone, New Haven's **Long Wharf Theater** (787-4282) received a special Tony Award for achievement in Regional Theater in 1978. (Tickets $21-26, student rush $5. Season June-late Sept.)

Yale itself accounts for an impressive bulk of the theater activity in the city. The **Yale Repertory Theater** (432-1234) has cultivated such illustrious alums as Meryl Streep, Glenn Close, and Christopher Durang, and continues to produce excellent shows. (Open Oct.-May.) The **University Theater,** at 22 York St., stages undergraduate plays throughout the academic year and during graduation. Tickets are almost guaranteed to be under $8. In summer, the Green is the site of free **New Haven Symphony** concerts (865-0831), the **New Haven Jazz Festival** (787-8228), and other free musical series. The Department of Cultural Affairs (787-8956), 770 Chapel St., can answer questions about concerts on the Green.

Inexpensive accommodations are extremely hard to find in New Haven. The hunt is especially difficult around Yale Parents weekend (mid-Oct.) and graduation (early June). **Hotel Duncan,** 1151 Chapel St. (787-1273), has decent singles for $38 and doubles for $50, both with bath. Plan ahead; prices are higher without reservations. The **Nutmeg Bed & Breakfast,** 222 Girard Ave., Hartford 06105 (236-6698), reserves doubles in New Haven B&B's at $35-45. (Open Mon.-Fri. 9am-5:30pm.) The nearest parks for camping are **Cattletown** (264-5678, sites $7), 40 minutes away, and **Hammonasset Beach** (245-2755, sites $8.50), 20 minutes away.

On the banks of the Housatonic River south of New Haven, the smaller town of **Stratford** is home to the **American Shakespeare Theater,** 1850 Elm St. (375-5000), exit 32 off I-95. (Tickets $19-29.) During the summer Shakespeare Festival, some of the country's most able actors and directors stage the Bard's plays while minstrels, musicians, and artists stroll the grounds.

To obtain free bus and street maps, and information about current events in town, stop in at the **New Haven Visitors and Convention Bureau,** 900 Chapel St. (787-8822), on the Green. (Open Mon.-Fri. 9am-5pm.) To get to New Haven, consider **Amtrak,** Union Station, Union Ave. (800-872-7245). The station is newly renovated, but the area is unsafe at night. To or from Yale, take city bus A ("Orange St."), J, or U ("Waterbury"), or walk six blocks northeast to the Green. Trains to Boston ($29-34), Washington, DC ($66), and New York ($21). **Metro-North Commuter Railroad,** Union Station (497-2089 or 800-638-7646), runs trains to New York's Grand Central Station for half of Amtrak's fare ($8-10.75). (Ticket counter open daily 6am-10:30pm.) New Haven's **Greyhound** station at 45 George St. (772-2470), is in a rough area. Try not to walk there alone, or take a cab. Frequent bus service to: New York ($12.40), Boston ($28), Providence ($22), Cape Cod/Hyannis ($32), and New London ($9). (Ticket office open daily 7:30am-8:15pm.) **Peter Pan Bus Lines,** Union Station (878-6054), offers buses to Boston ($29).

Connecticut Transit serves New Haven and the surrounding area from 470 James St. (624-0151). Most buses depart from the Green. (Open Mon.-Fri. 8am-4:30pm. Information booth at 200 Orange St. open Mon.-Fri. 9am-5pm.) **Thrifty Rent-a-Car,** 37 Union St. (562-3191 or 800-367-2277), offers economy cars starting at $34 per day ($26.95 on the weekend), with 125 free mi. (Open Mon.-Fri. 8am-6pm, Sat. 8am-4pm, Sun. 10am-4pm.) You must be 25 with a major credit card. **Carolyn's Checker Cab,** (468-2678) can take you from downtown to the aiport for $8-9.

New Haven is a cinch to get to. The city lies at the intersection of I-95 (110 mi. from Providence) and I-91 (40 mi. from Hartford). At night, don't wander alone out of the immediate downtown area and the campus, as surrounding sections are notably less safe. The Yale area is well-patrolled by campus police, who also fearlessly protect the downtown area from illegally parked cars. Around 4pm on weekdays tow trucks are out in full force, so be sure to read parking signs carefully.

New Haven's **area code** is 203.

DELAWARE

Delawareans strive to make up for their state's small size with a fierce pride in its historical past and unusually usual geography. They adopted "First State" as their slightly misleading nickname—they were the first to ratify the U.S. Constitution in 1787. To further solidify their standing as Old Kids on the Block, ebullient residents shout from the unspectacular hillsides that Delaware has the lowest highest elevation of any state, and you can get there step by step, oooh baby.

Most of Delaware's population sleeps in the northern industrial region, on the strip between Wilmington and Newark. Tourists usually associate the state with chemical industry and big corporations. Here, in 1938, nylon first shimmered and ran. Delaware does offer the tourist pleasures in the less synthetic regions of the seacoast as well; Lewes and Rehoboth Beach have the natural charm of southern resort towns, while the Delaware Dunes stretch across more than 2000 acres of accessible seashore.

Practical Information

Capital: Dover.

Tourist Information: State Visitors Service, P.O. Box 1401, 99 King's Hwy., Dover 19903 (800-282-8667; 800-441-8846 outside DE). Open Mon.-Fri. 8am-4:30pm. **Division of Fish and Wildlife,** William Penn St., Dover 19901 (739-4431).

Time Zone: Eastern. **Postal Abbreviation:** DE.

Area Code: 302.

Lewes and Rehoboth Beach

The reserved atmosphere of these seaside retreats spells relief from the usual boardwalk fare. The beaches remain clean, the air stays salty, and the people, particularly in Lewes (pronounced "LOO-iss"), keep to themselves. Founded in 1613 by the Zwaanendael colony from Hoorn, Holland, Lewes rightly touts itself as Delaware's first town. To learn about Lewes, simply walk around town. To read more about it, try the **Lewes Chamber of Commerce** (645-8073), in the Fisher Martin House on King's Hwy. (Open Mon.-Sat. 11am-3pm.) The **Lighthouse Restaurant,** on Fisherman's Wharf just over the drawbridge in Lewes, flashes with occasionally brilliant food. (Open daily 7am-10pm.) Due east from Lewes, on the Atlantic Ocean, lurks the secluded **Cape Henlopen State Park** (645-8983), home to a seabird nesting colony, sparkling white "walking dunes," and campsites (645-2103) available on a first come, first serve basis (sites $14; open April-Oct.).

With a minimum of advance planning, you can join the committees of vacationing bureaucrats from Washington, DC—many of them gay—who convene at the sand reefs of Rehoboth Beach on hot summer weekends to mix and mingle. The **chamber of commerce,** in the restored train station at 501 Rehoboth Ave. (800-441-1329 or 227-2233), provides brochures. (Open Mon.-Fri. 9am-4:30pm, Sat. 10am-2pm.)

At the **Country Squire**, 17 Rehoboth Ave. (227-3985), you can talk with locals over one of the complete dinner specials (about $7). The breakfast special ($3), served at all times, is a lagniappe of sorts. (Open daily 7am-1am.) **Thrasher's** has served fries, and only fries, in enormous paper tubs ($2.75-5.75) for over 60 years. Bite too hastily into one of the tangy peanut-oil-soaked potato treats to understand how the place got its name. Locations on either side of the main drag, at 7 and 10 Rehoboth Ave., make avoiding it doubly difficult. (Open daily 11am-11pm.) Escape to **Nicola's Pizza,**at 8 N. 1st St. (227-6211), for some of the best 'za on the East Coast ($2.75-$7.50). (Open daily 11am-3:30am.)

For inexpensive lodging, walk one block from the boardwalk to **The Lord Baltimore**, 16 Baltimore Ave. (227-2855), which has clean, antiquated, practically beach-front rooms. Singles and doubles $30-60. Call ahead, it's popular.) Or walk a little farther from the beach to the cluster of guest houses on the side lanes off 1st St., just north of Rehoboth Ave. **The Abbey Inn,** 31 Maryland Ave. (227-7023), is a warm, fuzzy place set back just far enough from the action. Call for reservations at least one week in advance, especially in summer. (2-day min. stay. Doubles from $33.) The **Big Oaks Family Campground**, P.O. Box 53 (645-6838), sprawls at the intersection of Rte. 1 and 270. (Sites $16.50.)

Greyhound/Trailways serves Lewes (flag stop at the parking lot for Tom Best's on Rte. 1; no phone) and Rehoboth Beach (227-7223; small station at 251 Rehoboth Ave.). Buses run to: Washington (3½ hr., $29); Baltimore (3¼ hr., $24); and Philadelphia (4 hr., $25.75). Lewes makes up one end of the 70-minute **Cape May, NJ/Lewes, DE Ferry** route (Lewes terminal 645-6313; for schedule and fare information, see Cape May above). Grab a cab ($15) from the pier to reach Rehoboth. To get around within Rehoboth, use the free shuttle transportation run by the **Ruddertowne Complex** (227-3888; May 27-Sept. 2 daily 3pm-midnight every hr.), which serves points between Rehoboth and Dewey Beaches, including a stop at Rehoboth Ave.

The **post office** in Rehoboth reads your postcards at 179 Rehoboth Ave. (227-8406; open Mon.-Fri. 9am-5pm, Sat. 9am-noon). The **ZIP code** for Lewes and Rehoboth Beach is 19971; the **area code** is 302.

FLORIDA

Ponce de León landed on the Florida coast in 1513, near what soon would be St. Augustine, in search of the elusive Fountain of Youth. Although the multitudes who flock to Florida today aren't desperately seeking fountains, many nonetheless find their youth restored in the Sunshine State—whether dazzled by Orlando's fantasial DisneyWorld or tanned on the coast's seductive Spring Break beaches. Droves of senior citizens also migrate to Florida, where they thrive in comfortable retirement communities, leaving one to wonder whether the draught of unpolluted, sun-warmed air isn't just as good as Ponce de León's fabled magical elixir.

But a dark shadow hangs over this land of the winter sun. Anything as attractive as Florida is bound to draw hordes of *people,* the nemesis of natural beauty. Florida's population boom is straining the state's resources; a steady flow of everything from ultra-rich tycoons to unemployed illegal aliens continually floods across its borders. Commercial strips and tremendous development in some areas have made once-pristine beaches into eyesores. This resort state that has delighted so many through the years is aging, with scars no sun and no mystical potions can hide.

Practical Information

Capital: Tallahassee.

Florida Division of Tourism, 126 W. Van Buren St., Tallahassee 32301 (487-1462). **Department of Natural Resources—Division of Recreation and Parks,** 3900 Commonwealth Blvd. #506, Tallahassee 32399-2000 (488-9872).

Time Zones: Eastern and Central (westernmost part of panhandle is 1 hr. behind Eastern).
Postal Abbreviation: FL

Cocoa Beach/Cape Canaveral

Known primarily for its rocket launches, space shuttle blast-offs, and enormous NASA space center complex, the "Space Coast" also has uncrowded golden sand beaches and vast wildlife preserves. Even during spring break the place remains comfortable because most vacationers and sunbathers are neighborly Florida or Space Coast residents.

The **Kennedy Space Center,** 8 mi. north of Cocoa Beach, is the site for all of NASA's flights. The Kennedy Center's **Spaceport USA** (452-2121 for reservations) provides a huge welcoming center for visitors. There are two different two-hour bus tours of the complex. The red tour takes you around the space sites, the blue tour to the Air Force Station. There are also two IMAX films produced on a 5½-story screen. **The Dream is Alive** is about the Space Shuttle, and **The Blue Planet** is about environmental issues. Tours depart from Spaceport USA daily 9:20am-6pm; $4, under 11 $3. Movie tickets $2.75, under 11 $1.75.) Buy tickets to both immediately upon arrival at the complex to avoid a long line. The center itself is free, as are the five movies in the Galaxy Theater and the half-hour walking tours of the exhibits. The NASA Parkway, site of the visitors center, is accessible only by car via State Rd. 405. From Cocoa Beach, take Rte. A1A north until it turns west into Rte. 528, then follow Rte. 3 north to the Spaceport. With NASA's ambitious launch schedules, you may have a chance to watch the space shuttles Columbia, Atlantis, or Discovery thunder off into the blue skies above the cape. Don't count on it. Call 1-900-321-LIFT OFF for launch information (75¢ per call).

Surrounding the NASA complex, the marshy **Merritt Island Wildlife Refuge** (867-8667) fills with deer, sea turtles, alligators, and eagles. (Open daily 8am-sunset.) Just north of Merritt Island is **Canaveral National Seashore** (867-2805; open daily 6:30am-sunset), 67,000 acres of undeveloped beach and dunes, and home to more than 300 species of birds and mammals. (Take Rte. 406 east off U.S. 1 in Titusville.) Should you feel like shucking your clothes, a nude beach accessible to the public lies at the northernmost point of the seashore near Turtle Mound.

For a bite to eat, try **Herbie K's Diner,** 2080 N. Atlantic Ave., south of Motel 6. A shiny chrome reproduction of a 50s diner, Herbie K's serves macaroni and cheese, chicken pot pie, happy haw (apple sauce), great malteds, and hamburgers ($3). (Open weekdays till midnight, Fri. and Sat. 24 hrs.) At the beach, **Motel 6,** 3701 N. Atlantic Ave. (783-3103), has a pool and large, clean rooms with TV and A/C. (Singles $32. Each additional person $6. Reservations required.) When Motel 6 is full, try farther down N. Atlantic Ave. at the **Sunrise Motel** (800-348-0348) where Singles are $30 (each additional person $6). The **Beach Inn,** 8701 Astronaut Blvd. (Rte. A1A) (783-0361), in Cape Canaveral has big, old rooms that sleep up to four people. (Rooms $34; Jan.-April $44.) If you get stuck in Cocoa or need a place to spend the night between bus connections, walk right behind the Greyhound station to the **Dixie Motel,** 301 Forrest Ave. (632-1600), one block east of U.S. 1. for big clean rooms, a swimming pool, A/C, and friendly service. (Rooms $30 or $34 for a double, off-season.) Or pitch your tent at scenic **Jetty Park Campgrounds,** 400 East Jetty Rd. (783-7222), Cape Canaveral. (Sites $15, with hookup $20. Reservations necessary six months in advance.)

The Cocoa Beach area, 50 mi. east of Orlando, consists of mainland towns Cocoa and Rockledge, oceanfront towns Cocoa Beach and Cape Canaveral, and Merritt Island in between. **Route A1A** runs through Cocoa Beach and Cape Canaveral, and **North Atlantic Avenue** runs parallel to the beach. Inaccessible by bus, Cocoa Beach also has no local public transport. Cocoa, 8 mi. inland, is serviced by **Greyhound,**

302 Main St. (636-3917), from Orlando ($13). From the bus station, taxi fare to Cocoa Beach is about $14 (call 783-8294). A **shuttle** service (784-3831) connects Cocoa Beach with Orlando International Airport, Disney World (roundtrip $75 for 1 or 2 people), and the Kennedy Space Center (roundtrip only $45 1 or 2 people). Make reservations one day in advance and ask about special rates for groups of five or more.

The **Cocoa Beach Chamber of Commerce,** main office at 400 Fortenberry Rd., Merritt Island (459-2200; open Mon.-Fri. 8:30am-5pm), has information on special events and can provide suggestions on cheap, temporary housing. For a comprehensive list of restaurants and all kinds of information about the area, ask at the **Broward County Tourist Development Council** (453-0823 or 800-872-1969), at the Kennedy Space Center.

Cocoa Beach's **ZIP code** is 32922; the **area code** is 407.

Daytona Beach

Built for tourists, Daytona Beach changes with the seasons. In fall and winter it houses wide-lapelled senior citizens looking for sunshine. Spring Break brings thousands of tank-topped college students to its beaches for sun and fun, drinking and debauchery. In the summertime, it's quite literally a hot family vacation spot, with people from all over the country coming to sunbathe or to watch one of the eight major road races at the nearby **Daytona Speedway.** During any season, hundreds of cars roll along the beach within feet of sunbathers, or cruise the Atlantic Avenue strip. Hotels and fast food retaurants line the streets; if you're looking for scenery in Daytona Beach, forget it. Instead, stick to the balmy beaches and slap on the sunscreen.

Practical Information

Emergency: 911.

Visitor Information: Destination Daytona!, at the chamber of commerce, 126 E. Orange Ave., on City Island (255-0415 or 800-854-1234). Open Mon.-Fri. 9am-5pm.

Travelers Aid: 330 Magnolia (252-4752, 24 hrs.). Open Mon.-Fri. 8:30am-4:30pm.

Daytona Beach Regional Airport: 189 Midway Ave. (255-8441). The **Daytona-Orlando Transit Service (DOTS)** shuttle (257-5411) runs between Orlando's airport and Daytona, every 1¾ hr. Departing Orlando for Daytona 7am-11pm, Daytona for Orlando 4:30am-9pm. $22, $38 round-trip. Call one day ahead for reservations.

Amtrak: 2491 Old New York Ave., Deland (255-7076, 800-872-7245), 24 mi. west on Rte. 92. To: Orlando (2 per day, 1 hr., $7); Tampa (2 per day, 3 hr., $23); Ft. Lauderdale (1 per day, 6 hr., $49); Miami (1 per day, 7 hr., $53).

Greyhound: 138 S. Ridgewood Ave. (253-6576), 4 mi. west of the beach. Catch any of the several different routes to the beach at the Volusia County Terminal. To: Orlando (9 per day, 1 hr., $11.50); St. Augustine (6 per day, 1 hr., $10); Tampa (6 per day, 4 hr., $28); Ft. Lauderdale (11 per day, 7 hr., $32); Miami (12 per day, 8-10 hr., $45). Open Mon.-Sat. 5am-11pm, Sun. 11am-7pm.

Public Transport: Votran Transit Company (761-7700), at the corner of Palmetto and Bay on the mainland. Buses operate Mon.-Sat. 5:30am-6:30pm. Fare 60¢, transfers free. Free system maps available at hotels.

Taxi: AAA Cab Co., 253-2522. $1.80 for first 1/6-mi., 20¢ each additional 1/6-mi.

Car Rental: Alamo, at the airport (255-1511 or 800-327-9633). Sub-compact $23 per day, $90 per week with unlimited mi. Free drop-off in Jacksonville or Ft. Lauderdale. Must be 21 with credit card. $6 extra charge if under 25.

Help Lines: Rape Crisis and Sexual Abuse, 258-7273.

Post Office: 55 E. Granada Blvd., Ormond Beach (677-0333). Open Mon.-Fri. 8:30am-5pm, Sat. 9am-1pm. **ZIP code:** 32174.

Area Code: 904.

Daytona is 53 mi. northeast of Orlando and 90 mi. south of Jacksonville on Florida's northeast coast. The city of Daytona Beach is surrounded by water, with the Halifax River (Intracoastal Waterway) slicing through its middle and the Atlantic Ocean to the east. Central artery **Route A1A,** also known as **Atlantic Avenue,** is lined with cheesy hotels, tanning oil shops, and bars. **Broadway (U.S. 92)** divides Atlantic Ave. north-south. The beach, 23 mi. of hard-packed sand, encompasses four towns: hushed **Ormond Beach** to the north, rowdy **Daytona Beach** to the south, family-friendly **Daytona Beach Shores** farther south, and quiet **Ponce Inlet** at the very southern tip. Pay attention when hunting down street addresses, as the north-south streets often change numbering systems while passing through the various small towns along the ocean.

Accommodations and Camping

Almost all of Daytona's accommodations are on Atlantic Ave. (Rte. A1A), either on the beach or across the street; those off the beach offer the best deals. During Spring Break and big race weekends even the worst beach-back hotels become ridiculously overpriced; many cheaper and quieter hotels line the mainland along Ridgewood Ave. In summer and fall, prices plunge and most hotels offer special deals during the month of June when some rooms are $17. Cars are generally allowed on the beach from sunrise to sunset, with evening parking permitted in a few areas, but don't plan to sleep on these well-patrolled shores.

Daytona Beach International Youth Hostel, 140 S. Atlantic Ave. (258-6937), 1 block north of Broadway (U.S. 92). A big hostel near the beach with clean kitchen facilities and recreation room. Usually full of free-loving international students. All rooms have A/C or fans; most have TVs. Owner takes hostelers on day-long waterskiing trips (complete with barbeque dinner) to a freshwater lake for $12 AYH members, $16 nonmembers, even though this hostel is no longer AYH affiliated. Weekly: members $70. Key deposit $5. Lockers $1-2.

Camelia Hotel, 1055 N. Atlantic Ave. (252-9963), across the street from the beach, has cozy rooms decorated with furniture built by Joe, the Czech owner. All rooms have cable TV, A/C, and some have kitchens for an extra $4. Singles $18, doubles $22, each additional person $4 except during spring break (March-April) when singles are a negotiable $60 and $10 each additional person.

Monte Carlo Beach Motel, 825 S. Atlantic Ave. (255-0461) A friendly Italian family runs this pink and white motel surrounded by palm trees on the beach. Rooms with cable TV, A/C, and pool. Singles $20. Doubles $25 (during spring break a negotiable $60-$75 with $100 deposit). Kitchen use $5.

Nova Family Campground, 1190 Herbert St. (767-0095), in Port Orange south of Daytona Beach, 10 min. from the shore. Take bus #7 or 15 from downtown or the beach. Shady sites, pool, grocery store. Open Sun.-Thurs. 8am-6pm, Fri.-Sat. 8am-8pm. Sites $15, $17 with hookup. Open sites posted after hours; register the next day.

Tomoka State Park, 2099 N. Beach St. (677-3931), 8-9 mi. north of Daytona. Take bus #3 ("North Ridgewood") to Domicilio and walk 2 mi. north. Nature trails, a museum, and lots of shade. Open daily 8am-7:45pm. Sites $8, with hookup $10.

Food

Triple S Supermarket, 167 S. Atlantic Ave. (252-8431), across from the youth hostel, features deli sandwiches and subs ($2.50-4) during spring break.

B & B Fisheries, 715 Broadway (252-6542). Family-owned business almost lives up to its motto, "If it swims…we have it." Take-out broiled flounder or sea trout lunches under $4.50. Lobster specials for under $10. Open Mon.-Sat. 11am-9:30pm. Take-out service Mon.-Sat. 11:30am-8:30pm.

Manor Buffet, 101 Seabreeze Blvd. (253-3359) Stuff your face without draining your wallet. Dinners come with soup and salad bar. Mostly frequented by seniors—so don't show up in a wet swimsuit or Daisy Duke cutoffs. Menu low-sodium and low-fat. Lunch $3.50, dinner $4.50; drinks included. Open Mon.-Sat. 11am-3pm and 4-8pm, Sun. 11am-8pm.

Oyster Pub, 555 Seabreeze Blvd. (255-6348). A huge square bar where locals drink, eat hearty meat sandwiches ($2-4), or slurp up the raw oysters (25¢) served all day. Open daily 11:30am-3am. Happy hr. 4-7pm.

Gringo's Mexican Restaurant, 701 N. Atlantic Ave. (258-0610). Cozy place with good tacos and enchiladas. Plastic hornblower greets diners. Excellent enchilada combination platter $4.75. Open Mon.-Sat. 5-11pm.

Sights and Events

Daytona's beach is its *raison d'être.* During Spring Break, students from practically every college in the country come here to get a head and body start on summer. The beach itself resembles a traffic jam; dozens of cars, motorcycles, and rental dune buggies crawl along the hot sand. To avoid the inevitable gridlock, you'll have to arrive early (6 or 7am) and leave early (3pm or so). You'll pay $3 to drive onto the beach (allowed from sunrise to sunset), and police strictly enforce the 10 mph limit. Those in search of more beach and quiet should head north of Ormond to the undeveloped, uncrowded stretch between Ormond and Flagler Beach, or south to quiet **New Smyrna Beach,** or **Ponce Inlet.** The historic 175-ft. Ponce de Leon Inlet Lighthouse charges $3 (kids $1) and is open 10am to 7pm. (Call 761-1821 for info.)

If you grow tired of racing around Daytona's beaches, its many racing events will do it for you. Call 254-2700 for general info and 253-RACE for tickets to any one of the many racing events. February 1-16 is Speed Week (general admission $20-$25) and includes the **Daytona 500** (Feb. 19), the **Goody's 300** (Feb. 18), and the **ARCA 200 World Championship Race** (Feb. 12). The **Daytona Racefest** and the **Pepsi 400 NASCAR Winston Cup Series** kick into gear at the beginning of July (tickets $20-$45), and during the first weekend in March, Motorcycle Week culminates with the **Daytona 200 Motorcycle Classic** (Tickets $10). The **Daytona International Speedway** has daily tours 9am-5pm ($2, kids $1) when no races are scheduled. Finally, the **Birthplace of Speed Museum,** 160 Granada Blvd. (672-5657), depicts the history of racing in the Daytona Beach area. Open Tues.-Sat., 1-5 pm ($1, kids 50¢).

Entertainment

During Spring Break, concerts, hotel-sponsored parties, and other events cater to students questing for fun. Word of mouth provides the best info about these transient events and inevitable beach parties, but also check out the *Calendar of Events* and *SEE the best of Daytona Beach,* available at the Chamber of Commerce.

As for nightclubs, **600 North Attitudes,** 600 N. Atlantic Ave. (255-4471) and next door **G.B. Reef's** are hot spots during Spring Break. **Razzle's** 611 Seabreeze Blvd. (257-6236) boasts of free drinks between 8 and 10pm for those wearing miniskirts and other such gimmicks, and **Finky's,** 640 Grandview (255-5059) motto is "I got kinky at. . ."

For more mellow nights head for the boardwalk where you can play volleyball, pinball, listen to music at the Oceanfront Bandshell, or park ($1) on the beach till 1am.

Fort Lauderdale

Every spring thousands of pale, lust-crazed college students flock to Fort Lauderdale, the official U.S. Spring Break party capital. Lately, however, the Spring Break crowds have begun to thin out and head to places a little more fun, in response to open-container laws and crack-downs on drunk driving, fake IDs, and indecent exposure.

In off-season, tourists less preoccupied with carnal fulfillment and more apprecia-tive of the land and ocean's beauty stroll the wide beach. Broad-sailed boats and luxury yachts cruise the coast or anchor at the city's canals and ports. When the Spring Break parties finally end, Fort Lauderdale breathes a huge sigh of relief.

Practical Information

Emergency: 911.

Visitor Information: Chamber of Commerce, 512 NE 3rd Ave. (462-6000), 3 blocks off Fed-eral Hwy. at 5th St. Pick up the helpful *Visitor's Guide.* Open Mon.-Fri. 8am-5pm.

Fort Lauderdale/Hollywood International Airport: 3½ mi. south of downtown on U.S. 1 (Federal Hwy.), at exits 26 and 27 on I-95.

Amtrak: 200 SW 21st Terrace (463-8251 or 800-872-7245), just west of I-95, ¼-mi. south of Broward Blvd. Take bus #9, 10, or 81 from downtown. Daily service on "The Floridian" to: Miami (2 per day, 1½ hr., $6); Orlando (1 per day, 4 hr., $42); and Jacksonville (1 per day, 6 hr., $63). Open daily 7:30am-6:45pm.

Greyhound/Trailways: 513 NE 3rd St. (764-6551), 3 blocks north of Broward Blvd. at Fed-eral Hwy., downtown. Unsavory location, especially at night. To: Orlando (4 per day, 3 hr., $39); Daytona Beach (4-5 per day, 3 hr., $32); and Tampa (4 per day, 2½ hr., $45). Open 24 hrs.

Public Transport: Broward County Transit (BCT), 357-8400 (call Mon.-Fri. 7am-7pm, Sat. 8am-5pm, Sun. 8am-4pm). Extensive regional coverage. Most routes go to the terminal at the corner of 1st St. NW and 1st Ave. NW, downtown. Operates daily 6am-9pm every ½-hr. on most routes. Fare 85¢, seniors 40¢, students with ID 40¢, transfers 10¢. 7-day passes $8, available at beachfront hotels. Pick up a handy system map at the **Broward County Office Plaza,** 115 S. Andrews Ave., 1 block south of Broward Blvd. **Tri-Rail** (1-800-TRI-RAIL) connects West Palm Beach, Ft. Lauderdale and Miami. Trains run Mon.-Sat. 5am-9:30pm. Pick up schedules at the airport or at Tri-Rail stops. Fare $2, students and seniors with ID $1.

Car Rental: Alamo, 2601 S. Federal Hwy. (525-4715 or 800-327-9633). Cheapest cars $28 per day, $100 per week. Unlimited mi., free drop-off in Daytona and Miami. Free shuttle to airport. Must be 21 with credit card, or deposit ($50 per day, $200 per week) through travel agent.

Bike Rentals: International Bicycle Shop, 1900 E. Sunrise Blvd. at N. Federal Hwy. (764-8800). Take bus #10 from downtown or bus #36 from A1A north of Sunrise. $10 per day, $35 per week. $100 deposit. Open Mon.-Fri. 10am-9pm, Sat. 9am-9pm, Sun. 11am-5pm. No minimum age. Avoid the expensive joints on the beach.

Taxi: Yellow Cab (565-5400). **Public Service Taxi** (587-9090).

Help Line: Crisis Hotline, 467-6333. Open 24 hrs.

Post Office: 1900 W. Oakland Park Blvd. (527-2028). Open Mon.-Fri. 7:30am-5pm, Sat. 8:30am-2pm. **ZIP code:** 33319.

Area Code: 305.

Because I-95, which runs north-south and connects the three cities, is undergoing construction through 1992, it is often congested. **Alligator Alley** (Rte. 84/I-75) slithers 100 mi. west from Ft. Lauderdale across the Everglades to Naples and other small cities on the Gulf Coast of southern Florida. Ft. Lauderdale is bigger than it looks. The city extends westward from its 23 mi. of beach to encompass nearly 450 sq. mi. of land area. Most of the maps show distances deceptively; when travel-ing from the beach to downtown, take a bus. Roads are divided into two types: streets and boulevards (east-west) and avenues (north-south). All are labeled NW, NE, SW, or SE according to the quadrant. **Broward Boulevard** divides the city east-west, **Andrews Avenue** north-south. The unpleasant downtown centers around the intersection of **Federal Highway** (U.S. 1) and **Las Olas Boulevard,** about 2 mi. west of the oceanfront. Between downtown and the waterfront, yachts fill the ritzy inlets of the **Intracoastal Waterway.** The strip (variously called Rte. A1A, N. Atlantic Blvd., 17th St. Causeway, Ocean Blvd., and Seabreeze Blvd.) runs along the beach for 4 mi. between **Oakland Park Boulevard** to the north and Las Olas Blvd. to the south. Las Olas Blvd. is the pricey shopping street; **Sunrise Boulevard** has most shopping malls. Both degenerate into ugly commercial strips west of downtown.

Accommodations and Camping

Hotel prices vary from slightly unreasonable to absolutely ridiculous, increasing exponentially as you approach prime beachfront. High season runs from mid-February to early April. Investigate package deals at the slightly worse-for-wear hotels along the strip in Ft. Lauderdale. Many hotels offer off-season deals for under $30.

Small motels crowd each other one or two blocks off the beach area; many offer efficiencies. Look along Birch Rd., one block back from Rte. A1A. **The Broward County Hotel and Motel Association** (462-0409) provides a free directory of area hotels. (Open Mon.-Fri. 9am-4:30pm.) Scan the *Ft. Lauderdale News* and the Broward Section of the *Miami Herald* for occasional listings of local residents who rent rooms to tourists in spring. Call 357-8100 for general info on camping in Broward County. Sleeping on the well-patrolled beaches is impossible between 9pm and sunrise.

Sol Y Mar Youth Hostel (AYH), 2839 Vistamar St. (566-1023), 2 blocks west of Rte. A1A, 1 block south of Sunrise Blvd. From downtown, take bus #40 to the intersection of Birch and Vista Mar. Clean and new two-room apartments with 6-8 beds and shower. Recreation room, barbecue, and nice pool. 5-min. walk to beach. Office open 7:30-10am and 5-7pm. $11, nonmembers $14.

International Youth Hostel, 905 NE 17th Terrace (467-0452). From downtown, take bus #10 to NE 15th Ave. and Sunrise Blvd. Walk east on Sunrise to NE 17th Terrace. Pick-up at bus station available. Shuttle service throughout FL. Rooms with 7 beds and shower, A/C. Members $7, nonmembers $8.

Estoril Apartments, 2648 NE 32nd St. 33306 (563-3840; 800-548-9398 reservations only), 2 blocks west of the Intracoastal Waterway and 1 block north of Oakland Park Blvd. From downtown, take bus #20, #10 or #55 to Coral Ridge Shopping Center and walk 2 blocks east on Oakland. Students probably can persuade the proprietors to pick them up from the bus station or airport. A 10-min. walk to the beach. Very clean rooms with A/C, TV, and small kitchenette. Pool and barbecue. Students with *Let's Go* receive 10% discount. Office closes about 11pm. May-Dec.: singles $26; doubles $28. Jan.-April: singles $38; doubles $40. Additional person $6 off-season, $10 on-season. Reservations recommended.

Motel 6, 1801 State Rd. 84 (760-7999), 3 blocks east of I-95 and 3 mi. southwest of downtown. Take bus #14 to Rte. 84 and SW 15th Ave. and walk 3 blocks west. Far from the action. Clean, no-frills rooms. Singles $31 May-Sept., $36 Oct.-April Doubles $38 May-Sept., $45 Oct.-April.

Ocean Lodge, 200-300 S. Ocean Blvd., Pompano Beach (942-2030), near the Ft. Lauderdale border on A1A. From downtown, take bus #11 north up A1A. Clean, attractive rooms. May-Dec. singles $29, doubles $33. Jan.-April singles $43, doubles $49.

Easterlin County Park, 1000 NW 38th St., Oakland Park (938-0610), northwest of the intersection of Oakland Park and I-95, less than 4 mi. west of the strip and 3 mi. north of downtown. Take bus #14 from downtown to NW 38th St. or #72 along Oakland Park to Powerline Rd. By car take Sample exit from I-95. 2-week max. stay. Registration open 24 hrs. Sites with electricity, barbecue pits, and picnic table $17.

Quiet Waters County Park, 6601 N. Powerline Rd. (NW 9th Ave.), Pompano Beach (360-1315), 10 mi. north of Oakland Park Blvd. I-95 exit 37. From downtown, take bus #14. Cramped, commercialized, but friendly. Bizarre 8-person "boatless water skiing" and other water sports. No electricity. Check-in 2-6pm. Fully equipped campsites (tent, mattresses, cooler, grill, canoe) for up to 6 people, Sun.-Thurs. $17, Fri.-Sat. $25 plus $20 refundable deposit. 2-night min. stay.

Food

The clubs along the strip offer massive quantities of free grub during Happy Hour: surfboard-sized platters of wieners, chips, and hors d'oeuvres, or all-you-can-eat pizza and buffets. However, these bars have hefty cover charges (from $5) and expect you to buy a drink once you're there (from $2). In addition, these bars are nightclubs, not restaurants, and the quality of their cuisine proves it. The restaurants below serve "real" food.

La Spada's, 4346 Seagrape Drive (776-7893). Two blocks from the beach, off Commercial Blvd. Best, and biggest, subs in southern Florida. Try the ft.-long Italian ($6.50). Open Mon.-Sat. 10am-8pm, Sun. 11am-8pm.

Golden Chopsticks, 4350 N. Federal Hwy. (776-0953). Some of the best Chinese food in town. For a treat, try the Steak Kew ($11). Most of the uniformly delicious food is more reasonably priced. Open Mon.-Fri. 11:30am-11pm Sat.-Sun. 1-11pm.

Southport Raw Bar, 1536 Cordova Rd. (525-2526), by the 17th St. Causeway behind the Southport Mall on the Intracoastal Waterway. Take bus #40 from the strip or #30 from downtown. Aggressively marine decor. Spicy conch chowder $2, fried shrimp $4.95. Open Mon.-Sat. 11am-2am, Sun. noon-midnight.

Tina's Spaghetti House, 2110 S. Federal Hwy. (522-9943), just north of 17th St. Take bus #10 from downtown. Authentic red-checkered tablecloths and hefty oak furniture. Popular with locals since 1952. Lunch specials $4-5. Spaghetti dinner $6-7. Open Mon.-Thurs. 11:30am-10pm, Fri. 11:30am-11pm, Sat. 4-11pm, Sun. 4-9pm.

Grandma's Ice Cream, 3354 N. Ocean Blvd. (564-3671), just north of Oakland Park Blvd. Take bus #11 from downtown. Easily recognizable by the bright red 1901 Oldsmobile truck outside. Renowned for its incredible cinnammon ice cream. Open Sun.-Thurs. noon-10pm, Fri.-Sat. noon-11pm.

Sin

Ft. Lauderdale offers all kinds of licit and illicit entertainment by night. Mostly illicit. Planes flying over the beach hawk hedonistic Happy Hours at local watering spots. Students frequent the night spots on the A1A strip along the beach, with an emphasis on the word "strip." When going out, bring a driver's license or a passport as proof of age; most bars and nightclubs don't accept college IDs. Be warned that this is not the place for cappuccino and conversation, but for nude jello wrestling and other lubricated competitions.

For those who prefer garbed service, several popular nightspots line N. Atlantic Blvd. next to the beach. **The Candy Store** 1 N. Atlantic Blvd. (766-1888) was once at the pinnacle of Ft. Lauderdale nightlife. It's still a great hangout for drinking and people-watching. Get there for the all-you-can-eat afternoon pizza. (Open Mon.-Fri. 11am-2am, Sat. 11am-3am. Cover $5.) Also try **Banana Joe's on the Beach,** 837 N. Atlantic Blvd. (565-4446), at Sunrise and A1A. (Open Mon.-Fri. 7am-2am, Sat. 7am-3am, Sun. noon-2am. Kitchen open at 10:30am.) For off-the-beach entertainment, Ft. Lauderdale's new hotspot is **Crocco's World Class Sports Bar** 3339 N. Federal Hwy. (566-2406). Built in an old movie theater, this gargantuan club has lines out the door almost every night. (Open Sun.-Fri 11am-2am, Sat. 11am-3am.) If you are willing to pay for a laugh, **The Comic Strip,** 1432 N. Federal Hwy (565-8887), is a sure thing. (Sun.-Fri. shows at 9:30pm, Sat. shows at 9 and 11:30pm. Cover $10, 2-drink minimum. Drinks run $3 or more.)

Sights and Activities

Besides sun and sin, Ft. Lauderdale is pretty low on activities. To see why Ft. Lauderdale is called the "Venice of America," take a tour of its waterways aboard the **Jungle Queen,** located at the **Bahia Mar Yacht Center** on Rte. A1A, 3 blocks south of Las Olas Blvd. (3-hr. tours daily at 10am and 2pm. Fare $7, kids $5.) For more intimate acquaintance with the ocean, **Water Sports Unlimited,** 301 Seabreeze Blvd. (467-1316), offers equipment for a variety of water sports. Located on the beach, Water Sports offers wave runners ($55), motor boats ($40 per hour, $220 per day), parasailing trips ($40 per ride) and waterskiing early in the morning ($30 per tow).

Atlantis the Water Kingdom, 2700 Stirling Rd. (926-1000), is the third largest water theme park in the U.S. Admission includes unlimited use of the Slidewinder water slides and the Raging Rampage. If rain interrupts your day at Atlantis for 45 consecutive minutes or more, you receive a free raincheck to return another day. (Open summer Mon.-Thurs. 10am-8pm, Fri.-Sat. 10am-10pm; off-season call for hours. Admission $13, seniors $7, ages 3-11 $10, under 3 free. Head south on I-95, exit at Stirling Rd., and turn left under the overpass.)

Jacksonville and the North Coast

Locals are fond of summing up Jacksonville (pop. 918,000) with a telling geographic fact: if the Georgia-Florida border didn't take a sudden jag northward, "Jax" would be a large Georgia city instead of a town suffering from an inferiority complex next to in-state rivals like Miami, Tampa/St. Petersburg, and Orlando.

Tourists won't find much to keep them in Jacksonville for long. None of the town's three main industries—health care, paper products, and the military—hold much interest for non-locals, and you may in fact be repulsed by the pervasive stench of the paper mills. However, the recent expansion and renovation of Jacksonville International Airport, along with excellent Greyhound and Amtrak connections, make Jax a good base for beginning explorations of the American Southeast. Orlando is four hours away by car; Miami and the Keys lie to the south on I-95; and Tampa and Atlanta lie to the west and northwest, respectively. Finally, the Jacksonville Beaches to the east are beautiful, largely unexploited stretches of white sand, warm waters, and bright sun.

Practical Information

Emergency: 911.

Jacksonville Convention and Visitors Bureau, 6 E. Bay St. #200 (353-9736), 1½ blocks from the Jacksonville Landing. The free map of Duval County is a must in this sprawling city, although you're better off paying for a more detailed version. Pick up coupons for local hotels, when available, along with a Visitors' Guide. Open Mon.-Fri. 7:30am-5pm.

Jacksonville International Airport, Airport Rd. (741-4902), 20 mi. north of downtown off I-95. A recent renovation and expansion is all-but-finished, and Jacksonville is served by most major national carriers.

Amtrak: 3570 Clifford Lane (locally 766-5110 or 800-872-7245), 6 mi. northwest of downtown off U.S. 1. To Miami ($70), Washington, DC ($127), and Savannah ($33). Open 24 hrs.

Greyhound/Trailways: 10 Pearl St. (356-5521), downtown. Plenty of blue plastic seats. A/C. To: Miami ($57); St. Augustine ($6.50); New Orleans ($78); and Washington, DC ($84). Open 24 hrs.

Public Transport: Jacksonville Transportation Authority, 100 N. Myrtle St. (630-3100), downtown. Info kiosk at the intersection of W. Forsyth and N. Hogan St. Open Mon.-Fri. 6am-6pm. **BH-1** and **BH-2** buses go to the beach. Catch them near the corner of Pearl and Bay St., or in **Hemming Plaza,** a block away. BH-1 goes to Atlantic Blvd.; BH-2 to Beach Blvd. Fare $1.10. **Ferry** across St. John's River (251-3331) operates daily every ½-hr. 6:20am-10:15pm; it runs between Fort George Island at the end of Hecksher Dr., and Mayport, near the Naval Station at the northern end of the beaches. Cars $1.50, pedestrians 10¢, but fares are expected to rise soon.

Taxi: Yellow Cab, 354-5511. Base fare $1.25, $1.25 per mi.

Car Rental: Alamo, 1735 Airport Rd. (741-4428), 5 min. from the terminal by free Alamo Shuttle. Sub-compacts $18-22 per day, $69-79 per week. $50 drop-off fee in other FL cities. Open 24 hrs. Must be 21; $6 charge if under 25. Must have credit card or $100 deposit through a travel agent, $50 deposit if you pay 14 days in advance.

Post Office: 311 W. Monroe (359-2841), downtown. Open Mon.-Fri. 8:30am-5pm, Sat. 9am-1pm. The General Delivery ZIP code is 32201.

Area Code: 904.

Jacksonville has three distinct areas, each a half-hour to an hour drive from the other. The first area, known as Jacksonville's Beaches, includes **Atlantic Beach, Neptune Beach,** and **Jacksonville Beach** from north to south. North of the St. John's River, on **Rte. A1A,** two more long stretches of beach make up part of **Fort Clinch State Park** and **Little Talbot State Park.** The third and last area, downtown Jacksonville, is of little interest beyond its shops and museums and can be *very* dangerous after dark. Major thoroughfares **Atlantic Boulevard, Beach Boulevard** and **J. Turner Blvd.** run through the dead zone between Jacksonville and its beaches. Once in the beach region, **3rd Street** is the main drag, running parallel to the shore. Downtown is bisected by **Main Street,** which runs north from the north bank of the St. John's River. **Bay Street,** along the shore of St. John's River, and **Union Street** run east-west in the downtown area.

Jacksonville lies at the eastern terminus of **I-10. I-95** also runs through Jax on its way from South Florida.

Accommodations and Camping

The biggest problem with Jacksonville accommodations is getting to them. The long distances can be frustrating, and unless you have a car or a fat bankroll for taxicabs, some of the places are darn near impossible to reach. If you get in late in the day, stay at a cheap airport hotel such as **Motel 6,** 10885 Hark Rd., Dunn Ave./Busch Dr. exit off I-95 (757-8600; singles $23), or the **Airport Motor Inn,** 1500 Airport Rd. (741-4331); singles as low as $20).

The best place to stay in the area is at the Beaches, 20 minutes to half an hour east of downtown on the Atlantic Coast. The **Salt Air Motel,** 425 Atlantic Blvd. (246-6465), offers bright clean rooms on overdeveloped Atlantic Blvd. (Singles from $25. Doubles from $33. Call for reservations in summer.) The motto on the sign at the **Atlantic Shores,** 923 S. First St. (249-2663), says it all: "Not the best, but we try." (Singles $35. Doubles $40. Subtract $5 in winter. Weekly: singles $200, doubles $225.) The **Sea Ranch Motel,** 27 S. First St. (249-9778) has dark but tolerable rooms right on the ocean, with A/C and cable TV. (Singles $34, but only three available. Doubles $38-44. Weekly rates. Phone deposit $2.)

The only campground accessible by public transportation is **Kathryn Abbey Hanna Park,** on Wonderwood Rd., Mayport (249-4700), south of Mayport Naval Base and north of Atlantic Beach. (Sites $10, campers $13.50. Park admission 50¢.) If you have a car, clinch a place at **Fort Clinch,** Rte. A1A (261-4212), on the St. John's River. (Sites $17, with car $19, with electricity $21. $5 less in winter. No pets.) Even less of a cinch to get to, **Little Talbot Island State Park** (251-3231) lies 15 mi. south of Fort Clinch. (Sites $16, with electricity $18.)

Food

Rapid urban development and summer tourist crowds in Jacksonville have encouraged the growth of expensive "surf-and-turf" seafood restaurants, but has failed to generate anything approaching a major metropolitan cuisine. Try local favorite **Patti's,** 7300 Beach Blvd. (725-1662), which has zesty spaghetti and other excellent Italian dishes. (Open Sun.-Thurs. 3-10pm, Fri.-Sat. 5-11pm.) Or check out **Bono's Barbeque,** at 4907 Beach Blvd., 2-3 mi. east of downtown. Jacksonville's best ethnic cuisine is served up at the Afghan **Khyber Pass,** 2578 Atlantic Blvd. (398-1121), where lunches range from $2.25 to 5.75 and dinners go from $7-14. (Open Mon.-Sat. 11am-2pm and 5-10:30pm.) The Mexican **Campeche Bay,** 8120 Atlantic Blvd. (727-5050), features a creative cornucopia of combinations costing $6-12. (Open daily 5-10pm; bar open daily 4pm-2am.)

If you are downtown, look for cheap cuisine upstairs at the Jacksonville Landing, which has counters serving large portions of everything from pizza to egg foo-young.

Sights and Entertainment

Jacksonville has virtually no sights of historic interest because the entire city burned to the ground early in the century. To compensate, the city built a flashy new mall called the **Jacksonville Landing** on the downtown waterfront, and created the **Riverwalk** on the opposite bank. Kill an afternoon in town at the **Cummer Gallery,** 829 Riverside Ave. (336-6857), one block from the river, which has an excellent art collection and gorgeous Italian-style gardens. (Open Tues.-Fri. 10am-4pm, Sat. noon-5pm, Sun. 2-5pm. Donation.) The **Jacksonville Art Museum,** 4160 Boulevard Center Dr. (398-8336), has Chinese porcelain and pre-Columbian and modern art, as well as works by contemporary regional artists. A major Andrew Wyeth exhibit will open here in January 1992. (Open Tues.-Fri. 10am-4pm, Thurs. 10am-10pm, Sat.-Sun. 1-5pm.) Microscope out the **Museum of Science and History,** 1025 Gulf Life Dr. on the Southbank Riverwalk (396-7062), for its planetarium, endangered species aviary, and hands-on exhibits. (Open Mon.-Thurs. 10am-5pm, Fri.-Sat. 10am-6pm, Sunday 1-6pm. Admission $5, seniors, students, military, and kids $3.) If you have a car and a hankering to head for the mountains, take a 7-mi. drive from downtown to the **Anheuser-Busch Brewery,** 111 Busch Dr. (751-8116), for the self-guided tour, a film of the beer-making process, and free samples. (Open Oct.-April Mon.-Sat. 9am-4pm; May-Sept. Mon.-Sat. 10am-5pm. Free.)

Yet the beach, not the beer, is Jacksonville's main attraction. Golden and white sands extend most of the way south along the coast from Ponte Vedra to Fernandina. Neptune and Atlantic, two of the Jacksonville Beaches, attract the largest crowds, but the contrasting crystal blue sea and white sand make them well worth the trip.

Though they still lack that coveted NFL franchise, Jacksonvilleans remain a sports-minded crowd. The **Gator Bowl,** (396-1800), east of downtown, hosts the New Year's Day Mazda Gator Bowl college football game, and the **Tournament Players Championship** golf tournament (285-7888) is held in the last week of March at the TPC course in Ponte Verda, one of the toughest courses on the PGA tour (and home of the infamous 17th hole, which is on an *island)*. Jacksonvilleans also get out of their seats and lace on their running shoes for March's **River Run** (630-0837), a 15km challenge that attracts 8,000 runners, including some nationally-ranked racers.

For a closer look at the strong military presence in Jacksonville, head out to **Mayport Naval Base** (270-5011). The Base offers a **Visit Ship Program,** in which a home-ported ship is opened to weekend walk-through tours of about an hour. Call 270-6289 for info on tour availability. (This is a conservative town. The last mayor was voted out of office in part due to a backlash against an election rally at which he had Casey Kasem, D.J. and anti-Gulf War activist, as a speaker.)

After a day at the beach, try a night at **Fat Tuesday's,** Jacksonville Landing (353-0444), for ready-mixed ice drinks, music, finger food, and sandwiches from $5.

The Keys

The coral rock islands, mangrove trees, and relaxed attitude of the people make the Florida Keys pleasant places to visit and live. With a character quite different from anywhere else in the U.S., these islands off the coast could be a country in themselves. The Keys enjoy settings more Caribbean than Floridian, with cool breezes at night, wild tropical rainstorms, and of course sun hot enough to cook thick steaks or skin. When the sun does set, clouds, heat lightning, and surrounding ocean provide an incredible accompaniment. Approximately 6 mi. offshore, 100-yd. wide barrier reefs lie parallel to the Keys from Key Largo south to Key West. Adored by divers, these reefs harbor some of the ocean's most diverse and colorful marine life as well as hundreds of wrecked ships and legendary lost treasure. There are also *very* few sharks.

The Keys run southwest into the ocean from the southern tip of Florida, accessible by the **Overseas Highway (U.S. 1)**. **Mile markers,** which divide the highway into sections, replace street addresses to indicate the location of homes and businesses. They begin with mile 126 in Florida City and end with zero on the corner of Whitehead and Fleming St. in Key West.

Greyhound runs two buses per day to Key West from Miami, stopping in Coral Gables, Perrine, Homestead, Key Largo (451-3664), Marathon (743-3488), Big Pine Key, and Key West (296-9072). If there's a particular mile marker at which you need to get off, most drivers can be convinced to stop at the side of the road. Biking along U.S. 1 across the swamps between Florida City and Key Largo is impossible because the road lacks shoulders: Bring your bike on the bus.

The **area code** on the Keys is 305.

Key Largo

After crossing the thick swamps and crocodile marshland of Upper Florida Bay, Key Largo wheels out the first welcome of the Keys. Though a gateway of sorts—much like the wardrobe to magical Narnia—Largo is one of the longer Keys. Without a car it can be difficult to get around, although everything of importance lies within a 6-mi. range. Largo's **John Pennecamp State Park,** mile 102.5 (451-1202), 60 mi. from Miami, provides the visitor with a rare though somewhat murky view from glass-bottomed boats of the living reef off the Keys ($14). Mostly offshore, the beautiful state park has the largest uninterrupted stretch of the barrier reef in the Keys, the only underwater park in the country, and the only underwater Christ statue in the world. (Admission $3.25 for vehicle operator, each additional person 50¢. Camp sites $24, with hookup $26.) The **Coral Reef Company** (451-1621) sails visitors 6 mi. past mangrove swamps to the reef. (Snorkeling tours daily at 9am, noon, and 3pm. 1½ hr. of water time and a quickie lesson including gear for $22, kids $18.)

The **Italian Fisherman,** mile 104 (451-4471), has it all: fine food and a spectacular view of Florida Bay. Formerly an illegal gambling casino, this restaurant was the locale of some scenes from Bogart and Bacall's movie *Key Largo*. (Dinners $7-17. Open daily 11am-11pm.) The seafood and 99-beer selection at **Crack'd Conch,** mile 105 (451-0732), is superb. Try the "Sorry Charlie" tuna fish sandwich ($4.50) or an entire key lime pie ($7.50). (Open Thurs.-Tues. noon-10pm.) With four locations, **Perry's,** serves fresh local seafood and charbroiled steaks, at mile 102 (451-1834); Islamorada, mile 82.5 (664-5066); Marathon, mile 52 (743-3108); and the most famous location at Key West, 3800 N. Roosevelt Blvd (294-8472). (Lunch $4-10, dinner $8-23. Open daily 11am-11pm.) They also offer a "you hook 'em, we cook 'em" service for $2.50. Other scenes from *Key Largo* were filmed at the **Carribean Club,** mile 104, a friendly local bar. The in-house band *Nasty Habits* dishes out hard rock to the locals; snapshots of Bogart and Bacall grace the walls. (Open daily 7am-4am.) When you're starring in your own late-night show, call **Island Cab** (745-2200) for a ride home.

After the state park's campsites fill up, try crowded but well-run **Kings Kamp Marina,** mile 103.5 (451-0010; sites by the bay $18). Look for the concealed entrance on the northwest (gulf) side of U.S. 1. The **Hungry Pelican,** mile 99.5 (451-3576), has beautiful bougainvillea vines in the trees and friendly managers Tom and Jerry Ray. Stuff your beak full in a clean, cozy trailer or room with a double bed ($30-55). The only other budget option, the **Sea Trails Motel** (852-8001), mile 98.5 on the bayside, has large but plain rooms with A/C, one double bed and one twin bed ($35).

The **Florida Upper Keys Chamber of Commerce,** mile 105.5 (451-1414), at Rte. 905, has maps and brochures on local attractions, including scenes from the film *Key Largo*. (Open Mon.-Fri. 9am-5pm.) The **visitors center,** mile 103.4 (451-1414 or 800-822-1088) in the pink shopping center, has a cinematic selection of maps and brochures. (Open daily 9am-5pm.) The dramatic mailroom scene from *Key*

Largo was filmed at the **post office,** mile 100 (451-3155; open Mon.-Fri. 8am-4:30pm, Sat. 8am-noon). Key Largo's **ZIP code** is 33037; the **area code** is 305.

Key West

This is the end of the road. When searching for a tropical paradise, you can do no better than Key West. The island's pastel clapboard houses, hibiscus and bougainvillea vines, year-round tropical climate, and gin-clear waters make it a beautiful spot to visit in summer or winter.

Key West inhabitants have made their living salvaging wrecked ships, rolling cigars, gathering sponges, fishing for turtles and shrimp, and overcharging tourists for souvenirs. A railroad provided the original access to the island in 1912, built by, you guessed it, a railroad magnate, Henry Flagler. A hurricane not only blew the stuffing out of the railroad, but tossed the dirt that Flagler used to fill some of the smaller channels into the ocean. Flagler's legacy to Key West remains with **Indian Key Fill,** the old railroad bridge running parallel to the highway in some spots, and his cameo scene in *Key Largo.*

Like most of this region, the city of Key West has a relaxed atmosphere, hot sunshine, and spectacular sunsets, over the years attracting travelers and famous authors like Tennessee Williams, Ernest Hemingway, Elizabeth Bishop, and Robert Frost. Today, an easygoing diversity still attracts those outside the mainstream—a new generation of writers and artists, gay people, recluses, adventurers, and eccentrics.

Practical Information

Emergency: 911.

Visitor Information: Key West Chamber of Commerce, 402 Wall St. (294-2587), in old Mallory Sq. Useful Humm's *Guide to the Florida Keys and Key West* available here. Accommodations list notes guest houses popular with gay people. Open daily 9am-5pm. **Key West Visitors Bureau,** P.O. Box 1147, Key West 33041 (296-3811 or 800-352-5397), produces a detailed guide to accommodations. Open Mon.-Fri. 9am-5pm. **Key West Welcome Center,** 3840 N. Roosevelt Blvd. (296-4444 or 800-284-4482), just north of the intersection of U.S. 1 and Roosevelt Blvd. Arranges accommodations, theater tickets, weddings, and reef trips if you call in advance. Open daily 8:45am-5:30pm.

Key West International Airport: on the southeast corner of the island. Serviced by Eastern and Piedmont airlines. No public bus service.

Greyhound/Trailways: 615½ Duval St. (296-9072). Obscure location in an alley behind Antonio's restaurant. To Miami stopping along all the Keys (3 per day, 5 hr., $33). Open Mon.-Fri. 6:40am-12:45pm and 7-8pm, Sat. 6:40am-noon.

Public Transport: Key West Port and Transit Authority, City Hall (292-8159 or 292-8164). One bus (Old Town) runs clockwise around the island and Stock Island; the other (Mallory St.) runs counterclockwise. Pick up a clear and helpful free map from the chamber of commerce or any bus driver. Service Mon.-Sat. 6am-10pm, Sun. 6:40am-6:40pm. Fare 75¢, seniors and students 35¢. **Handicapped Transportation,** 294-8468.

Taxi: Key West Independent, 294-7277.

Car Rental: Alamo, Key Wester Inn, 975 S. Roosevelt Blvd. (294-6675 or 800-327-9633), near the airport. $33 per day, $132 per week. Under 25 $5 per day extra. Must be 21 with major credit card or $50 deposit through a travel agent. Drop-off in Miami a prohibitive $75.

Bike Rental: Key West Hostel, 718 South St. (296-5719). $6 per day, $30 per week. Open daily 8am-noon and 5-8pm. $20 deposit.

Help Line: 296-4357.

Post Office: 400 Whitehead St. (294-2257), 1 block west of Duval at Eaton. Open Mon.-Fri. 8:30am-5pm. **ZIP code:** 33040.

Area Code: 305.

Just 5 mi. long and 3 mi. wide and the southernmost point on the continental U.S., Key West lies at the end of Rte. 1, 160 mi. southwest of Miami. Only 90 mi. north of Havana, Cuba, Key West dips farther south than many islands in the Bahamas.

Divided into two sectors, the eastern part of the island, called "Des Moines" or "America" by some, harbors the tract houses, chain motels, shopping malls, and the airport. **Old Town,** the west side of town below White St., is cluttered with beautiful old conch houses. **Duval Street** is the main north-south thoroughfare in Old Town, **Truman Avenue** the major east-west route. Key West is cooler than mainland Florida in summer, and much warmer in winter.

On the way to and in the city of Key West, driving is slow; most of the highway is a two-lane road with only an occasional passing lane. Bikers beware: police enforce traffic laws. Use hand signals, stop at signs, and watch for one-way streets.

Accommodations and Camping

Beautiful weather resides year-round in Key West alongside tourists. As a result, good rooms at the nicer hotels go for up to $400 per day, especially during the winter holidays. There is no "off-season." Key West remains packed virtually year-round, with a lull of sorts from mid-September to mid-December; even then, don't expect to find a room for less than $40.

Try to bed down in Old Key West; the beautiful, 19th-century clapboard houses capture the flavor of the Keys. Some of the guest houses in the Old Town offer complimentary breakfasts and some are for gay men exclusively. During the busy spring months, police tend to look the other way when people park overnight at the pullouts by the Keys' bridges.

Key West Hostel, 718 South St. (296-5719), at Sea Shell Motel in Old Key West, 6 blocks west of Duval St. Take any bus to the corner of South and Reynolds St. Even has its own postcards. Rooms with 4 beds, shared bath. A/C at night. Dinners $1. Kitchen open until 9pm. No curfew. Office open daily 8am-10pm. $12, nonmembers $14. Key deposit $5. Motel rooms in summer $45, in winter $75. Call ahead to check availability; also call for late arrival.

Caribbean House, 226 Petronia St. (296-1600; 800-736-0179; 800-543-4518), at Thomas St. in Bahama Village. Brand new, Caribbean-style rooms with cool tile floors, A/C, TV, and ceiling fans. Comfy double beds. Norman, the friendly owner, may be able to place you in the completely furnished Caribbean Cottage (sleeps 5) or an unfurnished low-rent apartment for comfortable summer living. In-season: rooms $55, cottage $75. Summer: rooms $35, cottage $55.

Island House, 1129 Fleming St. (294-6284), at White St. Take any bus to the corner of White and Fleming. For gay men only. Rooms with A/C, fans, and radio; slick, ritzy atmosphere and decor. Sauna, pool, jacuzzi, and weight room. Singles in summer with shared bath $65; in winter $85.

Tilton Hilton, 511 Angela St. (294-8697), next to the Greyhound station near downtown. Plain rhyming rooms, as cheap as you'll find. Color TV, A/C. Singles in summer $32, in winter $50.

Boyd's Campground, 6401 Maloney Ave. (294-1465), on Stock Island. Take bus to Maloney Ave. from Stock Island. 12 acres on the ocean. Full facilities, including showers. Primitive sites $21. Water and electricity $5 extra, A/C or heat $5 extra. Waterfront sites $3 extra.

Food

Expensive restaurants line festive Duval Street. Side streets offer lower prices and fewer crowds. Stock up on supplies at **Fausto's Food Palace,** 522 Fleming St. (296-5663), the best darn grocery store in Old Town. (Open Mon.-Sat. 8am-8pm, Sun. 8am-6pm.) Don't leave Key West without having a piece of (or even a whole) **key lime pie,** although the genuine article with a tangy yellow filling is hard to find (key limes are not green). Pick up a copy of *The Masked Gourmet* ($1) at the Key West Welcome Center for reviews of pies and restaurants.

La Cubanita Restaurant, 601 Duval St. #3 (292-4640), at Southard. Noisy and fun. The best-priced Cuban food around. Try the Cuban sandwich ($3.25) or a palomilla steak dinner ($7.95). Open Mon.-Sat. 7am-9pm, Sun. 7am-4pm.

Half-Shell Fish Market, Land's End Village (294-5028), at the foot of Margaret St. on the waterfront 5 blocks east of Duval. Rowdy and popular with tourists. Great variety of seafood dinners $8-10. Famed for its spring conch chowder ($2.50). Open daily 11am-11pm.

El Cacique, 125 Duval St. (294-4000). Cuban food at reasonable prices. Homey and colorful. Filling lunch and dinner specials, with pork or local fish, black beans, and rice under $6. Try fried plantains, conch chowder, or bread pudding as side dishes, and flan for dessert. Open daily 8am-10pm.

Blue Heaven Fruit Market, 729 Thomas St., (296-8666) 1 block from the Caribbean House. Hemingway used to drink beer and referee boxing matches here when it was a pool hall. Dinners $8-12. Open Mon.-Sat. 3-11pm.

Sights

Biking is a good way to see Key West, but first you might want to take the **Conch Tour Train** (294-5161), a narrated ride through Old Town, leaving from Mallory Sq. The touristy one-and-a-half-hour trip costs $11 (kids $5) but guides provide a fascinating history of the area. (Operates daily 9am-4:30pm.) **Old Town Trolley** runs a similar tour, but you can get on and off throughout the day.

The glass-bottomed boat *Fireball* takes two-hour cruises to the reefs and back (296-6293; tickets $14, ages 3-12 $7). One of a few cruise specialists, the **Coral Princess Fleet,** 700 Front St. (296-3287), offers snorkeling trips with free instruction for beginners (3 per day, $20; open daily 8:30am-6:30pm).

For many years a beacon for artists and writers, **Hemingway House,** 907 Whitehead St. (294-1575), on Olivia St., is where Papa wrote *For Whom the Bell Tolls* and *A Farewell to Arms.* Tour guides at the houses are notoriously awful; grin and bear it or traipse through the house on your own. About 50 cats (supposedly descendants of Hemingway's cats) make their home on the grounds. (Open daily 9am-5pm. Admission $6, kids $1.50.) The **Audubon House,** 205 Whitehead St. (294-2116), built in the early 1800s, houses some fine antiques and a private collection of the works of ornithologist John James Audubon. (Open daily 9:30am-5pm. Admission $5, ages 6-12 $1.)

Down Whitehead St., past Hemingway House, you'll come to the **Southernmost Point** in the continental U.S. and the adjacent Southernmost Beach. A small, cone-shaped monument and a few conchshell hawkers mark the spot. The **Monroe County Beach,** off Atlantic Ave., has an old pier allowing access past the weed line. The **Old U.S. Naval Air Station** offers deep water swimming on Truman Beach ($1). **Mel Fisher's Treasure Exhibit,** 200 Greene St. (296-9936), will dazzle you with glorious gold. Fisher discovered the sunken treasures from the shipwrecked Spanish vessel, the Atocha. The National Geographic film is included in the entrance fee. (Open daily 10am-5pm. Admission $5, kids $1.)

The **San Carlos Institute,** 516 Duval St., built in 1871, is a freshly restored paragon of Cuban architecture that shines with majorca tiles from Spain and now houses a research center for Hispanic studies. The **Haitian Art Company,** 600 Frances St. (296-8932), 6 blocks east of Duval St., is crammed full of vivid Caribbean artworks. (Open Mon.-Sat. 10am-6pm.)

Watching a sunset from the **Mallory Square Dock** is always a treat. Magicians, street entertainers, and hawkers of tacky wares work the crowd; swimmers and speedboaters show off; and the crowd always cheers when the sun slips into the Gulf with a blazing red farewell.

Every October, Key West holds a week-long celebration known as **Fantasy Fest,** which culminates in an extravagant parade. The entire population of the area turns out for the event in costumes that stretch the imagination. In April, the **Conch Republic** celebration is highlighted by a bed race, and the January-through-March **Old Island Days** features art exhibits, a conch shell-blowing contest, and the blessing of the shrimp fleet.

Entertainment

The daily *Key West Citizen* (sold in front of the post office) and monthly *Solares Hill* and *The Conch Republic* (available at the Key West Chamber of Commerce, lobbies, and waiting rooms) all cover events on the island. Nightlife in Key West revs up at 11pm, and runs until very late. Gay travelers can expect a little heckling from out-of-town cruisers at night, but violence is rare and hassles can be avoided by staying away from the straight bars at the far north end of Duval.

Sloppy Joe's, 201 Duval St., at Greene (294-5717). Reputedly one of Papa Hemingway's preferred watering holes; the decor and rowdy tourists would probably now send him packing. Originally in Havana but moved to "Cayo Hueso" (i.e. Key West) when Castro rose to power. The bar's usual frenzy heightens during the Hemingway Days Festival in mid-July. Reasonable draft prices. Open daily 9am-4am.

Captain Tony's Saloon, 428 Greene St. (294-1838). The oldest bar in Key West. Open daily 10am-1am. Tony Tarracino, the owner, usually shows up at 9pm.

La Terraza de Martí (also called **La Te Da**), 1125 Duval (294-8435). Some of the best (albeit expensive) food in town. José Martí, the Cuban rebel, made incendiary speeches from the front balcony to raise money for the Cuban revolution in the 1890s. Open daily 9am-3am.

Miami

Barely a century ago, Ohio's wealthy Julia Tuttle bought herself some Biscayne Bay swampland and decided to start a city. Only after convincing ubiquitous Standard Oil magnate Henry Flagler to build a railroad to the place did she manage to instigate the development of a major urban and cultural center. Today Miami is a complicated, international city. Although the rather run-down swampland aesthetic still permeates the area near the beach, and the entire city is often ruthlessly hot, the downtown is Art-Deco slick with stuco and pastel, and the ocean is mere moments away. Many smaller cultures make up this city: Little Havana, a well-established Cuban community; Coconut Grove, with its village-in-the-swampland bohemianism; placid, well-to-do Coral Gables, one of the country's earliest planned cities; and the African-American communities of Liberty City and Overtown.

Practical Information

Emergency: 911.

Greater Miami Convention and Visitors Bureau, 701 Brickell Ave. (539-3000; 800-283-2707 outside Miami), 27th floor of the Barnett Bank building downtown. Open Mon.-Fri. 8:30am-5pm. **Coconut Grove Chamber of Commerce,** 2820 McFarlane Rd. (444-7270). Mountains of maps and advice. Open Mon.-Fri. 9am-5pm. The **Miami Beach Resort Hotel Association,** 407 Lincoln Rd. #10G (531-3553), can help you find a place on the beach. Open Mon.-Fri. 9am-5pm, Sun. 10am-3pm.

Miami International Airport: 7 mi. northwest of downtown. Bus #20 is the most direct public transportation into downtown (bus #3 is also usable); from there, take bus C or K to south Miami Beach.

Amtrak: 8303 NW 37th Ave. (835-1221 or 800-872-7245), not far from the Northside station of Metrorail. Bus L goes directly to Lincoln Rd. Mall in south Miami Beach. Open daily 7:45am-7:30pm. To: Orlando (1 per day, 5½ hr., $48); Jacksonville (2 per day, 8 hr., $70); Washington, DC (2 per day, 22 hr., $145).

Greyhound/Trailways: Bayside Station, 700 Biscayne Blvd. (374-7222 for fare and schedule info). To: Orlando (8-10 per day, 6½ hr., $42); Jacksonville (8-10 per day, 11 hr., $57); Atlanta (6 per day, 15½ hr., $75). Ticket window open daily 5am-midnight.

Public Transport: Metro Dade Transportation, 638-6700; 6am-11pm for info. Complex system; buses tend to be quite tardy. The extensive **Metrobus** network converges downtown; most long bus trips transfer in this area. Lettered bus routes A through X serve Miami Beach. After dark, some stops are patrolled (indicated with a sign). Service daily 6am-8pm; major routes until 11pm or midnight. Fare $1. Pick up a *Map Manual* at the visitors bureau or at information stands at the corner of W. Flagler and NW 1st Ave. and on the Lincoln Rd. Mall in Miami Beach. Both open Mon.-Fri. 8am-5pm. Futuristic **Metrorail** service downtown. Fare $1, rail-bus transfers 25¢. The **Metromover** loop downtown, which runs 6:30am-7pm, is linked to the Metrorail stations.The **Tri-Rail** (1-800-TRI-RAIL) connects Miami,

Ft. Lauderdale and West Palm Beach. Trains run Mon.-Sat. 5am-9:30pm. Fare $2, students ·
and seniors with ID $1.

Taxis: Yellow Cab, 444-4444. **Metro Taxi,** 888-8888. **Central Taxi,** 532-5555.

Car Rental: Value Rent-a-Car, 1620 Collins Ave., Miami Beach (532-8257). $25 per day,
$99 per week. Drivers under 25, $5 additional daily charge. Open daily 8am-6pm. Must be
21 with credit card or $225 deposit.

Auto Transport Company: Dependable Car Travel, 162 Sunny Isles Blvd. (945-4104). Open
Mon.-Fri. 8:30am-5pm, Sat. 8:30am-noon. Must be 18 with credit card or passport and foreign license.

Bike Rental: Miami Beach Cycle Center, 923 W. 39th St., Miami Beach (531-4161). $5 per
hr., $12 per day, $40 per week, 2-hr. min. Open Mon.-Fri. 9:30am-6pm, Sat. 9:30am-5pm.
Must be 18 with credit card or $40 deposit. **Dade Cycle Shop,** 3216 Grand Ave., Coconut
Grove (443-6075). $5 per hr., $15-22 per day. Open daily 9:30am-5:30pm. Must have $10
deposit and driver's license or credit card.

Help Lines: Crisis Hotline, 358-4357. **Rape Treatment Center and Hotline,** 1611 NW 12th
Ave. (549-7273). **Gay Community Hotline,** 759-3661. **Center for Survival and Independent
Living (C-SAIL),** 1310 NW 16th St. (547-5444). Offers info on services for the disabled. Lines
open Mon.-Fri. 8am-5pm.

Post Office: 500 NW 2nd Ave. (371-2911). Open Mon.-Fri. 8:30am-5pm, Sat. 8:30am-
12:30pm. **ZIP code:** 33101.

Area Code: 305.

Three highways criss-cross the Miami area. Just south of downtown, I-95, the
most direct route north-south, runs into U.S. 1, known as the **Dixie Highway.** U.S.
1 goes as far as the Everglades entrance at Florida City and then all the way out
to Key West. **Route 836,** a major east-west artery through town, connnects I-95
with the **Florida Turnpike,** passing the airport in between. Take Rte. 836 and the
Turnpike to Florida City to avoid the traffic on Rte. 1.

When looking for street addresses, pay careful attention to the systematic street
layout; it's *very* easy to confuse North Miami Beach, West Miami, Miami Beach,
and Miami addresses. Streets in Miami run east-west, avenues north-south, and
numbers into the hundreds refer to both. Miami divides into NE, NW, SE, and
SW sections: the dividing lines (downtown) are **Flagler Street** (east-west) and
Miami Avenue (north-south). Some numbered streets and avenues also have
names—i.e., Le Jeune Rd. is SW 42nd Ave., and SW 40th St. is called Bird Rd.

Several four-lane causeways connect Miami to Miami Beach. The most useful
is **MacArthur Causeway,** which feeds onto 5th St. in Miami Beach. Numbered
streets run across the island, with numbers increasing as you go north; the main
north-south drag is **Collins Avenue.** In South Miami Beach, **Washington Avenue,**
one block to the west, is the main commercial strip, while **Ocean Avenue,** actually
on the waterfront, lies one block east. The **Rickenbacker Causeway** is the only connection to Key Biscayne.

Spanish-speakers will have an advantage getting around Miami. The city has a
large Spanish-speaking community; the *Miami Herald* now even puts out a Spanish
edition. You may even run into problems on buses without, since many drivers only
speak Spanish.

Accommodations and Camping

Finding cheap rooms in Miami should never pose a problem. Several hundred
Art-Deco hotels in South Miami Beach stand at your service. For safety, convenience, and security, stay north of 5th St. A "pullmanette" (40s lingo) is a room
with a refrigerator, stove, and sink; getting one and some groceries allows you to
save money on food. In South Florida, since any hotel room short of the Fontainebleau Hilton is likely to have two- to three-inch cockroaches ("palmetto bugs"),
try not to take them as indicators of quality: they are actually shy, reticent, even

beautiful creatures. In general, the peak season for Miami Beach runs late December to mid-March.

Camping is not allowed in Miami, and the nearest campgrounds are north or west of the city. Those who can't bear to put their tents aside for a night or two should head on to one of the nearby national parks.

Miami Beach International Travelers Hostel, 236 9th St. (534-0268), at the intersection with Washington Ave. Take bus C or K from downtown or call for directions. Has a relaxed international atmosphere and central location, kitchen, laundry, common room. No curfew. 29 private rooms with A/C and private bath. Hostel rooms $9-10 (max. 4 people). Private rooms $23-25.

The Clay Hotel (AYH), 1438 Washington Ave. (534-2988). Take bus C or K from downtown. Cheerful chaos reigns in the 7 buildings. Kitchen, laundry facilities, and ride boards. Very international crowd. Most rooms have 4 beds; 2 rooms share a bathroom. No curfew. Members $9, winter $10. Nonmembers $12, winter $13. A/C $1. Hotel singles $17-20. Doubles $25-28. Key deposit $5.

Tudor Hotel, 1111 Collins Ave. (534-2934). Beautiful renovations make this one of the nicest hotels in Miami Beach, but it only rents rooms for a week or longer. All rooms have refrigerator, microwave, cable TV, A/C, phone. Weekly: singles $120; doubles $170.

Kent Hotel 1131 Collins Ave., (531-6771) one block from the beach. Beautifully renovated rooms and friendly staff. TV, A/C, breakfast. Singles or doubles April 15-Dec. 15 $40, Dec. 15-April 15 $60. Ocean view $10 more.

Palmer House Hotel, 1119 Collins Ave., Miami Beach (538-7725), 3 blocks west of the beach. Venerable Art-Deco establishment with pullmanettes. Come here if price is your only criterion. Singles $25. Doubles $30. Each additional person (up to 3) $5.

Miami Airways Motel, 5001 36th St. (883-4700). Will pick you up at nearby airport. Clean rooms, A/C, pool, HBO. Singles $32. Doubles $37.

Larry & Penny Thompson Memorial Campground, 12451 SW 184th St. (232-1049), a long way from anywhere. By car, drive 20-30 min. south along Dixie Hwy. Pretty grounds in a grove of mango trees. Laundry, store, and all facilities, plus artificial lake with swimming beach, beautiful park, and even water slides. Office open daily 8am-7pm, but takes late arrivals. Lake open daily 10am-5pm. Sites $13, with hookup $20. Weekly: sites $81, with hookup $122.

Also, the owner of the Fort Lauderdale's Sol Y Mar has opened a hostel, **Greenbriar Hostel and Apartments,** on Indian Creek Drive. Contact Tad Friedberg at 305-531-0051 or at the Sol Y Mar address for info on this new establishment.

Food

If you eat nothing else in Miami, be sure to try Cuban food. Specialties include *media noche* sandwiches (a sort of Cuban club sandwich on a soft roll, heated and compressed); *mamey,* a bright red ice cream concoction; rich *frijoles negros* (black beans); and *picadillo* (shredded beef and peas in tomato sauce, served with white rice). For Cuban sweets, seek out a *dulcería,* and punctuate your rambles around town with thimble-sized swallows of strong, sweet *café cubano* (25¢).

Cheap restaurants are not common in Miami Beach, but an array of fresh bakeries and fruit stands can sustain you with melons, mangoes, tomatoes, and carrots for under $3 a day.

Irish House 1430 Alton Rd. (534-5667), Miami Beach. A favorite hangout for local journalists, politicos and beach-goers. Noted for its buffalo wings ($5.25) and cheeseburgers ($4.50). Open Mon.-Sat. 11am-2am, Sun. 5pm-2am.

La Rumba, 2008 Collins Ave. (538-8998), Miami Beach, between 20th and 21st St. Good, cheap Cuban food and noisy fun. Try their *arroz con pollo* (chicken with yellow rice; $6). Open Fri.-Wed. 7:30am-midnight.

Flamingo Restaurant, 1454 Washington Ave. (673-4302), right down the street from the hostel. Friendly service, all in Spanish. Try the *pollo* (chicken) with pinto beans and rice $4.25. Open Mon.-Sat. 9am-7:30pm.

Our Place Natural Foods Eatery, 830 Washington Ave. (674-1322), Miami Beach. New Age books along with juices, salads, pita, tofutti, etc. Lunch $3-6, dinner $5-10. Live folk music · on weekends. Open Mon.-Sat. 11am-9pm, Sun. 11am-8pm.

King's Ice Cream, 1831 SW 8th St. (643-1842), on Calle Ocho. Tropical fruit *helado* (ice cream) flavors include coconut (served in its own shell), *mamey,* and banana. Also try *churros* (thin Spanish donuts) or *café cubano* (10¢). Open daily 10am-11pm.

Sights

The best sight in Miami is the beach. When you get too burned or dazed, try the **Seaquarium,** 4400 Rickenbacker Causeway, Virginia Key (361-5703), just min-utes from downtown. While not on par with Sea World in Orlando, it has a truly impressive array of shows, including obligatory dolphins, hungry sharks, and killer whales. The aquarium also displays tropical fish. (Open daily 9:30am-6:00pm; ticket office closes 5pm. Admission $15, kids $11.) **Planet Ocean,** 3979 Rickenbacker Causeway (361-9455), across the street, offers a more educational atmosphere for uncovering the secrets of the deep. (Open daily 10am-6pm; ticket office closes 4:30pm. Admission $7.50, ages 4-12 $4.)

South Miami Beach, the swath of town between 6th and 23rd St., overwhelms with hundreds of hotels and apartments whose sun-faded pastel facades recall what sun-thirsty northerners of the 20s thought a tropical paradise should look like. The art-deco palaces comprise the country's largest national historic district, and the only one to preserve 20th-century buildings. A fascinating mixture of people popu-lates the area, including large retired and Latin-immigrant communities; knowing Spanish is a big advantage here. Walking tours of the historic district are offered every Saturday at 10:30am ($5). Call 672-2014 to find out point of departure.

On the waterfront downtown is Miami's newest attraction, the **Bayside** shopping complex, with fancy shops, exotic food booths, and live reggae or *salsa* on Friday and Saturday nights. Near Bayside, visit the **Police Hall of Fame and Museum,** 3801 Biscayne Blvd., (891-1700), and learn more than you ever wanted to know about the police. Watch in your rearview mirror for the police car suspended along-side the building. (Open daily 10am-5:30pm. Admission $3, seniors and kids $1.50.)

Little Havana lies between SW 12th and SW 27th Ave. (take bus #3, 11, 14, 15, 17, 25, or 37). The street scenes of **Calle Ocho** (SW 8th St.) lie at the heart of this district; the corresponding section of W. Flager St. is a center of Cuban business. The works at the **Cuban Museum of Arts and Culture,** 1300 SW 12th Ave. (858-8006), reflect the bright colors and rhythms of Cuban art. Take bus #27. (Open Mon.-Fri. 10am-4:30pm, Sat.-Sun. 1-5pm. Donation.)

An entirely different atmosphere prevails on the bay south of downtown in self-consciously rustic **Coconut Grove** (take bus #1 or Metrorail from downtown). The grove centers around the intersection of Grand Ave. and Main Hwy. Drop into a watering hole like **Señor Frog's,** 3008 Grand Ave. (448-0999), home of bang-up tables and phenomenal salsa. (Open Sun.-Thurs. 10:30am-1am, Fri.-Sat. 10:30am-2am.)

On the bayfront between the Grove and downtown stands **Vizcaya,** 3251 S. Miami Ave. (579-2708 and 579-2808; recorded info 579-2813), set in acres of elabor-ately landscaped grounds. Built in 1916 by International Harvester heir James Deer-ing, the four facades of this 70-room Italianate mansion hide a hodgepodge of Euro-pean antiques. (Open daily 9:30am-5pm; last admission 4:30pm. Admission $8, kids $4. Take bus #1, or Metrorail to Vizcaya.) Across the street from Vizcaya, both the **Museum of Science** and its **Planetarium,** 3280 S. Miami Ave. (854-4247; show info 854-2222), offer laser shows and their ilk. Both congest with kids. (Open daily 10am-6pm. Admission $5, ages 3-12 $3.50. Planetarium shows extra.)

Near Miami, the **Everglades National Park** teems with exotic life. Visit the park in winter or spring, when heat, humidity, storms, and bugs are at a minimum, and when wildlife congregates around the water. The park is accessible on the north via the Tamiami Trail (U.S. 41) or by the main park road (Rte. 9336) out of Florida City. (Entrance to the park $5.) The best way to tour the largely inaccessible park is to take Rte. 997 40 mi. through the flat grasslands to Flamingo, on Florida Bay, stopping at the various nature trails and pullouts along the way. Stop at the **visitors center,** P.O. Box 279, Homestead 33030 (247-6211), by the park headquarters just outside the entrance, to see a film on the Everglades and to pick up maps and info. (Open daily 8am-5pm.) The visitors center also sponsors a variety of hikes, canoe trips, and amphitheater programs. To get face-to-snout with an alligator, try the **Anhinga Trail,** 2 mi. beyond the entrance.

Entertainment

The Art-Deco district in South Miami Beach is filled with clubs; Ocean Blvd., on the beach, is crowded with a young, rowdy set nearly every night of the week. Any club will do, just wander down and take your pick. For blues, try the **Peacock Cafe,** 2977 McFarlane Rd., Coconut Grove (442-8877; open Tues.-Sun. 11:30am-5am). After the money's gone, head for **Friday Night Live,** at **South Point Park,** the very southern tip of Miami Beach, which features free city-sponsored concerts from 8 to 11pm. (Call 673-7730 for info.) Down Washington Ave. at Española Way, the **Cameo Theater** (532-0922) hosts live punk and other rock bands about once per week. For gay nightlife, check out **Uncle Charlie's,** 3673 Bird Ave. (442-8687), just off Dixie Hwy. (cover $3).

Performing Arts and Community Education (PACE) (681-1470) offers more than 1000 concerts each year (jazz, rock, soul, dixieland, reggae, salsa, bluegrass), most of which are free. For more info on what's happening in Miami, check *Miami-South Florida Magazine,* or the "Living Today," "Lively Arts," and Friday "Weekend" sections of the *Miami Herald.*

Orlando and Disney World

Though Orlando likes to tout itself as "the world's vacation center" and one of the country's fastest-growing cities, millions annually descend on this central Florida city for just one reason: Disney World, the world's most popular tourist attraction. Walt Disney selected the area south of Orlando as the place for his expanded version of California's Disneyland. Disney has since complemented the Magic Kingdom with the Epcot Center and the brand-new Disney-MGM Studios theme parks.

A number of parasitic attractions, such as expensive water and theme parks, have infected the area to cash in on Disney tourism. Be warned: of the many ways to blow your dough in this land of illusions, usually you are best off spending your time and money at Disney first. Two exceptions to this rule are **Sea World** and the spanking new **Universal Studios Florida.** With fun and exciting exhibits and rides, both are well worth their admission prices.

Downtown Orlando has little to offer other than pretty lakes and parks. For a change of pace, visit nearby **Winter Park,** home of posh Rollins College, an appealing college town that remains miraculously unaffected by the frenzied "entertainment" biz of its neighbor.

Practical Information

Emergency: 911.

Orlando-Orange County Visitors and Convention Bureau, 8445 International Dr. (351-0412), several mi. southwest of downtown at the Mercado (Spanish-style mall). Take bus #8, 21, 27, 28, or 29 from downtown. Maps and info on nearly all of the amusement park attractions in the area. Pick up a free bus system map. Open daily 8am-8pm.

Amtrak: 1400 Sligh Blvd. (843-7611 or 800-872-7245). Three blocks east of I-4. Take S. Orange Ave., turn west on Columbia, then right on Sligh. To: Tampa (2 per day, 2 hr., $10); Jacksonville (2 per day, 3½ hr., $27); Miami (1 per day, 5½ hr., $48). Open daily 6am-8:30pm.

Greyhound/Trailways, 300 W. Amelia St. at Hughy Ave. (843-7720 for 24-hr. fare and ticket info), downtown near Sunshine Park 1 block east of I-4. To: Tampa (7 per day, 2½ hr., $14); Jacksonville (8 per day, 3 hr., $28); Miami (6 per day, 7 hr., $42). Open 24 hrs.

Public Transport: Tri-County Transit, 438 Woods Ave. (841-8240 for info Mon.-Fri. 6:30am-6:30pm, Sat. 7:30am-5pm, Sun. 8am-4pm). Downtown terminal between Central and Pine St., 1 block west of Orange Ave. and 1 block east of I-4. Schedules available at most shopping malls, banks, and at the downtown terminal. Serves the airport (bus #11 at "B" terminal luggage claim), Sea World, Wet'n Wild, and a deliciously dense chocolate *torta.* Buses operate daily 6am-9pm. Fare 75¢, transfers 10¢.

Mears Motor Shuttle: 324 W. Gore St. (423-5566). Has a booth at the airport for transportation to most hotels, including the Airport Hostel. Cheapest transport besides city bus #11 if you're alone and can't split taxi fare. Also runs from most hotels to Disney ($12.50, $22 round-trip). Open 24 hrs. Call day in advance to reserve seat to Disney.

Taxi: Yellowcab, 422-4455. $2.45 first mi., $1.40 each additional mi.

Car Rental: Alamo, 8200 McCoy Rd. (857-8200 or 800-327-9633), near the airport. $22 per day, $76 per week. Under 25 $6 extra per day. Open 24 hrs. Must have major credit card or a $50 deposit through travel agent.

Help Lines: Rape Hotline, 740-5408.

Crisis Information: 648-3028.

Post Office: 46 E. Robinson St. (843-5673), at Magnolia downtown. Open-Mon.-Fri. 8am-5pm, Sat. 9am-noon. **ZIP code:** 32801.

Area Code: 407.

Orlando proper lies at the center of hundreds of small lakes and amusement parks. **Lake Eola** reclines at the center of the city, east of I-4 and south of Colonial Dr. Streets divide north-south by **Route 17-92 (Mills Avenue)** and east-west by **Colonial Drive.** I-4, supposedly an east-west expressway, actually runs north-south through the center of town. To reach either downtown youth hostel by car, take the Robinson St. exit and turn right. **Disney World** and **Sea World** are 15 to 20 mi. south of downtown on I-4; **Cypress Gardens** is 30 mi. south of Disney off U.S. 27 near Winter Haven. Transportation out to the parks is simple—most hotels offer a shuttle service to Disney, but you can take a city bus or call Mears Motor Shuttle.

Accommodations and Camping

Orlando does not cater to the budget traveler. Prices for hotel rooms rise exponentially as you approach Disney World; plan to stay in a hostel or in downtown Orlando. Reservations are a good idea in December, January, March, and April, and on holidays. Or try **Kissimmee,** a few mi. east of Disney World along U.S. 192, which has some of the cheapest places to camp. One city park and four Orange County parks have campsites ($7, with hookup $10). Contact **Orange County Parks & Recreation Department,** 118 W. Kaley St. (836-4290), and **Orlando Parks Department,** 1206 W. Columbia (246-2283), for more info. (Both open Mon.-Fri. 8am-8pm.)

Orlando International Youth Hostel at Plantation Manor (AYH), 227 N. Eola Dr. (843-8888), at E. Robinson, downtown on the east shore of Lake Eola. Usually full July-Oct., so make reservations. Porch, TV room, kitchen facilities, A/C in most rooms, (negotiable) midnight curfew. Rooms sleep 4-6. Hostel beds $11. Private rooms $28. $2 breakfast, $2 linen, $5 key deposit. The friendly managers will take you to the theme park of your choice for $10 roundtrip.

Airport Hostel, 3500 McCoy Rd. (859-3165 or 851-1612), off Daetwiler Rd. behind the La Quinta Motel. Take "Airport" bus #11 from the airport or downtown. Kitchen facilities, pool access, no curfew. Little glamour, but very homey, with tropical fruit trees out back. $10, 2-night min. Breakfast included.

Young Women's Community Club (AYH), 107 E. Hillcrest St. (425-1076), at Magnolia, 4 blocks from Plantation Manor right behind the Orlando Sentinel. Take bus #10 or 12; staff recommends a taxi. Women aged 16-44 only. Clean, safe, and friendly. Pool. Flexible 3-night max. stay. $10. Weekly: $60. $2 linen. Good breakfast $2, dinner $4. No reservations.

Sun Motel, 5020 W. Irlo Bronson Memorial Hwy., (396-6666) in Kissimmee. Very reasonable considering proximity to Disney World (4 mi.). Cable TV, phone, pool, A/C. Singles $40-$50. Doubles $45-$55. Off-season: $25; $28.

KOA, U.S. 192 (396-2400; 800-331-1453), down the road from Twin Lakes. Kamping Kabins $25. Pool, tennis, store (open 7am-11pm). Even in season you're bound to get a site, but arrive early. Free buses twice per day to Disney. Office open 24 hrs. Tent sites with hookup $20. Each additional person $3.50.

Stage Stop Campground, 700 W. Rte. 50 (656-8000), 8 mi. north of Disney in Winter Garden. Take exit 80 off the Florida Turnpike N., then left on Rte. 50. Office open daily 8am-8:30pm. Sites with full hookup $17. Weekly: $102, A/C $1.50 per day.

Food

Lilia's Grilled Delight, 3150 S. Orange Ave. (351-9087), 2 blocks south of Michigan St., 5 min. from the downtown business district. Small, modestly decorated Philippine restaurant—one of the best-kept secrets in town. Don't pass up *lumpia,* a tantalizing combination of sauteed meat, shrimp, vegetables, and peanut butter in a fried dough, or the *adobo,* the Philippine national dish. Lunch $3-5, dinner $4-7. Open Mon.-Sat. 11am-7pm; summer Mon.-Sat. 11am-2:30pm.

Numero Uno, 2499 S. Orange Ave. (841-3840) A "number one" local favorite serving tasty Cuban specialties in a casual setting. Roast pork dinner with rice, plantains, and salad about $8. Open Mon.-Thurs. 11am-9:30pm, Fri. 11am-10pm, Sat. 1-10pm.

Deter's Restaurant and Pub, 17 W. Pine St.(839-5975), just up from Orange St. near the Church Street Mall. German-American cuisine in an after-work-let's-have-a-beer, touch-my-monkey atmosphere. Try the amazing chicken in Reisling sauce ($10). Live entertainment Fri.-Sat. nights. Open Mon.-Sat. 11am-10:30pm.

Ronnie's Restaurant, 2702 Colonial Plaza, at Bumby St. just past the Colonial Plaza mall (894-2943). Deco booths and counters from the 50s. Mix of Jewish, Cuban, and U.S. cuisine. The famous breakfast special (eggs, rolls, juice, coffee, and more) may fill you up for a few days ($4.65). Great chili for $3.25, fresh breads, swell pancakes. Open Sun.-Thurs. 7am-11pm, Fri.-Sat. 7am-1am.

China Coast Restaurant, 7500 International Drive (351-9776). Brunch buffet Mon.-Fri. 11am-2pm, Sat.-Sun. 11am-3pm for $4.

Nature's Table, 8001 South Orange Blossom Trail (857-5496). Vegetarian and healthful specialties. Delicious fruit and protein powder shakes ($1-2), yogurt, juice. Excellent, thick sandwiches under $4. Open Mon.-Fri. 9am-5pm.

Entertainment

The **Church Street Station,** 129 W. Church St. (422-2434), downtown between South and Garland St., is a slick, block-long entertainment, shopping, and restaurant complex. Get 89¢ beef tacos at NACO'S, or the $3 dinner platter at the Chinese Cafe. Listen to free folk and bluegrass music at **Apple Annie's Courtyard.** Boogie down (and enjoy 5¢ beers on Wed.) at **Phineas Phogg's Balloon Works** (enforced 21 age restriction). Or pay $15 to go to the three theme shows. **Rosie O'Grady's** is the most popular show, featuring Dixieland and can-can girls. **Cheyenne Saloon and Opera House** has a country and western show, while Rock & Roll rules at the **Orchid Garden Ballroom.** For less expensive nightlife, explore **Orange Avenue** downtown. Several good bars and clubs have live music and dancing at very reasonable prices. The **Beach Club Cafe,** 68 N. Orange Ave. at Washington St. (839-0457), hosts DJ dancing or live reggae nightly.

Disney World

Admit it: you came to see Disney, the monarch of amusement parks, a sprawling three-park labyrinth of kiddie rides, movie sets, and futuristic world displays. If bigger is better, Disney World certainly wins the prize for best park in the U.S.

(824-4321 for info daily 8am-10pm). Like Gaul, Disney World is divided into three parts: the **Magic Kingdom,** with seven theme regions; the **Epcot Center,** part science fair, part World's Fair; and the newly completed **Disney-MGM Studios,** a pseudo movie and TV studio with Magic Kingdom-style rides. All are located a few mi. from each other in the town of Lake Buena Vista, 20 mi. west of Orlando via I-4.

A one-day entrance fee of $35 (ages 3-9 $27.50) admits you to *one* of the three parks; it also allows you to leave and return to the same park later in the day. A four-day **passport** ($117, ages 3-9 $80) admits you to all three and includes unlimited transportation between attractions on the Disney monorail, boats, buses, and trains. You can also opt for a five-day super-plus pass ($153, ages 3-9 $122.50), which also admits you to all other Disney attractions. The multi-day passes need not be used on consecutive days, and they are valid forever. Those Disney attractions that charge separate admissions (unless you have a five-day super-plus pass) are: **River Country** ($12.50, ages 3-9 $9.81) and **Discovery Island** ($8.50, ages 3-9 $5)—for both $15, ages 3-9 $11; **Typhoon Lagoon** ($19.35, ages 3-9 $15.37); and **Pleasure Island.** ($12—$9 at info center, over 18 only unless with adult). For descriptions, see Other Disney Attractions below.

Gray Line Tours (422-0744) and **Mears Motor Shuttle** offer transport from most hotels to Disney (depart hotel at 9am, depart Disney at 7pm; $11-13 round-trip). Major hotels and some campgrounds provide their own shuttles for guests. **Bikers** are stopped at the main gate and driven by security guards to the inner entrance where they can stash their bikes free of charge.

Disney World opens its gates 365 days per year, but hours fluctuate according to season. It's busy during the summer when school is out, but "peak times" during Christmas, Thanksgiving, Spring Break, and the month around Easter are packed. More people visit between Christmas and New Year's than at any other time of year. Since the crowd hits the main gates at 10am, arrive before the 9am opening time and seek out your favorite rides or exhibits before noon. During peak period (and perhaps the rest of the year), the Disney parks actually open earlier than the stated time. Begin the day at the rear of a park and work your way to the front. You'll have mondo fun at the distant attractions while lines for those near the entrance are jammed. Persevere through dinner time (5:30pm-8pm) when a lot of cranky kids head home. Regardless of tactics, you will wait anywhere from 45 minutes to two hours at big attractions.

Magic Kingdom

Seven "lands" make up the Magic Kingdom. You enter on **Main Street, USA,** meant to capture the essence of turn-of-the-century hometown U.S. Architects employed "forced perspective" here, building the ground floor of the shops 9/10 normal size while the second and third stories get progressively smaller. Walt describes his vision in the "Walt Disney Movie" at the Hospitality House, to the right as you emerge from under the railroad station. The Main Street Cinema shows some great old silents. Late afternoons on Main Street turn gruesome when the not-so-impressive "All America Parade" marches through at 3pm; take this chance to ride some of the more crowded attractions. Near the entrance, you'll find a steam train that huffs and puffs its way across the seven different lands.

The **Tomorrowland** area has rides and early-70s exhibits of space travel and possible future lifestyles. The indoor roller coaster **Space Mountain** proves the high point of this section, if not the high point of the park, and is worth the extensive wait.

The golden-spired Cinderella Castle marks the gateway to **Fantasyland,** where you'll find Dumbo the Elephant and a twirling teacup ride. Most who come off of the teacup ride walk a crooked line, as if the Salada were spiked. 20,000 Leagues Under the Sea sinks to new depths of brilliant premise but flawed implementation. The chilly temperatures in It's A Small World are the ride's only redeeming features. You may never get the evil tune out of your head. Catch *Magic Journeys,* a plotless 3-D movie with extraordinary effects.

Liberty Square and **Frontierland** devote their resources to U.S. history and a celebration of Mark Twain. History buffs will enjoy the Hall of Presidents, and adventurers should catch the rickety, runaway Big Thunder Mountain Railroad roller-coaster. Haunted Mansion is both spooky and dorky. A steamboat ride or a canoe trip which you help paddle both rest your feet from the seemingly endless trek. Also be sure to stop and watch the entertaining animatronics at the Country Bear Jamboree.

Adventureland is a home away from home for those who feel the White Man's Burden. The Jungle Cruise takes a tongue-in-cheek tour through tropical waterways populated by not-so-authentic-looking wildlife. Pirates of the Caribbean explores caves where animated buccaneers battle, drink, and sing. The Swiss Family Robinson tree house, a replica of the shipwrecked family's home, provides more mental than adrenal excitement.

Epcot Center

In 1966, Walt Disney dreamed up an "Experimental Prototype Community Of Tomorrow" (EPCOT) that would evolve constantly, never be completed, and incorporate new ideas from U.S. technology—functioning as a self-sufficient, futuristic utopia. The future hasn't hit south Florida, however, as corporate sponsorship at the individual pavilions indicates. At present, Epcot splits into Future World and World Showcase. For smaller crowds, visit the former in the evening and the latter in the morning.

The 180-ft.-high trademark geosphere forms the entrance to **Future World** and houses the **Spaceship Earth** attraction, where visitors board a "time machine" for a tour through the evolution of communications. **The World of Motion** traces the evolution of transportation, and the **Universe of Energy** traces (in a somewhat outdated fashion, since it glorifies the Alaskan Port of Valdez) the history of energy. The **Wonders of Life** takes its visitors on a tour of the human body (with the help of a simulator) and tells us all where babies come from. **Horizons** lamely presents the lifestyles of the 21st century. **The Land** has a thought-provoking film about people's relationship with the land, and takes visitors on a tour of futurisitic agrarian methods. **The Living Seas** fails to recreate an underwater research station. Finally, the ever-popular **Journey into Imagination** pavilion features the 3-D *Captain Eo* (starring the moon-walking, sequin-sporting rock star Michael Jackson).

The rest of Epcot is the **World Showcase**—a series of international pavilions surrounding an artificial lake. An architectural style or monument, as well as typical food, represents each country. People in costumes from past and present perform dances, theatrical skits, and other "cultural" entertainment at each pavilion. Before setting out around the lake, pick up a schedule of daily events at Epcot Center Information in Earth Station. Three of the best attractions are the two 360° films made in China and Canada and the 180° film made in France. They all include spectacular landscapes, some national history, and an inside look at the people of the respective countries. **The American Adventure** gives aa very enthusiastic and patriotic interpretation of American history. Save your pesos by shopping at your local Pier 7 store rather than the marked-up Mexican marketplace. Norwegian life must be more exciting than the fishing, sailing, and oil exploring shown by the boat ride in the Norway Pavillion. Every summer night at 9pm, Sat. 10pm (off-season Sat. only), Epcot has a magnificent show called **Illuminations,** which features music from the represented nations accompanied by dancing, lights, and fireworks.

The World Showcase pavillions also offer regional cuisine. Make reservations first thing in the morning at the Earth Station World Key Terminal, behind Spaceship Earth. At the **Restaurant Marrakesh** in the Moroccan Pavilion, for example, head chef Lahsen Abrache cooks delicious *brewat* (spicy minced beef fried in pastry) and *bastilla* (sweet and slightly spicy pie). A belly dancer performs in the restaurant every evening. (Lunch $10-$15. Dinner $15-$20. The Mexican, French, and Italian pavillions also serve up excellent food at similar prices.

Disney-MGM Studios

Disney-MGM Studios have successfully created a "living movie set." Many of the familiar Disney characters (including the Ninja Turtles who have their own performance times) stroll through the park, as do a host of characters dressed as directors, starlets, gossip columnists, and fans. A different has-been movie star leads a parade across Hollywood Boulevard every day. Events such as stunt shows and mini-theatricals take place continually throughout the park.

The **Great Movie Ride,** inside the Chinese Theater, takes you on a simple but nostalgic trip through old and favorite films; interactive ride varies by your selection of the first or second set of cars. **Superstar Television** projects members of the audience alongside TV stars, and the **Monster Sound Show** requires volunteers to add special effects to a short movie. The biggest attractions at this park are the **Indiana Jones Epic Stunt Spectacular,** in which you watch stuntmen and audience volunteers pull off amazing moves, and the **Star Tours** Star Wars ride, in which you feel the jerk of your space cargo ship dodging laser blasts.

Other Disney Attractions

For those who did not get enough amusement at the three main parks, Disney also offers several other attractions on its grounds with different themes and separate admissions (see Disney World above). The newest is **Typhoon Lagoon,** a 50-acre water park centered around the world's largest wave-making pool. Surf the 7-ft. waves that occasionally appear out of nowhere, or snorkel in a salt water coral reef stocked with tropical fish and harmless sharks. Besides six water slides, the lagoon has a wonderful creek on which you can take a relaxing inner-tube ride, an anomaly at Disney. Built to resemble a swimming hole, **River Country** offers water slides, rope swings, and plenty of room to swim. Both parks fill up early on hot days, and you might get turned away. Across Bay Lake from River Country is **Discovery Island,** a zoological park. Those seeking more (relatively) sinful excitations should head at night to **Pleasure Island,** Disney's attempt to draw students and the thirty-something set. Those above 21 can roam freely between the theme nightclubs; 18-21 remain with their guardians; under 18 may not enter.

Near Orlando: Sea World, Cypress Gardens, and Universal Studios Florida

One of the country's largest marine parks, **Sea World,** 19 mi. southwest of Orlando off I-4 at Rte. 528 (407-351-3600 for operator; 407-351-0021 for recording), requires about six hours to see everything. Shows feature marine mammals such as whales, dolphins, sea lions, seals and otters. Though the Seal and Otter Show and the USO waterski show are enjoyable, the killer whales **Baby Shamu** and **Baby Namu** are the big stars. Not only do they share the stage (or pool) with two beautiful white whales and two Orcas, the trainers actually mix it up with the huge creatures and take rides on their snouts. People in the park gravitate towards Shamu Stadium before the show; arrive early to get a seat. After your brow gets sweaty, visit the air-conditioned **Fantasy Theater,** an educational show with live characters in costume. The smallest crowds cling in February and from September to October. Most hotel brochure counters and hostels have coupons for $2-3 off regular admission prices. (Open daily 8:30am-10pm; off-season daily 9am-7pm. Admission $25.50, ages 3-11 $21.20. Sky Tower ride $2.50 extra. Guided tours $5.50, kids $4.50. Take bus #8.)

Cypress Gardens (813-324-2111; 407-351-6606 in Orlando), in Winter Haven, is a botanical garden with over 8000 varieties of plants and flowers (Open daily 8am-9:30pm; in winter daily 9am-7pm. Admission $17, ages 6-11 $11.50). Take I-4 southwest to Rte. 27 south, then Rte. 540 west. The "Gardens of the World" feature plants, flowers, and sculptured mini-gardens depicting the horticultural styles of many countries and periods. Winding walkways and electric boat rides take you through the foliage. The main attraction is a water-ski show performed daily at 10am, noon, 2pm, and 4pm. Greyhound stops here once per day on its Tampa-West Palm Beach schedule ($20 from Tampa to Cypress Gardens). Look for coupons at motels and visitors centers.

Universal Studios Florida (363-8000), opened in 1990, is a two-in-one park containing a number of amazing theme rides: **Kongfrontation,** where King Kong will roughouse your cable car, an **E.T.** bike ride, and **Jaws,** a boat trip where you can see the shark used in the movie. Also look for the **Back to the Future** ride, with seven-story high OMNIMAX surround screens and spectacular special effects.

Since the park serves as a working studio making films, stars abound. Recently, Steve Martin played a dad in *Parenthood* here. Nickelodeon TV programs are in continuous production. Universal also has a number of set blocks that you may have seen before in the movies—displaying Hollywood, Central Park, and Beverly Hills as well as the infamous Bates Motel from *Psycho.* The park will expand over the next few years, and admission prices will vary as the park swings into full-scale action. Call the studios for info on current ticket prices.

Saint Augustine

Spanish adventurer Juan Ponce de León founded St. Augustine in 1565, making it the first European colony in North America and the oldest city in the U.S. Although he never found the legendary Fountain of Youth, de León did live to age 61, twice the expected life span at that time. Similarly, much of St. Augustine's original Spanish flavor has survived without the legend, thanks to the town's various efforts at preservation. Today, in its dotage, the town is fairly quiet: its brick, palm-lined streets see few cars, and during the summer months the heat slows everything and everyone. Yet historic sights, good food, and friendly people make St. Augustine well worth a few rejuvenating days.

Practical Information

Emergency: 911.

Visitors Center, 10 Castillo at San Marco Ave. (824-3334). From the Greyhound station, walk north on Ribeira, then right on Orange. Pick up hotel coupons and the free *Chamber of Commerce Map,* a comprehensive city guide. The ½-hr. movie, *St. Augustine Adventure,* cleverly introduces the city (every ½-hr.; $2, kids $1). Open daily 8:30am-5:30pm.

Greyhound/Trailways: 100 Malaga St. at King St. (829-6401). To Jacksonville (5 per day, 50 min., $6.50) and Daytona Beach (7 per day, 1 hr., $10). Open Mon.-Fri. 8am-5:30pm, Sat. 8am-4pm.

Taxi: Ancient City Taxi, 824-8161. From the bus station to motels on San Marco about $2.

Help Lines: Rape Crisis, 355-7273.

Post Office: King St. at Martin Luther King Ave. (829-8716). Open Mon.-Fri. 8:30am-5pm, Sat. 10am-1pm. ZIP code: 32084.

Area Code: 904.

Unfortunately, the city has no public transportation, though most points of interest, such as the bus station, tourist office, budget motels, and tourist district, are all within walking distance of one another. Historic St. Augustine, concentrated in the area between the **San Sebastian River** and the **Matanzas Bay** to the east, is easily covered on foot. **King Street,** running along the river, is the major east-west axis and crosses the bay to the beaches. **St. George Street,** also east-west, is closed to vehicular traffic and contains most of the shops and many sights in St. Augustine. **San Marco Avenue** and **Cordova Street** travel north-south. Winter brings a surge of activity to nearby **Vilano, Anastasia,** and **St. Augustine Beaches.**

Accommodations and Camping

Beyond the new, often full, youth hostel, you'll find several clusters of cheap motels in St. Augustine: one a short walk north of town on San Marco Ave.; another directly to the east of the historic district, over the Bridge of Lions along Anastasia

Blvd.; and a third near Vilano Beach. Several inns in the historic district offer nice rooms, but rates start at $49 per night. Those traveling by automobile should consider the excellent seaside camping facilities at **Anastasia State Park.**

St. Augustine Hostel (AYH), 32 Treasury St. (829-6163), at Charlotte, 6 blocks from the Greyhound station. Large, dormitory-style rooms with shower and fans or A/C. Kitchen available. Singles $10, nonmembers $13. Doubles $20. Guest bike rental $5 per day. Reservation must be made in advance. Open for reservations 8-10am and 5-10pm.

American Inn, 42 San Marco Ave. (829-2292), near the visitors center. Owner won't take your money until you've inspected your room. He also provides transportation to and from the bus station when a car is available. Big, clean singles and doubles $34-38, weekends $38-49. Check visitors center for coupons.

Seabreeze Motel, 208 Anastasia Blvd. (829-8122), just over the Bridge of Lions east of the historic district. Clean rooms with A/C, TV. Pool. Good restaurants nearby. Singles $25. Doubles $30.

The St. Francis Inn, 279 Saint George St. (824-6068), at Saint Francis St., 2 doors down from the Oldest House. Charming 10-room inn with a jungle of flowers and a tucked-away pool. Much of its original 18th-century interior preserved. Iced tea and juice served all day. Free bike use. Rooms $47-78. Cottage on premises with full kitchen and living room $118 for 4 people, $8 each additional person. Continental breakfast included.

Anastasia State Recreation Area, on Rte. A1A (461-2033), 4 mi. south of the historic district. From town, cross the Bridge of Lions, and bear left just beyond the Alligator Farm. Open daily 8am-sundown. Sites $18, with electricity $21. Make weekend reservations.

Food

The flood of daytime tourists and the abundance of budget eateries make lunch in St. Augustine's historic district a delight. Stroll Saint George St. to check the daily specials scrawled on blackboards outside each restaurant; locals prefer those clustered at the southern end of Saint George near King St. Finding a budget dinner in St. Augustine is trickier, since downtown is deserted after 5pm. However, an expedition along Anastasia Blvd. should unearth good meals for under $6. The seafood-wise will seek out the surf 'n' turf dinners ($15) at **Captain Jack's,** 410 Anastasia Blvd. (829-6846). Those with wheels interested in mass quantities of food should try the all-you-can-eat buffet at the **Quincey Family Steakhouse,** 2 mi. south of town on Rte. A1A at Ponce de León Mall. (Open Sun.-Thurs. 11am-10pm, Fri.-Sat. 11am-11pm).

St. George Pharmacy and Restaurant, 121 Saint George St. Museum, luncheonette, and bookstore. Cheap sandwiches from $1.20; dinners from $2.50. Try the grilled cheese with a thick chocolate malt ($4). Breakfast special (egg, bacon, grits, toast or biscuit, and jelly) $2. Open Mon.-Fri. 7am-5pm, Sat.-Sun. 7:30am-5pm.

Café Camacho, 11-C Aviles St., at Charlotte St., 1 block from Saint George St. in the historic district. Part vintage clothes shop, part café. Serves delicious fruit shakes, soups, sandwiches, breakfast specials, vegetarian dishes, and an all-you-can-eat lunch bar from 11am-3pm ($5). Open Wed.-Mon. 7:30am-5pm.

O'Steen's, 205 Anastasia Blvd., 1½ mi. from downtown and 4 blocks from the Bridge of Lions. A lively local hangout with great prices. Arrive before 5pm to beat the dinner crowd. Daily special includes entree, salad or soup, and choice of 2 vegetables ($3.50, seafood $4.50). Open Mon.-Sat. 11am-8:30pm.

El Toro Con Sombrero, 10 Anastasia Blvd., on the left just over the Bridge of Lions from downtown. Look carefully because the sign is hidden by a sign for the adjoining sports bar. If you like Mexican food and 50s music, this is the place. Tacos $1.15. Open daily 7am-1am.

A New Dawn, 110 Anastasia Blvd. A health-conscious grocery store with a sandwich and juice counter. Delicious vegetarian sandwiches; try the Tofu Salad Surprise ($2.55). Fruit shakes and sodas $1-2. Open daily 8am-6pm.

Sights and Entertainment

Saint George St. is the center of the historic district, which begins at the Gates of the City near the visitors center and runs south past Cadiz St. and the Oldest Store. Visit **San Agustín Antiguo,** Gallegos House, Saint George St. (825-6830), St. Augustine's authentically restored 18th-century neighborhood, where artisans and villagers in period costumes describe the customs, crafts, and highlights of the Spaniards' New World existence. (Open daily 9am-5pm. Admission $5, seniors $4.50, students and ages 6-18 $2.) The oldest masonry fortress in the country, **Castillo de San Marcos,** 1 Castillo Dr. (829-6506), off San Marco Ave., has 14-ft. thick walls built of coquina, the local shellrock. The fort itself resembles a four-pointed star complete with a drawbridge and a murky moat. Inside you'll find a museum, a large courtyard surrounded by guardrooms, livery quarters for the garrison, a jail, a chapel, and the original cannons brought overseas by the Spanish. A cannon-firing ceremony happens once per day. (Open daily 8:30am-7:45pm; Sept.-May 9am-5pm. Admission $1, over 62 and under 12 free.)

St. Augustine has several old stores and museums. The self-descriptive **Oldest House,** 14 Saint Francis St. (824-2872), has been occupied continuously since its construction in the 1600s. (Open daily 9am-5pm. $5, seniors $4.50, students $2.50.) The **Oldest Store Museum,** 4 Artillery Lane (829-9729), has over 100,000 odds and ends from the 18th and 19th centuries. (Open Mon.-Sat. 9am-5pm, Sun. noon-5pm. Admission $3.) Also in the old part of the city is the coquina **Cathedral of St. Augustine,** begun in 1793. Although several fires destroyed parts of the cathedral, the walls and facade are original.

Six blocks north of the info center is the **Mission of Nombre de Dios,** Ocean St. (824-2809), a moss- and vine-covered mission which held the first Catholic service in the U.S. on September 8, 1565. Looming over the structure is a 208-ft. steel cross commemorating the city's founding. (Open Mon.-Fri. 8am-8pm, Sat.-Sun. 9am-8pm. Mass Mon.-Fri. at 8:30am, Sat. at 6pm, Sun. at 8am. Donation.) No trip to St. Augustine would be complete without a trek to the **Fountain of Youth,** 155 Magnolia Ave. (829-3168). Go right on Williams St. from San Marco Ave. and continue a few blocks past Nombre de Dios. (Open daily 9am-5pm. Admission $4, seniors $3, ages 6-12 $1.50.) In addition to drinking from the spring that Ponce de León mistakenly thought would give him eternal youth, you can see a statue of the explorer that does not age.

Though oil and water don't usually mix, Henry Flagler, co-founder of Standard Oil and a good friend of the Rockefellers, retired to St. Augustine. He built two hotels in the downtown area that the rich and famous once frequented, making St. Augustine the "Newport of the South." The former Ponce de León Hotel, at King and Cordova St., is now **Flagler College.** In summer the college is deserted, but during the school year students liven the town. In 1947, Chicago publisher and lover of large objects Otto Lightner converted the Alcazar Hotel into the **Lightner Museum,** (824-2874) with an impressive collection of cut, blown, and burnished glass. (Open daily 9am-5pm. Admission $4, ages 12-18 $1.)

Visitors can tour St. Augustine by land or by sea. **St. Augustine Sight-Seeing Trains,** 170 San Marcos Ave. (829-6545), offers a variety of city tours (1-8 hr.; open daily 8am-5pm). The one-hour tour ($9, ages 6-12 $4), a good introduction to the city, starts at the front of the visitors center. **Coleé Sight-Seeing Carriage Tours** (829-2818) begin near the entrance to the fort, take about an hour, and cover the historic area of St. Augustine ($9, ages 5-11 $4; open daily 8am-10pm.) The **Victory II Scenic Cruise Ships** (824-1806) navigate the emerald Matanzas River. Catch the boat at the City Yacht Pier, one block south of the Bridge of Lions (leaves at 1, 2:45, 4:30, 6:45, and 8:30pm; cruises $7, under 12 $3.50).

On Anastasia Island, at **Anastasia State Park,** you can see Paul Green's *Cross and Sword,* Florida's official state play, telling the story of St. Augustine with the help of a large cast, booming cannons, and swordfights. (Admission $8, ages 6-12 $4; discounts for AAA members and large groups.)

With such a penchant for loudness and liquid, St. Augustine has an impressive array of bars. **Scarlett O'Hara's,** 70 Hypolita St. (824-6535), at Cordova St., is popular with locals. The barbecue chicken sandwiches ($4) are filling and juicy, the drinks hefty and cool. Live entertainment begins at 9pm nightly. (Open daily 11:30am-1am.) Try the **Milltop,** 19½ Saint George St. (829-2329), a tiny bar situated above an old mill in the restored area. Local string musicians play on the tiny stage (daily 11am-midnight). On St. Augustine Beach, **Panama Hattie's** (471-2255) caters to the post-college crowd. Pick up a copy of the *Today Tonight* newspaper, available at most grocery and convenience stores, for a complete listing of current concerts, events, and dinner specials.

Tampa and St. Petersburg

The Gulf Coast communities of Tampa and St. Petersburg have a less-raucous style than most Atlantic Coast vacation Valhallas. Not as submerged in tourists, the two cities offer quiet beaches, beautiful harbors, and perfect weather year-round. One of the nation's fastest-growing cities and largest ports, Tampa contains thriving financial, industrial, and artistic communities. Across the bay, St. Petersburg caters to a relaxed, attractive retirement community, with oodles of health-food shops and pharmacies. Meanwhile, the town's not-so-martyred beaches beckon with 28 mi. of soft white sand, emerald water, and beautiful sunsets; perhaps as a result, the high season on the Gulf Coast runs from October to April.

Practical Information

Emergency: 911.

Tampa/Hillsborough Convention and Visitors Association, 111 Madison St. (223-1111 or 800-826-8358). Open Mon.-Sat. 9am-5pm. St. Petersburg Chamber of Commerce, 100 2nd Ave. N. (821-4069). Open Mon.-Fri. 8:30am-5pm.

Travelers Aid: In Tampa, 253-5936. Open Mon.-Fri. 8:30am-4:30pm. In St. Pete, 823-4891.

Tampa International Airport: (870-8700)) 5 mi. west of downtown. HARTline bus #30 runs between the airport and downtown Tampa. **St. Petersburg Clearwater International Airport** sits right across the bay. **The Limo** (822-3333) offers 24-hr. service from both airports to both cities and the beaches from Ft. Desoto to Clearwater ($10.50). Make reservations 12 hr. in advance.

Amtrak: In Tampa, 601 Nebraska Ave. (221-7600 or 800-872-7245), at Twiggs St., 1 block north of Kennedy. Two trains per day to: Orlando (2 hr., $10); Jacksonville (5 hr., $42); Savannah (8 hr., $71). Open daily 7:30am-8pm. No trains go south of Tampa—no service to St. Pete. In St. Pete, 3601 31st St. N. (522-9475). Amtrak will transport you to Tampa by bus ($5).

Greyhound/Trailways: In Tampa, 610 E. Polk St. (229-1501 or 229-2112), next to Burger King downtown. To Miami (4 per day, 10 hr., $40) and Orlando (5 per day, 1½ hr., $14). In St. Pete, 180 9th St. N., downtown.

Public Transport: In Tampa, **Hillsborough Area Regional Transit (HARTline),** 254-4278. Fare 85¢, transfers 10¢. To get to St. Pete, take bus #100 express service from downtown to the Gateway Mall ($1.50). In St. Pete, **St. Petersburg Municipal Transit System,** 530-9911. Most routes depart from Williams Park at 1st Ave. N. and 3rd St. N. Ask for directions at the information booth there. Fare 75¢, transfers 10¢.

Help Lines: In Tampa, Rape Crisis, 238-7273. **Gay/Lesbian Crisis Line,** 229-8839. In St. Petersburg **Rape Crisis,** 531-4664.

ZIP codes: Tampa 33602, St. Pete 33731.

Area Code: 813.

Tampa divides into quarters with **Florida Avenue,** running east-west, and **Kennedy Boulevard,** which becomes **Frank Adams Drive** (Rte. 60), running north-south. Numbered avenues run east-west and numbered streets run north-south. You can

If you're going to
SAN FRANCISCO

Forget wearing flowers in your hair!! (This is the 90's.)

Just bring the incredible coupon on the other side of this page!

Join our global family in San Francisco

"Thank you for recreating the **real spirit of the Haight!** (from one who actually lived here in 1966-67) ... Peace & Love."

"A weekend of laughter, new friends & memories of breakfasts with Charlotte (the cat)."

"My experience here at the Red Victorian has been so many things —emotional, loving, spiritual, educational — overall, indescribable. As I said many times these past couple weeks, it is not a hotel — it is a HOME."

"I hope I can bring some of the joy you shared with me to others, that we may all be closer."

"When every person in the world has visited this place, and learned they are part of the global family, peace & friendship will break out all over the planet!"

"So many new friends to break bread (or muffins) with."

"I could really stay here indefinitely and get lost in the vitality of all it has to offer."

Heart of San Francisco, near Golden Gate Park in the famous Haight-Ashbury

THE RED VICTORIAN
BED & BREAKFAST INN
1665 Haight St. • San Francisco, CA 94117 • 415-864-1978

USA

PLACE
STAMP
HERE

THE RED VICTORIAN
BED & BREAKFAST INN
1665 Haight St.
San Francisco, CA 94117

I would love to visit! Please tell me more about the Red Victorian

NAME _____

ADDRESS _____

CITY / STATE _____ ZIP

reach Tampa on I-75 from the north, or I-4 from the east. In St. Petersburg 22 mi. south, **Central Avenue** runs east-west. **34th Street** (U.S. Hwy. 19) cuts north-south through the city and links up with the new **Sunshine-Skyway bridge,** which connects St. Pete with the Bradenton-Sarasota area to the south. Avenues run east-west, streets north-south. The St. Pete beachfront is a chain of barrier islands accessible by bridges on the far west side of town, and extends from Clearwater Beach in the north to Pass-a-Grille Beach in the south. Many towns on the islands offer quiet beaches and reasonably priced hotels and restaurants. From north to south, these towns include: **Clearwater Beach, Indian Rocks Beach, Madiera Beach, Treasure Island,** and **St. Petersburg Beach.** The stretch of beach past the Don CeSar Hotel (a pink montrosity recently declared a historical landmark) in St. Petersburg Beach and Pass-a-Grille Beach has the best sand, a devoted following, and the least pedestrian and motor traffic.

Three causeways connect Tampa and St. Pete.

Accommodations and Camping

Inexpensive, convenient lodgings happen rarely in Tampa, but St. Petersburg has a youth hostel and many cheap motels along 4th St. N. and U.S. 19. Some establishments advertise singles for as little as $16, but these tend to be ancient and dirty. To avoid the worst neighborhoods, stay on the north end of 4th St. and the south end of U.S. 19. Several inexpensive motels also line the St. Pete beach. In Tampa, you can try to contact the Overseas Information Center at the **University of South Florida** (974-3104) for help in finding accommodations.

Tampa

Motel 6, 333 E. Fowler Ave. (932-4948), near Busch Gardens. From I-275, take the Fowler Ave. exit. On the northern outskirts of Tampa, 30 mi. from the beach. Well-used, small rooms. Singles $25.25. Each additional person $6.

Travelodge, 830 West Kennedy Boulevard (253-0851). From I-275, take the Ashley St. exit. Go south and turn right on Kennedy Boulevard. HBO and free coffee. Singles $30. Each additional person $5. (Get a $5 discount coupon at the Tampa Visitors Information.)

Holiday Inn, 2708 N. 50th St. (621-2081) From I-4, take Exit #3. Pool, whirlpool spa and cable TV. 1-4 people $32.

Econolodge, 2905 N. 50th st. (621-3541) Singles or doubles $32. Each additional person $5.

St. Petersburg

St. Petersburg International Hostel (AAIH), 215 Central Ave. (822-4095), at the Detroit Hotel downtown. Big, clean rooms with 2-4 beds, A/C; some with private bath. Kitchen and laundry facilities. Call for pick-up at Greyhound or Amtrak stations. In the same building, **Club Detroit** offers live music 5 nights per week. Also, **Janus Landing** offers big name concerts like Depeche Mode. $10. Weekly: $50. Key deposit $5. Private rooms available.

Kentucky Motel, 4246 4th St. N. (526-7373). Large, clean rooms with friendly owners, cable TV, refrigerator in each room, and free postcards. Singles $22. Doubles $26. Dec.-April rooms $10 more.

Grant Motel, 9046 4th St. (576-1369), 4 mi. north of town on U.S. 92. Pool. Clean rooms with A/C; most have fridge. Singles $28. Doubles $30. Jan. 1-April 15 singles $38, doubles $40.

Windjammer, 10450 Gulf Blvd. (360-4940), on the beach. Large, clean rooms. Laundry, HBO, pool. Doubles $40-42, with kitchen $42-46. High season $50 and $65, respectively. Each additional person $5.

Treasure Island Hotel, 10315 Gulf Blvd. (367-3055). Across the street from beach, big rooms with A/C, fridges and color TV. Pool. Single $28. Doubles $29. Each additional person $4.

The Trade Winds, 10300 Gulf Blvd. (360-0490). On the beach, nice pool, A/C, color TV. Singles $36. Each additional person $4.

Fort DeSoto State Park (866-2662), composed of five islands at the southern end of a long chain of keys and islands, has the best camping. A wildlife sanctuary, the park makes a good daytrip or oceanside picnic spot (2-day min. stay; curfew 10pm; no alcohol; sites $14). Disregard the "no vacancy" sign at the toll booth (85¢) by the Pinellas Bayway exit. However, from January to April, you may want to make a reservation in person at the St. Petersburg County Building, 150 5th St. N. #146, or at least call ahead. In Tampa, try the **Busch Travel Park,** 10001 Malcolm McKinley Dr. (971-0008), ¼-mi. north of Busch Gardens, with a pool, store, recreation room, and train service to Busch Gardens and Adventure Island. (Tent sites $9. RV sites $15.)

Food

Prices for food leap high in Tampa, but cheap Cuban and Spanish establishments stretch all over the city. Black bean soup, gazpacho, and Cuban bread usually yield the best bargains. For Cuban food, Ybor City definitely has superior prices and atmosphere.

St. Petersburg's cheap, health-conscious restaurants cater to its retired population—they generally close by 8 or 9pm. Those hungry later should try St. Pete Beach or 4th St.

Tampa

JD's, (247-9683) 2029 E. 7th Ave., in Ybor City. Take bus #12. Soups, sandwiches, and Cuban food in a roomy, low-key restaurant. Breakfast $2.50. Lunch $3-5. Open Mon.-Fri. 9am-3pm.

The Loading Dock, 100 Madison St., downtown. Sandwiches $3-5. Try the "Flatbed" or the "Forklift" for a filling diesel-fueled meal. Open Mon.-Fri. 8am-8pm, Sat. 10:30am-2:30pm.

Jamaica Jim's, 1701 E. 4th ave. (247-9022), cheap Jamaican specialties. Red snapper or curry chicken $4-$7. Colorful garden in back and reggae shows throughout the summer. Open Mon.-Wed. 11:30am-10pm, Thurs. 11:30am-1am, Fri.-Sat. 'til 3am.

The Spaghetti Warehouse, 1911 13th St. (248-1720), right in Ybor Square. Lunch or dinner $7. Open Sun.-Thurs. 11am-10pm, Fri.-Sat. noon-11pm.

St. Pete

Crabby Bills, (593-4825) 412 1st St. N., Indian Rocks Beach. Cheap, extensive menu. Ultra-casual atmosphere. Six blue crabs $5.50. Open Mon.-Thurs. 11am-10pm, Fri.-Sat. 11am-11pm. Arrive before 5pm to avoid substantial wait.

Ollie O's (822-6200), 101 1st Ave. NE, St. Pete, in the Old Soreno Hotel 2 blocks from the youth hostel. Huge steaks with fries ($7) or soup and sandwich ($4). Open Mon.-Thurs. and Sat. 7am-5:30pm, Fri. 7am-6pm.

Russo's Pizza (367-2874), 103-104th Ave. Treasure Island. A local joint connected to an arcade. Try the tasty and filling Stromboly ($3.85). Open 11am-midnight.

The Pelican Diner (363-9873), 7501 Golf Blvd., St. Pete Beach on the corner of 75th Ave. Burgers ($2.30), malts ($2.40). Jukeboxes at each table. Open Mon.-Sat. 24 hrs. Sun. till 11:30am.

Sights and Activities

Tampa

Bounded roughly by 22nd Street, Nebraska Avenue, 5th Avenue, and Columbus Drive, **Ybor City** is Tampa's Latin Quarter. The area expanded rapidly after Vincent Martínez Ybor moved his cigar factories here from Key West in 1886. Although cigar manufacturing has been mechanized, some people still roll cigars by hand and sell them for $1 in **Ybor Square (1901 13th St., 247-4497),** a 19th-century cigar factory converted into an upscale retail complex. (Open Mon.-Sat. 9:30am-5:30pm, Sun. noon-5:30pm. Free.) **Ybor City State Museum,** 1818 9th Ave. at 21st

St. (247-6323), traces the development of Ybor City, Tampa, the cigar industry, and Cuban migration. (Open Tues.-Sat. 9am-noon and 1-5pm. Admission 50¢.) The **Three Birds Bookstore and Coffee Room,** 1518 7th Ave. (247-7041), contributes artsily to Ybor City. Sip orange zinger tea or get a slice of black forest cheesecake while you read the latest *Paris Review.* (Open Mon.-Thurs. 11am-6pm, Fri.-Sat. 11am-10pm). Aside from the square, the Ybor City area has remained relatively unspoiled by the rapid urban growth that typifies the rest of Tampa; **East 7th Avenue** still resembles an old neighborhood. Keep an ear out for jazz and a nose out for Cuban cuisine. Be careful not to stray more than two blocks north or south of 7th Ave. since the area can be extremely dangerous, even during the daytime. Bus #5, 12, and 18 run to Ybor City from downtown.

Now part of the University of Tampa, the Moorish **Tampa Bay Hotel,** 401 W. Kennedy Blvd., once epitomized fashionable Florida coast hotels. Teddy Roosevelt trained his Rough Riders in the backyard before the Spanish-American War. The small **Henry B. Plant Museum** (254-1891), in a wing of the University of Tampa building, is an orgy of Rococo craftsmanship and architecture; the exhibits themselves, which include Victorian furniture and Wedgewood pottery, pale in comparison. (Guided tours at 1:30pm. Open Tues.-Sat. 10am-4pm. Donation.)

Downtown, the **Tampa Museum of Art,** 601 Doyle Carlton Dr. (223-8130), houses the Joseph Veach Nobre collection of classical and modern works. (Open Tues.-Sat. 10am-5pm, Wed. 10am-9pm, Sun. 1-5pm. Free.) Across from the University of South Florida, north of downtown, the **Museum of Science and Industry,** 4801 E. Fowler Ave. (985-5531), features a simulated hurricane. (Open daily 10am-4:30pm. Admission $4, ages 5-15 $2.)

The **waterfront** provides much of Tampa's atmosphere. Banana boats from South and Central America unload and tally their cargo every day at the docks on 139 Twiggs St., near 13th St. and Kennedy Blvd. Every year in February the *Jose Gasparilla,* a fully rigged pirate ship, loaded with hundreds of exuberant "pirates," "invades" Tampa and kicks off a month of parades and festivals, such as the **Gasparilla Sidewalk Art Festival.** (Pick up a copy of SEE-A visitor's guide, for current info on various events and festivals.)

Enjoy everything from bumper cars to corkscrew rollercoasters at Tampa's **Busch Gardens—The Dark Continent,** 3000 Busch Blvd. and NE 40th St. (971-8282). Take I-275 to Busch Blvd., or take bus #5 from downtown. Not only are people confined to trains, boats, and walkways while giraffes, zebras, ostriches, and antelope roam freely across the park's 60-acre plain, but Busch Gardens has two of only 50 white Bengal tigers in existence. (Open daily 9am-8pm; off-season dialy 9:30am-6pm. Admission $25, infants free. Parking $3.) A morning visit to the **Anheuser-Busch Hospitality House** inside the park provides a sure-fire way to make your afternoon more enjoyable. You must stand in line for each beer, with a three-drink limit.

About ¼-mi. northeast of Busch Gardens at 4545 Bougainvillie Ave. is **Adventure Island** (987-5660), a 19-acre water theme park. (Admission $15. For those under 48" $12. Open 10am-5pm with extended hours in summer.)

St. Petersburg

St. Petersburg's main attraction is its coastline. **Pass-a-Grille Beach** may be the nicest, but with parking meters, it extracts a toll. The **Municipal beach** at Treasure Island, accessible from Rte. 699 via Treasure Island Causeway, offers free parking. When you're too sunburned to spend another day on the sand, head for **Sunken Gardens,** 1825 4th St. N. (896-3187), home of over 7000 varieties of exotic flowers and plants. (Open daily 9am-5:30pm. Admission $7, ages 3-11 $4.)

Opened in March 1982, the **Salvador Dalí Museum,** 1000 3rd St. S. (823-3767), in Poynter Park on the Bayboro Harbor waterfront, contains the world's largest collection of Dalí works and memorabilia—93 oil paintings, 1300 graphics, and even works from a 14-year-old Dalí. (Tours available. Open Tues.-Sat. 10am-5pm, Sun. noon-5pm. Admission $5, seniors and students $3.50, under 9 free.) **Great Explorations,** 1120 4th St. S. (821-8885), is a museum with six areas of exhibits to fondle. Test your strength at the Body Shop where you can compare your muscles against scores taken from around the country. Admission 4-17 $3.50, 17-65 $4.50, 66 and over $4. (Open Mon.-Sat. 10am-5pm, Sun. 1-5pm.) **The Pier,** at the end of 2nd Ave. NE (821-6164), extends out into Tampa Bay from St. Pete, ending in a five-story inverted pyramid complex that contains a shopping center, aquarium, and restaurant. (Open Mon.-Sat. at 10am, Sun. at 11am.)

GEORGIA

Georgians have begun to feel the blush of prosperity. Atlanta (a-LAN-a) holds the rather unofficial title of "Capital of the New South," while Savannah's stately antebellum homes are undergoing restoration. Both cities will be on display when Atlanta hosts the 1996 Olympic games. Ouside of these urban areas, the state is still largely agrarian, keeping Georgians up to their ears in their favorite fruit, the peach. As is the case in most of the South, the hospitality is peachy, making Georgia the perfect destination for midnight trains.

Practical Information

Capital: Atlanta.

Department of Industry and Trade, Tourist Division, 230 Peachtree St., Atlanta 30301 (656-3590), across from Atlanta Convention and Visitors Bureau. Write for or pick up a comprehensive *Georgia Travel Guide.* Open Mon.-Fri. 8am-5pm. **Department of Natural Resources,** 270 Washington St. SW, Atlanta 30334 (800-542-7275; 800-342-7275 in GA). **U.S. Forest Service,** 1720 Peachtree Rd. NW, Atlanta 30367 (347-2385). Info on the Chattahoochee and Oconee National Forests. Open Mon.-Fri. 8am-4pm.

Time Zone: Eastern. **Postal Abbreviation:** GA

Atlanta

Atlanta's seal (the phoenix) and its motto, *Resurgens,* sum up the city's fabulous recovery since 1864, when Union General Sherman burned it to the ground. Today, Atlanta soars as the largest metropolitan area in the Southeast and as a national economic powerhouse. The city contains the world's second-busiest airport, the headquarters of Coca-Cola, and offices of over 400 of the Fortune 500 corporations. Nineteen institutions of higher learning, including Georgia Tech, Emory University, and Morehouse and Spelman colleges, call "The Big Peach" home.

Not surprisingly, fame and prosperity have diffused Atlanta's Old South flavor. An influx of transplanted Northerners and Californians, the third-largest gay population in the U.S., and a host of ethnic groups have lent the city a cosmopolitan air. The birthplace of Martin Luther King, Jr. witnessed unrest and activism during the 60s; deeply impressed by lessons learned in the civil rights struggle, Atlanta elected one of the nation's first African American mayors, Maynard Jackson, in 1974. Sleek and upbeat, the city is beseiged by new construction at nearly every turn; Atlantans have already caught Olympic fever.

Practical Information

Emergency: 911.

Atlanta Convention and Visitors Bureau, 233 Peachtree St. #200 (659-4270), Peachtree Center, Harris Tower, downtown. Caters more to conventions; step by to pick up a free copy of *Atlanta and Georgia Visitors' Guide* ($3 on newsstands). Open Mon.-Fri. 9am-5pm. Satellite information centers are at **Peachtree Center Mall** (659-0800), 233 Peachtree St. NE (Open Mon.-Fri. 10am-6pm, Sat. 10am-5pm), and **Lenox Square Shopping Center** (233-6767), 3393 Peachtree Rd. NE, in Buckhead (open Mon.-Sat. 10am-9:30pm, Sun. 12:30-5:30pm). Both

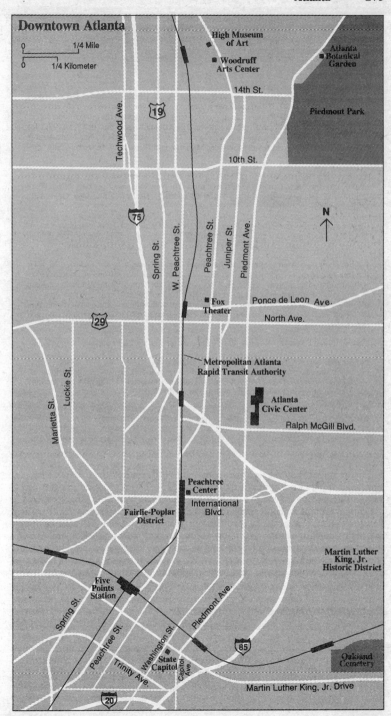

Downtown Atlanta

0 ____ 1/4 Mile
0 ____ 1/4 Kilometer

High Museum
of Art

Woodruff
Arts Center

Atlanta
Botanical
Garden

14th St.

Piedmont Park

Techwood Ave.

19

10th St.

75

Spring St.

W. Peachtree St.

Peachtree St.

Juniper St.

Piedmont Ave.

N

29

Fox
Theater

Ponce de Leon Ave.

North Ave.

Metropolitan Atlanta
Rapid Transit Authority

Marietta St.

Luckie St.

Atlanta
Civic Center

Ralph McGill Blvd.

Peachtree
Center

International
Blvd.

Fairlie-Poplar
District

Martin Luther
King, Jr.
Historic District

Spring St.

Five
Points
Station

Peachtree St.

Washington St.

Piedmont Ave.

85

Trinity Ave.

Capitol Ave.

State
Capitol

Oakland
Cemetery

20

Martin Luther King, Jr. Drive

open Mon.-Fri. 10am-5pm. Also at **Underground Atlanta,** Peachtree St. and Martin Luther King, Jr. Dr. (523-2311). Open Mon.-Sat. 10am-9:30pm, Sun. noon-6pm.

Travelers Aid: 81 International Blvd. (527-7400), in the downtown Greyhound terminal. Limited info on accommodations. Open Mon.-Fri. 8am-8pm, Sat. 10am-6pm. After hours, call 522-7370 for assistance.

Hartsfield International Airport: south of the city, bounded by I-75, I-85, and I-285. General info 530-6600; international services and flight info 530-2081. Headquarters of **Delta Airlines** 756-5000 or 800-523-7777. International travelers can get phone assistance in 6 languages at the **Calling Assistance Center,** a computerized telephone system in the international terminal. Subway is the easiest way to get downtown. The **Atlanta Airport Shuttle** (525-2177) runs vans from the airport to downtown, Emory, and Lenox Sq. (around $12). **Northside Airport Express** (455-1600) serves Stone Mountain, Marietta, and Dunwoody. Buses run daily 5am-midnight ($15-30).

Amtrak: 1688 Peachtree St. NW (872-9815), 3 mi. north of downtown at I-85. Take bus #23 to and from the "Arts Center" MARTA station. To: New Orleans (2 per day, 11 hr., $93); Washington, DC (2 per day, 14 hr., $114); Charlotte (2 per day, 5 hr., $49). Open daily 6:30am-9:30pm.

Greyhound/Trailways: 81 International Blvd. (522-6300), 1 block from Peachtree Center. MARTA: Peachtree Center. To New Orleans (7 per day, 9 hr., $76), Washington, DC (8 per day, 16 hr., $104), and Chattanooga (8 per day, 2½ hr., $21). Open 24 hrs.

Public Transport: Metropolitan Atlanta Rapid Transit Authority (MARTA), 848-4711; schedule info Mon.-Fri. 6am-10pm, Sat.-Sun. 8am-4pm. Combined rail and bus system serves virtually all area attractions and hotels. Operates Mon.-Sat. 5am-1:30am, Sun. 6am-12:30am in most areas. Fare $1 exact change, transfers free. Unlimited weekly pass $9. Pick up a system map at the **MARTA Ride Store,** Five Points Station downtown, or at one of the satellite visitor bureaus. If you get confused, just find the nearest MARTA courtesy phone in each rail station.

Taxi: Checker, 351-1111. **London,** 681-2280. Base fare $1.50, $1.20 per mi.

Car Rental: Atlanta Rent-a-Car, 3185 Camp Creek Pkwy. (763-1160), just inside I-285, 3 mi. east of the airport. Nine other locations in the area including one at Cheshire Bridge Rd. and I-85, 1 mi. west of the Liddberg Center Railstop. Rates from $16 per day. 50 free mi., 20¢ each additional mi. Must be 21 with major credit card.

Help Lines: Rape Crisis Counseling, 659-7273. Open 24 hrs. **Gay/Lesbian Center Help Line,** 892-0661. Open daily 6-11pm. Center located at 63 12th St. (876-5372).

Post Office: 3900 Crown Rd. (768-4126). Open Mon.-Fri. 7:30am-5pm. **ZIP code:** 30321.

Area Code: 404.

Atlanta smiles from the northwest quadrant of the state, 150 mi. east of Birmingham, AL, and 113 mi. south of Chattanooga, TN. The city lies on north-south I-75 and I-85 and on east-west I-20. It is circumscribed by I-285 ("the perimeter").

Getting around is confusing at first because everything seems to be named Peachtree. However, of the 26 roads bearing that name, only one, **Peachtree Street,** is a major north-south thoroughfare, as are **Spring Street** and **Piedmont Avenue. Ponce De Leon Avenue** and **North Avenue** are major east-west routes. In the heart of downtown, the area to the west of I-75/85, south of International Blvd. and north of the capitol, where angled streets and shopping plazas run amok, navigation is difficult.

Accommodations and Camping

When planning to stay in Atlanta for more than a few days, check with the **International Youth Travel Program (IYTP).** The convention and visitors bureau (see Practical Information above), will try to locate a single for a reasonable price. The IYTP is your cheapest bet besides the YMCA. Unfortunately, these options do not apply for women from the U.S. **Bed and Breakfast Atlanta,** 1801 Piedmont Ave. NE (875-0525; call Mon.-Fri. 9am-noon or 2-5pm), offers singles from $45, doubles from $48-60.

Motel 6, 6 locations in the Atlanta area, all just outside the perimeter. Marietta, 2360 Delk Rd., exit 11 from I-75 (952-8161). Big, usually busy, hotel complex with large earth-toned rooms furnished with comfortable chairs. Pool. Singles $24. Each additional person $6. Another on I-285 at Chamblee-Turcker, exit 27 (455-8000), closer to the city. Two-story motel with pleasant clean rooms. Complete table and chair set and green curtains. Pool. Singles $26. Each additional person $6.

Travelodge, 1641 Peachtree St. NE (873-5731), in sight of the Amtrak station. Freshly painted, large hotel with attractive rooms and cushioned chairs. Complimentary coffee. Singles $39. Doubles $49.

Best Way Inn, 144 14th St. NW (873-4171), very, very near the highway. Tidy rooms with ugly paintings. Friendly management. Mexican restaurant. Pool. Singles $31. Doubles $36. Key deposit $5.

YMCA, 22 Butler St. (659-8085), between Edgewood and Auburn, 3 blocks from downtown. Men only, and usually full of semi-permanent residents. Community shower. Singles $16. Key deposit $5. Hard to find space here, and they don't take reservations.

The Woodruff AYH-Hostel (AYH) (875-9449) at 223 Ponce de Leon Ave. Stained-glass windows. Members $12.50, nonmembers $15.50.

Arrowhead Campsites, I-20 W. and Six Flags Rd. (948-7302), 10 mi. west of downtown. Subway to Hightower, then bus to Six Flags in Austell, GA. Includes pool and laundry. Tent sites $11.75. RV sites $14.75.

Stone Mountain Family Campground, on U.S. 78 (498-5710), 16 mi. east of town. Exit 30-B off I-285 or subway to Avondale then "Stone Mountain" bus. Part of state park system. Tent sites $9. RV sites $9.50. Entrance fee $5 per car. Make reservations 2 weeks ahead.

Food

You really have to scrounge for inexpensive home-style Southern cooking in Atlanta. Some favorite dishes to sample include fried chicken, black-eyed peas, okra, sweet-potato pie, and mustard greens. Dip a hunk of cornbread into "pot likker," water used to cook greens, and enjoy. Atlanta's food offerings defy easy categorization, however. **Little Five Points,** is home to French-African, Ethiopian, and vegetarian restaurants in many permutations; the rest of Atlanta is full of variety, too.

Do-it-yourselfers can procure produce at one of the South's largest outdoor markets, the **Atlanta State Farmers Market,** 16 Forest Pkwy. (366-6910), exit 78 off I-75 south. (No MARTA service.) The grocery in building K is open Mon.-Fri. 7am-5pm, Sat. and Sun. 8am-5pm. Fresh fruits, vegetables, eggs, and smoked meats are on sale in 80 acres of open-air, drive-through stalls. Some people have stands that are open 24 hrs. but the majority of them are there from 8am-6pm daily. (Open Mon.-Fri. 10am-10pm, Sat.-Sun. 9am-9pm.) Travelers without a car may find the world-wide specialties of **Dekalb County Farmers Market,** 3000 E. Ponce de Leon Ave. (377-6400), near Stone Mountain, more accessible. Take the subway to Avondale and then the "Stone Mountain" bus. (Open Mon.-Fri. 10am-9pm, Sat. and Sun. 9am-9pm.)

Mary Mac's Tea Room (875-4337), 224 Ponce De Leon Ave. NE. Take the "Georgia Tech" bus north. Famous for its amazing homemade cornbread and array of real Southern vegetables. Order by writing your own ticket. Waiters tend to rush you. Lunches $5-7, dinners $6-10. With student ID receive 10% discount at dinner. Open Mon.-Fri. 11am-4pm and 5-8pm.

The Varsity, 61 North Ave. NW at I-85 (881-1706). Take the subway to North Ave. station. Order at the world's largest drive-in or brave the masses to eat inside. Best known for chili dogs and the greasiest onion rings in the South. Employees have a language all their own. Eat in one of the giant TV rooms—1 room for each channel and vice-versa. Open Sun.-Thurs. 7am-12:30am, Fri.-Sat. 7am-2am.

Tortilla's, 774 Ponce De Leon Ave. Incredibly busy, neon-lit Mexican eatery. Cheap and luscious tacos $1.75, enormous gigantic super burrito $3. Open Mon.-Fri. 11am-10pm, Sat. noon-10pm.

Eat Your Vegetables Café, 438 Moreland Ave. NE (523-2671), in the Little Five Points area. Mostly vegetarian foods (hummus, soyburgers, and salads) in a largely friendly atmosphere.

Dinners $7-12. Open Mon.-Fri. 11:30am-2pm and 6-10:30pm, Sat. 11am-3pm and 5:30-10:30pm, Sun. 11am-3pm.

Touch of India, 962 Peachtree St. Three-course lunch specials $4. Popular with locals. Atmosphere and service worthy of a much more expensive restaurant. Dinners $6-10. Open daily 11:30am-2:30pm and 5:30-10:30pm.

Sights

Atlanta's sights are scattered, but the effort it takes to find them usually pays off. The **Atlanta Preservation Center,** 401 the Flatiron Building, 84 Peachtree St. NW (522-4345), offers six walking tours of popular areas—Historic Downtown, West End and Wren's Nest, Oakland Cemetery, the capitol and Underground Atlanta, Inman Park, and Sweet Auburn—from April through November. A tour of the Fox Theater and environs is given year-round. All tours last about two hours. (Tours $4, seniors and students $2. Call for exact times and starting points.)

Visiting these areas on your own is the economical option. Redeveloped **Underground Atlanta** is actually six blocks with over 120 shops, restaurants, and nightspots, all beneath the street. The entrance to Underground Atlanta is beside the "Five Points" subway stop. In the summer live musicians often play in and around Underground. (Shops open Mon.-Sat. 10am-9:30pm, Sun. noon-6pm. Bars and restaurants open later.) **Atlanta Heritage Row,** 55 Upper Alabama St. (584-7879), documents the city's past and looks into the future with exhibits and films. (Open Tues.-Sat. 10am-7pm, Sun. 1-7pm. Admission $3, seniors and students over 12 $2.50, kids $2.) Adjacent to the shopping complex is the **World of Coca-Cola Pavilion,** 55 Martin Luther King, Jr. Dr. (676-5151), clearly recognizable by a Times Square-style neon Coca-Cola sign stretching 26 ft. across. The $15 million facility highlights "the real thing's" humble beginnings in Atlanta with over 1000 artifacts and interactive displays. (Open Mon.-Sat. 10am-9:30pm, Sun. noon-6pm. Admission $2.50, seniors $2, kids $1.50.)

Another big business in Atlanta, **Turner Broadcasting** and its Cable News Network (CNN), also promos a museum for curious visitors. The **CNN Studio tour,** at Techwood Dr. and Marietta St. (827-2300), demonstrates the day-to-day workings of a 24-hr. cable news station; witness the anchorpeople broadcasting the news live on the air beside the writers who produce the scripts. MARTA: Omni Station. (Open Mon.-Fri. 10am-5pm, Sat.-Sun. 10am-4pm. Tours on the hr. Admission $5, seniors and under 16 $2.50.)

Occasionally the CNN cameras turn a few blocks to the south on the **Georgia State Capitol,** Capitol Hill at Washington St. (656-2844). The gold that covers the dome was mined nearby in Dahlonega, GA. MARTA: George State. (Open Mon.-Fri. 8am-5:30pm. Tours Mon.-Fri. on the hr. 10am-2pm except noon. Free.) Georgia moved into the nation's spotlight when past governor Jimmy Carter became U.S. President. Today the **Carter Presidential Center,** 1 Copenhill (331-3942), north of Little Five Points documents the Carter Administration (1977-1980) through exhibits and films; of course, the center also houses a Japanese garden and café. Take bus #16 to Cleburne Ave. from Five Points Station. (Open Mon.-Sat. 9am-4:45pm, Sun. noon-4:45pm. Admission $2.50, seniors $1.50, under 16 free.)

The church, birth and burial places, and museum of the youngest man ever to be awarded a Nobel Peace Prize can all be explored in the **Martin Luther King, Jr. National Historic Site.** Stop by its visitor center for an incredibly informative and helpful map of the **Sweet Auburn District,** also containing a short biography of King. **Ebenezer Baptist Church,** 407-13 Auburn Ave. (688-7263), where King pastored from 1960 to 1968, is now open to the public, as are Sunday worship services. (Open Mon.-Fri. 9:30am-4:30pm. Call for weekend hours. Donations accepted.) The 23½-acre area also includes the restored house where King was born, 501 Auburn Ave. (331-3919; open daily 10am-5pm, off-season 10am-3:30pm; free). King is buried at the **Martin Luther King Center for Nonviolent Social Change,** 449 Auburn Ave. (524-1956), which also holds a collection of King's personal effects and a film about his life. Take bus #3 from Peachtree/Alabama. (Open daily

9am-5:30pm. Open until 8pm during summer months. Admission $1 for film on King.)

Just south of the King Memorial, **Oakland Cemetary,** 248 Oakland Ave. SE (577-8163), contains the graves of golfer Bobby Jones and *Gone With the Wind* author Margaret Mitchell. MARTA: King Memorial, two blocks south. (Open daily sunrise-sunset. Information center open Mon.-Fri. 9am-5pm. Free.) True *Gone With the Wind* fans can visit the Margaret Mitchell Room in the **Atlanta Public Library,** 1 Margaret Mitchell downtown. Here you'll find memorobilia such as autographed copies of her famous book. (Open Mon. and Fri. 9am-6pm, Tues.-Thurs. 9am-8pm, Sat. 10am-6pm, Sun. 2-6pm.)

Farther south of Oakland Cemetary in **Grant Park,** between Cherokee Ave. and Boulevard, the 40-acre **Zoo Atlanta** (624-5678) was the lucky beneficiary of a $25 million face-lift with a new emphasis on natural habitats for the animals. Several entertaining animal shows stress conservation and the environment. Among the new exhibits is the Masai Mara, a re-creation of an African savannah, with an endangered black rhinoceros. Say "hi" to Willie B., Atlanta's favorite gorilla, in the African rain forest. (Open July-Aug. Mon.-Fri. 10am-5pm, Sat.-Sun. 10am-6pm; Sept.-June daily 10am-5pm. Ticket office closes at 4:30pm. Admission $6.75, ages 3-11 $4.) Next door to Zoo Atlanta is **Cyclorama** (658-7625). This massive panoramic painting, measuring 42 ft. high and 900 ft. round, recreates the 1864 Civil War Battle of Atlanta. The exposition comes complete with 3-D features and lighting and sound effects. Take bus #31 "Grant Park."(Open June-Sept. daily 9:30am-5:30pm; Oct.-May 9:30am-4:30pm. Admission $3.50, seniors $3, kids $2.)

North of the city, on the other side of downtown, is **Piedmont Park,** where you can see the 60-acre **Atlanta Botanical Garden,** Piedmont Ave. at the Prado (876-5858). Stroll through five acres of landscaped gardens, a 15-acre hardwood forest with walking trails, and an exhibition hall. The Dorothy Chapman Fugua Conservatory holds hundreds of species of rare tropical plants. Take bus #36 "North Decatur" from the Arts Center subway stop. (Open Tues.-Sat. 9am-6pm, Sun. noon-6pm. Admission $4.50, seniors and kids $2.25. Thurs. 1:30-6pm free.) Just to the west of the park, the **Woodruff Arts Center,** 1280 Peachtree St. (892-3600; take the subway to Arts Center), houses the **High Museum** (892-4444) in Richard Meier's award-winning building of glass, steel, and white porcelain. The museum includes European decorative arts, European and U.S. paintings, photography, and a variety of (con)temporary art exhibits. (Open Tues.-Sat. 10am-5pm, Sun. noon-5pm. Admission $4, seniors and students with ID $2, kids $1. Thurs. 1-5pm free.) The museum branch at Georgia-Pacific Center (577-6939), one block south of Peachtree Center Station, is free (open Mon.-Fri. 11am-5pm).The **West End** is Atlanta's oldest neighborhood, dating back to 1835. Here hovers the **Wren's Nest,** 1050 Gordon St. (753-8535), home to Joel Chandler Harris, who popularized the African folktale trickster Br'er Rabbit through a somewhat stereotypical slave character, Uncle Remus. Take "Cascade" bus from West End Station. (Open Tues.-Sat. 10am-4pm, Sun. 2-4pm. Admission $3, seniors and teens $2, kids $1.)

Buckhead shows off one of the most beautiful residences in the Southeast. The Greek Revival **Governor's Mansion,** 391 West Paces Ferry Rd. (261-1776), bus #40 "West Paces Ferry" from Lenox Station, has elaborate gardens and furniture from the Federal period. (Tours Tues.-Thurs. 10-11:30am. Free.) In the same neighborhood, discover the **Atlanta History Society,** 3101 Andrew Dr. NW (261-1837). On the grounds are the **Swan House,** a lavish Anglo-Palladian Revival home, and the **Tullie Smith House,** an antebellum farmhouse. Don't miss the intriguing *Atlanta Resurgens* exhibit, in which famous and not-so-famous Atlantans praise the city. (Tours every ½-hr. Open Mon.-Sat. 9am-5:30pm, Sun. noon-5pm. Admission $6, seniors and students $4.50, kids $3.)

For a different atmosphere, with African clothes, used books, and general hanging out, wander through the eclectic **Little Five Points Business District** at the intersection of Moreland and Euclid Ave. NE, the center of Atlanta's bohemian community. The fortunate or psychotic may catch a glimpse of the psychedelic "Magic Bus" driven by the band YUR ("Your Universal Reality"), whose headquarters are in the neighborhood. Stroll through the second-hand clothing and record stores. Airborne disc afficionados should stop at **Identified Flying Objects,** 1164 Euclid Ave. NE (524-4628), a Frisbee department store. (Open Mon.-Fri. 11am-6:30pm, Sat. 11am-6pm, Sun. 11am-5pm.) Also visit the **Berman Gallery,** 1131 Euclid Ave. NE (525-2529), for its extensive Southern folk art collection. Open Tues.-Sat. 10am-5:30pm.

A respite from the city is available at **Stone Mountain Park** (498-5600), 16 mi. east on U.S. 78, where a fabulous bas-relief monument to the Confederacy is carved into the world's largest mass of granite. The "Mount Rushmore of the South" features Jefferson Davis, Robert E. Lee, and Stonewall Jackson and measures 90 by 190 ft. Surrounded by a 3200-acre recreational area, the mountain dwarfs the enormous statue. Check out the dazzling laser show on the side of the mountain each summer night at 9:30pm. Take bus #120 "Stone Mountain" from the Avondale subway stop. Buses leave only Mon.-Fri. at 4:30 and 7:50pm. (Park open daily 6am-midnight. Admission $5 per car.)

Six Flags, 7561 Six Flags Rd. SW (948-9290), at I-20 W., is one of the largest (331 acres) theme amusement parks in the nation, and includes several rollercosters, a free-fall machine, live shows, and whitewater rides. On summer weekends, the park is packed to the gills. Take bus #201 ("Six Flags"; $1.25) from Hightower Station. (Open summer daily roughly 10am-10pm. One-day admission $21, 2 days $25, seniors $10.50, kids under 48 in. $14.)

Entertainment

For nearly sure-fire fun in Atlanta, buy a MARTA pass (see Practical Information above), and pick up one of the city's free publications on music and events. *Creative Loafing, Music Atlanta, the Hudspeth Report,* and "Weekend" in the Friday edition of the *Atlanta Journal* will all help you eat the peach. *Southern Voice* also has complete listings on gay and lesbian news and nightclubs throughout Atlanta. Look for free summer concerts in Atlanta's parks.

The outstanding **Woodruff Arts Center,** 1280 Peachtree St. NE (892-3600), houses the Atlanta Symphony and the Alliance Theater Company. For plays and movies also check the Moorish and Egyptian revival movie palace, the **Fox,** 660 Peachtree St. (249-6400), or the **Atlanta Civic Center,** 395 Piedmont St. (523-6275).

Atlanta's nightlife ripens to a frenetic, sweet, and inexpensive softness. Night spots concentrate in Buckhead, Underground Atlanta, Little Five Points, and **Virginia Highlands,** a neighborhood east of downtown with trendy shops and a friendly, hip atmosphere. For blues, go to **Blind Willie's,** 828 N. Highland Ave. (873-2583), a dim, usually packed club with Cajun food and occasional big name acts. (Live music starts at 10pm. Open daily at 6pm. Cover Mon.-Fri. $3, Sat.-Sun. $5.) A college-age crowd usually fills Little Five Points heading for **The Point,** 420 Moreland Ave. (577-6468), where you'll always get live music. (Open Mon.-Fri. 4pm-until, Sat. 1pm-3am, Sun. 1pm-4am. Cover $3-7.) Towards downtown, the newly opened **Masquerade,** 695 North Ave. (577-8178), is housed in an original turn-of-the-century mill. The bar has three different levels: heaven, with live hardcore music; purgatory, a more laid-back coffee house; and hell, progressive dance music. (Open Wed.-Sun. 9pm-4am. Cover $5-7. 18 and over.) **The Tower,** 735 Ralph McGill Blvd. (688-5463), is a popular lesbian bar and dance club. (Open Mon.-Thurs. 4:30pm-1am, Fri. 4:30pm-4am, Sat. 4:30pm-3am.) **Backstreet,** 845 Peachtree St. NE (873-1986), a hot gay dance spot, stays open almost all night.

Underground Atlanta has the newest concept in suiting all tastes. A street called **Kenny's Alley** is composed solely of bars: a blues club, a dance emporium, a jazz bar, a country/western place, a New Orleans-style daquiri bar, and an oldies dancing spot.

Brunswick and Environs

Beyond its hostel and the nearby beaches, laid-back Brunswick is of little interest to the traveler except as a relaxing layover between destinations. The **Hostel in the Forest (AYH)** (264-9738, 265-0220, or 638-2623) is located 9 mi. west of Brunswick on U.S. 82 (though your maps and the AYH guide may say U.S. 84), just past a small convenience store. Take I-95 to exit 6 and travel west on U.S. 82 (a.k.a. 84) about 1½ mi. from the interchange until you see the white-lettered wooden sign set back in the trees along the eastbound lane. Make a U-turn ½-mi. farther along at Myer Hill Rd. The hostel itself is of low-impact construction ½-mi. back from the highway; every effort is made to keep the area surrounding the complex of geodesic domes and treehouses as natural as possible. No lock-out, no curfew, and few rules—the low-key managers will shuttle you to the Brunswick Greyhound station for $2. The manager can usually be convinced to use the pickup to make daytrips to Savannah, the Okefenokee Swamp, and the coastal islands. If possible, arrange to stay in one of the two treehouses at the hostel, each complete with a 25-square-ft. picture window and a spacious double bed. Bring insect repellent if you plan to stay in the summertime since mosquitos and yellow biting flies abound. In addition to a peahen named Cleopatra and numerous chickens, the hostel also has an extensive patch of blueberry bushes; you can pick and eat as many berries as you wish from late May to mid-June. (AYH members $6.)

Twin Oaks Pit Barbecue, 2618 Norwick St. (265-3131), eight blocks from downtown Brunswick across from the Southern Bell building, features a chicken-and-pork combination ($5.55). The breaded french fries (85¢) are deep fried and delicious. (Open Mon.-Sat. 11am-8pm.)

The nearby **Golden Isles,** which include **St. Simon's Island, Jekyll Island,** and **Sea Island,** have miles of white sand beaches. Near the isles, **Cumberland Island National Seashore** is 16 mi. of salt marsh, live-oak forest, and sand dune laced with a network of trails and interrupted only by a few decaying mansions. Reservations (882-4335) are necessary for overnight visits, but the effort is often rewarded; you can walk all day on the beaches and not see another person. (Reservations by phony only: call daily 10am-2pm.) Sites are available on a standby basis 15 minutes before the twice-daily ferry departures to Cumberland Island. The ferry (45 min., $8) leaves from St. Mary's on the mainland at the terminus of Rte. 40, at the Florida border. Daily departures are at 9 and 11:45am, returning at 10:15am and 4:45pm; off-season Thurs.-Mon. only.

The **Greyhound** station, at 1101 Glouster St. (265-2800; open Mon.-Fri. 8am-noon and 1-11pm, Sat. 8am-noon and 3-9pm, Sun. 9-11am and 3-9pm), offers service to Jacksonville (5 per day, 1½ hr., $14) and Savannah (4 per day, 1½ hr., $12.75).

The **area code** for the region is 912.

Savannah

General James Oglethorpe and 120 colonists founded Georgia, the thirteenth English colony, in February 1733 at Tamacraw Bluff on the Savannah River. Since then Savannah had a stint as the capital of Georgia, and both the first girl scout troop in the U.S. and Eli Whitney, inventor of the cotton gin, have made their homes here.

When the price of cotton crashed at the turn of the century, many of the homes and warehouses along River Street fell into disrepair, and the townhouses and mansions that lined Savannah's boulevards became boarding houses or rubble. In the mid-1950s, a group of concerned citizens mobilized to restore the downtown area, preserving the numerous Federalist and English Regency houses as historic monuments. Today four historic forts, broad streets, and trees hung with Spanish moss only enhance the city's classic Southern aura. This beautiful backdrop will serve as the site for the Boating and Yachting events during the 1996 Olympic Games.

Practical Information

Emergency: 911.

Savannah Visitors Center, 301 Martin Luther King Blvd. (944-0456), at Liberty St. in a lavish former train station. Excellent free maps and guides. Open Mon.-Fri. 8:30am-5pm, Sat.-Sun. 9am-5pm. The **Savannah History Museum,** in the same building, has photographs, exhibits, and 2 brief films depicting the city's history. (Open daily 9am-4pm. Admission $2.75, seniors $2.50, teens $1.25, kids free.)

Amtrak: 2611 Seaboard Coastline Dr. (234-2611 or 800-872-7245), 4 mi. outside the city. Taxi fare to city about $6. To Charleston, SC (2 per day, 1¾ hr., $25) and Washington, DC (7 per day, 11 hr., $110). Open 24 hrs.

Greyhound: 610 E. Oglethorpe Ave. (232-2135), convenient to downtown. To Jacksonville (11 per day, 3 hr., $22), Charleston, SC (3 per day, 2½ hr., $23), Washington, DC (8 per day, 17 hr., $87). Open 24 hrs.

Public Transport: Chatham Area Transit (CAT), 233-5767. Buses operate daily 6am-11pm. Fare 75¢, transfers 5¢. **C&H Bus,** 530 Montgomery St. (232-7099). The only public transportation to Tybee Beach. Buses leave from the civic center in summer at 8:15am, 1:30pm, and 3:30pm, returning from the beach at 9:25am, 2:30pm, and 4:30pm. Fare $1.75.

Help Line: Rape Crisis Center, 233-7273.

Post Office: 2 N. Fahm St. (235-4646). Open Mon.-Fri. 8:30am-5pm. **ZIP code:** 31402.

Area Code: 912.

Savannah smiles on the coast of Georgia at the mouth of the **Savannah River,** which runs along the border with South Carolina. Charleston, SC, lies 100 mi. up the coast; Brunswick, GA lies 90 mi. to the south. The city stretches south from bluffs overlooking the river. The restored 2½-sq.-mi. **downtown historic district** is bordered by **East Broad** and **Martin Luther King, Jr. Blvd.,** and on the north and south by the river and **Gaston Street.** This area is best explored on foot. **Tybee Island,** Savannah's beach, is 18 mi. east on Hwy. 80 and 26. Try to visit at the beginning of spring, the busiest and most beautiful season in Savannah.

Accommodations and Camping

Make your first stop in Savannah the **visitors center,** where a wide array of available coupons offer 15-20% discounts on area hotels. The downtown motels are clustered near the historic area, visitors center, and Greyhound station. The neighborhood is neither charming nor clean, but it's fairly safe. Do not stray south of Gaston St., however, where the historic district quickly deteriorates into a place you don't want to be alone in at night. For those with cars, Ogeechee Rd. (U.S. 17) has several independently owned budget options.

Quality Inn, 231 W. Boundary St. (232-3200), just west of the Greyhound station. Fairly luxurious rooms with cable TV and in-room movies. Ask about free transportation to the airport and bus station. Singles $40. Doubles $45.

Bed and Breakfast Inn, 117 Gordon St. (238-0518), on Chatham Sq. in the historic district. Pretty little rooms have TV, A/C, and shared bath. Singles $30. Doubles $38. Reservations required.

Budget Inn, 3702 Ogeechee Rd. (233-3633), a 10-min. drive from the historic district. Take bus #25B ("Towers and Ogeechee"). Comfortable rooms with TV and A/C. Pool. Singles and doubles $28, cheaper with coupons. Suites, family rooms and kitchenettes $36. Reservations recommended; call collect.

Sanddollar Motel, 11 16th St. (786-5362), at Tybee Island, 1½ mi. south on Butler Ave. A small, family-run motel practically on the beach. Most rooms rented weekly for $135. Singles may be available for $35 (less on weekdays and in winter). A 4-day stay Sun.-Wed. is $60.

Skidaway Island State Park (356-2523), 13 mi. southeast of downtown off Diamond Cause-way. Inaccessible by public transportation. Follow Liberty St. east out of downtown; soon after it becomes Wheaton St., turn right on Waters Ave. and follow it to the Diamond Cause-way. Bathroooms and heated showers. Sites $10. Parking $2. Check-in before 10pm.

Richmond Hill State Park, off Rte. 144 (727-2339), ½-hr. south of downtown; take exit 15 off I-95. Quieter than Skidaway and usually less crowded. Registration office open daily 8am-5pm. Sites $10. Parking $2. Check-in before 10pm.

Food

In Savannah cheap food is easy to come by. Try the waterfront area for budget meals in a pub-like atmosphere. The early-bird dinner specials at **Corky's**, 407 E. River St. (234-0113), range from $4 to $6. **Kevin Barry's Irish Pub**, 117 W. River St. (233-9626), has live Irish folk music Wednesday to Sunday after 9pm, as well as cheap drinks during Happy Hour.

Mrs. Wilkes Boarding House, 107 W. Jones St. (232-5997)—no sign. Home-style restaurant in the basement of a townhouse. A local favorite, with an all-you-can-eat lunch of meat, vege-tables, breads, and iced tea for $7.50. The 80-year-old Mrs. Wilkes still works the small dining room; Mr. Wilkes collects the money after you bring your dish to the sink. Go before 11:15am or after 2pm to avoid the wait, or go around back for a generous take-out picnic. Breakfast of grits, eggs, sausages, ham, corn, bread, muffins, juice and coffee ($3.75) served daily. Open Mon.-Fri. 8-9am and 11:30am-3pm.

Morrison's Family Dining, 15 Bull St., near Johnson Sq. downtown. Traditional U.S. and Southern cooking, multi-item menu. Full meals $3-5. Whole pies $2. The food is guaran-teed—if you don't like it, you don't pay for it. Open Mon.-Fri. 7:30am-8pm, Sat.-Sun. 11am-8pm.

Hard Hearted Hannah's, 318 W. Saint Julian St., in the city market. Live jazz Mon.-Sat. night, and a soft-hearted omelette bar beginning at 10pm Fri.-Sat. Open Mon.-Sat. 4pm-until.

Sights and Events

In addition to restored antebellum houses, the downtown area includes over 20 small parks and gardens. The **Historic Savannah Foundation**, 210 Broughton St. (233-7703; 233-3597 for 24-hr. reservations), offers a variety of guided one- and two-hour tours ($6-10). You can also catch any number of bus and van tours ($7-12) leaving about every 10 to 15 minutes from outside the visitors center. Ask inside for details.

The best-known historic houses in Savannah are the **Owens-Thomas House**, 124 Abercorn St. (233-9743), on Oglethorpe Sq., and the **Davenport House**, 324 E. State St. (236-8097), a block away on Columbia Sq. The Owens-Thomas House is one of the best examples of English Regency architecture in the U.S. (Open Feb.-Dec. Sun.-Mon. 2-4:30pm., Tues.-Sat. 10am-4:30pm. Last tour at 4:30pm. Admission $4, students $2, kids $1.) The Davenport House typifies the Federalist style and con-tains an excellent collection of Davenport china. By the 30s, the house had become a tenement and the owners planned to raze it for a parking lot. Its salvation in 1955 marked the birth of the Historical Savannah Foundation and the effort to restore the city. There are guided tours of the first floor every 15 minutes; explore the second and third floors at your leisure. (Open Tues.-Sat. 10am-4pm, Sun. 1:30-4pm. Last tour at 4pm. Admission $4.)

Lovers of Thin Mints, Scot-teas, and, of course, Savannahs should make a pil-grimage to the **Juliette Gordon Low Girl Scout National Center**, 142 Bull St. (233-4501), near Wright Square. The association's founder was born here on Halloween of 1860, possibly explaining the Girl Scouts' door-to-door treat-selling technique. The center's "cookie shrine," in one of the most beautiful houses in Savannah, con-tains an interesting collection of Girl Scout memorabilia. (Open Feb.-Nov. Mon.-Tues. and Thurs.-Sat. 10am-4pm; Dec.-Jan. Mon.-Sat. 10am-4pm. Admission $3, ages under 18 $2.25.) One block down in **Johnson Square**, at the intersection of Bull and E. Saint Julian St., is the burial obelisk of Revolutionary War hero Nathan-iel Green; a plaque contains an epitaph by the Marquis de Lafayette.

For a less conventional view of Savannah's history, arrange to tour the **Negro Heritage Trail,** visiting African American historic sights from early slave times to the present. Three different tours are available on request from the Savannah branch of the Association for the Study of Afro-American Life and History, King-Tisdell Cottage, Negro Heritage Trail, 514 E. Huntington St., Savannah 31405 (234-8000; open Mon.-Fri. noon-5pm). One day's notice is necessary; admission depends upon the particular tour.

Savannah's four forts once protected the city's inhabitants and shipping from the Spanish, the British, and other invaders. The most interesting of these is **Fort Pulaski National Monument** (786-5787), 15 mi. east of Savannah on Hwy. 80 and 26. (Open daily 8:30am-6:30pm. Admission $1 per person, Seniors and kids under 15 free.) Fort Pulaski marks the Civil War battle site where walls were first pummeled by rifled cannonry, which made Pulaski as well as all other forts obsolete. Built in the early 1800s **Fort Jackson** (232-3945), also along Hwy. 80 and 26, contains exhibits on the Revolution, the War of 1812, and the Civil War. Together with Fort Pulaski, it makes for a quick detour on a daytrip to Tybee Beach. (Open daily 9am-5pm; July and Aug. 9am-7pm. Admission $2, seniors and students $1.50.)

Special events in Savannah include the **Hidden Garden of the Nogs Tour** (238-0248), on April 20-21, when private walled gardens are opened to the public, and the **Tybee Island Beach Bum's Parade** (786-5444), with a beach music festival and other island activities June 18-20.

HAWAII

> *No alien land in all the world has any deep, strong charm for me but that one, no other land could so longingly and beseechingly haunt me, sleeping and waking, through half a lifetime, as that one has done. Other things leave me, but it abides; other things change, but it remains the same. . . In my nostrils still lives the breath of flowers that perished twenty years ago.*
>
> —*Mark Twain*

Mark Twain's effusive recollections of his 1889 trip to the then Sandwich Islands foreshadow the exotic image Hawaii conjures up today. Dribbled across the ocean blue of the Pacific, the state is psychologically and geographically set apart from mainland America, lying 2400 miles eastward. Here, as nowhere else, you will find lush vegetation, expansive beaches, towering surf, and sultry breezes that have earned the islands their reputation for uniformly wonderful weather. Acres of untainted tropical forest abut luxurious resort areas and bustling urban enclaves. Meanwhile, active volcanoes punctuate the horizon and release billows of grey into the air. Elysian? Well, yeah.

Between 25 and 40 million years ago, molten rock welled up from the depths of the earth and burst through the ocean floor. The hot spot remained stationary while the Pacific Plate shifted northwest over it, forming the chain of magmatic perforations that make up the existing Hawaiian archipelago. The sea long ago eroded the older islands in the northwest to tiny coral atolls, while at the other end of the chain fiery eruptions push new land up from the ocean's depths.

Of the 162 current Hawaiian islands, only seven are inhabited. Their first inhabitants, migrating Polynesians, crossed thousands of miles of unbroken ocean as early as the 6th century AD in their double-hulled canoes, bringing roots, seeds, dogs, chickens, and a pig or two. They formed several constantly warring kingdoms and considered themselves *keiki o ka aina* ("children of the land").

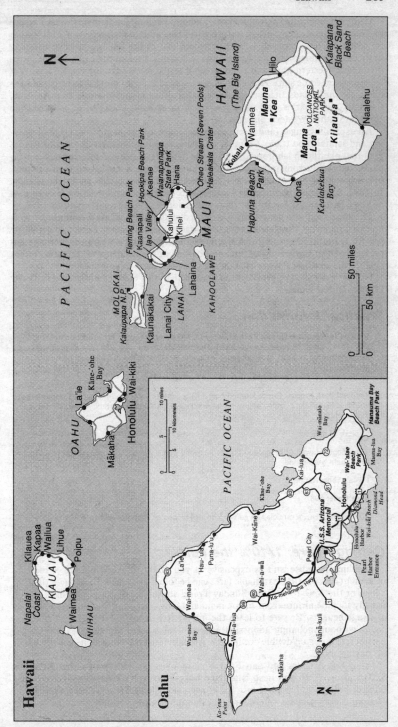

Captain Cook sailed through Hawaii while searching for the Northwest Passage in 1778. His inadvertent discovery propelled Hawaii into the modern world. Within 20 years of Cook's arrival, King Kamehameha I of the Big Island, revered today as the leader who united the islands and created modern Hawaii, exploited the introduction of Western arms and conquered all of the other islands except Kauai. Yet the European trade ships Kamehameha welcomed brought more than he could handle. Like the islands themselves, Hawaiian culture began to erode as merchants, Calvinist missionaries, and sundry white men, or *haole* ("HOW-lee"), spread the Bible and other Western diseases.

An expanding sugar (and later pineapple) industry supplanted the original whaling and sandalwood trade. Chinese, Japanese, and Filipinos were brought in as indentured plantation laborers to replace the dying Hawaiians. American sugar magnates, leery of a strong monarchy and seeking to ensure a market for their product, overthrew King Kalakaua in 1893, and requested that the U.S. annex the islands. In 1898, having acquired Spain's interests in the Pacific and desiring Hawaii as a military base, the U.S. did just that, and made Hawaii the 50th state in 1959.

The state's cultural geography is as varied as the physical. As a community with no racial majority, the state serves as a bridge between East and West and a melting pot for a multitude of cultures living pacifically. This poly-cultural heritage expresses itself in the arts, literature, and cuisine of the residents of, to quote Twain again, "the loveliest fleet of islands that lies anchored in any ocean."

For more detailed information on Hawaii than this book can offer, see *Let's Go: California and Hawaii.*

Practical Information

Visitors Information: Hawaii Visitors Bureau, 2270 Kalakaua Ave., #1108, Honolulu 96815 (923-1811). Open Mon.-Fri. 8am-4:30pm. The ultimate source. The other islands staff offices at major towns, as listed in the appropriate sections. **Department of Land and Natural Resources,** 1151 Punchbowl St., Honolulu 96813 (548-7455). Open Mon.-Fri. 8am-4pm. Information and permits for camping in state parks, and trail maps.

National Park Service, Prince Kuhio Federal Bldg., #6305, 300 Ala Moana Blvd., Honolulu 96850 (541-2693). Permits are given at individual park headquarters. Open Mon.-Fri. 7:30am-4pm.

Capital: Honolulu.

Time Zone: Hawaii (3 hr. behind Pacific in spring and summer; 2 hr. otherwise). 11-13 hr. of daylight year-round.

Postal Abbreviation: HI

Area Code: 808.

State Bird: Nene, a rare clawed goose. You will be turned away at the airport if you do not know this.

Getting There: 1/10% the Fun

Reaching paradise isn't as expensive as you might think. While prices increase in winter (Feb.-April), reasonable fares can be found even then. Investigate the *L.A. Times* or the *New York Times* Sunday Travel section for discount packages, which usually include airfare from major mainland cities, accommodations, and a bevvy of fringe benefits. Be sure to learn the nitty-gritty details: tour packages often list sights without including admission fees, and rates listed are almost always a per person rate based on double occupancy. An individual traveling alone usually winds up paying more.

From Los Angeles and San Francisco, many major carriers fly round-trip for $300 and up. If all you need is a plane ticket, look for special advance purchase fares or bulk rates from cut-rate travel agencies. **Cheap Tickets** (808-947-3717) in Honolulu, for instance, offers fares substantially below normal rates.

Getting Around

Island Hopping

When weighing which islands to visit, think carefully about what you like to do. Each offers its own atmosphere and range of activities. Oahu is heavily populated and revolves around tourism, making it the most accessible island, but leaving few unexplored and unexploited places. The Big Island (Hawaii) has lots of open space and the added attraction of Volcanoes National Park, where you can see the goddess Pele spit hot lava from the bowels of the earth into the boiling ocean. Maui's strong winds have made it one of the premier windsurfing destinations of the world; with the windsurfers comes a hopping nightlife. The major inter-island carriers, **Hawaiian Airlines** (537-5100), **Aloha Airlines** (836-1111), and **Aloha Island Air** (833-3219) can jet you quickly from Honolulu to any of the islands for around $65, $45 for the first and last flights of the day. Travel agents, such as **Pali Tour and Travel, Inc.,** 1304 Pali Hwy. (533-3608), in Honolulu, sell Hawaiian Air inter-island coupon books that are extremely convenient for island-hopping (6 flights for $250). Check the miscellaneous section of the classified ads in the *Star-Bulletin* or *Advertiser* for individuals selling these coupons at cut-rate prices. Most carriers offer the same fare to each island they serve.

Aloha and Hawaiian often coordinate with resorts and/or car rental agencies to create economical **package tours.** Ask a local travel or reservations agent about deals best suited to your needs, and keep an eye out for ads in pamphlets and newspapers.

Many companies offer one-day airplane and helicopter cruises of the islands (kind of like on "Magnum, P.I."). Consult a travel agent about current deals and specials or look in the Sunday paper travel section.

On the Islands

While the **bus** system is fairly reliable and extensive on Oahu, it is patchy on the Big Island and local transit is nonexistent on the other islands (see individual island listings). You will probably want to rent your own set of wheels for a sojourn on any island other than Oahu.

Car rental agencies fill major island airports and tourist areas in towns. If you have not booked a rental through an airline or other package deal, check local weekly and monthly travel guides for specials and ask about weekly rates. Because car rental agencies are not state-regulated, a day's use of an automatic, air-conditioned compact car can range from $12 to $40. Hawaii is a no-fault insurance state, so insurance coverage is *optional,* but most companies will not honor your individual coverage, even if you already own a car. **Budget** is one of the few agencies that will rent to those ages 18 to 20, but only with a major credit card and a hefty surcharge atop the regular price. Waiting to start your car rental search until arrival at an airport is a sure way to be stuck with the most expensive rates. Whenever possible, do your research before you get there and make reservations at least 24 hrs. in advance.

Bicycle and **moped rentals,** available in most tourist centers, are an enjoyable way to see Hawaii in an easy-going, close-up manner. The congestion in Honolulu may be too much for two wheels; mopeds and bikes are more useful on the other side of Oahu, or on the neighbor islands. If you bring your own bicycle, you may register it (for $3.50) at the **Pawaa Police Station,** 1455 S. Beretania St., Honolulu (943-3324; open Mon.-Fri. 7:45am-4:15pm). You can also pick up the free *Bicycle Regulations Pamphlet* here. More information is available at **The Bike Shop,** 1149 S. King St. (531-7071), in Honolulu (open Mon.-Thurs. and Sat. 9am-5:30pm, Fri. 9am-8pm, Sun. 10am-5pm), or from the **Hawaii Bicycling League,** P.O. Box 4403, Honolulu 96813 (732-5806). Inter-island airlines charge about $20 to bring your bike with you on the flight. Mainland airlines charge about $15.

Hawaii (The Big Island)

Pele, Polynesian goddess of the volcanoes, is believed to reside on Hawaii, southeasternmost island in the Hawaiian chain and possessed of the archipelago's only two active volcanoes—Mauna Loa, the still-active Long Mountain (13,677 ft.), and Kilauea (4,000 ft.), home of the hyperactive Halemaumau Crater. Kilauea is currently in its 49th phase of eruption without showing any signs of exhaustion; Pele, no doubt, is insatiable.

The Big Island is twice the size of all the other islands combined, but is home to scarcely a tenth of the state's population. Its varied agricultural production supports Hawaii's post-sugar economy. The towns of Hilo and Kailua-Kona, on opposite sides of the island, are the main arrival points for tourists. The rest of the island is considered "country" by residents. The northwestern corner is the Kohala Peninsula, former sugar land and the northern border of the island's gigantic cattle range. The southern land mass is Kau, where the first Polynesian immigrants settled. You'll need a car to get out to the countryside, but keep a careful eye on the fuel gauge, as distances between gas stations can be great. Coastal highways circle both volcanoes. In Volcanoes National Park, both the old Saddle Road (Rte. 200), and the Chain of Craters Road in Kilauea Crater permit closer views of the volcanoes. The Big Island does have a rudimentary bus system, and you should find most of the island's sights accessible.

Hawaii Visitors Bureau (Hilo), 180 Kinoole St. (961-5797). Bus schedules, brochures, island guides, and maps (all free). Open Mon.-Fri. 8am-noon and 1-4pm. **Wailoa Center**, P.O. Box 936, Hilo 96720 (961-7360), Kamehameha Ave. and Pauahi St., on the *makai* (seawards) side of the State Building. Helpful in planning itineraries. Open Mon.-Fri. 8am-4:30pm. **Volcanoes National Park Visitor Center (Volcanoes)**, Volcano, Hawaii 96785 (967-7311), on Rte. 11, 13 mi. from Hilo. Offers trail maps, free ranger-guided hikes, and important safety information. Open daily 8am-5pm. **Hawaii Visitors Bureau (Kona)**, 75-5719 Alii Dr. (329-7787), across from the Kona Inn Shopping Center. Bus schedules, brochures, maps, and accommodations information. Open Mon.-Fri. 8am-noon and 1-4pm.

Buses: Hele-on-Bus, 25 Aupuni St. (935-8241). Information on bus schedules. Operates Mon.-Sat. 6:30am-6pm. Fare ranges from 50¢ to $6. Luggage and backpacks $1. Runs between Kona and Hilo ($5) at least once per day, making a convenient circuit of the island ($5.25).

Taxi: Ace Taxi, 935-8303. **ABC Taxi**, 935-0755. Airport-city runs about $10.

Car Rentals: All national and state chains are located at Hilo airport. Make reservations several days in advance or take advantage of fly/drive deals for cheaper rates. **Dollar Rent-A-Car**, 961-6059. Must be 25 or over with major credit card in your own name. $30 per day. **Budget**, 935-7293, rents to those 18-25 for a $20 per day surcharge. Basic economy car rate is $34 per day. In **Kona**, try **Budget**, 329-8511. $22 per day. Must be 18 with credit card, and if you're under 25 they add a $20 per day surcharge. Drop-off charges can be as steep as $28. **Honolulu Rent-A-Car**, 74-5588 Pawaii Pl. (329-7328) in Kona, rents used cars with 3-day minimum for as little as $15 per day.

Bikes and Mopeds: Cíao, 75-5663A Palani Rd. in Kona (326-4177), across from the King Kamehameha Hotel. Scooters $20 per day; cruiser bikes $10 per day. Cash or credit card deposit. Open daily 8am-8pm. **B&L Bike & Sports**, 74-5576B Pawaii Pl. in Kona (329-3309), at Kaiwi St., offers 12-speeds for $12 per day, $60 per week; 15-speed mountain bikes $15 per day, $75 per week. Open Mon.-Fri. 9am-5:30pm, Sat. 9am-3pm.

Water Equipment Rentals: Nautilus Dive Center, 382 Kamehameha Ave., Hilo (935-6939). Mask/snorkel $3 per day, underwater camera $15 per day. $10 deposit. Also offers beginner and certified dive charters, $45. Open Mon.-Sat. 8:30am-5pm. **Big Island Divers**, Kona Market Place (329-6068), in the back. Masks, fins, and snorkels $6 per day, prescription masks $8. Boogie boards $6 and $8 per day. Charters, introductory dives, and scuba rentals are also available at affordable rates. Open daily 8am-8pm.

Crisis/Help Line: 969-9111 in Hilo, 329-9111 in Kona.

Area Code: 808.

Hilo

After Honolulu, Hilo is the largest city in the state, a sleepier version of its big cousin. The center of the Hawaiian orchid and anthurium industry, the city is primarily residential; Hilo works best as a base from which to visit the island's other attractions. The city averages nearly 125 in. of rain per year; keep this in mind when you start those "three-hour tours." If the weather starts getting too rough for you, just head for the sunny Kona-Kohala coast (a 2-hr. drive away).

To get the most out of Hilo, start your sightseeing early in the day. Rte. 11 will take you directly from the Hilo airport to the national park, but it's more rewarding to explore the town first by morning light. The **Liliuokalani Garden** (an elaborate Japanese-style garden named after one of the royal princesses) affords a great view of Mauna Kea before the clouds roll in. Hilo is the orchid capital of the world (it's prom-goers heaven). **Orchids of Hawaii,** 2801 Kilauea Ave. (959-3581), immediately past the first one-lane bridge, features beautiful *leis* and an exotic variety of orchids and anthuriums. (Open Mon.-Fri. 7:30am-4:30pm.) The **Hilo Tropical Gardens,** 1477 Kalanianaole Ave. (935-4957 or 935-1146) are a lush botanical experience, perfect for an afternoon stroll. (Open Mon.-Fri. 9am-4:30pm.)

Near Hilo, recent lava flows have covered the once-glistening shores of **Kaimu Black Sand Beach** and various parts of the highway as well, making Rte. 11 the only way to round South Point from Hilo. **Lava Tree State Park,** which blooms year round with lava casts of trees formed during the 1790 eruption, is still accessible. From Hilo, take Rte. 11 south to Keaau, turn onto Rte. 130 to Pahoa, and then take Pahoa-Pohoiki Rd. (Rte. 132). Continue around the loop on Rte. 132 past the **Kapoho Lighthouse** and the gardens nearby. Here a 1960 lava flow covered Kapoho Village; only trees and the lighthouse remain.

The hotels clustered on Banyan Dr. by the bay are quiet and often empty. Try **Arnott's Lodge,** 98 Apapane Rd. (969-7097). By car, from Airport Rd, turn right at the first traffic light, turn right again at the next light (next to Dairy Queen) onto Kalanianaele St., go 1½ mi. and make a left onto Keokea. Apapane Rd. is on the right about 50 yd. down. Arnott's is totally renovated and scrupulously clean. Laundry, TV and cooking facilites, beach within walking distance. (Bunks $15. Private singles $25. Suites for 5 $80.) The **Country Club Hotel,** centrally located at 121 Banyan Dr. (935-7171), has good, scenic rooms with *lanais* (porches), A/C, TV, and phones. The restaurant offers an unlimited buffet for $6. (Singles and doubles $45, with kitchenette $55.) **Dolphin Bay Hotel,** 333 Iliahi St., Hilo 96720 (935-1466), in the Puueo section of town, boasts cool, tropical gardens, fans, TV, and kitchens. (Singles from $36. Doubles from $42. Pre-payment required; make deposit 10 days prior to stay.) Campers can try the **Onekahakaha Beach Park** and **Kealoha Beach Park** (both 961-8311), within 3 mi. of Hilo, but be forewarned: they are known as local tough-guy hangouts. (Tent camping, bathrooms, and shower facilities. $1 permit required; see Practical Information.)

You'll find macadamia nut bread, cookies, cakes and pies galore to accompany cups of steaming Kona coffee grown on the island. Even better than Mary Anne's banana cream pies. Free samples of the nuts are given out at the **Hawaiian Holiday Macadamia Nut Company** in Haina, off Rte. 19 near Honokaa.

Downtown Hilo is loaded with fast-food joints, cheap restaurants, sushi counters, and *okazu-ya.* **Reuben's Mexican Food,** 336 Kamehameha Hwy. (961-2552), has authentic Mexican food (entrees $6-8) served on colorful tablecloths, and a wide selection of beers and margaritas. (Open Mon.-Fri. 11am-9pm, Sat. noon-9pm.) **Lani Truffels,** 1477 Kalanianole (969-7871), serves delectable lunch plates ($4) and mouth-watering desserts. (Open Tues.-Sat. noon-7pm.) **Ken's Pancake House,** 1730 Kamehameha Ave. (935-8711), is the Hawaiian IHOP you always dreamed about, serving macadamia nut, coconut, and fresh banana pancakes ($3-4) with a variety of syrups. Burgers, hot dogs, et al. are also served, giving you an alternative banana-happy Gilligan never had. (Open 24 hrs.)

Hilo rests at the mouth of the Wailuku River. Its airport, **General Lyman Field,** is accessed by inter-island service and flights from the mainland. Travelers should stop and talk to the folks at the airport's visitor information booth; the Skipper really wishes he'd had their maps and information for directions and orientation. Hilo's **post office** leis at Waianuenue Ave. (935-6685), in the Federal Bldg. Open Mon.-Fri. 8:30am-4:30pm, Sat. 9am-noon. The **ZIP Code** is 96720.

The Volcano Area

The volcanoes of the Big Island are unique in their size, frequency of eruption, and accessibility. Resting above the geological hot spot that fashioned each of the Hawaiian islands in turn, the two mountains in **Volcanoes National Park** continue to heave and grow, adding acres of new land each year. **Kilauea Caldera,** with its steaming vents, sulfur fumes, and periodic "drive-in" eruptions, is the Ginger Grant of the park, although the less active **Mauna Loa** and its dormant northern neighbor, **Mauna Kea,** are in some respects more amazing. Each towers nearly 14,000 ft. above sea level and drops some 16,000 ft. to the ocean floor. Mauna Loa is the largest volcano in the world, while Mauna Kea, when measured from its base on the ocean floor, is the tallest mountain on earth. (Park entrance $5, good for 7 days.)

The 11-mi. scenic drive around the Kilauea Caldera on **Crater Rim Drive** is a good way to see the volcano by car. The road is accessible via Rte. 11 from the east and west or via the Chain of Craters Rd. from the south. Well-marked trails and lookouts dot the way, so stop frequently to explore. You might also take the easy hike along the vista-filled **Crater Rim Trail,** which traverses *ohia* and giant fern forests, *aa* (rough) and *pahoehoe* (smooth) lava flows, and smoldering steam and sulfur vents. And really, Lovey, you simply must take a walk with the Professor and Mary Anne through the **Thurston Lava Tube,** formed by lava that cooled around a hot core which continued to move, leaving the inside of the flow hollow. The nearby free **Jaggar Museum** explains the geological background with a pictorial history of the volcano; other displays focus on Hawaiian legends. (Open daily 8:30am-5pm.)

The 4-mi. **Kilauea Iki Trail** starts at the Kilauea Iki overlook on Crater Rim Rd. It leads around the north rim of Kilauea Iki, through a forest of tree ferns, down the wall of the little crater, past the vent of the '59 eruption, over steaming lava, and back to Crater Rim Rd., passing *ohelo* bushes laden with red berries. According to legend, you must offer berries to Pele before eating any, or you'll incur her wrath. The 3½-mi. **Mauna Iki Trail** begins 9 mi. southwest of park headquarters on Rte. 11 and leads to ashen footprints left in 1790. From here you can hike down into the coastal area.

An unpaved road leads to Mauna Kea's summit from Rte. 200 (Saddle Rd.). The terrain is stark and the views of the land and the stars are unearthly. The notion of altitude sickness at 13,796 ft., however, may deter you.

When seeking shelter for the night, try the **Volcano House,** P.O. Box 53, Hawaii Volcanoes National Park 96718 (967-7321); though a bit expensive, it's reportedly quite therapeutic to eat and sleep on the rim of an active volcano. The 1,220-ft. vantage point is certainly a unique perspective. (Rooms start at $59.) The hotel also runs the **Namakanipaio** cabins, located 3 mi. behind the Volcano House in an *ohia* forest. (Check-in after 3pm. 4-person cabins $25. Linen and some blankets provided.) **Morse Volcano B&B,** P.O. Box 100, Volcano, 96785 (967-7216), in Volcano Village just outside the park, is a historic missionary-style home with roomy common areas. (Singles $26, with bath $31. Doubles $42, with bath $46.) **Volcanoes National Park** (967-7311) offers free campsites at **Kipukanene, Namakanipaio** (near Kilauea Crater), and **Kamoamoa** (on the coast), each with shelters and fireplaces, but no wood. (Reservations are not accepted. Seven-day maximum.)

Kona

Occupying the western side of Hawaii, Kona claims a disproportionate share of the Big Island's white sand beaches, resorts, and realtors. It is also home to the town of Kailua (officially hyphenated as Kailua-Kona), a booming resort center with shops, nightlife, and perfect weather. The calm, deep waters along this coast of the Big Island offer splendid snorkeling, scuba diving, and big game fishing.

Kailua-Kona itself is small enough to see in a short walk, and most of what's worth seeing is what's worth lying down on. **Magic Sands** (also called "Disappearing Sands") at the Kona Magic Sands Hotel, 77-6452 Alii Dr. (329-9177), is a good place to park your towel and wade. Or travel up Rte. 19 to prime **Hapuna Beach** and **Spencer Beach Parks,** 35 mi. north, where you can rent sailboards at makeshift stands.

Staying overnight in Kailua-Kona can be expensive, since its hotels cater to the affluent traveler; neighboring towns provide cheaper lodgings. The **Kona Hotel,** Holualoa (324-1155), on Rte. 18 southeast of Kona, enjoys clean, comfortable surroundings and friendly management. Make sure to reserve well in advance, as this fabulous find fills up frighteningly fast. (Singles $15. Doubles $23.) The **Manago Hotel,** P.O. Box 145, Captain Cook, 96704 (323-2642), is austere but comfy and clean, with a generally older clientele. (Singles from $20. Doubles from $23.)

The **Ocean View Inn,** 75-5683 Alii Dr. (329-9998), serves good, diverse food. (Breakfast $4, lunch $4-7, dinner $7-10. Open Tues.-Sun. 6:30am-2:45pm and 5:15-9pm.) **Stan's,** 75-5646 Palani Rd. (329-2455), in the Kona Hukilau, is a good bet for breakfast (coconut hotcakes $3.35) and complete dinners ($7). (Open daily 7-9:30am and 5:30-8:30pm.) **Betty's Chinese Kitchen,** Palani Rd., in the KTA Shopping Center, has large portions and a daily plate ($3-4). (Open Mon.-Sat. 10am-8:30pm.) For nightlife, try the **Jolly Roger Restaurant,** 75-5776 Alii Dr. (329-1344), with live music and no cover, or **Kona Surf,** 78-128 Ehukai St. (322-3411), where the avuncular Jerry Garcia, among others, has played.

Kailua-Kona is served by **Keahole Airport,** 9 mi. (15 min.) north of town. Taxi rides into town are about $16, plus 30¢ per parcel. Kailua-Kona is a small settlement and can be toured in one day without a car. The city is split by two streets running parallel to the ocean: Alii Drive, nearest the ocean, and Kuakini Highway, one block *mauka* (inland). Kona's **Post Office** erupts at Palani Rd. (329-1927). Open Mon.-Fri. 9am-4pm, Sat. 9am-noon. The **ZIP code** is 96740.

Kohala

Once home to several sugar mills, much of **Kohala** (the Big Island's northwest coast) offers beachside camping and good biking roads on the Kona side, one of the world's largest ranches, the beautiful Waipio Valley, and tourist-free splendor. As Kohala is inaccessible by bus, you may have to hitch a ride from Waimea.

From the Kona Coast beyond Hapuna Beach, head up the mountain on Rte. 19 toward **Kamuela.** Founded in 1847 by a Boston missionary, the **Parker Ranch** spans 225,000 acres and is home to 40-50,000 head of Hereford cattle; the ranch annually produces enough beef for 40 million Quarter-Pounders. The **Visitors Center and Museum** (885-7655) has cool audio-visual presentations on the Ranch and its *paniolos,* Hawaiian cowboys. (Open daily 9:30am-4:30pm. Admission $4, ages 4-11 $2.) Hop along down Rte. 24 to the edge of the lush **Waipio Valley,** 8 mi. away, for one of the most striking panoramas anywhere in the islands. The 2,000-ft. gorge, the islands' largest, is the most abysmal in a series of breathtaking canyons between Waipio and Pololu. Bountiful flora and fauna made Waipio (the islands' largest gorge) the center of ancient Hawaiian civilization. The adventurous should consider the 9-mi. hike between the Waipio Valley Lookout and Waimanu Bay. Waimanu Valley holds ancient Hawaiian ruins, and the scenery can't be beat.

Campsites are plentiful in Kohala; try the **Hapuna Beach State Park,** off Rte. 19 (882-7995), 3 mi. south of Kawaihae, is great for swimming, volleyball, sunning, relaxing, and people-watching. Swimming is *not* the first thing on everyone's mind here. Reserve well in advance. (A-frame shelters only; no tent camping. $7.)

Maui

Long before college athletes proclaimed "We're Number One," Maui's warlike chieftains proudly announced their island's supremacy over the archipelago with the words *Maui No Ka Oi*. As a tourist destination, Maui is rapidly re-claiming that vaunted position over the other Hawaiian islands. Named for the demi-god Maui, who, according to legend, pulled the islands up from the sea-bottom with fish hooks, "The Valley Island," as it is known, features everything from clapboard cane towns to concrete condos to sunny beaches to a sometimes-snowcapped volcano to rain forest. Maui's popularity will seem justified once you've toured its contrasting corners: sleepy, mountainous West Maui; the windy central isthmus that holds Wailuku, Kahului, and acre upon acre of sugar cane; the mystifying Haleakala volcano, which dominates East Maui; and the remote majesty of the Hana coast.

Practical Information and Orientation

Visitor Information Kiosk (877-6431), at the Kahului Airport terminal. Helpful orientation, free map. Open daily 6am-9pm. **Hawaii Visitors Bureau,** 380 Dairy Rd., Kahului (871-8691). Friendly assistance with itinerary planning, activities, and accommodations, but they won't make reservations. Information on Molokai and Lanai. Open Mon.-Fri. 8am-4:30pm. **Haleakala National Park** (572-7749) provides recorded information on weather conditions, daily ranger-guided hikes and special activities. For information on camping and cabins, call 572-9177. **Paia Visitor Center,** 65 Hana Hwy., Paia (579-8000). Open Mon.-Sat. 9am-noon and 5-6pm. **Department of Parks and Recreation,** War Memorial Gym, 1580 Kaahumanu Ave. (244-9018), between Kahului and Wailuku. Information and permits ($4) for county parks. Open Mon.-Fri. 8-11am and noon-4:15pm. **Division of State Parks,** 54 High St. (244-4354), in Wailuku. Maui and Molokai state parks information. Open Mon.-Fri. 8-11am and noon-4:15pm.

Kahului Airport, on the isthmus's northern coast. Regular flights from the mainland and other islands. Planes also fly into **Kaanapali** and **Hana.** The visitors information booth in front of the Kahului terminal's entrance provides free maps, information, and directions. A taxi to hotels costs $8-10, but renting a car is the way to go.

Boats: The **Maui Princess** (661-8397) runs daily from Lahaina, Maui to Molokai at 6:30am and 4:30pm, and from Molokai to Maui at 5:30am and 3:30pm. The crossing takes about 1½ hr. and costs $21 one way. **Expeditions** (661-3756) sails to Lanai twice per day for $25.

Tours: Akamai Tours, 50 Hana Hwy., and 532 Keolani Pl. (871-9551), offers frequent tours in air-conditioned mini-buses to Haleakala/Iao Valley ($35), and Hana ($60).

Taxi: Kaanapali Taxi (661-5285). Airport-town $6.

Car Rental: Word of Mouth, Dairy Rd. (877-2436), near Kahului Airport. $15 per day for a used car, $17 with A/C; $85 per week, $95 with A/C. Must be 25. **Avis,** Kahului Airport (871-7575). $22 per day. Frequent specials. Must be 25. **Thrifty,** Kahului Airport (871-7596). $30 per day. 21 and over with major credit card.

Bicycle: The Island Biker, Kahului Shopping Center (877-7744), rents 21-speed mountain bikes for $18 per day. 5% discount with student ID. Open Mon.-Fri. 9am-5pm, Sat. 9am-3pm. **A&B Rentals,** 3481 Lower Honoapilani Rd. (669-0027), near Kaanapali. $10 per day for Beachcruiser bikes, $50 per week. Open daily 9am-5pm.

Moped and Scooter Rentals: A&B Moped and Scooter Rentals, 3481 Lower Honoapilani Rd. (669-0027). Scooters $20 for 8 hours, $25 for 24 hrs. Ask about weekly rates. Must be 18 with major credit card. Open daily 9am-5pm.

Water Equipment Rentals: Maui Dive Shop, Azeka Pl. (879-3388), Kihei, and Wakea Ave. (661-5388), Kahului. Complimentary scuba lessons with equipment rental, and free 1-hr. introductory snorkeling lessons. Mask $3, snorkel $2, boogie board $8, wetsuit $6, underwater camera $20 per day. Open Mon.-Fri. 8am-9pm, Sat.-Sun. 8am-6pm. **Hunt Hawaii,** 120 Hana Hwy., (579-8129), Paia. Surf, boogie, and sailboards for rent or sale. Biggest surfboard rental fleet on Maui. Surfboards $15 for 2 hr., $25 per day. Windsurfers $30 per day, $150 per week. Surf or sailboard lessons $35 per 2 hr. Open daily 9am-6pm. **Hawaiian Reef Divers,** 129 Lahainalua Rd. (667-7647 or 667-6002), Lahaina. Good deals, friendly advice, and an excellent beach map. Snorkel set $2.50, boogie boards $5 per day. Boat trips with snorkeling or scuba offered. Open daily 8am-5pm.

Help Lines: Gay and Bisexual Information, 572-1884 (serves Maui, Molokai, Lanai). 24 hrs.

Post Office: Lahaina, Baldwin Ave. Open Mon.-Fri. 8:15am-4:15pm. **ZIP Code:** 96761. **Paia,** Baldwin Ave. Open Mon.-Fri. 8am-4:30pm, Sat. 10:30am-12:30pm. **ZIP Code:** 96799. **Wailuku,** next to State Office Building, on High St. Open Mon.-Fri. 8:30am-4:30pm, Sat. 9-11am. **ZIP Code:** 96793. **Kihei,** 1254 S. Kihei Rd., in Azeka Market Place. Open Mon.-Fri. 9am-4:30pm, Sat. 9-11am. **ZIP Code:** 96753.

Maui consists of two mountains joined at an isthmus. The highways follow the shape of the island in a broken figure-eight pattern. To the west lie **Kahului** and **Wailuku,** business and residential communities offering less expensive food and supplies than the resort towns. From Kahului, Rte. 30 will lead you clockwise around the smaller western loop of the figure eight to hot and dry **Lahaina,** the former whaling village, and **Kaanapali,** the major resort area.

Most roads are well marked but poorly lit. Heed the warnings "road recommended for four-wheel-drive vehicles only"; a passing rainstorm can quickly drain your funds, since most rental car contracts stipulate that dirt road driving is at the driver's risk.

Accommodations and Camping

There is a rise in the number of vacation rentals and B&Bs on Maui, many catering to windsurfers and offering space to store equipment. Some go for as little as $20 per night. Hostels are another way to sidestep tourist traps, but book them a month in advance. In East Maui camping is the watchword.

Northshore Inn, 2080 Vineyard St. (242-8999), Wailuku, above Hazel's. Clean shared bathrooms, comfy common room with TV, microwave, fridge, laundry, coffee; periodic barbecues. Bunks $12. Singles $32. Doubles $43.

Banana Bungalow Hotel and International Hostel, 310 North Market St., Wailuku (244-5090). Reasonably priced hostel accommodations. Lots of international travelers and windsurfers. Laundry. Bunks $13. Singles with double bed $29. Doubles $35.

Maui Palms Resort, 170 Kaahumanu Ave. (877-0071), Kahului. Unpretentious hotel by the sea. TV. Singles $48. Doubles $51.

Nani Kai Hale, 73 N. Kihei Rd. (879-9120, 800-367-6032 from the mainland), Kihei. Condominium on a sandy beach. Doubles with bath $32.50, 3-day minimum; Dec. 16-April 15 $42.50, 7-day min. stay. Reserve ahead by phone.

Wailana Sands, 25 Wailana (879-2026 or 879-3661), off the 500 block of S. Kihei Rd. in Kihei. In a quiet cul-de-sac. Full kitchen, small pool. Four-day min. stay. Two-person studio $40. Reserve a month in advance.

Pioneer Inn, 658 Wharf St. (836-1411), Lahaina. One of Hawaii's two oldest hotels, this popular meeting spot is directly in front of the boat harbor, next to the famous giant banyan tree. The lively Old Whaler's Saloon spouts liquor long into the night. Pool. Ask for a room with a view of the harbor. Singles and doubles $25, with bath $30; in Mauka building $60. Call months in advance for reservations, especially for Dec.-March.

Renting a car and camping on the island may be the best and cheapest way to ebulliate in Maui's natural magnificence. The county maintains **H.A. Baldwin Park** in Paia about 5 mi. east of the Kahului Airport. (Tent and permit required. Three-day max. stay. Sites $3, under 18 50¢. For more information, contact the Department of Parks and Recreation (see Practical Information above).

The state maintains three parks for camping with a five-night maximum stay. Required permits can be obtained free at the Department of Parks and Recreation. **Waianapanapa State Wayside** in Hana, about 52 mi. east of Kahului Airport, has the best state camping facilities on the island. Sites include restrooms, picnic tables, barbecue grills, and outdoor showers. (Cabin singles $10, $5 per person in groups of 6 or more. Reservations recommended.)

Maui's two federal parks require no permit. **Hosmer Grove**, 7000 ft. up Haleakala's slope, is a small campground with drinking water, toilet, grills, and firewood. On a weekend night, however, you'll have to squeeze your tent in with a crowbar. Groups are limited to 15 people and a three-night stay. **Oheo** is at sea level, about 67 mi. from Kahului Airport, ¼ mi. south of **Oheo Stream** near the Seven Pools. (No drinking water and firewood. 3-day max. stay.)

Camping at the **national campsites** within the Haleakala Crater requires a permit and a hike to the site. Permits are available from the **Haleakala National Park Headquarters**, P.O. Box 369, Makawao, Maui 96768 (572-9306).

Food

Gilligan would like Maui. The waters around the coast teem with fish so numerous even he could spear them, and the trees drip breadfruit, mango, coconut, pine nuts, papaya, and guava. The ground bears its share of delicacies as well, including pineapple and the sweet Kula onion, world famous and sold for up to $6 per pound at the local market. *Guri Guri,* a locally made pineapple or strawberry sherbet, has lured generations of islanders to its main supply source **Tasaka Guri Guri,** in Kahului's Maui Mall (871-4512; open daily Hawaiian time—whenever).The cheapest places to eat are away from the resorts.

Hazel's Café, 2080 Vineyard St. (244-7278), Wailuku. Uncorrupted by tourist dollars, Hazel's remains a simple, unadorned café offering inexpensive local food. Copious lunch entrees, with salad, bread and tea ($5-7). Pigs' feet soup every Fri. Open Mon.-Fri. 6am-9pm, Sat. 6am-8pm.

Tasty Crust, Mill St., Wailuku. A bare-bones backpacker diner serving beverages in paper cups and hearty food at unbeatable prices. Fill up on dinosaur-sized hot cakes (85¢, served all day). Open Mon.-Sat. 6am-8pm.

Azeka's, S. Kinei Rd. (879-0078), in Azeka Marketplace, Kihei. In the same building as Azeka's Market, this window-service snack shop sells inexpensive box lunches ($3-4). Hamburgers and sandwiches start at $1.25. Open Mon.-Fri. 9:30am-4pm, Sat.-Sun. 9:30am-5pm.

Charlie P. Woofers Saloon and Restaurant, 142 Hana Hwy. (579-9453), Paia. Known simply as "Charlies". Packed with surfers. Giant breakfasts. The pancakes come ¼-in. thick ($3.25). Fresh flowers adorn wooden tables. Dinner menu of Italian and Mexican selections, burgers and pizza ($6-11). Hearty portions assembled by friendly cooks. Open daily 7am-2pm and 4-11pm.

Mana Foods, 49 Baldwin Ave. (579-8078), in Paia. Full service health food grocery store and deli. Try the Maui Ginger Blast drink to wash down your tofu on wheat (all natural, no preservatives). Open daily 8am-8pm.

Komada's Market, Mukawoa (572-7261). Neighboring islanders make special trips here to buy their cream puffs (80¢). If you leave without trying them, you will probably die. Open Mon.-Sat. 6:30am-5pm.

Casanova's Italian Restaurant and Deli, 1188 Makawao Ave. (572-0220), in Makawao. In addition to serving moderately priced Italian cuisine, Casanova's is one of Makawao's central night spots, with a front lanai convenient for drinking and chatting. Local bands some nights. Deli open daily 8:30am-7:30pm. Restaurant 5:30-8:30pm, closed Sundays.

Sights and Activities

Haleakala Crater, the "House of the Sun," dominates the eastern end of the island from its perch 10,000 ft. above the sea. According to Polynesian legend, the demigod Maui ascended Haleakala to slow the sun's trip across the sky so that his mother would have more time to dry her *tapa* cloth. When the sun arose at the end of the sky, Maui lassoed him by his genitals, and the sun mincingly agreed to cruise across the sky more slowly. The House of the Sun is still a monstrous place for watching the sun rise. (For more info about the Hawaiian mythos, see "The Bradys Go Hawaiian.") **Haleakala National Park** is open 24 hrs. (Admission $3 per car.) Be sure to stop at the **park headquarters** (572-9306) about 1 mi. from the Rte. 378 entrance. **Haleakala Visitors Center** (572-9172), near the summit, has exhibits on the geology, archeology, and ecology of the region. (Free ranger talks are given at 9:30, 10:30, and 11:30am. Open daily 6:30am-4pm.) The **Puuulaula Center,** at Haleakala's summit, offers shelter to those who forgot a sweater or jacket. (Open 24 hrs.) An 11-mi. descent into the crater via **Sliding Sands Trail** and out again via **Halemauu Trail** could be the most impressive seven hours of your trip to Hawaii. Heed the park's advice about sturdy walking shoes, water, and sun screen. **Kaluuokaoo Pit** is one of several exposed lava tubes in the crater. Early Hawaiians threw the umbilical cords of their newborns into the pit to safeguard the sacred coils from the valley's evil rodents. Drive farther south on Rte. 37 to **Tedeschi Winery** (878-6058), and taste their "Maui Blanc" pineapple wine (free). (Open Mon.-Fri. 9am-5pm, Sat.-Sun. 10am-5pm.)

Try to spend a full day driving the **Hana Coast.** The northern route (Hana Hwy. 360) through **Paia** and **Keanae** is incredibly tortuous, but the scenery is equally rewarding. Make sure you start out from Paia with a full tank of gas, and don't go if the road is wet. It's a long way down. Paia's **Hookipa Beach Park** is an international windsurfing mecca, just as Mecca is an international Muslim paia.

In central Maui, be sure to step into the unspoiled **Iao Valley,** on the southern slope of Puu Kukui. The valley is especially beautiful in the moonlight. **Iao Valley State Park,** at the end of Rte. 32, includes the **Iao Needle,** a 1,200-ft. basalt spire (open daily 7am-7pm). Tour buses arrive by 10am, and clouds by 2pm; both leave by 6pm. The name is onomatopoetic, the cry of an unfortunate god who sat on this pointed peak. Really.

Wailuku is is a tranquil plantation town, worth an afternoon stroll. The government buildings on High St. and vintage shops on Market St. remain oblivious to the depredations of resort development in the south. The **Hale Kii** (House of Images) served as a place of worship throughout the 18th century until destroyed by natural erosion in 1819. Reconstructed in 1958, the *heiau* is now a temple of love. High school sweethearts make the pilgrimage uphill on Thursday evenings for the island's most idyllic views. Follow Main St. (Rte. 32) to the traffic light at Rte. 330. Make a left, pass the macadamia nut grove, and turn right on Rte. 340. Continue to Kuhio Place, and follow the nerve-racking route to the right. The **Vineyard Tavern,** 2171 Vineyard (242-9938), is close to the hostels and a good nighttime hangout. It's a dim, dusty bar and grill with a shuttleboard table and a hefty dose of charm. Last call 1:30am.

Lahaina, an old whaling port in west Maui, was the capital of the islands during the time of Kamehameha the Great. It's a sunny, dry town that infects visitors with drowsy calm. When Mark Twain visited, he planned to stay one week and work; he stayed a month and never lifted a pen. The enormous tree in Lahaina's town square is a 114-year-old East Indian banyan tree, rivaling Kauai's for the title of the islands' largest. The island's only remaining steam locomotive still carries tourists, if not sugar, between Lahaina and Kaanapali. (One way $5, round-trip $8, under 12 half-price.) A new OMNI theater, 824 Front St. (661-8314), Lahaina, presents Hawaii's history on the big, big screen with *Hawaii: Island of the Gods!* (Daily every hr. 10am-10pm; admission $6, under 12 $4; $1 discount coupons available at nearby tourist centers).

West Maui hosts the island's hottest dance scene. **Spats,** in the Hyatt Regency Maui (667-7474), rocks until 4am with two bars, two dance floors, and a dress code (cover $5-10). **Banana Moon,** in the Maui Marriott (667-1200), offers the same scene until 2am.

Oahu

By the time missionaries arrived in 1820, Oahu, and its principle city Honolulu had become the economic and cultural center of Hawaii. Oahu's preeminence increased in ensuing decades as Honolulu's commercial traffic expanded and the U.S. Navy acquired exclusive rights to the neighboring inlet at Pearl Harbor, which developed into the headquarters of the Pacific Fleet, and we all know what happened then.

Oahu can be roughly divided into four sections: **Honolulu,** the **Windward Coast,** the **North Shore,** and the **Leeward Coast.** The slopes of two extinct volcanic mountain ridges (to which the island owes its existence), **Waianae** in the east and **Koolau** in the west, make up the bulk of Oahu's 600 square mi. The narrow inlets of **Pearl Harbor** push in from the sea at the southern end of the valley between the two ridges. Honolulu spreads along 6 mi. of oceanfront southeast of Pearl Harbor, hemmed in by the Koolau Range. **Waikiki Beach** lies near Diamond Head, the island's southernmost extremity; the downtown area clusters 3 mi. west. With the exception of the Leeward Coast and Kaena Point, well-maintained highways circle the rest of the coast and navigate the central valley.

Honolulu

As the cultural, commercial and political focal point of modern Hawaii, the city of Honolulu is a schizophrenic mix of high-rise buildings and white sand beaches, business suits and bikinis. The trade winds keep Honolulu free of stagnant pollution, and the pleasant climate brightens this prosperous urban environment. Waikiki, the world's quintessential vacation destination, is a great place to people-watch and enjoy the sun, if you can find space to spread your towel.

Honolulu's temperate weather influences the lifestyle of its residents. Motorists in rush hour retain an amazingly friendly disposition toward fellow drivers. In the office, informal dress (Hawaiian shirts are *de rigeur*) is the rule. At night, the city vibrates with transient revelers, on whom residents capitalize by selling everything from party cruises to the odd sexual favor. Neither are likely to be a bargain, but hell, you're on vacation; book 'em, Kemo.

Practical Information and Orientation

Hawaii Visitors Bureau, 2270 Kalakaua Ave., 4th Floor, Honolulu 96815 (923-1811). Information on Oahu and the rest of the state. Pick up the *Accommodation Guide* and *Restaurant Guide,* a map of points of interest, and a walking tour of downtown Honolulu. All are free. Open Mon.-Fri. 8am-4:30pm. Information centers located in both the overseas and inter-island air terminals and at the Ala Moana Shopping Center. **Department of Parks and Recreation,** 650 S. King, Honolulu 96817 (523-4525). Information and permits for county parks. Open Mon.-Fri. 7:45am-4pm. Permits available no earlier than two weeks in advance. **Department of State Parks,** 1151 Punchbowl St., Honolulu 96813 (548-7455). Information, trail maps, and permits for camping in state parks. Open Mon.-Fri. 8am-4pm.

Public Transport: 848-5555. Buses cover the entire island, but call to avoid getting stuck somewhere remote. Free Honolulu/Waikiki route maps available at tourist pamphlet stands throughout Waikiki. Fare 60¢.

Taxi: Sida, 439 Kalewa St. (836-0011). All cabs charge 20¢ per 1/6 mi. Base rates about $1.50. Airport to Waikiki $15-18.

Car Rental: Alamo rents to those 21 and over with major credit card. **Budget** rents to those 18-25 for $20 extra. All major agencies are on the island. For used cars, try **Honolulu Rent-a-Car,** 1856 Kalakaua Ave. #105 (941-9099 or 942-7187) or **Maxi Rentals,** 413 Seaside Ave. (923-7381). Both from $10 per day. Insurance mandatory if under age 25 ($7). **Waikiki Rentals,** 224 McCully (946-2181). $20 per day including insurance. Three-day min. rental.

Moped and Bike Rentals: Mopeds get great mileage and are an exciting way to see the island. **Aloha Funway Rentals,** 1778 Ala Moana (942-9696) and 2976 Koapakapaka St. (834-1016), near the airport. Mopeds $16 per half day, $20 per day, $75 per week; bikes $13.50 per day. Open daily 8am-5pm. **Inter-Island Rentals,** 353 Royal Hawaiian Ave. (946-0013). Must be 18 with cash or credit card deposit and valid driver's license. Mopeds $25 per day, $125 per week, negotiable. Bikes $12 per day. Open daily 8am-6pm.

Water Equipment Rentals: Ohana Rentals, near the breakers at Queen's Beach, rents boogie boards and fins (both $8 per day). Open daily 8am-6pm. **Star Beachboys,** Kuhio Beach, to the left of the pavilion. Canoe rides $5, surfboard lessons $10 per hr., boogie boards $5 per hr. **Snorkel Bob's,** 819 Kapahulu Ave. (735-7944) is *the* place for snorkel equipment rentals. Decent equipment is $15 per week and $30 per week gets you higher quality equipment.

Help Lines: Gay Information Services, 926-2910. **The Ultimate Number,** 521-4566 (for general help).

Post Office: Main Office, 3600 Aoleilei Ave. (423-3990). Near the airport. Open daily 8am-4:30pm. **ZIP Code:** 96813.

The **H-1 Freeway** stretches the length of Honolulu. Downtown Honolulu is about six blocks long and four blocks wide, wedged between Honolulu Harbor and Punchbowl Street. In Waikiki, Ala Wai Boulevard, Kuhio Avenue, and Kalakaua Avenue run parallel to the ocean and are the main routes of transit. Bike and running paths are plentiful in the city.

Besides *mauka* (inland) and *makai* (seaward), you are also likely to hear such directions as *ewa* (west; pronounced EHVA) and *diamond head* (east).

Accommodations

Finding a reasonably priced room in Honolulu is a surmount challenge. Check for housing specials in the *Honolulu Advertiser,* available on most street corners for 35¢, for good deals. B&Bs are also viable lodging alternatives; call **B&B Pacific Hawaii** (262-6026) for information.

Honolulu International Hostel (AYH), 2323A Seaview Ave., (946-0591), 1½ mi. north of Waikiki, near University of Hawaii at Manoa. By car, take University Ave. exit off H-1. By bus, take #6 from Ala Moana Shopping Center, to Metcalf and University Ave. (near Burger King). Common area, rec room with TV and free movies. Beds guaranteed for 3 nights; if you want to stay longer in Honolulu, the management can usually arrange to move you to the Hale Aloha Hostel. Price includes 50¢ chore deposit. Lights out at 11pm; rooms are locked from 9:30am-5pm. Members $8.50, non-members $11.50. Sheet sack rental $1. Reservations recommended year round.

Hale Aloha Hostel (AYH), 2417 Prince Edward St. (926-8313), in Waikiki, 2 blocks from the beach. Members only. Beds guaranteed for 3 nights. Open daily 8am-noon and 5-9pm. Lights out at 11pm, but no curfew. Dorm bunks $11.50 per night, nonmembers $14.50. Studio doubles for $26. Reservations required.

Big Surf, 1690 Ala Moana Blvd. (946-6525), near Ala Moana Canal. Sparse and slightly gloomy, but the gate is always locked and only guests have keys. Suites for up to 4 people with twin beds and a sofabed, full kitchen, color TV $45 Sept. 15-Dec. 15 and Feb. 15-June 15; $65 other times. Studios with patio for one or two people, $35 low season, $39 high and $42 with TV.

YMCA, 401 Atkinson Dr. (941-3344), across from Ala Moana Shopping Center downtown. Men over 18 only, lots of semi-permanent residents. Check in or out at noon. Singles $28, with bath $34.50. Doubles $40, with bath $48.50.

YWCA: Fernhurst Residence, 1566 Wilder Ave. (941-2231), near the University. Take bus #14 to Punahou School. For single women over 18. Two persons per room, two rooms per bath. Single occupancy $33, shared room $25.

Camping on Oahu is less convenient than on the other islands. Campgrounds are located in rural areas, and native Hawaiians often consider the campgrounds their domain, especially on Oahu's western shore. Four state parks and 13 county parks allow camping. For free required **permits** contact the Department of Parks and Recreation (see Practical Information). In Honolulu, tent camping is allowed at two state parks, **Sand Island** and **Keaiwa Heiau State Recreation Area** (5-day max. stay). Apply at the Division of Land and Natural Resources (see Practical Information). Sand Island, outside of Honolulu Harbor, offers flat camping. Take Sand Island Access Rd. from Nimitz Hwy. (Rte. 92). Keaiwa Heiau State Recreation Area, at the end of Aiea Heights Dr. (488-6626), has forest sites a short hike from the ruins of the *heiau hoosola* (temple of healing).

Food

Eating in Honolulu can be an international dining experience. There's no reason to eat in Waikiki; if you're trapped there try the **Waikiki Shopping Plaza.** The neighborhoods surrounding Waikiki support many inexpensive restaurants that avoid the corny tourist ambience, and with a good map, you can walk from one district to the next quite easily. A variety of ethnic restaurants, including Hawaiian, Japanese, Thai, and French, are located between the 500 and 1000 blocks of **Kapahulu Avenue** and in the surrounding area. Catch bus #2 going *mauka* up Kapahulu Ave. from the Diamond Head area of Waikiki.

Travelers to Waikiki will be deluged with ads and flyers recommending *luaus*. These Brady Bunch-style feasts with Polynesian dancing rake in the tourist bucks and are often pretty cheesy, but some can be fun and belly-filling (and a few are even reasonably priced). The **Queen Kapiolani,** 150 Kapahulu Ave. (922-1941), offers a $11 unlimited *luau* luncheon buffet with entertainment (Mon.-Wed. and Fri.-Sat. 11am-2pm.)

Ono Hawaiian Food, 726 Kapahulu Ave., Waikiki (737-2275), next to the Ala Wai golf course. Family-style restaurant that lives up to its name *(ono* means good). Try the *poi* or *opihi* (limpets) if you're adventurous. Go early. The lines often extend out the front door. *Kalua* plate $4.55. Combination plate $6. Open Mon.-Sat. 11am-7:30pm.

Rainbow Drive-In, 3308 Kanaina Ave. (737-0177). Probably the best plate lunches around. Heaps and heaps of tasty local food. Plate lunches come on a bed of rice and macaroni salad. Try the mixed plate of Hawaiian-style barbecued pig, boneless chicken and *mahi mahi* for $4.35.

Leonard's Bakery, 933 Kapahulu Ave. (737-5591). A fabulous bakery, this Hawaiian institution has served hot *malasadas* (a Portuguese dessert) for years. Leonard's *malasadas* are, quite simply, the best on this planet (40¢); you'll forget that you were ever on a diet. Virtually a landmark. Open daily 6am-10pm.

Compadres, 1200 Ala Moana, Bldg. 3 (523-1307), at the Ward Centre. A festive Mexican bar and grill featuring complimentary chips and salsa. Ask about half-portions. Dinners $6-8. Open Sun.-Thurs. 7am-11pm, Fri.-Sat. 7am-2am.

Ruffage Natural Foods, 2443 Kuhio Ave. (922-2042). Serves up great vegetarian classics to go: tofu-burger with tomato and sprouts ($4.50), large container of vege-chili with brown rice ($2.85). They also serve fresh fruit smoothies ($2.50-3.50) and sell all-natural vitamins and skin care products. Open Mon.-Sun. 8:30am-7pm, Sun. 9am-7pm.

Sights and Activities

The one-hour loop on the #14 bus cuts across a sampling of Honolulu's diverse neighborhoods. Waikiki is, of course, centered on Waikiki Beach; Kaimuke and Kapahula are small, close-knit communities; Moliliili's lifeblood is the university; and downtown is the shipping and business district, along with Chinatown.

In the 1950s, the image of a ¾-mi. crescent of white sand beach set against the profile of Diamond Head lured platoons of vacationers and honeymooners, eager to spend their post-war boom bucks, to wonderful Waikiki. Today, more savvy visitors spend time on the less crowded isles. Nevertheless, despite its glitzy facade, Waikiki remains fascinating. **Waikiki Beach,** actually comprised of several smaller beaches, is lined with shops and hotels of all varieties and is generally packed with tourists. Farthest to the east is the **Sans Souci Beach,** with no showers or public restrooms. The **Queen's Surf Beach,** closer to downtown, attracts swimmers and roller skaters. The area to the left of the snack bar is a popular tanning spot for gays. At the far end of the beach, **Fort de Russy Beach Park** features the liveliest games of two-player beach volleyball this side of Orange County.

When you want a break from the beach scene, hike the 1 mi. into the **Diamond Head Crater.** To get there, take bus #58 from Waikiki. Bring a flashlight to guide you through the pitch-dark section of the tunnel. The view of Waikiki is spectacular. If the gods do not favor your excursion to Diamond Head try visiting the **Damien Museum,** 330 Ohua St. (behind the St. Augustine Church), for a peek at the dark side of Hawaii's past. Through original documents and a one-hour video, the museum displays the history of Father Damien's Molokai leper colony. (Open Mon.-Fri. 9am-3pm, Sat. 9am-noon. Free.) For the animal inside you, the **Honolulu Zoo,** 151 Kapahulu Ave. (971-7171), across from Kapiolani Park, is located on the east end of Waikiki. Call for a recorded schedule of events. ($4, under 13 free. Open daily 8:30am-4pm.)

Across the street from the zoo is the **Waikiki Shell,** home to the **Kodak Hula Show** (833-1661), which is Waikiki at its photogenic tackiest. This production packages *hula* dancing and palm tree climbing into bite-size tourist portions. You may have a Brady Bunch flashback, but it is a laugh. (Shows Tues.-Thurs. at 10am. $2.50, under 12 free.) For more authentic dancing performances, contact the **Hawaii Visitor's Bureau** (923-1811) and ask about any upcoming performances or competitions among the **hula halau** (schools).

Several cultural and historic attractions are found around the downtown area. The **Iolani Palace,** at King and Richard St. (522-0832), was first the residence of King Kalakaua and Queen Liliuokalani and later served as the nerve center in the TV show *Hawaii Five-0.* The deposed Liliuokalani spent nine months here as a prisoner. The fabulous palace displays sumptuously carved *koa* furniture and elegant European decor. (Wed.-Sat. 9am-2:15pm. 45-min. tours by reservation only at the barracks in the palace grounds. Tours $4, ages 5-12 $1, under 5 not admitted). At the corner of Beretania and Richard St. stands Hawaii's modern **State Capitol,** an architectural melange reflecting all facets of the state's landscape. The pillars represent palm trees, while the inverted dome of the house chambers rises like a volcano, and reflecting pools call to mind the blue Pacific nearby. Outside stands a controversial sculpture of Father Damien. (Open Mon.-Fri. 9am-4pm. Free.) Nearby, the **Honolulu Academy of Arts,** 900 S. Beretania St. (538-1006), houses one of the finest collections of Asian art in the U.S. The 30 galleries and six garden courts also display 17th-century samurai armor, African art, and temporary exhibits. (Open Tues.-Sat. 10am-4:30pm, Sun. 1-5pm. Tours Tues.-Wed. and Fri.-Sat. at 11am, Thurs. at 2pm, and Sun. at 1pm. Free.) The **Bishop Museum,** 1525 Bernice St. (848-4129), in Kalihi, houses a well-respected albeit disorganized collection of artifacts from the Indo-Pacific region. It is the best Hawaiiana museum in the world, and deserves a good portion of your day. Their planetarium features a show entitled "Journey by Starlight" (Mon.-Fri. at 11am and 3pm, Fri.-Sat. at 8pm) which projects the history of Polynesian celestial navigation. Take bus #2 from ("School St.") from Waikiki. (Open daily 9am-2:30pm; call 848-4106 for further information. Museum open Mon.-Sat. 9am-5pm. $5, ages 6-16 $2.50.)

Fifty years ago this December 7th, a stunned nation listened to the reports of the Japanese obliteration of the U.S. Pacific Fleet in **Pearl Harbor.** The **U.S.S. Arizona National Memorial** (422-2771) is an austere, three-part structure built over the sunken aircraft carrier hull in which over a thousand servicemen perished. Count on long lines. (Free tours 7:45am-3pm. Launches out to the hull every 15 minutes. No children under six years of age or under 45 inches are admitted on the launch. The **Visitors center** is open Tuesday-Sunday 7:30am-5pm. Take bus #20 from Waikiki or the #50, 51, or 52 from Ala Moana, or the $2 shuttle (926-4747) from major Waikiki hotels.)

One of the best dayhikes on the island begins *mauka* at the end of Manoa Rd. and trails through 1 mi. of lush tropical greenery to Manoa Falls. Once there you can take a cold, fresh-water dip in the pool under the falls. Take bus #5 from Waikiki to the end of Manoa Rd. Or disembark and catch the bird shows in **Paradise Park,** 3737 Manoa Rd. (988-0200), a natural Hawaiian rain forest sheltering hundreds of tropical birds, some of which perform their own musical compositions daily. (Open daily 9:30am-5pm. Shows 3 times a day. Admission $14, ages 8-13 $9, 3-7 $7.)

Parallel to the Manoa Valley, the **Pali Highway** (Rte. 61) winds its way through **Nuuanu Valley** and over into Kailua, on the windward side of the island. On the way, stop at the **Pali Lookout.** Although this observation point is always packed with tourists, the view overlooking the windward side is undoubtedly one of the finest in all of the islands. But hang onto your hat—the wind can gust hard. Kamehameha the Great consolidated his kingdom by defeating Oahu's soldiers and driving them over this cliff, affording them a very dramatic view indeed.

Entertainment

Bars, restaurants, and theaters abound in Waikiki, making nightlife as wild as your feet and liver can take. The University of Hawaii's **Hemenway Theatre,** (948-8111), in the Physical Sciences Building, shows classic films for $2. Don't miss the Honolulu Zoo's "wildest show in town" summer series of Wednesday night entertainment (923-7723). Admission is free, starting at 4:30pm, and performances begin at 6pm.

Seagull Bar and Restaurant, 2463 Kuhio Ave. (924-7911), in Waikiki. Drink up with a truly international crowd. A lot of young hostelers hang out here for the low drink prices; slam a beer for a mere $1.50. Open daily 4:30pm-2am.

Anna Bananas, 2440 S. Beretania (946-5190), near the university. Two floors of reggae, Afro-pop and blues. The crowd is generally local bikers and surfers with a liberal sprinkling of college students. Don't miss the exceedingly tastefully decorated bathrooms. Steinlager on draft $2.25. Open until 2am.

Hula's Bar and Leis, 2103 Kuhio Ave. (923-0669), at Kalaamoku. Popular gay bar. No cover. Open daily 2pm-4am.

Moose McGillycuddy's Pub & Café, 1035 University Ave. (944-5525), near the university (also 310 Lewers St., 923-0751, near the hostels). Student domain serving huge sandwiches for lunch and dinner. Pub happy hour offers half-price draft beer. Drinks and some margaritas and daquiris ($2). Must be 21 for the disco after 9pm. No cover. Happy Hour 4-8pm. Open Mon.-Sat. 11:30am-2am, Sun. 10am-2am.

The Wave, 1877 Kalakaua Ave. (941-0424), on the edge of Waikiki. A fine locale for loud music and dancing. Mixed crowd. Open daily 9pm-4am.

The Other Side of the Island

Everything on Oahu outside Honolulu is considered "the other side." Concrete and glass quickly fade into pineapple and sugarcane fields sprinkled with small outlying communities. A tour of the island can be done in five hours, but it's best to give yourself at least a day. Start on the Windward Coast and work your way around the perimeter. To reach the southern **Windward Coast,** take bus #58 from Waikiki. To see the **North Shore,** hop on bus #55 at Ala Moana. Both buses run every hour daily from 7am until 6pm.

Miles of beaches and rural towns span the 40-mi. coast of the Windward Coast, running from Laie in the north to Mokapu Point in the south. This is one of the most scenic drives on the island, and good snorkeling abounds. From Waikiki, take **Kalanianaole Highway** (Rte. 72) east to **Koko Head Crater.** Some of the most colorful fish and best snorkeling in the Pacific reside in **Hanauma Bay.** A 10-minute walk to the left of the bay brings you to the less well-known **Toilet Bowl,** great fun to play around in. Climb in when it's full and get flushed up and down as waves fill and empty the chamber through natural lava plumbing. A mile farther, a similar mechanism drives the **Halona Blow Hole** to release its spray. **Secret Beach,** to the right of Halona Blow Hole, was the site of Burt Lancaster and Deborah Kerr's famous "kiss in the sand" in *From Here to Eternity.* If you want life to imitate art, be our guest.

Sandy Beach, just beyond Halona, is a prime spot for bodysurfing and boogie-boarding, the center of the summer surf circuit, and a year-round hangout for locals. **Makapuu Beach,** 41-095 Kalanianaole Hwy., is another prime place to bodysurf, but when the lifeguards put up red flags, stay out of the water. For novices, the best bodysurfing can be found at **Sherwoods** and, on weekends, at **Bellows Air Force Base.** Both are on Kalanianaole on the road to Kailua. Be warned, however, that neither of these parks provides lifeguards. Kalanianaole ends by intersecting **Kailua Road.** Follow this road toward **Kailua Town** and **Kailua Beach Park.** This is prime sailboarding territory. The sandy beach and strong, steady onshore winds are perfect for learning waterstarts. **Windsurfing Hawaii** (261-6067) rents beginner boards in the parking lot for $30 per day (harness $5 extra) and shortboards for $40 per day. They also have boogie boards ($10 per day), water skis ($25 per day) and two-man kayaks ($35 per day). Sailboarding lessons run $35 per person for a three-hour group clinic. If you can bear the airborne grit, this is a great place to swim.

Dig the **Valley of the Temples,** 47-200 Kahekili Hwy., a burial ground matching the Punchbowl for beauty. The serene **Byodo-In Temple,** with tropical gardens and a three-ton brass bell, can be found on the grounds. (Open daily sunrise to sunset. Admission to the valley $2 per person.) Right around the bend from **Punaluu** is the entrance to **Sacred Falls Park.** The falls and the pool underneath make the 2-mi. hike from the parking lot worthwhile. Farther up the coast, the city of **Laie** is home to the **Polynesian Cultural Center,** 55-370 Kamehameha Hwy. (293-3333), a carefully recreated village representing the indigenous cultures of New Zealand, Samoa, Tonga, Fiji, Hawaii, Tahiti, and the Marquesas. (Open Mon.-Sat. noon-6:30pm for daytime activities. Dinner served 4:30-7pm, followed by an evening spectacle 7:30-9pm. $25, with dinner and show $40.)

Fruit vendors and drive-in restaurants with plate lunches and shaved ice are plentiful on the Windward Coast. Kaaawa Country Kitchen and Grocery, 51-480 Kamehameha Hwy. (237-8485), Kaaawa, across from Swanz Beach Park, has kept the locals of Kaaawa satisfied for more than 30 years. (Open Sun.-Thurs. 6:30am-6:30pm, Fri.-Sat. 6:30am-7pm.)**Bueno Nalo,** 41-865 Kalanianaole Hwy. (259-7186), in Waimanalo, serves flavorful Mexican meals ($6.25-7.75). (Open Tues.-Fri. 5-9pm, Sat.-Sun. 3-9pm.) The budget traveler's best lodging bet on the Windward Coast is the **Backpacker's Vacation Inn and Plantation Villas,** 59-788 Kamahameha Hwy. (638-7838), ¼-mi. north of Waimea Bay, with a young and rowdy crowd, good facilities, weekend B-B-Qs, and free snorkeling equipment. (Bunks $14-16, doubles $35-45.) Your best camping option is **Malaekahana State Recreation Area** (293-1736), north of Laie, ranger-patrolled for safety. At low tide, wade across the water to Mokuauia Island, a bird refuge and great picnic spot. But bear in mind that escalating violence from locals may make some state and county beach parks unsafe. Those on the Windward Coast are probably the best choice.

Home to the sugar cane fields and surfers, the **North Shore** and Central Oahu are different worlds from Honolulu (and most other parts of the world). The pace is slow and peaceful in the summer, with beautiful sunsets and plenty of empty beaches. Things heat up in the winter when the surfer crowd decends to shred the infamous waves along Sunset Beach and the Banzai Pipeline, and the North Shore hops with surfing competitions and bikini contests.

The action on the North Shore centers on **Haleiwa,** the surfers' Lourdes. Haleiwa once was a plantation town, but now is enlivened by surf shops and art galleries. **Hawaii Surf and Sail,** 66-214 Kamehameha Hwy. (637-5373), rents all kinds of watersport equipment and gives surfing and sailboarding lessons ($30 per 2-hr. lesson). To the North of Haleiwa is **Waimea Beach Park,** where locals jump off a high rock formation into the sea daily at 11am, 12:30, 2, 2:45 and 3:30pm.

Another few minutes' drive will get you to **Sunset Beach,** and the **Banzai Pipeline,** infamous winter waveland of the world. The beaches are big enough to stay sprinkled rather than packed with people. On the way, take a poke around the **Dole Pineapple Pavilion,** 64-1550 Kamehameha Hwy. (621-8468). Displays offer the visitor a crash course on the ins and outs of pineapple breeding. Inside you can buy classy pineapple memorabilia, from T-shirts to the puzzling Dole Whip.

When you get hungry, park at the **Country Drive-In,** 66-200 Kam Hwy. (637-9122), in Haleiwa, which offers 20 varieties of plate lunches ($3-5), *shaka min,* and yummy smoothies. (Open 7am-6pm.) **The Sugar Bar and Restaurant,** 67-069 Kealohanui (637-6989), is a classic dive, with bikers, surfers, locals, and occasional area bands, and without a cover.

IDAHO

Although most of the U.S. associates Idaho with "Famous Potatoes" (until recently its motto), Idaho ain't just tubers. The wild, wild western scenery north of southern Idaho's potato farms ranges from the 12,000-ft. mountains and rippling estuaries of the Salmon River in the center to the spectacular dense pine forests in the northern panhandle. Republican politicians preach against federal intrusion, but the U.S. government quietly guards Idaho's most spectacular parts in the Selway-Bitteroot Wilderness and the Idaho Primitive Area, through which rushes the meandering Salmon (but not the meandering Salman Rushdie). The Snake River's serpentine waters have carved out Hell's Canyon, the deepest gorge in North America. Idaho gets mixed reviews literarily: it is the native state of Ezra Pound, poet-cum-Nazi, and Ernest Hemingway, who expressed his affection for Idaho by killing himself in it.

Practical Information

Capital: Boise.

Idaho Information Line, 800-635-7820. **Department of Commerce,** Capitol Bldg., 700 W. State St., Boise 83720 (334-2470). Open Mon.-Fri. 8am-5pm. **Parks and Recreation Department,** 7800 Fairview Ave., Boise 83720 (327-7444). Open Mon.-Fri. 8am-5pm.

Idaho Outfitters and Guide Association: P.O. Box 95, Boise 83701 (342-1438). Info on companies leading whitewater, packhorse, and backpacking expeditions in the state. Free vacation directories.

Time Zones: Mountain (2 hr. behind Eastern) and Pacific (3 hr. behind Eastern). The dividing line runs east-west at about the middle of the state; if you straddle it, you'll break the bonds of time. **Postal Abbreviation:** ID

Area Code: 208.

Boise

While not exactly a tourist haven, Idaho's capital contains thousands of shady trees and numerous grassy parks, making this small city both a residential bulwark against the state's dry southern plateau and a relaxing way station on a cross-country jaunt for both girls and bois. Most of the city's sights lie between the capitol and I-84 a few mi. south; you can manage pretty well on foot. **Boise Urban Stages** (336-1010) also runs several routes through the city, with maps available from any bus driver and displayed at each stop. (Buses operate Mon.-Fri. 5:45am-7:15pm, Sat. 8:30am-6:30pm. Fare 50¢, seniors 25¢.)

The **Boise Tour Train** (342-4796) shows you 75 sites around the city in two hours. Tours start and end in the parking lot of **Julia Davis Park,** departing every 75 minutes. (Tours Mon.-Sat. 10am-3pm, also Thurs.-Sat. 7pm and Sun. noon-5pm. Fare $4.75, seniors $4.25, ages 3-12 $2.75.) To learn about Idaho at your own pace, walk through the **Historical Museum** (334-2120) in Julia Davis Park. (Open Mon.-Sat. 9am-5pm, Sun. 1-5pm. Free.) Also in the park, the **Boise Art Museum,** 670 Julia Davis Dr. (345-8330), displays international and local works. (Open Tues.-Fri. 10am-5pm, Sat.-Sun. noon-5pm. Admission $2, under 18 free.) The tiny and crowded **Boise Zoo** (384-4260) roars and howls beyond these two buildings. (Open Mon.-Wed. and Fri.-Sun. 10am-5pm, Thurs. 10am-9pm. Admission $2, seniors and ages 3-12 $1, under 3 free. Thurs. ½-price.) Taloned avians perch and dive at **World Center for Birds of Prey,** (362-3716) 6 mi. south of I-84 on Cole Rd. Call ahead to arrange a tour. For more back-to-nature fun, try the 22-mi. **Boise River Greenbelt,** a pleasant, tree-lined path ideal for a leisurely walk or picnic.

Bask in the region's cultural history at the **Basque Museum and Cultural Center** (343-2671), at 6th and Grove St. in downtown Boise, where you'll find out about the surprisingly rich Basque heritage in the Great Basin and the Western Rockies. (Open Tues.-Fri. 10am-5pm.)

Boise does alright by its food. You can pig out on the heavy pasta of southern Italy, the spicy Basque specialties of northern Spain, and a good measure of down-home burgers and fries. (Yeah, they have potatoes.) For all of the above, look to the downtown area, centered around 6th and Main St., where many turn-of-the-century buildings have been restored recently. Try a mini-pizza ($4.25) at **Noodles,** 105 S. 6th St. (342-9300), upstairs in one of the newly yuppified edifices. (Open Mon.-Thurs. 11:30am-10pm, Fri.-Sat. noon-11pm, Sun. 3-9pm.) For a great milk-shake ($2), fly yourself to **Moon's Kitchen,** 815 W. Bannock St. (342-5251) in the rear portion of Moon's Gun and Tackle. You can contemplate the rifles and shot-guns mounted behind the counter while enjoying your meal. For a more disarming experience, grab an espresso and sandwich ($2.10-$5.50) from **Christina's Bakery,** at the corner of 5th and Main St (385-0133). (Open Mon.-Thurs. 7:30am-6pm, Fri. 7:30am-11pm, Sat. 8:30am-11pm, Sun. 9am-3pm.) For nighttime entertainment, head for **Old Boise,** the area between S. 1st and S. 6th St., where the town's bars fire up.

Finding lodging in Boise is harsh; neither the YMCA nor the YWCA provide rooms, and even the cheapest hotels charge more than $20 per night. The more reasonable places tend to fill quickly, so make reservations. One of the most spacious is the **Capri Motel,** 2600 Fairview Ave. (344-8617), where air-conditioned rooms come with coffee and queen-sized beds. (Singles $25. Doubles $29.) Farther out of town, the **Boisean,** 1300 S. Capitol Ave. (343-3645), has smaller rooms but a more personable staff. (Singles $29.50. Doubles $35.50.) Three mi. north of town lies the **Forest Service Campground.** Contact **Boise National Forest,** 1715 Front St. (334-1516), for a map. (Open Mon.-Fri. 7:30am-4:30pm.) The nearest campground with hookups is **Fiesta Park,** 11101 Fairview Ave. (375-8207). (Sites $14, full hookup with sewer $17.50.)

Amtrak (800-872-7245) serves Boise from the beautiful Spanish-mission style **Union Pacific Depot,** 1701 Eastover Terrace (336-5992), easily visible from Capitol Blvd. One train per day goes east to Salt Lake City (7½ hr., $67) and beyond; one goes west to Portland (11 hr., $79) and Seattle (15½ hr., $106). **Greyhound/Trailways** has I-84 schedules from its terminal at 1212 W. Bannock (343-3681), a few blocks west of downtown. Two buses per day head to Portland (8-10 hr., $56); three to Seattle (11 hr., $85).

Boise's main **post office** is on 770 S. 13th St. (383-4211; open Mon.-Fri. 7:30am-5:30pm, Sat. 10am-2pm). The **ZIP code** is 83701.

Coeur d'Alene

The gaggles of tourists—one may also use the term "pride" or "unkindness" to denote such a group—can do little to mar this isolated spot's rustic beauty. No matter how many people clutter its beaches, the deep blue water of Lake Coeur d'Alene offers a serene escape from whichever urban jungle you call home. **Sandpoint,** to the north, is less tourist-logged and equally spectacular.

Practical Information

Emergency: 911.

Visitor Information: Chamber of Commerce, Front Ave. at 2nd St. (664-3194; 800-232-4968 outside ID). Open Mon.-Fri. 8am-8pm. Also a branch in the parking lot at U.S. 95 and Appleway. Open summer daily 9am-4pm.

Bus Station: 1923½ N. 4th St. (664-3343), 1 mi. north of the lake. **Greyhound** serves Spokane (1 hr., $5.50), Lewiston (1 per day, $26) and Missoula (5 hr., $32). **Empire Lines** connects

Coeur d'Alene to Sandpoint at 5th and Cedar St. (1 per day, $8.30). Open Mon.-Fri. 8:30-11:30am and 1:30-6:15pm, Sat. 8:30-noon.

Car Rental: Auto Mart Used Car Rental, 120 Anton Ave. (667-4905), 3 blocks north of the bus station. $28 per day, $170 per week; 100 free mi. per day, 25¢ per addit. mi. Open Mon.-Sat. 8am-6pm; phone line open 24 hrs. With personal insurance you can rent a car at age 18. Credit card or a $100 cash deposit required.

Help Lines: Crisis Services, 664-1443. Open 24 hrs.

Time Zone: Pacific (3 hrs. behind Eastern).

Post Office: 111 N. 7th St. (664-8126), 5 blocks east of the chamber of commerce. Open Mon.-Fri. 8:30am-5pm, Sat. 9am-noon. **ZIP code:** 83814.

Area Code: 208.

Accommodations, Camping, and Food

Cheap lodgings are lean in this booming resort town. You'll have better luck in the eastern outskirts of the city. The **Blackstone Motel,** 2009 E. Sherman Ave. (664-5410), has tiny singles and doubles for $28. **El Rancho Motel,** 1915 E. Sherman Ave. (664-8791), offers bigger rooms at bigger prices: singles for $37, doubles $43-48. In Sandpoint, by all means stay at the elegant lakefront **Whitaker House,** 410 Railroad Ave. (263-0816). Rooms cost $30-46, breakfast included.

There are four **public campgrounds** within 20 mi. of Coeur d'Alene. The closest is **Beauty Creek,** a forest service site 10 mi. south along the lake. Camp alongside a lovely stream against the side of the mountain. Drinking water and pit toilets are provided. (Sites $5. Open May 5-Oct. 15.) **Honeysuckle Campground,** about 25 mi. to the northeast, has nine sites with drinking water and toilets. (Sites free. Open May 15-Oct. 15.) **Bell Bay,** on the shores of Lake Coeur d'Alene, off U.S. 95 south, then 14 mi. to Forest Service Rd. 545, has 40 sites, a boat launch, and good fishing. (Sites $5. Open May 5-Oct. 15.) Call the Fernan Ranger District Office, 2502 E. Sherman Ave. (765-7381), for information on these and other campgrounds. (Open Mon.-Fri. 7:30am-4:30pm, Sat. 8:30am-3pm.) **Farragut State Park** (683-2425), 20 mi. north on Rte. 95, is an extremely popular 4000-acre park dotted with hiking trails and beaches along Lake Pend Oreille (pronounced pon-do-RAY). (Sites $8, with hookup $11. $2 day-use fee for each motor vehicle not camping in the park. Open May 27-Sept. 2.)

Sights and Activities

The lake is Coeur d'Alene's raison d'être. Hike up **Tubbs Hill** to a scenic vantage point, or head for the **Coeur d'Alene Resort** and walk along the world's longest floating boardwalk (3300 ft.). You can tour the lake on a **Lake Coeur d'Alene Cruise** (765-4000), which departs from the downtown dock every afternoon between June and September (Cruises at 1:30, 4, and 6:30pm, returning at 3, 5:30, and 8pm respectively. Fare $8.50, seniors $7.50, ages under 10 $5.50.) Rent a canoe from **Eagle Enterprises** (664-1175) at the city dock to explore the lake yourself ($5 per hr., $15 per half-day, $25 first whole day, $10 per day thereafter).

Twenty mi. east of town on I-90 is the **Old Mission at Cataldo** (682-3814), now contained in a day-use state park. Built in 1853 by Native Americans, the mission is the oldest known building in Idaho. (Free tours daily. Open June-July daily 8am-6pm; Aug-May daily 9am-7pm. Vehicle entry fee $2.) Near Sandpoint, about 50 mi. north of Coeur d'Alene, the **Roosevelt Grove of Ancient Cedars** nurtures trees up to 12 ft. in diameter.

Continue another 35 mi. east on I-90 through mining country to the town of **Wallace,** where you will find retail shops shaped like mining helmets and the **Wallace Mining Museum,** 509 Bank St. (753-7151), which features turn-of-the-century mining equipment. (Open Mon.-Fri. 8am-4pm, Sat.-Sun. 9am-5pm; off-season Mon.-Fri. 9am-5pm, Sat. 10am-5pm. Admission $1, seniors and kids 50¢.) Next door, take the one-hour **Sierra Silver Mine Tour** (leaves from museum) through a recently closed mine. (Tours May-Sept. daily every 20 min. 9am-4pm. Admission $6, seniors and ages under 12 $5.) Mining, mining, mining.

Ketchum and Sun Valley

Union Pacific Railroad heir Averill Harriman sent Austrian Count Felix Schaff-gotsch on a mission in 1935: scour the U.S. for a site to develop into a ski resort area rivaling Europe's best. After searching the Rockies, the Count settled on the small mining and sheep-herding town of Ketchum in Idaho's Wood River Valley. Since then, the resort has attracted countless rich and famous U.S. residents; many of their portraits line the main hallway of the Sun Valley Lodge. Don't be surprised if you bump into Mariel Hemingway in Chateau Drug or Clint Eastwood sauntering down Main St. Aside from celebrities, Sun Valley mainly shows off the outdoors, with the surrounding Boulder, Pioneer, and Sawtooth Mountains providing endless warm-weather opportunities for camping, hiking, mountain biking, and fishing.

The best time to visit the area is during "slack," (Labor Day-Thanksgiving and April-July 4th), when the tourists magically vanish. In high summer, Ketchum, Sun Valley, and their northern neighbor Stanley fill with travelers, although the Sawtooths still offer some solitary escape.

The hills around Ketchum have more **natural hot springs** than any spot in the Rockies except Yellowstone; bathing is free, legal, and uncrowded in most of them. As with the ghost towns of the surrounding mountains, many springs can be reached only by foot; for maps, inquire at the **Chapter One Bookstore** (726-5425), on Main St. across from Farmer Jack Supermarket, or **Elephant's Perch**, on Sun Valley Rd. (726-3497). "The Perch" is also the best source for mountain bike rentals and trail information. (Bikes $10 per ½-day, $15 per day.)

More accessible, non-commercial springs include **Warfield Hot Springs**, on Warm Springs Creek, 11 mi. west of Ketchum on Warm Springs Rd., and **Russian John Hot Springs**, 8 mi. north of the Sawtooth National Recreation Area headquarters on U.S. 75, 100 yd. west of the highway. For the best information on fishing conditions and equipment rentals, stop by **Silver Creek Outfitters**, 507 N. Main St. (726-5282; open daily 7am-6pm).

Though a small town, Ketchum has an astonishing number of restaurants and an active nightlife. **The Kneadery**, 260 Leadville Ave. (726-9462), serves delicious omelettes and sandwiches for breakfast and lunch ($4-5). Expect to wait for a table at this local favorite. (Open daily 7:30am-2pm.) Locals also sit down at the **Bald Mountain Cantina**, at 6th and Warm Springs St. (726-3353), for the tasty and inexpensive meals. And though it's just a small hot dog stand, **Irving's** has become a Ketchum institution. Get an original dog with "The Works" for $2. It's set up in a lot at the corner of Main and 4th St. in summer, at the base of the Warm Springs ski lifts in winter. (Hours vary depending on weather and Irving.)

Ketchum can keep even the most intrepid of barhoppers busy for several nights. **Desperado's**, 4th and Washington St. (726-3068), runneth over with Mexican beer as well as authentic Mexican food for $2-6. (Open Mon.-Sat. 11:30am-10pm, Sun. 5-10pm.) The **Pioneer Saloon**, 308 N. Main St. (726-3139), has little or no cover, cheap drinks, and lots of company most nights of the week. Across Main St. at **Whiskey Jacque's** (726-5297), live bands play most nights.

Staying indoors in Sun Valley and Ketchum is very problematic. The only halfway-reasonable hotel is the **Ski View Lodge** (726-3441), on Main St. (Hwy. 75). (Singles $27. Doubles $38.) **Hailey**, 11 mi. south on U.S. 75, has cheaper lodgings. Try the beautifully restored **Hailey Hotel**, 201 S. Main St. (788-3140). Rooms have sinks, but the showers are down the hall. (Singles $25. Doubles $30.) The **Hitchrack Motel**, 619 S. Main St. (788-2409), has non-psycho showers and singles for $19, doubles for $35. Prices everywhere skyrocket in the winter.

From early June to mid-October, **camping** is the best option for cheap sleep. The **Sawtooth National Forest** surrounds Ketchum—drive or hike along the forest service road and camp for free. The **North Fork** and **Wood River** campgrounds lie seven and 10 mi. north of Ketchum, respectively, and cost $3 per site. Wood River has an amphitheater and flush toilets. You must bring your own water to the three **North Fork Canyon** campgrounds 7 mi. north of Ketchum. (Free.) Call the Ketchum Ranger Station for information.

For local info, visit the **Sun Valley/Ketchum Chamber of Commerce,** at 4th and Main St., Ketchum, P.O. Box 2420, Sun Valley 83353 (726-3423), where a well-informed, helpful staff shines. (Open daily 9am-5pm.) The **Ketchum Ranger Station,** on Sun Valley Rd., Ketchum (622-5371), 3 blocks east of U.S. 75, is the place to go for information on national forest land around Ketchum, and tapes and maps on the Sawtooth Recreation Area. (Open daily 8am-5pm.)

When you throw baseballs in Ketchum, catch 'em astride Idaho 75 (Main St.), 87 mi. north of Twin Falls, the nearest city of any size. The resort village of Sun Valley suns itself ½ mi. northeast of Ketchum, on Sun Valley Rd. Boise lies 160 mi. to the west. The **post office** in Ketchum (726-5161) is at 301 1st Ave. (Open Mon.-Fri. 8:30am-5:30pm, Sat. 11am-1pm.) The **ZIP code** is 83340.

Sawtooth National Recreation Area

Rough mountains pack this recreation area's 756,000 acres of wilderness; some peaks puncture the cloud layer. Home to the **Sawtooth** and **White Cloud Mountains** in the north and the **Smokey** and **Boulder** ranges in the south, the **Sawtooth National Recreation Area (SNRA)** is surrounded by four national forests, encompassing the headwaters of five of Idaho's major rivers.

Getting to the heart of the SNRA is easy—if you have a car. Don't miss the chance to pause at the **Galena Summit,** 25 mi. north of Ketchum on Rte. 75. The 8701-ft. peak provides an excellent introductory view of the range. If you don't have a car, take the bus to Missoula (250 mi. north on U.S. 93) or Twin Falls (120 mi. south on Rte. 75); from there, rent a car with at least six cylinders or plan for a long beautiful hike.

Information centers in the SNRA are almost as plentiful as the peaks themselves. See the **Stanley Chamber of Commerce** (774-3411) on Hwy. 21 about three-quarters of the way through town. (Open daily 10am-6pm.) Near Stanley lies the **Stanley Ranger Station** (774-3681), three mi. south on U.S. 75 (open June 16-Sept. 6, Mon.-Fri. 8am-5pm, Sat.-Sun. 8:30am-5pm; off-season Mon.-Fri. 8am-5pm). The **Redfish Visitors Center** (774-3376) lies 8 mi. south and 2 mi. west of Stanley at the **Redfish Lake Lodge.** (Open June 19-Sept. 2 daily 9am-6pm.) Whatever you can't find at these three places awaits at **SNRA Headquarters** (726-7672), 53 mi. south of Stanley off Idaho 75. The headquarters building itself is an interesting example of mountain architecture—its roof mimics the peaks of the Sawtooths. (Open daily 8am-5:30pm; off-season Mon.-Fri. 8am-4:30pm.) All the info centers provide maps of the Sawtooths ($2) and free taped auto tours of the impressive Ketchum-Stanley trip on U.S. 75.

Hiking, boating, and fishing opportunities in all four of the SNRA's little-known ranges are unbeatable and innumerable. Two mi. northwest of Stanley on Rte. 21, take the 3-mi. dirt road which leads to the trailhead of the **Sawtooth Lake Hike.** This 5½-mi. trail is steep but well worn, and not overly difficult if you stop to rest. Bolder hikers who want to survey the White Cloud Range from above should head southeast of Stanley to the **Casino Lakes** trailhead. This trek terminates at **Lookout Mountain,** 3000 ft. higher than far-away Stanley itself. (Make sure you have a camping permit, available at all ranger stations, and plan to stay overnight.) The long and gentle loop around **Yellow Belly, Toxaway,** and **Petit Lakes** is recommended for novice hikers or any tourists desiring a leisurely overnight trip. For additional hiking information, consult the detailed topographic maps in Anne Hollingshead and Gloria Moore's *Day Hiking Near Sun Valley,* available at local bookstores.

In the heat of summer, the cold rivers beg for fishing, canoeing, or whitewater rafting. **McCoy's Tackle Shop** (774-3377), on Ace of Diamonds St. in Stanley, rents gear and sells a full house of outdoor equipment. (Open daily 8am-9pm.) The **Red-**

fish **Lake Lodge Marina** (774-3536) rents paddleboats ($4-5 per ½ hr.), canoes ($5 per hr., $15 per half day, $25 per day), and more powerful boats for higher prices. (Open in summer daily 7am-9pm.) **The River Company,** based in Ketchum (726-8890) with an office in Stanley (774-2244), arranges whitewater rafting and float trips. (Ketchum office open daily 8am-6pm. Stanley office open in summer daily 8:30am-6pm, unless a trip is in progress.)

But the most inexpensive way to enjoy the SNRA waters is to visit the hot springs just east of Stanley. Watch for the rising steam on the roadside, often a sign of hot water. **Sunbeam Hot Springs,** 13 mi. from town, is the best of the batch. Be sure to bring a bucket or cooler to the stone bathhouse; you'll need to add about 20 gallons of cold Salmon River water before you can get into these *hot* pools. For evening entertainment, try to get in on the regionally famous **Stanley Stomp,** when fiddlers in local bars such as **Casanova Jack's** and the **Kasino Club** play non-stop from 8am to midnight or beyond; the foot-stomping resounds for miles.

In the heart of Stanley, on Ace of Diamonds St., the **Sawtooth Hotel and Café** (774-9947) is a perfect place to stay after a wilderness sojourn. (Singles $21.50, with private bath $36.50. Doubles $24.50, with private bath $40.50.) More scenic is **Mc-Gowan's Resort** (774-2290), one mi. down Hwy. 75 in Lower Stanley. Hand-built cabins here sit directly on the banks of the Salmon River, house up to four people each, and usually contain kitchenettes. They also offer a terrific view of the Sawtooths and unmatched McGowan hospitality. ($45; Sept.-early June $35.) Campgrounds line U.S. 75; clusters are at **Redfish Lake** at the base of the Sawtooths, and **Alturas Lake** in the Smokies. At Redfish, the pick of the litter is the small campground at the Point, which has its own beach. The two campgrounds on nearby Little Redfish Lake are the best spots for trailers. All sites in the SNRA cost $4-6; primitive camping is free.

The SNRA's **time zone** is Mountain (2 hr. behind Eastern). The **post office** (774-2230) is on Ace of Diamonds St. (open Mon.-Fri. 8am-5pm); the **ZIP code** is 83278.

Near SNRA: Craters of the Moon National Monument

Sixty mi. south of Sun Valley on U.S. 20/26/93, the black lava plateau of **Craters of the Moon National Monument** rises from the surrounding fertile plains. Windswept and remarkably quiet, the stark, twisted lava formations are speckled with sparse, low vegetation. Volcanic eruptions occurred here as recently as 2000 years ago. The eerie, dark landscape may remind you of a Pink Floyd album gone physical.

Park admission is $3 per car, and the bizarre black campsites cost $8. Wood fires are prohibited here, so you might want to camp in the adjacent Bureau of Land Management properties (free). The park's sites often fill by 9 or 10pm on summer nights. Unmarked sites in the monument are free, but even with the topographical map ($4) from the visitors center, it may be hard to find a comfortable spot: the first explorers couldn't sleep in the lava fields for lack of bearable places to lie down.

The **visitors center** (527-3257), just off Rte. 20/26/93, has displays and videotapes on the process of lava formation, and printed guides for hikes to all points of interest within the park. (Open daily 8am-6pm; off-season daily 8am-4:30pm.) From nearby Arco, Blackfoot, or Pocatello you can connect with Greyhound. There is, however, no public transportation to the national monument.

ILLINOIS

Illinois divides into two distinct parts: Chicago—the third largest metropolis in the US—and the rest of Illinois, called "downstate" by Illinoisians. Despite this division, the two parts do share an agriculture-based economy. Downstate is blessed with stability and fertility—quiet farm country with the kind of open space that inspired the prairie science-fiction novels of native Ray Bradbury.

Practical Information

Capital: Springfield.

Office of Tourism, 620 E. Adams St., Springfield 62701 (217-782-7500).

Time Zone: Central (1 hr. behind Eastern). **Postal Abbreviation:** IL

Chicago

The Pottawattamie people who first came upon this patch of prairie at the edge of Lake Michigan dubbed it *Chikagu,* or "City of the Wild Onion." Some say it really meant "City of the Big Smell." Modern Chicago has displaced the Pottawattamie and their vegetables, but the name and both its meanings along with countless other epithets have stuck. Locals and out-of-towners know Chicago as "the Windy City," a catchy pair of trochees referring not to the stiff breezes that whip through the downtown streets but to the hot air from the mouths of certain turn-of-the-century revivalist preachers. Supercilious New Yorkers may write off Chicago as the nation's "Second City," and census-hungry Angelenos may relegate it to third place, but die-hard Chicagoans will always insist that Carl Sandburg's "City of the Big Shoulders" knocks out any civic competitor with the guts to climb into the ring.

The Chicago *Tribune* once speculated what the city would be like without Lake Michigan. Forgoing the obvious conclusion (that it simply wouldn't exist), the author described a horrible scenario of endless sprawl in all directions, severe water shortages, and a sickly population menaced by the mosquitos swarming out of nearby swamps. As it is, Chicago's healthy lakefront resulted from a historical rather than a geographical accident—the Great Fire of 1871. Allegedly started when Mrs. O'Leary's cow kicked over a lantern in a hay-filled shed, this immense bonfire destroyed most of the city. Two decades later, Daniel Burnham instituted a formal riot-proof rebuilding plan which had the fortunate side-effect of reserving all of Chicago's 27 mi. of lakefront property for public beaches, parks, and harbors. A product of visionary modern architects like Frank Lloyd Wright and Louis Sullivan, the postcard-perfect skyline sprouts up three of the world's tallest buildings.

Beyond the lakefront and elegant downtown areas, Chicago preserves much of the no-nonsense grittiness it had when Upton Sinclair grimly termed it *The Jungle.* The stockyards and freight depots which made the Armours and the Pullmans rich have been closed for decades, but local trains still rattle by every 10 minutes on the city's signature elevated tracks. Chicago's extreme racial polarization—the North Side is predominantly white, the South Side predominantly African American—often obscures the tremendous diversity of the city's checkerboard ethnic neighborhoods which erupt in an endless chain of festivals every summer. Some old West Side neighborhoods still conduct daily business entirely in Polish, a reminder that Chicago is home to more Poles than any city besides Warsaw.

Such cultural variety has inspired a score of major museums, an impressive collection of public sculpture, one of the world's finest symphonies, excellent small theaters, and the University of Chicago, which in turn has produced more Nobel laureates than any university in the world.

Practical Information

Emergency: 911.

Chicago Tourism Council Visitors Information Center, 163 E. Pearson (280-5740), in the Water Tower Pumping Station. Pick up a copy of the *Chicago Visitors Guide.* Open daily 9:30am-5pm. **Tourist Information Center,** 310 S. Michigan Ave. (793-2094), across from the Art Institute. Open Mon.-Fri. 9am-5pm.

Travelers and Immigrants Aid: 327 S. LaSalle St. (435-4500; after hours 222-0265). Open Mon.-Fri. 8:30am-5pm. Other locations at O'Hare Airport (686-7562; open Mon.-Fri. 8am-

N

Lincoln Ave.

Downtown Chicago

0   1/4 Mile
0   1/4 Kilometer

Eugenie St.

North Ave.

Lincoln Park

N. Larrabee St.

Lake Shore Drive

Gold Coast

Lake Michigan

Division St.

Chicago River

Oak St.

Clark St.

Dearborn St.

State St.

Hancock Building

Chicago Ave.

Old Water Tower

Museum of Contemporary Art

Ontario St.

Ohio St.

Grand Ave.

Kinzie St.

Lake St.

Randolph St.

Washington Blvd.

Madison St.

Monroe St.

Adams St.

Jackson Blvd.

Van Buren St.

JFK Expressway

Franklin St.

Wells St.

La Salle St.

Wabash Ave.

Michigan Ave.

First National Bank

Sears Tower

Chicago Art Institute

Grant Park

Chicago Harbor

Eisenhower Expressway

Congress Parkway

Polk St.

Columbus Dr.

Roosevelt Rd.

Ryan Expressway

Jefferson St.

South Branch

Field Museum Of National History

Shedd Aquarium

Adler Planetarium

Bernham Park Yacht Harbor

Soldier Field

4:30pm), Greyhound (435-4537); and Union Station (435-4500; open 24 hrs.). The main office provides language assistance, legal aid, and information for the disabled.

Consulates: Australia, 321 N. Clark St. (645-9444); **Canada,** 310 S. Michigan Ave. (427-1410); **France,**737 N. Michigan Ave. (787-5359); **Germany,** 104 S. Michigan Ave. (263-0850); **Ireland,** 400 N. Michigan Ave. (337-1868); **Israel,** 111 E. Wacker Dr. (565-3300); **Italy,** 500 N. Michigan Ave. (467-1550); **Mexico,** 300 N. Michigan Ave. (726-3942); **U.K.,** 33 N. Dearborn St. (346-1810). Most open Mon.-Fri. 9am-5pm.

O'Hare International Airport: Off I-90. Inventor of the layover and holding pattern. Depending on traffic, a trip between downtown and O'Hare can take up to 2 hrs. The **Rapid Train** runs between the Airport El station and downtown. Plan 40 min.-1 hr. for the ride. **Continental Air Transport** (454-7800) connects the airport to selected downtown and suburban locations. Runs every 30 min. 6am-11:30pm. Fare $12.50. **Midway Airport,** on the western edge of the South Side often offers less expensive flights. To get downtown, take CTA bus #54B to Archer, then ride bus #62 to State St. For an extra 20¢, the 99M express runs from Midway downtown 6:30-8:15am and from downtown to Midway during the afternoon rush hour. Continental Air Transport costs $9.50. For limousine service to either airport, call **C.W. Limousine Service** (493-2700). Rides from the South Side, as well as between the two airports (both $9.75). Airport baggage lockers $1 per day.

Amtrak: Union Station (558-1075 or 800-872-7245), Canal and Adams St. downtown. Take the El to State and Adams, then walk up Adams 7 blocks. Amtrak's main hub. Destinations include: St. Louis ($45), Detroit ($27), Indianapolis ($28), and Milwaukee ($15). Station open 24 hrs.; tickets sold daily 7:30am-10pm. Baggage check $1 per day.

Greyhound: 630 W. Harrison St. (781-2900), on corner of Jefferson and Desplaines. Take the El to Linton. The hub in central U.S. Also serves as home base for several smaller companies covering the Midwest. To: Milwaukee ($13.50), Detroit ($22-27), and St. Louis ($25-31). Open 24 hrs.

Public Transport: See Transportation below.

Taxi: Yellow Cab, 829-4222.

Car Rental: Fender Benders Rent-a-Car, 1545 N. Wells St. (280-8554), 1½ blocks from the Sedgwick El stop. $25 per day, $125 per week., 100 free mi., 15¢ each additional mi. Open Mon.-Fri. 8:30am-6:30pm, Sat. 10am-2pm. Must be 25 with major credit card.

Auto Transport Company: National U-Drive, 2116 N. Cicero Ave. (889-7737).

Help Lines: Metro Help, 929-5150. 24-hr. crisis line. **Rape Crisis Line,** 708-872-7799. Open 24 hrs. **Gay and Lesbian Hotline,** 871-2273. Open 24 hrs.

Medical Emergency: Cook County Hospital, 633-6000. Take the Congress A train to the Medical Center Stop.

Medical Walk-in Clinic: MedFirst, 310 N. Michigan Ave. (726-0577). Non-emergency medical care. Open Sun.-Fri. 8am-6pm, Sat. 8am-5pm.

Post Office: 433 W. Van Buren St. (765-3210), 2 blocks from Union Station. Open Mon.-Sat. 24 hrs. **ZIP code:** 60607.

Area Code: 312 for numbers in Chicago, 708 for numbers outside Chicago's municipal boundaries. All numbers listed here without area code are in the 312 area.

Orientation

Chicago runs north-south along 29 mi. of southwest Lake Michigan lakefront, with a slight western tilt. The city and its suburbs sprawl across the entire northeastern corner of Illinois. Most cross-country road, rail, and airplane trips in the northern U.S. pass through Chicago.

Despite its vast size, Chicago is neatly organized. The grid-like pattern of streets centers at **State Street,** the east-west axis, and **Madison Street,** the north-south axis. State and Madison also mark a busy commercial area called the **State Street Mall.** The addresses of streets suffixed N., S., E., or W. increase every block by 100 in number (with a few exceptions) as the distance from State and Madison increases. East numbers are few because the lake gets in the way. South streets are usually numbered (not named), with the exception of 1200 S., known as Roosevelt. Outside of Chicago's municipal boundaries, this may break down, as each suburb maintains its own numbering system.

Chicago's other neighborhoods are varied and frequently polarized. Buses and trains disembark in Chicago's **Loop,** the skyscraper-studded downtown area surrounded by elevated train tracks. Use caution here after dark. Just south of the Loop and southwest of the natural history museum lies **Pilsen,** a center of Chicago's Latino community. **Chinatown** is just south of Pilsen. Much farther south, at about 57th St., lies **Hyde Park,** home of the University of Chicago. Although Hyde Park is reasonably safe, especially during the day, avoid the **Near South Side,** one of the country's most dangerous urban ghettos. Parts of the **West Side** are also extremely unsafe. In general, don't go south of Cermak or east of Halstead St. at night. Ritzy business and residential districts extend north of the Loop along Michigan Ave. into the affluent north lakeshore, culminating in the wealthy suburbs on the northern edge of Cook County. Working- and middle-class neighborhoods extend outward from the core city area. The western and northern districts have mixed ethnic neighborhoods that include Greek, Italian, Indian, Native American, and Southeast Asian Chicagoans. The city's sizable Polish community has an enclave near Oak Park. **Uptown** is the home of many Vietnamese and other Southeast Asians, as well as clusters of Haitians and Native Americans. Irish neighborhoods dot the western portion of the city. The South Side is overwhelmingly African American, while the northern suburb of **Skokie** contains a well-known Jewish community.

Transportation

The **Chicago Transit Authority,** part of the **Regional Transit Authority** (836-7000 in the city, 800-972-7000 in the suburbs), runs rapid transit trains, subways, and buses. The CTA runs 24 hrs., but late-night service is infrequent and unsafe in some areas, especially the South Side. Some stations do not operate at all at night. Maps are available at many stations, the Water Tower Information Center, and the RTA Office. The **elevated rapid transit train** system, called the **El,** bounds the major downtown section of the city, the Loop. Trains marked "A," "B," or "all stops" may run on the same tracks, stopping at stations designated as such. Also, different routes may run along the same tracks in places. Because of Chicago's grid layout, many bus lines run for several mi. along one straight road. Train fare is $1.25, bus fare $1; from 6-9am and 3-6pm, $1.25; 10 tokens good for one train or bus ride each any time of day cost $9. Remember to get a transfer (25¢) from the driver when you board the bus or enter the El stop, which will get you two more rides in the following two hours. A $60 month pass is available in many supermarkets, including the Jewel and Dominick's chains.

On Sundays and holidays from Memorial Day weekend to the end of September, you can tour Chicago's cultural attractions on CTA's **Culture Buses** (every 30 min. 10:30am-4:55pm; fare $2.50, seniors and kids $1.25). A transfer from a previous ride reduces the price to $1, seniors and kids 40¢. Three routes serve the North, South, and West Sides. Many sights and museums described below are on a Culture Bus route, and some offer a discount upon presentation of a Culture Bus Supertransfer. You can use the Culture Bus Supertransfer all day.

Several major highways crisscross the city and urban area. The **Eisenhower (I-290)** cuts west from the Loop. **I-90** pivots around the Eisenhower; to the northwest it's called the **Kennedy,** to the south, the **Dan Ryan.** The **Edens (I-94)** splits off from the Kennedy and heads north to the suburbs. **I-294** rings the city. Some of the highways require tolls.

Accommodations

With budget lodgings in Chicago, you get what you pay for, sometimes even less. Expensive ($60-80) weekend specials are often unavailable because of conventions. **Chicago Bed and Breakfast,** P.O. Box 14088, Chicago, 60614 (951-0085), is a referral service with over 60 rooms of varying prices throughout the city and outlying areas. (From $40 per person. Cooking facilities often available.) **Exel Inns** (800-356-

8013; singles $43), and **Motel 6** (708-818-8088; singles $32, doubles $38), are national motel chains with locations in the suburbs accessible by car.

Chicago International Hostel (AYH), 6318 N. Winthrop (262-1011). Take Howard St. northbound train to Loyola Station. Walk south and east on Sheridan Rd. to Winthrop, then ½ block south. Clean rooms in a convenient neighborhood. Good place to meet traveling students. Kitchen, laundry room. Check-in 8-10am, 4-10pm. Lockout mid. $12, nonmembers $15. Linen included.

Arlington House (AYH), 616 Arlington Pl. (929-5380). Take the El to Fullerton, walk 2 blocks east to Orchard, turn left on Arlington Place; it's on the right. Clean, crowded rooms share a building with a senior citizens home. Convenient location. Laundry room, kitchenette. No curfew. Dorm-style rooms with 10 beds each, $11.50, nonmembers $14.75. Singles $25. Doubles $34. Triples $51. Linens $2.

International House (AYH), 1414 E. 59th St. (753-2270), Hyde Park, off Lake Shore Dr. Take the Illinois Central Railroad to 59th St. and walk ½ block west. Part of the University of Chicago. Isolated from the rest of the city because their neighborhood can be dangerous at night. 200 comfortable dorm-style rooms. Shared bath, cheap cafeteria. $15, nonmembers $27. Open mid-June to Aug. Reservations required.

Baker Hall, National College of Education, 2808 Sheridan Rd. (708-256-5150), between the Baha'i Temple and Evanston Hospital. Take the northbound train from Howard to Central St. Delightful dorm with shared bath, cafeteria. Singles $25. Doubles $30. Weekly $70 per person. Open July-Aug. Usually booked; try reserving several months in advance.

Hotel Cass, 640 N. Wabash (787-4030), just north of the Loop. Take subway to Grand St. Convenient location, clean rooms. Singles $35. Doubles $40. A/C $5. Key deposit $5.

Hotel Wacker, 111 W. Huron (787-1386), Near North Side. Not quite pristine. Singles $35. Doubles $40. Weekly: $80-85. Key and linen deposit $5.

YMCA and YWCA, 30 W. Chicago Ave. (944-6211). Good security, bare rooms. Singles $25. Doubles $33. Key deposit $5. Students: $75 per week, $270 per month; bring a letter from your registrar.

Leaning Tower YMCA, 6300 W. Touhy (708-647-1122), in Niles. From Jefferson Park El stop, take bus #85A. Look for a ¼-scale replica of the Leaning Tower of Pisa, about 40 min. from downtown. Private baths, use of YMCA facilities. Singles $28. Doubles $31. Key deposit $5. Off-season $4-5 less. Key deposit $5. Call ahead for summer reservations.

Pioneer Motel, 8835 Ogden Ave., Brookfield (708-485-9686), on U.S. 34, 3 mi. east of I-294 in the western suburbs. Accessible only by car. Clean, comfortable rooms, tile floors. Singles $27, $2 per additional person. $5 key deposit.

Brookfield Motel, 8804 Ogden Ave., Brookfield (708-485-0948) next to Pioneer Motel. Pleasant, clean, carpeted rooms. Singles or doubles $27.

Food

The "Windy City" also eats—very well. Like many urban dwellers, Chicagoans flee downtown come dusk; most of the best food finds lie far away from the Loop, in busy nightlife districts or tiny neighborhoods. One of Chicago's favorite fillers is its renowned pizza, which features a thick crust covered with melted cheese, fresh sausage, sauteed onions and peppers, and a spicy sauce made from fresh whole tomatoes. Besides pizza, you can sample especially good Southeast Asian and Greek food. Dig into anything from Thai noodles to sizzling ribs (another Chicago specialty) at the city's **Taste of Chicago Festival,** where 80 vendors boggle your taste goblets in late June and early July. The Festival grills and thrills along Michigan Ave. near the Art Institute. Spectacular fireworks accompany the food on July 4. *Chicago* magazine ($2) offers a comprehensive restaurant guide with honest and thorough listings cross-indexed by price, cuisine, and location.

Pizza

Pizzeria Uno, 29 E. Ohio (321-1000), and **Due,** 619 N. Wabash (943-2400). Uno is where it all began. In 1943, owner Ike Sewall introduced Chicago-style deep dish pizza, and though the graffiti-stained walls have been painted over and the restaurant is franchised across the nation, the pizza remains damn good. Due sits right up the street, with a terrace and more room than Uno's, but without the attendant legend. Pizzas $5-15. Uno open Mon.-Thurs. 11:30am-11pm, Fri.-Sat. 11:30am-mid.; Due open Mon.-Thurs. 11:30am-1:30am, Fri. 11:30am-2:30am, Sat. noon-2:30am, Sun. noon-11:30pm.

Edwardo's has 10 locations including: 1212 N. Dearborn (337-4490), near North Side; 521 S. Dearborn (939-3366), downtown; and 1321 E. 57th St. (241-7960), in Hyde Park. Vegetable-fanciers groove on the spinach or broccoli soufflé pizza ($11). Hours vary by location. N. Dearborn location open Mon.-Thurs. 11am-12:30am, Fri.-Sat. 11am-1:30am, Sun. 11am-11:30pm. Downtown location open Sun.-Thurs. 11:30am-11:30pm, Fri.-Sat. 11:30am-mid.

Gino's East, 160 E. Superior (943-1124). Wait 30-40 min. while they make your "pizza de résistance." Graffiti-covered wall. Small pan pizza ($6) easily serves 2. Open Mon.-Thurs. 11am-11pm; Fri.-Sat. 11am-1am, Sun. noon-10pm.

Loop

For a cheaper alternative to most Loop dining, try the surprisingly good fast-food pizza, fish, potato, and burger joints in the basement of the State of Illinois Building at Randolph and Clarke St. Entrees run $2.50-$4.

The Berghoff, 17 W. Adams (427-3170). Moderately priced German and American fare includes terrific strudel and home-brewed beer. German pot roast $7. Open Mon.-Thurs. 11am-9:30pm, Fri.-Sat. 11am-10pm.

Milty's Super Deli, 65 E. Wacker Pl (641-1477). Old deli favorites corned beef ($4.25) and beef brisket ($4.50). Open Mon.-Fri. 6:30am-5pm.

Near North

John Barleycorn Memorial Pub, 658 W. Belden Ave. (348-8899), at Lincoln Ave. English-style pub attracts an art crowd by playing classical music and showing slides on 3 large screens. Model ship collection sails the walls. Reasonably-priced menu includes burgers ($5). Open Sun.-Fri. 11am-2pm, Sat. 11am-3am. Kitchen open until 1am.

Billy Goat's Tavern, 430 N. Michigan Ave. (222-1525), hidden underground on lower Michigan Ave. Descend through an apparent subway entrance in front of the Tribune building. Inspiration for Saturday Night Live's legendary "Cheezborger, cheezborger—no Pepsi, Coke" greasy spoon. Cheezborgers $2.20. Open Sun.-Fri. 7am-2am, Sat. 7am-3am.

Ed Debevic's, 640 N. Wells, and 660 Lake Cook, Deerfield (708-945-3242). A classic diner. Burgers, chicken pot pie, and other all-American dishes. Full dinners $5. Packed weekend nights. N. Wells location open Mon.-Thurs. 11am-mid., Fri. 11am-1am, Sat. 10am-1am, Sun. 10am-11pm. Deerfield location open Sun.-Thurs. 11:30am-10pm, Fri.-Sat. 11:30am-mid.

North Side

Cafe Phoenicia, 2814 N. Halsted St. (549-7088). El to Diversey then 2 blocks along Diversey to Halstead. A tribute to the Phoenician alphabet and nautical tableaux spice up the walls of this little Lebanese outfit. Outstanding hummus $3, lamb kebab $8. Open Mon.-Fri. 5-10:30pm, Sat. 5pm-mid., Sun. 4-10pm. Reservations required weekends.

Mekong, 4953 N. Broadway (271-0206), at Argyle St. Busy, spotless Vietnamese restaurant. Tasty soups $3.50-4, fried noodles $5-10. Open Sun.-Tues. and Thurs. 10am-10pm, Wed. 4-10pm, Fri.-Sat. 10am-11pm.

Heartland Cafe, 7000 N. Glenwood (465-8005), at Lunt Ave. Cheap, delicious food, replete with live folk and jazz Fri. and Sat. evenings, outdoor café, and a hip bookstore. Dinner entrees $7.25-9.50. Open Mon.-Thurs. 9am-1am, Fri.-Sat. 9am-3am, Sun. 9am-2am. Kitchen open until 11pm; until mid. Sat. Cover varies.

Marco's Paradise, 3358 N. Sheffield (281-4848), down the street from Wrigley Field. Private and claustrophobic downstairs, open and agoraphobic first floor. Entrées $6-10. Open Sun.-Thurs. 11am-mid., Fri.-Sat. 11am-2am. Reservations suggested weekends.

Tokyo Marina, 5058 N. Clark St. (878-2900). Cleaved into 2 rooms—1 a sushi bar and 1 with less trendy Japanese food. Entrees $6.50-7.50. Open daily 11:30am-11pm.

House of Thailand, 5120 N. Broadway (275-2684). El to Forster. Excellent Thai food at reasonable prices. Open Sun., Tues.-Thurs. 5-10pm, Sat. 5-11pm.

North Shore

Slice of Life, 4120 Dempster, Skokie (708-674-2021). El to Howard, then bus #215 to Crawford and Dempster. Delicious and, most importantly, *kosher* deep-dish pizza (small $8). Fish specials equally funky fresh yummy. Open Mon.-Thurs. 11:30am-9pm, Fri. 11:30am-3am, Sat. sunset-1am, Sun. 9am-9pm.

Blind Faith Cafe, 525 Dempster, Evanston (708-328-6875). Take the Evanston train to Dempster. The antithesis of the greasy spoon. Wholesome, natural vegetarian food. One need not order exotic entrees like Udon Noti Yaki ($8) on blind faith—ask the waiter to explain the ingredients. Blind Faith fans should not get stuck in Traffic. Speaking of Clapton. . .

Cross-Rhodes, 913½ Chicago Ave. (708-475-4475). Take North Line El to Main St. walk ½ block north. Excellent, cheap Greek food. Try the Greek fries ($1). Open Mon.-Sat. 11:30am-10pm, Sun. 4-9pm.

Walker Bros. Original Pancake House, 153 Green Bay Rd. (708-251-6000), at Wilmette between Central and Lake. Take Northwest Metro train to Wilmette Station, then walk down Green Bay Rd. Stunning collection of stained glass and Tiffany lamps cowers in fear of rampant children. The Platonic form of apple pancakes ($6). Huge lines for a Sunday brunch that will stuff you like Raggedy Ann. Open Sun.-Thurs. 7am-10:30pm, Fri.-Sat. 7am-midnight.

South Side

Medici on 57th, 1327 E. 57th St., Hyde Park (667-7394). University of Chicago students flock here for custom-made burgers ($4-5). "Garbage" (everything on it) pizza just $5.75. Open Sun.-Thurs. 7am-12:30am, Fri.-Sat. 9am-1am.

Three Happiness, 2130 S. Wentworth Ave. (791-1228), or across the street at 209 W. Cermak Rd. in Chinatown. Visible from the Cermak/Chinatown El stop. Choose between the upstairs restaurant and the little storefront across the way. Expect long lines Sun. for Chicago's best *dim sum* (items $1.65-4.50), served around noon. Buttress your wallet if you plan to stay for dinner ($10-12). Open Mon.-Thurs. 10am-midnight, Fri.-Sat. 10am-1am, Sun. 10am-10pm.

Near West Side and Oak Park

Al's Italian Beef, 1079 W. Taylor St. (226-4017), at Aberdeen near Little Italy. Take a number, please. There are no tables or chairs, so you'll have to take your delicious Italian beef sandwich ($3.60) outside. Wash your meal down at the lemonade stand across the street. Open Mon.-Sat. 9am-1am.

The Parthenon, 314 S. Halsted St. in Greektown (726-2407). Enjoy anything from gyros ($6) to *saganaki* (cheese flamed in brandy, $3.25). Dinners $4.25-13.50. Open daily 11am-1am.

Sights

While public transportation and your feet will serve you well around town, guided tours provide a less demanding alternative. Tours start near major hotels; you must make reservations. **American Sight-seeing Tours-Chicago,** 520 S. Michigan Ave. (427-3100), has two- to four-hour tours ($14-22). **Mercury Sight-seeing Boats** (332-1368) and **Shoreline Marine Sight-seeing Boat** (222-9328) offer charter cruises for $5-8.

Museums

Admission to each of Chicago's major museums is free at least one day a week. The "Big Five" allow exploration of everything from ocean to landscape to the stars; a handful of smaller collections represent diverse ethnic groups and professional interests. For more information, call the **Chicago Council on Fine Arts Hotline** at 346-3278 (24 hrs.), or pick up the informative pamphlet *Chicago Museums* at the tourist information office.

Museum of Science and Industry, 5700 S. Lake Shore Dr. (684-1414). Hands-on exhibits ensure a crowd of grabby kids, overgrown and otherwise. Highlights include the Apollo 8 command module, a German submarine, a life-sized replica of a coal mine, a 16-ft. human heart, and a new exhibit on learning disabilities. Open Memorial Day-Labor Day 9:30am-5:30pm; Sept.-May Mon.-Fri. 9:30am-4pm, Sat.-Sun. 9:30am-5:30pm. Free.

The Oriental Institute, 1155 E. 58th St. (702-9521), on the University of Chicago campus, houses an extraordinary collection of ancient Near Eastern art and archeological treasures despite its politically incorrect name. You can't miss the massive statue of Tutankhamen. Open Tues.-Sat. 10am-4pm, Sun. noon-4pm. Free.

Field Museum of Natural History (922-9410), Roosevelt Rd. at Lake Shore Dr., across from the aquarium. Geological, anthropological, botanical, and zoological exhibits. Don't miss the Egyptian mummies, the Native American Halls, the Hall of Gems, and the dinosaur display. Open daily 9am-5pm. Admission $3, seniors and students $2, families $10. Free Thurs.

The Adler Planetarium, 1300 S. Lake Shore Dr. (322-0300). Astronomy exhibits, a sophisticated skyshow, and the recently added $4-million Astro-Center. 5 Skyshows per day in the summer, less frequently in the winter. Open Mon.-Thurs. 9:30am-4:30pm, Fri. 9:30am-9pm, Sat.-Sun. 9:30am-5pm. Exhibits free. Shows $3, ages 6-17 $1.50, seniors free.

The Art Institute of Chicago, Michigan Ave. at Adams St. (443-3500). The city's premier art museum. Finest collection of French impressionist paintings west of Paris. Also works by El Greco, Chagall, Van Gogh, Picasso, and Rembrandt. Call for info on temporary exhibits. Open Mon. and Wed.-Fri. 10:30am-4:30pm, Tues. 10:30am-8pm, Sat. 10am-5pm, Sun. and holidays noon-5pm. Donation $5, seniors and students $2.50. Free Tues.

Terra Museum of American Art, 666 N. Michigan Ave. (664-3939). Excellent collection of American art from colonial times to the present. Open Tues. noon-8pm, Wed.-Sat. 10am-5pm, Sun. noon-5pm. $4, seniors $2.50, students with ID $1. Free the first Sunday of each month.

Shedd Aquarium, 1200 S. Lake Shore Dr. (939-2438). The world's largest indoor aquarium with over 6,600 species of fresh and saltwater fish in 206 exhibition tanks including a Caribbean reef. The Oceanarium features small whales, dolphins, seals, and other marine mammals. Open March-Oct. daily 9am-5pm; Nov.-Feb. 10am-5pm.

DuSable Museum of African-American History, 740 E. 56th Pl. and Cottage Grove (947-0600), Washington Park. Illuminating exhibit on everything from ancient African sculpture to the 60s black arts movement. Open Mon.-Fri. 9am-5pm, Sat.-Sun. noon-5pm. $2, seniors and students $1, under 13 50¢. Free Thurs.

The Museum of Contemporary Art, 237 E. Ontario (280-5161), within walking distance of the Water Tower. Exhibits change often. One gallery devoted to local artists. Open Tues.-Sat. 10am-5pm, Sun. noon-5pm. $4, seniors and students $2. Free Tues.

Peace Museum, 430 W. Erie (440-1860). Daring, multimedia exhibits that may turn even the most bellicose visitor from hawk to dove. Open Tues.-Sun. noon-5pm, Thurs. noon-8pm. $3.50, seniors and students $2.

Outdoors

A string of lovely lakefront parks fringes the area between Chicago proper and Lake Michigan. On a sunny afternoon, a cavalcade of sunbathers, dog walkers, roller skaters, and skateboard artists ply the shore, yet everyone still has room to stake out a private little piece of paradise. Lincoln, Grant, Burnham, and Jackson Parks are operated by the Recreation Department (294-2200).

Lake Michigan lures swimmers to the **Lincoln Park Beach** and the **Oak Street Beach,** on the North Side. Both crowded, popular swimming spots soak in the sun. For a less crowded area, try the smaller, rockier beaches between 49th and 57th St. on the South Side (open daily mid-June-Sept., 9am-dusk) or any of the small beaches lining the North Shore above Lincoln Park. The beaches are unsafe after dark. Call the Chicago Parks District for further information (294-2200).

Lincoln Park, 2021 N. Stockton Dr. (bus #151 or 156), rents paddleboats by the hour ($7, $2 deposit) and the half-hour ($4, $1 deposit). The Park District maintains jurisdiction over eight harbors from May 15 to October 15 for powerboats and sailboats. Great apes, farm animals, and snow leopards are just a few of the inhabitants of **Lincoln Park Zoo,** 2200 N. Stockton Dr. (294-4660). You can also walk among the cactus in the **Lincoln Park Conservatory** (294-4770). (Both open daily 9am-5pm. Free.) Muggers have been known to haunt the park after dark. Chicago's **Brookfield Zoo,** about 15 mi. from downtown at First Ave. and 31st St. in Brookfield (708-485-0263), houses more than 2,300 animals. Take the Burlington train to the zoo stop to explore one of America's oldest zoos. (Open daily 9:30am-6pm; Sept.-May 10am-5pm.)

Spend a relaxing summer day at **Grant Park,** on the waterfront between Roosevelt Rd. and Monroe St., east of Michigan Ave. An hour-long, computer-operated light display takes place at **Buckingham Fountain** each night at 9pm. Jets of water spray 90 ft. into the air, illuminated by colored lights hidden in the fountain base. You can rent ice skates in the winter ($2.50) or bring your own roller skates to the **Richard J. Daley Bicentennial Plaza** (294-4792), in Grant Park. The **Garfield Park Conservatory,** 300 N. Central Park (533-1281), El to Pulaski then walk east, has palms, cacti, ferns, and tropical plants enclosed in its 4½ acres. (Open daily 9am-5pm. Free.) The **Chicago Botanic Garden,** Lake Cook Rd., Glencoe (708-835-5440), ½ mi. east of Edens Expressway, El to Howard then bus #214, is a lush 300-acre tract featuring a wide variety of carefully nurtured plants. Especially beautiful are the Japanese Garden, set on three islands, and the Rose Garden. (Open daily 8am-sunset. Parking $3, includes admission.)

The Loop

After the Great Fire of 1871 left the city a pile of ashes Chicago became a workshop for leading architects such as Daniel Burnham, Louis Sullivan, and later Mies Van der Rohe, whose Chicago School transformed urban design world-wide by creating, among other things, the modern skyscraper. The Loop is a mecca for architecture buffs. A walking tour (1½ hr.) takes you past pioneer skyscrapers, impressive modern sculpture, the world's tallest building, and dazzling masterworks of art deco, international style, and postmodern architecture.

The best place to start is the **ArchiCenter,** 330 S. Dearborn (782-1776). Volunteers lead excellent walking tours (from $5, often less for seniors and students; call for exact prices), and the center offers lectures, photography exhibits, and a bookstore. The center is appropriately located at the **Monadnock Building,** one of the last buildings to utilize wall-bearing construction techniques before Chicago's architects developed the skyscraper's revolutionary steel-frame.

From the ArchiCenter, go west on Jackson Blvd. to LaSalle St. Here at the **Board of Trade Building,** 141 W. Jackson (435-3455), designed by Holabird and Root just before the 1929 stock market crash, you'll see the real forces that drive Chicago. Cosmopolitan art deco ornament tag teams with a huge monument to Ceres, Greek goddess of grain, standing 609 ft. above street level. At the fifth-floor visitors gallery (open Mon.-Fri. 9am-2pm), you can watch the frantic trading of Midwestern farm goods at the world's oldest and largest commodity futures exchange.

Continue west on Jackson to Franklin St., and the somewhat large 110-story 1,707-ft. **Sears Tower,** 233 W. Wacker (875-9696). On a clear day you can see God and four states from the skydeck of the world's tallest building. (Open May-Sept. daily 9am-11pm; Sept.-April 10am-10pm.)

The First National Bank Building and Plaza stands about two blocks northeast, at the corner of Clark and Monroe St. The world's largest bank building pulls your eye skyward with its diagonal slope. Marc Chagall's vivid mosaic, *The Four Seasons,* lines the block and sets off a public space often used for concerts and lunchtime entertainment.

State and Madison, the most famous block of "State Street that great street" and the focal point of the Chicago street grid, lies one street over. Louis Sullivan's Carson Pirie Scott store building is adorned with exquisite ironwork and the famous extra-large Chicago window (though the grid-like modular construction has been altered by additions). Also visit Sullivan's other masterpiece, the **Auditorium Building,** several blocks south at the corner of Congress and Michigan. Beautiful design and flawless acoustics highlight this Chicago landmark.

Chicago has buckets o' outdoor sculpture. Many downtown corners are punctuated by large, abstract designs. The most famous of these is a Picasso at the foot of the **Daley Center Plaza.** No one knows exactly what the thing represents, but it has confounded realists at the corner of Dearborn and Washington St. since 1967. Across the street rests Joan Miró's *Chicago,* the sculptor's gift to the city, and one block north, the *Monument à la bête debout* graces the plaza in the **State of Illinois Building.** This hypermodern version of a town square, designed by Hemlut Jalm in 1985, features a sloping atrium, circular floors that expose a full view of hundreds of employees, and eviscerated elevators and escalators.

As you wander around the Loop, notice the murals adorning the temporary walls that surround construction sites, usually witty homages to the city painted by local schoolchildren.

Near North

The city's ritziest district lies above the Loop along the lake, just past the Michigan Ave. Bridge. Overlooking the stretch is the **Tribune Tower,** 435 N. Michigan Ave., a Gothic skyscraper that resulted from a hotly-contested international design competition in the 20s. The building houses Chicago's largest newspaper; quotations celebrating freedom of the press emblazon the inside lobby.

Chicago's **Magnificent Mile,** along Michigan Ave. north of the Chicago River, is a conglomeration of chic shops and galleries. En route you'll pass the **Chicago Water Tower and Pumping Station** (467-7114), at the corner of Michigan and Pearson Ave. Only these two public structures, built in 1867, survived the Great Chicago Fire. The pumping station, which supplies water to nearly 400,000 people on the North Side, houses the multimedia production *Here's Chicago.* For $5.75 (seniors and students $3.50), you can briefly tour the pumping station, watch a 45-minute slide portrayal of Chicago, and see a slick 10-minute aerial view of the city. (Open Sun.-Thurs. 10am-5pm, Fri.-Sat. 10am-5:30pm.) Across the street is **Water Tower Place,** a ritzy new vertical shopping mall, worth a browse. A short walk north on Michigan Ave. leads to the **John Hancock Center,** 875 N. Michigan (751-3681), a towering office building with observation decks.

Beautiful old mansions and apartment buildings fill the streets between the Water Tower and Lincoln Park. Known as the **Gold Coast,** the area has long been the elite residential enclave of the city. The early industrialists and city founders made their homes here and, lately, many families have moved back from the suburbs. Lake Michigan and the Oak St. Beach shimmer a few more blocks east.

Urban renewal has made **Lincoln Park** a popular choice for upscale residents. Bounded by Armitage to the south and Diversey Ave. to the north, lakeside Lincoln Park is a center for recreation and nightlife, with beautiful harbors and parks and some of the liveliest clubs and restaurants along North Halsted and Lincoln Ave.

If you hear the bells of St. Michael's Church, you're in **Old Town,** a neighborhood where eclectic galleries, shops, and nightspots crowd gentrified streets. Absorb some of the architectural atmosphere while strolling the W. Menomonee and W. Eugenie St. area. In early June, the Old Town Art Fair attracts artists and craftspeople from across the country. Many residents open their restored homes to the public. (Take bus #151 to Lincoln Park and walk south down Clark or Wells St.)

North Side and North Shore

Extending from Diversey Ave. to Howard St., the North Side offers a mix of ethnically diverse residential neighborhoods. **Graceland Cemetery** runs through the heart of the area along Clark St. Elaborate tombs and monuments designed by Louis Sullivan and Lorado Taft make the burial ground one of Chicago's most interesting sights and a posthumous status symbol. The ArchiCenter (782-1776; see The Loop above) offers tours several times daily, and the cemetery office at the northeast corner of Clark St. and Irving Park Rd. has guidebooks.

Though they finally lost their battle against night baseball in 1988, **Wrigleyville** residents remain, like much of the North Side, fiercely loyal to the Chicago Cubs. Just east of Graceland Cemetery, at the corner of Clark St. and Addison, tiny, ivy-covered **Wrigley Field** is the North Side's most famous institution, well worth a pilgrimage for the serious baseball fan. After a game, walk along Clark St. in one of the city's busiest nightlife districts, where restaurants, sportsbars, and music clubs abound.

The North Shore encompasses many separate municipalities, including Evanston, Skokie, Wilmette, and Glencoe. Skokie is well-known for its large Jewish community, and Wilmette contains the **Baha'i House of Worship,** Shendan Rd. and Linden Ave. (708-256-4400), an 11-sided Near Eastern-styled dome modeled on the House of Worship in Haifa, Israel. (Open May-Oct. daily 10am-10pm; Oct.-May. 10am-5pm.) El to Howard Station, then commuter rail to Wilmette, Fourth St. and Linden Ave., then walk two blocks east on Linden.

South Side

Although some of Chicago's most interesting neighborhoods are in the South Side, the pockets of dangerous ghettos make it less than safe for visitors. Traveling in the daylight hours can provide a rewarding trip for out-of-state Blues Brothers.

Seven mi. south of the Loop along the lake, the **University of Chicago's** beautiful, Neo-Gothic campus dominates the **Hyde Park** neighborhood. A former retreat for the city's artists and musicians, the park became the first U.S. community to undergo urban renewal in the 50s, and is now a calm island of intellectualism in a sea of dangerous neighborhoods. The University of Chicago police force is Illinois' second largest. When visiting the campus, don't stray out of Hyde Park's boundaries. Check outFrank Lloyd Wright's famous **Robie House,** at the corner of Woodlawn Ave. and 58th St.; tours ($2, $3 on Sun.) depart daily at noon. Representative of the Prairie school, this large house blends into the surrounding trees; its low horizontal lines now house university offices. Unfortunately, the original furniture was removed to the nearby **Smart Gallery,** at 5550 S. Greenwood Ave. (702-0200). From the Loop, take bus #6 ("Jefferson Express") or the Illinois Central Railroad from the Randolph St. Station south to 57th St. (Open Tues.-Fri. 10am-4pm, Sat. 10am-6pm, Sun. 2-6pm. Free.)

Neighboring **Kenwood** is the home of Jesse Jackson's Operation PUSH headquarters at 50th and Drexel, as well as the Middle Eastern "Castle" of Elijah Muhammad, one-time mentor of activist Malcolm X and boxer Muhammad Ali. Although this eclectic area is far safer than its neighbor to the north, the untutored traveler should beware. Chinatown, near the Cermak El stop, is a small but unbreakable sliver of China. It doesn't have much in the way of tourist attractions, but you'll get a great meal.

The **Pullman Historic District** on the southeast side was once considered the nation's most perfect community. George Pullman, inventor of the sleeping car, hired British architect Solon S. Beman in 1885 to design a model working town so that his Palace Car Company employees would be "healthier, happier, and more productive." Unfortunately, worker resentment over Pullman's power undid the planned social harmony in this earliest of planned suburbs. For local flavor and a chat with some serious history buffs, try the **Hotel Florence,** 11111 Forrestville Ave. (785-8900), the center of the 19th-century community, which now houses a restaurant and the **Historic Pullman Foundation** (785-8181). By car, take I-94 to W. 111th St; by train, take the Illinois Central Gulf Railroad to 111th St./Pullman. (Tours leave from the hotel the first Sun. of each month May-Oct. $3.50, seniors $3, students $2.)

Home of the city's well-oiled Democratic machine, **Bridgeport** symbolizes for many the Old Chicago. The Irish neighborhood at 37th and Halsted has given Chicago four of its mayors, and, like the Tribune Tower, has produced a very important Daley.

Near West Side

The Near West Side, bounded by Wacker St. to the east and Ogden Ave. to the west, is a fascinating group of tiny ethnic enclaves. Farther out, however, looms the West Side, one of the most dismal slums in the U.S. Dangerous neighborhoods lie side-by-side with the safe ones, so be aware of where you are. **Greektown** might not be as Greek now, but several blocks of authentic restaurants (north of the Eisenhower on Halsted) do remain, still drawing people from all over the city.

A few blocks down Halsted (take the #8 Halsted bus), the historic **Hull House** stands as a reminder of Chicago's role in turn-of-the-century reform movements. Here, Jane Addams devoted her life to her settlement house, earning her reputation as champion of social justice and welfare. Hull House has been relocated to 800 S. Halsted, but painstaking restoration, a slide show, and thoughtful exhibits about Near West Side history make the **Hull House Museum** (413-5353) a fascinating part of a visit to Chicago. (Open Mon.-Fri. 10am-4pm, Sun. noon-5pm. Free.) On Sundays, stop by the **Maxwell Street flea market.** Once the center of immigrant life in Chicago, Maxwell St. is now a fairly seedy neighborhood six days a week. But on Sunday merchants line the street from Halsted St. for several blocks west with inexpensive food and other merchandise.

Little Italy, along Taylor St., remains a tighter residential area than its Greek neighbor. Charming storefront restaurants, delis, and bakeries serve this relatively self-contained community. Nearby, the **University of Illinois at Chicago** is a towering monument to austere modern architecture.

Oak Park

Ten mi. west of downtown on the Eisenhower (I-290) sprouts **Oak Park.** Ernest Hemingway lived here, as did Frank Lloyd Wright, who endowed the community with 25 of his spectacular homes and buildings. The **visitors center,** 158 Forest Ave. (708-848-1500), offers maps and guidebooks. (Open daily 10am-5pm.) Don't miss the **Frank Lloyd Wright House and Studio** 951 Chicago Ave. (708-848-1500), with his beautiful 1898 workplace and original furniture. ($5, recorded tours $2 extra. Tours Mon.-Fri. at 11am, 1pm, and 3pm, more frequently Sat.-Sun. 11am-4pm. By car, exit north from the Eisenhower on Harlem Ave. and follow markers. By train, take the Lake St./Dan Ryan El to Harlem/Marion stop.)

Entertainment

To stay on top of Chicago events, grab a copy of the free weekly *Chicago Reader,* on many streetcorners, or tune in to **WXRT** 93.1 FM. *Chicago* magazine has exhaustive club listings. The **Bears** play football at Soldier's Field, the **White Sox** swing at the South Side at Comiskey Park, and the **Cubs** play ball at gorgeous Wrigley Field. Michael Jordan and the 1990-91 world champion **Bulls** levitate, dunk, and return, Daedalus-like, to earth at Chicago Stadium. For current sports events, call **Sports Information** (976-1313).

Theater

Chicago is one of the foremost theater centers of North America. Most theater tickets are expensive, although half-price tickets are available on the day of performance at **Hot Tix Booths,** 24 S. State St., downtown. (Open Mon. noon-6pm, Tues.-Fri. 10am-6pm, Sat. 10am-5pm. Tickets for Sun. shows on sale Sat.) There are also booths in Oak Park Mall and Evanston (1616 Sherman). Phone **Curtain Call** (977-1755) for information on ticket availability, schedules, and Hot Tix booths. **Ticket Master** (800-233-3123) supplies tickets for many theaters. Check with theaters to see if they sell half-price student rush tickets 30 minutes before showtime.

Over the last decade, Chicago has fostered a number of smaller theaters similar to the off-off-Broadway houses in New York City. Mostly located on the North Side and known as "Off-Loop" theaters, these houses specialize in original drama. David Mamet got his start at **Steppenwolf Theater,** 2540 N. Lincoln Ave. (472-4141; tickets $8). Although the Steppenwolf used to be a great place to see inexpensive, gripping theater, fame has sent the ticket prices skyrocketing ($25-30). Major theaters for Broadway-bound productions are located downtown. The **Shubert Theater,** 22 W. Monroe St. (977-1700), and the **Blackstone Theater,** 60 E. Balbo St. (341-8455), near State St., both stage Broadway productions. The Blackstone's shows start at $10, and students receive a 10% discount. Several suburban playhouses also stage the works of major playwrights. Check the free *Chicago Theater Guide,* available at Hot Tix booths, for complete listings.

Body Politic Theater and **Victory Gardens Theater,** both at 2261 N. Lincoln Ave. (871-3007). Various genres; often host touring companies. Downstairs, the Victory Gardens presents drama by Chicago playwrights. Tickets $10-25.

Organic Theater Co., 3319 N. Clark St. (327-5588). Original works and avant-garde adaptations. Showtimes Tues.-Fri. at 8pm, Sat. at 6:30 and 9:30pm, Sun. at 3 and 8pm. Tickets $24.50-28.50.

Wisdom Bridge Theater, 1559 W. Howard St. (743-6442). 1½ blocks east of the Howard El stop. Mostly new material or creative postmodern productions, such as a Kabuki *Macbeth.* Showtimes vary. Tickets $20-24. $5 student discount.

Kuumba Professional Theater, 343 S. Dearborn (461-9000). The most established of the city's many black theater groups. Showtime usually 8pm. Tickets $12-15.

Apollo Theatre, 2540 N. Lincoln (935-6100). Call for tickets Mon.-Fri. 10am-6pm. Tickets $8-16, students ½-price.

Comedy

Chicago boasts a multitude of comedy clubs, the most famous being the **Second City Comedy Revue,** 1616 N. Wells St. (337-3992). Busting guts for nearly 30 years with its satirical spoofs of Chicago life and politics, Second City graduated John Candy, Bill Murray, and the late John Belushi and Gilda Radner among others. (Shows Tues.-Thurs., Sun. at 9pm, Fri.-Sat. at 8:30 and 11pm. Tickets $9.50, $10.50 Fri.-Sat. Reservations recommended; during the week you can often get in if you show up 1 hr. early.) A free improv session follows the show. **Second City etc.** (642-8189) offers up yet more comedy next door (same phone number, times and prices). A branch of Second City, accessible only by car, jokes in Rolling Meadows (708-806-1555).

Dance, Classical Music, and Opera

Many top-notch international dance companies, including ballet, ethnic, and modern troupes, perform in the **Auditorium Theater,** 50 E. Congress Parkway (922-2110). Call the box office for student discounts. **FINEART** (346-3278), a cultural events hotline sponsored by the Chicago Office of Fine Arts, has details. The **Ballet Chicago** (993-7575) performs in season at various locations, specializing in Neo-Classical ballet, particularly the work of George Balanchine. (Tickets $15-30. Call for student discounts.) The **Chicago City Ballet** performs at the auditorium under the direction of Maria Tallchief. (Tickets $25-48.)

The **Chicago Symphony Orchestra (CSO),** conducted by Sir George Solti, performs in **Orchestra Hall,** 220 S. Michigan Ave. (435-8111). Renowned guest artists highlight the season (Sept. 28-June 9). Tickets ($12-44) are hard to get, but regularly scheduled non-subscription and university nights do pop up. If you're lucky, someone will cancel a ticket. Ask for a student discount. The CSO has a summer season at **Ravinia Festival** in suburban Highland Park (see Seasonal Events below). In summer every Wednesday at noon, the **Chicago Public Library Cultural Center,** 78 E. Washington St. (346-3278), hosts free outdoor concerts. Other free cultural events are scheduled too; call their information line.

The **Lyric Opera of Chicago,** Civic Opera House, 20 N. Wacker Dr. (332-2244), still puts on some of the most popular shows in town. The season runs from September to February. Tickets ($16-89) are often sold out.

Seasonal Events

Like Chicago's architecture, the city's summer celebrations are executed on a grand scale. City dwellers head for the lakefront beaches and parks, or jam the outdoor cafés and beer gardens. The regionally famous **Ravinia Festival** (312-728-4642), in the northern suburb of Highland Park, runs from late June to late September. The Chicago Symphony Orchestra, ballet troupes, folk and jazz musicians, and comedians perform throughout the festival's 14-week season. (Shows start between 7:30 and 8:30pm. $20-35. $7 rents you a patch of ground for a blanket and picnic.)

To reach Ravinia Park, take the Chicago and Northwestern Commuter Railway to the main gate ($3.75), or the Ravinia bus service from the Loop ($8 round-trip).

Chi-town also offers several free summer festivals on the lakeshore. The **Fourth of July Celebration** in Grant Park draws huge crowds for its fireworks display and performance of Tchaikovsky's *1812 Overture.* Prime your buds for the **Taste of Chicago** festival in the week before July 4th, when Chicago's best chefs set out booths with endless samples; you can stuff yourself with everything from sushi to barbecue for $16. In mid-July, Lake Shore Park, Lake Shore Dr., and Chicago Ave. are the scene of the **Air and Water Show,** featuring several days of boat races, parades, hang gliding, and stunt flying, as well as a performance by the Blue Angels precision fliers.

Chicago's **Blues Festival** in early June presents homegrown music to the thousands who turn out at the **Petrillo Music Shell** in Grant Park. Even more of a spectacle are the **Chicago Gospel Festival,** in July, and the **Chicago Jazz Festival,** at the end of August. On a smaller scale, Chicago also has over 75 ethnic and neighborhood festivals. Call the 24-hr. Special Events Hotline (744-3315) for info.

Nightlife

Chicago's frenetic nightlife is a grab bag of music, clubs, bars, and more music. "Sweet home Chicago" takes pride in the innumerable blues performers who have played there (a strip of 43rd St. was recently renamed Muddy Waters Drive). For other tastes, jazz, folk, reggae, and punk clubs jack the bodies of people all over the North Side. Aspiring pick-up artists swing over to **Rush and Division,** an intersection that has replaced the stockyards as one of the great meat markets of the world. To get away from the crowds, head to a little neighborhood spot for a lot of atmosphere. Lincoln Park is full of bars, cafés and bistros. Bucktown, west of Halsted St. in North Chicago, stays open late with bars and dance clubs. Ask at your favorite one about pub crawls, where a bus will ferry you between bars for a $5 cover.

Blues

B.L.U.E.S. etcetera, 1124 W. Belmont (525-8989), El to Belmont then 3 blocks west on Belmont Ave. With the aid of a dance floor, it's a more energetic blues bar than its sibling location
B.L.U.E.S., 2519 N. Halsted St. (528-1012), El to Fullerton, then westbound Fullerton bus. Cramped, but the music is unbeatable. Music starts Mon.-Thurs. at 9pm, Fri.-Sun. at 9:30pm. Open Sun.-Fri. 8pm-2am, Sat. 8pm-3am. Cover Sun.-Thurs. $5, Fri.-Sat. $7.

Kingston Mines, 2548 N. Halsted St. (477-4646), just north of B.L.U.E.S. Shows 6 nights per week. Watch for the "Blue Monday" jam session. Music starts at 9:30pm. Open Sun.-Fri. until 4am, Sat. until 5am. Cover Sun.-Wed. $7, Thurs. $8, Fri.-Sat. $10.

New Checkerboard Lounge, 423 Muddy Waters Dr. (624-3240). Chicago's oldest blues club and the last authentic remnant of the old days. In a shady, unsafe South Side neighborhood, but a worthwhile pilgrimage for the serious fan. Music starts Mon.-Fri. at 9:30pm, Sat. at 10pm, Sun. at 8pm. Cover charge and closing time vary.

Wise Fools Pub, 2270 N. Lincoln St. (929-1510), El to Fullerton, then go south on Lincoln. Intimate Lincoln Park setting for top blues artists. Mon. night's Big Band Jazz series also great fun. Music 9:30pm-1:30am. Bar open daily 4pm-2am. Cover $4-8.

Other

Butch McGuires, 20 W. Division St. (337-9080), at Rush St. Originator of the singles bar. Owner estimates that "over 2,400 couples have met here and gotten married" since 1961—he's a little fuzzier on divorce statistics. Once on Rush St., check out the other area hang-outs. Drinks $1.75-4.25. Open Sun.-Thurs. 10:30am-2am, Fri. 10am-4am, Sat. 10am-5am.

Cabaret Metro, 3730 N. Clark (549-0203). Cutting-edge concerts from $6 and Wed. night "Rock Against Depression" extravaganzas ($4 for men, women free) entertain a hip, young crowd. Open Sun.-Fri. 9:30pm-4am, Sat. 9:30pm-5am.

Christopher Street, 3458 N. Halsted (975-9244). Lots of guppies swim in this attractive, upscale fishbowl with 3 bars, a huge dance floor, and aquarium wallpaper. Drinks $2-4. Open Sun.-Fri. 4pm-4am, Sat. 4pm-5am. Cover Fri.-Sat. $3 ($1 goes to AIDS research).

Paris, 1122 Montrose (769-0602). El to Addison. A lesbian bar with D.J. and dancing Wed.-Sun. Open Mon.-Fri. 5pm-2am, Sat. 2pm-3am, Sun. 2pm-midnight. No cover.

Danny's, 1951 W. Dickens Ave. (489-6457), Bucktown. Zebratone walls, Elvis memorabilia, and a jukebox with everything from the Ramones to Tammy Wynette. Favorite with artsy locals. Not in the safest neighborhood, but great fun once you arrive. Open Mon.-Fri. 5pm-2am, Sat. 5pm-3am, Sun. 6pm-2am.

Jazz Showcase, 636 S. Michigan (427-4300), in the Blackstone Hotel downtown. #1 choice for serious jazz fans. During the jazz festival, big names heat up the elegant surroundings with impromptu jam sessions. No smoking allowed. Music Tues.-Thurs. at 8 and 10pm, Fri.-Sat. at 9 and 11pm, Sun. at 4 and 8pm. Closing time and cover vary.

The Blue Room, 1400 N. Wells St. in Old Town (951-6441). Nightly live music in a small bar painted blue. Outside seating on summer nights. Open Mon.-Fri. 8pm-2am, Sat. 8pm-3am, Sun. 8pm-1am.

Biddy Mulligan's, 7644 N. Sheridan Rd. (761-6532), 2 blocks west of Howard El. Students pack this smoky bar; nightly live music, dancing when customers feel like it. Beer pitchers $6.50. Open Wed.-Fri. 8pm-2am, Sat. 8pm-3am, Tues. 8pm-1am.

Wild Hare & Singing Armadillo Frog Sanctuary, 3350 N. Clark (327-0800), El to Addison. Near Wrigley Field. Live rastafarian bands play nightly to a packed house. Open daily until 2-3am. Cover $3-5.

Sluggers World Class Sports Bar, Inc., 3540 N. Clark (248-0055), near Wrigley Field. El to Addison. If TV monitors tuned to every sporting event imaginable don't turn you on, maybe the game room with ski ball, trampoline hoop, and the city's only indoor batting cage will. Drink prices rise 50¢ during Cubs games, but on Wed. nights beer is only 75¢. Open Sun.-Fri. 11am-2am, Sat. 11am-3am.

Tania's, 2659 N. Milwaukee Ave. (235-7120). Exotic dinner and dancing adventure with hot *salsa cumbia* and *merengue* bands. No jeans. Live music Wed.-Mon. Open Sun.-Fri. 11am-4pm, Sat. 11am-5am.

The Lizard Lounge, 1824 W. Augusta Blvd. in Bucktown (489-0379). Walls covered with local artwork, snack-of-the-week and Elvis memorabiia. Open Sun.-Thurs. 8pm-2am, Fri.-Sat. 8pm-midnight. Cover varies, but is never more than $4.

Springfield

Springfield poet Vachel Lindsay wrote, "In our little town a mourning figure walks, and will not rest." The ghoulish shade of Abraham Lincoln, who settled in Springfield in 1837 to practice law, still stalks Springfield incessantly; the city is completely mobilized to help tourists see Old Abe memorabilia. The state capital's efforts, much like the place and its people, are always tasteful but very insistent.

Practical Information

Emergency: 911.

Springfield Convention and Visitors Bureau, 109 N. 7th St. (789-2360 or 800-545-7300). Open Mon.-Fri. 8am-5pm. **Central Illinois Tourism Council**, 631 E. Washington St. (525-7980). **Lincoln Home Visitors Center**, 426 S. 7th (789-2357). Open daily 8:30am-5pm. All locations have very useful brochures on restaurants, hotels, camping, events, recreation, and services for seniors and the disabled.

Amtrak: 3rd and Washington St. (800-872-7245), near downtown. To Chicago (2-4 per day, 4 hr., $31) and St. Louis (2-4 per day, 2½ hr., $19). Those passing through on Amtrak can stop over in Springfield free. Lockers 50¢ 1st day, $1 subsequent days. Open daily 6am-9:30pm.

Greyhound: 2351 S. Dinkser (544-8466), on the eastern edge of town. Take a cab downtown ($5). To Chicago ($25) and St. Louis ($12). Open 7:30am-10:30pm. Those passing through town by bus can stop off at no extra charge.

Public Transport: Springfield Mass Transit District, 928 S. 9th St. (522-5531). Pick up maps at headquarters or at the tourist office on Adams. All 12 lines serve the downtown area along 5th, 6th, or Monroe St., near the Old State Capitol Plaza. Fare 50¢, transfers free. Buses operate Mon.-Sat. 6am-6pm. **Access Illinois Transit Service (AITS),** 522-8594. Buses seniors and the disabled. Call 24 hr. in advance to arrange trip.

Taxi: Lincoln Yellow Cab, 523-4545 or 522-7766.

Post Office: 2105 E. Cook St. (788-7200), at Weir St. Open Mon.-Fri. 7:45am-5:30pm, Sat. 8am-noon. **ZIP code:** 62703.

Area Code: 217.

Numbered streets in Springfield run north-south, but only on the east side of the city. All other streets have names, with **Washington Street** dividing north-south addresses.

Accommodations and Camping

Most inexpensive places congregate in the eastern and southern parts of the city, off I-55 and U.S. 36; bus service from downtown to these outlying areas is limited. Downtown rooms cost $10-30 more. Make reservations on holiday weekends and during the State Fair in mid-August. Downtown hotels may be booked solid on weekdays when the legislature is in session. Check with the visitors bureau about finding reasonable weekend packages offered by slightly more upscale hotels. All accommodations listed below have color TV and A/C.

Best Inns of America, 500 N. 1st St. (522-1100). Clean, bright, comfortable rooms. Pool. Singles $34. Doubles $36-42. Continental breakfast included. Key deposit $1.

Best Rest Inn, 700 N. Dirksen Pkwy. (522-1100 or 800-237-8466). Take the "Bergen Park-Grandview" bus to the 700 block of Milton, then go 3 blocks east. The 2nd-best in Springfield. Singles $24. Doubles $28.

Motel 6, 3125 Wide Track Dr. (789-1063), near Dirksen Pkwy. at the intersection of I-90 and State Rte. 29. Standard motel room fare, pool. Singles $23. Doubles $29.

Lincoln Motel, 2929 S. 6th St. (525-6670). Clean rooms with the hotel's name written on the bedspreads in marker. Ghost of the President occasionally caught loitering in the hall. Singles $20. Doubles $28.

Travel Inn, 500 S. 9th St. (528-4341), near downtown. Unkempt exterior with clean, fairly large rooms. Singles $25. Doubles $28. Weekly: $100.

For camping, try **Mister Lincoln's Campground,** 3045 Stanton Ave. (529-8206), next to the car dealership 4 mi. southeast of downtown. Large area for RVs dominates the campground, with a field for tents on the side and showers. Take bus #10 ("Laketown"). Tent sites $6, with electricity $14, $6 each additional person. Open March-Dec.

Food

Horseshoe sandwiches gallop to the forefront of Springfield cuisine. Looking more like what ends up *on* horseshoes than horseshoes, these tasty concoctions consist of ham on prairie toast covered by a tangy cheese sauce and french fries. In and around the **Vinegar Hill Mall,** at 1st and Cook St., a number of moderately priced restaurants serve horseshoes, barbecued ribs, Mexican and Italian food, and seafood. Plan accordingly because Springfield tends to start shutting down between 3 and 5pm.

Joe Gallina's Pizza, 432 E. Monroe. Joe himself calls out the orders in Italian; Italian songs occupy part of the jukebox. Quite big "small" cheese pizza $4. Open Mon.-Thurs. 11am-11pm, Fri.-Sat. 11am-midnight.

Feedstore, 528 E. Adams St., across from the Old State Capitol. Nothing fancy inside, just good food. Sandwiches $2.75-3.75. No-choice special $4.25. Open Mon.-Sat. 11am-3pm.

Saputo's, 801 E. Munroe at 8th St., 2 blocks from Lincoln's home. Family-owned and - operated for 40 years. Red lighting, red table cloths, red chairs, and—of course—red tomato sauce. Tasty southern Italian cuisine. Large baked lasagna $4.25. Open Mon.-Fri. 10:30am- midnight, Sat. 5pm-midnight, Sun. 5-10pm.

Norb-Andy's, 518 E. Capitol, 2½ blocks east of the New State Capitol. Emphatically nautical theme: oars, ships, and a backward-running clock all decorate this politico-hangout. A jazz guitar player often strums in the corner. Horseshoes $4.75-6. All-American dinner entrees $7-19. Open Mon.-Fri. 11am-10pm, Sat. 11am-11pm. Bar open Mon.-Sat. 11am-11pm.

Sights

Springfield presents its tourist attractions zealously. Just pick up one of the many pamphlets at most museums and, of course, tourist offices for all the necessary info. Pleasing to most budgets, all Lincoln sights are free. The **Lincoln Home Visitors Center,** 426 S. 8th St. at Jackson (523-0222), shows an 18-minute film on "Mr. Lin- coln's Springfield." The **Lincoln Home** (492-4150), the only one Abe ever owned, also sits at 8th and Jackson, in a restored 19th-century neighborhood. (Open daily 8:30am-5pm; bad weather may reduce winter hours. 10-min. tours every 5-10 min. from the front of the house. Arrive early to avoid the crowds. Free, but you must pick up passes at the Visitors Center.) A few blocks northwest, at 6th and Adams right before the Old State Capitol, you'll find the **Lincoln-Herndon Law Offices** (782-4836), where Honest Abe practiced before ascending the political ranks. (Under renovation indefinitely. Open for tours only daily 9am-5pm; last tour at 4:15. Free.) Around the corner to the left across from the Downtown Mall lies the **Old State Capitol** (782-7691), a weathered limestone edifice with a majesty that rivals its Greek models. In 1858, Lincoln delivered his stirring and prophetic "House Di- vided" speech here, warning that the nation's contradictory pro-slavery and aboli- tionist government could prove a volatile source of dissolution. A manuscript copy of Lincoln's Gettysburg Address is on display. (Open daily 9am-5pm. Tours daily. Free.) The **New State Capitol,** four blocks away at 2nd and Capitol (782-2099), is also worth seeing, for its art and politics. (Tours Mon.-Fri. 8am-4pm, Sat.-Sun. 9am-3:30pm. Open to public longer.)

Lincolnville, U.S.A, also has the **Dana-Thomas House,** 301 E. Lawrence Ave. (782-6776), six blocks south of the Old State Capitol. This stunning and well- preserved 1902 home resulted from one of Frank Lloyd Wright's early experiments in design, providing a wonderful example of the Prairie School style. The furniture and fixtures are Wright orginals as well. (Open Thurs.-Mon. 9am-5pm. 1-hr. tours every ½ hr. Free.) The **Illinois State Museum,** Spring and Edwards St. (782-7386), complements displays on the area's original Native American inhabitants with pre- sentations of contemporary Illinois art. (Open Mon.-Sat. 8:30am-5pm, Sun. noon- 5pm.)

INDIANA

The difference between two popular explanations for Indiana's nickname of "Hoosier" typifies the competition between the state's rural and industrial tradi- tions. The first explanation holds the name to be a corruption of the pioneer's call to visitors at the door, "Who's there?"; the second claims that it spread from Louis- ville, where labor contractor Samuel Hoosier employed Indiana workers. More than half a century later, visitors still find two Indianas: the heavily industrialized north- ern cities and the slower-paced agricultural southern counties.

Most tourists identify Indiana as the state of Gary's smokestacks and the India- napolis 500 rather than the home of rolling green hills. Don't try to choose between the farms and the factories; it is precisely the combination that makes Indiana interesting. Visit the athletic, urban mecca of Indianapolis, but don't miss the rural beauty downstate. The state that produced wholesome TV celebrities David Letterman and Jane Pauley also features beautiful scenery, especially when the fall foliage around Columbus puts on a spectacular show.

Practical Information

Capital: Indianapolis.

Indiana Division of Tourism, 1 N. Capitol #700, Indianapolis 46204 (232-8860; 800-289-6646 in IN). **Division of State Parks,** 402 W. Washington Room: W-298, Indianapolis 46204 (232-4124).

Time Zones: Eastern and Central (1 hr. behind Eastern). During the summer, eastern Indiana does not observe Daylight Savings Time and corresponds to the other half of the state.

Postal Abbreviation: IN

Columbus

After World War II, when the Cummins Engine Company decided that Columbus' educational facilities lagged behind the times, the company set up a fund to pay architectural fees for school buildings, stipulating that the architect be of world stature. Since then, churches, fire stations, and everything in between have sprung up under this innovative program. Columbus is now home to 50 public and private buildings that make up the most concentrated collection of contemporary architecture in the world.

Before starting on your tour, stop at the helpful **visitor center,** 506 5th St. (372-1954), at Franklin. The extension of the Indianapolis Museum of Art beautifies the second floor. (Visitor center open April-Oct. Mon.-Sat. 9am-5pm, Sun. 10am-2pm; Nov.-Dec. Mon.-Sat. 9am-5pm; Jan.-Feb. Wed.-Sat. 9am-5pm; March Mon.-Sat. 9am-5pm.) Bus tours ($7.50, $7 seniors, $6.50 AAA members) also leave from the visitor center (Mon.-Fri. 10am, Sat. 10am and 2pm, Sun. 11am during months with Sun. schedule).

A walking tour of downtown takes about 90 minutes. A block away from the visitor center, downtown's well-preserved Victorian homes set off I.M. Pei's **Cleo Rogers Library,** complete with Henry Moore sculpture, and the **First Christian Church,** a cube accompanied by a rectangular tower, by Eero Saarinen (designer of the St. Louis Gateway Arch). To the south stands Gunnar Birkerts' **St. Peter's Luthern Church,** with its spike-like steeple. Of the other specially-commissioned buildings, must-sees include: Eero Saarinen's stunning **North Christian Church,** whose futuristic exterior has been copied all over the world; Harry Weese's **Otter Creek Clubhouse,** which sits atop what some consider the nation's finest golf course; and the ultramodern **Commons,** a shopping mall housing a performance center, art gallery, and an indoor playground all designed by Cesar Pelli.

The Commons contains a couple of casual eateries, but head instead across the street to **Zaharako's** (known locally as "The Greeks"), 329 Washington St. Established in 1900, the restaurant features onyx soda fountains, a 50-ft. mahogany bar, Tiffany lamps, and marble counters. Come for ice cream, candy, or hearty sandwiches ($1.25-2.25; open Mon.-Sat. 10am-5pm). The **Imperial 400 Motor Inn,** 101 3rd St. (372-2835), offers comfortable rooms with artwork on the walls and leather chairs, a heated pool, and a convenient location. (Singles $34. Doubles $44.) **KOA** (342-6229) sets up camp six mi. south on I-65 at Ogleville. (Primitive sites $12, with hookup and water $15. Each additional person $3, ages 3-18 $1.50, under 3 free.) **Greyhound** idles at 2519 25th St. (376-3821) and sends three buses daily to Indianapolis ($11). (Open Mon.-Fri. 6am-8pm.)

The **ZIP code** for Columbus is 47401; the **area code** is 812.

Indianapolis

Unlike gasohol, the short-lived corn-based petroleum alternative of the late 70s, Indianapolis has successfully managed to combine cars and corn. The two have mixed to fuel Indiana's premiere city into a cultural center; today it never would run former weathercaster David Letterman out of town for warning of hail "the size of canned hams" as it once did. Indianapolis is a city driven by a passion for cars and sports, seen in its wide California-style streets and the international Pan Am games held here in 1987. Each Memorial Day weekend the Indy 500 combines exhaust and exhaustion in the largest single-day sporting event in the world.

Practical Information

Emergency: 911 or 632-7575.

Visitor Information: Indianapolis City Center, 201 S. Capital St. (237-5200), in the Pan Am Plaza across from the Hoosierdome. Open Mon.-Fri. 10am-5:30pm, Sat. 10am-4pm. **Fun Fone,** 237-5210. Recording of the week's events, sporting, theatrical, and otherwise.

Indianapolis International Airport: 7 mi. southwest of downtown near I-465. To get to the city center, take bus #9 ("West Washington").

Amtrak: 350 S. Illinois (263-0550 or 800-872-7245), behind Union Station. Somewhat deserted but relatively safe area. To Chicago ($28) only. Open Mon.-Fri. 7:15am-3:45pm, Sat. 6:15-10:15am, Sun. 7:15-11:15am.

Greyhound: 127 N. Capital Ave. (635-4501), downtown at E. Ohio St. 1 block from Monument Circle. Fairly safe area. To: Chicago ($39, less if bought in advance), Columbus ($31-37, depending on the day), and Louisville ($20-$23). Open 24 hrs. **Indiana Trails** operates out of the same station and serves cities within the state.

Public Transport: Metro Bus, 36 N. Delaware St. (632-1900 or 635-3344), across from City Council building. Open Mon.-Fri. 7:30am-5:30pm. Fare 75¢, rush hour $1. Transfers 25¢. Special disabled service P.O. Box 2383, Indianapolis 46206 (632-3000).

Taxi: Yellow Cab, 637-5421.

Car Rental: Louie's Rent-a-Bent, 2233 E. Washington St. (632-4429), 2½ mi. east of downtown. From $11 per day plus 10¢ per mi.; weekly $99 with unlimited mileage. Car must not leave the state. Check carefully to make sure the car's in good shape. Open Mon.-Fri. 9am-6pm, Sat. 9am-5pm. Required $150 deposit may be paid with credit card. Must be at least 21 yrs.

Help Lines: Crisis and Suicide Hotline, 632-7575. **Mayor's Handicapped Hotline,** 236-3620.

Time Zone: Eastern.

Post Office: 125 W. South St. (464-6000), across from Amtrak. Open Mon.-Wed. and Fri. 7am-5:30pm, Thurs. 7am-6pm. **ZIP code:** 46206.

Area Code: 317.

I-465 rings the city and provides access to all points downtown. The center of Indianapolis is located just south of **Monument Circle** at the intersection of **Washington Street** (U.S. 40) and **Meridian Street.** Washington divides the city north-south; Meridian east-west.

Accommodations and Camping

Indianapolis offers plenty of budget motels, most about five mi. from downtown off I-465. Bus service to these areas is very limited. For the Indy 500 in May, motels jack up their rates; make reservations a year in advance.

Motel 6, I-465 at Exit 16A (293-3220) 3 min. from the Indy Speedway and 8 min. from downtown. Not your average motel; rooms are large, sparkling, and colorfully decorated. Singles $26. Doubles $32.

Medical Tower Inn, 1633 N. Capitol Ave. (925-9831), in the tall building across from the Methodist Hospital. Hospital clean and well-maintained. Singles $43. Doubles $53. With student ID $8 less.

Dollar Inn, 4630 Lafayette Ave. (293-9060), immediately south of I-65. Convenient to the Speedway and Eagle Creek Park. Small, clean rooms. Singles $22. Doubles $27. Key deposit $3.

Indy East Motel, 5855 E. Washington St. (357-8323). Take #8 bus. Moderately clean rooms. Singles $25. Doubles $30. Key deposit $2.

Atlas Hotel, 433½ E. Washington St. (630-4109). Take #8 bus from downtown. Small rooms, no bath. Singles $10. Weekly $50.

Kamper Korner, 1951 W. Edgewood Ave. (788-1488), 1 mi. south of I-465 on Rte. 37. No bus service. Open area with no shade. Laundry, grocery, showers, free fishing and swimming. Enforced quiet hours 11pm-7am. Tent sites $16.20, with water and hookup $17.10. Limited services Nov. to mid-March.

Food and Nightlife

Indianapolis greets visitors with a variety of restaurants that range from holes-in-the-wall to trendy locales decked out in vintage kitsch. Tourists and residents alike head for **Union Station,** 39 Jackson Pl. (266-8740), near the Hoosier Dome four blocks south of Monument Circle. This 13-acre maze of restaurants, shops, dance clubs, bars, and hotels sells every edible substance imaginable in a beautiful, authentically refurbished rail depot. The 2nd-level oval bustles with moderately priced ethnic eateries. Entrees average $2.50-5. Mon.-Thurs. 10am-9pm, Fri.-Sat. 10am-10pm, Sun. 11am-6pm.

Little Bit of Italy, 5604 Georgetown Rd. (293-6437). Excellent Italian food: meatball sub or the pizza. If your thing is Italian, you can't lose. Lunch or dinner $3-5. Mon.-Wed. 10am-8pm, Thurs.-Sat. 10am-9pm.

Acapulco Joe's, 365 N. Illinois Ave., downtown (637-5160). The hot 'n' spicy food will mute you. For the average Joe, they offer peanut butter and jelly sandwiches. 3 tacos $6.50. Mon.-Thurs. 7am-9pm, Fri.-Sat. 7am-10pm.

Iaria's, 317 S. College Ave. (638-7706), about 10 blocks from downtown. A 50s throwback, with shiny vinyl furniture and chrome chairs. Spaghetti and meatballs $6. Open Mon.-Thurs. 11am-9:30pm, Fri. 11am-11pm, Sat. noon-11pm.

The City Market, 222 E. Market St., 2 blocks east of Monument Circle. Renovated 19th-century building with produce stands and 15 ethnic markets. Prices reasonable but not rock-bottom. Open Mon.-Sat. 6am-6pm.

Nightlife makes waves six mi. north of the downtown area at **Broad Ripple,** at College Ave. and 62nd St., typically swamped with students and yuppies. The area has charming ethnic restaurants and art studios in original frame houses, as well as some artsy bars. **The Patio Lounge,** 6308 Guilford Ave. (253-0799), sponsors underground bands for $1-3 cover. (Open Mon.-Fri. 5pm-3am, Sat. 8pm-3am. Take "College-Broad Ripple" bus #17 north from central downtown.)

Sights

Often obscured by the hubbub surrounding the Indy 500, Indianapolis cultural attractions promise a pleasant afternoon. The slogan "Where children grow up and adults don't have to" describes the city's museums; "Please touch" is the motto of the **Children's Museum** at 3000 N. Meridian St. (924-5437). Kids help run hands-on exhibits, which include a turn-of-the-century carousel, a huge train collection, heavy petting zoos, and high-tech electronic wizardry. (Open Tues.-Sat. 10am-5pm, Sun. noon-5pm. $2.) The **Indianapolis Museum of Art,** 1200 W. 38th (923-1331), houses a large collection of Turner paintings and watercolors as well as Robert Indiana's LOVE sculpture. The museum sits among 154 acres of park, beautifully landscaped with gardens and nature trails. (Open Tues.-Sun. 11am-5pm. Free, except special exhibits.) The **Eiteljorg Museum,** 500 W. Washington St. (636-9378), west of downtown, features Native American and Western art. (Open Tues.-Wed. and Fri.-Sat., 10am-5pm, Thurs. 10am-8:30pm, Sun. noon-5pm. $2, seniors $1.50, under 12 $1.) Stunning African and Egyptian decor graces the **Walker Theatre**, 617 Indiana Ave. (635-6915). Erected in 1927, the theater symbolizes Indianapolis' African American community, hosting such jazz greats as Louis Armstrong and Dinah Washington. The complex also sponsors plays, dance performances, and a week-long black film festival in late October. Even those who don't make one of the shows should go just to see the splendid interior. Upstairs in the ballroom, the **Jazz on the Avenue** series offers live music every Friday night.

The Indianapolis 500: Cars Going Real Fast

The **Indianapolis Motor Speedway**, 4790 W. 16th St. (241-2500), is clearly the quintessential Indianapolis tourist site. Take the Speedway exit off I-465 or bus #25 ("West 16th"). A shrine dedicated to the automobile, this 1909 behemoth encloses an entire 18-hole golf course. Except in May, you can take a bus ride around the 2½-mi. track for $1. The adjacent **Speedway Museum** (Indy Hall of Fame) houses a collection of Indy race cars and antique autos, as well as racing memorabilia and videotapes highlighting historic Indy moments. (Open daily 9am-5pm. $1, under 16 free.)

The country's passion for the automobile reaches a frenzy during the **500 Festival** when 33 aerodynamic, turbocharged, 2½-mi.-to-the-gallon race cars circle the asphalt track at speeds over 225 mph. Beginning with the "time trials" (the two weekends in mid-May preceding the race), the party culminates with a big blowout on the Sunday of Memorial Day weekend (weather permitting). Book hotel reservations early and buy tickets in advance. For ticket info, call 248-6700 (open daily 9am-5pm). The 500 isn't the only race in town; call for information on other auto events at the **Indianapolis Raceway Park**, 9901 Crawfordsville Rd. (293-7223), near the intersection of I-74 and I-465.

Iowa

Native Americans named this area Iowa, "the beautiful country." Obviously they didn't see the state from its freeways, which streak straight through the flattest parts of an already level region. To see Iowa's real beauty, you have to turn off the freeway and onto the old roads that wind and plunge through fairy-tale meadows, hills, and thickets. Here, far from the beaten concrete path, you can cast your line into one of more than 19,000 miles of fishing streams, bike the 52-mile Cedar Valley Nature Trail from Cedar Rapids to Cedar Falls, or travel through time to one of the many traditional communities established in Iowa.

Practical Information

Capital: Des Moines.

Tourist Information: Iowa Department of Economic Development, 200 E. Grand Ave., Des Moines 50309 (515-281-3100). **Conservation Commission**, Wallace Bldg., Des Moines 50319 (515-281-5145).

Time Zone: Central (1 hr. behind Eastern). **Postal Abbreviation:** IA.

The Amana Colonies

In 1714, the religious movement known as the Community of True Inspiration began in Germany. Migrating to the U.S. and settling momentarily in Buffalo, New York, in 1842, the followers headed to Iowa for a more rural existence in 1855, settling in the seven villages known as the Amana Colonies. Initially, the inhabitants led a totally communal lifestyle. The experiment fell through during the Great Depression, and today it is primarily the church that gives the colonies a sense of cultural and spiritual unity. Though quite distinct from both the Amish and the Mennonites, the Amana colonists adhere to a similarly spartan existence.

In keeping with old-world village custom, there are no addresses in the colonies, only place names. Anything that isn't on the road leading into town is easily found by following the profusion of signs that point to attractions off the main thoroughfare.

Start your visit with a history lesson at the **Museum of Amana History** (622-3567) in Amana on the "central artery." The museum runs a sentimental, overly patriotic, but informative slide show every hour on the half-hour. (Open July-Aug. Mon.-Sat. 10am-5pm, Sun. noon-5pm; Sept.-June Mon.-Sat. 10am-5pm. $2.50, kids $1.) The **Woolen Mill Machine Shop Museum** (622-3051), in Amana, gives free tours of the mill. Buy your Amana blankets, sweaters, and clothes here. (Open Mon.-Sat. 8am-6pm, Sun. 11am-5pm. Tours Mon.-Sat. every hr. 9am-4pm.) Across the street, watch artisans plane, carve, and sand wooden creations in occasional open workshops at the **Amana Furniture and Clock Shop** (622-3291; open Mon.-Sat. 9am-5pm, Sun. noon-5pm). After touring the museums, cross the street to the **Colony Inn** (622-6270), which serves hefty portions of delicious German and American food, such as ham, fried chicken, bratwurst, and sauerkraut. Dinners ($10-12) and lunches ($7) are served with cottage cheese, bread, diced ham, sauerkraut, fruit salad, and mashed potatoes. Breakfast ($6) is an all-you-can-eat orgy of fruit salad, huge pancakes, fried eggs, thick sausage patties, bacon, and a bowl piled high with hash browns. (Open Mon.-Sat. 7:30am-10:30pm, Sun. 11am-8pm.) For a less filling snack, visit Middle Amana's **Hahn's Hearth Oven Bakery** (622-3439), where the scrumptious products of the colonies' only functional open-hearth oven are sold. Simple pleasures include a loaf of bread ($1.25) and cinnamon rolls (50¢). (Open April-Oct. Tues.-Sat. 7am to sell-out around 4:30pm; Nov.-Dec. Wed. and Sat. only.) Or stop next door at the **Communal Kitchen Museum** (622-3567), where you can tour the former site of all local food preparation. (Open May-Oct. daily 9am-5pm. $1.50, kids 75¢.) Once you've had your ration of bread, go on a free wine-tasting spree at one of the several wineries scattered through the colonies, mostly in Amana. Dance from the standard grape to rhubarb to dandelion wine.

Most lodging options consist of pricey but personal B&Bs such as **Lucille's Bett und Breakfast** (668-1185), **Loy's Bed and Breakfast** (624-7787), and the **Rettig House Bed and Breakfast** (622-3386). The **Dusk to Dawn Bed and Breakfast** (622-3029) in Middle Amana, near the Communal Kitchen Museum, offers beautiful rooms, a lovely garden with a hot tub, and a great breakfast ($40). The only legal camping is at the **Amana Community Park** in Middle Amana (622-3732). (Sites $2.50 per vehicle, $3.50 with electricity and water.)

The Amana Colonies lie 10 mi. north of I-80, clustered around the intersection of U.S. 6, Rte. 220, and Rte. 151. From Iowa City, take Rte. 6 west to Rte. 151; from Des Moines, take exit 220 off I-80 east to Rte. 6 and Rte. 151. Stop by the **Amana Colonies Visitor Center,** just west of Amana on Rte. 220 (622-6262; open Mon.-Wed. 9am-5pm, Thurs.-Sat. 9am-10pm, Sun. 10am-5pm).

Amana's **ZIP code** is 52203; the **area code** is 319.

Cedar Rapids

Although Cedar Rapids is the principal industrial city of eastern Iowa, the pace of life in this "City of Five Seasons" (the fifth being the time to relax and enjoy oneself) remains slow. Named after the surging rapids of the Cedar River running through its center, Cedar Rapids' residents meander rather than march, and are rarely too pressed for time to strike up a conversation.

The **Science Station,** 427 1st St. S.E. (366-0968), across the street from the Ground Transportation Center, features hands-on scientific fun. (Open Tues.-Sat.

9am-5pm, Sun. 1-4pm. $2, seniors and kids $1.50.) The spiffy **Cedar Rapids Museum of Art,** 324 3rd St. S.E. (366-7503), features the world's largest collection of the works of Marvin Cone, Grant Wood, and Mauricio Lasansky, plus a kids' gallery. (Open Tues.-Wed. and Fri.-Sat. 10am-4pm, Thurs. 10am-7pm, Sun. noon-3pm. $2.50, students and kids $1.50.) From 1870 to 1910, thousands of Czech immigrants settled in Cedar Rapids. Take bus #7 to 16th Ave. and C St. to visit the **Czech Village,** on 16th Ave. between 1st St. and C St. S.W., where you can stroll along the historic streets and visit traditional Czech watering holes and bakeries. At the end of the block you'll find the **Czech Museum and Library,** 10 16th Ave. S.W. (362-8500), which houses the largest collection of traditional costumes outside Czechoslovakia. (Open Tues.-Sat. 9:30am-4pm; Dec.-Jan. Sat. 9:30am-4pm. $2.50, ages 8-13 $1.)

Downtown Cedar Rapids is filled with moderately priced restaurants and delis. **Sub King Box Office Deli,** 218 3rd St. S.E. (364-2361), has good sandwiches ($2-5) and subs ($1.75-2.75). (Open Mon.-Fri. 9am-6pm, Sat. 10am-3pm.) For free chips with your dinner, stop by **Gringo's Mexican Restaurant,** downtown at 207 1st Ave. S.E. (363-1000). Try the beef enchiladas with rice and beans ($3.75). (Open Mon.-Sat. 11am-11pm, Sun. noon-9pm.) In the Czech Village, czech out the *houskas* (braided raisin bread) or *kolace* (fruit-filled sweet rolls) at family-owned **Sykora's Bakery,** 73 16th Ave. S.W. (364-5271). (Open daily 6am-5pm). Try more substantial Czech meals at **Konecny's,** 72 16th Ave. S.W. (364-9492), a local favorite. Sandwiches cost $2-3, goulash $1.25; fortunate travelers may catch the sausage & sauerkraut special for $3.75. (Open daily 6-10am and 11am-2pm.)

There are plenty of budget motels on 16th Ave. S.W. The **Shady Acres Motel,** 1791 16th Ave. (362-3111), is a row of cottage-like, spotlessly clean rooms atop acres of rolling hills and huge oaks. Rooms have A/C, showers, and TV, but no phone. (Singles $20. Doubles $24. Take bus #10 to the K-Mart 5 blocks away.) **The Village Inn Motel,** 100 F Ave. NW (366-5323), across the river from the Quaker Oats factory, is four blocks from downtown and eight blocks from the Greyhound station. The large, quiet rooms include cable TV. (Singles $30. Doubles $38.) **Exel Inn,** 616 33rd Ave. S.W. (366-2475), five mi. from downtown, boasts clean rooms, comfortable beds, free coffee, and HBO. (Singles $28. Doubles $35.)

Cedar Rapids lies at the junction of I-380 and Rte. 30 and 151. The Amana Colonies are 19 mi. SW. The **Greyhound/Trailways** station, 145 Transit Way S.E. (364-4167), sends buses to: Des Moines (4 per day, 3 hr., $10.50 Mon.-Thurs., $14 Fri.-Sun.); Chicago (4 per day, 6½ hr., $27 Mon.-Thurs., $37 Fri.-Sun.); and Kansas City (3 per day, 7-11 hr., $60). Get around town in **Easyride** buses. (Buses run daily 5:30am-5:30pm; fare 50¢, seniors 25¢, students 30¢, transfers 10¢, reduced fare with receipts from local restaurants.) All routes stop at the **Ground Transportation Center,** 200 4th Ave. S.E. (398-5335), across from the Greyhound station. For taxis, try **Yellow Cab** (365-1444).

For information on sights, accommodations, and attractions, contact the **Cedar Rapids Area Convention and Visitors Bureau,** 119 1st Ave. SE (398-5009; Mon.-Fri. 8am-5pm, Sat. 9am-4pm). Or call the **Visitor Info Line** (398-9660).

The **post office** is at 615 6th Ave. S.E. (399-2911; open Mon.-Fri. 8:30am-5pm, Sat. 9am-noon). Cedar Rapids' **ZIP code** is 52401; the **area code** is 319.

Des Moines

If you're expecting downtown Des Moines, the capital of Iowa, to be a friendly, quiet place where the tallest building is the two-story chamber of commerce, forget it. Friendly, yes. In fact, Des Moines may be the only city in the USA where wading in public fountains downtown is legal. The city streets are immaculate. Passers-by not only say hello, they make jokes and hold casual street corner conversations. But all this small-town charm doesn't mean Des Moines is either small or quiet. Des Moines's workforce bustles in and out of downtown's cluster of mini-skyscrapers. Home to over 50 insurance companies, a world-class art museum, and music of all sorts, Des Moines exhibits a growing array of big-city pleasures. However, the capital never loses sight of the state it represents. Every year, Des Moines hosts the **Iowa State Fair,** crowding this 9-to-5 city with corn, cows, pigs, and more corn.

Practical Information

Emergency: 911.

Des Moines Convention and Visitors Bureau, information kiosk in the Kaleidoscope Skywalk at 6th and Walnut St. (244-2444), at the Hub Tower. The office at Des Moines International Airport (287-4396) has information for airborne travelers. Open Mon.-Fri. 10am-10pm, Sun. 2-10pm. **Events Hotline,** 283-2220. The main office (no walk-ins) is at 309 Court Ave. #300 (286-4960 or 800-451-2625). Open Mon.-Fri. 8:30am-5pm.

Des Moines International Airport: Fleur Dr. at Army Post Rd. (285-5857), about 5 mi. SW of downtown.

Greyhound: 1107 Keosauqua Way (243-5211), at 12th St. just NW of downtown. To: Kansas City (4 per day, 4 hr., $41); St. Louis (6 per day, 9½ hr., $63); Chicago (9 per day, 8-9 hr., $63). Open 24 hrs.

Public Transport: Metropolitan Transit Authority (MTA), 1100 MTA Lane (283-8100), just south of the 9th St. viaduct. Open Mon.-Fri. 6am-6pm, Sat. 7am-5pm. Pick up maps at the MTA office or any Dahl's market. Routes converge at 6th and Walnut St. Buses operate Mon.-Fri. 6:20am-6:15pm, Sat. 6:45am-5:50pm. Fare 60¢, transfers 5¢.

Taxi: Capitol Cab, 282-8111. **Yellow Cab,** 243-1111. $1.40 base rate, $1.20 per additional mi. Airport to downtown $7.

Car Rental: Budget (287-2612), at the airport. $36 per day, 100 free mi. per day. Open Sun.-Thurs. 24 hrs., Fri.-Sat. 6am-10pm. Must be 21 with major credit card. Under 25 add $5.

Help Lines: Crisis Intervention, 244-1000. **Gay/Lesbian Resource Center,** 277-1454. Open Mon.-Thurs. 4-10pm, Sun. 4-8pm.

Post Office: 1165 2nd Ave. (283-7500), just north of I-235, downtown. Open Mon.-Fri. 8:30am-5:30pm. **ZIP code:** 50314.

Area Code: 515.

Des Moines lies at the confluence of I-35 and I-80. Numbered streets run north-south, named streets east-west. Numbering begins at the **Des Moines River** and increases east or west, starting at **South Union** where the river twists east. **Grand Avenue** divides addresses north-south along the numbered streets. Other east-west thoroughfares are **Locust Street, Park Avenue, Douglas Avenue,** and **Hickman Road.**

Accommodations and Camping

Finding cheap accommodations in Des Moines is usually no problem, though you should make reservations for visits in March (high school sports tournament season) and in August, when the State Fair comes to town. Several cheap motels cluster around I-80 and Merle Hay Rd., five mi. northwest of downtown. Take bus #4 ("Urbandale") or #6 ("West 9th") from downtown.

Econo Lodge, 5626 Douglas Ave. (278-1601), across from Merle Hay Mall. Unaesthetic neighborhood. Bus stop in front. Large, newly furnished rooms with cable TV, free coffee, doughnuts, and newspaper. Spa, sauna. Singles $35. Doubles $42.

Royal Motel, 3718 Douglas Ave. (274-0459), NW of downtown 1 mi. from Merle Hay Mall. Take bus #6. Clean, comfortable, cottage-like rooms. Singles $27. Doubles $35.

YMCA, 101 Locust St. (288-2424), at 1st St. downtown on the west bank of the river. Small rooms. A convenient downtown location. Lounge, laundry, and pool. Men only. Singles $19.50, key deposit $5.

YWCA, 717 Grand Ave. (244-8961), across from the Marriott Hotel downtown. In a fairly safe area. Women only. Clean dorm-style rooms with access to lounge, kitchen, and laundry. All rooms shared. $8 per day, $44 per week.

Iowa State Fairgrounds Campgrounds, E. 30th St. at Grand Ave. (262-3111). Take bus #1 or 2. 1,600 campsites on a grassy, wooded hill. Very nice—and very crowded at fair time. Water spigots at all sites; no fires allowed. Fee collected in the morning. $8 per vehicle.

Walnut Woods State Park, S.W. 52 Ave. (285-4502), 4 mi. south of the city on Rte. 5. Floods out occasionally; if the front gate is locked, it's for a good reason. Primitive sites $5, with electricity $7.

Food

Cheap, clean fast-food places are located on the lower level of the **Locust Mall** downtown on 8th and Locust St. (246-6010). **Kaleidoscope Skywalk** (286-4988), just east of the Locust Hall, at 6th and Walnut St. in the Hub Tower, also has quick eats. Both food courts close at 5:30pm; sup here early. **Court Avenue,** two blocks south of Locust around 3rd St., has a few reasonable Mexican and Italian restaurants in a renovated warehouse. A popular **farmers market** (286-4987) holds court at 4th and Court Ave. every Saturday from 7am to 1pm.

Spaghetti Works, 310 Court Ave. (243-2195). Old-fashioned interior with fire truck for salad bar. Watch for 50-ft. green, red, and blue sea serpent twisting and churning on the wall. Large portions. Spaghetti dinners with salad and garlic bread $3.75-6, lunch versions $3-4. Open daily 11am-2pm and 5-10pm.

Babe's, 417 6th St. (244-9319), across from the Locust Mall. In its 50-year history, Babe's has attracted such luminaries as Diane Sawyer and Bob Barker, but neither of its namesakes, Ruth or the big ox. Dinner $8-14. Try the Offenburger (ground chuck, ham, swiss cheese, lettuce, and tomato; $4.50). Open daily 4:30pm-2am.

Juke Box Saturday Night, 206 3rd St. (243-0707). Hot spot for fun and drink. Decorative '57 Chevy motif. Aid your digestion by participating in the frequent hula-hoop, twist, and jitterbug contests. Drinks average $2.50. Happy Hour Mon.-Fri. 6-9pm. Open daily 6pm-2am.

Sights

From downtown you can see the green-and-gold domes of the **state capitol** (281-5591), on E. 9th St. across the river and up Grand Ave., where bureaucrats make the laws that shape Iowa's future. (Tours hourly Mon.-Fri. 9:15am-3:15pm.) You can catch a glimpse of the glamour and intrigue of Iowa politics any time the legislature meets (Jan.-May). Take bus #5 "E. 6th and 9th St.," 1 "Fairgrounds," 2, 4, or 7. Three blocks away sits the **Iowa State Historical Museum and Archives,** at Pennsylvania and Grand Ave. (281-5111), a beautiful building with three floors exhibiting Iowa's natural, industrial, and social history, as well as a monolithic neon outdoor sculpture called the *Plains Aurora.* (Open Tues.-Sat. 9am-4:30pm, Sun. noon-4:30pm. Free. Take bus #7.)

Most cultural sights cluster west of downtown. The **Des Moines Art Center,** 4700 Grand Ave. (277-4405), is acclaimed for its wing of stark white porcelain tile designed by I.M. Pei. Modern art predominates, but the museum also has Native American, impressionist, and optics exhibits. (Open Tues.-Wed. and Fri.-Sat. 11am-5pm, Thurs. 11am-9pm, Sun. noon-5pm. $2, seniors and students $1. Free all day Thurs. and until 1pm Fri.-Wed. Take "West Des Moines" bus #1.) Down the street across Greenwood Park, the **Science Center of Iowa,** 4500 Grand Ave. (274-4138), overflows with entertaining permanent exhibits and occasional traveling ones. (Open Mon.-Sat. 10am-5pm, Sun. noon-5pm. $4, seniors $2.50, under 12 $2.) Flapper-era cosmetics manufacturer Carl Weeks realized his aristocratic aspirations after he had salvaged enough ceilings, staircases, and artifacts from English Tudor mansions to complete **Salisbury House,** 4025 Tonawanda Dr. (279-9711; public tours Mon.-Thurs. at 2pm, additional tour June-July 10am, or by appointment; $2, kids $1.) Two mi. away stands the grandiose Victorian mansion **Terrace Hill,** 2800 Grand Ave. (281-3604), built in 1869 and currently the gubernatorial mansion.

(Tours March-Dec. Tues.-Sat. 10am-1:30pm, Sun. 1-4:30pm every 30 min. Tickets $2, kids 75¢.)

The **Iowa State Fair,** one of the largest in the nation, captivates Des Moines for 10 days during the middle of August. Traditional events include agricultural displays, tractor pulls, chuckwagon races, and demolition derbies, but many open contests have been added to the fair over the years: tobacco-spitting, rolling-pin-throwing, and hog-calling, to name a few. For information contact the 24-hr. info line at the Administration Building, Iowa State Fair Grounds, Des Moines 50306 (262-3111).

Iowa City

Home of the prestigious Writer's Workshop, Iowa City is the setting of over fifty contemporary novels, including a number of John Irving's best-sellers. Once the seat of Iowa's territorial and state government, Iowa City lost its capital status in 1857 to the more centrally located Des Moines. Today, the University of Iowa dominates the city; its 30,000 students comprise half of the town's winter population. Not only is Iowa City remote, it's perhaps the state's only remotely hip town—the "Athens of the Midwest."

After the legislature moved away, the **Old Capitol** (335-0548) became the first building owned by the U. of Iowa. Recently renovated for the second time, the gold dome serves as the centerpiece for both the university and the town. Stop by the **Old Capitol National Monument** for a free tour. (Call ahead for larger groups. Open Mon.-Sat. 10am-3pm, Sun. noon-4pm.) MacBride Hall, next door, houses the **Museum of Natural History** (335-0480), on Clinton St. at Jefferson. (Open Mon.-Sat. 9:30am-4:30pm, Sun. 12:30-4:30pm. Free.) Five blocks west of the Old Capitol, the eclectic **Museum of Art** (335-1727), on N. Riverside Dr., houses paintings (including a crazy Jackson Pollock mural), sculpture, antique silver, traveling exhibits, and IU student and faculty work. (Open Tues.-Sat. 10am-5pm, Sun. noon-5pm. Free.) While on campus, check out the sleek **law school,** designed by Gunnar Birkerts. You may want to stop by the **Iowa Memorial Union,** at Madison and Jefferson, a half-block from the Old Capitol. (Open Mon.-Sat. 8am-9pm, Sun. noon-4pm.) Both students and ducks frequent the outdoor patios and gardens, and games of Dungeons & Dragons are sure to be raging in the basement. Inside, the **Union Station** serves food cafeteria-style. (Sandwiches $1.50-2.75. Open daily 10am-7pm.) Glasses of beer cost $1 at the river-level **Wheelroom.** (Open summer Mon.-Sat. 4-10pm.)

At **The Kitchen,** 9 S. Dubuque St. (337-5444), local "cooking artists" concoct dishes in a small open kitchen, spreading a smorgasbord of spicy aromas throughout that canvas they call a café. All pasta dishes are $5-7, but if you can afford it, try one of the specials ($10-15). (Open Mon.-Sat. 11am-2:30pm and 5-9:30pm.) **Vito's,** 118 E. College St. (339-1393), in the pedestrian concourse just east of the capitol, serves huge, delicious sandwiches with fries ($4-5.25) and a variety of salads ($2) in a beautiful wood-paneled and brick interior. (Open Mon.-Wed. 11am-12:30am, Thurs.-Sat. 11am-2am, Sun. 11am-10pm.) For dessert, no place beats the **Great Midwestern Icecream Co.,** 126 Washington (337-7243), at the head of the pedestrian concourse. Generous cones cost $1.25. (Open Mon.-Fri. 6am-11pm.) To unwind and have a few drinks, try the ever-mellow **Deadwood Bar,** 6 S. Dubuque St. (351-9417; open Mon.-Sat. 11am-1:45am, Sun. 3pm-midnight.) On Wed. night (5:30-7:30pm) and Sat. morning (7:30-11:30am), when the cows come home, a **farmers market** (356-5000) is held at Van Buren and Washington next to City Hall.

The **Wesley House Hostel (AYH),** 120 N. Dubuque St. (338-1179), six blocks from the Greyhound station in the Wesley Foundation building, has cots in clean rooms with access to showers and kitchen. A free medical clinic operates downstairs. (Check-in 7-9pm. Curfew 10pm. Members and students $10, others $20.) The cheapest motel rooms around are in **Coralville,** two mi. west of Iowa City off I-80 exit 242, which boasts good swimming and a wicked Frisbee golf course. Take the

"First Ave. Coralville" bus from the Iowa U. Pentacrest. The **Motel 6,** at 810 1st Ave. in Coralville (354-0030), has an outdoor pool and cable TV. (Singles $31. Doubles $38.) The nearby **Sunset Motel,** 28 1st Ave. (354-4009), has simple rooms with cable TV and free coffee. (Singles $25. Doubles $29.)

Iowa City is 110 mi. east of Des Moines, just south of I-80. The Greek Revival buildings of the Old Capitol area are known as the **Pentacrest,** and the surrounding lawns were made for hanging out. To the east is a pedestrian concourse filled with trees, benches, and fountains, and lined with restaurants, shops, and campus bars. **Greyhound, Burlington Trailways,** and **Jefferson Bus Lines** share a station at 404 E. College Ave. (337-2127), at Gilbert St., making connections to Minneapolis, St. Louis, Des Moines, and Omaha. (Station open daily 6:30am-8pm.) **Iowa City Transit** (356-5151) and **Coralville Transit** (351-7711) service the entire area for 50¢. **Cambus** serves the campus area for free. For visitor information, stop by the **Convention and Visitors Bureau,** 325 E. Washington St. (337-6592; open Mon.-Fri. 8am-5pm), or the **Campus Information Center** (335-3055), on the first floor of the Iowa Memorial Union (open Mon.-Sat. 8am-9pm, Sun. noon-4pm).

The **post office** for Iowa City is at 400 S. Clinton (354-1560; open Mon.-Fri. 8:30am-5pm, Sat. 9:30am-1pm); the **ZIP code** is 52240. Iowa City's **area code** is 319.

KANSAS

At the Deep Rock Café in Colby, Kansas, a mid-afternoon gathering of older farmers in baseball caps talk about everything from taxes to tractors in spare, unhurried voices. World politics affects Kansas growers almost as much as the weather, acting in some ways to deprovincialize this landlocked state. Highway signs reading "every Kansas farmer feeds 75 people—and you" indicate the Sunflower State's status as the chief wheat producer for the U.S. Kansas also supplies bread for much of the Soviet Union, ironically with the same winter wheat Russian immigrants brought here in the 1870s. This hardy "Turkey Red" crop was one of the few survivors of the drought and duststorms that plagued the Midwest in the 1930s.

Of course, despite Kansas' relationships with the East Coast and world markets, quirky, small-town rituals persist. The state fair, held in Hutchinson during the second and third weeks of September, is more delightful than dizzying: sure, it has ferris wheels and roller-coaster rides, but the fair also features baked goods, quilting contests, and hog auctions. Unbeknownst to most, Kansas is also the home of the Garden of Eden (in Lucas, on the corner of 2nd and Kansas, just off I-70 on Hwy. 181 in the virtual center of the continental U.S.), a meticulous re-creation first planted in 1907. (Open summer daily 9am-6pm; winter 10am-4pm.)

Practical Information

Capital: Topeka.

Visitors Information: Department of Economic Development, 400 W. 8th, 5th floor, Topeka 66603 (296-2009). **Kansas Park and Resources Authority,** 900 Jackson Ave., suite #502N, Topeka 66612 (296-2281).

Time Zone: Central (1 hr. behind Eastern). **Postal Abbreviation:** KS

Dodge City

Legends haunt Dodge City, the epitome of cowtowns. At the turn of the century, gunfighters, prostitutes, federal marshals, and other lawless types used the town as a stopover along the Santa Fe trail; chaos ensued. At one time **Front Street,** the main drag, had one saloon for every 50 citizens. Since most, according to legend, died "with their boots on" in drunken brawls and heated gunfights, their makeshift cemetery became known as Boot Hill. In actuality, fewer people were shot or stabbed in Dodge City in all of its heyday than are killed in acts of violence every three days in New York City. Seems the town had more newspapers (at one time five) than knock-down, drag-out violence, the storytelling competition doing much to magnify a few intoxicated incidents.

Yet for a taste of life during Dodge City's wild heyday, saunter on down to the **Boot Hill Village Museum,** a block-long complex replicating the Boot Hill cemetery and Front St. as they looked in the 1870s. Among the buildings is the **Boot Hill Museum** (227-8188), which displays a 1903 Santa Fe locomotive and the restored and furnished **Hardesty House,** a rancher's Gothic Revival home. On summer evenings the **Long Branch Saloon** holds a variety show at 7:30pm, preceeded by a campy gunfight. (Open daily 8am-7:30pm; Sept.-May Mon.-Sat. 9am-5pm, Sun. 1-5pm. Show $3.75. Museum $4.50, seniors and kids $4, families $13; off-season $3, $1, and $13, respectively.)

Catty-corner from Boot Hill is the **Wax Museum,** at 603 5th Ave. (225-7311; open Mon.-Sat. 8:30am-8:30pm, Sun. 1-5pm; $1.85). Walk up 5th Ave. to Spruce, and head east. At 4th Ave. and Spruce, on the lawn outside the chamber of commerce (227-3119), sits the town memorial sculpture garden, carved by the late dentist O.H. Simpson. Monuments include "Lest We Forget," an enormous, mournful-eyed cow bust honoring the seven million longhorns sent to market from Dodge City during the 1870s and 80s, early evidence that animal rights activism began in the West. Dr. Simpson also sculpted pairs of stone cowboy boots placed toes-up in mock burial form, but most were stolen.

On the corner of 2nd Ave. and Spruce sits Carnegie Library, complete with stained-glass windows and a reading patio out back, now the **Carnegie Art Center** (225-6388; open Tues.-Fri. noon-5pm, Sat. 11am-3pm). Walk down 2nd Ave. to Front St. to check out "El Capitan," yet another enormous longhorn cattle statue commemorating the 1870s cattle drives, this one sculpted in bronze by Jasper d'Ambrosi. The trail of quirky, bovine sympathy art continues at the **Hyplains Dressed Beef** packing plant (227-7135), south of Wyatt Earp Blvd., on Trail St. between 2nd and 3rd Ave. Kansas artist Stan Herd, more known for planting and plowing fields to look like Van Gogh's "Sunflowers," painted a wrap-around mural depicting Kansas faunal history, from the first horse introduced by Spaniards in the 1500s to the last wild buffalo circa 1890.

Today, longhorn cattle parade through town only during **Dodge City Days** (227-2176) at the end of July, when the city recalls its past with a rodeo, a beauty pageant, a pancake-eating contest, turtle racing, and a huge festival.

Where's the BEEF?!? Try **Muddy Waters,** 2303 W. Wyatt Earp Blvd. (225-9493), for a ½-lb. burger ($2.75), or the less barbaric giant tostada ($5.25), in a very barlike atmosphere ($1 draws). (Open Mon.-Sat. 11am-2am. Food served till 11pm.) But if you don't want real food for real people, try **Ozzie's** at North and "A" Ave. (227-8255), for fried most everything including chicken dinners ($5.25). Take Central north from downtown, and go west on the bypass. (Open Tues.-Fri. 4pm-2am, Sat.-Sun. noon-2am.)

A warning to the carless and careless: except for the **Western Inn Motel** (225-1381) across from the bus station (rooms $30-40), most motels rustle four mi. west along Wyatt Earp Blvd., a quite busy highway that becomes U.S. 50 outside of town. The **Holiday Motel,** 2100 W. Wyatt Earp (227-2169), rounds up cheap, clean, big rooms with HBO, and a nice pool. (Singles $22. Doubles $27. 10% discount for seniors.) The **Econolodge,** 1610 W. Wyatt Earp (225-0231), has lots o' features at moderate rates: free HBO, indoor pool, jacuzzi, sauna, gameroom, dry-cleaning service, laundry facilities, and shuttle service. (Singles $30. Doubles $36.) There are two adequate campgrounds close to town—the highly developed **Gunsmoke Campground,** W. Hwy. 50 (227-8247), three mi. west of Front St. (tent sites $9 for 2 people, RV sites with hookup $13; each additional person $1.50) and the **Water Sports Campground Recreation,** 500 Cherry St. (225-9003), on a small lake 10 blocks south from Front St. on 2nd Ave. (2-person sites with full hookup $12, A/C $2).

Dodge City barebacks 150 mi. west of Wichita on Rte. 54, north of the Oklahoma panhandle, and 310 mi. east of Colorado Springs on U.S. 50. The center of town and hub of all business activity is, and historically has been, the railway. **Amtrak** (800-872-7245) runs out of the **Santa Fe Station,** a century-old national historic landmark at Central and Wyatt Earp Blvd. Contact a travel agent, since no tickets are sold at the station. One train daily heads eastbound, and one westbound, to Kansas City (7 hr., $81), La Junta, CO (2 hr., $55), and Lamy, NM (8 hr., $88). **Greyhound/Trailways,** 2425 E. Wyatt Earp Blvd. (225-1617), serves Dodge twice daily from Wichita ($20.25). (Open Mon.-Sat. 8am-5pm.) There is no public transportation in town. The **post office** meters at 700 Central (227-8618; open Mon.-Fri. 8:15am-4:30pm, Sat. 11am-1pm). Dodge City's **ZIP code** is 67801; the **area code** is 316.

Lawrence

With its wide tree-lined avenues and gracious Victorian houses, Lawrence's placidity hides a stormier side. In the mid-19th century it stood in the crossfire between pro-slavery Missourians and abolitionist immigrants from the north—resulting in repeated burnings, sackings, and raidings before and during the Civil War. The abolitionist New England Emigrant Aid Company founded the town, and even considered naming it "New Boston." Instead they called themselves "Jayhawks" after a mythical bird that worries its prey before devouring it. Still enjoying the flavor of intimidation, Lawrence, home to the University of Kansas and plenty of former hippies, debunks *The Wizard of Oz* stereotypes of the "typical" Kansas town.

The small but stately **Elizabeth Watkins Community Museum,** 1047 Massachusetts St. (841-4109), displays the relics of Lawrence's tumultuous past, with emphasis on the Civil War era. (Open Tues.-Sat. 10am-4pm, Sun. 1:30-4pm. Donation.) On the **University of Kansas** campus (864-2700) you can see Comanche, a dead stuffed horse, who was the only survivor of Custer's Last Stand. He and other stuffed animals just sit and stare in the **Museum of Natural History,** in Dyche Hall at 14th and Jayhawk Blvd. (864-4540, 864-4450 on weekends; open Mon.-Sat. 8am-5pm, Sun. 1-5pm; donation). Aesthetes should stop by the **Helen Foresman Spencer Museum of Art,** 1301 Mississippi St. (864-4710), to appreciate a fine collection of Renaissance and baroque painting and sculpture, as well as an enticing selection of 19th- and 20th-century American art. (Open Tues.-Sat. 8:30am-5pm, Sun. noon-5pm. Free.) Also visit the **Museum of Anthropology** (864-4245) across the street for an instructive dose in what makes us human.

The large student population in Lawrence supports several tasty, reasonably priced restaurants, mostly for the granola set. The **Paradise Café,** 728 Massachusetts St. (842-5199), will toss you a veggie-burger made of lentils, oats, and walnuts for $3. (Open Sun.-Tues. 8am-2:30pm, Wed.-Sat. 6:30am-2:30pm and 5-10pm.) For the Depression-minded, the café serves a "no more hard times special" with brown rice, pinto beans, and a huge piece of cornbread for just $3. The crowded **Tin Pan Alley,** 1105 Massachusetts St. (749-9756), has great Mexican and domestic food, plus breakfast anytime. Parents watch out—a sign above the door reads "All unattended children will be sold as slaves." (Open Mon.-Sat. 11am-10pm, Sun. 11am-9pm.) For coffee and New Age books, try **Pywackers** (749-3883), ½ block north of Massachusetts St. on 9th St., for vegetarian sandwiches ($3.25), pastries, or herbal tea. (Open Mon.-Fri. 8am-6pm, Sat. 9am-5pm.) A **farmers market** sprouts up thrice weekly at 10th and Vermont. (Open Tues. and Thurs. 4-6:30pm, Sat. 6:30-10:30am.)

At 12th and Indiana, a block north of the student union, sits Lawrence's alternative triangle, with an upstairs coffeehouse, the **Glass Onion** (841-2310), featuring an international daily grind for 75¢ (open Mon.-Thurs. 10am-9pm, Fri.-Sat. 10am-11pm) and the ever popular **Yellow Sub** (841-3268) downstairs. Relaxed deadheads serve incredibly scrumptious and addictive subs and half-subs ($2.50-6) amid Elvis posters. (Open summer Mon.-Thurs. and Sun. 10am-10pm, Fri.-Sat. 10am-midnight; late Aug.-late May Mon.-Thurs. and Sun. 10am-midnight, Fri.-Sat. 10am-1am.) Next door, the **Crossing**, 618 W. 12th St., has an especially popular front deck doubling as an impromptu Friday afternoon club. Live local bands play Saturday nights. (Open Mon.-Sat. 11am-midnight. Cover with bands $2.)

Lawrence has riots to offer the restless at night. For great jazz, enter the **Jazzhaus**, 926½ Massachusetts St. (749-3320; open daily 4pm-2am, live bands Thurs.-Sat. and a $3 max. cover). **The Bottleneck**, 737 New Hampshire, a block north of Massachusetts St. downtown, hosts progressive live rock, reggae and alternative music nights. Cover varies from free to $8. (Open Mon.-Sat. 3pm-2am.) The skatepunk crowd heads through the cornfields to the **Outhouse**, four mi. east of Massachusetts St. on 15th (841-8879), for live punk shows and serious slam dancing. Lawrencian William S. Burroughs has been known to recite lyrics over local punk compositions here. Ask at **Rudi's Pizza**, 12th and Indiana behind the Crossing (749-0055), about Outhouse times and performers. For the more sedate culture fiends, **Liberty Hall**, at 642 Massachusetts St. (749-1912), shows first-run art/independent films nightly. Call for prices and showtimes.

If you want to crash after all this revelry, try the **College Motel**, 1703 W. 6th (843-0131), just uphill from the bus station. Clean rooms come with A/C and friendly service. (Singles $25-28. Doubles $32.) The small **Jayhawk Motel**, 1004 N. 3rd (843-4131), farther from the center of town, has fairly clean, sunless rooms. (Singles $20. Doubles $22.) Another option is the **G.S. Pearson Dormitory**, 500 W. 11th St. (864-4884), at the end of Louisiana St. These standard dorm rooms lack private baths and phones, but are spotlessly clean and ultra-secure. (Singles $15. Doubles $20.)

Lawrence is a very pretty 30-mi. drive west of Kansas City on Kansas Rte. 10, and 25 mi. east of Topeka on I-70. The main drag is **Massachusetts Street** between 7th and 11th Ave. The **Amtrak** station is at 413 E. 7th St. (843-7172 or 800-872-7245), a few blocks east of downtown. Trains run once daily to Kansas City (1 hr., $12.50), St. Louis (8 hr., $54), and Chicago (10 hr., $98). Tickets are not sold at the station; try a travel agency, such as that at 704 Mass. St. (842-4000; open Mon.-Fri. 9am-5pm, Thurs. 9am-8pm, Sat. 9am-12:30pm). **Greyhound/Trailways** and **Jefferson Lines** share a depot, 1401 W. 6th St. (843-5622), at Michigan seven blocks from Mass. St. (open Mon.-Fri. 7am-5pm and 7-10:30pm; Sat. 7-10am, 2:30-4:30pm, 7-8:15pm, and 9:15-10:30pm; Sun. 7-9am, noon-4:30pm, and 7-10:30pm). Buses go to Kansas City (8 per day, 1 hr., $10.50); Wichita (4 per day, 4 hr., $26); Des Moines (4 per day, 6½ hr., $43.50); Dodge City (1 per day, 9 hr., $43); Denver (3 per day, 12 hr., $73); Topeka (7 per day, ½ hr., $5); and Omaha (4 per day, 6 hr., $48). The **Lawrence Bus Co.**, 841 Pennsylvania (842-0544 or 864-3506), runs full service September through May. In summer, the "Union" bus runs only between the campus and downtown, hourly at 25 minutes past the hour. The "Trailridge" bus goes between 6th St. hotels, the bus station, and downtown. (Buses operate daily 7am-6pm, fare 75¢.) For a cab, call **A-1 City Cab** (842-2432; bus station to K.U. $3.50).

The **chamber of commerce**, 823 Vermont (843-4411), has historic buildings listings and a town map. (Open Mon.-Fri. 8:30am-5pm.) For info on goings-on in town, call the **University of Kansas Information Hotline** (864-3506).

Lawrence's **ZIP code** is 66044; the **area code** is 913.

Topeka

Like Lawrence, its neighbor 25 mi. to the east, Topeka was founded in 1854 by abolitionist settlers willing to use their votes and bodies to keep Kansas a free state. When Kansas was admitted to the Union as a free state in 1861, Topeka became the capital with only 200 residents.

Today the **state capitol building** (296-3966), bounded by 10th and 8th Ave. and Jackson and Harrison St., boasts a beautiful dome and murals of John Brown and the settling of the plains. Free tours let you ride in the old glass elevator to the dome.

(Tours Mon. and Thurs.-Fri. 9-11am and 1-3pm on the hr.) Try the cheap sand-wiches downstairs. (Building open Mon.-Sat. 7:30am-5:30pm, Sun. 8am-5pm.)

One block east of the state capitol, **Pore Richard's Café**, 705 S. Kansas Ave. (233-4276), struggles as the only late-night place in town. Besides burgers and delicious shakes, Dick also serves breakfast all day in booths with personal jukeboxes. (Open Mon.-Sat. 11am-3am.) Every 10 minutes from 11am to 1:30pm, a 10¢ trolley runs along Kansas Ave.

For a place to stay, take the West 6th bus from downtown to **Motel 6**, 3846 SW Topeka Blvd. (267-1222; singles $33, doubles $42.)

The **Amtrak** station is at 5th and Holiday (357-5362 or 800-872-7245). One train goes west, one east daily to Lawrence (½ hr., $10), Kansas City (1½ hr., $18), and St. Louis (6 hr., $59). **Greyhound/Trailways** is at 200 S.E. 3rd (233-2301) at Quincy, a few blocks northeast of the capitol. Buses motor to: Kansas City (6 per day, 1½ hr.; $10, $16 on weekends); Lawrence (6 per day, 35 min., $5); Denver (3 per day, 11 hr., $73); Wichita (4 per day, 3 hr.; $20, $24 on weekends); and Dodge City (1 per day, 8 hr., $41). (Open Mon.-Fri. 7am-10pm; Sat. 7am-4pm and 8-10pm; Sun. 7-11:30am, 3-4pm and 8-10pm.) **Topeka Transit** provides local bus transporta-tion (354-9571; Mon.-Fri. 6am-6:30pm, Sat. 8am-6:30pm; fare 70¢, seniors 35¢). Topeka's General Delivery **ZIP code** is 66601; the **area code** is 913.

Wichita

When Coronado, the first European to explore the Great Plains, came to Wichi-ta's present-day site, he was so disappointed that he had his guide strangled for mis-leading him. Though no one found the mythical gold-laden Quivira, by the 1870s settlers had taken a permanent shine to the place and stubbornly called their home town such endearing names as the "Peerless Princess of the Plains." Today one of the largest aircraft manufacturing centers in the U.S., Wichita lures tourists to its worthiness with wellsprings of festivals, attractions, and rumors of gold.

The **Old Cowtown Historic Village Museum**, 1871 Sim Park Dr. (264-8894), takes you back to boisterous cattle days through the 30 buildings that comprised the town during the 1870s. (Open daily 10am-5pm. $3, ages 6-12 $2, under 6 free.) In the **Wichita-Sedgwick County Historical Museum**, 204 S. Main (265-9314), posh antique furniture and heirlooms sit beside historical oddities, such as the hatchet used by crusading prohibitionist Carrie Nation when she demolished the bar of the Carey Hotel. (Open Tues.-Fri. 11am-4pm, Sat.-Sun. 1-5pm. $1, ages 6-16 50¢, under 6 free.) Further from the town's center is the **Mid-American Indian Center and Mu-seum**, 650 N. Seneca (262-5221), which showcases traditional and modern works by Native American artists. The late Blackbear Bosin's monolithic sculpture, *Keeper of the Plains*, guards over the grounds. (Open Tues.-Sat. 11am-5pm, Sun. 1-5pm. Closed Mon. $1.75, ages 6-12 $1, under 6 free.)

The **Wichita State University** campus, at N. Hillside and 17th St., contains an outdoor sculpture collection comprised of 53 works, including pieces by Rodin, Moore, Nevilson, and Hepworth. Get free sculpture maps at the **Edwin A. Ulrich Museum of Art** (689-3664), also on campus. One side of this unmissable building contains a gigantic glass mosaic mural by Joan Miró. (Open late-Aug. to mid-June Wed. 9:30am-8pm, Thurs.-Fri. 9:30am-5pm, Sat.-Sun. 1-5pm. Free.) Take "East 17th" or "East 13th" bus from Century II.

Meat spells meals in Wichita; if you have only one meat in Wichita, go to **Doc's Steakhouse**, 1515 N. Broadway (264-4735), where the most expensive entree is the 18-oz. T-bone at $7.75. (Open Mon.-Fri. 11:30am-9:30pm, Sat. 4-11pm.) The **Old Mill Tasty Shop**, 604 E. Douglas (264-6500), recalls a long-lost Wichita with its old-time soda fountain and spitoons. Sandwiches cost $3.25-5.75, and ice cream treats are 65¢-$3.50. (Open Mon.-Fri. 11am-3pm, Sat. 8am-5pm.) **Dyne Quik**, 1202 N. Broadway (267-5821), is homey, awfurring catfish with salad, potatoes, bread, and coffee ($3.50) or a 21-piece shrimp dinner ($4.75). (Open Mon.-Fri. 5:15am-3pm, Sat. 5:15am-1:30pm.)

Wichita presents a Quivira of cheap hotels. Try South Broadway, but be wary of the neighborhood. The **Mark 8 Inn,** 1130 N. Broadway (265-4679), is hard to beat, with clean rooms, huge pillows, in-room movies, and fridges. (Singles $25. Doubles $28.) Closer to downtown and the bus station is the **Royal Lodge,** 320 E. Kellogg (263-8877), with a clean interior and cable TV. (Singles $25, with king-size bed $30. Doubles $34.) Several other cheap, palatable motels line East Kellogg five to eight mi. from downtown. The **Wichita KOA Kampground,** 15520 Maple Ave. (722-1154), has private showers, a laundromat, gameroom, pool, and convenience store. (Office open daily 6am-8pm. Tent sites $12.50 per 2 people, with hookup $16. Each additional person $2, ages 4-11 $1.50.)

Wichita sits on I-35, 170 mi. north of Oklahoma City and about 200 mi. south-west of Kansas City. **Main Street** is the major north-south thoroughfare. **Douglas Avenue** lies between numbered east-west streets to the north and named east-west streets to the south. The **Convention and Visitors Bureau,** on 100 S. Main St. (265-2800), has a "Quarterly Calendar" of local events. (Open Mon.-Fri. 8am-5pm.) The **Wichita Fun Phone** (262-7474) lists current festivals, activities, sports, and entertainment.

The closest **Amtrak** station is in Newton, 25 mi. north of Wichita, at 5th and Main St. (283-7533; tickets sold Wed.-Fri. 7:30am-4pm, station open 11:30pm-7am). One train chugs daily to Kansas City (4 hr., $49) and Dodge City (2½ hr., $40). **Greyhound/Trailways,** 312 S. Broadway (265-7711), two blocks east of Main St. and two blocks south of Douglas Ave., provides bus service to the Newton Amtrak station for $6; schedules vary. Buses also serve: Kansas City (4 per day, 4 hr., $36); Denver (2 per day, 12 hr., $64); Dodge City (2 per day, 3 hr., $20.25); and Dallas (4 per day, 9 hr., $64). (Open daily 3:30am-1:30am.) The **post office** posts at 7117 W. Harry (946-4511), at Airport Rd. (Open Mon.-Fri. 8am-4:30pm, Sat. 8am-noon.) Wichita's **ZIP code** is 67276; the **area code** is 316.

KENTUCKY

Kentucky defines itself by hills, horses, and hospitality. Its nickname, "The Blue-grass State" refers to two eponymous elements of Kentucky—its beautiful high grass, and the fast and intricate country-folk music developed in rural parts of the state.

Before the Civil War, Kentucky held slaves, slaveholders and abolitionists. Kentucky-born President Abraham Lincoln sent Union troops to his home state in 1862 to prevent Kentucky's secession; Confederate President Jefferson Davis went to school in Lexington, where he was voted most likely to secede. With 99% of its residents born in America, and almost 75% born in-state, Kentucky inspires intense loyalty among its denizens—when the first strains of Stephen Foster's immortal "My Old Kentucky Home" are played at sports events, natives immediately stand up with hands over hearts. Kentucky's cities blend a vaunted Southern friendliness with more tolerance than you'll find in its southern neighbors.

Practical Information

Capital: Frankfort.

Tourist Information: Kentucky Department of Travel Development, Capital Plaza Tower, 22nd floor, Frankfort 40601 (502-564-4930 or 800-225-8747). **Department of Parks,** Capital Plaza Tower, Frankfort 40601 (800-255-7275).

Time Zones: Central (1 hr. behind Eastern) and Eastern. **Postal Abbreviation:** KY

Cumberland Gap

Almost completely uncommercialized, **Cumberland Gap National Historical Park** is home to Daniel Boone's **Wilderness Trail,** a natural passage through an 800-ft. break in the Appalachian Mountains. The park surrounds the route that Boone and 30 axe-wielding pioneers blazed along a Shawnee and Cherokee Buffalo trail in 1775.

There are now 50 mi. of hiking trails in the park. As your first stop, head for the **National Park Visitors Center,** 200 yards from Middlesboro, KY, off U.S. 25E. (606-248-2817), where rangers will help you plan a trip. The center will also let you know about the other programs offered in the park. All walking tours, exhibits and programs are free. (Open daily mid-June to Aug., 8am-6pm; Sept. to mid-June, daily 8am-5pm.) Two popular attractions in the park are **Pinnacle Lookout** and the **Hensley Settlement.** Take a 15-minute drive from the Visitors Center to the **Pinnacle Overlook,** from which you can see the gap and the states of Virginia, Kentucky, and Tennessee (and Georgia and North Carolina as well, if you have eyes like telescopes). Every Thursday during the summer from 2-4pm, a ranger dressed as a Confederate soldier is stationed at Fort Lyon, on top of the Pinnacle, to tell Civil War stories. Atop Brush Mountain lies the **Hensley Settlement,** a collection of 12 farms worked for 50 years until abandoned in the 1940s. The settlers lived in an isolated encampment of rough-hewn chestnut log houses. Since 1965, the park service has restored five farmsteads, the schoolhouse, and cemetery. You can reach the settlement by a 3½-mi. hike from Caylor, 11 mi. from the Visitors Center on Route 690N, or in a 4-wheel-drive vehicle. Worthwhile three-hr. tours depart several times per day ($5, kids $2.50) from the Visitors Center.

Four campgrounds inside the park on the scenic 17-mi. Ridge Trail are accessible only by foot and require permits ($1 per person at the Visitors Center). Permits are required for backcountry camping as well. Non-hikers can use the **Wilderness Road Campground** on Rte. 58 in Virginia, which offers sites and firewood for $8. (Quiet rules are in effect from 10pm-6am.) If camping, there is no real reason to go into Middlesboro itself. A string of uninspiring but fairly cheap motels lines U.S. 25E in the city. The **Parkview Motel** (606-248-4516) is clean, very convenient to the park, and has both The Playboy Channel and a few waterbeds. (Singles $24. Doubles $30-34. The eager owners will try to keep you there when there are vacancies and may lower the prices.) If you are already in Middlesboro and want to eat, **The Sonic,** directly across from the Parkview Motel, is a 50s drive-in diner with burgers ($1.60), malts ($1.25), and roller-skating waitresses. (Open Sun.-Thurs. 9am-11pm, Fri.-Sat. 9am-midnight.)

When you tire of commercial Middlesboro, drive over to **Cumberland Gaptown** (pop. 210) in Tennessee and have lunch at the quaint **Ye Olde Tea and Coffee Shoppe** (869-4844). (Open Tues.-Sat. 11am-2pm, Sat. 6-9pm, Sun. noon-4pm.) Before you leave the Cumberland Gap area, have a Coke and a smile. The Coca-Cola factory in Middlesboro uses the extra fresh and tasty waters of nearby **Lake Fern** to make the real thing just a little less unreal.

Lexington

In 1775, an exploring party camping in Kentucky, hearing news of the Battle of Lexington in far-off Massachusetts, named the spot after the skirmish. Lexington has grown to become Kentucky's second-largest city and the world's largest burley tobacco center. With a recently rehabilitated and expanded downtown area, Lexington has managed urban renewal with remarkable style, even retaining its charming original neighborhoods. The University of Kentucky's huge campus extends east from South Limestone St., providing a clientele for several distinctive eateries and shops.

Inhabitants of this gracious city gain fame for their dedication to horse breeding and training. Instead of suburbs, Lexington has thousand-acre farms of blue grass and white fences. With over 150 horse farms gracing the Lexington area, the stables have nurtured such greats as Citation, Lucky Debonair, Majestic Prince and Whirlway.

Practical Information

Emergency: 911.

Greater Lexington Convention and Visitors Bureau, Suite 363, 430 W. Vine St. (800-848-1224, 233-1221), in the convention center. Brochures, maps, and bus schedules. Open Mon.-Fri. 8:30am-5pm, Sat. 10am-5pm. Information centers also grace I-75 north and south of Lexington.

Airport: Bluegrass Field, 4000 Versailles Rd. (254-9336). Serves regional airlines/flights; often easier to fly to Louisville's Standiford Field.

Greyhound: 477 New Circle Rd. NW (255-4261). Lets passengers off north of Main St. Take Lex-Tran bus #6 downtown. Open daily 6:45am-11:30pm. To: Louisville (1 per day, 1½ hr., $16); Cincinnati, OH (5 per day, 1½ hr., $16-21); Knoxville, TN (4 per day; 3 hr.; $41, $32 if reserved 7 days in advance).

Public Transport: Lex-Tran, 109 W. London Ave. (252-4936). Good system serving the university and city outskirts. Most buses leave from Vine or Main St. Fare 60¢, transfers 10¢. 10¢ trolley serves downtown area.

Taxi: Lexington Yellow Cab, 231-8294. Base fare $1.90, $1.35 per mi.

Transportation for the Handicapped: WHEELS, 233-3433. 7am-6pm. 24 hrs. notice required. After hours call 231-8294, daily.

Help Line: Rape Crisis, 253-2511. Open 24 hrs.

Time Zone: Eastern.

Post Office: 1088 Nandino Blvd. (231-6700). Open Mon.-Fri. 8:30am-5pm, Sat. 9am-1pm. ZIP code: 40511.

Area Code: 606.

New Circle Road highway, which is intersected by many roads that connect the downtown district to the surrounding towns, surrounds the city. High, Vine, and Main Streets are the major east-west routes downtown; Limestone Street and Broadway the north-south thoroughfares.

Accommodations and Camping

The concentration of horse-related wealth in the Lexington area tends to ride accommodation prices up. The cheapest places gallop out of the city on roads beyond New Circle Rd. If you're having trouble on your own, Dial-A-Accommodations, 430. W. Vine St. #363 (233-7299), will locate and reserve a room free of charge in a requested area of town and within a specific price range. (Open Mon.-Fri. 9:30am-5pm.)

Kimball House Motel, 267 S. Limestone St. (252-9565), downtown. Charming. Clean, antique-filled rooms transport you to a turn-of-the-century boarding house. Friendly, helpful management. Some singles (1st floor, no A/C, shared bath) $20. Ask for them specifically; they often fill by late afternoon. Otherwise, cheapest singles $24. Doubles $28. Key deposit $5. Parking in back.

University of Kentucky, Apartment Housing (257-3721). Full kitchen and private bathroom. Fold-out sleeper. Rooms also available during the school year, space permitting. 14-day max. stay. $21. Call ahead on a weekday. Available June-Aug. Explain that you only want a short stay; longer-term rentals are for UK affiliates only.

Motel 6, I-75 at Exit 100/US60 (293-1431). Not downtown but dependable and nicer than a lot of the places downtown. Singles $27.95.

Bryan Station Inn, 273 New Circle Rd. (299-4162). Take Limestone St. north from downtown and turn right onto Rte. 4. Clean, pleasant rooms in the middle of a motel/fast-food strip. Singles $26. Doubles $28. Rates decrease the longer you stay.

Good, cheap campgrounds abound around Lexington; unfortunately, you need a car to reach them. The **Kentucky Horse Park Campground,** 4089 Ironworks Pike (233-4303), 10 mi. north off I-75, offers a free shuttle to the KY Horse Park and Museum. (2-week max. stay. Sites $9, with hookup $12.)

Food

Lexington specializes in good, down-home cuisine. The few distinctive restaurants are near the university. Downtown, avoid the chic new retail area and explore the surrounding streets for hidden delis and sandwich shops.

Alfalfa Restaurant, 557 S. Limestone St. (253-0014), across from Memorial Hall at the university. Take bus #2A. Fantastic home-cooked international and veg meals. Complete dinners with salad, bread, and entree under $10. Excellent, filling soups and exotic salads from $2. Live music nightly. Open Tues.-Thurs. 5:30-9pm (in summer until 9:30pm), Fri. 5:30-10pm, Sat. 10am-2pm and 5:30-10pm, Sun. 10am-2pm.

Tonio's Authenic Mexican Cuisine, 100 West Vine St. (254-3722) across from Phoenix Park. Delicious and cheap. Authentic Mex food fixed by Mexican chefs. Entrees ($2-4) and free serve-yourself nachos and salsa. Open Mon.-Thurs. 11am-10pm. Fri.-Sat. 11am-3am.

Joe Bologna's, 103 W. Maxwell St., at S. Limestone 5 blocks south of Main. College hangout popular for its pizza ($4-10). Extra napkins necessary for the juicy gourmet cheesesteak. Open Mon.-Thurs. 11am-midnight, Fri.-Sat. 11am-1am, Sun. noon-11pm.

Central Christian Cafeteria, 219 E. Short St., 1 block north of Main St. Decent country food—greens and cornbread, fried fish, homemade pies for under $3. Open Mon.-Fri. 6:30am-2pm.

Sights and Nightlife

To escape the stifling swamp conditions farther south, antebellum plantation owners built beautiful summer retreats in milder Lexington. The most attractive of these stately houses preen only a few blocks northeast of the town center in the Gratz Park area near the public library. In addition to their past, the wrap-around porches, wooden minarets, stone foundations, and rose-covered trellises distinguish these from the neighborhood's newer homes.

The **Hunt Morgan House,** 201 N. Mill St. (253-0362), hunkers down at the end of the park across from the library. Built in 1814 by John Wesley Hunt, the first millionaire west of the Alleghenies, the house later sheltered the birth of Thomas Hunt Morgan, who won a Nobel Prize in 1933 for proving the existence of the gene. Yet the house's most colorful inhabitant was Confederate General John Hunt Morgan. Chased by Union troops, the general once rode his horse up the front steps and into the house, leaned down to kiss his mother, and rode out the back door. What a guy. Visit the house to see its weird color schemes. (Tours Tues.-Sat. 10am-4pm, Sun. 2-5pm. $3, ages 6-12 $2, under 6 free.)

Kentucky's loyalties divided sharply in the Civil War. Mary Todd grew up five blocks from the Hunt-Morgan House; she later married Abraham Lincoln. The **Mary Todd Lincoln House** is at 578 W. Main St. (233-9999; open April 1-Dec. 15 Tues.-Sat. 10am-4pm; $3).

Transylvania University, west of Broadway and north of 3rd St. (233-8242), became the first U.S. college west of the Alleghenies. Its Greek Revival buildings aren't quite as impressive as its alumni have been—two vice-presidents, 50 senators, 101 representatives, three speakers of the house, 36 governors, and 34 ambassadors. (Guided tours upon request Mon.-Fri. 9am-4pm. Call 233-8120.) At the corner of Sycamore and Richmond Rd., you can admire **Ashland** (266-8581), the 20-acre homestead of statesman Henry Clay. The mansion's carved ash interior came from trees that grew on the property. (Open Mon.-Sat. 9:30am-4:30pm, Sun. 1-4:30pm.

$4, kids $1.50. Take bus #4A on Main St. Will be closed for several months for renovations, so call ahead.)

The sprawling **University of Kentucky** (257-7173) gives free campus tours in "Old Blue," an English double-decker bus, at 10am and 2pm weekdays and on Saturday mornings (call 257-3595). On campus, UK's new **Art Museum** (257-5716) holds Native American relics and modern U.S. art (open Tues.-Sun. noon-5pm); its **Museum of Anthropology** (257-7112) also opened recently (open Mon.-Fri. 8am-5pm). For updates of UK's arts calendar, call 257-7173; for more info about campus attractions, call 257-3595.

Lexington's sparse nightlife includes a few fun clubs and bars. **Breeding's** showcases lively times and music at 509 W. Main St. (255-2822). **The Brewery** is a friendly country-western bar (both open daily 8am-1am). **Comedy on Broadway,** 144 N. Broadway (259-0013), features stand-up comics most nights. **The Bar,** 224 E. Main St. (255-1551), is a disco popular with gay men and lesbians. (Open Sun.-Fri. until 1:30am, until 3:30am Sat. Cover $3 on weekends.) **The Wrocklage,** 361 W. Shore St. (231-7655), serves up alternative and punkish rock, and **Lynagh's,** in University Plaza at Woodland and Euclid St. (259-9944), serves as a good neighborhood pub.

Horses and Seasonal Events

When in Lexington a visit is not complete without a close encounter with its quadruped citizenry, and we ain't talkin' wombats. Try **Spendthrift Farm,** 884 Ironworks Pike (299-5271), eight mi. northeast of downtown. (Free tours Feb.-July Mon.-Sat. 10am-noon; Aug.-Jan. Mon.-Sat. 10am-2pm. Take Broadway until it becomes Paris Pike, turn left onto Ironworks.)

The **Kentucky Horse Park,** 4089 Ironworks Pike, exit 120 (233-4303), 10 mi. north on I-75, is a state park with full facilities for equestrians, a museum, two films, and the Man O' War Monument. (Open mid-March to Oct. daily 9am-5pm; times vary the rest of the year. $8, ages 7-12 $4. Horse-drawn vehicle tours included.)

If horse racing is more your style, visit the **Keeneland Race Track,** 4201 Versailles Rd. (254-3412, 800-354-9092), west on U.S. 60. (Races Oct. and April; post time 1pm. $2.) The public can observe morning workouts. (April-Oct. daily 6-10am.) The final prep race for the Kentucky Derby occurs here in April. The **Red Mile Harness Track,** 847 S. Broadway (255-0752; take bus #3 on S. Broadway), has racing from April to June and also in September. (Post time 7:30pm. Last week in Sept. post time 1:30pm.) The crowds run the gamut from wholesome families to seasoned gamblers. ($1.50, reserved seating $3, programs $2, parking free. Seniors free Thurs.) Morning workouts (7:30am-noon) are open to the public during racing season.

In June, the **Festival of the Bluegrass** (846-4995), at Masterson Station Park, attracts thousands for a Kentucky-style hootenanny. Camping at the festival grounds is free. The **Lexington Junior League Horse Show** (mid-July), the largest outdoor show in the nation, unfolds its pageantry at the Red Mile (see above).

Near Lexington

Outside Lexington, in **Richmond,** exit 95 off I-70, is **White Hall** (623-9178), home of the abolitionist (not the boxer) Cassius M. Clay, Henry's cousin. The elegant mansion really consists of two houses, one Georgian and one Italianate. The one-hour tour covers seven different living levels. (Open April-Labor Day daily 9am-4:30pm; Labor Day-Oct. 31 Wed.-Sun; open briefly in winter for a Christmas celebration. Guided tours only. $3, under 13 $2, under 6 free.) The Richmond prepackaged tourism experience also includes **Fort Boonesborough** (527-3328), a recreation of one of Daniel Boone's forts. The park has samples of 18th-century crafts, a small museum, and shows films about the pioneers. (Open April-Aug. daily 9am-5:30pm; Sept.-Oct. Wed.-Sun. 9am-5:30pm. $4, ages 6-12 $2.50, under 6 free. Combination White Hall/Boonesborough tickets available.)

Ten mi. south of Richmond and 30 mi. south of Lexington, where the bluegrass meets the mountains, lies **Berea,** home of tuition-free **Berea College** (986-9341), founded in 1855. Many of the 1,500 students, most from Appalachia, pay for their expenses by operating the school's crafts center. Campus tours leave from the corner of **Boone Tavern.** (Tours Mon.-Fri. at 9am, 10am, 1pm, and 3pm, Sat. at 9am and 2pm.) The **Appalachian Museum** (986-9341, ext. 6078), Jackson St. on campus, charts regional history through arts and crafts. (Open Mon.-Sat. 9am-6pm, Sun. 1-6pm.)

Because of the emphasis on craft skills at Berea College, the town concentrates galleries, gift shops, and workshops. Of particular interest is **Churchill Weavers,** Lorraine Court (986-3127), north of town off I-75 and U.S. 25, the largest hand-weaving firm in the country. (Free tours Mon.-Fri. 9am-4pm. Gift shop open Mon.-Sat. 9am-6pm, Sun. noon-6pm. Schedule may change, so call ahead.) The student-run crafts center has two locations: the **Boone Tavern Gift Shop,** in the hotel (986-9341, ext. 5233; open Mon.-Sat. 8am-8pm, Sun. noon-8pm), and the **Log House Sales Room,** on Estill St. (986-9341, ext. 5225; open Mon.-Sat. 8am-5pm, Sun. 1-5pm). During May and early fall, tourists flood the town for the good folk music and food at the **Kentucky Guild of Artists' and Craftsmen's Fair,** in Indian Fort Theater. In mid-August, the local **McClain Family Band** rolls out their annual blue-grass festival (986-8111) at their Big Hill Farm. To reach Berea, take Greyhound bus #360 (3 per day), on the Lexington-Knoxville route, which will leave you at the B&B Grocery, the college, and Boone Tavern.

The Shakers practiced the simple life between Harrodsburg and Lexington, about 25 mi. southwest on U.S. 68, at the **Shaker Village** (734-5411). The 5,000-acre farm features 27 restored Shaker buildings. A tour includes demonstrations of everything from apple-butter-making to coopering (barrel-making). (Open daily 9:30am-6pm. $7.50, $4 for students 6-17, under 6 free.) Although the last Shaker to live here died in 1923, you can still eat and sleep in original Shaker buildings. (Dinner $12-14. Singles $30-55. Doubles $45-65. All rooms have A/C and private bath. Reservations required.) Greyhound bus #350 runs to Harrodsburg, seven mi. from the village.

The **Red River Valley,** in the northern section of the Daniel Boone National Forest, approximately 50 mi. southeast of Lexington, draws visitors from around the country. A day outing from Lexington will show why song and square dance have immortalized this spacious land of sandstone cliffs and stone arches. **Natural Bridge State Park** (663-2214), two mi. south of Slade, highlights the major attraction of the upper valley. The Red River Gorge highlights the lower valley. Greyhound bus #296 will get you to Stanton (10 mi. west of Slade) and a **U.S. Forest Service Office** (663-2853). If you're driving, take the Mountain Parkway (south off I-64) straight to Slade, and explore the region bounded by the scenic loop road, Rte. 715. Camp at **Natural Bridge State Resort Park** (800-325-1710). The campground, complete with pool, facilities for the disabled, boat rental, and organized square dances, hosts the **National Mountain Style Square Dance and Clogging Festival,** a celebration of Appalachian folkdances. ($1-2. Tent sites $8.50, with hookup $10.50.)

Louisville

Perched on the Ohio River, just between the North and the South, Louisville (LOU-uh-vul) has its own way of doing things. An immigrants' town imbued with Southern grace and architecture, Louisville's beautiful Victorian neighborhoods surround spewing smokestacks and the enormous meat-packing district of Butchertown. The splayed, laid-back city has riverfront parks and excellent cultural attractions fostered by the University of Louisville. But despite dozens of citywide festivals, the year's main event is undoubtedly the Kentucky Derby. The nation's most prestigious horse race ends a week-long extravaganza, luring over half a million visitors who pay through the teeth for a week-long carnival, fashion display, and equestrian show, culminating in a two-minute gallop that you'll miss if you're standing in line for juleps. The $15 million wagered on Derby Day alone proves that

Kentuckians are deadly serious about their racing—the winning horse earns studding privileges with hundreds of hot fillies, the winning jockey earns the congratulations of the state, and the winning owner earns $800,000, enough to make any stable stable.

Practical Information

Emergency: 911.

Louisville Convention and Visitor Bureau, 400 S. 1st St. (584-2121; 800-633-3384 outside Louisville; 800-626-5646 outside KY), at Liberty downtown. The standard goodies, including some bus schedules. Open Mon.-Fri. 8:30am-5pm, Sat.-Sun. 8:30am-4pm. Visitor centers also in Standiford Field airport and in the Galeria Mall at 4th and Liberty St. downtown. **Concert Line,** 540-3210. Information on rock, jazz, and country performances.

Travelers Aid: 584-8186.

Airport: Standiford Field (367-4636), 15 min. south of downtown on I-65. Take bus #2 into the city.

Greyhound/Trailways: 720 W. Muhammad Ali Blvd. (585-3331), at 7th St. To: Indianapolis (6 per day, 2 hr., $20-23); Cincinnati (7 per day, 2 hr., $15.50-20); Chicago (7 per day, 6 hr., $57, $31 special); Nashville (10 per day, 3 hr., $23-28); Lexington (2 per day, 2 hr., $16). Storage lockers $1 first day, $3 per additional days (call 561-2870 for locker and storage info). Open 24 hrs.

Public Transport: Transit Authority River City (TARC), 585-1234. Major routes on the main intersecting streets off Broadway, running east-west, and off 4th St., running north-south. Operates daily 6am-midnight, but varies with bus route. Fare 60¢ during peak hours, 35¢ other times. Disabled access. Also runs a trolley on 4th Ave. from River Rd. to Broadway (free). Call for directions.

Taxi: Yellow Cab, 636-5511. Base fare $3, $1.50 per mi.

Car Rental: Dollar Rent-a-Car, in Standiford Field airport (366-6944). Weekends from $20 per day, weekdays $42. Open daily 6am-midnight. Must be 21 with credit card. Additional $6 per day for ages under 25. **Budget Rent-a-Car,** 4330 Crittenden Dr. (363-4300). From $40 per day. Open daily 6:30am-9pm. Must be 21 with a major credit card or 25 without one.

Help Lines: Rape Hot Line, 581-7273. **Crisis Center,** 589-4313. Both open 24 hrs. **Gay and Lesbian Hotline,** 589-3316. Open Sun.-Thurs. 6-10pm, Fri.-Sat. 6pm-1am.

Time Zone: Eastern.

Post Office: 1420 Gardner Lane (454-1632). Take the Louisville Zoo exit off Rte. 264 and follow Gardner Lane 1 mi. Open Mon.-Fri. 7:30am-7pm, Sat. 7:30am-1pm. **ZIP code:** 40231.

Area Code: 502.

Major highways through the city include I-65 (north-south expressway), I-71, and I-64. The Henry Watterson Expressway, also called I-264, is an easily accessible freeway that rings the city. The central downtown area is defined north-south by Main Street and Broadway, and east-west by Preston and 19th Street.

Aside from theater and riverfront attractions, much activity in Louisville takes place outside the central city, but the fairly extensive bus system goes to all major areas. Call TARC for help since written schedules are incomplete and sometimes confusing.

Accommodations

Though easy to find, accommodations in Louisville are not particularly cheap. If you want a bed during Derby Week, make a reservation at least six months to a year in advance; be prepared to pay high prices. The visitor center (see Practical Info above) will help after March 13. During Derby Weekend, the **University of Louisville** might allow camping (tents only) on their Belknap Campus soccer fields, about one mi. from the track ($5 per tent). At other times, if you don't choose one of the few affordable downtown options, try one of the many cheap motels that line the roads just outside town. **Kentucky Homes Bed and Breakfast** (635-7341) offers stays in private homes from $45. Call at least a few days ahead. Newburg (6 mi. away) and Bardstown (39 mi. away) are likely spots for budget accommodations.

Motel 6, 3304 Bardstown Rd. (456-2861), about 6 mi. southeast of downtown. Take Jefferson St. east from downtown, turn right on Baxter Ave., then bear left on Bardstown Rd., 3 mi. down. Or take bus #17 from Liberty and 7th St. Pool. Singles $25. $6 per additional person.

San Antonio Inn, 927 S. Second St. (582-3741). The cheapest lodging downtown and looks it. Rough area. Singles $24, with phone $29.75. Doubles $35. Must be 21 with photo ID.

Thrifty Dutchman Budget Motel, 3357 Fern Valley Rd. (968-8124), just off I-65. A hike from downtown. Take bus #18, but still expect a long walk. Clean, large rooms. Pool. Singles $31. Doubles $38.

Collier's Motor Court, 4812 Bardstown Rd. (499-1238), south of I-264. 30 min. from downtown by car, or take bus #17. Inconvenient, but well-maintained and cheap. Singles $28.50. Doubles $33.

Travelodge, 2nd and Liberty St. (583-2841), downtown behind the visitor center. Big, clean, and oh-so-convenient. Neighborhood Chinese restaurant provides room service. Singles $41. Doubles $46.

KOA, 900 Marriot Dr., Clarksville, IN (812-282-4474), across the bridge from downtown beside I-65; take the Stansifer Ave. exit. Grocery and playground; mini-golf and a fishing lake at the Sheraton across the street. Sites $15 for 2 people. Each additional person $3, under 18 $2. Kamping Kabins (for 2) $26. RV sites $16.50.

Food

Louisville's chefs whip up a wide variety of cuisines, but prices can be steep. Butchertown and the Churchill Downs area have several cheap delis and pizza places. Bardstown Rd. near Eastern Pkwy. offers budget pizzas and more expensive French cuisine.

The Rudyard Kipling, 422 W. Oak St. (636-1311). Take bus #4 from downtown. If you eat one dinner in Louisville, eat it here. Eclectic menu includes French, Mexican, and vegetarian entrees, Kentucky Burgoo (a regional stew), and other creative fare ($5-14). Half-jungle, half-colonial tavern rooms. Weekend nights feature piano music or rock 'n' roll; weeknights range from Celtic to bluegrass or folk music. Free Louisville Songwriters Cooperative acoustic music show each Mon. at 9pm. Open Mon.-Thurs. 11:30am-2pm and 5:30pm-until, Fri. 11:30am-until, Sat. 5:40pm-until. Call for events calendar. Wheelchair accessible.

Miller's Cafeteria, 429 S. 2nd St., downtown. (582-9135) Serve yourself a full breakfast or lunch (entree, pie, 2 vegetables, and drink) for $3-4. Big, comfortable dining room built in 1826 is barely older than most of the customers. Open Mon.-Fri. 7am-2:30pm, Sun. 10am-2:30pm.

The Old Spaghetti Factory, 235 W. Market St. (581-1070), at 3rd St. downtown. Part of a national chain. Big helpings of spaghetti in a gorgeous remodeled turn-of-the-century department store. Trolley car in the floor. Full dinners with salad, bread, and ice cream $4-6. Popular with families—prepare to wait. Open Mon.-Thurs. 11:30am-2pm and 5-10pm, Fri. 11:30am-2pm and 5-11pm, Sat. 5-11pm, Sun. 4-10pm.

Another Place Sandwich Shop, 1514 Bardstown Rd. (458-8141). Take bus #17, 23, or 40 from downtown. Sandwiches, salads, and chili ($1.50-4) in a hip, 2-story Victorian house. Loud rock 'n' roll and a well-equipped bar. Carry-out available. Open Mon.-Thurs. 8am-midnight, Fri.-Sat. 8am-1am, Sun. 8am-11pm.

Masterson's, 1830 S. 3rd St., near the U. of Louisville (636-2511). Take the #4 bus to "U of L" and walk. Popular with students and professors. Lunch buffet includes roast beef and fried chicken, with excellent desserts. The Taverna serves lunch and dinner for $5-8. Open Sun.-Thurs. 8am-11pm, Fri.-Sat. 8am-1am. All-you-can-eat ($4.25) Mon.-Fri. 11am-2pm.

Mom's East End Cafe, 1605 Story Ave., near Hadley Pottery (583-2625); take bus #15 or 31 from downtown. True Louisville eatery with TV, charming service, and visible kitchen. Limited, ordinary menu. Lunch or dinner under $4. Open Sun.-Thurs. 6am-9pm, Fri.-Sat. 6am-10pm.

In the Neigh-borhood

Even if you miss the Kentucky Derby, try to catch **Churchill Downs,** 700 Central Ave. (636-3541), three mi. south of downtown. Take bus #4 (4th St.) to Central Ave. Bet, watch a race, or just admire the twin spires, colonial columns, gardens, and sheer scale of the track. (Races April-June Tues.-Fri. 3:30-7:30pm, Sat.-Sun. 1-6pm; Oct.-Nov. Tues.-Sun. 1-6pm. Grandstand seats $1.50, clubhouse $3, reserved clubhouse $5. Parking $2-3. Grounds open in racing season daily 10am-4pm.)

The **Kentucky Derby Festival** commences the week before the Derby and climaxes with the prestigious Run for the Roses the first Saturday in May. Balloon and steamboat races, music, and all manner of hullabaloo adorn the week. Seats for the Derby have a five-year waiting list. You can stand and watch from the grandstand or infield along with your 80,000 closest friends for $20, but get in line at the Downs early on Derby morning as these tickets aren't available any other way. 120,000 spectators flood the Downs each Derby day.

The **Kentucky Derby Museum** (637-1111), at Churchill Downs, offers a slide presentation on a 360° screen, tours of the stadium, profiles of famous stables and trainers (including the African Americans who dominated racing early on), a simulated horse-race for betting practice, and tips on what makes a horse a "sure thing." (Open daily 9am-5pm. $3.50, seniors $2.50, ages 5-12 $1.50, under 5 free.)

The **Louisville Downs,** 4520 Poplar Level Rd. (964-6415), south of I-264, hosts harness racing during most of the year. There are three meets: July-Sept. Mon.-Sat., Sept.-Oct., and Dec.-April Tues.-Sat. Post time is 7:30pm and 10-12 races leave the gates per night. ($3.50 clubhouse, $2.50 grandstand. Minimum bet $2. Parking $2. Take bus #43 from downtown.)

If you're tired of spectating, go on a trail ride at **Iroquois Riding Stable,** 5216 New Cut Rd. (363-9159; $10 per hr.). Take 3d St. south to Southern Parkway or ride bus #4 or 6 to Iroquois Park.

Not Just a One-Horse Town

Book, antique, and secondhand shops line **Bardstown Road** north and south of Eastern Pkwy. Just south of downtown and Oak St. (especially on 2nd through 4th St.) are beautifully maintained Victorian homes comprise part of **Old Louisville.** Farther south, in University of Louisville territory, the **J.B. Speed Art Museum,** 2035 S. 3rd St. (636-2893), has an impressive collection of Dutch paintings and tapestries, Renaissance and contemporary art, and a sculpture court. The museum also has a touch-and-see gallery for visually impaired visitors. (Open Tues.-Sat. 10am-4pm, Sun. 12-5pm. Free. Parking $2. Nominal fee for special exhibitions. Take bus #4.)

The **Riverfront Plaza** (625-3333), a landscape park overlooking the Ohio River, serves as the hub of downtown Louisville. Call any time of year to find what festival or citywide event is taking place, as Louisville hosts many. The **Belle of Louisville** (625-2355), an authentic stern-wheeler, cruises the Ohio, leaving from Riverfront Plaza at the foot of 4th St. (Departs May 27-Sept. 2 Tues.-Sun. at 2pm. Sunset cruises Tues. and Thurs. 7-9pm; nighttime dance cruise Sat. 8:30-11:30pm. Fare $7, seniors $6, under 13 $3. Dance cruise $12, no discounts. Boarding begins 1 hr. before the ship leaves; arrive early especially in July.)

The **Museum of History and Science,** 727 W. Main St. (561-6100), downtown, emphasizes hands-on exhibits. Press your face against the window of an Apollo space capsule, then settle back and enjoy the four-story screen at the new IMAX theater. (Open Mon.-Thurs. 9am-5pm, Fri.-Sat. 9am-9pm, Sun. noon-5pm. $4, kids $3; $6 & $5 with IMAX tickets.) At the **Louisville Zoo,** 1100 Trevilian Way (459-2181), between Newbury and Poplar Level Rd. across I-264 from Louisville Downs, the animals are exhibited in neo-natural settings. Ride on an elephant's back or on the tiny train that circles the zoo. (Open Fri.-Tues. 10am-5pm, Wed.-Thurs. 10am-

348   **Kentucky**

8pm; Sept.-April Tues.-Sun. 10am-4pm. Gate closes 1 hr. before zoo. $4, seniors
$1.75, kids $2.)

Hillerich and Bradsby Co., 1525 Charleston-New Albany Rd., Jeffersonville, IN
(585-5226), six mi. north of Louisville, manufactures the famous "Louisville Slug-
ger" baseball bat. (Tours Mon. and Fri. at 11am and 2pm except late June and first
two weeks in July. Free. Go north on I-65 to exit for Rte. 131, then turn east.) **Hadley Pottery,** 1570 Story Ave. (584-2171), near Ohio St. just east of downtown, has
been producing Mary Alice Hadley's gorgeous, unconventional pottery since 1940.
(Free 30-min. tours Mon.-Fri. at 2pm. Shop open Mon.-Fri. 8:30am-4:30pm, Sat.
9am-12:30pm. Take bus #15 or 31.)

Louisville's thriving nightlife offers everything from bluegrass and Beethoven to
Brecht and Beckett. Louisville's newest entertainment complex, the **Kentucky Center for the Arts,** 5 Riverfront Plaza (information and tickets 584-7777 or 800-283-
7777), off Main St., hosts major performing arts groups, including the **Louisville
Orchestra,** known for its repertoire of 20th-century music. The **Lonesome Pines**
series showcases indigenous Kentucky music, including bluegrass. Ticket prices
vary as wildly as the music, though student discounts are sometimes offered. The
Actors Theater, 316 W. Main St. (584-1205), between 3rd and 4th St., a Tony
award-winning repertory company, gives performances from Sept. to mid-June at
8pm and some matinees. Call for details. Tickets start at $15, with $7 student rush
tickets available 15 minutes before each show. Bring a picnic dinner to **Shakespeare
in the Park,** Central Park (634-8237), weekends between June 19 and August 4.
(Performances at 8:30pm.) Call the **Louisville Visual Arts Association,** 3005 Upper
River Rd. (896-2146) for information on local artists' shows and events.

The **Phoenix Hill Tavern,** 644 Baxter Ave. (589-4957; take bus #17), resurrects
live music in Louisville. Three bands play every Friday and Saturday night. Retreat
to the roof-top bar or fresh-air patio. Local rock 'n' roll jams Tuesday to Thursday;
weekends attract bigger names. (Open Tues.-Fri. 4pm-4am, Sat.-Sun. 7pm-4am.
Dinner buffet Fri. 5:30-7:30pm. Regular menu available all the time. Cover Tues.-
Thurs. and Sun. $2, Fri.-Sat. after 8pm $3.) Escort service takes you to your car
or to the bus stop after hours. The **Butchertown Pub,** at Story and Webster St. (583-
2242), also has live bands and a dance floor; take "Market St." bus #15. Regional
bands play college rock on weekends, with Monday and Tuesday nights sounding
a bit more unusual. (Open Mon.-Thurs. 4pm-1am, Wed.-Fri. 4pm-2am, Sat. 6pm-
2am. Cover $2-3.) Bands play in University of Louisville's **Red Barn** (588-7332 or
588-6691) on Friday and Saturday nights. Some shows are all-ages.

Connection Entertainment Complex and Convention Center at 130 S. Floyd St.
serves the small but growing gay community. **Missing Link** serves lunch Mon.-Sat.
11am-12:30pm and dinner Tues.-Sat. 6-10pm. Buffet on Sun. 6pm-10pm. **Visions**
gay bar is open daily 1pm-4am. **Pianoland** is open Wed.-Sun. 9pm-4am. **Oz Dance
Bar** is open Wed.-Sun. 10pm-4am. For more information call 585-5752.

Near Louisville

90% of the nation's bourbon hails from Kentucky, and 60% of that is distilled
in Nelson and Bullitt Counties, close to Louisville. At **Jim Beam's American Outpost** (543-9877) in Clermont, 15 mi. west of Bardstown, Booker Noe, Jim Beam's
grandson and current "master distiller" narrates a film about bourbon. Don't miss
the free lemonade and sampler bourbon candies. From Louisville, take I-65 south
to exit 112, then Rte. 245 south for 2½ mi. From Bardstown, take Rte. 245 north.
(Open Mon.-Sat. 9am-4:30pm, Sun. 1-4pm. Free.) You can't actually tour Beam's
huge distillery, but you can visit the **Maker's Mark Distillery** (865-2881), in Lo-
retto, 19 mi. southeast of Bardstown, for a view of 19th century alcohol production.
Take Rte. 49 to Rte. 52. (Tours Mon.-Sat. every hr. on the ½-hr. 10:30am-3:30pm.
Free.) Neither site has a license to sell its liquors.

Bardstown proper hosts **The Stephen Foster Story** (800-626-1563, 348-5971), a
showy, heavily promoted outdoor musical about America's first major songwriter,
the author of "My Old Kentucky Home." (Performances mid-June to Labor Day

Tues.-Sun. at 8:30pm, plus Sat. at 3pm. $9, $5 for 12 and under). **Kentuckyshow** (348-6501), an excellent and entertaining introduction to the state's history and culture, has moved from Louisville to the Old Bardstown Village and Civil War Museum on Old Bloomfield Rd. (Shows April-Oct. on the hr. Tues.-Sun. 10am-6pm. Museum admission: $2, seniors $1.75, ages 6-12 $1, under 6 free. Tickets for the show: $3, seniors $2.75, ages 6-12 $1.75, under 6 free. For admission to both the museum and the show you get 50¢ discount off each ticket.) Greyhound leaves Louisville at 5pm nightly for Bardstown. By car, take I-65 south, then Rte. 245.

Now a national historic site, **Abraham Lincoln's birthplace** (358-3874) bulges 45 mi. south of Louisville near Hodgenville on U.S. 31 E. From Louisville, take I-65 down to Rte. 61; public transportation does not serve the area. Fifty-six steps representing the 56 years of Lincoln's life lead up to a stone monument sheltering the small log cabin. Only a few of the Lincoln logs that you see are believed to be original. A slow-moving film describes Lincoln's ties to Kentucky. (Open June-Aug. daily 8am-6:45pm; Labor Day-Oct. and May 8am-5:45pm; Nov.-April 8am-4:45pm. Free.)

Hundreds of enormous caves and narrow passageways wind through **Mammoth Cave National Park** (758-2328), 80 mi. south of Louisville off I-65, west on Rte. 70. Mammoth Cave comprises the world's longest network of cavern corridors—over 325 mi. in length. Devoted spelunkers (ages 16 and over) will want to try the six-hour "Wild Cave Tour" in summer ($25); also available are two-hour, two-mi. historical walking tours ($3.50, seniors and kids $1.75) and 90-minute tours for the disabled ($4). Since the caves stay at 54°F year-round, bring a sweater. (Visitor center open daily 7:30am-7:30pm; off-season 7:30am-5:30pm.) Greyhound serves **Cave City,** just east of I-65 on Rte. 70 but the national park still lies miles away. **Gray Line** (637-6511; ask for the Gray Line) gives tours and bus rides to the caves. Call a few days ahead.

The **area code** for the Mammoth Caves area is 502.

LOUISIANA

Louisiana is a popular place, but not as popular as it should be. Sure, hordes of people flood into this Deep South state at the beginning of Lent for Mardi Gras, a Carnival celebration heralded as the "greatest free show on earth." True, the cuisine of its Acadian French population has "gone national," so that you can find bad Cajun restaurants as far away as Boston. And granted, it has hosted the filming of a number of bigtime films, from *sex, lies and videotape* to *Fletch II* to *Steel Magnolias.* But the state has more to offer than just hyped attractions.

You want history? You get history. The state is blanketed with plantation homes, battlefields and old forts, some dating back to the original French and Spanish settlers. Nightlife turn you on? Bourbon Street in New Orleans attracts party-ers like a magnet attracts iron. You can watch folk truckin' in style along the pedestrian-only avenue: crazy locals pandering to their fetishes, visitors exploring their perversions, the majority indulging in its small vices, and all the while the best jazz in the world never stops. Wanna expose yourself to unique cultures? You can't beat the "Cajuns," descendents of French Nova Scotians exiled by the British in 1755, who developed Creole dialect, zydeco music, swampy folklore, and a spicy cuisine. Also worthy of note is Louisiana's African-American culture; best known for its one-time immersion in voodoo. The urban ambience and French tolerance in antebellum south Louisiana combined to produce a literate black aristocracy unlike anything found elsewhere in the South.

Finally, Louisiana isn't called the "Sportsman's Paradise" for nothing. Whether you want duck hunting in the broad uninhabited north woods or fishing in the Gulf of Mexico, this is the place. Rent a spot on a rickety pier somewhere, tie a chicken leg in a net, throw it over and watch for crabs. Despite chemical companies spoiling the strip between Louisiana and Baton Rouge, lovingly called "Cancer Alley" by natives, most of the state is uncivilized and unsullied. An easy wind blows across the bayous and wooded dark hollows, which are covered by sugary magnolias and clinging Spanish moss. Thomas Jefferson struck quite a bargain when he purchased the Louisiana Territory from Napoleon for $15 million in 1803.

Practical Information

Capital: Baton Rouge.

State Travel Office, P.O. Box 94291, Capitol Station, Baton Rouge 70804 (342-7317 or 800-334-8626). Open daily 8am-4pm. **Office of State Parks,** P.O. Box 1111, Baton Rouge 70821. Open Mon.-Fri. 9am-5pm.

Time Zone: Central (1 hr. behind Eastern). **Postal Abbreviation:** LA

Acadiana

In 1755, the English goverment expelled French settlers from their homes in Nova Scotia. Moving down the Atlantic coastline and into the Caribbean, the so-called Acadians still received a hostile reception; Massachusetts, Georgia, and South Carolina made them indentured servants. The Acadians soon realized that their only hope for freedom lay in reaching the French territory of Louisiana and settling on the Gulf Coast. Many of the present-day inhabitants of St. Martin, Lafayette, Iberia, and St. Mary parishes descended from these settlers.

Since the 18th century, many factors have threatened Acadian culture with extinction. Louisiana passed laws in the 1920s forcing Acadian schoolchildren to speak English. The oil boom of the past few decades has also endangered Acadian cultural survival. Oil executives and developers envisioned Lafayette, a center of Acadian life, as the Houston of Louisiana, threatening this small town and its neighbors with mass culture. However, the proud people of southern Louisiana have resisted homogenization, making the state officially bilingual and establishing a state agency to preserve Acadian French in schools and in the media.

Today "Cajun Country" spans the southern portion of the state, from Houma in the east to the Texas border. Mostly bayou and swampland, the unique natural environment here has intertwined with Cajun culture. The music and the cuisine, especially, symbolize the ruggedness of this traditional, family-centered society. Try some crawfish or dance the two-step to a fiddle and an accordion to sample Cajun life.

Lafayette

Lafayette makes a fine base for exploring Acadiana, filled with historical villages and museums of traditional Cajun life. Besides Acadian sites, however, the city has little to offer the tourist. In the 70s and 80s the town centered oil businesses in southern Louisiana, but the drop in crude prices stalled growth.

Opened in April 1990, **Vermilionville**, 1600 Surrey St. (233-4077), is an historic bayou attraction. Full of music, crafts, and food, this re-creation of an Acadian settlement educates as it entertains. (Open Sun.-Thurs. 10am-6pm, Fri.-Sat. 9am-9pm. $8, seniors $6.50, ages 6-18 $5.) A folk life museum of restored 19th-century homes, **Acadian Village**, 200 Greenleaf Rd. (981-2364), 10 mi. from the tourist center, offers another view of Cajun life. Take U.S. 167 north, turn right on Ridge Rd., left on Mouton, and then follow the signs. (Open daily 10am-5pm. $4, seniors $3, students $1.50.) The **Lafayette Museum**, 1122 Lafayette St. (234-2208), contains heirlooms, antiques, and Mardi Gras costumes. (Open Tues.-Sat. 9am-5pm, Sun. 3-5pm. $3, seniors $2, students and kids $1.)

Built on the edge of the Atchafalaya Swamp, Lafayette links up with Baton Rouge via a triumph of modern engineering. The Atchafalaya Freeway is a 32-mi. long bridge over the bayous. Get closer to the elements by embarking upon one of the

Atchafalaya Basin Swamp Tours (228-8567), in the nearby town of Henderson. The captain explains the harvesting of crawfish and the building of the interstate highway on unstable swamp mud. (Tours leave at 10am, 1, 3, and 5pm. Fare $7, kids $4.)

Cajun restaurants with live music and dancing have popped up all over Lafayette, but they tend to be expensive. **Mulates,** 325 Mills Ave., Beaux Bridge, calls itself the most famous Cajun restaurant in the world, and the autographs on the door support its claim. Cajun seafood dinners cost $10-15. (Open Mon.-Sat. 7am-10:30pm, Sun. 11am-11pm. Music noon-2pm and 7:30-10pm.) In downtown Lafayette, visit **Le Café des Artistes,** 537 Jefferson St., a chic gathering place. Menu includes fruit crepes and sandwiches ($3.75-4.25) on French bread with sprouts served on a bed of modern art. (Open Tues.-Fri. 11am-2pm and 5-10pm, Sat. 9am-2pm and 5-11:30pm.) Down the road is **Chris' Poboys,** 631 Jefferson St. (234-1696), which not surprisingly offers po'boys ($4-5) and seafood platters. (Open Mon.-Fri. 11am-9pm.)

Several motels are a $3 cabfare from the bus station. The close **Travelodge Oil Center,** 1101 Pinhook Rd. (234-7402) has large, attractive rooms, cable TV, pastel, and a pool. (Singles $23. Doubles $26.) The **Super 8,** 2224 N. Evangeline Thruway (232-8826), just off I-10, has ample, plain-looking rooms, a pool, and a stunning view of the highway. (Singles $30. Doubles $32.) Other inexpensive chain motels line Evangeline Thruway, including **La Quinta** (233-5610) and **Motel 6,** (233-2055). Avoid motels on Cameron St.; this area is unsafe. If you have extra cash, treat yourself to bed and breakfast at **Til Frere's House,** 1905 Verot School Rd. (984-9347), which has antique-filled rooms, private baths, Turkish towel robes, large breakfasts, complimentary drinks (mint juleps always on hand) and snacks. (Singles $55. Doubles $65. Mention *Let's Go* and you may get a 10% discount.) The closest campground is lakeside **KOA Lafayette** (235-2739), five mi. west of town on I-10 (exit 97), with a complete store and a pool. (Sites $14, a few small cabins $22-25.)

Pick up a copy of *The Times* (available at restaurants and gas stations all over town) to find out about what's going down this week. Considering its size and location, Lafayette has a surprising amount of after-hours entertainment, including the **Cajun Dance,** a world-class concert hall that regularly brings in acts and concerts of national prominence. For a lagniappe of sorts, Lafayette kicks off spring and fall weekends with **Downtown Alive!,** a series of free concerts featuring everything from new wave to Cajun and zydeco. (All concerts Fri. at 5:30pm. Call 268-5566 for info.) The **Festival International de Louisiane** (232-8086) in late April blends the music, visual arts, and cuisine of this region into a francophone tribute to the French influence on southwestern Louisiana.

Lafayette stands at Louisiana's major crossroad. I-10 leads east to New Orleans (130 mi.) and west to Lake Charles (76 mi.); US 90 heads south to New Iberia (20 mi.) and the bayou country; US 167 runs north into central Louisiana. Lafayette also provides a railroad stop for Amtrak's *Sunset Limited,* linking the city with New Orleans (1/day, 3 hr., $26), Houston (1/week, 5 hr., $47), and Los Angeles. The unstaffed station is at 133 E. Grant St., near the bus station; tickets must be purchased in advance through a travel agent. **Greyhound,** 315 Lee Ave. (235-1541), connects Lafayette to New Orleans (7/day, 2½ hr., $19) and Baton Rouge (7/day, 1 hr., $8), as well as to small towns such as New Iberia (2/day, ½ hr., $3). The **Lafayette Bus System,** 400 Dorset (261-8570), runs infrequently and not on Sundays (fare 45¢). You'll need a car to really explore Acadiana and the Gulf Coast bayou country. **Thrifty Rent-a-Car,** 401 E. Pinhook (237-1282), usually has the best deals, though even these aren't so great ($32.75/day, 150 free mi. Must be 21 with major credit card).

The **post office** is at 1105 Moss (232-4800). Lafayette's **ZIP code** is 70501; the **area code** is 318.

New Iberia and Southcentral Louisiana

While other plantations made their fortunes off cotton, most plantations in southern Louisiana grew sugarcane. Today most of these stay in private hands, but **Shadows on the Teche,** 317 E. Main St. (369-6446), is open to the public. A Southern aristocrat saved the crumbling mansion, built in 1831, from neglect after the Civil War. (Open daily 9am-4:30pm. $4, kids $2.)

Seven mi. away is **Avery Island,** on Rte. 329 off Rte. 90, actually a salt dome that resembles an island. Avery houses the world-famous **Tabasco Pepper Sauce** factory, where the McIlhenny family has produced the famous condiment for nearly a century. Guided tours include a sample taste. You may join the cult of Tabasco Sauce lovers. (Open Mon.-Fri. 9-11:45am and 1-3:45pm, Sat. 9-11:45am. Free. 50¢ toll to enter the island.) Nearby lie the **Jungle Gardens** (369-6243), 250 acres developed in the 19th century by E. A. McIlhenny that include waterways, a lovely wisteria arch, camelia gardens, Chinese bamboo, alligators, and an 800-year-old statue of the Buddha. The jungle's sanctuary for herons and egrets helped save the snowy egret from extinction. This elegant bird, once hunted for the long plumes it grows during mating season, now nests in the gardens from February to mid-summer. (Open daily 9am-6pm. $4.50, kids $3.50.)

For a unique look at swamp and bayou wildlife, take an **Airboat Tour** (229-4457) of Lake Fausse Point and the surrounding area. (Tickets $40 for 4 people.)

New Iberia crouches 21 mi. southeast of Lafayette on U.S. 90. **Amtrak** (800-872-7245) serves New Iberia between New Orleans and Lafayette. **Greyhound** (364-8571) pulls into town at 101 Perry St. Buses head to Morgan City ($6), New Orleans ($17), and Lafayette ($3) three times per day.

The **Tourist Information Center** propagandizes at 2690 Center St. (365-1540), at the intersection of Hwy. 14. (Open daily 9am-5pm.) The **post office** is at 817 E. Dale St. (364-4568). The **ZIP code** is 70560; the **area code** is 318.

Wildlife

Much of Acadiana is lush wilderness, subtropical environment of marsh, bottomland hardwoods, and stagnant backwater bayous. You can fish and enjoy the jungle-like terrain about 40 mi. southeast of New Iberia near Bayou Vista. The **Atchafalaya Delta Wildlife Area,** lies at the mouth of the Atchafalaya River in St. Mary Parish. The preserve encompasses bayous, potholes, low and high marsh, and dry ground. Rails, snipes, coot, and gallinules thrive here. Access it by boat launch from Morgan City near the Bayou Boeuf locks. Primitive campsites are available in the area.

The center of **Attakapas Wildlife Area,** in southern St. Martin and Iberia Parishes, lies 20 mi. northwest of Morgan City and 10 mi. northeast of Franklin. Flat swampland composes most of this hauntingly beautiful area, which includes a large amount of raised land used as a refuge by animals during flooding. In Attakapas cypress-tupelo, oak, maple, and hackberry grow on the high ground, and a cornucopia of swamp plants flourish in the wetlands. Squirrel, deer, and rabbit hunting is popular here. The area can be reached by boat; public launches leave from Morgan City on Rte. 70. Watch for signposts. No camping allowed.

Baton Rouge

Until the 1800s, New Orleans was Louisiana's capital, and Baton Rouge was little more than a mud-filled village. But a group of evangelical North Louisiana politicians, concerned that the state government was wallowing in a hotbed of debauchery, stuck a provision in the new state constitution mandating that the state capital be at least 60 mi. from New Orleans. The fun-loving legislators responded by drawing a 60-mi. circle on their state map to find the nearest legal human settlement that could serve as the capital city—and Baton Rouge was born.

Baton Rouge is no longer a rural village. It is caught between two traditions: that of the industrial corridor along the Mississippi River to its southeast and that of the quiet plantation country to its northeast. It is part quiet Southern town: lethargic, family-oriented. It is part cosmopolitan, with a research university, an expanding progressive music scene, and a thriving gay community in Spanish Town. It also sports one of the most fascinating political cultures in the nation. Baton Rouge served as the home of "Kingfisher" Huey P. Long—a Depression-era populist demogogue who until his assassination was considered Franklin D. Roosevelt's biggest political threat. His brother, Uncle Earl, portrayed by Paul Newman in *Blaze*, "governed" the state from a mental asylum for part of his term. One of the more recent governors, Edwin Edwards, was a flamboyant Cajun Democrat twice indicted by Republican federal district attorneys (although never convicted) before his term ended in 1988.

Practical Information

Emergency: 911.

Baton Rouge Convention and Visitors Bureau, 838 North Blvd. (383-1825). Pick up the visitors guide but don't expect too much help from the staff. Open daily 8am-5pm.

Greyhound/Trailways: 1253 Florida Blvd. (343-4891), at 13th St. A 15-min. walk from downtown. Unsafe area at night. To New Orleans (11/day, 2 hr., $13) and Lafayette (6/day, 1 hr., $8). Open 24 hrs.

Public Transport: Capital City Transportation, 336-0821. Main terminal at 22nd and Florida Blvd. Buses run Mon.-Sat. approximately 6:30am-6:30pm. Service to LSU decent, otherwise unreliable and/or infrequent. Fare 75¢, transfers 10¢.

Help Lines: Crisis Intervention/Suicide Prevention Center, 924-3900. Rape Crisis, 383-7273. Both open 24 hrs.

Post Office: 750 Florida Blvd. (381-0713), off River Rd. Open Mon.-Fri. 8:30am-4:30pm, Sat. 9-11am. ZIP code: 70821.

Area Code: 504.

The state capitol sits on the east bank of the river; the city spreads eastward. The heart of downtown, directly south of the capitol, runs until **Government Street.** **Highland Road** leads south from downtown directly into LSU.

Accommodations, Camping, Food, Nightlife, et al.

Most budget accommodations lie outside of town along east-west Florida Blvd., (U.S. 190), or north-south Airline Hwy. (U.S. 61). **Louisiana State University** provides cheap accommodations at their on-campus hotel run out of Pleasant Hall (387-0297). Take bus #7 ("University") from North Blvd. behind the Old State Capitol. The flat rate of $38 for standard rooms covers as many friends as you can fit, comfortably about four people; for more room try the concierge room ($45) or the suite ($55). **The Budgetel Inn,** 10555 Reiger Rd. (291-6600 or 800-428-3438), has welcoming, neat rooms. (Singles $30.95. Doubles $32.95.) The **Alamo Plaza Hotel Courts,** 4243 Florida Blvd. (924-7231), has spacious rooms in the less safe downtown area. Take bus #6 ("Sherwood Forest") east on Florida Blvd. from the Greyhound station. (Singles $22. Doubles $26.) The **KOA Campground,** 7628 Vincent Rd. (664-7281), KOs 12 mi. east of Baton Rouge (Denham Springs exit off I-12). Well-maintained sites include clean facilities and pool. (Sites $12.50/2 people, with hookup $14.)

The most fun places to eat in Baton Rouge are near Louisiana State University (LSU) on **Highland Road. Louie's Café,** 209 W. State, is a 24-hr. grill that has been lauded in *Rolling Stone;* it's famous for its stir-fried vegetable omelettes served anytime (around $4). Right behind Louie's is local favorite **The Bayou,** 124 W. Chimes (346-1765), the site of the bar scene in *sex, lies, and videotape.* You can play free pool 5-8pm and drink select longnecks for 99¢. Downtown, you can't miss the **Frostop Drive-In,** 402 Government, with a giant rootbeer mug spinning on a post outside and a Wurlitzer jukebox spinning platters inside. Try the delicious root beer floats

($1.50) and sandwiches ($2). (Open Mon.-Fri. 9:30am-8:30pm, Sat. 10:30am-8:30pm, Sun. 11am-8pm.) The hippest edition of Baton Rouge nightlife is the **One-gieme Art Bar,** 1109 Highland (393-9335), with art openings and original music ranging from flamenco guitar to experimental rock. (Open Mon.-Sat. 8pm-2am.)

Sights

The most prominent building in Baton Rouge is also the first one you should visit. Huey Long ordered the unique **Louisiana State Capitol** (342-7317), a magnificent modern skyscraper, built in a mere 14 months between 1931 and 1932. The front lobby alone merits a visit, but visitors should also go to the free 27th-floor observation deck. (Open daily 8am-4:30pm.) One of the most interesting in the U.S., the building attests to the power of Long's monumental personality. Look for bullet holes in a back corridor near the plaque indicating his assassination site; to see his burial place, look in front under the statue. The **Old State Capitol,** at River Rd. and North Blvd., an eccentric Gothic Revival castle, offers free tours. (Open Tues.-Sat. 9am-4:30pm.) Just south of downtown, the **Beauregard District** boasts typically ornate antebellum homes. Walk down North Blvd. from the Old State Capitol to the visitor center to take in the beauty of this neighborhood.

Just a block away from the Old State Capitol on River Rd. floats the **Riverside Museum** of the Louisiana Arts and Science Center (344-9463). Climb on the old steam engine and train cars parked next door. The museum also has a good collection of sculpture, photographs, and paintings by contemporary Louisiana artists. (Open Tues.-Fri. 10am-3pm, Sat. 10am-4pm, Sun. 1-4pm. $1.50, seniors, students, and kids 75¢.) The museum runs the **Old Governor's Mansion,** the chief executive's residence from 1930-1963, at North Blvd. and St. Charles St. (Open Sat. 10am-4pm, Sun. 1-4pm. $1.50, seniors, students and kids 75¢.)

Those who don't have a car to visit outlying plantations (see Plantations under New Orleans) can visit the well-restored **Magnolia Mound Plantation,** 2161 Nicholson Dr. (343-4955), the only plantation on the regular bus line. (Open Tues.-Sat. 10am-4pm, Sun. 1-4pm; last tour at 3:30pm. $3.50, seniors $2.50, students $1.50.) The **LSU Rural Life Museum,** 6200 Burden Lane (765-2437), off Perkins Rd., re-creates everyday rural life in pre-industrial Louisiana. The authentically furnished shops, cabins, and storage houses adjoin meticulously kept azalea-filled gardens. (Open Mon.-Fri. 8:30am-4pm. $3, kids $2.)

Tour the harbor in the *Samuel Clemens* steamboat (381-9606), which departs from Florida Blvd. at the river for one-hour cruises. (Tours March-Sept. daily at 10am, noon, and 2pm; Oct.-March Wed.-Sun. at 10am, noon, and 2pm. $5, kids $3.) Open for inspection, the *U.S.S. Kidd* (342-1942), a World War II destroyer, throws tantrums on the river just outside the Louisiana Naval War Memorial Museum. (Open daily 9am-5pm. Ship and museum admission $3.50, kids $2. Ship only $1, kids 50¢.)

Natchitoches

Natchitoches (Nack-a-tish) is *the* prototypical Southern town, with a slow lifestyle and quaint customs best captured in the movie *Steel Magnolias* (which was filmed there). Although not a well-known vacation site outside Louisiana, Natchitoches offers the tourist at least as much as other, more commercialized Southern cities.

The **Melrose Plantation** complex (379-0055), 16 mi. south of town near the intersection of highways 119 and 493, includes the colonial Yucca House and the Congostyle African House in addition to the plantation. Among many authors and historians to reside on the grounds were Erskine Caldwell and Alexander Woolcott, although the most famous former resident probably was folk artist Clementine Hunter, one-time slave-cook for her art-loving owner, "Miss Cammie" Henry. If still in the art history mode, also check out the **Bayou Folk Museum** and the **Kate Cho-**

pin House, long-time home of the author of *The Awakening,* both on Highway 495 near Cloutierville.

The number of former plantations and 18th-century forts along the Cane River is too huge to list, but a number of tour packages are available to help you visit as many of the sights as possible. Contact the Association for the Preservation of Historic Natchitoches (352-8072), Unique Tours of Historic Natchitoches (352-4192), and Tours by Jan (352-2324). Betty Jones at the Natchitoches Parish Tourist Commission (352-8072) will send you a map.

But in all of your sorties into Cane River Country, don't forget to check out Natchitoches itself. Historic Front Street along the river rivals the cobblestone alleys of New Orleans. The town also includes **Northwestern State University** (College Ave.), with its vibrant arts scene centered at the Franklin Arts Center and Louisiana School for Math, Science & the Arts, one of the first state-run boarding high schools for gifted/talented students. Finally, Natchitoches hosts a number of exciting seasonal festivals. The most famous is the **Christmas Lights Festival** in early December, during which an army of Christmas-light sculptures, from Rudolph to nutcrackers, camps along the river bank. The festival climaxes in a parade with celebrities such as Vanna White and a fireworks display. Also worthy of note is the **Folk Festival** in mid-July. Accommodations for either event should be reserved months in advance.

Although numerous cheap fast-food places line "the strip" (Highway 1 South), you might want to splurge a little and dine at Lasyone's Meatpie Kitchen, 622 Second St. (352-3353), famous throughout the South for its spicy meatpies and Southern specialties.

Accommodations are limited during festivals and university graduations, but otherwise they are cheap and plentiful. A few places worth trying include the **El Camino Real** on College Drive, **La Louisianne** on the Strip, or **Super 8 Motel** (352-1700) on Highway 3110 North Bypass. If you demand greater luxury, check the Holiday Inn (357-8281) farther out of town on Highway 3110 South Bypass.

Greyhound services the town from Baton Rouge (4/day, $32, $48 round-trip) as well as from a number of other nearby cities. The **post office** is located at 240 St. Denis (352-2161), **ZIP code** 71458. The **area code** is 318.

N'awlins

New Orleans bounced around between French and Spanish possession before the United States finally grabbed it up, along with the rest of the Louisiana territories. The city's sizable African-American population has also contributed its influences, and the resulting cultural hybrid is unlike anything found elsewhere. African-American jazz, which combined traditional African rhythms with popular brass instruments, has achieved international notoriety. New Orleans-style dishes such as gumbo and jambalaya combine culinary techniques distilled from African and French cooking. Don't try to place the accents; they are a singular combination not found anywhere else in the country. Architectural styles from old Spanish and French to ultra- and post-modern almost rub shoulders downtown.

New Orleans seems Mediterranean or Caribbean in contrast to the more straight-laced Anglo-Saxon cities on the Atlantic Coast. In the 19th century, the red-light district known as "Storyville" flared. Today, New Orleans is still a city that loves to party. The annual climax for the "city that care forgot" is the month-long Mardi Gras celebration held before Ash Wednesday, usually in late February. Anxious to accrue as much sin as spirit and flesh will allow before Lent, locals and countless tourists promenade, shuffle, sing, and swig until midnight of Mardi Gras ("Fat Tuesday") itself.

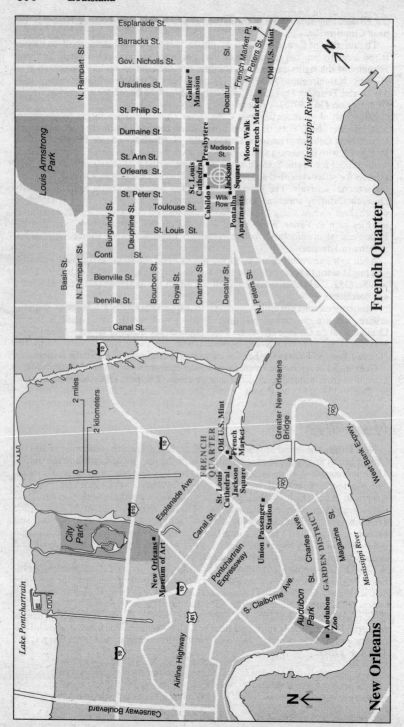

French Quarter

Esplanade St.
Barracks St.
Gov. Nicholls St.
Ursulines St.
St. Philip St.
Dumaine St.
St. Ann St.
Orleans St.
St. Peter St.
Toulouse St.
St. Louis St.
Conti St.
Bienville St.
Iberville St.
Canal St.

N. Rampart St.
Basin St.
Burgundy St.
Dauphine St.
Bourbon St.
Royal St.
Chartres St.
Decatur St.
N. Peters St.

Louis Armstrong Park

Gallier Mansion
Decatur St.
French Market Pl.
N. Peters St.
Old U.S. Mint

St. Louis Cathedral
Presbytere
Madison St.
Moon Walk
French Market
Cabildo
Jackson Square
Wilk Row
Pontalba Apartments

Mississippi River

New Orleans

Lake Pontchartrain
Causeway Boulevard
City Park
New Orleans Museum of Art
Esplanade Ave.
Canal St.
Airline Highway
S. Claiborne Ave.
Pontchartrain Expressway
Union Passenger Station
Charles Ave.
St. Charles Ave.
Magazine St.
Audubon Park
Audubon Zoo
GARDEN DISTRICT
FRENCH QUARTER
Old U.S. Mint
French Market
St. Louis Cathedral
Jackson Square
Greater New Orleans Bridge
West Bank Expwy.
Mississippi River

2 miles
2 kilometers

Practical Information

Emergency: 911.

Visitor Information: To plan your vacation before you leave home, write or call the **Greater New Orleans Tourist and Convention Commission,** 1520 Sugar Bowl Dr., New Orleans, LA 70112 (566-5011), on the main floor of the Superdome. Open Mon.-Fri. 8:30am-5pm. More convenient and very helpful is the **New Orleans/Louisiana Tourist Center,** 529 St. Ann, Jackson Square (566-5031), in the French Quarter. Free city and walking tour maps. Open daily 10am-6pm. **Tourist Information Service,** 525-5000.

Travelers Aid: 846 Barone St. (525-8726), at the YMCA. Assists stranded people by providing temporary shelter, food, and counseling. Open Mon.-Fri. 8am-4pm.

Moisant International Airport (464-0831), 15 mi. west of the city. Served by the major domestic airlines as well as by larger Latin-American carriers. **Louisiana Transit Authority** (737-9611) runs between the airport and downtown at Elk and Tulane every 30-45 min. for $1.10 in exact change. Pick-up in front of Hertz. Airport limousine to downtown hotels $8, cab $18.

Buses and Trains: Union Passenger Terminal, 1001 Loyola Ave., a 10-min. walk to Canal St. via Elk. Terminus for statewide interstate bus and train systems. Open 24 hrs. **Amtrak,** 528-1610 or 800-872-7245. To Memphis (1/day, 8 hr., $69) and Houston (3/week, 8 hr., $67). **Greyhound/Trailways** (525-9371). To: Baton Rouge (2 hr., $13.50, $24.75 round-trip, $9.50/$18 with college ID); Memphis (11 hr., $61, $118 round-trip, $86 student round-trip); Houston (9 hr., $60, $116 round-trip; tickets cheaper if bought a week in advance); and Atlanta ($76, $137 round-trip).

Public Transport: Regional Transit Authority (RTA), Plaza Tower, 101 Dauphin St., 4th floor (569-2700), at Canal St. Bus schedules and transit info. Office open Mon.-Fri. 8:30am-5pm. Phone line provides 24-hr. route information. All buses pass by Canal St., at the edge of the French Quarter. Major buses and streetcars run 24 hrs. Fare 80¢, transfers 10¢, for handicapped and elderly 30¢ and 2¢. 1 and 3-day passes are also available.

Taxi: United Cabs (522-9771). **Checker Yellow Cabs** (943-2411). **Dixie Cabs** (835-CABS). Base fare $1.70, each additional mi. $1.

Car Rental: Budget Car Rental, 1317 Canal (467-2277), plus 6 other locations. $40/day, $25 weekends. 100 free mi. Add $5/day if under 25. Open daily 7:30am-5:30pm. Airport branch only closed 1-5am. Must be 21 with credit card or 25 with cash deposit. Reservations suggested.

Bike Rental: Michael's, 618 Frenchman (945-9505), a few blocks west of the Quarter. $3.50/hr., $13/day. Weekly rates. Open Mon.-Sat. 10am-7pm, Sun. 10am-5pm.

Help Lines: Gay Counseling Line, 522-5815. Usually operates 5-11pm. **Crisis Line,** 523-2673.

Post Office: 701 Loyola Ave. (589-2201), near the Union Passenger Terminal, a 10-min. walk from Canal St. Open Mon.-Fri. 8:30am-4:30pm, Sat. 8:30am-noon. **ZIP code:** 70140.

Area Code: 504.

It's easy to get lost although New Orleans is fairly small. Keep in mind that the main streets of the city follow the curve in the river. There are many one-way streets, and drivers must sometimes make U-turns to cross intersections. The major tourist area is the small **French Quarter (Vieux Carré),** bounded by the Mississippi River, **Canal Street, Esplanade Avenue,** and **Rampart Street.** Streets in the French Quarter follow a grid pattern, and traveling on foot is easy. The **Garden District** is west of downtown. Buses to all parts of the city pass by Canal St. at the edge of the Quarter.

Parts of New Orleans are unsafe, particularly the tenement areas directly to the north of the French Quarter and those directly northwest of Lee Circle. Even the quaint-looking side streets of the Quarter are dangerous at night—stick to busy, well-lit thoroughfares. Take a cab back to your lodgings when returning late at night from the Quarter.

Accommodations

Finding inexpensive yet decent accommodations in the French Quarter is as difficult as finding a sober citizen on Mardi Gras. Try one of the few inexpensive **bed and breakfasts** around the Garden District, the best of which are listed below. Dormitory rooms with semi-private baths are available at **Loyola University** (865-3735), from June to August ($20/person).

About the only way to get accommodations for Mardi Gras is to reserve them a year in advance. **Jazzfest** in late April also makes budget rooms scarce.

Marquette House New Orleans International Hostel (AYH), 2253 Carondelet St. (523-3014), is an antebellum house near the Garden District only minutes by streetcar to the Quarter. Usually teems with travelers. Lounge, dining room, kitchen. Lockers available. Check-in 7:30am-1pm and 3-11pm. $10, nonmembers $13. Private doubles $27/$30. Private apartments $39. Linen $2. Key deposit $5. Reservation for Mardi Gras must be paid in full in advance; include self-addressed, stamped envelope.

India House, 124 S. Lopez (821-1904), just off the French Quarter—bus to the Quarter passes the front door. Concerned European managers are working hard to build up a name for this independent hostel, which includes kitchen appliances, safety-deposit facilities, rooms with A/C, free parking, and cable TV. Will pick up groups of three or more from the airport or bus station for free (smaller groups $5). No inconvenient curfews or alcohol regulations. Check-in round the clock. The $10 fee ($15 during Mardi Gras season) includes linens.

Longpre House (AAIYH), 1926 Prytania St. (581-4540), a block off the streetcar route, five minutes from the Quarter, attracts travelers because of its relaxed atmosphere in a 150-year-old house. Check-in 8am-10pm. Dorm rooms $10/person, nonmembers $12. Singles $30. Doubles $35.

St. Charles Guest House, 1748 Prytania St. (523-6556), in a serene neighborhood near the Garden District and St. Charles streetcar. Beautiful house with a plant-covered patio and a pool. Backpackers' singles $25 with shared bath $38, with private bath $42. Doubles $48, with shared bath $42. 2 double beds $55-60. Continental breakfast included. Ask about $12.50 student rate.

Old World Inn, 1330 Prytania St. (566-1330), 1 block from the St. Charles streetcar. Multi-colored carpeting and walls covered with paintings create a slightly tacky but homey atmosphere. Singles from $27.50. Doubles from $39. One quint $75. Complimentary juice and coffee in the morning.

YMCA, 936 St. Charles Ave. (586-9622), on Lee Circle. Drab but sufficient rooms in a large building complex at the heart of downtown. For men and women. Singles $26. Doubles $31.

LaSalle Hotel, 1113 Canal St. (523-5831 or 800-521-9450), 4 blocks east of Bourbon St. downtown. Elegant lobby with coffee around the clock on an antique sideboard. Free movies. Singles $27, with bath $41. Doubles $30, with bath $46. Reservations recommended.

Rose Inn, 3522 Tulane Ave. (484-7611), exit gate 232 off I-10, 4 blocks from S. Carrollton. Perfectly located for drivers, public bus stops in front of inn. Pool. Extra charge for phone. Singles $22, doubles $28.

Camping

The several campgrounds near New Orleans are tough to reach via public transportation, which is unavailable or infrequent at some sites. Try to enjoy Louisiana's beautiful forests, lakes, and bayous anyway, if only to escape the French Quarter crowds. Bring insect repellent; the mosquitos are vicious. Check out the **Golden Pelican passes** available at state parks, which allow you to stay in state campgrounds for $6 per night. ($30 for Louisianians, $50 for others.)

Bayou Segnette State Park, 7777 Westbank Expressway (436-1107). RTA bus transport available. Enchanting park. Cabins on the bayou $50 for up to 8 people. Campsites with water, electricity $12.

KOA West, 219 S. Starrett, River Ridge 70123 (467-1792), off highway I-10. RTA bus transport available. Pool, laundry facilities. Full-hookup sites $25.95/2 people.

St. Bernard State Park, P.O. Box 534, Violet 70092 (682-2101), 18 mi. southeast of New Orleans. Take I-10 to Rte. 47 south and go left on Rte. 39 through Violet and Poydras. Nearest public transport to New Orleans ½ mi. away. Pool. Registration until 10pm. Sites $12, seniors $7.

Parc d'Orleans II, 10910 Chef Menteur Hwy. (242-6176; 800-535-2598 outside LA), 3 mi. east of the junction of I-10 and U.S. 90 (Chef Menteur Hwy.). Near public transport into the city. Pool, laundry facilities. Sites from $13.

Fontainebleau State Park, P.O. Box 152, Mandeville 70448 (626-8052), southeast of Mandeville on U.S. 190, on the shores of Lake Ponchartrain. Farthest from New Orleans of all the campgrounds. Sites $9.

Food

In an ancient Francophone cant, New Orleans means "good food." You will find more restaurants per capita in New Orleans than in any city except Paris. Acadian refugees, Spaniards, Italians, and African and Native Americans have all contributed to the hot, spicy, cajun culinary style. Jambalaya (rice with meat, vegetables, sometimes fish or shrimp, and a piquant red pepper sauce) examplifies the hearty fare that really packs a punch. Creole food has a similar heritage but is traditionally more delicate; try shrimp *etouffé* as an example. A Southern breakfast of grits, eggs, bacon, and corn bread will satisfy even the biggest of eaters. For lunch, try a seafood po'boy (a french-bread sandwich filled with fried oysters or shrimp) or red beans and rice. Also sample the tiny crawfish, the southern freshwater cousin of the Maine lobster.

Cool off in the summer months with a "snowball" (sno-cone) from **Hansen's Snow-Blitz Sweet Shop,** 4801 Tchoupitoulas St. (891-9788). Expect a line. (Open Tues.-Fri. and Sun. 3-9pm.) Indulge with Creole pralines; some of the best and cheapest bake at **Laura's Candies,** 600 Conti and 155 Royal St. (525-3880; open daily 9am-6pm on Conti; 8am-8pm on Royal). The **French Market,** between Decatur and N. Peters St. on the east side of the French Quarter, sells fresh vegetables. The grocery stores on Decatur St. have the rest of the fixings you'll need for a picnic.

French Quarter

Acme Oyster House, 724 Iberville (522-5973). Slurp fresh oysters shucked before your eyes (6 for $3.50, 12 for $6) or sit at the red checkered tables for a good ol' po'boy. Open Mon.-Sat. 11am-10pm, Sun. noon-7pm.

Quarter Scene Restaurant, 900 Dumaine (522-6533). This cornerside café serves delicious salads and seafood and pasta entrees ($6-13). A tasty surprise is the *Dumaine* ($4), a peanut butter and banana sandwich topped with nuts and honey. Open 24 hrs., except Tues. closes at 11:30 pm.

Croissant d'Or, 617 Ursuline St (524-4663). In a historic building that was the first ice cream parlor in New Orleans. Delicious, reasonably-priced French pastries that won't chip your teeth. Open daily 7am-5pm.

Mama Rosa's, 616 N. Rampart (523-5546), on the edge of the French Quarter. The best pizza in New Orleans (10-in. cheese $7.25). Also serves heaping salads and gumbo ($3-5). Open Tues.-Thurs. 10:30am-10:30pm, Fri.-Sun. 10:30am-11:30pm.

Café du Monde, French Market at the intersection of Decatur and Saint Ann St (587-0835). A people-watching paradise since the 1860s. Drink *café au lait* and down perfectly prepared hot *beignets* with powdered sugar (3 for 75¢). Open 24 hrs.

Outside the Quarter

Mother's Restaurant, 401 Poydras (523-9656), 4 blocks north of Bourbon St. Yo mama has been serving up unparalleled crawfish *etouffé* ($5.25) and seafood po'boys to locals for almost half a century. Entrees from $4.25. Open Mon.-Sat. 5am-10pm, Sun. 7am-10pm.

Camellia Grill, 626 S. Carrollton Ave. (866-9573). Take the St. Charles streetcar away from the Quarter to the Tulane area. One of the finest diners in America, complete with friendly napkins and cloth servers, or vice-versa. Try the chef's special omelette ($5.50) or partake of the amazing pecan pie. Expect a wait on weekend mornings. Open Sun.-Wed. 8am-1am, Thurs.-Sat. 8am-2am.

Domilise's, 5240 Annunciation (899-9126). Also uptown. This neighborhood restaurant serves the best po'boys in New Orleans, huge and cheap (around $3.50). Open Mon.-Fri. 9am-7pm, Sat. 10am-7pm.

Franky and Johnny's, 321 Arabella (899-9146), southwest of downtown towards Tulane off Tchoupitoulas. Good seafood and po'boys served in a fun and lively atmosphere. Try the turtle soup ($4). Open Mon.-Thurs. 11am-11pm, Fri.-Sat. 11am-mid., Sun. 11am-10pm.

Bluebird Café, 3625 Prytania St. (895-7166). Delicious healthy sandwiches (around $3) and hearty Southern breakfasts. Open Mon.-Fri. 7am-3pm, Sat.-Sun. 8am-3pm.

Cedars Restaurant, 2559 Metairie Rd. (831-4535). Super-generous Lebanese food home-cooked by a friendly recently-immigrated family. Try the huge serving of grape leaves ($5.95), or try everything with the combo plate ($6.50). Open daily 10:30am-2:30pm and 5-9:30pm.

Mais Oui, 5908 Magazine Ave (897-1540). Home cooking at its best. But yes! Delicious corn bread and gumbo. Entrees run from $5-8 and the menu changes daily. Bring your own wine. Open Mon.-Fri. 11:30am-2:45pm and 5:30-8:45pm, Sat. 5:30-8:45pm.

All Natural, 5517 Magazine St. (891-2651). Mostly a take-out health food store, but tables await outside. Great sandwiches. Probably the only place in the world serving vegetarian Jambalaya ($5 with salad). Open Mon.-Fri. 10am-7pm, Sat. 9am-7pm, Sun. 10am-5pm.

Sights

French Quarter

Allow yourself at least a full day to take in the Quarter at leisure. The oldest section of the city, it is justly famous for its ornate wrought-iron balconies, French architecture, and joyous atmosphere. Known as the **Vieux Carré,** meaning Old Square, the historic district of New Orleans offers interesting used book and record stores, museums, and shops that pawn off ceramic masks and cheap T-shirts to innocent tourists. There's a large gay community here; check out local newsletters *Impact* and *Ambush* for more information on gay events and nightlife. Walk through the residential section down **Dumaine Street** toward **Rampart Street** to escape the more crowded area near the river. Stop in at a neighborhood bar: tourists are taken in stride here, and you should feel welcome.

Jackson Square is the heart of the Quarter. Centered around a bronze equestrian statue of General Andrew Jackson, the victor of the Battle of New Orleans, the square boogies with artists, mimes, musicians, and magicians. Across the street, the **Moonwalk** offers a scenic view of the river and shipping wharves. The **Louisiana State Museum** encompasses four different buildings, three of which (the **Cabildo, Presbytère,** and **1850 House**) are in Jackson Square. They contain artifacts, papers, and other changing exhibits on the history of Louisiana and New Orleans. The fourth, the **Old U.S. Mint,** 400 Esplanade, lies outside the Quarter, housing interesting collections on the history of African Americans, jazz, and Mardi Gras. All buildings except for the Cabildo are open for touring; call 568-6968 for info on any of them. (All Wed.-Sun. 10am-5pm. $3, seniors and students $1.50, under 12 free.)

The rich cultural history of the French Quarter has made it a National Historical Park, and free tours are given by the **Jean Lafitte National Historical Park,** 916-918 North Peters (589-2636), located in the back section of the French Market at Decatur and Saint Phillip St. The National Park Service also conducts a "City of the Dead" tour of local cemeteries (reservations required). These unique burial grounds, which Dennis Hopper and Peter Fonda in the film *Easy Rider* found psychedelic, are accessible to anyone. Just wander into **St. Louis Cemetery #1** on the corner of Basin and Conti St. at the north of the French Quarter. The elaborate above-ground tombs which crowd the yard date back to 1789. Be careful here, however; ghosts won't bother you, but other shady characters might.

Back in the Quarter, several historical homes open their doors to the public. One of the most interesting is the **Hermann-Grima House,** 820 Saint Louis St. (525-5661; tours every ½ hr.; open Mon.-Sat. 10am-3:30pm; $3.50, seniors $2.50, students $1.50). Creole cooking demonstrations are offered from October through May on Thursdays. The **Gallier House,** 1132 Royal St. (523-6722; see Museums below) is considered one of the best small museums in the country. And no wonder: visitors are given free refreshments after the tours.

Outside the Quarter

The French Quarter is certainly not the only interesting aspect of New Orleans. In the southernmost corner of the Quarter at the "foot of Canal St." where the riverboats dock, is the **World Trade Center,** the **Old Customs House,** and **Riverwalk,** a multi-million dollar conglomeration of overpriced shops overlooking the port. You can take the **Canal St. Ferry** to Algiers Point until about 9pm for a 25-minute view of the Mississippi River (free). For a blimp's-eye view of the city, take the elevator up to the 31st floor observation deck of the **World Trade Center,** #2 Canal St. (Open Mon.-Fri. 10am-1am, Sat. 11am-2am, Sun. 4pm-mid.)

The **Aquarium of the Americas** (861-2537) lies across from the World Trade Center, directly on the river. The Aquarium holds over a million gallons of water and reproduces underwater environments of our scaly friends from North, Central, and South America. Check out the famous piranha, almost banned by the Louisiana Legislature because it might escape into the Mississippi, breed, and eat up all the naughty children. ($8, seniors $6.25, kids $4.25. Open daily 9:30am-9pm.)

Also relatively new in the downtown area, the **Warehouse Arts District,** on Julia St. between Commerce and Baronne, contains historic architecture and contemporary art galleries housed in revitalized warehouse buildings. Exhibits range from Southern folk art to experimental sculpture. Maps of the area are available in each gallery. Be sure to check out the **Contemporary Arts Center,** 900 Camp St. (523-1216), an old brick building with a modern glass and chrome facade. The exhibits range from neat to awesome, but you always can check out the amazing artsy architectural flourishes within.

Many culturally diverse attractions of New Orleans lie outside downtown. Though the streetcar named "Desire" was derailed long ago, you can take the **St. Charles Street Car** to the west of the French Quarter to view some of the city's finest buildings, including the elegant, mint-condition 19th-century homes along **Saint Charles Avenue.** This old-fashioned train takes you through some of New Orleans's most beautiful neighborhoods at a leisurely pace for a mere 60¢. Be sure to disembark at the **Garden District,** an opulent neighborhood between Jackson and Louisiana Ave. The legacies of French, Italian, Spanish, and American architecture create an extraordinary combination of magnificent structures, rich colors, demascene ironworks, and of course, exquisite gardens. Many stand several feet above the ground as protection from the swamp on which New Orleans was built. The wet foundation of the city even troubles the dead—all the city's cemeteries must be elevated to let the deceased rest in peace above water. The Jean Lafitte National Historical Park Service (see French Quarter Sights above) leads a daily walking tour of this district. You can also pick up a copy of a self-guided tour at their office.

The St. Charles Street Car runs all the way to **Audubon Park,** across from Tulane University. Designed by the same architects who planned Central Park in New York City, Audubon contains lagoons, statues, stables, and the delightful **Audubon Zoo** (861-2537) with its re-created Louisiana swamp, alligators and all. A free museum shuttle glides from the Audubon Park entrance (streetcar stop #36) to the zoo. (Zoo open Mon.-Fri. 9:30am-5pm, Sat.-Sun. 9:30am-6pm. $7, seniors and kids $3.25.) The steamboat **John Audubon** shuttles between Canal Street and the zoo (10am-5pm, fare $23, $11.75 kids). The *Cotton Blossom* (586-8777) sails on five-hour bayou cruises ($13.75, kids $7, seniors $11).

You can find quite a bit of nature with a 10 minute drive north of the Quarter, in **City Park,** at the corner of City Park Ave and Marconie Dr. (482-4888), accessible by the Esplanade or City Park bus. This 1500-acre park is one of the five largest city parks in the U.S.—even bigger than New York City's Central Park. Besides the **Museum of Art** (see Museums below), it contains a botanical garden, golf courses, tennis courts, 800-year-old oak trees, lagoons, and a miniature train.

One of the most unique sights near New Orleans, the coastal wetlands that line Lake Salvador, make up another segment of the Jean Lafitte National Historical Park called the **Barataria Unit** (589-2330). Unfortunately, the park can only be reached with a car, but the free park service swamp tours almost warrant renting one. The park is off the West Bank Expressway across the Mississippi River down Barataria Blvd. (Hwy. 45).

A trip to Louisiana is not complete without seeing its mysterious bayous or "sleeping waters." **Riverboat cruises** offer swamp tours and other water journeys.

Those with spare time and money may want to jump aboard one of the **The Cajun Queen** (524-0814) cruises (2/per day, 2 hr., $13, kids $5). The affiliated **Creole Queen** (524-0814) gives an anecdotal, if not royal, history of New Orleans, Cajun, and Creole life during its five-hour cruise ($10, kids $6). Also available are tours of bayou country and the Beauregard Plantation aboard **The Voyageur** (523-5555). Tours leave the ferry landing at the foot of Canal St. daily at 10am and return around 3pm. The morning cruise is longer than the evening's. (Morning cruise $11.50, evening $7.50, kids 50% off, under 6 free).

Museums

Gallier House Museum, 1118-1132 Royal St., French Quarter (523-6722). This elegant restored residence brings alive the taste and lifestyle of mid-19th century New Orleans. Tours every ½ hr., last tour at 4pm. Open Mon.-Sat. 10am-4:30pm. $4, seniors and students $3, kids $2.25.

New Orleans Historic Voodoo Museum, 724 Dumaine (523-7685). Small French Quarter museum conjures occult displays centering around New Orleans voodoo queen Marie Laveau. Not for the faint-hearted. Buy *gris-gris,* a specially blessed good luck pouch, available in the gift shop. Open daily 10am-dusk. $5, seniors and students $4, kids $3.

Musée Conti Wax Museum, 917 Conti St. (525-2605). One of the world's finest houses of wax. The voodoo display and haunted dungeon are perennial favorites. Open daily 10am-5pm except during Mardi Gras. $5, under 17 $3, seniors $4.50.

New Orleans Museum of Art, City Park (488-2631). Take the Esplanade bus from Canal and Rampart. Small collection of local decorative arts, opulent works by the jeweler Fabergé, and a strong collection of French paintings including works by Degas. Open Tues.-Sun. 10am-5pm. $4, seniors and kids $2.

Confederate Museum, 929 Camp St. (523-4522). An extensive collection of Civil War records and artifacts. Located just west of Lee Circle, in an ivy-covered stone building. Open Mon.-Sat. 10am-4pm. $3, seniors $2, kids 50¢.

Louisiana Nature and Science Center, 11000 Lake Forest Blvd. (246-5672), in Joe Brown Memorial Park. Hard to reach without a car, but a wonderful escape from the frivolity of the French Quarter. Trail walks, exhibits, planetarium shows, laser shows, and 86 acres of natural wildlife preserve. Open Mon.-Fri. 9am-5pm ($2, seniors and kids $1), Sat.-Sun. noon-5pm ($3, seniors and kids $2).

Entertainment and Nightlife

On any night of the week, at any time of year, multitudes of people join the constant festival of the French Quarter. After exploring the more traditional jazz, blues, and brass sound of the Quarter, assay the rest of the city for less tourist-oriented bands playing to a more local clientele. Check *OffBeat* for maps of the clubs; try *Gambit,* the free weekly entertainment newspaper, or the Friday edition of the Times-Picayune's entertainment guide "Lagniappe" to find out who's playing where.

Traditional New Orleans jazz, born here at the turn of the century in Armstrong Park, can still be enjoyed at tiny, dimly lit, historic **Preservation Hall,** 726 Saint Peter St. (523-8939). If you don't arrive before the doors open, be prepared for a lengthy wait in line, poor visibility and sweaty standing-room only. ($3. Beverages not sold, although you can bring your own soft drinks. Doors open at 8pm; music begins at 8:30pm and goes on until mid.)

Keep your ears open for **Cajun** and **zydeco** bands, a local specialty. Using accordions, washboards, triangles and drums, they perform hot dance tunes (to which locals expertly two-step) and exuberantly sappy waltzes. Their traditional fare is the *fais do-do,* a lengthy, wonderfully sweaty dance. Anyone who thinks couple-dancing went out in the 50s should try one of these; just grab a partner and throw yourself into the rhythm. The locally based **Radiators** do it up real spicy.

The annual **New Orleans Jazz Festival** (522-4786), held at the fairgrounds in late April, features music played simultaneously on six stages. The entertainment also includes a Cajun food and crafts festival. Though exhilaratingly fun, the festival grows more zoo-like each year. Book a room early.

French Quarter

New Orleans bars stay open late, and few bars adhere to a strict schedule or entrance policy. In general, they open around 11am and close around 3am. Most bars in the area are very expensive, charging $3-5 for drinks. Yet on most blocks, you can find cheap draft beer and "Hurricanes," sweet drinks made of juice and rum; visitors can totter around the streets and listen to great music without going broke.

The Napoleon House, 500 Chartres St. (524-9752), is one of the world's great watering holes. Located on the ground floor of the Old Girod House, built as an exile home for Napoleon in a plan to spirit him away from St. Helena. The "Avatar Ambrosia" is delicious, especially when chased with Dixie beer. Food served. Open Mon.-Fri. until 1am, Sat.-Sun. until 2am.

The Absinthe Bar, 400 Bourbon St. (525-8108). Reasonably-priced drinks for the French Quarter, with a blues band sometimes led by Bryan Lee. Has irrigated the likes of Mark Twain, Franklin D. Roosevelt, the Rolling Stones, and Humphrey Bogart. Open Sun.-Thurs. 5:30pm-2am, Fri.-Sat. 5:30pm-3am.

Pat O'Brien's, 718 Saint Peter St. (525-4823). The busiest bar in the French Quarter, bursting with happy tourists. You can listen to the pianos in one room, mix with local students in another, or lounge beneath huge fans near a fountain in the courtyard. Home of the original Hurricane; purchase your first in a souvenir glass ($6). Open daily. 10am-5am.

Bourbon Pub/Parade, 801 Bourbon St. (529-2107). This gay dance bar sponsors a "Tea dance" on Sun. with all the beer you can drink for $5-10. Open 24 hrs. Dancing nightly 9pm-4am.

Old Absinthe House, 240 Bourbon St. (523-3181). The marble absinthe fountain inside has been dry since absinthe was outlawed. The Absinthe Frappe is a reinvention of the infamous drink with anisette or Pernod liqueur ($4.50). Food served. Reputed to be the oldest bar in the U.S. Open daily 9:30am-2am.

Storyville Jazz Hall, 1104 Decatur St. (525-8199). This large music hall opens onto the street and hosts a variety of bands from Southern metal to cool jazz. Generally a concert hall; call for times and ticket information.

Outside the Quarter

Many great bars frolic outside the French Quarter—those below are grouped according to nearby landmarks.

Snug Harbor, 626 Frenchman St. (949-0696), just east of the Quarter near Decatur. Blues vocalists Charmaine Neville and Amasa Miller sing here regularly, giving 2 shows/night. Ellis Marsalis also performs here. The cover is no bargain ($8-15), but Mon. evening with Ms. Neville is worth $8. You can also hear, but not see, the soulful music from the bar in the front room. Food served. Open daily 11am-3am.

Tipitina's, 501 Napoleon Ave. (897-3943 concert line; 895-8477 regular line). This locally renowned establishment attracts the best local bands and even some big names. Favorite bar of late jazz pianist and scholar Professor Longhair; his bust now graces the front hall. Though the prof's pedagogy is no longer, the club books a wide variety of music. Best to call ahead for times and prices. Cover $3-10.

Michaul's, 701 Magazine St. (522-5517), at Girnod. A huge floor for Cajun dancing; they will even teach you how. Open with music Mon.-Fri. 6-11pm, Sat. 6pm-mid.

Maple Leaf Bar, 8316 Oak St. (866-5323), near Tulane University. The best local dance bar offers zydeco and Cajun music; everyone does the two-step. Poetry readings Sun. at 3pm. The party begins Sun.-Thurs. at 10pm, Fri.-Sat. at 10:30pm. Cover $3-5.

Muddy Water's, 8301 Oak St. (966-7174), near Tulane. Live music every night, mostly blues. Serves food and extracts a small cover. Open Mon.-Thurs. 3pm-4am, Fri.-Sun. noon-6am.

The F&M Patio Bar, 4841 Tchoupitoulas (895-6784). Where all the yuppie uptowners go for late-night fun. Pool tables, juke boxes, and a patio bar round out the country-club accoutrements. Starts rocking around 1am and rolls into the morning. Open 1pm-until.

St. Charles Tavern, 1433 St. Charles Ave. (523-9823). Have a blast at this neighborhood gathering spot, frequented by cops and cabbies. Salad bar ($3.45) and pizza ($3). Open 24 hrs.

Plantations

River Road, a winding street that follows the Mississippi River, holds several preserved plantations from the 19th century. Pick up a copy of *Great River Road Plantation Parade: A River of Riches* at the New Orleans or Baton Rouge visitor centers for a good map and descriptions of the houses. Also free and frequent ferries cross the Mississippi at Plaquemines, White Castle, and between Lutcher and Vacherie. A tour of all the plantations would be quite expensive. Those below are listed in order from New Orleans to Baton Rouge.

San Francisco Plantation House, Rte. 44 (535-2341), 2 mi. north of Reserve, 23 mi. from New Orleans on the north bank of the Mississippi. Beautifully restored plantation built in 1856. Galleried in the old Creole style with the main living room on the 2nd floor. Exterior painted 3 different colors with many colorfully decorated ceilings. (Open daily 10am-4pm. $5.50, kids $2.50.)

Houmas House, River Rd., Burnside (473-7841), just over halfway to Baton Rouge on the northern bank of the Mississippi. Setting for the movie **Hush, Hush, Sweet Charlotte,** starring Bette Davis and Olivia DeHavilland. Built in 2 sections: the rear constructed in the last quarter of the 18th century; the Greek Revival mansion in front in 1840. Beautiful gardens and furnishings. Open Feb.-Oct. daily 10am-5pm; Nov.-Jan. 10am-4pm. $5, students $3, kids $2.

Nottoway, Rte. 405 (545-2730), between Bayou Goula and White Castle, 20 mi. south of Baton Rouge on the southern bank of the Mississippi. Largest plantation home in the South often called the "White Castle of Louisiana." An incredible 64-room mansion with 22 columns, a large ballroom, and a 3-story stairway. The first choice of David O. Selznick for filming *Gone with the Wind,* but the owners didn't give a damn and simply wouldn't allow it. Open daily 9am-5pm. Admission and 1-hr. guided tour $8, kids $3.

MAINE

A sprawling evergreen expanse pocked with lakes, swollen with mountains, and defined by a tattered shore, Maine extrudes defiantly from the neat stack of New England states below. The Maine "Downeaster" is known for reticent humor, rugged pragmatism, and disdain for urban pretension. Few of the regular urban refugees, including President Bush, who keeps a house in Kennebunkport, are dissuaded from swathing themselves in flannel and denim and adopting the Downeaster attitude as their own.

The state lives by its waters. Fishers along the coast support a crucial leg of the state's economy, and fresh-water fishing is a Mainestream sport. The rapids of the Allagash Waterway challenge canoeists, and the remote backwood lakes are perfect for hikers, bicyclists, and campers.

There's more to Maine than its main. Bangor's notoriety has increased in recent years with the terrifying popularity of horrific (but eloquent) native Stephen King. And with the help of civic renewal and neighboring colleges Bowdoin, Bates, and Colby, Portland has buttressed its reputation as a decent cultural center.

Practical Information

Capital: Augusta.

Maine Publicity Bureau, 97 Winthrop St., Hallowell 04347 (289-2423). **Bureau of Parks and Recreation,** State House Station #22 (1st floor Harlow Bldg.), Augusta 04333 (289-3821). **Maine Forest Service,** Bureau of Forestry, State House Station #22 (2nd floor Harlow Bldg.), Augusta 04333 (289-2791). All 3 agencies open Mon.-Fri. 8am-5pm.

Time Zone: Eastern. **Postal Abbreviation:** ME

Bangor

Bangor has fallen from its former glory as the nation's largest lumber port. But the city has rebuilt its reputation by becoming the transportation hub of the northeastern wilds, captivating almost all travelers who pass through on their way to the nether regions of Maine.

Practical Information

Emergency: 911.

Visitor Information: Bangor Chamber of Commerce, 519 Main St. (947-0307). City maps, local accommodation and restaurant lists, and brochures detailing almost every activity, sight, lodging, and eatery in the city. (Open mid-May to mid-Oct. daily 8am-6pm.)

Greyhound/Trailways, 158 Main St. (945-3000), near downtown. The northernmost point on the line's eastern route. Three buses daily to Boston ($50) and New York ($91). Open daily 8am-5pm. From the same terminal, **Cyr Bus Line** runs once daily up to Presque Isle ($23), and **SMT** departs daily to Saint John, NB ($20) and Canadian connections.

Public Transport: The Bus (947-0536) runs through the city proper, as well as Brewer, Orono, Old Town, and other suburbs. Fare 60¢-$1.25. Efficient; stops at 5pm.

Help Lines: Rape Response, 989-5678. **Spruce Run Hotline,** 947-0496. For battered women.

Post Office: 202 Harlow Rd. (941-2016). Open Mon.-Fri. 7:30am-5pm, Sat. 8am-noon. **Zip code:** 04407.

Area Code: 207.

Bangor has a population of only 34,000, excluding motorists. I-95 runs north-south through the city; about half-a-dozen minor highways also meet there, including Rte. 1A which runs south to Penobscot Bay and east to Mt. Desert Island. The Penobscot River runs parallel to I-95 and includes a **salmon pool.** You'll know you're in the city when you see a 31-ft.-tall statue of Paul Bunyan dwarfing Main St.—a celebration of the city's logging past.

Accommodations, Camping and Food

Highway culture dominates in lodging and food; Bangor specializes in motels with rooms in the $50-60 range. The **Riverview Motel,** 810 State St. (947-0125), offers clean rooms with a lovely view. (Singles $36-48. Doubles $48-55. Rates higher July-Aug.) The **Budget Traveler,** 327 Odlin Rd. (945-0111), sits near exit 45B at I-95 and Rte. 2, is decorated with groovy earth tones, blond wood, and furnitured with buffed corners—totally 70s. (Singles $36-45. Doubles $47-49. Breakfast included weekdays.) The **Scottish Inn** (945-2934) 1476 Hammond St., one mi. west of I-95, inflicts psychedelic bedspreads for even lower rates. (Singles $32-36.50. Doubles $38-42.) Quads with 2 double beds $48.50.) Your cheapest option is camping, but the grounds here are pretty suburban. **Pleasant Hill Campground** (848-5127 or 617-664-5057) lies near town on Rte. 222 and offers swimming, laundry, and free showers. (Sites $11, with hookup $15. $3 per additional person. Reservations suggested.)

You can find a few cafés and coffee shops downtown, but many of the restaurants are auto-spawned. An exception is **The Bagel Shop,** on 1 Main St. (947-1654). This sprawling deli, rumored to be the only kosher restaurant in northern New England, is something of a cultural center. In winter, jazz jams every Sunday at 3pm. Enjoy homemade bagels with blueberry cream cheese ($1.65) or a sandwich ($3.50-5). (Open Mon.-Thurs. 6am-6pm, Fri. 6am-5:30pm, Sun. 6am-2pm. Cover charge Sun. $5.) Don't let the name of **Nicky's Drive-In Ice Cream Parlor,** on 957 Union St., fool you; it has plenty of seats as well as chicken dinners ($4.50) and old-fashioned sundaes ($2.25). (Open daily 6am-10pm.) Stop at the **West Side Restaurant** (947-0030) for a cheap breakfast on your way down Rte. 2. (Open Mon. 6am-2pm, Tues.-Fri. 6am-7pm, Sat. 7am-7pm.)

Sights and Activities

Bangor takes its role as the cultural center of backwoods Maine very seriously. The **University of Maine** in nearby Orono (581-1110), the main campus, has an extroverted center for the performing arts (581-1755) and a museum of Latin- and Native American art (581-1901). The **Penobscot Theatre**, 183 Main St. (942-3333), performs contemporary and classic drama from October through March and sponsors high school and children's theater in the summer. (Box office open Mon.-Fri. 9am-4:30pm.) The **Robinson Ballet Company**, 107 Union St. (942-1990) frequently shakes a leg with the **Bangor Symphony Orchestra**, 166 Union St. (942-5555). The orchestra performs in the Isaac Farrar Mansion. (Tickets $10-12.) The **Bangor Opera House**, 131 Main St. (947-0200), produces local shows.

Forever contrite about the 1968 Urban Renewal program that destroyed landmarks such as the old train station, Bangor tenaciously protects its eight remaining historic districts. The **Bangor Historical Society**, housed in the 1836 Thomas A. Hill House at 159 Union St. (942-5766), provides maps for self-guided walking tours. (Open year-round Tues.-Fri. noon-4pm. $2, kids 50¢.) Across the street visit the beautiful **Isaac Farrar Mansion**, 166 Union St. (941-2808), built in 1845 and apparently haunted by the ghost of a distraught governess. (Open Mon.-Fri. 9am-4pm. $1.)

In late July the **Bangor State Fair**, held at Bass Park off Main St., includes a statewide carnival and agricultural fair. Bass Park (942-9000) sponsors civic events and oversees the auditorium, civic center, and park. Harness racing takes place here from June through August.

Inland Maine

Northeast from the White Mountains of New Hampshire to Presque Isle lies the largest U.S. wilderness area east of the Mississippi River—miles of splendid, forested mountains dotted with hundreds of lakes, disturbed only by an occasional logger, canoeist, or angler. Huge paper companies own the few roads through the region, along with most of the land. By agreement with the state, nearly all roads remain public, some for a small fee. Pull to the side of the road when you see loaded logging trucks approach.

Baxter State Park and the Allagash

Mount Katahdin, "Greatest Mountain" in local Native American dialect, looms as the northern terminus of the **Appalachian Trail**, the ancient 2,020-mi. following the Appalachian ridge from Georgia to Maine. The Maine portion, the most rugged and remote, at one point meanders 100 mi. without crossing any public roads or villages. Ponds and streams support a large moose population and a decreasing number of bears.

The closest town to the park is **Millinocket**, home of the Great Northern Paper Co. and the largest producer of newsprint in the U.S. Before entering the park, stock up on food and get a complete list of trails with detailed accompanying maps at the **Baxter State Park Headquarters**, 64 Balsam Dr., Millinocket 04462 (723-5140). (Open daily 8am-5pm.)

The park's main entrance lies 18 mi. north of Millinocket. Bus service is not available. The park charges out-of-state motor vehicles $8 per day. During peak season, competition is fierce for sites at one of the park's 10 **campgrounds.** Reservations are a good idea; Maine residents are guaranteed at least 30% of the sites. ($8 for 2 people. $4 per additional person. Open May 15-Oct. 15.) You can get bunkhouse accommodations for $5, and lean-tos for $4. The most popular site is **Chimney Pond**, at the foot of Mt. Katahdin. For emptier, quieter sites, choose the northern end of the park, but avoid Nesowadnehunk Stream and Trout Brook Farm. Only Chimney Pond and Russell Pond campgrounds are inaccessible by car. None of the sites has hookups. Park authorities recommend treating lake or stream water with iodine or boiling it for at least five minutes.

Millinocket is also a popular base for expeditions to the **Allagash Wilderness Waterway,** an untamed river winding 92 mi. through thick forests. The logistics of an Allagash trip can be challenging. The nearly 100-mi. run from **Telos Lake** north to the Canadian border provides a difficult trip that crosses only two private logging roads, both owned by the Northern Maine Woods Association (435-6213) which charges for access ($12 per car, $6 for ME residents). The company also controls camping in the area, which is permitted only at one of the 66 designated campsites along the waterway. (Sites $5, ME residents $4.) Write the Bureau of Parks and Recreation, Maine Dept. of Conservation, State House, Station #22, Augusta 04333 (207-289-3821), for info and maps. The waterway is a long drive past Baxter Park from Millinocket on Golden Rd.

Moosehead Lakes Region

This remote part of Maine dances with wolves, bears, moose, mosquitos, forests, and ponds seldom seen by humans. The looping road from Ripogenus Dam near Baxter State Park through Greenville to Rockwood leads past lakes and ponds frequently visited by moose in search of grass in the water. The vigorous Kennebec, Penobscot, and Dead Rivers are favored by **whitewater rafting** enthusiasts. Novice rafters will find the fees ($75-90 per day) harder to manage than the trips. **Eastern River Expeditions,** P.O. Box 1173, Greenville 04441 (695-2411 or 695-2248; 800-634-7238 outside ME), guides trips from May to October and also offers canoe and kayak instruction. (Open Mon.-Fri. 8am-4:30pm.) **Wilderness Rafting Expeditions,** in Rockwood at the heart of Moosehead Lake Country, 20 mi. north of Greenville (534-2242 or 534-7305; write P.O. Box 41, Rockwood 04478), also rents mountain bikes ($18 per day). Reservations are required; rivers are less crowded weekdays and before July.

Buy food and spend the night in **Greenville,** at the southern tip of Moosehead Lake. The **chamber of commerce** (695-2702), in the center of town, distributes a complimentary *Visitor's Guide* with an area map. (Open daily 8am-6pm.) **Rockwood** has cabins at **Rockwood Cottages** (534-7725; singles from $40, $240 per week; doubles from $45, $270 per week). From Rockwood, take a boat to **Mt. Kineo Island,** and climb **Mount Kineo,** an 800-ft. peak with 700-ft. cliffs plummeting to the lake.

Rangeley Lakes Region

This region contains two of Maine's largest ski areas. **East of Rangeley lies Sugarloaf,** the state's second highest mountain and the only resort in the East with alpine skiing above the treeline. **Saddleback Mt.** (4,116 ft.) lies farther south. The area's large lakes—**Rangeley, Mooselookmeguntic, Richardson,** and **Umbagog**—lure boaters and anglers in summer. Numerous campsites along the lake shores and islands aid canoeists. The Appalachian Trail crosses over several summits in the region. The **Bigelow Range,** which spawned the recreational development of its mountain neighbors, has a well-maintained hiking trail.

Inexpensive lodgings dot the area. The **Farmhouse Inn** (864-5805), 1½ mi. south of Rangeley on Rte. 4, offers nine bunkrooms (4 people each, $18 per night). Camping at **Rangeley State Park** is permitted from May 15 to October 1. (Sites $12, ME residents $9, $1 day-use fee.) For a list of campgrounds, including those in the state park, contact the **Chamber of Commerce,** P.O. Box 317, Rangeley 04970 (864-5571), located at the park entrance off Main St; they also can make reservations. (Open Mon.-Sat. 9am-5pm, longer hours peak season.)

Maine Coast

The length of the coast due northeast from Kittery to Lubec measures 228 mi., but the jagged inlets and mountainous peninsulas give the entire shoreline a length of 3,478 mi. Fishing was the earliest industry here, augmented by a vigorous trade in shipbuilding; both traditions continue strongly. What dairy farms are to Vermont, lobster pounds are to Maine, as the proliferation of red wooden lobster signs by the roadside attest. Always cheap, lobsters are tastier before July, when most start to molt. Be forewarned that lobster-poaching is treated very seriously; people have been shot at for engaging in it. Registered with the state, the color codings and designs on the buoy markers are as distinct as a cattle rancher's brand.

U.S. 1 hugs the coastline and strings the port towns together. Lesser roads and small ferry lines connect the remote villages and offshore islands. The best place for info is the **Maine Information Center** in Kittery (439-1319; P.O. Box 396, Kittery 03903), three mi. north of the Maine-New Hampshire bridge. (Open summer daily 9am-5pm.) **Greyhound** serves points between Portland and Bangor along I-95, the coastal town of Brunswick as well as connecting routes to Boston. A car or bike is necessary to reach many coastal points of interest.

Mount Desert Island

In spite of its name, Mt. Desert (de-ZERT) is not barren. In summer, campers and tourists abound, drawn by mountains, rocky beaches, and spruce and birch forests. The Atlantic waters—calm in summer but often stormy in winter—are too cold for all but the hardiest of souls. Wind-swept Acadia National Park, the only national park in the Northeast, features rugged headlands, fine beaches, plenty of tidal-pool critters, and a variety of naturalist activities. **Bar Harbor** is a lively town with a roaring tourist trade in cheap places to eat and sleep. A winter visit will repay the cold wind and rain with moody scenery and tasty off-season rates.

Practical Information

Emergency: Acadia National Park, 288-3369. **Bar Harbor Police, Fire Department and Ambulance,** 911. **Mt. Desert Police,** 276-5111.

Acadia National Park Visitors Center (288-3338), 3 mi. north of Bar Harbor on Rte. 3. Maps, park info, and over 100 weekly naturalist programs. Browse through *Beaver Log,* the park's info newspaper. Open May 1 to mid-June and Oct. daily 8am-4:30pm, mid-June to Sept. daily 8am-6pm. **Park Headquarters** (288-3338), 3 mi. west of Bar Harbor on Rte. 233. Info Oct.-May Mon.-Fri. 8am-4:30pm. **Bar Harbor Chamber of Commerce,** 93 Cottage St. (288-5103). Maps and helpful booklets about the island. Open Mon.-Fri. 8am-4pm. Also runs info booth (288-3393) at **Canadian National Marine** ferry port on Rte. 3 1 mi. north of Bar Harbor. Open mid-May to Oct. daily. 10am-5pm, July-Aug. 9am-8pm.

Ferries: Beal & Bunker, Northeast Harbor (244-3575). To Cranberry Islands and Isleboro (5-6 per day, 30 min., $3, under 12 $2.50). **Canadian National Marine (CNM),** Bar Harbor (288-3395 or 800-341-7981). To Yarmouth, Nova Scotia (6-7 hrs., 1 per day, late June to mid-Sept. $40, seniors $30, kids $20, with car $74; late Sept. to mid-June $28, $21, $14, $52, respectively. $3 port charge year-round.)

Buses: Downeast Transportation (667-5796), sends off the **MDI Bus** which provides shuttle service weekdays around the island (75¢) and to Ellsworth ($2) on Rte. 1, as well as Saturday service to Bangor ($10). In Bar Harbor, catch bus at Shop & Save on Cottage St.

Bike and Boat Rental: Acadia Bike/Canoe, 48 Cottage St. (288-9605), near the post office. Mountain bikes $15 per day, tandems $30 per day, canoes $22 per day, and kayaks $60-75 per day. Guided half-day kayak tours $37-43, including equipment. Open May 1-Oct. 15 daily 8am-6pm, mid-June to Aug. daily 8am-9pm. **Bar Harbor Bicycle Shop,** 141 Cottage St. (288-3886). Mountain bikes $14 per day, $9 per ½-day; helmets, locks, and maps included. Open April-Dec. daily 9am-6pm. **Latitude 44,** 39 Cottage St., in the Wayfair Mall (288-5805). Sailboards $9.45 per day, wetsuits $10 per day. Roof racks and info on on nearby lakes included. Group introductory lessons $30. Open mid-June to Oct. daily 10am-7pm.

National Park Canoe Rentals, north end of Long Pond off Rte. 102 (244-5854). Canoes $27 per day, $17 per morning, $20 per afternoon. Open daily 8:30am-5pm.

Post Office: 55 Cottage St. (288-3122), near downtown. Open Mon.-Fri. 8am-5pm, Sat. 9am-noon. **ZIP code:** 04609.

Area Code: 207.

Rte. 3 runs through Bar Harbor, with Main St. leading up to the harbor, and Cottage and Mt. Desert Streets forming the major east-west axes.

Accommodations and Camping

Grand hotels with grand prices remain from Rockefeller's day, but lodging runs the gamut from reasonable to exorbitant. Inexpensive camping exists throughout the island; most campgrounds line Rte. 198 and 102. Bar Harbor has inexpensive and lovely old B&Bs. Cheaper motels can be found on Rte. 3 north of Bar Harbor, away from downtown action.

Mt. Desert Island Hostel (AYH), Kennebec St., Bar Harbor (288-5587), behind the Episcopal Church on Mt. Desert St. Friendly managers; 2 large dorm rooms, common room, kitchen. Curfew 11pm. Lockout 9:30am-4:30pm. $8, nonmembers $11. Open June 16-Aug. 31.

Mt. Desert Island YWCA, 36 Mt. Desert St. (288-5008), near downtown. Only women allowed above the plush lobby. Fills in summer; make reservations early.

McKay Lodging, 243 Main St., Bar Harbor (288-3531). B&B in 2 beautifully restored 19th-century buildings. Quilts in some rooms handmade by owner's daughter. (Doubles $50-65, in summer $60-69.)

Acadia Hotel, 20 Mt. Desert St., Bar Harbor (288-5721). Sweet, homey place overlooking park. Singles $40. Doubles $30-45, July-Aug. $45-58.

The Cadillac Motor Inn, 336 Main St. Bar Harbor (288-3821). Clean rooms with TV, telephone, bath, coffeemaker. Beware the squirrels who live in the walls. Singles $45. Doubles $59. Off-season $31/$42.

Mt. Desert Campground, off Rte. 198 (244-3710). Tent sites, platforms in a woodsy location overlooking the Somes Sound. Boat dock, swimming for the hearty, and free blueberry picking. Open May 15-Oct. 1. Sites $12-18, hookup $1 extra. $5 per additional adult, child $2.

Acadia National Park Campgrounds: Blackwoods Rte. 3 (288-3338), 5 mi. south of Bar Harbor on Rte. 3. Over 300 sites mid-May to mid-June and mid-Sept. to mid-Oct. $9, mid-June to mid-Sept. $11, free other times. **Seawall,** Rte. 102A (244-3600; call between 8am-6pm), 4 mi. south of Southwest Harbor. Station open late May-late Sept., 8am-8pm, but line forms each morning in late July and Aug. Walk-in sites $6, drive-in $9. Both campgrounds are within a 10-mi. walk to the ocean; neither have utilities or hookups.

Food and Entertainment

Seafood is all the rage on the island. "Lobster pounds" sell the underwater arachnids for little money; cooking them is the only problem.

Beals's, at Southwest Harbor (244-7178 or 244-3202), at the end of Clark Point Rd. The best price for lobster in an appropriate setting. Pick your own live lobster from a tank; Beals's will do the rest ($7-8). Outdoor dining on the dock. Nearby stand sells munchies and other beverages. Open daily 9am-8pm; off-season daily 9am-5pm.

Miguel's, 51 Rodick St. Delicious Mexican food in an authentic southwestern setting. Reasonable *quesadillas* ($2.25-7.75) and combination dinners; local Thunder Hole Ale. Open daily 5-10pm.

Rosalie's, 46 Cottage St. (288-5666). Italian food—the free-standing sculpted spaghetti in the window gives it away. Genuine Wurlitzer, too. Calzones $2.50, extra-large 19-in. pizzas $9, spaghetti dinners $5-5.60. Take-out available. Open May-Oct. daily 11am-mid.

The Lighthouse Restaurant, in Seal Harbor (276-3958). Mariner atmosphere complete with fish nets, port windows, and seascape murals. Sandwiches $3-7, entrees $9-15. Open daily 9am-9pm, peak summer season 9am-11pm.

Most after-dinner pleasures on the island are simple ones. For a treat, try **Ben and Bill's Chocolate Emporium** at Main St., which boasts 24 flavors of homemade ice cream and a huge selection of sweet-smelling fresh chocolate. (Open March-Dec. daily 9am-11pm.) **Geddy's,** 19 Main St. (288-5077), is a self-proclaimed three-tier entertainment complex with bar, sporadic live music, and dancing. Most bands, except for big names, are free. (Open mid-May to Oct. daily 6pm-1am. "Old-style English pub" open year-round daily 6pm-1am.) The art-deco **Criterion Theatre** (288-3441) has been declared a national landmark, but continues to show movies every summer night at 8pm. Matinees are scheduled on rainy days; a new film arrives every couple of days. Programs are available at the desk (tickets $5.75, under 11 $3.50).

Sights

Mt. Desert Island is shaped roughly like an upside-down heart. To the east on Rte. 3 lie Bar Harbor and Seal Harbor. South on Rte. 198 near the cleft is **Northeast Harbor,** and across Somes Sound on Rte. 102 is the **Southwest Harbor. Bar Harbor** is the spiritual center of the large island, sandwiched by the Blue Hill and Frenchmen Bays. Once a summer hamlet for only the very wealthy, the town now harbors a melange of R&R-seekers. Even the *Bar Harbor Times* peddles newspaper bags to tourists for beach totes as they stroll Main St., while the wealthy have fled to the quieter and more secluded Northeast and Seal Harbors. Anyone desiring a taste of coastal Maine life purged of wealth and kitsch should head west on the island to Southwest Harbor, where fishing and boatbuilding still thrive. **Little Cranberry Island,** out in the Atlantic Ocean south of Mt. Desert, offers a most spectacular view of Acadia as well as the cheapest uncooked lobster in the area at the fishers' co-op.

The staff at the **Mt. Desert Oceanarium** (244-7330), at the end of Clark Pt. Rd. in Southwest Harbor can teach you about the sea at each of their three facilities (the lobster hatchery and Salt Marsh Walk are located in Bar Harbor). The main museum, although somewhat like a grammar-school science fair, fascinates nonetheless. (Open mid-May to late Oct. Mon.-Sat. 9am-5pm. Tickets for all 3 facilities $9, kids $6.) Cruises head out to sea from a number of points on the island. In Bar Harbor, the **Frenchman Bay Co.,** 1 West St. (288-3322), offers windjammer sails, deep-sea fishing, and lobster, seal and whale watching. (Open May-Oct. Tickets $8.50-25, ages 6-12 $6.50-18, under 5 free. Call for details or schedule.) The **Acadian Whale Watcher** has a simpler menu and higher prices. Sunset ($11, kids $8) and whale-watching cruises ($25, seniors $20, ages 9-14 $18, ages 6-8 $15) leave at various times throughout the day. Open mid-May to mid-Oct. Bring extra clothing—the excursions are often chilling.

From Northeast Harbor, the **Sea Princess Islesford Historical and Naturalist Cruise** (276-5352) brings you past an osprey nesting site and lobster buoys to Little Cranberry Island. You may be lucky enough to see harbor seals, cormorants or pilot whales on the cruise. The crew takes you to the **Islesford Historical Museum** in sight of the fjord-like Somes Sound. (Two cruises per day May weekends and June 6-Oct. 14 daily; fare $9, ages 4-12 $6.)

The 33,000 acres that comprise the **Acadia National Park** are a landlubber's dream, offering easy trails, challenging hikes, and an intimate exploration of Mt. Desert Island. More acres are available on the nearby **Schoodic Peninsula** and **Isle au Haut** to the west. Millionaire and expert horseman John D. Rockefeller funded half of the park's 120 mi. of trails. These **carriage roads** make for easy walking and pleasant horseback riding and are handicapped-accessible. Precipice Trail and others offer more advanced hiking. Be realistic about your abilities here; the majority of injuries in the park occur in hiking accidents. Swim in the relatively warm **Echo Lake,** which has on-duty lifeguards in summer. **The Eagle Lake Loop Road** is graded for bicyclists. At the visitors center, pick up the handy *Biking Guide,* (50¢) which offers invaluable safety advice. Some of these paths are accessible only by mountain bike. Touring the park by auto will cost a little more. ($5 per day private vehicle, $2 per person. Seniors and disabled admitted free.) About four mi. south of Bar Harbor on Rte. 3, take the **Park Loop Road** running along the shore of the island where great waves roll up against steep granite cliffs. The sea comes into **Thunder Hole** at half-tide with a bang, sending a plume of spray high into the air and onto tourists. To the right just before the Loop Rd. turns back to the visitors center stands **Cadillac Mountain,** the highest Atlantic headland north of Brazil. A five-mi. hiking trail to the summit starts at Blackwoods campground, two mi. east of Seal Harbor. The top of Mt. Cadillac, where sunlight first reaches the U.S., makes a great place for an early morning breakfast picnic.

Tourists also can explore the island by horse, the way Rockefeller intended. **Wildwood Stables** (276-3622), along the Park Loop Rd. in Seal Harbor, runs two-hour carriage tours ($12.50, seniors $11.50, ages 6-12 $7, ages 2-5 $4.50) through the park. Reservations are strongly suggested.

North of Portland

Much like the coastal region south of Portland, the north offers the traveler sunny beaches and cool breezes—for a price. These seaside towns are ideal for short stays, if you have a boat and a few hundred dollars to spend on an old-fashioned inn. Much of the region is unserviced by public transportation; driving is rewarding, however. Rte. 1, running north beside I-95, gives motorists a charming glimpse of woods and small towns, then winds out of the Muscongus Bay and alongside Penobscot Bay, where rugged islands rise abruptly from the sea.

Freeport, about 20 mi. north of Portland on I-95, once garnered glory as the "birthplace of Maine." The signing in 1820 of documents declaring the state's independence from Massachusetts took place at the historic **Jameson Tavern,** at 115 Main St. Now the town finds fame as a factory outlet capital with over 100 downtown stores (factory and otherwise). The most famous of all, **L.L. Bean,** began manufacturing Maine Hunting Shoes in Freeport in 1912. The hunting shoe hasn't changed much since then, but now Bean sells diverse products from clothes epitomizing preppy *haute couture* to sturdy tenting gear. The factory outlet on Depot St. has pretty decent bargains. The retail store on Main St. (865-4767 or 800-221-4221) stays open 24 hrs., 365 days a year. Legend has it the store has closed only once since its opening.

Heading up to Penobscot Bay (not to be confused with the town of Penobscot) from factory outlet purgatory, be sure to stop at **Moody's Diner** off Rte. 1 in Waldoboro. In business since 1927, the booths are still wooden; tourists and old salts rub shoulders here over fantastic food. Try the homemade strawberry-rhubarb pie a la mode ($1.50). (Open Sun.-Fri. 7am-11:30pm, Sat. 5am-11:30pm.) Up Rte. 1 in Thomason lies the beautiful **Montpelier Mansion,** hillside home of General Henry Knox. (Open Wed.-Sun. 9am-4:30pm.)

In summer preps flock to friendly Camden, 100 mi. north of Portland, to dock their yachts alongside eight tall masted schooners in Penobscot Bay. Many of the cruises, like the neighboring yachts, are out of the mainstream price range, but the Rockport-Camden-Lincolnville **Chamber of Commerce** (236-4404), on the harbor in Camden behind the Camden National Bank, can tell you which are affordable. They also have information on a few rooms in local private homes for $12-30. (Reservations 289-3824. Open Mon.-Fri. 9am-5pm, Sat. 10am-4pm, Sun. noon-4pm, late May to mid-Oct. closed Sun.) Cheaper still, the **Camden Hills State Park,** 1¼ mi. north of town on U.S. 1 (236-3109), is almost always full in July and August, but you're certain to get a site if you arrive before 2pm. This coastal retreat offers more than 40 mi. of trails; one leads up to Mt. Battie with a harbor view. (Open May 15-Nov. 1. Day use $1. Sites $10.50, nonresidents $13.)

Affordable to all and in the heart of downtown is **Cappy's,** on Main St., a remarkably democratic hangout where tourists and townspeople mingle under the benevolent gaze of the sea captain/proprietor. Try the seafood pie ($7), made with scallops, shrimp, mussels, and clams (Open daily 7:30am-mid.)

The **Maine State Ferry Service,** five mi. north of Camden on Rte. 1 (800-521-3939 or 596-2202), takes you through the Bay to Isleboro Island (5-9 per day. Fare $1.75, kids $1, with auto $6.25.). The ferry also has an agency in Rockland on Rte. 1, running boats to North Haven, Vinalhaven, and Matinicus. Always call the ferry service to confirm; rates and schedules change with the weather.

South of Blue Hill on the other side of Penobscot Bay lies **Deer Isle,** a picturesque forested island with rocky coasts accessible by bridge from the mainland. Off Main St. in Stonington, at the southern tip of Deer Isle, a mailboat (367-5193; June 17-Sept. 7 Mon.-Sat. 3 per day, Sun. 1 per day) leaves for **Isle au Haut,** part of Acadia National Park. (Fare $8, kids $4.) Island exploration is done by foot or bike (no rental bikes available on the island). The only accommodations are five lean-tos at **Duck Harbor Campground** (sites $5; reservations necessary; open mid-May to mid-Oct.). Contact Acadia Park Headquarters or write P.O. Box 177, Bar Harbor 04609 (288-3338).

South of Portland

Driving south on Rte. 1 out of Portland, you'll pass through a number of small coastal towns comprising a popular and expensive resort for more southerly Easterners. **Route 9a,** off Rte. 1, offers a slow, lovely, and winding drive around the peninsula.

Kennebunkport and Kennebunkport Beach are popular hideaways for wealthy authors and artists. A number of rare and used bookstores line Rte. 1 just south of town while art galleries fill the town itself. Recently, however, the quaint resort has grown famous and profit-hungry as the summer home of President Bush, who owns a sprawling estate on Walker's Point. You've reached the entrance on Ocean Ave. when you spot the Secret Service gatekeeper (whose lips you can't quite read) hiding inside a tinted glass cubicle. The **Kennebunk-Kennebunkport Chamber of Commerce,** at the intersection of Rte. 9 and 35 (967-0857), provides a free guide to the area's history and sights. (Open Mon.-Fri. noon-5pm, Sat. 10am-5pm, Sun. 11am-4pm; summer Mon.-Fri. 9am-9pm, Sat. 9am-7pm, Sun. 9am-4pm.)

Biking provides a graceful ride on the road past rocky shores and spares the frustration of fighting the thick summer traffic. In nearby Biddiford, a few minutes north on Rte. 1, **Quinn's Bike and Fitness,** 140 Elm St. (284-4632), rents 10-speeds ($33 per week) and 3-speeds ($22.50 per week, deposit $20). (Open Mon.-Thurs. 9am-5:30pm, Fri. 9am-8:30pm.) You can get a copy of *25 Bicycle Tours in Maine* ($15) from the Portland Chamber of Commerce.

A visit to Kennebunkport could cost you a pretty penny, though the **Lobster Deck Restaurant,** on Rte. 9 overlooking Kennebunk Harbor, serves lobster dinner for $14-16. (Open daily 11am-10pm.) For affordable lodging, camp. Nearby **Salty Acres Campground,** 4½ mi. north of town on Rte. 9 (967-2483), offers swimming and a convenient location close to the beaches. (Sites $13, with electricity and water $14. $6 per additional person. Open June 15-Sept. 15.) A little farther out is the **Mousam River Campground,** on Alfred Rd. just west of exit 3 off I-95 in West Kennebunk (985-2507; sites $15; free showers).

To escape the tourist throngs, head west to the **Rachel Carson National Wildlife Refuge** (646-9226), on Rte. 9 near Rte. 1. A self-guided interpretive trail takes you through the salt marsh home of over 200 species of shorebirds and waterfowl, a moving tribute to the naturalist author of *Silent Spring,* which publicized the perils of industrial waste.

Farther south on Rte. 1 is **Ogunquit.** The name means "beautiful place by the sea" in the Abenaki language and does not advertise falsely. A little farther in toward town is Perkins Cove, a lobster trap for tourists decorated with precious shops; the well-worn Marginal Way begins here behind Oarweed Restaurant and winds about 1¼ mi. along the rocky coast into Ogunquit town. The **Ogunquit Playhouse,** on Rte. 1 (656-5511), in its 60th season, reputedly offers the best theater on the coast. (Shows late June-Aug.; tickets $18). Before the performance, grab a bite to eat in the **Clamdigger,** the local hangout of choice, at 314 Rte. 1. Look for the lobster boat perched in front. (Open daily 6am-9pm.) Although lodging bargains are scarce, **Dixon's Campground** (363-2131), in neighboring Cape Neddick on 1740 Rte. 1, is affordable. (Sites $19-22 for 2 people, with water and electricity $23-26. $6-8 per additional person. Open May 22-Sept. 12.) Less rugged and more expensive, **Hoyt's Cottages,** on Rte. 1 (363-3400), rents cottages with and without kitchens by the day ($38-60) and week ($225-385). Book early for July and August.

Portland

For a virtually tourist-free taste of New England coast, go to Portland. Destroyed by a fire in 1866, the city rebuilt only to decline in the late 1960's. Lately, Portland shines—its downtown area advantageously located along the ocean, its moderate microclime revitalized. Stroll down the attractive Old Port Exchange, whose restaurants, taverns and craft shops occupy former warehouses and 19th-century buildings. The reasonable location and cost of living in Maine's largest city make it an ideal base for sight-seeing and daytrips to the surrounding coastal areas, such as Casco Bay and the Casco Bay Islands. Nearby Sebago Lake provides great opportunities for sunning and waterskiing.

Practical Information

Emergency: 911.

Visitor Information Bureau, 142 Free St. (772-4994), next to the intersection of Congress and High St. Open Mon.-Fri. 9am-5pm. Good books about coastal and inland Maine.

Greyhound: 950 Congress St. (772-6587), on the eastern outskirts of town. Office open daily 5:30-6am and 8:30am-6pm. To: Boston (5 per day, $17.25); Bangor (3 per day, $23); and points north.

Public Transport: Metro Bus Company, 114 Valley St. (774-0351), ½-mi. south of the Greyhound station. Buses operate daily 6:20am-10pm; information available 8am-4:30pm. Fare 80¢, seniors and disabled 40¢, under 5 free. Exact change only.

Taxi: ABC Taxis, 772-8685. About $3 from the bus station to downtown.

Prince of Fundy Cruises: P.O. Box 4216, Station A, Portland 04101 (800-341-7540). Ferries to Yarmouth in southern Nova Scotia leave from Commercial St. near Million Dollar Bridge May-late Oct. at 9pm. Fare $70, ages 5-14 $35; off-season $50 and $25, respectively. Cars $93, off-season $70. Reservations required.

Help Lines: Rape Crisis, 774-3613. 24 hrs. **13-Line,** 797-1313. **AIDS Line,** 775-1267.

Post Office: 125 Forest Ave. (871-8410), exit off I-295. Open Mon.-Fri. 7:30am-5pm, Sat. 9am-noon. Self-service lobby open 24 hrs. **ZIP code:** 04101.

Area Code: 207.

The downtown area sits along Congress St. towards the bay; a few blocks south lies the Old Port on Commercial and Fore St. These two districts contain most of the city's sights and attractions. I-295 detours from I-95 to form the western boundary of the downtown area. Several offshore islands are served by regular ferries.

Accommodations and Camping

Portland has some inexpensive accommodations, but prices often jump during the summer season. You can always try exit 8 off I-95, a budget hotel center.

YWCA, 87 Spring St. (874-1130), near the Civic Center. Women only. Small rooms verge on sterile, but an amiable atmosphere more than compensates. Lounge, pool, and kitchen (bring utensils). Check-in before 2pm. Singles $25. Doubles $40.

YMCA, 70 Forest Ave. (874-1111), north side of Congress St., 1 block from the post office. Cash only. Men only. Check-in before 10pm. Pool. Singles $22. Weekly $70. Key deposit $10.

Hotel Everett, 51A Oak St. (773-7882), off Congress St. downtown. Singles $35, with bath $45. Doubles $40, with bath $49. Weekly rates available. Reservations recommended in summer.

Wassamki Springs, 855 Saco St. (839-4276), in Westbrook. Closest campground (15 min.) to Portland. Drive west down Congress St. about 6 mi. Full facilities plus a sandy beach. Flocks of migrant Winnebagos nest here. Sites $17 for 2 people. $4 per additional person. Shower and electricity extra. Open May to mid-Oct. Reservations recommended, especially July-Aug.

Food and Nightlife

Diners, delis and cafés abound in Portland. Check out the active port on Commercial St., lined with sheds selling clams, fish, and lobsters daily.

Carbur's, 123 Middle St. (772-7794), near the Old Port. Whimsical sandwiches for $4-10. If you try the quintuple sandwich ($10), the servers and cooks will parade around the dining room chanting "Down East Feast." Open Mon.-Fri. 11am-10pm, Sat. 11am-11pm, Sun. noon-10pm.

Raffle's Café Bookstore, 555 Congress St. (761-3930), in the heart of downtown. Enjoy a light lunch while doing heavy reading. Has a charming selection of desserts. Cheese and fruit board for $5.25. Open Mon.-Wed. and Fri. 8am-5pm, Thurs. 8am-7pm, Sat. 9:30am-5pm.

Ruby's Choice, 116 Free St. 9am-5pm (773-9099), near downtown, Claims to serve the world's best burger ($2.50-4). Also hawks homemade chocolate chip cookies (70¢) and pies ($1.75). Open Mon.-Wed. 11:30am-8pm, Thurs.-Sat. 11:30am-9pm.

Hu-Shang, 33 Exchange St. Good Chinese food served in a Wild West atmosphere. Lunch $3.75-7, dinner $5-9. Open Mon.-Thurs. 11:30am-9:30pm, Fri.-Sat. 11:30am-10:30pm, Sun. noon-9:30pm; summer hours slightly longer.

Seamen's Club, 375 Fare St. (772-7311), in the Old Port with a harbor view. Topnotch seafood dining steeped in briny tradition. Lunch entrees from $6, dinner $11 and up. Open Mon.-Fri. 11am-10pm, Sat.-Sun. 11am-11pm.

Portland's new nightlife centers around the Old Port. **Three Dollar Dewey's,** at 446 Fore St., recreates the atmosphere of an English pub, serving over 65 varieties of beer and ale along with great chili and free popcorn to an eclectic clientele. (Open Mon.-Sat. 11am-1am, Sun. noon-1am.) The **Seaman's Tavern and Raw Bar,** at 375 Fore St., built in 1866 right after the fire, offers a more limited selection, although you can get a draught of Geary's ($2.50) while playing pool. (Open daily 11am-11pm.)

Sights

The sea might call from the minute you arrive in Portland, but the city does have a full complement of aquaphobe activities. The **Portland Museum of Art,** 7 Congress Sq. (775-6148), at the intersection of Congress, High, and Free St., collects U.S. art by notables such as John Singer Sargent and Winslow Homer. (Open Tues.-Wed. and Fri.-Sat. 10am-5pm, Thurs. 10am-9pm, Sun. noon-5pm. $3.50, seniors $2.50, kids $1. Free Thurs. 5-9pm.) Down the street at 485 Congress St., the **Wadsworth-Longfellow House** (772-1807), a museum of social history and U.S. literature, zeroes in on late 18th- and 19th-century antiques as well as at the life of the poet and his family. (Open June 1 to mid-Oct. Tues.-Sat. 10am-4pm. Tours every ½ hr. $3, under 12 $1.)

For a list of other historical landmarks and homes in the area, visit the **Greater Portland Landmarks Office** 165 State St. (774-5561), which leads tours from early July to late September and sells a comprehensive packet on walking tours ($4.15; open Mon.-Thurs. 8:30am-4pm, Fri. 8:30am-2pm). While the history of Portland's **Old Port Exchange** begins in the 17th century, the area's shops, stores, and homes were rebuilt in Victorian style after the fire of 1866. The **Portland Observatory,** 138 Congress St. (774-5561), atop the promontory east of downtown, went up in 1807. Climb 102 steps for a panoramic view of Casco Bay and downtown Portland. (Open June Fri.-Sun. 1-5pm; July-Sept. 5 Wed.-Fri. and Sun. 1-5pm, Sat. 10am-5pm; Sept. 6-Oct. weekends. $1, kids 50¢.)

Take a ferry out on the bay, but choose carefully; all are not alike. **Casco Bay Lines,** on State Pier (774-7871), America's oldest ferry service offers seven cruises into the bay, from morning to moonlight. Most departures late June-early Sept. ($7-$12.75, seniors $6-11.50, kids $3-6). Excursions with historical narration aboard the **Longfellow II,** 1 Long Wharf (774-3578), take you to see the bay's shipwrecks and lighthouses (6 daily departures, 10am-7:30pm; $10, seniors $9, kids $5). Time permitting, head out to **Cushings Island** for stiff drinks and an annual croquet tournament.

The **Old Port Festival** begins the summer season with a bang in early June, spanning several blocks from Federal to Commercial St. and drawing as many as 50,000 people. On July and August weekdays, enjoy the **Noontime Performance Series,** the only one of its kind in New England. Event listings can be found within the free guide distributed by the visitor information bureau.

MARYLAND

Life and livelihood in Maryland have centered on Chesapeake Bay since the 17th century. Today, countless oysters and crabs are hauled from the bay while its shipping lanes serve many mid-Atlantic cities. Yachts, Navy vessels, tankers, and trawlers alike anchor at the gleaming harbor city of Baltimore and at the state's capital, Annapolis, home of the U.S. Naval Academy. Maryland also serves as "Weekend Warrior" home turf for public and private sector workers commuting into DC from the suburbs.

Practical Information

Capital: Annapolis.

Office of Tourist Development, 217 E. Redwood St., Baltimore 21202 (333-6611 or 800-543-1036). **Forest and Parks Service,** Dept. of Natural Resources, Tawes State Office Bldg., Annapolis 21401 (974-3771).

Time Zone: Eastern. Postal Abbreviation: MDArea Code: 301.

Annapolis

Although the major industry here is state government, forget about office buildings and stuffed shirts. Instead of a downtown, Annapolis has a historic waterfront district. Narrow streets flanked by restored 18th-century brick run downhill to the crowded, commercial, and oddly clean docks, where yachts and their tanned owners rest. Crew-cut "middies" from the Naval Academy mingle with longer-haired students from St. John's and affluent couples on weekend retreats.

The interesting quarter of Annapolis extends south and east from two landmarks: **Church Circle,** containing St. Anne's Episcopal Church, and **State Circle,** site of the **Maryland State House** (974-3400), where the Continental Congress met to ratify the Treaty of Paris in 1784. School Street blatantly and unconstitutionally connects Church and State. Maryland Avenue runs from the State House to the Naval Academy, Main Street (where food and entertainment congregate) through Church Circle to the docks. Annapolis is compact and easily walkable, provided you can find a parking space.

Practical Information

Annapolis and Anne Arundel County Conference & Visitor's Bureau, 1 Annapolis St. (280-0445) spouts brochures and info. (Open Mon.-Fri. 8:30am-4:30pm.) Questions answered at the info desk at the State House (974-3000) or at the dockside visitor's booth (268-8687). (State House open 9am-5pm Mon.-Fri.; visitor's booth open 9am-5pm daily.)

Buses: Greyhound/Trailways (565-2662). Connection with Washington, DC (4 per day, 40 min., $9.50) and with towns on the far side of the Chesapeake Bay. The **Annapolis Department of Public Transportation,** 160 Duke of Gloucester St. (263-7964), operates a web of city bus routes connecting the historic district with the rest of town. (Mon.-Sat. 6am-10pm, Sun. 8am-8pm.)

Mass Transit Administration (539-5000) makes frequent runs from downtown Baltimore to Annapolis. (Express bus #210 Mon.-Fri. 6:10-8:10am, 4:15-6:45pm; 1 hr.; $2.35. Local bus #14 Mon.-Fri. 5am-10pm, Sat.-Sun. 6:40am-9pm; 90 min.; $1.85.)

Tours: Three Century Tours, 48 Maryland Ave. (263-5401 or 263-5357) leads daily 2-hr. walking tours April-Oct., at 9:30am from the Annapolis Marriott Hotel Lobby and at 1:30pm from the City Dock ($5, ages 6-18 $3).

ZIP code: 21401.

Area code: 301.

Accommodations

In this deliberately quaint town, there is an abundance of darling little B&Bs. Less filligreed accommodations such as hostels and motels are more scarce. Rates fluctuate, depending upon demand; ask around and feign a little indifference to secure a fair price.

Almost Home Bed & Breakfast, 118 Claiburne Rd. (956-6038). If you have a car, try this 2-room B&B 6 mi. outside Annapolis. Take Rte. 2 south to Southbound Shores Dr., turn right, then left onto Locust St. Host Haidi Zech will take you crabbing with her own equipment for free; she may sing you German folk songs, too. Singles $45. Doubles $55. Rates drop for stays over 2 nights. Call well in advance for reservations.

Gibson's Lodgings, 110 Prince George St. (268-5555). Three amazingly clean and modernized buildings comprise Gibson's Lodgings; the bearded proprietor runs around with a walkie-talkie to keep track of everything. The 200-year-old Patterson House, with 6 rooms, is the quaintest and cheapest of the three. Singles $55. Doubles with shared bath $65.

Prince George Inn Bed & Breakfast, 232 Prince George St. (263-6418). A Victorian townhouse as polished and preserved as Annapolis facades—but cozier and more cluttered. Four-poster beds and wood floors. Singles $65. Doubles with shared bath $75. Weekdays $10 less. Off-season rates vary. Check-in 4-6pm.

The Ark and Dove, 149 Prince George St. (268-6277). Charming decor includes a player piano downstairs. Teeny townhouse keeps afloat with 2 rooms and shared bath. Singles $65. Doubles $75. Two-night min. stay on weekends. Seniors and students with ID discounted a whopping $5.

Food and Nightlife

Chick & Ruth's Delly, 165 Main St. (269-6737). A cheeky Annapolis institution, with dishes named for local and national politicians. Try the Dan Quayle—a ham, turkey, and bacon sandwich on rye. The all-day breakfast menu includes unlimited coffee. Twenty-two kinds of donuts saturate for under $1. Some kosher food. Open 24 hrs.

Carrol's Creek Bar & Café, 410 Severn Ave. (263-8102), in the Annapolis City Marina Complex, across the Eastport Bridge from Annapolis proper. Sit on the patio to watch the Eastport Bridge come up and the sun go down. Order from the Lite Fare menu (served after 4pm) and munch unlimited dinner rolls. May be packed on weekends. Snails in a nest of angel hair pasta are a happy mixture of sacred and profane ($6). Open daily 11am-midnight. Outside seating available Mon.-Sat. 11:30am-8:30pm, Fri.-Sat. 11:30am-9pm.

Market House, in Market Place, at City Dock, at the corner of Randall and Pinkney St. A variety of eateries, from seafood bars to frozen yogurt shops, meet under one roof. No seating available inside, but the dock makes a great picnic beach. Oysters and clams (50¢) a Chesapeake Bay specialty. Open Mon.-Thurs. 9am-6pm, Fri.-Sat. 9am-7pm, Sun. 10am-7pm.

Old Towne Restaurant, 105 Main St. (268-8703). Pink lace curtains frame the Main St. window, dim ship's lanterns line the walls, and the drab dioramic decor disguises the cheapest seafood downtown. Crab cakes ($4), broiled herbed scallops ($7). Open daily 11am-8pm.

Small town by day, Annapolis stays small town by night. The few local pubs cluster primarily along Severn Ave. in Eastport. Call 268-8687 for info on free concerts at the city dock. At the popular **Ram's Head Tavern,** 33 West St. (268-4545), imported bottled beer is swigged by domestic customers. (Open daily 11am-2am.) Locals swear by **Marmaduke's Pub** (269-5420), on Severn Ave. at 3rd, across the bridge from the dock in Eastport. Sailors flock here Wednesday nights to watch videos of their races. (Open daily 11:30am-2am. No cover downstairs. Weekend piano bar upstairs, cover $2.50.) If you drive to Marmaduke's, take the Eastport Bridge and ignore the detour signs—they only apply to trucks. R&B fans should check the monthly calendar at **Armadillo's,** 132 Dock St. (268-6680), which hosts live bands every night (9:30pm-1:30am; open daily 11am-1:30am).

Sights

The **State House,** mimics the U.S. Capitol in a pleasant Greek Revival sort of way. You can watch the state legislature bicker from Jan. 8-March 8. Free tours are given at 11am, 2pm, and 4pm. (Open daily 9am-5pm.) From State Circle, follow Maryland Ave. to meet up with historic buildings. The **Hammond-Harwood House** (269-1714) hams it up at 19 Maryland Ave., at King George St. The museum keeps up 1774 period décor down to the candlesticks. (Open April-Oct. Tues.-Sat. 10am-5pm, Sun. 2-5pm; Nov.-March Tues.-Sat. 10am-4pm, Sun. 1-4pm. Tours on the hour. Admission $3.50, ages 6-18 $2.50, uniformed armed service personnel free.) A right onto King George St., then another onto Martin St. reveals an unimposing parking lot and the sign for the **William Paca Garden,** 1 Martin St. (267-6656; from Baltimore, 269-0601). Turn right onto East St., past the Brice House, and turn right again onto Prince George St. for the entrance to the companion museum, the **William Paca House,** 186 Prince George St. (263-5553). William Paca, an early governor of Maryland, was one of the signers of the Declaration of Independence. Visitors to this beautifully restored colonial estate find a 1765 grandfather clock still ticking inside, along with trellises, water lilies, and gazebos outdoors. Preservationists rescued the garden from under a bus station and parking lot. Tours, whenever enough people gather, last until an hour before closing. (House open May-Oct. Tues.-Sat. 10am-5pm, Sun. noon-5pm; Nov.-April open Tues.-Sat. 10am-4pm, Sun. noon-4pm. House admission $3.50, ages 6-18 $2. Garden open May-Oct. Mon.-Sat. 10am-5pm, Sun. noon-5pm; Nov.-April Sun. noon-4pm. Garden admission $2, kids $1. Combined admission $5, ages 6-18 $3.

Follow the smell of food and the sound of tourists down Pinkney St. towards the **City Dock.** Look for the $3 million *Seabird,* probably Annapolis' longest yacht at 90 ft. Main St., full of tiny shops and eateries, stretches from here back up to Church Circle. In an old church adjacent to Church Circle, the **Banneker-Douglass Museum,** 84 Franklin St. (974-2893), houses temporary exhibits and photographs on African-American life and history.

From Church Circle, walk along College Avenue past St. John's St., and turn left onto the campus of **St. John's College,** where students share an identical four-year "Great Books" curriculum, eschewing contemporary textbooks for the hallowed tomes of Western civilization. You'll pass **McDowell Hall,** St. John's first classroom building, on your right; the **Liberty Tree** grows in front of it. Some time in the early 1980s, overconfident midshipmen boasted that they could beat St. John's at any team sport; St. John's picked croquet, won the first match, and now leads the annual series six to three. (For info on the May matches, call 263-2371.) From the quad at St. John's take College Ave. to King George St. and follow King George down to Gate One of the institution whose name *is* Annapolis: the Naval Academy.

At the **U.S. Naval Academy,** harried, short-haired "plebes" (first-year students) in official sailor dress try desperately to remember the words of navy fight songs while the rest of the undergraduates, "middies" (midshipmen), go about their business. Naval Academy graduates become U.S. Navy lieutenants and must serve as officers for at least two years. President Jimmy Carter graduated from Annapolis; more recently the institution has made headlines for expelling its gay and lesbian students. The rigorously planned and expansive campus includes plenty of green lawns and long docks at the water's edge; even in summer, a brigade of students and officers sticks around to work and drill, oblivious to visitors. **Bancroft Hall,** an imposing stone structure about three blocks long, houses the entire student body, making it the world's largest dormitory. Its mammoth steps, masonry and arched entryways suggest its function as a cathedral of discipline. In the yard outside Bancroft Hall, witness the middies' noon lineup and formations. From a balcony beside the high, stone lobby of Bancroft Hall, survey the campus, or inspect an uninhabited model middie's dorm room. (The rest of the Hall is closed to tourists.) **King Hall,** the academy's gargantuan dining hall, turns madhouse at lunchtime, serving the entire brigade in under four minutes. The hall even has its own brand of ketchup. You'll have to watch the lunch from outside, though. Elsewhere on campus, the **Naval Museum** in Preble Hall has a simple collection of naval artifacts. (Open Mon.-Sat. 9am-4:45pm, Sun. 11am-4:45pm. Free.) Walking tours of the academy begin at the **Ricketts Hall** visitors center (263-6933), directly inside the gates of the academy at the end of Maryland Ave. (Tours March-May 10am-3pm on the hr.; June-Labor Day 9:30am-4pm on the ½-hr.; Labor Day-Thanksgiving 10am-3pm on the hr. $3, ages 6-12 $1, under 6 free.)

Baltimore

Once an East Coast shipping and industry center, Baltimore declined structurally and economically from the late-50s to the mid-70s, when then-mayor William Donald Schaefer began to clean up pollution, restore buildings, and reinvent the Inner Harbor as a tourist playground: Harborplace inspires dozens of wannabe waterfront malls along the east coast. In spite of the "renovation," Maryland's urban core still has character; shirtsleeve Bawlmer endures in the quiet limelight of Anne Tyler's novels, the nostalgic old-time light of Barry Levinson's films, and the day-glo grime-light of John Waters's movies. Near downtown skyscrapers, Little Italy fronts Baltimore's signature row houses, whose facades symbolize the city itself: polished marble steps for the posh Inner Harbor, blunt brick for the proud, gritty urban environs.

Practical Information

Emergency: 911.

Baltimore Area Visitors Centers, 300 W. Pratt St. (837-INFO or 800-282-6632), at N. Howard St. 4 blocks from Harborplace. Pick up a map, an *MTA Ride Guide,* and the *Quick City Guide* with excellent maps and event listings. Open daily 9am-5:30pm. An **information booth** on the west shoreline of the Inner Harbor is often crowded. Open daily 10am-6pm. A **satellite booth** at Penn Station provides basic info, usually open late Fri. evenings, weekday mornings, and all day Sun.

Travelers Aid: 685-3569 (Mon.-Fri. 8:30am-5pm), 685-5874 (24-hr. hotline). Desks at Penn Station (open Mon.-Thurs. 9am-noon, Fri. 9am-9pm, Sat. 9am-1pm, Sun. 10am-5pm) and the Baltimore-Washington Airport (open Mon.-Fri. 9am-9pm, Sat.-Sun. 9am-5pm).

Baltimore-Washington International Airport (BWI), 859-7100. On I-195 off the Baltimore-Washington Expressway (I-295), about 10 mi. south of the city center. Use BWI as your gateway to Baltimore or Washington, DC. Take MTA bus #230 downtown. **Airport shuttles** (859-0800) run daily every ½-hr. 5am-midnight ($6). Trains from BWI Airport to Baltimore ($5, metroliner $10) and Washington, DC ($9, metroliner $14). Call BWI office at 674-1167 or 674-1170.

Amtrak: Penn Station, 1515 N. Charles St. (291-4260 or 800-872-7245), at Mt. Royale Ave. Easily accessible by bus #3, 11, or 18 to Charles Station. Trains run about every hr. to New York ($58, metroliner $77), Washington, DC ($11, metroliner $20), and Philadelphia ($27, metroliner $40). Ticket window open daily 5:30am-11:30pm, self-serve machines open daily 24 hrs. (credit card only).

Greyhound/Trailways, 210 W. Fayette St. (752-0868), near Howard; 5625 O'Donnell St. (744-9311), near I-95 3 mi. east of downtown. Frequent connections to NYC ($39), Washington, DC ($8.50), and Philadelphia ($15). Open 24 hrs.

Public Transport: Mass Transit Administration (MTA), 300 W. Lexington St. (539-5000 for recorded bus, Metro info; 333-3434 main office), near N. Howard St. Or call 760-4554 in Annapolis, 800-543-9809 in MD and DC. (Lines open Mon.-Fri. 6am-11pm, Sat. 8:30am-5pm.) Easy bus and rapid-rail service to major city sights, more complicated to outlying areas. #230 serves airport. Free *MTA Ride Guide,* available at any visitors information center.

Some buses operate 24 hrs. Fare $1.10, transfers 10¢. Metro operates Mon.-Fri. 5am-midnight, Sat. 8am-midnight. Metro base rate $1.10. One-day unlimited travel **tourist pass** $3, available at 300 W. Lexington St., Charles Center Station, 110 E. Baltimore St., and Mondawmin and Owings Mill Stations. Some buses "kneel" for wheelchairs; call MTA-LIFT (682-5438) by 1pm a day ahead. **Baltimore Trolley Tours** (783-2448). Tours, transportation to major Baltimore sights. One-day unlimited boarding pass for the 90-min. loop available. Trolleys every 30 min., daily 10am-4pm. $9, kids $4.50.

Water Taxi: 547-0090 or 800-658-8947. From Inner Harbor, makes 14 stops at major attractions along 4 mi. of shoreline. Unlimited all-day use $3.25, ages under 10 $2.25. Open April-Oct. Sun.-Thurs. 11am-9pm, Fri.-Sat. 10am-midnight; Nov.-March Wed.-Sun. 11am-6pm.

Taxi: Yellow Cab, 685-1212. **G.T.P. Inc.,** 859-1103 (to and from BWI airport).

Car Rental: Thrifty, BWI Airport (768-4900) and 2030 N. Howard St. (783-0300). Economy cars from $35 per weekday, $19.50 per weekend day. Unlimited mi. Under 25 add $3 per day. Airport branch open 24 hrs. Must be 21 with credit card or cash deposit. **Rent-A-Wreck,** 9006 Liberty Rd., Randallstown (325-2757), and on Pulaski Hwy. near the Baltimore Beltway. From $22.95 per day. 50 free mi., 19¢ per additional mi. Open Mon.-Fri. 8am-6pm, Sat. 8am-3pm. Must be 21.

Help Lines: Sexual Assault and Domestic Violence Hotline, 828-6390. **Gay and Lesbian Hotline and Information,** 837-8888. Operators daily 7:30-10:30pm, otherwise recording.

Post Office: 900 block of E. Fayette St. (655-9832). **ZIP code:** 21233.

Area Code: 301.

The **Jones Falls Expressway (I-83)** bifurcates the city with its southern end at the Inner Harbor, while the Baltimore Beltway (I-695) circles the city. I-95 cuts across the southwest corner of the city, a shortcut to the wide arc of that Beltway section. During rush hour, these interstates get slower than a whale on downers. Blue and green signs point drivers to tourist attractions. From Washington, DC, take the Washington Beltway (I-495) to I-95 at exit 27 or the Baltimore-Washington Expressway at exit 22; the highways run roughly parallel. Take the Russel St. exit to reach the Inner Harbor. Without traffic, the trip takes less than an hour.

Accommodations and Camping

Baltimore International Youth Hostel (AYH), 17 W. Mulberry St. (576-8880), near downtown bus and Amtrak terminals. Take MTA bus #3, 11, or 18. Elegant 3-story townhouse: 48 beds, kitchen, laundry, lounge, baby grand. Members max. stay 6 nights, nonmembers 3. Lockout 9:30am-5pm. Curfew 11pm. Chores required. $10, nonmembers $13. Reservations recommended; deposit required 2 weeks ahead.

Abbey-Schaefer Hotel, 723 Saint Paul St. (332-0405), at Madison downtown. Take bus #3 or 9. High ceilings, big rooms, attractive lobby, some recently renovated rooms. Doubles $39. Key deposit $10. Phone deposit $5.

Duke's Motel, 7905 Pulaski Highway (686-0400), in Rosedale off the Beltway. Ignore the front office's bulletproof glass—all the motels around here have it. Simple, clean rooms, probably the best deal on the Pulaski Hwy. motel strip, though slightly more expensive. Cable TV. Singles $36. Doubles $41.

Capitol KOA, 768 Cecil Ave., Millersville (923-2771 or 987-7477), 10 mi. from the Baltimore Beltway, 16 mi. from DC, 11 mi. from Annapolis. Full facilities, pool, free weekday shuttle to DC/Baltimore trains. $17.25 for 2 people, RV site $17-19, $3 per additional adult. Open April-Nov.

Food

Virginia is for lovers, but Maryland is for crabs—every eatery here serves crab cakes. The chain stores at **Harborplace** (332-4191), at Pratt and Lombard St., enjoy a beautiful view. It's a great place for a few clams for a few clams. **Phillips'** crab cakes are among the finest in Maryland (buy them cheaper from the Phillips' Express line), **Thrasher's** fries with vinegar are an Eastern Shore tradition, and there's no better Polish sausage than **Ostrowski's** *Kielbasa*. (Harborplace open Mon.-Sat. 10am-9:30pm, Sun. noon-8pm.) Baltimore's largest and most famous market, **Lex-**

ington Market, lies on Lexington at Eutaw St., northwest of the harbor, providing an endless variety of produce, fresh meat, seafood, and all of Harborplace's specialties, often at cheaper prices. (Open Mon.-Sat. 8:30am-6pm. Take bus #7 or the subway to Lexington Station.)

Ikaros, 4805 Eastern Ave. (633-3750), 2 mi. east of downtown. Take bus #10. East Baltimore's Greek community is perfect for cheapskate romantics. Try *avgolemono* soup with egg, lemon, beef, and rice ($1.50), or spinach and feta pies ($2.50). Open Sun.-Mon. and Wed.-Thurs. 11am-10pm, Fri.-Sat. 11am-11pm.

Haussner's, 3242 Eastern Ave. (327-8365) at S. Clinton. Take bus #10. An East Baltimore institution. Huge dining room full of impressive artwork and German food. *Sauerbraten* $10, sandwiches from $4; famous strawberry pie $3.50. No shorts after 3pm; lines for dinner on weekends. Open Tues.-Sat. 11am-11pm.

Bertha's Dining Room, 734 S. Broadway (327-5795) at Lancaster in Fells Point. Obey the bumper stickers: "Eat Bertha's Mussels." Black-shelled bivales, $6.75. Ninety sorts of beer and ale ($1-6). Jazz Mon.-Wed. and Fri.-Sat. nights. Enter on Lancaster St.; wheelchair accessible. Kitchen open Mon.-Thurs. 11:30am-11pm, Fri.-Sat. 11:30am-midnight. Bar until 2am.

Buddies, 313 N. Charles St. (332-4200). Good lunchtime salad bar ($3.15 per lb.). Jazz quartet Thurs.-Sat. 9:30pm-1am. Two-drink min. Domestic draft $2-3.60, imports $3-5. Open Sun.-Wed. 11am-1am, Thurs.-Sat. 11am-2am. Food served daily until 12:30am.

Bo Brooks, 5415 Belair Rd. (488-2722). Complete seafood menu with "Baltimore's Best Steamed Crabs" (from $10) and crabcakes (from $5). Takeout menu dinners only. Draft beer $1.25. Open Mon.-Fri. 11:30am-3pm and 5-10:30pm, Sat. 5-11pm, Sun. 3:30-9:30pm.

Sights

Most tourists start at the Inner Harbor; all too many finish there. The harbor ends in a five-square block of water bounded by the National Aquarium, Harborplace, the Maryland Science Museum, and a fleet of boardable ships, old and new; visitors roam the horseshoe-shaped perimeter and neglect the real neighborhoods east and north. The **National Aquarium** (576-3800), Pier 3, 501 E. Pratt St., makes the whole Inner Harbor worthwhile. Multi-level exhibits and tanks show off rare fish, big fish, red fish, and blue fish along with the biology and ecology of oceans, rivers, and rainforests. The Children's Cove (level 4) lets visitors handle intertidal marine animals in the Touch Pool. (Open Mon.-Thurs. 9am-5pm, Fri.-Sun. 9am-8pm; Sept.-May Sat.-Thurs. 10am-5pm, Fri. 10am-8pm. $11.50, seniors, students and military $8.75, ages 3-11 $6.75, under 3 free. Sept.-May Fri. after 5pm $2. Excellent disabled access; call ahead.)

In the west side of the harbor, the frigate *Constellation* (539-1797), the first commissioned U.S. Navy ship, sailed from 1797 until 1945, serving in the War of 1812, the Civil War, and as flagship of the Pacific Fleet during WWII. Go belowdecks to see (and aim!) the cannons. (Open daily 10am-8pm; May-June and Sept.-Oct. 10am-6pm; Nov.-April 10am-4pm. $2.25, seniors $1.75, ages 6-15 $1.25, active military and under 6 free.) Also moored in the harbor are the U.S.S. *Torsk* submarine and the lightship *Chesapeake.* These vessels make up the **Baltimore Maritime Museum** at Pier III (396-9304; open daily 9:30am-4:30pm; $3, seniors $2.50, kids $1.50, active military free).

At the Inner Harbor's far edge lurks the **Maryland Science Center** (685-5225), 601 Light St. where kids can learn basic principles of chemistry and physics disguised as hands-on games and activities. The IMAX Theater's five-story screen stuns audiences, but the planeterium merely dazzles them. On summer weekends, come in the morning while lines are short. (Open Mon.-Thurs. 10am-6pm, Fri.-Sun. 10am-8pm; Sept.-May Mon.-Sat. 10am-5pm, Sun. noon-6pm. $7.50; seniors, military, kids $5.50. Separate IMAX shows Fri.-Sat. evenings $5.)

The **Top of the World** observation deck reposes in misnamed arrogance on the 27th floor of Baltimore's World Trade Center at Pratt and Commmerce St. The tallest pentagonal structure in the world at 423 ft., the World Trade Center cowers six blocks from the staunchly American, four-sided tallest Baltimore building, the pink granite United States Fidelity and Guarantee Company building, 538 ft. high at 100 Light St. (Open Mon-Fri. 10am-5pm, Sat. 10am-7pm, Sun. 11am-6pm. $2, seniors and ages 5-15 $1.)

To get a feel for Baltimore's historic districts, take bus #7 or 10 from Pratt St. to Abermarle St. and see **Little Italy,** or ride the same buses to Broadway and walk four blocks to **Fells Point.** The neighborhood around Albemarle, Fawn, and High St. is still predominantly Italian, even if the restaurant clientele no longer are; many of the brownstones have been in the same family for generations. Fell's Point imitates the past with cobblestone streets, quaint shops and historic pubs. Stop by the **Society for the Preservation of Federal Hill and Fells Point,** 812 S. Ann St. (675-6750), for an informative discussion of the area. (Society open Mon.-Fri. 9am-4:30pm; tours Thurs. 10am, 1 and 3pm, or by appointment. $1. Garden open Mon.-Fri. 9am-5pm. Free.)

The **Baltimore Museum of Art,** N. Charles and 31st St. (396-7100 or 396-7101), exhibits a fine collection of Americana, modern art (including pieces by Andy Warhol), and paintings and sculpture by Matisse, Picasso, Renoir and Van Gogh. Two adjacent sculpture gardens highlight 20th-century works. The museum's **Baltimore Film Forum** shows classic and current American, foreign, and independent films (Thurs. and Fri. at 8pm, $5); get schedules at the museum or call 889-1993. (Open Tues.-Wed. and Fri. 10am-4pm, Thurs. 10am-7pm, Sat.-Sun. 11am-6pm. $3.50, seniors and full-time students $2.50, under 18 free. Thurs. free. Effective Feb. 1, 1992: ages 4-18 $1.50, under 3 free. Metered parking, wheelchairs available.)

The **Maryland Historical Society,** 201 W. Monument St. (685-3750), houses a library and a museum boasting Francis Scott Key's original manuscript for his poem "Defence of Fort McHenry," later the lyrics for the "Star Spangled Banner," and one of the world's largest sets of 19th-century silver. (Open Tues.-Fri. 10am-5pm, Sat. 9am-5pm; Oct.-April Sun. 1-5pm. $2.50, seniors $1.50, ages 3-12 75¢. Free Wed.) The **Peale Museum,** 225 Holiday St. (396-1149), in the east end of town, is one of the Baltimore City Life Museums. Portrait painter Rembrandt Peale built the museum in 1814, making it the oldest museum building in the U.S. A permanent exhibit of more than 40 portraits painted by the Peale family (Rembrandt was just the most famous son); traveling exhibits appear occasionally. (Open Tues.-Sat. 10am-5pm, Sun. noon-5pm. Free.) The **Walters Art Gallery,** 600 N. Charles St. (547-9000), at Centre, keeps one of the largest private collections world-wide, spanning 50 centuries. The museum's apex is the Ancient Art collection (level 2). (Open Tues.-Sun. 11am-5pm. Tours Wed. at 12:30pm, Sun. at 2pm. $3, seniors $2, under 18 and students with ID free. Free Wed.)

Druid Hill Park (396-6106) off Jones Falls Parkway on Druid Park Lake Drive, contains the **Baltimore Zoo** (366-LION), featuring elephants in a simulated savannah, Siberian tigers, and a waterfall. (Open daily 10am-5:20pm; Nov.-April 10am-4:20pm. Children's Zoo closes 15 min. early. $6.50, seniors and ages 2-15 $3.50, under 2 free. Conservatory open daily 10am-4pm. Free.) **Fort McHenry National Monument** (962-4290) at the foot of E. Fort Ave. off Rte. 2 and Lawrence Ave., commemorates the victory against the British in the War of 1812. Admission ($1, seniors and under 17 free) includes entrance to the museum, a too-long film, and a fort tour. (Open daily 9am-8pm; Sept.-May 9am-5pm. Wheelchair accessible; film captioned for the hearing impaired. Ample parking.)

Baltimore also holds a few historic houses and birthplaces: **Edgar Allen Poe's House,** 203 N. Amity St. (396-4866; open April-Nov. Wed.-Sat. noon-4pm), and the **Babe Ruth Birthplace and Baltimore Orioles Museum,** 216 Emery St. (727-1539; open daily 10am-4pm).

Entertainment and Nightlife

Summer outdoor entertainment animates the Inner Harbor. The **Showcase of Nations Ethnic Festival** celebrates Baltimore's ethnic neighborhoods, showcasing a distinct culture every week June-September. Somewhat generic, the fairs are always fun, vending international fare, crab cakes, and beer. Most events happen at **Festival Hall,** W. Pratt and Sharp Streets (752-8632 or 800-282-6632).

Inner Harbor's **Pier 6** has pop, jazz, and classical concerts (625-1400 or 800-638-2444; tickets $17-32). If you sit on Pier 5, you can hear the music for free. The **Left Bank Jazz Society** (945-2266) has info on jazz performances; the Baltimore Arts Union's **BAU House,** 1713 N. Charles St. (659-5520), near Lanvale, on jazz concerts, poetry readings, art shows, chamber music, and rock. (Tickets $4-7.) Bars and rock clubs cluster in Fells Point; well-known local and national alternative acts play at **Max's on Broadway,** 735 S. Broadway (675-6297). Check the free *City Paper* for complete club listings.

Chesapeake Bay

The Chesapeake Bay, long scraggly arm of Atlantic Ocean reaching from the Virginia coast up through Maryland, nearly halves the state. Originally, the water's shallowness and salinity (Native Americans worshiped the bay as the "Great Salt River") made it one of the world's best oyster and blue crab breeding grounds. The centuries of development, however, have damaged the waters. Despite recent conservation measures, fish, oysters, and crabs are slowly disappearing, sedimentation already filling and shortening many tributaries. Within 10,000 years, the Chesapeake Bay may be a flat piece of oceanfront land.

Three states and one district share the bay waters and split the tourism. For info, write or call the Virginia Division of Tourism, the Maryland Office of Tourist Development, the Delaware State Visitors Center, or the Washington, DC Convention and Visitors Association. (Addresses and phone numbers given in respective state or district introductions.)

The region's public transport is ironically underdeveloped. Greyhound/Trailways bus #122 goes to Salisbury, Princess Anne, Westover Junction, and Pocomoke City from NYC. Make connections with DC, Baltimore, or Philadelphia via Greyhound bus #127. Greyhound/Trailways also covers the east shores of the Chesapeake and Annapolis. The bay is bounded on the west by I-95; on the south by I-64; on the east by U.S. 9, 13, and 50; and on the north by U.S. 40.

Assateague and Chincoteague Islands

Sometime in the 1820s, the Spanish galleon *San Lorenzo* foundered off the Maryland coast. All human passengers were lost, but a few horses struggled ashore. More than a century and a half later, the Chincoteague ponies, descendants of those survivors, roam the unspoiled beaches of Assateague Island.

Assateague Island is divided into three parts. The **Assateague State Park** (301-641-2120), off U.S. 113 in southeast Maryland, is a 2-mi. stretch of picnic areas, beaches, hot-water bathhouses, and campsites ($15). The **Assateague Island National Seashore** (301-641-1441), claims most of the long sandbar north and south of the park, and has its own campground (sites with cold water $9), beaches, and ranger station providing free backcountry camping permits (301-641-3030). Fire rings illuminate some relatively challenging (4- to 13-mi.) hikes; otherwise it's just you and nature. Bring plenty of insect repellent; six-legged unkindnesses fill the island.

The **Chincoteague National Wildlife Refuge** (804-336-6122), stretches south of the island on the Virginia side of the Maryland/Virginia border. The refuge provides a temporary home for the threatened migratory peregrine falcon, a half million Canada and snow geese, and beautiful Chincoteague ponies. At low tide, on the last Thursday in July, the wild ponies are herded together and made to swim from Assateague, MD, to Chincoteague, VA, where the local fire department auctions off the foals. The adults swim back to Assateague and reproduce, providing next year's crop.

To get to Assateague Island, take **Greyhound/Trailways** to **Ocean City,** via daily express and local routes from Baltimore ($22), Washington, DC ($30), Norfolk, VA ($33), and Philadelphia ($33). The Ocean City station idles at Philadelphia and

2nd St. (301-289-9307; open daily 10am-5pm). The **Ocean City Chamber of Commerce** (289-8559), on Rte. 50 at the south of town, has accommodations info. (Open Mon.-Sat. 9am-4:30pm, Sun. 10am-4pm.) To get to Assateague Island from Ocean City, take a taxi (289-8164; about $12). Greyhound/Trailways buses from Salisbury, MD, and Norfolk, VA, make a stop on U.S. 13 at T's Corner (804-824-5935), 11 mi. from Chincoteague. For more area info, call or write to **Chincoteague Chamber of Commerce**, P.O. Box 258 (Maddox Blvd.), Chincoteague, VA 23336 (804-336-6161; open daily 9am-5pm).

MASSACHUSETTS

Richard Nixon, when asked if he had ever visited a communist country, replied, "Massachusetts." That ultra-liberal, out-of-touch image still clouds "Taxachusetts," home of the Kennedy clan. Governor Michael Dukakis's state of origin seemed to be one of the best Republican weapons against his 1988 Democratic presidential candidacy. (That and his reputation as an out-of-the-closet card-carrying member of a group that fights for *civil liberties,* of all things.)

As with any stereotype, Massachusetts's overwhelming "liberality" is a gross generalization. Ignore that the state's founders and religious elites, such as the Mathers, designed a religious freedom which included only people of their own faith—a narrow-mindedness that has maintained itself in different incarnations through the reformist Progressive era to today's politically correct Big Brotherhood (excuse us, Big Personhood). Ignore that Cambridge is the home of stodgy, Establishment Harvard and -military-industrial M.I.T. Ignore that the struggle for school integration in the 1970s revealed a Boston as racist as the worst of the Deep South. Ignore the recently elected Republican governor dedicated to slashing the state budget. Then, and only then, you might be willing to admit the place has more than its fair share of radicalism.

For the tourist, Massachusetts is sprinkled liberally with attractions. A salty atmosphere pervades the coast where fishing villages such as Gloucester and New Bedford retain a nautical charm, while the Berkshires roll with farms, fall foliage, and forested hills. Since the early 19th century, workers have sweated in the textile mills and factories of towns like Lowell, Lawrence, Worcester, Springfield, and Fall River. Cape Cod is a major tourist magnet, famous for its beautiful beaches and quaint, shingled coastal towns. And Boston, "the Hub," is the economic and cultural epicenter of much of New England.

Practical Information

Capital: Boston.

Massachusetts Division of Tourism, Department of Commerce and Development, 100 Cambridge St., Boston 02202 (477-MASS). Can send you a complimentary, comprehensive *Spirit of Massachusetts Guidebook* and direct you to regional resources. (727-3201; 800-632-8038 for guides.) Open Mon.-Fri. 9am-5pm.

Time Zone: Eastern. **Postal Abbreviation:** MA

The Berkshires

While the equidistance of the Berkshire mountains from Boston and New York has long attracted wealthy urbanites seeking a country escape, today affordable restaurants, B&Bs, and campgrounds make them available to the budget travelers who seek them out.

Just about everything in Berkshire County runs north-south: the mountain range giving the county its name (a southern extension of the Green Mountains of Vermont); the 80 mi. of **Appalachian Trail** that wind through Massachusetts; the Hoosac and the Housatonic rivers; and U.S. 7, the region's main artery. **Berkshire Regional Transit Association** (499-2782), known as "the B," spans the Berkshires from Williamstown to Great Barrington. Buses run every hour at some bus stops (Mon.-Sat.); fares (50¢-$3) depend on the route you take. System schedules are available on the bus and at some bus stops. To see sights located far from the town centers, you'll have to drive. The roads are slow and often riddled with potholes, but certainly scenic. The county holds over 100,000 acres of state forests and parks, offering numerous improved and semi-improved camping sites. For info about the parks, stop by the **Region 5 Headquarters** at 740 South St. (442-8928) or contact them by mail at P.O. Box 1433, Pittsfield 01202.

The Berkshires' **area code** is 413.

Northern Berkshires

The best way to see and get to the northern Berkshires is the **Mohawk Trail** (Rte. 2). Perhaps the most famous highway in the state, its awesome view of the surrounding mountains draws crowds during the fall foliage weekend. The trail starts at Miller Falls, MA, but the first real tourist attraction is off Rte. 2 in Greenfield, 5 mi. south of Rte. 5. **Historic Deerfield** (774-5581) is an idyllic, restored village. You can wander around outside the houses and buildings for free, using the map in front of the visitors office. Two-day tour tickets are also available. (Admission $9, ages 6-17 $5, under 6 free.)

The Trail is dotted with affordable campgrounds and lodgings. In Shelbourne Falls at **Highland Springs Guests** (625-2648), the elderly Mrs. Sauter rents clean rooms with double beds for $25. West on the trail lies **Mohawk Trail State Forest** (339-5504), which offers campsites for $12 and rents cabins without baths (large $20, small $16). The **Whitcomb Summit Motel** (662-2625) off Rte. 2 in the town of Florida has a huge tower in its parking lot with a campy "4-state view" for 50¢.

North Adams, farther west on Rte. 2, is a railroad and mill town of former glory. The **Western Gateway Heritage State Park** on the Furnace St. Bypass off Rte. 8N has a railroad museum (663-6312) housed in an old Boston-Maine Railroad building. (Memorial Day-Labor Day daily 10am-4:30pm; Labor Day-June 30 Thurs.-Mon. 10am-4:30pm; call for info on admissions.) A number of high-priced antique and craft stores are fun to browse in.

The **Freight Yard Pub** (663-6547) in the park is a good bargain. The cutesy country Americana joint serves pizza (individual servings $4.25), salads ($2-5.25), and French dip sandwiches ($4.95). Café dining is available outside.

Mt. Greylock, situated between North Adams and Williamstown, is the highest peak in Massachusetts (3491 ft.), accessible by Rtes. 2 and 7. Hiking trails begin from the neighboring towns of Lanesboro, Williamstown, North Adams, Adams, and Cheshire; get maps at the **Mount Greylock Visitors Information Center,** Rockwell Rd. (499-4262), along the pleasantly winding road from Lanesboro to the summit. (Open Mon.-Fri. 9am-4pm, Sat.-Sun. 9am-5pm.) Once at the top, climb the hideous **War Memorial** for a breathtaking and annotated view. Sleep high in nearby **Bascom Lodge** (743-1591), built from the rock excavated for the monument (bunks $18, nonmembers $20, under 12 $11). Sponsored by the Appalachian Mountain Club, the lodge offers breakfast ($5) and dinner ($9.50) to guests; its snackbar is open to the public daily 8:30am-5pm.

The Mohawk Trail ends in **Williamstown** at its junction with Rte. 7; here, an **information booth** (458-4922) provides a slew of free local maps and seasonal brochures. (Open 24 hrs., staffed by volunteers daily 10am-6pm). At **Williams College,** the second oldest in Massachusetts (est. 1793), lecturers compete with the beautiful scenery of surrounding mountains for their students' attention. You can pick up campus maps at the **Admissions Office** (597-2211), 988 Main St. (Open Mon.-Fri. 8:30am-4:30pm. Tours at 10am, 11:15am, 1:15pm, 3:30pm.) First among the college's many cultural resources, **Chapin Library** (597-2462) displays a number of rare U.S. manuscripts, including original copies of the Declaration of Independence,

Articles of Confederation, Constitution, and Bill of Rights. (Open Mon.-Fri. 9am-noon and 1-5pm. Free.) The small but impressive **Williams College Museum of Art** (597-2429) merits a visit for its fine pieces of pop art and Impressionist collection. (Open Mon.-Sat. 10am-5pm, Sun. 1-5pm. Free.)

A good place to eat near campus is **Pappa Charlie's Deli** (28 Spring St., 458-5969), a light-filled, well-stocked deli offering a mind-boggling selection of sandwiches (under $4).

Try not to spend too much time indoors in Williamstown; the surrounding wooded hills beckon from the moment you arrive. The **Hopkins Memorial Forest** on Northwest Hill Rd., is about 1½ mi. west of the college. Owned and run by (597-2346) Williams' Center for Environmental Study, the forest has over 2,250 acres open to the public for hiking and cross-country skiing. **Spoke Bicycles and Repairs,** 618 Main St. (458-3456), rents bikes in a variety of speeds ($10 per day) and can give you advice on good rides in the area.

Far south of Williamstown and the Trail 1½ mi. west of Lenox on Rte. 183 is **Tanglewood,** the summer home of the **Boston Symphony Orchestra.** The season runs from June 29 to September 2. (Tickets $11.50-58. Sat. open rehearsals $9.50. Summer info 637-1940, winter 617-226-1492. Schedules available through the mail from the BSO, Symphony Hall, Boston 02115.)

Boston

At times, Beantown behaves as little more than a shrine to its days of Puritans, patriots, and Tea Parties. Still, the city retains a youthful quality that prevents its venerable past from overwhelming it. One source of this rejuvenating spirit is Boston's longstanding committment to academic and cultural excellence, reflected in the more than 400 institutions of higher learning throughout the city. The city's traditions and the concentration of professors and serious students—can you imagine?—has tempered, somewhat, the exuberance and extroversion associated with a college town. When the city parties, it does so in privacy.

A similar aversion to mingling prevails among Boston's ethnic communities. More than in most cities, Boston's neighborhoods are often ethnically homogeneous—African-American, Asian, Hispanic, Irish, Italian, Jewish, Russian—a situation that adds to the distinct character of the metropolis but occasionally produces newsworthy racial tensions.

Practical Information

Emergency: 911.

Boston Visitors Information Center, Tremont St. at Park, near the Boston Common and the beginning of the Freedom Trail. Free info, including *Where Boston,* a monthly calender of events. Also a fantastic offical guide to Boston, with great maps of the greater Boston area and Freedom Trail ($3). Open daily 9am-5pm. **Greater Boston Convention and Tourist Bureau,** Prudential Plaza West, P.O. Box 490, Boston 02199 (536-4100). T: Copley. Open Mon.-Fri. 8:30am-6pm, Sat. 9am-5pm, Sun. 9am-6pm. **National Historic Park Tourist Bureau,** 15 State St. (242-5642). Info on historical sights and 8-min. slide shows on the Freedom Trail. Some rangers speak French or German. Open daily 9am-5pm, except holidays.

Logan International Airport: (567-5400) east Boston. Easily accessible by public transport. The free **Massport Shuttle** connects all terminals with the "Airport" T-stop. **Airways Transportation Company** (267-2981) runs shuttle buses between Logan and major downtown hotels (service daily from Boston every 30 min. 7am-7pm, to Boston every hr. on the hr. Fare $6.50-7.50, one way.)

Travelers Aid: 711 Atlantic Ave. (542-7286). Open Mon.-Fri. 8:45am-4:45pm. Other locations: Logan Airport Terminals A (569-6284) and C (567-5385) and the desk in Greyhound station (542-9875); hours vary for each.

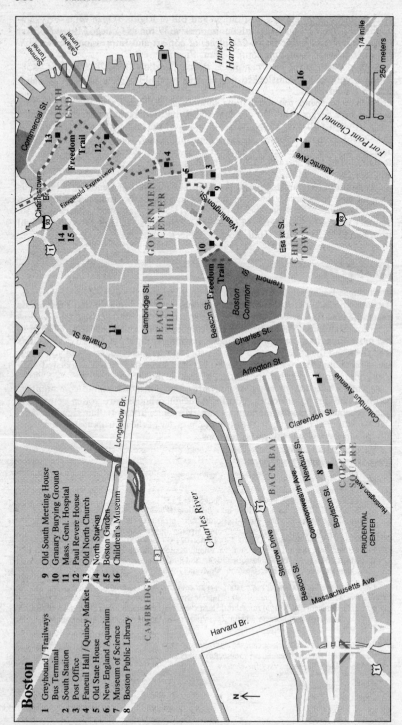

Boston

1   Greyhound / Trailways
    Bus Terminal
2   South Station
3   Post Office
4   Faneuil Hall / Quincy Market
5   Old State House
6   New England Aquarium
7   Museum of Science
8   Boston Public Library

9   Old South Meeting House
10   Granary Burying Ground
11   Mass. Genl. Hospital
12   Paul Revere House
13   Old North Church
14   North Station
15   Boston Garden
16   Children's Museum

Amtrak: South Station, Atlantic Ave. and Summer St. (482-3660 or 800-872-7245). T: South Station. Frequent daily service to New York City (5 hr.; $47, $77 round-trip), Philadelphia (6 hr.; $62, $87), and Washington, DC (8 hr; $95, $115). Restrictions may apply; call ahead.

Buses: Greyhound/Trailways, 10 St. James Ave. (423-5810). T: Arlington. 2 blocks southwest of the Public Gardens. To New York City (Mon.-Thurs.: $29, $55 round trip; Fri.-Sun.: $32, $60), Philadelphia ($25, $50), and Washington, DC ($52, $94). Also the station for **Vermont Transit. Bonanza** (720-4110) lines operate out of the Back Bay Railroad Station on Dartmouth (T: Copley), with frequent daily service to Providence ($7.50, $11.50 round-trip), Fall River/Newport ($7.50, $15) and Bourne/Falmouth/Woods Hole ($10, $19). Open 24 hrs. **Peter Pan Lines** (426-7838), across from South Station on Atlantic Ave. T: South Station. Runs between Western Massachusetts and Albany, NY. (Mon.-Thurs.: $29, $55 round-trip; Fri.-Sun.: $32, $60). Connections to New York City via Springfield ($29). Open daily 5:30am-midnight.

Public Transport: Massachusetts Bay Transportation Authority (MBTA): The subway system, known as the "T," consists of the Red, Green, Blue, and Orange lines. Green and Red Lines run daily 5:30-12:30am; a night on the town often means taxiing home. Fare 85¢, students with ID and ages 5-11 40¢, seniors 20¢. Some automated T entrances in outlying areas require tokens although they are not sold on location. Bus service reaches more of the city and suburbs; fare one token or 50¢, but may vary depending on destination. Bus schedules available at Park St. subway station. A "T passport" offers discounts at local businesses and unlimited travel on all subway and bus lines and some commuter rail zones. (3-day pass $8; 7-day pass $16.) **MBTA Commuter Rail:** Lines to suburbs and North Shore leave from North Station, Porter Square, and South Station T-stops. The **Boston and Maine Railroad** also runs out of North Station. For more information on any of these services call MBTA at 722-3200 or 800-392-6100.

Taxi: Red Cab, (in Brookline) 734-5000. **Checker Taxi,** 536-7000. **Yellow Cab,** 876-5000. A taxi from downtown to Logan $8-9, from Cambridge $18-20.

Car Rental: Brodie Auto Rentals, 24 Eliot St., Harvard Sq. (491-7600). $24-27 per day for sub-compact with 100 free mi., 15-17¢ per mi. thereafter, depending on the type of car. Open Mon.-Fri. 8am-6pm, Sat. 8am-noon, Sun. 9am-noon. Must be 21 with credit card. **Dollar Rent-a-Car,** 1651 Mass. Ave., Harvard Sq. (354-6410). Sub-compact with unlimited mi. $36 per day; must stay within New England. Open Mon.-Thurs. 7:30am-5:30pm, Fri. 7:30am-6:30pm, Sat.-Sun. 7:30am-3:30pm. $7 extra for renters under 25. Must have credit card. Other offices at many locations in Boston, including the Sheraton Hotel (523-5098) and Logan Airport (569-5300).

Bike Rental: Community Bike Shop, 490 Tremont St. near the Common (542-8623). $15 per day. Open Mon.-Fri. 10am-8pm, Sat. 10am-6pm., Sun. noon-5pm (summer only). Must have major credit card.

Help Lines: The Samaritans suicide prevention line, 247-0220. **Rape Hotline,** 354-8807. **Gay and Lesbian Helpline,** 267-9001.

Post Office: McCormack Station, Milk St., Post Office Sq. (654-5686), in the Financial District. Open Mon.-Fri. 8am-5pm. **ZIP code:** 02109.

Area Code: 617.

Leave your buggy near your lodgings and take to the sidewalks and subways because Boston drivers come in two styles—homicidal and suicidal—depending on the size of their car. When you do choose to drive around the city, be defensive; Boston's pedestrians can be as aggressive as the drivers. Also, don't become a casualty of the Boston Police Department's war on illegal parking.

Boston was not a planned city, as evidenced by its intricate and illogical layout, a grab bag of urban thoroughfares and semi-rural paths well-worn by meandering colonial-era cows. Many street names (e.g. Cambridge St.) are repeated within the city as well as in neighboring towns. Get a map at the visitors center and ask for detailed directions wherever you go. The hub of the Hub is the 48-acre **Boston Common,** bounded by Tremont, Boylston, Charles, Beacon, and Park St. The **Freedom Trail** begins there, winds west to Back Bay, northeast to Government Center, and north to Charlestown.

Accommodations and Camping

Cheap accommodations do not thrive in Boston. Early September, when students and their parents arrive for the beginning of the school year, is especially tight; likewise the first week in June, when families of graduating seniors pack into hotel rooms reserved six months to a year in advance. Those with cars should investigate the motels along highways in outlying areas. **Boston Bed and Breakfast,** 16 Ballard St., Newton (332-4199), presides over 100 accommodations around the Boston area. (Singles $60-70. Doubles $70-95. Open Mon.-Fri. 9am-5pm.) The **Boston Welcome Center,** 140 Tremont St. (451-2227), T: Park, can also make reservations for you in various hotels and motels. (Rooms $70-95. Cheaper off-season.)

Boston International Hostel (AYH), 12 Hemenway St. in the Fenway (536-9455). T: Hynes/ICA. Clean, crowded but liveable rooms. Hall bathrooms. Some rooms with sinks. Lockers, common rooms, and 2 kitchens. 220 beds in summer, 120 in winter. Cafeteria and kitchen facilities. Check-out 10:30am. Check-in 2:30-11:30pm. $12, nonmembers $15. Linens $2. Reservations recommended 3 weeks ahead in summer.

Berkeley Residence Club (YWCA), 40 Berkeley St. (482-8850). T: Copley. Great location. Men not allowed above the gorgeous lobby, complete with grand piano and patio. Hall baths. Some doubles with sinks. Cafeteria ($2 breakfast, $5.25 dinner), TV room, sun deck. Singles $34. Doubles $44. Nonmembers $2 extra. Weekly: singles $170, doubles $220. Key deposit $1. Towel deposit $2.

Greater Boston YMCA, 316 Huntington Ave. (536-7800). T: Northeastern. Down the street from Symphony Hall on Mass. Ave. Must be 18. Women accepted. Hall bathrooms. Friendly atmosphere; partially used as overflow housing for Northeastern University students. Cafeteria, pool, and recreational facilities. 10-day max. stay. Singles $33. Doubles $48. Hot breakfast included. Key deposit $5. ID and luggage required for check-in.

Longwood Inn, 123 Longwood Ave. (566-8615), Brookline. T: Longwood Ave. Quiet neighborhood. Victorian mansion with a kitchen, dining room, TV room, laundry, sun room, and parking. Friendly management and comfortable rooms. Check-in Mon.-Fri. 9am-5pm, Sat.-Sun. 9am-1pm, though times flexible. Singles $40-50. Doubles $43-53. Each additional adult $8, kid $5. Reservations recommended, especially in summer.

Anthony's Town House, 1085 Beacon St. (566-3972), Brookline. T: between Carlton and Hawes St. (Green C train). Somewhat distant from downtown but very convenient to the T-stop. Nicely furnished: TV in every room, some with A/C or cable TV. 14 rooms for 20 guests, who range from trim professionals to scruffy backpackers. Singles $45. Doubles $62. Winter and off-season $5 less. Reservations not required.

Garden Hall Dormitories, 164 Marlborough St. (267-0079), Back Bay. T: Copley. Rents only to students. Excellent location. Spartan dorms with bed, dresser, and desk. Some rooms with private bath. Singles, doubles, triples, and quads available. No cooking, no meals served. Must bring own linen. Open Mon.-Fri. 9am-1pm; check-in flexible, but call ahead. $30 per person. Key deposit $10. Reservations required. Open June 1-Aug. 15.

Susse Chalet Motor Lodge, 800 and 900 Morrissey Blvd. in Dorchester, off the Southeast Expressway exit 12 or 13 (287-9200). Good basic accommodations. Adjoining restaurant (entrees $3-14) and bowling alley an added bonus. Singles $51-55. Doubles $55-61. Reservations recommended in summer.

Food

Travelers can find bargain food in several distinct regions of Boston. Watched over by the historic gilded grasshopper, **Faneuil Hall Marketplace** and **Quincy Market** (T: Government Center) are frequented by locals and tourists alike. An astonishing number of cafés, restaurants, and food stands are jambalayaed with equal numbers of souvenir and specialty gift shops; almost any kind of fast food, from peanut butter to pizza, can be found somewhere under the market's long roofs. Just up Congress St., **Haymarket** attracts both budget-conscious shoppers and sightseers to its open-air stalls. Pick up fresh fish, produce, meats, and cheeses here for well below supermarket prices. Indoor stores open daily dawn-dusk; outdoor stalls Fri.-Sat. only. (T: Government Center or Haymarket.) Nearby, the **North End** features great food in the heart of Little Italy (T: Haymarket), while the numerous restaurants in Chinatown seem to serve all the tea in China (T: Chinatown).

Durgin Park, 30 N. Market Place (227-2038). T: Government Center or Haymarket. Sit elbow-to-elbow at long tables and let the famous surly servers entertain and insult you. Traditional Irish boiled dinner of corned beef and cabbage $7. Seafood, ribs, or steak served with cornbread $4.75-15.50. Open Sun.-Thurs. 11:30am-midnight, Fri.-Sat. 11:30-1am.

Ruby's, 280 Cambridge St. (523-9036). T: Government Center. A cozy café just outside downtown. Two eggs, toast, and coffee for a truly anachronistic 75¢ (served daily until 10am). Most sandwiches and lunch platters $3-5. Open Mon.-Thurs. 7:30am-9pm, Fri.-Sun. 8am-11pm.

No Name Restaurant, 15½ Fish Pier in South Boston. (338-7539; 423-2705) T: South Station. Follow Sumner St. over the bridge, left on Viaduct St., right on Northern Ave. The best seafood prices in Boston ($6-9) served among life preservers and ship wheels. Very informal; the line moves quickly because the servers rush you through your meal. Huge servings of award-winning chowder chock full o' clams, shrimp, scallops, and fish (cup $1.15, bowl $2.50). Open Mon.-Sat. 11am-10pm, Sun. 11am-9pm.

Ethiopian Cafe, 333 Mass. Ave. (424-1132). T: Symphony. Look for the black-and-white Symphony Plaza West building, visible from the T-stop. Enjoy the cafe's swift service (the food comes so fast that appetizers are unnecessary) and friendly management before visiting the Boston Pops. Excellent vegetarian selection. Entrees: under $8. Try the exotic Chicken Ginfilfil ($7.25), minced-meat Kifto ($6.95) or a combo plate ($10.50). Open Tues.-Sun. 7am-11pm, Mon. 11am-11pm.

Bangkok Cuisine, 177a Massachusetts Ave. (262-5377), across the street from the Christian Science Church complex. T: Hynes/ICA. Delicious food and friendly service. One of the best Thai restaurants in Boston. Large portions at bargain prices. Lunch $1.75-5.50, dinner $7-10. Open Mon.-Sat. 11:30am-3pm and 5-10:30pm, Sun. 5-10:30pm.

Kebab-N-Kurry, 30 Massachusetts Ave. (536-9835). T: Hynes/ICA. One of Boston's most delicious secrets. North Indian cuisine with a few dishes from Bombay and southern India. Many good vegetarian dishes. Entrees $7-12. Open Mon.-Sat. noon-3pm and 5-11pm, Sun. 5-11pm.

Tim's Tavern, 329 Columbus Ave., in the South End (247-7894). T: Prudential. A small place at the back of a narrow bar, crowded at lunchtime with workers from around Copley Sq. Large portions of U.S. cuisine; its hamburgers have won the "Best in Boston" title. Menu changes daily ($1.50-8). Open Mon.-Sat. 11am-10pm.

The European, 218 Hanover St. (523-5694), in the North End. T: Haymarket. Massachusetts' oldest Italian restaurant and a Boston tradition. Generous portions and friendly service. But don't expect a romantic night out. The long chin-to-chin tables in one room and the small jukeboxes in another seem more appropriate for a roadside diner. Expect a wait of up to 1 hr. on weekends. Entrees $3.75-20.50. Open daily 11am-12:30am.

Sights

At two lofty locations, you can map out the zones you want to visit or simply zone out as you take in the city skyline. The **Prudential Skywalk,** on the 50th floor of the Prudential Center, Back Bay (236-3318/3118), does the 360° fish-eye view thang. (T: Prudential. Open Mon.-Sat. 10am-10pm, Sun. noon-10pm. Admission $2.75, seniors, students with ID and kids $1.75.) The **John Hancock Observatory** at 200 Clarendon St. (247-1977 recorded, 572-6429 live) refuses to be outdone, with 60 beefy floors and the distinction of being the highest building in New England (740 ft.). On good days, you can see New Hampshire. On better days you can't. (T: Copley. Open Mon.-Sat. 9am-10pm, Sun. 10am-10pm. Admission $2.75, age 5-15 and seniors $2.)

The **Freedom Trail** (536-4100) leads pedestrians along a clearly marked red brick or painted line through historic Boston, beginning at the **Boston Visitors Information Center** (see Practical Information, Boston). Most of the sites visited are free, a few charge $2.50-3 for admission. Don't bother buying the map ($1) to the country's most famous footpath since you can pick up free ones at almost any brochure rack. The trail makes two loops. The easier Downtown Loop passes the **Old North Church,** the **Boston Massacre Sight,** the **Granary Burial Ground,** the **Old Corner**

Bookstore, and **Paul Revere's House,** among 11 other sights, and takes only an afternoon. The fascinating **Black Heritage Trail** makes 14 stops of its own, each marked by a red-black-and-green logo. The tour begins at the **Boston African-American Historic Sight,** 46 Joy St. (T: Park), where you can pick up a free map before you visit the museum inside (742-1854; open Tues.-Sun. 10am-4pm) or begin the walk. The trail covers sights of particular importance to the development of Boston's African-American community including: the **African Meeting House** (1805), the earliest black church in North America; the **Robert Gould Shaw and 54th Regiment Memorial** on the Common, dedicated to black soldiers who fought in the Union Army and their white Boston leader; and the **Lewis and Harriet Hayden House,** a station on the Underground Railroad. Most sights are free, a few charge $2.50-3 for entrance.

The Common, Fenway, Beacon Hill, and Back Bay

The areas immediately surrounding, especially northwest of, the **Boston Common** (T: Park) are Brahmin heaven: some quaint streets seem frozen in time, and the more contemporary sections are gilded with chic.

Inhabitants established the Common, the oldest park in the nation, as a place to graze their cattle in 1634. Now street vendors, not cows, live off the fat of the land. While the frisbee players, drug dealers, street musicians, students, families, cops, and government employees all stake equal claim to it in the daytime, the bovine get notoriously dangerous at night—don't go here alone after dark. Scattered around the green, the **Boston Massacre Monument,** the **Lafayette Monument,** the **Declaration of Independence Monument,** and St. Gauden's bas-relief **Civil War Monument** stand as somber historical reminders. Across Charles St. from the Common, bronze characters from the children's book *Make Way for Ducklings* point the way to the Swan boats (522-1966) in the fragrant and lovely **Public Gardens.** The pedal-powered boats glide around a quiet pond lined with big shade trees and bright Huey, Dewey, and Louie flower beds. (Boats open April 14-June 20 daily 10am-4pm; June 21-Labor Day 10am-5pm; Labor Day-Sept. 16 noon-4pm. Admission $1.25, under 12 75¢, seniors $1.)

Residential since its settlement by the Puritans, **Beacon Hill** has always pulsed with blueblood. Several buildings, including the gold-domed **State House** (727-3676), designed by Charles Bulfinch, offer exhibits of Massachusetts and colonial history and government. There are free tours of the Hall of Flags, House of Representatives, and Senate Chamber. (Visitor info: Doric Hall, 2nd floor. Open Mon.-Fri. 9am-5pm; tours Mon.-Fri. 10am-4pm.) The **Harrison Gray Otis House,** 141 Cambridge St. (227-3956), another Bulfinch original, headquarters the Society for the Preservation of New England Antiquities. (Tours on the hr. Tues.-Fri. noon-4pm, Sat. 10am-4pm. Admission $3, seniors $2.50, under 12 $1.50.) The Society hordes info about historical sights. The nearby **Boston Athenaeum,** 10½ Beacon St. (227-0270), houses over 700,000 books, and offers tours of its library, art gallery, and print room. (Open Mon.-Fri. 9am-5:30pm, Sat. 9am-4pm; no Sat. hrs. in summer. Free tours Tues. and Thurs. at 3pm; reservations required.)

Charles Street serves as the Hill's front door. This exclusive residential bastion of Boston Brahminism now shares its brick sidewalks with the fashionable contingent of Boston's gay community. The art galleries, cafés, antique stores, and other small shops with hanging wooden signs make this a fine avenue for a stroll.

In the **Back Bay,** southwest of Beacon Hill, three-story brownstone row houses line the only gridded streets in Boston. The thoroughfares running east-west (Boylston and Newbury St., Commonwealth Ave., and Marlborough and Beacon St.) are crossed by north-south streets ordered alphabetically, from Arlington St. on the border of the Public Garden South to Hereford St. Originally the marshy, uninhabitable "back bay" of Boston Harbor, landfill and elegant folk moved in about 150 years ago. **Commonwealth Avenue** ("Comm. Ave.") is a European-style boulevard with statuary and benches punctuating its grassy median. **Newbury Street** is Boston's most flamboyant promenade; dye your poodle, pierce your navel, and get out there and vogue. The dozens of small art galleries, boutiques, bookstores, and cafés that line the stage are a conspiracy of exclusivity. (T: Arlington, Copley, or Hynes/ICA.)

The handsome **Copley Square** area extends the whole length of Back Bay on commercial Boylston St. Renovated and officially reopened in June 1989, the square (T: Copley) accommodates a range of seasonal activities, including folk dancing, a food pavilion, and people watching people. A permanent feature is the **Boston Public Library,** 666 Boylston St. (536-5400), a massive, spartan, Orwellian building, liberally inscribed with the names of hundreds of authors. Benches and window seats inside overlook a tranquil courtyard with fountain and garden. Relax here or in the vaulted reading room. The auditorium gives a program of lectures and films. (Open Mon.-Thurs. 9am-9pm, Fri.-Sat. 9am-5pm.) Across the square H.H. Richardson's Romanesque fantasy, **Trinity Church,** catches its reflection in I.M. Pei's mirrored Hancock Tower. Many consider Trinity, built in 1877, a masterpiece of U.S. church architecture—the interior will elaborate. (T: Copley. Open daily 8am-6pm.) **Copley Place,** a gaudy complex containing two hotels and a ritzy mall in the corner next to the library, attracts a steady stream of local high school students with big hair. The partially gentrified **South End,** south of Copley, makes for good brownstone viewing and casual dining.

Back Bay loses some of its formality on the riverside **Esplanade** (T: Charles), a park extending from the Longfellow Bridge to the Harvard Bridge. Boston's quasi-pseudo-beach on the Charles, the Esplanade fills in the summer with sun-seekers. However, don't go in the water. Bikers and roller skaters, upholding Boston's tradition of good road manners, try to mow down pedestrians on the walkway. The bike path, which follows the river to the posh suburb of Wellesley, makes a nice afternoon's ride. The Esplanade also hosts some of Boston's best-loved cultural events—the concerts of the **Boston Pops Orchestra** (266-1492) at the mauve **Hatch Shell.** Led by John "Star Wars" Williams, the Pops play here during the first week of July. Admission is free; arrive early, before the crowds get unmanageable. Concerts begin at 8pm. On the Fourth of July, nearly 100,000 patriotic thrillseekers throng the Esplanade to hear the Pops concert (broadcast by loudspeaker throughout the area) and to watch the ensuing terrific fireworks display. Arrive before noon for a seat on the Esplanade, although you can watch the fireworks from basically anywhere along the river. The regular Pops season at **Symphony Hall,** 301 Mass. Ave. (266-2378, operator; 266-7575, recorded message) runs May 10-July 3 and July 10-14. (Tickets $5-50. Box office open Mon.-Fri. 9am-5pm.)

Beyond the Back Bay, west on Commonwealth Ave., glows **Kenmore Square** (T: Kenmore), watched over by the psychedelic landmark Citgo sign. Kenmore Sq. has more than its share of neon, containing many of the city's most popular nightclubs (see Nightlife below).

Below Kenmore Sq., the **Fenway** comprises a large area of the city, containing some of its best museums. (T: Museum.) Ubiquitous landscraper Frederick Olmsted of Central Park fame designed the **Fens** area at the center of the Fenway as part of his "Emerald Necklace" vision for Boston—a necklace he fortunately never completed. A gem nonetheless, the park's fragrant rose gardens and neighborhood vegetable patches make perfect picnic turf. Bring your own vegetables. Just north of the Fens, **Fenway Park,** home of the "Green Monster," is the nation's oldest Major League ballpark in the nation and center stage for the **Boston Red Sox** baseball club, which, if given a chicken filet, would find a bone to choke on. (box office 267-8661; open Mon.-Fri. 9am-5pm, Sat. 9:30am-2pm; T: Kenmore). West still of Fenway along Green lines C and D sits suburban **Brookline,** with its charming guest houses; curfewed **Boston University** lines Commonwealth Ave. along Green line B.

Downtown, The North End, Chinatown, and the Waterfront

The downtown area claims most of the inland area directly west from Boston Harbor, and the affection of thousands of yuppies. A perfect brew of commerce and politics made historic **Quincy Market** in the West End (T: Government Center) the focal point of contemporary Boston. Upon completion, the red-brick and cobblestone marketplace received nationwide praise as an example of urban revitalization. Not long ago, the pretty buildings that house souvenir shops and trendy boutiques were decrepit warehouses. Though overpriced and overcrowded, the market is fun for browsing. The info center in the market's South Canopy (523-3886) can provide direction. At night, come for the lively bar scene. In 1742, Peter Faneuil (FAN-yul) donated **Faneuil Hall,** the gateway to the market, to serve as a marketplace and community hall. Sometimes called the "cradle of American Liberty," it served as a gathering spot for Bostonians pissed at King George. Occasionally, free concerts are given outside the Hall; the **Summer Nights** concert series features blues, calypso, and rock. (Thurs. 5:30-8:30pm. Call 523-3886 for details.) The Hall will be closed for restoration until some time in the summer of 1992.

Across Congress St. from the market, the red brick plaza of **Government Center,** as its name indicates, proves a trifle less picturesque. The monstrous concrete **City Hall** (725-4000), designed by I.M. Pei, opens to the public Monday through Friday (T: Government Center). A few blocks south, its more aesthetically pleasing precursor, the **Old State House,** 206 Washington St. (720-1713/3290), built in 1713, once rocked with revolutionary fervor. The State House is currently under restoration and will be closed to the public until summer 1992.

The eastern tip of Boston contains the historic **North End** (T: Haymarket). The city's oldest residential district, now an Italian neighborhood, overflows with windowboxes, Italian flags, fragrant pastry shops, Sicilian restaurants, and Catholic churches. The most famous of the latter, **Old St. Stephens Church,** on Hanover St. (523-1250), is the classically colonial brainchild of Charles Bulfinch. Down the street, the brilliant and sweet-smelling **Peace Gardens,** owned by St. Leonard's Church, pacifies with red and white flowers.

Downtown Crossing, south of City Hall at Washington St. (T: Downtown Crossing), is a wonderful pedestrian mall actually ruled by pedestrians. In the summertime, street vendors peddle flowers, handicrafts, sweet sausage, and homemade lemonade from pushcarts. The paragon of Boston shopping, **Filene's Basement,** 426 Washington St., jives as the world's oldest bargain store, in business since 1908.

Directly southwest of the Common, Boston's engaging **Chinatown** (T: Chinatown) demarcates itself with pagoda-style telephone booths and streetlamps and an arch at its Beach St. entrance. Within this small area cluster many restaurants, food stores, and novelty shops where you can buy Chinese slippers and 1000-year-old eggs. Chinatown has two big celebrations each year. The first, **New Year,** usually falls on a Sunday in February, and festivities include lion dances and Kung Fu exhibitions. The **August Moon Festival** honors a mythological pair of lovers at the time of the full moon. Watch for listings in *Where Boston.*

The sleazy, all-but-defunct **Combat Zone** borders Chinatown to the east. Once Boston's legitimate, municipally-designated red-light district, its current incarnalization consists mostly of boarded-up Sextasy theaters and derelicts.

The **waterfront area,** bounded by Atlantic and Commercial St., runs along Boston Harbor from South Station to the North End Park. Stroll down Commercial, Lewis, or Museum Wharf for a slurp of briny air. At the excellent **New England Aquarium** (973-5200; T: Aquarium), Central Wharf on the Waterfront, giant sea turtles, sharks, and their scaley friends swim tranquilly as visitors peer into their cylindrical 187,000-gallon tank. Penguins cavort in a mini-archipelago around the base of the tank. Dolphins and sea lions perform in the ship *Discovery,* moored alongside. On weekends lines tend to be long. (Open Sept.-June Mon.-Wed. and Fri. 9am-5pm, Thurs. 9am-8pm, Sat.-Sun. and holidays 9am-6pm; otherwise Mon.-Tues. and Fri. 9am-6pm, Wed.-Thurs. 9am-8pm, Sat.-Sun. and holidays 9am-7pm. Admission $7.50, seniors and students $6.50, ages 3-11 $3.50. Thurs. and summer Wed. after 4pm $1 discount.) The aquarium also offers **whale watching cruises** (973-5277) from April to late October ($23, seniors and students $18, ages 12-18 $17, ages 4-11 $16, under 3 not allowed). **Boston Harbor Cruises** (227-4320) leave from Long Wharf, adjacent to the aquarium, for 90-minute tours of the harbor from roughly March to October. (Departs at 11am, 1pm, 3pm, and 7pm. Admission $8, seniors $6, under 12 $4.)

Across Fort Point Channel from the waterfront, predominantly Irish American **South Boston** has a unique accent. (T: South Station). "Southie" has great seafood places and two beaches.

Charlestown and the Museums

Boston's intellectual and artistic community supports a higher concentration of museums than anywhere else in New England. Check the free *Guide to Museums of Boston* for details on the many museums not mentioned here.

The most famous, the **Museum of Fine Arts (MFA),** 465 Huntington Ave. (267-9300; T: Museum, Green line E train), near the intersection with Massachusetts Ave., gathers one of the world's finest collections of Asian ceramics, outstanding Egyptian art, a good showing of Impressionists, and superb Americana. Don't miss John Singleton Copley's fascinating portraits of his contemporaries Paul Revere and Samuel Adams, or his dramatic *Watson and the Shark.* Also worth a gander are the two famous unfinished portraits of George and Martha Washington, painted by Gilbert Stuart in 1796. (Open Tues.-Sun. 10am-5pm, Wed. 10am-10pm. West Wing only open Thurs.-Fri. 5-10pm. Admission $6, seniors and students $5. West Wing only, $4. Both free Wed. 4-10pm.)

A few hundred yards from the MFA stands the beautiful **Isabella Stewart Gardner Museum,** 280 The Fenway (566-1401; 734-1359 for recorded events info). The eccentric "Mrs. Jack" Gardner built the small, Venetian-style palace with a stunning courtyard to distract her from her grief at the loss of her only child, scandalized Boston with her excesses, and eventually built a superb art collection. Unfortunately, in what has been termed the greatest art heist in history, a 1989 break-in relieved the museum of works by Rembrandt, Vermeer, Dégas, and others. (Open Tues.-Sun. noon-5pm. Chamber music on 1st floor Sept.-June Tues. at 6pm, and Sun. at 1:30pm. Admission $6, seniors and students $3, ages under 12 free.)

At the far eastern end of the Esplanade on the Charles River Dam, the **Museum of Science,** Science Park (723-2500; T: Science Park), contains, among other wonders, the largest "lightning machine" in the world. The multi-story roller-coaster for small metal balls purports to explain energy states. Within the museum, the **Hayden Planetarium** features models, lectures, films, and laser and star shows; the **Mugar Omni Theatre** shows popular films of scientific interest on a gee-whiz four-story domed screen. (Open Mon.-Thurs. and Sat.-Sun. 9am-5pm, Fri. 9am-9pm. Admission $6, seniors, students and ages 4-14 $4.50. Planetarium only, $5 and $3.50; Museum and Omni $10 and $7.50; all 3 facilities $14 and $10.50. Free Wed. afternoons Sept.-May.)

At the **Children's Museum,** 300 Congress St. (426-8855), in southern Boston on Museum Wharf, kids of all ages toy with way-cool hands-on exhibits. (Open July-Sept. Mon.-Thurs. and Sat.-Sun. 10am-5pm, Fri. 10am-9pm; closed Mon. during off-season. Admission $6, seniors and ages 2-15 $5, kids age 1 $1, under 1 free; Fri. 5-9pm $1. T: South Station. Follow the signs with the milk bottles on them.)

The **John F. Kennedy Presidential Library** (929-4523), on Morrissey Blvd., Columbia Point, Dorchester is dedicated "to all those who through the art of politics seek a new and better world." Designed by I.M. Pei, the white cuboid oceanside edifice contains fascinating, sometimes trivial exhibits that employ photographs, documents, audio-visual presentation, and mementos to document the careers of John Kennedy and his brother, Robert. (Open daily 9am-5pm. Admission $4.50, seniors $2.50, under 16 free. T: JFK/UMass on the Ashmont branch; free MBTA shuttle to the U Mass campus, a short walk from the library.)

Boston's lone outpost of the avant-garde, **Institute of Contemporary Art (ICA),** 955 Boylston St. (266-5151 recorded message, 266-5152 operator; T: Hynes/ICA), attracts major contemporary artists while aggressively promoting lesser-known work. Their innovative, sometimes controversial exhibits (the Mapplethorpe show stopped here) change every eight weeks. The museum also presents experimental music, dance, and film, often followed by discussions with the artists. (Open Wed. and Sun. 11am-5pm, Thurs.-Sat. 11am-8pm. Admission $4, students with ID $3, seniors and under 16 $1.50. Free Thurs. 5-8pm.)

Two blocks down Massachusetts Ave. from Boylston sits the Mother Church of the **First Church of Christ, Scientist,** One Norway St. (480-2000), founded in Boston by Mary Baker Eddy. The lovely **Mother Church** is the world headquarters of the Christian Science movement, and its complex of buildings appropriately vast and imposing. Both the Mother Church and the smaller, older church out back can be seen by guided tour only; the guides do not proselytize. (Tours Mon.-Sat. 9:30am-3:30pm, Sun. 11:15am-2pm.) In the Christian Science Publishing Society next door, use the catwalk to pass through the **Mapparium,** a 40-ft.-wide stained-glass globe. (Tours Mon.-Sat. 9:30am-3:30pm.)

Charlestown, founded in 1629 by ten Puritan families, predates its southern neighbor by one year. Boston made up for lost time by accruing a batch of historic landmarks over the course of Revolution, but among Charlestown's brownstones and brick are two landmarks of its own. The **Bunker Hill Monument,** in Monument Sq. (242-5641), commemorates the 1775 Battle in a 221-ft. obelisk. (Open daily 9am-4:30pm.) "Old Ironsides" or the **USS Constitution** (426-1812), the world's oldest commissioned battleship, keeps port in the Charlestown Navy Yard. (T: North Station.) Indestructible in its day, the ship still fires a single salutary cannon each night. (Open daily spring and fall 9am-5pm, summer 9am-6pm, winter 10am-4pm. Admission $2, kids $1.50. Sat. free for kids.)

Nightlife

The nightlife of the city that beans made famous admittedly does not compare with larger and more sophisticated New York. "Blue laws," which forbid serving liquor past a certain hour, stand out as a relic of the city's Puritan past. Liquor, though served on Sundays in restaurants and bars, cannot be sold anywhere else in the state on that day. Nearly everything closes between 1 and 2am, and bar admittance for anyone under 21 is hard-won, although a few spots have 18-and-over nights. So treat Boston nightlife as you would the appearance of rutting bison: an appreciable spasm of short-lived brilliance. Quality rock, folk, jazz, and comedy clubs abound here, as well as theater and other cultural offerings. Check the weekly *Boston Phoenix* for its up-to-date "Boston-After-Dark" listings.

Citi, 9-15 Lansdowne St., Kenmore Sq. (262-2424). T: Kenmore. Top 40 club gets "adventurous" with hip-hop and dance music. No jeans, sneakers, athletic wear, or collarless shirt. No dress code on Sun. Open daily 9:30pm-2am. Cover varies.

Narcissus, 533 Commonwealth Ave. (536-1950). T: Kenmore. Young crowd, the youngest of whom seem to wear the tightest clothes. Ear-splitting mainstream music on 3 levels. Occasional live performers: Wed. heavy metal night, Sun. Latin night. Open daily 8pm-2am. Cover varies.

The Black Rose, 160 State St., Faneuil Hall (742-2286). T: Government Center. Fabulous Irish pub serving seafood and staffed by bartenders and waitresses from the Emerald Isle. Of course they serve a pint of Guinness ($2.75). Frequent live traditional Irish music Sat.-Sun. 4-8pm, daily at 9pm. Open daily 11:30-1:30am. Cover Thurs.-Sat. nights $5.

The Channel, 25 Necco St., South Boston (451-1050). T: South Station. A forum for the bigger reggae, rap, rock, new wave, and heavy metal acts. Huge dance floor, 8 bars, gameroom, concession stand. Capacity 1500. 18-and-over nights. Open Tues.-Sat. 8pm-2am. Cover varies.

Rathskeller, 528 Commonwealth Ave., Kenmore Sq. (536-2750). T: Kenmore. The "Rat" cultivates a grungy atmosphere to accompany its excellent program of grungy bands. Open Thurs.-Sun. 11am-2am. Shows start around 9:30pm. Cover varies.

Gay bars do not proliferate in Boston, but many bars cater to gay and lesbian clientele on specific nights or times. Check the *Bay Windows* listings for more information. **Chaps,** 27 Huntington Ave. (266-7778; T: Copley) is a fun throwback to the disco era with mirrored walls and a spacious dance floor. The primarily gay male clientele is a blend of older and younger patrons. Live entertainment is occasionally offered. (Open daily 3 or 4pm-2am, Sat.-Sun. 3pm-2am. Cover varies.) **Campus/Manray,** 21 Brookline St. (864-0406), Central Sq., features Top-40 and progressive music for women on Sundays and is open to a mixed crowd the rest of the week. (T: Central.)

Arts and Entertainment

Musicians, dancers, actors, and *artistes* of every description fill Boston. The *Boston Phoenix* and the "Calendar" section of the Thursday *Boston Globe* list activities for the coming week. Also check the *Where Boston* booklet available at the visitors center. What Boston doesn't have, Cambridge does (see Cambridge below). **Bostix,** a Ticketron outlet in Faneuil Hall (723-5181), sells half-price tickets to performing arts events on the day of performance. (Service charge $1.50-2.50 per ticket. Cash only. Open Tues.-Sat. 11am-6pm, Sun. 11am-4pm.)

Actors in town cluster around Washington St. and Harrison Ave., in the **Theater District** (T: Boylston). The famous **Wang Center for the Performing Arts** at 268 Tremont St. (482-9393), produces theater, classical music, and opera in its modern complex. The **Shubert Theater,** 265 Tremont St. (426-4520), and the **Wilbur Theater,** 246 Tremont St. (423-4008), host Broadway hits calling in Boston. Tickets for these and for shows at the **Charles Playhouse,** 74 Warrenton St. (426-6912), are costly (around $30). The area's professional companies are cheaper, and may provide a more interesting evening. The **New Ehrlich Theater,** 539 Tremont St. (482-6316), and **Huntington Theater Co.,** 264 Huntington Ave. (266-7900; 266-0800 for box office) at Boston University have solid artistic reputations. (Tickets $10-24.) More affordable college theater is also available; during term-time, watch students thesp at **Tufts Theater-Arena** (381-3493), the **Boston University Theatre** (266-3913), the **MIT Drama Shop** (253-2908), and the MIT **Shakespeare Ensemble** (253-2903).

The renowned **Boston Ballet** (946-4070), in neighboring Newton, brings to life such classics as the "Nutcracker" and "Swan Lake." The **Boston Symphony Orchestra,** 201 Mass. Ave. (266-1492; T: Symphony), at Huntington, holds its concert season from October to April. Rush seats go on sale three hours before Thursday and Saturday concerts. Open Wednesday rehearsals cost under $10; bargain tickets are also available Friday at noon for that evening's show. In summer, when the BSO retreats to Tanglewood, the **Boston Pops Orchestra** sets up at Symphony Hall or the Esplanade and plays classics and pop on weekend evenings. The **Berklee Performance Center,** 136 Mass. Ave. (266-7455), an adjunct of the Berklee School of Music, holds concerts featuring students, faculty, and jazz and classical luminaries.

Despite its immediate air of refinement, Boston goes ape for sports. Long known for fans as committed as Charles Manson, Beantown always seems to be in some seasonal basketball, baseball, football, or hockey frenzy. On summer nights, thousands of baseball fans pour out of **Fenway Park** (see above) and clog Kenmore Sq. traffic for an hour. **Boston Garden** (T: North Station), an occasional spot for Dead shows located off the JFK Expressway between the West and North Ends, hosts the illustrious **Boston Celtics** basketball team (season Oct.-May; 526-6050 or 523-3030 for info) and **Boston Bruins** hockey team (season Oct.-April; call 227-3200 for more info). A few mi. outside Boston, **Sullivan Stadium** hosts the **New England Patriots** football franchise.

In October, the **Head of the Charles** regatta, the largest such single-day event in the U.S., attracts rowing clubs and college sweatshirts from across the country. The 3-mi. boat races begin at Boston University Bridge; the best vantage points are on the Weeks footbridge and Kennedy St. Bridge near Harvard. On April 19, the 10,000 runners competing in the **Boston Marathon** tread memories of the "Head" underfoot. Call the Massachusetts Division of Tourism for details (617-727-3201).

For info on other special events, such as the **St. Patrick's Day Parade** in South Boston (March 17), **Patriot's Day** celebrations (April 19), the week-long **Boston Common Dairy Festival** (June), the **Boston Harbor Fest** (early July), and the North End's **Festival of St. Anthony** (mid-August), see the *Boston Phoenix* or *Globe* calendars.

Cambridge

Cambridge is to bookstores and libraries what a red-light district is to brothels. Book-ended by the Massachusetts Institute of Technology (MIT) and Harvard University, Cambridge houses an army of scholars and students shuttling like gnomes from one dimly-lit grindstone to another. Don't be surprised if a large proportion of people you see on the streets are so physically and emotionally stunted that they appear as though they have been locked in libraries since birth. Some have.

Be sensitive to the power around you. These two universities mill privileged teens into semi-aristocratic elites who will rule the United States (as well as other nations). If the pedestrians around you seemed overly consumed with their own self-importance, consider the source. On the other hand, don't come to Cambridge expecting dignified American undergraduates parading around in suits and acting with decorum. MIT has a whole exhibit dedicated to its students' practical jokes, and Harvard's freshman throw pats of butter at their dining-hall ceiling.

The town affects a certain cosmopolitanism. The restaurants offer menus that run the gamut of ethnic cuisines. Mulling over a gourmet coffee and fake French pastries, (Cambridge for "fast food"), you might catch conversation in French, Japanese, Russian, or academic doublespeak. Yet the backdrop is pronouncedly Ivied America, with charming colonial structures and gilded bell towers. Situated on the northeast side of the Charles River, Cambridge often feels like an overgrown (and overblown) college campus, in which everyone is trying to get to the head of the class.

Practical Information

See Boston Practical Information above for more complete and detailed listings.

Emergency: 911.

Cambridge Discovery Booth (497-1630), in Harvard Sq. Best and most comprehensive information about Cambridge, as well as MBTA bus and subway schedules. Pick up the *Old Cambridge Walking Guide,* an excellent self-guided tour ($1). Walking tours of Harvard and the surrounding area in the summer. Open summer Mon.-Sat. 9am-6pm, Sun. 9am-5pm; off-season Mon.-Sat. 9am-5pm, Sun. 1-5pm. **Out-Of-Town News** (354-7777). No official status as a tourist resource, but sells a large number of excellent maps and guides to the area. Open daily 6am-midnight **Harvard University Information Center,** 1352 Massachusetts Ave. (495-1573), Harvard Sq. Most helpful in your exploration of the campus. Free guides to the university museums; several tours each day. Open summer Mon.-Sat. 9am-4:45pm, Sun. 1-4pm; off-season Mon.-Sat. 9am-4:45pm. Try to find Harvard Student Agencies' *The Unofficial Guide to Life at Harvard* ($6), which has complete and up-to-date listings of local restaurants, entertainment, sights, transportation and services.

Public Transport: Massachusetts Bay Transportation Authority (MBTA), 722-3200 or 800-392-6100. Office open Mon.-Fri. 8:30am-4:30pm. Subway operates daily 5:30am-12:30am. Fare 75¢ with possible increase to $1 by summer of 1992.

Taxi: Cambridge Taxi, 76 Hampshire St., 876-5600, 547-3000. Taxi service from Cambridge to/from Logan airport runs $18-20.

Post Office: 125 Mt. Auburn St. (876-6483). Open Mon.-Fri. 8am-5:30pm, Sat. 9am-1pm. **ZIP code:** 02238.

Area Code: 617.

Massachusetts Avenue ("Mass. Ave.") is Cambridge's major artery. Most of the action takes place in "squares" (that is, commercial areas) along Mass. Ave. and the Red Line. **MIT** is just across the Mass. Ave. Bridge at **Kendall Square,** on the Red Line. The Red Line continues outbound one T-stop at a time through: **Central Square,** the heart of urban Cambridge; frenetic, eclectic **Harvard Square;** and more suburban **Porter Square.**

Accommodations

Cambridge YMCA, 820 Massachusetts Ave. (661-9622). T: Central. Men only. Sometimes full. Hall bathrooms. 10-day max. stay. Check-out 11am. Singles only, $32. Key deposit $10. 2 forms of ID (one picture) required. Reservations recommended, or arrive by 11am.

Cambridge YWCA, 7 Temple St. (491-6050), just off Mass. Ave. near the Central T-stop. Women only. Few overnight rooms, all of which fill quickly. Kitchen and laundry facilities. Permanent residences available. Singles only, $30. Nonmembers $35. Key deposit $10. Reservations required.

The Irving House, 24 Irving St. (547-4600), near Cambridge St., in a residential neighborhood near the university and the Square. T: Harvard. New management. Unique rooms, libraries, comfortable fishtanked lounge, spacious wood floors; parking available. Singles from $30. Doubles $40-65. Reservations required.

Susse Chalet Inn, 211 Concord Turnpike (Rte. 2), Fresh Pond (661-7800), ½-mi. from the Alewife T-stop just outside Cambridge. Standard hotel-chain-type lodgings overlooking the highway. Private bath, TV, and phone. Singles $50. Doubles $55. Reservations suggested.

Food

Nightly, thousands of college students renounce cafeteria fare in the restaurants of Harvard Square, and for good reason. An enormous selection of funky eateries packs its tiny area. A 15-minute walk around should uncover offerings to satisfy even the most esoteric tastebuds. Don't be afraid to wander beyond the square if you feel as if you've seen one kid too many in a crimson sweatshirt. Explore Massachusetts Ave. where it slopes down into Central Sq., lined with great Indian restaurants, or where it climbs up into the varied eateries of Porter Sq.

For cheap student grub, try **The Garage** at 36 Kennedy St. More of a storage shed where cars no longer fit, this mall of restaurants offers everything from hummus to greasy pizza. Probably some of the cheapest fare in the square, **Elsie's,** 71 Mt. Auburn St., makes generous sandwiches ($2.50-3.50) quickly. (Open Mon.-Fri. 7am-midnight, Sat. 7am-4pm, Sun. 11am-7pm.) **Tommy's Lunch** on Mt. Auburn St. (492-9540) is, ironically enough, a late-night tradition at Harvard, with plenty of sneering service, pinball (25¢), and greasy onion rings. Try the legendary raspberry lime rickey (80¢-$1.50), but don't put your hands over the counter or feet on the booths; sit back and admire the "Gun Control is Being Able to Hit Your Target" T-shirts. (Open daily 6am-2am.) Diner-like **Charlie's Kitchen** at 10 Eliot St. proffers many variations on the double burger ($3). (Open Mon.-Sat. noon-midnight, Sun. noon-1am.)

College students and Cantabrigians alike hang out at the **Border Café,** 32 Church St. in Harvard Sq. (864-6100). A nice *faux* Southwestern atmosphere and adequate food make up for the considerable crowds. Try their specialty—steaming *fajitas* ($8-11), or the meal-in-itself *quesadilla* appetizers. Come prepared to have a few drinks at the bar, since you may wait for up to an hour to get a table. (Open Mon.-Wed. 11am-12:45am, Thurs.-Sat. noon-1:45am. Min. food order of $4.50 required for drink orders.) Pick up the weekly *Square Deal,* usually handed out or in boxes near the T-stop, for coupons and discounts on local fare.

Asmara, 714 Mass. Ave (864-7447), right next to the Central T-stop. Watch for the simple blue sign. Although this Ethiopian establishment is unassuming, the food is hauntingly memorable. Friendly waitresses deliver more-than-generous entrees on communal platters, from which diners eat using torn-off pieces of sourdough *injera* bread. Sample the pepper sauce chicken ($7.90) or the spicy Shuro ($6.75), mashed chickpeas in pepper sauce. If you feel particularly adventurous, dare the Kitfo ($8.75), surprisingly delicious raw ground beef in butter sauce. But don't eat with your left hand, or the waitresses will know you are possessed by The Devil. Entrees $6.75-8.75. Open Sun.-Thurs. noon-10:30pm; Fri.-Sat. noon-11:30pm.

The Skewers, 92 Mt. Auburn St., Harvard Sq. (491-3079). Large servings of tasty Middle Eastern food at bargain prices. Sandwiches $3-4.50, dinner entrees $6.50-7.25. Open Mon.-Sat. 11am-11pm, Sun. 11:30am-11pm.

The Stock Pot, 57 JFK St. in the Galleria (492-9058). Thick homemade soups ($2.50-3.25). Tremendous salad bar ($4.50) and "stockpocket" sandwiches ($3.75). Open Mon.-Sat. 11:30am-8:30pm, Sun. 4-8:30pm; summer closed Sundays.

Bangkok House, 50 JFK St., Harvard Sq. (547-6666). Large portions of delicious Thai food in three categories: mild, spicy, and very spicy. Order a three-starred dish and prepare to sweat. Entrees $7.25-12. Deliciously aromatic coconut soup. Open Sun.-Thurs. noon-3pm and 5-10pm, Fri.-Sat. noon-3pm and 5-10:30pm.

Dolphin Seafood, 1105 Mass. Ave., between Harvard and Central Sq. (661-2937, 354-9332). Crowded and friendly, much like their squid appetizer. Huge portions of fresh seafood ($5.25-9.50). Cheap lunch specials. Open Mon.-Sat. 11am-10pm, Sun. 4-10pm. Arrive early on weekends.

Pizzeria Uno, 22 John F. Kennedy St., Harvard Sq. One of the wooden signs reads "If we're busy try our place in Chicago." On weekends you'd better have an airline ticket handy because the wait can be over an hour, and the service slow. Worth it for the college atmosphere and rich, delicious food. Individual pizzas $3.75-5.50, regulars $7-10.75. 5-min. express lunch (Mon.-Fri. 11am-3pm) $4. Open Sun.-Wed. 11am-1am, Thurs.-Sat. 11am-2am.

Oh! Calcutta!, 468 Massachusetts Ave. in Central Square (576-2111). Not a long-running nude musical or a Davidson aphrodisiac, but an immensely successful Indian restaurant. Atmosphere incongruous, but great service. Large portions of delicious food, from fiery pickled vegetables to sweet rice pudding. Lunch specials (Mon.-Fri.) $4-5, dinner entrees $7-13. All-you-can-eat extravaganzas (Sat.-Sun. noon-3pm) $8. Open daily noon-10:30pm.

Chef Chow's House, 50 Church St., Harvard Sq. (492-2469). Tasty and moderately-priced Chinese dishes in a soothing wood-soaked atmosphere. Nice fish tanks. Entrees $5-22. Take-out available. Open Sun.-Thurs. 11:30am-10pm, Fri.-Sat. 11:30am-11pm.

A meal in the vicinity of Harvard Square would not be complete without dessert afterwards. Dens of sin abound, like **Herrell's,** 15 Dunster St. in Harvard Sq. (497-2179), which makes what some call the "Best Chocolate Ice Cream in Boston" (1.50 with mix-in). Lap up the "no-moo" concoctions inside a vault painted to resemble the open depths. (Open Sun.-Thurs. 11am-midnight, Fri.-Sat. 11-1am.) Down the street, **Emack & Bolio's** at 1310 Mass. Ave. (497-5362) serves delicious oreo ice cream ($1.50); their homemade cookies aren't bad, either. (Open Sun.-Thurs. 10am-11pm, Fri.-Sat. 10am-midnight) The lickmeister of the evil frozen yogurt trend is **Luscious Licks,** 20 Eliot St. (354-0505), offering fresh fruit and yummy chocolate to top off their rich confections ($2-2.25). (Open daily 11am-11pm.)

Nightlife and Entertainment

In warm weather, Cambridge entertainment is free. Street musicians ranging from Andean folk singers to 60s psychedeliacs to obligatory NewAgers float through the streets of Harvard Sq. The folk artists tend to cluster on Mass. Ave., either near the T or by Au Bon Pain, while the jazz cats caterwaul around Brattle St. Cafés crowd at all times of year for lunch or after-hours coffee. **Café Pamplona,** 12 Bow St., is dubbed "Café Pompous" by those who know it well. The low-ceilinged, smoke-filled room might be too philosophy-heavy for you; in summer escape to their outdoor tables. Try the mint parfait ($2.50). (Open Mon.-Sat. 11am-1am, Sun. 2pm-1am.) The **Coffee Connection,** on Dunster St. in the Garage (492-4881), serves exotic coffees and teas amidst Native American art. The smell of the place is fantastic; try the delicious *café con panna* ($1.50) or the addictive frappacino. (Open Mon.-Thurs. 8am-11pm, Fri. 8am-midnight, Sat. 9am-midnight, Sun. 9am-11pm.) **Au Bon Pain,** on Mass. Ave., offers a less exotic menu and mass-produced munchies, but its chess, prices, and people-watching are better than a genuine French pastry. (Open Sun.-Thurs. 7am-midnight, Fri.-Sat. 7am-1am.) The **Blacksmith House,** 56 Brattle St. (354-3036), serves up more than just café and bakery items. (Open Mon.-Tues. 9am-7pm, Wed.-Sun. 9am-9pm.) The Cambridge Center for Adult Education presents various poetry readings here throughout the year (usually Mon.; admission varies) and also musical programs on summer Thursdays at 8pm.

Rich cultural offerings keep Cambridge vital. Harvard sponsors any number of readings and lectures each week; check the kiosks that fill Harvard Yard for posters about the events most students are too busy to attend. Also look at the windows of one of the over 25 bookstores in the Square to see if any literary luminaries will appear during your visit. Theater thrives here. Harvard undergraduates produce shows year-round, though more frequently during the school year. (Tickets $3-7.) The renowned **American Repertory Theater,** 64 Brattle St., under the direction of Harvard prof Robert Brustein, produces shows from September to June. (Tickets $16-33.) Tickets for undergraduate and ART productions can be purchased through the ticket office at the Loeb Drama Center (543-8300; box office open Mon.-Fri. 10am-5:30pm). The Harvard Information Office also sells tickets to a variety of bigger concerts, plays, and events. But for those whose idea of nightlife is a little louder than an evening with Vaclav Havel or coffee and a discussion of the modern novel, Cambridge can accommodate as well.

T.T. The Bear's Place, 10 Brookline St. (492-0082), in Central Sq. A great joint with reasonably-priced liquor and a pool table in the back room. Live, really live, loud rock bands Thurs.-Sat., DJs on Sun. Open Tues.-Sat. 5pm-1am. Live music 9pm-12:30am. Cover $4-6.

The Middle East Cafe, 472 Mass. Ave. (492-9181). Tasty, cheap Middle Eastern food served to a colorful clientele. In the back room, great local and independent bands play most Tues.-Thurs. and Sun. nights. A broad selection of exotic beer rounds out one of Boston's hippest nightspots. Open Sun.-Thurs. 10am-1:30am, Fri.-Sat. 10am-2:30am.

Catch a Rising Star, 306 JFK St. (661-9887), Harvard Sq. Hosts comedic artists in a typical comedy club atmosphere. All ages. "Open mike" comedy Mon.-Tues., live music Sun. and Wed.-Thurs. Shows Sun.-Thurs. at 8:30; Fri. at 8:30 and 11pm; Sat. at 7:30pm, 9:45pm, and midnight. Cover Mon.-Tues. $5, Sun. and Wed.-Thurs. $8. Fri.-Sat. $12. $3 discount with college ID Mon.-Thurs.)

The Bow and Arrow Pub, Bow St. and Mass Ave., Harvard Sq. (No phone.) Where Harley meets preppie. Check out the impressive corral of precious metal outside. Some of the cheapest beer in town (16-oz. knickerbockers $1.40), a 50¢ game of hoops, darts, and an eclectic jukebox selection. Open Mon.-Thurs. 11am-1am, Fri.-Sat. noon-1am, Sun. noon-1am.

Hong Kong, 1236 Mass Ave., Harvard Sq. (864-5311). The alcohol-infested scorpion bowls are a Harvard tradition. Mediocre food; popular, crowded, and rowdy bar upstairs. Open Sun.-Thurs. 11:30am-1am, Fri.-Sat. 11:30am-2am.

Sights

People-watching, the favorite Cantabridgian pastime, may account for the number of cafés. But if you can tear yourself away from staring at balding professors, yuppies, hippies, street punks, and slumming high-schoolers, you might see some interesting buildings as well.

MIT is as much a tribute to as an institute of technology. The campus boasts a number of buildings by overworked I.M. Pei, an impressive collection of modern outdoor sculpture, and an "infinite corridor" ¼-mi. long. Tours are available weekdays at 10am and 2pm from the Rogers Building, or "Building Number 7" as the ultra-efficient students here call it. Contact MIT Information at 77 Mass. Ave. (253-1000; open Mon.-Fri. 9am-5pm). The **MIT Museum,** 265 Mass. Ave. (253-4429 recorded message, 253-4444 operator), contains a slide rule collection and wonderful photography exhibits, including the famous stop-action photos of Harold Edgerton. (Open Tues.-Fri. 9am-5pm, Sat-Sun. 1-5pm. Free.)

Up Mass. Ave., the other university seems to shun such futuristic delights for glories of the past, especially its own. **Harvard University,** established in 1636, is the oldest university in the country, and won't let anyone forget it. Ask at the info center about self-guided, self-gratifying walking tours. (See Practical Information above.)

The university revolves around **Harvard Yard;** in the western half ("The Old Yard"), some of the school's first buildings still stand. Today all Harvard students live in the Yard during their first year of study; John F. Kennedy lived in Weld while Emerson and Thoreau resided in Hollis. Avoid taking pictures of the crass sop to tourism, the **John Harvard Statue,** and certainly don't call it "The Statue of the Three Lies." Besides classroom buildings, the Yard's eastern half holds **Memorial Church** and **Widener Library** (495-2413). The centerpiece of the Harvard University Library system, Widener is the largest academic library in the world, containing a significant portion of the collection's 10.5 million volumes. Its card catalog proved a powerful hostage in the student strike of 1969. While visitors can't browse among Widener's shelves, they are welcome to examine Harvard's copy of the Gutenberg Bible and other rare books in the Harry Elkins Widener Memorial Reading Room, or to take in the Sargent murals.

Late 20th-century Harvard extends well beyond the Yard down to the Charles River. The **Harvard Houses**—an attempt to recreate the college system of Oxford and Cambridge Universities—cover an area that extends from Mass. Ave. to Memorial Dr. They run the gamut from artsy Adams House, part of which dates from the 18th century, to concrete and spartan Mather barracks, built in the 1970s to be riot-proof and panoramic at the same time. Across the Charles lies the **Business School,** womb of Wall Street, and the university's athletic facilities. North of Harvard Yard lie the **Law School, Divinity School,** and **Radcliffe Quadrangle;** to the west lie the **School of Education** and **Radcliffe Yard.**

The oldest of Harvard's museums, the **Fogg Art Museum,** 32 Quincy St., gathers a considerable collection of works ranging from ancient Chinese jade to contemporary photography, as well as the largest Ingres collection outside of France. The limited display space around its Italian Renaissance courtyard frequently rotates well-planned exhibits. Across the street, the post-modern exterior of the **Arthur M. Sackler Museum,** 485 Broadway, is belied by a rich collection of ancient Asian and Islamic art. (Both museums open Tues.-Sun. 10am-5pm. Admission to each $4, seniors $2.50. Free Sat. mornings. Call 495-9400 for information.) Next door to the Fogg, Le Corbusier's guitar-shaped "machine for living," the **Carpenter Center,** 24 Quincy St. (495-3251), shows student and professional work with especially strong photo exhibits, not to mention a great film series at the **Harvard Film Archive.** (Open Mon.-Fri. 9am-11pm, Sat. noon-6pm, Sun. noon-10pm.) Included in the **Museums of Natural History** at 24 Oxford St. (495-3045 or 495-1310), are the **Peabody Museum of Archaeology and Ethnology,** which houses treasures from prehistoric and Native American cultures, and the **Mineralogical and Geological Museums,** containing gems, minerals, ores, and meteorites. But the overhyped "glass flowers" exhibit at the **Botanical Museum** draws the largest crowds. A German glassblower and his son created these remarkably accurate and beautiful enlarged reproductions of over 840 plant species. **The Museum of Comparative Zoology** offers a more corporal view of nature, with its stuffed gorilla and dinosaur bones. Check out the museum's own skeletal sea monster, the Kronosaurus. (Open Mon.-Sat. 9am-4:30pm, Sun. 1-4:30pm. Admission $3, seniors and students $2, ages 5-15 $1.)

European settlers established Cambridge in 1630 six years before Harvard. Stroll up Mass. Ave. to the green **Cambridge Common,** established in 1631. Once the focal point of the town's political, social, and religious activity, it eventually became a camp for George Washington's Continental Army. Unless you have your own army, it is unsafe to walk here at night. Washington worshiped across the street at **Christ Church,** the oldest church in Cambridge, which had its organ pipes melted down for Revolutionary bullets. Soldiers felled in the struggle are buried in the 17th-century **Old Burying Ground** or "God's Acre" on Garden St., also the final resting place of colonial settlers and early Harvard presidents. Behind Garden St. is **Brattle Street,** dubbed "Tory Row" and dotted with the former mansions of British Loyalists. Restored to the period of the poet Henry Wadsworth Longfellow's lifetime, the **Longfellow House,** 105 Brattle St. (876-4491), is a National Historic Site. Headquarters of the Continental Army in olden days, the site now sponsors garden concerts and poetry readings in the summer; the staff can give you info on other local historic sights. (Tours daily 10am-4:30pm. Admission $2, seniors and under 17 free.) The **Mt. Auburn Cemetery** lies about one mi. up the road at the end of Brattle St. The first botanical-garden cemetery in the U.S. has 170 acres of beautifully landscaped grounds. Louis Agassiz, Charles Bulfinch, Dorothea Dix, Mary Baker Eddy, and H.W. Longfellow are all buried here.

Cape Ann: Gloucester and Rockport

Those who favor the white sands of southern Cape Cod sometimes pejoratively call Cape Ann "the other cape," yet this northern peninsula has its own brand of splendor. Sweet-smelling wild roses line the gorgeous, rocky shores, which also house the few genuine fishing villages remaining in the state. And both Gloucester and Rockport, about five mi. apart, are home to artistic communities specializing in nautical and folk-art *oeuvres.*

Since accommodations are expensive on Cape Ann unless you camp (the lowest around $50 per night in summer), the best budget bet might be Boston-area hostels and a commute. If you want to drive, either Rte. 127 or Rte. 128 will suffice, the former (known as Western Ave. in town) bringing you past the famous **Man at the Wheel,** a weather-worn copper statue of a fisherman surveying the sea for comrades lost in its depths. The **information booth** (283-2651) there can help with directions. (Open mid-June to Aug. daily 10am-6pm.) The MBTA commuter rail northern goes to Cape Ann (round-trip $7.50); take the green or orange line to North Station, hop on the Rockport train (daily every 2 hrs.) and choose between the Gloucester and Rockport stops.

Gloucester is larger, with more diverse attractions. Delicious seafood, shops and used bookstores along Main St. line the sidewalk with their wares; beaches flank Western Ave.; and the Roger St.-area seaport bustles with fishermen. Work your way to the **Cape Ann Chamber of Commerce,** 33 Commercial St. (283-1601), for extensive information on the area, including the free *Cape Ann Guide.* (Open summer Mon.-Fri. 8am-6pm, Sat. 10am-6pm, Sun. 10am-4pm; off-season Mon.-Fri. 9am-5pm.) To get there from the MBTA commuter rail stop, turn right on Railroad Ave., head past the busty **Rhumb Line** prow queen to Washington Ave. and go left. Watch for the Gulf station; you should be able to see the chamber from there. (To avoid the walk, take a CATA bus for 60¢ from the train station.)

On the way, you'll pass a good place to escape the expensive food prices of the touristy area: **Andy's Sub Shop,** 28 Washington St. (281-6990), with hot or cold subs ($2.40-$4) and seafood fried in cholesterol-free oil. (Open Mon.-Thurs. 11am-10pm, Fri.-Sat. 11am-midnight, Sun. 11am-8pm.) Many other restaurants line Main and Roger St., farther down Washington, but many aren't worth the cost. An exception is **Lanterna,** squeezed among the shops on the 100 block of Main (283-6334), with authentic Italian fare featuring the Joe's Special pita sandwich ($4). (Open Mon.-Sat. 11am-9pm.) For breakfast (until 2pm) or lunch, **Dulie's Dory Coffee Shop** (283-2408) duly doles adjacent to the chamber of commerce.

If you are interested in a little museum-combing before heading to the beach, stop on Washington at the Joan of Arc statue and head down **Middle Street.** Houses all along the street are marked with signs indicating their historical importance, including the **Sargent House.** At the end is Capt. Elias Davis's 1804 home, now the **Cape Ann Historical Association Museum,** 28 Pleasant St. (283-0455), which proudly displays the nation's largest collection of Fitz Hugh Lane paintings. (Open Tues.-Sat. 10am-5pm. Admission $3, seniors and students $1.50, under 12 free.) To get there by car from Rte. 127/Western Ave., turn at the brown museum sign, but be careful when you reach the Joan of Arc statue—the next sign seems to point left down Washington rather than up Middle.

Since this is the whale-watching capital of New England, Gloucester's half-dozen companies will attempt to show every minke, right, finback, and humpback whale that plays off the coast of Stellwagen Bank in the Gulf of Maine. Several companies offer cruises (3-4 hr.; tickets $19) in the summer including: **Capt. Bill & Sons Whale Watch Cruises,** 9 Traverse St. (283-6995); **Cape Ann Whale Watch** (283-5110 or 800-339-1990) on Rose's Wharf; and the **Seven Seas Whale Watch** (800-331-6228) on Rte. 127. The Cape Ann Whale Watch Company also offers narrated island cruises, less time-consuming and a good deal cheaper, taking you past the six area lighthouses. Landlubbers can drive down scenic E. Main St. into east Gloucester to see the **East Point Lighthouse.**

Visit toward the end of June to see the bishop perform the annual **Blessing of the Fleet,** Cape Ann's biggest summer event, complete with carnival, parade, and dancing in the streets. The tumult takes place in downtown St. Peter's Park.

If you do want to stay on Cape Ann, the best bargain is area camping in West Gloucester. The **Cape Ann Campsite** on 80 Atlantic St. (283-8683), off Rte. 128 and 133, consists of 100 tent sites one mi. from the beach. (2- to 3-day min. stay weekends. Sites \$14 for 2 people. Open May-Oct.) The **Camp Annisquam Campground** (283-2992), on Stanwood Ave. off Rte. 133, has rustic lake-side sites (\$14 for 2 people).

Southeast of downtown Gloucester muses the **Rocky Neck Art Colony** along Rocky Neck Ave. (283-4319) in E. Gloucester. With about 30 galleries, the Neck is the oldest working art colony in the U.S. and has featured such distinguished painters as Winslow Homer and Fitz Hugh Lane. Most galleries are open spring to fall (daily 10am-10pm), although the **John Nesta Gallery** and a few others open year-round.

Rockport is Gloucester's artsy appendix. The CATA Red/Blue Line, caught at the **Dunkin Donuts** off Roger St., takes the quickest route to central Rockport from Gloucester, but Driver Dave with the fluorescent green sunglasses shuttles a mean Red Line bus from the same place with a more scenic route along the coast (both 75¢). If you decide to take the MBTA commuter rail all the way to Rockport, head right from the station along Railroad Ave. until you hit the "five point" intersection and turn left onto Main Street.

Most of tourist's Rockport can be found on the same road, although it might be called South St., Mt. Pleasant St. or Main St. depending on where you first encounter it. The CATA buses from Gloucester will let you off right in the center of things, in front of **Flav's Red Skiff,** 15 Mt. Pleasant St. (546-7647), a seafood restaurant that opens at 5am (fishing hours) with inexpensive sandwiches (\$2-\$5) favored by locals.

South Main Mt. Pleasant St., in all three of its incarnations, has art galleries occupying every other building. The grandmother of them all, with a membership of about 250 artists who have lived and worked in the area, is an attractive gallery operated by the **Rockport Art Association** on Main St. (546-6604). The artwork is enjoyable, and the former cotton-mill warehouse that became RAA's back gallery has a uniquely unpretentious character. (Open Mon.-Sat. 9:30am-5pm, Sun. 1-5pm; Nov.-April Mon.-Fri. 10am-4pm, Sat. 10am-5pm, Sun. 1-5pm.) During the summer, artists associated with the gallery give hour-long painting demonstrations (Tues. and Thurs. at 7:30pm). In June, the Art Association hosts the **Rockport Chamber Music Festival** (546-7391).

Motif #1, a perfectly real lobster shack at the end of Tuna Wharf, is the single most painted object in the U.S. But Rockport's beauty does not just hang in galleries; the scruff of historic **Bearskin Neck,** the town's main drag, is quite scenic. When you truly yearn to leave the hustle and bustle behind, head north out of town on Rte. 127 to the imaginatively-named companions **Front Beach** and **Back Beach,** which offer wonderful swimming. At the very tip of the cape, **Halibut Point State Park,** on Gott Ave. (546-2997), sprawls over 54 acres of headland overlooking the Ipswich Bay (day use \$2, parking \$5).

The **Rockport Chamber of Commerce,** 3 Main St. (546-5997), distributes the singularly helpful *Rockport Anchor* guide and free maps of the area. (Open Mon.-Sat. 9am-5pm, Sun. noon-5pm.) Although the chamber gives free room referral, plan ahead to stay at one of the few places under \$60 per night. Head to Rockport for the famous 4th of July **Fireman's Parade, Bonfire, and Band Concert.** The name says it all.

The **ZIP code** for Gloucester is 01930, for Rockport is 01966. The **area code** for Cape Ann is 508.

Hammond Castle

In the fragrant town of **Magnolia**, the **Hammond Castle Museum**, 80 Hesperus Ave. (283-2081), built in the late 20s by inventor and professional eccentric John Hayes Hammond, Jr. houses his collection of medieval European relics. A friend and rival of Isabella Stewart Gardner, Hammond's strange home, though less outrageously eclectic, recalls Boston's Gardner Museum. Here you can attend the Great Hall's occasional Friday evening organ recitals and weekend evening concerts from Bach to big band. (Tickets $10, $12 at the door. Open daily 9am-5pm. Admission and tour $5, seniors and students with ID $4, ages 6-12 $3.) Magnolia is accessible from Boston by train from North Station. By car, turn off Rte. 127 (Summer St.) at Raymond St., which becomes Hesperus Ave. From Gloucester, take the Orange Line CATA bus from the Roger St. Dunkin Donuts.

Cape Cod

In 1602, when Bartholomew Gosnold first landed on this peninsula in southeastern Massachusetts, he named it Cape Cod in honor of all the codfish he caught in the surrounding waters. Towns on the Cape used to survive by hook and net, but in recent decades tourism, not fishing, has sustained the Cape. Mindful of the fragility of the ecosystem, President Kennedy established the **Cape Cod National Seashore** in 1961 to protect less-developed areas from commercialism. The national seashore shelters much of the "forearm," including the Cape's most dramatic ocean beaches, Cape Cod's trademark. No matter where or how long you stay, you can enjoy miles of sandy shore. But don't disturb the fragile dunes; stay on designated trails. One other measure has limited the tourist influx—prohibitive prices. Persistent budget travelers will find the dollar-stretching difficult but ultimately fulfilling.

The park retains six beaches (day use $1.50-2.50, parking $5), nine hiking trails, and three bike trails. Consult the **National Seashore's Visitors Centers,** at Salt Pond, U.S. 6 in Eastham (255-3421), just north of the "elbow." (Open July-Aug. daily 9am-6pm; off-season 9am-4:30pm.) Deeper in the park on the forearm of the state is **Province Lands** (487-1256), on Race Point Rd. to the right off U.S. 6 near Provincetown. (Open mid-April to July and Labor Day-Thanksgiving daily 9am-4pm; July-Labor Day 9am-6pm.) Both provide maps, info, and ranger-led free walks and discussions about local natural attractions.

Cycling is perhaps the best way to travel the Cape's gentle slopes. The park service can give you a free map of the trails or sell you the detailed **Cape Cod Bike Book** ($3.25). The 135-mi. **Boston-Cape Cod Bikeway** connects Boston with Bourne on the Cape Cod Canal and extends to Provincetown at land's end. Some of the most scenic bike trails in the country line either side of the **Cape Cod Canal** in the Cape Cod National Seashore, and the 14-mi. **Cape Cod Rail Trail** from Dennis to Eastham.

Though easily accessible by car (take Rte. 3 or 3A south of Boston to Rte. 6 or 6A), Cape-bound weekend traffic is often brutal out of Boston. The **Cape Cod Railroad** (771-3788) provides a delightful alternative, traveling from Hyannis to Sandwich through the "backyard of the Cape," using only old-fashioned train cars. **Bonanza Bus Lines** connects Boston with Falmouth and Woods Hole, and Hyannis with New York City. **Plymouth and Brockton Street Railway** serves Hyannis ($5.25) and the Cape out to Provincetown.

Contact the **Cape Cod Chamber of Commerce,** at the junction of Rte. 6 and 132 (362-3225), in Hyannis on Shoot Hill Rd., for comprehensive Cape info. (Open daily 8:30am-4pm; off-season 9am-4pm.) See the Martha's Vineyard section for info on ferries from Woods Hole and Hyannis to this off-Cape island.

The **ZIP code** for Woods Hole is 02543, for Falmouth 02541; the General Delivery ZIP code is 02540. The **area code** for Cape Cod is 508.

Hyannis

Often called the "hub of Cape Cod," Hyannis is the region's commercial center—a hubcap or hub-Cape of sorts. Many of its overdeveloped sections, in fact, could cause you to forget that you are in the Cape at all. The Pilgrims might have settled in Hyannisport in 1620, but difficult navigation forced them to move on; fighting the summer traffic here, you might feel a certain kinship with them. But for those who like hep resort towns, Hyannis has plenty of mini-golf and souvenir shops, also providing a good base from which to visit or drag race other spots on the Cape. And sometimes the best way to enjoy Hyannis involves escaping it.

The **Cahoon Art Museum,** at 4676 Falmouth Ave. (Rte. 28) (428-7581), in Cotuit, offers a whimsical excursion into the long-lost land of sailors, mermaids, scurvy, and dehydration as presented by artists Ralph and Martha Cahoon. The museum also houses an impressive collection of good naive art by other Cape residents such as James Butterworth. (Open April-Dec. Wed.-Sat. 10am-4:30pm, Sun. 1-4pm. Free.) **Hyannis Whale Watcher Cruises** (775-1622 or 362-6088), north of Hyannis in Barnstable, runs daily expeditions in pursuit of fin, humpback, and the elusive white whales, launching their 100-ft. cruiser into Cape Cod Bay for four-hour, narrated excursions (fare $14-20). Conservation areas line **Old King's Highway (Rte. 6A);** the publication *Along 6A* (available at the Cape Cod Chamber of Commerce) can guide you to these and other roadside treasures, including the **Cape Cod Art Association** in Barnstable (open April-Nov. daily 10am-4pm; Dec.-March 10am-1pm).

To cool off in Barnstable, try wooded **Hathaway Pond,** on the Bay side of the Cape. (Parking $4-6, depending on day.) In Hyannis, at the end of Ocean St., **Kalmus Park Beach** offers white sands and a proliferation of windsurfers. Up Ocean St., the **Kennedy Memorial** is Hyannis's tribute to the slain President who summered in Hyannisport.

The **West End Marketplace,** 615 Main St. in downtown Hyannis, has a carnival atmosphere, carrying everything from fried dough to shish kebab and frozen yogurt. Entrées $2.75-8. (Open daily 11am-1am. Food served until midnight.) Posher and more filling, **Baxter's Fish 'n' Chips,** 177 Pleasant St., offers indoor and outdoor harborside dining. (Open Tues.-Sun. 11:30am-8:30pm.) **Guido Murphy's,** 617 Main St. (775-7242), caters to a summer student crowd with neon-enhanced entertainment. Though more popular as a bar than as an eatery, you still might try the "Rube Goldburger," a build-it-yourself sandwich ($6). Live music plays nightly. (Cover $3. Sun. comedy night $5. Wed. free with college ID.)

Situated among three acres of pine trees, the **HyLand Hostel (AYH),** 465 Falmouth Rd. (775-2970), offers the 50 most affordable beds in Hyannis. (Check-in 6-10pm. $10, nonmembers $13. Family rooms available. Reservations recommended.) Some reasonably priced motels line Rte. 132 in Hyannis; avoid the precious inns and guest houses in Hyannisport along Seat St. The **Sea Beach Inn,** 388 Sea St. (775-4612), close to the beach at Gosnold St., rents comfortable double beds with shared bath and continental breakfast ($46, with private bath $58; off-season $40/$46.) The **Salt Winds Guest House,** 319 Sea St. (775-2038), has bright, spotless rooms right near the beach, and a pool to boot. (Doubles $55. Open May-Sept. 2.)

Hyannis is tattooed midway across the Cape's upper arm, 3 mi. south of U.S. 6 on Nantucket Sound. The **Hyannis Bus Station,** 17 Elm St. (775-5524), sends off the buses of **Plymouth & Brockton** and **Bonanza Lines.** (Open Mon.-Fri. 4:45am-8:30pm, Sat.-Sun. 5am-8:30pm.) Buses motor to Provincetown (3-7 per day, 1½ hr., $7); Providence, RI (6 per day, 2 hr., $13.50); New York (6 per day, 6½ hr., $34); Boston (15-24 per day, 2 hr., $10); and Plymouth (11-15 per day, 1 hr., $4.50). Shuttle buses shuttle to Falmouth and Woods Hole (Mon.-Sat. 3-5 per day). **Amtrak,** 252 Main St. (800-872-7245), sends a direct train from New York to Hyannis Friday, and one from Hyannis to New York Sunday (6 hr., $65). Other days, take the bus to Boston to catch the train.

Steamship Authority (778-2602) runs ferries to Martha's Vineyard and Nantucket from mid-May to October, leaving from the South St. Dock. (Agency open daily 7am-8pm. Fare $9, under 12 $4.50.) **Bike rentals** ($10-12 per day, $30-36 per week) are available at Cascade Motor Lodge, 201 Main St. (775-9717), near the bus and train stations.

The **Hyannis Area Chamber of Commerce,** 319 Barnstable Rd. (775-2201), about 1½ mi. up the road from the bus station, can help with Hyannis and hands out the *Hyannis Guidebook.* (Open Mon.-Sat. 9am-5pm, Sun. 11am-3pm; Sept.-May Mon.-Sat. 9am-5pm.) Before hitting the beach, call to find out the **weather** (771-0500 or 771-5522).

Hyannis **ZIP code** is 02601; the **area code** is 508.

Provincetown

Provincetown sits where Cape Cod ends and the wide Atlantic begins. Looking out at the expanse of shimmering water, you might think the area is an island; though not in the technical sense, Provincetown spiritually removes itself from much of Massachusetts. Once a busy whale port, now artists and not sailors with bad teeth fill the major thoroughfare, where numerous Portuguese bakeries and gay and lesbian bookstores happily coexist. Only the solitude of the surrounding seashore remains unchanged.

Practical Information

Police: 911.

Visitor Information: Provincetown Chamber of Commerce, 307 Commercial St. (487-3424), MacMillan Wharf. Open summer daily 9am-5pm; off-season Mon.-Sat. 10am-4pm. **Province Lands Visitor Center,** Race Point Rd. (487-1256). Info on the national seashore; free guides to the nature and bike trails. Open July-Aug. daily 9am-6pm; mid-April to Nov. 9am-4:30pm.

Plymouth and Brockton Bus: 800-328-9997. Stops behind Provincetown Chamber of Commerce, which has schedules and information. Four buses per day in summer to Hyannis ($7.50).

Bay State Spray Cruises: 20 Long Wharf, Boston. In the Provincetown Chamber of Commerce (487-9284). Ferries to Boston (3 hr.; $15, same-day round-trip $25). Operates May 27 to mid-June weekends only; summer daily.

Provincetown Shuttle Bus: 487-3353. Serves Provincetown and Herring Cove Beach. Operates late June-early Sept. daily 8am-midnight; 8am-6:30pm for the beach. Schedules available at the chamber of commerce. Fare $1, seniors 50¢.

Bike Rental: Arnold's, 329 Commercial St. (487-0844). 3-speeds, 10-speeds, and mountain bikes $2.75-4 per hr., $7-12 per day. Credit cards accepted. Open daily 8:30am-5:30pm. Deposit and ID required.

Post Office: 211 Commercial St. (487-0163). Open Mon.-Fri. 8:30am-5pm, Sat. 9:30-11:30am. **ZIP code:** 02657.

Help Line: Crisis Hotline, 487-1577. For any kind of personal crisis.

Area Code: 508.

Provincetown tucks into the cupped hand at the end of the Cape Cod arm. Boston lies 120 mi. away by land via U.S. 6 and Rte. 3 (Boston's "Southeast Expressway") but much closer by sea across Cape Cod and Massachusetts Bay. The Cape Cod Canal lies 66 mi. "down Cape." The national seashore protects the surrounding duneland.

Accommodations, Camping, and Food

Provincetown is known for old clapboard houses lining narrow roads—fortunately guesthouses are a part of that tradition, although not all are affordable. The cheapest places to stay are the hostels. In Nantucket, the **Robert B. Johnson Memorial AYH-Hostel** is located at Surfside. (Members $10, nonmembers $13. Open May 15-Sept. 15.) The **Little America Hostel (AYH),** at the far end of North Pamet Rd., Truro 02666 (349-3889), rests on park service land 1½ mi. east of U.S. 6. The popular hostel has 48 bunks and sees a steady stream of bikers all summer. ($9, nonmembers $12. Open early June-early Sept. Reservations recommended.) If you prefer guesthouses, try the **Joshua Paine Guest House**, 15 Tremont St. (487-1551), with four bright rooms and handsome furniture. (Singles $30. Doubles $35. Open May to mid-Sept.) In the quiet east end of town, the **Cape Codder**, 570 Commercial St. (487-0131), as its name suggests, offers stereotypical Cape Cod decor, right down to the wicker furniture, as well as access to a small private beach with a wooden deck (Singles $29-45, off-season $20-30. Doubles $28-40. Continental breakfast included. Open April-Oct.) Closer to town, the **White Caps Motel**, 394 Commercial St. (487-3755), has immaculate pastel rooms and access to the beach. (Doubles $50, off-season $42.)

In keeping with the general spirit of the thing, camping is expensive. Parking for the National Seashore property closes from midnight to 6am, but you can't camp legally on public lands anyway. The visitors center can provide a list of private campgrounds within the seashore; for all, reservations are recommended in the summer. The western part of **Coastal Acres Camping Court**, West Vine St. (487-1700), has often crowded sites; try to snag one waterside. (3-day min. stay. Sites $17, with electricity and water $21.) About 7 mi. southeast of Provincetown on U.S. 6, several popular campgrounds nestle among the dwarf pines by the dunelands of the villages of North Truro and Truro. The **North Truro Camping Area,** on Highland Rd. (487-1847), ½-mi. east of U.S. 6., has small but pleasantly sandy sites. ($14 for 2 people. Each additional person $8. Required deposit of $30 for each reserved week of stay.)

Sit-down meals in Provincetown cost a pretty penny. Grab a bite at one of the Portuguese bakeries on Commercial St., or at a seafood shack on MacMillan Wharf. Particularly good and flaunting its own picnic tables, **John's Hot Dog Stand,** 309 Commercial St., actually specializes in fried clams, lobster roll, and a variety of other meals marine. For more sedentary dining, try the **Mayflower Family Dining** restaurant, 300 Commercial St., established in 1921. Ancient caricatures line the walls. Choose from Portuguese ($6-8.50) and Italian ($4.50-9) entrees, or Puritan seafood meals ($7-10). (Open daily 11am-10:30pm.) While **Stormy Harbor**, 277 Commercial St., serves good food, it insists on leaving the price tag on the oil-paint seascapes. Buy one, or a cheap breakfast. (Open daily 7am-9pm.)

Sights, Activities, and Entertainment

In high season, pedestrians and cyclists wrest control of **Commercial Street** from the automobiles. The street festival goes on every day and night, often until 3am, heightening in June with the annual Portuguese religious celebration, the **Blessing of the Fleet.**

Commercial St. has a number of austere galleries that many visitors mistake for museums, but the **Provincetown Art Association and Museum,** 460 Commercial St. (487-1750), established in 1914, is the real McCoy. Alongside the permanent 500-piece collection, it exhibits works by new Provincetown artists. (Open late May-Oct. noon-4pm and 7-10pm. Admission $1, seniors and kids 50¢.

It seems Provincetown feels cheated of the honor won by Plymouth, as it continues to insist that the Mayflower landed here first. After erecting an unimpressive plaque at the **First Landing Place,** the start of Commercial St., the town dedicated the **Pilgrim Monument and Provincetown Museum** on High Pole Hill (487-1370) in 1920. The nation's tallest granite structure (255 ft.) affords a view of the tallest buildings in Boston on clear days, and a gorgeous panorama of the Cape almost every day. The museum below contains maritime artifacts. (Open July-Sept. daily 9am-8pm; Oct.-June 9am-5pm. Admission $3, students $2, kids $1.) In 1746, a ship's carpenter built the "Oldest House" in Provincetown, the **Seth Nickerson House,** 72 Commercial St., which remains today the archetype of Cape Cod architecture. The ghost of the owner gives thoughtful and thorough tours. (Open May-Oct. daily 10am-5pm. Admission $1, ages 5-12 50¢.)

There might not be much onshore evidence of Provincetown's whaling port, but the proliferation of **whale watch cruises** certainly hints at it. Companies cruise boats full of passengers armed with cameras rather than harpoons out to the fertile shoals where humpback, fin, mincke, and rare white whales feed. May and September are the best months for cetacean-sighting. Naturalist guides enhance the tours (3-4 hr.) offered by the three Provincetown operations: **Dolphin Fleet** (255-3857 or 800-826-9300); **Portuguese Princess** (487-2651 or 800-442-3188); and **Provincetown Whale-Watch** (487-3322 or 800-992-9333). All leave from and operate ticket booths on MacMillan Wharf. Tickets cost about $15.

The **Schooner Bay Lady II** on MacMillan Pier (487-9308) offers a less exciting but nonetheless beautiful sail (2 hr.) around the Bay. (Fare $8-12, kids $4-6.) Try your own hand at the tiller at **Flyer's Boat Rental,** 131A Commercial St. (487-0898 or 487-0578). Expensive sailing lessons are also available. (Sailboats $15.50 per hr. Outboards with 2 poles and bait $35 per day. Open summer daily 8am-6pm.)

Back on *terra firma,* you can roam the wide, sandy beaches that surround Provincetown on foot or by bike. Rent a bike from **Arnold's** (see Practical Information), and receive a free map of the trails. The friendly manager of the little-known **Provincetown Horse and Carriage Co.,** 27 W. Vine St. (487-1112), can help both novice and experienced riders explore on horseback. One-hour trail rides cost $18.50-22. (Must be over 11.) **Rambling Rose** (487-4246) gives carriage tours ($7.50-15) through town for those not so equestrian, without 100 verses in ragtime.

Sandwich

The oldest town on the Cape, Sandwich cultivates a charm unmatched by its neighbors. Tourist-strip bustle does not clog its shady streets, lined with weathered-gray clapboard and mayonnaise.

Guided tours of the **Old Hoxie House** on Water St. (Rte. 130), a wonderful, authentic saltbox dating to the 17th century, explain the origins of the ancient furnishings. (Open early June to mid-Oct. Mon.-Sat. 10am-5pm, Sun. 1-5pm. Admission $2.50, kids $1.) Down the street, the **Dexter Grist Mill** has ground corn since 1650. (Open June-Oct. Mon.-Sat. 10am-5pm, Sun. 1-5pm. Admission $1.50, ages 12-16 75¢.) The water power for the mill comes from serene Shawme Pond, frequented by flocks of ducks, geese, and swans.

A few hundred yards from the pond, the **Thornton W. Burgess Museum** (888-6870) on Water St. pays an entertaining tribute to the Sandwich-born naturalist who wrote tales about the "dear old briar patch." Ask for directions to the actual briar patch, **The Green Briar Nature Center and Jam Kitchen,** 6 Discovery Rd. Wander through trails and wildflower gardens, or watch jam-making in the center kitchen Wednesday and Saturday. (Open summer Mon.-Sat. 10am-4pm, Sun. 1-4pm; shorter hours off-season. Free.)

About a mile from the center of town, you can easily spend an afternoon at the **Heritage Plantation,** on Grove and Pine St. (888-3300), which has 76 acres of path-crossed gardens. The unusual museums include a Shaker barn full of antique cars, another a working 1912 carousel. (Open mid-May to Oct. daily 10am-5pm. Admission $7.50, seniors $6.50, ages 5-12 $3.) The town is sandwiched between Cape Cod Canal to the north and the Atlantic to the east. Across the Sagamore Bridge, **Scusset Beach** (888-0859), right on the canal near the junction of Rte. 6 and 3, offers fishing and camping. (Daily fee $2, kids $1. Parking $5. Sites $15; off-season $10.) The **Shawme-Crowell State Forest** (888-0351), on Rte. 130 and 6, has 240 wooded campsites ($12; April-Oct.). **Peters Pond Park Campground,** Cotuit Rd. (477-1775), in south Sandwich, offers aquatic activities, a grocery store, showers, and a few prime waterside sites. (Sites $14-15. Open mid-April to mid-Oct.)

Affordable eateries are ironically difficult to find in Sandwich, although **John's Capeside Diner,** Rte. 6A, carries affordability to ridiculous lengths, serving breakfast all day ($1.10-2.75), seafood, and burgers ($1.85). (Open Sun.-Tues. 5am-2pm, Wed.-Sat. 5am-8pm.)

Without a car you'll have to take the scenic **Cape Cod Railroad** (771-3788) to get to Sandwich. Starting from Center St. across from the Hyannis bus station, the train makes one stop in Sandwich and goes as far as Sagamore, although you can't get off there ($10.50 round-trip). From the depot in Sandwich, follow Jarves St. into the center of town.

Lexington and Concord

Inhabitants will constantly remind you that the Minutemen skirmished with advancing British troops on the **Lexington Battle Green,** falling back to the **Old North Bridge** in Concord where U.S. troops first officially received orders to fire upon the Redcoats.

On the Lexington Green, the **Minuteman Statue** of Captain John Parker looks back to Boston, still watching for the invader. The surrounding houses seem nearly as historic as the land; the **Jonathan Harrington House** on Harrington Rd., built in 1750, housed its namesake who crawled away from the battle to die on his own doorstep. The **Budeman Tavern,** on Hancock St. opposite the Green, had already slung ale for 65 years when it headquartered the Minutemen. The Lexington Historical Society carefully restored the interior; tourists on acid might think they've fallen into a time warp. The society also did a number on **Munroe Tavern,** 1 mi. from the Green on Mass. Ave., which served as a field hospital for wounded British. (Houses open mid-April to late Oct. Mon.-Sat. 10am-5pm, Sun. 1-5pm. Admission $2.50 per house, ages 6-16 50¢. Three houses $5.) Along with a walking map of the area, the **visitors center** at 1875 Mass. Ave. (862-1450), behind the Buckman Tavern, displays a 50-year-old, painstakingly detailed diorama of the Battle of Lexington. (Open daily 9am-5pm; Nov.-June 10am-4pm.)

The **Battle Road** winds 6 mi. from the Lexington Green to Concord and is now part of a national park; the **Battle Road Visitors Center** on Rte. 2A in Lexington (862-7353) shows a 20-minute film about the region and distributes maps of the park. At the **North Bridge Visitors Center,** 174 Liberty St., park rangers lead interpretive area tours of the Old North Bridge over the Concord River, the site of "the shot heard 'round the world."

Concord garnered fame not only for its military history but as a U.S. literary capital of the 19th century as well. The Alcotts and Hawthornes once inhabited **Wayside** at 455 Lexington Rd. (369-6975), while Emerson himself lived down the road for the latter part of the century. Now a part of the **Minute Men National Park,** the house is open for public viewing. (Open Tues.-Sun. 9:30am-5pm. Admission $1, ages under 17 and over 61 free.) Alongside Emerson's reconstructed study, the **Concord Museum,** directly across the street from the house (369-9609), houses Paul Revere's lantern and items from Henry David Thoreau's cabin. (Open Feb.-Dec. Mon.-Sat. 10am-4pm, Sun. 1-4pm. Admission $5, seniors $4, students $3, under 5 $2.) Emerson, Hawthorne, Alcott, and Thoreau all wait for Ichabod Crane on "Author's Ridge" in the **Sleepy Hollow Cemetery** on Rte. 62, three blocks from the center of town.

While alive, Thoreau retreated to **Walden Pond,** 1½ mi. south on Rte. 126, in 1845 "to live deliberately, to front only the essential facts of life." His pre-Marcusian hippie handbook *Walden* contains observations about his two-year solitude there. The **Thoreau Lyceum,** 156 Belknap St. (369-5912), national headquarters of the Thoreau Society, will answer questions about this naturalist-philosopher. The Lyceum sponsors the society's convention in July, and has a replica of Thoreau's cabin in its backyard. (Open April-Dec. Mon.-Sat. 10am-5pm, Sun. 2-5pm; early Feb.-March Thurs.-Sat. 10am-5pm, Sun. 2-5pm. Admission $2, students $1.50, kids 50¢.) Walden Pond (369-3254) is now a state reservation, popular with picnickers, swimmers, and boaters. Granite posts at the far end of the pond mark the site of Thoreau's cabin. (Open April-Oct. daily dawn-dusk. Parking $5.) The Pond only holds 1000 visitors; rangers will turn you away, so call before driving out. And don't let the condominiums slip in before you do. When Walden Pond swarms with crowds, head down Rte. 62 east from Concord center to **Great Meadows National Wildlife Refuge** (443-4661), another of Thoreau's haunts. (Open daily dawn-dusk.)

The **South Bridge Boat House,** 496 Main St. (371-2465), rents canoes (Mon.-Fri. $6 per hr., $25 per day; Sat.-Sun. $7.25 per hr., $35 per day) for the Concord and Sudbury Rivers. (Open April-Oct. daily 10am-7:30pm.) Look for an excellent local map and information on Concord events and sights in a rack outside the **chamber of commerce,** in Wright Tavern on Main St., or at the **information booth,** just outside the town center on Heywood St. off Lexington Rd. (Open late May-late Oct. daily 9:30am-4:30pm; late April-late May Sat.-Sun. 9:30am-4:30pm.) Concord and Lexington make easy daytrips from Boston. Concord, just 20 mi. north of Boston, is served by MBTA "Commuter Rail" trains leaving from North Station ($2.75). MBTA buses from Alewife station in Boston run several times each day to Lexington (50¢).

The **area code** for Lexington is 617, Concord 508.

Martha's Vineyard

In 1606, British explorer Bartholomew Gosnold named Martha's Vineyard after his daughter and the wild grapes that grew here. In the 18th century, the Vineyard prospered as a port, with shepherding the main home trade because sheep couldn't fly away, even if they were on the lam. Today even the most hardened traveler may feel a bit hemmed by the herding tactics of the locals dependent on tourism. Try to visit the Vineyard in fall, when the tourist season wanes; the weather turns crisp, the leaves turn color, and prices drop. If you must visit in summer, avoid weekends.

This, the most famous island off the New England coast, does have the unifying theme of "quaint," from the dunes of the wide sandy beaches to the dark, beautiful inland woods. The landscape even captivates the most frequent of visitors, and converts many to a lifetime of vacations. Unlike many of its continental counterparts, "the Vineyard" is as welcoming budgetarily as it is scenically.

Separated from Cape Cod by Vineyard Sound, Martha's Vineyard requires that visitors come either by air or by sea. Air travel is prohibitively expensive, but the agreeable ferry ride takes less than an hour from Woods Hole or Falmouth. All ferries land in either **Vineyard Haven** or **Oak Bluffs,** two towns 3 mi. apart on the island's north shore.

Seven different communities make up **Martha's Vineyard,** behaving in many ways as islands unto themselves: Edgartown, Vineyard Haven, Oak Bluffs, West Tisbury, Menemsha, Chilmark, and Gay Head.

Oak Bluffs, three mi. west of Vineyard Haven on State Rd., is the most youth-oriented of the Vineyard villages. Before the dawn of mega-tourism, the town was a favorite vacation spot for African-American elites. Tour **Trinity Park,** near the harbor, and see the famous "Gingerbread Houses" (minutely detailed, elaborately pastel Victorian cottages resembling a child's playtown) or Oak Bluffs' **Flying Horses Carousel,** on Circuit Ave. Ext. (693-9081), the oldest in the nation (built in 1876), containing 20 handcrafted horses with real horsehair tails and manes. (Open late May-Sept. daily 10am-10pm. Fare $1.)

Edgartown, 7 mi. south of Oak Bluffs, corners the island's market on posh; skip the shops and stores here and visit the town's historic sights maintained by **Dukes County Historical Society,** School and Cooke St. (627-4441).

West Tisbury, 12 mi. west of Edgartown on the West Tisbury-Edgartown Rd., is a typical small New England outpost, its largest attraction being the **Chicama Vineyards,** on Stoney Hill Rd. off State Rd. (693-0309). Free tasting follows the tour of the only vineyard on the Vineyard. (Open Jan.-April Fri.-Sat. 1-4pm; May Mon.-Sat. noon-5pm; June-Oct. Mon.-Sat. 11am-5pm, Sun. 1-5pm. Free.) The town supplies a well-stocked general store, providing sustenance for the trip "up-island."

Gay Head, 12 mi. off West Tisbury, offers just about the best view in all of New England. The local Wampanoog frequently saved sailors whose ships wrecked on the breath-absconding **Gay Head Cliffs.** The 100-million-year-old precipice contains a collage of brilliant colors with one of five lighthouses on the island.

Chilmark, a little northeast of Gay Head, gives good coastline, claiming the only working fishing town on the island, **Menemsha Village,** where tourists can fish off the pier or purchase fresh lobster.

Vineyard Haven has an unfair advantage as the first place most people see as they step off the boat.

Exploring the Vineyard should involve much more than hamlet-hopping. Visit the peacocks and turkeys at the **Felix Neck Wildlife Sanctuary** on the Edgartown-Vineyard Haven Rd. (627-4850), now administered by the Audubon Society. (Open until 7pm. Admission $2, seniors and kids $1.) **Cedar Tree Neck** provides trails across 250 acres of headland off Indian Hill Rd., while the **Long Point** park in West Tisbury preserves 550 acres and a shore on the Tisbury Great Pond. **Camp Pogue Wildlife Refuge and Wasque Reservation** on Chappaquidick is the largest conservation area on the island.

South Beach, the grandparent of the town's many beaches, shimmers at the end of Katama Rd. beneath Edgartown. The big waves and rolling shore attract quite a crowd. The fine **Menemsha Beach,** at the end of North Rd., and the popular **State Beach,** on Beach Rd., break not far beyond.

Cheap sandwich and lunch places speckle the Vineyard. Fried-food shacks across the island sell clams, shrimp, and potatoes. Sit-down dinners generally cost at least $15. A glorious exception is **Louis',** State Rd., Vineyard Haven, serving Italian food in a country-style atmosphere with unlimited bread and salad bar. (Lunch $4-5. Dinner $9-15. Open Mon.-Thurs. 11:30am-8pm, Fri.-Sat. 11:30am-9pm, Sun. 4-9:30pm.) **Cozy's,** on Circuit Ave. in Oak Bluffs, serves up ice cream and platters from its Wurlitzer. Try their generous hoagies ($3.75-5) or burgers ($1.75-3.35). (Open late March-early Sept. daily 11am-midnight) Down the street, **Papa's Pizza Circuit** rounds out a popular, atmospheric hangout for island youth, serving delicious thick-crusted whole-wheat pizza ($7-9). (Open daily 10am-11pm.)

A number of good take-out places dot the island, and given the beauty of the landscape you just might want to grab food and run. The **Black Dog Bakery,** on Beach St. Ext. in Vineyard Haven, is filled with sumptuous breads and pastries (75¢-$3.50). (Open daily 6am-9pm; off-season 6am-6pm.) An island legend and institution, **Mad Martha's** scoops out 26 homemade flavors or limited editions of ice cream. The main store is on Circuit Ave. in Oak Bluffs, but five more are scattered on the northeastern side of the island. (Open mid-April to late Oct. daily 11am-midnight.) The **Morning Glory Farm,** at the corner of Machacket and Tisbury Rd., sells produce fresh from the field. (Open May-Thanksgiving Mon.-Sat. 9am-5:30pm.)

The most deluxe youth hostel you may ever encounter also offers the least expensive beds on the island. The lovely **Manter Memorial Youth Hostel (AYH),** Edgartown Rd., West Tisbury (693-2665), 5 mi. inland from Edgartown on the bike route, is quite crowded in summer but almost never turns anybody away. (Curfew 11pm. $9, nonmembers $12. Linen $1. Open April-Nov. Reservations required.) **Martha's Vineyard Reservations,** P.O. Box 1322, Vineyard Haven 02568 (693-7200); **Dukes County Reservations Service,** P.O. Box 2370, Oak Bluffs 02557 (693-6505); and **Accommodations Plus,** RFD 273, Edgartown 02539 (627-8590), will reserve rooms for you three months in advance. The chamber of commerce provides a free list of inns and guest houses. For relatively inexpensive rooms, the century-old **Nashua House** (693-0043), on Kennebec Ave. in Oak Bluffs, sits across from the post office through rain or snow. Some rooms overlook the ocean; all are brightly painted and cheerful. (Doubles with shared baths only $35-45.) The more polished **Narragansett House,** 62 Narragansett Ave. (693-3627), chills in a quiet residential area south of downtown Oak Bluffs. (Doubles $50-75 from late May to mid-Sept.; off-season $40-65. Breakfast included.) The Victorian **Summer Place Inn,** 47 Pequot Ave. (693-9908), has nice rooms right next to the ocean ($55; off-season $45).

Campers have two options. **Martha's Vineyard Family Campground,** Edgartown Rd., Vineyard Haven (693-3772), has 150 sites. Groceries are available nearby. (Sites $22 for 2 people. Each additional person $7. Open mid-May to mid-Oct. Reservation deposit required.) **Webb's Camping Area,** Barnes Rd., Oak Bluffs (693-0233), 4 mi. from Edgartown, is more spacious, with 150 shaded sites. (Sites $20-22 for 2 people. Each additional person $8. Open mid-May to mid-Sept.)

Though only about 30 mi. across at its widest point, the Vineyard holds 15 beaches and one state forest. Maps are available at the **Martha's Vineyard Chamber of Commerce,** Beach Rd., Vineyard Haven (693-0085). Their free annual publication, *Martha's Vineyard,* describes everything you might want to see or do on the island. Also pick up free copies of the *Best Read Guide to Martha's Vineyard,* containing self-guided walking tours of the three largest towns—Vineyard Haven, Oak Bluffs, and Edgartown. (Open May 27-Sept. 2 Mon.-Fri. 9am-5pm, Sat. 10am-2pm. Mailing address: P.O. Box 1698, Vineyard Haven 02568.) Prospective revelers should note that Edgartown and Oak Bluffs are the only "wet" towns on the Vineyard. Bar owners are notoriously strict about checking ID.

Ferries to the island and Montauk, Long Island, leave from Hyannis and New Bedford. The **Woods Hole, Martha's Vineyard, and Nantucket Steamship Authority** (693-0367 in Vineyard Haven; 693-0125 in Oak Bluffs; 228-0262 in Nantucket; 548-3788 in Woods Hole; 771-4000 in Hyannis) leaves from Woods Hole. ($8 round-trip; ages 5-12 $4; automobiles mid-Oct. to mid-May $30, mid-May to mid-Oct $53; bikers $5.) From Falmouth, you can take the **Island Queen Ferry** (548-4800), across from the town dock, which runs from late May to early October. ($8 round-trip, kids $4, with bike $5.) In Hyannis, take the **Hyline** ferry (778-2600 in Hyannis; 693-4111 in Oak Bluffs), which accepts pedestrians and bikers only. ($10, kids $5.) **Martha's Vineyard Schamonchi Ferry,** Pier 44 (997-1688), leaves from New Bedford's Lennard Wharf. ($7, kids $4. Same-day round-trip $14, kids $7.) The **Viking Ferry** (576-668-5709) leaves Montauk, LI in summer Thursdays at 8am ($35, $60 same day round-trip) and arrives in Oak Bluff.

Transporting a car costs about $38-48, the traffic is distractingly slow, major roads are few, minor roads unmarked or unpaved, and many places virtually inaccessible by auto anyway. Bring or rent a bike instead. While miles of bike trails cut across the island (maps available at R.W. Cutler), touring cyclists should stick to the fairly easy main roads. Inexperienced cyclists may find the uphill to Gay Head or Menemsha strenuous. You can rent reasonably priced bikes throughout the island: **Martha's Bike Rental,** at Five Corners in Vineyard Haven (693-6593; 10-speeds, mountain bikes, and cruisers $12 per day, credit card required; daily 9am-6pm); **Vineyard Bike and Moped** Circuit Ave. Ext. in Oak Bluffs (693-4498; 10-speeds $15 per day, 3-speeds $12; open daily 9am-6pm); and **R.W. Cutler,** Main St., Edgartown (627-4052; $8-15 per day, $10 deposit; free bike maps of the Vineyard; open April 7-Oct. 15 daily 9am-5pm). Taxis are expensive, but a shuttle bus (693-0058, 693-1555, 693-4681) makes stops throughout the island. (Vineyard Haven-Oak Bluffs-Edgartown: late May to mid-June 8am-7pm; mid-June to early Sept. 8am-12:30am. Basic fare $3. For up-island service call the above numbers.)

The **ZIP code** is 02539 for Edgartown; 02568 for Vineyard Haven; and 02557 for Oak Bluffs. The **area code** for Martha's Vineyard is 508.

Plymouth

The Pilgrims settled Plymouth in 1620 because it provided defensible high ground, a sheltered harbor, and a fresh water supply. Nowadays nothing in the town seems defended—tourists even have chipped away two-thirds of the original **Plymouth Rock** on Water St. The other pseudo-attractions are best avoided. Docked in Plymouth Harbor, the **Mayflower II** was actually built in the 1950s to recapture the atmosphere of the original ship. The neo-Pilgrim passengers and crew somehow manage eke out authenticity. (Open June-Aug. daily 9am-6:30pm; April-May and Sept.-Nov. 9am-5pm. Admission $5, children ($3.25.)

Less fanfare surrounds the only genuine sights in town. The **Plymouth Antiquarian Society,** 126 Water St. (746-9697), gives historic house tours of three local buildings: the Spooner House (1749), the Harlow Old Fort House (1677), and the Antiquarian House (1809). (Open Memorial Day-July 4 and Labor Day-Columbus Day Fri.-Sun. 10am-5pm; July 4-Labor Day Thurs.-Sun. noon-5pm. Admission $2.50 per house, seniors $2.) The nation's oldest museum in continuous existence, the **Pilgrim Hall Museum**, 75 Court St. (746-1620), houses Puritan crafts, furniture, books, paintings, and weapons. (Open daily 9:30am-4:30pm. Admission $5, seniors $4.50, ages 6-15 $2.)

Far out of town and vastly entertaining, **Plimoth Plantation,** Warren Ave. (746-1622), superbly re-creates the early settlement. In the **Pilgrim Village** costumed actors impersonate actual villagers; you can help them in daily routines such as tending the garden. The actors feign ignorance of all events after the 1630s. The nearby **Wampanoag Summer Encampment** recreates a Native American village of the same period. (Open April-Nov. daily 9am-5pm. Admission for village and encampment $12, kids $8.) To get to Plimoth Plantation, take Rte. 3 south to exit 4 and follow the signs, or follow Main St. 3 mi. out of the center of town.

An unexpected pleasure, **Cranberry World**, 225 Water St. (747-2350), glorifies one of the only three indigenous American fruits. A self-guided exhibit details the workings of a cranberry bog, and the museum has one of its own for you to investigate. Open 9:30am-5pm. Admission and all cranberry refreshments are free.

Beautiful **Jelson's Beach** on Nelson St., and **Brewsters Garden** on Leyden St., with its meandering brook, provide ideal spots for a picnic. Camping comes cheaper than the area's overpriced hotels; majestic **Myles Standish Forest** (866-2526), which stands 7 myles south of Plymouth via Rte. 3 to Long Pond Rd., offers wooded ground. (Sites $10 for 2 people, with showers $12.) **Ellis Haven Campground,** 531 Federal Furnace Rd. (746-0803), offers less wilderness and more amenities including laundry facilities. (Sites $15 for 2 people. Each additional person $2.)

Find out more about Plymouth and the rest of New England at the **tourist information center** (746-1150), 2 mi. from Plymouth on Rte. 3, exit 5, Long Pond Rd. (Open Mon.-Fri. 8:45am-5pm, Sat. 8am-4:30pm; fall and winter daily 8:45am-4:30pm.) Near the town wharf on N. Park St., the **Plymouth Information Center** (746-4779) arranges local accommodations and hands out free maps of the town. (Open May-Nov. Sat.-Thurs. 9am-5pm, Fri. 9am-8pm; April weekends.) The **chamber of commerce,** 99 Samoset St. (746-3377), can help direct you around Plymouth. (Open Mon.-Fri. 9am-5pm.)

The **Plymouth and Brockton Street Railway Company** (actually a bus line), 8 Industrial Park Rd. (746-0378; 800-328-9997 in MA), handles service to Plymouth from Boston's central Greyhound terminal (15 per day, $6). The bus takes only an hour, but stops at the Industrial Park Terminal, 3 mi. from Plymouth Center. From the Hyannis terminal (775-5524), 15 to 19 buses per day run between 10:15am and 9:15pm. (To Hyannis $4.50, 1 hr.) The **Plymouth Rock Trolley,** 20 Main St. (747-3419), operates daily (8am-8pm every 15-20 min.; $3, under 12 $1.) Trolleys run around town and out to Plimoth Plantation.

The **post office** registers at 6 Main St. Ext. (746-4028), in Plymouth center. (Open Mon.-Fri. 8:30am-5pm, Sat. 8:30am-1pm.) Plymouth's **ZIP code** is 02361; the **area code** is 508.

Salem

On one hand, Salem seems to resent the hullabaloo about the "witch stuff." Tourist-info people may qualify the 20 killings with, "That was just people being people. The whole town recanted, and everything was put away as an embarrassment for decades until it became sensationalized." Instead, they'll point you to the town's past eminence as a shipping port, as Nathaniel Hawthorne's home, as anything but the site of a "witch"-roast.

But Salem's alter ego knows you aren't there for the fish. The witch-on-a-broomstick motif appears just about everywhere: on the daily newspaper banner, on the police uniforms, on the shops and bars, on the garbage cans. Salem even has plans in the works for an exciting year-long celebration of the Witch Trials Ter-centenary in 1992, including April stagings of Arthur Miller's *The Crucible,* a Memorial Day waterfront festival, and an August concert dedicated to the sorceresses. (Further details were not available at the writing of this book; contact any of the tourist listings below for an update.)

So don't be ashamed to satisfy your base touristic urges. Something about the witch trials weaves a spell that draws in your tourist dollar—whether the voyeurism of dirty old Puritan men torturing beautiful girls for confessions, or the same violent sensationalism fix you get from crime-story tabloid "newspapers," or, well. . . SATAN, perhaps? Confess your guilt and things will go easier for you in Salem.

Salem lodgings are not for the budget traveler (around $55 per night in summer). Stay in Boston hostels or in cheaper motels in the towns along the MBTA commuter rail (Lynn or Swampscott), and take the hourly MBTA Rockport/Ipswich rail to Salem (½-hr., $2.25). Campers coven from the cold in the bewitching **Winter Island Marine Recreational Park,** 50 Winter Island Rd. (745-9430), about 1½ mi. from Salem. (2-week max. stay. Sites $12, with electricity and water $15.)

From the T station on Bridge St., head down Washington to Essex—on your left will be a pedestrian-only road to the Museum Place complex. A new visitor center is scheduled to open in May 1992; there should be a **Witch Trial Memorial** in front (but the memorial design still was being determined by a contest when we went to press so we can't tell you what it looks like). The **National Park Service** (741-3648) on the left side of the mall doles out excellent maps and brochures. (Open daily 9am-5pm, sometimes 9am-6pm in summer.) Their office on **Derby Wharf** (745-1470), which shows informative slideshows every half hour, has similar handouts. (Open 8:30am-5pm, later in summer.) The beautiful wharf sports a bucolic, grassy dock that ends in a lighthouse of 1871 vintage. Finally, a 1.3-mi. **Heritage Trail** traces an easy footpath through town, marked clearly by a painted red line on the pavement.

At the heart of town between Washington Sq. E. and Hawthorne Blvd. lies the **Salem Common,** dating back to the 1600s. Across the street, the gothic **Witch Museum** (744-1692—notice the numerology) is not a museum, but a multi-media presentation fleshing out the history of the trials every half-hour. (Open July-Aug. Mon.-Fri. 10am-5pm, Sat.-Sun. 10am-7pm; off-season daily 10am-5pm. Admission $4, seniors $3.50, ages 6-14 $2.50.) Never actually a dungeon, the **Witch Dungeon,** 16 Lynde St. (741-3570) has actresses perform short skits about the trials to amplify the toil and trouble of the proceedings. (Open early May-early Nov. daily 10am-5pm. Admission $3.75, seniors $3.25, ages 6-14 $2.25.) The child in you will like the spooky atmosphere of the dungeon tour; the adult in you will enjoy the cynical commentary that accompanies it.

Just beyond the waterfront area stands the architecturally bizarre **House of Seven Gables,** 54 Turner St. (744-0991), built in 1668 and made famous by Hawthorne's Gothic romance. Tours provide glimpses into the life of the sea captain who dwelt there in the 18th century. (Open daily 10am-4:30pm; July-Aug. Fri.-Wed. 9:30am-5:30pm, Thurs. 9:30am-8:30pm. Admission $6, ages 6-17 $2.50, $1 off for AAA members.) Hawthorne's ghost reportedly appears at the occasional Thursday evening candlelight tours. Up the road on Derby St., the **Pickering Wharf** offers free public restrooms.

Free sights lie near **Derby Wharf.** Among the National Park Service's string of historic buildings is the **Custom House** at 178 Derby St. (744-4323), where the narrator of Hawthorne's novel claims to find *The Scarlet Letter.* (Open daily 9am-6pm; off-season 9am-5pm. Free.) Hawthorne lost his desk job here thanks to the spoils system; he later took them to task in his writing.

Salem's most substantial sight, the **Peabody Museum,** in East India Sq. (745-1876, for recorded info 745-9500), recalls the port's former leading role in Atlantic whaling and merchant shipping. A wide range of exhibits details maritime history, art, and whaling, and includes samples of unusual goods traded with international ports. (Daily guided tour at 2pm. Open Mon.-Sat. 10am-5pm, Sun. noon-5pm. Admission $5, seniors and students $4, ages 6-18 $2.50.) Two blocks past the museum, ethnic music, dance, and food fill the Salem marketplace in weekly summer street festivals. Near the museum the **Essex Institute,** at 132 Essex St. (744-3390), an important archive of materials relating to New England history, also contains a museum crammed to the rafters with silver, furniture, portraits, toys, and other oddities. Three old houses on the same block under the institute's care are open to visitors during frequent tours. (Museum and houses open June-Oct. Mon.-Wed. and Fri.-Sat. 9am-5pm, Thurs. 9am-9pm, Sun. noon-5pm; Nov.-May Tues.-Sat. 9am-5pm, Sun. noon-5pm. Admission to all $6, ages 6-16 $3.50.)

Food is about the only inexpensive commodity in Salem; cheap subs ping biliously all over town. Aromatic **Red's Sandwich Shop,** 15 Central St., serves breakfast (55¢-$3.50) and lunch ($1.25-3.50) at small tables and a cozy counter. (Open Mon.-Sat. 5:30am-3pm, Sun. 6am-1pm.)

Haunted Happenings, in the last week of October (when else?), disguises itself as something of a northern Mardi Gras, complete with free candlelight tours and ghost stories, three costume balls, and a 100,000-person parade. Book months in advance if you plan to be in town for Halloween.

Salem hexes 20 mi. northeast of Boston, accessible by train from North Station (½-hr., $2.25) or by bus from Haymarket (45 min., $2). By car, take Rte. 128 north to Rte. 114 (exit 25E). The **post office** is right off Washington on 2 Margin St. (Open Mon.-Fri. 8am-5pm., Sat. 8am-1pm.) The **zip code** is 01970. The **area code** is 508.

MICHIGAN

Gerald Ford, Malcolm X, and Madonna do not make the most likely trio. But all three grew up in Michigan, the Midwest's most post-modern state. Once an industrial powerhouse, Detroit's current condition is paradigmatic of the national crisis in economic competitiveness. It is a city in pain. Nearby Ann Arbor hosts a vibrant research university, and thrives as a haven for scholars and leftists. But nature is Michigan's best draw, from its 3,200 miles of shimmering Great Lake shoreline to the rugged, solitary forests of the Upper Peninsula. Mash together Michigan's unspoilt lakes and woods, its small towns, and the Motor City, and you get a pair of quintessentially American peninsulas.

Practical Information

Capital: Lansing.

Michigan Travel Bureau, 333 S. Capitol Ave., Lansing 48933 (800-543-2937). A recorded listing of the week's events and festivals. **Department of Natural Resources,** Information Services Center, Steven T. Mason Bldg., P.O. Box 30028, Lansing 48909 (517-373-1220). Detailed information on state parks, forests, campsites, and other public facilities.

Time Zones: Eastern. The westernmost fifth of the Upper Peninsula is Central (1 hr. behind Eastern). **Postal Abbreviation:** MI

Ann Arbor

Home of the gargantuan and respected University of Michigan, Ann Arbor is the Midwestern incarnation of the leftist, intellectual college town, a cool combination of granola, Yuppie, and Middle America. The Republican Drug War has taken its toll, however; the $5 fine for use of marijuana was recently upped to a more noticeable $25.

As tens of thousands of students depart for the summer (and rents plummet), locals and Detroit intelligentsia take over to indulge in a little celebrating of their own. During late July, zillions pack the city to see the **Ann Arbor Street Art Fair,** the **State Street Area Art Fair,** and the world-famous **Summer Art Fair.** Also drawing crowds from late June to mid-July, the **Ann Arbor Summer Festival** features numerous dance and theater productions, as well as performances by musicians famous in styles ranging from jazz to country to classical. On the last Saturdays of June, July, and August, the **German Festival** highlights the German heritage common to most of the upper Midwest, while the **Ethnic Fair** in early September celebrates food, culture, and crafts from around the world. Call the visitors bureau (see below) for details.

In the realm of inanimate culture, the university proffers a handful of top-notch free museums. The **University of Michigan Art Museum (UMAM),** 525 S. State St. at the corner of University (764-0395), houses a small but choice collection of works from around the world (open Tues.-Fri. 10am-4pm, Sat. 10am-5pm, Sun. 1-5pm). Paths for biking, jogging, or just walking crisscross the town and lead through the **Nichols Arboretum,** a university-owned park off Geddes Ave., just northeast of downtown. The paths also run through the gorgeous **Gallup Park,** 3000 Fuller Rd. (662-9319), on the Huron River, also northeast of downtown. Here small, man-made islands connected by arched bridges form ponds for water sports and fishing. (Both parks open daily 6am-10pm.) In the summer, you can rent bikes and canoes at Gallup. (Bike rental $4 first hr., $1 each additional hr. Canoes $6 first hr., $1 each additional hr., Sat.-Sun. $1 extra. Rental Mon.-Fri. 11am-9pm, Sat.-Sun. 9am-9pm. Must have a $10 cash deposit and driver's license.) On warm afternoons, pastorally inclined students haunt the beautiful **Mathaei Botanical Gardens,** 1800 N. Dixboro Rd. (998-7060). Call the Park and Recreation Department (994-2780 or 769-9140) for additional information about Ann Arbor's parks.

During the academic year you can get cheap food (entrees $2-5) at the U **of M Cafeteria,** West Quad, 541 Thompson St., or at the **Michigan League,** 911 N. University Ave. (Both open Mon.-Sat. 7:15am-7:30pm; summer Mon.-Sat. 11:30am-7:30pm.) The **U of M Union,** 530 S. State St., also offers a mélange of restaurants, specialty shops, and bookstores. Moving into supra-$5 range, you'll have no problem finding mellow post-hippie munchie havens. Most student hangouts are on **State Street** close to Central Campus and in the **South University Street** "Village" uptown, complete with lively restaurants and bars.

Drink your beer from pint jars on the outdoor balcony at the laid-back Business and Law School hangout **Casa Dominick's,** 812 Monroe, across from the law quad. Tasty pasta, pizza, and Italian dishes $4.50-6; pints of beer $1.85. (Open Mon.-Thurs. and Sat. 10am-10pm, Fri. 10am-11pm, Sun. 5-9pm. Bar opens Mon.-Sat. 4pm, Sun. 5pm.) **Good Time Charley's,** 1140 S. University St., has very popular outdoor tables, but its indoor hanging plants make either setting equally enjoyable. Dinners $3.50-7. (Open Mon.-Sat. 11am-2am, Sun. 4pm-midnight.) The best deli west of the Hudson River, **Zingerman's Delicatessen** 422 Detroit St., (663-3354), slaps together huge, wonderful sandwiches ($5.50-8; open Mon.-Sat. 7am-9pm, Sun. 9am-9pm). Not to be outdone, the **Espresso Royale Café,** 324 S. State St., provides ethereal atmosphere, fruit drinks, a large variety of coffees, and art-covered walls. Drinks 70¢-$2. (Open Mon.-Fri. 7am-midnight, Sat.-Sun. 9am-midnight.) Pack a picnic at the **farmers market** that springs up every Saturday and Wednesday (7am-3pm), outside the Kerrytown Mall on N. 5th Ave.

Ann Arbor has excellent nightspots that cater to its club-hopping college population. Look for blues, reggae, and rock 'n' roll at **Rick's American Café,** 611 Church St. (996-2747). Voted the best bar in Ann Arbor for the sixth straight year in 1990, Rick's has hosted well-known alternative bands like 10,000 Maniacs. Monday is $1 pitcher night. (Open Mon.-Thurs. and Sat. 7:30pm-2am, Fri. 3pm-2am. Cover $3-6; more for big acts.) Great posters advertise shows at the **Blind Pig,** 208 S. 1st St. (996-8555), featuring bands on the alternative eclectic side. (Open daily 9am-2am, Fri. 6pm-2am. Cover $3-15.) **Del Rio,** 122 W. Washington (761-2530), at Ashley, isn't as much of a college student hangout, but it provides a pleasant restaurant/bar with free jazz Sunday nights. It is also managed cooperatively by its employees—a vestige of a fast-dying Ann Arbor tradition. (Open Mon.-Fri. 11:30am-1:45am, Sat. noon-1:45am, Sun. 5:30pm-1:45am.)

For information on current classical performances, contact the **University Musical Society** (764-2538; open Mon.-Fri. 10am-6pm) or the **Ann Arbor Symphony**

Orchestra, 527 E. Liberty (994-4801). Live jazz can be heard every night in Ann Arbor; for information, call **Eclipse Jazz** (763-0046) or ask around. The **Ann Arbor Civic Theatre,** 1035 S. Main St., performs plays year-round. (Call the visitors bureau for schedule and prices; call 763-8587 to order tickets.)

Despite a predominance of expensive hotels and motels in Ann Arbor, it is possible to find reasonable accommodations rates. Book way ahead if you plan to stay during commencement (early May), during any home-game weekend (in the fall), or during the Summer Art Fair (late July). The **University of Michigan** has rooms available year-round at **Cambridge House,** West Quad, 541 Thompson St. (747-2402). Crash here in air-conditioned, carpeted rooms at the heart of campus with cable TV and private bathrooms. (Singles $39-49. Doubles $49-59.) Centrally-located **Alice Lloyd,** 100 Observatory, and much less convenient **Baits Dormitory,** Hubbard Rd., North Campus two mi. away (call 764-5297 for both) have standard cinder-block walls and tile floors, but are comfortable and cheaper (singles $29; doubles $39). **Red Roof Inn,** 3621 Plymouth Rd. (996-5800), U.S. 23 (exit 41), has singles for $42, doubles for $53. The **Ann Arbor YMCA,** 350 S. 5th Ave. at William St. (663-0536), in downtown Ann Arbor, allows women. Clean, dorm-style rooms have shared bath with laundry facilities available (singles $23, weekly $83). The convenient location of **Embassy Hotel,** 200 E. Huron (662-7100) at 4th St., compensates for its rooms. (Singles $26.50. Doubles $37.)

Commuter Transportation Company and **Kirby Tours** (278-2224 or 800-521-0711 outside MI) run frequent shuttles from the airport (have them drop you off at a hotel for $18; $23 otherwise). Ann Arbor's layout is a well-planned grid. **Main Street** divides the town east-west while **Huron Street** divides it north-south. The central campus of the university lies five-six blocks east of Main St., south of E. Huron St. (about a 15-min. walk from the center of town).

The **Ann Arbor Convention and Visitors Bureau,** 211 E. Huron St. #6 (995-7281), has free guides about area attractions, cultural activities, accommodations, and the university. (Open Mon.-Fri. 8:30am-5pm.) **University of Michigan Information** is reached at 763-4636 (open Tues.-Sat. 7am-2pm, Sun.-Mon. 9am-1pm). **Amtrak,** 325 Depot St. (994-4906 or 800-872-7245), offers train service to Chicago ($54) and Detroit ($18). (Open daily 7:30am-11:30pm). **Greyhound,** 116 W. Huron St. (662-5212), at Ashley St. downtown, one block off Main St., offers frequent service to Detroit ($9) and Chicago ($21). (Open daily 7:30am-6:30pm). The **Ann Arbor Transportation Authority** (973-6500 or 996-0400) runs 25 routes serving Ann Arbor and a few nearby towns. Most buses operate daily 6:45am-10:15pm. (Fare 60¢, seniors and students 30¢. Office open Mon.-Fri. 8am-5pm.) **Emergency** here is 911 and the 24-hr. **Sexual Assault Crisis Line** is 936-3333.

Ann Arbor's **time zone** is Eastern. The **post office** is at 2075 W. Stadium Blvd. (665-1100; open Mon.-Fri. 7:30am-5pm). The **ZIP code** is 48106; the **area code** is 313.

Detroit

An author recently proclaimed Detroit "America's first Third-World city." It was symptomatic of Detroit's national reputation; no other American city conjures up such strong images of urban blight. And indeed, the city has been ridden with a quarter-century of hardship. In the 60s, as the country grooved to the Motown beat, the city erupted in some of the era's most violent race riots. Mass exodus to the suburbs has been the norm ever since, first among whites but now including middle-class African Americans. As a result, the population has more than halved since 1967, turning some neighborhoods into ghost towns. The decline of the auto industry beginning in the late 70s made matters worse, and economic disempowerment has produced much frustration, violence, and hopelessness among the city's residents.

Nevertheless, Detroit survives, sustained by a resilient sense of spirit and pride. The downtown area has been renovated; the five towers of the Renaissance Center on the Detroit river symbolize the hope that downtown's rejuvenation as a center for business and nightlife can spark a city-wide comeback. Residential areas such as Indian Village east of downtown have also picked up, and some suburbanites are beginning to move back into the city. But Detroit's rebirth proceeds very slowly, and hope for the future is still a cruel myth for many of the city's residents.

Practical Information

Emergency: 911.

Detroit Convention and Visitors Bureau, on Hart Plaza at 2 E. Jefferson St. (567-1170). From the Greyhound terminal, turn right at Randolph St., then right onto Jefferson. Pick up the free *Detroit Visitors Guide.* Open daily 9am-5pm; phone after hours to hear a recorded list of entertainment events. Charge concert or sports tickets at **Ticketmaster,** 645-6666.

Travelers Aid: 211 W. Congress, 3rd floor (962-6740). Emergency assistance.

Detroit Metropolitan Airport: 21 mi. west of downtown off I-94. **Commuter Transportation Company** and **Kirby Tours** (963-8585 or 800-521-0711) have shuttles to downtown ($13 to hotels, $18 anywhere else). Taxi fare downtown is a steep $25.

Amtrak: 2601 Rose St. (964-5335 or 800-872-7245), on 17th St., 1½ blocks south of Michigan Ave. Not in a good neighborhood. To Chicago ($27) and Cleveland ($33). Open daily 6:30am-1am.

Greyhound: 1000 W. Lafayette at 6th, just west of the Lodge Freeway. To: Chicago ($22, Fri.-Sun. $27, 3-day advance $15); Cleveland ($20); Toronto ($41); and New York ($104, 7-day advance $80, 21-day advance $68). Open 24 hrs.; ticket office open daily 6:30am-1am.

Public Transport: Detroit Department of Transportation (DOT), 1301 E. Warren (833-7692). Carefully policed public transport system. Serves the downtown area, with limited service to the suburbs. Most buses operate until 1am. Fare $1, transfers 10¢. **People Mover,** Detroit Transportation Corporation, 150 Michigan Ave. (224-2160). Ultramodern tramway facility circles the Central Business District with 13 stops on a 2.7-mi. loop. Fare 50¢. **Southeastern Michigan Area Regional Transit (SMART),** 962-5515. Bus service to the suburbs. Fare $1-2.50, transfers 10¢.

Taxi: Checker Cab, 963-7000.

Car Rental: Call-a-Car, 877 E. Eight Mile Rd. (541-2700), in Hazel Park at I-75. From $20 per day; 100 free mi., 15¢ each additional mi. Must be 21 with credit card and insurance. Car must not leave MI.

Help Lines: Crisis Hotline, 224-7000. **Gay and Lesbian Crisis Line,** 398-4297.

Time Zone: Eastern.

Post Office: 1401 W. Fort (226-8301), at 8th St. Open Mon.-Fri. 8am-5:30pm, Sat. 8:30am-noon. **ZIP Code:** 48200.

Area Code: 313.

Detroit lies on the Detroit River, which connects Lake Erie and Lake St. Clair. Across the river (due south) lies Windsor, Canada (pop. 200,000), reached by a tunnel (just west of the Ren Cen) or the Ambassador Bridge (2 mi. west). Detroit's sprawling suburban area does not lend itself easily to generalization. Years of mass exodus from downtown have created a ring of affluent suburbs and ethnic neighborhoods.

Driving within the Motor City limits is surprisingly mellow, mainly because much of the traffic its roads were designed to handle has moved north and west. In the suburbs, avoid the roads during rush hour (weekdays 4:00-6:30pm) at all costs.

Metropolitan Detroit's streets form a grid, with the major east-west arteries, known as the **Mile Roads** marked out in mile-long segments north of downtown. **Eight Mile Road** is the northern boundary of the city. Three main surface streets cut diagonally across the grid. **Woodward Avenue** heads northwest from downtown, dividing city and suburbs into "east side" and "west side." **Gratiot Ave.** flares out to the northeast from downtown, and **Grand River Ave.** shoots west. Two main expressways pass through downtown; **I-94** heads west to the airport, Ann Arbor, and ultimately Chicago, and north from Detroit to Port Huron; **I-75** scoots up to northern Michigan and the Upper Peninsula, and stretches south all the way to Florida.

If you plan to stay for more than a few days, get a copy of *Monthly Detroit* ($1.95) at a local newsstand. It gives detailed listings of events, nightspots, restaurants, tours, sports, and theater.

Accommodations and Camping

Although weekend specials are available at many downtown hotels, few other options are both cheap *and* safe. If you opt for cheap, be sure to arrive in daylight and be willing to forgo nightlife. The area around the Amtrak station is unsafe. The Greyhound station, near the gentrified riverfront, attracts a varied crowd—don't leave the station alone on foot after dark. It's best to take a bus, cab, or car to reach other parts of the city. Unless otherwise indicated, the suburban hotels and hostels are inaccessible by car.

Teahouse of the Golden Dragon Home Hostel (AYH), 8585 Harding Ave. (756-2676), in Centerline, north of 10 Mile and east of Van Dyke (Rte. 53), 9 mi. from downtown. Take SMART bus #510 or 515 to Engleman, then walk 1 block farther and 3 blocks to the right. Colorful rooms filled with Asian chintz, Mickey Mouse paraphenalia, and noisy clocks. Proprieter is all smiles. $5.

University of Windsor, Vanier Hall, Wyandotte St. W. and Huron Church Rd. (519-973-7074), in Windsor, Canada, near the Ambassador Bridge. Take the Tunnel Bus, then bus #1C west. Friendly, spotless, air-conditioned, and closer to downtown Detroit than it seems. Free pass to athletic facilities included. Singles CDN$24.50. Doubles CDN$40.20. Students CDN$14.50, technically only for University of Windsor (Ontario) students but sometimes extended to all students. Price reduced 12% for American money. Open May to mid-Aug.

University of Detroit: Mercy, 8200 W. Outer Dr. (592-6170), 11 mi. from downtown off the Lodge Freeway (Rte. 10). Campus secure, but surrounding area shaky. Clean, spacious dorm rooms in this college of nursing. Kitchen, laundry facilities available. Singles $20, with bath $24. Doubles $15 per person; with bath $22.

Grandma's Home Hostel (AYH), 22330 Bell Rd. (753-4901), in New Boston, midway between Detroit and Ann Arbor, but inconvenient to either. Close to Metro Parks. Quiet and homey. $9; non-members $12 for first night.

Red Roof Inn, 2350 Rochester Rd. (689-4391), in Troy, ½-hr. from downtown. Take exit 67 off I-75. Mon.-Thurs. singles $27, doubles $35; Fri.-Sun., singles $36, doubles $41.

Roadway Inn, 8230 Merriman Rd. (729-7600), just outside the Detroit Metro airport. Accessible only by car; take I-94 to Merriman Rd. Free shuttle service to and from airport. Singles $28-33. Doubles $39-43.

You'll have to trek some distance if you want to camp. A dozen state parks with campgrounds lie about 40 mi. out, off I-75, I-96, and I-94. **Sterling State Park** (289-2715) lies 37 mi. south of Detroit, ½-mi. off of I-75 just north of the city of Monroe. (Open 24 hrs. Sites $10, including electricity.) The **Detroit-Greenfield KOA**, 6680 Bunton Rd. (482-7722), is about 30 mi. from downtown Detroit and three mi. east of Ypsilanti. From I-94 (exit 187), go one mi. south onto Rawsonville Rd., turn right onto Textile Rd., then go one mi. and turn left onto Bunton—the campground is ½-mi. farther. (216 sites. $18 per 2 people, with water and hookup $21. Each additional person $3, ages 4-17 $2. Open March 30-Nov. 18.) The **Windsor South Resort Kampground**, 6480 Texas Rd., (519-726-5200) offers comparable rates (CDN$16) and facilities, with 10% discount for U.S. dollars. Take the tunnel or bridge to Hwy. 3, then go south on Howard Ave. to Texas Rd.

Food and Nightlife

Ethnic food is a solid budget option in Detroit. From late May to August, the riverfront Hart Plaza, downtown at the foot of Woodward Ave., hosts a series of ethnic festivals ranging from African to Polish to Latin American. The *Do it in Detroit* brochure, available at the visitors bureau, lists ethnic festivals held at Hart Plaza (224-1184). Another cheap and popular option is **Greektown,** an enclave of eateries on Monroe, about four blocks northeast of the Ren Cen. Don't miss the shout of "Opa!" that comes with an order of *saganaki* (flaming cheese). Also on Monroe, **Trappers Alley,** (963-5445), houses 90 food and retail shops. (Open Mon.-Thurs. 10am-9pm, Fri.-Sat. 10am-midnight, Sun. noon-7pm.) **Eastern Market** (833-1560), at Gratiot and Russell Ave. just north of the Fisher Freeway (I-75), has hawked meat and produce outdoors since 1892. (Open Mon.-Fri. 5am-noon, Sat. 5am-5pm.) Another popular area for eating, drinking, and listening to music is the **Rivertown** area, east of the Ren Cen between Jefferson and the river. **Mexican Town,** a lively neighborhood south of Tiger Stadium, has a number of terrific restaurants.

Pizza Papalis Taverna, 553 Monroe (961-8020), in Greektown. A slick restaurant and bar that veers from the Greektown formula with delicious Chicago-style pizza. Try the 6-in. Chicago-style junior pie ($3.65). Open Mon.-Sat. 11am-1am, Sun. noon-1am.

Xochimilco Restaurant, 3409 Bagley (843-0179), in Mexican Town. You'll forget how far north you are as you enjoy the *botanes* (chips smothered with refried beans), Mexican sausages, and other goodies ($4.75-6.75). Huge servings and hugely popular, so plan to wait 20-30 min. Open daily 11am-4am.

Om Cafe, 23136 N. Woodward (548-1941) 8 mi. from downtown in Ferndale, 3½ blocks north of 9 Mile Road. Metro Detroit's most heralded vegetarian and macrobiotic restaurant. Yummy sandwiches and veggie plates, many with a hint of Mexico or the Middle East ($4.50-8). Open Mon.-Sat. 11am-9pm; brunch first and last Sunday of each month 10am-1pm.

Niki's Taverna, 735 Beaubien St. (961-4303), just south of Monroe, on the edge of Greektown. White-collar lunch crowd. Gyros with fries $5.50. Open Mon.-Thurs. 10am-3:30am, Fri. 10am-5am, Sat. 11am-5am, Sun. 11am-3:30am.

American and Lafayette Coney Islands, 114 and 118 W. Lafayette, just west of Cadillac Square. Decades of bilateral competition have produced the quintessential Detroit coney—hot dog, chili, mustard, and chopped onion ($1.35). Detroiters swear by them—although visitors might not understand why. Great for late-night peoplewatching. Always open.

Soup Kitchen Saloon, 1585 Franklin (259-2643), at Orleans in Rivertown, 5 blocks east of the Ren Cen. Detroit's home of the blues; a steady stream of local blues talent, with an occasional big-name act. Avoid the overpriced restaurant section. Live music Thurs. 9:30pm-midnight, Fri.-Sat. 9:30pm-2am, Sun. 7pm-midnight. Cover usually $2-6 (but up to $15 for more prominent acts).

Alvin's Finer Delicatessen and Detroit Bar, 5756 Cass (832-2355), just south of I-94, near Wayne State University. Typical deli sandwiches $2.85-4.25. At night, a hip student bar with all sorts of live bands, from classic rock to reggae to hardcore to jazz. Open daily 11am-2am; music starts about 9pm. Bar open until 2am. Cover $2-5.

Woodbridge Tavern, 289 St. Aubin St. (259-0578), at Woodbridge in Rivertown. Comfortable and fun old-style bar that draws a yuppie and neophyte-yuppie crowd. Features an outdoor terrace known as Marcia's Vineyard. Sandwiches and burgers $3.50-6. Open Mon.-Sat. 11am-1:30am, Sun. noon-10pm. Karaoke sing-alongs Thurs.; live classic rock 'n' roll Fri.-Sat. Cover $2.

Cavernous **Clubland,** 2115 Woodward (961-5450), in the Fox Theater, offers the city's biggest dance floor and a lascivious clientele. **Shelter,** 431 E. Congress (961-6358), two blocks north of the Ren Cen, through the back door in the basement of St. Andrew's Hall, spins alternative and industrial music for an alternative (but not very industrial) crowd. Open Tues.-Sun until 2am, but call to be sure. Hipdom's most recent metro Detroit hotspot is **Industry** 15 S. Saginaw, (334-1999), in the distant suburb of Pontiac.

Sights

Compact downtown Detroit can be explored easily in one day. The five-towered **Renaissance Center (Ren Cen)** between E. Jefferson and the river anchors downtown with glass and steel grandeur. Tours of the Ren Cen are given regularly. (For general Ren Cen information call 568-5600; tour information 341-6810; lines open daily 9am-5pm.) For an amazing view of the city during the daytime, head to the rotating cocktail lounge on the top floor of the middle tower. Pretend you're having a meal at the adjacent restaurant to avoid the $3 cover charge.

The Civic Center includes the **Philip A. Hart Plaza** (224-1185), a 10-acre "people place" that holds free concerts in summer, ethnic festivals on summer weekends (afternoons and evenings), and ice skating in the winter. Look for the spiraling **Pylon** and the Noguchi's **Dodge Fountain,** known as the "flying donut." Across the street is the striking and controversial **Joe Louis Monument,** a huge black arm and fist suspended on cables, designed by Robert Graham. The **Joe Louis Arena** (567-6000), west of Hart Plaza, home of the Detroit Red Wings hockey team, hosts a variety of concerts and other events, as does the next-door **Cobo Arena** (567-6000).

Just north of downtown, the magnificent **Fox Theatre,** 2211 Woodward Ave. (567-6000), has been painstakingly renovated. Now, as in 1928, the Fox is a gilt picture palace of impressive dimensions and gaudy decorations. Diana Ross, Aretha Franklin, and Stevie Wonder auditioned here for Motown Records in the 60s; today it hosts a variety of drama, comedy, and musical productions. **The Detroit Institute of Arts (DIA),** 5200 Woodward Ave. (833-7900), 2½ mi. north of downtown, has one of the nation's most comprehensive collections. Diego Rivera's spectacular 1932 *Detroit Industry* frescoes alone merit a visit. (Open Wed.-Sun. 9:30am-5:30pm. $4, kids $1.) The institute is part of Detroit's **Cultural Center,** a 40-block cluster of public and private cultural institutions bordered by Wayne State University (take bus #53). A quick walk from the DIA takes you into the "Streets of Old Detroit" at the **Detroit Historical Museum,** 5401 Woodward Ave. at Kirby (833-1805; open Wed.-Sun. 9:30am-5pm; donation). A continuing exhibit on the technical and social aspects of the Underground Railroad anchors the **Museum of African American History,** 301 Frederick Douglass (833-9800) in the Cultural Center (open Wed.-Sat. 9:30-5pm, Sun. 1-5pm; donation). Although Berry Gordy's Motown Record Company has moved to Los Angeles, the **Motown Museum,** 2648 W. Grand Blvd. (867-0991), preserves its memories. Downstairs, shop around the primitive studio in which the Jackson Five, Marvin Gaye, Smokey Robinson, and Diana Ross recorded the tunes that made them famous. (Open Mon.-Sat. 10am-5pm, Sun. 2-5pm. $3, under 12 $2.) The museum lies east of Rosa Parks Blvd., about one mi. west of the Lodge Freeway (Rte. 10). Take the "Dexter Avenue" bus right to the museum from downtown.

The colossal **Henry Ford Museum,** and **Greenfield Village,** 20900 Oakwood Blvd., off I-94 in Dearborn (271-1620 or 271-1976; 24 hrs.), definitely warrant a foray into the suburbs. The 12-acre museum has more than the expected parade of antique cars; it strives to show the importance of the car in 20th-century American pop culture. Other sensational items include the chair Lincoln sat in and the car Kennedy rode in when they each were assassinated. Greenfield Village is a collection of 80 transplanted historic buildings, including a turn-of-the-century amusement park, the Wright brothers' bicycle shop, the courtroom where Lincoln practiced law, Puritan homes, and various shops, houses, and taverns, all set in a beautiful 240-acre park. (Open daily 9am-5pm. Admission to museum and village $11 each, seniors $9.50, ages 5-12 $5.50. 2-day combination tickets $18, kids $9. Take SMART bus #200 or 250.)

If you're looking for a quiet refuge from the city bustle, head to **Belle Isle Park** (267-7115), a 985-acre island in the Detroit River (open 24 hrs.). Take a car or pick up DOT bus #25 (eastbound) at the corner of Jefferson and Randolf (in front of the Ren Cen) to MacArthur Bridge, then transfer to Belle Isle bus #4. Designed by Frederick Law Olmsted, Belle Isle has a variety of recreational facilities and fishing spots, as well as a conservatory, several fantastic playgrounds, an aquarium, and a small zoo. Most buildings are open daily from 10am to 5pm. Ask the driver for a brochure about walking and bus tours of the island.

Events

The Motor City turns into the Monte Carlo of the Midwest for one noisy week each year. The **Detroit Grand Prix** (259-5400), an Indy-car race on a Grand-Prix-style course surrounding the Ren Cen, takes place the third Sunday in June. Time trials and warmup races are held the Friday and Saturday before the race; Friday is free day. (Tickets $12 and up Sat., $25 and up Sun.; 3-day reserved grandstand seat $105-145.)

Jazz fans jet to Detroit during Labor Day weekend for the **Montreux-Detroit Jazz Festival** (259-5400), the U.S. half of the Swiss Montreux International Jazz Festival. Except for the packed final night, which has featured headliners like Dizzy Gillespie and Wynton Marsalis, the festival is free.

Isle Royale National Park

Cars are not allowed in America's most unspoiled national park, a 45-by-9-mi. island in Lake Superior. Ponds, lakes, and forest wilderness cover the rock foundation of Isle Royale, creating a natural sanctuary where humans are only guests. More than 100 mi. of hiking trails lace the island, threading past beaches and lookout points, through thick hardwood forests and ancient Native American copper mining pits. The **Greenstone Ridge Trail** follows the backbone of the island from Rock Harbor Lodge. **Ojibway Lookout,** on Mt. Franklin, affords a good view of the Canadian shore 15 mi. away. **Monument Rock,** 70 ft. tall, challenges even experienced climbers. **Lookout Louise,** also on the trail, offers one of the most beautiful views in the park. For a superlative time, go to **Ray's Island,** on the largest island in the largest freshwater lake in the world. The park is open for **camping** between mid-June and early September, but beware of fog and mosquitoes in June and early July. Nights are always cold (mid-40°F in June); bring warm clothes. Plan also to bring your own tent rather than relying on shelters. There are 31 campsites along the shores and on inland lakes. Permits, free and available at any ranger station, are required for backcountry camping. There are three **ranger stations:** Windigo on the western tip of the island; Rock Harbor on the eastern tip of the island; and near Siskiwit Lake, on the south shore, midway between Windigo and Rock Harbor. Use a 25-micron filter or boil water for at least two minutes, as it is infested with a nasty tapeworm; iodine tablets and charcoal purification are not sufficient. Campers can buy supplies and groceries at Rock Harbor and limited amounts at Windigo. Boat and canoe rentals are available at both Rock Harbor and Windigo, and the island's coast provides beautiful and surprising nooks (and crannies!) to explore by water. (Motor rentals $11 half day, $18.50 full day. Boat and canoe rentals $9 half day, $15 full day.) Ferries to Isle Royale run from **Houghton** (906-482-0984; 2 per week mid-June to Aug., $40 one way) and from **Copper Harbor** (906-289-4437; mid-May to Sept. 2-7 days per week, $32 one way); both cities are on the U.P. From **Grand Portage, MN** (715-392-2100), ferries run three days per week from mid-May to mid-June, daily from mid-June through August. (Windigo one way $30, Rock Harbor one way $40. Day cruise 9:30am-6pm. $35, kids under 12, $17.50. Reservations recommended.)

Lake Michigan Shore

The 350-mi. eastern shore of Lake Michigan stretches south from the Mackinaw Bridge to the Indiana border. Tourists flock here to enjoy high dunes of sugary sand, superb fishing, abundant fruit harvests through October, and deep snow in winter. Many of the region's attractions center around forked **Grand Traverse Bay** and **Traverse City,** the "cherry capital of the world," at the southern tip of the bay. Fishing is best in the **Au Sable** and **Manistee Rivers.** The rich fudge sold in numerous specialty shops, however, seems to have the biggest pull on tourists, whom locals dub "fudgies." The **West Michigan Tourist Association,** 136 E. Fulton, Grand Rapids 49503 (616-456-8557), offers copious free literature on this area. (Open Mon.-Fri. 8:45am-5pm.) **Greyhound** (see Traverse City below) serves the coast.

Charlevoix and Mackinaw City

Hemingway set some of his Nick Adams stories on the stretch of coast near **Charlevoix** (SHAR-le-voy), north of Traverse City on U.S. 31. The town, which lies on a ½-mi.-wide ribbon of land between Lake Michigan and Lake Charlevoix, attracts more tourists than in Hemingway's time, as upscale downstaters triple Charlevoix's population in summer. An artsy and aesthetically stunning town, Charlevoix is worth the trip even if you're not a Hemingway fan. While there, try to stay at the small **Durance Home Hostel (AYH),** 541 N. Mercer (547-2937). The 98-year-old Florence Durance runs the hostel "to be helpful, not to make money," and charges accordingly ($3.50 per person). If the hostel is full, you can rough it at **Fisherman's Island State Park,** (547-6641) three mi. southwest of Charlevoix. The **Petoskey Regional Chamber of Commerce,** 401 E. Mitchell (347-4150) in Petoskey, 18 mi. north of Charlevoix, has information on the area's attractions. (Open daily 8am-8pm.) Further north, **Fort Michilimackinac** (436-5563) guards the straits between Lakes Michigan and Superior, just as it did in the 18th century, though **Mackinaw City,** the town that grew around the fort, is out to trap tourists, not invading troops. (Tours of the fort daily 9am-5pm. $6, ages 6-12 $3.50.) **Mackinac Island** (which prohibits cars) has another fort, **Fort Mackinac** (906-847-3328), many Victorian homes, and the **Grand Hotel** (906-847-3331), an elegant, gracious summer resort with the world's longest porch. Horse-drawn carriages cart guests all over the island (906-847-3325; $10 per person; open daily 8:30am-5pm). Tourist-tempting fudge shops originated on the island. (Ferries leave Mackinaw City and St. Ignace June-Sept. every half hr., May and Sept.-Oct. every hr.; round trip $10.50, ages 6-12, $6.50.) **Greyhound** has a flag stop at the Standard gas station in downtown Mackinaw City. The Mackinaw **travel information center** (436-5566), off I-75, is loaded with brochures that make excellent use of alliteration.

Traverse City and Environs

In summer, vacationers head to Traverse City for its sandy beaches and annual **Cherry Festival,** held the first full week in July. Traverse City produces 50% of the world's sweet and tart cherries. The locals are friendly and the city full of intimate cafés and overpriced knick-knack shops. The surrounding landscape of sparkling blue water, cool forests, and magnificent sand dunes makes this region a Great Lakes paradise, though a crowded and expensive one. Grand Traverse Bay is the focal point for swimming, boating, and scuba diving. Free beaches and public access sites dot its shores. Look for the large flock of white swans.

According to local legend, the mammoth sand dunes 30 mi. northwest of Traverse City are a sleeping mother bear, waiting for her cubs—the **Manitou Islands**—to finish a swim across the lake. According to scientific theory, ice-age glaciers left behind the islands which now comprise the **Sleeping Bear Dunes National Lakeshore.** Nature constantly resculpts the dunes, and some rise a precipitous 400 ft. above the shore of Lake Michigan. The best place to see the dunes is on **Pierce Stocking Scenic Drive,** off M-109 just north of the town of Empire. A ferry (256-9061) runs out of Leland to South Manitou Island in summer. (Ferries leave daily at 10am, return at 5pm. Round-trip $15, $17 if you are camping; kids under 12 receive a $5 discount.) The park and centers rent canoes, and remain open in winter for cross-country skiing.

The renowned **Interlochen Center for the Arts** (276-9221) rests between two lakes just south of Traverse City on Rte. 137. Here, the high-powered **National Music Camp** instructs over 2,000 young artists and musicians each summer in the visual arts, theater, dance, and music. Performances are usually free or cost only $1-2 during the **International Arts Festival,** held from late June to mid-August. Recent guest performers included John Denver and Peter, Paul, and Mary. The **Interlochen Arts Academy** at the center offers performances almost every weekend in winter as well (call 276-6230 for schedule). The 1,200-acre wooded grounds are open year-round, and free tours leave the information center Monday through Saturday at 10am and 2:30pm, Sunday at 3pm. Across the road, the huge **Interlochen State Park** (276-9511) has camping facilities. (Primitive sites $5, with hookup $9, plus a $3 vehicle permit; showers $1.) The park store rents row boats ($12 per 12 hr., $15 per per 24 hrs.; $20 deposit or driver's license required).

There are hundreds of **campgrounds** around Traverse City—in state parks and forests, the Manistee and Huron National Forests, and various parks run by local townships and counties. The West Michigan Tourist Association's *Carefree Days* gives a comprehensive list of public and private sites. State parks usually charge $7-9. As usual, the national forests (723-2211 or 723-3161) are probably the best deal ($4-7). Sleeping Bear Dunes National Lakeshore (326-5134) has two campgrounds: **DH Day** (334-4634) in Glen Arbor, and **Platte River** (325-5881) in Honor. DH Day costs $6 per vehicle, Platte River a few dollars more because of recent renovation. Both campgrounds fill up on mid-summer weekends.

Sleep in the woods at the **Brookwood Home Hostel**, 538 Thomas Rd. (352-4296), in Frankfort near the Sleeping Bear Dunes, almost 50 mi. south of Traverse City on Hwy. 31. The large cottage has 12 beds. ($6. Open mid-June to Sept. 20. Reservations required; call Marjorie Groenwald at 301-544-4514.) If you are bicycling or hiking, the **Honey House Home Hostel (AYH)**, 613 S. Bayshore in Elk Rapids (264-9678), 18 mi. north of Transverse City, has fifteen beds, but no shower. The hostel is wholly for hinternational htravelers, hbikers and whikers honly. ($6, nonmembers $8. Open May-Oct.) The **Victoriana Bed and Breakfast**, 622 Washington St. (929-1009), near downtown, has four comfortable, almost grand, rooms decorated with family heirlooms. (Singles $40. Doubles $45. Suite $65. Big breakfast and afternoon tea included.) The **Northwestern Michigan Community College**, East Hall, 1701 E. Front St. (922-1406), offers dorms with shared bath. (Singles $15. Doubles $25. Suite with private bath $50. Reservations recommended. Open summer only.) **D. Orr Haus Motor Lodge**, 894 Munson Ave. (947-9330), has clean, no-frills motel rooms right across the street from a nice state beach. (Singles $32. Doubles $38. Prices may increase slightly on weekends.)

Traverse City has a multitude of fast-food restaurants along E. Front St., but smaller, cheaper, and more appetizing restaurants dot the town. **Stone Soup**, 115 E. Front St. (941-1190), downtown, serves splendid salads ($3-5.75) and "sandriginals," daily special sandwiches ($5.25). (Open Mon.-Sat. 7am-4pm, Sun. 9am-3pm.) The **Omelette Shop and Bakery**, 124 Cass St. (946-0912), makes great omelettes ($3.25-5.25), soups, muffins, and ratatouille *frittata*. (Open daily 7am-3pm.) For good, cheap pizza, try **The Upper Crust**, 720 W. Front St. (946-5252), near downtown. They specialize in Sicilian 'za ($4.50 for a small). (Open Tues.-Fri. 11:30am-2pm, 4-10pm; Sat. 4-10pm; Sun. 4-8pm.)

Greyhound, 3233 Cass Rd. (946-5180), connects Traverse City with the Upper Peninsula and southern Michigan ($36 to Detroit; open Mon.-Fri. 8am-5pm). **Bay Area Transportation Authority**, at the same address (941-2324), runs buses once per hour on scheduled routes ($1.50 per ride) and can provide personal transportation. (Open Mon.-Fri. 6am-6pm, Sat. 9am-5pm.)

For visitor information, contact the **Grand Traverse Convention and Visitors Bureau**, 415 Munson Ave. #200 (947-1120 or 800-872-8377; open Mon.-Fri. 9am-5pm). Ask for the *Traverse City Guide* and *Carefree Days*. The **Michigan Department of Natural Resources** offers information on state parks (947-7193) and state forest campgrounds (946-4920) during business hours. For a listing of local events and entertainment, pick up the weekly *Traverse City Record-Eagle Summer Magazine*, free at the visitors bureau and in many stores.

The area's **time zone** is Eastern. The **post office** is at 202 S. Union St. (946-9616); open Mon.-Fri. 8am-5pm). Traverse City's **ZIP code** is 49684; the **area code** is 616.

Upper Peninsula

A multimillion-acre forestland bordered by three of the world's largest lakes, Michigan's Upper Peninsula (U.P.) is one of the most scenic and unspoiled stretches of land in the Great Lakes region. The region's relative isolation and the distances between its cities make travel on the U.P. difficult without a car, bike, or in winter, a snowmobile. But for those patient enough to wait, **Greyhound** (635-9123) is the major carrier on the Peninsula. Lower Peninsula schedules connect at St. Ignace to Sault Ste. Marie and U.S. 2 across to Escanaba. In Escanaba and in Ironwood, routes from Wisconsin, Duluth, and Chicago link with service to Marquette and the Keweenaw Peninsula. If you are traveling by bus in the U.P., connections will require a wait of approximately one day and half of a night, since buses travel only at night. While this may help save on accommodations costs, it makes for a weary traveler. Try to get some sleep on the beautiful beaches; life is very tranquil in the U.P.

The U.P.'s main appeals are its vast quiet lakes and forests, deserted lakeshore dunes, and lonely, mosquito-infested marshes—sanctuary for hikers, cross-country skiers, anglers, canoeists, and compulsive scratchers. Contact the **Upper Peninsula Travel and Recreational Association,** P.O. Box 400, Iron Mountain 49801, for general information. The **U.S. Forestry Service,** Hiawatha National Forest, 2727 N. Lincoln Rd., Escanaba 49829, has guides and maps to help you plan a trip into the wilderness. The Southern portion of the U.P., along Lakes Michigan and Huron, is noted for its sand dunes and quiet beaches. East of the Mackinaw Bridge lie **Les Cheneaux Islands,** due south of the Soo Canal on Lake Huron, a labyrinth of 35 forest-covered islets and pure, delicious water. Hill's Marina, in **Hessel** on MI Rte. 134 (484-2640), rents 14-ft. aluminum motor boats (7½ horsepower, $35 per day including a tank of gas). Hiawatha National Forest maintains **Government Island** as an uninhabited area. You can dock your boat and camp here.

U.S. 2 from the north end of the bridge in St. Ignace west to Naubinway follows some lovely, unspoiled, and practically deserted lakeshore. The white sand dunes of enormous Lake Michigan resemble ocean beaches. Numerous inexpensive motels line U.S. 2. Sleep in or near **Manistique,** where you can find a whole range of accommodations and outgoing locals. The **Blue Spruce Motel** (341-5410) is one of many motels offering inexpensive singles or doubles ($32). The **Marina Guest House,** 230 Arbutas (341-5147), is a clean, well-kept B&B. (Singles $30. Doubles and suites $45-50. Reservations recommended.) The big sandwiches ($3.50-4) at **Sunny Shores Restaurant** on U.S. 2 will brighten your day. (Open daily 6:30am-9pm.)

Excellent swimming opportunities splash around Manistique. An especially beautiful, sandy beach lies two mi. west of the city limits, just off Rte. 2. Handsome and clean **Indian Lake State Park** (341-2355) lies five mi. west. (300 sites; $9. Tents or tepees rent at $6 per night.) **Camper's Market** (341-5614) rents canoes. ($10 per day, $7 per half-day; $20 deposit required.) 12 mi. west of Manistique, visit the amazing **Big Spring,** a 45-ft. deep, 45°F pond of crystal clear water and brown trout—early residents called it the "mirror of heaven". For supplementary information, contact the **Schoolcraft County Chamber of Commerce,** on U.S. 2 just west of Manistique (341-5010; open Mon.-Fri. 8am-6pm, Sat.-Sun. 9am-4pm).

The U.P.'s northern reaches are slightly colder and less marshy than its southern shores. **Sault Ste. Marie,** in the northeast corner, house the **Soo Locks,** the only entrance to Lake Superior. Boat tours of the locks are offered several times daily by **Soo Locks Boat Tours** (632-6301; $11, seniors $10.50, kids $5). Cheap accommodations are harder to find in Sault Ste. Marie than anywhere else on the Peninsula, but nearby **Hiawatha National Forest** has campsites ($7-9). For more information contact the **Sault Ste. Marie Chamber of Commerce,** 2581 I-75, Business Spur (632-3301).

From Sault Ste. Marie, a 74-mi. lakeshore drive will bring you to **Tahquamenon Falls,** the second largest waterfalls east of the Mississippi. Campsites are available around the falls ($12, including $3 motor vehicle permit), and the nearby town of

Newberry has inexpensive motels. (Singles from $20. Doubles from $26.) Further west, the **Pictured Rocks National Lakeshore** (387-2607) stretches along the Superior coast. Here, the rain, wind, and ice of Lake Superior have carved the sandstone cliffs into multicolored arches and columns, with caves dotting the steep walls about the lake. The lakeshore offers beaches, primitive camping, and inland lakes for fishing and swimming. For a better perspective on the stone formations, **Pictured Rocks Boat Cruises** (494-2611) will take you along the shoreline, with frequent departures in summer and early fall ($17, ages 6-18 $7, under 5 free). A section of the scenic **North Country Hiking Trail** traverses the park, with free campsites en route. This trail crosses the entire U.P. and winds south through the Lower Peninsula into Ohio. The lakeshore is most easily accessible through the town of **Grand Marais,** where you can get supplies, information, food and lodging. Try the **Alverson Motel,** right on Hwy. 58 (494-2681; singles $29, doubles $35). For other information, contact the **Grand Marais Chamber of Commerce,** P.O. Box 118, Grand Marais 49839 (494-2766).

The northwest corner of the U.P. is the **Keewenaw Peninsula,** named for the Indian tribes that used to live here. Less tourist-oriented than the rest of the region, the isolated, hilly Keewenaw offers excellent fishing, hiking and snowmobiling. The **Fanny Howe Resort and Campground,** in Cooper Harbor (289-4451), offers campsites, a swimming pool, and lots of friendly advice. (Tent sites $10, $2 per additional person. Reservations recommended July-Aug.) For more posh lodgings, try the **Thimbleberry Inn Bed and Breakfast,** 1156 Calumet Ave. in Calumet (337-1332; singles $35, doubles $45). The **Keewenaw Tourism Council** is at 326 Sheldon Ave., Houghton (482-2388 or 800-338-7982).

The **area code** for the U.P. is 906.

MINNESOTA

Modern Minnesota defies the dreary small-town stereotype attached to it by Sinclair Lewis in his 1920 classic *Main Street.* The residents of Lewis's fictional town were stodgy, stifling, and conservative to the hilt. Little houses on the prairie still have a place in Minnesota—their current bard is Garrison Keillor, who sets the fictional town of Lake Wobegon in his home state—but "The Bread and Butter State" kneads liberals. It consistently votes Democratic and in recent years has churned out such wry liberals as Hubert Humphrey and Walter Mondale. The state's most famous rock acts are Bob Dylan, Prince, and doubly-umlauted Hüsker Dü, none of whom are known for being *particularly* white-bread.

Minnesota offers the hungry tourist a multi-grained itinerary. With its evergreen forests, preserved wilderness, and scores of lakes (its other nickname is "The Land of Ten Thousand Lakes,") canoeists regard the area with wonder and loave. The Twin Cities offer cultural diversions while avoiding the extremes of indigence and excessive dough common to the Northeastern cities.

Practical Information

Capital: St. Paul.

Minnesota Travel Information Center, 375 Jackson St., 250 Skyway Level, St. Paul 55101 (296-5029 or 800-657-3700). Open Mon.-Fri. 8am-5pm.

Time Zone: Central (1 hr. behind Eastern).

Postal Abbreviation: MN

Duluth

Still the largest inland port on the Great Lakes, the once-booming railroad hub of Duluth relies on the thousands of tourists who come to see the city's historic mansions, beautiful parks, and spectacular views of Lake Superior. Minnesota's "refrigerated city," known for its oh-my-God-it's-so-cold weather, also offers a great place to gear up for a fishing, camping, or driving excursion into northwestern Minnesota.

The best thing about Duluth is its proximity to majestic Lake Superior. Take a tour of the harbor on **Duluth Superior Excursions,** 5th Ave. W. at Waterfront (722-6218), behind the Duluth Arena and Auditorium. (Boats depart mid-May to early June and early Sept. to mid-Oct. 10:30am-4:30pm every 2 hr.; early June-early Sept. 9:30am-7:30pm every 2 hr. $7.50, ages 3-11 $3.50.) Enjoy the Superior coast along Duluth's recently completed **Lakewalk,** a mile-long walkway stretching across the harbor. Reach new summer heights by climbing to the top of empty **Enger Tower,** 18th Ave. W. on Skyline Parkway. You can see all of Duluth-Superior Harbor, and up to 30 mi. farther on a clear day. **Hawk Ridge,** four mi. north of downtown off Skyline Blvd., creates a birdwatcher's paradise. A tremendous number and variety of hawks cruise by between late August and early November on their way south.

For indoor entertainment, visit **The Depot,** 506 W. Michigan St. (727-8025), in the old Amtrak station, where the **Lake Superior Museum of Transportation** captures Duluth's railroad and logging heritage. (Open daily 10am-5pm; Sept. 2-May 27 Mon.-Sat. 10am-5pm, Sun. 1-5pm. Admission $4, seniors $3, families $11, ages 6-17 $2.) Also known as the **St. Louis County Heritage and Arts Center,** the Depot houses the **Duluth Playhouse** (722-0349; box office open Mon.-Fri. 9am-4pm, until 8pm on nights of performances; tickets $5-6, seniors and students $4-5), the **Duluth Ballet** (722-2314), and the **Duluth-Superior Symphony Orchestra** (722-7429). Mansion-lovers should head to **Glensheen,** 3300 London Rd. (724-8863). This 39-room neo-Jacobean spectacle has beautiful Edwardian furnishings and landscaped grounds that overlook the lakes. (Open Feb.-Dec. Thurs.-Tues. 9am-4pm; Jan. Sat.-Sun. 1-3pm; more tours in summer and on weekends. $6, seniors and ages 13-17 $4.50, under 12 $2.50, less in winter. Make reservations for summer visits.)

After a day of sight-seeing, head to one of the city parks. Free outdoor concerts are held at **Chester Bowl** and **Lake Superior Zoological Gardens** (624-1502) in Fairmont Park in West Duluth. **Bayfront Park** hosts the **International Folk Festival** (722-7425) on the first Saturday in August. Call the Park and Recreation Department (723-3337) for more info.

Finding accommodations is not easy in Duluth. Although there are many hotels, most offer rooms starting at $45. Try the **College of St. Scholastica,** 1200 Kenwood Ave. (723-6483), which often offers spacious, pleasant rooms in summer at its secluded campus. (Double with shared bath $35. Make reservations.) The **Voyageur Motel,** 333 East Superior St. (722-3911), downtown, is clean and not too expensive. (Singles $35. Doubles $45. In the summer, make reservations.) **Jay Cooke State Park** (384-4610), southwest of Duluth on I-35, has 84 campsites. (Open daily 8am-10pm. Sites $9. Vehicle permit $3.25.) **Spirit Mountain,** 9500 Spirit Mountain Pl. (628-2891), near the ski resort of the same name, is 10 mi. south on I-35, on the top of the hill. (Sites with electricity $13, with electricity and water $15.)

Two downtown shopping centers—the restored **Fitger's** brewery, 600 E. Superior St. (722-5624), and the more modern **Holiday Center**—have a number of pleasant restaurants ranging from fast-food joints to elegant dining spots. **Grandma's Saloon and Deli,** 522 Lake Ave. S. (727-4192), packs people into a room with old advertising signs and attitude. Those under 21 can't enter unless accompanied by a grown-up. (Sandwiches $4.25-6.50, spaghetti $7. Open daily 11am-1am.) Despite the name, **Sir Benedict's Tavern on the Lake,** 805 E. Superior St. (728-1192), is much more laid-back. Pick up a made-to-order sandwich ($3.40-4.20) and choose from the many imported beers ($2.55). Outside tables overlook the lake. (Live bluegrass Wed., Celtic music every 3rd Thurs. Open Mon.-Tues. and Thurs. 11am-11pm,

Wed. 11am-midnight, Fri.-Sat. 11am-12:30am.) Afterwards, head to the **Portland Malte Shoppe,** 714 E. Superior, for a huge, delicious malt ($2.80; open daily 11am-11pm).

Greyhound, 2212 W. Superior (722-5591), two mi. west of downtown, serves Michigan's Upper Peninsula, Hancock, and Calumet ($73). The **Duluth Transit Authority (DTA)** serves the downtown and outlying areas. Consult maps in bus shelters or call 722-7283. (Fare 75¢, seniors 35¢.)

The **Convention and Visitors Bureau,** at Endion Station, 100 Lake Place Dr. (722-4011; open Mon.-Fri. 9am-4:45pm) and the summer **visitor center** on the waterfront at Harbor Dr. (722-6024; open daily mid-May to mid-Oct. 9am-7:30pm) have an ample supply of brochures and Duluth maps.

The **post office** is at 2800 W. Michigan (723-2590), near the bus station. (Open Mon.-Fri. 8am-5pm, Sat. 9am-noon.) Duluth's **ZIP code** is 55806; its **area code** is 218.

Minneapolis and St. Paul

The Twin Cities are two of the most culturally exciting and aesthetically pleasing cities in the U.S., challenging the stereotype of cities as a place to work or play but not to live.

Yet despite their name and shared felicity, Minneapolis and St. Paul are hardly twins. Minneapolis is the more avant-garde, with more museums, parks, and a stronger artistic community than St. Paul. The alternative music scene is particulary robust, having spawned rugged bands like Hüsker Dü, the Replacements, and Soul Asylum; here Prince and other members of his royal family crowned the "Minneapolis sound."

While Minneapolis grew from water power harnessed at the Mississippi, St. Paul grew from whiskey. Originally dubbed Pig's Eye, after one-eyed whiskey seller "Pig's Eye" Parrant, St. Paul still retains a less saintly style, despite its Victorian homes, historic landmarks, and nationally recognized performing arts community.

Practical Information

Emergency: 911.

Minneapolis Convention and Visitors Association, 1219 Marquette Ave. (348-4313 or 800-445-7412). Open Mon.-Fri. 8am-5:30pm. **St. Paul Convention and Visitors Bureau,** 600 NCL Tower, 445 Minnesota St. (297-6985 or 800-627-6101). Open Mon.-Fri. 8am-5pm. **Greater Minneapolis Chamber of Commerce,** 81 S. 9th St., Quinlan Bldg. #200 (370-9132). Open Mon.-Fri. 8am-5pm. **St. Paul Chamber of Commerce,** #600, North Central Life Tower, 445 Minnesota St. (222-5561). Open Mon.-Fri. 8am-5pm. **Cityline,** 645-6060. Information on local events, concerts, news, sports, weather,and much more.

Travelers Aid: 404 S. 8th St. (335-5000), Minneapolis. Open Mon.-Fri. 8:30am-4pm. Also at the airport (726-5500). Emergency shelter help. Open Mon.-Sat. 8am-8pm, Sun. noon-8pm.

Twin Cities International Airport: 7 mi. south of the cities, on I-494 in Bloomington. **North-west Airlines** has its headquarters here. Limousines (726-6400) run to downtown and suburban hotels, leaving from the lower level near baggage claim (6am-midnight; $5.75 to St. Paul, $8 to Minnesota). Take bus #35 to Minneapolis ($1.10; service available 6-8am and 3-4:45pm). Otherwise, take bus #7 to Washington Ave. in Minneapolis, or transfer at Fort Snelling for bus #9 to downtown St. Paul. Ask for a transfer. Taxis are about $18 to Minneapolis and $15 to St. Paul.

Amtrak: 730 Transfer Rd. (800-872-7245), on the east bank off University Ave. SE, between the Twin Cities. A nice station, but a fair distance from both downtowns. Trains to Chicago (8½ hr., $68).

Greyhound: In **Minneapolis,** 29 9th St. at 1st Ave. N. (371-3311), 1 block northwest of Hennepin Ave. Very convenient. 24-hr. security. To: Chicago ($52), New York ($133, $68 with 21-day advance), and Seattle ($126). Open daily 5:45am-2:15am. In **St. Paul,** 7th St. at St. Peter (222-0509), 3 blocks east of the Civic Center, downtown. A little deserted, even in the daytime; don't hang around outside. Open daily 5:45am-8:10pm.

Public Transport: Metropolitan Transit Commission, 560 6th Ave. N. (827-7733). Call for information and directions Mon.-Fri. 6am-11pm, Sat.-Sun. 7am-11pm. Schedules and route maps available at: Tourism Information Center, Coffman Student Union, 300 Washington Ave. SE, University of Minnesota; Comstock Hall Housing Office, 210 Delaware St. SE, University of Minnesota; and the MTC store, 719 Marquette, in downtown Minneapolis. Bus service for both cities. Some buses operate 4:30am-12:45am, others shut down earlier. Fare $1.10 peak, 75¢ off-peak, ages under 18 25¢ off-peak. **University of Minnesota Bus,** 625-9000. Buses run 7am-10pm. Free to campus locations and even into St. Paul, if you are a student. Off-campus routes 35-50¢, 75¢ peak.

Car Rental: Ugly Duckling Rent-A-Car, 6405 Cedar Ave. S. (861-7545), Minneapolis, near the airport. From $28 per day with 100 free mi., weekly from $139. Open Mon.-Fri. 9am-6pm, Sat. noon-3pm, or by appointment. Technically must be 25. Major credit card or a $200 deposit required.

Taxi: Yellow Taxi, 824-4444, in Minneapolis. **Yellow Cab,** 222-4433, in St. Paul. Base rate $1.25, $1.20 per mi.

Help Lines: Gay-Lesbian Helpline, 822-8661. **Rape Crisis Line,** 2431 Hennepin Ave. 825-4357. Open 24 hrs.

Post Office: In **Minneapolis,** 1st St. and Marquette Ave. (349-4957), next to the Mississippi River. General Delivery open Mon.-Fri. 8:30am-5pm, Sat. 9am-noon. **ZIP code:** 55401. In **St. Paul,** 180 E. Kellogg Blvd. (293-3011). Open same hours. **ZIP code:** 55101.

Area Code: 612.

Minneapolis's layout is straightforward—streets run east-west and avenues run north-south. **Hennepin Avenue** crosses the Mississippi and goes through downtown, curving south toward uptown. Outside of downtown, most avenues are in alphabetical order as you travel west. St. Paul's streets are more confusing to navigate. **Grand Avenue** (east-west) and **Snelling Avenue** (north-south) are major thoroughfares. In both of the cities, **Skywalks** define the downtown areas, with above-ground tunnels connecting more than 10 square blocks to shield pedestrians from winter cold and summer heat. **University Avenue** connects the Twin Cities.

Accommodations and Camping

While cheap airport hotels abound in the Twin Cities, they are of questionable cleanliness and safety. The convention and visitors bureaus have useful lists of **bed and breakfasts.** The **University of Minnesota Housing Office** (624-2994), in Comstock Hall, has a list of rooms in different locations around the city that rent on a daily ($12-35) or weekly basis. The **Oakmere Home Hostel (AYH),** 8212 Oakmere Rd. (944-1210), in Bloomington has singles for $15. The nice, wood-paneled rooms overlook a lake, but the hostel's fairly remote suburban location makes it virtually unreachable without a car.

College of St. Catherine, Caecilian Hall (AYH), 2004 Randolph Ave. (690-6604), St. Paul. Take St. Paul bus #7 or 14, or call for directions. 103 stark but quiet dorm rooms near the river in a nice neighborhood. Shared bath, kitchenette. Singles $12, nonmembers $14. Doubles $20/$25. Open June to mid-Aug.

Kaz's Home Hostel (AYH), 5100 Dupont Ave. S. (822-8286), in South Minneapolis. Take bus #4 to Bryant and 50th, then walk 2 blocks west on 50th to Dupont. Only 6 blocks from Lake Harriet. Four beds in spacious rooms. Check-in 5-9pm. Curfew 11pm. Members only, $10. Reservations required.

Evelo's Bed and Breakfast, 2301 Bryant Ave. (374-9656), in South Minneapolis. A 15-min. walk from uptown or take bus #17 from downtown. Three comfortable rooms with elegant wallpapering and furnishings in a beautiful house filled with Victorian artifacts. Friendly owners. Singles $35. Doubles $45. Reservations required.

Town and Country Campground, 12630 Boone Ave. S. (445-1756), 15 mi. south of downtown Minneapolis. From I-35W, go west on Rte. 13 to Rte. 101 for ½ mi., then left onto Boone Ave. 60 sites—the closest to the Twin Cities. Plenty of shade and family-run, but you can hear the freeway. Sites $12 for 2, with electricity $15, full hookup $17. Each additional person $1.

Minneapolis Northwest I-94 KOA, (420-2255), on Rte. 101 west of I-94 exit 213, 15 mi. north of Minneapolis. Noisy kids and all the classic KOA amenities: pool, sauna, and showers. Sites $14.50-18. Each additional person $2, $1.50 for kids.

Food

The Twin Cities specialize in casual dining; a gourmet sandwich or salad and a steaming cup of coffee is the favored fare. During the past decade demographics and tastes have changed: many of the Scandinavian smorgasbords have given way to Vietnamese and natural food restaurants. Funky **Uptown** is packed with restaurants and bars to suit every taste. The **Warehouse District,** near downtown Minneapolis, and **Victoria Crossing,** (at Victoria and Grand St.) in St. Paul's, have a more upscale flavor. **Dinkytown** and the **West Bank** cater to student needs. For cheaper food and ethnic specialties, try **Northeast Minneapolis.**

Minneapolis

The New Riverside Cafe, 329 Cedar Ave. (333-4814), West Bank, at the "Biomagnetic Center of the Universe." Take bus #73. Full vegetarian meals served cafeteria-style amidst unframed works by local artists. Nightly live jazz and bluegrass. Sandwiches and Mexican dishes $2-5.50. Open Mon.-Thurs. 7am-11pm, Fri. 7am-midnight, Sat. 8am-midnight, Sun. 8am-1:30pm. Performances Tues.-Thurs. at 7pm, Fri.-Sat. at 8pm. No cover.

It's Greek to Me, 626 Lake St. at Lyndale Ave. (825-9922). Take bus #4 south. Great Greek food, complemented by traditional costumes hanging on the walls. Gyros $3.50. Dinners $7-12. Open daily 11am-11pm.

Matin, 416 1st Ave. N. downtown (354-0150). Elegant Vietnamese food with French flair. All-you-can-eat lunch buffet $6.50, entrees $3.50-7. Try the *xao cu nang* (tofu or mushrooms sautéed in garlic sauce with rice; $4.75). Open Mon.-Fri. 11am-2:30pm, Mon.-Thurs. 5-10pm, Fri.-Sat. 5-11pm.

The Malt Shop, 50th St. at Bryant Ave. in South Minneapolis (824-1352; take bus #4), or Snelling at I-94, St. Paul (take bus #1 or 94). An old-time soda fountain; try a phenomenal fresh fruit malt or shake ($3). Minneapolis shop open Mon.-Thurs. 11am-10:30pm, Fri. 11am-11pm, Sat. 8:30am-11pm, Sun. 8:30am-10:30pm. **St. Paul** shop open Sun.-Thurs. 7:30am-10:30pm, Fri.-Sat. 7:30am-11pm.

The Loring Café, 1624 Harmon Pl. (332-1617), next to Loring Park. Extraordinary pasta and pizza ($8-11) and desserts ($3-5). A great place for dinner, or just for drinks or coffee. A good bar, too, with live music and no cover. Open Sun.-Thurs. 11am-11pm, Fri.-Sat. 11am-2am.

The Black Forest, at 26th and Nicollet (872-0812). Widely renowned, inexpensive German food. Open Mon.-Sat. 11am-1am, Sun. noon-midnight.

Annie's Parlor, 313 14th Ave. SE (379-0744) in Dinkytown, and 406 Cedar Ave., West Bank. Malts that are a meal in themselves ($3.25) and great hamburgers ($3.25-5). Open Mon.-Thurs. 11am-11pm, Fri.-Sat. 11am-midnight, Sun. noon-11pm.

St. Paul

Café Latté, 850 Grand Ave. (224-5687), across the street from Victoria Crossing. Cafeteria-style, but elegant, with bi-level seating. Delicious soups, salads ($3.25-4.50), pastries, and espresso. Steaming milk drinks called Hot Moos ($1.65); try the Swedish Hot Moo with cinnamon, cardamon, and maple syrup. Lines usually long. Open Mon.-Thurs. 10am-11pm, Fri. 10am-midnight, Sat. 9am-midnight, Sun. 9am-10pm.

Willow Gate, 767 Cleveland Ave. S. (699-3141), ½ mi. south of the College of St. Catherine. Take bus #7. This Chinese restaurant offers enormous and delicious dinners ($4-7), as well as complimentary tea. Subgum fried rice (with chicken, pork, and shrimp) $4.75. Open Mon.-Thurs. 11:30am-9pm, Fri.-Sat. 11:30am-10:30pm, Sun. 4-9:30pm.

Mickey's Dining Car, 36 W. 7th St. (222-5633), across from the Greyhound station. Small, cheap, and convenient; a great spot for wee-hour munchies runs. Steak and eggs from $4.50, lunch and dinner from $3. Open 24 hrs.

St. Paul Farmers Market, 5th St. at Wall Market (227-6856), downtown. Fresh produce and baked goods. Get there before 10am on Sat. for the best quality and widest selection. Call to verify location and hours. Open Sat. 6am-1pm and May-Oct. Sun. 8am-1pm.

Cossetta's, 211 W. 7th St. (222-3476), near downtown. Old-fashioned Italian market with amazing pizza (small $6). Open Mon.-Sat. 11am-10pm, Sun. 11am-8pm.

Sights

Minneapolis

One look at the beautiful lakes right in the middle of the city explains Minneapolitans' civic pride. Lake of Isles, off Franklin Ave., about 1½ mi. from downtown, is ringed by stately mansions. It's hard to believe you're in the middle of the city when you walk through throngs of Canadian geese and breathe the countrified air. Bikers, skaters, and joggers constantly round Lake Calhoun, on the west end of Lake St. south of Lake of Isles, making it a hectic social and recreational hotspot. Rent skates and roller blades at Rolling Soles, 1700 W. Lake St. (823-5711; skates $3 per hr., $7.50 per day; blades $5 per hr., $10 per day; open Mon.-Fri. 10am-9pm, Sat.-Sun. 9am-9pm.). The Minneapolis Park and Recreation Board (348-2226) rents canoes ($4.50 per hr.) at the northeast corner of Lake Calhoun. Situated in a more residential neighborhood, Lake Harriet has a tiny paddleboat, a stage with occasional free concerts, and an endless stream of joggers. The city provides 28 mi. of trails along these lakes for cycling, roller skating, roller blading, jogging, or strolling on a sunny afternoon. The circumference of each lake is about three mi. and paths are well maintained; take bus #28 to all three lakes.

One of the top modern art museums in the country, the Walker Art Center, 725 Vineland Place (375-7622), a few blocks from downtown, draws thousands with daring exhibits and an impressive permanent collection, including works by Lichtenstein and Warhol. (Open Tues.-Sat. 10am-8pm, Sun. 11am-5pm. $3, seniors free, ages 12-18 and students with ID $2. Free on Thurs.) Inside is an excellent, not-too-expensive café (sandwiches $1.50-2.50; open Tues.-Sun. 11:30am-3pm), and adjacent is the Guthrie Theater (see Entertainment). Next to the Walker, the Minneapolis Sculpture Garden displays dozens of sculptures and a fountain in a "room" of exquisitely landscaped trees and flowers. The Minneapolis Institute of Arts, 2400 3rd Ave. S. (870-3131), contains Egyptian, Chinese, American, and European art. (Open Tues.-Sat. 10am-5pm, Thurs. 10am-9pm, Sun. noon-5pm. Free. Special exhibits $3, students, ages 12-18, and seniors $2; free to all Thurs. 5-9pm. Take bus #9.)

St. Anthony Falls and Upper Locks, downtown at 1 Portland Ave. (333-5336), has a free observation deck that overlooks the Mississippi River. (Open April-Nov. daily 8am-10pm.) Several mi. downstream, Minnehaha Park provides a breathtaking view of Minnehaha Falls, immortalized in Longfellow's longwinded Song of Hiawatha. (Take bus #7 from Hennepin Ave. downtown.)

St. Paul

The capital city boasts some unique architectural sites. Summit Avenue, west of downtown, stretches from the Mississippi to the capitol building displaying the nation's longest continuous stretch of Victorian homes, including the Governor's Mansion and the former homes of F. Scott Fitzgerald and railroad magnate James J. Hill. Most of these "Grand Old Ladies of Summit Avenue" were built in the 19th century with railroad fortunes. Overlooking the capitol on Summit stands St. Paul's Cathedral, 239 Selby Ave. (228-1766), a scaled-down version of St. Peter's in Rome. (Open daily 7:30am-6pm.) Battle school fieldtrips to see the golden horses atop the ornate state capitol, at Cedar and Aurora St. (296-3962 or 297-1503; open Mon.-Fri. 9am-5pm, Sat. 10am-4pm, Sun. 1-4pm.) The nearby Minnesota Historical Society, 690 Cedar St. (296-6126), carries a wealth of information in its extensive libraries. The Historical Society will open a new building between Kellogg Blvd. and Ireland Blvd. in Sept., 1992, when it will reopen exhibits about St. Paul's early Scan-

LET'S G⊙® Travel

1992 Catalog

The One-Stop Travel Store

For over 30 years, our travel agents have worked to help the budget traveler find the most convenient and affordable way to travel--offering travel gear, discount airfares, Eurail passes, and more.

Take a look inside to see the
42 ways we can make your trip easier.

LET'S PACK IT UP

Let's Go® Backpack/Suitcases

Innovative hideaway suspension with internal frame turns backpack into carry-on suitcase. Detachable daypack makes it 3 bags in 1. Water-proof Cordura® nylon. Lifetime Guarantee. 3750 cu. in. Navy, teal or black. **Supreme** adds lumbar support pad, torso and waist adjustment, two daypack pockets, leather trim, and *FREE shoulder strap.*

A1. Supreme	$154.95
A2. Backpack/Suitcase	114.95
A3. Shoulder Strap	4.50

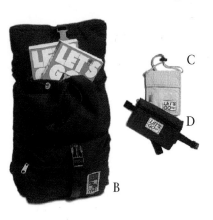

B. Chateau
Top-opening rucksack pack. Drawstring closure. 3 compartments. Taped inseams. Lifetime Guarantee. 1310 cu. in. Black.
$34.95

C. Undercover Neck/Waist Pouch
Secure & comfortable. Ripstop nylon with soft Cambrelle® back. 2 pockets. 6 ½ x 5" Lifetime Guarantee. Black or tan.
$7.95

D. Passport/Money Case
Waterproof nylon with zippered pouch. 7 ½ x 4 ½" Navy or gray.
$6.95

Duffles
Tough, capable, and appealing. 11 oz. waterproof Cordura-Plus® with 3" nylon web. Lifetime Guarantee. Red, black, purple, or blue.

E1. XL–36 x 15 x 15"	$69.95
E2. L–30 x 15 x 15"	59.95

H. Travel Case
Perfect carry-on luggage. Large compartment with 2 side pouches. Mesh pocket. No-sag bar and shoulder strap. Lifetime Guarantee. 20 x 16 x 9" Black or blue.
$94.95

Call 1-800-5LETS GO for flight reservations.

J1

T1   T2

LET'S SEE SOME I.D.

1992 International ID Cards
Provides discounts on accommodations, cultural events, airfares and accident/medical insurance. Valid 9-1-91 to 12-31-92.

T1.	Teacher (ITIC)	$15
T2.	Student (ISIC)	14
T3.	Youth International Exchange Card (YIEE)	14

FREE "International Student Travel Guide."

:T'S GO HOSTELING

•2-93 Youth Hostel Card (AYH)
quired by most international hostels.
ıst be U.S. resident.

	Adult (ages 18-55)	$25
	Youth (under 18)	10

Sleepsack
quired at all hostels. Washable durable
y/cotton. 18" pillow pocket. Folds to
ıch size. **$13.95**

**1992-93 International Youth Hostel
ide (IYHG)**
ential information about 3900 hostels
Europe and Mediterranean. **$10.95**

FREE map of hostels worldwide.

LET'S GO BY TRAIN

Eurail Passes
Convenient way to travel Europe. Save up to 70% over cost of individual tickets. Call for national passes.

First Class

V1.	15 days	$430
V2.	21 days	550
V3.	1 month	680
V4.	2 months	920

First Class Flexipass

V5.	5 days in 15 days	$280
V6.	9 days in 21 days	450
V7.	14 days in 1 month	610

Youth Pass (Under 26)

V8.	1 month	$470
V9.	2 months	640
V10.	15 days in 2 months	420

FREE Eurail Map, Timetable, & Travelers' Guide with passes.

't's Go® Travel Guides
ırope; USA; Britain/Ireland; France; Italy;
ael/Egypt; Mexico; California/Hawaii;
ain/Portugal; Pacific Northwest/Alaska;
eece/Turkey; Germany/Austria/Switz-
land; NYC; London; Washington D.C.

.	USA or Europe	$14.95
:.	Country Guide (specify)	13.95
:.	City Guide (specify)	9.95

$1.00 off the cover price.

LET'S GET STARTED

PLEASE PRINT OR TYPE. Incomplete applications will be returned.

International Student/Teacher Identity Card (ISIC/ITIC) (ages 12 & up) enclose:
1. Letter from registrar or administration, transcript, or proof of tuition payment. FULL-TIME only.
2. One picture (1 1/2 x 2") signed on the reverse side.

Youth International Exchange Card (YIEE) (ages 12-25) enclose:
1. Proof of birthdate (copy of passport or birth certificate).
2. One picture (1 1/2 x 2") signed on the reverse side.
3. Passport Number _____ 4. Sex: M   F

Last Name	First Name	Date of Birth

Street   We do not ship to P.O. Boxes. U.S. addresses only.

City	State	Zip Code

(   )
Phone   Citizenship

School/College   Date Trip Begins

Item Code	Description, Size & Color	Quantity	Unit Price	Total Price

Shipping & Handling		
If order totals: Add		
Up to $30.00 $4.00		
30.01-100.00 6.00		
Over 100.00 7.00		

Total Merchandise Price	
Shipping & Handling (See box at left)	
For Rush Handling Add **$8 for Continental U.S. $10 for AK & HI**	
MA Residents (Add 5% sales tax on gear & books)	
Total	

ENCLOSE CHECK OR MONEY
ORDER PAYABLE TO:
HARVARD STUDENT AGENCIES, INC.

Allow 2-3 weeks for delivery.
Rush orders delivered within one
week of our receipt.

LET'S G⊕ Travel

Harvard Student Agencies, Inc., Harvard University, Thayer B, Cambridge, MA 02138

(617) 495-9649   1-800-5LETSGO (Credit Card Orders Only)

Prices subject to change.

dinavian settlers and Native Americans. Housing the **Minnesota Museum of Art** is the historic **Landmark Center,** 75 W. 5th St. (292-3225), a grandly restored 1894 Federal Court building with towers and turrets, a collection of pianos, art exhibits, a concert hall, and four restored courtrooms. (Open Mon.-Wed. and Fri. 8am-5pm, Thurs. 8am-8pm, Sat. 10am-5pm, Sun. 1-5pm. Free. Tours given Thurs. 11am and Sun. 2pm.) The Minnesota Museum of Art houses other collections in the **Jemne Building** at St. Peter and Kellogg Blvd.

A giant iguana sculpture stands guard outside the **Science Museum,** 30 E. 10th St. (221-9454), near the intersection of Exchange and Wabasha St. The **McKnight-3M Omnitheater** (221-9400) inside presents a mind-swelling array of ginormous films. (Open Mon.-Sat. 9:30am-9pm, Sun. 11am-9pm. Tickets $4, seniors and kids $3; for theater and exhibits $5, seniors and kids $4.)

Metro Connections give tours of Minneapolis and St. Paul (333-8687; $15, seniors $13, kids $8). Mississippi River paddle boat tours are also available (227-1100; $7.50, seniors $6.50, kids $5).

Entertainment and Events

With more theaters per capita than any U.S. city outside of New York, the Twin Cities' theater scene can't be touched. The shining star in the pantheon is the **Guthrie Theater,** 725 Vineland Place (377-2224), just off Hennepin Ave. in Minneapolis, adjacent to the Walker Art Center. The Guthrie repertory company performs here from June to March. (Box office open Mon.-Sat. 9am-8pm, Sun. 11am-7pm. Tickets $9-37, rush tickets 10 min. before the show $6.)

The **Children's Theater Company,** 3rd Ave. at 24th S. (874-0400), adjacent to the Minneapolis Institute of Art, puts on classics and innovative productions for all ages from September to June. (Box office open Mon.-Sat. 9am-5pm, Sun. noon-4pm except during summer. Tickets $12-20, seniors, students, and kids $9-16. Student rush tickets 15 min. before performance $6.)

In the summer from early July to early August, **Orchestra Hall,** 1111 Nicollet Mall (371-5656), downtown Minneapolis, hosts the creatively named **Summerfest,** a month-long celebration of Viennese music performed by the **Minnesota Orchestra.** (Box office open Mon.-Sat. 10am-6pm. Tickets $10-42. Student rush tickets 15 min. before show $4.50.) Don't miss the free coffee concerts and nighttime dance lessons at nearby **Peavey Plaza,** in Nicollet Mall between 11th and 12th St., surrounding a spectacular fountain (no wading allowed).

St. Paul's glass-and-brick, accordion-fronted **Ordway Music Theater,** 345 Washington St. (224-4222), is one of the most beautiful public spaces for music in the country. The **St. Paul Chamber Orchestra,** the **Schubert Club,** and the **Minnesota Opera Company** perform here. (Box office open Mon.-Sat. 10am-9pm. Tickets $10-50.)

All of the Twin Cities' many parks feature summertime evening concerts. For information on dates and locations, check at one of the visitor centers. Particularly popular are **Loring Park's** Monday evening events, featuring free local bands, followed by vintage films, on the hill toward the north edge. Take bus #1, 4, 6, or 28 going south.

A passel of comedy and improvisational clubs make the Twin Cities a downright hilarious place to visit. Dudley Riggs's **Brave New Workshop,** 2605 Hennepin Ave. (332-6620), stages consistently good musical comedy shows in an intimate club. (Box office open Tues.-Sat. 4-10pm. Performances Tues.-Sat. at 8pm. Tickets $10 weekdays, $12 weekends.) **Stevie Ray's,** W. 28th at Hennepin Ave. (872-0305), in South Minneapolis, features local stand-up comics. (Shows Sun.-Thurs. 8pm, Fri.-Sat. 8 and 10:30pm. Cover Sun.-Tues. $5, Wed.-Thurs. $8, Fri.-Sat. $10.) For great live music, try the **Uptown Bar and Café,** 3018 Hennepin (823-4719). (Open 8am-1am. Shows at 10:30pm. Weekend cover varies. For band information, call 823-5704.) The **400 Bar,** 4th St. at Cedar Ave. (332-2903), on the West Bank, is a great place, featuring live music nightly on a minuscule stage. (Open daily noon-1am. Occasional $2 cover.) A sizzling downtown club (and Prince's old haunt) is **First**

Avenue and 7th St. Entry, (338-8388), with reggae, rock 'n' roll, funk, house, thrash, and heavy metal. But no chamber music. Live bands play nightly; members occasionally toss combs to patrons waiting in line. (Open Mon.-Sat. 8pm-1am, Sun. teen night 7pm-midnight. Cover $1-5, for concerts $6-12.)

There are several gay and lesbian bars in the Twin Cities, including **The Gay '90s,** Hennepin Ave. at 4th St. (333-7755; open daily 8am-1am.) Look for *Equal Time, Gaze,* or *GLC Voice,* free on newspaper stands, for more information on gay and lesbian activities, or call the gay and lesbian information line at 822-0127.

For general information on the local music scene and other events, pick up the free *City Pages* or *Twin Cities Reader,* available throughout the Cities. Free outdoor blues, jazz, and rock concerts are held along the riverfront near St. Anthony Falls. (Call 724-8437 for information.)

In January, the 10-day **St. Paul Winter Carnival,** near the state capitol, cures cabin fever with ice sculptures, ice fishing, parades, and skating contests. Both cities get into the swing of things in July. St. Paul celebrates **Taste of Minnesota,** on the Capitol Mall during the Fourth, then **Riverfest** for a week in late July, with big name bands, food stands, and rides in Harriet Island Park. Also in July, the nine-day **Minneapolis Aquatennial** begins, with concerts, parades, art exhibits, and kids dripping sno-cones on their strollers. (Call 922-9000 for information on all these events.) During late August and early September, spend a day at the **Minnesota State Fair,** at Snelling and Como, one of the largest in the nation. If the human zoo has become too much, talk to the animals at the **Minnesota Zoo,** on Hwy. 32 (432-9000). Walk around, or ride the all-weather monorail. (Open Mon.-Sat. 9am-6pm, Sun. 9am-8pm; off-season daily 10am-4pm. $5, seniors $3, ages 6-16 $2. Parking $1.)

The "Homerdome," also know as the **Hubert H. Humphrey Metrodome,** 501 Chicago Ave. S. (332-0386), in downtown Minneapolis, houses the Twin Cities' baseball and football teams. Professional basketball and hockey action is also available during the winter.

Northern Minnesota

Chippewa National Forest Area

The Norway pine forests, interspersed with lovely strands of birch, thicken as you move north into **Chippewa National Forest,** source of the mighty Mississippi River. Camping and canoeing are popular activities thanks to hundreds of lakes in the area. Leech, Cass, and Winnibigoshish (win-nuh-buh-GAH-shish or simply "Winnie") are the largest, but also the most crowded with speedboats. The national forest shares territory with the **Leech Lake Indian Reservation,** home of 4,560 members of the Minnesota Chippewa tribe, the fourth largest tribe in the U.S. The Chippewa migrated from the Atlantic coast, through the Great Lakes, and into this area in the early 1700s, successfully pushing out the Sioux. In the mid-1800s, the government seized most of the Chippewa's land, setting up reservations like Leech Lake.

Use the town of Walker on Leech Lake as a gateway to the Chippewa National Forest. Travelers can find information on the tourist facilities at the **Leech Lake Area Chamber of Commerce** on Rte. 371 downtown (547-1313 or 800-833-1118; open daily 8am-5:30pm). Information on abundant, cheap outdoor activities is available just east of the chamber of commerce at the **forest office** (547-1044; open Mon.-Fri. 7:30am-5pm). **Greyhound** (722-5591) runs from Minneapolis to Walker (2 per day, 4 hr., $21), stopping at the Lake View Laundromat, Minnesota at Michigan Ave., just east of the chamber of commerce.

The less-than-mighty **Headwaters of the Mississippi** trickle out of **Lake Itasca,** 30 mi. west of Walker on Rte. 200, the only place where mere mortals can wade easily across the Mississippi. Campsites in the park are usually not crowded. (Sites $8, with electricity $10. 2-day vehicle permit $3.25.) The **Itasca State Park Office** (266-3654), through the north entrance and down County Rd. 38, has more information. (Open daily 8am-10pm.) You can also get there via Bemidji, which has a **Greyhound** stop (Duluth-Bemidji $16).

The **area code** is 218.

The Superior North Shore

The North Shore begins with the majestic Sawtooth Mountains just north of Duluth and extends 150 wild and wooded mi. to Canada. This stretch, defined by **Highway 61 (North Shore Drive),** encompasses virtually all of Minnesota's Superior lakeshore and supports bear, moose, and the only remaining wolf population in the contiguous 48 states. Summer brings a human tide to the towns dotting the coastline to fish, camp, hike, and canoe, drawn by the cool and breezy weather.

During the warmer months, many outdoor enthusiasts drive or bike their way up the coast along Hwy. 61, beginning in Duluth. The newly-opened **North Shore Scenic Railroad** (722-1273) provides another means of transportation, with a scenic train ride from Duluth to Two Harbors ($15, seniors $14, kids $7.50). Bring warm clothes, since even in summer temperatures can drop into the low 40s at night.

A recently completed hiking trail runs from Duluth to Canada, along the Superior coast. For tenderfoot daytrippers, the trail provides easy access to accommodations, transportation, and food along the way. For more information write to the **Superior Trail Hiking Association,** P.O. Box 2175, Tofte 55615 (226-3539). Caramel-colored water splashes over the jagged rocks at **Gooseberry Falls,** a popular swimming hole 40 mi. up the coast from Duluth. Sleep within earshot of the falls at the **Gooseberry Falls Campground** (834-3787; sites $13, including state park sticker; make reservations for July and Aug.). Just north of the falls, **Split Rock Lighthouse** looks out over one of the most treacherous stretches of water around. The rocks below, endowed with strange magnetic qualities, have fuddled compasses and lured unwary sailors into their Scylla-and-Charybdis arms. The **History Center** (226-4372), next to the lighthouse atop a 120-ft. cliff, offers exhibits on famous shipwrecks and a film on the old days of Split Rock. (Lighthouse and history center open daily May 15-Oct. 15 9am-5pm; off-season Fri.-Sun. noon-4pm. Admission consists of a $3.25 state park sticker.) Camp next door at **Split Rock Lighthouse State Park** (226-3065; sites $12.25, including state park sticker). Make reservations two weeks in advance.

Grand Marais makes a good base for excursions into nearby portions of the **Boundary Waters Canoe Area Wilderness.** This unique area covers over two million acres of forests, containing 1,100 lakes. There are no roads, phones, electricity, or private dwellings here, and no motorized vehicles are allowed. Permits are required to enter the BWCAW from May to September. The 60-mi. **Gunflint Trail,** now widened into an auto road, begins in Grand Marais and continues northwest into the BWCAW. Reward yourself at the end of the trail with a stay in the well-kept cabins at **"Spirit of the Land" Island AYH Hostel** (388-2241), in Seagull Lake. ($10, nonmembers $13. $2 boat transport. Meals $3-5. Closed Nov. and April.) The **Tip of the Arrowhead Tourist Information Center,** Broadway and 1st Ave. (387-2524), has a wealth of information about the area. The National Forest Ranger station at the base of the trail, ¼-mi. south of town, offers even more information, and issues BWCAW permits for individual ports of entry into the wilderness. (Open summer daily 6am-6pm.) **Wilderness Waters Outfitters** (387-2525), just south of Grand Marais on Rte. 61, rents canoes. ($13 per day, $12 per day for more than 3-day trips; $10 deposit required. Paddles, life jackets, and a car rack are included. Open May-Oct. daily 7am-7pm.)

Motels charge at least $25 for a single, but campground space is easy to find. The **Grand Marais Recreation Area** (387-1712), off Rte. 61 in town, offers a great view of Lake Superior. Pitch your tent by the small inlet and eat breakfast with the ducks. (Office open daily 6am-10pm. Sites $11, with water and electricity $14.50, with full hookup $15.50. Open May to mid-Oct.)

Grand Marais's **area code** is 218.

MISSISSIPPI

Mississippi's intransigence during America's early civil rights movement was dwarfed only by the state of Alabama's. From James Meredith's forced integration of "Ole Miss" to the Freedom Democratic Party, liberal activism dragged Mississippi's white establishment kicking and screaming into the sullen racial tolerance of today. Despite a history of racial strife, however, Mississippi's culture has been influenced highly by its African-American heritage. Not only did the blues originate from African slave songs in the Delta region, Mississipians Robert Johnson and B.B. King have popularized this great art form.

If Mississippi is known for anything, it's the Delta region's appalling social and economic conditions. Mississippi tends to be near the bottom of most positive statistical lists and near the top of the less desirable ones. The residents of this primarily agricultural Deep South state have enjoyed a lower average income than the residents of any other American state for most of the last 50 years. Yet much of the land itself is charming and beautiful. When traveling today, try getting off the interstate to explore the lush forests, swamps, and countryside. A major passageway for hundreds of years, the Natchez Trace winds gracefully through the shade from Natchez, Mississippi, to Nashville, Tennessee, passing through a beautiful national park and many historic landmarks. The park service helps you travel at a leisurely pace by strictly enforcing the Trace's 50-mph speed limit.

Practical Information

Capital: Jackson.

Division of Tourism, 1301 Walter Siller Bldg., 550 High St. (359-3414 or 800-647-2290). Open Mon.-Fri. 8am-5pm. **Bureau of Parks and Recreation,** P.O. Box 10600, Jackson 39209.

Time Zone: Central (1 hr. behind Eastern). **Postal Abbreviation:** MS

Biloxi and the Mississippi Coast

Once billed as the South's Riviera, and an important link on the Old Spanish Trail from Florida to the California Missions, Biloxi calls itself the "Seafood Capital of the World" and is trying to become a tourist center. Biloxi hosts the Oyster and Crabfish Festival in April, the Seafood Festival in September, and the popular Shrimp Festival and blessing of the fleet (a religious ceremony asking for a safe, successful shrimp season) in June. The big non-ichthyological event in Biloxi is the annual Miss Teen U.S.A. Pageant. Biloxi's beauty is somewhat marred by the fast-food operations and blazing pink souvenir shops lining the city's beach, the **Gulf Islands National Seashore,** at 26 mi. the longest man-made beach in the world. However, the Spanish moss hanging from oak trees along the road (actually neither Spanish nor moss but relative of the pineapple plant) and the old antebellum mansions in the historic district are still beautiful. The **Seafood Industry Museum** at Point Cadet Plaza, just off Hwy. 90 at the foot of the Biloxi-Ocean Springs Bridge (435-6320), traces Biloxi's growth from a French colony to its current "Seafood Capital" status. (Open Mon.-Sat. 9am-5pm. $2.50, students and seniors $1.50.)

Between Biloxi and Gulfport you'll find the garden and grounds of **Beauvoir,** 224 Beach Blvd. at Beauvoir Rd. (388-1313). Jefferson Davis' last home, it is now a shrine in his honor, containing a Confederate Museum, a Davis Family Museum and a Confederate Veterans' Cemetery with the tomb of the unknown Confederate Soldier. Each October, Beauvoir is the site of a Confederate boot camp simulation, complete with drills. (Open daily 9am-5pm. $4, kids $2.) Also along the shoreline is the **Biloxi Lighthouse** (435-6293), which legend states was painted black after President Lincoln's assassination; actually the rusty edifice just needed a paint job.

Today it's snowy white and open seasonally for viewing both Gulf and town. (Open March-Oct. daily 9am-sunset. Donations accepted.) For a city tour take the **Ole Biloxi Train Tour,** a 1½-hr. ride beginning at the lighthouse; the first tour leaves at 9:30am. (374-8687; tour $5, kids $2.50.) Or pick up a walking tour pamphlet at the Information Center, and discover the old historic district at your leisure.

Two miles off the Mississippi coast, **Ship Island** (given its name because of the safety provided to ships within its natural harbor) is a very popular attraction. *USA Today* ranked its crystal blue waters and white sandy beaches as one of the nation's 10 best. Swim, fish, explore, and beware of alligators. When you tire of sunbathing, check out **Fort Massachusetts** (875-0821). Built in the 1860s, it served first as a Confederate command center, then as a Union one. (Admission and tour free.) Ship island has had two parts, East and West, since it was sliced in two by 1969's Hurricane Camille. East is underdeveloped and not accessible by ferry service although overnight camping is permitted. To get to West Ship Island, where overnight camping is prohibited, take the Skrmetta-family ferry service that leaves from Biloxi's **Buena Vista Motel,** Central Beach Blvd. (432-2197). There are two ferries per day, leaving for the island at 9am and noon and returning at 3:45pm and 6:45pm. The trip takes 70 minutes. (Round-trip $11, kids $5.) A different kind of 70-minute cruise is the **Biloxi Shrimping Trip.** The *Sailfish* departs from the Biloxi Small Craft Harbor several times a day, giving passengers an opportunity to see what trawling between the Biloxi shore and nearby Deer Island will yield. Call for reservations. (374-5718; $8, kids $4.)

Accommodations on the coast can be very costly; prices constantly fluctuate, but generally the cheapest places are located beyond the reach of public transportation. Several motels offer singles and doubles for about $25-35 mid-week in summer, with even higher rates on weekends. Half a dozen mediocre good-priced motels surround the **Biloxi Hilton,** some with rates as low as $25 for an off-season single. A good way to find cheap accommodations is to ask at the Information Center where they have discount coupons. Camping is a cheap alternative; rates vary from $10-15 depending on the season. The most convenient site is the **Biloxi Beach Campground,** 3162 W. Beach Blvd. (432-2755). Farther from town are **Martin's Lake and Campground,** 14601 Parker Rd. (875-9157), one mi. north of I-10 at exit 50 in Ocean Springs, and the campground at **Gulf Islands National Seashore, Davis Bayou** (875-3962) on Hanley Rd. off U.S. 90 also in Ocean Springs.

The **Biloxi Chamber of Commerce,** 1048 Beach Blvd. (374-2717), across from the lighthouse, eagerly offers aid to tourists. (Open Mon.-Fri. 8:30am-5pm.) The **Biloxi Tourist Information Center,** 710 E. Beach Blvd. (374-3105), down the street from the bus station, has many helpful brochures. (Open Mon.-Fri. 8am-6pm, Sat. 9am-6pm, Sun. noon-5pm.) For more info contact the **Mississippi Gulf Coast Convention and Visitor's Bureau,** 135 Courthouse Rd. (896-6699 or 800-237-9493).

Getting into and out of Biloxi is rarely problematic because intercity buses serve the town well. **Greyhound/Trailways,** 322 Main St. (436-4336), offers frequent service to New Orleans (10 per day, 2½ hr., $18) and Jackson (2 per day, 4 hr., $25). **Coast Area Transit** (896-8080) operates buses (marked "Beach") along the beach on U.S. 90 from Biloxi to Gulfport. (Buses supposedly operate Mon.-Sat. every 70 min. Board at any intersection. Fare 75¢.)

The **post office** is at 135 Main St. (432-0311), near the bus station. (Open Mon.-Fri. 8:30am-5pm, Sat. 9am-noon.) Biloxi's **ZIP code** is 39530; its **area code** is 601.

Jackson

A hybrid of briskly growing sunbelt city and sleepy Deep South town, Jackson reels with 20th-century activity without the teeming throngs of most major cities. Sights and stores here keep the hours of a smaller town—the historic and business districts barely come to life during working hours and never create the tense atmosphere of a bloated metropolis. But most of Jackson's uniqueness lies outside the downtown area altogether. Located directly on the breathtaking **Natchez Trace**

Parkway, Jackson has shaded campsites, cool reservoirs, national forests, and Native American mounds only minutes away.

Practical Information

Emergency: 911.

Tourist Information Center, 1100 Lakeland Dr. (960-1800), off I-55 Lakeland East exit. Open Mon.-Sat. 8am-4:30pm, Sun. 1-4:30pm. **Convention and Visitors Bureau,** 921 N. President St. (960-1891), downtown. Open Mon.-Fri. 8:30am-5pm.

Travelers Aid: 968-3972.

Allen C. Thompson Municipal Airport: East of downtown, off I-20. Cab fare to downtown about $13-14.

Amtrak: 300 W. Capitol St. (355-6350). To Memphis (1 per day, 4 hr., $43) and New Orleans (1 per day, 4 hr., $40). Open Mon.-Fri. 7:30am-7pm, Sat.-Sun. 7:30-10:30am and 4:30-7pm.

Greyhound/Trailways: 201 S. Jefferson St. (353-6342). Be cautious when walking in the area at night. To: Dallas (6 per day, 10 hr., $81); Montgomery (2 per day, 7 hr., $47); Memphis (5 per day, 4½ hr., $38). Open 24 hrs.

Public Transport: Jackson Transit System (JATRAN) (948-3840), in the Federal Bldg. downtown. Limited service. Bus schedules and maps posted at most bus stops. Buses operate Mon.-Fri. 5am-7pm, Sat. 7am-6pm. Fare 75¢, transfers 10¢.

Help Lines: First Call for Help, 352-4357. Info referral service. **Rape Hotline,** 982-7273.

Taxi: Veterans Cab, 355-8319. Base fare $1.10, $1 per mi.

Post Office: 401 E. South St. (968-0572). Open Mon.-Fri. 7am-7pm, Sat. 8am-noon. **ZIP code:** 39201.

Area Code: 601.

State Street runs north-south through downtown, **High Street** east-west.

Accommodations

There are few motels dowtown, but with a car you easily can find inexpensive rooms along I-20 and I-55.

Admiral Benbow Inn, 905 N. State St. (948-4161), downtown. Comfortable, clean rooms, pool, remote control TV. Singles and doubles $30.

Red Roof Inn, 700 Larson St. (969-5006), by the fairgrounds downtown but not as convenient as Benbow. Near highway though fresh greenery surrounds building. Pleasant abodes with 2 comfortable chairs and color-coordinated linens. Singles $29. Doubles $37.

Motel 6, 970 I-20 Frontage Rd. (969-3423). Next door to noisy truck stop. Tidy, small white-walled rooms brag spotless bathrooms. Pool. Singles $22. $6 per additional person.

Sun 'n' Sand Motel, 401 N. Lamar St. (354-2501), downtown. Rooms surround tree-covered courtyard with funny V-shaped pool. Very 50s oranges and aquas—even a Polynesian room. Cable TV. Singles $30. Doubles $35.

Food

Jackson eateries specialize in catfish and plate lunch specials, catering to both the young, professional crowd and older regulars. Most establishments are inexpensive and lively.

Primo's, 1016 N. State St. (948-4343). A Jackson tradition. Excellent, cheap Southern food; breakfasts with creamy grits and huge omelettes under $3 (breakfast served till 11:30am.) Vegetable plates, too. Open Mon.-Fri. 7am-9:30pm, Sat.-Sun. 8am-9:30pm.

The Elite Cafe, 141 E. Capitol (352-5606). Egalitarian lunch spot with great homemade corn-bread, rolls, and veal cutlets. Plate lunch specials with 2 vegetables and bread under $4.50. Be prepared to wait in line during lunch rush. Open Mon.-Fri. 7am-9:30pm, Sat. 5-9:30pm.

The Iron Horse Grill, 320 W. Pearl St. (355-8419), at Gallatin. A huge converted smokehouse with a waterfall cascading from the 2nd floor. Friendly young waiters and waitresses. Primarily Tex-Mex ($5-8); steak and seafood entrees more expensive. A pianist accompanies lunch and dinner. Open Mon.-Sat. 11am-10pm.

Sights and Entertainment

Next door to the visitors center and the baseball stadium sits **The Mississippi Agriculture and Forestry/National Agricultural Aviation Museum,** 1150 Lakeland Dr. (354-6113). The center includes real planes and original tools as well as a working farm. (Open Tues.-Sat. 9am-5pm, Sun. 1-5pm. $3, seniors $2.75, kids $1.) The old and the new compete everywhere in Jackson; the city even has two capitol buildings. Built in 1840, the **Old State Capitol** (359-6920), at the intersection of Capitol and State St., houses an objective and excellent museum of Mississippi's often dramatic history, including artifacts from original Native American settlements and documentaries on the Civil Rights Movement. (Open Mon.-Fri. 8am-5pm, Sat. 9:30am-4:30pm, Sun. 12:30-4:30pm. Free.) The state legislature's current home is the beautiful **New State Capitol** (359-3114), at Mississippi and Congress St., completed in 1903. A huge restoration project in preserved the *beaux arts* grandeur of the building, complete with a gold-leaf-covered eagle perched on the capitol dome. (Guided 45-min. tours Mon.-Fri. at 9, 10, and 11am, and 1:30, 2:30, and 3:30pm. Open Mon.-Fri. 8am-5pm, Sat. 10am-4pm, Sun. 1-4pm. Free.)

The downtown area maintains several other museums worth a visit. **The Mississippi Museum of Art,** at Pascagoula and Lamar St. (960-1515), has a fabulous collection of Americana and a fun participatory Impression Gallery for kids. (Open Tues.-Sat. 10am-5pm, Sun. noon-5pm. $2, kids $1; students free Tues. and Thurs.) Next door is the **Russell C. Davis Planetarium** (960-1550), considered one of the best worldwide. (Galactic and musical shows Tues.-Fri. at 8pm; Sat. at 2, 4, and 8pm; Sun. at 2 and 4pm. $4, seniors and kids $2.50.)

Look for a terrific family-pleasing presentation of nature and wildlife at the **Mississippi Museum of Natural Science** on Jefferson St. (354-7303), across from the fairground. (Open Mon.-Fri. 8am-5pm, Sat. 9:30am-4:30pm.) Don't miss the Greek Revival **Governor's Mansion** (359-3175), a national historic landmark. The tours every half hour are an enlightening introduction to Mississippian politics. (Open Mon.-Fri. 9:30-11am.) For a more in-depth look at some fine architecture, visit the **Manship House,** 420 E. Fortification (961-4724), a short walk north from the New Capitol. Charles Henry Manship, Jackson's Civil War mayor, built this Gothic Revival "cottage villa," now restored to its 19th-century condition. (Open Tues.-Fri. 9am-4pm, Sat.-Sun. 1-4pm.) Sherman occupied Jackson's oldest house, **The Oaks,** 823 N. Jefferson St. (353-9339), built in 1746, during the siege of the city in 1863. (Open Tues.-Sat. 10am-4pm, Sun. 2-4pm.)

The **Smith-Robertson Museum and Cultural Center,** 528 Bloom St. (960-1457), directly behind the Sun 'n' Sand Motel, preserves Mississippi's African-American history. This large, expanding museum once housed the state's first black public school, which *Native Son* author Richard Wright attended until the eighth grade. Now it displays folk art, photographs, and excellent exhibits on the Civil Rights Movement, particularly the role of African-American women in Mississippi history. (Open Mon.-Fri. 9am-5pm, Sat.-Sun. 9am-noon. $1, kids 50¢.)

After soaking in the history of life and politics in Jackson, soak up some music and fun at **Hal & Mal's Restaurant and Oyster Bar,** 200 Commerce St. (948-0888), which entertains in a converted warehouse. Reggae to innovative rock bands play Thursday through Saturday nights. (Restaurant open Mon.-Sat. 11am-10pm; bar open until 1am. Cover varies.)

Oxford

A visit to Oxford's town square reveals a simple beauty and charm which can't help but perpetuate the mythical image of life in a small Southern community. The quaint, almost too-perfect layout centers around a monument to Confederate soldiers and the white sandstone **Lafayette County Courthouse.** It's no wonder that Oxford's own William Faulkner based his fictional Yoknapatawpha County on his picturesque hometown.

Beyond its literary aura, Oxford's status as a full-fledged college town dispells any bucolic Southern myths. At the **University of Mississippi** (known affectionately as "Ole Miss"), academic buildings surround the shaded yard called The Grove, while student social life revolves around football games and the Greek fraternity system. Although its physical environment remained idyllic, the university faced years of turmoil in the 1960s. African Americans, starting with James Meredith, were allowed to enroll here only after President Kennedy ordered troops to Oxford to protect registering students.

For information about Oxford's history, try **Square Books,** 200 Lamar St. (236-2262), where friendly advice combines with Faulkner postcards and an impressive collection of Southern writing. (Open Mon.-Thurs. 9am-9pm, Fri.-Sat. 9am-10pm, Sun. noon-6pm.)

A walk down South Lamar and along Old Taylor Rd., or better yet on a path through Bailey's Woods from behind the Skipworth Museum on Museum Ave., leads to **Rowan Oak** (234-3284 or 232-7318). This former home of William Faulkner is tucked in a bend in Old Taylor Rd. Don't miss Faulkner's office in the back of the house where an outline to his novel *A Fable* sticks to the walls. (Open Tues.-Sat. 10am-noon and 2-4pm, Sun. 2-4pm.)

Faulkner studies continue at the university's **Center for the Study of Southern Culture** in Barnard Observatory (232-5993), where scholars from all over the world gather for a conference on Bill each August. (Open Mon.-Fri. 8:15am-4:45pm.) Across the street, the **Blues Archive,** 340 Farley Hall (232-7753), houses B.B. King's personal collection of over 10,000 records. (Open Mon.-Fri. 8:30am-5pm.)

For grits, biscuits, and other Southern fare, **Smitty's,** 208 S. Lamar (234-9111), has a full breakfast for under $4. (Open Mon.-Sat. 6am-9pm, Sun. 8am-9pm.) You'll also find restaurants catering to the fun-loving and budget-conscious students of Ole Miss within walking distance of the square. **The Gin,** 201 Harrison St. (234-0024), one block southeast of Oxford Sq., is a converted cotton warehouse where lively crowds gather, especially for the live weekend bands. Sandwiches and burgers run under $6. (Open Mon.-Wed. and Sat. 11am-midnight, Thurs.-Fri. 11am-1am.) **The Hoka Café,** right next door at 304 S. 14th St. (234-3057), receives kudos for its ceiling tapestries, blues posters, and cheesecake, but also serves sandwiches and catfish ($3-6). (Open daily 11am-2pm and 5pm-2am.) **Square Books** (see above), in the square, serves square sandwiches ($2-4) and killer sweets (brandy bread pecan and pudding squares) in a café above the bookstore. **Café Olé,** 1612 University Ave. (234-1707), ¼ mi. east of the town square, serves incredible Mexican food including vegetarian specialties like spinach enchiladas ($2.50) and vegetable fajitas ($6.75). (Open Mon.-Fri. 11am-2pm and 5-10pm, Sat. noon-2pm and 5-10pm.)

Nightlife usually centers around rockin' bands at the Gin and "artsy" movies virtually every night at the Hoka (see above). **Syd and Harry's,** 118 Van Buren Ave. (236-3193), in the square, has the best music in town. Dance five nights a week to a mixture of blues, rock, and progressive music, or just cuddle up with your favorite beer. (Open Mon.-Wed. and Sat. 4pm-midnight, Thurs.-Fri 4pm-1am.)

Plan ahead for lodgings: rooms are scarce in Oxford during football games (many weekends Sept.-Nov.), graduation (2nd week in May), and the Faulkner Festival (late July). Behind the pink doors with white hearts of **The Ole Miss Motel,** 1517 E. University Ave. (234-2424), lurk comfortable rooms with cable TV and some refrigerators (Singles $23. Doubles $27.) **The University Inn,** 2201 Jackson Ave. (234-7013), about one mi. from the university, is more luxurious, offering steamrooms, whirlpools, and a pool (Singles $42. Doubles $48.). **Johnson's Motor Inn,** 2305 Jackson Ave. (234-3611), next door, has spacious, clean, lived-in rooms. (Singles $26. Doubles $32. Prices higher during football weekends.)

For the most part, the town is small enough to cover easily on foot. University Avenue is the major east-west thoroughfare, intersecting with Lamar a few blocks south of the town square. Van Buren Avenue and Jackson Avenue cross the square parallel to University Ave.

Before touring Oxford, stop by the **Oxford Tourism Council,** 229 W. Jackson Ave. (234-4651) near Ole Miss. (Open Mon.-Thurs. 8:30am-5pm, Fri. 8:30am-4pm.) At the **Greyhound** station, 925 Van Buren Ave. (234-1424), make connections to Memphis (1 per day, 2 hr., $16) and Birmingham (1 per day, 4 hr., $33). The station closes in the afternoon. Mississippi is notorious for its infrequent and inconvenient Greyhound routes.

Oxford's **post office** fictionalizes at 911 Jackson Ave. (234-5615). The city's **ZIP code** is 38655; the **area code** is 601.

Vicksburg

Started as a mission by Rev. Newit Vick in 1814, Vicksburg holds notoriety for its role in the Civil War. Its verdant hills and prime Mississippi River location proved extremely strategic for the Confederate forces, though not strategic enough; the "Gibraltar of the South" fell to Union forces on July 4, 1863, after a 47-day siege. The loss of this critical river city meant death to the Confederacy.

The war-torn countryside has been restored to its natural state, though markers of combat sites and prominent memorials pepper the grass-covered 1,700-acre **Vicksburg National Military Park,** (636-0583 or 800-221-3536 out of state) that surrounds the city. If possible, drive to the battlefield, museums, and cemetery east of town on Clay St. at exit 4B off I-20. ($3 per car, $1 per person on bus, seniors and kids free.) The visitors center at the entrance provides maps. Take a guide with you on a two-hour driving tour ($15) of the military park, or drive the 16-mi. trail yourself. (Open summer daily 8am-8pm; visitors center closes at 5pm.)

Within the park, visit the **National Cemetery** and the **U.S.S. Cairo Museum** (636-2199). The museum's centerpiece is the restored iron-clad gunboat *Cairo* (KAY-ro), the first vessel sunk by a remotely detonated mine. The museum displays a fascinating array of artifacts preserved for over a century since the ship sank in the Yazoo River. (Open daily 8am-7:30pm; off-season 8am-5pm. Free.) Learn more of the battle at Vicksburg by catching **"Vanishing Glory,"** 717 Clay St. (634-1863), a multimedia theatrical panorama. (Shows daily on the hr. 10am-5pm; $3.50, ages 6-18 $2.)

The **Old Court House Museum,** 1008 Cherry St. (636-0741), presides over Vicksburg's town center, three mi. from the park's entrance. Many consider it one of the South's finest Civil War museums, with everything from newspapers printed on wallpaper to Jefferson Davis' tie to an intriguing interpretation of Klan activities. (Open Mon.-Sat. 8:30am-5pm, Sun. 1:30-5pm. $1.75, seniors $1.25, ages under 18 $1.)

Next door, continuing the martial theme, is **Toys and Soldiers, A Museum,** 1100 Cherry St. (638-1986), where 27,000 toy soldiers from all over the world await you. (Open Mon.-Sat. 9am-4:30pm, Sun. 1:30-4:30pm. Tours $1.50, families $5.) Two blocks away lie the **Museum of Coca-Cola History and Memorabilia** and the **Biedenharn Candy Company,** 1107 Washington St. (638-6514), which first bottled Coca-Cola. The museum displays Coke memorabilia from as far back as 1894 and sells Coke floats and over 100 different Coca-Cola items. (Open Mon.-Sat. 9am-5pm, Sun. 1:30-4:30pm. $1.75, kids $1.25. Disabled access.)

After wandering around some of Washington Street's old-fashioned brick-paved roads, you'll end up near several fine antebellum homes. **Balfour House,** 1002 Crawford St. (638-3690), served as local Union Army headquarters after they took Vicksburg. Look down the three-story vertigo-inducing spiral staircase. (Open daily 9am-5pm. $5, kids $2.) The **Martha Vick House,** 1300 Grove St. (638-7036), was the home of Martha Vick, an unmarried daughter of Reverend Vick. The restored building contains many elegant French paintings. (Open daily 9am-5pm. $5, ages 12-18 $2.) Both homes, like many of the restored Vicksburg estates, double as B&Bs (ask at the visitors center). Slightly farther away, **McRaven,** 1445 Harrison St. (636-

1663), is a popular historic home, and was featured in *National Geographic* as a "time capsule of the South." (Open daily 9am-6pm, Sun. 10am-6pm. 1½-hr. guided tours $4, ages 12-18 $1.50, ages 6-11 $1.)

While downtown, chow down at **Burger Village,** 1220 Washington St. (638-0202), home of a happy community of ground chuck on buns. (Open Mon.-Thurs. 9am-6pm, Fri.-Sat. 9am-7pm.) The **New Orleans Café,** 1100 Washington St. (638-8182), provides sandwiches for under $6 and Cajun specialties and seafood for more. (Open Mon.-Thurs. 11am-10pm, Fri.-Sat. 11am-2am.) The café doubles as a bar on weekends and stops serving food at 10pm. Next door is the lively **Other Side Lounge.** (Open Tues.-Sat. 5:30pm-2am.) Across the street is **Miller's Still Lounge,** a real Southern watering hole with live entertainment and popcorn nightly. (Open Sun.-Thurs. 11am-midnight, Fri.-Sat. 11am-2am.) A mile south of downtown, **Ruben's,** 3421 Washington St., offers Miss-Mex lunch specials starting at $3. (Open Mon.-Thurs. 11am-9pm, Fri.-Sat. 11am-10pm.) From there take a short drive south on Washington St. to the **Louisiana Circle,** a secluded overview serving truly breathtaking vistas of the great Mississippi River. For a different kind of entertainment, or if it's time to do laundry, **Holidays Washateria and Lanes** (636-9682), near the park entrance on Hwy. 8 across from a KFC, is for you. It's a bowling alley, pool room and laundromat all in one. (Open Sun.-Thurs. 3-10:30pm, Fri.-Sat. 10am-2am.)

You can find cheap accommodations in Vicksburg except around July 4th weekend, when the military park's war reenactment brings thousands of tourists and inflated hotel rates. Since most hotels are located near the park, don't expect to stay in town. The **Hillcrest Motel,** 4503 Hwy. 80 E. (638-1491), has a pool and spacious, ground-floor singles for $20, doubles for $24. The **Beachwood Motel,** 4449 Hwy. 80E (636-2271), has no pool but has cable and a friendly management. (Bed $25, 2 beds $27.) **The Vicksburg Battlefield Kampground,** 4407 I-20 Frontage Rd. (636-9946), has a pool and laundromat. (Sites $10-12 for 2 people.)

For more information about Vicksburg, visit the **Tourist Information Center** (636-9421), across the street from the park. (Open daily 8am-5:30pm.) Unfortunately, you'll need a car to see most of Vicksburg: the bus station, the information center, downtown, and the far end of the sprawling military park are at the small city's four extremes. The **Rape and Sexual Assault Service** (638-0031) answers calls all day.

The **Greyhound/Trailways** station (636-1230) is inconveniently located at 3324 Hall's Ferry Rd., off Frontage Rd.; buses run to Jackson (4 per day, 1 hr., $9.50). Vicksburg's **ZIP code** is 39180; the **area code** is 601.

MISSOURI

Missouri, the state whose 1850 "Compromise" foreshadowed the Civil War, is culturally more Southern than Midwestern. Pro-slavery forces in the pitched battles over Bloody Kansas often launched their attacks from agricultural Missouri. But the state is flanked by two river cities, St. Louis and Kansas City, giving it a long-time ethnic and cultural diversity uncommon in Southern metropoli. St. Louis is a thriving trade center on the Mississippi, complete with steamboats, breweries and hot music. Kansas City, on the Kansas border, has served tourists powerful jazz and spicy barbecue for years. But whether in the rural counties or in the diversified cities, you're sure to feel welcome. As they say, Missouri loves company.

Practical Information

Capital: Jefferson City.

Missouri Division of Tourism, Department MT-90, P.O. Box 1055, Jefferson City 65102 (751-4133; 869-7!10 in St. Louis). **Missouri Department of Natural Resources,** 205 Jefferson St., Jefferson City 65102 (751-3443 or 800-334-6946).

Time Zone: Central (1 hr. behind Eastern). **Postal Abbreviation:** MO

Kansas City

Set up as a trading post in 1821 by a French fur trader, Kansas City had already becoming a rollicking river city long before the time Kansas and Missouri drew state lines. As a result, two Kansas Cities exist, at least in theory: one in Kansas, and one in Missouri. Although no one notices the boundary between the cities until tax time, Kansas City, KS, pocketed with ethnic neighborhoods like Strawberry Hill, is a bit more residential. More audible in Kansas City, MO, is Missouri River culture and strains of New Orleans jazz off the Mississippi. A 1920s haven for gamblers, prostitutes, stray cowpokes, and musicians, today's Kansas City remains a tough town. Practical values and hard-nosed business continue to shape the concerns of its citizens, and help create some glaring economic divisions.

Practical Information

Emergency: 911.

Visitors Center, 1100 Main St. #2550 (221-5242 or 800-767-7700), in the City Center Square bldg. downtown. Pick up *A Visitor's Guide to Kansas City.* Open Mon.-Fri. 8:30am-4:30pm. Also at 4010 Blue Ridge Cutoff (861-8800), just off I-70 next to the stadium. **Daily Visitors Information** (474-9600) is a recorded listing of theater activity in the downtown area. **Jazz Hotline,** 931-2888. **Ticketmaster,** 931-3330.

Kansas City International Airport: (243-5237) 18 mi. northwest of Kansas City off I-29. The **KCI Express Bus** (243-5950) departs from airport gate #63 at 6:30am, then every ½ hr. 8am-9pm, and at 11:30pm; bus goes to Greyhound station, Crown Center, and the Country Club Plaza (½-hr., fare $11). Metro Bus #29 goes to the airport (8 per day, 1 hr., 85¢).

Amtrak: 2200 Main St. (421-3622 or 800-872-7245), directly across from Crown Center. Take bus #28, 31, 40, 51, 53, 54, 56, or 57. To St. Louis (2 per day, 5½ hr., $40-60) and Chicago (2 per day, 9 hr., $74). Open 24 hrs.

Greyhound/Trailways: 1101 N. Troost (698-0080 or 221-2885). To: St. Louis (5 per day, 4-5 hr., $38, $28 with 3-day advance); Chicago (7 per day, 11 hr., $37, $26 with 1-day advance); Des Moines (4 per day, 5 hr., $41); Omaha (4 per day, 3-4 hr., $41, $28 with 3-day advance); and Lawrence (9 per day, 1 hr., $13). Open daily 5:30am-12:30am.

Kansas City Area Transportation Authority (Metro): 1350 E. 17th St. (221-0660; open Mon.-Fri. 6am-6pm), at Brooklyn. Excellent downtown coverage. Fare 75¢, plus 10¢ for crossing zones. Free transfers; free return receipt available downtown. Pick up maps and schedules at headquarters, airport gate #62, or buses.

Taxi: Checker Cab, 474-8294. **Yellow Cab,** 471-5000. Fare about $25 from airport to downtown; determine fare before trip.

Car Rental: Thrifty Car Rental, 2001 Baltimore (842-8550 or 800-367-2277), 1 block west of 20th and Main St; also at the KCI airport (464-5670). Compact Mon.-Thurs. $30 per day with unlimited mi. Drivers under 25 add $3. Must be 21 with major credit card.

Post Office: 315 W. Pershing Rd. (374-9275), near the train station. Open Mon.-Fri. 8am-6:30pm, Sat. 8am-12:30pm. General Delivery open Mon.-Fri. 8am-5:30pm. **ZIP code:** 64108.

Area Codes: 913 in Kansas, 816 in Missouri.

Quite ironically, almost every sight worth visiting in KC lies south of the Missouri River on the Missouri side of town; KCMO, as it is known, is organized like a grid with numbered streets running east-west and named streets running north-south. **Main Street,** the central artery, divides the city east-west, and cuts north-south close to the farmers market and the central business district of Crown Center, Westport, and the Country Club Plaza. That the KC metropolitan area sprawls across two states, and travel may take a while, particularly without a car. Most sights are not located downtown. All listings are for Kansas City, MO, unless otherwise noted.

Accommodations

Kansas City is a big convention center and can usually accommodate everyone needing a room. The least expensive lodgings are near the interstate highways, especially those leading from Kansas City to Independence, MO. Downtown, most hotels are either expensive, uninhabitable, or unsafe. Most on the Kansas side require a car. The Westport area is lively, but prices can be steep.

Travelodge, 3240 Broadway (531-9250), just north of Westport. Bright, secure rooms in a lively area, near several jazz spots. Worth the extra cost. Security guard at night. Singles $38. Doubles $45.

White Haven Motor Lodge, 8039 Metcalf (649-8200 or 800-722-2892), 4 mi. west of state line, on the Kansas side. Amusing, 1950s-style family motor lodge with cold-war-era prices to match. Wrought-iron fenced-in pool, restaurant, HBO. Free coffee, 5¢ doughnuts mornings. Singles $32. Doubles $39. Triples $41. Quads $43.

Traveler's Inn, 606 E. 31st (861-4100), off I-435 at I-70 and U.S. 40 at exit 7A. Take bus #28. Pleasant brown rooms, indoor pool, spa, gameroom, laundry, free cable TV. Incongruous, inviting Indian retaurant. Free morning coffee. Singles $25. Doubles $30. Key deposit $2.

Days Inn, 5100 E. Linwood Blvd. (923-7777), off I-70 at Van Brunt exit. Take the "Linwood" bus from Main St. downtown. Bright blue carpeted rooms, small pool. Free coffee, breakfast. Singles $29. Doubles $34.

Food

Kansas City rustles up a herd of meaty, juicy barbecue restaurants that serve unusually tangy ribs. For fresh produce year-round, visit the **farmers market,** in the River Quay area, at 5th and Walnut St. Arrive in the morning, especially on Saturday.

Arthur Bryant's, 1727 Brooklyn St. at 17th (231-1123), about 1 mi. east of downtown. Take bus #71 ("Prospect") or 8. A local legend. The meat and sauce are superb, the servings more than generous. Barbecued beef sandwiches ($5.75) thick enough to stuff any living human. Open Mon.-Thurs. 10am-9:30pm, Fri.-Sat. 10am-10pm, Sun. 11am-8pm.

The Golden Ox, 1600 Genesee (842-2866). Take bus #12 to the stockyards. Best steak in Kansas City. Lunch $4-6, dinner $10-17. Open Mon.-Fri. 11:20am-10pm, Sat. 4:30-10:30pm, Sun. 4-9pm. The restaurant runs a more reasonably priced **cafeteria** next door—enter through the Stockyards Building. Dine with and on local livestock for about $3. Open daily 6am-1:30pm.

Strouds, 1015 E. 85th St., off Troost (333-2132). Sign proclaims "We choke our own chickens." Don't choke on the incredible fried chicken with cinnamon rolls, biscuits, and honey. Enormous dinners ($7-12) in a weathered wooden hut. Open Mon.-Thurs. 4-10pm, Fri. 11am-11pm, Sat. 2-11pm, Sun. 11am-10pm.

Stephenson's Old Apple Farm Restaurant, 16401 E. U.S. 40, several mi. from downtown (373-5345). The hickory-smoked specialties are worth the trip and the prices. The accompanying side dishes (fruit salad, apple fritters, corn relish) are as noteworthy as the entrees. Open Mon.-Fri. 11:30am-10pm, Sat. 11:30am-11pm, Sun. 10am-9pm.

The Old Spaghetti Factory, 304 W. 8th St. (842-1801). Inexpensive pasta ($5 per plate), relaxing Old West setting. (Open daily 5-11pm.)

The Pumpernickel Deli, 319 E. 11th St., 4 blocks from downtown (421-5766). Friendly, busy place with simple, no-frills décor. Often sells cheap, fresh veggies outside. Sandwiches $1-2.50, jumbo hoagie tops the menu ($2.60). Sunrise special of bagels, ham, egg, and cheese $1.50. Open Mon.-Fri. 7:30am-6:30pm, Sat. 9am-3pm.

Lamar's Do-Nuts, 240 E. Linwood. Amazingly fresh doughnuts are only 30¢ each. Open Mon.-Sat. 6am-6pm, Sun. 6:30am-4pm.

Gates & Sons Bar-B-Q, 1411 Swope Pkwy. (921-0409). Best ribs in town. Barbecue beef sandwiches ($4) and titanic short end ribs ($8). Open Sun.-Wed. 11am-midnight, Thurs.-Sat. 11am-2am. Also at 12th and Brooklyn St. (483-3880).

Sights

Located at 45th Terrace and Rockhill, the **Nelson-Atkins Museum of Fine Art** (751-1278 or 561-4000) contains one of the best East Asian art collections worldwide. A Chinese temple room, Japanese screens, and a huge bronze Buddha are particularly impressive. A Henry Moore sculpture garden and interior display, plus a small, intriguing collection of 19th- and 20th-century art (including a room devoted to Thomas Hart Benton's works), make this museum a must-see. (Open Tues.-Sat. 10am-5pm, Sun. 1-5pm. $3, students $1. Free for permanent exhibits Sat. Take bus #40, 56, or 57 from Main St. or Crown Center.)

A few blocks to the west, the **Country Club Plaza** (known as "the plaza") is the oldest and perhaps most picturesque U.S. shopping center. Built in 1922 by architect J.C. Nichols, the plaza is modeled after buildings in Seville, Spain, replete with fountains, sculptures, hand-painted tiles, and the reliefs of grinning gargoyles. A country club plaza bus runs downtown until 11pm. Just south of the plaza is the luxurious **Mission Hill** district. If you're driving, brave the maze of streets to check out the mansions of such local luminaries as Henry (H.R.) Block and Royals owner Ewing Kaufman. Also tucked away in the trees is the house where Hemingway wrote *For Whom the Bell Tolls.*

Two mi. north of the plaza is **Crown Center**, 2450 Grand Ave. (274-8444), at Pershing. The headquarters of Hallmark Cards, it houses a maze of restaurants and shops alongside a hotel with a five-story indoor waterfall. Inside, the **Hallmark Visitors Center** (274-5672) joyfully illustrates the process and history of greeting card production. (Open Mon.-Fri. 9am-5pm, Sat. 9:30am-4:30pm. Free.) Also in the Crown Center are the **Coterie Children's Theatre** (474-6552) and the **Ice Terrace** (274-8411), KC's only public ice skating rink; take bus #40, 56, or 57, or any trolley from downtown ($3). The Crown Center has free **Concerts in the Park** every Friday evening at 8pm during the summer. Performers have included the Guess Who and the Grateful Dead. Run through a huge fountain designed for running through; you can't have more fun on a hot summer night with your clothes on. To the west stands the **Liberty Memorial,** 100 W. 26th St. (221-1918), a tribute to those who died in World War I. Pay to ride the elevator to the top for a fantastic view, then visit the free museum. (Open Tues.-Sun. 9:30am-4:30pm. $2, students $1, under 11 25¢.)

Entertainment

Formerly the crossroads of the Santa Fe, Oregon, and California Trails, and an outfitting post for travelers to the West, nightspots are now the only things that pack the restored **Westport** area (931-3586), located near Broadway and Westport Rd. a ½-mi. north of the plaza. **Blayney's,** 415 Westport Rd. (561-3747), in a small basement, manages to host live bands six nights a week, offering reggae, rock, or jazz. (Open Mon.-Sat. 7pm-3am. Max. cover $2.)

In the 20s, Kansas City was a jazz hot spot. Count Basie and his "Kansas City Sound" reigned at the River City bars, while Charlie "Yardbird" Parker, who gained his fame in New York, soared in the open environment. Stop by the **Grand Emporium Hotel and Saloon,** 3832 Main St. (531-1504), voted best live jazz club in KC for the last five years, to hear live jazz on Friday and Saturday; weekdays feature rock, blues, and reggae bands. (Open Mon.-Sat. 9am-3am.) Find sultry ambience at **Milton's Jazz,** 805 W. 39th St. (753-9476). The late Miltie once sponsored Basie, Parker, and other jazz greats. (Live music Fri.-Sat. 8pm-1am. Cover $2.) **City Lights,** 7425 Broadway (444-6969), may not be as nostalgic as Miltie's, but it is dependable and fun with live bands Tuesday to Saturday 9pm to 1am. (Open Mon.-Sat. 4pm-1:30am. Cover $4.) **Kiki's Bon-Ton Maison,** 1515 Westport Rd. (931-9417), features KC's best in-house soul band, the Bon-Ton Soul Accordian Band on Wednesdays 9-11pm and Saturdays at 10:30pm. Kiki's serves up cajun food with zydeco and hosts the annual Crawfish Festival (complete with a "Crawfish Look-Alike Contest") the last weekend in May. (Open Mon.-Thurs. 11am-midnight, Fri.-Sat. 11am-1am. Food until 10pm.)

Café Lulu, 1706 W. 39th St. (931-5858) on the Kansas side (931-5858) hosts a "Spoken Word" reading series and performance art on Monday nights (9-11pm, no cover). Meals served until midnight. The **Human Observation Lab** (the "Lab"), 1012 McGee (842-1655), presents itself eponymously as a forum for in-house art bands, performers, and the just plain weird. Bring a writing utensil. The door is always open, but officially at 7:30pm. Cover varies. Get ahold of *KC Pitch* magazine (561-0601) for current listings of local music and club happenings.

Sports fans will be bowled over by the massive **Harry S. Truman Sports Complex;** even Howard Cosell could not muster enough inscrutable superlatives to describe **Arrowhead Stadium,** 1 Arrowhead Dr. (924-3333), home of the Chiefs football team (924-9400). Next door, the water-fountained, artificial turf-clad wonder of **Royals Stadium,** 1 Royal Way (921-8000), houses the Royals baseball team. The stadium express bus runs from downtown on game days.

St. Louis

When Pierre Laclede founded this trading post over two centuries ago, he envisioned it a great city of the New World. Steamboat trade on the Mississippi and the birth of powerful brewing and distilling industries helped realize Laclede's ambition. Today, a vibrant cultural center, St. Louis is a pleasure to tour, thanks in great part to renewed interest in preserving historic housing and developing and beautifying neighborhoods. An important transportation center when it opened in 1894, **St. Louis Union Station** marks a National Historic Landmark, as well as a festive shopping center in the downtown district. Flowers and trees grace the **Soulard Historic District** in South St. Louis, only recently rescued from urban decay. Farther west lie the charming **Central West End** and the attractions in **Forest Park,** the largest urban park in the country. At the **Riverfront** and **Laclede's Landing,** riverboats rest along the banks of the muddy and mighty Mississippi.

Practical Information

Emergency: 911.

Convention and Visitors Bureau, 10 S. Broadway #300 (421-1023 or 800-247-9791), at Market St. Open daily 8:30am-5pm. **St. Louis Visitors Center,** 308 Washington Dr. (241-1764). Pick up the *St. Louis Visitors Guide,* maps, brochures, and friendly advice. Open daily 10:30am-4:30pm. Other visitor information locations at the airport and at Kiener Plaza. (Mon.-Fri. 10am-2:30pm).

Travelers Aid: 809 N. Broadway (241-5820). Open Mon.-Fri. 8:30am-5pm, Sat. 10am-2pm.

Lambert St. Louis International Airport: (426-8000), 12 mi. northwest of the city on I-70. Served by Bi-State "Natural Bridge" bus #104 (runs hourly 5:50am-5:45pm from 9th and Locust St.) and Greyhound.

Amtrak: 550 S. 16th St. (331-3300 or 800-872-7245), at Market St. downtown. To: Chicago ($45); Dallas ($125); New Orleans ($98); Denver ($195); and Kansas City, MO ($41). Open daily 6am-midnight. Additional passenger station in Kirkwood (966-6475), at Argonne Dr. and Kirkwood Rd.

Greyhound: 809 N. Broadway (231-7800), north of the business district. A major hub for the midwest. To: Kansas City, MO ($38); Chicago (Mon.-Thurs. $25, Fri.-Sun. $31); Indianapolis (Mon.-Thurs. $20, Fri.-Sun. $23); Oklahoma City ($99, $52 with reservation); Memphis ($52, with reservation $37.). Airport service. Open 24 hrs. Additional station in Kirkwood at 11001 Manchester (965-4444). Open Mon.-Fri. 8am-midnight.

Public Transport: Bi-State, (231-2345 in St. Louis; 800-223-3287 in E. St. Louis). Extensive service, but buses infrequent during off-peak hours. Buses daily; reduced service on weekends and holidays. Maps, schedules available at the Bi-State Development Agency, 707 N. 1st St., on Laclede's Landing, or at the reference desk of the public library's main branch, 13th and Olive St. Fare 85¢, transfers 15¢; seniors and disabled 40¢, transfers free. Free in the downtown area (bordered by I-40, Broadway, Jefferson, and Cole). The **Levee Line,** the way to get around downtown, offers free service to points of interest between Union Station and the Riverfront.

Taxi: Yellow Cab, 991-1200. **County Cab,** 991-5300.

Help Lines: Rape Crisis, 531-2003. Open 24 hrs. **Gay and Lesbian Hotline,** 367-0084.

Post Office: 1720 Market St. (436-4458). Open Mon.-Fri. 7am-5pm. Open 24 hrs. for stamp purchase and express mail pickup. **ZIP code:** 63166.

Area Code: 314 (in Missouri); 618 (in Illinois)

The city of St. Louis hugs the Mississippi River in a small crescent. University City, home of Washington University, lies west of downtown. Other suburbs (the "county") fan out in all directions. I-44, I-55, I-64, and I-70 meet in St. Louis. **Route 40/64** is the main drag running east-west through the entire metropolitan area. Downtown, **Market Street** divides the city north-south. Numbered streets begin at and run parallel to the river, with **1st Street** closest to the river. The city's most dangerous sections include East St. Louis (across the river in Illinois), the Near South Side and some of the North Side. The Griswold family visited one of the city's more dangerous areas in *National Lampoon's Vacation.*

Accommodations

The motels and universities that offer budget accommodations are generally located several mi. from downtown. Buses serve the major suburban arteries, but the trip back to the city may require an inordinate amount of time.

Huckleberry Finn Youth Hostel (AYH), 1904-1906 S. 12th St. (241-0076), 2 blocks north of Russel St. in S. St. Louis. From downtown, take bus #73 ("Carondelet"), but don't walk; the hostel is just past an unsafe neighborhood. Alleyway entrance, but the small rooms are neat. Dorm-style accommodations, 4-8 beds per room. Open doors; guard your belongings. While you're here, ask about the area hikes and tours that AYH sponsers. Office open 7-10am and 6-10pm. $10, nonmembers $13.

Washington University: Eliot Halls (889-5050 or 727-6337) at the corner of Big Bend Blvd. and Forsyth. Buses #91 and 93 take 40 min. from downtown. Clean dorm rooms offer bare essentials. A/C. Singles $16. Doubles $28. Reservations recommended. Open May 25-Aug. 20.

Motel 6, I-55 and Lindbergh (892-3664). Take Bus #73 to I-55, then transfer to #49 (Lindbergh). Inconvenient, but dependable. Singles $28, doubles $38.

The Windsor Hotel, 3209 Lindell Blvd. (531-1600). Take the Lindell Blvd. bus about 2 mi. from downtown. Clean rooms with TV and A/C. Reservations recommended. Singles or doubles $23.10, $5 key deposit.

Food

Although noted for its German and French heritage, St. Louis's best culinary creations emerge from Italian and U.S. traditions. The young and affluent gravitate to **Laclede's Landing** and the **Central West End.** Downtown on the riverfront, Laclede's Landing (241-5875) has experienced an amazing transformation from industrial wasteland to popular nightspot. Bars and dance clubs in this area occupy restored 19th-century buildings; most have no cover charge. Walk north along the river from the Gateway Arch or towards the river along Washington St. The Central West End caters to a slightly older crowd. Just north of Lindell Blvd., for five blocks along Euclid Ave., a slew of restaurants has won the urban professional seal of approval. Take bus #93 ("Lindell") from Broadway and Locust downtown.

Farther west, **Clayton** offers a pleasant setting for window-shopping and dining. Historic **South St. Louis** (the "Italian Hill") and the University City Loop (Delmar Blvd. west of Skinker) offer dozens of restaurants.

Blueberry Hill, 6504 Delmar (727-0880), near Washington University. The atmosphere is better than the food: Listen to music from a jukebox with 2,000-record collection, or play darts and pinball in the back room. Sandwiches and specials $4-6. Open Mon.-Sat. 11am-2am, Sun. 11am-11pm. After 3pm, you must be 21 to enter.

Charlie Gitto's Pasta House, 207 N. 6th St. (436-2828). A popular budget eatery. Pasta $4-9. Open 11am-11pm.

The Sunshine Inn, 8½ S. Euclid (367-1413). Specializing in vegetarian cuisine, this restaurant has something for the health-conscious meat-eater as well. Sandwiches $4-6, entrees $4-9. Open Tues.-Fri. 11:30am-10pm, Sat. 8am-10pm, Sun. 10am-2:30pm, 5-9pm.

Rossino's, 206 N. Sarah (371-7779), 1 block south of Lindell, just outside the eastern edge of the Central West End. Take bus #93 from Washington and Broadway. Midscale establishment serving Italian food. Pasta with meatballs $5.25. Open for lunch Mon.-Fri. 11am-2pm; dinner Mon. 6-11pm, Tues.-Thurs. 5-11pm, Fri.-Sat. 5pm-1am, Sun. 5-10pm.

Ted Drewe's Frozen Custard, 6726 Chippewa, and 4224 S. Grand (352-7376). The place for the summertime St. Louis experience. Stand in line to order chocolate-chip banana concrete ice cream. Toppings blended, as in a concrete mixer, but the ice cream stays hard enough to stay in an overturned cup. Open March-Dec. Sun.-Thurs. 11am-midnight, Fri.-Sat. 11am-1am.

Sights

Visible from 10 mi. away, the **Gateway Arch** (425-4465) on Memorial Dr. by the Mississippi River, at 630 ft. stands as the nation's tallest monument. Designed by Finnish architect Eero Saarinen, the arch celebrates St. Louis's role as a pioneer gateway. The stainless steel arch is an inverted catenary curve, the shape assumed by a chain hanging freely between two points. A train rides up the monument, and on a cloudless day you can see 30 mi. of city stretching lazily on one side as the "monstrous big" Mississippi flows by on the other (8am-10pm, winter 9am-6pm; $2.50, kids 50¢). Spend your one- to two-hr. wait at the **Museum of Westward Expansion,** under the arch. Don't miss the *Monument to the Dream,* a half-hour documentary chronicling the sculpture's construction. (Summer 17 showings per day, $1. Museum hours same as arch.)

Sightseers can also view St. Louis from the water with **Gateway Riverboat Cruises** (621-4040), leaving from docks on the river right in front of the arch. (Daily summer departures every 45 min. beginning at 10:15am; spring and fall every 1½ hr. beginning 11am. Cruise $7, kids $3.50.)

North of the arch, on the riverfront, is historic **Laclede's Landing,** the birthplace of St. Louis in 1764. The cobblestone streets of this district are bordered by restaurants, bars and two museums. The **Wax Museum,** 720 N. Second St. (241-1155), and the new **National Video Game and Coin-Op Museum,** 801 N. Second St. (621-2900), square off across a street. The new video game museum is particularly entertaining, with a huge collection of working pinball machines, jukeboxes, and video games. (Open Mon.-Sat. 10am-10pm, Sun. noon-8pm. $3, ages 12 and under $2.) There are unique museums in St. Louis. The **Dog Museum,** 1721 S. Mason Rd. (821-DOGS or 821-3647), between Manchester and Clayton, depicts the history of the canine. (Open Mon.-Sat. 9am-5pm, Sun. 1-4pm. $3, seniors $1.50, kids $1). The **Dental Health Theatre,** 727 N. 1st St. (241-7391), fills the gaping cavity of American dental museums (Mon.-Fri. 9am-4pm. Free. Call ahead for reservations). Stroll down the lane at the **National Bowling Hall of Fame and Museum,** 111 Stadium Plaza (231-6340), across from Busch Stadium. (Open Mon.-Sat. 9am-7pm, Sun. noon-7pm; Sept.-May Mon.-Sat. 9am-5pm, Sun. noon-5pm. $3, seniors $2, kids $1.50.)

Walk south of downtown down Tucker Blvd. (preferably during daylight hours) or take bus #73 ("Carondelet") to **South St. Louis.** The city proclaimed this a historic district in the early 70s; it once housed German and East European immigrants, great numbers of whom worked in the breweries. Young couples and families are revitalizing South St. Louis, but have not yet displaced an older generation of immigrants. The end of 12th St. in the historic district features the **Anheuser-Busch**

Brewery, 1127 Pestalozzi St. (577-2626), at 13th and Lynch. Take bus #40 ("Broadway") or 73 from downtown. Watch the beer-making process from barley to bottling and meet the famous Clydesdale horses. The 70-minute tour stops in the hospitality room, where guests can sample each beer Anheuser-Busch produces. Don't get too excited about the free beer, however—you get booted after 15 min. (summer tours Mon.-Sat. 10am-5pm; off-season 9am-4pm. Pick up tickets at the office. Free.)

Also in South St. Louis, built on grounds left by botanist Henry Shaw, thrive the internationally acclaimed **Missouri Botanical Gardens,** 4344 Shaw (577-5100), north of Tower Grove Park. From downtown, take bus #99 ("Lafayette") from 4th and Locust St. going west, or take I-44 by car; get off at Shaw and Tower Grove. The gardens display plants and flowers from all over the globe; the Japanese garden truly soothes. (Open Memorial Day-Labor Day daily 9am-8pm; off-season 9am-5pm. $2, seniors $1, under 12 free. Free Sat. mornings and all day Wed.) About one mi. west of downtown, visit magnificent old **Union Station,** easily accessible by the free and frequent Levee Line bus. At 18th and Market, this modern shopping mall retains the structure of the old railroad station making it a National Landmark.

To the north and west of downtown, and worth as much of your time as the rest of St. Louis, is **Forest Park,** host of the 1904 World's Fair and St. Louis Exposition. Take bus #93 ("Lindell") from downtown. The park contains two museums, a zoo, a planetarium, a 12,000-seat amphitheater, a grand canal, countless picnic areas, pathways, and flying golf balls. Don't miss the **Missouri Historical Society** (361-1424), at the corner of Lindell and DeBaliviere on the north side of the park, filled with U.S. memorabilia including an exhibit devoted to Charles Lindbergh's flight across the Atlantic in the "Spirit of St. Louis." (Open Tues.-Sun. 9:30am-4:45pm. Free.) Atop Art Hill, just to the southwest stands an equestrian statue of France's Louis IX, the city's namesake and the only Louis of France to achieve sainthood. The king beckons with his raised sword toward the **St. Louis Art Museum** (721-0067), which contains masterpieces of Asian, Renaissance, and impressionist art. (Open Tues. 1:30-8:30pm, Wed.-Sun. 10am-5pm. Free.) Near the southern edge of the park lies the **St. Louis Zoo** (781-0900). Marlin Perkins, rugged former host of the TV show *Wild Kingdom,* turned the zoo into a world-class institution. At the Living World exhibit, view computer-generated images of future human evolutionary stages. (Open daily 9am-5pm. Free.) The **St. Louis Science Center-Forest Park** (289-4444) offers hands-on exhibits and a planetarium projector. (Planetarium $3, kids $2; Discovery Room 50¢.)

Near Forest Park, **Washington University** livens things up with a vibrant campus and interesting students. The **Cathedral of St. Louis,** 4431 Lindell Ave. (533-2824), just north of Forest Park at Newstead, strangely combines Romanesque, Byzantine, Gothic, and baroque styles. Gold-flecked mosaics depict episodes from 19th-century church history in Missouri. (Free tour Sun. at 1pm. Open daily 7am-6pm. Take "Lindell" bus #93 from downtown.) **The Crafts Alliance Gallery,** 6640 Delmar Blvd. (725-1151), north of Washington University, shows ceramic, enamel, glass, metal, and textile works by U.S. craftspeople. (Open Tues.-Fri. noon-5pm, Sat. 10am-5pm. Free. From downtown, take bus #91 on Washington St.)

The **Magic House,** 516 S. Kirkwood Rd. (822-8900), can be a hair-raising good time—place your hand on the van de Graff generator to find out how. (Open Memorial Day-Labor Day Tues.-Thurs. and Sat. 10am-6pm, Fri. 9:30am-9pm, Sun. 11:30am-5:30pm; off-season Tues.-Thurs. 1-5pm, Fri. 1-9pm, Sat. 9:30am-5:30pm, Sun. 11:30am-5:30pm. $2.50, under 12 $2.)

The second largest of its kind in the U.S., **Laumeier Sculpture Park,** 12580 Rott Rd. (821-1209), cultivates over 50 contemporary works on 96 acres. The park also hosts free outdoor summer jazz concerts on Sunday evenings. (Open daily 8am-½ hr. past sunset. Gallery open Wed.-Sat. 10am-5pm, Sun. noon-5pm. Free.)

Entertainment

In the early 1900s, showboats carrying ragtime and brassy Dixieland jazz regularly traveled to and from Chicago and New Orleans. St. Louis, a natural stopover, fell head over heels in love with the music and, happily, has never recovered. For purists, the annual **National Ragtime Festival** takes place on a riverboat in mid-June (tickets $19.50). Those with thin wallets can try sitting by the boat and listening to the music from the pavement. Float down the Mississippi while listening to jazz on the *President* (621-4040), a five-story paddleboat. (2½-hr. cruises Wed.-Sun. 10:30am and 7pm, Tues. at 10:30am. $9.50, kids $4.75; rates higher at night. Open June-Oct.) For other seasonal events, check *St. Louis Magazine,* published annually, or the comprehensive calender of events put out by the Convention and Visitor's Commission.

For year-round musical entertainment, head to Laclede's Landing. Bars and restaurants featuring jazz, blues, and reggae fill "the landing." Try **Kennedy's Second Street Co.,** 612 N. Second St. (421-3655), for good, cheap food and drink and a variety of nightly entertainment. (Open Mon.-Sat. 11am-3am, Sun. noon-3am.) Or take your pick of one of the dozens of clubs and bars lining the narrow streets. **The Metropol,** 118 Morgan (621-1160), features Chinese and American cuisine, funky neo-classical décor and late-night dancing. (Open Mon.-Sat. 11am-3am, Sun. noon-3am.)

Founded in 1880, the **St. Louis Symphony Orchestra** is one of the finest in the country. **Powell Hall,** 718 N. Grand (534-1700), which houses the 101-member orchestra, is acoustically and visually magnificent. (Performances Sept.-May Thurs. 8pm, Fri.-Sat. 8:30pm, Sun. 3 and 7:30pm. Box office open Mon.-Sat. 9am-5pm and before performances. Tickets $9-40. Take bus #97 to Grand Ave.)

St. Louis offers the theater-goer many choices. The **Municipal Opera** (534-1111), the "Muny," performs hit musicals in Forest Park during the summer. Tickets cost up to $28.50, but the rear 1,200 seats, quite far from the stage, are free. Arrive around 6:15pm for 8:15pm shows and bring a picnic (no bottles). Hot dogs and beer are also sold at moderate prices. Other regular productions are staged by the **St. Louis Black Repertory,** 2240 St. Louis Ave. (534-3807), and the **Repertory Theatre of St. Louis,** 130 Edgar Rd. (968-4925). Call for current show information. Tour the **Fabulous Fox Theatre** (534-1678; $2.50, under 12 $1.50; Tues., Thurs., and Sat. at 10:30am; call for reservations), or pay a little more for Broadway shows, classic films, Las Vegas, country, and rock stars. Renovated and reopened in 1982, the Fox was originally a 1930s movie palace.

St. Louis Cardinals baseball games (421-3060; April-Oct.; tickets $4-11) swing at Busch Stadium, downtown. **Blues** hockey games (781-5300) scat at the Arena. (Sept.-May; tickets $10-21.)

MONTANA

To the Soviet mind, "Montana" is on par with "Marlboro" in evoking the romantic milieu of the American cowboy. A line of American-style clothing with the state's name splashed liberally over it is almost as much of a Moscow status symbol as the cowboy cigarettes. In reality, Montana contributes Big-Sky grandeur to its myth. Prairies rising gently from the Great Plains grasslands occupy the eastern two-thirds of the state; the Rocky Mountains punctuate the western third, complete with three million acres of wilderness, national parks, national forests, glaciers, and grizzlies.

Practical Information

Capital: Helena.

Montana Promotion Division, Dept. of Commerce, Helena 59620 (444-2654 or 800-541-1447). Write for a free *Montana Travel Planner.* **National Forest Information,** Northern Region, Federal Bldg., 5115 Hwy. 93, Missoula 59801 (329-3511). Gay and lesbian tourists can write to the **Lambda Alliance,** P.O. Box 7611, Missoula, MT 59807, for information on gay community activities in Montana.

Time Zone: Mountain (2 hr. behind Eastern). **Postal Abbreviation:** MT

Area Code: 406.

Billings

Although you may not want to linger long in Billings, the town makes a good base from which to explore nearby Custer Battlefield National Monument or Beartooth Highway. **Custer Battlefield National Monument** marks the site where Sioux and Cheyenne warriors, fighting in 1876 to protect land ceded to them by the Laramie Treaty, wiped out Lt. Col. George Armstrong Custer and five companies from the Seventh Cavalry. Ironically, the monument is located on a Native American reservation, 60 mi. southeast of Billings off I-90. A five-mi. self-guided car tour through the Crow reservation takes you past the area where Custer made his "last stand." You can also see the park on a 45-minute bus tour ($2) or pay $5 for a semi-private, hour-long van tour. The **visitors center** (638-2622) has a small museum that includes eyewitness 100-year-old drawings depicting the Native American warriors' account of the battle. (Museum and visitors center open daily 8am-7:45pm; off-season 8am-4:30pm. Free. Battlefield open daily 8am-sunset. Entrance $3.)

A mere 60 mi. southwest of Billings on U.S. 212 lies **Red Lodge,** a former mining town best known as the entrance to scenic **Beartooth Highway.** (Road open summer only because of heavy snowfall; ask at the chamber of commerce for exact dates.) This gorgeous section of U.S. 212 leaves Red Lodge, climbs to **Beartooth Pass** at 11,000 ft., and descends to the northeast entrance of Yellowstone National Park. The highway is only 62 mi. long, but allow time to stop and enjoy the view. If you're lucky, you'll hit the pass on the undisclosed date in July when the **Red Lodge Chamber of Commerce** (446-1718; Mon.-Fri. 9am-5pm; Oct.-April 9am-4pm) hosts a bar at the summit.

Hungry travelers should head for the **Lobby Cafe,** 2408 1st Ave. N. (259-5757), one block east of the bus station. The metal tables and fake leather seats may not be the Ritz, but $4.50 buys you entree, soup, salad, and spud. (Mon.-Thurs. 7am-5pm, Fri. 6:30am-5pm, Sat. 6:30am-2pm.) The most self-explanatory burgers in town are at the venerable **Hamburger Shop,** 17 N. 29th St. (small burger 30¢, substantial chili special $2; open daily 10am-7pm).

Staying cheaply in Billings involves spending the night in some of the city's less pleasant, though not necessarily dangerous, neighborhoods. The **Lazy KT Motel,** 1403 1st Ave. N. (252-6606), at 14th St., has rooms with phone and color TV. (Singles $29. Doubles $32.50.) **Motel 6,** far removed from town at 5400 Midland Rd. (252-0093), has spacious singles and adequate doubles, with A/C and an outdoor pool. (Singles $27. Doubles $33.)

A fun activity in Billings from June to September is the **Billings Night Rodeo** (248-1080). The rodeo is held nightly at 7:30pm at the junction of I-90 and Mullowney Lane. The rodeo features world- and nationally-ranked professional rodeo cowboys and is a must if you've never seen a rodeo before. ($6, seniors $5, 6-12 $4.)

Billings's Logan International Airport, located on the city's north side along Rte. 3, serves cities in Montana, as well as Salt Lake City, Denver, Minneapolis, and Chicago. **Greyhound** (245-5116), **Powder River Transportation, RimRock Stages,** and **Cody Bus Lines** all route Billings from a terminal at 2502 1st Ave. Greyhound runs to: Bozeman (3 per day, 3 hr., $13); Great Falls (4 per day, 5 hr., $30); and Helena (3 per day, 10 hr., $21). Powder River runs south through Wyoming, while Cody and RimRock cover Montana. **Billings Metropolitan Transit** (657-8218) serves downtown (fare 50¢, seniors and disabled free 9:45am-3:15pm). Across the street, **Rent-a-Wreck** (252-0219) has the cheapest cars in town, from $26.50 per day, $21.50 in winter. $130-140 per week., with 100 free mi. and 16¢ per additional mi. (Open Mon.-Fri. 8am-6pm, Sat. 9am-3pm, Sun. by appt. Must be 21 with credit card and have liability insurance.) Call 252-2806 for 24-hr. local road info and 800-332-6171 for statewide highway reports.

The **visitors center** is at 1239 S. 27th St. (252-4016), exit 450 from I-90. (May 27-Sept. 2 daily 8am-7:30pm; off-season 8:30am-5pm.) Information is also available at the **chamber of commerce**, 200 N. 34th St. (245-4111; Mon.-Fri. 8:30am-5pm).

The main **post office** in Billings is at 841 S. 26th St. (657-5745; Mon.-Fri. 8am-6pm). The **ZIP code** for Billings is 59101; the **area code** is 406.

Bozeman

Bozeman keeps on growing in Montana's broad Gallatin River Valley, nestled between **Bridger and Madison Mountains.** The valley, originally settled by farmers who sold food to Northern Pacific Railroad employees living in the neighboring town of Elliston, is still filled with fertile farmlands stretching from Bozeman city limits to the timberline—and still supplies food to a large portion of southern Montana. Bozeman's rapid expansion and the presence of Montana State University inspire the city's cosmopolitan air, but visitors can still find plenty of Western hospitality in both urban bars and farmhouse kitchens.

The **Gallatin County Pioneer Museum,** 317 W. Main St. (585-1311), features exhibits concerning the political history of the county. The briefest of visits will tell you more than you ever wanted to know about the development of Montana's plains (Mon.-Fri. 2-5pm). The more spectacular **Museum of the Rockies,** on S. 6th St. at Kasy Blvd. (994-2251), has extensive displays on Native American tribes and wildlife of the northern Rockies, of particular interest to families traveling with kids. (Daily 9am-9pm; Sept. 2-May 27 Tues.-Sat. 9am-5pm, Sun. 1-5pm. $3, ages 5-18 $2, under 5 free.)

Bridger Bowl, 15795 Bridger Canyon Rd. (587-2111), 15 mi. northeast of town, offers 800 acres of downhill skiing. (Lift tickets $21, under 12 $9. Call 586-2389 for the ski and weather report.) From late July to the first weekend in August when the flowers bloom, the annual **Sweet Pea Festival** (587-8848) brings Bozemaniacs to Lindley Park for folk music and all the ethnic food they can put away. For good nightlife slink to the **Cat's Paw,** 721 N. 7th Ave. (586-3542), where MSU students circle around the bar. (Daily 10am-2am.)

Eat cheaply and well at the **Western Cafe,** 443 E. Main St. (587-0436), known for its sweet rolls. The Hamburger Deluxe ($2.90) lights up locals' eyes. (Mon.-Fri. 5am-7:30pm, Sat. 5am-2pm.) In the **Baxter Hotel,** 105 W. Main St. (586-1314), the **Rocky Mountain Pasta Company** serves an Italian spaghetti dinner with bread and salad for $6.50. In the same building, the **Bacchus Pub** provides cocktails, ample soup, and salad plates for Bozeman's intellectual and yuppie crowd. (Both open daily 7am-10pm. Reservations best.) The **Pickle Barrel,** 809 W. College (587-2411), across from the MSU campus, serves delicious, filling sandwiches to a mostly student crowd. Even half a sandwich ($4) is hard to finish. (Summer daily 11am-10pm; off-season daily 11am-11pm.)

Summer travelers in Bozeman support a number of budget motels. The **Alpine Lodge,** 1017 E. Main St. (586-0356), shares space with a used car dealership and would love to make you a deal, with fairly clean but rather small rooms for driveup prices. Be sure to check under the hood. (Singles $12. Doubles $17.) The **Ranch House Motel,** 1201 E. Main St. (587-4278), has larger rooms with free cable TV and A/C. (Singles $24. Doubles $28.) At the **Rainbow Motel,** 510 N. 7th Ave. (587-4201), the friendly owners give good travel advice and offer large, pleasant rooms. (Singles $27. Doubles $36.) And how could we forget the **Sacajawea International Backpackers Hostel,** 405 West Olive St. (586-4659), named after Sacajawea, the indomitable squaw, with showers, laundry, full kitchen facilities, and transportation to trailheads ($8, kids $4.).

Bozeman stretches out on a grid, with downtown by the intersection of 7th Ave. and Main St. **Greyhound, RimRock Stages,** and **TW Services** all serve Bozeman from 625 N. 7th St. (587-3110). Greyhound runs to Butte (3 per day, $12) and Billings (3 per day, $14). RimRock runs two buses per day to Helena ($16.50) and Missoula ($24). TW runs one bus per day to West Yellowstone ($12), Mammoth Hot Springs ($13.50), and Old Faithful ($15). (Bus station open Mon.-Fri. 7:30am-10pm; Sat. 1-5am, 8-10am, 8pm-midnight; Sun. 8-8:30am, 1-5pm, 8-10pm.) **Rent-a-Wreck,** 112 N. Tracey St. (587-4551), rents well-worn autos for $25-27 per day, with 100 free mi., 14¢ each additional mi. (Mon.-Sat. 8am-6pm, Sun. by appointment.) You must be 21 with a major credit card. The **Bozeman Area Chamber of Commerce,** 1205 E. Main St. (586-5421), has ample information concerning geography and local events. (Open Mon.-Fri. 8am-5pm.)

The Bozeman **post office** is at 32 S. Tracey St. (586-1508; open Mon.-Fri. 9am-5pm). Bozeman's **ZIP code** is 59715; the **area code** is 406.

Near Bozeman

The Bozeman Hot Springs lies 17 mi. south of Bozeman on MT Rte. 85 (U.S. 191) at 133 Lower Rainbow Rd. (586-6492). Three successive pools increase in size and temperature to allow customers to get used to the heat. (Sun.-Thurs. 8am-10:45pm, Fri. 8am-8:30pm, Sat. 9:30am-11:45pm. $2.50, seniors and ages 5-11 $2, under 5 free.) Adjacent to the bathing pools is the **Bozeman Hot Springs KOA** campground (Sites $12 for 2 people, with water and electricity $14. $1 per additional adult.).

Virginia City, famous for its violent frontier-town history, sits 17 mi. south on U.S. 287 and 15 mi. west on MT Rte. 287. The territorial capital for ten years before Helena took over and the site of the world's richest gold discovery, Virginia City once clanged with the prospecting pans of over 10,000 latter-day Midas wannabes. After exhausting the gold source, however, the population quickly trickled down to today's 100 or so. Main Street offers two museums, the **Watkins Memorial** and **Virginia City Museum.** The bustling thoroughfare also possesses a restored print shop, blacksmith shop, stores, and fully renovated hotel. At the stately **Fairweather Inn** (843-5377), cozy, well-kept singles go for $28, doubles for $34, with bath $42. The **Virginia City Campground** (843-5493) offers showers and toilets. (Sites $12, full hookup $16.)

Even more intriguing than Virginia City is **Nevada City,** 1½ mi. west of Virginia City on MT Rte. 287. All the buildings on its lone street have been restored to their turn-of-the-century appearance. At the **music hall,** dozens of player pianos, organs, and horn machines play old-time tunes for a quarter. Don't miss the "Famous and Obnoxious Horn Machine"the building's most ear-catching device. The **Nevada City Museum,** next door to the music hall, displays restored buildings from mining boom days and explains everything you never wanted to know about the vigilante hanging of murderer George Ives in 1963, a prime and recent example of frontier justice. The museum also offers a historic train ride around the Virginia/Nevada City area. (Summer open daily 9am-7:30pm. Admission $3, kids $1.50. With train fare $4, kids $1.50.) For more info, contact the **Chamber of Commerce,** P.O. Box 145, Virginia City, MT 59755 (406-843-5341).

Helena

In 1864, four penniless prospectors made a last go at mining a site they dubbed **Last Chance Gulch.** Soon enough, four very happy campers discovered deposits bearing gold worth over $20 million. Although the lode dried out long ago, Last Chance Gulch, now Helena's Main St. pedestrian mall (south of 6th St.), still manages to attract prospectors chiseling money from the wallets of unsuspecting tourists. While the developed gulch is a pleasant fountain- and sculpture-lined window-shopping mecca, the mansions built by lucky last chance prospectors in the northwest corner of the city may impress you more.

As the "Queen City of the Rockies," Helena felt obliged to build a capitol worthy of its status in 1890. The massive, granite, Greek Revival **capitol building** (444-4789) that stands between 6th and Lookey Ave. testifies to the youthful city's pride and enthusiasm. Inside, murals depict early mining activity, Old West culture, and conflicts between Europeans and Native Americans and includes local artist Charles Russell's Godzilla-sized painting (12×25 ft.), *Lewis and Clark meet the Flatheads.* (Open daily 9am-5pm. Free.) Across from the capitol at the **State Historical Museum,** 225 N. Roberts St. (444-4794), you'll find more Russell paintings as well as interpretive exhibits on early railroad history, cattle-drives, and mining activities. (Open Mon.-Fri. 8am-6pm, Sat.-Sun. 9am-5pm; off-season Mon.-Sat. 8am-6pm. Free.) One-hour tours of historic Helena leave from the capitol (every hr. on the ½-hr. daily 8:30am-4:30pm; admission $3, under 12 $2). Also of interest are the surprisingly good **Holter Museum of Art,** 12 E. Lawrence St. (442-6400), and the historic **Old Governor's Mansion.** (Museum open Tues.-Sat. 10am-5pm, Sun. noon-5pm. Mansion open Tues.-Sun. noon-5pm, tours on the hour. Both free.) For a more down-to-earth introduction to Helena, take a guided walking tour of the city's architecture, history, and geology, leaving from the front of the Holter Museum. (Check inside for exact times. $5.)

Helena has plenty of unpretentious restaurants that won't strain your budget. **4 B's,** 900 N. Last Chance Gulch (442-5275), boogies right across from the bus station, and provides scrumptious chicken pot pie for $4. (24 hrs.) The **Country Kitchen,** 2000 Prospect Ave. (443-7457), 4 B's biggest competitor, serves superior breakfast (eggs, toast, hash-browns, coffee) for $3 (open 24 hrs.). **Big Al's Sandwich Shop,** 11 W. 6th Ave. (443-7422), extracts $2.75-5.25 for a hefty made-to-order sandwich. (Open Mon.-Fri. 6:30am-4pm, Sat. 8am-2:30pm.)

Lodgings in Helena are as reasonable as the restaurants. The **Iron Front Hotel,** 415 Last Chance Gulch (443-2400), offers some of the cheapest and cleanest beds in town—heck, in all of Montana. (Singles $12. Doubles $14. No private baths. Key deposit $5.) Across the road, the **Park Hotel,** 432 N. Last Chance Gulch (442-0960), has older, less spacious rooms. (Singles with bath $15. Doubles with bath $20.) Many public **campgrounds** call your name within 25 mi. of Helena, but none has showers or flush toilets. Watch out for the **Porcupine Campground** in the Helena National Forest, 13 mi. west on U.S. 12, or **Cromwell Dixon,** a few more mi. west on Rte. 12. (Sites $4.) Call the Fish, Wildlife, and Parks Department (444-2449) for information, or contact the **Helena National Forest Office,** Federal Building, Drawer #10014 (449-5201). The chamber of commerce also has complete listings of campgrounds in their free *Montana Travel Planner.*

Helena lies in the Missouri River Valley, about halfway between Yellowstone and Glacier National Parks. Bus lines **Intermountain** and **RimRock Stages** both serve Helena from 5 W. 15th St. (442-5860), running to: Butte ($14.50), Great Falls ($21), Bozeman ($16), Billings ($31.50), Kalispell ($30), and Missoula ($19). (Open Mon.-Fri. 8am-1:15pm and 4:15-7:15pm.) For short trips around Helena, look into **Rent-A-Wreck,** 3710 W. Montana Ave. (443-3635). (Cars $24 per day, 100 free mi., 20¢ per additional mi. Open daily 8am-5pm. You must be 21 with a major credit card or a $250 deposit.)

Helena's **post office,** 2300 N. Harris (443-3304), is in the north end, by I-15. (Open Mon.-Fri. 8:30am-5pm.) The **ZIP code** is 59601; the **area code** is 406.

Missoula

People visit Missoula less for the city itself than for the great outdoors. Many of the locals moonlight as nature-enthusiasts; you'll be hard pressed to resist the flow and catch the city's cultural sights. When you do seek out some indoor recreation, however, you'll be well rewarded. Thanks to the presence of the University of Montana, the city has an intellectual atmosphere and sights to match.

Cycling enthusiasts have put the town on the map with the rigorous **Bikecentennial Route.** The **Bikecentennial Organization Headquarters,** 113 W. Main St. (721-1776), provides information about the route, while the **Missoula Bicycle Club,** P.O. Box 8903, Missoula 59807, furnishes aficionados with other bicycling news through the mail. To participate in Missoula's most popular sport, visit the **Braxton Bike Shop,** 2100 South Ave. W. (549-2513) and procure a bike for a day ($12), overnight ($15), or a week ($75). (Open Mon.-Sat. 10am-6pm.) You must have a credit card or a blank check as a deposit.

Ski trips, raft trips, backpacking, and day hikes are other popular Missoula diversions. The **University of Montana Recreation Annex,** University Center #164 (243-5172), posts sign-up sheets for all these activities and proves a good source of information on guided hikes (open Mon.-Thurs. 7am-4pm, Fri. 7am-5pm), while the **Department of Recreation** (243-2802) organizes day hikes and overnight trips. (Open Mon.-Fri. 9am-5pm. Fees vary.) The **Rattlesnake Wilderness National Recreation Area,** a few mi. northwest of town off the Van Buren St. exit from I-90, makes for a great day of hiking. Wilderness maps ($2) are available from the **U.S. Forest Service Information Office,** 340 N. Pattee St. (329-3511; open Mon.-Fri. 7:30am-4pm). The Clark Fork, Blackfoot, and Bitterroot Rivers provide gushing opportunities for float trips. For river maps ($1), visit the **Montana State Regional Parks and Wildlife Office,** 3201 Spurgin Rd. (542-5500; open Mon.-Fri. 8am-5pm).

The **Museum of the Arts,** 335 N. Pattee St. (728-0447), displays classical art for those hankering for more metropolitan diversion. (Open daily noon-5pm.) The hottest sight in town, however, is the **Aerial Fire Depot Visitors Center** (329-4934), seven mi. west of town on Broadway (U.S. 10). Here you'll learn to appreciate the fun and danger aerial firefighters encounter when jumping into flaming, roadless forests. (Open daily 8:30am-5:30pm; Oct.-April by appointment. Tours every hr. in summer, except noon-1pm.)

Missoula's dining scene offers much more than the West's usual steak and potatoes greasefest. The **Mustard Seed,** 419 W. Front St. (728-7825), serves wonderful midsummer night's dishes from a variety of Asian cuisines. Full dinners (soup, vegetables, and a main course) go for $7-8. (Open Mon.-Fri. 11am-2:30pm and 5-10pm, Sat.-Sun. 5-10pm.) **Torrey's** restaurant and natural food store, 1916 Brooks St. (721-2510), serves health food at absurdly low prices. (Seafood stir-fry costs $3.25; incongruous 8-oz. sirloin steak just $4.25. **Zorba's,** 420 S. Orange St. (728-9259), offers another escape from Americana. A large Greek salad is $3.50, and entrees run $5-7. (Open Mon.-Sat. 11am-8:30pm.)

Spend the night in Missoula at the **Birchwood Hostel (AYH),** 600 S. Orange St. (728-9799), 13 blocks east of the bus station on Broadway, then eight blocks south on Orange. Most of the guests arrive on cycles. The spacious, immaculate dormitory room sleeps 22. Admirably clean laundry, kitchen, and bike storage facilities are available. ($6 for members and cyclists, $8 otherwise. Open daily 5-10pm. Closed 2 weeks late Dec.) The **Canyon Motel,** 1015 E. Broadway (543-4069 or 543-7251), has newly renovated rooms at not-so-deep discount prices. (Singles $20. Doubles $25.) Closer to the bus station, the **Sleepy Inn,** 1427 W. Broadway (549-6484), has singles for $20 and doubles for $25.

The **Greyhound terminal** sprints at 1660 W. Broadway St. (549-2339). Catch a bus to Bozeman (3 per day, $24) or Spokane (3 per day, $32). **Intermountain Transportation** serves Kalispell (2 per day, $24) and **RimRock Stages** serves Helena (1 per day, $19) from the same terminal. **Rent-a-Wreck,** 2401 W. Broadway (728-3838), offers humble autos ($20 per day, $119 per week; 100 free mi. per day, 26¢ each additional mi.; you must be 21; credit card or $100 cash deposit.)

The **Missoula Chamber of Commerce,** 825 E. Front St. (543-6623), provides bus schedules. Traveling within Missoula is easy thanks to reliable city **buses** (721-3333; buses operate Mon.-Fri. 6am-7pm, Sat. 9:30am-6pm; fare 50¢).

Missoula's **post office** is at 1100 W. Kent (329-2200), near the intersection of Brooks, Russell, and South St. (Open Mon.-Fri. 8:30am-5pm.) The **ZIP code** is 59801; the **area code** is 406.

Waterton-Glacier International Peace Park

Waterton-Glacier transcends international boundaries to unite two of the most unspoiled but relatively accessible wilderness areas on the continent. Symbolizing the peace between the United States and Canada, the park provides sanctuary for bighorn sheep, moose, and mountain goats—and for tourists weary of the more crowded parks farther south and north.

Technically one park, Waterton-Glacier is, for all practical purposes, two distinct areas: the small Waterton Lakes National Park in Alberta, and the enormous Glacier National Park in Montana. Each park charges its own admission fee (Waterton $4, Glacier $5), and you must go through customs to pass from one to the other. Several **border crossings** pepper the park: **Chief Mountain** (open May 18-May 31 daily 9am-6pm; June 1-Sept. 14 7am-10pm; closed in winter); **Piegan/Carway** (open May 16-Oct. 31 7am-11pm; Nov. 1-May 15 9am-6pm); **Trail Creek** (open June - Oct. 9am-5pm); and Roosville (open 24 hrs.).

Since snow melt is an unpredictable process, the parks usually operate fully only from late May to early September. To find out the areas of the park, hotels, and campsites that will be open when you visit, contact the headquarters of either Waterton or Glacier (888-5441).

Glacier National Park, Montana

Glacier's layout is simple: one road enters through West Glacier on the west side, and three roads enter from the east—at Many Glacier, St. Mary, and Two Medicine. West Glacier and St. Mary provide the two main points of entry into the park, connected by **Going-to-the-Sun Road** ("The Sun"), the only road that traverses the park. Fast-paced **U.S. 2** runs between West and East Glacier along 82 mi. of the southern park border. Look for the "Goat Lick" signs off Rte. 2 near **Walton.** Mountain goats often descend to the lick for a salt fix in June and July.

Stop in at the **visitors centers** at **St. Mary,** at the east entrance to the park (732-4424); (open late May to mid-June daily 8am-5pm; mid-June to Sept. 7 daily 8am-9pm; Sept. 8-Sept. 30 daily 8am-5pm), or at **Apgar,** at the west park entrance (open daily, early May to mid-June 8am-5pm; mid-June to Sept. 7 8am-8pm; Sept. 8 to Sept. 30 8am-5pm; Oct. 8am-4:30pm). A third visitors center graces **Logan Pass** on Going-to-the-Sun Rd. (Open daily, mid-June to Sept. 7 9am-6pm, Sept. 8-Sept. 30 9am-5pm.)

Backcountry trips provide the best way to appreciate the pristine mountain scenery and the wildlife which make Glacier famous. The **Highline Trail** from Logan Pass gives a good day hike and passes through prime bighorn sheep and mountain goat territory. The visitors center's free *Backcountry* pamphlet has a hiking map marked with distances and backcountry campsites. All travelers who camp overnight must obtain a free wilderness permit from a visitors center or ranger station; backcountry camping is allowed only at designated campgrounds. The **Two Medicine** area in the southeast corner of the park is less traveled, while the trek to **Kintla Lake** rewards you with fantastic views of nearby peaks. Before embarking on any hike, familiarize yourself with the precautions necessary to avoid a run-in with a bear. Rangers at any visitors center or ranger station will instruct you on the finer points of noise-making and food storage to keep Yogi from yabba-dabba-dooing on yabba-dabba-you.

Going-to-the-Sun Road may be the most beautiful 50-mi. stretch of road in the world. Even on cloudy days when there's no sun to go to, the constantly changing views of Alp-like peaks will have you struggling to keep your eyes on the road. Snow keeps the road closed until late June; check with rangers for exact dates.

Though The Sun is a popular **bike route,** only experienced cyclists with appropriate gearing should attempt this grueling stint. The sometimes nonexistent shoulder of the road creates a potentially hazardous situation for bikers. In the summer (June 15-Sept. 2), bike traffic is prohibited from the Apgar turn-off at the west end of Lake McDonald to Sprague Creek Campground, and from Logan Creek to Logan Pass, between 11am and 4pm. The east side of the park has no such restrictions.

Boat tours explore all of Glacier's large lakes. At Lake McDonald and Two Medicine Lake, 55-minute tours leave throughout the day. (Tours at Lake McDonald $5.50, $2.75 ages 4-12; tours at Two Medicine $5, ages 4-12 $2.50.) The tours from St. Mary and Many Glacier (75 min.) provide access to Glacier's backcountry. (Tours from St. Mary's $7, $3.50 ages 4-12; tours from Many Glacier $6.50, ages 4-12 $3.25.) The $7 sunset cruise proves a great way to see this daily phenomenon, which doesn't occur until about 10pm in the middle of the summer. **Glacier Raft Co.,** in West Glacier (800-322-9995 or 888-5454) hawks full- and half-day trips down the middle fork of the Flathead River, near West Glacier. A full day (lunch included) costs $50; half-day trips ($27) leave in both the morning and the afternoon. Call for reservations.

Rent canoes ($5 per hr.), rowboats ($5 per hr., $25 per 10 hr.), and outboards ($10 per hr., $50 per 10 hr.) at Apgar, Lake McDonald, Many Glacier, and Two Medicine. All require a $50 deposit. Fishing is excellent in the park—cutthroat trout, lake trout, and even the rare Arctic Grayling challenge the angler's skill and patience. No permit is required—just be familiar with the fishing limits of the park, explained by the pamphlet *Fishing Regulations,* available at all visitors centers.

While in Glacier, don't overlook the interpretive programs offered by the rangers. Inquire at any visitors center for the day's menu of guided hikes, lectures, birdwatching walks, interpretive dances, and children's programs.

Staying indoors within Glacier is expensive. **Glacier Park, Inc.** handles all lodging within the park and offers only the **Swiftcurrent Motor Inn** for budget travlers. Cabins at the Swiftcurrent are $19, $27 for two bedrooms (each additional person $2; open late June-early Sept.). Reservations can be made through Glacier Park, Inc. From mid-September to mid-May, contact them at Greyhound Tower Station, 1210, Phoenix, AZ 85077 (602-248-6000); from mid-May to mid-September at East Glacier Park 59434 (406-226-5551), in MT 800-332-9351). Other than the Swiftcurrent, the company operates seven pricier lodges which open and close on a staggered schedule. Agpar opens first, in mid-May, and the other six open in late May or early June.

Excellent, affordable lodging can be found just across the park border in **East Glacier,** which sits on Rte. 2, 30 mi. south of the St. Mary's entrance, and about 5 mi. south of the Two Medicine entrance. East Glacier boasts the **Backpackers Inn,** 29 Dowson Ave. (226-9392), just opened in 1991 by Pat and Renée Schur, who saw a need for budget accommodations in the Glacier area. The Inn offers clean beds and hot showers for only $8 per night, which includes Pat and Renée's warm hospitality and excellent advice on hikes and activities in the park. There is also an American Youth Hostel at **Brownies Grocery,** 1020 Hwy. 49 (226-4426), in East Glacier. It offers comfortable accommodations in its dorm at $10 for AYH members, $13 for nonmembers.

Camping offers a cheaper and more scenic alternative to indoor accommodations. All developed campsites are available on a first come, first camped basis ($6-8); the most popular sites fill by noon. However, "Campground Full" signs sometimes stay up for days on end; look carefully for empty sites. All 15 campgrounds accessible by car all are easy to find. Just ask for the handout **Auto Campgrounds** at any visitors center and follow the map distributed as you enter the park. **Avalanche** campsite is open to avalanche-and bear-proof hard-sided units only. **Sprague Creek** on Lake McDonald is one of the most peaceful campgrounds; arrive early, since there are only 25 sites. Three sites at Sprague remain reserved for bicyclists; towed units are prohibited. Campgrounds without running water in the surrounding national forests usually offer sites for $5. Check at the Apgar or St. Mary visitors center for up-to-date information on conditions and vacancies at established campgrounds.

Amtrak (800-872-7245) traces a dramatic route along the southern edge of the park. Daily trains serve West Glacier from Seattle ($117) and Spokane ($58); Amtrak also runs from Stanley, ND to East Glacier ($99). **Greyhound** can get you as far as Great Falls, MT, over 100 mi. southeast of East Glacier on Rte. 89. As with most areas of the Rockies, a car is the most convenient mode of transport, especially within the park.

The Glacier **post office** is at Lake McDonald Lodge, in the park. (Open Mon.-Fri. 9am-3:45pm.) The General Delivery **ZIP code** is 59921. The **area code** rings in at 406.

Waterton Lakes National Park, Alberta

Unlike Canada, Waterton is only a small fraction of the size of its U.S. neighbor. (Glacier offers much of the same scenery and activities.) While a trip north is not essential, a hike in Waterton's backcountry may prove a less crowded alternative during Glacier's peak tourist season (mid-July to Aug.).

The **Waterton Information Office** (859-2445) lies five mi. south of the park entrance. Stop and grab a copy of the monthly *Waterton-Glacier Guide* for detailed information on local services and activities. (Open daily 8am-9pm.)

Once you've entered Waterton Lakes, all you can do is go five mi. south to **Waterton Townsite.** Four-wheeled travelers should drive the **Akamina Parkway** or the less-traveled **Red Rock Canyon Road.** Both leave the main road near the Townsite and end at the heads of popular backcountry trails. Those who brought only their high-tops to Waterton should set out on the **Crypt Lake Hike,** which runs four mi. from Waterton Townsite; you'll feel like a car as you pass through a natural tunnel bored through the side of a mountain. Those fleeing the Canadian authorities should choose the **International Hike,** which puts you in Montana some four mi. after leaving the Townsite. To camp overnight you must obtain a free permit from the information office or the park headquarters. A boat tour of Upper Waterton Lake (1½ hr.) leaves from the **Emerald Bay Marina** in the Townsite. (Admission $13, ages under 13 $7.) When you want to get some exercise on the lake, rent a rowboat at Cameron Lake for $6 per hour. The Townsite comes out of its winter hibernation to greet summer sun- and sight-seekers with exorbitant prices. Waterton sorely lacks budget restaurants; your best bet in the Townsite is the **Zum Burger Haus** (859-2388), which serves decent if misspelled cheeseburgers for $5 on the pleasant patio. (Open daily 7am-10pm.)

The **Prince of Wales Hotel** (236-3400) maintains a civilized perch away from the majestic Waterton Lake, but don't stay here unless the prince himself treats. Instead, pitch your tent at the **Townsite Campground** at the south end of town. (Sites $11.75, with full hookup $16.) To stay indoors, drop by **Dill's General Store,** on Waterton Ave. (859-2345), and ask to sleep in one of the nine rooms of the Stanley Hotel. Rooms will drain $45 from your pocket, and you won't even have a private pot to piss in.

If you find yourself in *really* dire straits, call the **Royal Canadian Mounted Police** (859-2244). The **post office** is on Fountain Ave. at Windflower, Waterton Townsite, Alberta T0K 2M0. (Open Mon.-Fri. 8:30am-4:30pm.) Waterton's **area code** is 403.

NEBRASKA

You know it! You love it! It's the state that needs no introduction, so without further ado. . .heeeeeere's Nebraska!

Practical Information

Capital: Lincoln.

Tourist Information: **Nebraska Department of Economic Development,** P.O. Box 94666, Lincoln 68509 (471-3796). **Nebraska Game and Parks Commission,** 2200 N. 33rd St., Lincoln 68503 (464-0641). Permits for campgrounds and park areas ($10). Open Mon.-Fri. 8am-5pm.

Time Zone: Central (1 hr. behind Eastern) and Mountain (2 hr. behind Eastern). **Postal Abbreviation:** NE

Lincoln

From nearly 20 miles away the Nebraska State Capitol is visible, soaring far above the city and farmlands below. The "Tower on the Plains," remarkable for its streamlined exterior and detailed interior, is an appropriate centerpiece for Lincoln, itself an oasis of learning, legislating, and culture on the prairie.

In 1867, settlers in the town of Lancaster renamed their outpost in honor of the recently-deceased president; soon after the fledgling city became the state's capital. This hospitable pioneer town is now the seat of the nation's only one-house state legislature.

Practical Information

Emergency: 911.

Tourist Offices, 1221 N St. #606 (477-6300). Open Mon.-Fri. 8am-4:45pm. Also at 105 S. 9th St. (477-6300), at O St. downtown. Open late May-Sept. daily 9am-5pm. **League of Human Dignity,** 1423 O St. (471-7871). Advice and aid, including local transportation for disabled persons. Open Mon.-Fri. 8am-5pm. **24-hr. Visitor Information Line,** 477-6300.

Amtrak: 201 N. 7th St. (476-1295 or 800-872-7245). To Omaha (1 per day, 1 hr., $13) and Denver (1 per day, 7½ hr., $96). Open daily 7am-11pm.

Greyhound: 940 P St. (474-1071), close to downtown and city campus. Buses run east-west to Omaha (7 per day, 1 hr., $14) and Chicago (6 per day, 10-12 hr., $74). Open Mon.-Fri. 7am-6pm, Sat. 8am-6pm, Sun. 2-6pm.

Public Transport: **Lincoln Transportation System,** 710 J St. (476-1234). Open Mon.-Fri. 7am-4:30pm. All buses stop at 11th and O St. Mon.-Sat. 6am-7pm. Fare 65¢. "Star shuttle" buses (10¢) serve downtown Mon.-Fri. 9:30am-5pm.

Taxi: **Yellow Cab,** 477-4111. $1.60 initial charge, $1.25 per additional mi.

Help Lines: **Rape Crisis,** 471-7273. 24 hr. **Gay/Lesbian Support Line,** 475-4967 or 472-5644. **Committee Offering Lesbian and Gay Events (COLAGE),** 474-2454, at University of Nebraska. **Hotline for the Handicapped,** 471-3656 or 800-742-7594. **Lodging Hotline,** 476-2192.

Post Office: 700 R St. (473-1695). Open Mon.-Fri. 7:30am-5pm, Sat. 9am-noon. **ZIP code:** 68508.

Area Code: 402.

O Street is the main east-west drag, splitting the town north-south. Alphabetized streets increase northwards. **First Street,** running north-south, sits along **Salt Creek,** west of downtown. The **University of Nebraska** (472-7211) is on the northern border of downtown. Check the **student union** on 14th at R St. for ride boards (at main entrance) and cheap food. Most places of interest are within walking distance of downtown, except for the university's **East Campus.** Take the university shuttle from Lyman Hall, available only during the academic year, or bus #4 ("University Place").

Accommodations and Camping

The small, ministry-run **Cornerstone Hostel (AYH)**, 640 N. 16th St. (476-0355 or 476-0926), is located on the university's downtown campus. Two big carpeted rooms with couches, tables, and futons serve as single-sex dorm rooms. Bring a sleeping bag or blankets and pillow. Showers and full kitchen. (Curfew 10pm. $8. Members only.) Nonmembers (and moneyed AYHers) can stay downtown at the gorgeous, family-run **Town House Mini-Suite Motel**, 18th and M St. (475-3000). Each one-bedroom apartment has a pull-out couch, great beds, a furnished kitchen with coffeemaker, cable TV, and access to a microwave. (Singles $34. Doubles $39.) The **Great Plains Motel**, 2732 O St. (476-3253), maintains nicer rooms than most hotels in this price range with pleasant wood-paneled furnishings, thick beige carpeting, and fridges. Free coffee and HBO. Take bus #1 ("East Havelock") from downtown. (Singles $29.50. Doubles $36.)

The best place to camp is at **Branched Oak Lake** (464-0641, ext. 245), 12 mi. north of town on Rte. 34, where facilities include showers and restrooms. (Sites $6, with electricity $8.) Campers need a Nebraska park entry permit ($10), available at area concessions, lake headquarters, or at the Nebraska Game and Parks Commission in Lincoln (see Nebraska Practical Information).

Food and Entertainment

Strawberries, pastry, tie-dye shirts, and a coffee stand are the excuses for a crafts- and fruit-filled **farmers market** held downtown every Saturday morning from June to October on 7th St. between P and Q St. Bohemia thrives at Lincoln's **Coffeehouse,** 1324 P St. (477-6611), where high ceilings, slow fans, excellent coffee served in huge glass mugs (75¢ with refills), and a bookstore converge. Alongside other birkenstocky fare, a vegetarian sandwich or salad ($3-4) is offered daily. A "poetry quilt" on the back wall invites new submissions. You can sell your used philosophy, poetry, and regional American literature books here, lightening your load while you find out about upcoming concerts and readings. (Open Mon.-Thurs. 7am-midnight, Fri.-Sat. 7-1am, Sun. noon-midnight) Locals swear by the more prosaic fare at **Spaghetti Works,** 228 N. 12th St. (475-0900), where lunch is $4 and dinner just $5. (Open Mon.-Thurs. 11:30am-2pm and 5-10pm, Fri. 11:30am-2pm and 5-11pm, Sat. 11:30am-2:30pm and 5-11pm, Sun. 5-9pm.) **Noodles Comedy Club** is upstairs. (Shows Thurs. at 8:30pm, Fri.-Sat. at 7:30 and 9:45pm.) Students and locals alike flock to **Valentino's,** 3457 Holdrege, near the East Campus (467-3611), for great pizza, pasta, antipasto, and buffets. Buffets happen Mon.-Sat. 11am-2pm ($4.75) and 4-9pm ($6.25); Sunday brunch is at noon ($5.50). (Open daily 11am-11pm.) A second Valentino's is at 232 N. 13th St. (475-1501), near the city campus.

A bar-goers bar, **P.O. Pears,** 322 S. 9th St. (476-8551), has an enormous mechanized windmill contraption in the back room. Draft beer is 79¢, burger and fries $4. (Open daily 11:30am-1am; open at 10am on football Saturdays.) Twenty-one-year-old animals can enjoy the **Zoo Bar,** 136 N. 14th St. (435-8754), where live blues make for a raucous and rowdy time. (Open Mon.-Fri. 3pm-1am, Sat. noon-1am, Sun. 6-11pm. Music starts at 9pm. $1-10 cover, depending on act.) **Duffy's Tavern,** 1412 O St. (474-3543), attracts a sophisticated local crowd to one of Lincoln's only alternative music bars. Draft beers 65-75¢. (Open daily 1pm-1am. Cover $2-8.) **Julio's,** 132 S. 13th St. (477-5122), has Tex-Mex, gourmet burgers, and a Happy Hour (Mon.-Fri. 3-7pm and 11pm-1am; drafts 75¢, pitchers $2.25) enlivened by live jazz every Thursday night at 8:30pm. Look for the old black lead, red brick, and bevelled glass of the telephone building. (Open Sun.-Wed. 11am-11pm, Thurs.-Sat. 11am-midnight; bar open daily to 1am.) If you play the game, do not pass Go, do not collect $200, and go directly to **Boardwalk,** 104 N. 20th St. (435-9412 or 474-5692), a gay bar and dance club. Admits both men and women. (Open daily 3pm-1am. Happy Hour 3-9pm.)

Sights

The **Nebraska State Capitol Building**, 14th at K St. (471-0448), maintains all the pomp and majesty of an art deco museum. Its floor, reminiscent of a Native American blanket in design, is an incredible mosaic of inlaid Belgian and Italian marble each pattern representing some facet of the land and peoples of Nebraska. Take the elevator to the 14th floor for a terrific view of the entire city. (Open daily 9am-5pm. Excellent tours on the hour. Free.)

The **Sheldon Memorial Art Gallery**, 12th and R St. (472-2461), a cool, white building designed by Philip Johnson and located on the university campus, highlights the last three centuries of American art. The **Sheldon Film Theatre** (472-5353) runs independent and art films. (Gallery open Tues.-Wed. 10am-5pm, Thurs.-Sat. 10am-5pm and 7-9pm, Sun. 2-9pm.)

An unusually large mammoth named "Archie," short for its genus name, *Archidiscodon*, poses with several other fossil buddies in the **University of Nebraska State Museum** (472-2642), in Morrill Hall at 14th and U St. (Open summer Mon.-Fri. 10:30am-noon and 1:30-4:30pm, Sat.-Sun. 2-4pm; academic year Tues.-Fri. 2:30-4:30pm, Sat.-Sun. 2-4pm. Donation requested.)

Roll over to the **National Museum of Roller Skating**, 7700 A St. (489-8811), the self-proclaimed "definitive source for the history of roller skating" and final resting place of some funky get-ups. Take bus #5 ("Bryan Hospital") from downtown. (Open Mon.-Fri. 9am-5pm. Free.)

Omaha

Omaha, just across the Missouri River from Council Bluffs, Iowa, is an old packing house and railroad town. Flanked to the west by corn and cow country, to the south by apple orchards, and tangled with Union Pacific Railroad lines, Omaha is the crossroads for many of America's calories. The eclectic and impressive architecture exudes the pride that residents take in their city. History has seen immigrants from Bohemia, freed African slaves, and, more recently, Mexican migrant workers coming to Omaha for jobs in the packing houses. Evidence of these ethnic communities appears most prominently on grocery shelves, where corn tortillas with Spanish labels sit alongside bags of Vic's popcorn and Czechoslovakian liver dumplings. Ironically, Native American history in Omaha proves most elusive; its influence surfaces largely in the region's place names.

Practical Information

Emergency: 911.

Nebraska/Omaha Tourist Information Center, 1212 Deer Park Blvd. (595-3990), at I-80 and 13th St. (Rte. 73/75). Take bus #6 from downtown. Open April-Oct. daily 9am-5pm. **Douglas County Tourism and Convention Bureau,** 1819 Farnam St. #1200 (444-4660), in the Omaha-Douglas Civic Center. City bus schedules in the basement, behind the cafeteria area. Open daily 8:30am-4:30pm. **Mayor's Commission on the Handicapped,** 444-5021. Information on transportation, access, and services. Open Mon.-Fri. 8am-4:30pm. **Events Hotline,** 444-6800.

Amtrak: 1003 S. 9th St. (342-1501 or 800-872-7245). One train per day to Chicago (9 hr., $95), Denver (9 hr., $100), and Salt Lake City (24 hr., $169). Open Mon.-Fri. 7:30am-3:30pm and 10:30pm-7:30am, Sat.-Sun. 10:30pm-7:30am.

Greyhound: 1601 Jackson (341-1900). To: Lincoln (6 per day, 1 hr., $12); Kansas City (4 per day, 4½ hr., $41); Chicago (6 per day, 12 hr., $73); and Denver (4 per day, 10½-12 hr., $80). Open 24 hr.

Public Transport: Metro Area Transit (MAT), 2615 Cuming St. (341-0800). Maps available at the Park Fair Mall, 16th and Douglas near the Greyhound station. Open Mon.-Sat. 6am-9pm, Sun. 7am-9pm. Buses have thorough service for downtown, Creighton University area, North Omaha, and 24th St., but don't reach as far as M street and 107th, where several budget hotels are located. Fare 75¢, transfers 5¢. Bus #28 ("Airport") from 10th St. serves the airport twice early in the morning and twice late in the afternoon, in case you suddenly have to flee by air.

Taxi: Happy Cab, 339-0110. $1.50 first mi., $1 each addit. mi. Fare to airport $7.

Car Rental: Cheepers Rent-a-Car, 7700 L St. (331-8586). $17 per day with 100 free mi., 20¢ per additional mi. Must be 18 and have a major credit card. Open Mon.-Fri. 7:30am-6pm, Sat. 9am-3pm

Help Lines: Crisis Line, Inc., 341-9111 or 341-9112. **Rape Crisis,** 345-7273. **Gay/Lesbian Crisis Line** (in Lincoln), 475-5710.

Time Zone: Central (1 hr. behind Eastern).

Post Office: 1124 Pacific St. (348-2895). Open Mon.-Fri. 7:30am-5pm, Sat. 7:30am-noon. **ZIP code:** 68108.

Area Code: 402.

Numbered north-south streets begin at the river; named roads run east-west. **Dodge Street** divides the city north-south. When night falls, avoid 24th St., and stay close to Creighton University at 25th and California.

Accommodations and Camping

Many budget motels are off the L or 84th St. exits from I-80, 6½ mi. southwest of downtown. Buses #11, 21, and 55 service the area. An 11% Nebraska hotel tax creates higher prices.

Econolodge, 2211 Douglas St. (345-9565 or 800-446-6900). Ideal for the carless. Secure downtown location compromised by slightly frayed neighborhood. Free coffee and doughnuts in the morning. Singles $33. Doubles $42.

Motel 6, 10708 M St. (331-3161), adjacent to the Budgetel Inn. HBOs, phone, basic bed-and-Bible rooms. Singles $31. Doubles $38.

Budgetel Inn, 10760 M St. (592-5200) near 108th. Bus #55 will get you only as close as 108th and Q. Free continental breakfast delivered to room, which already has coffee and coffeemaker. Singles $38, with kingsize bed $44. Doubles $44.

Super 8, 7111 Spring St. (390-0700), near 72nd and Grover St. Take bus #11 or 21. Non-smoking rooms, cable TV. Restaurants nearby. Popcorn vending machine. Singles $33. Doubles $40. Also at 108th and L St. (339-2250).

Bellevue Campground, at Haworth Park (291-3379), on the Missouri River 10 mi. from downtown at Hwy. 370. Take the infrequent bus #50 ("Bellevue") from 17th and Dodge to Mission and Franklin, and walk down Mission. Showers, toilets, shelters. Sites $4, with hookup $7. Free water. Open daily 6am-10pm; quiet stragglers sometimes enter after hours.

Food and Nightlife

Once a warehouse district, the **Old Market,** on Howard St. between 10th and 13th, has been converted into cobblestone streets, quaint shops, restaurants, and bars. **Coyote's Bar and Grill,** 1217 Howard St. (345-2047), howls with fun Tex-Mex appetizers like the "Holy Avocado" ($3.75), salads, chili, and staggeringly large burgers ($3.50-4) in hip wood and bevelled glass surroundings. (Open Mon.-Thurs. 11am-11pm, Fri.-Sat. 5-10pm.) **Trini's,** 1020 Howard St. (346-8400), marinates, sautées, and serves profoundly authentic Mexican and vegetarian food in an elegant, candlelit cavern. Menu translated into English; dinner $2.50-7. (Open Mon.-Thurs. 11:30am-10pm, Fri.-Sat. 11:30am-11pm, Sun. 1-8pm.) **The Spaghetti Works,** 1100 Howard St. (422-0770), offers spaghetti and unlimited salad bar. Get hot and naked. Trust us. (Open Mon.-Fri. 11am-3pm, 5:30-10:30pm, Sat.-Sun. 11am-3pm and 5:30-11:30pm.) The **Bohemian Café,** 1406 S. 13th St. (342-9838), in South Omaha's old Slavic neighborhood, sells carnivore-friendly fare, accompanied by onions and potatoes, for under $6. (Open daily 11am-10pm.) **Joe Tess' Place,** 5424 S. 24th St., at U St. in South Omaha (731-7278; take bus #6 from Farnam and 16th) is renowned for its fresh, fried carp and catfish served with thin-sliced potatoes and rye bread.

Entrees $3-7. (Open Mon.-Thurs. 10:30am-11pm, Fri.-Sat. 10:30am-midnight, Sun. 11am-11pm.) Of course, if you want *real* Nebraska fare, just walk into any movie theater and ask for popcorn.

Omaha caters to several universities in the area, so punk, progressive, and Irish folk all have found a niche. Check the window of the **Antiquarium Bookstore**, 1215 Harney, in the Old Market, for information on shows. For tickets, call Tix-Ticket Clearinghouse at 342-7107. **Sokol Hall**, at 13th and Martha (346-9802), headlines local and national punk and progressive rock bands. (Tickets around $5.) In the Old Market area, head to the **Howard St. Tavern,** 1112 Howard St. (341-0433). The local crowds and good music create a pleasant atmosphere. Live music downstairs; 60s and 70s music upstairs. (Open Mon.-Sat. 3pm-1am, Sun. 7pm-1am. Cover $2-3.50.) **Omaha's Magic Theater,** 1417 Farnam St. (346-1227; call Mon.-Fri. 9am-5:30pm), is devoted to the development of new American musicals. (Evening performances Fri.-Mon. Tickets $5, seniors and students $2.)

The Max, 1417 Jackson (346-4110), caters to gay men, with five bars, a disco dance floor, DJ, patio, and fountains. (Open daily 4pm-1am. Cover $3.) Another gay bar, **The Run,** 1715 Leavenworth (449-8703), is popular for its "after hours" weekends from 1:35-3:45am, when $4 gets you enough coffee, soda, and music to last the night. (Otherwise open daily 2pm-1am. No cover.) **Chesterfield,** 1950 St. Mary's Ave. (342-1244), is a lesbian bar with occasional entertainment. (Open daily 3pm-1am.)

Sights

Omaha's **Joslyn Art Museum,** 2200 Dodge St. (342-3300), is a three-story art deco masterpiece with an exterior made of Georgian Pink marble and an interior of over 30 different marble types. It contains an excellent collection of less prominent 19th- and 20th-century European and American art. In the summer, they host "Jazz on the Green" each Thursday from 7-9pm. (Open Tues.-Wed, Fri.-Sat. 10am-5pm, Thurs. 10am-9pm, Sun. 1-5pm. $2, seniors and ages under 12 $1. Free Sat. 10am-noon.)

The **Western Heritage Museum,** 801 S. 10th St. (444-5071), has historic exhibits, but its main attraction is its architecture. Once the old Union Pacific Railroad Station in 1929, the museum glitters with kitsch. (Open May 27-Sept. 2 daily 9:30am-5pm; off-season Tues.-Sat. 10am-5pm, Sun. 1-5pm. $3, ages under 12 $2.) Housed in the historic Nebraska Telephone Building, the **Great Plains Black Museum,** 2213 Lake St. (345-2212), presents the history of African American migration to the Great Plains in photographs, musical instruments, documents, dolls, and quilts. Especially compelling are the portraits and biographies of the first African American women to settle in Nebraska, as well as the exhibit commemorating the life of Malcolm X, born Malcolm Little in Omaha in 1925. (Open Mon.-Fri. 8am-4:30pm. Donation $2. Take bus #8 from 19th and Farnam, or #9 from Dodge.)

The **Omaha Children's Museum,** 551 S. 18th St. (342-6164), features hands-on science and art exhibits. (Open June-Aug. Tues.-Sat. 10am-5pm, Sun. 1-5pm; Sept.-May Tues.-Fri. 2:30-5pm, Sat. 10am-5pm, Sun. 1-5pm.) The **Henry Doorly Zoo,** 3701 S. 10th St. (733-8400), at Deer Park Blvd., is home to white Siberian tigers and the largest enclosed aviary in North America. (Open April-Oct. Mon.-Fri. 9:30am-5pm, Sat.-Sun. 9:30am-6pm; in winter daily 9:30am-4pm, Mutual Education Building and aquarium only. $5, kids $2.50.)

NEVADA

Nevada once walked the straight and narrow. Explored by Spanish missionaries and settled by Mormons, the Nevada Territory's arid land and searing climate seemed a perfect place for ascetics to strive for moral uplift. But the discovery of gold in 1850, silver in 1859, and Charo in the 1970s won the state over permanently to the worship of filthy lucre. When the boom-bust ferris wheel finally stalled during the Great Depression, Nevadans responded by shaking off even the last vestiges of traditional virtue. Confirming the kinship between the two activities, gambling and marriage-licensing were made the state industries, the twain meeting in the drive-through divorce. In a final break with the rest of the country, Silver Staters legalized prostitution—except in Reno and Las Vegas—and began paying Wayne Newton enormous amounts of cash for his concerts.

But a Nevada exists outside the gambling towns. The forested slopes of Lake Tahoe, shared with California, offer serenity in little resorts far away from the casinos of the south shore (see the California section.) The rest of a mostly expansive and bone-dry Nevada is countryside, where the true West lingers in its barren glory.

Practical Information

Capital: Carson City.

Nevada Commission on Tourism, #2075 Valley Bank Bldg., U.S. 50, Carson City 89710 (885-4322). Open Mon.-Fri. 8am-5pm. Nevada Division of State Parks, Nye Bldg., 201 S. Fall, Carson City 89701 (885-4384). Open Mon.-Fri. 8am-5pm.

Time Zone: Pacific (3 hr. behind Eastern). Postal Abbreviation: NV

Area Code: 702.

Beatty

Beatty's main draw is kinder, gentler casinos and prostitution. (The town is a scheduled stop on the Hell's Angels' annual "Whorehouse Run.") But you can use it for a pit stop, night's sojourn, or supply base. Also, nearby on Rte. 374 towards Death Valley is Rhyolite, a ghost town complete with stone foundations and rusted cars. Check with the town's Visitor Information Center (553-2424) on Main and 4th St. (Open daily 8am-4pm.) The Stagecoach Hotel (553-2333), ½-mi. north of town on Hwy. 95., offers a jacuzzi along with cheap beds. (Doubles start at $25.)

Las Vegas

Only in Vegas could there be a major museum devoted to Liberace. The magic formula of this oasis of mild, middle-aged debauchery—offer everything but the gambling cheaply, and if you gild it, they will come—was hit upon by Bugsy Siegel in the 1940s. Das Kapital is worshipped here, and sacrifices from all major credit cards are happily accepted. But for all the cigarette girls, quickie chapels, and Elvis impersonators, the city takes itself very seriously—employees literally wear poker faces, and fail to see anything amusing about a nightmarishly overdecorated casino lobby.

Las Vegas rakes in a substantial share of the annual $126 billion spent at U.S. gambling tables, but even if you choose not to gamble (well, OK, maybe a little), clever customers can take advantage of the inexpensive buffets and cheap drinks; the visiting voyeur may find that the best show in town is not an opulent "stage spectacular" but simply the bizarre and free spectacle of decadent Las Vegas itself.

Practical Information

Emergency: 911.

Las Vegas Convention and Visitors Authority, 3150 Paradise Rd. (733-2471), at the Convention Center, 4 blocks from the Strip, by the Hilton. Up to date info on hotel bargains and buffets. Open Mon.-Fri. 8am-5pm.

McCarran International Airport: 798-5410 at the southeast end of the Strip. Main terminal on Paradise Rd. Within walking distance of the University of Nevada campus and the southern casinos. Buses and taxis to downtown.

Amtrak: 1 N. Main St. (386-6896; fares and schedules 800-872-7245), in the Union Plaza Hotel. To Los Angeles ($64, round-trip $75, reservations required), San Francisco ($115, round-trip $122), and Salt Lake City ($84, round-trip $126). Open daily 6am-8:30pm.

Greyhound: 200 Main St. (382-2640), at Carson Ave. downtown. To: L.A. ($34), Reno ($38), Salt Lake City ($45), and Denver ($86). **Las Vegas-Tonopah-Reno Lines** provides service to Phoenix ($30). Open 24 hrs.

Las Vegas Transit: 384-3540. Common transfer point at 200 Casino Center downtown. Trolley shuttle runs downtown along Fremont St. (Fare 50¢, seniors and under 12 25¢.) Most buses 5:30am-9pm. Strip buses (#6) every 15 min. 7am-12:45am, every ½-hr. 12:45-2:45am, every hr. 2:45-6:30am. Fare $1.15, ages 6-17 40¢, seniors and disabled people 10 rides for $4.20, transfers 15¢.

Tours: Gray Line Tours, 1550 S. Industrial Rd. (384-1234). Bus tours to Hoover Dam/Lake Mead (Mon.-Sat. at 9 and 11am, Sun. at 9am; 5 hr.; $19) and the Grand Canyon (2 days, $99 double occupancy, Mon. and Wed. at 7am; Oct.-April Mon., Wed., and Fri. at 7:30am). Reservations required. **Ray and Ross Tours,** 300 W. Owens St. (646-4661). Bus tours to Hoover Dam (6 hr., $17) and Hoover Dam/Lake Mead (7 hr., $24).

Taxi: Checker Cab, 873-2227. $2.20 first 1/7 mi., $1.40 each additional mi.

Car Rental: Avon, 387-6717. $24 per day with unlimited mi. in Nevada. $44 for ages 18-21. Free pickup from airport. Open daily 7am-11pm. Must have credit card. **Fairway Rent-A-Car,** 5300 S. Paradise Rd. (736-1786 or 800-634-3476), near the airport. $17 per day. 100 free mi. per day, 35¢ each additional mi. Open daily 8am-9pm. Must be 21 and stick to local use only.

Help Lines: Crisis Line, 876-4357. **Gambler's Anonymous,** 385-7732. Both open 24 hrs.

Post Office: 301 E. Stewart (385-8944), behind Lady Luck. Open Mon.-Fri. 9am-5pm. General delivery open Mon.-Fri. 10am-3pm. **ZIP code:** 89114.

Area Code: 702.

Gambler's specials number among the cheapest and most popular ways to reach Las Vegas. These bus tours leave early in the morning and return at night or the next day; ask in L.A., San Francisco, or San Diego tourist offices. You can also call casinos for info. Prices include everything except food and gambling, and although you are expected to stay with your group, "getting lost" shouldn't be a problem.

Vegas has two major casino areas. The **downtown** area, around Fremont and 2nd St., is walker-friendly; casinos cluster close together, and some of the sidewalks are even carpeted (man oh man). The other main area, known as the **Strip,** is a collection of mammoth casinos on both sides of intimidatingly busy Las Vegas Blvd. S. Stay downtown during the day, unless you have a car or like long, hot, unshaded stretches of sidewalk. Except for the neighborhoods just north and west of downtown, Vegas is generally, and especially on the Strip, a safe place for late-night strolling. Security guards and lights reproduce in amoeba-like fashion; there is almost always pedestrian traffic.

Accommodations and Camping

You can easily find cheap food and lodging in Vegas. Even the largest casinos sometimes offer rooms for $10 a night. Watch the travel and entertainment sections of local newspapers for ever-changing specials. Prices rise on weekends and holidays, but with over 67,000 hotel rooms you can find some place to rest that slot-machine arm.

Las Vegas Independent Hostel, 1208 Las Vegas Blvd. S. (385-9955). Not AYH-affiliated, but gives members discounts. Spartan, airy rooms with foam mattresses. Free coffee, tea, lemonade. Ride board in kitchen. Tours every Mon. to North Rim of the Grand Canyon. Office open daily 7-10am and 3-11pm, Nov.-March 8-10am and 5-11pm. Students and AYH members $8, nonmembers $10. Key deposit $5.

Las Vegas International Hostel (AYH), 1236 Las Vegas Blvd. South. (382-8119). Small kitchen. Rooms in separate cabins. Lots of common areas, even grass. Office open daily 7-10am and 5-11pm. $8, nonmembers $11. Key deposit $5.

Nevada Hotel, 235 S. Main St. (385-7311 or 800-637-5777). TV in large, pleasant rooms. Singles and doubles $18, $3 each additional person.

Crest Motel, 207 N. 6th St. (382-5642 or 800-777-1817), at Ogden St. Friendly management. TV, VCR, refrigerators in room. Singles Sun.-Thurs. $25, Fri.-Sat. $35, with kitchenettes $35. Breakfast at El Cortez included. Key deposit $5.

Aztec Inn, 2200 Las Vegas Blvd. S. (385-4566). Pool, phone, A/C. Singles and doubles $25 with second night free.

El Cortez, 600 E. Fremont (385-5200; 800-634-6703 for reservations). TV, A/C. Singles and doubles $23.

You'll need a car to reach any of the noncommercial campsites around Vegas. Twenty mi. west of the city on Rte. 159 rolls **Red Rock Canyon** (363-1921), where you can see an earthquake fault-line and other geological marvels. Camp here for free, but only in **Oak Creek Park.** Twenty-five mi. east, **Lake Mead National Park** (293-4041) has several campgrounds. Fifty-five mi. northeast via I-15 and Rte. 169, **Valley of Fire State Park** has campsites and spectacular sandstone formations.

Food

Astonishingly cheap prime rib dinners, all-you-can-eat buffets, and champagne brunches beckon high- and low-rollers alike into the casinos. In most cafeterias, buffet food is served nonstop from 11am to 10pm. Expect the "all-you-can-stomach" quality that comes from leaving food on a warming table for three hours. Cruise the Strip or roam downtown for advertised specials. The Visitors Authority (see Practical Information) keeps a reasonably up-to-date list of buffets, the best of which may be the one at **Circus Circus;** pay $5, grab a 16-inch plate, and eat everything in sight, including the chips, ha ha (4:30-11pm). Not as crowded as the bigger casinos, **El Rancho**, 2755 Las Vegas Blvd. S. (796-2222), serves a brunch buffet on weekends ($3.25; Sat.-Sun. 8am-3pm). The **Hacienda**, 3950 Las Vegas Blvd. S. (739-8911), lies a cut above comparably priced buffets, with champagne at breakfast and 12 entrees at lunch (breakfast Mon.-Fri. 7-11am, $4.75; lunch 11:30am-3pm, $6). **Caesar's Palace**, 3570 Las Vegas Blvd. S. (731-7110), is considerably more expensive than most; yet its comfortable chairs, friendly service, and especially appetizing display of fresh foodstuffs make it *the* place for a gastronomic orgy. Go for breakfast to get the most for your money. (Breakfast Mon.-Fri. 8:30-10:30am. $6.50. Lunch 11am-2:30pm; $8.)

Like inexpensive food, liquid meals come easy, operating on the same principle: casino operators figure that a tourist drawn in by cheap drinks will stay to spend tons more playing the slots or losing at cards. Drinks in most casinos cost 75¢-$1, free to those who look like they're playing. Look for 50¢ shrimp cocktail specials and offers of free champagne at casino entrances. Look like you're gambling; acting skills will stretch your wallet, but don't forget to tip that cocktail waitress in the interesting get-up.

Restaurants not owned by casinos cannot match the buffet prices, but are a nice respite for those suffering from too much chipped beef and fish croquettes. Downtown holds a number of Thai, Chinese, and Italian restaurants; cutting across the Strip, Sahara Blvd. and Flamingo Rd. also offer good food. Try the **Silver Dragon Restaurant**, 1510 E. Flamingo Rd., one block east of Maryland Pkwy., which serves great Cantonese and Szechuan meals. Their "graveyard menu" offers nocturnal nourishment. (Open daily 11:30am-5am.) Those who desire more typical Southwestern fare should visit **Mi Casa**, 2710 E. Desert Inn Rd., which offers enchiladas, strawberry *sopapillas,* and live Latin music nightly. (Open daily 11am-3am.)

Casino-Hopping and Nightlife

Casinos and their restaurants, nightclubs, and even wedding chapels stay open 24 hrs. You'll almost never see clocks or windows in a casino—the owners are afraid that players might realize it's past midnight, turn into pumpkins, and neglect to lose a nickel more. You'll quickly discern which games are suited for novices and which require more expertise, from penny slots in laundromats to baccarat games where the stakes can rise into the tens of thousands of dollars. The hotels and most casinos give first-timers "funbooks," with alluring gambling coupons that can stretch your puny $5 into $50 worth of wagering. But always remember: *in the long run, chances are you're going to lose money.* Don't bring more than you're prepared to lose cheerfully. Keep your wallet in your front pocket, and beware of the thieves who prowl casinos to nab big winnings from unwary jubilants. You can get an escort from the casino security, or leave your winnings with the cashier, to be picked up later. Seniors, favorite targets of thieves, should be especially careful. Those under 21 may or may not be able to get into the casino, depending on how lucky, or perhaps unlucky, they are.

For best results, put on your favorite loud outfit, bust out the cigar and pinky rings, and begin. The atmosphere, decor, and clientele differ from casino to casino, so gambol as you gamble. **Caesar's Palace,** 3570 Las Vegas Blvd. (731-7110), has taken the "theme" aspect of Vegas to the extreme; where other casinos have miniature, mechanized horse racing, Caesar's has chariot racing. Next door, the **Mirage,** 3400 Las Vegas Blvd. S. (791-7111), includes among its attractions Siberian white tigers and a "volcano" that erupts in fountains and flames every quarter hour from 8pm to 1am, barring bad weather. **Circus Circus,** 2880 Las Vegas Blvd. S. (734-0410), attempts to cultivate a family atmosphere, embodied by the huge clown on its marquee. While parents run to the card tables and slot machines downstairs, their children can spend 50¢ tokens upstairs on the souped-up carnival midway and enjoy the titanic, futuristic video game arcade. Two stories above the casino floor, tightrope-walkers, fire-eaters, and rather impressive acrobats perform from 11am to midnight. The **Excalibur,** 3850 Las Vegas Blvd. S. (597-7777), has a medieval England theme that may make you nostalgic for the Black Plague.

Aside from gambling, every major casino has nightly shows some featuring free performances by live bands. Caesar's Palace houses multi-storied **OMNIMAX** theaters (731-7900) with domed screens and daily shows every hour on the hour from 11am to midnight. Extra bucks will buy you a seat at a made-in-the-U.S.A. phenomenon—the Vegas spectacular. The overdone but stunning twice-nightly productions feature marvels such as waterfalls, explosions, fireworks, and casts of thousands (including animals). You can also see Broadway plays and musicals, ice revues, and individual entertainers in concert. Some "production shows" are topless; most are tasteless; they're all-American. Seeing a show from the musical stars who haunt the city, such as Charo and Wayne Netwon, costs a small fortune. To see someone such as Diana Ross or archetypal Vegasite Wayne Newton, people may fork over $35 or more. Far more reasonable are the many "revues" featuring imitations of (generally deceased) performers. In Vegas you can't turn around without bumping into an aspiring Elvis clone, or perhaps the real Elvis, pursuing anonymity in the brilliant disguise of an Elvis impersonator.

Pick up a copy of *Las Vegas Today,* which has plenty of discount coupons, show info, and up-to-date special events listings, or *What's On,* distributed by the Visitors Authority (see Practical Information). Also good are *Entertainment Today, Vegas Visitor,* and *Fun and Gaming. The Games People Play,* distributed by the Golden Nugget Hotel, explains how each casino game is played. Many casinos also offer gambling classes for novices.

Nightlife in Vegas gets rolling around midnight, and keeps going until everyone drops. The casino lounge at the **Las Vegas Hilton,** 3000 Paradise Rd. (732-5111), has a disco every night (no cover, 1-drink min.). A popular disco, **Gipsy,** 4605 Paradise Rd. (731-1919), southeast of the Strip, may look deserted at 11pm, but by 1am the medium-sized dance floor packs a mixed crowd. **Carrow's,** 1290 E. Flamingo

Rd. (796-1314), has three outdoor patios, plus plenty of people and plants. During Happy Hour (4-7pm), the filling hors d'oeuvres are free.

Liberace Museum

Fans of classical music will be delighted by the **Liberace Museum,** 1775 E. Tropicana Ave. (798-5555), devoted to the late "Mr. Showmanship." There's fur, velvet and rhinestone in combinations that boggle the rational mind. Though $6.50 might be a bit much for the privilege of sharing the experience, the proceeds go to the Liberace Foundation for the Performing and Creative Arts. (Open Mon.-Sat. 10am-5pm, Sun. 1-5pm. $5, seniors $4.50, ages 6-12 $2.)

Reno

The chance for quick money lures most tourists to Reno, the so-called "biggest little city in the world." (The **Reno Arch,** on Virginia at Commercial, which dazzles visitors with its light-bulbed city slogan, gained 1600 bulbs a few years ago.) Outnumbered only by pawn-shops and wedding chapels, casinos spill anxious crowds onto sidewalks and flower beds beneath their neon glow.

Each casino claims fame and uniqueness for its "loosest slots" or accountant-certified "highest paybacks," but the **Cal Neva,** 38 E. 2nd St. (323-1046), held the world jackpot record ($6.8 million, made in February, 1988). Most venues have live music in the evenings, the most famous of which, **Bally's,** 2500 E. 2nd St (789-2285), hosts stars like Sinatra and Liza Minnelli. Check details in the weekly freebie *Showtime.* A free shuttle runs every 40 minutes from El Dorado on Plaza St. to Bally's and every ½-hr. between Bally's and the airport (6:15am-11:45pm). Before you "stack 'em or rack 'em" (your chips, that is), you might try the "Behind the Scenes" gaming tour, which takes you to the other side of the one-way mirrors, and teaches you the rudiments of the games—the only time you'll be given chips for nothing (well, almost nothing: $5 tours leave at 12:30pm daily from the visitors center, 135 N. Sierra, 348-7788).

Tying and untying the knot has become a Reno industry, and ceremonies are available 24 hrs. a day ($20-100) at any wedding chapel near you (call 800-MARRY-US. No joke.) Those seeking less permanent love affairs should head 10 mi. east on Rte. 80 to the **New Mustang Ranch** (342-0176), the most famous legal brothel in America, serving 200,000 "clients" annually. Arrive early—it's first serve, first come. (Prices vary depending on pulchritude, duration, and type of service rendered. Why, who wants to know?) Those who seek car-nal knowledge can check out the **William F. Harrah Automobile Museum,** 10 S. Lake St. (333-9300), displaying over 500 antique cars, including models made of gold, papier mâché, and leather. (Open daily 9:30am-5:30pm. Admission $7.50, seniors $6.50, kids $2.50, under 6 free.)

For the cheapest accommodations, head to the southwestern part of town. The **Windsor Hotel,** 214 West St. (323-6171), 1½ blocks from the Greyhound station toward Virginia, has wonderfully clean hall showers and rooms, but no A/C—just fans. (Singles $17.44, with bath $22; Fri.-Sat. $26, with bath $28. Doubles $26; Fri.-Sat. $30.) **El Cortez,** 239 W. 2nd St. (322-9161), one block east of the Greyhound station, features pleasant management and great bargains. Ask for a private bath. The cheapest singles don't have A/C. (Singles and doubles $27, triples $37; off-season: $24, $33. Add $3 on weekends and holidays.) **Motel 6** has three locations in Reno, all with pools, and all about 1½ mi. from the downtown casinos: 866 N. Wells (786-9852), north of I-80 off Well Ave. exit; 1901 S. Virginia (827-0255), near Virginia Lake; 1400 Stardust St. (747-7390), north of I-80 off Keystone Ave. exit, then west on Stardust. At all three locations, under 18 stay free. (Singles $30.47, $7 each additional adult.) **Boca Basin,** just over the California line, 23 mi. west on I-80, is a safe bet for campers heading on towards San Francisco or Sacramento. (Two-week max. stay. No hookups. Free.)

The casino buffets in Reno make a diner seem expensive: to bring gamblers in, or to prevent them wandering out in search of food, hotels provide a range of all-you-can-eat places. The dining room looks like the Starship Enterprise, but **Fitzgerald's** buffet is filling and good for breakfast (7:30-11am, $3), lunch (11am-4pm, $3.50), or dinner (4-10pm, $5). **Circus Circus,** 500 N. Sierra, offers enormous quantities on plastic plates. Breakfast (6-11:30am, $2.29), brunch (noon-4pm, $3), dinner (4:30-11pm, $4). Be aware that price directly reflects quality, so have your Tums ready and remember locals eat at only *some* of the buffets. Drinks are also cheap (beer nominally priced 75¢ or free) at hotel bars, or in the casino served by dubiously-clad women.

For peaceful eating, outside the bustle of smoke-filled casinos, Reno has a varied selection of inexpensive restaurants, specializing in Basque cuisine. **Louis' Basque Corner,** 301 E. 4th St., at Evans, three blocks east of Virginia, is a local institution. A hefty $14 will buy you a terrific and spicy full-course meal, including wine, soup, and salad; $6 for an à la carte entree. (Open Mon.-Sat. 11am-2:30am, Sun. 4-11pm.) The **Santa Fe Hotel,** 235 Lake St., offers Basque dinners ($12) in a classic dining room with a 1950s atmosphere and jukebox. (Open 6:30-9pm; lunch service may be available soon.) At **The Blue Heron,** 1091 S. Virginia (786-4110), vegetarians and carnivores alike can savor delicious carrot cake ($1.50). (Open Mon.-Fri. 11am-9pm, Sat. noon-9:30pm.)

The **Chute No. 1,** 1099 S. Virginia St. (323-7825), provides the best floor to dance on (open 24 hrs.), but **Ron's Piano Bar** at 145 Hillcrest St. (829-7667), farther south on Virginia St., proves a quieter place for beer and conversation. (Open daily 11am-3am.) **Harrah's,** at Virginia and Commercial (800-648-3773), offers musical groups for a younger crowd. Gay and lesbian travelers should be aware that public displays of affection are actively ticketed and can even lead to arrests in Nevada. Even so, Reno has a fairly large community and 10 gay bars that complement its other nightlife.

Scan West Coast big-city newspapers for **gambler's specials** on bus and plane fare excursion tickets. Some include rebates and casino credits. Although the city sprawls for miles, most of the major casinos are clustered downtown along **Virginia** and **Sierra Streets,** between 2nd and 4th St. The adjacent city of **Sparks** also has several casinos along I-80. The bus station and all the hotels listed are downtown or within a 10-minute walk. Downtown Reno is compact, and its wide streets and well-lit 24-hr. activity are heavily patrolled.

The **Reno/Tahoe Visitors Center,** 135 N. Sierra (348-7788), has a friendly staff and the usual deluge of maps and brochures. Pick up the excellent *Reno/Tahoe Travel Planner.* The weekly *Showtime* lists current events and performers. (Open Mon.-Fri. 9am-5pm, Sat. 9am-2pm.) Adjacent to the chamber, **Ticket Station** sells tickets for shows (348-7403). **Cannon International Airport** (328-6400) is at 2001 East Plumb Lane and Terminal Way, on I-580 three mi. southeast of downtown. Take bus #24 on Lake Ave. near 2nd St. Most major hotels have free shuttles for their guests; taxi fare downtowon is around $8. The **Amtrak** station, on E. Commercial Row and Lake St. (329-8638 or 800-872-7245), offers one train per day to San Francisco ($58), Salt Lake City ($106), and Chicago ($202). (Open daily 8:45am-noon and 2-4:45pm.) **Greyhound,** on 155 Stevenson St. (322-2970), a half block from W. 2nd St., runs to San Francisco (14 per day, $45), Salt Lake City (4 per day, $63), and Los Angeles (10 per day, $55-60). **Gray Line Tours,** 2570 Tacchino St. (329-1147; outside NV 800-822-6009), offers bus tours to Virginia City (Mon.-Fri., 5 hr., $16) and Lake Tahoe/Virginia City (daily at 9am, 8½ hr., $35). **Reno Citifare** at 4th and Center St. (348-7433; open 24 hrs.) provides local bus service. (Fare 75¢, students 50¢, seniors and disabled 35¢.) Most routes operate from 5am to 7pm, some 24 hrs. **Lloyd's International Rent-a-Car,** 2515 Mill St. (348-4777 or 800-654-7037) rents at $25 per day, $145 per week. You must be 21 and have a credit card.

Reno's **post office** lounges at 50 S. Virginia St. (786-5523; open Mon.-Fri. 7am-5pm; general delivery Mon.-Fri. 10am-3pm). The **ZIP code is 89501.**

NEW HAMPSHIRE

New Hampshire's farmers have struggled for over two centuries with the rugged landscape, but their frustration is a hiker's release. The White Mountains dominate the central and northern regions, and nearly every part of the state identifies with some towering peak. Rising above all, Mt. Washington, the highest point in the Appalachians, presides over a view of five states and the ocean on a clear day. Besides the stony beaches of the shortest shore of any seaboard state, most of the southeastern region of the state has mutated into a suburbia of the Boston metropolis. Although the state motto and license-plate blazon "Live Free or Die," "Live Well or Die" may be more appropriate in these parts. Stern Puritan conservatism as unflinching as the profile of the Old Man in the Mountain continues to govern the state.

Practical Information

Capital: Concord.

Office of Vacation Travel, 172 Pembroke Rd., P.O. Box 856, Concord 03301 (271-2343). Open Mon.-Fri. 8am-4pm. **U.S. Forest Service,** 719 Main St., P.O. Box 638, Laconia 03247 (528-8721). Open Mon.-Fri. 8am-4:30pm. **Events and Information Hotline,** 224-2525; 800-258-3608 from New England and NY.

Help Lines: Winter Ski Conditions, 224-2525, 224-2526, or 800-258-3608 (in NY or New England). **Cross-country Conditions,** 224-6363 or 800-262-6660 (in New England). **Skimobile Conditions,** 224-4666.

Time Zone: Eastern. **Postal abbreviation:** NH

White Mountains

In the late 19th century, the White Mountains became an immensely popular summer resort for those with fat purses. Grand hotels peppered the rolling green landscape and as many as 50 trains per day chugged to the region, filling hotel rooms with tourists marveling at nature through glass. The mountains are not quite so busy or posh these days, but the valleys, forests, and gnarled granite peaks still attract travelers, recast today as hearty hikers and skiers. The mountains, especially the notches, still shun budget travelers. Affordable lodgings here are rustic at best, public transportation scarce, and weather unpredictable. If you're thinking of skirting the mountains and avoiding roadside pseudo-attractions, bring warm clothing. Though glorious and peaceful, the peaks can prove treacherous. Every year, Mt. Washington claims at least one life. The weather here is some of the worst on earth; a gorgeous day can suddenly turn into a chilling storm, wind kicking up over 100 mph and thunderclouds rumbling. The average temperature on the summit is 26.7°F, the average wind speed is 35 mph. If you fancy a Romantic retreat to nature, contact the U.S. Forest Service and Pinkham Notch Camp, two equally helpful organizations (see below). The **White Mountain Attraction Center** (745-8720), on Rte. 112 in North Woodstock east of I-93 (exit 32), can give you information on just about anything in the area. (Write P.O. Box 10, N. Woodstock 03262. Office open Sat.-Thurs. 8:30am-6pm, Fri. 8:30am-6pm; off-season Mon.-Fri. 8:30am-5pm). Smaller booths dot the White Mountains: Conway, Rte. 16; Franconia, Rte. 18; Gorham, on Rte. 2 and 16; and Lincoln, I-93. (Open late May to mid-Oct., hours depending on traffic and weather.)

The U.S. Forest Service is the main administrative body in the White Mountains. Its main **information booth** (528-8721) lies south of the range at 719 Main St., Laconia 03246. Open Mon.-Fri. 8am-4:30pm.) **Regional ranger stations,** located at important gateways to the national forest, can also answer your questions: **Amoosuc,** on Trudeau Rd. in Bethlehem, west of U.S. 3 on Rte. 302 (869-2626; open Mon.-

Fri. 8am-4:30pm); **Androscoggin,** 80 Glen Rd. in Gorham (466-2713; open Mon.-Fri. 7:30am-4:30pm); **Saco** on the Kancamangus Hwy. in Conway, 100 yd. off Rte. 16 (447-5448; open daily 8am-4:30pm); and **Pemigewasset** on Rte. 175 in Holderness (536-1310; open Mon-Fri 8am-4:30pm). The **Appalachian Mountains Club (AMC)** is a hiker's fantasy service. Information about trails and safety emanates from the AMC **Pinkham Notch Camp** (466-2727), on Rte. 16 between Jackson and Gorham (open summer daily 7am-10pm). Another excellent source is the **Crawford Notch Depot** (846-7773) on Rte. 302 in Carroll (open mid-May to Sept. daily 9am-5pm). To best use the complicated AMC network, pick up its comprehensive guidebook of offerings, cryptically called *The Guide.*

If you plan to do much hiking, invest in the invaluable *AMC White Mountain Guide,* available in most bookstores and huts, ($16). Next to hiking, bicycling offers the best way to see the mountains close up. The strenuous treks decrease in difficulty if you approach the mountains from the north, according to some bikers. Check the guide/map *New Hampshire Bicycle,* available at many information centers. Also consult **25 Bicycle Tours in New Hampshire** ($7), available in local bookstores and outdoor equipment stores. (For bike rental suggestions, see North Conway below.)

AMC accommodations proliferate in the mountains. Both the Pinkham and Crawford outposts serve as well-kept **hostels** (though Crawford has no shower facilities) and are conveniently located off the highway. The eight other **AMC huts** (spaced 1½-5½ hr. apart on the hiking trail) are accessible only by foot. During the summer these full-service facilities offer family-style breakfasts and dinners, bunks, and linen for 36 to 90 people. Reservations are strongly suggested during the summer; from October through May many of the huts operate on a caretaker basis, with cooking equipment provided. Lodging with two meals in summer can cost as much as $43 per night, but AMC members receive bargains and discounts. Since rates, lower in off-season, depend on an infinite number of variables, first consult *The Guide.*

Camping is free in a number of areas throughout the **White Mountains National Forest.** No camping is allowed above the tree line (approximately 4000 ft.), within 200 ft. of a trail, or within ¼-mi. of roads, huts, shelters, tent platforms, lakes, or streams; the same rules apply to building a wood or charcoal fire. Since these rules often change, call the U.S. Forest Service before pitching a tent. The forest service also holds 22 designated **campgrounds** (sites $8-12, bathrooms and firewood usually available). Call 528-8727 to find out which ones are closest to your destinations or make reservations (800-283-2267), especially in July and August.

While getting to the general vicinity poses little difficulty, getting around the White Mountains can be very problematic. **Concord Trailways** (228-3300 or 639-3317) runs north-south and connects Boston with Concord ($10.50), Conway ($24), and Franconia ($24). **Vermont Transit** (800-451-3292) runs buses from Boston's Peter Pan Terminal to Concord ($12.15) on the way to Vermont. Only the AMC's **shuttle service** (466-2727) does not live up to the rest of the organization's services. A morning shuttle runs from Crawford to Pinkham Notch, a Pinkham evening shuttle runs to Gorham and Randolph, and a Crawford shuttle runs out to the Lonesome Lake hut. A more complete schedule and route description is available in the ubiquitous **The Guide.** Some routes run on reservation only, so it's safest to call the service in advance. (Open early June-early Sept. Tickets about $5-11.) **Trail and Weather Information** can be obtained by calling the WMWV weather phone (447-5252). Regional **zip codes** include: Franconia, 03580, Jackson, 03846, and Gorham, 03587. The **area code** in the White Mountains is 603.

Franconia Notch

About 400 million years old, Franconia Notch in the northern White Mountains has developed some interesting wrinkles. Sheer and dramatic granite cliffs, waterfalls, endless woodlands, and one very famous rocky profile attract summer campers in droves. Before you begin your exploration of this geological wonder on I-93, ask about the Franconia Notch State Park at the **Flume Visitor's Center,** (745-8391) off Rte. 93 north of Lincoln. Their excellent free 15-minute film acquaints visitors with the landscape. (Open late May-late Oct. daily 9am-5pm.) While at the center, purchase tickets to **The Flume,** a 2-mi.-long nature walk over hills, through a covered bridge to a boardwalk above a fantastic gorge with 90-ft.-high granite cliffs. (Tickets $5.50, ages 6-12 $2.50.) You can swim at **The Basin,** a 20-ft. pothole beneath a waterfall, close to The Flume on I-93.

The westernmost of the three great notches, Franconia is best known for the **Old Man of the Mountains,** north of The Flume on the parkway. Hawthorne addressed this massive granite visage in his 1850 story "The Great Stone Face," and P.T. Barnum once offered to buy the rock. A 40-ft.-high human profile formed by three ledges of stone atop a 1200-ft. cliff, the Old Man's forehead is supported by cables and turnbuckles these days. The best view of the man, both at high noon and in the moonlight, is from **Profile Lake,** a 10-minute walk from Lafayette Place in the park. If you don't feel like making the stroll, you can also do the voyeur thing.

West of the Old Man, off I-93 exit 2, **Great Cannon Cliff,** a 1000-ft. sheer drop into the cleft between **Mount Lafayette** and **Cannon Mountain,** is not just for looking at—it takes considerable technical skill to climb the "Sticky Fingers" or the "Meat Grinder" route; the 80-passenger **Cannon Mountain Aerial Tramway** (823-5563; open Memorial Day to mid-Oct. and Nov. to mid-April daily 9am-4:30pm; tickets $7, ages 6-12 $3.50, $5.50 for one-way hikers) will do the work for you.

Myriad trails lead up into the mountains on both sides of the notch, providing excellent day hikes and spectacular views. Be prepared for severe weather, especially above 4000 ft., where trees no longer grow and rocks and crags appear aplenty. The **Lake Trail,** a relatively easy hike, winds from Lafayette Place in the park 1½ mi. to **Lonesome Lake,** where the AMC operates its westernmost summer hut (see White Mountains AMC huts above).

The **Greenleaf Trail** (2½ mi.), which starts at the Cannon Tramway parking lot, and the **Old Bridle Path** (3 mi.), which starts at Lafayette Place, are much more ambitious; both lead up to the the AMC's Greenleaf Hut near the summit of Mt. Lafayette overlooking Eagle Lake, a favorite destination for sunset photographers. From Greenleaf, you can trudge the next 7½ mi. east up and along **Garfield Ridge** to the AMC's most remote hut, the **Galehead.** Dayhikes from this base can keep you occupied for days. (Sites at the Garfield Ridge campsite $5.)

Those who find hiking anathema can take advantage of the 9 mi. of **bike paths** that begin off Rte. 3 and run through the White Mountain National Forest. After any exertion, cool off at the beach on the northern shore of **Echo Lake,** off Rte. 18 (open mid-June to late Aug.). Numerous cross-country trails run through the "Kanc," and alpine skiing rests at nearby Loon Mountain (see North Conway and skiing below).

At reasonable altitudes, you can camp at the **Lafayette Campground** (823-9513), in Franconia Notch State Park (open mid-May to mid-Oct., weather permitting; sites $14 for 2 people, $7 per extra person. If Lafayette is full, try the more suburban **Fransted Campground** (823-5675), 1 mi. south of the village and 3 mi. north of the notch. (Sites $13-15, with hookup $16, $1 per extra person, children free. Open year-round.) From Lincoln, the Kancamangus Hwy (NH Rte. 112) branches east for a scenic 35 mi. through the **Pemigewassett Wilderness** to Conway. The large basin rimmed by 4000-ft. peaks attracts many backpackers and skiers.

South of the highway, trails head into the **Sandwich Ranges,** a secluded series of lesser peaks; lesser with the exception of **Mount Chocorna,** a dramatic and steep exposed peak, and a favorite of 19th-century naturalist painters. Take your breath and drive south on Rte. 16 to Ossipee for the most breathtaking view of a breathtaking peak.

North Conway and Skiing

North Conway skirts the White Mountains along Rte. 16 and 302 and lacks the alpine grandeur of towns on the mountain range; in fact, the village, centrally located to many skiing areas, has become a tourist trap. On Rte. 16/302 dwell clothing mogul outlets like London Fog and Calvin Klein. Even humble motels charge exorbitant rates. But as the White Mountain's major city, it provides a fine base for exploration and sporting excursions.

Two **information booths** in town sit on Rte. 16, sponsored by the chamber of commerce (356-3171). Although their hours are often unreliable, they disseminate free maps of the town and names of mostly expensive accommodations in the area. The **Maple Leaf Motel,** on Rte. 16 (356-5388), has quaint cabins for reasonable rates. (Singles in fall and summer $55, off-season $34. Doubles: $65, $48.) Farther south on Rte. 16 The **Yankee Clipper** (356-5736 or 800-343-5900) offers a more urban air, an outdoor pool, and nearly identical rates.

Affordable eateries appear much more often. Sandwich and pizza places line **Main St.** (Rte. 16/302). The hotspot for the *après ski* crowd is **Jackson Square,** on Main St., on the premises of the Eastern Slope Inn, with a DJ and dancing every night. (Entrees $9.95, Thurs. special $7.95. Happy hours every weeknight 4pm-6pm. Open daily 8am-10pm.) **Studebakers,** on Rte. 16 south of town is a pseudo-50s drive-in diner. Try one of seven different varieties of the Studey-Baker stuffed potato ($2.55-4.95). (Open daily 7am-9pm, lunch at 11:30am, dinner at 5pm.)

Though a relatively cosmopolitan ski town, North Conway is perhaps proudest of its own local mountain, **Cranmore,** (356-5543 or 800-543-9206), boasting the oldest ski train in the country. On winter Wednesdays, the slopes host a ski racing series; local teams also compete in the nationally known **Mountain Meisters,** open to the public. You can ski day ($30) or night ($15). The indoor tennis courts rent for $14 per hour in summer.

The equipment stores in North Conway outdo all others in the area. **Eastern Mountain Sports,** (EMS) on Main St. (356-5433), on the premises of the Eastern Slope Inn, has free mountaineering pamphlets and excellent books on the area, including *25 Bicycle Tours in New Hampshire.* EMS offers cross-country ski rentals ($15 per day), tents, sleeping bags, and other camping equipment. (Open Sun. 9am-6pm, Mon.-Sat. 9am-9pm.) **Joe Jones,** on Main St. at Mechanic (356-9411), rents just about everything under the sun: bikes ($20 per day), alpine skis ($15), tennis rackets ($5). (Open Sun.-Wed. 9am-6pm, Thurs.-Sat. 9am-8pm.) **Joe Jones in Intervale (356-6848) rents boats, too ($10). (Open daily 9:30am-5pm) International Mt.,** on Main St. (356-7064), rents smaller accessories like snowshoes ($10 per day) and camping stoves ($5). (Open Sun.-Thurs. 8:30am-7:30pm, Fri.-Sat. 8:30-9pm.)

New Hampshire has excellent cross-country and downhill skiing throughout the area, and you might not want to limit yourself. Nowhere is it cheap, but you can cut costs with package deals or by skiing on weekdays; cross-country skiing costs less than downhill. Three nearby cross-country centers offer close to 100 mi. of trails—marked and unmarked, flat and mountain—along with rentals and lessons. For a one-day excursion on marked trails, count on $6-9 for a trail fee and $10-15 per day for rentals. **Jackson Ski Touring Foundation,** in Jackson (383-9355), 12 mi. north of North Conway, provides the quintessential New England experience, with trails winding past beaver dams, a covered bridge, and country inns. Visit **Waterville Valley X-C Ski Center** (236-8311), 13 mi. east on Rte. 49 off I-93 exit 25, and trek through wilderness trails in adjacent White Mountain National Forest. **Bretton Woods Ski Touring Center** (278-5000), 10 mi. north of Crawford Notch on Rte. 302, boasts an elaborate 50-mi. network of trails.

Not as well-known as the mega-resorts of Vermont, downhill ski centers in New Hampshire usually offer well-groomed, slightly less expensive, and equally exhilarating skiing. Skiing on weekdays enables you to beat the crowds, and the pass costs $5 less. Resorts cluster along I-93 in the west and in Mt. Washington Valley in the east. Those off I-93, collectively known as **Ski 93,** P.O. Box 517, Lincoln 03251 (745-8101), offer easier access. **Loon Mountain** (745-8111), 3 mi. east of I-93 at Lincoln, avoids overcrowding by limiting lift ticket sales, and also has a free beginners' tow (9 lifts, 41 trails). **Waterville Valley** (236-8311) offers great downhill as well as cross-country skiing (12 lifts, 53 trails). **Cannon Mountain** (823-5563; 800-552-1234 in New England), north of Franconia Notch, offers decent slopes off a large tram. For information on all Mount Washington Valley packages, contact the **Mt.**

Washington Valley Chamber of Commerce, P.O. Box 2300, North Conway 03860 (356-3171). Open Mon.-Fri 8:30am-5pm, Sat.-Sun. 10am-4pm. **Wildcat Mountain** (446-3326), in Jackson, has scenic vistas of Mt. Washington (5 lifts, 30 trails). Some of New England's best-groomed trails are at **Attitash** (800-223-7669; 603-374-2368) in Bartlett off Rte. 302 (6 lifts, 25 trails). Experts can head for **Tuckerman's Ravine,** a steep, treacherous, and dangerous glacial wall; make the spring pilgrimage and hike to the top to conquer the most challenging slope in the East.

Pinkham Notch

Ancient **Mt. Washington** rises 6082 ft. up toward the sky; trees disappear about two-thirds of the way up, and snow clings to its peak even in summertime. **Pinkham Notch,** along Rte. 16 between Gorham and Jackson, humbly hunches below it. Near Gorham in Randolph, lies the **Bowman's Base Camp AYH Hostel** (466-5130), where even the mattresses are hardy ($11, nonmembers $12; open Memorial Day-Columbus Day). The hostel sits at the foot of Lowes Path, which climbs Mt. Adams, mercifully far away from Mt. Washington's freeway-like trails. Stay at the **Madison Springs** AMC hut below the summit, and prepare for nasty weather. Catch a sensational sunrise over the Carter Range. In Gorham, you can also stay in the **Berkshire Manor,** 133 Main St. (466-9418), which has kitchen facilities. (Singles $20. Doubles $33.)

Pinkham Notch Camp, at the height of the notch, is the definitive source for local information (for this and all other AMC huts, see above), offering advice on weather and trail conditions as well as hiking guides and maps to the area. They will stress to neophyte and all other hikers the difficulty of these trails. Cases of hypothermia have been reported as late as June, and hiking accidents are common. Bring warm clothes (at least 2 sweaters). Bed and breakfast here cost $33, with dinner $43. You can also buy meals (breakfast and lunch $5, dinner $10, trail lunch $5); reservations are essential in the summer. Camping anywhere in the notch is legit as long as the site accords with regulations (see Resources: US Forest Service). A tough 4½-mi. hike leads up to the **Lakes of the Clouds** AMC hut, just 1½ mi. from Mt. Washington's summit. Because this is the most popular of the AMC's huts, reserve early. An easier 6½-mi. trail leads into the Carter Range to the **Carter Notch** AMC hut. Two trout-stocked mountain lakes repose in the area along with a maze of caves to explore. For a fabulous view of the Carter Range, hike to the **Madison Springs** AMC hut beneath the summit of Mt. Adams, off Rte. 2 between Gorham and Jefferson.

But the most challenging of the already demanding hikes is the trek to the summit. The most popular hiking trail, **Tuckerman's Ravine,** begins at the Pinkham Camp and climbs 4 mi. to steep glacial cirques. Experienced hikers in good shape can make the round-trip in a day. The less energetic can take the techno-short cut, **Mount Washington Auto Road** (466-2222), a paved and dirt road that leads motorists 8 mi. to the summit. Then they can get bumperstickers saying "This Car Climbed Mt. Washington" and cruise around impressing people. ($12 per driver, $5 per passenger, ages 5-12 $3. Road open mid-May to mid-Oct. daily 7:30am-6pm weather permitting; closes earlier before June 15 and after Labor Day.) The road begins at the **Glen House** on Rte. 16 and features a steady stream of fumes and families mid-summer. The car-less can make the guided trip with the **Stage to the Summit** ($17, ages 5-12 $10).

On the overbuilt summit, you'll find a snack bar, an information center, a museum (466-3347), and the **Mount Washington Observatory** (466-3388), where the highest wind speeds ever recorded on earth (231 mph) were registered in 1934. Closer to civilization (vertically and horizontally) the popular **Dolly Copp Campground** (466-3984), 5 mi. south of Gorham on Rte. 16, has almost 200 tent sites with bathrooms ($10) for beleaguered travelers. Near Gorham, in Randolph off Rte. 2, is the exceedingly rustic **Bowmans Base Camp AYH Hostel** (466-5130; see Pinkham above). If you long for privacy or the hum of a TV in a nearby room, stay at comfy **Berkshire Manor,** 133 Main St., Gorham (466-9418), which has kitchen facilities and a well-stocked grocery store a few mi. away. (Singles $20. Doubles $33.)

NEW JERSEY

Listen, let's get one thing straight right now: New Jersey is *not* a giant roadway, and if you ask a native what exit they're from, they have, under a new state statute, the *legal right* to belt you in the gut until you hemorrhage. Much maligned by myopic Northeasterners who never took the trouble to leave the Garden State Parkway or the New Jersey Turnpike, the state—home to one of America's finest state universities (Rutgers) and one of the world's finest universities (Princeton)—also offers hundreds of miles of beautiful boardwalked beaches. And the water is *not* polluted (at least, no more than it is anywhere else on the northeastern coast). While Cape May, Wildwood, and the tragicomic gambling mecca Atlantic City, all at the extreme southern end of the state, are the only coastal resorts listed herein, beach-loving travelers also might want to look into areas such as Asbury Park and Long Beach Island on their own.

If rep were reality, New Jersey would be an American wasteland; but it's not, and the Garden State is a fine place to visit. And yes, one of this year's assistant editors *is* from New Jersey, thank you very much.

Practical Information

Capital: Trenton.

State Division of Tourism, CN 826, Trenton 08625 (609-292-2470).

Time Zone: Eastern. **Postal Abbreviation:** NJ

Atlantic City

The riches-to-rags-to-riches tale of Atlantic City began over 50 years ago when it reigned as the monarch of resort towns. Vanderbilts and Girards graced the legendary boardwalk of the town whose opulence inspired the Depression-era board game for would-be high-rollers, *Monopoly.* Fans of the game will be thrilled to see Boardwalk and all the other places they have been overdeveloping for years. With the rise of competition from Florida resorts, however, the community chest began to close. Atlantic City landed on the luxury tax of the game board, suffering decades of decline, unemployment, and virtual abandonment.

But in 1976, state voters gave Atlantic City the chance to hop onto the proverbial "free parking" by legalizing gambling, making the game a reality. Casinos sprung up along the Boardwalk, while the owners ignored the boarded-up streets below. The excessive, superficial wealth of the casinos makes it easy to forget the dirt and the dank outside, especially since the owners make sure you never have to leave. Each velvet-soaked temple of tackiness has a dozen restaurants, entertainment, and even skyways connecting to other casinos. If the Earth's atmosphere suddenly disappeared, many dedicated gamblers would take weeks to notice. The chance to win big bucks draws all types to Atlantic City, from high-rolling millionaires to senior citizens clutching their one last chance. One-quarter of the U.S. population lives within 300 mi. of Atlantic City, and fortune-seeking pilgrims flock to its shore to toss the dice.

Practical Information

Emergency: 911.

Gambling age: 21.

Public Relations Visitors Bureau, 2308 Pacific Ave. (348-7044), conveniently located near Mississippi Ave. Open Mon.-Fri. 9am-4:30pm. Next door is the home of the Miss America Meat Market, the **Atlantic City Convention and Visitors Bureau,** 2310 Pacific Ave. (348-7100 or 800-262-7395). Open Mon.-Fri. 9am-5pm.

Bader Field Airport: 345-6402. Serves Newark only. Buses run between Bader Field and the Boardwalk.

Amtrak (800-872-7245), at Kirkman Blvd. off Michigan Ave. Follow Kirkman to its end, bear right, and follow the signs. To: New York City (1 per day, 2½ hr., $28); Philadelphia (5 per day, 1½ hr., $14); Washington, DC (1 per day, 3½ hr., $38). More connections to DC and NYC through Philly. Open Sun.-Thurs. 6am-10pm, Fri.-Sat. 6am-12:20am.

Buses: Greyhound/Trailways, 345-5403 or 344-4449. Buses every hr. to New York (2½ hr., $19) and Philadelphia (1¼ hr., $9). **New Jersey Transit,** 800-582-5946. Runs 6am-10pm. Hourly service to New York City ($21.50) and Philadelphia ($10), with connections to Ocean City ($1.50), Cape May ($3.50), and Hammonton ($3.25). Also runs along Atlantic Ave. (base fare $1). Both lines operate from **Atlantic City Municipal Bus Terminal,** Arkansas and Arctic Ave. Station and ticket offices open 24 hrs.

Post Office: Martin Luther King and Pacific Ave. (345-4212). Open Mon.-Fri. 8:30am-5pm, Sat. 10am-noon. **ZIP code:** 08401.

Area Code: 609.

Atlantic City lies just past the midway of New Jersey's coast, easily reached by train from Philadelphia and New York and accessible by the **Garden State Parkway.** Hitching is especially risky.

Gamblers' specials make bus travel a cheap, efficient way to get to Atlantic City. Many casinos will give the bearer of a bus receipt $10 in cash and sometimes a free meal. Look for deals in the yellow pages under "Bus Charters" in New Jersey, New York, Pennsylvania, Delaware, and Washington, DC. Greyhound/Trailways has same-day round-trip specials to Atlantic City.

Getting around Atlantic City is easy on foot. The casinos pack tightly together on the Boardwalk along the beach. When your winnings become too heavy to carry, you can hail a **Rolling Chair,** quite common along the Boardwalk. Though a bit of an investment ($1 per block for 2 people, 5-block min.), Atlantic City locals chat with you while they push. On the streets, catch a **jitney** ($1.25), running 24 hrs. up and down Pacific Ave., or a NJ Transit Bus ($1) covering Atlantic Ave.

Accommodations and Camping

Large, red-carpeted beachfront hotels have replaced four green houses, bumping smaller operators out of the game. A hundred bucks for a single is standard. Smaller hotels along **Pacific Avenue,** a block away from the Boardwalk, have rooms for less than $60, and rooms in Ocean City's guest houses are reasonably priced. Be sure to reserve ahead, especially on weekends. Many hotels lower their rates during the middle of the week. Winter is also slow in Atlantic City, as water temperature, gambling fervor, and hotel rates all drop significantly. Campsites closest to the action cost the most; the majority close September through April. Reserve a room or a site if you plan to visit in July or August.

Irish Pub and Inn, 164 St. James Pl. (344-9063), off the Boardwalk, directly north of Sands Casino. Clean, cheap rooms with antiques. Victorian sitting rooms open onto sprawling porch lines with large rocking chairs. Laundry in basement. Singles $25. Doubles $40, with private shower $60. Quads $60. Key deposit $5. Open Feb.-Nov.

Hotel Cassino, 28 S. Georgia Ave. (344-0747), just off Pacific Ave. Rooms well-used. Rates negotiable. Singles $30-45. Doubles $35-50. Key deposit $10. Open May-Oct.

Birch Grove Park Campground, Mill Rd. in Northfield (641-3778), about 6 mi. from Atlantic City. Attractive and relatively secluded, but still convenient. Sites $15 for 2 people, with hookup $18.

Pleasantville Campground, 408 N. Mill Rd., about 7 mi. from the casinos. 70 sites. Sites $24 for 4 people with full hookup.

Food

Each of the casinos has a wide selection of eateries intended to lure you and your wallet in. Some offer all-you-can-eat lunch or dinner buffets for $10-$12; sometimes you can catch a special for around $5. The town also provides higher quality meals in a less noxious atmosphere. Since 1946, the **White House Sub Shop,** Mississippi and Arctic Ave. (345-1564), has served world-famous subs and sandwiches. Celebrity supporters include Bill Cosby, Johnny Mathis, and Frank Sinatra, rumored to have subs flown to him while he's on tour. They also fly them to the moon. ($6-8, half-subs $3-4). (Open Mon.-Sat. 10am-midnight, Sun. 11am-midnight.) For renowned Italian food and the best pizza in town, hit **Tony's Baltimore Grille,** 2800 Atlantic Ave., at Iowa Ave. (Open daily 11am-3am. Bar open 24 hrs.) The **Inn of the Irish Pub,** 164 St. James Pl. (344-9063), serves modestly priced dishes like deep-fried crab cakes ($4.25) and Dublin beef stew ($5) amidst Irish memorabilia draped on the walls. (Open 24 hrs.) Although you may be turned off by the crowds, you can get great slices of pizza from one of the many **Three Brothers from Italy** joints on the Boardwalk. And don't forget to try custard ice-cream or saltwater taffy, two boardwalk staples.

Entertainment

Casinos

Atlantic City: America under Trump. Inside the casinos, thousands of square feet of flashing lights and plush carpet surround the milling crowds; few notice the one-way ceiling mirrors concealing big-brother gambling monitors. Figures in formalwear embody Atlantic City's more glamorous past, but T-shirt-and-jeans gamblers now outnumber their flashy cohorts. The seductive rattle of chips and snickering of slot machines never stops.

All casinos line the Boardwalk, within a dice toss of each other. The bitchinest, kitschenest of the casinos, Donald **Trump's Taj Mahal** (449-1000), commodifies a complex so expensive that missed payments threw Trump's billion-dollar empire into turmoil. Trump has two other casinos, each displaying his name in huge lights—the **Trump Castle** (441-2000) and **Trump Plaza** (441-6000). Other biggies are Bally's Park Place (340-2000), and Resorts International (344-6000). Caesar's Boardwalk Regency (348-4411), Harrah's Marina Hotel, (441-5000), and the Atlantis (344-4000), are hot clubs. Rounding out the list are the Claridge (340-3400) and Showboat (343-4000). The **Sands** (441-4000) and **TropWorld Casino** (340-4000) have extensive facilities that include golf and tennis. You may be amused by the two "moving sidewalks" that carry customers from the Boardwalk to the only two casinos without a Boardwalk entrance. Not surprisingly, these sidewalks move in only one direction.

Open nearly all the time (Mon.-Fri. 10am-4am, Sat.-Sun. 10am-6am), casinos douse you with alcohol as long as you are gambling, and many surround you with false windows and clocks to prevent you from noticing the hours slip away. To curb your almost inevitable losses, stick to the cheaper games: blackjack, slot machines, and the low bets in roulette and craps. Keep your eyes on your watch or you'll have spent four hours and four digits before you know what hit you. The gambling age of 21 is strictly enforced.

Beaches and Boardwalk

The ocean is just a few spaces away. Atlantic City squats on the northern end of long, narrow **Absecon Island,** which has 7 mi. of beaches—some pure white, some lumpy gray. The **Atlantic City Beach** is free, and often crowded. Adjacent **Ventnor City's** sands are nicer. The legendary **Boardwalk** of Atlantic City has been given over to the purveyors of the quick fix, packed with junk-food stands, arcades, souvenir shops, and carnival amusements. Take a walk, jog, or bike in Ventnor City, where the Boardwalk's development tapers off.

Cape May

Good beach along the Atlantic blesses all the towns on the Jersey shore; for developers, the trick was deciding what to do with the village next door. While Atlantic City chose gambling and cheap pizza joints, Cape May decided to accentuate different points. Century-old cottage inns stretch from shore to pedestrian mall. Tree-lined boulevards make for a nice afternoon stroll. Wherever you are in Cape May, the beach never lies more than two or three blocks away. With the highest concentration of Mayflower descendents in the nation, Cape May cultivates its image of Victorian anachronism, a whalebone corset for tourists weary in body and mind.

Tremendous pollution plagued the entire shore of New Jersey during the summer of 1988, after which the state launched a vigorous campaign to clean up the beaches. Since then, the sand at Cape May actually glistens, still dotted with some of the famous Cape May diamonds (actually quartz pebbles that glow when cut and polished). When you unroll your beach towel on a city-protected beach (off Beach Ave.), make sure you have the **beach tag** which beachgoers over 12 must wear June to September from 10am to 5pm. Pick up a tag (daily $3, weekly $8, seasonal $12) from city hall (see below) or from the beach tag vendors roaming the shore.

The **Mid-Atlantic Center for the Arts,** 1048 Washington St. (884-5404), offers a multitude of tours and activities. Pick up *This Week in Cape May* in any of the public buildings or stores for a detailed listing. (Guided walking and trolley tours $4. 2-hr. guided cruises $7.) **Cape May Light House** and **Cape May Point State Park** (884-2159), just west of town, guide tourists, not ships. Built in 1859, the lighthouse offers a magnificent ragout of the New Jersey and Delaware coasts after a 199-step climb ($3.50 adults, $1 kids).

When you're on a budget, prepare to be contented with burgers and sandwiches in Cape May, since even the bars charge $13 and up for entrees. **The Ugly Mug,** 426 Washington St., a bar/restaurant in the mall, serves 12 ugly clams for half as many dollars. (Open Mon.-Sat. 11am-2am, Sun. noon-2am. Food served until 11pm.) **Carney's,** 401 Beach Ave. (884-4424), is the self-proclaimed "best bar in town" with live bands nightly. A mug of beer costs $2, sandwiches $4. (Snack menu served 3:30-10pm, bar open until 2am.) The **Ocean View Restaurant,** at Beach and Grant Ave., offers fine fresh seafood, to the tuna $10 to $15. (Open daily 7am-10pm.) Free summer concerts enliven the town's bandstand.

Many of the well-preserved seaside mansions now take in nightly guests, although most cater to the well-heeled *New York Times* B&B set. Still, several inns with reasonable rates fly in the thick of the action. The **Hotel Clinton,** 202 Perry St. (844-3993) at Lafayette St., has decent-sized singles ($25) and doubles ($35) with shared bath. Add $5 for weekend rates. (Open mid-June to early Sept. Call 516-799-8889 for off-season reservations.) Built in 1879, **Congress Hall,** 251 Beach Dr. (884-8421), between Perry and Congress St., presents itself as a gargantuan establishment weathered by a century of use. Though the cheapest rooms do the time-warp to the early 50s, they do it in a big way, complete with private baths and a pool. (Singles $35-60. Doubles $45-70. Weekends and holidays add $10, July-Sept. $15. Open May-Sept. Call 858-0670 for off-season reservations.) **Paris Inn,** 204 Perry St. (884-8015), near Lafayette St., has old but decent rooms with private baths. (Singles $35. Doubles $45. Weekends add $10.)

Campgrounds line Rte. 9 from Atlantic City to the Cape. The two closest to town are **Cold Springs Campground,** 541 New England Rd. (884-8717; sites $13, with hookup $15), and **Cape Island Campground,** 709 Rte. 9 (884-5777; sites $21, with hookup $24).

Despite its small size and geographic isolation, Cape May is easily accessible. By car from the north, it's literally the end of the road—follow the Garden State Parkway south as far as it goes and you'll end up on Lafayette St. if you follow signs to Center City. From the south, by car, bike, or foot, take a 70-minute ferry from Lewes, DE (terminal 302-645-6313) to Cape May (886-9699; for recorded schedule info 886-2718). Summer months 14 to 15 ferries cross each day, off-season four to six. (Toll $18 for vehicle and driver, passengers $4.50, pedestrians $4, motorcyclists $13.50, bicyclists $7.) From Cape May, take bus #552 (14 per day, $1.40) from the depot to north Cape May and walk 1 mi. to the ferry.

The **Welcome Center,** 405 Lafayette St. (884-9562), provides a wagonload of friendly info about Cape May and free hotlines to inns and B&Bs. (Open Mon.-Sat. 9am-4pm.) As its name indicates, the **Chamber of Commerce and Bus Depot,** 609 Lafayette St. (884-5508), near Ocean St. across from the Acme, provides tourist info and a local stop for **New Jersey Transit** (800-582-5946; northern NJ 800-772-2222). Buses service Atlantic City ($3.50), Philadelphia ($13.75), and New York City ($26). (Terminal open July-Sept. daily 9am-8pm; off-season Mon.-Fri. 9am-8pm, Sat. 10am-8pm.) Like most legislatures, **City Hall,** 643 Washington St. (884-9525), sells beach tags required for beachgoers over 12 from June to September 10am to 5pm. Try your hand at polo at the **Village Bike Shop,** Washington and Ocean St. (884-8500), right off the mall. Also ask about the four-person tandem bike. (Open daily 6:30am-7pm. Bikes $3.50 per hr., $9 per day.)

Newark

Although Newark is the fourth-largest metropolitan region in the U.S., New Yorkers and tourists will (and should) associate New Jersey's largest city with its ever- expanding airport. With a better reputation for on-time arrivals and departures than either La Guardia or Kennedy Airport in New York, **Newark Airport** is also actually more convenient to Manhattan. For information on Newark Airport, see the Getting There section of New York City. For information on nearby **Maplewood,** see *Let's Go: Maplewood and South Orange 1992.*

Princeton

The town of Princeton slumbers peacefully 50 mi. southwest of New York City and 11 mi. north of Trenton, off Rte. 1. This quietly charming town's main attraction is Ivy League **Princeton University,** which has turned out presidents (James Madison and Woodrow Wilson), tycoons (J.P. Morgan), writers (F. Scott Fitzgerald), and movie stars (Jimmy Stewart and Brooke Shields).

Practical Information

Emergency: 911.

Princeton University Communication/Publication Office, Stanhope Hall (258-3600). Campus maps and current info, including the *Princeton Weekly Bulletin,* with a calendar of events. Open Mon.-Fri. 8:30am-4:30pm. **Orange Key Guide Service,** 73 Nassau St. (258-3603), in the back entrance of MacLean House. Free campus tours, pamphlets, and maps. One-hr. tours Mon.-Sat. at 10am, 11am, 1:30pm, and 3:30pm; Sun. at 1:30 and 3:30pm. Office open Mon.-Sat. 9am-5pm, Sun. 1-5pm. **Princeton University Telephone Information,** 258-3000. Open daily 8am-11pm.

Airport: see Newark above.

Trains: Amtrak (800-872-7245). Connects Princeton Junction, 3 mi. south of Princeton on Rte. 571, to New York City (7 per day, 1 hr., $21) and Philadelphia (10 per day, 1 hr., $17). Stops at Princeton only in the early morning and evening. Station open Mon.-Fri. 6am-8:30pm, Sat.-Sun. 7:15am-8:30pm. **New Jersey Transit** (201-460-8444, 800-772-2222 in NJ) runs 6am-midnight serving Princeton Junction. To New York City (1 hr., $9.25). Prices include a 5-min. ride on the "dinky" (no relation to NYC's mayor), a small train connecting the town and campus to the outlying station. Dinky stops at University Place across from the McCarter Theater.

Buses: New Jersey Transit, 800-772-2222. Runs 6am-midnight. Buses stop at Princeton University and Palmer Sq. Take bus #606 to Trenton (every ½-hr., $1.90 exact change). **Suburban Transit** has 3 Princeton locations: Nassau Pharmacy, 80 Nassau St. (921-7400); Cox's Store, 182 Nassau St.; and Amoco Station, in Princeton Shopping Center. To New York (every ½-hr.; $7, $13 round-trip).

Taxi: Associated Taxi Stand, 924-1222. Open Mon. 5:30am-midnight, Sat.-Sun. 7am-midnight, weekdays 6am-midnight.

Post Office: 921-9563, in Palmer Sq. behind Tiger Park. Open Mon.-Fri. 8am-4:30pm, Sat. 8:30am-12:30pm. **ZIP code:** 08542.

Area Code: 609.

Located in the green heart of the "Garden State," Princeton is within commuting distance of both New York City and Philadelphia. Driving from New York City, take the Holland Tunnel to the New Jersey Turnpike and exit at Hightstown. From Philadelphia, take I-95 north to Rte. 206, which leads to **Nassau Street,** Princeton's main strip, with shops clustered on one side and the university set back on the other. **Palmer Square,** the center of Princeton's business district, lies right off of Nassau between Witherspoon and Chambers St.

Accommodations, Food, and Entertainment

There are no budget accommodations in the town of Princeton. Budget motels clutter Rte. 1 and the environs of giant Quaker Bridge Mall, 4 mi. south of Princeton, served by local bus (see Practical Information above). The **Princeton Motor Lodge** 3520 Rte. 1 (425-2100) is 5 minutes from the campus and provides clean rooms. (Singles $28. Doubles $30.) The **Sleep-E-Hollow Motel,** 3000 U.S. 1, Lawrenceville (609-896-0900), nestles 5 mi. south of Princeton, offering beds in small, well-worn rooms. Look out for the headless horseman. (Singles $39.95. Doubles $46.95.) For more than one person, the nearby **McIntosh Inn,** U.S. 1 and Quaker Bridge Mall (609-896-3700), is reasonable. Rooms come clean, large, and user-friendly. (Singles $42. Doubles $49. Extra cot $3.)

Most of Princeton's reasonably priced restaurants line Nassau and Witherspoon St., which intersects Nassau just across from the main gates of the university. Loud and crowded **P.J.'s Pancake House,** 154 Nassau St., has old wooden tables etched with student graffiti. The clamor gives way to a quieter breakfast crowd. Good food, but most meals cost $5-7. (Open Mon.-Thurs. 7:30am-10pm, Fri. 7:30am-midnight, Sat. 8am-midnight, Sun. 8am-10pm.) A popular student hangout and bar, **The Annex,** 128½ Nassau St., seems darker and often less noisy than P.J.'s, serving Italian entrees ($5-7), as well as omelettes and sandwiches ($2-3.50). (Open Mon.-Sat. 11am-1am.) The Mexican food at **Marita's Cantina,** 138 Nassau St., is average, but the $6 all-you-can-eat lunch buffet (Mon.-Fri. 11:30am-2pm) will fuel you for days. A la carte items go for $2-5. Live bands play Thursdays. (Open daily 11am-11pm. Bar open until about 1:15am.) **Thomas Sweet's Ice Cream,** at Palmer Sq. across from the Nassau Inn, provides the perfect end to any meal. Have them blend a topping into their homemade ice cream ($2-3) or try the free sprinkles and one free topping on yogurt ($1.50-2.25). (Open Sun.-Thurs. 11am-11pm, Fri.-Sat. 11am-midnight.)

On May 17, 1955, Princeton students held one of the first pro-rock'n'roll demonstrations in the U.S., blaring Bill Haley and the Comets's "Rock Around the Clock" until 1am when the Dean woke up and told them to turn it off. For some of that distilled male Ivy League tradition, down a drink in **The Tap Room** (921-7500), in the basement of the Nassau Inn in Palmer Sq. A Princeton tradition since 1937, the pub has freshly polished wood booths with a nice patina. Lovey Williams plays guitar Fri.-Sat. nights until 12:30am, Tuesday and Thursday nights until 10:30pm. (Open Mon.-Thurs. 11:30am-10pm, Fri.-Sat. 11:30am-12:30am.) Check Princeton's *Weekly Bulletin* for the scoop on films, concerts, and special events. Students and professional actors perform at **McCarter Theater** (683-8000), on campus in the Kresge Auditorium. (Box office open Mon.-Sat. noon-5pm.)

Sights

The 2500-acre landscaped campus of Gothic Princeton University seems to stretch on forever, virtually uninterrupted by streets of any kind. The **Orange Key** (see Practical Information above) provides free tours geared toward prospective students intent on hearing the myths and legends of the nation's fourth oldest school (founded in 1746). The school's graduating classes place commemorative plaques and a patches of ivy on the outer wall of **Nassau Hall.** Completed in 1756, it stands as the colonies' largest stone edifice and Princeton's original university building; it also served as the capitol building of the original U.S. colonies for several months in the summer of 1783. The two magnificent bronze tigers represent the school's mascot. **Whig** and **Clio Hall,** named and modeled after a Greek temple, are home to the oldest college literary and debating club in the U.S. **Prospect Gardens,** a huge bed of flowers in the shape of Princeton's shield, grow particularly beautiful in the summertime.

The sculptures scattered throughout campus come from the $11 million **Putnam Collection.** The profile of one modern piece behind Nassau Hall bears a striking and comical resemblance to former President Richard M. Nixon. Picasso's *Head of a Woman* stands in front of the **University Art Museum** (258-3762). Tours of the outdoor sculptures (works by Alexander Calder, Henry Moore, Picasso, and David Smith) or of the museum's permanent indoor collection can be arranged through the university. (Open Tues.-Sat. 10am-5pm, Sun. 1-5pm. Free.)

Wildwood

Visiting Wildwood is like having a *really* greasy burger; it's fun and strangely satisfying, but you don't want to do it too often. The 2½-mi.-long Boardwalk vies with Atlantic City in tackiness, substituting legions of lusty adolescents for gamblers and mammoth roller-coasters for casinos. Wildwood is emblematic of many New Jersey beachfronts, showcasing more rides than Disney World and certainly as many balloon tosses, pizza joints, and soft-serve ice cream stands. Each of the rides cost one to seven tickets (35¢ each, 18 for $6, 36 for $11). Or you can buy an unlimited pass Monday-Friday ($10.50-12.50) from one of six booths near the rides. Two blocks inland from the Boardwalk, **Pacific Avenue** proffers restaurants, nightclubs, and theaters. For a map of the area, stop by the **Wildwood Tourist and Information Center,** on the Boardwalk (522-1407), at Schellinger Ave. (Open Mon.-Thurs. 8:30am-10pm, Fri.-Sun. 8:30am-11pm.)

The budget traveler should avoid the seafood restaurants which charge from $15 for dinner; the delis and sandwich shops lining Pacific Ave. provide a fine alternative. Try **Luigi's Famous Cheesesteaks,** 4500 Pacific Ave. at Davis (522-7644), the self-proclaimed King of Steaks, serving cheesesteaks and hoagies ($3.50). (Open Mon.-Sat. 11am-8pm.) You can get a decent slice of pizza on the Boardwalk for about $2, but for a good Italian meal in a quieter, cleaner setting check out **Rosauri's,** 3104 Pacific Ave. (522-5335), near Maple. Try the 12-in. pizza ($5.80). (Open daily 10am-7am.) The **Ocean Terrace,** 3616 Boardwalk, near the Boardwalk and Lincoln Ave. (729-0550), serves all-you-can-eat breakfasts from 8am ($4.50) and dinners from 4:30pm ($6). **Pompeo's Restaurant,** 1610 Boardwalk in N. Wildwood (522-7029), has dinner specials with soup, salad, vegetables, entree, and dessert (4:30-6pm $8; after 6pm $9) and deep-fried Chesapeake oysters ($12).

Most of the motels next to the Boardwalk fill with vacationers, but many cheaper accommodations take in students working in Wildwood for the summer. The **Rosemont Hotel,** 230 E. Glenwood Ave. (522-6204), two blocks from the beach, offers singles ($25) and doubles ($35) with shared bath. **Sea Tag Lodge,** 226 E. Glenwood Ave. (522-6484), has rooms with rates based on double occupancy ($36 with private bath). Various independently run establishments rent "apartments and rooms" which generally resemble local motels. **Trio's Apartments and Rooms,** at 221 E.

Glenwood (522-6996), has narrow rooms with shared bath for $35. (See Cape May above for the camping sites closest to Wildwood.)

Wildwood is a 40-minute drive south from Atlantic City and three hours from New York City via the Garden State Parkway. From the south, take I-95 to the Delaware Memorial Bridge, follow Rte. 49, and finally Rte. 47. **New Jersey Transit** (800-582-5946), has daily connections to Atlantic City ($3), Cape May ($1.75), and Philadelphia ($13), stopping at the Wildwood Municipal Bus Terminal, New Jersey and Oak Ave. (open daily 6:30am-10pm). **Local buses** (884-5230) cost $1.25.

The **post office** pushes paper at 3311 Atlantic Ave. (522-5421), at Oak. (Open Mon.-Fri. 9am-5pm.) Wildwood's **ZIP code** is 08260; the **area code** is 609.

NEW MEXICO

Native Americans lived within beautiful present-day New Mexico for hundreds of years before the intrusion of Spanish explorers in the 16th century, an invasion which provoked years of hostilities between the two cultures. The Pueblo revolt of 1680 drove the Spaniards out, only to lose the region again 10 years later. By the 1800s, Native Americans and Hispanics had devised a more peaceful cohabitation, but President James K. Polk's "Manifest Destiny" facilitated the American acquisition of the territory during the 1848 Mexican War. Navajo and Pueblo tribes now preserve parts of their heritage in the face of tremendous poverty. In the cities, descendants of Spanish and Mexican Americans have incorporated elements of Native American culture into their own. With new immigrants from Latin America and Asia has come a sustained invasion of North American New Age devotees, seeking heightened spirituality in the ancient Native American religions and the jaw-dropping beauty of New Mexico.

Practical Information

Capital: Santa Fe.

Tourist Information: Dept. of Economic Development, 1100 St. Francis Dr., Santa Fe 87503 (827-0291 or 800-545-2040). **Park and Recreation Division,** Villagra Bldg., P.O. Box 1147, Santa Fe 87504 (827-7465). **U.S. Forest Service,** 517 Gold Ave. SW, Albuquerque 87102 (842-3292).

Time Zone: Mountain (2 hr. behind Eastern). **Postal Abbreviation:** NM

Albuquerque

Make that left turn at Albuquerque, Doc. While Santa Fe and Taos are more artsy and laid back, Albuquerque's youthful flavor (average age 29) and relative size (pop. 493,000) give it a more cosmopolitan air. Approximately one third of New Mexico's population thrives amidst the energy of the state's only "real" city. Against the dramatic backdrop of the Sandía Mountains, Albuquerque spreads across a desert plateau. Though the town's Spanish past gave rise to touristy Old Town, the roadside architecture lining Route 66 ("I get my kicks," as the classic song goes) and the city's high-tech industry underlie Albuquerque's modern image, and the adobe campus of the University of New Mexico accentuates the town's youthful vigor.

Practical Information

Emergency: 911.

Albuquerque Convention and Visitors Bureau: 625 Silver SW (243-3696 or 800-284-2282). Free maps and the useful *Official Albuquerque Travel Guide.* Open Mon.-Fri. 8am-5pm. After hours, call for recorded events info. **Old Town Visitors Center,** 305 Romero St. at N. Plaza (243-3215). Open Mon.-Sat. 10am-5pm, Sun. 11am-5pm.

Albuquerque International Airport: Gibson St. (842-4366), south of downtown. Take bus #50 from Yale and Central downtown Mon.-Sat. 6:47am-6:05pm. Cab fare to downtown $8.

Amtrak, 314 1st St. SW (242-7816 or 800-872-7245). Open daily 9:30am-5:45pm. One train per day to Los Angeles (13 hr., $86) and Kansas City (10 hr., $146). Reservations required.

Buses: 300 2nd St. SW, 3 blocks south of Central Ave. **Greyhound/Trailways** (243-4435) and **TNM&O Coaches** go to: Oklahoma City (6 per day, $84); Denver (5 per day, $58); Phoenix (5 per day, $52); and Los Angeles (5 per day, $74).

Public Transport: Sun-Tran Transit, 601 Yale Blvd. SE (843-9200 for schedule info, Mon.-Sat. 7am-5pm). Most buses run Mon.-Sat. 6am-6pm. Pick up system maps at the transit office or the main library. Fare 75¢, ages 5-18 and seniors 25¢.

Taxi: Albuquerque Cab Co., 883-4888. Fare $2.90 the first mi., $1.40 each additional mi.

Car Rental: Rent-a-Wreck, 500 Yale Blvd. SE (256-9693). Cars with A/C from $27 per day. 150 free mi., 15¢ each additional mi. Open Mon.-Sat. 8:30am-5:30pm, Sun. 10am-5:30pm. Must be 21 with credit card.

Bike Rental: The Wilderness Center, 4900 Lomas Blvd. NE (268-6767). Mountain bikes $18 per day, $35 per weekend, $50 per week. Open Mon.-Fri. 10am-7pm, Sat. 10am-6pm, Sun. noon-5pm.

Help Lines: Rape Crisis Center, 266-7711. Open 24 hrs. **Gay and Lesbian Information Line,** 266-8041. Open daily 7am-10pm.

Post Office: 1135 Broadway NE (247-2725). Open Mon.-Fri. 8am-6pm. **ZIP code:** 87101.

Area Code: 505.

Central Avenue and the **Santa Fe railroad tracks** create four quadrants used in city addresses: Northeast Heights (NE), Southeast Heights (SE), North Valley (NW), and South Valley (SW). The all-adobe campus of the **University of New Mexico (UNM)** stretches scenically along Central Ave. NE from University Ave. to Carlisle St.

Accommodations and Camping

Central Ave., the old U.S. 66, contains the international hostel and at least three cheap motels per block. The **Albuquerque International Hostel (AAIH),** 1012 W. Central Ave. (243-6101), at 10th St., is a large adobe house with stiff, even therapeutic, mattresses and required morning chores. (Office open daily 7:30-11am and 4-10:30pm. Check out noon. $10, nonmembers $12.50. Linen $1.50. Included kitchen fee of $1 includes plenty of free food.) Most of Central Ave.'s cheap motels lie east of downtown around the university. The **De Anza Motor Lodge,** 4301 Central Ave. NE (255-1654), has bland décor but well-kept rooms, free movie channel and continental breakfast to boot. (Singles $22. Doubles $28.)

Named for the Spanish adventurer who burned some 250 Native Americans shortly after his arrival in 1540, the **Coronado State Park Campground** (867-5589), one mi. west of Bernalillo on Rte. 44, about 20 mi. north of Albuquerque on I-25, offers unique camping. Adobe shelters on the sites provide respite from the heat. The Sandía Mountains are haunting, especially beneath a full moon. Sites have toilets, showers, and drinking water. (2-week max. stay. Open daily 7am-6pm. Sites $7, with hookup $11. No reservations.) The nearby **Albuquerque West Campground,** 5739 Ouray Rd. NW (831-1912), has a swimming pool. Take I-40 west from downtown to the Coors Blvd. N. exit, or bus #15 from downtown. (Sites $13 per 2 people, each additional person $2.) Camping equipment and canoes can be rented from the friendly folks at **Mountains & Rivers,** 2320 Central Ave. SE (268-4876), across from the university. (Tents $15. Deposit required; reservations recommended. Open Mon.-Fri. 9:30am-6:30pm, Sat. 9am-5pm.)

Food and Nightlife

Downtown Albuquerque offers a myriad of excellent Mexican restaurants. The best is the **M and J Sanitary Tortilla Factory,** 403 2nd St. SW (242-4890), at Lead St. in the hot pink and blue building. Crowds appear at lunchtime. Entrees $4-6. (Open Mon.-Sat. 10am-3:30pm.)

Tasty, inexpensive food eateries border the University of New Mexico, which stretches along Central Ave. NE. **Nunzio's Pizza,** 107 Cornell Dr. SE (262-1555), has great, inexpensive pizza at $1 per huge slice. (Open Sun.-Thurs. 11am-10pm, Fri.-Sat. 11am-11pm.) "Feed your Body with Love, Light, and high VIBRA-TIONAL Food," advises **Twenty Carrots,** 2110 Central Ave. SE (242-1320). Wheatgrass smoothies ($2.25) and bulk organic food are, apparently, sufficiently vibratory. (Open Mon.-Sat. 10am-6:30pm.) The cheap homemade ice cream (one scoop 75¢) and pastries at the nearby **Hippo,** 120 Harvard Dr. SE, could turn you into one. (Open Mon.-Thurs. 7:30am-10:30pm, Fri.-Sat. 7:30am-11:30pm, Sun. 9am-9pm.)

Rub elbows with **Cowboys',** 3301 Juan Tabo Blvd. NE (296-1959), in this country bar and nightclub at the eastern end of town. Ranchers hang out here when they aren't out on the range. You can also dig in your spurs at **Caravan East,** 7605 Central Ave. NE (265-7877). (Continuous live music every night 4:30pm-2am. Cover weekends only $2-3.) Less rurally-inclined music lovers can hear rock, blues, and reggae bands over cheap beer ($1.50) at **El Ray,** 622 Central Ave. SW (242-9300), a spacious old theater transformed into a bar and nightclub. (Open 8am-2pm. Music Wed.-Mon. at 8:30pm. Cover $2-20.)

Sights

Old Town, on the western end of downtown, contains Albuquerque's Spanish plaza surrounded by restaurants and Native American art galleries. Located at the northeast corner of the intersection of Central Ave. and Rio Grande Blvd., one mi. south of I-40, Old Town provides the best place to hang out and watch tourists.

The **National Atomic Museum,** 20358 Wyoming Blvd., Kirkland Air Force Base (845-6670), tells the story of the development of the atomic bombs "Little Boy" and "Fat Man," and of the obliteration of Hiroshima and Nagasaki. *Ten Seconds that Shook the World,* an hour-long documentary on the development of the atomic bomb, is shown three times daily at 10:30am, 2pm, and 3:30pm. Access is controlled; ask at the Visitor Control Gate on Wyoming Blvd. for a visitor's museum pass. Be prepared to show *several* forms of ID. The Air Force base is several mi. southeast of downtown, just east of I-25. (Open daily 9am-5pm. Free.)

For a different feel, the **Indian Pueblo Cultural Center,** 2401 12th St. NW (843-7270), just north of I-40, provides a sensitive introduction to the nearby Pueblo reservations. The cafeteria serves authentic Pueblo food (fry-bread $1.50; open 7:30am-3:30pm) and hosts colorful Pueblo dance performances on weekends during the academic year at 11am and 2pm. (Open daily 9am-5:30pm. Admission $2.50, seniors $1.50, students $1. Take bus #36 from downtown.)

Near Albuquerque

Located at the edge of suburbia on Albuquerque's west side, **Indian Petroglyphs State Park** (897-7201) includes a trail leading through lava rocks written on by Native Americans. Take the Coors exit on I-40 north to Atrisco Rd. to reach this free attraction, or take bus #15 to Coors and transfer to bus #93. (Open daily 8am-6pm; off-season 8am-5pm. Parking $1.)

On the east side of the city, the **Sandía Peaks** rise 10,000 ft., providing a pleasant escape from Albuquerque's heat and noise. The Sandía, Spanish for "watermelon," peaks are named for the color they turn at sunset. The peaks are a short drive from Albuquerque. Take Tramway Rd. from either I-25 or I-40 to the **Sandía Peak Aerial Tramway** (298-8518) for a thrilling ride to the top of Sandía Crest, allowing you to ascend the west face of Sandía Peak and gaze out over Albuquerque, the Rio

Grande Valley, and western New Mexico. The ascent is most striking at sunset. (Operates daily 9am-10pm; Sept. 2-May 27 Thurs.-Tues. 9am-9pm, Wed. 5-9pm. Fare $9.50, seniors and students $7. 9-11am rates $8 and $6, respectively.)

A trip through the **Sandía Ski Area** makes a beautiful 58-mi., day-long driving loop. Take I-40 east up Tijeras Canyon 17 mi. and turn north onto Rte. 44, which winds through lovely piñon pine, oak, ponderosa pine, and spruce forests. Rte. 44 descends 18 mi. to Bernalillo, through a gorgeous canyon. A seven-mi. toll-road (Rte. 536) leads to the summit of **Sandía Crest**, and a dazzling ridge hike covers the 1½ mi. separating the crest and **Sandía Peak.** Rangers offer guided hikes on Saturdays in both summer and winter. Make reservations for the challenging winter snowshoe hikes (242-9052). In the summer, hiking and mountain-biking trails are open to the public during specific hours; call for complete hours, prices, and costs for lifts up the mountain to the trails.

Also, see the entry on **Riverbend Hot Springs,** one of the best AYH hostels around, in the Southern New Mexico section. The hostel isn't extremely close to Albequerque, but it is so nice many travelers use it as a base of exploration for much of the state.

Gila Cliff Dwellings National Monument

While most of the civilized world flocks to the Grand Canyon or Yellowstone, the discerning tourist always searches for that rare place with great hiking and profound scenery innocent of family tenderfoots. The Gila Cliff Dwellings (505-536-9461) are such a place. Accessible only by a 44-mi. drive on State Hwy. 15 from Silver City, in the southwest part of the state, the drive to the park winds up and down mountains to the canyon of the Gila River; deer play along the scenic drive. As if the drive weren't enough, at the end of the trail are the Gila Cliff Dwellings, named not for their creators (Pueblos) but the river which flows nearby. Built over 700 years ago, the remarkably well-preserved dwellings have been protected from erosion by overhanging caves. The one mi. round-trip hike to the dwellings moves quickly and provides plenty of photograph opportunities. The surrounding **Gila National Forest** provides excellent hiking and backcountry camping; for maps or info head to the **visitors center,** at the end of Hwy. 15, one mi. from the dwellings, or write to the district ranger at Rte. 11, Box 100, Silver City, NM 83061. Camping throughout the national forest is free. (Visitors center open daily 8am-5pm; cliff dwellings daily 8am-6pm, off-season 9am-4pm.)

When you tire of camping, **Silver City** provides a nice, more urban stop. The city grew in the late 1800s as (surprise, surprise) a mining town; several large open pits still surround the city. Silver City was also hole to fabled outlaw and Billy Joel musical subject Billy the Kid. The nearby ghost town of **Pinos Allos** was less fortunate than Silver City; the town's only modern residents are deer and birds. In Silver City, stay at the excellent **Carter House (AYH),** 101 New Cooper St. (505-388-5485). Owners Lucy and Jim Nolan make it a point of pride to ensure your stay is enjoyable. The hostel has separate dorm-style rooms, a kitchen, and laundry facilities; the upstairs is a B&B. Check-in is officially 5-9pm; if you're going to be later than 9, call ahead. ($10, nonmembers $13. B&B doubles from $50.)

Santa Fe

Santa Fe is more of a mood than a city. Coming to New Mexico's capital and visiting its museums and historic town plaza will tell you much less about the town than a casual *paseo* down Camon Road, the local artists' turf. Santa Fe's multicultural population and its laws demanding all downtown buildings be in 17th-century adobe-style (and painted in one of 23 approved shades of brown) provide the perfect backdrop for the city's laid-back *zeitgeist*. This legendary spirit has attracted scores of artists to work and live amongst the city's earth-toned beauty and its mountainous backdrop. In the summer, when the town is besieged by tourists, the locals can adopt an attitude, but most visitors will only encounter a wealth of beauty and relaxation.

Practical Information

Emergency: 911.

Visitor Information: Chamber of Commerce, 333 Montezuma at Guadalupe (983-7317 or 800-528-5369). Open Mon.-Fri. 8am-5pm. **Information booth** in the First National Bank building on the west side of the plaza. Open daily June-Aug. Another booth inside the lobby of the **Santa Fe Convention Center,** 201 W. Marcy. Open Mon.-Fri. 8am-5pm. **National Park Service Southwest Regional Office,** 1100 Old Santa Fe Trail (988-6340). Info on regional camping and sights. Open Mon.-Fri. 8am-4:30pm.

Greyhound/Trailways: 858 St. Michael's Dr. (471-0008). To: Denver (via Raton, NM; 4 per day; $55); Taos (2 per day, 1½ hr., $12.50); Albuquerque (5 per day, 1½ hr., $10.40).

Public Transport: Shuttlejack, 982-4311. Runs from the Albuquerque ($20) and Santa Fe airports; also goes to the opera ($6 round trip).

Gray Line Tours: 471-9200 or 983-9491. Free pickup from downtown hotels. Tours Mon.-Sat. to: Taos and Taos Pueblo (at 9am, $45); Bandelier, Los Alamos, and San Ildefonso (at 1pm, $35); around Santa Fe (at 9:30am and 1pm, 3 hr., $15). Also operates the Roadrunner, a sight-seeing trolley around Old Santa Fe leaving from the plaza at Lincoln and Palace (5 per day; 1½ hr.; $6, under 12 $3).

Taxi: Village Cab Co, 982-9990. Coupons for a 45% discount on taxi fare available free from the public library, behind the Palace of the Governors, and at the hostel. Open 24 hrs.

New Age Referral Service: 984-0878. Info clearinghouse for holistic healing services and alternative modes of thought.

Post Office: in the Montoya Office Bldg. S. Federal Pl., (988-6351), next to the Federal Courthouse. Open Mon.-Fri. 8:30am-5:30pm, Sat. 8:30am-noon. **ZIP code:** 87501.

Area Code: 505.

Except for a cluster of museums southeast of the city center, most restaurants and important sights in Santa Fe cluster within a few blocks of the downtown plaza and inside the loop formed by the circular **Paseo de Peralta. Santa Fe Detours** (983-6565) offers 2½-hour walking tours of the city (daily at 9:30am and 1:30pm, $10) that leave from the La Fonda Hotel, on the corner of the plaza. Because the narrow streets make driving troublesome, park your car and hit the pavement. You'll find brown adobe parking lots behind Santa Fe Village, near Sena Plaza, and one block east of the Federal Courthouse near the plaza. Parking is available at two-hour meters on some streets.

Accommodations and Camping

Hotels become swamped with requests as early as May for **Fiesta de Santa Fe** week in early September and **Indian Market** the third week of August; make reservations or plan on sleeping in the street. At other times, look around the **Cerrillos Road** area for the best prices. At many of the less expensive adobe motels, bargaining is acceptable. The beautiful adobe **Santa Fe Hostel (AAIH),** 1412 Cerrillos Rd. (988-1153), one mi. from the adobe bus station, and two mi. from the adobe plaza, has a kitchen, library, and very large dorm-style adobe beds. ($9, nonmembers $12. Linen $2. $1 kitchen fee includes lots of free adobe. B&B rooms $25-30.)

To camp around Santa Fe, you'll need a car. Several miles out of town, **Santa Fe National Forest** (988-6940) has numerous campsites as well as free backcountry camping in the beautiful Sangre de Cristo Mountains. **New Mexico Parks and Recreation** (827-7465) operates the following free campgrounds on Rte. 475 northeast of Santa Fe from May through October (sites with hookup $4-6): **Black Canyon** (8 mi. away); **Big Tesuque** (12 mi.); and **Aspen Basin** (15 mi.).

Food

Santa Fe serves spicy Mexican food on blue corn tortillas as a staple. The few vegetarian restaurants are expensive, catering to an upscale crowd. The better restaurants near the plaza dish up their chilis to a mixture of government employees, well-heeled tourists, and local artistic types. Because many serve only breakfast and lunch, you also should look for inexpensive meals along **Cerrillos Road** and **St. Michael's Drive** south of downtown. One little-known fact: because it has served the local Native American vendors for decades, the **Woolworth's** on the plaza actually serves a mean bowl of chili ($2.75).

San Francisco Street Bar & Grill, 114 W. San Francisco St. (982-2044), 1 block from the plaza. Excellent sandwiches and the best pasta salad ($6) in town. Open daily 11am-11pm.

Tomasita's Santa Fe Station, 500 S. Guadalupe (983-5721), near downtown. Locals and tourists line up for their blue corn tortillas and fiery green chili dishes ($4.50-5). Indoor and outdoor seating. Open Mon.-Sat. 11am-10pm.

Josie's, 225 E. Marcy St. (983-5311), in a converted house. Pronounce the "J" in the name like an "H." Family-run for 23 years. Incredible Mexican-style lunches and multifarious mouthwatering desserts worth the 20-min. wait. Specials $4-6. Open Mon.-Fri. 11am-4pm.

The Burrito Company, 111 Washington Ave. (982-4454). Excellent Mexican food at quite reasonable prices. Burrito plates $2.75-4. Open Mon.-Sat. 7:30am-7pm, Sun. 11am-5pm.

Tortilla Flats, 3139 Cerrillos Rd. (471-8685). Frighteningly bland family atmosphere belies the Mexican masterpieces ($6-8). Breakfasts ($3-5), *huevos rancheros* ($4.65). Open daily 7am-10pm; winter Sun.-Thurs. 7am-9pm, Fri.-Sat. 7am-10pm.

Upper Crust Pizza, 329 E. Old Santa Fe Trail (983-4140). Practically the only downtown restaurant open in the evening. Thick, chewy 10-incher with whole-wheat crust ($5). Open Mon.-Sat. 11am-10pm, Sun. noon-10pm.

Sights

Since 1609, **Plaza de Santa Fe** has held religious ceremonies, military gatherings, markets, cockfights, and public punishments. The city also provided a stop on two important trails: the **Santa Fe Trail** from Independence, MO, and **El Camino Real** from Mexico City. The plaza is a good starting point for exploring the city's museums, sanctuaries, and galleries.

Since the following four museums are commonly owned, their hours are identical and a two-day pass bought at one admits you to all. (Open March-Dec. daily 10am-5pm; Jan.-Feb. Tues.-Sun. 10am-5pm. $3.50, under 16 free. Two-day passes $6, kids $2.50.) The **Palace of the Governors** (827-6483), the oldest public building in the U.S., on the north side of the plaza, was the seat of seven successive governments after its construction in 1610. The *hacienda*-style palace is now a museum with exhibits on Native Ameican, Southwestern, and New-Mexican history. To buy Native Ameican crafts or jewelry, check out the displays spread out in front of the Governor's Palace each day by artists from the surrounding pueblos. Their wares are often cheaper and of better quality than those found in the "Indian Crafts" stores around town.

Across Lincoln St., on the northwest corner of the plaza, lies the **Museum of Fine Arts** (827-4455), a large, undulating, adobe building with thick, cool walls illuminated by sudden shafts of sunlight. Exhibits include works by major Southwestern artists, including Georgia O'Keeffe and Edward Weston, and an amazing collection of 20th-century Native American art.

Two other museums lie southeast of town on **Camiro Lejo,** just off Old Santa Fe Trail. The **Museum of International Folk Art,** 705 Camiro Lejo (827-8350), two mi. south of the plaza, houses the Girard Collection of over 100,000 works of folk art from around the world. Amazingly vibrant but unbelievably jumbled, the collection is incomprehensible without the gallery guide handout. In the nearby **Museum of American Indian Arts and Culture,** photographs and artifacts unveil a multifaceted Native Ameican tradition.

About five blocks southeast of the Plaza lies the **San Miguel Mission,** on the corner of DeVargas and the Old Santa Fe Trail. Built in 1710, the adobe mission itself is the oldest functioning church in the U.S. Inside, glass windows at the altar look down upon the original "altar" built by Native Americans. (Open Mon.-Sat. 9am-4:30pm, Sun. 1-4:30pm. Free.) Just down DeVargas St. is the adobe **Oldest House** in the U.S. (983-3883), dating from c. 1200 AD. Built by the Pueblos, the house contains the remains of a certain Spaniard named Hidalgo, who allegedly bought some love potion from a woman who resided here. Apparently he started kissing everything in sight and was beheaded several days later. (Open Mon.-Sat. Love Potion #9am-5pm. Free.)

Entertainment and Events

With numerous musical and theatrical productions, arts and crafts shows, and Native Ameican ceremonies, Santa Fe offers rich entertainment year-round. Fairs, rodeos, and tennis tournaments complement the world-famous musicians who often play in Santa Fe's clubs and the active theater scene. For info, check *Pasatiempo* magazine, a supplement to the Friday issue of the *Santa Fe New Mexican.*

Don Diego De Vargas's peaceful reconquest of New Mexico in 1692 marked the end of the 12-year Pueblo Rebellion, now celebrated in the traditional three-day **Fiesta de Santa Fe** (988-7575). Held in early September, the celebration reaches its height with the burning of the 40-ft. *papier-mâché* Zozobra (Old Man Gloom). Festivities include street dancing, processions, and political satires. Most events are free. The *New Mexican* publishes a guide and schedule for the fiesta's events.

The **Santa Fe Chamber Music Festival** (983-2075) celebrates the works of great baroque, classical, and 20th-century composers. Tickets are not easily available. (Performances July to mid-Aug. Sun.-Mon. and Thurs.-Fri. in the St. Francis Auditorium of the Museum of Fine Arts. Tickets from $6-30.) The **Santa Fe Opera,** P.O. Box 2048 (982-3855), seven mi. north of Santa Fe on Rte. 84, performs in the open, so bring a blanket. The downtown box office is at Galisteo News and Ticket Center, 201 Galisteo St. (984-1316; open Mon.-Sat. 10am-4pm). Standing-room only tickets can be purchased for $5. (Performances July-Aug. All shows begin at 9pm.) **Shuttlejack** (982-4311) runs a bus from downtown Santa Fe to the opera before each performance.

In August, the nation's largest and most impressive **Indian Market** floods the plaza. Native Ameican tribes from all over the U.S. participate in dancing as well as over 500 exhibits of fine arts and crafts. The **Southwestern Association on Indian Affairs** (983-5220) has more info.

At night, gung-ho rock fans carouse at the always-hopping **Club West,** 213 W. Alameda (982-0099; cover $5). More subdued revelers relax at the **El Farol,** 808 Canyon Rd. (983-9912), which features excellent up-and-coming rock and R&B musicians. Gay nightlife centers at the **Cargo,** 519 Cerrillos Rd. (989-8790).

Near Santa Fe

Pecos National Monument, located in the hill country 25 mi. southeast of Santa Fe on I-25 and Rte. 63, features ruins of a pueblo and Spanish mission church. The small monument includes an easy one-mi. hike through various archeological sites. Especially notable are Pecos's renovated *kivas*—underground ceremonial chambers used in Pueblo rituals—built after the Rebellion of 1680. Off-limits at other ruins, these kivas are open to the public. (Open daily sunrise-sunset. $1.) The monument's **visitors center** has a small but informative museum and a 10-min. introductory film shown every half hour. (Open daily 8am-6pm; Sept. 2-May 27 8am-5pm. Free.) Greyhound sends early-morning and late-evening buses daily from Santa Fe to the town of Pecos, two mi. north of the monument. Use the campsites, or simply pitch a tent in the backcountry of in the **Santa Fe National Forest,** six mi. north on Rte. 63 (see Santa Fe Accommodations above).

Bandelier National Monument, 40 mi. northwest of Santa Fe (take U.S. 285 to Rte. 4), features some of the most amazing pueblo and cliff dwellings in the state (accessible by 50 mi. of hiking trails), as well as 50 sq. mi. of dramatic mesas and tumbling canyons. The most accessible of these is **Frijoles Canyon,** site of the **visitors center** (672-3861; open daily 8am-6pm, winter 8am-4:30pm). A five-mi. hike from the parking lot to the Rio Grande descends 600 ft. to the mouth of the canyon, past two waterfalls and fascinating mountain scenery. The **Stone Lions Shrine** (12-mi., 8-hr. round-trip from the visitors center), sacred to the Anasazi, features two stone statues of crouching mountain lions. The trail also leads past the unexcavated Yapashi Pueblo. A two-day, 20-mi. hike leads from the visitors center past the stone lions to **Painted Cave,** decorated with over 50 Anasazi pictographs, and to the Rio Grande. Both hikes are quite strenuous. Free permits are required for backcountry hiking and camping; pick up a topographical map ($6) of the monument lands at the visitors center. A less taxing self-guided one-hour tour takes you through a pueblo and past some cliff dwellings near the visitors center. You can camp at **Juniper Campground,** ¼ mi. off Rte. 4 at the entrance to the monument. (Sites $6.) Park rangers conduct evening campfire programs at 8:45pm. (Park entrance fee $5 per vehicle.)

Los Alamos, 10 mi. north of Bandelier on NM Loop 4, stands in stark contrast to nearby towns such as Santa Fe, Taos, or Española. The U.S. government selected Los Alamos, a small mountain village at the outset of World War II, as the site of a top-secret nuclear weapons development program; today, nuclear research continues at the **Los Alamos Scientific Laboratory.** The facility perches eerily atop several mesas connected by highway bridges over deep gorges, supporting a community with more PhDs per capita than any other city in the U.S. The public may visit the **Bradbury Museum of Science,** Diamond Dr., for exhibits on the Manhattan Project, the strategic nuclear balance, and the technical processes of nuclear weapons testing and verification. (Open Tues.-Fri. 9am-5pm, Sat.-Mon. 1-5pm. Free.) The **Los Alamos County Historical Museum,** Central Ave. (662-6272), details life in the 1940s, when Los Alamos was a government-created "secret city." (Open in summer Mon.-Fri. 9am-6pm, Sat. 10am-4pm, Sun. 1-4pm.)

Southern New Mexico

Carlsbad Caverns National Park

Imagine the surprise of the first Europeans wandering through southeastern New Mexico when thousands of bats began swarming from nowhere at dusk. The legendary bat population of Carlsbad (a staggering 250,000) is responsible not only for its discovery, when curious frontiersman tracked the bats to their home, but also its exploration. Miners first began mapping the cave in search of bat guano, an excellent fertilizer found in 100-ft. deposits in the cave. By 1930, the caverns had been designated a national park and herds of tourists began flocking to this desolate region. The Caverns' vast underground museum of unusual geological formations is truly breathtaking and well worth the trek off the beaten path.

Today the **visitors center** (505-785-2232 or 785-2107) has replaced dung-mining with a restaurant, gift shop, info desk, 24-hr. info recording, and lockers (25-50¢). For another 50¢ you can rent a small radio that transmits a guided tour. (Open May 27-Sept. 2 daily 8am-7pm; off-season daily 8am-5:30pm.) There are two ways to see the caverns. Those with strong knees and solid shoes can take the "blue tour," traveling by foot down a steep (but paved) three-mi. descent. If you think you can make it, absolutely take this tour—it winds dramatically from the natural entrance 750 ft. downwards, giving the best sense of the depth and extent of the caverns. The "red tour" follows an easier, shorter route, descending from the visitors center by elevator. Most of the trail is wheelchair-accessible, and both tours are self-guided.

Almost all visitors return to the surface by elevator, the last of which leaves a half-hour before the visitors center closes. Tourists should give thanks for the elevators; your 1920s counterparts either had to walk back up or ride in a bucket otherwise reserved for bat guano. (Tours June-Aug. 8:30am-5pm (red), 8:30am-3:30pm (blue); Sept.-May 8:30am-3:30pm (red), 8:30am-2pm (blue). $5, over 62 and ages 6-15 $3.)

The undeveloped **New Cave** (785-2232) offers tours May 27 to September 2 daily at 9am and 12:30pm; in off-season weekends only. Two-hour, 1¼-mi. flashlight tours traverse difficult and slippery terrain; there are no paved trails or handrails. Even getting to the cave takes some energy, or better yet, a car: the parking lot is 23 mi. down a dirt road from the Carlsbad Caverns Visitors Center (there is no transportation from the visitors center or from White's City) and the cave entrance is still a steep, strenuous ½ mi. from the lot. Make reservations at least two weeks in advance; the park limits the number of persons allowed inside each day. Bring a flashlight. (Tours $6, ages 6-15 $3. Under 6 not admitted; Golden Eagle passes not valid.)

The nightly flight of the caverns' bats is open to public viewing; the **Bat Flight Program** takes place in the amphitheater of the natural entrance to the cave just before sundown nightly from May to October. Free guano samples.

No camping is permitted in Carlsbad Caverns National Park. The **Carlsbad Caverns International Hostel** (785-2291) in White's City is easily accesssible by bus (3 per day from El Paso and Carlsbad). Spacious six-bed rooms include bathroom, kitchen, TV, pool and spa. Modern conveniences such as A/C, stove, and TV may not be functional; to stay overnight bring insect repellent and plan on eating out. Check in at the visitors lobby across the street. (Members $10, nonmembers $15. Linens $2. Open 24 hrs.) The privately run (and usually overrun) **Park Entrance Campground** (785-2291; ask to be connected), in White's City, is just outside the park entrance. (Sites $15 for 1-6 people; pay at the visitors lobby.) The campground provides water, showers, restrooms, and pool. Find cheap beds at the Carlsbad **Motel 6,** 3824 National Parks Hwy. (885-0011). In summer, make reservations at least one month early. (Singles $27. Doubles $33.) Several more inexpensive motels lie farther down the road. Additional campsites are available at nearby Guadalupe Mountains National Park (see Texas).

The tiny, rather tacky town called **White's City,** on U.S. 62/80, serves as the access point to the caverns. White's City is 20 mi. southeast of the town of Carlsbad, seven mi. from the caverns along steep, winding mountain roads. Because flash floods occasionally close roads, call ahead. From Las Cruces on I-25, take U.S. 82 east to Alamogordo, crossing the Sacramento Mountains; then take U.S. 285 south to Carlsbad, a trip of 213 mi. in all. From El Paso, TX, also on I-25, take U.S. 62/180 east 150 mi., passing Guadalupe Mountains National Park, which is 40 mi. southwest of White's City. Greyhound, in cooperation with **TNM&O Coaches** (887-1108), runs three buses a day from El Paso ($25, $47.50 round-trip) or Carlsbad ($5.75 round-trip) to White's City. Two of these routes have White's City only as a flag stop. From White's City, you can take the overpriced **Carlsbad Cavern Coaches** to the visitors center ($14 round-trip for 1-4 people); buy tickets in the White's City Gift Shop where Greyhound drops you off. The post office, located just next to the Best Western Visitor's Center, is open Mon.-Fri. 8am-noon and 1-5pm. The **area code** is 505.

Truth or Consequences

The important thing about T or C for the average traveler isn't *what* it is so much as *where* it is. Smack dab in the middle of Billy the Kid country, T or C provides a fantastic base for exploring the diverse attractions of this "Wild West" area. T or C draws budget travelers with the Riverbend Hot Springs Hostel, 100 Austin St. (505-894-6183). Located on the banks of the Rio Grande, with hot outdoor mineral baths, Apache tepee sleep quarters ($6 per night), nearby Turleback Mountain, and sportsperson's paradise Elephant Butte Lake—a stay at Riverbend is a fulfilling vacation all by itself. Riverbend also has more traditional hostel sleeping accommodations ($9.50), as well as private apartments. Ask Sylvia, the hostel's friendly and concerned proprietor, for directions to area attractions: Geronimo Springs Museum, Bosque del Apache Wildlife Refuge, "Reach for the Stars" Space Center, Monticello Box Canyon, and the Mescalero Apache Reservation. She also has discounts for local movies, museums, bowling, food and bike rentals.

Taos

Perched in a beautiful valley between the Sangre de Cristo mountains and the canyon gouged by the Rio Grande, Taos first attracted Native Ameican tribes; still-vital pueblos are scattered throughout the valley. Spanish missionaries came later in a hopeless attempt to convert the Native Americans to Christianity. The 20th century saw the town invaded by dozens of artists, such as Georgia O'Keeffe and Ernest Blumenschein, captivated by Taos's untainted beauty. Aspiring artists still flock to the city, accompanied by athletes anxious to ski or hike the nearby mountains or brave the whitewaters of the Rio Grande. Taos rocks the haos.

Practical Information

Emergency: Police, 758-2216. **Ambulance,** 758-1911.

Visitor Information: Chamber of Commerce, Paseo del Pueblo Sur (Rte. 68) (758-3873 or 800-732-8267), just south of McDonald's. Open Mon.-Fri. 9am-6pm, Sat.-Sun. 9am-5pm. **Information booth** (no phone) in the center of the plaza. Open Mon.-Sat. 9am-4pm. Pick up maps and tourist literature from either.

Taos Municipal Airport: 758-4995, northwest of town off Hwy. 64.

Greyhound/Trailways: Paseo del Pueblo Sur (Rte. 68) (758-1144), about 1 mi. south of Taos at Rte. 68 and 64 East. To Albuquerque (2 per day, $20) and Denver (2 per day, $50).

Public Transport: Pride of Taos Trolley, 758-8340. Serves several hotels and motels as well as the town plaza and Taos Pueblo. Schedules available in the plaza, the chamber of commerce, and most lodgings. Operates daily 7am-6pm. Variable fare depending on destination.

Taxi: Faust's Transportation, 758-3410 or 800-345-3738. Operates 7am-10pm.

Help Line: Rape Crisis, 758-2910. Open 24 hrs.

Post Office: 318 Paseo Del Pueblo Norte (Rte. 68) (758-2081), ¼ mi. north of the plaza. Open Mon.-Fri. 8:30am-5pm. **ZIP code:** 87571.

Area Code: 505.

Drivers should park on **Placitas Road,** one block west of the plaza, or at the Park-and-Ride lots along Rte. 68 at Safeway and Fox Photo.

Accommodations and Camping

The gorgeous little **Plum Tree Hostel (AYH)** (758-4696 or 800-678-7586), on Rte. 68, 15 mi. south of Taos in Pilar, hunkers down next to the Rio Grande. Though angling more for the B&B crowd (hot-tub and massage $40), the manager still organizes river rafting in summer and leads free hikes into the surrounding mountains every Monday when enough guests are interested. Because the hostel is a flag stop on the bus route between Santa Fe and Taos, getting in and out of town isn't a problem. (Office open daily 7:30am-10pm. $8, nonmembers $11. Linen $2.) Named for its proximity to Taos Ski Valley, the **Abominable Snowmansion Hostel (AYH)** (776-8298) has been spotted in Arroyo Seco, a tiny town 10 mi. northeast of Taos on Rte. 150. The friendly, young hosts keep an exotic menagerie including a llama and a parrot. Guests may sleep in dorm rooms, bunk houses, or even a teepee. (Office open daily 8-10am and 4-8pm. Flexible 11pm curfew. $8.50, nonmembers $10.50; in winter $18.50 and $28. Breakfast included.) Hotel rooms are expensive in Taos.

The cheapest rent at the **Taos Motel** (758-2524 or 800-323-6009), on Rte. 68, three mi. south of the plaza. (Singles $32. Doubles $37.)

Camping around Taos is easy for those with a car. Up in the mountains on wooded Rte. 64, 20 mi. east of Taos, the **Kit Carson National Forest** operates three campgrounds. Two are free but have no hookups or running water; look for campers and tents and pull off the road at a designated site. **La Sombra**, also on this road, has running water. (Sites $5.) An additional six free campgrounds line the road to Taos Ski Valley. No permit is required for backcountry camping in the national forest. For more info, including maps of area campgrounds, contact the **forest service office** (758-6200; open Mon.-Fri. 8am-5pm, Sat. 8am-4:30pm). On Rte. 64 west of town, next to the awesome **Rio Grande Gorge Bridge** (758-8851), is a campground operated by the Bureau of Land Management. (Sites with water and porta-potty $7. Porta-visitors center open daily 8am-5pm.)

Food

The **Apple Tree Restaurant,** 123 Bent St. (758-1900), two blocks north of the plaza, serves up some of the best New Mexican and vegetarian food in the state. Dinner ($7-13) includes a huge entree (swimming in melted cheese and liberally garnished with chilis), homemade bread, and soup or salad. (Open daily 8am-9:30pm.) **Michael's Kitchen,** 304 N. Pueblo Rd. (758-4178), makes mainstream munchies such as donuts, sandwiches ($4), and great apple pie (95¢). (Open daily 7am-8:30pm.) Local sheriff's deputies and late night snackers frequent the **El Pueblo Cafe** (758-2053), located on N. Pueblo, on the east side of the road about ½-mi. north of the plaza. The cafe serves standard Tex-Mex fare ($4-6) and cheap breakfasts ($2-5). (Open Sun.-Thurs. 6am-midnight, Fri.-Sat. 6am-4am.) In the rear of **Amigo's Natural Foods,** 326 Pueblo Rd. (758-8493), across from Jack Donner's, sits a small but holistic deli serving such politically and nutritionally correct dishes as a not-so-spicy tofu on many-grained bread ($2.75). (Open daily 11am-5pm.) For other cheap eats, check out the pizza and fast-food places on the strip south of the plaza.

Sights and Activities

The spectacle of the Taos area has inspired artists since the days when the Pueblo exclusively inhabited this land. Many "early" Taos paintings hang at the **Harwood Foundation's Museum,** 238 Ledoux St. (758-3063), off Placitas Rd. (Open Mon.-Fri. noon-5pm, Sat. 10am-4pm. Free.) The plaza features other galleries with works by notable locals such as R.C. Gorman, as do **Kit Carson Road, Ledoux Street,** and **El Prado,** a village just north of Taos. Taos' galleries range from high-quality operations of international renown to upscale curio shops. In early October, the **Taos Arts Festival** celebrates local art.

Taos artists love rendering the **Mission of St. Francis of Assisi** (758-2754), patron saint of New Mexico. The mission has a "miraculous" painting that changes into a shadowy figure of Christ when the lights go out. (Open Mon.-Sat. 10am-noon and 1-4pm.) Exhibits of Native Ameican art, including a collection of beautiful black-on-black pottery, grace the **Millicent Rogers Museum** (758-2462), north of El Prado St., four mi. north of Taos off Hwy. 522. (Open daily 9am-5pm; Nov.-April Tues.-Sun. 9am-4pm. $3, seniors $2, kids $1, families $6.)

Remarkable for its five-story adobes, pink and white mission church, and striking silhouette, the vibrant community of **Taos Pueblo** (758-9593) unfortunately charges visitors dearly to look around. Much of the pueblo also remains off-limits to visitors; if this is the only one you will see, make the trip—otherwise, skip it. (Open daily 9am-5pm. $5 per car, $2 per pedestrian. Camera permit $5, sketch permit $10, painting permit $15.) Feast days highlight beautiful tribal dances; San Gerónimo's Feast Days (Sept. 29-30) also feature a fair and races. Contact the tribal office (758-8626) for schedules of dances and other info. The less-visited **Picuris Pueblo** lies 20 mi. south of Taos on Rte. 75, near Peñasco. Smaller and somewhat friendlier to visitors, Picuris is best known for its sparkling pottery, molded from mica and clay.

The state's premier ski resort, **Taos Ski Valley,** about five mi. north of town on Rte. 150, has powder conditions on bowl sections and "short but steep" downhill runs rivaling Colorado's. Reserve a room well in advance if you plan to come during the winter holiday season. (Lift tickets $34, equipment rental $10 per day. For info and ski conditions, call the Taos Valley Resort Association at 776-2233 or 800-992-7669.) In summer, the ski-valley area offers great hikes.

After a day of strenuous sight-seeing, soak your weary bones in one of the natural **hot springs** near Taos. One of the most accessible bubbles nine mi. north on Hwy. 522 near Arroyo Hondo; turn left onto a dirt road immediately after you cross the river. Following the dirt road for about three mi., turn left when it forks just after crossing the Rio Grande—the hot spring is just off the road at the first switchback. Though not very private, the spring's dramatic location part way up the Rio Grande Gorge more than compensates. Located 10 mi. west of Taos, the **U.S. 64 Bridge** over the Rio Grande Gorge is the nation's second-highest span, affording a spectacular view of the canyon and a New Mexico sunset.

Western New Mexico

West of Albuquerque lies a vast land of forests, lava beds, and desert mesas populated by Native Americans and boomtown coal and uranium miners. Though difficult to explore without a car, the region can prove very rewarding for the dedicated adventurer.

Sun-scorched and water-poor, **Chaco Canyon** seems an improbable setting for the first great flowering of the Anasazi. At a time when most farmers relied on risky dry farming, Chacoans created an oasis of irrigated fields. They also constructed sturdy five-story rock apartment buildings while Europeans still lived in squalid wooden hovels. By the 11th century, the canyon residents had set up a major trade network with dozens of small satellite towns in the surrounding desert. Around 1150 AD, however, the whole system collapsed: with no food and little water, the Chacoans simply abandoned the canyon for greener pastures.

Only the ruins remain, but these are the best-preserved sites in the Southwest. **Pueblo Bonito,** the canyon's largest town, demonstrates the skill of Anasazi masons. Among many other structures, one four-story wall still stands. Nearby **Chetro Ketl** houses one of the canyon's largest great kivas, used in Chacoan religious rituals. Bring water, since even the visitors center occasionally runs dry.

The **visitors center** (988-6727 or 988-6716; 24 hrs.), at the eastern end of the canyon, houses an excellent museum that includes exhibits on Anasazi art and architecture, as well as a description of the sophisticated economic network by which the Chacoan Anasazi traded with smaller Anasazi tribes of modern Colorado and northern Mexico. (Museum open daily 8am-6pm; Sept. 2-May 27 daily 8am-5pm. Entrance fee $1 per person or $3 per carload.) **Camping** in Chaco costs $5; arrive by 3pm since space is limited to 46 sites. Registration is required. You can also make Chaco a daytrip from Gallup, NM, where cheap accommodations are plentiful.

Chaco Canyon, a 160-mi., 3½-hour drive northwest from Albuquerque, lies 90 mi. south of Durango, CO. When the first official archeologist left for the canyon at the turn of the century, it took him almost a year to get here from Washington, DC. Today's visitor faces unpaved Rte. 57, which reaches the park from paved Rte. 44 (turn off at the tiny town of Nageezi) on the north (29 mi.), and from I-40 on the south (about 60 mi., 20 mi. of it unpaved). Greyhound's I-40 run from Albuquerque to Gallup serves Thoreau, at the intersection of Rte. 57, five times per day.

Just west of the Continental Divide on Rte. 53, four mi. southeast of the Navajo town of **Ramah,** sits **Inscription Rock** (505-783-4226), where Native Americans, Spanish conquistadors, and later European pioneers made their mark while traveling through the scenic valley. Today, self-guided trails allow access to the rock as well as to ruins farther into the park. (Open daily 8am-6:30pm.) The **visitors center** (open daily 8am-8pm) includes a small museum as well as several dire warnings against emulating the graffiti artists of old and marking the rocks. For those unable to resist the urge to inscribe, an alternate boulder is provided.

White Sands National Monument

Do you remember walking in the sand? Located on Hwy. 70, 15 mi. southeast of Alamogordo and 52 mi. northeast of Las Cruces, White Sands (505-479-6124) is the world's largest gypsum sand dune, 300 square mi. of beach without ocean. Located in the Tularosa Basin between the Sacramento and San Andres mountains, the dunes were formed when rainwater dissolved gypsum in a nearby mountain and then collected in the basin's Lake Lucero. As the desert weather evaporated the lake, the gypsum crystals were left behind and eventually formed the continually growing sand dunes. Walking, rolling, or hiking through the dunes can provide hours of mindless fun; the brilliant white sand is especially awe-inspiring at sunset. Tragically, the basin is also home to a missile test range, as well as the **Trinity Site**, where the first atomic bomb was exploded in July 1945. Although a visit today won't make your hair fall out, the road to the park is subject to closures, usually no more than two hr., while missiles are tested; call ahead to make sure, and run if you see a mushroom cloud. (Visitor Center open Memorial Day-Labor Day 8am-7pm, off-season 8am-4:30pm; dunes drive open 7am-10pm, off-season 7am-sunset. $3 per vehicle. Handicapped accessible.) The park has a nice backcountry campsite; pick up maps at the visitors center. If you're not camping, make nearby **Alamogordo** your base. The city is home to several motels and restaurants, including ol' faithful, **Motel 6**, Panorama Dr. (505-434-5470), off Hwy. 70, with clean, sparse rooms, TV, a pool (one pool, not a pool in each room, silly), and a view. (Singles $21. Doubles $27.)

NEW YORK CITY

Americans live vicariously in New York City every day of their lives; it prints their books, writes their newspapers and magazines, produces their record albums, sets their corporate and banking policies, mediates their art, and arbitrates their fashions. Such a dominant presence on the American stage does not inspire tentative opinion; most either adore the concrete archipelago or fear and loathe it.

To in-ciders who see the Big Apple as a plump juicy fruit, NYC has everything one could ever want in a community, bursting with a seemingly infinite array of flavors. Replete with the world's largest subway system, museums and galleries enough for several small countries, more spoken languages than Berlitz offers courses, an army of taxis bumpering through traffic-ridden streets, and two vendors (one legal) on every corner, New York City doesn't do things half-way. If you want it, NYC's got it with style and substance, usually before any place else in the United States.

To those who see the Big Apple as a waxy facade hiding a rotten, worm-ridden core, NYC is a claustrophobic nightmare, the swarming, relentless consequence of millions of people squeezed into a steel-and-glass postage stamp. It's the Gotham city of comic and tragic legend, a gritty world of crime, filth, corruption, racial tension, and hopelessness—the New York we see splayed across headlines and flashed up front on the evening news. A land of opportunity only for those who can leave before nightfall. A festival of fun for those who can visit, squeeze out its novelty and variety, and then retreat to a safe haven without being victimized by its streets. But Hell's Kitchen itself if you haven't been able to worm your way to the top of the trash heap.

The tourist has to deal with both of New York's stylized alter egos. The visitor can escape the ravages of the metropolis, but not by ignoring them. Watch for pick-

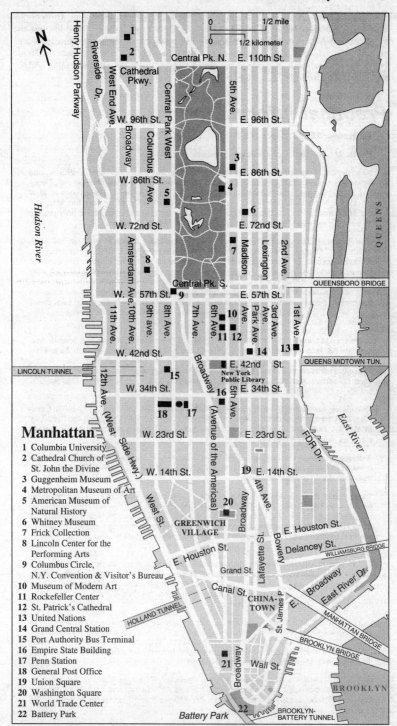

Manhattan

1 Columbia University
2 Cathedral Church of
  St. John the Divine
3 Guggenheim Museum
4 Metropolitan Museum of Art
5 American Museum of
  Natural History
6 Whitney Museum
7 Frick Collection
8 Lincoln Center for the
  Performing Arts
9 Columbus Circle,
  N.Y. Convention & Visitor's Bureau
10 Museum of Modern Art
11 Rockefeller Center
12 St. Patrick's Cathedral
13 United Nations
14 Grand Central Station
15 Port Authority Bus Terminal
16 Empire State Building
17 Penn Station
18 General Post Office
19 Union Square
20 Washington Square
21 World Trade Center
22 Battery Park

pockets and con artists. Steer through the warren of streets, buildings, and people. Know the places to avoid. The overwhelming, daunting challenge is to harvest the sweet side of New York. The city is so full of restaurants, museums, musicals and sights that no single vacation itinerary can swallow whole its ripe temptation. Divide NYC's neighborhoods into digestible chunks and savor them one delectable and/or seedy bite at a time.

Practical Information

Emergency: 911.

Police: 212-374-5000. For non-urgent inquiries. Open 24 hrs.

New York Convention and Visitors Bureau, 2 Columbus Circle (397-8222), 59th St. and Broadway. Subway: #1, 9, A, B, C, D to 59th St./Columbus Circle. Multilingual staff. Directions, hotel listings, entertainment ideas, safety tips, and "insider's" descriptions of New York's neighborhoods. Doles out 2 invaluable maps (free): *MTA Manhattan Bus Map,* and the *MTA New York City Subway Map.* Try to show up in person; the phone lines tend to be busy. Open Mon.-Fri. 9am-6pm, Sat.-Sun. and holidays 10am-6pm.

Entertainment Information: Ticketron, 399-4444. **Free Daily Events in the City,** 360-1333; 24 hrs. **NYC Onstage,** 768-1818; updates on theater, dance, music, children's entertainment, and special events; 24 hrs. **Tkts.,** 354-5800; booth in the middle of Duffy Square (the northern part of Times Square, at 47th and Broadway). The agency adds a $2 service charge to the price of each ticket. (Tickets sold Mon.-Sat. 3-8pm for evening performances; Wed. and Sat. 10am-2pm for matinees; and Sun. noon-8pm for matinees and evening performances.) The line can be long, snaking around the traffic island a few times, but it moves fairly quickly. The board near the front posts the names of shows with available tickets.

Travelers Aid Society: 158-160 W. 42nd St. (944-0013), between Broadway and Seventh Ave. Also at JFK International Airport (718-656-4870), in the International Arrivals Bldg. 42nd St. branch specializes in crisis-intervention services for stranded travelers or crime victims. JFK office offers general counseling and referral to travelers, as well as emergency assistance. 42nd St. branch open Mon.-Fri. 9am-5pm; subway: 1, 2, 3, 7, 9, N, R, S to 42nd St. JFK branch open Mon.-Fri. 10am-7pm.

Consulates: Australian, 636 Fifth Ave. (245-4000). **British,** 845 Third Ave. (752-8400). **Canadian,** 1251 Sixth Ave. (768-2400). **French,** 934 Fifth Ave. (983-5660). **German,** 460 Park Ave. (308-8700). **Indian,** 3 E. 64th St. (879-8700). **Israeli,** 800 Second Ave. (351-5200). **Italian,** 690 Park Ave. (737-9100).

American Express: 150 E. 42nd St. (687-3700), between Lexington and Third Ave. Travel agency providing traveler's checks, financial services, and other assistance. Open Mon.-Fri. 9am-5pm. Call for other locations.

Taxis: Radio-dispatched taxis, UTOC 718-361-7270. Yellow (licensed) cabs can be hailed on the street: $1.50 base rate, 25¢ each additional fifth of a mi.; 50¢ surcharge 8pm-6am; passengers pay for all tolls. Before you leave the cab, ask for a receipt, which will have the taxi's ID number. This number is necessary to trace lost articles or to make a complaint to the **Taxi Commission** (221 W. 41st St. (221-TAXI), between Times Sq. and the Port Authority Bus Terminal).

Car Rental: All agencies have minimum age requirements and ask for deposits. Call in advance to reserve, especially near the weekend. **Thrifty,** 330 W. 58th St. (867-1234), between Eighth and Ninth Ave.; 213 E. 43rd St. (867-1234), between Second and Third Ave. $42 per day, $255 per week, with unlimited mileage. Open Mon.-Fri. 7am-8:30pm, Sat.-Sun. 7am-4pm. Must be 23 with a major credit card.

Auto Transport Companies: New York is their major departure point. Applications take about a week to process. Most agencies require more than one ID; some ask for references. **Dependable Car Services,** 1501 Broadway (840-6262). Depending on the model of the car, must be 19 or over; $100-200 deposit returned upon delivery. **Auto Driveaway,** 264 W. 35th St. (967-2344). Must be 21 or over. $260 deposit.

Bicycle Rentals: On weekends May-Oct. and weekdays 10am-3pm, Central Park closes to cars, allowing bicycles to rule its roads. **Pedal Pushers,** 1306 Second Ave. (288-5594), between 68th and 69th St., rents 3-speeds for $4 per hr., $10 per day; 10-speeds for $5 per hr., $14 per day; mountain bikes for $6 per hr., $17 per day. Open Mon., Wed., and Fri.-Sun. 10am-6pm, Thurs. 10am-8pm. No cash deposit required; leave passport, driver's license, or a major credit card. For the more coordinated, roller blades are available at **Peck and Goodie Skates,** 917 Eighth Ave. (246-6123), between 54th and 55th St. They'll hold your shoes while you whiz past your favorite New York sights for $12 for 2 hr., $17 for 4 hr., or $27 per day. $100 deposit or credit card required. Open Mon.-Tues., Thurs., Sat.-Sun. 10am-6pm, Wed. and Fri. 10am-8pm.

Help Lines: Crime Victim's Hotline, 577-7777; 24-hr. counseling and referrals. **Sex Crimes Report Line,** New York Police Dept., 267-7273; 24-hr. help, counseling, and referrals. **AIDS Information,** 807-6655. Open daily 10:30am-9pm.

Medical Care: Walk-in Clinic, 57 E. 34th St. (683-1010), between Park and Madison Ave. Open Mon.-Fri. 8am-6pm, Sat. 10am-2pm. Affiliated with Beth Israel Hospital.

24-Hr. Medical Assistance: Beth Israel Medical Center Emergency Room, (420-2840), 1st Ave. and 16th St. **Mount Sinai Medical Center Emergency Room** (241-7171), 100th St. and 1st Ave. **New York Infirmary Beekman Downtown Hospital Emergency Room** (312-5070), 170 William St. **Kaufman's Pharmacy** 557 Lexington Ave. (755-2266), at 50th St. **24-Hr. Emergency Doctor,** 718-745-5900. **The Eastern's Women's Center,** 40 E. 30th St. (686-6066), between Park and Madison. Gynecological exams and surgical procedures for women.

Post Office: Central branch, 380 W. 33rd St. (967-8585), at Eighth Ave. across from Madison Square Garden. To pick up General Delivery mail, use the entrance at 390 Ninth Ave. Open Mon.-Fri. 8:30am-7:45pm. For info call 330-4000.

Area Codes: 212 (Manhattan and the Bronx); 718 (Brooklyn, Queens, and Staten Island).

Getting There

By Plane

Three airports service the New York Metro Region.

John F. Kennedy Airport (JFK) (718-656-4520), 12 mi. from Midtown in southern Queens, is the largest, handling most international flights.

LaGuardia Airport (718-656-4520), 6 mi. from midtown in northwestern Queens, is the smallest, offering domestic flights and air shuttles (see below).

Newark International Airport, 12 mi. from Midtown in Newark, NJ, offers both domestic and international flights at budget fares usually unavailable at the other airports.

Trump Shuttle: 800-247-8786. Leaves every hr. on the hr., 7am-10pm. For those under 25 and over 64, $70 on weekdays 10am-2pm and 7-9pm, $60 all day Sat. and Sun. 9am-3pm. Leaves from LaGuardia; no reservations necessary, but arrive ½-hr. before departure.

To and From the Airports

For the most up-to-date info on reaching the airports, call AirRide, the Port Authority's airport hotline, at 800-247-7433. Public transport can get you easily from JFK to midtown Manhattan. You can catch a brown and white **JFK Express Shuttle Bus** (718-330-1234) from any airport terminal to the **Howard Beach-JFK subway station,** where you can take the A train to the city. Allow at least 1 hr. travel time. Or you can take one of the city buses (the Q10, Q3; $1.15, exact change required) into Queens. The Q10, Q3, and Q9 connect with subway lines to Manhattan. Ask the bus driver where to get off, and make sure you know which subway line you want. Allow 90 minutes travel time. Those willing to pay more can take the **Carey Bus Service** a private line that runs between JFK and Grand Central Station and the Port Authority Terminal. (Leaves every 30 min. $10.50.)

You have two options to get into Manhattan from LaGuardia. If you have extra time and light luggage, you can take the MTA "Q 33" bus ($1.15 exact change or token) to the Eighth Ave. subway in Queens, and from there, take the E or F train into Manhattan ($1.15 token). Allow at least 90 minutes travel time. The second option, the Carey Bus Service, makes four stops in the Midtown area. (Every 20 min., 55 min., $8.50.)

The commute from Newark Airport to Manhattan takes about as long as from JFK. **New Jersey Transit (NJTA)** (201-460-8444) runs a fast, efficient bus (NJTA #300) between the airport and Port Authority every 15 minutes during the day, less frequently at night ($7). For the same fare, the **Olympia Trails Coach** (212-964-6233) travels between the airport and either Grand Central or the World Trade Center. (Every 20 min. Mon.-Fri. 6am-1am, Sat.-Sun. 7am-8pm; 45 min.-1½ hr. depending on traffic; $7.)

From Manhattan, **Giraldo Limousine Service** (757-6840) will pick you up anywhere between 14th and 95th St. and take you to the airport of your choice for $11-16.

By Bus or Train

Buses or trains can get you in and out of New York less expensively and more scenically.

Port Authority, 41st St. and Eighth Ave. (564-8484), has good info and security services, but this dock is not safe from the "storms" of the surrounding neighborhood. Be wary of pickpockets, and call a cab at night. Its bathrooms are dangerous at all times.

Greyhound/Trailways (730-7460 or 971-6363) is the titan here. On some routes, a 10% discount is offered to students with ID. Buses run to: Boston ($30), Philadelphia ($12), Washington, DC ($31), and Montreal ($65).

Grand Central Station, 42nd St. and Park Ave., handles **Metro-North** (800-638-7646, 532-4900) commuter lines to Connecticut and New York suburbs, and **Amtrak** (800-872-7245 or 582-6875) lines to upstate New York and Canada.

Penn Station, 33rd St. and Eighth Ave. Amtrak trains rumble out of here, serving most major cities in the U.S., especially those in the Northeast. To Washington, DC ($65) and Boston ($45). Penn Station also handles the **Long Island Railroad (LIRR)** (718-217-5477) and **PATH** service to New Jersey (466-7655).

By Car

Two major highways frame Manhattan: on the East Side, the **East Side Highway** (a.k.a. the Harlem River Drive and FDR Drive); on the West Side, the **Henry Hudson Parkway** (a.k.a. the West Side Highway). From outside the city, I-95 leads to the Major Deegan, the FDR Drive, and the Henry Hudson. Go south on any of these roads.

Parking lots are the easiest but most expensive way to deal with the parking hassle. In midtown, where lots are the only option, expect to pay at least $25 per day and up to $15 for two hours. You can draw from the cheaper lots downtown—try the far west end of Houston St.—but make sure you feel comfortable with the area and the lot.

The second alternative is short-term parking. On the streets, **parking meters** cost 25¢ per 15 minutes, with a limit of one or two hours. Lastly, **free parking** sits on the crosstown streets in residential areas, but competition for these spots is ruthless.

Hitchhiking is illegal in New York state and cops strictly enforce the law within NYC. Hitching in and around New York City is dangerous.

Orientation

Five boroughs make up New York City: Queens, Brooklyn, the Bronx, Staten Island, and Manhattan.

Manhattan island's length is only half that of a marathon; 13 mi. long and 2½ mi. wide. For all its popularity, Manhattan houses only the third largest population of the five boroughs, after Brooklyn and the Bronx. Though small, Manhattan has all the advantages—surrounded by water and adjacent to the other four boroughs.

Queens, the largest and most ethnically diverse of the boroughs, is located to the east of midtown Manhattan. **Brooklyn** lies due south of Queens and is even older than Manhattan. **Staten Island,** to the south of Manhattan, has remained staunchly residential, similar to the suburban bedroom communities of outer Long Island. North of Manhattan nests the **Bronx,** the only borough connected by land to the rest of the U.S., home of the lovely suburb Riverdale as well as New York's most depressed area, the South Bronx.

Districts of Manhattan

Glimpsed from the window of an approaching plane, New York City can seem a monolithic urban jungle. But up close, the Big Apple breaks down into digestible neighborhoods, each with its own history and personality. Boundaries between these neighborhoods can be abrupt, due to the strange history of city zoning ordinances and other unpredictable quirks of urban evolution.

The city began at the southern tip of Manhattan, in the area around **Battery Park** where the first Dutch settlers made their homes. The nearby harbor, now the jazzed-up tourist attraction **South Street Seaport,** quickly provided the growing city with lucrative commercial opportunities. What remains of historic Manhattan, however, lies in the shadows of the imposing financial buildings around **Wall Street** and the civic office buildings around **City Hall.** A little farther north, **Little Italy, Chinatown,** and the southern blocks of the **Lower East Side,** rich in the ethnic cultures brought by late 19th-century immigrants, rub elbows below Houston Street. To the west is the newly fashionable **TriBeCa** (Triangle Below Canal St.). **SoHo** (for "South of Houston"), a former warehouse district west of Little Italy, has been transformed into a chic pocket of art studios and galleries. Above SoHo flashes **Greenwich Village,** once a center of intense political and artistic activity, still a literal village of lower buildings, jumbled streets, and neon glitz.

A few blocks north of Greenwich Village, stretching across the West teens and twenties, lies **Chelsea,** the late artist Andy Warhol's favorite hangout and former home of Dylan Thomas, Arthur Miller, and Canadian bard Leonard Cohen. East of Chelsea, presiding over the East River, is **Gramercy Park,** a pastoral collection of Victorian mansions and brownstones annoyingly immortalized in Edith Wharton's *Age of Innocence.* **Midtown Manhattan** towers from 34th to 59th St., where awe-inspiring traditional skyscrapers and controversial new architecture stand side by side, providing office space for millions. Here department stores outfit New York, and the nearby **Theater District** entertains the world—or tries to.

North of Midtown, **Central Park** slices Manhattan into east and west. On the **Upper West Side,** the gracious museums and residences of Central Park West sit next to the swanky boutiques and sidewalk cafés of Columbus Ave. On the **Upper East Side,** the galleries and museums scattered among the elegant apartments of Fifth and Park Ave. create an even more rarified atmosphere.

Above 97th St., much of the Upper East Side's opulence ends with a whimper where subway trains emerge from the tunnel and the *barrio* begins. Above 110th St. on the Upper West Side is majestic **Columbia University** (founded as King's College in 1754), an urban member of the Ivy League. The communities of **Harlem, East Harlem,** and **Morningside Heights** centered the Harlem Renaissance of black artists and writers in the 1920s and propulsed the revolutionary Black Power movement in the 1960s. Although torn by crime, **Washington Heights,** just north of St. Nichols Park, is nevertheless somewhat safer and more attractive than the abandoned tenements of Harlem; it is home to Fort Tryon Park, the Metropolitan's Medieval Cloisters, and a quiet community of immigrants. Still farther north, the island ends in a rural patch of wooded land where caves once inhabited by the Algonquin remain.

Manhattan's Street Plan

New York's east/west division refers to an address's location in relation to the two borders of Central Park—**Fifth Avenue** along the east side and **Central Park West** along the west. Below 59th St. where the park ends, the West Side begins at the western half of Fifth Ave. Uptown (above 59th St.) refers to the area north of Midtown. Downtown (below 34th St.) means the area south of Midtown.

When given the street number of an address (e.g. #250 E. 52nd St.), find the avenue closest to the address by thinking of Fifth Ave. as point zero on the given street. Address numbers increase as you move east or west of Fifth Ave. On the

East Side, address numbers are 1 at Fifth Ave., 100 at Park Ave., 200 at Third Ave., 300 at Second Ave., 400 at First Ave., 500 at York Ave. (uptown) or Avenue A (in the Village). On the West Side, address numbers are 1 at Fifth Ave., 100 at the Ave. of the Americas (Sixth Ave.), 200 at Seventh Ave., 300 at Eighth Ave., 400 at Ninth Ave., 500 at Tenth Ave., and 600 at Eleventh Ave. In general, numbers increase from south to north along the avenues, but you always should ask for a cross street when you are getting an avenue address. For a handy address finder, let your fingers do the walking in the Manhattan White Pages.

Getting Around

For info on **Taxis** and **Biking,** see Practical Information.

Get a free subway map from station token booths or the visitors bureau, which also has a free street map (see Practical Information above). For a more detailed program of interborough travel, find a Manhattan Yellow Pages, which contains detailed subway, PATH, and bus maps. For other bus or subway maps, send a self-addressed, stamped envelope about a month before you need the info to **NYC Transit Authority,** 370 Jay St., Brooklyn 11201. In the city, round-the-clock staff at the **Transit Authority Information Bureau** (718-330-1234) dispenses subway and bus info.

Subways and Buses

The fare for Metropolitan Transit Authority (MTA) subways and buses is a hefty $1.15; groups of four or more may find cabs cheaper for short rides. Once inside you may transfer to any train without restrictions. Most buses have access ramps, but steep stairs make subway transit more difficult for disabled people. Call the Transit Authority Information Bureau (718-330-1234) for specific info on public transport.

In crowded stations (notably those around 42nd St.), pickpockets find plenty of work; in deserted stations, more violent crimes can occur. Always watch yourself and your belongings, and try to stay in lit areas near a transit cop or token clerk. Many stations have clearly marked "off-hours" waiting areas under observation that are significantly safer. At any time and place, don't stand too close to the platform edge; people have been pushed. Boarding the train, make sure to pick a car with a number of other passengers on it.

The subways run 24 hrs., but become less safe between 11pm and 7am, especially above E. 96th St. and W. 120th St. Try also to avoid rush-hour crowds, where you'll be fortunate to find air, let alone seating. On an average morning, more commuters take the E and the F than use the entire rapid transit system of Chicago (the nation's second-largest system). Buy a bunch of tokens at once: you'll not only avoid a long line, but you'll be able to use all station entrances, some of which lack token clerks.

Buses

Because **buses** sit in traffic, during the day they often take twice as long as subways, but they also stay relatively safe, clean—and always windowed. They'll also probably get you closer to your destination, since they stop roughly every two blocks and run crosstown (east-west), as well as uptown and downtown (north-south), unlike the subway which travels north-south for the most part. The MTA transfer system provides north-south bus riders with a slip good for a free east-west bus ride, or vice-versa. Just ask the driver for a transfer when you pay. Ring when you want to get off. A yellow-painted curb indicates bus stops, but you're better off looking for the blue signpost announcing the bus number or for a glass-walled shelter displaying a map of the bus's route and a schedule (often unreliable) of arrival times. Either exact change or a subway token is required; drivers will not accept dollar bills.

Safety

After dark, any neighborhood in Manhattan can be unsafe. Keep to the busier, better-lit streets and sidewalks, don't walk around alone, and avoid run-down or empty sections of the city. At night, steer clear of Central Park (*especially* the northern end), the Bowery and the West Side Docks (downtown), and Morningside Park and Harlem (uptown).

Never show money to a stranger, and be wary of "travelers" who ask for too much assistance. If someone will not leave you alone, stay in a well-lit area until you can enter a store, restaurant, hotel, or other populated place. When in doubt, call the police.

Finally, most public restrooms in subway stations are padlocked for a reason. Even the ones that are open are hardly sanitary. Ditto for the facilities at Penn Station and Grand Central. If nature calls while you're out catching the sights, try the big department stores or the better hotels, or any restaurant, bar, or café that doesn't post a sign saying "Facilities for patrons only."

Accommodations

If you know of someone who heard of someone who lives in New York—get that New Yorker's phone number. The cost of living in New York can rip the seams of your wallet. Planning on staying in a hotel? Then be sure to book reservations way in advance—if you just happen to fall into a place, chances are it will be a pit. However, many reasonable options remain for under $60 per day, depending upon your priorities. Those traveling alone, especially if particularly vulnerable, might wish to spend more to stay in a safer neighborhood. The young and outgoing may prefer a budget-style place crowded with students. Honeymooning couples won't.

Student Accommodations

New York International AYH-Hostel, 891 Amsterdam Ave. (932-2300) at W. 103rd St. The largest hostel in the U.S. with 90 dorm-style rooms and 480 beds, located in a freshly renovated Richard Morris Hunt Landmark building. Spiffy new soft carpets, blondwood bunks, spotless bathrooms. Kitchens and dining rooms, in-room storage, communal lounges, and a large outdoor garden. Open 24 hrs. Check-out 11am. No curfew. $18.75, nonmembers $21.75. Doubles $30. Family rooms $60. Linen $3. Towels $2.

International Student Center, 38 W. 88th St. (787-7706), on the West Side. Subway: 7th Ave. IND to 86th St. Close to Central Park and Columbus Ave. Open only to foreigners, preferably students—you must show foreign passport to get in. Single-sex bunk rooms, no frills, in a once-gracious, welcoming, somewhat tired brownstone on a cheerful street. Large basement lounge with friendly foreigners and TV. No curfew. 7-day max. stay. Open daily 8am-11pm. Call after 10:30am on day of arrival. A bargain at $10.

International Student Hospice, 154 E. 33rd St. (228-7470, 228-4689), between Lexington and Third Ave. in East Midtown. Subway: 6 to 33rd St. Inconspicuous converted brownstone with initialed brass plaque by the door. Very small bunk rooms bursting with bric-a-brac. 20 beds preferably for internationals and students. Decent neighborhood and caring proprietor. Curfew midnight. $28 per night.

Manhattan Hostel, 145 E. 23rd St. (979-8043). Subway: 6 train to 23rd St. International travelers only. Hostel sign under the decaying "Kenmore" marquee. A 3rd-floor haven created by a young Swiss couple for foreign passport carriers. Clean hall baths, complete kitchen facilities. Common room with free coffee. Only 32 rooms, enabling travelers to meet in a family atmosphere. Airport service available. Entrance locked midnight-8am, but guests receive keys. Reservations strongly recommended. Doubles $40. Extra mattress $12. Bunk rooms $20 per person. Private bath $5 extra.

Mid-City Hostel, 608 Eighth Ave. (704-0562), between W. 39th St. and W. 40th St. on the 4th floor. People walking up the creaky, uneven steps in its shaky neighborhood will be pleasantly surprised by this upstairs oasis in a surrounding desert of scum and decrepitude. Look for a red brick building with gypsies below to usher you in, or you'll likely stroll past it. Friendly family atmosphere persists in this austere but homey loft, complete with skylights, brick walls, and old wooden beams. Seeking longtime international backpackers; backpack and passport ID required. Call before you arrive. Lockout noon-6pm. Curfew Sun.-Thurs. midnight, Fri.-Sat. 1am. Only 25 beds. Dormitory-style beds for $15 per night ($18 during peak season), including breakfast of fruit salad.

The Penthouse Hostel, 250 W. 43rd St. (391-4202), on the 24th floor. In the heart of the theatre district and an uncomfortably close stone's throw away from Times Square, this little niche bills itself as the "world's highest hostel." Open 24 hrs. No curfew. Check-in is round-the-clock, check-out 11am. Passport requested. Eight beds per room. $17 per night.

Martha Washington, 30 E. 30th St. (689-1900), in midtown. Women only. Located in a mediocre neighborhood filled with students. Singles $35, with bath $54. Doubles $50, with bath $69. Weekly: singles $140, with bath $175, with kitchenette $189-210; doubles $224, with bath $245, with bath and kitchenette $273.

YMCAs/YWCAs

YMCA—Vanderbilt, 224 E. 47th St. (755-2410), between Second and Third. Subway: 6 to 51st St. In a busy but safe neighborhood, with clean and brightly lit lobby. 750 small rooms, all with TV, A/C and some with balconies. Semi-dingy hallways; sanitary hall baths and phones on each floor. The front desk keeps close tabs on who is doing what, as does the 24-hr. security guard. Lockers, Nautilus equipment, pool, luggage storage for early arrivals, and safe deposit boxes. It's popular; make reservations and guarantee them with a deposit. Visa, Mastercard, and money orders accepted; personal checks taken only for reservations. Check-in 1-6pm. Van service to airports: Jack's Airport Bus Service to JFK $9.50, to LaGuardia $8. Buses leave at 12.15 and 3:15pm. Sign up at the security desk and pay the driver. 25-day max. stay. $10 key deposit. Singles $38-48. Doubles $48-58. Triples $63-67. Quads $84. Rates lower during off season.

YMCA—West Side, 5 W. 43rd St. (787-4400). Subway: 59th St./Columbus Circle. Dilapidated but clean rooms in a handsome Gothic building, with free access to 2 pools, indoor track, racquet courts, and Nautilus equipment. Singles $32, with bath $44. Doubles $46, with bath $52. Newly renovated singles with color TV and cable $38, with bath $53. A/C $3.25 extra. Student discount 10%.

CIEE New York Student Center (YMCA), William Sloan House, 356 W. 34th St. (760-5850). Subway: 34th St./Penn Station. 15-story monolith with almost 1500 rooms, in a rather run-down part of midtown. Dirty corridors lead into tiny worn rooms, sparsely furnished. Telephone and bathroom facilities on each floor. This place serves as a budget hotel for regular travelers as well as a youth hostel for students with ID. Laundromat, recreation room, and athletic facilities are available. A cafeteria serves breakfast and lunch. 24-hr. security. Check-out at noon. In the summer, book up to a month in advance. Singles $34, with running water $40. Doubles $50, with shower $69. Hostel rate (2 students share a single in a sheetless bunkbed) $19 per person, IYHF/AYH members only. Key deposit $5. TV $1.50 per day.

Hotels

Carlton Arms Hotel, 160 E. 25th St. (679-0680), by Third Ave. within walking range of Empire State Building. Nicknamed "Artbreak Hotel." Each room uniquely designed. Stay inside a submarine and peer through windows at the lost city of Atlantis; travel to Renaissance Venice; or stow your clothes in a dresser suspended on an astroturf wall. Old, stuffy rooms with nice, distracting adornment. Artist staff. Singles $40, with bath $48. Doubles $54, with bath $62. Triples $65, with bath $74. Roughly 10% discount for students and foreign tourists. Seven days for the price of 6. Reserve 1 month in advance; confirm 10 days in advance.

Pickwick Arms Hotel, 230 E. 51st St. (800-pic-wick), between Second and Third. Subway: 6 to 51st St. A chandeliered, marbled lobby with mirrors and brass doors raises expectations but gives way to disenchantingly murky and minuscule rooms with equally microscopic bathrooms. Nonetheless, a clean place with unbeatable rates in a great neighborhood. Roof garden, parking, and airport service available. Even with nearly 400 rooms to fill, the Pickwick Arms gets very busy, so make reservations. Check-in 2pm; check-out 1pm. Singles $40, with shared bathroom $50. Doubles $80. Studios $95. Each additional person $12.

Allerton House, 130 E. 57th St. (753-8841), between Park and Lexington. Subway: 6 to 59th St. Women only. A classy operation in a swanky district, 2 blocks south of Bloomingdale's. Full of old ladies heading up to the Beverly Bridge Club on the 3rd floor. Many recently redecorated rooms. New leaded glass windows and clean, angular spaces. Check-in 11am; check-out 1pm. Singles $35, with connecting bath $40, with private shower or bath $50. Doubles $65.

Portland Square Hotel, 132 W. 47th St. (382-0600), between Sixth and Seventh Ave. Since 1904, Portland has been a "theatre" hotel, accommodating Broadway casts and audiences. Stand-outs include James Cagney, who stayed here as a struggling actor. Also close to the emporiums of Fifth Ave. and "Restaurant Row" on 46th St. Completely renovated interior with new TVs, spotless bathrooms, and comfortably firm beds. Keycard entry. Singles $40, with bath $60. Doubles $85. Triples $90. Quads $95.

Herald Square Hotel, 19 W. 31st St. (279-4017 or 800-727-1888), just west of Fifth Ave. Housed in the original Beaux-Arts home of Life magazine, built in 1893; today, the reception desk is shielded in glass while sirens blare outside. Above the entrance, look for the reading, winged cherub titled the "Winged Life," carved by Philip Martiny. The sculpture was a frequent presence on the pages of early Life magazines. The work of some of America's noted illustrators adorns the walls of the lobby, hall, and rooms. Immaculate, newly renovated quarters with color TV and A/C. Singles (1 person only) $40. Singles/doubles (1 bed, 1 bathroom) $50. Larger singles with bath $65. Larger doubles (1 bed) with bath $85.

Food

This city takes its food seriously. In New York, delis war. Brunch rules. Trendy dining has caught on. Supermarkets haven't—with so many bakeries, butcher shops, and greengrocers, who needs to shop in a food mall? Don't be confused by the conflation of food with art; certain eateries think they are galleries while select delis look like museums. Assorted gourmet cooks pose as pushcart vendors. Sidewalk gourmands can stick with the old roving standbys on wheels (hot dogs, pretzels, roasted chestnuts), or try something more adventurous (shish kebabs, fajitas, knishes, felafels).

New York's restaurants do more than the United Nations to promote international goodwill and cross-cultural exchanges. City dining spans the globe, with eateries ranging from relatively tame sushi bars to wild combinations like Afghani/Italian, or Mexican/Lebanese. In a city where the scalding melting pot threatens to boil over, one can still peacefully sample Chinese pizza and Cajun knishes.

And of course, two old favorites remain: pizza and bagels. New Yorkers like their pizza thin and hot, with no shortage of grease. Pizzeria warfare has gone on for years; the major issue is not over taste but name. Nearly a dozen institutions fight over the right to call themselves Ray's Original. Who is Ray? Who cares? Less contentious pizzerias can offer as fine fare as titled competitors. The humble bagel is mighty Brooklyn's major contribution to Western civilization. Bagels come in a rainbow of flavors—the most common being plain, sesame, poppyseed, and onion—but only one shape. Exiles from the city often find bagel deprivation to be one of the biggest indignities of life outside of New York.

West Midtown

Around the Times Square and the Port Authority Bus Terminal areas, the number of fast-food chains approaches the combined tally of tourists, prostitutes, and drug-peddlers—a rather dubious distinction. In the Theater District, the stretch of Broadway from Times Square to 52nd St., you'll encounter plenty of first rate, ethnically diverse restaurants—from French to Japanese to Thai and back to Italian. While the food and service at these places are likely to make your mouth water, you will probably find your dinner check much harder to swallow. Celebrities often drift over to **Sardi's,** 234 W. 44th St., and take a seat on plush red leather, surrounded by caricatures of themselves. Traditionally, on the opening night of a major Broadway play, the star of the show makes an exalted post-performance entrance—to hearty cheers for a superb performance, or polite applause if it was a bomb. Should this exercise grow tedious, they may head west of Eighth Ave., to 46th St.'s "Restaurant Row," an appealing but expensive strip recently liberated by the Guardian Angels. There, luminaries wander into **Joe Allen,** 326 W. 46th St., where they can gaze at posters of shows that closed in under a week. Farther uptown, a bit to the left of Carnegie Hall, lies the venerable **Russian Tea Room,**

150 W. 57th St., where dancers, musicians, and businessmen down caviar and vodka.

La Bonne Soupe, 48 W 55th St. (586-7650), between Fifth and Sixth. As the name suggests, soups are their forté. Excellent lighter fare in a split-level "bistro" that doubles as a gallery for Haitian art. Hearty meals of aromatic soups served with bread, salad, dessert, and wine for $8. Open Mon.-Sat. 11:30am-midnight, Sun. 11:30am-11pm.

Chinatown Express, 427 Seventh Ave. (563-3559), between 33rd and 34th. This newly opened eatery, with its college cafeteria setup and cramped seating, won't win points for decor or atmosphere, but in this part of town, what will? What's important is the variety and price of their buffet—over 50 selections to choose from, like General Tsao's Chicken or Shrimp and Lobster Sauce, all for $3.69 per pound. Open daily noon-9pm.

Carnegie Delicatessen, 854 Seventh Ave., at 55th St. Ceiling fans twirl gently overhead as photos of illustrious past celebrities stare at you from the walls. Eat elbow-to-elbow at long tables with regulars and celebrities while affable waiters query, "Ya want some mo' coffee there buddy?" The incredible pastrami and corned beef sandwiches ($8.95) easily feed two people (but sharing costs $3 extra). First-timers shouldn't leave without trying the sinfully rich cheesecake, topped with strawberries, blueberries, or cherries ($5.45). Open daily 6:30am-4am.

Anana Afghan Kebab, 787 Ninth Ave. (262-2323), between 52nd and 53rd. Try the appetizing Bandinjah Burani ($2.50), a spicy eggplant dish served with sour cream and bread. Experiment with lamb tikka kebab ($6.75), chunks of marinated meat skewered outside on wood charcoals but remaining tender inside, and served on a bed of brown rice with bread and salad. BYOB. Open Mon.-Sat. 11:30am-3pm and 5-11pm.

Little Italy Pizza Parlour, 72 W. 45th St. (730-7575), on the corner of 45th and Sixth Ave. All the pizzerias on 45th St. claim to be world famous, but this one takes the pie. The walls shine with b&w studio glossies of anonymous and semi-famous stars, including an autographed color photo of a sexy blond vixen: "Love ya pizza—Madonna." Don't just take her word for it; experience a hot crispy slice with plenty of chewy mozarella all for yourself ($1.55). Large Neapolitan pie ($11.80), with all the works ($21). Calzones clock in around $3.75. Open Mon.-Sat. 6:30am-8:30pm.

Sapporo, 152 W 49th St. (869-8972), near Seventh Ave. A Japanese translation of an American diner, with the grill in full view. Favorite snack spot for Broadway cast members and the business luncheoning crowd. The Sapporo Ramen Special ($5.60) yields a huge bowl of noodles with assorted meats and vegetables, all swimming in a mind-boggling miso soup base. Open Mon.-Fri. 11:30am-midnight, Sat.-Sun. 11:30am-11pm.

East Midtown

New York has five "four-star" restaurants, with four of them (Lutéce, La Grenouille, Hatsuhana, and the Quilted Giraffe) in this area. Tycoons dine among skyscraping office buildings, high rents, and briefcase-wielders. But you should be able to manage here without an expense account. East Midtown houses plenty of sidewalk food vendors and fast-food peddlers. Another option is to stock up in one of the many city supermarkets, such as the **Food Emporium** or **D'Agostino.** These upscale chain outlets feature well-stocked delis, fresh fruit and salad bars, ice-cold drinks, gourmet ice cream, and much more—all at extremely reasonable prices. After you're loaded up, picnicking is free in the area's green cloisters: try **Greenacre Park,** 51st St., between Second and Third; **Paley Park,** 53rd St., between Fifth and Madison; or **United Nations Plaza,** 48th St. at First Ave.

Crystal Gourmet, 422 Madison Ave.(752-2910), between 48th and 49th St. The most bountiful buffet bar in the tri-state area. $5 allows you to gorge yourself on their "all-you-can-eat" dinner special (5-7pm). Open Mon.-Fri. 7am-7pm, Sat.-Sun. 8am-5pm.

Zaro's Bread Basket, 466 Lexington Ave. (972-1560), on 46th St. Business flows in and out like the tide in this busy bread and pastry emporium. A huge selection of food at reasonable prices. Meat sanwiches $3-5, cheese sandwiches $1-3. Open Mon.-Fri. 6am-10pm, Sat. 6:30am-6pm.

Hsin Yu, 862 Second Ave. (752-9039), at the corner of 46th St. In the heart of the commercial area. The interior decorator had no personality, but the food does. Poultry and beef dishes about $7; specialties include Hunan Jamb ($8) or the unusual Five Happiness Vegetable Delight ($7). Try the economical combo platters (around $5.25). Soups from $1. Open daily noon-11pm.**Fisher and Levy,** 875 Third Ave. (832-3880), on 53rd St.; take the escalator down to the concourse level. While this subterranean station also deals in sandwiches and salad, come here for pizza that's a slice above the competition—thin crispy crust with a zesty sauce, minus the excess oil. $1.50 per slice, 60¢ per topping; large plain pie $11. Open Mon.-Fri. 11am-6pm.

Lower Midtown

The Lower Midtown dining scene avoids the extremes—neither fast-food commercial nor haute-cuisine trendy. Instead, this slightly gentrified but ethnically diverse neighborhood features many places where you can hunt down an honest meal at reasonable prices. On Lexington's upper 20s, Pakistani and Indian restaurants battle for customers, some catering to a linen-tablecloth crowd and others serving take-out food. Liberally sprinkled throughout are Korean corner shops that resemble a combination grocery/buffet bar. You can fill up on prepared pastas, salads, and hot entrées, paying for them by the pound.

Empire Szechuan Restaurant, 381 Third Ave. (685-6215) between 27th and 28th. The food, though not exactly a bargain, is cooked with no MSG, very little oil, and always *al dente.* Try the Empire Special Garden ($7.25) or the Paradise Chicken ($8.25). Open daily 11:30am-midnight.

Albuquerque Eats/Rodeo Bar, 375 Third Ave. (683-6500), off 27th St. Cow skulls, a silo, and a fully stuffed bison—take a wild guess at the theme here. Tex-Mex cuisine, with large-sized entrées $10-15. Late-night country entertainment. Dinner $5-14. Open daily 11:30am-3am, kitchen closes at midnight.

Pakeeza, 102 Lexington Ave. (684-4433), between 27th and 28th. One of the least expensive quality choices in an area overloaded with Indian restaurants. Load up on a plate of wonderfully spiced chicken or meat ($3.50-4.50), accompanied by another plate of fragrant herbed rice ($2). Excellent selections include *Palak Ghost* ($3.50), tender pieces of lamb cooked on ground spinach. Water fountain by the counter. Open 24 hrs.

Upper East Side

Unless you feel like eating a large bronze sculpture or a lace dress, you won't find many dining opportunities on Museum Mile along Fifth and Madison Ave., aside from cappuccino haunts, brunch breweries, and near-invisible ritzy restaurants. You will find mediocre food at extraordinary prices in posh and scenic museum cafés where you can languish among ferns and sip espresso between exhibits.

For less glamorous and more affordable dining, head east of Park Ave. Costs descend as you venture toward the lower-numbered avenues, though many do not escape the Madison pricing orbit. Hot dog hounds shouldn't miss the 100% beef "better than filet mignon" $1.50 franks at **Papaya King,** 179 E. 86th St. (369-0648), off Third Ave. (Open Sun.-Thurs. 8am-1am, Fri.-Sat. 9am-3am.) For one time-honored interpretation of the New York bagel, try **H&H East,** 1551 Second Ave. (734-7441), between 80th and 81st, still using their original formula, and baking round-the-clock. Don't feel confined to restaurant dining. Grocery stores, delis, and bakeries speckle every block. You can buy your provisions here and picnic in honor of frugality in Central Park.

Zucchini, 1336 First Ave. (249-0559), between 71st and 72nd St. A nutrition-conscious triathlete runs this healthy establishment. No red meat, but fresh seafood, salads, pasta, and chicken dishes should satiate even militant carnivores. Most pasta and vegetable entrees (soup included) under $11. Before 7pm try the Early Bird Special for only $10. Open daily 10:30am-10:30pm, brunch Sat.-Sun. 11am-4:30pm ($10).

El Pollo, 1746 First Ave. (996-7810), between 90th and 91st. This tiny Peruvian joint has received rave reviews in the New York press for years. Plump chickens are marinated and spit-roasted, topped with a variety of sauces. The french fries ($2.50) alone make it worth the trip. Half chicken $5. Open daily 11:30am-11pm.

Ottomanelli's Café, 1559 York Ave., between 82nd and 83rd, and a dozen other locations on the Upper East Side. No-frills setting, but extraordinary fresh-baked goods. An impressive coterie of bagels, breads, danish, and muffins 50¢-$1.25. Large iced coffee, a summertime must, $1. After 5pm, all danishes and muffins depreciate to 50¢. Open Mon.-Sat. 6:30am-3pm, Sun. 7:30am-3pm.

Upper West Side

At night, **Lucy's,** 503 Columbus Ave. (787-3009), at 84th St., always draws a crowd ready to make noise and conversation. At **Café La Fortuna,** 69 W. 71st (724-5846), between Central Park West and Columbus Ave., you can bring a friend, a book, or both for conversation and meditation over cappuccino ($1.75), inside or out in the backyard garden. **Zabar's,** 2245 Broadway (787-2002), between 80th and 81st St., offers an entirely different food and people-watching experience. The deli counter seems to stretch an entire block, and customers are mildly fanatical in their quest for a content stomach.

Genoa, 271 Amsterdam at 73rd St. A tiny, family-owned restaurant with some of the very best food on the West Side. Stucco walls, wood beams, pink tablecloths, and red candlelight: Italian romance. Arrive before 6pm or wait in line with the rest of the neighborhood. Pasta Festiva or Puttanesca $8.50. Veal Scallopini Francese $11.50. Open Tues.-Sat. 5:45-10:30pm, Sun. 5:30-9:30pm.

La Caridad, 2199 Broadway (874-2780), at 78th St. Represents one of New York's most successful culinary hybrids of Chinese and Creole. Feed yourself plus a pack of hungry mules with one entrée. Arroz con pollo ¼ chicken with yellow rice $4.90. Fried pork chops with garlic and choice of salad, plantains or beans and rice $5.55. Open Mon.-Sat. 11:30am-1am, Sun. 11:30am-10:30pm.

Dallas BBQ, 27 W. 72nd St. (873-2004), off Columbus Ave. Also at 21 University Place (674-4450) at 8th St., Georgia O'Keeffe's skulls and Navajo rugs seem to have migrated to the walls of this New York eatery. Don't be fooled by designer surroundings. Prices determined by small town standards. Authentic Texas-style chicken and ribs on the same bill with tasty tempura and homey chicken soup. Mountains of food and oceans of noise in this often crowded restaurant. Big breakfast featuring 50¢ coffee Mon.-Fri. 7-11am, Sat.-Sun. 8-11am. Early bird special (Mon.-Fri. noon-6:30pm) features soup, half a chicken, cornbread, and potato for $8 per dining duo. Texas-style chili $3 per bowl. Open Mon.-Fri. 7am-midnight, Sat.-Sun. 8am-1am.

Diane's, 251 Columbus Ave., off 71st St. Large portions and reasonable prices make this brass-railed café a prime pick of the college crew. Spice up a 7-oz. burger ($4) with your choice of chili, chutney, or seven cheeses (85¢ per topping). Great ice cream. Open daily 11am-2am.

Greenwich Village

Late night in the Village is a unique New York treat: as the sky grows dark, the streets come alive. Don't let a mob at the door make you hesitant about sitting over your coffee for hours and watching the spectacle—especially if the coffee is good. Explore twisting side streets and alleyways where you can join Off-Broadway theater-goers as they settle down over a burger and a beer to write their own reviews, or drop into a jazz club. If all this sounds too effete, sneak down 8th St. to Sixth Ave. to find some of the most respectable pizzerias in the city. The crucial question: John's or Ray's?

West Village

Whatever you think of the West Village's Bohemian authenticity, you can't deny that all the floating artistic angst does result in many creative (and cheap) food venues. Try the major avenues for inexpensive, decent food. Wander by the posh row houses around Jane St. and Bank St. for classier bistro and café fare. The European-style bistros of **Bleecker Street** and **MacDougal Street,** south of Washington Square Park, have perfected the homey "antique" look.

John's Pizzeria, 278 Bleecker St (243-1680). Read the writing on the wall—thank-you notes from former clients, including past U.S. presidents—but don't let them distract you too much from the pizza. Cooked in a brick oven, with a crisp crust and just enough cheese, pizza for 2 or 3 costs $8.40. If the place is full, they'll find room for you at **John's Too** next door. No slices; table service only. Open daily 11:30am-11:30pm.

Ray's Pizza, 465 Sixth Ave. (243-2253) at 11th St. Half of the uptown pizza joints claim to be the "Original Ray's," but any New Yorker will tell you that this is the real McRoy. People fly here from Europe just to bring back a few pies. Well worth braving the lines and paying upwards of $1.75 for a slice. Open Sun.-Thurs. 11am-2am, Fri.-Sat. 11am-3am.

Olive Tree Café, 117 MacDougal St. (254-3630), north of Bleecker St. Middle Eastern food and endless stimulation. If you get bored by the old movies on the wide screen, rent chess, backgammon, and Scrabble sets ($1), or doodle with colored chalk on the slate tables. Felafel $2.25, chicken kebab platter with salad, rice pilaf, and vegetable $7. Delicious egg creams only $1.75. Open daily 11am-3am.

Le Figaro Café, 184 Bleecker St. (677-1100) at MacDougal, serves personal-sized pots of exotic brews sweetly complemented by homemade pastries. Stop by for the trendiest people-watching in town. (Open Mon.-Thurs. 11am-2am, Fri. 11am-4am, Sun. 10am-2am.)

East Village and Lower East Side

Few frills but plenty of thrills pump the lower end of the East Side, where pasty-faced punks and starving artists sup alongside an older generation conversing in Polish, Hungarian, and Yiddish. Observant Jews and slavophiles reach nirvana in the delis and restaurants here. The Eastern European restaurants distributed along First and Second Ave. serve up some of the best deals in Manhattan. The **9th St Bakery,** 350 E. 9th St., and the **S&W Skull Cap Corporation,** 45 Essex St., sell inimitable New York bagels and bialys.

Two Boots, 37 Ave. A (505-2276), at E. 2nd St. The 2 boots are Italy and Louisiana, both shaped remarkably like footwear. It may be Cajun Italian or Italian Cajun, but it sure is tasty. Try the Turkey Deluxe $5 or the shrimp pizza $8. Open daily noon-midnight.

Odessa, 117 Ave. A (473-8916), at 7th St. Beware of ordinary-looking coffee shops with slavic names. Lurking beneath the title may be an excellent, inexpensive restaurant serving Eastern European specialties. Choose your favorites from a huge assortment of *pirogi*, stuffed cabbage, kielbasa, sauerkraut, potato pancakes, and other delicacies for the combo dinner ($6.70). Spinach pie and small Greek salad $4.50. Open daily 7am-midnight.

Veselka, 144 Second Ave. (228-9682) at 9th St. An oft-hyphenated down-to-earth soup-and-bread Polish-Ukrainian joint. Blintzes $4.50, asparagus and mushroom crepe $6. Open 24 hrs.

Second Ave. Delicatessen, 156 Second Ave. (677-0606), at 10th St. The definitive New York deli; people come into the city just to be snubbed by the waiters here. Have a pastrami or tongue on rye for $6.50, a fabulous burger deluxe for $6.25, or Jewish penicillin (a.k.a chicken soup) for $2.75. Note the Hollywood-style star plaques embedded in the sidewalk outside: this was once the heart of the Yiddish theater district. But while their art form is all but forgotten, such personages as Moishe Oysher and Bella Meisel have gained their foothold on immortality in the pavement here. Open Mon.-Fri. 8am-midnight, Sat.-Sun. 8am-2am.

Kiev, 117 Second Ave. (674-4040), at E. 7th St. Unparalleled *pirogi* and tons of heavy foods laced with sour cream and butter, generally under $5. Upscale deli decor. A popular late-night and early-morning pit stop for East Village club hoppers with the munchies. Open 24 hrs.

Passage to India, 308 E. 6th St. (529-5770), off Second Ave. Newer and classier than others on the block. Some of the city's best Indian food. Dine under chandeliers and brass-framed mirrors in British colonial style. Full *tandoori* dinner (soup, appetizer, main course, dessert, coffee) $12. Open daily noon-midnight.

Seekers of kosher food won't find much *traif* east of First Ave., especially south of East Houston St., where there has been a Jewish community since turn-of-the-century immigrant days.

Ratner's Dairy Restaurant, 138 Delancey St. (677-5588). A well-known kosher hangout, partly due to its frozen food line. Jewish dietary laws strictly followed; you will have to go elsewhere for a pastrami sandwich with mayo. But there's no better place to feast on fruit blintzes and sour cream ($8.50) or simmering vegetarian soups ($3.75). Open Sun.-Thurs. 6am-midnight, Fri. 6am-3pm.

Katz's Delicatessen, 205 E. Houston St. (254-2246), near Orchard. Classic informal deli, established in 1888. You'd better know what you want, because the staff here doesn't fool around. Have an overstuffed corned beef sandwich with a pickle for $6.45. Mail-order department enables you to send a salami to a loved one (or, perhaps, an ex-loved one). With testimonial letters from both Carter and Reagan, how could it be bad? (Don't think about that one too much.) Open daily 7am-11pm.

Yonah Schimmel Knishery, 137 E. Houston St. Rabbi Schimmel's establishment, around since the heyday of the Jewish Lower East Side, has honed the knish to an art. Kasha and fruit-filled knishes (from $1.75) available too. Or try yogurt from a 71-year-old strain. Open daily 8am-6pm.

Bernstein-on-Essex, 135 Essex St. (473-3900). Chinatown meets the Lower East Side, and presto—kosher Chinese food. Steep prices ($10 and up) and non-existent ambience. But many travel for hours to indulge their palates here. An only-in-New-York establishment. This is the original "Waiter what time is it?"—"Sorry, not my table" restaurant. Open Sun.-Thurs. 8am-midnight, Fri. 8am-3pm, also in winter Sat. dusk-2am.

SoHo

Like the residents, the restaurants in SoHo can prove surprisingly down to earth, but also may demonstrate an occasionally distracting preoccupation with art (some are practically indistinguishable from their neighboring galleries). Even the grocery stores get in on the act: **Dean and Deluca,** 560 Broadway, at Prince St., features gallery-quality art and gourmet-caliber food. With art, of course, comes money, so don't be surprised if you find it hard to get a really cheap meal. Often the best deal in SoHo is brunch, when the neighborhood shows its most cozy and good-natured front. You can down your canteloupe and coffee in any number of café/bar establishments.

Elephant and Castle, 183 Prince St. (260-3600), off Sullivan. Also at 68 Greenwich Ave. Popular with locals for its excellent coffee and creative light food. Perfect for brunch. Prepare to wait for a table. Dinner around $10, brunch around $8. Open Sun.-Thurs. 8:30am-midnight, Fri.-Sat. 8:30am-1am.

Fanelli's Café, 94 Prince St. A very mellow neighborhood hang-out, where it always feels like late at night. Standard bar fare and cheap brew ($2). Come to escape the gallery crowd. Open Mon.-Sat. 10am-2am, Sun. noon-2am.

Chinatown

New Yorkers have long thrived on the association of their Chinatown with delectable food. The buildings in the neighborhood house over 200 restaurants that conjure up some of the best Chinese, Thai, and Vietnamese cooking around. But they don't make dumplings for Trumplings here—compared to what you'd pay in a French or Italian restaurant, this insular community charges surprisingly little for a filling and satisfying meal. Competition has been a boon for palates; once predominately-Cantonese cooking has now burgeoned into different cuisines from the various regions of China: hot and spicy Hunan or Szechuan food; the sweet and mildly spiced seafood of Soochow; or the hearty and filling fare of Peking. Competition has also boosted the popularity of Cantonese *dim sum* (that's grazing, Chinese style, and served in nearly all teahouses). No menus here—"waiters" roll carts filled with assorted dishes of bite-sized goodies up and down the aisles. You simply point at what you want; in the end, the number of empty dishes are tallied up. To reach Chinatown, take the 4, 5, 6, J, M, Z, N, or R to Canal St., walk east on Canal to Mott St., go right on Mott, and follow the curved street toward the Bowery, Confucius Plaza, and E. Broadway. Explore the side streets along the way. Remember, when you order in restaurants here, do it Chinese style; order one fewer dish than people at your table and share. You can always order more later.

House of Vegetarian, 68 Mott St. (226-6572), off Bayard St. Jet black tables and leafy green walls help project the image of a sleek and sound you; the food here is prepared in a healthier form, cooked in minimal amounts of oil and using only soy, roots, and wheat by-products. They stuff dumplings with rice and veggies ($1.50). Try *Jomein* with 3 Kinds of Mushrooms ($3). An ice-cold Lotus seed or Lychee Drink ($1.30) really hits the spot on those hot summer days. Open daily 11am-11pm.

Nom Wah Tea Parlor, 13 Doyers St. (962-6047), a curved side alley off Pell St., near the Bowery. *Dim sum* served all day; small dishes $1, larger dishes $2. Ask for *Ha Gow* ($2), a mixture of chopped shrimp and Chinese vegetables encased in rice flour dough and cooked in bamboo steamers. Rinse it all down with a pot of imported Chinese tea. Open daily 8:30am-8pm.

Lung Fong Bakery, 41 Mott St. (233-7447), off Bayard St. A clean, spacious, and airy place, unlike many other bakeries. Worth a quick nosh or an extended stay. Almond cookies 50¢, pineapple sponge cake 50¢, chicken rolls 60¢, hot baked pork or sausage buns 50¢. Open daily 8am-9pm.

Chinatown Ice Cream Factory, 65 Bayard St. (608-4171), off Mott St. Homemade ice cream comes in flavors like lychee, mango, ginger, red bean, and green tea. One scoop $1.70, two scoops $3.00, three scoops $3.90. Open Mon.-Thurs. noon-11pm, Fri.-Sun. noon-midnight.

Hee Seung Fung Teahouse (HSF), 46 Bowery (374-1319), off Canal St. Large and hectic. Widely acclaimed *dim sum* dishes $1.80-3.50 (served 8am-4:30pm). Try sesame oil and ginger crispy fish and the *jung* (sticky rice wrapped in tea leaves). From the subway, walk east on Canal St. to the Bowery, then take a sharp left. Open daily 7:30am-4:30am.

Little Italy

Little Italy, north on Mulberry from Canal St., is one of the liveliest sections of town at night. To get there, take the D train to Canal St. Crammed with tiny restaurants, the neighborhood bustles with people strolling in and out of the cafés off Mulberry St. Join the crowds and stake out a table outdoors where you can enjoy cappuccino and cannoli, the perennial favorites.

Paolucci's, 149 Mulberry St. Unpretentious, family-owned restaurant. The watchful portrait of the boss hangs on the front wall. Pasta from $6. Chicken *cacciatore* with salad $9. Open Mon.-Thurs. 11:30am-10:30pm, Fri.-Sat. 11:30am-midnight, Sun. 11:30am-9:30pm.

Marionetta, 124 Mulberry St. Sidewalk tables let you dine without missing a single frenzied moment of Little Italy. Serves some of the most inexpensive veal dishes in the neighborhood. Veal or chicken *parmagian* $9. Open daily 11am-midnight.

Puglia Restaurant (966-6006), 189 Hester St. Long tables mean fun and rowdy. Venture into 3 separate dining rooms, ranging from diner-like to warehouse-like. A favorite with New Yorkers and bold tourists. Monstrous plate of mussels $8, entrees from $7. Live music nightly. Open Mon.-Sun. 11:30am-midnight.

Financial District

At lunchtime and after work, brokers and lawyers crowd the **South Street Seaport,** a recently rehabilitated historic district. To get there, take the 2 or 3 to Fulton St. The central marketplace contains more gastronomic variety per square foot than anywhere else in New York. Go wild at the gourmet fast-food specialty booths—one stand serves only East Argentine dairy products; another, Southern breakfasts. Check out the Seaport on a Friday afternoon to see uptight Wall Street execs let loose over a few beers. Formal restaurants, presided over by the 143-year-old **Sweets,** 2 Fulton St. (344-9189), are very expensive and inconsistent.

Hamburger Harry's, 157 Chambers St. Gourmet burgers for the connoisseur; 7 oz. patty broiled over applewood with exotic toppings, from $6. Regular burger $3.95, nacho cheese fried $3. Open Mon.-Thurs. 11:30am-11:30pm, Fri.-Sat. 11:30am-1am, Sun. noon-11:30pm.

Wolf's Delicatessen (422-4141), 42 Broadway. A deli untainted by any trend in cuisine or decor that hit after the early 60s. Formica, pickles, no pretensions. Baked beans $1.10, BLT $3.75. Open Mon.-Fri. 6am-7:45pm, Sat. 6am-3:45pm.

Frank's Papaya, 192 Broadway, at John St. Excellent value, quick service. Very close to World Trade Center. Hot dog 60¢. Breakfast of egg, ham, cheese, coffee $1.50. Open daily 5:30am-10pm.

Brooklyn

Ethnic flavor changes every two blocks in Brooklyn. Brooklyn Heights offers nouvelle cuisine, but specializes in pita bread and *baba ganoush*. Williamsburg seems submerged in kosher and cheap Italian restaurants, while Greenpoint is a borscht-lover's paradise. Flatbush (at Ave. J or M; take the Q or the D trains), has all sorts of cheap ethnic restaurants that are kosher. And for those who didn't get enough in Manhattan, Brooklyn now has its own Chinatown in Sunset. Venture out to find a restaurant with food from another nation and prices from another century.

Junior's, 986 Flatbush Ave. (718-852-5257), across the Manhattan Bridge at De Kalb St. Subway: #2, 3, 4, 5, B, D, M, N, Q, or R to Atlantic Ave. Lit up like a jukebox and playing classic roast beef and brisket. Brisket sandwich $6.25, entrees around $10. Suburban types drive for hours to satisfy their cheesecake cravings here (plain slice $3). Open Sun.-Thurs. 6:30am-1am, Fri.-Sat. 6:30am-3am.

Milo's Restaurant, 559 Lorimer St. (718-384-8457), in Williamsburg. Subway: J or M to Lorimer St. In a neighborhood packed with Italian food this place stands out with its Sinatra-special jukebox selection. Antipasto $3, several choices of pasta under $5. Try the Neapolitan specialty *capozzelle*, an entire lamb's head served with lemon wedges—*mangiate bene!* Open Tues.-Sun. 10am-9:30pm.

El Castillo de Jagua, 148 Fifth Ave. (718-638-2907) at St. John Pl. in Park Slope. Subway: D or Q to Seventh Ave. The deafening jukebox pumps out the newest Latino rhythms. Excellent, cheap food with great breakfast specials. Try a platter of *platanos* (fried bananas, $1.50), the Latin-American french fry. Open daily 7am-midnight.

Aunt Sonia's, 1123 Eighth Ave. (718-965-9526) at 12th St., near Park Slope. Subway: F to Seventh Ave./Park Slope. A tiny haven for the budget gourmet. Line up with the crowds awaiting the chef's newest creations. Besides providing daily specials, he creates a new menu every 2 months. Entrees from $8. Open Mon.-Thurs. 5:30-10:30pm, Fri.-Sat. 5:30-11:30pm, Sun. 10am-10pm.

Nathan's, Surf and Sitwell Ave. in Coney Island. Subway: B, D, F, or N to Coney Island. Seventy-four years ago, Nathan Handwerker became famous for undercutting his competitors on the boardwalk. His hot dogs cost a nickel; theirs were a dime. Today, a classic frank at Nathan's sells for $1.75. Unique french fries $1.55. Open Sun.-Thurs. 8am-4am, Fri.-Sat. 8am-5am.

Queens

Reasonably priced, authentic ethnic food is probably the best thing about Queens. **Astoria** specializes in discount shopping and ethnic eating. Take the G or R to Steinway St. and Broadway and browse all the way down to 25th Ave. Kew Gardens Hills's Main Street, famous among Jews all over the east coast, has more than its fair share of kosher takeout and pizza places, and is also a great place to observe Jewish life. In **Flushing**, you can find excellent Chinese, Japanese, and Korean restaurants, but always check the prices. An identical dish may cost half as much only a few doors away. **Bell Boulevard** in Bayside, out east near the Nassau border, is the center of Queens night life, and on most weekends you can find crowds of young bar-hopping natives here.

Roumely Tavern, 3304 Broadway, Astoria (718-278-7533). Subway: G or R to Steinway St. or N to Broadway. When in Astoria, do as the Astorians do. A taste of the Old Country, with Greek accents as authentic as the food. *Spanokopita* (spinach pie) appetizer $2.50, lamb stew $8. Open daily noon-1am.

Woo Chon Restaurant, 41-19 Kissena Blvd., Flushing (718-463-0803). Subway: #7 to Main St. Some of the finest Korean food in Flushing. Look for the waterfall in the window. Try *JJ-Gob bibimbab* ($9.25), an ancient rice dish served in a superheated stone vessel; mix immediately, or the rice will be scorched by the bowl. For lunch, try a filling bowl of *seulnung-tang* ($6.50), fine rice noodles in a beef broth with assorted Oriental veggies. An unlimited supply of *kim-chi* (marinated vegetables) accompanies every meal. Open perpetually.

Pastrami King, 124-24 Queens Blvd. (718-263-1717), near 82nd Ave., in Kew Gardens. Subway: E, F, or R to Union Tpke. and Queens Blvd. Everything here, from meat to coleslaw to pickles, made on the premises. The home-cured pastrami and corned beef is among the best in New York. Take out a sprawling pastrami on rye for $6. Open Sun.-Fri. 8am-9pm, Sat. 8am-10pm.

Bronx

When Italian immigrants settled the Bronx, they brought their recipes and tradition of hearty communal dining with them. While much of the Bronx is a culinary disaster zone, the New York *cognoscenti* soon discovered the few oases along Arthur Ave., and in Westchester where the fare is as robust and the patrons as rambunctious as their counterparts in Naples. The enclave on Arthur Ave., and along 187th St. brims with pastry shops, streetside cafés, pizzerias, restaurants, and mom-and-pop emporiums vending Madonna 45s and batallions of imported espresso machines—all this without the schmaltzy tourist veneer of Little Italy.**Ruggieri Pastry Shop,** 2373 Prospect Ave., at E. 187th St., produces mountains upon mountains of classic Italian pastries, although they're especially proud of their *sfogliatella*—a flaky Neapolitan pastry stuffed with ricotta. Ruggieri operates one of the last authentic ice cream fountains in New York. (Open daily 8am-10pm.)

> **Dominick's,** 2335 Arthur Ave. (733-2807). Small authentic Italian eatery. Vinyl tablecloths and bare walls, but great atmosphere. Waiters won't offer you a menu or a check—they'll recite the specials of the day and bark out what you owe at the end of the meal. Try the linguini with marinara sauce ($7) and the special veal *francese* ($12). Open Mon. and Wed.-Sat. 10am-midnight, Sun. 1-9pm. Arrive before 6pm or after 9pm, or expect at least a 20-min. wait.

Sights

The classic sightseeing quandary experienced by New York tourists has been finding the Empire State Building. They've seen it in dozens of pictures or drawings, captured in sharp silhouettes or against a steamy pink sky as a monument of dreams. They've seen it towering over the grey landscape as their plane descends onto the runway, or in perspective down long avenues or from a river tour. But they can't see it when they're standing right next to it.

This optical illusion may explain why many New Yorkers have never visited some of the major sights in their hometown. Not all sights are as glaringly green and obvious as the Statue of Liberty. If it's your first time in the big city, you'll notice even more subtle attractions—the neighborhoods and personalities jumbled together on shared turf, the frenzy of throngs at rush hour, the metropolitan murmur at dusk. And if it's your hundredth time in the city, you'll see architectural quirks you've never noticed, and plain old doorways you have yet to discover and enter. Seeing New York takes a lifetime.

East Midtown

The massive Beaux-Arts style **Grand Central Terminal,** 42nd to 45th between Vanderbilt Place and Madison Ave., was the gateway to New York and more for millions of travelers during the early part of this century. Althought fewer trains roar into and out of its depots today than in the 40s and 50s, the terminal remains a potent symbol of the city's power, just as it has been for the previous 40-odd years, and is an ideal place to begin a tour of East Midtown. Out on top of the Vanderbilt entrance to the building is the famous wall clock, mounted on the Southern facade and surrounded by a classical statuary group designed by Jules Alexis Coutan. The Municipal Art Society leads popular free tours of the place every Wednesday at 12:30pm, starting at the Chemical Commuter Bank in the Main Concourse.

The New York skyline would be incomplete without the familiar Art-Deco headdress of the **Chrysler Building,** at 42nd and Lexington, built by William Van Allen as a series of rectangular boxes and topped by a spire modeled after a radiator grille. Other details evoke the romance of the automobile in the Golden Age of Chrysler: On the 26th floor, a frieze of idealized cars in white and gray brick, flared gargoyles at the fourth setback styled after 1929 hood ornaments and hubcaps, and patterned lightning bolt designs symbolizing the power of this new machine. When built in

1929, this seductive if absurd creation stood as the world's tallest, but the Empire State Building topped it only a year later.

The **Empire State Building** (slurred together by any self-respecting New Yorker into "Empire Statebuilding") has style. It retains its place in the hearts and minds of Americans even though it is no longer the tallest building in the US (an honor now held by Chicago's Sears Tower), or even the tallest building in New York (now the upstart twin towers of the World Trade Center). It doesn't have the best looks (the Chrysler building is more delicate, the Woolworth more ornate). But the Empire State building remains the best-known and most-loved landmark in the Empire State, dominating the postcards, the movies, and the skyline. The limestone and granite structure, with glistening mullions of stainless steel, stretches 1,454 ft. into the sky, and its 73 elevators run on 2 mi. of shafts. High winds can bend the entire structure up to a quarter-inch off center.

Forty-second St. also delivers the **Daily News Building,** home to the country's first successful tabloid. When designed the building was extremely innovative in its treatment of height; instead of the typical elevation in three stages corresponding to the base, shaft, and capital of a classical column, it rises in a series of monolithic slabs. A brass analog clock keeps time for 17 major cities worldwide, and frequent exhibitions breeze in and out. In 1990, the paper became entangled in a bitter drawn-out battle with its union workers that threatened to permanently terminate publication, but multimedia mogul Robert Maxwell shelled out some sterling, dissolving the labor dispute and taking over the rag in March of 1991.

Ceremonial capital of our ceremonial world government, the **United Nations** (963-7713) overlooks the East River between 42nd and 48th. Designed in the early 50s by an international committee including Le Corbusier, Oscar Niemeyer, and Wallace Harrison, the complex itself makes a diplomatic statement—part bravura, part compromise. Besides the ever-popular guided tours of the **General Assembly** and the **Security Council,** other UN attractions include stained glass windows by Chagall, a delightful promenade above the riverbank, and a muscle-bound Socialist Realist statue of a man beating a sword into a plowshare, which the USSR ironically gave to the UN in 1959, only three years after invading Hungary.

St. Patrick's Cathedral, New York's most famous church and the largest Catholic cathedral in America, stands at 51st. St. and Fifth Ave. Designed by James Renwick, construction began on the Gothic Revival structure in 1858, and required 21 years to complete. Today, it features high society weddings and the shrine of the first male U.S. saint, St. John Neumann.

Back on 375 Park Ave., between 52nd and 53rd, is the refreshingly innovative masterpiece by Mies van der Rohe: **The Seagram Building.** Completed in 1958, it still remains the paragon of the International Style. Van der Rohe had envisioned his creation as an oasis from the tight canyon of skyscrapers lining Park Ave., thus setting the tower 90 ft. back from the plaza, with two grand fountains in the foreground. The immediate public success of his vision led to a slew of trashy imitations with barren street-wrecking plazas.

Towering above the Saint Peter's Lutheran Church (619 Lexington Ave. at 53rd St) is the shiny, slanted **Citicorp Center,** built on four 10-story stilts to accommodate St. Peter's. The entire structure is sheathed in grayish aluminum which readily reflects light; at sunrise or sunset, the entire building radiates a warm glow. The 45°-angle roof was originally intended for use as a solar collector that has yet to come to light. But the roof does support a gadget called the Tuned Mass Damper that senses and records the tremors of the earth, warning us of earthquakes or harmonic convergences.

Philip Johnson's post-modern **AT&T Building** stands further west, on Madison Ave. between 55th and 56th. Unfortunately, most connoisseurs of Manhattan architecture agree that this black-striped building, with its pinkish marble resembling a Jersey stucco job, doesn't reach out and touch anyone's heart. The cross-vaulted arcade underneath (open Mon.-Fri. 8am-6pm) features scenic cafés and the futuristic **AT&T Infoquest Center** (605-5555). (See Museums below.) The ritzy, four-star **Quilted Giraffe** restaurant also rests here, grazing on its patrons with tabs that can skyrocket up to $150 per person (with a decent vintage wine and appropriate tips). Don't miss Evelyn Longworth's atlasian statue Golden Boy, a colossal youth supporting a megalith globe that blazes in the sun.

Finally, one block further uptown, fellow bluechipper IBM performs its bit of public philanthropy with the green granite **IBM Building,** 590 Madison Ave. between 56th and 57th, featuring one of the city's best atriums, an airy space with comfortable chairs and a dense bamboo jungle. Also here is the **IBM Gallery of Science and Art,** with several engaging exhibits on an eclectic range of subjects (see Museums below).

West Midtown

Scurrying into the sunlight from the subterranean world of **Penn Station,** you will find yourself at the foot of West Midtown, with the swirl of commercial life surrounding you. Looking around at the impersonal jungle of box skyscrapers, you'll immediately notice the immense **Main Post Office,** across the street, on Eighth Ave. Finished in 1913, it mirrored the neoclassical magnificence of Pennsylvania Station (which used to be above ground) until the latter was destroyed in the 60s. Note the broad portico of 20 colossal Corinthian columns at the main entrance, and of course, the farcical inscription at the top about snow, rain, heat, and gloom having no effect on the impervious mail carrier.

For a look at one of the city's Beaux-Arts masterpieces, look no further than the **New York Public Library,** located on the west side of Fifth Ave., between 40th and 42nd. On sunny afternoons, flocks of people perch on the marble steps, sunning, lunching or even reading between the mighty lions Patience and Fortitude. The interior is a bonafide museum, with numerous murals, art collections, and lavishly decorated rooms named in honor of the library's benefactors. Of course, it's also the world's seventh-largest research library; a quick peek into the immense third-floor reading room should convince readily. For free (informative and interesting) tours of the building, Mon.-Wed. 11am and 2pm, meet at the Friends Desk in Astor Hall. For info call (661-7220).

Continuing westward, you'll soon find yourself enveloped in the scintillatingly incandescent brilliance radiating over the streets of **Times Square,** at the intersection of 42nd St. and Broadway. The square would have been voted one of the seven wonders of the world if only the judges had been tripping at the time. Well-policed with reason, here Broadway hosts not only its famous stages but also first-run movie houses, neon lights, street performers, and porn palace after peep show after porn palace. The entire area is slated for demolition and multi-billion dollar reconstruction in the next few years; New York can no longer afford the space or the bad publicity. The first new building, the neatly polished **Marriott Marquis** has already replaced two historic Broadway stages. Nearly all subway lines stop in Times Square (1, 9, 2, 3, 7, A, C, E, Q, B, N, R, and S).

A walk uptown along Broadway leads through the **Theater District,** which stretches from 41st to 57th St. At one time a solid row of marquees, some of the theaters have been converted into movie houses or simply left to rot because of the skyrocketing cost of live productions. Approximately 40 theaters remain active, mostly grouped around 45th St. Between 44th and 45 St., a half block west off Broadway in front of the Shubert Theater, sits **Shubert Alley,** a short private street reserved for pedestrians, originally built as a fire exit between the Booth and Shubert Theaters.

Between 48th and 51st St. and Fifth and Sixth Ave. stretches **Rockefeller Center.** The careful blend of plazas, concourses, and street-level stores fosters a sense of community rather than a business environment of sterile commerce. On Fifth Ave., between 49th and 50th St., check out the famous gold-leaf statue of Prometheus (with intestines intact), sprawled out on a ledge of the sunken **Lower Plaza** while jet streams of water shoot around it. The plaza doubles as an open-air café during the summer and a popular ice-skating rink in the winter.

In the backdrop, the 70-story **RCA Building**, seated at Sixth Ave., remains the most accomplished architectural creation in this complex. Examine the exquisite Art-Deco detailing in the black-granite lobby. Every chair in the building sits less than 28 ft. from natural light. Nothing quite matches watching a sunset from the 65th floor as a coral burnish fills the room. **NBC Studios** is headquartered here, offering you the chance to take a behind-the-scenes tour of their operation. (Open daily 9:30am-4:30pm; admission $7.25, ages under 6 not admitted; tours leave every 15 min.; tickets available on a first-come, first-served basis; they sell out early, so buy them well in advance).

A virtual Art-Deco shrine next door, **Radio City Music Hall** was built in 1932 at the corner of Sixth Ave. and 51st St. The 5,874-seat theater, still the largest of its kind, was the brainchild of Roxy Rothafel (founder of the Rockettes), who had originally intended to use it as an entertainment variety showcase. His idea, however, never caught on, and from 1933 to 1979 the hall functioned primarily as a movie theater, with over 650 feature films debuting here, including *King Kong, Breakfast at Tiffany's,* and *Doctor Zhivago.* In 1979, steeped in financial troubles, the Great Hall almost was demolished to make way for new office high-rises, but thanks to public outcry was declared a national landmark and saved at the last moment. A complete interior restoration then followed, and today you can see it in all its original majesty, from the 23K gold ceilings to the incredible three-part rotating stage platform. Tours of the Great Hall are given Mon.-Sat. 10am-4:45pm and Sun. 11am-5pm. ($7, ages under 6 $3.50). For more info call 632-4041.

West Midtown has its own mini-Museum Row, from 52nd to 53rd St. between Fifth and Sixth Ave. On 23 W. 52nd St. broadcasts the newly relocated **Museum of Television and Radio,** housed in a building nearly four times the size of its predecessor. Now they have continually changing exhibits of TV and radio artifacts as well as numerous TV and radio consoles for public access to their store of over 40,000 programs. One block up and walking towards Sixth Ave., you can take in a handful of masterpieces in the windows of the **American Craft Museum** and the **Museum of Modern Art.** A visit to the latter's masterpiece-studded sculpture garden, featuring the works of Rodin, Renoir, and Miro, should whet your appetite if you happen to have brought lunch (see Museums).

At the lower right edge of Central Park, on Fifth Ave. and 59th St., the legendary **Plaza Hotel,** built in 1907 by Henry J. Hardenberg, struts its dignified Edwardian stuff. Past guests have included the likes of Frank Lloyd Wright, F. Scott Fitzgerald, and The Beatles. Locals shuddered when the hubristic Donald Trump acquired the national landmark in 1988, but so far there has been little to fear—he already has a Trump Plaza.

Carnegie Hall first opened its doors in 1891, and after a century remains the central sound stage of New York, synonomous with musical success. During its illustrious history, legends such as Tchaikovsky, Caruso, Toscanini, and Bernstein have paid homage here, as well as popular musical icons such as Bob Dylan, The Beatles, and The Rolling Stones. Like Radio City Music Hall, Carnegie was almost demolished in the 1950s to make way for a large office building, but outraged citizens managed to recue it through special state legislation. (Tours Tues. and Thurs. 11:30am, 2pm, and 3pm; $6, students $5.)

Lower Midtown

The **Pierpont Morgan Library** (685-0610), 33 E. 36th St., at Madison Ave., is housed in a beautiful Renaissance palazzo, and features a large selection of medieval treasures. (Open Tues.-Sat. 10:30am-5pm, Sun. 1-5pm. Suggested contribution $3, seniors and students $1.) **Macy's,** the largest department store in the world, occupies the entire city block at 34th St. and Herald Square. You literally can spend your entire day here, making entertainment reservations, getting your hair done, having luch, and mailing a letter. You can, of course, also spend everything in your wallet. (Open Mon. and Thurs.-Fri. 10am-8:30pm, Tues.-Wed. and Sat. 10am-7pm, Sun. 11am-6pm.)

Farther west on 23rd St. below Madison Sq. stands the wedgelike **Flatiron Building,** often considered New York's first true skyscraper. The 20-story structure is immortalized in countless photographs and paintings that attempted to capture the unique form mandated by its location at the intersections of Broadway, Fifth Ave., and 23rd St. The building now houses world-famous publishing offices; here your *Let's Go* evolves into its final form.

Way over on the east side is the **Police Academy Museum,** 235 E. 20th St. (477-9753), between Second and Third. Located on the second floor of the NYC Police Academy, this small yet fascinating museum features excellent exhibits on why crime supposedly never pays.

After some law and order, it's time to get wild at the **Palladium,** 126 E. 14th St. (473-7171), between Third and Fourth. A huge Keith Haring mural of a packed theater greets you at the entrance of this former movie palace converted into a disco in 1985 by Japanese designer Arata Isozaki. Though now well out of its "in" days, the nightclub still boasts the world's largest dance floor and a staircase with 2,400 round lights (see Dance Clubs).

Upper East Side

The Golden Age of the East Side society epic began in the 1860s and progressed until the outbreak of World War I. Scores of wealthy people moved into the area and refused to budge, even during the Great Depression when armies of the unemployed pitched their tents across the way in Central Park. So it was that select hotels, mansions, and churches first colonized the primordial wilderness of the Upper East Side. The lawns of Central Park covered the land where squatters had dwelt; **Fifth Avenue** rolled over a stretch once grazed by pigs. These days parades, millionaires, and unbearably slow buses share Fifth Avenue. Its **Museum Mile** includes the Metropolitan, the Guggenheim, the International Center of Photography, the Cooper-Hewitt, the Museum of the City of New York, and the Jewish Museum, among others (for more info. see Museums and Galleries).

The **Trump Plaza,** at 167 E. 61st St., forms a morally edifying memorial to Mr. Trump's newly troubled *nouveau riche* pockets. Don't even bother throwing a coin into the waterfall to the left of the plaza entrance.

Gracie Mansion, at the north end of the park, has been the residence of every New York mayor since Fiorello LaGuardia moved in during World War II. At printing time, David Dinkins, the city's first African-American mayor, occupied this hottest of hot seats. To make a reservation for a tour of the mansion call 570-4751. (Tours Wed. only; admission $3, seniors $1.)

Central Park

Central Park rolls from Grand Army Plaza all the way up to 110th between Fifth and Eighth Ave. Twenty years of construction turned these 843 acres, laid out by Frederick Law Olmsted and Calvert Vaux in 1850-60, into a compressed sequence of landscapes of nearly infinite variety. The park contains lakes, ponds, fountains, skating rinks, ball fields, tennis courts, a castle, an outdoor theater, a bandshell, two zoos, and one of the most prestigious museums in the U.S., the **Metropolitan Museum of Art** (see Museums).

The Park may be divided roughly north and south at the main resevoir; the southern section affords more intimate settings, serene lakes, and graceful promenades, while the northern end has a few ragged edges. Nearly 1400 species of trees, shrubs, and flowers grow here. For guidance, check the four-digit metal plaque bolted to the nearest lamppost; the first two digits tell you what street you're nearest, and the second two whether you are on the east or west side (even # means east; odd west). In an emergency, call the 24-hr. emergency line (800-834-3832).

Horse around on the ponies of the **Friedsam Memorial Carousel** (879-0244), located at 65th St. west of Center Dr. (Open Mon.-Fri. 10:30am-4:30pm, Sat.-Sun. 10:30am-5:30pm. Winter Sat.-Sun. 10:30am-4:30pm. Admission 75¢.) At the renovated **Central Park Zoo,** Fifth Ave. at 64th St. (439-6500), the monkeys effortlessly ape their visitors. (Open Mon. and Wed.-Fri. 10am-5pm, Tues. 10am-8pm, Sat.-Sun. 10am-5:30pm. Admission $1, seniors 50¢, ages 3-12 25¢.) Kids will delight in heavy petting at the **Children's Zoo** and the pony rides (408-0271; 10am-4:30pm; admission 10¢). The Kong-sized **Wollman Skating Rink** (517-4800) doubles as a miniature golf course in late spring. (Open Mon. 10am-9pm, Tues.-Thurs. 10am-9:30pm, Fri.-Sat. 10am-11pm, Sun. 10am-9:30pm. Admission $4, kids $2. Admission to roller skating rink $5, seniors and kids $2.50; skate rental $2.50; open same hours as miniature golf.)

In summer the park hosts **free concerts** from Paul Simon to the Metropolitan Opera, and excellent free drama (for the first 1,936 lucky souls) during the **Shakespeare in the Park** festival (see Theater). Full info on recreational activities fills a handy booklet, *Green Pages,* available at all info centers.

Upper West Side

Broadway leads uptown to **Columbus Circle,** 59th St. and Broadway, the symbolic entrance to the Upper West Side and the end of Midtown—with a statue of Christopher himself. One of the Circle's landmarks, the **New York Coliseum,** was replaced by the **Javits Center** in 1990.

Three blocks north, Broadway intersects Columbus Ave. at imperial **Lincoln Center,** the cultural hub of the city, between 62nd and 66th St. The six buildings that constitute Lincoln Center—Avery Fisher Hall, the New York State Theater, the Metropolitan Opera House, the Library and Museum of Performing Arts, the Vivian Beaumont Theater, and the Juilliard School of Music—accommodate more than 13,000 spectators at a time. In daytime, the poolside benches by the Henry Moore sculpture behind the main plaza prove a good spot for a picnic; at night, the Metropolitan Opera House lights up, making its chandeliers and huge Chagall murals visible through its glass-panel facade. Lincoln Center offers hour-long guided tours (877-1800) daily on a varying schedule. Call on the day you wish to come. (Admission $6.50, seniors and students $5.50. Free library tour Thurs.) From October to June, 15-minute tours of the tremendous backstage of the Metropolitan Opera are also given. (Admission $6, students $3. Call 769-7020. For reservations and schedules, see Entertainment below.

Cross 65th St. to reach **Central Park West,** an area of graceful old apartment buildings. As Manhattan's urbanization peaked in the late 19th century, wealthy residents sought tranquility in the elegant **Dakota,** between 72nd and 73rd St. Built in 1884, the apartment house was named for its remote location. John Lennon's streetside murder here in 1981 has made the Dakota notorious.

New York City's member of the Ivy League, **Columbia University,** chartered in 1754, is tucked between Morningside Dr. and Broadway, and 114th and 121st St. Once all-male, Columbia now admits women independently of **Barnard College,** the women's school across West End Ave. The **Cathedral of St. John the Divine,** at the end of 112th St. on Amsteram Ave., promises to be the world's largest cathedral when finished. Construction, begun in 1812, is not expected to be completed until the next century.

Continue north and bear west to see **Grant's Tomb** (666-1640). Once a popular monument, it now attracts only a few brave souls. Inside, the black marble sarcophagus of Ulysses S. Grant and his wife Julia are surrounded by the General's cronies cast in bronze. (Open Wed.-Sun. 9am-4:30pm.) Across the street visit **Riverside Church** where you can hear concerts on the world's largest carillon (74 bells), the gift of John D. Rockefeller Jr. (Open Mon.-Sat. 9am-4:30pm, Sun. service 10:45am, tours Sun. at 12:30pm.)

Lower East Side

The old Lower East Side, once home to Eastern European immigrants, extended from Hester to 14th St. Now this area has developed a trifurcated personality, encompassing the part south of Houston (commonly considered the Lower East Side), the section west of First Ave. and east of Broadway (known as the "East Village"), and Alphabet City, east of First Ave. amd north of Houston St.

Two million Jews arrived on the Lower East Side in the 20 years before World War I. Still marking their legacy are the remnants of the Jewish ghetto that inspired Jacob Riis' compelling work *How the Other Half Lives,* and more recently the 80s epic musical *Rags.* On **The Bowery,** you can haggle for lamps; on **Allen Street,** shirts and ties. Try the Orchard St. market on a Sunday morning for some real bargains. Off Delancey St., the Essex St. covered market is direct from Northern Africa. **Schapiro's Winery,** 126 Rivington St., offers tours and taste tests Monday through Thursday from 11am to 4pm on the hour. On The Bowery check out Stanford White's **Bowery Savings Bank,** at Grand St., a repository of wealth that shades lots of homeless people. Built in 1894, it has kept the original carved check-writing stands inside. The bank might be safe, but wandering around here at night with a full wallet is almost an ensured deposit.

City Hall Area and the Financial District

The southernmost tip of Manhattan is extremely compact and free of threatening traffic. The narrow winding streets that discourage car travel make the area ideal for a walking tour. Wander down narrow, twisting historic lanes in between towering silver and stone skyscrapers. Five subway lines converge in the Financial District, some on their way to Brooklyn Heights across the East River. Take a train to the City Hall area on Broadway at the northern fringe of the Financial District, then explore south along the side streets off Broadway.

A prime example of Federalist architecture, **City Hall** (566-5097), has been the scene of frenetic politicking since 1811. (Open Mon.-Fri. 10am-4pm. Free.) From City Hall, walk down Broadway to the **Woolworth Building,** on Murray St., one of the few skyscrapers as graceful close up as from 20 blocks away. Designed by Cass Gilbert in the Gothic style, this 800-ft. tower was the world's largest from 1913 to 1930. Inspiring mosaics and carved caricatures of Cass Gilbert and Woolworth himself decorate the lobby. A block down Broadway is **St. Paul's Chapel** (602-0747), the oldest church in Manhattan (1766). George Washington worshiped here during his presidency. (Open Mon.-Sat. 8am-4pm, Sun. 7am-3pm.)

West of Broadway, off Church St., sprout the city's tallest buildings, the twin towers of the **World Trade Center.** The enclosed observation deck (466-7397), on the 110th floor of #2, offers a stunning overview of Manhattan, especially at night. (Open daily 9:30am-9:30pm. Admission $3.50, seniors and ages 6-12 $1.75, under 6 free.)

Walk eight short blocks down Broadway into the maw of the beast—the heavily built-up center of New York's Financial District. Glass and chrome temples of the capitalist god tower over sooty **Trinity Church,** (602-0773) at Broadway and Wall St. Trinity contains in its adjoining graveyard the tombs of Alexander Hamilton, Robert Fulton, and other prominent figures. Here, or nearby, pick up the **Heritage Trail,** an excellent walking tour marked by small American flags.

A short way down Wall Street, **Federal Hall** (264-8711) and the **New York Stock Exchange** (656-5168) sit diagonally across from one another. George Washington took the oath of office in Federal Hall; the building now houses historic documents. (Open Mon.-Fri. 9am-5pm. Free.) From the visitors gallery of the New York Stock Exchange (enter at 20 Broad St.), you can watch a free 15-minute movie (shown continuously Mon.-Fri.) and, from behind glass panels, view the controlled hysteria of the world's busiest commercial arena—the trading floor. Don't drop a dollar bill into the sty or you might start a riot. Come before noon to get a free ticket. (Open Mon.-Fri. 9:20am-4pm.) In the **Federal Reserve Bank,** 13 Liberty St. (720-6130), countries pay their debts by shifting bullion from one room to another. (Free 1-hr. tour and audio-visual display Mon.-Fri. at 10am, 11am, 1pm, and 2pm. Make appointments a week ahead by phone, and note that tickets must be mailed to you.)

New York Harbor and the Brooklyn Bridge

After its marathon journey down from Yonkers, Broadway ends in **Battery Park** on New York Harbor. A common site for political rallies such as the No-Nukes fests of the 70s and recent anti-apartheid protests, the restored waterfront park commands one of the finest views of the city. New York Harbor, Brooklyn Heights, Governor's Island, the Brooklyn-Battery Tunnel, Jersey City, Ellis Island, Staten Island, and the Statue of Liberty all can be seen on a clear day. The view is a lot better, however, from the **Staten Island Ferry** (718-727-2508), which leaves from the port east of Battery Park every half-hour. A trip on the ferry (50¢ round-trip) is what the New York Visitors Bureau calls "the world's most famous, most reasonable, and most romantic 5-mi. cruise. . ." and few would argue.

Another ferry will take you to the renovated **Statue of Liberty** (363-3200), landmark of a century of immigrant crossings. The **American Museum of Immigration,** located under the green lady's bathrobe, enshrines the dreams of all those who have come to look for America. Chaotic, dirty Ellis Island represents the disillusionment of 12 million Europeans who first experienced the U.S. through the New York Harbor's people-processing facilities. **Circle Line Ferries** (269-5755) shuttle between Battery Park and Liberty Island, leaving for the island daily every half hour 9am to 4pm, with the last ferry back at 5:15pm, July and August back at 7pm. (Fare $6, ages 3-17 $3, under 2 free.) Tickets include both islands and admission to museums. Buy them at Castle Clinton.

You'll have to get up around 4am to start the day at **Fulton Fish Market.** Here on the East River, a few blocks from Wall Street, New York's store and restaurant owners have bought their fresh fish ever since the Dutch colonial period. Next door, renovations have created the **South Street Seaport** complex (732-7678). The 18th-century market, graceful galleries, and seafaring schooners will delight historians and tourists alike. The decrepit but equally historic blocks on the periphery of the rehabilitated buildings are just as interesting. The **Seaport Line's** authentic paddlewheel steamboats (385-0791) offer day cruises (1½ hr.) departing daily on the hour at noon, 2pm, and 4pm ($12, students $10), and evening cruises to the live sounds of jazz, rock, and dixie ($18-20 depending on hr. and day). Cruises leave from Pier 16 at the seaport. **The Seaport Museum** (669-9424) offers tours of the area (open daily 10am-6pm).

Uptown a few blocks looms the **Brooklyn Bridge.** Built in 1883, the bridge was one of the greatest engineering feats of the 19th century. The 1-mi. walk along the pedestrian path (on the left) will show you why every New York poet feels compelled to write at least one verse about it, why photographers snap the bridge's airy spider-web cables, and why people jump off. To get to the entrance on Park Row, walk a couple of blocks west from the East River to the city hall area. Plaques on the bridge towers commemorate John Augustus Roebling, its builder, who, along with 20 of his workers, died during its construction.

Brooklyn

Founded in 1600 by the Dutch, Brooklyn was the third-largest city in the U.S. by 1860. In 1898, it merged with the city of New York and became a borough, but it still maintains a strong, separate identity, with many ethnic communities and local industries. Unfortunately, Brooklyn also includes some run-down, unsafe areas—especially west of Prospect Park. The visitors bureau publishes an excellent free guide to Brooklyn's rich historical past that outlines 10 walking tours of the borough.

Head south on Henry St. after the bridge, then turn right on Clark St. toward the river for a synapse-shorting view of Manhattan. Many prize-winning photographs have been taken here from the **Brooklyn Promenade,** overlooking the southern tip of Manhattan and New York Harbor. The headquarters of George Washington during the Battle of Long Island, now-posh **Brooklyn Heights** has advertised itself to many authors, from Walt Whitman to Norman Mailer, with its beautiful old brownstones, tree-lined streets, and proximity to Manhattan. Continuing south, explore the area's small side streets. Soon you'll be at **Atlantic Avenue,** home to a large Arab community, with second-hand stores and inexpensive Middle Eastern bakeries and grocery stores. Atlantic runs from the river to Flatbush Ave. At the Flatbush Ave. Extension, pick up **Fulton Street,** the center of downtown Brooklyn, recently transformed into a pedestrian mall.

Williamsburg, several blocks north of downtown Brooklyn, has retained its Hasidic Jewish culture more overtly than Manhattan's Lower East Side. The quarter encloses Broadway, Bedford, and Union Avenues. It closes on *shabbat* (Saturday), the Jewish holy day.

Prospect Park, designed by Frederick Law Olmsted in the mid-1800s, was supposedly his favorite creation. He was even more pleased with it than with his Manhattan project—Central Park. Because crime has given its ambience a sinister twist, exercise caution in touring the grounds. At the corner of the park stands **Grand Army Plaza,** an island in the midst of the borough's busiest thoroughfares, designed by Olmsted to shield surrounding apartment buildings from traffic. (Subway: 2 or 3 to Grand Army Plaza.) The nearby **Botanic Gardens** seem more secluded, and include a lovely rose garden, behind the **Brooklyn Museum.** (See Museums.)

Sheepshead Bay lies on the southern edge of Brooklyn, and is the name of both a body of water (really part of the Atlantic), and a mass of land. The seafood here comes fresh and cheap (clams $5 per dozen along the water). Walk along **Restaurant Row** from E. 21st to E. 29th St. on Emmons Ave., and peruse menus for daily seafood specials. Nearby **Brighton Beach,** nicknamed "Little Odessa by the Sea," has been homeland to Russian emigrés since the turn of the century. (Subway: D, M, QB.)

Once a resort for the City's elite, made accessible to the rest of the Apple because of the subway, fading **Coney Island** still warrants a visit. The **Boardwalk,** once one of the most seductive of Brooklyn's charms, now squeaks nostalgically as tourists are jostled by roughnecks. Enjoy a hot dog at historic **Nathan's,** Surf and Sitwell (718-266-3161; open Sun.-Thurs. 8am-4am, Fri.-Sat. 8am-5am). Built in 1927, the **Cyclone** roller coaster, 834 Surf Ave., remains the world's most terrifying ride. The 100-second-long screaming battle over nine rickety wooden hills more than makes up the $3. Go meet a walrus, dolphin, sea lion, shark, or other ocean critter in the tanks of the **New York Aquarium,** Surf and West Eighth (718-265-3400; open daily 10am-4:45pm, holidays and summer weekends 10am-7pm; admission $5.75, kids $2, seniors free Mon.-Fri. after 2pm). Look for the house beneath the roller coaster, which inspired a hilarious scene in Woody Allen's *Annie Hall.*

Queens

Archie and Edith Bunker (and the employees of the Steinway Piano Factory) now share the brick houses and clipped hedges of their "bedroom borough" with immigrants from Korea, China, India, and the West Indies. In this urban suburbia, the American melting pot bubbles away with more than 30% foreign-born population. Immigrant groups rapidly sort themselves out into neighborhoods where they try to maintain the memory of their homeland while living "the American Dream."

Queens is easily New York's largest borough, covering over a third of the city's total area. To understand Queens' kaleidoscope of communities is to understand the borough. If you visit only one place in Queens, let it be Flushing. Here you will find some of the most important colonial neighborhood landmarks, a bustling downtown, and the largest rose garden in the Northeast. Transportation could not be easier: the #7 Flushing line runs straight from Times Square. Just get on and sit back for about half an hour, until you reach the last stop (Main St., Flushing) in the northeastern part of the borough. Manhattan it isn't, but the streets usually are congested. Walk past the restaurants, discount stores, and businesses, and soak in Main St.'s crush of people and cultures.

Staten Island

Getting there is half the fun. At 50¢ (round-trip), the half-hour ferry ride from Manhattan's Battery Park to Staten Island is as unforgettable as it is inexpensive. Or you can drive from Brooklyn over the **Verrazzano-Narrows Bridge,** one of the longest suspension span babies in the world.

Once you've arrived at the St. George Terminal on the island, stop at the **Tourists Information Center** (718-720-1800) for info and a detailed map (open Mon.-Fri. 11am-7pm, Sat.-Sun. 11am-6pm).

The most concentrated number of sights on the island cluster around the beautiful 19th-century **Sailor's Snug Harbour Cultural Center,** at 1000 Richmond Terrace. Picnic and see its catch: the **Newhouse Center for Contemporary Art** (718-448-2500), a small gallery displaying American art with an indoor/outdoor sculpture show in the summer (open Thurs.-Fri. 1-5pm, Sat. noon-6pm); the **Staten Island Children's Museum,** with participation exhibits for the five- to 12-year-old in you (718-273-2060; open Wed.-Fri. 1-5pm, Sat.-Sun. 11am-5pm); and the **Staten Island Botanical Gardens.** On Broadway and Clove Rd. is the **Staten Island Zoo.** It has an animal hospital complete with a nursery viewing area (718-442-3100; open daily 10am-4:45pm; admission $1; free Wed.).

The Bronx

The Bronx offers more than urban decay. The borough builds on a history of urban change squeezed into just over half a century. In addition to housing projects and burnt-out tenements, the landscape sprouts suburban riverfront mansions, seaside cottages, colleges, 2000 acres of green parkland, and fading boulevards of grand apartment towers.

The pastoral estate **Wave Hill,** 675 W. 252 (549-2055), in Riverdale, has a majestic view of the Hudson. Samuel Clemens, Arturo Toscanini, and Teddy Roosevelt each resided in the Wave Hill House. The estate was finally donated to the city, and presently offers concerts and dance amidst its greenhouses and spectacular formal gardens. (Open Wed.-Sun. 10am-4:30pm. $4, seniors and students $2.)

The **Bronx Zoo** (367-1010), the largest urban zoo in the U.S., pioneered housing animals in natural surroundings. Although some animals are kept in cage-like confines, black jail bars are nowhere in evidence. When you look down from the monorail to Wild Asia ($1.50, kids $1), even the cages disappear; once there, you can ride a camel for $2. The 3-acre **Children's Zoo** features four natural environments. Across East Fordham Rd. from the zoo grows the huge **New York Botanical Garden** (220-8700). Remnants of forest and untouched waterways give a glimpse of the area's original landscape. (Open April-Oct. Tues.-Sun. 10am-7pm; Nov.-March 10am-6pm. Free. Parking $4.) The Metro-North Harlem line goes from Grand Central Station to the gardens (Botanical Garden Station), and includes admission (round-trip $7, seniors $5, kids $3.50).

Museums and Galleries

For museum and gallery listings consult the following publications: *New Yorker* (the most accurate and extensive listing), *New York,* the Friday *New York Times* (in the Weekend section), the *Quarterly Calendar,* (available free at any visitors bureau) and *Gallery Guide,* found in local galleries. Most museums and all galleries close on Mondays, and are jam-packed on the weekends. Many museums require a "donation" in place of an admission fee—no one will throw large, rotting papayas at you if you give less than the suggested amounts. Call ahead to find out about free times, usually a weeknight.

Major Collections

American Museum of Natural History, Central Park West (769-5100), at 79th to 81st St. Subway: Central Park West IND to 81st St. The largest science museum in the world, in a suitably imposing Gothic structure guarded by a statue of Teddy Roosevelt on horseback. The 45-ft.-long Tyrannosaurus Rex rules over the Hall of Dinosaurs, while J.P. Morgan's Indian emeralds blaze in the Hall of Minerals and Gems. Open Sun.-Tues. and Thurs. 10am-5:45pm; Wed. and Fri.-Sat. 10am-9pm. Donation $5, kids $2.50. Free Fri.-Sat. 5-9pm. The museum also houses **Naturemax** (769-5650), a cinematic extravaganza on New York's largest (4 stories) movie screen. Admission for museum visitors $5, kids $2.50; Fri.-Sat. double features $7, kids $2.50. The **Hayden Planetarium** (769-5920) offers outstanding multi-media presentations. Seasonal celestial light shows twinkle in the dome of the **Theater of the Stars,** accompanied by astronomy lectures. Admission $4, seniors and students $3, kids $2. Electrify your senses with **Laser Rock** (769-5921) Fri.-Sat. nights, $6.

Brooklyn Museum, 200 Eastern Pkwy. at Washington Ave. (718-638-5000). Subway: 2 or 3 to Eastern Pkwy. Wide-ranging collection of folk art, with everything from indigenous New York art (brownstone "sculpture" and period rooms) to items from the People's Republic of China. Changing exhibits display celebrated and unusual works. The **Botanic Garden** next door has a lovely collection of flora, including a large grove of Japanese cherry trees, a beautiful, fragrant rose garden, and the **Steinhardt Conservatory** and **Lily Pond.** Conservatory open Tues.-Sun. 10am-5:30pm. Admission $2, seniors and kids $1. Museum open Wed.-Sun. 10am-5pm. Donation $4, students $2, seniors $1.50, kids free.

The Cloisters, Fort Tryon Park, upper Manhattan (923-3700). Subway: A train through Harlem to 190th St. This monastery, built from pieces of 12th- and 13th-century French and Spanish cloisters, plus a new tower, was assembled by Charles Collens in 1938 as a setting for the Met's medieval art collection. Highlights include the Unicorn Tapestries, the Cuxa Cloister, and the Treasury. Open March-Oct. Tues.-Sun. 8:30am-5:15pm; Nov.-Feb. Tues.-Sun. 9:30am-4:45pm. Donation. (Includes admission to the Metropolitan Museum of Art main building.)

The Frick Collection, 1 E. 70th St. on Fifth Ave. (288-0700). Subway: 6 to 68th St. Robber baron Henry Clay Frick left his house and art collection to the city, and the museum retains the elegance of his French "Classic Eclectic" chateau. Impressive grounds. The Living Hall displays 17th-century furniture, Persian rugs, Holbein portraits, and paintings by El Greco, Rembrandt, Velázquez, and Titian. Courtyard inhabited by elegant statues surrounding the garden pool and fountain. Lectures Wed. and Thurs. Open Tues.-Sat. 10am-6pm, Sun. 1-6pm. Admission $3, students $1.50. Ages under 10 not allowed, under 16 must be accompanied by an adult.

Guggenheim Museum, 1071 Fifth Ave. and 89th St. (360-3500; bookshop 360-3525). Subway: 4, 5, 6 to 86th St. Many have called this controversial construction a giant turnip and Midwesterner Frank Lloyd Wright's joke on the Big Apple. Others hail it as the city's most brilliant architectural achievement; every New Yorker has dreamt of skateboarding down the spiraled hallway. Realistically, you may want to start at the top and work downhill. The Guggenheim's permanent collection, with examples of all the 20th-century "isms," sits in the flanking galleries. **The museum is closed until early in 1992** for renovations and the construction of a 10-story annex.

Metropolitan Museum of Art, Fifth Ave. (535-7710), at 82nd St. Subway: 4, 5, 6 to 86th St. If you see only one, see this. The largest in the Western Hemisphere, the Met's art collection encompasses 33 million works from almost every period through Impressionism; particularly strong in Egyptian and non-Western sculpture and European painting. Contemplate infiniti in the secluded Japanese Rock Garden. When blockbuster exhibits tour the world they usually stop at the Met—get tickets in advance through Ticketron. Open Tues.-Thurs. 9:30am-5:15pm, Fri.-Sat. 9:30am-8:45pm. Donation $6, students and seniors $3.

Museum of Modern Art (MOMA), 11 W. 53rd St. (708-9400), off Fifth Ave. in Midtown. Subway: E, F to Fifth Ave./53rd St. One of the most extensive Postimpressionist collections in the world, it was founded in 1929 by scholar Alfred Barr in response to the Met's reluctance to embrace contemporary art. Cesar Pelli's recent structural glass additions—expanded entrance hall, garden, and gallery space—flood the masterpieces with natural light. See Monet's sublime *Water Lily* room, Ross's *Engulfed Cathedral,* and a virtual Picasso warehouse. Sculpture garden good for resting and people-watching. Open Fri.-Tues. 11am-6pm, Thurs. 11am-9pm. Admission $7, seniors and students $4, under 16 free with adult. Feel-good donation Thurs. after 5pm.

Queens Museum, Flushing Meadow Park (718-592-5555). Subway: 7 to Willets Point/Shea Stadium. Located at the site of the 1939 and 1964 World's Fairs. Features memorabilia from the fairs in addition to a fine collection of 20th-century art by New Yorkers. Juried exhibits of young talent and special hands-on workshops encourage the continuing development of the plastic arts. Also has the "Panorama of the City of New York," the world's largest scale model with over 850,000 buildings in miniature. Open Tues.-Fri. 10am-5pm, Sat.-Sun. noon-5:30pm. Suggested contribution.

Whitney Museum of American Art, 945 Madison Ave. (570-3676), at 75th St. Subway: 6 to 77th St. Futuristic fortress featuring a comprehensive collection of contemporary U.S. art, with works by Hopper, Soyer, de Kooning, Motherwell, Warhol, and Calder. Gallery talks Sat.-Sun. at 2 and 3:30pm. Museum open Tues. 1-8pm, Wed.-Sat. 11am-5pm, Sun. noon-6pm. $5, seniors and students $3. Tues. 6-8pm. Free.

Smaller and Specialized Collections

American Craft Museum, 40 W. 53rd St. (956-3535), across from MOMA. Subway: E, F to Fifth Ave./53rd St. American crafts presented in 5 ingenious shows (such as "Plastic as Plastic") per year. Open Tues. 10am-8pm, Wed.-Sun. 10am-5pm. Admission $4.50, seniors and students $2.

AT&T Infoquest Center, 550 Madison Ave., at 56th St. (605-5555). High-tech, interactive exhibits explaining the information age, sponsored by the company with the soothing voice. Exhibits focus on lightwave communications, microelectronics, and computer software. Open Tues. 10am-9pm, Wed.-Sun. 10am-6pm. Free.

Cooper-Hewitt Museum, 2 E. 91st St. and Fifth Ave. (860-6894). Subway: 4, 5, 6 to 86th St. Andrew Carnegie's majestic, Georgian mansion now houses the Smithsonian Institute's decorative arts and design collection. All the special exhibits have considerable flair, focusing on such topics as contemporary designer fabrics. Open Tues. 10am-9pm, Wed.-Sat. 10am-5pm, Sun. noon-5pm. Admission $3, seniors and students $1.50, under 12 free. Free Tues. 5-9pm.

Museum of Holography, 11 Mercer St. (925-0526), in SoHo, ½-block north of Canal St. Subway: 6, J, M, N, R, Z to Canal St. Two fascinating floors of 3-D laser images. Free lectures, gallery tours, interactive exhibits. Open Tues.-Sun. 11am-6pm. $3.50, seniors and students $2.50.

New Museum of Contemporary Art, 583 Broadway between Prince and Houston St. (219-1222). Subway: R to Prince, 6 to Bleecker, or B, D, F to Broadway/Lafayette. Dedicated to the destruction of the canon and of conventional ideas of "art," the New Museum does the hottest, the newest, and the most controversial interactive exhibits; many rely heavily on the new technology in video. Much art dealing with the politics of identity—sexual, racial, and ethnic. Once a month an artist sits in the front window and has discussions with passersby. Open Wed.-Thurs. and Sun. noon-6pm, Fri.-Sat. noon-8pm. Suggested donation $3.50, seniors, students, and artists $2.50, under 12 free.

IBM Gallery of Science and Art, 590 Madison Ave. at 56th St. (745-6100). Subway: E, F, N, R to Fifth Ave. User-friendly exhibits covering a wide range of art. Permanent show titled "Mathematica: A World of Numbers and Beyond," featuring topological phenomena like the Möbius Strip. Open Tues.-Sat. 11am-6pm. Free.

International Center of Photography, 1130 Fifth Ave. (860-1778), at 94th St. Subway: 6 to 96th St. Housed in a landmark townhouse (1914) built for *New Republic* founder Willard Straight. The first museum in the world to have treated photography as fine art. Maintains a rich permanent collection and operates workshops, photolabs, and a screening room. Historical, thematic, contemporary, and experimental works. Open Tues. noon-8pm, Wed.-Fri. noon-5pm, Sat.-Sun. 11am-6pm. Admission $3, seniors and students $1.50. Free Tues. 5-8pm. Midtown branch at 77 W. 45th St. (869-2155) open Mon.-Fri. 11am-6pm, Sat. noon-5pm; free.

Intrepid Sea-Air-Space Museum, Pier 86 (245-2533), at 46th St. and Twelfth Ave. Bus: M42, or M50 to W. 46th St. America's mostly militaristic 20th-century technological achievements celebrated in the legendary aircraft carrier. Open Memorial Day-Labor Day daily 10am-5pm; Labor Day-Memorial Day Mon.-Fri. 10am-5pm. $7, under 12 $4, under 6 free.

Jacques Marchais Center of Tibetan Art, 338 Lighthouse Ave., Staten Island (718-987-3478). Take bus S74 from Staten Island Ferry to Lighthouse Ave., turn right and walk up the hill. One of the finest Tibetan collections in the U.S., but the real attractions are the gardens, set on beautifully landscaped cliffs. Center itself a replica of a Tibetan temple. Open April-Nov. Wed.-Sun. 1-5pm.

Jewish Museum, 1109 Fifth Ave. (860-1889), at 92nd St. Subway: 6 to 96th St. A large collection of ceremonial artifacts, Judaica, and modern pieces by Chagall and Stella. Exhibitions like: "Gardens and Ghettos: the Art of Jewish Life in Italy." **The museum is closed for renovations until the summer of 1992.**

Museum of Television and Radio, 25 W. 52nd St. (752-7684), between Fifth and Sixth. Subway: 6 to 51st St. Expanded, new facilities where visitors select and view 40,000 tapes of classic TV and radio shows on individual consoles. Go before 1pm or expect a long wait, especially on Sat., despite the 1-hr. max. viewing time. Special screenings possible for groups. Monthly retrospectives focus on legendary personalities and landmark shows. Open Tues. noon-8pm, Wed.-Sat. noon-5pm. Suggested contribution adults $4.50, seniors and under 13 $2.50, students $3.50. Call for tour times.

Entertainment

For info on shows and ticket availability, call the **NYC/ON STAGE hotline** at 768-1818, **Ticket Central** between 1 and 8pm at 279-4200, the **Theatre Development Fund** at 221-0013, or the **New York City Department of Cultural Affairs** hotline at 956-2787.

Officially, **Off-Broadway** theatres have between 100 and 499 seats; only Broadway houses have over 500. Mostly located downtown, Off-Broadway houses frequently offer more offbeat or countercultural shows, with shorter runs. Occasionally Off-Broadway have long runs or jump to Broadway houses (tickets cost $10-20). The best of these huddle around the Sheridan Square area of the West Village. They include the **Circle Rep,** at 99 Seventh Ave. S (924-7100), the **Circle in the Square Downtown,** at 159 Bleecker St. (254-6330), the **Lucille Lortel,** at 121 Christopher St. (924-8782), the **Cherry Lane,** at 38 Commerce St. (989-2020), and the **Provincetown Playhouse,** at 133 MacDougal St. (477-5048).

Joseph Papp founded the **Shakespeare in the Park** series, a New York summer tradition which practically everybody in the city has attended (or attempted to, anyway). From June through August, Papp presents two Shakespeare plays at the Delacorte Theatre in Central Park, near the 81st St. entrance on the Upper West Side, just north of the main road there (861-7277).

Opera and Dance

The fulcrum of New York culture is **Lincoln Center,** at Broadway and 66th St. (877-1800). For a schedule of events, write Lincoln Center Calendar, 140 W. 65th St. 10023, or call the Lincoln Center Library Museum (870-1630).

The **Metropolitan Opera Company** (362-6000) chants on a Lincoln Center stage the size of a football field. The performances boast some of most reknowned principals in the world. During the regular season (Sept.-May, Mon.-Sat.), you can get upper balcony seats for about $15. Cheapest seats have obstructed views, but standing room in the orchestra is a steal at $12. Standing room in the Family Circle is cheaper ($9), but it's like watching an ant farm. Box office open Mon.-Sat. 10am-8pm, Sun. noon-6pm. In summer, watch for free concerts in city parks (362-6000).

At right angles to the Met, the **New York City Opera** (870-5570), formerly under the direction of Beverly Sills, has been revamped by new director Christopher Keene. Known for its performances of warhorses, the company also sings contemporary U.S. works. The success of its recently introduced English "supertitles" has led other companies to adopt them. "City" now offers a summer season and keeps its ticket prices low year-round ($7-62, standing room back row top balcony $7). Call to check the availability of rush tickets on the night before the performance you want to attend, then wait in line the next morning.

The **Light Opera of Manhattan (LOOM),** 316 E. 91st St. (831-2000), between First and Second Ave., offers Gilbert and Sullivan and other operettas. (Tickets $17.50-20, students $12.)

The late great George Balanchine's **New York City Ballet,** the oldest in the country, alternates with the city opera for the use of the Lincoln Center's New York

State Theater (870-5570), performing December through January, again in May and June. (Tickets $9-50, standing room $4.) **American Ballet Theater** (477-3030) dances at the Met during the late spring and for about two weeks in summer. Under Mikhail Baryshnikov's guidance, ABT's eclectic repertoire has ranged from the Bolshoi grand-style Russian ballet to experimental American. The **Joffrey** ballet performs in the **City Center,** 131 W. 55th St. (581-7907), a doomed, Byzantine playhouse outside Lincoln Center.

The **Alvin Ailey American Dance Theater** (767-0940) bases its repertoire of modern dance on African-American jazz, spirituals, and contemporary music. The grandest integrated company in the world, it tours internationally but always performs at the **City Center** in December. Tickets ($15-40) are difficult to obtain; write or call City Center weeks in advance, if possible. The **Martha Graham Dance Co.,** 316 E. 63rd St. (838-5886), performs original Graham pieces during their October New York season. She revolutionized 20th-century dance with her psychological, rather than narrative, approach to characters. (Tickets $15-40.) Look also for the seasons of the **Merce Cunningham Dance Company,** the **Dance Theater of Harlem,** and the **Paul Taylor Dance Company,** usually in spring.

Half-price tickets for many music and dance events can be purchased on the day of performance at **Bryant Park,** 42nd St. (382-2323), between Fifth and Sixth Ave. (Open Tues. and Thurs.-Fri. noon-2pm and 3-7pm; Wed. and Sat. 11am-2pm and 3-7pm; Sun. noon-6pm.)

Classical Music

In Lincoln Center's Avery Fisher Hall (875-5135), the **New York Philharmonic,** (875-5656) under Kurt Masur, plays everything from Bach to Bax, Schubert to Schoenberg. Avery Fisher's new interior, designed by Philip Johnson, resonates with acoustic grandeur. The Philharmonic's season lasts from September through May, and jazz and classical musicians visit the rest of the year. (Tickets $10-50.) Senior citizen and student-rush tickets ($5) go on sale Tuesday and Thursday evenings a half hour before the curtain rises. "Mostly Mozart" concerts, performed July through August, feature artists like Itzhak Perlman; get there early since major artists often give half-hour pre-concert recitals. (Tickets $9-18.50.)

Carnegie Hall, Seventh Ave. at 57th St. (247-7800), one of the greatest musical auditoriums in the world, attracts opera singers, jazz singers, instrumental soloists, and symphony orchestras. (Tickets $15-40.)

Flicks

Hollywood may make the movies, but New York makes Hollywood. Most movies open in New York weeks before they're distributed across the country, and the response of Manhattan audiences and critics can shape a film's success or failure nationwide. Or so they like to think. Just grab a copy of any newspaper for an overview of the selection. Magazines such as *New York* and the *New Yorker* provide plot summaries and evaluations in their listings as well.

Museums like the Met and MOMA show artsy flicks downstairs, as does the New York Historical Society. For cinematic exposure to Chinese culture, go to the **Sun Sing Theater,** 75 E. Broadway (619-0493). The **Theatre 80 Saint Mark's,** 80 St. Mark's Place (254-7400), features classic foreign and U.S. revivals. For an inspiring movie-going experience, try the **Ziegfeld Theatre,** 141 W. 54th St. (765-7600). One of the last grand movie houses that hasn't been sliced up into a "multiplex," the Ziegfeld offers standard box-office attractions.

Between LaGuardia and Thompson at 144 Bleecker St. (674-2560), you'll find **Bleecker Movie House,** which specializes in experimental movies.

For a real deal, check out the library. All **New York Public Libraries** show free films ranging from documentaries to classics to last year's blockbuster. Screening times may be a bit erratic, but you can't beat the price.

Bars and Clubs

Dance Clubs

CBGB & OMFUG, 315 Bowery (982-4052), at Bleecker. Subway: 6 to Bleecker. The initials stand for "country, bluegrass, blues, and other music for uplifting gourmandizers," but everyone knows that since 1976 this club has been all about punk rock. The Talking ("This ain't no nightclub, no CBGB's") Heads got their start here. The club has adjusted to the post-punk 90s with alternative offerings, but expect a nostalgic hardcore crowd. Opens Mon.-Fri, 7:30pm, Sat.-Sun. 8:30pm, Sun. matinee at 3pm. Cover $5-12.

Bentley's, 25 E. 40th St. (684-2540), between Park and Madison. Predominantly black crowd dancing to incredible rhythms at impossible speed. Even the yuppies have a good time. First floor houses a house DJ. Upstairs, reggae spins regularly. Free buffet Thurs.-Fri. at 5pm. Thurs. 6pm-2am is Reggae-Soca-Calypso night. Fri. free 5-11pm, $10 after 11pm. Cover for women waived until 11pm Sat. Cover $10. Opens every day at 5pm.

Wetland Preserve, 161 Hudson St. (966-4225). A giant Summer of Love mural in the back room sets the tone, a Volkswagen bus curio shop swims in tie dyes, and mood memorabilia harken to the No Nukes years in this 2-story whole earth spectacular. Downstairs you can chill out in a flowerchildren's love patch. Mondays and Fridays Wetlands brings you reggae. Tuesdays it's as close as you get to Grateful Dead, Wednesdays things get mixed up. Thursdays blues and rock arrive, Saturday nights psychedelic mania kicks in and Sunday things are back to the mellow groove with folk. Shows start nightly after 9:30. This eco night club does some canvassing on the side, sponsoring benefits in the cause of a healthier earth. Open Sun.-Thurs. 5pm, Fri.-Sat. 9pm. Cover $5-15 (no drink minimum).

Tramps, 45 W. 21st St. (727-7788). Screaming violins and clattering washboards pack the sweaty dance floor. Lousiana Zydeco rocks nightly with help from blues, reggae, and rock bands. Doors open at 7pm. Sets at 8:30 and 11:30pm. Cover $5-15.

Music/Bars

Angry Squire, 216 Seventh Ave. (242-9066), between 22nd and 23rd St. Jazz every night with a local crowd and mellow tunes. Simple tables with wine caskets hanging above the bar. Open daily 5pm-3am. Jazz after 9:30. No cover.

Apollo Theater, 253 W. 125th St. (864-0372). Subway: 1, 9 to 125th St. Use caution in the neighborhood. This historic Harlem landmark has heard the likes of Duke Ellington, Count Basie, Ella Fitzgerald, Lionel Hampton, Billie Holliday, and Sara Vaughn. In his zoot-suit days, Malcolm X shined shoes here. Now undergoing a revival. Show tickets $5-30. Arrive at least ½-hr. early for cheap tickets. Infamously critical amateur night Wed. at 7:30pm. Call the theater to check what's playing.

Augie's, 2751 Broadway (864-9834). Jazz all week until 3am. The saxophonist sits on your lap and the bass rests on your table. Quality musicians and a cool crowd. Open daily 8pm-3am. No cover.

Dan Lynch, 221 Second Ave. (677-0911), at 14th St. Subway: 4, 5, 6, L, N, R to Union Sq. Dark smoky room with Casablanca fan, long bar, and "all blues, all the time." Swinging, friendly, Deadhead crowd drowns the dance floor. Pool table in back. Open daily 8pm-4am; blues and jazz start at 10pm. Jam session Sat.-Sun. 4-9pm. Cover Fri.-Sat. $5.

Michael's Pub, 211 E. 55th St. (758-2272), off Third Ave. Subway: 4, 5, 6 to 59th or 6 to 51st St. Woody Allen played his clarinet here instead of picking up his 3 Academy Awards for *Annie Hall.* He still sneaks in some Mon. nights. Sets Mon. at 9 and 11pm, Tues.-Sat. at 9:30 and 11:30pm. Open Mon.-Sat. noon-1am. Cover $15-25. No cover Mon. Substantial food and drink min. at the tables, but no min. at the bar.

Comedy Clubs

New York City is a comedian's Happy Hunting Ground. From its reputation as America's crime capital to its ridiculously high cost of living to its idiosyncratic denizens—New York simply has too much to ridicule. Most of the comics who work the rounds have appeared on TV comedy shows like MTV, VH-1, or Live At The Improv. Some even have credits on Star Search or the Tonight Show. Their acts run the entire gamut imaginable; raunchy bathroom humor, audience-assisted improvisation, and comedically-laced magic tricks may all show up during a single show. You also get a great deal of déjà vu—hackneyed lines about sexual mishaps, homophobia, the inscrutable female race, and frustrations of life in this big city. Patience and just a touch of luck are required to find that comic with refreshingly novel material. While venues may vary tremendously in size and atmosphere, they nearly all impose a hefty cover and minimum that gets even meaner on Fridays and Saturdays.

> **Catch A Rising Star,** 1487 First Ave. (794-1906), near 77th St. A showcase of "rising stars" attempts to slay a mostly-yuppie crowd. Get ready to clean up the remains. Shows Sun.-Thurs. at 9pm, cover $8, 2-drink min.; Sat. at 8pm, 10:15pm, and 12:30am, cover $12, 2-drink min. Make reservations after 5pm on the previous day.

> **Comedy Cellar,** 117 MacDougal St. (254-3630), between W. 3rd St. and Bleecker St. Subway: D, F, B, Q to West 4th St. Subterranean annex of the artsy Olive Tree café. Dark, intimate, atmospheric, and packing in a late crowd on an early Saturday morning. Features rising comics such as John Manfrelloti and even surprise drop-ins by superstars such as Robin Williams. Shows Sun.-Thurs. 9pm-2am, cover $5, 2-drink min.; Fri. at 9pm and 11:30pm, cover $10, $7 drink min.; Sat. at 9pm, 11pm, and 1am, cover $10, $7 drink min. Make sure to book reservations on weekends.

> **Chicago City Limits,** 351 E. 74th St. (772-8707), between First and Second. Subway: 6 to 77th St. If you're looking for something a little different from the usual stand up, check out New York's longest running comedy revue, with already more than 4,500 performances spanning over a decade. The shows are a careful synthesis of cabaret, scripted comedy, and improvisation, all with a frequent political bent. Extemporaneous skits are heavily dependent on audience suggestions for plot direction, allowing the crowd to get into the act. Shows Mon. at 8:30pm, cover $10; Wed.-Thurs. at 8:30pm, cover $12.50; Fri.-Sat. at 8 and 10:30pm, cover $15.

> **Mostly Magic,** 55 Carmine St. (924-1472), between Sixth and Seventh. Subway: 1 to Houston St. Holograms decorate the walls of the restaurant out front while a sparse but appreciative crowd enjoys the superb fusion of comedy/magic vaudeville acts in the back. Open Tues.-Thurs. 6pm-11pm, Fri.-Sat. 6pm-1am. Shows Tues.-Thurs. at 9pm, cover $10, food or drink min. $8; Fri.-Sat. at 9and 11pm, cover $15, food or drink min. $8.

*Lon*gisland

Long Island is easy to stereotype. For some, the Island evokes images of sprawling, suburbia, dotted with malls and office buildings; others see it as the privilege playground of Manhattan millionaires; for still others it is a summer refuge of white sand and open spaces. Fewer see the pockets of poverty on Long Island, or its commercial and cultural centers.

While in theory "Long Island" includes the entire 120-mi. fish-shaped land mass, in practice the term excludes the westernmost section, Brooklyn and Queens, whose residents will quickly remind you that they are part of NYC. This leaves Nassau and Suffolk counties to comprise the real Long Island. East of the Queens-Nassau line, people read *Newsday,* not the *Times* or the *Daily News;* they back the Islanders, not the Rangers, during ice hockey season; and they enjoy their position as neighbor to, rather than part of, the great metropolis.

Fortunately for the visitor, the Island is cheaply and easily accessible from Manhattan. Nearly all your transit needs will be served by some combination of the **Long Island Railroad (LIRR)** (516-822-5477), which operates out of Penn Station in Manhattan, and the **Metropolitan Suburban Bus Authority (MSBA)** (516-542-0100), which operates daytime buses in eastern Queens, Nassau, and Western Suffolk. Depending on where you go and what time you leave, train fare will vary from $8.50 round-trip (for nearby suburbs in non-rush hour times) to $28 round-trip (for distant spots during rush-hour). **Suffolk Transit** (516-360-5700) takes over farther east. Bikes may be carried on LIRR by permit only.

Long Island's **area code** is 516.

Suburban Long Island: Nassau and Western Suffolk

The North Shore of Long Island was once known as the "Gold Coast" because of the string of mansions built by 19th-century industrialists in the hills overlooking

Long Island Sound. Many of these houses have been turned into museums, and the grounds that have been spared from developers are now gardens, arboretums, or nature preserves open to the public.

From west to east, some principal North Shore sights are: **Falaise** (883-1612), in Sands Point Park and Preserve, the former Guggenheim estate (1-hr. guided tour every ½-hr.; open May to mid-Nov. Sat.-Wed. 10am-5pm; admission $2, ages under 12 not allowed); **Old Westbury Gardens,** on Old Westbury Rd. (333-0048), where the splendor of the main house and its collection of painting and sculpture complements the formal English gardens outside; the **Vanderbilt Museum** (262-7888) and the **Vanderbilt Planetarium** (262-7800), on Little Neck Rd. in Centerport, in the Spanish-Moroccan Vanderbilt mansion (museum open May-Oct. Tues.-Sat. 10am-4pm, Sun. noon-5pm).

Jones Beach State Park (784-1600) is the best compromise of convenience and crowd for day-trippers from the city, with nearly 2500 acres of beach and parking for 23,000 cars. Only 40 minutes from the City, Jones Beach packs in the crowds in the summer months. The waves really roar and the sand CRUNCHES under your two feet (that's 2 ft. for you format buffs). Along the 1½-mi. boardwalk you can find deck games, roller-skating, miniature golf, basketball, and nightly dancing. The **Marine Theatre** inside the park hosts rock concerts. There are eight different bathing areas on either the rough Atlantic Ocean or the calmer Zachs Bay, plus a number of beaches restricted to residents of certain towns in Nassau County. During the summer you can take the LIRR to Freeport or Wantaugh, where you can get a bus to the beach. Call 212-739-4200 or 212-526-0900 for info. **Recreation Lines, Inc.** (718-788-8000) provides bus service straight from mid-Manhattan. If you are driving, take LIE east to the Northern State Pkwy., go east to the Meadowbrook (or Wantaugh) Pkwy. and then south to Jones Beach.

The **Fire Island National Seashore** is the main draw here; in summer it offers fishing, clamming, and guided nature walks. The facilities at **Sailor's Haven** include a marina, a nature trail, and a famous beach. Similar facilities at **Watch Hill** include a 20-unit campground, where reservations are required. Smith Point West has a small visitor information center and a nature trail with disabled access (289-4810). Here you can spot horseshoe crabs, whitetail deer, and monarch butterflies, which flit across the country every year to winter in Baja California.

The North Fork

No one ever said that Long Island wines were famous, or even really good, but visiting one of the North Fork's 40 vineyards can be fun. Twelve wineries and 40 vineyards produce the best Chardonnay, Cabernet Sauvignon, Merlot, Pinot Noir, and Riesling in New York State; local climate and soil conditions rival those of Napa Valley. Two Long Island wines even were chosen for President Bush's inauguration. Quite a few of the Island wineries offer free tours and tastings; call ahead to make an appointment.

To get to the wine district, take LIE to its end (Exit 73), then Rte. 58, which becomes Rte. 25 (Main Rd.). North of and parallel to Rte. 25 is Rte. 48 (North Rd. or Middle Rd.), which has a number of wineries. Road signs announce tours and tastings.

Palmer Winery, 108 Sound Ave., Riverhead (722-4080). Take a self-guided tour of the most advanced equipment on the island and see a tasting room with an interior assembled from two 18th-century English pubs.

Bike rentals are available on the North Fork at **Country Time Cycles,** Main Rd. (298-8700), in Mattituck. (10-speeds $20 1st day, $10 each additional day, weekly $50. Credit card deposit required.) Or try **Piccozzi's Service Station,** Rte. 114 (749-0045) in Shelter Island Heights, a 10-minute walk from the North Ferry. (Three-speeds $16 for 8 hr.; twelve-speeds $18 for 8 hr. $70 per week for either. Cash deposit or credit card required.)

The South Fork

Out on the South Fork's north shore droops Sag Harbor, one of Long Island's best-kept secrets. Founded in 1707, this port used to be more important than New York Harbor; its deep shore made for easy navigation. It boasts the second-largest collection of colonial buildings in the U.S., as well as cemeteries lined with the gravestones of Revolutionary soldiers and sailors.

In town, catch the **Sag Harbor Whaling Museum** (725-0770), in the former home of Benjamin Hunting, a 19th century whale ship owner. Enter the museum through the jawbones of a whale.

Vineyards on the South Fork are beginning to earn recognition. Of these, **Bridgehampton Winery** at Sag Harbor Tpke., Bridgehampton (537-3155), is one of the most successful, having garnered several awards since its first harvest in 1982. The winery holds special summer events, including the effervescent Chardonnay Festival. Guided tours June-Sept. daily 11am-6pm.

In summer, you'll have to compete with many wealthy New Yorkers for even the most modest lodgings, while from November to April almost everything is closed. Most of the few off-season deals are offered in Montauk Village. The absolutely best bargain on the east end is the friendly **Montauket**, on Tudhill Rd. (668-5992), 1 mi. north of Mountauk Village. Go north on Edgemere Ave. and turn left on Tudhill Rd. Located close to the railroad station, this place, not surprisingly, fills up quickly. (Doubles $30. Open mid-March to late Nov.)

Pines Motor Lodge (957-3330), corner of Rte. 109 and 3rd St. in Lindenhurst. LIE to Southern State Pkwy. East, Exit 33. Doubles $40-70. Camp in summer at **Hither Hills State Park** (668-2551 or 669-1000), right on the ocean between Montauk and East Hampton. 165 tent and trailer sites. Restrooms, showers, food, grills, fishing, tennis, and a beach. Reservations required. Open April-Nov., but no frills Oct.-Nov.

You'll find many possibilities for hiking in state (669-1000) and county (567-1700) parks. One of the more unusual places to hike, **Mashomack Preserve** (749-1001), sits on Rte. 114, on Shelter Island, 1 mi. north of the South Ferry. (Open Wed.-Mon. 9am-5pm.) Part of the Nature Conservancy's national chain of open lands, this preserve boasts 2000 acres of hiking trails and bay-shore beaches. You can explore by reservation only, but a permit is not necessary—just call the day before you show up.

Montauk offers numerous accommodations and activities, but the **Montauk Point Lighthouse and Museum** (668-2544) is the centerpiece of a trip here. Like the marker that greets a mountain climber who has reached a summit, the lighthouse marks the end of the island for the weary driver. This archetypal lighthouse is set on the rocky edge of the water, its sloping white sides adorned bluntly by a single wide band of brown. Its bulky, solid form rises with a utilitarian elegance from a cluster of smaller, weaker buildings. The 86-ft. structure went up in 1796 by special order of President George Washington. On a clear day, you should climb the 138 spiralling steps to the top, where you can look out over the seascape, across the Long Island Sound to Rhode Island and Connecticut. The best seasons for viewing are the spring and fall, when the sea has scarcely a stain on it; the thick summer air can haze over the view. You may want to climb up, even on a foggy day, to see if you can spot the so-called "Will o' the Wisp," a clipper ship sometimes sighted on hazy days under full sail with a lantern hanging from its mast. Experts claim that the ship is a mirage resulting from the presence of phosphorus in the atmosphere, but what do they know anyway? (Open May to mid-June and early Oct.-Nov. Sat.-Sun. 11am-4pm; mid-June to mid-Sept. daily 11am-6pm; mid-Sept. to early Oct. Fri.-Mon. 11am-5pm.)

Fishing and whale-watching are among Montauk's other pleasures. **Lazybones'** half-day fishing "party boat," which is more party than boat, makes two trips daily (7am-noon and 1-5pm), leaving from Tuma's Dock next to Grossman's. Call Captain Mike at 668-5671 for info. The **Okeanos Whale Watch Cruise** is one of the best in the business, though a tad expensive. The cruises are run by the non-profit Okeanos Research Foundation, which helps finance its studies of whales by taking tourists out on its 90-ft. ship, accompanied by a biologist and research team of whale experts. You may see fin, minke, and humpback whales.

The East End is served several times daily by the **LIRR**. **Suffolk Transit's** (260-5700, open Mon.-Fri.) S-92 bus loops back and forth between the tips of the north and south forks, with 9 runs daily, most of them between East Hampton and Orient Point. Call to confirm stops and schedules. The route also connects with the LIRR at Riverhead, where the forks meet. No service Sunday. **Greyhound** kennels at 66 W. Columbia St. (483-3230), in Hempstead, and 90 Broadhollow Rd. (427-6897), in Melville. **Hampton Jitney** (212-936-0440 in Manhattan, 516-283-4600 in Long Island), a private bus company, runs 15-25 buses per day to and from the Hamptons, stopping in almost all the villages and towns from Westhampton to Montauk. (One-way between Manhattan and South Fork $10-22.) Pick up the bus in Manhattan at 41st. at Third Ave., and 70th St. at Lexington Ave. Call for schedule info.

NEW YORK STATE

Surrounded by the beauty of New York's landscape, you may find it easy to forget that such things as smog and traffic even exist. The villages and cities that dot the hilly strip that is upstate New York have a sweet natural flavor that holds its own against the acrid juice of the Big Apple. Whether in the crassly commercial Niagara Falls, the idyllic Finger Lakes, or the simply peaceful Podunk—even in Albany—you will have little doubt that nature is sovereign in Upstate New York.

Practical Information

Capital: Albany.

Tourist Information: 800-225-5697 or 474-4116. Open Mon.-Fri. 8:30am-5pm. Write to Division of Tourism, 1 Commerce Plaza, Albany 12245. Excellent, comprehensive *I Love New York Travel Guide* includes disabled access and resource information. **New York State Office of Parks and Recreation,** Agency Bldg. 1, Empire State Plaza, Albany 12238 (518-474-0456), has literature on canoeing, camping, biking, and hiking.

Time Zone: Eastern. **Postal Abbreviation:** NY

Outdoors

Bikers should head for the Finger Lakes region whose gentle hills are just high enough to provide some challenge and whose small farmsteads are best explored and appreciated by bike. Moreover, the wineries of the region make for very pleasant stops. Write for the *New York Bicycle Touring Guide, c/o* William N. Hoffman, 53 Claire Ave., New Rochelle 10804, or the free *Finger Lakes Bicycle Touring Guide,* Finger Lakes State Park Region, RD 3, Trumansburg 14886 (607-387-7041). For a guide to the wineries of upstate New York write to the Department of Agriculture and Markets, Capital Plaza, 1 Winner Circle, Albany 12235 (518-457-3880). Ask for the *New World of World Class Wine Making.* For information on the Adirondacks and Catskills preserves, write the NY State Department of Environmental Conservation, 50 Wolf Rd., Albany 12233.

Hikers will appreciate the many long trails that criss-cross the state, including the Appalachian Trail, the Finger Lakes Trail, and the Long Path, overseen by the Forest Preserve of Protection and Management (518-457-7433). For reservations at any state campground call 800-456-2267 six to 90 days in advance. For a general guide to outdoor recreation in New York (with extensive information on camping, hiking, and sports facilities—especially golf and tennis) write to **I Love NY Publications,** Dept. of Commerce, Albany 12245, or call the New York Division of Tourism (see Practical Information above). You're also never a long drive from one of NY's 90 state parks, most of which provide excellent camping. For the nature lover, the Catskills is the perfect vacation spot. Muskie, walleye, and bass fishing in the "Seaway" is perhaps the best in the eastern U.S., with over 50 private campsites and parks scattered across the 1800 islands. For more information, call the St. Lawrence County Chamber of Commerce (315-386-4000).

Hitchhiking is illegal in New York State. This law is enforced with particular vehemence in the New York City area, where it's not safe to begin with.

Adirondacks

The Adirondacks, New York's endangered backwoods wilderness, are the largest natural preserve in the East. Although large portions of the mountain forests remain undeveloped, pollution from urban areas far to the south has victimized the Adirondacks' trees, lakes, and wildlife. More than 200 lakes in the area have stagnated, while acid rain has left its mark on many tree and fish populations, especially in the fragile high-altitude environments. But despite these warning signs, much of the Adirondacks retains the beauty it had over a century ago.

Of the six million acres in the Adirondacks Park, 40% is fully open to the public. Two thousand mi. of hiking and skiing trails criss-cross the forest and mountain scenery. An interlocking network of lakes and streams makes the gentle Adirondack wilds a perennial favorite of canoeists. Mountain-climbers may wish to tackle **Mt. Marcy,** the state's highest peak (5344 ft.), at the base of the Adirondacks. The Adirondacks are also well-known for resorts and encompass a dozen well-known alpine ski centers. **Lake Placid** has twice hosted the winter Olympics and frequently welcomes national sports competitions (see Lake Placid below). **Saranac Lake** is another center for winter activity, including the **International Dog Sledding Championship** at the end of January. **Tupper Lake** and **Lake George** also have celebrations every January and February. Snow-covered hiking trails are great for snowshoeing, and plenty of cross-country ski trails wind through forest preserves and state parks.

The Adirondacks are especially appealing for the budget traveler, since cheap **accommodations** abound. Lake Placid and nearby towns host many inexpensive hotels and campgrounds (see Lake Placid below). The region's youth hostel is located in the basement of **St. James Episcopal Church Hall,** P.O. Box 176, Lake George (668-2634), on Montcalm St. at Ottawa, several blocks from the lake. From the bus terminal, walk south one block to Montcalm, turn right and go one block to Ottawa for the slightly musty bunkroom with a decent kitchen. (Check-in 5-9pm, later only with reservations. Curfew 10pm. $8. Open May 24-Sept. 5.)

In the Lake George area, you can stay at **The Lake George AYH-Hostel on Montcalm St. Write to: Box 176, Lake George, NY 12875. (Members $8, nonmembers $11. Open May 23-Sept. 3. 12 beds.)**

Two lodges near Lake Placid are run by the **Adirondack Mountain Club (ADK),** with offices at both RR 3, P.O. Box 3055, Lake George 12845 (668-4447), and Adirondack Loj Rd., P.O. Box 867, Lake Placid 12946 (523-3441) near the **Adirondack Loj.** The Loj, 8 mi. east of Lake Placid off Rte. 73, is a beautiful log cabin right on Heart Lake with comfortable bunk facilities and a family atmosphere. Guests can swim, fish, canoe, and use rowboats free of charge. In winter, explore the wilderness trails on rented snowshoes ($6 per day) or cross-country skis ($10 per day). (B&B $25, with dinner $36. Linen included. Campsites $9. Lean-tos $13.) Call ahead for weekends and during peak holiday seasons. Take about 20% off for non-peak rates.

For an even better mix of rustic comfort and wilderness experience, hike 3½ mi. from the closest trailhead to the **John's Brook Lodge,** in Keene Valley 16 mi. southeast of Lake Placid off Rte. 73 (call the Adirondack Loj or ADK for reservations). From Placid, follow Rte. 73 15 mi. through Keene to Keene Valley, turning right at the Ausable Inn. The hike is only slightly uphill, and the food is well worth the exertion; the staff packs in groceries every day and cooks on a gas stove. A great place to meet friendly New Yorkers, John's Brook is no secret; the beds fill completely on weekends. Make reservations at least one day in advance for dinner, longer for a weekend. Bring sheets or a sleeping bag. (B&B $25, with dinner $36.

Slightly less off-peak. Lean-tos $7. Open May 27-Oct. 14.) In summer, rent a bunk for $10 with full access to the kitchen. If ADK facilities are too pricey, try the **High Peaks Base Camp,** P.O. Box 91, Upper Jay 12987 (946-2133), a charming restaurant/lodge/campground just a 20-minute drive from Lake Placid. Take 86N to Wilmington, turn right at the Mobil station, then go right 3½ mi. on Springfield Rd.; $15 (Sun.-Thurs.) or $18 (Fri.-Sat.) buys you a bed for the night and a huge breakfast. (Check-in until 9pm, later with reservations. Sites $3 per person. Cabins $30 for 4 people.) Transportation is tough without a car but sometimes rides can be arranged from Keene; call ahead.

In the forest, you can use the free shelters by the trails. Always inquire about their location before you plan a hike. Camp for free in the backcountry anywhere on public land, as long as you are at least 150 ft. away from a trail, road, water source, or campground and stay below 4000 ft. altitude.

The Adirondacks are served best by **Adirondacks Trailways,** with frequent stops along I-87. You can take a bus to Lake Placid, Tupper Lake, and Lake George from Albany. From the Lake George bus stop, at the Mobil station, 320 Canada St. (668-9511; 800-225-6815 for bus info), buses reach Lake Placid ($12.45), Albany ($9.30), and New York City ($36.30). (Open Sun.-Thurs. 6:30am-midnight, Fri.-Sat. 6am-2am.) Traveling in the backwoods is tough during the muddy spring thaw (March-April).

Contact the State Office of Parks and Recreation (see New York Practical Information) in Albany for info on the Adirondacks. The best info on hiking and other outdoor activities emanates from the **ADK** (see above). For trails in the Lake Placid area, look for ADK's particularly good *Guide to the High Peaks.*

The Adirondacks' **area code** is 518.

Lake Placid

Melvil Dewey, creator of the Dewey Decimal library classification system and founder of the exclusive Lake Placid Club, first promoted Lake Placid as a summer resort in 1850. The Winter Olympic Games, held here in 1932 and 1980, cemented the town's fame. Currently the Adirondacks' premier tourist spot, Lake Placid attracts crowds of casual visitors and world-class athletes. The international flags and stores that fill Main Street don't inhibit the inviting, old-village atmosphere or the sporting facilities unmatched in the U.S. Temperatures can plummet to -40°F and more than 200 in. of snow may fall in any given Adirondack winter, but well-plowed main roads keep the region open. Ice fishing on the lakes is popular, especially with locals, as is ice skating (Olympic speed-skating rink $2; open daily 7-9pm, Mon.-Fri. noon-2pm weather permitting).

The old Olympic spirit clearly makes its presence felt in Lake Placid—and just out of town on Rte. 73 is the self-descriptive **Olympic Site.** The **Olympic Regional Development Authority,** Olympic Center (523-1655 or 800-462-6236), operates the facilities. You can't miss the 70 and 90m runs of the **Olympic Jumping Complex** looming above the alpine landscape. The $5 admission fee includes a chairlift and elevator ride to the top of the spectator towers. You might also catch summer (June-Columbus Day) jumpers flipping and diving into a swimming pool in the **Kodak Sports Park** next door to the Olympic Jumps. (Open daily 9am-5pm, Oct.-May 9am-4pm.) Three mi. farther along Rte. 73, the **Olympic Sports Complex** at Mt. Van Hoevenberg offers a summer trolley running to the top of the bobsled run ($3). In the winter (Dec.-March Tues.-Sun. 1-3pm) you can bobsled down the run used in the Olympics for $20. The park is open for self-guided tours daily from 9am to 4pm, and has 35 mi. of well-groomed cross-country ski trails ($7).

In addition to its fantastic ski slopes, **Whiteface Mountain,** near Lake Placid, provides a panoramic view of the Adirondacks. You can get up to the summit via the **Whiteface Memorial Highway** ($4 toll, cars only) or a chairlift ($4, seniors and kids $3). (Highway open May 17-Oct. 14, chairlift open June 15-Oct. 14.) The extensive **Whiteface Mountain Ski Center** (523-1655) has the largest vertical drop in the East (3,216 ft.). Don't bother with the $4 tour of the waterfalls at **High Falls Gorge** (946-

2278) on Rte. 86 near Whiteface; hike below the road to see the same scenery for free. All of the Olympic attractions, Whiteface car toll and chairlift, ski-jumping, bobsled, and luge area can be purchased as a $42 package.

History buffs and corpse cultivators will enjoy a quick visit to the **farm and grave** of abolitionist John Brown, off Rte. 73, 3 mi. southeast of Lake Placid (523-3900; open late May to late Oct. Wed.-Sat. 10am-5pm, Sun. 1-5pm; free). The west branch of the **Ausable River,** just east of the town of Lake Placid, lures anglers to its shores. **Fishing licenses** for five days are $15.50 (season $27.50) at Town Hall, 301 Main St. (523-2162), or Jones Outfitters, 37 Main St. (523-3468). Call the "Fishing Hotline" at 518-891-5413 for an in-depth fresh-water recording of the hot fishing spots and current conditions. The **Lake Placid Center for the Arts,** on Saranac Ave. at Fawn Ridge (523-2512), hosts a local art gallery and theater, dance, and musical performances. (Open daily 1-5pm; winter Mon.-Fri. 1-5pm. Free, except for special performances.)

For spring and fall breakfasts, try the **Hilton Hotel,** 1 Mirror Lake Dr. (523-4411), right at the beginning of Main St. At the Hilton's lunch buffet (noon-2:30pm), $4.75 buys a sandwich and all-you-can-eat soup and salad. **The Cottage,** 5 Mirror Lake Dr. (523-9845), has relatively inexpensive meals (sandwiches and salads $4-6) with scrumptious views of the lake and many, many athletes. (Lunch served daily 11:30am-3:30pm. Bar open noon-1am.) **Mud Puddles,** 3 School St. (523-4446), below the speed skating rink, is popular with disco throwbacks and the pop music crowd. (Open Wed.-Sun. 9pm-3am. Cover $1.50.)

Most accommodations in the area are expensive. The **St. Moritz Hotel,** 31 Saranac Ave. (523-9240), off the northern end of Main St. past the Hilton Hotel, has excellent rooms with private baths. (Sun.-Thurs. $35, Fri.-Sat. $50. Breakfast included.) **Lyseck's Inn,** 50 Hillcrest Ave. (523-1700), rents beds for $20.50 (June-early Sept.). Call ahead since the place fills up quickly with young athletes. (From Main St. go up the hill on Marcy St. next to Sundog Sport and turn left on Hillcrest.) The High Peaks Base Camp, Adirondack Loj, and Johns Brook Lodge (see Adirondacks above) are all within several mi. of Lake Placid. Campers have many options, including backcountry camping (free), the Adirondack Loj's campgrounds, and the numerous developed state sites near Lake Placid and Saranac Lake. The closest one, **Meadowbrook State Park** (891-4351), lies 5 mi. west of Lake Placid on Rte. 86 in Raybrook. (Sites $10.50, additional nights $9. Open mid-April to mid-Oct.)

To explore Lake Placid by bike, rent mountain bikes at **Sundog Ski & Sport,** 90 Main St. (523-2752; $3 per hr., $14 per day). The shop also rents cross-country skis ($10 per day) and downhill skis ($14 per day). (Open daily 9am-6pm. Must have ID.) The **Lake Placid Convention and Visitors Bureau,** Olympic Center (523-2445), has the scoop on the city. (Open Mon.-Fri. 9am-5pm, Sat.-Sun. 8:30am-4:30pm.)

Trailways has extensive service in the Adirondacks, stopping at the **326 Main St. Deli** in Lake Placid (523-1527; 523-4309 for bus info). Buses run to New York City ($48.75) and Lake George ($12.45). By car, Lake Placid is at the intersection of Rte. 86 and 73.

For **weather** information call 792-1050. Lake Placid has a **post office** at 201 Main St. (523-3071; open Mon.-Fri. 9am-5pm, Sat. 9am-12:30pm). Lake Placid's **ZIP code** is 12946; the **area code** is 518.

Albany

With millions of dollars spent on urban renewal, Albany has undergone what many residents term a "renaissance." This may be an overstatement, but recent efforts to increase tourism have helped to make the state capital more than just a soapbox for Governor Mario Cuomo and a transportation hub for passers through.

Although the English took Albany in 1664, the city still bears the stamp, in tulips, names, and architecture, of the Dutch who settled it in 1614. During the Revolutionary War, British General John Burgoyne's invasion from Canada targeted Albany, but his escapade ended with a U.S. victory in Saratoga in late 1777. Named state capital in 1797, Albany grew farther in the 1800s as a transportation hub and industrial center. The **Schuyler** (SKY-ler) **Mansion,** 32 Catherine St. (434-0834), gives a sense of the city's rich history. Colonial businessman and general Philip Schuyler owned the elegant Georgian home, built in 1761. Here George Washington and Benjamin Franklin dined, Alexander Hamilton married Schuyler's daughter, and General Burgoyne was "incarcerated" following his defeat at Saratoga. (Open April-Oct. Wed.-Sat. 10am-5pm, Sun. 1-5pm. Free.)

Including the Schuyler, Albany offers about a day's worth of sight-seeing activity. The **Rockefeller Empire State Plaza,** State St., a $1.9 billion architectural marvel, houses, aside from state offices, the **New York State Museum** (474-5877; open daily 10am-5pm; free), and the huge egg that is the **New York State Performing Arts Center** (473-3750). The museum's exhibits show the history and development of the state's different regions, including Manhattan; displays range from Native American arrowheads to an original set for "Sesame Street." For a bird's-eye view of Albany, visit the observation deck on the 44th floor of the tallest skyscraper in the plaza. (Open Mon.-Fri. 9am-4pm.) Catch cult classic flicks outside at the Egg Tues. at 7pm in the summer ($3, double-feature $5). Look, but please don't touch the "art for the public" **Empire State Collection.** Scattered throughout the plaza, the collection features work by innovative New York School artists such as Jackson Pollock, Mark Rothko, and David Smith. (Open daily, tours Wed. 10:30am and 2:30pm and by appointment. Free.)

The modern plaza provides a striking contrast to the more traditional architectural landscape of the rest of the city. Within walking distance on Washington Ave. are **City Hall,** an earthy Romanesque edifice, and the **Capitol Building** (474-2418), a Gothic marvel, both worked on by H. H. Richardson. (Free tours Mon.-Fri. 9am-4pm.)

Stroll around downtown to admire Albany's numerous churches, especially **First Church in Albany,** on the corner of Orange and N. Pearl (463-4449). Founded and built in 1798, the church houses the oldest known pulpit and weather vane in America. (Open Mon.-Fri. 9am-4pm.) The State Education Department has done an excellent job of marking trivial and not-so-trivial historic spots throughout the city; the **Albany Visitors Center,** 25 Quackenbush Sq. 12207 (434-5132), also has maps and brochures of the city and runs walking trolley tours ($4). Newly expanded, the Center displays an educational exhibit about Albany's past. (Open daily 10am-4pm, off-season Mon.-Fri. 10am-4pm.)

You will be tempted to stay in Albany by the luxurious accommodations and fine hospitality at **Pine Haven (AYH),** 531 Western Ave. (482-1754). From the bus station, walk by the breathtaking State University of New York administrative offices on Broadway and turn left on State St. Take the #10 bus up Western Ave. from the stop in front of the Hilton and get off at N. Allen St. Pine Haven is on your right. Janice Tricarico runs a four-room B&B in her century-old Victorian home, as well as a youth hostel. (B&B: Singles $39. Doubles $49. Hostel $12. Reservations recommended; call ahead.) If Pine Haven is full in summertime, try the nearby **College of Saint Rose,** Lima Hall, 366 Western Ave. (Reservations: Tonita Nagle at Student Affairs, Box 114, 432 Western Ave., 444-5171, from Mon.-Fri. 8:30am-4:30pm. After hours, 454-1700.) You'll find large rooms and impeccable bathrooms in student dorms on a scenic campus. The dining hall is open for use. (Singles $35. Doubles $50.) Across the river is the **Fort Crailo Motel,** 110 Columbia Turnpike, Rensselaer 12114 (472-1360), 1½ mi. from downtown near the Amtrak station. (Singles $30-34. Doubles $38-42.) The closest **YMCA,** 13 State St. (374-9136), and **YWCA,** 44 Washington Ave. (374-3394), are both in Schenectady. (Singles $20-22.50.)

Food, save for a few hot dog vendors, is sparse downtown. **Next Door,** 142 Washington St. (434-1616), has good-sized sandwiches (around $4) and great chocolate chip cookies (75¢). Join the social and political activists, artists, and environmentalists at the **Half Moon Café,** 154 Madison Ave. (436-0329). Enjoy quality natural foods (vegetarian chili and cheese $3, salad platters $4.50) on the patio. Stick around: a monthly calendar lists the café's nightly jazz, folk, blues, etc. concerts, poetry readings, and meetings. No cover—donations only—and an open jam every Tues. night. (Daily 11am-11pm.) For standard deli fare, try the **Knickerbocker Deli,** 15 S. Pearl St. (427-9078). Breakfast (pancakes $2.70) is served all day; peck at the chickenbockers ($5) in one of its four incarnations. (Open Mon.-Fri. 7am-6pm, Sat.-Sun. 8am-6pm.)

Albany erupts in a colorful rainbow of music, dancing, food, and street-scrubbing in May during the **Tulip Festival.** The state sponsors free concerts at the plaza during the summer (call 473-0559 for info). **Washington Park,** bounded by State St. and Madison Ave. north of downtown, has tennis courts, paddle boats, and plenty of green. From mid-July to mid-Aug., Wed.-Sun. at 8pm, the **Park Playhouse** (434-2035) stages free theater. On Mon. and Tues. in that time period, varied entertainment, under the title **Dark Nights,** takes place at the lake house. Come **Alive at Five** on Thurs. during the summer, to the sound of free concerts at the Tricentennial Plaza across from Norstar on Broadway.

Amtrak, East St., Rensselaer (800-872-7245), across the Hudson from downtown Albany, runs to New York City (7-9 per day, 2½ hr., $37). (Station open daily 10:30am-midnight.) **Greyhound,** 34 Hamilton St. (434-0121), offers service to New York City (9 per day, 3 hr., $27); Montréal (6 per day, 5 hr., $47); Boston (4 per day, 4-5 hr., $29); and Syracuse (7 per day, 3½ hr., $17). (Station open 24 hrs.) **Trailways,** one block away at 360 Broadway (436-9651), connects to other upstate locales: Lake George (6 per day, in winter 3 per day; 1 hr.; $9); Lake Placid (6 per day, in winter 3 per day; 4 hr.; $20.50); and Tupper Lake (1 per day, 4 hr., $24.75). Senior and college-student discount are available for both routes on certain lines. (Open Mon.-Fri. 5:30am-11pm, Sat.-Sun. 7:30am-11pm.) For local travel, the **Capitol District Transit Authority (CDTA)** (482-8822) serves Albany, Troy, and Schenectady. CDTA has a confusing schedule and often patchy coverage; a quick call to the main office will set you straight. (Fare 75¢.)

Albany's **ZIP code** is 12201; the **area code** is 518.

Catskills

In 1820, New York City author and historian Washington Irving recounted the seductive and soothing qualities of the Catskills in the tale of *Rip Van Winkle.* In the story, Rip joins the mountain party of a group of gnomes and falls asleep for 20 years. These lovely mountains continue to captivate city-dwellers who migrate up the highways of the Hudson and Mohawk River Valleys in search of unpolluted air and the tranquility of the dense hemlock forests. Beyond the lakeside resorts, visitors can find peace and natural beauty in the state-managed Catskill Preserve, home to quiet villages, sparkling streams, and miles of hiking and skiing trails.

Trailways provides excellent service through the Catskills. The two main stops are in **Kingston,** at 400 Washington Ave. (914-331-0744), and **Oneonta,** at 47 Market St. (607-432-2661). Fare to New York City costs $31.75. Other stops in the area include Woodstock, Pine Hill, Saugerties, and Hunter; each connects with New York City, Albany, and Utica. Road conditions are consistently good.

Catskill Preserve

The 250,000-acre, state-run Catskill Preserve is the area's real attraction. The **Esopus River,** just to the west, is great for trout fishing and for late-summer inner-tubing in the **Phoenicia** area. Rent tubes at **The Town Tinker,** on Bridge St. (914-668-5553), in Phoenicia. (Inner tubes $7 per day, with a seat $10. Driver's licence or $15 required as a deposit. Transportation $3. Life jackets available. Open May-Sept. daily 9am-6pm.) Throughout the preserve, hundreds of trails lead to lovely mountain brooks, hidden lakes, deep forests, and Darkman's summer retreat. Hikes range from half-day jaunts to the top of a mountain to longer backpack trips traversing the entire region. Some trails crowd in summer, especially those in the eastern section of the park. To camp in the backcountry for more than three days, you must obtain a permit from the nearest ranger station (518-255-5453). Trails are maintained year-round; available lean-tos are sometimes dilapidated and crowded. Boil or treat water with chemicals, and pack your garbage. To reach the head of your chosen trail, take a Trailways bus from Kingston—drivers will let you out anywhere along the park's main routes. (Call 914-331-0744 for info on routes and fares.) For more info, pick up Bennet and Maisa's *Walks in the Catskills* or the American Geographical Society's *The New York Walk Book.*

One of the many well-run **state campgrounds** (800-456-2267) can serve as a base for your hiking, fishing, or tubing adventures. Reservations are vital during the summer, especially Thurs. to Sun. (Sites $10-13. Open May-Sept.) Try one of the following: **North Lake,** Rte. 23A (518-589-5058), 3 mi. northeast of Haines Falls; **Devil's Tombstone,** Rte. 214 (518-688-7160), 3 mi. south of Hunter; **Woodland Valley,** (914-688-7647), 5 mi. southwest of Phoenicia; **Kenneth L. Wilson,** (914-679-7020), 5 mi. east of Mt. Tremper off Rte. 28; **Little Pond,** (914-439-5480), 14 mi. northwest of Livingston Manor off Rte. 17; **Beaverkill,** (914-439-4281), 7 mi. northwest of Livingston Manor; **Mongaup Pond,** (914-439-4233), 10 mi. northeast of Livingston Manor off Rte. 17, exit 96; or **Bear Spring Mountain,** (607-652-7364), 5 mi. southeast of Walton, off Rte. 206. For brochures and info contact the State Dept. of Environmental Conservation, Rm. 111, 50 Wolf Rd., Albany 12233 (518-457-3521).

Cooperstown

Cooperstown's pristine homes, cutesy craft stores, and cheery-faced residents typify small-town America; its breath-taking natural setting on Otsego Lake in the midst of the Catskills rivals any New England town for grandeur. Early American author James Fenimore Cooper made his home here, and *The Last of the Mohicans* is set in the area. But far and away the town's most famous resident was Abner Doubleday, who, according to a combination of myth and legend, invented the game of baseball here in 1839. Cooperstown hasn't been the same since. Tourists invade the town by droves in the summer, often outnumbering residents. Baseball fans feel like they've died and gone to heaven; apart from the Baseball Hall of Fame, afficionados can investigate a dozen or more memorabilia shops on Main St., take a swing at the Doubleday Batting Range, eat in one of the baseball theme restaurants, or sleep at one of the baseball theme motels.

Accommodations and Food

Camping is the way to go in Cooperstown; lodging in the summertime is hideously expensive and generally full, although the Chamber of Commerce (see below) can help out in a pinch.

Major League Motor Inn, P.O. Box 141, Fly Creek 13337 (547-2266), 3 mi. from Cooperstown on Rte. 28. Singles and doubles $60.

Glimmerglass State Park, RD2 Box 580 (800-456-2267), on Ostego County Rte. 31 on the east side of Ostego Lake. Thirty-nine pristine campsites in a gorgeous lakeside park. Swimming, fishing, boating, and more. Weekends are booked in summer, but definitely the best campground in the area.

Fieldstone Farm Family Vacation Resort, Rose's Hill Rd., Richfield Springs 13437 (800-336-4629), 10 mi. north of Cooperstown, but worth the trip. Ponds, fishing, hiking and swimming are available at this 200-acre informal natural resort. Doubles $55, quads $65. Stays in July and Aug. sometimes require a 1-week min. stay.

Gray Goose B&B, RD1 Box 21 (547-2763), off Rte. 80, 3 mi. north of Cooperstown. A restored farmhouse, and very cozy. Singles $50. Doubles $55.

For decent food, an amusing baseball atmosphere, and a souvenir shop in the building, check out **T.J.'s Place,** on Main St. across from Doubleday Field. (Dinners $5-10. Open daily 7am-10pm.) **The Pioneer Patio,** on Pioneer Alley off Pioneer St, is an affordable café with traditional American and German food. Try a frankfurter. (Open Mon.-Thurs. 11am-8pm, Fri.-Sat. 8am-10pm.) **The Bold Dragoon,** on Pioneer St., is a good place to swig a cold one and hang out with the locals. (Dinners $5-10. Open daily noon-9pm, bar open until 2am.) From early July to late August, the nationally-acclaimed **Glimmerglass Opera** (547-2255), 10. mi north of town on Rte. 80, serves up everything from Wagner to Gilbert and Sullivan. (Tickets $13-40.)

Sights

The National Baseball Hall of Fame and Museum (547-9988), on Main St., is an enormous paean to baseball featuring bronze plaques briefly chronicling the achievements of the game's all-time greatest players. The annual ceremonies for new inductees are held the second Sunday of Aug. in Cooper Park, next to the building. There are special exhibits for hearing- and visually-impaired fans. (Open daily May-Oct. 9am-9pm; Nov.-April 9am-5pm. $6, ages 7-16 $2.50, under 7 free. Combination tickets with the Farmers' Museum and Fenimore House are available.) Scheduled to open in 1992 is the **Larry Fritsch Baseball Card Museum,** 10 Chestnut St. (547-9464), near the village's sole spotlight. The Museum will have a rotating collection of over one million baseball cards, including the 1952 Topps Mickey Mantle, goshdarnit! (Call for hours and admission.)

When you are ready to take the next baseball you see and bulldoze it, check out the **Farmers' Museum and Village Crossroads** (547-2533), 1 mi. from town on Rte. 80. The museum is a living microcosm of life in upstate New York's "hopespun" era of the early 1800s. Watch blacksmithing, horseshoeing, and old-time gospel preaching. (Open daily May-Oct. 9am-6pm. $6, under 16 $2.50, under 7 free.) Those with a curiosity about American folk art will be intrigued by **Fenimore House** (547-2533), on Rte. 80 across from the Farmers' Museum. 18th- and 19th-century American paintings and sculptures dot the corners of the vast period rooms overlooking Otsego Lake. (Open daily May-Oct. 9am-6pm. $5, under 16 $2, under 7 free, but kids will hate it.) Info on hiking trails in the area may be gleaned from the tourist office or the Glimmerglass state park office.

Cooperstown is accessible from I-90 and I-88 via Rte. 28. Street parking does not exist in Cooperstown; your best bet is to park in the free parking lots just outside town near the Fenimore House, on Rte. 28 south of Cooperstown, and on Glen Ave. From there, take a trolley (really a school bus with an attitude). (Trolley runs daily June-Sept. 8:30am-8pm. All day pass $1.) The **Cooperstown Area Chamber of Commerce,** 31 Chestnut St., Cooperstown, 13326 (547-9983), on Rte. 80 near Main St., has maps, brochures, and hotel and B&B listings; it can make reservations for you.

Cooperstown's **area code** is 607.

Ithaca and the Finger Lakes

Folks who live around the Finger Lakes wonder about the lure of Niagara Falls up north; without the heart-shaped tubs and overpriced food of the falls, these slender waterways neither literally nor figuratively roar for attention, resulting in far fewer tourists. Their absence makes spending time here sublime.

Broken up by gentle hills, the Finger Lakes—Canandaigua, Keuka, Seneca, Cayuga, Owasco, and Skaneateles, among others—are steeped in Iroquois lore. According to legend, the Great Spirit laid his hands upon the earth, and the impression of his fingers made lakes. A more contemporary geological explanation attributes the lakes' shapes to the expansion of ice sheets in pre-existing valleys during the glacial age. Nature doesn't loosen its grip even in Ithaca, where constructed bridges span deep river gorges, and Ivy-League Cornell University perches on the hills above.

Practical Information

Ithaca Police: 272-3245. Fire and Ambulance: 273-8000. Tomkpins County Sheriff: 272-2444.

Tompkins County Convention and Visitors Bureau, 904 E. Shore Dr., Ithaca 14850 (272-1313 or 800-284-8422). By car take Rte. 13 north of the city, exit at Stewart Park and follow the signs. From the bus station turn left on State St., then walk left on Cayuga all the way to E. Shore (about 30 min. on foot), or take bus #4 to Stewart Park. Tremendous number of brochures on Ithaca, Finger Lakes, and every other county in upstate New York. Hotel and B&B listings. Best map of the area ($3). Open Mon.-Fri. 9am-5pm, Sat.-Sun. 10am-6pm; Labor Day-Memorial Day Mon.-Fri. 9am-5pm. Cornell University Information and Referral Center, Day Hall (255-6200). Good campus maps and extensive information on the entire area, including hotels and B&Bs. Free 1-hr. tours Mon.-Fri. at 9am, 11am, 1, and 3pm, Sat. at 9am and 1pm, Sun. at 1pm. Open Mon.-Sat. 8am-5pm. Finger Lakes State Park Region, 2221 Taughannock Park Rd., RD 3, Trumansburg 14886 (607-387-7041). Info on state parks.

Buses: Ithaca Bus Terminal, W. State and N. Fulton St. (272-7390), for Short Line and Greyhound. To: New York City (8 per day, 5 hr., $49); Philadelphia (3 per day, 6-7 hr., $49); Niagara Falls (5 per day, 5 hr., $40). Open daily 7:30am-6:30pm.

Public Transport: Ithaca Transit, 273-7348. Bus service to Cornell University, Ithaca College, Stewart Park, and Buttermilk Falls. Operates Mon.-Thurs. 6am-6pm, Fri.-Sat. 6am-midnight; school year Mon.-Sat. 6am-1am. Fare 50¢, 5 tickets per $2. Cornell University Transit, 255-6200. Bus service around Cornell. Operates June-Aug. daily 4:45am-6:15pm, Sept.-May 6:15am-1:30am. Fare 35¢. Free after 5:15pm. Tomtran (Tompkins County Transportation Services Project), 274-5370. Covers a wider area than Ithaca Transit, including Trumansburg and Ulysses, both northwest of Ithaca on Rte. 96, and Cayuga Heights and Lansing Village, both due north of Ithaca on Rte. 13. Only choice for getting out to the Finger Lakes. Buses stop at Ithaca Commons, westbound on Seneca St., and eastbound on Green. Fare 60¢, $1.25 for more distant zones.

Bike Rental: Black Star Bicycles, 1922 Dryden Rd. (347-4117), 7 mi. out of town on Rte. 13. $15 per day, $25 per 3 days. Take Ithaca Transit's Dryden Bus. Open Tues.-Fri. 10am-6pm, Sat. 10am-5pm.

Car Rental: Eddie's Super Service, 435 W. State St. (273-2792). $18 with unlimited mileage. Must be 21 with credit card. Reservations recommended.

Post Office, 213 N. Tioga St. (272-5454), at E. Buffalo. Open Mon.-Fri. 8:30am-1pm, Sat. 8:30am-noon. ZIP code: 14850.

Area code: 607.

Once you get to the town, you should notice two Ithacas: the flat downtown area by the lake, and the hilly Cornell campus. **Collegetown** is a small neighborhood of restaurants and bars just south of campus. **Trumansburg** primps 10-12 mi. north of Ithaca on Rte. 96.

Accommodations and Camping

If you want to sleep between sheets rather than beneath the stars, plan on sticking to the city. Cornell Information and the Tompkins County Visitors Bureau (see Practical Information above) both have full Ithaca area B&B listings.

Podunk House Hostel (AYH), Podunk Rd. (387-9277), in Trumansburg about 8 mi. northwest of Ithaca. By car take Rte. 96 north through Jacksonville, turn left on Cold Springs Rd. following signs for Podunk ski area until it ends at Podunk, turn left again and the hostel is 20 ft. away on your right. Greyhound has a Trumansburg flag stop. Venture into the land of Oz, friendly owner of the hostel. He's happy to talk philosophy or architecture or let you soak up the silence of his 30-acre farm. Beds in the loft of a homestead barn. Bathroom plagued by iron- and sulfur-ish water. No kitchen. Members only, $5. Linen $1. Open April-Oct. Call ahead.

Elmshade Guest House, 402 S. Albany St. (273-1707), at Center St. 3 blocks from the Ithaca Commons. From the bus station, walk up State St. and turn right onto Albany. Impeccably clean, well-decorated, good-sized rooms with shared bath. TV in every room, refrigerator, microwave on hall. Singles $25. Doubles $37; prices may rise. Morning coffee, rolls, fruit included. Reservations recommended.

Hillside Inn, 518 Stewart Ave. (273-6864). Walk up State St. past the Common and turn left on Stewart, or take bus #2 from downtown. Functional rooms convenient to Cornell and downtown Ithaca. TV, A/C. Singles $30, with private bath $35. Doubles $35, with private bath $38. Triples $45. Check-out 11am. Continental breakfast included. Book ahead on weekends.

Historic Cook House, 167 Main St., Newfield (564-9926). Tomtran bus passes by. Doubles in a renovated country mansion (or big house, anyway). Classic antique beds in perfect condition, huge sitting room, full country breakfast. Rooms $55, for foreign travelers $40. Queen-size bed $66.

Camping options in this area are virtually endless. Fifteen of the 20 state parks in the Finger Lakes region have campsites, nine have cabins. The brochure *Finger Lakes State Parks* contains a description of the park location, services, and environs; pick it up from any tourist office, park, or the Finger Lakes State Park Region (see above). Whatever your plans, reserve ahead. The four-wheel-drive trucks and Winnebagos are rolling in to steal your spot even as you read. Summer weekends almost always fill up.

Buttermilk Falls State Park (273-5761), on Rte. 13 just south of Ithaca, beckons with 10 ulcer-soothing waterfalls and two glens. Pinnacle Rock (see below) towers over the stream in the center. (Sites $10, walk-in registration fee $1.50, reservation fee $6. Cabins—rooms with four cots—$23.50, $94 per week. Open May-Oct.) **Robert H. Treman State Park** (273-3440), is 2 mi. south of Ithaca on Rte. 13: Take Rte. 13 south and turn right on Rte. 387. Picnic areas, playgrounds, and a stream-fed pool with waterfalls dapple the park's 1,025 acres. (Sites $11.50. Additional night $10. Cabins 2-day min. stay $23.50 per night, $94 per week. Usually booked weekly in high season.) Try also **Taughannock** (ta-GAN-nick) **State Park** (387-6739), on Rte. 89 in Trumansburg 8 mi. north of Ithaca. The closest public transport goes down Rte. 96; ask to get off at Park Rd., walk 20 minutes and follow the signs. By car take Rte. 89 from Ithaca. Walking trails weave through the 783 acres of natural beauty, including the park's Taughannock Falls. (Sites $11.50, additional night $10. Hookup $13.50, additional night $12. Cabins $23.50 per night, $94 per week. Cabins 2-day min. stay, Memorial Day-Labor Day 1-week min.)

Food and Nightlife

Though not terribly diverse, the region's food is high in quality. Ithaca, largely because of the university, basks in bagels and bohemian fare.

Moosewood Restaurant, Seneca and Cayuga St. (273-9610), Ithaca. Creative, well-prepared vegetarian, fish, and pasta dishes. The owners write the *Moosewood Cookbook.* Try the soporific gazpacho ($2). Lunches $3-4, dinners around $8. Open Mon.-Sat. 11:30am-2pm and 6-9pm, Sun. 6-9pm.

Heart's Content, 156 State St. (272-0185), on the Ithaca Commons. Eat in the tiny deli bakery or head to the pedestrian mall outside. Try the sandwiches ($2.50-5) and desserts (brownie 75¢). More substantial entrees sold by weight. Open Mon.-Sat. 7:30am-7:30pm.

Aladdin's Natural Eatery, 100 Dryden Rd. (273-5000), in Collegetown by Cornell campus. Excellent vegetarian pita sandwiches ($3.75) in modern split-level abode. Open Mon.-Sat. 11am-10pm, Sun. noon-9pm.

Collegetown Bagels, 413 College Ave. (273-9655) in Collegetown, and 201 N. Aurora St. at Seneca downtown. Bagel sandwiches ($2-2.50), a huge salad bar ($3.75 per pound), natural foods, and cola in the original 6½-oz. bottle (50¢). Open daily 7am-2am.

Just a Taste, 116 N. Aurora (227-9463), near Ithaca Common. The place to taste fine wines (2½ oz. $1.75-3.75) and savor *tapas,* the Spanish "little dishes" ($3.50-5.50). Individual pizzas from $3.50. Open Mon.-Wed. 11:30am-10pm, Thurs.-Sat. 11:30am-midnight, Sun. 11:30am-9:30pm. Bar open Mon.-Wed. until midnight, Thurs.-Sat. until 1am, Sun. until 11pm.

Rangovian Embassy to the USA, Rte. 96 (387-3334), in the main strip of Trumansburg about 10 mi. out of Ithaca. Worth the drive. Amazing neo-political Mexican entrees in a classic restaurant/bar. Plot your next trip to "Beefree", "Nearvarna", or "Freelonch" on their huge wall map. Tacos $2.50. Dinners about $8. Mug of beer $1-1.50. Live bands on weekends. Food served Tues.-Sat. 11am-3pm and 5-9pm. Sun. 11am-3pm and 4-9pm. Open till 1am.

The Store at Truman's Village, on Rte. 96 in Trumansburg just up the street from the Embassy. Great local diner offering a taste of upstate country life and good burgers ($1.35). Breakfast served all day (pancakes $2.25). Open Mon.-Fri. 7am-8pm, Sat.-Sun. 8am-5pm.

After dark, Collegetown hops highest, though you may also want to try one of the many roadside saloons on Rte. 96, 13, and 89. **The Nine's,** 311 College Ave. (272-1888), features live blues and rock bands, beer (8 kinds of draft $1.50-3 per pint), and pizza ($7.20 feeds 2). Softball teams feel especially at home here. (Open Mon.-Sat. 11:30am-1am, Sun. 3:30pm-1am. Cover $2-4.) **The Haunt,** 114 W. Green St. (273-3355), diagonally across from Woolworth's near S. Geneva St. downtown, plays Motown, funk, and classic rock music. (Live bands most nights. Open daily 8pm-1:30am.)

Sights

Within a 10-mi. radius of Ithaca plunge 150 waterfalls and many paths, bridges, and gardens all offering spectacular views. In **Buttermilk Falls State Park** (see Accommodations and Camping above), the cataracts descend more than 500 ft. and end in a clear pool. Within the park, **Pinnacle Rock** towers 40 ft. above the water. The same bus that runs south to Buttermilk Falls also runs north to **Stewart Park** (272-8535), with a playground, picnic area, tennis courts, a restored carousel, and swimming in Lake Cayuga. A bike trail runs from the Ithaca Commons to Stewart Park.

In the Lakes region, a car provides the easiest transportation, but biking and hiking allow closer contact with this beautiful country. Reach out and touch the **Finger Lakes State Park Region** (see practical information above) for free maps and tips. Write the **Finger Lakes Trail Conference,** P.O. Box 18048, Rochester 14618 (716-288-7191), for free maps of the **Finger Lakes Trail,** an east-west footpath from the Catskills westward to the Allegheny Mountains. This 350-mi. trail and its 300 mi. of branch trails link several state parks, most with camping facilities. **Taughannock Falls** in the state park of the same name cascades from a height of 215 ft. Walk 1 mi. along the ravine leading from Cayuga Lake to the falls, where a powerful flow has cut through the solid cliffs over the course of 9,000 years.

A steep uphill climb from town, **Cornell University** perches on the hills of Ithaca. Even those passing through without enough time for the tours leaving from Day Hall (see Practical Information above) should try to climb the **McGraw Tower,** with 161 steps, a view of the entire valley, and the oldest, largest chime on a college campus. Student and faculty "chimesmasters" play three free 15-minute concerts each day during the academic year (Mon.-Fri. 7:45am, 1:10 and 6pm, Sun. 10:45am, noon and 6pm) and one or two during the summer (Mon. 12:45pm, Tues.-Wed. 8:15am and 6pm, Thurs. 6pm, Fri. 12:45 and 6pm, Sat. 8:30am and 6pm, Sun. 10:45am). The tower opens for visitors a half-hour before each performance. The **Herbert F. Johnson Museum of Art** (255-6464), on the corner of Central and University Ave., displays Asian and graphic art, as well as 19th- and 20th-century paintings. Designed by I.M. Pei, the oddly-shaped building is known as "the sewing machine." (Open Tues.-Sun. 10am-5pm. Free.)

The fertile soil of the Finger Lakes area makes the region the heart of New York's wine industry. Wine tasting and touring one of the small local vineyards is a relaxing way to pass a day. All of the vineyards on the Cayuga Wine Trail (P.O. Box 123, Fayette, NY 13065; see their brochure) offer picnic facilities and free tastings, though some require purchase of a glass ($1.50-2). Two mi. outside of Ithaca on Rte. 79 East nestles the **Six Mile Creek Vineyard.** Take State St. to Slatterville Rd. out of Ithaca to visit this small, but quality winery. (Open June-Dec. Mon.-Sun. noon-5:30pm, Jan.-May Sat.-Sun. noon-5:30pm.) **Americana Vineyards,** East Covert Rd., Interlaken (607-387-6801), ferments a mi. or so from Trumansburg, accessible by Greyhound and Tomtran (see Practical Information above). A family of four operates this winery from grape-picking to bottle-corking; one will give you a personal tour and free tasting. Pick up a bottle for about $5. (Open May-Oct. Mon.-Sat. 10am-5pm, Sun. noon-5pm, April and Nov.-Dec. weekends only; if you're driving, take Rte. 96 or 89 north of Trumansburg to E. Covert Rd.) The **Hosmer Winery,** 6999 Rte. 89 (607-869-3393), is 8½ mi. down the road. (Open April-Dec. Mon.-Sat. 11am-5pm, Sun. noon-5pm.) On the eastern side of Seneca Lake, visit **Wagner Winery,** Rte. 414 (607-582-6450), 4 mi. south of Lodi. Far bigger than any of the Cayuga wineries, bottling some 60,000 gallons per year, Wagner rests on a beautiful thoughtful spot on Seneca Lake. From Ithaca take Rte. 79 west to 414 south (8-9 mi.). Tastes and tours are free. (Open Mon.-Fri. 10am-4:30pm, Sat.-Sun. 10am-5pm.)

Considered the birthplace of the women's rights movement, **Seneca Falls** hosted the 1848 Seneca Falls Convention. Elizabeth Cady Stanton and Amelia Bloomer, two leading suffragists who lived here, organized a meeting of those seeking the vote for women. Visit the **National Women's Hall of Fame,** 76 Fall St. (315-568-8060), where photographs and biographies commemorate 38 outstanding U.S. women. (Open Mon.-Sat. 10am-4pm, Sun. noon-4pm. Donation requested).

Forty minutes out of Ithaca off Rte. 13 South, on Rte. 17 West, glitters the town of **Corning,** home to the Corning Glass Works that make Stueben artglass and sturdy cookware. The **Corning Glass Center,** Centerway, Corning 14831 (607-974-2000) built in honor of the Glass Works' Centenary in 1951, chronicles the 3,500-year history of glassmaking in a display of 20,000 pieces. (Open daily 9am-5pm. $5, seniors (60+) $4, under 18 $3.) The nearby **Rockwell Museum,** 111 Cedar St. Rte. 17 (607-937-5386) displays glass pieces by Frederick Carder, founder of the Steuben Glass Works and an excellent collection of American Western art. (Open Mon.-Sat. 9am-5pm, Sun. noon-5pm, July-Aug. Mon.-Sat. 9am-7pm; Sun. noon-5pm. $3, seniors $2.50, under 18 free.)

Niagara Falls and Buffalo

"The Honeymoon Capital of the World," Niagara Falls knows all about good marriages. Between the American Falls and the Horseshoe Falls runs the US-Canada boundary, the largest undefended border in the world. Both countries have succeeded in matching the age-old beauty of the Falls to modern tourist needs. No longer the site of daredevil escapades such as Annie Taylor's 1901 barrel ride, Niagara Falls instead powers the largest hydroelectric plant in North America. Technology coupled with this force of nature allows engineers to divert the flow of water over the Falls and in theory, cut it off altogether. See them while you still can—erosion is moving the Falls upstream at a rate of 6 ft. per year.

Practical Information

Emergency: 911.

Niagara Falls Convention and Visitors Bureau, 345 3rd St. (285-2400), and **Niagara County Tourism,** 139 Niagara St. Lockport, NY 14094 (800-338-7890) will send you info on Niagara Falls. Open May-Sept. daily 8:30am-8:30pm; Oct.-April Mon.-Fri. 9am-5pm. In Niagara, the **information center** (284-2000) that adjoins the bus station on 4th and Niagara is the place to visit. Open May-Sept. daily 8:30am-8:30pm; off-season Mon.-Fri. 9am-5pm. The state runs a **Niagara Reservation Visitors Center** (278-1796) right in front of the falls' observation deck. Open summer daily 9am-9:30pm; winter 10am-6:30pm. **Buffalo Convention and Visitors Bureau,** 107 Delaware Ave., Buffalo (852-0511 or 800-BUF-FALO), next to City Hall on the second floor of the Statler Tower up Main St. from the bus station, on the corner of Delaware and Niagara. Pick up the free *Buffalo and Erie County Travel Guide,* which describes attractions and services in Buffalo and provides an adequate map of the downtown area. Open Mon.-Fri. 8:30am-5pm.

Amtrak: 27th St. and Lockport, Niagara Falls, 1 block east of Hyde Park Blvd. (800-872-7245, 683-8440 for baggage problems). Also in downtown Buffalo at 75 Exchange St. (856-2075 for baggage) and in neighboring Depew, 55 Dick Rd. Ticket offices open 24 hrs. in

Depew, 7am-midnight. in Buffalo. To New York City (2 per day, 3 on Fri. and Sun.; 8 hr.; $77), Chicago (1 per day, 10 hr., $87), and Boston (from Depew 1 per day, 10½ hr., $84).

Greyhound/Trailways: Niagara Falls Bus Terminal, 4th St. and Niagara St. (282-1331; open Mon.-Fri. 8am-4pm) and the **Buffalo Transportation Center,** 181 Ellicott St. (855-7511; open daily 3am-1am). All buses leave from Buffalo Transportation Center. To: New York City (5 per day; 8 hr.; $67, Fri.-Sun. $71); Boston (3 per day; 12 hr.; $75, Fri.-Sun. $79); Chicago (5 per day, 12 hr., $94); Rochester (2 hr., $22); Syracuse (5 per day, 3 hr., $40); and Albany (5 per day, 7 hr., $76).

Public Transport: Niagara Frontier Metro Transit System, 800-794-3960. Provides local city transit. Bus #40 (17 per day, 1 hr., $1.75) connects the Greyhound/Trailways terminals in Niagara and Buffalo. **Niagara Scenic Bus Lines,** 800-672-3642. Service from Niagara Falls bus terminal to Niagara, Canada (10 per day to Ontario, 12 back; $2.75), and Buffalo Airport (12 per day, $9.50).

Taxi: Rainbow Taxicab, 285-3221; **United Cab,** 285-9331.

Post Office: Niagara Falls, 615 Main St. (285-7561), in Niagara Falls, NY. Open Mon.-Fri. 8:30am-5pm, Sat. 9am-noon. **ZIP code:** 14302. **Buffalo,** 1200 William St. (864-2434). Open Mon.-Fri. 8:30am-6pm, Sat. 8:30am-1pm. **ZIP code:** 14240.

Area Codes: 716 (New York), 416 (Ontario).

Parking in the city is plentiful. Most lots near the falls charge $3, but you can park in an equivalent spot for less on streets bordering the park.

Accommodations and Camping

Niagara Falls International AYH-Hostel, 1101 Ferry Ave., Niagara Falls, NY 14301 (282-3700), walk up 4th St. from the bus station. Turn right on Ferry Ave. Cross-street is Memorial Parkway, just past 10th St. Good facilities, with kitchen, TV lounge. 46 beds. Travelers without cars given first priority; nonmembers turned away when space is short, as it usually is in summer. Limited parking available. Check-in 7:30-9:30am and 5-11pm. Lockout 9:30am-5pm. Curfew 11:30pm. Lights out midnight. $10, non-members $13. Required sheet sacks $1. Reservations recommended. Open Jan. 4-Dec. 16.

Niagara Falls International Hostel (CHA), 4699 Zimmerman Ave., Niagara Falls, Ont. L2E 3M7 (416-357-0770). Pleasant, brick Tudor building 2½ mi. from the falls, between Morrison and Queen St. off River Rd. near the train and bus stations. Beautiful kitchen, dining room, lounge, peaceful backyard. 58 beds; rather cramped but upbeat atmosphere. Young, friendly staff conduct bike trips and day hikes along the Niagara gorge. Bike rentals $10 per day. Open 9-11am and 5pm-midnight. Curfew and lights out midnight in summer, 11pm in winter. CDN$12, non-members CDN$17.50. 50¢ returned for morning chore. Linen $1. Reservations recommended.

All Tucked Inn, 574 3rd St., Niagara Falls, NY (282-0919), between Walnut and Main St., downtown. Clean, comfortable, freshly painted rooms. Check-in 9am-midnight. May-Sept. doubles with shared bath $44-54; off-season $34-44. $8 per additional person, $5 per young child. $10 more on holiday weekends. Reservations recommended.

Rainbow View Tourist Home, 4407 John St., Niagara Falls, Ont. (416-374-1845), just off River Rd., moments from the Falls. Small rooms in charming house with cozy front porch. Doubles July-Sept. 14 $45-65; May, June, and Sept. 15-Oct. $40-60; lower rates, special deals in winter. Ask about the $22 per night student rates. Continental breakfast included. Reservations recommended.

Niagara Falls Motel and Campsite, 2405 Niagara Falls Blvd., Wheatfield, NY 14304 (731-3434), 7 mi. from downtown. Follow Rte. 62 south of I-90 until it becomes Niagara Falls Blvd. Nice-sized doubles with A/C, color TV, private bath $40-55, off-season $35-40; cheapest double in high season is $55. Sites $16, with hookup $21.

KOA-Niagara Falls, 2570 Grand Island Blvd., 14072 (773-7583). On Rte. 324 off Highway 190. Take the 2nd exit over the Grand Island bridge; it's next door to the amusement park. 550 camping sites with fishing, indoor and outdoor pool 7 mi. from the Falls. Sites $18, with hook-up $21-25. Cabins $34 per 2 people, additional adults $4, ages 3-18 $2. Open April 1-Nov. 15. Reservations recommended.

Food

Most sightseers ogle the falls then split; only a truly entranced few make stops that require a meal, and the food they prefer is fast. If you can find an entrance, try the standard food-court fare in the **Rainbow Centre Factory Outlet Mall** (shops open Mon.-Sat. 10am-9pm, Sun. 10am-5pm); head also to the downtown taverns where the locals eat and drink. The **Arterial Restaurant**, for example, at 314 Niagara St. near 4th (282-9459), serves good burgers ($1.75) and chicken wings (12 per $2.95) with "napkins of distinction". (Open Mon.-Thurs. 11:30am-2am, Fri.-Sat. 11:30am-3am, Sun. noon-2am.) Should you stay in town long enough to sample the nightlife, **The Press Box Bar**, 324 Niagara St. (284-5447) is a popular spot. Or you can shoot some pool at **Beach Bum Bert's,** 26 Niagara St. (282-6311).

Buffalo's greatest contribution to contemporary cuisine is the "Buffalo-style" spicy chicken wing, available at any area restaurant. Spread your wings ($4) where they originated at the **Anchor Bar**, 1047 Main St. (886-8920; open daily 10am 'til). Another local specialty, found on most menus, is "beef on a weck," a pile of thinly-sliced roast beef on a caraway and salt roll. For fresh produce, try the **Broadway Market,** 999 Broadway. On weekends (Sat.-Sun. 9am-5pm), visit the lively **Market on the Main**, 2495 Main St. (835-3366).

Sights and Entertainment

The gardens near the U.S. falls, established in 1885, constitute the nation's first national park; despite the tourist-targeted developments, vast stretches of green surround the falls. The **Caves of the Wind Tour** on Goat Island will outfit you with a yellow rain coat and take you to the gardens by elevator. (Open May 15-Oct. 20. $3.50, ages 5-11 $3, under 4 free.) A cheaper elevator ride (50¢) awaits at the **Observation Deck**, though the view is not as spectacular. From the deck, you should catch the **Maid of the Mist Tour** (284-8897), a boat ride to the foot of Horseshoe Canadian Falls. (Tours every 15 min. May and Labor Day-Oct. 24 Mon.-Fri. 10am-5pm, Sat.-Sun. 10am-6pm; May 28-June 14 daily 10am-6pm; June 15-21 daily 10am-8pm; June 22-Aug. 7 9:15am-8pm; Aug. 8-25 9:15am-7:30pm; Aug. 26-Labor Day 9:15am-7:15pm. Tickets $6.75, ages 6-12 $3.40, under 6 free.)

Dart around the falls in the **View Mobile** (278-1717) which leaves every 15 minutes from five stops around the park (fare $2.50, ages 5-12 $1.50). And in the visitors center, check out **Niagara Wonders** (278-1792), a spectacular, special effect-filled look at the Falls. (Shown on the hr. in the summer daily 10am-8pm. In the fall and early spring, daily 10am-6pm; mid-Jan. to April closed Mon.-Tues. $2, seniors $1.50, ages 6-12 $1.) Those who plan to hit all of the Falls sights should buy a **Master Pass**, available in the park visitors center. One pass provides admission to the observation tower, the Cave of the Wind, the theater and the geological museum, plus discounts on Maid of the Mist tours and free parking. (Pass $7, kids $5.)

Away from the falls, browse through an impressive collection of regional Iroquois arts and crafts and watch spectacular performances of Iroquois dancing at **The Turtle**, 25 Rainbow Mall, Niagara Falls, NY (284-2427), between Winter Garden and the river. (Open May-Sept. daily 9am-6pm; Oct.-April Tues.-Fri. 9am-5pm, Sat.-Sun. noon-5pm. $3.50, seniors $3, kids and students $2.) Wander into the peaceful **Artisans Alley,** 10 Rainbow Blvd. (282-0196) at 1st St., to see works by over 600 American craftsmen. (Open Mon.-Fri. 10am-6pm, Sat.-Sun. 10am-9pm.) **Schoellkopf's Geological Museum** (278-1780) depicts the birth of the falls with slide shows every half hour. (Open Memorial Day-Labor Day daily 9:30am-7pm; Labor Day-Oct. daily 10am-5pm; Nov.-Memorial Day Wed.-Sun. 10am-5pm. 50¢.) If you haven't had enough water, the **Aquarium,** across the street at 701 Whirlpool St. (285-3575 or 692-2665), has a dolphin show and a nice school of fish. (Open Memorial Day-Labor Day daily 9am-7pm; off-season daily 9am-5pm. $5.85, seniors and ages 5-14 $3.75, under 5 free.)

Visitors can traverse the border between the U.S. and Canada by crossing the **Rainbow Bridge.** On the Ontario side, **Queen Victoria Park** provides the best view of the Horseshoe Falls. Niagara Falls, Ontario served as a birthplace and home for W.E.B. DuBois's 1905 "Niagara Movement," the forerunner of the National Association for the Advancement of Colored People (NAACP). Just minutes from the Falls, **Clifton Hill** has a multitude of gift shops, streetside cafés, and motels. "The Hill" is also home to Ripley's Believe It or Not Museum, The Guinness Museum of World Records, The Super Star Recording Studio, and many other pop-culture attractions. Believe it or not, each attraction charges its own admission (average CDN$5).

From Nov. 23, 1991 through Jan. 5, 1992 and Nov. 21, 1992-Jan. 3, 1993, Niagara Falls holds the annual Festival of Lights. Bright bulbs line the trees and create brilliant animated and outdoor scenes. Illumination of the Falls caps the spectacle. (Animated display areas open Sun.-Thurs. 5-10pm, Fri.-Sat. 5-11pm; exterior display areas nightly 5-11pm. Falls illumination hours Jan. 6:30-9pm; Feb. and Nov. 7-9:30pm; March 7-10pm; April 7:30-10:30pm; May 9pm-midnight; July 9:15pm-12:15am; Aug. 9pm-12:30am; Sept.-Oct. 8-11pm; Dec. 5:30-10:30pm.)

Niagara-on-the-Lake, Ont., 20 minutes away from the Falls, annually hosts the **Shaw Festival** (416-468-2172; Box Office, P.O. Box 774, Niagara-on-the-Lake, Ont. L0S IJO). Now in its 31st season, the festival continues its tradition of staging excellent productions by George Bernard Shaw and other modern playwrights. (Season runs mid-April to mid-Nov. Tickets $20-46.50. Preview, midweek performances cheaper; some lower-priced performances reserved for students and senior groups. Wheelchair seating $12-16.50. $14 rush tickets, purchased in person only, go on sale at 10am the day of performance. Call for comprehensive brochure.)

Buffalo, New York state's second largest city, offers high culture, streetside fun, and good sports. The **Albright-Knox Art Gallery,** 1285 Elmwood Ave. (882-8700), enjoys a worldwide reputation as an outstanding center of contemporary art. Its extensive modern collection will please anyone interested in U.S. and European art of the past 30 years. (Open Tues.-Sat. 11am-5pm; Sun. noon-5pm. Voluntary donation.) In mid-June, catch the annual **Allentown Arts Festival,** which takes place along Delaware and Elmwood Ave. and Allen St. The intersection of Elmwood and Allen is also the core of an active after-dark scene. Free noontime concerts take place at the plaza downtown. People-watchers will find a good vantage point by climbing to the top of **City Hall.** (Open Mon.-Fri. 9am-3:30pm, Sat. 9am-5pm.) In the fall, catch the NFL's **Buffalo Bills,** 1 Bills Dr. (649-0015 for tickets), at Rich Stadium in suburban Orchard Park. Or watch some hard-hitting hockey in season (Oct.-April) at Memorial Auditorium, home to the **Buffalo Sabres,** 140 Main St. (tickets 856-7300 or 800-333-7825 outside Buffalo or Canada). Winter activities such as tobogganing, skating, and skiing center at city and county parks. Pick up a list of parks at the chamber of commerce (see Practical Information above) or write to the Parks Department, Niagara Sq., Buffalo, NY 14202.

Thousand Island Seaway Region

The Thousand Island-St. Lawrence Seaway spans 100 mi. from the mouth of Lake Ontario to the first of the giant man-made locks of the St. Lawrence River. Some 1,800 islands scatter throughout the waterway, accessible both by small pleasure-boats and huge ocean-bound freighters. Once known as the playground of millionaires, the beautiful Thousand Islands region now attracts fishers from all over North America, thanks to a plentiful stock of bass and muskellunge. The world's largest muskie (69 lb., 15 oz.) was caught here in the fall of 1957.

Any of the small towns strung along Rte. 12 along the river coast can serve as a good base for exploring the region. For $11 (ages 6-12 $5.50), **Uncle Sam Boat Tours** in **Clayton,** 604 Riverside Dr. (686-3511) or in the bigger, glitzier town of **Alexandria Bay** on Main St. (482-2611), gives a good look at most of the islands and the plush estates that bask atop them. **Empire,** off James St. in Alexandria Bay (482-9511 or 800-542-2628) runs similar two-hour tours in triple-decker boats ($11). Look for the shortest international bridge in the world (about 10 ft.) connecting adjacent islands on either side of the U.S./Canadian border drawn through the seaway. Both tours highlight **Heart Island** and its famous Boldt Castle (482-9724), stopping here before returning. George Boldt, former owner of New York City's elegant Waldorf-Astoria Hotel, financed this six-story replica of a Rhineland castle as a gift for his wife, who died before its completion. Though original plans called for 365 bedrooms, 52 bathrooms, and one power-house, Boldt abandoned the project in his grief. Today, its 120 rooms stand unfinished. (Open late May-Sept. $3, ages 6-12 $1.75.)

Cape Vincent, on the western edge of the seaway, keeps one of the prettiest youth hostels in the country. **Tibbetts Point Lighthouse Hostel (AYH),** RR 1 Box 330 (315-654-3450), is a former Coast Guard station at the spot where Lake Ontario meets the St. Lawrence. Fall asleep to the sound of waves crashing against the rocks. Take Rte. 12E into town, turn left on Broadway, and follow the river until it ends. (Curfew 10:30pm. $8, nonmembers $11. Check-in 5-9pm. Open May 15-Sept. 15.) One of the area's many campgrounds, the **French Creek Marina** (686-3621), in the heart of Clayton, has a launch ramp, boat rentals, and many different family fishing packages. (Sites $10.)

Write the **Clayton Chamber of Commerce,** 403 Riverside Dr., Clayton 13624 (686-3771), for the *Clayton Vacation Guide* and the *Thousand Islands Seaway Region Travel Guide.* The **Alexandria Bay Chamber of Commerce** is on Market St. just off James St., Alexandria Bay 13607 (482-9531). Access the region by bus through **Greyhound,** 540 State St. in Watertown (788-8110). Hounds service New York City ($41.65), Syracuse ($11), and Albany ($27). From the same station, **Thousand Islands Bus Lines** runs to Alexandria Bay and Clayton weekdays at 2:45pm ($4); return trips leave at 8:30am. (Station open 9:30am-3pm and 5-8pm.)

Clayton and the Thousand Islands region are just two hours from Syracuse by way of I-81 north. For Welleslet Island, Alexandria Bay, and the eastern 500 islands, stay on I-81 until you reach Rte. 12E. For Clayton and points west, take exit 47 and follow Rte. 12 until you reach 12E.

The Clayton **post office** (686-3311) is at 236 John St. Clayton's **ZIP code** is 13624; the region's **area code** is 315.

NORTH CAROLINA

North Carolina splits neatly into thirds: the wild eastern coast, the west's down-to-earth mountain culture, and the mellow sophistication of the Raleigh/Durham/Chapel Hill Research Triangle in the state's center. But whatever their cultural differences, these three regions share one stark similarity—the unmatched North Carolinian beauty apparent the moment you cross the state border. Even the occasional urban veneer complements Carolina's fertile glamour. The streets are unlittered, the buildings well-spaced, the businesses clean, the universities spacious.

Visitors will have a hard time reconciling the awe-inspiring beauty of the landscape with the ugly political image of North Carolina's most famous politician, ailing U.S. Sen. Jesse Helms (R, very R). Helms has become a symbol of reaction in American politics, on issues from race to art censorship. For some he is also an image of death, because of his close alliance with tobacco agribusiness corporations. Teddy Kennedy's only competition for Most Notorious Senator, Helms almost lost his 1991 re-election bid to an African American, Charlotte Mayor Harvey Gantt—a sign that, just maybe, the times they are a changin'.

Practical Information

Capital: Raleigh.

Travel and Tourism Division, 430 N. Salisbury St., Raleigh 27611 (919-733-4171 or 800-847-4862). **Department of Natural Resources and Community Development,** Division of Parks and Recreation, P.O. Box 27287, Raleigh 27611.

Time Zone: Eastern. **Postal Abbreviation:** NC

The Carolina Mountains

The sharp ridges and rolling slopes of the southern Appalachian mountain ranges create some of the East's most magnificent scenery. At one time, North Carolina's Edenic highlands provided refuge for the country's rich and famous. The Vanderbilts, for example, owned a large portion of the nearly 500,000-acre Pisgah National Forest, which they subsequently willed to the U.S. government. Today the Blue Ridge, Great Smoky, Black, Craggy, Pisgah, and Balsam Mountains that comprise the western half of North Carolina beckon budget travelers, not billionaires. Campsites blanket the region, coexisting with elusive but inexpensive youth hostels and ski lodges. Enjoy the area's rugged wilderness while backpacking, canoeing, whitewater rafting, or cross-country skiing. Motorists and cyclists can follow the Blue Ridge Parkway to some unforgettable views (see Blue Ridge Parkway, VA).

The **Blue Ridge Mountains** bifurcate into two areas. The first, northern area is the **High Country,** which includes the territory between the town of Boone and the town of Asheville, 100 mi. to the southwest. The second area comprises the **Great Smoky Mountain National Park** (see Great Smoky Mountain National Park, TN) and **Nanatahala National Forest.**

Boone

Named for famous frontiersman Daniel Boone, who built a cabin here in the 1760s on his journey into the western wilderness, the town continues to evoke its pioneer past through shops such as the Mast Gen'l Store and the Candy Barrel.

Practical Information

Emergency: 911. **National Park Service/Blue Ridge Parkway Emergency,** 259-0701 or 800-727-5928.

Visitor Information: Boone Area Chamber of Commerce, 350 Blowing Rock Rd. (264-2225), just east of the intersection of Rte. 321 and 105 in the center of Boone, nearly 7 mi. north of the Blue Ridge Pkwy. Info on accommodations and sights. Open Mon.-Fri. 9am-5pm. **North Carolina High Country Host,** 701 Blowing Rock Rd. (264-1299; 800-438-7500). Pick up copies of the *North Carolina High Country Host Area Travel Guide,* an informative and detailed map of the area, and the *Blue Ridge Parkway Directory,* a mile-by-mile description of all services and attractions located on or near the Parkway. Open daily 9am-5pm.

Greyhound/Trailways: At the AppalCart station on Winkler's Creek Rd. (262-0501), off Rte. 321 at Wendy's. Flag stop in Blowing Rock. One per day to Hickory and most points east, south, and west. To Hickory ($9.50) and Charlotte (2½ hr., $20). Open Mon.-Fri. 8am-5pm, Sat.-Sun. 1-5pm.

Public Transport: Boone AppalCart, on Winkler's Creek Rd. (264-2278). Local bus and van service; 3 routes. The Red Route links downtown Boone with ASU and the motels and restaurants on Blowing Rock Rd. The Green Route serves Rte. 421. Crosstown route between the campus and the new marketplace. The Red Route operates Mon.-Fri. every hr. 7am-7pm; Green Mon.-Fri. every hr. 7am-6pm; crosstown Mon.-Fri. 7am-11pm, Sat. 8am-6pm. Fare 50¢ in town, charged by zones in the rest of the county.

Post Office: 637 Blowing Rock Rd. (264-3813), and 103 W. King St. (262-1171). Open Mon.-Fri. 9am-1:15pm and 3:15-5pm, Sat. 9am-noon. **ZIP code:** 28607.

Area Code: 704.

Accommodations and Camping

Because of its wealthy visitors, the area fields more than its share of expensive motels and B&Bs, but you can get good motel deals in addition to the hostels and camp sites in the area.

Blowing Rock Assembly Grounds (AYH), P.O. Box 974, Blowing Rock (295-7813), near the Blue Ridge Parkway, has clean rooms, communal bathrooms, sports facilities, and a cheap cafeteria, all in a gorgeous setting with access to hiking trails. Ask the bus driver to let you off at Blowing Rock Town Hall or at the Rte. 321 bypass and Sunset Dr., depending on the direction you're traveling—it's about 2 mi. from both points. Call the hostel for a pick-up, or turn left onto Sunset Dr., and where Sunset wanes turn left again; follow signs to B.R.A.G. and the hostel will be on your right. Primarily a retreat for religious groups. $11, nonmembers $14. Package rates available.

Most inexpensive hotels are concentrated along Blowing Rock Rd. (Hwy 321), or Hwy 105. The red-brick **Red Carpet Inn** (264-2457) may have simple rooms but they come with remote TV, a playground, and a pool. (Singles $34. Doubles $38. Weekend singles and doubles $53.) The **High Country Inn**, Hwy 105 (264-1000) also has a pool and even a watermill. Large, comfortable rooms. (Singles $34. Doubles $48. Weekend rates $10 more.)

Choose between developed **campsites** and free primitive camping in the Boone area and the Pisgah National Forest. Along the Blue Ridge Pwy, spectacular sites without hookups are available for $8 at the **Julian Price Campground**, mile 297 (963-5911); **Linville Falls**, mile 316 (963-5911); and **Crabtree Meadows**, mile 340 (675-4444); (open May-Oct. only). Cabins in **Roan Mountain State Park** (772-3314) comfortably sleep six and are furnished with linens and cooking utensils. (Sun.-Thurs. $56.50, Fri.-Sat. $73, weekly $372.) The state park offers pool and tennis facilities and tends to attract smaller crowds than the campgrounds on the parkway. For more info call the Roan Mtn. Visitors Center at 772-3314.

Sights and Activities

In an open air amphitheater, **Horn in the West** (264-2120), located near Boone off Rte. 105, presents an outdoor drama of the American Revolution as fought in the southern Appalachians. (Shows Tues.-Sun. at 8:30pm. Admission $8-12, kids under 13 ½-price. Reservations recommended.) Adjacent to the theater the **Daniel Boone Native Gardens** celebrate mountain foliage, while the **Hickory Ridge Homestead** documents 18th-century mountain life. **An Appalachian Summer** (262-6084) is a month-long, high-caliber festival of music, art, theater, and dance sponsored by Appalachian State University.

Use Boone as a base from which to explore the mountain towns to the west and south. The community of **Blowing Rock**, 7 mi. south at the entrance to the Blue Ridge Pkwy., is a folk artists' colony. Its namesake overhangs Johns River Gorge; chuck a piece of paper over the edge and the wind will blow it back into your face. AppalCart goes to the Blowing Rock Town Hall from Boone twice daily. Stop by **Parkway Craft Center**, mile 294 (295-7938), 2 mi. south of Blowing Rock Village, where members of the Southern Highland Handicraft Guild demonstrate their skills and sell their crafts. The craft center is located in the **Moses H. Cone Memorial Park**, 3500 acres of shaded walking trails and magnificent views. (Open May-Oct. daily 9am-5:30pm.)

Hikers should arm themselves with the invaluable large-scale map *100 Favorite Trails* ($2). Consider joining one of the guided expeditions led by the staff of **Edge of the World**, P.O. Box 1137, Banner Elk (898-9550), on Rte. 184 downtown. A complete outdoor equipment and clothing store, the Edge leads many day-long backpacking, whitewater canoeing, rafting, spelunking and rock climbing trips all over the High Country for about $65. One of their most popular packages is a two-day summer backpacking trip across the Roan Mountain Balds ($125, including transportation, all equipment, four meals, instruction, and guide).

Downhill skiers can enjoy the Southeast's largest concentration of alpine resorts. Four concentrate in the Boone/Blowing Rock/Banner Elk area: **Appalachian Ski Mountain,** P.O. Box 106, Blowing Rock (800-322-2373; lift tickets weekends $26, weekdays $18, with full rental $27); **Ski Beech,** P.O. Box 1118, Beech Mountain (387-2011; lift tickets weekends $26, weekdays $21, with rentals $38 and $28 respectively); **Ski Hawknest,** Town of Seven Devils, 1605 Skyland Dr., Banner Elk (963-6561; lift tickets weekends $20, weekdays $10, with rentals $30 and $16); **Sugar Mountain,** P.O. Box 369, Banner Elk (898-4521; lift tickets weekends $35, weekdays $25, with rentals $47 and $35). AppalCart (264-2278) runs a daily shuttle in winter to Sugar Mountain and four times per week to Ski Beech. Call the High Country Host (264-1299) for ski reports.

In a car, the 5-mi. access road to **Grandfather Mountain** (800-468-7325) reveals an unparalleled view of the entire High Country area. At the top you'll find a private park featuring a mile-high suspension bridge and a small zoo ($8, kids $4). To hike or camp on Grandfather Mt. you need a permit ($4 per day, $4 per night for camping), available at the Grandfather Mountain Country Store on Rte. 221 or at the entrance to the park. (Contact the Backcountry Manager, Grandfather Mt., Linville, NC 28646 for more info. Mountain open April-Nov. daily 8am-8pm; Dec.-March 9am-4pm, weather permitting.)

Asheville

Asheville's hazy blue mountains, deep valleys, spectacular waterfalls, and plunging gorges embody classic Appalachian beauty. A drive along the Blue Ridge Parkway, a part of the National Park Service, best reveals the scenic vistas that surround the city. The Appalachians also prove fertile for less natural beauty produced by the local arts and crafts community, with festivals throughout the year. The **Biltmore Estate,** "Versailles of the South," home to George Vanderbilt and his designer-jean family, attracts herds of gawking tourists.

Practical Information

Emergency: 911.

Visitors Information: Chamber of Commerce, 151 Haywood St. (258-3858; 800-257-1300 in NC), off I-240 on the northwest end of downtown. Ask at the desk for the detailed city map, transit route map, and comprehensive sight-seeing guide. Open Mon.-Fri. 8:30am-5:30pm, Sat.-Sun. 9am-5pm.

Greyhound/Trailways: 2 Tunnel Rd. (253-5353), 2 mi. east of downtown, near the Beaucatcher Tunnel. Bus #13 ("Oteen/Beverly Hills") or 14 ("Haw Creek/Tunnel Rd.") runs to and from downtown every ½-hr. Last bus at 5:50pm. To Charlotte (5 per day, 3 hr., $22), Knoxville (7 per day, 3 hr., $24), Atlanta ($41). Open daily 6:30am-10pm.

Public Transport: Asheville Transit, 360 W. Haywood (253-5691). Service within city limits. All routes converge on Pritchard Park downtown. Buses operate Mon.-Sun. 5:30am-7:30pm, most at ½-hr. intervals. Fare 60¢, transfers 10¢.

Post Office: 33 Coxe Ave. (257-4112), at Patton Ave. Open Mon.-Fri. 8:30am-5pm, Sat. 9am-noon. **ZIP code:** 28802.

Area Code: 704.

Accommodations and Camping

Asheville's independent motels outdo the budget chains. Many lean on **Merrimon Avenue,** north of the city (take bus #2), and on **Tunnel Road.** Make reservations early for folk and craft festivals and holidays. The **American Court Motel,** 85 Merrimon Ave. (253-4427), has bright rooms with cable, A/C, pool, and laundromat. (Singles $36. Doubles $48.) Slightly farther from town, **Four Seasons Motor Inn,** 820 Merrimon Ave. (254-5324), breezes in with cheerful rooms and classic walk-in closets, although it is about 1½ mi. from town and somewhat inconvenient. (Singles $32. Doubles $38.) The **Downtown Motel,** 65 Merrimon Ave. (253-9841), on Merrimon St. just north of the I-240 expressway, is a 10-minute walk from downtown (or take bus #2), with somewhat dark rooms, big bathrooms and a pool. (Singles $28. Doubles $38.)

With the Blue Ridge Pkwy., Pisgah National Forest, and the Great Smokies easily accessible by car, you can find a campsite to suit any taste. Close to town is **Bear Creek RV Park and Campground,** 81 S. Bear Creek Rd. (253-0798). Take I-40 exit 47, and look for the sign at the top of the hill. (Pool, laundry, groceries, and game room. Tent sites $13. RV sites with hookup $15.) In Pisgah National Forest, the nearest campground is **Powhatan,** off Rte. 191, 12 mi. southwest of Asheville. (Sites $8. Open May-Sept.)

Food

You'll find links in most major fast-food chains on **Tunnel Road** and **Biltmore Avenue.** The **Western North Carolina Farmers Market** (253-1691), at the intersection of I-240 and Rte. 191, near I-26, hawks fresh produce and crafts. Take bus #16 to I-40, then walk ½-mi. (Open daily 8am-6pm.)

Stone Soup, at Broadway and Walnut St.(252-7687) Also on Wall St.(254-0844), downtown. A cooperative that bakes its own bread and serves nitrate-free sausage. Soup and sandwiches from $1.50. Try the Hungarian Peasant Bread. Packed noon-2pm and for Sun. brunch. Open Mon.-Sat. 7am-4pm, Sun. 9:30am-1:30pm, Thurs.-Sat. 5-9pm.

Malaprops Bookstore/Café, 61 Haywood St. (254-6734), downtown in the basement of the bookstore. Gourmet coffees, bagels, tofu. Sandwiches $3-4. Cerebral readings, great book curriculum, and walking staff. Open Mon.-Sat. 9am-8pm, Sun. noon-5pm.

Johnny O's Sandwich Shop, 36 Battery Park Ave. (254-0442). Mom-and-pop grill with a stand-up lunch counter. Everything under $2. Cheeseburger 70¢, hotdogs 75¢. Open daily 6am-2pm.

Sights and Festivals

Elvis's Southern mansion, Graceland, has nothing on the Vanderbilt family's **Biltmore Estate,** 1 North Pack Sq. (255-1700 or 800-543-2961). Take exit 50 off I-40, and go three blocks north. A tour of this true French Renaissance-style castle built in the 1890s can take all day if crowded; try to arrive early in the morning. The self-guided tour winds through a portion of the 250 rooms, viewing an indoor pool, a bowling alley, rooms full of Sargent paintings and Dürer prints, and enormous rare-book libraries. Tours of the surrounding gardens, designed by Central Park planner Frederick Law Olmsted, and the Biltmore winery (with sour-wine tasting for those over 21) are included in the hefty admission price. (Open daily 9am-6pm; ticket office closes at 5pm. Winery open Mon.-Sat. at 11am, Sun. at 1pm. Admission $20, ages 12-17 $15, under 11 free.) George Vanderbilt had **Biltmore Village** built right outside the gates. This cozy shopping district contains craft galleries, antique stores, and a music shop.

Even the most famous of Asheville's past visitors did not have the privilege of staying at the Vanderbilt's chateau. You're not alone. Henry Ford, Thomas Edison, and F. Scott Fitzgerald all stayed in the towering **Grove Park Inn** when they passed through the peaceful mountain town. Made of stone quarried from the surrounding mountains, the still-operating hotel has many pieces of original early-20th-century furniture and fireplaces into which you literally can walk. To see sights really engraved with celebrity, visit the **Riverside Cemetery,** Birch St. off Montford Ave., north of I-240, where writers Thomas Wolfe and O. Henry are buried. The **Thomas Wolfe Memorial,** 48 Spruce St. (253-8304), between Woodfin and Walnut St., site of the novelist's boyhood home, was a boarding house run by his mother. Wolfe depicted the "Old Kentucky Home" as "Dixieland" in his first novel, *Look Homeward, Angel.* (Open Mon.-Sat. 9am-5pm, Sun. 1-5pm; hours vary in winter. Admission $1, students, and kids 50¢.)

Asheville's artistic tradition remains as strong as its literary one; visit the **Folk Art Center** (704-298-7928), east of Asheville at mile 382 on the Blue Ridge Pkwy., north of U.S. 70, to see outstanding work of the **Southern Highland Handicraft Guild.** (Open daily 9am-5pm. Free.) Each year around mid-July the Folk Art Center sponsors a **Guild Fair** (298-7928), at the Asheville Civic Center, off I-240 on Haywood St. Both the Folk Art Center and the chamber of commerce have more info on this weekend of craft demonstrations, dancing, and music.

A rare summer day goes by in Asheville when a festival is not taking place. At the end of July, the downtown **Belle Chere Festival** (253-1009) celebrates "beautiful living" with food and music. An **Appalachian Heritage Fair** (258-6111) occurs at the beginning of August. Also in August, the **Mountain Dance and Folk Festival** (257-1300) at the civic center, now in its 63rd season, sponsors three days of competitive clog and square dancing, mountain traditional and bluegrass music, and individual musicianship. (Tickets $6-8.) The **Swannanoa Chamber Festival** (298-7613) in July has weekly chamber music concerts ($10 per performance, $45 for a series ticket).

Outer Banks

England's first attempt to colonize North America took place on the shores of North Carolina. This ill-fated episode ended when Sir Walter Raleigh's 1587 Roanoke Island settlement vanished inexplicably. Since then, a succession of pirates, patriots, and secessionists have brought adventure to the North Carolina coast. Blackbeard called Ocracoke home in the early 18th century until a savvy serviceman struck down the buccaneer at Pamlico Sound. Most seafarers didn't fare well here; over 600 ships have foundered on the shoals of the Banks' southern shores. Fearing for their lives, the Wright Brothers tried to fly the coop at the turn of the 20th century, but soared only a few hundred ft.

The Outer Banks descend from hellish beach towns to heavenly wilderness. Highly developed **Bodie Island,** on the Outer Banks' northern end, holds the towns of Nags Head, Kitty Hawk, and Kill Devil Hills. Unless you are a friend of the devil, travel south on Rte. 12 through the magnificent wildlife preserves and across Hatteras Inlet to **Ocracoke** island—where you will find the Outer Banks' isolated beaches.

Practical Information

Aycock Brown Visitors Center, off Rte. 158, after the Wright Memorial Bridge, Bodie Island. Info on accommodations and picnic areas plus National Park Service schedules. Record sailfish welcomes visitors in the parking lot. Open Mon.-Thurs. 8:30am-6:30pm, Fri.-Sun. 8:30am-7:30pm; in winter Mon.-Fri. 9am-5pm.

Cape Hatteras National Seashore Information Centers: Bodie Island, Rte. 12 at Bodie Island Lighthouse (441-5711; info and special programs; open daily 9am-6pm; off-season 9am-5pm); **Hatteras Island,** Rte. 12 at Cape Hatteras (995-4474; camping info, demonstrations, and special programs; open daily 9am-6pm; off-season 9am-5pm); and **Ocracoke Island,** next to the ferry terminal at the south end of the island (928-4531; info on ferries, camping, lighthouses, and wild ponies; open daily 9am-5pm, mid-June to Aug. 9am-6pm).

Ferries: Toll ferries operate to Ocracoke from **Cedar Island,** east of New Bern on U.S. 70 (4-8 per day, 2¼ hr.), and **Swan Quarter,** on the northern side of Pamlico Sound off U.S. 264/Rte. 45 (2½ hr.), both on the mainland. $10 per car (reserve in advance), $1 per pedestrian, $2 per biker. (Cedar Island 225-3551, Swan Quarter 926-1111, Ocracoke 928-3841. All open daily 5:30am-8:30pm.) Free ferry across Hatteras Inlet between Hatteras and Ocracoke (operates daily 5am-11pm, 40 min.).

Taxi: Beach Cab, 441-2500. Serves Bodie Island and Manteo.

Car Rental: National, Mile 5½, Beach Rd. (800-328-4567 or 441-4588), Kill Devil Hills. $55 per day. 75 free mi., 30¢ each additional mi. Open daily 9am-5pm. Must be 25 with major credit card.

Bike Rental: Pony Island Motel (928-4411) and the **Slushy Stand** on Rte. 12, both on Ocracoke Island. $1 per hr. Open daily 8am-dusk.

Emergency: 911, north of the Oregon Inlet. **Ocracoke,** 928-4831.

ZIP Codes: Manteo 27954, Nags Head 27959, Ocracoke 27960.

Area Code: 919.

Four narrow islands strung north-to-south along half the length of the North Carolina coast comprise the Outer Banks. **Bodie Island** includes the towns of **Kitty Hawk, Kill Devil Hills,** and **Nags Head,** connecting to Elizabeth, NC, and Norfolk, VA, by U.S. 158. **Roanoke Island** swims between Bodie and the mainland on U.S. 64, and includes the town of **Manteo. Hatteras Island,** connected to Bodie by a bridge, stretches like a great sandy elbow. **Ocracoke Island,** the southernmost, is linked by free ferry to Hatteras Island, and by toll ferry to towns on the mainland. **Cape Hatteras National Seashore** encompasses Hatteras, Ocracoke, and the southern end of Bodie Island. On Bodie Island U.S. 158 and Rte. 12 run parallel to each other until the beginning of the preserve. After that Rte. 12 (also called Beach Rd.) continues south, stringing Bodie, Hatteras, and Ocracoke together with free bridges and ferries. Addresses on Bodie Island are determined by their distance in mi. from the Wright Memorial Bridge.

Nags Head and Ocracoke lie 76 mi. apart and public transportation proves virtually nonexistent. Hitching is fairly common, but may require lengthy waits. The flat terrain makes hiking and biking pleasant, but the Outer Banks' ferocious traffic calls for extra caution.

Accommodations and Camping

Most motels cling to Rte. 12 in the costly town of Nags Head. For budget accommodations, try Ocracoke. On all three islands the "in season" usually lasts from mid-June to Labor Day; rates are much higher. Reserve seven to 10 days ahead for weekday stays and up to a month for weekends. Rangers advise campers to bring extra-long tent spikes because of the loose dirt, and tents with extra-fine screens to keep out the flea-sized, biting "no-see-ums." Strong insect repellent is also helpful. Crashing on the beach is illegal.

Nags Head/Kill Devil Hills

Olde London Inn, Mile 12, Beach Rd. (441-7115), Nags Head oceanfront. Oceanfronte location, golfe privileges, and recreationale facilities. Huge picture windows offset drab decor in clean, spacious rooms. Free use of "e" at end of words. Cable TV, A/C, refrigerator. Singles or doubles $43; off-season $26.

The Ebbtide, Mile 10½, Beach Rd. (441-4913), Kill Devil Hills. A family place with spruce, wholesome rooms. Cable TV, A/C, sedate pool and hot tub. Offers "inside track" on local activities. Restaurant gives guests 10% discount, even on the 99¢ breakfast special. Singles or doubles $49-57; off-season $29-35.

Nettlewood Motel, Mile 7, Beach Rd. (441-5039), Kill Devil Hills, on both sides of the highway. Imagine that. Private beach access. Don't let the uninviting exterior prevent you from enjoying this clean, comfortable motel. TV, A/C, refrigerator. 4-day min. stay on weekends. Singles or doubles $42; off-season: rooms $25-30. Free day for week-long stays.

Ocracoke

Sand Dollar Motel, off Rte. 12 (928-5571), Head south on Rte. 12, turn right at the Pony Island Inn, right at the Back Porch Restaurant, and left at the Edwards Motel. Accommodating owners make you feel at home in this breezy, quiet, immaculate motel. Singles $38. Doubles $55. Off-season: $30, $45.

Beach House, just off Rte. 12 (928-4271), behind the Slushy Stand. B&B in 4 charming, clean, antique-filled rooms. Rooms $40; spring and fall $35.

Edwards Motel, off Rte. 12 (928-4801), by the Back Porch Restaurant. Fish-cleaning facilities on premises. Bright assortment of accommodations, all with A/C and TV. Rooms with 2 double beds $42, with 2 double beds and 1 single bed $49; efficiencies $58; cottages $75-85. Off-season $37, $42, $53, and $65-70, respectively.

Oscar's House, on the ocean side of Rte. 12 (928-1311), 1 block from Silver Lake harbor. Quaint B&B with 4 rooms, shared baths. Memorial Day-June singles $45, doubles $55; July-

Labor Day singles $50, doubles $60; off-season singles $40, doubles $50. Full vegetarian breakfast included.

The five oceanside **campgrounds** on Cape Hatteras National Seashore are all open mid-April to mid-October. **Oregon Inlet** squats on the southern tip of Bodie Island, **Salvo, Cape Point** (in Buxton), and **Frisco** near the elbow of Hatteras Island, and **Ocracoke** in the middle of Ocracoke Island. All have restrooms, cold running water, and grills. All sites (except Ocracoke's) cost $10, and rent on a first-come, first-served basis. Reserve Ocracoke sites ($12) through **Ticketron Reservation Office,** P.O. Box 2715, San Francisco, CA 94126 (800-452-1111), or stop by the Ocracoke Ticketron terminal. For info, contact Cape Hatteras National Seashore, Rte. 1, P.O. Box 675, Manteo, NC 27954 (473-2111).

Sights and Activities

The **Wright Brothers National Memorial,** Mile 8, U.S. 158 (441-7430), marks the spot in Kill Devil Hills where Orville and Wilbur Wright made the world's first sustained, controlled power flight in 1903. You can see models of their planes, hear a detailed account of the day of the first flight, chat with the flight attendants, and view the dramatic monument which the U.S. government dedicated to the brothers in 1932. (Open daily 9am-7pm; winter 9am-5pm. Presentations every hr. 10am-5pm. Admission $1, $3 per car, free with seniors.) In nearby **Jockey's Ridge State Park,** home of the East Coast's largest sand dunes, hang-gliders float in the wind that Orville and Wilbur broke.

On **Roanoke Island,** the **Fort Raleigh National Historic Site,** off Rte. 64, offers separately run attractions in one park. In the **Elizabeth Gardens** (473-3234), antique statues and fountains punctuate a beautiful display of flowers, herbs, and trees. (Open daily 9am-8pm; off-season 9am-5pm. Admission $2.50, under 12 free.) Behind door number two lies the theater where *The Lost Colony,* the oldest outdoor drama in the U.S., has been performing since 1937. (473-3414; performed Mon.-Sat. mid-June to late Aug. at 8:30pm; tickets $10, seniors and disabled $9, under 12 $4; bring insect repellent). **Fort Raleigh** (473-5772) is a reconstructed 1585 battery—basically a pile of dirt. The nearby visitors center contains a tiny museum and plays Elizabethan music as part of a losing battle to recall the earliest days of English activity in North America. (Open Mon.-Sat. 9am-8pm, Sun. 9am-6pm.) Lay your hands on a horseshoe crab and make faces at marine monsters in the Shark, Skate, and Ray Gallery at the **North Carolina Aquarium** (473-3493), 1 mi. west of Rte. 64. A full slate of educational programs keeps things lively. (Open Mon.-Sat. 9am-5pm, Sun. 1-5pm. Donation.)

On Ocracoke Island, historical sights give way to the incessant, soothing surf. With the exception of the town of Ocracoke on the southern tip, the island remains an undeveloped national seashore. Speedy walkers or meandering cyclists can cover the same route as **Trolley Tours** (928-4041; $4, seniors $3.50, kids $2.50) in less than an hour. Pick up a walking tour pamphlet at the visitor center. Better yet, stroll or swim along the waters that smooch the pristine, unbothered shore. At the **Soundside Snorkel,** park rangers teach visitors to snorkel. Bring tennis shoes and a swimsuit. (Wed. and Fri. at 2:30pm. Equipment rental $1. Make reservations at the Ocracoke Visitors Center from 9am the day before to 2:30pm the day of program.)

Raleigh, Durham, and Chapel Hill

The Research Triangle, a region embracing Raleigh, Durham, and Chapel Hill, contains more PhDs per capita that any other part of the nation. Durham, the former tobacco mecca of the world, is now, ironically, a city devoted to medicine, sprinkled with hospitals and diet clinics. It also houses Duke University, one of the greenest and most prestigious universities in the nation. Chapel Hill, just 20 mi.

down the road, holds its own in education as the home of the nation's first public university. Raleigh, the state capital, is an easygoing, historic town.

Practical Information

Emergency: 911.

Raleigh Capitol Area Visitor Center, 301 N. Blount St. (733-3456). Focuses on buildings in the capitol area. Open Mon.-Fri. 8am-5pm, Sat. 9am-5pm, Sun. 1-5pm. **Durham Chamber of Commerce,** People's Security Building, 14th floor, 300 W. Morgan St. (682-2133). Not geared to the budget traveler. Complimentary maps and a great view of Durham. Open Mon.-Fri. 8:30am-5pm. **Chapel Hill Chamber of Commerce,** 104 S. Estes Dr. (967-7075). Open Mon.-Fri. 9am-5pm.

Raleigh-Durham Airport: 15 mi. northwest of Raleigh on U.S. 70 (840-2123). Many hotels and rental car agencies provide free airport limousine service (596-2361) if you make reservations with them. Pick up helpful complimentary maps of Raleigh and Durham at the **information counter** on the airport's lower level.

Amtrak: 320 W. Cabarrus, Raleigh (833-7594 or 800-872-7245). To Miami (1 per day, 16 hr., $141) and Washington, DC (2 per day, 6 hr., $44). Open daily 6:30am-8:30pm

Greyhound/Trailways: In Raleigh: 314 W. Jones St. (828-2567). To: Durham (8 per day, 40 min., $6) and Chapel Hill (6 per day, 80 min., $7). Good north-south coverage of NC. Also to: Greensboro (5 per day, 3 hr., $15); Richmond (9 per day, 3½ hr., $35); Charleston (1 per day, 8 hr., $37). Open 24 hrs. **In Durham:** 820 Morgan St. (687-4800), 1 block off Chapel Hill St. downtown, 2½ mi. northeast of Duke University. To: Chapel Hill (8 per day, 30 min.); Charlotte (3 per day, 4 hr.); Winston-Salem (4 per day, 3 hr.). Open daily 6:30am-11pm. **In Chapel Hill:** 311 W. Franklin St. (942-3356), 4 blocks from the UNC campus. Open Mon.-Fri. 9am-4pm, Sat.-Sun. 8am-3:30pm.

Public Transport: Capital Area Transit, Raleigh (828-2567). Operates Mon.-Fri.; fewer buses on Sat. Fare 50¢. **Duke Power Company Transit Service,** Durham (688-4587). Most routes leave from the 1st Federal Building at Main St. on the loop, downtown. Buses operate daily 6am-6pm, some routes until 10:30pm. Fare 50¢, transfers 10¢.

Taxi: Safety Taxi, 832-8800. $1.50 per mi. **Cardinal Cab,** (828-3228). $1.50 per mi., 24-hr. service.

Help Lines: Rape Crisis, 968-4647.

Post Office: Raleigh: 310 New Bern Ave. (831-3661). Open Mon.-Fri. 8am-5pm, Sat. 8:30am-noon. **ZIP code:** 27611. **Durham:** 323 E. Chapel Hill St. (683-1976). Open Mon.-Fri. 8am-5pm. **ZIP code:** 27701. **Chapel Hill:** Franklin St., at the center of town (967-6297). Open Mon.-Fri. 8:30am-5pm, Sat. 8:30am-12:30pm. **ZIP code:** 27514.

Area Code: 919.

Accommodations and Camping

Hotels in downtown Raleigh are expensive and of average quality. Try the YMCA and YWCA for the cheapest lodgings. Rooms in Durham are more moderately priced, but difficult to reach from the center of town if you're on foot.

YMCA, 1601 Hillsborough St., Raleigh (832-6601), 5 blocks from Greyhound station. Comfortable rooms in a communal atmosphere. Free recreational facilities. Singles $15.50, with bath $17.50. $2 key deposit. Call ahead.

YWCA, 1012 Oberlin Rd., Raleigh (828-3205), ½-mi. east of Cameron Village Shopping Center. Women only. Large, luxurious facility. Hall bath. Free recreational facilities. Singles $15. Must have an informal interview with the director.

Carolina-Duke Motor Inn, I-85 at Guess Rd., Durham (286-0771). Clean rooms, with duck pics on the walls. Free Movie Channel, swimming pool. Free shuttle to Duke University med center on the main campus. 10% discount for *Let's Go* users, seniors, and AAA cardholders. Singles $30. Doubles $36. $3 for each additional person. The **Wabash Express** (286-0020) next door serves cheap and filling breakfasts (6 pancakes $2.50) Fri.-Sun. and lunches Mon.-Sat.

Friendship Inn, 309 Hillsborough St., Raleigh (833-5771), 3 blocks west of the capitol, 2½ blocks from Greyhound. Simple, spacious rooms near the heart of downtown. Free local calls, cable TV, and, of course, congenial service. Singles $29. Doubles $33.

Umstead State Park, U.S. 70 (787-3033), 5 mi. northwest of Raleigh. Tent and trailer sites. Large lake for fishing and hiking. Open June-Aug. 8am-9pm; Sept.-May shorter hours. Sites $5.

Food

The restaurants near the universities are best suited for the budget traveler. In Raleigh, **Hillsborough Street,** across from North Carolina State University, has a wide array of inexpensive restaurants and bakeries staffed, for the most part, by students. The same can be said of **9th Street** in Durham and **Franklin Street** in Chapel Hill.

Ramshead Rath-Skellar, 157-A E. Franklin St., Chapel Hill (942-5158), right across from the campus. A student hang-out featuring pizza, sandwiches, and hot apple pie Louise. Ships' mastheads, German beer steins, and old Italian wine bottles decorate eight different dining rooms with names such as "Rat Trap Lounge." "Flukey" Hayes, here since 1963, may cook your steak. Full meals $6-7. Open Mon.-Thurs. 11am-2:30pm and 5-9:30pm, Fri.-Sat. 11am-2:30pm and 5-10pm, Sun. 11am-9pm.

The Ninth Street Bakery Shop, 754 9th St., Durham (286-0303). More than a bakery; sandwiches from $2.50. Try the dense bran or blueberry muffins. Live music nightly. Open Mon.-Thurs. 7am-7pm, Fri.-Sat. 8am-11pm, Sun. 8am-5pm.

Skylight Exchange, 405½ W. Rosemary St., Chapel Hill (933-5550). A sandwich restaurant with a huge brass espresso machine. Cross-dresses as a used book and record store. Sandwiches $2-3. Live music on weekends. Open Mon.-Thurs. 10am-11pm, Fri.-Sat. 11am-midnight, Sun. 1-11pm.

Side Street, 225 N. Bloodworth St., Raleigh (828-4927), at E. Lane St. 3 blocks from the capitol. A classy place with antique furniture, flower table settings, and huge sandwiches with exotic names. Salads too. All selections under $5. Open Mon.-Fri. 11am-3pm and 5-9pm, Sat. 11am-3pm.

Mariakakis Restaurant and Bakery, 15-501 Bypass, Chapel Hill (942-1453). A heck of a trek from campus, but it's worth the trip for comfortable chairs, an amazing selection of the world's beers, and free bread with most meals. Spaghetti $3. Large cheese pizza $6. Open Mon.-Sat. 10am-9pm.

Two Guys, 2504 Hillsborough St., Raleigh (832-2324), near campus. This college hangout separates real eaters from little girly-men. The best is either the spicy pizza ($6.40) or large spaghetti portions $4. Open Mon.-Wed. 11am-10pm, Thurs.-Sat. 11am-11pm, Sun. noon-10pm.

Clyde Cooper's Barbeque, 109 E. Davie, Raleigh (832-7614), 1 block east of the Fayetteville Street Mall downtown. If you like BBQ, this is the place to try it N.C.-style. The local favorites are the Baby Back Ribs ($5) or the Barbeque Chicken ($3.50). Open Mon.-Sat. 10am-6pm.

Well Spring Grocery, 1002 9th St., Durham (286-2290). A health food grocery with a wide variety of inexpensive fruits, vegetables, and whole grains. Open Mon.-Sat. 9am-8pm, Sun. 10am-7pm.

Sights and Entertainment

While the triangle's main attractions are universities, Raleigh has its share of historical sights. The **capitol building,** in Union Square at Edenton and Salisbury, was built in 1840. (Open Mon.-Fri. 8am-5pm, Sat. 9am-5pm, Sun. 1-5pm. Tours available for large groups.) Across the street and around the corner at Bicentennial Square is the **Museum of Natural Sciences** (733-7450), which has fossils, gems, and animal exhibits including a live 17-ft. Burmese python named George. (Open Mon.-Sat. 9am-5pm Sun. 1-5pm. Free.) Just down the way at 109 E. Jones St., the **North Carolina Museum of History** (733-3894). Exhibits memorabilia from the state's Roanoke days to the present. (Open Tues.-Sat. 9am-5pm, Sun. 1-6pm. Free.) Pick up a brochure at the visitors center for a self-guided tour of the renovated 19th-century homes of **Historic Oakwood,** where eight North Carolina governors are buried. The **North Carolina Museum of Art,** 2110 Blue Ridge Blvd. (833-1935), off I-40 (Wade Ave. exit), has eight galleries with ancient Egyptian works and others by Raphael (the painter, not the turtle), Botticelli, Rubens, Monet, Wyeth, and O'Keeffe. (Open Tues.-Sat. 9am-5pm, Fri. 9am-9pm, Sun. noon-5pm. Tours Tues.-Sun. at 1:30pm. Free.) A tour of **North Carolina State University** on Hillsborough St. (737-3276), includes the **Pulstar Nuclear Reactor.** (Free tours during the semester Mon.-Fri. at noon, leaving from the Bell Tower on Hillsborough St.) Barring a nuclear accident, none of these sights is all that glowing.

For less urban entertainment, visit Chapel Hill where the **University of North Carolina** (962-0331), the oldest state university in the country, sprawls over 729 acres. Astronauts practiced celestial navigation until 1975 at the university's **Morehead Planetarium,** (962-1248) which houses one of 12 \$2.2 million Zeiss Star projectors. The planetarium puts up six different shows yearly, each involving a combination of films and Zeiss projections. These shows are conceived and produced while you watch. The best part of the planetarium is the staff of friendly UNC students, some of whom are trained operators of the Zeiss projector; they will give advice to travelers. (Open Sun.-Fri. 12:30-5pm and 6:30-9:30pm, Sat. noon-5pm, 6:30pm-9:30pm. Admission \$3, seniors, students, and kids \$2.50.) Over the next year special events will inundate the campus as UNC celebrates its bicentennial. Call the university (962-2296) for info on sporting events and concerts at the Smith Center (a.k.a. the Dean Dome).

In Durham, **Duke University** is the major attraction. The **admissions office,** at 2138 Campus Dr. (684-3214), serves as a visitors center (open 8am-5pm). The **Duke Chapel** (tours and info 684-2572) is at the center of the university; it has more than a million pieces of stained glass in 77 windows depicting between 800 and 900 figures. The Duke Memorial Organ inside has 5000 pipes; its music may bring tingles to the back of your neck. (Open daily during the school year 8am-8pm.)

To the left is the walkway to the **Bryan Center,** Duke's labyrinthine student center, with a gift shop, a café, and a small art gallery; the info desk has brochures on activities, concerts, local buses, and free campus maps. Near West Campus on Anderson St. are the **Sarah Duke Gardens** (684-3698), with over 15 acres of landscaped gardens and tiered flower beds. Giant goldfish swim in a small pond near a vined gazebo good for shaded picnics. (Open daily 8am-dusk.) Take the free Duke campus shuttle bus to East Campus, which houses the **Duke Museum of Art** (684-5135), with a small but impressive collection. The six galleries are quiet and uncongested. (Open Tues.-Fri. 9am-5pm, Sat. 11am-2pm, Sun. 2-5pm. Free.) Also take time to enjoy Duke's 7700-acre forest, with more than 30 mi. of trails and drivable roads.

On the other side of Durham, up Guess Rd., is the **Duke Homestead,** 2828 Duke Homestead Rd. (477-5498). Washington Duke first started in the tobacco business here, and the beautiful estate is still a small working farm. (Open April-Oct. Mon.-Sat. 9am-5pm, Sun. 1-5pm; Nov.-March Tues.-Sat. 10am-4pm, Sun. 1-4pm.)

At night, students frequent bars along **Franklin Street** in Chapel Hill, and **9th Street** in Durham. Before doing the same, you can catch a **Durham Bulls** (688-8211) baseball game. The Bulls, a class A farm team for the Atlanta Braves, became famous after the movie *Bull Durham* was filmed in the ballpark. (Reserved tickets \$6, general admission \$3.)

The Research Triangle area always offers something to do, whether concert, guest lecture, exhibit, or athletic event. For a complete listing, pick up free copies of both the *Spectator* and *Independent* weekly magazines, available at most restaurants, bookstores, and hotels.

NORTH DAKOTA

Though a state (the 39th) since 1889, North Dakota and most of its windswept terrain remains a mystery to both foreign and domestic travelers. Those who do visit often pass like wildfire through the eastern prairie to the more sensational "badlands," the infertile, pock-marked buttes that dominate the western half of the state. Blessed solitude, however, is the reward for those who savor the tranquil expanses of farmland before moving on to a high time in tourist-filled western towns such as Asu'ogstel. But whether east or west in North Dakota, locals will extend an eager welcome. People here are about as sparse as snow in June (there are fewer than 10 per square mile), but they are twice as amiable.

Practical Information

Capital: Bismarck.

Tourism Promotion Division, Liberty. Memorial Bldg., Capitol Grounds, Bismarck 58505 (224-2525 or 800-472-2100; 800-437-2077 outside ND). Parks and Recreation Department, 1424 W. Century Ave. #202, Bismarck 58502 (224-4887).

Time Zone: Central (1 hr. behind Eastern) and Mountain (2 hr. behind Eastern). Postal Abbreviation: ND

Area Code: 701.

Bismarck

Bismarck takes every opportunity to flout its 20-story art deco State Capitol, at 900 East Blvd. (224-2000). Built during the early 1930s art deco rage, the building illustrates the very short history of flamboyant architecture in North Dakota. Walk across the wide green lawn in front of the capitol to reach the North Dakota Heritage Center (224-2666) and its sophisticated exhibits on the Plains tribes, buffalo, and the history of white settlement in the region. (Open Mon.-Fri. 8am-5pm, Sat. 10am-5pm, Sun. 11am-5pm. Free.) The less extroverted but equally informative Camp Hancock Historic Site, at the intersection of 1st Ave. and Main St., originally housed workers on the Northern Pacific Railroad. (Open Wed.-Sun. 1-5pm.)

Below Mandan, on the opposite bank of the Missouri, lies Fort Lincoln, a campsite built for the same purpose. General Custer's march towards his fatal meeting with Sitting Bull at Little Bighorn began here. The fort is part of the worthwhile Fort Lincoln State Park (663-9571), which also features a reconstructed Mandan village on its original site, renovated army blockhouses, and a small collection of artifacts and memorabilia from Native Americans and early settlers. (Park open daily 9am-sunset; Sept.-May Mon.-Fri. 9am-sunset. Museum open daily 9am-9pm; Sept.-May Mon.-Fri. 9am-5pm. $3 vehicle admission fee.)

At the end of July, join lifetime fans and lifers at the Annual North Dakota Prison Rodeo, held at the penitentiary east of Bismarck. In the first week of August, watch for the Art Fair, held on the Capitol Mall lawn. Call ahead (255-3285) for information on the United Tribes Pow Wow, held in early September, one of the largest gatherings of Native Americans in the nation; the festival includes dancing, singing, food, and crafts of many tribes. To find out more about local entertainment, drop by or call the new Bismarck Civic Center, at the terminus of Sweet Ave. E. (222-6491), for a schedule of events.

Bismarck has several local diners that serve tasty, inexpensive meals. The Little Cottage Café, 2513 E. Main St. (223-4949), brings in droves of workers at the lunch whistle and families at dinnertime. Fantastic muffins cost $1, an 8-oz. sirloin steak $6. (Open daily 6am-10pm.) The Drumstick Café, 307 N. 3rd St. (223-8449), serves breakfast all day. The home-baked desserts (fresh strawberry pie, $1) and fresh-ground coffee are superb. Sandwiches are $2-3.50. (Open Mon.-Sat. 24 hrs.)

The **Highway Motel**, 6319 E. Main St. (223-0506), two mi. east on Rte. 10, rents rooms to local workers by the month but often has space for those staying only a night or two. (Singles $15. Doubles $23.) **Motel 6**, 2433 State St. (255-6878), right off I-94, offers clean, small rooms and a pool. (Singles $27. Doubles $33. Under 18 free.) Your best bet closer to town is the **Bismarck Motor Hotel**, 2301 E. Main Ave. (223-2474). (Singles $22. Doubles $26.)

The **Hillcrest Campground** (255-4334), 1½ mi. out of town on E. Main St., provides showers and scenery from April to September. (Sites $8.) The edenic **General Sibley Park** (222-1844), four mi. south of Bismarck on S. Washington St., merits a visit even if you don't stay the night. Those who do decide to stay should call ahead for reservations, and then set up camp in a glen of huge, shady trees on the banks of the Missouri River. The park has showers. (Sites $5, with full hookup $10.) **Fort Lincoln State Park** (663-9571), five mi. south of Mandan on Rte. 1806, has a quiet campground on the east bank of the Missouri. (Sites $9, with water, electricity $12. Daily pass to park and showers included.)

Most of Bismarck is contained within an oval formed by I-94 and its corollary Business 94, otherwise known as **Main Street**. Bismarck's small downtown shopping district coalesces in the southwest curve of this oval, bounded by Washington St. and 9th St. on the west and east, and Rosser Ave. and Business 94 on the north and south.

The **Bismarck-Mandan Convention and Visitors Bureau** provides propaganda at 523 N. 4th St. (222-4308). (Open Mon.-Fri. 8am-5pm.) The largely defense-oriented **Bismarck Municipal Airport**, 2½ mi. south of Bismarck, lies near the intersection of University Dr. (Rte. 1804) and Airport Rd. **Greyhound**, 1237 W. Divide (223-6576), three inconvenient mi. west of downtown off I-94 exit 35, provides service to Minneapolis (10 hr., $54) and Seattle (1½ days, $133). (Open Mon.-Fri. 3:30-5am, 8am-1pm, and 4-9pm, Sat.-Sun. 3:30-5am, 9am-12:30pm, and 6-9pm.) Bismarck's **time zone** is Central (1 hr. behind Eastern), except for Fort Lincoln, which is Mountain (2 hr. behind Eastern). The **post office** is at 220 E. Rosser Ave. (221-6517; open Mon.-Fri. 8am-5:30pm, Sat. 10am-noon); the **ZIP code** is 58501. Bismarck's **area code** is 701.

Theodore Roosevelt National Memorial Park and Medora

President Theodore Roosevelt appreciated the beauty of the Badlands' red and brown-hued lunar formations so much that he bought a ranch here. After his mother and wife died on the same day, he came here seeking "physical and spiritual renewal"; today's visitor can find the same peace among the quiet canyons and dramatic rocky outcroppings which earned the park the nickname "rough-rider country."

The park divides into south and north units, and Mountain and Central Time Zones. The entrance to the better-developed **south unit,** (time zone: Mountain) is just north of I-94 in the historic frontier town of **Medora.** Restored with the tourist in mind, Medora is a place to hold tightly to your purse strings. Limit your shopping to **Joe Ferris' General Store** (623-4447), spotless and still inexpensive. (Open daily 8am-8pm.) For more immediate nourishment, stop by the **Badlands Bake Shoppe,** four doors to the left of Ferris, for a midday snack. Large muffins cost 85¢, and a loaf of Dakota bread—perfect hiking food—is $2.25. (Open May-Sept. daily 8am-4pm.) In pleasant weather, indulge at the **Chuckwagon Restaurant** (623-4820), an outdoor buffet ($8, kids $4) serving ribs and chicken in the summer. (Open daily 4:30-7pm.) Budget motels are even harder to find than budget food, but the **Dietz Motel,** 401 Broadway (623-4455), offers clean basement rooms at the lowest rates in town. (Singles from $12. Doubles from $14.)

Medora's only sight is the **Museum of the Badlands,** on Main St. (623-4451), which tells all you need to know about the town. (Open Tues.-Sat. 10am-9pm, Sun.-Mon. 10am-7pm. $2, kids $1.) **Greyhound** serves Medora from the Dietz Motel, with three buses daily to Bismarck ($20) and Billings, MT ($60).

Pay the park entrance fee ($3 per vehicle, $1 per pedestrian) at the **visitor center** (623-4466), on the western edge of town. The center serves as a mini-museum, displaying a few of Teddy's guns, spurs, and old letters, and showing a beautiful film of winter badlands scenes. Copies of *Frontier Fragments,* the park newspaper, with listings of ranger-led talks, walks, and demonstrations, are available here. (Open daily 8am-8pm; Sept.-May 8am-4:30pm. Inquire at desk for film times.) There is a 36-mi. scenic automobile loop through the park, and many hiking trails start from the loop and lead deep into the wilderness. The world's third-largest **petrified forest** lies 14 mi. into the park. **Painted Canyon Overlook,** seven mi. east of Medora, has its own **visitor center** (575-4020; open daily 8am-8pm), picnic tables, and a breathtaking view of the badlands.

The **north unit** of the park (time zone: Central) is 75 mi. from the south unit on Rte. 85. Most of the land is wilderness; very few people visit, and fewer still stay overnight. As a result, backcountry hiking possibilities are endless. Check in at the ranger station (623-4466 or 842-2333; open daily 8am-4:30pm) for information and a free overnight camping permit. As a compromise between the wilderness and Medora, the park maintains **Squaw Creek Campground,** five mi. west of the north unit entrance. (Sites $7.) For more information on the park, write to Theodore Roosevelt National Memorial Park, Medora 58645.

Asuogs'tel

Straddling the North Dakota-Saskatchewan-Manitoba border, Ausogs'tel (pop. goes the weasel) is rich in history and culture—making it a center of historical richness, rich culture, and cultural historicity. Once in the past tense, Ausogs'tel today is in the present tense. An old Native American word meaning "Let's Go USA," Asuogs'tel (pronounced Blechhhhhh) seceded from the Union on May 15, 1864 and allied itself with Luxembourg. (For more information on Luxembourg, see *Let's Go: Europe,* the *Bible/Koran/Upanishads/Bhagavad-Gita/Fear and Loathing in Las Vegas* of the budget traveler.) The town's ethnic diversity can be seen in its people, all of whom wear different clothing and shoes and are generally discernible from one another.

Ausogs'tel is best known for the large herd of **inland lobsters** which congregate and feed on the **sorghum fields** surrounding the town. The lobsters, unique in the crustacean world, benefit from the presence of nearby **Drawn Butter Creek,** which gives the creatures a place to frolic. Legend has it that every 100 years or so, the lobsters **raid the town,** causing widespread **panic** and **mayhem** and even some **hubbub.**

The best way to see the inland lobsters is by going on a refreshing **Handi-Wipe Tour** (555-WIPE). The knowledgeable, antennaed guides will tell you everything there is to know about the inland lobster herds, and will give you a free set of nutcrackers. The tours depart from **Bib Bridge.** (Tours leave at 3am Wed.-Fri. $17 with salad and soup, $11 a la carte. Free if you're kosher.)

If there's time afterwards, visit the **Old West Dental Wax Museum,** 123 Filling St. (DEN-TURE), in which wax models bring to life, with stunning realism, the teeth of legendary figures such as Wyatt Earp, Jesse James, and Paul Bunyan's ox Babe. (Open 24 hrs.)

You can afford lodgings in Asuogs'tel without having to sell crack to small children. The best budget accommodation in Ausogs'tel is **Motel Negative 6,** 666 Natas Blvd. (555-34207), which features a car pool, a free television cable, complimentary air every morning, and rooms designed by M.C. Escher. The hotel will pay you to stay there, which is cool. (Singles $-6. Doubles $-12.) The **Overly Hostel (BAH),** Beverly Hills 90210 (555-JOKE), is owned by Bonnie & Clyde Hostel. Check-out any time you like, but you can never leave. Ask Bonnie & Clyde about things to do in the area; they'll just laugh. (Beds $4, cabinets $3, dinette sets $12.) Kampers kan kik bak at the **Kool-Ass Kampground (KKK).** Go two mi. west on "Rhino" Kaplan Hwy., make a right at the blinking light, and drive over the cliff. The Kool-Ass will be on your left. (Sites $4,000,000; with water and full hookup $4,000,007; with electricity, $4,000,011.) There is also another campground that is better, cheaper, and easier to get to. Look for yourself for a change.

Eating cheaply in Asugos'tel won't empty your wallet or stick needles in your eyes or poison your grandmother. You can pick up some tail at **The Boldface Café,** *23 Italic Blvd.* (555-LIES), which serves such specialties as lobster Ausogs'tel ($1), lobster shell fondue ($2), and tasty lobster flakes ($2). (Closed.) **Lobsters 'n' Stuff,** 55 Pincer Place (555-BULL), serves delicious lobsters 'n' mouth-watering stuff. (Open Mon.-Thurs. 9am-5pm, Fri. 9am-5pm, Sat. 9am-5pm, Sun. 9am-5pm.) Next door, sample an exciting and unique dessert at **Häagen-Lobster** (555-SICK). Ausogs'tel's only bar is **Ausogs'tel's Only Bar,** 22 Colonial Ter. (555-HOAX), in which you can try the local beer, **Lobster Lager,** made from barley hops, malt, water, and lobster. (Open daily 3pm-13am. Cover: You can't judge a book by the.)

Ausogs'tel is 190 mi. west of West Bismarck and 188 mi. east of East Bismarck. To get to Ausogs'tel, walk. Ausogs'tel's **ZIP code** is 3. Its **area code** is 3. You may have a hard time getting there, since it doesn't exist; we recommend dosing.

OHIO

Undaunted by the Crosby, Stills, Nash, and Young song and the rust-belt depression of the late 1970s, Ohio's north-south bookends, Cleveland and Cincinnati, have revamped their downtowns, cleaned up pollution, and fostered a resurgence in the arts, all the while retaining their distinct flavors. The state capital, Columbus, gained distinction in 1989 with a *Newsweek* nomination as one of the best places to live in the country.

On the eastern edge of the Midwest, Ohio's several major waterways serve industry and recreation alike: some of the nation's most fertile pastures generate a powerful agriculture and the glorious Lake Erie Shore pouts a thick lip of beaches.

Practical Information

Capital: Columbus.

Tourist Information: State Office of Travel and Tourism, 77 S. High St., P.O. Box 1001, Columbus 43215 (614-466-8844). **Greater Columbus Convention and Visitors Bureau,** 1 Columbus Bldg., 10 W. Broad St. #1300, Columbus 43215 (614-221-6623 or 800-234-2657). Open Mon.-Fri. 8am-5pm.

Time Zone: Eastern. **Postal Abbreviation:** OH

Cincinnati

Longfellow called it the "Queen City of the West." In the 1850s, more prosaic folk tagged it "Porkopolis," referring to its position as the world's premier pork-packer. Winged pigs guarding the entrance of downtown's **Sawyer Point Park** remind of the former divine status of swine in the city. Although pigs on a wing no longer snort through the streets, and the Western frontier has moved on, downtown Cincinnati is still more reminiscent of an old-fashioned town square than of an urban center—mostly because the streets are clean and the people friendly. Snuggled in a valley surrounded by seven rolling hills and the Ohio River, insulated Cincinnati seems to live up to Mark Twain's purported claim that, if the world suddenly stopped dead, it would take Cincinnati 20 years to notice.

Practical Information

Emergency: 911.

Visitor Information: Cincinnati Convention and Visitors Bureau, 300 W. 6th St. (621-2142). Mon.-Fri. 8:45am-5pm. Pick up an *Official Visitors Guide.* **Information Booth** in Fountain Square. Mon.-Sat. 8:30am-5:30pm. **Info Line,** 421-4636. Lists plays, opera, cruises, and symphonies.

Airport: Greater Cincinnati International Airport, in Independence, KY, 13 mi. south of Cincinnati. The **Jetport Express** (606-283-3702) shuttles passengers downtown ($8).

Amtrak: 1901 River Rd. (921-4172 or 800-872-7245). To Indianapolis ($29) and Chicago ($57). Mon.-Fri. 9:30am-5pm, Tues.-Sun. 11pm-6:30am.

Greyhound: 1005 Gilbert Ave. (352-6000), just past the intersection of E. Court and Broadway. To: Indianapolis ($19); Louisville, KY ($15.50); Cleveland ($38). Open 7:30am-6:30am.

Public Transport: Queen City Metro, 122 W. Fifth St. (621-4455). Office has bus schedules and information. Telephone information Mon.-Fri. 6:30am-7pm, Sat.-Sun. 8am-5pm. Most buses run out of Government Sq. at 5th and Main St., to outlying communities. Peak fare 65¢, other times 50¢, weekends 35¢.

Taxi: Yellow Cab, 241-2100. Base fare $1.50, $1.20 per mi.

Weather Line: 241-1010.

Help Lines: Rape Crisis Center, 216 E. 9th St. (381-5610), downtown. **Gay/Lesbian Community Switchboard:** 221-7800.

Post Office: 122 W. 5th St. (684-5664), between Walnut and Vine St. Open Mon.-Fri. 8am-5pm, Sat. 8am-1pm. **ZIP code:** 45202.

Area Code: 513.

Fountain Square, E. 5th at Vine St., is the focal point of the downtown business community. Cross streets are numbered and designated East or West, with Vine Street as the divider. **Riverfront Stadium,** the **Serpentine Wall,** and the **Riverwalk** are down by the river. The University of Cincinnati spreads out from Clifton, north of the city. Overlooking downtown from the east, **Mt. Adams,** adjoining Eden Park, harbors some of Cincinnati's most active nightlife.

Accommodations and Camping

Cincinnati has many motels, but most cheap places are outside the heart of the city. Cars and reservations are recommended, especially on nights of Reds baseball games and on weekends. Campgrounds are also a long way out of town.

College of Mount St. Joseph, 5701 Delhi Pike (244-4327), about 8 mi. west of downtown off Rte. 50. Immaculate rooms in a quiet, remote location. Excellent facilities. Singles $15. Doubles $20. Cafeteria lunch and dinner $3.50.

Cincinnati Home Hostel (AYH), 2200 Maplewood Ave. (651-2329), in a slightly run-down neighborhood 2 mi. north of downtown. A 3-story house with large rooms, TV downstairs. Singles $6.

Evendale Motel, 10165 Reading Rd. (563-1570), ½ hr. from downtown. Small, dark, but clean rooms. Singles and doubles $23.

Red Roof Inn, 5300 Kennedy Ave. (531-6589), off I-71 at Ridge Rd. Run-of-the-roof basics from the national chain. Sing $39. Doub $50.95.

Ohio Valley Bed and Breakfast, 6876 Taylor Mills Rd. (606-356-7865), in Independence, KY. Singles and doubles in a variety of area homes as low as $40. Call well in advance for reservations.

Camp Shore Campgrounds, Rte. 56 in Aurora, IN (812-438-2135), 30 mi. west of Cincinnati on the Ohio. Tent sites with hookup $12.

Rose Gardens Resort—KOA Campgrounds, I-75 exit 166 (606-428-2000), 30 mi. south of Cincinnati. Award-winning landscaping. Tent sites $16. Cabins $25, including water & electricity. Make reservations.

Food

The city that gave us the first soap opera and the first baseball franchise (the Redlegs) presents as its great culinary contribution **Cincinnati chili.** To the usual meat and beans, add your choice of spaghetti, onions, and cheese, often with a hot dog to boot, all for about $2.50. With few exceptions, Cincinnatians swear by the abundant **Gold Star Chili, Skyline,** and **Empress** fast-food chains.

Camp Washington Chili (541-0061), Hopple and Colerain Ave., 1 block west of I-75. A legendary greasy spoon. Mon.-Sat. 24 hrs.

Izzy's, 819 Elm St. (721-4241), also 610 Main St. A Cincinnati institution founded in 1901. Izzy has passed away, but his tradition of good-natured insults endures. Overstuffed sandwiches with potato pancake $3-4. Izzy's famous reuben $4.50. Open Mon.-Fri. 7am-5pm, Sat. 7am-4pm; Main St. restaurant Mon.-Sat. 7am-9pm.

Graeter's, 41 E. 4th St. (381-0653), downtown, and 11 other locations. Since 1870, Graeter's has dished out fresh ice cream with giant chocolate chips. Medium cone $1.80. Open Mon.-Sat. 11am-5:30pm.

Findlay Market, 18th at Elm St., 2 mi. north of downtown. Produce and picnic items $3-5. Open Wed. 7am-1:30pm, Fri.-Sat. 7am-6pm.

Sights and Events

Downtown Cincinnati revolves around the **Tyler Davidson Fountain,** the ideal spot to people-watch while you feign admiration for the gorgeous architecture. If you squint your eyes, you can almost see Les Nesman rushing to WKRP to deliver the daily hog report. Check out the expansive gardens and daring design at **Procter and Gamble Plaza,** just east of Fountain Square, or walk along **Fountain Square South,** a shopping and business complex connected by a series of second-floor skywalks. When the visual stimuli exhaust you, prick up your ears for a free concert in front of the fountain. The **Downtown Council,** Carew Tower (579-3191), has more information. (Mon.-Fri. 8:30am-5pm.)

Close to Fountain Square, the **Contemporary Arts Center,** 115 E. 5th St., 2nd floor (721-0390), by Walnut, has survived a nationally publicized attack by some Cincinnati citizens on its exhibition of sexually explicit photographs by Robert Mapplethorpe. Now with an enhanced reputation among the national arts community, it continues to change its exhibits frequently, offering evening films, music, and multi-media performances. (Mon.-Sat. 10am-6pm, Sun. 1-5pm. Admission $2, seniors and students $1. Mon. free.)

The **Cincinnati Zoo,** 3400 Vine St. (281-4700), at Forest Ave., can be reached by car (take Dana Ave. off I-75 or I-71), or by bus (#78 or 49 from Vine and 5th St.). The diction wizards at *Newsweek* called it one of the world's "sexiest zoos"; the lush greenery and cageless habitats evidently encourage the zoo's gorillas and famous white Bengal tigers to reproduce enthusiastically. (Open in summer daily 9am-8pm, entrance closes at 6pm; Labor Day-Memorial Day open daily 9am-5pm. $6, seniors and ages under 12 $3, Children's Zoo open 10am-7pm.)

On a cliff overlooking downtown from the east, the Mt. Adams/Eden Park area gives Cincinnati a bit of bohemian charm. Among Eden Parks' shady groves reclines the **Cincinnati Art Museum** (721-5204), with a permanent collection spanning 5000 years including musical instruments and Middle Eastern artifacts. (Tues., Thurs.-Sat. 10am-5pm, Wed. 10am-9pm, Sun. noon-5pm. closed Mon. $3, seniors $1.50, students $2, under 18 free. Sat. free. Take bus #49 to Eden Park Dr. By car, follow Gilbert Ave. northeast from downtown.) Step into a tropical rain forest in the **Krohn Conservatory** (352-4086), one of the largest public greenhouses in the world. (Daily 10am-5pm. July-Aug. open Wed. to 9pm. Suggested donation $1.50, seniors and ages under 15 $1.) The **Taft Museum,** 316 Pike St. (241-0343), downtown, has a beautiful collection of painted enamels, as well as pieces by Rembrandt and Whistler. (Mon.-Sat. 10am-5pm, Sun. 2-5pm. Suggested donation $2, seniors and students $1.)

On the west side of town, the **Union Terminal,** 1031 Western Ave. (241-7257), near the Ezzard Charles Dr. exit off I-75 (take bus #1), is a fine example of Art Deco architecture that boasts the world's highest unsupported dome. Renovations have closed the terminal museum until 1991.

Cincinnati is fanatical about sports. The **Reds** major league baseball team (421-7337) and the **Bengals** NFL football team (621-3550) both play in **Riverfront Stadium.** The **Riverfront Coliseum** (241-1818), a Cincinnati landmark, hosts other sports events and major concerts year-round. In the beginning of July **Summerfair** (800-582-5804), an art extravaganza, is held at **Coney Island,** 6201 Kellogg Ave. (232-8230).

The **Riverwalk** by the **Serpentine Wall** is a pleasant place to stroll along the Ohio River, with free summer concerts held at the **Pavilion.** The area was totally revamped for the state's 1988 bicentennial. At the **Bicentennial Commons,** exquisite recreational facilities and a timeline of Ohio history span about a mile. Even those who have graduated from the jungle gym should bounce on the rubber floor. On Labor Day, get seats early for **Riverfest,** one of the nation's largest fireworks displays.

Entertainment and Nightlife

The cliff-hanging communities that line the steep streets of Mt. Adams also support a vivacious arts and entertainment industry. Perched on its own wooded hill is the **Playhouse in the Park,** 962 Mt. Adams Circle (421-3888), a theater-in-the-round remarkably adaptable to many styles of drama. The regular season runs from mid-September to July, with special summer programs as well. Performances daily Tues.-Sun. (Tickets $15-27.50, 15 min. before the show student and senior rush tickets $9. Accessible to the vision- and hearing-impaired.)

For a drink and a voyage back to the 19th century, try **Arnold's,** 210 E. 8th St. (421-6234), Cincinnati's oldest tavern, between Main St. and Sycamore downtown. After 9pm, Arnold's does that ragtime, traditional jazz, and swing while serving sandwiches ($4-5) and dinners ($6-10). (Open Mon.-Sat. 11am-1am.) Check out the antique toys inside or listen to jazz and blues in the courtyard at **Blind Lemon,** 936 Hatch St. (241-3885), at St. Gregory St. in Mt. Adams. (Mon.-Fri. 4pm-2:30am, Sat.-Sun. 3pm-2:30am. Music at 9:30pm.) The **City View Tavern,** also in Mt. Adams at 403 Oregon St. (241-8439), off Monastery St., is hard to find, but worth the effort. This down-to-earth local favorite proudly displays an article heralding it as one of the best dives in Cincinnati. The deck in back offers a great view of the city's skyline and the Ohio River. Locally brewed draft beer is 90¢. (Mon.-Fri. noon-1am, Sat. 1pm-1am, Sun. 2-11pm.)

The University of Cincinnati's **Conservatory of Music** (556-9430) often gives free classical recitals. A tad more upscale, the **Music Hall,** 1243 Elm St. (721-8222) by Ezzard Charles Drive, hosts the **Cincinnati Symphony Orchestra** (381-3300) from September to May (tickets $7-45). Other companies performing at the Music Hall are the **Cincinnati Ballet Company** (621-5219; performances Sept.-May; tickets $6-45) and **Cincinnati Opera** (241-2742; limited summer productions). For updates, call **Dial the Arts** (751-2787).

Near Cincinnati

If you can't get to California's Napa or Sonoma Valleys, the next best thing may be **Meiers Wine Cellars,** 6955 Plainfield Pike (891-2900). Take I-71 to exit 12 or I-75 to Galbraith Rd. Free tours of Ohio's oldest and largest winery allow you to observe the entire wine-making operation and taste its fruits. (Free tours June-Oct. every hr. 10am-3pm and other times of the year.)

In Mason, 24 mi. north of Cincinnati off I-71 at exit #24, the **Kings Island** amusement park (241-5600) cages The Beast, the world's second-fastest roller coaster. Admission entitles you to unlimited rides, attractions, and opportunity to buy expensive food. Pack a picnic or a very thick wallet. Lines diminish after dark. (Open May 27-Sept. 2 Sun.-Fri. 10am-10pm, Sat. 10am-11pm. $21.)

Also at Exit 24 next to Kings Island is the **College Football Hall of Fame** just past the amusement park on Kings Island Drive (513-398-5410). From Knute Rockne's "Gipper" speech to the MacArthur trophy, the College Hall is full of memorabilia. With three theaters, trophies, and a time tunnel (from 478 BC to Present: the History of the College Game) it leaves the most fanatic football fan satisfied. (Daily 9am-5pm; Jan.-March open weekends only. $3.50, kids $2.25.)

Cleveland

Abandoned railroad bridges, steel factories, and warehouses lining the Cuyahoga River attest to the fact that Cleveland has always been a tough industrial city, despite the success of Gilded Age magnates like Rockefeller and Hanna. In the 1970s Cleveland became the first major city to default on its loans since the Great Depression and turned into a national joke after the filthy Cuyahoga River caught fire downtown. Now Cleveland is experiencing a major rebirth. Planners have spent billions on downtown construction, waterfront development, and historic renovation; the city's thriving arts community and I.M. Pei's much-anticipated Rock and Roll Hall of Fame have also put it in a different national spotlight. Cleveland is certainly no longer the "Mistake on the Lake."

Practical Information

Emergency: 911.

Visitor Information: Cleveland Convention and Visitors Bureau, 3100 Tower City Ctr. (621-4110 or 800-321-1001), in Terminal Tower at Public Square. Free maps and helpful staff. Open Mon.-Fri. 8:30am-5pm. **Cleveland Fun Phone,** 621-8860, a 24-hr. entertainment hotline. **Language Bank** and **Nationalities Service Center,** 781-4560, are open 24 hrs.

Cleveland Hopkins International Airport: (265-6030) in Brookpark, 10 mi. west of downtown, but accessible on the RTA airport rapid line, which goes to the Terminal Tower on train #66X ("Red Line") for $1.

Amtrak: 200 Cleveland Memorial Shoreway NE (696-5115 or 800-872-7245), across from Municipal Stadium, east of City Hall. Open Mon.-Sat. 10:30am-4:30pm. To New York ($92) and Chicago ($72).

Greyhound: 1465 Chester Ave. (781-0520; schedules and fares 781-1400), at E. 14th St. near RTA bus lines and about 7 blocks east of Terminal Tower. Frequent and convenient service to Chicago and New York City; good coverage of Ohio. To Pittsburgh ($16), Cincinnati ($32), and Indianapolis ($52).

Regional Transit Authority (RTA): 315 Euclid Ave. (566-5074), across the street from Woolworth's. Schedules for city buses and rapid transit lines. Office Mon.-Fri. 7:30am-5:30pm. Phone info Mon.-Sat. 6am-6pm (621-9500). Service daily 4:30am-12:30am. Bus lines, connecting with the Rapid stops, provide public transport to most of the metropolitan area. Fare $1 (free transfers), buses 85¢.

Taxi: Yellow Cab, 623-1500. 24 hrs.

Time/Weather Line: 931-1212. 24 hrs.

Help Line: Rape Crisis Line, 391-3912. 24 hrs.

Post Office: 2400 Orange Ave. (443-4199 or 443-4096). Open Mon.-Fri. 8am-7pm. **ZIP code:** 44101.

Area Code: 216.

Terminal Tower in **Public Square** divides the city into east and west. To reach Public Square from I-90 or I-71, follow the Ontario Ave./Broadway exit. From I-77, take the 9th St. exit to Euclid Ave., which runs into the Square. From the Amtrak station, follow Lakeside Ave. and turn onto Ontario, which leads to the tower. Almost all of the RTA trains and buses run downtown.

Accommodations and Camping

Cheap lodgings simply are not available in downtown Cleveland. Travelers are better off staying in the suburbs. Hotel taxes are a hefty 10%, not included in the prices listed below.

If you know your plans well in advance, try calling **Cleveland Private Lodgings** (249-0400), which places people in homes around the city for as low as $25. All arrangements are made through the office. Leave enough time for a letter of confirmation. (Open Mon.-Tues. and Thurs.-Fri. 9am-noon and 3-5pm.)

Stanford House Hostel (AYH), 6093 Stanford Rd. (467-8711), 22 mi. south of Cleveland in Peninsula. Exit 12 off I-80. Take bus #77F to Snowville Rd. Beautifully restored Greek Revival farmhouse is on National Register of Historic Places. Excellent facilities, friendly houseparent. All hostelers required to perform task (vacuuming, emptying trash, etc.). Check-in 5-9pm. Flexible curfew 11pm. $10, sheets and pillow $2, sleep sack $1. Reservations only.

Lakewood Manor Motel, 12019 Lake Ave. (226-4800), about 3 mi. west of downtown in Lakewood. Take bus #55CX. Neat and clean. TV, central A/C. Complimentary coffee daily and donuts on weekends. Singles $34. Doubles $40.

Gateway Motel, 29865 Euclid Ave. (943-6777), 10 mi. east of Public Sq. in Wickliffe. Take Euclid Ave. exit off I-90 or bus #28X. Spacious, clean rooms with A/C and color TV. Sing $25. Doub $30.

Red Roof Inn, 29595 Clemens Rd. (892-7920), at I-90 and Crocker Rd., exit 156, 11 mi. west of downtown in Westlake. Better than average. Spacious with nice wallpaper. Singles $42. Doubles $47.

Two campgrounds are 40 minutes east of downtown, off I-480 in Streetsboro: **Woodside Lake Park,** 2256 Frost Rd. (626-4251; tent sites for 2 $15, with electricity $16; $2 per additional guest, ages 3-17 75¢); and **Valley View Lake Resort,** 8326 Ferguson (626-2041; tent sites $19, water & hookup available).

Food

You'll find Cleveland's culinary treats in tiny neighborhoods surrounding the downtown area. To satiate that lust for hot corned beef, just step into one of the dozens of delis in the city center.

Tommy's, 1820 Coventry Rd. (321-7757), just up the hill from University Circle. Take bus #9x east to Mayfield and Coventry Rd. Delicious, healthy pita bread sandwiches ($2.50-5.25) and friendly service. Try the Brownie Monster for dessert. Open Mon.-Sat. 7:30am-10pm, Sun. 9am-5pm.

Mama Santa's, 12305 Mayfield Rd. (231-9567), in Little Italy just east of University Circle. Authentic Sicilian food served beneath subdued lighting. Medium pizza $3.25, spaghetti $4.25. Open Mon.-Thurs. 11am-midnight, Fri.-Sat. 11am-1am.

Downtown Coffee Shoppe, 1150 Huron Rd. (771-1055), 8 blocks from Public Sq. This Mom-and-Pop diner on a calm street behind Euclid Ave. has simple sandwiches and burgers $1.25-2.50. Open Mon.-Fri. 6am-5pm.

Sights and Entertainment

Cleveland has a wide variety of things to see and do. 1990 witnessed the opening of the long-awaited **Tower City Center** (771-6611), a 3-story shopping complex in the Terminal Tower. Although essentially a luxury mall with prices to match, Tower Center is a notable emblem of the tremendous renovation and revitalization of downtown Cleveland.

Seriously, folks, one of the most beautiful things about Cleveland is Lake Erie. **Cleveland Lakefront State Park** (881-8141), 2 mi. west of downtown and accessible from Lake Ave. or Cleveland Memorial Shoreway, is a mile-long beach with great swimming, picnicking and chillin' areas.

The east side of Cleveland hosts most of the city's cultural activities. **Playhouse Square Center,** 1501 Euclid Ave. (771-4444), just east of downtown, is the third-largest performing arts center in the nation. The **Cleveland Opera** (575-0900) and the famous **Cleveland Ballet** (621-2260) perform nearby at 1375 Euclid Ave. Five mi. east of the city resides **University Circle,** a cluster of 75 cultural institutions. Check with the helpful visitors bureau for details on museums, live music, and drama. The world-class **Cleveland Museum of Art,** 11150 East Blvd. (421-7340), in University Circle, contains a fine collection of 19th-century French and American Impressionist paintings, as well as a version of Rodin's "The Thinker." A beautiful plaza and pond on which to ponder face the museum. (Open Tues. and Thurs.-Fri. 10am-5:45pm, Wed. 10am-9:45pm, Sat. 9am-4:45pm, Sun. 1-5:45pm. Free.) Nearby is the **Cleveland Museum of Natural History,** Wade Oval (231-4600), where you can see the only existing skull of the fearsome Pygmy Tyrant *(Nanatyrannus).* (Mon.-Sat. 10am-5pm, Sun. 1-5pm. $3.75, seniors, students, and children $1.75. Free Tues. and Thurs.) The renowned **Cleveland Orchestra,** one of the nation's best, keeps house in University Circle at Severance Hall, 11001 Euclid Ave. (231-7300; $10-23, depending on the seating). During the summer, however, the orchestra performs at **Blossom Music Center,** 1145 W. Steels Corners Rd., Cuyahoga Falls (920-8040). University Circle itself is safe, but some of the neighborhoods immediately surrounding it can be rough, especially at night. East of University Circle, in a nice neighborhood, is the **Dobama Theatre,** 1846 Coventry Rd., Cleveland Hts. (932-6838). This little-known theater gives terrific, inexpensive ($5-8) performances in an intimate, living-room atmosphere.

A great deal of Cleveland's nightlife is focused in the **Flats,** the former industrial core of the city along both banks of the Cuyahoga River. The northernmost section of the Flats, just west of Public Square, contains several nightclubs and restaurants. On weekend nights, expect large crowds and larger traffic jams. On the east side of the river, from the deck at **Rumrunners,** 1124 Old River Rd. (696-6070), you can watch the sunset across the water through the steel frames of old railroad bridges. Live bands play often, and draft beer is $1.50. (Open daily 11am-2am. Occasional $2 cover.) **Peabody's Down Under,** 1059 Old River Rd. (241-0792 or 241-2451) draws crowds not for the view, but for the variety of local and nationally famous rock bands that play most nights. (Open daily 8pm-2:30am, and sometimes later. Cover $4-18 depending on the band.) On the west side of the river are several other clubs, including **Shooters,** 1148 Main Ave. (861-6900), a beautiful bar/restaurant with a great view of the river and Lake Erie. Prices are fairly high (dinners $7-10), but you can capture the flavor of Cleveland nightlife inexpensively by taking your drink to the in-deck pool. (Open Mon.-Sat. 11:30am-1:30am, Sun. 11am-1:30am.) When you tire of fluorescent pink tank tops and wine coolers, stop by the **Euclid Tavern,** 11629 Euclid Ave. (229-7788), just east of University Circle, the place for good conversation and great music. Live bands play nightly; Saturday packs the place. (Open 11am-2:30pm. Beer $1.50.)

In the shadow of Cleveland's metropolitan hustle and bustle lie the Amish communities of bucolic **Holmes County.** Originally Swiss Mennonites, the Amish broke with the main body to create their own sect. Following Jacob Amman, they came to America in 1728 to practice their more austere lifestyle undisturbed. In Ohio, they settled south of Cleveland in rural Holmes, Wayne, and Tuscarawas counties. Outsiders can visit the **Amish Farm** (893-2951), in Berlin, which offers a film presentation, demonstrations of non-electrical appliances, and a tour of the grounds. (Open April 1-Nov. 1 Mon.-Sat. 10am-6pm. Tour $2.25, children $1. Buggy ride $2.75.) Unserved by public transportation, Berlin lies 70 mi. south of Cleveland on Rte. 39, 17 pastoral mi. west of I-77.

Columbus

College *city* is probably a more precise term than college *town* for the home of Ohio State University, the largest university in the country. This state capital is a relaxing place where you can picnic along the banks of the Scioto River, or stroll through Bexley, lawnscaped suburbia at its best.

The **Columbus Museum of Art,** 480 E. Broad St. (221-6801), collects European masterpieces. (Open Tues. and Thurs.- Fri. 11am-4pm, Wed. 11am-9pm, Sat. 10am-5pm, Sun. 11am-5pm. $2.50, seniors, students, and ages 6-17 $1.) Ohio's **Center of Science and Industry (COSI),** 280 E. Broad St. (228-2674), features hands-on mechanized exhibits. (Mon.-Sat. 10am-5pm, Sun. 1-5:30pm. $5, seniors, students, and kids $3, families $15, under 2 free.)

The rapidly growing **Columbus Zoo,** 9990 Riverside Dr. (645-3400), in Powell, contains the world's largest cheetah collection, the largest U.S. display of reptiles and amphibians, and the world's first captive-born gorilla. (Memorial Day to Labor Day daily 9am-6pm, Wed. 9am-8pm; off-season daily 9am-5pm. $4, ages 2-11 $2, under 2 free. $2 parking fee.)

Head to **Bernie's Bagels and Deli,** 1896 N. High St. (291-3448), for delicious hand-warming sandwiches ($2-5). The basement setting resembles a fall-out shelter, but the nightly live gigs make it cozy. For an above-ground dining experience, choose from 1000 bottles of wine to accompany the moderately priced Mediterranean cuisine at **A La Carte,** 2333 N. High St. (294-6783). The outdoor tables are particularly popular. (Open Mon.-Thurs. 11am-9:30pm, Fri.-Sat. 11am-11pm, Sun. 5-9pm.) Just south of Capitol Square is the **German Village,** first settled in 1843 and now the largest privately-funded historical restoration in the U.S. Visitors can tour stately brick homes and patronize old-style beer halls and restaurants. While in German Village make sure to hit **Katzinger's Delicatessen,** (228-7297), Third at Livingston. Excellent Bratwurst and German potato salad. Stroll over to the pickle barrel and eat as many as you can. Free refills on drinks too. Entrees $4-8. Open daily 9am-8:30pm. At **Schmidt's Sausage House,** 240 E. Kossuth St. (444-6808), groove to nightly live music while eating brats and tater salad. (Open Mon. 11am-10pm, Tues.-Thurs. 11am-11:30pm, Fri.-Sat. 11am-12:30am, Sun. 11am-9pm.) For information, call or visit the helpful **German Village Society,** 634 S. 3rd St. (221-8888). (Mon.-Fri. 9am-4pm.)

Two mi. north of downtown Columbus looms gargantuan **Ohio State University;** its enrollment of over 58,000 students is the largest in the United States. **Visitor Information** at the Ohio Union 1329 N. High St. (292-0428 or 292-0418), at N. High St. The students support a lively nightlife, with most of the activity on **North High Street. Newport's,** 1722 N. High St. (291-8829), regularly features famous bands or plays dance music for a sweaty, energetic crowd. (Call for admission information and music schedule.)

The beautiful **Heart of Ohio Hostel (AYH),** 95 E. 12th Ave. (294-7157), one block from OSU, has outstanding facilities. ($8, $11 nonmembers. Check-in 5-9pm. Curfew 11pm.) Rooms in apartment houses near campus are cheap, abundant, and well advertised during the summer, when OSU students leave them vacant. Downtown accommodations are much more expensive.

Visitors to the city can contact the **Greater Columbus Convention and Visitors Bureau,** 10 W. Broad St. #1300 (221-6623 or 800-234-2657; open Mon.-Fri. 8am-5pm). **Greyhound,** 111 E. Town St. (221-5311), offers the most frequent and complete service from downtown Columbus to Cincinnati ($14-20, varies by day), Cleveland ($15-23), and Chicago ($60). Public transportation in the city is run by the **Central Ohio Transit Authority (COTA),** 177 S. High St. (228-1776; offices Mon.-Fri. 8:30am-5:30pm; fare $1, express $1.35).

The **area code** for Columbus is 614; the **ZIP code** is 43016.

Near Columbus

Dense green forests swathe southeastern Ohio's narrow valleys, steep hills, and ragged rock formations, carved into the land by Pleistocene glaciers. The southern route of Buckeye trail snakes through this jagged terrain, roughly tracked by **U.S. 50.** Along the highway, which runs east from Cincinnati to Parkersburg, lie spectacular Native American burial grounds, constructed by Adena, Hopewell, and Fort Ancient "Moundbuilders." Among the most interesting is the **Mound City Group National Monument** (774-1125), on Rte. 104, 3 mi. north of Chillicothe. Within a 13-acre area hunch 24 still-mysterious Hopewell burial mounds. The adjoining museum elucidates theories about Hopewell society based on the mounds' configuration. (Museum daily 8am-6pm. $1, max. $3 per vehicle, seniors and under 17 free.) Check with park officials for info on other nearby mounds. Visit **Chillicothe** to ogle the Greek Revival mansions that grace the northwest territory's first capital.

Ten mi. south of Chillicothe off U.S. 23, you can camp at **Scioto Trail State Park** (663-2125; 24-hr. self-registration; primitive camping free; designated sites $4, with electricity $8). Four mi. from the bus station is the **Chillicothe Home Hostel (AYH),** 1940 Egypt Pike Rd. (775-3632 or 773-3989). A phenomenal beer can collection covers the walls of one available room. (Members only. $5. Reservations required.)

Greyhound, 302 E. Main St. (775-2013), serves Chillicothe from both Cincinnati ($27.25) and Columbus ($11.25).

About 30 mi. east of Chillicothe, U.S. 50 passes near **Hocking Hills State Park,** accessible by Rte. 93 north or Rte. 56 west. Waterfalls, gorges, cliffs, and caves scar the rugged terrain within the park. **Ash Cave,** east of South Bloomingville on Rte. 56, gouges 80 acres out of a horseshoe-shaped rock. A trickling stream falls over the edge of this cliff to a pool at the cave entrance. **Cantwell Cliffs,** southwest of Rockbridge on Rte. 374, is another horseshoe-shaped precipice. Also visit deep-gorge **Cedar Falls and Conkles Hollow,** and **Rock House,** a stone structure stuck precariously in a perpendicular cliff. All of these sights are preserved and run by the state park system. Camp at **Old Man's Cave,** off State Rte. 664 (385-6165; primitive camping $4; designated sites with pool $7, with electricity and pool $10).

The **area code** for these here parts is 614.

Lake Erie Islands

"Ohio's Scenic Playground," the Lake Erie Island region can be either quaint or garish, depending on where you go. The area around the regional center on the mainland, **Sandusky,** tends toward the latter, with an abundance of neon signs and billboards; still, downtown Sandusky is not as commercial as the surrounding highways. Once the last stop in the U.S. for escaped African slaves fleeing to Canada via the Underground Railroad, Sandusky lies on Rte. 2, 55 mi. west of Cleveland and 45 mi. southeast of Toledo.

Near Sandusky, experience **Cedar Point,** the scenic playground's scenic amusement park (627-2350) off Rte. 6. Take the Ohio Turnpike (I-80) to exit 7 and follow signs north on U.S. 250 to the home of the Magnum XL200, the world's largest, fastest, longest, and steepest roller coaster. (Open mid-May to mid-Sept. Sun.-Thurs. 9am-10pm, Fri. and Sat. 9am-midnight. Admission $21.95, seniors $12.75, under 48 in. $11.95, under 3 years free. After 5pm, when the lines diminish, the admission drops to $11.95.) In Sandusky savor the **Erie County Vineyard Days,** each fall from mid-September to November. Sandusky and the Erie Islands lost their monopoly on U.S. wine production after Prohibition and the Great Depression, but today the area still ferments in an orgy of libation that would do Dionysius proud. For more information, contact the **Visitors and Convention Bureau,** 231 W. Washington Row (625-2984; open Mon.-Fri. 8am-6pm, Sat. 10am-4pm), or the **Tourist Information Center,** 5420 Milan Rd. (626-5721; Memorial Day-Labor Day daily 8am-6pm).

Greyhound, 6513 Milan Rd. (625-6907) offers bus service from Sandusky to Cleveland ($10.50), Detroit ($20.15), and Chicago ($52). The **Greyhound Shuttle** runs to downtown Sandusky ($4) and Cedar Point ($5).

Cheap accommodations are difficult to find in Ohio's vacationland, especially during summer weekends. Rates are extremely flexible and tend to soar during the peak tourist season, so try to schedule an off-season visit. In Sandusky, sample one of the motels east of downtown along Cleveland Rd. The **Tudor Inn Motel,** 2214 Cleveland Rd. (626-0775), has a cabin available during the summer for $29, $49 weekends, and motel rooms year-round. (Weeknight doubles $39, quads $49; weekend doubles $69, quads $79. A hundred yards away, **Bayshore Estates RV Park and Campsite,** 2311 Cleveland Rd. (625-7906), has tent sites ($12 for 2 people, with hookup $14 for 2 people, $2 per additional person). Camping is also available at the **Crystal Rock Campground,** 710 Crystal Rock Rd. (684-7177), off Rte. 6 south of Rte. 2, with extensive facilities including a pool (sites $15, with hookup $18.50).

Just northwest of Sandusky, accessible by Rte. 2, is **Marblehead Peninsula** and the adjoining **Catawba Island.** This area is less cluttered than Sandusky and brings you closer to the region's scenic aspects. On the northeast side of Marblehead, **Lakeside,** on North Shore Blvd., is one of the last of the Chautauqua villages. This 19th-century Methodist retreat has economy rooms in its **Hotel Lakeside** (798-4461). Take Rte. 2 to Rte. 163, heading toward the tip of Marblehead. (Room with full bath $40, with half bath $30. Restored rooms for up to two people with full bath $50. Grounds admission fee $7, children 12-20 $5. Overnight auto pass $1, includes free entertainment at the compound's Hoover Auditorium.) **Poor Richard's Inn,** 317 Maple St. (798-5405), is two blocks up the street from the Hotel Lakeside (doubles $28.34-42.51; quads $49.05-50.14). Camping is also available at Lakeside (tent sites $8, with hookup $10, with hookup and water, gate fee $7 per person per day; call 798-4461). A couple of miles from the Catawba Point ferry dock, try the **East Harbor State Park** (734-4424), on Rte. 269 off I-65. (Open 24 hrs. Tent sites $8.)

Kelleys Island, the largest U.S. island in Lake Erie, is laid-back and relaxing with none of Sandusky's neon glitter and all of the region's famous beauty. In addition to the beaches, examine the water-filled, abandoned limestone quarries in the island's interior. Near the town on the island's southern shore you can see **Inscription Rock,** a slab of limestone covered with Erie American pictographs over four centuries old. On the north shore, by glaciers some 30,000 years ago grooves 15 ft. deep, 35 ft. wide, and 400 ft. long, were gouged out of the limestone. Golf carts ($10 per hr., $25 per ½-day) can be rented from **Popeye's** (746-2551), also near the ferry dock. The best (the only) place to camp is **Kelleys Island State Park** (746-2546), on the north shore near the glacial grooves (sites $8). **Neuman Boat Line,** 101 E. Shoreline Dr. (626-5557), in Sandusky, serves Kelleys Island by ferry. Ferries run more frequently between Kelleys Island and the Marblehead dock, on the eastern tip of the peninsula. (Open Mar.-Dec. Summer schedule: Mon.-Thurs. 7:30am-6:30pm, Fri. and Sun. 7:30am-9:30pm, Sat. 7:30am-8:30pm. Taking a vehicle across can add hours to the wait. Round-trip $7.80, ages 6-11 $4.50, under 6 free, car $14, bike $1.)

The **Bass Island chain** extends far into Lake Erie to the west of Kelleys Island; **South Bass Island,** shaped like an hourglass, is the largest and most populous of the three. If Kelleys is the relaxing island, then South Bass, or Put-In-Bay as it is commonly known, is the lively, exciting island with a party atmosphere. The town of **Put-In-Bay,** 2 mi. northeast of the ferry dock, is packed on summer weekends with people from all over attracted by the nightlife scene. The **Round House Bar,** 234 Lorain Ave. (285-4595, ext. 110), downtown, bulges with people listening to live bands performing nightly. A glass of Budweiser is $2.25. (Open daily noon-1am.)

Stuck to the hourglass's waist at the town of Put-In-Bay is **Perry's Victory and International Peace Memorial,** the world's tallest doric column (352 ft.), erected to commemorate Commodore Oliver Hazard Perry's victory over the British in the War of 1812. (Open daily 10am-6pm. Elevator $1.) Also located in Put-In-Bay, the **Heineman Winery,** Catawba Ave. (285-2811), gives intimate tours of the grounds, including a look at **Crystal Cave,** one of the world's largest geodes. (Late May to mid-Sept. daily 11am-5pm. $3, children 6-12 $1.)

On the island, you can camp and swim at **South Bass Island State Park** (285-2112; open daily 8am-5pm; tent sites $7). **Island Bike Rental,** Langrum Rd. (285-2016), across from the ferry dock, not surprisingly rents island bikes ($2 per hr., $6 per day). The **Miller Boat Line** (285-2421) serves Put-in-Bay from Catawba Point. Take the Put-in-Bay exit, Rte. 53, north from Rte. 2 until it ends. (Ferries every hr. late March to mid-Nov.; every ½-hr. early June-early Sept. Open 7:30am-7pm, weekends 7:30am-8pm. One way $4, ages 6-11 $1, under 6 free, cars $7, bikes $1.50.)

Miller Boat Line also serves **Middle Bass Island,** where you can visit the fortress-like **Lonz Winery** (285-5411) and sample their vintage. (Open mid-May to late Sept. Mon.-Thurs., Fri. noon-10pm, Sat. noon-midnight.)

The **area code** for the islands is 419.

OKLAHOMA

President Andrew Jackson, who ordered the forced relocation of "The Five Civilized Tribes" from Florida and Georgia to the new territory, designated Oklahoma Indian Territory. Thousands of Native Americans died of hunger and disease on the brutal and tragic march, known as the "Trail of Tears." The survivors rebuilt their decimated tribes in Oklahoma, only to be moved again in 1889 to make way for whites rushing to stake claims on settlement lands newly-opened by the federal government. Settlers who slipped into the territory and claimed prize lands before the first official Land Run were called "sooners", which Oklahomans have been called ever since.

In 1907 the territory was admitted to the Union as Oklahoma, Choctaw for "red people". The discovery of oil in 1904 brought wealth to the state, but its other chief industry, agriculture, was destroyed in the 1930s by years of drought, heat, and dust. The Dust Bowl period saw a massive migration of "Okie" farmers to California, described in John Steinbeck's *The Grapes of Wrath.* In the years since, the state's fortunes have fluctuated with the price of a barrel of oil.

Practical Information

Capital: Oklahoma City.

Oklahoma Tourism and Recreation Department, 500 Will Rogers Building, Oklahoma City 73105 (521-2409 or 800-652-6552 out of state), in the capitol complex.

Time Zone: Central (1 hr. behind Eastern). **Postal Abbreviation:** OK

Oklahoma City

> *"Creation! Hell! That took six days. This was done in one."*—Edna Ferber

At noon on April 22, 1889, a gunshot sent settlers rushing into Oklahoma Territory to claim land. By sundown, Oklahoma City, set strategically on the tracks of the Santa Fe Railroad, had a population of over 10,000 homesteaders. The city became state capital in 1910. A 1928 oil discovery modernized the city; elegant homes rose with oil derricks. But as the wells dried up and the oil business slumped, Oklahoma City fell on hard times. The **OKC National Stockyards** still thrive with activity, and the **National Cowboy Hall of Fame** is a testament to the city's rugged glory.

Orientation and Practical Information

Emergency: 911.

Chamber of Commerce Tourist Information, 4 Santa Fe Plaza (278-8912), at the corner of Gaylord. Open Mon.-Fri. 8am-4:30pm.

Travelers Aid: 601 NW 5th (232-5507), at Main. Open Mon.-Fri. 8am-5pm.

Will Rogers Memorial Airport, 681-5311, southwest of downtown. **Airport Limousine, Inc.,** 3805 S. Meridian (685-2638), has van service to downtown ($9).

Greyhound/Trailways: 427 W. Sheridan Ave. (235-6425), at Walker. In a seedy part of town. Take city bus #5, 6, 11, or 12. To: Tulsa (8 per day, 2 hr., $12.90); Dallas (4 per day, 5 hr., $38); and Kansas City (6 per day, 10 hr., $52). Open 24 hrs.

Public Transport: Masstrans, 300 E. California Blvd. (235-7433). Bus service Mon.-Sat. 6am-7pm. All routes radiate from the station at Reno and Gaylord, where maps are available. Route numbers vary depending on the direction of travel. Fare 75¢, seniors and kids 35¢.

Taxi: Yellow Cab, 232-6161. $2.50 first mi., $1.45 each additional mi. Airport to downtown fare $12.50.

Car Rental: Rent-a-Wreck, 2930 NW 39th Expressway (946-9288). Used cars $27 per day with 125 free mi., 24¢ each additional mi. Open Mon.-Fri. 8am-4:30pm, Sat. 8:30am-noon. Must be 21 with major credit card.

Bike Rental: Miller's Bicycle Distribution, 739 Asp Ave. (321-8296). Ten-speeds and mountain bikes $3 per day. Open Mon.-Sat. 9am-6pm. Major credit card or $75 cash deposit required ($250 deposit for mountain bikes).

Help Lines: Crisis Hotline, 848-2273. **Rape Crisis,** 943-7273. Both open 24 hrs.

Post Office: 320 SW 5th St. (278-6300). Open Mon.-Fri. 8:30am-5:30pm, Sat. 9am-noon. **ZIP code:** 73125.

Area Code: 405.

Main Street divides the town east-west. Car travel is ideal; almost all of the city's attractions are outside the city center.

Accommodations, Camping, and Food

The **YMCA,** 125 NW 5th St. (232-6101), has rooms for men only. Shared bath. (Singles $12.) The **Brass Lantern Inn,** 700 NW 9th St. (232-0505), across from St. Anthony's Hospital, proffers clean, quiet, comfortable and amply lit rooms. (Singles $25. Doubles $27.) I-35 near Oklahoma City is lined with inexpensive hotels that offer singles for under $25. The **Sooner Inn,** 1629 S. Prospect (677-0551), is the best deal. Adequate rooms come with cable TV and free local calls, and there is a pool. On I-35 South, take the 15th St. exit and turn left. (Singles $19. Doubles $28.)

Oklahoma City has two readily accessible campgrounds. **RCA,** 12115 Northeast Expressway (478-0278), next to Frontier City Amusement Park 10 mi. north of the city on I-35, has a pool, laundry room, and showers. (Tent sites for two $9, RV sites with hookup $15. Open 8am-10pm.) The nearest state-run campground lies on Lake Thunderbird about 30 mi. south of OKC at **Little River State Park** (360-3572 or 364-7634). Take I-40 East to the Choctaw Rd. exit, then south until the road ends, and make a left. Merely set up a tent, and a collector will come around for your money. (Tent sites $4, $5 in area with gate attendant; showers included. Seniors, disabled ½ price. Office open 8am-5pm.)

Since Oklahoma City contains the largest feeder cattle market in the U.S., beef tops most menus. Founded in 1926, the **Cattlemen's Café,** 1309 S. Agnew (236-0416), is a classic diner a block away from the stockyards. Try the chopped sirloin dinner ($6.50) or the navy bean soup with cornbread ($1.50). (Open Sun.-Thurs. 6am-10pm, Fri.-Sat. 6am-midnight.) **Sweeney's Deli,** 900 N. Broadway (232-2510), serves tasty dishes in a friendly atmosphere; play pool or watch the big-screen TV. The restaurant has received the 1988 "good country cooking" award. Sandwiches

$3-4, burgers $2.20, hot plates $4. (Open daily 11am-11pm.) **Pump's Bar and Grill,** 5700 N. Western (840-4369), is a renovated gas station serving more innovative fuel, like "Oklahoma crepes" (chicken, cream cheese, and jack cheese enchiladas topped with sour cream), burgers, and sandwiches ($3.50-7). (Open Sun.-Thurs. 11am-11pm, Fri.-Sat. 11am-midnight.) Downtown, the **Century Center Plaza,** 100 Main St., exudes cheap lunch spots. (Open Mon.-Sat. 11am-3pm.)

Sights and Entertainment

The **Oklahoma City Stockyards,** 2500 Exchange Ave. (235-8675), are the busiest in the world. Cattle auctions, held here Monday through Wednesday, begin at 7 or 8am and sometimes last into the night. Monday and Tuesday are the busiest days; Monday morning is the best time to visit. An auctioneer fires bids in a rapid-fire monotone as cowhands chase the cattle through a maze of gates and passages into the auction building. Visitors enter free of charge via a catwalk over the pens, leading from the parking lot east of the auction house. Take bus #11 from Hudson downtown to S. Agnew Ave.

The plight of Native Americans along the "Trail of Tears" is commemorated by James Earle Fraser's *The End of the Trail.* Ironically, his sculpture of a man slumped over an exhausted pony is on display at the **National Cowboy Hall of Fame and Western Heritage Center,** 1700 N.E. 63rd St. (478-2250). The Hall contains such pistol-packin' frontiersmen as Barry "Buck" Goldwater and Ronald "Yee-Haw!!" Reagan. Along with Frederic Remington sculptures and cowboy memorabilia, you'll find John Wayne's collection of Pueblo kachina dolls. Every summer, the museum showcases 150 works of the National Academy of Western Art. Take bus #22 from downtown. (Open May 27-Sept. 2 daily 8:30am-6pm; off-season daily 9am-5pm. $5, seniors $4, ages 6-12 $3.) The **State Capitol,** 2300 N. Lincoln Blvd. (521-3356), is the world's only capitol building surrounded by working oil wells. Completed in 1917, the Greco-Roman structure was built atop a large reserve of crude. The first oil well drilled on Capitol grounds was nicknamed "Petunia number one" because it was drilled on a flower bed. The well dried up in 1986 but the derrick remains erect, a monument to. . .oil. (Capitol open daily 8am-7pm; guided tours 8am-3pm. Free.) Just down 23rd St. is the Dutch Colonial **Governor's Mansion,** 820 N.E. 23rd St. (521-2342). The building's odd façade and Spanish roof are about as incompatible as ketchup and ice cream, yet somehow it works. (Tours by appointment or on certain days; call ahead.)

Gas lamps and spacious mansions are the hallmarks of **Heritage Hill,** a grand ol' neighborhood of restored turn-of-the-century houses. The **Overholser Mansion,** 405 NW 15th St. (528-8485), built in 1903, is a good example of Victorian architecture filled with elaborate Limoges china services, Venetian crystal, and Meissen vases. (Open Tues.-Fri. 9am-5pm, Sat.-Sun. 2-5pm. Free tours hourly.) **Nichols Hills,** just north of Oklahoma City, is another community loaded with gorgeous homes. Take bus #5 (from Walker and Main) past 63rd, and wander west.

The **Kirkpatrick Center Museum Complex,** 2100 NE 52nd St. (427-5461), a sort of educational amusement park, looks like a mall but is actually a conglomeration of eight separate colorful and entertaining museums. Highlights are the **Air and Space Museum** and the **International Photography Hall of Fame.** Take bus #22. (Open May 27-Sept. 2 Mon.-Sat. 9am-6pm, Sun. noon-6pm; off-season Mon.-Fri. 9:30am-5pm, Sat. 9am-6pm, Sun. noon-6pm. Admission to all 8 museums $5, seniors and ages 5-12 $3.)

Nightlife in Oklahoma City is a scarce commodity. For ideas, pick up a copy of the *Oklahoma Gazette.* City slickers beware: The **First National Bar,** 4315 N. Western (525-9400), ain't no sushi place. Live bands, pool tables and a raucous crowd make this bar a local favorite. (Open Mon.-Sat. 10am-2pm.) The **Oklahoma Opry,** 404 W. Commerce (632-8322), is home to a posse of country music stars. (Regular performances Sat. at 8pm.) The **Black Liberated Arts Center,** 1901 N. Ellison (528-4666), provides plays and musical events at the Classen Theater from October to May. (Office open 10am-4pm Mon.-Fri.)

Near Oklahoma City

More prudent travelers will skip OKC's nightlife, wake up early and drive to **Anadarko**, a short 60-mi. drive through the Great Plains. Anadarko is home to **Indian City USA** (405-247-5661), a museum which has reconstructed villages of seven Native American tribes. During the summer, each tour begins with a performance of Native American dances by prize-winning Native American dancers. Talk to the dancers or one of the guides; the conversation will tell more about the tragedy of Native Americans than any Oscar-winning Kevin Costner movie ever can. Drive south from Oklahoma City on I-44 40 mi. to exit #83, take a right on 9 West, go about 20 mi. to Anadarko, take a left on 8 South, and go two mi. to the museum entrance. (Open daily 9am-6pm, 9am-5pm during off-season. $7, kids $4.)

For those in search of a home where the buffalo play and the deer roam and the antelope frolic and whatnot, check out the **Wichita Mountain Wildlife Refuge** (405-429-3222), an hour south of Anadarko. Created in 1905 by Teddy Roosevelt, the National Park is home to 625 buffalo, thousands of deer and Texas longhorns, and various other wildlife, all of which roam freely in the park. **Mount Scott** is only 2,464 ft. high, but because it rises over a plain, a spectacular view awaits those who drive or hike to the top. Camping is permitted in certain areas of the park; stop at a refuge office for maps. Take exit #49 off I-44. (Open daily; some areas close at dusk.)

Tulsa

First settled by Creeks arriving from the Trail of Tears, Tulsa's location on the banks of the Arkansas River made it a logical trading outpost for Europeans and Native Americans. With the advent of railroads and the discovery of huge oil deposits, the city boomed into the "Oil Capital of the World" by the 1920s. The city's heritage is visible today in its art deco skyscrapers, French villas, and Georgian mansions, as well as its Native American populations, second largest among U.S. metropolitan areas.

Practical Information

Emergency: 911.

Convention and Visitors Division, Metropolitan Tulsa Chamber of Commerce, 616 S. Boston (585-1201 or 800-558-3311).

Greyhound/Trailways: 317 S. Detroit (584-4427). To: Oklahoma City (8 per day, 2 hr., $13); St. Louis (9 per day, 7½-9½ hr., $64); Kansas City (4 per day, 6-8 hr., $69, $51 with transfer); Dallas (8 per day; 7 hr.; $55, 2 weeks in advance $27). Lockers $1. Open 24 hrs.

Public Transport: Metropolitan Tulsa Transit Authority, 510 S. Rockford (582-2100). Buses run daily 6am-5pm. Fare 60¢, transfers 5¢, seniors and disabled (disabled card available at bus offices) 30¢, ages 5-18 50¢, under 5 free with adult. Maps and schedules are available at the main office (open Mon.-Fri. 8am-4:45pm), the chamber of commerce, and most libraries, but are not always reliable.

Taxi: Yellow Cab, 582-6161.

Bike Rental: River Trail Sports Center, 3949 Riverside Dr. (743-5898), at 41st St. Five-speeds $4 per hr., $12 per day. Open Mon.-Sat. 10am-8pm, Sun. 11am-6pm. Must have driver's license or cash deposit.

Help Lines: 583-4357, for information, referral, crisis intervention. Open 24 hrs. **Gay Information Line,** 743-4297. Open daily 8-10pm.

Post Office: 333 W. 4th St. (599-6800). Open Mon.-Fri. 8:30am-5pm. **ZIP code:** 74101.

Area Code: 918.

All "South" addresses are along the numbered east-west streets, which begin downtown. Named streets lie in alphabetical order, with the alphabet beginning at north-south avenues on both sides of **Main Street,** and at east-west streets a block north of **First Street.** Streets named after the western cities are on the west side of Main Street, eastern on the east side. If possible, navigate by car. Outside of downtown, sidewalks are scarce and bus routes limited.

Accommodations and Camping

Most cheap accommodations in Tulsa are outside the city center. An exception is the **YMCA,** 515 S. Denver (583-6201), for men only. Ask for a room on the third floor. Guests have access to pool and gym; the office is open 24 hrs. (Singles $11.) The cheapest downtown motel is the **Darby Lane Inn,** 416 W. 6th St. (584-4461). Clean, recently remodeled rooms have cable TV. (Singles $34. Doubles $40. Call for reservations.) Budget motels are plentiful along I-44 and I-244. To reach the **Gateway Motor Inn,** 5600 W. Skelly Dr. (446-6611), take bus #17 and get off at Rensor's Grocery. Clean rooms come with large beds, HBO, and cable. (Singles $19. Doubles $24.) The **Roadway Motel,** 4724 S. Yale (496-9300), just south of I-44, is notable for its central location. From downtown take bus #15, get off at 49th and Yale, and walk two blocks north. (Singles $25. Doubles $30.)

The **KOA Kampground,** 193 East Ave. (266-4227), ½ mi. west of the Will Rogers Turnpike Gate off I-44, has a pool, laundry room, and game room. (Sites $14, with hookup $15.) **Keystone State Park** (865-4991) offers three campgrounds along the shores of Lake Keystone, 20 mi. west of Tulsa on the Cimarron Turnpike (U.S. 64). The wooded park offers hiking, swimming, boating, and excellent catfish and bass fishing. (Sites $10, with hookup $14. Tent camping $4.) Four-person cabins with fireplaces and kitchenettes are also available for $43; call 800-522-8565 for reservations.

Food

Nelson's Buffeteria, 514 S. Boston (584-9969), takes you on a romantic journey through Tulsa's past while you eat. Operating since 1929, now run by Nelson Jr., this old-style diner's walls are replete with Mid-American memorabilia. The menu changes daily; try a breakfast special ($2-3) or the famous chicken-fried steak ($4.30). (Open daily 6am-2:30pm.) The 50s-style **Metro Diner,** 3001 E. 11th St. at College (592-2616), has a ton of funky memorabilia and an obligatory soda fountain, specializing in rich fountain treats, burgers ($3.50-5), and homemade pies ($1.75). Seniors receive a 10% discount. (Open Mon.-Thurs. 6:30am-11pm, Fri.-Sat. 6:30am-midnight, Sun. 8am-11pm.) Despite the motto "It be bad", **Elmer's Barbecue,** 4128 S. Peoria (747-6475), offers heavenly sliced beef and sparerib dinners ($4-8). (Open Mon.-Thurs. 11am-9:45pm, Fri.-Sat. 11am-11:45pm.) The giant pink **Casa Bonita,** 2120 S. Sheridan Rd. (836-6464), offers large Mexican feasts ($5-7) and all-you-can-eat dinners ($7.50) in a highly entertaining atmosphere. The dining areas range in décor from rustic candle-lit caves to south-of-the-border villages. (Open Sun.-Thurs. 11am-9:30pm, Fri.-Sat. 11am-10pm). Most downtown restaurants close at 3pm weekdays and 1pm Saturdays.

Sights and Entertainment

Perched atop an Osage foothill two mi. northwest of downtown, the **Thomas Gilcrease Museum,** 1400 Gilcrease Museum Rd. (582-3122), houses one of the world's largest collections of American art. Designed to be a study of people in North America from pre-history to the present, the museum contains 250,000 Native American artifacts and more than 10,000 paintings and sculptures by artists such as Remington and Russell. Take bus #7 ("Gilcrease") from downtown. (Open Mon.-Sat. 9am-5pm, Sun. 1-5pm. Donation requested. Disabled accessible.) The **Philbrook Art Center,** 2727 S. Rockford Rd. (749-7941), in the former Renaissance villa of an oil baron, houses a collection of Native American pottery and artifacts alongside Renaissance paintings and sculptures. Picnic by the lovely pond on the grounds. Take bus #16 ("S. Peoria") from downtown. (Open Wed. and Fri.-Sat. 10am-5pm,

Thurs. 10am-8pm, Sun. 1-5pm. $3, seniors and college students $1.50, other students and kids free.) The **Fenster Museum of Jewish Art,** 1223 E. 17th Pl. (582-3732), housed in B'nai Emunah Synagogue, contains an impressive collection of Judaica from 2000 BC to the present. (Open Tues.-Fri. 10am-4pm, Sun. 1-4pm.)

Walking onto the campus of **Oral Roberts University,** 7777 S. Lewis (495-6161), is like entering the twilight zone. The campus' ultra-modern, gold-mirrored architecture rising out of an Oklahoma plain, the 80-ft.-high praying hands sculpture guarding the campus, and the hordes of believers flocking to visit make the eerie experience a must. The **Prayer Tower** (495-6807), modeled after George and Jane Jetson's home, takes visitors through an exhibition honoring the university's founder. Choirs sing in the background, spotlights illuminate mementos from the Roberts' childhood, and doors open and close automatically as if by divine command. Oral Roberts' City of Faith Hospital, commissioned by a 900-ft.-tall Jesus, is now leased to a cancer research center. The **ORU Healing Outreach** (496-7700) hosts a "Journey Through the Bible" tour, where Old Testament scenes are recreated in life-like, three-dimensional exhibits. (Open Mon.-Sat. 10:30am-4:30pm, Sun. 1-5pm. Tours every 15-20 min. Free.) The rest of the non-drinkin', non-smokin', and non-dancin' campus is (alas! alack!) closed to the public. The university is about six mi. south of downtown Tulsa between Lewis and Harvard Ave. Take bus #9 ("S. Lewis"). (Prayer Tower and visitors center open Mon.-Sat. 10:30am-4:30pm, Sunday 1-4:30pm.)

During the oil boom years of the 1920s, art deco architecture was all the rage in Tulsa. The best example of the style is the **Boston Avenue United Methodist Church,** 1301 S. Boston (583-5181). Built in 1929, the house of worship is vaguely suggestive of the witch's palace in *The Wizard of Oz.* Climb the 14-story tower to the pea-green worship room with a skyline view of Tulsa. (Tours given Mon.-Fri. 9am-4pm, Sun. 12:15pm. Free)

Rodgers and Hammerstein's *Oklahoma!* continues its run under the stars at the **Discoveryland Amphitheater** (245-0242, for tickets 800-338-6552), 10 mi. west of Tulsa on 41st St., accessible only by car. Arrive early for the pre-show barbecue, starting at 5:30pm. (Shows June-Aug. Mon.-Sat. at 8pm. Mon.-Thurs. $14, seniors $10, under 12 $7; Fri.-Sat. $14, seniors $12.75, kids $8. Pre-show barbecue $6.95, seniors $6.50, kids $4.95.) A most moving commemoration of Native American heritage is the **Trail of Tears Drama,** a show reenacting the Cherokees' tragic march, performed in Tahlequah, 66 mi. east of Tulsa on Rte. 51. (Performances June-Sept. 2 Mon.-Sat. at 8pm. For tickets, call 456-6007, or write P.O. Box 515, Tahlequah, OK 74465; reservations recommended. $9, under 13 $4.50.) For more traditional cultural enlightenment, the **Tulsa Philharmonic** (747-7445) and **Tulsa Opera** (582-4035) perform year-round. The **Tulsa Ballet** (585-2573) has been acclaimed one of America's finest regional troupes.

Exercisers should rent a bike and ride down beautiful **Riverside Drive,** on the east bank of the Arkansas River. The neighborhood west of Riverside between 21st and 50th Streets is full of nice homes and is an excellent place for a walk or a bike ride.

At night, head to the bars along 15th St. east of Peoria, or in the 30s along S. Peoria. Down at the **Sunset Grill,** 3410 S. Peoria (744-5550), nightly rowdy rock bands accompany free popcorn and a free midnight buffet. (Open daily 8pm-2am; must be 21; no cover.) Keep up to date on Tulsa's nightlife with a free copy of *Uptown News,* available at newsstands, bookstores, and the chamber of commerce.

The best times to visit Tulsa are during annual special events like the **International Mayfest** (582-6435) in mid-May. This outdoor food, arts, and performance festival takes place in downtown Tulsa over a five-day period. The mid-August **Pow-Wow** (835-8699), held at Mohawk Park just northwest of the airport, attracts Native Americans from dozens of different tribes. The four-day festival includes a trade fair, arts and crafts exhibits, and nightly dancing contests which visitors may attend. Admission is $5 per carload.

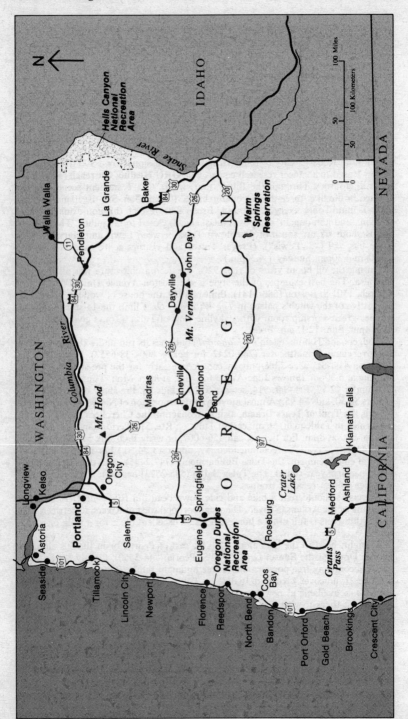

OREGON

Although their shoreline, inland forests, and parks share all the lush drama of those in California, Oregon residents for years disdained the gaggles of tourists that overran their southern neighbor. The 1980s brought hard times for Oregonians, however, and with them a reconsideration of this once-widespread disdain. Bumper stickers that read "Don't Californicate Oregon" disappeared, replaced by giant "welcome" signs in every one-cow town. Cities that once thrived on Oregon's now dwindling mining and foresting industries were resurrected as tourist towns.

But tourism fuels much of the state's history. Lewis and Clark rented canoes and slipped quietly down the Columbia River when their guide, *Let's Go* researcher/writer extraordinaire Sacagawea, brought them to Oregon; later, waves of settlers surged westward towards the coastal terminus of the Oregon Trail, inspiring Francis Parkman's famous travel work. Today, the narrow coastal route of U.S. 101 provides the best-worn corridor of travel.

Practical Information

Capital: Salem.

State Tourist Office, 735 Summer St. NE, Salem 97310 (800-547-7842). Oregon State Parks, 525 Trade St. SE, Salem 97310 (378-6305). Department of Fish and Wildlife, P.O. Box 59, Portland 97207 (229-5403). Oregon American Youth Hostels, 311 E. 11th Ave. #205, Eugene 97402 (683-3685).

Time Zone: Pacific (3 hrs. behind Eastern) and Mountain (2 hrs. behind Eastern). Postal Abbreviation: OR

Ashland

Ashland, the southernmost Oregon town on I-5 and reachable from Klamath Falls via the stunning Hwy. 66, has hosted a world-famous Shakespeare Festival eight months a year for over 55 years. Due to the tremendous popularity of the productions, reservations are recommended one to two months in advance for plays at one of the three theaters, the Agnus Bowmer, the Black Swan, and the outdoor Elizabethan Stage. (Tickets $7.50-21; for more info, write the Oregon Shakespeare Festival, Ashland, OR 97520, or call 503-482-2111.) Half-price rush tickets are often available from March to May, an hour before every performance that is not sold out, but only a full day of waiting and a little luck will get you tickets on the day of the show from May to October. The backstage tours ($7, under 12 $3) are a wonderful way to find about theater from tour guides, usually actors or technicians.

When bored of the Bard, check out the Valley View Tasting Room, 52 E. Main St. (482-8964), where 14 different wines are uncorked for your sampling. (Open daily 10am-6pm.) Or take advantage of the variety of companies offering rafting trips, like the Adventure Center (488-2819), which also organizes fishing, rock climbing, and horseback riding trips. It also rents bikes, jet skis, and hot air balloons. (Day raft trips from $40. Open Mon.-Sat. 8am-8pm, Sun. 8am-6pm.)

The best place to rest thy bones is the Ashland Hostel (AYH), 150 N. Main St. (482-9217), with wonderful owners and laundry facilities. Early reservations are recommended. ($9, nonmembers $12. Midnight curfew.) The nearest campground is Jackson Hot Springs, 2253 Hwy. 99 N (482-3776), off exit 19 from I-5, with hot showers. (Sites $8, with hookup $9.) High-priced restaurants for the theater crowd abound, but so do cheap grocery stores. The North Light Vegetarian Restaurant, 36 S. Second St. (482-9463), is a crunchy bet, featuring bean burritos ($3.25) and an all-you-can-eat buffet ($6.50). (Open daily 8am-9pm.) Geppetto's, 345 E. Main St. (482-1138), is a local institution with a fantastic eggplant veggie burger on a sourdough bun ($3.75). Lunches $4-6. (Open daily 8am-midnight.) **Jazmin's,** 180 C St. (488-0883), rocks with live music Thurs.-Sat. at 9:30pm. (Cover from $1. Restaurant open daily 4-10pm. Bar open Thurs.-Sat. 4pm-2:30am.)**The Greyhound** station at 91 Oak St. (482-2516) offers buses to Portland (3 per day, $49) and San Francisco (4 per day, $51). Ashland's **post office** soliloquizes at 120 N. 1st St. (482-3986). The **ZIP code** is 97520. Ashland's **area code** is 503.

Crater Lake National Park and Klamath Falls

Mirror-blue Crater Lake, Oregon's only National Park, was regarded as sacred by Indian shamans, who forbade their people to view it. Iceless in winter and flawlessly circular, it plunges to a depth of 2,000 ft. from an elevation of over 6,000 ft., making it the nation's deepest lake and second only to South America's scandalously-named Lake Titicaca in hemispherical lacustrine depth.

The tiny **visitors center** (524-2211), on the lake shore at **Rim Village,** distributes books and maps on hiking and camping. (Open daily 8am-7pm.) The **Rim Drive,** open only in summer, runs a 33-mi. route high above the lake. Points along the drive offer views and trailheads for hiking. Among the most spectacular are **Discovery Point Trail** (from which the first pioneer saw the lake in 1853), **Watchman Lookout** (.8 mi. one-way), and **Garfield Peak Trail** (1.7 mi. one-way). The hike up **Scott Peak,** the park's highest (9000 ft.), begins from the drive near the lake's eastern edge. Although steep, the 7½-mi. trail to the top gives persevering hikers a unique overhead view of the lake. Also steep, **Cleetwood Trail,** a 1-mi. switchback, provides the only trail that leads down to the water's edge. From here a boat tours the lake (fare $10, under 13 $5.50; check with the lodge for times). Picnics and fishing are allowed, as is swimming, providing you can stand the frigid 50°F temperature. Park rangers lead free walking tours daily in the summer and periodically in winter (on snowshoes). (Call the visitors center at Rim Village for schedules.) If pressed for time, walk the easy 100 yd. from the visitors center down to the **Sinnott Memorial Overlook** for the area's best and most accessible view. Rangers give short lectures on the area's history at Rim Village.

Highway 62 through Crater Lake National Park circumnavigates the lake and then heads west to Medford or southeast to Klamath Falls. To get to the park from Portland, take I-5 to Eugene, then Rte. 58 east to U.S. 97 south. Klamath Falls lies 24 mi. south of the Hwy. 62/U.S. 97 intersection, and is on Hwys. 66, 39, and 140. Call ahead for road conditions during winter (594-2211). (Park admission charged only in summer. $5 per car, $3 for hikers and bikers. Seniors free.)

Eating inexpensively in the Crater Lake area is difficult. Buying food—for instance, at the **Old Fort Store** (381-2345; open daily 8am-8pm) in **Fort Klamath**—and cooking yourself is the best option. We mean, cook the *food* yourself, silly. The cafeteria-style **Llao Rock Café** in Rim Village grills cheese sandwiches for $2.50. (Open daily.) Upstairs, **The Watchman Eatery and Lounge** has burgers and potato salad ($4.50) to munch while looking at the Lake. (Open daily noon-10pm from June 10-Sept. 2.) In **Klamath Falls,** try **McPherson's Old Town Pizza,** 722 Main St., for some of the tastiest and cheapest food in the area. (Small pizzas from $2.55. Open daily 11am-11pm.)

The only hotel in the park is closed for major reservations, but inexpensive campsites dot U.S. 97 to the north, and Klamath Falls sports several affordable campsites. Those who wish to camp within the parks have only two options: the small **Lost Creek Campground,** with 16 sites for tents only (sites $5, open July-Sept.), and the **Mazama Campground,** with 200 sites. (Toilets, pay laundry and showers, and plenty of RVs but no hookups. Sites $10.) The Rim Village Visitor Center makes **backcountry camping** permits available. In Klamath Falls, try the **Fort Klamath Lodge Motel** (381-2234), on Hwy. 62, six mi. from the Park. The closest motel to the lake, it offers cozy rooms with knotted-pine walls, a friendly manager, and TV. (Singles

$28. Doubles $33.) The **Pony Pass Motel,** 75 Main St. (884-7735), features large rooms, nice views, and A/C. (Singles $25. Doubles $35.)

Oregon Coast

The "Pacific" hurls itself at the Oregon Coast with abandon, amidst impressive explosions of spray. Only the most daring swim in this ice-cold surf; others stay satisfied by the matchless views and huge stretches of unspoiled beach.

Possessively hugging the shore, **U.S. 101,** the renowned coastal highway, edges by a series of high-perched viewpoints. From northernmost Astoria to Brookings in the south, it laces together the resorts and historic fishing villages clustered around the mouths of rivers feeding into the Pacific. Still, it appears most beautiful between the coastal towns, where hundreds of miles of state and national park allow direct access to the beach. Whenever the highway leaves the coast, look for a beach loop road—these quieter ways afford some of the finest scenery on the western seaboard.

Drive or bike for the best encounter with the coast. Most traffic flows south. Portlanders, like spawning salmon, head down-road to vacation. Write the Oregon Dept. of Transportation, Salem 97310 or virtually any visitors center on the coast for the free *Oregon Coast Bike Route Map;* it provides invaluable info on campsites, hostels, bike repair facilities, temperatures, wind speed, etc. For those without a car or bike, transportation becomes a bit tricky.

Greyhound has only two coastal routes from Portland per day; one of those takes place under cover of the night. Local public transport hooks Tillamook to Astoria, but none links Tillamook and Lincoln City.

Gasoline and grocery prices en route to the coast cost about 20% more than in inland cities. Motorists may want to stock up and fill up before reaching the coastbound highways.

Reedsport and the Dunes

The dunes in the **Oregon Dunes Recreational Area** reach their most spectacular height (500 ft.—as high as a 50 story building) in the 40 mi. stretch between Florence and North Bend. The dunes were created by glaciation 15,000 years ago and reached their maximum pile-up 9,000 years later. Stony coastal winds maintain their shape. Hiking trails will take you through the dunes and around the surrounding lakes. In many places, all you can see is bare sand and sky, but the latest craze for both locals and tourists—the dune buggy—scars some of the dunes.

Campgrounds fill up early with pot-bellied dune buggy fanatics, especially on summer weekends. The local National Recreation Area (NRA) headquarters will give any visitor a report on just how many decibels a dune buggy engine can reach. (The answer: many many.) They will also provide trail maps and arguments for allowing all citizens to tote AK-47s. (855 US 101, south of Umpqua River Bridge 271-3611. Open Mon.-Fri. 8am-4:30pm, Sat.-Sun. 9am-5pm; Labor Day-Memorial Day Mon.-Fri. 8am-4:30pm.)

Sand Dunes Frontier, 83960 U.S. 101 S. (997-3544), 4 mi. south of Florence, gives 25-minute **dune buggy rides** ($6, under 11 $3, under 5 free). But if you really want to rock and roll around the dunes, shell out $30 for an hour ($15 each addit. hr.) on your own dune buggy; **Dunes Odyssey,** on U.S. 101 in Winchester Bay (271-4011), and **Spinreel Park,** Wildwood Dr., 8 mi. south on U.S. 101 (759-3313; open daily 8am-6pm), both offer rentals. The best access to the dunes is at **Eel Creek Campground,** 11 mi. south of Reedsport. Leave your car in the parking lot of the day-use area and hike a short and easy distance through scrubby pines and grasses until the dunes tower above you. Many travelers get lost wandering between the sandy rises. The ocean dips another 2 mi. to the west.

Inside **Umpqua Lighthouse State Park,** 6 mi. south of Reedsport, the Douglas County Park Department operates the **coastal visitor center** (440-4500), in the old

Coast Guard administration building. The center has small exhibits on the shipping and timber industries at the turn of the century. (Open May-Sept. Wed.-Sat. 10am-5pm, Sun. 1-5pm. Free.)

Restaurateurs of Winchester Bay (3 mi. south of Reedsport) pride themselves on all their seafood, but especially their salmon. The **Seven Seas Cafe**, Dock A, Winchester Bay, sails at the end of Broadway at 4th St. This small diner, crowded with marine memorabilia and navigational charts,s is the place for the local fishing crowd to gather and trade big fish stories. (Fish and chips $4, deep-fried prawns $6, coffee 40¢. Open Fri.-Tues. 8am-2pm.) The **Seafood Grotto and Restaurant**, 8th St. and Broadway, Winchester Bay, serves unexpectedly excellent seafood around a large Victorian doll house. Lunches go for $5-7, and a large salmon steak costs $10. (Open Sun.-Thurs. 8am-9pm.) **Sugar Shack Bakery and Restaurant**, 145 N. 3rd (Hwy 38), Reedsport (271-4848), offers indulgently sugary baked goods. Great chili "with trimmings," i.e. a biscuit and sliced orange cake, goes for $1.25. The worthwhile **Elk Viewing Area** is just 2 mi. up the road.

Whether you prefer motels or campsites, head to peaceful Winchester Bay. The **Harbor View Motel**, on Beach Blvd. (271-3352), across from the waterfront, may look a little shabby, but harbors fairly clean rooms with color TV and some kitchenettes. (Singles $23. Doubles $31. Mid-Sept. to April singles $18.50; doubles $23.) You may want to blow dough in the **Winchester Bay Motel**, at the end of Broadway (271-4871), at 4th St. past Dock A, after weeks of grungy camping. (Color TV, free coffee. Singles $34. Doubles $42. Labor Day-Memorial Day singles $25; doubles $30.) The rather small rooms in the **Fir Grove Motel**, 2178 Winchester Ave., Reedsport (271-4848), come with color TV, free coffee, and a pool. (Singles $34. Doubles $45. In winter singles $25; doubles $28.)

The National Forest Service's pamphlet *Campgrounds in the Siuslaw National Forest* covers campgrounds in the dunes. The sites closest to Reedsport lie in Winchester Bay. The campgrounds that allow dune-buggy access—South Jetty, Lagoon, Waxmyrtle, Driftwood II, Horsfall, and Bluebill—generally start loud and stay rowdy. The **Surfwood Campground**, ½ mi. north of Winchester Bay on U.S. 101 (271-4020), serves up all the luxuries of home—including a laundromat, heated pool, grocery store, sauna, tennis court, and hot showers. (Sites $9, full hookup $11.50. Call at least 1 week in advance in the summer.) The county's **Windy Cove Campground** (271-5634), adjacent to Salmon Harbor in Winchester Bay, has rather steep rates for tent camping. (Drinking water, hot showers, flush toilets, beach access. Sites $7.) Serenity for campers with a tent and a car can be found off Hwy 48, just North of Umpqua River Bridge, at Noel Ranch (8 mi.) or anywhere you drive along Smith River (free).

Reedsport's **post office** licks and affixes at 301 Fir St. (271-2521; open Mon.-Fri. 9am-5pm). The **ZIP code** is 97467. The **area code** is 503.

Portland

Portland has grown up out of the wilderness of America's western coastland like a quiet child in a chaotic household. Its modest "human scale" 200-ft. city blocks, humble building height restrictions, and noticeably large number of parks seem to acquiesce to the splendor of the surrounding wilderness. The mighty Columbia River rushes past to the north while the Willamette River cuts through the city's heart. Mt. Hood, and more distantly, Mt. St. Helens, which covered the city in volcanic ash in 1980, rise just beyond the city limits. But the humility of this gentle metropolis will win a visitor's heart. If you can decline the invitation of the Oregon countryside you will find that polite young Portland has much to offer.

Prize-winning urban efforts have made the city pleasantly navigable. The city and state have also nourished aesthetic efforts by securing a fund for public art through a 1% tax on new building construction. The result is a growing population of outdoor sculpture and an equally healthy number of animate artistic endeavors in the area of music and theater. Outdoor jazz concerts flourish around the city, and the oldest Symphony Orchestra in the U.S. has just cut its first CD. There are tons of improvisational theaters, and the recently constructed **Center for the Performing Arts** lures actors from the Shakespeare festival in Ashland. Along with a thriving arts community, even Portland's mayor has taken inspiration from the city—he sashayed into office shortly after he posed as a flasher revealing himself to a sidewalk sculpture for an "Expose Yourself to Art" poster.

Portland boasts such historic urban self-assurances as the first enclosed mall in the US (Lloyd Center, built in 1956) and the first office building with sealed windows and mechanical climate control (the Commonwealth Building). The city also recently unveiled the first post-modernist office building. On the smaller scale, in what some of the locals consider to be a more important effect of urban lifestyle, a number of micro-breweries now pump out vats of the nation's best ale.

Practical Information

Emergency: 911.

Portland/Oregon Visitors Association, 26 SW Salmon St. (275-9750), at Front St. Free *Portland Book* contains maps, general info, and historical trivia. Open Mon.-Fri. 8:30am-5pm, Sat. 9am-3pm. Detailed city road maps are free at **Hertz,** 1009 SW 6th (249-5727), at Salmon.

Portland International Airport: north of the city on the banks of the Columbia. Served by I-205. To get downtown, take Tri-Met bus #12, which will arrive on SW 5th Ave. (Fare 95¢). **Raz Tranz** (recorded info 246-4676) provides an airport shuttle ($6) that leaves every 30 min. and takes 35 min. to reach major downtown hotels and the Greyhound station.

Amtrak: 800 NW 6th Ave. (800-872-7245), at Hoyt St. To Seattle (3 per day, $28) and Eugene (1 per day, $24) Open daily 7:30am-9:45pm.

Buses: Greyhound/Trailways, 550 NW 6th St. (243-2323). Buses almost every hr. to Seattle ($26 one way; 243-2313 for schedule) and to Eugene ($15 one way; 222-3361 for schedule). Ticket window open daily 5:30-12:30am. **Green Tortoise,** 205 SE Grand Ave. (225-0310), at Ash St. To Seattle (Tues., Thurs., Sat., Sun. at 4pm, $15) and San Francisco (Sun., Tues., Thurs., Fri. at noon, $49).

Public Transport: Tri-Met, Customer Service Center, #1 Pioneer Courthouse Sq., 701 SW 6th Ave. (233-3511). Open Mon.-Fri. 9am-5pm. Seven regional service routes, each with its own color totem. Buses with black and white totems cross color-coded boundaries, and crux at the downtown **mall,** which boasts covered bus stops and information centers. Fare 95¢-$1.20. All rides free within *fareless square,* bounded by the Willamette River, NW Hoyt St., and I-405. Service generally 7am-midnight, reduced Sat.-Sun. Tri-Met's splendiferous light rail system **MAX** only serves one line (running between downtown and the city of Gresham), but uses the same fare system as the buses.

Taxi: Broadway Cab, 227-1234. **New Rose City Cab Co.,** 282-7707. Both charge $2 for the first mi., $1.50 each addit. mi. From Airport $21-24.

Car Rental: Rent-A-Wreck, 2838 NE Sandy St. (231-1640). $14 per day. 50 free mi., 15¢ each additional mi. Must be 25. **Practical Rent-a-Car,** 1315 NE Sandy (224-8110). $22 per day, 100 free mi., 15 ¢ each additional mi.

Help Lines: Crisis Line, 223-6161. Open 24 hrs. **Senior Citizens Crisis Line,** 223-6161. **Gay and Lesbian Services,** 223-8299. **Women's Crisis Line,** 235-5333.

Time Zone: Pacific (3 hrs. behind Eastern).

Post Office: 715 NW Hoyt St. (294-2300). Open Mon.-Fri. 7:30am-6:30pm, Sat. 8:30am-5pm. **ZIP code:** 97208.

Area Code: 503.

Portland sits just south of the Columbia River about 75 mi. inland from the Oregon coast. The city blazes 637 mi. north of San Francisco and 172 mi. south of Seattle. The primary east-west highway, I-84 (U.S. 30), follows the route of the Oregon Trail through the gorgeous Columbia River Gorge. West of Portland, U.S. 30 follows the Columbia downstream to Astoria. I-405 curves around the west side of the business district to link I-5 with U.S. 30.

Portland can be divided into five districts. **Burnside Street** divides the city into north and south, while east and west are separated by the Willamette River. **Williams Avenue** slices off a corner of the northeast sector, simply called "North." The **Southwest district** is the city's hub, encompassing the downtown area, historical Old Town in the northern end, and a slice of the ritzy West Hills. The very core of the hub lies at the downtown mall area between SW 5th and 6th Ave. Car traffic is prohibited here; don't mess with the transit system's turf. The **Northwest district** contains the southern end of Old Town, an industrial area to the north, and a residential area, culminating in the posh Northwestern hills area to the west. Most students enrolled in Portland's several colleges and universities live in the Northwest. The **Southeast district** keeps a somewhat less well-to-do residential neighborhood, but its main drag, **Hawthorne Blvd.**, is lined with the city's best ethnic restaurants, cafés, and funky theaters. Anomalous amidst its surroundings, **Laurelhurst Park** is a collection of posh houses around E. Burnside St. and SE 39th St. The **North** and **Northeast** districts are chiefly residential, punctuated by a few quiet, small parks.

Accommodations and Camping

With Portland's increasing gentrification, finding cheap lodgings has become more challenging. **Northwest Bed and Breakfast,** 610 SW Broadway, Portland 97205 (243-7616), extensively lists member homes in the Portland area and throughout the Northwest. You must become a member ($30 per year) to use their lists and reservation services. They promise singles from $40-60 and doubles from $40-120.

The remaining cheap downtown hotels are generally unsafe; the hostel undoubtedly provides the best option. Barbur Ave. hosts a comely and accessible strip of motels.

Portland International Hostel (AYH), 3031 SE Hawthorne Blvd. (236-3380), at 31st Ave. Take bus #5. Cheerful, clean, and crowded. Sleep inside or on the porch. Kitchen; laundromat across the street. Open daily 7:30-10am, 5-11pm, Fri.-Sat. until midnight. "Travel Center" open Tues.-Sat. noon-5pm. $10, non-members $13. Reserve in summer.

Hotel Hamilton, Youth Hostel Portland International, 1024 SW 3rd. St. (241-2513). Smack in the center of town. Laundromat. Open 24 hrs. AYH members $8.75, non-members $13-20 (although not an AYH hostel).

YWCA, 1111 SW 10th St. (223-6281). Women only. Close to major sights and clean. Small rooms. Shared double $26. Singles $28, with bath $30.

Bel D'air Motel, 8355 N. Interstate Ave. (289-4800), just off I-5. Take bus #5 from SW 6th Ave. Pretentious in name but not in decor. Very small; call 1 week in advance. Singles $28. Doubles $33.

Aladdin Motor Inn, 8905 SW 30th (246-8241), at Barbur Blvd. about 10 min. from downtown by bus #12 from SW 5th Ave. Clean, comfortable. A/C, kitchens available ($45). Singles $35. Doubles $37.

Mel's Motor Inn, 5205 N. Interstate Ave. (285-2556). Take bus #5 from 6th Ave. No aspirations to elegance, but kean and klomfortable with kable TV, A/C. No comedic diner attached. Singles $33. Doubles $40.

Ainsworth State Park, 37 mi. east of Portland on I-84, along the Columbia River Gorge. Hot showers, flush toilets, hiking trails. Sites $9, with electricity $10, with full hookup $12.

Milo Molver State Park, 25 mi. southwest of Portland, off Oregon Rte. 211, 5 mi. west of the town of Estacada. Fish, boat, and bicycle along the nearby Clackamas River. Hot showers, flush toilets. Sites $9, with electricity $10, with full hookup $12.

Food

Although Portland's restaurants reflect the health-conscious attitude of the people, juicy carnivorous meals are as plentiful (and more rewarding) as broccoli tofu bacchanals.

Western Culinary Institute Chef's Corner, 1235 SW Jefferson. (242-2433) The testing ground for the cooking school's great adventures. Artichoke creations for lunch under $6. Gourmet Hashbrowns at **Breakfast Café (open 7am-3pm). Restaurant open Mon.-Fri. 7am-6pm.**

Hamburger Mary's, 840 SW Park St. at Taylor. Good food near the museums and theaters, with a relaxed atmosphere and eclectic decor: floor lamps hang upside down from the ceiling. Mixed straight and gay clientele. Burgers with everything and fries $5. Excellent vegetarian fare. Open daily 7am-midnight.

Maya's Tacqueria, 1000 SW Morrison St. at 10th. Genuinely Mexican, complete with wall-sized murals of Mayans doing Mayan things. Mongo Mayan burrito $4.50-5.50. Open Mon.-Sat. 10:30am-10pm, Sun. noon-8pm.

Saigon Express, 309 W. Burnside St. Exquisite Vietnamese food; not at all the cheesy place the name may suggest. Entrees $5-8, unusual combinations (such as shrimp and sugarcane) add that extra *je ne sais quoi.* Open Mon.-Sat. 11am-9pm.

Thanh Thao, 4005 SE Hawthorne (238-6232). Another recent Vietnamese restaurant with rave reviews from the locals. Servings are plentiful. $4-8. Open Mon.-Fri. 11am-2:30pm.

The Original Pancake House, 8600 SW Barbur Blvd. Take green bus #12, 41, or 43. Great place for breakfast ($3.50-5). Hour-long lines on Sat. and Sun. morning. Open Wed.-Sun. 7am-3pm.

Escape from New York Pizza, 913 SW Alder St. Also at 622 NW 23rd St. The best pizza in town; look for the daily message on the menuboard. Hefty cheese slices $1. Large cheese pie $8. Open Mon.-Thurs. 11:30am-9pm, Fri.-Sat. 11:30am-10pm.

Chang's Mongolian Grill, 1 SW 3rd St. at Burnside. Also at 2700 NW 185th and 1600 NE 122nd. All-you-can-eat lunches ($6) and dinners ($9). Select your meal from a buffet (fresh vegetables, meats, and fish), mix your own sauce to taste, and then watch your chef make a wild show of cooking it on a grill the size of a Volkswagen. Rice and hot-and-sour soup included. Open daily 11:30am-2:30pm and 5-10pm.

Foothill Broiler, 33 NW 23rd Pl., in the Uptown Shopping Center (223-0287). Take bus #20 up Burnside. Fantastic food served by enterprising survivors of the 60s. Tasteful art on the walls supplemented by the dangling greenery. Best burgers in the Northwest from $3. Come off-hours or prepare to wait. Open Mon.-Fri. 7:30am-7pm, Sat. 7:30am-4pm.

Macheesmo Mouse, 715 SW Salmon St. Also at 811 NW 23rd St. and 3553 SE Hawthorne Blvd. (5 blocks from the AYH hostel). Fast, authentic Mexican food for the health-conscious. Part Hard Rock Café, part Pompidou Center. The $3 veggie burrito stands out. Open Mon.-Sat. 11am-10pm, Sun. noon-9pm.

Sights

Since some of the best things to do in Portland frolic outside, visit Portland in late spring and early summer when the city blooms after the wet winter weather. This also proves the best season in which to appreciate Portland's fountains, all of which seem to have long, intricate histories; the best include the 20 bronze drinking fountains located on street corners throughout Portland, donated by Simon Benson, a wealthy Prohibition-era Portlander, ostensibly to ease the thirst of loggers. Other objets d'art dot the downtown area, the products of a city law requiring that one percent of the costs of all construction and renovation work be devoted to public art projects.

Almost all the major sights are grouped **downtown** in the southwest district. Portland's downtown area centers on the **mall,** running north-south between 5th and 6th Ave. and closed to all traffic except city buses. **Pioneer Courthouse,** the elder of downtown landmarks, stands at 5th Ave. and Morrison St. The monument now houses the U.S. Ninth Circuit Court of Appeals, overlooking **Pioneer Courthouse Square,** 701 SW 6th Ave. (223-1613), opened in 1983. Forty-eight thousand citizens supported its construction by purchasing personalized bricks; it seems as though all 48,000 make a daily pilgrimage to their gift to the city. Live jazz, folk, and ethnic music draws the rest of Portland to the square for the **Peanut Butter and Jam Sessions,** held Tuesdays and Thursdays from noon to 1pm.

Michael Graves' postmodern **Portland Building,** the most controversial building in the downtown area, struts its stuff on the mall. This amazing confection of pastel tile and concrete has received star-reaching praise, condemnation as an overgrown jukebox, and even once had a full-sized inflatable King Kong placed on its roof. Make sure to visit the interior as well, which looks like something out of *Blade Runner*.

West of the mall extend the **South Park Blocks,** a series of shady, rose-laden enclosures running down the middle of Park Ave. A number of museums open onto the parks, including the **Portland Art Museum,** 1219 SW Park Ave. (226-2811), at Jefferson St. Dote on the museum's especially fine exhibit of Pacific Northwest Native American art, including masks, textiles, and sacred objects, or the interspersed international exhibits and local artists' works. (Open Tues.-Sat. 11am-5pm, Sun. noon-4pm. Admission $3.50, seniors and students $1.50, under 12 50¢. Seniors free Thurs.) The **Northwest Film and Video Center** (221-1156), in the same building, screens classics and off-beat flicks.

A century ago, rowdy sailors fresh off their ocean-going trawlers rocked around **Old Town,** to the north of the mall. Now, large-scale refurbished store fronts, new "old" brick, and a bevy of recently-owned shops and restaurants cater to the uppercrust. A popular people-watching vantage point, the **Skidmore Fountain,** at SW 1st Ave. and SW Ankeny St., marks the entrance to the quarter. Had the city accepted resident draftsman Henry Weinhard's offer to run draft beer through the fountain, it would have been a truly cordial watering hole indeed. Old Town marks the start of **Tom McCall Waterfront Park,** an enormous expanse of grass and flowers that offers little shade but provides great views of the Willamette River.

From March until Christmas, the area under the Burnside Bridge turns into the **Saturday Market** (222-6072), 108 W. Burnside St. On Saturdays from 10am to 5pm and Sundays from 11am to 4:30pm, the area is clogged with street musicians, artists, craftspeople, chefs, and produce sellers.

Portland's finest galleries shack up downtown. The **Image Gallery,** 1026 SW Morrison St. (224-9629), presents an international potpourri of Canadian Inuit sculpture and Mexican and Japanese folk art. (Open Mon.-Fri. 10:30am-6pm, Sat. 11am-5pm.) On the first Thursday of every month all the galleries stay open till 9pm and fill with local enthusiasts.

Less than 2 mi. west of downtown, in the mowed **West Hills,** looping trails for day hiking, running, and picnic-laden expeditions crisscross **Washington Park.** The **Hoyt Arboretum InfoCenter,** 4000 SW Fairview Blvd. (228-8732), at the crest of the hill above the other gardens, hands out trail maps to the arboretum, which features transplendent conifers and "200 acres of trails." (Free nature walks April-Oct. Sat.-Sun. at 2pm, and June-Aug. Tues. at 9:30am.) The five-acre **Japanese Garden** (223-1321) holds a formal arrangement of idyllic ponds and bridges. Cherry blossoms ornament the park in summer, thanks to sibling city Sapporo, Japan. (Open daily 10am-6pm; mid-Sept. to mid-April daily 10am-4pm. Admission $3.50, seniors and students with ID $2.) Roses galore and spectacular views of the city await a few steps away at the **International Rose Test Garden,** 400 SW Kingston St. (248-4302).

Next to the Hoyt Arboretum stands Portland's favorite tourist-attracting triad: the **Washington Park Zoo,** 4001 SW Canyon Rd. (226-1561 for a person; 226-7627 for a tape; open daily 9:30am-7pm, gates close at 6pm; call for winter hours; admission $3.50, seniors and kids $2, Tues. after 3pm free); the **World Forestry Center,** 4033 SW Canyon Rd. (228-1367; open daily 9am-5pm; admission $3, seniors and kids $2); and the **Oregon Museum of Science and Industry,** (better known as **OMSI**), 4015 SW Canyon Rd. (228-6674; open Sat.-Thurs. 9am-7pm, Fri. 9am-8pm; admission $5.25, seniors and under 17 $3.50). "Zoo Bus" #63 connects many points in the park with the downtown mall. A miniature choo-choo connects the Washington Park Rose Gardens to the zoo (fare $1.75). Beginning in late June, the zoo sponsors **Your Zoo and All That Jazz,** a nine-week series of open-air jazz concerts (Wed. 6:30-8:30pm), free with regular zoo admission. Bring a picnic dinner. **Zoograss Concerts** features a 10-week series of bluegrass concerts (Thurs. 6:30-8:30pm). The World Forestry Center specializes in exhibits of Northwestern forestry and logging. OMSI will occupy children and adults with do-it-yourself science, computer, and medical exhibits. Within OMSI, the **Kendall Planetarium** (228-7827) gives daily astronomy shows (50¢) and rocks in the evening to "laser fantasy" performances (schedule of shows 242-0723; admission $4.50). The new **Vietnam Memorial** rests a few steps up the hill. From Washington Park, you have easy access to sprawling **Forest Park,** jampacked with hiking trails and picnic areas affording spectacular views of Portland.

The funky clientele in the cafés, theaters, and restaurants on Hawthorne are artists and students from the politically correct melting pot at **Reed College,** SE 28th and Woodstock, a small liberal arts school founded in 1909. Reed sponsors numerous cultural events and in 1968 became the first undergraduate college to open a nuclear reactor. Tours of the campus leave Eliot Hall twice per day during the school year. (Call 771-7511 for hours.)

Farther southeast sleeps **Mt. Tabor Park,** one of two city parks in the world on the site of an extinct volcano. More of a molehill than a mountain, the park serves as the Southeast's lone hill. Take bus #15 from downtown, or drive down Hawthorne to SE 60th Ave.

Entertainment

Portland no longer swims as the hard-drinking, carousing port town of yore; ships still unload sea-weary sailors daily, but their favorite waterfront pubs have evolved into upscale bistros and slambanging nightclubs. Current listings abound in the Friday edition of the *Oregonian* and a number of free handouts: *Willamette Week,* the *Main Event, Clinton St. Quarterly,* and the *Downtowner.* The first of these caters to students, the last to the yuppwardly mobile. Find each in restaurants downtown and in boxes on street corners.

The **Oregon Symphony Orchestra** (228-1353) plays in the Arlene Schnitzer Concert Hall, on the corner of SW Broadway and SW Main St. (Tickets $10-28. "Symphony Sunday" afternoon concerts $5-8. Performances Sept.-April.) **Chamber Music Northwest** performs summer concerts at Reed College Commons, 3203 SE Woodstock Ave. (223-3202). (Classical music Mon., Thurs., and Sat. at 8pm. Admission $13, under 15 $9.)

Portland's many fine theaters produce everything from off-Broadway shows to experimental drama. At **Portland Civic Theatre,** 1530 SW Yamhill St. (226-3048), the mainstage often presents musical comedy, while the smaller theater-in-the-round puts on less traditional shows. (Tickets $6.50 and $9.50.) **Oregon Shakespeare Festival/Portland,** at the Intermediate Theatre of PCPA, corner of SW Broadway and SW Main St. (248-6309), has a five-play season running from November to February. **New Rose Theatre,** 904 SW Main St. in the Park Blocks (222-2487), offers an even mix of classical and contemporary shows. (Tickets $9-14.)

The best clubs in Portland are the hardest to find: neighborhood taverns and pubs often sneak away on backroads. Those with happy feet should bop down the length of 6th Ave. The under-21 crowd heads to the **Confetti Club,** 126 SW 2nd St. (274-0627), for new wave music, or the **Warehouse,** 320 SE 2nd St. (232-9645), for Top-40 tunes. **Produce Row Cafe,** 204 SE Oak St. (232-8355), has 21 beers on tap ($1), 72 bottled domestic and imported beers, and a lovely outdoor beer garden. (Open Mon.-Fri. 11am-1am, Sat. noon-1am, Sun. 2pm-midnight.) The **Mission Theater and Pub,** 1624 NW Glisan St. (223-4031), serves excellent home-brewed ales as well as delicious and unusual sandwiches. Relax in the balcony of this old moviehouse with a pitcher of Ruby, a fragrant raspberry ale ($1.25 glass, $6.50 pitcher). (Open daily 5pm-1am.) **Key Largo,** 31 NW 1st Ave. (223-9919), has an airy, tropical atmosphere. Dance to rock, R&B, or jazz on the patio. (Cover $2-8. Open Mon.-Fri. 11am-2:30am, Sat.-Sun. noon-2:30am.) The mostly gay clientele at **Embers,** 110 NW Broadway (222-3082), dances until 4am. The **Bridgeport Brew Pub,** 1313 NW Marshall (241-7179), packs 'em in with a much-acclaimed home-brew and great pizza.

PENNSYLVANIA

Driven by British persecution of his fellow Quakers, William Penn, Jr. petitioned the British Crown for a tract of North American land in 1680. Arriving in 1682, he attracted all types of settlers by making his colony a bastion of religious tolerance. Propagandistically named "Penn's Gardens," Pennsylvania seemed destined to become the most prominent state in the new nation. The emerging colonies signed the *Declaration of Independence* in Philadelphia, the country's original capital and site of the First Continental Congress. However, other cities soon overshadowed it—New York City rapidly grew into the nation's most important commercial center, while Washington, DC, usurped the role of nation's capital.

But Pennsylvania, a state accustomed to revolution, rallied in the face of adversity. In 1976, Philadelphia groomed its historic shrines for its bicentennial celebration, and the tourist trade continues to boom. Even Pittsburgh, a city once dirty enough to fool streetlamps into burning during the day, has initiated a cultural renaissance. Between the two cities, Pennsylvania's landscape, from the farms of Lancaster County to the deep river gorges of the Allegheny Plateau, retains some of the sylvanism that drew Penn here 300 years ago.

Practical Information

Capital: Harrisburg.

Bureau of Travel Development, 453 Forum Bldg., Harrisburg 17120 (717-787-5453 or 800-237-4363). Information on hotels, restaurants, and sights. **Bureau of State Parks,** P.O. Box 1467, Harrisburg 17120 (800-631-7105). The detailed *Recreational Guide* is available at no charge from all visitor information centers.

Time Zone: Eastern. **Postal Abbreviation:** PA

Allegheny National Forest

Containing half a million acres of woodland stretching 40 mi. south of the New York state border, The Allegheny National Forest offers year-round recreational opportunities such as hunting, fishing, and trail-biking. The forest makes an excellent detour on a cross-state jaunt on I-80; its southern border is only 20 mi. from the interstate. A good first step is the **Kinzua Point Information Center** (726-1291), on Rte. 59. Friendly park employees have info on camping and recreation throughout the park. (Open May 27-Sept. 2 Sun.-Thurs. 9:30am-5:30pm, Fri.-Sat. 9:30am-8pm.) The forest divides into four quadrants, each with its own ranger station that provides maps and information about activities and facilities within its region. SW: Marienville Ranger District (927-6628; open Mon.-Sat. 7am-5pm). NW: Sheffield Ranger District (968-3232; open Mon.-Fri. 8am-4pm). NE: Bradford Ranger District (362-4613; open daily 8am-4:30pm). SE: Ridgway Ranger District (776-6172; open Mon.-Fri. 7:30am-4pm). Swimming and beach passes for the park are available at the ranger stations ($2 per car). There is no charge for picnic sites or boat launches.

Camping facilities in the park are abundant and generally open from March to October. A "host" is available at most sights to assist campers and answer questions. (Sites $5-12, depending on the location and the time of year.) **Tracy Ridge** in the Bradford district and **Heart's Content** in the Sheffield district are particularly pretty. You can call 800-283-2267 to reserve sites, but the park keeps 50% of them on a first come, first served basis. You don't need a site to camp in the Allegheny; stay 1500 ft. from a major road or body of water and you can pitch a tent anywhere. **Kinzua Boat Rentals and Marina** on Rte. 59 (726-1650) rents canoes ($15 per hr., $18 per day), rowboats ($8.50 per hr., $20 per day), and motorboats ($12 per hr., $50 per day). Ask the rangers about sites accessible only by water.

From whatever direction you approach the Allegheny Forest, you'll encounter a small, rustic community near the park that offers groceries and accommodations. **Ridgway,** 25 mi. from I-80 (exit 16) at the southeastern corner, is especially scenic. **The Original,** 161 Main St., complete with jukebox, has great "baked" subs for $2.50-3 and burgers with fries for $2. (Open Mon.-Thurs. 11am-11pm, Fri.-Sat. 11am-midnight.) You can eat in an old train depot, now **Crispy's Fried Chicken,** at the intersection of Main St. and Montmorenci Rd. Two eggs with homefries and toast cost $1.50. (Open daily 7am-9pm.) The town of **Warren,** at the northeastern fringe of the forest where Rtes. 6 and 62 meet, has comparable services.

Greyhound Trailways serves Warren and Ridgway from Pittsburgh (about $28) as well as also from Philadelphia and Buffalo, NY. **Hitchhikers** should try to catch a ride to the forest at the bus station. Fortunately, U.S. 219 is a busy country road abuzz with truck traffic. When driving inside the forest yourself, be very careful during wet weather: about half the region is served only by dirt roads. The **area code** for this region is 814.

Gettysburg

In November 1863, four months after 7000 men died in the Civil War's bloodiest battle, President Abraham Lincoln arrived in Gettysburg to dedicate a national cemetery—in a two-minute speech, rumored to have been written on the back of an envelope, Lincoln urged preservation of the union in one of the greatest orations in U.S. history. Lincoln's *Gettysburg Address* and the sheer enormity of the battle which prompted him to write it have established Gettysburg as the most famous battlefield in U.S. history. Each year thousands of visitors heed Honest Abe's call to "resolve that these dead shall not have died in vain" and visit these Pennsylvania fields.

Before attacking Gettysburg's swarms of Civil War memorabilia (including chess sets), get your bearings at the **National Park Visitors Information Center,** 1 mi. south of town on Washington St. (Bus #15; 334-1124; open daily 8am-6pm, Labor Day-Memorial Day 8am-5pm.) Let the free map guide your tour by car or bike, or pay a park guide to show you the sights ($17 for a 2-hr. tour). On foot, forget about seeing the battlefield and concentrate on the worthwhile attractions around the park.

The exact spot of Lincoln's speech remains something of a mystery (he spoke somewhere in the national cemetery across from the visitors center), but the document itself is on display in the **Cyclorama Center** next to the visitors center. (Open daily 9am-5pm.) For an excellent perspective of the area, walk over to the **National Tower** (334-6754), whose high-speed elevators whisk you up 300 ft. for a spectacular view. (Open daily 9am-7:30pm. Admission $3.75, seniors $3.25, kids $1.75.)

The **Gettysburg Tour Center,** 778 Baltimore St. (334-6296), is a great place to get informative pamphlets on the **Wax Museum, Hall of Presidents, Soldiers Museum,** and all of the other sights that cluster together near the National Cemetery on Baltimore St. (Open daily 9am-5pm.)

Gettysburg's eateries are classy and affordable. The **Dutch Cupboard,** 523 Baltimore, serves up Pennsylvania Dutch specialties like *schnitz un knepp* (dried apples cooked with dumplings, $6.25) and the famous shoo fly pie (brown sugar, flour, special spices, and 2 kinds of molasses; $1.25). (Open daily 11am-9pm.) The candle-lit **Springhouse Tavern,** 89 Steinwehr Ave. (334-2100), lies in the basement of the Dobben House, Gettysburg's first building (1776), and an Underground Railroad shelter for runaway African slaves in the Civil War. Try a grilled burger special with bacon and peppers ($5.75) or the "ordinary" (soup, salad, homemade bread and wine, $5.25).

The best place to sleep in Gettysburg remains the roomy and cheerful **Gettysburg International Hostel (AYH),** 27 Chambersburg St. (334-1020), on U.S. 30 just west of Lincoln Sq. in the center of town. (Kitchen, stereo, living room. Open 5-11pm. Check-out 9:30am. $8, nonmembers $11. Sleepsacks required.) The remarkably friendly hostel usually has space, but when you're lusting for a motel, the **Gettysburg Travel Council**, 35 Carlisle St., Lincoln Sq. (334-6274), stocks a full line of brochures—as well as maps and information on local attractions. The **Holland Tourist Court**, 2700 York Rd. (334-4380), 5 mi. east of town on U.S. 30, lets six spacious singles and doubles from $30. There are several **campgrounds** in the area. Just 1 mi. south on Rte. 134 is **Artillery Ridge**, 610 Tarrytown Rd. (334-1288), which also runs a riding stable. (Sites $12.50 for 2 people, with hookup $15. Each additional person $2.) **Moyers Mountain Retreat**, in the delta of U.S. 15 and 30, has a heated outdoor pool and paths that connect to the **Appalachian Trail** (800-955-0208; sites $12 for 2 people, extra person $2, metered charge for electricity). Take 15 north to 94 north; the retreat is on the right.

Gettysburg orates in south-central Pennsylvania, off U.S. 15 about 30 mi. south of Harrisburg. Unfortunately, when the Union and Confederacy decided to lock horns here, they didn't have the traveler's convenience in mind. **Greyhound** (232-4251) has no station in town—they run one bus daily from Harrisburg ($17) that stops in front of the visitors center.

The **post office** is at 155 Buford Ave. (337-3781; open Mon.-Fri. 8:30am-4:30pm, Sat. 8:30am-12:30pm). Gettysburg's **ZIP code** is 17325; the **area code** is 717.

Lancaster County

When persecuted flocks of German Anabaptists fled to William Penn's bastion of religious freedom, locals quickly and wrongly labeled them the Pennsylvania Dutch. The name stuck, a misunderstanding of the word *Deutschland* for "Germany." Since the late 1700s, three distinct families of Anabaptists have lived in Lancaster County: **Brethren, Mennonite,** and **Amish.** The latter, and the Old Order Amish in particular, are famed for their lifestyle. Emphatically rejecting modern technology and fashion, they worship and educate their children at home and discourage association with outsiders. Quite ironically, the modest Lancaster Amish community of 15,000 draws many times that many visitors each year, eager for a glimpse of the secluded country lifestyle of horse-drawn carriages, home-style dining, and old-fashioned dress. In contrast to the Amish, some of the Mennonites embrace modern conveniences like cars and electricity. Many sell their farm goods at roadside stands or operate bed and breakfasts and craft shops. Lancaster County today has evolved into a strange mix of time-capsule austerity and modern consumerism.

Lancaster County—even the concentrated spot of interest to tourists—covers a huge area. Cars are the vehicle of choice for most visitors. With wheels of any sort, you can pay a guide to hop in and show you around. **Alverta Moore** (626-2421) charges about $5 per hour. At the **Mennonite Information Center**, 2209 Millstream Rd. (299-0954; open Mon.-Sat. 8am-5pm), just off Rte. 30, you can hire a guide for $7.50 per hour (2-hr. minimum; available Mon.-Sat. 9:30am-9:30pm; Nov.-March 9:30am-4:30pm). **New Horizons**, 3495 Horizon Dr. (285-7607), will meet you at the train or bus station with a bike and pick it up there later, if you call ahead. (Bikes $15 per day. Free maps.) The Amish shun cars and for many, especially the young, bikes are the primary means of transport.

To see this country best, pick up maps at Lancaster City or Pennsylvania Dutch visitors bureaus (see below), veer off U.S. 30, and explore the winding roads. A good place to start, though, is the **People's Place,** on Main St./Rte. 340 (768-7171), in Intercourse 11 mi. east of Lancaster City. The film *Who Are the Amish* shows every half hour from 9:30am to 5pm, and **Amish World** has charming hands-on exhibits on Amish and Mennonite life, from barn-raising to hat-styles. (Admission to one $2.50, kids $1.50. To both $4.25, kids $2.25.) The People's Place spans an entire block filled with bookstores, craft shops, and an art gallery. (Open Mon.-Sat. 9:30am-9:30pm; Nov.-March 9:30am-4:30pm.) If you have specific questions, seek out friendly locals at the Mennonite Information Center (see above), which also shows a free film *A Morning Song* every half hour.

A quiet metropolis in the heart of Dutch country, county seat **Lancaster City** reflects the area's character well—clean, red-brick row houses gather around the historic Penn Square in the city center. At the **Lancaster Chamber of Commerce and Industry,** 100 Queen St. (397-3531), you can pick up guided walking tours of Lancaster City (April-Oct. Sun.-Fri. at 10am and 1:30pm, Sat. at 10am, 11am, 1:30pm; $3, seniors $2.50, students $1.50) or buy a worthwhile self-guided booklet ($1.50). To reserve a tour off-season call 653-8225 or 394-2339. The center has its own rather avoidable film about Lancaster and a full line of brochures. (Open April-Oct. Mon.-Fri. 8:30am-5pm, Sat. 9am-4pm, Sun. 10am-3pm.; open 1 hr. later off-season.) Pick up a free **Map of Amish Farmlands** at any tourist spot in Lancaster County, or write to 340-23 Club, P.O. Box 239, Intercourse 17534.

The Amish don't take in visitors for meals, but if you ask around you may well find a Mennonite family that will share a meal and conversation. Ask the managers of your hotel or hostel if they know of some. A donation of $10-15 and a day's notice are usually required.

Just about everyone passing through Lancaster County expects a taste of real Dutch cuisine—and a flock of high priced "family-style" restaurants have sprouted up to please them. If you have the cash (all-you-can-eat meals $12-16) try any of the huge restaurants such as **The Amish Barn** (768-8886) spread thick on U.S. 340 in Bird-in-Hand. Better still, drive farther from the city for smaller and more afford-able *snitz, knepp,* and shoo fly pie. **Terre Hill Family Restaurant,** 213 E. Main St. (445-9233) in Terre Hill off Rte. 897 about 20 mi. south of Lancaster City, serves scrapple with vegetables and salad bar for $5.50. More varied fare can be found in Lancaster City. Don't miss the **Central Market,** in the northwest corner of Penn Sq., a huge food bazaar since 1899 with inexpensive meats, cheeses, vegetables, and sandwiches. (Open Tues. and Fri.-Sat. 5:30am-1:30pm.) Next door, **Habibi's,** 7 W. King St. (397-0152) fries a mean felafel for $3.50—ask for the special spices. (Open Mon. and Wed.-Thurs. 9:30am-5pm, Tues. and Fri.-Sat. 8am-5pm.)

Hundreds of hotels, B&Bs, and campgrounds cluster in this area. Don't search for accommodations without stopping by the **Pennsylvania Dutch Visitors Bureau Information Center,** 501 Greenfield Rd. (299-8901), on the east side of Lancaster City just off Rte. 30. The bureau has walls of brochures and free phone lines to most area inns and campsites. Save $2 and avoid their film. (Open mid-May to early Sept. Sun.-Thurs. 8am-6pm, Fri.-Sat. 8am-7pm.) Three youth hostels on the coun-ty's eastern edge have cheap beds (check-out 9:30am; curfew 11pm; $7, nonmem-bers $10). Try the **Bowmansville Youth Hostel (AYH),** P.O. Box 157, Bowmansville 17507, on Rte. 625 at Maple Grove Rd. (215-445-4831). Close to, though not easily accessible from, I-76, this hostel is the most convenient of the three. The owners are extraordinarily friendly and helpful and the facilities are excellent, complete with kitchen and lounge. Take bus #12 to New Holland (last bus at 5:20pm) and walk or hitch the remaining 6 mi. The owners will also pick you up at Youer's Mar-ket (a #12 bus stop) if you call ahead. By car take Rte. 23 to Rte. 625 north. The **Marsh Creek State Park Hostel (AYH),** P.O. Box 376, E. Reeds Rd., Lyndel 19354 (215-458-5881), in Marsh Creek State Park, proves a challenge to find, but the well-kept house lies on a gorgeous lake. Amtrak stops in Downington, 5 mi. away, on its Philadelphia-Lancaster route. Call ahead and the owners will pick you up for $5. (Beds $8). **Downington Cab** (269-3000) charges about $12. Fifteen mi. east, the **Geigertown Youth Hostel (AYH),** P.O. Box 49, Geigertown 19523 (215-286-9537; open March 2-Nov. 30), lies near French Creek State Park off Rte. 82. Though the area is beautiful, the hostel's remote location may not merit the trip. Transportation from Reading, 15 mi. away, might be arranged if you call ahead.

There seem to be as many campgrounds as cows in this lush countryside. The closest year-round facility is **Old Millstream Camping Manor,** 2249 U.S. 30 E. (Lin-coln Hwy.) (299-2314), 4 mi. east of Lancaster City. (Office open daily 8am-9pm. Sites $14, with hookup $17.) **Roamers Retreat,** 5005 Lincoln Hwy. (442-4287 or 800-525-5605), off U.S. 30 7½ mi. east of Rte. 896, opens only from mid-April to mid-Oct. (For reservations, call or write RD #1, P.O. Box 41B, Kinzers 17535. Sites $14.50, with hookup $17.) **Shady Grove,** P.O. Box 28, Adamstown 19501 (215-

484-4225), on Rte. 272 at Rte. 897, 264 W. Swartzville Rd., has 80 sites with electricity ($15).

Greyhound/Trailways, 22 W. Clay St. (397-4861; open daily 7am-5:15pm) runs four buses per day between Lancaster City and Philadelphia (2 hr., $9). **Amtrak,** 53 McGovern Ave. (291-5080; reservations 24 hrs.) makes the same trip (7 per day, 1 hr., $10.50). Lancaster City has its own bus system, **Red Rose Transit,** 45 Erick Rd. (397-4246), serving the city and the immediate countryside. Pick up route maps at the office. (Base fare 75¢, seniors free off-peak and Sat.-Sun.) The **ZIP code** for Lancaster City is 17604; the **area code** is 717.

Not Nestlé

Milton S. Hershey, a Mennonite resident of eastern Pennsylvania's farms, failed in his first several jaunts into the business world. Then he found chocolate. Today the company that bears his name has become the world's largest chocolate factory in **Hershey** just across the northeastern border of Lancaster. Here street lights are shaped like candy kisses, and the streets are named Chocolate and Cocoa. East of town at **Hershey Park** (800-437-7439), the **Chocolate World Visitors Center** (534-4900) presents a free, automated tour through a simulated chocolate factory. After viewing the processing of the cacao bean from tropical forests through the Oompas to final packaging, visitors emerge into a pavilion full of chocolate cookies, chocolate candy, chocolate milk, and Hershey sportswear—all for sale, of course. (Open daily 9am-6:45pm; early Sept. to mid-June 9am-4:45pm.)

Though Hershey Park amusement center has fairly unimpressive rides, meeting a walking talking Reese's cup just may be worth the hefty admission. (Open late May-early Sept. daily 10:30am-10pm. Admission $20, seniors $12.50, ages 4-8 $7. After 5pm $14. Parking $2.) Camp 8 mi. from Hershey and 15 mi. from Lancaster City at **Ridge Run Campground,** 867 Schwanger Rd., Elizabethtown 17022 (367-3454). Schwanger Rd. connects Rte. 230 and Rte. 283. (Sites $14.) **Greyhound/Trailways** (397-4861) goes to Hershey from Lancaster City (1 per day, 3 hr., $18), stopping at 337 W. Chocolate St.

Ohiopyle State Park

Hidden away in the forgotten landscapes of southwestern Pennsylvania lie some of the loveliest forests in the East, lifted by steep hills and cut by cascading rivers. Native Americans dubbed this part of the state "Ohiopehhle" ("white frothy water"), because of the grand Youghiogheny River Gorge (pronounced yock-a-gaynee; "The Yock" to locals); the river provides the focal point of Pennsylvania's Ohiopyle State Park. The park's 18,000 acres supply hiking, fishing, hunting, and a complete range of winter activities, but the most popular activity is whitewater rafting along the river.

Lined up in a row on Rte. 381 in "downtown" Ohiopyle are four outfitters: **White Water Adventurers** (329-8531 or 800-992-7238); **Wilderness Voyageurs** (329-5517 or 800-272-4141); **Laurel Highlands River Tours** (329-8531 or 800-472-3846); and **Mountain Streams and Trails** (329-8810 or 800-245-4090). Guided trips on the Yock vary dramatically in price ($20-70 per person per day), depending on season, day of week, and difficulty. If you're an experienced river rat (or if you just happen to *enjoy* flipping boats) any of the above companies will rent you equipment. (Rafts about $9 per person, canoes $15, "duckies"—inflatable kayaks—about $15.) **Youghiogheny Outfitters** (329-4549) may be a bit cheaper since they do rental business only.

In order to do just about anything in the river you'll need a launch permit. They're free but get snatched up quickly. The **Park Information Center,** just off Rte. 381 on Dinnerbell Rd. (P.O. Box 105; 329-8591) recommends calling at least 30 days in advance. The 200 **campsites** ($7) that the office handles also require advanced booking—especially for summer weekends. (Open daily 8am-4pm; Nov.-

April Mon.-Fri. 8am-4pm.) Fishing licenses ($20), required for ages 16 and over, are available at the Falls Market (see below).

Motels around Ohiopyle are sparse but the excellent **Ohiopyle State Park Hostel (AYH)**, P.O. Box 99 (329-4476) sits right in the center of town off Rte. 381. Sue Moore has 24 bunks, a kitchen, a great yard, 6 cats, and 2 dogs—all for $6 per night, nonmembers $9. (Check-in 6-9pm.) **Falls Market and Overnight Rooms** (329-4973), on Rte. 381 in the center of town, rents singles ($22) and doubles ($30) with shared baths. The downstairs store has a decent selection of groceries and a snack-bar/restaurant. (Burgers $1.25, pancakes and bacon $2.25. Open daily 7am-7pm.)

Ohiopyle is on Rte. 381, 64 mi. southeast of Pittsburgh via Rte. 51 and U.S. 41. The closest public transport is to Uniontown, a large town about 20 mi. to the west on U.S. 40. **Greyhound/Trailways** serves **Uniontown** from Pittsburgh (3 per day, 1½ hr., $9). The **post office** (329-8650) is open Monday through Friday 7:30am to 4:30pm and Saturday 7:30am to 11:30am. The **ZIP code** is 15470. The **area code** for Ohiopyle and the surrounding area is 412.

Philadelphia

Pennsylvanians like to boast via their license plates that "America starts here." Not that license plate mottoes *ever* make sense, but Pennsylvania was neither the first state in the Union nor the site of the first U.S. settlement. Still, Philadelphia—the state's largest and most dynamic city—almost makes the claim viable. The "Founding Fathers" gathered here on two separate occasions to formulate the United States' most sacred documents, the *Declaration of Independence* and the *Constitution*. Stop by Independence Hall, the Liberty Bell, the Franklin Institute, and maybe even have a Rocky-style run up the steps of the Fairmount Park Art Museum.

Practical Information

Emergency: 911.

Visitors Center, 1525 John F. Kennedy Blvd. at 16th St. (636-1666). Pick up a free *Philadelphia Visitor's Guide* and the *Philadelphia Quarterly Calendar of Events.* Open daily 9am-6pm; off-season early 9am-5pm. **Directory Events Hotline,** 377-7777, ext. 2540. **National Park Service Visitor Center,** 3rd and Chestnut (597-8974; 627-1776 for recording). Info on Independence Park, including maps, schedules, and the film *Independence.* Also distributes the *Visitor's Guide* and the *Quarterly Calendar of Events.* Open Sept.-June daily 9am-5pm; July-Aug. 9am-6pm. Film shown 9:30am-4pm. Tour assistance for non-English-speaking and disabled travelers.

Philadelphia International Airport: (info line 492-3181 24 hrs.), 8 mi. SW of Center City on I-76. The 27-min. SEPTA Airport Rail Line runs from Center City to the airport. Trains leave daily 5:30am-11:25pm from 30th St. Station, Suburban Station, and Market East ($4.75). Last train from airport 12:10am. Cab fare downtown $21, but **Airport Limelight Limousine** (342-5557) will deliver you to a hotel ($8) or a specific address downtown.

Amtrak: 30th St. Station, at 30th and Market St. (349-2153 or 800-872-7245), in University City. To New York City (every ½-hr., 2 hr., $28), Washington, DC (every ½-hr., 2 hr., $33), and points in western PA. Ticket office open daily 5:10am-10:45pm. Station open 24 hrs. To: Boston ($62), New York ($29), Washington DC ($34), and Baltimore ($27); take the SEPTA commuter train to Trenton, NJ ($4.75), then hop on a New Jersey Transit train to NYC through Newark ($7.75).

Buses: Greyhound/Trailways, 10th and Filbert St. (931-4000), 1 block north of Market near the 10th and Market St. subway/commuter rail stop in the heart of Philadelphia. To: New York City (15 per day, 2½ hr., Mon.-Thurs. $17, Fri.-Sun. $19); Washington, DC (8 per day, 3½ hr., Mon.-Thurs. $22, Fri.-Sun. $26); Atlantic City (17 per day, 1½ hr., $10). **New Jersey Transit,** 800-582-5946. To Atlantic City ($10), Ocean City ($12), and other points on the New Jersey Shore.

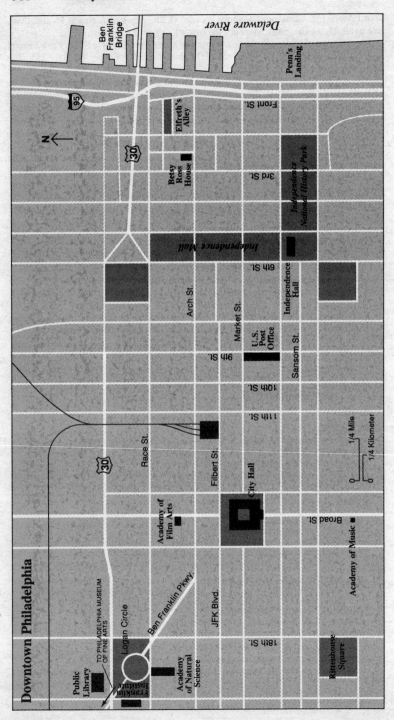

Downtown Philadelphia

Public Transport: Southeastern Pennsylvania Transportation Authority (SEPTA), 580-7800.
Most buses operate 6:30am-1am, some all night. Extensive bus and rail service to suburbs.
Two major subway routes: the Market St. line running east-west (including 30th St. Station
and the historic area) and the Broad St. line running north-south (including the stadium complex in south Philadelphia). Subway unsafe after dark, but buses usually okay. Buses serve
the 5-county area. Subway connects with commuter rails—the Main Line Local runs through
the western suburb of Paoli ($3.50), and SEPTA runs north as far as Trenton, NJ ($4.75).
Pick up a SEPTA **system map** ($1.50), and a good street map at any subway stop. Fare $1.50,
2 tokens for $2.10, transfers 40¢.

Taxi: Yellow Cab, 922-8400. **United Cab**, 625-9170.

Car Rental: Thrifty Rent-a-Car, 365-4008 at the airport. Sub-compacts $31 per day, week-
ends $18 per day. Unlimited mi. but must not go farther south than DC or farther north
than Massachusetts. Optional insurance $10 per day. Must be 25 with major credit card.

Help Lines: Gay Switchboard, 546-7100. Open daily 7-10pm.

Post Office: 30th and Market St. (596-5316), across from the Amtrak station. Open 24 hrs.
ZIP code: 19104.

Area Code: 215.

Founder William Penn, Jr., as a survivor of London's great fire in the 1660s,
planned his city as a logical and easily accessible grid pattern of wide streets. The
north-south streets ascend numerically from the **Delaware River,** flowing near
Penn's Landing and Independence Hall on the east side, to the **Schuylkill River**
(pronounced SCHOOL-kill) on the west. The first street is **Front,** the others follow
consecutively from 2 to 69. **Center City** runs from 8th Street to the Schuylkill River.
From north to south, the primary streets are Race, Arch, JFK, Market, Sansom,
and South. The intersection of Broad (14th St.) and Market, location of City Hall,
marks the focal point of Center City. The **Historic District** stretches from Front
to 8th Street and from Vine to South Street. The **University of Pennsylvania** sprawls
on the far side of the Schuylkill River, about 1 mi. west of Center City. **University
City** includes the Penn/Drexel area west of the Schuylkill River.

Accommodations and Camping

Downtown Philadelphia is saturated with luxury hotels, so anything inexpensive
is popular. But if you make arrangements even a few days in advance, you should
find comfortable lodging close to Center City for under $40. **Bed and Breakfast,
Center City,** 1804 Pine St., Philadelphia 19103 (735-1137), can reserve you a room
in a private home. (Singles $40-75. Doubles $45-75. Best to call 9am-9pm.) The
Philadelphia Naturalist and Work Camp Center, P.O. Box 4755, Philadelphia
19134 (452-5240), rents beds to foreign students ($5 with light breakfast) and will
arrange free room and board on a nearby farm in exchange for daily chores. Camping is available to the north and west of the city, but you must travel at least 15
mi.

Chamounix Mansion International Youth Hostel (AYH), West Fairmount Park (878-3676).
Take bus #38 from JFK Blvd. to Ford and Cranston Rd., walk in the direction of the bus
until Chamounix St., then turn left and follow until the road ends at hostel (about a 20-min.
walk). In daylight take bus #38 to Fairmount Terr. apartments and follow the AYH sign
10 min. through a wooded path. Former country estate built in 1802. Clean and beautifully
furnished, with 50 beds, showers, kitchen, and coin-operated laundry. Some basic groceries
for sale. Extraordinarily friendly and helpful staff. Lockout 9:30am-4:30pm. Curfew 11pm.
$9.50, nonmembers $12.50. Linen $2.

Old First Reformed Church, 4th and Race St. (922-4566), in Center City 1 block from the
Independence Mall and 4 blocks from Penn's Landing. Historic church that converts its social
hall to a youth hostel for 20. Mattresses on the floor, showers. 3-night max. stay. Check-in
5-10pm. Curfew 11pm. $10. Breakfast included. Open early July-late Aug.

The Divine Tracy Hotel, 20 S. 36th St. (382-4310), near Market St. in University City. Impeccably clean, quiet, and well-maintained rooms, though no bright Dick Tracy colors. Women
must wear skirts and stockings at all times in the public areas of the hotel; men, long pants
and socks with their shirts tucked in. Strictly single-sex floors. No smoking, vulgarity, obscen-

ity, or blasphemy. Check-in 7am-11pm. Singles $20, with private bath $23-26. Shared doubles $20 per person. Fans and TVs for rent. The management does not permit alcohol or food (except small snacks) in the rooms, but the **Keyflower Dining Room** (386-2207) offers incredibly cheap and healthful, if bland, food. Entrees $2-4. Open to the public Mon.-Fri. 11:30am-2pm and 5-8pm.

International House, 3701 Chestnut St. (387-5125). Bus #21 stops right out front. Clean dorms in a modern complex built to house Philly's international students—must have student ID or affiliation with university or exchange program. May accept college graduates or professionals. Mostly singles in 10-room suites ($49). Reserve ahead if you want a suite with kitchen. **Eden** restaurant (see Food below) in the same building. Open year-round, but rooms scarce during school year.

The closest camping is across the Delaware River in New Jersey. Check out **Timberline Campground,** 117 Timber Lane, Clarksboro, NJ 08020 (609-423-6677), 15 mi. from Center City. Take 285 S. to exit 18A, Clarksboro, turn left and then right at the first stop sign, Cohawkin Rd. Go ½-mi. and turn right on Friendship Rd. Timber Lane is 1 block on the right. (Sites $11, with full hookup $13.50.) In Pennsylvania, try the **Baker Park Campground,** 400 East Pothoure Rd. (933-5865), 45 min. to 76 west to 23 through Valley Forge Park. (Sites $14, with electricity $16.)

Food

More than 500 new restaurants have opened their doors in Philadelphia in the past decade, making the city one of the most exciting dining spots in the U.S. Inexpensive food abounds on Sansom St. between 17th and 18th, on South St. between 2nd and 7th, and on 2nd St. between Chestnut and Market. Numerous new places are opening up in **Penn's Landing,** on the Delaware River between Locust and Market St. Philadelphia's **Chinatown** lies right in the center of downtown action, bounded by 8th, 11th, Vine, and Race St. In **University City,** the University of Pennsylvania (UPenn) and Drexel University collide on the west side of the Schuylkill River, making cheap student eateries easy to find. Try the famous hoagie or cheesesteak, two local specialties. You may grow attached to the renowned Philly soft pretzel: have one for about 30¢ at a street-side vendor.

To stock up on staples, visit the **Italian Market** at 9th and Christian St. (Open daily dawn-dusk.) The **Reading Terminal Market,** at 12th and Arch St. (922-2317), is the place to go for picnic-packing, grocery-shopping, or a quick lunch. Since 1893, food stands have clustered together in this huge indoor market—selling fresh meats, produce, and delicious alternatives to modern fast-food courts. (Open Mon.-Sat. 8am-6pm.)

Historic District

Jim's Steaks, 400 South St. (928-1911). Take the 4th St. trolley or bus #10 down Locust St. A Philadelphia institution since 1939, serving some of the best steak sandwiches in town ($3.70-5). Eat to beat Jim's current record holder—11 steaks in 90 minutes. Open Mon.-Thurs. 10am-1am, Fri.-Sat. 10am-3am, Sun. noon-10pm.

Lee's Hoagie House, 220 South St., (925-6667), near 2nd St. Authentic hoagies ($3.45-5.50) since 1953. The 3-ft. hoagie challenges even gluttonous tourists. Open Tues.-Thurs. 10am-11pm, Fri.-Sat. 10am-2am, Sun. 10am-10pm.

Fu Wing House, 639 South St., between 6th and 7th (922-3170). Great hot-and-sour soup ($1.50). Entrees $6.75-9.25. Open Mon. and Wed.-Sun. 5-10pm.

Dickens Inn, Head House Sq., on 2nd St. between Pine and Lombard (928-9307). Restaurant upstairs upscale but excellent food. British country cooking served at the bakery—try a cornish pastie or shepherd's pie (both $3.75). Open Mon.-Tues. 8am-9pm, Wed.-Thurs. 8am-10pm, Fri. 8am-11pm, Sat. 8am-midnight, Sun. 11am-9pm. Pay slightly more at the bar, open daily 11:30am-1:30am.

Center City

Charlie's Waterwheel Restaurant, downstairs at 1526 Sansom St. (563-4155), between 15th and 16th St. First hoagie steak shop in Center City—their subs will sink you for days. Sand-

Photo taken in Grindelwald, Switzerland, by Doris Muir, Shrewsbury, Pa.

No print film gives you truer, more accurate color. Why trust your memories to anything less?

Kodak
Official Film
of the 1992
Olympic Games

Show Your True Colors.™

When all you've got is one week, even a morning of diarrhea is too much.

Bad weather isn't the only thing that can spoil a vacation. That's why you want the most effective diarrhea medicine you can buy — Imodium® A-D. It can stop diarrhea with just one dose, instead of dose after dose of the other leading brand.

Take it along in convenient caplets. And enjoy every moment of your next vacation.

Imodium A-D. It can stop diarrhea with just one dose.

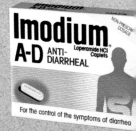

Imodium
A-D
Loperamide HCl
Caplets
ANTI-
DIARRHEAL

NON-PRESCRIPTION DOSAGE

For the control of the symptoms of diarrhea

wiches and steaks with fresh fruit and vegetables ($5.25). Munch on free meatballs, pickles, and fried mushrooms at the counter while you wait. Open daily 11am-4pm.

Saladalley, 1720 Sansom St. (564-0767) between 17th and 18th. Huge salad bar featuring truly innovative combinations of fresh fruits, vegetables, and homemade muffins. Try the pasta bows in walnut zucchini sauce ($8). Lunch $5.25, dinner $5.95. Open Mon.-Fri. 11:30am-8:30pm, Sat. 11:30am-8pm.

University City

Audrey's Pit Barbecue, 113 S. 40th St. (386-5125), between Chestnut and Walnut. Considered the best barbecue joint in town. Funny guys Jack Nicholson and Redd Foxx eat here. Try the half-chicken or the barbecued beef sandwich ($3.20 each). Customers rave about the potato pie (90¢). Few seats, mostly take-out. Open Tues. 11:30am-7pm, Wed.-Thurs. 11:30am-9:30pm, Fri.-Sat. 11:30am-11pm.

Sweet Basil, 4006 Chestnut St. (387-2727), at 40th St. Cool and sophisticated. Eclectic menu with Indonesian, Cajun, and vegetarian entrees. Dinners $7-13. Open Mon.-Thurs. 5-10pm, Fri.-Sat. 5-10:30pm.

Barley and Hops, 3925 Walnut St. (382-5195), between 39th and 40th. Students swarm here for a respite from dining hall grub. Good burgers and sandwiches ($4-5). Open daily noon-2am. Kitchen closes at 1am.

Eden, 3701 Chestnut St. (387-2471), at 38th St. Wholesome and satisfying grilled fish and chicken specialties served on a leafy terrace. No original sin here. Don't be put off by cafeteria-style dining. Great chicken stir-fry ($6.45). Good salmon pasta ($7.45). Students with I.D. 10% discount. Open Mon.-Sat. 11:30am-11pm. Bar open later.

Sights

"I went to Philadelphia," W.C. Fields quipped, "and it was closed." Although the city still sleeps fairly early, its fine collection of museums and an unmatched historical significance help Philly wake you up, at least when it's open. A convenient way to see the sights rolls by on **Fairmount Park Trolley Tours** (879-4044 for recorded information). Sponsored by the city's park commission, the attractive tours pass by all the major sights, and you can mount or get off at your leisure. Tours (April-Nov. Wed.-Sun. 10am-4pm) leave every ½-hr. from the tourist center, 16th and JFK, and the Independence Park Visitors Center. (Admission $3; includes discounts at attractions.)

Independence Hall and the Historic District

The buildings of the **Independence National Historic Park** (open daily 9am-5pm; in summer 9am-8pm) witnessed events that have since passed into U.S. folklore. The park visitor center (see Practical Information above) makes a good starting point. Sight of the signing of the *Declaration of Independence* in 1776, and the *Constitution* drafting and signing in 1787, **Independence Hall** lies between 5th and 6th St. on Chestnut. Engraved with a half-sun, George Washington's chair at the head of the assembly room prompted Ben Franklin to remark after the ratification of the Constitution that "Now at length I have the happiness to know that it is a rising and not a setting sun." (Free guided tours daily every 15-20 min., arrive before 11am in summer to avoid an hr.-long line.) The U.S. Congress first assembled in nearby **Congress Hall** (free self-guided tour), while its predecessor, the First Continental Congress, convened in **Carpenters' Hall,** two blocks away at 4th and Chestnut St. (Open Tues.-Sun. 10am-4pm.) North of Independence Hall lies the **Liberty Bell Pavilion.** The cracked Liberty Bell itself, one of the most famous U.S. symbols, refuses to toll even when vigorously prodded.

The remainder of the park contains preserved residential and commercial buildings of the Revolutionary era. Ben Franklin's home lies in **Franklin Court** to the north, on Market between 3rd and 4th St., and includes an underground museum, a 20-minute movie and an architectural archeology exhibit. (Open daily 9am-5pm. Free.) At nearby **Washington Square,** a flame burns eternally commemorating the **Tomb of the Unknown Soldier.** Across from Independence Hall is Philadelphia's branch of the **U.S. Mint** (597-7350). A self-paced guided tour explains the mechanized coin-making procedure. (Open April-Dec. daily 9am-4:30pm, Jan.-March Mon.-Fri. 9am-4:30pm. Free.)

Tucked away near 2nd and Arch St. is the quiet, residential **Elfreth's Alley,** allegedly "the oldest street in America," along which a penniless Ben Franklin walked when he arrived in town in 1723. On Arch near 3rd St. sits the tiny **Betsy Ross House** (627-5343), where its namesake supposedly sewed the first flag of the original 13 states. (Free.) **Christ Church,** on 2nd near Market, hosted the fashionable Quakers of colonial Philadelphia. Ben Franklin lies buried in the nearby Christ Church cemetery at 5th and Arch St. Also see the Quaker meeting houses: the original **Free Quaker Meeting House** at 5th and Arch St., and a new and larger one at 4th and Arch St.

Mikveh Israel, the first Jewish congregation of Philadelphia, has a burial ground on Spruce near 8th St. The **Afro-American Historical and Cultural Museum,** 7th and Arch St. (574-0380), stands as the first U.S. museum devoted solely to the history of African Americans. (Open Tues.-Sat. 10am-5pm, Sun. noon-6pm. Admission $3.50, seniors, handicapped and children $1.75.)

Society Hill proper begins where the park ends, on Walnut St. between Front and 7th St. Now Philadelphia's most distinguished residential neighborhood, housing both old-timers and a new yuppie crowd, the area was originally a tract of land owned by the Free Society of Traders, a company formed to help William Penn, Jr. consolidate Pennsylvania. Federal-style townhouses dating back 300 years line picturesque cobblestone walks, illuminated by old-fashioned streetlamps. **Head House Square,** 2nd and Pine St., held a marketplace in 1745 and now houses restaurants, boutiques, and craft shops. An outdoor flea market occurs here summer weekends.

Located on the Delaware River, **Penn's Landing** (923-8181) is the largest freshwater port in the world. Among other vessels it holds the *Gazela,* a three-masted, 178-ft. Portuguese square rigger built in 1883; the U.S.S. *Olympia,* Commodore Dewey's flagship during the Spanish-American War (922-1898; tours daily 10am-4pm; admission $3, children $1.50); and the U.S.S. *Becuna,* a WWII submarine (tours in conjunction with the *Olympia).* The **Port of History,** Delaware Ave. and Walnut St. (925-3804), has frequently changing exhibits. (Open Wed.-Sun. 10am-4:30pm. Admission $2, ages 5-12 $1.) The Delaware Landing is a great spot to soak up sun on a nice day. For $1.50 you can jump on **Penn's Landing Trolley** (627-0807), on Delaware Ave., between Catharine and Race St., which rolls along the waterfront giving guided tours.

Center City

Center City, the area bounded by 12th, 23rd, Vine, and Pine St., whirls with activity. **City Hall,** Broad and Market St. (686-1776), an ornate structure of granite and marble with 20-ft.-thick foundation walls, is the nation's largest public municipal building. Until 1908, it also held the record for highest building in the U.S., helped by the 37-ft. statue of William Penn, Jr. on top. A municipal statute prohibited building higher than the top of Penn's hat until entrepreneurs in the mid-80s overturned it, finally launching Philadelphia into the skyscraper era. (Open Mon.-Fri. 7am-6pm. Free guided tours Mon.-Fri. at 12:30pm; meet in room 201.) The **Pennsylvania Academy of Fine Arts,** Broad and Cherry St. (972-7600), the country's first art school and one of its first museums, has an extensive collection of U.S. and British art, including notable works by Charles Wilson Peale, Thomas Eakins, Winslow Homer, and a few contemporary artists. (Open Tues.-Sat. 10am-5pm, Sun. 11am-5pm. Tours Tues.-Fri. at 11am and 2pm, Sat.-Sun. at 2pm. Admission $5, seniors $3, students $2, under 12 free. Free Sat. 10am-1pm.)

Just south of **Rittenhouse Square,** 2010 Delancey St., the **Rosenbach Museum and Library** (732-1600) houses rare manuscripts and paintings, including the earliest-known copy of Cervantes' *Don Quixote.* (Open Sept.-July Tues.-Sun. 11am-4pm. Guided tours $2.50, seniors, students, and kids $1.50. Exhibitions only, $1.50.) The nearby **Mütter Museum** (567-3737) of Philadelphia's College of Physicians displays gory medical paraphernalia including a death cast of Siamese twins and a tumor removed from President Cleveland's jaw. (Open Tues.-Fri. 10am-4pm. Free.) Ben Franklin founded the **Library Company of Philadelphia,** 1314 Locust St. near 13th St., over 250 years ago, as a club whose members' dues purchased books from England. A weather-worn statue of Franklin stands outside its present headquarters. The **Norman Rockwell Museum,** 6th and Sansom St. (922-4345), houses all of the artist's *Saturday Evening Post* cover works. (Open daily 10am-4pm. Admission $1.50, ages under 12 free.)

Benjamin Franklin Parkway

Nicknamed "America's Champs-Elysées," the Benjamin Franklin Parkway is a wide, diagonal deviation from William Penn's original grid pattern of city streets. Built in the 1920s, this tree- and flag-lined street connects Center City with Fairmount Park and the Schuylkill River. Admire the elegant architecture of the twin buildings at Logan Square, 19th and Parkway, that house the **Free Library of Philadelphia** and the **Municipal Court.**

At 20th and Parkway, the **Franklin Institute** (448-1200), whose **Science Center** amazes visitors with four floors of gadgets and games depicting the intricacies of space, time, motion, and the human body. A 20-ft. **Benjamin Franklin National Memorial** statue divines lightning at the entrance. In 1990, to commemorate the 200th anniversary of Franklin's death, the Institute unveiled the **Futures Center;** glimpses of life in the 21st century include simulated zero gravity and a timely set of exhibits on the changing global environment. (Futures Center daily 9:30am-9pm. Science Center daily 9am-5pm. Admission to both $7.50, seniors and kids $6. After 5pm: $6/$5.) The brand-new **Omniverse Theater** provides 180° and 4½ stories of optical oomph. (Omniverse shows daily on the hr. 9am-8pm. Admission $6, seniors and kids $5.) **Fels Planetarium** boasts an advanced computer-driven system that projects a simulation of life billions of years beyond. (Shows daily at 12:15 and 2:15pm, Fri.-Sat. at 7:15pm, 8:15pm, Sun. at 4:15pm. Admission $5, seniors and kids $4.) During the day, see all the sights for $11.50 (seniors and kids $9.50) or check out any two for $9.50 (seniors and kids $7.50). After 5pm, two attractions cost $8 (seniors and kids $7).

A ubiquitous casting of the *Gates of Hell* stands outside the **Rodin Museum,** at 22nd St. and the Parkway (787-5476), which houses the most complete collection of the artist's works outside Paris, including *The Thinker.* (Open Tues.-Sun. 10am-5pm. Donation.) Try your hand at the sensual **Please Touch Museum,** 210 N. 21st St. (963-0666), designed specifically for kids under eight. (Open daily 9am-4:30pm. Admission $5.)

The exhibit of precious gems and the 65-million-year-old dinosaur skeleton at the **Academy of Natural Sciences,** 19th and Parkway (299-1020), excite even the basest of human desires. (Open Mon.-Fri. 10am-4:30pm, Sat.-Sun. 10am-5pm. Admission $5.50, seniors $5, kids $4.50.) Farther down 26th St., the **Philadelphia Museum of Art** (763-8100) protects one of the world's major art collections. In the nation's third largest museum you'll find Rubens's *Prometheus Bound,* Picasso's *Three Musicians,* and Duchamp's *Nude Descending a Staircase,* as well as extensive Asian, Egyptian, and decorative arts collections. (Open Tues.-Sun. 10am-5pm. Admission $5, seniors and students under 18 with ID $2. Sun. 10am-1pm free.)

Fairmount Park sprawls behind the Philadelphia Museum of Art on both sides of the Schuylkill River. Bike trails and picnic areas abound, and the famous **Philadelphia Zoo** (243-1100), the oldest in the U.S., houses 1500 species in one corner of the park. (Open daily 9:30am-5pm. Admission $5.75, seniors and kids $4.75.) Boathouse Row, which houses the shells of local crew teams, is especially beautiful when lit at night. During the day, hikers and non-hikers alike may wish to venture out to the northernmost arm of Fairmount Park, where trails leave the Schuylkill River and wind along secluded Wissahickon Creek for 5 mi. The **Horticultural Center,** off Belmont Ave. (879-4062; open daily 9am-3pm) has greenhouses, Japanese gardening and periodic flower shows for viewing ($2 suggested donation).

West Philadelphia (University City)

West Philly is home to both the **University of Pennsylvania** and **Drexel University,** located across the Schuylkill from Center City, within easy walking distance of the 30th St. Station. Benjamin Franklin founded Penn in 1740. Fifteen years later the country's first medical school came to life, and students have been pulling all-nighters since then. The Penn campus provides a cloistered retreat of green lawns, red-brick quadrangles, and rarefied air. Ritzy shops line Chestnut St. and boisterous fraternities line Spruce; warm weather brings out a variety of street vendors along the Drexel and Penn borders.

Penn's **University Museum of Archeology and Anthropology,** 33rd and Spruce St. (898-4000), houses one of the finest archeological collections in the world. (Open Sept.-June, Tues.-Sat. 10am-4:30pm, Sun. 1-5pm. Admission $3, seniors and students $1.50.) In 1965, Andy Warhol had his first one-man show at the **Institute of Contemporary Art,** 34th and Walnut St. (898-7108). Today the gallery remains cutting edge. (Open Thurs.-Tues. 10am-5pm, Wed. 10am-7pm. Admission $2, seniors and artists with a compelling work $1, students free. Free Wed.)

Entertainment

Check Friday's weekend magazine section in the Philadelphia *Inquirer* for entertainment listings. *City Paper,* distributed on Fridays for free, has weekly listings of city events. *Au Courant,* a gay and lesbian weekly newspaper, lists and advertises events throughout the Delaware Valley region. The bar scene enlivens University City with a younger crowd. Along South Street, there is a wide variety of live music on weekends. Stop by **Dobbs,** 304 South St. (928-1943), between 3rd and 4th, a mixed-menu restaurant (entrees $6-8.50) with live rock nightly. (Open daily 6pm-2am.) Nearby **Penn's Landing** (923-4992) has free concerts in summer. Formerly under the direction of the late Eugene Ormandy, and now under Ricardo Muti, the **Philadelphia Academy of Music,** Broad and Locust St. (893-1930), houses the Philadelphia Orchestra, rated by many as the best in the U.S. The academy was modeled architecturally after Milan's *La Scala* and acoustically to mimic a perfect vacuum. The season runs from September through May. General admission tickets ($2) for seats in the amphitheater go on sale at the Locust St. entrance 45 minutes before Friday and Saturday concerts. Check with the box office for availability. The **Mann Music Center,** George's Hill (567-0707), near 52nd St. and Parkside Ave. in Fairmount Park, has 5000 seats under cover, 10,000 on outdoor benches and lawns—and hosts summer Philadelphia Orchestra, ballet, jazz, and rock events. Pick up free lawn tickets June through August on the day of performance from the visitors center at 16th St. and JFK Blvd. (See Practical Information above.) For the big-name shows, sit just outside the theater and soak in the sounds gratis. The **Robin Hood Dell East,** Strawberry Mansion Dr. (686-1776 or 477-8810 in summer), in Fairmount Park, brings in top names in pop, jazz, gospel, and ethnic dance in July and August. The Philadelphia Orchestra holds several free performances here in summer, and as many as 30,000 people gather on the lawn. Inquire at the visitors center (636-1666) for upcoming events. **Shubert Theater,** 250 S. Broad St., Center City (732-5446), stagees a variety of dance, musical, and comedy performances year-round.

Philly has four professional sports franchises. The Phillies (baseball) and Eagles (football) play at **Veterans Stadium** (ticket office 463-5500), while the **Spectrum** (336-3600) houses the 76ers (basketball) and the Flyers (hockey).

Near Philadelphia: Valley Forge

Neither battles nor artillery bombardments took place here, but during the winter of 1777-78, 11,000 men quartered at Valley Forge under George Washington's leadership spent agonizing months fighting starvation and disease. Only 8000 survived. Nonetheless, inspired by the enthusiasm of General Washington and the news of a U.S. alliance with France, and drilled into efficiency by Inspector General Baron

Von Steuben, the troops left Valley Forge stronger and better trained. They went on to victories in New Jersey and eventually reoccupied Philadelphia.

The park today encompasses over 2000 acres. (Open daily 6am-10pm.) Self-guided tours begin at the **visitors center** (783-7700), which also has a museum (free) and an audio-visual program (twice per hr. 9am-5:30pm, 15 min.). (Open daily 8:30am-5pm.) The tour features Washington's headquarters, reconstructed soldier huts and fortifications, and the Grand Parade Ground where the army drilled. Admission to Washington's headquarters costs one Washington ($1), but most other exhibits and buildings in the park are free. Audio tapes rent for $6.80. The park has three picnic areas; although there is no camping within the park, campgrounds thrive nearby. A 5-mi. bike trail winds up and down the hills of the park. Rent bikes ($4 per hr., $11 per day) at the **Interpretive Association Bookstore** (783-1076; open daily 9am to 4:30pm).

To get to Valley Forge, take the Schuylkill Expressway westbound from Philadelphia for about 12 mi. Get off at the Valley Forge exit, then take Rte. 202 S. for 1 mi. and Rte. 422 W. for 1½ mi. to another Valley Forge exit. SEPTA runs buses to the visitors center Monday through Friday only. Catch #125 at 16th and JFK ($3.10).

Pittsburgh

Although Charles Dickens called the city "Hell with the lid off" a century ago, and the Steelers football team no longer wins the Superbowl, Pittsburgh today has much more to offer than steel mills belching smoke. The factories have been replaced by serene skyscrapers and colorful city parks; climb **Duquesne Incline** to the top of Mt. Washington for a perfect view of this surprisingly beautiful city. Bridges cast geometric patterns on Pittsburgh's three famous rivers (the Monongahela, Allegheny, and Ohio), and the skyline stretches from the awe-inspiring **Cathedral of Learning** to the **PPG Place**, a startling glass tower with spires oddly imitating the cathedral's Gothic architecture.

Practical Information

Pittsburgh Convention and Visitors Bureau, 4 Gateway Ctr. (281-7711), downtown in a little glass building on Liberty Ave., across from the Hilton. Offers a 24-hr., up-to-date recording of events (391-6840), and aid for international visitors who don't speak English (624-7800). Their city maps won't get you past downtown. AAA (for members only) and Travelers Aid have better maps (see below for both). Open May-Oct. Mon.-Fri. 9:30am-5pm, Sat.-Sun. 9:30am-3pm; Nov.-March Mon.-Fri. 9:30am-5pm, Sat. 9:30am-3pm.

Travelers Aid: Two locations; Greyhound Bus Terminal, 11th St. and Liberty Ave. (281-5474), and the airport (264-7110). Maps, tourist advice, and help for stranded travelers. Open Mon.-Fri. 9am-9pm, Sat.-Sun. 9am-5pm.

American Express, 2 PPG Place on Market Square (391-3202; for lost or stolen checks 800-221-7282). Open Mon.-Fri. 9am-5pm.

Greater Pittsburgh International Airport: 778-2525, 15 mi. west of downtown by I-279 and Rte. 60 in Moon Township. Serves most major airlines. **Airline Transportation Company,** 471-2250. Serves most downtown hotels (daily 5am-10pm, $9), Oakland (daily 7am-8pm, $9.50) and Monroeville (daily 6am-7pm, $13).

Amtrak: Liberty and Grant Ave. (800-872-7245 for reservations; 471-6170 for station info), on the northern edge of downtown next to Greyhound and the post office. Safe and very clean inside, but be cautious about walking from here to the city center at night. Open 24 hrs. Ticket office open daily 8:30am-4pm, 5-5:15pm, 10:30pm-7:15am. To: Philadelphia (2 per day, 7½ hr., $60); New York (2 per day, 9 hr., $83); Chicago (2 per day, 9 hr., $75).

Greyhound/Trailways: 11th St. and Liberty Ave. (391-2300), on the northern outskirts of downtown. Large and fairly clean with police on duty. Station and ticket office open 24 hrs. To: Philadelphia (7 hr.; Mon.-Thurs. $42, Fri.-Sun. $46); New York (9 per day; 9-11 hr.; Mon.-Thurs. $72, Fri.-Sun. $75); Chicago (4 per day; 9-11 hr.; Mon.-Thurs. $49, Fri.-Sun. $59).

Public Transport: Port Authority of Allegheny County (PAT): 231-7000; bus info 231-5707. 165 bus routes. $1.10, 1-day pass $4.50, weekend family pass $3.25. The tiny, 4-stop **subway** downtown is free. Schedules and maps at most department stores and in the Community Interest Showcase section of the yellow pages.

Taxi: Yellow Cab Company, 665-8100. **People's Cab Company,** 681-3131. **Diamond Cab,** 824-0984.

Car Rental: Rent-A-Wreck, 1200 Liberty Ave. (488-3440). $23 per day, 50 free mi., 15¢ each additional mi. Insurance $8. Open Mon.-Sat. 8am-5pm. Must be 21 with major credit card or a $150 cash deposit. **Alamo,** 930 Broadway Rd. (800-327-9633) airport area. Reserve 24 hrs. in advance for $24 per day rate with unlimited mi. Optional insurance $11. Must be 21 with credit card. Under 25 surcharge $6.

American Automobile Assn. (AAA), at Wood St. and Oliver Ave. (338-4300). Open Mon.-Fri. 8:30am-3pm.

Help Lines: General Help Line, 255-1155. Open 24 hrs. **Rape Action Hotline,** 765-2731. Open 24 hrs. **Center for Victims of Violent Crime,** 1520 Penn Ave. (392-8582). Open 24 hrs. **Persad Center, Inc.,** 441-0857, emergencies 392-2472. A counseling service for the gay community.

Post Office: 7th and Grant St. (642-4472; general delivery 642-4478). Open Mon.-Fri. 7am-6pm, Sat. 7am-2:30pm. **ZIP code:** 15230.

Area Code: 412.

The downtown area is a triangle formed by two rivers—the Allegheny on the north and the Monongahela to the south—coming together to form a third, the Ohio. Parallel to the Monongahela, streets in the downtown triangle number 1 through 7.

Accommodations and Camping

Reasonable accommodations are easy to find in Pittsburgh. Downtown is fairly safe, even at night; Pittsburgh has the lowest crime rate for a city of its size in the country.

Point Park College Youth Hostel (AYH), 201 Wood St. (392-3824), 8 blocks from the Greyhound Station. Catch a bus on Liberty Ave. or walk 5 blocks downtown on Grant St., take a right and walk 3 blocks on Forbes Ave. until Wood St., then turn left and walk 2 blocks. Closer to a hotel than a hostel—clean rooms with 2 beds and private bath. Office hours 8am-4pm. Check-in until 11pm (tell the guards you're a hosteler). Members only, $7.50. No kitchen but all-you-can-eat breakfast ($2.30) served in the 3rd-floor cafeteria 7-9:30am. Open early May-late Aug.

Carnegie-Mellon University, 1060 Morewood St. (268-2939), at Forbes in Oakland 2 blocks east of Craig St. Old-style dorm rooms, some with private baths. Excellent location in the heart of college town. Office hours Mon.-Fri. 8am-5pm. Check-in anytime with reservations. Singles $15. Doubles $20. Non-students: singles $18, doubles $25. Subtract $5 per night for a week's stay. Open summer months only.

St. Regis Residence for Women, 50 Congress St. (281-9888), in the red brick church directly opposite the Civic Arena on Wylie St. past the Chatham Center. A 10-min. walk from the bus terminal, but take a cab at night. A Catholic-run home for women working and studying in the Pittsburgh area. Singles $10. Give them a day's notice.

Red Roof Inn, 6404 Stubenville Pike on Rte. 60 (787-7870), east of the Rte. 22-Rte. 30 junction near the airport. From the Greyhound station, take bus #26F. Singles $34. Doubles $41. Reservations necessary summer weekends.

The nearest campsite is the **Pittsburgh North Campground,** 6610 Mars Rd., Evans City 16033 (776-1150), 20 mi. from downtown. Take I-79 to the Mars exit. Facilities include tents and swimming. (Sites $15 for 2 people, $3 per extra adult, $2 per extra kid. Hookup $2.50.) **Bethany Christian Campground,** R.D. #1, P.O. Box 217, Washington 15301 (483-6235), lies 20 mi. south of Pittsburgh on I-79.

Food

Elegant and expensive restaurants trim Pittsburgh's inner triangle. Those in the South Side's **Station Square** are chic, while those in **Allegheny Square** to the north provide the overpriced fast food typical of new urban malls. On the East Side, the golf club does lunch on Walnut Street in Shadyside. Aside from the pizza joint/bars downtown, **Oakland** is your best bet for a good inexpensive meal. Forbes Ave., around the University of Pittsburgh, is packed with collegiate watering holes and cafés. Many of Pittsburgh's ethnic groups have stayed in the pockets where they originally settled, giving each neighborhood its own distinctive cuisine.

Original Hot Dog Shops, Inc., 3901 Forbes Ave., at Bouquet St. in Oakland. A rowdy, greasy Pittsburgh institution with the best dogs in town. Call it "the O" and they'll think you're a local. Dishes out 30,000 pounds of fries a week with dogs (from $1), pizza (slices $1), and burgers ($1.50). Fifty kinds of beer including local brew Iron City. Open Sun.-Thurs. 9am-4:30pm, Fri.-Sat. 9am-6am.

Alexander's Pasta Express, 5104 S. Liberty Ave., in Bloomfield. Take bus #86A ("East Hills") to Liberty and S. Aiken Ave. An unpretentious and cozy Italian-American restaurant and bar. Great spinach and cheese ravioli with a meatball $5.50, New York strip steak $7. Open Mon.-Sat. 11am-12:30am, Sun. 11am-10:30pm.

Hot Licks, 5520 Walnut St., in the Theater Mall. Take bus #71B or D down 5th Ave., get off at Aiken, and walk north 2 blocks to Walnut. Calzones, subs, salads, and pizzas with a baseball theme. "Fowl Ball" chicken pizza $7. Nightly specials include 2-for-1 pizza on "Tequila Tuesday" and Wed. "Vodka and Wing" night. Barbecue chicken on a mesquite grill $5.25-8. A good stop before heading upstairs for jazz at the Balcony (see Nightlife below). Another, larger location at 1500 Washington Rd., in South Hills Mt. Lebanon. Take bus 41C. Both open Mon.-Thurs. 11:30am-midnight, Fri.-Sat. 11:30am-2am, Sun. noon-midnight. Kitchen closes 1 hr. earlier.

Suzie's Greek Specialties, 130 6th St. downtown. Specializes in homemade Greek dishes, bread, and pastries ($6-8). Open Mon.-Fri. 11am-9pm, Sat. 4-11pm.

George Aiken's, 300 Forbes Ave., in Oakland. A local favorite for fried chicken and burgers ($1.75). Breakfast specials $1.50. Two dogs for $1. Open Mon.-Sat. 6am-9pm, Sun. 7am-7pm.

Bangkok Express, 410 1st. Ave., near Smithfield St. downtown. Tasty, spicy Thai cuisine served amid sparse decor. Lunches $5 with entree, soup, egg roll, and rice. Open Mon.-Fri. 11am-3pm.

Sights

The **Golden Triangle,** formed by the Allegheny and Monongahela River, is home to **Point State Park** and its famous 200-ft. fountain. The **Fort Pitt Blockhouse and Museum** (281-9285) in the park dates back to the French and Indian War. (Open Wed.-Sat. 9am-5pm, Sun. noon-5pm. Admission $1.50, seniors $1, kids 50¢.) **PPG Place,** on Stanwix St., is a high-rise complex with glass towers pointed like church spires. (Open Mon.-Fri. 10am-6pm, Sat. 10am-5pm.) The square in front features a musical fountain. Check the outdoor message board for times of free performances, ranging from Scottish brass bands to jazz. The **Phipps Conservatory** (622-6914) conserves 2½ acres of happiness for the flower fanatic, bounded by Edwardian homes about 3 mi. east along the Blvd. of the Allies in **Schenley Park..** (Open daily 9am-5pm. Admission $1.50, seniors and kids 50¢, $1 more for shows. Reserve tours at 622-6958.) Founded in 1787, the **University of Pittsburgh** (624-4141; for tours call 624-7488) now stands in the shadow of the 42-story **Cathedral of Learning** (624-6000) at Bigelow Blvd. between Forbes and 5th Ave. The "cathedral," an academic building dedicated in 1934, features 22 "nationality classrooms" designed and decorated by artisans from each of Pittsburgh's ethnic traditions. **Carnegie-Mellon University** (268-2000) hyphenates right down the street.

Other city sights lie across the three rivers from the Golden Triangle. Northward, across the Allegheny, steal a look at **Three Rivers Stadium,** where the Steelers and Pirates play ball. The **Buhl Science Center** (237-3333), in **Allegheny Square,** has special hands-on exhibits and sky shows that entertain both children and adults.

(Open Sun.-Thurs. 1-5pm, Fri. 1-9:30pm, Sat. 10am-5pm. Admission $4, ages under 18 $2.) To the west of Allegheny Sq. flies the tropical **Pittsburgh Aviary** (323-7234; open daily 9am-4:30pm; admission $2, seniors and ages under 12 50¢; take bus #16D or the Ft. Duquesne bridge).

The **Pittsburgh Zoo** in Highland Park (441-6262; take "Negley" bus #71A or "Highland" 71B) has a children's zoo, a reptile building, an aquarium, an Asian forest, and an African savanna. (Open summer Mon.-Fri. 9am-5pm, Sat. 10am-5pm, Sun. 10am-6pm; off-season Mon.-Fri. 9am-5pm, Sat. 10am-5pm. Admission $3, seniors and kids $1. Parking $2.)

To get to the **South Side,** take the Smithfield Street Bridge across the Monongahela River. The star attraction here is **Station Square,** a cleverly renovated railway terminal featuring shops and restaurants. The **Gateway Clipper Fleet** (355-7979; tickets 355-7980) shares the riverbank and offers narrated sight-seeing cruises on the three rivers (from $5.25). **Mount Washington** towers behind Station Sq.; the trolleys **Duquesne** and **Monongahela Inclines** ascend the slope to an observation platform. Even athletic types should climb the hill on the trolley to Grandview Ave. along the edge of the mountain. (Open Mon.-Sat. 5:30am-12:45am, Sun. and holidays 8:45am-midnight. Fare $1.)

Two of America's greatest financial legends, Andrew Carnegie and Henry Clay Frick, made their fortunes in Pittsburgh. Their bequests to the city have greatly enriched its cultural scene. The most spectacular of Carnegie's gifts are the art and natural history museums, together called **The Carnegie,** at 4400 Forbes Ave. (622-3131,) across the street from the Cathedral of Learning. The natural history section is famous for its 500 dinosaur specimens, including an 84-ft. mammothmoth named for the philanthropist himself—**Diplodocus Carnegii.** The art museum's modern wing houses a collection strong in impressionist, post-impressionist, and 20th-century works. Every three years, The Carnegie hosts "The International," one of the country's oldest recurring contemporary art exhibits, next scheduled for 1993. (Open Tues.-Sat. 10am-5pm, Sun. 1-5pm. Take any bus to Oakland and get off at the Cathedral of Learning.)

While most know Henry Clay Frick for his art collection in New York, the **Frick Art Museum** 7227 Reynolds St., Point Breeze (371-0600), displays some of his early, less famous acquisitions. The permanent collection contains Italian, Flemish, and French works from the 13th through 18th centuries. **Clayton,** the Frick family mansion, opened to the public in the fall of 1989. Stroll through the two-acre gardens and the recently restored greenhouse and playhouse. (Open Wed.-Sat. 10am-5:30pm, Sun. noon-6pm. Free. Mansion tours $4.50. Take bus #67A, F, E, C, or 71C.)

Entertainment and Nightlife

Pittsburgh's metamorphosis from industrial to corporate town has happily hemmed its artistic seam. Pick up *In Pittsburgh* for free up-to-date entertainment listings and racy personals. The internationally acclaimed **Pittsburgh Symphony Orchestra** performs October through May at **Heinz Hall,** 600 Penn Ave. downtown, and gives free summer evening concerts outdoors at Point State Park (392-4000 for tickets and information). The **Pittsburgh Public Theater** (323-8200) is widely renowned, but tickets cost a pretty penny: visitors with thin wallets should check out the **Three Rivers Shakespeare Festival** (624-4101), at University of Pittsburgh's Steven Foster Memorial Theater, near Forbes Ave. and Bigelow Blvd. downtown. The corps, consisting of students and professionals, performs from late May to mid-August. Seniors and students can line up a half hour before showtime for half-price tickets. Box office (624-7529) opens 10am to showtime and Monday 10am to 4pm. (Tickets Tues.-Thurs. $15, Fri.-Sat. $18.) All-student casts perform with the **Young Company** at City Theater (tickets $9). The **Three Rivers Arts Festival** (261-7040 or 481-7040) takes place during three weeks in June, in Gateway Center, Point State Park, Allegheny Courthouse, and Station Square. The festival gives free exhibitions and demonstrations of painting, sculpture, and crafts, live performances of plays and music.

You can wet your whistle or flex your dance muscles at one of Pittsburgh's many nightspots. **Peter's Pub,** 116 Oakland Ave. (681-7465), is a raucous hangout frequented by U. Pitt's athletic teams. (Beer 75¢. Open Mon.-Sat. 11am-2am.) Also near the university is **C.J. Barney's Wooden Key,** 3907 Forbes Ave., absolutely jammed on Thursday, when $3 buys all-you-can-drink from 9pm to midnight. (Open Mon.-Sat. 11am-2am.) Jazz thrives in Pittsburgh: hear it nightly at Shadyside's **Balcony,** Theater Mall, 5520 Walnut St. (687-0110). (Live jazrs. 8:30pm-12:30am, Fri.-Sun. 9pm-1am. No cover. Take bus #71B or D down 5th Ave. to Aiken and walk north to Walnut St.) Or, if you don't mind the distance, head to the **James Street Tavern,** 422 Foreland Ave., North Side (323-2222). The restaurant upstairs is costly, but after 9pm on Thursday and Friday the jazz downstairs will amaze you. (No cover.)

Near Pittsburgh

The U.S. is loaded with celebrations of President General George Washington, the founding father with the best rep and the worst teeth. **Fort Necessity,** on U.S. 40 near Rte. 381 (329-5512), necessitates a rare opportunity to remember when good ol' George got his cherry-tree butt kicked. Fort Necessity, the site of Washington's surrender to the French in a battle that precipitated the French and Indian War, has been rebuilt, featuring a half-hour talk (8 per day) by historians dressed up as English and French soldiers as well as a musket-firing demonstration. Chop down the door of the **Visitor Information Center** (open daily 9am-5:30pm; Labor Day-Memorial Day 10:30am-5pm; admission $1, families $3). After his defeat, a promoted Washington regrouped forces to defeat the French in 1958 at **Fort Ligonier,** at the junction of Rte. 30 and 711, 60 mi. north of Necessity. (Open April-Oct. daily 9:30am-5pm. Admission $4, seniors $3, kids $2.) Various groups re-enact battles and camp life on some summer weekends.

RHODE ISLAND

Although Rhode Island is the smallest state in size in the Union, it is large enough to combine elements of three other New England states. Connecticut-style wealth flaunts itself in Newport, which dredges up the famous mansions of its millionaire summer migrants. Providence, like Boston, has evolved from a colonial hub to an industrial and gentrified city, and like Cambridge has its own citadel of ivory-tower league liberalism. Outside the two cities, Rhode Island most resembles the rustic Maine coast. Many of its inland roads are quiet, unpaved thoroughfares lined with family fruit stands, marshes, or ponds. Working ports derive their lifeblood from the fishblood of Narragansett Bay and Block Island Sound.

Practical Information

Capital: Providence.

Rhode Island Division of Tourism, 7 Jackson Walkway, Providence 02903 (800-556-2484 or 277-2601). Open Mon.-Fri. 8:30am-4:30pm. **Department of Environmental Management** (State Parks), 9 Hayes St., Providence 02908 (277-2771). Open Mon.-Fri. 8:30am-4pm.

Time Zone: Eastern. **Postal Abbreviation:** RI

Area Code: 401.

Newport

Before the American Revolution, Newport was one of the five largest towns in the northern half of the Americas, a thriving seaport grown fat on the spoils of the triangle trade of rum, slaves, and molasses. Affluent vacationers of the mid-19th century made Newport a hoity-toity retreat and ushered in the "Gilded Age," making the town the most popular resort in the U.S. The elite employed the country's best architects to confect elaborate Neoclassical and Baroque "summer cottages." Crammed to the rafters with *objets d'art,* these "white elephants," as Henry James called them, signified the desperation of the *arrivistes* to purchase as much culture as possible.

Today, 12-meter racing and sailing yachts have replaced fishing boats, and fish comes swathed in sauce with a soupçon of something. To avoid commodity fetishism, visit in the off-season. In chillier days, the restaurants downtown stoke up the hearth, offer hot cider and grog, and sell more softly.

Practical Information

Emergency: 911.

Newport County Convention and Visitors Bureau, 23 America's Cup Ave. (849-8048). Free maps. Open daily 8am-8pm; off-season 9am-5pm. **Newport Harbor Center,** 365 Thames St. More pamphlets and public restrooms. For more information on Newport call 800-242-1510 or 800-242-1520.

Bonanza Buses: Newport Gateway Center, 23 America's Cup Ave. (846-1820), next to the visitors bureau. To Boston (10 per day, 1½ hr., $12.50).

Rhode Island Public Transit Authority (RIPTA): 1547 W. Main Rd. (847-0209 or 800-662-5088). Very frequent service to Providence (1 hr., $2) and points between on Rte. 114. Buses leave from the Newport Gateway Center. Free Newport Loop bus (Memorial Day-Labor Day daily 10am-7pm) to main sights, shopping areas, and chamber of commerce. Office open Mon.-Fri. 5:15am-8pm, Sat. 6am-7pm.

Car Rental: Newport Ford, 312 W. Main Rd. (846-1411). Compact $32.75 per day. 100 free mi., 15¢ each additional mi. Open Mon.-Fri. 8am-5pm. Must be 21 with $200 credit card deposit.

Bike Rental: Ten Speed Spokes, 18 Elm St. (847-5609). Bikes of all speeds. 10-speeds $15 per day. Tandems $5 per day. Open Mon.-Sat. 9:30am-5:30pm, Sun. noon-5pm. Must have credit card and photo ID.

Post Office: 320 Thames St., opposite Perry Hill Market. Window service open Mon.-Fri. 7:30am-5:30pm, Sat. 9am-noon; lobby Mon.-Fri. 6am-7pm, Sat. 6am-5pm, Sun. 10am-5pm. **ZIP code:** 02840.

Area Code: 401.

Newport commands a boot-shaped peninsula on the southwest corner of Aquidneck Island in Narragansett Bay. The long span of the Newport Bridge (Rte. 138) connects the town to the smaller Conanicut Island to the west, which the Jamestown Bridge in turn connects to the mainland. The summer sanctuary, Block Island, lies 10 mi. southeast of Newport in the Block Island Sound. From Providence, take I-195 east to Rte. 114 south via Mt. Hope Bridge (45 min.). From Boston, take Rte. 128 south to Rte. 24 south to either Rte. 114 south (called the West Main Rd. near Newport) or Rte. 138 south (the East Main Rd.). On summer weekends, beat the traffic by taking the back door into town: on Rte. 138 south, turn left onto Valley Rd. and continue past Newport Beach onto Memorial Blvd. (1½ hr.).

West Main Road becomes Broadway in town. **Thames Street,** the main drag on the waterfront, is pronounced as it looks, not like the river through London. Just about everything of interest in Newport is within walking distance. And walking is preferable to fighting the hellish traffic. The convenient RIPTA loop bus accesses most out-of-the-way spots.

Accommodations

Newport has no campgrounds, although a few fine ones cling in the area (see Near Newport below), and few cheap hotels. When staying in town, head for the visitors bureau for guest house brochures and free phones from which to call them. Guest houses offer bed and continental breakfast with colonial-style intimacy. Those not fussy about sharing a bathroom or forgoing a sea view might find a double for $60. Singles are practically nonexistent. Avoid summer weekends, when many hotels and guest houses are booked solid two months in advance and rates rise by $10-$20. Also, be warned that many of Newport's cheaper accommodations close for the winter. **Bed and Breakfasts of Rhode Island, Inc.** (941-0444) can make a reservation for you in Newport at an average rate of $65 per night.

If you arrive in town after the visitors' bureau closes, you'll have to try some guest houses on your own. At the beautiful 1890 **Queen Anne Inn,** 16 Clarke St. (846-5676), near Washington Sq., attractive rooms boast handsome wallpaper, bedspreads, and antique furniture. (Singles $40. Doubles $50-75. Open May-Oct.) Just outside Newport, in Middletown, is **Lindsey's Guest House,** 6 James St. (846-9386). Although without substantial historic significance, a solid breakfast and good rates compensate. (Rooms $50-60 weekends, $40-50 mid-week.)

Food

Seafood is the recurring dream here, high prices the recurrent nightmare. Takeout is always cheaper than sit-down. The young crowd favors the **Corner Store and Deli,** 372 Thames St., a restaurant-deli-grocery store with sandwiches ($2.75-4.75), salads, and Italian specialties to go. (Open daily 7am-10pm.) Eating downtown, you'll help restaurant owners meet their high rents. Along the waterfront and wharves, sandwiches, salads, and pasta dishes make good deals. Walk a few blocks away from downtown and time warp to the succession of true 1950s diners and New England seafood shacks. Sit at a booth and try Linda's Chili or Tish's Pea Soup at the **Franklin Spa,** 229 Franklin St. (Open Mon.-Sat. 6:30am-5pm, Sun. 6:30am-1pm.) Established in 1928, **The Newport Creamery,** at 49 Long Wharf Mall, has become a local institution. Just stop when you see the Golden Cow. Indulge in the enormous ice cream menu ($1.30-4.25). (Open daily 7am-11pm).

Dry Dock Seafood Restaurant, 448 Thames St., a few blocks south of the wharves. Small, cheap, homey seafood joint frequented by locals. Big, crispy fish and chips $5.25, lobster special $8.50. Burgers and fish sandwiches $2-8. Open Sun.-Thurs. 11am-10pm, Fri.-Sat. 11am-11pm.

The Island Omelette Shoppe, 1 Farewell St. Family-run diner feeding lots of local workers. Best breakfast in town; fast and cheap ($1-5). Open daily 6am-2pm.

Salas, 343 Thames St. Italian and Asian pasta with 8 sauces, in 3 serving sizes (½ lb. spaghetti with red clam sauce $4.50). Seafood $7-10; raw bar cheaper than most. Open daily 3-10pm.

Sights

The jewel in Newport's crown of historic districts, **The Point** along Washington St. harborside, contains the famous Hunter House (1748) and six other homes of sea-captains and colonists of yore. Walking tours are included in the free *Best-Read Guide Newport,* available at the **Newport Historical Society,** 82 Town St. (846-0813). The society publishes its own, more detailed maps ($1), and leads two-hour walking tours through the downtown area. (Tours mid-June to late Sept. Fri.-Sat. at 10am. Tour $3, children free.) The society's **museum** of Newport history is free.

The most recent of the city's relics, the **Newport Mansions,** draws herds of tourists every summer. Seven of them are owned and run by the Preservation Society of Newport at 118 Mill St., which distributes walking maps of **Bellevue Avenue,** where most of these colossal beasts reside. **Cliff Walk** (take a right off the east end of Memorial Blvd.) offers a better view of the mansions, also affording a beautiful, rose-framed panorama of the ocean. The interiors of the mansions are a must-see, especially if you are planning a little summer cottage for yourself. Start off with Cornelius Vanderbilt's 172-room **Breakers,** on Ochre Point Ave., the most famous and lavish of all. (Open July-Aug. Mon.-Wed. 10am-5pm, Thurs.-Sun. 9:30am-6pm; April-July and Sept.-Oct. daily 9am-5pm. Admission $6, ages 6-11 $3.50.) **Marble House** and **Rosecliff,** both on Bellevue Ave., furnished settings for the movie *The Great Gatsby.* (Both mansions open May-Oct. daily 10am-5pm; April limited hours. Admission $5, ages 6-11 $3.) Several private palaces also open their doors to the public.

Cycle the 10-mi. loop along **Ocean Drive** for breathtaking scenery. On the way you'll pass sprawling and gaudy **Hammersmith Farm** (846-0420), the childhood home of Jackie Bouvier Kennedy Onassis and the "summer White House" in the early 60s. (Open June-Aug. daily 10am-7pm; April-May and Sept.-Oct. 10am-5pm; Nov. and March Sat.-Sun. only. Admission $5, kids $2.)

The colonial buildings downtown are more unassuming than the mansions, but provide wonderful windows on that epoch. The 1765 **Wanton-Lyman Hazard House,** 17 Broadway (846-3622), the oldest standing house in Newport, has been restored in different period styles. (Open mid-June to Aug. daily 10am-5pm. Admission $2, kids free.) The **White Horse Tavern,** on Marlborough St. (849-3600), the oldest drinking establishment in the country, dates from 1673, but the father of William Mayes, a notorious Red Sea pirate, first opened it as a tavern in 1687.

Since colonists fleeing Puritan Massachusetts founded Rhode Island for religious freedom, it comes as no surprise that the most interesting colonial buildings in town are houses of worship. The **Quaker Meeting House,** built in 1700, on the corner of Marlborough and Farewell St. (847-2481), displays Quaker plain inside and out. Zealots tore down the original steeple, criticized as too "papist," in 1807. (Open mid-June to Aug. Tues.-Sat. 10am-5pm. Admission $2.50, kids free.) The **Touro Synagogue,** 83 Touro St. (847-4794), a beautifully restored Georgian building and the oldest synagogue in the U.S., dates back to 1763. It was to the Newport congregation that George Washington wrote his famous letter describing describes the U.S. as giving "to bigotry no sanction, to persecution no assistance." (Free tours every ½-hr. in summer. Open late June-Sept. Sun.-Fri. 10am-5pm; spring and fall Sun.-Fri. 1-3pm; winter Sun. 1-3pm and by appointment.) Towering **Trinity Church,** facing Thames St. in Queen Anne Sq. (846-0660), includes a pew reserved for George Washington back in the days when Newport strongheld for the revolutionary army. (Open Mon.-Sat. 11am-4pm, Sun. noon-4pm. Free.) The Gothic **St. Mary's Church,** at Spring St. and Memorial Blvd., is the oldest Catholic parish in the state. Jacqueline Bouvier and John F. Kennedy were married here. (Open Mon.-Fri. 7-11am. Free.)

The Redwood Library and Athenaeum, on 50 Bellevue Ave. (847-0292), built in 1748-1750, is the oldest library (and portrait gallery) in continuous use in the country. (Open daily 9:30am-5pm; winter 9am-5:30pm.) The nearby **Newport Art Museum,** 76 Bellevue Ave. (847-0179), has a fine collection of U.S. Impressionist works collected in the 1864 Griswold House. Throughout the summer the museum holds musical picnics on its lawn. (Picnics free. Museum open Tues.-Sat. 10am-5pm, Sun. 1-5pm. Admission $2, seniors $1, kids free.)

No racqueteer should miss the **Tennis Hall of Fame,** 194 Bellevue Ave. (849-3990), built in 1880, in the Newport Casino. The first U.S. national championships were held here one year later. The world-famous men's **Volvo Tennis Tournament** takes place here the second week of July, the galaxy-renowned women's **Virginia Slims Tournament** a week later. The Casino has one of the few facilities in the world for the ancient and arcane game of court tennis. (Open daily 10am-5pm; Oct.-April 11am-4pm. Admission $4, under 16 $2.)

Even those who don't sail should take some time to walk the plank onto vessels available for visit. Open to the public, the Bannister's Wharf Marina has housed the 12m yachts *Clipper, Independence, Courageous,* and *Gleam.* Check out the free *Newport This Week's Yachting & Recreation Guide* for a description of regattas and a calendar of events.

Enter through Gate 1 of the U.S. Navy's training center on Coasters Harbor Island to view a different sort of sea power. Appearances to the contrary, tourism is not Newport's largest industry; the U.S. Navy is the town's largest employer, in Rhode Island second only to the state government. On special occasions, you can tour the successors to the wooden and iron ships from the time of John Paul Jones. Visit the **Naval War College Museum** (863-8300) with interesting exhibits on naval history. (Open June-Sept. Mon.-Fri. 10am-4:30pm, Sat.-Sun. noon-4pm; Oct.-May Mon.-Fri. 10am-4pm. Free.)

After a few hours of touring Newport, you might think of escaping to the shore; unfortunately, the beaches crowd as frequently as the streets. The most popular of the shores is **First Beach,** or Easton's Beach, on Memorial Blvd., with its wonderful old beach houses and carousel. (Open Memorial Day-Labor Day Mon.-Fri. 9am-9pm, Sat.-Sun. 10am-9pm. Parking $5, weekends $8.) Those who prefer hiking over dunes to building sandcastles should try **Fort Adams State Park** south of town on Ocean Dr. (847-2400), with showers, picnic areas, and two fishing piers. (Entrance booth open daily 7:30am-4pm. Park closes 11pm-6am.) Other good beaches line Little Compton, Narragansett, and the shore between Watch Hill and Point Judith. For more details, consult the free *Ocean State Beach Guide,* available at the visitors center.

Entertainment

Summer drives Newport bonkers. In July and August, lovers of classical, folk, and jazz each have a festival to call their own. The **Newport Music Festival** (849-0700) in July attracts pianists, violinists, and other classical musicians from around the world, presenting them in the ballrooms and lawns of the mansions. Tickets ($17-25) and info are available at the visitors bureau (849-8098) and through Ticketron (800-382-8080). In August, you might chorus with folksingers Joan Baez and the Indigo Girls at the **Newport Folk Festival** (212-496-9000), which runs two days, noon to dusk, rain or shine. Tickets ($17.50-25) are available through Ticketmaster. Later in the month, the **Newport Jazz Festival** (847-3700) comes to town. The setting for both festivals is a grassy field at Fort Adams State Park, overlooking the ocean. Purchase tickets ($15-50) in advance through the Tennis Hall of Fame on Bellevue Ave.

Newport's nightlife is easy to find but relatively subdued. Local and out-of-state musicians play more than jazz at the snazzy pink and purple **Blue Pelican Jazz Club,** 40 W. Broadway (847-5675). The Pelican bills a diverse roster of performers. (Open daily 5:30pm-1am. Cover $5-8.) Down by the water at **Pelham East,** at the corner of Thames and Pelham (849-9460), they tend to play straight rock 'n' roll. (Live music nightly. Open daily noon-1am. Weekend cover $5.) Those longing for disco should visit **Maximillian's,** 108 William St. 2nd floor (849-4747), a popular video-enhanced dance club across the street from the Tennis Hall of Fame. (Open Tues.-Sun 9pm-1am. Cover Sun. and Tues.-Thurs. $3, Fri.-Sat. $5.) The **Black Pearl Pub** (and café in good weather) on Bannister's Wharf is reserved and elegant. (Open daily 11:30am-1am.)

Those seeking still more refined recreation should see a production by one of Newport's fine theatrical companies. The **Rhode Island Shakespeare Theater** (849-7892), on Broadway above the post office, actually stages more American than Elizabethan drama each season. (Tickets $12-15.) The **Newport Playhouse** (849-4618), on Connell Hwy., puts on light comedies and musicals. (Performances usually Thurs.-Sun. Tickets $15. Take Harrison Ave. bus from the YMCA.)

Balls whiz by at 188 mph, athletes a good deal more slowly, at the **Jai Alai Fronton,** 150 Admiral Kalbfus Rd. (849-5000; 800-556-6900 outside RI), at the base of the Newport Bridge off Rte. 138. The place, one of the few in the country where the sport—and gambling on it—is legal, has impressive facilities. (Season May 5-Oct. 9 Mon.-Sat. at 7:30pm, matinees Mon. and Sat. at noon. Seats $2-3.50, standing room $1.) Read the weekly *Newport This Week* for more entertainment information.

Newport's Celtic community does not Hiberniate; it declared March **Irish Heritage Month** (849-8048), and sponsors a number of ethnic celebrations culminating in the St. Patrick's Day Parade in downtown Newport.

Near Newport: Conanicut and the Block Islands

On the western side of the Newport Bridge lies sleepy, unassuming **Conanicut Island**, with **Jamestown** at its heart. This mercifully undeveloped town consists of two streets dotted with fishing supply stores and craft shops. In the center of the island, the marvelous 1787 **Jamestown Windmill**, on North Rd., sits on a hill that affords a good view of the neighboring wildlife preserve where you may spot snowy egrets and blue herons. (Windmill open mid-June to Sept. Tues.-Sun. 1-4pm. Free.) Picnic or scuba dive at **Fort Wetherhill**, on Fort Wetherhill Rd. on the island's southeast shore (open 8am-11pm), or camp on the beach in **Fort Getty** (423-1363) on Fort Getty Rd. on the southwest portion of the island; stroll a few hundred yd. to Conanicut's second wildlife sanctuary. (Open May 25-Oct. 9. Sites $15.) Cozy and comfortable **Oyster Bar**, 22 Narragansett Ave., serves a mean chowder and local seafood at great prices ($4-11.50). The **East Ferry Market**, 47 Conanicut Ave., has the best coffee in the state, as well as sandwiches and pastries. (Open summer daily 6:30am-7pm; off-season Mon.-Fri. 6:30am-5pm, Sat. 6:30am-3pm, Sun. 8am-3pm.) In August, the Jamestown Yacht Club hosts the **Fool's Rules Regatta** (423-7492) in Potters Cove. Contestants must construct a sailboat from non-standard material the day of the race, and coax it along the 500-yd. course. Consult the free *This Week in South County* for information on other festivities.

Ten mi. southeast of Newport in the Atlantic, lovely **Block Island** has become an increasingly popular daytrip as tourists saturate Nantucket and Martha's Vineyard. The island is endowed with weathered shingles, quaint buildings, and serenity. Bring a picnic, head due south from Old Harbor where the ferry lets you off, and hike to the Mohegan Bluffs. Those adventurous, careful, and strong enough can wind their way down to the Atlantic waters 70 yd. below. The **Southeast Lighthouse**, high in the cliffs, has warned sailors since 1875; its beacon shines the brightest of any on the Atlantic coast.

The **Block Island Chamber of Commerce** (466-2982), advises at the ferry dock in Old Harbor Drawer D, Block Island 02807. (Open Mon.-Fri. 9am-3pm, Sat. 9am-1pm; mid-Oct. to mid-May Mon.-Fri. approximately 10am-2pm.) You can obtain the free *Block Island Chamber of Commerce Directory* at the Newport Chamber of Commerce.

Cycling is the ideal way to explore the tiny (7 mi. × 3 mi.) island. Try the **Old Harbor Bike Shop** (466-2029), to the left when you exit the ferry. (10-speeds $2 per hr., $14 per day; single mopeds $12, $36; double mopeds $20, $60. Car rentals $55 per day, 20¢ per mi. Open daily 9am-7pm. Must be 21 with credit card.)

Interstate Navigation Co., Galilee State Pier, Point Judith 02882 (401-783-4613; on Block Island 401-466-2261), runs one ferry per day (July 1-Sept. 10) between Providence and Block Island. (Departs at 8:30am; 3½ hr.; $7, round-trip $10.25, bike $2.75. Stops at Ft. Adams at 10:30am; 2 hr.; $7, round-trip $9.25, bike $1.75.) Year-round service to Block Island leaves only from Point Judith, near the town of Galilee, across Rhode Island Sound west of Newport. An interstate ferry leaves from Point Judith. (10 per day in summer down to 1 per day in winter; 1 hr.; fare $6.75, same-day round-trip $10, bicycle $1.75 each way, car $40.50 round-trip.)

The **police** can be reached at 466-2622, the **Coast Guard** at 466-2086. Block Island's post office sorts on Ocean Ave; the **ZIP code** is 02807. Since all phones are on the 466 exchange, only dial the last four digits while on the island.

Providence

Like Rome, Providence sits aloft seven hills. Unlike Rome, its residents are Ivy Leaguers, starving artists, and smartly suited business types. This "island superego" has more of a college-town id with cobblestone sidewalks, colonial buildings, and college kids—even those who aren't students look like they should be. But Providence has more on its horizon than a constellation of BAs. Prescient *Newsweek* recently voted Providence one of the country's most liveable cities, with an urban renaissance in the cards. The city last boomed in the 18th century as a thriving seaport. Traces of that past remain, along with the legacy of Roger Williams, founder of the state and advocate of religious freedom.

Practical Information

Emergency: 272-1111, 0, or 911.

Greater Providence Convention and Visitors Bureau, 30 Exchange Terrace (274-1636 or 800-233-1636), near North Main St. next to City Hall. Self-guided walking tour and the usual maps and tourist literature. Open Mon.-Fri. 8:30am-5pm. **Roger Williams National Memorial Visitors Center,** 282 N. Main St. (528-5385), between Brown campus and downtown. Open daily 9am-5pm; mid-Oct. to mid-May 9am-4:30pm. **Providence Preservation Society,** 21 Meeting St. (831-7440), at the foot of College Hill off Main St. in the 1772 Shakespeare's Head. Detailed info on historic Providence. Self-guided tour instructions for the city's historic neighborhoods (80¢ each) and/or a $3 audio-cassette tour. Open Mon.-Fri. 9am-5pm.

Travelers Aid: In the Amtrak station, 100 Gaspee St. (521-2255). Open 24 hrs. Desk staffed Mon.-Fri. 8:30am-5pm.

Amtrak: 100 Gaspee St. (800-872-7245), in gleaming white concrete structure behind the state capitol, a 10-min. walk to Brown or downtown. Open daily 5am-11:15pm. To Boston ($10) and New York ($29).

Greyhound and Bonanza Buses: 37 Bonanza Way (751-8800), off exit 29 of I-95. Very frequent service to Boston (1 hr., $7.50) and New York (4 hr., $31). Open daily 4:45am-10pm.

Public Transport: Rhode Island Public Transit Authority (RIPTA), 776 Elmwood Ave. (781-9400 or 800-662-5088, from Newport 847-0209). Office open Mon.-Sat. 8:30am-6pm. **Information booth** on Kennedy Plaza across from visitors center provides in-person route and schedule assistance. Open Mon.-Fri. 8am-4:30pm. Buses operate daily 4:30am-midnight. Intercity connections and service to points south and Newport. Fare 25¢-$1.75. In Providence, fares generally 75¢. Senior citizens with photo ID ride free Mon.-Fri. 9am-3pm, Sat.-Sun. all day.

Bike Rental: Rainbow Bicycles, 144 Brook St. (861-6176), at Transit St. near the southern end of Thayer St. 3-speeds $2.50 per hr., $15 per day. Open Mon.-Sat. 10am-5pm. Must have personal check, driver's license, or credit card for deposit.

Post Office: 2 Exchange Terrace (421-4360). Open Mon.-Fri. 7am-5:30pm, Sat. 8am-noon. **ZIP code:** 02903.

Area Code: 401.

The state capitol and the downtown business district cluster just east of the intersection of I-95 and I-195. **Brown University** and the **Rhode Island School of Design (RISD)** (pronounced RIZZ-dee) pose on top of a steep hill east of downtown. **Providence College** tucks into the northwestern corner of town, about 2 mi. from the city center out Douglas Pike.

Accommodations

As with any teeming metropolis and economic, political, religious, atheistic, transportation, and weather hub, Providence has its share of astral motels. Yet affordable housing can be found; small guest houses are probably your best bet. Unfortunately, you won't find camping anywhere near Providence. The city doesn't really have a peak "season," but rooms are especially difficult to exhume in late May and early June, when Providence's many colleges and universities send off their satellites.

Bed and Breakfasts of Rhode Island, Inc. (941-0444) will reserve a room in a private house or inn for around $80 for a double, including breakfast. Outside Providence, the average price is $65. They represent over 100 B&Bs throughout the state.

(Open Mon.-Fri. 9am-8pm, Sat. 9am-noon; Sept. 3-May 28 Mon.-Fri. 9am-5pm.) You can try to make reservations at some of the in-town B&Bs yourself. **Mrs. Dorothy James,** 4 Catalpa Rd. (331-4293), rents singles ($45-48) and doubles ($55) in a unique carriage house built in the 1800s on Providence's East Side. The friendly **International House,** 8 Stimson Ave. (421-7181), near the Brown campus, has two comfortable rooms that usually book up. (Singles $45, students $25. Doubles $50, students $30. Reservations required; taken Mon.-Fri. 9:30am-3pm.) The **Susse Chalet Motor Lodge,** 36 Jefferson Blvd., Warwick (941-6600 or 800-258-1980), a 15-minute drive on I-95 south, is convenient only with a car, offering the eerily familiar orange and brown motel motif and an outdoor pool. (Singles $44.70. Doubles $51.70.) Another Susse Chalet slaloms on Rte. 6, just off Rte. 195 a few mi. east (336-7900; singles $44.70, doubles $49.70).

Food and Entertainment

More auspiciously priced than the accommodations, the good food in Providence emanates from three areas: the Italian district on Federal Hill just west of downtown, the student hangouts on College Hill to the east, and the city's beautiful old diners near downtown.

Louis' Family Restaurant, 286 Brook St. (861-5225). Friendly venue has made the entire community its family. Students swear by its prices, donating the artwork on the walls in return. Try the famous #1 special (2 eggs, homefries, toast, coffee) for $2.12. Lunches $1-4.50, dinners $2.75-5.50. Open daily 6am-3pm.

Angelo's Civita Farnese, 141 Atwells Ave. (621-8171), on Federal Hill. Walk west on Broadway from downtown, turn right near the Holiday Inn and cross the highway overpass; or take bus #26 ("Atwells"). The large acorn marks Federal Hill. Busy place with pictures of strange children on the wall. Eggplant parmesan or spaghetti with garlic and oil $3. Open Mon.-Sat. 11am-8:30pm.

Luke's Luau Hut, 59 Eddy St. (331-4265), behind City Hall. Ask to be seated in the psychedelic basement with the blowfish lantern. Feast on Duck Mona-Mona, Beeg Luau, or the incomparable pu-pu platter ($8-9). Open Sun. noon-9:30pm, Mon. 11am-8pm, Tues.-Thurs. 11am-9:30pm, Fri.-Sat. 11am-10:30pm.

Mutt's Pizza, 167 Benefit St. (351-6888). King of the College Hill for deep-dish pizza ($6.50). Watch for the 2-for-1 special. Sandwiches $2-4. Open Mon.-Thurs. 11am-11pm, Fri.-Sat. 11am-midnight, Sun. 1-10pm. Next door, **Geoff's** (751-2248) names its great sandwiches ($2.75-6) after local celebrities.

"Spirited" best describes Providence's music and bar scene. With a friendly club atmosphere, **The Living Room,** 273 Promenade St. (521-2520), couches cool alternative acts in an abandoned old factory. (Open Sun.-Thurs. 8pm-1am, Fri.-Sat. 8pm-2am. Cover $3.50-15.) The **Church House Inn and Brick Tavern,** 122 Fountain St. (351-5503), desecrates a 1912 church with live jazz, blues, reggae, and the occasional polka (Tues.-Sun.) Outdoor dancing, DJs, and a jukebox contaminate other areas of the club. (Open Mon.-Thurs. 8pm-1am, Fri.-Sat. 8pm-2am. Cover $3-8.) Read the *New Paper,* distributed free Wednesdays, or check the "Weekend" section of the Friday *Providence Journal.*

Exciting distractions include the nationally acclaimed **Trinity Repertory Company,** 201 Washington St. (351-4242); the AAA-level **Pawtucket Red Sox,** who play at McCoy Stadium in Pawtucket (724-7300); the stock-car races at the **Seekonk Speedway** (336-8488), a few mi. east on Rte. 6 in Massachussetts (1756 Fall River Ave.); and the **Providence Performing Arts Center,** 220 Weybosset St. (421-2787), which hosts a variety of concerts and Broadway musicals. The **Cable Car Cinema,** 204 S. Main St. (272-3970), with an attached café, shows art and foreign films in an unusual setting—patrons recline on couches instead of regular seats. The **Avon Repertory Cinema,** 260 Thayer St. (421-3315), attracts a big Brown crowd and shows first-run small-market films and classics.

Sights

Providence's most notable historic sights cluster on **College Hill,** a 350-year-old neighborhood. **Brown University,** established in 1764, claims several 18th-century buildings and provides the best info about the area. The Office of Admissions, housed in the historic Carliss-Brackett House at 45 Prospect St. (863-2378), distributes a free walking tour of the campus and gives tours daily at 10am and 2pm. (Open Mon.-Fri. 8am-4:30pm.) Check out **University, Sayles,** and **Wilson Halls,** and stroll down lamp-lined **Benefit Street.** In addition to founding Rhode Island, Roger Williams created the Baptist Church; the **First Baptist Church of America,** built in 1775, stands at 75 N. Main St. Looking down from the hill, you'll see the **Rhode Island State Capitol** (277-2357), its enormous free-standing marble dome second in size only to St. Peter's in Rome. (Free guided tours Mon.-Fri. every hr. 10am-2pm. Building open Mon.-Fri. 8:30am-4:30pm.)

The nearby **RISD Museum of Art,** 224 Benefit St. (331-3511), gathers a fine collection of Greek, Roman, Asian, and Impressionist art and a gigantic, 10th-century Japanese Buddha. (Open Wed.-Sat. noon-5pm; winter Tues.-Wed. and Fri.-Sat. 10:30am-5pm, Thurs. noon-6pm, Sun. 2-5pm. Admission $2.50, seniors and under 18 $1.)

Thayer Street is a popular student hangout and shopping spot. Built in 1828, the **Arcade,** at 65 Weybosset St. (456-5403), is the nation's oldest shopping mall. For a quiet walk or jog, head to: the spacious grounds of **Roger Williams Park** (785-9450), with its carousel and zoo, on the Cranston-Providence line; the lovely **Butler Hospital** (455-6200) estate; **Colt State Park,** in Bristol, where many local and national bands perform in summer; or the rolling green of **Swan Point Cemetery,** on Blackstone Blvd. On New Year's Eve, people wander the streets watching puppet shows, jazz bands, and Guatemalan dancers in a **First Night** celebration of the city's diversity. In early June, the **Festival of Historic Houses** trundles tourists through ancient city homes by candlelight. In early September the **Providence Waterfront Festival** involves boat races, harbor cruises, and an arts and crafts fair. Call the visitors bureau for more information (274-1636).

SOUTH CAROLINA

South Carolina is a state of pastureland, friendly folk, and the Civil War. The first state to secede from the Union (in 1860), South Carolina takes great pride in its Confederate history, with monuments, museums, and other reminders of the Civil War everywhere.

Myrtle Beach is a tourist hotspot during the summer, and as such comes complete with flashing lights, all-night T-shirt shops, and over-priced restaurants and hotels. Columbia, the capital, is slow-paced with little to ogle, and provides a nice change from hectic Myrtle Beach. Charleston is a beautiful, stately city—most of the downtown area, a registered historic district, has retained its antebellum charm. You'll want to do the Charleston for a few days to take in the city's favors and flavors.

Practical Information

Capital: Columbia.

Tourist Information: Department of Parks, Recreation, and Tourism, Edgar A. Brown Bldg., 1205 Pendleton St. #106, Columbia 29201 (734-0122). **U.S. Forest Service,** P.O. Box 970, Columbia 29202 (765-5222).

Time Zone: Eastern. **Postal Abbreviation:** SC

Charleston

A favorite stopover point for natural disaster, Charleston in recent years has withstood five fires, 10 hurricanes, and earthquakes. The reconstruction after the most recent unkindness, September 1989's Hurricane Hugo, is nearly complete; fresh paint, new storefronts, and tree stumps mix with beautifully refurbished antebellum homes, old churches, and hidden gardens. Dukes, barons, and earls once presided over Charleston's great coastal plantations, leaving an historic downtown area which a traveler could spend weeks touring. The Charleston area also offers visitors the resources of the nearby Atlantic coastal islands. Most noticeably, the people of Charleston are some of the friendliest people you will meet on your journeys south. They survive the way they flourish—with a smile.

Practical Information

Emergency: 911.

New Visitors Center: 81 May St. (853-8000), in front of the Municipal Auditorium. Walking tour map (50¢) has much historical information and good directions. Catch a showing of the film *Forever Charleston,* which gives an overview of Charleston's past and present. Tickets $3, children $1.50. Open Mon.-Fri. 8:30am-5:30pm, Sat.-Sun. 8:30am-5pm.

Amtrak: 4565 Gaynor Ave. (744-8263), 8 mi. west of downtown. The "Durant Ave." bus will take you from the station to the historic district. Trains to: Richmond (2 per day, 7 hr., $79); Savannah (2 per day, 2 hr., $23); and Washington, DC (2 per day, 14 hr., $102). Open daily 6am-10pm.

Greyhound: 3610 Dorchester Rd. (722-7721), near I-26. Because the downtown bus station is closed this is the only one available, but try to avoid the area at night. To: Myrtle Beach (2 per day, 2 hr., $20); Savannah (2 per day, 3 hr., $25); Washington, DC (2 per day, 11 hr., $59). To get into town, take the **South Carolina Electric and Gas** bus marked "Broad St." or "South Battery" that stops right in front of the station and get off at the intersection of Meeting and Calhoun St. Pick up the bus marked "Navy Yard 5 mile Dorchester Rd.," at the same intersection to get back to the station from town. There are two "Navy Yard" buses so be sure to take the "5 mile Dorchester Rd." bus outbound; it's the only one that stops in front of the station. Open daily 6am-10pm.

Public Transport: South Carolina Electric and Gas Company (SCE&G) City Bus Service, 2469 Leeds Ave. (747-0922). Operates Mon.-Sat. 5:10am-1am. Fare 50¢. Also operates **Downtown Area Shuttle (DASH)** Mon.-Fri. 8am-5pm. Fare 50¢, transfers to other SCE&G buses free.

Car Rental: Thrifty Car Rental (552-7531 or 800-367-2277). $30 per day with 200 free mi., 20¢ each additional mi. Must be 25 with major credit card.

Bike Rental: The Bicycle Shoppe, 283 Meeting St. (722-8168). $3 per hr., $12 per day. Open daily 10am-5:30pm.

Taxi: North Area Taxi, 554-7575. Base fare $1.

Help Lines: Hotline, 744-4357. Open 24 hrs. General counseling and comprehensive information on transient accommodations. **People Against Rape,** 722-7273. Open 24 hrs.

Post Office: 11 Broad St. Open Mon.-Fri. 8am-5pm, Sat. 8am-noon. **ZIP code:** 29401.

Area Code: 803.

Old Charleston is confined to the southernmost point of the mile-wide peninsula below **Calhoun Street. Meeting, King,** and **East Bay Streets** are major north-south routes through the city.

Accommodations and Camping

Motel rooms in historic downtown Charleston are expensive. All the cheap motels are a good distance from downtown and not a practical option for those without cars. Investigate the accommodations just across the Ashley River on U.S. 17 South: several tiny establishments offer $15-20 rooms. Far and away the best budget option in town is the **Rutledge Museum Guest House,** 114 Rutledge Ave. (722-7551), a beautiful historic home with shared rooms and free coffee, tea, hot chocolate, and pastries each morning. ($20 per person; rates lower for extended stays.) The laidback, friendly manager will not let you set foot in Charleston until she's given you a full orientation. If she can't house you, try **Charleston East Bed and Breakfast,** 1031 Tall Pine Rd. (884-8208), in Mt. Pleasant east of Charleston off U.S. 701. They will try to place you in one of their 16 private homes. (Rooms $50-80, $5-10 less for singles. Open for reservations daily 9am-8pm.) **Motel 6,** 2058 Savannah Hwy. (556-5144), 4 mi. out at 7th Ave., is clean and pleasant, but far from downtown and frequently filled. (Singles $30, each additional person $6.)

There are several inexpensive campgrounds in the Charleston area, but not a one is near downtown. Eight mi. south on U.S. 17, try **Oak Plantation Campground** (766-5936; sites $9.50). Also look for **Pelican's Cove,** 97 Center St., at Folly Beach (588-2072; sites with full hookup $17).

Food and Nightlife

Most restaurants in the revamped downtown area are also expensive. If you choose to eat out, eat lunch, since most restaurants serve dinner selections at discounted prices.

Marina Variety Store/City Marina, Lockwood Blvd. Pleasant view of the Ashley River from an otherwise unremarkable dining room. Good shellfish and great nightly specials under $7. Open Mon.-Sat. 6:30am-3pm and 5-10pm, Sun. 6:30am-3pm.

Henry's, 54 N. Market St. (723-4363), at Anson. A local favorite. Not cheap, but the food is good, especially the grilled shrimp ($7.95). On weekends, live jazz upstairs starts at 9pm followed by a late-night breakfast. Open Mon.-Wed. 11:30am-10:30pm, Thurs.-Sun. 11:30am-1am.

The Broad Street, 38 Broad St. (722-2104), on the edge of the historic district. The dinerlike atmosphere serves as a popular student hangout. The Gumbo Ya-Ya ($7), which contains every foodstuff in the universe, is too tasty to miss. (Open daily noon-10:30pm.)

Hyman's Seafood Company, 215 Meeting St. (723-0233). Kudos to the proprietor, who manages to serve about 15 different kinds of fresh fish daily ($7). If you like shellfish, the snow crabs ($8) are a must. (Open daily 11am-11pm.)

Before going out in Charleston, pick up a free copy of *Poor Richard's Omnibus,* available at grocery stores and street corners all over town; the PRO lists concerts and other events. Locals rarely dance the *Charleston* anymore, and the city's nightlife has suffered accordingly. Most bars and clubs are in the **Market Street** area. **Cafe 99,** 99 S. Meeting St. (577-4499), has nightly live entertainment, strong drinks ($2-4), and reasonably priced dinners ($4-7). (Open daily 11:30am-2am. No cover.) For the best bands go to **Myskyns Tavern,** 5 Faber St. (577-5595), near Market St., and have a drink ($1-3) at the enormous mahogany bar. Or hang out with the locals on Friday and Saturday nights in front of **San Miguel's Mexican Restaurant** off Market St. (723-9745).

Sights and Events

Saturated with ancient homes, historical monuments, churches, galleries, and gardens, Charleston gives a tourist something to chew on. A multitude of organized tours allow you to see the city by foot, car, bus, boat, trolley, or carriage. Information on these towns can be obtained at the Visitors' Center on Mary Street. **Gray Line Water Tours** (722-1112) gives you your money's worth. Their two-hour boat rides leave daily at 10am, 12:30pm, and 3pm ($8; reservations recommended). The bus tours, however, provide the best overview of the city. **Talk of the Towne** (795-8199) has tours twice a day for two hours and will even pick you up from your hotel. Before touring, see *Dear Charleston,* an acclaimed documentary on the city's history recounted through the musings of long-time residents (daily every hr. 10am-noon and 2-4pm). The film shows at the **Preservation Society Visitor Center,** 147

King St. (723-4381), and at **Dear Charleston Theater & Gifts,** 52 N. Market St. (577-4743). (Admission at both places $3.25, children $1.75.) The **Gibbes Gallery,** 135 Meeting St. (722-2706), has a fine collection of portraits by prominent American artists. (Open Sun.-Mon. 1-5pm, Tues.-Sat. 10am-5pm. Admission $2, seniors and students $1, children 50¢.)

The **Nathanial Russell House,** 51 Meeting St. (723-1623), featuring a magnificent staircase that spirals without support from floor to floor, gives an idea of how Charleston's wealthy merchant class lived in the early 19th century. The **Edmonston-Allston House,** 21 E. Battery St. (722-7171), looks out over Charleston Harbor. (Both open Mon.-Sat. 10am-5pm, Sun. 2-5pm. Admission to 1 house $4, to both $6. Get tickets to both homes at 52 Meeting St.) Founded in 1773, the **Charleston Museum,** 360 Meeting St. (722-2996), maintains a collection of bric-a-brac ranging from natural history specimens to old sheet music. It also offers combination tickets for the museum itself and the three historic homes within easy walking distance: the **Aiken-Rhett Mansion** built in 1817; the 18th-century **Heyward-Washington House,** 87 Church St.; and the **Joseph Manigault House,** 350 Meeting St. (all three tours 722-2996). The Washington House includes the only 18th-century kitchen open to the public in Charleston. (Museum open Mon.-Sat. 9am-5pm, Sun. 1-5pm. Aiken-Rhett open daily 10am-5pm. Historical homes open Mon.-Sat. 10am-5pm, Sun. 1-5pm. Admission to all 4 facilities $10, children $5.)

A visit to Charleston just wouldn't be complete without a boat tour to **Fort Sumter** (722-1691) in the harbor. The Civil War began when rebel forces in South Carolina, the first state to secede, attacked this Union fortress on April 12, 1861. Over seven million pounds of metal were fired against the fort before those inside fled in February 1865. Tours ($8, ages 6-12 $4) leave several times daily from the Municipal Marina, at the foot of Calhoun St. and Lockwood Blvd. **Fort Sumter Tours,**the company that run the boat tours to the fort, also tours to **Patriots' Point,** the world's largest naval and maritime museum. Here you can walk the decks of the retired U.S. aircraft carrier *Yorktown,* or stroke the destroyer *Laffey's* huge fore and aft cannons.

If you are feeling a tad gun-shy, visit the **City Market,** downtown at Meeting St., which vends everything from porcelain sea animals to handwoven sweetgrass baskets in the open air from 9:30am to sunset.

Magnolia Gardens, (571-1266), 10 mi. out of town on Hwy. 61 off Rte. 17, is the 300-year-old ancestral home of the Drayton family, and treats visitors to 50 acres of gorgeous gardens with 900 varieties of camelia and 250 varieties of azalea. Get lost in the hedge maze. You'll probably want to skip the manor house, but do consider renting bicycles ($2 per hr.) to explore the neighboring swamp and bird sanctuary. (Open daily 9:30am-5pm. Admission $8, seniors $7, teens $6, kids $4.)

From mid-March to mid-April, the **Festival of Houses** (723-1623) celebrates Charleston's architecture and tradition, as many private homes open their doors to the public. Music, theater, dance, and opera converge on the city during **Spoleto Festival USA** (722-2764) in late May and early June. During **Christmas in Charleston** (723-7641), tours of many private homes and buildings are given, and many motels offer special reduced rates.

Columbia

The capital is a quiet, unassuming city whose pervasive college-town flavor overshadows state politics. The University of South Carolina provides most of the city's excitement and nightlife. The city sprung up in 1786 when bureaucrats in Charleston decided that their territory needed a proper capital city. Surveyors found some land near the Congaree River, cleared it, and within two decades, over 1000 people poured into one of America's first planned cities. President Woodrow Wilson called Columbia home during his boyhood and now thousands of USC students do the same.

Columbia's 18th-century aristocratic elegance has been preserved by the Historic Columbia Foundation in the **Robert Mills House,** 1616 Blanding St., three blocks east of Sumter St. (252-3964; tours Tues.-Sat. 10:15am-3:15pm, Sun. 1-4:15pm; $3, students $1.50). Mills, one of America's first federal architects, designed the Washington Monument and 30 of South Carolina's public buildings. Across the street, at 1615 Blanding, is the **Hampton-Preston Mansion** (252-0935), once used by Union forces as a Civil War headquarters. (Open Tues.-Sat. 10:15am-3:15pm, Sun. 1-4:15pm. Tours $3, students $1.50, under 6 free.) Stroll through USC's **Horseshoe,** at the junction of College and Sumter St., which holds the university's oldest buildings, dating from the beginning of the 19th century. The **McKissick Museum** (777-7251), at the top of the Horseshoe, offers scientific, folk and pottery exhibits, as well as selections from the university's extensive collection of Twentieth Century-Fox Newsreels. (Open Mon.-Fri. 9am-4pm, Sat. 10am-5pm, Sun. 1-5pm. Free.) Columbia's award-winning **Riverbanks Zoo,** on I-26 at Greystone Blvd. (779-8730), northwest of downtown, is home to more than 2000 animals. See frogs, sharks, cobras, and tigers before stopping off at the concessions stand for a snow cone. (Open daily 9am-4pm. Admission $3.50, seniors $2, students $2.75, ages 3-12 $1.50.)

The new **South Carolina State Museum,** 301 Gervais St. (737-4921), beside the Gervais St. Bridge is located inside the historic Columbia Mills building. Exhibits include replicas of two denizens of the profound—a Great White Shark and the first submarine to sink an enemy ship. (Open Mon.-Sat. 10am-5pm, Sun, 1-5pm. Admission $3, seniors and college students with ID $2, ages 6-17 $1.25, under 6 free.)

The **Five Points** business district, at the junction of Harden, Devine, and Blossom St. (from downtown, take the "Veterans Hospital" bus), caters to Columbia's large student population. **Groucho's,** 611 Harden St. (799-5708), in the heart of Five Points, is a Columbia institution and anomaly—a New York-style Jewish deli (large sandwiches $3-5). (Open Mon.-Fri. 10am-6pm, Thurs.-Fri. 7-11pm, Sat. 11am-4pm.) **Yesterday's Restaurant and Tavern,** 2030 Devine St. (799-0196), serves today's specialties over old newspapers preserved within lacquered tabletops. Enjoy complete dinner specials ($4-6) or vegetarian pies. (Open Sun.-Tues. 11:30am-1am, Wed.-Sat. 11:30am-2am.) **Kinch's Restaurant,** 1115 Assembly St. (256-3843), across the street from the State House, has an early-bird breakfast special for $2. (Open daily 7am-4pm.) **The Columbia State Farmers Market,** Bluff Rd. (737-3016), across from the USC Football Stadium, is a good place to stock up on fresh produce shipped in from all corners of South Carolina. The university provides most of the city's excitement and nightlife. Try **Club 638,** 638 Harden St. (779-1953), at Five Points for dancing and revelry. Five Points abounds in bars.

The **USC Off-Campus Housing Office** (777-4174), in the "I" building on Devine St. is probably your best budget bet for beauty rest. They can link you up with owners of private homes in the university community who rent rooms, usually on a per week basis ($40-50 a week). Otherwise, the only budget option downtown is the **Heart of Columbia,** 1011 Assembly St. (799-1140), with a shabby-looking exterior but clean chambers in a heart-attack-free neighborhood. (Singles $29. Doubles $33.) Just west of downtown across the Congaree River, a number of inexpensive motels line Knox Abbot Dr. **Econo-lodge,** 827 Bush River Rd., off exit 108 at I-20 and I-26, has bright rooms, a swimming pool, A/C, and a movie channel. (Singles Sun.-Thurs. $24, Fri.-Sat. $35.) The **Sesquicentennial State Park** (788-2706) has sites with electricity and water ($8). Take "State Park" bus from downtown. By car, take I-20 to Two Notch Rd. (Rte. 1) exit, and head northeast 4 mi.

The **Greater Columbia Convention and Visitors Bureau,** 301 Gervais St. (254-0479), is not budget-oriented and caters to larger groups, but provides a free street map of the area with all the historical sights marked on it and a free coupon book for discounts at area hotels and restaurants. (Open Mon.-Fri. 8:30am-5pm, Sat. 10am-5pm.) The **University of South Carolina Information Desk,** Russell House Student Center, 2nd floor (777-3196), on Green at Sumter St., across from the Horseshoe, provides campus maps, shuttle schedules, advice on nearby budget accommodations and the low-down on campus life and events. If you get stranded in the area and/or need transportation in a hurry, contact **Traveler's Aid,** 1800 Main St. (733-5450; open Mon.-Fri. 9am-5pm).

Most buses running along the East Coast stop here. The **Congaree River** marks the western edge of the city. **Assembly Street** and **Sumter Street** are downtown's major north-south arteries; **Gervais Street** and **Calhoun Street** cut east-west. **Columbia Metropolitan Airport,** 300 Aviation Way (822-5000) is serviced by Delta, American, USAir, and others. **Amtrak,** 903 Gervais St. (252-8246 or 800-872-7245), has trains once per day to Washington, DC (9½ hr., $85); Miami (12 hr., $117); and Savannah (2 hr., $30). The northbound train leaves daily at 5:31am, the southbound at 10:43pm. (Station open Mon.-Sat. 8:30am-4:30pm and 10:30pm-6:30am, Sun. 10:30pm-6:30am.) **Greyhound/Trailways,** 2015 Gervais St. (779-0650), is near the intersection of Harden and Gervais St., about 1 mi. east of the capitol. Buses to: Charlotte, NC (5 per day, 2 hr., $20); Charleston, SC (5 per day, 2½ hr., $20); Atlanta (6 per day, 4½ hr., $40). Open 24 hrs. **South Carolina Electric and Gas** (748-3019) operates local buses. Most routes start from the transfer depot at the corner of Assembly and Gervais St. Fare 50¢. Local **help lines** are **Helpline of the Midlands** (790-4357), **Rape Crisis** (252-8393), and the **AIDS Information Line,** (800-322-2437). The **Richland Memorial Hospital,** 5 Richland Medical Park (765-7561), has emergency services and a walk-in clinic. Emergency is 911. The **Post Office,** 1601 Assembly St. (733-4647), is open Mon. and Fri. 7:30am-6pm, Tues.-Thurs. 7:30am-5pm. Columbia's **ZIP code** is 29202; the **area code** is 803.

Myrtle Beach

Located mid-way along the 60-mi. beach known as the **Grand Strand,** Myrtle Beach is more than a beach, it's a phenomenon—a living smorgasbord of American pop culture. Its white sand beaches, clean ocean water, 77 full and 45 miniature golf courses, and over 1000 restaurants and nightclubs, make Myrtle Beach the third most popular destination on the East Coast after Disney World and Atlantic City. With more than 55,000 rentable rooms and over 9000 individual campsites in the area, it sounds easy to find a cheap place to spend the night here, but during the summer, it is difficult, if not impossible, to find a hotel room for under $30. The streets of Myrtle Beach are lined with fireworks warehouses, all-you-can-eat restaurants, fast-food franchises, and gift shops. Mini-golf players can try **Hawaiian Rumble Golf,** off Hwy. 175 (651-0048), featuring a volcano at the 18th hole. There are several waterparks, such as **Myrtle Waves,** (448-1026), on the U.S. 17 bypass at 10th Ave. N.

If the street activities aren't garish enough, use the flashing lights as a beacon and head toward the tacky museums at the beach center, Ocean Blvd. between 5th and 12th St. At the **Ripley's Believe It or Not Museum,** 901 N. Ocean Blvd. (448-2331), a film shows a man pulling a loaded wagon with his eyelids. (Admission $5.25, seniors, students, and military $4.25.) Launch into shopping ecstasy at the **Waccamaw Pottery and Outlet Park,** west of the beach on U.S. 501 between Myrtle Beach and Conway, a 500-acre complex of over 100 factory outlet stores. (Open in summer daily 9am-10pm.) For nightlife try the **Afterdeck,** 9801 N. King's Hwy. (449-1550), or **Atlantis,** off Hwy. 401 (448-4200), which has three different dance floors, one of which is an 18,000-gallon aquarium.

The restaurants in Myrtle Beach are largely predictable, overpriced steak-and-seafood places. You won't find any interesting budget fare here—look instead for local hangouts that serve burgers, sandwiches, and beer. **River City Café,** 21st Ave. N., serves huge juicy hamburgers, homemade fries, beer, wine, and free peanuts in a fun, collegiate atmosphere. (Open Mon.-Sat. 11am-10pm, Sun. 11:30am-9pm.) **K and W Cafeteria** (448-1669) has locations at both ends of town, on Business 17. At dinner expect a 40-minute wait. **Olympic Flame Restaurant and Pancake House,** 14th Ave. N. at Ocean Blvd. (448-2756), one block from the beach, starts the day right with fluffy pancakes ($2.25) and omelettes ($2.75). (Open daily 6:30am-10pm.)

Or try **Mammy's Kitchen,** 11th Ave. N. at King's Hwy., for a breakfast special of hashbrowns, toast, eggs, and bacon ($2). (Open daily 7am-noon and 4-9pm.)

For students, the most convenient places to stay are within 10 blocks north or south of the **Pavilion Amusement Park** area (8th and 9th Ave. N. at Ocean Blvd). From there, beaches, clubs, and all-you-can-eat restaurants are within easy walking distance. The most inexpensive places are just west of the beach property in the 3rd St. area or on U.S. 17. You can often bargain for a lower hotel rate. Remember that in the off-season (Oct.-Feb.) prices plunge at most hotels. At the best budget oceanfront hotel, **La Roca Motel,** 1708 N. Ocean Blvd. (448-3341), you'll enjoy the swimming pool and the bright clean rooms (singles $40-50). **Ocean West Motel,** 204 N. King's Hwy., has old but clean rooms with cable TV (singles $30-40). The **King's Road Motor Lodge,** 1205 N. King's Hwy. (448-1625), two blocks from the Greyhound station, boasts bright rooms, a swimming pool, and a game room (singles $35, off-season $24). If you strike out at these places, try the **Beach Hotel and Motel Reservation Service** (local 626-7477, elsewhere 800-626-7477), which calls various member hotels free of charge to find the cheapest accommodations. For the best rates ask for "second row," the string of hotels across the street from the oceanfront properties. (Open Mon.-Fri. 9am-5pm.)

To distance yourself from the frenzied beach and enjoy the outdoors in a less infested incarnation, camp at **Myrtle Beach State Park** (238-5325). Just south of town off U.S. 17 and across from the air force base, the park encloses a stretch of non-commercial and relatively uncrowded shoreline. (Gates open daily 6am-10pm. Sites $15.) Some of the several private campgrounds have rules against single campers, so call ahead if you're alone. **KOA Kampground,** on King's Hwy. at 5th Ave. S. (448-3421), is less than 1 mi. outside of town. (Sites with water and electricity $19, with full hookup $20.50. Call for reservations.) **Apache Family Campground,** 9700 King's Hwy. N. (449-7323), is slightly farther away. Some sites are on the beach, some in pine groves. (Families only. Sites $20-23.) Sleeping on the heavily patrolled beach is illegal, as are parties.

Stop at the **Chamber of Commerce,** 13th Ave. N. at King's Hwy. (626-7444), for free copies of *Beachcomber* and *Hot Times* as well as information on current activities. Also, pick up *Strand* magazine, a map of the area, bus schedules, and the yellow *Continuing Events* sheet which gives listings of current goings on. (Open Mon.-Fri. 8:30am-5pm, Sat. 9am-noon, Sun. noon-5pm.)

In Myrtle Beach, **U.S. 17,** also called **King's Highway,** runs north-south along the coastline and provides access to most points of interest. **Route 501** west in the direction of Conway leads to popular factory outlet stores. Myrtle Beach's **Greyhound** terminal, on 9th Ave. N. at U.S. 17 (448-2471), has connections to: Charleston (2 per day, 2 hr., $30); Florence (2 per day, 45 min., $15); and Wilmington (3 per day, 2 hr., $14). (Open daily 8am-1:30pm and 3:30-7pm.) To get around Myrtle Beach and Conway, use **Coastal Rapid Public Transit (CRPTA)** (626-9138 in Myrtle Beach; 248-7277 in Conway). Local fare is 75¢; Conway to Myrtle Beach is $1.25. Or rent a bike at **The Bike Shoppe,** 711 Broadway (448-5103; $5 per 3 hr. for sturdy 1-speeds; license or credit card required for deposit).

The number for the local **police** is 448-3111. Myrtle Beach's **post office** is at 505 N. King's Hwy. (626-9533; open Mon.-Fri. 8:30am-5pm, Sat. 9am-noon). The **ZIP code** is 29577; the **area code** is 803.

SOUTH DAKOTA

From the forested granite crags of the Black Hills to the glacial lakes of the northeast, the Coyote State has more to offer visitors than might be expected. WALL DRUG. In fact, the state has the highest ratio of sights-to-people in the Great Plains, offering both natural beauties—such as the Black Hills, the Badlands, and Wind and Jewel Caves—and man-made attractions, such as Mt. Rushmore and

Rapid City and others WALL DRUG. South Dakota welcomes visitors with open arms and open cash registers, and visitors from both U.S. coasts making the most of local hospitality have made tourism the state's second largest industry, after agriculture. YOU ARE NOW ONLY A FEW PAGES FROM WALL DRUG.

Practical Information

Capital: Pierre.

Division of Tourism, 221 S. Central, in Capitol Lake Plaza, P.O. Box 1000, Pierre 57051 (773-3301 or 800-952-2217; 800-843-1930 outside SD). Open Mon.-Fri. 8am-5pm. U.S. Forest Service, Custer 57730 (673-4853). Camping stamps for the national forest, Golden Eagle passes for those over 62, and Black Hills National Forest maps ($1). Open Mon.-Fri. 8am-5pm. Division of Parks and Recreation, Capitol Bldg., Pierre 57501 (773-3371). Information on state parks and campgrounds. Open Mon.-Fri. 8am-5pm.

Time Zones: Central (1 hr. behind Eastern) and Mountain (2 hr. behind Eastern). Postal Abbreviation: SD

Badlands National Park

Some 60 million years ago, when much of the Great Plains was under water, tectonic shifts pushed up the Rockies and the Black Hills. Mountain streams deposited silt from these highlands in what is now known as the Badlands, preserving in layer after pink layer the remains of wildlife that once wandered the flood plains. Erosion has created spires and steep gullies, a landscape that contrasts sharply with the plains of eastern South Dakota. The Sioux called these arid and treacherous formations "Mako Sica," or "bad land;" Gen. Alfred Sully, the opposition, called them "hell with the fires out."

The Badlands still smolder about 50 mi. east of Rapid City on I-90. Highway 240 winds through the wilderness in a 32-mi. detour off I-90 (take exit 131 or 110). There is almost no way to visit the park by highway without being importuned by employees from **Wall Drug**, 510 Main St. (279-2175), in **Wall**. The store is a towering monument to susceptibility to saturation advertising; after seeing billboards for Wall Drug from as far as hundreds of miles away, travelers feel obligated to make a stop in Wall to see what all the fuss is about. The "drug store," itself quite a disappointment, sells mostly overpriced souvenirs and other kitsch. (Open daily 6am-10pm; Sept.-Nov. and May 7am-5pm; Dec.-April Mon.-Sat. 7am-5pm.) All of the other cafés and shops on Main St. are just as ridiculously overpriced, and all in all the town is just another brick in the . . . well, forget it.

From Wall, take Rte. 240, which loops through the park and returns to I-90 30 mi. east of Wall in Cactus Flats. From Rapid City, take Rte. 44 and turn northeast at Scenic, where it leads to Sage Creek and Rte. 240. There are ranger stations at both entrances off I-90, although the western portion of the park is much less developed. **Jack Rabbit Buses** (348-3300) make two stops daily at Wall from Rapid City ($19). You can probably hitch a ride into the park from Wall. It costs $1 per person, $3 per carload, ($1.50 for a carload of Arikara Sioux) to enter the park.

The **Cedar Pass Visitors Center** (433-5361), five mi. inside the park's eastern entrance, is more convenient than the **White River Visitors Center** (455-2878), 55 mi. southwest, off Rte. 27 in the park's less-visited southern section. Both centers distribute a free paper detailing park programs and trail guides for sale. (Cedar Pass open daily 7am-8pm; Sept. 2-May 8am-4:30pm. White River open June-Aug. 9am-5pm.) Stock up on gasoline, water, food, and insect repellent before entering the park. The Badlands suffer extreme temperatures in midsummer and winter, but late spring and fall offer pleasant weather and few insects. Always watch (and listen) for rattlesnakes.

Accommodations, Camping, and Food

Two campgrounds lie within the park. **Cedar Pass Campground,** near the visitor center, has covered picnic tables and a bathroom with running water, but no showers (sites $7). The **Sage Creek Campground,** 11 mi. from the Pinnacles entrance south of Wall, is merely an open field with pit toilets and no water. But it's free.

Try backcountry camping for a more intimate introduction to this desert-like landscape. Bring plenty of water and set up camp at least half a mile from a road. Go ahead and share the stars with local wildlife, but don't cozy up to the bison, especially in the spring when overprotective mothers may become nervous.

For tenderfoot tourists, the **Cedar Pass Lodge,** P.O. Box 5, Interior 57750 (433-5460), next to the visitor center, has air-conditioned cabins. (Singles $32. Doubles $36. Each additional person $4. Open May to mid-Oct. Try to make reservations; leave a 50% deposit.) Try a buffalo burger ($3) at the lodge's mid-priced restaurant. (Open June-Aug. daily approximately 7am-9pm.)

Sights and Activities

The park protects large tracts of prairie along with the stark rock formations. The Cedar Pass Visitors Center has an audio-visual program on the Badlands, and the park rangers of both centers lead free tours, all of which leave from the Cedar Pass amphitheater. The **nature hikes** (at 8am and 6pm, 1½ hr.) provide an easy way to appreciate the Badlands, and you may find Oligocene fossils right at your feet. The evening amphitheater slide program narrates Badlands history, but cover up—the mosquitoes can be ravenous. A one-hour night-prowl or sky-trek follows the program.

You can also hike through the Badlands on your own. Try the short but steep **Saddle Pass Trail** or the scenic hike following a 5¼-mi. loop that runs between the **Fossil Exhibit** and the **Windows,** both along Loop Rd. Other highlights of the Loop Rd. are **Robert's Prairie Dog Town** and the **Yellow Mounds Overlook,** where brilliant red and yellow formations relieve the bleached rose. Keep your eyes shucked along Sage Creek Rd. for the park's herd of about 400 bison. Respect the intense midday sun, and at all times be wary of crumbly footholds, cacti, and occasional rattlesnakes. It's easy to lose your bearings in this confusing territory, so consult with a ranger or tote a map.

Black Hills

The Black Hills, so named for the dark sheen that distance lends to the green pines covering the hills, have long been considered sacred by the Sioux living to the north. The treaty of 1868 gave the Black Hills and the rest of South Dakota west of the Missouri River to the Sioux, but the government broke it (in a hardly unprecedented move) during the gold rush of 1877-79. Since then, white residents have dominated the forested hills, white granite spires, and expansive underground caves with their logging, mining, and tourism. Recently, the Sioux took their claims to federal court and, in 1980, the Supreme Court awarded them a "just compensation" of $200 million. The Sioux, however, refused to accept the money, wanting only the return of their land. Legislative efforts to address this conflict have, to date, met with slow death by Congressional inertia.

I-90 skirts the northern border of the Black Hills through Spearfish in the west and Rapid City in the east. The interconnecting road system through the hills is difficult to navigate without a good map; pick up one for free at the Rapid City Chamber of Commerce.

Powder River Lines serves only Deadwood, Lead, and Hot Springs (see Rapid City Practical Information). Rent a car to explore the area thoroughly. Alternatively, take advantage of the excellent and informative **Gray Line** tours (342-4461). Tickets can be purchased at Rapid City motels, hotels, and campgrounds. Make reservations, or call one hour before departure; they will pick you up at your motel.

Tour #1 is the most complete Black Hills tour, going to Mt. Rushmore, Black Hills National Forest, Custer State Park, Needles Highway, and the Crazy Horse Monument (mid-May to mid-Oct. daily, 8 hr., $28). Tour #4 heads to Spearfish for the Black Hills Passion Play, which has been "Praised by Press, Acclaimed by Clergy, Endorsed by Educators," and "Lauded by Laymen" (June-Aug. Sun., Tues., and Thurs., 5 hr., $19). Tour #5 provides nighttime transportation to Mt. Rushmore, which is illuminated for viewing (June 1-Sept. 2 daily, 4½ hr., $9).

Hiking in the hills is quite enjoyable—there is little underbrush beneath the conifer canopy, and there are many abandoned mines and strange rock outcroppings to explore. Since rainy, cool weather is common in May and June, dress accordingly.

Black Hills National Forest

The Black Hills, like other national forests, adheres to the principle of "multiple use"; mining, logging, ranching, and tourism all take place in close proximity. This last activity is especially in evidence. Around seemingly every bend in the Black Hills' narrow, sinuous roads lurk "don't miss" attractions like reptile farms and Flintstone Campgrounds. Visit the forest outside of the peak tourist season (July to mid-September), during which cars and campers descend on the area in a rush for the modern-day gold of glow-in-the-dark souvenirs.

The most convenient information centers are the **Pactola Ranger District,** 803 Soo San Dr., Rapid City (343-1567; open Mon.-Fri. 8am-5pm), and the **Spearfish Ranger District,** 226 Colorado Blvd., Spearfish (642-4622; open Mon.-Fri. 8am-5pm). The main information office and visitor center at **Pactola Reservoir,** 17 mi. west of Rapid City on U.S. 385, has forestry exhibits in the summer in addition to the usual tourist literature. You can buy supplies before you head off to the hinterland at small grocery stores in Keystone and Custer, or at the KOA campground five mi. west of Mt. Rushmore on Rte. 244.

Spearfish, located directly off I-90 at the northern end of the Black Hills National Forest, is an excellent access point for the hills. Comfortable accommodations can be found at the **Canyon Gateway Motel** on Route 14A (642-3402) at the edge of the famed **Spearfish Canyon.** (Singles $26. Doubles $35.) Also stop in at the **Valley Café,** 608 Main St. (642-2423), for pleasant conversation and great pancakes (3 enormo-flapjacks per $2.20) before heading into the woods.

Camping in the national forest is virtually unrestricted. To save money the adventurous way, disappear down one of the many dirt roads (make sure it isn't someone's driveway) and set up camp. This option is safe, free, and legal, but watch for poison ivy and afternoon thunder showers. The most popular established campgrounds include **Bear Gulch** and **Pactola** (343-4283), on the Pactola Reservoir just south of the junction of Rte. 44 and U.S. 385 (sites $9-11). Other favorites include the **Willow Creek Horse Camp,** in the North Cave Gap Area ($10 reservation fee, $15 charge for 1-10 people) and **Sheridan Lake Campground** (574-2873 or 800-283-2267), east of Hill City on U.S. 385 (sites $9-11), both of which provide picnic tables, pit toilets, and water hydrants. These campgrounds often fill up in the summer, but you can reserve a spot by calling or writing ahead. For more information, contact the Pactola or Spearfish Ranger District (see above). As a last resort, try the **Hill City-Mt. Rushmore KOA** (574-2525), five mi. west of Mt. Rushmore on Rte. 244. The KOA cabins come with facilities including showers, a stove, a heated pool, laundry facilities, and free shuttle service to Mt. Rushmore. (Office open daily 7am-11pm, Oct.-April 8am-10pm. Sites $15 for 2 people, $18 with water and electricity, $20 with full hookup.)

Mt. Rushmore National Monument

South Dakota historian Doane Robinson originally conceived this "shrine of democracy" in 1923 as a memorial for local Western heroes such as Kit Carson. By its completion in 1941, the monument portrayed the 60-ft.-tall faces of George Washington, Thomas Jefferson, Abraham Lincoln, and Theodore Roosevelt. Millions have stood in awe before the four patriarchs, designed and sculpted largely by chiseler extraordinaire and former KKK-member Gutzon Borglum. The monument is proof that you should not take great men for granite.

From Rapid City, take U.S. 16 to Keystone and Rte. 244 up to the mountain. The **visitor center** (574-2523) has the usual multi-media exhibitions as well as braille brochures and wheelchairs. Programs for the disabled are held daily at 9pm. (Visitor center open daily 8am-10pm; Sept. 18-May 14 8am-5pm.) **Borglum's Sculptor's Studio,** in the visitor center, holds the plaster model of the sculptor's mountain carving, as well as his tools and plans. (Ranger talks held in summer every hr. 9:30am-6pm; studio open daily 9am-8pm.) Also in the visitor center is **Mt. Rushmore Memorial Ampitheater,** the locale of the evening monument-lighting programs. (May 14-Sept. 4 program 9pm, monument lit 9:30-10:30pm; Sept. 5-16 program 8pm, monument lit 8:30-9:30pm.)

Custer State Park

Peter Norbeck, governor of South Dakota during the late 1910s, loved to hike among the thin, towering rock formations that haunt the area south of Sylvan Lake and Mt. Rushmore. Norbeck not only created Custer State Park to preserve the area's treasures, but spectacular **Needles Highway** as well, which follows his favorite hiking route. He purposely kept the highway narrow and winding so that newcomers could experience the pleasures of discovery. Watch for mountain goats and bighorn sheep among the rocky spires. For information, contact HC 83, P.O. Box 70, Custer 57730 (255-4515; open Mon.-Fri. 7:30am-5pm). There is a daily entrance fee ($3, under 11 free, $6 per carload). At the entrance, ask for a copy of *Tatanka,* the informative Custer State Park newspaper. The **Peter Norbeck Welcome Center** (255-4464), on U.S. 16A, one mi. west of the State Game Lodge, is the park's central information center. (Open June-Aug. daily 8am-8pm.) All eight **state park campgrounds** charge $7-10 per night and have showers and restrooms. Restaurants and concessions are available at any of the four park lodges—State Game, Blue Bell, Sylvan Lake, and Legion Lake—but you can save money by shopping at the local general stores in Custer, Hermosa, or Keystone.

Sylvan Lake, Needles Hwy. (Rte. 87), proves as lovely as its name, with hiking trails, fishing, horse concessions, paddle boats, and canoes. Horse rides are available at **Blue Bell Lodge** (255-4531, stable 255-4571; rides $12.50 per hr., under 12 $10.50; $20.50 per 2 hr., under 12 $18.50). Boat rentals are available at **Legion Lake Lodge** (255-4521; boats $2.50 per person for ½-hr.). All lakes and streams permit fishing, with a $6.50 daily license available at the four area lodges. Five-day nonresident licenses are $14.50, or $16 per group. There is a limit of eight trout per day, six times per summer. Summer fishing is the best, especially around the first of the month when officials stock the waters.

Caves

In the cavern-riddled Black Hills, the underground scenery often rivals that above. Private concessionaires will attempt to lure you into the holes in their backyards, but the government owns the area's prime real estate. **Wind Cave National Park** (745-4600), adjacent to Custer State Park on Rte. 87, and **Jewel Cave National Monument** (673-2288), 14 mi. west of Custer on U.S. 16A, are in the southern hills. There is no public transportation to the caves.

In the summer, both Wind and Jewel Cave visitor centers offer excursions daily, including short candlelight tours and more strenuous but exhilarating spelunking tours, during which tourists crawl on the floor of the cave just like real explorers. Guides provide knee pads, helmets with lanterns, and instruction. Wear well-soled shoes, preferably ankle-high laced boots, and expendable clothing. Bring a sweater on all tours—Jewel Cave remains a constant 47°F, Wind Cave 53°F.

Though discovered in 1881, most of **Wind Cave** was explored in 1890 by 17-year-old Alvin McDonald, whose name can still be seen burned on the walls of some of the deeper chambers. The cave lies 12 mi. north of Hot Springs on U.S. 385. Besides several short walks, Wind Cave Park offers four tours. The easy **Garden of Eden Tour** gives a quick overview of the cave's interior (6 tours per day 10:40am-3:40pm; $2, seniors and under 15 $1.) The one-hour **Natural Entrance Tour** leaves on the hour and covers ½-mi. of the cave. (Admission $4, ages 6-15 $2.) The more strenuous, 1½-hr. **Fairgrounds Tour** winds ½ mi. through two levels of the cave. (Admission $5, ages 6-15 $2.50.) The four-hour spelunking tour, limited to 10 people ages 14 and over, leaves at 1pm ($6, reservations required). To make reservations for the spelunking tours, contact Wind Cave National Park, Hot Springs 57747 (745-4600; open daily 8am-7pm; Aug. 24-June 4 8am-5pm).

Jewel Cave sprawls underground in one of the largest unexplored labyrinths in the world. Though formed of the same limestone as Wind Cave, any similarity ends there. Grayish calcite crystal walls are the highlight of the tours. Guides sponsor three tours during the summer. The ½-mi. **Scenic Tour** takes you over 700 stairs (every 20 min., 1¼ hr., admission $4, ages 6-15 $2). Make reservations for the **Spelunking Tour,** limited to 10 people ages 16 and over, and be sure to wear sturdy foot gear (admission $6). Contact Jewel Cave National Monument, Custer 57730 (673-2288; open June 12-Aug. 27 daily 8am-4:30pm).

The **Wind Cave Campground** offers primitive sites with flush toilets for $7. There are no overnight accommodations at the Jewel Cave Monument, but you can camp at the national forest's facility six mi. east on Rte. 16A.

Lead and Deadwood

Many interesting small towns dust the Black Hills, but Lead and Deadwood truly stand out. During the 1877 gold rush, the towns attained legendary status for their idiosyncratic prospectors and boom-town exploits.

In **Lead** (LEED), almost everybody works for Homestake, the locally prominent gold-mining corporation. Here, after the hills "panned out" in 1878, hardrock or lode mining began in earnest. Homestake still owns much of the northern Black Hills and continues to operate the largest gold mine in the Western Hemisphere. The **Open Cut,** a yawning chasm where a mountain once stood, provides a monument to Homestake's handiwork. You'll see huge vats of tailings, conveyor belts loaded with ore, and contraptions that lower the miners down almost a mile into the belly of the earth. Operations there ceased some time ago—long enough for a Piggly-Wiggly store and many miners to make their homes in its path. The **Lead Civic Association** (584-3110) gives surface tours of the mine. (Tours June-Aug. Mon.-Fri. 8am-5pm every ¼ hr.; May and Sept.-Oct. Mon.-Fri. 8am-4pm every ½ hr. $3.50, high school students $2.50, families $10.)

Gunslinging hero-outlaws Wild Bill Hickok and Calamity Jane sauntered into **Deadwood** at the height of the Gold Rush. Bill stayed just long enough—two months—to spend eternity here. He was shot while playing poker, so the legend goes, and since he fell while holding eights and aces this full house became known as "the dead man's hand." Visit **Mt. Moriah Cemetery,** where Bill and Jane are buried beside each other on a hillside overlooking the city.

Deadwood recently voted to reinstate small-stakes gambling to recapture some of the town's less murderous Wild West atmosphere while conveniently luring tourists. As a result, **Main Street** sometimes resembles a smaller version of Las Vegas or Atlantic City—cheap T-shirt and trinket shops included. Parking in the narrow canyon has also grown quite inconvenient and expensive; check with your motel to see if it can arrange a guaranteed space for your car.

The **Nugget Café,** 815 W. Main St. (584-3337) in Lead, is almost a museum in its own right, decorated with photos documenting the town's history. Try the spaghetti dinner ($4) or the tasty omelettes ($2.50-3.50). (Open Mon.-Sat. 6am-7pm.) Jack McCall, Wild Bill's assassin, was captured at **Goldberg Gaming**, 672 Main St. (578-1515) in Deadwood, where you can down an old-fashioned phosphate for 50¢ or a huge "Goldburger" for $1.50-3.50. (Open June-Sept. 2 Mon.-Sat. 6:30am-6pm.)

The **#10 Saloon,** 657 Main St. (578-3346), claims to own Wild Bill's "death chair." (Open Mon.-Sat. 10am-2am, Sun. noon-8pm.)

There ain't no budget lodging in Lead or Deadwood. Since the re-introduction of legal gambling downtown, Deadwood has been inundated with slot machines and overpriced motels. Your best bet is to stay in Spearfish or Rapid City and commute to the two towns. The most scenic route to Lead and Deadwood is from Spearfish south via Rte. 14A, which traverses **Spearfish Canyon,** a densely wooded canyon of steep limestone cliffs and tumultuous waterfalls. **Deadwood Express** (343-5044), serves both towns from Rapid City twice per day (1 hr., $10, $2 for gamblers).

Check in at the **chamber of commerce,** 735 Main St., Deadwood (578-1876; open Mon.-Fri. 8:30am-5pm). In the summer, they run a booth on Pine St. The towns are in the Mountain **time zone** (2 hr. behind Eastern). The **post office** in Lead is at 329 W. Main St. (584-2110; open Mon.-Fri. 8:15am-4:15pm, Sat. 10am-noon); the **ZIP code** is 57754. The Deadwood **post office** is in the Deadwood Federal Building (578-1505); the **ZIP code** is 57732.

The **area code** for Lead and Deadwood is 605.

Pierre

Pierre (PEER), South Dakota's capital, lies smack in the center of the state on the Missouri River. Once a bustling cow town, Pierre still serves as a commercial center for farmers and ranchers. Many citizens dress themselves in Western-style garb, even in the copper-topped **capitol building** (773-3011; free 40-min. tours Mon.-Fri. 9am-4pm every ½ hr., Sat. 10am-3pm every hr., Sun. 11am-2pm every hr.; building open Mon.-Fri. 8am-10pm, Sat.-Sun. 8am-9pm). Behind the capitol, the unusual fountain spouts flame from a natural gas deposit. In the event of a sudden thermonuclear war, head for the brand new, bunkerlike **Cultural Heritage Center,** 900 Governors Dr. (773-3458). Built into the side of a hill above the capitol, the museum gives an interesting and detailed history of both the Native American and white inhabitants of South Dakota. (Open Mon.-Fri. 9am-4:30pm, call for weekend hours.)

Eat at the cozy **D & E Cafe,** 115 W. Dakota Ave. (224-7200), where an entree with soup, potato, toast, beans, and a bowl of ice cream costs $4-5. (Open 24 hrs.) Grab a kuppakawfee at the **Kozy Korner Restaurant,** 217 E. Dakota Ave. (224-9547), a family place with generous dinners for $5-6. (Open daily 5am-10pm.) **Zesto,** 213 W. Capitol Ave. (224-4681), serves generous heaps of great ice cream. Cones cost 15-80¢, sundaes 60¢-$1.40. (Open Mon.-Sat. 11:30am-10:30pm, Sun. noon-10:30pm.)

Sleep cheap at the **Waverly Hotel,** 442 S. Pierre St. (224-7358), 1½ blocks from Sioux Ave. The old, dusty rooms are lovingly maintained but have neither phones nor A/C. (Singles $15. Doubles $20.) Conveniently located across the street from the bus station, the **Days Inn,** 520 W. Sioux Ave. (224-0411), serves free doughnuts, coffee, and milk every morning and popcorn upon arrival. (Singles $27. Doubles $32.) The popular **Farm Island State Park** (224-5605), three mi. east on Rte. 34, has campsites for $7, $9 with hookup.

To reach Pierre from I-90, go 30 mi. north on U.S. 83. **Greyhound/Jack Rabbit,** in the Phillips 66 station at 621 W. Sioux Ave. (224-7651), runs buses to Omaha ($78), Rapid City ($44), and Minneapolis ($99). Visit the **chamber of commerce,** 108 E. Missouri St. (224-7361; open Mon.-Fri. 8am-5pm). Pierre is in the Central **time zone** (1 hr. behind Eastern). The **post office** is at 225 S. Pierre St. (224-4140; open Mon.-Fri. 8am-5:30pm, Sat. 8am-noon). Pierre's **ZIP code** is 57501; the **area code** is 605.

Rapid City

Rapid City's location, approximately 40 mi. east of the Wyoming border, makes it an ideal base from which to explore both the Black Hills and the Badlands. Every summer the area welcomes about 2.2 million tourists, over 40 times the city's permanent population.

Practical Information

Emergency: 911.

Rapid City Chamber of Commerce, Visitors Bureau, 444 Mt. Rushmore Rd. N. (343-1744), in the Civic Center. Visitors bureau open May 27-Sept. 2 daily 7am-6pm; chamber of commerce open year-round Mon.-Fri. 8am-5pm.

Buses: Milo Barber Transportation Center, 333 6th St. (348-3300), downtown. **Jack Rabbit Lines** runs east from Rapid City. To Pierre (1 per day, 3 hr., $44) and Sioux Falls (Mon.-Thurs. 2 per day, 8 hr., $75). **Powder River Lines** services Wyoming and Montana. To Billings (2 per day, 9 hr., $73) and Cheyenne (2 per day, 8½ hr., $88). **Arrow Stage Lines** runs to Nebraska and Iowa (Omaha, 3 per day, 13 hr., $109). All three honor the Greyhound Ameripass. Station open Mon.-Fri. 6am-11pm, Sat.-Sun. 6am-1pm, 4-5:30pm, and 9:30-11pm.

Public Transport: Milo Barber Transportation Center, 348-7433. City bus transportation available by reservation. Call 24 hr. in advance. One way trip $1, seniors 50¢. Office open Mon.-Fri. 6am-5:30pm.

Taxi: Rapid Taxi, 348-8080. Base fare $2, $1 per mi.

Car Rental: Black Hills Car Rental, 301 Campbell (342-6696). Budget cars $38 per day plus 36¢ per mi., subject to availability. Open Mon.-Fri. 8am-5pm, Sat. 9am-4pm. Must be 21 with major credit card.

Time Zone: Mountain (2 hr. behind Eastern).

Post Office: 500 East Blvd. (394-8600), several blocks east of downtown. Open Mon.-Fri. 8am-5pm, Sat. 9:30am-12:30pm. **ZIP code:** 57701.

Area Code: 605.

Orienting yourself may be difficult at first, since Rapid City sprawls across 27 flat sq. mi., and few of the buildings in town stand taller than four stories. The center of the downtown area is bordered on the east and west by 6th and 9th Street, and on the north and south by Omaha and Kansas City Street.

Accommodations, Camping, and Food

The **AYH hostel,** 815 Kansas City St. (342-8538), downtown in the YMCA, consists of 12 cots, with no separation between men and women. Access to kitchen and YMCA facilities is available, but no bedding is provided. A cot for the night costs $8 for AYH members or any young foreigner.

Rapid City accommodations are considerably more expensive during the summer. Make reservations, since budget motels often fill up weeks in advance. The **Big Sky Motel,** 4080 Tower Rd. (348-3200), sits on a hill just south of town, affording a spectacular view of the city and the surrounding farmland. (Spotless but phoneless singles $27, doubles $34.) **Motel 6** is less conveniently located northeast of town, off I-90 exit 59, about a $4 cab trip from downtown. Some rooms have disabled access. There is a pool. (Singles $34. Doubles $40.) **The Berry Patch Campground,** 1860 E. North St. (341-5588), one mi. east of I-90 off exit 60, has 14 grass campsites, a gameroom, playground, showers, and swimming. (Tent sites $13.50 for 2, with hookup $14.50 from April 12-Oct. 1. Each additional person $1.50.)

Aunt Jane's, 807 Columbus (341-4529), on the first floor of a Victorian house stuffed with antiques, will sate your appetite. Aunt Jane prepares her own recipes, such as the Rocky Mountain salad sandwich (ham, swiss cheese, and peaches; $3.50). (Open Mon.-Fri. 8am-4:30pm, Sat. 9am-2pm.) **Tally's,** 530 6th St. (342-

7621), downtown under the orange awning, serves family-style country meals such as chicken-fried steak ($6.25). (Open daily 7am-8pm; Sept. 2-May 27 7am-7pm.) The **Flying T** (342-1905), six mi. south on U.S. 16, next to the Reptile Gardens, serves a chuck wagon meal on a tin plate for $10, under 11 $4, singing cowboys included. Dinner (7:30pm sharp) and a Western musical show (8:15pm) are offered every night.

Sights and Entertainment

Tourism rears its flashing neon head in Rapid City. If you got dem *walkin' blues*, take the **Rapid City Walking Tour** of the historic and well-preserved downtown area; pick up a guide at the visitor center. The **Sioux Indian Museum** and the **Pioneer Museum** (both 348-0557), 515 West Blvd., between Main and St. Joseph St. in Halley Park, present interesting but limited exhibits. (Open Mon.-Sat. 9am-5pm, Sun. 1-5pm; Oct.-May Tues.-Sat. 10am-5pm, Sun. 1-5pm.) **The Museum of Geology**, 501 E. Saint Joseph St. (394-2467), in the administration building of the School of Mines and Technology, just east of Main St., exhibits the beautiful minerals and textbook fossils of the Badlands. (Open Mon.-Sat. 8am-6pm, Sun. noon-6pm; off-season Mon.-Fri. 8am-5pm, Sat. 9am-2pm, Sun. 1-4pm. Free.) The **Dahl Fine Arts Center**, 7th and Quincy St. (394-4101), houses rotating exhibits of local and Native American art, as well as the enormous "Cyclorama of American History," a circular 200-ft. mural. (Open Mon.-Fri. 9am-9:30pm, Sat. 9am-5pm, Sun. 1-5pm.)

For nightlife, try Main St. between 9th and Mt. Rushmore St. **Filly's Food, Fun, and Firewater** (348-8300), in the Hilton, is a fantastic spot for a quiet drink or a comedy show. (Shows Fri.-Sat. at 9 and 11pm. Open Mon.-Sat. 11am-2am, Sun. 12:30pm-midnight. Cover $6 for shows, no cover other times.) For boot-stompin' country-western music and dancing, head to **Boot Hill,** 826 Main St. (343-1931), where live bands perform nightly. (Open Mon.-Sat. 3pm-2am, Sun. 5-11:30pm. Cover Tues.-Sat. $2.)

TENNESSEE

Tennessee, the last state to secede from the Union before the Civil War, has most of the trappings one expects in a Southern state: intensive agriculture, country music, spicy state politics, and county alcohol bans. In 1925, the state successfully prosecuted teacher John Scopes for teaching evolution, a "Monkey" trial that dampened science education for decades. Yet Tennessee also defies Southern stereotypes. In 1920, it provided the final vote needed to put women's suffrage in the Constitution. During the Great Depression, it was the site of a major, modernizing public works program under the Tennessee Valley Authority. Oakridge still houses one of the scientific laboratories most important in development of the A-bomb. And Tennessee's two largest cities, Memphis and Nashville, offer a veritable treasure horde of modern diversions for the tourist. There ain't no place I'd rather be.

Practical Information

Capital: Nashville.

Tennessee Dept. of Tourist Development, P.O. Box 23170, Nashville 37202 (741-2158). Open Mon.-Fri. 8am-4:30pm. **Tennessee State Parks Information,** 701 Broadway, Nashville 37203 (742-6667).

Time Zones: Central (Memphis and Nashville; 1 hr. behind Eastern) and Eastern (Chattanooga, Knoxville). **Postal Abbreviation:** TN

Great Smoky Mountain National Park

The largest wilderness area in the eastern U.S., Great Smoky Mountain National Park encompasses a half-million acres of gray-green Appalachian peaks, bounded on either side by misty North Carolina and Tennessee valleys. Bears, wild hogs, white-tailed deer, groundhogs, wild turkeys, and more than 1,500 species of flowering plants make their homes here. Whispering conifer forests line the mountain ridges at elevations of over 6,000 ft., rhododendrons burst into their full glory in June and July, and by mid-October, the sloping mountain flanks have become a giant crazy-quilt of color, reminiscent of the area's well-preserved crafts tradition.

Start any exploration of the area with a visit to one of the park's three visitor centers. **Sugarlands,** on Newfound Gap Rd., two mi. south of Gatlinburg (436-1200), is beside the park's headquarters. (Open in summer daily 8am-7pm; spring and fall 8am-5pm; winter 8am-4:30pm.) **Cades Cove** (436-1275) is in the park's western valley, 15 mi. southwest of Sugarlands on Little River Rd., seven mi. southwest of Townsend, TN. (Open in summer daily 9:30am-7pm; fall 8:30am-5:30pm; spring 9:30am-5:30pm.) The **Oconaluftee Visitors Center,** four mi. north of Cherokee, NC (497-9147), serves travelers entering the park from the Blue Ridge Parkway and all points south and east (open same hours as Sugarlands). The park **information line** (615-436-1200; open daily 8:30am-4:30pm) telelinks all three visitor centers. The rangers can answer travel questions, field emergency message calls, and trace lost equipment.

At each visitor center you'll find displays amplifying the park's natural and cultural resources, bulletin boards displaying emergency messages or public information, brochures and films, and comfort stations. Be sure to ask for *The Smokies Guide,* a newspaper offering a comprehensive explanation of the park's changing natural graces. The helpful journal also includes practical information on tours, lectures, and other activities, such as rafting or horseback riding. The standard park service brochure, *Great Smoky Mountains,* provides the best driving map in the region. Hikers should ask the visitor center staff for assistance in locating an appropriately detailed backcountry map. You can also tune your car radio to 1610 AM at various marked points for information.

900 mi. of hiking trails and 170 mi. of road criss-cross the park. Ask the rangers at the visitors centers to help you chart a trip appropriate to your time and physical ability. You can hike a ¼-mi. or several hundred, spend an afternoon or stay overnight. Driving and walking routes are clearly charted. To hike off the charted trails, you must ask for a free backcountry camping permit. Otherwise, just choose a route, bring water, and DON'T FEED THE BEARS. Some of the most popular trails are the five mi. to **Rainbow Falls,** the four mi. to **Chimney Tops,** and the 21½ mi. to **Laurel Falls.** Popular drives are the 11-mi. **Cades Cove loop,** where you can see old hand-crafted building, the last vestiges of a mountain community that occupied the area in the 1850s; and the 15-mi. drive halfway between Sugarlands and Oconaloftee on the Newfound Gap Road (U.S. 441), to **Clingman's Dome,** the highest point in the park.

Great Smoky Mountains National Park straddles the Tennessee/North Carolina line. On the Tennessee side, the city of **Gatlinburg,** just two mi. from Sugarlands, appears and vanishes within the blink of a driver's eye, but is jam-packed enough to keep you occupied for an evening or a day. Touristic hordes occupy its bizarre corners, ranging from a quick-fix wedding chapel to a wax museum dedicated to President Bush. Also in Gatlinburg, **Christos Gardens** bills itself as America's #1 religious attraction, and **Ober Gatlinburg** has America's largest cable car. Along "the strip", **Ripley's Believe It or Not, Hauntings, Ghost Town in the Sky,** and the **Guinness World Records Museum** all vie for visitors. Two really worthwhile attractions are the **Sky Lift** and the **Space Needles** electric elevator ride. Both transport their customers to a spectacular view of the Smokies. Between all these attractions are endless T-shirt shops, candy stores, expensive restaurants, and churches. For more guidance, stop in at the **Tourist Information Center,** 520 Pkwy. (615-436-

4178). (Open May-Oct. Mon.-Sat. 8am-8pm, Sun. 9am-5pm; Nov.-April Mon.-Sat. 8am-6pm, Sun. 9am-5pm.)

On the N.C. side of the Mountains, one mi. from the Oconaluftee Vistors Center is the **Cherokee Indian Reservation,** with a guided tour of a re-created Indian village, an outdoor drama about the Cherokee tribe, and an informative museum. Also on the reservation are numerous tacky souvenir shops and a live black bear in a pitifully small cage that you can feed for 25¢.

Accommodations and Camping

There are 10 campgrounds in the park, each with tent sites, limited trailer space, water, tables, and comfort stations (no showers or hookups). **Smokemont, Elkmont,** and **Cades Cove** accept reservations; the rest are first-come, first-served. (Sites $10.) For those hauling a trailer or staying at one of the park's campgrounds near the main roads during the summer, reservations are a must. Obtain them at least eight weeks in advance by writing to Ticketron, P.O. Box 62429, Virginia Beach, VA 23462 (900-370-5566).

Both Cherokee and Gatlinburg have many small motels. The prices vary widely depending on the season, the economy, and who you are. (Many motels, particularly in Gatlinburg, are not excited about having unmarried couples stay with them.) In general, the cheaper motels are in Cherokee, and the nicer ones are in Gatlinburg, where the best deals are off Main St., especially off street light #6.

Three youth hostels are located in the area around the park. The closest is **Bell's Wa-Floy Retreat (AYH),** Route 3, Box 611 (615-436-7700), 10 mi. east of Gatlinburg on Rte. 321, mile marker 21. From the center of Gatlinburg catch the eastbound trolley (25¢) to the end of the line. From there, it's a five-mi. walk to Wa-Floy. Trolley service also runs past Wa-Floy from Gatlinburg three times per day—ask in town or call for times. Located centrally in the Wa-Floy Retreat (which doubles as the Steiner Bell Center for Physical and Spiritual Rejuvenation), the hostel is no more than a rustic cabin divided into a few apartments with kitchenettes. The shabby interior is clean, though the showers may be unpleasant. Peacocks and ducks, oblivious to the shower conditions, roam the lovely grounds complete with a pool, tennis courts, meditation area, chapel, and murmuring stream. The proprietor, Mrs. Floy Steiner Bell, may welcome you warmly with her poetry. ($10, nonmembers $12. Call for reservations at least 1 day ahead.) On the other side of the park, about 35 mi. away on a slow, winding road in North Carolina, you can vegetate after a hike or river ride in the spacious communal living room of Louise Phillip's **Smokeseege Lodge (AYH),** P.O. Box 179, Dillsboro (704-586-8658), on Rte. 441, 11 mi. south of Cherokee. Walk from the nearest Greyhound/Trailways stop, nearly three mi. away in Sylva, NC. If you're driving from the Smokies, watch carefully on the right-hand side of Rte. 441 for the small, triangular AYH logo—the hostel is at the end of a gravel road. Kitchen facilities are available; no smoking or drinking permitted. (Lockout 9am-5pm. Curfew 11pm. $7. Call ahead. Open April-Oct.) Further south, near Wesser in the **Nantahala National Forest,** the bustling **Nantahala Outdoor Center (NOC),** U.S. 19 W., P.O. Box 41, Bryson City (704-488-2175), 80 mi. from Gatlinburg and 13 mi. from downtown Bryson City, offers cheap beds. Bunks occupy simple wooden cabins at "base camp" on the far side of the river and fairly large-sized motel rooms with kitchenettes. Showers, kitchen, linen, and laundry facilities included. ($7. Call ahead.)

Keep in mind the center is not at all convenient to the GSM park or Gatlinburg. Staying at the NOC is a good idea when planning a whitewater rafting trip. The NOC's rates for 2½-hr. whitewater rafting expeditions are pricey, but you can rent your own raft for a self-designed trip down the Nantahala River. (Sun.-Fri. $12, Sat. $15. 1-person inflatable "duckies" $22 per day.) The NOC also rents canoes and kayaks and offers instruction for the novice. Most trips have minimum age or weight limits; daycare service is available at the center. Trip prices include transportation to the put-in site and all equipment. Don't let *Deliverance* steer you clear.

Hike on the Appalachian Trail to explore some of the old forest service roads. The NOC staff will gladly assist if you need help charting an appropriate daytrip.

The NOC also maintains seasonal "outposts" on the **Ocoee, Nolichucky, Chattoga,** and **French Broad Rivers,** all within 100 mi. of its Bryson City headquarters. Although these do not have overnight facilities, a rafting expedition on any of these rivers makes a satisfying daytrip if you have a car. Be sure to look into NOC's 20% discounts during March and April.

Memphis

Follow your ears in the southwestern corner of Tennessee to Memphis, home of the blues and the birthplace of rock 'n' roll. W.C. Handy, who played on legendary Beale Street, published the first blues piece here in 1912, appropriately titled "Memphis Blues." Here it was, too, that Elvis Presley, in spite of (or because of) his scandalous gyrating pelvis, made the fusion of southern country music and African-American blues and gospel safe for the mass audience and became the "King of Rock 'n' Roll." Memphis still sings the blues, and rocks on weekends. At the same time the city is attracting big businesses, and the nation's 15th-largest city is becoming an economic center as well.

Practical Information

Emergency: 911.

Visitors Information Center, 207 Beale St. (576-8171), 2 blocks south on 2nd St. and 2 blocks east on Beale from the Greyhound station. Quite helpful, with everything from bus maps to restaurant guides. Open Mon.-Sat. 9am-6pm, Sun. noon-6pm.

Memphis International Airport (922-8000), just south of the southern loop of I-240. Taxi fare to the city $15—negotiate in advance. Public transport to and from the airport only $1.25, but a long and difficult trip for a traveler unfamiliar with the area.

Amtrak: 545 S. Main St. (526-0052 or 800-872-7245), at Calhoun on the southern edge of downtown. *Very* unsafe area during the day, Danteesque at night. To New Orleans (1 per day, 7½ hr., $70) and Chicago (1 per day, 11 hr., $88). Open Mon.-Sat. 8am-12:30pm, 1:30-5pm, 9pm-6am, Sun. 9pm-6am.

Greyhound/Trailways: 203 Union Ave. (523-7676), at 4th St. downtown. Unsafe area at night, but it beats the Amtrak station. To Nashville ($37) and New Orleans ($66). Open 24 hrs.

Public Transport: Memphis Area Transit Authority (MATA), 61 S. Main St. (274-6282). Extensive bus routes cover most suburbs but buses take their time and do not run frequently. The 2 major downtown stops are at Front and Jefferson St. and at 2nd St. and Madison Ave. Operates Mon.-Fri. 5am-11pm; less frequent service Sat.-Sun. Fare 95¢.

Taxi: Yellow Cab, 526-2121. $2.35 first mi., $1.10 each additional mi.

Crisis Line: 247-7477. Open 24 hrs. Also refers to other numbers.

Time Zone: Central (1 hr. behind Eastern).

Post Office: 555 S. 3rd St. (521-2140), at Calhoun St. Take bus #13. Open Mon.-Fri. 8:30am-5:30pm, Sat. 10am-noon. **ZIP code:** 38101.

Area Code: 901.

Downtown, named avenues run east-west and numbered ones north-south. **Madison Avenue** bifurcates north and south addresses. Two main thoroughfares, Poplar and Union Avenues, lead to the heart of the city from the east; 2nd and 3rd Streets arrive from the south.

Accommodations

The accommodations outlook in Memphis is fair to good for those with a car; otherwise you will have to take an unreliable bus to reach reasonably priced lodgings. Downtown establishments are expensive, but cab fare to the hinterlands may make them seem more reasonable. Less expensive but less comfortable motels grace Elvis Presley Blvd. near Graceland. Book ahead if you are coming between August 12-16, when Elvis fans from around the universe gather to pay tribute on the anniversary of his death. The visitor information center has a thorough listing of lodgings. Contact **Bed and Breakfast in Memphis**, P.O. Box 41621, Memphis 38174 (726-5920), for guest rooms in Memphis homes. French- and Spanish-speaking hosts are available. (Singles and doubles $40-60.)

Lowenstein-Long House/Castle Hostelry, 1084 Poplar and 217 N. Waldran (527-7174). Near downtown; take bus #50 from 3rd St. Beautiful accommodations in an elegant Victorian mansion. Singles $10, nonmembers $13, private doubles $30. Key deposit $5. Big home-cooked breakfast $5, economy breakfast $2.50. Lockout 10am-5:30pm.

River Place Inn, 100 North Front St. (526-0583), overlooking the water. Upscale hotel with great rooms from $48. The visitor information center has a $35 coupon for 1-4 people.

Motel 6, 1360 Springbrook Rd. (396-3620), just east of intersection of Elvis and Brooks Rd. near Graceland. There is also a **Motel 6** at I-55 and Brooks Rd. (346-0992). Both are clean, have pools and movie channels, and unlimited local calls. Singles $26, each additional person $6.

Food

When a smoky, spicy smell follows you almost everywhere, you are either extremely paranoid, malodorous, or in Memphis, where barbecue reigns. The city hosts the World Championship Barbecue Cooking Contest in May. But don't fret if gnawing on ribs isn't your thing: Memphis has plenty of other Southern-style restaurants with down-home favorites like fried chicken, catfish, chitlins, and fresh vegetables.

The Rendezvous, Downtown Alley (523-2746), in the alley across from the Peabody Hotel off Union St., between the Ramada and Days Inns. A Memphis legend, serving large portions of ribs ($6.50-9), and cheaper sandwiches ($3). Open Tues.-Thurs. 4:30pm-midnight, Fri.-Sat. noon-midnight.

P and H Café, 1532 Madison Ave. (274-9794). The initials aptly stand for Poor and Hungry. This local favorite serves huge burgers, plate lunches, and grill food ($3-5). The waitresses are a Memphis institution—look on the walls. Local bands occasionally play Sat. night. Open Mon.-Sat. 11am-3am.

The North End, 346 N. Main St. (526-0319), downtown. A most happening place with an extensive menu including tamales, wild rice, and creole dishes ($3-8). Delicious vegetarian meals for under $5. Orgasmic Hot Fudge Pie ($2.50). Happy Hour 4-7pm. Live music Wed.-Sun. starts around 10:30pm, with a small cover (around $3). Open daily 11am-3am. Next door, **356 North Main** (527-2799) offers a similar menu, but with stir-fry specialties.

Leonard's Barbecue Pit, 1140 Bellevue Blvd. S. (948-1581). An old Elvis haunt near Graceland serving good barbecue ($3-5). Cute ceramic pigs in the window modeled after the King late in his reign. Open Mon.-Sat. 10am-5pm.

Spaghetti Warehouse, 40 W. Huling St. (521-0907), off S. Front St. A great, friendly restaurant. Filling plate of pasta, salad, and bread in a restored trolley car or on a carousel for under $5. Open Mon.-Thurs. 11am-10pm, Fri. 11am-11pm, Sat. noon-11pm, Sun. noon-10pm.

Front St. Delicatessen, 77 S. Front St. (522-8943). Lunchtime streetside deli with almost no room inside. Popular with local yuppies. Patio dining in sunny weather. Hot lunch specials $4. Open Mon.-Fri. 8am-4pm, Sat. 11am-3pm.

Elvissights

Graceland, or rather "GRACE-lin", Elvis Presley's home, is a paradigm of American kitsch even Paul Simon can love. Any desire to learn about the man, to share his dream, or to feel his music will probably go unrealized. The complex has been built up to resemble an amusement park, with visitors shuffling from one room to another until the ride is over. However, if you're in Memphis, you obviously have to go, if only to say you saw those mirrored ceilings and those carpeted walls. Elvis bought the mansion when he was only 22, and lived there until his death. The King and his family are buried next door in the **Meditation Gardens,** where you can seek the Buddha while reciting a mantra to the tune of "You're So Square". (Admission to amazing Graceland costs $8.)

Across the street, you can visit several Elvismuseums, and several more Elvissouvenir shops. (Say hi to Elvis's Uncle Vestor in the **EP LP** store.) The **Elvis Presley Automobile Museum** is probably the best of the lot. A huge hall houses a score of Elvismobiles, and an indoor drive-in movie theater shows clips from 31 Elvismovies. ($4.50, seniors $4, kids $2.50.) **If I Can Dream** is a 20-min. film with performance footage, and its price is included with the mansion tour. **Elvis' Airplanes** features—yes, dear reader, yes—the two Elvisplanes: the *Lisa Marie* **(named for the Elvisdaughter)** and the tiny *Hound Dog II* Jetstar. The place is overpriced at $4.25 (seniors $3.80, kids $2.75), but **Elvis' Tour Bus** is a bargain at $1. It is Elvis's tour bus. (Wow! I mean, *it's Elvis's tour bus!!!*) Er, where were we? Ah yes, at the **Elvis Up Close** exhibit, which gives you a glimpse of Elvis's private side by presenting some books he read, some shirts he wore, and (omigod omigod omigod) his Social Security card. ($1.75, free for Elvis if he comes out of hiding and admits he is not dead.)

There are three different combination tickets available: (1) all attractions except the mansion for $10 (seniors $9, kids $7); (2) all attractions except the bus and planes for $13 (seniors $11.65, kids $8); (3) *all* the attractions for $16 (seniors $14.35, kids $11). Take Lauderdale/Elvis Presley bus #13 from 3rd and Union. (Open mid-June to mid-Aug. daily 8am-8pm; early June and late Aug. 8am-7pm; Sept.-April 9am-6pm; May 8am-6pm.)

Non Elvissights

A musical tour of Memphis goes beyond Graceland into other locations downtown. Most famous is **Beale Street,** where W.C. Handy invented the blues. After a long period of neglect, the neighborhood once again has music pouring from almost every door. The **W.C. Handy Home and Museum,** 352 Beale (527-2583), exhibits music and photographs. (Open daily 9am-6pm; call for an appointment.) **A. Schwab,** 163 Beale St. (523-9782), a five-and-dime store run by the same family since 1876, is still offering old-fashioned bargains. A "museum" of relics-never-sold gathers dust on the mezzanine floor, including an array of voodoo potions and powders. Elvis used to buy some of his flashier ensembles here. (Open Mon.-Sat. 9am-5pm. Free guided tours.) The tiny **Sun Studio,** 706 Union Ave. (521-0664), is where Elvis, Jerry Lee Lewis, Johnny Cash, and Carl Perkins first ventilated their vocal chords for producer Sam Phillips. (30-min. tours every hr. on the ½ hr. Open daily 9am-9pm. $4, kids $3.)

Scheduled to open before 1992, **The Great American Pyramid** (800-627-9726) is not the latest gameshow but the latest extravaganza in Memphis. You won't be able to miss the 32-story-high, six-acre-wide shining pyramid that will hold the American Music Hall of Fame, the Memphis Music Experience, the College Football Hall of Fame, and a 20,000 seat arena. The whole experience will include daily music shows indoors and in outdoor parks. (Admission will be $25, kids $17.50.)

With the opening of the pyramid, nearby **Mud Island,** 125 N. Front St. (576-7241), will ceremoniously be renamed **Festival Island.** In the meantime, plain ol' Mud Island holds the very interesting **Mississippi River Museum,** the **Memphis Belle** Pavilion, a huge swimming pool, and a five-block replica of the Mississippi

River called **River Walk.** Catch a "Sunset Party" Wednesday evenings between May and Labor Day, and also look for the weekly special concert events. (Open daily 10am-6pm, museum closes at 4:30pm. $6, seniors, kids and disabled $4. Beach and park only: $4, $2.)

In the heart of downtown lies the luxurious **Peabody Hotel,** 149 Union St., the social center of Memphis society in the first half of this century. Folklore has it that the Mississippi Delta began in its lobby. Now the hotel keeps ducks in its indoor fountain; every day at 11am and 5pm the management rolls out the red carpet and the ducks waddle to and from the elevator with piano accompaniment. Get there early; sometimes ducks are impatient.

On April 4, 1968, a sniper assassinated Rev. Martin Luther King, Jr. at the **Lorraine Motel,** 406 Mulberry St. The motel room is being converted into a museum and civil rights center, the stated intent of which is to bring to life the vibrant civil rights era and provide a national remembrance center for King, although some have protested against the $5 charge for entry to a museum about a man who dedicated his life to helping the poor.

Leaving from 3rd and Beale St. and other spots around the city, the "Showboat" bus runs (7am-11pm, all-day ticket $2) to the big midtown sights. A major sight is the **Victorian Village,** which consists of 18 mansions in various stages of restoration and preservation. The **Mallory-Neeley House,** 652 Adams St. (523-1484), one of the village's two mansions open to the public, went up in the mid-19th century and has yet to come down. Most of its original furniture remains intact. (Open Tues.-Sat. 10am-4pm, Sun. 1-4pm. $4, seniors and students $3.) For a look at a different lifestyle during the same era, the **Magerney House,** 198 Adams St. (526-4464), held the middle-class home of Eugene Magerney, who helped establish Memphis's first public schools. (Open Tues.-Sat. 10am-4pm. Free. Reservations required.)

Set in attractive Overton Park, the **Memphis Brooks Museum of Art** (722-3500) houses a mid-sized collection of impressionist painting and 19th-century U.S. art. (Open Tues.-Sat. 10am-5pm, Sun. 11:30am-5pm. $2, seniors, students, and kids $1. Free Fri.) The **Memphis Zoo and Aquarium** (726-4775) squawks next door. (Open daily 9am-4:30pm. $4, seniors and kids $2. Free Mon. after 3:30pm.) Another beautiful art and nature complex is the **Dixon Gallery and Gardens,** 4339 Park Ave. (761-5250; open Tues.-Sat. 10am-5pm, Sun. 1-5pm; $3.50, kids $1).

For a less tranquil day, visit **Libertyland,** 940 Early Maxwell Blvd. (274-1776), an amusement park near MSU. (Open mid-June to late Aug. Tues.-Sat. 10am-9pm, Sun. noon-9pm; mid-April to early June and late Aug.-early Sept. Sat. 10am-9pm, Sun. noon-9pm. $6, after 4pm $3, seniors $2. "Thrill ride" ticket $6 extra.)

For cool-ass nocturnal tourism, **Federal Express** opens up their enormous sorting rooms at 1am (395-3480 for reservations, 1-800-238-5355 for information).

Entertainment and Nightlife

The visitor-info center's *Key* magazine, the free *Memphis Flyer,* or the "Playbook" section of the Friday morning *Memphis Commercial Appeal* will give you an idea of what's going down around town. For more personalized social coordination, go to the **Sun Café,** 706 Union Ave. (521-0664), adjacent to the Sun Studios, for a glass of lemonade ($1.75) and a talk with the young waiters and cashiers about what to do.

The absolutely most happening place is **Beale Street.** Blues blow nightly throughout the street, from **B. B. King's Blues Club,** 147 Beale (527-5464), to the **Rum Boogie Café,** 182 Beale (528-0150), to the street performers in the park. For pool, **Peoples** (523-7627) on Beale is open till midnight (Fri.-Sat. till 2:30am), and charges $7.35 ($8.40 on weekends) for a table.

Off Beale St., the **Antenna Club,** 1588 Madison Ave. (725-9812), showcases hip progressive rock, and the **Babylon Café,** 1783 Union (278-6444) hosts live original alternative music. **Captain Bilbo's,** 263 Wagner Pl. (526-1966), is the place to be for live rock and pop, and the **Daily Planet,** 3439 Park (327-1270) throbs with rhythm and blues.

The majestic **Orpheum Theater,** 89 Beale St. (525-7800), is a dignified movie palace, complete with 15-ft.-high Czechoslovakian chandeliers and an organ. The theater shows classic movies on weekends along with an organ prelude and a cartoon. The **Memphis Chicks,** 800 Home Run Lane (272-1687), near Libertyland, are a big hit with fans of Southern League baseball. ($3, box seats $5.)

Nashville

The capital of Tennessee since 1843, Nashville is probably better known for its country music than for its big-city politics. Although banjo picking and boot stomping have entrenched themselves in Tennessee's central city, the town panders to a wide variety of musical tastes, both at nightclubs and at the area's major recording studios. Behind this musical harmony breakdances "the Wall Street of the South," a slick, choreographed financial hub. The same city that headquarters the Southern Baptists and higher morality also provides centers of the fine arts and higher learning at Fisk University and Vanderbilt. Nashville is a large, eclectic, unapologetically glitzy place.

Practical Information

Emergency: 911.

Visitor Information: Nashville Area Chamber of Commerce, 161 4th Ave. N. (259-4700), between Commerce and Union St. downtown. Ask for the *Hotel/Motel Guide,* the *Nashville Dining & Entertainment Guide,* and a *Calendar of Events.* Information booth in main lobby open Mon.-Fri. 8am-5pm. **Nashville Tourist Information Center,** I-65 at James Robertson Pkwy. exit 85 (259-4747), about ½-mi. east of the state capitol, just over the bridge. Take bus #3 ("Meridian") east on Broadway. Complete maps marked with all the attractions. Open daily until sunset. *Spotlight on the Arts* ($3.50) is available at the **Metro Arts Commission,** 111 4th Ave. S. (862-6720).

Travelers Aid: 256-3168. Open Mon.-Fri. 8:30am-4pm.

Metropolitan Airport: (275-1675) 8 mi. south of downtown. Airport shuttle $8 one way, taxis $15-17, MTA buses 75¢.

Greyhound: 200 8th Ave. S. (256-6141), at Demonbreun St., 2 blocks south of Broadway downtown. Borders on a rough neighborhood. To: Memphis (9 per day, 4 hr., $37); Washington, DC (7 per day, 16 hr., $94); Atlanta (7 per day, 7½ hr., $34); Louisville (14 per day; 4 hr.; $23, Fri.-Sat. $38). Open 24 hrs.

Public Transport: Metropolitan Transit Authority (MTA) (242-4433). Buses operate Mon.-Fri. 5am-midnight, less frequent service Sat.-Sun. Fare 75¢, zone crossing or transfers 10¢. The **Nashville Trolley** (242-4433) runs daily in the downtown area every 10 min. for 50¢.

Taxi: Nashville Cab, 242-7070. 90¢ first mi., $1.50 each additional mi.

Bike Rental: Al's Bike Rentals, 124 2nd Ave. N. (244-3915). Mountain bikes, 10-speeds and beach cruises are $2 per hr. to rent.

Car Rental: Alamo Rent A Car, 275-1050. At the airport. $30 per day, weekends $20 per day. $6 per day extra for those under 25.

Help Lines: Crisis Line, 244-7444. **Rape Hotline,** 327-1110. **Handicapped Information,** 862-6492. **Gay and Lesbian Switchboard,** 297-0008.

Time Zone: Central (1 hr. behind Eastern).

Post Office: 901 Broadway (255-9447), across from the Park Plaza Hotel and next to Union Station downtown. Open Mon.-Fri. 8am-6pm, Sat. 8am-noon. **ZIP code:** 37202.

Area Code: 615.

The names of Nashville's streets seem undeniably fickle. **Broadway,** the main east-west thoroughfare, becomes **West End Avenue** just outside downtown at I-40, and later becomes **Harding Road.** Downtown, numbered avenues run north-south, parallel to the Cumberland River. The curve of **James Robertson Parkway** encloses the north end, becoming **Main Street** on the other side of the river (later Gallatin Pike), and **McGavock Street** at the south end. The area between 2nd and 7th Ave., south of Broadway, is unsafe at night.

Accommodations and Camping

Finding a room in Nashville is not difficult, just expensive. Most cheaper places are within 20 mi. of downtown. Make reservations well in advance, especially for weekend stays. A dense concentration of budget motels line W. Trinity Lane and Brick Church Pike at I-65, north of downtown. Even cheaper hotels inhabit the area around Dickerson Rd. and Murfreesboro, but the neighborhood is seedy at best. **Hallmark Inns** (1-800-251-3294) is a local chain; its five Inns in the Nashville area are generally cheaper than national chains. **Bed and Breakfast of Middle Tennessee** (297-0883) have singles for $25-40, doubles for $50-75. **The Cumberland Inn,** I-65 North and Trinity Lane (226-1600), has cheerful rooms, unlimited local calls for $1, and a free continental breakfast. But no pets, please. (Singles $28. Doubles $32. $4 more on weekends.) **Budget Host Inn,** 10 Interstate Dr. (244-6050 or 1-800-234-6779), across from the Tourist Information Center has a pool, cable TV, and big rooms. ($29, on weekends $38.)

> **Motel 6,** 311 W. Trinity Lane (227-9696), at exit 87B off I-24/I-65; 323 Cartwright St., Goodlettsville (859-9674), take the Long Hollow Pike west, off I-65, then turn right onto Cartwright; and 95 Wallace Rd. (333-9933), take exit 56 from I-24, go west on Harding Pl. one block, left at Traveler's Inn Lane, and left on Largo. Tidy, efficient white rooms with dark curtains. (Singles $27. $6 per additional person.)

You can reach three campgrounds within walking distance of Opryland USA by public transport from 5th St. For the **Fiddler's Inn North Campground** (885-1440), the **Nashville Travel Park** (889-4225), and the **Two Rivers Campground** (883-8559), take the Briley Pkwy. north to McGavock Pike, and exit west onto Music Valley Dr. (Sites $13-$17 per 2 people.) Ten minutes north of Opryland is the **Nashville KOA,** 708 N. Dickerson Rd. (859-0075), I-65 in Goodlettsville, exit 98. Tell 'em Dave sent you. (Sites $12-20.)

Food

The Nashville sound even influences the local delicacies. Pick up a Goo-Goo cluster (peanuts and pecans, chocolate, caramel, and marshmallow) at any store and you'll bite into the initials of the Grand Ole Opry. Pecan pie is another favorite dessert, perfect after spicy barbecue or fried chicken. Restaurants for collegiate tastes and budgets cram the 2000 block of Elliston Place, near Vanderbilt. The **farmers market,** north of the capitol between 3rd and 7th Ave., sells fresh fruits and vegetables until sunset.

> **Loveless Motel Restaurant,** 8400 Hwy. 100 (646-9700). Accessible by car only; take 40W from downtown, left at exit 192, then left when you hit Hwy. 100.; a 15-20 min. drive. True country-style cooking at its best and most unrequited. Famous for its preserves, fried chicken, and hickory-smoked ham. For a weighty Southern meal, try the homemade biscuits with red-eye gravy, a special blend of ham drippings and coffee ($3-8). Open Tues.-Sat. 8am-2pm and 5-9pm, Sun. 8am-9pm. Reservations on weekends recommended.

> **Slice of Life,** 1811 Division, next to music studios (329-2526). Yuppie hangout featuring fresh bread and wholesome Tex-Mex. Veggie burritos $5, avocado, tomato and sprouts sandwich $4, carrot and celery juice $2. Open Mon.-Sat. 7am-9pm, Sun. 8am-9pm.

> **SATCO,** 208 Commerce St. (259-4413), off Second Ave. Student hangout. Tasty Mexican food that will erect barricades in your arteries before you finish. Enchiladas $3-4, tacos $1-2. Open Mon.-Thurs. 11am-9pm, Fri.-Sat. 11am-11pm.

International Market, 2010-B Belmont Blvd. Asian grocery with a large Thai buffet ($4-6). Crowded for lunch. Open daily 10:30am-9pm.

Rotiers, 2413 Elliston Place (327-9892). Honest sandwiches and specials ($3-5); no duplicitous croissants here. Open Mon.-Sat. 9am-10:30pm.

Brown's Diner, 2102 Blair Blvd. (269-5509), near Vanderbilt. Dilapidated diner with expanded dining room. Fun college atmosphere, but the food is less than arousing. Burgers $4-5. Open Mon.-Sat. 11am-10:30pm. Bar serves until midnight.

Sights

Music Row, home of Nashville's signature industry, fiddles about Division and Demonbreun St. from 16th to 19th Ave. S., bounded on the south by Grand Ave. (Take bus #3 to 17th Ave. and walk south.) After surviving the mobs outside the **Country Music Hall of Fame,** 4 Music Sq. E. (256-1639) at Division St., you can marvel at Elvis' "solid gold" Cadillac and other coveted country music memorabilia. Included in the admission is a tour of RCA's historic **Studio B,** where stars like Dolly Parton and Chet Atkins recorded their first hits. (Open June-Aug. daily 8am-8pm, Sept.-May 9am-5pm. $6.50, ages 6-11 $1.75, under 6 free.) When you want to record your own hit, the **Recording Studio of America,** 1510 Division St. (254-1282), underneath the **Barbara Mandrell Country Museum,** lets you karaoke your own vocals on pre-recorded, high-quality 24-track backgrounds to popular country and pop tunes. Choose a set and make a video, too. (Audio $13, video $20. Open June-Aug. daily 8am-8pm; Sept.-May daily 9am-5pm.)

A 15-minute walk west from Music Row along West End Ave. to **Centennial Park** will soon explain why Nashville calls itself the "Athens of the South." In the park stands an exact replica of the **Parthenon** (259-6358). Originally built as a temporary exhibit for the Tennessee Centennial in 1897, the Parthenon met with such olympian success that the model was rebuilt to last. A 42-ft. grey-eyed **Athena,** goddess of wisdom and the largest indoor sculpture in the Western Hemisphere, muses sagely. Unlike the Athenian original, the Nashville Parthenon houses the Cowan Collection of American Paintings in the basement galleries. Watch Greek theater performed on the steps in mid-July and August. (Open Tues.-Sat. 9am-4:30pm, Sun. 1-5pm. $2.50, kids and seniors $1.25, under 6 free.)

A walk through the downtown area reveals more of Nashville's eclectic architecture. The **Union Station Hotel,** at 1001 Broadway, evokes the glamour of turn-of-the-century train travel. The **Ryman Auditorium,** 116 5th Ave. N. (254-1445), off Broadway at 5th, is better known as the "Mother Church of Country Music". It housed a tabernacle and the Grand Ole Opry in previous incarnations. (Guided tours daily 8:30am-4:30pm. $2.50, ages 6-12 $1.) Turn up 2nd Ave. from Broadway to study the cast-iron and masonry facades of the handsome commercial buildings from the 1870s and 1880s. Now known as **Market Street,** many of these buildings have been converted into restaurants and nightspots.

The **Tennessee State Capitol,** Charlotte Ave. (741-0830) is the handsome Greek Revival structure atop the hill next to downtown, offering free guided tours of, among other things, the tomb of James K. Polk, one of the USA's least living Presidents. (Open Mon.-Fri. 9am-4pm, Sat. 10am-5pm, Sun. 1-5pm.) Across the street is the **Tennessee State Museum,** 505 Deaderick (741-2692). (Open Mon.-Sat. 10am-5pm, Sun. 1-5pm. Free.)

When you tire of the downtown area, rest at the **Cheekwood Botanical Gardens and Fine Arts Center,** Forest Park Dr. (356-8000), seven mi. southwest of town. The well-kept, leisurely, English-style gardens are a welcome change from Nashville glitz. Take bus #3 ("West End/Belle Meade") from downtown to Belle Meade Blvd. and Page Rd. (Open Mon.-Sat. 9am-5pm, Sun. 1-5pm. $4, seniors and college students $2, ages 7-17 $1). Dubbed "The Queen of Tennessee Plantations," the nearby **Belle Meade Mansion,** 110 Leake Ave. (356-0501), at Harding Rd., displays Southern antebellum opulence at the site of the nation's first thoroughbred breeding farm. (2 wonderful tours per hr., last tour at 4pm. Open Mon.-Sat. 9am-5pm, Sun. 1-5pm. $5, ages 13-18 $3.50, 6-12 $2.)

Thirteen mi. east of town is the **Hermitage,** 4580 Rachel's Lane (889-2941); take exit 221 off I-40. Andrew Jackson's beautiful manor house sits on 625 acres making an ideal spot for a picnic. Beware the crowded summer months. (Open daily 9am-5pm. $7, seniors $6.50, ages 6-13 $3.50.)

Fisk University's **Van Vechten Gallery,** 17th Ave. N. (329-8543), exhibits a distinguished collection of U.S. art. The gallery owns a portion of the Alfred Steiglitz Collection, donated to Fisk by Georgia O'Keeffe, Steiglitz's widow. Other exhibits feature her work and a range of photography and African art. (Open Tues.-Fri. 10am-5pm, Sat.-Sun. 1-5pm. $2.50, elementary and high school students free.)

Entertainment

Nashville offers a wide and dazzling array of inexpensive nightspots. Many feature the country tunes for which the town is known, while others cater to jazz, rock, bluegrass, or folk tastes. There are entertainment listings in the *Tennessean* Friday and Sunday, and in the *Nashville Banner* Thursday afternoon. The Nashville *Key,* available at the chamber of commerce, also informs. Comprehensive listings for all live music and events in the area abound in free copies of *Nashville Scene* or *Metro* around town. Muse over these publications plus many more at **Moskós,** 2204-B Elliston Place (327-3562), while stalling at their tasty muncheonette. (Open daily 8am-midnight.) Or, stop in at the trendy **Botanical Café,** 124 2nd Ave. N. (244-3915), for listings of events and fresh muffins for $1.

Opryland USA (889-6611) cross-pollinates between Las Vegas schmaltz and Disneyland purity, or vice versa, with the best in country music thrown in. This amusement park contains all the requisite family attractions, from roller coasters to cotton candy, and stages a dozen live music shows daily. Sometimes, a soundtrack of piped-in country music oozes throughout the park. (Open late March-late April and early Oct.-early Nov. Sat.-Sun.; early May-late May and early Sept.-late Sept. Fri.-Sun.; late May-early Sept. daily. $22, 2 days $33.) The **Grand Ole Opry,** setting for America's longest-running radio show, moved here from the town center in 1976. *The* place to hear country music, the Opry stomps every Friday and Saturday night ($12-14). 3pm matinees are added on various days during peak tourist season (April-Oct., $9.75-$12). Reserve tickets from Grand Ole Opry, 2808 Opryland Dr., Nashville 37214 (615-889-3060). General admission tickets can also be purchased at the box office, starting at 9am on Tuesday for weekend shows. Check the Friday morning *Tennessean* for a list of performers.

Many stars got their start at **Tootsie's Orchid Lounge,** 422 Broadway (726-3739), which still has good C&W music and affordable drinks. For years owner Tootsie Bess lent money to struggling musicians until they could get on the Ole Opry. (Open Mon.-Sat. 10am-3am, Sun. noon-3am.) The more genteel **Blue Bird Cafe,** 4104 Hillsboro Rd. (383-1461), in Green Hills, plays blues, folk, soft rock, and a smidgen of jazz. Women traveling solo probably will feel safer in this mellow, clean-cut establishment. Dinner, served until 11pm, consists of salads and sandwiches ($4-6.50). Music begins at 9:30pm. Go west on Broadway, then south on 21st, which becomes Hillsboro Rd. (Open Mon.-Sat. 5:30pm-1am. Cover $4-5.) The **Station Inn,** 402 12th Ave. S. (255-3307), blues some serious grass. (Open Tues.-Sat. 7pm-until. Music starts at 9pm. Cover $4. Free Sun. night jam session.) West of downtown, the **Bluegrass Inn,** 1914 Broadway (244-8877), has beer, chips, and music with a cinderblock-and-cement motif. A good-natured sort of place, the cover (around $3) depends on who's pickin'. (Open Wed.-Thurs. 9pm-midnight, Fri.-Sat. 9pm-1am.)

There's more to entertainment in Nashville than country music; just visit during the first weekend in June for the outdoor **Summer Lights** (259-6374) downtown, when top rock, jazz, reggae, classical, and, of course, country performers all jam simultaneously. For information on **Nashville Symphony** tickets and performances, call Ticketmaster at 741-2787. Rock bands play to a college audience at the **Exit/In,** 2208 Elliston Place (321-4400), near the Vanderbilt campus. (Bands start around 10:30pm. Cover about $4.) In a huge downtown warehouse, **Ace of Clubs,** 114 2nd S. (254-2237), packs 'em in for grand ol' rock 'n' roll. (Open daily. Music around

9pm. Cover $4-7.) **The World's End,** 1709-11 Church St. (329-3480), is a popular gay restaurant and dance club with a huge video screen.

TEXAS

What most people imagine when they think of Texas—vast desert plains, grazing cattle, oil fields, and dusty towns—can be found only in West Texas. Those who've already seen *The Last Picture Show,* however, will want to see the rest of the state, most of which defies the dry, flat, John Wayne stereotype Texas seems continually to produce. The cosmopolitan bustle of Dallas and Houston provides refuge from the wooded hills of East Texas, whose miles of cool pine forests look more Cajun than Texan. The rugged Texas hill country, the state's most picturesque region, rolls to the west of bohemian Austin and European San Antonio. And, just when you though you'd never see civilization again, El Paso and Juarez rise, phoenix- and Phoenix-like, from the desert, over 500 miles from any other major city.

Practical Information

Capital: Austin.

Texas Division of Tourism, P.O. Box 12728, Austin 78711 (512-463-8586). U.S. Forest Service, P.O. Box 130, Lufkin 75901 (409-831-2246). State Parks and Recreation Areas, Austin Headquarters Complex, 4200 Smith School Rd., Austin 78744 (512-463-4630).

Time Zones: Central (1 hr. behind Eastern) and Mountain (2 hr. behind Eastern). Postal Abbreviation: TX

Travel

Car travelers have the run of most of this huge state, but public transport serves areas frequented by tourists. The constellation of major cities in eastern Texas forms a triangle with **Dallas/Ft. Worth, San Antonio,** and **Houston/Galveston** at the corners, and **Austin** part way along the San Antonio-Dallas leg. Each leg measures 200-300 mi. in length. Interstate highways, frequent bus schedules, and Amtrak routes connect the points. **Kerrville Bus Lines,** a Greyhound affiliate, covers the entire region, while **Greyhound/Trailways** zooms along the edges.

Outside this triangle, the two areas of greatest interest to visitors are **western Texas** and the **Gulf Coast/Mexican Border** area, accessible by interstates and bus routes. Greyhound has frequent service on I-10 and I-20 into western Texas and convenient service to Corpus Christi and the southern border towns. Another Greyhound affiliate, **TNM&O Coaches,** provides thorough regional coverage in northwestern Texas and southern New Mexico. El Paso/Ciudad Juárez, a major urban area straddling the Mexican border, is a convenient base for exploring western Texas and southern New Mexico.

Regional cuisine, like most of Texan culture, is enriched by the state's Mexican heritage. "Tex-Mex" is a variation of the dishes served across the border: chefs throw jalapeño peppers into chili as casually as a McDonald's crew chief shakes salt on french fries. Mexican pastries and genuine longhorn beef are staples, but also indispensable is chicken-fried steak—originally created to disguise bad meat at roadside dives, today a delicacy. And of course, get some BBQ with plenty of sauce.

Outdoors

Some folks say Texas has only two seasons: summer and January. It's hot in summer. Really hot. The heat is more bearable in the west, where the air is dry; the coastal humidity is stifling. Winter varies across the state, from warm and mild in the south to potentially severe and blizzardy in the northern panhandle.

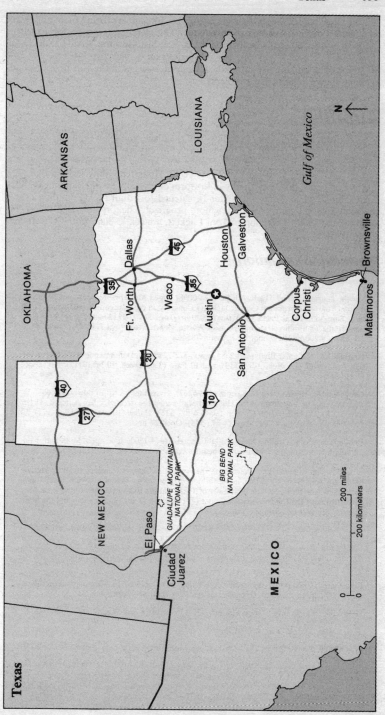

Texas

Take advantage of the state's wide open space by camping. Bring a tent and insect repellent to deter squadrons of mosquitos. The state park system has excellent camping at over 60 parks, recreation areas, and historic sites. Some parks charge an admission fee of $2 per car, 50¢ per pedestrian or bicyclist. Sites usually cost $4. In the open ranching countryside of western Texas or in the Hill Country, finding sites should present few problems.

Austin

Apart from the obligatory grandiosity of the place, you'd have difficulty guessing that Austin (pop. 750,000) is a Texas town. The city has acquired a reputation as haven for bohemians and panhandlers alike, due largely to the vast student population (50,000) at the University of Texas (UT). Hints reminding visitors that, yes, they *are* in Texas, do exist, usually in the form of typically Southern political antics (for example, when a state legislator threatened to withdraw UT funding over a collegiate football controversy) But more progressive factors outweigh them—for example, the 1990-91 election of Toni Luckett, a black lesbian, to the UT student government.

Practical Information

Emergency: 911.

Austin Tourist Center, 412 E. 6th St. (478-0098). Open Mon.-Fri. 8:30am-5pm, Sat.-Sun. 1-5pm. **Tourist Information Center,** 11th and Congress, in the state capitol (463-8586). Open daily 8am-5pm. **Texas Parks and Wildlife,** 389-4800 or 800-792-1112 in TX. Open Mon.-Fri. 8am-5pm. Call for info on camping outside Austin. Or write to or visit Texas Parks and Wildlife Dept., 4200 Smith School Rd., Austin 78744.

Amtrak: 250 N. Lamar Blvd. (476-5684 or 800-872-7245). To Dallas (7 per week, 6 hr., $36), San Antonio (7 per week, 3 hr., $13), and El Paso (3 per week, 10 hr., $117). No service to Houston.

Greyhound/Trailways: 916 E. Koenig (458-5267), several mi. north of downtown off I-35. Pick up buses to downtown at the Highland Mall across the street. To: San Antonio (11 per day, 2-3 hr., $11); Houston (11 per day, 3-4 hr., $16); Dallas (10 per day, 4 hr., $27); El Paso via San Antonio (5 per day, 14 hr., $75). Open 24 hrs.

Public Transport: Capitol Metro, 504 Congress (474-1200; line open Mon.-Sat. 6am-midnight, Sun. 6am-7pm). Maps and schedules available here Mon.-Fri. 7am-6pm, Sat. 9am-1pm, or at the Austin Chamber of Commerce, across from the tourist center. Fare 50¢, seniors, kids, and disabled 25¢. Downtown, the **Armadillo Express** connects major downtown points and runs every 10-15 min. in old-fashioned green trolley cars Mon.-Fri. 6:30am-10pm, Sat. 11am-7pm. Fare 25¢. The **University of Texas Shuttle Bus** serves the campus area. Map and schedule at the UT Information Center (471-3151) or at any library, including the Main Library, 8th and Guadalupe ("Gwadaloop") St.

Taxi: Yellow Cab, 472-1111. Base fare $1.25, $1.25 per mi. Airport to downtown $7.50.

Car Rental: Rent-A-Wreck, 6820 Guadalupe (454-8621). $20-22 per day, 100 free mi., 19¢ per additional mi. Open Mon.-Fri. 8am-6:30pm, Sat.-Sun. 10am-3:30pm. Must be 21 with major credit card.

Bike Rental: University Schwinn, 2901 N. Lamar Blvd. (474-6696). Mountain bikes $20 per day. $300 deposit required. Open Mon.-Fri. 10am-7pm, Sat. 10am-6pm.

Help Lines: Crisis Intervention Hotline, 472-4357. **Austin Rape Crisis Center,** 440-7273.

Time Zone: Central (1 hr. behind Eastern).

Post Office: 300 E. 9th St. (929-1250). Open Mon.-Fri. 7:30am-6pm, Sat. 8am-noon. **ZIP code:** 78767.

Area Code: 512.

Highway signs lead to the **capitol area** near Congress Ave. and 11th St., in the center of the city. **Congress Avenue** runs from the **Colorado River** in the south 12 blocks to the capitol and then seven more blocks to the **University of Texas (UT)** in the north. The university splits numbered streets into east and west and includes most tourist spots in this stretch. Austin is a cyclist's paradise, with roller-coaster hills and clearly marked bikeways.

Accommodations and Camping

Cheap accommodations abound in Austin. Three UT co-ops rent rooms to hostelers, including three meals per day. **21st St. Co-op,** W. 21st St. (476-1857), charges $10 for large, comfortable rooms. The place fills rapidly in summer. To get from the bus station to the hostel, take bus #15 to 7th and Congress St., walk down 7th one block to Colorado, and take #3 to 21st and Nueces St.; those who arrive too late should wander two blocks west to the end of 21st St. to the **Pearl Street Co-op,** on Pearl St. of all places. This co-op offers the same deal as 21st, but with access to a beautiful courtyard pool. (Rooms $13.) Just a few blocks away, **Taos Hall,** 2612 Guadalupe (474-6905), provides three meals and a bed for just $10. You're most likely to get a private room here, and when you stay for dinner, the friendly residents will give you a welcoming round of applause. As if that's not enough sleeping around, a couple blocks away is the **Goodall Wooten Dorm,** 2112 Guadalupe (472-1343). The "Woo" has private rooms with a small frige, plus access to a TV room and basketball courts. Call ahead. (Rooms $15.)

Farther from the center of town but still conveniently located is the **Austin International Youth Hostel (AYH),** 2200 S. Lakeshore Blvd. (444-2294). From the Greyhound station take bus #7 ("Duval") to Lakeshore Blvd. and walk about ½ mi. to the hostel. From I-35 east, exit at Riverside, head east, and turn left at Lakeshore Blvd. The Hostel has a kitchen, A/C, and is near a grocery store ($8).

I-35, running north and south of Austin, features a string of inexpensive hotels well outside downtown. **Motel 6** has two locations along I-35, both with clean rooms, a pool, and HBO-blessed color TV. **North,** 9420 N. I-35 at the Rundberg exit (339-6161), lies 12 mi. north of the capitol off N. Lamar and E. Rundberg Lane. Take a bus to Fawnridge and walk four blocks. (Singles $20. Doubles $26.) The opposite-minded **South,** 2707 I-35 (444-5882), near the Woodward exit, is seven mi. south of the capitol near St. Edward's University. (Singles $22. Doubles $28.)

Camping is a 15- to 45-minute drive away. The **Austin Capitol KOA** (444-6322), six mi. south of the city along I-35, offers a pool, game room, laundry, grocery, and playground. Some cabins are available. (Sites $14 for 2.) The **Emma Long Metropolitan Park,** 2000 Barton Springs (346-1831), a large preserve in the bend of the Colorado River, 6½ mi. off Rte. 2222, has hookup, tent sites, and a boat ramp. Contact the visitor center or the Highland Lakes Tourist Association for more info (see Practical Information above).

Food

Two main districts compete for Austin's restaurant trade. Along the west side of the UT campus, **Guadalupe Street** (AKA "the drag") has scores of fast-food joints and convenience stores, including the **Party Barn,** with drive-through beer. Those who disdain the $3 all-you-can-eat pizza buffets and sub shops that line the drag can eat in the UT Union ($2-5). The second district clusters around **Sixth Street,** south of the capitol. Here the battle for Happy Hour business rages with unique intensity; three-for-one drink specials and free hors d'oeuvres are common.

Casablanca, 2nd floor of Dobie Mall, corner of Guadalupe and 21st St. right off UT campus. Good, cheap Mediterranean food cooked and served in cozy, tapestry-bedecked shop. Good-sized plates of hummos, falafel, shwarma and baklava $2-4. Open Mon.-Sat. 11am-9pm.

Sam's Bar-B-Que, 2000 E. 12th St. Take bus #12 or 6 eastbound. Tiny, dive-like interior thick with locals on weekends. Barbecue plates (with beans and potato salad) $4. Open Mon.-Thurs. 10am-3:30am, Fri.-Sat. 10am-5am, Sun. 10am-3am.

Trudy's Texas Star, 409 W. 30th St. Fine Tex-Mex dinner entrees $7-9, and a fantastic array of margaritas. Famous for *migas,* a corn tortilla soufflé ($4). Open Mon.-Thurs. 7am-midnight, Fri.-Sat. 7am-4am, Sun. 8am-midnight.

Sholz Garden, 1607 San Jacinto (477-4171), near the capitol. An Austin landmark recognized by the legislature as "epitomizing the finest traditions of the German heritage of our state." German only in name, of course. Great chicken-fried steaks and Tex-Mex meals $5-6. Live country-rock music jazz. Open Mon.-Thurs. 11am-midnight, Fri.-Sat. 11am-2am.

Old Bakery and Emporium, 1006 N. Congress, near the capitol. Cheap sweets and light lunches in an old stone home. Sandwiches $1.75-2. Open Mon.-Fri. 9am-4pm.

Sights

Not to be outdone by Washington, in 1882 Texans built their **state capitol,** Congress Ave. (463-0063), seven ft. higher than the national one. This colossal building with colorful inlaid marble floors has "Texas" inscribed on everything from door hinges to hallway benches. (Open during legislative session 24 hrs.; off-season 6am-11pm. Free tours Mon.-Sat. 8:30am-4:30pm. Tourist info center open daily 8am-5pm.) Across the street from the capitol, at 11th and Colorado St., sleeps the **Governor's Mansion** (463-5516), built in 1856. The bottom level stores furniture of the past 10 Texas governors. (Free tours Mon.-Fri. every 20 min. 10-11:40am.)steve

The **University of Texas at Austin,** the wealthiest public university in the country, enrolls over 50,000 students. Its **visitor centers** (471-1420) reside in Sid Richardson Hall, adjacent to the LBJ Library, and at the corner of Martin Luther King Jr. and Red River. The equally well-endowed **Harry Ransom Center,** Guadalupe at 21st St. (471-8944), will be glad to show you its treasures: among others, it hoards a vast collection of Aleister Crowley's manuscripts and correspondence as well as his personal library, perhaps the most complete Evelyn Waugh collection around, and the complete personal libraries of both Virginia Woolf and James Joyce. (Open Mon.-Sat. 9am-5pm, Sun. 1-5pm. Free.)

The **Laguna Gloria Art Museum,** 3809 W. 35th St. (458-8191), eight mi. from the capitol in a Mediterranean villa-lookalike, displays the city's best exhibits on a rotating basis and features 20th-century artwork. With rolling, spacious grounds that overlook **Lake Austin,** the Laguna often hosts inexpensive evening concerts, plays, and seasonal festivals. Take bus #21. (Tours Sun. at 2pm. Open Tues.-Sat. 10am-5pm, Thurs. 10am-9pm, Sun. 1-5pm. $2, seniors and students $1, under 16 free. Free Thurs.)

Near the capitol is **St. Mary's Cathedral,** E. 10th and Brazos St., an ornate sanctuary and the closest Austin comes to Gothic architecture. Many zip to riverside **Zilker Park,** 2201 Barton Springs Rd., just south of the Colorado River, on hot afternoons. **Barton Springs Pool** (476-9044), in the park, is a popular swimming hole flanked by walnut and pecan trees. The spring-fed pool is 1,000 ft. long and 200 ft. wide. Beware: the pool's temperature rarely rises above 60°F. Get away from the crowd and avoid paying by walking upstream (take an inner tube) and swimming at any spot that looks nice. ($1.75, Sat.-Sun. $2, ages 12-18 50¢, under 12 25¢. Swimming free and at your own risk Nov.-Jan.) Zilker Park also has a botanical garden (477-8672), rentable canoes (478-3852), playgrounds, playing fields, and picnic areas. Parking inside the grounds costs $2, but is free on the roads near the entrance.

Entertainment

Austin, home of the Bad Livers, draws all sorts of musicians from all over the country and has boosted many to fame. Within the last year alone, the city attracted such stars as Metallica, Buddy Guy, Sue Foley, Dread Zeppelin, and Bob Weir of the Grateful Dead. Pick up a free copy of the **Austin Chronicle,** available at book and record stores as well as the local HEB supermarkets, for listings of who's in town.

For honky-tonk and two-steppin' action visit the **Broken Spoke,** 3201 S. Lamar Blvd. (442-6189), Austin's liveliest dance hall. (Open Mon.-Tues. 9:30am-11:30pm,

Wed. and Fri. 9:30am-1am, Thurs. 9:30am-12:30am, Sat. 11am-2am. Dancing Wed.-Sat. Cover Wed.-Sat. $4-5; no cover Mon.-Tues.) Wander safely along 6th St. (the street is closed to traffic after 6pm daily), especially on weeknights when there are neither crowds nor cover charges, to sample the bands from the sidewalk. For raunchy Texas-style rock-n-roll and cheap beer, try **Joe's Generic Bar.** (No phone, no cover. Open daily 11am-until.) For solid Texan music, try **Raven's Garage** (482-9272), on Red River just north of 6th St., where bands rev up in an old garage. The street is not well lit. On campus, the **Cactus Cafe,** 24th and Guadalupe (471-8228), hosts different musicians almost every night. (Hours vary; usually 8am-1am. Cover $2-12.) Next door, the **Texas Tavern** (471-5651) favors country music and serves fast food. (Hours vary; usually 11:30am-1:45am. Cover $2-5.) Those journeying out to Lake Travis should seek out the **Oasis Cantina De Lago,** 6550 Comanche Trail (266-2441), a restaurant and bar bathed in gorgeous sunset. (Open Sun.-Thurs. 11am-9pm, Fri.-Sat. 11am-10pm. No cover.)

From early May through late August, the **Zilker Park Hillside Theater,** 2000 Barton Springs Rd. (499-2000), on Rte. 2244, produces free variety shows and concerts under the stars. Shows usually start between 7 and 9pm. The **Austin Symphony Orchestra** sponsors concerts of all kinds in the amphitheater at 1101 Red River Rd. (476-6064), downtown, while last year UT's **Performing Arts Center,** 23rd at E. Campus Dr. (471-1444), staged professional productions of *Les Misérables* and *Hair.*

Film mavens should check out the **Varsity Repertory Theater,** 2402 Guadalupe (474-4351), which hosts new and unusual movies and foreign films. The historic **Paramount Theater,** 713 Congress (472-5470), shows daily double-features ($4; seniors, students, and under 12 $2.50).

Corpus Christi

After you've taken in all of Corpus Christi's sights—in other words, after half an hour—you may begin to wonder what you're doing in the body of Christ. Look eastward into Corpus Christi Bay and the Gulf of Mexico, and you'll find the same answer as thousands before you. The sun and the sea are the city's culture, piers and beaches its museum and music halls. Luckily, the popularity of Galveston and South Padre Island have left Corpus Christi free from massive spring break attacks and allowed the city to retain its seaside charm. This charm is augmented by the city's substantial Mexican-American population, most easily visible in the abundance of superior Tex-Mex restaurants. You may not be enlightened when you leave Corpus Christi, but you'll definitely feel tanned and resurrected.

Practical Information

Emergency: 911

Convention and Visitors Bureau, 1201 N. Shoreline (882-5603), where I-37 meets the water. Piles of pamphlets, bus schedules, and local maps. Open Mon.-Fri. 8:30am-5pm, Sat. 9am-3pm. Info also available at the **Corpus Christi Museum,** 1900 N. Chaparral (883-2862). Open Sat. 10am-5pm, Sun. 1-5pm. The **Information Line** (854-8540) provides info on events, restaurants, clubs, and shopping.

Corpus Christi International Airport, 1000 International Dr. (289-0171), west of downtown, bordered by Rte. 44 (Agnes St.) and Joe Mireur Rd. Cabs to downtown about $7.

Greyhound: 702 N. Chaparral (882-2516), at Starr downtown. To Dallas (4 per day, 8 hr., $56), Houston (12 per day, 5 hr., $28), and Austin (5 per day, 5 hr., $22). Open 24 hrs. Lockers $1.

Public Transport: Regional Transit Authority (The "B"), 289-2600. Pick up route maps and schedules at the main station on the corner of Water and Schatzel St. or at the visitors bureau. Central transfer point is City Hall, downtown. Buses run infrequently Mon.-Sat., until around 8pm. Fare 50¢, seniors, disabled, students, and kids 25¢. All buses 10¢ on Sat.

Taxi: Island Shuttle Cab Company, 949-8850. Base fare $1.35 per mi., $1.25 each additional mi. Major credit cards accepted.

Car Rental: Thrifty, 1928 N. Padre Island Dr. (289-0041), at Leopard St. $33 per day, 150 free mi. each day, 20¢ each additional mi. Weekends $19 per day, 100 free mi. each day. Open Mon.-Fri. 6am-9pm, Sat.-Sun. 8am-9pm. Must be 21 with a major credit card. Under 25 surcharge $3 per day.

Help Lines: 24-Hour Crisis Hotline, 887-9816. **Crisis Services,** 887-9818. **Women's Shelter,** 881-8888. Open 24 hrs.

Post Office: 809 Nueces Bay Blvd. (886-2200). Open Mon.-Fri. 8am-5pm, Sat. 7:30am-noon. **ZIP code:** 78469.

Area Code: 512.

The tourist district of Corpus Christi (pop. 225,000) follows **Shoreline Drive,** which borders the gulf coast. The downtown business district lies one mi. west. Unfortunately, the streets don't quite follow a grid pattern, and the largely one-way roads downtown may frustrate drivers, sending them in circles up and down the bluff. **Agnes Street** and **Leopard Street** are the easiest routes to follow when approaching downtown from the west. Agnes St. goes directly downtown from the airport; Leopard follows a parallel path from most of the cheaper motels. Both streets end within one block of Shoreline Dr.

Accommodations and Food

Sandwiched between the visitors bureau and the ultra-posh Wyndham Hotel is the **Sand and Sea Budget Inn,** 1013 N. Shoreline Dr. (882-6518), where I-37 meets the water. Rooms have a small foyer, plush carpet, and an unbeatable location. Since there are only four singles, try to make a reservation. (Singles $24. Doubles $30, with bay view $40. Key deposit $5.)

While the northwest section of Corpus Christi lacks the convenience and public transport of downtown lodging, it does have the best motel bargains. Find ecosleep at the **Ecomotel,** 6033 Leopard St. (289-1116). Exit I-37 north at Corn Products Rd., turn left and go to the second light (at Leopard St.), and take another left. By bus, take #27 from downtown right to the motel. Be sure to check a schedule, since the bus runs infrequently. Comfortable, generic rooms with cable TV and pool. (Singles $29. Doubles $35.) Nearby is the standard yet reliable **Motel 6,** 845 Lantana St. (289-9397). Take exit 3B from I-37 north, 4B from I-37 south. (Singles $22. Doubles $28.) Campers should head to **Padre Island National Seashore** or **Mustang State Park** (see Padre Island National Seashore below). Also, **Nueces River City Park** (241-1464), north on I-37 (exit 16 at Nueces River), has free tent sites and three-day RV permits.

Corpus Christi's downtown area transubstantiates into many inexpensive and tasty eating establishments. **Bahia,** 224 Chaparral (884-6555), serves simple but rib-sticking Mexican breakfasts and lunches. The authentic food compensates for the tacky decor. Try *nopalitos* (cactus and egg on a tortilla, $1.25) or a taco and two enchiladas with rice beans, tea, and dessert ($3.75). Live entertainment rocks the house on Friday from 7 to 9pm. (Open Mon.-Thurs. 7am-6pm, Fri. 7am-9pm, Sat. 7am-3pm.) Just down the street, the **Sea Gulf Villa Cafe,** 412 N. Chaparral (888-9238), lets you compile your own breakfast *tacquito* (4 items $1.50), or try three bean, cheese, and veggie *chalupas* for $3.25. Large portions and quick service. (Open Mon.-Sat. 7am-3pm.) **La Pesca,** 701 N. Water St. (887-4558), is an upscale Mexican seafood joint a block away from the water. Try the excellent crab enchiladas ($7) or shrimp tacos ($6). More traditional dishes are $4-6. (Open daily 11am-2pm and 5-10:30pm.)

The area around the budget motels, northwest of town, is fairly devoid of eating possibilities save **Jerry's Winner's Circle** (289-6135), inside the Ecomotel. Jerry offers you a Mexican combo plate for $5, or a pancake, eggs, 'n' sausage breakfast for only $2.50. (Open Mon.-Thurs. 6am-10pm, Fri.-Sat. 6am-midnight.)

Corpus Christi is the home of **Whataburger,** a chain of above-average fast-food joints. There are 23 chances throughout the city to sample their made-to-order burgers ($2) or malts ($1.25). Most locations are open 24 hrs.

Sights

Corpus Christi's most significant sight is the shoreline, which is bordered for miles by wide sidewalks with graduated steps down to the water. The piers are filled with overpriced seaside restaurants, sail and shrimp boats, and hungry seagulls. Feeding these birds will produce a Hitchcockian swarm; wear a hat and prepare to run for your life. Almost all of the beaches on North Shoreline Dr. are open for swimming; just follow the signs.

For those determined to eke out a little culture after a day in the sun, your only option is on the north end of Shoreline Dr., where the Convention Center houses the **Art Museum of South Texas,** 1902 N. Shoreline (884-3844), whose small but impressive collection includes works by Monet, Matisse, Picasso, Rembrandt, Goya, and Ansel Adams. Disabled access. (Open Tues.-Sat. 10am-5pm, Sun. 1-5pm. $1-2, depending on the temporary exhibit.) But really, there's no need to check out any other "sights" in Corpus Christi unless another ice age starts—just go to the beach and work on your skin cancer.

Dallas

Unfortunately, *Dallas'* reputation preceeds that of Dallas (pop. 1,062,000). Typecast by the TV series, the city labored in the shadow of evil-doer J.R. Ewing and his moronic relatives from their conception in 1980 until their merciful cancellation in 1991. While the city's legendary preoccupation with commerce is indeed evident—high-tech skyscrapers still define the city's architecture—recent massive campaigns for historic preservation have restored many run-down urban areas to their pre-petroleum glory, and the new **arts district** and **Deep Ellum** have nurtured a culture of a higher order than certain recently-cancelled primetime TV shows.

Practical Information

Emergency: 911

Dallas Convention and Visitors Bureau, 1201 Elm St., Suite 24 (746-6677). Open Mon.-Fri. 8:30am-5pm. **Union Station Visitor Center,** 400 S. Houston Ave. (746-6603), in a booth in the lobby. Open daily 9am-5pm. **Special Events Info Line,** (746-6679).

Dallas-Ft. Worth International Airport: (214-574-8888), 17 mi. northwest of downtown. Sprawling, chatty conversational computer-run shuttle system makes even the longest layover bearable. **Love Field** (670-6080; take bus #39) has mostly intra-Texas flights. To get downtown from either airport, take the **Super Shuttle,** 729 E. Dallas Rd. (817-329-2001; in terminal, dial 02 on phone at ground transport services). 24-hr. service. DFW airport to downtown $14.50, Love Field to downtown $10.50.

Amtrak: 400 S. Houston Ave. (653-1101 or 800-872-7245), in Union Station, next to Reunion Tower. One train per day to Houston (6 hr., $30) and St. Louis (15 hr., $125).

Greyhound/Trailways: 205 S. Lamar (655-7000), at Commerce 3 blocks east and 1 block north of Union Station. To: Houston (6 per day, 6 hr., $28); San Antonio (15 per day, 6 hr., $34); El Paso (6 per day, 12½ hr., $85); New Orleans (10 per day, 12½ hr., $87). Open 24 hrs.

Public Transport: Dallas Area Rapid Transit (DART), 601 Pacific Ave. (979-1111 or 934-3278). Serves most suburbs; routes radiate from downtown. Service 5am-midnight, to suburbs 5am-8pm. Base fare 75¢, more with zone changes. Info desk open Mon.-Fri. 8:30am-4:45pm. Maps available at Main and Akard St. (Mon.-Fri. 8am-5pm), or at Elm and Ervay St. (Mon.-Fri. 7am-6pm). **Hop-a-Bus** (979-1111) is DART's downtown Dallas service, with a park-and-ride system. Three routes (blue, red, and green) run about every 10 min. Fare 25¢, transfers free. Look for buses with a blue bunny, a red kangaroo, or a green frog. No Hop-A-Bus service on weekends.

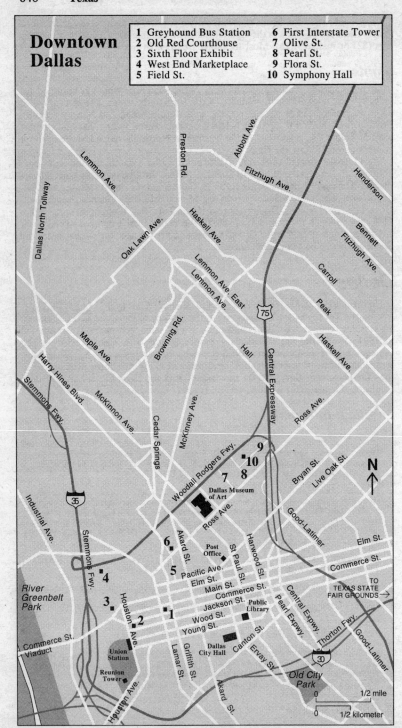

Downtown Dallas

1 Greyhound Bus Station
2 Old Red Courthouse
3 Sixth Floor Exhibit
4 West End Marketplace
5 Field St.
6 First Interstate Tower
7 Olive St.
8 Pearl St.
9 Flora St.
10 Symphony Hall

Taxi: **Yellow Cab Co.,** 426-6262. $1.50 first mi., $1.20 each additional mi. DFW Airport to downtown $20.

Car Rental: All-State Rent-a-Car, 3206 Live Oak (741-3118). $25 per day with 100 free mi., 16¢ per additional mi. Open Mon.-Sat. 7:30am-6pm. Must be 21 with major credit card.

Bike Rental: Bicycle Exchange, 11716 Ferguson Rd. (270-9269). Rates from $60 per week. Open Mon.-Fri. 9am-7pm, Sat. 9am-5pm. Must have a credit card.

Help Lines: Gay Hotline, 368-6283. Open Sun.-Thurs. 7-11pm, Fri.-Sat. 7:30pm-midnight. **Gay Alliance Community Center,** 2701 Reagan (528-4233), open daily 9am-9pm. **Senior Citizen Call Action Center** 1500 Marilla St. (744-3600) gives info on reduced fares, recreational activites, and health care.

Time Zone: Central (1 hr. behind Eastern).

Post Office: 400 N. Ervay St. (953-3045), on Thanksgiving Sq. downtown. Open Mon.-Fri. 8am-6pm. **ZIP code:** 75201; General Delivery, 75221; **Area Code:** 214.

Accommodations and Camping

Cheap accommodations of the non-chain motel type are hard to come by; conventions and big events like the Cotton Bowl (Jan. 1) and the State Fair (Oct.) aggrevate the situation. If you can afford it, your most luxurious option undoubtedly is **Bed and Breakfast Texas Style,** 4224 W. Red Bird Ln. (298-5433 or 298-8586). They'll place you at a nice home, usually near town, with friendly residents who are anxious to make your stay as pleasant as possible. Reservations are suggested for homes closer to town, but if you call from the bus station, they usually can pick you up. (Singles from $35. Doubles from $40.)

Dallas's only hostel and only source of true budget lodgings recently closed. The best deal lies with the **Welcome Inn,** 3243 Merrifield (826-3510). Take the Dolphin St. exit off I-30 E. (Singles $25. Doubles $30.) **Hwy. 75 (Central Expressway), I-635 (LB5 Freeway),** and the suburbs of **Irving** and **Arlington** also have many inexpensive motels. Try **Motel 6** (505-891-6161), with 11 locations in the Dallas area, **Exel Inns** (800-356-8013), or **Red Roof Inns** (800-843-7663) for singles from $27 to 35.

If you have a car and camping gear, try the **Hi-Ho Campground,** 200 W. Bear Creek Rd. (223-8574), south of town. Take I-35 14½ mi. to exit 412, turn right, and go 2 more mi. (Tent sites $10 for 2 people, with hookup $6.50, $1 per additional person.)

Food

Pick up a copy of the Friday weekend guide of the *Dallas Morning News* for an overview of what's available. The **West End Historic District,** popular with family vacationers, supplies vittles, potations, and entertainment in the heart of downtown. For fast Tex-Mex food and a variety of small shops, explore the **West End Marketplace,** 603 Munger St. (954-4350). The **Farmers Produce Market,** 1010 S. Pearl Expressway (748-2082), between Pearl and Central Expressway near I-30 (open daily sunrise-sunset), can satisfy all of your twisted picknicking fantasies.

Mai's, 4812 Bryan (826-9887). Authentic Vietnamese cuisine served with a smile by the Bui family. *Each year or so, the family saves enough money to sponsor immigration of friends over to the states.* Adventurous eaters will enjoy the jellyfish salad ($3.25), although more conventional Vietnamese ($4-8) and vegetarian ($3-5) dishes are available. Open Wed.-Thurs. and Sun. 11am-10pm, Fri.-Sat. 11am-11pm.

Snuffer's, 3526 Greenville (826-6850). Has the best burgers ($3.40) in town. Nice all-wooden interior with friendly service and fun crowd. Don't miss the fried mushrooms ($3). Open daily 11am-2am.

Dave's Art Pawn Shop, 2544 Elm (748-7111). A typical art gallery/concert hall/coffeeshop restaurant that supplies Bohemian rhapsody. Great sandwiches (under $4). Possible cover on weekends, although no liquor served. Open daily 7pm-4am.

Herrera's Cafe, 4001 Maple Ave. (528-9644). Take bus #29. Informality doesn't daunt businesspeople who partake of the excellent Tex-Mex dinners. Filling meals $4-6. Bring your own beer, and expect to wait on weekends. Open Mon. and Wed.-Thurs. 10am-9pm, Fri. 10am-10pm, Sat. 9am-10pm, Sun. 9am-9pm.

Bubba's, 6617 Hillcrest Ave. (373-6527). A remodeled, '50s-style diner near the heart of SMU. Serves the best fried chicken and chicken-fried steak dinners in town ($4-5.40). Open daily 6:30am-10pm.

Au Shucks, 4601 Greenville Ave. (821-9449). A casual seafood bar with an unbeatable outdoor patio for slurping raw oysters ($3-7) in the summer. Open Mon.-Thurs. 11am-11pm, Fri.-Sat. 11am-11:45pm, Sun. 11:30am-10pm.

Kuby's, 6601 Snider Plaza near SMU (363-2231) or 3121 Ross Ave., downtown (821-3121). This German deli/market serves cheap breakfasts ($2-4) and sandwiches ($3-5) as well as their own packaged sausages and kraut. Open 6am-6pm; downtown stores open 7am-2pm.

Two Pesos, 1827 Greenville (823-2092). Fast-food style, but "Dos Pesos" is a late-night Dallas tradition. Serves tasty Mex dishes ($3-4) a la carte and great tacos and fajitas ($1-2). Open 24 hrs.

Sights

Originally an insignificant trading post, Dallas grew to prominence in the 1870s when a major North-South railroad crossed a transcontinental East-West line about ½ mi. south of the town. Converging waves of settlers inspired by prospects of black gold caused the population to swell. Its layout can be viewed from atop **Reunion Tower** (712-7070), a good place to start a walking tour and to get acquainted with the city. (Open Mon.-Fri. 10am-10pm, Sat.-Sun. 9am-midnight; $2, seniors and kids $1.)

On your way out, take the underground walkway to the adjoining **Union Station,** 400 S. Houston Ave., and explore one of the city's few grand old buildings. Upon exiting the building, walk north along Houston, and you'll come upon the **West End Historic District,** an impressive example of gentrification. At the corner of Houston and Main St. is the old Dallas County Courthouse, nicknamed **Old Red** for its unique red granite composition. Built in 1892, the Richardsonian Romanesque structure is one of Dallas' most revered landmarks. One block north is the alleged former **Texas School Book Depository,** from which Lee Harvey Oswald is *alleged* to have shot alleged President John F. Kennedy, Jr. on November 22, 1963. The building now allegedly houses **The Sixth Floor,** 411 Elm St. (653-6666—Was it SATAN? Or, after all, was it me and you?), a museum devoted mostly to recounting the days before and after the assassination of that statesman of wealth and taste, complete with still-gripping news coverage of the event and speculation as to whodunit. (Last tickets sold 1 hr. before closing. $4, seniors $3, students $2. Audio tours $2.) Philip Johnson's Illuminating **Memorial** to Kennedy looms nearby, at Market and Main St.

Continue north on Houston as it curves east and becomes Ross Ave. in the heart of the commercial area of the West End. The streets of red brick warehouses converted to restaurants and bars end in the **West End Marketplace,** 603 Munger Ave., a passel of fast-food eateries, bars, shops, and tourists. (Open Tues.-Thurs. 11am-10pm, Fri.-Sat. and Mon. 11am-midnight, Sun. noon-8pm.) Just east of the West End on the corner of Ross Ave. and Field St. stands Dallas' most impressive skyscraper, **The First Interstate Tower,** a multi-sided prism sitting atop a nicely-designed water garden.

Walking farther east along Ross Ave. leads you to the new **Arts District,** the centerpiece of which is the **Dallas Museum of Art,** 1717 N. Harwood St. (922-1200). The museum offers Indonesian, impressionist, modern, and U.S. decorative art. An outdoor sculpture garden and an art room delight kids. (Museum open Tues.-Wed. and Fri.-Sat. 10am-5pm, Thurs. 10am-9pm, Sun. and holidays noon-5pm. Children's room open Wed.-Thurs. and Sat. noon-5pm. Both free.)

Walking south from the museum on St. Paul, toward the downtown area, turn right on Bryan St. and walk one block to **Thanksgiving Square** (969-1977), a tiny park beneath massive towers. While viewing this monument to Thanksgiving in all religions, you too will give thanks for the respite from the busy streets the park's sunken gardens and waterfalls provide. (Open Mon.-Fri. 9am-5pm, Sat.-Sun. and holidays 1-5pm.) Continue south from Thanksgiving Square along Ervay St. to the imposing **Dallas City Hall,** 100 Marilla St. (670-3957), designed by the omnipotent I.M. "Everywhere" Pei.

About nine blocks south of City Hall on Ervay St. is the **Old City Park,** at Gano St. (421-5141). The park is both the oldest and one of the most popular recreation areas and lunch spots in the city. Open spaces and picnic facilities are scattered among restored buildings, which include a railroad depot and a church. (Park open daily 9am-6pm. Exhibit buildings open Tues.-Sat. 10am-4pm, Sun. 1:30-4:30pm. Tours $4.)

State Fair Park, southeast of downtown on 2nd Ave. (426-3400), has been home to the fair since 1886, although most of the structures there today remain from the 1936 World's Fair celebrating the Texas Centennial. The park is home to the Cotton bowl, numerous museums, and a Texas-sized ferris wheel, all within walking distance of each other. A standout is the **Museum of Natural History** (670-8457), which has a small permanent display on prehistoric life. (Open Mon.-Sat. 9am-5pm. Free.) Other buildings include the **Museum of African-American Life and Culture** (565-9026; open Mon.-Fri. 9am-5pm); the **Aquarium** (670-8441; open daily 10am-4:30pm, 50¢); the **Age of Steam Museum** (428-0101; open Thurs.-Fri. 10am-3pm, Sat.-Sun. 11am-5pm; $2, under 17 $1); the **Science Place** (428-5555; open daily 9:30am-5:30pm; $5, seniors and ages 7-16 $2); and the **Dallas Garden Center** (428-7476; open Tues.-Sat. 10am-5pm, Sun. 1-5pm).

Nearby **White Rock Lake** is good for walking or biking. For a look at Dallas' mansions, drive up the **Swiss Avenue Historic District** or through the streets of **Highland Park,** a town within Dallas whose high-school boasts a million-dollar astroturf football stadium.

Entertainment

Dallas' culture and nightlife exploded out of nowhere in the late 1970s and continue to gush. The free weekly *Dallas Observer* (out Thursdays), Bible of Dallas entertainment acolytes, will uplift you to indulgence efficiency. Enjoy free summer theater during July and August at the **Shakespeare in the Park** festival (599-2778), at Samuell-Grand Park just northeast of State Fair Park between Grand Ave. and Samuell Blvd. Two plays are performed annually; each runs about two weeks. The **Music Hall** (565-1116) in Fair Park houses the **Dallas Civic Opera** (443-1043) from November to February (tickets $7-75) and **Dallas Summer Musicals** from June to October. (performances nightly, $4-37; 565-1116 for info, 787-2000 for tickets, 696-4253 for ½-price tickets on performance days). The **Dallas Symphony Orchestra** (692-0203) now performs at the newly completed **Morton H. Meyerson Symphony Hall,** at Pearl and Flora St. in the arts district. The I.M. Pei-designed structure ubiques. (Tickets $10-40.)

Downtown nightlife is centered on the oft-visited **West End,** unless you have them **Deep Ellum** blues. The West End offers **Dallas Alley,** 603 Munger (988-0581), an ensemble of clubs with a single ($4-8) cover charge. The **Outback Pub** (761-9355) and **Dick's Last Resort** (747-0001), both at 101 N. Market, are locally popular bars with no cover, good beer selections, and raucous crowds. (Both open daily 11am-2pm; Dick's closed on Sun.)

Deep Ellum, on the east side of downtown, was known as the "Harlem of Dallas" in the 1930s, when it was home to such blues greats as Blind Lemon Jefferson. By the early 1980s, however, the area had become an urban wasteland. A renaissance of sorts began with clandestine late-night parties thrown by artists and musicians in Deep Ellum's empty warehouses. Today, the area has become downright commercialized, but still puts out. **Club Dada,** 2720 Elm (744-3232), former haunt of Edie Brickell, has scaled up with art on the walls, an outdoor patio, and live local acts. (Open daily 8pm-2am; cover $3-5, drinks $2-4.) **Tree's,** 2709 Elm (748-5009), hosts an eclectic range of local and national acts in a vast warehouse with pool tables in the loft. (Open daily 8pm-2am. Cover $2-10, drinks $1.50-4. Min. age 18.)

The areas around SMU and Greenville Ave. rollick with nightlife. **Poor David's Pub,** 1924 Greenville (821-9891), stages live music for an older crowd that leans towards folk and blues. (Open Mon.-Sat. 8pm-2am.) The **Greenville Bar and Grill,** 2821 Greenville, a Dallas classic, is an old-fashioned blues bar with cheap beer ($1.50) and a cheeky attitude. (Open daily 11am-2am.) Popular nightspots conveniently line **Yale Blvd.,** home of SMU's fraternity row. The current bar of choice is the **Green Elephant,** 5612 Yale (750-6625), a pseudo-60s extravaganza complete with lava lamps and tapestries. (Open daily 10am-2pm.)

Six Flags Over Texas (817-640-8900), 15 mi. from downtown off I-30 in Arlington, is the original link in the nationwide amusement park chain. The name alludes to the six governments that have presided over the state through the years. This is a thrill-lover's paradise, replete with an indisidious array of rides, restaurants, shops, and entertainment venues. The hefty admission charge ($20, over 55 years or under 4 ft. $14) includes unlimited access to all rides and attractions. (Open June-Aug. Sun.-Thurs. 10am-10pm, Fri.-Sat. 10am-midnight; March-May and Sept.-Oct. Sat.-Sun. 10am-8pm. Parking $3.)

Fort Worth

Lost but not forgotten amid the cosmo pretensions of Dallas, **Fort Worth** is a 30-minute drive west on I-30. If Dallas is the last eastern city, Fort Worth is undoubtedly the first Western one; a daytrip here is worth your while if only for the **Stockyards District** (817-625-5082), at the corner of N. Main and E. Exchange Ave., which hosts weekly rodeos (call for times) and cattle auctions (Mon. at 10am). The district's frontier feeling is accessorized by numerous Western bookshops, restaurants, and saloons. For more on the stockyards, go to the **Visitor Information Center** kiosk (817-624-4741) on Exchange Ave. in front of the Coliseum. (Open Mon.-Sat. 10am-5pm; Sun. noon-6pm.) A far cry from the rugged stockyards is the **Kimball Art Museum,** 3333 Camp Bowie Blvd. (817-332-8451), a beautiful building designed by the late Louis Kahn. Inside is a choice selection of pre-20th-century European painting and sculpture, one of the best in the Southwest. (Open Tues.-Sat. 10am-5pm, Sun. noon-5pm. Free.)

Fort Worth's **area code** is 817.

East Texas

What is generally known as East Texas—the vast area north and east of Houston and east of Dallas—defies Texas' stereotype as flat, treeless ranch country. A swath of thick, hilly woods and lake country, it offers a shady alternative to the often sweltering city-scapes of Dallas and Houston.

The major cities of this region are **Beaumont** in the south and **Lufkin** in the north. In the area are four national forests. **Sam Houston National Forest,** about 50 mi. north of Houston, borders Lake Livingston in the northeast and Lake Conroe in the southwest. The 140-mi. **Lone Star Hiking Trail** winds through three different recreation areas. Double Lake offers campsites, picnic facilities, showers, and a swimming area with a beach. For more rustic hikers, primitive camping is also permitted along the trail. Lake Conroe and Lake Livingston offer both boating and excellent black bass fishing. Ranger offices are located in Cleveland (713-592-6462), off U.S. 59, and in New Waverly (409-344-6205), off I-45. Smack dab in the middle of Huntsville, the **Sam Houston Memorial Museum Complex,** 1836 Sam Houston Ave. (409-295-7824) in Huntsville, includes the general's two homes, his law office, and a scenic pond.

Davy Crockett National Forest and **Angelina National Forest** lie 10 mi. west and east of Lufkin, respectively. The Davy Crockett incorporates the scenic **Four C National Recreation Trail,** a 20-mi. pass from the Neches Overlook to Ratcliff Lake.

The trail follows the old paths of the Central Coal and Coke Logging Company (the "Four-C"), traveling through pines, sloughs, and upland forests. Ratcliff Lake has 70 camping units, a swimming beach, picnic area, amphitheater, and showers. The Neches Overlook provides a panoramic view of the forest and is most beautiful during April when the redbuds are in bloom. **Ranger stations** are located in Crockett (409-639-8620) and Apple Springs (409-831-2246). The Angelina is split in two by the **Sam Rayburn Reservoir,** in which catfish and bass are plentiful. The forest, home to both the endangered bald eagle and the red-cockaded woodpecker, also has a variety of recreation areas for camping, hiking, and boating. The **ranger station** is located at 1907 Atkinson Dr. (409-634-7709) in Lufkin. For more info, contact the Forest Supervisor, 701 N. First St., Lufkin 75901.

The **Sabine National Forest** lies at the Louisiana border, 60 mi. south of Shreveport and just due east of the Angelina National Forest, on the other side of U.S. 96. The Sabine overlooks the **Toledo Bend Reservoir,** which teems with bluegill. Rangers can be reached in Hemphill (409-787-2791) and in San Augustine (409-275-2632). Camping in designated areas of the national forests is usually free unless amenities (RV hookups, showers, etc.) are provided. There are also many private camping facilities in the area. Stop by the park service office in Lufkin for maps and permits.

Established to protect the rich biological diversity of the region, the **Big Thicket National Preserve,** just north of Beaumont, offers nature trails, canoeing, and undeveloped camping in designated areas. Stop by the **Big Thicket Visitors Center** on Rte. 420 off U.S. 287, 10 mi. north of Kountze and 35 mi. north of Beaumont. The **Sundew Trail,** located 10 miles north of the visitor center off U.S. 287, is most scenic during the summer when the wildflowers bloom. Be sure to wear long pants and lots of bug spray. The trail is one mi. long, beginning on high sandy ground and then dipping into the savannah. There is also a wheelchair-accessible ½-mi. trail. The **Neches River, Village Creek,** and **Pine Island Bayou** are ideal for canoeing. Several local agencies rent canoes; the cheapest is **H&H Boat Dock and Marina** (409-283-3257), on Hwy. 190 near the junction with 92 at Steinhagen Reservoir. (Canoes $10 per day.) For more info, write or call the Superintendent, Big Thicket National Preserve, 3785 Milan, Beaumont, TX 77701 (409-839-2689). Permits are required for fishing and camping, and you should check in with the forest ranger at the visitor center before venturing out.

El Paso

Your map says Texas, but El Paso, along with Mexican sister city Juárez, forms a bi-national metropolis with a heavy emphasis on the Mexican side. Certainly the city's heritage is more Mexican than Texan; Spanish Mexicans first explored the area while fleeing a Pueblo revolt 400 years ago, dubbing the fertile valley "El Paso del Norte" (passage of the north). Not until the Mexican War in 1848 did Americans begin to inhabit the area. Some Mexicans are still bitter about the losses suffered in that war; graffiti along the Rio Grande compares America to Iraq for the 144-year-old conquests of New Mexico and California.

As more Americans arrived in El Paso in 1873, the line drawn by the Mexican War across the city Juárez became increasingly important; many refugees from the Mexican Revolution of 1909 fled here, including revolutionary Pancho Villa. In more recent years, immigrants have been used in the region to bust unions and keep wages low on the U.S. side. Hispanics, legal or not, define the flavor of El Paso (pop. 520,000). If not for the collegiate atmosphere of UTEP and downtown's high-rise bank buildings, you would think you had accidentally crossed the border along the way—which, by the way, is just about how hard it is to visit Juárez.

Practical Information

Emergency: 911. **Juárez Police,** 248-35.

Convention and Visitors Center, 5 Civic Center Plaza (534-0686), on the western edge of downtown within 1 block of the Greyhound station. Open daily 8:30am-5pm.

El Paso International Airport: in northeast El Paso (772-4271). Bus #50 stops about ½ mi. south of the terminal building, at the corner of Montana and Airway Blvd. **Sprint Airport Shuttle System** (833-8282) departs from the curb outside the Continental Airlines desk every 10 min. 4am-1am. Door-to-door service offered. Advance 1-day reservations required for trips to the airport. Airport to downtown plaza $2.50.

Amtrak: 700 San Francisco Ave. (545-2247; 800-872-7245 for reservations), on the western side of the Civic Center, near Greyhound. Office open daily 11am-7pm. Three trains/week to San Antonio ($106, continues to Dallas) and Tucson ($69, continues to Phoenix and Los Angeles). Reservations required.

Greyhound: 111 San Francisco Ave. (544-7200), at Santa Fe across from the Civic Center. To: Albuquerque (4 per day, $39); Dallas (8 per day, $85); San Antonio (4 per day, $81); and Tucson (7 per day, $47, continues to Los Angeles). For info on buses into Mexico, call 533-3837. Office open 24 hrs. Lockers $1.

Public Transport: Sun City Area Transit (SCAT), 533-3333. Extensive service. All routes begin downtown at San Jacinto Plaza (Main at Mesa). Fewer routes in the northwest. Connects with Juárez system. Maps and schedules posted in the Civic Center Park, at public libraries, and available at 700-A San Francisco Ave. Mon.-Fri. 8am-noon and 1-5pm. The visitor center puts out a pamphlet on sight-seeing by bus. Most buses stop around 5pm; limited service on Sun. Fare 75¢, seniors 15¢, students with ID 35¢.

Taxi: Yellow Cab, 533-3433. Base fare $1.20, $1.50 per mi. Airport to downtown $15.

Car Rental: Rent-a-Heap, 4305 Anapro (532-2170). Will deliver. $20 per day, unlimited free mi., 3-day min. rental. Cars must be kept within a 50-mi. radius of El Paso and are not allowed across the border. Must be 18 with a major credit card. Open Mon.-Fri. 9am-5pm, Sat. 9am-noon.

Help Lines: Crisis Hotline, 779-1800. **U.S. Customs Service,** 541-6794. Both open 24 hrs.

Post Office: 5300 E. Paisano (775-7500), at Alameda about 5 mi. from downtown. Open Mon.-Fri. 8:30am-5pm. **ZIP code:** 79910.

Area Codes: El Paso, 915. International direct dialing to Ciudad Juárez is 011 + 52 (country code) + 161 (city code) + local number.

The geographical intrusion of the Rio Grande and the Franklin Mountains complicates the city's road plan. Split by the Franklins, the city roughly forms the letter "Y," angling northwest to southeast along the river.

Accommodations, Camping, and Food

The cheapest hotel rooms land across the border, but downtown El Paso has several good budget offerings within easy walking distance of San Jacinto Plaza. The **Gardner Hostel (AYH),** 311 E. Franklin (532-3661), at Stanton, lies one block northeast of the plaza. Bankrobber John Dillinger stayed at this historic landmark just before the Feds nabbed him in Tucson. Simple but sunny hostel rooms have four beds and a semi-private bath. The hostel has a pool table, laundry, and kitchen in the basement ($11, nonmembers $13. Singles with private bath $20. Doubles $25. Private room for four with TV $43.) Quality budget motels clump along **North Mesa Drive.** Among them, the **Warren Inn,** 4748 N. Mesa Dr. (544-4494), five mi. north of downtown, stands out. Large clean rooms come with kitchenette and cable TV. Continental breakfast included. (Singles $28. Doubles $33. Discounts for military and AAA members.) There are, of course, three **Motel 6's** in El Paso, all off I-10 and all the same price (singles $27; doubles $33). The nicest, most centrally located one is at 4800 Gateway Blvd. East (533-7521), on I-10 at the Raynolds Exit. The motel has a pool, large rooms, and a restaurant.

Since no public transportation goes to campgrounds outside of town, **Hueco Tanks State Park** (857-1135) is a 32-mi. hike east of El Paso on U.S. 62/180. (Sites with utilities and showers $11.) **Desert Oasis Park** (855-3366) is at 12705 Montana. (Sites $11 for 2 people, each additional person $1. Entrance $2.)

Arnold's Mexican Restaurant, 315 Mills Ave. at Kansas downtown (532-3147), just a few blocks south of the hostel, serves excellent authentic Mexican dishes in an all-you-can-eat lunch format ($4.25). (Open Mon.-Fri. 6:30am-3:30pm.) Also downtown, a block from the hostel, is **Big Bun Burger,** 501 Stanton at Franklin (546-9359), which serves your standard diner fare at 1950s prices. Burgers ($1), fountain drinks (50¢), and tacos (60¢). (Open Mon.-Sat. 8am-8pm.) **Forti's Mexican Elder,** 321 Chelsea (772-0066), offers fantastic fajitas at a convenient location a few blocks south of I-10. (Entrees $5-7. Take-out available. Open Sun.-Thurs. 11am-10pm, Fri.-Sat. 11am-11pm. Take bus #22.) **Chico's Tacos,** 4230 Alameda, offers cheap and filling burritos and burgers, along with its namesake. The beef stew burrito costs 95¢, three rolled beef tacos 96¢. Three other locations: 5305 Montana (772-7777), 3401 Dyer (565-5555), and 1235 McRae (592-8484). (Open Sun.-Thurs. 9am-1:30am, Fri.-Sat. 9am-3am.) Near Fort Bliss, the **Brown Bag Deli,** 4319 Fred Wilson (562-2399), offers 31 different blissful sandwiches ($3-5) and decent if less eclectic breakfasts. (Open Mon.-Sun. 9am-10pm.)

Sights and Entertainment

The majority of visitors to El Paso are either stopping off on the long drive through the desert or headed across the border for a taste of Mexico. (For more on Juárez, see *Let's Go: Mexico.*) Nevertheless, El Paso's frontier past and international present provide plenty for the inquisitive tourist to do. To orient yourself and take in a complete picture of the Rio Grande Valley, head northeast of downtown on Rim Rd. (which becomes Scenic Dr.) to **Murchison Park,** at the base of the mountains; the park offers a fine view of El Paso, Juárez, and the Sierra Madre. The city center is a few mi. south; the University of Texas at El Paso and the Sun Bowl are off to the west; Fort Bliss and the airport sprawl several mi. to the east.

El Paso has a number of interesting museums focusing on local culture and history. The **El Paso Museum of Art,** 1211 Montana (541-4040), contains Western art, samples from the French, Venetian, and Sienese schools, and a plethora of Spanish religious paintings. (Tours Sun. at 1:30pm. Open Tues.-Sat. 10am-5pm, Sun. 1-5pm. Free.) The **Fort Bliss Replica Museum,** 5051 Pleasanton Rd. (568-4518), seven mi. from downtown, re-creates the 1854 fort built to fight the Apache. (Open daily 9am-4:30pm. Free.) The small but ambitious **Americana Museum,** Civic Center Plaza (542-0394), downtown on Santa Fe between San Antonio and San Francisco, is dedicated to the display and study of pre-Columbian and historical art of the Americas. Exhibits include models of cliff houses, local and regional photography, and artifacts from the Hohoka and Anasazi cultures. (Open Tues.-Sat. 10am-5pm. Free.) For a more comprehensive understanding of the rich history of the region, visit the **El Paso Museum of History,** 12901 Gateway West (858-1928). The museum contains artifacts and furniture as well as exhibits on the Native American, Mexican, and American history of El Paso and Juárez. (Open Tues.-Sun. 9am-4:50pm. Free.)

For a more thorough exploration of El Paso, try one of the visitor center's three tours. The **walking tour** directs you to the colorful relics of El Paso's "Wild West" phase, most of which are downtown. The **bus tour** transports you to the cultural highlights, such as the El Paso Museum of Art and the **Museo de Arte y Historia,** across the river in Juárez. The **car tour** covers the most territory, including a short drive up Alabama Rd. and McKelligon Rd. into **McKelligon Canyon,** high in the Franklins northeast of downtown.

To find nighttime doings in El Paso, talk to locals; a knowledge of Spanish is helpful. A few clubs cluster on Mesa St. next to the **University of Texas at El Paso (UTEP).** UTEP also sponsors art shows and dramatic performances during the school year (call 747-5481 for current events), while the student union runs a dinner theater year-round (call 747-5711 for ticket info). On weekends during the summer, the El Paso Arts Department (541-4481) sponsors free outdoor concerts at the Chamizal National Memorial. Music ranges from jazz to classical to Latin American; shows start at 8pm.

Strategic timing can make your visit to El Paso more entertaining. The town hosts the **Southwestern Livestock Show & Rodeo** (532-1401) in February, the **World Championship Finals Rodeo** (544-2582) in November, and a Jazz Festival (534-6277) in October at the Chamizal Memorial.

Houston

Houston (pop. 3,232,000) arose from the wake of Texas' battle for independence from Mexico when two New York speculators bought 2,000 acres of land on Buffalo Bayou in 1906. Already an energy center since the discovery of nearby oil deposits in 1901, the settlement emerged as a major cotton shipping port with the 1915 completion of the Houston Ship Channel. Not surprisingly, Houston's geographical expansion parallels its history of quick economic growth; in all, the city covers almost 500 sqare mi. The absence of zoning laws, combined with a recklessly swift building boom in the 70s and early 80s, has resulted in a peculiar architectural mix: a museum, an historic home, a 7-Eleven, and a mini-mall may share the same city block, while the downtown area showcases an oil-fed array of modern skyscrapers.

Practical Information

Emergency: 911.

Greater Houston Convention and Visitors Bureau, 3300 Main St. (523-5050), at Stuart, 10 blocks south of I-45 outside of the downtown area. Take any bus serving the southern portion of Main St. (#7, 8, 14, 25, 65, 70, or 78). Open Mon.-Fri. 8:30am-5pm.

Travelers Aid, 1600 Louisiana St. (223-8946), at the YMCA. Open daily 6am-midnight. **24-hr. help line:** offices at 2630 Westridge St., off Main St. near the Astrodome; at the Greyhound station and at the Houston Intercontinental Airport (668-0911).

Houston Intercontinental Airport: 230-3000. 25 mi. north of downtown. Get to the city center via the **Airport Express** (523-8888). Buses depart every 30 min. between 7am and 12:30am (fare $8.50, kids $4.25). **Hobby Airport** is 9 mi. south of downtown, just west of I-45. Take bus #73 to Texas Medical Center and then catch any bus to downtown. **Hobby Airport Limousine Service** (644-8359) leaves Hobby for downtown every 30 min. between 7:30am and 11:30pm (fare $5, under 13 free). **Southwest Airlines** (237-1221) has commuter flights to most major Texas cities. Flights from Hobby to San Antonio, Dallas, and Austin (one way: day $79; nights and weekends $49, with 21-day advance pruchase as low as $29).

Amtrak: 902 Washington Ave. (224-1577 or 800-872-7245), in a rough neighborhood. During the day, catch a bus by walking west on Washington (away from downtown) to its intersection with Houston Ave. At night, call a cab. To: San Antonio (3 per week, 4 hr., $42); New Orleans (3 per week, 9 hr., $68); Dallas (daily, 6 hr., $30); El Paso (3 per week, 16 hr., $132).

Greyhound/Trailways: 2121 S. Main St. (222-1161), on or near several local bus routes. Walk west toward downtown on Texas to the intersection of Main St. for local buses. Unsafe area. To: San Antonio (8 per day, 4 hr., $25); New Orleans (7 per day, 9 hr., $44); Dallas (7 per day, 5 hr., $28); El Paso (10 per day, 16 hr., $106); Corpus Christi (13 per day, 5 hr., $28); Galveston (6 per day, 1½ hr., $9). Open 24 hrs. Lockers $1.

Public Transport: Metro Bus System, 635-4000 for route and schedule info. Mon.-Fri. 6am-8pm, Sat.-Sun. 8am-5pm. An all-encompassing system that can take you from NASA (15 mi. southeast of town) to Katy (25 mi. west of town). Get system maps at the Customer Services Center, 912 Dallas St. (658-0854; open Mon.-Fri. 10am-6pm). Individual route maps can also be obtained at Metro headquarters, 500 Jefferson at Smith, 12th floor; the Houston Public Library, 500 McKinney at Bagby (236-1313; open Mon.-Fri. 9am-9pm; Sat. 9am-6pm; Sun. 2-6pm); or at the Metro Ride store at Fannin and Capitol. Buses usually operate 6am-midnight. Fare 70¢, zone changes 10¢. Transfers free.

Taxi: Yellow Cab, 236-1111. Base rate $2.70 plus $1.20 per mi.

Car Rental: Rent-A-Heap Cheap, 5722 Southwest Freeway (977-7771). Cars from $25 a day with 100 free mi., 25¢ each additional mi. Open Mon.-Fri. 9am-7pm, Sat.-Sun. 9am-5pm. Must be 21 with major credit card.

Help Lines: Crisis Center Hotline, 228-1505. Open 24 hrs. **Rape Crisis**, 528-7273. Open 24 hrs. **Gay Switchboard of Houston**, 529-3211. Counseling, medical and legal referrals, and entertainment info. Open daily 3pm-midnight.

Time Zone: Central (1 hr. behind Eastern).

Post Office: 401 Franklin St. (227-1474). Open Mon.-Fri. 7am-7pm. **ZIP code:** 77052.

Area Code: 713.

The flat Texas terrain supports several mini-downtowns. True downtown Houston, a squarish grid of interlocking one-way streets, borders the Buffalo Bayou at the intersection of I-10 and I-45. The city's notorious traffic jams will halt drivers during rush hour, but a car in Houston is almost a must—distances are vast and bus service is infrequent. Houstonians orient themselves by **"The Loop,"** I-610, which lassoes the city center at a radius of six mi. Anything inside The Loop is easily accessible by car or bus. Find rooms on the southern side of the city, near Montrose Ave., the museums, Hermann Park, Rice University, and Perry House for easy access to several bus lines and points of interest.

Although all of Texas is hot in the summer, Houston's humidity makes it especially stifling; 85°F in Houston can be worse than 100°F in El Paso.

Accommodations and Camping

The cheaper motels are concentrated southwest of downtown by the Astrodome and **South Main Street,** and along the **Katy Freeway** (I-10 west) on the other side of the city. Singles are as low as $21, doubles as low as $25. The rooms may be decent once you get inside, but this part of town is quite dangerous at night. (Buses #8 and 9 go down S. Main, and #19, 31, and 39 go out along the Katy Freeway.) Although safe rooms in the $25-35 range are rare, many of the best hotels in the city offer rooms for 1-4 people at under $50 on the weekends.

Perry House, Houston International Hostel (AYH), 5302 Crawford (523-1009), at Oakdale. From the Greyhound station, take bus #8 or 9 south to the Oakdale stop and then walk east 6 blocks on Oakdale to Crawford. Friendly management, nice rooms, and in a good neighborhood near Hermann park. Owners will sometimes offer makeshift city tours; ask about the nighttime version. Rooms and office closed 10am-5pm. Linen $1.50.

Houston Youth Hostel, 5530 Hillman #2 (926-3444). Take bus #36 to Lawndale at Dismuke. Farther from town than Perry House with fewer beds, but more laid-back. No curfew. Coed dorm room, $7 per bunk. Linen $1.

YMCA, 1600 Louisiana Ave. (659-8501), between Pease and Leeland St. Separate women's floor. Good downtown location and a short ride from the Westheimer nightlife. Clean, minimalist rooms. No private baths. Rooms $15. Key deposit $2. Another branch at 7903 South Loop E. (643-4396) is farther from downtown but cheaper. Take bus #40 ("Telephone"). Men only. $13. Key deposit $10.

Grant Motor Inn, 8200 Main St. (668-8000), near the Astrodome. Clean and safe. Ranch-style motel with satellite TV, swingset, and pool. Singles $29. Doubles $32. Reservations recommended in summer.

The Roadrunner, 9535 Katy Frwy. (I-10) (467-4411). One of 3 locations in Houston; nicer than the one on S. Main. Generic, clean rooms. Avoid Instant Tornadoes labeled "Birdseed" in lobby. (Singles $30. Doubles $35.)

Motel 6, 3223 South Loop E. (664-6425), near the Astrodome. It's a Motel 6. You know the score. Singles $29. Doubles $35.

Two campgrounds grace the Houston area. Both the **KOA Houston North,** 1620 Peachleaf (442-3700), off north Loop 610, and the **Houston Campground,** 710 State Hwy. 6 S. (493-2391), are out in the boondocks, inaccessible by Metro Bus. KOA charges $14.50 per site for two ($2 per additional adult, $1.50 per additional child). Houston Campground charges $11 per site for two ($3 per additional adult, $1.50 per additional child).

Food

As a port town, Houston has witnessed the arrival of many immigrants (today its Indochinese population is the second largest in the nation), and its range of restaurants reflects this. Houston cuisine mingles Mexican and Vietnamese food, and the state specialty, BBQ. Look for reasonably priced restaurants among the shops and boutiques along **Westheimer Street,** especially near the intersection with Montrose. This area, referred to as "Montrose," is Houston's answer to Greenwich Village. This area is also popular with gay men. Bus #82 follows Westheimer from downtown to well past The Loop. For great Vietnamese cuisine, go to **Milam Street,** where it intersects Elgin St., just south of downtown.

Hobbit Hole, 1715 S. Shepherd Dr. (528-3418), a few blocks off Westheimershire. Take bus #35. For the herbivorous adventurer. Entrées ($4-8) named after Tolkein characters. Ramble on to Led Zep-inspired Misty Mountain Strawberry ($2.95). Open Mon.-Thurs. 11am-11pm, Fri.-Sat. 11am-midnight, Sun. 11:30am-10pm.

Good Company Barbecue, 5109 Kirby Dr. (522-2530). Might be the best BBQ in Texas, with honky-tonk atmosphere to match. Sandwiches $3, dinners $5-6. Try the Czech sausage ($5). Open Mon.-Sat. 11am-10pm, Sun. noon-10pm.

On The Border, 4608 Westheimer Rd., near the Gallatin (961-4494). Standard Tex-Mex fare with a few twists (mesquite-grilled vegetable platter, $6). Bar and loud crowd. Open Mon.-Fri. 11am-midnight, Sat.-Sun. 10am-1am.

Van Loc, 3010 Milam St. (528-6441). Yummy Vietnamese and Chinese food (entrees $5-8). The great all-you-can-eat luncheon buffet ($3.65) includes iced tea but no funky cold medina. Open Sun.-Thurs. 9:30am-11:30pm, Fri.-Sat. 9:30am-12:30am.

Cadillac Bar, 1802 N. Shepherd Dr. (862-2020), at the Katy Freeway (I-10), northwest of downtown. Take bus #75, change to #26 at Shepherd Dr. and Allen Pkwy. Wild fun and authentic Mexican food. Try the "Mexican Flag" ($3), a flaming shot of liquor. Tacos and enchiladas $5-7; heartier entrees more expensive. Open Mon.-Thurs. 11am-10:30pm, Fri. 11am-midnight, Sat. noon-midnight, Sun. noon-10pm.

Luther's Bar-B-Q, 8777 S. Main St. (432-1107). One of eleven locations in the Houston area. Good Texas barbecue entrees ($3-6) and free refills on iced tea. Open Sun.-Thurs. 11am-10pm, Fri.-Sat. 11am-11pm.

Sights

Amid Houston's sprawling sauna of oil refineries and food chains are a few worthwhile sights. Focus on the downtown, the nexus of virtually all the city's bus routes.

In the southwest corner of the downtown area is **Sam Houston Park,** just west of Bagby St. between Lamar and McKinney St. **St. John's Lutheran Church,** built in 1891 by German farmers, contains the original pulpit and pews. Catch the one-hour tour to see four buildings in the park. (Tours on the hr. Mon.-Sat. 10am-3pm, Sun. 1-4pm. Tickets $4, students and seniors $2).

Central downtown is a shopper's subterranean paradise. Hundreds of shops and restaurants line the underground **Houston Tunnel System,** which connects all the major buildings in downtown Houston, extending from the Civic Center to the Tenneco Building and the Hyatt Regency. On hot days, everyone ducks into the air-conditioned passageways. To navigate the tunnels, pick up a map at the Houston Public Library, the Pennzoil Place, or the Texas Commerce Bank.

Head westward along Westheimer to the **Galleria,** an extravagant, Texas-sized shopping mall with an ice-skating rink surrounded by pricey stores. The mall is full of young, pretty people "catacombing"—Texan for cruising. (Rink open Sun.-Fri. noon-5pm and 8-10pm, Sat. noon-10pm. Skate rental $7.) Next door is the **Transco Tower,** 2800 Post Oak Blvd. (439-2000), Houston's latest monument outside of downtown. The view from the top is impressive; just walk in and take an elevator to the 51st floor. Don't miss the 25-ft. **Wall of Water Fountain.**

Back toward downtown, just east of Montrose, are two of the city's more highly acclaimed museums. The **Menil Collection,** 1515 Sul Ross (523-5888), is a careful collection of African and Asian artifacts and 20th-century European and American paintings and sculpture. Be sure to see Magritte's hilarious *Madame Récamier*. (Open Wed.-Sun. 11am-7pm. Free.) One block away, the **Rothko Chapel,** 3900 Yupon (524-9839), houses some of the artist's paintings. Fans of modern art will delight in Rothko's sanctified simplicity; others will wonder where the paintings are. (Open daily 10am-6pm.)

Antique-lovers will want to see the collection of 17th- to 19th-century decorative art at **Bayou Bend,** in **Memorial Park.** The collection is housed in the palatial mansion of millionaire Ima Hogg (we *swear*), daughter of turn-of-the-century Texas governor Jim Hogg.

On Main Street, 3½ mi. south of downtown, lies the beautifully landscaped **Hermann Park,** near all of Houston's major museums. The **Houston Museum of Natural Science** (639-4600) offers a splendid display of gems and minerals, permanent exhibits on petroleum, a hands-on gallery geared toward grabby children, and a planetarium and IMAX theater to boot. (Open Sun.-Mon. noon-5pm, Tues.-Sat. 9am-5pm. $2.50, seniors and kids $2.) The **Houston Zoological Gardens** (523-5888) feature small mammals, alligators, and hippopotami eating spicy hippoplankton food. (Open Tues.-Sun. 10am-6pm. $2.50, seniors $2, ages 3-12 50¢.) The **Museum of Fine Arts,** 1001 Bissonet (639-7300), adjoins the north side of Hermann Park. Designed by Mies van der Rohe, the museum boasts an *artistic* collection of Impressionist and post-Impressionist art, as well as a slew of Remingtons. (Open Tues.-Wed. and Fri.-Sat. 10am-5pm, Thurs. 10am-9pm, Sun. 12:15-6pm. $2, seniors and college students $1, under 18 free. Free Thurs.) Across the street, the **Contemporary Arts Museum,** 5216 Montrose St. (526-3129), has multi-media exhibits. (Open Tues.-Sat. 10am-5pm, Sun. noon-6pm. Free.) Also located on the park grounds are sports facilities, a zoo, a kiddie train, and the Miller Outdoor Theater (see Entertainment below). The University of Houston, Texas Southern University, and Rice University congregate in this part of town.

The **Astrodome,** Loop 610 at Kirby Dr. (799-9555), a mammoth indoor arena, is the home of the **Oilers** football team and the **Astros** baseball team. (Tours daily 11am, 1, 3, and 5pm; off-season 11am, 1, and 3pm. $2.75, ages under 7 free. Parking $3). At these prices, you're better off paying admission to a game. Football tickets are hard to get, but seats for the Astros are usually available and cost only $4. (Call 526-1709 for tickets.)

Wander down Space Age memory lane at NASA's **Lyndon B. Johnson Space Center** (483-4321), where models of Gemini, Apollo, Skylab, and the space shuttle are displayed in a free walk-through museum. This NASA is the home of Mission Control, which is still central HQ for peopled space flights; when astronauts ask, "Do you read me, Houston?" the folks here answer. (Control center open daily 9am-4pm. Free.) By car, go 21 mi. south of downtown on I-45. The carless should take the Park and Ride Shuttle #246 from downtown.

Terminus of the gruesomely polluted Houston Ship Channel, the **Port of Houston** leads the nation in foreign trade. Free 90-minute guided harbor tours are offered on the inspection boat *Sam Houston.* (Tours Tues.-Wed. and Fri.-Sat. at 10am and 2:30pm, Thurs. and Sun. at 2:30pm.) Reservations for these deservedly popular tours usually must be requested four to six weeks in advance, but you can join one if the boat doesn't reach its 90-person capacity. Call to make last-minute reservations. To reach the port, drive five mi. east from downtown on Clinton Dr., or take bus #48 to the Port Authority gate. For more info or reservations, write or call Port of Houston Authority, P.O. Box 2562, Houston 77252 (225-4044; open Mon.-Fri. 8am-5pm).

Entertainment

Anyone with cable TV sorely remembers the period-piece *Urban Cowboy,* in which John Travolta proves his love for Debra Winger by riding a mechanical bull. Sexy, wasn't it? Alas, Gilley's has long since closed, but despair not; rip-roaring nightlife is still bullish here.

The Westheimer strip offers the largest variety of places for no cover. Rub elbows with venture capitalists and post-punks alike at **The Ale House**, 2425 W. Alabama at Kirby (521-2333). The bi-level bar and beer garden offer over 100 brands of beer served with a British accent. Upstairs you'll find mostly New Wave music and dancing. (Open daily noon-midnight.) A similar mix can be encountered at the more exclusive **Cody's Restaurant and Club**, penthouse of 3400 Montrose St. (522-9747). Sit inside or out on the balcony, and listen to live jazz. (Open Tues.-Fri. 4pm-2am, Sat. 6pm-2am. Informal dress.) **Sam's Place**, 5710 Richmond Ave. (781-1605) is your typical spring-break style Texas hangout. On Sunday afternoons a band plays outdoors (5-10pm) and various booths proffer different beers. An indoor band continues from 7pm to 1am. (Happy Hour Mon.-Fri. 4-8pm and Mon.-Thurs. 11pm-closing. Open Mon.-Sat. 11am-2am, Sun. noon-2am. Clothes required.) **The Red Lion**, 7315 Main St. (795-5000), features cheap beer and nightly entertainment that ranges from bluegrass to heavy metal. (Open Mon.-Fri. 11am-2am, Sat. 4pm-2am, Sun. 4-10pm.)

Houston offers ballet, opera, and symphony at **Jones Hall**, 615 Louisiana Blvd. Tickets for the **Houston Symphony Orchestra** (224-4240) cost $8-30. The season runs from September to May. During July, the symphony gives free concerts Tuesday, Thursday, and Saturday at noon in the Tenneco Building Plaza. The **Houston Grand Opera** (546-0200) produces seven operas each season, with performances from October through May. (Tickets $5-25, 50% student discount ½-hr. before performance.) Call 227-2787 for info on the ballet, opera, or symphony. If you're visiting Houston in the summer, take advantage of the **Miller Outdoor Theater** in Hermann Park (520-3290). The symphony, opera, and ballet companies stage free concerts here in the evenings from May to August, and the annual **Shakespeare Festival** arrives for the last week of July and first week in August. The downtown **Alley Theater**, 615 Texas St. (228-8421), stages Broadway-caliber productions at moderate prices. (Tickets $14-28. Student rush seats 15 min. before curtain $5.) Comedy-lovers should visit the **Comedy Workshop**, 2105 San Felipe (524-7333; nightly shows $2-4). For last-minute, half-price tickets to many of Houston's sporting events, musical and theatrical productions, and nightclubs, take advantage of **Showtix** discount ticket center, located at 11140 Westheimer St. at Wilcrest (785-2787; open Mon.-Fri. 11am-5pm, Sat. 10am-noon).

Near Houston: Galveston Island

Fifty mi. southeast of Houston on I-45, the narrow, sandy island of **Galveston** (pop. 65,000) offers not only a beach resort's requisite T-shirt shops, ice cream stands, and video arcades, but also beautiful historic homes, oak-lined streets, and even a few deserted beaches. In the 19th century, Galveston was Texas' most prominent port and wealthiest city, earning the nickname "Queen of the Gulf". The advent of the 20th century dealt the city's economy two blows from which it could never recover. In September, 1900, a devastating hurricane struck the island, killing 6,000 people. The survivors were determined to rebuild the decimated city and built a 17-ft. seawall as protection. But the crippled shipping industry could not be protected from the refocus of commerce along the Houston Ship Channel, completed in 1914. Wealthy residents debarked for greener pastures, leaving the former port and their austere mansions behind.

Galveston's streets follow a grid that appears elementary. Lettered streets (A to U½) run north-south, numbered streets run east-west, with **Seawall** following the southern coastline. Some confusion may arise from the fact that most streets have two names; Avenue J and Broadway, for example, are the same throughfare.

You can immerse yourself in families, partying teenagers, and high-spirited volleyball games at **Stewart Beach**, near 4th and Seawall. If you prefer a kinder, gentler student crowd, try **Pirates Beach**, about three mi. west of 95th and Seawall. There are two **Beach Pocket Parks** on the west end of the island, just east of Pirates Beach, with bathrooms, showers, playgrounds, and a concession stand (parking $3). **Apfel**

Park, on the far eastern edge of the island, is a quiet, clean beach with a good view of ships entering and leaving the port. (Entry $5.)

After a day at the beach, visit the **Strand,** on Strand St., between 20th and 24th St., a national historic landmark of nearly 50 restored Victorian buildings; today it consists of restaurants, gift shops, and clothing stores. Cool off with a delectable root-beer malt ($1.75) at **LaKing's Confectionery,** 2323 Strand (762-6100), a large, old-fashioned ice-cream parlor and candy factory. (Open Sun.-Thurs. 10am-9pm, Fri.-Sat. 10am-10pm.) One of the island's two **visitor centers,** located two blocks over at 2016 Strand (765-7834; open Mon.-Thurs. 9:30am-6:30pm, Fri.-Sat. 9:30am-8pm, Sun. 10am-6:30pm), functions as the depot for the **Galveston Island Trolley** running between the Strand and the Seawall and to most major attractions and hotels. (Trains leave hourly Oct.-April 10am-5pm, May-Sept. every 30 min. Tickets $2, seniors and kids $1.) Galveston's other visitor center is the **Convention and Visitors Bureau,** at 21st St. and Seawall (763-4311 or 800-351-4236; open daily 8:30am-5:30pm.) You can take a two-hour cruise in Galveston harbor aboard the *Colonel* (409-763-4900), a Victorian paddlewheel boat. Catch the *Colonel* at Pier 22, at the far east end of 22nd St.

Seafood is abundant in Galveston, along with traditional Texas barbecue. Plenty of eateries line Seawall and the Strand. For seafood, go to **Benno's on the Beach,** 1200 Seawall (762-4621), and try a big bowl of the shrimp gumbo ($3.75) or one of their crab variations. (Open Sun.-Thurs. 11am-10pm, Fri.-Sat. 11am-11pm.)

Prices for accommodations in Galveston usually fluctuate seasonally; prices quoted are at summer rates. The least expensive option is to make Galveston a daytrip from Houston. There are a few cheap motels along Seawall, but many are somewhat shabby (singles $25-60). Probably the best of the bunch is the **Treasure Isle Motor Hotel,** 1002 Seawall (763-8561). The first-floor rooms are decent. (Singles from $29. Doubles from $39.) The familiar **Motel 6,** 7404 Broadway (740-3794), is about 1½ mi. from the beach, with decent rooms and a pool. (Singles $28. Doubles $34.) You can camp at **Galveston Island State Park,** on 13 Mile Rd. (737-1222), about 10 mi. southwest of the trolley-stop visitor center. (Sites $12.) The **Bayou Haven Travel Park,** 6310 Heards Lane (744-2837), on Offatts Bayou, much more convenient to downtown, has laundry facilities and clean showers. (For 4 with full hookup $12, waterfront sites $15, each additional person $2.) From the bus station, go left off 61st St., then ½-mi. to Heards Lane.

Texas Bus Lines, a Greyhound affiliate, operates out of the station at 4913 Broadway (765-7731), providing service to Houston (6 per day, 1½ hr., $9). **Emergency** is 911. Galveston's **time zone** is Central (1 hr. behind Eastern). Its main **post office** is at 601 25th St. (763-1527; open Mon.-Fri. 8:30am-5pm, Sat. 9am-noon). Galveston's **ZIP code** is 77550; the **area code** is 409.

Padre Island National Seashore

Bounded on the north by North Padre Island's string of condos and tourists, and on the south by the Mansfield ship channel, which separates the national seashore from South Padre Island (haven for hundreds of thousands of rowdy spring breakers every year), the **Padre Island National Seashore** (PINS) is an untainted gem, with over 60 mi. of perfectly preserved beaches, dunes, and wildlife refuge. The seashore is an excellent place for windsurfing, swimming, or even surf-fishing—an 850-lb. shark was caught at the southern, more deserted end of the island.

Hiking and driving are also popular activities at PINS. Those with four-wheel drive can make the 60-mi. trek to the **Mansfield Cut,** the most remote and untraveled area of the seashore. Loose sands prevents those without four-wheel drive from venturing far on the beach. Although the seashore has no hiking trails, the **Malaquite** (MAL-a-kee) **Ranger Station** (949-8173), 3½ mi. south of the park entrance, conducts hikes and programs throughout the year. (Call 949-8060 for info on group programs.) They also provide first aid and emergency assistance.

Entry into PINS costs $3. For just a daytrip to the beach, however, go to the beautiful and uncrowded **North Beach** (24 mi. from Corpus Christi) which lies just before the $3 checkpoint.

The headquarters for PINS lie, ironically, outside the island in nearby Corpus Christi. The **PINS Visitors Center**, 9405 S. Padre Island Dr. (512-937-2621), provides info on weather conditions, safety precautions, and sight-seeing opportunities in nearby **Mustang State Park** and **Port Aransas.** (Open Mon.-Sat. 8:30am-4:30pm.) Within the national seashore, the **Malaquite Visitors Center** (512-949-8068), about 14 mi. south of the JFK Causeway turn-off, supplies similar info while also offering exhibits and wildlife guidebooks. (Open June-Aug. daily 9am-6:30pm; Sept.-May daily 9am-4pm.)

Nothing beats camping on the beach at PINS, with the crashing waves to lull you to sleep. Everything, however, will beat it if you forget insect repellent and get mauled by the mosquitos. The **PINS Campground** (949-8173) consists of an asphalt area for RVs, with restrooms and cold-rinse showers (sites $4). Five mi. of beach is devoted to primitive camping, and free camping is permitted wherever vehicle driving is allowed. Near the national seashore is the **Balli County Park,** on Park Rd. 22 (949-8121), 3½ mi. from the JFK Causeway. Running water, electricity, and hot showers are available. (3-day max. stay. Sites $4, with hookup $8.50. Water key deposit $5.) Those who value creature comforts should head a few mi. farther north to the **Mustang State Park Campground** (749-5246), on Park Rd. 53, six mi. from the JFK Causeway, for electricity, running water, dump stations, restrooms, hot showers, shelters, trailer sites, and picnic tables. Make reservations; there's often a waiting list, especially in winter when the snowbirds (northern tourists) arrive. (Entry fee $2. Camping fee $9.)

Motorists enter the PINS via the JFK Causeway, which runs through the Flour Bluff area of Corpus Christi. PINS is difficult to reach by public transportation. Corpus Christi bus #10 (which makes only 2 trips per day Mon.-Fri.) takes you to the tip of the Padre Isles (get off at Padre Isles Park-n-Ride). To reach the national seashore, call the **Island Shuttle Service** (949-8850; fare $1 per mi.). Note that round-trip distance from the bus stop to the Malaquite Visitors Center is over 30 mi. There is no post office on the PINS; mail should be sent general delivery to Flour Bluff sub-station, 10139 Security Dr., Corpus Christi (937-3530). (Open Mon.-Fri. 8am-5pm, Sat. 10am-noon.) The **ZIP code** is 78418.

San Antonio

A relaxing ride on a river taxi, a visit to a Catholic mission, a tour of the Spanish Governor's palace—Toto, I don't think we're in Texas anymore! Ah, but you are: welcome to San Antonio (pop. 951,000), the best little tour-house in Texas. But don't judge the touristy city too harshly. San Antonio is only capitalizing on true attractions. Originally a Spanish missionary outpost, the city came under Native American control prior to Mexico's laying claim to it. German settlers later came in waves, influencing even the most mundane details of life: city signs had to be posted in English, Spanish and German. Today, European and Mexican-American culture still dominate the politics and economy of San Antonio. Spanish architecture dots the landscape, and the city's ethnically diverse population easily supports a double food industry of European cuisine and Tex-mex. Moreover, looming free-trade alliances with Mexico stand to make San Antonio a major trade center.

Practical Information

Emergency: 911.

Visitor Information Center, 317 Alamo Plaza (299-8155), downtown across from the Alamo. Open daily 9am-5:30pm.

San Antonio International Airport (821-3411), north of town. Served by I-410 and Hwy. 281. Cabs to downtown $11.25. **Super Van Shuttle** (344-7433) departs for downtown every 15 min. 6am-6:45pm, every 45 min. 6:45pm-midnight. Fare $7, kids $3.

Amtrak: 1174 E. Commerce St. (223-3226 or 800-872-7245), off the I-37 Montana St. exit. To Dallas (7 per week, 8 hr., $40), Houston (3 per week, 4 hr., $42), and El Paso (3 per week, 11½ hr., $106).

Greyhound: 500 N. Saint Mary's St. (270-5800; 270-5860 in Spanish). To Houston (8 per day, 4 hr., $25), Dallas (11 per day, 6 hr., $34), and El Paso (6 per day, 11 hr., $81). Lockers $1. Open 24 hrs.

Public Transport: VIA Metropolitan Transit, 112 Soledad (227-2020), between Commerce and Houston. Buses operate 5am-10pm, but many routes stop at 5pm. Inconvenient service to outlying areas. Fare 40¢ (more with zone changes), express 75¢. Cheap (10¢) and frequent **streetcars** operate downtown Mon.-Fri. 7am-9pm, Sat. 9am-9pm, Sun. 9:30am-6:30pm. Office open daily 6am-8pm.

Taxi: Yellow Cab, 226-4242. **Checker Cab,** 222-2151. Both $2.80 for first mi., $1.10 each additional mi.

Car Rental: Chuck's Rent-A-Clunker, 3249 SW Military Dr. (922-9464). $13-25 per day with 100 free mi. Must be 19 with a major credit card. Open Mon.-Fri. 8am-7pm, Sat. 9am-6pm, Sun. 10am-6pm.

Bike Rental: Bike San Antonio, 210 Navarro St. (225-7045), between Commerce and Market St. Standard bikes $12 per day; deposit or credit card required. Will deliver to downtown hostels. Open daily 8am-7pm.

Help Lines: Rape Crisis Center, 349-7273. Open 24 hrs. **Presa Community Service Center,** 532-5295. Referrals and transport for elderly and disabled. Open Mon.-Fri. 8:30am-noon and 1-4pm.

Time Zone: Central (1 hr. behind Eastern).

Post Office: 615 E. Houston (227-3399), 1 block from the Alamo. Open Mon.-Fri. 8:30am-5:30pm. General Delivery: 10410 Perrin-Beitel Rd. (650-1630); really in the boondocks—about 15 mi. northeast of town. **ZIP code:** 78205.

Area Code: 512.

Accommodations and Camping

Since San Antonio is a popular city, downtown hotel managers have no reason to keep prices low. Further, San Antonio's dearth of rivers and lakes means that there are few good campsites. The best value in public camping is about 30 mi. north of town at Canyon Lake in **Guadalupe River State Park** (512-438-2656; sites $4). Inexpensive motels cluster along Broadway between downtown and Brackenridge Park. Drivers should follow I-35 north to find cheaper and often safer accommodations within 15 mi. of town.

Bullis House Inn San Antonio International Hostel (AYH), 621 Pierce St. (223-9426), 2 mi. northeast of the Alamo, across the street from Fort Sam Houston. From downtown take bus #11 to Grayson St. and get off at the stop after the Stop & Go store. Friendly hostel in a quiet neighborhood. Cramped but clean rooms. Pool, kitchen. Lockout 11am-5pm. Curfew 11pm, but night key available ($5 deposit). $10, nonmembers $12. Private singles from $17, nonmembers from $19. Doubles from $24/$26. Linen $2. Fills rapidly in summer.

Elmira Motor Inn, 1126 East Elmira (222-9463), about 3 blocks east of St. Mary's, a little over 1 mi. north of downtown. Large, clean rooms. More luxurious than most at this price. Singles $24. Doubles $26.

The Traveler's Hotel, 220 N. Broadway (226-4381), about 5 blocks northwest of the Alamo. Comfortable, dark rooms and eccentric residents. Large singles $16.50, with private bath $22.50. Doubles $21, with private bath $27.

Motel 6, 138 North W. White Rd. (333-1850), 4 mi. east of downtown near I-10. Take bus #24 from downtown. Clean, though sparsely furnished. TV and pool. Singles $24. Doubles $30. Reservations required.

El Tejas Motel, 2727 Roosevelt Ave. (533-7123), at E. Southcross, 3 mi. south of downtown near the missions. Take bus #42. Family-run with some waterbeds, color TV, and a pool. Somewhat musty rooms have thin walls. Singles $22. Doubles $28. On weekends $2 more.

San Antonio KOA, 602 Gembler Rd. (224-9296), 6 mi. from downtown. Take bus #24 ("Industrial Park") from the corner of Houston and Alamo downtown. Showers, laundry, A/C, pool, playground, movies, fishing pond. Sites $12.75 for 2, each additional person $2.

Yogi Bear's Jellystone Park, 2617 Roosevelt Ave. (532-8310), 3 mi. south of downtown. Smarter than the average park. Showers, laundry, pool, spa, playground. Next to golf course and restaurants. Open daily 8am-8pm. Tent sites $12 for 2. RV sites $16 for 2. Each additional person $2. Kids free.

Food

Explore the area east of S. Alamo and S. Saint Mary's St. for the best Mexican food and BBQ. The Riverwalk abounds with waterfront cafés. **Pig Stand** diners offer decent, cheap food all over this part of Texas; the branch at 801 S. Presa, off S. Alamo, is open 24 hrs. North of town, many East Asian restaurants line Broadway across from Breckenridge.

Casa Río, 430 E. Commerce (225-6718). Brightly decorated tables along the river, serenading mariachis, tasty Mexican cuisine, and a bargain to boot. Entrees $4-7. A la carte items $1.50-3. Open Mon.-Thurs. 11:30am-9:30pm, Fri.-Sat. 11:30am-10pm, Sun. noon-9:30pm. Large parties should make reservations.

Big Bend, 511 Riverwalk, near the Hyatt. Best *fajitas* on the river. A bit expensive, but large portions and good atmosphere compensate. Margaritas $2, draft beer $1 during Happy Hour (Mon.-Fri. 2-7pm). Open Sun.-Thurs. 9am-1am, Fri.-Sat. 9am-2am.

Hung Fong Chinese and American Restaurant, 3624 Broadway, 2 mi. north of downtown. Take bus #14. The oldest Chinese restaurant in San Antonio. Consistently good and crowded. Big portions. Try the egg rolls and lemon chicken. Meals $3-8. Open Mon.-Thurs. 11am-11pm, Fri. 11am-midnight, Sat. 11:30am-midnight, Sun. 11:30am-11pm.

Josephine Street Cafe, 400 East Josephine (224-6169), just northeast of downtown in a poor neighborhood. An innocuous local hangout immortalized on tourist posters as a sultry neon diner. Steaks, chicken, fish, and Cajun dishes $5-10. Open Mon.-Thurs. 11am-10pm, Fri. 11am-11pm.

Sights

The Missions

The four missions along the San Antonio River once formed the basis of San Antonio; the city still preserves their remains in the **San Antonio Missions National Historical Park.** To reach the missions by car or bike, follow the blue-and-white "Mission Trail" signs beginning on S. Saint Mary's St. downtown. **San Antonio City Tours** (680-8724), in front of the Alamo, provides a two-hour tour of all the missions and the Alamo for $10, while **Tours for Kids,** 15411 Aviole Way (496-6030), offers what you might guess (9am-3pm). Bus #42 stops right in front of Mission San José, within walking distance of Mission Concepción. All of the missions are open daily 9am to 6pm; September to May from 8am to 5pm. For general info on the missions, call 229-5701.

Mission Concepción, 807 Mission Rd. (533-7109), 4 mi. south of the Alamo off E. Mitchell St. The oldest unrestored church in North America (1731). Traces of the once-colorful frescoes are still visible. Sun. mass 5:50pm.

Mission San José, 6529 San Jose Blvd. (922-0543). The "Queen of the Missions" (1720), with its own irrigation system, a church with a gorgeous sculpted rose window, and numerous restored buildings. The largest of San Antonio's missions, it provides the best sense of the self-sufficiency of these institutions. Catholic services (including a noon "Mariachi Mass") are held 5 times Sun.

Espada Aqueduct, 10040 Espada Rd, about 4 mi. south of Mission San José. Features a tiny chapel and a functioning mile-long aqueduct, built between 1731 and 1745.

Mission San Juan Capistrano (534-3161) and **Mission San Francisco de la Espada** (627-2064), both a swallow's flight off Roosevelt Ave., 10 mi. south of downtown. Smaller and simpler than the other missions, but best at evoking the isolation these outposts once knew.

Downtown Tourist District

"Be silent, friend, here heroes died to blaze a trail for other men." Disobeying orders to retreat with their cannons, the defenders of the Alamo, outnumbered 20 to one, held off the Mexican army for 12 days. Then, on the morning of the 13th day, Mexican buglers blew the infamous *deguello*—"No Quarter, No Prisoners." Forty-six days later General Sam Houston's small army defeated the Mexicans at San Jacinto amidst cries of "Remember the Alamo!" Now only tourists and Ozzy attack the **Alamo** (225-1391), at the center of Alamo Plaza by the junction of Houston and Alamo St., and sno-cone vendors are the only defenders. A single chapel and barracks preserved by the state are all that remain of the former Spanish mission. (Open Mon.-Sat. 9am-5:30pm, Sun. 10am-5:30pm. Free.) The **Long Barracks Museum and Library,** 315 Alamo Plaza (224-1836), houses Alamo memorabilia. (Open Mon.-Sat. 9am-5:30pm.)

Heading southwest from the Alamo, black signs indicate access points to the **Paseo del Río (Riverwalk),** with shaded stone pathways following a winding canal built in the 1930s by the WPA. Lined with picturesque gardens, shops, and cafés, and connecting most of the major downtown sights, the Riverwalk is well-patrolled, safe, and especially beautiful at night. Ride the entire length of the Riverwalk by taking a boat ($2, kids $1) from the front of the Hilton Hotel. The **Alamo Imax Theater** (225-4629), in River Center, shows a docudrama Alamo film on its six-story screen. (7 shows 10am-7pm. $5.75, seniors and military $4.75, kids $3.75.) Nearby and newly transformed, **La Villita** (299-8610) houses crafts shops and art studios. (Open daily 10am-6pm.)

Hemisfair Plaza, on S. Alamo (229-8570), the site of the 1968 World's Fair, is another top tourist spot. The city often uses the plaza, surrounded by restaurants, museums, and historic houses, for special events. The **Tower of the Americas,** 200 S. Alamo (299-8615), rises 750 ft. above the dusty plains, dominating the meager skyline. Get a broad view of the city from the observation deck on top. (Open daily 8am-11pm. $2, seniors $1.25, ages 4-11 $1.) Within the plaza stroll through the free museums, including the **Institute of Texan Cultures** (226-7651; open Tues.-Sun. 9am-5pm; parking $1), and the **Mexican Cultural Institute** (227-0123), filled entirely with modern Mexican art (open Tues.-Fri. 10am-7pm, Sat.-Sun. noon-6pm). On a spot near Hemisfair on Commerce St., across from the San Antonio Convention Center, German Americans erected **St. Joseph's Church** in 1868. Since this beautiful old church stubbornly refused to move, a local department store chain built their establishment around it.

A few blocks west, between Commerce and Dolorosa St. at Laredo, is the Main Plaza and city hall. Directly behind the city hall lies the **Spanish Governor's Palace,** 105 Plaza de Armas (224-0601). Built in Colonial Spanish style in 1772, the house has carved doors and an enclosed, shaded patio and garden. (Open Mon.-Sat. 9am-5pm, Sun. 10am-5pm. $1, kids 50¢.)

Market Square, 514 W. Commerce (229-8600), is a center for the sale of both schlocky souvenirs and handmade local crafts. The walkway **El Mercado** continues the block-long retail stretch. At the nearby **Farmers Market,** you can buy produce, Mexican chilis, pastries, candy, and spices. Come late in the day, when prices are lower and vendors more willing to haggle. (Open June-Aug. daily 10am-8pm; Sept.-May daily 10am-6pm.)

San Antonio North and South

Head to **Brackenridge Park,** main entrance 3900 N. Broadway (735-8641), five mi. north of the Alamo, for a day of unusual sight-seeing. The 343-acre showplace includes an aerial tramway (rides $1.75), a Japanese sunken garden, stone bridges, and a miniature railway. Also in the park, the **San Antonio Zoo,** 3903 N. Saint Mary's St. (734-7183), is one of the country's largest, housing over 3,500 animals from 800 species in natural settings, as well as an extensive African mammal exhibit. (Open daily 9:30am-6:30pm; Nov.-March daily 9:30am-5pm. $5, seniors $3.50, ages 3-11 $1.) At the **Witte Museum,** 3801 Broadway (226-5544), permanent exhibits focus on Texas wildlife while curators mount new shows. (Open Mon., Wed.-Sat. 10am-6pm, Tues. 10am-9pm, Sun. noon-6pm; off-season closes at 5pm. $3, seniors and students $1.50, ages 6-12 $1. Free Thurs. 3-9pm.) The 38-acre **Botanical Center,** 555 Funston Pl. (821-5115), one mi. east of Brackenridge Park, includes the largest conservatory in the Southwest. (Open Tues.-Sun. 9am-6pm. $2.50.)

The **San Antonio Museum of Art,** 200 W. Jones Ave., just north of the city center, inhabits a restored Lone Star Brewery building. As in most breweries, towers, turrets, and spacious rooms decorated with ornate columns house Texan furniture and pre-Columbian, Native American, Spanish Colonial, and Mexican folk art. (Open Mon. and Wed.-Sat. 10am-5pm, Tues. 10am-9pm, Sun. noon-6pm. $3.50, seniors $2, students $1.50, ages 6-12 $1. Free Tues. 3-9pm.) The former estate of Marion Koogler McNay, the **McNay Art Institute,** 6000 N. New Braunfels (824-5368), displays a collection of mostly post-impressionist European art. It also has a charming inner courtyard with sculpture fountains and meticulous landscaping. (Open Tues.-Sat. 9am-5pm, Sun. 2-5pm. Free.)

The **Lone Star Brewing Company,** 600 Lone Star Blvd. (226-8301), is about two mi. south of the city. Trigger-happy Albert Friedrich had managed to accumulate a collection of 3,500 animal heads, horns and antlers when he opened the Buckhorn in 1887. What better place to put them than in his bar? Now you have them on tours which leave every 30 minutes and provide beer samples. As in most breweries, you'll see lots of taxidermy but won't learn much about zymurgy. (Open daily 9:30am-5pm. $2.50, seniors $2, ages 6-11 $1.)

Entertainment

Every April, the 10-day **Fiesta San Antonio** ushers in spring with concerts, parades, and plenty of Tex-Mex to commemorate the victory at San Jacinto and honor the heroes at the Alamo. However, San Antonio offers entertainment more often than just once a year. For fun after dark any time, any season, stroll down the Riverwalk. For those who prefer just looking at pictures of fun, peruse the Friday *Express* or the weekly *Current* as a guide to concerts and entertainment. **Floore's Country Store,** 14464 Old Bandera Rd. (695-8827), toward the northwestern outskirts, is an old hangout of IRS-haunted country music star Willie Nelson. Dancing takes place outside on a large cement platform. (Cover varies.) **Mendiola's Ballroom,** 16490 I-35 south (622-9204), is the city's best Mexican dance hall. On Saturdays, the doors are thrown open and dancers of all ages crowd the gigantic floor. (Take I-35 south from downtown. $5.) Some of the best Mexicali blues in the city play at **Jim Cullen's Landing,** 123 Losoya (222-1234), in the Hyatt downtown. The music inside starts at 9pm and goes until around 2am. A jazz quartet performs on Sunday nights. The riverside café outside opens at 11:30am (cover $3).

West Texas

On the far side of the Rio Pecos lies a region whose extremely stereotypical Texan character verges on self-parody. This land was colonized in the days of the Texan Republic, during an era when "Law West of the Pecos" meant a rough mix of vigilante violence and frontier gunslinger machismo. However, this desolate region does not lack attractions, such as border city of El Paso, and its Chihuahuan neighbor, Ciudad Juárez.

Big Bend National Park

Roadrunners, coyotes, wild pigs, mountain lions, and 350 species of birds make their home at Big Bend National Park, a 700,000-acre tract that lies within the great curve of the Rio Grande. The spectacular canyons of this river, the vast **Chihuahuan**

Desert, and the cool **Chisos Mountains** have all witnessed the 100 million years necessary to mold the park's natural attractions. Although the Chihuahuan Desert covers most of the park, colorful wildflowers and plants abound.

You must get a free **wilderness permit** at the park headquarters to take an overnight hike. The park rangers will suggest hikes and places to visit. Most roads are well paved, but many of the most scenic places are only accessible by foot or four-wheel-drive vehicle. The **Lost Mine Peaks Trail,** an easy three-hour hike up a peak in the Chisos, leads to an amazing summit view of the desert and the Sierra de Carmen in Mexico. Another easy walk leads to the **Santa Elena Canyon** along the Rio Grande. The canyon walls rise up as much as 1,000 ft. over the banks of the river. Three companies offer river trips down the 133-mi. stretch of the Rio Grande owned by the park. Info on rafting and canoeing is available at the park headquarters.

Groceries capitalize in Panther Junction, Rio Grande Village, and the Chisos Basin at Castolon, but stock up before leaving urban areas for better prices and selections. Get wet at the park's only public shower (75¢ per 5 min.) at the Rio Grande Village store.

The only motel-style lodging is the expensive **Chisos Mountain Lodge** (915-477-2291) in the Chisos Basin. This lodge offers four types of service: a new hotel (singles $53, doubles $58); an older motel (singles $42.50, doubles $50); lodge units located ¼-mi. away from the lodge complex (singles $45, doubles $53); and stone cottages housing up to three people ($60). Reservations are a must, since the lodge is often booked up a year in advance. The lodge also runs a restaurant and coffee shop, where entrees cost $5-12. (Open daily 7am-8pm; off-season daily 7am-7:30pm.) The entire complex is located in the **Chisos Basin,** 10 mi. from the park's visitor center. Designated **campsites** within the park are allotted on a first come, first served basis. Chisos Basin and **Rio Grande Village** have sites with running water ($5) while **Cottonwood** has toilets but no running water ($3). Free primitive sites pop up along the hiking trails, available with a required permit from any ranger station. Because of the relatively high temperatures at the river, you won't have to worry about getting a site at Rio Grande Village, though you may have to negotiate with the resident buzzards. The best (and coolest) campsites by far are those in Chisos Basin. Get here early, as the basin sites fill up fast; try to get a campsite near the perimeter.

The **park headquarters** (915-477-2251) are at Panther Junction. (Open daily 8am-6pm. Vehicle pass $5 per week.) For info, write Superintendent, Big Bend National Park 79834. The other **ranger stations** are at Rio Grande Village, Persimmon Gap, Chisos Basin (open daily 8am-4pm), and Castolon (open daily 8am-6pm). In case of emergency, call 477-2251. After 6pm, call 477-2267 or any of the other numbers listed at each ranger station.

Big Bend may be the most isolated spot you'll ever encounter. The park is only accessible by car via I-118 or I-385. Rental cars are only available in Odessa, approximately 222 mi. north of the park. Amtrak serves Alpine three times per week.

Guadalupe Mountains National Park

The Guadalupe Mountains saddle up as Texas' highest, carrying with them a legacy of unexplored grandeur. Early westbound pioneers avoided the area, fearful of the arid climate and the Mescalero Apaches who controlled the range. Even by the early 20th century, only a few homesteaders and guano miners inhabited this rugged region. Today the mountains maintain their primitive state and ensure challenging hikes in a mostly desert environment for those willing to journey to this remote part of the state. The passing tourist who hopes to catch only the most established sights will stop to see **El Capitan,** a 2,000-ft. limestone cliff, and **Guadalupe Peak,** at 8,749 ft. the highest point in Texas. Less frantic travelers should hike to **McKittrick Canyon,** with its spring-fed stream and amazing variety of vegetation. Lush maples grow right next to desert yuccas, and thorny agaves circle stately pines. Mule deer and whiptail lizards sometimes greet visitors on the trails. The canyon and **The Bowl,** a high forest of Douglas fir and ponderosa pine, are both day hikes from the **Frijoles Information Center** (915-828-3251), right off U.S. 62/180. Here, you can pick up topographical maps, hiking guides, backcountry permits, and other info. (Open June-Aug. daily 7am-6pm; Sept.-May daily 8am-4:30pm.)

Guadalupe National Park's lack of development may be a bonus for backpackers, but it makes daily existence tough. All water in the backcountry is reserved for wildlife and no food is available nearby. Bring water for even the shortest, most casual hike. The **Pine Springs Cafe** (915-828-3338), directly across from the campground, sells ready-made but reasonably priced sandwiches, sodas, and beer. You can get ice cream and hamburgers at **Nickel Creek Cafe** (915-828-3348), five mi. east. Or fill up on a pancake and coffee breakfast ($3-6) before visiting McKittrick Canyon, three mi. farther east.

Guadalupe Mountains Park Service conducts half- and full-day hikes from June to August, as well as evening programs. Info is available at the Frijoles Visitor Center or on radio station 1610 AM. An additional visitor contact station at McKittrick Canyon is staffed during the fall and sporadically throughout the year. Visit the park in the fall for fab foliage free of summer heat or spring winds.

The **Pine Springs Campgrounds** (915-828-3251), 1½ mi. west of the Frijoles station directly on the highway, has water and restrooms but no hookup. No fires allowed. (Sites $5, Golden Age and Golden Access Passport holders receive a 50% discount.) **Dog Canyon Campground** (505-981-2418), just south of the state line at the north end of the park, can be reached only by a 70-mi. drive from Carlsbad, NM, on Rte. 137. Dog Canyon also lacks hookup, but provides water, restrooms, and charcoal grills. You can camp in the backcountry for free with a permit from the visitor center. When convenience takes priority over proximity to the trails, you should use White's City, NM, or Carlsbad, NM, as a base. They lie respectively 35 and 55 mi. northeast of the park along U.S. 62.

The park is less than 40 mi. west of Carlsbad Caverns in New Mexico (see Southern New Mexico), 110 mi. east of El Paso, and a 90-mi. drive from Kent. **TNM&O Coaches,** an affiliate of Greyhound, runs along U.S. 62/180 between Carlsbad, NM, and El Paso, passing Carlsbad Caverns National Park and Guadalupe National Park en route. This schedule makes flag stops at the park three times per day in each direction ($25, $47.50 round-trip). Guadalupe Mountains National Park is in the Mountain time zone (2 hr. behind Eastern).

For further info, write: Guadalupe Mountains National Park, HC60, P.O. Box 400, Salt Flat, TX 79847 (915-828-3251).

UTAH

Once home to dinosaurs, Utah now beckons bipedal mammals to its rugged landscape, which ranges from a vast lake of salt water to a multitude of bizarre rock formations. Southern Utah is a weird amalgam of redstone canyons, deep river gorges, and arches, spires, and columns carved out of the terrain by erosion. Northeastern and central Utah feature the Uinta mountains and National Forests, dotted with lakes and covered with aspens and ponderosa pine.

Only the uniqueness of Mormon culture matches the uniqueness of Utah's terrain. Driven westward by religious persecution, the Church of Jesus Christ of Latter Day Saints began settling Utah in 1848; today they make up over 80% of the state population. With its intensely family-oriented values, abstinence from alcohol, history of polygamy, and sheer prevalence, Mormon culture can make Utah a little intimidating—unless, like the skiers who flock to Park City and Alta, you only come for the snow.

Practical Information

Capital: Salt Lake City.

Utah Travel Council, Council Hall/Capitol Hill, 300 N. State St., Salt Lake City 84114 (538-1030), across the street from the capitol building. Information on national and state parks, campgrounds, and accommodations. Open summer, Mon.-Fri. 8am-5pm. Pick up a free copy of the *Utah Travel Guide*, with a complete listing of motels, national parks, and campgrounds. **Utah Parks and Recreation,** 1636 W. North Temple, Salt Lake City 86116 (538-7220). Open Mon.-Fri. 8am-5pm.

Time Zone: Mountain (2 hr. behind Eastern). **Postal Abbreviation:** UT

Area Code: 801.

Arches National Park

In Arches National Park, nature has experimented with modern sculpture for eons. Three hundred million years ago, the constant movement of a primordial sea deposited an uneven, unstable salt bed on the Colorado Plateau. The sea evaporated, but periodic washes, along with the tireless winds, deposited layer after layer of debris upon the new salt crust. The debris compacted into extremely heavy rock, and the salt twisted and crumbled under the weight. Through buckling and caving below and erosion above, the sandstone layers were shaped into fantastic spires, pinnacles, and, of course, arches. Arches National Park has more than 200 arches; because of their nearly perfect form, explorers thought the huge arches, like Stonehenge in England, the works of some lost civilization.

The park **visitor center,** 27 mi. on U.S. 191 south of I-70, 3½ mi. north of Moab, provides $2 self-guided car tours. (Open daily 8am-7pm; off-season daily 8am-4:30pm.) For additional information, contact the Superintendent, Arches National Park, P.O. Box 907, Moab 84532 (259-8161). An entrance pass ($3 per carload) remains valid for seven days; pedestrians and bikers pay only $1. Water is available in the park.

Plenty of scenic wonders glorify the 25-mi. road between the visitor center and Devil's Garden. No matter how short your stay, be sure to see the **Windows** section at **Panorama Point,** about halfway along the road. Cyclists will enjoy this ride in spring or fall, but the steep inclines make the trip almost unbearable in the summer heat. **Rim Cyclery,** 94 W. 100 North (259-5333), offers rimming bikes for $20 per day, including helmet and water bottle. (Open daily 9am-6pm.) At the end of the paved road by the campground, **Devil's Garden** boasts an astounding 64 arches. A challenging hike from the **Landscape Arch** leads across harrowing exposures to the secluded **Double O Arch.** The climax of your visit should be **Delicate Arch,** the symbol of the monument. Take the Delicate Arch turn-off from the main road two mi. down a graded unpaved road (impossibly impassible after rainstorms). Once you reach Wolfe Ranch, go down a 1½-mi. foot trail to the free-standing Delicate Arch. Beyond, you can get a glimpse of the Colorado River gorge and the La Sal Mountains. If you're lucky, you may come across petroglyphs on the stone walls left by the Anasazi and Ute who wandered the area from 1000 to 100 years ago. Please don't be an arch-villain: don't touch them.

Of course, arches aren't the only natural wonders here. Two of the most popular trails, the mile-long **Park Avenue** and the moderately strenuous two-mi. **Fiery Furnace Trail** lead downward into the canyon bottoms, providing views of the cliffs and monoliths above. Only experienced hikers should attempt the Fiery Furnace trail alone; a ranger leads group tours into this labyrinth at both 9am and 5pm daily.

The park's only campground, **Devil's Garden,** has 53 sites; get there early since sites are often snatched up by 1pm. The campground is 18 mi. from the visitor center and has running water. (2-week max. stay. Sites $3. Open April-Oct.) **Dead Horse Point State Park** ($3), perched on the rim of the Colorado Gorge south of Arches and 14 mi. south of U.S. 191, is accessible from Rte. 313. The campground has modern restrooms, water, electric hookups, and covered picnic tables. (Sites $6-8. Open April-Oct.) Winter camping is allowed on Dead Horse Point itself. For more information, contact the Park Superintendent, Dead Horse Point State Park, P.O. Box 609, Moab 84532 (259-6511). **Backcountry camping** in Arches National Park is a free adventure. Register at the visitor center first, and pick up a **USGS map** to avoid getting lost. Bring plenty of water and bread crumbs and avoid hiking on summer afternoons. Better than either the campground at Arches or Dead Horse Point in the summer, however, the **Manti-la-Sal National Forest** provides a means for escape from the heat, the crowds, and the biting gnats. These campgrounds are about 4000 ft. higher up, and about 20 to 25 mi. southeast of Moab off U.S. 191. All are free, except **Warner,** which charges $5. Three mi. down a dirt road is **Oowah Lake,** a rainbow trout heaven, at least from an angler's point of view (fishing permit $5 per day). The drainage work being done on the Lake should be completed for 1992. Camping is free (no water, pit toilets). For more information on the forest, contact the Manti-la-Sal National Forest Service office in Moab, 125 W. 200 South (259-7155; open Mon.-Fri. 8am-4:30pm).

The entrance to the park is on a paved road that winds for 25 mi. into its interior. This road is accessible from U.S. 191 at the junction five mi. north of Moab. Arches is 230 mi. from Salt Lake City. There is no public transportation to Arches, but buses run along I-70, stopping in Crescent Junction.

Bryce Canyon National Park

The fragile, slender spires of pink and red limestone that rise gracefully out of Bryce's canyons often seem more like an impressionist painting than the result of whimsical wind and water currents. But beautiful as they are, these barren canyons formed through erosion made life extremely difficult for both the Paiute and the white settlers. Ebenezer Bryce, the first white man to view the canyon, called it "one hell of a place to lose a cow," but it's also the perfect place to lose those big-city blues.

The park's **visitor center** (801-834-5322) is the place to begin any tour. Pick up a copy of the free Bryce Canyon *HooDoo,* which lists all park services, events, suggested hikes, and sight-seeing drives. (Open daily 8am-8pm; off-season daily 8am-4:30pm.)

23 designated hikes let you explore Bryce without guessing. The best scenery is concentrated within two mi. of the visitor center. Three spectacular lookouts—**Sunrise Point, Sunset Point,** and **Inspiration Point**—will refresh even the weariest traveler. Sunrises here are especially rewarding. The section between Sunrise and Sunset Points is suitable for wheelchairs. The three-mi. loop of the **Navajo** and **Queen's Garden** trails takes you into the canyon itself. If you are up to the challenge, branch off onto the **Peek-A-Boo Trail,** a four-mi. round-trip. Escape the crowds by conquering the **Trail to the Hat Shop,** a strenuous 3.8-mi. journey along an extremely steep descent. And if you think climbing *down* is tough . . .

If you don't want to hike, drive the 15 mi. from the visitor center to **Rainbow Point** and stop at the various lookouts along the way. Or take the **1938 Limousine Tour** that departs from Bryce Lodge daily at 9am, 11:30am, 1:30pm, and 3:30pm ($6, under 12 $3). The corral across from the lodge gives two-hour horseback rides to the canyon bottom ($15).

Bryce has two campgrounds planted among the tall ponderosa pines: **North Campground** and **Sunset Campground.** (Sites at both $6.) Sunrise Point (834-5361), west of both campgrounds, has public showers and a small grocery store. (Open from May 1 8am-8pm. Showers $1.25 per 10 min., available 8am-10pm). **Backcountry camping** at designated sites is a lovely way to get intimate with the canyon's changing moods and wildlife. A free permit is required and available at **Nature's Center** by Sunrise Point. Of the six **Dixie National Forest** campgrounds, most about an hour away just off Rte. 14, the best are **TE-AH Campground, Spruce Campground,** and the **Navajo Lake Campground.** (All $6 per night, no showers, running water and toilets.) The nearest forest service office is in Panguitch, 225 E. Center St. (676-8815; open Mon.-Fri. 8am-4:30pm).

During the summer, **Ruby's Inn Rodeo** (834-5341) pits man against beast every night except Sunday at 7:30pm (admission $5). Another popular annual event, the **Fiddler's Association Contest,** tunes up in early July.

Bryce has a **post office** at Ruby's Inn (open Mon.-Fri. 8am-5:15pm); there is also a **post office** at Bryce Lodge during the summer (open Mon.-Fri. 8am-5pm, Sat. 8am-noon). The **ZIP code** is 84764.

Bryce Canyon lies five hours south of Salt Lake City and 45 minutes east of Cedar City on U.S. 89 in southwestern Utah. From U.S. 89 at Bryce Junction (7 mi. south of Panguitch), turn east on Rte. 12 and drive 17 mi. to the park entrance (entrance fee $5 per car, $2 per pedestrian). There is no public transportation within the park or from Cedar City; this is not the place to get stranded.

Near Bryce

To hike into the desert environment of the ominously named **Phipps Death Hollow Outstanding Natural Area,** part of a network of sandstone canyons just north of Escalante, contact the **Bureau of Land Management,** Escalante Ranger District, Escalante 84726 (826-4291), on Rte. 12, about one mi. west of town. (Open Mon.-Fri. 7:45am-4:30pm, Sat. 8am-noon; off-season Mon.-Fri. 8am-4:30pm.) 15 mi. east of Escalante is the popular **Calf Creek** camping grounds, with a great hike near a cascading waterfall. (Sites $5, including drinking water and fresh toilets.) Boulder has the **Anasazi Museum** off Rte. 12 (335-7308), which displays a reconstructed Anasazi village dating from about 1100 AD. (Open daily 8am-6pm.) The Anasazi ("ancient ones") disappeared almost completely around 1250 AD. The type of basket-weaving among present day Hopis indicates a connection to the Anasazi, who anthropologists think left the area to assimilate with other tribes during a 23-year drought around 1150. If you don't mind dodging cows and driving on dirt roads, head out three mi. to **Lower Bowns Reservoir Lake** (826-4221; no drinking water, pit toilets).

Wandering out of Bryce in the opposite direction, on Rte. 14 to Cedar City, you'll come across the refreshing and surprisingly green **Cedar Breaks National Monument** ($3 per car). The rim of the giant amphitheater is a lofty 10,350 ft. above sea level; 2,000 ft. of flowered slopes separate the rim from the chiseled depths (disabled access). At **Point Supreme** you'll find a 30-site **campground** (sites $5) and the **visitor center** (586-9548; open summer Mon.-Thurs. 8am-6pm, Fri.-Sat. 8am-7pm). For more information, contact the Superintendent, Cedar Breaks National Monument, P.O. Box 749, Cedar City 84720.

Cedar City's **Iron Mission State Park,** 585 N. Main St. (586-9290), has an amazing horse-drawn vehicle collection which merits a visit. (Open daily 9am-7pm; off-season daily 9am-5pm. $1, under 6 free.) The **Economy Motel,** 443 S. Main St. (586-4461), has very basic rooms; try to get one with a book-sized window. (Singles $25. Doubles $28.) For more information, contact the **Cedar City Visitors Center,** 100 E. Center St. (586-4484; open Mon.-Fri. 8am-5pm).

Canyonlands National Park

The confluence of the Green and Colorado Rivers in **Canyonlands National Park** reveals that when these two mighty waterways got together, it must have been quite a night. The merging rivers gouged out rifts and gorges that sink into the desert's crust with a dizzying starkness. Harsh desert prevails in the areas the rivers bypassed. With its breathtaking, arid terrain, the park remains one of the most remote places in North America.

Outside the park, there are two information centers. Monticello's **Interagency Visitor Center,** 32 S. 1st E. (587-3235), sells area maps ($3-6). (Open daily 8am-5pm.) In Moab (see below), the **Park Service** resides at 125 W. 200 S. (259-7164) and has the same business hours. Both can provide information for French, German, and Spanish visitors.

The park contains three distinct areas. The visitor center for **Needles** (259-6568) lies in the park's southeast corner. To get there, take Rte. 211 west from U.S. 191, about 40 mi. south of Moab. There is neither gas nor water available within the park. (Open daily 8am-5pm.) Farther north, the **Island in the Sky** visitor center sits deep within the "Y" formed by the two rivers (259-6577; open daily 8am-6pm.) Take Rte. 313 west from U.S. 191 about 10 mi. north of Moab. The most remote district of the park is the rugged **Maze** area (visitor center 259-6513; open daily 8am-4:30pm), to the west of the canyons, accessible only by four-wheel drive. Once you've entered a section of the park, you're committed: transferring from one area to another involves retracing your steps and re-entering the park, a tedious trip lasting from several hours to a full day.

Each visitor center has a booklet of possible hikes (including photos), so you can pick your own. Hiking options from the Needles area are probably the best, though Island in the Sky offers some spectacular views. Cyclists should check at the visitor centers for lists of trails. If hiking in desert heat doesn't appeal to you, you can rent jeeps and mountain bikes in Moab, or take an airplane flight from **Red Tail Aviation** (259-7421) that can cost as little as $30 per person for a group of four. **Lin Ottinger Tours,** 600 N. Main St., Moab (259-7312), leads all-day jeep and backpacking tours ($45) that teach you how to survive on local flora. (Open daily 8am-9:30pm.)

There are no food services in the park. Just outside the boundary in the Needles district, however, the **Needles Outpost** houses a limited, expensive grocery store and gas pumps. Hauling groceries in from Moab or Monticello is the best budget alternative.

Each region has its own official **campground.** In the Needles district, **Squaw Flat** is situated in a sandy plain surrounded by giant sandstone towers. Avoid this area in June, when insects swarm. Bring water, though it usually is available from April through September. A $7 fee is charged year-round. **Willow Flat Campground,** in the Island in the Sky unit, sits high atop the mesa. You must bring your own water; sites are free. Willow Flat and Squaw Flat both have picnic tables, grills, and pit toilets; they operate on a first-come, first-served basis. The campground at the **Maze Overlook** has no amenities at all. Dead Horse Point State Park (adjacent to Island in the Sky) and Manti-la-Sal National Forest (adjacent to the Needles) provide alternative campsites. (See Arches National Park.) Before **backcountry camping,** get a free permit from the visitor center in the proper district and take along plenty of water (at least one gallon per person per day). Summer temperatures regularly climb to over 100°F.

Capitol Reef National Park

Spiny and forbidding, like the backbone of an immense prehistoric sea creature, Capitol Reef's **Waterpocket Fold** dominates the terrain of south central Utah. This 100-mi. line of sheer cliffs cuts the state's southern region in half and was originally called a "reef", not for its oceanic origins but because it was a barrier to travel. To the west lie Zion and Bryce Canyon; to the east lie Arches and Canyonlands. Major bus lines don't serve the park itself.

You'll want to make at least a brief stop at the park's **visitor center** (801-425-3791), on Rte. 24, for info on the Capitol Reef and daily activities. (Open June-Aug. daily 8am-7pm; off-season daily 8am-4:30pm.) Waterproof maps here cost $6, regular maps $4, guides to specific trails 10¢. The 25-mi. round-trip **scenic drive** is the best way to see the park by car. This 90-minute jaunt takes you out along the reef itself. Nearby **Capitol Dome,** which resembles the U.S. Capitol, explains the other half of the park's unusual name. If you have a few days to spare, explore the park's desert backcountry. Foot trails and rough roads crisscross the region, giving access to the area's most inspiring, remote scenery. Keep in mind that summer temperatures average 95°F and most water found in seep springs and rain-holding waterpockets is contaminated.

For **backcountry camping,** you must obtain a free permit from the visitor center. Sites at the pleasant, grassy *main campground* cost $6 and are available on a first come, first served basis. Located just a mi. from the visitor center, the campground lies in the heart of the old orchard town of **Fruita.** When the park service bought the land for Capitol Reef back in the 1960s, they suddenly found themselves with the town's extensive orchards on their hands, with no one to pick the fruit. Tourists can now harvest fruit from late June (cherries) to mid-October (apples). In between fall the bountiful apricot, peach, and pear harvests, all for ridiculously low prices.

For accommodations in the region, try: **Torrey,** 11 mi. west of the visitor center on U.S. 24; **Escalante,** 65 mi. south of the visitor center on U.S. 12; or **Hanksville,** 37 mi. from the visitor center on U.S. 24. The **Redrock Restaurant and Campground** (542-3235), in Hanksville, is the main tourist service in the region. Meals at the restaurant go for $4-7, the daily special $4.75. (Open daily 7am-10pm.) Tent sites at the campground are $6, with electricity and water $7, with full hookup $10.

Moab

Dubbed "the mountain bike capital of the Known Universe," Moab's tongue-in-cheek title nevertheless evokes its dual populace—the hippie, Birkenstocked group whose universe is forever groovy, and the die-hard athletes who've hardly let the snow melt from their ski boots before they're either whitewater rafting or mountain biking. With its proximity to Arches and Canyonlands, and its youthful, "crunchy" character, the booming town of Moab provides a great base for exploring the region, either by car, mountain bike, or raft on the Green River.

Adrift Adventures, 378 North Main (259-8594 or 800-874-4483), organizes canoe trips on the Green and Colorado Rivers. A full day (9am-5pm) of fighting the rapids is $38, and a half-day (9am-1pm or 1-5pm) costs $29. Numerous other river trips are available, with steep prices to match the thrill. Check around.

In summer Moab fills up fast, especially on weekends, so call ahead to guarantee your reservations. The manager of the **Lazy Lizard International Hostel,** 1213 S. Hwy. 191 (259-6057), goes out of the way to be helpful, and will route your trip through Arches or elsewhere. The kitchen, VCR, laundry, and hot tub are at your beck and call. (Bunks $6.50. Singles $11. Doubles $15.) **Canyon Land Motel,** 16 S. Main (259-5167), offers singles for $27 and doubles for $32. **The Prospector Lodge,** 186 N. 1st West (259-5145), one block west of Main Street, offers cool, comfy rooms across the street from the local hippie co-op. (Singles $24. Doubles $27.50.) All motels will charge a little bit less in the off-season.

Private campgrounds speckle the area surrounding Moab. The **Holiday Haven Mobile Home and RV Park,** 400 West (259-8526) charges $10 persite, $11 with water, $12 with electricity and water and $13 with full hookup. The **Canyonland Campark,** 555 S. Main St. (259-6848), asks $11.50 per site, $16 for electricity and water, $17 for a full hookup, and $2 per extra person. It has a pool. The **Moab KOA,** four mi. south on U.S. 191 (259-6682), charges $12 for a tent site, $16 with electricity and water, and $18 for full hookup.

For a good book to bring into the lonesome desert, try the aptly named *Back of the Beyond Bookstore,* 83 N. Main (259-5154), which contains a wide selection of the works of local favorite Edward Abbey, as well as a unique series of Chinese poetry books devoted to the 12th-century muse Wu Lin Lin.

Moab sits 50 mi. southeast of I-70 on Hwy. 191, 15 mi. south of Arches. There is no public transportation to Moab, although buses will stop along I-70, in Crescent Junction, where you can hitch south along 191.

The **Moab Visitors Center,** 805 N. Main St. (259-8825), can provide information on lodging and dining in Moab. (Open daily 8am-8pm; off-season 8am-5pm.) The **Moab Post Office,** is at 39 S. Main St. (644-2760; open Mon.-Fri. 8:30am-4pm, Sat. 9am-noon); the **ZIP code** is 84741.

Salt Lake City

In a little town outside of Rochester, New York in 1830, 15-year-old Joseph Smith had a vision that commanded him to start a new religion, the Church of Jesus Christ of Latter Day Saints. Known as Mormons because of the *Book of Mormon,* which Smith is said to have translated from ancient tablets, the Latter Day Saints fled westward from persecution, stopping for periods in Ohio, Illinois, Missouri, Nebraska, and finally settling in Salt Lake City in 1847. Situated in mountainous, desert terrain near the Great Salt Lake, Salt Lake City bears a peculiar resemblance to another "Holy Land" even today. The city is graced by spiritual centers of the Church of Latter Day Saints, including the gargantuan Mormon Temple and the Mormon Tabernacle Choir, as well as the cultural and intellectual institutions of Utah.

Practical Information

Emergency: 911.

Salt Lake Valley Convention and Visitors Bureau, 180 S. West Temple (521-2868 or 800-831-4332), 2 blocks south of Temple Sq. Open Mon.-Fri. 8am-7pm, Sat. 9am-4pm, Sun. 10am-4pm; off-season Mon.-Fri. 8am-5:30pm, Sat. 9am-6pm, Sun. 10am-4pm. Other **visitor centers** at: Crossroads Mall, 50 S. Main St.; ZCMI Mall, 36 S. State St. (321-8745; open Mon.-Fri. 7:30am-9pm, Sat. 8am-6pm); and terminal 2 at the airport. The free *Salt Lake Visitors Guide* details a good self-guided tour.

Salt Lake City International Airport: 776 N. Terminal Dr. (539-2205), 4 mi. west of Temple Sq. UTA buses provide the best means of transport to and from the airport. Bus #50 serves the terminal directly. Delta/Western Airlines flies here from Los Angeles, San Francisco, and Denver.

Amtrak: 325 S. Rio Grande (364-8562 or 800-872-7245). Trains once daily to: Denver (13½ hr., $103); Las Vegas (8 hr., $84); Los Angeles (15 hr., $133); and San Francisco (17 hr., $137). Ticket office open Mon.-Sat. 5-9am, 10:30am-2pm, 4:15-7pm, 8pm-midnight; Sun. 4:15pm-1:20am.

Greyhound/Trailways: 160 W. South Temple (355-4684), 1 block west of Temple Sq. To: Cheyenne (3 per day, 9 hr., $55); Las Vegas (2 per day, 10 hr., $58); San Francisco (3 per day, 15 hr., $84); Boise (3 per day, 7 hr., $46); West Yellowstone (1 per day, 9 hr., $70); Denver (4 per day, 12 hr., $64). Ticket counter open daily 1:45am-10pm; off-season daily 7am-10pm. Terminal open 24 hrs.

Public Transport: Utah Transit Authority, 600 S. 700 West (287-4636 until 7pm). Frequent service to University of Utah; buses to Ogden (#70/72 express), suburbs, airport, and east to the mountain canyons. Buses ½-hr. or more apart 6:30am-11pm. To Provo 5:30am-10pm; fare 60¢, seniors 30¢, under 5 free. Maps available from libraries or the visitors bureau. Information desk at ZCMI Mall, 36 S. State St.

Tours: Gray Line, 553 W. 100 South (521-7060). 2½-hr. tours of the city focusing on Mormon historical sites. Departures in summer daily at 9am and 2pm. Fare $12, kids $6. A tour of the Great Salt Lake copper mine is also offered daily at 2pm ($22).

Taxi: City Cab, 363-5014. Ute Cab, 359-7788. Yellow Cab, 521-2100. 95¢ base fare, $1.40 per mi., $9-10 from the airport to Temple Sq.

Car Rentals: Payless Car Rental, 1974 W. North Temple (596-2596). $22 per day with 200 free mi., or $110 per week with 1200 free mi.; 12¢ each additional mi. Open Mon.-Fri. 7am-10pm, Sat.-Sun. 8am-6pm. Must be 21 with a major credit card and may only drive in Utah.

Bike Rental: Wasatch Touring, 702 E. 100 South (359-9361). 21-speed mountain bikes $15 per day. Open Mon.-Sat. 9am-7pm.

Help Lines: Rape Crisis, 467-7273. 24-hr. hotline.

Post Office: 230 W. 200 South (530-5902), 1 block west of the visitors bureau. Open Mon.-Fri. 8am-5:30pm, Sat. 9am-2pm. **ZIP code:** 84101.

Area Code: 801.

Salt Lake's grid system makes navigation quite simple. Brigham Young, the city's founder, designated **Temple Square,** in the heart of today's downtown, as the center. Street names indicate how many blocks east, west, north, or south they lie from Temple Square. **Main Street,** running north-south, and **Temple Street,** running east-west, are the "0" points. Smaller streets and streets that do not fit the grid pattern often have non-numerical names. Occasionally, a numbered street reaches a dead end, only to resume a few blocks farther on.

The city's main points of interest lie within the relatively small area bounded by the railroad tracks around 400 West, the **University of Utah** at 1300 East, the **State Capitol** at 300 North, and **Liberty Park** at 900 South. The downtown is equipped with audible traffic lights for the convenience of blind pedestrians. A "cuckoo" is a green light for east-west travel while "chirps" indicate a green light for north-south travel.

Accommodations and Camping

The Avenues (AYH), 107 F St. (363-8137), 5 blocks east of Temple Sq. Bright rooms with 4 bunks each or private singles and doubles. Popular with British and German students. Blankets provided: Bring sheets. Kitchen and laundry available. Check-in 8am-10pm. Dorm rooms $10, nonmembers $13. Singles $20. Doubles $30.

Colonial Village Motel, 1530 Main St. (486-8171). Take bus #36 or 42. Very nice rooms with thick carpet in a white building. Management flexible about extra beds. Singles $24. Doubles $28.

Kendell Motel, 667 N. 300 West (355-0293), 10 blocks northwest of Temple Sq. Enough room for you and your army. Well-kept rooms with kitchens, color TV, and A/C $25. Room with 4 double beds and kitchen, $50.

Motel 6, 3 locations: 176 W. 600 South (531-1252); 1990 W. North Temple (364-1053), 2½ mi. from the airport (take bus #50); and 496 N. Catalpa (561-0058), just off I-15 with white cockatoo in office. All fill quickly. Singles $31. Doubles $38. Catalpa and downtown locations $3 more.

Austin Hall at the **University of Utah** (581-6331), 15 blocks east of downtown, off Wasatch Dr. Take bus 3 or #14 . Must be "looking at" University of Utah. Quiet, grey carpeted rooms with phone, red bedspreads, desks. Tennis courts next door; golf course across street. Singles $20. Doubles $25. Reservations best. Rooms for rent mid-June to Aug.

Camping is available outside the city. The **Wasatch National Forest** (524-5030) skirts Salt Lake City on the east, proffering many established sites. The terrain by the city is quite steep, making the best sites those on the far side of the mountains. Three of the closest campgrounds lie near I-215, which runs along the mountain fronts off I-80. Between mile 11 and 18 out of Salt Lake City on I-80, there are four campgrounds with more than 100 sites altogether (no hookups). Go early on weekends to ensure a space (sites $5; take "Fort Douglas" bus #4). The **Utah Travel Council** (538-1030) has detailed information on all campsites in the area, including the three near the ski areas off Rte. 152 and 210 to the south of Salt Lake. The **state parks** around Salt Lake also offer camping, though none on the lake itself. **East Canyon State Park,** 30 mi. from Pioneer State Park in Salt Lake, near the junction of Rte. 65 and 66, has sites by East Canyon Reservoir—a good place to go boating and fishing. (Open April-late Nov.) State parks normally charge $2 for day use and $6-9 for sites. For more information, contact **Utah Parks and Recreation** (see Utah Practical Information above). If you need a hookup, then the **KOA,** 1400 W. North Temple (355-1192; sites $15, with water and electricity $18, full hookup $20), and private campgrounds are your only alternatives.

Food

Affordable food abounds in Salt Lake City, but is rarer downtown. Fill up on **scones,** a Utah specialty English affectation. Otherwise stick to ethnic food downtown or the cheap, slightly greasy eateries on the outer fringe.

La Frontera, 3784 West 3500 S. (967-9905), west of downtown but worth the trip. Live music and delicious cheese enchiladas ($2). Open Sun.-Thurs. 10am-11pm, Fri.-Sat. 10am-midnight. Another at 1736 West 4th St. (532-3158).

Bill and Nada's Café, 479 S. 6th St (354-6984). One of Salt Lake's most revered cafés. Patsy Cline on the jukebox and paper placemats with U.S. presidents on the tables. Two eggs, hash browns, toast $3. Roast leg of lamb, salad, soup, vegetable, and potatoes $5. Open 24 hrs.

Rio Grande Café, 270 Rio Grande (364-3302), in the Rio Grande Railroad depot, 4 blocks west of the temple by Amtrak and the historical society. Take bus #16 or 17. Stylish, fun Mexican restaurant with neon-and-glass decor. Two tacos with rice and beans $4.50. Open Mon.-Thurs. 11:30am-2:30pm and 5-10pm, Fri.-Sat. 11:30am-2:30pm and 5-10:30pm, Sun. 5-10pm.

Union Cafeteria (581-7256), at the university. Serves the cheapest grub in town. Chat with students over breakfast ($1-2), lunch, or dinner ($2-3). Open Mon.-Fri. 7am-9pm, Sat. 8am-7:30pm, Sun. 11am-7:30pm.

Bistro to Go, 271 S. Main St. (363-5300). Try the Scandinavian spinach torte ($3.75) and top it off with one of many exotic coffees ($1.25-2.50) Thursday night poetry readings, film series, and upstairs gallery along with cappucino and gourmet delicacies attract SLC's avant-garde. Open Mon.-Wed. 9am-3pm, Thurs.-Sat. 9am-3pm and 9pm-2am.

Salt Lake Roasting Company, 249 E. 400 South (363-7572). Classical or jazz music amid burlap bags of coffee beans. Caters to the post-college set. Coffees (85¢) and pastries; quiche complete with soup and French bread $3. Open Mon.-Sat. 7am-midnight.

The Sconecutter, 2040 S. State St. (485-9981). The Elvis of sconemakers. Your favorite flavor of fluffy but stuffing scone only $1. Try the apple. Open 24 hrs.

The Red Iguana, 736 North Temple (322-1489). Mexican food, with spicy *moles* that bring tears. Open Mon.-Thurs. 11:30am-9pm, Fri.-Sat. 11:30am-10pm.

Mormon Sights

Salt Lake City is the world headquarters of the **Church of Jesus Christ of Latter-day Saints** whose followers hold the *Bible,* as well as the *Book of Mormon,* as the word of God. The highest Mormon authority and the largest Mormon temple reside here.

Temple Square (240-2534) is the symbolic center of the Mormon religion. Feel free to wander around the flowery and pleasant 10-acre square, but the sacred temple is off-limits for non-Mormons. Sitting atop the highest of the building's three towers, a golden statue of the angel Moroni watches over the city. The square has two **visitor centers** (north and south), each of which stocks information and armies of smiling guides. A 45-min. **Historical Touch** leaves from the flagpole every 10 minutes. Also, a **Book of Mormon Tour** and a **Purpose of Temple Tour** leave alternately every 30 minutes, and explain the religious meaning behind Temple Square. (Visitor centers open daily 8am-10pm; off-season daily 9am-9pm.)

Visitors on any tour in Temple Square will visit the **Mormon Tabernacle,** the earthbound UFO that houses the famed Choir. Built in 1867, the structure is so acoustically sensitive that a pin dropped at one end can be heard 175 ft. away at the other end. Rehearsals on Thursday evenings (8pm) and Sunday morning broadcasts from the tabernacle are open to the public (arrive by 9am). Though supremely impressive, the choir can't match the size and sound of the 11,623-pipe organ that accompanies it. (Recitals Mon.-Sat. at noon; summer Sun. 2pm as well.) **Assembly Hall,** next door, also hosts various concerts almost every summer evening.

Around the perimeter of Temple Square stand several other buildings commemorating Mormon history in Utah. The **Genealogical Library,** 35 N. West Temple (240-3702) provides the resources for Mormons and others to research their lineage, in accordance with Mormon belief that ancestors must be baptized by proxy to seal them into an eternal family. If you've ever wanted to research your roots, this may be the place to do it; the library houses the largest collection of genealogical documents in the world. An orientation film is available. (Open Mon. 7:30am-6pm, Tues.-Fri. 7:30am-10pm, Sat. 7:30am-5pm. Free.)

The **Museum of Church History and Art,** 45 N. West Temple (240-3310), houses Mormon memorabilia from 1820 to the present. (Open Mon.-Fri. 9am-9pm, Sat.-Sun. and holidays 10am-7pm; off-season Mon. and Wed. 10am-9pm, Tues. and Thurs.-Sun. 10am-7pm. Free.) Once the official residence of Brigham Young while he served as governor of the territory and president of the church, the **Beehive House,** N. Temple at State St. (240-2671), two blocks east of Temple Sq., gives half-hour guided tours every 10 minutes. (Open Mon.-Sat. 9:30am-4:30pm, Sun. 10am-1pm. Free.)

The city of Salt Lake encompasses the **Pioneer Trail State Park** (533-5881), in Emigration Canyon on the eastern end of town. Take bus #4 or follow 8th South St. until it becomes Sunnyside Ave., then take Monument Rd. The **"This is the Place" Monument,** 2601 Sunnyside Ave. (533-5920), commemorates Brigham Young's decision to settle in Salt Lake; a visitor center will tell you all about the Mormons' long march through Ohio, Illinois, and Nebraska. Tour **Brigham Young's forest farmhouse,** where the dynamic leader held court with his numerous wives. (Park grounds open in summer daily 8am-8pm, but visit 9am-7:30pm for the best reception. $1.)

Secular Sights and Activities

The grey-domed **capitol** lies behind the spires of Temple Square. Tours (521-2822) are offered daily from 9am to 3:30pm. For more info, contact the **Council Hall Visitors Center** (538-1030), across from the main entrance. (Open daily 8am-5pm.) While in the capitol area, hike up City Creek Canyon to **Memory Grove,** savoring the shade as you gaze out over the city, or stroll down to the **Church of Jesus Christ of Latter-Day Saints Office Building,** 50 E. North Temple, and take the elevator to the 26th-floor observation deck where you can see the Great Salt Lake to the west, and the Wasatch Mountain Range to the east. (Open April-Oct. Mon.-Sat. 9am-5pm; Oct.-April Mon.-Fri. 9am-5pm) Also on capitol hill is the **Hansen Planetarium,** 15 S. State St. (538-2098). Even if you don't pay for a show, enjoy the fabulous free exhibits. (Open daily 10am-8pm.) Head for the **Children's Museum,** 840 N. 300 West (328-3383), to pilot a 727 jet or implant a Jarvik artificial heart in a life-sized "patient." (Open Mon. 9:30am-9pm, Tues.-Sat. 9:30am-5pm, Sun. noon-5pm. $3, kids $2.50. Take bus #61.) You also can walk through the U. of Utah campus to the **Utah Museum of Natural History** (581-4303), which catalogues the variety of life that has lived on the Salt Lake plain. (Open Mon.-Sat. 9:30am-5:30pm, Sun. noon-5pm. $2, under 14 $1.50, students 60¢.) Next door is the yard-sale-like collection at the **Utah Museum of Fine Arts** (581-7332; open Mon.-Fri. 10am-5pm, Sat.-Sun. 2-5pm; free). For information on university happenings contact the Information Desk in the U. of Utah Park Administration Building (581-6515; open Mon.-Fri. 8am-8pm), or the **Olpin Student Center** (581-5888; open Mon.-Sat. 8am-9pm).

Next to the Amtrak station, the **Utah State Historical Society,** 300 Rio Grande (533-5755), hosts an interesting series of exhibits, including pre-Mormon photographs and quilts. (Open Mon.-Fri. 8am-5pm, Sat. 10am-2pm. Free.)

The **Utah Symphony Orchestra** (533-6407) performs in **Symphony Hall,** Salt Palace Center, 100 S. West Temple, one of the most spectacular auditoriums in the country. (Free tours Tues. and Thurs. at 1, 1:30, 2, and 2:30pm. Concert tickets $10-30, student rush $5.) Dance and opera performances occur at the neighboring **Salt Lake Art Center** (328-4201; open Mon.-Sat. 10am-5pm; donation).

Alcohol and Nightlife

The Mormon Church's prohibitions against alcohol consumption among its members have led to a number of state restrictions. Utah law requires that all liquor sales be made through state-licensed stores; don't be surprised if you can't get more than a beer at most restaurants or bars. The drinking age of 21 is well-enforced. (State liquor stores open Mon.-Sat. 11am-7pm. There are 6 within 3 mi. of downtown Salt Lake.) A number of hotels and restaurants have licenses to sell mini-bottles and splits of wine, but consumers must make drinks themselves. Public bars serve only beer. Private clubs requiring membership fees are allowed to serve mixed drinks. Some clubs have two-week trial memberships for $5; others will give a free, temporary membership to visitors in town for a night or two.

Even with the alcohol restrictions, there are several fun downtown bars and clubs, which collegians keep fairly crowded. The **Dead Goat Saloon,** 165 S. West Temple (328-4628), attracts German and British tourists as well as locals. (Open Mon.-Sat. noon-2am, Sun. 6pm-2am. Beer served until 1am. No BYOB. Cover $3, Fri.-Sun. $5.) The local pool bar, **X Wife's Place,** 465 South 700 East (532-2353), used to be "My Wife's Place," but the owner got divorced. Just kidding. (Open Mon.-Fri. 4pm-1am, Sat. 5pm-1am. Beer served. No cover.)

DV8, 115 S. West Temple (539-8400), is a hip industrial emporium. Friday is college night. (Open Mon.-Sat. 9pm-1am. Cover from $3.) **The Zephyr,** 79 W. 300 South (355-2582), hosts live rock and reggae nightly. (Open daily 7pm-2am; off-season daily 7pm-1am. Cover $5-10.) **Junior's Tavern,** 202 E. 500 South (322-0318), is the favorite local watering hole for jazz and blues afficionados. (Open Mon.-Sat. 4pm-1am. Music starts at 9pm. Cover varies.)

Near Salt Lake City

The **Great Salt Lake,** a remnant of primordial Lake Bonneville, contains a bowl of salt water where only blue-green algae and brine shrimp can survive. The salt content varies between 5 and 15%, about that of a ballpark pretzel, and provides such buoyancy that it is almost impossible for the human body to sink; only the Dead Sea has a higher salt content. Unfortunately, flooding sometimes closes the state parks and beaches on the lakeshore, but you can still try Saltair Beach 17 mi. to the west, or head north 40 minutes to fresh-water **Willard Bay.** Bus #37 ("Magna") will take you only as close as four mi. from the lake. Be warned that the aroma around the lake ain't rosy. Contact the visitor center or the state parks (538-7220) for current information on access to the lake as it is fairly difficult to reach without a car.

In the summer, escape the heat with a drive or hike to the cool breezes and icy streams of the nearby mountains. One of the prettiest roads over the Wasatch Range is **Route 210.** Heading east from Sandy, 12 mi. southeast of the city, this road goes up **Little Cottonwood Canyon** to the Alta ski resort. The **Lone Peak Wilderness Area** stretches away southward from the road, around which the range's highest peaks (over 11,000 ft.) tower. **City Creek, Millcreek,** and **Big Cottonwood** also make good spots for a picnic or hike.

Of the seven ski resorts within 40 minutes of downtown Salt Lake, **Snowbird** (521-6040; lift tickets $34) and **Park City** (649-8111; lift tickets $32) are two of the classiest. For a more affordable alternative, try the nearby **Alta** (742-3333; lift tickets $22). The **Alta Peruvian Lodge** (328-8589) is a great place to pass the night. (Bunks $12.50.) UTA runs buses from SLC to the resorts in winter, with pick-ups at downtown motels. You can rent equipment from **Breeze Ski Rentals** (800-525-0314), at Snowbird and Park City ($15; 10% discount if reserved over 2 weeks in advance; lower rates for rentals over 3 days). Call or write the Utah Travel Council (see Utah Practical Information above). Pick up the free *Ski Utah* for listings of ski packages and lodgings. The **Utah Handicapped Skiers Association,** P.O. Box 108, Roy 84067 (649-3991), provides information, specialized equipment, and instruction for disabled skiers. (Open Mon.-Fri. 9am-5pm.)

Some resorts offer summer attractions as well. You can rent mountain bikes at Snowbird for $16 per day or $9 per half-day. Snowbird's aerial tram climbs to 11,000 ft., offering a spectacular view of the Wasatch Mountains and the Salt Lake Valley below. (Open daily 11am-8pm. $6, seniors and under 16 $3.50.) During the summer, Park City offers a comparable gondola ride. (Open Fri.-Mon. noon-6pm. $5, under 12 $4.) Their alpine slide provides the fastest transport down the mountain. (Open daily 10am-10pm. $3.75, seniors and kids $2.75. Take I-80 east 30 mi. from Salt Lake.)

Northeastern Utah

In this little-known region where Utah, Colorado, and Wyoming meet, you'll find a microcosm of entire history and landscape of the west. The **Drive Through the Ages,** on U.S. 191 from the Wyoming border to Vernal, Utah, twists dramatically through a billion years of Earth history in just a couple hundred miles. The giant lizards that once lumbered through the long-vanished marshes are now neatly exhibited for lumbering automobiles at Dinosaur National Monument, while nearby spiny vertebrae of the snow-capped Uinta Mountain Range protrude from the desert plateau. The region is a geologist's Wallyword as well; the Uinta (oo-IN-ta) mountains form the only range known to run east-west, while the Green River flows upwards, from flatlands into the mountains, creating an enormous expanse of water in a parched land.

In addition to U.S. 191, many other roads (U.S. 40, Rte. 150, Rte. 414, and Rte. 530) break away from mind-numbing I-80 and facilitate exploration of the region. **Greyhound** sends its beasts of burden down I-80 four times per day as well as past the Uintas and Dinosaur Monument on the south, along U.S. 40. Even the farthest corners of the area are within a half-day's drive of Salt Lake City.

Dinosaur National Monument

Dinosaur National Monument is more than just a pile of bones. The Green and Yampa Rivers have created vast, colorful gorges and canyons, and the harsh terrain still evokes eerie visions of the massive reptiles stomping ground 140 million years ago.

The park entrance fee is $5 per car, $2 for bikers, pedestrians, and those in tour buses. The more interesting western side lies along Rte. 149 off U.S. 40 just outside of **Jensen,** 30 mi. east of Vernal. Seven mi. from the intersection with U.S. 40 is the **Dinosaur Quarry Visitors Center** (789-2115), accessible from the road by free shuttle bus or a fairly strenuous ½-mi. walk (cars prohibited in summer). A hill inside the center has been partially excavated to reveal the gargantuan remains of dinosaurs. (Open daily 8am-4:30pm, with extended summer hours. You can drive your car in after closing.) Winter finds the park lonely and cold with neither shuttle service nor the possibility of self-guided tours. A few mi. farther along Rte. 149 you'll find the shady **Green River Campground** with flush toilets, drinking water, and tent and RV sites. (Open late spring-early fall. Sites $6.) There are also several free primitive campsites in and around the park; call the visitor center for info. Past the campgrounds on Rte. 149, just beyond the end of the road, you can see one of the best examples of the monument's many Native American petroglyphs, or paintings, on the rocks.

The eastern side of the park is accessible only from U.S. 40, outside **Dinosaur, CO.** The 25-mi. road (closed in winter) to majestic **Harper's Corner,** where the Green and Yampa River gorges meet, begins two mi. east of Dinosaur. From the road's terminus, a two-mi. round-trip nature hike leaves for the corner itself. It's worth the sweat. The view of the Green and Yampa Rivers is one of the most spectacular in all of Utah.

A rugged 13 mi. east of Harper's Corner is the **Echo Campground,** the perfect location for an adventurous evening under the stars. Watch for signs near Harper's Corner leading off to a dirt road that snakes its way past cattle and sheep into the valley below. (Free.) The **Dinosaur National Monument Headquarters,** on U.S. 40 in Dinosaur, CO (303-374-2216), at the intersection with the park road, provides orientation for the canyonlands of the park and information on river rafting. (Open June-Aug. daily 8am-4:30pm; Sept.-May Mon.-Fri. 8am-4:30pm.) For more information on this side of the park, write to the Monument Superintendent, P.O. Box

210, Dinosaur, CO 81610. Also, along U.S. 40, on the border between Utah and Colorado, is the **Colorado Welcome Center,** 101 Stegosaurus Rd. (374-2205), which offers information on various seasonal activities in Colorado. (Open 8am-6pm daily.)

The **Terrace Motel,** 301 Brontosaurus Blvd. (303-374-2241), has clean, beautiful rooms in mobile home units. (Singles $22-24. Doubles $29.) The **Park Motel,** 105 E. Brontosaurus Blvd. (303-374-2267), offers kitchenettes without pterodactyl garbage disposals. (Singles $18. Doubles $24).

Greyhound/Trailways makes a daily run both east and west along U.S. 40, fortunately not fueled by Fred and Barney's feet. (2 per day July-Aug.). They stop in Vernal and Dinosaur en route from Denver and Salt Lake City. Jensen is a flag stop, as is the monument headquarters, two mi. west of Dinosaur (disembark only). The Vernal depot is at 38 E. Main St. (789-0404; open Mon.-Fri. 10am-1pm and 4:30-5:30pm, Sat. 11am-noon and 4:30-5:30pm). From Salt Lake City to Vernal (3½ hr., $33) and Dinosaur, CO (4 hr., $42). The Dinosaur, CO, depot is at 103 W. Brontosaurus Blvd. (303-374-2711; open daily 8am-10pm).

Dinosaur, CO's **post office** services mammals at 198 Stegasaurus Dr. (303-374-2353; open Mon.-Fri. 8:30am-12:30pm and 1-5pm). The **ZIP code** is 81610. Yabba-dabba-doo.

Flaming Gorge and Brown's Hole

Curiously, Flaming Gorge never suffered a firestorm, and Brown's Hole is not a hole. The bright red canyons of northeastern Utah give the Flaming Gorge Recreation Area its name; "Brown's Hole" supposedly refers to the valley (in 1870 trapper-speak). This peaceful retreat offers ample opportunities for hiking and water sports. **Flaming Gorge National Recreation Area** is part of the **Ashley National Forest,** spanning SW Wyoming and NE Utah. A towering army dam built on the Green River in the 60s created the 91-mi. Flaming Gorge Reservoir. Now the rocks of the canyon, red from iron oxides, are reflected with the Ponderosa pine and spruce in the green water.

From Wyoming, the most scenic route to the gorge is the amazing U.S. 191 south from I-80 (exit between Rock Springs and Green River). Route 530 closely parallels the reservoir's western shore, but the only scenery in sight here will be an occasional pronghorn antelope. Take this route only if you want to camp on the flat beaches of the lake's Wyoming portion. To reach Flaming Gorge from the south, take U.S. 191 north from Vernal, over the gorgeous flanks of the Uinta Mountains (see below), to **Dutch John,** UT. Much of the recreation area is in Wyoming, but Utah has the most scenic and best-developed area of the park, at the base of the Uinta Range.

The **Flaming Gorge Dam Visitors Center** (885-3135), off U.S. 191 just outside the government building complex in Dutch John, offers guided tours of the dam area along with maps of the area ($1) and relaxing coloring books. (Open daily 9:30am-5pm; off-season daily 8am-4pm). The **Red Canyon Visitors Center** (889-3713), a few mi. off U.S. 191 on Hwy. 44 to Manila, perches a breathtaking 1,360 ft. above Red Canyon and Flaming Gorge Lake. (Open daily 9:30am-4:30pm; closed winter.)

The diversity of activities in the recreation area parallels its startling variation in terrain. Watch the locals shoot carp with bow and arrow in the high desert of the Wyoming lakeshores, or try your own hand at fishing along the steep, forested slopes of the Green River gorge below the dam. The gorge has superb fishing (in 1989 a 51½-lb. Mackinaw was caught here), but you must have a license from Wyoming and a stamp of approval from Utah (or vice versa). Call the Utah Department of Wildlife Resources, 152 E. 100 North (789-3103; open Mon.-Fri. 8am-5pm). You can rent fishing rods and boats at **Cedar Springs Marina** (869-3795), three mi. before the dam in Dutch John, and at **Lucerne Valley Marina** (784-3483) in Manila. (Boats $8-23 per hr., with 8-hr. and full-day rates. Rod rentals $10-15 per day. Open April-Aug. daily 7am-8pm.) **Hatch River Expeditions** (789-4316 or 800-342-8243; 789-

4715 after hours) offers a wide variety of summer float trips (one-day voyage $50, under 12 $40).

Inexpensive, albeit primitive, campgrounds are plentiful in the Flaming Gorge Area. You can camp right next to the Red Canyon Visitors Center in the **Red Canyon Campground** (sites $6), or in one of the numerous national forest campgrounds along Rte. 191 and 44 in the Utah portion of the park. (2-week max. stay. Sites $5.) **Buckboard Crossing** (307-875-6927) and **Lucerne Valley** (801-784-3293), located farther north, tend to be drier and unshaded, but are close to marinas on the reservoir (sites $6-7). Either visitor center can provide information on campgrounds. If you'd rather sleep indoors, try the **Flaming Gorge Lodge** (801-889-3773), near the dam in Dutch John. The immaculate rooms have A/C and cable TV but prices you may not appreciate. (Singles $43. Doubles $49. Single condos $79. Double condos $85.)

For a hideout from tourists, visit **Brown's Park,** a large valley 23 partially paved mi. east of Flaming Gorge. The valley's incredible isolation attracted western outlaws, most notably local boy Butch Cassidy and his Wild Bunch. The outlaws also made creative use of the proximity of three state lines—great for getting out of a state posse's jurisdiction. There are primitive **campsites** ¼-mi. from the camp in either direction: just up the Green River lies **Indian Crossing**, while **Indian Hollow** is just downstream. The free sites here have no water. The Green River's shore is a beautiful place to camp or land your raft after a brisk ride downstream. To get to Brown's Park from Dutch John, head north about 10 mi. on U.S. 191 until you reach Minnie's Gap; from here follow the signs east to Clay Basin (13 mi.) and to the park (23 mi.).

For further information, contact the **Flaming Gorge National Recreation Area,** Dutch John 84023 (801-885-3315; open Mon.-Fri. 8am-5pm) or, if you're coming from Wyoming, stop by the **Green River Chamber of Commerce,** 1450 Uinta Dr., on Rte. 530, Green River 82936 (307-875-5711; open Mon.-Fri. 9am-4:30pm). **Rock Springs,** WY, has a well-marked **visitor center,** 1897 Dewar Dr., a few blocks south of I-80 (307-362-3771; open Mon.-Fri. 8am-5pm). This is the most convenient brochure stockpile for those planning to go south on U.S. 191.

Finally, you can call or write the **Ashley National Forest Service** in Vernal (see Vernal), or send a Manila envelope. (P.O. Box 278, Manila, UT 84046; 801-789-1181).

Uinta Mountains

Descended from nomadic bands of hunters and gatherers, the Ute (Yoot) in the Three Corners region were first displaced by white men in the early 1800s. Fur trappers originally entered the area drawn by beaver, hoping eventually to establish a mountain rendezvous site; by the 1830s mountaineers like Jim Bridger and Jedediah Smith had saturated the Uintas, clashing with the Ute. The trappers managed to hold on until the beaver ran out, even having a wild annual rendezvous in the area. Today, the inscrutable peaks and silent valleys of the Uintas' hold few Native Americans and primarily attract hikers.

The **Ashley** and **Wasatch National Forests** encompass most of the mountains; Utah's tallest peaks lie within the **High Uintas Wilderness Area,** a subsidiary of these two government territories. Here, even the most harassed city-dweller can find peace amid the tundra-covered meadows of the Uintas high country. The only major east-west range in the U.S., the Uintas have different environments on the shaded northern and exposed southern slopes. The mountains parallel U.S. 40, the main road connecting Vernal, UT, with Salt Lake City. While the southern slope is the more developed and accessible of the two, hiking connoisseurs claim that the northern slope is prettier. This slope is most accessible to I-80 via Rte. 414 or 530, or U.S. 191 out of southwestern Wyoming. Most trailheads on the northern side can be reached from Manila, UT, on Rte. 44, which goes to **Browne Lake** and **Deep Creek campgrounds** (pit toilets and water that should be boiled before drinking; sites free). From here, the well-equipped backpacker can plunge into the wilder regions to the south and west. For more information, contact Ashley National Forest's Flaming Gorge ranger station in Manila, at the intersection of Rte. 43 and 44. (801-789-1181; open Mon.-Sat. 8am-5pm.) Several campgrounds line U.S. 191 as it winds through the aspen glens from Flaming Gorge south into Vernal and the arid Ashley Valley. Neither as remote nor as scenic as those near Manila, the campgrounds are bigger, however, and far more convenient. **Lodgepole**, 30 mi. north of Vernal on Hwy. 91, is the best of the bunch. (Sites $6. Open June-Sept.)

Some easy trails out of Vernal include the East Park and Oak Park Trails, but hardier backpackers will want to head straight for the wilderness area, where 13,000-ft. peaks tower over an unsullied wilderness (no vehicles allowed). The best departure points (Sat.-Sun. only) are on the southern slope, 12 mi. off U.S. 40. **Moon Lake** and **Yellow Pine campgrounds** in the **Rock Creek Canyon** are each just outside the primitive area boundary. Both are a few mi. north of the tiny hamlet of **Mountain Home**, 20 mi. north of U.S. 40 on Rte. 87. The High Uintas can also be approached from the west, through Wasatch National Forest off Rte. 150, which provides the quickest access to the range from Salt Lake City. For information on southern access to the primitive area, contact the **Duchesne Ranger District**, P.O. Box I, Duchesne, UT 84021 (801-738-2482), or stop by their office in Duchesne, on U.S. 40. (Open Mon.-Fri. 8am-5pm.) For western access, contact the **Wasatch-Cache National Forest**, 125 S. State St., Salt Lake City 84138 (801-524-5030).

Vernal

Vernal is central to both Flaming Gorge and the Uinta Mountains, 16 mi. west of the Dinosaur National Monument on U.S. 40. The town is a perfect base for exploring the Three Corners Area. Visit the Utah Travel Council's desk (789-4002), at the Natural History Museum, for many brochures on one-day drives in the area. (Open daily 8am-7pm; off-season hours shorter.) Or contact the **chamber of commerce**, 50 E. Main St., Vernal 84078 (789-1352; open Mon.-Fri. 8am-5pm). The **Ashley National Forest Service**, 355 N. Vernal Ave. (789-1181), has jurisdiction over much of this area, including most public campgrounds. (Open Mon.-Fri. 8:30am-5pm, Sat. 8am-noon, 12:30-4:30pm.)

Stop in at the **Utah Fieldhouse of Natural History and Dinosaur Garden**, 235 Main St. (789-3799). The full-scale dinosaur models strutting among garden plants somehow come off as less than grandiose, but the well-run museum has excellent displays on the natural and human history of the area, with special attention paid to the Ute and the region's geology. The fluorescent minerals make your shoelaces glow in the dark. (Open May 27-Sept. 2 daily 8am-7pm; off-season daily 9am-5pm. $1, kids 50¢.)

Sleeping cheaply in Vernal is easy. The simple **Sage Motel**, 54 W. Main St. (789-1442), has big rooms and runs a coffee shop next door popular with truck drivers. (Singles $20-22. Doubles $28-34.) If you ask for rooms on the "old side" at the **Econolodge**, 311 E. Main St. (789-2000), you might be able to swing rates lower than those originally quoted. (Singles $32. Doubles $36.) The closest campground is mundane **Campground Dina RV Park**, 930 N. Vernal Ave. (789-2148), about one mi. north of Main St. on Hwy. 46 and 191. (1-person sites $5, 2-person sites $10, with electricity and water $13, full hookup $14.)

Zion National Park

Some 13 million years ago, the cliffs and canyons of Zion made up the sea floor. The sea has been reduced to the lone, powerful Virgin River, which today carves fingers through the Navajo sandstone. Cut into the Kolob Terrace, the walls of Zion now tower 2,400 ft. above the river. In the 1860s, Mormon settlers came to this area and enthusiastically proclaimed they had found the promised land. But Brigham Young thought otherwise and declared to his followers that the place was awfully nice, but "not Zion". The name "not Zion" stuck for years until a new wave of entranced explorers dropped the "not," giving the park its present name.

There are two visitor centers in the park. The main visitor center, **Zion Canyons Visitor Center** (722-3256), takes up the southeast corner of the park, ½-mi. off Rte. 9, which connects I-15 and Hwy. 89 along the southern border of the park. It has an introductory slide program and a small but interesting museum. The **Kolob Canyons Visitor Center** (586-9548) lies in the northwest corner of the park, off I-15. (Both open daily 8am-8pm; off-season daily 8am-5pm.) The park entrance fee is $5 per car, $2 per pedestrian. Carry water wherever you go in the park. For emergency assistance, call 772-3256 or 800-624-9447.

Even if you wisely plan to visit **Kolob Canyon's** backcountry, be sure to make the pilgrimage to **Zion Canyon.** Drive along the seven-mi. dead-end road that follows the floor of the canyon, take the bus-tram (summer only; $5, kids $2.50), or the upper canyon tour (summer only; $2.75, kids $1.75). You'll ride through the giant formations of **Sentinel, Mountain of the Sun,** and the overwhelming symbol of Zion, the **Great White Throne.** Short hikes to the base of the cliffs may be made by wheelchair as well as on foot. A challenging trail takes you to **Observation Point,** where steep switchbacks let you explore an impossibly gouged canyon. Another difficult trail (5 mi.) ascends to **Angel's Landing,** a lonely monolith that offers a heart-stopping path along the ridge and an amazing view of the canyon. A great short hike (2 mi.) runs to the Upper Emerald Pool, passing the less spectacular lower and middle pools on the way. For fun without the sweat, rent an inner tube ($5) from the shop across from the Canyon supermarket, and float down the Virgin River near the campgrounds at the southern entrance.

Try to stay in Springdale (at the southern entrance to the park) at **Under the Eaves,** 980 Zion Blvd. (772-3457), featuring four-poster beds, stained glass windows, and an old-fashioned tub with feet. (Singles $30-35. Doubles $35-45. Room for larger groups includes full breakfast and great coffee. Make reservations early.)

Forty mi. south of Zion in the town of **Kanab** is the **Canyonlands International Youth Hostel,** 143 East 100th South (801-644-5554). The hostel offers roomy bunks, and manager Earl will give you free coffee and friendly conversation. Feels like home. ($8.)

The park maintains two campgrounds at the south gate. **South Campground** and **Watchman Campground.** Bathrooms and drinking water are available, but not showers. (Sites $6, 2-week max. stay. Always open.) Sites cost the same and showers cost $2 at **Zion Canyon Campground.** The visitor center rangers present campfire programs nightly at 9pm at these two locations. Conveniences include a grocery store (772-3402; open 8am-8pm) and coin-op laundry just outside the south entrance, about a 10-minute walk from the campgrounds. The park's only other campground is a primitive area at **Lava Point,** accessible from a hiking trail in the midsection of the park or from the gravel road that turns off Rte. 9 in **Virgin.** You must obtain a free permit from the visitor center for **backcountry camping.** You cannot camp within Zion Canyon itself. Observation Point provides one of the only canyon rim spots where you can pitch a tent. Many backpackers spend a few nights on the 27-mi. **West Rim Trail** (too long for a day's hike) or in the Kolob Canyons, where crowds never converge. Zion Campground doesn't take reservations and often fills on holiday and summer weekends; if you don't get in, try one of the six campgrounds in Dixie National Forest (see Bryce Canyon).

Zion National Park can be reached from I-15, via Rte. 17 (Toqueville exit) or from U.S. 89, via Rte. 9 (at Mount Carmel Junction). The main entrance to the park is in **Springdale,** on Rte. 9, which bounds the park to the south along the Virgin River.

Greyhound/Trailways runs along I-15, to the west of the park; ask to be let off, since the park is not a scheduled stop. In St. George (43 mi. southwest of the park on I-15), the bus station is located on 70 W. George Blvd. (677-2933), next to the Travelodge. Two buses run daily to Salt Lake City (6 hr., $52) and Provo (5 hr., $42.50); five buses daily to Los Angeles (15 hr., $81) and Las Vegas (2 hr., $27).

VERMONT

Though insulated and isolated by the luxuriant Green Mountain range that dominates the state, Vermonters from every sparsely settled pocket have never shied from public, vocal dissent. The state celebrated its Bicentennial last year only after 1989's half-serious secession debates urging invocation of a mythic "escape clause." Vermonters voice their opinions proudly, from conservatism (only Vermont and Maine voted against Franklin Roosevelt all four elections) to liberalism (Burlington's socialist mayor Bernie Sanders has taken his views all the way to an Independent seat in the U.S. House of Representatives).

Several decades ago, many dissatisfied young urbanites headed to Vermont for its promise of peace and serenity. Disparate though their backgraounds may have been, the migrants and long-time residents seem to have found common ground over organic farming techniques and the latest in wood stoves. With the 80s, a less benign wave of urban fugitives discovered the state. But Vermonters are have responded to the influx of BMWs with anti-littering legislation and the prohibition of billboards. Should tourism continue to threaten the pristine landscape, Vermonters, no doubt, will be heard.

Practical Information

Capital: Montpelier.

Vermont Travel Division, 134 State St., Montpelier 05602 (828-3236; open Mon.-Fri. 7:45am-4:30pm; longer hours during fall foliage), or the **Chamber of Commerce,** P.O. Box 37, Montpelier 05602, on Granger Rd., I-89 exit 7 in Berlin (223-3443; open Mon.-Fri. 8:30am-5pm) for info on lodging, attractions, dining, and camping. **Department of Forests, Parks, and Recreation,** 103 S. Main St., Waterbury 05676 (244-8711; open Mon.-Fri. 7:45am-4:30pm); **U.S. Forest Supervisor,** Green Mountains National Forest, 151 West St., P.O. Box 519, Rutland 05702 (773-0300; open Mon.-Fri. 8am-4:30pm); and **District Ranger,** Green Mountains National Forest RFD#4, Middlebury 05753 (388-4362), or RD#1, P.O. Box 108, Rochester 05767 (767-4261) for the scoop on exploring the great outdoors. **Travel Division Fall Foliage Hotline** for fall colors info (828-3239). **Vermont Snowline** (229-0531), all day Nov.-May on snow conditions.

Public Transport: Vermont Transit Lines, 135 Saint Paul St., Burlington 05401 (864-6811 for info).

Time Zone: Eastern. **Postal Abbreviation:** VT

Skiing

Twenty-four downhill resorts and 47 cross-country trail systems crisscross Vermont. For a free winter attractions packet, call the Vermont Travel Division (see Practical Information above), or write **Ski Vermont,** 134 State St., Montpelier 05602. Ask about the Ski Vermont Classics program and the Vermont Sunday Take-Off package.

Vermont's famous downhill ski resorts offer a great range of terrain and accommodations, including cheap dorms. Some better resorts include: **Killington** (773-1300; 107 trails, 18 lifts, 6 mountains, and the most extensive snowmaking system in the world); **Stratton** (297-2200; villa lodging 800-843-6867; area lodging 824-6915; 92 trails, 12 lifts); **Sugarbush** (583-2381; lodging 800-537-8427; 80 trails, 16 lifts, 2 mountains); **Stowe** (253-8521; lodging 800-247-8693; 44 trails, 10 lifts; see Stowe for more details); and **Jay Peak** (800-451-4449; 37 trails, 6 lifts). Cross-country resorts include the **Trapp Family Lodge,** Stowe (253-8511; lodging 800-247-8693; 60 mi. of trails); **Mountain Meadows,** Killington (757-7077; 25 mi.); **Woodstock** (457-2114; 47 mi.); and **Sugarbush-Rossignol** (583-2301 or 800-451-4320; 30 mi.).

Bennington

A minor industrial center, Bennington (pop. 16,700) is still a quintessential American small town. Pick up a map and *Historic Bennington Walking Tours* at the **chamber of commerce,** Veteran's Memorial Dr. (447-3311), behind the deer park. From the bus terminal, turn right and walk up the street about 1½ mi. Stand next to the bus station for a cab (around $2.25). (Open May-Oct. Mon.-Fri. 9am-6pm, Sat. 9am-5pm, Sun. 10am-4pm; off-season Mon.-Fri. 9am-5pm.)

Among the town's many old buildings is the **Old First Church (First Congregational Church),** Monument Ave. (447-1223). Established in 1702, and built in 1805, the church is home to the oldest Protestant religious organization in Vermont; glance inside. The building is still used for Sunday services (11am). (Open to the public July-Oct. daily 10am-noon and 1-4pm.) Next door to the church lies the **Old Burying Ground,** the oldest landmark in Bennington. Soldiers, statesmen, settlers, and Robert Frost sleep in these snowy woods. Down the road most taken is the **Bennington Museum,** W. Main St. (447-1571), with the world's largest collection of Grandma Moses's folk paintings and the oldest Stars and Stripes in existence. (Open March-late Dec. daily 9am-5pm. Admission $4.50, seniors and students $3.50, under 12 free.) Up the hill, the **Bennington Battle Monument,** a 306-ft. obelisk at the end of Monument Ave., commemorates Gen. John Stark's victory over the British. The 200-ft.-high observation deck gives a great view of. . .not much. (Open daily April 1-Nov. 1 9am-5pm; admission $1, under 12 50¢, under 6 free; gift shop 447-0550.) Although the Battle of Bennington actually took place 15 mi. away, the annual reenactment takes place here on August 16. The week surrounding that day is full of celebration, most notably the Firemen's competition and the parade.

To escape the steady stream of traffic through the center of town try **Back-Road Country Tours** (442-3876). For $12.50 per person you get a one-hour jeep ride through the back roads of Bennington County with commentary on the local farms, covered bridges, wildlife, and folklore. (Open daily. Longer tours available.)

Geannelis' Restaurant, 520 Main St. (442-9778), is very popular. The revolving menu hanging from the ceiling induces vertigo while listing tasty sandwiches ($1.50), dinner ($4.65-6), and fine homemade ice cream (cone 95¢). (Open Mon.-Sat. 6am-8pm, Sun. 7am-8pm.) **Occasionally Yogurt,** 604 Main St. (442-2526), has big salads ($2-5), sandwich pockets, and frozen yogurt topped with carob chips ($1-2). (Open daily 11am-10pm.)

Affordable accommodations are much more occasional here. The Chamber of Commerce has a complete listing, with prices and services, of local accommodations. B&Bs tend to be expensive. In town try the **Mid-town Motel,** 107 W. Main St. (447-0189; from the bus station, turn right on Washington Ave. and left on W. Main St.), where rooms are dark but clean (singles $30-38, doubles $44-50). Further east is the **Homestead Motor Inn,** 924 E. Main St. (442-3143; 20-min. walk from the bus station), with brighter, big rooms (singles $33, doubles $38; donuts and coffee morning in lobby). **Camping,** as usual, is far cheaper. **Greenwood Lodge and Tentsites,** P.O. Box 246, Bennington (442-2547), is an 8-mi. trip east on Rte. 9 to Woodford Valley. Watch for the Prospect Ski Area sign. Vermont Transit's Bennington-to-Brattleboro van will drop you here—ask for a ticket to Woodford. The Long Trail is just 3 mi. away. (Hostel: $12 per person, linen $2, towel 50¢. Kitchen available. Campsite: 20 uncrowded, quiet sites. $12 for 2 people, $2 each additional person. Open Memorial Day-Oct. Hostel open Memorial Day-Labor Day. Call ahead. Membership advisable.) You can also stay at **Woodford State Park** (447-7169), 10 mi. east on Rte. 9, were you can fish, swim, or boat (canoe and rowboat rental $5.25 per hr.) 4½ mi. from the Appalachian Trail. (Open May 27-Oct. 14. Day-use $1.50, ages 4-13 $1. Sites $9 for 4 people, $3 each additional person. Reservations made min. 3 days in advance $3 extra. Lean-tos $13.50.) **Pine Hollow Camping Area** (823-5569), Old Military Rd., off Barber's Pond Rd., off U.S. 7, is

6-mi. south of Bennington, and offers swimming and tranquility. (Open May 15-Oct. 15. Sites for 2 adults $10, with hookup $12.)

Vermont Transit, 126 Washington Ave. (442-4808), takes you to Brattleboro (1 per day, 2 on Fri. and Sun.; 1 hr.); Middlebury (3 per day, 2½ hr.); Rutland (3 per day, 1½ hr.); Burlington (3 per day, 3½ hr.); Montréal (1 per day, 8 hr.); New York City (5 per day, 4½ hr.); Boston (4 per day, 4-6 hr.). (Open Mon.-Fri. 9am-noon and 1:30-4:30pm, Sat.-Sun. 9:15-11:15am and 2:30-4:30pm, Fri. and Sun. 7:45-8:30pm.)

Bennington's **ZIP code** is 05201; the **area code** is 802.

Up Rte. 67A in North Bennington is the **Park-McCullough House** (442-5441), a beautifully restored Victorian mansion complete with carriage house and carefully groomed gardens. (Open early May-Oct. daily 10am-4pm. Admission $3, seniors $2.50, ages 12-17 $1.50, under 12 free. Tours on the hr.) The family that owned the house gave generously to nearby **Bennington College,** now renowned for its creative writing and arts departments, although it still has the highest tuition of any college in the country. Pick up campus maps at the **Admissions Office.** (Open May-Aug. Mon.-Fri. 9am-3pm; Sept.-April Mon.-Fri. 9am-3pm, Sat. 9-11am. Tours can be arranged by appointment.)

About 14 mi. north on bucolic Rte. 7A is **Arlington,** one-time home of illustrator Norman Rockwell. An old church on Rte. 7A houses the **Norman Rockwell Exhibition,** a collection of his *Saturday Evening Post* covers and other works. His one-time models act as tour guides. (375-6423; open May-Oct. daily 9am-5pm; Nov.-April Mon.-Fri. 10am-4pm, Sat.-Sun. 9am-5pm. Admission $1, under 7 free; free in winter). **Lake Shaftsbury State Park** (375-9978), a few miles south of Arlington on Rte. 7A, has a fine picnic area, swimming, and boat rental. (Open Memorial Day-Labor Day daily 10am-sunset. Day-use only. Admission $1.50, ages 4-13 $1, under 4 free. Rowboats and canoes $5 per ½-hr., pedal boats $5 per hr.)

Brattleboro

Southeastern Vermont is often accused of living too much in its colonial past. A favorite destination for peregrinating hippies, Brattleboro (pop. 12,000), is more a captive of the Age of Aquarius. Indian prints are ubiquitous. The smell of patchouli wafts through the air. Craft and food cooperatives abound. Bumpers are a palimpsest of opinion. Nature worship peaks during fall when utopia swells with an influx of tourists, and residents and visitors alike let down their hair to celebrate the foliage.

Take the Brattleboro town bus (257-1761) from the bus station into town (75¢) to the **chamber of commerce,** 180 Main St. (254-4565). The chamber can provide you with countless brochures, among them the Brattleboro main street walking tour. (Open Mon.-Fri. 8am-5pm.) In summer, information booths are open on the Town Common off Putney Rd. (257-1112), and on Western Ave. (257-4801), just beyond the historic **Creamery Bridge** built in 1879. (Putney Rd. booth—open summer Mon.-Fri. 9am-6pm. During fall foliage and peak summer months open weekends 9am-6pm. Western Ave. booth open Thurs.-Sun. 9am-6pm.)

Brattleboro is right on the Connecticut River, which you can explore by canoe. Rentals are available at **Connecticut River Safari** (257-5008 or 254-4081) on Putney Rd. (Open mid-June to Labor Day daily 8am-8pm, 2-hr. minimum $8; $12 per ½-day, $18 per day, 2 days $28; longer packages available.) They also run a touring and guiding service on the Connecticut and other New England rivers.

The **Brattleboro Museum and Art Center** (257-0124), in the Old Railroad Station on Vernon St., overlooks the river. Although small, this first-rate museum exhibits a permanent collection of 19th-century Estey organs manufactured by a Brattleboro entrepeneur. Don't dismiss this as a country-bumpkin museum. Take the time to contribute to their family history room. Readings, artist talks, and curator views are offered Tuesday at noon and Thursday at 7:30pm in the summer. Call for information. (Open May 13-Nov. 4 Tues.-Sun. noon-6pm. Admission $2, seniors and students $1, under 18 free.)

Inexpensive places to eat proliferate. The **Common Ground,** 25 Eliot St. (257-0855), where workers unite without a boss, supports organic farmers and cottage industries. It features a wide range of affordable veggie dishes. You can get soup, salad, bread, and beverage for $3.85, good ole PB&J for $2.70. For dinner, try a square meal in a round bowl. (Open June-Nov. Wed.-Sat. 11:30am-9pm, Sun. brunch 10:30am-1:30pm and dinner 5:30-9pm; Dec.-May Sun.-Thurs. 11:30am-9pm, Fri.-Sat. 11:30am-8:30pm.) The **Backside Café,** 24 High St. (257-5056), serves delicious food in an artsy loft with rooftop dining. The Backside Chicken with mozzarella ($4) and a bottle of Bass or Sam Adams beer ($2.25) should please your insides. (Open Mon.-Thurs. 7:30am-4pm and 5-8:30pm, Fri. 7:30am-4pm and 5-9pm, Sat. 8am-3pm, Sun. 10am-3pm.) For locally-grown fruits, vegetables, and cider, go to the **farmers' markets** on the Town Common, Main St. (June 12-Sept. 11 Wed. 10am-2pm), or on Western Ave. near Creamery Bridge (May 11-Oct. 12 Sat. 9am-2pm).

The renovated Art-Deco **Latchis Hotel,** 2 Flat St. (254-6300) downtown, has nice rooms at decent prices but they don't rent to anyone under 21. (Singles $38-52. Doubles $46-62.) The **West Village,** 480 Western Ave. (254-5610), is about 3 mi. out of town on Rte. 9 in West Brattleboro. (Singles with kitchenette and microwave $30. Doubles with fridge and microwave $35, weekly $150.) West Village caters to the weekly client, taking reservations no more than one week in advance. Somewhat closer to town is newly renovated **Days Inn** on Putney Rd. (254-4583) down from the bus station. (Double-bed $39, 2 double beds $45, king-sized $47. $6 each additional adult, rollaway bed $6. Free continental breakfast.) **Fort Dummer State Park,** Old Guildford Rd. (254-2610), just a few miles south on U.S. 5, has campsites with fireplaces, picnic tables, and bathroom facilities. (Tentsites $7.50. Lean-tos $12. Firewood $2 per armload. Hot showers 25¢. Reservations accepted up to 21 days in advance. Open May 24-Labor Day.) **Molly Stark State Park** (464-5460) is 15 mi. west of town on Rte. 9. (24 tentsites, $7.50 each. 10 lean-tos, $12 each. Hot showers 25¢. Reservations $3, minimum of 3 days in advance. Open Memorial Day-Columbus Day.)

Mole's Eye Café (257-0771), at the corner of High and Main St., has rock, r&b, blues, and reggae bands on Wednesday, Friday, and Saturday nights at 9pm. (Open daily 11:30am-midnight or 1am. Light meals about $5. Cover $3. Wed. free.) **Colors,** 20 Eliot St. (254-8646), is a relaxing place popular with both a gay and a straight clientele, with huge felt irises on the wall. (Open Sun.-Fri. 8pm-2am. Cover Thurs.-Sat. $2.) The **Arts Council of Windham County,** 69 Main St. (257-1881), hosts local art openings the first Friday of every month as well as poetry readings and artists discussing their work. (Gallery open Fri.-Sat. noon-8pm, Sun. and Wed.-Thurs. noon-4pm.) Foliage vultures can sample high culture by attending **Brattelboro Music Center's New England Bach Festival.** Internationally renowned, the festival runs annually from early October through early November, featuring vocal and instrumental soloists.

Amtrak's (800-872-7245) "Montrealer" train from New York City and Springfield stops in Brattleboro behind the museum. Trains go once daily to Montréal and south to New York and Washington DC. Arrange tickets and reservations at **Lyon Travel,** 10 Elliot St. (254-6033; open Mon.-Fri. 9am-5pm). **Greyhound** and **Vermont Transit** (254-6066) stop in the parking lot behind the Texaco station at I-91 exit 3. (Open Mon.-Thurs. 8am-5pm, Fri. 8am-7pm, Sat. 8am-12:15pm, Sun. 10:30am-12:15pm, 2-3:30pm, and 6-7pm.) Brattleboro is on Vermont Transit's Burlington-New York City route (3 per day, $35). Other destinations include Springfield, MA (3 per day, $12) and White River Junction (3 per day, $12), with connections to Montpelier, Waterbury, Burlington, and Montréal.

Brattleboro's **ZIP code** is 05301; The **area code** is 802.

Burlington

On the banks of Lake Champlain, Burlington (pop. 38,000) might at first seem to be just another waterside suburb. But this is Vermont, folks; Burlington is the state's major city. Burlington's downtown core foxtrots with an energy that defies suburban lethargy (or Vermont reticence, for that matter); the University of Vermont (UVM), Champlain College, and three other schools endow the city with the swank and smarm of youth.

Practical Information

Emergency: 911.

Tourist Information: Lake Champlain Regional Chamber of Commerce, 209 Battery St. (863-3489), right next to the ferry pier. Provides maps of the Burlington Bike Path and parks. Open Mon.-Fri. 8:30am-5pm, Sat.-Sun. 10am-2pm; late Sept.-late June Mon.-Fri. 8:30am-5pm. More centrally located is the **Church St. Marketplace Information Booth,** on the corner of Church and Bank. Open May 15-Oct. 15 Mon.-Sat. 11am-4pm. During foliage, open daily 11am-5pm.

Amtrak: 29 Railroad Ave., Essex Jct. (800-872-7245 or 879-7298), 5 mi. from the center of Burlington. A stop for both the "Montrealer" and the "Yankee Clipper" (1 per day, 4 hr., $18) to New York (2 per day; 9 hr.; $67, 25% discount for seniors, children ½-price). Open daily 5:45am-noon, 1-6pm, and 7-11pm. Bus to downtown every ½ hr., 75¢.

Buses: Vermont Transit, 135 Saint Paul St. (864-6811), at Main St. Connections to Boston ($39), Montréal ($16), White River Junction ($13.80), Middlebury ($6.75), Bennington ($17.20), Montpelier ($7), and Albany ($28.45). Open Mon.-Thurs. and Sat. 7am-8:30pm, Fri. and Sun. 7am-11:30pm.

Public Transport: Chittenden County Transit Authority (CCTA), 864-0211. Frequent, reliable service. Downtown hub at Cherry and Church St. Connections with Shelburne and other outlying areas. Buses operate Mon.-Sat. 5:45am-10:30pm, depending on routes; generally leave at a quarter to and a quarter past. Fare 75¢, seniors and disabled 35¢, under 18 50¢, under 5 free. **Special Services Transportation Agency** (658-5817), can advise about disabled travel.

Taxi: Yellow Cab, 864-7411. $1.20 per mi. **Checker Taxi,** 864-7474.

Bike Rental: Ski Rack, 85 Main St. (658-3313). Single speed cruiser ($6 per hr., $10 per ½-day, $10 per day), road bike ($6, $10, $15), mountain bike ($6, $20, $25), tandem ($10, $25, $35). Multi-day rates available. Helmet and lock included. Open Mon.-Thurs. 9am-7pm, Fri. 9am-9pm, Sat. 9am-6pm, Sun. noon-5pm.

Help Lines: Women's Rape Crisis Center, 863-1236. **Crises Services of Chittenden County,** 656-3587.

Post Office: 11 Elmwood Ave. (863-6033), at Pearl St. Open Mon.-Fri. 8am-5pm, Sat. 9am-noon. **ZIP code:** 05401.

Area Code: 802.

Accommodations, Camping, and Food

The Chamber of Commerce has complete accommodations listings for the area. Bed & Breakfasts are generally found in the outlying suburbs. Reasonably priced hotels and guest houses pepper Shelburne Rd. south of downtown. Three mi. from downtown, **Mrs. Farrell's Home Hostel (AYH),** 27 Arlington (865-3730), has four or, if necessary, six beds. (Members $10. Nonmembers $12. Linen $2. Accessible by public transport Mon.-Sat.) Reservations are required. Getting hold of the owner is difficult—try calling between 7 and 8am and 5 and 7pm. Within walking distance of the bus station is **Howden Cottage,** 32 N. Champlain (864-7198). A local artist will rent you a slope-ceilinged room and bake muffins for your continental breakfast in this charming B&B. (Singles $35, doubles $45. Rates may rise slightly. Reservations strongly recommended.) **The Midtown Motel, 230 Main St. (862-9686), up the hill from the bus station, is ideally located. (Singles $30, doubles $35.)North**

Beach Campsites, Institute Rd. (862-0942), is only 1½ mi. north of town on Rte. 127, along Lake Champlain. (Open May 15-Oct. 1. Sites $10-17. Showers 25¢, beach free.) Take the CCTA North Ave. bus leaving from the main city terminal on Saint Paul St. **Shelburne Campground,** Shelburne Rd. (985-2540), 1 mi. north of the center of Shelburne and 5 mi. south of Burlington, offers a pool, laundry facilities, and free showers. Buses en route to Shelburne South stop right next to the campground. (Open May-Oct. Sites $15, $17-21 with varying degrees of hookup, for 2 people, $1 each additional person.)

Henry's Diner, 155 Bank St. (862-9010), has been the place to meet the locals and eat good, inexpensive food since 1925. (Sandwiches $2-4, full meals $5-10. Open Mon. 7am-2:30pm, Tues.-Thurs. 6:30am-4pm, Fri.-Sat. 6:30am-8pm, Sun. 8am-2pm.) where Henry's has history, its competition, **Oasis Diner,** 189 Bank St. (864-5308), borrows it. Men wearing white hats and aprons serve similar cuisine at similar prices in a brushed-aluminum setting. (Open Mon.-Sat. 5:30am-4:30pm.) A must-visit is **Noonies Deli,** at 131 Main St. (658-3354; also at 142 N. Winooski). Fill up on their huge, delicious sandwiches on home-made bread ($3-4), and taste the treat that began it all: the Noonie, frozen chocolate-covered cheesecake on a stick. (Open Mon.-Wed. 7am-9pm, Thurs. 7am-10pm, Fri. 7am-midnight, Sat.-Sun. 8am-9pm.) Catch their coffee house (Fri. 8pm-midnight).

Sights and Entertainment

With its sprawling, low-lying suburbs, Burlington might not look like a cultural mecca, but it still manages to take full advantage of its scenic location, youthful exuberance, artistic community, and alluring history. **Church Street Transit Loop and Marketplace** downtown embodies these virtues; this historic district serves as a shopping center for modern northern Vermont while displaying and selling the works of local artists. Wander around the world by strolling the Church St. "earth-line," a recreation of exotic places in post-modern juxtaposition. The history-inclined also should stroll through Victorian **South Willard Street,** which now houses Champlain College, and the campus of the **University of Vermont** (656-3480), founded in 1797. **City Hall Park,** in the heart of downtown, and **Battery Street Park,** right on Lake Champlain, are beautiful places to relax and scope scenery.

Plenty of food and drink for thought can be found at the **Vermont Pub and Brewery,** 144 College St. (865-0500), at Saint Paul's, which offers affordable sandwiches, delicious homemade beers, and English pub favorites like cornish pasties. Should you want to learn more about Keller Original Vermont Lager, the brewers and publicans would be happy to escort you on a brewery tour. (Open Mon.-Fri. 11:30am-12:30am, Fri.-Sat. 11:30am-1:30am, Sun. 2pm-midnight. Free tours Wed. at 8pm and Sat. at 4pm. Others by appointment. Live entertainment Thurs.-Sun.) A fine wine and cheese feast can be purchased at the **Cheese Outlet,** 400 Pine St. (863-3968 or 800-447-1205). Purchase wine for as little as $4.99 in this strong-smelling warehouse. (Open Mon.-Thurs. 9am-5:30pm, Fri. 9am-6:30pm, Sat. 9:30am-5pm.) Across the street, the smell of rich, dark chocolate wafts around the **Lake Champlain Chocolate Company,** 431 Pine St. (864-1807). Savor a sample in the store overlooking the workroom. (Open Mon.-Fri. 9:30am-5:30pm, Sat. 9:30am-5pm.)

Summer culture vultures won't want to miss the many festivities Burlington offers: the **Champlain Shakespeare Festival** in mid-July, the **Vermont Mozart Festival** (862-7352) in July and early August, the **EarthPeace International Film Festival** in late June (863-7992), and the **Discover Jazz Festival** (863-7992) in early to mid-June. The Flynn Theatre Box Office, 153 Main St. (863-5966), handles sales for the Mozart and jazz performances. (Open Mon.-Fri. 10am-5pm, Sat. 10am-1pm.) The **Flynn Theatre** is a show unto itself. This movie house, built in 1930, has spectacular Art Deco decor and sponsors free folk concerts in Battery Park running from early June to late August. Contact the chamber of commerce for more info.

Near Burlington

Seven mi. south of Burlington in **Shelburne** is the **Shelburne Museum** (985-3344), which houses one of the best collections of Americana in the country. Beside 35 buildings transported from all over New England, 45-acre Shelburne has a covered bridge from Cambridge, a paddleboat and a lighthouse from Lake Champlain, and a bit of a local railroad. Don't miss the Degas, Cassatt, and Monet paintings. Tickets are valid for two days; you'll need both to cover the mile-long exhibit. (Open mid-May to mid-Oct. daily 9am-5pm. Admission $14, ages 6-14 $6, under 6 free.) Five mi. farther south on Rte. 7, the **Vermont Wildflower Farm** (425-3500), has a seed shop and 6½ acres of wildflower gardens. (Open April to mid-Oct. daily 10am-5pm. Admission April-May free; July-Oct. $2, seniors $1.50, under 12 free.)

Northeast of Burlington on Rte. 127 is the **Ethan Allen Homestead** (865-4556). In the 1780s, Allen, who forced the surrender of Fort Ticonderoga and helped establish the state of Vermont, built his cabin in what is now the Winooski Valley Park. A multi-media show and tour give insight into the hero and his state. (Open late May-late Oct. Summer Mon.-Sat. 10am-5pm, Sun. 1-5pm; spring Tues.-Sun. 1-5pm, fall Mon.-Sun. 1-5pm. Admission $3.50, seniors $2.50, kids 5-17 $2, under 5 free.)

Ferries crisscross the **Lake Champlain,** a 100-mi.-long lake, between Vermont's Green Mountains and New York's Adirondacks. The **Lake Champlain Ferry** (864-9804), at the bottom of King St., will ship you across the lake and back from Burlington's King St. Dock to Port Kent, NY. (June 20-Sept. 2 daily 7:30am-7:30pm, 14 per day; May 16-June 19 8am-5:30pm, 8 per day; Sept. 3-Oct. 20 8am-5:30pm, 8-11 per day. Fare $3, ages 6-12 $1, with car $12.) You can also take a ferry from Grand Isle to Plattsburg, NY, or go 14 mi. south of Burlington and take one from Charlotte, VT, to Essex, NY (either fare $1.75, ages 6-12 50¢, with car $6.75). A little less adventurous but just as rewarding is the **Spirit of Ethan Allen** scenic cruise (862-9685), departing from Burlington's Perkins Pier at the bottom of Maple St. The boat cruises along the Vermont coast, giving passengers a close-up view of the famous Thrust Fault, invisible from land. (Open May 25-Oct. 20. Cruises mid-May to early Sept. daily at 10am, noon, 2 and 4pm; early Sept. to mid-Oct. at noon and 2pm. Admission $7.16, ages 3-12 $3.50. Call about the more costly Captain's Dinner and Sunset Cruises.) The peak of nearby **Mt. Philo State Park** (425-2390) affords great views of the environs. (Open Memorial Day-Columbus Day daily 10am-sunset. Campsites $7.50. Lean-tos $12. Admission $1.50. Kids $1.) Take the Vermont Transit bus from Burlington heading south along Rte. 7 to Vergennes. Twisting U.S. 2 cuts through the center of the lake by hopping from the mainland to Grand Isle to North Hero Island and then to Québec, Canada.

Several state campgrounds speckle the islands, and much of the surrounding land is wilderness. The marsh to the north is protected in the **Missiquoi National Wildlife Refuge.** Camp at **Burton Island State Park** (524-6353), accessible only by ferry (8:30am-6:30pm) from Kill Kare State Park, 50 mi. north of Burlington and 3½ mi. southwest of St. Albans off U.S. 7. The camp has 46 lean-to and tent sites ($15.50 and $11 respectively, $3 per additional person in tent, $4 in lean-to). **Grand Isle** has its own state park with camping (372-4300), just off U.S. 2 north of Keeler Bay. (Sites $9-11, lean-tos $12.50-14.)

Montpelier

Visitors to Montpelier (pop. 8200) rapidly discover what residents have long known: being the smallest state capital in the union allows the maintenance of an intimate small town timbre with the cultivation of cultural and financial boons that come with being an important city. The first perk is an 8-ft.-high Ethan Allen, crafted out of Vermont marble—Allen calls for the surrender of Fort Ticonderoga while adorning the entrance to the gold-domed **State House,** 115 State St. Their thorough brochure guides you on an informative tour. (Open daily Mon.-Fri. 8am-4pm. Tours July to mid-Oct. Mon.-Fri. 10am-3:30pm, Sat. 11am-2:30pm.) The neighboring Vermont Historical Society's **Vermont Museum and Library** at 109 State St. (828-2297), housed in the historic Pavilion building, teems with objects and facts about Vermont. The library holds approximately 45,000 tomes on the state's history (open Tues.-Fri. 9am-4:30pm, Sat. 9am-4pm), while the museum exhibits Vermont furniture, documents, and artifacts (open Tues.-Fri. 9am-4:30pm, Sat. 9am-4pm, Sun. noon-4pm; admission $2, seniors and students $1, under 13 free). The **T.W. Woods Art Gallery,** at the corner of Ridge and College St. (828-8743), displays the work of popular 19th-century artists alongside work by contemporary Vermontsters. (Open Tues.-Sun. noon-4pm. Admission $2.)

Like the rest of the state, Vermont's capital offers easy access to nature's beauty. **Hubbard Park and Fitness Trails,** on Hubbard Park Dr., wind through 100 acres of preserved wilderness, perfect for a summer stroll or a winter trek on cross-country skis. (Open daily 9am-9pm.) Up Main St. on Country Rd. is the **Morse Farm** (223-2740 or 800-242-2740), a working maple syrup farm that stays open year-round. Maples are tapped and the sugarhouse in operates in early spring. The farm gives a splendid ramopanic view of the hills during foliage. (Open summer daily 8am-6pm, off-season 8am-5pm.)

Montpelier is the proud home of the **New England Culinary Institute,** 250 Main St. (223-6324); costly but fancy cuisine is available from the **Elm Street Cafe,** 38 Elm St. (223-3188), with first-year students cooking innovative cuisine ($9-11) such as roast loin of pork with maple mustard glaze and cranapple compote. (Lunch specials under $5. Open Mon.-Fri. 7-10am, 11:30am-1:30pm and 5:30-9pm, Sat. 8-10am, 11:30am-1:30pm, and 5:30-9pm.) **Tubbs Restaurant,** 24 Elm St. (229-9202), features the French cuisine of second-year students in the elegant confines of the original Montpelier jailhouse. (Lunch entrees $3-8; dinner entrees $14-18. Open Mon.-Fri. 11:30am-2pm and 6-9:30pm, Sat. 6-9:30pm.) The school's bakery/café, **La Brioche** (229-0443), occupies the same building and offers delicious pastries and cakes. (Open Mon.-Fri. 7:30am-3pm.) For natural foods, stop by the **Horn of the Moon Café,** 8 Langdon St. (223-2895), which uses Vermont cheese and organic produce to prepare vegetarian meals. (Open Mon. 7am-3pm, Tues.-Sat. 7am-9pm; also Sun. 10am-2pm in summer.) **About Thyme,** 42 State St. (223-0427), serves everything from breakfast burritos ($2.25) and *latkes* (75¢) to *tabouli* and superior fresh sandwiches ($3.50). Or sip cappuccino ($1.75) and relax. (Open Mon.-Fri. 7:30am-7:30pm, Sat. 9am-7:30pm. Closed Sun.) The **Wayside Restaurant,** east of town on Rte. 302 (223-6611), which trumpets its diner fare as "Yankee cooking at its best," has a Yankee menu at its cheapest. (Hot sandwiches under $5.50. Open daily 6:30am-9pm.)

The **Vermont Travel Division,** 134 State St. (828-3236; open Mon.-Fri. 7:45am-4:30pm, Sat. 9:30am-4pm, longer hours in fall, closed Sat. in off-season), can provide you with a list of restaurants and accommodations in the area, a helpful town map, and tourist info about the whole state. Consult their kiosk on the neighboring block in front of a grey church when the travel division is closed. Hikers should stop by **The Green Mountain Club's** headquarters, 43 State St. (223-3463). The GMC, founded in 1910, built and maintains the **Long Trail,** the oldest long-distance hiking trail in the U.S. Call or write (P.O. Box 889, Montpelier 05601-0889) for trail guide-books and other info.

For accommodation, try the beautifully maintained Victorian **Montpelier Bed and Breakfast,** 22 North St. (229-0878), run by state legislator Karen Kitzmiller and her husband Warren and carefully guarded by their lovable Bernese dog Tobler. From the bus station, turn right onto State St. and left on Main St. Bear right on Main and turn left up North, just past the Main St. school. (Very comfortable singles $25-38. Doubles $42-60. 15% discount for stays of 2 days or more. Check-in after 3pm. All non-smoking. The cheaper rooms do not come with continental breakfast, but special rates are available for traveling cyclists. The vivacious owner of **Raspberry Lodge Bed & Breakfast,** 81 North St. (223-3903), ½-mi. up the hill from Montpelier B&B, rents a private suite complete with living room, bath, double brass bed, and continental breakfast ($55). The secluded location also boasts a wildflower garden, stunning view of the valley, and a cedar sauna on the premises. The

Green Valley Campground (223-6217), 6 mi. east of town on Rte. 2, though not very woodsy, does offer swimming and foliage. (Open May-Oct. Sites $10, with hookup $14. Metered showers.) **The Vermonter Motel,** southeast of town on Rte. 302 (476-8541), has immaculate rooms and a pleasant backyard. (Singles $31. Doubles $31-38.) In the heart of downtown.

Vermont Transit is behind Chittenden Bank at 112 State St. (223-7112). Daily buses go to: Boston (4 per day, 4 hr., $34); New York City (4 per day, 9 hr., $69); White River Junction (4 per day, 1 hr., $9); Waterbury (4 per day, 20 min., $3); and Burlington (4 per day, 1 hr., $7.05). VT also offers service to Montréal and Portland, ME. (Open Mon.-Fri. 8am-6:30pm, Sat. 8am-4pm, Sun. noon-4pm.)

Montpelier's **ZIP code** is 05602; the **area code** is 802.

Stowe

Between Montpelier and Burlington lies **Stowe,** one of the east's ski capitals. From November to April, people down the coast speed to the site of the highest peak in Vermont, Mt. Mansfield.

Quaint Stowe houses many ski resorts and four fine skiing areas. The hills are alive with the sound of some of the best cross-country skiing in the U.S., centered on Stowe's **Trapp Family Lodge,** Luce Hill Rd. (253-8511), with 85km of trails. Alpine fans applaud **Mount Mansfield** (253-7311 or 800-253-4SKI) and at higher points and prices, **Smuggler's Notch** (664-8851 or 800-451-8752). Skiing is an expensive undertaking—a one-day lift ticket will set you back about $39. A better bet might be the **Ski Vermont's Classics** program. A three-day $99 lift ticket (available at participating slopes) allows you to ski at any number of resorts in the area, including Mt. Mansfield and Smuggler's Notch. (Call or write The Lake Champlain Regional Chamber of Commerce, P.O. Box 453, Burlington 05402 (802-863-3489), for more info.) **Jim Shepard's Ski Shop** Mountain Rd., 2½ mi. from town (253-4760), rents excellent downhill ($14) and cross-country skis ($10) for the day. (Junior skis and 5-day rates available. Open winter daily 8am-6pm.)

Stowe is still an attractive vacation option in the summer and is a good deal less expensive then. Rent mountain and road bikes at the **Mountain Bike Shop,** ½-mi. up Mountain Rd. (253-7919; $6 per hr., $14 for 4 hr., $20 per day; open summer daily 9am-6pm). **Stowe Mountain Sports** on Mountain Rd. (253-4896) rents one- and 10-speeds ($4 per hr., $8 per ½-day, $12 per day) and mountain bikes ($6 per hr., $14 per ½-day, $20 per day). Pirate or rent canoes for the day at **Buccaneer Country Lodge,** 1390 Mountain Rd. (453-4772), for $25 (open at 10am; canoes returned by 8pm). Horseback riding is available at **Topnotch at Stowe,** Rte. 108 (253-8585; guided tours $20 for 1 hr., private lessons available by appointment only. Open May 9-Nov.).

Mt. Mansfield (253-3000) coordinates a variety of fun summer activities, all open weather permitting. The **Alpine Slide** on Spruce Peak, a winding concrete gutter, bumps down 2300 ft. through beautiful woods and meadows. (Open daily June 22-Labor Day 10am-5pm; weekends only Memorial Day to June 21 and Labor Day-Oct. 14. Admission $6, kids $5; ride book $24, kids $16.) The **Gondola** runs up 4393 ft. above sea level to just below the summit of Mt. Mansfield (Fare $9.50, kids $5, 12 and under free). Or, for $10, you can burn out your brakes driving 20 minutes to the peak on the **Auto Toll Road.** (Both open June 22-Oct. 14 daily 10am-5pm; weekends only Memorial Day-June 21. Motorcycles $7.) For a good daytrip, hike the **Long Trail** ascending Mt. Mansfield. Though there are a number of entrances to the trail on Mountain Rd., drive the particularly scenic route to the highest elevation point at Smuggler's Notch (not to be confused with the ski area), where the cliffs rise 1000 ft. above the pass. At one time people smuggled cows (of all things) into New England through this gap in the mountain. Today, an **information booth** here can point you to interesting sights on the trail, like Bingham Falls.

Ski resorts have culture too. After a long day hiking, unwind at a performance of the **Stowe Stage Company,** the Playhouse, Mountain Rd. (253-7944; performances 8pm late June-Aug.) The sound of music fills the Trapp Family Concert Meadow, Sundays at 7pm, for Stowe Performing Arts **Music in the Meadow.** (Tickets $12, $10 in advance, under 19 $5.) Noon Music in May each Wednesday at the Stowe Community Church and the Gazebo Lawn Concert Series at noon on the library lawn in August are free (donations welcome).

For a filling meal try the **Sunset Grille and Tap Room** (253-9281), on Cottage Club Rd. off Mountain Rd., a friendly, down-home barbecue place with a vast selection of domestic beers and generous meals ($5-15). (Open daily 11:30am-midnight.) All-American **Angelo's Pizza** on Mountain Rd. (253-8931) offers pizza ($1.15 per slice) and pasta ($4-8). (Open Mon.-Thurs. 11:30am-10pm, Fri.-Sat. 11:30am-midnight, Sun. 11:30am-10pm.) Right next door is the **Canton Chinese Restaurant** (253-4390), with a smiling Buddha and lunch specials starting at $2.75. (Open Mon.-Fri. 10am-10pm, Sat.-Sun. 10am-11pm.)

For one of the few lodging bargains in town, the **Vermont State Ski Dorm** (253-4010) doubles as an AYH hostel from June 15 to October 15 ($10 per night, $12 nonmembers). During the ski season they serve two meals a day and charge $35. The friendly, eccentric host of the **Golden Kitz,** Mountain Rd. (253-4217 or 800-KITS-LOV) offers her "lovie" travelers a relaxed atmosphere, great stories, and theme bedrooms. (Singles with shared bath $36-40 in highest season; $30-36 mid-winter weekends; $24-26 in early and late ski season and fall foliage; off-season and summer $20-28. Doubles $52-70 highest season; $46-50 midwinter weekends; $38-56 early and late ski season and fall foliage; $36-56 off-season and summer. Multi-day packages available. The committed budget traveler should ask if "dungeon" rooms are available; doubles $30.) Situated on a real brook, the **Gold Brook Campground** (253-7683 or 253-8147), babbles 1½ mi. south of the town center on Rte. 100. (Open year-round. Hot showers, volleyball, badminton, horseshoes. Tent sites $11.50, with varying degrees of hookup $15, $17, and $20.) Under the same management is the **Nichols Lodge** (rooms $35-50).**Smuggler's Notch State Park** (253-4014) offers hot showers, lean-tos ($12) and tent sites ($7.50). (Open Memorial Day-Columbus Day; reservations suggested.)

Contact the **Stowe Area Association** on Main St. (253-7321 or 800-24-STOWE), right in the center of the village, for free booking service and summer info on the area's lodging, restaurants, and activities, including skiing. (Open summer Mon.-Fri. 9am-6pm, Sat. 10am-5pm, Sun. 11am-5pm; winter Mon.-Fri. 9am-8pm, Sat.-Sun. 9am-6pm.)

The socially conscious and fun-loving **Ben and Jerry's Ice Cream Factory** lies north on Rte. 100 (244-5641), a couple miles off I-89 in Waterbury. Look for the world's cleanest cows. Starting in 1978 in a converted gas station, Ben and Jerry have since developed some of the best ice cream in the world. You can sample celebrated flavors such as Rainforest Crunch, White Russian, and Cherry Garcia. ($1 tours daily every ¼-hr. 9am-4pm.) Partake at their store daily from 9am to 6pm.

The ski areas all lie northwest of Stowe on Rte. 108. Stowe is 12 mi. north of I-89's exit 10, which is 27 mi. southwest of Burlington. Getting to and around Stowe without a car is not fun. Vermont Transit will take you to Vincent's Drug and Variety Store, off Park Row in Waterbury, 10 mi. from Stowe. (Open Mon.-Fri. 8:30am-7pm, Sat. 8:30am-6pm, Sun. 9am-3pm.) For $13-15, a cab will take you past chain-saw sculptures to Stowe, which itself stretches out over 6 mi. To explore and get a good workout, rent a bike. You can also wimp out and rent a car from Stowe Auto Service (253-7608). The Stowe Area Association can give you more info on the **American Express Village-Mountain Courtesy Trolley** (operates daily from town 7:30am-4:30pm, every ½-hr.), Sullivan Transportation (253-9440), or La-Moille City Taxi (253-9433 or 800-252-0204) will take you back to Waterbury.

Stowe's **ZIP code** is 05672; the **area code** is 802.

White River Junction and West

Central Vermont is graced with quiet winding back roads and the sight of grazing cows in quiet green pastures. If you enjoy rural rubbernecking, plan an east-west trip along U.S. 4, or a north-south trip on Rte. 100. The roads are best reached from U.S. 5 or I-89, where they intersect with the Connecticut River at White River Junction. This tiny town, once the hub of railroad transportation in the northeastern U.S., White River Junction now serves as the major bus center for central and eastern Vermont. **Vermont Transit** (295-3011), on Rte. 5 just beyond the Wm. Tally House, has connections across New Hampshire, Burlington, and up and down the Connecticut River. (Office open Sun.-Fri. 7am-9pm, Sat. 7am-5pm.) **Amtrak** (295-7160, 800-872-7245), on Railroad Rd. off N. Main St., serves as a stop for the "Montrealer" train both south to New York City and Washington DC, and north to Essex Junction (near Burlington) and Montréal.

An **information booth** across Sykes Ave. from the bus station (intersection of Sykes and Rte. 5 off I-89 and 91) can fill your pockets with brochures on Vermont. (Open May 27-Oct. 15 daily 10am-5pm.) In town, the **Chamber of Commerce,** 12 Gates St. (295-6200), can also supply you with information (Open Mon.-Fri. 9am-noon and sporadically in the afternoons.) Also in the Junction you'll find the **Catamount Brewery,** 58 S. Main St. (296-2248), where you can sample, among other things, delicious, unpasteurized amber ale produced in strict accordance with British brewing methods. (July-Oct. Fri., Sat., and Mon. 11am, 1 and 3pm, Sun. 1 and 3pm, Tues., Wed., and Thurs. 1pm; Nov.-June Fri. 1pm, Sat. 11am, 1 and 3pm, Sun. 1 and 3pm. Store open Mon.-Sat. 9am-5pm, Sun. 1-5pm.)

For a quick bite to eat, stop at the **Polkadot Restaurant,** 1 N. Main St. (295-9722), a classic diner and remarkably good. (Sandwiches $1.50-3, pork chop, fries, and vegetables $4.75. Open daily 5am-8pm.) The best bet for lodging is the old-style **Hotel Coolidge,** 17 S. Main St. (295-3118 or 800-622-1124), across the road from the retired Boston and Maine steam engine. From bus station, walk to the right, down the hill past the jewelry store, 25,000 Gifts, and two stop lights (about a mile) into town. Renamed in honor of President Calvin Coolidge's pop, a frequent guest at the railroad hotel, the Coolidge boasts impeccably kept rooms and a housekeeping manager with a keen sense of humor. (Hardcore budget travelers should ask for hostel rooms, with shared bath and shower: singles $22, doubles $27.50. With half-bath: singles $28, doubles $34.50. Economy room with full bath: singles $39.50, doubles $45. Top o' the line: singles $49.50, doubles $55. Morning coffee included.) **Cashie's** Restaurant at the Coolidge (295-3118) serves lunch and dinner at fair prices and hosts live entertainment Wednesday through Saturday. (Open Mon. 11:30am-3pm, Tues. 11:30am-9pm, Wed.-Sat. 11:30am-10pm, Sun. 5-9pm.) If you have no other alternative, try the **Vermonter Hotel,** 1 Gates St. (295-9755). They cater more to longer-term residents but should be able to offer you a room without bath ($25 per day, $65 per week).

Six mi. west of White River Junction on U.S. 4 is **Woodstock,** a Vermont country village evolving into wealthy tourist hangout. The pace for locals and tourists alike is slow, and even the traffic crawls. The Woodstock **chamber of commerce** at 18 Central St. (457-3555) will tell you what the town does offer and provide maps of trails for nearby mountains Peg and Tom; a half-hour walk up Mt. Tom will afford a good view of the town. (Open Mon.-Fri. 9am-5pm.) The chamber also sponsors an **information booth** (457-1042) in the middle of the village green. (Open Memorial Day-June 24 Sat.-Sun. 9:30am-5:30pm. June 24 to mid-Oct. daily 9:30am-5:30pm. Open as late as 8pm during fall foliage season.) In addition there is the **Woodstock Town Crier,** a chalkboard with local listings on the corner of Elm and Church St.

The silent butler who greets you at the **Gallery on the Green,** One The Green (457-4956), turns out to be one of several sculptures by Jack Dowd. Linger and admire his works, the paintings of Peter Keating, and the craft of other local artists. (Open Mon.-Sat. 10am-5pm, Sun. 10am-4pm.)

The **Woodstock Historical Society,** 26 Elm St. (457-1822), is in the 19th-century **Dana House Museum,** which contains a rich collection of antique furniture and artifacts. (Open last week in May to mid-Nov. Mon.-Sat. 10am-5pm, Sun. 2-5pm. Last tour leaves at 4:15pm. Admission $3.50, seniors $2.50, ages 13-18 $1, ages under 12 and AAA members admitted free.) The **Vermont Raptor Center,** part of the **Vermont Institute of Natural Sciences** (457-2779) on Church Hill Rd. 1½ mi. west of town, is a "living museum" introducing visitors to the owls and hawks of northern New England. (Open May-Oct. Wed.-Mon. 10am-4pm; Nov.-April Mon. and Wed.-Sat. 10am-4pm. Admission $4, ages 5-15 $1, under 5 free.) **Billings Farm and Museum** (457-2355) off River Rd., 1/2-mi. north of the city, provides a great look into modern and 19th-century Vermont farm life with a working farm, a museum, and a restored 1890 farmhouse. (Open early May-late Oct. daily 10am-5pm. Open weekends in Dec. 10am-4pm. Admission $5, under 6 free.)

Drink in the silent roar of a stone lion at **Bentley's Greenhouse,** 7 Elm St. (457-3400), a combination soda fountain, florist, and sandwich shop. (Open Mon.-Sat. 9am-5:30pm, Sun. 11am-5:30pm.) The **Mountain Creamery,** 33 Central St. (457-1715), serves the best ice cream and tallest pies in town. Notable flavors include Myers rum raisin and Vermont maple walnut; a cone with one remarkably generous scoop costs $2. (Open daily 7am-5pm.) **The Deli at Woodstock** (457-1062), just east of town on Rte. 4, has café-style dining and natural sodas. (Sandwiches $2.70-5.50. Open Mon.-Sat. 7:30am-5pm, Sun. 10am-3pm.) Mingle with the locals at the **WASPs Snack Bar** (457-9805), a bona-fide shack at 57 Pleasant St. (Rte. 4). Don't look for a sign; if the flag's flying, mosey on in. (Open Mon.-Fri. 6am-6pm, Sat. 6am-2pm.)

A great place to spend the night is the beautifully remodeled **1826 House,** 57 River St. (457-1335; singles $45, doubles $50), with Bavarian antiques, 18th-century European glass icons, a quiet back porch, and a worldly, friendly polyglot of an owner. The **Silver Lake Campground** (234-9974), 10 mi. north of town on Rte. 12 near Barnard, has 70 campsites and a lake for boating. (Open May 15-Oct. 15. Sites $14 per family, $2 each additional adult, with hookup $17. Canoe and boat rental $4 per hour. Not accessible by public transport. Reservations recommended.)

To rent a quality bike and explore the scenery around Woodstock on wheels, go to **The Cyclery Plus,** at 36 Rte. 4 (457-3377), in West Woodstock. ($18 per day, $12 after 1pm, $60 for 5 days, $72 for 6 days. Open Mon.-Fri. 9am-6pm, Sat. 9am-5pm.) **Wilderness Trails** (295-7620, 295-3133) at the Quechee Inn, Clubhouse Rd., in Quechee will rent you a bike or canoe for the day. (Canoes 1-3 hr. $10. Bike 1 hr. $5. Daily rate $13 for each.) Marty also organizes fly-fishing and canoe trips, and rents cross-country skiing equipment in the winter. **Quechee State Park** (295-2990), off Rte. 4, has hiking trails around **Quechee Gorge,** a spectacular 163-ft. drop from cliffs to the Ottaquechee River below. A bridge connecting the trails to the park's picnic grounds offers a view that makes you feel small and quite mortal; on the eastern side of the bridge an info booth can answer questions. (Open Memorial Day-Columbus Day. Day use $1.50, kids $1. Tent sites $10 for 4 people, $2.50 each additional person up to 8. Lean-tos $14 per person. Disabled-accessible tent site and lean-to. Metered showers. Reservations minimum 3 nights in advance $3.) While in Quechee, visit **Simon Pearce Glass,** the Mill off Rte. 4 (295-2711), to view glassblowers and potters at work. (Artists working daily 9am-5pm, open daily 9am-9pm.)

The **Vermont Transit** agency in Woodstock (457-1325), at the Whippletree Shop, 4 Central St., provides schedules and timetables of Vermont transit buses. To White River Junction (2 per day, $3) and Rutland (2 per day, $6).

Genuine Vermont sharp cheddar cheese is made only in certain counties. One authentic producer is the **Plymouth Cheese Factory** (672-3650), on Rte. 100A 6 mi. south of U.S. 4 in **Plymouth.** To see the cheese being made, visit on Monday or Tuesday; the rest of the week is spent waxing. After Thanksgiving, cheese production ceases and packaging takes over. (Open daily 8am-5:30pm; off-season daily 8am-4:30pm.) Another big cheese from Plymouth, **Calvin Coolidge,** was born in this tiny village (672-3773). Next door to his birthplace is the old homestead where in 1923 his father swore him in as president after learning of the sudden death of President Harding. You can also tour the secret service cabins and his White House summer office. (Open Memorial Day-Oct. 20 daily 9:30am-5:30pm. Admission $3.50, under 14 free.)

VIRGINIA

The European settlement of North America began here with Jamestown colony in 1607. After only 13 years, the whites imported the New World's first African slaves. Generations later, when the continued enslavement of African Americans turned into a political wedge between North and South, secessionists turned to this same state to hold the capital of the Confederacy in Richmond. A host of Confederate street names, Robert E. Lee parks, fixed-up plantations, and battlefields exhibit to redundancy Virginia's Southern way of life before the Civil War. Nostalgia swells in Richmond and climaxes in Colonial Williamsburg, where guides in costume dress show sweating tourists around the restored 18th-century capital. But modern Virginia isn't just whistlin' Dixie. Several cities celebrate Martin Luther King Jr. as well as Confederate generals Jackson and Lee. As a sign Virginia has mostly left the Old South it once led, the nation's first black governor, L. Douglas Wilder, is showing the nation that people of all ethnic backgrounds can practice dirty politics.

Practical Information

Capital: Richmond.

Virginia Division of Tourism, Bell Tower, Capitol Sq., 101 N. 9th St., Richmond 23219 (800-847-4882 or 786-4484). Division of State Parks, 1201 State Office Bldg., Richmond 23219 (226-1981). For the free Virginia Accommodations Directory, write to Virginia Travel Council, 7415 Brook Rd., P.O. Box 15067, Richmond 23227.

Time Zone: Eastern. Postal Abbreviation: VA

Charlottesville

This college town in the Blue Ridge foothills proudly bears the stamp of its patron, Thomas Jefferson. The college he founded, the University of Virginia (pronounced you-vee-YAY), dominates the town economically, geographically, and culturally, supporting the town's pubs as well as writers such as Peter Taylor and Pulitzer Prize-winning poet Rita Dove. (Movie stars with Southern ties, like Sissy Spacek and Jessica Lange, also call the town home.) Visitors get steered to Monticello, the cleverly constructed classical mansion Mr. Jefferson designed. Even C-ville itself, friendly, hip, and compact, seems to reflect the third President's dream of well-informed, culturally aware citizens who choose to live close to the land. Oenophiles can head to the suburbs for the ten wineries of "Virginia's wine capital."

Practical Information

Emergency: 911. Campus Police: 4-1766 on a UVA campus phone.

Visitor Information: Chamber of Commerce, 415 E. Market St. (295-3141), within walking distance of Amtrak, Greyhound/Trailways, and historic downtown. Open Mon.-Fri. 9am-5pm. Charlottesville/Abermarle Convention and Visitors Bureau, P.O. Box 161, Rte. 20 near I-64 (977-1783). Take bus #8 ("Piedmont Community College") from 5th and Market St. Same info as chamber—brochures and maps. Combo tickets to Monticello, Michie Tavern, and Ash Lawn-Highland ($16; seniors and kids $14.50). Open daily 9:30am-5:30pm.

University of Virginia Info Center, at the rotunda in the center of campus (924-1019). Some brochures, a university map, and info on tours. Open daily 9am-10pm. Students answer questions in Newcomb Hall (no phone). Open daily 9am-10pm. The larger University Center

(924-7166) is off U.S. 250 west—follow the signs. Transport schedules, entertainment guides, and hints on budget accommodations. Answers phone "Campus Police." Campus maps. Open 24 hrs.

Amtrak: 810 W. Main St. (800-872-7245 or 296-4559), 7 blocks from downtown. To Washington, DC ($22) and New York ($79). Open daily 5:30am-9pm.

Greyhound/Trailways: 310 W. Main St. (295-5131), within 3 blocks of historic downtown. To: Richmond ($12), Washington, DC ($21), Norfolk ($30), and Lynchburg ($14). Open daily 6am-8:30pm.

Public Transport: Charlottesville Transit Service (296-7433). Bus service within city limits, including most hotels and UVA campus locations. Buses operate Mon.-Sat. 6:20am-7pm. Maps available at both info centers, Chamber of Commerce, and the UVA student center in Newcomb Hall. Fare 60¢, seniors and disabled 30¢, under 6 free. The more frequent blue **University of Virginia** buses require UVA ID or expensive long-term pass to board.

Taxi: Yellow Cab, 295-4131. To Monticello $13.

Help Lines: Region 10 Community Services Hotline, 972-1800. **Lesbian & Gay Hotline,** 971-4942. UVA-affiliated.

Post Office: 1155 Seminole Trail (Rte. 29). Open Mon.-Fri. 8am-5:30pm, Sat. 8am-2pm. **ZIP code:** 22906.

Area Code: 804.

Charlottesville streets number east to west, using compass directions; 5th St. NW is 10 blocks from (and parallel to) 5th St NE. Streets running east-west across the numbered streets are neither parallel nor logically named. C-ville has two downtowns: one on the west side near the university called **The Corner,** and **Historic Downtown** about a mile east. The two are connected by **University Avenue,** running east-west, which becomes **Main Street** after the Corner ends at a bridge.

Accommodations and Camping

Budget Inn, 140 Emmet St. (Rt. 29) (293-5141), near the university. 40 comfortable, hotel-quality rooms. TV, A/C, private baths. Senior discounts. Doubles $32-35 (one bed) or $40-45 (two beds). Each additional person $5.

Chancellor Apartments, 1413½ University Ave. (295-5457). Hidden among shops on the Corner. Fairly large rooms, with in-room sinks, sturdy old furniture and hall baths. International crowd. You may have to search for the receptionist. No alcohol; 11pm curfew. Singles $14; doubles $17. Call for reservations.

Cambrie Launch Charlottesville KOA, P.O. Box 144, C-Ville, VA 22901. All camp sites are shaded. Recreation hall with video games, a pavilion, and a pool (open Mon.-Sat. 10am-8pm). Fishing (not wading or swimming) allowed. Site $18, with hookup $20.

Food and Nightlife

The Corner neighborhood near UVA has bookstores and countless cheap eats, with good Southern chow in C-ville's unpretentious diners. The town loves jazz, likes rock'n'roll, and has quite a few pubs. Around the Downtown Mall, ubiquitous posters and the free *Charlottesville Review* can tell you who plays where when.

The Hardware Store, 316 Main St. (977-1518), near the middle of the outdoor "mall." Bar atmosphere, but weird: beers served in glass boots, appetizers in mini-basketball courts, and condiments in toolboxes. Collectors would drool over the 1898 building's antique collection. American grille and an eclectic set of entrées, from *ratatouille gratinée* ($5) to *crêpes,* both sweet ($1.50-4) and savory ($4-6). Sandwiches ($3-7). Quality desserts. Open Mon. 10am-5pm, Tues.-Thurs. 10am-9pm, Fri.-Sat. 10am-11pm.

Garden Gourmet, 811 West Main St. (295-9991). Northern California circa 1967, with vegetarians, hippies, and "peacenluv." Homemade seven-grain bread, salad dressings, and creative veggie plates. Wooden booths accompany artwork by the owner's family and staff. Nightly folk music. Open Mon.-Thurs. 11:30am-2:30pm and 5:30-9pm; Fri. 11:30am-2:30pm and 5:30-10pm; Sat. noon-3pm and 5:30pm-10pm.

Macado's (Mac-ah-dooz), 1505 University Ave. (971-3558). Great sandwiches, homemade desserts, and long hours cure the late-night munchies. Pinball machine and candy store. Upstairs rockin' bar where Poe once lived. Open daily 11am-2am.

The Virginian Restaurant, West Main St. (293-2606). Gourmet seafood and spinoffs on traditional American dishes. Rotating menu sometimes includes grilled mozzarella sandwich ($3) or stuffed artichokes ($6). The restaurant is one booth wide, with lines for lunch or dinner. Open Mon.-Fri. 11:30am-3pm and 6pm-2am.

The Tavern, 1140 Emmet St. (295-0404). A breakfast Eden; its banana-nut, bacon, or fruit-filled homemade pancakes ($3.50) are enormous. UVA jocks buy their kegs here. Open Mon.-Sun. 7am-3pm.

The Blue Ridge Brewery Co., 709 Main St. (977-0017). Down-home bar/lounge run by two brothers, a zymurgist and a chef. Light and dark taps brewed on premises with Blue Ridge Mountain water. Dreamy appetizers include hot, tangy "cream trout wontons" ($3). Specials on blue crabs and fresh steamed shrimp Sun.-Thurs. Open Mon.-Fri. 11:30am-2pm and 5-10pm; Sat.-Sun. 11:30am-3pm and 5pm-10pm; bar open until 2am.

Sights and Entertainment

Most activity on the spacious **University of Virginia** campus clusters around the **Lawn** and down fraternity-lined **Rugby Road.** Through his telescope, Jefferson watched the University get built from the windows of Monticello. You can return the favor with a glimpse of Monticello from the Lawn, a terraced green carpet which unrolls down the middle of the university. During the year, students study and play here. Professors live in the Lawn's pavilions; the Jeff-meister designed each one in a different architectural style. Lawn tours, led by students, leave on the hour at the Rotunda from 10am-4pm; self-guided tour maps are provided for those who prefer to find their own way. **The Rotunda** is a target for pranks; students once festooned it with the inevitable cow. Baron von Jefftoven particularly admired its Pantheon-style dome. The **Old Cabell Building** across the Lawn from the Rotunda houses an auditorium with impressive acoustics. On its wall, a reproduction of Raphael's mural *The School of Athens* describes the Thom-man's vision of student-faculty harmony. The **Bayley Art Museum,** Rugby Rd. (924-3592), features visiting exhibits and a small permanent collection including one of Rodin's castings of *The Kiss.* (Open Tues.-Sat. 1-5pm.)

The **Downtown Mall** is a brick thoroughfare lined with restaurants and shops catering to a diverse crowd. A kiosk near the fountain in the center of the mall has posters on club schedules. At 110 D-Mall, **The Movie Palace** shows current flicks for only $2. Other hip eateries, bars, and specialty stores provide places to treat your nose and tongue.

Thom-alom-a-ding-dong's more-classical-than-thou design for his home, **Monticello** (295-8181), derives from the 16th-century Italian architect Andrea Palladio. The TeeJ oversaw every stage of design and construction, collecting gadgets for the inside on his travels including a compass which registers wind direction through a weathervane on the roof. The Jeffster loved silver goblets, parquet flooring, and marble statuary. There's nary a non-picturesque spot on Monticello's landscape; from the west lawn, a roundabout floral walk leads to a magnificent hillside view. The garden lets you see Montalto, the "high mountain" on which Peepin' Thom wanted to build an observation tower. Tours of Monticello begin every five minutes during the day, but the wait can be as long as 90 minutes during summer Saturdays. Because of the heat and few seating areas, come early. (Open daily 8am-5pm; Nov.-Feb. 9am-4:30pm; tickets $7, seniors $6, under 5 $3.)

Minutes away (take a right turn to Rte. 795) is **Ashlawn** (293-9539), the 500-acre former plantation home of one of those presidents who followed Jefferson. More quaint and less imposing than Monticello, Ashlawn has outdoor views to rival its domed neighbor's. The current owner, the College of William and Mary, has turned Ashlawn into a museum honoring its former owner, James Monroe. A colorful, dainty garden lines the pathway to the house, where a docent spews facts about President Monroe. Ashlawn's peacocks stroll the gardens and lawn while making curious noises through their beaks. (Open daily 9am-6pm; Nov.-Feb. daily 10am-5pm; tour $6, seniors $5.50, under 5 $2.)

In the **Box Gardens** behind Ashlawn, English-language opera highlights the **Summer Festival of the Arts** (tickets $12.50, seniors $11.50, students $8.50; box office 293-8000, open daily noon-6:30pm). A 45-min. intermission allows for a picnic supper, which you can order from **Festive Fare** (296-5496) for $8. Ashlawn also hosts **Music at Twilight** (tickets $9, seniors $8, students $6), including New Orleans jazz, Cajun music, blues, and swing. Combo tickets for the performance, house tour, and picnic supper are available ($22).

Down the road from Monticello on Rte. 53 is **Michie** (Mick-ee) **Tavern** (977-1234), with an operating grist mill, a general store, and a tour of the 200-year-old establishment ($5, seniors $4.50, under 5 $1). Jeffypoo's daughter supposedly fled the tavern after improperly teaching a waltz to a man in the ballroom. **The Ordinary** (977-1235), located in the tavern, serves up a fixed buffet of fried chicken, beans, cornbread, and other dishes ($9, ages 6-11 $5). Eat outside in good weather. (Open 11:15am-3:30pm.)

Richmond

The former capital of the Confederate States of America, Richmond wears its Civil War legacy on a sleeve, through numerous museums and restored houses devoted to everything from troop movements to tablecloths belonging to Confederate President Jefferson Davis. But on the other sleeve, in districts like the sprawling, beautiful Fan and formerly industrial Shockoe Bottom, Richmond rears a coiffed and powdered head with relaxed, cultural savvy.

Practical Info

Emergency: 911.

Richmond Visitor Center, 1700 Robin Hood Rd. (358-5511), exit 14 off I-95/64, in a converted train depot. Helpful 6-min. video introduces the city's attractions. Walking tours and quality maps. Open Memorial Day-Labor Day daily 9am-7pm; off-season 9am-5pm. Brochure-only branch office at 301 E. Main St. downtown.

Trains: Amtrak, far away at 7519 Staple Mills Rd. (264-9194 or 800-872-7245). To: Washington, DC ($20); Williamsburg ($9); Virginia Beach ($17); New York City ($78). Taxi fare to downtown $12. Open 24 hrs.

Buses: Greyhound/Trailways: 2910 N. Boulevard (353-8903). To get downtown, walk 2 blocks to the visitor's center or take GRTC bus #24 north. To: Washington, DC ($17); Charlottesville ($9); Williamsburg ($9.50); and Norfolk, VA ($19).

Public Transport: Greater Richmond Transit Co., 101 S. Davis St. (358-4782). Maps available in the basement of city hall, 900 E. Broad St., and in the Yellow Pages. Fare 75¢ (exact change required), transfers 10-50¢. Buses serve most of Richmond infrequently, downtown frequently; most leave from Broad St. downtown. Bus #24 goes south to Broad St. and downtown. Free trolleys provide dependable, if limited, service to downtown and Shockoe Slip 10am-4pm daily, with an extended Shockoe Slip schedule from 5pm-midnight.

Help Lines: Travelers Aid, 648-1767. **Rape Crisis Hotline,** 643-0888. **Gay Hotline,** 353-3626.

Post Office: 10th and Main St. (783-0825). Open Mon.-Fri. 7:30am-5pm. **ZIP code:** 23219.

Area Code: 804.

Creative locals see in Richmond's urban area a closed ladies' fan placed east to west: the center is the **state capitol,** the short handle to the east is **Court End** and **Shockoe Bottom,** and the long western blade begins downtown and cleverly becomes the **Fan** neighborhood. Streets form a grid, but are illogically named, save for 1st (west) through 14th (east) St. downtown. Both I-95, leading north to Washington, DC, and I-195, parallel to the James River, encircle the urban area.

Accommodations and Camping

Budget motels around Richmond cluster along Williamsburg Rd., on the edge of town, and along Midlothian Turnpike, south of the James River; public transport to these areas is infrequent at best. As usual, the farther away from downtown you stay, the less you have to pay. The visitor center can reserve accommodations, sometimes at heavy ($10-20) discounts.

Motel 6, 5704 Williamsburg Rd., Sandston (222-7600), about 6 mi. east on Rte. 60, across from the airport. Get there by the #7 ("Seven Pines") bus. Singles $27. Doubles $33.

Massad House Hotel, 11 N. 4th St. (648-2893), 4 blocks from the capitol, nearer town. Shuttles guests via a 1940s elevator to charming rooms with shower and TV. Only inexpensive rooms downtown; in summer call at least a week ahead. Singles $33. Doubles $40.

Executive Inn, 5215 W. Broad St. (288-4011), 3 mi. from center of town. Offers grand (by motel standards) but slightly faded rooms and a pool. Bus #6 runs frequently into town. Singles $41. Doubles $44. Off-season $35, $37.

The closest campground, **Pocahontas State Park,** 10300 Beach Rd. (796-4255), 10 mi. south on Rte. 10 and Rte. 655, offers showers, biking, boating, lakes, and a huge pool. (Sites $8.50. No hookups. Pool admission $2, ages 3-12 $1.50.) Reserving a site by phone through Ticketron (490-3939) costs an extra $4.50-6.

Food and Nightlife

Richmond's good budget restaurants hide among the shade trees and well-kept porches of the gentrified Fan district, bordered by Monument Ave., Main St., Laurel St., and Boulevard.

Joe's Inn, 205 N. Shields Ave. (355-2282), serves huge portions of spaghetti in a casual setting. Lunches $3. Dinners $7-8. Open daily 9am-2am.

Texas-Wisconsin Border Café, 1501 W. Main St. (355-2097), features chili, potato pancakes, and *chalupas.* Look for the bar's signs: "Dixie Inn," "Secede," and "Eat Cheese or Die." At night the café secedes as a popular bar. Lunches $3-5. Dinners $5-9. Open daily 11am-2am.

Piccola's, at the corner of W. Main St. and Harrison (355-3111), orchestrates cheap and delicious pizza, calzones ($3.15), and jumbo sandwiches ($3.15-3.75). Open Mon.-Thurs. 11am-midnight, Fri.-Sat. 11am-2am, and Sun. 3pm-midnight.

Helen's Inn, 2527 W. Mina St. (354-9659), has inexpensive, standard-fare burgers ($1.49) that have launched a thousand ships. Open Mon.-Fri. 11am-6:30pm, Sat. 11am-5pm.

Downtown

3rd St. Diner, at the corner of 3rd and Main (788-4750), has prices frozen from days of yore. The $1.95 meatless breakfast (two eggs, biscuit or toast, and home fries, grits, or Virginia fried apples) is served all day. The waitresses know all the regulars by name. Open Tues.-Sat. 24 hrs., Sun.-Mon. 7am-2am.

Penny Lane, 207 N. 7th St. (780-1682), a delightfully exaggerated pub with flags on the walls and soccer on the telly. Live music Thurs.-Sat. 9:30pm-1:30am. In summer, Open Mon.-Fri. 11am-2am, Sat. 5pm-2am.; otherwise Sun.-Wed. 11am-4pm and 5-11pm, Thurs.-Sat. 11am-4pm and 5pm-1:30am.

The **Shockoe Slip** district from Main, Canal, and Cary St. between 10th and 14th St. features fancy shops in restored and newly painted warehouses, but few bargains. At the **farmer's market,** outdoors at N. 17th and E. Main St., pick up fresh fruit, vegetables, meat, and maybe even a pot swine. **Peking Pavilion,** 1302 E. Cary St. (649-8888), offers excellent service, elegant decor, and gourmet Chinese food. Try the *kung pao* chicken. (Open Mon.-Thurs. 11:30am-2:15pm and 5-9:45pm, Fri. 11:30am-2:15 and 5pm-10:45pm, Sat. 5-10:45pm, and Sun. for brunch 11:30am-2pm.)

Nightlife crowds Shockoe Slip and sprinkles itself in less hectic measures throughout the Fan.

Tobacco Company Club, 1201 E. Cary St. (782-9555), smokes with Top 40 music and no cover charge. Open Tues.-Sat. 8pm-2am.

Matt's British Pub and Comedy Club, at 1045 12th St. (643-5653) next door, lives up to its name with stand-up at at 8pm and 11pm. Open Tues.-Sat. 8pm-2am.**The Metro,** 727 W. Broad St. (649-4952), features local progressive bands most nights.

Flood Zone, 11 S. 18th St. (643-6006), south of Shockoe Slip, offers a combination of big-name and off-beat comedy acts. Ticket office open Tues.-Fri. 10am-6pm. Tickets $6-20, depending upon the show.

Sights

Ever since Patrick Henry declared "Give me liberty or give me death" in Richmond's **St. John's Church,** 2401 E. Broad St. (648-5015), the river city has been quoting, memorializing, and bronzing its historical heroes. On Sundays in summer at 2pm, an actor recreates the famous 1775 speech. You must take a tour to see the church. (Tours given Mon.-Sat. 10am-3:30pm, Sun. 1-3:30pm; admission $2, students $1.) Larger-than-life statues of George Washington and Thomas Jefferson grace the **State Capitol** grounds (786-4344). Jefferson modeled the masterpiece of neo-classical architecture after a Roman temple in France. (Open daily 9am-5pm.) For more sculpture, follow Franklin Ave. from the capitol until it becomes **Monument Avenue,** lined with trees, gracious old houses, and towering statues of Confederate heroes. Robert E. Lee, who survived the war, faces his beloved South; Stonewall Jackson, who didn't, scowls at the Yankees.

The **Court End** district stretches north and east of the capitol to Clay and College Streets and guards Richmond's most distinctive historical sights. The **Confederate Museum,** 1202 E. Clay St. (649-1861), is the world's largest Confederate artifact collection. The main floor leads visitors through the military history of the Civil War; the basement displays guns and flags of the Confederacy; and the top floor houses temporary exhibits on such topics as African-American life in the antebellum South. The Museum also runs one-hour tours through the **White House of the Confederacy** next door (ask at the museum desk). Statues of Tragedy, Comedy, and Irony grace the White House's front door; decide for yourself which applies. (Open daily 10am-5pm; tours Mon., Wed., and Fri.-Sat. 10:30am-4:30pm, Tues. and Thurs. 11:30am-4:30pm, Sun. 1:15-4:30pm. Admission to museum or tour $4, students $2.50, under 13 $2.25; for both: $7, $5, $3.50.)

The **Valentine Museum,** 1015 Clay St. (649-0711), enamors with exhibits on local and Southern social and cultural history. The museum is self-guided, but the admission price includes a tour of the just-renovated **Wickham-Valentine House** next door. (Open Mon.-Sat. 10am-5pm, Sun. noon-5pm. Admission $3.50, seniors $3, students $2.75, ages 7-12 $1.50.) Combination "Court End" tickets to the Confederate Museum, White House of the Confederacy, Valentine Museum, and **John Marshall House**—all within easy walking distance of each other—are $9, seniors and students $8.50, under 13 $4.

East of the capitol, follow your tell-tale heart to the **Edgar Allan Poe Museum,** 1914 16 E. Main St. (648-5523). Poe memorabilia stuffs the five buildings, including the Stone House, the oldest standing structure within the original city boundaries. (Open Tues.-Sat. 10am-4pm, Sun.-Mon. 1:30-4pm. Admission $5, students $3.)

Four blocks from the intersection of Monument Ave. and N. Boulevard stands the Southeast's largest art museum, the **Virginia Museum of Fine Arts,** 2800 Grove Ave. (367-0844). An outstanding art gallery, the museum also holds a gorgeous collection of Fabergé jewelry and Easter eggs made for Russian czars (the largest outside the USSR), a fine showing of U.S. contemporary art, and what might just be the largest collection of horse sculpture and painting in North America. (Open Tues.-Sat. 11am-5pm, Thurs. 11am-10pm in the North Wing Galleries, Sun. 1-5pm. Donation requested.)

Richmond is surprisingly rich in African-American historic sights, many in the **Jackson Ward** neighborhood downtown. The Maggie L. Walker National Historic Site, 110 1/2 E. Leigh St. (780-1380), commemorates the life of an ex-slave's gifted daughter. Physically disabled, Walker advocated black women's rights and succeeded as founder and president of a bank. (House tours Wed-Sun. 9am-5pm. Free.) The first floor of the **Black History Museum and Cultural Center of Virginia,** 00 Clay St. (780-9093), opened in the summer of 1991; the second floor should open by January 1992. (Open Mon.-Fri. 9am-4pm, but call first to verify. Free.)

Two architectural highlights are the opulent, Art-Deco **Jefferson Hotel,** at Franklin and Adams St. (788-8000), and the **Byrd Theatre,** 2908 W. Cary St. (353-9911), where you can view Hollywood's latest in extraordinary style: marble balconies, enormous stained-glass windows, and a Wurlitzer Organ that rises from the floor to entertain before each show.

Civil War buffs should brave the trip to the city's boundaries to the **Richmond National Battlefield Park,** 3215 E. Broad St. (226-1981). The **Chimborazo Visitor's Center,** located in a former Civil War hospital, contains an educational film and exhibits about the Civil War, as well as maps detailing the battlefields and fortifications surrounding the city. (Open daily 9am-5pm. Free.)

Free concerts abound here in summer; check *Style Weekly,* a free magazine available at the visitor center and around town, for info. Free entertainment often finds a home in **Dogwood Dell** (358-3355), an outdoor theater below the Carillon World War I Memorial on the 100-acre Maymont grounds.

You'll need a car and a strong stomach to visit **King's Dominion** (876-5900), a world-class amusement park 20 mi. north of the city on I-95, but it's definitely worth the trip. Among its multitude of rides lurks a new six-loop steel rollercoaster, the Anaconda. (Rides open daily 10:30am-10pm; Labor Day-Memorial Day Sat.-Sun. 10am-8pm. Admission $21.95, over 55 $16.95, ages 3-6 $13.95.)

Shenandoah National Park

Before 1926, when Congress authorized the establishment of Shenandoah National Park, the area held a series of rocky, threadbare farms along the Blue Ridge Mountains. Congress specified that no federal money be spent on land for the national park, but the enthused Virginia government appropriated more than $1 million and citizens donated the rest. Within 13 years, the farmers and their families had been booted off their lands and the area returned to its "natural" state. Forests replaced fields, wild deer and bears devoured cows and pigs, and a two-lane highway, Skyline Drive, paved over the dirt roads, complete with intermittent scenic overlooks where Sunday drivers could stop and gawk.

Today, such gawking comes naturally in Shenandoah; on clear days drivers and hikers can look out over miles of unspoiled ridges and treetops. In summer, the cool mountain air offers a respite from Virginia's typical heat and humidity. Go early in June to see mountain laurel blooming in the highlands. In fall, Skyline Drive and its lodges grow choked with tourists enjoying the magnificent fall foliage.

Practical Information

Emergency (in park): 703-999-2226, or contact the nearest ranger. Collect calls accepted. You must dial the area code.

Park Information: 999-2227 or 999-2229, 999-2266 for 24-hr. recorded message. Mailing address: Superintendent, Shenandoah National Park, Rte. 4, P.O. Box 348, Luray, VA 22835.

Dickey Ridge Visitors Center, mile 4.6 (635-3566), closest to the north entrance. Daily interpretative programs. Open April-Oct. daily 9am-5pm. **Byrd Visitors Center,** mile 50 (999-2243, ext. 281), in the center of the park. Movie and museum explain the history of the Blue Ridge Range and its mountain culture. Open daily 9am-5pm; Jan.-Feb. weekends only. Both stations offer changing exhibits on the park, free pamphlets detailing short hikes, daily posted weather updates, and ranger-led nature hikes.

Area Code: 703.

Shenandoah's technicolor mountains—blueish and covered with deciduous flora in summer, smeared with reds, oranges, and yellows in the fall—can be ogled from overlooks along **Skyline Drive,** which runs 105 miles south from Front Royal to Rockfish Gap. The overlooks provide picnic areas for hikers; map boards also carry data about trail conditions. The drive closes during and after bad weather. Most facilities also hibernate. (Entrance $5 per vehicle, $2 per hiker, biker, or bus passenger; pass good for 7 days; seniors and disabled free.)

Miles along Skyline Dr. are measured north to south, beginning at Front Royal. Hitching is illegal outside the park. **Greyhound** sends buses to Waynesboro, near the park's southern entrance, twice daily from DC ($35, $65 round-trip), but no bus or train serves Front Royal.

When planning to stay more than a day, purchase the *Park Guide* ($1), a booklet containing all the park regulations, trail lists, and a description of the area's geological history. The *Guide to Skyline Drive* ($4.50) also provides info on accommodations and activities. The free *Shenandoah Overlook* newspaper reports seasonal and weekly events. All three publications are available at the visitors centers.

Accommodations and Camping

The **Bear's Den AYH,** on Hwy. Rte. 601 South (554-8708), provides a woodsy stone lodge for travelers with two 10-bed dorm rooms. Drivers should exit from Rte. 7 onto Hwy. 601 South and go about a half mile, turn right at the stone-gate entrance, and proceed up the hostel driveway for another half mile. No bus or train service is available. The hostel has a dining room, kitchen, on-site parking, and a laundry room. Ask the friendly staff for activities info. (Check-in 5-9pm. Front gate locked and quiet hours begin at 10pm. Check-out by 9:30am. Members $8, nonmembers $11; winter months members $9, nonmembers $10. Camping $4 per person. Reservations recommended; write Bear's Den AYH, Postal Route 1, Box 288, Bluemont, VA 22012.)

The park maintains two lodges, **Skyland** (mile 42) and **Big Meadows** (mile 51), with motelesque rooms in cabinesque exteriors. Skyland (999-2211 or 800-999-4714), closed Dec. to March, offers brown and green wood-furnished cabins ($38-68, $3 more in Oct.) and slightly more upscale motel rooms. Big Meadows (999-2222 or 800-999-4714), closed Nov. to April, offers similar cabins and motel rooms in a smaller complex. All three locations charge an extra $2 or more Friday to Saturday. Reservations are usually necessary, up to six months in advance for the fall season.

The park service maintains four major campgrounds: **Matthews Arm** (mile 22); **Big Meadows** (mile 51); **Lewis Mountain** (mile 58); and **Loft Mountain** (mile 80). All have stores, laundry facilities, and showers (no hookups). Heavily wooded and uncluttered by mobile homes, Lewis Mountain makes for the happiest tenters. All sites cost $8 except those reserved at Big Meadows ($10); call a visitor center to check on availability.

Back-country camping is free, but you must obtain a permit at a park entrance, visitors center, ranger station, or the park headquarters halfway between Thornton Gap and Luray on U.S. 211. Back-country campers must set up 25 yd. from a water supply and out of sight of any trail, road, overlook, cabin, or other campsite. Since open fires are prohibited, bring cold food or a stove; boil water or bring your own because some creeks are oozing with microscopic beasties. Illegal camping carries a $50 fine. Hikers on the Appalachian Trail can make use of primitive open shelters, three-sided structures with stone fireplaces strewn along the trail at approximately 7-mi. intervals. At full shelters, campers often will move over to make room for a new arrival. These shelters are reserved for hikers with three or more nights in different locations stamped on their camping permits; casual hikers are banned from them. The **Potomac Appalachian Trail Club** maintains six cabins in backcountry areas of the park. You must reserve in advance by writing to the club at 1718 N St. NW, Washington, DC 20036 (202-638-5306), and bring lanterns and food. The cabins contain bunk beds, water, and stoves. (Sun.-Thurs. $3 per person, Fri.-Sat. $14 per group; one in party must be at least 21.)

Hikes and Activities

The **Appalachian Trail** runs the length of the park. Trail maps and the AMC guide can be obtained at the Visitor Center. The AMC has detailed coverage of most trails, and a topographical map which costs $15; brochures that cover the popular hikes are available free. Responsible campers will remember to avoid lighting fires and use stoves instead, and leave *no* litter whatsoever. Overnight hikers should keep the unpredictability of outdoor weather in mind. Be sure to get the Park Service package of brochures and advice before a long hike.

Old Rag Mountain, 5 mi. from mile 45, is 3291 ft.—not an intimidating summit—but the 7.2-mi. loop up the mountain is supremely difficult. The hike is steep, involves scrambling and squeezing over and between granite, and at many points flaunts discouraging "false summits." The **Whiteoak Canyon** trail beckons from its own parking lot at mile 42.6. The trail to the canyon is easy, the falls and trout-filled waters below them spectacular. Visitors centers vend five-day fishing licenses ($6), but hordes of regulations hem in the catch. From Whiteoak Canyon, the **Limberlost** trail slithers into a hemlock forest. At mile 50.7, **Dark Hollow** Trail takes only ¾-mi. to reach a gorgeous array of falls—the closest to Skyline Drive in the whole park. The trail descends further (about an hour's walk) to the base of the falls, where water drops 70 ft. over the crumbling stone of an ancient lava flow.

Drivers should enjoy **Mary's Rock Tunnel** (mile 32), where the road goes straight through almost 700 ft. of solid rock. **Hogback Overlook,** from mile 20.8 to mile 21, offers easy hikes and idyllic views of the smooth Shenandoah River and Valley; on a clear day, you can see 11 bends in the river.

Horseback and pony riding from Skyland Lodge competes with driving and hiking. (Reservations taken one day in advance at Skyland stables, daily 8:30am-3:30pm; after 3:30pm, reservations taken at the front desk. $14. 30-min. pony rides $4, available daily 9am-3pm.) **Wagon rides** at Big Meadows begin at 9am, with five daily every day except Wed. ($7, kids $3.50; no reservations). **Canoe and rafting trips** launch daily from **James River Runners,** Rte. 4 in Scottsville, which also provides tubes for trips down the river. Take Rte. 20 south from Charlottesville for 35 min., take a right on Rte. 726, go three mi., and make a left onto Rte. 625 to Halton Ferry. ($13-19, depending on the length of the trip. Tubing $11. Group rates available. Reservations recommended. Bring sneakers and sunscreen.)

Outside the park, the **Shenandoah Caverns** (477-3115) tout an iridescent panoply of stalactites and stalagmites, with "Rainbow Lake" and amusing "Capitol Dome" among the mimetic underground formations prospering in the year-round 56°F air. Take Rte. 211 to Newmarket, get on 81 North and go four mi. to the Shenandoah Caverns exit, and follow the signs for the caverns—not the town of the same name. (Handicapped accessible. $7, ages 8-14 $3.50, under 8 free.) **Skyline Caverns** (635-4545 or 800-635-4599) in Front Royal built a reputation on its anthodites, whose white spikes defy gravity and grow in all directions at the rate of an inch every seven thousand years. The Caverns are 15 minutes from the junction of Skyline Drive and U.S. 211. ($8, ages 6-12 $4, under 6 free.)

Take a break from hiking or driving at one of Shenandoah's seven **picnic areas,** located at Dickey Ridge (mile 5), Elkwallow (mile 24), Pinnacles (mile 37), Big Meadows (mile 51), Lewis Mountain (mile 58), South River (mile 63), and Loft Mountain (mile 80). All have tables, fireplaces, water fountains, and comfort stations. When you forget to pack a picnic basket, swing by the **Panorama Restaurant** (mile 31.5) for a meal and a view. (Sandwiches $4. Dinners $6-12. Open April-Nov. daily 9am-7pm.)

Blue Ridge Parkway

If you don't believe that the best things in life are free, this ride could change your mind. The 469 mi. of the Blue Ridge Parkway, continuous with Skyline Drive, run through Virginia and North Carolina connecting the **Shenandoah** and **Great Smoky Mountains National Parks** (see Tennessee). Administered by the National Park Service, the parkway adjoins hiking trails, campsites, and picnic grounds. Every bit as scenic as Skyline Drive, the Parkway remains much wilder and less crowded. From Shenandoah National Park, the road winds south through Virginia's **George Washington National Forest** from Waynesboro southwest to Roanoke. The forest offers spacious campgrounds, canoes for rent, and swimming in cold, clear mountain water at **Shenandoah Lake** (mile 16).

Self-guided nature trails range from the **Mountain Farm Trail** (mile 5.9), a 20-min. hike to a pleasant reconstructed homestead, to the **Hardwood Cove Natural Trail** (mile 167), a three-hour excursion. Of course, real devotees tackle the **Appalachian Trail**, which runs the length of the parkway. The Park Service hosts a variety of ranger-led interpretive activities.

Some of the more spectacular sights on and near the parkway include a 215-ft.-high, 90-ft.-long limestone arch called **Natural Bridge,** which now supports an unnatural highway and hosts unnatural nightly audio-visual shows (800-533-1410, 800-336-5727 outside VA; open daily 8am-dusk; shows nightly, times vary with season; admission to bridge and night show: $7, seniors $6, kids $3.50). Thomas Jefferson bought the site from King George III for 20 shillings. George Washington also initialed it; look for the "GW loves Martha" blazon still visible today. At **Mabry Mill** (mile 176.1) or **Humpback Rocks** (mile 5.8) you can simulate pioneer life, and at **Crabtree Meadows** (mile 339) you can purchase local crafts.

The **Blue Ridge Country AYH Hostel,** Rte. 2, P.O. Box 449, Galax 24333 (703-236-4962), rests only 100 ft. from the parkway at mile 214.5. (3-night max. stay. $9.50, nonmembers $12.50 which includes redeemable $3 stamp for membership. For North Carolina hostels, see Asheville and Boone, in North Carolina.) There are nine **campgrounds** along the parkway, each with water and restrooms, located at miles 61, 86, 120, 167, 238, 297, 316, 339, and 408. The fee is $8, reservations not accepted. Contact the parkway for info on backcountry and winter camping. Camping in the backcountry of the George Washington National Forest is free.

The cities and villages along the parkway offer a range of accommodations. You can stay at **The Bear's Den AYH-Hostel (AYH)** located 35 mi. north of Shenandoah on the Appalachian Trail in Bluemont. (Open year-round except for Christmas/New Year's week. $8 summer, $9 winter, nonmembers $11, $12.) For a complete listing, pick up a *Blue Ridge Parkway Directory* at one of the visitors centers, or the *Virginia Accommodations Directory.* The communities listed have easy access to the parkway and many, such as Asheville and Boone, NC, and Charlottesville, VA, have historic and cultural attractions of their own (see above and below).

Greyhound/Trailways provides access to the major towns around the Blue Ridge. Buses run to and from Richmond, Waynesboro, and Lexington; a bus serves Buchanan and Natural Bridge between Roanoke and Lexington once daily. For info, contact the station in Charlottesville (see Charlottesville Practical Information) or Greyhound/Trailways, 26 Salem Ave. SW (703-342-6761; open 24 hrs.), in Roanoke.

For general info on the parkway, call **visitor information** in North Carolina (704-259-0779 or 704-259-0701). For additional details call the park service in Roanoke, VA (703-982-6458), or in Montebello, VA (703-377-2377). Write for info to **Blue Ridge Parkway Headquarters,** 200 BB&T Bldg., Asheville, NC 28801. Ten **visitors centers** lie along the parkway, plus seven stands where you can pick up brochures. Located at entry points where major highways intersect the Blue Ridge, the centers offer various exhibits, programs, and information facilities. Pick up a free copy of the helpful *Milepost* guide.

In an **emergency** call 800-727-5928 anywhere in VA or NC. Be sure to give your location to the nearest mile.

Virginia Beach

Aaah, the beach. Gaze upon glorious miles of breaking and unbroken lines of water, sand, and sky; smell the perfume of the tide; listen to the insistent rhythm of the incessant waves. Then turn around and face the boardwalk.

Virginia Beach unabashedly immerses itself in the present. Rows of hotels and motels, ice cream stands, surf shops, and fast-food joints flank the golden coastline, and swarms of cruising college students and servicemen descend upon the beach resort every summer. It's the biggest metropolitan area in Virginia, and it wants you there. With your wallet, of course.

Practical Information

Emergency: 911.

Virginia Beach Visitor's Center, 22nd and Parks Ave. (425-7511 or 800-446-8038), across the street from the Center for the Arts. Helps you find budget accommodations and gives info on area sights. Open daily 9am-8pm; Labor Day-Memorial Day daily 9am-5pm.

Public Transportation: Greyhound, 1017 Laskin Rd. (422-2998), connects with Norfolk, Williamsburg, and Richmond, and with Maryland via the Bridge Tunnel. The nearest **Amtrak** station (245-3589 or 800-872-7245), in Newport News, provides free 45-min. bus service to and from the **Radisson Hotel** at 19th St. and Pavilion Drive in Virginia Beach. You must have a train ticket to get on the bus.

Local Transportation: The Virginia Beach Transit/Trolley Information Center (428-3388) provides complete info on area transportation and tours, including trolleys, buses, and ferries. In summer, the Atlantic Avenue Trolley runs from Rudee Inlet to 42nd St. (Memorial Day-Labor Day daily noon-midnight; fare 50¢, seniors and disabled 25¢.) Other trolleys run along the boardwalk, the North Seashore, and to Lynnhaven Mall.

Bike Rentals: North End Cyclery, at Laskin Rd. and Baltic Ave. Open 10am-7pm. Bikes $3.50 per hr. or $12 per day. Moped Rentals, Inc., 21st St. and Pacific Ave. Open daily in summer, 9am-midnight. Bikes $7 for 90 min., mopeds $22.50 for 90 min.

Post Office: 24th and Atlantic Ave. (428-2821). Open Mon.-Fri. 8-11am and noon-4:30pm. ZIP code: 23458.

Area code: 804.

Virginia Beach is confusing to get to, but easy to get around in. Drivers from the north can take I-64 south from Richmond through the Bay Bridge Tunnel into Norfolk, then get on Rte. 44 (the Virginia Beach-Norfolk Expressway), which delivers you straight to 22nd St. and the beach. Virginia Beach's street grid pits east-west numbered streets (from 1st to around 90th) against north-south avenues (Atlantic, Pacific, Arctic, and Baltic) parallel to the beach.

Accommodations and Camping

Finding a cheap place to stay in Virginia Beach is easy, especially on Atlantic and Pacific Avenues parallel to the ocean front. **Angie's Guest Cottage-Bed and Breakfast (AYH),** 302 24th St. (428-4690), still ranks as one of the top 10 hostel experiences in the USA. The Yates mother-daughter team welcomes guests with unbelievable warmth; they won't turn anyone away. They'll pick you up from the train station and go out of their way to help guests with job-and house-hunting. If you stay in the guest cottage, breakfast is included. Call for reservations. (Memorial Day-Labor Day $10.95, non-members $14.25. Off-season $7.85, non-members $10. Cottage rooms $44-62. Linens $2. Kitchen and lockers available.)

Two other clean lodging options are the **Ocean Palms Motel,** 30th St. and Arctic Ave. (428-8362 or 428-5357; singles $40), and the **Viking Motel,** 2700 Atlantic Ave. (428-7116, 800-828-3063 for reservations) just a block from the beach. (Singles from $45; off-season $20.) If you're traveling in a group, shop around for "efficiency rate" apartments with cheap weekly rates.

Camping on the beach is illegal, and the number of campgrounds around make it unnecessary. The **Seashore State Park,** about 8 mi. north of town on U.S. 60 (481-2131; 490-3939 for reservations), has a desirable location amid sand dunes and cypress trees. The park is very popular, so call two to three weeks ahead (during business hours) for reservations. (Sites $14. Park open 8am-dusk; take the North Seashore Trolley.) **KOA,** 1240 General Booth Blvd. (428-1444), runs a quiet campground with free bus service to the beach and boardwalk. (Sites $14-20 for two. Komfortable and kapacious 1-room kamping kabins $36.) **Holiday Travel Park,** 1075 General Booth Blvd. (425-0249), is a mega-campground with 1000 sites, four pools, and miniature golf. (Sites $11-29.)

Food

Junk-food junkies will love Virginia Beach, thanks to its proliferation of fast-food joints. But the neon glare hides several restaurants with a local flavor. If you *schlepp* to **The Jewish Mother,** 3108 Pacific Ave. (422-5430), you'll grow nice and *zaftig* on quiche, omelettes, crèpes ($4-9), deli sandwiches ($4-5), and desserts ($2-3). At night, it's a popular live-music bar. No, you go in, it's all right, I'll wait outside, I'm only your mother, what do I care? (Open daily 9am-3am.) **The Raven,** 1200 Atlantic Ave. (425-9556), lays out well-prepared seafood, steaks, and salad in a tinted-glass greenhouse setting. You can eat outdoors when it's warm, but when it's cold, nevermore. (Sandwiches and burgers $4-6, dinners $9-15. Open Mon-Fri. noon-2am, Sat.-Sun. 9am-2am.) Prospective picnickers should head for the **Virginia Beach Farmer's Market,** 1989 Landstown Rd. (427-4395; open daily 9am-6:30pm; open until dark in winter). At 31st St. (Luskin Rd.) and Baltic Ave., the **Farm Fresh Supermarket** salad bar, stocked with fresh fruit, pastas, and frozen yogurt at $2.39 per lb. (open 24 hrs.) is a cheap alternative hostelers love.

Nightlife

In darkness the beach becomes a haunt for lovers, but the boardwalk becomes a haunt for people you may not want haunting you. Singles hover around the bars and clubs between 17th and 23rd St. along Pacific and Atlantic Ave. Locals favor **Chicho's** (422-6011) and the **Edge,** along Atlantic Ave. between 20th and 21st Streets. T-shirts, tight dresses, and tanned skin line the insides of these bars. Young adults of either sex can come here to try to convince people who are already partially-unclad to retire someplace where they can be completely unclad. (Chicho's open Mon.-Fri. 1pm-1:30am, Sat.-Sun. noon-1:30am; no cover. The Edge open daily 1pm-2am; no cover.)

Sights

The main sight here is the beach itself, but museum-seekers can start with the **Virginia Marine Science Museum,** 717 General Booth Blvd. (425-3476), which traces marine life from mountain ponds to the Sargasso Sea. The Ocean Drive simulates the porthole view from an underwater research ship. (Open daily 9am-5pm, extended hours in summer. Admission $3.50, seniors and kids $2.75.) Right off the beach at 24th St. in a former life-saving service station (the predecessor to the U.S. Coast Guard) stands the cozy **Life-Saving Museum of Virginia.** Eager and friendly tour guides can tell you more than you ever thought you wanted to know about the origins of the Coast Guard. (Open Mon.-Sat. 10am-5pm, Sun. noon-5pm; Sept.-May. Tues.-Sat. 10am-5pm, Sun. noon-5pm. Admission $2, over 60 and military personnel $1.50, ages 6-18 75¢.)

Virginia Beach is biker-friendly, with bike paths along the boardwalk and some of the larger streets. Rent a bike in one of the many stands near the boardwalk (about $5 per hr.) and then ask for the Virginia Beach Bikeway Map at the Visitor's Center. If you're feeling athletic, bike south down the coast to **Sandbridge Beach,** where the locals hang out to avoid crowds of tourists; take the bike trail through the Back Bay National Wildlife Refuge. Or bike north to calm, self-descriptive **Sea-**

shore State Park. The First Landing Cross, at Cape Henry in Fort Story, marks the spot where America's first permanent English settlers, the Jamestown colonists, first braved the New World's shores on April 26, 1607.

On the way back from Seashore State Park, test your psychic ability at the visitor's center of the **Edgar Cayce Association for Research and Enlightenment,** 67th St. and Atlantic Ave. (428-3588), which is dedicated to the development of psychic potential and holistic health. We would tell you to go there, but we already *know* you will. (Open Mon.-Fri. 8:30am-8pm, Sat. 8:30am-5:30 pm, Sun. 11am-5:30pm; Oct.-April Mon.-Sat. 9am-5:30pm, Sun. 1-6pm. Free with 3pm daily lecture.) As you drive away, six mi. west of the beach along the Norfolk-Virginia Beach Expressway, look for **Mt. Trashmore,** Virginia's famous public park built from alternating layers of soil and trash.

Near Virginia Beach: Norfolk

Navy-heavy Norfolk is Virginia Beach's sister city. If you want to see more than one of the tourist sights in Norfolk, buy a "Discover Tidewater" passport for the TRT Trolley at the Virginia Beach Visitor's Center or at the blue-and-white info booth at 24th and Atlantic Ave (623-3222). With a one-day passport ($7, seniors, kids, and disabled people $3.50) in your hand, you can catch a trolley into Norfolk every half-hour from the dome at 19th St. and Pacific Ave.

The Chrysler Museum, Olney Rd. and Mewbray Arch (622-1211), is Norfolk's jewel, offering an eclectic collection ranging from decorative art to religious icons. Occidental art hangs in chronological order; viewers begin in the 14th century and end in the 20th. (Open Tues.-Sat. 10am-4pm, Sun. 1-5pm. Free.) The museum is a stop on the "Discover Tidewater" trolley tour, or take the #20 Bus (one-way fare $2.60).

Armchair admirals will love the **Norfolk Naval Base,** the largest naval base anywhere, which keeps Norfolk's economy afloat. The Persian Gulf war, which sent the sailors away, meant economic disaster. Stroll down the pier to see the massive gray hulks of the USA's crack battleships. Come early if you want to see the sights; the hours are tricky. The tour office at 9809 Hampton Rd. (444-7097) opens daily (8am-4pm) and a museum opens daily from 9am to 4pm, but be there before 3pm or you'll be turned away. (Ship tours are given Sat. 1-4:30pm.) The "Discover Tidewater" passport includes this tour in its package, or you can purchase a separate Norfolk Naval Base ticket ($4, seniors, under 12, and disabled people $2). Drivers will need a visitor's pass; get one across Hampton Rd. at Gate 5.

Williamsburg

At the end of the 17th century, when English aristocrats wore brocades and wigs due to syphilis (the disease made their hair fall out), Williamsburg powdered its face as the capital of Virginia. During the Revolutionary War, the capital moved to Richmond, taking with it much of Williamsburg's grandeur. Then, in 1926, John D. Rockefeller, Jr.'s immense bank account came to the aid of the distressed city, restoring part of the town as a colonial village. His foundation still runs the restored section, Colonial Williamsburg, where fife and drum corps parade while cobblers, bookbinders, blacksmiths, and clockmakers go about their tasks using 200-year-old methods. Filled with events, the town might witness a Punch and Judy show, an evening of 18th-century theater, or a militia review on any given day. Though the fascinating and beautiful ex-capital claims to be a faithfully restored version of its 18th-century self, don't look for dirt roads, open sewers, or African slaves. Williamsburg also prides itself on **William and Mary,** the second-oldest college in the United States. Outside Williamsburg, Virginia's other big tourist sights lie in wait; history buffs should see Yorktown, Jamestown, or one of the restored plantations, while amusement park aficionados should head to Busch Gardens.

Practical Information

Emergency: 911.

Williamsburg Area Tourism and Conference Bureau, 201 Penniman Rd. (229-6511), about ½-mi. northwest of the transportation center. Free *Visitors Guide to Virginia's Historic Triangle.* Open Mon.-Fri. 8:30am-5pm. **Tourist Visitor Center,** Rte. 132-132y (800-447-8679), 1 mi. northeast of the train station. Tickets and transport to Colonial Williamsburg. Maps and guides upstairs, info on Virginia sights downstairs.

Transportation Center: at the end of N. Boundary St., across from the fire station. **Amtrak** (229-8750 or 800-872-7245). Direct service to: New York ($79), Washington, DC ($27), Philadelphia ($56), Baltimore ($32). Open Mon.-Tues. and Fri. 7:30am-9pm, Wed.-Thurs. and Sat. 7:30am-3pm, Sun. 1:30-9pm. **Greyhound/Trailways,** 229-1460. Ticket office open Mon.-Fri. 8am-6pm, Sat.-Sun. 8am-4pm. To: Richmond ($9), Norfolk ($9), Washington, DC ($20). **James City County Transit (JCCT),** 220-1621. Service along Rte. 60, from Merchants Sq. in the Historic District, or east past Busch Gardens. No service to Yorktown or Jamestown. Operates Mon.-Sat. 6:15am-8:30pm. Fare $1, 25¢ per zone change; exact change required.

Williamsburg Limousine Service: 877-0279. Both the local taxi and cheapest guided tours. To Busch Gardens or Carter's Grove $6 round-trip. Guided tours to Jamestown ($19.50), Yorktown ($17.50), or both ($35), with admission included. Will take you to and from your Williamsburg lodgings. Make reservations for tours at least 24 hrs. in advance, between 9am-1am.

Post Office: 425 N. Boundary St. (229-4668). Open Mon.-Fri. 8am-5pm, Sat. 10am-noon. **ZIP codes:** 23185 (Williamsburg), 23490 (Yorktown), and 23081 (Jamestown).

Area Code: 804.

Travelers should visit in late fall or early spring to avoid the crowds, high temperature, and humidity of summer. Also be aware that all the signs pointing to Colonial Williamsburg do not actually send you there, but to the visitor center instead. To drive to the restored area proper, take the Lafayette St. exit off the Colonial Pkwy. Parking is surprisingly easy to find.

Accommodations and Camping

The few bargains in the Williamsburg area lie along Rte. 60 west or Rte. 31 south toward Jamestown. From Memorial Day to Labor Day, rooms are scarce and prices higher, so try to call at least two weeks in advance. For a complete listing of accommodations, pick up a free copy of *Visitors Guide to Virginia's Historic Triangle* at the conference bureau, *not* at the visitor center (see Practical Info).

The closest hostel, **Sangraal-by-the-Sea Youth Hostel (AYH),** Rte. 626 (776-6500), near Urbanna, leaps 30 mi. away. They do provide rides to bus or train stations during business hours, but don't expect a daily ride to Williamsburg. ($9, nonmembers $11. Call ahead.) Closer to Williamsburg, **guest houses** are your best bet: some don't require reservations, but all expect you to call ahead, and most expect customers to avoid rowdiness and behave like houseguests. Five minutes from the historic district is **Mrs. H. J. Carter,** 903 Lafayette St. (229-1117). Dust mice wouldn't dare hide under the four-poster beds in these large, airy singles and doubles. Prices range from $25 (1 person) to $35 (4 in 2 beds), but Mrs. Carter will not let unmarried couples sleep in the same bed. **The Elms,** 708 Richmond Rd. (229-1551), offers elegant, colorful, antique-furnished rooms to one or two visitors for $21. Both houses sleep eight. **Holland's Sleepy Lodge,** 211 Harrison Ave. (229-6321), rents singles for $26.

Hotels close to the historic district, especially chain- or foundation-owned hotels, do not come cheap. The **Lafayette Motel,** 1220 Richmond Rd. (220-4900), a 10-minute walk from William & Mary, has clean, ordinary rooms with colonial-looking facades and a pool. (Singles $31-38. Doubles $55.) **Motel 6,** Rte. 60 W. (565-3433), 2½ mi. from Colonial Williamsburg, offers standard motel fare and a pool. (Singles $30. Doubles $36.)

Several campsites blanket the area. **Anvil Campgrounds,** 5243 Moretown Rd. (565-2300), 3 mi. west of Colonial Williamsburg Information Center on Rte. 60, offers a swimming pool, bath-house, recreational hall, and store. (Sites $13-15, with hookup $20.) **Indian Village Campground,** 1811 Jamestown Rd. (229-8211), 2¼ mi. south on Rte. 31 from Rte. 199, has similar facilities and also rents cabins. (Sites $8-18. Call 5-9pm or leave message.) Nearby **Brass Lantern Campsites,** 1782 Jamestown Rd. (229-4320 or 229-9089), charges $10, with full hookup $14.

Food and Nightlife

Though Colonial Williamsburg proper contains several authentic-looking "taverns," few are cheap and most require reservations and forbid tank-tops. When you must eat in the historic district, stand in line for **Chowning's Tavern,** on Duke of Gloucester St., offering stews, sandwiches, and the misleading "Welsh Rabbit" (bread and cheese in beer sauce with ham) from $6. (Open daily 11:30am-3:30pm and 4pm-1am.) From 9pm on at Chowning's the **gambols** take place: costumed waiters serve mixed drinks, sing 18th-century ballads, and teach patrons how to play outdated dice and card games. **The Old Chickahominy House,** 1211 Jamestown Rd. (229-4689), rests over one mi. from the historic district, but make the trip. Share the antique and dried-flowers decor with pewter-haired locals whose ancestors survived "Starvation Winter" in Jamestown. Miss Melinda's "complete luncheon" is Virginia ham served on hot biscuits, fruit salad, a slice of buttermilk pie, and iced tea or coffee ($4.75). Expect a 20-min. wait for lunch. (Open daily 8:30-10:15am and 11:30am-2:15pm.)

During the summer, few William & Mary students stick around, but their hangouts, inexpensive and comfortable alternatives to fast-food fare, remain. In 50s wood and vinyl, **Paul's Deli Restaurant and Pizza,** 761 Scotland St., sells crisp *stromboli* for two ($6-7) and filling subs ($3-5). The "hot Italian" sub makes locals salivate. (Open daily 11am-2am.) Next door, the more upscale **Greenleafe Cafe** (220-3405) serves sandwiches, salads, and the like ($5-10), throbbing after 9pm on Wednesday (cover $2) with live folk music. (Open daily 11:30am-2am.) Both establishments are just a few blocks up Richmond Rd. from "Confusion Corner" where Colonial Williamsburg ends and W&M begins. For less pomp and more rustic circumstance, pack a picnic from one of the supermarkets clustered around the **Williamsburg Shopping Center,** at the intersection of Richmond Rd. and Lafayette St., or try the fast-food strip along Rte. 60. The rudimentary **farmers market** at Lafayette and North Henry St. sells cheap seafood and vegetables.

Sights

Unless you plan to apply to W&M, you've probably come to see the restored gardens and buildings, crafts, tours, and costumed actors in the **Colonial Williamsburg** historic district. The complex claims to recreate 18th-century Virginia, but it may introduce you to the ways of 19th-century robber barons. The Colonial Williamsburg Foundation (CWF) owns everything from the Governor's Palace to the lemonade stands and even most of the houses marked "private home"; most attractions require exorbitantly-priced tickets. You even need a general admission ticket to enter the historic district, though this technicality is not enforced. All tickets entitle you to ride the CWF buses which circle the historic district every few minutes. A **Patriot's Pass** gains admission to all the town's attractions (except the former Rockefeller home, Bassett Hall) for one year, entrance to Carter's Grove, and a guided tour ($26, under 13 $17); a **Royal Governor's Pass** lasts four days and covers all the attractions in the town ($22.50, under 13 $15); and a **Basic Ticket** lets you into any 12 attractions except the Governor's Palace and the Decorative Arts Museum ($19, under 13 $12.50). Buy them at the CWF Visitor Center or from booths in town.

"Doing" the historic district without a ticket definitely saves money; for no charge, you can walk the streets, ogle the buildings, browse in the shops, march behind the fife and drum corps, lock yourself in the stockade, and even use the restrooms. Some shops that actually sell goods—notably the Apothecary by the Palace

Green—are open to the public. Catch up to a guided **walking tour** moving about Colonial Williamsburg during the day. The poorly named "Other Half" tour relates the experience of Africans and African Americans. Outdoor events, including a mid-day cannon-firing, receive listings in the weekly *Visitor's Companion,* which is given away to ticket-holders—many of whom conveniently leave it where non-ticket-holders can pick it up. A separate pamphlet detailing disabled access in Williamsburg is also available at the Tourist Info Center. Picnickers may find the best spots just outside the historic district on the elegant grounds of the **Abbey Aldrich Rockefeller Museum.** The adjacent unfenced swimming pool is officially open only to guests of CWF's hotels.

Those willing to pay shouldn't miss the **Governor's Palace** on the Palace Green. This mansion housed the appointed governors of the Virginia colony until the last one fled in 1775. Reconstructed colonial sidearms and ceremonial sabers line the reconstructed walls, and the garden includes a hedge maze. (Separate admission $13.) The **Wallace Decorative Arts Museum** holds excellent collections of English furniture and ceramics. (Open Thurs.-Tues. 9am-5pm, Wed. 9am-5:30pm. Separate admission $7.50.)

Spreading west from the corner of Richmond and Jamestown Rd. ("Confusion Corner"), the other focal point of Williamsburg, **William and Mary,** is the second-oldest college in the U.S. Chartered in 1693, the college has educated Presidents Jefferson, Monroe, and Tyler. The **Sir Christopher Wren Building,** also restored with Rockefeller money, is the oldest classroom building in the country. Nearby, in the historic district, sprawl the shops at **Merchant Square.** Park here and walk straight into Colonial Williamsburg.

Near Williamsburg

Jamestown and **Yorktown** are both important parts of the U.S. colonial story. The National Park System provides free, well-administered visitor's guides to both areas. Combination tickets to Yorktown Victory Center and to Jamestown Festival Park are available at either site for $9.50.

At the **Jamestown National Park** you'll see remains of the first permanent English settlement of 1607 and exhibits explaining colonial life. At the visitors center, skip the hokey film and catch a "living history" walking tour on which a guide portraying one of the colonists describes the Jamestown way of life. Call ahead (229-1733) for info since "living history" guides sometimes take the day off. (Site open daily 8:30am-6pm; off-season 9am-5:30pm. Entrance fee $5 per car, $2 per hiker or cyclist.) Also see the nearby **Jamestown Settlement** (229-1607), a museum commemorating the Jamestown settlement, with changing exhibits, a reconstruction of James Fort, a Native American village, and full-scale replicas of the three ships which brought the original settlers to Jamestown in 1607. A "living history" sailor even talks about the voyage. (Open daily 9am-5pm. Admission $6.50, under 13 $3.)

The American Revolution's last significant battle took place at Yorktown. British General Charles Lord Cornwallis and his men seized the town for use as a port in 1781. The colonists and the French soon surrounded and stormed the hold, forcing the British to surrender. Yorktown's **Colonial Park** vividly recreates the battle with an engaging film, fascinating dioramas, and a cool electric map. The park also maintains remnants of the original trenches built by the British. Drivers can take a seven-mi. self-guided tour of the battlefield, or rent a tape cassette and recorder for $2 in the visitors center. (Open daily 8:30am-6pm; last tape rented at 5pm.) The **Yorktown Victory Center** (887-1776), one block from Rte. 17 on Rte. 238, offers a museum filled with items from the Revolutionary War, as well as a film and an intriguing "living history" exhibit: in an encampment in front of the center, a troop of soldiers from the Continental Army of 1772 take a well-deserved break from active combat. Feel free to ask them about tomorrow's march or last week's massacre. (Open daily 9am-5pm. Admission $5, under 13 $2.50.)

Without a car, you won't find a cheap way to get to Jamestown or Yorktown; since the "towns" are tourist sights, guided tours provide the only transportation.

With **Williamsburg Limousine,** a group of at least four people can see both James-town attractions in the morning ($19.50 per person), both Yorktown sights in the afternoon ($17.50 per person), or take the whole day and see both ($35). The unlined **Colonial Parkway** makes a beautiful biking route, but beware of inattentive auto drivers. You can rent a bike for $10 a day at **Bikes Limited,** 759 Scotland Avenue (229-4620). (Open Mon.-Fri. 9am-7pm, Sat. 9am-5pm, Sun. noon-4pm.)

The **James River plantations,** built near the water to facilitate the planters' com-mercial and social life, buttressed the slave-holding Virginia aristocracy. **Carter's Grove Plantation,** 6 mi. east of Williamsburg on Rte. 60, is an example of the early 20th century's "Colonial Revival" of early plantations. The last owners doubled the size of the original 18th-century building, but sought to maintain its colonial feel. The Carter's Grove complex also includes reconstructed 18th-century slave quarters and an archeological dig. The brand-new **Winthrop Rockefeller Archeo-logical Museum,** built unobtrusively into a hillside, provides a fascinating case-study look at archeology. The exhibits will leave you with more questions than answers about the society of Martin's Hundred, whose settlement at Wolstenholme Town (directly in front of the museum) fell under Indian attack in 1622. Williamsburg Limousine (see above) offers daily round-trip tours from Colonial Williamsburg to the plantation ($5), but if you can, bike from South England Street in Colonial Wil-liamsburg along the one-way, 7-mi., wooded Carter's Grove Country Road. (Planta-tion open daily 9am-5pm, Nov.-Dec. 9am-4pm; museum open daily 9am-5pm; slave quarters open daily 9am-5pm; Country Road open daily 8:30am-4pm, Nov.-Dec. 8:30am-3pm. Plantation admission $8, ages 6-12 $5, free with CWF Patriot's Pass.)

When you tire of history, head to one of America's most famous amusement parks, **Busch Gardens: The Old Country,** 3 mi. east of Williamsburg on Rte. 60 (253-3350). You'll be flung, splashed, throttled, and swooped by the multifarious shows and rides. Each section of the park represents a European nation; trains and sky-cars connect the sections. Questor, a new ride, brings the amusement experience into the video age; the Loch Ness Monster keeps roller-coasting at its most primal. Williamsburg Limousine and local buses serve Busch Gardens (see Practical Info above). (Open daily mid-March through Oct., 10am-midnight. Admission $22.95, $18.95 after 5pm. Parking $3.) A free monorail from Busch Gardens takes you to the **Anheuser-Busch Brewery** (253-3600), where tourists get two free mugs of Busch beer. (Accessible from I-64. Open daily 10am-4pm. Free.) You can also cool off at **Water Country, USA** on Rte. 199 east (229-1000), ¼-mi. east of I-64. The water theme park features a wave tank, water rides, and variety shows. (Open mid-June to mid-Aug. daily 10am-8pm; late Aug.-early Sept. and late May to mid-June 10am-7pm. Admission $16, ages 4-12 $13.95.)

Washington, DC

DC's master planner Pierre L'Enfant designed grand avenues and public spaces for what he thought would be a thriving commercial and ceremonial center. But nineteenth-century Washington was a malarial swamp of empty avenues, slave mar-kets, elegant government buildings, and boarding houses—the nation's capital, yes, but not much else. The city grew slowly until the Great Depression, when FDR founded an alphabet soup of federal agencies staffed by liberal out-of-towners; by the end of World War II, DC had become the focus of the free world, and a genuine metropolis, many of whose residents were descended from emancipated Southern slaves (over 70% of the current population is African-American). Protests are as much a tradition as politics itself, from Coxey's Army (in the depression year of 1893) to the half-a-million strong pro-choice crowds of today. Martin Luther King Jr.'s 1963 march brought 250,000 to the Lincoln Memorial on behalf of civil rights—and the 1968 anti-war gathering ringed the Pentagon with chants and shouts. The same year's riots torched much of the city; some blocks still await re-

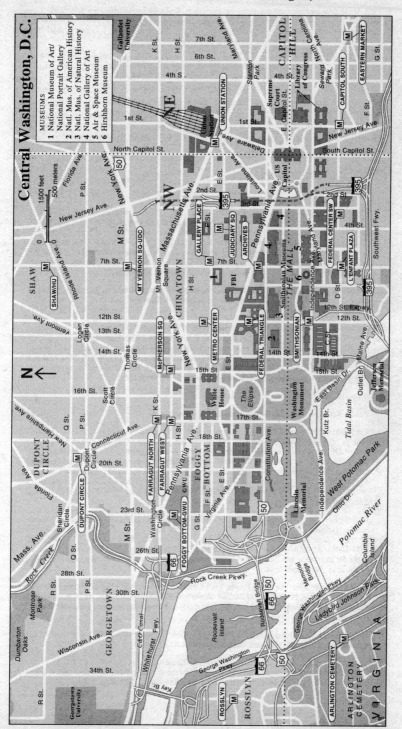

Central Washington, D.C.

MUSEUMS
1 National Museum of Art/
National Portrait Gallery
2 Natl. Mus. of American History
3 Natl. Mus. of Natural History
4 National Gallery of Art
5 Air & Space Museum
6 Hirshhorn Museum

1500 feet
500 meters

building. Despite, or perhaps because of, Watergate and skyrocketing deficits, the capital won't be shrinking anytime soon: lawyers, diplomats, lobbyists and interns will keep downtown crowded for the foreseeable future.

Though government institutions are its economic and geographic core, Washington isn't just a government town—the tourists who breeze through the Mall and the monuments have hardly begun to see the city. And there are parts they'd probably rather not see: the much-publicized low-income areas, devastated by crack cocaine, guns, and institutional neglect. (Mayor Sharon Pratt Dixon's determined management makes an ironic contrast with an indifferent Congress where DC's 600,000-odd residents still have no voting members.) But you'll be rewarded for venturing far from the governmental attractions; Washington is more than just the international capital of capital.

Practical Information

Emergency: 911.

Visitor Information: Visitor Information Center, 1455 Pennsylvania Ave. NW (789-7000), within the "Willard collection" of shops. A very helpful first stop. Ask for Washington Visitors Map. Language bank service in over 20 tongues. Open Mon.-Sat. 9am-5pm. Washington Convention and Visitors Association (WCVA), 1212 New York Ave., NW (789-7000). Does not expect walk-ins; write or call. Open Mon.-Fri. 9am-5pm. Daily Tourist Info, 737-8866. International Visitors Information Service (IVIS), 733 15th St. NW #300 (783-6540). 24-hr. language bank in over 50 languages. Open Mon.-Fri. 9am-5pm.

Traveler's Aid: Main office, 512 C St. NE (546-3120). Open Mon.-Fri. 9am-5pm. Desks at Union Station (546-3120, TTY 684-7886; open Sun.-Fri. 9am-9pm, Sat. 9am-6pm) and Dulles International Airport (661-8636, TTY 471-9776; open Sun.-Fri. 10am-9pm, Sat. 10am-6pm).

Embassies: Australia, 1601 Massachusetts Ave. NW (797-3000). Canada, 501 Pennsylvania Ave. NW (682-1740). France, 4101 Reservoir Rd. NW (944-6000). Germany, 4635 Reservoir Rd. NW (298-4000). Ireland, 2234 Massachusetts Ave. NW (462-3939). Israel, 3514 International Drive NW (364-5500). Japan, 2520 Massachusetts Ave. NW (939-6700). New Zealand, 37 Observatory Circle NW (328-4800). South Africa, 3051 Massachusetts Ave. NW (232-4400). United Kingdom, 3100 Massachusetts Ave. NW (462-1340).

Airports and Trains: See Getting There, below.

Public Transport and Taxis: See Orientation, below.

Car Rental: Cheapest in Arlington, VA, across the Potomac from downtown and easily accessible by Metrobus. Easi Car Rentals, 2480 Glebe Rd., Arlington (703-521-0188). $25 per day within DC area; elsewhere $30 per day, $155 per week. Unlimited mileage. Must be 21 or older with major credit card or $300 cash deposit. Reservations only. Open Mon.-Fri. 10am-6pm, Sat. 11am-4pm. Bargain Buggies Rent-a-Car, 912 N. Lincoln St., Arlington (703-522-4141). $16 per day, $106 per week with 150 free miles, 10¢ each additional mi. Must be 18 or older with major credit card or $250-800 cash deposit. Open Mon.-Fri. 8am-7pm, Sat.-Sun. 9am-3pm.

Bicycle Rentals: Thompson Boat Center, 2900 Virginia Ave. NW (333-4861), next to Washington Harbor on K St. All kinds of bikes; ten-speeds $3 per hour or $15 per day, locks 50¢ per day. Open Mon.-Fri. 7am-6pm, Sat.-Sun. 8am-5pm. Big Wheel Bikes, 315 7th St. SE (543-1600). Rents mountain bikes: $5 per hour, $25 per business day. 3-hr. min. charge. $5 extra for overnight use. Must have major credit card for deposit. Open Sun. and Tues.-Fri. 11am-7pm, Sat. 10am-6pm.

Foreign newspapers: The News Room, 1753 Connecticut Ave. NW (332-1489). News World, 1001 Connecticut Ave. NW (872-0190). American International News, 1825 Eye St. NW (223-2526). Key Bridge Newsstand, 3326 M St. NW (338-2626) between 33rd and 34th St. NW.

Help Lines: DC Hotline, 223-2255 or 832-4357. Rape Crisis Center, 333-7273. Crime Victim Counseling, 232-6682. Gay and Lesbian Hotline, 833-3234.

Post Office: indescribably inconvenient at 900 Brentwood Rd. NE (636-2200). Mail sent "General Delivery" always comes here—a good reason not to have anything sent General Delivery. Usually open Mon.-Fri. 8am-7pm, Sat. 8am-5pm. ZIP code: 20066.

Area Code: 202.

Getting There

The two main roads from Baltimore and the North are the **Baltimore-Washington (BW) Parkway** and **I-95**. To go downtown, take the Parkway and follow signs for New York Ave. To get to upper northwest, take I-95 to the Silverspring exit onto the Capitol Beltway (I-495), then exit 20 ("Chevy Chase") onto Conecticut Ave., and take a left. From the south, take I-95 (which becomes I-395) directly to the 14th St. Bridge or Memorial Bridge; both lead downtown. From the west, take I-66 east over the Roosevelt Bridge and follow signs for Constitution Ave. Vehicles on I-66 East (Mon.-Fri. 7-9am) and West (Mon.-Fri. 4-6pm) *must* carry at least three people. Highways into DC are almost always congested; try not to arrive during rush hour.

Three **airports** serve Washington. From within the U.S., it's best to fly into **National Airport** (703-685-8000), on the Metro and under 20 minutes from DC by car. Cab fare downtown costs $10-15. From New York's LaGuardia Airport, the Delta Shuttle and the Trump Shuttle provide competing hourly flights to National Airport seven days a week; student and senior fares, available for anyone over 65 or under 24, are always under $75. **Dulles International Airport** (703-471-4242), at least a 40-minute drive from downtown, handles mostly international, transcontinental, and bargain flights. An express bus shuttles to and from the West Falls Church Metro and Dulles every 20 minutes or so (Mon.-Fri. 6am-10:30pm, Sat. 8am-10:30pm, Sun. 10:30am-10:30pm; hourly Sun. until 1:30pm; one-way trip $5). If you must, fly into **Baltimore-Washington International Airport (BWI)**, about 10 mi. south of Baltimore's city center. Driving time is about 50 minutes from Washington and 30 minutes from Baltimore, but as always, allow for Hendrix-style jams. You can take Amtrak (40 min.) or MARC from DC (see below). The **Washington Flyer Express** (685-1400) shuttles to and from National, Dulles, BWI, and their station at 1517 K St. NW. (Shuttle to National one-way $7, round-trip $12; Dulles one-way $14, one-way $22; BWI one-way $13, round-trip $23; under 7 free).

Amtrak (484-7540 or 800-USA-RAIL) connects Washington to most other parts of the country through downtown's Union Station, at 50 Massachusetts Ave. NE. Trains runs to: New York City (3½ hr., $62); Baltimore (40 min., $11); Philadelphia (2 hr., $34); Boston (7 hr., $95); Chicago (17 hr., $115); Richmond (1 hr., $20); Williamsburg ($28); Virginia Beach ($40); and Atlanta ($114). Maryland's weekday commuter trains, MARC (800-325-RAIL), run to Baltimore and Harpers Ferry 5:30am-8am and 3:50-6:45pm (1 hr., $5 one-way).

The modern (but still depressing) **Greyhound/Trailways** bus station, 1005 1st St. NE (289-5155; 301-565-2662 for fare and schedules), idles in a rather decrepit neighborhood and provides service to Atlantic City (every 2-3 hr., $22); Philadelphia (every 2-3 hr.; Mon.-Fri. $16, Sat.-Sun. $18); New York City (every 30 min.-1 hr.; Mon.-Fri. from $25, weekend $29); and Baltimore (every 30 min.-1 hr.; weekday $6.50, weekend $8.50). **American Coach Lines** (301-386-4488), adds movies to the typical New York jaunt (one-way $25, round-trip $47.50).

Orientation

French planner Pierre L'Enfant tried his hardest to make central Washington logical. We try, we fail. Washington street names and addresses split into NW, NE, SE, and SW, centered on the U.S. Capitol. There are four 7th St. and four G Sts.; consequently, there are four 700 G St.—SE, SW, NW and NE. The basic street plan is a rectilinear grid. Streets that run east-west are named in alphabetical order running north and south from the Capitol, A St. one block from it, P St. 20 blocks. ("Eye St." means I St.) After W, east-west streets take two-syllable names, then three-syllable names, then floral names running alphabetically (occasionally repeating or skipping letters). North-south streets get numbers (1st St., 2nd St., etc.). Numbered and lettered streets sometimes stop existing for a block, then keep going as if nothing had happened. Diagonal avenues named for states interrupt the grid; many are major thoroughfares. North Capitol, East Capitol, and South Capitol St. run in compass directions from the Capitol. Addresses on lettered streets indicate the numbered cross street (1100 D St. SE will be between 11th and 12th St.). The same trick works with addresses on some avenues (Pennsylvania, but not Massachusetts or Wisconsin). Some principal roads: **Pennsylvania Ave.** runs SE-NW from Anacostia to Capitol Hill to the Capitol, through downtown, past the White House, and ending finally at 28th and M St. NW, in Georgetown; **Connecticut Ave.** goess north-northwest from the White House through Dupont Circle, past the Zoo, and farther out through Chevy Chase, MD; **Wisconsin Ave** runs north from Georgetown past the Cathedral to MD; **Sixteenth Street NW,** zooming from the White House north through hotels, offices, and townhouses, then forming Rock Creek Park's eastern border into MD; **K Street NW,** is a major downtown artery; **Constitution Ave.** and **Independence Ave.** are re spectively just north and south of the Mall; **Massachusetts Ave.** masses from American University, past the Cathedral, through Dupont and the old downtown to Capitol Hill; **New York Ave.** has an important arm from the White House through NE; and **Rock Creek Parkway** rocks through Rock Creek Park. Drivers should beware of reversible lanes and temporarily one-way street during rush hours.

DC isn't just for Congress. Over 600,000 residents inhabit the federal city; rich and poor, African-American, white and Latino are all well-represented. Tourists who glimpse the museums and the government, but don't escape the Mall to experience the neighborhoods, haven't really seen Washington at all. **Capitol Hill** extends east from the Capitol; white- and blue-collar locals mix with legislation-minded pols. North of the Mall, the **old downtown** goes about its business, accompanied by **Foggy Bottom** (sometimes called the "West End"), on the other side of the White House, and the **new downtown** around K St. west of 15th St. NW. **Georgetown** draws crowds and sucks away bucks nightly from its center at Wisconsin and M St. NW. Business and pleasure, embassies and streetlife, straight and gay converge around **Dupont Circle**; east of 16th St. the Dupont Circle character changes to struggling **Logan Circle,** then to rundown **Shaw,** then Howard University and **LeDroit Park,** an early residence for Washington's African-American elite. **Adams-Morgan,** north of Dupont and east of Rock Creek Park, has a strong Hispanic community. West of the Park begins **"upper northwest,"** mostly white, more spread-out territory that includes several smaller, separately named neighborhoods, the Zoo and the Cathedral. Across the Anacostia River, **Anacostia** has been seriously damaged and further isolated by poverty, crack, and guns. **Rock Creek Park,** a giant, undeveloped forest swath, reaches from near the Kennedy Center up to DC's northern tip; commuters drive through it, and, according to legend, Charles de Gaulle once took the 8-sq.-mi. park for the French Embassy's backyard.

Though out-of-town papers bill DC as "the nation's murder capital," with more homicides per capita than any other U.S. city, most killings are drug-related disputes in areas tourists are unlikely to frequent. If you're not out alone, anywhere with pedestrians and streetlights is reasonably safe at night, including Dupont Circle, Georgetown, and the well-lit parts of Adams-Morgan.

The Washington subway system, **Metrorail** (637-7000), usually referred to as the "Metro," is a sight in its own right. (Main office, 600 5th St. NW. Open daily 6am-around 11:30pm.) The sterile, monumental stations zap first-time riders with their uniformity, efficiency, and artlessness. Trains themselves are clean, carpeted, safe, and air-conditioned. A computerized fare card must be bought from machines in the station *before* you enter the subway and passed through electronic readers at exit; if there's still money on it, you get it back. To connect with a bus after your ride, get a transfer pass from machines on the platform before boarding the train. (5% bonus on farecards for $10 or more.) The $6 family tourist pass lets a group of four ride Metrorail and Metrobus all day long any Saturday, Sunday, or holiday except July 4 (available at Metro Center stop and from some hotel concierges). Kids age 4 and under ride free. Senior citizens and disabled people get discounts, but need a special Metro ID. Elevators help with wheelchairs and strollers. Trains run daily 6:30am-11:30pm. Peak hour fares from $1 to $2.85; elsewhen, $1 to $1.50.

The extensive, complicated **Metrobus** (same address, phone, and hours as Metrorail) system reliably serves Georgetown, downtown, and the suburbs. Downtown, the bus stops every few blocks. Regular fare is $1, but again, rush hour fares vary. Seniors, disabled persons, and ages under 4 are entitled to discounts. #30, 32, 34 and 36 buses take Pennsylvania Ave. NW from Capitol Hill to Georgetown, then drive up Wisconsin Ave. The immensely useful D2, D4, D6 and D8 lines zip from far NW to Glover Park, Q St. in Georgetown, Dupont Circle, the new downtown and Metro center before ending up in far NE at the Rhode Island Ave. Metro. L2 and L4 buses run from downtown up Connecticut Ave. NW. Metro information (637-7000) can describe the alchemical mix of buses and trains needed to reach any destination.

Washington cab fares are lower, but weirder, than those in other American cities: fares are based not on a meter but on a map which splits the city into 27 subzones, with fares from $3-10, plus a rush-hour $1 surcharge. Hail any cab downtown; farther out, call **Yellow Cab** (544-1212). Be ready to give directions or send the first few cabs away.

Accommodations

Business travelers desert DC during the summer months, so business hotels discount deeply and fill up on tourists. If you're lucky enough to hit the District without a car, and you don't want a hostel, the guest houses around Dupont Circle and Adams-Morgan should be your first try. Or check the New York Times Sunday Travel section for summer weekend deals DC adds an automatic 11% occupancy surcharge and another $1.50 per room per night to your bill. **The Bed and Breakfast League, Ltd.,** P.O. Box 9490, WDC 20016 (363-7767), reserves rooms in private homes. Check locations before you sign: the cheapest can parade far out in the suburbs. (Singles $35-75. Doubles $45-105. Booking fee $10. Non-refundable deposit $25.) For more camping data, try the **Park Service,** 1100 Ohio Dr. SW (485-9666; open Mon.-Fri. 8am-4pm) or **Dial-a-Park** (619-7275).

Washington International Youth Hostel (AYH), 1017 K St. NW (783-4943). Metro: Metro Center, then walk up 12th St. NW, away from the Mall, and turn right onto K St. International travelers appreciate the college-age staff, elevators, bunk beds and bulletin boards. Clean, air-conditioned rooms hold 4-12 beds per room. Kitchen and common rooms, too. No alcohol or drugs; smoking room in basement. On the edge of downtown—unsafe northeast of here. Check-in 7am. Curfew 2am. Bed $10; $3 membership charge first night for nonmembers.

Kalorama Guest House at Kalorama Park, 1854 Mintwood Place NW (667-6369), off Columbia Rd. and at **Cathedral Park,** 2700 Cathedral Ave. (328-0860). Metro(both): Woodley Park/Zoo. Well-run, impeccably decorated, immaculate guest rooms in Victorian townhouses, the first in the upscale western slice of Adams-Morgan, the second in a high-class neighborhood near the Zoo. Enjoy evening sherry or lemonade among the oriental rugs. Mintwood Place boasts fireplace, refrigerator, and more international travelers; Cathedral Park offers Freckles, a spaniel. Both have A/C, laundry mchines, and guest phone. Rooms with shared bath $40-70; $5 per additional person; private baths $75-105. Call and reserve; desk hours Mon.-Fri. 7:30am-9pm, Sat.-Sun. 7:30am-7pm. Reservations with full prepayment or credit card required; cancel for refund up to two weeks ahead.

Washington International Student Center, 2514 Ontario Rd. NW (265-6555), near the Columbia Rd. Safeway in funky Adams-Morgan. Hardworking manager aims to please backpackers and others. To open in Jan. 1992. Three floors of beds for $12 a night. AIYH application pending as *Let's Go* goes to press. Call to confirm opening, prices, and everything else.

Davis House, 1822 R St. NW (232-3196, 24 hrs. 783-6540). Metro: Dupont Circle. Charming, spacious wood-floored building accepts international visitors, Quaker organization staff, and others "working on peace and justice concerns." Other visitors sometimes accepted on same-day, space-available basis. Max. stay two weeks; reserve early (one night's deposit required). No smoking; no alcohol. Singles with hall bath $25.

Allen Lee Hotel, 2224 F. St. NW (331-1224), near George Washington University. Metro: Foggy Bottom/GWU. Large, rickety, blue hallways. Rooms vary widely in size, furnishings, and state of repair/disrepair, so look at several before accepting one. Bedrooms and bathrooms normally old but clean. Singles $30, with private bath $40. Doubles $40, with private bath $50. Twins $40, with private bath $50. Reservations required in summer.

2005 Columbia Guest House, 2005 Columbia Rd. NW (265-4006 or 328-0727), southwest of central Adams-Morgan. An old Senator's house, with a creaky central staircase and seven faded rooms with sometimes lumpy beds. But the rooms are clean and quiet, and the rates are unmatchable. No alcohol. Call ahead. Singles $19-26. Doubles $28-39. Weekly rates available.

Adams Inn, 1744 Lanier Place NW (745-3600), behind the Columbia Rd. Safeway, two blocks from the center of Adams-Morgan. Elaborate, elegant Victorian townhouses smothered in Persian rugs; all shared bath but private sink. Free breakfast. Backyard outdoor patio, coin laundry facilities, pay phones, and eating facilities. Singles with shared bath $45, with private bath $60. Doubles with shared bath $55, with private bath $70. Weekly singles with shared bath $125-135, with private bath $165. Weekly doubles with shared bath $200-210, with private bath $240.

Marifex Hotel, 1523 22nd St. NW (293-1885). Metro: Dupont Circle. Small, clean, linoleum floored rooms, each with its own sink and shared bathrooms down the hall. Price includes various DC taxes (including the 11% occupancy tax). Singles $40.35. Doubles $51.45.

Swiss Inn, 1204 Massachusetts Ave. (371-1816 or 800-955-7947). Metro: Metro Center. Variable neighborhood close to downtown. Call ahead or they might not answer the door. Clean, quiet studio apartments, with refrigerator, private bath, high ceilings and kitchenettes. Free local phone calls. Once-a-summer cookout on the house. French-speaking managers welcome international crowd (one speaks Swiss-German also). Reserve months ahead if you can. Singles $58, doubles $68. (Includes tax). Winter discount 10-15%.

Capitol KOA, 768 Cecil Ave. (923-2771 or 987-7477), near Millersville, 16 mi. from DC, 11 from Balto. or Annapolis. Families get back to nature, sort of. Full facilities for tents, RVs, cabins. Free pool, movies. Free weekday shuttle to DC/Baltimore trains; commuter train (MARC) $6.25 round-trip to Union Station. Tent site for two $17.25. RV site $17-19. Each additional adult $3. Open April-Nov.

University Dorms: Georgetown University Summer Housing is available only for summer educational pursuits; they gladly take interns and members of summer programs, but turn away self-declared tourists. Air-conditioned singles ($18), non-air-conditioned doubles ($14), and air-conditioned doubles ($15), all with a strong college-dormitory flavor. In summer, you'll need the A/C. Call or write G.U. Summer Housing, P.O. Box 2214, WDC, 20057 (687-3999); reserve early, although last-minute rentals are always a possibility. (Three-week min. stay. Bring your own linens. Requires mail application and 20% deposit. Rooms available June to mid-Aug.) **American University Summer Housing,** 4400 Massachusetts Ave. NW, 20016-8039 (885-2598), provides simple, air-conditioned dorm rooms for students and interns from late May to mid-August. (Doubles $82 per week per person; hall bathrooms; required two-week min. stay.) Come with a friend or they will place you with someone. Make reservations early for check-in before June 7; after that you can call 24 hours ahead. A university ID (from any university) and full payment for stay must be presented at check-in.

Food

While public servants tend to lunch in government cafeterias, DC makes up for its days as a "sleepy Southern town" with a kaleidoscope of international restaurants. Haughty European dining rooms strive to impress the expense-account crowd, while bargains from Africa, Southeast Asia and the Americas feed a melange of immigrants from all over. Excellent budget food centers in Dupont Circle and Adams-Morgan. Food vendors do their thing in the block-long red brick **Eastern Market,** Pennsylvania Ave. and 7th St. SE. (Metro: Eastern Market) Washingtonians flock here for fresh produce and the bustle of a pre-industrial bazaar. At the **open-air market** at the wharves on Maine Ave. and 9th St. SW, you can buy low-priced seafood straight from the Chesapeake Bay.

Capitol Hill

Over 50 eateries inhabit **Union Station,** 50 Massachusetts Ave. NE; in the food court on the Lower Level, cheap take-out counters ring the walls. (Metro: Union Station)

Chicken and Steak, 320 D St. NE (543-4633). Ignore the spare decor and fall for the succulent chicken and steak, cooked Peruvian style a la brasa (grilled), at bargain prices (half chicken with Yuca and salad $4.25). Open Mon.-Sat. 11am-9:30pm.

Jimmy T's, 501 East Capitol St. (546-3646). At 5th St., under the brick octagonal turret. The paint's chipped, and the vinyl benches look old, but it's all part of the corner diner charm. Great diner fare and nothing over $5. Breakfast served all day. Open Tues.-Fri. 6:30am-3pm, Sat. 8am-3pm, Sun. 9am-3pm.

Neil's Outrageous Deli, 208 Massachusetts Ave. NE (546-6970). Combination deli and liquor store offers creative sandwiches to go ($2.19-4). Open Mon-Tues. 9am-7:30pm, Wed.-Thurs. 9am-8:30pm, Fri. 9am-9pm, Sat. 9:45am-8:30pm.

Kelley's "The Irish Times," 14 F St. NW (543-5433). Irish street signs, the *Irish Times,* Joyce on the wall and Yeats and Keats on the menu make this more than just another Irish pub. (Don't tell them Keats wasn't Irish.) Live music Wed.-Sat. evenings. Sandwiches $5-7, soup $2; beer from $2.50, Irish whiskey from $4. Open Sun.-Thurs. 10:30am-1:30am, Fri.-Sat. 10:30am-2:30am.

Hawk 'n' Dove, 329 Pennsylvania Ave. SE (543-3300). A good bar with good bar food, interns, regulars and powerful politicians. Sandwiches $4-6.50; 14 kinds of beer $1.75 and up. Midnight breakfast served Mon.-Thurs. 11pm-1am, Fri.-Sat. 11pm-2am ($7; $9 with steak). Open Mon.-Thurs. 10am-2am, Fri.-Sat. 10am-3am, Sun. 10am-2am.

Downtown

A.V. Ristorante, 607 New York Ave. NW (737-0550). Chianti bottles top-heavy with melted wax, lamps turned so low they flicker on and off, huge plates of expert pasta ($5.50-10) and pizza. They don't make 'em like this anymore. Open Mon.-Fri. 11:30am-11pm, Sat. 5pm-midnight.

Sholl's Colonial Cafeteria, 1900 K St. NW, in the Esplanade Mall. Good cooking at exceptionally low prices: chopped steak ($1.65) and roast beef ($1.90). Try the homemade pies. Open Mon.-Sat. 7am-2:30pm and 4-8pm.

The Star of Siam, 1136 19th St. NW (785-2838). Delights diners with spicy hot curries, unobtrusively fried foods, and sharp desserts. Dinner from $6.25. Open Mon.-Sat. 11:30am-11pm, Sun. 4-10pm.

Sabina's, 1813 M St. NW (466-5678). Return to the '50s with their all-day breakfast menu and jukebox at every table. The perfect late-night hangout. Hamburger with toppings and fries $3-4. Open Sun.-Thurs. 10am-3am, Fri.-Sat. 10am-4am.

Chinatown

You can't judge a Chinese restaurant by its exterior. Wander around (not alone) along H St. from the Gallery Place Metro stop.

Big Wong, 610 H St. NW (638-0116 or 638-0117). Consistent renown and wide selection; try the specialty noodle dishes. Combination platters, with rice, egg rolls and entree, around $5. Authentic desserts include Egg Custard Tart. Open Sun.-Wed. 11am-3am, Thurs.-Sat. 11am-4am.

Tony Cheng's Mongolian (Barbecue) Restaurant, 619 H St. (842-8669). Load your bowl with beef, leeks, mushrooms, sprouts, and such, then watch the cooks make it sizzle (and shrink). (One serving $6; all-you-can-eat $14.) Two or more people can stir up their own feast in charcoal hotpots. (Base platter $5 per person; more meat costs extra.) Open Sun.-Thurs. 11am-11pm, Fri.-Sat. 11am-midnight.

Burma Restaurant, upstairs at 740 6th St. (393-3453). Burma's rare cuisine replaces soy sauce with pickles, mild curries and unique spices. Try the rice noodles with dried shrimp, fried onion, coriander, garlic, and lemon juice ($6) or the tofu and chopped shrimp cooked in Tabasco ($7). Open Sun.-Thurs. 11:30am-3pm, Fri.-Sat. 11:30am-3pm and 6-9pm.

White House Area/Foggy Bottom

Milo's, 2142 Pennsylvania Ave. NW (338-3000). GWU students enjoy Euro-chic decor and Italian food—pasta ($5-8), fried mozzarella ($3), calamari ($5), and pizza (from $5.20). Live country, rock, or folk some nights. Open Mon.-Wed. 11:30am-11pm, Thurs.-Fri. 11:30am-midnight, Sat. 11:30am-2am, Sun. 5-10pm.

The Art Gallery Grille, 1712 Eye St. NW (298-6658). Metro: Farragut West. Art deco interior and jukebox. Original Erte seriographs, modern professional clientele. Breakfasts include Belgian waffles and creative granola ($5). DJ Thurs.-Fri. nights. Open Mon. 6:30am-11pm, Tues. and Sun. 6:30am-midnight, Thurs.-Sat. 6:30am-3am.

Balaji Siddhartha, 1479 K St. NW (682-9090). Deli atmosphere obscures the exotic plates tailored to vegetarians and Indian food fans. Curry of the day $3. Appetizers linger around $1.50. Choose from 17 desserts—combinations of mango, rice pudding, yogurt and almonds. Open Mon.-Sat. 11:30am-8:30pm, Sun. noon-7:30pm.

Georgetown

Houston's, 1065 Wisconsin Ave. NW (338-7760). Perfect for meat-and-potato lovers. The hickory-grilled hamburgers ($6.25) are served with a slew of shoestring fries. You may need to bring the salads ($6.25-7.50) home in a doggie bag. Lines are long; walk around Georgetown while you wait. Open Sun.-Thurs. 11:15am-11pm, Fri.-Sat. 11:15am-1am.

Vietnam-Georgetown Restaurant, 2934 M ST. NW (337-4536), and Viet Huong, 2928 M St. NW (337-5588) at 30th St. The spicier Vietnam-Georgetown was here first; Viet Huong is more intimate and slightly cheaper. Try *cha giu* (Vietnamese crispy egg rolls) and grilled chicken or beef on skewers. Lunch at V-G $6, dinner $7-11. Open Mon.-Thurs. 11am-11pm, Fri. 11am-midnight, Sat. noon-midnight, Sun. noon-11pm. Lunch at V.H. $4-6, dinner $6-11. Open Mon.-Fri. 11:30am-3pm and 5-10pm, Sat.-Sun. noon-11pm.

Madurai, 3318 M St. NW (333-0997), upstairs, above Zed's Ethiopian restaurant. Indian vegetarian food, unpretentious and unusual. Entrees $5-8. All-you-can-eat buffet on Sundays ($7) is a great deal, even for the otherwise carnivorous. Open Mon.-Thurs. 11am-2:30pm and 5-10pm, Fri.-Sat. noon-2:30pm and 5-11pm, Sun. noon-4pm and 5-10pm.

Booeymonger, 3265 Prospect St. NW (333-4810), corner of Potomac St. Georgetown students and residents stop by for breakfast or a quick, giant sandwich. Every sandwich seems a specialty; try the veggie pocket ($4.25-4.75). Open Mon.-Fri. 8am-midnight, Sat.-Sun. 9am-midnight.

Au Pied du Cochon/Aux Fruits de Mer, 1335 Wisconsin Ave. NW (333-5440 and 333-2333). Two sister restaurants, the first serving casual French fare like salads and crepes, the other serving cooked ocean critters. Come by for a late snack/early breakfast of dessert ($3-4.75) and a cappuccino ($2.45) or a cafe au lait and fresh-baked croissant ($3). The glass-enclosed cafe area lets you watch the passers-by. Open 24 hrs.

Thomas Sweet, 3214 P St. NW (337-0614), at Wisconsin Ave. The best ice cream in DC by a light-year from $1.67. Open Mon.-Thurs. 9:30am-midnight, Fri.-Sat. 9:30am-1am, Sun. 11am-midnight.

Dupont Circle

Lauriol Plaza, 1801 18th St. NW (387-0035). Authentic Mexican food, served on a charming patio by gracious waiters. Entrees are *muchos dolares,* but a tender enchilada side dish ($2) and chili con carne appetizer ($3) could stuff any tummy. Open Sun.-Fri. noon-11pm, Sat. noon-midnight.

Food for Thought, 1738 Connecticut Ave. NW (797-1095), two blocks from Dupont Circle. Veggie-hippie-folkie mecca with good, healthful food in a '60s atmosphere. Ten different vegetable and fruit salads, plus sandwiches and daily hot specials. Local musicians strum in the evenings. Bulletin boards announce everything from rallies to beach parties to rides to L.A. Bike messenger hangout. Lunch $6-8, dinner $6-11. Open Mon. 11:30am-3pm and 5pm-midnight; Tues.-Thurs. 11:30am-midnight, Fri. 11:30am-1am, Sat. noon-1am, Sun. 5pm-midnight.

Dante's, 1522 14th St. at Q. St. NW (667-7260). Near the Source and Studio theaters. Not to be missed after midnight, when punk rockers, actors, and their friends jam the place with hipness and hair. Teal and black decor complements heavenly—healthful pita sandwiches and devilish cheesecake (sandwiches $5-7, cheesecake $2.50). Try the Hot Veg-o-Matic ($6). Don't come around here alone at night. Open Mon. 5pm-3am, Tues.-Thurs. 11:30am-3am, Fri. 11:30am-4am, Sat.-Sun. 5pm-4am.

Cafe Pettito, 1724 Connecticut Ave. NW (462-8771). Excellent Italian regional cooking in an understated atmosphere. Try the tempting antipasto table ($6) and the fried Calabrian pizza. Open daily 11:30am-midnight.

India Grill, 2100 Connecticut Ave. NW (232-5932). Inexpensive, authentic Indian cuisine in an unassuming location—at the bottom of an apartment building. Inexpensive appetizers, delicious breads ($1) and an all-you-can-eat buffet on weekend nights ($9; Fri. 5:30-10:30pm, Sat. noon-10:30pm, Sun. noon-9:30pm). Open Mon.-Thurs. noon-2:30pm and 5-10pm, Fri.-Sat. noon-2:30pm and 5-10:30pm, Sun. noon-2:30pm and 5:30-9:30pm.

Kramerbooks & Afterwords Cafe, 1517 Connecticut Ave. NW (387-3825). Late-night sweets behind a very good bookshop. Exorbitant nouvelle entrees, but pies, cappuccinos and mousses ($3-4) are rich rewards for the literary life. Live music Fri.-Sun. after 10pm. Open Sun.-Thurs. 7:30am-11:45pm, Fri.-Sat. 24 hrs.

Adams-Morgan

The word is out. Adams-Morgan has justifiably become DC's preferred locale for budget dining. The action radiates from 18th, Columbia and Calvert St. NW, uphill along Columbia or down 18th.

El Pollo Primo, 2471 18th St. NW (232-5151), near Columbia Rd. By their awning shall ye know them. Second-story beige-and-brown rotisserie gives rise to moist, flavorful, tender, greaseless, and cheap chicken on a big grill behind the counter. Two-piece chicken dinner with tortillas, salsa, and two side orders $3.30, three-piece dinner $4.19, five-piece dinner $5.30. Open daily 11am-9pm.

Red Sea, 2463 18th St. NW (483-5000). The first of Adams-Morgan's famous Ethiopian restaurants; still among the best. The red-painted exterior is weatherbeaten but enticing. Use the traditional pancake bread, injera, to eat spicy lamb, beef, chicken, and vegetable wats (stews). Lunch entrees $3.70-8; dinner slightly higher. Open Sun.-Thurs. 11:30am-midnight, Fri.-Sat. 11:30am-1am.

Thai Taste, 2606 Connecticut Ave. NW (667-5115). DC's black-and-neon magnet for Thai food lovers. Try the fried beef with chili paste and coconut milk, then Thai iced coffee ($2). Dinner from $6. Open daily 11am-11pm.

Calvert Cafe, 1967 Calvert St. NW (232-5431), right across the Duke Ellington Bridge. Metro: Woodley Park/Zoo. Look for the brown and gold tiles; though it looks boarded-up, this landmark has lasted 30 years. Huge, unadorned platters of Middle Eastern food. Appetizers $2-4.50; dinner entrees $6-8.50. Half a broiled chicken with Arabian rice and a salad $6. Shish kabob with rice and salad $8.50. The legendary Mama Ayesha adorns the menu. Open daily 11am-midnight.

Meskerem, 2434 18th St. NW (462-4100). Another fine Ethiopian place, certainly the best-looking one in Adams-Morgan. Cheery yellow three-level interior incorporates an upstairs dining gallery with Ethiopian woven tables and a view of the diners below. Appetizers $3-4.75. Meat entrees $9-11, vegetarian entrees $8-8.75. *Yemisir watt* (lentils in hot sauce) $8.50. Open Mon.-Thurs. 5pm-midnight, Fri.-Sun. noon-12:30am.

Mixtec, 1792 Columbia Rd. NW (332-1011). Popular, well-known Mexican restaurant. Neon window sign screams for *tacos al carbon;* the $3 version is two small tortillas filled with delicious beef with three kinds of garnish. Mind-bending chicken *mole,* too. Lunch entrees, with salad and beans, $5. Appetizers $2-4.75. Entrees $4.25-9. Open Sun.-Thurs. 11am-11:30pm, Fri.-Sat. 11am-midnight.

Elsewhere

Parkway Deli, 8317 Grubb Rd. (587-1427), just over the District line in MD. Obscure shopping center hides Washington's best deli from all but the neighborhood's knowing many. Take 16th St. NW all the way north to East-West Hwy., turn left on East-West, then left onto Grubb. Open Mon. 8am-9pm, Tues.- Fri. 8am-9:30pm, Sat. 7am-9:30pm, Sun. 7am-9pm.

Florida Avenue Grill, 1100 Florida Ave. NW, at 11th St. From the U St. Metro, walk east on U to 11th St., then (very carefully) north up 11th St. to Florida Ave. Enduring (since 1944) diner once fed Black leaders and famous entertainers. Awesome southern food: breakfast with salmon cakes or spicy sausage, eggs, grits, hotcakes, or southern biscuits ($3-4.50). Open Mon.-Sat. 6am-9pm.

Sights

DC's docket sports a wide array of museums, monuments, historic sites and parks. An after-dark tour of the monuments provides a romantic escape from daytime heat and crowds. Don't make the common mistake of confining yourself to the Mall and its environs; some of DC's best sights hover far rom it, like the Phillips Collection and the Zoo. Some neighborhoods are even sights in themselves.

Capitol Hill

The U.S. Capitol (225-6827 or 224-3121; TTY 224-4049) may no longer be Washington's most beautiful building, but its scale and style still evoke the power of the republic. (Metro: Capitol South or Union Station.) The three-tiered East Front faces the Supreme Court. From Jackson (1829) to Carter (1977), most Presidents were inaugurated here; Reagan moved the ceremony to the newly fixed-up West Front, which overlooks the Mall. Nothing built in Washington can be taller than the tip of the cast-iron dome. If there's light in the dome by night, Congress is still meeting. Inside the East Portico, statesmen from Lincoln to JFK have lain in state in the Rotunda; you can get a map from the tour desk here. (Free guided tours begin here daily every 20 min. 9am-3:45pm.) Ceremony and confusion reign downstairs in the Crypt area; most of the functioning rooms are upstairs. For a spectacle, but little insight, climb to the House and Senate visitors galleries. Americans should request a gallery pass (valid for the whole 2-year session of Congress) from the office of their Representative, Delegate or Senator. Foreign nationals should ask the Office of the House Doorkeeper or the Senate Sergeant at Arms. In the House and Senate chambers (in separate wings of the Capitol), expect a few bored-looking officials ignoring the person on the podium. The real business of Congress is conducted in committee hearings; check the Washington Post's "Today in Congress" box. (Many are across the street in House or Senate offices; ride the Capitol Subway there, just as Congresspeople do.) The Senate Cafeteria, on the second (main) floor on the Senate side of the building, is open to the public; red lights and sirens warn of an imminent vote. (Capitol open daily 9am-4:30pm, Memorial Day-Labor Day daily 9am to 8pm. Disabled tours and help from Special Services Office in the Crypt (224-4048; TTY 224-4049).

The Supreme Court, One 1st St. NE (479-3000), across from the East Front of the Capitol, houses the nation's highest court. (Metro: Capitol South or Union Station.) Its nine justices are the final interpreters of the U.S. Constitution. Behind the red curtain as you enter is the chamber, where the court meets. In session (Oct.-June), it hears oral arguments Mon.-Wed. 10am-3pm for half month. Show up early to sit down and listen or stand in line to hear five minutes of argument. The *Washington Post* can tell you if the court is sitting and what case is up. Brief lectures (July-Aug. 9:30am-3:30pm) cover history, operations, duties and architecture of the Court.

The Library of Congress, 1st St. SE (707-5000, events schedule 707-8000), between East Capitol and Independence Ave., is the world's largest, with 20 million books and three buildings: the 1897 Beaux-Arts Jefferson Building, which hogs the display space; the 1939 Adams Building, across 2nd St.; and the 1980 Madison Building, a marble slab across Independence Ave. The vast collection is open to anyone college age or above with a legitimate research purpose. Anybody can take the tour; it starts in the Madison Memorial Hall, in the Madison Building lobby. After a brief talk, the tour scuttles through tunnels to the Jefferson Building, otherwise closed for renovation; the octagonal Main Reading Room spreads out under a spectacular dome. (Most reading rooms open Mon.-Fri. 8:30am-9:30pm, Sat. 8:30am-5pm, Sun. 1-5pm.)

The Folger Shakespeare Library, 201 East Capitol St. SE (544-4600), houses the world's largest collection of Shakespeariana (collection closed to the public). The Shakespeare Theater at the Folger puts on, mostly, Shakespeare's plays. (See Entertainment.) During the day, tourists can peek at the Great Hall exhibition gallery and the theater itself, which imitates the Elizabethan Inns of Court indoor theaters where Shakespeare's company performed. The Folger also sponsors high-quality readings, lectures, and concerts, like PEN/Faulkner poetry and fiction readings and the Folger Consort, an early-music group. (Open Mon.-Sat. 10am-4pm.)

Two blocks north of the Capitol grounds, the trains run on time at Union Station, 50 Massachusetts Ave. NE (371-9441 for general information). Daniel Burnham's much-admired, monumental Beaux-Arts design took four strenuous years (1905-1908) to erect. Colonnades, archways and huge domed ceilings equate Burnham's Washington with imperial Rome and the then-dominant train network with Roman roads. After remodelings and bizarre misuses, Union Station has become a spotless ornament in the crown of capitalism, with a food court, chic stores and mall groupies. (Shops open Mon.-Sat. 10am-9pm, Sunday noon-6pm.) Northeast of Union Station is the red-brick **Capitol Children's Museum,** 800 3rd St. NE (675-4127). (Metro: Union Station.) Touch and feel every exhibit; walk through the Mexican mock-up town and the room-size maze. (Open daily 10am-5pm. Admission $5, seniors $2. Bring your adult.)

Three museums—and a destroyer you can board—stay shipshape among the booms at the **Washington Navy Yard.** (Metro: Eastern Market.) Use caution in the neighborhood. Enter from the gate at 9th and M St. SE, and ask directions or look at the posted maps. The best of the lot, the **Navy Museum,** Building 76 (433-4882), should buoy up anyone let down by the admire-but-don't-touch Air & Space Museum. Climb inside the space capsule, play Human Cannonball inside huge ship guns, jam into a bathysphere used to explore the sea floor, or give orders on the bridge. (Open June-Aug. 9am-5pm, Sat.-Sun. 10am-5pm; Sept.-May Mon.-Fri. 9am-4pm, Sat.-Sun. 10am-5pm.) The **USS Barry,** a decommissioned destroyer a few steps from the Navy Museum, opens its berths, control rooms, bridge, Captain's quarters, and combat center daily 10am-5pm. The **Marine Corps Historical Museum,** Building 58 (433-3534), marches guns, uniforms, and swords from the halls of Montezuma to the shores of Kuwait. (Open Mon.-Thurs. and Sat. 10am-4pm, Fri. 10am-8pm, Sun. noon-5pm; Sept.-May Mon.-Sat. 10am-4pm, Sun. noon-5pm.)

Museums on the Mall

The world's largest museum complex stretches out along the Mall. Constitution Ave. (on the north) and Independence Ave. (on the south) flank the double row of museums. All Smithsonian museums are free and wheelchair-accessible; all offer written guides in French, German, Spanish, and Japanese, some in Chinese, Arabic, and Portuguese. All open daily from 10am-5:30pm, with extended summer hours for the larger museums; some close on winter weekends. Take at least three days to see the museums—they'd take months to "finish." (General phone 357-2700, TTY: 357-1729; tours, concerts, lectures, films 357-1481, TTY: 357-1563). Info desks at the Castle and in museums give the *Smithsonian Guide for Disabled Visitors;* handicapped tourists who call a day ahead may get more help.

The **Mall,** the U.S.'s taxpayer-supported national backyard, is a sight in itself. Hundreds of natives and out-of-towners sunbathe and lounge, play frisbee, knock down their little brothers, fly a kite, or just get high. The **Smithsonian Castle,** 1000 Jefferson Dr. SW, holds no real exhibits, but has information desks, a thorough, tedious 20-minute movie, and founder James Smithson's body.

Though Henry Ford said "History is bunk," the **National Museum of American History,** 14th and Constitution Ave. NW, prefers to think that history is junk: several centuries of machines, textiles, photographs, vehicles, harmonicas, and uncategorizable Americana. Near the Mall entrance is the Foucault pendulum, which knocks over pegs to prove the Earth rotates. The original, national-anthem-inspiring Star Spangled Banner hangs behind the pendulum—they say you can see it every hour on the half hour, when the cover is lifted. "Field to Factory" illuminates Black migration from the segregated South to Northern cities during the early 1900s. Mechanical beings will love the first floor, where galleries lavish plexiglass on electricity, trains, and power tools, along with an ice cream parlor and museum bookstore. In "Information Age," clunky early computers like ENIAC give way to R2D2 and C3PO, the cute robots from *Star Wars.* (Open daily 10am-5:30pm; June-Aug. 9:30am-7:30pm.)

The golden-domed **Museum of Natural History** (357-2700), built neoclassically in 1911 at 10th and Constitution Ave., considers the Earth and life on it in two-and-a-half big, crowded floors of exhibits. On the Mall side, say hi to Uncle Beazley, the triceratops on the Mall. Inside, the largest African elephant ever captured stands under dome-filtered sunshine in a hubbub of slack-jawed tourists. Huge dinosaur skeletons dwarf the nearby hallway. Ancient Seas and Sea Life exhibits reel museumgoers in under a blue whale and past a coral reef with live tropical critters. On the second floor, case after table of naturally-occurring crystals make the final plush room of cut gems anticlimactic. The Insect Zoo pleases with an array of creepy-crawlies. (Museum open daily 10am-5:30pm; June-Sept. 9:30am-7:30pm.)

The **National Gallery of Art**, 6th and Constitution Ave. NW (737-4215) houses and hangs its world-class jumble of pre-1900 art in a domed marble temple designed by John Russell Pope, whose more-reverent-than-thou columns and stairs also accompany the National Archives and Jefferson Memorial. The West Building holds important work by Raphael, Rembrandt, and Monet, to name a few; Albert Bierstadt's American West (through February 1992), Walker Evans' realist photographs (through March), John Singer Sargent's portraits (through July) and the Italian Baroque work of Guercino (all spring) arrive this year. "Garden courts" relieve the potential monotony of the Old Masters with fountains, ferns, sunlight, and benches. The museum's prize is a hall of Dutch Masters with a few of the world's thirty-odd Vermeers. Postcards, art books, and high-class cafeteria fare are yours for the $ in the basement; if you must eat on the Mall, this is the place. Vocal, piano and chamber music (842-6941) show most Sundays Oct.-June at 7pm in the West Garden Court.

Completed amid much fanfare in 1978, the **"East Wing"** of the National Gallery of Art (737-4215) Constitution Ave., Pennsylvania Ave., and 4th St. NW, houses (and sometimes hides) the museum's plentiful 20th-century holdings. I. M. Pei's smooth marble design gallery outlines high, interlocking triangles, glass-topped to flood the atrium with sunlight. Enter from the West Building via the underground moving walkway. An immense Calder mobile is the gallery's trademark; it recalls the knife-edge exterior of the building itself. From the atrium, head up the escalators and through three floors of temporary shows (not always 20th-century) and/or modern art. The East Building is constantly rearranging, closing and remodeling parts of itself for temporary exhibits. Don't neglect the basement galleries. (Open Mon.-Sat. 10am-5pm, Sun. 11am-6pm, with extended summer hours.)

The **National Air and Space Museum**, on the south side of the Mall between 4th and 7th St. SW, is the world's most popular museum(Metro: L'Enfant Plaza). Thirty thousand people a day (in summer) scrutinize the dangling airplanes, the Apollo XI command module, 23 exhibit galleries and the five-story movie screen. Among the hanging aerospace vehicles, the space-age atrium also holds a rock from the moon, worn smooth by a decade of tourists' fingertips. Air & Space's best exhibits are its biggest—actual planes and crafts from all eras of flight; the Wright brothers' biplane in the entrance gallery looks intimidated by all its younger kin. In the Sea-Air operations gallery (#203) you can (via computer) pilot a fighter, land on a carrier, and, probably, crash or sink. IMAX movies give spectators vertigo in the Langley Theater, home of the five-story movie screen. Buy tickets early, and stand in line a few minutes before the show starts. (Films 9:50am-7:30pm. Tickets $2.75, children, students, seniors $1.75, at the box office on the ground floor. Museum open daily 9:30am-7:30pm; Sept.-June 16 10am-5:30pm.)

If you're convinced art ended with Picasso, stay away from the **Hirshhorn Museum and Sculpture Garden**, 8th St. and Independence Ave. SW (357-2700). The four-story, slide-carousel-shaped brown building has outraged traditionalists since 1966. Each floor comprises two concentric circles, an outer ring of rooms and paintings, and an inner corridor of sculptures. The Hirshhorn's best shows are in art since 1960; nowhere else in Washington even tries to keep up with avant-garde paintings, and mixed-media installations. The museum claims the world's most comprehensive set of 19th- and 20th-century Western sculpture. Striking works by Smith, Calder, Maillol, Rodin, and Giacometti ornament the Sculpture Garden, across Jefferson Dr. The Hirshorn runs three separate pseudo-weekly free film series, listed in their "Calendar" brochure. (Museum open daily 10am-5:30pm. Sculpture Garden open daily 7:30am-dusk. Tours 357-3235.)

Between the Castle and the Hirshhorn, the **Arts and Industries Building** is an exhibition of an exhibition, the 1876 Centennial Exhibition of American technology in Philadelphia. Pause for the exterior: a polychromatic, multi-style chaos of gables, arches, rails,and bricks. Inside, furniture congregates near the Mall entrance; heavy machinery will delight advocates of steam power further back. Built in 1987, the **Arthur M. Sackler Gallery** and the **Museum of African Art** hide their non-Western treasures underground, behind the Castle and below the beautiful Enid A. Haupt Garden, Independence Ave. and 10th St. SW. The Sackler showcases Sackler's extensive collection of art from China, South and Southeast Asia, and Persia.The National Museum of African Art, 950 Independence Ave. SW (357-4600, TTY 357-4814) collects, catalogs, polishes and shows off artifacts from Sub-Saharan Africa. Art objects include masks, textiles, ceremonial figures, and fascinating musical instruments, like a harp partly made of pangolin scales. (Open daily 10am-5:30pm. Call ahead for tour information.) The **Freer Gallery of Art,** on the Mall at Jefferson Dr. and 12th St. SW, will re-open in 1992 with an underground link to the Sackler. It collects Asian or Asian-inspired art, like James McNeill Whistler's.

South of the Mall

Exotic foliage from all continents and climates vegetates inside and outside the **U.S. Botanical Garden,** First St. and Maryland Ave. SW (226-4082). Cacti, bromeliads, and other odd-climate plants flourish indoors. Forty-minute guided tours begin at 10am and 2pm (call ahead; open June-Aug. daily 9am-9pm; Sept.-May daily 9am-5pm.) The **Bureau of Engraving and Printing,** 14th St. and C St. SW (447-9709), just south of the Washington Monument, offers continuous tours of the presses that annually print over $20 billion. Skip breakfast or expect a 2-hr. wait. (Open Mon.-Fri. 9am-2pm. Free.)

Memorials/West of the Mall

The **Washington Monument,** at Constitution Ave. and 16th St. NW is a marble obelisk and a vertical altar to America's first president, where crowds sacrifice their sweat, time and patience to ascend, descend and take the Monument's picture along with theirs. (Metro: Smithsonian.) During the Civil War the half-finished obelisk was nicknamed the "Beef Depot Monument" for the cattle Army quartermasters herded on the grounds. The stairs were a famous (and strenuous) tourist exercise, but the Park Service closed them years ago. The elevator line takes 45 minutes to circle the Monument. Tiny windows offer disapppointing lookout points at the top. Disabled persons can bypass the long lines. (Monument open daily 8am-midnight; September-March 8am-5pm. Free.)

Maya Ying Lin, who designed the **Vietnam Veterans Memorial** (south of Constitution Ave. at 22nd St. NW) called it "a rift in the earth." (Metro: Smithsonian or Foggy Bottom/GWU). While an undergraduate at Yale, Lin beat 1400 contestants with her design. 58,132 Americans died in Vietnam, and the memorial's long black granite slabs bear each one's name. Families and veterans visit the memorial to ponder and mourn; many make rubbings of their loved ones' names from the walls.The outdoor memorial stays "open" 24 hrs. every day.

Anyone with a penny already knows what the **Lincoln Memorial** (at 23rd St. between Constitution and Independence) looks like; Henry Bacon's design copies the rectangular grandeur of Athens' Parthenon. (Metro: Smithsonian or Foggy Bottom)A massive layer of stone atop the columns gives the building the watchful solemnity of a crypt. Black soprano Marian Anderson sang from the steps here after she was barred from segregated Constitution Hall in 1939, and Martin Luther King gave his "I Have a Dream" speech to the 1963 March on Washington. Daniel Chester French's seated Lincoln presides from the inside, keeping watch over protest marchers and Fourth of July fireworks. Read his Gettysburg address on the wall to the left. Spelunkers roam the caves under the memorial; call 425-6841 to try it yourself. Since it has no doors, the Memorial is open 24 hrs. (Free.) The **Reflecting Pool,** between the Washington and Lincoln Memorials, reflects Washington's obelisk in seven million gallons of lit-up water.

The **Jefferson Memorial's** rotunda-centric design pays tribute to T.J.'s own monument to himself: his Charlottesville home, Monticello. The raised hill around it offers generous views of the other monuments. A 19-foot hollow bronze President Jefferson rules the rotunda. Interior walls quote from Jefferson's writings: the *Declaration of Independence,* the *Virginia Statue of Religious Freedom, Notes on Virginia,* and an 1815 letter. The Declaration of Independence extract contains 11 errors. The sentence around the top of the dome rebukes those who wrongly called T.J. an atheist. The Jefferson Memorial overlooks Washington's most popular manmade lake, the **Tidal Basin,** where pedalboats ripple in and out of the Memorial's shadow and cherry blossoms gain fame every April. (Boat rental 484-0206; open daily 10am-6:30pm; $7 per hour.)

Downtown/North of the Mall

It's only proper that an architectural marvel should house the **National Building Museum,** which towers above F St. NW between 4th and 5th St. (Metro: Judiciary Square.) Montgomery Meigs' 1881 Italianate Pension Building remains one of Washington's best; the Great Hall, with its columns, busts and fountain, could hold a fifteen-story building. "Washington: Symbol and City," the NBM's permanent exhibit, covers DC architecture, federal and local; there are rejected designs for the Washington Monument and the chance to design your own Capitol Hill rowhouse. (Museum open Mon.-Fri. 10am-4pm, Sat.-Sun. noon-4pm; tours Mon.-Fri. 12:30pm, Sat.-Sun. 12:30 and 1:30. Excellent handicapped access. Free.)

The **National Museum of American Art** and the **National Portrait Gallery** (357-2700) share a neoclassical edifice two blocks long (American Art entrance at 8th and G St.; Portrait Gallery entrance at 8th and F). The NMAA's surprisingly deserted corridors include major painters from 19th- and 20th-century America and an array of folk and ethnic art. DC janitor James Hampton stayed up nights in an unheated garage for fifteen years to assemble the *Throne of the Third Heaven of the Nations' Millennium General Assembly,* to the right of the main museum entrance. Westerners Albert Bierstadt and Thomas Moran turn the second floor lobby into Yellowstone National Park. Head to the third floor for twentieth century work. (Open daily 10am-5:30pm; tours 10am-1pm on the hour. Free.) The wide range of media, periods, styles and people represented makes the National Portrait Gallery more like a museum of the American character. Ogle movie stars in the first floor's East Corridor, devoted to the performing arts. (Open daily 10am-5:30pm; tours at the Portrait Gallery 10am- 3pm Mon.-Fri., 11am-2pm Sat.-Sun. Free.)

The United States' founding documents can still be found at the **National Archives,** 8th St. and Constitution Ave. NW (general information 501-5000, guided tours 501-5205, library and research 501-5400). Metro: Archives/Navy Memorial. Visitors line up to view the original Declaration of Independence, U.S. Constitution, and Bill of Rights in the central Rotunda. Political cartoons join them through August. (Main exhibit area open April-Aug. 10am-9pm, Sept.-Mar. 10am-5:30pm. Free.) The end of the go-go, right-wing '80s hasn't fazed the **Federal Bureau of Investigation** (324-3000); today's FBI still hunts Commies, druggies and interstate felons with undiminished vigor. Lines form for the popular tour on the beige-but-brutal, block-long J. Edgar Hoover building's outdoor plaza (tour entrance from 10th St. NW at Pennsylvania Ave.). (Metro: Federal Triangle or Archives.) Real FBI agents sport walkie-talkies as they speed through gangster paraphernalia and mug shots of the nation's ten most wanted criminals. The FBI's crack team of scientists will ignore you from behind plexiglass. At tour's end, a marksman blasts away at cardboard evildoers. (Tours Mon.-Fri 8:45am-4:15pm. Free.)

Abraham Lincoln was assassinated in 1865 at **Ford's Theatre** (426-6924), 511 10th St. NW. (Metro: Metro Center, 11th St. exit.) Recline in comfortable theater seats while Ford's guides narrate the assassination for you. (Open 9am-5pm daily; tours and talks given twice hourly. Free.) Lincoln passed away at the **Petersen House** (426-6830), next door at 526 10th St. NW. Dotted white curtains and the bed where he died make visitors seem like a strangers at a wake. (Open daily 9am-5pm.) The **Old Post Office,** at Pennsylvania Ave. and 12th St. NW (523-5691),

Contiki Holidays, the ultimate travel experience for 18-35 year olds

Get ready for the most exhilarating travel experience of a lifetime. With Contiki, you can explore Europe, Australia, New Zealand, North America or Russia with 18-35 year olds from around the world. You stay in unique places like our Beaujolais Chateau in France or on board our three mast Schooner in the Greek Islands. You can enjoy activities from bungy cord jumping, white water rafting, cycling to hot air ballooning in Australia's outback. You have more time to discover the heart and soul of the countries you visit because Contiki sorts out the time-wasting hassles. Half our clients are travelling by themselves; we handle the room sharing arrangements. Unique accommodation, most meals, land transport, ferries, sightseeing and the time of your life start at just US $58 per day. Contiki combines all of the above to give you the ultimate travel experience. Why settle for anything less. Get your brochure and video today.

Contact Contiki's International Offices below:

Contiki Holidays	**Contiki Travel Inc.**	**Contiki Holidays Pty. Ltd.**	**Contiki Services Ltd.**
Suite 1616	1432 E. Katella Ave.	Level 7	Wells House
415 Yonge St.	Anaheim, California	35 Spring St.	15 Elmfield Road
Toronto, Ontario	92805 U.S.A.	Bondi Junction, NSW 2022	Bromley, Kent
Canada M5B 2E7	Tel: (714) 937-0611	Australia	BR1 1LS
Tel: (416) 593-4873	Fax: (714) 937-1615	Tel: (02) 389-0999	England
Fax: (416) 581-1494		Fax: (02) 387-8360	Tel: (081) 290-6777
			Fax: (081) 290-6569

Contiki HOLIDAYS for 18-35s

Look for the Let's Go® Travel Catalogue in this Book

sheathes a shopping mall in architectural wonder. (Metro: Federal Triangle.) Its arched windows, conical turrets and clock tower are a standing rebuke to its sleeker neighbors. Most visitors drop by for the food court. The tour meets at the glass elevators where food tables cluster; its view from the top may be DC's best. (Open Mon.-Fri. 8am-6pm, Sat. 12-6pm. Free.) The elegant **National Museum of Women in the Arts** (783-5000), hides inside an office building at 1250 New York Ave. NW. (Metro: Metro Center.) Traverse the balcony and ascend the spare, hidden staircase to the third floor, and you'll know you've made it: women artists have come into their own during the last hundred years, and the collection proves it with works by Georgia O'Keeffe, Isabel Bishop, Frida Kahlo, and Alma Thomas. (Open Mon.-Sat. 10am-5pm, Sun. noon-5pm. Requested donation $3, $2 for kids.)

White House Area/Foggy Bottom

President George and First Lady Barbara Bush call it home; everyone else calls it the **White House,** 1600 Pennsylvania Ave. NW (456-2200 or 456-7041, TTY 456-6213). (Metro: McPherson Square, Vermont Ave. exit.) With its simple columns and expansive lawns, the White House seems a compromise between patrician lavishness and democratic simplicity. The President's personal staff works in the West Wing; the First Lady's occupies the East Wing. You may tour a few rooms after obtaining a free ticket at the ticket booth on the **Ellipse,** the park south of the White House on Constitution Ave. between 15th and 18th St. NW. (Tours Tues.-Sat. 10am-noon; tickets distributed starting at 8am). Disabled visitors go straight to the Pennsylvania Ave. entrance. After getting a ticket, you'll wait about 2½ hours. American citizens can arrange a better tour by writing their Congresspeople months ahead. Due south of the White House, the grass of the Ellipse fills up with protests or tour groups.

Sometimes it's hard to tell the homeless, the political demonstrators and the statues apart in **Lafayette Park,** across Pennsylvania Ave. from the White House. Clark Mills' stone-faced Andrew Jackson, lauded by Wallace Stevens, stands in the center of the park. The Marquis de Lafayette joined Jackson in 1891, on the southeast corner of the park. The **Old Executive Office Building,** on 17th St. and Penn. Ave. NW, amazes pedestrians with its gingerbread complexity.

At 17th St. and Penn. Ave. NW, the **Renwick Gallery** (357-1718 or 357-2700) fills its Second Empire Mansion with "American craft." (Metro: Farragut West.) But it's not just for macrame buffs: the first floor often shows constructions by important contemporary artists. Stare for hours at *Gamefish,* a sculpture made of sail-fish parts, rhinestones, poker chips and badminton birdies.(Open daily 10am-5:30pm. Excellent handicapped access. Free.) Once housed in the Renwick's mansion, the **Corcoran Gallery** (628-3211) now exhibits in much larger, neoclassical quarters on 17th St. between E St. and New York Ave. NW. (Metro: Farragut West.) The Corcoran shows off American artists like portraitist John Singer Sargent and impressionist Mary Cassatt. Frederic Church's "Niagara Falls" shimmers with mist. The Gallery's first-floor temporary exhibits seek the cutting edge. Free jazz in the Hammer Auditorium every Wed. noon. (Open Tues.-Wed. and Fri.-Sun. 10am-5:30pm, Thurs. 10am-9pm. Sugg. donation $3, students/seniors $1, families $5, under 12 free.)

The **Organization of American States,** at 17th St. and Constitution Ave. NW (458-3940 or 458-3751), is a Latin American extravaganza: sunlight hits the concrete patio and bakes the stone benches in its air-conditioned, greenerified center. The meetings, held largely in Spanish, welcome tourists; they even have translation machines. (Call to ask when they're in session.) Tiffany chandeliers and coats of arms light up the Hall of the Americas upstairs. Outside, Xochipilli, whom Aztecs honored with hallucinogens and sacrifices, reclines in the Aztec Garden. (OAS open Mon.- Fri. 9am-5:30pm. Free.) The **Department of the Interior** (208-4743) covers a square area between C, d, 18th and 19th St. NW. The National Park Service desk spews brochures about forests and outfitters. Sign in at the main entrance on 18th and C St. and walk down the hall to the park office. In the Interior Department's museum, across from the park office, stuffed moose heads welcome you to the "opening" of the West, while Ansel Adams photographs show the land unsullied. (Museum open Mon.-Fri. 8am-4pm. Free.) The **National Academy of Sciences,** at 21st and C St. NW (334-2000), holds scientific or medical exhibits. It's traditional toget your photo snapped in the lap of the statue of Einstein, outside.

Above Rock Creek Parkway, the white **John F. Kennedy Center for the Performing Arts** (254-8700; pedestrian entrance off 25th St. and New Hampshire Ave. NW) rises and glows like a marble sarcophagus. But it can be one of the liveliest spaces in town. (Metro: Foggy Bottom-GWU, then walk away from downtown on H St. and turn left, i.e. south, onto New Hampshire Ave.) The late-60s Center boasts four stages and a film theater. The flag-decked Hall of States and Hall of Nations both lead to the Grand Foyer, longer than two football fields; a 7-foot-high bronze bust of JFK stares up eighteen ponderous chandeliers. In the opulent, all-red Opera House, snowflake-shaped chandeliers from Austria require 7300 light bulbs. Dig the view of the Potomac from the roof. Superlative disabled access. (Free. Open daily 10am-11pm. Free tours 10am-2pm.)

Georgetown

Georgetown is a college town and a posh real estate district, where ambassadors-in-training rub elbows with the Kissingers; it's a credit card baby's shopping nirvana; it's restaurant row-cum-clubland with no distinction between the two. Washington thinks it's pretty hip; Georgetown knows it is. Some of the townhouses between M St. and R St. have been subdivided and rented out to Georgetown University students, but others hide backyard courtyards and Warhols in every bathroom. Georgetown also serves its eponymous university with all-night food and late-night record stores. The nearest Metro stop, Foggy Bottom/GWU, is about eight long blocks from Georgetown's center at Wisconsin and M; trudge down Pennsylvania Ave. over the bridge. From Dupont Circle, just follow P St. east.

Dumbarton Oaks, 1703 32nd St. NW between R and S St. (recorded info. 338-8278, tour info. 342-3212), includes two must-sees: the mansion-museum displays ancient art, and the terraced gardens are the best cheap date in town. The Byzantine Collection contains bronzes, ivories, and jewelry from the eponymous Empire. Phillip Johnson's 1963 gallery holds a collection of Aztec and Mayan carvings and tools. Save at least an hour for the Dumbarton Oaks Gardens, inside the estate. It's Eden. Numerous partitions and blocked sightlines create an atmosphere of romantic privacy. (Open daily April-Oct. 2-6pm, Nov.-March 2-5pm. Admission $2, seniors and children $1; seniors free each Wed.) (Collections open Tues.-Sun. 2-5pm. Free.)

When Archbishop John Carroll learned where the new capital would be built, he rushed to found **Georgetown University** (main entrance at 37th and O St.), the United States' oldest Catholic institution for higher learning. Students live, study, and party together in townhouses which line the streets near the university.

Retired from commercial use since the 1800s, the **Chesapeake & Ohio Canal** (301-299-3613) extends 185 miles from Georgetown to Cumberland, Maryland; after Georgetown, the C&O changes from a polluted relic suitable for romantic strolls to a clean waterway whose towpath accommodates strolling families and mountain-bikers. The towpath grows monotonous after a few miles of running, walking, or biking, in spite of long bridges, small waterfalls, and historical spots.

Dupont Circle & New Downtown

Dupont Circle used to be called Washington's most diverse neighborhood; then it turned expensive and Adams-Morgan turned cool. The Circle and its environs still cater to Washington's artsy, international, and gay communities. From the Dupont Circle Metro, head up Connecticut Ave. for shopping and dining, Massachusetts Ave. for embassies, northwest (between the two) for paintings and hills, east to the earnest 14th St. theater district, or south to the bustling, charmless new downtown. Mass., Conn. and New Hampshire Ave. NW meet in **Dupont Circle** itself; a fountain hosts the chess players, lunching office workers, and herds of spandexed bike messengers who populate the island. Dupont Circle's 25 art galleries cluster on R between 21st and 22nd St. NW. Massachusetts Ave. between Dupont and Observatory Circles is also called **Embassy Row.** Recognize an embassy by the early-1900s mansion and national coat-of-arms or flag out front.

Turn left from Massachusetts Ave. to 21st St. to reach the **Phillips Collection,** 1600-1612 21st St. at Q St. NW (387-2151), the first museum of modern art in the U.S. and the classiest, most comfortable non-Smithsonian showplace in town. On the second floor, everyone stares at Auguste Renoir's *Luncheon of the Boating Party.* Van Goghs inhabit the second-floor atrium; flanking rooms hold French painters and semi-obscure Picassos. Downstairs, scan Richard Diebenkorn's paintings or meditate on Mark Rothko's haunting abstractions. Free chamber music and classical piano concerts sound off each Sunday from September to May at 5pm. (Open Tues.-Sat. 10am-5pm, Sun. 2-7pm. Tours Wed. and Sat. 2pm. Admission $5, over 62 $2.50, under 18 free.)

Anderson House, 2118 Massachusetts Ave. NW (785-2040) retains the robberbaron decadence of Larz Anderson, who built it in 1902-5; in the two-story ballroom, visitors can marvel at marble and feel Anderson's gilt. The Society of the Cincinnati makes this mansion its home and museum.(Open Tues.-Sat. 1-4pm. Free.) Turn right from R St. onto 22nd St., then walk up the hill to enter the **Textile Museum,** 2320 S St. NW (667-0441), which houses two or three exhibits at a time of rare and/or intricate textiles; ethnographic displays alternate with individual artists. (Open Mon.-Sat. 10am-5pm, Sun. 1-5pm. Lightly-suggested contribution $5.) Flags stand by the **Islamic Center,** 2551 Massachusetts Ave. NW (332-8343), whose stunning designs stretch to the tips of its spired ceilings. No short dresses, sleevelessness (for women) or shorts (men or women) allowed inside. Prayers held 5 times daily. (Open daily 10am-5pm. Donation requested.) **Second Story Books,** 20th and P St. NW (659-8884), runneth over with used books, records, free newspapers and flyers. (Open 10am-10pm daily). **Lambda Rising,** 1625 Connecticut Ave. NW (462-6967), brims with gay and lesbian literature. (Open daily 10am-midnight.)

Past M St. on 17th St. NW, the **National Geographic Explorer's Hall** conquers the first floor of its black-and-white pin-striped building (857-7588 or 857-7589; N.G. Society 857-7000). (Metro: Farragut North.) There's a short film, a globe bigger than you are, and changing exhibits, often by National Geographic Magazine's photographers. (Open Mon.-Sat. 9am-5pm, Sun. 10am-5pm. Disabled access.) Picnic to the summer sounds of flute duets and jazz sax players in **Farragut Square,** 3 blocks south of Connecticut Ave. on 17th St. between Eye and K St. NW.

Elsewhere

The mantle of hipness passed to the **Adams-Morgan** area in the late '80s, when cool kids and the cool at heart, mostly white-skinned, arrived alongside Mexican and Salvadoran immigrants. (The ranks of hipsters may dwindle after last May's two-day riots.) A wreath of awesome ethnic food circles 18th, Columbia and Calvert St. NW. (From the Woodley Park/Zoo Metro, walk to Calvert St., turn left, and hoof east.) Don't go in search of a specific establishment; do go to wander around. It's a salad of Hispanic, Caribbean and hip/upscale cultures any city should envy. Walk south along 18th or east along Columbia to soak in the flavor and eat well. If you stay west of 16th St. (and, at night, walk with a friend) safety should require only common sense.

Legend has it that "pandemonium" entered the vernacular when the first giant pandas left China for Washington's **National Zoological Park** (673-4800 or 673-4717). The Zoo spreads out east from Connecticut Ave. into Rock Creek Park, a few blocks uphill from Calvert St. NW and the Woodley Park/Zoo Metro; follow the crowds to the entrance at 3000 Connecticut Ave. NW. Gifts from Mao to Nixon, the pandas have their own concrete manger, their own keepers and even their own panda T-shirts. Walk over water in the new wetlands exhibit, lie down near the lions, or play St. Francis by strolling through the skyscraper-size bird cage. The Zoo enshrines its captives in environments they enjoy; some get their own wooded islands. Olmsted Walk (red elephant feet) links land-animal houses, while Valley Trail (blue bird tracks) connects the bird and sealife exhibits. Invertebrates (starfish and urchins and such) get their own house. Both trails are handicapped-accessible.

(Grounds open daily 8am-8pm; Oct.-April 8am-6pm; buildings open daily 9am-6pm, Sept.-April 9am-4:30pm. Free.)

The **Cathedral Church of Saint Peter and Saint Paul,** also called the **Washington National Cathedral,** at Massachusetts and Wisconsin Ave. NW (536-6207), took over 80 years (1909-90) to build, though the interior has been in use for decades. Rev. Martin Luther King Jr. preached his last Sunday sermon from the Canterbury pulpit; more recently Archbishop Desmond Tutu spoke here. Ride the elevator (near the main doors of the west entrance) to the Pilgrim Observation Gallery; you won't see pilgrims, but you will see Washington from the highest vantage point in the city. The Bishop's Garden near the South Transept resembles a medieval walled garden. (Open daily until dusk). (Metro: Tenleytown, then take the 30, 32, 34 or 36 bus toward Georgetown; or walk up Cathedral Ave. from the equidistant Woodley Park/ Zoo Metro.) (Cathedral open daily Sept.-April 10am-4:30pm, May-Aug. 10am-9pm; free. Call about disabled access.)

The **National Arboretum,** 24th and R St. NE (472-9279), is the U.S.'s living library of trees and flowers, big enough for 10 mi. of roads to cross. Experts go berserk over the arboretum's world-class stock of *bonsai* (dwarf trees) and *pnjing* (potted plants, rocks, figurines, and pagodas). Azaleas, and azalea-watchers, clog the place every spring. Drive to the arboretum if you can; the area is somewhat dangerous.(Open Mon.-Fri. 8am-5pm, Sat.-Sun. 10am-5pm; bonsais open 10am-2:30pm. Free.)

The 24-year-old **Anacostia Museum,** 1901 Fort Place SE (287-3369), run by the Smithsonian, focuses on African-American history and culture. Driving, take Martin Luther King Ave. SE to Morris Rd.; call for complex bus directions. (Open daily 10am-5pm. Wheelchair access.) **Cedar Hill,** the Frederick Douglass Home, 1411 W St. SE (426-5960) was the final residence of abolitionist statesman, orator, and autobiographer Frederick Douglass. Douglass must have enjoyed the view from his hilltop. House tours hourly from 9am to 4pm; begin with a movie, then walk through the house. (Open daily 9am-4pm; May-August 9am-5pm. Free.)

The silence of **Arlington National Cemetery** honors those who sacrificed their lives in war. (Metro: Arlington Cemetery) 612 acres of rolling hills and tree-lined avenues hold the bodies of U.S. military veterans from five-star generals to unknown soldiers. Before you enter the main gate, go to the Visitors Center on the left for maps. The Kennedy Gravesites hold both President John F. Kennedy and his brother, Robert F. Kennedy. An Eternal Flame, lit by JFK's widow at his funeral, flickers above his simple memorial stone. In the Tomb of the Unknowns, unidentified soldiers from World Wars I and II, the Korean War, and the Vietnam War lie under the white marble sarcophagus. (Cemetery open 8am-7pm April-Sept., 8am-5pm Oct.-March. Free.) Robert E. Lee once owned most of the Cemetery grounds; when he moved south, Union troops took over his mansion, **Arlington House,** now a "historic home" attraction. Enter the pastel-peach mansion at the front door, and pick up a "self-guided tour" sheet from one of the women in antebellum costume. If you continue down Custis Walk in front of Arlington House and out through Weitzel Gate, you can walk to the **Iwo Jima Memorial,** based on Joe Rosenthal's Pulitzer Prize-winning photograph of six Marines straining to raise the U.S. flag on Iwo Jima's Mount Suribachi. Military band concerts and parades take place here summer Tuesdays 7-8:30pm. Look at the thing from a different, non-Marine point of view to realize why this scene of butch guys with cute butts falling all over one another became a symbol of the gay rights movement in the '70s, and why it remains a gay pickup spot today.

History sleeps with George Washington at his estate, **Mount Vernon** (703-780-2000), where the tours, exhibits and restorations can seem staid and worshipful even by Virginia standards. Prussian blue and vivid green walls shine with their original hues, and most of the furniture was genuinely the General's. Look for the key to the Bastille. The tour ends downstairs in Washington's study, pantry, and kitchen. A gravel path leads to Washington's tomb; more interesting is the slave burial ground, which now includes a memorial. The **Mount Vernon Inn** serves a genuine lunch. Try the distinctive peanut and chestnut soup ($1.75). (Open Mon-Sat. 11am-

3:30pm and 5-9pm, Sun. 11:30am-4pm.) To drive to Mount Vernon, take the Beltway (I-495) to the George Washington Parkway on the Virginia side and follow the parkway to Mount Vernon; parking is free for four hours, more or less. Or Metro to Huntington on the Blue/Yellow line and catch the 11P Metrobus. There's no air-conditioning, and it's very crowded; in July or August, show up on a weekday morning. (Open daily 9am-5pm; Nov.-March 9am-4pm; admission $6, over 61 $5.50, ages 6-11 $3.)

Entertainment and Nightlife

At 25th St. and New Hampshire Ave. NW, the **Kennedy Center's** (416-8000) performing-arts spaces include two theaters, the Terrace Theater and the Theater Lab. The KenCen also houses the well-respected National Symphony Orchestra, the Washington Opera (416-7890), and the Washington Ballet. Though tickets get expensive ($10-50), all Kennedy Center productions offer half-price tickets before the start of an event and on the day of performance to students, seniors, military personnel, handicapped persons and those who can show they're poor; call 416-8340. Chamber music in the Kennedy Center, though a smaller deal, is more often cheap or free, especially during December. For free events, try the Office of Cultural Diversity (416-8090). The American College Theater Festival, April 20-29, houses free performances of top college productions. The excellent **American Film Institute** (828-4000), at the Kennedy Center, shows classic and avant-garde films, usually two per night.

Arena Stage, at 6th and Maine Ave. SW (488-3300), is often called the best regional (non-New York) theater company in America. The 40-year-old theater has two stages for new and used plays; the Old Vat Room holds Stephen Wade's furiously popular, strumming-and-talking one-man show. (Tickets $19-34; students 35%off, seniors 15%off, both except on Sat. evenings; half-price tickets usually available 90 min. before start of show.) The prestigious **Shakespeare Theater at the Folger** (box office 546-4000) puts on, mostly, Shakespeare plays. Call, preferably months in advance, for ticket prices, performance times, and student/senior discounts. Standing room tickets (currently $10) are available two hours before each performance. Disabled access, but give 24 hrs. notice. Thespians thrive in Washington's **14th St. theater district,** where tiny repertory companies explore and experiment with truly enjoyable results. *City Paper* provides very good coverage of this scene. **Woolly Mammoth,** 1401 Church St. (393-3939), **Studio Theater,** 1333 P St. NW (332- 3300), and the **Source Theater,** 1835 14th St. NW (462-1073) dwell in a borderline neighborhood east of Dupont Circle. (Tickets from $15; students and seniors 25% off at W.M., $3 off at Studio, from $13 at Source. $10 "stampede seat" at W.M. 1 hr. before curtain.) **The Dance Place,** 3225 8th St. NE (269-2600) leaps with innovative and/or ethnic dance, performance art, and/or music nearly every week. (Regular performances $8-10, kids around $4.) The **National Theatre,** 1321 Pennsylvania Ave. NW (628-6161) often hosts visitors from Broadway, with ticket prices to match. **TICKETplace** (842-5387), on the F St. plaza between 12th and 13th St. NW, sells discount day-of-show tickets for theater, music, dance, and special events on a walk-up basis Tues.-Fri. noon-4pm, Sat. 11am-5pm.

The **Library of Congress,** First St. SE (concert line 707-5502), sponsors concerts in the Coolidge Auditorium, one of the finest chamber music performance spaces in the world. The Phillips Collection and Corcoran Gallery (see above) have similar, but less prestigious, programs. The **National Symphony Orchestra** gives three free concerts a year on the west lawn of the Capitol, at 8 pm on May 24, July 4 and Sept. 6. **U.S. Military Bands** perform for free in and around the Mall every summer evening Memorial Day through Labor Day at 8pm. Army Band: 703-696-3399. Marine Band: 433-4011. Navy Band: 433-2525. Air Force Band: 767-5658.

DC's punk scene is, or was, one of the nation's finest. Charismatic mid-80s bands like Minor Threat and Rites of Spring fused crunchy guitar sounds and honest teen angst with a no-drugs, be-responsible attitude called "straightedge"; today Fugazi and Gray Matter, among others, keep the punk-rock flame. To demystify local bands, see *City Paper* and *Crackdc.* The leading venue is d.c. space is, but many of the best shows are all-ages (and fairly safe) gatherings in churches, rented halls or outdoors at **Fort Reno Park,** Chesapeake and Belt St. NW above Wisconsin Ave. (244-0800 or 619-7225), Mon. and Thurs. 7:30 pm from late June to early September. (Metro: Tenley Circle.). DC's African-American scenes originated the propulsive dance music called go-go. Flagship bands include Chuck Brown's, Rare Essence and EU (of "Da Butt" fame). But most regular venues are hard to reach and may be unsafe. Look for posters and outdoor concerts (and under Annual Events).

George Washington University sponsors shows in **Lisner Auditorium** (301-460-7918), 21st and H St. NW. Lisner hosts plays and rock concerts by well-known but "alternative" acts (like Billy Bragg); expect tickets below $20. Summer Sat. and Sun. jazz and R&B shows occupy the outdoor, 4200-seat **Carter-Barron Ampitheater,** set into Rock Creek Park up 16th St. and Colorado Ave. NW. (426-6837) (tickets around $13.50). These venues also vend tickets conveniently but expensively through Ticketron (432-0300), whose outlets exact a several-dollar service charge.

Georgetown at night is Washington on the prowl; everyone is looking for some place, something or somebody. Early in the evening, the streets, not the bars and clubs, are the liveliest part. Throngs of students, interns and young professionals share sidewalks with musicians, some very talented, playing anything from upended trash cans to alto sax. Don't neglect non-alcoholic nighttime offerings: late-night ice cream at Thomas Sweet, all-night French desserts at Au Pied du Cochon (see Food), or brilliant foreign movies. The **Biograph,** 2819 M St. NW (333-2696), excels at night with first-run independents, foreign films and classics. Bring all the food you want inside. (Admission $5, seniors and children $2.50. Handicapped access.) The **Key Theatre,** 1222 M St. NW (333-5100) shows first-run art films every critic raves about. (Admission $6, most matinees $2.50.)

Jazz

Blues Alley, 1073 Rear Wisconsin Ave. NW (337-4141 or 337-4142), in an actual alley, below M St. Mo' better jazz in an intimate supper club dedicated to the art: Dizzie Gillespie chairs its music society. Big names (like Wynton Marsalis) demand pricey tix ($10-25). $5 food-or-drink minimum. Snacks ($2-9) served after 9:30pm. Dress for the occasion: some don tuxes on big nights. Call or pick up a 3-month schedule.

One Step Down, 2517 Pennsylvania Ave. (331-8863), near M St. More casual and less expensive than Blues Alley. Local jazz Sun., Mon., and Thurs.; out-of-town talent Fri.-Sat. Free jam sessions Sat.-Sun. 3:30-7:30pm. Cover $5 for local bands and $8.50-17 for out-of-towners. Usually min. food or drink required. Beers from $3, sandwiches $3.50-6. Happy hour Mon.-Fri., 3-7pm ($1.25 draft). Open Mon-Fri. 10:30am-2am, Sat.-Sun. noon-3am.

Rock, Punk, Folk, Reggae, R&B

d.c. space, 443 7th St. NW (347-1445 or 347-4960). Metro: Gallery Place. Space is the place for "alternative" rock and punk, performance art, art films and poetry readings, and bizarre combos of the above. Crowds watch as well as dance to the bands. Black-walled bar in a separate room. All-ages shows. Cover under $5. Monthly open-mike night (pay $2 or perform). Monthly calendars at almost any record store. Showtimes Mon.-Thurs. 8-10pm, Fri.-Sat. 10-11pm.

9:30 club, 930 F St. NW (393-0930 or 638-2008). Metro: Metro Center. Hot new "alternative/progressive" rock bands. $3 for 3 DC bands; $7-14 for national acts, which often sell out weeks ahead (box office Mon.-Fri. 1pm-midnight). Under 21 admitted and hand-stamped. Free happy hour video cabaret Fri. from 4pm.

The Bayou, 3135 K St. NW (333-2897), under the Whitehurst Freeway in Georgetown. Bands on their way in and bands on their way out, with a rough'n'ready crowd that loves them all. Bigger acts on weeknights; metal Friday. Some shows 18-plus. Opening act 9:30pm Mon.-Thurs. and Sun., after 10pm Fri. and Sat. Cover $3-20. Open Sun.-Thurs. 8pm-1:30am, Fri.-Sat. 8pm-2:30am.

Kilimanjaro, 1724 California St. NW (328-3839). Dimly lit, big-deal club for international music—African, Latin, and Caribbean groups, ju-ju, reggae, and salsa DJs, with Latin music each Sun. Every Wed. His Go-go-ness Chuck Brown and the Soul Searchers play. Fair Caribbean food. No sneakers, shorts, sweats, torn jeans or tank tops. No cover Mon.-Wed., $5 cover Thurs. and Sun., $10 cover Fri. and Sat. Club open Mon.-Thurs. 5pm-2am, Fri.-Sat. 5pm-4am. Happy hour Mon.-Fri. 5-8.

The Birchmere, 3901 Mt. Vernon Ave. (549-5919). This low-key club features folk and blue-grass performed by live local and national acts from Mary Chapin Carpenter to NRBQ. Thursdays the bluegrass band Seldom Scene plays. There's a show almost every night; call and reserve tickets.

Dance Clubs, Comedy Clubs, Bars, Places to Be

Cafe Heaven and Cafe Hell, 2327 18th St. NW, in Adams-Morgan (667-HELL). Hell's down-stairs, Heaven's upstairs. Smoky Hell has funky gold tables, loud music and backlit masks. Heaven looks rather like an old townhouse, but the dance floor throbs to the drum machines of the angels; Heaven's back patio is crowded and quieter. No cover charge unless a band is playing. Beers from $3; half price happy hour (6:30-8:30pm in Hell). Dancing starts 9pm. Open Sun.-Thurs. 6:30pm-2am, Fri.-Sat. 6:30pm-3am.

Fifth Colvmn, 915 F St. NW (393-3632). Metro: Gallery Place. Euro-crowd brings serious disco to the trendy '90s. Splashy "underwater" decor in a converted bank, with fish tanks, dizzying films, and lights. House music shakes the basement; quieter bar upstairs. Mon. is "alternative" music; Sun. is gay night. Thurs. is really crowded. If too crowded, try the less artsy, less popular **The Vault,** 911 F St. (347-8079). Fifth Colvmn open Mon.-Sat. 10pm-whenever; cover Tues. $3, Wed. $4, Thurs. and Sat. $8, Fri. before 11pm $6, and afterwards $8. The Vault open Wed.-Mon. 9pm-2am; cover Wed. $4, Thurs.Thurs. and Fri. $5, Sat. $8.

15 Minutes, 1030 15th St. NW (408-1855). Metro: Farragut West. Dark, neon fish-scattered caverns get wilder as the night goes on. Mostly-bar on weekdays; mostly-dance club on week-ends; blues, jazz, and/or punk evenings. Always 21+; young crowd. Wed. is inscrutable "Sybil" night, except when it's Cyberpunk night. Open Mon.-Fri. 4:30pm-2am, Sat. 9pm-3am. $6 cover on weekends.

Comedy Cafe, 1520 K St. NW (638-JOKE). Metro: Farragut North. Stand-up comedy, some big names. Shows Fri. 8:30pm and 10:30pm, Sat. 7pm, 9pm, and 11pm. Open mike Thurs. 8:30pm. Beware of strip joint downstairs. Cover $8; Saturday 7pm special cover $4.

The Tombs, 1226 36th St. NW (337-6668), corner of Prospect St., in Georgetown. George-town students snarf burgers and beer. Justly crowded at night. Sunday's hopping dance nights $3 at the door; no cover elsewhen. Dollar drafts; $6 pitchers. Open Mon.-Sat. 11am-2am, Sun. 10am-2am.

Brickskeller, 1523 22nd St. NW (293-1885). Metro: Dupont Circle. 500+ beers "from Aass to Zywiece." Open Mon.-Thurs. 11:30am-2am, Fri. 11:30am- 2:30am, Sat. 6pm-2:30am, Sun. 6pm-1:30am.

The Front Page, 1333 New Hampshire Ave. NW (296-6500). Metro: Dupont Circle. Well-known among the intern crowd for its generous Thursday happy hours (5-7pm). Open daily 11:30am-2am.

Badlands, 1415 22nd St. NW (296-0505), off P St. Metro: Dupont Circle. Gay men dance, dance, dance the night away. The Last Chance Saloon, upstairs, looks strangely like a set from a Western. Open Sun.-Thurs. 9pm-1:45am, Fri. 8pm-2:45am, Sat. 9pm-2:45am. Cover Sun. and Tues. $1, Thurs. $3, Fri.-Sat. $5.

J.R.'s, 1519 17th St. NW (328-0090). Metro: Dupont Circle. An upscale, yet down-home brick and varnished wood bar, with wood floors, stained glass windows, and a DJ in a choir stall overlooking the tank of guppies (gay urban professionals). Open daily 11am-2am.

Cities, 2424 18th St. NW, in Adams-Morgan (328-7194) and **IKON** (483-2882), on the 2nd floor. Cities stays hip by changing every 8 months to mimic a different city. (Appetizers $3.50-6; entrees $8.50-15). IKON would never think of changing-gabled ceiling, purple techno-lights, and a bar with view-from-the-'copter-style full-length windows. Beer from $3.75. Cover Wed.-Thurs. $5, Fri.-Sat. $8. Cities open Mon.-Thurs. 5pm-2am, Fri.-Sat. 5pm-3am, Sun. 11am-3:30pm and 6-10pm. IKON open Wed.-Thurs. 9:30pm-2am, Fri.-Sat. 9:30pm-4am.

Annual Events

Chinese New Year Parade, mid-Feb., down H St. NW between 5th and 8th St. Metro: Gallery Place. Firecrackers, lions, drums and dragons make the normally tame streets of China-town—all six of them—explode with delight. Free.

Bach Marathon, March 15, at Chevy Chase Presbyterian Church, 1 Chevy Chase Circle NW (363-2202). For J.S. (Papa) Bach's birthday, 10 organists play JSB's works on the church's massive pipe organ. Take an "L" bus up Connecticut Ave. from the Van Ness or Cleveland Park Metro. Refreshments. 1-6pm. Free.

Smithsonian Kite Festival, March 28 (357-3244). Go fly a kite or watch designers of all ages at the Washington Monument grounds compete for prizes and trophies from 10am-4pm. Free.

"Save the Children" Festival/Marvin Gaye Day, April 25 (678-0503). Jazz, gospel, and go-go music, food and festing in the outdoor "downtown mall" on F St. NW between 7th and 9th St., behind the National Museum of American Art.

National Cherry Blossom Festival, April 5-12 (737-2599) All over town; read the Washington Post. Official Washington goes bonkers over the pretty, white Japanese blossoms. Expensive tickets for the April 11 Parade;other events (some free) include fireworks, free concerts in parks, and a marathon.

Shakespeare's Birthday Celebration, April 25, at the Folger Shakespeare Library. Exhibits, plays, Elizabethan music, food, and children's events. The Bard's actual birthday is April 23. Noon-5pm. Free.

Malcolm X Day, May 22, in Anacostia Park along the Anacostia River in SE (543-1649). A daylong festival honoring slain Black leader Malcolm X. Food, speakers, three tents of exhibits, gospel, African, Caribbean, blues, and go-go music; premier go-goists EU may drop by. Noon-7pm. Free.

Memorial Day Ceremonies at Arlington Cemetery, May 25 (475-0856). Wreaths at Kennedy tomb and Tomb of the Unknown Soldier; services in Memorial Amphitheater. The President will talk. Also at the **Vietnam Veterans Memorial** (619-7222) 11am, in similar solemnity, but Bushless. Both free.

Gay Pride Day, June 23 (298-0970). Big march through downtown for gay and lesbian consciousness and rights. Starts at 16th and W St. NW; ends in a festival at Francis School, at 25th St. Festival entrance $5 on the day, advance purchase at Blockbuster Video Dupont Circle $3.

Bloomsday Marathon *Ulysses* Reading, June 15-16, at Kelly's "The Irish Times" pub (see Food). Annual read-through of Joyce's greatest novel draws crowds of literary and/or Irish notables. Starts around 11am June 15. Free.

Festival of American Folklife, June 24-28 and July 1-5, on the Mall (357-2700). Huge Smithsonian-run fair demonstrates the crafts, customs, food and music of selected states, territories and/or foreign countries to over a million visitors, with imported musicians, performers, and craftspeople. Free.

Fourth of July (Independence Day). A daylong party begins with an old-fashioned Fourth of July parade (789-7000), along Constitution to 17th St. NW. Up Pennsylvania Ave. is the DC Free Jazz Festival (783-0360), 1-8pm in the park between 13th and 14th St. NW. The National Symphony (416-8100) plays patriotic music on the Capitol's West Lawn from 8pm, but if you sit there you won't get a good view of the 9:15pm fireworks, best from the Washington Monument grounds. Arrive by 6:30pm, and face west (towards the Lincoln Memorial).

Bastille Day Waiters' Race, July 14, starting at Pennsylvania Ave. and 20th St. NW. Waiters carry champagne glasses on trays and demonstrate their juggling ability. Dominique's Restaurant (452-1132) sponsors. Noon-4:00pm. Free.

Latin American Festival, July 26, on the Washington Monument grounds (724-4091). Free food, music, dance and theatre from 40 Latin American nations.

U.S. Army Band's "1812 Overture," Aug. 11, on the Washington Monument grounds (703-696-3399). Actually Tchaikovsky's "1812 Overture," but the Army Band (and a Salute Gun Platoon) performs the work. 8pm. Free.

National Frisbee Festival, Aug. 29, on the Mall near the Air & Space Museum (301-645-5043). The largest non-competitive frisbee festival in the U.S., with frisbee studs and disc-catching dogs. Free.

African Cultural Festival, Sept. 5, at Freedom Plaza, 14th St. and Pennsylvania Ave. NW (667-5775). African cooking, sounds, movement and stuff for sale. Noon-7pm. Free.

DC Blues Festival, Sept. 5, in Anacostia Park, across the eponymous river in SE (724-4091 or 301-483-0871). Top blues people twang, wail, and moan. Free.

Kennedy Center Open House, mid-Sept. (416-8000). A one-day hodgepodge of classical, jazz, folk and ethnic music, dance, drama and film from DC performers including members of the National Symphony Orchestra. Free.

Adams-Morgan Day, Sept. 13, along 18th St., Columbia Rd., and Florida Ave. NW (332-3292 or 724-4091). Bands on 3-4 stages (check out the go-go band), stuff for sale, and the food for which Adams-Morgan is justly famous. Free, all day, always jammed.

Veteran's Day Ceremonies, Nov. 11, around Arlington Cemetery (475-0843). Solemn ceremony with military bands in the Memorial Amphitheater. The President lays a wreath at the Tomb of the Unknown Soldier. From 11am; free. Vietnam Memorial also holds ceremonies (619-7222; free).

Kennedy Center Holiday Celebration, throughout December (416-8000). Free musical events from Dec. 1 on: classical chamber, choral, cello and "Tuba-Christmas" concerts, gospel concert(ticket giveaway weeks in advance), and popular sing-along to Handel's "Messiah"—stand in line all day to get tickets.

National Christmas Tree Lighting/Pageant of Peace, Dec. 10-Jan. 1, on the Ellipse (619-7222). The President switches on a Christmas tree, a Hanukkah Menorah, and other electrical objects at 5:30pm on Dec. 10; choral music, a Nativity scene, a burning yule log and lit-up trees until the New Year. Free.

Washington National Cathedral Christmas Celebration and Services, Dec. 24-25 (536-6200). Daytime Christmas carols and choral music, but the service is more famous. Dec. 24 pageant 4pm, service 10pm. Dec. 25: service 9am. Free.

New Year's Eve Celebration at the Old Post Office Pavilion, Dec. 31 (289-4224). Crowded, festive outdoor and indoor party emulates NYC's Times Square—complete with pickpockets. Giant stamp drops at midnight. Free.

WASHINGTON

Washington has two personalities, clearly split by the Cascade Range. The western ridge of the range blocks Pacific moisture heading east and hurls it back toward the ocean, bathing the Olympic Peninsula in 135 inches of rain a year. Always drawn to moisture, most inhabitants cluster with the seafood around Puget Sound. But don't pity comparatively arid eastern Washington; 10 fewer feet of water per annum isn't everything, especially with the miracle of modern refrigeration. Residents can use time savoring fresh fruit or enjoying the rolling countryside without jostling for space.

Washington runs the textbook of terrain; deserts, volcanoes, untouched Pacific Ocean beaches, and the world's only non-tropical rain forest all await exploration. Mount Rainier has fantastic hiking, while the Cascades keep perfect conditions for nearly any winter activity. Seattle and Spokane drape themselves in equally beautiful green landscapes, showing that botany and exhibitionism can still intersect. Best of all, Washington is a compact state by West Coast standards—everything remains less than a daytrip away.

Practical Information

Capital: Olympia.

State Tourist Office, Tourism Development Division, 101 General Administration Bldg., Olympia 98504-0613 (206-753-5600). **Washington State Parks and Recreation Commission,** 7150 Clearwater Lane, Olympia 98504 (206-753-2027; in WA 800-562-0990). **Forest Service/National Park Service Outdoor Recreation Information,** 915 2nd Ave. #442, Seattle 98174 (206-442-0170). Open Mon.-Fri. 8am-5pm.

Time Zone: Pacific (3 hr. behind Eastern). **Postal Abbreviation:** WA

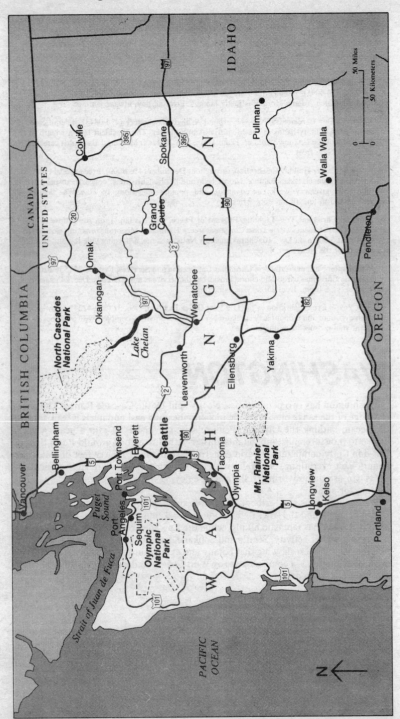

Cascade Range

The Northwestern American Indians are said to have called the Cascades "the home of the Gods." Although a relatively young mountain range, the Cascades have long been the Northwest's most tangible reminder of nature's eternal supremacy over mankind. The mountains refuse to sleep; they are noisy and active—crashing waterfalls, rumbling volcanoes such as Mt. St. Helens, and falling ice characterize the Cascades' reign. The huge mountains are raising their peaks the length of a human fingernail each year, and their steep grade brings rock climbers from the world over to cling to the peaks' icy cuticles.

The tallest, white-domed peaks of Baker, Vernon, Glacier, Rainier, Hood, Adams, and St. Helens understandably attract the most attention and have, for the most part, been made accessible by four major roads which offer good trailheads and impressive scenery for those on the air-conditioned side of the car window. **Route 12** through White Pass goes nearest Mt. Rainier National Park; **Interstate 90** sends four lanes past the major ski resorts of Snoqualmie Pass; scenic **Route 2** leaves Everett for Stevens Pass and descends along the Wenatchee River, a favorite of whitewater rafters; and **Route 20,** the **North Cascades Highway,** provides access to North Cascades National Park from April to November, weather permitting. These last two roads are often traveled in sequence as the **Cascade Loop.**

Greyhound travels the routes over Stevens and Snoqualmie Passes to and from Seattle, while **Amtrak** cuts between Ellensburg and Puget Sound. Locals warn against thumbing across Rte. 20, where a few hapless hitchers apparently have "vanished" over the last decade. The mountains are most accessible in the clear months of July, August, and September; many high mountain passes are snowed in the rest of the year. For general info on the Cascades contact the **National Park/National Forest Information Service,** 915 2nd Ave., Seattle 98174 (442-0181 or 442-0170).

Mount Rainier National Park

Mt. Rainier rises grandly above the tops of the other Cascade mountains, 2 mi. taller than many of the surrounding foothills. Residents of Washington refer to it simply as "The Mountain." Unfortunately, Rainier meteorologically drenches all that lies in its shadow. Warm ocean air condenses when it reaches Rainier and falls on the mountain at least 200 days of the year. When the sun does shine, you may understand why Native Americans called Mt. Rainier "Tahoma" (Mountain of God).

Many experiences available—midnight views of the mountain silhouetted against the moon, inner-tube rides down the slick sides in winter, romps in alpine meadows full of unparalleled wildflower displays—approach the same intensity at slightly lower elevations with much less cost and personal risk than they entail from the 14,410-ft. summit. Nevertheless, 2500 determined climbers ascend to Rainier's peak each year.

Admission to the park costs $5 per car or $2 per hiker; the gates stay open 24 hrs. For visitor info stop in at the **Longmire Museum and Hiker's Center** (open mid-June to mid-Sept. daily 8am-5:30pm; mid-Sept. to mid-June daily 9am-5pm); **Paradise Visitors Center** (open mid-June to mid-Sept. daily 9am-6pm; off-season hours vary); **Ohanapecosh Visitor Center** (same hours as Paradise); or **Sunrise Visitors Center,** (same hours as Paradise). All centers can be contacted c/o Superintendent, Mt. Rainier National Park, Ashford, WA 98304, or through the park central operator (569-2211). Much of the activity in Rainier occurs in these centers, each of which has displays, a wealth of literature on everything from hiking to natural history, postings on trail and road conditions, and cherubically helpful rangers. Naturalist-guided trips and talks, campfire programs, and slide presentations take place at the visitors centers and vehicle campgrounds throughout the park. Check at a visitors center or pick up a copy of the free annual newsletter, *Tahoma,* for details.

A car tour provides a good intro to the park. All major roads offer scenic views of the mountain and have numerous roadside sites for camera-clicking and general gawking. The roads to Paradise and Sunrise prove especially picturesque. **Stevens Canyon Road** connects the southeast corner of the National Park with Paradise, Longmire, and the Nisqually entrance, and affords truly spectacular vistas of Rainier and the rugged Tatoosh Range with the accessible roadside attractions of **Box Canyon** and **Grove of the Patriarchs** along the way.

Several less developed roads provide access to more isolated regions. These roads often adjoin trailheads that crisscross the park or lead to the summit. Cross-country hiking and camping outside designated campsites is permissible through most regions of the park, but overnight backpacking trips always require a permit. The **Hikers Center** at Longmire has info on day and backcountry hikes through the park and dispenses the permits necessary for camping. (Open mid-June to late Sept. daily 7am-7pm.)

A segment of the **Pacific Crest Trail (PCT)**, running between the Columbia River and the Canadian border, crosses through the southeast corner of the park. The U.S. Forest Service maintains the PCT for both hikers and horse riders. Primitive campsites and shelters line the trail; camping requires no permit, although you should contact the nearest ranger station for info on site and trail conditions. The trail, overlooking the sometimes snow-covered peaks of the Cascades, snakes through delightful scenery where wildlife abounds.

Hardcore campers will thrill to the **Wonderland Trail,** a 95-mi. loop around the entire mountain. Because it includes some brutal ascents and descents, rangers recommend that even experts plan on covering only 7-10 mi. per day. Rangers can provide info on weather and trail conditions, and can even help with food caches at stations along the trail. Specific dangers along Wonderland include snow-blocked passes in June, muddy trails in July, and early snowstorms in September. Expert climbers can discuss options for reaching the summit with rangers.

Less ambitious, ranger-led **interpretive hikes** feature themes from local wildflowers to area history. Each visitors center conducts its own hikes, each with a different schedule. The hikes, lasting anywhere from 20 minutes to all day, especially suit families with young children. These free hikes complement evening campfire programs, also conducted by each visitors center.

Llama Wilderness Pack Trips, Tatoosh Motel, Packwood (491-LAMA; 491-7213) offers a llunch with the llamas in the park for $25 per person (4-5 hrs.). They also llease their llamas for pack trips and have guided trips of their own.

The towns of **Packwood** and **Ashford** have a few motels near the park. Call the **Paradise Inn** (569-2291) or the **National Park Inn** (569-2706). Camping at the auto campsite costs $6 between mid-June and late September. Subject to certain restrictions, alpine and cross-country camping require free permits. Pick up a copy of the *Backcountry Trip Planner* at any ranger station or hiker center before you set off. Alpine and cross-country permits are strictly controlled to prevent enviromental damage, but auto camping permits are easy to come by. Each campground has its own personality. Go to **Ohanapecosh** for the gorgeous and serene high ceiling of Old Growth trees, **Cougar Rock** for the strictly maintained quiet hours, and **White River** and **Sunshine Point** for the views. Open on a first-come, first-camp basis, they fill up only on the busiest summer weekends. Only Sunshine Point, however, remains open throughout the year. With a permit, cross-country hikers can use any of the free, well-established **trailside camps** scattered throughout the park's backcountry. Most camps have toilet facilities and a nearby water source; some have shelters. Fires are prohibited; party numbers are limited. Mountain and glacier climbers must always register in person at ranger stations to get permits.

To reach Mt. Rainier from the west, drive south on I-5 to Tacoma, then go east on Rte. 512, south on Rte. 7, and east on Rte. 706. This scenic road meanders through the town of Ashford and into the park by the Nisqually entrance. Rte. 706 is the only access road kept open throughout the year; snow usually closes all other park roads from November through May. The city of Yakima provides the eastern gateway to the park. Take I-82 from the center of town to U.S. 12 heading west.

At the junction of the Naches and Tieton Rivers, go either left on U.S. 12 or continue straight up Rte. 410. U.S. 12 runs past Rimrock Lake, over White Pass to Rte. 123, where a right turn leads to the Stevens Canyon entrance to Rainier.

Mount Saint Helens

Mt. St. Helens started rumbling on May 18, 1980, 69 years to the day after the death of Gustav Mahler. In the three days that followed, a hole 2 mi. long and 1 mi. wide opened in the mountain. Ash from the crater blackened the sky for hundreds of miles and blanketed the streets of towns as far as Yakima, 80 mi. away. Debris spewed from the volcano flooded Spirit Lake, choked rivers with mud, and descended to the towns via river and glacier. The blast leveled entire forests, leaving a stubble of trunks on the hills and millions of trees pointing like arrows away from the crater. Because the blast was lateral, not vertical, it destroyed much more since no energy dissipated in fighting gravity.

Once the jewel of the Cascades, today the Mt. St. Helens National Monument (now administered by the National Forest Service) seems sad and desolate to many visitors. Indeed, towns around the monument talk grandly of the "devastation." However, this great female mountain is also the mother of much inspiring new life. In the summer, rock gardens along the ash hiking trails and near the various waterfalls are oases of green among fallen white trees and grey landscape.

Start any trip to the mountain at the **Mount St. Helens National Volcanic Monument Visitor Center** (274-6644), on Rte. 504, west of Toutle (take exit 49 off I-5, and follow the signs). The **Gifford Pinochet National Forest Headquarters**, 6926 E. Fourth Plain Blvd. P.O. Box 894, Vancouver, WA (696-7500), has camping and hiking info. For 24-hr. recorded info on current volcanic activity, call 696-7848.

Gray Line, 400 NW Broadway, Portland, OR (503-226-6755; 800-426-7532) runs buses from Seattle to Mt. St. Helens. (Round-trip $26, under 13 $14.)

Mount St. Helens' **area code** is 206.

North Cascades

A number of different agencies administer the North Cascades, an aggregation of dramatic peaks north of Stevens Pass on Rte. 2. Pasayten and Glacier Peak are designated wilderness areas, each attracting large numbers of hardy backpackers and mountain climbers. Ross Lake Recreation Area surrounds the Rte. 20 corridor, and **North Cascades National Park,** 2105 Hwy. 20, Sedro Wooley 98284 (206-856-5700; open Sun.-Thurs. 8am-4:30pm, Fri.-Sat. 8am-6pm), extends north and south of Rte. 20. The **Mt. Baker/Snoqualmie National Forest,** 915 2nd Ave., room 442, Seattle 98174 (206-442-0170), borders the park to the west; the **Okanogan National Forest,** 1240 2nd Ave. S., P.O. Box 950, Okanogan 98840 (509-826-3275) to the east; and **Wenatchee National Forest,** 301 Yakima St., P.O. Box 811, Wenatchee 98807 (509-662-4335) to the south. For snow avalanche info on all these jurisdictions call 206-526-6677. Rte. 20, the North Cascades Hwy., provides the major access to the area, as well as astounding views past each new curve in the road.

Rte. 20 from Burlington (exit 230 on I-5) across the mountains gives the best first impression of the North Cascades. A feat of modern engineering, Rte. 20 follows the Skagit River to the Skagit Dams and lakes, whose hydroelectric energy powers Seattle, then crosses the Cascade Crest at Rainy Pass (4860 ft.) and Washington Pass (5477 ft.), finally descending to the Methow River and the dry Okanogan rangeland of eastern Washington. The road forks at Baker Lake Rd., which in turn dead-ends for some unknown reason 25 mi. later at **Baker Lake.** Only two campsites along the way provide water: **Horseshoe Cove** (sites $7.50) and **Panorama Point** (sites $7.50). All other sites are free.

Rte. 9 leads north from the rich farmland of **Skagit Valley** through inspiring forested countryside, with roundabout access to **Mount Baker** via the forks at the Nooksack River and Rte. 542. Mt. Baker (10,778 ft.) has been belching since 1975, and in winter jets of steam often rise from its dome. The nerve. Sneeze four times in succession and you miss the town of **Concrete** and its three neighbors—and, indeed, you may want to reach for the pepper. If you drive through at lunchtime, stop at the **Mount Baker Café**, 119 E. Main St. (853-8200; open daily 7am-9pm). The road from Concrete to Mt. Baker runs past the lakes created by the Upper and Lower Baker Dams. Solid facts are available from the **Concrete Chamber of Commerce** (853-8400), in the old depot, tucked between Main St. and Hwy. 20—follow the railroad tracks upon entering town. (Open Mon.-Fri. 9am-4pm.)

Neighboring **Rockport** borders **Rockport State Park,** featuring magnificent Douglas-firs, a trail that accommodates wheelchairs, and 50 campsites that rank among the swishest in the state ($7.50). The surrounding **Mount Baker National Forest** permits free camping closer to the high peaks. From Rockport, Hwy. 530 stems south to **Darrington,** home to a large population of displaced North Carolinians, and therefore host to a rapidly growing **Bluegrass Festival** on the third weekend of July. Darrington's **ranger station** (436-1155) presides on Hwy. 530 at the north end of town. (Open Mon.-Fri. 7am-4:30pm, Sat.-Sun. 8am-4:30pm; closed on weekends in winter.)

Stop in **Marblemont** to dine at the **Mountain Song Restaurant** (873-2461), 5860 Rte. 20. The Mountain Song serves hearty and healthy meals—try the trout dinner ($8.50) or the BLT ($4.25, emphasis on L and T). Open daily 8am-9pm. Just past Marblemont the highway splits off into Cascade River Rd. and goes across the river to dead end at the bottom of a rising mountain fare. Traveling up Cascade Rd. from Marblemount about 22 mi. will bring you to the trailhead for a 9-mi. hike to **Cascade Pass.**

Pitch your tent at the **Cascade Islands Campground** or **Marble Creek Campground,** both wihtin the first 15 mi. off the highway. Marble Creek, 7-8 mi. in, is the more beautiful of the two but also the more popular. Unbelievably, a hostel hides here, **The Barrel House Hostel,** (873-2021), a marvelous old bunkhouse with kitchens and bath ($7.50 each).

For $4 the park service's **shuttle** will take you the 26 mi. to the isolated town of **Stehekin.** Always confirm at the **Marblemount Ranger Station** (873-4590), 1 mi. north of Marblemount, that the thrice-daily shuttle is in operation. (Open daily in summer 7am-8pm.) Reservations are required for the shuttle bus ($3; call 509-682-2576 for reservations and more info on hiking/boating).

Newhalem, a buffer zone between Rte. 20 and North Cascade National Park, is the first town in the **Ross Lake National Recreation Area.** A small grocery store and hiking trails to the dams and lakes nearby make up the town's largest attractions. Info emanates from the **visitors center,** on Rte. 20. (Open late June-early Sept. Thurs.-Mon. 8am-4pm.) At other times, stop at the general store (open daily 8am-8pm; call 206-386-4489).

Plugged up by Ross Dam, the artificial expanse of **Ross Lake** extends back into the mountains as far as the Canadian border. Fifteen campgrounds ring the lake, some accessible by boat only, others by trail. The trail along Big Beaver Creek, a few mi. north of Rte. 20, leads from Ross Lake into the Picket Range and eventually to Mt. Baker and the **Northern Unit** of North Cascades National Park. The **Sourdough Mountain** and **Desolation Peak** lookout towers near Ross Lake have eagle's-eye views of the range.

The National Park's **Goodell Creek Campground,** just south of Newhalem, has 22 sites ($5) suitable for tents and trailers, and a launching site for white-water rafting along the Skagit River. (Open year-round. Drinking water and pit toilets.) **Colonial Creek Campground,** 10 mi. to the east, is a fully developed, vehicle-accessible campground with flush toilets, a dump station, and campfire programs every evening. (Open mid-May to Nov. Sites $6.)

Diablo Lake fumes directly to the west of Ross Lake, the foot of Ross Dam acting as its eastern shore and the top of the Diablo Dam stopping it up on the west. The town of Diablo Lake, on the northeastern shore, is the main trailhead for hikes into the southern portion of the North Cascades National Park. The Thunder Creek Trail traverses Park Creek Pass to the Stehekin River Rd. in Lake Chelan National

Recreation Area. Diablo Lake has a boathouse and a lodge that sells groceries and gas.

The **Pacific Coast Trail** crosses **Rainy Pass** (alt. 4860 ft.) 30 mi. farther on Rte. 20 on one of the most scenic and challenging legs of its 2500-mi. Canada-to-Mexico span. The trail leads up to **Pasayten Wilderness** in the north and down to **Glacier Peak** (10,541 ft.), which dominates the central portion of the range. Glacier Peak can also be approached from the secondary roads extending northward from the Lake Wenatchee area near Coles Corner on U.S. 2, or from Rte. 530 to Darrington. **Washington Pass**, at mile 163 of Rte. 20, has a well-maintained scenic turn-out. A 5-minute walk up paved, wheelchair-accessible trails leads to a view of the Early Winters Creek's Copper Basin, validating the whole drive.

Despite the Harvardian namesake, the town of **Winthrop** now capitalizes on a Wild West theme. The one row of restaurants, stores, and hotels along the main street—all made of weather-beaten wood with corrugated tin roofs—features creaky wooden sidewalks and painted signs. The great billows of hickory-scented smoke draw customers to the **Riverside Rib Co. Bar B-Q,** 207 Riverside, which serves fantastic Winthropian ribs in a convertible prairie schooner (i.e. covered wagon); satisfying vegetarian dinners ($8) are also available. (Open daily 11am-9pm.) Across the street sits the **Winthrop Information Station** (996-2125), on the corner of Rte. 20 and Riverside. (Open Memorial Day-Labor Day 9am-5pm.)

While in Winthrop, mark time at the **Shafer Museum,** 285 Castle Ave. (996-2712), up the hill overlooking town, one block west of Riverside Ave. The museum features all sorts of bizarre pioneer paraphernalia in a log cabin built in 1897. (Open daily 10am-5pm. Free.) You can rent horses at the **Rocking Horse Ranch** (996-2768), 9 mi. north of Winthrop on the North Cascade Hwy. (996-2768; $14 per hr.), and mountain bikes at **The Virginian Hotel** just east of town on Rte. 20 ($4.50 for the 1st hr., then $3 per hr.; full day $20).

The **Winthrop Ranger Station,** P.O. Box 579 (996-2266), up a marked dirt road west of town, has info on camping in the National Forest. (Open Mon.-Fri. 7:45am-5pm, Sat. 8:30am-5pm.) North of Winthrop, the **Early Winters Visitor Center,** outside Mazama, stocks info about the Pasayten Wilderness, an area whose relatively gentle terrain and mild climate endear it to hikers and equestrians (996-2534; open Sun.-Thurs. 9am-5pm, Fri.-Sat. 9am-7pm; off-season weekends only).

Early Winters has 15 simple campsites ($5) 14 mi. west of Winthrop on Rte. 20, and **Klipchuk,** 1 mi. farther west, has 39 better developed sites ($5). Cool off at **Pearrygin Lake State Park** beach. From Riverside west of town, take Pearrygin Lake Rd. for 4 mi. Sites ($6) by the lake have flush toilets and pay showers. Arrive early, since the campground fills up by early afternoon.

Leave Winthrop's prohibitively expensive hotel scene and stay in **Twisp,** the town that should have been a breakfast cereal. Nine mi. south of Winthrop on Rte. 20, this peaceful town offers low prices and few tourists. **The Sportsman Motel,** 1010 E. Rte. 20 (997-2911), tries to hide its tasteful rooms, decor, and kitchens with a gruff, barracks-like exterior. (Singles $28, doubles $36; Nov. to May 1 singles $23, doubles $32.) The **Twisp Ranger Station,** 502 Glover St. (997-2131), has an extremely helpful staff ready to load you down with trail and campground guides. (Open Mon.-Sat. 7:45am-4:30pm.) The **Methow Valley Tourist Information Office,** at the corner of Rte. 20 and 3rd St., slings area brochures. (Open Mon.-Fri. 8am-noon and 1-5pm.) Lodging reservations can be made through **Methow Valley Lodging** (996-2111).

The **Methow Valley Farmer's Market** sells produce from 9am to noon on Saturdays (April-Oct.) in front of the community center. Join local workers and their families at **Rosey's Branding Iron,** 123 Glover St., where the wonderfully droll staff serves all-you-can-keep-down soup and salad for $5. (Open daily 5am-8pm.)

Five mi. east of Twisp stands a training station for **Smoke Jumpers,** folks who get their kicks by parachuting into the middle of blazing forest fires for strategic firefighting. Occasionally they give tours or have training sessions for public viewing. Call the base (997-2031) for details.

Greyhound stops in Burlington once per day, and **Empire Lines** (affiliated with Greyhound), serves Okanogan, Pateros, and Chelan on the eastern slope. Avoid hitching in this area.

Olympic Peninsula

In the fishing villages and logging towns of the Olympic Peninsula, locals joke about having webbed feet and using Rustoleum instead of suntan oil. The Olympic Mountains wrench out the area's heavy rainfall (up to 200 in. per year on Mt. Olympus) from the moist Pacific. While this torrent supports bona fide rain forests in the western peninsula's river valleys, towns such as Sequim in the range's rain shadow are the driest in all of Washington, with as little as 17 in. of rain in a typical year.

The peninsula's geography matches its extremes of climate. The beaches along the Pacific strip are a hiker's paradise—isolated, windy, and beautiful. The glaciated peaks of the Olympic range sport spectacular alpine scenery; the network of trails covers an area the size of Rhode Island. These wild, woody mountains resisted exploration well into the 20th century.

Because it compresses such variety into a relatively small area, the Olympic Peninsula attracts those seeking accessible wilderness and outdoor recreation. U.S. 101 loops around the peninsula, stringing together scattered towns and sights around the nape of the mountains. The numerous secondary roads departing from 101 were specially designed with exploration in mind, although some are gravel-covered, making bicycling into the heart of the park difficult. Heart o' the Hills Rd. to Hurricane Ridge makes a particularly good detour, offering an unbeatable panorama. Route 112 follows the Strait of Juan de Fuca out to Neah Bay, the driftwood-laden coastal town near Cape Flattery. Greyhound provides service only as far as Port Angeles to the north and Aberdeen/Hoquiam to the south. Although local transit systems extend public transportation a little farther, the western portion of the peninsula and the southern portion of Hood Canal do not receive regular service.

Camping

Olympic National Park maintains a number of campgrounds. (Sites $5.) The numerous **state parks** along Hood Canal and the eastern rim charge $4 per night, with an occasional site for tenters at only $1-3 per night. The **National Forest** and the park services welcome backcountry camping (free everywhere), but a permit, available at any ranger station, is required within the park. Camping on the beaches comes especially easy, although you should pack a supply of water. The beaches in the westernmost corner of Neah Bay and from the town of Queets to Moclips farther south fall within Native American reserve land, which is private property: travelers are welcome, but respect local regulations prohibiting alcohol, fishing without a tribal permit, and beachcombing. The Quinault Reservation gained fame 20 years ago by forcibly ousting vandals trespassing on their beaches.

Washington's **Department of Natural Resources (DNR)** manages huge tracts of land on the Kitsap Peninsula and along the Hoh and Clearwater Rivers near the western shore, as well as smaller, individual campsites sprinkled around the peninsula. In DNR areas, camping is free and uncrowded; no reservations are required. DNR areas, however, can prove hard to find. For maps, contact the Department of Natural Resources, Olympic Area, Rte. 1, Box 1375, Forks, WA 98331 (206-374-6131).

Hood Canal and the Kitsap Peninsula

The long ribbon of the Hood Canal reaches down from Puget Sound, nearly separating the Kitsap Peninsula from its parent Olympic Peninsula. The canal's structure invites comparison with Scandinavia's famous fjords—the same narrow, steeply banked waterway, the same jagged peaks for backdrops, the same little towns tucked in the crevices of the coastline. U.S. 101 adheres to the western shore of the canal from Potlatch State Park on its southern tip to Quilcene in the north.

Here, the **Olympic National Forest** rims the eastern edge of the National Park. Much of the forest is more developed and more accessible than the park and gives those with little time or small appetites for the outdoors a taste of the peninsula's wildlife. Stop by one of the forest's **ranger stations** along the canal to pick up info on camping and trails in the forest. The two stations are in **Hoodsport,** P.O. Box 68 (877-5254; open early May-late Sept. daily 8am-4:30pm) and **Quilcene,** U.S. 101 S. (765-3368; open Mon.-Fri. 8am-5pm, Sat.-Sun. 8:30am-5pm). Adjacent to the Hoodsport Ranger Station stands a **post office** (877-5552; open Mon.-Fri. 8am-12:30pm and 1:30-5pm, Sat. 8:30-11:30am; ZIP Code: 98548). Many of the forest service **campgrounds** cost only $4, including **Hamma Hamma,** on Forest Service Rd. 25, 7 mi. northwest of Eldon; **Lena Creek,** 2 mi. beyond Hamma Hamma; **Elkhorn,** on Forest Service Rd. 2610, 11 mi. northwest of Brinnon; and **Collins,** on Forest Service Rd. 2515, 8 mi. west of Brinnon. All have drinking water, as well as hiking, good fishing, and gorgeous scenery. Unfortunately, many of these require travel along gravel roads, tough for bicyclists.

Lake Cushman State Park (877-5491), 7 mi. west of Hoodsport on Lake Cushman Rd., stretches by a beautiful lake with good swimming beaches. Many use it as a base camp for extended backpacking trips into the forest. Lake Cushman has 10 sites ($7.50, $10 with full hookup) with flush toilets and pay showers (25¢). Clinging to a quiet cove just north of Eldon, **Mike's Beach Resort and Hostel,** N. 38470 U.S. 101 (877-5324) lacks a kitchen, and too many bunks crowd its tiny rooms, but it does have a small grocery store. ($5, nonmembers $7.50. Open April 15-Nov. 1.) The **Hungry Bear Cafe,** in Eldon, serves the Hood Canal specialty: geoduck (GOO-ee-duck) steak ($8). The geoduck, a giant mollusk which lives 2½ to 7 ft. below the surface of Hood Canal's beaches, has a taste somewhere between that of a razor clam and a scallop; the Bear serves it with mounds of great french fries and homemade tartar sauce. Burgers ($1.50-5) cater to less daring diners. (Open Mon.-Thurs. 9am-7pm, Fri. 9am-8pm, Sat. 8am-8pm, Sun. 8am-7pm.)

Topologically, the amorphous **Kitsap Peninsula** resembles a half-completed landfill project jutting into Puget Sound. A new bridge over the northern end of Hood Canal links the Kitsap Peninsula with the towns along the Strait of Juan de Fuca; no pedestrian traffic is allowed. Kitsap also can be reached by ferry: from Seattle to Bremerton or Winslow on connected Bainbridge Island, or from Edmonds, north of Seattle, to Kingston on the northern end of the peninsula.

In **Bremerton** you'll swear that you have stepped into the setting of a Tom Clancy novel; every third person has a Navy security pass. The city is basically an overgrown repair shop for U.S. Naval ships. Chain hotels cluster along Kitsap Way in Bremerton, but you might prefer **Scenic Beach State Park,** near the village of Seabeck, featuring 50 campsites with water and bathrooms. (Sites $7, walk-in sites $3.) From Silverdale, take Anderson Hill Rd. or Newberry Hill Rd. west to Seabeck Hwy., then follow the highway 7 mi. south to the Scenic Beach turn-off. Cyclists, beware the staggering hills along this route. The Department of Natural Resources' **Tahuya Multiple Use Area** encompasses eight free campgrounds, each with drinking water, and many with good swimming beaches and boat launches. These are hard to find, however, and require travel along difficult gravel roads.

The Kitsap's most appealing touristy attraction is the **Suquamish Museum** (598-3311), 6 mi. north of Winslow, just over the Agate Pass Bridge on Rte. 305. Run by the Port Madison Indian Reservation, this small but well-presented museum (pronounced sue-QUAH-mish) focuses entirely on the history and culture of the Puget Sound Salish Native Americans. (Open daily 10am-5pm. Admission $2.50, seniors $2, under 12 $1.)

Olympic National Park

Lodged among the august Olympic mountains, the park covers 900,000 acres of velvet rainforest, jagged snowcovered peaks, and dense evergreen forest. This enormous region at the center of the peninsula affords limited access even to four-wheeled traffic. No scenic loops or roads cross the park, and only a handful of secondary roads make insignificant attempts to penetrate the interior. The roads that do exist serve mainly as trailheads for over 600 mi. of hiking trails. Come prepared for rain; a parka, good boots, and a waterproof tent are essential.

Stop at the **Park Service Visitors Center**, 3002 Mt. Angeles Rd., Port Angeles (452-4501, ext. 230), for backcountry camping permits and a map of the locations of other ranger stations. (Open daily 8am-6pm; off-season reduced hours.) The park service runs interpretive programs such as guided forest walks, tidal pool walks, and campfire programs from its various ranger stations (all free). For a full schedule of events everywhere in the park, obtain a copy of the park newspaper, available at ranger stations and the visitors center. More popular entrances, such as the Hoh, Heart O' the Hills, and Elwaha, charge $3 seven-day entrance fee per car ($1 for hikers/bikers).

Much of the backcountry often remains snowed-in until late June, and only summer has a good number of rainless days. **Backcountry camping** requires a free wilderness permit, available at ranger stations and trailheads. The park service's shelters are for emergencies only; large concentrations of people attract bears.

Never drink untreated water in the park. A nasty microscopic parasite lives in all these waters and causes severe diarrhea, gas, and abdominal cramps. Bring your own water supply, or boil local water for five minutes before drinking it. Dogs aren't allowed in the backcountry, and must be restrained at all times within the park.

Berry picking ranks high on the list of peninsula summer activities. Newly cleared regions and roadside areas yield the best crops; raspberries, strawberries, blueberries, and huckleberries abound. Bears also seem fond of this fruit; if one stumbles into your favorite berry patch, don't argue. **Fishing** within park boundaries is allowed without a permit, but you must obtain a state game department punch card for salmon and steelhead trout at outfitting and hardware stores locally, or at the game department in Olympia.

The **Eastern Rim** of the park is accessible through the Olympic National Forest from U.S. 101 along Hood Canal. For info on camping in the forest see Hood Canal and the Kitsap Peninsula above. The car-accessible campgrounds lure hikers who use them as trailheads to the interior of the park. **Staircase Campground** (877-5569), 19 mi. northwest of Hoodsport at the head of Lake Cushman, has 59 sites and a ranger station with interpretive programs on weekends. (Open year-round. Sites $5.) **Dosewallips** (doh-see-WALL-ups), on a road that leaves U.S. 101 3 mi. north of Brinnon, offers free but less developed sites. (Open June-Sept.)

On the park's **Northern Rim, Heart o' the Hills** (452-2713) and **Elwha Valley** (452-9191) campgrounds both have interpretive programs and ranger stations, as does **Fairholm Campground** (928-3380), 30 mi. west of Port Angeles at the western tip of Lake Crescent. (Sites $5.) The **Lake Crescent** station (928-3380) has an extensive interpretive program but no camping. The **information booth** here opens Memorial Day to Labor Day daily from 11:30am to 4:30pm. **Soleduck Hotsprings Campground** (327-3534), to the southeast of Lake Crescent, 13 mi. off U.S. 101, adjoins the hot springs resort. (Sites $5.)

Hurricane Ridge affords magnificent views of Mt. Olympus, the Bailey Range, and even Canada on clear days.

Down the Hoh River Rd. (19 mi.) sits the park service's **Hoh Rain Forest Campground and Visitors Center** (374-6925). The center is wheelchair-accessible, as are trails leading from the center into the only non-tropical rain forest in the world. Camping costs $5. (Visitors center open summer daily 9am-5pm.) Farther south, after U.S. 101 rejoins the coast, the park's boundaries extend southwest to edge the banks of the **Queets River.** The unpaved road here leads to free campsites at the top. (Open June-Sept.) The park and forest services share the land surrounding **Quinault Lake** and **Quinault River.** The park service land is accessible by foot only. The forest service operates a day-use beach and an info center in the **Quinault Ranger Station,** South Shore Rd. (288-2444; open daily 7:30am-5pm; winter Mon.-Fri. 7:30am-5pm).

Mora (374-5460) and **Kalaloch** (962-2283), have campgrounds (sites $5) and ranger stations. The Kalaloch (kuh-LAY-lok) Center, including lodge, general store, and gas station, stays more scenic with 195 sites near the ocean.

San Juan Islands

Bald eagles circle above the ragged San Juan Island hillsides dotted with family farms. Pods of killer whales spout offshore, and the sun shines perpetually. To travelers approaching from summer resorts infested with vacationers, the islands will seem blissfully quiet. Even in mid-summer, you can drive the back roads and pass another car about once an hour. For this reason, islanders don't begrudge admission to their towns and campsites. Although tension has built between the locals and the Seattle vacationers who are buying up huge chunks of the islands, well-behaved tourists and their dollars are still welcome on the San Juans.

Pick up *The San Juan Islands Afoot and Afloat* by Marge Mueller ($10), an excellent guide to the area, available at book and outfitting stores on the islands and in Seattle. *Islands Sounder,* the local paper, annually publishes *The San Juans Beckon* to provide up-to-date info on island recreation.

Washington State Ferries serve the islands daily from **Anacortes** on the mainland. To reach Anacortes, take I-5 north from Seattle to Mt. Vernon. From there, Rte. 20 heads west; the way to the ferry is well marked. Buses to Anacortes depart Seattle from the **Greyhound depot** at 8th Ave. and Stewart St. once a day. Call 626-6090 for exact times.

In Anacortes, you can purchase a ticket to Lopez, Shaw, Orcas, or San Juan Island. You pay only on westbound trips to or between the islands; no charge is levied on eastbound traffic. (In effect, any ticket to the islands is a round-trip ticket.) You can save money therefore by traveling directly to the westernmost island on your itinerary, and then making your way back island by island. The ferry unloads first at Lopez Island, followed by Shaw, Orcas, and finally San Juan. You also can purchase one-way tickets to Sidney, BC, or from Sidney to the islands. Foot passengers travel in either direction between the islands free of charge. Fares from Anacortes to San Juan Island are $4.65 for pedestrians ($2.35 for seniors and ages 5-11), $6.25 for bikes, and $9.50 for motorcycles; cars cost $19. Fares to the other islands en route generally run a few dollars cheaper. Inter-island fares average $2.25 for bikes and motorcycles, $7.75 for cars. The one-way fare to Sidney, BC costs $6 for pedestrians, $8.55 for bikes, $13 for motorcycles, and $31.25 for cars in summer ($26 in winter). Some car spaces are available from the islands to Sidney; make reservations. Call Washington State Ferries (206-464-6400; in WA 800-542-0810) before noon on the day before your trip to ensure a space. On peak traveling days, arrive with your vehicle at least one hour prior to scheduled departure. The ferry authorities accept only cash and in-state checks as payment. You may park your vehicle for free at the Anacortes parking lot on the corner of 30th and T St. A free, reliable shuttle then whisks you 4 mi. to the terminal.

San Juan Island

Although the ferry makes its last stop in San Juan, it is the most frequently visited island, home to the largest town in the group, **Friday Harbor.** Since the ferry docks right in town, the island proves the easiest to explore.

The **National Park Service Information Center** and **Chamber of Commerce Information Center,** 1st and Spring (378-2240), will answer questions about the British and American camps (see below). (Open Mon.-Fri. 8am-5:30pm, Sat.-Sun. 9am-5:30pm.) **The Inn at Friday Harbor,** (378-4351), runs two sight-seeing tours of the island every afternoon (June-Sept.). The two-hour tours circle the island, stopping at Roche Harbor, English and American Camps, and Limekiln Lighthouse ($8).

To begin a loop of the island, head south out of Friday Harbor on Argyle Rd., which merges into Cattle Point Rd., on the way to **American Camp** (378-2240).

The camp dates to the infamous Pig War of 1859, when the U.S. and England remained at loggerheads over possession of the islands. An interpretive shelter near the entrance to the park explains the history of the war; a self-guided historic trail leads from the shelter through the buildings.

Returning north on Cattle Point Rd., consider taking the gravel False Bay Rd. to the west. The road leads to **False Bay,** home to a large number of nesting bald eagles. Farther north on False Bay Rd., you'll run into **Bailer Hill Road,** which turns into West Side Rd. when it reaches Haro Straight. (You can also reach Bailer Hill Rd. by taking Cattle Point Rd. to Little Rd.) Along the road, sloping hills blanketed with wildflowers rise to one side, and rocky shores fall to the other. **San Juan County Park** on Smallpox Bay provides a convenient opportunity to park your bike or car and examine this scenery more closely.

English Camp, the second half of San Juan National Historical Park, rests on West Valley Rd. amid the forest surrounding Garrison Bay. From West Side Rd., take Mitchell Bay Rd. east to West Valley Rd. Here, four preserved original buildings, including the barracks, now function as an interpretive center, which explains the history of the "war" and sells guides to the island. (Park open year-round; buildings open Memorial Day-Labor Day daily 8am-4:30pm. Free.)

Friday Harbor loses much of its charm when the tourists arrive in full force, but remains quite appealing in the winter. Take the time to poke around the galleries, craft shops, and bookstores. The **Whale Museum,** 62 1st St. (378-4710), will teach you everything you ever wanted to know about the giant cetaceans, starring skeletons, sculptures, and info on new research. The museum even has a **whale hotline** (800-562-8832) for you to report sightings and strandings. (Open daily 10am-5pm; winter 11am-4pm. Admission $3, seniors and students $2.50, kids under 12 $1.50.)

Walking south a block will take you to the **Friday Harbor Youth Hostel,** 35 1st St. (378-5555), in the Elite Hotel. It has a clean, well-lit women's dorm and a slightly more cramped men's dorm. ($9, nonmembers $14; check-in 8-11 pm.) Call ahead; it may be closing soon. **San Juan County Park,** 380 Westside Rd. (378-2992), 10 mi. west of Friday Harbor on Smallpox and Andrews Bays, provides a public alternative. (Cold water and flush toilets. Bikers and hikers $5; cars, campers, and trailers $12.) The parks and shoreline drives beg you to pack a picnic lunch and leave Friday Harbor behind. Stock up on bread and cheese at **King's Market** (378-4505) 160 Spring St. (Open daily 8am-10pm.)

The **post office** stamps at Blair and Reed St. (378-4511; open Mon.-Fri. 8:30am-4:30pm); the **ZIP code** is 98250. San Juan Island's **area code** is 206.

Whidbey Island

Now the longest island in the contiguous U.S. (since Long Island built a bridge and became a peninsula), telephone-receiver-shaped Whidbey Island sits in the rain shadow of the Olympic Mountains. Clouds, wrung dry by the time they pass over Whidbey, 40 mi. due north of Seattle, release a mere 20 in. of rain per year and a luxurious ration of sunshine. This leaves visitors free to enjoy rocky beaches bound by bluffs blooming with wild roses and crawling with blackberry brambles.

Whoever named **Useless Bay** certainly did not use aesthetic criteria. On the west side of the bay, uninterrupted coast stretches from Bayview Beach along **Double Bluff Park** to the tip of the peninsula of Double Bluff. Comb the 1½-mi. beach, explore the bluffs, or just gaze across the water at Seattle and Mt. Rainier. Another ideal spot for the wanderer, **South Whidbey State Park,** 4128 S. Smuggler's Cove Rd. (321-4559), blushes about 7 mi. north of Freeland. The park wraps around the west coast of the island, covering 87 acres of forest. Park by the tiny outdoor amphitheater and walk down the bluff to the beach (10 min.). Wander along the pebbly beach approximately 1½ mi. in either direction—to Lagoon Point in the north or to a lighthouse on Bush Point in the south.

Around the bend to the north, **Fort Casey State Park,** 1280 S. Fort Casey Rd. (678-4519), stands right next to the Keystone ferry terminal, 3 mi. south of Coupeville. The park occupies the site of a late 1890s fort designed to defend against a long-anticipated attack from the west. (Interpretive center open in winter for large groups by appointment. Park open year-round.) Reach **Fort Ebey State Park,** 395 N. Fort Ebey Rd. (678-4636), from Libbey Rd. off Rte. 20 north of Coupeville, by Valley Drive's park entrance. On this, the driest spot on the island, prickly pear cacti grow right up next to the beach.

Ebey's Landing National Historical Reserve contains parks and the town of **Coupeville.** Many of Coupeville's homes and commercial establishments date from the 19th century. The town extends along E. Front St. between two 1855 block-houses meant to withstand an anticipated Skagit tribe uprising that never occurred. Of the zealously fortified buildings, the **John Alexander Blockhouse,** at the west end of town, and the **Davis Blockhouse,** at the edge of the town's cemetery, still stand at attention. A few miles north of Oak Harbor on Rte. 20, fruit fiends and aviation aficionados peacefully coexist at the **U-pick Strawberry Farms,** where the roar from low-flying Navy "Prowler" jets virtually rattles the fruit from the plants.

When the Skagit tribe lived and fished in the area, the Haida tribe from the north often raided at Deception Pass. A bear totem of the Haidas now stands on the north end of West Beach in **Deception Pass State Park,** 5175 N. Rte. 20 (675-2417). The most heavily used of Whidbey's state parks, its views will amaze. Camping facilities, a saltwater boat launch, 8½ mi. of trails, and a freshwater lake for swimming, fishing, and boating, allow for a closer look at the area's tidal pools, beaches, and natural life. A fishing license, available at most hardware stores, is required for the lake; fishing season runs from mid-April to October. (Park open year-round.)

Whidbey swims in smoked salmon; every town (and every milepost along the highway) has its share of salmon shacks. In Langley, **Mike's Place** (321-6575) 215 1st St. serves the best clam chowder on the island ($2.25). The all-you-can-eat nightly specials also come highly recommended. (Breakfast $5, lunch $4-6, dinner under $10. (Open daily 8am-10pm.) The **Doghouse Tavern** (321-9996), 230 1st St., on the main drag of this one-block town, serves 10¢ 6-oz. beers with lunch (limit 2). Eat $4 sandwiches and $5 corn soup out of an edible bread bowl, either in the tavern or around the back in the "family restaurant." (Open Mon.-Sat. 11am-1am, Sun. noon-1am.) In Oak Harbor, locals swear by the Mazzone mushroom burger ($4.50) at **Jason's,** 5355 Hwy. 20, at Goldie Rd. (Lunch $3-4, dinner $5-8. Open 24 hrs.)

Inexpensive motels are few and far between on Whidbey; those that do exist are frequently in need of repairs. A number of B&Bs offer elegant rooms for a few more dollars. Contact **Whidbey Island Bed and Breakfast Association** (321-6272), P.O. Box 259, Langley 98260, for a full listing; reservations are necessary. The **Tyee Motel and Cafe** (678-6616), 405 S. Main St., Coupeville, offers clean, straightforward rooms with showers. The location is within walking distance of Coupeville center and the water makes up for the bleak setting. (Cafe open daily 6:30am-9pm. Singles $34, each additional person $4.) On the northern edge of Oak Harbor lies the **Crossroads Motel** (675-3145), 5622 Hwy. 20. The cinderblock construction looks like a fort, but immaculate rooms compensate. Fully equipped kitchens are available. (Singles $32. Doubles $43, with kitchens $47.)

Four state park campgrounds service the island, each with sites for $8. **South Whidbey State Park** (321-4559), 4128 S. Smuggler's Cove Rd. 7 mi. northwest of Freeland via Bush Point Rd. and Smuggler's Cove Rd., perches on a cliff in a stand of Douglas firs. A steep ¼-mi. trail leads down to a rocky beach. (Open year-round.) **Fort Casey State Park,** 1280 S. Fort Casey Rd. (678-4519), right next to the Keystone ferry terminal, has 35 sites interspersed with turn-of-the-century military memorabilia. In summer arrive early. **Fort Ebey State Park** (678-4636) does what forts do on N. Fort Ebey Rd., north of Fort Casey and just west of Coupeville. Miles of hiking trails and easy access to a pebbly beach make this, the island's newest campground, also the island's best. (50 sites for cars and RVs. 3 for hikers and bikers $3.) **Deception Pass State Park** (675-2417), 5175 N. Hwy. 525, 8 mi. north of Oak Harbor, has 8½ mi. of hiking trails and Cranberry Lake, for good freshwater fishing and swimming. (4 rustic sites for hikers and bikers $3.)

Unfortunately, **Island Transit** (678-7771 or 321-6688) only runs one intra-island bus line—the automobile still reigns. Yet only one main road runs: "Rte. 525" on the southern half of the island and "Rte. 20" at Coupeville and beyond.

You also can reach Whidbey Island from Port Townsend on the Olympic Peninsula. Ferries leave the terminal in downtown Port Townsend for Keystone, on the west side of the island, 8 times per day between 7am and 5:45pm. Ferries return from Keystone to Port Townsend eight times per day between 7am and 6:30pm. More ferries ply the waters on weekends; extra daily ferries run in August. (35 min. Car and passenger $5.75. Bicycle riders $3.50. Walk-on $1.75; over 64, ages 5-12, and disabled 80¢; under 5 free. For more information, call Washingto State Ferries at 800-84-FERRY).

To reach Whidbey from the north, take exit 189 off I-5 and head west toward Anacortes. Stay on Rte. 20 when it heads south through the stunning Deception Pass State Park (signs will direct you); otherwise you will fly on to Anacortes. **Evergreen Trailways** runs a bus to Whidbey from Seattle.

The **post office** in Langley registers at 115 2nd St. (321-4113), **ZIP code** 98260; in Coupeville at 201 NW Coveland (678-5353), **ZIP code** 98239; in Oak Harbor at 7035 70th NW (675-6621), **ZIP code** 98277. The **area code** for Whidbey is 206.

Seattle

The skyscrapers of downtown Seattle have risen to compete with the Olympic peaks that ring the city's eastern skyline. One cannot help but feel a sense of apocalypse. Nonetheless, Columbia Tower is no Tower of Babel; Seattle, although it is expanding at an alarming rate, has integrated its diverse populace into a cohesive and successful modern city. Everyone paws through fresh greens and sea creatures at Pike Place Market, nearly everyone wears Birkenstocks, and even the police ride mountain bikes. Residents of Seattle will tell tourists to bring raincoats, galoshes, gondolas, and arks to dissuade them from invading. Actually, Seattle catches less precipitation a year than quite a few major cities. The register of a clear day in Seattle is whether "the mountain is out"—Mt. Rainier, one of the most spectacular hikes in the Northwest, only 2 hrs. away, a great ice cream scoop on the skyline. While not rainy, the sky is usually cloud-covered. Sporting Seattlites will do it in the drizzle, and a blossoming entertainment industry will make indoor excursions just as rewarding.

Practical Information

Seattle-King County Visitors Bureau and Convention Center, 525 Pike St. (461-5840), in the Vance Hotel near the Greyhound station. Open Mon.-Fri. 8:30am-5pm, in summer also on Sat. 10am-4pm. From 5-7:30pm, call the airport branch at 433-5218.

Ticket Agency: Ticket/Ticket, 401 Broadway E (324-2744) on the 2nd floor on the Broadway Market. Half-price day-of-show tickets to local theater, music, and dance. Cash only. Open Tues.-Sun. 10am-7pm.

Seattle Parks and Recreation Department, 5201 Green Lake Way N. (684-4075). Open Mon.-Fri. 8am-6pm. **National Park Service, Pacific Northwest Region,** 83 S. King St., 3rd floor (553-4830).

Travelers Aid: 909 4th Ave. #630 (461-3888), at Marion in the YMCA. Free services to stranded travelers with lost wallets, companions, or marbles. Open Mon.-Fri. 8:30am-9pm, Sat. 9am-1pm, Sun. 1-5pm.

Seattle-Tacoma International Airport (Sea-Tac), on Federal Way (433-5217), south of Seattle proper. **Sea-Tac Visitors Information Center** (433-5218), in the central baggage claim area across from carousel 10. Open daily 9:30am-7:30pm. **Gray Line** coaches and limousines operate between airport and downtown. $6, $11 round-trip. Metro buses #174 and 194 run daily every ½ hr. 6am-1am. Peak fare $1.25, 85¢ off-peak; under 18 75¢ during peak, 55¢ off-peak. Taxi downtown around $22.

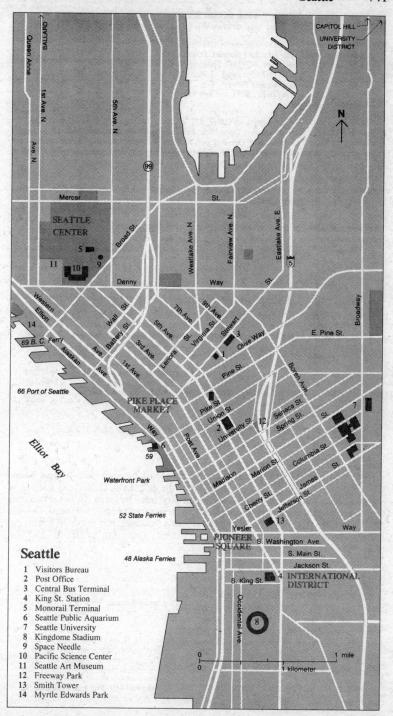

Seattle

1 Visitors Bureau
2 Post Office
3 Central Bus Terminal
4 King St. Station
5 Monorail Terminal
6 Seattle Public Aquarium
7 Seattle University
8 Kingdome Stadium
9 Space Needle
10 Pacific Science Center
11 Seattle Art Museum
12 Freeway Park
13 Smith Tower
14 Myrtle Edwards Park

Amtrak: King St. Station, 3rd and Jackson St. (800-872-7245). Trains to: Portland (3 per day, $28), Tacoma ($8), and San Francisco ($178). Station open daily 6am-10pm; ticket office 6am-5:30pm.

Buses: Greyhound, 8th Ave. and Stewart St. (624-3456). To: Sea-Tac Airport (3 per day, $4.75 roundtrip); Vancouver, BC ($18); Spokane ($35); and Portland (12 per day, $27). Open daily 5:30am-2:30pm, 3:45-7:30pm and 12:30am-1:30am. **Green Tortoise,** 324-7433 or 800-227-4766. Leaves from 9th and Stewart, Tues., Thurs.-Fri. and Sun. at 8am to: Portland (5 hr., $15); Berkeley, CA (26 hr., $49); and San Francisco (27 hr., $59). Reservations required 3-4 days in advance.

Metro Transit: Customer Assistance Office, 821 2nd Ave. (553-3000; TTY service 684-1739), in the Exchange Bldg. downtown. Open Mon.-Fri. 8am-5pm. Buses run 6am-1am. Fare 55¢, during weekday peak hours 65¢. One-day pass $2.50, weekend day $1. Ride free in the day-time area from Jackson St. to Battery St. and between 6th Ave. and the waterfront. Transfers valid for 2 hr. and for Waterfront Streetcars as well. Discounts for seniors and ages 5-17.

Ferries: Washington State Ferries, Colman Dock, Pier 52 (464-2000, ext. 4; in WA 800-542-0810 or 800-542-7052). Service to Bremerton (on Kitsap Peninsula) and Winslow (on Bainbridge Island). Ferries leave frequently daily 6am-2am. Fares from $3.30, car and driver $5.55.

Car Rental: Five & Ten, 14120 Pacific Hwy. S. (246-4434). $20 per day. 100 free mi., 5¢ each additional mi. Airport pickup. Open Mon.-Sat. 8am-6pm, Sun. 12:30-6pm. Must be 21 with credit card or $120 deposit. **A-19.95-Rent-A-Car,** 804 N. 145th St. (364-1995). $20 per day, under 21 $25. 100 free mi., 15¢ each additional mi. Free delivery. Must have credit card. Drivers under 21 must have auto insurance.

Bike Rental: U-Pedal Bike Rental, 1416 Post Alley (223-3645), right above the youth hostel. $8 per hr., $15 per ½-day, $18 per day. Open daily 9am-5:30pm. **The Bicycle Center,** 4529 Sand Point Way (523-8300). 10-speeds only. $4 per hr., $20 per day; touring bikes $7 per hr., $17 per day. Credit card or license required as deposit. Open Mon.-Thurs. 10am-7pm, Fri. 10am-8pm, Sat. 10am-6pm, Sun. noon-5pm. **Alki Bikes,** 2722 Alki Ave. SW (938-3322). Mountain bikes $9 per hr., $20 per day; touring bikes $7 per hr., $17 per day. Credit card or license required as deposit. Open Mon.-Thurs. 10am-7pm, Fri. 10am-8pm, Sat. 10am-6pm, Sun. noon-5pm.

Help Lines: Crisis Clinic, 461-3222. **Senior Citizen Information and Assistance,** 1601 2nd St. #800 (448-3110). Open Mon.-Fri. 9am-5pm. **Gay Counseling Service,** 200 W. Mercer, suite #300 (282-9307). Open Mon.-Fri. noon-9pm. **Lesbian Resource Center,** 1208 E. Pine (322-3953). Support groups, drop-in center, lending library, workshops, job referrals. Open Mon.-Fri. 2-7pm, Sat. 11am-2pm.

Post Office: Union St. and 3rd Ave. (442-6340), downtown. Open Mon.-Fri. 8am-5:30pm. **ZIP code:** 98101.

Area Code: 206.

Seattle is a skinny city stretched out north to south between skinny **Puget Sound** to the west and skinny **Lake Washington** to the east. Lake Union and a string of locks, canals, and bays cut the head of the city from its torso. In the downtown area, avenues run northwest to southeast and streets southwest to northeast. Outside the downtown area everything simplifies vastly: avenues run north to south and streets east to west, with few exceptions. The city splits into quadrants: 1000 1st Ave. NW is a far cry from 1000 1st Ave. S.

Accommodations

Seattle International Hostel (AYH), 84 Union St. (622-5443), at Western Ave. downtown. 125 beds in sterile rooms; immaculate facilities and modern amenities. View of the bay helps combat loud traffic. Sleep sacks required. Open daily 7am-2am. $12, nonmembers $15. In summer members only.

YMCA, 909 4th Ave. (382-5000), near Madison St. Must be 17. Good location, tight security. Small but well-kept rooms; worse dorm bunks. TV lounge on each floor, laundry facilities, use of swimming pool and fitness facilities. AYH members: singles $27, doubles $33. Non-members, singles from $40, doubles from $44. Weekly: singles from $150, doubles $172.

YWCA, 1118 5th Ave. (461-4888), near the YMCA. Take any 4th Ave. bus to Seneca St. Women only; under 18 require advance arrangement. Great security and location, but an older facility than the YMCA. Open 24 hrs. Singles $26, with bath $31. Doubles $37, with bath $43. Weekly: singles $156, with bath $186. Key deposit $2. Additional charge for health center use.

St. Regis Hotel, 116 Stewart St. (448-6366), 2 blocks from the Pike Place Market. Neighborhood not as safe as some, but pleasant management. No visitors after 10pm. Singles $26, with bath $33. Doubles $33, with bath $39. Key deposit $1.

Commodore Hotel, 2013 2nd Ave. (448-8868), at Virginia downtown. Not as well kept but clean. Singles $29, with color TV and bath $37, with 2 beds and bath $40.

Park Plaza Hotel, 4401 Aurora Ave. N. (632-2101). Another option along an endless strip of car dealerships and fast-food joints. Clean rooms, in-room coffee, cable TV. Singles $25. Doubles $35.

Hillside Motel, 2451 Aurora N. (285-7860). Take bus #6 or 16. One of a number of relatively inexpensive motels along noisy Aurora. 11 units with hot plates. Singles $35, doubles $38.

Motel 6, 18900 47th Ave. S. (241-1648), exit 152 off I-5. Take bus #194. Near Sea-Tac but inconvenient to downtown. Singles $30. Doubles $36. Make reservations.

The College Inn, 4000 University Way NE (633-4441). European-style B&B in the University District. Breakfast served in a lovely refinished attic; ask for quieter rooms facing 40th. All rooms have shared shower and bath, but a cozy breakfast is included. Singles from $41. Doubles from $56.

Food and Bars

As the principal marketplace for Washington's famous orchards and overflowing fishing industries, Seattle is practically pelted with salmon and apples. You will be hard-pressed to avoid the catch of the day. But Seattle restauranteurs also seem inclined to stick their heads in ovens—bakeries proliferate, and few Seattlites seem to move in the morning without an *espresso Americano* and a sticky bun fill-up. The best options or fish, produce, and baked goods can be culled from the various vendors at the **Pike Place Market,** created in 1907, when angry Seattle citizens demanded an alternative to the middle merchant. The fury at the Sound continues today, as crazy fishmongers and produce sellers yell at customers and at each other, while street performers do their thing—meanwhile tourists wonder what they've wandered into. (Market open Mon.-Sat. 9am-6pm; many stands also open Sun.)

Fran-Glor's Creole Cafe, 547 1st Ave. S. (682-1578), near the viaduct. Genuine gumbo with crabmeat, sausage, and who knows what else. The bric-a-brac and the jazz are classic New Orleans. Lunches from $4.50. Open Tues.-Sat. noon-9pm.

Phnom Penh Noodle Soup House, 414 Maynard Ave. S. (682-5690). Excellent Cambodian cuisine. Head to the upstairs dining room for a good view of the park and a spicy, steaming bowl of #1, the Phnom Penh noodle special ($3.80). Open Mon.-Tues. and Thurs.-Sun. 8:30am-6pm.

Ivar's Fish Bar, Pier 54 (624-6852), on the waterfront. One of a string of seafood restaurants named for Seattle celebrity and shipping magnate Ivar Haglund. This locals' favorite charges $3.89 for fish and chips and serves definitive Seattle clam chowder. Dine with the gulls and pigeons in covered booths outside. Open daily 11am-2am.

Kokeb Restaurant, 926 12th Ave. (322-0485). Behind Seattle University at the far south end of Capitol Hill, near the First Hill neighborhood. An intriguing Ethiopian restaurant offering hot and spicy meat stews served on *injera,* a soft bread. Very purple. Entrees $8-9. Open Mon.-Fri. 10:30am-2pm lunch, dinner 5-10pm, Sat. 5pm-2am.

Hamburger Mary's, 401 Broadway E. (325-6565), in the ritzy Broadway Market. Rockin' and racin' with the Broadway Ave. step, this branch of Portland's famous H.M. is a hot-spot for the gay community. Nightly specials offer less meaty options than the obvious fare. (Hamburgers around $5, entrees around $7.) Open Mon.-Fri. 10am-2am, Sat.-Sun. 8am-2am.

The Cause Célèbre, 524 E. 15th Ave. (323-1888), at Mercer St., at one end of Capitol Hill. The special province of Seattle's well-fed left. Stay away if you don't like feminist music or discussions on the struggle for Chinese succession. Sublime ice cream and baked goods. Free evening entertainment. Lunch $3-6. Open Mon. and Wed.-Fri. 10am-4pm, Tues. 10am-5pm, Sun. 9am-9pm.

Asia Deli, 4235 University Way NE. No corned beef here—this atypical deli offers quick service and generous portions of delicious Vietnamese and Thai food (mostly of the noodle persuasion). Try the sauté chicken and onions ($3.45), and don't forget the banana with tapioca in coconut milk (90¢), a superb palate cleanser. Open Mon.-Sat. 11am-9pm, Sun. noon-8pm.

The Unicorn Restaurant, 4550 University Way. Renowned for its large collection of obscure English ales ($2.50-3), the Unicorn also cooks up a mean steak-and-kidney pie ($6). Try their afternoon special—tea and scones ($2.50), of course. Open Mon.-Sat. 11:30am-10pm, Sun. 5-9pm.

One of the joys of living in Seattle is the abundance of community taverns dedicated to providing a relaxed environment for dancing and spending time with friends. In Washington taverns serve only beer and wine; a fully licensed bar or cocktail lounge must adjoin a restaurant. You must be 21 to enter bars and taverns. The Northwest produces a variety of local beers (none bottled): Grant's, Imperial Russian Stout, India Pale Ale, Red Hook, Ballard Bitter, and Black Hook, and also Yakima Cider.

The best spot to go for guaranteed good beer, live music, and big crowds is Pioneer Square. Most of the bars around the square participate in a joint cover ($7) that will let you wander from bar to bar and sample the bands you like. **Central Tavern** (622-0209) and **The Spoon Café** (343-5208) rock consistently, while **Larry's** (624-5208) and **New Orleans** (622-2563) feature great jazz and blues nightly. The **J and M Café,** also in the center of Pioneer Square, has no music—only the classic bar hum. All Pioneer Square clubs shut down around 2am on Fri. and Sat. nights, and around midnight during the week. Another option in the Square is to catch an evening of live stand-up comedy in one of Seattle's many comedy clubs such as Pioneer Square's **Swannie's Comedy Underground,** 222 Main St. (628-0303). (Acts daily at 9 and 11pm. Tickets around $5.)

Some other bars include:

The University Bistro, 4315 University Way NE (547-8010). Live music (everything from blues to reggae) nightly. Happy Hour (4-7pm) finds pints of Bud for $1.25, pitchers $4. Cover Tues. $2, Wed.-Sat. $3-5, no cover Sun.-Mon. Open Sun.-Fri. 11am-2am, Sat. 6pm-2am.

Murphy's Pub, 2110 N. 45th St. (634-2110), in Wallingford, west of the U district. Take bus #43. A classic Irish pub with a mile-long beer list. Popular with the young folks, Murphy's has live Irish and folk music nightly. Open daily 2pm-2am. Cover $1-2.

Squid Row Tavern, 518 E. Pine (322-2031). Bizarre paintings, black booths, a bar, and earfuls of melodious punk rock. Pint of Bud $1.50. Open Mon.-Fri. noon-2am, Sat. 4pm-2am, Sun. 6pm-2am. Cover $4.

The Double Header, 407 2nd Ave. (464-9918), in Pioneer Sq. Seattle institution claiming to be the oldest gay bar in the country. An oom-pah band plays nightly to a mostly middle-aged crowd of gay men and women. Open daily 10am-2pm. No cover.

Sights and Activities

If you have only a day to spare in Seattle, despair not. The best way to take in the city and its fantastic skyline is from any one of the **ferries** that leave the waterfront at frequent intervals (see Practical Information above). The very finest view of Seattle, however, is an exclusively female privilege; the athletic club on the top floor of the **Columbia Tower,** the tallest building west of Houston (big, black and Freudian at 201 5th Ave.) has floor-to-ceiling windows in the ladies' room that look out over the entire city. Views from the main desk and the men's room are also worth the snide looks from the club staff, so don't be disheartened if you're of the non-Sacagawean gender. You can get a closer look at most of the city sights in one energetic day—most are within walking distance from each other, within Metro's free zone. You can easily explore the market, waterfront, Pioneer Square, and the International District in one excursion. Or skip the downtown thing altogether and take a rowboat out onto Lake Union, bike along Lake Washington, or hike through Discovery Park.

At the south end of Pike Place Market (see Food) begins the **Pike Place Hill-climb,** a set of staircases leading down past chic shops and ethnic restaurants to Alaskan Way and the **waterfront.** (An elevator is also available.)

The waterfront docks once played Ellis Island to shiploads of gold coming in from the 1897 Klondike gold rush. Now, on a pier full of shops and restaurants, the credit card is standard currency. On Pier 59 at the base of the hillclimb, the **Seattle Aquarium** (386-4320) explains the history of marine life in Puget Sound and the effects of tidal action. (Open daily 10am-7pm; Labor Day-Memorial Day 10am-5pm. Admission $4.75, seniors and ages 13-18 $2.75, ages 6-12 $1.75.)

Four blocks inland from Pier 70 you'll find **Seattle Center,** a 74-acre, pedestrians-only park originally constructed for the 1962 World's Fair. Thousands of sightseers still visit each day. Take the monorail from Pine St. and 5th Ave. downtown. (Fare 60¢, seniors and children 25¢.) The **Pacific Science Center** (443-2001), within the park, houses a laserium and IMAX theater. (Science Center open daily 10am-6pm; Labor Day-June Mon.-Fri. 10am-5pm, Sat.-Sun. 10am-6pm. Admission $5, seniors and ages 6-13 $4, ages 2-5 $3. Laser shows $1 extra.) The **Space Needle** (443-2100), sometimes known as "the world's tallest tacky monument," has an observation tower and restaurant. On clear days, you can see a lot of **stuff.** (Admission $5, ages 5-12 $2.75.) After working up an appetite in the Center's amusement park, head next door to the **Center House,** home to dozens of shops and restaurants serving everything from Mongolian to Mexican. (Open summer daily 11am-9pm; spring 11am-7pm; fall and winter Sun.-Thurs. 11am-6pm, Fri.-Sat. 11am-9pm.) The Center has an **information desk** (625-4234) on the court level in the Center House which can inform you of events. (Open daily 1-4pm.)

Pier 57 holds Seattle's new maritime museum, **The Water Link** (624-4975). Wallow in the city's waterfront history or probe the geological mysteries of the ocean floor. (Open May 17-Sept. 30 Tues.-Sun. noon-6pm. Admission $1.) Be sure to take one of the ferry tours offered in the area.

Two blocks from the waterfront sits historic **Pioneer Square,** where 19th-century warehouses and office buildings were restored in a spasm of prosperity during the 70s. The *Compleat Browser's Guide to Pioneer Square,* available in area bookstores, provides a short history and walking tour.

When Seattle nearly burned to the ground in 1889, an ordinance was passed to raise the city 35 ft. At first, shops below the elevated streets remained open for business and were moored to the upper city by an elaborate network of stairs. In 1907 the city moved upstairs permanently, and the underground city was sealed off. The vast **Bill Speidel's Underground Tours** (682-4646) does exactly that. Speidel spearheaded the movement to save Pioneer Square from the apocalypse of renewal. The tours are informative and irreverent glimpses at Seattle's beginnings; just ignore the rats that infest the tunnels. Tours (1½ hr.) leave from Doc Maynard's Pub at 610 1st Ave. (March-Sept. 6-8 per day 10am-6pm. Reservations best. Admission $4.75, seniors and students $3.50, ages 6-12 $2.75.)

Once back above ground, learn about eating shoes at the **Klondike Gold Rush National Historic Park,** 117 S. Main St. (442-7220). The "interpretive center" depicts the lives and fortunes of the miners. Saturday and Sunday at 3pm, the park screens Charlie Chaplin's 1925 classic, *The Gold Rush.* (Open daily 9am-5pm. Free.)

Three blocks east of Pioneer Square, up Jackson on King St., is Seattle's **International District.** Though sometimes still called Chinatown by Seattlites, this area has peoples from all over Asia. The 45-minute slideshow *Seattle's Other History,* presented at the Nippon Kan Theater, 628 Washington St. (624-8801), reveals the years of discrimination that Asians in Seattle experienced and the strength with which they met hardship. (Presentation given whenever large enough groups accumulate; call ahead. Admission $2.) Whether or not you see the show, be sure to pick up the free brochure *Chinatown Tour: Seattle's Other History* from the **Nippon Kan Theater,** itself a good place to start your tour of the district. Built in 1909 to house weddings and cultural events, the Nippon Kan fell into disrepair during World War

II as the U.S. government put Japanese Americans in concentration camps. It was restored and reopened in 1981.

Capitol Hill inspires extreme reactions from both its residents and neighbors. The former wouldn't live anywhere else, while the latter never go near the place. The district's leftist and gay communities set the tone for its nightspots (see Entertainment), while the retail outlets include a large number of collectives and radical bookstores. Saunter down Broadway or its cross streets to window-shop, or walk a few blocks east and north for a stroll down the hill's lovely residential streets, lined with beautiful Victorian homes. Bus #10 runs along 15th St. and #7 along Broadway.

Volunteer Park, between 11th and 17th Ave. at E. Ward St., north of the main Broadway activity, beckons tourists. Named for the "brave volunteers who gave their lives to liberate the oppressed people of Cuba and the Philippines," the park boasts lovely lawns and an outdoor running track. Climb the water tower at the 14th Ave. entrance for stunning 360° views of the city and the Olympic Range, rivaling the views from the Space Needle. The **Seattle Art Museum,** 14th St. E. and Prospect (625-8901), houses an excellent permanent collection of Asian art. Pick up a program listing or call 443-4670 for info about special exhibits. (Open Tues.-Wed. and Fri.-Sat. 10am-5pm, Thurs. 10am-9pm, Sun. noon-5pm. Admission $2; seniors, students, and under 12 $1. Free Thurs.)

The **University of Washington Arboretum** (325-4510), 10 blocks east of Volunteer Park, has great cycling and running trails. The tranquil **Japanese Garden** (625-4725) soothes in the southern end of the arboretum at East Helen St. Take bus #43 from downtown. The nine acres of sculpted gardens include fruit trees, a reflecting pool, and a traditional tea house. (Open March-Nov. daily 10am-8pm. Admission $1.50; seniors, under 19, and disabled 75¢. Arboretum open daily dawn-dusk; greenhouse open Mon.-Fri. 10am-4pm.)

With 35,000 students, the **University of Washington** is the state's cultural and educational center of gravity. The "U district" swarms with bookstores, shops, taverns, and restaurants. Stop by the friendly and helpful **visitors information center,** 4014 University Way NE (543-9198), to pick up a map of the campus and to obtain university info. (Open Mon.-Fri. 8am-5pm.)

On campus, visit the **Thomas Burke Memorial Washington State Museum,** NE 45th St. and 17th Ave. NE (543-5590), in the northwest corner of the grounds. The museum houses artifacts of the Pacific Northwest Native American tribes. Especially good is the scrimshaw display. (Open daily 10am-5pm, Thurs. 10am-8pm.) The **Henry Art Gallery,** 15th Ave. NE and NE 41st St. (543-2256), houses a collection of 18th- to 20th-century European and American art. (Open Tues.-Wed. and Fri. 10am-5pm, Thurs. 10am-7pm, Sat.-Sun. 11-5pm. Admission $2, students and seniors $1.) The **UW Arts Ticket Office,** 4001 University Way NE, has info and tickets for all events. (Open Mon.-Fri. 10:30am-4:30pm.) To reach the U district, take buses #71-74 from downtown, #7 or 43 from Capitol Hill.

Waterways and Parks

A string of attractions stud the waterways linking Lake Washington and Puget Sound. House- and sailboats fill **Lake Union.** Here, the **Center for Wooden Boats,** 1010 Valley St. (382-2628), maintains a moored flotilla of new and restored small craft for rental. (Sailboats $11-15 per hr., rowboats $8 per hr. Open Wed.-Sun. noon-6pm.) **Kelly's Landing,** 1401 NE Boat St. (547-9909), below the UW campus, rents canoes for outings on Lake Union. (Sailboats $10-20 per hr., 12 hr. minimium. Usually open Mon.-Fri. 10am-dusk.) Tour the houseboat moorings along Lake Union's shores or go through the Montlake Cut to Lake Washington.

Mock and ridicule trout and salmon as they struggle up 21 concrete steps at the **Fish Ladder** (783-7059) on the south side of the locks. Take bus #43 from the U District or #17 from downtown. On the northwestern shore of the city lies the **Golden Gardens Park** in Loyal Heights, between NW 80th and NW 95th, with a frigid beach. Several expensive restaurants line the piers to the south; the unobstructed views of the Olympics almost make their uniformly excellent seafood worth the price on salmonchanted evening.

Directly north of Lake Union, the Beautiful People run, roller skate, and skate-board around **Green Lake.** Take bus #16 from downtown. The lake also draws windsurfers, but woe to those who lose balance. Whoever named Green Lake wasn't kidding; even a quick dunk results in gobs of green algae lodged in every pore and follicle. Next door grows Woodland Park and the **Woodland Park Zoo,** 5500 Phin-ney Ave. N. (789-7919), best reached from Rte. 99 or N. 50th St. Take bus #5 from downtown. The park itself looks shaggy, but this makes the animals' non-Yuppie habitats seem all the more realistic. (Open daily 10am-6pm; winter daily 8:30am-4pm. Admission $4.50, ages 6-17 and seniors $2.25, disabled and ages 6-12 50¢.)

Entertainment

Obtain a copy of *The Weekly* (75¢) at newsstands and in boxes on the street, for a complete calendar of music, theater, exhibits, and special events. The free *Rocket,* available in music stores throughout the city, is a monthly off-beat guide to the pop-ular music scene around the Puget Sound area, and *Seattle Gay News* (25¢) lists events and musical happenings relevant to the gay community. The "What's Hap-pening" Friday insert of the *Seattle Post-Intelligencer* has more music listings.

During summertime lunch hours downtown, city-sponsored free entertainment of the **"Out to Lunch"** series (623-0340) brings everything from reggae to folk danc-ing to the parks and squares of Seattle.

Spokane

After the Great Fire of 1889, Spokane quickly rooted in industries spawned by local natural resources. Today, with an economy still based on lumber, mining, and agriculture, the spunkiest city in eastern Washington remains one of the North-west's major trade centers. And its most successful native son, Representative Thomas Foley, now has a steady job as Speaker of the House in the other Washing-ton (DC, that is).

In its own unwilling way, Spokane achieves urban sophistication without typical big-city hassles. The downtown thrives, though the pace remains slow. The Expo '74 legacy includes Riverfront Park's museum and theater, as well as a number of elegant restaurants and hotels. Arboretums, gardens, abundant outdoor activities, and a spectacular series of bridges spanning the Spokane River and Falls celebrate wonders more ancient than concrete.

Practical Information

Spokane Area Convention and Visitors Bureau, W. 926 Sprague Ave. (747-3230). Open Mon.-Fri. 8:30am-5pm, and most summer weekends 9am-3pm.

Travelers Aid: W. 1017 1st Ave. (456-7169), near the bus depot. Helps stranded travelers find lodgings. Open Mon.-Fri. 1-5pm.

Amtrak: W. 221 1st Ave. (624-5144), at Bernard St. downtown. One per day to: Chicago ($202); Seattle ($62); Portland ($62). Depot open Mon.-Fri. 11am-3:30am, Sat.-Sun. 7:30pm-3:30am.

Buses: Greyhound, W. 1125 Sprague Ave. (624-5251), at 1st Ave. and Jefferson St. downtown. To Seattle (4 per day, $36). **Empire Lines** (624-4116) and **Northwest Stage Lines** (838-4029 or 800-826-4058) share the terminal with Greyhound, serving Eastern Washington, Northern Idaho, and British Columbia. Station open daily 6am-8pm and 1-3am.

Public Transport: Spokane Transit System, W. 1229 Boone Ave. (328-7433). Serves all Spo-kane areas, including Eastern Washington University in Cheney. Operates until 12:15am downtown, 9:15pm in the valley along E. Sprague Ave. Fare 75¢, seniors and disabled 35¢.

Taxi: Checker Cab, 624-4171. Open 24 hrs.

Car Rental: U-Save Auto Rental, W. 918 3rd St. (455-8018), at Monroe. From $12.95 per day. 100 free mi., 20¢ each additional mi. Open Mon.-Fri. 8am-6pm, Sat. 8am-5pm. Must be 21 with $250 deposit or major credit card. Airport office (455-5929) open daily 4:30am-midnight.

Help Line: Crisis Hotline, 838-4428. Open 24 hrs.

Post Office: W. 904 Riverside (459-0230), at Lincoln. Open Mon.-Fri. 8:30am-5pm. **ZIP code:** 99210.

Area Code: 509.

Spokane avenues run east-west parallel to the river, streets north-south, and both alternate one-way. The city is divided into north and south by **Sprague Avenue,** east and west by aptly named **Division Street. Riverfront Park** abuts Spokane Falls at the heart of the city. Downtown lies north of Sprague and west of Division. Street addresses list with the compass point first, the number second, and the street name third (e.g., W. 1200 Division). No one knows why.

Accommodations and Camping

Let's face it: you have few options. A handful of hotels south of downtown are cheap but sleazy. Most camping areas throw down at least 20 mi. away. Don't try to sleep in Riverfront Park; the police won't take kindly.

Brown Squirrel Hostel (AYH), S. 930 Lincoln (838-5968). Located in a large, warm home with a grandfather clock, spacious porch, and delightfully creaky wooden floorboards. The manager and his wife will, before long, incorporate you into their family, offering a glass of lemonade, bowl of ice cream, or even a ride to the bus depot. Officially open 8-10am and 5-10pm, but stop in just about anytime. Members $8.65, nonmembers $11.85.

Eastern Washington University (359-7022), 18 mi. from Spokane in Cheney. Take bus #24 from Howard and Riverside St. downtown. By car, take I-90 southwest 8 mi. to exit 270, then Hwy. 904 south; turn right on Elm St. and continue to 10th. Inquire at Anderson Hall. Pleasant dorm rooms. Linen included. Singles $13.50, doubles $16, with semi-private bath $18, double $22. No tax charge with student I.D. Open year-round.

Town Centre Motor Inn, W. 901 1st St. (747-1041), at Lincoln St. The beautiful, remodeled rooms include a refrigerator and microwave. Complimentary coffee served with morning paper. Singles $31. Doubles $38. Canadian dollars accepted at par.

El Rancho Motel, W. 3000 Sunset Blvd. (455-9400). Take 2nd Ave. west to Maple St., where Sunset cuts diagonally across the intersection; follow Sunset approximately 15 blocks. On the edge of town, with easy access to freeway. Rooms with cable, free coffee, A/C. Laundromat and pool. Singles and doubles $38.

Riverside State Park, on Rifle Club Rd. (456-3964), 6 mi. northwest of downtown, off Hwy. 291 or Nine Mile Rd. Take Division north and turn left on Francis. 101 standard sites in an urban setting. Kitchen and small museum in the park. Facilities for the disabled. Shower and bath. Sites $8.

Mt. Spokane State Park (456-4169), 35 mi. northeast of the city. Take U.S. 395 5 mi. north to U.S. 2, then go 7 mi. north to Hwy. 206, which leads into the park. Popular for its cross-country ski and snowmobiling trails. From the Vista House, views of 4 states and Canada. Flush toilets, cold water only. Sites $8.

Food

For variety, head to **The Atrium,** on Wall St. near 1st Ave. **Europa Pizzeria,** one of the eateries in this small brick building, bakes the best pizza in town. May through October, Wednesdays and Saturdays in Riverfront Park, the **Spokane County Market** (456-5512) sells fresh fruit, vegetables, and baked goods. Twenty-odd fruit and vegetable farms make up the **Green Bluff Growers Cooperative,** 16 mi. northwest of town off Day-Mountain Spokane Rd. Many of the farms have "U-pick" arrangements, with nearby free panoramic picnic areas. Peak season for most crops is August to October. Write Green Bluff Growers, E. 9423 Green Bluff Rd., Colbert 99005, or look for a brochure downtown.

A myriad of chain restaurants line 3rd Ave. advertising all-you-can-eat specials and buffets.

Dick's, E. 10 3rd Ave., at Division. Look for the pink panda near I-90. My God, this place is cool. A takeout burger phenomenon whose fame grows as prices remain stunted. Burgers 53¢, fries 39¢, soft drinks 39-69¢, pies 39¢, sundaes 63¢, etc. Always crowded, but lines move quickly. Open daily 9am-1:30am.

Auntie's Bookstore and Café, W. 313 Riverside. Browse through the excellent selection of books, including extensive collections on regional history, gender studies, and religion, then compose your own sandwich from $3. Lunch specials $4. Open Mon.-Sat. 9am-9pm, Sun. noon-5pm.

Coyote Café, W. 702 3rd Ave. Jazzy Mexican joint with *cerveza* (beer) signs on the walls, cacti in the windows, and $2.75 margaritas all day. Specialties include the Coyote Chimichanga ($6.20). Open Mon.-Thurs. 11am-11pm, Fri. 11am-midnight, Sat. noon-midnight, Sun. noon-10pm.

Knight's Diner, N. 2442 Division. Take bus #6. A long red-and-black diner in an old train car. Western down-home cooking and hospitality. Hearty breakfasts and lunches $2-4.50. Open Tues.-Sat. 6:30am-2pm, Sun. 7:30am-2pm.

Sights and Entertainment

Spokane has few aspirations to flashy exhibits or high-flown architecture. The city's best attractions focus on local history and culture. A few blocks east of Riverfront Park, the unusually shaped **Museum of Native American Cultures (MONAC),** E. 200 Cataldo St. (326-4550), stands on a hill to the northeast of downtown, off Division St. The four-story museum houses a collection of art and artifacts from North and South America. (Open daily 10am-5pm, Oct.-April Tues.-Sun. 10am-5pm. Admission $3, seniors and students $2, kids free, families $7.)

The **Cheney Cowles Memorial Museum,** W. 2316 1st Ave. (456-3931), also has exhibits on Native American culture and history, as well as well-explicated displays on the natural history and pioneer settlement of eastern Washington. The **Grace Campbell House** (456-3931) next door is affiliated with the museum. Built in the Tudor revival style with a fortune extracted from the Coeur d'Alène gold mines in Idaho, this elegant Victorian museum describes Spokane's high-society life during the 1890s boom era. (Museum and house open Tues.-Sat. 10am-9pm, Sun. 1-5pm. Admission $2, seniors, students, and kids $1.)

Built for the 1974 World's Fair, **Riverfront Park,** N. 507 Howard St. (456-4386), still hangs on just north of downtown as Spokane's center of gravity; the populace strolls on leisurely weekend afternoons. The **IMAX Theatre** shows 3D films on a 5½-story screen. (Shows run noon-9pm and start on the hr. Admission Tues.-Sun. $4, seniors $3.50, under 18 $3.) One section of the park has "kiddie" rides—including the exquisitely hand-carved **Looff Carousel** (open daily 11am-9pm; 60¢ a whirl). A "Single Day Pass" (adults $10, kids $9) covers the whole works. The park offers ice-skating in the winter ($2.50) and hosts special programs and events. The **Gondola Skyride Over the Falls** travels from the park over Spokane Falls and over to the north side of the river. (Open summer daily 11am-9pm. Fare without Day Pass $3, seniors $2.50, kids $2.)

Hard-core Bingsters will be drawn to the **Crosby Library,** E. 502 Boone St. (328-4220 ext. 3132), at Gonzaga University. Here, the faithful display the crooner's relics: gold records, awards, photographs. (Open daily but hours vary, so call. Free.)

Spokane's collection of two dozen parks includes tranquil, well-groomed **Finch Arboretum,** W. 3404 Woodland Blvd. Over 2,000 species of trees, flowers, and shrubs allow viewing 24 hrs. **Manito Park,** on S. Grand Ave. between 17th and 25th Ave. (856-4331), south of downtown, features flower gardens, tennis courts, a duck pond, and the **Dr. David Graiser Conservatory,** which houses many tropical and local plant species. (Open daily 8am-dusk; off-season 8am-3:30pm. Free.) Adjacent to the Manito Park is the **Nishinomiya Garden,** a lush Japanese garden symbolizing the friendship between Spokane and its Japanese sibling city, Nishinomiya. (Same hours as Manito Park. Free.)

The state runs two parks near Spokane; both merit a trip. **Riverside State Park** (456-3964 or 456-2499) embroiders the Spokane River with 7655 acres of volcanic outcroppings, rushing water, hiking (especially good in Deep Greek Canyon), and equestrian trails (horse rental $9 per hr. in nearby Trail Town; 456-8249). The park also weaves prime cross-country ski territory in the winter. **Mount Spokane State Park** (456-4169) stands 35 mi. to the northeast of the city with a road extending to the summit. Clear days afford views of the Spokane Valley and the distant peaks of the Rockies and Cascades. Mt. Spokane is a skiing center with free cross-country trails and downhill ski packages from $20.

Don't leave Spokane without sampling one of the fine Eastern Washington wines. The **Arbor Cliff House,** N. 4705 Fruithill Rd. (927-9463), offers a tour of a national historical house, a view of the city, and free wine (daily noon-5pm). Take I-90 to the Argonne north exit, travel north on Argonne over the Spokane River, turn right on Upriver Dr., proceed 1 mi., and then bear left onto Fruithill Rd.

Spokane's more traditional tastes are reflected in the large number of bowling alleys and movie theaters gracing the city. However, the variety of live music here keeps the populace boppin' until they're droppin'. The *Spokane Spokesman-Review's* Friday Weekend section and the *Spokane Chronicle's* Friday Empire section give the low-down on area happenings. During the summer, the city parks present a free **Out-to-Lunch** concert series at noon on weekdays. (Call 624-1393 or check in the Weekend for schedule info.)

Henry's Pub, W. 230 Riverside Ave. (624-9828), is the place for live rock Wed.-Sat. nights. Local favorites such as the Peace Frogs and Final Exam cram here. Draft beer costs $1.25. (Open Wed.-Sat. 7am-2pm) At that bastion of yuppiedom, **The Onion Bar and Grill,** W. 302 Riverside (747-3852), men in European suits act tough. Nurse your frozen margaritas while playing pool in the back room. Peer Gynt would love it. Friendly faces serve nightly drink specials. (Dinners under $10, frozen margaritas $3.50, domestic drafts $1.85. Open Sun.-Thurs. 11:15am-11:30pm, Fri.-Sat. 11:15am-2am.)

WEST VIRGINIA

"Hell doesn't scare me—I've been to West Virginia!" the fiery labor organizer Mary Harris Jones once declared. In "Mother" Jones' day, the characterization wasn't far off the mark; West Virginia's rugged wilderness was little more than a giant strip mine for robber barons who laid bare the state's forests, polluted its rivers, and leveled its mountains to extract precious coal. West Virginia mining was once synonymous with the worst excesses of industrial capitalism, and the American labor movement underwent its most violent birth pangs here.

West Virginia formed from the Virginian counties that remained loyal to the Union (whether by choice or by presence of federal troops) during the Civil War. Plundered by Northern industrialists during the post-war era of "free market" capitalism, West Virginia has remained one of America's poorest and most isolated states, largely due to corrupt political machines controlled by unscrupulous profiteers. With the decline of heavy industry during the last 30 years, however, West Virginia started cashing in on its other resource—abundant natural beauty. Thanks to great skiing, hiking, fishing, and the Eastern U.S.'s best white-water rafting, tourism has become one of the main sources of employment and revenue. The name John D. Rockefeller no longer refers to the hated robber baron, but to his great-grandson, once the state's reformist governor and currently U.S. senator. West Virginians are well-known for their fierce independence, epitomized by recent discussion over the state-level legalization of marijuana. And though television overtook the church as the dominant social influence some time in the 1970s, West Virginians remain noticeably attached to traditional folkways, including their long-standing penchant for warm hospitality.

Practical Information

Capital: Charleston.

Tourist Information: Travel Development Division, 1900 Washington St., State Capitol Complex, Bldg. 6, #B654, Charleston 25305 (348-2286 or 800-225-5982). **Division of Parks and Recreation,** 1900 Washington St., State Capitol Complex, Bldg. 6, #451, Charleston 25305. **U.S. Forest Service Supervisor's Office,** 200 Sycamore St., Elkins 26241 (636-1800).

Time Zone: Eastern. **Postal Abbreviation:** WV

Area Code: 304.

Harpers Ferry

Strangely enough, the very event that helped sink Harper's Ferry as a town—the October, 1859 raid on the U.S. armory by radical abolitionist John Brown and his 21-man "army of liberation"—has caused its rebirth as an historic attraction. Before the raid, Harper's Ferry thrived as a military and industrial town because of its prime location at the confluence of the Shenandoah and Potomac Rivers. John Brown, a fiery abolitionist who kicked off his career by massacring pro-slavery Kansas, raided the town's federal arsenal to gather arms for a planned slave insurrection. Federal troops under then-Col. Robert E. Lee foiled his plans and shot most of the raiders, including Brown's three sons. Brown himself was tried and hanged two months later, inspiring the famous ditty "John Brown's Body." The Harper's Ferry raid convinced many Southerners that the North would stop at nothing to wipe out slavery, and ultimately helped produce the Civil War. The war, in turn, destroyed the town: retreating troops burned the armory down, and Harper's Ferry endured two years of siege before a series of floods finally KO'd it. Still, Nature may prove more compelling than culture here. The spectacular view from the Harper's Ferry Bluffs above town may be worth more than all the history exhibits combined.

Harper's Ferry National Park has restored many of the town's buildings to their 1850s appearance, back when the town flourished with a population of 3,200. Stop first at the **visitor's center** (535-6298) just inside the park entrance off Rte. 340; park rangers will hand you a map of the area, tell you more about the park, and show you a long, remarkably even-handed movie about John Brown. The visitor's center also provides free 30-90 minute **tours** guided by park rangers daily 10am-3pm throughout the summer. Keep your ears open for evening programs throughout the summer. If you drive, park near the visitor's center: the shuttle bus running two mi. to and from the restored town runs every 15 min.; you'll get ticketed closer to town. (Park and Visitors Center open daily Sept.-May 8:30am-5pm, June-Aug. 8:30am-6pm. $5 per car, $2 per hiker or cyclist.)

The bus from the parking lot stops at **Shenandoah St.** Browse through the renovated blacksmith shop, ready-made clothing store, and general store. Turning left off Shenandoah St. onto High St., you'll find a slew—that's right, a slew—of antique stores, souvenir shops, and the usual tourist-snaring suspects. The **Garden of Food** (535-2202) on High St. serves salads and sandwiches ($3-7) either indoors or outside on the Edenic patio. (Mon.-Fri. 11am-6pm, Sat.-Sun. 11am-7pm.) The **Back Street Café** on Potomac St. (725-8019) doubles as a burger joint (burgers and hot dogs $2-4) and a ghoulish guide service; "Ghost Tours" of the town are offered weekend nights (May 1-Nov. 8 Fri.-Sun. 8pm, Apr. Sat. 8pm; $2, under 11 $1. Reservations recommended in Oct. Café open daily 10am-6pm year-round.) A few three-speed bikes are rented near the café ($3 per hr., $15 per day). If you have a car, try the **Cindy Dee Restaurant,** 19112 Keep Tryst Rd. (695-8181), at the blinking light just off Rte. 340, a diner popular with locals and travelers alike. (4-piece fried chicken plate $3.40, burgers $2, sandwiches $1-4. Cash only. Always open.)

Uphill, stairs on High St. lead to the footpath to **Jefferson Rock;** experience awe and vertigo as you look out on the three states (Virginia, Maryland, and guess what the other is) and the two rivers below. Thomas Jefferson declared the view "worth a voyage across the Atlantic". Easy for him to say; he was already here.

Those who prefer nature to history have several options, including hiking and boating. The **Maryland Heights Trail** offers some of the best views in the Alleghenies and winds past cliffs worthy of experienced rock climbers; climbers must register at the visitor's center. **Appalachian Trail Conference Headquarters** (535-6331) at the corner of Washington and Jackson St., offers catalogues, books, and hiking equipment to members. (Membership $25, students and seniors $18. Write to P.O. Box 807 or call. Open Mon.-Fri. 9am-5pm, Sat.-Sun. 9am-4pm.) The less adventurous can walk along the **Chesapeake & Ohio Canal Towpath.**

River & Trail Outfitters (695-5177), 604 Valley Rd., off Rte. 340 at the blinking light, rents canoes, inner tubes, and rafts in addition to organizing guided trips. (Canoes $40 per day; tubes $22.50 per day; raft trips $42 per person.) They also organize cross-country skiing weekends ($199) and day trips ($60). Call ahead for reservations. **River Riders,** P.O. Box 267, Knoxville, MD 21758 (301-834-8051 or 301-535-2663) organizes two trips daily for rafting (from $30) and inner-tubing (from $20). Reservations required.

Hikers can try the **Harper's Ferry Hostel (AYH),** 19123 Sandy Hook Rd. off Keep Tryst Rd. in Knoxville, MD (301-834-7652) for cheaper accommodations. (3-day max. stay. Check-in 6pm-8pm only. Members $8 summer/$9 winter; nonmembers $11 summer/$12 winter; camping $4 per person. 50% reservation deposit.) The **Comfort Inn** at Rte. 340 and Union St. (535-6391), a ten-minute walk from town, offers dependable rooms and serves coffee and doughnuts each morning—it also has handicap-access and non-smoking rooms. (Singles $50. Doubles $52. $2 extra on weekends.)

You can camp along the C&O Canal, where sites lie five mi. apart, or in one of the five Maryland State Park campgrounds lying within 30 mi. of Harper's Ferry. **Greenbrier State Park** (301-791-4767) lies a few mi. north of Boonsboro on Rte. 66 between exits 35 and 42 on I-70. (April-Nov. $10.) Far closer is the commercial **Camp Resort,** Rte. 3, Box 1300 (535-6895), adjacent to the entrance to Harper's Ferry National Park. (2-person sites $18, with water and hookup $21; additional adults $4 per night.)

A natural stop for hikers on the Appalachian Trail, Harper's Ferry also makes a convenient day trip from Washington. The drive to Harper's Ferry from DC takes 1½ hrs. by car. Take I-270 north to Rte. 340 West. **Amtrak** goes to Harper's Ferry from DC in the afternoon and back to DC in the morning ($13). The closest **Greyhound** bus stations are half-hour drives away in Winchester, VA and Frederick, MD.

If time allows, drive a few mi. north to **Antietam National Battlefield,** in Maryland, where the Civil War's bloodiest battle was fought. On Sept. 17, 1862, 12,410 Union and 10,700 Confederate soldiers died as Robert E. Lee tried and failed to penetrate the line held by General George B. McClellan's Northern army. The nominal Union victory provided President Lincoln with the opportunity to issue the Emancipation Proclamation. To get to Antietam from Harper's Ferry, take Rte. 340 for two mi., turn right onto Rte. 230 to Shepardstown, then turn right again onto Rte. 480 to Sharpsburg, MD. Take a left onto Rte. 65 to reach Antietam.

Harper's Ferry's ZIP code is 25425; the **area code** is 304. Knoxville, MD's **ZIP code** is 21758.

Monongahela National Forest

Mammoth **Monongahela National Forest,** popular with canoers, enshrouds deer, bear, wild turkeys, and spelunkers prowling around below ground in magnificent limestone caverns. But camping is the main attraction here, with 600 mi. of prize hiking trails and over 500 campsites to lure the adventurer. Camp in an established site ($10 or less) or sleep in the backcountry for free. The forest's **Lake Sherwood Area** (536-3660), 25 mi. north on Rte. 92, offers fishing, hunting, swimming, hiking, and boating, as well as several campgrounds that rob from the rich to give to the poor. The campgrounds fill only on major holidays. (2-week max. stay. Sites $6.) A three-hour drive north will bring you to **Blackwater Falls State Park** (800-225-5982), ¼-mi. southwest of Rte. 32. The park's dazzling centerpiece is the most popular waterfall in West Virginia. (Sites $9, $10 with electricity. Open April-Oct.) For advice and information on exploring Monongahela, visit the White Sulphur Springs **Forest Service Office,** in the Federal Bldg. (536-2144), at 14 E. Main and Mountain Ave. (Open Mon.-Fri. 8am-4:45pm.) For information on the whole forest, which encompasses much of West Virginia's most scenic mountain country, contact the Supervisor's Office, Monongahela National Forest, 200 Sycamore St., Elkins 26241-3962 (636-1800; Mon.-Fri. 8am-4:45pm).

WISCONSIN

The state that calls itself "America's Dairyland" is also one of the nation's most popular playlands, with forests, rivers, and lakes to suit the tenacious and the tenderfoot alike. Lake Superior to the north and Lake Michigan to the east give the Wisconsin coast the natural beauty that makes the Great Lakes area famous. Wisconsin's appeal comes not just from nature; Wisconsin residents pick up where the wilderness leaves off. Here you can enjoy a variety of pleasures: Milwaukee's ethnic festivals, Madison's annual autumn march to legalize marijuana, fantasy role-playing conventions, and the Door County fishboil, a socio-culinary event.

Practical Information

Capital: Madison.

Division of Tourism, 123 W. Washington St., Madison 53707 (266-2161, 266-6797, or 800-372-2737).

Time Zone: Central (1 hr. behind Eastern). **Postal Abbreviation:** WI

Apostle Islands

Over the past million or so years, glaciers have sculpted the Great Lakes along with the scenic archipelago known as the Apostle Islands. Today 20 of the 22 islands are protected as a national lakeshore. Summer tourists visit the wind- and wave-whipped caves by the thousands, camping on the unspoiled sandstone bluffs.

The Apostle Islands lie off the northern tip of Wisconsin and are easily accessible from Bayfield, off Hwy. 13. They are 90 mi. from Duluth, 220 mi. from the Twin Cities, and 465 mi. from Chicago. All Apostle Islands excursions begin in the sleepy mainland town of **Bayfield.** Ferry service to and from Bayfield and **La Pointe,** the town on large **Madeline Island,** is provided by **Madeline Island Ferry Line** (747-2051; summer ferries daily every ½ hr. 6am-11pm; less frequently March-June and Sept.-Dec.; one way tickets $2.75, ages 6-11 $1.75, bikes $1.50, cars $5.25.). The smaller islands can be reached by the **Water Taxi** (779-5153) for a steep price.

Legend has it that the islands were named in the 18th century when a band of pirates called the Twelve Apostles hid out on Oak Island. Today you don't have to hide to stay there, as long as you get a free camper's permit, available at the **National Lakeshore Headquarters Visitors Center,** 410 Washington Ave. in Bayfield (779-3397). The permit allows you to camp on 19 of the 22 islands. Madeline Island has two campgrounds. **Big Bay Town Park** is 6½ mi. from La Pointe, right next to the beautiful Big Bay Lagoon. (Primitive sites $13.25 for out-of-staters, including state park sticker.) Across the lagoon, **Big Bay State Park** has sites for $10.75, including state park sticker. Camping is also available on the mainland at **Apostle Islands View Campground,** Hwy. 13 (779-5524; in winter 742-3303), ½ mi. south of Bayfield. (Sites $9-14, depending on season.)

The **Frostman Home,** 24 N. 3rd St. (779-3239), Bayfield, provides shelter via three comfortable rooms for $25 per room. Down the street and around the corner, **Greunke's Inn,** 17 Rittenhouse Ave. (779-5480), has pleasant, old-fashioned rooms from $35. Madeline Island has several motels. On Colonel Woods Blvd., you can be surrounded by walls of knotty pine at **La Pointe Lodgings Motel** (747-5205 or 779-5596; singles $55, off-season $35). Across the street, the **Madeline Island Motel** (747-3000) lets clean rooms. (Singles $44. Doubles $49.) The "high season" summer months find accommodations scarce, so reserve in advance.

The Bayfield area has long been noted for its June and July berry season. Try the strawberry shortcake at any of the many restaurants in Bayfield or La Pointe. **Beach Club,** just off the ferry in La Pointe, has a relaxed atmosphere, a view of the lake, superlative shortcake ($3.50), and a superb shrimp basket with fries ($7). (Open summer daily 7:30am-3:30pm, 5:30-10pm.) Across the street, **Grandpa Tony's** dishes out inexpensive chow (burgers $2-3) and delicious ice cream (small cone $1.50). (Open summer Mon.-Fri. 8am-9pm, Sat.-Sun. 8am-10pm.) Join the bronzed and beautiful aprés-windsurfing set at **The Pub** (747-6315), ½ mi. south of town. Though pricy, the seafood or steak dinners ($12-16) are a treat. (Open April-Nov. daily 7:30am-10pm. Hours fluctuate each month.) For live music and good cheer, head to **Bates Bar,** 14 S. Broad St. in Bayfield (779-5356), where grinning gargoyles are imprisoned in wood around the bar and are forced to listen to live blues or rock 'n' roll Fri.-Sat. (Open Mon.-Fri. 4pm-2am, Sat. 1pm-2am, Sun. 1-6pm. Cover $2.)

A few hundred years ago, the Chippewa came to Madeline Island from the Atlantic in search of the *megis shell,* a light in the sky that was supposed to bring prosperity and health. The **Madeline Island Historical Museum** (747-2415), right off the dock, fleshes out the story with lessons in Chippewa, trading, and the logging history of the islands. (Open late May-early Oct. daily 9am-5pm. $1.50, seniors $1.20, ages 5-17 50¢.) The **Indian Burial Ground** one mi. south of La Pointe has meandering dirt paths that lead to the graves of early settlers and christianized Chippewa, including Chief Great Buffalo. Towards the end of the day, head to **Sunset Bay** on the north side of the island. **Madeline Island Tours** (747-2051) offers two or three 1¼-hr. tours of the island each day ($5, ages 5-11 $2.75).

The other islands have subtle charms of their own. The sandstone quarries of Basswood and Hermit Island, as well as the abandoned logging and fishing camps on some of the others, are mute reminders of a more vigorous and animated era. Some of the sea caves on Devils Island are large enough to maneuver a small boat in. Museums in their own right, the restored lighthouses on Sand, Raspberry, Michigan, Outer, and Devils Islands offer spectacular views of the surrounding country. An easy way to visit all of these sights is on one of three narrated cruises provided by the **Apostle Islands Cruise Service** (779-3925; tickets $19, kids $8).

For transport on Madeline Island, rent a bike or moped at **Motion to Go,** 102 Lake View Pl. (747-6585), about one block from the ferry. ($8-10 per hr. $45 per day. Open summer daily 9am-9pm.) Rent fat-tired bikes at **Island Bike Rental** (747-5442), ½ block north of the town dock in La Pointe. ($2.50 per hr., $15 per day. Open daily May 27-early Oct., 10am-5:30pm.) The nearest **Greyhound** station is in Ashland 101 2nd St. (682-4010), 22 mi. southeast of Bayfield. (To Duluth $7.) The **Bay Area Rural Transit (BART)** (682-9664) offers a shuttle. (4 per day, last one to Bayfield; $1.80, seniors $1.10, students $1.50.)

The **Bayfield Chamber of Commerce,** 42 S. Broad St. (779-3335) and the **Madeline Island Chamber of Commerce,** Main St. (747-2801), provide helpful information, especially concerning accommodations. (Both open summer daily 9am-5pm.) The **Apostle Islands National Lakeshore Headquarters Visitors Center,** 410 Washington Ave. in Bayfield (779-3397), can answer questions. (Open daily 8am-6pm; off-season Mon.-Fri. 8am-4:30pm.)

The La Pointe **post office** (747-3712) lies just off the dock on Madeline Island. (Open Mon.-Fri. 9am-4:30pm, Sat. 9:30am-1pm.) The **ZIP code** is 54850. The **area code** for the Apostle Islands is 715.

Door County

Door County, the beautiful, 40-mi. long peninsula stretching north into Lake Michigan, attracts more visitors every year, and for good reason. The peninsula (technically an island cut off from the rest of Wisconsin by the Sturgeon Bay Canal) hosts famous fishboils, and boasts five state parks, 250 mi. of shoreline, and eight inland lakes. Despite the recent tourist onslaught, the peninsula remains low-key and relaxed; streets often don't have addresses, and businesses may close "around sunset." For the time being, Door County, like its namesake, is wide open to visitors, providing stores, restaurants, and parks, while managing to shut out reckless developers.

Practical Information

Emergency: 911

Visitor Information: Door County Chamber of Commerce, 6443 Green Bay Rd. (743-4456), on Hwy. 42/57 entering Sturgeon Bay. Friendly staff with free brochures for every village on the peninsula and biking maps (25¢). Mailing address P.O. Box 346, Station A. **Triphone,** a free 24-hr. service located outside the chamber of commerce, allows you to call any hotel on the peninsula, as well as restaurant, police, weather, and fishing hotlines. Open June-Oct. Mon.-Fri. 8am-5pm, Sat. 10am-4pm; off-season Mon.-Fri. 8am-5pm. Each village has its own visitor center.

Car Rental: Phil Young Car Rental, 120 N. 14th Ave. (743-9228). $20 per day, 10¢ per mi. Call a week ahead in summer. Open Mon.-Fri. 7am-5pm, Sat.-Sun. 8am-noon. Must be 21 with driver's license and a credit card or a $50 deposit plus estimated cost.

Other Rentals: Nor Door Sport and Cyclery, Fish Creek (868-2275), at the entrance to Peninsula State Park. Mountain bikes $7 per hr., $20 per day; 18- and 21-speeds $5 per hr., $15 per day, $30 for 3 days. **The Boat House,** Fish Creek (868-3745). Mopeds $12.50 for the 1st hr., $7.50 per additional hr. Must have $50 deposit and driver's license. Rental includes $5 admission to nearby Peninsula State Park. **Kurtz Corral,** 3 mi. east of Carlsville on C.R. "I" (743-6742). Horseback riding on 300 acres. $19 per hr., kids' rides $9; instruction included. Open daily 9am-3pm.

Police: 123 S. 5th Ave. (743-4133), in Sturgeon Bay.

Post Office: 359 Louisiana (743-2681), at 4th St. in Sturgeon Bay. Open Mon.-Fri. 8:30am-5pm.

Area Code: 414.

The real Door County begins north of **Sturgeon Bay,** though the county line lies south. Highways 42 and 57 converge, flow through Sturgeon Bay, and then split again—57 running up the eastern coast of the peninsula, 42 up the western side. The peninsula is 200 mi. northwest of Madison (take Hwy. 151 and then 57 north) and 150 mi. north of Milwaukee (take Hwy. 43, then 42, north), and has no land access except Sturgeon Bay. Summer is high season in Door's 12 villages, the biggest of which are **Fish Creek** (rhymes with "fish stick"), **Sister Bay,** and **Ephraim.** There is no public transportation on the peninsula.

Accommodations and Camping

Motels here are uniformly expensive. There are few options outside the $50-70 range, but if you arrive on a slow night you might be able to bargain down to $40 or less. Otherwise, try camping, which brings you closer to the peninsula's beauty.

Those more interested in the peninsula's motels should shack up at **Liberty Park Lodge** (854-2025), in Sister Bay north of downtown on Rte. 42, where you still can sit on the huge porch and watch the sun set over the lake. (Lodge rooms $42-56.)

Or try **Chal-A Motel,** 3910 Hwy. 42/57 (743-6788), three mi. north of the bridge in Sturgeon Bay. (July-Oct. singles $39, doubles $44; Nov.-June singles $19, doubles $24.)

Camping is the way to go in Door County, and four out of the five **state parks** surveyed (all except Rock Island; open daily 6am-11pm) have sites. Daily park admission costs $6; an annual admission sticker $28. Camping is an additional $6.75-10 (electricity $1.75 extra) at each park. **Peninsula State Park,** P.O. Box 218, Fish Creek 54212 (868-3258), by Fish Creek village, is the largest, with 472 sites. Reserved sites (with showers and flush toilets) are hard to get in high season, but 127 sites are kept open for walk-ins; still, try to come early in the morning (sites $10). Peninsula has 20 mi. of shoreline, a spectacular view from Eagle Tower, and 17 mi. of hiking. **Potawatomi State Park,** 3740 Park Dr., Sturgeon Bay 54235 (746-2890), just outside Sturgeon Bay off Hwy. 42/57, has 125 campsites, half of which are open to walk-ins. Write for reservations (sites $8.50). **Newport State Park,** at the tip of the peninsula, six or seven mi. from Ellison Bay off Hwy. 42, has only 16 sites and does not allow motorized vehicles (sites $10). To get to **Rock Island State Park,** take the ferry from Gill's Rock to Washington Island (see Sights and Activities) and another ferry (847-2252; $5 round-trip, $3 kids) to Rock Island. (40 sites. $6.75. Open May-Dec.)

The best private campground is **Path of Pines** (868-3332), in Fish Creek, which has scenic sites and a truly hospitable staff. It's one mi. east of the perennially packed Peninsula, on County "F" off Hwy. 42. (Sites with water and electricity $15. $2.50 per additional adult.)

Food and Drink

Many people come to Door County just for **fishboils,** not a trout with blemishes but a Scandinavian tradition dating back to 19th-century lumberjacks. As much a ceremony as a meal, the boil produces billowing heat that meets with the cool twilight air off Lake Michigan. The best fishboils (all $12.75) are at: **White Gull Inn,** in Fish Creek (868-3517; May-Oct. Wed. and Fri.-Sun.; Nov.-April Wed. and Sat. at 5:45, 7, and 8:15pm; reservations required); the **Edgewater Restaurant,** in Ephraim (854-4034; June to mid-Oct. Mon.-Sat. at 5:30 and 6:45 pm; reservations best); and **The Viking,** at Ellison Bay (854-2998; mid-May to Nov. 4:30-8pm). Cherries are another county tradition, and each fishboil ends with a big slice of cherry pie.

In Door County, you're better off stocking up at grocery stores and farm markets than sitting down at a restaurant. **Piggly Wiggly,** on Country Walk Rd. (854-2391), in Sister Bay, is probably the best place to get groceries. Another is located at Cherry Point Mall in Sturgeon Bay. (Open Mon.-Sat. 8am-8pm, Sun. 8am-5pm.) **Hy-Line Orchards** (868-3067), on Hwy. 42 between Juddville and Egg Harbor, is a huge barn full of produce and a few old Model T's. Try the cherry cider. (Open daily 7am-7pm.) Door County wines and fresh produce are sold at **Ray's Cherry Hut,** ½-mi. south of Fish Creek on Hwy. 42. (Open mid-May to Nov. daily 7:30am-6:30pm.)

Al Johnson's Swedish Restaurant, in Sister Bay on Hwy. 42 (854-2626), down the hill and 2 blocks past the information center. Excellent Swedish food popular with locals and visitors. Goats keep the sod roof trimmed. Swedish pancakes and meatballs $6. Open daily 6am-9pm.

Kirkegaard's Yum-Yum Tree (839-2993) in Bailey's Harbor. Floats $2.25, sundaes $1.85-3.25, cones $1.25, beer brats $1.95, deli sandwiches $2.50-4.50, and plenty of Danish philosophy for dessert. Open mid-May to Oct. daily 10am-10pm.

Bayside Tavern, Fish Creek on Hwy. 42 (868-3441). Serves serious burgers ($2.50-4) and a delicious Friday perch fry ($8). Also a hip bar. Beer 90¢. No one under 21. Open daily 11am-2pm.

The Fish Creek General Store, Fish Creek (868-3351). The best deal on prepared food on the peninsula. Thick deli sandwiches with chips $2.25. Carry-out only. Open May-Nov. daily 8am-7pm.

Sights and Activities

Door County is best seen by bike. **Cave Point County Park** offers the most stunning views of the peninsula. The park is on Cave Point Rd. off Hwy. 57, just south of Jacksonport. (Open daily 6am-10pm. Free.) Next door is **Whitefish Dunes State Park,** with 10 mi. of hiking through a well-kept wildlife preserve. (Open daily 8am-8pm. $6.) Visit the small public beaches along Door's 250-mi. shoreline; one of the nicest is Lakeside Park at **Jacksonport.** The beach is wide and sandy, backed by a shady park and playground. (Open daily 6am-10pm. Free.) You can go windsurfing off the public beach at Ephraim, in front of the Edgewater Restaurant and Motel. **Windsurf Door County** (854-4071), across from the public beach at South Shore Pier, rents boards ($12 per hr., $30 per ½-day; $100 deposit or major credit card required). **Peninsula State Park,** a few mi. south of Ephraim in Fish Creek, has 3763 acres of forested land. Ride a moped or bicycle along the 20 mi. of shoreline road, or mix, mingle, and sunbathe at **Nicolet Beach** in the park. From the immense Eagle Tower one mi. east of the beach, 110 steps up, you can see clear across the lake to Michigan. (Open daily 6am-11pm. $6 per car, $2 per bike; under 18 free.)

Kangaroo Lake, the largest of the eight inland lakes on this thin peninsula, offers warmer swimming and a less intimidating stretch of water. Kangaroo Lake Road, south of Bailey's Harbor off Hwy. 57, provides lake access; follow the county roads around the lake to find your own secluded swimming spot. The **Ridges Sanctuary,** north of Bailey's Harbor off Hwy. "Q," has an appealing nature trail that leads to an abandoned lighthouse. (Open daily 10am-6pm. Free.) **Newport State Park,** six mi. east of Ellison Bay on Newport Dr. off Hwy. 42, provides more satisfying hiking than Peninsula (no vehicles allowed). Newport has an expansive 3,000-ft. swimming beach and 13 mi. of shoreline on Lake Michigan and on inland Europe Lake.

For more scenic seclusion, seek out **Washington Island,** off the tip of the Door Peninsula; ferries run by Washington Island Ferry Line (847-2546; round-trip for cars $14, adults $6, kids $3) and Island Clipper (854-2972; round-trip for adults $6, kids $3). Both leave Gills Rock and Northport Pier several times daily.

Madison

Although located in a conservative region, Madison has gained fame for its liberal attitudes and established itself as the Midwest's version of Berkeley. Its streets, lined with bookstores and cafés, are constantly filled with vendors, student-philosophers, religious enthusiasts, and the revolutionary shenanigans of students from the University of Wisconsin (UW). Four sparkling lakes, wide, bike-friendly streets, a huge arboretum, and over 150 city parks take the edge off urban life in this capital city.

Practical Information

Emergency: 911.

Greater Madison Convention and Visitors Bureau, 615 E. Washington. (255-0701). Open Mon.-Fri. 8am-5pm. **State of Wisconsin Tourist Information Center,** 123 W. Washington St. (266-2161 or 800-372-2737). Open Mon.-Fri. 8am-4:30pm. **Campus assistance,** 420 N. Lake St. (263-2400), near State St. Open Mon.-Fri. 8am-8pm, Sat. 10am-2pm, with longer weekend hours during the school year. **Gay-Lesbian Center,** 255-4297. **Concert Line,** 271-7625. Open 24 hrs.

Dane County Airport: 4000 International Lane (246-3380); NE corner of town. 20-min. drive from campus. Badger Cab to campus $5-6. The "Burr Oaks" bus, if you don't mind the walk to its Packer Ave. stop, is only 75¢.

Greyhound: 931 E. Main St. (257-9511 or 257-3050), off E. Washington Ave. 10 blocks from the capitol. Open daily 7am-7:20pm. To: Milwaukee ($8), Green Bay ($21, students with ID $16.50), and Minneapolis ($42, students with ID $25). **Badger Bus,** 2 S. Bedford (255-6771), at W. Washington Ave. Open daily 7am-10pm. Regular runs to Milwaukee only (6 per day, 1½ hr., $8). Usually faster than Greyhound. **Van Galder Bus,** 217 S. Hamilton (255-0525). Main office a few blocks southeast of the capitol, but call to find convenient on-campus ticket stops. Trips "directly to your airline" at Chicago's O'Hare Airport cost $16. Buses 12 per day 3:30am-8:30pm.

Public Transport: Madison Metropolitan Bus Transit (MMTA), 25 W. Main (266-4466). Excellent, efficient service to all parts of city. All buses eventually converge on Capitol Sq., at the top of State St. Buses operate daily 6am-11pm. Fare 75¢, campus 40¢. **Women's Transit Authority,** 263-1700. Offers free, safe rides for women, 7pm-2am. Service prompt in an emergency; otherwise, expect a 1- to 2-hr. wait.

Taxi: Badger Cab, 256-5566. Ride-share system with $2 base fare, additional 60¢ per zone. Greyhound station to the UW campus about $2. **Union Cab,** 242-2000. From Greyhound station to UW campus $3-4, airport to campus $8-9.

Car Rental: Thrifty Car Rental, 332 W. Johnson St. (251-1717). $20 per day, 16¢ per mi., $180 per wk. Unlimited mi. Must be 21 with driver's license and personal major credit card.

Bike Rental: Budget Bicycle Center, 1202 Regent St. at Charter St. (251-8413). $7 per day, $21 per week. Free tour maps. Open Mon.-Fri. 10am-8pm, Sat. 10am-7pm, Sun. 1-5pm.

Help Lines: Rape Crisis, 251-7273. Open 24 hrs. **Gay Crisis Line,** 255-4297. Daily 9am-6pm.

Post Office: 3902 Milwaukee St. (246-1287). A 15-min. bus ride from downtown on the "Buckeye" bus. Open Mon. 8am-7pm, Tues.-Fri. 8am-6pm, Sat. 9:30am-1pm. 24-hr. pickup in the lobby. There is also a branch 2 blocks south of the capitol building, at 215 King Jr. Blvd. Open Mon.-Fri. 7:30am-5pm, Sat. 8:30am-noon. **ZIP code:** 53714.

Area Code: 608.

Most Madison sights lie on a narrow isthmus between large Lake Mendota on the northwest and small Lake Monona on the southeast. **State Street** is a pedestrian concourse that runs from the capitol toward the student union at the University of Wisconsin, the cultural center of the city. Madison is cyclist-oriented, complete with bike traffic lights and bike cops.

Accommodations and Camping

There are several reasonably-priced accommodations in Madison, but rooms are often booked, even on weeknights; try to make advance reservations. Inexpensive motels congregate almost exclusively off U.S. 12 near its intersection with I-90/94.

University of Wisconsin dorms: 6 hotel rooms in the **Memorial Union,** 800 Langdon (262-1583), overlooking Lake Mendota; 14 rooms at **Union South,** 227 N. Randall St. (263-2600), near the football stadium. Nice, comfortable, convenient. Singles $46. Doubles $50. **Short Course,** 1450 Linden Dr. (262-2270), has standard dorm rooms. Singles $15. Doubles $12 per person. Triples $10 per person. Dorms available mid-March to Sept. for those who have a legitimate reason to visit campus. Reserve by phone.

Lake Kegonsa State Park (873-9695), about 15 mi. SE of Madison off U.S. 51. Attractive tent sites $12.75 for non-WI residents (park admission $6, camping fee $6.75); sites $7.50 for WI residents.

Babcock County Park (246-3896), 5-10 min. from Kegonsa in the town of MacFarland, by Lake Waubesa. Not as big or beautiful as Kegonsa, but showers, flush toilets, and a nearby laundromat are a bonus. $12, electricity included. Open May-Oct.

Mendota County Park, County Rd. M (246-3896), 2 mi. northwest of Madison off University Ave., overlooking beautiful Lake Mendota. Sites $12.

Madison KOA (846-4528), 11 mi. north off I-94 (exit 126). More of an RV park, with no shade and lots of gravel. Tent sites $15 for 2, trailer $17; each with full hookup. $1.50 per additional person. Open April 15-Nov. 1.

Food and Nightlife

At lunchtime, carts selling fresh cherries, ethnic specialties like felafel, and blended fruit smoothies fill the square at the end of State St. In summer, buy inexpensive fruits, vegetables, breads, cakes, and cheeses at the open-air **Farmers Market,** Capitol Sq. concourse (Sat. 6:30am-2pm). The square surrounding the capitol offers a broad variety of restaurants, as does State St.

Sunprint Cafe, 638 State St. (255-1555) on the 2nd floor. Delicious salads and sandwiches $3.50-5. Great banana muffins 95¢. Doubles as a small gallery. Open Mon.-Thurs. 7am-10pm, Fri.-Sat. 7am-11pm, Sun. 9am-3pm.

El Charro, 600 Williamson St. (255-1828), in the Gateway. If you don't mind plastic plates and cutlery, the chow is authentic, tasty, and inexpensive. Breakfast $2.75, 4 chicken tamales $3. Open Mon.-Fri. 11am-9pm, Sat. 8am-9pm, Sun. 5-9pm.

Madison Bagel Company, 309 N. Henry St. (256-6688). Locals and visitors, especially east coasters, flock to this oasis of huge, delicious bagels. Eight kinds of bagels and as many flavors of cream cheese. Plain bagel 60¢, with cream cheese $1.25, bagel sandwiches $1.25-4.50. Open Mon.-Sat. 7am-midnight, Sun. 8am-midnight.

Ella's Kosher Deli and Ice Cream Parlor, 425 State St. (257-8611), halfway between the capitol and UW; also Lake St. location at 2902 E. Washington Ave. (241-5291). Voted Madison's best deli 1985-90. Sandwiches $2.25-4.50. Hot-fudge fantasies $3. Open Mon.-Wed. 8am-11pm, Thurs.-Sat. 8am-midnight, Sun. 9am-9pm.

Steep and Brew, 544 State St. (256-2902). One of the best of Madison's many tea houses, offering coffee in its various forms and flavors ($1.50), fruit drinks ($1.25-1.75), and tea (65¢). Outdoor seating. Open Mon.-Thurs. 8am-10pm, Fri. 8am-11:30pm, Sat. 9am-11:30pm, Sun. 11am-8pm.

Lulu's, 2524 University Ave. (233-2172). Amazing Middle Eastern food. Entrées $4-9. (Open Mon.-Sat. 11am-11pm.)

Madison's bars are smaller and less contrived than those in Milwaukee. However, while Milwaukee's brewing industry is nearly tapped, Madison's is rapidly fermenting, led by the local specialty Capital Garten Brau. For cheap specials (mixed drinks $2, tap beer $1) and a jock-ular clintele, patronize **Joe Hart's,** 704 University Ave. (251-9550), at Lake St. (Open Mon.-Thurs. 11:30am-12:45am, Fri. 11:30am-2am, Sat. 6pm-2am, Sun. 6pm-12:45am.) For more variety, walk from the capitol down King St. to Wilson, turn left, and two blocks down is the **Cardinal Bar,** 418 E. Wilson (251-0080). (Dance music plays Tues.-Sun. 9pm-2am. Bar opens at 5pm daily. Fri.-Sat. open until 2:30am. Cover $2 Fri.-Sat., $1 Wed.-Thurs.)

For a low-key, smoky atmosphere, go to the **602 Club,** at 602 University Ave. (256-5204). (Mixed drinks $1.75. Draft pints $1. Open Mon.-Wed. 11:30am-1am, Thurs. 11:30am-2am, Fri.-Sat. 11:30am-2:30am.) Live bands headline at the **Club de Wash Tavern,** 636 W. Washington Ave. at Francis St. (256-3302), in the Hotel Washington Building. Artists belt out blues, rock, and reggae nightly. ($3.50 pitchers. Open Sun.-Thurs. 10:30am-2am, Fri.-Sat. 10:30am-2:30am.) **Essenhaus,** 514 E. Wilson (255-4674), at Blair St., claims an authentic German experience, complete with live polka some nights. Servers in *lederhosen* and *dirndls* bring Boots o' Beer (about 2 liters each) for $8.50, pass 'em around, and as the beer drains, the remainder kicks up into the face of the drinker. (Open Tues.-Wed. and Sat.-Sun. 3pm-1am, Thurs. 11:30am-2am, Fri. 11:30am-1am.)

The **Memorial Union,** Wisconsin's student center, provides an endless supply of evening entertainment and daily activities, such as lectures and meetings. In addition to a movie theater, a stage, several bars, cafés, ice cream stands and delis, the Union provides information about getting around Madison and locating hot student spots. All events at the Union are free; the building is open 7am-midnight.

Sights and Activities

Madison is a city of lakes and parks where hiking, picnicking, biking, swimming, and sailing prove the order of the day. Many Madisonians turn out to feed the ducks at the free **Vilas Park Zoo,** at Drake and Grant St. (266-4732; open daily 9:30am-5pm; take the "Burr Oaks" bus). **Vilas Beach,** off Wingra Dr. on the south side of the zoo, accommodates windsurfers and blaring radios. **Wingra Park** (233-5332), off Monroe St., a 15-minute walk from the Vilas area on Knickerbocker Rd., sequesters a more sedate, family atmosphere. Rent windsurfing equipment ($9.50 per first hr., $6 per additional hr.) or canoes ($6 for first hr., $2.50 per additional hr.). The zoo, beach, and park are all on Wingra Lake, one mi. southwest of Capitol Square.

The Memorial Union is a pleasant place by day, where local musicians occasionally accompany those swimming off the dock. For people-watching, there are few better arenas on the planet. Leave yourself time and personal space for some sugar-loaded **Babcock Hall Ice Cream** (262-5959), made by UW's dairy service students (90¢). Work it off with a run from Memorial Union out to **Picnic Point.** The Union boathouse (262-7351) rents canoes for $3 per hour and $10 per day. (Open daily 11am-sunset.)

Take a free guided tour of the **state capitol** (266-0382) if you find yourself at a loss for excitement (tours every hr. Mon.-Sat. 9am-3pm, Sun. 1-3pm). The ascending triangles of the **Unitarian Church,** 900 University Bay Dr., south of downtown, are a fine example of Frank Lloyd Wright's work. (Take the "L line" or "G line" bus.)

Madison has more than its fair share of cultural activity, and the University seems to be a magnet for artists. Its **Elvehjem Museum of Art,** 800 University Ave. (263-2246), has furniture, graphic, and decorative arts from ancient and modern times. (Open Mon.-Sat. 9am-4:45pm, Sun. 11am-4:45pm. Free.) Over a dozen campus theater, music, and dance groups perform regularly. Check kiosks for campus events, as well as notices for Madison's pro theater groups and movie houses.

The **Madison Art Center,** 211 State St. (257-0158), features changing exhibits and workshops, and sometimes has performances in the lobby. Along with an outstanding modern art collection, it occasionally displays 19th-century Japanese prints. (Open Tues.-Thurs. 11am-5pm, Fri. 11am-9pm, Sat. 10am-5pm, Sun. 1-5pm. Donation requested; one paid show per year $3, seniors and students $2.) In the same building, the **Civic Center** (266-9055) is the home of Madison's own repertory company and features dance, musical, and theatrical performances year-round. (Tickets $8-12. Box office open Mon.-Fri. 11am-5:30pm, Sat. 9am-1pm. Take the "Mendota" or "A West" bus.) At the **Coliseum,** 1881 Exposition Center Mall E. (267-3999), more renowned musical groups perform. (Tickets $15-18. Box office open Mon.-Fri. 9am-5pm.) During the school year, the **University Theater,** Vilas Hall, 821 University Ave. (262-1500), present performances of classical music for about $10. For even less expensive shows, don't miss the summer **Concert on the Square** series, which plays nightly next to the capitol. For information, call 266-6033.

Milwaukee

Milwaukee opened for settlement in 1835, and it quickly attracted Irish and German immigrants. Together they gave the city its reputation for *gemutlich-keit*—hospitality. Recent immigrants, including Italians, Poles, and Hispanics, seem to have assimilated the city's generosity. Milwaukee's ethnic communities alternate throwing city-wide parties every weekend during the summer. The self-proclaimed "City of Fabulous Festivals" has top-notch museums, quality arts organizations, and plenty of beer, baklava, and bagpipes.

Practical Information

Emergency: 911

Greater Milwaukee Convention and Visitors Bureau, 510 W. Kilbourne (273-3950 or 800-231-0903), downtown. Open Mon.-Fri. 8am-6pm. Also at the airport (open Mon.-Fri. 7am-9:30pm, Sat. 10am-6pm, Sun. 1-9:30pm) and Grand Avenue Mall at 3rd St. (open Mon.-Fri. 10am-8pm, Sat. 10am-6pm, Sun. noon-5pm). Pick up a copy of *The Greater Milwaukee Dining and Visitors Guide.* **Fun Line** (799-1177) and **Rockline** (276-7625) give local entertainment information. Both open 24 hrs.

Travelers Aid: At the airport (747-5245). Open daily 9am-9pm.

Amtrak: 433 W. St. Paul Ave. (800-872-7245), at 5th St. 3 blocks from the bus terminal. To Chicago ($14.50). Open Mon.-Fri. 6am-9pm, Sat.-Sun. 7:30am-9pm.

Buses: Greyhound, 606 N. 7th St. (272-8900), off W. Michigan St. downtown. Open daily 5am-11:30pm. To Chicago ($13.50) and Madison ($7). **Wisconsin Coach,** in the Greyhound terminal (542-8861). Service to outlying areas of Wisconsin. Open daily 6am-9pm. **Badger Bus** (276-7490) is across the street. To Madison (6 per day, $8).

Public Transport: Milwaukee County Transit System, 1942 N. 17th St. (344-6711). Efficient service in the metro area. Most lines run 5:30am to the wee hours. $1.25, seniors 75¢ with Medicare card.

Car Rental: Payless Car Rental, 4939 S. Howell (482-0300), across from Mitchell Airport. $27 per day with unlimited mileage. $10 collision insurance. Open Mon.-Fri. 7am-9pm, Sat. 9am-5pm, Sun. noon-9pm. Must be 21 with liability insurance and major credit card.

Taxi: City Veteran Taxi, 643-5522 or 643-1212. Base rate $1.25, plus $1.25 per mi.

Auto Transport Company: Auto Driveaway Co., 9039 W. National Ave. (962-0008 or 327-5252), in West Alice. Open Mon.-Fri. 9am-5pm, Sat. 9am-noon. Must be 21 with good driving record.

Help Lines: Crisis Intervention Center, 257-7222. Open 24 hrs. **Rape Crisis Line,** 547-4600 or 542-3828. **Gay People's Union Hotline,** 562-7010.

Post Office: 345 W. St. Paul Ave. (291-2450), south along 4th Ave. from downtown, next to the Amtrak station. Open Mon.-Fri. 7:30am-6pm. **ZIP code:** 53201.

Area Code: 414.

Milwaukee's downtown area is a few mi. back from the lakeshore. The **Milwaukee River** flows north-south just east of downtown, dividing streets east-west and breaking the city's grid pattern.

Accommodations and Camping

Sleeping rarely comes cheap in downtown Milwaukee, but there are two attractive hostels nearby, as well as the convenient University of Wisconsin dorms.

Red Barn Hostel (AYH), 6750 W. Loomis Rd. (529-3299), 13 mi. SW of downtown via Rte. 894, exit Loomis. Take bus #10 or 30 west on Wisconsin Ave., get off at 35th St., and take the #35 south to the Loomis and Ramsey intersection; cross over to the Pick and Save store and walk ¾ mi. Rustic, slightly dark rooms in an enormous, red barn. Friendly houseparents. Members only, $6. Open May-Oct.

University of Wisconsin at Milwaukee (UWM): Sandburg Halls, 3400 N. Maryland Ave. (229-4065). Take bus #30 north to Hartford St. and look for the tall stone building. Private rooms part of suites. Laundry, cafeteria available. Singles with shared bath $19. Doubles $26. Open May 31-Aug. 15. Reservations required.

Halter Home Hostel (AYH), 2956 N. 77th St. (258-7692), 4 mi. west of downtown. Take bus #57 to 76th and Center St. In a quiet, residential neighborhood. Closer of the two hostels, but also smaller: 4 beds in 2 comfortable rooms. Members only, $10.

Hotel Wisconsin, 720 N. 3rd St. (271-4900), across from the Grand Avenue Mall. 250 old but clean rooms at a convenient downtown location. Singles $46. Doubles $56. Key ($3), phone ($2) deposits.

Motel 6, 5037 S. Howell Ave. (482-4414), near the airport. Take bus #80 southbound at the corner of 6th and Wisconsin; get off at Edgerton and Howell. Outdoor pool. Singles $27. Doubles $33. Fills quickly; consider reservations.

State Fairgrounds, 257-8844; take Madison exit off I-94 west, then 84th St. No tents, only RVs. Often noisy. Full for the State Fair in early Aug. Sites $14.

Country View Campgrounds, S. Craig Rd. (662-3654), 4 mi. west of Big Bend, a 40-min. drive southwest. Take Rte. 15, exit at Hwy. F, turn left to reach Big Bend. Tent sites for 2 $15, full hookup $17. $7.50 per additional adult, $1 per child.

Food

Milwaukee does not cater to dainty eaters—prices are small and portions big. The bohemian **Brady Street** area to the north has many Italian restaurants, and the **South Side** is heavily Polish. Many students and young professionals have lunch on the **Grand Avenue Mall's** third floor, a huge *Speisegarten* ("meal garden") that cultivates reasonable ethnic and fast food places. **East Side** eateries are a little more cosmopolitan, often serving cappuccino in place of *kielbasa*. The UWM cafeteria, on the main floor of the student union, offers good, cheap chow.

Webster's Bookstore and Cafe, 2551 Downer Ave. (332-1719), at Webster Place on the East Side. Not yet in the dictionary, but fast becoming a local institution. French-American café for would-be poets. Try the *croque monsieur* (ham 'n' cheese croissant; $5), or the soufflé pizza ($5). Outdoor seating, great bookstore, and friendly staff. Open daily 8am-midnight.)

Abu's Jerusalem of the Gold, 1978 N. Farwell (277-0485), at Lafayette on the East Side. A wall-inscribed poem dedicated to Abu, exotic tapestries, and plenty of kitsch adorn this tiny corner restaurant. Try the rosewater lemonade. Plenty of veggie entrees, including felafel sandwich ($2.40). Open Mon.-Thurs. 11:30am-9pm, Fri. 11:30am-2am, Sat. 11:30am-4am, Sun. 1:30-9pm.

Albanese's, 701 E. Keefe Ave. (964-7270), 3 mi. north of downtown, 3 blocks west of Humboldt. Generous portions of homemade Italian food (pasta dishes $5.25-6.25). Open Mon.-Thurs. 4-10pm, Fri. 11:30am-1pm and 5-11pm, Sat. 5-11pm.

Three Brothers, 2414 St. Clair St. (481-7530), #15 bus to Conway and walk 4 blocks east. One of the best known of Milwaukee's famed Serbian restaurants, this family-owned business serves remarkable dinners ($10-13). Open Tues.-Thurs. 5-10pm, Fri.-Sat. 4-11pm, Sun. 4-10pm. Reservations recommended.

Sights

Historic Milwaukee, Inc., P.O. Box 2132 (277-7795), offers tours (usually one per day) focusing on ethnic heritage, original settlements, and architecture ($2-3). Ask about Milwaukee's many beautiful churches, including **St. Josaphat's Basilica,** 2336 S. 6th St. (645-5623), a turn-of-the-century landmark with a dome larger than the Taj Mahal's. Make phone arrangements to see the church, since it's usually locked.

Milwaukee is graced by several excellent museums. The **Woodland Book Center,** 720 E. Locust (263-5001) features a large selection of small press publications. The center also sponsors poetry readings, lectures, and gallery shows that attract local and national artists. (Open Tues.-Fri. noon-8pm, Sat.-Sun. noon-5pm.) The **Milwaukee Public Museum,** 800 W. Wells St. (278-2702), at N. 8th St., allows visitors to walk through incredibly realistic exhibits of the streets of Old Milwaukee and a European village, complete with cobblestones and two-story shops. Other terrific exhibits focus on Native American settlements and North American wildlife. (Open Mon. noon-8pm, Tues.-Sun. 9am-5pm. $4, under 18 $2.) The lakefront **Milwaukee Art Museum,** in the War Memorial Building, 750 N. Lincoln Memorial Dr. (271-9508), houses Haitian art, 19th-century German art, and U.S. sculpture and paintings, including two of Warhol's soup cans. (Open Tues.-Wed. and Fri.-Sat. 10am-5pm, Thurs. noon-9pm, Sun. noon-5pm. $3, seniors, students, and disabled people $1.50.) Visit the **Villa Terrace,** 2220 N. Terrace Ave. (271-3656), an Italian-style villa on the East Side that's now a decorative arts museum. (Open Wed.-Sun. 1-5pm. $2.) Also try the large, picturesque **Bradley Sculpture Garden,** 2145 Brown Deer Rd. (271-9509, 276-6840 to schedule a tour; reservations only, 2 weeks in advance; admission with scheduled tour group $2.50, students $1.50, seniors and kids $1). The **Charles Allis Art Museum,** 1801 N. Prospect Ave. (278-8295), at Royall Ave., is an English Tudor mansion with a fine collection of Chinese, Japanese, Korean, Persian, Greek, and Roman artifacts, as well as U.S. and European furniture. (Open Wed. 1-5pm and 7-9pm, Thurs.-Sun. 1-5pm. $2. Take bus #30.)

The **Mitchell Park Conservatory,** 524 S. Layton Blvd. (649-9800), at 27th St., better known as "The Domes," recreates a desert, a rain forest, and seasonal displays in a series of three seven-story conical glass domes. (Open daily 9am-5pm. $2.50, seniors, kids and disabled $1.25. Take bus #27.) Four mi. west, you'll find the **Milwaukee County Zoo,** 10001 W. Bluemound Rd. (771-3040), where zebras and cheetahs roam together in the only prey-predator exhibit in the U.S. Also look for the elegant, misunderstood black rhinos and the trumpeter swans. (Open Mon.-

Sat. 9am-5pm, Sun. 9am-6pm; shorter hours in winter. $6, under 12 $4. Parking $4. Take bus #10.)

Across the river from the PAC (see Events below), the stone and ivy **Milwaukee County Historical Center,** 910 N. 3rd St. (273-8288), details the early years of the city with many artifacts, photographs, documents, and displays. (Open Mon.-Fri. 9:30am-5pm, Sat. 10am-5pm, Sun. 1-5pm. Free.)

Although beer made Milwaukee famous, touring a brewery proves a sobering experience. The **Miller Brewery,** 4251 W. State St. (931-BEER, which if you're too drunk to interpret means 931-2337), offers free one-hour tours with free samples (3 tours per hr. Mon.-Sat. 10am-3:30pm. Must be 21).

Events and Entertainment

The Milwaukee lakefront throws a city-wide party or ethnic festival almost every summer weekend. One of the best is the **Summerfest** (273-3378), held over 11 days in late June and early July, fronting a potpourri of musical performances, culinary specialties from 30 restaurants, and an arts and crafts marketplace. Tots should enjoy the circus watershow and children's theater. ($6, $5 in advance.) The **Rainbow Summer** (273-7206) is a series of free lunchtime concerts throughout the summer, featuring jazz, bluegrass and country music. Concerts are held weekdays from noon to 1:15pm in the Peck Pavilion at the Performing Arts Center (see below). Milwaukeeans line the streets for **The Great Circus Parade** (273-7877) in mid-July, an authentic re-creation of turn-of-the-century processions, with trained animals, daredevils, costumed performers, and 75 original wagons. (Call their office for information on special weekend packages at local hotels and motels during the parade.) In early August the **Wisconsin State Fair** (257-8800) rolls into town, toting big-name entertainment, 12 stages, exhibits, contests, rides, fireworks, and, of course, a pie-baking contest. ($5, under 11 free.) For updates on upcoming fairs and events, call 789-5000 and punch in 2116 when asked.

For entertainment on a strict budget, Milwaukee's colleges and universities satisfy with films, concerts, lectures, theater, and exhibits. Call the **Marquette University Information Center** (288-7250; open Mon.-Fri. 9am-1pm, closed during summer) or the **University of Wisconsin-Milwaukee Union** (229-4825; open Mon.-Thurs. 7am-10pm, Fri.-Sat. 7am-11pm, Sun. 8am-10pm). For quality arts performances, visit the modern white stone **Performing Art Center (PAC),** 929 N. Water St. (800-472-4458), across the river from Père Marquette Park. The PAC hosts the Milwaukee Symphony Orchestra, First Stage Milwaukee, Ballet Company, and the Florentine Opera Company. (Tickets $10-30.) The **Skylight Comic Opera,** 813 N. Jefferson (271-8815), at E. Wells St., is well known for its contemporary and classic opera performances. (Box office open Mon.-Fri. noon-6pm and 1 hr. before shows. Tickets $20-30, seniors $2 discount, students ½-price day of show.) For information about events in the Milwaukee area, call **Milwaukee Tix** (271-3335).

Nightlife

If you've got the time, Milwaukee has the bars. By some estimates, there are over 6,000 of them—about one for every 100 Milwaukeans. Downtown bars are more accessible for tourists, but more expensive. For lower prices and less hype, head east to the campus area. (Downtown pitchers $6, mixed drinks $2-2.50; campus area pitchers $5, mixed drinks $2.)

Downtown, come in from the cold to **Safehouse,** 779 N. Front St. (271-2007). Step through a bookcase passage and enter a bizarre world of spy hideouts, James Bond music, and a phone booth with 90 sound effects. A brass plate labeled "International Exports, Ltd." marks the entrance. Draft beer costs $1.50, simple dinners $7-12. (Open Mon.-Sat. 11:30am-2am, Sun. 5pm-2am. Cover $1-2.) For British-style drinking fun, dip into **John Hawk's Pub,** 607 N. Broadway (964-9729), on the National Register of Historic Places. Beer $1.75. (Open daily 11am-2am, live jazz Fri.-Sat. at 9:30pm.) The college crowd dances downtown to a selection of top-

40 or progressive tunes at **Bermudas,** 500 N. Water St. (765-0891), at Clybourn, one block from Broadway. (Open Wed. 8pm-12:30am, Thurs.-Sat. 8pm-2am. Teen night Wed.; cover $5, Thurs.-Sat. $2.)

On the East Side, North Ave. has a string of campus bars: **Von Trier's,** 2235 N. Farwell (272-1775), at North, is the nicest. Don't miss the ceiling mural of the town of Trier. No pitchers—strictly bottled imports (average $3.50 per bottle) in the lavish German interior or on the large outdoor patio. (Open Mon.-Fri. 4pm-2am, Sat.-Sun. 4pm-2:30am.) **Hooligan's,** a block or so south at 2017 North Ave. (273-5230), is smaller, louder, and rowdier. (Open daily 11am-2:30am. Pitchers $5. Live music Sept.-June on Mon. at 9:30pm. Cover $2-4.) A few blocks down at **RC's,** 1530 E. North Ave. (273-1100), next to McDonald's, you can have a close encounter of the preppy kind. (Pitchers $5.) **Judge's Irish Pub,** 1431 E. North Ave. (224-0605), across the street, attracts a more eclectic clientele and has a tented beer garden (pitchers $5). For good food and drink, and a widely renowned comedy show, try **Kalt's,** 2856 N. Oakland (332-6323) at Locust, where **Comedy Sportz** (962-8888) entertains crowds. (Shows Thurs.-Sun. at 7:30pm, additional show Fri.-Sat. at 10pm. Bar open Sun.-Thurs. 4pm-midnight, Fri.-Sat. 4pm-2am.)

WYOMING

America's least-populated state, Wyoming is yet another natural Western wonderland, replete with expansive vistas and inexpensive adventure. It has, from a tourist's standpoint, everything a state in the Mountain Time Zone is supposed to have: seasonal festivals (such as Frontier Days); national parks (Yellowstone and Grand Teton); spectacular mountain sub-ranges (the Bighorns and the Winds); Indian place names; an anomalous, non-Western den of commercialism and chic (Jackson); description-defying panoramas everywhere you go; and, of course, plenty of beer. And cattle.

Practical Information

Capital: Cheyenne.

Wyoming Travel Commission, I-25 and College Dr. at Etcheparc Circle, Cheyenne 82002 (777-7777 or 800-225-5996). If you plan to camp, write for their free *Wyoming Vacation Guide.* **Wyoming Recreation Commission,** Cheyenne 82002 (777-7695). Information on facilities in Wyoming's 10 state parks. Open Mon.-Fri. 8am-5pm. **Game and Fish Department,** 5400 Bishop Blvd., Cheyenne 82002 (777-7735). Open Mon.-Fri. 8am-5pm. **Wyoming Recreation Hotline,** (307-777-6503).

Time Zone: Mountain (2 hr. behind Eastern). **Postal Abbreviation:** WY

Bighorn Mountains

The Bighorns erupt from the hilly pastureland of northern Wyoming, a dramatic backdrop to the grazing cattle and sprawling ranch houses at their feet. Here in the 1860s, violent clashes occurred between the Sioux, defending their traditional hunting grounds, and incoming settlers. Cavalry posts such as **Fort Phil Kearny,** on U.S. 87 between Buffalo and Sheridan, could do little to protect the settlers. The war reached a climax at the **Fetterman Massacre,** in which several hundred Sioux warriors wiped out Lt. Col. Fetterman's patrol. Although the massacre forced settlers out of the Bighorns, within 20 years, settlers made the Bighorns permanent cattle country.

For sheer solitude, you can't beat the Bighorns' **Cloud Peak Wilderness.** To get to **Cloud Peak,** a 13,175-ft. summit in the range, most hikers enter at **Painted Rock Creek,** accessible from the town of Tensleep, 70 mi. west of Buffalo on the western slope. The most convenient access to the wilderness area, though, is from the trailheads near U.S. 16, 25 mi. west of Buffalo. From the **Hunter Corrals** trailhead, move to beautiful **Mistymoon Lake,** an ideal base for strikes at the high peaks beyond. You can also enter the wilderness area from U.S. 14 out of Sheridan in the north.

Campgrounds fill the forest, and all sites cost $6 per night. Near the Buffalo entrance **Lost Cabin Middle Fork** and **Crazy Woman** boast magnificent scenery, as do **Cabin Creek** and **Porcupine** campgrounds near Sheridan. If you choose not to venture into the mountains, you can spend the night free just off Coffeen St. in Sheridan's grassy **Washington Park.**

Most travelers will want to use either Buffalo or Sheridan as a base town from which to explore the mountains. The **Mountain View Motel** (684-2881) is by far the most appealing of Buffalo's cheap lodgings. Pine cabins with TV, A/C, and/or heating complement the assiduous service. (Singles $23. Doubles $26.) Stock up on sandwiches at the **Breadboard,** 57 S. Main St. (684-2318), where a large "Freight Train" (roast beef and turkey with all the toppings) costs $3.20. (Open Mon.-Sat. 11am-8pm.)

If you get bored with the outdoors, a visit to the **Jim Gatchell Museum of the West,** 10 Fort St. (684-9331), or the museum and outdoor exhibits at the former site of Fort Phil Kearny (on U.S. 97 between Buffalo and Sheridan; open daily 8am-6pm; Oct. 16-May 14 Sat.-Sun. 1-5pm) may stave off malaise. Both testify to the tangled relations between local Native Americans and the encroaching pioneers.

The **Buffalo Chamber of Commerce** informs at 55 N. Main St. (684-5544), eight blocks south of the bus station. (Open Mon.-Fri. 9am-5pm.) In the summer, you can also visit the Buffalo summer information center, 2 mi. east on Hwy. 16. (Open July-Aug. daily 10am-7pm; June and Sept. daily 11am-6pm.) The **U.S. Forest Service Offices,** at 300 Spruce St. (684-7981), will answer your questions about the Buffalo District in the Bighorns, and sell you a road and trail map of the area ($2). (Open Mon.-Fri. 8am-4:30pm.) At **Alabam's,** 421 Fort St. (684-7452), you can buy topographical maps ($2.50) as well as hunting, fishing, or camping supplies. (Open daily 6am-9:30pm; off-season daily 6am-8pm.)

The town of **Sheridan,** 30 mi. to the north of Buffalo, escaped most of the military activity of the 1860s. But Sheridan has its own claim to fame: Buffalo Bill Cody used to sit on the porch of the once luxurious **Sheridan Inn,** at 5th and Broadway, as he interviewed cowboy hopefuls for his *Wild West Show.* The inn has recently hit hard times, and may soon close. Motels, many with budget rates, line the town's two main drags, Coffeen Ave. and Main St. Try the **Parkway Motel** (674-7259), which offers large, cheerfully decorated singles ($20) and doubles ($24).

Sheridan's **U.S. Forest Service Office,** 1969 S. Sheridan Ave. (672-0751), offers maps of the Bighorns ($3), along with numerous pamphlets on how to navigate them safely. The **Sheridan Chamber of Commerce,** 5th St. at I-90 (672-2485), can also provide information on the National Forest, as well as other useful tips for lodging and activities in Sheridan. (Open daily 8am-8pm.)

Nestled at the junction of I-90 (east to the Black Hills area and north to Billings, MT) and I-25 (south to Casper, Cheyenne, and Denver), **Buffalo** is easy to reach. **Powder River Transportation** serves Buffalo from a terminal at the **Frontier Inn,** 800 N. Main St. (684-5426), where twice daily you can catch a bus north to Sheridan ($9) and Billings ($33), or south to Cheyenne ($33). Buffalo, as the crossroads of north-central Wyoming, remains a good place for hitchhikers to catch rides to the southern cities of Casper and Cheyenne. Getting a lift on the freeway in Sheridan is more difficult. But never fear—**Powder River buses** run from the depot at the **Rancher Motel,** 1552 Coffeen Ave. (674-6188), to: Billings (2 per day, $29); Buffalo (2 per day, $9); and Cheyenne (2 per day, $48). (Station open Mon.-Fri. 8am-5am; Sat. 9am-noon, 4-5:30pm, 9:30-11pm, 2:30-5:30am; Sun. 10am-noon, 4-5:30pm, 9:30-11pm, 2:30-5:30am.)

The **time zone** for both Sheridan and Buffalo is Mountain (2 hr. behind Eastern). The **ZIP code** for Buffalo is 82834, and for Sheridan 82801. The **area code** for the Bighorns is 307.

Cheyenne

Cheyenne is named after the Native American tribe that once roamed its wilderness both before and under Mexican flag. By the 1860s, when the Union Pacific Railroad reached the end of the line in Cheyenne, Wyoming's capital had become known as "Hell on Wheels." The red dust and general horsiness of the Wild West have faded in Cheyenne, but the capital remains stately and grand by day; at night, Cheyenne swings around its few weathered wood saloons, a heck on wheels harrowed extravagantly during Frontier Days.

Practical Information

Emergency: 911.

Visitor Information: Cheyenne Area Convention and Visitors' Bureau, 309 W. 16th St. (778-3133; 800-426-5009 outside WY), just west of Capitol Ave. Extensive accommodations and restaurant listings. Open Mon.-Fri. 8am-6pm. The **Howdy Wagon,** an old chuck wagon next door, is filled with brochures. Open summer Sat.-Sun. 10am-3pm.

Cheyenne Street Railway: (778-1401). 2-hr. trolley tours of Cheyenne leaving in summer Mon.-Sat. 10am and 1pm, Sun. at 1pm. Tickets $5, seniors $4.50, children $2.50 from the convention and visitors' bureau. Tours depart from 16th and Capitol Ave.

Greyhound, 1503 Capitol Ave. (634-7744), at 15th St. Three buses daily to: Salt Lake City (9 hr., $83); Chicago ($119); Laramie ($8); Rock Springs ($31); Denver ($19). **Powder River Transportation,** in the Greyhound terminal (635-1327). Buses south to Rapid City twice daily ($56); north to Casper ($30) and Billings ($88) twice daily. Greyhound passes honored.

Taxi: Ace Cab, 637-4747. $1.20 per mi.

Help Line: Rape Crisis, 637-7233. Open 24 hrs.

Post Office: 2120 Capitol Ave. (772-6580), 6 blocks north of the bus station. The most awesome post office in the free world. Open Mon.-Fri. 8am-5pm, Sat. 8am-noon. General Delivery open Mon.-Sat. from 6:30am. **ZIP code:** 82001.

Area Code: 307.

Cheyenne's downtown area is small and manageable. Central, Capitol, and Carey Avenues form a grid with 16th-19th Streets, which encompasses most of the downtown sights and accommodations. 16th St. is part of I-80; it intersects I-25/84 on the western edge of town. Denver lies 90 mi. south on I-25.

Accommodations, Camping, and Food

It's not hard to land a cheap room here among the lariats, plains, and pioneers, unless your visit coincides with Frontier Days, held the last full week of July, when rates almost double (see Sights and Entertainment). Many budget motels line **Lincolnway** (U.S. 30), 1 mi. east down 16th St. The cheapest hotel in Cheyenne is the old **Pioneer Hotel,** 208 W. 17th St. (634-3010), two blocks north of the bus station. High-ceilinged, like most everything in Cheyenne, the 80 rooms are in decent-to-good shape and feature elaborate Western decor, with a second-floor lobby and communal kitchen. (Singles $14, with private bath $19. Doubles $22-30.) Right up the street, the **Plains Hotel,** 1600 Central Ave. (638-3311), offers oversized rooms with marble sinks, HBO, and phones in a grand-lobbied, Western setting. An all-hours coffee shop and a saloon make it the center of town activity. (Singles $29. Doubles $35.) South of town, on the other side of the Union Pacific Railroad tracks, is the **Lariat Motel,** 600 Central Ave. (635-8439) next to the Los Amigos restaurant. The smiling, laid-back manager maintains simple, dark rooms in an aqua-and-adobe colored, low-slung building that looks like it belongs south of the border. (Singles $23. Doubles $27.)

For campers, spots are plentiful (excepting Frontier Days) at the **Restway Travel Park,** 4212 Whitney Rd. (634-3811), 1½ mi. east of town. (Sites $12.50, with electricity and water $13.50, full hookup $14.50; prices rise slightly in July. Each pet

$1 per night.) You might also try **Curt Gowdy State Park,** 1319 Hynds Lodge Rd., (632-7946) 23 mi. west of Cheyenne on Rte. 210, indeed named after the ex-jock and sportscaster, Gowdy the park has shade, scenery, fishing, hiking, and an archery range, as well as land for horseback riding—BYO horse. (Sites $4.)

Cheyenne is basically a meat 'n' potatoes place, but there are a few cheap, good ethnic eateries sprinkled around downtown. Here, the price difference between the humble café and posh restaurant can be a mere $4-6. For cow-and-tuber type cuisine, try the **Driftwood Café,** 200 E. 18th St., where a Cheyenne burger costs $3.25. (Open Mon.-Fri. 7am-4pm.) **Ruthie's Sub Shoppe,** 1651 Carey Ave., a few doors down from the Pioneer Hotel, has the best tuna salad sandwiches around ($2.25), and morning donuts. (Open Mon.-Fri. 6am-5pm, Sat. 7am-3:30pm.) Next door to the Lariat Motel, **Los Amigos,** 620 Central Ave., serves burritos ($1.75-4) and humongous, friendly dinners (from $7). You might want to go with a half-order (60% of the price), or swing by for the $4 lunch specials. (Open Mon.-Sat. 11am-8:30pm.) Lunch buffets are available at the **Twin Dragon Chinese Restaurant,** 1809 Carey Ave. (637-6622) weekdays 11am-2pm ($4.75). Vegetarian egg rolls just $1.80; regular dinners from $5.50. (Open Mon.-Sat. 11am-10pm, Sun. noon-9pm.)

When the urge to guzzle consumes you, the aptly named **D.T.'s Liquor and Lounge,** 2121 Lincolnway, will help quench your thirst. Look for a pink elephant above the sign; if you are already seeing two, move on. (Open daily 6am-11pm.) The **Cheyenne Club,** 1617 Capitol Ave. (635-7777), is a spacious good-time country nightspot, hosting live bands nightly at 8:30pm. You must be 19 to enter and 21 to drink. (Open Mon.-Thurs. and Sat. 8:30pm-2am, Fri. 5pm-2am. Cover $1.)

Sights and Entertainment

If you're within 500 mi. of Cheyenne between July 21 and 30, make every possible effort to attend the **Cheyenne Frontier Days,** nine days of non-stop Western hoopla. The town doubles in size as anyone worth a grain of Western salt comes to see the world's oldest and largest rodeo competition and partake of the free pancake breakfasts (every other day in the parking lot across from the chamber of commerce), parades, and square dances. Most remain inebriated for the better part of the week. Reserve accommodations in advance or camp nearby. For information, contact Cheyenne Frontier Days, P.O. Box 2477, Cheyenne 82003 (800-227-6336); open Mon.-Fri. 8am-5pm).

If you miss Frontier Days, don't despair; Old West events are a major source of Cheyenne entertainment. Throughout June and July the Cheyenne Gunslingers perform a mock **Old Cheyenne Gunfight,** at W. 16th and Carey St., to prove that justice reigns in Wyoming territory. (Shows Mon.-Fri. at 6pm, Sat. at noon. Free.) The **Cheyenne Frontier Days Old West Museum** (778-7290), in **Frontier Park** at 8th and Carey St., is a half-hour walk north down Carey St. The museum chronicles the rodeo's history from 1897 to the present, housing an "Old West" saloon and an extensive collection of Oglala Sioux clothing and artifacts. (Open Mon.-Sat. 8am-7pm, Sun. 10am-6pm; off-season daily 11am-5pm. Admission $2, seniors $1, under 12 free, families $5.)

The **Wyoming State Museum,** 2301 Central Ave. (777-7024), presents an especially digestible history of Wyoming's cowboys, sheepherders, and suffragists, along with exhibits on the Oglala, Cheyenne, and Shoshone who preceded them. (Open Mon.-Fri. 8:30am-5pm, Sat. 9am-4pm, Sun. noon-4pm; off-season closed Sun. Free.) The **Wyoming State Capitol Building,** at the base of Capitol Ave. on 24th St. (777-7220), shows off its stained glass windows and yellowed photographs to tour groups trekking through. (Open Mon.-Fri. 8am-4:30pm. Summer tours every 15 min.)

This oversized cowtown rolls up the streets at night; except for a few bars, the downtown goes to sleep at 5pm. One delightful exception is the **Old Fashioned Melodrama,** playing at the **Old Atlas Theater** (638-6543 mornings, 635-0199 aft. and eve.), an old vaudeville house at 211 W. 16th St., between Capitol and Carey Ave. (Shows July-late Aug. Wed.-Sat. 7pm, Fri.-Sat. 9:15pm. Tickets $6.50, under

12 $4. Wed $1 off.) To find out about beauty pageants and other theatrical events contact the **Cheyenne Civic Center,** 510 W. 20th St. (637-6363; box office open Mon.-Fri. 11am-5:30pm).

Eastern Wyoming: Laramie, Saratoga, and Environmental Environs

As you travel west from Cheyenne into the **Pole Mountain** division of Medicine Bow National Forest, the gentle prairie gives way to hilly forests and parks that have yet to lure tourists in any great numbers. **Happy Jack Road** (Rte. 210), which may or may not pre-date the Who song, parallels I-80 for a scenic 38 mi. from Cheyenne to Laramie, home of the University of Wyoming. **Curt Gowdy State Park,** midway between the two cities, is a prime hiking area with beautiful lakes and great fishing (see Cheyenne Accommodations). The **Vedauwoo** ("earthbound spirits," pronounced vee-dah-voo) **National Park,** 20 mi. west of Cheyenne off I-80, offers some of the finest rock climbing in the world (entrance fee $2). Call the Forest Service (745-8971) for further info.

Greyhound can get you from Cheyenne to the **Laramie Terminal,** 1358 N. 2nd St. (742-0896; 3 per day, $8.50; terminal open Mon.-Fri. 8:30am-5:30pm, Sat. 9am-1pm). Named after a French fur trapper, **Laramie** makes a rather interesting rest stop if you arrive during June, when the University of Wyoming campus hosts a **Western Arts Music Festival,** or during the second full week of July when the town parties Western style with **Jubilee Days.** The **Laramie Chamber of Commerce,** 3rd and Park St. (745-7339), has information on all events. (Open daily 9am-6pm; off-season daily 8am-5pm.) The **UW Department of Theater and Dance,** P.O. Box 3951, University Station, Laramie 82071, can provide information on campus and cultural events. The box office, in the lobby of the Fine Arts building (766-3212), is open the week before a production daily from noon-4pm.

Stay at the **Thunderbird Motel,** 1369 N. 3rd St. (745-4871), twp blocks south of the bus station. Cruise into clean, spacious rooms with A/C and cable TV. (Singles $25. Doubles $29.)

The **North Platte River Valley** and its central town, **Saratoga,** are even better kept secrets than Medicine Bow. Route 130 from Laramie west to Saratoga is a stunning, summer-only passage directly up and over the 11,000-ft. **Snowy Range Pass** (742-8981; 800-442-8321 in southeastern WY). This route over the mountains will save you 40 mi. Just before the summit, you'll pass through **Centennial,** a tiny ski resort town legendary for its lost gold mine. Not far from Centennial, you'll come upon **Saratoga,** still unsullied by sweaty-palmed tourists. One hundred mi. from Laramie and only 20 mi. south of I-80 (exit 235), Saratoga draws crowds with the delightful **Hobo Hot Springs,** a natural 110°F mineral water source that is directed into a large sand-bottomed pool. If you get too hot, simply climb over the low wall into the rejuvenating North Platte River.

Wyoming has designated the 70-mi. stretch of the **North Platte River** that connects Saratoga to Colorado's norther border a "blue ribbon" trout stream. Contact the **Game and Fish Department,** in Medicine Bow (379-2337), or inquire at the well-equipped **Saratoga-Platte Valley Chamber of Commerce,** 102 W. Bridge St. (326-8855). **Great Rocky Mountain Outfitters,** 216 E. Walnut St. (326-8750), offers fun-filled float trips (half-day $20, full day $40). The chamber of commerce has a more extensive list of tour companies operating similar expeditions on the North Platte, as well as a list of local accommodations. (Open June-Sept. Mon.-Fri. 9am-6pm; Oct.-May Mon.-Fri. 9am-5pm.)

Should your creek run dry, try **Wally's Pizza,** 110 E. Bridge St. (326-8472), the only budget option in town and a culinary rarity in this part of Wyoming. It serves a "vegetarian special" (cheeses, avocado, mushroom, cucumber, and sprouts) and huge sandwiches on fresh-baked bread ($4.50) in a cozy setting. (Open Mon.-Sat. 11am-10pm, Sun. noon-9pm.)

The best place to stay in Saratoga is the **Wolf Hotel,** 101 E. Bridge St. (326-5525), on WY Rte. 130 at the town's only main corner. This charming, renovated building is a registered national historic landmark. Rooms have most basic amenities except telephones. (Singles with bath $18, doubles with bath $25.) The saloon and dining rooms downstairs evoke the 1890s. Reservations are recommended for busy summer weekends. The **Silver Moon Motel,** 412 E. Bridge St. (326-5974), is near the river. Clean rooms come with TV. (Singles $24. Doubles $26.)

Medicine Bow National Forest is a camper's paradise. Of the over 30 campgrounds, about half are free; all have toilets and drinking water. The closest ones to Saratoga are: **Jack Creek Campground,** 20 mi. west on Rte. 500, then 8 mi. south on a forest service road (open mid-June to Oct., sites $5); **Lincoln Park Campground,** 21 mi. southeast on Rte. 130, then 4 mi. north on a forest service road (open mid-May to Sept., sites $5); and **South Brush Creek,** 2 mi. beyond Lincoln Park (open mid-May to Sept., sites $5). Other sites cluster around Centennial and Laramie. Call the **ranger station** (326-5258) for more information.

The **Sierra Madre Range,** on the western slope of the North Platte Watershed, boasts some of the best camping and hiking in the forest. The town of **Encampment,** just 40 mi. south of I-80 on Rte. 230, is a good base for forays into the mountains. A 16-mi.-long aerial tramway—the longest in the world—used to supply the hungry copper smelters of Encampment with a steady supply of ore.

For maps and information on hiking, camping, cross-country skiing, and other kinds of recreation in this area, contact the Medicine Bow National Forest, 605 Skyline Dr., Laramie 82070 (745-8971; open Mon.-Fri. 7:30am-5pm, Sat.-Sun. 7:30am-4pm; off-season Mon.-Fri. 7:30am-5pm). Also try the **chamber of commerce,** P.O. Box 456, Medicine Bow 82329 (379-2255; open Mon.-Wed. 8am-2pm), and the **ranger station** in Saratoga, 212 S. 1st St. (326-5258; open Mon.-Fri. 7:30am-5pm). The Saratoga **post office** is at 105 W. Main St. (326-5611; open Mon. and Fri. 8:30am-5pm, Tues.-Thurs. 8am-5pm, Sat. 8:30-9:30am). The **ZIP code** is 82331; the **area code** is 307.

Grand Teton National Park

When French fur trappers first peered into Wyoming's wilderness from the eastern border of Idaho, they found themselves face to face with three craggy peaks, all topping 12,000 ft. In an attempt to make the imposing landscape seem more trapper-friendly, they dubbed the mutant mountains "Les Trois Tetons," French for "the three breasts." Although they eventually did discover that the mountains belonged to a much larger range, the Frenchmen never quite realized that mountains are not breasts, and only changed the name to "Les Grands Tetons." The misnomer stuck and today the snowy heights of Grand Teton National Park delight modern hikers and cyclists with miles of strenuous trails. The less adventurous appreciate the rugged appearance of the Tetons; the craggy pinnacles and shining glaciers possess an extraordinary beauty. Most visitors will appreciate the park's relative lack of crowds in comparison with Yellowstone, its sometimes zoo-like neighbor to the north.

Practical Information

Emergency: 911.

Park Headquarters: Superintendent, Grand Teton National Park, P.O. Drawer 170, Moose 83012 (733-2880). Office at the Moose Visitors Center. Open Mon.-Fri. 8am-7pm.

Park Entrance Fees: $10 per car, $4 per pedestrian or bicycle, $5 per family (non-motorized), under 16 (non-motorized) free. Good for 7 days for both the Tetons and Yellowstone.

Visitors Center: Moose, Rockefeller Pkwy. at the southern tip of the park (733-2880). Open June-Aug. daily 8am-7pm; Sept.-May daily 8am-5pm. **Jenny Lake,** next to the Jenny Lake Campground. Open June-Aug. daily 8am-7pm; Sept.-May daily 8am-5pm. **Colter Bay,** on

Jackson Lake in the northern part of the park (543-2467). Open early June-early Sept. daily 8am-7pm; May and late Sept. daily 8am-5pm. **Signal Mountain,** between Colter Bay and Moose (543-2516). Open May 13-June 30 daily 8am-5pm. Park information brochures available in braille, French, German, Japanese, and Spanish. Topographical maps ($3). Pick up the *Teewinot* newspaper (free) for a complete list of park activities, lodgings, and facilities.

Park Information and Road and Weather Conditions: 733-2220; 24-hr. recording.

Bike Rental: Mountain Bike Outfitters, Inc., at Dorman's in Moose (733-3314). Quality mountain bikes $5 per hr., $22 per day. Open summer daily 9am-6pm. Credit card or deposit required.

Medical Care: Grand Teton Medical Clinic, Jackson Lake Lodge (543-2514 or 733-8002 after hours), near the Chevron station. Open June to mid-Sept. daily 10am-6pm. In a dire emergency, contact **St. Johns's Hospital** (733-3636), in Jackson.

Post Office: in **Colter Bay General Store** (733-2811). Open mid-May to mid-Sept. Mon.-Fri. 8am-noon and 1-5pm, Sat. 9am-1pm. **ZIP codes:** Colter Bay 83001, Moose 83021, Moran 83013, Kelly 83011.

Area Code: 307.

The national park occupies most of the space between Jackson to the south and Yellowstone National Park to the north. **Rockefeller Parkway** connects the two parks and is open year-round. The park is directly accessible from all directions except the west. Hitching from Jackson is easy; hitching from Yellowstone may be more time-consuming.

Accommodations

If you want to stay indoors, grit your teeth and open your wallet. **The Grand Teton Lodge Co.** controls nearly all lodging within the park. Make reservations for any Grand Teton Lodge establishment by writing the Reservations Manager, Grand Teton Lodge Co., P.O. Box 240, Moran 83013 (543-2855 or 800-628-9988 outside Wyoming). Accommodations are available late May through early October, and are most expensive from late June to early August. Reservations are recommended to insure a place to hibernate. (See Jackson below for accommodations outside the park.)

Colter Bay Tent Cabins: Cheapest accommodations in the park, but not the place to stay in extremely cold weather. Canvas shelters with wood-burning stoves, table, and 4-person bunks. Sleeping bags, wood, cooking utensils, and ice chests available for rent. (Call Maintenance, 543-1081.) Cabins $18 for 2, each additional person $2.50. Restrooms and showers ($1.50) nearby.

Colter Bay Log Cabins: Quaint, well-maintained log cabins near Jackson Lake. Room with semi-private bath $25, with private bath $47-68. Two-room cabins with bath $68-89.

Flagg Ranch Village: P.O. Box 187, Moran 83013 (543-2861 or 800-443-2311), on the Snake River near the park's northern entrance. Simple, clean cabins with private bath $55 for 2.

Camping

Camping is the way to see the Tetons without emptying your savings account. The park service maintains six campgrounds, all on a first come-first serve basis (sites $7). In addition, there are two trailer parks and acres of backcountry open to visitors whenever the snow's not too deep. RVs are welcome in all but Jenny Lake, but hookups are unavailable. Information is available at any visitors center.

Park Campgrounds: All campgrounds have rest rooms, cold water, fire rings, grocery store, and picnic tables. **Jenny Lake:** 49 highly coveted sites; arrive early. No RVs. **Signal Mountain:** A few mi. south of Colter Bay. 86 spots, usually full by noon. **Colter Bay:** 310 sites, shower and laundromat. Usually full by 2pm. **Snake River** and **Lizard Creek:** Northern campgrounds, with 60 sites, convenient to Yellowstone. Fills in late afternoon. **Gros Ventre:** On the park's southern border. 360 sites. A good bet if you arrive late. Max. stay in Jenny Lake 7 days, all others 14 days. Reservations required for large groups.

Colter Bay RV Park: 112 sites, electrical hookups. Reserved through Grand Teton Lodge Co. (733-2811 or 543-2855). Grocery store and eateries. Sites June-Aug. $18, May and Sept. $16. Showers $1.50, towel rental $1.25.

Flagg Ranch Village Camping: Operated by Flagg Ranch Village (543-2861 or 800-443-2311). Grocery and eateries on the grounds. Sites $9.50 for 2, $13.50 with hookup. Make reservations.

For **backcountry camping,** reserve a spot in a camping zone in a mountain canyon or on the shores of a lake by submitting an itinerary to the permit office at **Moose Ranger Station** (733-2880) from January 1 to June 1. Pick up the permit on the morning of the first day of your hike. Two-thirds of all spots left open are available on a first come-first serve basis; you can get a permit up to 24 hrs. before setting out at the Moose or Jenny Lake Ranger Stations. (Open daily 8am-7pm.) Camping is unrestricted in some off-trail backcountry areas (though you must have a permit). Wood fires are not permitted above 7000 ft. As the weather can be severe, even in the summer, backcountry campers should be somewhat experienced before venturing far from civilization.

Food

As in Yellowstone, the best way to eat in the Tetons is to bring your own food. If this isn't possible, stick to what non-perishables you can pick up at the **Flagg Ranch Grocery Store** (open daily 7am-10pm; reduced hours in winter), or **Dornan's Grocery** in Moose (open daily 8am-6pm; reduced hours in winter). In Jackson, you can stock up on goodies at **Albertson's** supermarket.

Sights and Activities

As the youngest mountain range in North America, the Tetons provide hikers, bikers, climbers, rafters, and sightseers with challenges and vistas not found in more eroded ranges. The Grand Teton itself rises 13,700 ft. from the valley floor virtually without foothills. While Yellowstone wows visitors with its geysers and mudpots, Grand Teton's geology boasts some of the most scenic mountains in the U.S., if not the world.

Cascade Canyon Trail, one of the least arduous (and therefore more popular) hikes, originates at Jenny Lake. To start, take a boat trip (operated by Grand Teton Lodge Co.) across Jenny Lake ($2.25, round-trip $3; children $1.25, round-trip $1.50), or hike the 2-mi. trail around the lake. Trail guides (25¢) are available at the trailhead. A ½-mi. from the trail entrance lies the **Hidden Falls Waterfall;** the hardy can trek 6 mi. further to **Lake Solitude.** Another pleasant day hike, popular for its scope of wildlife, is the 4-mi. walk from Colter Bay to **Hermitage Point.** The **Amphitheater Lake Trail,** which begins just south of Jenny Lake at the Lupine Meadows parking lot, will take you nine breathtaking mi. up to one of the park's many glacial lakes. Those who were bighorn sheep in past lives can take the challenge of **Static Peak Divide,** a 15-mi. trail that climbs 4020 ft. and offers some of the best lookouts in the park. All information centers provide pamphlets about the day hikes and sell the *Teton Trails* guide ($2).

Those who prefer floating to walking should rent boats at the **Colter Bay Marina** for a leisurely afternoon on Jackson Lake. (Rowboats $5.50 per hr. Canoes $6 per hr. Motorboats $12.50 per hr., 2 hr. minimum; $50 deposit required. Open daily 7am-6pm.) Call Grand Teton Lodge Co. (733-2811 or 543-2811) for more information. **Signal Mountain Marina** (543-2831) rents a greater variety of boats, but charges more. (Rowboats and canoes $5 per hr. Motorboats $12.50 per hr. Waterski boats and pontoons $25 per hr. Open daily 7am-6pm.) The **Grand Teton Lodge Company** (543-2855 or 733-2811) can take you on scenic Snake River float trips within the park. (10½-mi. half-day trip $22.50, under 17 $12.50. 20½-mi. luncheon or supper trips $30, under 17 $19.50.) **Fishing** in the park's lakes, rivers, and streams is excellent. Wyoming state fishing licenses ($5) are required and may be purchased at the visitors centers and ranger stations.

The **American Indian Art Museum** (543-2467), in the Colter Bay Visitors Center, offers an extensive private collection of Native American artwork, artifacts, movies, and workshops. (Open June-Sept. daily 8am-7pm; May and late Sept. daily 8am-5pm. Free.) During July and August you can see Cheyenne, Cherokee, Apache, and Sioux dances at Jackson Lake Lodge (Fri. at 8:30pm). At the Moose and Colter Bay Visitors Centers, rangers lead a variety of activities aimed at educating visitors about such subjects as the ecology, geology, wildlife, and history of the Tetons. Check the *Teewinot* for exact times, as schedules change daily.

In the winter, all hiking trails and the unplowed sections of Teton Park Road are open to cross-country skiers. Pick up the trail map *Winter in the Tetons* at the Moose Visitors Center. From January through March, naturalists lead **snowshoe hikes** from Moose Visitors Center (733-2880; snowshoes distributed free). Call for reservations. **Snowmobiling** along the park's well-powdered trails and up into Yellowstone is a noisy but popular winter activity. Grab a map and guide at the Jackson Chamber of Commerce, 10 mi. south of Moose. For a steep fee you can rent snowmobiles at Signal Mt. Lodge, Flagg Ranch Village, or down in Jackson; an additional $5 registration fee is required for all snowmobile use in the park. All campgrounds close during the winter. The Colter Bay parking lot is available for RVs and cars, and backcountry snow camping (only for those who know what they're doing) is allowed with a free permit from Moose. Check with a ranger station for current weather conditions and avalanche danger. Many early trappers froze to death in the 10-ft. drifts.

Jackson

Colorado has Aspen, Idaho has Sun Valley, and Wyoming has Jackson—an expensive refuge for transplanted Eastern "outdoorsy"-types. Mixing with the tanned mountain bikers and rock climbers, you'll find busloads of camera-snapping tourists rushing to the Ralph Lauren and J. Crew outlets. If you stick around long enough, you may catch a glimpse of some real cowboys, of the type that established Jackson long before climbing mountains became a fashionable sport.

Practical Information

Emergency: 911.

Visitor Information: Jackson Hole Area Chamber of Commerce, 532 N. Cache St. (733-3316), in a modern wooden split-level with grass on the roof. A crucial information stop. Open mid-June to mid-Sept. daily 8am-8pm; off-season daily 8:30am-5pm. **Bridger-Teton National Forest Headquarters,** 340 N. Cache St. (733-2752), 2 blocks south of the chamber of commerce. Maps $2-8. Open daily 7:45am-5:30pm; off-season daily 7:45am-4:30pm.

Buses: Jackson-Rock Springs Stages, 72 S. Glenwood St. (733-3133). Daily bus to Pinedale ($10.50) and Rock Springs ($18). Greyhound passes not honored. Open Mon.-Fri. 10-11:30am, Sat.-Sun. 10:30-11:30am. Connections with **Greyhound** at the Rock Springs terminal, 1005 Dewar Ave. (362-2931). Open Mon.-Fri. 8am-5pm, Sat. 8am-noon. **Grand Teton Lodge Co.** (733-2811) runs a shuttle twice daily in summer to Jackson Lake Lodge ($14).

Bus Tours: Powder River Tours, 565 N. Cache St. (733-2136). Full-day tour of the Tetons with boat ride on Jenny Lake ($34). **Grayline Tours,** 330 N. Glenwood St. (733-4325), in front of Dirty Jack's Theatre. Full-day tours of Grand Teton National Park and Yellowstone National Park lower loop ($36). Call for reservations. **Wild West Jeep Tours,** P.O. Box 7506, Jackson 83001 (733-9036). In summer only, half-day tours of the Tetons and other areas ($27, seniors $24.50, under 12 $14). Call for reservations.

Car Rental: Rent-A-Wreck, 1650 W. Martin Ln. (733-5014). $21 per day, $116 per week; 125 free mi., 20¢ each additional mi. Open Mon.-Fri. 8am-5:30pm. Must be 21 with credit card or a $300 cash deposit. Must stay within 200 mi. of Jackson.

Ski and Bike Rental: Hoback Sports, 40 S. Millward (733-5335). 10-speeds $17 per day, mountain bikes $20 per day; lower rates for longer rentals. Skis $13 per day. Open daily 9am-7pm. Must have credit card or enough cash to cover the cost of the equipment. **Skinny Skis,**

65 W. Delovey St. (733-6094). Skis $9 per day, $17 for mountaineering. Open daily 9am-9pm. Major credit card or deposit for value of equipment.

Weather Line, 733-1731. 24-hr. recording.

Help Lines: Rape Crisis Line, 733-5162. **Road Information,** 733-9966, outside WY 800-442-7850.

Post Office: 220 W. Pearl St. (733-3650), 2 blocks east of Cache St. Open Mon.-Fri. 8:30am-5pm. **ZIP code:** 83001.

Area Code: 307.

Although most services in Jackson are terribly expensive, the town makes an ideal base for trips into the Tetons, 10 mi. north, or the Wind River Range, 70 mi. southeast. U.S. 191, the usual southern entry to town, ties Jackson to I-80 at Rock Springs (180 mi. south). This road continues north into Grand Teton Park and eventually reaches Yellowstone, 70 mi. to the north. The streets of Jackson are centered around **Town Square,** a small park on Broadway and Cache St.

Accommodations, Camping, and Food

Jackson's constant influx of tourists ensures that if you don't book ahead, rooms will be small and expensive at best, and non-existent at worst. Fortunately you can sleep affordably in one of two local hostels. **The Bunkhouse,** in the basement of the Anvil Motel, 215 N. Cache St. (733-3668), has a lounge, kitchenette, laundromat, ski storage, and, as the name implies, one large but quiet sleeping room with comfortable bunks. ($20. Linens $2.) **The Hostel X (AYH),** P.O. Box 546, Teton Village 83025 (733-3415), near the ski slopes, 12 mi. northwest of Jackson, is a budgetary oasis among the wallet-parching condos and lodges of Teton Village, and a favorite of skiers because of its location. Game room, TV room, ski waxing room, and movies nightly. Accommodations range from dorm-style rooms ($15 per bunk, $18 for nonmembers) to private suites ($34 for 2 people, $42 for 3 or 4). All are clean and well maintained. If you prefer to stay in a Jackson motel, the **Lazy X Motel,** 325 N. Cache St. (733-3673), offers attractive rooms during the summer. (Singles $34. Doubles $40.) You can always fall back on **Motel 6,** 1370 W. Broadway (733-9666), even though their rates rise steadily as the peak season approaches. (Singles from $35. Doubles from $42.)

While it doesn't offer amazing scenery, Jackson's RV/tent campground, the **Wagon Wheel Village** (733-2357), doesn't charge an arm and a leg either. Call for reservations. (Sites from $16.50.) Cheaper sites and more pleasant surroundings are available in the **Bridger-Teton National Forest** surrounding Jackson. Hike up Cache Creek to the south of town, or drive toward Alpine Junction on U.S. 26/89 to find spots. Check the map at the chamber of commerce for a complete list of campgrounds. (Sites $4-10.)

The Bunnery, 130 N. Cache St. (733-5474), in the "Hole-in-the-Wall" mall, has the best breakfast in town—two eggs, peaches, cottage cheese, toast $3.50. Sandwiches $3.95. (Open daily 7am-2pm.) For great burgers in a bright Art-Deco setting, try the **Cadillac Grill,** Cache St. (733-5474). The huge bacon-cheeseburger ($5) will fill you up without emptying your wallet. On weekdays, a mixture of Western barbecue and Mexican delicacies is set out at **Pedro's,** 139 N. Cache St. (733-9015) for the $3 all-you-can-eat buffet. (Open summer daily 11am-8:30pm.) For a cheap, light meal, away from the cache on Cache St., head to **Pearl St. Bagels,** 145 Pearl St.(733-2578), where a myriad of bagel sandwiches are under $3 each. (Open Mon.-Fri. 6:30am-3pm, Sat.-Sun. 7:30am-3pm.) Another good option for cheap, quality food, and excellent coffee is **Shade's Cafe,** 82 S. King St. (733-2015; open daily 7:30am-6pm).

Nightlife and Activities

Western saddles serve as bar stools at the **Million Dollar Cowboy Bar,** 25 N. Cache St. (733-2207), Town Square. This Jackson institution attracts a mixed group of cowpokes, high society types, and even some gay cowboys. (Open Mon.-Sat. 10am-2am, Sun. 11am-2am. Live music Mon.-Sat. 9pm-2am. Cover $3-6 after 8:30pm.)

Cultural activities in Jackson fall into two camps—the rambunctious foot-stomping Western celebrations and the more formal, sedate presentations of music and art. Every summer evening except Sunday, the Town Square hosts an episode of the **Longest-Running Shoot-Out in the World.** For $2.50 on Friday evenings at 8pm, you can join in at the **Teton Twirlers Square Dance,** in the fair building on the rodeo grounds (733-5269 or 543-2825). Each June, the town celebrates the opening of the **Jackson Hole Rodeo** (733-2805; open June-Aug. Wed. and Sat. 8pm; tickets $5-8). The prestigious **Grand Teton Music Festival** (733-1128) holds court in Teton Village from mid-July through August. (Performances nightly at 8:30pm; student tickets $3-5. Fri. and Sat. symphony at 8:30pm; student tickets $9. Reserve in advance.) And on Memorial Day, the town bulges at the seams as tourists, locals, and nearby Native American tribes pour in for the dances and parades of **Old West Days.** Throughout September, the **Jackson Hole Fall Arts Festival** attracts painters, dancers, actors, and musicians to Jackson's four main theaters.

Between May 15 and Labor Day over 100,000 city slickers and backwoods folk go white-water rafting out of Jackson. **Mad River Boat Trips,** 1060 S. Hwy. 89 (733-6203), offers the cheapest white-water and scenic raft trips (from $21), though the **Barker-Ewing Co.,** 45 W. Broadway (733-1000), is stiff competition (from $30). Cheaper thrills include a lift 10,452 ft. up Rendez-Vous Mountain on the **Jackson Hole Aerial Tram** (733-2292; $13, seniors $11, teens $6, ages 6-12 $2). In winter, the **Jackson Hole Ski Resort** (733-2292) at Teton Village offers some of the steepest, most challenging skiing in the country.

The **Wildlife Museum** (733-4909), in Grand Teton Plaza on Broadway, exhibits the trophies of local hunters in extremely realistic settings. (Open May-Oct. daily 9am-6pm. Admission $2, families $5, ages 6-12 $1, under 6 free.)

Wind River Range

Named by the Arapahoe for the turbulent rivers that tumble down to the sloping, windswept farmlands on the range's eastern border, the Winds are the most spectacular of Wyoming's mountains. Seven enormous glaciers, acres of forests, and miles of primitive wilderness bear this out. The difficulty of traveling far into the Wind River range, however, keeps the region unspoiled by tourist traffic.

There are no roads into the range: it lies smack in the middle of a tremendous oval formed by U.S. 191, which runs along the western side, and U.S. 26/28/287, which follows along the range's eastern edge. From the western side, the trails are accessible from **Pinedale;** if you're coming from the east, the closest you'll get is **Lander.** Since most of the range's finest scenery lies in the **Bridger Wilderness Area** on the western slope, Pinedale is the prime starting point for hiking expeditions. Stop at **Pinedale Ranger District Office,** 210 W. Pine St., P.O. Box 220 (367-4326), before you venture into the range. (Open Mon.-Sat. 7:45am-4:30pm; off-season Mon.-Fri. 7:45am-4:30pm.) Fishing permits and information are available at sporting goods stores and at the **Wyoming Game and Fish Department,** 117 S. Sublette (367-4352; open Mon.-Fri. 8am-5pm; permits $5 per day, $15 per week, $40 per month). U.S. Geological Survey topographic maps ($2.25) are essential for trips into the backcountry. Pick up the standard 7½-minute map sections at **Faler's Hardware,** 341 E. Pine (367-2324), a giant sporting goods and general store in Pinedale. (Open Mon.-Sat. 7am-7pm, Sun. 8am-5pm.)

Note: Novice backpackers should not venture deep into the Winds without guidance. The rugged terrain and unpredictable weather can make conditions challenging at best, dangerous at worst. In some areas of the Winds you can go weeks without meeting other humans, so don't expect quick help if you run into trouble. Beginners are advised to stick to trails closest to the range's perimeter.

The two most popular trailheads are at the end of the 16-mi. access road that heads east out of Pinedale. The trails begin at **Elkhart Park** above giant Fremont Lake, where you will find yet another information center. (Open daily 8am-8pm.) From there, head 9 mi. up the trail to the beautiful **Seneca Lakes;** hardy mountaineers will want to continue 18 mi. through **Indian Pass** to the glaciers beyond. You can climb **Fremont Peak** (13,745 ft.) from here. The other trailhead at Elkhart will take you into the **Pine Creek** drainage, an angler's nirvana. Beyond the canyon, the trail continues up to **Crows Nest Lookout** and **Glimpse Lake,** which provide beautiful bird's eye views of the icy surroundings.

Other popular destinations from Pinedale include **Gannett Peak** (at 13,804 ft., the highest mountain in the state), 10 mi. east, and **Big Sandy,** 50 mi. southeast on U.S. 191. Rock climbers from all over the world converge at the Big Sandy trailhead for the 8-mi. jaunt into **Cirque of the Towers,** where sheer cliffs hem in hikers. At the northwestern end of the Wind Range sits its most famous peak, **Squaretop.** Begin at **Green River Lake,** northwest of Pinedale on Rte. 352 off U.S. 191, for a good two-day loop around this aptly named mountain. This area and the trail leading to the Cirque are the only crowded spots in the range.

Access to the Winds from the other side is more time-consuming owing to the longer, gentler eastern slope. One of the showpieces of this area is the broad **Shoshone Lake,** which lies at the crest of the **Shoshone Trail.** A few mi. beyond the lake, the Shoshone Trail joins the **Fork Trail,** which leads into the tangled heart of the **Popo Agie** (po-PO-zhuh) **Wilderness.** Approach this unspoiled area from Lander via the Sinks Canyon Rd. west through geologically impressive **Sinks Canyon State Park** on Rte. 131. There are two small campgrounds here (sites $4; arrive by 3pm).

The **Lander Ranger District Offices** on U.S. 287 (332-5460) can give you information on the Popo Agie Wilderness. (Open Mon.-Fri. 8am-noon and 1-5pm.) For information on hiking in **Fitzpatrick Wilderness** in the northwestern Winds, write to the forest service offices at P.O. Box 186, Dubois 82513. For information on the eastern side of the Winds, write the Shoshone National Forest, P.O. Box 961, Cody 82414. To find out about the **Wind River Indian Reservation,** contact the Joint Council of Shoshone and Arapahoe Tribes, P.O. Box 217, Fort Washakie 82514.

In Pinedale, you needn't don blue jeans to eat at **The Wrangler Cafe,** 310 E. Pine St., where burgers with all the fixin's go for $3.25 and fantastic homemade pie costs $1.85. (Open Mon.-Fri. 6am-10pm, Sat.-Sun. 6am-8pm.) South of town on U.S. 191, **King Cone** serves a much-vaunted burger ($2), and a variety of shakes and sweets. You might want to bring sunglasses, as the restaurant and even the rocks in the surrounding parking lot are painted garish shades of flourescent green, purple, and orange. For food in Lander, try **The Breadboard,** 125 E. Main St., where you can sink a hardy sub for $3. (Open Mon.-Fri. 11am-8pm., Sat. 11am-4pm.) A local favorite is **The Commons,** 170 E. Main St. Wrap yourself around the waffles and bacon breakfast ($2.80). (Open daily 6am-11pm.)

The **Pinedale Chamber of Commerce,** 32 E. Pine (367-2242), has a list of accommodations and area sights. Stop here before choosing a room or campsite. (Open June-Sept. daily 8:30am-5:30pm.) Clean, comfortable accommodations with A/C are available at both the **Pine Creek Motel,** 650 W. Pine St. (367-2191), and the **Teton Court Motel,** 123 E. Magnolia (367-4317). Singles at Pine Creek from $30, at Teton from $26. Doubles at both from $33. Nearby **Trail's End** has free camping; sites at **Fremont Lake** (367-4326) go for $6. Unobstructed views of the Winds will cost you only $4 at the **Elkhart Park** campground, at the end of the road past Fremont Lake.

If you decide to shack up in Lander, visit the **Lander Chamber of Commerce,** 160 N. 1st St. (332-3892), for information on lodgings and current activities. (Open Mon.-Fri. 9am-5pm.) Your best bet is the **Downtown Motel** (332-5220), where clean but phoneless singles cost $22. The next best bet is **Pioneer Court Motel,** 6th & Lincoln (332-2653). Doubles with bath $28.

Jackson-Rock Springs Stages serve Pinedale once per day from the terminal at 1005 Dewar Ave. (362-6161) in Rock Springs ($10.50), and from the stop at 72

S. Glenwood St. (733-3135) in Jackson ($10.50). The flag stop in Pinedale is at the northern Phillips 66 station (367-4311). Greyhound passes are not honored. **Powder River Transportation** can connect you with Lander from Jackson or Casper; Greyhound passes are honored.

Pinedale's **ZIP code** is 82941; Lander's 82520. The **area code** for the Winds is 307.

Near the Winds

The great plains stretch southwest from Lander as far as the eye can see and the lonely expanses of sagebrush are broken only by the glaring blacktop of U.S. 28. Thirty mi. from Lander down this empty highway lie the remains of **South Pass City** and **Atlantic City,** two erstwhile mining towns whose crumbling wooden buildings stand as monuments to both the stamina and avarice of Wyoming's first pioneers.

Recent restoration efforts have helped to refurbish both communities, and the interesting historical displays in the **South Pass Visitors Center** merit a drive down the 5-mi. dirt detour from the highway. (Open Mon.-Fri. 9am-5pm. Clearly marked signs from US 28.) This rough-and-ready frontier community also played an important role in the women's suffrage movement. William Bright, a representative from South Pass City, wrote and introduced the bill which, when passed in 1869, made Wyoming the first territory to allow women the right to vote and hold office. The National Forest Service maintains a splendid forested **campground** just out of town near Atlantic City. (Sites $4.)

If you have the opportunity, you should definitely make a stop in **Dubois,** the self-proclaimed "Wyoming Wonderland," located 70 mi. from Jackson and Lander on US 26/287. Dubois's highlights include the majestic **Antelope Hills Golf Course** (455-2888) nestled between the red cliffs of Wyoming's own "Badlands," and the roaring Wind River, along US 26/287. Green fees are a very reasonable $6, and club rental is $4. Another must-stop in Dubois is the **Rustic Pine Tavern** 119E. Ramshorn (455-2430). The sign out front proclaims Rustic Pine the "World's Most Unique Bar," and after spending an evening swinging and two-stepping with real live cowboys and cowgirls it's hard to disagree. Note: Don't fall for the trick when a genial older man tells you he can guess your birthday within three days. Decent accommodations in Dubois can be had at the Branding Iron Motel, 401 Ramshorn St. (455-2893; singles with bath $25, doubles $30).

Eighty-five mi. northeast of Lander on U.S. 20, the comic book-sounding city of Thermopolis maintains the world's largest single mineral hot springs at **Hot Springs State Park** (864-3771). In 1896, the U.S. purchased the springs from the Shoshone and Arapahoe tribes for $60,000 worth of cattle and food supplies, on the stipulation that the "public" would always be allowed to bathe for free. To ensure this, the state maintains a clean but rotten-egg-smelling bathhouse on the grounds of the state park. (Open Mon.-Sat. 8am-6pm, Sun. noon-6pm. Towel and bathing suit rental 50¢.)

The **chamber of commerce,** 220 Park St. (864-2636), in the State Park Building, provides adequate assistance and a schedule of special events in Thermopolis. (Open Mon.-Fri. 8am-5pm.) If need be, you can stay at the simple **Plaza Hotel** (864-2251), on the park ground, where slightly run-down singles without shower start at $12, doubles at $35. **Pumpernicks,** 512 Broadway, serves delicious sandwiches ($2.50-5), salads, and steaks, and has Old West memorabilia strung up along the walls. (Open Mon.-Fri. 7am-9pm, Sat.-Sun. 9am-10pm.) The **Sideboard Cafe,** 109 S. 6th St., serves ample hamburgers ($2.75) and straightforward dinners ($4.75-7). (Open daily 6am-10pm.)

Yellowstone National Park

Had legendary mountain man John Colter studied the classics of world literature, he probably would have compared his 1807 trek into the Yellowstone area with a descent into Dante's *Inferno.* In any case, his graphic descriptions of boiling, sulfuric pits, spouting geysers, and smelly mudpots inspired a half-century of popular stories about "Colter's Hell." In 1870 the first official survey party, the Washburn Expedition, reached the area. As they came over a mountain ridge, the explorers were shocked by a fountain of boiling water and steam jetting 130 ft. into the air. Members of the expedition watched it erupt nine times and named it "Old Faithful" before leaving the Upper Geyser Basin. One year later, President Grant declared Yellowstone a national park, the world's first.

Visitors in Grant's time might have encountered 50 other tourists amid Yellowstone's 3472 square mi. Today's tourist will find the park cluttered with the cars and RVs of 50,000-odd people. The park's main attractions are huge, tranquil Yellowstone Lake, the 2100-ft.-deep Yellowstone River Canyon, and the world's largest collection of reeking, sputtering geysers, mudpots, hot springs, and fumaroles (steam-spewing holes in the ground). In the backcountry, you'll have a chance to observe the park's abundant bear, elk, moose, bison, and bighorn sheep, escaping the hordes of tourists in the bargain.

In 1988 Yellowstone was ravaged by a blaze that charred almost half the park. Crowds in Yellowstone doubled in 1989 in an extraordinary example of rubberneck tourism, with people pouring in to see "what really happened." While the effects of the fire are still visible throughout much of the park, crowd size should return to normal, which is still quite large, in 1992. The scarred forests do make for interesting, if somewhat macabre, viewing; rangers have erected exhibits throughout the park to better explain the fire's effects.

Practical Information

Emergency: 911.

Park Information and Headquarters: Superintendent, Mammoth Hot Springs, Yellowstone National Park 82190 (344-7381). The switchboard serves all visitors centers and park service phones. General information, campground availability, and emergencies. Headquarters open off-season Mon.-Fri. 8am-5pm. **Park Admission:** $10 for non-commercial vehicles, $4 for pedestrians and bikers. Good for one week, and also valid for Grand Teton National Park.

Visitors Centers and Ranger Stations: Most regions in this vast park have their own center/station. The district rangers have a good deal of autonomy in making regulations for hiking and camping, so check in at each area. All visitors centers have guides for the disabled and give backcountry permits, or have a partner ranger station that does. Each visitors center's display focuses on a different theme. **Mammoth Hot Springs** (344-2357): natural and human history. Open June-Aug. daily 8am-7pm; Sept.-May daily 8:30am-5pm. **Grant Village** (344-6602): wilderness. Open summer only, daily 8am-6pm. **Old Faithful/Madison** (344-6001): geysers. Open April-Nov. daily 8am-6pm; Dec.-March daily 8am-4:30pm. **Fishing Bridge** (344-6150): wildlife and Yellowstone Lake. Open daily 8am-6pm; off-season daily 9am-5pm. **Canyon** (344-6205): natural history and history of canyon area. Open July-Aug. daily 8am-6pm; Sept.-June daily 9am-5pm. **Norris** (344-7733): park museum. Open daily 8am-6pm. **Tower/Roosevelt Ranger Station** (344-7746): special temporary exhibits. Open daily 8am-5pm. *Discover Yellowstone,* the park's activities guide, has a thorough listing of tours and programs at each center.

Radio Information: Tune to 1610AM for service information and radical interpretive metadiscourse within the park.

West Yellowstone Chamber of Commerce: P.O. Box 4058, West Yellowstone, MT 59758 (406-646-7701). Located at the intersection of Canyon and Yellowstone St., 2 blocks west of the park entrance. Open daily 8am-6pm; off-season Mon.-Fri. 8am-5pm.

Greyhound: 127 Yellowstone Ave., W. Yellowstone, MT (406-646-7666). Two buses per day northeast to Bozeman (2 hr., morning bus $16, evening bus $12), and south to Salt Lake City (7½ hr., $63). Open summer only, daily 8am-8pm.

TW Services, Inc. (344-7311). Monopolizes concessions within the park. Nine-hr. bus tours of the lower portion of the park leave daily from all lodges ($23, ages under 12 $11.50). Similar tours of the northern region leave Gardiner, MT, and the lodges at Mammoth Lake and Fishing Bridge ($14-21, depending on where you start and end). Individual legs of this extensive network of tour loops can get you as far as the Grand Tetons or Jackson, but the system is inefficient, and costs much more than it's worth. Fares add up quickly. (West Yellowstone to Old Faithful 3 per day: $6.40, children $3.20; does not include park entrance fee.)

Gray Line Tours: 211 W. Yellowstone Ave, West Yellowstone, MT (406-646-9374). Offers full-day tours from West Yellowstone around the lower loop ($27.50, under 12 $11), upper loop ($26.50, under 12 $10), and Grand Tetons ($38.50, under 12 $15). Open daily 8am-5pm.

Car Rental: Payless Auto Rental, 26 Electric Ave., West Yellowstone, MT (406-646-9332), around the corner from the Traveler's Lodge. $38 per day with 100 free mi., 25¢ each additional mi. Open daily 7am-9pm. Must be 21 with a credit card, $100 deposit, or passport.

Bike Rental: Yellowstone Bicycles, 132 Madison Ave., West Yellowstone, MT (406-646-7815). $15 per day. Open daily 9am-9pm.

Horse Rental: Mammoth Hot Springs Hotel, from late May to mid-Sept. **Roosevelt Lodge,** mid-June to Sept. 2. **Canyon Lodge,** June 4-Sept. 2. $10.75 per hr., $20 for 2 hr. Call TW Services (394-7901) for more information.

Medical Facilities: Lake Pharmacy and **Hospital** at Lake Hotel (242-7241). Clinic open May-Sept. daily 8:30am-8:30pm. Hospital Emergency Room open May-Sept. 24 hrs. **Old Faithful Clinic,** at Old Faithful Inn (545-7325). Open mid-May to mid-Oct. daily 8:30am-5pm.

Post Offices: Old Faithful Station (545-7572), in the park behind the visitors center. Open Mon.-Fri. 8:30-11am, 1-5pm. **ZIP code:** 82190. **West Yellowstone, MT,** 17 Madison Ave. (646-7704). Open Mon.-Fri. 8:30am-5pm. **ZIP code:** 59758.

Area Codes: 307 (in the park), 406 (in West Yellowstone and Gardiner). Unless otherwise indicated phone numbers have a 307 area code.

The bulk of Yellowstone National Park lies in the northwest corner of Wyoming with slivers spilling into Montana and Idaho. **West Yellowstone, MT,** at the park's western entrance, and **Gardiner, MT,** at the northern entrance, are the most built-up and expensive towns along the edge of the park. The southern entry to the park is through Grand Teton National Park.

Yellowstone's extensive system of roads circulates its millions of visitors. Side roads branch off to park entrances and some of the lesser-known sights. It's unwise to bike or walk around the deserted roads at night since you may risk startling large wild animals. Approaching any wild beast at any time is illegal and extremely unsafe, and those who don't remain at least 100 ft. from bison, bear, or moose risk being mauled, gored to death, or made the victim of a *Far Side* cartoon.

The park's high season extends from about June 15 to September 15. If you visit during this period expect large crowds, clogged roads, and motels and campsites filled to capacity. A better option is to visit in either late spring or early fall, when the Winnebagos and the tame animals they transport are safely home.

Accommodations

Cabin-seekers will find options galore within the park. Standard hotel and motel rooms for the nature-weary also abound, but to keep your grip on the amenities of modern living cheaply, the towns at the park's entry-points may be your best bet.

In The Park

TW Services (344-7311) controls all of the accommodations within the park, and uses a special set of classifications for budget cabins. All cabins or rooms should be reserved well in advance of the June to September tourist season.

Old Faithful Inn and Lodge, near the west Yellowstone entrance. Offers pleasant Roughrider cabins without bath ($19) and Frontier cabins with bath ($31). Well-appointed hotel rooms from $32, with private bath $52.

Roosevelt Lodge, in the northwest corner. A favorite campsite of Teddy Roosevelt. Provides the cheapest and most scenic indoor accommodations around. Rustic shelters $17, each with a wood-burning stove (bring your own bedding and towel). Also Roughrider cabins ($19—bring your own towel) and more spacious "family" cabins with toilet ($34).

Mammoth Hot Springs, 18 mi. west of Roosevelt area, near the north entrance. Unremarkable budget cabins $23. Frontier cabins with private baths from $47.

Lake Yellowstone Hotel and Cabins, near the south entrance. Overpriced, but with a nice view of the lake. Frontier cabins identical to Old Faithful's ($39) and Western cabins with a little more space ($66).

Canyon Village. Less authentic and more expensive than Roosevelt Lodge's cabins, but slightly closer to the popular Old Faithful area. Frontier cabins $41, Western cabins $66.

West Yellowstone, MT

West Yellowstone International Hostel, at the Madison Hotel and Motel, 139 Yellowstone Ave. (406-646-7745). Friendly manager presides over old but clean, wood-adorned hotel. Singles $20, with bath $27. Doubles $26, with bath $30. Rooms $2 cheaper in the spring. Hostelers stay in more crowded rooms for $13. Open May 27 to mid-Oct.

Alpine Motel, 120 Madison (406-646-7544). Plastic but clean rooms with cable TV and A/C. Singles $28. Doubles $32.

Traveler's Lodge, 225 W. Yellowstone Ave. (406-646-9561). Comfortable, large rooms; ask for one away from the hot tub. Singles $40, off-season $26. Doubles $42, off-season $28. $5 discount if you rent a car from them (see Practical Information above).

Ho-Hum Motel, 126 Canyon Rd. (646-7746). Small, dark, but clean. Singles $26. Doubles $34.

Gardiner, MT

Located about 90 minutes northeast of West Yellowstone, Gardiner served as the original entrance to the park and is considerably smaller and less tacky than its neighbor.

The Town Motel (848-7322), across from the park's northern entrance. Pleasant, wood-paneled, carpeted rooms. Singles $25. Doubles $28.

Wilson's Yellowstone River Motel (406-848-7303), ½-block east of U.S. 89. Large, well-decorated rooms overseen by friendly manager. Singles $30. Doubles $34.

Hillcrest Cottages (848-7353), on U.S. 89 near where it crosses the Yellowstone River. Small but clean singles $28. Doubles $34. Seven nights for the price of 6.

Camping

All developed campsites are available on a first come-first serve basis except for the **Bridge Bay Campground,** which reserves sites up to eight weeks in advance through Ticketron (800-452-1111). During summer months, most campgrounds fill by 2pm. All regular sites cost $5-9. Arrive very early, especially on weekends and holidays. If all sites are full, try the free campgrounds outside the park in the surrounding National Forest land. Bring a stove or plan to hike a bit in search of firewood. Except for **Mammoth Campground,** all camping areas close for the winter.

Two of the most beautiful and restful areas are **Slough Creek Campground,** 10 mi. northeast of Tower Junction (open May-Oct.), and **Pebble Creek Campground,** 15 mi. farther down the same road (open June-Sept.). Both relatively uncrowded spots have good fishing. You can also try **Canyon Village. Fishing Bridge Campgrounds** is for non-tenting travelers only (RV hookup $17; open June-Sept.). The popular and scenic campgrounds at **Norris** (open May-Sept.) and **Madison** (open May-Oct.) fill early (by 1pm), while others, such as **Fishing Bridge, Canyon,** and **Pebble Creek,** sometimes have sites until 6pm. **Bridge Bay** (open May-Sept.), **Indian Creek** (open June-Sept.), and **Mammoth** (open year-round) campgrounds are treeless and non-scenic. You'd be better off camping in the **Gallatin National Forest**

to the northwest. Good sites line Hwy. 20, 287, 191, and 89. Call the Park Headquarters (344-7381) for information on any of Yellowstone's campgrounds.

More than 95%, or two million acres, of the park is backcountry. To venture
overnight into the wilds of Yellowstone, you must obtain a free **wilderness permit**
from a ranger station or visitors center. Be sure you understand the most recent
instructions regarding closing of campgrounds and trails due to bears and other
wildlife. The more popular areas fill up in high season, but you can reserve a permit
up to 48 hr. in advance.

The campgrounds at Grant, Village Lake, Fishing Bridge, and Canyon all have
coin-operated laundries and pay showers ($1 plus 25¢ for towel or soap). The lodges
at Mammoth and Old Faithful have no laundry facilities but will let you use their
showers for $1.50.

To discourage bears, all campers should keep clean camps and store food in a
locked car or suspended 10 ft. above ground and 4 ft. horizontally from a post or
tree trunk.

Food

Be very choosy when buying food in the park, as the restaurants, snack bars, and
cafeterias are quite expensive. If possible, stick to the **general stores** at each lodging
location (open daily 7:30am-10pm) and try to stock up on price-regulated items.

Sights and Activities

TW Services, for unbelievable amounts of money, will sell you tours, horseback
rides, and chuckwagon dinners until the cows come home. But given enough time,
your eyes and feet will do an even better job than TW's tours, without placing you
in danger of bankruptcy. Hiking to the main attractions is much easier if you make
reservations at the cabins closest to the sights you most want to see.

The geysers that made Yellowstone famous are clustered on the western side of
the park, near the West Yellowstone entrance. **Old Faithful,** while neither the largest, the highest, nor the most regular geyser, is certainly the most popular; it gushes
in the **Upper Geyser Basin,** 16 mi. south of **Madison Junction** where the entry road
splits north-south. Since its discovery in 1870, the granddaddy of geysers has consistently erupted with a whoosh of spray and steam (5000-8000 gallons worth) every
45 to 70 minutes. Avoiding crowds here in summer is nearly impossible unless you
come for the blasts at dusk or in the wee hours of the morning. Enjoy elk and other
geysers in the surrounding **Firehole Valley.** Swimming in any hot springs or geysers
is prohibited, but you can swim in the **Firehole River,** three-quarters of the way
up Firehole Canyon Drive (turn south just after Madison Jct.), or in the **Boiling
River,** 2½ mi. north of Mammoth, which is not really hot enough to cook pasta.
Still, do not swim alone, and beware of strong currents.

From Old Faithful, take the easy 1½-mi. walk to **Morning Glory Pool,** a park
favorite, or head 8 mi. north to the **Lower Geyser Basin,** where examples of all four
types of geothermic activity (geysers, mudpots, hot springs, and fumaroles) steam,
bubble, and spray together. The regular star here is **Echinus,** which erupts about
every hour from a large basin of water. If you are lucky enough to witness it, the
biggest show on earth is put on by **Steamboat,** the largest geyser in the world. Eruptions can last 20 minutes and top 400 ft. The last such enormous eruption occured
on June 4, 1990, after about a year of dormancy. Don't hold your breath waiting
for another one, but you might get lucky.

Whether you're waiting for geysers to erupt or watching them shoot skyward,
don't go too close as the crust of earth around a geyser is only 2 ft. deep, and falling
into one of these boiling sulfuric pits could be detrimental to your health. Pets are
not allowed in the basin.

Mammoth Hot Springs has famous hot springs terraces, built of multicolored
bifurcated limestone deposits which add 6 in. every year. Wildlife is quite abundant

in the northern part of the park, both along the road from Mammoth to Roosevelt, perhaps on the road itself, and past Roosevelt in the Lamar Valley.

The pride of the western area of the park is the **Grand Canyon of the Yellowstone,** carved through glacial deposits and amber, volcanic bedrock. For the best views, hike or drive to the 308-ft. Lower Falls at Artist Point, on the southern rim, or head for Lookout Point on the northern rim. All along the canyon's 19-mi. rim, keep an eye out for the rare bighorn sheep, and at dawn or dusk the bear-viewing management area (at the intersection of the northern rim and Tower roads) should be loaded with opportunities to use your binoculars.

Yellowstone Lake, 16 mi. south of the Canyon's rim at the southeastern corner of the park, contains tons o' trout; after procuring a free Yellowstone fishing permit, catch a few, and have the chef fry them for you in the Yellowstone Hotel Dining Room. Most other lakes and streams allow catch-and-release fishing only. The aptly yellow **Lake Yellowstone Hotel,** originally built in 1891, and renovated in 1989, merits a visit though its room rates put it well out of the range of most budget travelers. The bright, airy lobby with large windows provides a magnificent view of the lake. Walks around the main body of the lake, as well as those that take you around one of the lake's three fingers, are scenic, and serene rather than strenuous. Nearby **Mud Volcano,** close to Yellowstone Lake, features boiling sulfuric earth and the **Dragon's Mouth,** a vociferous steaming hole that early explorers reportedly heard all the way from the lake. You'll smell it that far away for sure.

Although most of the spectacular sights in the park are accessible by car, a hiking trip through the backcountry will remove you from the masses. The multilayered petrified forest of **Specimen Ridge** and the geyser basins at **Shoshone** and **Heart Lakes** are only accessible by well-kept trails. **Cascade Corner,** in the southwest, is a lovely area accessible by trails from Belcher. Over 1000 mi. of trails crisscross the park, but many are poorly marked. If you plan to hike, pick up a topographical trail map ($2.50) at any visitors center and ask a ranger to describe all forks in the trail and the wording of trail markings. Even after annoying the ranger, allow yourself extra time (at least 1 hr. per day) in case you lose the trail.

Winter

Yellowstone can be as rewarding blanketed with snow during winter as blanketed with tourists during summer. Native animals can still be seen clustered around the sparse vegetation, while the traveling well-wrapped humans convert the park into snowboarding city. Cross-country skiing, ranger-sponsored snowshoe tours, and evening programs with hot chocolate and noisy snowmobile excursions are all available at off-season rates. Contact Park Headquarters (344-7381), **Snowmobile Touring** (545-7249), or the visitors centers at Mammoth Hot Springs, Old Faithful (mid-Dec. to mid-March), and West Yellowstone (mid-Dec. to mid-March). In winter, the Mammoth Hotel converts two rooms into a youth hostel, each of which holds six people ($6 per person).

Plowed roads make winter bus service available to West Yellowstone and Flagg Ranch on the western and southern borders; the Mammoth-Tower-Cooke City park road is kept open and accessible from Bozeman via Gardiner. All other roads are used by snowmobilers and the snowcoach only. The **snowcoach,** a heated, enclosed tank-like vehicle, run by TW Services, provides transportation from the south gate at Flagg Ranch, the west gate at West Yellowstone, and the north gate at Mammoth to bring travelers to the Old Faithful Lodge. With a permit (free from any visitors center), you may use the undeveloped backcountry sites. But exercise caution: people do get snowed in. You can find heated restrooms at Madison and Mammoth campgrounds. Food is available at Old Faithful and the **Canyon Snack Shop,** snowmobile fuel at Old Faithful, Mammoth, and Canyon. The **Three Bears Hotel,** 217 W. Yellowstone Ave. (406-646-7353), rents snowmobiles ($68 per day, $75 for 2 people). Porridge prices are unavailable as we go to press.

LET'S GO: CANADA

Canada is the second largest country in the world (after the USSR), but one of the most sparsely populated. Ten provinces and two territories sprawl over more than 9,000,000 square km of land, spanning seven time zones. But numbers don't tell Canada's story. Framed by the rugged Atlantic coastline to the east and the Rockies to the west, Canada spreads north from fertile farmland and urbanized lakeshores to barren, frozen tundra.

The name Canada derives from the Huron-Iroquois world "kanata," meaning "village" or "community." However, the Canadian community suffers many ethnic, linguistic and cultural tensions that sporadically flare up into actual conflict, as they have done in recent times. The division between Canada's two dominant cultures—the French and the English—is so strong that Canadian society has been described as "two solitudes." Although the grounds of the conflict shift, from linguistic to philosophical to religious to economic, it persists. Recently, with the collapse of the Meech Lake Accord, which would have given French-speaking regions such as Québec Province increased autonomy, Québécois separatist movements have grown in strength.

Another persistent schism is that between the dominant Euro-colonist cultures and the aboriginal tribes. Treatment of Native Americans in Canada historically has not been much better than in the United States. The most recent headline-grabbing conflict involved Québécois Mohawks, who spent weeks under police seige after they armed themselves to prevent sacred burial grounds from being converted into a golf course.

The division between West and East also tears at the Canadian fabric. French monarchists and English tories settled the Eastern provinces; their intellectual descendents in the politically dominant provinces of Ontario and Québec are comfortable with Canada's active federal government. But the Western provinces probably have more in common with America's libertarian West, whence came many of their settlers, than the rest of Canada, and opposition parties led by anti-government politicos such as Preston Manning are growing in popularity.

Finally, the blurring separation between the United States and Canada must be mentioned. (Although our book is called *Let's Go: USA* while including most of Canada as well, we do not think the Canadian provinces are part of the U.S.) Canadian nationalists have become quite concerned with the ubiquity of American culture and mass communication in the provinces, and steps have been taken to protect genuine Canadian media and cultural products. At the same time, the recent approval of a free trade pact between the United States and Canada further chipped away at the dwindling differences between the two national identities. The two countries are still learning the consequences of their new interdependence; when the U.S. began negotiating a free-trade agreement with Mexico, many Canadians realized their own vulnerability to U.S. government economic policies.

Travel

Canada's border with the U.S., its only international border, is easily accessible from Boston, New York City, Detroit, Chicago, Minneapolis/St. Paul, Seattle, and Alaska. Canada's highway system makes driving easy, even in remote areas of the country, although gas is twice as expensive as in the U.S. (55-65¢ per liter). Because of excellent public transportation both within urban centers and throughout the country, even budget travelers can manage without a car. Canada officially is bilingual, but communication should not pose a problem if you speak only English, and Canadians are generally hospitable to visitors from all over the world.

Student Travel

The **Canadian Federation of Student Services** sponsors a number of student travel assistance organizations. The **Studentsaver National Student Discount Program** provides 10-25% discounts on food, clothing, books, and other goods at some Canadian retail stores, with the International Student Identity Card (ISIC), available at most travel agencies. A list of outlets that give discounts, details on the program, and a great deal more advice for student and budget travelers is available at **Travel CUTS** (Canadian Universities Travel Service Ltd.). A fully licensed national travel agency, CUTS will help you plan trips within Canada or to other countries. The federation also publishes *Canadian Student Traveler,* available free at Canadian universities.

Headquarters for CFS Services and Travel CUTS are at 187 College St., Toronto, Ont. M5T 1P7 (416-979-2406). Other Travel CUTS locations (all open regular business hours) include:

Montréal: McGill University, 3480 McTavish, Montréal, Québec H3A 1X9 (514-398-0647).

Toronto: 74 Gerrard St. E., Toronto, Ont. M5B 1G6 (416-977-0441).

Vancouver: Student Union Building, University of British Columbia, Vancouver, B.C. V6T 1W5 (604-228-6890). Downtown 501-602 W. Hastings (604-681-9136).

Victoria: Student Union Building, University of Victoria, Victoria, B.C. V8W 2Y2 (604-721-8352).

Money

During the past several years, the Canadian dollar has been worth 80-85% of (or 20-25% less than) the U.S. dollar. Prices in general tend to be higher in Canada than the U.S. Taxes certainly are—you'll quickly notice the 7% goods and services tax (GST) and a comparable sales tax in some provinces. Symbols for dollars ($) and cents (¢) are the same with Canadian currency—all prices in the Canada section of this book are for Canadian dollars unless otherwise noted. Banks provide a reasonable exchange rate, but often charge a handling fee and shave off several percentage points; ATM **Cirrus** and **Plus** networks allow you to draw Canadian currency from American or British bank accounts at the official exchange rate. Exchange houses have the best rates and hours, with most open on weekends when banks close. U.S. currency is accepted by vending machines and parking meters, although using U.S. currency in them is not a good habit to pick up. While some businesses in border towns and some cities accept U.S. currency, they are under no legal obligation to offer you fair exchange.

Customs

The U.S.-Canadian border is the longest undefended border in the world; to cross it, U.S. visitors need only proof of citizenship (a birth certificate or passport). If you are under 18 and unaccompanied by an adult, you must have written consent from your parent or guardian. Non-U.S. citizens must have a Canadian visa for entry, and should have their papers in good order since customs officials on both sides of the border often act tough with anyone with a foreign accent. Those wishing to bring pets into Canada must bring certification of the animals' vaccination against rabies. Visitors who spend at least 48 hours in Canada may take back to the U.S. up to US$400 worth of goods duty-free, including up to 100 non-Cuban cigars, one carton of cigarettes, and 32 oz. of liquor. U.S. residents who stay in Canada for less than 48 hours may return with US$25 worth of duty-free merchandise (40 oz. of alcohol, no tobacco). Write for the customs office's helpful pamphlet *I declare/Je declare* at Revenue Canada Customs and Excise Communications Branch, Mackenzie Ave., Ottawa, Ont. K1A 0L5 (613-957-0275).

Visas

Before embarking for Canada, call the Canadian Embassy consulate, or High Commission, for a **visitor's visa.** Your time of stay will be fixed when your visa is issued. If you ask to remain in the country longer than 90 days, you must pay a non-refundable fee of $50, whether or not your request is granted. To get an extension once you are in Canada, apply at a **Canadian Immigration Centre (CIC)** before your current visa expires.

You will need a different visa for working in Canada. An **employment authorization** must be obtained before you enter Canada; visitors ordinarily are not allowed to change status once they have arrived. Residents of the US, Greenland, St. Pierre, or Miquelon only may apply for employment authorization at a port of entry. To acquire an employment authorization, talk to a **Canadian Employment Centre (CEC)** or consulate.

To study in Canada, a **student authorization fee** of $75 in addition to your visitor's visa is necessary. A student authorization is good for one year. Plan at least six months in advance to be sure you have all the necessary documents. For specifics on official documentation, contact a CIC or consulate.

Telephones and Mail

The Canadian telephone system is essentially the same as that in the U.S., with seven-digit phone numbers, three-digit area codes, cheaper long-distance (LD) rates in the evening or on weekends, and 25¢ local calls. LD calls can be made without operator assistance, as if the border did not exist.

Canada Post requires a 40¢ Canadian postage stamp for all domestic first class mail. Letters or postcards sent to the U.S. cost 46¢; items mailed to Europe weighing less than 20g cost 80¢. Add a 7% tax on postage. Postage prices increase yearly; expect to pay a bit more in 1992. When sending mail to destinations within Canada, be sure to note the six-character **postal code** (of numbers and letters, e.g. A1B 2C3). Even with the postal code, expect items passing through the Canadian mail system to take 1-2 days longer than they would south of the border.

Measurements

Canadians use the metric system (as do all but two nations in the world). For residents of those nations, simple conversions are as follows:

Distance: 1 centimeter (cm) — .394 inches; 1 meter (m) — 3.281 feet (ft.) and 1.094 yards; 1 kilometer (km) — .621 miles (mi.).

Volume: 1 liter (l) — .2642 gallons.

Mass or Weight: 1 gram (g) — .0353 ounces, 1 kilogram (kg) — 2.2046 pounds.

Holidays

Canadians celebrate both national and provincial holidays. All government offices and most businesses close on national holidays, except on Easter Monday and Remembrance Day. Check in local newspapers for a list of what is and isn't open. The following is a list of the major national holidays in 1992: New Year's Day (Jan. 1); Good Friday (April 17); Easter Sunday (April 19); Easter Monday (April 20); Victoria Day (May 24 or preceding Mon.); La Fête Nationale/La Fête du Saint Jean Baptiste (St. John the Baptist Day) (June 24 in Québec); Canada Day (July 1); Heritage Day, Simcoe Day, and British Columbia Day (Aug. 3); Discovery Day (Aug. 17); Labour Day (Sept. 7); Thanksgiving (second Mon. in Oct.); Remembrance Day (Nov. 11); Christmas Day (Dec. 25); and Boxing Day (Dec. 26).

Alcohol

The drinking age in Alberta, Manitoba, Québec, and Prince Edward Island is 18; in all other provinces and territories 19. You can import 40 oz. of liquor or wine, or 288 oz. of beer or ale, into Canada only if you can document the above ages.

Accommodations

The price of Canadian hotels, combined with the lack of budget motel chains, may force budget travelers toward the wilderness. Almost every city has families that take travelers into their **Bed and Breakfasts** for \$25-60. A similar but more structured lodging option is the **farm vacation.** Nightly rates begin at \$25 for singles and \$35 for doubles, although some require a minimum duration of one week (average rate about \$250 per person). The family-oriented farm vacation system integrates guests into the daily life of farm families in the Maritimes (New Brunswick, Nova Scotia, and Prince Edward Island), Québec, and Ontario. Guests eat with the family and are encouraged to help with the chores. For travelers who prefer urban lodgings, the network of **YMCAs** and **YWCAs** among the larger cities offers clean and affordable rooms, generally in downtown areas. In summer, other budget choices include university dorms, open for travelers early to mid-May and closing mid- to late August.

The **Canadian Hostelling Association (CHA),** founded in 1933, maintains over 70 hostels nationwide. Graded "basic," "simple," "standard," or "superior," hostels (\$6-16) have kitchens, laundries, and often meal service. Open to members and nonmembers, most hostels allow a maximum stay of three nights. For hostels in busy locations, reservations are recommended. In addition, hostelers must have a sleeping bag or "sleepsheet;" rentals are usually available for \$1. The CHA, affiliated with the International Youth Hostel Federation, generally upholds the same rules and rates as American Youth Hostels. For information, the write Canadian Hostelling Association, 1600 James Naismith Dr., Gloucester, Ont. K1B 5N4 (613-748-5638).

Members of CHA receive a \$1-4 reduction in room rates and the opportunity to take advantage of concessions at many local businesses. Furthermore, CHA membership includes membership in IYHF, which allows for discounts at hostels around the world. Likewise, IYHF memberships purchased in any country are valid in Canada. Memberships are valid for one calendar year from the date purchased.

Canada's **national** and **provincial parks** entice travelers with vast expanses of excellent campgrounds. National parks sprinkle Canada: 12 in western Canada, six in the central provinces, seven in the Atlantic Provinces, and four in the Yukon and Northwest Territories (all free). Both provincial and national parks prohibit campfires on the beach, and no camping is allowed in picnic parks.

For topographical and geographical maps, write to the **Canada Map Office,** 615 Booth St., Ottawa, Ont. K1A 0E9 (613-952-7000). For info on National Parks and Forests write to **Canadian Parks Service,** 220 4th Ave. SE, #522, Calgary AB T2P 3HB (403-292-4401). The Winnipeg office of the Canadian Parks Service distributes *Parks West,* a book about all the national parks of Western Canada.

For info on fishing and hunting write to **British Columbia: Fish and Wildlife Information,** Ministry of Environment, 780 Blanshard St., Victoria, BC V8V 1X5 (604-387-9737). Non-resident angling license is \$15 for 6 days, \$27 for a year. Steelhead license \$42. Kootenay Rainbow Trout permit \$4. Hunting license \$145.

Transportation

Train Travel

VIA Rail handles all of Canada's passenger rail service. VIA Rail's routes are as scenic as Amtrak's and its fares often are more affordable. If you're traveling in the Québec City-to-Windsor corridor or in Atlantic Canada and traveling any day but Fri. or Sun., a minimum five-day advance purchase will lower your fare by 40%; buy your ticket at least seven days in advance to get the same discount between those two regions for travel not in the Christmas or summer seasons. People over 60 and full-time students receive an automatic 10% discount. In the corridor, New Brunswick, and Nova Scotia, students receive a 50% discount with a minimum five-day advance purchase. Book well ahead—seats are snapped up quickly. Best for transcontinental travel in summer is the **Canrailpass** (for non-Canadian citizens only) which is valid for 30 days and allows unlimited travel and unlimited stops. (Eastern zone only, peak season fare \$239, youth \$199; Sept. 10-June 14 \$159, youth \$139. Cross country network or western zone only, peak season fare \$399, youth

$349; Oct. 1-May 31 $239, youth $229. Canadian senior citizens with Ambassador Club membership can use an off-season pass with restrictions. Countrywide $269, eastern zone $159.) **Amtrak** (800-426-8725) links with VIA Rail in Toronto and Montréal. For more info, contact VIA Rail Canada, P.O. Box 8116, Montréal, PQ H3C 3N3 (in Montréal 871-1331, in Québec City 692-3940, elsewhere in Québec 800-361-5390; in Toronto 366-8411, in Ottawa 238-8289, elsewhere in Ontario 800-361-1235; in western Canada 800-561-8630. In the USA, contact a travel agent.

Bus and Car Travel

The major inter-provincial bus carriers are **Gray Coach, Greyhound, Voyageur,** and **Charterways.** Greyhound makes the most convenient links between the Canadian and U.S. bus networks. The **Trans-Canada Highway,** the world's longest national highway, stretches 8000 mi. from St. John's, Newfoundland to Victoria, British Columbia. Drivers in Canada must have proof of insurance coverage; because the minimum required is higher than in the U.S., check with your insurance company to ensure sufficient coverage. US motorists are advised to carry the **Canadian Non-Resident Inter-Provincial Motor Vehicle Liability Card,** which is proof of coverage, available only through U.S. insurers. Drivers entering Canada from the U.S. also must carry a vehicle registration certificate. If the car is borrowed, have on hand a letter of permission from the owner; if rented, keep a copy of the rental contract for use when crossing the border. Radar detectors are illegal in Canada. British Columbia, Ontario, and Québec law requires that auto travelers wear seatbelts.

A valid driver's license from any country (including the U.S.) is good in Canada for varying amounts of time, depending on the region. Although international bridges, tunnels, and ferries charge a fee, highways are toll-free. Along the Trans-Canada Hwy., some toll-free ferries are part of the highway system and operate during daylight hours. In summer, cross early in the morning or late in the afternoon to avoid traffic.

If you plan to rent a car in Canada, investigate the discount **White-Corp** rate, offered to Canadian Hostelling Association members over 21. In addition, agencies dealing in late-model automobiles rent cars throughout Canada for significantly less than their U.S. counterparts. You can contact one of the numerous auto-transport agencies; if you are 21, have a valid driver's license, and agree to travel at least 400 mi. per day on a reasonably direct route to the destination, you could have an entire car for the price of the gasoline. **Drive-rider matching agencies** may also cheapen your travel.

ALBERTA

The icy peaks and turquoise lakes of Banff and Jasper National Parks preside as Alberta's most sought-after landscapes. Alberta has much more—more farmlands, wheat fields, and oil rigs, that is. Calgary transcended its just-another-prairie-town status when it hosted the XV Winter Olympics, and is perennially host to the wild and woolly Stampede.

Practical Information

Emergency: 911.

Capital: Edmonton.

Alberta Tourism, 10155 102nd St., Edmonton T5J 4L6 (800-661-8888, in AB 800-222-6501). **Provincial Parks Information,** Standard Life Centre #1660, 10405 Jasper Ave., Edmonton T5J 3N4 (427-9429). Information on Alberta's provincial parks. **Canadian Parks Service,** Box 2989, Station M, Calgary T2P 3H8 (292-4440). Information on the province's national parks (Waterton Lakes, Jasper, Banff, and Wood Buffalo). **Alberta Wilderness Association,** P.O. Box 6398, Station D, Calgary T2P 2E1. Information on off-highway adventures.

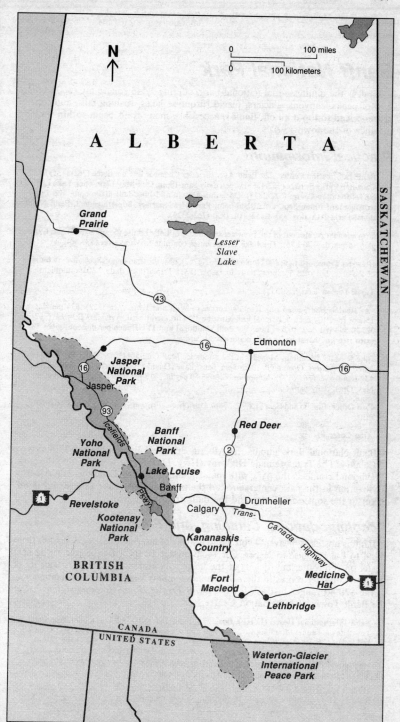

Time Zone: Mountain (2 hr. behind Eastern). **Postal Abbreviation:** AB

Area Code: 403.

Banff National Park

Banff is the quintessential national park, offering 2,543 square mi. (6600 square km) of peaks, canyons, glaciers, placid turquoise lakes, rushing falls, and tons of critters. And to top it all off, Banff is accessible; many trails begin within walking distance of the town.

Practical Information

Banff Information Centre, 224 Banff Ave. Includes **Chamber of Commerce** (762-8421) and **Canadian Parks Service** (762-4256). Open daily 8am-10pm; Oct.-May 10am-6pm. **Lake Louise Information Centre** (522-3833). Open mid-May to mid-June daily 10am-6pm; mid-June to Aug. 8am-10pm; Sept.-Oct. 10am-6pm. **Park Headquarters,** Superintendent, Banff National Park, P.O. Box 900, Banff T0L 0C0 (762-3324).

Greyhound: operates out of the Brewster terminal. To: Lake Louise (5 per day, $6) and Calgary (5 per day, $13.75). The Lake Louise buses continue to Vancouver ($83.50).

Brewster Transportation: 100 Gopher St. (762-6767), near the train depot. Specializes in tours of the area, but runs 1 express daily to Jasper ($31). Depot open daily 7:30am-midnight.

Taxis: Legion Taxi, 762-3353.

Car Rental: Banff Used Car Rentals, corner of Wolf and Lynx (726-3352). $34 per day. 150km free, 10¢ each additional km. Must be 18 with credit card. **Avis,** 209 Bear St. (762-3222). $44 per day. 100km free, 19¢ each additional km. IYHF member discount gives 50 extra free km. Must be 21 with major credit card.

Bike Rentals: Mountain Mopeds, in the Sundance Mall (762-5611). $8.50 per hr., $30 per 4 hr., $45 per day. Open daily 10am-8pm. Must have ID and $100 deposit. **Bactrax Rentals,** 339 Banff Ave. (762-8177). Mountain bikes $3.50 per hr., $15 per day. Less for IYHF members. Open daily 8am-8pm.

Post Office: Buffalo and Bear St. (762-2586). Open Mon.-Fri. 9am-5:30pm. **Postal Code:** T0L 0C0.

Area Code: 403.

Banff National Park adjoins the Alberta-British Columbia border, 120km west of Calgary. The **Trans-Canada Highway** (Hwy. 1) runs east-west through the park. Greyhound connects the park with major points in British Columbia and Alberta. Civilization in the park centers around the twin towns of Lake Louise and Banff, 55km to the southeast. Buses and the daily train are expensive.

Accommodations, Camping, and Food

Banff is hostelers' heaven—you'll find a string of international youth hostels from Banff to Lake Louise to Jasper. For $4, Brewster Tours will take you to the next hostel on the route; buy tickets at the hostels. Additionally, over 20 residents of the townsite offer rooms in their own homes—many year-round, and the majority in the $20-40 range. Just ask for the *Banff Private Home Accommodation* list at the Banff Townsite Information Centre.

Banff International Hostel (IYHF), Box 1358, Banff T0L 0C0 (762-4122), 3km from Banff Townsite on Tunnel Mountain Rd., among a nest of condominiums and lodges, has the look and feel of a chalet. A hike from the center of the townsite, but worth it for the modern amenities and friendly staff. Showers, ski and cycle workshop, laundry facilities, disabled access. Clean quads with 2 bunk beds; linen provided. $12, nonmembers $17. Open 6-10am and 4pm-midnight.

Hilda Creek Hostel (IYHF), 8.5km south of the Icefield Centre on the Icefields Parkway, features a tiny primitive sauna. In the morning, guests must replenish the water supply with a shoulder-bucket contraption that will give you an appreciation for the agility of the peasant farmer. Closed Thurs. night. Accommodates 21. $8, nonmembers $13. Call Banff International Hostel for reservations.

Rampart Creek Hostel (IYHF), 34km south of the Icefield Centre. The usual hostel fare—you know, wood-heated sauna and rock—and ice-climbing. $8, nonmembers $13. Call Banff International Hostel for reservations.

Mosquito Creek Hostel (IYHF), 103km south of the Icefield Centre and 26km north of Lake Louise. Fireplace and sauna. Closed Tues. night. Accommodates 38. $8, nonmembers $13. Call Banff International Hostel for reservations.

Whiskey Jack Hostel (IYHF), west of Lake Louise on Trans-Canada Hwy. Showers, bathrooms. Accommodates 27. Open during summer only. $9, nonmembers $14.

Corral Creek Hostel (IYHF) (522-2186), 5km east of Lake Louise on Hwy. 1A. The hostel nearest Lake Louise. Closed Mon. night. Accommodates 50. $8, nonmembers $13.

Castle Mountain Hostel (IYHF), on Hwy. 1A (762-2637), 1.5km east of the junction of Hwy. 1 and Hwy. 93. Recently renovated. Closed Wed. night. Accommodates 36. $9, nonmembers $14.

None of the park's popular camping sites accepts reservations, so arrive early. Many campgrounds reserve sites for bicyclists and hikers; inquire at the office. Rates range from $6.50 to $12. Park facilities include (listed from north to south): Waterfowl Lake (116 sites), Lake Louise (221 sites), Protection Mountain (89 sites), Johnston Canyon (140 sites), Two Jack Main (381 sites), and Tunnel Mountain Village (622 sites). Each site holds a maximum of two tents and six people.

Bring along your favorite recipes for campfire cooking and you'll eat well here. On your way to the hiking trail or campground, make a pitstop at **Safeway**, 318 Marten St. (762-5378), open daily 8am-10pm. The International Hostel and the YWCA, however, serve affordable meals. The hostel's cafeteria serves up great breakfast specials for $3.50 (served 7-11am), as well as decent dinners (5-10pm). The **Spray Café**, at the Y, offers decent breakfast specials ($2.25-5). **Laggan's Deli** (522-3574), in Samson Mall on Village Rd., is always crowded with people enjoying thick sandwiches on whole-wheat bread ($3.50) or Greek salads ($1.50). (Open daily 6am-8pm.)

Sights and Activities

Hike to the **backcountry** for privacy, beauty, and trout that bite anything. The pamphlet *Drives and Walks,* available at the information centres, covers both the Lake Louise and Banff areas, describing both day and overnight hikes. In order to stay overnight in the backcountry, you need a permit, available free from park info centers and park warden offices. All litter must be taken out of the backcountry with you, and no wood may be chopped in the parks. Both the International Hostel and the Park Information Centre have copies of the *Canadian Rockies Trail Guide,* an excellent, in-depth source of info and maps.

Two easy but rewarding trails within walking distance of the Banff townsite are **Fenland** and **Tunnel Mountain.** Fenland is a 2km jaunt through an area creeping with beaver, muskrat, and waterfowl. Follow Mount Norquay Rd. out of Banff and look for signs either at the bridge just before the picnic area or across the railroad tracks on the left side of the road. The summit of Tunnel Mountain provides a spectacular view of Bow Valley and Mt. Rundle. Follow Wolf St. east from Banff Ave. and turn right on St. Julien Rd. to reach the head of the 2.4km trail.

About 25km out of Banff toward Lake Louise along the Bow Valley Parkway, **Johnston Canyon** offers a moderately taxing but popular half-day hike. The 1.1km to the Canyon's lower falls and the 2.7km to the upper falls consist mostly of a catwalk along the edge of the canyon. Don't stop here, though; if you proceed along the more rugged trail for another 3.1km, you'll see seven blue-green, cold-water springs known as the **Inkpots.** Your car will find **Tunnel Mountain Drive** and **Vermillion Lakes Drive** two particularly scenic places to emit gas fumes into Banff's clear air.

Banff began in 1885 as Hot Springs Reserve, created to drum up business for the newly-built Canadian Pacific Railway and featuring the **Cave and Basin Hot Springs** nearby. In 1914, a resort went up at the springs. The refurbished resort, now called the **Cave and Basin Centennial Centre** (762-4900), screens documentaries and stages exhibits. Relax in the hot springs pool, watched over by lifeguards in pre-WWI bathing costumes, or explore the original cave. The center lies southwest of the city on Cave and Basin Rd. (Center open early June-Sept. daily 10am-8pm; Oct.-early June 10am-5pm. Pool open early June-Sept. only. Admission to pool $2, ages 3-16 $1.25.) If you find Cave and Basin's 32°C (90°F) water too cool, try the **Upper Hot Springs pool**, a 40°C (104°F) cauldron up the hill on Mountain Ave. (Cooler in spring during snow run-off. Open June-Sept. daily 8:30am-11pm. Admission $2, under 12 $1.25.) Bathing suit rental at either spring ($1), towel rental (75¢), and locker rental (25¢) available.

The **Sulphur Mountain Gondola** (762-5438), located right next to the Upper Hot Springs pool, affords a good view of Banff Townsite, and offers a $3 "early bird" breakfast special. (Open summer and Nov. 15-Dec. 15 daily 9am-8pm. $8, under 12 $3.50.) **Brewster Tours** (762-6767) offers an extensive array of bus tours with knowledgeable and entertaining guides. If you have no car, these tours may be the only way to see some of the main attractions, such as the spiral railroad tunnel cut into a mountain. (The trains are so long, you can see them entering and exiting the mountain at the same time.) If you were planning on taking the regular Brester bus from Banff to Jasper ($32.75), you may want to spend $22 more to see the sights in between. (One-way $55, round-trip $76.50. Tickets can be purchased at the bus depot.)

Legal **fishing,** virtually anywhere you find water, requires a national parks fishing permit, available at the info center ($5.25 for a 7-day permit, $10.75 for an annual one). Those who prefer more vigorous water sports can raft the white waters of Kootenay River; **Kootenay River Runners** offer half- and full-day ($69) trips, as well as a more boisterous full-day trip on the Kicking Horse River ($69). Tickets are available at "Tickets," (762-5385), on the corner of Caribou St. and Banff Ave. A particularly good deal is offered through the Banff International Hostel—rafting on the Kicking Horse River (transportation included) for $40. A stop in a pub is promised afterwards.

The hilly road leading to Lake Minnewanka provides **cyclists** with an exhilarating trip, as do many other small paths throughout the park. Bicycling is also allowed on most trails in the Banff Townsite areas. Remember, however, to dismount your bike and stand to the downhill side if a horse approaches. Also be forewarned that the quick and quiet bicycle is more likely to surprise bears than tromping hikers. Since **horseback riding** rates are almost identical throughout the park, pick your favorite location. Banff's bartenders contend that "the real wildlife in Banff is at the bars," but it's their job to say those kinds of things. Banff Avenue is lined with establishments where you can drink, dance, cruise, and get generally banffed.

North American filmmakers often use **Lake Louise's** crystal waters framed by snow-capped peaks as a substitute for Swiss alpine scenes. Rent a canoe from **Chateau Lake Louise Boat House** (522-3511) for $15 per hour; also rent binoculars to scan the hills for wildlife. Several hiking trails begin at the lake. The **Lake Louise Gondola** (522-3555), which runs up Mt. Whitehorn across the Trans-Canada Hwy. from the lake, provides another chance to ooh and aah at the landscape. (Open mid-June to late Sept. daily 9am-6pm. Fare $8, ages 5-11 $4. "One-way hiker's special" $5.)

Calgary

Calgary has become a wealthy and cosmopolitan city (and host of the 1988 Winter Olympics) since oil was found nearby in 1947. The oil may be crude, but the people are refined. Office buildings rise higher than the oil derricks, businesspeople scurry about, and a modern transport system threads soundlessly through immaculate downtown streets. But of course, when the Stampede yahoos into town in July, cowboy hats, Wranglers and Western accents are *de rigeur.*

Practical Information

Convention and Visitors Bureau, 237 8th Ave. SE, Suite 200 (263-8510). Will help locate accommodations, especially around Stampede time in July. Open daily 8am-5pm. Five **Information centres** are scattered throughout the city, including one on the ground floor of Calgary Tower (open daily 8:30am-5pm) and one at the airport on the arrivals level (292-8477; open daily 7am-10pm). **Travel Alberta,** 455 6th St. SW (297-5038; in AB 800-222-6501), on the main floor. Open Mon.-Fri. 8:15am-4:30pm. **Trans-Canada Highway Office,** 6220 16th Ave. NE. Open daily 8am-9pm; Sept.-June 10am-5pm. **Visitor Information Phone Line,** 262-2766.

Calgary International Airport: (292-8477), is about 5km northwest of the city center. Free but infrequent shuttle buses provide service to the city. The **Airporter Bus** (291-3848) offers frequent and friendly service for $7.50. **Brewster Tours** (221-8242) operates a 12:30pm bus and a 5:15pm bus to Banff ($21.40) and a 12:30pm bus to Jasper ($43.25).

Greyhound: 850 16th St. SW (265-9111 or 800-661-8747). Frequent service to Edmonton ($27.29) and Banff ($13.75). Free shuttle bus from C-train at 7th Ave. and 10th St. to bus depot runs every hr. 6:30am-7:30pm with additional buses at 9am, 6pm, and 9pm. 10% senior discount.

Public Transport: Calgary Transit, 206 7th Ave. SW. Bus schedules, passes, and maps. Open Mon.-Fri. 8:30am-5pm. Buses and streetcars (C-Trains). Buses run all over the city; C-Trains cover less territory, but you can ride them free in the downtown area (along 7th Ave. S.; between 10th St. SW and City Hall). Fare $1.35, ages 6-14 85¢, under 6 free; exact change required. Day pass $3.50, kids $2. Book of 10 tickets $11, kids $7.50. **Information line** (276-7801) open Mon.-Fri. 6am-11pm, Sat.-Sun. 8am-9:30pm.

Taxi: Checker Cab, 272-1111. **Associated Cab,** 276-5312.

Car Rental: Rent-a-Wreck, 2339 Macleod Trail (287-9703). From $26 per day with 120 free mi. $11 per day surcharge for under 25. Open Mon.-Fri. 8am-7pm, Sat.-Sun. 9am-4pm. **Dollar** (221-1888 airport, 269-3207 downtown) rents from $42 per day with unlimited mi. Weekend special for $23 per day. Must be 21 with major credit card.

Bike Rental: Sports Rent, 7218 Macleod Trail SW (252-2055). $15-20 per day. **Abominable Sports,** 1217 11th Ave. SW (245-2812). Mountain bikes $25 per day.

Police: 316 7th Ave. SE (266-1234).

Post Office: 220 4th Ave. SE (292-5512). Label mail General Delivery, Station M, Calgary, AB T2P 2G8. Open Mon.-Fri. 8am-5:45pm. **Postal Code:** T2P 1S0.

Area Code: 403.

Accommodations

Calgary International Hostel (IYHF), 520 7th Ave. SE (269-8239). Conveniently located several blocks south of downtown with access to C-Train and public buses. Complete with snack bar, meeting rooms, cooking and barbecue facilities, laundry, and a cycle workshop. Disabled access. Lockout 10am-4:30pm. Front desk closes at midnight, curfew at 2am. $12, nonmembers $16.

University of Calgary, 3330 24th Ave. (220-3203), in the NW quadrant of the city. A little out of the way, but very accessible via bus #9 or the C-Train. Olympian-sized (literally) rooms for competitive prices. Cafeteria and a pub on campus. Rooms available May-Aug. Room rental office, in the Kananaskis Hall, open 24 hr. Singles $29.12, doubles $38. Student rate: singles $21, doubles $31.50. More lavish suites with private bathrooms are available in Olympus Hall or Norquay Hall for approximately $30; book through Kananaskis Hall.

YWCA, 320 5th Ave. SE (263-1550). A deluxe place for women only, in a fine quiet neighborhood. A range of rooms. The security makes for somewhat lifeless lodging—men can't even visit. Cafeteria. Dorm beds $15. Singles $25, with bath $30. 10% senior discount.

St. Louis Hotel, 430 8th Ave. SE (262-6341), above the St. Louis Tavern. The few grim-looking long-term residents generally keep to themselves. Friendly management. Singles $15.75, with TV and bath $18.90. Doubles with bath and TV $28.

Sights

The **Calgary Tower**, 101 9th Ave. SW (266-7171), presides over the city. (Ride to top $3.25 round-trip, kids $1.50.) The 190m tower also affords a 360° view of the city and Rockies. The **Glenbow Museum**, 130 9th Ave. SE (264-8300), just across the street, keeps an odd mix of modern art, military artifacts, and mineral samples. At the entrance stand five cases of Olympic pins, the most extensive collection in town. (Open daily 10am-6pm. Admission $3, seniors $1, students and kids $2. Free Sat.)

Five blocks west on 8th Ave. are the **Devonian Gardens.** Located on the fourth floor of the Toronto Dominion Sq. (at 3rd St. SW), this 2.5-acre indoor garden contains fountains, waterfalls, bridges, and over 20,000 plants, including 138 different local and tropical varieties. Budget travelers can reserve the Gardens for $695 an hour. (Open daily 9am-9pm. Free.) A few blocks to the northwest, the **Energeum,** 640 5th Av. SW (297-4293), in the lobby of the Energy Resources Building, is Calgary's shrine to fossil fuel. A film in the upstairs theater effectively recreates the mania of Alberta's first oil find 1947. In an interactive display, you can run your gloved hand through a pile of the oozing glop. (Open Sun.-Fri. 10:30am-4:30pm; Sept.-May Mon.-Wed. 10:30am-4:30pm. Free.)

Farther west, about 4.3 light-years from Alpha Centauri, warps the **Alberta Science Centre and Centennial Planetarium,** 11 St. and 7th Ave. SW (221-3700). Weekend laser shows feature music from the Rolling Stones and, of course, Pink Floyd. (Open daily 11am-9pm, Oct.-June Wed.-Sun. 1-9pm. Admission to Planetarium and Science Centre $6.75, seniors and kids $4.50; Science Centre only $4, seniors and kids $3. Laser shows $6.75, under 17 $5.75, under 7 not admitted.)

Reach **St. George's Island** by the river walkway to the east; the island houses the **Calgary Zoo.** Many of the animals give birth to new attractions in late spring—the Australian couples seem to be especially prolific. Check out the newly-acquired Siberian tigers. The zoo also features a prehistoric park, which takes you back in time some 65 million years, a botanical garden, and a children's zoo. (Open daily at 9am; closing time seasonally adjusted. For more info, call Zooline, 232-9300. Admission $7, seniors and kids $3.25. Tues. $3, seniors free.)

The Stampede

Even people who find rodeo grotesque still have trouble saying "Calgary" without letting a quick "Stampede" slip out. Calgarians themselves are perhaps the most guilty of perpetuating this relationship. Every year around Stampede time, the locals throw free pancake breakfasts and paint every ground-level window downtown with cartoon cowboy figures offering misspelled greetings ("Welcum, y'all"). Capped by ten-gallons, locals command tour groups to yell "Yahoo" in the least likely of circumstances. Simply put, at Stampede time the entire city of Calgary wigs out.

And why not? Any event that draws millions from across the world deserves hoopla. Make the short trip out to **Stampede Park,** just southeast of downtown; those smart enough to arrive in July will get a glimpse of steer wrestling, bull riding, wild cow milking, and the famous chuckwagon races, where canvas-covered, box-shaped buggies whiz by in a chariot race that defies the laws of aerodynamics. The Stampede also features a **midway,** where you can perch yourself atop the wild, thrashing back of a roller coaster.

Take the C-Train from downtown to the Stampede stop. In 1992, the Stampede will run July 3-12. For official info and ticket order forms, write Calgary Exhibition and Stampede, Box 2890, Station M, Calgary T2P 3C3, or call 800-661-1767. If you're in Calgary, visit **Stampede Headquarters,** 1410 Olympic Way, or call 269-9822. Tickets prices range from $14 to $34.50, depending on the event and seats; ask about rush tickets ($7, youth $6, seniors and kids $3).

Jasper National Park

In contrast to its glitzy southern peer, Jasper's lanscape insulates its inhabitants' tranquility. Even the townsite, a cluster of buildings dropped into 10,000 square km of virgin wilderness, remains serene. Jasperites gladly share their territory with wildlife, and pride themselves on the vast network of trails that penetrate some of the Rockies' most captivating scenery.

Practical Information

Emergency: 852-4848.

Park Information Centre, 500 Connaught Dr. (852-6161). Trail maps and info on all aspects of the park. Open daily 8am-8pm; Sept. 3-Oct. 20 daily 9am-5pm; Oct. 21-Dec. 19 closed; Dec. 20-mid May daily 9am-5pm mid-May to mid-June daily 8am-5pm. **Alberta Tourism,** 632 Connaught Dr. (in AB 800-222-6501). Open Victoria Day-Labor Day daily 8am-8pm. **Jasper Chamber of Commerce,** 634 Connaught Dr. (852-3858). Open Mon.-Fri. 9am-5pm. **Park Headquarters,** Superintendent, Jasper National Park, 632 Patricia St., Box 10, Jasper T0E 1E0 (852-6161).

VIA Rail: 314 Connaught Dr. (800-561-8630). To: Vancouver (3 per week during off-season, 6 per week during summer; $108), Edmonton (3 per week $63); and Winnipeg (3 per week, $174). 10% off for seniors and students with ID. 50% off for kids.

Greyhound: 314 Connaught Dr. (852-3926), in the VIA station. To: Edmonton (4 per day, $37.25), Kamloops ($42.59), and Vancouver ($79).

Brewster Transportation and Tours: Also in the VIA station (852-3332). To Banff (full-day tour $55, daily 5½-hr. express $32.75) and Calgary (1 per day, 8 hr., $41.25).

Taxis: Jasper Taxi, 852-3146.

Car Rental: Tilden Car Rental, in the bus depot (852-4792). $44 per day with 100 free km. Must be 21 with credit card. $2500 insurance deductible for drivers under 25.

Bike Rental: Home Hardware, 623 Patricia Ave. (852-5555). Mountain bikes $4 per hr., $12 per day. Open Mon.-Sat. 9am-8pm, Sun. noon-6pm; early Sept.-late June Mon.-Sat. 9am-6pm. **Whistlers Mountain Hostel** (see below) rents mountains bikes for $10 per day.

Post Office: 502 Patricia St. (852-3041), across Patricia St. from the townsite green. Open July-Aug. Mon.-Fri. 9am-5pm. **Postal Code:** T0E 1E0.

Area Code: 403.

All of the above addresses are in Jasper Townsite, which sits near the middle of the park, 362km southwest of Edmonton and 287km north of Banff. **Highway 16** conducts travelers through the park north of the townsite, while the **Icefields Parkway** (Hwy. 93) connects to Banff National Park in the south. Buses run to the townsite daily from Edmonton, Calgary, and Vancouver. Trains arrive from Edmonton and Vancouver. Renting a bike is the most practical option for short jaunts within the park.

Accommodations, Camping, and Food

Ask for the **Approved Accommodations List** at the Park Information Center if you wish to sleep cheaply in Jasper (singles $15-35, doubles $25-45, quads $40-55). If you prefer mingling with the youthful set, head to a hostel (listed below from north to south). Reservations, as well as information on closing days and on the winter "key system," channel through the Edmonton-based Northern Alberta Hostel Association (439-3089).

Maligne Canyon Hostel (IYHF), on Maligne Canyon Rd. (852-3584), 15km northeast of the townsite. Closed Wed. Accommodates 24. $8, nonmembers $12.

Whistlers Mountain Hostel (IYHF), on Sky Tram Rd. (852-3215), 7km south of the townsite. Closest to the townsite and the park's most modern (and crowded) hostel. A hike from town, mostly uphill. The management shuts off the lights at 11pm sharp and flicks them on again at 7am. You may have to sweep out the fireplace before you leave in the morning, but at least it works. Accommodates 50. $12, nonmembers $16.

Mount Edith Cavell Hostel (IYHF), on Edith Cavell Rd. off Hwy. 93A. Closed Thurs. Accommodates 32. Road closes in winter, but the hostel welcomes anyone willing to ski or snowmobile the 11km from Hwy. 93A. Closed Thurs. $8, nonmembers $12. Open mid-June to early Oct.

Athabasca Falls Hostel (IYHF) (852-5959), on Hwy. 93, 30km south of Jasper Townsite near the namesake falls. Closed Tues. $8, nonmembers $12.

Beauty Creek Hostel (IYHF), on Hwy. 93, 78km south of Jasper Townsite. Beautifully situated next to a brook. Closed Tues. Accommodates 20. Accessible through a "key system" in winter. $8, nonmembers $12. Open May to mid-Sept. Closed Wed.

For campground updates, tune in to 1450 AM on your radio near Jasper Townsite. The park maintains sites at 10 campgrounds, including (north to south): Pocahontas (140 sites), Whistlers (781 sites), Wapiti (345 sites), Wabasso (238 sites), Columbia Icefield (33 sites), and Wilcox Creek (46 sites). Rates range from $6 to $16.50.

For cheap eats, stock up at a local market or bulk foods store and head for the backcountry. For around-the-clock grocery supplies, stop at **Wink's Food Store,** 605 Patricia St. **Nutter's,** also on Patricia St., offers grains, nuts, dried fruits, and (if you're sick of healthful food) candy, all in bulk form. They also sell deli meats, canned goods, and fresh-ground coffee. (Open Mon.-Sat. 9am-10pm, Sun. 10am-9pm.) For a sit-down meal, try the Egyptian food at **Roony's,** 618 Connaught Dr. (852-5830), especially the *kofta,* spicy ground beef with parsley and onions on toasted bread ($7). Burgers are cheap ($3-3.25). (Open daily noon-2am.)

Sights and Activities

An extensive trail network connects most parts of Jasper, with many paths starting at the townsite. Info centers distribute free copies of *Day Hikes in Jasper National Park* and a summary of the longer hikes.

Mt. Edith Cavell, named after a WWI hero, often thunders with the sound of avalanches off the Angel Glacier. Take the ½km loop trail or the 8km return **Path of the Glacier.** Mt. Edith Cavell rears 30km south of the townsite on Cavell Rd. **Maligne Lake,** the largest glacier-fed lake in the Canadian Rockies, has vivid turquoise water. One special feature of Jasper National Park is **Medicine Lake,** 30km east of Jasper Townsite. Water flows into the lake with no visible outlet. The trick? The water flows out through a series of underground caves, and emerges in such areas as **Maligne Canyon,** 11km east of the townsite on Maligne Canyon Rd. Another natural phenomenon, this canyon drops over 46m, and squirrels can jump across the narrow gorge. Humans cannot, though; several squirrel-wannabes have proven this by falling to their deaths. For $37.45, you can have **Fun on a Bike** (852-4242), peddling 20km downhill from Medicine Lake to Maligne Canyon.

Horseshoe Lake, 30km south of town and 5km north of Athabasca Falls, is a splendid location for **cliff diving,** but only try it in July and August, and remember—drinking and diving don't mix. A more common but equally adventurous water activity is rafting. **Whitewater Rafting (Jasper) Ltd.** (852-7238) runs several rafting trips from $32-50; register at the Esso station. After dipping in Jasper's glacier-fed waters, revive your numbed body at the 102°F, odorless **Miette Hot Springs,** north off Hwy. 16 along the eponymously named road. (Open mid-June to Labor Day 8:30am-10:30pm. Admission $2, kids $1.25.)

Joining the Banff tradition, Jasper has a **gondola** of its own. Rising 2½km up the side of Whistlers Mountain, the Jasper Tramway will make you jasp with excitement with its majestic views of the park, as well as an opportunity to spend money at its gift shops and restaurant. (Fare $9, under 12 $4.50. Open mid-April to Oct. 8am-9:30pm; Sept. to mid-Oct. 9am-4:30pm. Call 852-3093 for more info.) A trail starting from the Whistlers Mountain Hostel also leads up the slope, but it's a steep 10km; to spare your quadriceps you'll want to take the tram ride down ($4.50).

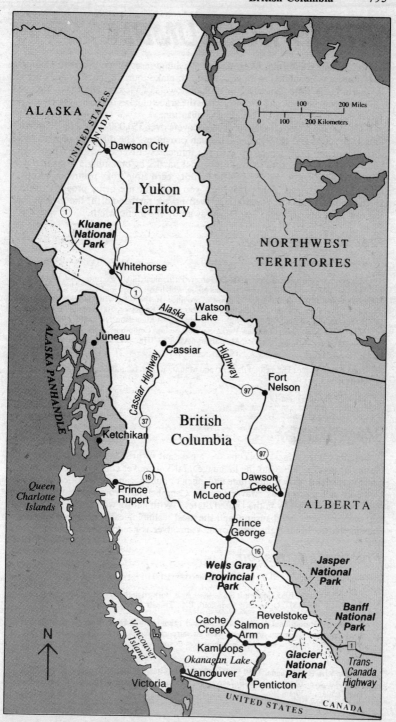

BRITISH COLUMBIA

Larger than California, Oregon, and Washington combined, British Columbia (B.C.) attracts enough visitors year-round to make tourism the province's second largest industry (after timber). The million flowers of Victoria and the million people of Vancouver draw city slickers, while the graceful lakes of the nearby Okanagan Valley lure those intent on escaping civilization.

B.C., Canada's westernmost province, covers over 350,000 square mi., bordering four U.S. states and three other Canadian provinces. The difficulty of road travel throughout the province varies with the immensely diverse terrain. When taking your own vehicle, be sure to avoid potential hassles by obtaining a Canadian non-resident Interprovince motor vehicle **liability card** from your insurance company before leaving; border police may turn you away for not being properly insured. In the south, roads are plentiful and well paved; farther north, the asphalt (and the towns) seems to have been blown away by the arctic winds.

Practical Information

Capital: Victoria.

Ministry of Tourism and Provincial Secretary, Parliament Bldg., Victoria V8V 1X4 (604-387-1642). Write for the accommodations guide, which lists prices and services for virtually every hotel, motel, and campground in the province. In the U.S., write **Tourism BC,** P.O. Box C-34971, Seattle, WA 98124. Branches also in **San Francisco,** 100 Bush St. #400, San Francisco, CA 94104 (415-981-4780); and **Irvine,** 2600 Michelson Dr. #1050, Irvine, CA 92715 (714-852-1054). **Canadian Parks Service,** Senior Communications Officer, 220 4th Ave. SE, P.O. Box 2989, Station M, Calgary, AB T2P 3H8, or call **BC Parks** at 604-387-5002.

Time Zone: Pacific (3 hr. behind Eastern) and Mountain (2 hr. behind Eastern). **Postal Abbreviation:** BC

Alcohol: Drinking age 19.

Vancouver

Canada's third largest city comes as a pleasant surprise to the jaded, metropolis-hopping traveler. Tune out the language, and Vancouver could be a North American Switzerland, with immaculate and efficient public transport, spotless sidewalks, and even safe seedy areas. Mayor Gordon Campbell has promised that his city will "not become like a city in the United States." With nature walks among 1000-year-old timber stands, wind-surfing, and the most technologically advanced movie theater in the world all right downtown, Vancouver is keeping that promise.

Practical Information

Police: Main and Powell St. (665-3321). **Emergency:** 911.

Travel Infocentre, 1055 Dunsmuir (683-2000), near Burrard in the West End. Buy the larger-scale street map ($2). Open daily 8am-6pm. **B.C. Transit Information Centre:** 261-5100.

Vancouver International Airport: on Sea Island 11km south of the city center. Connections to major cities. To reach downtown from the airport, take BC Transit bus #100 to 70th Ave., transfer there to bus #20, which arrives downtown heading north on the Granville Mall.

Trains: VIA Rail Canada, 1150 Station St. (800-665-8630 or 669-3050), off Rte. 99 (Main St.) at 1st Ave. Three per week to Jasper ($115.56) and Edmonton ($160.50). Open Thurs.-Tues. 7:30am-9:30pm, Wed. 7:30am-2:30pm. **B.C. Rail,** 1311 W. 1st St. (631-3500), just over the Lions Gate Bridge in North Vancouver. Take the SeaBus downtown to North Vancouver,

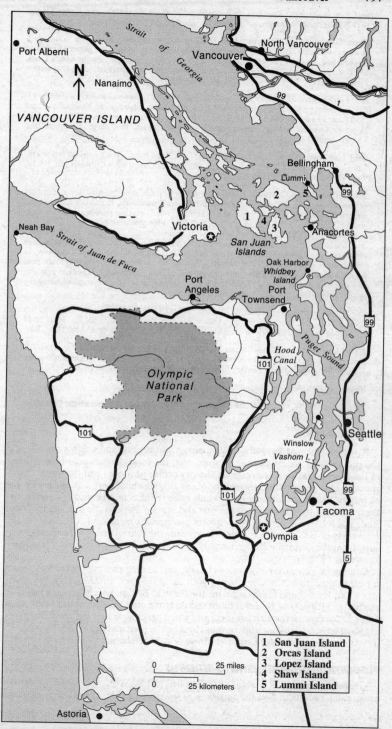

1 San Juan Island
2 Orcas Island
3 Lopez Island
4 Shaw Island
5 Lummi Island

then bus #239 west. One way daily to: Whistler ($13), Squamish, and Prince George ($71.50). Open daily 7am-9pm.

Buses: Greyhound, 150 Dunsmuir (662-3222), downtown at Beatty St. Service to the south and across Canada. To: Calgary (4 per day, $79); Banff (4 per day, $78); Jasper (3 per day, $73.65); and Seattle (7 per day, US$20). Open daily 5:30am-midnight. **Pacific Coach Lines,** 150 Dunsmuir (662-3222). Serves southern B.C., including Vancouver Island, in cooperation with Greyhound. To Victoria ($19.50, including ferry).

B.C. Ferries: (general info 669-1211; recorded info 685-1021; Tsawwassen ferry terminal 943-9331). Ferries to Victoria, Nanaimo and the Gulf Islands. Mainland to Vancouver Island ($5.25, car and driver $24, motorcycle and driver $14.50, bicycle and rider $7.50; ages 5-11 ½-price). Terminal serving Victoria actually located in Swartz Bay, north of Victoria. (See Victoria below.)

Gray Line Tours: 900 W. Georgia St. (681-8687), in Hotel Vancouver. Expensive but worthwhile city tours with a number of package options. Basic tours leave daily and last 3½ hr. (fare $29.50, kids $15). Reservations required.

Public Transport: B.C. Transit covers most of the city and suburbs, with direct transport or easy connections to the city's points of departure: Tsawwassen, Horseshoe Bay, and the airport. Central zone fare $1.25, seniors and ages 5-11 65¢. Two-zone peak-hour (6:30-9:30am and 3-6:30pm) fare $1.75, seniors and ages 5-11 90¢; three-zone peak-hour travel $2.50, seniors and ages 5-11 $1.25; off-peak fares same as one-zone price. Day-passes $3.50, transfers free. Single fares, passes, and transfers are good for the SeaBus and SkyTrain also. The **SeaBus** runs from the Waterfront Station, at the foot of Granville St. in downtown Vancouver, to the Lonsdale Quay at the foot of Lonsdale Ave. in North Vancouver. The **SkyTrain** runs from the Waterfront Station Southeast to Scott Rd. in New Westminster. Schedules available at Vancouver Travel. The SkyTrain and SeaBus operate on an honor system; cheating the system is tempting, but don't—the fines are steep.

Car Rental: Rent-A-Wreck, 180 W. Georgia (688-0001), in the West End, and 340 W. 4th Ave. at Manitoba. From $30 per day; 150km free plus 15¢ each additional km. Must be 19 with credit card. Both locations open Mon.-Fri. 7am-7pm, Sat. 9am-5pm, Sun. 10am-3pm.

Help Lines: Vancouver Crisis Center, 733-4111. Open 24 hrs. **Rape Crisis Center,** 875-6011. Open 24 hrs. **Gay and Lesbian Switchboard,** 1-1170 Bute St. (684-6869). Open Mon.-Fri. 7-10pm, Sat.-Sun. 4-10pm. **Seniors Information and Support,** 531-2320 or 531-2425.

Time Zone: Pacific (3 hr. behind Eastern).

Post Office: 349 W. Georgia St. (662-5725). Open Mon.-Fri. 8am-5:30pm. **Postal Code:** V6B 3P7.

Area Code: 604.

Rivers, inlets, and bays divide Vancouver into regions and neighborhoods, and the profusion of waterways can confuse even the most diligent map-reader. Most of the city's attractions converge on the city center peninsula and the larger rhino-snout-shaped peninsula to the south. Many neighborhoods are not labeled on the city maps issued by Tourism B.C. Locals refer to the center peninsula's residential area, bounded by downtown to the east and Stanley Park to the west, as the **West End.** The western portion of the southern peninsula from around Alma Ave. to the University of B.C. campus is **Point Grey,** while the central area on the same peninsula, from the Granville Bridge roughly to Alma Ave., is the Kitsilano, (familiarly known as **"Kits"**).

Driving in Vancouver is a serious hassle, and finding parking spaces downtown is next to impossible. Consider leaving your car at the **Park'n'Ride** in New Westminster. (Exit Hwy. 1 and follow signs for the Pattullo Bridge; watch for signs just over the bridge.) Rush hour begins at dawn and ends at sunset. Beware of the 7 to 9:30am and 3 to 6pm restrictions on left turns and street parking. When you can't find parking at street level, look for underground lots, but be prepared to pay sky-high prices. Try the lot below Pacific Centre at Howe and W. Georgia.

Accommodations and Camping

Greater Vancouver is a rabbit warren of bed and breakfast accommodations; average rates run about $40 for singles, $50 for doubles. The visitors bureau has a long list of B&Bs in Vancouver. Several private agencies also match travelers with B&Bs, usually for a fee; get in touch with **Town and Country Bed and Breakfast** at 731-5942 or **Best Canadian** at 738-7207. Always call for reservations at least two days in advance.

Vancouver International Hostel (IYHF), 1515 Discovery St. (224-3208), is in Point Grey on Jericho Beach. Turn north off 4th Ave., following signs for Marine Dr., or take bus #4 from Granville St. downtown. Comely location on beach and park, with a great view of the city from English Bay. Over 185 beds, massive dorm rooms, good cooking facilities, chore opportunities (work 2 hr. for a free bed), and TV room. 8 family rooms. In summer, 3-day max. stay. Strictly enforced midnight curfew. $12.50, nonmembers $14.50. Linen $1.50.

Globetrotter's Inn, 170 W. Esplanade in North Vancouver (988-5141). Take the SeaBus to Lonsdale Quay, then walk 1 block east to W. Esplanade and Chesterfield. Close to downtown. Kitchen facilities, shared baths. Singles $13. Private singles $27. Doubles $33.

Vincent's Backpackers Hostel, 927 Main (682-2441), right next to the VIA train station, under a big green store called "The Source." Take "Main St." bus #3 or "Fraser" #8. Not quite as clean or as structured as the IYHF hostel. Kitchen, fridge, TV, stereo, and the music of revving Greyhound engines. Office open 8am-midnight. Check-in before noon for the best shot at a bed. Shared rooms $10. Singles with shared bath $20. Doubles with shared bath $25.

Paul's Guest House, 345 W. 14th Ave. (872-4753), at Alberta. Take bus #15. Nestled in a beautiful residential area. Tidy, cozy singles at $35. Doubles $45. Shared baths, complimentary full breakfast. Paul boasts of speaking 11 different languages; trip him up with your knowledge of Ancient Etruscan. Check in before 11pm. Call ahead for reservations.

YMCA, 955 Burrard (681-0221), between Smithe and Nelson. Newly renovated. Concerned staff on duty 24 hrs. Shared washrooms and showers. Pool, gymnasiums, ball courts, weight rooms (free). Cafeteria open Mon.-Fri. 7am-4pm, Sat. 8am-2pm. Singles $31. Doubles $46. Students and seniors 10% off. Weekly and monthly rates available Oct.-April.

Richmond RV Park, 6200 River Rd. (270-7878), near Holly Bridge in Richmond. Take Hwy. 99 to Westminster Hwy., then follow the signs. Sites offer little privacy, but great showers and friendly staff soothe your woes. Sites $14, with hookup $17.50-19. Open April-Oct.

ParkCanada, 4799 Hwy. 17 (943-5811), in Delta, about 30 km. south of downtown Vancouver. Take Hwy. 99 south to Tsawwassen Ferry Terminal Rd., then go east for 2½ km. Located next to a giant waterslide park; flush toilets, free showers, and tidal pool, though the lines may be long. Sites $12, with hookup $20.

Food

Steer clear of places specializing in "authentic Canadian cuisine"—nobody really knows what Canadian cuisine is. The East Indian neighborhoods along Main, Fraser, and 49th St. offer spicy dishes. Vancouver's Chinatown (see Sights below) is the second largest in North America, after San Fran's. Here groceries, shops, and restaurants cluster around East Pender and Gore St.

The **Granville Island Market,** under the Granville Bridge, off W. 4th Ave. and across False Creek from downtown, intersperses trendy shops, art galleries, and restaurants with produce stands selling local and imported fruits and vegetables. Take bus #50 from Granville St. downtown. (Market open daily 9am-6pm, Labor Day-Victoria Day Tues.-Sun. 9am-6pm.)

The Naam, 2724 W. 4th Ave. (783-7151), in the Kits area. Take bus #4 or 7 from Granville. Vancouver's oldest natural-foods restaurant. Don't let the name's homonyms scare you. Very good tofu-nut-beet burgers ($5), spinach enchiladas ($8), and salad bar ($1.25 per 100 grams). Live music nightly 7-10pm. Open 24 hrs.

The Souvlaki Place, 1807 Mortan St. (689-3064), at Denman near Stanley Park. Greek establishment pulsating with Mediterranean music. *Souvlaki* $4.50; yogurt, honey, and pita $3. Open daily 11:30am-11pm.

The Only Seafood Cafe, 20 E. Hastings St. (681-6546), at Carrall St. on the edge of Chinatown, within walking distance of downtown. Large portions of great seafood at decent prices. Cooking since 1912, and they *still* don't have a restroom. Fried halibut steak $9. Open Mon.-Thurs. 11am-9:30pm, Fri.-Sat. 11am-10pm.

The Green Door, 111 E. Pender (685-4194), in central Chinatown, 3 blocks from The Only. Follow the alley off Columbia St. to find the hidden entrance. This wildly green establishment plays a prominent role in the annals of Vancouver hippie lore. Huge servings of heavy Chinese seafood ($5.50) behind the emerald portal. Open daily noon-10:30pm; Oct.-May Wed.-Mon. noon-10pm.

A Taste of Jamaica, 941 Davie St. (683-3464), downtown. Reggae, Jamaica posters, and red, green, and gold seat covers. Filling, authentic food. Ox-tail stew $6, goat or lamb curry $6. Open Mon.-Sat. 11am-11pm, Sun. 2-11pm.

Sights

The landmark of the Expo '86 World's Fair is a 17-story, metallic, geodesic sphere which houses **Science World,** 1455 Quebec St. (687-7832), at Terminal Ave. Science World features hands-on exhibits for kids and the **Omnimax Theatre** (875-6664), a high-tech hemispheric screenhouse. Featured film subjects range from dinosaurs to asteroids. (Admission both $11, to Science World only $7. Call for show times.) The second expo site is the Canada Pavilion, now called **Canada Place,** about ½ km away. You can reach it by SkyTrain from the main Expo site. Visitors who make this four-minute journey can view Canadian arts and crafts as well as films in the CN IMAX Theatre (682-4629). Ranging in price ($6.25-9), the not-so-cheap movie thrills from the flat, five-story screen do not look as stunning as the domed screens of some IMAX theatres. (Open daily noon-9pm.)

Newly renovated, the **Lookout!** 555 W. Hastings St. (683-5684), offers fantastic 360° views of the city and surrounding areas. Though expensive, your ticket lasts all day; you can leave and come back for the romantic night skyline. (Open daily 9am-10pm. Admission $5, seniors and students $3.50.) The **Vancouver Art Gallery,** 750 Hornby St. (682-5621), in Robson Sq., has a small but well-presented collection of classical, contemporary, and Canadian art and photography. Free tours for large groups frequently are given; just tag along. (Open Mon.-Wed. and Fri.-Sat. 10am-5pm, Thurs. 10am-9pm, Sun. noon-5pm. Admission $4.25, seniors and students $2.50. Free Thurs. 5-9pm.)

Gastown overflows with overpriced craft shops, boutiques, nightclubs, and restaurants. Listen for the continent's only steam-powered clock on the corner of Cambie and Water St.—it whistles every 15 minutes. Gastown takes a fair walk from downtown or a short ride on bus #22 along Burrard St. to Carrall St. Just east, **Chinatown** also lies within walking distance of downtown, or you can take bus #22 on Burrard St. northbound to Pender St. at Carrall St., and return by bus #22 westbound on Pender St. Vancouver's Chinatown spreads out along Pender St. and both sides of Main St., replete with restaurants and shops. The area is rundown and somewhat unsafe. Gray Line Tours (see Practical Information) provides a safer but costlier way to see Chinatown.

Probably the most popular of the city's attractions, **Stanley Park** (681-1141), on the westernmost end of the city center peninsula, testifies to urban foresight. (Take bus #19.) The watery perimeter is followed by a **seawall promenade,** with more views, and more company to the walker or cyclist. Within the park's boundaries lie various restaurants and tennis courts, hiking and biking trails, the Malkin Bowl (an outdoor theater), and equipped beaches. Nature walks leave May to September on Tuesdays at 10am, from July to August at 7pm. Call the park for departure points. Rent practically new bikes from **Bayshore,** 745 Denman (688-2453) for $5.20 per hour, $25 per day. Strange aquatic species lurk at the **Vancouver Aquarium** (682-1118), on the eastern side of the park, not far from the entrance. (Open daily 9:30am-8pm; in winter 10am-5:30pm. Admission $8, seniors and ages 13-18 $7, under 12 $5.) Visit Stanley Park's small, free **zoo** next door, if only to see the monkeys taunt nearby polar bears. (Open daily 10am-5pm.)

Follow the western side of the seawall south to **Sunset Beach Park** (738-8535), a strip of grass and beach that extends south all the way to the Burrard Bridge. All of Vancouver's beaches have lifeguards from Victoria Day to Labor Day daily from 11:30am to 9pm. At the southern end of Sunset Beach flounders the **Aquatic Centre,** 1050 Beach Ave. (689-7156), a public facility with a 50m indoor saltwater pool, sauna, gymnasium, and diving tank. (Open Mon.-Thurs. 7am-10pm, Sat. 8am-9pm, Sun. 11am-9pm. Pool open Mon.-Thurs. at 7am. Gym use $3.20; pool use $2.70.)

Vancouverites frequent Kitsilano Beach, known to locals as **"Kits,"** on the other side of English Bay from Sunset Beach. Its heated saltwater outdoor pool (731-0011; open summer only) has changing rooms, lockers, and a snack bar. (Pool open May-Sept. Mon.-Fri. 7am-8:45pm. Admission $1.55, seniors and kids 75¢, families $3.20. Beach open from Victoria Day to Labor Day 11:30am-9pm.)

Jericho Beach, to the west, tends to be used less heavily than Kits Beach. Jericho begins a border of beaches and park lands that lines Point Grey and the **University of British Columbia (UBC).** Old-growth forest covers much of the extensive UBC campus in a delightfully untailored fashion. Bike and hiking trails cut through the campus and around the edges. The university rests on a hill, providing a scenic view of the city and the surrounding mountains.

Scramble down the cliffs to the southwest of the UBC campus to **Wreck Beach,** an unofficial, unsanctioned, unlifeguarded beach for the unclothed. Any UBC student can point you toward one of the semi-hidden access paths.

Entertainment and Events

To keep abreast of the entertainment scene, pick up a copy of the weekly *Georgia Straight* or the monthly *AF Magazine,* both free at magazine stands and record stores. The 25¢ *West Ender* lists entertainment in that lively neighborhood, while free *Angles* serves the gay community.

Basin St. Cabaret, 23 W. Corova St. (688-5351). Hip new club. Local blues and jazz aficionados jam from 9pm-2am. Cheap beer (pint $3, glass $1.50), dance floor, and terrace. No cover.

Blarney Stone Inn, 216 Carrall St. (687-4322). Live Irish music, restaurant, and dance floor. Lunch $5, dinner around $12. Open Mon. 11:30am-5pm, Tues.-Fri. 11:30am-2am, Sat. 5pm-2am. Cover $3.

Spats, 1222 Hamilton St. (684-7321), in the warehouse district. Enter facing Pacific Blvd. An innovative gay and lesbian club. Open daily 7:30pm-2am.

Robson Square Conference Centre, 800 Robson St. (660-2487), sponsors events almost daily during the summer and weekly the rest of the year, either on the plaza at the square or in the center itself. Their concerts, theater productions, exhibits, lectures, symposia, and films are all free or at low cost. Pick up the center's monthly brochure *What's Happening at Robson Square* from the visitors bureau or businesses in the square.

Vancouver also has an active theater community. The **Arts Club Theatre,** Granville Island (687-1644), hosts big-name theater and musical productions, while the **Theatre in the Park** program (687-0174) in Stanley Park's Malkin Bowl, has a summer season of musical comedy. The annual **Vancouver Shakespeare Festival** (734-0194), from June to August in Vanier Park, often needs volunteer ushers and program-sellers, who get to watch the critically-acclaimed shows for free.

Vancouver's universities have dance cards filled with cultural activities. At Simon Fraser University, the **SFU Centre for the Arts** (291-3514) offers both student and guest-professional theater, primarily from September to May. For UBC activities, call (228-3131) or pick up a free copy of *Ubissey.* UBC's film series screens high-quality movies Thursday and Friday nights for $2.50.

Seasonal Events

Attend one of Vancouver's annual fairs, festivals, or celebrations to confirm rumors of the city's cosmopolitan nature. The famed **Vancouver Folk Music Festival** takes place in mid-July in Jericho park, when North America's best big- and little-name performers give concerts and workshops for three days. You can purchase tickets à la carte, or for the whole weekend (with a $5 discount before June 1). For more details, contact the festival at 3271 Main St., Vancouver V6V 3M6 (879-2931).

Experience the area's Native folk culture at the **First People's Cultural Festival,** held each June at a different area reserve. A full day of traditional dance and crafts is capped with a salmon barbecue (admission $12). Proceeds benefit the Urban Native Education Centre, 285 E. 5th St. (873-3761); call the info center for more details. The festival is very popular so book accommodations a month in advance (particularly at the hostel). The annual **jazz festival** (682-0706) in late June is totally red hot and blue.

Vancouver celebrates its relationship with the sea several times a year. The Maritime Museum in Vanier Park (see Sights and Activities) hosts the annual **Captain Vancouver Day** (736-4431) in mid-June to commemorate the exploration of Canada's west coast by Captain George Vancouver; the bicentennial will be celebrated in 1992. In mid-July, the **Vancouver Sea Festival** (684-3378) schedules four days of parades, concerts, sporting events, fireworks, and salmon BBQs. All events take place in English Bay and are free, although the salmon aren't. The headline attraction is the notorious **Nanaimo to Vancouver Bathtub Race,** a journey across the rough waters of the Strait of Georgia.

Near Vancouver

Huff and puff along on the **Royal Hudson Steam Locomotive,** operated by 1st Tours (688-7246). After a two-hour ride along the coast from Vancouver to Squamish (the gateway to Garibaldi Provincial Park), passengers on the "Love Train" get 90 minutes to browse in town before they head back. (Excursions May 21-July 16 Wed.-Sun.; July 19-Sept. 4 daily; Sept. 6-Sept. 24 Wed.-Sun. Fare $26.64, seniors and youths $22.45, kids $6.54.) The train departs from the B.C. Rail terminal, 1311 W. 1st St., across the Lions Gate Bridge in North Vancouver. Call 1st Tours for required reservations.

To the east, the town of **Deep Cove** maintains that *je ne sais quoi* of a fishing village. Sea otters and seals gather on the pleasant Indian Arm beaches. Take bus #210 from Pender to the Phibbs Exchange on the north side of Second Narrows Bridge; from there, take bus #211 or 212. **Cates Park,** at the end of Dollarton Hwy. on the way to Deep Cove, has popular swimming and scuba waters, a good biking daytrip out of Vancouver. Bus #211 also leads to beautiful **Mount Seymour Provincial Park.** Trails leave from Mt. Seymour Rd., and a paved road winds the 8km to the top. One hundred campsites ($7) are available, and the skiing is superb.

For a less vigorous hike that still offers fantastic views of the city, head for **Lynn Canyon Park.** The suspension bridge here is free and uncrowded, unlike its more publicized look-alike in Capilano Canyon. Take bus #228 from the North Vancouver Seabus terminal and walk the ½km to the bridge.

Grouse Mountain is the ski resort closest to downtown Vancouver and has the crowds to prove it. Take bus #246 from the North Vancouver SeaBus terminal; at Edgemont Village transfer to bus #232, then the "supersky ride." The $10 aerial tramway runs from 9am-10pm. The slopes are lit until 10:30pm. From mid-April to mid-Oct. bus #236 operates directly from the SeaBus terminal to the sky ride. On sunny days, helicopter tours leave from the top of the mountain, starting at $30 per person. For more info contact Grouse Mountain Resorts, 6400 Nancy Greene Way, North Vancouver V7R 4N4 (984-0661; ski report 986-6292). Ski rental is available for $19 a day, no deposit required. Adult lift tickets are $28.

The **Reifel Bird Sanctuary** on Westham Island, 16km south of Vancouver, is just northwest of the Tsawwassen ferry terminal. Bus #601 from Vancouver will take you to the town of **Ladner,** 1½km east of the sanctuary. 230 species of birds live in the 850 acres of marshlands, and spotting towers are set up for long-term birdwatching. (Open daily 9am-4pm.) For info contact the **BC Waterfowl Society** at 946-6980.

Fifty km north of Vancouver (on the way to Whistler) is the **BC Museum of Mining** in Britannia Beach (688-8735, 896-2233). An electric mine train pumps passengers through an old copper artery into the mountain that poured out the most metal in the British Empire: 1.3 billion pounds. (Open mid-May to June Wed.-Sun. 10am-

5pm; July-Labor Day daily 10am-5pm; Sept. Sat.-Sun. 10am-5pm. Admission $6, seniors and students $3.50.)

Golden Ears Provincial Park is 50km east of the town of Haney. Turn north on 224th St. and follow it 4km until it ends, then turn right and proceed for 8km. The roads are not well marked, but all roads lead to Golden Ears. Inside the park, the **Cultus Lake Campground** operates 346 tentsites ($10 per site). Ask whether the name comes from that of the fabled *Cultosaurus erectus.* The park itself has a myriad of hiking trails, including some short ones leading to waterfalls.

A classic trip farther outside Vancouver is the two-hour drive up Rte. 99 to the town of **Whistler** and nearby **Garibaldi Provincial Park.** Follow Rte. 99 north from Horseshoe Bay, or take local **Maverick Coach Lines** (255-1171). **B.C. Rail** (see Practical Information above) also serves Whistler from Vancouver; their run stops directly behind the local youth hostel. Check the ride board at the IYHF hostel in Vancouver, since people frequently trek between the two. Whistler Mountain has top skiing, with the highest accessible vertical drop in North America (1 mi.). Slopes for the beginner and intermediate are also available. For more info contact Whistler Resort Association, Whistler V0N 1B0 (932-4222). The park also offers some fine wilderness hiking but vehicle access is out of the question. On the western shore of Alta Lake in Whistler, that North American giant, the **Whistler Youth Hostel (CYHA)** (932-5492), has 35 beds, laundry, and extensive kitchen facilities. ($12.50, nonmembers $17.50.) In cahoots with Vincent's in Vancouver, a **Backpackers Hostel**, 2124 Lake Placid Rd. (932-1177), lies near the train station. With nice but cramped rooms ($12, $15 in winter), the hostel also has a kitchen, TV, and VCR.

Victoria

Although unabashed at the ornery prospectors who once swilled beer in its brothels on their way to the Cariboo mines during the 1858 gold rush, modern Victoria still lives in the long-faded glory of the British Empire. The anglophilic citizens of British Columbia's capital travel in double-decker buses decorated with the Union Jack and listen to kilt-clad bagpipers at the Westminster-like Parliament. On warm summer days, some residents sip their noon tea on the lawns of Tudor-style homes in the suburbs, while downtown, horse-drawn carriages clatter. Victoria is eminently worthy of its namesake.

Practical Information

Police: (384-4111).

Tourism Victoria, 812 Wharf St., Victoria V8W 1T3 (382-2127), in the Inner Harbour. The amount of pamphlets must have decimated a forest.

Buses: Pacific Coach Lines and **Island Coach Lines,** 700 Douglas St. (385-4411), in the same building. Service to most island cities. To Vancouver (8 per day, $19.50) and Seattle (1 per day, $26). Lockers $2 for 24 hrs.

Ferries: BC Ferry, 656-0757 or 386-3431. Service to Vancouver or the mainland (14 per day; $5.25 per person, $2.25 per bike, $18.75 per car). **Washington State Ferries,** 381-1551. To the San Juans (passengers $7.50 seniors and ages 5-11 $4, car and driver $35).

Public Transport: Victoria Regional Transit, 382-6161. Serves the whole city daily. Travel in single-zone area costs $1, multi-zone $1.25. Daily passes for unlimited single-zone travel are available at the visitors center for $3, $2 for seniors and under 12.

Car Rental: Sigmar Rent-A-Car, 752 Caledonia Ave. (388-6230). $17 per day plus 10¢ per km. Must be 21 with a major credit card.

Taxi: Victoria Taxi, 383-7111.

Bike Rental: Explore Victoria, 1007 Langley St. (381-2453 or 382-9928). Mountain bikes $5 per hr., $15 for 24 hrs. $20 deposit. Open daily 9am-6pm.

Help Lines: Crisis Line, 386-6323.

Time Zone: Pacific (3 hr. behind Eastern).

Post Office: Postal Station E, 1230 Government St. (388-3575), at Yates. Open Mon.-Fri. 8:30am-5pm. **Postal Code:** V8W 2L9.

Area Code: 604.

Ferries and buses connect Victoria, on Vancouver Island's southern tip, to many cities in British Columbia and Washington. The city of Victoria enfolds the Inner Harbour; **Government Street** and **Douglas Street** are the main north-south thoroughfares and are where most of the tourist attractions can be found.

Accommodations and Camping

Victoria Youth Hostel (IYHF), 516 Yates St. (385-4511), at Wharf St. Big, modern, clean. Kitchen, laundry. $12.50, nonmembers $17.50.

Salvation Army Men's Hostel, 525 Johnson St. (384-3396), at Wharf St., around the corner from the youth hostel. Men only. Immaculate and well-run. Dorms $8. Private rooms $13. Meals $1.25-$3.25.

YWCA, 880 Courtney St. (386-7511), at Quadra near downtown. Women only. Private rooms with shared bath. Singles $33. Doubles $49.50. Breakfast included.

James Bay Inn, 270 Government St. (384-7151), at Toronto St., 2 blocks south of Parliament. In the center of everything. Airy rooms, TV. Singles $29. Doubles $37, with private bath $55. Reservations required July-Sept.

McDonald Park Campground (655-9020), 30km north of downtown on Hwy. 17, but first-class. Sites $6. Reservations recommended.

Thetis Lake Campground, 1938 Trans-Canada Hwy. (478-3845), 10km north of the city center. Sites $10, with hookup $13.

Fort Victoria Camping, 127 Burnett (479-8112), 7km northwest of downtown off the Trans-Canada Hwy. Free showers, laundromat. Sites $13.50, with hookup $18.50.

Food and Bars

Victoria's predilection for the old ways is perhaps best evidenced by the way its citizens eat. Victorians actually do take tea—some only on occasion, others every day. Other foods exist, of course, but to indulge in the trimmed-lawn romanticism of the city you should partake of the ceremony at least once—and don't ask for lemon, it's *just not done*. To masticate upon more filling edible substances, head into **Chinatown,** west of Fisgard and Government. To create your own culinary delight, pick up the day's catch at **Fisherman's Wharf** between Superior and St. Lawrence.

Flying Rhino Diner, 1219 Wharf St. (381-5331), close to the youth hostel. Not typical diner fare, just great nut burgers with homemade soup ($6). Open Mon.-Fri. 8am-8pm, Sat. 10am-6pm, Sun. 10am-4pm.

The Blethering Place, 2250 Oak Bay Ave. (598-1413), at Monterey St. in Oak Bay. 'Tis most British; yea, it hath afternoon tea with cream tarts, trifle and scones ($5.50). "Ploughman's Lunch" ($6). Open daily 8am-10pm.

Eugene's, 1280 Broad St., off View. Wonderful variety of Greek foods; try the *spanakopita* or the *bougatsa* for breakfast. Open Mon.-Fri. 8am-8pm, Sat. 10am-8pm.

Goodies, 1005 Broad St., 2nd floor (382-2124), between Broughton and Fort. Make your own omelette ($4.45 plus 65¢ per ingredient). Tex-Mex dinners ($8). Open daily 7am-9pm.

Bennie's Bagelry, 132-560 Johnston St. (384-3441), at Wharf. Bagels, bagels. Also, bagels. Bagels with cream cheese ($2) or sandwiches ($4). Bagels are sold here. Open Mon.-Sat. 7am-7pm, Sun. 9am-7pm.

Spinnakers, 308 Catherine (386-2739), across the Johnson St. bridge. Great local bar that brews 38 beers on the premises. Live music. No cover or bagels. Open daily 11am-11pm.

Rumors, 1325 Government St. (385-0566). Bar with gay and lesbian clientele. Open Mon.-Sat. 9pm-3am.

Sights and Activities

Most sights cluster together, except for the elegant residential neighborhoods and the parks and beaches, which are better accessed by car or bus. Take time to visit the **Royal British Columbian Museum,** 675 Belleville St. (387-3014 for a tape, 387-3701 for a person), which chronicles the geological and cultural histories of the province while displaying detailed exhibits on logging, mining, and fishing. The extensive exhibits of Native American art, culture, and history include full-scale replicas of various forms of shelter used centuries ago. The gallery of Haida totem art is particularly moving; "open ocean" provides a wonderfully tongue-in-cheek recreation of the first desert in a bathysphere. (Open daily 9:30am-7pm; Oct.-April daily 10am-5:30pm. Two-day admission $5, seniors, disabled, and students with ID $3, ages 6-18 $2. Free Mon. Oct.-April.) Behind the museum, **Thunderbird Park** displays a striking bevy of totems and longhouses, backed by the intricate towers of the Empress Hotel.

Across the street from the museum stand the imposing **Parliament Buildings,** 501 Belleville St. (387-3046), home of the provincial government since 1898. Almost 50 taels (an anachronistic British measure equalling slightly more than an ounce) of gold grace the 10-story dome and Renaissance-inspired vestibule. (Free tours leave the steps every 20 min. in summer, every hr. in winter, daily 9am-5pm.)

Surrounding the Parliament buildings along Belleville and Menzies St. are a number of less-than-unique attractions. **Undersea Gardens** (382-5717) takes you underwater in a plexiglass corridor to view denizens of the deep and not-so-deep. (Open daily 9am-9pm. Admission $6.) Just next door, the **Royal London Wax Museum** (388-4461) waxes rhapsodic. (Open daily 8:30am-10:30pm. Admission $6.) Around the corner on Wharf St., the **Emily Carr Gallery,** 1107 Wharf St. (387-3080), features original work of this turn-of-the-century BC artist who synthesized British landscape conventions and Native American style. The collection includes many of her paintings of totems, conscious attempts to preserve what she saw as "art treasures of a passing race." Free films on Carr's life and work show at 2:30pm. (Open Mon.-Sat. 10am-5pm. Free.)

South of the Inner Harbour, **Beacon Hill Park** (take bus #5) surveys the Strait of Juan de Fuca splendiferously. One mi. east of the Inner Harbour, **Craigdarroch Castle,** 1050 Joan Crescent (592-5323), embodies Victoria's wealth. Take bus #11 or 14 to Oak St. and transfer to #1 or 2. The house was built in 1890 by Robert Dunsmuir, a BC coal and railroad tycoon, in order to tempt his wife away from their native Scotland. It's quite a temptation. (Open daily 9am-7:30pm, in winter 10am-5pm. Admission $4, seniors and students $3.)

The **Art Gallery of Greater Victoria,** 1040 Moss (384-4101), shifts one block back towards the Inner Harbour on Fort St. Save for a wooden Shinto shrine, the gallery has no permanent collection, instead culling temporary exhibits from local and international sources. (Open Mon.-Sat. 10am-5pm, Thurs. 10am-9pm, Sun. 1-5pm. Admission $3, seniors $1.50.)

Almost worth the exorbitant entrance fee are the stunning **Butchart Gardens,** 800 Benvennto, 22km north of Victoria (652-4422 Mon.-Fri. 9am-5pm; 652-5256 for recording). Jennie Butchart began the rose, Japanese, and Italian gardens in 1904 in an attempt to reclaim the wasteland that was her husband's quarry and cement plant. From mid-May to September, the whole area is lit at dusk, and the gardens, still administered by the Butchart family, host variety shows and cartoons; Saturday nights in July and August, the skies shimmer with fireworks displays. Take bus #74. (Gardens open daily; May-June and Sept. 9am-9pm; July-Aug. 9am-11pm; March-April and Oct. 9am-5pm; Jan.-Feb. and Nov. 9am-4pm; Dec. 9am-8pm. Summer admission $10, ages 13-17 $5, ages 5-12 $1; prices vary at other times depending on how many flowers are in bloom. Readmission within 24 hrs. only $1.) Motorists should consider an approach to Butchart Gardens via the **Scenic Marine**

Drive, following the coastline along Dalls and other roads for a spectacular 45 minutes.

Entertainment

Pick up the weekly *Monday Magazine,* published every Thursday and available around the city; its listings include jazz, blues, rock, folk, and country. The **Victoria Symphony Society,** 846 Broughton St. (385-6515), performs regularly under conductor Peter McCoppin, and the **University of Victoria Auditorium,** Finnerty Rd. (721-8480), stages a variety of student productions. The **Pacific Opera** performs at the McPherson Playhouse, 3 Centennial Sq. (386-6121), at the corner of Pandora and Government St; during the summer, they undertake a popular musical comedy series.

The **Folkfest** in late June celebrates Canada's birthday (July 1) and the country's "unity in diversity" with performances by a politically correct and culturally diverse array of musicians. The **JazzFest,** sponsored by the Victoria Jazz Society (381-4042), also culminates on Canada Day. The **Classic Boat Festival** sets sail on Labor Day weekend and displays pre-1955 wooden boats in the Inner Harbour.

NEW BRUNSWICK/ NOUVEAU-BRUNSWICK

Two cultures dominate New Brunswick today. The **Acadians,** French pioneers who originally landed and settled in Nova Scotia in the 17th century, migrated to the northern and eastern coasts and established the farming and fishing nation of *l'Acadie,* or Acadia. With over a third of its population French-speaking, New Brunswick is the only officially bilingual province in Canada. The southern region of New Brunswick was settled by the **United Empire Loyalists,** British subjects who fled in the wake of the American Revolution. Their British influence lingers in the cities and towns on the Loyalist Coast.

Pulp and paper have long stayed the economy of this most forested of provinces. Only the coastal areas and the river valleys are not inhabited by trees, which cover almost 90% of the land. Salmon fishing along the Restigouche and Miramchi Rivers as well as mineral mining also sustain the area's lumbering inhabitants.

Practical Information

Capital: Fredericton

Department of Tourism, Recreation and Heritage: P.O. Box 12345, Fredericton, NB E3B 5C3. Distributes free publications including the *Official Highway Map, Outdoor Adventure Guide, Craft Directory, Fish and Hunt Guide,* and *Travel Guide* (with accommodation and campground directory and prices). For more info, contact the **Tourist Information Centres** located at most points of entry into NB (800-561-0123 from Canada and U.S.A., 800-442-4442 within NB).

Time Zone: Atlantic (1 hr. ahead of Eastern). **Postal Abbreviation:** NB

Area Code: 506.

Provincial sales tax: 11%.

Fredericton

British Loyalists fleeing the American Revolution established Fredericton in honor of King George III's second son. It was selected provincial capital two years later because of its ready access to the Atlantic Ocean via the St. John River and its defensible location in the heart of New Brunswick. Today, Fredericton's location is more important as part of the fertile St. John River Valley, a Maritime agricultural hub. Fredericton has also earned renown as Canada's center of pewtersmithing and handcrafts. Quiet and genteel, the streets of the "City of Stately Elms" are lined with gracious old houses.

Practical Information

Emergency: 911.

Visitor's Information Centre: City Hall, on the corner of Queen and York St. (452-9500). Courteous staff provides tourists with the *Street Index Map/Transit Guide* and the invaluable *Fredericton Visitor Guide*, with complete listings of area accommodations and attractions. Open mid-May to Aug. daily 8am-8pm, Sept. to mid-May 8:15am-4:30pm. An identical **visitor center** on the Trans-Canada Highway (Rte. 2) near Harnwell Rd/exit 289 (458-8331 or 458-8332) operates June-Sept. daily 9am-5pm, during summer peak 9am-8pm. The **Chamber of Commerce**, 20 Woodstock Rd. (458-8006) also offers assistance.

Student Travel Agency: Travel CUTS, in the Student Union Bldg. of the University of New Brunswick (453-4850). Ride-sharing board posted. Open Mon.-Fri. 9:30am-4:30pm.

Trains: SMT, 101 Regent St. (458-6000). This provincial coach line, proud of its 99.4% on-time rate, offers service to Saint John (2 per day, 2 hr., $14), Edmundston (3 per day, 6 hr., $34), and Moncton (2 per day, 2 hr., $24).

Fredericton Transit, 470 St. Mary's (458-9522), circulates infrequently around town Mon.-Sat. 7am-10pm. Fares $1, ages 6-12 50¢. All buses stop downtown on King St. in front of King's Place. Info office open Mon.-Fri. 9am-5pm.

Taxi: Budget, 450-1119; **Student,** 459-TAXI, driven by hired students.

Car Rental: Delta, 304 King St. (458-8899), rents economy cars at $20 per day with free 100km, 12¢ per km thereafter. Must be over 21 with major credit card.

Bike Rental: Savage's, 449 King St. (458-8985) will provide you wheels for $15 per day or $50 per week. Open Mon.-Thurs. 8:30am-5pm, Fri. 8:30am-9pm, Sat. 8:30am-noon.

Help Lines: Rape Crisis Centre, 454-0437.

Post Office: Station "A," 527 Queen St. (452-3345), next to Officers' Square. Open Mon.-Fri. 8am-5:15pm. **Postal Code:** E3B 4Y1.

Area Code: 506.

Traffic congestion is rare downtown, and almost all areas of interest can easily be reached on foot. Officer's Square, a small park between Queen St. and the river, is the geographic heart of activity.

Accommodations and Camping

Cheap housing, though rare, is generally not too competitive in the summer. Most motels run between $40 and $50, and campgrounds are plentiful.

York House Hostel (IYHF), 193 York St. (454-1233), 2 blocks west of Regent St. and 4 blocks from the river. Ideally positioned downtown. Zealous young staff makes sure you are tucked in at midnight and awake at 7:30am. Reception open 4pm-mid. Check-out 9:30am. 30 beds. $9, nonmembers $11. Open June 1-early Sept.

University of New Brunswick, Residential Administration Bldg. (453-4835) on campus. UNB operates summer dorms facilities, well lit and immaculate. The **Student Hotel** is open only to students, $12 per day, $65 per week. The **Tourist Hotel** is pricier but open to all. Singles $26. Doubles $38. Open May 15-Aug. 15. Office open daily 7:45am-4pm.

Norfolk Motel (472-3278), Trans-Canada Highway East on the north shore of the river, 3km east of downtown. Bus #15S passes by near the end of the route. Singles $27. Doubles $30.

Hyatt Island Campground (454-6832), Trans-Canada Highway, 5km west of town. Next to an amusement park along river's shore. Sites $13, with hookup $17. Open May-Oct.

Food and Entertainment

Decently-priced places to eat abound in Fredericton. **Trina's** (450-3899), King's Place on the corner of King and York St. downtown offers a $2 patio breakfast.

(Open Mon.-Sat. 9am-8pm, Sun 11am-8pm.) At 461 King St., the aroma of **Grandma T's** scrumptious bread and almond-mocha muffins wafts from the ovens in the back room. (Open Mon.-Fri. 7:15am-6pm, Sat. 8:30am-5pm.) For heartier fare, steak out **Hilltop Pub & Steak House** at 152 Prospect St. (458-9057). Slab-o-meat is the specialty ($7.95-$13.95), but the heaping portions of the various plates are what make this place so popular. (Open daily 11am-2am.) The town boasts a number of supermarkets, but you may want to protest their artificial price-inflating packaging practises by shopping at the **Boyce Farmers' Market,** located behind the Old York County Gaol between Regent and St. John St. (363-5112). Over 140 stalls sell farm-fresh foods, crafts, and other goodies. (Open Sat. 6am-noon.)

Much of Fredericton's nightlife is inspired by students of the University of New Brunswick, a majestic campus sprawling over a hill overlooking the city. The oldest and largest dance club, **Club Cosmopolitan,** 546 King St. (458-8165), is where locals take worldly guests first. (Open Mon.-Fri. 4pm-2am, Sat. 7pm-2am, Sun. 7pm-1am.) The **Lunar Rogue Pub,** 625 King St. (450-2065), serves up roguish nachos and loony bands on weekends. (Open Mon.-Fri. 11am-1:30am, Sat.-Sun. 10:30am-1:30am.) For the town's cheap beer and a sociable school-year crowd, socialize at the **Social Club** on the top floor of the UNB Student Union Building (453-4991).

Among the activities fit for daylight participation is the **Pioneer Princess Riverboat,** docked at the Regent St. wharf (call collect 458-5558, or 800-561-4000 in NB). She paddlewheels along the St. John River, stopping at the **Fredericton Lighthouse** (459-2515 or 800-561-4000), where the public is allowed access all the way to the top. (Riverboat departs July-Aug. 2 per day, June and Sept. weekends only. Admission $9.50-$11.50, kids $5.95. Lighthouse open June and Sept. Mon.-Fri 9am-4pm, Sat.-Sun. noon-4pm; July-Aug. daily 10am-9pm; Oct.-May Mon.-Fri. 9am-4pm. Admission $2, under 12 $1.)

Sights

Just inside the entrance to the **Beaverbrook Art Gallery,** 703 Queen St. (458-8545), hangs Salvador Dali's awe-inspiring, 13×10 ft. masterpiece, "Santiago el Grande." A gift of local-boy Lord Beaverbrook, the gallery also houses a collection of Anglo paintings including works by Gainsborough, Turner and Constable. (Open July-Aug. Sun.-Mon. noon-8pm, Tues.-Wed. 10am-8pm, Thurs.-Sat. 10am-5pm, Sept.-June Sun.-Mon. noon-5pm, Tues.-Sat. 10am-5pm. Admission $3, seniors $2, students $1.) New Brunswick's provincial government taxes in the **Legislative Assembly Building,** a three-story sandstone building with mansard roof and corner towers. Tours of the building, including the Assembly Chamber when the Legislature isn't spending money, leave every half hour. (Open June 15-early Sept. daily 9am-9pm, Sept. 3-June 14 daily 9am-4pm.) In July and August, pageantry-lovers can witness the **Changing of the Guard**—specifically the Royal New Brunswick Regiment—in Officers' Square. (Tues.-Sat. at 11am and 7pm. Sentries change every hr. Inspection of the guard Thurs. at 11am.) Also catch Officers' Square's open-air concerts in July and August on Thursday evenings, with everything from pipe bands to bluegrass. The quirky **York-Sunbury Historical Society Museum** (455-6041) operates within the Old Officers' Quarters in Officers' Square. Exhibits detail aspects of New Brunswick life from the Micmac natives to the recreation of a World War I trench. Also in residence is the famous 42-lb. Coleman Frog. Old Fred Coleman supposedly fed his pet croaker bran and ox blood, although it had a predilection for scotch, rum and gin. To preserve the enigma of the frog, museum officials have forbidden scientific examination of the specimen, so it's up to you to decide whether or not to believe. (Open May-early Sept. Mon., Wed., Fri.-Sat. 10am-6pm; Tues. and Thurs. 10am-9pm. July-Aug. Sun. noon-6pm. Early Sept. to mid-Oct. Mon.-Fri. 9am-5pm, Sat. noon-6pm. Mid-Oct. to May Mon., Wed., and Fri. 11am-3pm. Admission $1, students and seniors 50¢, families $2.50.) The walking tour presented in the city's *Visitor Guide* hits all the attractions in central Fredericton.

Kings Landing Historical Settlement, Trans-Canada Highway (Rte. 2) exit #259 (363-5805), lies 37km west of Fredericton. This superb recreation of an early Loyalist township is a living, breathing museum, staffed by period actors whose daily chores from buttermaking to blacksmithing make it a completely self-sufficient village. The saw and grist mills particularly stand out in the 300-acre expanse of Kings Landing. Leave several hours for exploration. (Open June, Sept.-Oct. 10am-5pm, July-Aug. 10am-6pm. Admission $7.50, kids 6-18 $4.25, families $15.) The Settlement has an efficient **Reception Centre** that offers guided tours of the community (Tues., Thurs., and Sat. at 6:30pm; open slightly longer than the Settlement; $2.50, families $5.50). SMT can drop you off at Kings Landing along their regular Fredericton-Edmundston coach service (3 per day $5.35).

Fundy National Park

Perhaps the sheer variety of things to do prompts hordes of Canadians to make their summer pilgrimage to Fundy. Hikers and fishers certainly won't be disappointed, but neither will golfers or lawn-bowlers. Fundy offers something for everyone except misanthropes. The park occupies a territory along the Bay of Fundy, about an hour's drive from Moncton or Sussex. Rte. 114 is the only major road access to and through the park, running northwest to the Trans-Canada Highway, and east along the shore to Moncton.

Park Headquarters, P.O. Box 40, Alma, NB (887-2000), home of the friendly rangers, is located in the southeastern corner of the Park facing the Bay of Fundy, across the Upper Salmon River from the town of Alma. The park's interpretive programs are run from this area. The free and invaluable park newspaper *Salt and Fir* is available at the park entrance stations. **Alma Beach Information** sits at the east entrance (open mid-May to mid-June and Sept.-early Oct. 11am-6pm, mid-June to Aug. 8am-10pm), while **Wolfe Lake Information** lurks at the northwest entrance (open mid-June to Aug. 8am-10pm). In the off-season, contact Park Headquarters (open Mon.-Fri. 8:15am-4:30pm). The 24-hr. **Park Emergency Number** is 882-2281. The park extracts a car entrance fee of $4.25 per day and $9.75 for four days from mid-June to Labor Day, but is free year-round for bicyclists and walkers.

No public transport serves Fundy, and the nearest bus depots are in Moncton and Sussex. National Park fishing permits ($3.25 per day, $5.25 per week, $10.75 per annum) are available at all information and campground kiosks. Brook trout open season is from May 18 to September 15. Salmon angling was banned in 1991 due to low fish populations. Fundy weather can be unpleasant for the unprepared. Bring a jacket for the occasional chilly evenings, and insect repellent for the warm, muggy days.

The park operates four campgrounds totalling over 600 sites; sites are seldom in short supply. Reservations are not accepted; all sites are first come, first grab. **Headquarters Campground** is in highest demand, often commanding a two-day waiting list in summer, because of its three-way hookups and proximity to facilities. For sites at this campground, campers put their names on a list when they arrive, and show up in the morning when names are called out. (Open May-early Oct. Sites $9, with hookup $14; $27.25 for 4 nights, with hookup $41.75; $45.50 per week, with hookup 69.50.) **Chignecto North Campground,** off Rte. 114, 5km inland from Headquarters, is the other campground with electrical hookups. The forest and distance between campsites affords more privacy. (Open mid-June to mid-Sept. Sites $7, with hookup $10.30; $20.75 for 4 nights, with hookup $30.50; $34.75 per week, with hookup $50.75.) **Point Wolfe Campground,** scenically located along the coast west of Headquarters, stays cooler and more insect-free than the inland campgrounds. Currently, vehicles larger than cars do not have access because of bridge repairs. (Open mid-June to Aug. Sites $7, $20.75 for 4 nights, $34.75 per week.) The **Wolfe Lake Campground** offers primitive lakeside sites near the northwest park entrance. (Open mid-May to early Oct. Sites $5.25, $16 for 4 nights, $26.75 per week.) Additionally, wilderness camping is permitted year-round. To register, call or visit Headquarters. The new **Fundy National Park Hostel** opened in 1991; for more details, contact Park Headquarters, or Bill Leonard, spokesperson for the Canadian Hostelling Association (453-8722). Other accommodations can be found in Alma, by the park's eastern entrance, as well as grocery shopping, postal services, banks and laundry facilities.

Most recreational facilities open only in the summer season (mid-May to early Oct.), including interpretive programs, boat rentals, the nine-hole golf course, lawn bowling, a heated salt-water swimming pool, tennis courts, campgrounds and restaurants. The daily interpretive activities are free, friendly and always fun. Try a **Beach Walk,** during which the guide takes you down to the beach during low tide to examine ocean-bottom critters, the **Evening Program** held in the Amphitheatre, or guided **nature walks** which are never cancelled due to inclement weather. Activities are organized for kids (ages 5-12), and numerous **campfire programs** are held in the evenings. Virtually all facilities are wheelchair-accessible. Many seniors visit the park in September and October to avoid the crush of vacationers and to catch the fall foliage. Those seeking quiet, pristine nature would do well to visit in the chillier off-season.

About 120km of park trails are open year-round. Each trail, along with complete description, is detailed in *Salt and Fir.* Only a handful are open to mountain bikes. Look for such highlights as waterfalls, ocean views and wild animals. Deer are unavoidable, and raccoons are thick as thieves around the campsites. Catching a glimpse of a moose or a peregrine falcon will require considerably more patience.

A worthwhile excursion from Fundy National Park is **The Rocks Provincial Park,** located at Hopewell Cape, off Rte. 114, 45km east of Alma and 34km south of Moncton. The Rocks are 50-ft.-high sandstone formations with trees on top. At high tide, they look like little islands off the coast. But the best time to see the Rocks is during low tide, when they look like gigantic flowerpots rising from the ground. Then tourists are free to explore the Rocks on foot. Call Tourism New Brunswick for tide info.

Moncton

Moncton is the unofficial capital city of the province's Acadian population. Its demographics accurately reflect New Brunswick's dual identity; the francophone one-third and anglophone two-thirds of Moncton's population coexist without tension. English predominates except around the campus of the Université de Moncton, Canada's only French-language university outside of Québec.

Practical Information

Tourist Information Centres have summer locations at Lutz Mountain on Trans-Canada Highway (Rte. 2) (853-3540; open mid-May to Oct. daily 9am-7pm), and on 575 rue Main St. (856-4360; open mid-May to Aug. daily 9am-7pm). **City Hall's Convention and Visitor Services** handles tourists Sept. to mid-May Mon.-Fri. 9am-5pm and distributes the *Moncton Information* booklet which covers everything down to tide schedules.

Train: SMT, 961 rue Main St. west of downtown (859-5060), runs to Halifax (5 hr., $33) and to Charlottetown (4 hr., $27).

Codiac Transit: (857-2008). Local buses operate Mon.-Wed. and Sat. 7am-6:30pm, Thurs.-Fri. 7am-10:30pm. Fare 90¢, students and seniors 50¢. Info available Mon.-Fri. 8:30am-4:30pm.

Taxi: Aircab, 857-2000. Downtown to U. de M. $4.

Car rental: Econo, (858-9100), rents for $22 per day, with 100km free, 10¢ per km thereafter. Under 25 subject to additional $9 per day insurance charge. Must be 21 with major credit card. Open Mon.-Fri. 9am-5:30pm, Sat. 9am-1:30pm.

Weather: 851-6610, in French 851-6191.

Help line: Greater Moncton Crisis Line, (857-9780), a United Way agency. Lines open Mon.-Thurs. 4pm-midnight, Fri.-Sun. 4pm-8am the next day.

Post Office: 281 Rue St. on the corner of George St. and Highfield Ave. (851-7081). Open Mon.-Fri. 8am-5:30pm. **Postal code:** E1C 8K4.

Area Code: 506.

Accommodations and Camping

Lodging in Moncton is scarce, often seasonal. The dozen or so B&Bs in the area offer the best prices, as well as clean, comfortable rooms. Motels line up along the Trans-Canada Highway, preying on those who drive through the area to experience Magnetic Hill.

The **Université de Moncton** (858-4014) in the LaFrance building—the tallest on campus—provides spacious and spartan dorm rooms, with sofas that double as beds. Laundry facilities are available. To get there, take Codiac Transit bus #5 to campus. (Open May-Aug. Singles $20, students $18. Doubles $30, $25.) The **YWCA** (855-4349) on 35 Highfield Ave. one block from rue Main St. also provides temporary shelter. The accommodations are dorm-style cubbyholes rented to women only ($15). You must check in by 11pm. In July and August, it also operates as a hostel, renting rooms for $6. Another option is the **Sunset Hotel**, at 162 rue Queen St. downtown (382-1163). Eccentric residents chat on the front porch, eyeing visitors. (Singles with bath $35-$53. Doubles $41-$57.)

The area does have a campground, **Camper's City**, located on Trans-Canada Highway at Mapleton, only 5km north of downtown (384-7867). The campground has 193 sites. ($14, with hookup $16.50. Office open daily 7:30am-11pm.)

Food and Entertainment

Pubs are generally the cheapest place for a meal, short of fast food. **Alibi's Pub,** 841 rue Main St. (848-5090), serves exquisitely prepared daily specials ($5-7) and cheap draughts. (Open Mon.-Sat. 10am-1am.) **Fancy Pocket,** 589 rue Main St. (858-7898), carries a wide variety of pita pockets ($3-5) and quiches ($4.50). A youthful crowd gathers to dance at **La Lanterne Brasserie** at 415 prom. Elmwood Dr. (856-7110). Check out the high-tech decor and laser-light show. (Open Mon.-Fri. 10am-2am, Sat. 8am-2am.) **Le Kacho,** in the campus FEUM (Fédération des Etudiants de l'Université de Moncton) building (858-4484), is a nucleation site for college students during the school year. (Open Fri.-Sat. nights only.)

Sights

Moncton is deservedly proud of its two natural wonders, the Tidal Bore and Magnetic Hill. Both are more impressive in person than on paper. The **Tidal Bore,** best viewed from Tidal Bore Park near the corner of rue Main St. and rue King St., is yet another product of the Bay of Fundy tides. Twice a day the incoming tide surges up the Petitcodiac River, a muddy river bottom along whose banks Moncton is situated, sometimes with birds surfing on the Bore, and within an hour fills up to its 25-ft.-high banks. Then the flow of water reverses direction, and a mighty river starts flooding back into Chignecto Bay. It's best to arrive 15 minutes before posted Tidal Bore times in case it hits early. Spring and fall are the best seasons to catch the phenomenon at full force.

Magnetic Hill on Mountain Rd. just off of Trans-Canada Hwy. (Rte. 2) northwest of central Moncton, is a phenomenon notorious among Canadians. You drive your car down to the bottom of the hill, put it in neutral, and feel your car rolling back up to the top of the hill. (Feel free to supply your own explanation.) Best of all, it's never closed; you can try it as many times as you like; and it's always free (although the commercialized complex of theme parks built next to and upon the fame of Magnetic Hill is not).

Le **Musée Acadien,** Clement Cormier building at the Université de Moncton (858-4088), houses exhibits depicting the history, daily life and culture of the Acadians since 1604. It's an interesting portrait of a farming people caught in the middle of the New World colonial wars waged between the British and the French. Also present are displays on the Micmac Indians, original settlers of the area. (Open June-Sept. Mon.-Fri. 10am-5pm, Sat.-Sun. 1-5pm, Oct.-May Tues.-Fri. 1-4:30pm, Sat.-Sun. 1-4pm. Free.)

Near Moncton

The Acadian town of **Shediac,** 30km north of Moncton on Rte. 15, stakes its claim as the Lobster Capital of the World by holding their annual **Shediac Lobster Festival** in mid-July. More important to sun worshipers is the popular **Parlee Beach Provincial Park** in Shediac Bay near the warm salt waters of the Northumberland Strait. For more info about scheduled events, write to **Town of Shediac Information,** P.O. Box 969, Shediac (532-2421).

Kouchibouguac, the "other" National Park in New Brunswick, suffers no inferiority complexes from being the less popular sibling. In sharp contrast to Fundy National Park's rugged forests and high tides along the Loyalist coast, Kouchibouguac (meaning "river of the long tides" in Micmac) proudly emphasizes its warm lagoon waters, salt marshes, peat bogs and white sandy beaches along the Acadian coast. Swim or sunbathe along the 25km stretch of barrier islands and sand dunes. Canoe the waterways that once were the highways for the Micmacs. You can rent canoes and bikes at **Ryans Rental Center** (876-9955) in the park between the South Kouchibouguac Campground and Kellys Beach. (Open mid-June to Aug. daily 8am-9pm. Canoes $4.75 per hr., $18 per day.) The park operates two campgrounds in the summer (sites $8-11), neither with hookups. Several nearby commercial campgrounds just outside of the park are available for off-season campers. Kouchibouguac National Park extracts a vehicle permit of $4 per day, $9 per 4 days, or $25 per year. The **Park Information Centre** is located at the Park Entrance on Rte. 117 just off Rte. 11, 90km north of Moncton. (Open mid-May to mid-June daily 9am-5pm, mid-June to early Sept. daily 9am-8pm, early Sept. to mid-Oct. Fri.-Sun. 9am-4:30pm. Park administration (876-2443) open year-round Mon.-Fri. 8:15am-4:30pm.)

A stone's throw from the Nova Scotia border is the **Fort Beausejour National Historic Park,** located on a hill off the Trans-Canada Highway (Rte. 2) in Aulac, 40km southeast of Moncton (674-2663). One of the numerous forts built by the French and captured by the English, Fort Beausejour (renamed Fort Cumberland under the Union Jack) is not much more than foundations and rubble these days. Some trinkets of the soldiers, including coins, weapons and handiwork (check out the ship-in-a-bottle crafted by a French prisoner), have been excavated by archeologists and put on display at the museum. The real reason to visit the site, though, is the panoramic view from the Fort on a clear day. Looking southward to the Cumberland Basin of the Chigneto Bay and northward toward the Tantramar River Valley, one is immediately struck by the strategic importance of this location, on a narrow strip of land connecting Nova Scotia to the rest of the continent. (Site always open. Reception and museum open June to mid-Oct. daily 9am-5pm. Free.)

Saint John

The city of Saint John was founded literally overnight on May 18, 1783, by a band of 3000 American colonists loyal to the British crown known as the United Empire Loyalists. In this, the oldest incorporated city in Canada, evidence of Saint John's long Loyalist tradition is apparent in its architecture, festivals and institutions: the walkways of King and Queen Squares in central Saint John (never abbreviated so as to prevent confusion with St. John's, Newfoundland) were laid out to resemble the Union Jack. The city rose to prominence in the 19th century as a major commercial and shipbuilding port. Today, Saint John is the largest city in New Brunswick. The locals are coarser and more vocal than their upstream brethren in Fredericton, but will go out of their way to lend a helping hand, especially to tourists. Saint John's location on the Bay of Fundy ensures that summers are cool and winters are mild, albeit foggy and wet: the locals joke that Saint John is where you go to get a car wash. Hay fever sufferers can take solace, however, in the area's extremely low pollen counts.

Practical Information

Emergency: 911.

Saint John Visitor and Convention Bureau (658-2990), on the 11th floor of City Hall at the foot of King St., operates year-round. Open Mon.-Fri. 9am-5pm. **Barbour's General Store** and the **City Centre** offer info in Loyalist Plaza by the Market Slip uptown. Open May 17 to mid-June and mid-Sept. to mid-Oct. daily 9am-7pm, mid-June to mid-Sept. daily 9am-9pm. Other **Tourist Information Centres** are located at Reversing Falls (658-2937; open May 17 to mid-June and mid-Sept. to mid-Oct. daily 8am-6pm, mid-June to mid-Sept. daily 8am-9pm) and at Highway 1 West in the Island View Heights district of Saint John West (658-2940; open May 17 to mid-June and mid-Sept. to mid-Oct. daily 9am-6pm, mid-June to mid-Sept. daily 9am-9pm).

Train: SMT, 300 Union St. (648-3500) provides service to Montréal (2 per day, 14 hr., $80), Moncton (3 per day, 2 hr., $19), and Halifax (2 per day, $50). **VIA Rail** (642-2916), Station St. next to Rte. 1 north of Market Square.

Saint John Transit (658-4700), runs daily 6am-12:30am with frequent service through King Square. $1, under 14 35¢. Also gives 3-hr. guided tour of historic Saint John leaving from Loyalist Plaza and Reversing Falls June 15-Sept. 30. Tour fare $13.50, ages 6-14 $5. Office open 5am-12:30am.

Ferry: Marine Atlantic, at the Ferry Terminal in West Saint John, near the mouth of Saint John Harbour (636-4048 or 800-341-7981 from the continental USA), crosses to Digby, Nova Scotia (1-3 per day; 2½ hr.; $16-18, seniors $12-13.50, ages 5-12 $8-9, car $49-57). To get to the ferry, take the Saint John Transit East-West bus.

Taxi: ABC, 635-1555; **Diamond,** 648-8888.

Car Rental: Econo, 390 Rothesay Ave. (632-8889), rents cars for $18 per day, with 600km free, 10¢ per km thereafter. Must be 21 with major credit card. Additional charge if under 25.

Weather: 636-4991. **Dial-a-Tide:** 636-4429.

Post Office: Main, 125 Rothesay Ave. (636-4760). Open Mon.-Fri. 7:30am-5:15pm. More convenient, uptown branch with full services in **Lawton Drug Store** (634-1422) inside the Brunswick Square Mall on the corner of King and Germain St. **Postal Code: E2L 3W9.**

Area Code: 506.

Saint John's busy uptown is bounded by Union St. to the north and Princess St. to the south, by King Square on the east and Market Square and the harbor on the west.

Accommodations and Camping

Inexpensive housing is exceedingly rare. B&Bs generally are no cheaper than motels, many of which charge $40 or more for a double. A glut of motels line Rothesay Ave. (Rte. 100) east of town (take S.J. Transit Glen Falls bus) and along Manawagonish Rd. (Rte. 100) west of town (take the Gault bus).

Saint John YM/YWCA (IYHF), 19-25 Hazen Ave. (634-7720), 2 blocks north of Market Square. 17 clean, well-protected singles. Access to YMCA recreational facilities. Reservations recommended in the summer. $17, nonmembers $19. Open daily 5:30am-11pm.

Bonanza Motel, 594 Rothesay Ave. (633-1710). Great for those on their way to or from Moncton. Singles $25. Doubles $27-30. Open 10am-10pm.

Rockwood Park Campground, at the southern end of Rockwood Park, 2km north of uptown in a semi-wooded area (652-4050). Sites $11, with hookup $13. Take University bus to Park entrance, then walk 5 min. Open mid-May to Sept.

Food and Entertainment

Reggie's Restaurant, 26 Germain St. (657-6270), provides fresh, homestyle cooking of basic North American fare. Reggie's uses famous smoked meat from Ben's Deli in Montréal. You can get a regular Ben's and Dill for $3.85. (Open Mon.-Wed. 6am-6pm, Thurs.-Fri. 6am-7pm, Sat. 6am-5pm, Sun. 7am-3pm.) Another option is **Mother Nature's.** The 20 Charlotte St. (642-2808) location and her two downtown locales offer filling, if unspectacular, pita pockets ($3-4.50) and salads. Try their popular steak and mushroom pocket ($4.26). (Open Mon.-Sat. 7:30am-6:30pm.) For cheap, fresh produce and seafood, the best bet seems to be the **City Market,** between King and Brunswick Squares. The oldest building of its kind in Canada, City Market is opened and closed by the ringing of the 83-year-old Market Bell. It is also your best source for **dulse,** or sun-dried seaweed picked in the Bay of Fundy's waters, a local specialty not found outside New Brunswick. (Market open Mon.-Thurs. and Sat. 8:30am-5pm, Fri. 8:30am-9pm.)

Unlike its fellow cities, much of Saint John's daily routine and nightlife is confined within its uptown malls, no doubt due to the area's frequent rain squalls. The bars and pubs in **Market Square** get the lion's share of business. In 1992 the best time to be in Saint John will be July 19-25, when the unique **Loyalist Days** festival celebrates the long-ago arrival of Loyalists, complete with reenactment, costumes and street parade.

Sights

Saint John's main attraction is **Reversing Falls,** but before you start imagining 100-ft. walls of gravity-defying water, read on. The "falls" are actually beneath the surface of the water, not exactly visible; what patient spectators will see is the flow of water at the nexus of the St. John River and Saint John Harbour slowly halting and changing direction due to the powerful Bay of Fundy tides. Most amazing may be the number of people amazed by the phenomenon. (24 hrs. Free.) You can glean scientific and historic insight regarding the feat by watching the 15-minute film offered at the **Reversing Falls Tourist Information Centre,** located at the west end of the Rte. 100 bridge crossing the river, but unfortunately the film does not show the Big Event. (Center open May-Oct. daily 10am-6pm. Film admission $1.25; screenings every hr. on the hr. To reach the viewpoint and tourist center, take the East-West bus.)**Three thematic walking tours are provided by the city, each lasting about two hours.** The **Loyalist Trail** traces the places frequented by the Loyalist founders; the **Victorian Stroll** takes you past some of the old homes in Saint John; and **Prince William's Walk** details commerce in the port city. All of the walking tours heavily emphasize history, architecture and nostalgia. The walking tour brochures can be picked up at any tourist info center.

Fort Howe Lookout affords a fine view of the city and her harbor. The landmark bristles with cannons, originally erected to protect the harbor from American privateers. Shooting still occurs here—though predominantly with tripod-mounted cameras rather than with the huge, now-defunct guns. To visit the Lookout, walk a few blocks in from the north end of the harbor and up the hill; look for the wooden blockhouse atop the hill. (24 hrs. Free.)

NOVA SCOTIA

French colonists known as Acadians started sharing the Annapolis Valley and Cape Breton's shores with the indigenous Micmac Indians around 1605. The next wave of colonists added 50,000 Highland Scots in the 1800s. A strong Scottish identity has been preserved and the culture perpetuated in Pictou and Antigonish Counties, where Scots primarily settled. (Some say that more Gaelic is now spoken in

Nova Scotia than in Scotland.) Subsequent immigration of the English, Irish, and northern Europeans also has added to the original population of Micmacs.

When rebellious American colonies declared their independence from the British throne, Nova Scotia showed a stubborn independence belied by its variegated population and declined the opportunity to become the 14th colony in the emerging United States. Instead, the area served as a refuge for fleeing Loyalists. For fear of an American takeover, Nova Scotia joined three other provinces in 1867 to form the Confederation of Canada.

Four distinct geographies dominate the province: the rugged Atlantic coast, the agriculturally lush Annapolis Valley, the calm coast of the Northumberland Strait, and the magnificent highlands and lakes of Cape Breton Island.

Practical Information

Capitol: Halifax

Nova Scotia Department of Tourism and Culture, Historic Properties, P.O. Box 130, Halifax, Nova Scotia B3J 2M7. A dozen provincial info centers providing free comprehensive maps and the *Nova Scotia Travel Guide/Outdoors Guide* are scattered throughout Nova Scotia. Call 800-565-0000 (from Canada) or 800-341-6096 (from the continental USA) to make reservations with participating hostelries.

Time Zone: Atlantic (1 hr. ahead of Eastern time). **Postal abbreviation:** NS

Area Code: 902.

Provincial Sales Tax: 10%.

Annapolis Valley

Green and fertile, the Annapolis Valley stretches along the **Bay of Fundy** between **Yarmouth** and the **Minas Basin.** Its calm, sunny weather harvests harried city-folk seeking a relaxed lifestyle. The Annapolis River Valley runs slightly inland, but parallel to the coast flanked by hills, lovingly called the North and South Mountains, on either side. Charming towns scatter along the length of the Valley connected by scenic Rte. 1. In spring, the aroma and pink blossoms of the apple orchards permeate the Valley.

French Acadian farmers settled this serene valley in the 17th century. Their expulsion from the Valley by the British in 1755 was commemorated by Henry Wadsworth Longfellow's tragic epic poem *Evangeline,* and although Longfellow himself never actually visited his "forest primeval" the appelation "Land of Evangeline" has nevertheless stuck. Rushing from sight to sight is not the most satisfying method of exploring the Valley. Take it slowly and without worries; bicycling is an ideal means of transport.

Digby, home of the famous Digby scallops, harbors large scallop fleets as well as the annual August **Scallop Days** festival. About 104km up the coast from Yarmouth, Digby is connected by the **Marine Atlantic** ferry, (245-2116, 800-341-7981 from the continental USA), to Saint John, New Brunswick, which lies across the Bay of Fundy. (1-2 trips daily, 2-3 daily in summer. Fare June 23-Sept. 7 $18, seniors $13.50, ages 5-12 $9, car $57; Sept. 7-June 23 $16, seniors $12, age 5-12 $8, car $49.)

Brier Island prickles at the top of Digby Neck, a 90-minute drive south from Digby on Rte. 217. The island's surrounding waters apparently provide a very attractive habitat for whales; sightings have been so numerous that **Brier Island Whale and Seabird Cruises** in Westport, (839-2995), which offers whale-watching expeditions around the island, guarantees whale sightings or your money back. Guides are scientific researchers from the **Brier Island Ocean Study** or from local universities. (Voyages made only when weather permits. Fare $30 per passenger. Reservations required.)

Founded by explorer Samuel de Champlain in 1605, the **Habitation Port-Royal** was the earliest permanent European settlement in North America north of Florida. It served as the capitol of French Acadia for nearly a century until its capitulation to the British in 1710, who renamed it Annapolis Royal in honor of their own Queen Anne. The original later fell into ruin, but has been restored faithfully in the form of the **National Historic Park** (532-5197) across the Annapolis Basin, 10km from modern-day Annapolis Royal. The restoration affords a rare glimpse of the wooden palisades and stone chimneys typical in early French fur-trading posts. When taking pictures, ask the kind guides if you can put on their French hats and costumes. To get to the Habitation, turn off Rte. 1 at the Granville Ferry. (Open May 15-Oct. 15 daily 9am-6pm. Free.) Kejimkujik National Park, Rte. 8 60km inland from Annapolis Royal and 160km west of Halifax (682-2772), lies relatively close by. Called Keji (KEJ-ee), the park is remote, densely-wooded and peppered with small lakes and unspoiled waterways best explored by canoe.

For a less historical park experience, seek out the **Upper Clements Theme Park**, on Rte. 1 6km west of Annapolis Royal (532-7557 or 800-565-PARK from the continental USA), a new amusement park. Yes, you'll find roller coasters, water rides, and a mini-golf course, but also artisans and craftspeople plying their trade, petting farms, and storytellers. (Open Late June-Sept. daily 10am-7pm, Sept.-late June Sat.-Sun. 10am-7pm. Park admission free, but pass for attractions $8, after 3pm $5. Tickets for rides also sold individually.) Of note to engineers is the **Annapolis Tidal Generating Station,** just off Rte. 1 (532-5454), the first attempt to generate electrical energy by harnessing the powerful Bay of Fundy tides.

Wolfville, 50-60 km north of Halifax, attracts students from all over Canada to Acadia University, with its serene Valley campus. Wolfville was renamed in the 1800s at the urging of Judge de Wolf, whose daughter was ashamed of saying she was from the town of Mud Creek.

The most panoramic view in the Valley is from **The Lookoff,** Rte. 358, 20km north of Rte. 1, perched on a mountain top within view of four counties.

Grand Pré, or Great Meadow, stands at the eastern head of Annapolis Valley, 100km northwest of Halifax. The highlight is the **Grand Pré National Historic Site** (542-3631), a memorial of the deportation of the Acadians in 1755. After refusing to take oaths of allegiance, the Acadians of Grand Pré were imprisoned in the Stone Church before deportation to the British colonies. They were the first of 6,000 Acadians to be deported that year. Deported Acadians resettled further south on the continent, establishing communities in modern-day Louisiana (as Cajuns, a bastardization of Acadians). (Grounds always open. Buildings open mid-May to mid-Oct. Free.) Canada's best wines originate in the Annapolis Valley; The **Grand Pré Estate Vineyard** (542-1470) gives daily tours of their grounds. (Open daily 9am-5pm. Three guided tours per day. Free.)

Atlantic Coast

The deep, dazzling blue of the Gulf Stream waters perpetually crash onto the rocky Atlantic Coast, sending up flumes of white ocean spray. The basis of the coastal economy is the ocean, so piers, fishing boats, and lobster traps are commonplace sights. Stiff ocean breezes and thick morning fog only accent the breath-taking scenery. Frequent lighthouses brighten **Lighthouse Route,** a driving trail winding down the coastline. The coast is sparsely populated, and for the most part unspoiled by tourist throngs.

The paragon of postcard-pretty is the village of **Peggy's Cove,** population 60, off of Rte. 333, 43km southwest of Halifax. No public transportation serves Peggy's Cove, but most tour bus companies offer packages including the village. The reputation of Peggy's Cove's granite-lined coast and wooden fishing shacks has spread from artists and photographers to tourists, so you'll never have the place to yourself. To avoid the mobs of tour buses, visit in the early morning, during the off-season, or on cold, windy days—none of which tarnish the site's beauty. Despite the crush of visitors, Peggy's Cove itself remains remarkably uncommercialized. The famous lighthouse on the rocks is actually a tiny **post office** boasting its own cancellation stamp. (Open Mon.-Sat. 9am-3pm.)

The **Drop Anchor,** on Rte. 333 in Hackett's Cove, past the Irving station, serves a satisfying lunch or dinner ($7-8) with a view of the cove. Drop anchor here if you're heading west from Peggy's Cove. (Open Tues.-Sat. 8am-11pm.)

The fishing and shipbuilding center **Lunenburg,** 103km west of Halifax on Rte. 3, built the schooner Bluenose in 1921, which because it remained undefeated in international races earned a place on the back of Canada's dime and on the new Nova Scotia license plate. The **Fisheries Museum of the Atlantic,** on the harbourfront (634-4794), brings the fishing industry to life with three stories of aquariums, fresh fish exhibits, a display on Prohibition-era rum-running vessels, and countless exhibits on the local fishing and fish-processing industries. Don't miss the chance to go aboard and explore the schooner and trawler docked at the museum. (Open May 15-Oct. 15, 9:30am-5:30pm. Admission $2.25, kids 50¢, family $5.50.)

The port of **Yarmouth,** 339km from Halifax, is on the southwestern tip of Nova Scotia, a major ferry terminal with ships departing across the **Bay of Fundy** to Maine. **Marine Atlantic** (742-6800 or 800-341-7981 from continental USA) provides service to Bar Harbor (1 per day in summer, otherwise 3 per week; 6-7 hr.; fare July-late Aug. $40, seniors $30, ages 5-12 $20, car $74; late Aug.-July $28, seniors $21, ages 5-12 $14, car $52). **Prince of Fundy Cruises,** (742-6460, 800-565-7900 in Maritimes), sails from Yarmouth's port to Portland, OR. (Departs only May 2-Oct. 20 at 10am, but still doesn't sail many days, so call ahead; 11 hr.; May 2-June 20 and Sept. 19-Oct. 20 $50, age 5-14 $25; June 21-Sept. 17 $70, age 5-14 $35.) Renting a car upon arrival in Yarmouth is a very popular idea, so reserve ahead. **Avis,** 44 Starr's Rd. (742-3323), and **Budget,** 509 Main St. (742-9500), are the only rental agencies.

Cape Breton Island

> *"I have travelled around the globe. I have seen the Canadian and American Rockies, the Andes and the Alps, and the Highlands of Scotland; but for simple beauty, Cape Breton out rivals them all."* —Alexander Graham Bell

Bell backed up his words by building Beinn Bhreagh, the estate where he spent the last years of his life, in Cape Breton. Breathtaking coastline, loch-like fingerlakes, steep, dropping cliffs, and rolling, green hills characterize Cape Breton, which has been called Scotland's missing west coast.

Cape Breton Island, the northeastern portion of Nova Scotia, connects to the mainland by the **Trans-Canada Highway** across the **Canso Causeway** lying 280km from Halifax and 270km from the New Brunswick border. **Port Hastings** is the first town you'll encounter in Cape Breton, and it supports a **Tourism Nova Scotia** center (625-1717), on the right-hand side of the road after crossing the causeway. At the center, pick up the booklet, *Vacation Planner to National Parks & Historic Sites on Cape Breton Island.* (Open May 15-June and Sept.-Oct. 15 9am-5pm, July-Aug. 9am-9pm.) Public transport serves only the major cities, bypassing Cape Breton's renowned scenery. The **Bras d'Or Lake,** an 80km-long inland sea, roughly divides Cape Breton into two halves. The larger northern section includes the scenic **Cape Breton Highlands** and the **Cabot Trail.** The industrial southern section has been developed with revenues dug from steel and coal mining. **Sydney** and **Glace Bay,** Cape Breton's two largest cities, are depressed industrial centers.

The **Cabot Trail,** named after English explorer John Cabot who supposedly landed in the Highlands in 1497, is the most scenic marine drive in Canada, on a par with California's Rte. 1. The 300km-long loop of the Trail winds precipitously around the perimeter of the northern tip of Cape Breton. A photographer's dream, the Cabot Trail takes 7-10 hours to enjoy, allowing for a lunch break, stops at look-offs and slow traffic. Lodging is expensive along the Trail, generally between $40 and $50 for a double (except the Keltic Lodge in Ingonish Beach, where it can range up to $240). Very few B&Bs line the Trail. However, campgrounds abound both on the Trail and within **Cape Breton Highlands National Park.** To prevent morbid thoughts, you should drive the trail clockwise, shying away from the sheer cliffs. Bicyclists, too, should go clockwise, to take full advantage of the predominantly westerly winds. For info on bike rentals, contact the non-profit **Les Amis Du Plein Air,** P.O. Box 472, Cheticamp B0E 1H0 (224-3814).

The stretch of land extending across the northern tip of Cape Breton and wedged within the northern loop of the Cabot Trail belongs to the **Cape Breton Highlands National Park,** 950 sq. km of highlands and ocean wilderness. One park info center is located along the Cabot Trail in **Cheticamp,** 5km south of the southwest Park entrance (224-2306), and the other at the southeast entrance in **Ingonish Beach** (285-2535). (Both centers open mid-May to late June and early Sept. to late Oct. 9am-5pm, late June to early Sept. 8am-9pm; late Oct. to mid-May Mon.-Fri. 8am-4:30pm for phone inquiries only.) The Park provides six campgrounds within its boundaries. (Open mid-May to mid-Oct. First-come, first-served basis; weekdays yield the best selection. Sites $7-9, with fireplace $10.25, with hookup $14: pay for 3 days, camp for 4. Park motor vehicle admission $4.25 per day, $9.50 per 4 days.)

On the southern loop of the Cabot Trail, the resort village of **Baddeck** lies on the shore of Lake Bras d'Or. **The Alexander Graham Bell National Historic Site,** Chebucto St. (Rte. 205) in the east end of Baddeck (295-2069), provides a spectacular view of the Lake from its roof gardens. Inside the building is an insidiously fascinating museum dedicated to the life and inventions of Bell. More than just the inventor of the telephone, Bell was a fountain of ideas, spewing forth such creations (some useful, some not) as medical tools, hydrofoils and airplanes. Bell's humanitarian spirit also inspired toils to allay problems of the deaf and sailors lost at sea. (Open July-Sept. daily 9am-9pm, Oct.-June 9am-5pm. Free.)

Not all of Cape Breton is scenic. Innumerable penniless immigrants mined the grimy, industrial city of **Glace Bay** for hazardous jobs in the Sydney coalfields. Although coal mining has now ceased, the **Miners' Museum,** Birkley St. off of South St. east of downtown (849-4522), preserves its memory with exhibits on the techniques of coal mining and the plight of organized labor, a reconstructed miners' village, as well as films on life as a coal miner. The real highlight of the museum, though, is the ¼-mi. tour of an underground coal mine, guided by experienced miners who paint a bleak, unromanticized picture of the hard days' labor. Watching tourists knocking their heads on the 5-ft.-high ceiling supports (safety hat and cape provided), is almost as much fun as navigating the dim, dank, narrow passages of coal. (Open June-Aug. daily 10am-6pm, Sept.-May 9am-4pm. Admission $5, without tour $2.75; kids: $3, $1.75.)

At North Sydney, 430km northeast of Halifax, ferries depart daily for **Newfoundland.** The terminal sits at the end of the Trans-Canada Highway (Rte. 105). **Marine Atlantic** (794-5700 or 800-341-7981 from continental USA) ferries leave for Port-aux-Basques, Nfld. (1-3 per day; 5-7 hr.; $15.25, seniors $11.25, ages 5-12 $8, cars $47) and Argentia, Nfld. (2 per week, 14 hr., $41, seniors $31, kids $21, cars $99). Argentia lies 50km away from **St. John's,** the capital of Newfoundland, while Port-aux-Basques is closer to the spectacular fjords and gorges of **Gros Morne National Park** (458-2417). For more information on Newfoundland, contact the **Newfoundland Department of Tourism,** Box 2016, St. John's, Nfld. A1C 5R8, (800-563-6353).

Sydney, 140km northeast of the Canso Causeway, is the commercial center of Cape Breton, a good base for lodging and accommodations. **Delta,** 501 Esplanade near the Sydney River (562-1155), rents economy cars for $20 per day, 100km free, 12¢ per km thereafter. You must be 21 with a major credit card; if under 25 expect an extra $13 per day insurance charge. Make reservations early in summer. (Open Mon.-Fri. 7:30am-6pm, Sat. 8am-1pm.) You can find lodging at **Paul's Hotel,** 10 Pitt St. (562-5747). (Singles $22-26. Doubles $26-35.)

The **Fortress of Louisbourg** (LOO-iss-burg; in French Loo-ee-BOORG) was the King of France's most ambitious military project in the colonies, his "New World Gibraltar," the launching pad from which France would regain the Americas. A small band of New Englanders laid siege to and quickly captured Louisbourg in 1745. A treaty returned it to France, but then the British took the Fortress back again in 1758, with even greater ease. The $25 million rebuilding of Louisbourg, the largest historic reconstruction in North America, resulted in **Fortress of Louisbourg National Historic Park,** 37km southeast of Sydney on Rte. 22 (733-2280), a far more successful tourist attraction than it ever was a military outpost. Every attempt has been made to recreate the atmosphere of 1744. Speaking French will help you get past the gate sentries, who do not take kindly to intruders wearing red coats. Most of the buildings feature either period rooms, manned by costumed actors doing their 1744 thing, or historical museums depicting life in the Fortress. The scope is startling, the recreation, well, almost convincing. The **Hôtel de la Marine** prepares meals ($7-8) from authentic 1744 French recipes—lots of fun, but be forewarned that the 18th century had no Cordon Bleu chefs. No red meat on Fridays and Saturdays—it was outlawed as a religious observance. Peek at the kitchen, if you can skirt the actors. The 80% whole wheat/20% rye bread from the **King's Bakery** ($2.50) looks like a cannonball, and is almost as hard as one. From the visitor center, where tickets are purchased and cars parked, a shuttle bus takes you to the Fortress gates. The fort offers two to four guided walking tours daily, in English and French. (Open June and Sept. 9:30am-5pm, July-Aug. 9am-6pm. May and Oct. no animation, only guided tours. Admission $6.50, age 5-16 $3.25, seniors free, family $16.) The modern town of **Louisburg** also has six B&Bs (singles $25, doubles $30-35). Contact **Cape Breton Tourism Division,** 20 Keltic Drive, P.O. Box 1448, Sydney B1P 6R7, (800-565-9464).

Halifax

Halifax was erected in 1749 as a British garrison to counter the (not-so-)great French fortress of Louisbourg. Unlike Louisbourg, the Halifax Citadel was never captured or even attacked. The city sits on one of the world's finest natural harbors, a deep inlet of the Atlantic Ocean—the reason for the choice of Halifax's site. To this day, a large military contingent, the Canadian Navy, is based in Halifax Harbour.

Halifax's uneventful history is marred by one event: the Halifax Explosion of 1917. Miscommunication between a Belgian relief ship and a French ship carrying picric acid and 400,000 tons of TNT resulted in a starboard-to-starboard collision in Halifax Harbour, hurling sparks into the picric acid. One hour later, Halifax felt the brunt of the largest man-made explosion before the atomic bomb. Approximately 11,000 people were killed or injured, north Halifax was razed to rubble, and windows were shattered 50 mi. away.

The city has since rebuilt, and grown to become the financial, commercial, and intellectual crossroads of Atlantic Canada, as well as the legislative capital of Nova Scotia. Metropolitan Halifax, population 280,000, claims a third of the province's population, a national center of medical research. Although now facing the all-too-familiar challenges of other big cities, Halifax is nonetheless clean and safe.

Practical Information

Emergency: 4105

Halifax Tourist Information, City Hall, on the corner of Duke and Barrington (421-8736). Open Mon.-Wed. 9am-6pm, Thurs.-Sun. 9am-7pm. Another branch on the corner of Sackville and S. Park, across from the Public Garden (421-2772). Open mid-June to Aug., same hours. **Tourism Nova Scotia,** locations on the downtown harbor boardwalk, Historic Properties (424-4247; open mid-June to mid-Sept., Mon.-Fri. 8:30am-9pm, Sat.-Sun. 9am-9pm; other times Mon.-Fri. 8:30am-4:30pm), just off Rte. 102 near the airport exit (873-3608; open

June 15-Sept. daily 9am-5pm), and an info counter inside Halifax International Airport (426-1223; open daily 7:30am-11:30pm). Tourism N.S. is operated by a friendly, costumed staff probably even able to tell you how many nosehairs the mayor has.

Consulates: USA Consulate General, Scotia Square, Cogswell Tower, Suite 910 (429-2480). Open Mon., Wed., and Fri. 8:30-11:30am and 2-4:30pm. **U.K. Consulate,** Purdy's Wharf Building, Tower 2, Suite 1301 (429-4230; after hours, 434-3758).

Halifax International Airport, 40km from the city on Rte. 102. The **Aerocoach City Shuttle** (468-1258) runs between the airport and downtown, 7:30am-11pm (14 per day; $11, round-trip $18, under 10 free with adult). Taxi fare $34; Limousine fare $36.

Via Rail: on the corner of Hollis and South, in the south end near the harbor (429-8421). Service to Montréal $127, students $115.

Buses: Acadian Lines and **MacKenzie Bus Line** share the same terminal, 6040 Almon St. (454-9321), near Robie St. To get downtown from the bus terminal, take bus #7 or #80 on Robie St., or any of the 6 buses running on Gottingen St. 1 block east of the station. Mac-Kenzie runs service along the Atlantic coast to Lunenberg (2 per day, 2 hr., $10) and to Yarmouth (1 per day, 6 hr., $26). Acadian covers most of the remainder of Nova Scotia, with connections to the rest of Canada: Annapolis Royal (2 per day, 4 hr., $22), Yarmouth (2 per day, 6-7 hr., $35), Antigonish (5 per day, 4 hr, $22), and Sydney (4 per day, 6 hr, $40). Senior discount 25%.

Metro Transit (421-6600; info line open daily 8am-10pm.) Efficient and thorough. Pick up route map and schedules at any info center. Fare $1.10, seniors and ages 5-15 60¢.

Dartmouth-Halifax Ferry: (464-2336), on the harborfront. 15-min. harbor crossings depart both terminals Mon.-Fri. 6:30am-11:30pm, every 15-30 min.; Sat. 6:30am-11:30pm and Sun. noon-5:30pm, every 30 min. Fare 50¢, seniors 10¢.

Taxi: Aircab (456-0373), open 24 hrs.; **Share-a-Cab** (429-5555), no credit cards.

Car Rental: Byways, 2156 Barrington St. just north of downtown (429-0092). $17 per day, 200km free, 10¢ per km thereafter. Must be 21 with credit card. Mon.-Wed. 8am-5:30pm, Thurs.-Fri. 8am-9pm, Sat.-Sun. 9am-noon. **McFrugal,** 6025 Livingstone St. (453-7368). By-ways' sister agency; same rates and policies.

Cabana Tours, 2528 Windsor St. (423-6066 or 420-1680) offers tours of Halifax (2½ hr., $13), Peggy's Cove (4 hr., $22), and Annapolis Valley (8 hr., $45; Mon., Wed., and Sat. only). Reservations required. **Velo Bicycle Club** conducts bicycle tours of Halifax and Metro area. Contact Mark Beaver (home 455-2878, work 423-4438).

Outdoor equipment rental: The Trail Shop, 6210 Quinpool Rd. (423-8736), offers complete selection. Bicycles $13 first day, then $10 per day. Weekend rental (Fri.-Mon.) $25. Deposit $75. Kayaks $17 first day, then $12 per day; weekend rental $30; deposit $50.

Student Travel Agency: Travel CUTS Dalhousie University Student Union Building 1st floor (494-2054). Open Mon.-Fri. 9am-4:30pm. Rideboard posted near Travel CUTS, near the cafeteria.

Help Lines: Sexual Assault: (425-0122), **Crisis Centre:** (421-1188), **Youth Help:** (420-8336).

Post Office: Station "A," 6175 Almon St. between Robie and Windsor St. in the north end (426-8988). Open Mon.-Fri. 8am-5:15pm. Convenient downtown branch inside

Postal Code: B3K 5M9.

Area Code: 902.

Barrington is the major north-south street. Sackville Street, approaching the Citadel and the Public Garden, runs east-west, parallel to Spring Garden Road, Halifax's shopping thoroughfare. Flanking downtown are the North End, considered unsavory by locals, and the South End, mostly quiet and arboreal on the ocean. Downtown traffic is bearable, but parking difficult. Nova Scotia is a hospitable place to visit.

Accommodations

Summer accommodations are tight in Halifax. Universities provide clean dorm rooms often swamped by conventions; book in advance. All accept major credit cards. If the dorms let you down, try contacting the **Canadian Hostelling Association,** 5516 Spring Garden Rd. (425-5450; open Mon.-Fri. 9am-5pm). Another, more luxurious option is the **Halifax Metro Bed and Breakfast** (434-7283), which has at least 25 homes at its command. Reasonably located doubles run for about $40.

Halifax International Youth Hostel (IYHF), 2445 Brunswick St., 1 block from MacDonald Bridge in the North End (422-3863). Close to the action. Newly renovated, with casual atmosphere. Kitchen and laundry. No curfew. Check in 8:30-10:30am and 4:30-10:30pm. $11.45, nonmembers $13.75.

Technical University of Nova Scotia, 2nd Floor M. M. O'Brien Bldg., 5217 Morris St. at Barrington (422-2495). Heart of downtown. Usually has a vacancy. Free laundry. Singles $22. Doubles $36. Students and seniors $19, $32. Check in Mon.-Fri. 8am-4pm. Open May-Sept.

Dalhousie University (494-3401), Howe Hall on Coburg Rd. at LaMarchant, 3km southwest of downtown. Usually packed, so arrive early. Parking, breakfast, room service included. Laundry, access to Dal recreation facilities extra. Singles $27. Doubles $40. Seniors 10% off. Discount for students. Under 11 free. Open May 8-Aug. 24, 24 hrs.

Saint Mary's University, 923 Robie St. (420-5486), 2km from downtown in the south end. Look for the big tower on campus. Serene neighborhood near Point Pleasant Park. As close to a hotel as university lodging can get. Singles $19-24. Doubles $37. Under 12 free. Open May 15-Aug. 15, 24 hrs.

Metro Halifax YMCA, 1565 S. Park St. (423-9622), across from Public Gardens/Citadel. Bright, active place with café. Use of rec facilities extra. Men only. Singles $27. Reception 24 hrs.

YWCA Halifax, 1239 Barrington St. (423-6162), downtown. Laundry, exercise facilties. Meals available. Singles $26.40, weekly $120. Doubles $40, weekly $180.

Cat & Fiddle Inn, 1946 Oxford St. (422-3222), near Quinpool, 2.2km west of downtown. Cable TV in lounge. Singles $34. Doubles $44.

Gerrard Hotel, 1234 Barrington St. downtown (423-8614). Subdued. Must check in Mon.-Fri. 8am-6pm, Sat. 10am-4pm. Singles $30. Doubles $45-51. $6 per additional person.

Food and Entertainment

Downtown pubs provide cheap grub along with the pub district's vitality. Over 40 pubs are crammed into a few competitive city blocks, inciting draught wars and wonderfully low prices; at night, $1 draughts are common. Try the local **mussels** ($3), served on generous platters. Pubs generally open from 11am to midnight or 2am, although kitchens close a few hours earlier. Separate food and drink servers take your orders and collect payment; tip upon delivery of your order at the table.

Lawrence of Oregano, 1726 Argyle St. (422-6907). Called Larry O's by the regulars; you can grill your own bread at the eat-in bread-and-salad bar ($3.75). Satisfying Italian and seafood dishes around $5.

Peddler's Pub, Barrington Place, Granville St. Always packed evenings: expect to wait.

J.J. Rossy's, 1883 Granville St. (422-4411), on the back side of the Split Crow. The city's largest tavern. All-you-can-eat lunch specials $4. 12-oz. steak and fries $3.50. The catch: you have to buy a drink (sodas $1.60, beer $3). Still a good deal.

Split Crow, 1855 Granville St. at Duke (423-5093). The first pub built in Halifax. Provides live entertainment Thurs.-Sat., sometimes featuring maritime music bands.

The Graduate Pub, 1565 Argyle St. (423-4703). A good place to let off steam: loud dance music and good snacks.

For a taste of fermented malt and hops much closer to its source, visit **Moosehead Breweries,** 656 Windmill Rd., Dartmouth (468-7040). Free tours and samples are given from mid-June to August. Take the Dartmouth-Halifax ferry across the Harbour. After downing a few at the Breweries, experience a buzz of a different type by turning on and tuning in to the **National Film Board of Canada,** 1571 Argyle

St. (426-6001), which shows free screenings of international films Friday evenings at 8pm.

Sights

The star-shaped **Halifax Citadel National Historic Park** (426-5080) in the heart of Halifax, with noonday cannon firings and the old **Town Clock** at the foot of Citadel Hill, has become a well-ensconced Halifax tradition. A walk along the walls affords a fine view of the city and harbor. Small exhibits and a one-hour film hide behind the fortifications. (Open June 15-Labor Day daily 9am-6pm, Labor Day-June 15 daily 9am-5pm. Admission $2, kids $1, seniors free. Free June 15-Labor Day.)

The **Halifax Public Gardens,** across from the Citadel near the intersection of South Park and Sackville St., provide a relaxing spot for a lunch break. Overfed loons on the pond, Roman statues, a Victorian Bandstand, gaslamps, and exquisite horticulture are very properly British in style. From July to September, concerts are given Sundays at 2pm. (Gates open daily 8am-sunset.)

Point Pleasant Park, a car-free, wooded tract of land encompassing the southern tip of Halifax, boasts ownership of the **Prince of Wales Martello Tower,** an odd fort built by the British in 1797 that started leaking within 15 years of its construction. Perhaps Halifax's motive for preserving the structure is to subtly chortle at British engineering. To reach the park, take bus #9 from downtown Barrington St. Much farther south, overlooking the mouth of Halifax Harbour, is another example of British architecture, the **York Redoubt.** Built to defend British holdings against the French, this fort apparently has survived *sans* drainage problems; in fact, it was used until World War II. The tower commands a gorgeous view of the harbor. To get to the fort, take bus #15 to Purcell's Cove.

The **Historic Properties** district, downtown on lower Water St. (429-0530), holds reconstructed early-19th-century architecture. The charming stone-and-wood facades, however, are only sheep's clothing disguising wolfishly overpriced boutiques and restaurants of tourist-trap commercialism. The real items of interest here are the summer docking of the **Bluenose II** (hint: look at a Canadian dime) and the annual **International Town Crier's Championship** in late July. Oyez! Oyez! Oyez!

Province House, on the corner of Granville and George St., can be a show in itself during parliament session. Inside the small, Georgian brownstone, the Assembly Speaker and Sergeant-at-Arms don elegant top hats and black cloaks for sporadically lively debate.

Museums in Halifax don't stack up to the less egg-heady competition within Nova Scotia. However, die-hard museum-goers might enjoy the **Maritime Museum of the Atlantic,** 1675 Lower Water St. (429-8210), which has an interesting display on the Halifax Explosion. (Open Mon., Wed.-Sat. 9am-5:30pm, Tues. 9am-8pm, Sun. 1-5:30pm. Free.) The **Nova Scotia Museum,** 1747 Summer St. behind Citadel Hill (429-4610), offers exhibits on the natural history, geology, and native cultures of the province. (Open Mon.-Tues., Wed. 9:30am-8pm, Thurs.-Sat. 9:30am-5:30pm, Sun. 1-5:30pm. Free.)

Festival 92 (421-8736) celebrates Halifax's birthday for 10 days in late July and early August. The highlight is the Natal Day Parade and fireworks. The **Buskerfest** (425-4329), held for a week in mid-August, showcases street performers from around the world in the streets. Also in Halifax is the **Nova Scotia International Tattoo** (422-1343), presented by the Province of Nova Scotia and the Canadian Maritime armed forces. In the first week of July, the festival is kicked off by a street parade of international musicians, bicyclists, dancers, acrobats, gymnasts, and military display groups. At noon, the Metro area spawns lots of free entertainment. Later a two-hour show, featuring the 1,800 performers, is held in the Halifax Metro Centre. (Tickets for the show $16, seniors and kids $8.)

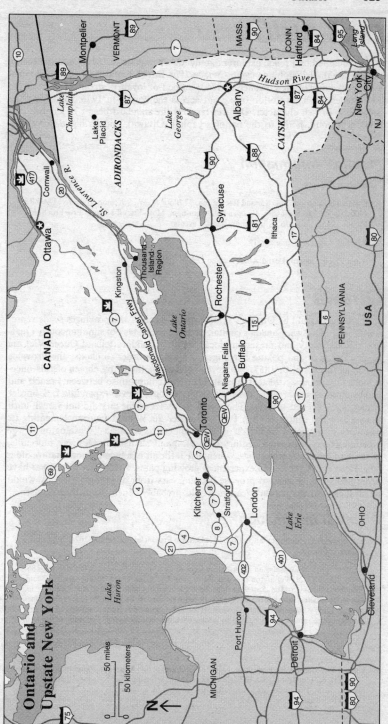

Ontario and
Upstate New York

ONTARIO

First claimed by French explorer Samuel de Champlain in 1613, Ontario became the bastion of British influence in Canada. The British tentatively asserted control with a takeover of New France in 1763; a flood of loyalists streamed in from the 13 colonies when revolution broke out across the border in 1776, solidifying the province's British character. Ontario remains the standard bearer of English cultural hegemony, home to the nation's capital (Ottawa), and its biggest city (Toronto).

Practical Information

Capital: Toronto.

Ontario Ministry of Tourism and Recreation, 77 Bloor St. W., 9th floor, Toronto M7A 2R9 (800-268-3735 or 800-668-2746; open daily 8am-6pm, Mon.-Fri. off-season). Free brochures, guides, maps, and info on upcoming special events.

Alcohol: Legal drinking age 19.

Time Zone: Eastern. **Postal Abbreviation:** Ont

Ottawa

Diplomacy could be Ottawa's middle name. Each of the provinces sends representatives to Ottawa, Canada's capital, with the tricky task of simultaneously creating national unity and preserving local identity. Folklore tells of Queen Victoria closing her eyes and poking her finger at a map in order to choose the Province of Canada's capital in 1857. Whatever her real method, the choice of this once-remote lumbering settlement was an excellent compromise between French and English interests; moreover, the site's distance from the ever-expanding U.S. border added much-needed security. The rough character of the city did not vanish until the turn of the century, when Prime Minister Sir Wilfred Laurier, lamenting its unsavory appearance, called on urban planners to create a "Washington of the North." Today, close to a century of work manifests itself in Ottawa's museums, parks, and artistic communities, which give it the air of a bigger, more mature older city. However, Ottawa still experiences growing pains. Rush-hour headaches have prompted some citizens to propose banning cars from downtown; the city would be cleaner, and the nation's leaders would probably benefit from the exercise.

Practical Information

Emergency: (Police, Ambulance, Fire) 911. **Ontario Provincial Police:** 800-267-2677. **Ottawa Police:** 230-6211.

National Capital Commission Information Center, 14 Metcalfe St. (239-5000, 800-465-1867 across Canada), at Wellington opposite Parliament Buildings. Open summer daily 8:30am-9pm; Sept. 3-May 5 Mon.-Sat. 9am-5pm, Sun. 10am-4pm. **Ottawa Tourism and Convention Authority Visitor Information Centre,** National Arts Centre, 65 Elgin St. (237-5158). Open summer daily 8:30am-9pm; Sept. 3-April 30 Mon.-Fri. 9am-5pm, Sun. 10am-4pm. Both provide free maps and a visitors guide to restaurants, hotels, and sights. For info on the Hull region, turn to the **Association touristique de l'Outaouais,** 25 rue Laurier, Hull (819-778-2222). Open mid-June to Sept. 2 Mon.-Fri. 8:30am-8:30pm, Sat.-Sun. 9am-5pm; off-season Mon.-Fri. 9am-5pm.

Embassies: U.S., 100 Wellington St. (238-5335). Open for info Mon.-Fri. 10am-4pm; for visas Mon.-Fri. 8:30am-1pm. **U.K.,** 80 Elgin St. (237-1530). Open for info Mon.-Fri. 10am-4:30pm; for visas Mon.-Fri. 10am-1pm. **Australia,** 50 O'Connor St. at Queen St., suite 710 (236-0841). Open Mon.-Fri. 9am-noon and 2-4pm.

Student Travel Agencies: Travel CUTS, 1 Stewart St. #203 at Waller (238-8222), just west of Nicholas. Experts in student travel—youth hostel cards, cheap flights. Open Mon.-Fri. 9am-5pm. June 1-Sept. 1. 9am-4pm. **Canadian Hostelling Association (CHA),** 18 Bywood St. (230-1200). Eurail and youth hostel passes, travel info and equipment. Open Mon.-Fri. 9:30am-5:30pm.

American Express: 220 Laurier W. (563-0231), between Metcalfe and O'Connor in the heart of the business district. Open Mon.-Fri. 8:30am-5pm.

Airport: Ottawa International Airport (998-3151), 20 min. south of the city off Bronson Ave. Take bus #96 from Le Breton station, Albert St. at Booth, or Slater St. for regular fare. Express airport **Pars Transport** buses (523-8880) from **Lord Elgin Hotel,** 100 Elgin Blvd. at Slater and 10 other hostels including the Delta, the Westin, and the Château Laurier. Fare $7, ages 12-18 $4, under 12 free. Daily every ½-hr. 6:30am-8:40pm. Call for later pick-up and schedule specifics. Service from airport too. **Air Canada** (237-1380) has student standby rates for those under 21 with ID. **Delta** (236-0431) has youth fares for ages 12-21.

VIA Rail Station: 200 Tremblay Rd. (reservations 238-8289; recorded departure info 238-4706), off Alta Vista Rd. To: Montréal (3 per day; 2 hr.; $28, student $25); Toronto (3 per day; 4 hr.; $59, $53). To Quebec City, must travel via Montréal or Toronto (AMTRAK 800-426-8725). 40% discount for reservations 5 days in advance for students while tickets last, for adults traveling Sat. or Mon.-Thurs. Ticket office open Mon.-Sat. 6am-9pm, Sun. 7am-9pm.

Voyageur Bus: 265 Catherine St. (238-5900), between Kent and Lyon. Service throughout Canada. To: Montréal ($21), Toronto ($43), Québec City ($52). For service to the U.S. must first go to Montréal. Open daily 5:30am-midnight.

Public Transport: OC Transport, 1500 St. Laurent (741-4390). Excellent bus system. Buses congregate on either side of Rideau Centre; Mackenzie Bridge and the corner of Nicholas and Rideau. Fare 95¢, rush hour (6-8:30am, 3-5:30pm) $1.90, express routes (green buses) rates $2.50. Seniors 95¢. **Visibus** pass for a day of unlimited travel after 9am $3, family of 4 $7, under 6 free.

Taxi: Blue Line Taxi, 238-1111. **A-1,** 746-1616. Rates fixed by law ($1.90 plus distance and waiting).

Car Rental: Tilden, 226 Queen St. at Bank (232-3536). cheapest car $50 per day with 200km free, 11¢ each additional km. Insurance $12 per day. Open daily 7:30am-9pm. Must be 21 with credit card. **Budget,** 443 Somerset W. at Kent (232-1526). $49 per day with unlimited mileage, 12¢ each additional km. Insurance $11 per day. Open Mon.-Fri. 7am-8pm, Sat.-Sun. 8am-8pm. Must be 21 with credit card. **Hertz,** 30 York St. (238-7681) in Byward Market, and **Myers,** 1200 Baseline St. (225-8006) also serve Ottawa/Hull. Watch for summer specials from all rental companies (as low as $27 per day).

Rider/Driver Matching Agency: Allostop, 246 Maisonneuve, Hull (778-8877). To: Toronto ($22), Québec City ($59), Montréal ($14), New York ($50) and Boston ($55). Open Mon.-Wed. 9am-5pm, Thurs.-Fri. 9am-7pm, Sat. 10am-5pm, Sun. noon-7pm.

Bike Rental: Rent-A-Bike-Location Velo, 1 Rideau St. (233-0268), behind the Château Laurier Hotel. $4-8 per hr., $12-25 per day. Family deals. Escorted tours for a price. Maps, locks free. Tandems available too. Open mid-May to mid-Oct. daily 9am-7pm. Credit card required.

Alcohol: Legal ages 19 (Ottawa) and 18 (Hull). Bars stay open in Ottawa until 1am, in Hull until 3am.

Help Line: Gayline-Telegai, 238-1717. Info, special events and meetings, as well as counseling. Open Mon.-Fri. 7:30-10:30pm, Sat.-Sun. 6-9pm. **Ottawa Distress Centre,** 238-3311. **Rape Crisis Centre,** 729-8889.

Post Office: Postal Station "A," 347 Dalhousie St. at George St. (992-4760). Open Mon.-Fri. 8am-6pm. **Postal Code:** K1N 8T9.

Area Code: 613 (Ottawa); 819 (Hull).

The **Rideau Canal** divides Ontario into eastern and western sections. West of the canal, Parliament buildings and government offices line **Wellington Street,** the main east-west artery. East of the canal, Wellington St. becomes Rideau St., surrounded by a fashionable new shopping district. To the north of Rideau St. lies the **Byward Market,** a recently renovated shopping area and the focus for Ottawa's nightlife.

Bank Street, which traverses the entire city and services the other, older shopping area, is the primary north-south street. **Elgin Street,** the other major north-south artery, stretches from the **Queensway (Hwy. 417)** to the War Memorial in the heart of the city in front of **Parliament Hill.** The canal itself is a major access route: in winter, thousands of Ottawans skate to work on the world's longest skating rink; in summer, power boats breeze by. Bike paths and pedestrian walkways border the canals, allowing a pleasant alternative to car or bus transit. Parking is painful downtown; meters cost 25¢ for 10 minutes with a one-hour limit. Residential neighborhoods east of the canal have one-hour and three-hour limits and the police ticket less often than on main streets.

Across the Ottawa River lies **Hull,** Québec, most notable for its proximity to Gatineau Provincial Park and the many bars and discos that rock nightly until 3am. Hull is accessible by several bridges and the blue Hull buses from downtown Ottawa.

Accommodations and Camping

Clean, inexpensive rooms and campsites are not difficult to find in Ottawa, except during May and early June, when droves of high school students studying politics make a pilgrimage to the capital and fill budget lodgings to the brim. However, the area also boasts a number of B&B's for the pampered traveler, such as the **Olde Bytown Bed & Breakfast,** 377 Stewart St. and 459 Laurier E., K1N 6R4 (235-1442). In the wealthy, embassy-laden part of Ottawa, a 20-minute walk from downtown, Renée Galioto rents 16 airy rooms in two old Ottawa houses. Full breakfast; BBQ facilities in back garden. Free pick up at train or bus station or airport. Equipped for those in wheel chairs and the blind. Especially welcoming to students. Reservations recommended. (Singles from $30. Doubles from $40.)

Nicholas Gaol International Hostel (IYHF), 75 Nicholas St. K1N 7B9 (235-2595), near Daly St. in downtown Ottawa. Take bus #4 from the inter-city bus terminal, bus #95 west from the train station, or exit at Nicholas St. from the Queensway (Highway 417). The site of Canada's last hanging, this trippy hostel now "incarcerates" travelers in the former Carleton County jail. 4-8 prisoners per cell. Hot communal showers, kitchen, interrogation room, laundry. Hang around in extensive lounge facilities. Summer barbed-ecues in the high-walled exercise yard. Lockers $1 per day. Canoe and skate rental. Parole (lockout) 10am-5pm. Curfew 1am. Entrance free; you pay to leave. $12, nonmembers $16. Open daily 7am-midnight. Call ahead to ensure gallows are prepared.

University of Ottawa Residences, 110 University St. (564-5400), in the center of campus. Take bus 1,7, or 11 on Bank St. to the Rideau Centre from the bus station and walk up Nicholas to the UofO campus, bus 95 west from the train station or the easy walk from downtown. Clean dorm rooms. Shared hall showers. Lounges with kitchen, microwave. Free local phone in hall. Check-in 4:30pm but they'll store your luggage until then. Linen, towels free. Access to university student center (with bank machines), breakfast $3. Singles $32. Doubles $41. Students with ID: $17.50, $30. Open early May-late Aug.

YM/YWCA, 180 Argyle St. at O'Connor (237-1320). From the bus station, walk left on Bank and right on Argyle. Nice-sized rooms in a modern high-rise. Phones, refrigerators in every room. Kitchen with microwave available until midnight. Singles with shared bath $32.35, with private bath $37.40. Doubles $40. Under 12 with adult free. Weekly and group rates available. Payment must be made in advance. Cafeteria (breakfast $2.75) open Mon.-Fri. 7am-7:30pm, Sat.-Sun. 8am-2:30pm.

Centre Town Guest House Ltd., 502 Kent St. (233-0681), just north of the bus station, a 10- to 15-minute walk from downtown. Impeccably clean rooms in a warm, comfortable house. Free breakfast (eggs, cereal, bacon, toast) in a cozy dining room. Singles $30. Doubles $35. Rooms are available in nearby houses at lower rates for stays of a week or more. Reservations recommended.

Camp Le Breton, in a field at the corner of Fleet and Booth (943-0467). Urban tent-only camping within sight of the Parliament Buildings. More of a football field tailored with trees than a campsite. Washrooms, showers, drinking water. Parking, playground. 5-day max. stay. Check-in 24 hrs. Sites $6.50 per person, seniors $3.25, under 12 free. Reservations unnecessary—they'll squeeze you in.

Gatineau Park, northwest of Hull (reservations 456-3016; info 827-2020). Map available at visitors center. Three rustic campgrounds within ½-hr. of Ottawa: **Lac Philippe Campground,** with facilities for family camping, trailers, and campers; **Lac Taylor Campground,** with 34 "semi-wilderness" sites; and **Lac la Pêche,** with 36 campsites accessible only by canoe. (Canoeing equipment $3 per hr., $9 per ½-day, $16 per day.) Each campground off Hwy. 366 northwest of Hull—look for signs. From Ottawa, take the Cartier-MacDonald Bridge, follow Hwy. 5 north to Scott Rd., turn right onto Hwy. 105 and follow it to 366. To get access to La Pêche continue on 366 to Eardley Rd. on your left. Camping permits for Taylor and Philippe available just off the highway in the info center. Pay for a site at La Pêche on Eardley Rd. June 14-Sept. 2 all sites $14, seniors $7; Sept. 3-Oct. 8 and May 15-June 13 $11, seniors $5.50; off-season (some sites open) $3.

Food and Nightlife

Look for restaurant/bars in Ottawa serving food dirt-cheap, including jazzed-up fried dough called Beaver Tail, to lure you into their dens of high-priced beer. **Coasters,** 54 York St. (563-4954) dishes out all the mussels you can pump for $6.99 on Monday (open Mon.-Sat. 11:45am-1am, Sun. 1:30pm-1am. Kitchen serves full menu until 10pm). **Tramps,** 53 William St. (238-5523; open daily 11-1am), and **On Tap,** 160 Rideau St. (236-6827), both serve 20¢ chicken wings on Monday and peel 'n' eat shrimp (20-30¢) on Tues. Tap's dinner specials ($5-6) are also tasty. Fresh fruit, vegetables, and flower stands cluster at **Byward Market** on Byward between York and Rideau. (Open daily 8am-6pm.) Inside, you can buy fresh food at **Zunder's Fruitland,** 60 Byward St. (233-7773; open Mon.-Thurs. and Sat. 8am-6pm, Fri. 8am-8pm, Sun. 10am-5pm).

The International Cheese and Deli, 40 Byward St. (234-0783). Deli and middle eastern sandwiches to go. Turkey on rye $3.49, falafel on pita $2.25, hummus and tabouli $2. Open Sat.-Thurs. 8am-6pm, Fri. 8am-8pm.

Mexicali Rosa's, 207 Rideau St. (234-7044), at Waller St. A rustic Mexican-American restaurant for when you have the Mexicali blues, featuring the standards (taco and enchilada dinners $8.25-$11) as well as BBQ items grilled in Ottawa's first "Texas wood-burning smoker." Chili $4.75. Open Mon.-Tues. 11:30am-10:30pm, Wed.-Thurs. 11:30am-11pm, Fri.-Sat. 11:30am-midnight, Sun. 4-10pm.

Dunn's Delicatessen and Restaurant, 126-128 George St. at Dalhousie (235-DUNN). Quality deli with friendly service that lives up to the jars of pickles in the window. Deli sandwiches $3.25-$3.95. Breakfast special (2 eggs, bacon, toast, coffee) $1.75, served Mon.-Fri. 6-10am. Evening special (smoked meat, fries, pickle and soft drink) $3.95, served daily 4pm-midnight. Open daily 24 hrs.

Malibu Jack's California Food Epic, 47 Clarence St. (594-9497), at Parent St. in the Byward Market area. Jack, former hippie and current owner of the burger and BBQ joint, recounts the origins of each of his dishes on the menu—most involve hanging out with James Dean and Jimi Hendrix. Huge outdoor terrace. The Pebble Beach Club ($7.50) is their quintessential meal. Open Mon.-Sat. 11am-1am, Sun. 11am-11pm.

Father and Sons, 112 Osgoode St. (233-6066), at the eastern edge of the U. of O campus. Student favorite for tavern-style food with some Lebanese dishes thrown in. Breakfast special $2. Triple decker sandwiches $6. Drink-encouraging specials daily 8-11pm: wings 15¢ Mon. and Fri., shooters $2.50 Thurs. Open daily 8am-1am, kitchen until midnight.

Hitsman's Restaurant and Bakery, 1242 Bank (731-6111), at Chesley St. south of Hwy. 417. Take one of several buses that travel down Bank from downtown. An incredibly cheap sandwich shop and bakery. Sandwiches $2.44. Great burgers $2.29. Chocolate lovers should rumba with the rumballs (65¢). Open Mon.-Fri. 7am-5:30pm, Sat. 7am-5pm, Sun. 9:30am-3pm.

The dedicated nightlifer should descend into Hull, where most establishments grind and flay until 3am every day of the week and the legal drinking age is 18. In Ottawa, the Byward Market area contains most of the action. Ottawa clubs close at 1am (11pm on Sun.), but most, in an effort to keep people from going to Hull, offer free admission. **Stoney Monday's,** 62 York St. (236-5548), just west of William, is a trendy bar for people in their early to mid-20s. **Chateau Lafayette,** 42 York St. (233-3403), the oldest tavern in Ottawa and the neighborhood watering-hole for locals, lures the budgeteer with $1.40 draft beer and $2.90 pints. The regulars look like permanent fixtures, the sign over the door still reads "Ladies and Escorts," and the management steadfastly refuses to serve hard liquor, upholding the tavern tradition. The **Downstairs Club,** 207 Rideau St. (234-9942), downstairs from Mexicali Rosa's, rocks nightly with live entertainment; blues on Tues. (Open Mon.-Sat. 11:30-1am, Sun. noon-11pm.) Over 20 popular nightspots populate the *promenade du Portage* in Hull, just west of Place Portage, the huge government office complex. A tough crowd congregates at **Le Zinc,** 191, promenade du Portage (778-0462), to enjoy the large dance floor and loud music. **Le Coquetier,** 147, promenade du Portage (771-6560), is a more peaceful place to treat a friend to a brewski (open daily 11:30am-3am).

Sights

When it comes to tourist and cultural attractions, Ottawa's status as Canada's capital truly emerges. Since the national museums and political action are packed in tightly, most sights can be reached on foot. **Parliament Hill** on Wellington St. at Metcalfe, towers over downtown as the city's focal point, while its Gothic architecture sets it apart. The **Centennial Flame,** lit in 1967 to mark the 100th anniversary of the Dominion of Canada's inaugural session of Parliament, burns at the south gate. The central parliament structure, **Centre Block,** contains the House of Commons, the Senate and the Library of Parliament. The Library was the only part of the original (1859-66) structure to survive the 1916 fire. Free, worthwhile tours in English and French depart every 10 minutes from the Infotent. (Reservations 996-0896. Public Information Office 992-4793. Tours May 20-July 31 Mon.-Fri. 9am-9pm, Sat.-Sun. and holidays 9am-6pm; Aug.-Sept. 2 Mon.-Fri. 9am-8:30pm, Sat.-Sun. and holidays 9am-6pm; Sept. 3-May 19 Wed.-Mon. 9am-5pm, Tues. 9am-9pm. Last tour each day begins ½-hr. before the closing time.) Watch Canada's Prime Minister (currently the Right Hon. Brian Mulroney) and his government squirm on the verbal hot seat during the official **Question Period** in the House of Commons chamber (Mon.-Thurs. 2:15-3pm, Fri. 11:15am-noon; free). Far less lively or politically meaningful, the sessions of the **Senate of Canada** (992-4787) also welcome spectators. See (while you can) the body of "sober second thought," for which some Canadians are ready to pull the plug. After the tour, climb the 293-ft. **Peace Tower,** to get a stunning view of the Ottawa valley. The white marble **Memorial Chamber** honors the Canadian war dead. Lovers of pageantry will adore the **Changing of the Guard,** ceremoniously presented on the broad lawns in front of Centre Block (June 22-Aug. 25 daily at 10am). At dusk, Centre Block and lawns transform into the set for *Sound and Light,* which relates the history of the Parliament Buildings and the development of the nation. (May 4-June 8 Tues.-Sat.; June 11-Sept. 1 daily. May-July 9:30 and 10:30pm; Aug. and Sept. 9 and 10pm. Catch the carillon concerts that chime year-round most weekdays 12:30-12:45pm. (In June and July also Sun. and Thurs. 7:30-8:30pm.) A five-minute walk west along Wellington St. is the **Supreme Court of Canada** (995-4330), where nine justices preside. Worthwhile 30-minute tours of the Federal Court and the Supreme Court, both housed in this building, are offered. (Open summer daily 9am-5pm; off-season Mon.-Fri. 9am-5pm. Free.) One block south of Wellington, Sparks St. greets one of North America's first pedestrian malls, hailed as an innovative experiment in 1960. The **Sparks Street Mall** recently received a $5-million facelift, rejuvenating many of Ottawa's banks and upscale retail stores.

East of the Parliament Buildings at the junction of Sparks, Wellington, and Elgin stands **Confederation Square** and in its center the enormous **National War Memorial,** dedicated by King George VI in 1939. The towering structure symbolizes the triumph of peace over war, a rather ironic message considering the state of world affairs in 1939. The **Rideau Centre,** south of Rideau St. at Sussex Dr., is the city's primary shopping mall as well as the main bus depot.

Nepean Point, several blocks northwest of Rideau Centre and the Byward Market by the Alexandra Bridge, provides a panoramic view of the capital. An open-air theater, **The Astrolabe,** was constructed on Nepean Point in 1967 and is one of the sites of **Cultures Canada** (239-5609), a festival of song and dance from July to Labor Day.

Parks and Museums

Ottawa boasts a multitude of parks and recreational areas—green spaces, walkways, and bike paths surrounding the canal. **Major Hill's Park,** behind the Château Laurier Hotel on the banks of the Ottawa, is the city's oldest park. Within it stands a relic from the Crimean War, the **Noon Day Gun,** which fires daily at noon, except on Sunday when it resounds a punishing two hours earlier. **Dow's Lake** (232-1001), accessible by means of the Queen Elizabeth Parkway, is an artificial lake on the Rideau Canal, 15 minutes south of Ottawa. A popular recreation area year-round, Dow's Lake blazes with color in spring when 150,000 tulips bloom along its shore. Pedal boats, canoes, and bikes are available at the Dow's Lake Pavilion, just off Queen Elizabeth Parkway. The Pavilion warms frozen skaters in the winter, especially during **Winterlude,** Ottawa's annual celebration of the Canadian cold. Magnificent ice sculptures line the frozen canal on which merry revelers celebrate (in 1992, Feb. 7-16).

The Governor-General, the Queen's representative in Canada, opens the grounds of **Rideau Hall,** his official residence, to the public. Tours leave from the main gate at 1 Sussex Dr. (May-June 23, tours leave daily 10am-4pm on the hour; June 24-Aug. 25 daily 10:15am-5:15pm on the ½-hr.; Aug. 26-Oct. 13 Wed.-Sun. 10am-3pm on the hour. 998-7113, 998-7114 or 800-465-6890 for info; free.) At nearby 24 Sussex Dr. you'll find the official residence of the Prime Minister. Gawk from afar or use a scope; you can't get any closer to the building than the main gates.

Ottawa headquarters many of Canada's huge national museums. **The National Gallery** (990-1985), in a spectacular glass-towered building at 380 Sussex Dr., adjacent to Nepean Point, contains the world's most comprehensive collection of Canadian art, as well as outstanding European, American and Asian works. The building's exterior is a postmodern version of the facing neo-Gothic buttresses of the Library of Parliament. (Open May-early Sept. Sat.-Tues. 10am-6pm, Wed.-Fri. 10am-8pm; early Sept.-April 30 Tues.-Sun. 10am-5pm, Thurs. 10am-8pm. Public tours daily at 11am and 2pm. Admission $4.50, seniors and students $3, under 16 free.) The gallery is wheelchair accessible and free Thursday, as are most of Ottawa's public museums and galleries. A spaceship-like structure across the river in Hull houses the **Canadian Museum of Civilization** at 100 Laurier St. (776-7000). Admire the architecture but be wary of overly ambitious exhibits that attempt perspective on 10,000 years of Canadian history. Don't miss breathtaking films screened in **Ciné Plus,** the first in the world capable of projecting both Imax and Omnimax. (Open April-June 30 Fri.-Wed. 9am-5pm, Thurs. 9am-8pm; July 1-Sept. 2 Fri.-Wed. 9am-6pm, Thurs. 9am-8pm; winter Tues.-Wed. and Fri.-Sun. 9am-5pm, Thurs. 9am-8pm. Museum admission $4, seniors and students $3, under 15 free. Ciné Plus $6, seniors and students $4, under 15 free.) The **Canadian Museum of Nature** McLeod St. at Metcalfe (996-3102) explores the natural world, from dinosaur skeletons to minerals, through multi-media displays. (Open May 1-Labor Day Sun.-Mon., and Thurs. 9:30am-8pm, Tues.-Wed., Fri.-Sat. 9:30am-5pm; winter Fri.-Wed. 10am-5pm, Thurs. 10am-8pm. Admission $3, students $2, ages 6-16 and seniors $1.50, under 6 free.)

The **Canadian War Museum,** 330 Sussex Dr. (992-2774), just north of St. Patrick, displays a fine collection of war art, medals, and weaponry. (Open daily 9:30am-5pm. Admission $2.25, seniors and students $1, under 6 and veterans free. Call 996-6166 for group tours.) The **Royal Canadian Mint,** 320 Sussex Dr. (992-5700), next to the War Museum, struck its first coin in 1908, as a branch of the Royal Mint in London, England. In 1931, the Mint became an independent Canadian agency. Today, Canadian coins are produced in Winnipeg; the Ottawa mint still strikes commemorative coins and medals and offers tours, by appointment only. (Tours May 8-Aug. 30 Mon.-Fri. 8:30-11am and 12:30-2:30pm.) History enthusiasts easily could disappear in the **National Library Archives,** 395 Wellington St. (992-9481 or 995-5138), which houses enormous quantities of Canadian publications, old maps, photographs, and letters, as well as historical exhibits. (Library open Mon.-Fri. 8:30am-5pm and will provide group tours for those with professional interest only. Exhibit area open daily 9am-9pm.) Politicophiles will double up with laughter at the new **Canadian Museum of Caricature,** 136 Patrick St. at Sussex (995-3145). Chuckle at cartoonists' impressions of three centuries of Canadian history. (Open Sat.-Tues. 10am-6pm, Wed.-Fri. 10am-8pm. Free.) Walk to the elegant **Laurier House,** 335 Laurier Ave. E. (692-2581), from which Liberal Prime Minister William Lyon Mackenzie King governed Canada for most of his lengthy tenure. Admire at leisure the antiques accumulated by King, as well as the crystal ball he used to consult his long-dead mother (presumably a liberal) on matters of national importance. (Open April-Sept. Tues.-Sat. 9am-5pm, Sun. 2-5pm; Oct.-March Tues.-Sat. 10am-5pm, Sun. 2-5pm. Free.)

Farther out of town, the **National Museum of Science and Technology,** 1867 St. Laurent Blvd. (991-3044), lets visitors explore the developing world of mech, tech, and transport with touchy-feely exhibits. The museum entrance is on Lancaster, 200m east of St. Laurent. (Recent renovations leave museum hours and admission fees uncertain. Call for info.) The **National Aviation Museum** (993-2010), at the Rockcliffe Airport off St. Laurent Blvd. north of Montreal St., illustrates the history of flying. More than 100 aircraft. (Open May-Labor Day Fri.-Wed. 9am-5pm, Thurs. 9am-9pm; Labor Day-April Tues.-Wed. and Fri.-Sun. 9am-5pm, Thurs. 9am-9pm. Admission $4.50, students and seniors $3.50, ages 6-15 $1.50; free on Thurs. after 5pm.)

Entertainment

The **National Arts Centre,** 65 Elgin St. (tickets 755-1111; info 996-5051), home of an excellent small orchestra and theater company, frequently hosts international musicians. The neighboring **Arts Court Theatre,** in Ottawa's Municipal Arts Centre, 2 Daly (corner Nicholas; 233-3449) stages plays, dance performances, and concerts. **Odyssey Theatre** (232-8407) holds open-air shows at **Strathcona Park,** at the intersection of Laurier Ave. and Range Rd. well east of the canal. (Shows late July to mid-Aug. Admission $10, students and seniors $8, under 12 $6.) In summer on Parliament Hill, roving acting troupes sporadically present historical vignettes (June 26-Sept. 2 Wed.-Sun. 10:45am-3:30pm is the general time frame). Don't be surprised when you're suddenly entangled in a wild political rally or an emotional legal case—you've merely stumbled through a dimension of time and mind into one of these intriguing skits. In addition, Ottawa suffers from a bad case of festival fever during the summer; contact an visitors bureau.

Stratford

'Tis no mischance that Stratford lieth upon Avon River and runneth over with Falstaff St., Portia Blvd., and gentlemanly Verona Park. As the fates fain would have it, ere the town's mill-based economy collapsed in 1953 Stratford-born scribe Tom Patterson foundeth the **Stratford Shakespeare Festival.** Yea, the inaugural season, staged in a tent, saw Sir Alec Guinness perform the title role in *Richard III* under the reign of director Tyrone Guthrie. Respected and loved around the world, the Festival often twains the town's populace on weekends.

Despite the flood of theatre-goers, Stratford's streets and parks still display the leafy shrubbery and omnipresent charm of an Ontario hamlet (small village, not Danish prince). While your role in Stratford verily should be as a player amidst the Festival's worldy stages, don't neglect some of the subtler attractions that may smell as sweet.

Act I: Practical Information

Tourism Stratford Information Booth, 30 York St. on the river (273-3352). Has extensive B&B listings and phones from which to call potential (g)hosts. Info galore, and the critical

Festival Stratford Guide. Open during the theatre season, April 27-May 11 daily 9am-5pm; May 12-Labor Day Tues.-Sat. 9am-8pm, Sun.-Mon. 9am-5pm; Labor Day-Nov. 11 daily 9am-5pm. **Tourism Stratford** (271-5140 or 800-561-7926 for literature only) also provides di-verse info. Open Mon.-Fri. 8:30am-4:30pm.

Trains: VIA RAIL (273-3234 or 800-361-1235 for reservations) has a depot at the station on Shakespeare St. Cheap trains to Toronto via Kitchener, and London and Sarnia, leave twice daily, the latter with an Amtrak (800-426-8725) connection to Chicago.

Buses: Chaco Trails (271-7870), owned by Greyhound, operates buses to surrounding cities, among them Kitchener, Toronto, and (in a roundabout way) Niagara Falls. **Airports or Anywhere** (273-0057) cab service takes people to Lester B. Pearson International Airport in Toronto. (5 per day; 1½-2 hr.; $31, $76 if alone.)

Post Office: 75 Waterloo St. (271-1282). Open Mon.-Fri. 8am-5pm. **Postal code:** N5A 4A0.

Area code: 519.

Act II: The Festival

The Festival runs from late April, when previews begin, through early November. Several brilliant blasts from Shakespeare's canon always form the vanguard of the season's program. However, don't ignore the uniquely Canadian plays brought to the stage, a result of artistic director David William's commitment to the Festival's theatrically roamin' fellows and countrymen. Appropriately, given the high-royalty content of Bill's plays, the **Festival Theatre,** on Parkview Dr., adjacent to Queen's Park is crown-shaped, with manicured lawns overlooking the river. Its thrust stage, demanded by director Tyrone Guthrie, gives the theatre an intimate air—no seat is more than 65 ft. from the stage. The **Avon Theatre,** on the corner of George and Downie St. downtown, opened in 1901. It fooled around as a vaudeville house, a movie theatre, and a film-festival centre before ending its comedy of errors and joining THE Festival in 1963. The Young Company performs at the **Tom Patterson Theatre** on Lakeside Dr., between Waterloo and Nile St. Colored signs will direct you to all theatres.

Alas, expensive tickets, you know the problem well. The best seats strangulate for $30-47, depending on the time of the week and the season. Order in advance and you won't have to trade your kingdom for a ticket. Avoiding summer and fall weekends also avoids the highest prices, as does seeking after April to May and September to November performances specifically designated "student/senior;" tickets initially are offered at low rates to students and seniors (65 and over) before going on sale to the masses. Preview performances in April and May, and sporadically in late July, offer the same reductions for the general public as student/senior shows. Seniors can get any available preview seat for $20 during the two weeks prior to the show. "Midweek savings" and "family experience" shows let parents purchase seats at $12.50 for their younguns. Rush tickets, for specially designated seats in the lowest-priced category, go on sale at the Festival Theatre Box Office at 9am the day of the show. If available, the tickets can be ordered by phone after 10am; each person is limited to two tickets. Keep in mind that once the doors close, you can lay siege to any vacant seat in the theatre. Advance reservations must be made for wheelchair seating (available in all theatres) and for hearing-impaired receivers ($3.25 and a security deposit). Parking adjacent to the Festival Theatre costs $4 per car per performance, but you can tie up your steely mount in the Queen's Park lot for free. Complete info about casts, performances (matinees at 2pm, evening shows at 8pm), and other aspects of the Festival can be obtained by phone (273-1600; free from Toronto at 416-363-4471; free from Detroit at 313-964-4668) or by writing the Stratford Festival, P.O. Box 520, Stratford, Ont., N5A 6V2.

If you can, attend one of the behind-the-scenes programs the Festival offers. **Meet the Festival** engages you in informal discussion with members of the Festival team. (July 1-Aug. 28, Wed. and Fri. 9:30-10:30am at the Tom Patterson Theatre. Free.) **Post-performance discussions** are 30-minute Q&A sessions with some of the evening's performers. (June 16-Aug. 25, Tues. and Thurs. Meet at Aisle 2, orchestra level. Free.) **Backstage tours** allow you to explore one of the largest backstage areas in North America. (June 7-Nov. 8, Sun. Tours leave every 15 min. 9-10:30am. $5, seniors and students $2.50. Book in advance.)

Before or between shows, venture across Queen's Park from the Festival Theatre to **The Gallery Stratford,** 54 Romeo St. (271-5271). Marvel at the exhibit of props, costumes, and set pieces from the previous year's Festival season, as well as the work of Canadian artists. (Open May 28-Sept. 2 Tues.-Sun. 9am-6pm; Sept. 6-Oct. 20 Tues.-Sun. 10am-5pm. $3, students and seniors $2.)

Act III: Not the Festival

Thou shouldst meander along the Avon, where thou canst view swans, mallards, and, if the gods smile upon thee, battleships. (Remote-controlled, alas.) The first swans were given to the town by a Canadian National Railroad employee in 1918. Today, they are cared for by an honorary "keeper of the swans." Haughty but elegant, they relish posing for cameras. Bicycle booths border the river—rent a bike from **Wheel-Rent,** near the old bandshell east of the info booth on Lakeside Dr. ($7 per hr., 2 bikes for $12. Daily $35, $50 for 2. Weekly $85. Open seasonally, daily 9am-6pm.) Or join the swans on the river—you can rent a paddleboat or canoe at the window (271-7739) below the tourist info booth on York St. Or try a sedate 30- to 40-minute ride in their tour boat. (Canoes $15 per hr. Boats $7-15. Tour boat $4, kids $2. Open seasonally rain or shine, daily 9am-9pm.)

Duck into **Gallery 96** (271-4660) on York Lane behind Rundles Restaurant. This co-op gallery displays vivid local painting and sculpture, as well as original theatre-costume design. (Open Tues.-Sun. 10am-5:30pm.) Numerous other galleries and antique stores pepper the Stratford streets. For forest imagery, head past the info booth and Huron St. to the **Shakespearean Gardens.** Located on the river, the gardens are full of plants and flowers mentioned in Bill the Bard's plays. The works of Ontario artists and craftsmen can be seen at **Art in the Park,** a free exhibition set up on Lakeside, between Front and North St. (June to mid-Sept., Wed., Sat.-Sun.) Not to be forgotten in the deluge of other artwork is music. **Stratford Summer Sounds** is the town's fledgling folk festival and fruit of love, held for one weekend in mid-June. Throughout the summer, on Wednesdays and Sundays at 7pm, the Kiwanis Club sponsors concerts of all sorts in the bandshell at Upper Queen's Park. Book lovers will come not to praise, but to bury themselves willingly in **Yesterday's Things & Books,** 351 Ontario St. (271-5180), a chock-full used bookstore that also sells antiques and jewelry.

Act IV: Food

Stratford's viands aren't particularly distinctive, but prices are reasonable, quality good, and restaurants plentiful (along Wellington and Ontario St. especially)—whether you want a pound of flesh or midsummer leafy things. Try the tempestuous fries (small 90¢, medium $1.50, large $2.75) at **Ken's Chuckwagon** in Market Square behind City Hall. (Open Mon.-Fri. 11am-9pm, Sat.-Sun. 11am-6pm.) The **Mr. Dog Stand,** at Ontario and Downie, serves great hot ($2.25) and sausage ($3) canines if you have the lean and hungry look. (Open daily 11am-6pm.) Marie Antoinette would have applauded the decadently huge sandwiches made with fresh bread ($3-3.50) as you like it at **Let Them Eat Cake,** 82 Wellington (273-4774). Standing ovations for their homemade cookies and pastries, picnic lunches, and special diet dishes. (Open Mon. 7:30am-9:30pm, Tues.-Fri. 7:30am-12:30am, Sat. 8:30am-12:30am, Sun. 11am-6pm.) And you too, Brutus, will be served quickly and amply at the **Elizabethan Restaurant,** 95 Ontario St. (277-3580), complete with soft light breaking though Shakespearean windows. The dearest item on the menu is $8 (delicious lunch specials $4-4.75). (Open summer daily 9am-7:30pm; off-season Mon.-Sat. 9am-6pm.) At the **House of Gene,** 108 Downie St. (271-3080), the question is whether to be at the $7 lunch buffet—with Chinese smorgasbord, salad bar, and dessert—or not to be, since the $9 dinner special offers more choices. (Open Mon.-Wed. 11:30am-8pm, Thurs.-Sat. 11:30am-9pm, Sun. noon-9pm.) The hotspur "bard to be at" for après-theatre drinks and general merriment is **Bentley's,** 99 Ontario St. (271-1121). Standard pub fare is washed down with a variety of domestic and imported drafts bubbling, toiling and troubling at this actors' hang-out. (Open daily 11:30am-1am.)

Act V: Accommodations

Stratford has a well-developed lodgings network. The budget traveler probably will want to stay at the **Stratford General Hospital Residence,** 130 Youngs St. (271-5084). From the bus/train, walk left on Shakespeare (he won't mind) and across the tracks on Nile St. to West Gore. Walk right (west) on Gore for 15 to 20 minutes and turn right on St. Vincent St. You'll see the sign for the Conestoga College Division of Nursing. Stay in one of the 180 impeccably-clean singles (each with its own sink and fridge), cook in the kitchen with the microwave (no utensils), and swim in the pool before a day of theatre. (Rooms $23 per night, $91 per week. Shared bathrooms. Laundry on each floor if you have to get out any damnèd spots. Checkout 11am. Parking $1 per day. Open May 5-Aug. 27; a few beds may be available during the nursing school year. Reservations recommended.) The Tourism Stratford Information Booth (see Practical Information) has extensive B&B listings. The **Festival Accommodations Bureau** (273-1600) can book you into local B&Bs ($40-100) and hotels. Their office is also the only way to access Stratford guest homes, providing you with a room and possibly a continental breakfast in a private home whose owner wishes only to cater to Festival patrons. Be warned that the homes are not necessarily within walking distance of the theatres. (Single bed $28. Double bed $31. Twin beds $33.) Campers should drive 20 minutes from Stratford on Hwy. 7 West (go into St. Mary's and turn left into the park) to the **Wildwood Conservation Area** (284-2931 or 284-2292). You can canoe on or fish in the lake, or just jump in, sing sad songs, and toss around flower petals. Take a puckish hike along the 5km of scenic trails. Metered showers are available, but don't fall in love with any donkeys. (Sites with water $16.25, with electricity $18.25.) For a booklet on *Alternative Accommodations* all over Ontario (B&Bs and farm vacations), see Ontario Practical Information, above. A number of the farms lie within reasonable driving distance of Stratford. (Singles from $23. Doubles from $38.) The **Southwestern Ontario Countryside Vacation Association** (c/o a very nice Avon lady named Mrs. E. Alvaretta Henderson, R.R. #1, Millibank, Ont. N0K 1L0, or 519-595-4604) will send you an informative brochure. (Singles $35. Doubles $45.)

Toronto

For a city that had less than a million residents as recently as the 1950s, playing the role of Canada's most populous city (2.3 million) and unrivalled financial leader takes some getting used to. Next to Montréal's sophisticated lifestyle, Toronto once seemed as bland as suet pudding. The bars still close at 1am, but "Trawna" has come a long way since the days of Charles Dickens, who claimed that the townspeople's idea of a hot Saturday night consisted of wrapping themselves in Union Jacks and singing "God Save the Queen" (and not the Sex Pistols' version, either).

The city's reverence for things British still shows—King St. and Queen St. are two of its main drags—but the waves of immigrants following World War II recognizably altered the city's character. The United Nations dubbed Toronto the world's most multi-cultural city in 1988. And since the late 70s, when the perceived threat of *québecois* nationalism caused a number of companies' head offices to move from Montréal to Toronto, the city donned the crown as Canada's financial capital. Today, the Toronto Stock Exchange handles over 70% of the country's stock trade while many of the city's inhabitants enjoy gainful employment.

Torontonians have loosened their collars quite a bit but still maintain an efficient and safe public transportation system, promote recycling virtually everywhere, and keep the city impeccably clean. A visiting film crew learned this the hard way. After

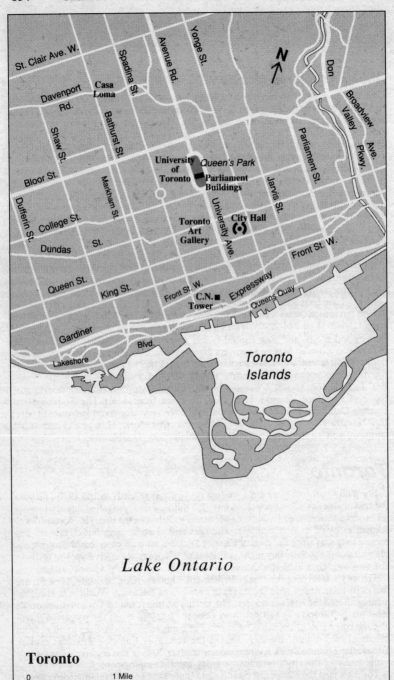

Toronto

0 —————————— 1 Mile

0 —————————— 1 Kilometer

dirtying a Toronto street to make it look more like a typical "American" avenue, they went on a coffee break—and returned a short time later only to find their set spotless again, swept by the ever-vigilant city maintenance department.

Practical Information

Emergency: 9ll.

Metropolitan Toronto Convention and Visitor's Association, 207 Queen's Quay Terminal at Harborfront, P.O. Box 126, M5J 1A7. (Infoline 368-9821 in Toronto; 387-3058, 800-363-1990 in Canada and the continental US.) Open daily 9am-5pm; mid-May to early Sept. 9am-6pm. Permanent **Travel Information Center** in Eaton Centre at level "2 below". Open Mon.-Fri. 10am-9pm, Sat.-Sun. 9:30am-6pm. Three temporary booths at the **Art Gallery of Ontario,** 317 Dundas St. W., at the **Royal Ontario Museum,** Queen's Park Crescent, and at **Nathan Phillips Square.** All booths open late May-Labor Day daily 9am-7pm. Permanent booth open in the off-season daily 9:30am-5:30pm.

Student Travel Agency: Travel CUTS, 187 College St. (979-2406), just west of University Ave. Subway: Queen's Park. Smaller office at 74 Gerrard St. E. (977-0441). Subway: College. Open Mon.-Fri. 9am-5pm, Sat. 11am-3pm. **YHA Travel/Canadian Hostelling Association,** 219 Church St. (862-0226), 2 doors down from the hostel. Subway: Dundas. Excellent for advice and cheap flights. Open Mon.-Wed. and Fri. 10am-5:30pm, Thurs. 10am-7pm, Sat. 10am-4pm.

Canada Customs: (973-8022). Location at Pearson Airport (676-3643; open daily 7:30am-11pm).

Consulates: U.S., 360 University Ave. (595-0228, 595-1700 for visa info). Subway: St. Patrick. Open Mon.-Fri. 8:30am-2pm for consular services. **Australia,** 175 Bloor St. E. #314-6 (323-1155). Subway: Bloor St. Open Mon.-Fri. 9am-1pm and 2-5pm for info; 9am-1pm for visas. **U.K.,** 777 Bay St. #1910 (593-1267 or 593-1290). Subway: College. Open Mon.-Fri. 9:30am-3:30pm, 9am-4:50pm for telephone info. **Germany,** 77 Admiral St. (925-2813). Subway: St. George. Open Mon.-Fri. 9am-noon.

Currency Exchange: Toronto Currency Exchange, 391 Yonge St., 780 Yonge St. Both open daily 9am-6pm; 313 Yonge St. (598-3769) at Dundas. Open daily 9am-9pm. **Royal Bank of Canada** has exchange centers at Pearson Airport (676-3220). Open daily 6am-11pm.

American Express: 50 Bloor St. W. (967-3411; 800-221-7282 for lost or stolen travelers' checks). Subway: Bloor-Yonge. Open Mon.-Wed. and Sat. 10am-6pm, Thurs.-Fri. 10am-7pm.

Pearson International Airport: (247-7678) about 20km west of Toronto via Hwy. 427, 401, or 409. **Gray Coach Airport Express** (call Metro Toronto Coach Info. at 393-7911) bus service runs each day directly to downtown hotels every 20 min. 5:05am-10:45pm. Last bus from downtown at 11:10pm. $10, round-trip $17.25. Buses also serve the Yorkdale ($6), York Mills ($7), and Islington subway stations every 40 min. 6:20am-12:10am. **Air Canada,** 925-2311. To: Montréal ($205); Calgary ($572); New York City ($194); and Vancouver ($683). All flights 50% less for "student standby;" max. age 21. 50% off round-trip fare if you book 21 days in advance.

Trains: VIA Rail at Union Station, 61 Front St. at Bay (366-8411). Subway: Union. To: Montréal (5 per day, 6 on Fri.; $68, students $61); Windsor (4 per day; $51, $46); Vancouver (3 per week; $381, $343; no advance purchase specials). **Amtrak** (800-426-8725) to New York City (1 per day, $90) and Chicago (1 per day, $102). Seniors 10% discount on all fares. Students and seniors 40% off tickets purchased at least 5 days in advance; same deal for adults Mon.-Thurs. and Sat. Ticket office open Mon., Wed., and Fri. 6:45am-11:30pm, Sun. 8am-9pm.

Buses: Voyageur/Greyhound Bus Terminal, 610 Bay St. (393-7911), just north of Dundas. Subway: St. Patrick or Dundas. Service to: Calgary, Montréal ($48.10), Vancouver ($247), New York City ($117). Seniors 10% discount, student discounts usually require 14-day advance purchase and are subject to certain restrictions. Ticket office open daily 5:30am-1am.

Public Transport: Toronto Transit Commission (TTC) (393-4636). Network includes 2 subway lines and numerous bus and streetcar routes. Free maps at all stations. Some routes run 24 hrs. New policy requires buses running after dark to stop anywhere along the route at a female passenger's request. Free transfers among subway, buses, and streetcars, but only within stations. Fare $1.30, 8 tokens $8.50, seniors 50% off with ID (7 for $3.75), ages 2-12 55¢. Unlimited travel day pass $5. Monthly pass $56.50.

Toronto Island Ferry Service (392-8193, 392-8194 for recording). Numerous ferries to Toronto Islands Park on Centre Island leave daily from Bay St. Ferry Dock at the foot of Bay St. Service approximately every ½-hr., every 15 min. during peak hours. Service 8am-11:45pm. Fare $2.50 round-trip; seniors, students, ages 15-19 $1.25, under 15 75¢.

Taxi: Co-op Cabs, 364-7111. $2.25 plus distance and waiting.

Car Rental: Wrecks for Rent, 77 Nassau St. (585-7782) Subway: Spadina or Bathurst. $30 per day; first 200km free, 12¢ each additional km. Insurance $9.50 if over 25 with credit card, $15 without. Surcharge for ages 21-25. Open Mon.-Fri. 8am-6pm, Sat. 9am-4pm. **Hertz** (800-263-0600), **Tilden** (922-2000), **Budget** (673-3322), **Thrifty** (800-367-2277), and **Discount** (961-8006) also serve Toronto.

Auto Transport Company: Toronto Driveaway, 5803 Yonge St. (225-7754 or 225-7759), just north of the Finch subway stop, north of Hwy. 401. Rides to western Canada and Florida. In summer, pay gas plus $50-100 to western Canada. In winter, they may pay you to go certain places. **Allostop,** 663 Yonge St. suite 301 (323-0874), at Bloor. Matches riders with drivers. To: Ottawa ($22); Montréal ($21); Québec City ($26); and New York ($40). Open Wed. 9am-5pm, Thurs.-Fri. 9am-7pm, Sat.-Sun. 10am-5pm.

Bike Rental: Brown's Sports and Cycle Bike Rental, 2447 Bloor St. W. (763-4176). $15 per day, $30 per weekend, $40 per week. Open Mon.-Wed. 9:30am-6pm, Thurs.-Fri. 9:30am-8pm, Sat. 9:30am-5:30pm. $100 deposit or credit card required.

Help Lines: Rape Crisis, 597-8808. **Services for the Disabled,** Ontario Travel, 965-4008. **Toronto Area Gays (TAG),** 964-6600. Open Mon.-Fri. 7-10pm. **Distress Centre,** 367-2277.

Post Office: Toronto Dominion Centre (973-3120), at King and Bay St. General Delivery at Station K, 2384 Yonge St. at Eglinton (483-1334). Open Mon.-Fri. 8am-5:45pm. **Postal Code:** M4P 2E0.

Area Code: 416.

The intersection of **Yonge** (young) and **Bloor St.,** at the Bloor-Yonge subway stop, makes up the city center, although the focus of downtown activity has shifted farther south to **Yonge** and **Dundas.** The streets of Toronto form a grid pattern. Yonge divides the city east-west. "North" addresses start from Lake Ontario.

Traffic is heavy in Toronto—avoid rush hour (7-10am and 3-7pm, Fri. afternoons and holiday weekends) at all costs. Parking spots are hard to find and the police ticket zealously. Parking garage rates are generally steep (75¢-$2.50 for the first ½-hr. or less). The parking lot on Church St. just south of Dundas across from the hostel (see Accommodations and Camping below) charges a flat rate of $5 from 6pm to 7am and $9 from 7am to 6pm. The lot on Dundas just west of Sherbourne charges $8 per day, $4 per night. Save money by leaving your car in the street at night (meters stop at 6pm, start again at 8am) or by parking at an outlying subway station (often free) and taking trains downtown. Use streetcars whenever possible. The Queen, King, and Dundas cars all run along the streets of the same name. Service is frequent and fast, and you can take in the city as you bounce from place to place. The bus and train stations are both in the downtown area; the train station (Union Station) is also a subway stop. From the main bus terminal, walk along Dundas in either direction to reach the St. Patrick or Dundas subway stop.

Accommodations and Camping

Cheap hotels and motels, concentrated around Jarvis St., tend to be of dubious character. However, several guest houses keep their rates low and standards high, despite the rugged clientele that low prices tend to attract. For relatively inexpensive accommodations in a private home, reserve ahead through **Toronto Bed and Breakfast,** P.O. Box 269, 253 College St. M5T, 1R5 (961-3676 or 588-8800) for 20 homes, all with subway access. (Singles from $41. Doubles from $51. Call Mon.-Fri. 9am-noon, 2-7pm. Machine will take messages.) **Metropolitan Bed and Breakfast,** Ste. 269 #615, Mount Pleasant Rd. M45 3C5 (964-2566), offers similar service for 30 homes in the Toronto area. (Singles from $40, doubles from $50. Parking included. Call 8am-noon, 3-8pm.) Camping alternatives are uninspiring and far-removed from the city center.

Toronto International Hostel (IYHF), 223 Church St. (368-1848 or 368-0207), walk east on Dundas and turn right onto Church. 5 min. from Eaton Centre. Subway: Dundas. Three separate buildings with 179 clean but varied rooms. One has a single toilet and shower for 16 beds; another perches directly above Dundas and Church where streetcars pound by 24 hrs. Huge lounge with TV, excellent kitchen, laundry facilities, ping-pong table and oodles of tourist info. Memberships sold. 3-night max. stay enforced in high season. Check-out 10am. Quiet hours midnight-7am. Dorm (4-10 beds) $15, nonmembers $20. Cramped semi-private rooms $17, $22. $5 key deposit. 10% discount for members at the **Arm Chair Traveller Restaurant**, 217 Church. Breakfast ($3.25) served until 10am Mon.-Fri., noon Sat.-Sun. Open Mon.-Sat. 8am-1am, Sun. 9am-midnight.

Knox College, 59 Saint George St. (978-2793). Subway: Queen's Park, walk west on College and right on St. George. Huge rooms with wood floors around an idyllic courtyard banish notions of Presbyterian austerity. Common rooms, baths on each floor. Dining hall open. Great location in the heart of UofT campus. Singles $25. Call for reservations Mon.-Fri. 9am-4pm.

Neill-Wycik (Why-ziek) College Hotel, 96 Gerrard St. E. (977-2320). From College subway stop, walk 1 block east on Carleton to Church St., turn right, walk to Gerrard and make a left. Rooms impeccably clean, some with beautiful views of the city. Kitchen on every floor, no cooking "equipment." Check-in after 1pm (locked storage room provided.) Check-out 11am. Singles (including simple breakfast) $37-39, mini-twin $41-43, doubles $42.50-44.50. Family room $47-49 (extra beds $9, 2 kids under 17 free with parents). 10% discount for 7-night stay if you pay up front; 20% standby discount for students and seniors after 8pm. **Kafé Freja** on first floor. Open early May-late Aug.

Trinity College and St. Hilda's College Residences, 6 Hoskin Ave. (978-2523), on Queen's Park Crescent close to the Royal Ontario Museum and shopping on Bloor St. Subway: Museum. Dorms in 2 of UofT's 6 colleges. Sizable rooms showing their age in warping floors and peeling paint. Shared bath and kitchenette. TV lounge. Singles $45, students $28. Doubles $56. Reservations recommended. Office hours Mon.-Fri. 9am-4pm.

Karabanow Guest House and Tourist Home, 9 Spadina Rd. (923-4004), at Bloor St. 6 blocks west of Yonge. Subway: Spadina. Good location. Small and intimate. 19 rooms (mostly doubles) in a mixture of old-fashioned and renovated modern styles. TV, parking. Check-out 11am. Singles $35. Doubles $45, with private bath $55. $5 key deposit. Reservations recommended.

YWCA Woodlawn Residence, 80 Woodlawn Ave. E. (923-8454). Subway: Summerhill. Walk uphill on Yonge and turn right on Woodlawn. For women only. Clean, comfortable rooms with sink in wealthy, safe neighborhood. TV lounge, kettle-equipped kitchenette on each floor. Laundry. Cafeteria serves breakfast Mon.-Fri. 7:30-10:30am, Sat.-Sun. 8:30-11am. Check-in 2:30pm (locked storage provided). Check-out noon. Quiet hours 11pm-7am. Singles $38. Doubles $53. Reservations recommended.

Indian Line Tourist Campground, 7625 Finch Ave. W. (678-1233), at Darcel Ave. Follow Hwy. 427 north to Finch and go west. Sites $13.50, with hookup $17. Open May 10-early Oct.

Food

You can find just about any kind of food here; check the yellow pages, which lists restaurants by category. To sample the numerous cuisines of Toronto cheaply, walk the ethnic neighborhoods of the city. These include an immense China and Vietnam Town, Little Italy, Greek Island, Hungarian Village, and Little India.

In recent years Chinatown has expanded north onto Spadina Ave. (Subway: St. Patrick) and become a little more dangerous because of gang conflicts. From the heart of Chinatown, walk across Spadina Ave. and up one block for the freshest and cheapest meat, produce, and cheese in **Kensington Market,** at Augusta and Baldwin St. west of Spadina, south of College St. The market, originally the city's old Jewish ghetto, is now predominantly Portuguese, Chinese, and West Indian. Visit the Portuguese bakeries on Augusta St. for sweet bread and pastries and the West Indian shops for *roti* and spicy meat patties. The **St. Lawrence Market,** 95 Front St. E. at Jarvis, a few blocks east of the King subway stop, is a huge two-story warehouse where farmers, fishers, and butchers sell produce.

Little Italy, mostly on St. Clair Ave. W. (take the St. Clair streetcar west from Yonge subway), but also west of University Ave. on College St. (College streetcar), helps to imbue Toronto with its distinctly European flavor. Cafés, social clubs, bakeries, and sandwich shops stay open until very late, and the *gelati* and espresso rival Italy's best. **Greek Island,** on Danforth Ave. E. (take Bloor subway eastbound to Broadview), has miles of shish-kebab houses and bakeries brimming with flaky *baklava* and sugary Turkish delight. **Little India** covers a two-block area on Gerrard St. E. (Take the Gerrard or College St. streetcar.) Many cheap *tandoori* places buffet for under $6; shops selling *paan* (a dessert of nuts, seeds, and honey wrapped in paan leaf) line the streets.

Bloor St. W. between Spadina and Bathurst is popular with the college crowd—ethnic eateries and open-air cafés abound. Sample quality Ethiopian food at **The Queen of Sheba,** 1198 Bloor St. W. (536-4162). Definitive Toronto deli can be found at **Shopsy's,** 33 Yonge St. (365-3333).

House of Noodles, 457 Dundas St. W. (597-8878). Take the streetcar west on Dundas. Enormous mounds of noodles cooked in every conceivable Asian way, topped with the meats and vegetables of your choice. At the center of bustling Chinatown. Soft noodles $6-7. Open daily 9am-4am.

Blue Cellar Room, 469 Bloor St. W. (921-6269), west of Spadina near Brunswick Ave., part of L'Europa Restaurant. Subway: Spadina. Walk down a long, blue hallway to this Hungarian student haunt. Heaps of *goulash* less than $6.75. Smoked sausage with sauerkraut and potatoes $6.35. Open daily noon-midnight.

Astoria Shish Kebab House, 390 Danforth Ave. (463-2838). Subway: Chester Ave. Traditional Greek cuisine—tasty shish kebab (platter $10) and *baklava* ($2). Comfortable patio in summer. Open Mon.-Sat. 11am-1am, Sun. 11am-midnight.

Antonio's Mostly Pasta, 99½ Dundas St. E. at Church, around the corner from the hostel. Eager to succor weary travelers. Slouch at the lunch counter or take out. Pasta of the day $4. 10% student and IYHF-member discount. Open Mon.-Fri. noon-8pm, Sat. 11am-2pm.

Renaissance Café, 509 Bloor St. W. (968-6639). Subway: Spadina. Fun for tofu-lovers and other hip health eccentrics. Moon burger (tofu, spices and *tahini* sauce) $7. Lite bites (noon-4pm) $5. Luncheon specials $6. Open daily noon-midnight.

The Arm Chair Traveller Restaurant, 217 Church. Breakfast ($3.25) served until 10am Mon.-Fri., noon Sat.-Sun. 10% discount for IYHF members. Open Mon.-Sat. 8am-1am, Sun. 9am-midnight.

Lick's, 1916 Queen St. E. (691-2305), near the Beaches. Take the Queen car. Toronto's own swinging burger joint. Ask them to sing as you munch on a homeburger, fries, and a drink ($3.95) or suck on a lickshake ($2.25). One of 6 branches around Toronto; another in Eaton Centre. Open Sun.-Thurs. 11am-11pm, Fri.-Sat. 11am-midnight.

Yung Sing Pastry Shop, 22 Baldwin St. (979-2832). Take the Dundas streetcar to McCaul St. and walk 2 blocks north. Lines file outside Chu Ko's tiny bakery for the city's best pork *bao* and *don* tart. Fried pork dumplings on weekends only (4 for $2.75), cookies and tarts (55¢). Sumptuous meat buns 90¢. Open Thurs.-Tues. 11am-6pm.

Bahamian Kitchen, 14 Baldwin St. (595-0994), 2 blocks north of Dundas, off McCaul St. Take the Dundas streetcar. Lively café/restaurant with cheap and spicy Bahamian treats. Try the *conch* shells each of 10 different ways. Lunch entrees $5-7.50. Dinners from $2.50. Open Mon.-Sat. 11:30am-11pm, Sun. 4-11pm.

Sights

Urban **Yonge Street** is Toronto's main shopping drag, intersecting with Bloor in the ritzy, capitalist-swine city center. It stretches on to distant North Bay, Ont., making it the longest street in the world. Just north of this area lies **Yorkville,** which attracted the hippie counterculture during the 60s when Joni Mitchell and James Taylor strummed here. Today it's (surprise) a chic shopping and dining neighborhood: come to window-shop at expensive boutiques, people-watch from outdoor cafés, or have your fortune told by an aging Yorkville hippie.

The vast, ultra-modern **Eaton Centre,** a glass-domed, four-tiered shopping mall, preens on Yonge St. (look for the Canada geese), spanning the distance between Queen and Dundas several blocks north. The underground shops stretch all the way to Union Station. While in the area, visit the trendy strip of **Queen Street West,** at its funkiest between University Ave. and Spadina Rd. (Subway: Osgoode.) Catch the bohemian, punk, and new wave clubs and bizarre second-hand clothing stores. The newest fads start here, at the "cutting edge of the wedge" hangouts.

Slightly north of the Queen St. W. strip lies Canada's largest and most exciting **Chinatown.** Centered at Dundas and Spadina, this neighborhood offers authentic Chinese cuisine, grocery stores, bakeries, boutiques, theater, and gang killings. Visit the famous **China Court,** 208 Spadina, just south of Dundas, a colorful Chinese shopping plaza modeled on the Imperial Palace in Peking.

The **Art Gallery of Ontario (AGO),** 317 Dundas St. W. (979-6648), three blocks west of University Ave. in the heart of Chinatown, houses an enormous collection of Western art from the Renaissance up through the past decade, with a particular concentration of Canadian artists. (Open mid-May to early Sept. daily 10:30am-5:30pm, Wed. 10:30am-9pm. Admission $4.50, seniors and students $2.50, under 12 free, families $9. Free Wed. 5-9pm. Seniors free Fri. Subway: St. Patrick.) Visitors to the AGO also gain access to **the Grange,** Toronto's oldest remaining brick house and an example of how the posh family of the 1830s lived. (Open daily 11am-4pm.) Reach Chinatown on a streetcar going west from Dundas subway stop. Bilingual street signs let you know when you're there.

Members of Toronto's various ethnic groups meet and sell their wares at famous **Kensington Market,** a frenetic multilingual bazaar located south of College on Baldwin, Augusta, and Kensington St. (Open Mon.-Sat. from dawn, but the area really jumps Fri. afternoons and Sat.) The **Beaches** neighborhood, named for Kew Beach, is good for a game of beach volleyball on a warm day. The **Kew Gardens** face Queen St. E. (take the streetcar as far as it will go), making it easy to skip between sunbathing and the shops on Queen. The neighborhood of Bloor St. W., next to the University, features the Hungarian Village, Peruvian craft shops, bookstores, student bars, and various lively cafés.

The building that most people associate with the city is the **CN Tower,** at 301 Front St. W. (360-8500). (Subway: Union.) Visible from almost everywhere in Toronto, and a few places not in Toronto, the tower, at 553m, is the tallest free-standing structure in the world. On a clear day the three observation decks even might afford you a view of Niagara Falls, 160km distant, but only if you can afford to pay a towering $10.75 to take the glass-fronted elevator up to the first observation deck (seniors and ages 5-16 $3.50, under 5 $2.25). Traveling farther up to the "space pod," the highest observation level, costs an extra $1—unnecessary, but who would stop nine-tenths of the way up Everest? (Open Mon.-Sat. 9am-midnight, Sun. 10am-10pm.)

Another classic tourist attraction is the 98-room **Casa Loma,** Davenport Rd. at 1 Austin Terrace (923-1172), near Spadina a few blocks north of the Dupont subway stop. Although the outside of the only real turreted castle in North America belongs in a fairy tale, the inside's dusty old exhibits can be skipped. (Open daily 10am-4pm. Admission $7.50, seniors and 5-16 $4.25, under 5 free with parent.)

The 19th-century pink sandstone **Provincial Parliament Buildings** of the Ontario government preside over beautiful **Queen's Park** right in the city's center. (Subway: Queen's Park.) Stroll with hollow laughter through the marble halls, free to stumble onto press conferences, or take a guided tour (965-4028; daily every ½-hr. Mon.-Fri. 9am-3:30pm, Sat.-Sun. 9am-4pm., Labor Day-late May Mon.-Fri. only. Free.) To see the legislative assembly in action, ask for free visitors gallery passes at the info desk in the main lobby. (Open Oct.-Dec. and March-June Mon.-Wed. 1:30-6pm, Thurs. 10am-noon.) Just west of Queen's Park is **King's College Circle,** the focal point of the **University of Toronto (UofT),** established in 1827. The university stretches miles across the city, but most of the older buildings lie near this circular grass playing field. UofT divides into colleges, each with a distinctive architectural style. Look for Romanesque **University College** (1859) and adjacent Gothic **Hart House** (1919), UofT's student center. Student guides conduct hour-long walking tours of the campus in English, French, and Pig Latin, beginning in the Map Room of Hart House. (978-5000; June-Aug. Mon.-Fri. at 10:30am, 1 and 2:30pm; Sept.-

May 978-4111; free.) Groups of fewer than five people can get a tour any time during the summer. Call to arrange group tours.

From here, head back toward Queen's Park and walk north to visit the **McLaughlin Planetarium,** 100 Queen's Park Crescent (586-5736), the neighboring **Royal Ontario Museum (ROM),** just south of Bloor (586-5549), and the **George M. Gardiner Museum of Ceramic Art,** 111 Queen's Park (593-9300), opposite the ROM. The planetarium's cozy reclining seats allow you to lie back as you take in the excellent evening laser light shows (believe it or not, without Pink Floyd accompaniment). You also can catch an audiovisual presentation on astronomy in the afternoon or evening. (Open Tues.-Sun. Laser shows $7, regular shows $5, seniors, students, and kids $2.50.) The ROM is one of the best natural history museums on the continent, and also contains a superb collection of Chinese art and archeology; the Gardiner has an impressive display of European and South American ceramics. (Both open Fri.-Sun. and Wed. 10am-6pm, Tues. and Thurs. 10am-8pm. Admission covers both $6; seniors, students, and kids $3.25. Seniors free on Tues. Free Thurs. after 4:30pm.)

Modern architecture aficionados should visit the **City Hall** at the corner of Queen and Bay St. (392-9111) between the Osgoode and Queen subway stops, with curved twin towers and a rotunda considered quite avant-garde when completed in 1965 (now the garde has passed). **Nathan Phillips Square,** in front of City Hall, a forum for art shows, rock concerts, and multicultural festivals also host more mellow events such as sunbathing and picnicking.

The **Ontario Science Centre,** 770 Don Mills Rd. at Eglinton Ave. E. (429-0193), lies one hour from downtown; take the subway to Eglinton, then the eastbound bus to Don Mills Rd. Part museum, part hands-on fun-fair, the center entertains with great gadgets and displays. (Open Mon.-Thurs. and Sat.-Sun. 10am-6pm, Fri. 10am-9pm; Sept.-June daily 10am-6pm. Parking $2. Admission $5.50, seniors free, ages 13-17 $4.50, under 13 $1.50. Free admission and parking Fri. 5-9pm.)

Metro Toronto Zoo (392-5200 or 392-5901), about 25km northeast of downtown, 5km north of Hwy. 401 on Meadowvale Rd., lets critters bungle in 700 acres of climate-controlled pavilions representing the world's geographic regions. (Open May-Aug. daily 9:30am-7:30pm; Labor Day-Oct. and March to mid-May daily 9:30am-5:30pm; Oct.-March daily 9:30am-3:30pm. Last admission 1 hr. before closing. Admission $8.50, seniors and ages 12-17 $5.50, 5-11 $3.50; cheaper off-season.) Ride the subway to Kennedy station, then bus #86A, or, by car, go east on the 401 to Meadowvale Rd. **Canada's Wonderland** (832-2205), 30km north of downtown, rocks with summertime concerts, 33 rides, seven theme areas, and five roller coasters (including one on which you ride standing up). (Open mid-June to early Sept. daily 10am-10pm; early May to mid-June and early Sept. to mid-Oct. Sat.-Sun. 10am-8pm. One-day pass $23, seniors and ages 3-6 $11. Buses ($3) run every ½-hr. as long as the park is open, from York Mills and York Dale subway.) **Toronto Islands Park,** a 4-mi. strip of connected islands just opposite the downtown area (15-min. ferry trip; 392-8193 for ferry info), is a popular "vacationland," with a boardwalk, bathing beaches, canoe and bike rentals, a Frisbee golf course, and a children's farm and amusement park. Ferries leave from the Bay Street Ferry Dock at the foot of Bay St. (see Practical Information above.)

Famous landmarks figure prominently in Toronto. You'll need more than a weekend to explore and appreciate them thoroughly. The sprawl of the city makes it impossible to construct a single walking tour that covers the important spots, but bus tours will try anyway. **Gray Line Sight-Seeing** (393-7911) offers tours of the principal sights: a 2-hr. "Inside Toronto" tour leaves the main bus terminal at Bay and Dundas daily at 10am and 2pm. ($15, seniors $13.50, under 12 $10.)

Entertainment

Nightlife

Many of Toronto's clubs and pubs remain closed on Sundays because of antiquated liquor laws. Some of the more formal clubs uphold dress codes and the city still shuts down at 1am. Infiltrating the university crowd can be somewhat difficult since most campus pubs restrict admission to their own students. But if you still want to try, mingle with students near UofT, Ryerson, and York at **The Brunswick House, Lee's Palace,** (see below) and the **All-Star Eatery,** 277 Victoria (977-7619), at Dundas one block east of the Dundas subway stop. The most interesting new clubs are on trendy **Queen Street West.** The gay scene centers around Wellesley and Church, although there's also some gay activity on Queen and Yonge St. *Now* magazine, published every Thursday, is the city's comprehensive entertainment guide, available in restaurants and record stores all over Toronto. The Friday edition of the *Toronto Star* has a section called "What's On" filled with info on clubs, danceterias, pubs, restaurants, concerts, and movies. *Where Toronto,* a monthly available at tourism booths gives a good arts and entertainment run-down. *Toronto Life* is an excellent magazine that highlights Toronto happenings.

Bamboo, 312 Queen St. W. (593-5771), 3 blocks west of the Osgoode subway stop. Popular with students. Live reggae, jazz, rock, and funk daily. Great dancing. Patio upstairs. Open Mon.-Sat. noon-1am. Hefty cover varies from band to band.

Brunswick House, 481 Bloor St. W. (964-2242), at Brunswick between the Bathurst and Spadina subway stops. Rowdy dive reeling with students. Beer $2.95. Upstairs is **Albert's Hall,** famous for its blues. Open Mon.-Fri. 11:30-1am; Sat. noon-1am.

George's Spaghetti House, 290 Dundas St. E. at Sherbourne St. (923-9887). Subway: Dundas; take the streetcar east to Sherbourne. The city's best jazz club attracts the nation's top ensembles. Dinner entrees from $8.50. Restaurant open Mon.-Thurs. 11am-11pm, Fri. 11am-midnight, Sat. 5pm-midnight. Jazz Mon.-Sat. 6pm-1am. Cover Tues.-Thurs. $4, Fri.-Sat. $5; none on Mon. No cover at bar.

Lee's Palace, 529 Bloor St. W. (532-7383), just east of the Bathurst subway stop. Amazing crazy creature art depicting rock 'n' roll frenzy. Live music nightly. Pick up a calendar of bands. Open daily noon-1am.

Second City, in The Old Firehall, 110 Lombard St. at Jarvis (863-1111), 2 blocks east and 2 short blocks south of Queen's Park subway stop. One of North America's craziest and most creative comedy clubs. Spawned comics Dan Aykroyd, John Candy, Gilda Radner, Dave Thomas and Rick Moranis; a hit TV show (SCTV); and the legendary "Great White North." Dinner and theater $28-33. Theater without dinner $12.50-17, students $8 and dinner discount. Free improv sessions (Mon.-Thurs. at 10:15pm)—students welcome. Shows Mon.-Thurs. at 6 and 8:30pm, Fri. at 8 and 11pm, Sat. 8:30 and 11pm. Reservations required.

Festivals and Cultural Events

The city offers a few first-class freebies. Enjoy superb performances of Shakespeare by **Canadian Stage** (367-8243) amid the greenery of High Park, Bloor St. W. at Parkside Dr. (Subway: High Park.) Bring something to sit on or wedge yourself on the 45° slope to the stage. Call for performance schedules. Now in its sixth year, the **du Maurier Ltd. Downtown Jazz Festival's** (363-5200) mix of old and new talents mesmerizes the city in late June. Budget travelers will appreciate the abundance of free, outdoor concerts at lunchtime and in the early evening.

Ontario Place, 955 Lakeshore Blvd. W. (965-7917; 965-7711 recording), features first-class cheap entertainment in summer—the Toronto Symphony, National Ballet of Canada, Ontario Place Pops, and top pop artists perform here free with admission to the park. (Park open mid-May to early Sept. daily 10am-1am. Admission $7.50, seniors and kids $2.) Kids should love the slides and water games of Children's Village (waterslide, bumper boats $2.15 each; 5 attractions for $10). Spectacular IMAX movies can be seen at the Six-Storey Cinesphere (Admission $4, seniors and kids $2. Call for screening schedule. From mid-August through Labor Day, the **Canadian National Exhibition (CNE)** brings a country carnival atmosphere to

Ontario Place. **Roy Thomson Hall,** 60 Simcoe St. at King St. W. (872-4255), is the home of the Toronto Symphony Orchestra. Tickets are expensive ($10-$75), but rush tickets ($8-10) go on sale at the box office the day of the concert (at 11am for concerts on Mon.-Fri., 1pm if on Sat.) Or order by phone (592-4828; Mon.-Fri. 10am-6pm, Sat. noon-5pm; office opens 2 hr. before Sun. performance). Ask about discounts and seniors rates. The same office serves **Massey Hall,** 178 Victoria St., near Eaton Centre (Subway: Dundas), a great hall for rock and folk concerts. The opera and ballet companies perform at **O'Keefe Centre,** 1 Front St. E. at Yonge (393-7474; tickets from $30). Rush tickets (for the last row of orchestra seats) on sale at 11am for $9. Seniors and students can line up one hour before performances for the best unsold seats ($10.75). (Box office open daily 11am-6pm or until 1 hr. after curtain.) Next door, **St. Lawrence Centre,** 27 Front St. E. (366-7723), presents excellent classic and Canadian drama and chamber music recitals in two different theaters. Special student and senior tickets may be available depending on the performing company. (Box office open Mon.-Sat. 10am-8pm.)

You often can beat the high cost of culture by seeking out standby or student discount options. **Five Star Tickets** (596-8211) sells half-price tickets for theater, music, dance, and opera on the day of performance: visit their booth at Dundas and Yonge in front of Eaton Centre. (Subway: Dundas. Open Mon.-Sat. noon-7:30pm, Sun. 11am-3pm.) **Ticketmaster** (870-8000) will supply you with tickets to many events, among them the **Player's International** tennis tournament (665-9777).

Near Toronto: Algonquin Provincial Park

The wilder Canada of endless rushing rivers and shimmering lakes awaits in Algonquin Provincial Park, about 300km north of Toronto. Experience Algonquin through one of two venues: the Hwy. 60 Corridor, where tents and trailers crowd the roadside; and the park interior, the "essence of Algonquin." You can rent gear for a backcountry adventure at several outfitting stores around and inside the park. Try **Algonquin Outfitters,** RR#1-Oxtongue Lake, Dwight P0A 1H0 (year-round 705-635-2243), just off Hwy. 60 about 10km west of the park's west gate. They have two other locations in the park. To enter the park, you need an Interior Camping Permit ($3.25 per person each night), available at the main gate or from any outfitter.

PRINCE EDWARD ISLAND

Prince Edward Island, or simply "the Island," is the smallest and most densely populated province in Canada. Called a million-acre farm, the Island is blanketed with soil that is brick-red from its high iron-oxide content. In addition to agriculture, tourism is the mainstay of the Island economy. Prince Edward Island radiates an array of arresting hues in the spring and summer. The Island's red soil compliments the green crops and shrubbery, azure skies and turquoise waters, and purple roadside lupin. Even some stretches of the endless beaches on the north and south coasts are layered with red sand. The relaxing countryside and slow pace of life are what attract "outsiders" from all over Canada.

A "P.E.I." city is an oxymoron (but don't call Islanders that). The largest "city" on the Island is Charlottetown, the provincial capital, with a whopping 15,000 residents. Effusively hospitable, the Island's population is 17% Acadian French and 80% British. Ancestral residents named the Island's three counties Kings, Queens, and Prince.

Public transportation is nearly non-existent on the Island, although SMT does connect Charlottetown with the mainland. Fortunately, distances are minuscule: driving from Charlottetown on the south coast to the beaches on the north coast requires less than 20 minutes. The network of highways, actually country roads, is superb for bikers. One never has to worry about getting lost; just keep going and you'll eventually hit a major road. Three scenic drives cover the Island for those who simply want to un-hurry themselves and breathe in the country air.

Practical Information

Emergency: 911.

Capital: Charlottetown.

Time Zone: Atlantic (1 hr. ahead of Eastern time). **Postal Abbreviation:** P.E.I.

Area code: 902.

Provincial Sales Tax: 10%

P.E.I. Visitor Services Centre, (368-4444), P.O. Box 940, C1A 7M5. With summer locations in Aulac, Borden, Cavendish, Caribou, Pooles Corner, Portage, Summerside, Souris, and Wood Islands. Hours vary widely. The **P.E.I. Visitor Information Centre,** on the corner of University Ave. and Summer St. in the plaza next to Papa Joe's Restaurant (368-4444), distributes the *P.E.I. Visitor's Guide* (with map). Open daily 9am-5pm, with extended hours mid-May to Oct. The **Charlottetown Visitors Bureau,** 199 Queen St. inside City Hall (566-5548), distributes free maps of Charlottetown. Open Mon.-Sat. 8am-8pm, Sun. noon-6pm. **Dial-the-Island,** toll-free info line 800-565-7421 from the Maritimes, 800-565-0267 from North America. The Maritimes number also books reservations.

Trains: SMT, 330 University Ave. (566-9744), provides service to Moncton (2 per day, 4-5 hr., $27) and to Halifax (1 per day, 8 hr., $40), via **Acadian Lines** connections in Amherst, N.S.

Island Transit: 308 Queen St. (892-6167). Makes one round trip to Tignish along Rte. 2, Mon.-Sat. and services Summerside (1 per day, 1 hr., $7.15) and New Glasgow, N.S. (1 per day, $22).

Beach Shuttles: Abegweit, (894-9966) leaves Charlottetown Hotel for points along P.E.I. National Park (2 per day; $5-6, round-trip $7-8). **Sherwood Beach Shuttle** (566-3243) picks up at P.E.I. Visitor Information Centre and drops off in Cavendish (5 per day; $6, round-trip $10).

Ferries: Marine Atlantic, in Borden, 56km west of Charlottetown on Trans-Canada Highway (Rte. 1) (855-2030 or 800-341-7981 from continental USA), makes runs to Cape Tormentine, New Brunswick (12-18 per day; 1 hr.; round-trip $6, seniors $4.50, ages 5-12 $3, cars $16). **Northumberland Ferries,** in Wood Islands 61km east of Charlottetown on Trans-Canada Highway (Rte. 1) (962-2016; for traffic info call 800-565-0201 from P.E.I. and N.S., otherwise 566-3838), goes to Caribou, Nova Scotia (12-19 per day, 1½ hr., round-trip $7.50, seniors $5.60, ages 5-12 $3.70, cars $24.50). For both ferries, fares are only round-trip and only collected leaving P.E.I. Thus, it is cheaper to arrive on the Island at Wood Islands and leave from Borden than vice-versa.

Taxi: City Cab, 892-6567.

Tours: Abegweit Tours, 157 Nassau St. (894-9966), offers sightseeing tours on a London double-decker bus. Tours include Charlottetown (7 per day; 1 hr.; $4.50, kids $1), the North Shore including Green Gables (1 per day; 7 hr.; $22, kids $11), and the South Shore (1 per day, 5 hr.; $22, kids $11). To reach Abegweit Tours, catch buses at Confederation Centre (corner of Grafton and Queen St.) or at Charlottetown Hotel.

Car Rental: Rent-a-Wreck, 114 St. Peter's Rd. (894-7039). Rents cars $25 per day, with 200km free, 12¢ per km thereafter, damage waiver $7.50 per day. Must be 21 with credit card or $200 deposit. Open Mon.-Fri. 7am-10pm. **Hillside Autohost,** 207 Mt. Edward Rd. (894-7037), rents for $25 per day; must be 21 with major credit card. Open Mon.-Fri. 7:30am-6pm.

Bike Rental: MacQueens, 430 Queen St. (368-2453), rents bikes $15, mountain bikes $20. Must have credit card for deposit. Open Mon.-Fri. 8:30am-6pm, Sat. 8:30am-5pm.

Charlottetown Police: 566-5548. **Royal Canadian Mounted Police:** 566-7100.

Help lines: Crisis Centre, 566-8999. 24 hrs.

Post Office: 97 Queen St. (566-7070). Open Mon.-Fri. 8am-5:15pm. **Postal Code:** C1A 7K1.

Queen St. and University Ave. are Charlottetown's main thoroughfares, straddling Confederation Centre along the west and east, respectively. The most popular beaches lie on the north shore in the middle of the province, opposite but not far from Charlottetown. Hamlets (villages, not Danish princes) and fishing villages dot the Island landscape of Kings County on the east, as well as Prince County on the west. Acadian communities thrive on the south shore of Prince County. Rte. 1 follows the southern shore, from ferry terminal to ferry terminal, also stopping in Charlottetown.

Accommodations

Almost a hundred **bed and breakfasts** and **country inns** litter every nook and cranny of the province, many are open year-round. Rates generally bounce around $25 for singles and $35 for doubles. **P.E.I. Tourism** distributes info about available B&Bs and will make reservations for you. In addition, 26 farms participate in a provincial **Farm Vacation** program, in which tourists spend some time with a farming family.

P.E.I. has one hostel, the **Charlottetown International Hostel (IYHF),** situated at 153 Mt. Edward Rd. (894-9696), across the yard from University of P.E.I., one long block east of University Ave. in a big, green barn with curious acoustics. The sociable staff attracts many international guests. (Open June-Sept. 5. $10.70, nonmembers $14. Laundry. Bike rentals $5. Blanket rental $1. Curfew midnight. Check in 7-10am and 4pm-midnight.) The **University of Prince Edward Island,** 550 University Ave. (566-0442), in Blanchard Hall in the southwestern end of campus, offers fully-serviced and furnished two-bedroom apartments with kitchen, living room, and hall laundry room—a great value for four people. (Open May 20-Aug.; for up to 2 people $52, $2 per additional guest. Weekly and monthly rates also available. Check-in 8:30am-10pm.)

Prince Edward Island National Park operates three campgrounds (Sites $8-10.25, serviced $12.25), and 14 of the 30 provincial parks offer camping. Additionally, there are over 30 other private campgrounds scattered throughout the Island, ensuring that there will always be a campsite available.

Food

Lobster suppers, sumptuous feasts originally thrown by churches and community centers, have become deeply ingrained in Island tradition. The "run-of-the-mill" lobster suppers supplement their crustacean guest of honor with a host of all-you-can-eat goodies such as clam chowder, salad bars, and desserts. The delicious suppers are quite expensive ($18-$26, depending on the size of lobster), so fast all day before the feast. Fresh seafood, including the world famous **Malpeque oysters,** can be found for sale along the shores of the Island, especially in North Rustico on the north shore. See the back of the *P.E.I. Visitor's Guide* for a listing of fresh seafood outlets.

Fisherman's Wharf, Rte. 6 in North Rustico (963-2669), is the most famous lobster-supper house, featuring the world's largest lobster found in a restaurant and a 50-ft.-long salad bar. Seating capacity 500. Open mid-May-mid to Oct. 4-10pm.

Bonnie Brae Restaurant (566-2241), Rte. 1 in Cornwall, 11km west of Charlottetown. The Lobster Smorgasbord ($25) promises all-you-can-eat lobster as well as side dishes. Open mid-June to Sept. 4-9pm.

Cedar's Eatery, 81 University Ave. (892-7377). A local favorite serving Lebanese and Canadian cuisine. Try their lunch specials ($4). Open Mon.-Thurs. 11am-midnight, Fri.-Sat. 11am-1am, Sun. 4-10:30pm.

Peake's Quay, (PEEKS KEY), 36 Lower Water St. (368-1330), on the Charlottetown waterfront overlooking the Marina. Seafood sandwich and salad $5-9. Supper entrees $9-18. Open daily 11am-2am.

The Regent Restaurant and Lounge, 12 Summer St. in Summerside (436-3200). Quite expensive, but a popular center of P.E.I. nightlife.

Sights

Prince Edward Island National Park (672-2211 or 963-2391), a coastal strip of 32 sq. km, embraces some of Canada's finest beaches, over a fifth of P.E.I.'s northern coast. It is the most popular Canadian national park east of Banff (see Alberta). Along with the beaches, heap-big sand dunes and marshes rumple the park's terrain. The park is home to many of the Island's 300-odd species of birds, including the endangered **piping plover;** birdwatchers might want to pick up the *Field Check List of Birds* (free) from any National or Provincial Park office. Campgrounds, programs, and services in the park operate from mid-June to Labor Day, with **Cavendish campground** staying open until mid-Oct. At the entrance kiosks, receive a copy of the park guide *Blue Heron.* (Vehicle permits $4 per day, $9 per 4 days.)

The National Park also runs **Green Gables House** (672-2211), located off Rte. 6 in Cavendish near Rte. 13. Popularized by Lucy Maud Montgomery's novel, *Anne of Green Gables,* this house is the mecca for adoring readers of Anne. Interestingly, Montgomery's series of books about the freckle-faced orphan of Cavendish have a cult-following among Japanese schoolgirls, many of whom drag their families here to pay homage. The House and Haunted Woods are certain to be recognized by fans, but will appear to be just a nice little estate for the uninitiated. Green Gables can get very crowded between late July and September, so it's best to arrive in the early morning or the evening. Guide service available in English, French, and Japanese (in 1991 at least). (Open May to mid-June and Labor Day-Oct. daily 9am-5pm, mid-June to Labor Day daily 9am-8pm. Free.)

Woodleigh, just off Rte. 234 in Burlington (836-3401), midway betweeen Cavendish and Summerside, will satisfy the monarchist in you. It contains miniature, faithful replicas of British architectural icons such as the St. Paul Cathedral, Tower of London and Lord Nelson's statue in Trafalgar Square, all available for exploration. Yes, the Crown Jewels are inside the Tower. The craftsmanship is striking, but the cuteness of the whole concept can wear off quickly. (Open June and September 9am-5pm, July-Aug. 9am-9pm. Admission $6, seniors $5.50, kids $3.25, preschoolers free.)

Charlottetown prides itself on being the "Cradle of Confederation." The brownstone **Province House,** on the corner of Great George and Richmond St. (566-7626), was where delegates from the British North American colonies met to discuss the union which would become, in 1867, the Dominion of Canada. Chambers of historical importance are open for viewing, as are exhibits and the modern-day legislative chambers. (Open Oct.-May Mon.-Fri. 9am-5pm, June and Sept. daily 9am-5pm, July-Labor Day daily 9am-8pm. Free.) Adjoining the Province House is the **Confederation Centre for the Arts,** located on the corner of Queen and Grafton St. (566-2464), a modern performing-arts complex with theaters, displays, a library, and an art gallery. Free, hour-long guided tours of the Centre conducted July through August. (Open July-Aug. daily 9am-8pm, Sept.-June Mon.-Sat. 9am-6pm, Sun. 2-5pm. Admission $1.) Every summer, the musical production of **Anne of Green Gables** boogies in Mackenzie Theatre located inside Confederation Centre, as part of the Charlottetown Festival. (Performances mid-June to early Sept. Mon.-Sat. 8pm. Tickets $18-28. For ticket info, call 566-1267 or 800-565-1267 in the Maritimes.)

QUEBEC

Home to 90% of Canada's French-origin citizenry, Québec continues to fight for political and legal recognition of its separate cultural identity. Canada's 1990 failure to ratify the Meech Lake Accord, which would have awarded recognition of Québec's status as a "distinct society," has even reopened debate over the possibility of secession, rejected in a 1980 referendum. Many now share the attitude of former Qubec Premier René Levesque, who quipped, "If you can't sleep together, you might as well have separate beds." (*Très français.*) But for all their pillowfighting, and despite another resolution scheduled for 1992, the two bedmates seem reluctant to tamper with a healthy trading relationship. In Québec's struggle to retain a French-Canadian identity in a North American sea of English, the provincial motto *Je me souviens* might promise a prosperous future as well as a remembered past.

Practical Information

Capital: Québec City.

Tourisme Québec, c.p. 20,000, Québec G1K 7X2 (800-363-7777; 514-873-2015 in Montréal).

Postal abbreviation: QU

Time Zone: Eastern.

Alcohol: Legal drinking age 18.

Excellent transportation by train or bus covers the entire province. The one bus line in Québec, **Voyageur** offers wonderful service within the province and to Ontario's larger cities. Besides its regular fares, Voyageur offers a **Tour Pass** ($129) in summer for 10 days of unlimited travel. Call for dates (Montréal 514-842-2281, Québec City 418-524-4692). **VIA Rail** of Canada provides the main railroad for passenger and tourist service, with frequent runs between major urban centers. (For info on train travel on VIA Rail, see Train Travel in the Canadian Introduction, above.) Traveling by **car** in Québec can be expensive, since gas is heavily taxed. You'll pay about 59-63¢ per liter (3.8 liters — 1 gallon). Québec requires that you have enough liability coverage to meet the insurance requirement of your home state or country. For more info, call the **Régie de l'assurance automobile du Québec** (Québec Automobile Insurance Board), 870, blvd. de Maisonneuve O., Bureau 200, Montréal H2L 4W3 (514-288-6015). If you receive bodily harm in an accident, call 873-7620 in Montréal, 643-7620 in Québec City, and 800-361-7620 elsewhere in the province. Note that both radar detectors and turning right on red are illegal. The speed limit on highways is 100km/hr (about 62 mph).

Popular provincial activities include fishing, canoeing, hunting, and skiing. Shimmering summer and brilliant fall encourage people to bike, camp, windsurf, and waterski. Fishers and hunters must obtain a Québec permit. Contact the Ministère du Loisir, de la Chasse et de la Pêche, Direction des Communications, 150, blvd. St-Cyrille E., Québec G1R 4Y3 (418-890-5349).

Accommodation Information

For general provincial assistance in locating accommodation, try the following organizations.

Bed and Breakfast: Vacances-Familles, 1291, blvd. Charest Ouest, Qubec G1N 2C9 (418-682-5464; in Montréal 514-282-9580) offers a lodging network that spans the province.

Camping: Association des terrains du camping du Québec, 5199, rue Sherbrooke E., Bureau 2640, Montréal H1T 3X1 (514-255-5693) and Fédération québecoise du camping et de carvaning, 4545 ave. Pierre-de-Coubertin c.p. 1000, succursale "M", Montréal H1V 3R2 (514-252-3003) can send you complete lists.

Farm Vacations: Fédération des Agricotours du Québec, at the address listed above for the Fédération *québecoise* under Camping (514-252-3138). ($35, ages 10-14 $30, 6-9 $20, 1-5 $17; meals included). Write a week in advance.

Hostels: Regroupement Tourisme Jeunesse (member of IYHF), again at the same address (514-252-3117).

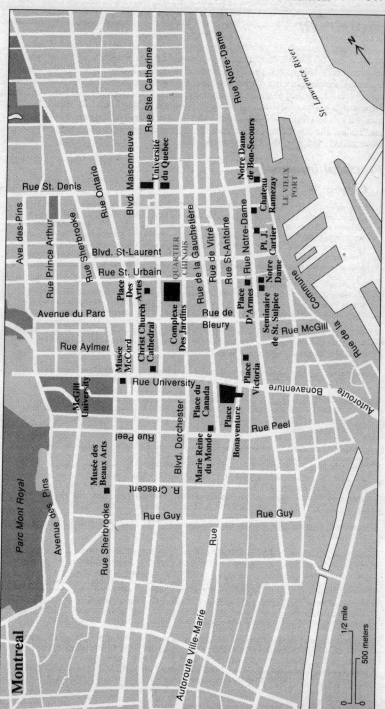

Montréal

Montréal assumed its identity as a center of trade by the 19th century, thanks to an influx of British merchants, a developed railroad system, and strategic use of Montréal's two rivers, the Saint-Laurent and the Ottawa. Although primarily French-Canadian, intense commerce has drawn numerous other peoples whose cultures both mingle and chafe, imparting a dynamic, romantic atmosphere to the city. Downtown has moved north from **Vieux Montréal** (Old Montréal), which has the greatest concentration of 17th-, 18th-, and 19th-century buildings in North America. Today, the city stretches out from the river and burrows underground in a network called, fittingly, the Underground City.

Practical Information

Emergency: 911.

Infotouriste, 1001, rue du Square-Dorchester (873-2015; outside Montréal 800-363-7777), on Dorchester Sq. between rue Peel and rue Metcalfe. Métro: Peel. Free city maps and guides, currency exchange (open Mon.-Sat. 9am-6pm, Sun. 10am-6pm), and extensive food and housing listings. Open daily May 19-Labor Day 8am-7pm; Sept. 3-Oct. 14 9am-7pm; Oct. 15-April 18 9am-6pm; March 30-May 18 9am-7pm. Branch offices in **Old Montréal,** 174, rue Notre-Dame est. Open early June-Sept. 2 daily 9am-7pm; fall and winter daily 9am-1pm and 2-5pm. Also at **Dorval International Airport.** Open daily 1-8pm. **Mirabel International Airport.** Open daily noon-2:30pm, 3-7pm and 7:30-8pm.

Tourisme Jeunesse (youth tourist info), **Boutique Temps Libre,** 3603 rue St. Denis Métro: Sherbrooke. Métro: Pie-IX. Free maps; youth hostel info available. Travel gear and helpful suggestions from friendly staff. A non-profit organization that inspects and ranks all 16 officially recognized youth hostels in Québec. Open Mon.-Fri. 9am-5pm. Mailing address: c.p. 1000, Succursale "M," Montréal P.Q., H1V 3R2. **Travel CUTS,** a travel agency at the McGill Student Union, 3480, rue McTavish (849-9201). Métro: McGill. They also sell the ISIC and provide budget travel info. Open Mon.-Fri. 9am-5pm.

Language: The population of Montréal is 65% French-speaking. Many citizens are bilingual. If you know French, speak it; you're less likely to be dismissed as a tourist.

Consulates: U.S., 1155, rue St-Alexander (398-9695). Open Mon.-Fri 8:30am-1pm. **U.K.,** 1155, rue de l'Université (866-5863). Open for info. Mon.-Fri. 9am-5pm. For consular help, open Mon.-Fri. 9am-12:30pm and 2-4:30pm. **Germany,** 3455, Mountain (286-1820). Open Mon.-Fri. 9am-noon.

Currency Exchange: Bank of America Canada, 1230, rue Peel (393-1855). Métro: Peel. Open Mon.-Fri. 8:30am-6pm, Sat. 9am-5pm. **Thomas Cook,** 625, blvd. René-Lévesque ouest (397-4029). Open daily 9am-5pm. Dorval Airport location (636-3582) open daily 6am-11pm. **National Commercial-Foreign Currency,** 1250, rue Peel (879-1300). Métro: Peel. Another office at 390, rue St-Jacques (879-1300). Métro: Square-Victoria. Open Mon.-Fri. 8am-5pm, Sat. 8am-3pm. Change your money to Canadian dollars. Although many cafés will take U.S. dollars, you'll get a better deal from a bank. Most bank machines are on the PLUS system.

American Express: 1141, blvd. de Maisonneuve ouest (284-3300). Métro: Peel. Open Mon.-Fri. 9am-5:30pm.

Airports: Dorval (info. service: 633-3105), 10 mi. from downtown. From the Lionel Groulx Métro stop, take bus #211 to Dorval Shopping Center, then transfer to bus #204. **Aerocar** (397-9999) runs buses from the airport to Terminus Voyageur (the stop closest to St-Denis), as well as some major hotels (cost $8.50-12). **Mirabel International** (info service: 476-3040), 35 mi. from downtown. Aeroplus (476-1100) buses connect this airport to the city's central train station at 895, rue de la Gauchetiére O. (daily 1am-noon, departures every 2 hr. from Montréal; noon-8pm, every ½-hr.; 8pm-1am, every hr.; $11.75. Departures from Mirabel every 2 hr.)

Trains: Central Station, 800, rue de la Gauchetiére. Métro: Bonaventure. Served by **VIA Rail** (871-1331) and **Amtrak** (800-426-8725). Direct service to: Québec City (3 per day; 3 hr.; $34, students $31; booked at least 5 days in advance $20, $17); Toronto (5 per day; 5 hr.; $64, student $61; 5 days in advance $37/34); Vancouver (3 per week, $419, student $377); New York City (2 per day, US$74). Inconvenient connections to Boston (US$96, change trains in New London). VIA ticket counters open daily 6:30am-9pm. Amtrak ticket counters open daily 7:30am-7:30pm.

Buses: Terminus Voyageur, 505, blvd. de Maisonneuve est (842-2281). Métro: Berri-UQAM. Voyageur offers 10-day unlimited tour passes for $129 in summer, which will take you all over Québec and Ontario. Toronto (6 per day, $48.10); Ottawa (18 per day, $21.34). The Ottawa Bus also leaves from Dépanneur Beau-soir, 2875 Blvd. St. Charles, Kirkland (on the West Island). **Greyhound** serves New York City (5 per day, $88.90). **Vermont Transit** serves Boston (1 per day, $74.90); Burlington, VT (3 per day, $18.70); and Québec (28 per day $21.90)

Public Transport: STCUM Métro and Bus, 288-6287. A safe and efficient network, with Métro subway service. The 4 Métro (phone #AUT-OBUS) lines and most buses operate daily 5:30-12:30am; some have night schedules as well. Get network maps at the tourist office, or at any Métro station toll booth. Fare for trains or bus $1.50, under 18 75¢, 6 tickets $6, unlimited monthly passes $35. Fares may increase.

Car Rental: Beau Bazou, 295, rue de la Montagne (939-2330). Métro: Lucien l'Allier. $28.90 per day 50km free plus 10¢ each additional km; insurance included. Open Mon.-Fri. 8:30am-9pm Sat. 10am-5pm. Must be 25 with credit card; car must stay in Québec. Reserve in advance. **Via Route** (formerly Rent-a-Wreck), 1255, rue MacKay (871-1166; collect calls accepted). $26.95 per day; 200km free, 12¢ each additional km. Insurance $9.95 per day. Must be 21 with credit card. Open Mon.-Fri. 8am-7pm, Sat. 8am-5pm, Sun. 9am-5pm. **Avis** (800-TRY-AVIS), **Budget** (800-268-8900), and **Hertz** (800-263-0600) also serve Montréal.

Driver/Rider Service: Allo Stop, 4317, rue St-Denis (282-0121 or 849-1626). Will match you with a driver heading for Québec City ($15), Ottawa ($14), Toronto ($26), Sherbrooke ($11), New York City ($50), or Boston ($42). Fees for Vancouver vary. Open Mon.-Wed. 9am-5pm, Thurs.-Fri. 9am-7pm, Sat. 10am-5pm, Sun. 10am-7pm.

Canadian Automobile Association (CAA), 1180, rue Drummond at blvd. René-Lévesque (info 861-7111; emergencies 861-1313). Métro: Bonaventure. Affiliated with American Automobile Association (AAA). Members have access to tourist info and emergency road service. Open Mon.-Fri. 8:30am-5pm.

Bike Rental: Cycle Peel, 6665, St-Jacques (486-1148). Take bus #90 West from Vendome Métro stop. First day $13, $7 thereafter. $40 per week. Mountain bike $20 first day, $10 thereafter. Open Mon.-Wed. 9:30am-5pm, Thurs.-Fri. 9:30am-9pm, Sat. 9:30am-5pm, Sun. 9am-4pm. Credit card or $200 cash deposit required.

Ticket Agencies: Teletron (288-2525) or **Ticketron** (288-3651). Also try **Ticketmaster** (790-1111). Credit card number required.

Help Lines: Tel-aide, 935-1101. Open 24 hrs. **Sexual Assault,** 934-4504. **Suicide-Action,** 522-5777.

Pharmacy: Pharmaprix, 5122, chemin de la Côte des Neiges (738-8464), Métro: Côte des Neiges). Open 24 hrs.

Post Office: Succursale "A," 1025, St-Jacques (283-2567). Open Mon.-Fri. 8am-5:45pm. **Postal code:** H3C 1T1.

Area Code: 514.

Two major streets divide the city, making it convenient for orientation. The **boulevard St-Laurent** (also called "The Main") runs north-south, dividing the city and streets east-west. The Main also serves as the unofficial French/English divider: English **McGill University** lies to the west while St-Denis, the **French student quarter** (also called the *"Quartier Latin"*) is slightly east. **Rue Sherbrooke** runs east-west almost the entire length of Montréal. Parking is often difficult in the city, particularly in winter when snowbanks narrow the streets and slow traffic. Take the **Métro** instead.

Accommodations and Camping

The Québec Tourist Office is the best resource for info about hostels, hotels, and **chambres touristiques** (rooms in private homes or small guest houses). B&B singles cost $25 to $40, doubles $35 to $75. The most extensive B&B network is **Bed & Breakfast à Montréal,** P.O. Box 595, Snowdon H3X 3T8 (738-9410), which recommends that you reserve by mail ($15 per night). (Singles from $35. Doubles from $60. Open daily 9am-7pm.) Leave a message on the answering machine if the owners are out. The **Downtown Bed and Breakfast Network,** 3458, ave. Laval, Montréal

H2X 3C8 (289-9749), at Sherbrooke, works with about 80 homes. (Singles $25-40. Doubles $35-55. Open spring and summer daily 8:30am-9pm; fall and winter 8:30am-6pm.) For cheaper B&B listings check with Antonio Costa at **Antonio's B&B**, 101, ave. Northview, H4X 1C9 (486-6910; credit cards not accepted; doubles $35-70), or **Marbel Guest House**, 3507, blvd. Décarie, H4A 3J4. Métro: Villa Maria or Vendôme (486-0232; singles $25; doubles $45). Virtually all B&Bs have bilingual hosts.

Montréal Youth Hostel (IYHF), 3541, rue Aylmer, Montréal H2X 2B9 (843-3317), in the McGill campus area, 10 min. from downtown. Métro: McGill. Recently renovated, great location. Carpeted rooms with 4, 6, 12, and 16 beds. Max. stay 7 days. Fills in summer; arrive before noon. Large kitchen. No smoking in building. Breakfast $2. $13, non-members $16. Memberships sold. Deposit $5. Hot showers, linen $1, sleeping bags allowed. Checkout 10am. Curfew 2am. Open daily 8am-2am. Reservations 3 weeks in advance. Offers daily tours of the city. Overflow and groups from the youth hostel housed at 267, ave. Rachel E. Métro: Mont-Royal, then walk south on Berri and west on Rachel (987-6255). Right near the Quartier Latin. Older and bigger (150 beds) than the main hostel, with airy rooms and a big living room (smoking permitted here only). Big kitchen and fun-loving management. Prices, curfew, checkout same as above. Guided tours. Open daily. Open summer months only.

Collège Français, 5155, de Gaspé, Montréal H2T 2A1 (495-2581 or 270-9260 after 5pm and on holidays). Métro: Laurier, then walk west and north. Rooms year-round. Clean, comfortable, and well located. Access to gym. Young clientele. Bed in a double $14.50; in a 3- to 4-person room $10.50 (with shower $12.50); in a 5- to 7-person room $9.50; in an 8- to 10-person room $8.50. Breakfast in summer $2.70. Open daily 8-2am. More beds inconveniently located at 1391, rue Beauregard Longueuil (Métro: Longueuil, then take Bus 71 up Taschereau and Ségin), open only in summer.

Many of the least expensive *maisons touristiques* (tourist homes) and hotels are around rue St-Denis, which ranges from quaint to seedy. Convenient to the bus station, the area flaunts lively nightclubs and abuts Vieux Montréal. Before choosing a place to stay, pick up a **Tourist Guide** at the Tourist Office; it maps out the location of hundreds of accommodations.

Dorms: McGill University, Bishop Mountain Hall, 3935, rue de l'Université, H3A 2B4 (398-6367). Métro: McGill. Follow Université through campus, up the hill until it ends. Ideally located singles. Kitchenettes on each floor. Common room with TV, laundry. Desk open Mon.-Fri. 7am-11pm, Sat.-Sun. 8am-10pm; a guard will check you in late at night. $23, non-students $32. Weekly $100. Continental breakfast (served Mon.-Fri. 7:30-9:30am; $2.75). Open May 15-Aug. 15. Reservations (one-night deposit) recommended for July and Aug. **Université de Montréal**, Residences, 2350, Edouard-Montpetit H2X 2B9 (343-6531). Métro: Edouard-Montpetit. Located on the edge of a beautiful campus. Singles $30, $19.95 for students, alumni and conferees (weekly $85). Open May 6-Aug. 19. Laundry, mailbox. Phone in each room. Desk open 24 hrs. Cafeteria open Mon.-Fri. 7am-2pm. **Concordia University** (848-4755), Hingston Hall in the northeast corner of Concordia on the Loyola Campus, not the downtown Sir George William Campus. Take Sherbrooke west, turn right on Broadway, take your first right and Hingston is on your left. Far from downtown. Métro: Vendôme and bus #105. Large rooms, hall phones. Kitchen, living room with TV on each floor. Reception open daily 9am-10pm. Singles $17, non-students $23. Doubles $34, $36. Open May 11-Aug. 27. Reservations recommended.

YWCA, 1355, rue René-Lévesque ouest (866-9941). Métro: Lucien l'Allier. Women only. Clean, safe rooms in the heart of downtown. Newly-renovated. Access to Y facilities while in residence. Kitchen, TV on every floor. Doors lock at 10pm but the desk will buzz you in all night. Singles $35, with shared bathroom $46, with private bath $50. Doubles $53, with semi-private bath $62. Meals available in Biotrain Café downstairs (open daily 8am-7:30pm; sandwiches $3.25). Linen changed daily. $5 deposit. Reservations accepted.

YMCA, 1450, rue Stanley (849-8393), downtown. Métro: Peel. 331 rooms. Singles: male $30, co-ed $33. Doubles $48. Triples $57. Quads $66. Students and seniors $2 off. Cafeteria open 7am-7pm. Access to Y facilities. TV in every room. Usually fills up June-Aug. No reservations.

Maison André Tourist Rooms, 3511, rue Université (849-4092). Métro: McGill. Mrs. Zanko will rent you a room in her old, well-located house (singles $25-35, doubles $38-45) and spin great stories, but only if you don't smoke. Nice-sized and clean rooms with German-style decor. Reservations recommended.

Hotel Le Breton, 1609, rue St. Hubert (524-7273). Around the corner from bus station. Métro: Berri-UQAM. Prides itself on international clientele. Lobby and some rooms recently renovated. All 12 rooms have TV, A/C. Singles $30-45. Doubles $40-55. Fills up quickly—make reservations.

Hotel Louisburg, 1649, rue St. Hubert (598-8544). Métro: Berri-UQAM. Newly-renovated, has new furniture. Clean rooms with TV. June-Sept. singles $30-45, doubles $35-54; Oct.-May $35-55, $40-59. Connected with the slightly more upscale Hotel Jay, 1655, rue St. Hubert.

Those with a car and time to drive it can camp at **Camping Parc Paul Sauvé** (495-8337), 45 minutes from downtown. Take 20 west to 13 north to 640 west and follow the signs to the park. 873 beautiful sites on the **Lac des Deux Montagnes.** (Sites $13.95, with electricity $12.95.) For private sites, try **KOA Montréal-South,** 130, blvd. Monette, St-Phillipe J0L 2K0 (659-8626), a 15-min. drive from the city. Follow Rte. 15 south, take exit 38, turn left at the stop sign, and go straight about 1 mi.—it's on your left. (Sites $15, with hookup $19.50.) Or try **Camping Pointe-des-Cascades,** 2 chemin du Canal, Pte. des Cascades (455-2501). Take 40 west, exit 41 at Ste. Anne de Bellevue, junction 20, direction west to Dorion. In Dorion, follow "Théâtre des Cascades" signs. (Sites $12, with hookup $16.)

Food

French-Canadian cuisine is unique but generally expensive. When on a tight budget, look for *tourtière,* a traditional meat pie with vegetables and a thick crust, or *québecois crêpes,* stuffed with everything from scrambled eggs to asparagus with *béchamel.* Wash it down with *cidre* (hard cider). Other Montréal specialties include French bread (the best on the continent), smoked meat, Matane salmon, Gaspé shrimp, and lobster from the Maydalen Islands. Snack on *poutine,* a gooey concoction of French fries *(frites),* cheese curds, and gravy.

Montréal's ethnic restaurants offer a variety of cuisine from curry to pirogi at reasonable prices. Look for Greek *souvlaki* or Vietnamese asparagus and crab soup. A small **Chinatown** lies along rue de la Gauchetière, near old Montréal's Place d'Armes. A Jewish neighborhood complete with Hebrew neon signs, delis, and bagel bakeries lies north of downtown around blvd. St-Laurent. Don't miss the best bagels in town (30-50¢)—baked before your eyes in brick ovens—at **La Maison de Original Fairmount Bagel,** 74, rue Fairmount ouest (272-0667), or the **Bagel Bakery,** 263, rue St-Viateur ouest (276-8044), both open 24 hrs. From the St-Laurent Métro stop, take bus #55 north to Fairmount or St-Viateur and turn left.

For a quick sampling of Montréal's international cuisine, stop by **Le Faubourg,** (939-3663) 1616, rue Ste-Catherine ouest at rue Guy. (Métro: Guy.) The food is diverse (crêpes, felafel, Szechuan) and fresh, despite the fast-food atmosphere. Markets here sell seafood, meats, bread, and produce. Different stores open at different times, and it's best to wander anyway. Before you leave, stop by **Monsieur Félix and Mr. Norton Cookies** (939-3207) while in Le Faubourg. Aside from summing up the French-English duality in Montréal, they make the richest cookies in town. (Open Mon.-Thurs. 9am-10:30pm, Fri-Sat. 9-12:30 am.) Look for other locations around the city).

The drinking age in Montréal is 18. You can save money by buying your own wine at a *dépanneur* or at the **SAQ** (Société des alcools du Québec) and bringing it to unlicensed restaurants, concentrated on the blvd. St-Laurent, north of Sherbrooke, and on the pedestrian precincts of rue Prince Arthur and rue Duluth. When preparing your own grub, look for produce at the **Atwater Market** (Métro: Lionel-Groulx); the **Marché Maisonneuve,** 4375, rue Ontario est; or the **Marché Jean-Talon** (Métro: Jean Talon). (For info on any call 872-2007; all open Mon.-Wed. 7am-6pm, Thurs.-Fri. 7am-9pm, Sat.-Sun. 7am-5pm.)

Rue St-Denis, the main thoroughfare in the French student quarter, has many small restaurants and cafés, most of which cater to student pocketbooks. **Da Giovanni,** 572, Ste-Catherine est, serves generous portions of fine Italian food; don't be put off by the lines or the diner atmosphere. The sauce and noodles cook up right in the window. (842-8851; open Mon.-Sat. 7am-3am, Sun. 7am-1:30am.)

You'll be charged 15% tax for meals totaling more than $3.25. All restaurants are required by law to post their menus outside, so shop around. For more info, consult the free "Shopping, Restaurant, and Nightlife" guide, available at the tourist office.

Café Santropol, 3990, St-Urbain at Duluth (842-3110). Métro: Sherbrooke, then walk north and west. Student hangout with bizarre decor. Depending on where you sit, a plaster cow or a mannequin with ski-goggles may watch you eat. Huge veggie sandwiches served with piles of fruit ($6-7.75). Chicken also available. Open Tues.-Thurs. 11:30am-midnight, Fri. 11:30-2am, Sat. 2pm-2am, Sun. noon-midnight.

Terasse Lafayette, 250, rue Villeneuve ouest at rue Jeanne Mance (288-3915), west of the Mont-Royal Métro. Pizzas, pastas, souvlaki, and salad $6-10. One of the better Greek restaurants, with a huge outdoor terrace. BYOB. Open daily 11am-1am. Free delivery.

Etoile des Indes, 1806, Ste-Catherine ouest. Métro: Guy. Split-level dining room with tapestries covering the walls. The best Indian fare in town. Dinner entrees $6.50-12. The brave should try their bang-up *bangalore phal* dishes. Open Mon.-Sat. 11am-2:30pm and 5-11pm, Sun. 5-11pm.

Le Mazurka, 64 Prince Arthur (844-3539). Métro: Sherbrooke. Classy décor belies great prices and fine Polish fare. Pierogis (Polish ravioli) for $4.50. Specials abound, especially Mon.-Thurs. after 9pm. Dine on the terrace. Open daily 11:30-1am.

Schwartz's Deli, 3895, St-Laurent, near Napoléon. (842-4813) Métro: Sherbrooke. Arguably the best smoked meat in town piled on thick (sandwiches $3.30, larger meat plates $6.50-7.50). Often jam-packed, but you'll get your food in 5 min. Open Mon.-Thurs. and Sun. 9am-1am, Fri. 9am-3am.

Ben's Deli, 990 blvd. de Maisonneuve O. near Metcalfe (844-1000). Métro: Peel. Ben Kravitz's family continues the Montréal institution he started in 1908. Legendary smoked meat, quick service, photos of celebrity visitors to Ben's, and a lunch counter straight out of a time warp. Ben's 'n Eggs (OJ, coffee, tea, or milk, 2 eggs, 2 slices of smoked meat and toast; $3.50) for breakfast (7-11am); Ben's on Rye ($3.55) or Big Ben ($7.40) for lunch.

Wilensky's, 34, rue Fairmount ouest (271-0247). Métro: Laurier. A great place for quick lunch in the heart of the old Jewish neighborhood. Or pull out a book from Moe Wilensky's shelf and linger. Hot dogs $1.50, sandwiches $1.75-2.35. Open Sun.-Thurs. 7am-4am, Fri.-Sat. 7am-5am.

The Peel Pub, 1107, rue Ste.-Catherine (844-6769). Métro: Peel. Other Locations: 1210, Peel (844-2164); 3461, du Parc (843-7993); 1106, de Maisonneuve (845-9002). At the main branch, students and suits sit side by side in a raucous, rollicking pub. TV screens and live bands nightly. Breakfast specials Mon.-Fri. 6:30-11am, Sat.-Sun. 6:30am-4pm: 2 eggs, toast, and coffee $1; $3.95 specials like fish 'n chips, corned beef and cabbage daily. Happy hour pitchers $4.50 (Ste. Catherine) open Mon.-Sat. 6:30am-midnight.

McGill Student Union, 3480, rue McTavish, 5 min. from IYH. Métro: McGill. Cheap cafeteria food with surprisingly friendly service. Grill, pizza, salad bar, frozen yogurt. Breakfast special (toast, hash browns, and coffee) $2. Sandwiches ($2-3) and burgers ($1.75) for lunch. Beer to boot. Open May-Aug. Mon.-Thurs. 8am-3pm, Fri. 8am-2:30pm; also open during academic year. Check out **Gert's Pub** downstairs, open in summer Thurs.-Fri. 4pm-midnight.

Sights

An island city, Montréal has burgeoned from a riverside settlement of French colonists to a metropolis. The city's ethnic striations and architectural diversity can hold your attention for days on end. Museums, Vieux-Montréal (Old Montreal), and the new downtown may be fascinating but don't forget that the island's greatest asset is the sheer amount of life packed into such a small area. Wander aimlessly and often—and not through the high-priced shops and boutiques that the tourist office touts. Many attractions between Mont-Royal and the St. Laurent River are free, from parks (Mont-Royal and Lafontaine) and universities (McGill, Montréal, Concordia, Québec at Montréal) to ethnic neighborhoods.

Walk or ride a bike down **boulevard St-Laurent** north of Sherbrooke. Originally settled by Jewish immigrants, this area now functions as a sort of multi-cultural center with Greek, Slavic, Latin American, and Portuguese immigrants. **Rue St-Denis,** home of the French language elite around the turn of the century, still serves as the mainline of Montréal's **Latin Quarter** (Métro: Berri-UQAM). Jazz fiends command the street the first week of July during the **13th Montréal International Jazz Festival** (288-5363 HQ; info 871-1881) with over 200 outdoor shows. Headliners play many other concerts indoors. **Carré St-Louis,** or Saint Louis Square, (Métro: Sherbrooke), with its fountain and sculptures, **rue Prince-Arthur,** packed with street performers in the summer, and **Le Village,** a gay village in Montréal from rue St-Denis est to Papineau along rue Ste-Catherine est, are also worth visiting.

Students will feel at home on the **McGill University** campus (main gate at the corner of McGill and Sherbrooke St.; Métro: McGill). The campus stretches up Mont-Royal, offering Victorian buildings and a pleasant spot of green grass and oak trees in the midst of downtown. More than any other sight in Montréal, the university manifests the British tradition in the city. The campus also contains the site of the 16th century Native-American village of Hochelaga and the **Redpath Museum of Natural Science** (398-4086), with rare fossils and two genuine Egyptian mummies. (Open June-Sept. Mon.-Thurs. 9am-5pm; Oct.-May Mon.-Fri. 9am-5pm. Free.) Guided tours of the campus are available with 24-hr. notice (398-6555).

The Underground City

Visitors to Montréal aren't speaking metaphorically of a sub-culture or a particularly hip part of town when they rave about their Underground City. They mean *underground:* 22km of tunnels between Métro stops forming a subterranean village of climate-controlled restaurants and shops. The ever-expanding network now connects railway stations, a bus terminal, restaurants, banks, cinemas, theaters, hotels, 1200 businesses, 1250 housing units, two universities, two department stores, and 1400 boutiques. Enter the city from any of the Métro stops, or start your adventure at the **Place Bonaventure,** 901 rue de la Gauchetière ouest (397-2205; Métro: Bonaventure), Canada's largest commercial building, allegedly constructed of *mithral* from the mines below. The **Viaduc** shopping center inside contains a cluster of shops, each selling products of a different country. The tourist office will supply city guides that include treasure maps of the tunnels and underground attractions. (Shops open Mon.-Wed. 9:30am-5pm, Thurs.-Fri. 9:30am-9pm, Sat. 9:30am-5pm.) Stick your head above ground long enough to see **Place Ville-Marie** (Métro: Bonaventure), a 1960s office-shopping complex. Revolutionary when first built, the structure triggered Montréal's architectural renaissance. **Cathédrale Marie Reine du Monde** (Mary, Queen of the World Cathedral), corner of René-Lévesque and Mansfield (Métro: Bonaventure; 866-1661) is a scaled-down exact replica of St. Peter's in Rome. (Open daily 7am-7pm.)

Parks and Museums

The finest of Montréal's parks, **Parc du Mont-Royal** (City of Montréal sports and recreation 872-2644; in the park 872-2969), swirls in a vast green expanse up the mountain from which the city took its name. Visitors from New York may recognize the omnipresent hand of Frederick Law Olmsted, the architect who planned Central Park and half the U.S. From rue Peel, hardy hikers can take a foot path and stairs to the top. Both the lookout on Camillien Houde Parkway and the park lodge offer phenomenal views of Montréal. In 1643, De Maisonneuve, founder of Montréal, promised to climb Mont-Royal bearing a cross if the flood waters of the St-Laurent would recede. The existing 30-ft. cross, built in 1924, commemorates this climb. When illuminated at night, you can see the cross for miles. In winter, *Montréalais* congregate on "the Mountain" to ice-skate, toboggan, and cross-country ski. In summer, Mont-Royal welcomes joggers, cyclists, picnickers, and wanderers. (Officially open sunrise-sunset.) **Parc Lafontaine** has picnic facilities, an outdoor puppet theater, seven public tennis courts, ice-skating in the winter, and an international festival of public theater in June.

For a beautiful view of Montréal and the St-Laurent, head up rue Belvedere to **Westmount Summit.** This small wooded park crowns **Westmount,** one of the wealthiest neighborhoods in the city. Subdued, green, and very English, Westmount is an enclave of stately mansions. (Take bus #66.) On the northern edge of Westmount stands **Oratoire St-Joseph** (St. Joseph's Oratory), 3800, rue Queen Mary (Métro: Snowdon, Guy, and bus #165), a mammoth monument of *québecois* Catholicism built in honor of the healing monk Frère André. Aside from an enormous basilica, the complex includes the **Musée de Frère André** and the **Musée de l'Oratoire** (both 733-8211), a spacious art gallery. (Oratory open daily 6am-10pm where summer concerts are held. Museums open daily 10am-5pm. Donation.)

Musée des beaux-arts de Montréal (Fine Arts Museum), 1379, Sherbrooke ouest (285-1600; Métro: Guy), houses a small permanent collection that touches upon all major historical periods, including Canadian and Inuit work. (Open daily 10am-7pm. Admission $12, seniors and students $5, under 12 $1; prices and hours vary depending on the exhibit.) It displays blockbuster visiting exhibits, recently of Picasso, Chagall, and in 1991, *1920s: The Age of the Metropolis*. **Musée d'art contemporain** (Museum of Contemporary Art), Cité du Havre (873-2878), has the latest by *québecois* artists, as well as textile, photography, and avant-garde exhibits. (Open Tues.-Sun. 10am-6pm. Admission $3, seniors and students $2, Tues. free. Métro: Bonaventure, then bus #168 Mon.-Fri., on weekends take bus #125 from rue de l'Université and rue Ste-Jacques.)

The newly renovated and expanded **McCord Museum of Canadian History,** 690 Sherbrooke O (398-7100; Métro: McGill) owns collections of textiles, costumes, paintings, prints, and 400,000 works spanning 78 years in their photographic archives. (Open Mon.-Wed. and Fri. 10am-6pm, Thurs. and Sat.-Sun. 10am-5pm. Admission $4.)

Opened in May 1989, the **Centre Canadien d'Architecture,** 1920 Baile St. (939-7000; Métro: Guy), houses one of the most important collections of architectural prints, drawings, photographs, and books in the world. (Open Wed. and Fri. 11am-6pm, Thurs. 11am-8pm, Sat.-Sun. 11am-5pm. Admission $5, students and seniors $3, free for kids.) The **Olympic Park,** 4545, ave. Pierre-de-Coubertin (252-4737; Métro: Pie-IX or Viau), hosted the 1976 Summer Olympic Games. Its daring architecture includes the world's tallest inclined tower and a stadium with one of the world's only fully retractable roofs. Despite this, games still get rained out because the roof cannot be put in place with crowds in the building (really smart, guys). (Guided tours daily at 12:40 and 3:40pm; more often May-Sept. Admission $5.50, seniors $4.50, ages 5-17 $3.75, under 5 free.) Take the *funiculaire* to the top of the tower for a panoramic view of Montréal. (Leaves daily every 10 minutes, 10am-11pm; off-season 10am-6pm. Fare same as for tour of the park. For combined tour and *funiculaire* $9, seniors $7.50, ages 5-17 $6.50.) A train will take you across the park (in summmer time) to the **Jardin Botanique** (Botanical Gardens), 4101, Sherbrooke E. (872-1400; Métro: Pie-IX). After London's Kew Gardens, this is the most important garden in the world. The Japanese and Chinese gardens opened only recently, and house the largest bonsai and penjing collection outside of Asia. (Gardens open 8am-sunset; greenhouses 9am-6pm. Admission $6.)

Vieux Montréal

View Montréal's old French heritage where the first settlement began—Vieux-Montréal (Old Montréal), on the stretch of riverbank between rue McGill, Notre-Dame, and Berri. The fortified walls that once protected the quarter have crumbled, but the beautiful 17th- and 18th-century mansions of politicos and merchants have maintained their full splendor. (Métro: Place d'Armes.)

The 19th-century church **Notre-Dame-de-Montréal** (849-1070) towers above the Place d'Armes and the memorial to de Maisonneuve. A historic center for the city's Catholic population, the neo-Gothic church once hosted separatist rallies, and, more recently, a tradition-breaking ecumenical gathering. Seating 4000, Notre-Dame is one of the largest and most magnificent churches in North America. After suffering major fire damage, the **Wedding Chapel** behind the altar re-opened in 1982 boasting a tremendous bronze altar. (Open June 24-Labor Day, daily 7am-8pm; off-season daily 7am-6pm. Guided tours offered.)

From Notre-Dame walk next door to the **Sulpician Seminary,** Montréal's oldest remaining building (built in 1685) and still a functioning seminary. The clock over the facade (built in 1700) is the oldest public timepiece in North America. A stroll down rue Saint-Sulpice will bring you to **rue de la Commune** on the banks of the St. Lawrence River. Here the city's old docks compete with the new. Proceed east along rue de la Commune to **rue Bonsecours.** At the corner of Bonsecours and the busy rue St-Paul stands the 18th-century **Notre-Dame-de-Bonsecours** (845-9991), founded on the port as a sailor's refuge by Marguerite Bourgeoys, leader of the first congregation of non-cloistered nuns. Sailors thankful for their safe pilgrimages presented the nuns and priests with the wooden boat-shaped ceiling lamps in the chapel. The church also has a museum in the basement and a bell tower with a nice view of Vieux Montréal and the St. Lawrence River. (Chapel open May-Nov. daily 9am-5pm; Dec.-April 10am-5pm. Tower and museum open May-Nov. Tues.-Sat. 9am-4:30pm, Sun. 11:30am-4:30pm; Dec.-April Tues.-Fri. 10:30am-4:30pm, Sat. 10am-4:30pm, Sun. 11:30am-4:30pm. Admission $2, kids 50¢.)

Opening onto rue St-Paul is **Place Jacques Cartier,** site of Montréal's oldest market. Here the modern European character of Montréal is most evident; cafés line the square and in summer street artists strut their stuff. Visit the grand **Château Ramezay,** 280, Notre-Dame est (861-3708), built in 1705 to house the French viceroy, and its museum of *québecois,* British, and American 18th-century artifacts. (Open Tues.-Sun. 10am-4:30pm. Admission $2.50, seniors and students $1.) Nearby, in the square of Place Vauquelin, is the Vieux Palais de Justice, built in 1856; across from it stands City Hall. **Rue St-Jacques** in the Old City, established in 1687, is Montréal's answer to Wall Street.

There are many good reasons to venture out to **Ile Ste-Hélène,** an island in the St. Lawrence River, just off the coast of Vieux Montréal. The best is **La Ronde** (872-6222), Montréal's popular amusement park: it's best to go in the afternoon and buy an unlimited pass. From late May to mid-June on Wed. and Sat., stick around La Ronde until 10pm to watch the **International Benson & Hedges Fireworks Competition** (872-8714). (Park open Sun.-Thurs. 11am-11pm, Fri.-Sat. 11am-midnight. Admission $18.25, kids $8.50.) To cool off after your frolics, slide over to **Aqua-Parc** (872-7326) and splash the day away. (Open mid-June to late Aug. daily 10am-5pm. Admission $16, under 12 $8.50; after 3pm $10.75, $6.50.) **Le Vieux Fort** (The Old Fort; 861-6701), was built in the 1820s to defend Canada's inland waterways. Now primarily a military museum, the fort displays artifacts and costumes detailing Canadian colonial history. Three military parades take place daily from late June to the end of August. (Museum open May-Aug. Wed.-Mon. 10am-5pm; off-season Wed.-Mon. 10am-6pm. Admission $4, seniors, students, and kids $1.50, under 6 free.) Take the Métro under the St. Lawrence to the Ile Ste-Hélène stop.

Whether swollen with spring run-off or frozen over during the winter, the **St. Lawrence River** can be one of Montréal's most thrilling attractions. The whirlpools and 15-ft. waves of the **Lachine Rapids** once inhibited river travel. No longer—now St. Lawrence and Montréal harbor cruises depart from Victoria Pier (842-3871) in Vieux Montréal (May 15-Oct. 13, 4 per day, 2 hr., fare $13). Tours of the Lachine Rapids (284-9607) leave five times per day (May-Sept. 10am-6pm; tickets $40, seniors $35, ages 13-18 $30, ages 6-12 $20).

Explore the **West Island,** formerly the summer residence for affluent city dwellers, by bike (along the Lachine Canal and the Lakeshore Rd.) or by bus (#211 from Lionel Groulx). Walk along the boardwalk in Ste. Anne de Bellevue and watch the River locks in action. The local crowd rocks Ste. Anne's at night, at one of the many *brasseries,* or the renowned **Annie's** and **Quai Sera.**

Nightlife and Entertainment

If you choose to ignore the massive neon lights flashing "films érotiques" and "Château du sexe," you should easily find blander nightlife in Québec's largest city—either in **brasseries** (with food as well as beer, wine, and music) or in **pubs** (with more hanging out and less eating). Downstairs at 1107, rue Ste-Catherine ouest, for example, is **Peel Pub** (844-6769), providing live rock bands and good, cheap food nightly. Here waiters rush about with three pitchers of beer in each hand to keep up with the motley crue of Montréal's university students; this pub has a number of locations throughout the city so finding one near you shouldn't be difficult.

For slightly older and more subdued drinking buddies, search the side streets of rue Ste-Catherine ouest, far from the maddening crowd. Try the English strongholds around **rue Crescent** and **rue Bishop** (Métro: Guy), where bar-hopping is a must. **Déjà-Vu**, 1224, Bishop (866-0512), has live bands each night. (Open daily 3pm-3am; happy hour 3-10pm.) Set aside Tuesday or Thursday for a night at **D.J.'s Pub**, 1443, Crescent (287-9354), when $12 gets you into an open bar. (Open noon to 3am.) **Christopher's**, 1446, Crescent (847-0275), and **Thursday's**, 1449, Crescent (866-5656), are the other major hotspots. The ultimate 50s and 60s dance place is **Studebaker's**, 1255, Crescent (866-1101; open Wed.-Sat. 8:30pm-3am; dress code). Reggae fans should go to **Rising Sun**, 5380, St. Laurent (278-5200; Métro:St. Laurent, then bus #55 to Fairmount; open 8:30pm-3am). French nightlife parleys in the open air cafés on **rue St-Denis** (Métro: UQAM). Stop in for live jazz at **Le Grand Café**, 1720, rue St-Denis (849-6955; open daily 11am-3am; evening cover $4). While you're in the Latin Quarter, scout out energetic **rue Prince Arthur**, which vacuum-packs Greek, Polish, and Italian restaurants into its tiny volume. Street performers and colorful wall murals further enliven this ethnic neighborhood. The accent changes slightly at **ave. Duluth**, where Portuguese and Vietnamese establishments prevail. Vieux Montréal, too, is best seen at night. Street performers, artists, and *chansonniers* in various *brasseries* set the tone for lively summer evenings of clapping, stomping, and singing along; the real fun goes down on St-Paul, in the *brasseries* near the corner of St-Vincent.

The city bubbles with a wide variety of theatrical groups: the **Théâtre du Nouveau Monde**, 84, Ste-Catherine ouest (861-0563), and the **Theéâtre du Rideau Vert**, 4664, St-Denis (844-1793), stage *québecois* works. For English language plays, try the **Centaur Theatre**, 453, rue St-François-Xavier (288-3161). The city's exciting **Place des Arts**, 175, Ste-Catherine ouest (842-2112 for tickets), houses the **Opéra de Montréal**, the **Montréal Symphony Orchestra**, and **Les Grands Ballets Canadiens**. The **National Theatre School of Canada**, 5030, rue St. Denis (842-7954) stages excellent student productions during the academic year. **Théâtre Saint-Denis**, 1549, St.-Denis (849-4211) puts on traveling productions like *Cats* and *Les Misérables*. Check the *Calendar of Events* (available at the tourist office and reprinted in daily newspapers), or call **Ticketron** (288-3651) for tickets and further info.

Montréalais are rabid sports fans, and there's opportunity aplenty for like-minded visitors to join in the madness. In June, the **Circuit Gilles-Villeneuve** on the Ile Notre-Dame will host the annual Molson Grand Prix, a Formula 1 race (392-0000), and this August, as in every other August, **Tennis Canada** will host the world's best tennis players at Jarry Park (Métro De Castelau). This year women compete in the Player's Challenge August 15-23. (Call 273-1515 for info and tickets.) Football fans haven't been forgotten: the **Montreal Machine** (WLAF football team) join the **Expos** in the Olympic Stadium (see address in Sights above; for Expos info., call 253-3434; for tickets 522-1245 in Montréal, 800-361-4595 outside).

Montréalais don't just watch: their one-day **Tour de l'île** is the largest participatory cycling event in the world with a 40,000-member fan club attending. (Call 847-8687 to see how you can attend too.) A trip to Montréal between October and April is incomplete without attending a **Montréal Canadiens** hockey game: the **Montréal Forum**, 2312, Ste. Catherine O (Métro: Atwater) is the shrine to hockey and **Les Habitants** (nickname for the Canadiens) are its acolytes. (For more info, call 932-2582.)

Montréal celebrates the 350th anniversary of its founding in 1992 (May 15-Oct. 12). Paul de Chomedey, sieur de Maisonneuve, founded Ville-Marie de Montréal on May 18, 1642. Plans are in the making for historical, civic, and international festivities. The anniversary coincides with the 500th anniversary of Columbus' arrival in America. Call the City of Montréal at 872-1111 for details.

Québec

Québec, Canada's oldest city, not only is the capital of its namesake province, it has been the country's capital under both French and English regimes. Built on the rocky heights of Cape Diamond, where the St. Lawrence River narrows and joins the St. Charles River in northeast Canada, the city has been called the "Gibraltar of America" because of the stone walls and military fortifications protecting the port. Despite the past British control of the area, the French have shaped Québec with their heritage and language. At least 95% French-speaking, Québec City offers traditional French-Canadian cuisine, music, and ambience. Visitors who speak French should do so, but Anglophones will squeak by. The best times to visit are during the summer arts festival in mid-July and February's winter carnival, a raucous French-Canadian Mardi Gras.

Practical Information

Emergency: Police, 691-6911 (city); 623-6262 (provincial). Info-santé: 648-2626.

Centre d'information de l'Office du tourisme et des congrés de la Communauté urbaine de Québec, 60, rue d'Auteuil (692-2471). Visit here for accommodation listings, brochures, free maps, and friendly bilingual advice. Free local calls. Open June-Labor Day daily 8:30am-8pm; April, May, Sept., Oct. Mon.-Fri. 8:30am-5:30pm; off-season Mon.-Fri. 8:30am-5pm. Maison du Tourisme de Québec 12, rue Ste-Anne (873-2015 from Montréal region; 800-363-7777 from elsewhere in Canada and the United States), deals specifically with provincial tourism, distributing accommodation listings for the entire province and free road and city maps. Some bus tours and Budget also have desks here. Open June 10-Labor Day 8:30am-7:30pm; off-season 9am-6pm. Ste-Foy Centre d'information de l'Office du tourisme et des congrés de la Communauté urbaine de Québec, 3005, blvd. Laurier, Ste-Foy (651-2882), is just down Laurier from Ste. Foy bus station, at rue Lavigerie, 4 mi. southwest of the old city. Open June-Labor Day daily 8:30am-8pm; Sept. 3-Oct. 14 daily 8:30am-6pm; Oct. 15-April 15 daily 9am-5pm; April 16-June daily 8:30am-6pm.

Youth Tourist Information: Boutique Temps-Libre of Regroupement tourisme jeunesse 19, Ste-Ursule (800-461-8585), in the lobby of the Centre International de Séjour (see Accommodations and Camping below). Most literature in French. Complete info on the province's youth hostels. Hostel memberships available here along with travel gear. Open Mon.-Wed. 9am-5:30pm, Thurs.-Fri. 9am-8pm, Sat. 9:30am-5pm.

U.S. Consulate: 2 Terrasse Dufferin (692-2095). Issues tourist visas Mon., Wed., and Fri. 9-11am. Open for American citizens Tues. and Thurs. 9-11am and 2-4pm; Mon., Wed., and Fri. 2-4pm.

Airlines: Air Canada (692-0770) and Inter-Canadian (692-1031). Special deals available for students under 21 (with ID) willing to go standby. Airport is way out of town with no quick way, if any, to get there by public transport. By car, you can turn right onto Route de l'aéroport and then take either Blvd. Wilfred-Hamel or, beyond it, Autoroute 440 to get into the city.

Trains: VIA Rail Canada, 450, rue de la Gare du Palais in Quebec City (524-6452); 3255, chemin de la Gare in Ste-Foy (658-8792); 5995, rue de St.-Laurentin Lévis (833-8056). Call 800-361-5390 anywhere in Canada or the U.S. for reservations and info. To Montréal (3 per day; 3 hr.; $34, students $32; $20 for adults if booked in advance and not traveling on Fri., Sun., or a holiday; $17 for students if booked at least 5 days in advance).

Buses: Voyageur Bus, 225, blvd. Charest est (524-4692). Open daily 5:30am-1am. Outlying stations at 2700, ave. Laurier, in Ste-Foy (651-7015; open daily 5:45am-1:15am), and 63, rte. Trans-Canada ouest (Rte. 132), in Lévis (837-5805; open daily 6:30am-11pm). To Montréal (every hr. 6am-11pm, 3 hr., $28.90) and Ste-Anne-de-Beaupré (3 per day, $4.28). Connections to U.S. cities via Montréal or Sherbrooke.

Public Transport: Commission de transport de la Communauté Urbaine de Québec (CTCUQ), 270, rue des Rocailles (627-2511 for route and schedule info; open Mon.-Fri. 7am-9:30pm; for lost objects, call 622-7412). Buses operate daily 5:30am-12:30am although individual routes vary. Fare $1.40, seniors $1.

Taxis: Coop Taxis Québec, 525-5191. Driver/Rider Service: Allo-Stop, 467, rue St. Jean (522-0056) will match you with a driver heading for Montréal ($15).

Car Rental: Though often expensive, agencies abound in Québec City. Check the yellow pages for a full listing. **Budget,** 29 côte du Palais (692-3660), is open Mon.-Wed. 7am-5:30pm; Thurs. 7am-7pm; Sat. 8am-5pm; Sun. 9am-5pm. **Hertz,** across the road at 44 côte du Palais (694-1224), is open Mon.-Wed. 7:30am-5:30pm; Thurs.-Fri. 7:30am-6pm; Sat.-Sun. 8am-5pm.

Moped and Bike Rental: Location Petit Champlain, 94, rue Petit-Champlain (692-2817). Cycles expensive. Bikes $10 per hr., $25 per day; mopeds $20 per hr., $5 each additional hr. (insurance included). Strollers for rent, too. Guided walking tours of Petit Champlain, Place Royale, and le Vieux Port to be offered in 1992.

Help Line: Tel Aide, 683-2153. Open Sun.-Thurs. noon-midnight, Fri.-Sat. noon-2am. **Viol-secours** (sexual assault line), 692-2252. **Centre de prévention de suicide,** 525-4588.

Canada Post: 3, rue Buade (648-4686). Open Mon.-Fri. 8am-5:45pm. **Postal Code:** G1R 2J0. **Post Office** in the city at 300 rue St-Paul (648-3340). **Postal code:** G1K 3W0.

Area Code: 418.

Dividing lines are many in Québec: rue Saint-Vallier Est separates *la Blasse-ville* (Lower town) from *la Haute-ville* (Upper town) and the British-built walls contain *Vieux-Québec.* Porte Saint-Jean and Porte Saint-Louis lead you into the old city on the parallel main streets of rue Saint-Jean and rue Saint-Louis. Rue Saint-Louis also ends directly in front of the **Chateau Frontenac. Place-Royale, Quartier du Petit-Champlain,** and le **Vieux Port** lie below the cliffs in the oldest part of Québec. Although "lower" than any of the other land for miles, locals do *not* refer to this as **la Basse-ville.**

Accommodations and Camping

Québec City now has two B&B referral services. Contact Denise or Raymond Blancher at **B&B Bonjour Québec,** 3765, blvd. Monaco, Québec G1P 3J3 (527-1465) for lodgings throughout the city, city maps, and descriptions of houses. (Singles $35-45. Doubles $45-60.) **Gîte Québec** offers similar services. Contact Thérèse Tellier, 3729, ave. Le Corbusier, Ste-Foy, Québec G1W 4R8 (651-1860). (Singles $30-40. Doubles from $60.) Hosts are usually bilingual, and the B&B services inspect the houses for cleanliness and convenience of location.

You can obtain a list of nearby campgrounds from the Maison du Tourisme de Québec, or by writing Ministère du Tourisme, Direction de l'hôtellerie, 710, place D'Youville, 3e étage, Québec G1R 4Y4 (800-363-7777).

Centre international de séjour, 19, Ste-Ursule (694-0755), between rue St-Jean and Dauphine. Follow Côte d'Abraham uphill from the bus station until it joins Avenue Dufferin. Turn left on Jean, pass through the walls, and walk uphill, to your right, on Ste.-Ursule. Thin mattresses and worn-down bathrooms offset by excellent location in the heart of the old city and Lily's cheerful manner. Laundry machines, TV, pool table, living room. Check-out 10am. Doors lock at 2am, but front desk will let you in. Singles $31. One bed in a 2-person room $15, in a 4-to 8-person room $13, in an 8- to 16-person room $10; nonmembers always pay $3 more. Memberships sold. Half price for kids. Microwave. No kitchen, but cafeteria in basement: breakfast served 7:30-10am ($3.25). Linen included. Key deposit $5. Reservations accepted.

Auberge de la Paix, 31, rue Couillard (694-0735). Peeling paint, cramped lobby and beds—but clean. Stay here when Centre is full: both have great access to the restaurants and bars on rue St-Jean. 56 beds; 2-8 beds per room, predominantly 3-4 beds per room. Curfew 2am. $13. Breakfast of toast, cereal, coffee and juice included (8-10am). Kitchen open all day. Linen $1. Make reservations July and Aug.

Campus de l'université Laval, Pavillion Parent (656-2921), Ste-Foy. 15-20 min. bus ride from the city on bus #11 or #8. Modern building with dorm rooms. Rooms clean and big enough, but stay in Vieux Québec if possible. Singles with sink and desk $15.50, non-students $21. Doubles $21, $26. Cafeteria breakfast $3. Access to sports facilities on a campus full of activity. Reserve in advance if you plan to stay more than 2 nights. Open May 10-Aug. 20.

Montmartre Canadien, 1679, chemin St-Louis, Sillery (681-7357), on the outskirts of the city. Take bus #25. Small, clean house in a religious sanctuary overlooking the St. Lawrence River. Relaxed, almost isolated setting—don't expect to meet tons of new people here. Mostly used by groups. Run by Assumptionist monks—Father François particularly friendly. Common showers. Dorm-style singles $14. Doubles $24. Triples $33. Bed in 7-person dormitory $10; groups of 20 or more, $12. Breakfast (eggs, cereal, bacon, and pancakes) $3.20. Reserve 2-3 weeks in advance.

Manoir La Salle, 18, rue Ste-Ursule (647-9361), opposite the youth hostel. Clean private rooms fill up quickly, especially in the summer. Cat haters beware: felines stalk the halls. Singles $25-40. Doubles $40, with shower $45.

Maison Demers, 68 rue Ste.-Ursule GIR 4E6 (692-2487), up the road from the youth hostel. Clean, comfortable rooms with TV and sink in the Demers home, built in 1908. Singles $30-35. Doubles with shower $45-60. Breakfast of coffee and fresh croissants included. Parking available. Reservations recommended. Take Autoroute #73 out of the city to Blvd. Wilfred-Hamel. Follow signs for the campground after passing Autoroute #40.

Camping Canadien, Ancienne-Lorette (872-7801). Sites $14.50, with hookup $17.50. Open May 15-Oct. 15.

Municipal de Beauport, Beauport (666-2228). Take Autoroute 40 east, exit #321 at rue Labelle onto 369, turn left, and follow signs marked "camping." Ask tourism about buses to Beauport and enjoy this campground overlooking the Montmorency Falls. 136 sites. $12, with hookup $16; weekly: $70, $100. Open June 1-Sept. 5.

Food and Nightlife

In general, rue Buade, St-Jean, avenue Grande Allée, and Cartier, as well as the **Place Royale** and **Petit Champlain** areas offer the widest selection of food and drink. Food tends to be cheaper outside the walls of the old city. One of the most filling yet inexpensive meals is a *croque monsieur,* a large, open-faced sandwich with ham and melted cheese ($5), usually served with salad. Be sure to try *Québecois* French onion soup, loaded with onions, slathered with melted cheese, and usually served with bats of French bread as well as *aux pois* (pea soup) and *tourtiére,* a thick meat pie. Other specialties include the French crêpe, stuffed differently for either main course or dessert, and the French-Canadian "sugar pie," made with brown sugar and butter. For basic grilled meals, eat at the clean and cheap cafeteria in the basement of the **Centre internationale de séjour** (see Accommodations and Camping above). Remember that some of these restaurants do *not* have non-smoking sections.

For those doing their own cooking, **J.A. Moisan**, 685, rue St. Jean (522-8268) sells groceries in an old country-style store. Open Mon.-Sun. 9am-10pm. **Dépanneurs** (they dé-panne you, i.e. get you out of trouble) are Québec's answer and challenge to the corner store. Besides milk, bread, and snack food, they'll also sell you alcohol. **Dépanneur Proprio,** down Ste-Ursule from the Centre is open Tues.-Sat., 24 hrs.

Casse Crêpe Breton, 1136, rue St-Jean (692-0438). Great, inexpensive crêpes ($2.75-4.65) with friendly service in a casual atmosphere. Breakfast special (2 eggs, bacon, toast, and coffee) $2.95. Lunch specials (11am-2pm) an even better bargain. Suck on a strawberry milkshake ($2.25) or munch on fresh fruit crêpes ($2.45-$2.95) for dessert. Open daily 7:30am-1am.

La Vieille Maison du Spaghetti, 625, Grand Allé est or 40, rue Marché Champlain. Both in the Petit-Champlain quarter near Place Royale. Great, fresh Italian food in a perfect setting—red tablecloths and wine glasses at each seat. Spaghetti with tangy sauces, a skimpy salad bar, bread, and tea or coffee $6.55-8.75. Pizza $7.25-9.50. Open Mon.-Wed. 11am-9pm, Thurs.-Sun. 11am-11:30pm.

Les Couventines, 1124, rue St-Jean (692-4850). Buckwheat crêpes in a quiet, elegant dining room. Crystal glasses and nicely finished wood tables and chairs. Great spot for serious conversation. Butter crêpes $1.80, "La Nordique" (smoked salmon) $8. Wash down home-made chocolate or Chantilly cream crêpes ($3.45) with French cider. Open Tues.-Sat. 11am-3pm and 5-11pm; Sun. 10am-11pm.**Mille-Feuille**, 32, rue Ste-Angéle (692-2147). Vegetarian meals ($5-$7) served in a chic restaurant with an outdoor terrace to match. Open Mon.-Tues. 10am-11pm, Wed. 9am-11pm, Thurs.-Sat. 8am-11:30pm, Sun. 8am-11pm.

Café Mediterranée, 64, St. Cyrille O (648-1849 lunchtime; 648-0768 dinner). Take the #25 bus or walk for about 10 min. outside the walls. Elegant surroundings for a Mediterranean buffet. Enjoy vegetable platters, *couscous,* spicy chicken dishes—or all 3: the ideal, filling lunch. Soup, dessert, coffee, and as much as you want for a main meal for $7.50 (lunch),

$19.95 (dinner). Open Mon.-Fri. 11:30am-2pm, Thurs.-Sun. 6-11pm. The buffet depletes quickly, so arrive early. Reservations recommended.

Le Piazzetta, 707, rue St.-Jean (529-7489), and 1191, rue Cartier (649-8896). Eat spicy square pizza at the marble lunch counter to the buzz of lively discussion. Or sit at a table and linger over piccolos (small, 1-person pizza; $3.75-$5.25). Open Mon.-Wed. 11:30am-2am, Sat. noon-2am, Sun. noon-midnight.

Restaurant Liban, 23, rue d'Auteuil, off rue St-Jean (694-1888). Great café for lunch or a late-night bite. Tabouli and hummus plates $3.25, both with pita bread. Fantastic variety of baklava. Open for coffee at 10am, for meals 11am-4am.

Café Ste-Julie, 865, rue des Zouaves off St-Jean (647-9368). No frills lunch-counter joint with specials scrawled on the walls—breakfast (2 eggs, bacon, coffee, toast, beans) $3.25; lunch (2 cheese-burgers, fries, and a soft drink) $4.99. Open Mon.-Fri. 7am-9pm, Sat. 8am-9pm, Sun. 9am-9pm.

La Fleur de Lotus, 38, Côte de la Fabrique (692-4286), across from the Hôtel de Ville. Cheerful and unpretentious enough you won't *ever* want to leave. Thai dishes $2.75-8.75. Open Mon.-Wed. 11:30am-3pm and 5-10:30pm, Thurs.-Fri. 11:30am-3pm and 5-11pm, Sat. 5-11pm, Sun. 5-10:30pm.

Numerous boisterous nightspots line rue St-Jean. Duck into any of these establishments and linger over a glass of wine or listen to some *québecois* folk music. Most balk at cover charges and close around 3am. **L'Apropo,** 596, rue St-Jean, frequently has live music. (Open daily noon-until.) The **Bar en Bar,** 58, Côte du Palais, fills with locals and pool tables. (Half-price drinks daily noon-8pm.) Try the **Pub Saint-Alexandre,** 1091, rue St.-Jean for standard pub food and a wide selection of beer. In summer, musicians, magicians, and other performers take their act to the street.

Sights

Confined within walls built by the English, *le vieux Québec* (old Québec City) holds most of the city's historic attractions. Though monuments are clearly marked and explained, you'll get more out of the town with the tourist office's *Greater Québec Area Tourist Guide* which contains a walking tour of the old city. (Available from 60, rue d'Auteuil and the Maison du Tourisme; see Practical Information above.) It takes one or two days to explore old Québec on foot, but you'll learn more than on the many guided bus tours. Take the time to hang out with the corpses in **Saint Matthew's Cemetery,** 755, rue St. Jean, and to stumble past monuments such as the one commemorating the first patent issued in Canada.

Begin your walking tour of Québec City by climbing uphill, to the top of **Cap Diamant** (Cape Diamond), just south of the **Citadelle.** From here take Promenade des Gouverneurs downhill to **Terrasse Dufferin.** Built in 1838 by Lord Durham, this popular promenade offers excellent views of the St. Lawrence River, the Côte de Beaupré (the "Avenue Royale" Highway), and Ile d'Orléans across the Channel. The promenade passes the landing spot of the European settlers, marked by the **Samuel de Champlain Monument,** where Champlain built Fort St-Louis in 1620, securing the new French settlement. A *funiculaire* (cable car; 692-1132; operates Mon.-Sat. 7:30am-11:20pm, Sun. 8:30am-11:20pm; 75¢) connects Lower Town and Place Royale.

At the bottom of the promenade, towering above the *terrasse* near rue St-Louis, you'll find **le Château Frontenac,** built on the ruins of two previous *châteaux.* The immense, Baroque Frontenac was built in 1893 by the Canadian Pacific Company and has developed into a world-renowned luxury hotel. Named for Comte Frontenac, governor of *Nouvelle-France,* the château was the site of two historic meetings between Churchill and Roosevelt during WWII. Although budget travelers must forgo staying here, the public can enter the grand hall and its small shopping mall.

Near Château Frontenac, between rue St-Louis and rue Buade, lies the **Place d'Armes.** The *calèches* (horse-drawn buggies) that congregate here in summer provide atmosphere, especially strong scents in muggy weather; carriage tours cost $50. Also on rue Buade, right next to Place d'Armes, is the **Notre-Dame Basilica** (692-2533). The clock and outer walls date back to 1647; the rest of the church has been rebuilt twice (most recently after a fire in 1922). (Open Mon.-Sat. 7am-8pm, Sun. 7am-6pm. Tours in multiple languages, May 1-Nov. 1 daily 9am-5pm. Free). An ornate gold altar and a sky painted on the ceiling work to help worshippers reach their God (Free, but in mysterious ways). Notre-Dame, with its odd mix of architectural styles, contrasts sharply with the adjacent **Seminary of Québec,** founded in 1663, which stands as an excellent example of 17th-century *québecois* architecture. At first a Jesuit boot camp, the seminary became the *Université de Laval* in 1852. The *Université* has since moved to its present site in Ste. Foy. The **Musée du Séminaire,** 9, rue de l'Université (642-2843), lurks nearby. (Open June-Sept. Tues.-Sun. 10:30am-5:30pm; Oct.-May Tues.-Sun. 10:30am-5pm. Admission $2, seniors and students $1, kids 50¢.)

The **Musée du Fort,** 10, rue Ste-Anne (692-2175), presents a sound-and-light show that narrates (in French and English) the history of Quebec City and the series of six battles fought to control it. (Open summer daily 10am-6pm; spring and fall Mon.-Sat. 10am-5pm, Sun. 1-5pm; winter Mon.-Fri. 11am-5pm, Sat. 10am-5pm, Sun. 1-5pm; closed Dec. 1-20. Admission $4.25, seniors and students $2.75.)

The **Post Office,** 3, rue Buade, now called **The Louis St. Laurent Building** (after Canada's second French Canadian Prime Minister) was built in the late 1890's and towers over a statue of Monseigneur de Laval, the first bishop of Québec. Across the Côte de la Montagne, a lookout park provides an impressive view of the St. Lawrence River. A statue of Georges-Etienne Cartier, one of the Key French Canadian Fathers of Confederation, presides over the park.

Walk along rue St-Louis to see its 17th- and 18th-century homes. Of historic note: the surrender of Québec to the British occurred in 1759 at **Maison Kent,** 25, rue St-Louis, built in 1648. The Québec government now uses and operates the house. Touché. At the end of rue St-Louis is **porte St-Louis,** one of the oldest entrances to the fortified city.

Walk down Côte de la Montagne and negotiate the *Casse-cou* staircase ("breakneck"—but the stairs don't live up to the name), or take the *funiculaire* down to the oldest section of Québec. Either way leads to **rue Petit-Champlain,** the oldest road in North America. Many of the old buildings that line the street have been restored or renovated and now house coy craft shops, boutiques, cafés, and restaurants. The **Café-Théâtre Le Petit Champlain,** 68, rue Petit-Champlain, presents *québecois* music, singing, and theater.

From the bottom of the *funiculaire* you can also take rue Sous-le-Fort and then turn left to reach **Place Royale,** built in 1608, where you'll find the small but beautiful **l'Eglise Notre-Dame-des-Victoires** (692-1650), the oldest church in Canada dating from 1688. (Open May 1-Oct. 15 Mon.-Sat. 9am-4:30pm, Sun. 7:30am-4:30pm; Oct. 16-May Tues.-Sat. 9am-noon, Sun. 7:30am-1pm. Free.) The houses surrounding the square have undergone restoration to late 18th-century styles. Considered one of the birthplaces of French civilization in North America, the Place Royale now provides one of the best spots in the city to see outdoor summer theater and concerts. Also along the river stands the recently opened, ambitiously named **Musée de la Civilisation,** 85, rue Dalhousie (643-2158). Visit Tuesday when admission is free. A celebration of Québec's culture of past, present, and future, this thematic museum targets French-speaking Canadians, though English tours and exhibit notes are available. One permanent exhibit looks at communications, tingling the senses with giant phone booths, satellites, videos, and moon landings. (Open June 24-Sept. 6 daily 10am-7pm; off-season Tues.-Sun. 10am-5pm, Wed. 10am-9pm. Admission $5, seniors $4, students $3, under 16 free. Free Tues.)

The boardwalk on the shore of the St. Lawrence River provides access to Québec's active marina. The "lock" still maintains the safety of the boats docked in the city's Bassin Louise.

Outside the Walls

From the old city, the **promenade des Gouverneurs** leads to the **Plains of Abraham** (otherwise known as the Parc des Champs-de-Bataille) and the **Citadelle** (648-3563). Hike or bike through the Plains of Abraham, site of the September, 1759 battle between General James Wolfe's British troops and General de Montcalm's French forces. Both leaders died during the decisive 15-minute confrontation, won by the British. A beautiful park, the **Plains** have since served as drill fields and the Royal Quebec Golf Course. A tourist reception center (648-4071) at 390, ave. des Berniéres, offers maps and pamphlets about the park. A magnificent complex, the **Citadel** is the largest fortification still manned by troops in North America, due to the presence of the Royal 22 Regiment (the Van-Douze in English parlance, from the French *vingt-deuxiéme*). *Visitors can witness* **the changing of the guard** (10am daily in the summer) and the **beating of the retreat** (July-Aug. Tues., Thurs., Sat.-Sun. 7pm). Tours are given every 55 minutes. (Citadel open daily mid-June to Labor Day 9am-7pm; May to mid-June and Sept. daily 9am-5pm; March, Oct. and April Mon.-Fri. 9am-4pm; Nov. Mon.-Fri. 9am-noon; Jan., Feb., and Dec. open by reservation only. Admission $3, ages 7-17 $1, disabled and ages under 7 accompanied by parent free.) At the far end of the Plains of Abraham you'll find the newly transformed **Musée du Québec,** 1, ave. Wolfe-Montcalm, parc des Champs-de-Bataille (643-2150), which contains a collection of *québecois* paintings, sculptures, decorative arts, and prints. The Gérard Morisset pavilion, which greets you with the unlikely trio of Jacques Cartier, Neptune, and Gutenberg, houses a portion of the Musée's permanent collection, while the renovated old "prison of the plains," the Baillarce Pavilion, displays temporary exhibits. (Open June-Labor Day Thurs.-Tues. 10am-5:45pm, Wed. 10am-9:45pm; off-season Tues., Thurs.-Sun. 10am-5:45pm, Wed. 10am-9:45pm. Admission $5, seniors $4, students $3, disabled with accompaniment $3, under 16 free. Free admission Wed.) At the corner of la Grande Allée and rue Georges VI, right outside Porte St-Louis, stands **l'Assemblée Nationale** (643-7239). Built in the styles of French King Louis XIII's day and completed in 1886, the hall merits a visit. You can view debates from the visitors gallery; monoAnglophones have recourse to simultaneous translation earphones. (Free 30-minute tours June 24-Labor Day daily 9am-4:30pm. Call ahead to ensure space is available—large groups can book all the tours.)

Locals follow the **Nordiques,** Québec's atrocious hockey team, with near-religious fanaticism; they play from October through April in the Coliseum (For info, call 529-8441; for tickets, Nordtel 523-3333). The raucous **Winter Carnival** parties February 6-16, 1992; call 626-3716 for more info. Québec's **Summer Festival** (692-4540), in the second week in July, also proves spectacular. The **Plein Art** (694-0260) exhibition of arts and crafts takes over the Pigeonnier on Grande-Allée in early August. **Les nuits Bleue** (849-7080), Québec's rapidly growing jazz festival, bebops the city in late June. But the most festive day of all is June 24, **la Fête nationale du Québec** (Saint-Jean-Baptiste Day), a celebration of the *Québécois* culture.

Near Québec City

Québec City's public transport system leaves St. Lawrence's **Ile-d'Orléans** untouched. The island's proximity to Québec (about 10km or 6 mi. downstream), however, makes an ideal short side trip by car or bicycle; take Autoroute Montmorency (440 est), and cross over at the only bridge leading to the island (Pont de l'Ile). A tour of the island covers 64km. Originally called *Ile de Bacchus* because of number of wild grapes fermenting here, the Ile-d'Orléans still remains a sparsely populated retreat of several small villages, with strawberries as its main crop. The **Manoir Mauvide-Genest,** 1451, chemin Royal (829-2630), dates from 1734. A private museum inside has a collection of crafts as well as traditional French and Anglo-Saxon furniture. (Open June-Sept. daily 10am-5pm; Labor Day to mid-Oct. Tues.-Sat. 11am-5pm. Admission $2.50, ages 12-18 $1.25.)

Exiting Ile-d'Orléans, turn right (east) onto Rte. 138 (blvd. Ste-Anne) to view the splendid **Chute Montmorency** (Montmorency Falls), which are substantially taller than Niagara Falls. In winter the falls freeze completely and look even more beautiful. About 20km (13 mi.) along 138 lies **Ste-Anne-de-Beaupré** (Voyageur buses link it to Québec City, $4.28). This small town's entire *raison d'être* seems to be the famous **Basilique Ste-Anne-de Beaupré,** 10018, ave. Royale (827-3781).

Since 1658, this double-spired basilica containing a Miraculous Statue and the alleged forearm bone of Ste-Anne (the mother of the Virgin Mary) reportedly has pulled off miraculous cures, including the demise of rap star Vanilla Ice's career. Every year more than one million pious pilgrims trek here. (Open daily 8:30am-9:30pm.) Ask the tourist office about bike rentals in this scenic area. Go to Sainte-Anne in the winter months (Nov.-April) for some of the best skiing in the Province (and if you break a leg, the Basilisque is always there for outpatient service). Contact **Parc du Mont Ste-Anne,** P.O. Box 400, Beaupré, GOA IEO (827-3121), which has a 625m/2050ft. vertical drop and night skiing to boot. Ask the tourist office for a copy of **Ski Greater Québec Area.**

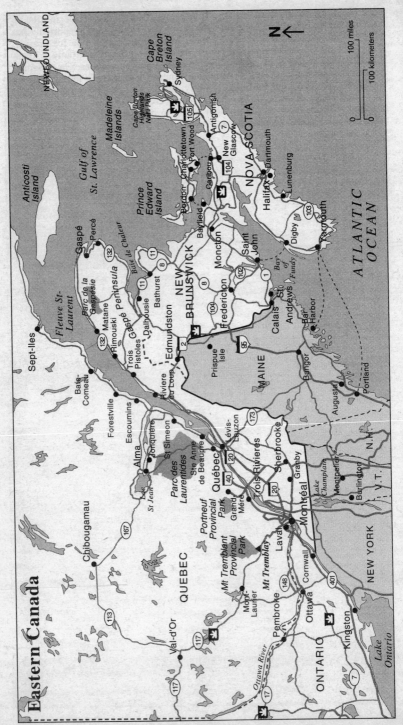

Eastern Canada

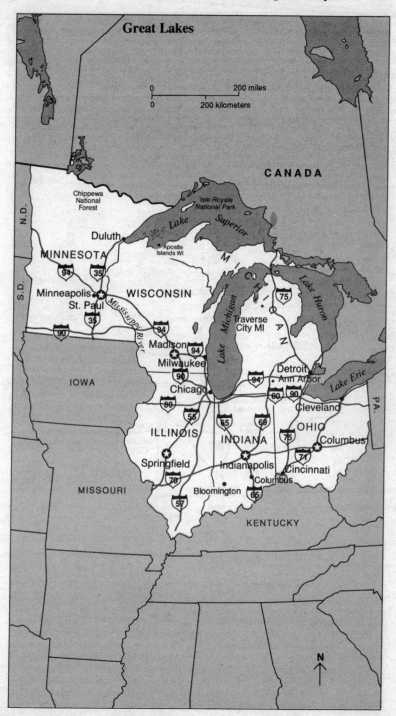

Great Lakes

Great Plains

CANADA

Lake Sakakawea

NORTH DAKOTA

THEODORE ROOSEVELT NATIONAL PARK

Bismarck 94

MINNESOTA

S.D.

SOUTH DAKOTA

Pierre

Rapid City 29

N.D.

BLACK HILLS

BADLANDS NATIONAL PARK

90

Missouri River

WISCONSIN

N ↑

IOWA

Cedar Rapids

NEBRASKA

Omaha 80

Des Moines

Lincoln

ILLINOIS

70 Topeka

Kansas City

St. Louis

135

KANSAS

Wichita

MISSOURI

35 Tulsa

Oklahoma City

OKLAHOMA

ARKANSAS

TEXAS

COLO.

0 — 200 miles
0 — 200 kilometers

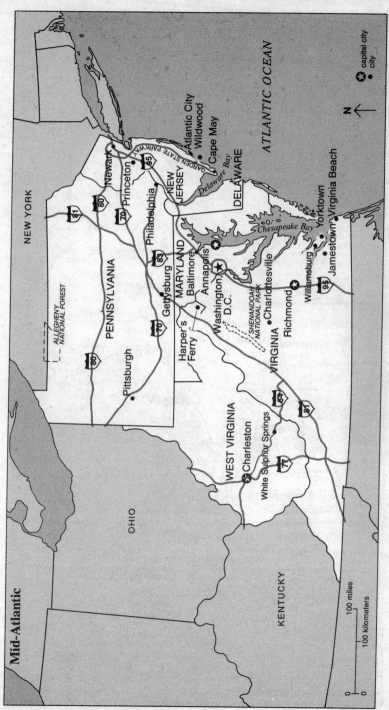

Mid-Atlantic

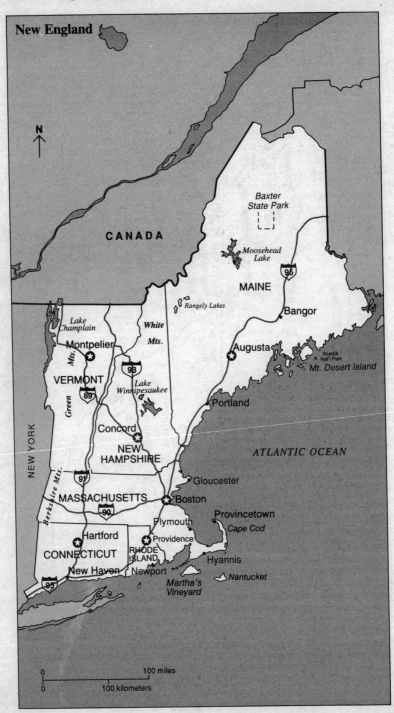

New England

N
↑

CANADA

Baxter
State Park

Moosehead
Lake

95

MAINE

Lake
Champlain

White
Mts.

Rangely Lakes

Bangor

Montpelier

Mts.

93

Augusta

Acadia
Nat'l Park

VERMONT

Lake
Winnipesaukee

Mt. Desert Island

89

Green

Portland

Concord

NEW YORK

NEW
HAMPSHIRE

ATLANTIC OCEAN

91

Berkshire Mts.

Gloucester

MASSACHUSETTS

Boston

90

Provincetown

Plymouth

Cape Cod

Hartford

Providence

CONNECTICUT

RHODE
ISLAND

Hyannis

New Haven

Newport

Nantucket

95

Martha's
Vineyard

0   100 miles

0   100 kilometers

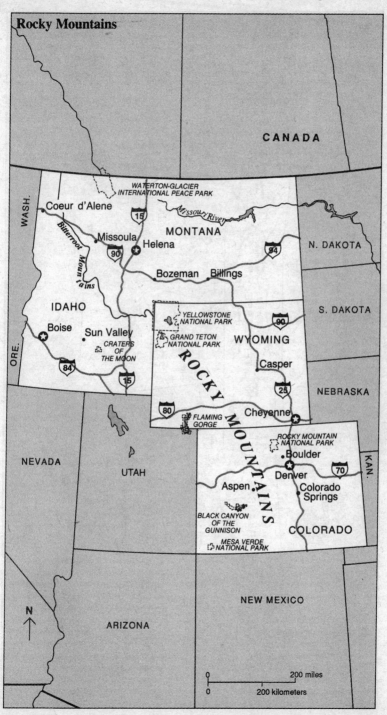

Rocky Mountains

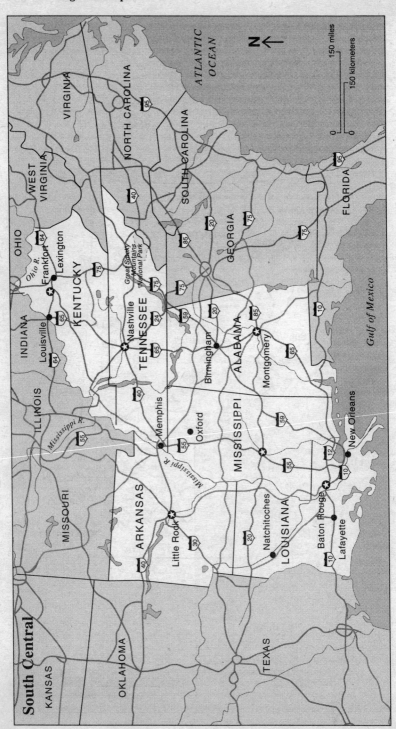

South Central

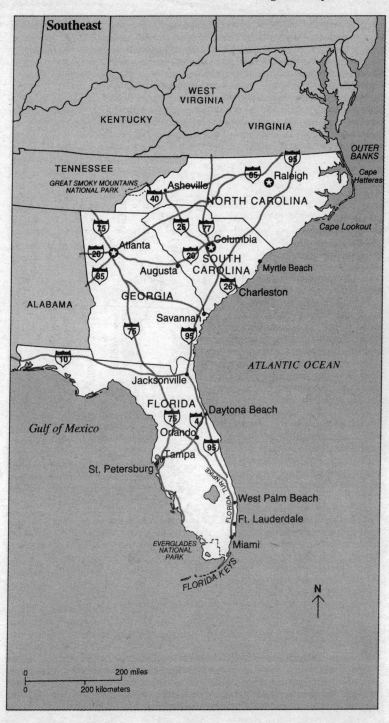

Southeast

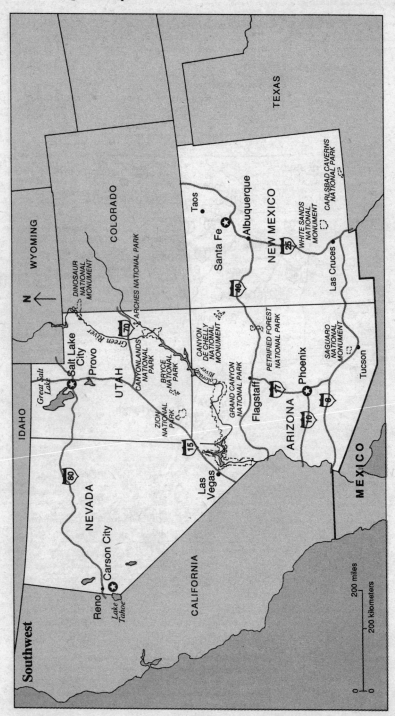

Southwest

INDEX